PURNELL'S COMPLETE COOKERY

PURNELL'S COMPLETE COOKERY

PURNELL

EDITOR-IN-CHIEF
ANNE LONDON
Director, Homemakers Research Institute

EDITORIAL CONSULTANT
Marion Howells

ASSISTANT EDITORS
Ann Currah
Elizabeth Evans
Susan Hughes
Miranda Kelsey
Vivienne Menkes
José Northey
Eileen Turner

EDITORIAL PRODUCTION
Robert Yeatman Ltd.

First published in the U.K. 1974 by Purnell Books,
Berkshire House, Queen Street, Maidenhead, Berkshire.

SBN 361 02477 0

Made and printed in Great Britain by Purnell & Sons Ltd., Paulton, Nr. Bristol.

FOREWORD

In the limited space of my introduction, I can only begin to praise adequately this masterpiece among cookery books, which must surely be unique in its scope and value. If you can only find room on your shelves for one comprehensive book, purely devoted to this most important of all domestic arts, *Purnell's Complete Cookery* is the obvious choice. It is a superb compendium of knowledge, unrivalled by any other I have seen published in this country, setting out every recipe clearly, giving basic essentials in detail, and rising to the realms of *haute cuisine*. Within its covers there are over 8,000 recipes as well as much other useful information on culinary techniques and food presentation. There are literally thousands of illustrations, some in full colour, of step-by-step preparation and finished dishes.

The index, often more of a stumbling block than an aid in large recipe books, is astonishingly detailed and helpful, and should be freely used. This index alone runs to about 40 pages, and from my own experience the careful cross-referencing enables one to look up and locate the information required with speed and certainty. All housewives have had at some time, when particularly busy, to grapple with an index more baffling than enlightening so this easy method of reference is a particular advantage. It is so useful to find the basic recipe for Popovers at a glance with an indication that there are variations, and yet to know that a little further on in the index, under the letter 'Y' (just where you would expect to find it) there is reference to an authentic and slightly different recipe for Yorkshire Pudding. Danish Beef Stew is listed under Danish, Beef, and Stew — so you are sure to find it.

The word encyclopedia, which can truly be used in speaking of the book, often seems to have rather scientific connotations; one expects it to be hard to read, and more of a duty than a pleasure. This encyclopedia makes colourful and compelling reading, opening out comfortably to lie flat on the table and, by the style of presentation, giving you the choice of as many as 12 recipes, some with variations, at a time. It is up-to-date in acknowledging that the housewife's horizon has widened to include many dishes from other lands, not only to impress occasional important guests, but as an integral part of day-to-day family catering.

Take a quick glance through the sections into which the recipes are divided. Although they are arranged in alphabetical order the less experienced cook would be wise to study 'Facts about food and cooking' and 'Special helps' first. This makes it all the easier to choose any dish in the book you feel you would like to try, confident of success. The selection of recipes, the testing and retesting, has been so meticulous that you really can rely on producing an appetising result every time. Most cooks have their own favourites; featherlight cakes which always turn out perfectly, or savoury stews which never fail to bring the family quickly to the table as the delicious aroma wafts from the kitchen. But, they also appreciate interesting additions to the well-loved repertoire. I have tested recipes at random from this book and I have been delighted with all of them.

The sections under their separate headings are self-explanatory and even the list of contents reveals an original and fascinating approach to cooking which suits today's style of living. For instance, many variations are included using packet cake mixes and other convenience foods. Very concise directions are given in a highly condensed section on home freezing, ending with hints on using commercially frozen foods.

Whether you are searching for ideas for hot soups made in a jiffy, ways to use the economical minced beef to better advantage, or a vast variety of salads for dieters, you will find appropriate recipes at your command. No skipping through vast sections of little-used recipes to find the few that are relevant to your needs! In short, this is the kind of cookery book housewives of today and tomorrow will find invaluable.

The highest compliment I can pay to *Purnell's Complete Cookery* is to tell you that it now has a treasured place in my own personal collection of cookery books.

Audrey Ellis

CONTENTS

APPETIZERS & FIRST COURSES

An appetizer, by its very name, should tempt the appetite, not destroy it. As a starter for a meal it should be a complement and contrast to the dishes which follow it, and may run the gamut of hot or cold appetite-provoking foods including fruit cups, seafood cocktails, small salads, canapés, and hors d'oeuvres. The latter is a French term which literally means "outside of work", hence served before a meal. In French, hors d'oeuvre means any appetizer. Canapé is culinary French for an individual appetizer on a bread or other edible base in a one-bite finger form. Canapés may be the same tasty concoctions as hors d'oeuvres but they are not usually served at the table.

Parties, whether in the afternoon or evening, also call for canapés and hors d'oeuvres. How many they will be and in what variety depends upon the type of party. If your party is to be an open-ended affair that is likely to last for several hours, your guests will be craving substantial fare, especially if it's a cocktail party that often spans the dinner hour.

In such cases the "menu" should be hearty enough to substitute for a meal. It should include four to six cold appetizers, and two or three hot ones. Include some meat, cheese, relishes, a dip, a spread, a finger food—things that can be made in advance and refrigerated or popped into the oven just a few minutes before your guests arrive. Make choices from among appetizers that can be kept warm for several hours in a chafing dish or in a casserole over a candle warmer.

The recipes in this book are ex-tremely varied and give specific methods and seasonings. Nevertheless these recipes should in the last analysis serve only as a guide. They are offered with the suggestion that each be sampled and seasoned to taste as they are made. We believe they will stimulate your imagination and that you will want to elaborate on them and create your own favourites. With these recipes as a base, you can evolve many hundreds of variations with contrasts in colours, textures, designs, and seasonings. They include so many favourite flavours and foods that when the impromptu occasion arises anyone can find enough ingredients on the larder shelf to make up a delectable array of dainties.

Dips

Give your guests a bit of something crisp, and a bowl of something spicy to dip it in and serving is simplified. Arrange a choice of dips on platters or trays large enough to hold an assortment of hors d'oeuvres and biscuits as well as the containers holding the dips.

Nothing is better to dunk than raw vegetables. Surround dips with a variety including celery, raw carrot cut in thin strips or very long slices curled in iced water, kohlrabi or turnips cut paper-thin, cauliflower broken and sliced in flowerets, asparagus tips, slices of cucumber and courgette, as well as spring onions, crisp radishes, and tiny cherry or plum tomatoes.

Many savoury mixtures are adaptable as dips. Before making your choices, see not only the recipes that follow but check also canapé spreads in this section and the sandwich fillings in the sandwich section. Some of these make excellent dips if thinned with mayonnaise or sour cream. Prepared spreads are a convenience, but they may need more seasoning.

ROQUEFORT COTTAGE CHEESE DIP

2½ ounces Roquefort cheese
8 ounces cottage cheese
½ teaspoon onion juice
About 6 tablespoons sour cream

Crumble Roquefort cheese and add to cottage cheese, mixing well. Stir in onion juice. Add enough sour cream to give good dipping consistency.

Serve with potato crisps, savoury biscuits, or crisp raw vegetables.

CHEESE AND CLAM DIP

1 clove garlic, cut in half
8 ounces cream cheese
2 teaspoons lemon juice
1½ teaspoons Worcestershire sauce
½ teaspoon salt
Dash of freshly ground pepper
1 7-ounce can minced clams, drained
4 tablespoons clam liquid

Rub a small mixing bowl with cut clove of garlic. Place remaining ingredients in bowl. Blend well.

For a thinner dip, add more clam liquid.

For an appealing hors d'oeuvre idea that is easy to prepare and very interesting to serve, try fresh vegetable relishes accompanied by a cold dip or a hot one such as cheese fondue.

SPICY DIP FOR SEAFOOD

8 fluid ounces mayonnaise
1 tablespoon anchovy paste
½ teaspoon dry mustard
½ teaspoon Tabasco sauce
¼ teaspoon garlic salt
2 tablespoons tarragon vinegar
3 hard-boiled eggs, finely chopped
3 tablespoons finely chopped, stuffed olives
3 tablespoons finely chopped gherkins
1 tablespoon chopped parsley
1 teaspoon finely chopped onion

Combine ingredients in order given and mix well.

Serve with chunks of lobster meat, prawns, or other seafood on sticks.

PINK DIP FOR PRAWNS

8 fluid ounces mayonnaise
1 teaspoon chilli sauce
3 tablespoons tomato ketchup
2 tablespoons horseradish
2 tablespoons vinegar or lemon juice
Few grains of cayenne pepper or dash of Tabasco sauce

Combine ingredients and chill thoroughly.

SARDINE AND CHEESE DIP

About 6½ ounces canned sardines
2 3-ounce packets cream cheese
1 clove garlic, finely chopped
3 tablespoons finely chopped onion
¼ teaspoon salt
2 tablespoons Worcestershire sauce
1 tablespoon lemon juice
Strips of pimiento

Mash drained sardines with cheese and blend with other seasonings. Chill several hours before serving to blend flavours.

Serve garnished with pimiento strips. Use as a dip for savoury biscuits or potato crisps.

AVOCADO-CHEESE DIP

Mashed pulp of 1 large avocado
8 ounces cream cheese
3 tablespoons lemon juice
Dash of Worcestershire sauce
½ bunch spring onions, finely chopped
1 teaspoon salt
Savoury biscuits

Gradually add the avocado to the cream cheese, blending until smooth. Add the lemon juice, Worcestershire sauce, onions, and salt and mix until thoroughly blended.

Place in a bowl on a tray or round plate, and surround with crackers.

SOUR CREAM-CAVIAR DIP

1 3-ounce packet cream cheese
Dash of Tabasco sauce
12 fluid ounces sour cream
½ teaspoon grated onion
2 ounces caviar or smoked cod's roe

Soften cream cheese with fork. Add Tabasco, sour cream, and onion. Mix well. Put in serving dish. Sprinkle caviar or roe over top.

Serve as dip for potato crisps, savoury biscuits, or Melba toast.

ANCHOVY-CELERY COCKTAIL DIP

8 ounces cream cheese
Dash of paprika
½ teaspoon celery salt
2 teaspoons finely chopped onion
1 tablespoon lemon juice
2 teaspoons anchovy paste
2 tablespoons cream

Cream the cheese until smooth. Add the remaining ingredients and blend until fluffy.

Serve with potato crisps or biscuits.

WINE AND CHEESE DIP

8 ounces grated Cheddar cheese
1 ounce butter
2½ fluid ounces port or sherry

Combine cheese, butter, and wine; beat with spoon until blended. Pack in small container and chill well.

Serve as dip for savoury biscuits or Melba toast.

GUACAMOLE

This avocado dish is of Mexican origin; it may be used as a cocktail dip, canapé spread, or as a salad. If this must be made long before serving time, it's a good idea to put a thin layer of mayonnaise over it to be sure it will not darken. Stir in the mayonnaise before you serve the guacamole.

1 large clove garlic, crushed
1 small onion, grated
1 teaspoon salt
¼ teaspoon pepper
1 avocado
1 tomato, skinned
1 teaspoon olive oil

Combine garlic, onion, salt, and pepper. Cut avocado in half and remove stone. Scoop out pulp; mash. Add to first mixture along with mashed tomato and oil.

Serve in the scooped-out skins with salty biscuits.

ZESTY EGG DIP

4 hard-boiled eggs, finely chopped
3 rashers cooked, crisp bacon, crumbled
1 teaspoon finely chopped onion
1 teaspoon Worcestershire sauce
1 teaspoon horseradish
Mayonnaise, enough to give good spreading consistency

Mix ingredients thoroughly; heap into bowl and chill before serving.

VEGETABLE-COTTAGE CHEESE DIP

8 ounces cottage cheese
2 fluid ounces double cream
1 ounce grated raw carrot
½ bunch spring onions, finely cut
6 radishes, sliced very thin
1 ounce chopped green pepper

Mix ingredients thoroughly; heap into bowl and chill before serving.

Nowadays dips and dunks and nibblers on sticks are favourites for most parties. Guests love making their own "sticks and picks" while the hostess takes care of last-minute preparations, or greets her guests, then joins in the fun.

Bases for Canapés

PREPARED BASES FOR CANAPÉS

A variety of ready-to-use bread, biscuit, pastry, and many novelty bases may be purchased. Thin crackers, biscuits or wafers of all types, potato chips, and various types of crispbread make simple, attractive bases for canapés.

All bases other than untoasted bread should be crisp. If it is necessary to crisp or freshen them, spread them on baking sheet and heat in a moderate oven (350°F. Mark 4) about 10 minutes.

TOASTED BREAD CANAPÉ BASES

Slice bread ¼-inch thick and cut into dainty shapes (rounds, stars, crescents, triangles, strips, etc.) with pastry cutters.

Toast bread on one side. Brush toasted side with melted butter, if desired. Spread canapé mixture on untoasted side.

CANAPÉ TOAST ROUNDS

For quickly prepared toast rounds, use small bread rolls, and slice each into several thin slices. Toast the slices as directed above.

This is quicker and less wasteful than cutting rounds from slices of bread.

FRIED (SAUTÉED) BREAD BASES

Method 1: Cut bread into desired shapes. Sauté on one side in a little butter or margarine in a heavy frying pan over very low heat. Drain on absorbent paper. Spread plain side with desired canapé spreads.

Method 2: Cut bread into desired shapes. Toast on one side. Sauté untoasted side as in Method 1 above. Drain. Spread untoasted side.

Hints: Most people find that sautéed canapé bases have more flavour than ordinary toasted bread bases.

All canapé bases should be spread as close to serving time as possible. Allowing them to stand too long will ruin them. If possible, don't spread them more than ½ hour before serving.

PUFF PASTRY BASES

Use recipe for puff pastry. Roll very thin (about ⅛ inch). Cut into small rounds (one with a hole in the centre), put 2 together to form cases and bake. Fill with any canapé filling, such as cheese, fish, or fruit.

Or roll puff pastry slightly thicker and cut into small, fancy shapes. Bake, and use with any canapé spreads, such as cheese, fish, meat, poultry, or seasoned caviar.

PASTRY CANAPÉ BASES

Use shortcrust pastry recipe or any of its variations. Roll very thin (about ⅛ inch). Cut into fancy shapes and bake in very hot oven (450°F. Mark 8) until lightly browned.

For variety, sprinkle, before baking, with allspice, cardamom, caraway seed, coriander, cayenne, curry powder, mace, mustard, paprika, or grated cheese. Use with desired canapé spreads.

COCKTAIL TURNOVERS

Roll out puff pastry on a floured board to ⅛-inch thickness. Cut in 3-inch squares or circles for each turnover.

Fill with desired filling. Lift one corner of a square and fold over the filling to the opposite corner, making a triangle tart. Moisten edges to seal. Press edges together with the prongs of a fork. Cut vent in each to permit escape of steam.

Bake on baking sheet in very hot oven (450°F. Mark 8) for about 12 to 15 minutes.

PASTRY COCKTAIL SLICES

Roll out shortcrust pastry. Spread lightly with anchovy paste or a ham spread mixed with melted butter, or very finely chopped ham.

Cover with sheet of greaseproof paper. Roll lightly to press spread into pastry. Remove paper. Roll Swiss roll fashion and slice. Or leave flat and cut in sticks or fancy shapes.

Bake in very hot oven (450°F. Mark 8) until lightly browned.

CANAPÉ PANCAKES

2 ounces plain flour
½ teaspoon salt
2 egg yolks, beaten
8 fluid ounces water

Mix and sift flour and salt. Mix egg yolks and water. Gradually combine the two mixtures, beating until smooth.

Cook on a greased griddle or large heavy frying pan. Cool and spread with desired canapé filling and roll. Makes about 20 very thin pancakes.

SAVOURY CRACKER CANAPÉ BASES

Any of the large variety of crisp savoury crackers may be used. Brush them lightly with melted butter and place in a moderate oven (350°F. Mark 4) until delicately browned.

For variations, sprinkle before browning with caraway seeds, celery salt, garlic salt, grated cheese, paprika, or onion salt.

Fill tiny cream puffs or eclair shells with chopped cooked prawns mixed with mayonnaise, or with chicken, lobster, prawn, or crabmeat salad, or with cream cheese blended with Roquefort and beaten with a little double cream.

MACARONI SHELL CANAPÉ BASES

Cook macaroni shells as directed on packet until tender but not soft. Drain on paper towels.

Fill the shells with desired filling when quite dry. If giant macaroni shells are used, they may be cut in half. Different manufacturers use different Italian names for giant macaroni shapes.

CREAM CHEESE PASTRY BASES

3 ounces plain flour
Pinch of salt
4 ounces butter
2 3-ounce packets cream cheese
1 tablespoon cold water

Mix and sift flour and salt. Cut in butter and cheese with a round-bladed knife. Stir in water and chill thoroughly.

Roll very thin and cut into rounds or sticks. Bake in very hot oven (450°F. Mark 8) until lightly browned, about 6 minutes. Spread with canapé fillings. Makes about 60 to 70 canapé bases.

You can give variety to your hors d'oeuvre tray by using different fillings and garnishes with one cheese pastry recipe.

Butters for Canapés

To prepare any of the following butters, combine softened butter and other ingredients as directed below. Blend thoroughly and store in a covered container in the refrigerator until ready to use.

If hard, leave at room temperature about 1 hour, or cream the mixture until of spreading consistency.

Savoury butters add flavour to canapés; if desired, some may be used alone without additional spreads. Just spread on canapé bases and garnish.

Anchovy Butter: To 2 ounces butter add 1 tablespoon anchovy paste, or mashed anchovy fillets, and ½ teaspoon lemon juice.

Caper Butter: To 2 ounces butter add 1 tablespoon finely chopped capers.

Caviar Butter: To 2 ounces butter add 2 teaspoons caviar, ¼ teaspoon grated onion, and a few drops lemon juice.

Cheese Butter: To 2 ounces butter add 2 ounces soft cheese.

Chilli Butter: To 2 ounces butter add ¼ teaspoon chilli sauce.

Chives Butter: To 2 ounces butter add 1 tablespoon finely chopped chives and 1 teaspoon lemon or lime juice.

Crabmeat Butter: To 2 ounces butter add 3 tablespoons finely shredded crabmeat and ½ teaspoon lemon juice.

Curry Butter: To 2 ounces butter add ¼ teaspoon curry powder.

Egg Butter: To 2 ounces butter add 2 mashed hard-boiled egg yolks, ½ teaspoon lemon juice, a dash of Tabasco sauce, salt and cayenne to taste.

Garlic Butter: To 2 ounces butter add 1 small clove of garlic, finely chopped.

Green Savoury Butter: To 2 ounces butter add 3 tablespoons spinach purée, 1 tablespoon anchovy paste, a dash of paprika, 1 teaspoon capers, and salt to taste. Put through a sieve.

Green Pepper Butter: To 2 ounces butter add 2 tablespoons grated green pepper, well-drained, and a few drops lemon juice.

A popular trend is the serving of only two or three kinds of canapés, with plenty of each. Preparation is certainly easier, and the results more appealing than an overwhelming array.

Herring Butter: To 2 ounces butter add 2 teaspoons minced smoked herring or herring paste, and a few drops lemon juice.

Honey Butter: To 2 ounces butter add 3 ounces honey. Use on hot biscuits, griddlecakes, and waffles.

Horseradish Butter: To 2 ounces butter add 2 tablespoons drained horseradish.

Ketchup Butter: To 2 ounces butter add 2 to 3 tablespoons tomato ketchup.

Lemon Butter: To 2 ounces butter add ½ teaspoon grated lemon rind and 1 tablespoon lemon juice. (Lime and orange rind and juice may be substituted.)

Liverwurst Butter: To 2 ounces butter add 2 tablespoons mashed liverwurst sausage and ½ teaspoon finely grated onion.

Lobster Butter: To 2 ounces butter add 2 tablespoons lobster paste, ½ teaspoon lemon juice, and a dash each of dry mustard and paprika.

Mint Butter: To 2 ounces butter add 2 tablespoons chopped mint leaves and 1 teaspoon lemon juice. Colour light green with food colouring.

Mustard Butter: To 2 ounces butter add 1 tablespoon prepared mustard.

Nut Butter: To 2 ounces butter add 2 tablespoons finely ground salted nuts.

Olive Butter: To 2 ounces butter add ⅛ cup finely chopped green or stuffed olives and a few drops onion juice.

Olive-Pimiento Butter: To 2 ounces butter add 1 pimiento rubbed through a sieve, and 4 finely chopped stuffed olives.

Onion Butter: To 2 ounces butter add 1 teaspoon onion juice.

Parmesan Butter: To 2 ounces butter add 2 tablespoons grated Parmesan cheese.

Parsley Butter: To 2 ounces butter add 2 tablespoons finely chopped parsley and 1 teaspoon lemon juice.

Peanut Butter: To 2 ounces butter add 2 tablespoons peanut butter, 1 teaspoon honey, and salt to taste.

Pimiento Butter: To 2 ounces butter add 2 tablespoons mashed pimiento and 1 teaspoon finely chopped pickles.

Prawn Butter: To 2 ounces butter add 2 tablespoons chopped cooked or canned prawns and ¼ teaspoon each lemon juice and onion juice.

Roquefort Butter: To 2 ounces butter add 1 tablespoon Roquefort cheese.

Salmon Butter: To 2 ounces butter add 1 tablespoon salmon paste, or mashed smoked salmon (1 ounce), and 1 teaspoon lemon juice.

Sardine Butter: To 2 ounces butter add 1 tablespoon sardine paste, or mashed sardines, and ½ teaspoon each of lemon and onion juice.

Arrange hors d'oeuvres in contrasting shapes and colours.

Tarragon Butter: To 2 ounces butter add 2 or 3 tarragon leaves, finely chopped, and a few drops tarragon vinegar.

Watercress Butter: To 2 ounces butter add 2 tablespoons finely chopped watercress, 1 teaspoon lemon juice, and a few drops Worcestershire sauce.

Worcestershire Butter: To 2 ounces butter add ¼ teaspoon Worcestershire sauce.

HERB BUTTERS — HINTS

Herb butters are excellent to use on piping hot steaks, chops, hamburgers, pot roasts, and grilled fish. Or the mixture is used as a savoury cracker or sandwich spread.

Try one herb at a time, then try blending two herbs to give distinction to your cookery.

HERB BUTTERS WITH FRESH HERBS

Combine chopped tender leaves of such fresh herbs as chives, chervil, fennel, marjoram, and tarragon and a few crumbs of dry bread in a mortar.

Add a drop or two of brandy or an aromatic liqueur and grind with a pestle.

Then blend with butter or margarine and force through a fine sieve. The crumbs and liqueur help distribute and hold the flavour of the herbs in the butter.

Place in covered jar and chill the mixture.

HERB BUTTERS WITH DRIED OR POWDERED HERBS

To 4 ounces butter or margarine add 1 teaspoon dried herb or ½ teaspoon powdered herb. A half teaspoon of lemon juice may be added, too.

Combine with a fork and keep in a covered jar at room temperature for about 2 hours to get the full bouquet of flavour.

Then keep in a covered jar in the refrigerator for use within two or three days.

Canapé "Pies" and "Cakes"

Canapé pies are deservedly very popular because they can be prepared well in advance of a party; they encourage the use of your imagination; they can often be made from ingredients in your refrigerator and cupboard; they are fun to make. The base for it is a large round loaf of rye bread, which you can slice crosswise into big circles. You spread each slice with softened butter or margarine or a thin layer of mayonnaise or cream cheese, and then let your fancy dictate how you finish it.

It should consist of circles of various appetizing mixtures that blend well in flavours and contrast in colours. Each spread may be separated by rings of seasoned cream cheese rippled from a decorating tube. The cream cheese, too, may be divided up and tinted in various contrasting shades with food colouring.

CANAPÉ PIE

1 round loaf of rye bread
2½ ounces softened butter or margarine
4 tablespoons mayonnaise
Caviar
Sieved egg yolk
Cream cheese
Sardine paste
Shrimp or prawn paste
Salmon paste
Pickled onions

Cut a slice horizontally (½ inch thick) from the widest part of the loaf of bread. Trim off the crusts.

Mix the butter or margarine and mayonnaise and spread generously on the slice of bread. Mark the slice in concentric circles, using cutters and bowls of various sizes.

Fill the centre ring with caviar, marking the centre point with a sieved egg yolk. Fill the next ring with cream cheese pressed through a pastry tube. Fill the next rings with sardine paste, shrimp or prawn paste, and salmon paste, separated by cream cheese.

Pipe an edge of cream cheese around the outer edge. Line the rim of the plate with tiny pickled onions.

Cut the canapé in wedges like pie. Serve cold.

APPETIZER PIE

Cut a large round loaf of rye bread in circular slices ¼ inch thick. Spread with soft butter.

Place a teaspoon of caviar in centre. Surround with a ring of cream cheese, then with a ring of rolled anchovies, a ring of chopped black olives, and another ring of cream cheese.

Garnish outer edge with small pickled onions, whole stuffed green olives, and halves of cooked or canned prawns, alternating the foods.

Chill and serve in pie-shaped wedges.

SANDWICH "CAKE"

1 round loaf, about 8 inches in diameter

Filling No. 1
12 ounces luncheon meat, mashed
1 tablespoon sweet pickle or chutney
2 tablespoons mayonnaise

Filling No. 2
4 hard-boiled eggs
½ teaspoon salt
Pinch of pepper
¼ teaspoon celery salt
1 tablespoon chopped parsley

Filling No. 3
12 ounces luncheon meat, mashed
½ teaspoon chilli sauce

Topping
2 cans devilled ham
8 ounces cream cheese
Milk
Sliced stuffed olives
Pitted black olives

Cut the loaf into four layers and trim off the side crusts.

Spread each layer with softened butter, margarine or mayonnaise.

Combine ingredients for each filling, as given above, and put layers together, with filling No. 1 on the bottom layer, No. 2 on the second layer, and No. 3 on the third layer. Spread top of loaf with devilled ham.

Cover sides with cream cheese which has been softened to spreading consistency with milk.

Decorate with cream cheese forced through a pastry tube and garnish with slices of stuffed and black olives.

To make umbrella, cut pimiento in half and use a strip of green pepper for the handle; make scallops with halves of sliced stuffed olive and tube "seams" on umbrella using cream cheese.

APPETIZER "CAKE"

The appetizer "cake" may be made from a commercial bakery loaf if you use one of the small round loaves of rye or pumpernickel which are sold in delicatessens and continental bakers' shops. You may prefer, however, to bake your own loaf in a deep round cake tin. After baking, cool and remove crusts with sharp knife.

Cut the loaf into 4 slices to form 4-inch "layers" of the appetizer "cake".

Spread the individual layers with sticky sandwich fillings. For example, chicken salad, alternating with vegetable salad, egg salad alternating with

Canapé Pie

fish salad. Put the spread slices together to form original shape of loaf.

Cover the loaf with softened cream cheese. Garnish as desired with sliced olives, pickles, radishes, etc.

Chill thoroughly in refrigerator. To serve, cut into individual wedges as you would a cake.

HALLOWE'EN CANAPÉ PIE

Cheese Spread: Cream together 6 ounces cream cheese and 1½ ounces blue cheese. Season to taste with Worcestershire sauce and chopped parsley. Mix in enough milk or cream to make it spreading consistency. Spread in an even layer in bottom of 8-inch pie plate.

Ham Layer: Spread 4½ ounces devilled ham over cheese layer.

Egg Layer: Chop 4 hard-boiled eggs. Season to taste with salt, pepper, pimiento, and mayonnaise. Spread on top of ham layer. Cover with greaseproof paper. Chill in refrigerator several hours or overnight.

To Decorate and Serve: Make Jack O'Lantern face with pimiento strips. Cut pie in thin wedges for serving and accompany with crisp savoury biscuits.

Sandwich "Cake"

Pecan Cheese Ball

Cheese Canapés and Spreads

PECAN CHEESE BALL

1 pound cream cheese
1 8¾-ounce can crushed pineapple, drained
8 ounces pecans or walnuts, chopped
2 tablespoons chopped green pepper
2 tablespoons chopped onion
1 tablespoon celery salt
Pineapple slices
Maraschino cherries
Parsley

Soften cream cheese; gradually stir in crushed pineapple, half the nuts, green pepper, onion, and salt. Chill well.

Form into a ball and roll in remaining nuts. Chill until serving.

Garnish with twists of pineapple slices, maraschino cherries, and parsley. Serve with assorted crackers.

GORGONZOLA OR ROQUEFORT SPREAD

Soften Gorgonzola cheese and butter (about half and half) and mix it together into a soft paste.

If Roquefort is used, unsalted butter is advisable if the cheese is very salty. Season with sweet Italian vermouth and spread on rounds of toast or bread.

GREEN PEPPER-CHEESE SPREAD

Blend 1 3-ounce packet cream cheese with 4 tablespoons finely chopped green pepper, 2 tablespoons finely chopped onion, 1 teaspoon French dressing, and a few grains cayenne.

COTTAGE CHEESE SLICES

8 ounces cottage cheese
1 ounce crumbled blue cheese
4 stuffed olives, chopped
1 tablespoon chopped parsley
1 pimiento, chopped
1 tablespoon finely chopped green pepper
1½ ounces creamed butter
¼ teaspoon paprika

Mix cheeses together until well blended. Add remaining ingredients and form into a roll 2 inches in diameter. Chill thoroughly. Slice and serve on savoury biscuits.

LIPTAUER CHEESE

This is sometimes referred to as Liptauer Käse or Hungarian cheese; it is a classic appetizer and like any classic dish it usually appears in many versions. In some parts of Europe, goat's milk pot cheese is often used. Other versions may include part cottage cheese and part cream cheese. Some delicatessens sell a ready-to-serve packaged mixture. A popular version is given below:

8 ounces cottage cheese
8 ounces butter
1 tablespoon crushed or whole caraway seeds
1 tablespoon finely chopped chives or onion
1 tablespoon finely chopped capers
1 tablespoon mild prepared or dry mustard
1 anchovy, chopped, or ½ teaspoon anchovy paste
1 tablespoon Hungarian paprika

Put the cheese through a fine sieve. Cream the butter with caraway seeds, chives or onion, capers, mustard, anchovy, and half the paprika, then gradually stir in the cheese.

Shape mixture into a mound; sprinkle with remaining paprika and garnish with lettuce. Serve as an appetizer with rye and pumpernickel bread. Serves 8 to 10.

Note: If chives are used, serve within 6 hours as the taste of the chives may grow strong.

STUFFED EDAM

1 Edam cheese
2 teaspoons onion juice
½ teaspoon Worcestershire sauce
¾ teaspoon prepared mustard
2 to 3 fluid ounces cream

Cut a small section off the top of the cheese. Hollow out inside.

Grate cheese and combine with other ingredients. Beat until smooth. Refill cheese shell with mixture. Refrigerate 3 hours to blend seasonings. Serve at room temperature.

ROQUEFORT-COTTAGE CHEESE SPREAD

1 pound cottage cheese
2 3-ounce packets cream cheese
4 ounces Roquefort cheese spread
2 tablespoons Worcestershire sauce
2 ounces butter, melted
2 tablespoons cream
2 tablespoons finely chopped onion

Mix all ingredients together and beat well. Cover and chill overnight to permit flavours to blend.

Serve in lettuce-lined bowl with savoury biscuits or Melba toast.

COCKTAIL CHEESE LOG

1 3-ounce packet cream cheese
3 ounces butter
1 teaspoon capers
1 teaspoon paprika
½ teaspoon caraway seed
⅛ teaspoon anchovy paste
1 tablespoon finely chopped onion

Blend cheese and butter. Add remaining ingredients. Shape into roll. Wrap in greaseproof paper. Chill thoroughly.

Let your guests cut and spread it on savoury biscuits, Melba toast, or thinly sliced bread.

TOMATO AND CREAM CHEESE SPREAD

1 cut clove garlic
2 very ripe tomatoes, peeled
8 ounces cream cheese
1 teaspoon Worcestershire sauce
1 teaspoon grated onion
½ teaspoon salt

Rub a chopping bowl with garlic. Chop tomatoes in same bowl until completely mashed.

Add remaining ingredients. Beat until smooth. Serve with savoury biscuits and potato crisps.

CHEESE-ANCHOVY SPREAD

2 3-ounce packets cream cheese
2 tablespoons anchovy paste
1 tablespoon lemon juice
1 teaspoon Worcestershire sauce
1 teaspoon finely chopped onion

Mix all ingredients together and chill to blend flavours.

Use as spread for biscuits, potato crisps, or as canapé topping.

A large tray of assorted biscuits and cheese, as well as crisp, cold vegetable sticks and spicy bite-size fruits are the main ingredients for a "serve yourself" snack assortment.

PROVOLONE AND SALAMI SPREAD

- 4 ounces Provolone cheese
- 4 ounces salami
- 2 small sweet pickles
- 7 tablespoons mayonnaise

Put cheese, salami, and pickles through mincer, using medium blade. Add mayonnaise, and mix well. Store mixture in covered jar in refrigerator.

Flavour improves after spread has stood a day or two. Especially good on rye bread.

Variations: Muenster, Cheddar, or Gruyère cheese may be substituted for Provolone.

CREAM CHEESE COCKTAIL MOULD

- 2 3-ounce packets cream cheese
- 2 ounces soft butter
- ½ teaspoon caraway seed
- 1 tablespoon anchovy paste
- 1 teaspoon paprika
- 1 tablespoon chopped chives
- ½ teaspoon salt
- 1 teaspoon capers

Cream the cheese and butter together until fluffy. Add remaining ingredients and mix well.

Pack into small mould. Chill several hours. Unmould on tray or plate. Serve with potato crisps and crackers.

SAGE-CHEESE SPREAD

Blend thoroughly 8 ounces cream cheese, ¼ teaspoon salt, and ¾ teaspoon ground sage.

Chill overnight in refrigerator. Spread on crackers, thin toast, or Melba toast.

WINE-CHEESE SPREAD

Combine grated mature Cheddar cheese with enough sherry to make a smooth spread. Add half as much chopped stuffed olives. Mix well.

PICKLE-CREAM CHEESE SPREAD

Mix finely chopped sweet pickles with cream cheese. Spread on canapé bases and garnish with slices of stuffed olives.

PISTACHIO-CHEESE SPREAD

Combine 1 3-ounce packet of Roquefort cheese and 1 3-ounce packet cream cheese with 1 tablespoon double cream, 1 teaspoon finely chopped onion, 2 tablespoons chopped black olives, and 2 ounces blanched pistachio nuts. Mix well and chill.

SOUR CREAM-CHEESE SPREAD

Blend cream cheese with sour cream. Season with salt and pepper.

WATERCRESS-CHEESE SPREAD

Cream 1 3-ounce packet cream cheese. Dry and chop ½ bunch watercress. Blend together with 1 teaspoon Worcestershire sauce and ¼ teaspoon salt.

CHUTNEY-CHEESE SPREAD

Blend 1 3-ounce packet cream cheese with 2 tablespoons chutney.

ONION-CHEESE SPREAD

Mince and mix together equal parts of Gruyère cheese and Spanish onions. Spread on rounds of buttered white or rye bread.

CHEESE-STUFFED ROLL SLICES

Cut off ends of frankfurter rolls. Scoop out centres with fork, and stuff rolls with any cheese spread. Wrap in greaseproof paper; chill. To serve, cut in ½ inch slices.

NUT AND CHEESE SPREAD

Blend cream cheese with chopped nuts. Sweeten to taste with icing sugar.

OLIVE-CHEESE SPREAD

Put 2 parts Cheddar cheese and 1 part stuffed or pitted olives through the mincer, using a fine blade. Mix together well.

DEVILLED HAM-CREAM CHEESE SPREAD

- 4 3-ounce packets cream cheese
- 4 fluid ounces single cream
- 2 tablespoons devilled ham
- 1 teaspoon finely chopped chives

Soften cream cheese with cream. Blend with remaining ingredients. Pile into a bowl.

HORSERADISH-CHEESE SPREAD

Combine 1 3-ounce packet of cream cheese with 1½ teaspoons drained horseradish, ½ teaspoon scraped onion, and a pinch of salt.

Blend thoroughly and spread on toast bases. Top with bits of crisp bacon.

GARLIC CREAM CHEESE SPREAD

Rub a salad bowl with a cut clove of garlic. Moisten cream cheese with a bit of cream and work in the bowl until cheese is softened and has absorbed some of the garlic aroma.

Garnish the spread canapés with a piping of finely chopped parsley.

CAMEMBERT SPREAD

Blend Camembert cheese with half as much cream cheese.

TOMATO-PARMESAN CANAPÉS

Place thin slices of tomato on toasted canapé bases. Sprinkle with grated Parmesan cheese and then with chopped parsley.

OLIVE AND SHARP CHEESE SPREAD

Combine 1 ounce grated soft sharp cheese with 2 ounces butter. Add 8 finely chopped green or stuffed olives. Season to taste with salt and pepper.

COMMODORE'S CHEESE

- 8 ounces sharp Cheddar cheese
- 4 ounces Roquefort or blue cheese
- 1 3-ounce packet cream cheese
- Finely chopped chives
- Double cream
- Paprika

Put Cheddar and blue cheese through a mincer, or grate finely and blend with cream cheese, chives, and cream. Beat until fluffy. Mound on a serving plate and sprinkle with paprika to serve.

(Try this as dessert sometime with preserved fruit and crisp biscuits.)

One savoury cheese spread may be used in different variations of hors d'oeuvres: ham pinwheels, triangular bologna stacks; salami cornucopias, and tiny filled tartlet cases. A versatile spread is made by blending 8 ounces cream cheese with 2 fluid ounces cream and 1 tablespoon Worcestershire sauce.

Egg Appetizers

HINTS ABOUT STUFFED EGGS

Hard-boiled eggs are, in fact, badly named, for eggs are not cooked properly if they are "boiled". They should be cooked in water just below the boiling point for 12 to 15 minutes.

If the eggs are taken directly from the refrigerator start them in cold or luke-warm water. Hot water may crack the shells. When done, chill in cold water to prevent darkening of the yolks and to make shelling easier.

Cut the eggs in half lengthwise, or if you want to cut them crosswise, cut a small piece off the bottom to form a flat base so they won't roll over.

Remove the yolks and put through a sieve or mash with a fork. Combine with seasonings and refill the whites of eggs. To get a more decorative effect, use a pastry tube.

Garnish the filled eggs with slices of stuffed olives, tiny pearl onions, chopped chives, chopped parsley, bits of pimiento, or paprika.

How To Centre Egg Yolks for Stuffed Eggs

If eggs are allowed to remain in one position while being hard-boiled there is a tendency for the yolks to sink to the bottom. For stuffed eggs it is desirable to have egg yolks in the centre of the eggs.

To obtain such a result gently stir the eggs in the pan, keeping them in motion for the first 6 or 7 minutes of cooking.

Devilled Eggs With Scalloped Edge

DEVILLED EGGS

6 hard-boiled eggs, shelled
1 tablespoon cream or mayonnaise
1½ teaspoons vinegar
Dash of pepper
¾ teaspoon prepared mustard
½ teaspoon Worcestershire sauce (optional)
¼ teaspoon salt

Cut eggs in halves lengthwise. Remove yolks; force through sieve. Add seasonings and beat until smooth and fluffy.

Fill egg whites with mixture. Garnish tops with dash of paprika, chopped parsley, or chopped chives.

Hot Devilled Eggs: If desired, substitute cream or evaporated milk for mayonnaise. To serve, heat eggs in top of double boiler and serve with hot cheese or tomato sauce.

Serve on buttered hot toast or arrange around boiled rice ring.

STUFFED EGG VARIATIONS

Follow method for Devilled Eggs. The ingredients given are used with 6 hard-boiled eggs unless otherwise indicated.

Anchovy Stuffed Eggs: For 6 eggs use 2 tablespoons anchovy paste, 1 tablespoon finely chopped chives, and 1 teaspoon lemon juice.

Bacon Stuffed Eggs: Cook bacon until crisp. Chop and mix with mashed egg yolk and finely chopped parsley. Moisten with mayonnaise.

Caviar Stuffed Eggs: For 6 eggs use 2 ounces caviar, 3 tablespoons mayonnaise, ¼ teaspoon salt, and a pinch of pepper. Garnish tops with caviar.

Celery Stuffed Eggs: Chop celery very finely. Mix with mashed egg yolk and moisten with mayonnaise or salad dressing.

Cheese Stuffed Eggs: For 6 eggs use 2 tablespoons creamed butter, 1½ ounces grated Gruyère cheese, and salt and pepper to taste.

Chicken or Veal Stuffed Eggs: Chop cooked chicken or veal very finely. Mix with equal amounts mashed egg yolk. Season to taste.

Chicken Livers Stuffed Eggs: Sauté chicken livers. Chop finely and mix with mashed egg yolk.

Crabmeat Stuffed Eggs: For 6 eggs use 2 ounces flaked crabmeat, 2 ounces finely chopped celery, 1 tablespoon chopped green pepper, ½ teaspoon dry mustard, and 2 tablespoons mayonnaise.

Devilled Ham or Liver Sausage Stuffed Eggs: Blend devilled ham or liver sausage with the mashed yolks. Smooth to a paste with mayonnaise.

Ham Stuffed Eggs: For 6 eggs use 2 ounces minced ham, 1 teaspoon dry mustard, about ½ teaspoon salt, and enough mayonnaise to form a smooth paste with the mashed egg yolks.

Mushroom and Onion Stuffed Eggs: Sauté chopped mushrooms and onions in butter. Mix with mashed egg yolk.

Pickle Stuffed Eggs: Mix finely mashed egg yolks with finely chopped pickle. Moisten with mayonnaise.

Sardine Stuffed Eggs: Mash sardines. Season with salt and lemon juice. Mix with mashed egg yolk. Moisten with mayonnaise.

Prawn Stuffed Eggs: Marinate small whole cooked or canned prawns in French dressing for ½ hour. Place a whole prawn in the cavity of each egg half.

Cover with mashed egg yolk mixed with mayonnaise and a little lemon juice.

Stuffed Eggs En Casserole: Place stuffed eggs in a casserole. Cover with cheese, tomato, mushroom, or other desired sauce. Sprinkle with buttered crumbs or grated cheese.

Bake in moderate oven (350°F. Mark 4) until browned on top and heated through.

Devilled Egg Faces: To make, first stuff the egg whites. Fasten a gherkin with a toothpick at the rounded end of the egg. Cut two tiny pimiento squares for the eyes and a 1 x ¼-inch strip for the mouth. Place these on the filling. Spread the top of the pointed end of the egg with mayonnaise. Dust mayonnaise with chopped parsley. Chill.

Shepherd's Pie (above) and Meat Roll (below)

Chicken Brunswick Stew (above) and Steak and Kidney Pie (below)

TOMATO-EGG CANAPÉS

Toast rounds of bread on one side. Spread untoasted sides with mayonnaise. Add thin slices of tomato, then slices of hard-boiled egg.

Sprinkle lightly with salt. Garnish with a slice or two of olive.

EGG AND SALMON CANAPÉS

Blend hard-boiled egg yolks, flaked salmon, and mayonnaise or salad dressing to a smooth paste.

Toast sliced bread on one side. Spread salmon mixture on untoasted side.

Garnish with finely chopped parsley and hard-boiled egg white.

BACON AND EGG SPREAD

Mash 2 hard-boiled eggs; combine with 4 rashers finely crumbled cooked bacon. Moisten with 1 tablespoon mayonnaise.

Season with 1 tablespoon of any dried herb and 1 tablespoon wine or herb vinegar. Mix to a smooth spread.

ZESTY EGG SPREAD

Mash 4 hard-boiled egg yolks; season with 1 teaspoon tomato ketchup, 1 teaspoon onion juice, 1 teaspoon prepared mustard, ¼ teaspoon salt, pinch of pepper, and 3 drops Worcestershire sauce.

EGG AND CHEESE SPREAD

3 3-ounce packets cream cheese
1 ounce blue cheese
2 hard-boiled eggs, chopped
1 teaspoon onion juice
1 tablespoon Worcestershire sauce
Cream to moisten
Salt and pepper to taste

Combine all ingredients. Mash with fork, adding enough cream to moisten.

Form into ball. Chill until firm. Serve with crackers or Melba toast.

WATERCRESS-EGG SPREAD

Mash hard-boiled eggs; combine with finely chopped watercress. Moisten with mayonnaise.

Fish and Shellfish Canapés and Spreads

FLAKED FISH SPREADS

Cook, cool, and flake fillets or use canned flaked fish. Serve in any of the three following ways:

1. Mix equal quantities of flaked fish and chopped pearl onions. Mix with mayonnaise and chilli sauce. Serve on whole-wheat biscuits.

2. Mix equal quantities of flaked fish and chopped mustard pickle. Serve on biscuits or toast strips.

3. Moisten flaked fish with cream and horseradish. Serve on biscuits or toast strips, garnished with green pepper.

SARDINE AND EGG SPREAD

Combine mashed sardines with mashed hard-boiled egg yolk. Season to taste with lemon juice. Add enough butter to form a smooth paste.

Spread on toasted canapé bases. Garnish with shredded egg white. Sprinkle with chopped parsley.

CHOPPED HERRING SPREAD

Wash, clean, bone and chop salted herring which has been soaked in cold water for several hours.

For each herring use 1 onion, 1 tart apple, 1 slice of toast soaked in vinegar or lemon juice. Chop all together very finely.

Add 1 teaspoon salad oil, and a dash each of cinnamon and pepper.

Serve garnished with finely chopped hard-boiled egg.

ANCHOVY-EGG SPREAD

Mash and blend 4 hard-boiled egg yolks and 4 anchovies. Moisten to spreading consistency with mayonnaise. Season with grated onion and freshly ground black pepper.

Spread and garnish with chopped egg white.

CRABMEAT OR LOBSTER SPREAD

Make a paste of canned or cooked seafood. Moisten with mayonnaise. Season with lemon juice and grated onion.

KIPPER SPREAD

1 kipper, boned and mashed
1 chopped hard-boiled egg
2 tablespoons finely chopped cucumber
Mayonnaise to moisten
2 drops lemon juice

Blend ingredients to a smooth spread.

DEVILLED LOBSTER SPREAD

4 ounces cooked or canned flaked lobster
½ teaspoon grated onion
2 tablespoons mayonnaise
1 tablespoon Worcestershire sauce
½ teaspoon prepared mustard
Salt and pepper to taste

Blend ingredients to a smooth spread.

KIPPER-CHEESE SPREAD

1 kipper, boned and flaked
6 ounces grated Cheddar cheese
½ medium-sized Spanish onion, grated

Blend to a smooth spreading consistency. Spread and garnish with slices of stuffed olives.

CLAM-CHEESE SPREAD

1 7-ounce can minced clams, drained
1 3-ounce packet cream cheese
1 tablespoon Worcestershire sauce
About 1 tablespoon onion juice
Pinch of dry mustard
Salt to taste

Mix thoroughly and use as spread for canapé bases.

SMOKED SALMON FINGERS

Spread pumpernickel or dark rye bread with unsalted butter. Cut into fingers. Cover with thin slices of smoked salmon. Sprinkle with finely chopped parsley.

Serve with lemon wedges. If desired, season with olive oil and freshly ground black pepper.

OYSTER CANAPÉS

Use round canapé bases toasted on one side. Spread untoasted side with mustard butter. Dip chilled raw oysters in mayonnaise and press one into each round.

Garnish with sieved hard-boiled egg yolk mixed with finely chopped chives.

PICKLED HERRING CANAPÉS

Place small slices of Spanish onion on squares of rye or pumpernickel bread.

Top each with small squares of pickled herring. Sprinkle with chopped parsley or watercress.

CHEESE AND SMOKED SALMON CANAPÉS

Split small hard rolls. Spread with cream cheese. Top with thinly sliced smoked salmon.

Cut into bite-size wedges.

QUICK PRAWN CANAPÉS

Spread untoasted side of canapé bases with mayonnaise. Place a whole cooked prawn on each.

Garnish with finely chopped parsley.

You'll be sure of compliments when you serve a colourful, attractive array of canapés and hors d'oeuvres.

CAVIAR SERVING HINTS

Caviar sounds extravagant but a little of it goes a long way, and to many people it represents absolute perfection as an appetizer. If you can't afford the best quality, such as Beluga, use pressed caviar or red caviar, which are less expensive.

To serve caviar by itself, bed the jars in a bowl of crushed ice and serve with accompaniments of dark rye bread, Melba toast, sour cream, finely chopped onion, and lemon wedges.

It is wise not to make caviar canapés too far ahead of time because caviar has a tendency to soak through ordinary bread or toast.

It is usually preferable to use the packaged kind of canapé base because these ready-made bases do not become as soaked as the usual homemade bases. However, if a layer of cream cheese is spread over toasted bread bases, the soaking can be prevented.

The simple traditional caviar canapé is made as follows: Spread toast squares or rounds with caviar; sprinkle lightly with grated onion and lemon juice. Decorate with finely chopped whites and yolks of hard-boiled eggs.

RED CAVIAR CANAPÉS

2 3-ounce packets cream cheese
1 tablespoon chopped onion
1 tablespoon chopped parsley
Few leaves sage, shredded
1 medium-sized jar red caviar
Mayonnaise
Toasted canapé bases

Mix cream cheese with onion, parsley, and sage. Cover half of each toast round with cream cheese mixture. Cover other half with caviar.

With a piping tube place a garnish of mayonnaise between the caviar and cheese and around the edges.

Always a favourite — an attractive tray of cooked prawns with a spicy cocktail sauce dip.

RED AND BLACK CAVIAR CANAPÉS

Use black and red caviar. Spread diamond or round canapé bases with cream cheese seasoned with onion juice. Divide the canapé down the middle with a ridge of cream cheese, finely chopped parsley, or chives.

Put red caviar on one side and black caviar on other side.

If desired, border canapés with grated hard-boiled egg yolk or white, or with finely chopped parsley.

WAGON-WHEEL CANAPÉS

Remove seed sections from small slices of tomatoes. Place on buttered toast rounds.

Fill alternate sections with chopped hard-boiled egg and black caviar.

CAVIAR-CHEESE SPREAD

Soften cream cheese with cream. Spread on small crackers. Dot with caviar.

CAVIAR-EGG SPREAD

Combine 2 finely chopped hard-boiled eggs with 2 tablespoons caviar; moisten with mayonnaise.

SALMON-AVOCADO CANAPÉS

2 ounces flaked cooked or canned salmon
2 tablespoons mayonnaise
1½ tablespoons lemon juice
¼ teaspoon salt
Dash of pepper
8 large toast rounds
1½ ounces softened butter
1 small or ½ large avocado, mashed
8 strips pimiento

Mix salmon, mayonnaise, ½ tablespoon lemon juice, salt, and pepper.

Spread toast rounds with softened butter. Spread half of each round with salmon mixture, the other half with avocado mixed with remaining lemon juice.

Mark the division with a pimiento strip.

EGG AND LOBSTER CANAPÉS

3 tablespoons lobster paste
1½ ounces butter
6 small rounds of toast
2 hard-boiled eggs
3 stuffed olives

Cream together the lobster paste and butter. Spread evenly on toast rounds. Arrange thick slices of hard-boiled egg in centre.

Cut olives in halves and press a half into the centre of egg slices, cut side up.

SARDINE SPREAD

Mash and blend together 3 sardines and 1 3-ounce packet cream cheese. Season with lemon juice to taste.

SARDINE-CUCUMBER CANAPÉS

Soak thin slices of cucumber in salted iced water to crisp. Cut canapé bases to size of cucumber and spread with cream cheese. Top each with a cucumber slice.

Top cucumber with chopped sardines mixed with mayonnaise and lemon juice. Garnish with a bit of pimiento.

CRABMEAT OR LOBSTER AND DEVILLED EGG SPREAD

1 6- or 7-ounce can crabmeat or lobster
2 hard-boiled eggs
½ teaspoon mustard
2 tablespoons mayonnaise
1 tablespoon lemon juice
About 1 teaspoon curry powder

Drain and bone the seafood. Mash and blend with remaining ingredients to a smooth spread.

CRABMEAT SPREAD

1 6-oz. can finely flaked crabmeat
2 tablespoons chopped parsley
1 tablespoon finely chopped onion
3 tablespoons mayonnaise
¼ teaspoon curry powder
1 teaspoon lemon juice

Blend ingredients to a smooth spread.

PRAWN-AVOCADO CANAPÉS

Peel and mash a small avocado. Season with 1 teaspoon lemon juice, 1 teaspoon finely chopped onion, and a dash of salt.

Spread on crackers or savoury biscuits and top each with a whole prawn.

EGG-SARDINE CANAPÉS

Mix equal parts of yolks of hard-boiled eggs and sardines and a little lemon juice. Spread on toast bases.

Sprinkle with chopped egg whites mixed with finely chopped parsley.

HERRING AND SALMON CANAPÉS

Spread canapé bases with lemon butter. Arrange thin strips of smoked salmon and buckling on the bases.

Decorate with chopped hard-boiled egg yolk. Sprinkle with finely chopped parsley.

PRAWN AND TOMATO CANAPÉS

Marinate cleaned, cooked prawns in French dressing for 1 hour. Cover each toast round with a slice of tomato.

Place a marinated prawn in centre. Top with a bit of mayonnaise.

ANCHOVY CANAPÉS

Spread rounds of Melba toast with cream cheese. Cover with slice of hard-boiled egg. Top each with rolled anchovy fillet.

Meat and Poultry Canapés and Spreads

PÂTÉ DE FOIE GRAS

Genuine pâté de foie gras (literally, a pâté of fat livers) is imported. It is made from the oversized marbled livers of geese that have been fattened by being confined to pens and stuffed with food; they are cooked with madeira, seasonings, and usually truffles. The forced feeding of geese to obtain the necessary fat livers is not legal in some countries. However, pâtés of chicken livers properly prepared make a more than acceptable substitute.

MOCK PÂTÉ DE FOIE GRAS
(Pâté of Chicken Livers)

8 ounces chicken livers
1 teaspoon salt
Pinch of cayenne
4 ounces rendered chicken fat,
**   goose fat, or softened butter**
¼ teaspoon nutmeg
1 teaspoon dry mustard
⅛ teaspoon ground cloves
2 tablespoons finely chopped onion

Cover chicken livers with water; bring to a boil, reduce heat and simmer in covered saucepan 15 to 20 minutes. Drain and put the hot livers through a mincer, using finest blade, or chop finely.

Mix with remaining ingredients until thoroughly blended. Pack in a crock or jar and chill in refrigerator.
Note: A few canned truffles may be added to above.
Blender Pâté: Cook and chop the livers as above, then whip in electric blender until very smooth. Mix with 4 ounces rendered chicken or goose fat or with 4 ounces softened butter. Season very lightly with salt and 1 tablespoon port or sherry. If desired, a few truffles may be added.

CHICKEN OR TURKEY SPREAD

Chop or mince cooked chicken or turkey. Moisten with mayonnaise. Add finely chopped celery or almonds. Season to taste. Garnish with watercress.

CURRIED CHICKEN SPREAD

6 ounces finely chopped cooked
**   chicken and giblets**
2 ounces chopped browned almonds
1 teaspoon grated onion
¼ teaspoon curry powder
About 4 tablespoons mayonnaise

Mix ingredients thoroughly; using just enough mayonnaise to moisten spread.

HAM-CHEESE-PINEAPPLE SPREAD

Combine equal parts of finely minced cooked ham, cream cheese, and drained crushed pineapple.

LIVER SAUSAGE PINEAPPLE

This is a popular centrepiece for a buffet spread. Use 1½ to 2 pounds cold, firm liver sausage. Remove covering and mould it into shape like a fresh pineapple.

Spread surface with a little soft butter or brush with lemon juice. Cover surface with slices of stuffed olive to resemble "eyes" of pineapple.

If desired, top with 3 or 4 spring onions or leaves from fresh pineapple. Serve surrounded with savoury biscuits and potato chips.
Note: The Liver Sausage Pineapple may be wrapped in greaseproof paper or aluminium foil and stored in the refrigerator 2 to 3 days before serving.

HAM SPREAD

Moisten finely chopped cooked ham with mayonnaise. Add a little chopped dill or sweet pickle and pimiento. Season to taste with salt and pepper. Spread on bases and garnish with stuffed olive slices.

CRUNCHY HAM SPREAD

6 ounces finely chopped cooked
**   ham**
1 ounce chopped walnuts or almonds
2 tablespoons finely chopped celery
2 ounces chopped pineapple
Mayonnaise to moisten

Mix ingredients thoroughly.

DEVILLED HAM AND EGG SPREAD

2 ounces devilled ham
1 tablespoon finely chopped celery
1 hard-boiled egg, chopped
¼ teaspoon curry powder
½ teaspoon olive oil
Mayonnaise to moisten
Salt to taste

Mix ham, celery, and egg. Combine curry powder and olive oil. Add to ham mixture and moisten with mayonnaise. Add salt to taste.

HAM-CHICKEN-OLIVE SPREAD

3 ounces chopped cooked ham
3 ounces chopped cooked chicken
8 green olives, chopped
Mayonnaise to moisten

Mix ingredients thoroughly.

CHICKEN LIVER AND EGG SPREAD

Mix 3 ounces chopped, cooked chicken livers and 2 hard-boiled eggs, chopped. Season with 1 teaspoon finely chopped onion and salt and pepper to taste. Moisten with cream.

DEVILLED HAM AND CHEESE SPREAD

Combine 6 ounces devilled ham with 2 ounces pimiento cheese spread and 2 tablespoons chopped sweet pickle. Moisten with mayonnaise.

DEVILLED HAM AND EGG SPREAD

Mix devilled ham and chopped hard-boiled egg; season with horseradish. Spread on canapé base and garnish with watercress.

ROAST BEEF OR VEAL SPREAD

Moisten finely minced cooked meat with mixture of horseradish and mayonnaise. Season to taste.

CHOPPED CHICKEN OR CALVES' LIVER

½ pound chicken or calves' liver
1 or 2 hard-boiled eggs
½ small onion
2 ounces finely chopped celery,
**   optional**
Salt and pepper

Lightly fry the chicken livers in a little chicken fat or butter.

Chop together with the other ingredients until fine. Season to taste with salt and pepper.

Moisten with melted chicken fat or butter.

A tray of "self-service" spreads with a variety of breads, biscuits, and vegetable hors d'oeuvres simplifies service.

BEEF OR STEAK TARTARE

2 pounds raw finely minced, fresh
    lean steak
2 raw egg yolks
1 medium onion, finely chopped
4 anchovies, mashed
Finely chopped watercress, parsley,
    or other desired herbs
Salt and pepper, to taste
Worcestershire sauce, to taste
Capers, to taste

Combine steak, egg yolks, onion, and anchovies. Add watercress or parsley, salt, pepper, Worcestershire sauce, and capers to taste.

Serve in a mound as an hors d'oeuvre with squares of pumpernickel or rye bread. Or shape the mixture into small balls and roll in chopped parsley.
Note: The same beef mixture may be served as a main dish.

LIVERWURST AND BACON SPREAD

Chop cold crisp bacon very finely. Combine 1 part bacon with 3 parts liverwurst.

Season with salt, pepper, Worcestershire, and Tabasco sauce to taste.

SPICY SNACKING TREE

3 hard-boiled eggs
2 4½-ounce cans devilled ham
1 tablespoon grated onion
¼ teaspoon Tabasco sauce
1 teaspoon Worcestershire sauce
1 3-ounce packet cream cheese,
    softened
Chopped chives
Pimiento

Chop hard-boiled eggs. Combine with devilled ham, grated onion, Tabasco, and Worcestershire. Chill.

Shape into tree form. Decorate around the edge of the tree with softened cream cheese, then top edging with chopped chives. Cover "tree trunk" with pimiento. Serve with assorted crackers and toast rounds. Serves 20 to 30.

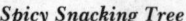

Spicy Snacking Tree

HAM HOURGLASS

1 pound minced cooked ham
3 ounces raisins
1 medium onion, shredded
½ teaspoon curry powder
9 tablespoons mayonnaise
2 3-ounce packets cream cheese,
    softened
2 tablespoons milk
2 tablespoons pimiento, chopped
2 tablespoons black olives, chopped

In a bowl thoroughly blend ham, raisins, onion, curry powder, and mayonnaise. Shape mixture into an hourglass, approximately 10 inches long on a tray. Chill.

Blend softened cream cheese and milk. Cover ham mixture with the cream cheese mixture. Make sand effect with chopped pimiento and black olives. Make frame of hourglass using assorted crackers.

HAM AND ONION CANAPÉS

6 ounces minced cooked ham
1 sweet red onion
1 tablespoon sour cream
1 tablespoon mayonnaise
Freshly ground pepper
Toasted canapé bases

Mince the ham with medium-sized onion and make a light smooth spread with the other ingredients. Spread on small pieces of buttered toast.

SALAMI AND EGG CANAPÉS

8 ounces hard salami
3 hard-boiled eggs
7 tablespoons salad dressing
Bread, sliced thin

Put salami and hard-boiled eggs through mincer 2 or 3 times, or chop finely. Blend with salad dressing.

Trim crust from bread and cut into small squares. Toast on one side. Spread untoasted side with salami mixture. Sprinkle with chopped parsley and garnish with pimiento strips.

CHOPPED LIVER AND MUSHROOMS

8 ounces chicken or calves' liver
1 ounce sliced raw mushrooms
1½ ounces chicken fat or butter
Salt and pepper
Onion juice

Lightly fry the liver in a little fat, then remove and fry the mushrooms in the same fat for about 5 minutes.

Chop liver and mushrooms finely and add the fat in which they were fried. Season to taste with salt, pepper, and onion juice.

Moisten, if necessary, with a little additional melted chicken fat or butter.

Ham Hourglass: A tasty spread for a New Year's party is this combination of ham, raisins, and curry powder shaped into an hourglass and covered with cream cheese.

BAKED BEAN AND FRANKFURTER CANAPÉS

Mash baked beans and spread on toasted canapé bases. Garnish with slices of frankfurters and stuffed olives.

PARSLEY ROUNDS

Spread edges of toast rounds with softened butter; roll in chopped parsley.

Combine chopped cooked chicken or flaked tuna fish with butter, onion juice, salt, and pepper. Spread on toast.

BACON AND TOMATO CANAPÉS

Toast rounds of bread the size of tomato slices. Spread with crisp, chopped bacon blended with mayonnaise.

Top with very thin tomato slice, cucumber slice, and stuffed-olive slice.

HAM AND EGG CANAPÉS

Combine yolks of 2 hard-boiled eggs, ½ teaspoon dry mustard, 1 teaspoon mayonnaise, and 1½ tablespoons devilled ham. Mix until smooth.

Spread on rounds of rye bread. Top with ring slices of hard-boiled egg white. Sprinkle with paprika.

HAM AND CHEESE SPREAD

6 ounces finely chopped cooked ham
1 ounce Cheddar cheese, grated
½ teaspoon finely chopped onion
1 teaspoon chilli sauce or
    tomato ketchup
Mix ingredients thoroughly.

LIVERWURST AND ONION CANAPÉS

Spread very thin slices of mild onion with liverwurst which has been mashed and moistened with mayonnaise.

Place on toast rounds. Garnish edges with sieved hard-boiled egg.

HAM AND RELISH SPREAD

Combine 6 ounces minced cooked ham and 4 tablespoons pepper relish.

Fruit and Vegetable Hors d'Oeuvres

Many raw fresh vegetables are delicious appetizers. Some of the best are carrots, cauliflower, celery, cucumber, spring onions, tiny whole tomatoes, and turnips. They must be of top quality. Cut the vegetables in small, attractive pieces or slices and have them crisp and well-chilled. Provide salt for those who prefer to eat them without sauce. Some cooked vegetables are also excellent, especially cooked or canned artichoke hearts and asparagus tips. Drain these and marinate in French dressing.

STUFFED BRUSSELS SPROUTS

Drain cooked Brussels sprouts. Cut out centres and stuff with favourite canapé spread to which may be added the chopped centres of sprouts.

BEETROOTS

Use tiny canned beetroots, plain or pickled. Provide a bowl of sour cream for dipping.

CARROT STICKS

Carrot sticks, if they are crisp, make an excellent appetizer by themselves, or accompanied by a dip.

CAULIFLOWERETS

Break cauliflower into small flowerets. Crisp in iced water. Drain and sprinkle with paprika.

Or, pre-cook flowerets for just a few minutes, then marinate in sharp French dressing until serving time.

MARINATED CELERIAC

Chill cooked celery root or celeriac and cut into oblongs. Marinate in French dressing for several hours.

STUFFED MUSHROOM CAPS

Wash and drain small fresh mushroom caps. Fry gently in a little butter until tender. Remove while still firm, drain on paper towels, chill and fill with chosen filling.

SHERRIED MUSHROOMS

Use small mushrooms. Remove skin and stems. Cover with sherry and soak several hours.

Drain and fill with Roquefort cheese or caviar. Serve each on a cocktail stick.

STUFFED TOMATO SLICES

Cut medium-sized tomatoes in eighths and cut out centres, leaving ½-inch thick piece.

Chop 2 hard-boiled eggs finely; add ½ teaspoon salt, a little finely chopped celery, 1 tablespoon mayonnaise, and 1 teaspoon mustard-with-horseradish. Fill the tomato boats and garnish with parsley.

PICKLED COCKTAIL MUSHROOMS

About 8 ounces canned button mushrooms
8 fluid ounces white wine or cider vinegar
1 tablespoon sugar
1 teaspoon salt
1 shredded bay leaf
3 cloves
3 whole black peppercorns
1 clove garlic, sliced
1 slice lemon

Combine vinegar, seasonings, and mushroom liquid. Boil 3 to 4 minutes. Add mushrooms. Turn into a jar and let stand overnight.

Letting them stand from 1 to 2 weeks will improve the flavour. Serve whole on sticks or chop and use as a canapé spread.

STUFFED RAW CARROTS

Make raw carrots into cylinders by hollowing out centres with an apple corer.

Or raw carrots may be shaped into troughs or cones hollowed for fillings.

STUFFED PLUM TOMATOES

Select firm cherry or plum tomatoes. Cut out centres and stuff with a favourite fish, seafood, or meat mixture.

GARLIC OLIVES

Drain green or black olives; place in a bowl. Add 6 to 12 peeled cloves of garlic. Cover with salad oil. Cover and store in refrigerator for 24 hours.

Drain and use the oil for salad dressing. Sprinkle the olives with chopped parsley.

STUFFED RADISHES

Hollow out good-sized radishes with a small sharp-pointed knife. Crisp in iced water.

Stuff with a mixture of caviar, finely chopped parsley, mayonnaise, lemon juice, and onion juice, seasoned to taste. Or fill with softened cheese.

STUFFED CUCUMBER

Remove centre of peeled cucumber with vegetable corer.

Stuff with a mixture of 4 ounces flaked tuna fish or salmon, 2 tablespoons mayonnaise, ½ teaspoon each of onion and lemon juice, a dash of Worcestershire sauce, and salt and pepper to taste.

Chill and cut into ½-inch slices.

GHERKIN FANS

Slice gherkins to within ½ inch of top. Spread the finger-like slices fan shape. This can also be done with half a gherkin cut lengthwise.

Vegetable Hors d'Oeuvres with Dipping Sauce.

CUCUMBER SLICES

Peel cucumber. Score it by running a fork lengthwise down the surface of the cucumber. Cut into very thin slices. Chill in a tray of ice. Drain and sprinkle lightly with chopped parsley.

When skin is tender, score without peeling and slice, thus adding a touch of colour.

CUCUMBER STICKS

Peel cucumber. Cut in half. Remove seeds. Cut solid part into narrow strips about 3 inches long.

Cover with damp cloth. Chill well before serving. Sprinkle with paprika.

MARINATED ONIONS

Skin and slice Spanish onions. Soak in a brine made of 10 fluid ounces water to 1 tablespoon salt. Drain and soak in vinegar for 20 to 30 minutes. Drain again. Chill thoroughly.

CUCUMBER CUPS

Scoop out centres of 2-inch lengths of cucumbers. Fill with a mixture of 4 ounces flaked tuna fish, 1 tablespoon chopped sweet pickle, 1 tablespoon lemon juice, ½ teaspoon onion juice, and salt and pepper to taste. Chill.

Serve garnished with slices of stuffed olives.

ITALIAN OLIVE MIXTURE

8 ounces green olives
8 ounces black olives
3 stalks celery, chopped
1 green pepper, chopped
1 red pepper, chopped
1 clove garlic, crushed
4 fluid ounces olive oil
4 fluid ounces vinegar
Black pepper, to taste
Oregano, to taste

Crack the olives with a hammer until the stones show. Combine with remaining ingredients. Let stand at room temperature 2 days. Store in refrigerator in sealed, sterilized jars. Serves 8 to 10.

STUFFED CELERY

Use only the tender white stalks showing no discolouration. The inside stalks are preferable.

Wash and leave tips of leaves on stalks or remove leaves from coarser stalks. Crisp in iced water. Dry on paper towels before stuffing.

Use a pastry tube or a knife and fill grooves with one of the following fillings.

Garnish with chopped parsley, green pepper, chives, pimiento, or a dash of paprika. Chill before serving.

STUFFED CELERY FILLINGS

Almond-Cream Cheese Filling: Combine 1 ounce finely chopped almonds, 1 3-ounce packet cream cheese, ¼ teaspoon chilli sauce, ¾ teaspoon curry powder, and a dash of salt.

Avocado Filling: Mash ripe avocado pulp. Sprinkle with lemon juice. Season to taste with salt and pepper. If desired, mix with finely chopped olives. Moisten slightly with mayonnaise.

Stuff and garnish with bits of pimiento.

Avocado-Roquefort Filling: Mash avocado pulp. Combine with Roquefort or other blue cheese and make a smooth paste, adding lemon juice and onion juice to taste.

Stuff and garnish with bits of pimiento.

Chicken-Cream Cheese Filling: Blend 6 ounces minced cooked white chicken meat, 1 3-ounce packet cream cheese, 2 tablespoons lemon juice, ½ teaspoon salt, and a few grains cayenne pepper.

Clam-Cream Cheese Filling: Drain 1 small can minced clams (about 7-ounce size) and combine with 1 3-ounce packet cream cheese, 1 tablespoon lemon juice, and 3 tablespoons butter. Chill slightly before filling celery stalks.

Cottage Cheese Filling: Season cheese with salt, and spread into grooves. Garnish with thin slices of radish with red edge showing.

Cottage Cheese Filling 2: Mix creamy cottage cheese with chopped sweet pickles, minced pimiento, or chopped chives.

Snappy Cheese Filling: Combine 2 ounces grated cheese, 1½ teaspoons mustard-with-horseradish, 1½ teaspoons mayonnaise, and a pinch of paprika. Press firmly into celery stalks. Sprinkle with paprika.

Crabmeat-Cream Cheese Filling: Remove cartilage from 1 6-ounce can crabmeat. Mash and combine with 1 3-ounce packet cream cheese, adding just enough sherry to bind mixture. Season to taste.

Cream Cheese Filling: Mix cream cheese with finely chopped nuts. Spread in celery grooves.

Or mix cheese with finely chopped, stuffed olives.

Cream Cheese Filling 2: Season cream cheese with prepared horseradish.

Egg Filling: Chop hard-boiled eggs fine. Moisten with mayonnaise. Season with salt and pepper. Stuff, and sprinkle with paprika or finely chopped parsley.

Devilled Ham Filling: Combine devilled ham, cream cheese, and mayonnaise to taste. Season with prepared mustard and horseradish.

Pimiento Cheese Filling: Blend pimiento cheese with chopped crisp bacon and chopped sweet pickle.

Roquefort Filling: Combine Roquefort or other blue cheese with a little butter or cream cheese. Season with grated onion.

Seafood Filling: Combine crabmeat, tuna fish, or other flaked, cooked, or canned seafood with a little lemon juice to flavour and mayonnaise to moisten.

Stuffed Celery with Sardines: Stuff lengths of celery cut to sardine size with cream cheese blended with a little onion juice and parsley.

Lay a whole sardine (small one) on each stuffed celery stalk and garnish with a strip of pimiento.

Stuffed celery and devilled eggs are always a treat. Put your imagination to work on fillings; their variety is infinite.

Celery Pinwheels

CELERY PINWHEELS

Blend cream cheese with Roquefort-type cheese. Add mayonnaise or cream until firm spreading consistency. Season with Worcestershire sauce.

Separate stalks of celery. Wash and dry. Fill stalks with cheese mixture and press stalks back into original form of the bunch.

Roll in waxed paper and leave overnight in refrigerator. Just before serving, slice celery crosswise forming pinwheels. Arrange on chilled Webb's Wonder lettuce cups. Two or 3 slices make 1 serving.

STUFFED PEPPER SLICES

Select long thin peppers in a variety of shades of green and red. Remove seeds and stuff so that all corners are filled with a seasoned cream cheese mixture. Chill 2 to 3 hours.

To serve, cut with a very sharp knife into ⅓-inch slices.

STUFFED ARTICHOKE HEARTS

Remove centres from drained canned artichoke hearts leaving ⅛ inch wall.

Chop centres and add equal amount of chopped pimiento and ½ quantity chopped browned almonds or peanuts. Fill artichoke hearts.

AVOCADO SPREAD

Peel avocados and mash pulp with a fork. Season with lemon or lime juice and salt. Spread on canapé bases.

Garnish with finely chopped parsley and strips of green pepper.

GREEN PEPPER AND EGG SPREAD

Mix finely chopped green pepper and finely chopped hard-boiled egg. Moisten with mayonnaise.

Season to taste with salt, pepper, and a tiny bit of dry mustard.

SPICED PINEAPPLE

Sauté pineapple chunks in a little butter or margarine.

Sprinkle with brown sugar, spices, and a dash of vinegar. Stir gently until glazed.

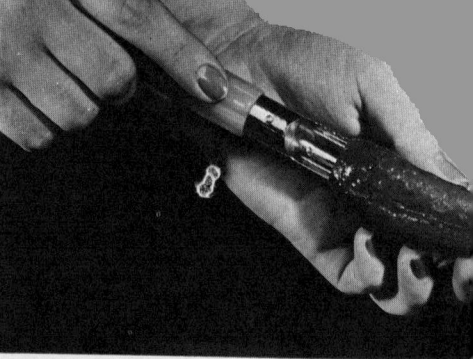

AUBERGINE "CAVIAR"

1 medium-sized aubergine
2 small onions, finely chopped
2 cloves, finely chopped
1 clove garlic, finely chopped
1 ripe tomato, peeled and chopped
Salt and pepper
Vinegar
Olive oil

Grill the whole aubergine over direct flame, or under a grill for 15 to 20 minutes, turning to cook evenly on all sides. Test with a fine skewer to see if it is soft all through.

Remove the skin and mash the pulp; mix with the onions, cloves, and garlic. Add the tomato, and season to taste with salt, pepper, vinegar, and oil.

Serve on lettuce, garnished with quartered tomatoes and black olives or use as a canapé spread.

STUFFED PRUNES

Stuff steamed or soaked plump prunes with a mixture of highly seasoned cream cheese or other suggested fillings.

1. Cottage cheese seasoned with chilli sauce.
2. Very crisp chopped celery.
3. Anchovy, shrimp, salmon, tuna fish, or sardine canapé fillings.
4. Roquefort cheese softened with cream.
5. Roquefort moistened with mayonnaise.
6. Mature Cheddar cheese finely grated and mixed with softened cream.
7. Cream cheese and chopped chives.
8. Finely chopped ham, seasoned with prepared mustard, finely chopped pickle, moistened with mayonnaise.
9. Cream cheese and chopped nuts, moistened with pineapple juice.

MILWAUKEE CANAPÉS

8 ounces well-drained sauerkraut
9 tablespoons mayonnaise
Rounds of rye bread
Stuffed olives

Chop sauerkraut very fine and mix with 1 tablespoon mayonnaise.

Spread on rye bread rounds which have already been spread with remaining mayonnaise. Garnish with sliced olives.

TOMATO-EGG CANAPÉS

3 slices peeled tomato, chopped
1 hard-boiled egg, chopped
2 tablespoons finely chopped pickle
2 tablespoons finely chopped onion
Pinch of salt
Dash of pepper
1 ounce softened butter

Combine ingredients and use as spread for toasted bread canapés or crackers.

STUFFED DILL PICKLE SLICES

Remove centres from dill pickles with a vegetable corer.

Stuff pickles with a flavoured cheese spread, well-seasoned minced cooked meat, mock pâté de foie gras, devilled ham, or liver sausage.

Chill thoroughly and cut them crosswise into ⅓-inch slices.

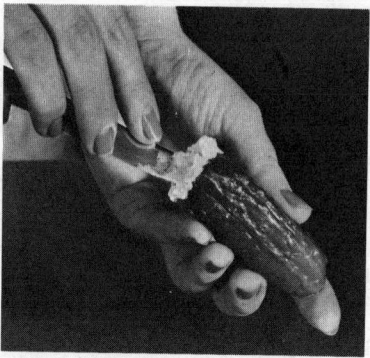

ONION AND EGG SPREAD

Combine 1 finely chopped medium-sized mild onion and 1 finely chopped hard-boiled egg. Moisten with about 4 tablespoons melted chicken fat. Season with salt and pepper to taste.

Serve on crackers or squares of dark rye or pumpernickel bread.

SPRING ONION AND BUTTER SPREAD

Cream 4 ounces butter or margarine until soft. Add a bunch of spring onions, finely chopped, and beat with a rotary beater until light and fluffy.

Store in covered jar in refrigerator.

WATERCRESS SPREAD

Combine ½ bunch watercress, chopped, 3 tablespoons cream cheese, ½ teaspoon Worcestershire sauce, 1 tablespoon French dressing, and salt and pepper to taste.

Spread on crackers or potato crisps.

STRAWBERRIES

Serve whole, perfect strawberries with the stems on, arranging them around a bowl of sour cream.

AVOCADO-CREAM CHEESE SPREAD

3 3-ounce packets cream cheese
4 fluid ounces single cream
1 large avocado, peeled, stoned, and mashed
1½ teaspoons lemon juice
1½ teaspoons onion juice
1 teaspoon salt

Avocado pulp and cream cheese should be about equal in amount. Soften cream cheese with cream. Blend with remaining ingredients. Chill thoroughly.

PIMIENTO ROLLS

Drain pimientos on paper towels and use as a base for filling. Roll and fasten with cocktail sticks.

Chill, then slice into bite-size portions.

WHOLE RADISHES

Select firm red radishes. Wash and scrub thoroughly. Leave enough stem on to serve as a handle.

Wrap in damp cloth. Chill thoroughly in refrigerator.

ASPARAGUS ROLL CANAPÉS

Roll tiny canned asparagus tips in thinly sliced boiled ham.

Serve on toasted canapé bases which have been spread with mustard butter.

MUSHROOM SPREAD

Wash and chop or mince mushrooms finely. Fry lightly in butter for 5 minutes. Cool and season to taste with lemon juice, salt, and pepper.

SURPRISE RADISHES

Cut small radishes in half lengthwise. Put together with cheese spread. Chill.

It's nice to let a bit of the stem and leaves remain on each radish.

MUSHROOMS WITH PÂTÉ

Sauté mushrooms in butter. Cool and fill caps with pâté de foie gras. Chill and serve on crisp crackers.

OLIVES IN FRENCH DRESSING

Place green or black olives in a bowl. Cover with a well-seasoned French dressing to which a cut clove of garlic has been added.

Let stand several hours or overnight in a cold place. Drain and serve.

Cold Skewered Tidbits

The hostess can place cocktail sticks in the food before the party begins or leave the guests to do it as they serve themselves. In the latter case, place the sticks in small glasses and arrange them in convenient places. The thoughtful hostess also provides a receptacle for disposing of used sticks.

Sometimes edible sticks like raw carrot sticks or celery sticks may be used, in which case the hostess will make holes in the food cubes with a skewer, before stringing them.

PORCUPINE SERVERS FOR SNACKS ON STICKS

An attractive way to serve snacks on sticks that not only saves space but also creates colourful centrepieces for platters and trays is to use the wooden or metal figures made especially for this purpose and frequently referred to as "porcupine servers".

If you don't have any use a large grapefruit, a big red apple, a large orange, an aubergine, a cantaloupe or other melons. These may be left whole and studded with the snacks on sticks, porcupine fashion.

Some fruits such as melons, apples, grapefruit, and pineapples may be cut in halves, placed flat side down on the platters or trays and studded with the snacks on sticks. Seeds should, of course, be removed from melons. Or melons such as honeydew or cantaloupe may be placed cut side up, the centres filled with fruit balls or such snacks as ripe or stuffed olives, cheese balls, and radish roses, and the edges used for the hors d'oeuvres' base.

Any sort of sticks may be used but an assortment of coloured wooden or plastic sticks is most attractive. Surround the porcupine servers with assorted canapés.

Colourful cocktail sticks make for convenience in service and are appreciated by your guests.

BOLOGNA-CHEESE STACKS

4 tablespoons cream cheese
¼ teaspoon finely chopped onion
Pinch of salt
1 teaspoon horseradish
3 ¹⁄₁₆-inch thick slices large
**   bologna sausage**
2 ⅛-inch thick slices Cheddar cheese

Blend together first 4 ingredients. Alternate slices of sausage with Cheddar cheese, putting cream cheese mixture between slices; chill.

When cheese is firm, cut into strips, wedges, or cubes. Stick each with a cocktail stick.

HAM AND CHEESE STACKS

Have ham and Gruyère cheese cut into very thin slices. Cream butter with horseradish-mustard and curry powder to taste.

Spread a slice of ham with seasoned butter. Cover with slice of cheese. Spread with butter and continue in this way until stack is ½ inch thick.

Wrap tightly in greaseproof paper. Chill thoroughly. To serve, cut into cubes or small wedges. Place one cube and a tiny pickled onion on each stick.

STUFFED FRANKFURTERS

Cut frankfurters in half lengthwise. Spread cut surface of half the frankfurters generously with a cheese spread.

Top each spread half with an unspread half, pressing back into original shape. Scrape off excess cheese.

Wrap in greaseproof paper. Chill. Cut into ½-inch pieces and serve on cocktail sticks.

APPLES AND CHEESE

Cut firm red eating apples into ½ inch slices, after coring. Do not peel. Dip in orange juice to prevent darkening.

Spread with softened Roquefort or blue or other sharp cheese and cut into wedges. Spear each wedge with a stick.

ARTICHOKE HEARTS

Marinate tiny canned artichoke hearts in highly seasoned French dressing to which a clove of garlic has been added. Drain well.

HAM AND CHEESE

Alternate cubes of boiled ham and Gruyère or Cheddar cheese on sticks.

HAM AND MELON

Cut fresh cantaloupe or other melon into cubes. Dip in lemon juice. Spear each cube with a cube of ham or canned spiced meat.

SAUSAGE AND CHEESE

Spear short pieces of Vienna or other sausage and cubes of Cheddar or Gruyère cheese.

A grapefruit makes a handy porcupine server for nibblers on sticks.

CHEESE AND DILL PICKLE

Cut Cheddar cheese into ½-inch cubes. Put between 2 thin slices of dill pickle, and skewer with a stick.

SAUSAGE AND PICKLED BEETROOTS

Spear cubes of bologna or other sausage and cubes of pickled beetroots.

CHEESE AND PINEAPPLE

Spear a cube of fresh pineapple, then a cube of sharp Cheddar cheese and top with a cherry.

CHEESE STUFFED OLIVES

Fill large stoned olives with cream cheese spread. Serve on sticks.

ROAST BEEF AND CHUTNEY BALLS

Mix 6 ounces minced leftover roast beef with 4 tablespoons chutney, 1½ ounces ground almonds, ¼ teaspoon curry powder, and 1 to 2 tablespoons mayonnaise to bind.

Shape into balls and chill.

COTTAGE CHEESE BALLS

Mix dry cottage cheese with just enough milk or cream to form a smooth paste. Season with salt, pepper, and finely chopped onion.

Chill, then form into balls. Roll in chopped parsley.

HAM AND PEANUT BUTTER BALLS

Add enough peanut butter to 6 ounces minced cooked ham to give a good shaping consistency.

Form into small balls and roll in chopped fresh parsley. Chill thoroughly.

LIVER SAUSAGE BALLS

Mash liver sausage with a fork. Form into small balls. Roll in finely chopped parsley.

Or scoop about a heaped tablespoon of the mashed sausage onto palm of left hand. Pat to flatten, then place a stuffed olive or a piece of dill pickle in the centre. Roll into a ball to cover the olive or pickle. Roll in chopped parsley.

BACON-CELERY-CHEESE BALLS

Combine about 6 ounces crisp bacon broken into bits, with 2 ounces finely chopped celery, ½ medium-sized apple diced finely, and 1 3-ounce packet cream cheese. Add just enough mayonnaise to bind.

Shape into balls and roll in chopped walnuts.

HAM AND CREAM CHEESE BALLS

Combine 6 ounces minced cooked ham, 1 3-ounce packet cream cheese, 1 teaspoon prepared horseradish, ½ teaspoon prepared mustard, and just enough mayonnaise to bind if needed.

Form into small balls and roll in chopped fresh parsley. Chill thoroughly.

GREEN BALLS

2 ounces grated Gruyère cheese
3 ounces minced cooked ham
½ teaspoon prepared mustard
1 egg yolk
¼ teaspoon salt
Dash of pepper
Minced chives or parsley

Blend first 6 ingredients together and chill thoroughly. Form into balls and roll in finely chopped chives or parsley.

CHEESE-ONION BALLS

Blend 4 ounces grated Cheddar cheese with 2 tablespoons grated onion. Add enough thick sour cream to bind.

Shape into small balls. Roll in chopped parsley and chill thoroughly.

CHICKEN-CHEESE BALLS

Mash a small can (about 6-ounce size) chicken with 6 ounces grated Gruyère cheese and blend well. There is usually enough jelly in canned chicken to act as a binder.

Shape into small balls, then roll in chopped almonds. Chill thoroughly.

An attractive and easy cheese tidbit tray is made with coloured sticks, skewered stuffed olives and little white pearl onions, topping Cheddar cheese cubes.

LOBSTER TAIL PICK 'N' DIP

8 fluid ounces mayonnaise
1 tablespoon anchovy paste
½ teaspoon dry mustard
½ teaspoon Tabasco sauce
¼ teaspoon garlic salt
2 tablespoons tarragon vinegar
3 hard-boiled eggs, finely chopped
3 tablespoons finely chopped stuffed olives
3 tablespoons finely chopped gherkins
1 tablespoon chopped parsley
1 teaspoon finely chopped onion
2 12-ounce lobster tails

Blend mayonnaise, anchovy paste, mustard, Tabasco sauce, and garlic salt. Stir in vinegar. Add hard-boiled eggs, stuffed olives, gherkins, parsley, and onion. Mix well.

Boil lobster tails; remove meat, chill and cube, saving 1 shell to serve sauce in. Place a wooden stick in each cube and arrange around sauce-filled shell.

Decorate platter with watercress or parsley. Makes about 24 appetizers.

ROQUEFORT CHEESE BALLS

2 3-ounce packets cream cheese
2 ounces Roquefort cheese
2 tablespoons finely chopped celery
1 tablespoon finely chopped onion
Dash of cayenne
Salad dressing
1½ cups finely chopped walnuts

Blend cream and Roquefort cheeses. Add celery, onion, cayenne, and salad dressing. Chill, then form into small balls. Roll in nuts.

APPLE AND CHEESE BALLS

Peel large eating apples and with a vegetable ball scoop make as many small apple balls as possible. Soak the balls in lemon juice to keep from discolouring. Drain on paper towels.

Spread with a seasoned softened cheese moistened with mayonnaise to get a spreading consistency. Roll each cheese-spread ball in chopped nuts.

CREAM CHEESE-CARROT BALLS

Blend 1 3-ounce packet cream cheese with 2 ounces grated raw carrot, and a few grains cayenne pepper.

Shape into small balls. Roll in chopped parsley and chill thoroughly.

BURNING BUSH

Season 1 3-ounce packet of cream cheese with ½ teaspoon finely chopped onion. Chill, then form into balls. Roll in paprika.

CREAM CHEESE "STRAWBERRIES"

Form seasoned cream cheese to resemble strawberries in shape. Chill.

Dust with paprika. Stick pieces of parsley in the ends.

Lobster Tail Pick 'n' Dip: As appealing to your guests as a dish of candy to a child is this offering of chilled lobster tail with its spicy sauce.

LIVER SAUSAGE BALLS

8 ounces liver sausage
1 tablespoon finely chopped parsley
2 teaspoons grated onion
2 teaspoons celery seeds
½ teaspoon Worcestershire sauce
Finely grated raw carrot
36 to 40 pretzel sticks

Mash liver sausage; add parsley, onion, celery seeds, and Worcestershire sauce; mix well.

Form into 36 to 40 small balls. Roll in grated carrot. Insert pretzel sticks for handles.

TONGUE AND CHEESE STACKS

Spread 2 slices of smoked boiled tongue with cream cheese softened with cream. Stack together and top with an unspread slice of tongue.

Trim edges (use trimmings in spreads) and cut into cubes. Stick each with a cocktail stick.

SAUSAGE WITH PICKLED ONION

Spear cubes of chipolatas or cocktail sausages and top with pickled onion.

PICKLES IN BLANKETS

Roll thin slices of roast beef, tongue, smoked salmon, strips of anchovy, or strips of pickled herring around tiny sour-sweet or other gherkins. Secure the rolls with cocktail sticks.

WATERMELON PICKLE

Spear cubes of watermelon pickle on cocktail sticks with pieces of ham.

SALAMI AND OLIVES

Alternate bite-size cubes of salami or other sausage and olives on sticks.

CHEESE AND ONION

Place a ½-inch square of Cheddar cheese, a tiny slice of pickle, and a tiny pickled onion on each stick.

Miscellaneous Cold Hors d'Oeuvres

PRAWN RÉMOULADE

1 large clove garlic
3 tablespoons olive oil
1 tablespoon vinegar
⅛ teaspoon chilli sauce
3 tablespoons tomato ketchup
¼ teaspoon salt
Few grains of pepper
Pinch of paprika
½ teaspoon dry mustard
1½ teaspoons prepared horseradish
2 cans large prawns

Mince garlic very finely; add olive oil, vinegar, chilli sauce and seasoning; mix well.

Remove black vein from prawns. Add prawns to sauce. Let stand in refrigerator several hours.

Pierce prawns with cocktail sticks; remove from sauce and arrange on serving platter. Pour remaining sauce over prawns. Serves 8.

ROAST BEEF-COTTAGE CHEESE ROLLS

8 ounces cottage cheese
2 teaspoons finely chopped parsley
2 teaspoons prepared horseradish
Pinch of paprika
Mayonnaise
12 small cooked beef slices

Combine cottage cheese, parsley, horseradish, paprika, and mayonnaise.

Spread on beef slices and roll. Fasten with sticks. Chill thoroughly.

PARSLEY ROLLS

White bread, fresh
Olive-pimiento cheese spread
Parsley

Cut the bread in thin slices; trim the crusts and spread each slice with the cheese spread softened at room temperature.

Roll up each slice and garnish the ends with small sprigs of parsley.

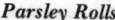

Parsley Rolls

PICKLE-FILLED HAM ROLLS

About 4½ ounces liver pâté
2 tablespoons mayonnaise
2 teaspoons prepared mustard
¼ teaspoon salt
6 slices boiled ham, cut ⅛-inch thick
2 large dill pickles

Combine liver pâté, mayonnaise, mustard, and salt; blend well. Spread each ham slice with part of liver mixture.

Cut pickles in thirds, lengthwise, and place a pickle strip crosswise on the end of each ham slice.

Roll up each slice crosswise starting from the pickle end. Fasten with sticks. Chill thoroughly. Cut in halves and serve as finger food. Makes 12.

GLAZED COCKTAIL PRAWNS

1 8-ounce can tomatoes
6 tablespoons water
2 tablespoons chopped celery
1 carrot, sliced
1 tablespoon chopped green pepper
1 whole clove
¼ teaspoon salt
Pinch of pepper
¾ tablespoon gelatine
1½ teaspoons lemon juice
1 pound fresh cooked, cleaned prawns, chilled

Put tomatoes and 4 tablespoons water in saucepan. Add vegetables and seasoning and bring to boiling point on high heat. Reduce heat and cook 15 minutes; strain.

Soften gelatine in 2 tablespoons cold water 5 minutes. Add to hot tomato juice and stir until gelatine is dissolved. Stir in lemon juice. Chill in refrigerator until of syrupy consistency.

Dip cold prawns in gelatine mixture. Drain on cake rack and chill. Repeat several times to build up heavy coating of aspic on prawns.

SALAMI CORNUCOPIAS

Spread thinly sliced salami with mustard. Roll into cornucopias and fasten with cocktail sticks.

Serve plain or place a small pickle, a stuffed olive, or a small ball of cream cheese mixed with chopped chives in the centre as a filling, or roll each round a few stalks of watercress.

HAM AND ASPARAGUS ROLLS

Spread small strips of thinly sliced boiled or baked ham with mayonnaise seasoned with mustard.

Roll each prepared ham slice around a cooked or canned asparagus tip. Fasten with a cocktail stick.

Or marinate asparagus tips in French dressing before rolling them in the ham slices.

Pickle-filled Ham Rolls

CHEESE "CARROTS"

1 3-ounce packet cream cheese
1½ ounces grated carrot
¼ teaspoon salt
Dash of cayenne
4 drops Worcestershire sauce
1 tablespoon chopped chives or onion
Sprigs of parsley

Mix cream cheese and carrot; season with salt, cayenne, Worcestershire sauce, and chives. Roll into miniature carrot shapes. Chill until firm.

Stick a tiny sprig of parsley into each "carrot" to resemble tops.

CHEESE "CARROTS" 2

1 teaspoon gelatine
2 tablespoons cold water
4 ounces smoked cheese spread
¼ teaspoon Worcestershire sauce
2 medium-sized carrots, grated
Parsley

Soften gelatine in cold water 5 minutes. Melt over hot water. Cool slightly. Blend with cheese and Worcestershire sauce.

Place in refrigerator until of pliable consistency. Divide into 1 teaspoon portions. Shape into cones.

Roll in grated carrots, and stick sprig of parsley in large end to represent carrot top.

HAM ROLLS

Spread thin slices of ham with cottage cheese mixed with piccalilli; roll up tightly and spear with cocktail sticks.

ROQUEFORT LETTUCE ROLLS

Mix and cream well 3 parts Roquefort cheese with 1 part cream cheese. Chill.

Wrap small portions in small, crisp lettuce leaves. Fasten with sticks.

CHICKEN ROLLS

Soften cream cheese with brandy and season with salt. Spread on thin slices of chicken meat and roll. Fasten with cocktail sticks and chill.

SMOKED SALMON-CAVIAR CORNUCOPIAS

Roll thin slices of smoked salmon into cone shape. Fasten with sticks.

Fill each with caviar seasoned with lemon juice, or caviar mixed with shredded hard-boiled eggs seasoned with lemon juice and paprika.

CHEESE AND PRETZELS

Form small balls from tasty cheese. Place a cheese ball at each end of a small pretzel stick.

HAM PINWHEELS

3 slices boiled ham
2 tablespoons olive-pimiento cheese spread
About 12 small stuffed olives

Spread each slice of ham with 2 teaspoons cheese spread. Cut into ¾-inch strips. Place an olive at end of each strip and roll. Secure with stick and chill.

When cheese is firm, remove sticks and cut each roll in half to form 2 pinwheels. Serve with cut side up.

MELON AND HAM ROLLS

Wrap small chilled wedges of honeydew melon with very thin slices of Italian prosciutto ham. Fasten with cocktail sticks.

CHEESE-BOLOGNA ROLLS

2 ounces Cheddar cheese
½ ounce softened butter
1 large stuffed olive, chopped fine
6 slices large bologna sausage
4 large stuffed olives, cut into lengthwise strips

Cream the cheese and butter together. Stir in chopped olive. Spread each round of sausage with 2½ teaspoons of cheese mixture.

Cut rounds crosswise into 4 triangular parts. Beginning at point of triangle, roll and secure with stick. Garnish ends of roll with slice of olive. Chill.

HAM STICKS

Spread ham with prepared mustard. Wrap around bread sticks allowing 1 inch of bread stick to be free as a handle.

QUICK SNACK TRAY

To make gay pinwheels, just spread slices of boiled ham with pasteurized processed cheese spread; roll up Swiss roll fashion and chill well. Slice and serve on round savoury biscuits.

For ribbon loaf, spread 12 slices of processed Cheddar cheese with canned devilled ham and stack them up. Cut through the centre of the stack to make two "loaves". Chill well and slice off as needed. Serve with crackers.

LOBSTER TAIL, PAN AMERICAN STYLE

4 to 6 (6-ounce) lobster tails
8 fluid ounces tomato sauce
2 fluid ounces olive oil
2 tablespoons vinegar
2 tablespoons finely chopped onion
1 ounce finely chopped celery
8 stuffed olives, chopped
1 teaspoon salt
1 teaspoon aromatic bitters

Cook lobster tails as directed on packet, or see index. Drench with cold water, drain. Cut down both sides of undershell with kitchen scissors, peel off undershell. Insert thumb between shell and meat, gently pull meat from shell, in one piece. Reserve shells. Chill meat and cut in large cubes.

Mix tomato sauce with remaining ingredients. Add lobster meat and allow to marinate several hours. Serve in shells, with sticks, as appetizer.

Note: The lobster meat may be heated after marinating, and served as a main course with boiled rice. Serves 4 to 6.

ROAST BEEF PINWHEELS

Spread thin slices of roast beef with garlic butter. Roll each prepared slice, then wrap individual rolls in greaseproof paper.

Chill thoroughly and when ready to serve slice with a sharp knife into bite-size pinwheels. Spear each with a stick.

Variations: Use liver paste or Roquefort cheese thinned with butter instead of the garlic butter.

SMOKED SALMON ROLLS

Spread thin slices of smoked salmon with cream cheese seasoned with horseradish, salt, and black pepper. Roll carefully, skewering with sticks.

TONGUE-ASPARAGUS ROLLS

Season mayonnaise with dry mustard to taste. Spread on small slices of tongue or beef.

Roll each slice round an asparagus tip. Secure with a stick.

Lobster Tail, Pan American Style

SMOKED SALMON CORNUCOPIAS

12 thin slices smoked salmon
4 ounces cottage cheese
⅛ teaspoon onion juice
¼ teaspoon salt
Dash of pepper
Paprika
Watercress or parsley

Shape very thinly sliced smoked salmon into cornucopias; fasten with cocktail sticks.

Combine cheese, onion juice, salt, and pepper. Fill each cornucopia with some of the mixture.

Garnish with a dash of paprika, a sprig of parsley or watercress. Chill.

Variations: Salami or other sausage may be used instead of smoked salmon. Roquefort cream cheese, cream cheese seasoned with chopped chives, or well-seasoned chicken salad may be used as the filling.

CHEESE-FILLED HAM ROLLS

1 3-ounce packet cream cheese
6 chopped stuffed olives
1 teaspoon prepared horseradish
2 tablespoons cream
Salt and pepper
Boiled ham slices

Combine cheese, olives, horseradish, and cream; season to taste. Spread on slices of boiled ham. Roll and fasten with cocktail sticks.

Fish and Shellfish First Courses

HINTS ABOUT SEAFOOD COCKTAILS

Chilled crabmeat, lobster, prawns, tuna fish, etc. with a sharp cocktail sauce are always a perfect at-table beginning for a dinner. They are traditionally served in cocktail glasses, lined with lettuce. Other ways to serve them include the following:

1. Arrange seafood on small plates with a round lettuce leaf filled with cocktail sauce in centre of each plate.

2. Pile seafood in green pepper rings placed on small plates; cover with sauce.

3. Hollow out small tomatoes; place on beds of watercress or lettuce on small plates. Fill tomatoes with seafood which has been dipped into sauce.

OYSTER OR CLAM COCKTAIL

Drain small oysters or clams and chill thoroughly. Place 5 or 6 oysters in each lettuce-lined cocktail glass.

Cover with cocktail sauce. Serve with wedge of lemon.

LOBSTER COCKTAIL

Cut cooked or canned lobster in pieces. Serve in lettuce-lined cup with cocktail sauce or with very highly seasoned mayonnaise.

PRAWNS IN MUSTARD SAUCE
(Prawns New Orleans)

1½ pounds fresh prawns, cooked, or two 6½-ounce cans prawns
2 tablespoons vinegar
2½ fluid ounces salad oil
Salt and pepper
2 tablespoons prepared mustard
1 teaspoon paprika
2 spring onions with tops finely chopped
1 celery heart, finely chopped

Clean prawns, or drain canned ones. Combine remaining ingredients and pour over prawns. Toss lightly. Chill 2 hours.

Serve on shredded lettuce or in scallop shells. Serves 6.

LOBSTER TAIL COCKTAILS

4 small lobster tails, boiled
4 tablespoons tomato ketchup
2 tablespoons lemon juice
1 tablespoon vinegar
2 tablespoons mayonnaise
1 teaspoon prepared mustard
Pinch of celery salt
3 drops Tabasco sauce

Remove meat from cooked lobster tails. Chill, dice and refill individual shells.

Top with sauce made by combining remaining ingredients. Serve icy cold with lemon wedges. Serves 4.

PRAWN COCKTAIL

Clean fresh-cooked prawns, removing black line from back. Drain canned prawns. Chill.

Serve in lettuce-lined cocktail cups with cocktail sauce or with very highly seasoned mayonnaise. Finely chopped celery may be added.

CANNED CRABMEAT COCKTAIL

Flake canned crabmeat, remove bony tissue and combine with chopped celery. Chill. Serve in lettuce-lined cocktail glasses with cocktail sauce.

FRESH CRABMEAT COCKTAIL

Combine equal quantities cooked fresh crabmeat and Russian dressing. Toss well. Serve from salad bowl or in individual lettuce-lined cups.

SCALLOP COCKTAIL

Clean scallops and cook in boiling water until they begin to shrivel, about 5 minutes. Drain and chill.

Serve in lettuce-lined cocktail cups with desired sauce.

SEAFOOD AND AVOCADO COCKTAIL

Use half and half avocado cubes and pieces of tuna fish, lobster meat, crabmeat, prawns.

Serve in lettuce-lined cocktail cups with cocktail sauce.

SEAFOOD AND GRAPEFRUIT COCKTAIL

Arrange cooked, cleaned prawns, pieces of lobster meat, or chilled tiny oysters in alternate layers with grapefruit segments in lettuce-lined glasses.

Top with mayonnaise seasoned with lemon juice and Tabasco sauce.

Seafood Cocktails: If you like, combine two or more kinds of seafood such as canned or cooked crabmeat, lobster, or prawns in each seafood cocktail. Use 2-3 ounces of seafood for each serving. Mix with cocktail sauce or serve the sauce separately. Put the seafood on lettuce or watercress in chilled dessert glasses.

Lobster Tail Cocktails

STANDARD COCKTAIL SAUCE

9 tablespoons chilli sauce or tomato ketchup
1½ tablespoons lemon juice
1 tablespoon Worcestershire sauce
1 tablespoon prepared horseradish
Few drops of Tabasco sauce
¼ teaspoon salt
1 teaspoon grated onion

Mix ingredients and chill thoroughly. Yield: about 8 fluid ounces.

CREAM COCKTAIL SAUCE

2 tablespoons tarragon vinegar
1 teaspoon dry mustard
Juice of ½ lemon
1 teaspoon prepared horseradish
8 fluid ounces chilli sauce
4 fluid ounces double cream, whipped
1 tablespoon mayonnaise
½ teaspoon Worcestershire sauce

Mix the mustard in the vinegar. Add other ingredients and mix well. Yield: about 16 fluid ounces.

CELERY COCKTAIL SAUCE

9 tablespoons tomato ketchup
1½ tablespoons lemon juice
1 teaspoon Worcestershire sauce
1 ounce chopped celery
Dash each of salt and cayenne

Mix ingredients and chill thoroughly. Yield: about 8 fluid ounces.

COCKTAIL DRESSING

7 tablespoons mayonnaise
1 tablespoon lemon juice
1 tablespoon tomato ketchup
1 tablespoon horseradish
3 drops Worcestershire sauce
2 drops Tabasco sauce
Salt and paprika to taste

Mix ingredients and chill thoroughly. Yield: about 6 fluid ounces.

CURRY COCKTAIL DRESSING

8 fluid ounces mayonnaise
½ teaspoon curry powder
1 tablespoon finely chopped onion
2 tablespoons chutney
1 tablespoon lemon juice

Mix ingredients and chill thoroughly. Yield: about ½ pint.

Fruit Cocktails

Normandy Fruit Cocktail

HINTS ABOUT FRUIT CUPS

Simple combinations of fruit make excellent first courses for they stimulate the appetite. Mixtures of almost any fruits may be used, canned, fresh or frozen. Choose combinations that contrast in colour, texture, and taste; dice them in attractive sizes, not too small. Prepare them in advance and chill in the refrigerator so the flavours will mingle. If canned ready-mixed fruit cocktail is used, it is frequently advisable to add some fresh, slightly sour fruit to vary the texture and flavour.

Sweetening: Canned fruits are usually sweet enough without additional sweetening. If fresh, sour fruits are used a little thin sugar syrup may be added; however, appetizer fruit cups must never be too sweet. The addition of a little lemon or lime juice will usually improve a fruit cup, whether fresh or canned fruits are used.

A simple lemon sauce may be made by mixing lemon juice with icing sugar to the consistency of a sauce.

Sugar Syrup: Boil 8 ounces sugar and 4 fluid ounces water gently for 5 minutes. Cool and dilute with juices from canned or fresh fruits or berries. Lemon or orange juice may be added.

Colouring: For variety, the syrup may be delicately coloured with a little red or green food colouring. Or, add colour by using the syrup of maraschino or mint cherries or a little crème de menthe or grenadine syrup.

Garnishing: Fruit cups may be garnished with a sprig of mint, a red or green cherry, a whole strawberry, or a small scoop of water ice.

Crushed Mints: Crushed after-dinner mints are an interesting addition to some fruit cups, especially those made of citrus fruits and other sour combinations.

Preserved Ginger: With sour fruits try syrup from preserved ginger and chopped ginger. Use 1 tablespoon syrup and 1 tablespoon chopped ginger with 3 cups fruit mixture.

Wine Cocktail Sauce: Mix 4 ounces sugar, 6 fluid ounces sherry, and 2 tablespoons lemon juice or Madeira. Chill and serve with any fruit cocktail.

Serving Cups: Serve fruits in cocktail glasses, dessert glasses, glass bowls, or in shells from grapefruit, oranges, melons, or pineapples. When shells are used, part of the fruit removed from the shells should be one of the ingredients in the fruit cup mixture.

Ginger Ale Fruit Cup: Pour small amount of chilled ginger ale over any combination of canned fruits.

MELON BALL COCKTAILS

Cut balls from cantaloupe, honeydew, watermelon, or other melons, using melon-ball cutter or half-teaspoon measure.

Serve very cold, alone or in combination with other fruits. Sweeten to taste with thin sugar syrup.

HONEYDEW MELON COCKTAIL

Cook 4 ounces sugar and 6 fluid ounces water 5 minutes; cool and add 2 tablespoons each of lemon, lime and orange juice. Pour over chilled melon balls.

PEACH COCKTAIL

6 fresh peaches, peeled and diced
1 tablespoon lemon juice
2 tablespoons sugar
Chilled ginger ale
Fresh mint

Combine peaches, lemon juice, and sugar. Fill fruit cocktail glasses. Add 1 to 2 tablespoons ginger ale to each glass. Garnish with sprig of mint. Serves 4.

GRAPE-MELON COCKTAIL

Mix equal amounts seedless grapes, diced honeydew melon, and diced orange sections. Flavour with lemon juice. Sweeten with sugar.

CANTALOUPE SALAD COCKTAIL

1 cantaloupe
4 ounces honeydew melon cubes
2 fresh peaches, peeled and sliced
8 ounces white grapes, seeded and cut in halves
2 fluid ounces fruit French dressing

Have all ingredients thoroughly chilled. Peel cantaloupe and cut into 8 wedges. Combine remaining ingredients.

Arrange 2 cantaloupe wedges on each salad dish to form circle or oval. Fill centres with salad mixture. Serves 4.

FRUIT SORBET CUP

Fill dessert glass half full with combined diced orange and grapefruit sections. Top with scoop of lemon or other fruit sorbet. Arrange fruit sections around sorbet. Garnish with mint leaves.

PINEAPPLE BOATS

Trim ⅔ from leafy top of large pineapple and chill. Cut into 8 lengthwise wedges. Cut out cores. Peel off skin in one piece, leaving it in place.

Cut pulp downward into 5 or 6 slices, retaining shape. Serve each portion garnished with whole berries and icing sugar.

NORMANDY FRUIT COCKTAIL

4 ounces granulated sugar
¼ teaspoon ground cloves
4 fluid ounces water
6 fluid ounces port
4 ounces melon balls
8 ounces sliced, seeded white grapes
3 bananas, sliced

Combine sugar, cloves, and water and bring to a boil. Boil 5 minutes.

Cool; add port and pour over melon and grapes and place in refrigerator for several hours. Add bananas just before serving. Serves 4 to 5.

BANANA-ORANGE COCKTAIL

Cut ripe bananas into thin slices. Place in cocktail glasses and cover with chilled orange juice.

Decorate tops with orange sections. Sprinkle lightly with icing sugar. Garnish with a sprig of mint, a cherry, or a strawberry.

SEMI-TROPIC COCKTAIL

3 oranges, diced
8 ounces diced pineapple
3 bananas, diced
3 tablespoons icing sugar
4 ounces grated coconut
16 fluid ounces grape juice

Mix together the fruit, sugar, and coconut. Fill cocktail glasses about ⅔ full. Chill thoroughly.

When ready to serve, pour the chilled grape juice over each cocktail and garnish with pieces of candied orange peel or the grated rind of oranges. Serves 6.

FRESH PINEAPPLE COCKTAIL

1 fresh pineapple
8 ounces sugar
3 fluid ounces water
4 fluid ounces chilled orange juice
3 tablespoons lime juice

Peel, core, and dice the pineapple. Chill thoroughly. Combine sugar and water; boil 1 minute.

Chill syrup and add orange and lime juices. Place pineapple in cocktail glasses and pour syrup mixture over it. Serves 6.

These citrus fruit cups are made by combining fresh, frozen, or chilled grapefruit sections with sliced bananas and diced apple (leave red peel on for colour contrast); with finely cut dates and shredded coconut; with diced avocado and chopped pimiento (omit sugar); with sliced strawberries; with orange or lime sorbet.

GRAPEFRUIT IN COCKTAIL GLASSES

Allow one-half grapefruit per person. To remove whole segments, a very sharp knife is essential. Peel off the yellow skin, then peel off the white skin so that none shows on whole fruit.

Remove segments by cutting the first few from the outside toward the centre. The remainder are usually easy to remove by cutting from the core toward the edge.

Place grapefruit segments and juice in glasses and fill the glasses with a dessert wine, orange juice, or ginger ale.

STRAWBERRY COCKTAIL

Cover chilled hulled strawberries with chilled pineapple juice. Add, if desired, icing sugar.

Variation: Sprinkle strawberries with lemon juice and icing sugar. Garnish with mint leaves.

PINEAPPLE-MINT COCKTAIL

6 ounces canned pineapple cubes
8 ounces halved and seeded white grapes
8 fluid ounces ginger ale
2 ounces mild, white mints

Drain pineapple and add grapes, ginger ale, and mints. Chill thoroughly.

GRAPE-SHERRY COCKTAIL

Wash small white seedless grapes; remove stems and cut in halves. Place shaved ice in bottom of each dessert glass and fill with grapes.

Pour 3 tablespoons sherry on each serving. Serve at once.

Fruit in Orange or Grapefruit Shells: Orange or grapefruit shells filled with grapes, berries, or other assorted fruits make a colourful and refreshing first course appetizer, or arranged on a silver platter, a beautiful addition to your punch party table.

For the fluted shells, choose clean-skinned oranges and grapefruit. Halve the orange or grapefruit by making zigzag cuts to centre as shown in illustration. Separate the halves and remove fruit from shells.

GRAPE-FILLED AVOCADOS

1½ pounds seeded and halved red grapes
3 ripe avocados
Lemon juice
Madeira wine

Cut avocados in halves and remove stones. Rub avocados with lemon juice to prevent darkening. Chill thoroughly.

Fill avocado halves with grapes. Pour wine over. Serves 6.

AVOCADO COCKTAIL

4 avocados, cut into cubes or balls
4 tablespoons tomato ketchup
1 teaspoon prepared horseradish
1 teaspoon Worcestershire sauce
2 tablespoons lemon or lime juice
1 tablespoon mayonnaise
¼ teaspoon salt
Dash of Tabasco sauce

Arrange the avocado cubes or balls in cocktail glasses. Combine ketchup, horseradish, Worcestershire sauce, lemon or lime juice, mayonnaise, salt, and Tabasco sauce; blend and pour over fruit. Serve chilled. Serves 6.

Variations: Add half as much of any of the following as the amount of avocado used: asparagus tips; balls or cubes of cooked celeriac; diced tomato and cucumber; diced celery; seafoods such as lobster, prawns, tuna fish, salmon, and crab. Oysters require a very nippy sauce.

PINEAPPLE GRAPE FREEZE

2 ounces caster sugar
1 pint pineapple juice
1 egg white
12 ounces halved, seeded red grapes

Dissolve sugar in pineapple juice. Beat egg white until stiff and fold in. Pour into refrigerator freezing tray.

Freeze to mush-like consistency and fold in grapes. Serve immediately. Serves 6.

WATERMELON COCKTAIL

This is a good way to use the ends of watermelon. Make balls with melon-ball scoop, or cut in 1-inch cubes, removing seeds.

Sprinkle melon with lemon juice and caster sugar, using ½ tablespoon lemon juice and 1 tablespoon caster sugar for each portion. Cover and chill. Serve in cocktail glasses. Garnish with fresh mint.

BRAZILIAN GRAPEFRUIT COCKTAIL

Cut grapefruit into halves. Remove seeds and pulpy centre. With a sharp knife remove membrane between segments. Sprinkle tops with finely chopped Brazil nuts and finely cut fresh mint. Add light cover of caster sugar. Chill.

Just before serving, pour a teaspoonful of sherry in the centre of each half.

If the fresh mint cannot be obtained, take a little of the grapefruit juice which will form in the hollow of the fruit and flavour with a few drops of oil, or essence, of peppermint.

Pour this over the fruit before adding the caster sugar. Sherry may be omitted.

Deep-Fried Hot Appetizers

If you can solve the service problem and get this type of hors d'oeuvre to your guests while hot and just out of the fryer, nothing is more delicious. Consider the suggestions given in this chapter plus other dishes such as deep-fat fried prawns and other shellfish, bite-size croquettes, etc.

BATTER DIPPED HORS D'OEUVRES

Make fritter batter (see Index) and use as suggested below and for other simple batter-dipped deep-fried appetizers.

Cocktail Frankfurters: Dip cocktail frankfurters in batter; drain and fry in hot deep fat (375°F.) 2 to 3 minutes.

Corned Beef Fingers: Cut corned beef into finger length strips. Dip in batter; drain and fry in hot deep fat (375°F.) 2 to 3 minutes.

Chicken Livers: Prick chicken livers well with a fork. Dip in batter; drain and fry in hot deep fat (375°F.) 2 to 3 minutes.

Surprise Cheese Balls: Cut processed cheese into small cubes or roll small spoonfuls of ready-spread cheese into balls.

Spear each ball or cube with a wooden cocktail stick. Dip in batter. Fry in hot deep fat (375°F.) 2 to 3 minutes.

Pineapple Frank Kebobs: Alternate drained pineapple cubes and cocktail frankfurters on skewers.

Dip in batter; drain and fry in hot deep fat (375°F.) 2 to 3 minutes.

CHEESE BOURAG
(Armenian)

8 ounces plain flour
¼ teaspoon salt
3 teaspoons baking powder
1½ ounces unsalted butter
About 4 fluid ounces milk
8 ounces sharp cheese, grated
3 tablespoons finely chopped parsley
¼ teaspoon salt

Sift flour, salt, and baking powder together. Cut in butter with a round-bladed knife and mix to a dough with milk, handling as little as possible.

Roll out very thin on a floured board; cut into 2-inch squares.

Mix remaining ingredients together. Put squares together by pairs with tablespoon of cheese mixture between. Seal edges well by pressing with the prongs of a fork.

Fry until brown in deep hot fat (365° to 375°F.). Drain and serve.

TURKISH CHEESE APPETIZERS
(Beureks)

Cut 8 ounces Gruyère cheese into small pieces. Put into a saucepan with 2 fluid ounces thick white sauce. Stir until cheese is melted and mixture is thick.

Spread on a platter to cool. Chill in refrigerator if necessary. Shape into small sausage-like shapes.

Wrap each in a thin piece of short-crust pastry and fry in deep hot fat (385°F.) until golden brown. Drain. Serve hot or cold.

FRIED PARSLEY

1 egg yolk
4 fluid ounces milk
4 ounces plain flour
¼ teaspoon salt
Sprigs of parsley

Beat egg yolk; add milk, then add sifted flour and salt.

Dip sprigs of parsley in the batter and fry in hot deep fat (365°-375°F.) until crisp. Serve with a dip.

CHEESE AND NUT BALLS

2 teaspoons plain flour
Pinch of cayenne
¼ teaspoon salt
4 ounces Cheddar cheese, grated
1 egg white, stiffly beaten
1 ounce finely chopped nuts

Mix sifted flour, cayenne, salt, and grated cheese. Fold egg white lightly into cheese mixture until well blended. Form into small balls and roll in chopped nuts.

Fry in hot deep fat (375°F.) until golden brown. Drain on paper towels. Serve hot on cocktail sticks. Makes about 15 balls.

MEAT AND SAUERKRAUT BALLS
(German)

¼ pound lean ham
¼ pound lean pork
¼ pound corned beef
1 medium-sized onion
1 teaspoon finely chopped parsley
1½ ounces fat
8 ounces plain flour
1 teaspoon salt
1 teaspoon dry mustard
16 fluid ounces milk
2 pounds sauerkraut, cooked and drained
Flour
2 slightly beaten eggs
Dry breadcrumbs

Put ham, pork, corned beef, and onion through mincer, using medium blade. Add parsley and blend well.

Sauté in fat until browned. Add flour, salt, mustard, and milk. Blend thoroughly. Cook, stirring constantly, until thick.

Add sauerkraut and put entire mixture through mincer. Mix thoroughly.

Cook in frying pan, stirring constantly, until thick. Cool, then form into balls the size of a walnut.

Roll balls in flour. Dip in beaten egg. Roll in crumbs. Fry in deep fat (370°F.) until browned. Serve hot on sticks.

BEEF BURGUNDY BALLS

½ pound topside of beef, minced
1 egg
2 tablespoons plain flour
2 teaspoons finely chopped onion
¼ teaspoon Worcestershire sauce
1 tablespoon burgundy
Salt and pepper to taste

Combine all ingredients; mix well; form in small balls. Roll balls in fine dry breadcrumbs.

Fry in hot deep fat (375°F.) until brown. Drain. Serve hot on sticks.

A tray of hot hors d'oeuvres will be welcomed by your guests—try it and wait for the compliments.

FRIED RICE BALLS

Form 4 ounces of soft cheese into small balls not over a ½-inch in diameter. Spread lightly with a tangy prepared mustard.

Then roll each ball in salted, cooked rice. The rice should not be blanched or fluffed; kernels should stick together. Roll balls in hands to make them firm and compact.

Drop into hot deep fat (375°F.) and fry until golden brown. These may be reheated in the oven. Serve hot on sticks.

Variations:

1. Substitute cooked prawns for cheese.
2. Substitute ball of anchovy paste for cheese.
3. Substitute stuffed olive for cheese.

COD-POTATO BALLS

About 6 ounces salt cod
1 pound potatoes
¼ ounce butter
1 egg, well beaten
Pinch of pepper

Wash fish in cold water. Pick in very small pieces or cut, using scissors.

Wash, peel and soak potatoes, cutting in pieces of uniform size.

Cook fish and potatoes in boiling water to cover until potatoes are nearly soft.

Drain throughly through strainer and return to pan in which they were cooked. Shake over heat until thoroughly dry.

Mash thoroughly and add butter, egg, and pepper. Beat with fork 2 minutes. Add salt if necessary.

Take up by spoonfuls and sauté in butter or fry 1 minute in hot deep fat (385°F.) until brown. Drain on paper. Serve hot on sticks.

CAVIAR RISSOLES

Roll puff pastry ¼-inch thick and cut in small rounds. Place 1 teaspoon caviar, seasoned with lemon juice, in the centre of each.

Moisten edges and cover with a second round. Press edges together with the prongs of a fork.

Fry in hot deep fat (370°F.) 3 to 4 minutes, or until golden brown. Drain on paper towels.

SAUSAGE-POTATO BALLS

Form seasoned sausage meat in ¾-inch balls. Coat with mashed potatoes. Roll in beaten egg diluted with 1 tablespoon cold water, then in fine dry breadcrumbs.

Let stand for an hour to dry. Fry in hot deep fat (370°F.) until golden. Serve hot on sticks.

TUNA BALLS

2 7-ounce cans tuna fish
1 tablespoon flour
5 fluid ounces milk
1 teaspoon finely grated onion
½ teaspoon salt
Pinch of pepper
Few grains of cayenne
1 beaten egg

Drain and shred tuna fish, saving the oil. Heat 1 tablespoon of the tuna oil in a saucepan. Blend in flour until smooth.

Remove from heat and slowly add milk, stirring until well blended. Add onion, salt, pepper, and cayenne.

Return to heat and, stirring constantly, cook until smooth and thick. Remove from heat; add beaten egg and tuna fish.

Chill until firm then form into ¾-inch balls. Roll in flour.

Fry in hot deep fat (375°F.) until golden brown. Serve on sticks with a dipping sauce. Makes 30 to 36 balls.

CLAM CAKE HORS D'OEUVRES

8 ounces plain flour
1 teaspoon baking powder
½ teaspoon salt
2 eggs, well beaten
8 fluid ounces milk
4 fluid ounces clam liquid
4 cans clams
Deep fat for frying

Sift flour with baking powder and salt. Add well beaten eggs, milk, and clam liquid slowly; stir well and add drained clams which have been finely minced.

Drop by spoonfuls into hot deep fat (375°F.). When nicely browned, remove from pan and drain. Serve hot. Provide a dipping sauce.

CORNED BEEF BALLS

1 pound finely chopped corned beef
1 egg, slightly beaten
2 tablespoons tomato ketchup
About 1 tablespoon Worcestershire sauce

Mix ingredients and form into ¾-inch balls. Roll in fine dry bread or biscuit crumbs, then in a beaten egg diluted with 1 tablespoon cold water, and again in crumbs.

Fry in hot deep fat (375°F.) until golden brown. Serve hot on sticks with a dipping sauce. Makes about 36 to 40 balls.

Ham Balls: Use finely chopped cooked ham instead of corned beef.

SOYED CHICKEN LIVERS

Cut chicken livers into small strips. Dip in soy sauce then in a very light batter made of egg and flour. Fry in hot deep fat (375°F.).

OYSTER BALLS—FRENCH FRIED

1 pound oysters
1 teaspoon grated onion
1 teaspoon finely chopped parsley
¼ teaspoon salt
¼ teaspoon pepper
Dash of Tabasco sauce or cayenne
Pinch of mace
3 ounces fresh white breadcrumbs
2 eggs
1 ounce butter
Fine dry breadcrumbs

Pour 1 quart of boiling water over drained oysters then drain well and chop finely.

Season with onion, parsley, salt, pepper, cayenne, and mace.

Add fresh breadcrumbs and mix to stiff paste with 1 beaten egg and the butter. Form into small balls.

Roll in beaten egg, then in dry crumbs. Fry in hot deep fat (350°F.) until browned. Drain on absorbent paper. Serve hot on sticks.

CHEESE BISCUIT BALLS

Knead 4 ounces grated Cheddar cheese and ⅛ teaspoon cayenne pepper into 8 ounces scone dough.

Shape into tiny balls and fry in hot deep fat (365°F.) until lightly browned. Serve hot on sticks. Makes about 24.

CHEESE BALLS

Blend 6 ounces grated Cheddar cheese with ½ green pepper chopped very finely, and 1 beaten egg. Season with ¼ teaspoon salt.

Shape into small balls. Roll in biscuit crumbs or dry breadcrumbs. Fry in hot deep fat (365°F.).

CHEESE AND RICE BALLS

Mix 6 ounces grated Cheddar cheese, 2 ounces dry cooked cold rice, 2 egg whites, ¼ teaspoon cayenne pepper, and a pinch of salt.

Shape into 1-inch balls. Fry in hot deep fat (375°F.). Drain on absorbent paper.

The chafing dish is an invaluable aid for serving almost any hot hors d'oeuvre at any time.

Hot Cheese Appetizers

HAM-CHEESE CANAPÉS

4 ounces freshly grated Cheddar cheese
4 ounces finely chopped ham
2 tablespoons single cream
1 teaspoon prepared mustard
Dash of cayenne
¼ teaspoon Worcestershire sauce
Toasted bread bases
Grated Cheddar cheese

Combine cheese, ham, cream, and seasoning. Heat in top of double boiler until cheese melts.

Spread warm mixture on bases. Sprinkle with grated cheese. Grill lightly. Serve hot.

TOMATO-CHEESE CANAPÉS

Cut white bread into small rounds with pastry cutter. Toast on 1 side and butter untoasted side.

Cut slices of small firm tomatoes ¼-inch thick. Place tomato slices on buttered side. Season with salt and a speck of grated onion.

Pile grated Cheddar cheese on tomato and grill until cheese is melted. Serve hot.

AMERICAN CHEESE CANAPÉS

Spread toast fingers or squares with mustard butter. Spread with a mixture of equal parts of finely chopped parsley and finely chopped olives. Top each with a thin slice of Cheddar cheese.

Grill under moderate heat until cheese melts. Sprinkle with paprika and serve hot.

PARMESAN-ONION CANAPÉS

Make circles of crustless bread with a round pastry cutter. Blend grated Parmesan cheese and mayonnaise until the mixture is very thick. Place a paper-thin slice of onion on the bread circle.

Heap with the cheese-mayonnaise mixture. Dust with paprika. Place under the grill until the bread is toasted and the top is bubbly.

CREAM CHEESE PUFF CANAPÉS

1 3-ounce packet cream cheese
2 tablespoons mayonnaise
1 tablespoon finely chopped onion or other seasoning
2 tablespoons chopped nuts, optional

Soften cream cheese with mayonnaise and add seasoning and nuts. Spread ¼-inch thick on salted crackers.

Brown quickly under grill and serve hot.

OLIVE-CHEESE-BACON ROLLS

Cut large stuffed olives into halves and put together with Cheddar cheese spread. Wrap in bacon. Grill until crisp.

OLIVE SURPRISE PUFFS

4 ounces grated processed Cheddar cheese
2 tablespoons melted butter or margarine
2 ounces plain flour
1 teaspoon dry mustard
Dash of cayenne
3 tablespoons sherry
3 ounces stuffed green olives

Combine ingredients except olives. Pat mixture round each drained olive to cover completely.

Arrange on greased baking sheet and bake in hot oven (400°F. Mark 6) 10 minutes. Serve hot. Makes 16 to 18.

ROQUEFORT-CREAM CHEESE PUFFS

1 3-ounce packet cream cheese
1½ ounces or more Roquefort cheese
1 ounce chopped pecans or walnuts
Thin bread slices

Mix the two cheeses and the nuts; season to taste. Cut crusts from bread slices.

Spread the cheese mixture between slices and cut into squares or triangles. Toast under grill and serve very hot.

CHEESE-OLIVE FINGERS

Cut bread into thin strips, lengthwise. Spread with butter. Sprinkle with grated cheese and season with salt and cayenne.

Bake until delicately browned in moderate oven (350°F. Mark 4).

Sprinkle with finely chopped black olives and serve.

CHEESE PASTRY TWIRLS

1 pound shortcrust pastry
5 ounces Cheddar cheese spread
2 tablespoons sherry
¼ teaspoon Worcestershire sauce
Dash of cayenne

Roll pastry into a rectangle about 10 by 15 inches. Cut crosswise in halves to make two smaller rectangles.

Blend cheese spread, wine, and seasonings; spread evenly over pastry. Roll Swiss-roll fashion, from one wide side to the other. Wrap in greaseproof paper; chill 1 hour or longer.

With a sharp knife, cut in slices about ⅜ inch thick. Place on greased baking sheet. Bake in hot oven (425°F. Mark 7) about 15 minutes or until golden brown. Serve hot. Makes about 36.

SWISS-ONION CANAPÉS

Cover toast rounds with a thin slice of onion, then with mayonnaise and top with a circle of Gruyère cheese.

Melt cheese under grill.

HOT CANAPÉ PUFFS

Soften 1 8-ounce packet of cream cheese at room temperature and cream it until it is soft. Add 1 teaspoon grated onion, ½ teaspoon baking powder, 1 egg yolk, and salt and pepper to taste. Blend all ingredients thoroughly.

Toast 18 small bread rounds. Spread 2 2¼-ounce cans devilled ham or ham spread on the bread rounds.

Place a heaped spoonful of the cream cheese mixture on top of the ham spread.

Place in a moderate oven (375°F. Mark 5) until heated through, lightly browned, and puffy, about 8 to 10 minutes.

Hot Canapé Puffs

APPETIZER FILLING ON BRIDGE ROLLS

Put 1 small onion, half of a medium-sized green pepper, and 6 slices of grilled bacon through a mincer.

Cut 8 ounces processed cheese into quarters lengthwise. Put the processed cheese through the mincer and add it to the chopped onion, pepper, and bacon. Add 4 fluid ounces condensed tomato soup, ½ teaspoon salt, a dash of cayenne, and a dash of Worcestershire sauce.

Split bridge rolls and spread half of each with 1 tablespoon of the filling; cover with the other halves. Bake in moderate oven (350°F. Mark 4) until rolls are hot and filling is melted.

Serve hot as an appetizer. This filling may also be used in frankfurter rolls and cut in inch pieces before baking.

Appetizer Filling on Bridge Rolls

HOT CHEESE BALLS

    8 ounces sharp Cheddar cheese,
        grated
    4 ounces butter
    4 ounces plain flour
    Pinch of salt
    ¼ teaspoon dry mustard
    ¼ teaspoon paprika

Blend cheese and butter; add flour, salt, mustard, and paprika. Roll into balls the size of marbles.

Place on greased baking sheet and bake in moderate oven (350°F. Mark 4) for 10 minutes.

PIMIENTO CHEESE AND BEEF ROLLS

Use 2 ounces pimiento flavoured cheese for filling. Spread 12 thin bread slices (crusts removed) with mayonnaise, using 3 tablespoons. Cover with cheese and top with a slice of roast beef.

Roll and cut each in half. Fasten with cocktail sticks.

Toast under grill and serve hot. Makes 2 dozen rolls.

BACON, BREAD AND CHEESE ROLLS

Place thin slices of cheese on thin slices of bread. Roll up and wrap in bacon rashers. Grill slowly until bacon is done.

PUFFY CHEESE AND BACON CANAPÉS

    1 egg yolk, well beaten
    2 ounces grated cheese
    1 tablespoon cream
    Salt and pepper
    1-inch strips of bacon
    Bread squares

Combine egg yolk, cheese, and cream. Season to taste.

Toast bread squares or rounds on one side and spread mixture on un-toasted side. Top each with a bacon strip.

Bake in moderate oven (350°F. Mark 4) until bacon is crisp.

TOASTED CHEESE ROLLS

    4 ounces cheese spread
    1 ounce butter
    ½ loaf unsliced fresh bread

Cream the cheese and butter together until very soft. Slice bread very thin and remove crusts.

Place slices on a damp cloth and spread each slice with some of the cheese mixture. Roll Swiss-roll fashion tightly and fasten with sticks.

Cover with greaseproof paper and chill in refrigerator.

Brush each roll with melted butter and toast in very hot oven (450°F. Mark 8) or under grill and serve hot. Makes 12 to 15 canapés.

Toasted Anchovy-Cheese Rolls: Substitute 1 3-ounce packet cream cheese, 1 tablespoon anchovy paste, and 1½ tablespoons double cream for the cheese and butter.

Toasted Pimiento-Cheese Rolls: Substitute pimiento flavoured cream cheese for the cheese spread and cream it with the butter.

CHEESE PUFFS

    4 ounces butter
    8 ounces shredded Cheddar cheese
    4 ounces plain flour
    Pinch of salt
    ¼ teaspoon paprika

Cream butter; add cheese and cream well. Sift flour with seasonings and add to creamed mixture. Shape in 1-inch balls.

Freeze on baking sheet and when frozen, store cheese balls in freezer bag.

If you do not want to freeze them, chill for several hours before baking.

Place on baking sheet in moderate oven (350°F. Mark 4) for about 15 minutes or until puffed and brown. Makes 30 puffs.

CHEESE CRACKER PUFFS

    24 round crackers
    2½ ounces grated processed
        Cheddar cheese
    ¼ teaspoon Worcestershire sauce
    Dash of dry mustard
    Dash of paprika
    1 stiffly beaten egg white

Sprinkle top of each cracker with cheese, then stack 3 together. Fold Worcestershire sauce, mustard, and paprika into egg white.

Place a small mound of egg-white mixture on top of each stack of crackers.

Bake on ungreased baking sheet in very hot oven (450°F. Mark 8) about 4 minutes or until cheese melts and meringue browns. Makes 8.

ST. REGIS CHEESE CANAPÉS

    4 ounces processed Cheddar
        cheese
    2 ounces butter
    2 ounces plain flour
    ¼ teaspoon salt
    Paprika

Cream the cheese and butter together. Blend in flour and salt. Form into small balls the size of marbles.

Place on an ungreased baking sheet and flatten with the prongs of a fork to make a waffle design. Dust lightly with paprika. Chill in refrigerator for 2 to 3 hours.

Bake in very hot oven (450°F. Mark 8) until browned, 8 to 10 minutes. Makes about 24 to 30 canapés.

PARMESAN SQUARES

Moisten grated Parmesan cheese with cream. Spread on toast squares or crackers.

Toast in moderate oven until cheese melts.

Toasted Cheese Dreams: Rolled hot canapés to delight your family as well as your friends.

TOASTED CHEESE DREAMS

8 ounces Cheddar cheese, grated
1 3-ounce packet cream cheese
1 ounce butter, melted
1 egg, beaten
1 tablespoon cream
1 whole loaf white bread (unsliced)

Combine grated cheese with softened cream cheese, melted butter, and beaten egg, adding cream to moisten.

Slice bread lengthwise or crosswise of loaf, as preferred.

Spread lengthwise slices with the cheese mixture. Roll up like a Swiss roll and slice ⅜ inch thick.

Spread thin crosswise slices with the mixture and roll from corner to corner, fastening with a cocktail stick.

Sliced bread may be cut in rounds or other shapes and spread with cheese mixture, if wished.

Toast under grill until golden brown. Serve hot. Makes about 2½ to 3 dozen.

CHEESE DREAMS AMERICAN

2 egg whites
Pinch of salt
4 ounces grated Cheddar cheese
1 teaspoon Worcestershire sauce
Bread squares or rounds, toasted on one side
Tiny pieces of bacon

Beat egg whites with salt until very stiff. Fold in grated cheese seasoned with Worcestershire sauce.

Spread untoasted sides of bread bases with cheese-egg mixture. Top each with a tiny piece of bacon.

Grill under moderate flame until cheese is lightly browned and puffed.

AMERICAN CHEESE CANAPÉS

Cut a packet of 8 slices of pasteurized processed Cheddar cheese in half and then in quarters.

Place the 32 squares of cheese on assorted crackers arranged on a baking sheet. Place in moderate oven or under low grill until cheese is melted.

Garnish each cheese square with an olive slice, an anchovy curl, or a cocktail onion.

Arrange the canapés on a round tray and garnish the centre with olives.

CHEESE PUFFS

4 ounces Cheddar cheese, grated
2 ounces butter or margarine
2 ounces plain flour
Pinch of salt

Place all ingredients in bowl. With fingers, blend all ingredients together until smooth; chill ½ hour.

Form into ½-inch balls. Place on baking sheet. Chill. Bake in moderate oven (350°F. Mark 4) 10 to 15 minutes. Makes 2½ dozen.

WAFFLED TEASERS

Place a very thin slice of Gruyère cheese or ham or both between thinly sliced buttered bread. Spread lightly with horseradish mustard.

Make sandwiches very small. Toast in waffle iron or under grill.

ROQUEFORT PUFF CANAPÉS

Beat 1 egg white until stiff. Cream 2 ounces Roquefort cheese spread and fold into egg white. Heap on crackers or bread rounds.

Bake in slow oven (300°F. Mark 2) until browned (about 15 minutes). Garnish with paprika. Makes 8 2-inch puffs.

CHEESE-NUT CANAPÉS

Mix grated Cheddar cheese, paprika, and onion juice. Spread on toast rounds. Place under grill to melt cheese.

Sprinkle with chopped Brazil nuts.

TOASTED CREAM CHEESE ROLLS

Trim crusts from unsliced loaf of bread with a very sharp knife. Cut into extremely thin slices. If necessary, flatten slices with rolling pin.

Spread with softened butter, then with cream cheese. Roll up and place on baking sheet with open end at bottom.

Toast under moderate grill heat until delicately browned. Serve hot.

Variations: Cheese spreads or other fillings may be substituted for cream cheese.

TOASTED CHEESE ROLLS

3 ounces grated Cheddar cheese
1 beaten egg yolk
2 teaspoons Worcestershire sauce
2 tablespoons ketchup

Mix ingredients thoroughly into a paste and spread evenly on slices of fresh bread, cut thin the long way of the loaf.

Roll bread like a Swiss roll and wrap tightly in greaseproof paper. Store in refrigerator about 3 hours.

Remove paper with hot, sharp knife. Cut off thin slices. Place on pan and toast under grill on one side, then on the other.

PIMIENTO CHEESE PUFFS

8 ounces pimiento flavoured cheese spread
1 well-beaten egg
Salt and pepper
Bread bases

Blend cheese and egg; season to taste. Make bread cutouts in various shapes with a pastry cutter. Toast on one side; brush other side with melted butter.

Spread with cheese mixture. Just before serving, grill until brown and puffed. Makes about 35.

CHEESE AND CHUTNEY CANAPÉS

Spread round crackers or toast with chutney. Top with a thin slice of Cheddar cheese. Grill to melt cheese. Serve hot.

ONION-CHEESE PASTRY ROLLS

1 recipe shortcrust pastry
2 ounces grated cheese
1 medium-sized onion, chopped
Salt and pepper

Roll pastry into a thin sheet and cut strips 4 inches long and ½ inch wide.

Sprinkle with cheese, onion, salt, and pepper. Roll Swiss-roll fashion and fasten with sticks.

Place on baking sheet, cut side down. Bake in very hot oven (450°F. Mark 8) until done, 12 to 15 minutes. Makes about 4 dozen.

American Cheese Canapés

Hot Fish and Shellfish Appetizers

ANGELS ON HORSEBACK

For each angel, lay a medium-sized oyster on a thin slice of bacon. Salt and pepper the oyster; sprinkle with paprika and finely-chopped parsley. Roll the bacon around the oyster, securing it with a cocktail stick.

Place in a shallow pan and brown slowly in moderate oven (375°F. Mark 5) until bacon is crisp. Serve very hot. **Note:** It's a good idea to precook the bacon slightly to shorten the baking time, as oysters should not be overcooked. Cook bacon only long enough to remove some of the fat. It should be very limp.

OYSTER-ROQUEFORT CANAPÉS

Toast rounds of bread on one side. Spread untoasted side with anchovy butter.

Cook oysters in white wine until edges curl, about 1 minute.

Place an oyster on each round. Cover with Roquefort cheese which has been creamed with unsalted butter and seasoned with pepper.

Sprinkle with paprika. Grill until bubbly and lightly browned.

OYSTER TURNOVERS

Marinate small oysters for about 3 hours in French dressing to which a piece of garlic clove has been added. Drain oysters well and dry on paper towels.

Roll out shortcrust pastry very thin; cut into 2½-inch rounds. Place an oyster in each round; fold over and seal the edges with the prongs of a fork. Prick each with fork to make vents.

Bake in very hot oven (450°F. Mark 8) about 15 minutes. Serve very hot.

EASY OYSTER CANAPÉS

Place small oysters on small toast rounds. Sprinkle with salt, pepper, and lemon juice, then with grated cheese.

If desired, add a tiny piece of bacon. Grill just until cheese melts. Serve immediately.

LOBSTER-BACON ROLLS

Use canned or freshly cooked lobster meat. Season with salt and paprika. Brown in melted butter in which a little finely chopped onion is cooked.

Roll when brown in slices of uncooked bacon. Fasten with cocktail sticks. Grill until bacon is crisp.

Serve on toast squares or rounds with coating of tartar sauce. Garnish with pimiento strips.

HERRING ROE WITH BACON

Wrap small pieces of herring roe in small pieces of bacon. Fry until crisp. Spear each with a stick.

LOBSTER RUMAKI

Remove the shells from raw lobster tails and cut the meat into pieces about ½ inch thick. Marinate (soak) in equal parts of soy sauce and sherry.

Drain and combine each piece with a slice of water chestnut. Wrap each in bacon and secure with a cocktail stick. Bake in hot oven (400°F. Mark 6) until bacon is crisp.

FINNAN HADDOCK CANAPES

½ tablespoon finely chopped onion
2 tablespoons finely chopped
    mushrooms
1½ ounces butter
2 tablespoons flour
5 fluid ounces single cream
2 tablespoons grated cheese
2 egg yolks, slightly beaten
About 6 ounces finnan haddock,
    soaked and flaked
Salt and cayenne
Bread rounds, toasted on 1 side
Grated cheese
Buttered breadcrumbs

Fry onion and mushrooms in butter for 5 minutes. Blend in flour. Add cream gradually and heat to boiling, stirring constantly.

Remove from heat and stir in 2 tablespoons cheese, egg yolks, and finnan haddock. Season with salt and cayenne.

Heap mixture on untoasted side of bread rounds. Sprinkle with cheese and buttered crumbs. Brown lightly in hot oven (400°F. Mark 6).

PUFFY PRAWN CANAPÉS

12 canned or cooked prawns
1 egg white
1 ounce grated cheese
Pinch of salt
Pinch of paprika
Dash of pepper
7 tablespoons mayonnaise

Cut the cleaned prawns in half lengthwise. Beat egg white until stiff; fold in remaining ingredients.

Pile this mixture on toast rounds or crackers. Top each canapé with a prawn half.

Grill under moderate heat until puffy and delicately browned. Serve hot.

DEVILLED HERRING ROE CANAPÉS

1 ounce melted butter
⅓ teaspoon mustard
1¼ teaspoons Worcestershire sauce
¼ teaspoon salt, about
4 pieces canned herring roe

Mix first 4 ingredients. Drain the roe and roll in this mixture. Mash the roe and spread on toast squares.

Bake in oven (425°F. Mark 7) for 5 minutes. Serve with lemon wedges.

Hot Seafood Hors d'Oeuvres: To make these hot bites of seafood, melt 4 ounces butter or margarine; add ½ teaspoon garlic salt, 1 teaspoon tarragon, and 2 fluid ounces sherry. Cook bite-size pieces of seafood in the wine-butter mixture. Use lobster tails, fish sticks, bacon-wrapped prawns, or bacon-wrapped white fish, cut in bite-sized pieces. Keep hot and serve with assorted wafers or crackers.

ANCHOVY STICKS

4 ounces plain flour
2½ ounces butter
2 tablespoons anchovy paste
Cold water

Cut the butter into the flour with a pastry blender or round-bladed knife. Rub in the anchovy paste and add enough water to make a dough that will roll.

Cut into sticks and bake in a very hot oven (450°F. Mark 8) about 5 minutes.

To form rings, fasten the ends of the sticks together or cut with a ring cutter, then bake.

ANCHOVY-TOMATO ROUNDS

1 ounce butter
2 tablespoons anchovy paste
8 toast rounds
8 tomato slices
3 tablespoons grated Cheddar cheese

Mix butter and anchovy paste. Spread on toast rounds. Place a thin slice of tomato on top of each. Sprinkle with grated cheese.

Place under moderate grill until cheese is melted. Serve at once very hot, garnished with chopped parsley.

ANCHOVY-CHEESE PUFFS

1 3-ounce packet cream cheese
4 ounces butter or margarine
4 ounces plain flour
Anchovy paste

Blend cheese and butter. Mix with flour. Chill.

Roll very thin and cut with 2-inch pastry cutter. Spread with anchovy paste.

Fold over and bake in hot oven (400°F. Mark 6) 10 minutes. Serve hot. Makes about 48.

MINCED CLAM CRISPETS

2 3-ounce packets cream cheese, at room temperature
4 ounces canned drained minced clams
1 teaspoon Worcestershire sauce
Dash or two of Tabasco sauce
¼ teaspoon salt

Mix together above ingredients. Remove crusts from bread slices and cut in squares or rounds. Brown in butter on moderately hot griddle, or in a frying pan, on 1 side only.

Spread other side heavily with clam mixture. Place on baking sheet.

Just before ready to serve, place under grill or in hot oven (400°F. Mark 6) until topping is puffed and browned. Serve at once.

How many appetizers it will make depends upon how large bread is cut and how generously the spread is used.

Variations: 1. Serve cold as spread for crisp crackers.

2. Add 2 or 3 tablespoons of liquid drained from minced clams to make consistency for dipping. Serve with large potato crisps or very thin slices of rye or pumpernickel bread toasted in slow oven.

3. This mixture is good used on an open sandwich, following the Crispet directions, or as topping for stuffed baked potatoes; bake in moderately hot oven to heat through and brown top.

SARDINE TURNOVERS

Roll shortcrust pastry thin. Cut into squares the length of sardines. Cut each square diagonally to form triangles.

Have small sardines drained on absorbent paper. Lay a sardine on each piece of pastry. Sprinkle with lemon juice.

Fold point of triangle opposite diagonal over sardine. Press tightly to opposite side. Prick with fork to form vent. Place on ungreased baking sheet. Store in refrigerator until ready to use. Bake in very hot oven (450°F. Mark 8) 15 to 20 minutes.

CRABMEAT-CHEESE CANAPÉS

Moisten flaked canned crabmeat with mayonnaise. Toast bread bases on one side.

Spread untoasted side with crabmeat. Cover thickly with grated mild cheese. Sprinkle with a little paprika.

Toast under moderate grill until cheese melts and is lightly browned.

PRAWN-VEGETABLE KEBAB

Alternate on a skewer whole cleaned prawns, tomato wedges, okra, and bacon. Grill until done.

Fried prawns are always a favourite appetizer. Your only problem is to keep the tray replenished.

TUNA- OR CRABMEAT-CUCUMBER CANAPÉS

1 7-ounce can tuna fish, drained and flaked
4 tablespoons mayonnaise
1 tablespoon tomato ketchup
1 tablespoon vinegar
Few grains of cayenne
¼ teaspoon salt
¼ teaspoon Worcestershire sauce
1 cucumber
Paprika
Bread rounds, toasted on 1 side

Combine the drained and flaked tuna with mayonnaise, ketchup, vinegar, cayenne, salt, and Worcestershire.

Peel the cucumber and flute it by scraping the sides lengthwise with the prongs of a fork. Slice very thin and dip edges in paprika.

Place a slice of cucumber on untoasted side of each bread round. Heap a little of the tuna mixture in centre of each. Brown lightly under the grill. Serve hot.

CRABMEAT-MUSHROOM CANAPÉS

4 ounces canned flaked crabmeat
About 5 fluid ounces condensed cream of mushroom soup
1 tablespoon finely chopped green pepper
1 tablespoon finely chopped pimiento
¼ teaspoon salt
Few grains of cayenne
1 tablespoon sherry, optional
Bread rounds, toasted on 1 side
Buttered breadcrumbs

Combine crabmeat, soup, pepper, pimiento, salt, and cayenne; heat through. Remove from heat and add sherry.

Spread untoasted side of canapé bases with crabmeat mixture. Sprinkle with breadcrumbs. Brown lightly under grill and serve hot.

Lobster or Prawn-Mushroom Canapés: Substitute flaked cooked or canned lobster or prawns for the crabmeat in the above recipe.

TUNA OR CRABMEAT CANAPÉS

Combine drained, mashed tuna fish or crabmeat with enough mayonnaise or French dressing to make a creamy paste.

Spread on toast rounds. Sprinkle with grated cheese. Brown lightly under grill.

PRAWN-PINEAPPLE KEBAB

Marinate cooked, cleaned prawns in soy sauce. Spear a small whole prawn and a cube of canned pineapple on each stick. Bake or grill until hot.

HOT PRAWNS WITH DIPPING SAUCE

2 ounces butter
6 tablespoons lemon juice
3 pounds cooked prawns

Melt butter in heavy frying pan; add lemon juice. When mixture bubbles add prawns. Keep heat very low.

This can be done in a chafing dish at buffet table. Serve with prawn dipping sauce (below).

Prawn Dipping Sauce:
12 fluid ounces ketchup
2 fluid ounces lemon juice
½ teaspoon salt
1 tablespoon Worcestershire sauce
1 tablespoon prepared horseradish
1 teaspoon finely chopped celery
Few drops onion juice
Few drops Tabasco sauce

Combine and chill ingredients.

FRIED BABY SCALLOPS

1 pound scallops
1 ounce flour
¼ teaspoon salt
Pinch of pepper
2 ounces butter or margarine

Wipe scallops with a damp paper towel. Roll in flour seasoned with salt and pepper.

Melt butter in a frying pan. Add scallops and cook only 5 minutes over high heat, turning constantly to brown evenly. Serve at once on sticks. Serve with a dipping sauce.

If large sea scallops are used, cut in small pieces.

Fried Baby Scallops

TUNA-CHEESE CANAPÉS

Mix flaked canned tuna fish with chopped stuffed olives and mayonnaise or salad dressing. Season with Worcestershire sauce.

Spread on small squares, strips, or rounds of toast. Sprinkle with grated Cheddar cheese.

Place under grill until cheese is melted. Serve hot.

SMOKED SALMON FINGERS

Spread toast fingers with lemon butter. Place ¼-inch slice smoked salmon on toast.

Cover with buttered crumbs and brown under grill.

SARDINE CANAPÉS WITH CHEESE

Drain and bone skinless sardines. Mash and season with finely chopped celery, tomato ketchup, finely chopped onion, and pepper.

Add enough mayonnaise to make a paste of spreading consistency. Spread lightly on thin slices of rye bread.

Sprinkle with Parmesan cheese. Grill until well heated throughout.

WHOLE SARDINE CANAPÉS

Mix 1 ounce soft butter with 1 teaspoon dry mustard and a few drops Worcestershire sauce.

Drain large sardines and brush with mixture. Dip in biscuit crumbs. Grill quickly.

Serve on toast strips and sprinkle with lemon juice. Garnish with finely chopped parsley.

SARDINE ROLLS

Drain oil from sardines; mash sardines and mix with horseradish and lemon juice to taste.

Spread on thin squares of very fresh bread (crusts removed). Roll up and secure with a cocktail stick.

Brush with melted butter and toast in a hot oven (400°F. Mark 6) until lightly browned. Serve at once.

Scallop Soufflé Snacks

DEVILLED CRABMEAT CANAPÉS

2 ounces flaked canned crabmeat
1 ounce butter
1 tablespoon onion juice
1 teaspoon Worcestershire sauce
¼ teaspoon mustard
2 fluid ounces thick white sauce

Combine ingredients and heat thoroughly. Season with salt and pepper.

Serve hot on crackers or toasted bread rounds.

CLAM CANAPÉS

Combine finely chopped, drained canned clams with enough mayonnaise to hold together. Season to taste with chilli sauce and salt and pepper.

Toast bread rounds on one side and spread clam mixture on untoasted side. Sprinkle with grated mild cheese. Top with a dash of paprika.

Toast under grill until cheese is melted and canapés are lightly browned.

GRILLED PRAWN-BACON ROLLS

Wrap cleaned, cooked or canned prawns in small slices of bacon. Fasten with cocktail sticks.

Brown slowly in frying pan, or grill, or bake in hot oven until bacon is done.

Replace burnt sticks with fresh ones.

ANCHOVY-BACON ROLLS

Place one or two anchovy fillets on each slice of bacon. Roll tightly Swiss-roll fashion. Secure with a stick. Grill until bacon is crisp. Replace burnt sticks with fresh ones and serve hot.

SCALLOP SOUFFLÉ SNACKS

1 pound sea scallops (about 12), fresh or frozen
4 tablespoons mayonnaise
2 tablespoons drained pickle relish
1 tablespoon finely chopped parsley
1½ teaspoons lemon juice
Pinch of salt
¼ teaspoon Worcestershire sauce
Few grains pepper
1 egg white

Defrost scallops, if frozen. Cook scallops in about ½ pint water in covered saucepan, keeping water below boiling point, until just tender (about 10 minutes). Drain, cool, cut in halves.

Combine all remaining ingredients except egg white; mix well. Beat egg white stiff; fold into mayonnaise mixture.

Place scallop halves on baking sheet or in shallow tin; top each with mayonnaise mixture. When ready to serve, place under grill. Grill about 3 minutes or until golden brown. Serve at once, as hot hors d'oeuvres. Makes 24.

HERRING ROE AND BACON CANAPÉS

Herring roe
Butter
2 or 3 rashers of bacon
Salt and pepper
Few drops of lemon juice
Toast rounds

Fry the herring roe a few minutes in a little butter, then mash it. Chop the bacon and fry until crisp; drain and add to the roe.

Season to taste with the lemon juice, salt and pepper. Spread on toast rounds and grill a few seconds before serving hot.

GRILLED BREADED OYSTERS

Roll fresh oysters in mixture of half bread and half biscuit crumbs. Press flat with hands.

Grill 2 minutes on each side. Salt lightly and brush with melted butter. Serve on buttered hot toast rounds.

LOBSTER, PRAWN, or CRAB-MEAT CANAPÉS

Season finely chopped cooked or canned lobster, prawns, or crabmeat with salt, cayenne, and a few drops of lemon juice.

Moisten with thick white sauce. Spread on toasted bread rounds. Sprinkle with cheese. Brown in the oven.

CLAM-CREAM CHEESE ROUNDS

1 large can (8 ounces) minced clams
8 ounces cream cheese
2 tablespoons lemon juice
Garlic to taste

Drain clams and combine with other ingredients. Spread on rounds of toast. Sprinkle with paprika.

Toast under grill until thoroughly heated and slightly browned.

OYSTER AND MUSHROOM CANAPÉS

Peel large mushrooms and remove stems. Dip in melted butter or olive oil.

Put a fresh oyster in each mushroom. Season to taste with salt, pepper, paprika, and celery salt, if wished.

Grill under moderate heat. Serve on hot toasted canapé bases or in the oyster shells.

SCALLOP-BACON ROLLS

Parboil scallops in their own liquid for 3 minutes. Drain and dry with paper towels.

Cut scallops into bite-size pieces. Wrap each in a piece of bacon. Fasten with a cocktail stick.

Grill or bake in a hot oven until bacon is crisp. Serve hot with a bowl of cocktail sauce.

Hot Meat and Poultry Appetizers

SWEDISH MEAT BALLS WITH RED WINE SAUCE

1 pound twice-minced beef
4 ounces fine dry breadcrumbs
1 teaspoon cornflour
1 teaspoon salt
¼ teaspoon pepper
Dash of allspice or mace
1 beaten egg
8 fluid ounces creamy milk or
   single cream
1 small onion, finely chopped
Fat or oil
3 tablespoons flour
16 fluid ounces water
5 fluid ounces red wine
Salt and pepper

Add breadcrumbs, cornflour, salt, pepper, allspice or mace, beaten egg and milk to the minced meat. Sauté onion lightly in fat or oil. Mix with minced meat mixture. Blend ingredients thoroughly.

Shape into tiny balls 40 to 42 in all. Brown lightly in a little oil or fat. Remove balls from pan.

Make gravy by slowly blending the flour into the fat in pan and then slowly adding the water and the wine. Add salt and pepper to gravy to taste. Return meat balls to pan; simmer 20 minutes.

ROQUEFORT-BEEF BALLS

4 ounces minced beef
¼ teaspoon salt
Pinch of pepper
1 teaspoon Worcestershire sauce
1 ounce Roquefort cheese
1 ounce butter

Mix meat and seasonings. Divide into 12 portions. Press flat into rounds about 1½ inches in diameter.

Place a piece of cheese in centre of each round; form into balls in palms of hands.

Brown on all sides in butter. Serve hot on cocktail sticks.

Use a chafing dish, a candle warmer, or electric frying pan to keep Swedish Meat Balls warm in their wine sauce.

BEEF FONDUE OR FONDUE A LA BOURGUIGNONNE

Your guests cook their own bite-sized morsels of tender beef in hot vegetable oil, then dip in a choice of tasty sauces from among a variety set out. A deep metal chafing dish, which narrows at the top, is preferable to keep the fat from sputtering. Since everything is pre-assembled this sumptuous dish makes entertaining easy. And it's a good choice to help people get acquainted; they just have to be friendly sharing the same central cooking dish and then personally dipping the meat into succulent sauces.

Allow for each person about ⅓ to ½ pound fillet of beef, trimmed and cut in ¾-inch cubes. Less tender cuts of beef may be used if prepared with instant meat tenderizer following directions on label.

Use smaller tid-bits of meat to serve as an hors d'oeuvre, larger ones when it is to be the main course. Have beef cubes at room temperature.

Have ready 2 to 4 sauces: such as Tomato Dipping Sauce, Horseradish Cream Sauce, Garlic Butter. Make other selections such as a curry sauce or a sweet-sour sauce from sauce section.

Heat 1½ inches cooking oil in saucepan. (You may use deep fryer or electric frying pan; bring to 425°F.) Each guest holds beef cube in hot oil with fork until cooked to taste. Special forks, though attractive, are not essential; improvise with your kitchen utensils. It even adds to the fun to use skewers.

The cooked meat is dipped into one of the sauces. Or each guest may arrange servings of sauces on individual plates. Compartmented plates are desirable for main course use but not necessary. Serve with crusty French bread or rolls and a tossed salad.

Tomato Dipping Sauce: Combine 1 8-ounce can tomato sauce, 2 fluid ounces bottled steak sauce, 2 tablespoons brown sugar, and 2 tablespoons vegetable cooking oil. Bring to a boil. Serve hot.

Horseradish Cream Sauce: Combine 8 fluid ounces sour cream, 2 tablespoons prepared horseradish, and ¼ teaspoon salt. Serve chilled.

Garlic Butter: Beat 4 ounces softened butter and 1 finely chopped clove of garlic until light and fluffy.

HAM ON STICKS

This one's easy. Cube cooked ham, spear on sticks, heat, and serve in a bath of hot kirsch, red wine, pineapple juice with mustard in it, or sweet-sour sauce, in the chafing dish.

Beef Fondue: Your guests cook their own bite-sized morsels of tender meat, then dip them in a choice of tasty sauces.

HOT PORK CUBE HORS D'OEUVRES

Cut fresh pork shoulder into small, even cubes and sprinkle with salt and pepper. Cook on a baking sheet in a preheated very slow oven (200°F. Mark ¼) until the cubes are crisp, 1½ to 2 hours. Serve on cocktail sticks.

COCKTAIL SAUSAGES OR FRANKFURTERS

Grill or sauté cocktail-size sausages or larger ones cut into 1-inch lengths. Serve hot on cocktail sticks.

Provide a small bowl of heated barbecue sauce in which to dunk them.

CHICKEN BALLS

1 pound finely chopped cooked
   chicken
½ teaspoon finely chopped onion
¼ teaspoon salt
2 tablespoons mayonnaise

Combine ingredients and form into small balls. Roll balls in flour; dip in melted butter or margarine.

Brown quickly in hot oven (400°F. Mark 6). Serve hot.

HAM AND CREAM CHEESE PUFFS

8 ounces minced cooked ham
3 tablespoons finely chopped green
   pepper
1 tablespoon prepared mustard
¼ teaspoon Worcestershire sauce
4 fluid ounces thick white sauce
1 3-ounce packet cream cheese
1 beaten egg yolk
1 teaspoon grated onion
¼ teaspoon baking powder
18 2-inch toast rounds

Combine ham, green pepper, mustard, and Worcestershire sauce. Stir in white sauce and mix well. Combine cheese, egg yolk, onion, and baking powder.

Spread toast rounds with ham mixture. Top with cheese mixture. Grill under moderate heat until topping puffs and browns. Serve hot. Makes 18.

PASTRY WRAPS

Roll grilled or fried cocktail sausages, or short lengths of any cooked spicy sausage, in ketchup, prepared mustard, or barbecue sauce and wrap in shortcrust pastry.

Bake in a hot oven at (425°F. Mark 7) 8 minutes, or enough to brown the pastry lightly.

Transfer to chafing dish and keep hot. Provide guests with cocktail sticks. These sausages can be prepared in advance and reheated in the chafing dish.

HAMBURGER CANAPÉS

½ pound lean minced beef
1 teaspoon finely chopped onion
½ teaspoon salt
Pinch of pepper
Dash of Worcestershire sauce

Mix ingredients thoroughly and spread in a thin layer on toasted canapé bases.

Grill until done. Makes about 24 2-inch canapés.

BEEF AND PINEAPPLE KEBABS

1 pound minced beef
2 fluid ounces soured cream
1 teaspoon celery salt
1 can (about 15 ounces) pineapple chunks, drained
Teriyaki sauce (below)

Have the beef minced twice. Mix beef, sour cream, and celery salt. Form into 56 small balls (about 1 teaspoon of mixture for each).

Place 2 meat balls and 1 pineapple chunk on a wooden cocktail stick, with pineapple in centre. Marinate kebabs 1 hour or more in Teriyaki sauce or other sauce of choice. Grill 3 minutes on each side. Makes 28 kebabs.

Teriyaki Sauce: Combine 4 fluid ounces soy sauce, 2 ounces sugar, ½ teaspoon monosodium glutamate, 1 tablespoon salad or olive oil, 1 teaspoon grated fresh ginger or ½ chopped clove of garlic (optional), and 2 fluid ounces sherry (optional). Stir until blended.

BEEF BITS EN BROCHETTE

2 pounds topside of beef or pork fillet
8 fluid ounces soy sauce
1 tablespoon Worcestershire sauce
1 clove garlic, mashed
2 fluid ounces sherry
1 teaspoon sugar

Cut meat into thin ¼-inch slices. Cut slices into small 1½-inch squares. Combine remaining ingredients. Blend well. Pour mixture over meat, stirring well to coat. Marinate for several hours, or overnight.

Spear 5 or 6 pieces of meat on a skewer. Grill over an indoor barbecue, alcohol burner, or under an electric grill until brown, about 5 minutes. Turn occasionally. Serve with hot mustard and sweet-sour sauce. Serves 6.

BEEF BALLS IN BACON BLANKETS

Season freshly minced beef with salt, pepper, and grated onion. Shape into balls.

Rub half rashers of bacon with a piece of cut garlic. Roll a piece of bacon round each meat ball and secure with a stick. Grill until the meats are cooked.

COCKTAIL SAUSAGE RISSOLES

Make puff pastry and roll out ⅛-inch thick. Cut into rounds.

Place a tiny cooked sausage in the centre. Fold pastry over. Press edges together with prongs of a fork or a pastry marker. Prick top.

Brush tops lightly with a mixture of 1 egg yolk beaten with 1 teaspoon cold water.

Bake in very hot oven (450°F. Mark 8) 10 minutes. To vary, substitute small sardines or rolled anchovy fillets for sausage. Serve hot.

CHEESE AND HAM COCKTAIL BISCUITS

1½ ounces plain flour
½ teaspoon salt
6 tablespoons grated Cheddar cheese
1 ounce butter
2 to 3 tablespoons milk
Devilled ham or ham spread

Mix and sift flour with salt. Rub in the cheese and butter. Add milk to form dough. Roll out ⅛ inch thick. Cut into tiny rounds.

Spread devilled ham on alternate rounds. Cover with unspread rounds. Pinch edges together. Bake in very hot oven (450°F. Mark 8) 12 to 15 minutes.

For variety, you may want to try other fillings.

◄

Piping hot beef and pineapple kabobs may be grilled or your guests could cook their own on an indoor barbecue.

Beef Bits en Brochette: Get your guests cooking their own snacks and you have a perfect party icebreaker.

HOT HAMBURGER APPETIZERS

4 ounces bologna or any smoked sausage
1 small onion
½ pound minced beef
¼ teaspoon salt
¼ teaspoon pepper
1 ounce fine, dry breadcrumbs
4 fluid ounces milk
1 egg

Put sausage and onion through medium blade of mincer. Combine with remaining ingredients. Pack into 9-inch pie dish.

Bake in moderate oven (350°F. Mark 4) about 45 minutes. Then cut in ¾-inch squares. Insert a stick in each.

Serve with sour cream mixed with horseradish or with mustard relish. Good, too, with chilli sauce, or tomato ketchup. Serves 6 to 8.

HAM AND CHEESE ROUNDS

10 baps
1 2¼-ounce can devilled ham or ham spread
1 tablespoon mayonnaise
1 teaspoon salt
5 slices processed Cheddar cheese
Stuffed olives, sliced

Split the baps in half.

Combine devilled ham, mayonnaise, and salt. Spread on bap halves. Cut cheese in quarters and place a square on each bap half. Decorate with a slice of olive.

Grill at low heat until cheese melts, about 4 minutes. Serve hot. Makes 20.

PINEAPPLE WITH BACON

Wrap pineapple chunks in narrow rashers of bacon. Fasten with sticks.

Grill or bake in moderate oven (375°F. Mark 5) until bacon is done, turning to brown on all sides. Serve hot.

BOLOGNA CURLS

Spread thin slices of bologna sausage, or any smoked sausage, with the casings on, with any cheese spread. Grill until sausage curls. Serve on sticks.

CHUTNEY-HAM ROUNDS

Spread toasted or sautéed rounds of bread with a mixture of equal parts of chutney sauce and ham spread or minced boiled ham.

Sprinkle with grated Parmesan cheese or other well-flavoured cheese. Brown in a hot oven (400°F. Mark 6). Serve hot or cold garnished with parsley.

LIVER SAUSAGE CANAPÉS

Toast bread canapé bases on one side. Spread untoasted side with mustard butter. Cover thickly with mashed liver sausage which has been seasoned with a little grated onion.

Grill under moderate heat until hot and puffy, 8 to 10 minutes. Garnish with stuffed olive slices before serving. Serve hot.

PORK SAUSAGE TEMPTERS

1   **pound pork sausage meat**
1   **small onion, finely chopped**
2½ **fluid ounces water**
2   **fluid ounces lemon juice**
2   **tablespoons vinegar**
2   **teaspoons Worcestershire sauce**
2   **tablespoons sugar**
½   **teaspoon salt**
1   **teaspoon prepared mustard**
Dash of cayenne or Tabasco sauce

Form sausage meat into ¾-inch balls. Brown slowly on all sides. Remove balls and drain off all but 1 tablespoon fat.

Brown onion lightly, stirring frequently. Add remaining ingredients. Simmer until thickened, about 20 minutes. Pour sauce into a chafing dish or top of double boiler.

Stick each ball with a cocktail stick and stand up in sauce. Makes about 4 dozen balls.

SAVOURY BOLOGNA ROLLS

Cut thin slices of bologna sausage or any smoked sausage. Spread with mixture of cream cheese, chopped pickles, chopped chives, and chopped olives.

Roll slices and fasten each with sticks. Dip in salad dressing seasoned with tomato ketchup and Worcestershire sauce. Grill a few minutes. Serve hot.

CHICKEN GIBLET CANAPÉS

Cover squares or rounds of toast with chopped cooked chicken giblets seasoned to taste.

Sprinkle generously with grated Parmesan cheese. Grill under moderate heat until cheese melts.

HAM AND BRAZIL NUT FINGERS

Cut slices of rye bread into finger-length sandwiches.

Spread with prepared mustard, then with a mixture of 4 ounces minced ham mixed with 1 tablespoon chilli pickle and 1 ounce thinly sliced Brazil nuts.

Toast and serve hot.

CHICKEN LIVERS WITH MUSHROOMS AND BACON

Cut livers in bite-size pieces. Cut rashers of bacon in 1-inch pieces.

Fill skewers with alternate pieces of chicken liver, bacon, and small button mushrooms.

Dip in melted butter and roll in breadcrumbs.

Grill under moderate heat until browned on all sides. Season with salt and pepper.

DEVILLED FRANKFURTERS

Grill cocktail frankfurters, then slit halfway down on one side. Spread with mixture of mustard and horseradish.

Use in proportion of 1 tablespoon prepared mustard to ½ teaspoon horseradish. Fasten with cocktail sticks.

LIVER SAUSAGE SURPRISES

Mash liver sausage and roll it round stuffed olives, pickled onions, or cubes of sharp cheese.

Roll in chopped parsley, finely chopped nuts, or toasted fine breadcrumbs. Bake or deep-fry until hot, then keep warm in a chafing dish.

RUMAKI

12 **ounces (20) chicken livers**
Salt and pepper
½ **teaspoon Aromat**
2 **tablespoons butter or margarine**
2 **tablespoons finely chopped onion**
10 **rashers bacon, cut in half**
20 **walnut halves or 20 slices water chestnut**
Wooden cocktail sticks

Cut livers in half; sprinkle with salt, pepper, and Aromat.

Melt butter; add onion; cook until soft but not brown. Add chicken livers; cook until just tender.

Fry bacon half done but not crisp; drain. Place a liver in centre of bacon rasher with a walnut half. Wrap bacon around both; secure with wooden stick.

Grill under moderate heat until bacon is crisp. Makes 20.

DEVILLED HAM PASTRY SNAILS

3 ounces plain flour
Pinch of salt
2 ounces fat
About 2 tablespoons cold water
1 2¼-ounce can devilled ham or ham spread

Sift flour and salt, cut in fat, then add water to make a stiff dough.

Roll very thin into oblong shape. Spread with devilled ham or ham spread. Roll up Swiss roll fashion.

Wrap in greaseproof paper and chill thoroughly. Slice thin and bake in hot oven (400°F. Mark 6) 15 minutes. Serve hot or cold. Makes 36.

Pastry Snail Variations: You may want to experiment with many of the fillings suggested for canapé spreads such as the cheese, fish, and seafood fillings, or try the suggestions given below.

Anchovy-Cheese: Soften cream cheese and blend with equal amount of anchovy paste or anchovy fillets mashed to a paste.

Cheddar Cheese: Spread with grated Cheddar cheese seasoned to taste.

Cottage Cheese: Season cottage cheese with salt and pepper to taste and a little paprika, if wished.

Cream Cheese: Soften cream cheese with just a little cream. Season with salt and paprika.

Devilled Ham and Cheese: Spread with devilled ham or ham spread. Season with mustard and salt. Sprinkle with grated cheese, then with a little paprika.

Roquefort Cheese: Crumble Roquefort or blue cheese and blend with equal amount cream cheese which has been softened with just a bit of cream.

HAM AND PINEAPPLE ON STICKS

Place chunks of pineapple and cubes of ham on sticks. Brush with golden syrup. Grill until golden brown.

Chicken livers, water chestnuts, and bacon, blend flavours in the Japanese appetizer, Rumaki.

SAUSAGE TEMPTERS

A chafing dish can do the heating of these little tempters while the guests arrive.

Cut cooked pure pork sausages in half-inch pieces.

Pour pineapple juice into the chafing dish pan. Add the sausage pieces. Stab a pineapple chunk on a cocktail stick and then stick the point into a piece of sausage. Just heat and let the guests help themselves.

FRANKFURTER AND CHEESE CANAPÉS

Simmer frankfurters until thoroughly heated. Drain and remove casings. Put through mincer, using medium blade. Season to taste with prepared mustard. Add a little piccalilli and enough mayonnaise to give spreading consistency.

Spread on toasted bread bases. Sprinkle with grated Cheddar cheese. Just before serving, heat under moderate grill until cheese melts. Serve hot.

If wished, the frankfurter mixture may be used as a cold spread.

DEVILLED HAM WITH MUSHROOMS

Spread canapé base with a mixture of devilled ham, or ham spread, chopped pickle, and mayonnaise.

Top each canapé with a fresh or canned button mushroom and place under grill to brown mushroom. Sprinkle with paprika. Serve hot.

CHILLI-HAMBURGER CANAPÉS

1 pound minced beef
1 teaspoon chilli powder
1 teaspoon salt
Dash of Tabasco sauce
4 tablespoons tomato ketchup
12 slices toast, buttered and crusts cut off
Chilli sauce

Stir and heat meat, chilli powder, salt, Tabasco, and tomato ketchup in skillet until red colour disappears and mixture becomes spreadable. Spread on hot buttered toast.

At serving time, cut toast into 8 triangles or 9 squares. Bake in very hot oven (450°F. Mark 8) 10 minutes. To serve, garnish with a dash of chilli sauce.

CHICKEN-CHEESE CANAPÉS

Whip a packet of flavoured cheese spread until creamy. Add an equal amount of boned canned chicken or turkey. Season with Worcestershire sauce. Mix lightly but do not mash.

Spread on cocktail crackers. Place on baking sheet. Bake in very hot oven (450°F. Mark 8) or grill until cheese melts, about 5 minutes. Serve hot.

FRANKFURTER TOP-NOTCHERS

Slit frankfurters lengthwise down the middle without cutting all the way through. Insert a stick of cheese.

Cut into 1-inch pieces and wrap each piece in bacon. Secure with a cocktail stick.

Grill to heat and crisp the bacon. Keep hot under grill or in a dish set over hot water.

HAM AND CHEESE TARTLETS

8 ounces plain flour
2 teaspoons baking powder
½ teaspoon salt
2½ ounces butter and lard mixed
4 ounces grated cheese
About 8 fluid ounces milk
1 pound minced cooked ham
1 beaten egg
Sour or single cream

Mix and sift flour, baking powder, and salt. Cut in fat with a round-bladed knife, then add the cheese. Add just enough milk so the pastry can be rolled out, handling it as little as possible. Roll very thin and cut into small rounds.

Moisten the ham with the egg and a little cream so that it is stiff but smooth. Put a rounded teaspoonful on one round and cover with another. Press down the edges with a fork.

Bake in a moderate oven (375°F. Mark 5) about 15 minutes. Serve hot.

Variations: Other fillings may be used such as creamed finely chopped mushrooms, prawns, or crabmeat.

FRANKFURTERS AND MUSH-ROOMS ON STICKS

Place small canned mushrooms and 1-inch pieces of frankfurter on sticks. Brush with melted butter. Grill.

WAFFLED WAFERS

8 ounces plain flour
3 teaspoons baking powder
1 teaspoon salt
1-2 ounces fat
5-6 fluid ounces milk
3-4 ounces ham spread or other spread or sandwich filling

Sift together flour, baking powder, and salt. Cut or rub in fat. Add milk to make a soft dough.

Turn out on lightly floured board and knead gently ½ minute. Roll out pastry to ¼-inch thick. Cut with biscuit cutter.

Spread half the rounds with sandwich spread. Cover with another round.

Place a "sandwich" in each section of a hot waffle iron and bake until well browned, about 3½ minutes. Serve hot. Makes 9 sandwich wafers.

Frankfurter Top-Notchers

BACON AND CHEESE CANAPÉS

8 ounces grated cheese
2 ounces crisp finely chopped bacon
1 tablespoon Worcestershire sauce
Few grains of cayenne
Toasted canapé bases

Mix cheese with bacon, Worcestershire sauce, and cayenne. Spread untoasted side of canapé bases.

Grill under moderate heat until cheese melts.

BACONWICHES

Have bacon cut into rashers ⅛ inch thick. Cut the rashers into quarters.

Place ½ teaspoon softened Cheddar cheese in the centre of each small cracker. Cover with a quarter rasher of bacon.

Grill until bacon is hot and crisp at edges. Serve on toast bases.

BACON-PEANUT BUTTER CANAPÉS

Method 1: Mix peanut butter with diced, crisp bacon. Toast rounds or squares of bread on one side. Spread untoasted side with mixture.

Place under grill just long enough to heat slightly. Serve warm.

Method 2: Spread untoasted side of canapé bases with peanut butter. Cover with small thin pieces of bacon.

Grill until bacon is crisp. Serve warm.

Waffled Wafers

Miscellaneous Hot Appetizers

MUSHROOM CANAPÉS
(Italian Style)

Olive oil
3 cloves garlic
1 pound small mushrooms
Salt and pepper
1 tablespoon onion juice
1 tablespoon lemon juice
Chopped parsley

Mash the garlic in the olive oil in an iron frying pan. Add washed mushrooms and fry over low heat until tender, adding salt and pepper to taste. Add onion and lemon juice.

Serve hot or cold on toasted bread bases. Garnish with parsley.

MUSHROOM-HAM CANAPÉS

2 ounces chopped mushrooms
1 ounce butter
4 ounces minced cooked ham
1 tablespoon sweet pepper or tomato relish
1 tablespoon salad dressing
Bread rounds, toasted
Stuffed olives
Pimiento

Fry mushrooms in butter over low heat 5 minutes. Add ham and cook 3 minutes.

Stir in the pepper or tomato relish and salad dressing. Spread on toast rounds.

Bake in very hot oven (450°F. Mark 8) 3 to 5 minutes.

Garnish with sliced olives and pimiento strips. Makes about 30 canapés.

STUFFED MUSHROOM CANAPÉS

Spread toast rounds with savoury butter. Top with sautéed mushroom cap filled with cooked minced meat or fish mixed with relish and salad dressing.

Bake in very hot oven (450°F. Mark 8) about 5 minutes.

CHILLI-OLIVE-CHEESE SNACKS

3 ounces chopped black olives
3 ounces grated Cheddar cheese
¼ teaspoon chilli powder
Shortcrust pastry (made with 6 ounces flour)

Combine olives with cheese and chilli powder. Roll pastry thinly and cut with 2-inch pastry cutter.

Place a teaspoon filling on one half of each round. Moisten edges and fold other half over filling in half-moon shape. Pinch edges to seal.

Place on baking sheet and bake in very hot oven (450°F. Mark 8) about 10 to 12 minutes. Serve hot. Makes about 36 snacks.

SCRAMBLED EGG ROLLS

Scramble eggs until thick but not dry; season with salt, pepper, and Worcestershire sauce.

Pile on thin bread slices (crusts removed). Roll and fasten with cocktail sticks. Grill.

ASPARAGUS-CHEESE FINGERS

Heat tiny canned asparagus tips in melted butter until hot throughout. Place on toast fingers.

Sprinkle heavily with grated Cheddar cheese. Grill under moderate heat until cheese melts.

ASPARAGUS IN BREAD ROLLS

Slice fresh bread in ¼-inch slices. Spread with creamed butter or with anchovy paste. Remove crusts. Roll 1 canned asparagus tip in each slice.

Wrap in greaseproof paper and chill several hours. Remove paper and toast in hot oven. Serve hot.

BACON-TOMATO ROUNDS

Cover rounds of buttered toast with thick slices of tomato. Season tomato slices with salt, paprika, and brown sugar.

Cover with small thin bacon rashers. Grill until bacon is crisp.

FRUIT BITS AND BACON

Roll in small bacon slices, 1-inch squares of watermelon, peach, pear, or any spiced fruit.

Fasten with a cocktail stick and grill, browning all sides. Serve hot.

BAKED BEAN ROLLS

Season ½ cup baked beans with 1 tablespoon chilli sauce. Pile on thin slices of bread. Roll and fasten with cocktail sticks.

Wrap in rasher of bacon and grill until bacon is crisp, browning on all sides. Serve hot.

BACON-AVOCADO FINGERS

Mash avocado pulp with fork. Season with salt, paprika, and lemon juice to taste.

Spread on toast strips. Sprinkle with chopped bacon. Grill until bacon is crisp.

ASPARAGUS-HAM ROLLS

Trim crusts from thin slices of fresh bread. Trim ham slices to fit bread slices and spread with mustard.

Dip cooked or canned asparagus tips in mayonnaise and place one tip at end of prepared slice of bread and ham.

Roll Swiss-roll fashion. Fasten with cocktail sticks. Grill, browning evenly all round. Serve hot.

Hot and Bubbly Appetizers: No one will deny the appeal of a hot appetizer—a little more work perhaps, but worth it. Many of the hot appetizers presented in this book may be assembled in advance, ready to pop into the oven when guests arrive.

And of course an electric tray, chafing dish, or electric frying pan really becomes a valuable asset for keeping hot appetizers hot until the last bite.

ANCHOVY AND EGG ON FRENCH TOAST

4 anchovies, chopped
2 hard-boiled eggs, finely chopped
6 small squares French toast
3 stuffed olives
Melted butter

Mix anchovies and eggs. Spread on French toast. Press a half of stuffed olive into centre. Brush with melted butter and place under grill 3 minutes.

SCRAMBLED EGG AND MEAT CANAPÉS

2 eggs, slightly beaten
3 tablespoons chopped ham, cervelat, salami, or other sausage
1 teaspoon finely chopped parsley
Salt and pepper
Butter or margarine
Bread bases, toasted on 1 side
Grated cheese

Combine eggs with ham or sausage and parsley. Season to taste and cook in butter or margarine over low heat until thick but not dry. Mix with fork while cooking.

Spread on untoasted side of bread bases. Sprinkle with cheese. Just before serving, grill under moderate heat until cheese melts. Serve hot.

EGG AND SALAMI CANAPÉS

8 ounces minced hard salami
4 to 6 eggs, depending on size
1 onion, minced
Salt and pepper

Beat all ingredients together until frothy. Drop by spoonfuls into a well-greased hot frying pan. Serve on canapé bases spread with mustard.

EGG AND MUSHROOM CANAPÉS

2 ounces sliced mushrooms
2 tablespoons finely chopped onion
4 ounces butter or margarine
4 hard-boiled eggs, finely chopped
2 tablespoons finely chopped
    parsley
Salt and pepper
1 slightly beaten egg
Canapé bases toasted on 1 side
Grated cheese

Sauté mushrooms and onion in melted butter or margarine. Add hard-boiled eggs, parsley, and salt and pepper to taste. Add beaten egg and cook only until thick.

Spread on untoasted sides of canapé bases. Sprinkle with grated cheese. Grill until cheese melts. Serve hot.

OLIVES IN PASTRY BLANKETS

Prepare shortcrust pastry. Roll out ⅛ inch thick on a slightly floured board. Cut into 2-inch squares.

Place a medium-sized stuffed olive in each square and fold pastry round it. Roll lightly between the palms of hands to form balls.

Bake on ungreased baking sheet in very hot oven (450°F. Mark 8) until crisp and delicately browned, about 15 minutes.

These snacks may be prepared in advance and kept in refrigerator until ready to be baked.

AVOCADO AND BACON SNACKS

Cut a peeled ripe, but firm, avocado into cubes. Dip in chilli sauce, then roll each cube in ⅓ to ½ inch rasher of bacon.

Fasten with a cocktail stick and grill. Serve hot when bacon is crisp.

COCKTAIL ONION AND BACON

Wrap cocktail onions in small slices of bacon. Fasten with cocktail sticks. Grill until bacon is crisp. Serve hot.

Serve Chilli Corn Quaso from a chafing dish with crackers or tortillas.

SHASHLIK TYPE HORS D'OEUVRES

1½ pounds luncheon meat
2 fluid ounces olive oil
2 medium-sized onions
Juice of 1 lemon or 3 tablespoons
    wine vinegar
Dash of salt
¼ teaspoon coarsely ground pepper
½ teaspoon Worcestershire sauce
1 pound cocktail sausages
Small whole onions

Cut meat in 1-inch cubes and oblongs. Put olive oil in bowl; add coarsely grated onions, lemon juice, and seasonings. Mix thoroughly.

Add meat, sausage, and small whole onions. Rub sauce mixture into meat and place covered in refrigerator for 4 to 5 hours or overnight.

When nearly ready to serve, remove meats to shallow flameproof dish and place under grill to brown lightly. Keep hot in chafing dish. Have cocktail sticks conveniently at hand for serving.

WATERMELON PICKLES AND BACON

Cut watermelon pickles into cubes and wrap each piece in a rasher of bacon which has been precooked just enough to shrink it slightly and remove excess fat.

Skewer with sticks and bake until hot in moderate oven (350°F. Mark 4). Serve hot.

FAT RASCALS

Stone and stuff small steamed or partially cooked prunes with a piece of Cheddar or processed cheese. Wrap in rasher of uncooked bacon, fastened with a wooden stick.

Grill on all sides until bacon is crisp. Serve hot.

PINEAPPLE-CHEESE CANAPÉS

Place a thick slice of pineapple on a toasted bread base. Sprinkle with grated cheese.

Top with small pieces of bacon. Grill until bacon is crisp. Serve hot.

CHILLI CORN QUASO

Small onion, finely chopped
1 clove garlic, finely chopped
½ ounce butter or margarine, melted
1 pound Cheddar cheese, grated
1 6-ounce can tomato paste
1 11½-ounce can sweetcorn with
    sweet peppers, drained
½ teaspoon Worcestershire sauce
1 teaspoon chilli powder

Sauté onion and garlic in melted butter or margarine in large heavy saucepan. Add cheese; melt over low heat, stirring frequently. Stir in remaining ingredients. Serve from chafing dish with crackers or tortillas.

Shashlik Type Hors d'Oeuvres

PICKLE AND CHEESE ROUNDS

Top untoasted sides of canapé rounds with slices of pickle. Sprinkle liberally with grated cheese.

Bake in moderate oven (350°F. Mark 4) until cheese melts.

OLIVES AND BACON

Wrap ½-inch rashers of bacon round large stuffed olives. Fasten with a cocktail stick. Place on rack in shallow pan.

Bake in hot oven (400°F. Mark 6) until bacon is crisp, 12 to 15 minutes. Serve hot.

OLIVE-STUFFED PRUNES

Steam prunes until tender. Remove stones. Fill each prune with a stuffed olive.

Wrap in a thin rasher of bacon and fasten with a cocktail stick.

Bake in a very hot oven (450°F. Mark 8) until bacon is crisp, turning to crisp all sides. Remove sticks and insert fresh ones. Serve hot.

FRIED BRUSSELS SPROUTS

Cook Brussels sprouts until just tender.

Drain well and dip in egg which has been beaten with a dash of salt and a few grains of cayenne pepper. Then dip in breadcrumbs and fry in bacon or sausage fat until golden brown.

Serve hot on sticks with a dip of thinned mayonnaise.

ARTICHOKE HEARTS

Drain canned artichoke hearts well and slowly fry in butter until lightly browned.

Sprinkle with salt, pepper, chopped parsley, and lemon juice. Serve hot on cocktail sticks.

HOT MEXICAN ROLLS

Combine 2 fluid ounces tomato sauce, ½ teaspoon oregano, 1 teaspoon Worcestershire, ¼ teaspoon chilli powder, ¾ teaspoon garlic salt, ½ teaspoon sugar, dash of Tabasco, and 1 can cocktail sausages, drained.

Heat to serving temperature. Serve on tiny bridge rolls.

BARBECUE COOKING

More and more women are discovering that it is more fun to cook over an outdoor grill with a husband than over an indoor stove alone.

The jointed chicken, the two-inch steak, and the rack of pork spareribs are natural and popular candidates for roasting over a bed of coals. Experts enlarge the scope of barbecuing beyond grilling and roasting over open coals. Many of your favourite recipes may be "moved out of the kitchen" into the patio or garden.

Here you'll find a large variety of recipes to keep grill, spit, and skewers busy for many months, plus numerous side dishes, hints, and sauces to give outdoor meals variety and flavour.

TOOLS AND EQUIPMENT

Have a work table near the grill, so tools, pots, pans, and ingredients can be handy. Here is a check-list of articles you will want to have handy before you plan your first outdoor meal:

Paper and kindling
Charcoal or dry wood
Poker to tame fire
Matches in small jar with
  screw top
Paper towels and napkins
Bib-type apron
Canvas or asbestos gloves
  and pot holders
Grilling grid
Long-handled fork and spoon
Skewers of various lengths
Tongs for turning food
Hinged, long-handled
  wire grill
Dutch oven
Platter or dish for cooked meat

Small saucepan for barbecue
  sauce
Swab or brush for barbecue
  sauce
Large coffee pot
Condiment kit of salt, pepper,
  tomato ketchup, Worcester-
  shire sauce, and mustard
Bottle opener
Can opener
Big carving board and a very
  sharp, sturdy carving knife

FUEL AND FIREMAKING HINTS

If you have some dry hardwood stacked away, even if it's only fallen branches, you're in luck. This is good fuel, especially if it's oak, maple, or walnut; these burn slowly and make a long-lasting bed of coals. If you picnic in the woods, you'll probably find plenty of wood with a little hunting. But for most barbecues, including those on the beach, or at lakeside, it is best to carry your own fuel. Most convenient and satisfactory are charcoal or the more condensed "briquettes". The latter costs more but burns longer and more evenly. Both provide an unmistakable outdoor aroma. Plenty of dry paper and kindling are needed to ignite this fuel.

Place crumpled newspapers and kindling in the fire pit first, then arrange the fuel on top loosely so that air can circulate freely throughout. Petrol and paraffin are almost as dangerous as dynamite, so never use them. For a quick-starting fire of charcoal or briquettes, use charcoal lighting fuel or several stubs of candles. Fan the fire gently.

The main points are:

1. Build your fire early enough so that it will have burned down to glowing coals by the time you are ready to cook the meal. If you use charcoal or briquettes, start the fire an hour ahead. Allow 1½ hours for wood.

2. Build a big enough fire to provide heat for cooking food for all your guests at one time. A shallow bed of coals will do for chops, hamburgers, or hot dogs. Roasts and thick meats need a deeper bed.

3. Replenish fuel occasionally but avoid flames.

4. Low, even heat from a flameless fire is the secret of outdoor cooking. Once the coals have burned down to a grey colour, lit by a ruddy glow, you will have the steady even heat necessary for barbecuing.

5. Keep a poker and a bulb syringe (or child's water pistol) to hand, and if the fire blazes up from meat drippings, extinguish flames with a few drops of water.

6. Keep the fire near the front of the grill for cooking meat. There will be enough heat at the back of the grill for making coffee and warming foods.

7. If your grill is movable, the temperature can be controlled by changing the distance between grill and coals. If your grill is stationary, you can increase the temperature by adding fuel, and reduce it by removing a few coals or pushing them away from the cooking area of the grate.

8. Put the fire out when finished. Always keep a bucket of water by the fireplace ready to use in case the fire threatens to get out of control completely.

OUTDOOR MENU HINTS

Choose a menu to suit grill space. Keep it simple, tasty, and portable. Plan the meal so that first grilling feeds all guests. Try out your barbecue menu on the family before inviting anyone else.

Serve some help-yourself appetizers to keep appetites from getting out of hand, so that the chef can carry on undisturbed.

Don't overload the menu with fancy frills. The centre of attraction should be the grill-cooked meat or poultry. Another hot dish such as baked beans in a casserole can be prepared on the grill, or other casserole dishes such as creamed potatoes, scalloped potatoes, or vegetables in a cheese sauce may be prepared in advance in the kitchen and kept hot by the barbecue fire or a candle warmer.

A tossed salad, some devilled eggs, potato crisps or sizzling chips, toasted split rolls or hot garlic bread or cheese bread chunks, mixed pickles, and olives round out a good barbecue menu.

Salads and Relishes: Green salads, which must be kept crispy-cool, are better prepared just before eating. Relishes such as carrot sticks, celery sticks, olives and tiny spring onions should be kept crisp and chilled in crushed ice or a vacuum container until serving time. Potato salad is very popular, but, of course, it requires at-home preparation and must be kept cold. A simple cole slaw may be prepared at home and served at the barbecue site.

Beverages: Individual cold drinks should be set out in serve-yourself form in a tub of ice. Include a variety of drinks in individual bottles as well as individual servings of milk drinks and lemonade poured in advance into small jars. Instant coffee is a time saver at a picnic for both iced and hot coffee.

Picnic Coffee: Heat 2 quarts freshly drawn cold water to boiling. Combine 4 ounces medium-ground coffee, 1 egg, and 3 tablespoons cold water. Pour the boiling water over coffee in coffee pot. Heat just to boiling. Cover and let stand 12 minutes over very low heat. Strain to serve.

Desserts: Individual pies and cakes are easy to serve. If whole cakes or pies are taken on a picnic, they should be carried in a basket with separate shelves to keep them intact. Apple or cherry pie can be warmed at the side of the grill in heavy foil plates. Marshmallows can be toasted. Ice cream, especially in individual cups, is popular, but keeping it can be a problem. Arrange to pack it in natural or dry ice so that it will keep firm.

After the Meal: Roast nuts (pecans, chestnuts, walnuts, etc.) in the shell over the fire. Place the nuts in a wire basket and shake over the heat to roast evenly.

Finally, be sure to have food that appeals to all tastes and pack it so that it can be set out and served without too much fuss or bother. After all, a barbecue or any outdoor meal should be a "picnic".

SETTING THE OUTDOOR TABLE

Take fire, smoke, sun, and wind into consideration when setting the outdoor table. The equipment for an outdoor meal should be in harmony with the setting.

Fine linens, silver, and glassware should be left in the home. Use sturdy plastic dinnerware or paper plates (or plastic-surface) and cups.

Inexpensive knives, forks, and spoons may be purchased and kept for this purpose.

Heavy paper spoons are a good choice because they can be destroyed, but the use of paper forks is inadvisable since they are difficult to use for cutting purposes, as for a meat loaf.

Paper napkins and a paper table cloth are very satisfactory. Don't use white, for it dazzles in the sun.

Candle warmers to keep coffee and casseroles hot are convenient and attractive. Use extra-large salt and pepper shakers.

Beef Steaks for the Barbecue

Think of charcoal grilling and almost everyone thinks first of steaks. This is not for lack of imagination but rather that they are so good. Though a plain and perfectly grilled steak is beef perfection, even that delight may pall if served too often. Therefore we include variations—classic recipes that taste even better outdoors.

Steak chefs are a divided clan, starting with stubborn preferences as to the cut and the method of cooking. Some char the steak, then grill it slowly; some do it the other way around. And among steak purists the charcoal grill vs. the wood fire can start an argument comparable to a major breach of the peace.

HOW TO BUY AND CHARCOAL-GRILL A STEAK

When Buying Beefsteak: Two things on which chefs do agree are that steak must be thick ($1\frac{1}{2}$ to 2 inches) for open fire cooking and of top quality.

Prime quality is the best you can buy but very often a porterhouse or sirloin from choice or good-quality beef is a good buy.

If you grill rump steaks, however, they should be prime quality. You can, of course, use a meat tenderizer with some cuts.

Amount to Buy: Consider the number of people to be served, the cooking area of your grill and the amount of money you intend to spend. For the average appetite $\frac{1}{2}$ to 1 pound of steak is not too much to allow. You'll find that most people have hearty outdoor appetites.

If your grill is small and your party

large, cook one large thick steak so that it can be sliced to make the rounds. If grill is large, individual steaks are in order.

The Fire: A wood fire for steak grilling should be built just big enough to burn down to a 4-inch-deep bed of coals, which, when spread out evenly, is only slightly larger than the steak. The fire is ready when the coals are glowing but have a light film of white ash.

Grilling with charcoal takes much less time than grilling over wood fire. Although many like to use fruit woods to give flavour to the steak, small uniform charcoal briquettes of top quality give the best performance. A good charcoal fire needs fewer briquettes than most amateur chefs use.

Preliminaries: Take steak out of refrigerator before grilling—but not more than 1 hour ahead.

Trim, leaving minimum of fat so that drippings won't blaze up too much. Gash edges.

Spear steak trimmings on fork and rub hot grill or folding wire grill to keep steak from sticking.

Optional Before Grilling: If desired, rub the steak with garlic or spread with prepared mustard, or rub with a mixture of 1 tablespoon flour, 1 tablespoon mustard, ¼ teaspoon salt, and a pinch of pepper.

Grilling: The time it takes to cook a steak over an open fire depends not only on how thick the steak is but also on four highly variable conditions: the temperature of the steak, how hot the fire is, the temperature of the air, the draughts or breezes.

As a rule of thumb, if a 1½-inch sirloin steak is at room temperature and placed about 6 inches from a good bed of coals, it should be rare after 6 minutes on each side, medium rare at 7 minutes, medium at 9 minutes, and well done at 12 minutes per side.

A 2-inch steak may require as much as 16 minutes each side for rare, 18 minutes for medium, and 20 for well done.

Grill on one side, then turn carefully without sticking fork into meat so as not to lose juices.

If drippings flare up, put out the blaze with a sprinkle of water. Salt and pepper the browned side.

To Test: Surest method is to test the steak before the allotted time is up by making a small cut near the centre and judging by the colour.

Since meat continues to cook for 5 to 10 minutes after it is removed from the fire, the stickler for an exact degree of rareness should stop when the colour is still a bit too red.

STEAK SPREADS

Mustard Spread: Cream 2 ounces butter with 2 tablespoons prepared mustard. Spread over cooked steak.

Horseradish-Tabasco Spread: Cream 2 ounces butter with 1½ teaspoons horseradish and ⅛ teaspoon Tabasco sauce. Spread over cooked steak.

Roquefort Spread: Cream 1 ounce butter with 3 ounces Roquefort cheese. Spread over cooked steak.

MUSHROOM TOPPING FOR STEAKS

½ pound fresh mushrooms
Flour
1½ ounce butter or margarine
½ teaspoon soy sauce
Salt and pepper

Wash mushrooms gently in a little cold water (don't soak). Drain thoroughly.

Cut off tip of stem and leave mushrooms whole or slice. Sprinkle lightly with flour.

Melt butter in a frying pan; add mushrooms, cover and cook over low heat until tender, 7 to 10 minutes, turning occasionally.

Add soy sauce and season to taste with salt and pepper. Serve over steak or hamburgers. Serves 4.

PEPPER TOPPING FOR STEAKS

1 clove garlic, finely chopped
2 fluid ounces salad oil
5 green peppers, very thinly sliced
2 tablespoons wine vinegar
½ teaspoon salt

Cook garlic in oil until golden; add peppers and cook gently until tender, stirring frequently.

Season with vinegar and salt. Serve over steak or hamburgers.

INDIVIDUAL STEAK SANDWICHES

Count on at least ½ pound steak per person. Let the steaks stand at room temperature for at least ½ hour.

Rub both sides with salt and pepper; spread with a thin layer of prepared mustard. Grill until brown on one side.

Turn and brown on second side until cooked to taste. Remove from heat; top with a piece of butter.

Butter a split loaf of French bread, split hamburger buns, or baps, or slices of white bread.

Place steaks on half the buttered bread or buns. Top other half with onion and tomato slices. Put together to form sandwiches.

Slice the French bread diagonally to make individual servings.

Trim steaks, leaving minimum of fat so that drippings won't blaze up too much. Gash edges at intervals to prevent curling.

SALT-GRILLED STEAK

Sirloin steak, 2 inches thick
Coarse salt
Water
Barbecue sauce

Remove the steak from the refrigerator long enough before cooking to completely remove chill.

When fire is very hot, moisten salt until it is like a thick paste. Spread over both sides of steak.

Grill 7 to 12 minutes for each side. Knock off salt; slice browned steak and serve on French bread with hot barbecue sauce.

MARINATED RIB STEAKS

Pound finely crushed or chopped garlic into the steaks. Cover with wine vinegar and let stand several hours at room temperature. Drain and cook over hot coals.

BLUE CHEESE GRILLED STEAK

Crush a clove of garlic; add ½ pound blue cheese and mash well.

Grill a thick steak on one side until browned, turn and spread with cheese. When steak is done on the bottom, cheese should have melted to a savoury sauce.

STEAK ROSEMARY

Cover both sides of steak with rosemary pressed in with your hand.

Grill as usual and season just before serving. Top each serving with a pat of butter.

Individual Steak Sandwiches

WINE-BARBECUED STEAK

4   fluid ounces salad oil
4   fluid ounces red wine
2   tablespoons grated onion
1   garlic clove, slashed
1½ teaspoons salt
1   teaspoon Aromat
Few drops Tabasco sauce
1   sirloin steak, cut 1 to 1½-inches
      thick

Combine all ingredients except steak. Cover; chill several hours or overnight.

At the barbecue, heat the sauce. Use to brush steak as it grills, turning steak and brushing frequently.

To serve, cut steak in slices ½ inch thick, from bone to edge. Serve in toasted frankfurter rolls. Serves 8.

STUFFED ROLLED FLANK STEAK

2   ounces butter or margarine
1   clove garlic, crushed
2   ounces chopped celery
1   small can drained mushrooms
¼   teaspoon ground black pepper
8   ounces dry breadcrumbs
1   ounce crumbled blue cheese
2   fluid ounces water
2   flank steaks

Melt butter or margarine; add garlic, celery, mushrooms, and pepper. Cook until celery is tender. Stir in crumbs, cheese, and water.

Pound flank steaks lightly to flatten. Spread ½ of the stuffing on each steak. Roll up and tie with twine.

Grill over low fire turning frequently until cooked, about ½ hour. Makes 8 to 10 servings.

Stuffed Rolled Flank Steak: Make the stuffing in the morning, roll the steak and chill until cooking time. Serve with cold, crisp vegetables and bacon-wrapped corn on the cob roasted in foil.

STEAK WITH GARLIC OIL

Soak 2 cut cloves of garlic in 8 fluid ounces olive oil the night before the barbecue.

Prepare 1-inch-thick steak by gashing around the edges to prevent curling during grilling.

Pour the oil in a shallow pan; remove the garlic. Dip the steak in the oil, coating both sides. Grill as usual and season with salt and pepper when it is about done.

STUFFED STEAK

1½ pounds steak, cut ¼-inch thick
4½ ounces breadcrumbs
3   tablespoons finely chopped onion
3   tablespoons finely chopped
      parsley
1½ ounces melted butter or
      margarine
Salt and pepper
8   rashers of bacon
8   bread rolls

Cut steak into 8 (2×4-inch) strips. Spread with dressing made by combining breadcrumbs, onion, parsley, melted butter, and seasonings. Roll up and wrap in bacon. Fasten with wooden sticks.

Grill over hot coals until bacon is crisp, turning frequently.

Serve sizzling on buttered rolls. If desired, make hollows in centres of rolls (using the crumbs in the dressing) so that finished sandwiches won't be too "fat" to bite. Makes 8.

SOYED STEAK

Chop 1 clove garlic very finely and combine with 2-4 fluid ounces soy sauce in a shallow pan.

Marinate steak in this sauce for about 15 minutes, turning frequently to thoroughly impregnate the steak with the sauce. Then grill as usual.
Note: Do not use a metal utensil for the marinade as it may affect the taste. The same marinade may be used for other meats.

LONDON GRILL

This requires aged top-quality steak, quick grilling, and thin serving slices. Do not attempt this method of cooking unless you are sure of the quality of the steak. When in doubt, braise it.

Have a 2- to 3-pound top-quality steak trimmed of excess fat and membrane and, if desired, scored on both sides.

Brush well with salad oil or bottled sauce for gravy.

Grill over hot coals until brown but still rare, about 5 minutes on each side.

Season with butter, salt, and pepper. Cut into very thin slices diagonally across the grain.

Blue Cheese Topped: Cover the steak with a mixture of 8 fluid ounces salad oil, 2 tablespoons vinegar, and 1 mashed, peeled clove of garlic; let stand in refrigerator 8 to 24 hours, turning 2 or 3 times.

Remove from marinade and grill on 1 side; turn, cover with mashed blue cheese for the last few minutes of grilling.

MARINATED GIANT SIRLOIN STEAK

Select a sirloin steak at least 2½ inches thick.

Marinate (soak) 1 hour in 3 fluid ounces salad oil to which has been added 3 finely chopped cloves garlic.

Place in folding wire grill. Season with salt and pepper.

Grill over hot coals 6 to 10 minutes, 1 minute at a time on each side.

Remove from wire grill and place right on hot coals until charred, at least 6 minutes per side. Slice ¾ inch thick (the meat will look raw).

Meanwhile, heat ½ pint water with ½ pound butter or margarine in a roasting pan. Place steak slices in pan. Simmer ½ minute per side—no longer —or 15 seconds for rare. Lift out and serve as it is or in bread rolls.

MARINATED CUBE STEAKS

Use top-quality sirloin, or fillet steak, ⅛ inch thick. Have it scored.

Marinate (soak) 15 minutes in barbecue sauce or in 4 fluid ounces soy sauce with 1 clove garlic, finely chopped.

Let guests cook their own on long sharp-pointed green sticks or long-handled forks, or cook several on a wire grill.

RIB ROAST OR STEAK

1 3-rib roast, separated into steaks
    or 1 4-pound steak
4 cloves garlic, crushed in salt
6 fluid ounces olive oil

Rub both sides of meat well with garlic salt. Brush generously with olive oil. Grill 10 to 15 minutes on each side.

BARBECUE COOKING

Aluminium Foil Cooking

Many foods take an exciting new flavour when slowly roasted in foil over or in the coals. All the flavour and food value are wrapped right in and seasonings can be added at the beginning. An additional advantage of foil-packet cooking is that the food stays hot and moist longer if there is a delay in serving.

It is best to use 18-inch heavy-duty aluminium foil. If the regular 12-inch-wide household foil is used, cut off twice the length required to wrap food and wrap double. Always be sure to wrap securely and seal edges tightly.

The following timing directions will serve as a general guide for your own recipes cooked directly on hot coals; turn each packet halfway through cooking.

Thick Steak: 20 minutes per pound.
Hamburgers, Medium Thin: 10 to 12 minutes.
Frankfurters: 5 to 8 minutes.
Chicken: Whole, 1 to 1½ hours; very small pieces, in individual packets, 30 to 35 minutes.

MASTER METHOD FOR CHICKEN-IN-FOIL DINNERS

Many combinations of chicken with vegetables and other ingredients may be cooked in foil. The way to prepare these easy eat-from-the-foil dinners is as follows:

Have chicken cut in half or in quarters; rinse. Small protruding and easily removed bones are pulled out.

Sufficient chicken for one serving is placed skin side down in the centre of a double thickness of regular household foil or one thickness of heavy-duty foil measuring about 12×14 inches. Vegetables, butter or margarine, seasonings, and a little liquid are added.

Bring the foil up over the food and seal the edges together with a double fold. Seal the ends the same way, turning them up to hold in the juice.

Place the bundles on the grate over an outdoor fire and cook, chicken side down, for about 40 to 50 minutes. Have a good fire when the chicken starts cooking, so that the chicken will brown through the foil. Eat straight from the foil. Delicious gravy is formed from the juice of the chicken mingled with the butter and other ingredients.

CHICKEN, SWEET POTATO AND APPLE IN A FOIL PACKAGE

Prepare chicken according to master method. Place on pieces of foil and season with salt and pepper.

Peel and slice thinly sweet potatoes or yams and place around chicken, allowing about ½ potato to each serving. Add 4 ½-inch slices of apple to each serving.

In a small bowl, combine 2 tablespoons lemon juice, a little grated lemon rind, 4 tablespoons light brown sugar, and ½ ounce softened butter or margarine. Spread over apples and potatoes.

Seal in a package and cook on a grate over an open fire as described above.

CHICKEN, SEASONED RICE AND TOMATO IN A FOIL PACKAGE

Prepare chicken according to master method, placing each quarter chicken in centre of a piece of aluminium foil.

In a frying pan, fry 2 rashers of bacon until crisp. Drain bacon and lightly brown the chicken liver in fat. Dice liver and bacon.

Pour off all but 1 tablespoon bacon fat from pan and add 8 ounces of quick-cooking rice (uncooked) to pan.

Add 1 8-ounce can of tomatoes, half juice and half pulp, cut up so that tomato is equally mixed through. Stir in bacon and liver, 1 teaspoon finely chopped onion, ½ teaspoon salt, a dash of pepper and garlic salt.

Spoon one-quarter of this mixture over each chicken piece. Seal packages and cook on grill as described.

CHICKEN, COURGETTE AND SAVOURY TOMATO SAUCE IN A FOIL PACKAGE

Prepare chicken according to master method. Place each piece skin-side-down on foil. Season with salt, pepper, a little fresh tarragon and chives, finely chopped.

Have ready sliced tender young courgettes and sliced onion and add a generous serving to each portion of chicken.

Season vegetable with salt and pepper, then add 1 tablespoon canned tomato sauce to each serving and top with a generous piece of butter or margarine. Seal packages and cook on grill as described.

CHICKEN DINNER IN FOIL

For each serving:
  2 or 3 pieces frying chicken
  1 peeled potato
  1 tomato
  1 peeled onion
  2 mushroom caps
  2 green pepper rings
  2 tablespoons rice
  1 tablespoon Worcestershire sauce
  ¾ teaspoon salt
  Dash of pepper
  Sprinkling of paprika
  Small pat of butter or margarine

Use a large piece of heavy-duty aluminium foil or a double thickness of regular household foil.

Arrange chicken, potato, tomato, onion, mushrooms, and green pepper neatly on the foil.

Sprinkle with rice and seasonings. Dot with butter.

Fold the foil to make a neat package, securing the ends well.

Cook over glowing coals until all is tender, about 1¼ hours, turning package every 20 or 30 minutes. Serve in the foil. Serves 1.

For very easy and delicious outdoor cooked meats, try chicken-in-foil dinners. Make them up the night before, wrap securely in aluminium foil and store in the refrigerator. Corn on the cob, too, can be prepared ahead and wrapped in foil. Cook over an outdoor fire, then eat it from the foil.

Frankfurter and Bean Rolls: Partially fill split rolls with canned baked beans or chilli con carne. Wrap each filled roll in a double thickness of foil and seal securely. Heat rolls for 10 minutes, turning frequently, on the cooler side of the grill. Grill frankfurters over hot coals until heated through. To serve, open roll packages and place a grilled frankfurter in each.

CHICKEN BREASTS IN FOIL

6   chicken breasts
1½ teaspoons salt
Pinch of pepper
1   can condensed cream of
       mushroom soup
1   clove garlic, finely chopped
1   tablespoon finely chopped spring
       onions
2   tablespoons finely chopped
       parsley
Dash of thyme
½   teaspoon dried tarragon

Season chicken with salt and pepper. Combine remaining ingredients and mix well. Spread equal portions on the surface and in the cavities of the 6 chicken breasts.

Put each breast on a square of aluminium foil; bring edges together and seal, folding corners under.

Cook over hot coals until tender, turning once. Total time about 40 to 45 minutes. Serves 6.

Note: Use heavy-duty aluminium foil or a double thickness of regular household foil.

PORK CHOP DINNER IN FOIL

Pork chops
Sweet potatoes, peeled
Sharp eating apples, peeled
Onion slices
Seasonings

Use heavy-duty foil or a double thickness of ordinary household foil. In the centre of each large square of foil place a pork chop which has been lightly browned in a frying pan.

Add two or more thick slices of

apple, sweet potato, and onion. Season each dinner well with salt, pepper, and a little thyme.

Bring foil up over food and seal into tight packages by double folding edges together. Place on grill over medium heat and cook about 1 hour.

STEAK DINNER IN FOIL

Red pepper relish or chilli pickle
Flour
Celery, cut into 3-inch lengths
Carrots, scraped and quartered
Small onions, peeled
Baking potatoes, peeled and
       quartered
1-inch cubes of steak
Aromat, salt, pepper

Use heavy-duty foil or double thickness of regular household foil.

For each serving, combine 2 tablespoons pepper relish or chilli pickle and 2 teaspoons flour; spread in centre of a large square of foil.

On sauce arrange several pieces of celery, 1 scraped and quartered carrot, 3 peeled onions, and 2 pieces peeled and quartered potato.

Top with about ¼ pound steak cubes; sprinkle with ⅛ teaspoon salt, dash of pepper, and ½ teaspoon Aromat.

Fold the foil into a secure package, and fasten ends underneath securely.

Cook over glowing coals until all is tender, about 1 hour.

INDIVIDUAL HAM DINNERS IN FOIL PACKAGES

1-inch thick gammon steaks (ready-
       to-cook-type)
Brown sugar
Prepared mustard
Whole cloves
Pineapple slices
Butter or margarine
Sweet potatoes, peeled and
       quartered

Use heavy-duty foil or a double thickness of ordinary household foil. In each large square of foil place a serving portion of ham; spread each serving with 2 tablespoons brown sugar and 1 teaspoon prepared mustard.

Stick a clove or two into drained pineapple slice and place on ham. Dot with butter.

Place 2 pieces of peeled and quartered sweet potato at side of ham.

Fold the foil into a secure package and fasten the ends underneath securely.

Cook over glowing coals until potato is tender, about 1 hour. Serve in the package.

FRANKFURTERS IN FOIL

Wrap individual frankfurters with 2 tablespoons any barbecue sauce in foil. Heat on hot coals 10 minutes.

FISH DINNER IN FOIL

Use a square of heavy-duty aluminium foil (or a double thickness of regular foil) for each serving.

In the centre place a slice of halibut, salmon, or other fish (fresh or thawed frozen). Season to taste with salt and pepper.

Cover with thin slice of peeled small aubergine, bay leaf, 1 thin slice each of tomato, onion, and lemon.

Wrap, double folding the edges. Place on hot greyish coals. Cook about 8 minutes, turning once.

FISH DINNER IN FOIL 2

Place on a piece of heavy-duty foil, 1 to 2 pounds of fish with 2 medium onions, thinly sliced; 2 tomatoes, cut in quarters; 4 ounces mushrooms, sliced, and 1 green pepper, finely chopped.

Add 1½ ounces butter, salt and pepper to taste.

Wrap tightly in foil and secure the edges well. Cook 10 to 15 minutes near the coals, turning halfway through cooking.

FOIL-PACKAGED KEBABS

Let your guests skewer their own assortment of cubes of steak, onion slices, tomato halves, small frankfurters, mushroom caps, and squares of bacon.

Place the filled skewers on squares of heavy-duty foil, brush with a hot barbecue sauce and sprinkle with salt and pepper. Close the foil by twisting it at the ends to hold it secure.

Place the kebabs on the grate over a good charcoal fire and cook, turning once or twice. It takes up to 40 minutes depending on size of pieces.

To serve, place the skewers on paper plates and, with a pot holder, push the foil-wrapped food off the skewer. Open the foil and savour the well cooked food with delicious juices intact.

Individual packaged dinners to cook on the grill can be prepared ahead of time, ready to be carried outdoors. French bread, sliced and buttered and wrapped in foil, can heat during the last 15 minutes.

Skewer Cookery

Skewer cookery is spectacular and never fails to intrigue guests, but actually it's not at all new and may be the earliest form of cookery. Centuries ago Armenian shepherds placed their food on sticks and cooked it over open fires. The dish Armenians made famous, shish kebab, consists of marinated lamb alternated on a skewer with pieces of green pepper and onion and grilled until done and crispy brown.

Some restaurants have popularized a flaming version by serving it on long swords tipped with cotton which can be ignited for an impressive parade to the table of the diner.

Your skewers may be green twigs, wires, or metal spikes. Your food may be almost anything: meat, game, fish, poultry, fruit, vegetables, alone or in combination. Sometimes they are marinated, sometimes merely brushed with oil or sauce—always succulent, delicious.

BEEF OR LAMB KEBABS
(Basic Recipe)

2 pounds boneless lean meat (lamb shoulder or leg, or sirloin beef steak)
¾ pound fresh mushrooms
2 medium-sized onions
3 medium-sized firm tomatoes
2 green peppers

Marinade and Basting Sauce:
2 bay leaves, crumbled
6 black peppercorns, crushed
6 fluid ounces vinegar
3 fluid ounces water
1½ teaspoons sugar
3 tablespoons olive or salad oil
1 medium-sized onion, chopped
1 clove garlic, finely chopped

Marinade: Combine bay leaves, peppercorns, vinegar, water, and sugar in small pan. Bring to boil; boil slowly 3 to 4 minutes.

Cool and pour into pint jar with the oil. Shake well before using.

Meat: Cut meat into 1½-inch cubes and put in 2-quart bowl. Sprinkle with chopped onions and garlic. Pour on marinade and stir well.

Cover and let stand in refrigerator 3 to 4 hours or longer, stirring occasionally.

Vegetables: Wash mushrooms quickly in cold water. Dry with towel; remove stems. Peel onions, quarter, ready to separate into layers. Wash tomatoes and peppers. Cut tomatoes into 6 wedges each. Cut de-seeded peppers into 1½-inch squares.

Fill Skewers: Drain marinade from meat; keep for basting. Slide a piece of meat on skewer, then pieces of green pepper, a whole mushroom, a layer of onion. Continue to alternate meat and vegetables, ending with meat.

Press filled skewers at ends so that ingredients will fit together tightly. Brush with marinade.

Grill: Grill until meat is cooked to taste, turning several times to brown evenly on all sides. Baste often with marinade. Sprinkle with salt and pepper and push from skewers with fork onto serving plates.

About Tomatoes: Since tomatoes cook more quickly than the meat and other ingredients, be sure to grill them separately.

Cut the tomatoes into 4 to 6 wedges, depending upon their size, then thread the pieces on a skewer and grill only until heated through and lightly browned.

Variations: Squares of luncheon meat or quarters of frankfurters may be used instead of beef or lamb. Keep in marinade only an hour or two, or just brush with salad oil.

Grilling on a Spit: To prepare in the spit, just lay the filled skewers across a shallow roasting pan and grill slowly, turning and basting as they cook.

SHISH KEBAB

1 leg of lamb (5 or 6 pounds), boned
½ pound onions, sliced
1 tablespoon salt
½ teaspoon pepper
2½ fluid ounces sherry
2 tablespoons oil
1 teaspoon oregano

Remove all fat and gristle from the leg of lamb. Bone it and cut meat into 1-inch squares.

Mix meat with sliced onions, seasonings, and other ingredients. Let meat marinate in sauce at least 1 hour, and preferably overnight.

Put on skewers and grill over charcoal fire or under gas grill until crisply brown on all sides. Serves 8.

STEAK KEBABS WITH RED WINE

1 pound steak, cut in cubes
12 large fresh mushrooms
4 fluid ounces claret or Burgundy
1 teaspoon Worcestershire sauce
4 fluid ounces salad oil
2 tablespoons tomato ketchup
1 tablespoon sugar
1 tablespoon vinegar
½ teaspoon powdered marjoram
½ teaspoon powdered rosemary

Marinate steak cubes and mushrooms 2 hours in a marinade made by blending wine, salad oil, Worcestershire, ketchup, sugar, vinegar, and herbs.

Arrange 4 beef cubes and 3 mushrooms alternately on skewers.

Grill, turning to brown well on all sides. Baste frequently with remaining marinade. Serves 4.

SKEWERED LAMB INTERNATIONAL

4 fluid ounces pineapple juice
2 fluid ounces soy sauce
2 teaspoons brown sugar
½ teaspoon Worcestershire sauce
½ small garlic clove, finely chopped
¼ teaspoon ground ginger
½ teaspoon Aromat
⅛ teaspoon thyme
1 pound boned lamb shoulder
6 bacon rashers
8 mushroom caps
8 pineapple chunks

Combine first 8 ingredients; mix well.

Cut lamb into 12 cubes. Cut bacon rashers in halves, fold each piece in two.

On each of 4 long skewers, alternately string 3 pieces of lamb, 3 bacon folds, 2 mushroom caps, and 2 pineapple chunks, beginning and ending with lamb.

Place in shallow pan; pour pineapple juice mixture over. Chill several hours.

Drain, saving sauce. Grill 10 minutes, with surface of meat 3 inches from heat; brush twice with sauce.

Turn, grill 10 minutes longer, brushing twice with sauce. Serve on rice. Heat any remaining sauce and pour it over kebabs and rice. Serves 4.

Lamb on skewers appears under many names and with many flavours. It is the shish kebab of the Near East, the shashlik of Russia, the brochette d'agneau of France, the souvlakia of Greece. And each nationality adds a distinctive flair by way of flavour in the sauce in which meaty squares of lamb are soaked before stringing on skewers.

The rules for kebab cookery are simple. Select foods that cook in the same length of time and are complementary in flavour. Of course, the meats must be the grilling type and, therefore, tender and cut for relatively quick cooking.

TERIYAKIS

**About 20 ounces canned pineapple
    chunks**
**1 pound topside or fillet of beef,
    cut ¾-inch thick**
2 fluid ounces soy sauce
1 clove garlic, finely chopped
¼ teaspoon ground ginger
1 small jar stuffed olives (about 22)
**22 short skewers (about 4 inches
    long)**
**   Aromat**

Drain pineapple; reserve 4 fluid ounces of the syrup.

Cut beef into cubes about the size of pineapple chunks.

Combine reserved pineapple syrup, soy sauce, garlic, and ginger. Add meat cubes and pineapple chunks; marinate at least 1 hour.

Alternate meat cubes and pineapple on skewers, ending with an olive. Grill to taste. Sprinkle with Aromat. Serve hot.

LAMB AND PINEAPPLE KEBABS

1½ pounds lamb, ½ inch thick
6 slices canned pineapple
Salt and pepper
**2½ ounces butter or margarine,
    melted**
3 ounces fine dry breadcrumbs

Choose steak from shoulder or leg; cut meat and pineapple in 1-inch squares.

Alternate pieces on skewers and sprinkle with salt and pepper; dip in melted butter and roll in crumbs.

Grill with moderate heat, turning often; serve on toast. Serves 6.

HAM AND PINEAPPLE KEBABS

Spear 1½-inch cubes of ham and canned pineapple chunks, allowing 3 cubes of ham and 2 of pineapple to each skewer.

Grill for 8 minutes, turning frequently, basting with pineapple juice.

LIVER AND BACON KEBABS

Cut calf, lamb, or veal liver into 1-inch cubes.

Alternate liver and rashers of bacon which have been folded into quarters on metal skewers. Brush liver with melted fat.

Brown about 5 inches from heat, turning to brown evenly. Grill until bacon is crisp and liver is browned, 10 to 15 minutes. Season with salt and pepper.

Variations: Alternate mushroom caps or small whole boiled onions with the liver and bacon. Chicken livers cut in half may be used. Sliced canned water chestnuts are a good combination with the chicken livers.

SPICED HAM AND POTATO KEBABS

Cut 1-pound can of ham into 12 cubes. Score each cube on sides. Insert on skewer, alternating with small cooked or canned potatoes.

Baste with your favourite barbecue sauce and grill 8 to 10 minutes, turning and basting with additional sauce throughout the grilling period.

Variations: Proceed as above, substituting canned spiced crabapples, canned sweet potatoes, and pineapple chunks for potatoes.

Baste with glaze of equal parts of brown sugar and pineapple syrup.

QUICK BEEF FILLET KEBABS

Buy beef fillet in one piece. Cut into 1½ × 2-inch cubes.

Place on skewers alternately with fresh mushroom caps and chunks of onion.

Brush with melted beef fat (your butcher will supply the suet to melt).

Grill quickly over coals until meat is browned but still rare and juicy inside, about 4 to 7 minutes.

CAUCASIAN SHASHLIK

**1 leg of lamb (about 6 pounds),
    boned**
16 fluid ounces Burgundy
16 fluid ounces olive oil
Juice of 2 lemons
Salt and pepper
½ Spanish onion, finely chopped
Vegetables of choice

Cut lamb in 2-inch squares.

Combine Burgundy, oil, lemon juice, seasonings, and onion. Place mixture in earthenware crock or in deep china or glass dish; do not use metal. Marinate 3 days in the refrigerator.

When ready to cook, use 12-inch skewers. On each skewer alternate pieces of lamb with ⅓ tomato, ⅓-inch slice of onion (1 inch in diameter) and a ring of green pepper, if desired.

Each 12-inch skewer will take about 5 cubes of lamb, 2 tomatoes and 2 onion slices.

To cook: Grill on both sides gently, about 8 minutes on each side, depending on thickness of meat. If possible, finish off in a moderate oven for 10 minutes.

For indoor service, make this quick, appetizing sauce:

Blend ¼ cup Burgundy or tarragon vinegar with 2 to 3 tablespoons melted warm butter; pour over each serving as a sauce.

Serve with hot steamed rice and a green vegetable or salad. Serves 8.

STEAK AND MUSHROOM KEBABS

**1½ pounds fillet or rump steak, cut
    in 1½ inch cubes**
**½ pound mushroom caps, washed
    and drained**
Sauce:
1 teaspoon Worcestershire sauce
½ teaspoon Aromat
1 clove garlic
⅛ teaspoon rosemary
4 fluid ounces red wine
4 fluid ounces oil
1 tablespoon horseradish

Remove mushroom stems and save for another dish. Marinate steak and mushrooms in combined sauce ingredients for several hours.

Arrange steak cubes and mushrooms alternately on skewers. Allow 3 cubes of steak and 2 mushrooms per skewer.

Grill over hot coals, basting frequently with sauce. Serve with remaining sauce. Serves 4.

Hamburgers for the Barbecue

TIPS FOR BETTER HAMBURGERS

● Freshly minced beef is bright red in colour and should have a little fat for flavour.

● When meat is minced to order, check the leanness of the meat and if it is very lean have 2 to 3 ounces suet minced with each pound of meat.

● Medium or coarsely minced meat (minced only once) gives extra juicy, light-textured hamburgers.

● For improved flavour, add ½ teaspoon Aromat or monosodium glutamate to each pound of minced beef.

● When shaping hamburger rounds, handle the meat lightly; the less handling minced beef gets, the more juicy and tender it will be.

● To avoid sticking, spread hamburgers with soft butter or margarine before grilling.

● While cooking, turn hamburgers only once. Don't flip back and forth.

● Don't pack hamburgers down with the spatula.

● If the grids on the grill are too widely spaced to hold hamburgers and if there is no frying pan or wire grill available, place a piece of aluminium foil on the grill.

● For extra juicy hamburgers, serve them with a spicy sauce. While the hamburgers cook over the grill, melt 1½–2 ounces butter or margarine in a frying pan for each 4 hamburgers. Season with Worcestershire sauce. When the hamburgers are cooked, put into frying pan and turn once so that both sides are coated; serve piping hot with the sauce.

● Always have hot toasted rolls or bread ready for serving when the hamburgers are done.

DOUBLE HAMBURGERS

1 pound minced beef
1 teaspoon salt
1 egg
2 fluid ounces milk
2 tablespoons prepared mustard
6 thin slices onion
2 tablespoons sweet pepper relish or chilli pickle

Combine the beef, salt, egg, and milk. Mix well. Make 12 small flat rounds. Spread mustard on 6 rounds. Top each with an onion slice and a teaspoon of relish.

Place remaining hamburger rounds on top of relish. Press hamburgers together, sealing well around the edges.

Grill 3 inches from heat source about 5 minutes on each side or pan-fry in 1 tablespoon fat in a heavy frying pan.

Makes 6 hamburgers.

HAMBURGERS WITH EVERYTHING

2 pounds lean minced beef
2 teaspoons salt
½ teaspoon pepper
Relishes

Combine minced meat, salt, and pepper. Shape into 12 rounds. Grill to taste turning once. Serve with choice of relishes.

Hot and Sharp Sauce: Mix 6 tablespoons mayonnaise, 4 tablespoons prepared mustard, and 2 tablespoons horseradish. Top with sliced dill pickle.

Green and Red Relish: Mix 1 cup chilli pickle and a dash of Tabasco. Put in serving dish and top with 2 tablespoons pepper relish.

Sweet and Sour Sauce: Fry 2 rashers bacon. Remove from pan. Stir 2 tablespoons flour into fat. Add 4 fluid ounces water, 4 fluid ounces vinegar, 2 tablespoons sugar, ½ teaspoon salt, and ½ chopped red pepper. Cook until thickened. Add the bacon, crumbled.

Minted Cucumber: Peel and dice 1 medium-sized cucumber. Sprinkle with ½ teaspoon salt and 1 tablespoon sugar. Add 2 tablespoons each of wine vinegar and chopped fresh mint.

Green Onion with Caraway: Mix 1 bunch sliced spring onions with a few caraway seeds and 2 tablespoons vinegar. Add salt and pepper to taste.

Herbed Sour Cream: Mix 8 fluid ounces sour cream, 2 tablespoons chopped spring onion tops, and 1 tablespoon chopped fresh herbs or 1 teaspoon dried herbs.

HAMBURGER PICNIC "PIZZA"

Fry 1 pound lean minced beef until brown. Add 5 fluid ounces tomato sauce, ¾ teaspoon salt, ¼ teaspoon garlic salt, 8 sliced stuffed olives, and 4 ounces diced Mozzarella or Muenster cheese.

Cut deep slits into top of 8 oblong crusty rolls. Fill rolls and sprinkle with oregano.

Wrap in aluminium foil. Cook on rack over hot coals about 15 minutes, turning frequently. Serves 4.

CAMPFIRE HAMBURGER-BACON SPECIALS

For each serving, shape around the end of a green stick ¼ pound lean minced beef seasoned with finely chopped onion, salt, and pepper.

Wrap diagonally with a rasher of bacon; fasten with a cocktail stick.

Cook slowly over hot coals, turning often, until bacon is crisp.

Remove sticks. Slip meat from stick into a split toasted frankfurter roll. Serve with piccalilli.

For Cheeseburger Stacks: Season minced beef with salt and pepper. Shape into thin rounds, using 2 ounces meat per round and flatten into 4 inch circles. Between each two rounds, place a thin slice of processed cheese; press edges together to seal cheese inside. Grill over the coals on both sides. Serve in heated baps or rolls.

JUICY PICNIC HAMBURGERS

Season each pound of minced beef with 1 teaspoon salt and a pinch pepper. Add 2 fluid ounces cold water per pound of meat.

Shape into patties and wrap in grease-proof paper before taking to the picnic spot.

JUICY PICNIC HAMBURGERS 2

Season each pound of beef with 1 teaspoon salt and a pinch of pepper.

Pat out into thin rounds. Dot half the rounds of meat with 4 or 5 bits of chipped ice in centre. Top with a second round and press gently to seal edges.

As the hamburgers cook, the ice melts and steam forms.

BARBECUE-STYLE HAMBURGER

Shape a pound of lean minced beef into 4 rounds and cook to taste.

Meanwhile heat quick barbecue sauce prepared at home by combining 6 fluid ounces chilli pickle, 2 tablespoons piccalilli, and a dash each of Tabasco and garlic salt.

Put each hamburger in a split heated roll and cover generously with sauce. Serves 4.

MINCED BEEF-OLIVE HAMBURGERS

1 pound minced beef
12 stuffed olives, sliced
1 small onion, finely chopped
½ teaspoon salt
Pinch of pepper

Combine minced beef, olives, onion, salt, and pepper. Shape into rounds.

Grill hamburgers with surface of meat 2 inches from heat. When one side is browned, turn and finish cooking on second side.

Serve each hamburger topped with an onion and tomato slice. Serves 4 to 6.

STUFFED HAMBURGER OBLONGS

1½ pounds minced beef
Salt and pepper
Prepared mustard
4 ounces processed Cheddar cheese
1 dill pickle
8 frankfurter rolls

Season minced beef with salt and pepper and divide into 8 equal portions. Pat each portion into a thin oblong and spread with prepared mustard.

Cut cheese into 8 sticks; cut pickle into 8 strips.

Place one cheese stick and one pickle strip on each portion of meat.

Roll up and grill over hot charcoal until cheese melts and meat is cooked.

Serve in toasted frankfurter rolls. Serves 8.

NUTBURGERS

1½ pounds minced beef
1 teaspoon salt
Pinch of pepper
1 small onion, to be chopped
1 ounce walnuts, to be chopped
8 sprigs parsley, to be chopped
4 hamburger rolls or baps

Season meat with salt and pepper; blend, then form into 8 thin rounds.

Chop and combine onion, walnuts, and parsley; spread mixture on 4 rounds of meat. Cover with remaining rounds; press edges of meat together so that filling is sealed in.

Grill until brown; serve on split rolls or baps. Makes 4 sandwiches.

CHEESEBURGERS

1 pound minced beef
1 teaspoon salt
Pepper
1 tablespoon Worcestershire sauce
Slices of sharp cheese
Hot buttered toasted rolls

Combine beef and seasonings; mix thoroughly. Shape into 4 to 6 rounds, depending upon how thick they are wanted.

Grill or pan fry. Lay a slice of cheese over the top of each hamburger for the last few minutes to melt cheese.

Serve in buttered toasted rolls or baps.

HAMBURGER-PEPPER STEAK

Cut 3 large sweet peppers (1 red and 2 green) into chunks. Fry in a little oil until tender.

Shape a pound of lean minced beef into a steak 1½ inches thick and 3 inches wide. Grill on rack over coals to taste. Cut into 8 slices.

Cut loaf of French bread into 4-inch pieces. Split and butter each and fill with 2 slices of steak and ¼ of the peppers. Season to taste. Serves 4.

BARBECUED HAMBURGERS IN FOIL

1½ pounds minced beef
1½ teaspoons salt
Chilli pickle
Prepared mustard
Tomato ketchup
Thick steak sauce

Mix meat and salt; shape into 8 large thin rounds. Spread with prepared condiments.

Wrap each hamburger in aluminium foil, and freeze in freezer or freezing compartment of refrigerator.

To cook, put wrapped hamburgers directly on hot coals; cover with more coals and cook for 8 to 10 minutes. Serves 4.

MUSHROOM-HAMBURGERS

Mix 1 pound lean minced beef with 1 teaspoon salt, ¼ teaspoon pepper, 1 ounce finely chopped fresh mushrooms (or finely chopped drained canned mushrooms), and 2 ounces grated Cheddar cheese.

Shape into 4 to 6 rounds. Grill or fry to taste. Serve in toasted hamburger rolls or baps. Serves 4.

SURPRISE CHEESEBURGERS

1 pound minced beef
½ teaspoon salt
About 4 ounces cheese-biscuit crumbs
2 tablespoons tomato ketchup

Blend all ingredients together well. Divide mixture into 8 equal parts; form into hamburgers.

Grill until well browned on both sides. Serve on toasted rolls. Makes 8 cheeseburgers.

CARNATZLACH
(Rumanian Hamburger Rolls)

1½ pounds lean minced beef
1 onion, grated
1 garlic clove, finely chopped
1 carrot, grated
Dash of cayenne (optional)
1 teaspoon salt
About 1½ teaspoons mixed herbs.
2 slightly beaten eggs
3 tablespoons flour
Pinch of paprika

Combine minced beef, onion, garlic, carrot, cayenne, salt, herbs, and eggs; mix well.

Form into 1-inch thick rolls, 3 to 4 inches long, tapering at the ends. Or form into smaller rolls, if wished. The former are called carnatzei; the latter are called by the diminutive, carnatzlach.

Roll the hamburgers in flour seasoned with paprika and grill under or over moderate heat. These are traditionally cooked over charcoal. Serves 6.

HOT STUFFED PICNIC ROLLS

1 ounce fat
1 chopped onion
1 ounce chopped green pepper
2 ounces chopped celery
1 pound minced beef
4 tablespoons tomato ketchup
1 teaspoon salt
¼ teaspoon pepper
1 tablespoon Worcestershire sauce
4 ounces grated mature Cheddar cheese
6 frankfurter rolls
Butter or margarine
Prepared mustard

Melt fat in heavy frying pan. Add onion, green pepper, and celery. Cook and stir 5 minutes. Add minced beef and cook until redness is gone.

Add ketchup, salt, pepper, Worcestershire sauce, and cheese. Cook slowly 10 minutes. Chill.

Split rolls and hollow out inside. Spread inside surface with butter and mustard. Fill each roll with hamburger mixture. (These are easier to fill if mixture is chilled.)

Wrap individually in aluminium foil.

At serving time, heat wrapped rolls on outdoor picnic grate or in moderate oven (350°F. Mark 4) 30 minutes.

Serve with pickles, cole slaw, and potato crisps. Makes 6 rolls.

JUMBO CHEESE-ONION BURGERS

2 pounds minced beef
2 tablespoons prepared horseradish or ½ teaspoon Worcestershire sauce
½ teaspoon mixed herbs
Salt and pepper
1 medium onion, cut in 4 slices
4 slices processed cheese
1 tablespoon olive or salad oil

Combine minced beef, horseradish or Worcestershire sauce, mixed herbs, and salt and pepper. Mix lightly and shape into 4 thick rounds.

Cover each onion slice with a slice of cheese; press slightly so they hold together.

Grill the hamburgers on 1 side about 5 minutes. Turn and grill on other side about 4 minutes.

Cover each with a cheese-onion slice; brush with oil and grill again, just long enough to melt the cheese. Serve with fresh hamburger rolls and sliced tomatoes. Serves 4.

HAMBURGER-PICKLE DOGS

Divide 1 pound minced beef into 4 parts. Shape each part over a long dill pickle strip.

Cook over slow fire to taste. Serve in toasted split frankfurter rolls with mustard and chilli sauce, or tomato ketchup. Serves 4.

Ham Steaks and Pork Chops

GRILLED HAM SLICE

Cut rind off slice of smoked ham and cut edges of fat in several places to prevent curling. Brush with melted butter or margarine.

Place in hinged wire grill and grill over moderate heat 10 to 30 minutes according to thickness of slice, turning frequently. Allow 10 minutes for slice ¼ inch thick; 15 to 20 minutes for slice ½ to ¾ inch thick, and 20 to 30 minutes for slice 1 inch thick. Tenderized ham slices require from ⅓ to ½ less time.

Serve with grilled pineapple and sweet potato slices, or with sautéed apples if desired. Allow ¼ to ⅓ pound per portion.

Fruited Ham Steak: Prepare as above and while grilling over moderate heat, baste with pineapple juice, white wine, or vermouth from time to time. To serve, slice in thin strips.

HAM STEAK WITH SOY-SHERRY SAUCE

Prepare grilled ham steak and, while grilling, brush both sides frequently with a mixture of 4 fluid ounces each soy sauce and sherry.

Serve with pineapple slices which have been brushed with the same sauce and grilled.

BARBECUED PORK CHOPS

Combine 8 fluid ounces soy sauce and 1 crushed clove of garlic. Marinate 6 1-inch thick pork chops in mixture for 1 hour, turning frequently.

Grill chops for 45 minutes, turning and basting often with Barbecue Chilli Sauce (see sauces). Serves 6.

HERB PORK CHOPS

Cover loin chops or cutlets with tomato juice which has been seasoned with salt, pepper, and a generous amount of fresh or dried basil. Marinate for several hours.

Remove chops carefully so that basil clings to them. Grill over low heat until well done. A 1-inch chop will take 15 to 20 minutes on each side.

Serve with a sauce made out of tomato juice, using 1 clove garlic, 1 tablespoon olive oil, and 1 tablespoon flour to 8 fluid ounces of tomato juice.

GRILLED HAM WITH PINEAPPLE SAUCE

6 ounces brown sugar
4 fluid ounces vinegar
2 tablespoons dry mustard
8 fluid ounces pineapple juice
Thin ham slices

Combine sugar, vinegar, and mustard; simmer gently for 3 minutes. Remove from heat and add pineapple juice.

Grill the thin ham slices. When slightly browned, baste with the sauce, then baste occasionally while they cook until tender and well seasoned.

BARBECUED HAM STEAKS

2 ounces melted butter or margarine
16 fluid ounces sherry
2 teaspoons powdered cloves
1½ ounces brown sugar
1 tablespoon dry mustard
2 teaspoons paprika
3 to 4 cloves garlic, finely chopped
3 ham slices, 1-inch thick

Combine sauce ingredients and marinate ham slices in it for 2 hours, turning once.

Drain ham slices and grill about 20 minutes, turning often and basting with the sauce. Serves 6.

HAM STEAKS WITH MUSHROOM SAUCE

2 ham steaks, ½-inch thick
3 tablespoons vinegar
1½ teaspoons dry mustard
½ teaspoon sugar
2 tablespoons redcurrant jelly
½ pound fresh mushrooms, peeled and sliced
Butter or margarine as needed
Salt, pepper, paprika

Score fat edges of ham steaks to prevent curling. Put ham in a frying pan; add a little water, cover and let steam 10 minutes.

Mix vinegar, mustard, sugar, and redcurrant jelly in saucepan and heat, but do not boil.

Grill ham in hinged wire grill. Lightly brown the mushrooms in butter and combine with sauce.

Place grilled ham on a heated platter; pour mushroom sauce over. Salt, pepper, and paprika may be added to sauce if desired. Serves 4.

GLAZED-GRILLED THICK HAM SLICE

1 1½- to 2-inch slice gammon
2 tablespoons orange or peach marmalade, honey, or brown sugar mixed with a tablespoon of mustard

Slash fat edges to prevent curling. Grill ham slice 3 inches from heat source for 10 minutes. Turn with tongs and grill until brown.

Spread with orange or peach marmalade or other sweet topping. Serve hot. Serves 6.

Note: Slices of ready-to-eat picnic ham or cooked boneless shoulder butt or Canadian style bacon may be grilled in this way.

QUICK AND EASY HAM BARBECUE

Use a fully cooked boneless ham. It may be left whole and skewered from end to end or cut into 1-inch serving portions to speed heating.

A tasty sauce is made by combining 4½ ounces brown sugar, 3 tablespoons vinegar, 2 fluid ounces pineapple juice, 4 fluid ounces apricot juice, ¼ teaspoon powdered cloves, and ¼ teaspoon powdered garlic.

Brush ham liberally with sauce, using a long-handled brush or cloth on a stick. Continue to brush on sauce as the ham heats. Constant turning over hot coals should heat the ham in 20 to 30 minutes. Because fully-cooked ham is used, there's no worry about under-cooking. When the slices are lightly browned, they are ready to serve.

Quick and Easy Ham Barbecue

Barbecued Spareribs

SPEEDY BARBECUED SPARERIBS

Barbecued spareribs are an outdoor favourite, but because of the necessity for thorough cooking of pork, many people prefer this method.

Cut 4 pounds spareribs into 3 to 4 rib sections. Simmer in 16 fluid ounces water until almost tender (about 1 hour) or pressure cook in 8 fluid ounces water at 15 pounds pressure for 20 minutes, according to manufacturer's directions.

Dip each piece in Texas barbecue sauce (see sauces) and grill over hot coals, turning often to brown well. Brush with more Texas barbecue sauce frequently during grilling. Serves 3 to 4.

"SMOKY" BARBECUED SPARERIBS

3 pounds spareribs, cut in pieces
Hickory salt or smoke-flavoured Aromat
1 clove garlic, chopped
1 medium onion, chopped
Few sprigs parsley, chopped
Pinch each of black pepper, ginger, and rosemary
4 fluid ounces dry sherry
2 tablespoons sugar
2 tablespoons tomato purée

Rub the ribs with hickory salt or flavoured Aromat and place in shallow roasting tin. Sprinkle with a mixture of garlic, onion, parsley, pepper, ginger, and rosemary.

Cover pan with foil or greaseproof paper and leave overnight.

To cook, remove ribs from pan and cook over coals until tender, basting occasionally with a mixture of sherry, sugar, and tomato purée. Serves 3 to 4.

SWEET AND SOUR SPARERIBS

3½ to 4 pounds spareribs
Salt
16 fluid ounces master barbecue sauce (see sauces)
8 fluid ounces crushed pineapple
4 tablespoons orange marmalade

Cut ribs into serving-size pieces. Season with salt. Brown over hot coals. When golden, place in frying pan.

Combine barbecue sauce, pineapple, and marmalade. Pour over spareribs. Brown, basting often, until tender, 1 to 1½ hours. Serves 4.

Just-right ribs are crispy-brown outside, tender and juicy inside. Lean shows no pink when cut. Long slow cooking and frequent turning are required.

BARBECUED SPARERIBS

8 fluid ounces tomato ketchup
4 tablespoons vinegar
2 to 4 tablespoons dark brown sugar
Few drops Tabasco or other hot sauce
4 tablespoons prepared mustard
3 to 4 pounds spareribs

Mix sauce ingredients well and use to baste spareribs often during cooking. If a thinner sauce is desired, add a little tomato juice.

Have the spareribs cracked down the middle and cut into 6-inch serving pieces. Sprinkle with salt and pepper.

Grill over low heat until tender, 1 to 1½ hours, turning and basting often with this sauce or with barbecue chilli sauce, or special hot barbecue sauce. Serves 4.

SPICY BARBECUED SPARERIBS

1½ ounces brown sugar
1 teaspoon salt
1 tablespoon celery salt
1-2 teaspoons chilli powder
1 teaspoon paprika
2½ to 3 pounds spareribs
2 fluid ounces vinegar
1 8-ounce can tomato sauce

Mix dry ingredients and rub about ⅓ into the ribs.

Combine remaining mixture with vinegar and tomato sauce.

Let the ribs stand an hour, if possible, before cooking. Then cook over moderate heat until tender, basting occasionally with the sauce. Serves 3 to 4.

GOURMET BARBECUED SPARERIBS

5 pounds spareribs
8 fluid ounces soy sauce
8 fluid ounces Cointreau
12 ounces honey
1 can (about 15 ounces) crushed pineapple
2 lemons, sliced
4 teaspoons powdered ginger
8 fluid ounces white wine vinegar
8 cloves garlic, finely chopped

Combine sauce ingredients. Marinate ribs in mixture for ½ hour, turning once.

Grill until done, 1 to 1½ hours, basting with this same sauce or with special hot barbecue sauce or with barbecue chilli sauce. Serves 5 to 6.

GARLIC SPARERIBS

4 to 5 pounds spareribs
4 cloves garlic
8 fluid ounces stock or consommé
8 ounces orange marmalade
2 fluid ounces vinegar
4 tablespoons tomato ketchup
1 teaspoon salt

Marinate (soak) the whole racks of ribs in a mixture of crushed or finely chopped garlic and all remaining ingredients for 12 hours or more in refrigerator.

Then lift ribs from the liquid and weave the bony strips onto a spit.

Grill 1 to 1½ hours or until meat is tender and glazed. Baste with the marinade during the cooking period. Serves 4 to 5.

Lamb and Veal for the Barbecue

LAMB CHOPS WITH LEMON

4 thick (1½ inches) loin lamb chops
Grated rind of 1 lemon
Juice of 1 lemon

Cut little pockets in the fat of each chop. Stuff pockets well with grated lemon rind.

Arrange chops on grilling rack or in hinged wire grill and cook on one side for about 10 minutes, then turn and grill second side for the same length of time.

For well done lamb, cook a little longer on both sides. Season with salt and pepper. Serve on heated dishes, with a little lemon juice poured over each chop. Serves 4.

MINTED SHOULDER LAMB CHOPS

4 fluid ounces orange juice
2 fluid ounces lemon juice
1 tablespoon sugar
½ teaspoon marjoram
½ teaspoon rosemary
½ teaspoon Aromat
¼ teaspoon salt
Few grains nutmeg
Bouquet of fresh mint
4 double shoulder lamb chops,
    boned and rolled

Combine all ingredients except mint and chops. Let stand 1 hour.

Tie mint bouquet in muslin.

Dip chops in sauce; place on grill. Turn frequently, brushing each time with sauce, using mint "switch" as a brush.

Grill 15 to 25 minutes, according to taste. Serves 4.

Lamb Shanks: Always a good buy and highly favoured by men. Although they are usually braised, they can be barbecued on the grill—with delicious results.

GRILLED VEAL CHOPS AND STEAKS

Veal needs long, slow cooking over moderate heat.

For steaks, use cuts from the leg, 1 to 1½ inches thick. Have kidney chops cut 1 to 1½ inches thick.

Season to taste as they cook. As veal is improved with extra seasoning, serve with well heated barbecue sauce.

GRILLED LAMB STEAKS

Lamb steaks about 1 inch thick, cut from the leg, may be cooked in much the same way as beef steaks. Grill slowly, turning often, and season to taste just before serving.

Many people like them seasoned with tarragon or rosemary. The rosemary should be rubbed into the steak before cooking. If tarragon flavour is preferred, sprinkle a little on the steak as it cooks.

BARBECUED LAMB SHANKS

4 fluid ounces olive oil
1 tablespoon lemon juice
1 teaspoon salt
½ teaspoon thyme
1 tablespoon tomato purée
1 teaspoon dry mustard
1 small onion, grated
4 garlic cloves
4 lamb shanks
4 whole red peppers

Combine first seven ingredients for marinade. Insert split garlic clove in each lamb shank. Arrange shanks on long skewers, alternately with whole de-seeded peppers. Prick meat all over with fork, then pour marinade over it. Let meat stand in marinade about 2 hours, then remove.

Roast directly over coals 4 to 5 inches from heat for about 1 hour or until meat is tender. Serves 4.

BARBECUED LEG OF LAMB

Leg of lamb, boned, flattened (about
    6 pounds)
2 tablespoons vinegar
4 fluid ounces olive oil
1 clove garlic, crushed
1 teaspoon salt
½ teaspoon pepper

Combine vinegar, oil, garlic, salt, and pepper. Marinate lamb in this sauce for 2 hours or more, turning often.

When ready to cook, lift lamb from marinade and place on a basket-grill. Flatten and shape, then lock the racks firmly in place. Grill over coals 1½ to 2 hours, turning often and brushing every 5 minutes with special hot barbecue sauce. Serves 6 to 8.

STUFFED BREAST OF LAMB CUTLETS

Get the butcher to remove the breast bone, cut off the first 2 or 3 ribs from point end of breast, and remove the boneless flank end. Have a pocket cut in the breast.

Cut meat and some fat from the trimmings; add an extra pound of lamb shoulder and put through the mincer. Season the minced meat with salt, pepper, and ½ teaspoon mace.

Stuff the lamb breast tightly with minced meat. Chill, if possible, then cut between ribs to make cutlets. Grill over hot coals.

LAMB CUTLETS WITH SPICY SAUCE

1 strip of lamb breast or cutlets
Garlic salt
2 fluid ounces chilli pickle
Pinch of celery salt
Dash of Tabasco sauce
Juice of 1 lemon

Cut breast into one-rib pieces. Sprinkle cutlets with garlic salt. Combine remaining ingredients.

Grill until cutlets are browned. Brush with sauce and grill until cutlets are tender. Serves 3.

LAMB CHOPS AND KIDNEY GRILL

4 lamb loin or shoulder chops
2 lamb kidneys, split
Butter or oil
Salt and pepper
2 tomatoes, cut in halves crosswise
4 whole cooked carrots

Place chops and kidneys on grill rack or in hinged wire grill. Brush kidneys with oil or butter. Grill about 7 minutes or until chops are well browned.

Season with salt and pepper. Turn and arrange tomatoes and carrots on grill, first seasoning with salt and pepper and brushing with oil or butter. Grill about another 7 minutes and serve hot. Serves 4.

MARINATED BREAST OF LAMB

1 large lamb breast (3 pounds)
8 fluid ounces orange juice
4 fluid ounces lemon juice
2 tablespoons sugar
About 1 ounce chopped mint leaves

Cut up the breast into cutlets or leave whole. Cover with mixture of the juices and sugar. Place in refrigerator overnight.

The next day add the chopped mint to the marinade 2 hours before cooking.

Remove the meat from the marinade; rub with oil and cook over a slow fire for 1 to 1¼ hours, or until tender on the inside and rather crisp outside. While cooking, baste with a sauce made from 4 fluid ounces of the marinade mixed with 2 fluid ounces salad oil.

Heat remaining marinade and serve as a sauce. Serves 4 to 6.

Marinated Lamb Shanks: Place 4 to 6 pounds lamb shanks in a heavy pan. Add a little water; cover and simmer gently until partially tenderized.

Drain, cool, and cover with above marinade and proceed as directed in recipe for marinated lamb breast.

MARINATED BREAST OF LAMB 2

8 fluid ounces lemon juice
2½ fluid ounces olive or salad oil
1 medium onion, thinly sliced
Breast of lamb (about 3 pounds)
½ teaspoon Aromat
½ teaspoon salt
Dash of pepper

Mix lemon juice, oil, and onion. Pour over lamb and let stand for 1 hour at least, longer if possible.

Lift meat from marinade and thread on spit. Sprinkle with Aromat, salt, and pepper.

Grill over a slow fire for 1 to 1¼ hours or until tender on the inside, rather crisp outside. Serves 4 to 6.

MARINATED LAMB STEAKS

Use steaks about 1 inch thick from leg or shoulder. Rub with garlic and salt.

Marinate in both white wine and tarragon leaves (to 8 fluid ounces wine, add 1½ teaspoons dry tarragon). Let steak absorb this for about 2 hours, turning frequently.

Remove to piece of absorbent paper.

Melt 3 ounces butter in saucepan; add the wine and tarragon; heat and save.

Put steak over medium-hot coals, brushing from time to time with the wine-tarragon mixture. A 1-inch steak

will take 4 to 6 minutes per side to cook to medium rare.

GRILLED LAMB CHOPS

Have lamb loin chops or shoulder chops cut about two inches thick. Place the chops in a hinged wire grill over a good bed of coals.

Brown on one side, turn and brown on second side. It will take about 30 to 40 minutes to cook these chops. Serve on heated plates.

LAMB BARBECUE — HUNGARIAN

Before barbecuing a roast of lamb or chops, rub with salt in which garlic has been crushed.

Then place a layer of sliced onion in the bottom of a pan or crock. Put in the meat and pile sliced lemon and sliced onion on top and around sides.

Cover and let stand in a cool place overnight, or longer if possible.

Before cooking, sprinkle lots of paprika over the meat. The meat is then ready for roasting or grilling.

BARBECUE VEAL CHOPS

4 veal chops, 1 inch thick
2 fluid ounces oil
2 tablespoons lemon juice
½ teaspoon salt
¼ teaspoon pepper
1 clove garlic, crushed
Pinch of marjoram
2 tablespoons Worcestershire sauce
2 tablespoons tomato ketchup

Combine ingredients for barbecue sauce. Place chops in a wire folding grill and brown chops near the coals.

Remove to a higher position. Turn and baste with sauce frequently until tender. This should take about 35 minutes. Serve on hot plates with remaining warm barbecue sauce. Serves 4.

HERB VEAL CHOPS OR STEAKS

Roll veal chops or steaks in oil or butter, then in a mixture of chopped chives, parsley, and tarragon. Let stand for an hour.

Grill over low heat until cooked through. A 1-inch steak will take about 15 minutes on each side.

LAMB WHIRLS

½ pound bacon rashers
1½ pounds minced lamb
1 teaspoon salt
Pinch of pepper
¼ teaspoon marjoram
1 tablespoon Worcestershire sauce
2 ounces cornflakes
2 tablespoons water

Arrange bacon in overlapping rashers on a sheet of paper about 10 inches wide.

Combine remaining ingredients, pat out on bacon.

Roll as for a Swiss roll, wrap tightly in greaseproof paper and chill thoroughly.

Before slicing, place wooden sticks through roll at inch intervals to hold bacon in place. Cut 1-inch slices.

Grill over hot coals 6 to 7 minutes on each side, turning when brown. Serves 6.

CURRIED LAMB STEAKS

Combine 6 fluid ounces soy sauce with 1 tablespoon curry powder, 1 crushed clove of garlic, and a little ground ginger.

Soak lamb steaks in this mixture for 1 hour before grilling.

Economy-wise housewives choose lamb breast for the barbecue. It makes a delicious dish when marinated and prepared in much the same way as barbecued pork spareribs. Prepare the breast whole, cut between the ribs for lamb cutlets, or cut in 2- or 3-rib portions.

Spit Barbecued Meats

SELECTING THE JOINT

Make a friend of a good butcher. He will advise about best cuts for barbecues. These are popular cuts for roasting on a spit: rib roasts of beef, rolled ribs, top-quality rump, sirloin or fillet of beef; leg, rolled shoulder, or saddle of lamb; fresh or smoked ham, loin of pork or double loin of pork (2 loins boned and tied together so fat is all on the outside), and sweet-cured bacon.

Meat for spit barbecuing should be at room temperature; remove from refrigerator 1 to 2 hours before you start the fire.

HOW TO SPIT A ROAST

The object is to have the meat secured to the spit so that, as nearly as possible, it is in balance and it is compact and well fastened. If one side of the roast is much heavier than the other, which it usually is in rib roasts, run the spit through diagonally. A rolled roast or leg of lamb is spitted directly through the centre.

USE A MEAT THERMOMETER

Use a meat thermometer when roasting and you won't have to guess when your roast is done. After the meat has been spitted, insert the thermometer at an angle into the heaviest end to the centre of the roast so that it won't strike coals or heating element as the roast turns. The tip must not touch bone, fat, or the metal spit.

The thermometer probably won't register a change for the first hour, or until the heat penetrates centre of the joint.

ROASTING HINTS

A fairly slow fire should be used. If the roast has a good covering of fat it will acquire a beautiful glaze as it evenly bastes itself with its own juices.

Lean cuts of meat are best basted with butter or oil while they cook. Or you can baste the roast with a herb-seasoned or barbecue sauce.

In either type, lean or fat, basting will add to the flavour and improve the glaze.

A drip pan made of aluminium foil can be set in place before or after you build the fire. Put it in front of the coals directly under meat on spit. The juices caught that way make a far better gravy, just as they are, than the usual flour and water variety.

Timing of cooking periods will vary with the size of firebox, degree of heat, amount and direction of wind, and type of grill used.

WHOLE BEEF FILLET ON A SPIT

Ask the butcher to roll the whole fillet in a thin sheet of rounded suet and tie securely.

Spit it through the centre and season with salt and pepper. Other seasonings such as garlic or a little rosemary may be used, if wished.

Roast until it is crisp on the outside but still rare in the centre, about 35 to 45 minutes. Slice and serve with a wine or mushroom sauce.

STUFFED TOPSIDE

2 pounds topside of beefsteak cut about ½-inch thick
½ pound minced beef
2 to 3 slices liverwurst, mashed
4 mushrooms, chopped
4 tablespoons cream, tomato juice, or meat stock
2 teaspoons salt
Dash of pepper
6 bacon rashers

Ask the butcher to pound the steak, or pound it yourself with a meat mallet.

Mix minced beef with liverwurst, mushrooms, cream, salt, and pepper to make the stuffing.

Spoon mixture onto steak, shaping it down the centre in a narrow strip.

Roll sides of steak over stuffing and tie tightly with string.

Wrap bacon rashers around the roll at even intervals and fasten bacon ends securely with wooden sticks.

Insert spit in centre of the meat and grill over hot coals or in an electric unit 30 to 45 minutes. Serves 4 to 6.

BARBECUED BOLOGNA ROLL

Remove casing from a large piece of round bologna sausage or any smoked sausage. Score surface crosswise at 1-inch intervals to depth of ¼ inch.

Insert spit through the centre and grill over coals or in rotisserie about 30 minutes, basting frequently with barbecue sauce.

A few minutes before sausage is done, split and toast sandwich rolls. Slice sausage, and serve between rolls with additional sauce, if wished.

RUMP ROAST ON A SPIT

Rump of beef
1 pint vinegar
1 pint water
3 onions, sliced
1 lemon, sliced
12 whole cloves
2 or 3 bay leaves
6 black peppercorns
1½ tablespoons salt

Because rump of beef is a less tender cut it is best to marinate it 2 or 3 days in the refrigerator before roasting.

Combine the marinade ingredients in a bowl and let stand at room temperature for several hours before adding meat.

Then add the meat and, for a mild flavour, let it stand in the refrigerator for only 24 hours.

Remove the meat from the refrigerator about 4 hours before roasting on a spit over coals or in a rotisserie, until tender, 1½ to 2 hours.

Baste the joint with barbecue sauce several times during cooking.

Note: You can keep the chilled marinade for the next roast.

STUFFED LEG OR SHOULDER OF LAMB

Leg or shoulder of lamb, boned and rolled, but not tied

Stuffing:
2 medium onions, finely chopped
2 cloves garlic, finely chopped
2 ounces butter or margarine
¼ pound pork sausage meat
4½ ounces fresh white breadcrumbs
1 teaspoon tarragon

Cook onions and garlic in butter until onions look limp.

Cook sausage meat in a little hot water about 5 minutes; drain thoroughly.

Combine all stuffing ingredients; mix well. Spread on lamb; roll up and tie securely.

Insert spit and roast over coals or in rotisserie, basting occasionally with pan juices, mixed, if wished, with a little white wine. Season the roast with salt just before removing from spit.

Kind of joint	ROTISSERIE ROASTING GUIDE		Thermometer reading
	Approximate cooking time*		
Beef			
Rare	2 to 2½ hours		140°F.
Medium	2½ to 3 hours		160°F.
Well-done	3 to 4 hours		170°F.
Pork	2 to 3½ hours		185°F.
Lamb			
Medium	1½ to 2 hours		175°F.
Well-done	2 to 2½ hours		180°F.

*For a 4- to 6-pound joint at room temperature.

ROAST SUCKLING PIG

Suckling pigs range in size from 10 to 30 pounds and it takes a rather large spit to roast one.

Choose the largest pig your equipment will hold. The smallest pigs will be nothing but skin and bones when cooked. Sprinkle the inside with salt, pepper, and a little oregano or sweet basil. Rub the skin well with oil, salt, and a little of the same herb.

Head and feet can be cut off before or after cooking; however, it won't look much like a pig if they are removed before cooking. Insert a piece of wood in the mouth to simplify adding an apple later.

Tie the legs in a kneeling position and arrange the pig on the spit so that it is perfectly balanced.

Place over a deep bed of hot coals arranged in such a way to allow for a pan to be placed in the centre to catch the drippings from the roasting meat. These should be used for basting. The pig may be basted with oil but will lose much of its flavour.

Like all pork, the pig must be roasted until thoroughly done. The skin should be very crisp. The time will be about 2½ hours for a very small pig, up to 6 to 10 hours for a large stuffed suckling pig, depending on the fire.

If the pig is stuffed with a sage or fruit dressing, stuff loosely to allow for expansion, and sew or lace up closely and tightly.

When done, remove from the spit, place a red apple in the mouth and cranberries or currants in the eyes.

MARINATED TOPSIDE OF BEEF

4 pounds topside of beef
1 tablespoon meat tenderizer
1½ pints dry white wine
6 fluid ounces salad oil
1 teaspoon rosemary
Pinch of sage
Pinch of thyme
1 tablespoon black pepper
2 onions, thinly sliced
1 ounce butter or margarine, melted
1 teaspoon celery seeds

Pierce surface of the meat in many places with a fork or skewer and sprinkle with meat tenderizer.

Put beef in a deep bowl and pour in marinade mixture of wine, oil, rosemary, sage, thyme, pepper, and onions.

Cover and let stand for 24 hours at room temperature, turning the meat occasionally to season and tenderize all over.

Drain meat, saving the marinade, and insert spit through centre.

Roast over coals or in rotisserie, about 1½ hours, basting frequently with a mixture of 16 fluid ounces of the reserved marinade combined with melted butter or margarine and celery seeds.

BARBECUED LOIN OF PORK

Have the backbone removed from pork loin. Tie securely. Insert spit through centre and cook over moderate heat, basting frequently with a barbecue sauce.

If the cooking is done over coals instead of in rotisserie, place a drip pan made of aluminium foil under it to catch drippings. It should take about 2 to 2½ hours over moderate coals.

ROLLED RIB OF BEEF

Make several incisions in the surface of the roast and insert small pieces of peeled onion and fresh thyme.

Rub lightly with hickory salt or smoke-flavoured Aromat.

Place on spit and roast, basting frequently with barbecue sauce. When done, slice in rounds and serve on buttered rolls.

BARBECUED LEG OF LAMB 2

Leg of lamb, 5 to 6 pounds
4 cloves garlic
Salt and pepper
2½ fluid ounces dry vermouth
2½ fluid ounces olive or salad oil

Cut little slashes in lamb and tuck in slivers of garlic.

Rub surface with salt and pepper and insert spit in centre of meat.

Roast over coals or in rotisserie until heated through, then start basting with the mixture of vermouth and oil.

Roasting time is about 1½ to 2 hours for medium to well-done meat.

Variations: If wished, the leg of lamb may be boned, rolled, and tied. Instead of the vermouth-oil basting sauce, it may be basted with pan juices mixed with a little white wine.

BARBECUED SHOULDER OF LAMB

Shoulder of lamb, boned and rolled, can be prepared in ways suggested for leg of lamb.

Here is a popular spicy basting sauce:
4 fluid ounces salad oil
Juice of 1 lime or lemon
1 small onion, finely chopped
1 clove garlic, finely chopped
1 teaspoon salt
¼ teaspoon pepper
1 teaspoon ground ginger
¼ teaspoon rosemary

Combine ingredients to make sauce.

Insert spit through centre of tied 3- to 4-pound lamb shoulder. Roast over coals or in rotisserie, basting frequently with the sauce.

BARBECUED LEG OF LAMB, HAWAIIAN

Have the leg of lamb boned but not rolled and tied. Sprinkle the inside with curry powder and salt. Add a light sprinkling of small strips of pineapple.

Roll up and tie securely. Insert spit and roast over coals or in rotisserie, basting occasionally with pineapple juice mixed with salad oil, and seasoned with a little curry powder.

A roasted joint is a top choice for entertaining out-of-doors if you have a grill with a revolving spit. The sight of it turning over the fire fascinates everyone and stimulates the appetite. But most important, a joint actually tastes better cooked this way.

Poultry

BARBECUED CHICKEN, DUCK, GOOSE, TURKEYS
(Basic Recipe)

The birds should be halved beforehand, washed, drained, and kept chilled.

Brush them with all-purpose barbecue sauce and lay on grill with skin side up.

Use two forks or fork and spoon to turn halves occasionally. Avoid piercing the meat as this lets the juices drain away.

Baste with brush, spoon, or, best of all, a green stick or long fork wrapped on one end with clean cloth to make a "daubing" stick.

Keep fire or coals very low so that the birds won't scorch or cook too quickly.

Place sauce near fire to keep warm and for convenience.

Serve the birds, cut according to size, on paper plates, or on warmed serving plates, if preferred, at small barbecues. Half of an average-size chicken suits most people. A quarter is enough for children.

Birds that weigh more than $3\frac{1}{2}$ pounds may be quartered, if wished, for serving to a group. Ducks may be served in halves or quarters. Small turkeys may be quartered. A goose halved for barbecuing may be disjointed, then sliced for serving.

The remaining sauce may be simmered down and poured over the warm birds just before serving, or it may be passed round.

Test by cutting into thick part of drumstick. If it cuts easily and no pink shows, the bird is done.

LEMON-BARBECUED TURKEY

1 4- to 6-pound turkey
2 lemons
1½ ounces fat, melted
1 teaspoon salt
Pinch of pepper
¼ teaspoon paprika
1 teaspoon sugar

Have turkey split in half lengthwise. Break the joints of the drumsticks, leg and wing. Skewer the legs and wings into position.

Rub both sides of turkey pieces with cut lemon, squeezing lemon to obtain plenty of juice. Brush with melted fat. Sprinkle with a mixture of salt, pepper, paprika, and sugar.

Place turkey halves in a large folding wire grill and cook slowly for about an hour. Turn every 15 minutes, brushing with melted fat each time.

The turkey is done when the meat on the thickest part of the drumstick cuts easily and there is no pink colour visible. Serves 8.

HOW TO ROAST CHICKEN OR TURKEY ON A SPIT

You can't beat a fine plump chicken, capon, or turkey cooked over coals.

Select chicken or capon weighing 4 to 8 pounds. The spit should enter through the backbone about 1 inch above the tail and come out through extreme front end of breast bone.

Any size turkey may be roasted on a spit provided it is young and tender. Large birds require a longer cooking time, of course, and frequent basting. The new small turkeys (4- to 8-pound ready-to-cook) are popular for spit roasting; however, the 15- to 18-pound turkeys are also ideal.

They should first be trussed, having legs and wings tied close to body and neck skin fastened to back with a skewer.

Insert spit as for chicken (a hammer may have to be used to drive the spit); fasten holding forks securely and balance.

It is important that the bird be spitted so that it is balanced well.

Stuffing: Either chicken or turkey may be stuffed before roasting. In this case the spit must emerge a little farther forward to compensate for the added off-centre weight. Also the cooking time is longer.

Roasting: Roast over a moderate fire, basting or not as you wish with a barbecue or basting sauce. Chicken is good basted with a mixture of melted butter and white wine.

You may test by pulling the leg; if it moves easily at the joint, it is done. A turkey of 14 to 16 pounds will take about 3 hours to cook; a 5-pound chicken may take as long as 1 hour and 40 minutes.

The insertion of a meat thermometer in the thickest part of the thigh of a very large chicken or a turkey will eliminate any guessing about when the bird is done.

Spit roasting may be done with charcoal, electricity, or gas supplying the heat. All methods roast meats equally well under properly controlled conditions. The choice may depend upon the convenience, the location, and the cost.

SPIT ROASTED DUCK WITH ORANGE GLAZE

Brush duck inside and out with undiluted frozen orange juice concentrate.

Follow directions for chicken in putting on spit and roasting; baste with orange juice. A 4- to 6-pound duck takes about 1 to 1½ hours.

TURKEY STEAKS

Ask the butcher to cut whole frozen turkey on electric meat saw in crosswise slices 1 inch thick. When turkey is completely sliced, cut each slice in half at the centre. Reserve end pieces for soups, salads, etc.

Place frozen steaks on grill over medium fire. Salt and baste steaks well with all-purpose barbecue sauce.

Grill slowly about 20 minutes on each side, turning once.

SPIT ROASTED ORANGE-STUFFED DUCK

1 duck, about 6 pounds
3 unpeeled oranges, quartered
2 fluid ounces olive oil
4 fluid ounces orange juice
1 tablespoon grated orange rind
4 ounces butter or margarine, melted
1 tablespoon chopped watercress

Stuff duck with quartered oranges. Place on spit. Brush with oil. Grill 1½ to 2 hours, turning often.

Serve with sauce made by combining remaining ingredients and heating until just below boiling point. Do not boil. Serves 6.

For Eating Pleasure: Spit barbecued poultry (duckling, chicken, Cornish hens, turkey) — a delight to the most discerning gourmet when rotisserie roasted over charcoal. To simplify the task, line grill with aluminium foil. It reflects heat upward, increases cooking efficiency, and keeps grill clean. Make a drip pan from foil to catch and hold juices.

To Make Foil Drip Pan for Rotisserie Roasting: Prepare this from 18 inch wide heavy-duty aluminium foil. Tear off a sheet about 5 inches longer than the food on the spit. Fold this in half lengthwise, then turn up edges all around 1½ inches and mitre corners to seal them and make the sides firm. Place this pan in front of the hot charcoal and under the meat; juices will fall into it.

Barbecued Baby Turkey Halves: When showing off your mastery of grilling, don't overlook this delicacy.

WINE BARBECUED STUFFED TURKEY

4 to 5-pound turkey
1¼ pints red wine
½ pound chestnuts, canned or fresh
1 medium potato
1 pound minced pork
1 teaspoon salt
¼ teaspoon pepper
½ pound sliced salt pork

Put turkey in a large bowl. Pour over the wine and marinate (soak) for 24 hours in refrigerator. Turn bird occasionally.

To make stuffing: Cook fresh chestnuts in boiling water for about 20 minutes or until tender, then remove shells and inner brown coating. Just drain liquid from canned chestnuts.

Cook potato until tender.

Fry minced pork until lightly browned.

Chop chestnuts and potato very finely; mix with ground pork, salt, and pepper.

Lift turkey from marinade; fill the cavity with stuffing.

Sew or skewer opening in turkey and truss tightly.

Arrange strips of salt pork over breast and back of bird and fasten the ends with wooden sticks.

Insert spit in centre of turkey; fasten holding forks securely.

Roast over hot coals or in rotisserie 2 to 2½ hours, or until tender. During the last 15 minutes of roasting, baste with the wine marinade.

Remove salt pork, wooden sticks, and string before serving. Serves 8.

WINE BARBECUED CHICKEN

Combine 2 parts olive oil to 1 part dry white wine.

Add 1 chopped onion, crushed or finely chopped clove of garlic, tarragon, and salt and pepper to taste.

Marinate (soak) the cut-up prepared chickens in this mixture for 2 to 3 hours, turning several times.

Remove from marinade and grill,

basting with the sauce while the chickens cook.

MARINATED BARBECUED CHICKEN

Cut ready-to-cook roasting chickens into serving pieces. Marinate them in any of the barbecue sauces 8 to 24 hours, or as long as possible.

Grill over hot coals slowly, about 25 minutes or until tender, turning often. Baste frequently with additional barbecue sauce.

Marinated Barbecued Turkey: Prepare and grill as for chicken (above), using 3- to 6-pound ready-to-cook turkeys.

SAVOURY CHICKEN ON A SPIT

2 roasting chickens (2½ to 3 pounds)
4 fluid ounces white wine
4 fluid ounces salad oil, melted butter, or margarine
1 teaspoon dried tarragon or rosemary
1 teaspoon salt
Dash of pepper

Fasten chickens on the spit. Mix wine, salad oil or melted butter or margarine, tarragon or rosemary, salt, and pepper together.

Brush or baste chickens every 15 minutes with sauce.

Cook until tender, 45 to 60 minutes. Serve with remaining sauce poured over. Serves 4.

SPIT ROASTED STUFFED DUCK

1 5-pound duck
3 teaspoons aniseeds
4 teaspoons ground coriander
1 medium onion, chopped
¾ pound minced beef
½ ounce butter or margarine
8 ounces raisins
1 teaspoon salt
Dash of pepper

Put the clean singed duck in a deep bowl. Sprinkle with 3 teaspoons each of aniseeds and coriander. Cover with water. Soak for 2 hours at least, then remove from water and drain.

To make the stuffing: Cook chopped onion and minced beef in butter or margarine until slightly browned.

Stir in raisins, 1 teaspoon coriander, salt, and pepper.

Spoon the stuffing into duck cavity and sew or skewer the opening. Insert spit through centre of birds and fasten holding forks securely.

Roast over hot coals or in rotisserie for 2 to 2¼ hours or until tender. Serves 4.

CHICKEN CANTONESE ON A SPIT

2 whole roasting chickens (about 2½ pounds each ready-to-cook)
4 stalks celery, coarsely chopped
2 fluid ounces soy sauce
2 fluid ounces sherry
1 clove garlic, crushed or finely chopped
1 teaspoon dry mustard
¼ teaspoon pepper
¼ teaspoon ginger
2 teaspoons Worcestershire sauce
3 tablespoons salad oil

Spoon celery into chicken cavities; close openings securely with skewers. Place on spit.

Combine remaining ingredients and use as basting sauce.

Brush chickens with sauce; cook over coals, basting frequently with sauce, about 45 to 50 minutes. Serves 4.

GRILLED CHICKEN OR DUCKLING

2 roasting chickens or ducklings (not over 2½ pounds each, ready-to-cook weight)
4 fluid ounces salad oil
2 teaspoons salt
½ teaspoon pepper
½ teaspoon Aromat

Cut chickens in halves lengthwise. Break the drumstick, wing joints, and hip so birds stay flat during grilling.

Brush with oil. Season with salt, pepper, and Aromat. Lay on grill with skin side up or inside nearest the hot coals.

When inside is well browned, turn without piercing the meat as this lets the juices drain away. Brown skin side, brushing with fat.

Test by cutting into thick part of drumstick. If it cuts easily and no pink shows, chicken is done. Serves 4.

Barbecue a turkey for a bountiful summer buffet supper. A hearty macaroni casserole and crusty French bread are ideal additions to the meal.

Frankfurters

RELISHES FOR FRANKFURTERS

1. Sliced mild, raw onion, separated into rings and then marinated in French dressing.
2. Hot seasoned sauerkraut plus caraway seeds or grated cheese.
3. Hot canned baked beans.
4. Strips of red and green pepper, fried lightly in oil for a few minutes.
5. Chutney or pickle relish.
6. Chopped onions and cucumbers, vinegar-dressed.
7. Chilli pickle and chopped pickles.
8. Cheese spread or sauce.
9. Mayonnaise mixed with chutney and spiked with a generous amount of cayenne or Tabasco sauce.
10. Cole-slaw or potato salad.
11. Bottled meat sauce.
12. Prepared mustard with a teaspoon of horseradish and a few celery seeds.
13. Hot apple sauce.
14. Hot crushed pineapple.
15. Chive cream cheese.
16. A sweet-sour bacon relish, made by heating equal parts of vinegar and brown sugar to boiling point, then adding chopped, crisp, cooked bacon. Serve hot.

GLAZED FRANKFURTERS

Slash 1 pound frankfurters. Combine 6 ounces brown sugar and 3 tablespoons prepared mustard. Spread into slashes and on frankfurters. Grill 3 to 5 minutes or until golden. Serves 4 to 6.

WIENER CANOES

Slit frankfurters lengthwise, not quite through. Stuff with fillings like those suggested below.

Wrap filled frankfurters in double thickness of foil, sealing edges together with a tight double fold. Heat on grill over medium fire 6 to 8 minutes. Do not turn. Remove foil and serve in warm rolls.
1. Slice spring onions, sautéed in butter and dotted with pimiento.
2. Cooked macaroni and cheese.
3. Horseradish, chopped stuffed olives, and cheese cubes.
4. Chopped celery, chopped onions, and pickle relish.

Wiener Canoes

Everybody's Favourite: Flavoured frankfurters wrapped in bacon. Slash frankfurters lengthwise without cutting all the way through. Fill with mustard (or tomato ketchup or pickle relish, or strips of cheese). Wrap bacon around filled frankfurters, fastening bacon ends with cocktail sticks. Arrange, cut side up, on grill rack. Grill until bacon is light brown.

FRANKFURTER TOASTIES

1 pound frankfurters (about 8 frankfurters)
8 slices thinly sliced sandwich bread
Melted butter or margarine
Prepared mustard
Wooden cocktail sticks

Pour boiling water over frankfurters and let stand 8 minutes. Drain.

Spread bread with softened butter and mustard. Place frankfurter cornerwise on bread and fasten the opposite corners together with wooden sticks.

Brush each toastie with melted butter and grill until toast is golden brown. Serve with barbecue sauce. Serves 8.

FRANKFURTERS WITH BLUE CHEESE TOPPING

2½ ounces crumbled blue cheese
2 tablespoons prepared mustard
1 pound frankfurters

Mash cheese with fork. Add mustard and combine thoroughly. Slice frankfurters lengthwise.

Spread cut surface with cheese and mustard mixture. Grill until cheese is bubbly and brown. Serves 6 to 8.

FRANKFURTER KEBABS WITH QUICK BARBECUE SAUCE

½ pound frankfurters
½ pound processed cheese
4 ounces canned whole mushrooms

Cut frankfurters into quarters. Cube processed cheese. Alternate frankfurter quarters, cheese cubes, and mushrooms on skewers and grill 3 to 4 minutes on each side.

Serve with quick barbecue sauce. Serves 8.

Quick Barbecue Sauce:
8 fluid ounces ketchup
2 tablespoons prepared mustard
2 tablespoons Worcestershire sauce
½ teaspoon onion salt

Combine ingredients and simmer 5 minutes.

FRANKFURTERS AND BEANS

Heat canned green lima beans, broad, or baked beans. Stir in sliced frankfurters.

If wished, season with mustard, tomato ketchup, or a little shredded cheese.

CONEY ISLAND HOT DOGS

1 can chilli con carne
3 ounces tomato purée
1 teaspoon prepared mustard
½ teaspoon salt
8 frankfurters
8 frankfurter rolls
Butter or margarine

Mix the chilli con carne, tomato purée, mustard, and salt in a pan. Heat thoroughly.

Slit frankfurters diagonally in 4 or 5 places; grill until brown.

Split rolls, spread with butter, and then toast.

Place a frankfurter in each roll and cover generously with chilli con carne. Makes 8 sandwiches.

FRANKFURTERS IN BLANKETS

About 1 pound scone dough
8 frankfurters
8 cocktail gherkins
Prepared mustard

Roll out the scone dough to ⅛-inch thickness on floured board. Cut into four 3½-inch squares.

Split the frankfurters and gherkins lengthwise. Spread centre of each frankfurter with mustard and insert 2 gherkin halves.

Place 1 filled frankfurter on each dough square and roll it so that the centre portion of frankfurter is encased. Cook slowly over coals until dough is browned on all sides. Makes 8.

STUFFED FRANKFURTERS

Split 1 pound frankfurters lengthwise and stuff with a mixture of 14 ounces hot seasoned mashed potatoes mixed with 2 ounces grated cheese and 4 tablespoons finely chopped onion. Grill 10 to 15 minutes. Serves 4 to 6.

FRANKFURTER KEBABS

Thread small salted tomatoes, onions, and frankfurters alternately on skewers. Rotate over coals until brown.

Put pieces between split rolls or slices of bread.

Fish and Shellfish for the Barbecue

BARBECUED WHOLE FISH

Any fish can be cooked over the fire whether it's a small smelt or the largest salmon your grill can accommodate. For large fish, have more moderate fire than for smaller ones.

Sprinkle the inside of the cleaned fish with salt, pepper, and lemon juice before grilling. Large fish may be split.

Put in a greased hinged wire grill and brown carefully on both sides.

If desired, baste the fish as it cooks with equal parts of melted butter and white wine or with melted butter flavoured with lemon juice and thyme or tarragon. Fish with substantial skin and rich in fat need not be basted.

A fish weighing about 5 or 6 pounds will take from 20 to 45 minutes, or until the fish flakes easily with a fork. Small whole fish will cook in 15 minutes.

BARBECUED FISH FILLETS AND STEAKS

Have both fish and hinged wire grill well oiled to prevent sticking. If fish is thick it will take a more moderate fire for a longer time than if it is thin.

A fish steak 2 inches thick takes about 15 minutes, one 1½ inches thick takes about 12 minutes, and one an inch thick about 7 minutes.

Fillets cook in 5 to 7 minutes, depending on size.

Brush fish well with softened butter or oil; heat the hinged wire grill and grease it.

Brush fish while cooking with melted butter to which lemon juice or herbs have been added. Season with salt and pepper.

Barbecued Fish Steaks

FISH KEBABS

2 pounds frozen fish fillets
6 fluid ounces ketchup
1 teaspoon Worcestershire sauce
Few drops Tabasco sauce
¾ teaspoon salt
¾ teaspoon Aromat
Few grains pepper
4 rashers of bacon
Dill pickle slices

Cut fish, while frozen, into 1½-inch cubes.

Combine ketchup, Worcestershire sauce, Tabasco, salt, Aromat, and pepper. Pour over fish cubes; let stand 1½ hours at room temperature, stirring occasionally with fork. Drain, saving sauce.

Cut each rasher of bacon in four. Cut dill pickle crosswise into 16 slices.

On each of 8 skewers string a fish cube, a square of bacon, and a pickle slice; repeat, ending with a third fish cube.

Place in folding wire grill and grill with medium heat 8 to 10 minutes, turning once and brushing several times with ketchup mixture.

Garnish with lemon wedges dipped in parsley. Makes 8 fish kebabs.

FISH KEBABS 2

2 pounds cod or other white fish, cut in 1-inch cubes
2 cucumbers, cut in 1-inch slices
1 large jar stuffed olives

Sauce:
6 fluid ounces olive oil
2½ fluid ounces lemon juice
1 bay leaf, broken
4 drops Tabasco sauce

Combine sauce ingredients. Marinate fish for ½ hour.

On a skewer, alternate kebab ingredients. Grill 10 minutes, basting with marinade. Serves 6.

FISH FRY

Small fish may be cleaned and fried whole. Larger fish are boned and cut into steaks or fillets before frying.

Dip cleaned fish in water, then in a mixture of 2 ounces flour, 2 ounces yellow corn meal, and 1 tablespoon salt.

Fry in ¼ inch hot fat until brown on 1 side; turn and brown other side. Cook until fish flakes easily when tested with a fork. Do not overcook.

For Sandwiches: Heat sliced buttered rolls in a foil picnic plate over grill. Insert a fried fish fillet and a serving of cole-slaw in each roll. Serve immediately.

Racks and skewers for fish kebabs can usually be bought at hardware stores. Or you can make your own from green wooden sticks.

SOYED GRILLED FISH FILLETS

1 pound fish fillets
Salt and pepper
2 teaspoons soy sauce
2 tablespoons salad oil
2 tablespoons lemon juice
2 tablespoons finely chopped parsley

Cut fillets into serving pieces; sprinkle with salt and pepper. Combine soy sauce and oil.

Place fish in oiled hinged wire grill and cook until golden brown, about 5 to 8 minutes on each side. Baste frequently with soy-oil mixture.

Place on warm platter. Heat remaining soy-oil mixture; add lemon juice and parsley; pour over fish. Serves 4.

TROUT GRILLED IN BACON

Wrap cleaned trout in bacon. Cook in folding wire grill over coals, turning to cook on both sides. Serve when bacon is done.

There are all kinds of tempting ways of preparing sea and fresh water fish, but none surpasses the outdoor fish fry. Shredded cabbage and tomato wedges combined with a tartare sauce can be added to the fried fillets served in buttered rolls for a big bite sandwich.

SHELLFISH IDEAS TO COOK ON SKEWERS

1. Scallops with partially cooked strips of bacon woven on skewers around the scallops. Secure at ends with wedges of lemon.

2. Scallops alternated with mushroom caps. Brush with butter while grilling.

3. Scallops dipped in melted butter to which lemon juice, chopped parsley, and crushed garlic have been added. Grill quickly.

4. Raw oysters, dipped in melted butter, then rolled in mixture of half crumbs and half grated Parmesan cheese.

5. Small raw oysters dipped in butter, each put in a mushroom cap and strung on skewers.

6. Raw oysters, each rolled in bacon which has first been sprinkled with chopped spring onion.

7. Raw prawns, shelled, cleaned, then marinated in melted butter, olive oil, chopped garlic, and curry powder, alternated with squares of green pepper.

8. Raw prawns, shelled and cleaned, with pineapple chunks, and sausage.

9. Use fresh or frozen prawns; do not shell. Dip in barbecue sauce. Spear on long fork or skewer.

Hold over fire until shells are brown-tinged. Pull shell off prawn and eat.

Scallops en Brochette: Skewer whole scallops, medium size mushrooms, and squares of bacon. Grill over charcoal about 10 minutes, turning often and brushing with highly seasoned French dressing throughout the cooking.

GRILLED LOBSTER TAILS

Split lobster tails along the top. Place on grill grid or in hinged wire grill.

Grill with the meat side up at the start; finish cooking with shell side up. Total cooking time about 12 minutes for medium-sized tails, 13 to 15 minutes for large tails.

While cooking, brush frequently with melted butter. Serve with additional melted butter and lemon wedges.

GRILLED LOBSTERS

Split live lobsters with a heavy knife or cleaver. Remove intestinal vein and stomach. Crack the claws with a hammer.

Brush meat well with melted butter and cook for a few minutes, flesh side up, then turn.

Baste lavishly with melted butter and finish cooking with shell to the fire. This will take about 15 minutes, depending on size of the lobsters.

After cooking, the empty part of the shell may be filled with hot toasted buttered crumbs. Serve with melted butter and lemon wedges.

GRILLED CRABS

2 ounces melted butter or margarine
1 tablespoon lemon juice
Dash of salt
Few grains pepper
6 soft-shelled crabs, cleaned
Flour

Combine butter, lemon juice, salt, and pepper. Roll crabs in mixture, then in flour.

Place in hinged wire grill and cook over hot coals 5 minutes on each side, brushing often with butter mixture. Serve in toasted bread rolls with tartare sauce.

Grilled Lobster Tails

Skewers threaded through the lobster tails will keep tails flat during cooking.

PRAWN AND PINEAPPLE KEBABS

3 pounds prawns, fresh or frozen
8 fluid ounces soy sauce
4 fluid ounces lemon juice
1 can (15-20 ounces) pineapple chunks
1 pound bacon, cut in half rashers

Shell prawns, cut down back and remove vein.

Marinate prawns in mixture of soy sauce and lemon juice for ½ hour.

On skewers, alternate prawns, pineapple, and bacon (½ rasher folded). Grill until bacon is crisp. Serves 6.

BACON AND SCALLOPS

8 rashers bacon
½ pound scallops
3 slices white bread, cut into 1-inch cubes

Using one slice of bacon for each skewer, thread alternately with scallops, bread cubes, and bacon (beginning and ending with bacon).

Grill 5 inches from heat source for 3 minutes on each side. Serve immediately. Serves 4.

ROAST OYSTERS

Scrub 1 dozen unshelled oysters per person, changing water several times.

Place on grill or wire mesh put across hot coals. Or wrap in aluminium foil and place on coals.

Turn occasionally and serve when shells open with melted butter or barbecue sauce for dipping.

Barbecue Sauces and Marinades

HINTS ON CHOOSING A SAUCE

Fish, meat, or poultry grilled out-of-doors over charcoal or wood should be basted frequently or they may dry out. There are sauces of an infinite variety of flavours, colours, and consistencies. One that is cool to one person's tongue may scorch that of another. But most people agree that barbecue sauce should have some sort of spice and kick, with more than a hint of woody, out-door flavour. It need not be fiery or fierce, but it should have a barbecue flavour.

A sauce recipe should be selected that will best suit the fish, meat, or poultry with which it will be served.

Fish and chicken call for a sauce that is delicately seasoned – mostly oil and herbs.

Barbecue sauce for pork chops and spare-ribs should have little oil or other fat, lots of chilli sauce (see Index) or tomato ketchup.

Lamb calls for a sauce with a liberal amount of oil and garlic.

Thick steaks and other thick beef cuts such as thick cubes on skewers require a well seasoned sauce fairly rich in oil.

The all-purpose barbecue sauce which follows teams up well with all kinds of poultry cooked on outdoor pits or in ovens. It has been tested and retested for years at small and large barbecues in home kitchens, hotel kitchens, restaurants, church kitchens, and elsewhere over a large part of the United States. Spooned or brushed over cooking meat, it browns to a tasty, reddish brown crust full of flavour. In roasting tins it cooks down with the drippings into a rich, thick gravy to be served over the meat or separately.

The recipes for sauces given here should be only a beginning for the outdoor chef. The range and variety of vinegars (wine, cider, distilled, herb-flavoured), fats, oils, spices, herbs, juices, and vegetables you may put into your sauce are limitless. So, use your imagination and experiment until you find the "Perfect Sauce", if there is one. There is certainly no set rule. If you don't have one ingredient, try another similar one. But taste frequently while mixing the ingredients. If your sauce is underflavoured, you can quickly correct that. Make plenty of sauce. Left-over sauce keeps well in the refrigerator.

ALL-PURPOSE BARBECUE SAUCE

To Serve 6 with 3 Chickens:

¾ teaspoon salt
½ teaspoon pepper
¾ teaspoon paprika
2 teaspoons sugar
¼ teaspoon garlic salt
2½ fluid ounces tomato ketchup
2½ fluid ounces tomato juice
1 small onion, finely chopped
5 fluid ounces water
2 fluid ounces vinegar or lemon juice
½ teaspoon Worcestershire sauce
1 ounce butter, margarine, or salad oil

To Serve 24 with 12 Chickens:

1 tablespoon salt
1¾ teaspoons pepper
1 tablespoon paprika
3 tablespoons sugar
1 teaspoon garlic salt
½ pint tomato ketchup
½ pint tomato juice
3 medium onions, finely chopped
1 pint water
8 fluid ounces vinegar or lemon juice
2 teaspoons Worcestershire sauce
4 ounces margarine, or salad oil

To serve 50 with 25 Chickens:

2 tablespoons salt
2½ teaspoons pepper
2 tablespoons paprika
2½ ounces sugar
2 teaspoons garlic salt
1½ pints tomato ketchup
1½ pints tomato juice
1¼ pounds onion, finely chopped
2¼ pints water
¾ pint vinegar or lemon juice
1½ tablespoons Worcestershire sauce
½ pound butter, margarine, or salad oil

Method: Measure all ingredients in pan. Heat to boiling. Keep hot for basting on grill.

Oven Barbecuing: Pour sauce over halved birds in roasting tin to about 1 inch deep. If sauce becomes too thick, add a little hot water.

The success secret of tasty barbecued ribs is the barbecue sauce. Choose your favourite from the recipes given here.

BARBECUE CHILLI SAUCE

1 medium-sized onion, finely chopped
1 green pepper, finely chopped
4 cloves garlic, finely chopped
3 ounces butter or margarine
2 pounds canned tomatoes
6 fluid ounces red wine
6 fluid ounces stock
1½ tablespoons salt
¼ teaspoon pepper
2-3 teaspoons chilli powder
1½ tablespoons cornflour
1½ teaspoons sugar

Cook onion, green pepper, and garlic in butter until soft.

Add remaining ingredients and bring to the boil. Reduce heat and cook until thickened, stirring constantly.

Cover and simmer gently 10 minutes longer. Serve with frankfurters, ham, pork, and spare-ribs.

TEXAS BARBECUE SAUCE

16 fluid ounces water
½ teaspoon black pepper
4 tablespoons brown sugar
1 teaspoon garlic salt or 2 cloves garlic, finely chopped
2 teaspoons salt
8 fluid ounces cider vinegar
1 5-ounce bottle Worcestershire sauce
Juice of 4 lemons
2 ounces butter (see note below)

Bring water to boil in a large 2-quart saucepan; add pepper and simmer 5 minutes.

Add brown sugar; stir until dissolved, then add garlic salt or chopped garlic, salt, and vinegar, and stir.

Add ½ the bottle of Worcestershire sauce; simmer for a few minutes, then add lemon juice and stir. Then add remainder of the Worcestershire sauce and stir while heating.

Add butter as sauce heats during use.

Note: In making up this sauce it is easier to make it in a larger quantity than you need for a single barbecue. By omitting the butter, it will keep for weeks in the refrigerator. When ready to use, heat slowly with the butter. Omit butter when barbecuing pork.

CHINESE BASTING SAUCE FOR PORK, SPARE-RIBS, HAM STEAKS

4 fluid ounces chicken stock or consommé
3 ounces honey
2 fluid ounces soy sauce
½ clove garlic, crushed
⅛ teaspoon ground ginger
2 tablespoons tomato ketchup

Combine ingredients and cook over low heat for 8 to 10 minutes.

SPECIAL HOT BARBECUE SAUCE

2 large onions, finely chopped
2 cloves garlic, finely chopped
1 bay leaf
1 teaspoon crushed chilli
1 teaspoon dry mustard
1 teaspoon salt
1 tablespoon brown sugar
1 pint chilli sauce (see Index)
6 fluid ounces olive oil
2½ fluid ounces lemon juice
2 tablespoons tarragon vinegar
2 teaspoons Tabasco sauce
2½ fluid ounces water

Combine all ingredients in saucepan; bring to the boil. Reduce heat and simmer 15 minutes. Serve with chicken, lamb, or spare-ribs.

BARBECUED STEAK SAUCE

5 fluid ounces water
½ teaspoon dry mustard
8 fluid ounces tomato juice
5 fluid ounces vinegar
1½ ounces butter or margarine
1 tablespoon Worcestershire sauce
3 tablespoons dried mixed peppers
1 teaspoon paprika
1 teaspoon salt
¼ teaspoon black pepper

Combine in saucepan and simmer 10 minutes.
Grill steak over coals. Brush with barbecue sauce as steak cooks. Serve with remaining sauce.

WINE MARINADE AND BASTING SAUCE

2 fluid ounces salad oil
4 fluid ounces red or white wine
1 clove garlic, grated
1 teaspoon onion, grated
½ teaspoon salt
1 tablespoon Worcestershire sauce
½ teaspoon black pepper

Mix oil and wine; add rest of ingredients and chill several hours.
Pour over poultry or meat; chill for 3 hours. Baste again with sauce during cooking.

Note: Use red wine for steaks or lamb; white wine for chicken or veal.

MASTER BASTING SAUCE

4 fluid ounces salad oil
4 fluid ounces wine vinegar
4 fluid ounces lemon juice
2 fluid ounces soy sauce
½ teaspoon Aromat
Salt, pepper, herbs to taste

Mix ingredients and store in covered jar in refrigerator.
This master sauce is used by many barbecue experts for basting all types of meat and poultry while cooking over hot coals or in rotisserie.

TARRAGON MARINADE FOR STEAK

1 large onion, sliced
1 lemon
5 cloves garlic
1 whole bay leaf
½ teaspoon dry mustard
Salt
Freshly ground black pepper
8 fluid ounces oil
3 tablespoons tarragon vinegar
4 fluid ounces dry red wine

Line a shallow glass baking dish with whole onion slices. Squeeze lemon juice over onion, toss in lemon rinds.
Add 4 split garlic cloves, spices, ½ teaspoon salt, and ½ teaspoon pepper. Pour in oil, vinegar, and wine.
Lay the steak in the marinade and spread the rest of the onion slices on the steak.
Squeeze the juice of another clove of garlic over all, and sprinkle with additional salt and pepper. Marinate for 3 hours, basting occasionally.
This amount is enough for 2 pounds of 2-inch sirloin. Serve the marinated onions raw with the cooked steak.

HERB BARBECUE SAUCE FOR CHICKEN

4 fluid ounces salad oil
2 fluid ounces olive oil
2 fluid ounces lemon juice
½ teaspoon salt (part garlic salt if desired)
⅛ teaspoon marjoram
⅛ teaspoon thyme
⅛ teaspoon black pepper
⅛ teaspoon Aromat
Pinch of oregano

Mix ingredients well and leave for several hours to blend flavours.
Use a sprig of fresh rosemary or marjoram for a "basting brush" if you have some growing in your garden. This will be enough sauce for basting chickens to serve 6.

MINT MARINADE FOR LAMB KEBABS

6 sprigs fresh mint
2 tablespoons vinegar
2½ fluid ounces salad oil
1 teaspoon salt
¼ teaspoon pepper
2 tablespoons finely chopped onion
¼ teaspoon paprika

Wash the mint and finely chop the leaves. Add chopped mint to remaining ingredients.
Mix well, pour sauce over lamb cubes and place in refrigerator for 2 to 4 hours.
Thread on skewers and grill.
Use the sauce for basting during the grilling process.

QUICK NO-COOK SAUCE FOR CHICKEN

½ teaspoon pepper
1 teaspoon salt
1 teaspoon onion salt, or 1 medium onion, grated
1 teaspoon prepared mustard
2 teaspoons sugar
1 can (10½ ounces) condensed tomato soup
8 fluid ounces vinegar
8 fluid ounces water
1 tablespoon Worcestershire sauce
2 fluid ounces cooking oil

Blend dry ingredients in a mixing bowl. Add remaining ingredients in order given. Mix thoroughly.
Barbecues 4 chickens outdoors and 3 indoors.
For oven barbecuing, add 4 fluid ounces water to sauce and pour over chicken halves in roasting tin.

After marinating the meat, pour the marinade in a handy jug for easy basting as the meat cooks.

Outdoor Ways with Vegetables

FROZEN VEGETABLES IN FOIL

Thaw vegetables until they can be broken into chunks.

Make individual packets of chunks, or place on large sheet of heavy foil or 2 sheets light foil.

Add salt, pepper, a little Aromat, and plenty of butter or margarine.

Shape into a long, flat package with edges tucked under.

Cook on grill over hot coals about 5 minutes longer than package label directs. If fire is too hot, move packages over to side of grill. Serve from foil with edges folded back.

MUSHROOMS IN FOIL

Put 5 or 6 mushrooms on a square of foil; add a pat of butter and salt and pepper.

Wrap in tight secure packet and grill about 8 minutes, turning once.

SAVOURY VEGETABLE COMBO IN FOIL

Slice aubergine, onion, tomato, and mushroom. Place a portion of each on a square of foil.

Brush with oil; season with salt, pepper, and oregano.

Fold and seal edges securely. Cook on hot coals about 12 minutes.

CORN ROASTED IN FOIL

Remove husks and silk from fresh corn or use frozen corncobs. Brush with butter or margarine; season with salt, pepper and maybe chilli seasoning or oregano.

Wrap in foil. Bake in coals, turning 2 or 3 times. Takes about 15 to 20 minutes.

Or cream together softened butter or margarine, finely chopped parsley, paprika, and a bit of salt, and freshly ground pepper. Spread this mixture liberally over each ear of corn before wrapping in foil.

Serve either with plenty of butter or margarine to brush over corn as it is being eaten.

CORN ROASTED ON THE COB

Pull back husks from corn; remove silk. Replace husks and tie in place.

Soak corn in salted water 5 minutes; drain.

Roast on grill over hot fire for about 10 to 12 minutes, turning frequently.

Remove husks, and serve corn with butter or margarine and salt.

To Roast in Coals: After draining corn, bury it in hot coals for 10 to 12 minutes.

To preserve the natural flavour and colour of vegetables, prepare them in aluminium foil packages.

TOMATOES AND BACON

Cut a thick slice of tomato, sprinkle with salt and pepper, and wrap with a thin strip of bacon. Place in a wire toaster and cook over the hot coals.

PEANUT BUTTER GRILLED CORN

Remove husks from ear of corn and spread lightly with peanut butter. Wrap each corn in a bacon rasher; fasten with a wooden stick.

Place on grill over hot coals and cook 10 minutes, turning often. Or grill on long skewers.

WESTERN-STYLE ONIONS

Cut peeled Spanish onions in ⅓-inch slices. Fry slowly in butter or margarine until yellow, turning often. Season and serve with hamburgers.

TOMATO-CORN-ONION BARBECUE

Simmer small whole onions and fresh corn on the cob until just underdone. Break ears of corn into halves or thirds.

String onions, corn, and small whole fresh tomatoes on heavy skewers. Brush with garlic butter.

Lay on grill of hot coals to finish cooking and brown lightly. Turn and baste with additional garlic butter during the barbecuing.

GRILLED AUBERGINE SLICES

This vegetable is especially good with barbecued meats. Peel aubergine and cut in ¾-inch slices.

Sprinkle lightly with flour; dot with butter or brush with oil.

Place in hinged wire grill and cook, turning once during the cooking.

Brush again with oil after turning and season with salt and pepper.

With Cheese: Sprinkle lightly with grated cheese before grilling.

VEGETABLE IDEAS TO COOK ON SKEWERS

1. Alternate green pepper squares, small onions, tomatoes, mushroom caps, and courgette slices. Brush with barbecue sauce before grilling.

2. Aubergine cubes, wrapped in bacon, alternated with pieces of green peppers and onions.

3. Aubergine cubes, small onions, and cherry tomatoes or tomato wedges. Marinate in olive oil seasoned with crushed garlic and oregano before grilling.

4. Small tomatoes and mushroom caps. Brush with m lted butter or olive oil while grilling.

5. Chunks of carrots, parboiled onions, and slices of courgette. Marinate in garlic-flavoured olive oil before grilling.

ONIONS ROASTED IN FOIL

Method 1: Wrap onions, peeled or not, in foil and bake until tender, about 30 minutes. Serve with butter, salt, and pepper.

Method 2: Stuff onions before wrapping with chopped apples, chicken livers, ripe olives, or nuts.

GRILLED ONION SLICES

Put large slices of Spanish onion in a hinged wire grill. Brush with butter and grill until golden brown. Leave them a little underdone in the centre and still crunchy.

TOMATOES AND ONION IN FOIL

Choose medium, firm tomatoes (one per serving). Cut each in half crosswise. Sprinkle cut surfaces with salt and pepper.

Put together with a thin slice of onion between halves. Fasten with a wooden cocktail stick.

Wrap each tomato in a square of foil and bake at edge of grill 15 to 20 minutes.

Skewered Vegetable Barbecue

SKEWERED VEGETABLE BARBECUE

1 pound courgettes
1 bunch carrots, scraped and cut into 1½-inch lengths
6 small potatoes (¾ pound), peeled
2 green peppers, washed and seeded, cut into 1½-inch squares
¾ pound plum tomatoes
2 fluid ounces cooking oil
½ teaspoon salt
¼ teaspoon pepper
¼ teaspoon Aromat

Simmer courgettes, carrots, and potatoes separately ahead of time (each in 4 fluid ounces water, ½ teaspoon salt, and ¼ teaspoon Aromat) until vegetables are just underdone. Drain and cool.

Combine vegetables, including whole tomatoes, in large bowl with oil, salt, pepper, and Aromat. Toss lightly to coat. Leave 1 hour to marinate.

Thread vegetables alternately on long skewers.

Grill over hot coals 4 to 5 minutes, turning 4 times and basting with warm butter mixture. Remove from skewer. Serve as accompaniment to main dish. Serves 6.

Individual cups of aluminium foil add new interest to traditional baked beans. Two thicknesses of aluminium foil are formed over coffee cups. Canned beans are heated and served in the attractive foil containers. Or home-baked beans can be prepared in these containers in the oven.

POTATOES BAKED IN CANS

Scrub baking potatoes; place in coffee cans. Put on lids loosely. Bake on grill when heat is low until tender, rolling the cans occasionally. They take about 1 hour and 15 minutes.

When potatoes are done, cut slit in each, season with salt, pepper, and butter or margarine.

QUICK CHIPS

Place thawed frozen chipped potatoes in corn popper or similar container. Shake over hot coals until piping hot. Season with salt.

Or heat a little fat or salad oil in heavy frying pan. Add potatoes and toss until hot.

POTATOES ROASTED IN FOIL

Method 1: Potatoes may be baked peeled or not. Scrub unpeeled baking potatoes well.

Brush with oil, melted butter or margarine; sprinkle with salt and pepper.

Wrap each securely in a square of foil. Bake on the grill or right on top of coals, or in hot ashes. It will take about an hour for good-sized potatoes. Press with finger to test to tell when ready to eat.

To serve, cut crisscross with fork in top; add a pat of butter.

Method 2: Scrub baking potatoes but do not peel. Cut each potato into 3 or 4 lengthwise slices. Brush with butter; season with salt and pepper.

Reassemble potato and wrap in foil. Bake in coals or at edge of grill about 45 to 60 minutes.

Method 3: Pare and slice potatoes. Season with salt, pepper, and butter or margarine. Wrap individual portions securely in foil and bake as in Method 1 above.

Method 4: Scrub baking potatoes well. Remove a lengthwise piece from each potato with an apple corer but do not cut clear to the other end.

Put a spoonful or two of evaporated milk into the hole. Seal the hole with outer ½-inch piece of the potato removed with the corer.

Wrap each potato securely in foil and bake on grill until tender.

RODEO POTATOES

Scrub new potatoes well. Cook in jackets in heavily salted water (3 tablespoons salt to 1½ pints water).

Drain and peel potatoes. Season with salt and pepper.

Brown well in hot bacon fat over medium heat. Keep turning potatoes carefully so they become crusty brown all over.

PAN-FRIED POTATOES

Peel and cut potatoes into ¼-inch strips. Cover with cold salted water (1 tablespoon salt to 8 fluid ounces water). Leave to stand about 25 minutes.

Drain and dry with paper towelling. Cook, covered, in small amount of hot fat in a heavy frying pan. Uncover and cook until brown, turning often.

SWEET POTATOES

Pan-Fried (Sautéed): Fry canned or cooked sweet potatoes in a little hot salad oil in a frying pan until golden brown on all sides.

Baked in Foil: Follow method for potatoes baked in foil.

Grilled: Cut peeled, cooked potatoes in halves lengthwise. Spread with butter or margarine. Cook in hinged wire grill over hot coals, turning often, until bubbly. Top with butter, salt, and pepper.

POTATO BAKE —OUTDOORS OR INDOORS

8 baking potatoes
½ pound butter, melted
2½ fluid ounces Worcestershire sauce
½ ounce chopped parsley, dill, or chives

Bake potatoes until half baked (about 40 minutes). Cool.

Cut potato into ½-inch slices leaving slices joined at the bottom. Combine butter, Worcestershire sauce and chopped herbs.

Place each sliced potato on a square of foil. Spoon about 3 tablespoons of the butter mixture over each potato. Wrap tightly in foil, sealing all edges.

Bake over grey coals, turning occasionally for 30 to 40 minutes or until potatoes, when pierced, are tender. Serves 8. Indoors: Bake in moderate oven (375°F. Mark 5) 30 to 40 minutes.

Potato Bake—Outdoors or Indoors

Outdoor Ways with Fruit

FRUIT MIXED GRILL

Brush tomato or pineapple slices, or peeled banana or peach halves, with melted butter, margarine, or salad oil.

Sprinkle with salt, pepper, and, if wished, lemon juice, nutmeg, etc.

Cook in hinged wire grill over hot coals, turning to brown.

FRUIT KEBABS

1 large can peach halves, halved
3 bananas, thickly sliced
2 apples, cut in wedges
1 fresh pineapple, cubed
3 grapefruits, in segments

Sauce:
8 fluid ounces grapefruit juice
2 tablespoons Cointreau
6 ounces honey
½ teaspoon chopped mint

Combine sauce ingredients and marinate the fruit for ½ hour.

Alternate fruit on skewer and grill 5 to 8 minutes, basting with marinade.

FLAMED BANANAS

Peel firm, ripe bananas and rub with sugar. Arrange in folding wire grill and sprinkle with lemon juice.

Grill until just delicately browned but not mushy.

Place on a flameproof dish. Sprinkle with a little more sugar. Pour 2 fluid ounces rum over them; ignite the rum and serve while flaming.

BACON, BANANA AND ORANGE GRILL

3 ounces brown sugar
½ teaspoon cinnamon
4 bananas
Lemon juice
4 rashers of bacon
3 oranges

Mix sugar and cinnamon. Peel bananas; roll in lemon juice, then in sugar mixture.

Wrap a bacon rasher around each banana; fasten with wooden sticks.

Peel oranges; slice and sprinkle with remaining sugar mixture.

Place fruit in hinged wire grill and cook over moderate heat 8 minutes, turning bananas once. Serves 4.

BANANA-HAM ROLLUPS

Cut peeled bananas in lengthwise halves, then crosswise.

Roll each in a very thin cooked ham slice. Cook in folding wire grill, turning to cook both sides.

Let your family and guests help themselves to cool eating from a deep salad bowl filled with chilled fruits served with wedges of lime or lemon.

SKEWER-COOKED FRUITS

1. Apple quarters, dipped in melted butter and sprinkled with sugar.
2. Halves of orange slices alternated with pieces of banana. Brush with honey, then grill and serve sprinkled with toasted coconut.
3. Dip pineapple chunks in butter, then roll in macaroon crumbs before serving.

FRESH PINEAPPLE IN FOIL

Cut off top and the bottom slice. Set aside. Cut around inside of shell.

Push out fruit in one piece; cut into sticks, discarding core. Return to shell. Replace top and bottom.

Wrap in foil. Bake on medium coals, turning once, about 30 minutes.

ROASTED BANANAS

Wash firm bananas (yellow with green tips), allowing at least one for each person.

Roast them on the grill grid. It will take 10 to 15 minutes for them to cook through and don't be alarmed when they darken as they cook.

Serve hot as a vegetable, same as a baked potato. Let each person split his own banana lengthwise and eat the rich fruit out of skin with a fork. No need to add butter, but some people like a bit of lemon juice.

BANANAS ROASTED IN FOIL

Method 1: wrap unpeeled bananas in foil. Put them around the edge of coals, turning once or twice during cooking. They take 10 to 15 minutes.

Method 2: Slit banana skins lengthwise. Insert brown sugar and wrap in foil. Bake 8 minutes over hot coals, turning once.

Method 3: Remove peels from bananas and place each in a section of foil cut large enough to wrap bananas securely.

Sprinkle 1 tablespoon granulated sugar and 1 teaspoon cinnamon on each banana.

Wrap securely and nestle them into hot but not flaming coals; cook 10 to 15 minutes, depending on heat of coals. Serve with spoons and eat directly from foil cases.

APPLES ROASTED IN FOIL

Method 1: Wrap whole apples each in a piece of foil and put them around the edge of coals, turning them once or twice during the cooking. Test with a fork through the foil and serve in the foil. They take about 30 minutes.

Method 2: Core the apples and fill the centres with sugar, cinnamon, and butter before roasting. Or fill the centres with peppermints before roasting.

CAMPFIRE APPLES

Stick an apple through the stem end on the end of a stick (one for each person).

Roast over coals until the skin can be easily peeled off. Tear off the peel and roll the hot apple in a pan of brown sugar.

Turn the sugared apple slowly over the coals until the sugar melts into the apple.

TOFFEE APPLES

½ pound toffees
2 tablespoons water
Apples, cut in quarters

Fold up sides of a double square of aluminium foil to serve as a disposable pan.

Place toffees and water in this; put on grill to melt. Stir until smooth.

Remove cores from quartered apples. Hold over fire on sticks or long-handled forks to heat slightly. Then dip in melted toffee; twirl to coat with toffee. Cool and eat from stick.

BEVERAGES

Beverages take the spotlight at the beginning and at the end of a well-planned meal. A chilled juice, tart and refreshing, makes a good start for any meal. From this liquid first course to after-dinner coffee, you'll find a broad selection of beverage ideas to complement your dinner or party menus.

The recipes given here, except for some variations of coffee, are non-alcoholic. Alcoholic drinks of all types are in a separate section, **Drinks.**

Juice Cocktails

Juice cocktails, except the hot varieties, should always be served thoroughly chilled. Fruit juices to be served as a starter should never be too sweet. Many of the canned juices may be improved by the addition of a little lemon or lime juice to give zest and to offset the natural sweetness of the fruit.

Innumerable interesting flavours may be created by combining two or more juices before chilling. Some suggestions are given below.

Many of the fruit and vegetable cocktails may be enriched in texture and food value if they are prepared in the liquidizer.

FROSTED GLASSES FOR COCKTAILS

Method 1: Just before filling cocktail glasses, dip rims in lemon or orange juice to depth of half an inch, then dip immediately into granulated sugar. If time permits, place the glasses in the refrigerator to frost for about 20 minutes.
Method 2: Dip rims into unbeaten egg white, then in granulated sugar. Allow glasses to dry before serving.

CHILLED FRUIT JUICE SUGGESTIONS

1. Mix pineapple juice, fresh or canned, with orange or lemon juice.
2. Mix equal parts unsweetened grapefruit juice and apricot juice.
3. Mix equal parts unsweetened pineapple or orange juice and prune juice.
4. Mix one part grape juice and two parts unsweetened pineapple juice.
5. Mix equal parts pineapple juice and orange juice and flavour with a dash of fresh lime juice.
6. Mix equal parts grape juice and unsweetened grapefruit juice.
7. Mix 4 parts sweet cider, 1 part pineapple juice, and 1 part orange juice.
8. Flavour cranberry juice with a dash of lemon juice, and sweeten to taste.
9. Mix equal parts of grapefruit and cranberry juices.
10. Mix equal parts of loganberry juice and pineapple juice.
11. Add chopped mint or 1 or 2 drops of oil of peppermint to canned or fresh grapefruit juice.
12. Mix 2 parts grape juice and 1 part ginger ale, and add lemon juice to taste.

SPARKLING FRUIT COCKTAILS

Method 1: Combine equal parts canned fruit juices (apple, cranberry juice cocktail, orange, whole fruit nectar) with chilled ginger ale.
Method 2: Reconstitute frozen juice concentrates (grape, grapefruit, lemonade, limeade, orange) with chilled ginger ale instead of water. Serve at once.

GRAPE JUICE COCKTAIL

1 pint grape juice
4 tablespoons lemon juice
1 pint chilled ginger ale

Combine grape and lemon juices and chill thoroughly. Just before serving add the ginger ale. Serve in frosted glasses. Serves 6.

PINEAPPLE-GRAPEFRUIT COCKTAIL

4 ounces sugar
4 fluid ounces water
14 fluid ounces pineapple juice
8 fluid ounces grapefruit juice

Heat sugar and water together 5 minutes, stirring until sugar is dissolved. Add fruit juices to the cooled syrup. Chill. Serves 6.

SPICED CIDER COCKTAIL

16 fluid ounces cider
$\frac{1}{8}$ teaspoon salt
3 whole cloves
3 whole allspice berries
2 cinnamon sticks
2 fluid ounces lemon juice
6 fluid ounces orange juice
8 fluid ounces chilled ginger ale

Combine cider, salt, and spices; bring to a boil, then simmer about 5 minutes. Cool and strain.

Add lemon and orange juices. Sweeten slightly if desired. Chill thoroughly. Just before serving add ginger ale. Serves 8.

SAUERKRAUT COCKTAIL

1 pint 4 fluid ounces canned sauerkraut juice
$\frac{1}{2}$ teaspoon Worcestershire sauce
$\frac{1}{4}$ teaspoon prepared French mustard
Dash of ground black pepper

Combine and chill thoroughly. Shake well before serving. Serves 6.

TOMATO JUICE COCKTAIL

1 pint 4 fluid ounces tomato juice
$\frac{1}{8}$ teaspoon ground black pepper
$\frac{3}{4}$ teaspoon salt
$\frac{1}{4}$ teaspoon sugar
5 teaspoons lemon juice
5 drops Tabasco sauce

Shake ingredients together and chill thoroughly before serving. Serve with tiny wedges of lemon. Serves 6.

CLAM JUICE COCKTAIL

1 pint 4 fluid ounces clam juice
3 tablespoons lemon juice
2 tablespoons tomato ketchup
1 or 2 drops Tabasco sauce

Combine and chill thoroughly. Shake well before serving. Serves 6.

Variations: Other seasonings such as horseradish, Worcestershire sauce, grated onion, celery salt, etc. may be used as desired.

LIQUIDIZER STARTER COCKTAILS

In each of the following recipes, combine all ingredients in the liquidizer. Cover and turn on liquidizer. Run until all ingredients are blended and smooth. Serve immediately. Each recipe makes about 1 pint 4 fluid ounces.

EMERALD JUICE COCKTAIL

8 fluid ounces grapefruit juice
8 fluid ounces pineapple juice
1 tablespoon lemon juice
2 ounces frozen spinach, unthawed, cut up
3 ounces crushed ice

FRUIT AND VEGETABLE COCKTAIL

8 fluid ounces orange juice
8 fluid ounces grapefruit juice
6 ounces shredded green cabbage
¼ green pepper
1 tablespoon lemon juice
6 ounces crushed ice

GOLDEN JUICE COCKTAIL

8 fluid ounces canned apricot nectar
8 fluid ounces grapefruit juice
4 fluid ounces frozen pineapple juice, unthawed
½ carrot, cut up
1 tablespoon lemon juice
3 ounces crushed ice

MINTED PINEAPPLE CUCUMBER COCKTAIL

8 fluid ounces pineapple juice
1 tablespoon lemon juice
4 ounces unpeeled diced cucumber
Few sprigs mint
6 ounces crushed ice

TOMATO JUICE CHEESE COCKTAIL

12 fluid ounces canned tomato juice
4 fluid ounces cottage cheese
6 ounces crushed ice
½ teaspoon Worcestershire sauce
Chives
Few celery leaves

VEGETABLE COCKTAIL

16 fluid ounces canned tomato juice
½ carrot, cut up
¼ small onion
Few celery leaves
Few sprigs parsley
6 ounces crushed ice

CRANBERRY JUICE COCKTAIL

8 ounces cranberries
1 pint 4 fluid ounces water
4 ounces sugar

Cook cranberries in water until skins pop; strain through muslin.

Cook juice and sugar until sugar is dissolved, about 2 minutes.

Chill and add lemon juice, orange juice, unsweetened pineapple juice, or pale ginger ale to suit taste. Serves 6.

CLAM AND TOMATO JUICE COCKTAIL

Combine equal amounts of clam juice and tomato juice or use two-thirds clam juice and one-third tomato juice.

Season to taste with lemon juice, a dash of Tabasco sauce, and salt and pepper. Chill thoroughly before serving with a wedge of lemon.

FROZEN FRUIT COCKTAIL

Freeze ginger ale to a mush in freezing trays. Spoon into sorbet glasses and top with well-chilled and drained tinned fruit cocktail.

FROZEN GRAPE JUICE

16 fluid ounces grape juice
1 tablespoon lemon juice

Combine and turn into freezing tray. Freeze to a mush, stirring once. Turn into a chilled bowl and beat with a fork. Serve at once. Serves 4.

FROSTED JUICE COCKTAILS

Add a tiny ball of any fruit water ice to each cocktail glass of fruit juice just before serving. Add a sprig of mint for garnish.

Two popular combinations are: (1) lime ice on pineapple juice; (2) cranberry sorbet on pineapple juice.

FROZEN TOMATO JUICE

Season tomato juice as desired. Turn into freezing tray. Freeze to mush, stirring once.

Turn into a chilled bowl and beat with a fork. Serve at once.

TOMATO JUICE FRAPPÉ

18 fluid ounce can tomato juice
1 small onion, sliced
Few celery leaves
Dash of Tabasco sauce
½ teaspoon salt
1 teaspoon gelatine
1 tablespoon cold water

Combine tomato juice, onion, celery leaves, Tabasco, and salt in saucepan. Bring to boil and simmer about 5 minutes. Strain.

Sprinkle gelatine over cold water and leave for 5 minutes. Add to hot tomato mixture and stir until dissolved. Cool.

Pour into refrigerator tray and freeze to a mush, stirring occasionally. Serve in sorbet glasses. Serves 6.

BEETROOT JUICE COCKTAIL

8 fluid ounces of liquid drained from canned beetroots
12 fluid ounces water
2½ fluid ounces lemon juice
½ teaspoon salt
Dash of cayenne pepper

Combine and chill thoroughly. Shake well before serving. Serves 6.

Tomato juice—winter style: serve in hot cups or in soup bowls. Some favourite garnishes for hot juice are: a slice of clove-spiked lemon; a generous spoonful of whipped cream; a slice of stuffed olive; a sprinkling of chopped chives; a few pieces of popcorn.

SPICED TOMATO COCKTAIL

16 fluid ounces tomato juice
4 ounces sugar
2 lemons, sliced
¼ teaspoon cinnamon
⅛ teaspoon nutmeg
6 whole cloves
4 fluid ounces lemon juice
16 fluid ounces iced water

Combine tomato juice, sugar, sliced lemons, cinnamon, nutmeg, and cloves; heat to boiling point.

Strain, chill thoroughly and add lemon juice and iced water. Serve in cocktail glasses, garnished with bits of candied ginger. Serves 6.

SAUERKRAUT-TOMATO JUICE COCKTAIL

No. 1: Combine equal parts of sauerkraut juice and tomato juice. Season to taste with Worcestershire sauce. Chill thoroughly before serving with lemon wedges.

No. 2: Combine 1 part sauerkraut and 3 parts tomato juice. Season to taste with lemon juice and salt and pepper. Chill thoroughly before serving.

FRESH MINT COCKTAIL

2-3 ounces fresh mint leaves
8 ounces sugar
4 fluid ounces water
Green food colouring
Crushed ice cubes
8 fluid ounces ginger ale
4 sprigs fresh mint

Crush mint leaves in pan with sugar. Add water. Mix thoroughly and boil 10 minutes. Strain. Add food colouring to make syrup a delicate mint green.

Half fill cocktail glasses with crushed ice. Add 2 tablespoons mint syrup and fill to top with ginger ale. Garnish with sprig of mint. Serves 4.

Coffee

COFFEE

The coffee bean grows on an evergreen tropical shrub or small tree believed to be native to Ethiopia. Popular in Arabia probably since the 15th century, coffee was not introduced into Europe until late in the 17th century. It quickly became a fad, and coffeehouses—the forerunners of modern clubs—were the meeting places of social, literary, and political leaders.

The flavour and aroma of the coffee bean are not released until it is roasted. Instant coffee is made by dehydrating brewed coffee. Despite its stimulating properties, coffee by itself has no food value.

The French word for coffee (and also for coffeehouse or restaurant serving light refreshments) is café.

Café Au Lait: Equal parts of strong hot coffee and hot milk, usually poured simultaneously from separate pots into the cup.

Café Brûlot, Café Diable, Café Diabolique: Black coffee prepared with spices and orange peel, served in a demitasse (small cup) with flaming brandy.

Café Creole Bourbon: A carefully filtered, strong, fragrant coffee, which takes over an hour to prepare.

Café Glacé: A mixture of coffee, water, sugar, and boiled milk, frozen and served in cups.

Café Liégeois: Café Glacé to which whipped cream has been added.

Café Noir: Black coffee.

The Italian word for coffee and coffeehouse is caffè. Italian coffee is roasted very dark, almost charred, which gives it a pungent flavour.

Caffè Espresso: Coffee made in a special machine that forces steam through finely ground (pulverized) coffee identified as "espresso" on the container. To make at home, use the recipe which comes with your equipment. Serve espresso after dinner in a small coffee cup (demitasse) or in an espresso glass with or without a twist of lemon peel. Some fanciers add a dash of brandy.

Caffè Latte: Coffee with milk, usually half and half.

Cappucino: Either black coffee topped with whipped cream and cinnamon or coffee served in a tall, narrow glass or cup with frothy boiled milk.

Caffè Borgia: Equal parts of hot espresso and hot chocolate, topped with whipped cream and sprinkled with grated orange rind.

In the Near East, finely powdered (pulverized) coffee is used and the beverage is drunk unfiltered and heavily sweetened. This is commonly known in Western countries as Turkish coffee.

RULES FOR MAKING GOOD COFFEE

1. Measure coffee and water accurately. Use 2 level standard measuring tablespoons to each half pint of water.

2. Use fresh water for making coffee. For best results, start with freshly drawn cold water. Water that has been pre-heated or drawn from the hot water tap may impart an undesirable taste to the brew.

3. Serve as soon as possible after brewing. If necessary to let brewed coffee stand any length of time, hold at serving temperature by placing pot in pan of hot water or over very low heat on asbestos pad. Keep coffee hot but do not boil. Coffee that has cooled cannot be reheated without loss of flavour.

4. For best results always brew coffee at full capacity of the coffee maker.

5. Consistent timing is important. After you find the exact timing to secure the results desired with your method of coffee-making, stick to it in order to get uniform results.

6. Never boil coffee.

7. Never re-use coffee grounds.

8. Never allow cloth filters to become dry. Keep immersed in cold water. Never use soap in washing cloth filters.

9. Keep coffee maker immaculately clean. Wash thoroughly after each use and rinse with clear hot water.

10. Always heat coffee maker with hot water before using.

PERCOLATOR COFFEE METHOD

1. Measure required amount of fresh cold water into percolator and place on heat.

2. When water boils, remove from heat.

3. Measure required amount of ground coffee into basket and insert basket into percolator.

4. Cover, return to heat and allow to percolate slowly for 6 to 8 minutes.

5. Remove coffee basket and serve.

STEEPED COFFEE METHOD

1. Preheat pot by scalding with hot water.

2. Measure required amount of ground coffee into pot.

3. Pour on measured amount of fresh boiling water.

4. Stir coffee and water for at least half a minute. Let stand 5 to 10 minutes, depending on grind of coffee used and strength of brew desired.

5. Pour coffee off grounds, through a strainer if desired, and serve.

STORING COFFEE

Coffee in bean form retains its flavour longer than in ground form.

Roasted coffee, whether in whole bean or ground, should be kept in a container as nearly air tight as possible. If market containers are not air tight, the coffee should be transferred to a tight-sealing fruit jar.

Refrigerate for best flavour retention. Approximate time limit for storage for opened ground coffee is 14 days at room temperature, considerably longer in the refrigerator.

If it becomes weak, use more. If it becomes bitter, it's usable if the bitterness is not objectionable.

VACUUM-MADE COFFEE

1. Measure required amount of fresh cold water into lower bowl; place on heat.

2. Place filter into upper bowl, and add measured quantity of ground coffee, but *do not* insert in lower bowl. If you have a vacuum maker with a vented stem (a small hole in the side of the tube above the hot water line) the pot may be completely assembled before placing on heat. In this type of vacuum maker the water in the lower bowl will not start to rise until the water boils. When water starts to rise, reduce heat and follow the regular procedure.

3. When water in lower bowl boils actively, reduce heat. (If electricity is used, turn it off.)

4. Insert upper bowl with a slight twist to ensure a tight seal.

5. When the water has risen into upper bowl (some water will always remain in the lower bowl) stir water and coffee thoroughly.

6. In 1 to 3 minutes (depending on grind—finer grinds require the shorter time) turn off heat. (If electricity is used remove coffee maker from unit.)

7. When all coffee has been drawn into lower bowl, remove upper bowl and serve.

8. Cloth filters should be washed in cold water immediately after being used and kept immersed in cold water until used again. Never use soap in washing cloth filters.

FILTERED COFFEE METHOD

1. Preheat pot by scalding with hot water.
2. Measure required amount of ground coffee into filter section.
3. Measure required amount of fresh boiling water into upper container, then cover.
4. When filtering is completed remove upper section immediately.
5. Stir brew and serve.
6. Cloth filters should be washed in cold water immediately after using and *kept immersed in cold water* until next used. Never use soap in washing filters.

PICNIC COFFEE

Use 1 pound coarsely ground coffee to 13 pints water. Tie coffee rather loosely in a sugar sack or muslin bag. There must be room for swelling of grounds, and for the water to circulate.

Bring water to the boil, and when boiling rapidly, push pan away from highest heat, so that water is held just under boiling point. Add sack of coffee and use a stick or paddle to agitate it. Slosh it up and down frequently for a 12 to 15 minute brewing period.

Lift sack out, let it drain, then discard it. Do not allow coffee to boil.

URN COFFEE

Use 1 pound coffee to 13 pints water. Fill water jacket of urn with water until glass gauge registers ¾ full and heat just to boiling point. Put coffee in basket or filter, and pour briskly boiling water over it. Cover.

When water has dripped through, remove coffee container immediately. One pound of coffee will make 32 standard cups (8 fluid ounces each).

TURKISH COFFEE

6 rounded tablespoons pulverized coffee
6 tablespoons sugar
1 pint 4 fluid ounces cold water
Rosewater (optional)

Place coffee, sugar, and water in a lidless coffee pot or pan. Heat until mixture comes to a brisk boil, stirring constantly.

Remove from heat and let the froth subside. Replace pot on very hot heat and repeat process 3 more times.

Add a little cold water to pot just before serving to settle brew. Add a few drops of rosewater, if desired, to each cup. Serve in demitasses.

IRISH COFFEE

Put in a pre-warmed 7 fluid ounce goblet or coffee cup 1½ fluid ounces Irish whiskey and 1 teaspoon sugar. Fill the glass with freshly made strong coffee. Stir until sugar is dissolved. Top with a spoonful of whipped cream.

CAFÉ BRÛLOT OR DIABLE
(French Flaming Coffee)

Peel of 1 orange
4 sticks cinnamon
12 whole cloves
6 lumps sugar
4 fluid ounces brandy or Cognac
1 pint 12 fluid ounces freshly made coffee

Slice orange peel thinly and place in a silver bowl or chafing dish with cinnamon, cloves, and sugar.

Pour brandy over sugar mixture and ignite; ladle it until the sugar is dissolved. Add freshly made coffee. Serve in demitasse cups. Serves 6 to 8.

ICED COFFEE

Method 1 (With crushed ice): Prepare double-strength coffee by any method. Pour hot freshly made coffee over crushed ice in tall glasses.

The double-strength will make up for dilution by the ice without loss of flavour.

Serve iced coffee with sugar and plain or whipped cream.

Method 2 (Precooled): Prepare regular strength coffee by any method. Pour into earthenware, enamel, or glass container. Cool and place, securely covered, in refrigerator.

Freshly made coffee can be kept in the refrigerator many hours without seriously impairing the flavour.

Method 3 (With coffee cubes): Prepare regular strength coffee by any method. Cool and pour into refrigerator trays. Freeze.

To serve, pour freshly made regular strength hot coffee over coffee ice cubes in tall glasses.

CINNAMON CHOCOLATE COFFEE

2 ounces cooking chocolate
8 fluid ounces double-strength freshly made coffee
3 tablespoons sugar
⅛ teaspoon salt
1 pint 4 fluid ounces milk
Crushed ice
Powdered cinnamon

Melt chocolate in coffee in top of double boiler. Add sugar and salt. Keep over hot water; add milk gradually and stir to blend.

Chill and pour over crushed ice in tall glasses. Sprinkle generously with powdered cinnamon. Serves 4.

ICED CHOCOLATE-CAFÉ

Combine and beat thoroughly 8 fluid ounces double-strength coffee, 1 tablespoon chocolate syrup, 2 tablespoons whipped cream, and 3 tablespoons crushed ice. Serve immediately.

Spiced Iced Coffee

SPICED ICED COFFEE CONCENTRATE

1 pint 12 fluid ounces warm water
2 ounces instant coffee
¼ teaspoon ground cloves
1 teaspoon cinnamon

To make concentrate: Empty instant coffee as it comes from the jar into suitable container or jar. Add cloves and cinnamon. Slowly add water. Stir or shake to dissolve coffee and spices. Cover and stir before using. Makes about 20 servings.

To use concentrate: For each serving pour 3 tablespoons concentrate over ice cubes into an 8 fluid ounce glass. Add cold water. Sweeten to taste. If desired, serve with plain or whipped cream. Garnish with nutmeg.

VIENNESE ICED COFFEE

Half fill tall glass with crushed ice. Sprinkle with icing sugar to taste. Add 1 tablespoon whipped cream. Fill with hot double-strength coffee.

MEXICAN ICED COFFEE

Chill 1 pint 12 fluid ounces double-strength coffee. To serve add 6 tablespoons sugar and 2 teaspoons vanilla essence. Stir well to dissolve sugar.

Pour into glasses about ¼ full of crushed ice. Add cream as desired. Serves 6.

SPANISH CREAM COFFEE

Caramelize 8 ounces sugar by melting in frying pan, stirring constantly. Add 8 fluid ounces boiling water and stir until sugar is dissolved. Boil 2 minutes and add 1 pint 12 fluid ounces double-strength coffee.

Add 1 cup single cream and serve in tall glasses with crushed ice. Garnish with small spoonful of ice cream.

MOCHA ICED COFFEE

Combine freshly made double-strength coffee with an equal amount of cooled cocoa.

Pour into tall glass filled with ice. Add icing sugar and cream to taste.

RUM ICED COFFEE

Pour precooled regular-strength coffee over ice in glass. Serve with whipped cream topping to which rum flavouring has been added.

Tea and Tea Base Beverages

RULES FOR BREWING TEA

Use spotlessly clean teapot made of glass, china, or earthenware. Scald teapot with boiling water and drain.

Measure tea into teapot, using one teaspoon tea leaves, or one teabag, for each measuring cup of water, plus one extra teaspoon or bag "for the pot".

Bring measured cold water to a rolling boil and pour over tea leaves. Steep 4 to 5 minutes to develop full flavour. Dilute to the desired strength with clear, boiling water.

Variations: Serve tea with sugar, honey, fruit preserves, cream, lemon or orange slices, crystallized ginger, or cloves.

RUSSIAN TEA

Scald an earthenware teapot with boiling water and drain. Put in 2 teaspoons of tea leaves for each cup of water. Pour boiling water over the tea leaves.

Cover tightly and keep warm for 5 minutes. Strain into another scalded pot.

To serve, pour ¼ cup of tea infusion into each cup. Fill with boiling water and serve with lemon and sugar.

BOHEMIAN TEA

5 pints boiling water
8 ounces sugar
1 teaspoon whole cloves
1 stick cinnamon
2 tablespoons black tea
6 fluid ounces orange juice
Juice of 2 lemons

Tie spices loosely in muslin bag and add with sugar to hot water. Boil 10 minutes. Turn off heat and add tea tied in another bag.

Cover and leave to stand 5 minutes. Remove spices and tea bag. Add fruit juices and serve hot. Serves 20.

ICED TEA

Method 1: Make double-strength hot tea, allowing 2 teaspoons of tea for each cup of boiling water. Pour hot over crushed ice in tall glasses.

Method 2: Make regular-strength tea. Freeze in refrigerator trays. To serve, pour freshly made regular-strength hot tea over tea cubes in tall glasses.

Method 3: Cool regular-strength tea to room temperature and place in refrigerator to chill. Serve over crushed ice in tall glasses.

ICED TEA CONCENTRATE

Pour 2½ pints boiling water over 4 ounces tea leaves. Steep 6 minutes. Strain concentrate into glass or earthenware container (**Note:** one pint of water will be absorbed by the tea leaves), and dissolve 8 ounces sugar in it.

To serve, dilute concentrate with 7 parts cold water and add ice and lemon. The concentrate is best when made fresh.

HOT FRUIT PUNCH

3 tablespoons tea leaves
3¾ pints boiling water
12 ounces sugar
8 fluid ounces lemon juice
2 pints fresh or canned orange juice, or orange and pineapple juice or apricot juice

Steep tea in boiling water. Add sugar and bring to boiling point. Add fruit juices and heat until just hot, but do not boil.

Garnish punch in bowl with sliver-thin slices of lemon and orange. Serves 30.

HOT MINTED TEA

4 sprigs fresh mint
4 teaspoons tea
1 pint 12 fluid ounces boiling water
Lemon or lime slices

Add fresh mint to dry tea. Pour boiling water over tea. Cover and allow to steep 3 to 5 minutes.

Strain and serve hot with slice of lemon or lime.

One tablespoon mint jelly may be substituted for fresh mint. Serves 4 to 6.

HAWAIIAN TEA — HOT OR COLD

4 fluid ounces water
8 ounces sugar
10 fluid ounces lemon juice
1 20-ounce can pineapple juice
3¼ pints freshly brewed black tea (3 tablespoons tea for 3¼ pints boiling water)
1 8-ounce bottle maraschino cherries and syrup

Boil sugar and water together 5 minutes. Combine with remaining ingredients and serve hot. Or pour over crushed ice and serve cold. Serves about 18.

ICED SPICED TEA

3 tablespoons tea leaves
1 pint 12 fluid ounces boiling water
12 whole cloves
12 allspice berries
1 2-inch cinnamon stick
Lemon wedges

Put tea leaves in a heated pot and add boiling water. Add spices and let stand 5 minutes.

Pour through a strainer into tall glasses filled with ice. Serves 4.

SPICED TEA FROST

5 ounces granulated sugar
16 fluid ounces cold water
Grated rind of 1 lemon
8 whole cloves
2 1-inch cinnamon sticks
¼ teaspoon ginger
2 pints freshly made hot tea
Lemon sections

Combine all ingredients but the tea and lemon sections, and boil 15 minutes. Strain and cool.

Add tea, mix well, and pour over ice in tall glasses. Serve with lemon sections. Serves 6.

MOCK CLARET PUNCH

3 lemons
5 oranges
8 fluid ounces redcurrant juice
Small stick cinnamon
16 fluid ounces water
8 fluid ounces tea infusion
Sugar or golden syrup
¼ cup stemmed fresh redcurrants

Squeeze juice from lemons and oranges and add to redcurrant juice. Chill.

Grate rind of 1 lemon and 1 orange, and add with cinnamon stick to water. Boil together 10 minutes, then strain and cool.

Add fruit juices and tea infusion to water. Sweeten to taste with syrup. Garnish with redcurrants. Serves 6 to 8.

STORING TEA

Whether bulk or package, tea should be kept in a moderately cool, dry place, away from foods of distinctive flavours.

Dampness will spoil tea by starting secondary fermentation.

Exposure to air will cause tea to lose flavour, strength, and aroma.

Do not keep tea more than nine months to a year.

A parfait pie and iced tea strike a cool note for summer patio gatherings.

Milk Drinks

COCOA

2 to 3 ounces sugar to taste
6 tablespoons cocoa
Dash of salt
8 fluid ounces water
2 pints milk

Combine sugar, cocoa, and salt in a pan. Add water slowly and boil 2 minutes, stirring until thickened. Add milk and heat slowly to just below boiling point.

Before serving, beat with rotary beater until frothy. Serve topped with whipped cream or marshmallow. Serves 6.

HOT CHOCOLATE

2 ounces cooking or plain chocolate
8 fluid ounces cold water
⅛ teaspoon salt
3 tablespoons sugar
1¼ pints milk

Heat chocolate and water together, stirring until chocolate is melted and blended. Add salt and sugar and boil 4 minutes, stirring constantly.

Place over hot water and gradually stir in milk. Heat thoroughly. To serve, beat with rotary beater until light and frothy. Serves 6.

ICED BRAZILIAN CHOCOLATE

2 ounces cooking or plain chocolate
8 fluid ounces strong coffee
3 tablespoons sugar
⅛ teaspoon salt
1¼ pints milk

Add chocolate to coffee in top of double boiler. Place over low heat and stir until chocolate is melted and blended. Add sugar and salt and boil 3 minutes, stirring constantly.

Place over boiling water. Add milk gradually, stirring constantly, then heat. Beat with rotary beater until light and frothy. Pour over ice in tall glasses. Serves 4.

ICED MINTED COCOA

6 tablespoons cocoa
2 sprigs fresh mint, crushed
8 fluid ounces boiling water
4 ounces sugar
1 pint 12 fluid ounces scalded milk
½ teaspoon vanilla essence

Add cocoa to well crushed mint and pour boiling water over all. Let stand until cold.

Add sugar to scalded milk, stirring until dissolved. Add to cocoa mixture and strain. Cool and add vanilla essence.

Serve well chilled in tall glasses with whipped cream topping. Serves 4 to 6.

EGGNOG
(Master Recipe)

1 egg
Few grains salt
1 tablespoon sugar
¼ teaspoon vanilla essence
8 fluid ounces cold milk
Dash of ground nutmeg

Beat egg, salt, and sugar. Add vanilla and milk. Beat thoroughly. Pour into glass and sprinkle lightly with nutmeg. Serves 1.

Almond Eggnog: Omit vanilla essence and flavour eggnog with 6 drops almond essence.

Chocolate Eggnog: Omit sugar. Add 1½ tablespoons chocolate syrup and 1 tablespoon malted milk (optional). Beat well. Top with whipped cream.

Fruit Juice Eggnog: Flavour eggnog with 2 tablespoons fresh or canned fruit juice.

Honey Eggnog: Substitute 2 tablespoons honey for sugar.

Malted Milk Eggnog: Add 1 to 2 tablespoons malted milk to eggnog.

Sherry Eggnog: Flavour eggnog with 2 tablespoons sherry or other favourite wine.

MEXICAN COCOA

3 egg whites
3 ounces cocoa
1 teaspoon cinnamon
2 ounces sugar or more
8 fluid ounces cold milk
3¾ pints scalded milk

Make thin paste of egg whites, cocoa, cinnamon, sugar, using cold milk.

Slowly add scalded milk to paste over low heat, beating constantly with rotary beater. Serve when thoroughly hot and foamy. Serves 10 to 12.

FRENCH CHOCOLATE MIX

2½ ounces cooking or plain chocolate
4 fluid ounces water
6 ounces sugar
¼ teaspoon salt
4 fluid ounces cream, whipped

Place chocolate and water in saucepan and cook over low heat until thick, stirring frequently. Add sugar and salt and bring to boil. Let cool, then fold in whipped cream. Store in covered jar in refrigerator. Makes nearly 1 pint. To serve as hot chocolate, pour hot milk over 1 or 2 tablespoons of mixture in cup.

To serve as cold chocolate milk, stir 1 or 2 tablespoons of mix into glass of milk with fork or use rotary beater.

The idea of a "home soda fountain" offers fun for the whole family—children love "make-your-own" drinks and milk drinks are real energy builders.

FRUIT MILK SHAKES

Use thoroughly chilled milk, fruit juice, or fruit pulp. Shake or beat with fruit or syrup until well blended. Sweeten to taste. Garnish with whipped cream if desired.

Evaporated milk diluted with an equal amount of water may be used instead of fresh milk.

Each of the following makes 4 generous servings.

Banana Shake: Combine 3 mashed ripe bananas with 1¼ pints milk.

Fruit Juice Shake: Combine 1 pint 12 fluid ounces milk with 4 fluid ounces fruit syrup from cooked or canned fruit. Use apricot, peach, plum, pineapple, prune, or fruit juice.

Grape Juice Shake: Combine 1 pint milk, 12 fluid ounces grape juice, and 1 teaspoon lemon juice.

Orange Shake: Combine 16 fluid ounces milk, 16 fluid ounces orange juice, and ¼ teaspoon almond essence.

Prune Shake: Combine 16 fluid ounces milk, 16 fluid ounces prune juice, and 1 teaspoon lemon juice.

Strawberry Shake: Combine 1 pint 12 fluid ounces of milk and 6 ounces crushed sweetened strawberries.

LIQUIDIZER MILK DRINKS

In recipes given below, pour 8 fluid ounces milk into container. Add fruit, 6 ounces finely crushed ice, and if a richer drink is desired, 2 or 3 marshmallows or 1 scoop ice cream. Blend until smooth.

Banana: Use 1 ripe medium-sized banana.

Chocolate-Mint: Use chocolate syrup to taste, 4 drops peppermint essence, and 4 marshmallows.

Peach: Use 6 ounces fresh or canned sliced peaches or frozen peaches and 2 tablespoons sherry.

Pineapple: Use 6 ounces fresh or canned, diced or crushed pineapple.

Prune: Use 4 ounces soaked pitted prunes and 1 tablespoon treacle.

Strawberry: Use 12 ounces fresh strawberries and 4 tablespoons sugar or frozen berries.

CHOCOLATE MILK SHAKE

Add 2 tablespoons or more chocolate syrup to 8 fluid ounces milk. Beat with rotary beater. Top with ice cream — vanilla or chocolate.

Frosted Chocolate: Beat into the chocolate and milk mixture a scoop of ice cream. Malted milk may be added.

Maple Milk Shake: Use 2 to 3 tablespoons of maple syrup instead of chocolate.

Minted Chocolate Shake: Flavour each chocolate milk shake with 3 drops of peppermint essence. Garnish with whipped cream and sprig of fresh mint.

CHOCOLATE MALTED MILK

    4 fluid ounces cold chocolate syrup
    3 tablespoons malted milk powder
    16 fluid ounces chilled milk
    1 large scoop vanilla or chocolate
        ice cream
    Dash of salt

Put all ingredients into mixer and shake or beat until well mixed and frothy. Serve at once. Serves 2.

COFFEE MALTED

    6 tablespoons malted milk powder
    16 fluid ounces fresh, hot double
        strength coffee
    5-6 ounces sugar
    12 fluid ounces milk
    4 fluid ounces single cream

Combine coffee with malted milk powder and beat until smooth. Add sugar to mixture and stir until dissolved. Add milk and cream.

Chill thoroughly and serve with plenty of crushed ice. Serves 6.

CHOCOLATE-MOCHA SHAKE

Mix 2 fluid ounces hot, double-strength coffee, 8 fluid ounces milk, and 2 tablespoons chocolate syrup.

Cool, and pour over crushed ice in glasses. Top with whipped cream. Serves 2.

Flavoured Milk Drinks
There's practically no end to the variety that can be made. The nice part of such a versatile concoction is that, provided with the ingredients, each person can create his own.

Mint Delight

MINT DELIGHT

    2 pints 8 fluid ounces milk
    4 tablespoons caster sugar
    1½ teaspoons peppermint essence
    5 to 6 drops green food colouring
    Few grains salt
    1 pint vanilla ice cream
    Maraschino cherries and pineapple
        chunks

Add sugar, peppermint, food colouring, and salt to cold milk, stirring to blend. Pour into cold glasses. Top with vanilla ice cream.

Garnish with maraschino cherries and pineapple chunks on straws. Serves 6.

TREACLE SHAKE

    2 tablespoons golden syrup
    2 tablespoons lemon juice
    1 teaspoon caster sugar
    ¼ teaspoon grated lemon rind
    8 fluid ounces milk
    1 large scoop vanilla ice
        cream

Combine ingredients in shaker. Shake or beat until frothy. Makes 12 fluid ounces.

BLACK BOTTOM COMBO

    4 fluid ounces chocolate flavoured
        syrup
    5-6 fluid ounces milk
    2 large scoops vanilla ice cream
    Dash of cinnamon
    1 egg white
    ¼ teaspoon vanilla essence
    2 tablespoons caster sugar

Pour 2 fluid ounces chocolate syrup into each of 2 10-ounce glasses. Put milk, ice cream, and cinnamon in deep 1½-pint bowl. Beat with rotary beater until ice cream is well blended and mixture is thick.

Pour slowly over syrup. Beat egg white until foamy. Add vanilla. Gradually beat in sugar, beating until mixture forms stiff peaks. Fill glasses with beaten egg white and garnish with maraschino cherries. Makes 2 10-ounce servings.

BLACKBERRY MILK SHAKE

    3 ounces crushed blackberries
    4 ounces caster sugar
    Few grains salt
    3 tablespoons grated lemon rind
    6 tablespoons lemon juice
    2½ pints cold milk
    1 pint vanilla ice cream.

Mash fresh blueberries and add sugar, salt, lemon rind, and juice. Blend thoroughly and add cold milk. Pour into cold glasses and top with vanilla ice cream.

Garnish with fresh blueberries or thin lemon slices. Serves 6.

SLIMMER'S COFFEE MILK SHAKE

Combine 8 fluid ounces skimmed milk, 1 teaspoon instant coffee, and saccharin to taste. Add an ice cube and blend until creamy.

BANANA MILK SHAKE

    1 fully ripe banana
    8 fluid ounces milk

Peel banana. Slice into a bowl and beat with a rotary egg beater or electric mixer until smooth and creamy. Add milk; mix well. Serve immediately. Makes 1 large or 2 medium-sized drinks.

Variations:

Banana Chocolate Milk Shake: Add 1 tablespoon chocolate syrup before mixing milk shake.

Banana Chocolate Malted Milk Shake: Add 4 teaspoons chocolate malted milk and ¼ teaspoon vanilla essence before mixing milk shake.

Banana Orange Milk Shake: Use 4 fluid ounces orange juice in place of half of the milk. Add ½ teaspoon caster sugar before mixing milk shake.

Banana Pineapple Milk Shake: Use 2 fluid ounces canned, unsweetened pineapple juice in place of a quarter of the milk before mixing milk shake.

Banana Spiced Milk Shake: Sprinkle ground nutmeg or cinnamon on top of milk shake just before serving.

Banana Vanilla Milk Shake: Add ½ teaspoon vanilla essence before mixing milk shake.

Banana Frosted Milk Shake: Add 3 tablespoons vanilla ice cream before mixing milk shake.

Important: For a colder drink, add about 2 tablespoons of crushed ice, and ice cream if desired, before mixing milk shake.

For a sweeter drink, add ice cream or plain sugar syrup. (See p. 70.)

Fruit Drinks

LEMONADE

10 fluid ounces sugar syrup (or to taste)

Juice of 7 lemons

2 pints water

Combine sugar syrup, juice, and water. Chill. Pour over crushed ice in tall glasses.

Variations: Substitute mineral water, ginger ale, grape juice (reduce sugar syrup to taste), or orange juice. To serve, garnish with lemon or orange slices, mint leaves, fresh berries, crushed fruit, etc.

LIMEADE

Use 10 fluid ounces lime juice, 10 ounces caster sugar syrup, and 2 pints water.

ORANGEADE

Use juice of 6 oranges, juice of 1 lemon, 10 fluid ounces sugar syrup, and 2 pints water.

LEMONADE READY-MIX

16 fluid ounces lemon juice

4 teaspoons grated lemon rind

8 ounces caster sugar, or 12 ounces honey, maple or golden syrup

Combine and stir until sugar dissolves. Store in covered glass (not metal) jar in refrigerator or cool place until ready to use.

For each serving of lemonade, combine 2 fluid ounces lemonade mix with iced water. Makes 8 to 10 large glasses.

GRAPEFRUIT JUICE FRAPPÉ

1½ teaspoons gelatine

2 tablespoons cold water

4 fluid ounces boiling water

2½-3 ounces sugar

16 fluid ounces grapefruit juice

2 fluid ounces lemon juice

Ginger ale

Soften gelatine in cold water. Dissolve in boiling water. Add sugar and cool. Add fruit juices and freeze to mush in refrigerator tray.

To serve, half fill tall glasses with frozen mixture and top up with ginger ale. Garnish with cherries and orange slices. Serves 4.

Lemonade-Mint Punch

ORANGE FROSTED

8 fluid ounces orange juice, fresh, frozen, or canned

2 scoops vanilla ice cream

Blend orange juice and ice cream with egg beater, electric beater, or liquidizer until ice cream is dissolved. Serves 1.

SPICED LEMONADE

Combine 10 fluid ounces sugar syrup with 13 whole cloves and 1 3-inch cinnamon stick. Cook 5 minutes. Strain.

Add juice of 7 lemons and 2 pints water. Chill. Serve over crushed ice.

MOCK MINT JULEP

6 ounces sugar

8 fluid ounces water

Juice of 3 lemons

4 sprigs of mint, bruised

16 fluid ounces ginger ale

Boil sugar and water. Cool. Add lemon juice, mint, and ginger ale. Serve in glasses half filled with crushed ice. Garnish each with 2 sprigs of mint. Serves 4.

ORANGE PEACH FREEZE

For each serving, put 2 tablespoons frozen orange juice concentrate in tall glass. Add 3 or 4 ice cubes. Fill glass ¾ full with ginger ale. Add a scoop of orange water ice.

Garnish with fresh peach slices dipped in orange juice to prevent discolouration.

FRUIT VELVET

1 6-ounce can frozen fruit juice concentrate

½ pint vanilla ice cream

2 6-ounce cans cold water

2 6-ounce cans ginger ale

Empty can of frozen orange, grape, or pineapple juice concentrate, add ½ pint vanilla ice cream into small mixer bowl and beat at a medium speed until well blended.

Using the frozen juice can as a measure, add 2 cans of cold water and 2 cans of ginger ale and beat at slow-to-medium speed until well blended and frothy. Serve immediately. Makes 4 to 6 servings.

LEMONADE-MINT PUNCH

1 6-ounce can frozen lemon juice concentrate

4 tablespoons green mint jelly

1 large bottle ginger ale

Ice cubes

Combine concentrate for lemonade (undiluted) and mint jelly; mix well until jelly has softened in the concentrate for lemonade.

Add ginger ale and ice cubes and stir well. Serve immediately. Makes 1 pint 12 fluid ounces.

GRAPE RICKEY

1¾ pints grape juice

1¾ pints water

2 fluid ounces lemon or lime juice

10 fluid ounces orange juice

Sugar syrup to sweeten

Combine ingredients and pour over crushed ice in tall glasses. Serves 10.

Syrups

An endless variety of drinks may be made by using as a foundation fruit syrup and juices which can easily be made in the home, bottled, and kept for future use. Syrups left over from preserved or pickled fruit may be used.

SUGAR SYRUP

Boil 1 pound sugar and 16 fluid ounces water 5 minutes. Cool and keep well chilled.

To substitute syrup for sugar, use 1¼ tablespoons syrup for each tablespoon sugar called for in recipe.

Fruit Syrups: (Strawberry, pineapple, raspberry, grape, apricot, etc.) Combine ½ pint fruit juice, 2 pints sugar syrup, and juice of 1 lemon.

COCOA SYRUP

4 fluid ounces hot water

6 tablespoons cocoa

18 ounces golden syrup or 8 tablespoons sugar

⅛ teaspoon salt

1 teaspoon vanilla essence

Pour hot water over cocoa and stir until smooth. Add golden syrup or sugar, and salt. Simmer 10 minutes, stirring constantly. Add vanilla.

Serve hot or cold over ice cream or other sweet. Syrup may be covered and stored 4 to 6 weeks in refrigerator.

Chocolate Syrup: Substitute 2 ounces cooking or plain chocolate for cocoa.

To make cocoa or chocolate: Add 1½ to 2 tablespoons of cocoa syrup or chocolate syrup to each cup hot or cold milk. Serve iced drinks over crushed ice in tall glass. Top with whipped cream.

Variations: Flavour with cinnamon, ginger, a drop of peppermint essence or crushed mint leaves.

COFFEE SYRUP

8 fluid ounces strong coffee

8 ounces sugar

1 teaspoon vanilla essence

Small pinch salt

Cook coffee and sugar together 5 minutes; add vanilla and salt. Cool.

Keep in covered jar to use as needed. Makes about 8 fluid ounces.

Party Punches

TEA PUNCH
(Master Recipe)
1 pint hot tea infusion (pour 1 pint boiling water over 1 teaspoon tea leaves)
3 pints fruit juice
2 pints ginger ale or mineral water
Sugar

Just before serving, combine, sweeten to taste, and pour over ice block in punch bowl. Makes 30 4-fluid-ounce servings.

California Punch: Use 1¼ pints loganberry juice, 1 pint orange juice, and 4 fluid ounces lemon juice as the fruit juice.

Golden Punch: Use ½ pint lime juice, 1 pint orange juice, and 1½ pints pineapple juice as the fruit juice.

Royal Punch: Use 2 pints grape juice and 1 pint grapefruit juice as the fruit juice.

COFFEE PUNCH
1 2-ounce jar instant coffee
1 pint 12 fluid ounces warm water
8 ounces sugar
5 pints cold water
3 pints vanilla, chocolate, or coffee ice cream

Combine coffee, warm water, and sugar; stir until sugar is dissolved. Chill.

Pour mixture into punch bowl. Stir in cold water. Beat 2 pints ice cream into coffee mixture. Spoon remaining ice cream over top. Makes about 50 servings.

LEMONADE-CIDER PUNCH BOWL
4 6-ounce cans lemonade concentrate
6½ pints cider

Combine concentrate for lemonade with chilled cider (instead of water) and place in punch bowl, over a chunk of ice or with ice cubes.

Purple Cow Punch

STRAWBERRY PUNCH
2 pints water
10 ounces sugar
1 pint golden syrup
2 pints grapefruit juice
1 pint lemon juice
1 pound strawberries
1 bunch mint
2 pints ginger ale

Cook water, sugar, and golden syrup together to make a syrup. Chill and add to fruit juices.

Wash strawberries and mint. Reserve half the strawberries to decorate each punch cup. Mash remaining strawberries and add to fruit juice mixture. Add ginger ale just before serving. Makes 8-9 pints.

FRUIT PUNCH
10 ounces sugar
1 pint water
2 pints lemon juice
1½ pints orange juice
2 pints grape juice
7 pints water

Make syrup of sugar and 1 pint water. Cool. Add strained fruit juices and water. Pour over block of ice in punch bowl. Makes about 55 small servings.

Variations: Ginger ale may be used instead of part of water. Pineapple juice may be used in place of part or all of grape juice. Garnish with thin wedges of orange and lemon.

ROSY LEMONADE PUNCH
3 12-ounce packets frozen strawberries or raspberries
4 6-ounce cans frozen lemon juice concentrate
2 large bottles ginger ale
2 large bottles soda water
Sliced bananas for garnish

Let berries thaw and put through sieve if you wish.

Combine concentrate for lemonade with berries and berry juice and add ginger ale and soda water just before serving. Pour over ice in punch bowl.

Sliced bananas make an interesting garnish for this rosy lemonade punch. Makes about 36 4-ounce servings.

PURPLE COW PUNCH
3¼ pints chocolate milk
1 25-ounce bottle blackberry soda
4 teaspoons aromatic bitters
Chocolate sprinkles or grated plain chocolate

Have chocolate milk and soda well chilled. At serving time, combine all ingredients in a punch bowl. Sprinkle chocolate sprinkles on top, if desired. Makes 17 servings.

Frosty Sorbet Punch

FROSTY SORBET PUNCH
3 cans (2 pints 6 fluid ounces each) orange-grapefruit juice
3 cans (2 pints 6 fluid ounces each) pineapple juice
3 cans (12 ounces each) apricot juice
5 pints ginger ale
5 pints lemon water ice

Have juices and ginger ale thoroughly chilled. Empty one can of each juice and 1½ pints of ginger ale into punch bowl. Add 1½ pints of water ice. Spoon the liquid over the water ice until partly melted. Serve.

When supply runs low, repeat the process adding another unit of each ingredient. Makes about 20 pints.

GRAPE PUNCH
1 pint 4 fluid ounces boiling water
3 tablespoons tea leaves
4 ounces sugar
Ice cubes
6 fluid ounces lemon juice
1 6-ounce can frozen concentrated grape juice, plus 18 fluid ounces water or 16 fluid ounces bottled grape juice
1 12-ounce bottle water

Pour boiling water over tea leaves. Cover and steep 5 minutes. Strain. Add sugar.

Pour hot over ice cubes in large punch bowl or pitcher. Add juices and water. Mix thoroughly. Makes 3¼ pints.

CREAMY SPICED MILK PUNCH BOWL
2 pints milk
2½ teaspoons cinnamon
1¼ teaspoons nutmeg
⅛ teaspoon salt
2 pints vanilla ice cream
½ pint whipping cream
1½ teaspoons vanilla essence
5 tablespoons grated orange rind

Pour milk into cold punch bowl; mix in seasonings. Add half the ice cream, stirring until partially melted.

Whip cream until stiff and fold in vanilla. Place remaining ice cream and whipped cream on top of spiced milk. Sprinkle with grated orange rind. Serve in mugs with stick cinnamon stirrers. Serves 12-14.

Easy Party Punch

EASY PARTY PUNCH

1 46-ounce can grapefruit juice, chilled
1 46-ounce can orange juice, chilled
1 18-ounce can tangerine juice, chilled
1¾ pints ginger ale, chilled

Combine chilled citrus juices in punch bowl with ice cubes. Add ginger ale.

If desired, garnish with grapefruit sections, lime slices, mint, and cherries. Makes about 7 pints or 36 4-fluid-ounce servings.

ORANGE SORBET FLOAT

8 pints orange water ice
16 pints chilled ginger ale
2 pints chilled fresh orange juice (10 to 13 oranges)

Turn orange water ice into large punch bowl. If the ice is very hard, let stand in cartons at room temperature to soften somewhat.

Add orange juice and ginger ale. Stir to blend. No ice is required. Makes 75-80 servings.

GOLDEN FRUIT PUNCH

2 20-ounce cans apricots
8 fluid ounces lemon juice
16 fluid ounces orange juice
4 28-ounce bottles ginger ale
Fresh mint

Put apricots through sieve. Add fruit juices.

Mix with ginger ale before serving and pour over ice cubes in tall glasses. Garnish with slices of lemon and mint. Serves 25.

HOLIDAY PARTY PUNCH

2½ pints apple juice
1¾ pints ginger ale
Lemon and lime slices
Maraschino cherries

Chill apple juice and ginger ale. Combine just before serving. Pour into punch bowl over ice cubes.

Garnish with lemon and lime slices topped with quarters of cherries. Allow about 4 fluid ounces per serving. Makes 10 to 12 servings.

FRUIT AND MINT PUNCH BOWL

Freeze water with sprigs of fresh mint in 2½ pint ring mould or loaf tin. Mix 1 46-ounce can each chilled orange drink and pineapple juice and 1 can frozen lemonade concentrate in punch bowl.

Shortly before serving, add 1 28-ounce bottle ginger ale and the ice ring. Garnish with orange and lemon slices. Makes 15 large or 30 small glasses.

Hot Holiday Punches

HOT MULLED CIDER

6½ pints sweet cider
6 cinnamon sticks, broken in 1-inch pieces
1 tablespoon whole cloves
1 tablespoon allspice berries
2 pieces whole mace
1 pound 2 ounces brown sugar
1 20-ounce can of spiced crab apples

Put cider in large pan. Add cinnamon. Tie other spices in muslin bag, and drop into cider. Stir in sugar. Heat slowly and simmer 20 minutes. Add apples 5 minutes before serving.

Remove spice bag before serving. Serve hot in earthenware mugs with an apple in each mug. Makes nearly 6 pints.

HOT BUTTERED PUNCH

4½ ounces brown sugar
¼ teaspoon salt
¼ teaspoon nutmeg
½ teaspoon cinnamon
½ teaspoon allspice
¾ teaspoon cloves
1 pint 12 fluid ounces water
2 1-pound cans jellied cranberry sauce
1 pint 12 fluid ounces unsweetened pineapple juice
2 ounces butter

Mix brown sugar, salt, spices, and 1 pint 4 fluid ounces water in saucepan and bring to a boil.

Add 8 fluid ounces water to cranberry sauce; beat with rotary beater until smooth.

Add pineapple juice and cranberry mixture to hot syrup; heat to just below boiling.

Serve hot with a small knob of butter in each cup. Makes about 24 4-fluid-ounce servings.

HOT CRANBERRY PUNCH

½ pint apple juice
1½ pints cranberry juice
5 fluid ounces strained orange juice (1 large orange)
Juice of 1 lemon, strained
3 whole cloves
1 small stick cinnamon (about 1½-inch thick)
3 to 4 tablespoons sugar
1 orange, sliced
1 lime, sliced
Cloves to stud orange and lime slices

Combine apple juice, cranberry juice, orange juice, lemon juice, cloves, cinnamon, and sugar in a 3 pint saucepan; stir to dissolve sugar and blend ingredients.

Cover and heat on a low heat until punch comes to boil. Carefully strain punch into punch bowl. Serve while hot.

Slice orange and lime and stud with cloves. Float for a garnish on top of punch. Makes about 1¾ pints or about 16 servings.

Note: This recipe can be multiplied successfully. Heat punch in 12 pint container on medium heat until punch comes to boil.

HOT SPICED GRAPE JUICE

1¾ pints grape juice
4.5 ounces sugar
2 short pieces stick cinnamon
12 whole cloves
⅛ teaspoon salt

Mix all the ingredients and bring to boiling point. Cool, and allow to stand several hours.

When ready to serve, reheat, remove spices, and add lemon juice if desired. Serve hot. Serves 6.

HOT CALYPSO CIDER

3¼ pints apple cider or juice
1½ ounces brown or maple sugar
3 slices orange
3 slices lemon
2 tablespoons aromatic bitters

Heat cider with sugar. Stir until sugar is dissolved. Add orange slices and lemon slices. Simmer 10 minutes. Add bitters, stir, and serve. Makes about 3¼ pints.

Hot Calypso Cider

BREADS AND ROLLS MADE WITH YEAST

WHAT TO KNOW BEFORE YOU START

Baking with yeast is one of the most rewarding forms of the culinary art. Mixing yeast doughs and batters is fascinating, and not at all difficult when you understand the hows and whys. Shaping the dough is more play than work. Baking produces the fragrant, delicious treats that bring you compliments by the baker's dozen.

If you are just starting your yeast-baking "career," or if you want to know how to improve your yeast breads, the following instructions cover everything you need to know.

INGREDIENTS

Really good bread begins with good ingredients. The amounts and flavourings in different breads vary, but the basic ways of mixing are the same.

Yeast

Active yeast in compressed or dry form is a living plant especially suited to breadmaking. It is responsible for the fermentation action which produces the light, porous grain and unusual texture of baked yeast products. One of the most important functions of yeast is that during the fermentation process carbon dioxide gas is formed which causes yeast doughs and yeast batters to rise. This process results in light porous baked products and is partly responsible for their delicious flavour and aroma.

There is also another type of yeast which is dry but inactive, sometimes called primary grown or brewers' yeast. It is used as a source of protein and

vitamin B complex factors in pharmaceuticals, animal and special dietary foods. But it will not raise bread.

Dry Yeast: For those who bake at home, dry yeast is fast replacing baker's yeast. Dry yeast in air-tight, moisture-proof packets stays fresh for many months on any cool shelf and gives uniformly fine results until the expiration date on packet.

Dry yeast can be used in place of baker's yeast in any recipe when dissolving directions are followed. ½ ounce baker's yeast is equivalent to 2 teaspoons dry yeast.

No-Dissolve Dry Yeast

No-dissolve and instant blend yeasts can be used according to manufacturers' general directions (blending undissolved yeast with flour) or can be used in the traditional way (dissolving yeast in warm water). We have provided recipes following the traditional and the more recently developed no-dissolve methods.

Baker's Yeast: Perishable baker's yeast must be kept in the refrigerator —and for not longer than a week or two. Baker's yeast can be frozen but must be defrosted at room temperature and used immediately. To determine whether baker's yeast is usable, crumble it between the fingers. If it crumbles easily, even though there is slight browning at the edges due to drying, it is still good.

Baker's yeast can be bought by the ounce from some bakers, Health Food Stores or Supermarkets.

Research shows that in dissolving yeast, the best results are obtained when the water temperature is 95°F. to 105°F. with the ideal temperature near 95°F. for baker's yeast and near 105°F. for dry yeast. In using dry or baker's yeast, too much heat can kill the action of the yeast. Not enough heat, however, can retard its action.

For best results, dissolve dry yeast in warm, not hot, water (105°F. to 115°F.), baker's yeast in lukewarm water (85°F. to 95°F.).

Flour

Wheat flour is used for breadmaking because it contains a particular protein called gluten which has unique physical properties. The gluten stretches to form an elastic framework capable of holding the bubbles of gas produced by the yeast. Without gluten, you cannot make satisfactory yeast-raised breads. The amount and quality of gluten vary with different flours. The variety of wheat, where grown, and the milling process all influence the character of the flour and the amount and kind of gluten which in turn influence the volume and texture of the yeast-raised products. Yeast recipes usually specify approximate instead of exact amounts of flour and do not indicate an exact number of minutes for kneading the dough or beating the batter. The amount of flour required and the time and manipulation necessary are determined by the character of the flour, particularly its absorptive property, amount and quality of gluten. For best results, follow recipe directions. But also learn to recognize good consistency in a mixture and proper kneading in a dough.

Plain flour is generally used for bread-making in the home, but when available a "strong" flour (with high gluten content) gives the best results.

Self-raising flour is sometimes used but does not produce the same result. Rolled oats, bran, corn meal, and rye flour are sometimes used in combination with wheat flour to make special breads and rolls.

Liquid

Milk and water are the liquids ordinarily used in making yeast breads. Occasionally other liquids such as fruit juices are added for special flavour. The milk may be fresh, evaporated, or dry. When using fresh milk to make yeast breads and rolls, it should be scalded to obtain best grain and texture. Whatever the liquid, it should be lukewarm when mixed with the dissolved yeast because too much heat kills the yeast.

Water is the best and fastest liquid medium for yeast rehydration. So for best results, use only water when dissolving dry yeast. In a recipe using liquid other than water for dissolving the yeast, substitute 4 tablespoons warm, not hot, water for 4 tablespoons of the liquid in the recipe. Dissolve dry yeast in the water and then proceed with the recipe.

Bread and rolls made with all water have a wheaty flavour and crisp crust, while those made with milk have a more velvety grain and a creamy white crumb. Milk breads also keep better and make better toast.

Sugar and Salt

Yeast and sugar work together to form the carbon dioxide gas which causes the dough—or batter—to rise. Salt helps control this rate of rise. The right proportion of sugar and salt contributes to flavour of the product, and, in addition, sugar helps give a golden brown colour to the crust.

The usual sugar is white, but brown sugar, treacle or molasses, honey, and golden syrup are sometimes used depending upon the type of product being made. Salt may be plain or iodized.

Fat

Some type of fat or oil is included in nearly all yeast-raised products. It conditions the gluten, making a dough or batter that stretches easily as the bubbles of gas expand. Fat also adds flavour, contributes to a tender crust and an attractive sheen. Hydrogenated fats, lard, vegetable oils, margarine, and butter are all suitable fats when used in tested recipes specifying these fats.

Eggs

Eggs give extra flavour and richness and make the product more nutritious. They also help produce a fine and delicate texture and, like sugar, encourage a golden brown crust. Sometimes, before baking, a beaten-egg mixture is brushed on the surface of the rolls or bread to give them a shiny golden sheen.

Other Ingredients

Spices and herbs, fruits, nuts, and other tasty ingredients are added for flavour, variety, and extra food value.

Utensils for Yeast Breads

Scales and spoons to weigh or measure ingredients accurately.

Select a bowl big enough to allow room for easy mixing and fermentation, and a wooden mixing spoon that is comfortable to handle.

Ordinarily, a clean towel is used to cover the dough or batter—or the shaped bread or rolls—when they are set to rise. But you can cover them just as efficiently with greaseproof paper, paper towelling, or even a plate for the bowl rise.

The utensils shown in the photographs throughout this book are good examples to follow. Do try to use tins of the same size called for in the recipes. The sizes given are inside measurements.

BASIC MIXING METHODS

When you combine a yeast mixture, you automatically follow a basic pattern or method. It may be one of several such as the time-saving batter method, the straight-dough method, or the sponge method. The yeast used may be either baker's or dry. Understanding the various basic ways of combining yeast mixtures makes any yeast recipe easier to follow.

The Batter Method

The Batter Method is a relatively new way to bake with yeast. Because yeast batter breads and rolls are so quick to make, the batter recipes in this book are sure to become favourites. As the name implies, this type of yeast mixture is a batter rather than the usual yeast dough. And not only is it lighter and easier to handle but also requires no kneading or shaping. These quick and easy yeast batters may be quite thin or fairly thick, depending on what you are making; for example, a casserole bread or yeast-raised waffles. But in any case, the yeast batter is merely mixed and then allowed to rise in a bowl or in the baking tin.

The Straight-Dough Method

The Straight-Dough Method is the one with which you may be most familiar. The mixing is done in continuous operation. The time it takes a dough to rise by the Straight-Dough Method is affected by the amount of yeast. More yeast (as specified in recipes) produces an Action-Quick Dough and speeds up the rising time.

The Sponge Method

The Sponge Method is one of the very oldest ways of combining yeast mixtures. The mixing is done in two operations. First a sponge is made by combining the dissolved yeast, some sugar, and part of the flour and liquid, and allowing it to ferment until it is raised, bubbly, and spongelike. The other ingredients are added with the remaining flour to make a dough that can be kneaded.

During the three rising periods, characteristic flavour and special lightness develop.

What About Refrigerator Dough?

If you have wondered about keeping doughs in the refrigerator, the answer is not to refrigerate any dough unless the recipe has been designed for refrigeration.

A refrigerator dough should have sugar and salt in the proportions that will extend the action of the yeast over several days.

A satisfactory refrigerator dough recipe specifies amounts that are carefully worked out according to a tested formula.

Temperature Is Important

Temperature plays an important role in the preparation of any yeast product. Because yeast is a living plant, too much heat can kill the action of the yeast, and not enough heat can slow down the action of the yeast.

For best results, dissolve dry yeast in warm, not hot water (105°F.) and baker's yeast in lukewarm water (95°F.). To test the temperature of the water, drop a little water on the inside of your wrist. Warm, not hot, water feels comfortably warm. Lukewarm water feels neither warm nor cool.

Before combining any mixture—such as scalded milk mixed with sugar, salt, and fat—with dissolved yeast, the mixture must be cooled to lukewarm.

STEPS IN MIXING STRAIGHT-DOUGH METHOD

Mixing a yeast dough is a simple step-by-step process that goes along quickly. Few special techniques are involved. Here are the steps for mixing by the Straight-Dough Method. To make bread and rolls by other methods, follow the recipes.

Step 1: Pour milk into saucepan and heat to the scalding point (this is just below boiling or at about 180°F.). Turn off heat. Stir in sugar, salt and fat. Let mixture cool to lukewarm to protect the action of the yeast.

Step 2: Measure water into a large mixing bowl. Test for warm, not hot, for dry yeast; lukewarm for baker's yeast (see above). Sprinkle dry yeast or crumble baker's yeast into the water. Stir until dissolved.

Step 3: Test the milk mixture to make sure it is lukewarm. When lukewarm, add to dissolved yeast. If the recipe calls for eggs, stir them in.

Step 4: Stir in half of the flour (previously sifted and carefully measured) or the amount called for in the recipe. Beat or mix until smooth.

Step 5: Add the remaining half of the sifted flour. You may need a little less or a little more flour, depending on the characteristics of the flour, to make a yeast dough that has a rough dull appearance and will be a bit sticky to handle.

Step 6: Continue to stir until an irregular ball forms and comes away from the bowl, leaving only a small amount sticking to the sides. The mixed dough is now ready to be turned out on a lightly floured breadboard or cloth.

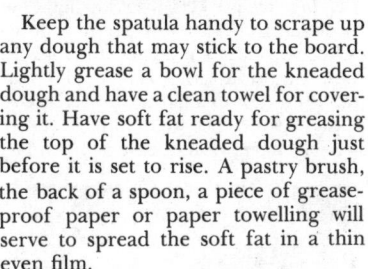

HOW TO KNEAD

Kneading is part of the process of mixing yeast dough during which the rough uneven texture of the dough changes to a smooth elastic ball. You can actually feel this fascinating change take place as you work the responsive dough with your hands.

Kneading helps blend ingredients. It improves flavour, and it develops the gluten which, in turn, develops good grain and texture in the bread and rolls. As you knead, the manipulation of the dough makes the gluten flexible and pliable so that it will stretch when the leavening gas expands, and trap the bubbles of gas produced by the yeast.

Getting Ready to Knead: Before you turn the dough out on the floured board, get out the things you'll need, such as extra flour, fat, spatula, pastry brush, and a clean towel. You'll get better results and kneading will go along smoothly.

You can knead on a large board, a cloth, or a table top, whichever is most convenient. Measure out 2-4 ounces of flour to be used on the board as you knead the dough. How much of this flour you will use is determined by the amount the dough requires.

Keep the spatula handy to scrape up any dough that may stick to the board. Lightly grease a bowl for the kneaded dough and have a clean towel for covering it. Have soft fat ready for greasing the top of the kneaded dough just before it is set to rise. A pastry brush, the back of a spoon, a piece of greaseproof paper or paper towelling will serve to spread the soft fat in a thin even film.

Now that you're all set, flour the board very lightly and turn the dough out on the board. With floured hands, flatten the dough very slightly by pressing it firmly, and shape it into a round, rather flat ball. Now you are ready to knead the dough.

As you knead, sprinkle the extra flour little by little onto the board and knead it into the dough. Enough has been added when the dough no longer sticks to your hands or the board. Work the dough firmly. This will make a smooth, springy ball and produce better results than too gentle handling. In fact, some like to give the dough an occasional slap against the board while kneading. Vigorous handling will give you a livelier dough and one that is easier to shape.

Kneading

Fold, push, and turn the dough, working in a rocking motion. At first kneading may be a little awkward, but once you get used to the 1-2-3 steps kneading becomes easy and you will develop a rhythm. The rough and slightly sticky dough changes to a smooth ball. The ball of dough becomes more elastic and as you knead you can feel the springiness develop. Generally, a dough is kneaded enough in about 8 to 10 minutes. The time may vary depending on the type of flour used, and the speed and energy with which you knead. The characteristics of the dough—the look and feel—tell you when the dough is kneaded enough.

The Kneaded Dough

Pick the dough up in your hands. Look at it and feel it. The dough itself tells you when it is well kneaded and is a better guide than any set time for kneading. A well kneaded dough looks full and rounded, smooth, satiny, and tightly stretched. By looking at it closely, you can see tiny gas bubbles under the surface. They have many sizes and shapes due to the stretching of the dough during kneading. The surface of the dough appears slightly irregular although it has a satiny sheen.

In your hands, the dough feels springy and elastic. Press it firmly with your fingers and you will feel the springiness gently pushing back. When the dough has been kneaded enough, place it in the greased bowl and spread the top with soft fat.

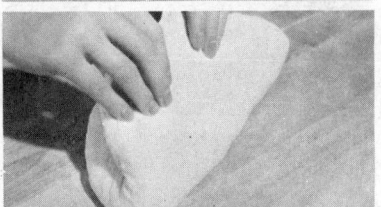
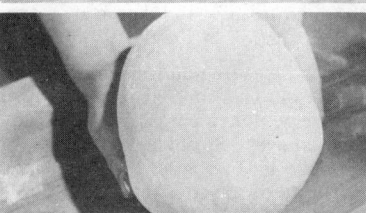
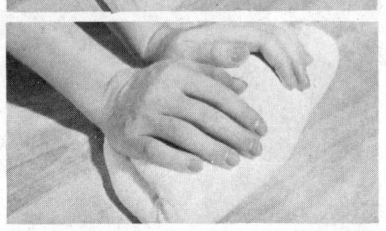

THE YEAST AT WORK

The yeast batter or dough rises as a result of the changes produced by the fermentation of the yeast. While the carbon dioxide gas bubbles are forming, the gluten is becoming more pliable allowing the batter or dough to expand. These changes within the batter or dough contribute to the characteristic flavour and texture of yeast products.

Temperature Is Important In Rising

For proper fermentation, yeast batters and doughs should be placed to rise at a temperature of about 85°F. In summer this means you have to be careful about too much heat, and in winter, find a way to keep the batter or dough warm and cosy. Yeast is a living plant that likes an atmosphere neither too hot nor too cold. Maintain steady warmth during this rising period.

(1) Rising: Always grease the surface of the dough and cover the bowl with a clean towel or cloth—or with greaseproof paper. Set the bowl in a warm place, free from draught. In hot weather, keep it out of the direct sunlight and away from the extra heat of the kitchen. In cold weather, warm the bowl before putting in the dough. Place it in a warm place—near a range or radiator, but never on top of either. If the room is cold, you can place the dough in an unheated oven with a large pan of hot water on the shelf beneath it, or on the grill rack with hot water in the grill pan. Or set the bowl of dough in a deep pan of water just warm enough so your hands feel comfortable in it.

(2) Doubled in Bulk: When the dough looks double its original size, called "doubled in bulk," the proper fermentation changes have taken place. The time varies with temperature, the amount of yeast, kind of flour, and the other ingredients in the recipe. The time given in recipes for double in bulk is approximate, a useful guide to tell you when to test the dough. To test for

double in bulk, press two fingers deeply into the dough. If the holes remain when the fingers are withdrawn, the dough has probably doubled in bulk. Doughs that are bubbly and that collapse are overfermented.

(3) Punch Down: When the dough has doubled in bulk, it is ready for punching down. Punching the dough down after the first rising releases some of the gas in the dough, thus speeding up the rate of fermentation by accelerating yeast activity. It also breaks up the big air pockets into smaller ones, producing a fine-textured product. After you punch it down with your fist, pull the sides into centre and turn dough out onto a lightly floured board, pastry cloth, or table top. A resting period makes dough easier to handle.

Step 1: With floured hands, flatten the dough very slightly by pressing it into a round, rather flat ball.
Step 2: Fold the dough toward you with a rolling motion, using the fingers of both hands.
Step 3: Push the ball of dough away from you, using the heels of your hands.
Step 4: Turn the dough one-quarter way around on the board. Repeat steps 2, 3, and 4.
Step 5: The dough should look full and rounded, smooth, satiny, and tightly stretched.

(4) Shaping: The dough, ready for shaping, feels warm and is easy to handle. If any flour is needed on the board for shaping, use it in small amounts. Shape the dough as desired, following the recipe-shaping directions. After the dough is shaped, it is ready for a second and final rising in a warm place.

(5) Ready to Bake: When the shaped dough is puffy and light, press very gently with your finger tip. If the slight indentation remains, it is ready to bake. Dough shaped for bread is ready to bake when the centre of the loaf is slightly higher than the edge of the tin.

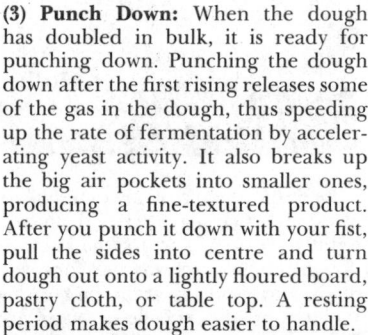
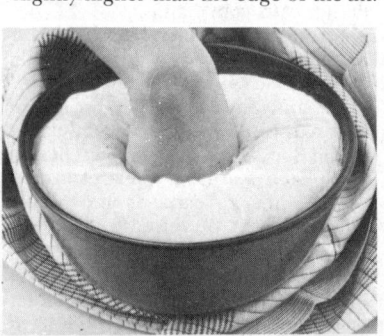

Yeast Bread in Loaves

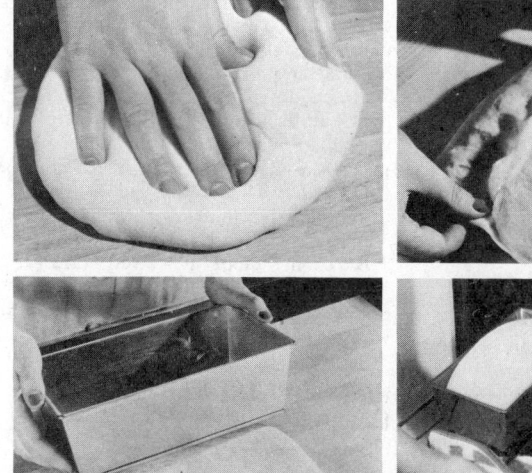

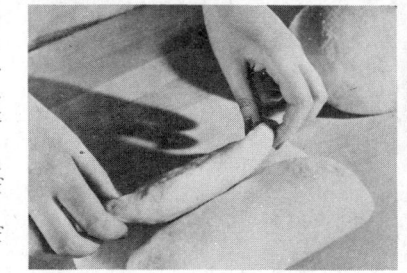
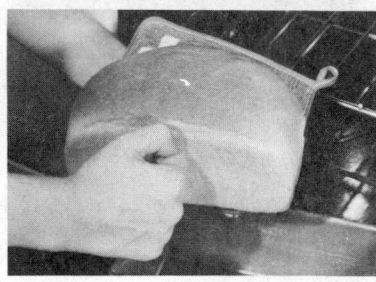

SHAPING AND BAKING THE LOAF

1. Form the dough into a smooth round ball on the pastry cloth or breadboard. Cut it in half with a sharp knife. With the fingers flatten one half of the dough.

2. Press the flattened dough into an oblong about 9×7×1 inches. The width will be about the same as the length of your bread tin.

3. Fold each end of the oblong to the centre, overlapping slightly. Press each side down firmly. Working with both hands, help to shape it evenly.

4. To seal the dough into shape, pinch the centre fold and ends. Place the loaf, sealed edge down, in a greased tin, 9×5×3 inches.

5. When baking two loaves, place tins on the centre shelf with 2 inches between them to allow heat to circulate. For four loaves use two shelves. Place at right front, left back, left front and right back.

6. Using pot holders, remove a tin from the oven and tip the loaf out of the tin.

Tap the bottom or sides of the loaf for a hollow sound.

If not done, return it to the oven for a few minutes for more baking.

WHITE BREAD
(Straight-Dough Method)

- **8 fluid ounces milk**
- **2 tablespoons sugar**
- **2 teaspoons salt**
- **3 ounces fat**
- **8 fluid ounces warm (not hot) water**
- **½ ounce baker's or 2 teaspoons dried yeast**
- **12 ounces sifted plain flour**
- **Additional 12 ounces sifted flour (approximately)**

Scald milk. Stir in sugar, salt, and fat. Cool to lukewarm.

Measure warm water into bowl (cool to lukewarm for baker's yeast). Sprinkle or crumble in yeast and stir until dissolved. Stir in lukewarm milk mixture.

Add 12 ounces flour and beat until smooth. Stir in additional flour. Turn out on lightly floured board. Knead until smooth and elastic. Place in greased bowl; brush with fat.

Cover. Let rise in warm place, free from draught, until doubled in bulk, about 1 hour. Punch down, turn out on board.

Divide in half, let rest 15 to 20 minutes. Shape into loaves. Place in greased bread tins 9×5×3 inches.

Cover. Let rise in warm place, free from draught, until centre is slightly higher than edge of tin, about 1 hour.

Bake in hot oven (400°F. Mark 6) about 50 minutes. Makes 2 loaves.

For Faster Bread (Action-Quick Dough): Use double the amount of yeast; bowl rise about 30 minutes, tin rise about 45 minutes.

Note: For 1 loaf use ½ ounce yeast and ½ of all other ingredients; bowl rise about 30 minutes, tin rise about 45 minutes.

For 4 loaves use double the amount of each ingredient; bowl rise about 1 hour, tin rise about 1 hour.

WHITE BREAD
(Sponge Method)

- **12 fluid ounces warm (not hot) water**
- **4 tablespoons sugar**
- **½ ounce baker's or 2 teaspoons dry yeast**
- **8 ounces sifted plain flour**
- **8 fluid ounces milk**
- **2½ teaspoons salt**
- **1½ ounces fat**
- **Additional 1¼ pounds sifted plain flour (approximately)**

To Make Sponge: Measure warm water and 2 tablespoons sugar into bowl. (Cool to lukewarm for baker's yeast.) Sprinkle or crumble in yeast and stir until dissolved. Add flour and beat until smooth.

Cover. Let rise in warm place, free from draught, until light and spongy, about 1 hour.

To Make Bread: Scald milk. Stir in 2 tablespoons sugar, salt, and fat. Cool to lukewarm.

Stir sponge down. Stir in lukewarm milk mixture. Stir in additional 1¼ pounds flour.

Turn dough out on lightly floured board. Knead until smooth and elastic. Place in greased bowl; brush with fat.

Cover. Let rise in warm place, free from draught, until doubled in bulk, about 45 minutes.

Punch down and turn out on lightly floured board.

Divide in half, let rest 15 to 20 minutes.

Shape into loaves. Place in greased bread tins 9×5×3 inches.

Cover. Let rise in warm place, free from draught, until centre is slightly higher than edge of tin, about 1 hour.

Bake in hot oven (400°F. Mark 6) about 50 minutes. Makes 2 loaves.

WHOLE WHEAT BREAD
(Straight-Dough Method)

6 fluid ounces milk
2 tablespoons sugar
3 teaspoons salt
3 ounces fat
4 ounces black treacle
12 fluid ounces warm (not hot) water
1 ounce baker's or 4 teaspoons dried yeast
1 pound 2 ounces whole wheat flour
8 ounces sifted plain flour

Scald milk. Stir in sugar, salt, fat, and treacle. Cool to lukewarm.

Measure into bowl 12 fluid ounces warm water (cool to lukewarm for compressed yeast). Sprinkle or crumble in yeast and stir until dissolved. Stir in lukewarm milk mixture.

Add ½ mixture of whole wheat flour and plain flour. Beat until smooth. Stir in remaining flour mixture. Turn dough out on lightly floured board. Knead until smooth and elastic. Place in greased bowl; brush top with soft fat.

Cover. Let rise in warm place, free from draught, until doubled in bulk, about 1 hour and 15 minutes.

Punch down and turn out on lightly floured board. Divide in half; shape into loaves. Place in greased bread tins 9×5×3 inches.

Cover. Let rise in warm place, free from draught, until centre is slightly higher than edge of tin, about 1 hour.

Bake in hot oven (400°F. Mark 6) about 50 minutes. Makes 2 loaves.

100% WHOLE WHEAT BREAD
(No-Dissolve Method)

2¼-2½ pounds unsifted whole wheat flour
3 teaspoons salt
4 teaspoons dry yeast
12 fluid ounces milk
12 fluid ounces water
6 ounces honey
3 ounces butter or margarine

In a large bowl thoroughly mix ¾ pound flour, salt, and undissolved dry yeast.

Combine milk, water, honey, and margarine in a saucepan. Heat over low heat until liquids are warm. (Margarine does not need to melt.) Gradually add to dry ingredients and beat 2 minutes at medium speed of electric mixer, scraping bowl occasionally. Add 4 ounces flour, or enough to make a thick batter. Beat at high speed 2 minutes, scraping bowl occasionally. Stir in enough additional flour to make a soft dough. Turn out onto lightly floured board; cover dough with bowl and let rest for 10 minutes. Then knead until smooth and elastic, about 8 to 10 minutes.

Place in greased bowl, turning to grease top. Cover; let rise in warm place, free from draught, until doubled in bulk, about 50 minutes.

Punch dough down; turn out onto lightly floured board. Divide dough in half; shape each half into a loaf. Place in 2 greased 8½×4½×2½-inch loaf tins. Cover; let rise in warm place, free from draught, until doubled in bulk, about 50 minutes.

Bake in moderate oven (375°F. Mark 5) about 35 to 40 minutes, or until done. Remove from tins and cool on wire racks. Makes 2 loaves.

NO-KNEAD WHITE BREAD
(Master Recipe)

12 fluid ounces scalded milk
4 ounces fat
2 ounces sugar
1 tablespoon salt
12 fluid ounces water
1½ ounces baker's yeast
3 eggs
2¼ pounds sifted plain flour

Combine milk, fat, sugar, and salt. Cool to lukewarm by adding 12 fluid ounces water.

Add yeast and mix well. Blend in eggs.

Add flour slowly. Mix until dough is well blended.

Place in large, greased bowl and cover if the dough is to be chilled.

Shape into 3 loaves on well-floured board. Place in greased tins, 9×4×3 inches, and cover.

Let rise in warm place until doubled in bulk, about 2 hours for chilled dough and 1 hour for unchilled dough.

Bake in moderate oven (375°F. Mark 5) 1 hour. Makes 3 loaves.

Variations:

Cheese Bread: Blend in 8 ounces grated cheese when flour is added.

Cinnamon Loaves: Roll ⅓ the dough into 16×8 inch rectangle. Sprinkle with 2 ounces sugar and 1 teaspoon cinnamon.

Roll as for Swiss roll, starting with 8-inch edge and sealing edges. Place in greased tin.

Use remaining dough plain or make 2 more cinnamon loaves from it.

Nut Bread: Blend in 4 ounces chopped nuts before flour is added.

WHITE BREAD
(No-Dissolve Method)

1¼-1½ pounds plain flour
2 tablespoons sugar
1½ teaspoons salt
2 teaspoons dry yeast
12 fluid ounces water
4 fluid ounces milk
1½ ounces margarine or butter

In a large bowl thoroughly mix 8 ounces flour, sugar, salt, and undissolved dry yeast.

Combine water, milk, and margarine in a saucepan. Heat over low heat until liquids are warm. (Margarine does not need to melt.) Gradually add to dry ingredients and beat 2 minutes at medium speed of electric mixer, scraping bowl occasionally. Add 3 ounces flour, or enough flour to make a thick batter. Beat at high speed 2 minutes, scraping bowl occasionally. Stir in enough additional flour to make a soft dough. Turn out onto lightly floured board; knead until smooth and elastic, about 8 to 10 minutes. Place in greased bowl, turning to grease top. Cover; let rise in warm place, free from draught, until doubled in bulk, about 1 hour.

Punch dough down; turn out onto lightly floured board. Cover; let rest 15 minutes. Divide dough in half and shape into loaves. Place in 2 greased 8½×4½×2½-inch loaf tins. Cover; let rise in warm place, free from draught, until doubled in bulk, about 1 hour.

Bake in hot oven (400°F. Mark 6) about 25 to 30 minutes, or until done. Remove from tins and cool on wire racks. Makes 2 loaves.

ONE BOWL ANADAMA BREAD
(No-Dissolve Method)

1¼-1½ pounds plain flour
2 teaspoons salt
5 ounces yellow corn meal
4 teaspoons dry yeast
2 ounces softened margarine or butter
16 fluid ounces very hot water
6 ounces molasses or treacle (at room temperature)

In a large bowl thoroughly mix 10 ounces flour, salt, corn meal, and undissolved dry yeast. Add softened margarine.

Gradually add very hot tap water and molasses to dry ingredients and beat 2 minutes at medium speed of electric mixer, scraping bowl occasionally. Add 2 ounces flour, or enough to make a thick batter. Beat at high speed 2 minutes, scraping bowl occasionally. Stir in enough additional flour to make a soft dough. Turn out onto lightly floured board; knead until smooth and elastic, about 8 to 10 minutes. Place in greased bowl, turning to grease top. Cover; let rise in warm place, free from draught, until doubled in bulk, about 1 hour.

Punch dough down; turn out onto lightly floured board. Divide dough in half and shape into loaves. Place in 2 greased 8½×4½×2½-inch loaf tins. Cover; let rise in warm place, free from draught, until doubled in bulk, about 45 minutes. Bake in a moderate oven (375°F. Mark 5) about 35 minutes, or until done. Remove from tins and cool on wire racks. Makes 2 loaves.

SALT-RISING BREAD

A type of bread leavened by micro-organisms which have a yeast-like effect and produce a distinctive flavour.

8 fluid ounces milk
2 tablespoons sugar
1½ teaspoons salt
2 ounces white corn meal
8 fluid ounces lukewarm water
1 pound 2 ounces sifted flour
2 tablespoons melted fat

Scald the milk, remove from the heat, and stir in 1 tablespoon of the sugar, the salt, and the corn meal. Mix thoroughly and place the mixture in a large jar.

Cover the container and place it in a pan of water which is hot to the hand (120°F.).

Allow it to stand in a warm place for 7 or 8 hours, or overnight, or until it has fermented.

Make a soft sponge by adding to the fermented mixture the water, 8 ounces of the flour and the remaining sugar.

Beat thoroughly, using an electric mixer if available.

Place the sponge in the container (120°F.) and allow it to rise until it is very light and full of bubbles.

Turn the sponge into a large, warm mixing bowl and gradually stir in the remaining flour, or enough to make a fairly stiff dough which does not stick to the hands and can be kneaded. Knead for 10 minutes.

Divide the dough in half, shape into loaves, and place in generously greased bread tins.

Brush the loaves with melted fat; cover the loaves with a light, clean towel, and allow them to rise in a warm place until the dough is twice its original size.

Bake in hot oven (400°F. Mark 6) for 10 minutes; reduce oven temperature to 350°F. Mark 4 and bake for another 30 minutes. Makes 2 loaves.

Note: Salt-rising bread has a disagreeable odour while it is rising and baking. This odour is diffused in the baking. It is never as light as other breads, but is close-grained and has a distinctive flavour. It dries out quickly, but it makes excellent toast.

SWEDISH LIMPE

Sometimes spelled limpa, this is a famous cake-like bread.

16 fluid ounces water
3 ounces brown sugar
2 teaspoons caraway seed
½ ounce fat
1 teaspoon chopped orange peel or
    1 scant teaspoon aniseed
¼ ounce compressed yeast
About 12 ounces sifted plain flour

1 teaspoon salt
About 8 ounces rye flour

Boil together water, sugar, caraway seed, fat, and orange peel (or aniseed) for 3 minutes. Let mixture become lukewarm.

Add yeast. Stir thoroughly, gradually adding sufficient white flour to make a soft dough.

Place dough in a warm place and let rise for 1½ hours. Then add salt and enough rye flour to make a stiff dough. Let rise again for 2 hours.

Knead slightly and shape into loaf. Put into greased loaf tin, 9×5×3-inches. Let rise again for half an hour.

Bake in moderate oven (350°F. Mark 4) for 1 hour. Makes 1 loaf.

RYE BREAD
(No-Dissolve Method)

10 ounces unsifted rye flour
10 ounces unsifted white flour
    (about)
1 tablespoon sugar
1 tablespoon salt
1 tablespoon caraway seeds
    (optional)
½ ounce dry yeast
8 fluid ounces milk
6 fluid ounces water
2 tablespoons honey
1 tablespoon margarine or butter
2 ounces corn meal
1 egg white
2 tablespoons water

Combine flours; in a large bowl thoroughly mix 6 ounces flour mixture, sugar, salt, caraway seeds, and undissolved dry yeast.

Combine milk, 6 fluid ounces water, honey, and margarine in a saucepan. Heat over low heat until liquids are warm. (Margarine does not need to melt.) Gradually add to dry ingredients and beat 2 minutes at medium speed of electric mixer, scraping bowl occasionally. Add 4 ounces flour mixture, or enough flour mixture to make a thick batter. Beat at high speed 2 minutes, scraping bowl occasionally. Stir in enough flour mixture to make a soft dough. (If necessary, add additional white flour to obtain desired dough.)

Turn dough out onto lightly floured board; knead until smooth and elastic, about 8 to 10 minutes. Place in greased bowl, turning to grease top. Cover; let rise in warm place, free from draught, until doubled in bulk, about 1 hour.

Punch dough down; turn out onto lightly floured board. Divide in half; form each piece into a smooth ball. Cover; let rest 10 minutes. Flatten each piece slightly. Roll lightly on board to form tapered ends. Sprinkle 2 greased baking sheets with corn meal. Place breads on baking sheets. Combine egg

white and 2 tablespoons water; brush breads. Let rise, uncovered, in warm place, free from draught, 35 minutes.

Bake in hot oven (400°F. Mark 6) about 25 minutes, or until done. Remove from baking sheets and cool on wire racks. Makes 2 loaves.

CHEESE POTATO BREAD
(Italian)

½ ounce baker's or 2 teaspoons dry
    yeast
4 fluid ounces scalded milk or 2
    fluid ounces lukewarm water
    and 2 fluid ounces scalded
    milk
12 ounces sifted plain flour
1 teaspoon sugar
1 teaspoon salt
4½ ounces riced or mashed potatoes
5 tablespoons melted butter or
    margarine
3 ounces grated Gruyere or other
    firm cheese
2 unbeaten eggs

Soften baker's yeast in 4 fluid ounces scalded milk, cooled to lukewarm. If dry yeast is used, dissolve in 4 tablespoons lukewarm water; decrease amount of scalded milk to 4 tablespoons. Let stand 5 minutes.

Sift together flour, sugar, and salt. Combine potatoes, melted butter or margarine, cheese, and eggs in large bowl. Beat until well combined. Blend in yeast-milk mixture and dry ingredients; mix thoroughly.

Knead on well floured board until smooth and satiny, 5 to 8 minutes. Place in greased bowl and cover. Let rise in warm place (85° to 90°F.) until doubled in bulk, about 1 hour.

Punch down dough by plunging fist in centre. Knead gently on floured board about 2 minutes. Shape into long roll and fit into well-greased 9-inch ring cake tin. Pinch ends together to seal. Let rise in warm place until light, about 30 minutes.

Bake in moderate oven (375°F. Mark 5) 25 to 35 minutes. Serve warm. Makes 1 9-inch bread ring.

Cheese Potato Bread

ONE BOWL WHEAT GERM CASSEROLE BREAD
(No-Dissolve Method)

12-14 ounces unsifted plain flour
2 teaspoons salt
2 ounces wheat germ
4 teaspoons dry yeast
2 tablespoons softened margarine
½ pint very hot tap water
2 tablespoons treacle or molasses (at room temperature)

In a large bowl thoroughly mix 4 ounces flour, salt, wheat germ, and undissolved dry yeast. Add softened margarine.

Gradually add very hot tap water and molasses to dry ingredients and beat 2 minutes at medium speed of electric mixer, scraping bowl occasionally. Add 2 ounces flour, or enough to make a thick batter. Beat at high speed 2 minutes, scraping bowl occasionally. Stir in enough additional flour to make a stiff batter. Cover; let rise in warm place, free from draught, until doubled in bulk, about 45 minutes.

Stir batter down. Beat vigorously, about ½ minute. Turn into a greased 2½-pint casserole. Bake in moderate oven (375°F. Mark 5) about 45 minutes, or until done. Remove from casserole and cool on wire rack. Makes 1 loaf.

IRISH FRECKLE BREAD
(No-Dissolve Method)

1¼-1½ pounds unsifted plain flour
4 ounces sugar
1 teaspoon salt
4 teaspoons dry yeast
8 fluid ounces potato water or water
4 ounces margarine or butter
2 eggs (at room temperature)
3½ ounces mashed potatoes (at room temperature)
6 ounces seedless raisins

In a large bowl thoroughly mix 6 ounces flour, sugar, salt, and undissolved dry yeast.

Combine potato water or water and margarine in a saucepan. Heat over low heat until liquid is warm. (Margarine does not need to melt.) Gradually add to dry ingredients and beat 2 minutes at medium speed of electric mixer, scraping bowl occasionally.

Add eggs, potatoes, and 2 ounces flour, or enough to make a thick batter. Beat at high speed for 2 minutes, scraping bowl occasionally.

Stir in raisins and enough additional flour to make a soft dough. Turn out onto lightly floured board; knead until smooth and elastic, about 8 to 10 minutes.

Place in greased bowl, turning to grease top. Cover; let rise in warm place, free from draught, until doubled in bulk, about 1 hour and 15 minutes.*

Punch dough down; turn out onto lightly floured board. Divide dough into 4 equal pieces. Shape each piece into a slender loaf, about 8½ inches long.

Put 2 loaves, side by side, in each of 2 greased 8½×4½×2½-inch loaf tins. Cover; let rise in warm place, free from draught, until doubled in bulk, about 1 hour.

Bake in moderate oven (350°F. Mark 4) about 35 minutes, or until done. Remove from tins and cool on wire racks. Makes 2 loaves.

*Note: If plain water is used, rising time will be about 1 hour 45 minutes.

ONE BOWL LOW CHOLESTEROL BREAD
(No-Dissolve Method)

1¾-2 pounds plain flour
2 tablespoons sugar
2 teaspoons salt
2 teaspoons dry yeast
1 tablespoon softened margarine
1 pint very hot tap water

In a large bowl thoroughly mix 10 ounces flour, sugar, salt, and undissolved dry yeast. Add softened margarine.

Gradually add very hot tap water to dry ingredients and beat 2 minutes at medium speed of electric mixer, scraping bowl occasionally. Add 3 ounces flour, or enough to make a thick batter. Beat at high speed 2 minutes, scraping bowl occasionally. Stir in enough additional flour to make a soft dough. Turn out onto lightly floured board; knead until smooth and elastic, about 8 to 10 minutes. Place in greased bowl, turning to grease top. Cover; let rise in warm place, free from draught, until doubled in bulk, about 1 hour.

Punch dough down; turn out onto lightly floured board. Divide dough in half; shape each half into a loaf. Place in 2 greased 9×5×3-inch loaf tins. Cover; let rise in warm place, free from draught, until doubled in bulk, about 1 hour.

Bake in hot oven (400°F. Mark 6) about 40 to 45 minutes, or until done. Remove from tins and cool on wire racks. Makes 2 loaves.

GLUTEN BREAD

Gluten is a nutritious substance found in wheat flour; the component that gives dough its elasticity. When isolated it is grey and sticky. Gluten flour is low in starch and high in gluten. Gluten powder strengthens the dough.

8 fluid ounces milk
1 tablespoon sugar
1 teaspoon salt
½ ounce baker's yeast
8 fluid ounces lukewarm water
1 pound plain flour
1 ounce gluten powder
1 tablespoon melted fat

Scald milk. Add sugar and salt. Cool to lukewarm. Dissolve yeast in lukewarm water and add to lukewarm milk. Mix flour and gluten powder together.

Add half the flour and beat until smooth. Add melted fat and remaining flour, or enough to make easily handled dough.

Knead dough quickly and lightly until smooth and elastic. Place dough in greased bowl. Cover and set in warm place, free from draught. Let rise until doubled in bulk, about 1¾ hours.

When light, divide into 2 equal portions and shape into loaves. Place in greased bread tins. Cover and let rise until doubled in bulk, about 1 hour.

Bake in hot oven (400°F. Mark 6) 45 minutes. Makes 2 loaves.

PUMPERNICKEL BREAD (SWEET)

German name for a coarse-textured, black or dark-brown bread, also called schwarzbrod, or black bread.

⅗ pint cold water
3 ounces corn meal
⅗ pint boiling water
1½ tablespoons salt
1 tablespoon sugar
2 tablespoons fat
1 tablespoon caraway seed
14 ounces cooled mashed potato
½ ounce baker's yeast
4 tablespoons lukewarm water
1½ pounds rye meal or rye flour
about 8 ounces whole wheat flour

Stir cold water into corn meal. Add to boiling water and cook, stirring constantly until thick. Add salt, sugar, fat, and caraway seed. Let stand until lukewarm.

Add potato and the yeast which has been softened in the lukewarm water. Add rye meal or rye flour and enough whole wheat flour to form a soft dough. Stir in at first with a spoon and then with the hand.

Turn out on a lightly floured board. Knead until it is smooth and elastic and does not stick to board. Place in greased bowl. Grease surface and let stand in a warm place (85°F.) until doubled in bulk.

Divide dough into 3 portions; form into balls. Let rest a few minutes. Roll 1 ball at a time, about twice the length and twice the breadth of loaf tins.

Fold in both ends so they overlap at centre. Press sides to seal and then fold in the pressed sides so they overlap at centre. Roll the loaf under the hands until it fits the tin.

Place in greased tin with seam-side of loaf underneath. Grease surface; let rise until doubled in bulk. Bake in moderate oven (375°F. Mark 5) about 1 hour. Makes 3 loaves.

BUTTERMILK BREAD
(No-Dissolve Method)

1 pound 6 ounces to 1 pound ten ounces plain flour
3 tablespoons sugar
2 teaspoons salt
¼ teaspoon bicarbonate of soda
2 teaspoons dry yeast
8 fluid ounces buttermilk or sour milk
8 fluid ounces water
3 ounces margarine

In a large bowl thoroughly mix 8 ounces flour, sugar, salt, bicarbonate of soda, and undissolved dry yeast.

Combine buttermilk, water, and margarine in a saucepan. Heat over low heat until liquids are warm. (Margarine does not need to melt.) Mixture will appear curdled. Gradually add to dry ingredients and beat 2 minutes at medium speed of electric mixer, scraping bowl occasionally. Add 4 ounces flour, or enough to make a thick batter. Beat at high speed 2 minutes, scraping bowl occasionally. Stir in enough flour to make a soft dough.

Turn out onto lightly floured board; knead until smooth and elastic, about 8 to 10 minutes. Place in greased bowl, turning to grease top. Cover; let rise in warm place, free from draught, until doubled in bulk, about 1 hour.

Punch dough down; turn out onto lightly floured board. Divide dough in half. Shape each half into a loaf. Place in 2 greased 8½×4½×2½-inch loaf tins. Cover; let rise in warm place, free from draught, until doubled in bulk, about 1 hour.

Bake in a moderate oven (375°F. Mark 5) about 35 minutes, or until done. Remove from tins and cool on wire rack. Makes 2 loaves.

ONE BOWL WHITE SALT-FREE BREAD
(No-Dissolve Method)

9-13 ounces plain flour
1 tablespoon sugar
2 teaspoons dry yeast
8 fluid ounces very hot tap water
2 tablespoons peanut oil

In a large bowl thoroughly mix 4 ounces flour, sugar, and undissolved dry yeast.

Gradually add very hot tap water and peanut oil to dry ingredients and beat 2 minutes at medium speed of electric mixer, scraping bowl occasionally. Add 1 ounce flour, or enough to make a thick batter. Beat at high speed 2 minutes, scraping bowl occasionally. Stir in enough additional flour to make a soft dough.

Turn out onto lightly floured board; knead until smooth and elastic, about 8 to 10 minutes. Place in greased bowl,

turning to grease top. Cover; let rise in warm place, free from draught, until doubled in bulk, about 45 minutes.

Punch down dough; turn out onto lightly floured board. Shape into a loaf and place in greased 9×5×3-inch loaf tin. Cover; let rise in warm place, free from draught, until doubled in bulk, about 45 minutes.

Bake in hot oven (400°F. Mark 6) about 30 minutes, or until done. Remove from tin and cool on wire rack. Makes 1 loaf.

CASSEROLE WHITE BREAD
(Batter Method)

8 fluid ounces milk
3 tablespoons sugar
3 teaspoons salt
1½ ounces fat
8 fluid ounces warm (not hot) water
4 teaspoons dry or 1 ounce baker's yeast
1 pound 2 ounces plain flour

Scald 8 fluid ounces milk. Stir in sugar, salt, and fat. Cool to lukewarm.

Measure into bowl 8 fluid ounces warm water (cool to lukewarm for baker's yeast). Sprinkle or crumble in yeast. Stir until dissolved. Stir in lukewarm milk mixture.

Add flour and stir until well blended, about 2 minutes. Cover. Let rise in warm place, free from draught, about 40 minutes or until more than doubled in bulk.

Stir batter down. Beat vigorously, about ½ minute. Turn into greased 2½ pint casserole. A square pan 8×8×2 inches or an 8 inch tube tin may also be used.

Bake uncovered in moderate oven (375°F. Mark 5) about 1 hour. Makes 1 loaf.

SOUR DOUGH BREAD
(No-Dissolve Method)

Starter:
7 ounces plain flour
1 tablespoon sugar
2 teaspoons salt
2 teaspoons dry yeast
1 pint warm water

Dough:
1¼-1½ pounds flour
3 tablespoons sugar
1 teaspoon salt
2 teaspoons dry yeast
8 fluid ounces milk
1 ounce margarine or butter
6 ounces starter

To make starter, combine the flour, sugar, salt, and undissolved dry yeast in a large bowl. Gradually add warm water to dry ingredients and beat 2 minutes at medium speed of electric mixer, scraping the bowl occasionally. Cover; let stand at room temperature (78°-80°F.) 4 days. Stir down daily.

To make dough, combine 4 ounces

flour, sugar, salt, and undissolved dry yeast in a large bowl.

Combine milk and margarine in a saucepan. Heat over low heat until liquid is warm. (Margarine does not need to melt.) Gradually add to dry ingredients and beat 2 minutes at medium speed of electric mixer, scraping bowl occasionally.

Add 6 ounces starter and 4 ounces flour, or enough to make a thick batter. Beat at high speed 2 minutes, scraping bowl occasionally. Stir in enough additional flour to make a soft dough. Turn out onto lightly floured board; knead until smooth and elastic, about 8 to 10 minutes. Place in greased bowl, turning to grease top. Cover; let rise in warm place, free from draught, until doubled in bulk, about 1 hour.

Punch dough down; turn out onto lightly floured board. Let rest 15 minutes. Divide dough in half. Shape each half into loaf and place in greased 9×5×3-inch loaf tin. Cover; let rise in warm place, free from draught, until doubled in bulk, about 1 hour.

Bake in hot oven (400°F. Mark 6) about 30 minutes, or until done. Remove from tins and cool on wire racks. Makes 2 loaves.

To Re-use Starter: Add 12 fluid ounces lukewarm water, 3 ounces flour, and 1½ teaspoons sugar to unused starter. Beat for 1 minute at medium speed of electric mixer. Cover and let stand until ready to make bread again. Stir down daily.

RAISIN BREAD
(Batter Method)

5 fluid ounces hot water
4 ounces sugar
1 teaspoon salt
2 ounces fat
4 fluid ounces warm (not hot) water
4 teaspoons dry or 1 ounce baker's yeast
1 egg, beaten
13 ounces plain flour
6 ounces raisins — seedless

Mix together water, sugar, salt and fat. Cool to lukewarm.

Measure into bowl 4 fluid ounces warm water (cool to lukewarm for baker's yeast). Sprinkle or crumble in yeast. Stir until dissolved. Stir in lukewarm water mixture.

Add beaten egg, flour, and raisins. Stir until well blended, about 2 minutes.

Let rise in warm place, free from draught, about 50 minutes or until more than doubled in bulk. Stir down. Beat vigorously about ½ minute. Turn into greased 2½ pint baking dish.

Bake uncovered in hot oven (400°F. Mark 6) about 45 minutes. Makes 1 loaf.

HIGH PROTEIN BREAD
(Rich Flour Formula Health Bread)

2   teaspoons dry or ½ ounce baker's
    yeast
4   tablespoons warm water (luke-
    warm for baker's yeast)
1¼ pounds sifted plain flour
1   tablespoon salt
2   ounces sugar
1½ ounces full-fat soy flour
2   ounces nonfat dry milk solids
1   ounce wheat germ
1   tablespoon melted fat
14 fluid ounces water

Dissolve yeast in 4 tablespoons water. Combine dry ingredients in mixing bowl. Add dissolved yeast, melted fat, and water, mixing to blend well.

Knead dough until smooth and satiny, then place in well greased bowl. Cover and allow to rise in warm place for about 1½ hours.

Punch down by plunging fist in centre of dough, then fold over edges of dough and turn whole mass upside down. Cover and allow to rise again for 15 to 20 minutes.

Shape into 2 loaves and place in greased tins. Cover and allow to stand about 55 to 60 minutes in warm place or until dough rises and fills tins.

Bake in hot oven (400°F. Mark 6) 45 minutes. Makes 2 loaves.

SALLY LUNN
(No-Dissolve Method)

¾-1 pound plain flour
3   ounces sugar
1   teaspoon salt
2   teaspoons dry yeast
4   fluid ounces milk
4   fluid ounces water
4   ounces margarine
3   eggs (at room temperature)

In a large bowl thoroughly mix 5 ounces flour, sugar, salt, and undissolved dry yeast.

Combine milk, water, and margarine in a saucepan. Heat over low heat until liquids are warm. (Margarine does not need to melt.) Gradually add to dry ingredients and beat 2 minutes at medium speed of electric mixer, scraping bowl occasionally. Add eggs and 4 ounces flour, or enough to make a thick batter. Beat at high speed 2 minutes, scraping bowl occasionally. Stir in enough additional flour to make a stiff batter. Cover; let rise in warm place, free from draught, until doubled in bulk, about 1 hour.

Stir batter down and beat well, about ½ minute. Turn into a well-greased and floured 9-inch tube tin. Cover; let rise in warm place, free from draught, until doubled in bulk, about 1 hour.

Bake in slow oven (325°F. Mark 3) about 45 to 50 minutes, or until done. Remove from tin and cool on wire rack. Best when served warm.

CHALLAH OR HALLAH

A Jewish term for twisted loaves of yeast-raised white bread prepared originally for the Jewish Sabbath. The dough is usually braided, but a variety of forms are made for the various holidays of the year.

16 fluid ounces hot water
1   tablespoon salt
1   tablespoon sugar
2   tablespoons vegetable oil
½ ounce baker's or 2 teaspoons dry
    yeast
3   tablespoons lukewarm water
    (warm for dry yeast)
2   beaten eggs
2   pounds plain flour

Pour the hot water over salt, sugar, and oil in mixing bowl. When lukewarm, add the yeast which has been dissolved in the 3 tablespoons lukewarm water.

Add eggs and flour gradually. Mix and stir, then knead until smooth and elastic. Cover and let rise in a warm place until double in bulk.

Turn half of the dough onto a board and cut into 4 equal parts. Roll each part 1½ inches thick and form 3 into a braid. Fasten the ends well and place in a floured bread tin.

Cut remaining ¼ into 3 parts and roll each part ½ inch thick. Form into a braid and place on top of braid in tin.

Let rise until doubled in bulk. Brush with beaten egg yolk; sprinkle with poppy seed, if desired.

Bake in hot oven (400°F. Mark 6) 1 hour then reduce heat to moderate (350°F. Mark 4) and bake 15 minutes longer. To form a hard crust, let cool in a draught. Makes 2 loaves.

ITALIAN CHRISTMAS BREAD
(Panettone)

1   ounce baker's or 4 teaspoons dry
    yeast
8   fluid ounces warm (not hot)
    water
4   ounces butter, melted
1½ teaspoons salt
4   ounces sugar
2   beaten eggs
3   beaten egg yolks
About 1 pound 6 ounces plain flour
3   ounces thinly sliced citron
6   ounces seedless raisins

Soften dry yeast in warm water (cool to lukewarm for baker's yeast).

Mix butter, salt, sugar, eggs, and egg yolks. Add yeast and butter mixtures to 1¼ pounds flour and stir until blended.

Knead on floured board until smooth and no longer sticky, adding more flour as needed. The dough should be soft. Knead in citron and raisins.

Place dough in greased bowl. Grease surface and cover with cloth towel. Let rise in warm place (80°F.) until doubled in bulk, about 2 hours.

Knead dough again until smooth. Place in greased 2½ pint round baking tin. Brush top with melted butter. Cover and let rise until doubled in bulk, about 40 minutes.

With a sharp knife, cut deep cross in top of loaf. Bake in hot oven (425°F. Mark 7) until surface begins to brown, about 9 minutes. Lower oven temperature to slow (325°F. Mark 3) and bake until done, about 1 hour longer. Makes 1 large loaf.

BARM BRACK
(No-Dissolve Method)

The Irish are famous for many types of breads—Irish soda bread, gingerbread, and their own special crusty whole wheat bread. One of their most popular loaves is Barm Brack. This bread is filled with candied fruits and acquired its name from "barm" the Gaelic word for yeast.

1-1½ pounds plain flour
4   ounces sugar
1   teaspoon salt
1   teaspoon grated lemon peel
6   teaspoons dry yeast
6   fluid ounces water
4   fluid ounces milk
2   ounces margarine
2   eggs (at room temperature)
8   ounces sultanas
2   ounces chopped mixed
    crystallized fruits

In a large bowl thoroughly mix 6 ounces flour, sugar, salt, lemon peel, and undissolved dry yeast.

Combine water, milk, and margarine in saucepan. Heat over low heat until liquids are warm. (Margarine does not need to melt.) Gradually add to dry ingredients and beat 2 minutes at medium speed of electric mixer, scraping bowl occasionally. Add eggs and 3 ounces flour, or enough to make a thick batter. Beat at high speed 2 minutes, scraping the bowl occasionally. Stir in enough additional flour to make a soft dough. Turn out onto lightly floured board; knead until smooth and elastic, about 8 to 10 minutes. Place in greased bowl, turning to grease top. Cover; let rise in warm place, free from draught, until doubled in bulk, about 40 minutes.

Punch dough down; turn out onto lightly floured board. Knead in sultanas and crystallized fruits. Divide in half. Shape into loaves. Place in 2 greased 8½×4½×2½-inch loaf tins. Cover; let rise in warm place, free from draught, until doubled in bulk, about 50 minutes.

Bake in a moderate oven (375°F. Mark 5) about 30 to 35 minutes, or until done. Remove from tins and cool on wire racks. Makes 2 loaves.

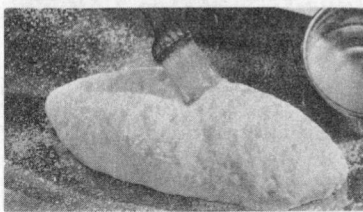

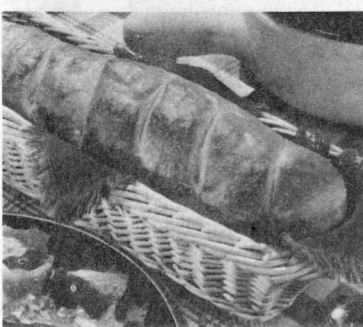

French Bread

FRENCH BREAD

½ pint warm, not hot, water (lukewarm for baker's yeast)
½ ounce baker's or 2 teaspoons dry yeast
1 teaspoon salt
½ ounce soft fat
1 tablespoon sugar
14 ounces sifted plain flour

Measure water into a large mixing bowl (warm, not hot, water for dry yeast; lukewarm water for baker's yeast). Sprinkle or crumble in yeast. Stir until dissolved.

Add salt, fat, and sugar. Stir in flour.

Turn dough out on lightly floured board. Knead 8 to 10 minutes or until dough is springy and elastic and does not stick to the board.

Place in greased bowl and brush top lightly with melted fat. Cover with a cloth. Let rise in a warm place, free from draught, until doubled in bulk, about 40 minutes.

Punch dough down. Let rise again until almost doubled in bulk, about 30 minutes.

Punch down, turn out on floured board and cut dough into two equal portions.

Roll each half into an oblong about 8×10 inches. Beginning with the wide side, roll up tightly. Seal edges by pinching together.

With hands on each end of roll, roll gently back and forth to lengthen loaf and taper ends.

Place loaves on a greased baking sheet sprinkled lightly with yellow corn meal. Brush loaves with cornflour glaze. Let rise, uncovered about 1½ hours.

Brush again with cornflour glaze. With a sharp knife, make ¼-inch slashes in dough at 2-inch intervals. Bake in hot oven (400°F. Mark 6) 10 minutes.

Remove from oven, brush again with cornflour glaze. Return and bake about 30 minutes or until golden brown. Makes 2 loaves.

Cornflour Glaze: Mix 1 teaspoon cornflour with 1 teaspoon cold water. Combine with 4 fluid ounces boiling water. Cook until smooth. Let cool slightly.

WHITE BATTER BREAD
(No-Dissolve Method)

1-1¼ pounds plain flour
3 tablespoons sugar
2 teaspoons salt
4 teaspoons dry yeast
8 fluid ounces milk
8 fluid ounces water
1 ounce margarine

In a large bowl thoroughly mix 6 ounces flour, sugar, salt, and undissolved dry yeast.

Combine milk, water, and margarine in a saucepan. Heat over low heat until liquids are warm. (Margarine does not need to melt.) Gradually add to dry ingredients and beat 2 minutes at medium speed of electric mixer, scraping bowl occasionally. Add 4 ounces flour, or enough to make a thick batter. Beat at high speed 2 minutes, scraping bowl occasionally. Stir in enough additional flour to make a stiff batter. Beat until well blended. Cover; let rise in warm place, free from draught, until doubled in bulk, about 40 minutes.

Stir batter down. Beat vigorously, about ½ minute. Turn into a greased 9×5×3-inch loaf tin.

Bake in a moderate oven (375°F. Mark 5) about 40 to 50 minutes, or until done. Remove from tin and cool on wire rack. Makes 1 large loaf.

Herb Batter Bread: Combine ¼ teaspoon basil leaves, ¼ teaspoon oregano leaves, and ¼ teaspoon thyme leaves with the 6 ounces flour, sugar, salt, and yeast. Then proceed with recipe as directed. Makes 1 large loaf.

RUSSIAN BLACK BREAD
(No-Dissolve Method)

1 pound rye flour
12 ounces white flour
1 teaspoon sugar
2 teaspoons salt
8 ounces whole bran cereal
2 tablespoons caraway seed, crushed
2 teaspoons instant coffee
2 teaspoons onion powder
½ teaspoon fennel seed, crushed
4 teaspoons dry yeast
1 pint water
3 tablespoons vinegar
3 ounces dark molasses or black treacle
1 ounce plain chocolate
2 ounces margarine
1 teaspoon cornflour
4 fluid ounces cold water

Combine rye and white flours. In a large bowl thoroughly mix 9 ounces flour mixture, sugar, salt, cereal, caraway seed, instant coffee, onion powder, fennel seed, and undissolved dry yeast.

Combine 1 pint cold water, vinegar, molasses, chocolate, and margarine in a saucepan. Heat over low heat until liquids are warm. (Margarine and chocolate do not need to melt.) Gradually add to dry ingredients and beat 2 minutes at medium speed of electric mixer, scraping bowl occasionally. Add 2 ounces flour mixture, or enough mixture to make a thick batter. Beat at high speed 2 minutes, scraping bowl occasionally. Stir in enough additional flour mixture to make a soft dough. Turn out onto lightly floured board. Cover dough with bowl and let rest 15 minutes. Then knead until smooth and elastic, about 10 to 15 minutes (dough may be sticky). Place in greased bowl, turning to grease top. Cover; let rise in warm place, free from draught, until doubled in bulk, about 1 hour.

Punch dough down; turn out onto lightly floured board. Divide dough in half. Shape each half into a ball, about 5 inches in diameter. Place each ball in the centre of greased 8-inch round cake tin. Cover; let rise in warm place, free from draught, until doubled in bulk, about 1 hour.

Bake in a moderate oven (350°F. Mark 4) about 45 to 50 minutes, or until done.

Meanwhile, combine cornflour and 4 fluid ounces cold water. Cook over medium heat, stirring constantly, until mixture boils; continue to cook, stirring constantly, 1 minute. As soon as bread is baked, brush cornflour mixture over tops of loaves. Return bread to oven and bake 2 to 3 minutes, or until glaze is set. Remove from tins and cool on wire racks. Makes 2 loaves.

Yeast Rolls

ROLL DOUGH
(Straight-Dough Method)

6 fluid ounces milk
2 ounces sugar
1½ teaspoons salt
2½ ounces fat
6 fluid ounces warm (not hot)
  water
½ ounce baker's or 2 teaspoons
  dry yeast
9 ounces plain flour
**Additional 9 ounces plain flour
  (about)**

Scald milk. Stir in sugar, salt, and fat. Cool to lukewarm.

Measure 6 fluid ounces warm water into bowl (cool to lukewarm for baker's yeast). Sprinkle or crumble in yeast. Stir until dissolved. Stir in lukewarm milk mixture.

Add 9 ounces flour. Beat until smooth. Stir in additional flour.

Turn out on lightly floured board. Knead until smooth and elastic. Place in greased bowl; brush with fat.

Cover. Let rise in warm place, free from draught, until doubled in bulk, about 1 hour.

Punch down and turn out on lightly floured board.

Proceed according to directions for shapes.

For Faster Roll Dough (Action-Quick Dough): Use double the quantity of yeast; bowl rise about 40 minutes.

WHOLE WHEAT ROLLS
(Batter Method)

½ pint milk
2 ounces sugar
2 teaspoons salt
2 ounces fat
3 ounces honey*
3 tablespoons warm (not hot)
  water
1 ounce baker's or 4 teaspoons
  dry yeast
14 ounces whole wheat flour

Scald milk. Stir in sugar, salt, fat, and honey. Cool to lukewarm.

Measure into bowl 4 tablespoons warm water (cool to lukewarm for baker's yeast). Sprinkle or crumble in yeast. Stir until dissolved. Stir in lukewarm milk mixture.

Add flour. Stir until well blended, about ½ minute. Cover. Let rise in warm place, free from draught, until doubled in bulk, about 45 minutes.

Stir batter down. Beat vigorously about ½ minute. Fill greased deep bun tins or darioles about ⅔ full.

Bake in hot oven (400°F. Mark 6) about 25 minutes. Makes 12 rolls.

*Corn syrup, molasses or treacle may be substituted, if necessary.

REFRIGERATOR ROLL DOUGH
(Straight-Dough Method)

6 fluid ounces milk
6 tablespoons sugar
2 teaspoons salt
2½ ounces fat
4 fluid ounces warm (not hot)
  water
1 ounce baker's or 4 teaspoons
  dry yeast
1 egg beaten
1 pound 2 ounces plain flour

Scald milk. Stir in sugar, salt, and fat. Cool to lukewarm.

Measure into bowl 4 fluid ounces warm water (cool to lukewarm for baker's yeast). Sprinkle or crumble in yeast and stir until dissolved. Stir in lukewarm milk mixture.

Add beaten egg and 8 ounces flour. Beat until smooth. Stir in remaining flour.

Place dough in greased bowl; brush top with soft fat. Cover tightly with waxed paper or aluminium foil. Store in refrigerator at least 2 hours or until needed.

To use, punch down and cut off dough needed.

Proceed according to directions for shapes selected.

May be kept 2 to 3 days in refrigerator.

WHOLE WHEAT ROLL DOUGH
(Straight-Dough Method)

8 fluid ounces milk
3 tablespoons molasses or treacle
2 tablespoons sugar
2 teaspoons salt
2 ounces fat
4 fluid ounces warm (not hot) water
½ ounce baker's or 2 teaspoons dry
  yeast
9 ounces whole wheat flour
9 ounces plain flour

Scald milk. Stir in molasses, sugar, salt, and fat. Cool to lukewarm.

Measure warm water into bowl (cool to lukewarm for baker's yeast). Sprinkle or crumble in yeast and stir until dissolved. Stir in lukewarm milk mixture.

Add ½ mixture of whole wheat flour and plain flour. Beat until smooth. Stir in remaining flour mixture.

Turn dough out on lightly floured board. Knead until smooth and elastic. Place in greased bowl; brush top with soft fat.

Cover. Let rise in warm place, free from draughts, until doubled in bulk, about 1 hour and 20 minutes. Punch down and turn out on lightly floured board.

Proceed according to directions for shapes desired.

ONE BOWL DINNER ROLLS
(No-Dissolve Method)

¾-1 pound plain flour
2 ounces sugar
½ teaspoon salt
2 teaspoons dry yeast
2½ ounces softened margarine
6 fluid ounces very hot tap water
1 egg (at room temperature)
Melted margarine

In a large bowl thoroughly mix 3 ounces flour, sugar, salt, and undissolved dry yeast. Add softened margarine. Gradually add very hot tap water to dry ingredients and beat 2 minutes at medium speed of electric mixer, scraping bowl occasionally. Add egg and 2 ounces flour, or enough to make a thick batter. Beat at high speed 2 minutes, scraping bowl occasionally. Stir in enough additional flour to make a soft dough.

Turn out onto lightly floured board; knead until smooth and elastic, about 8 to 10 minutes. Place in greased bowl, turning to grease top. Cover; let rise in warm place, free from draught, until doubled in bulk, about 1 hour.

Punch dough down; turn out onto lightly floured board. Proceed according to directions for desired shape. Cover; let rise in warm place, free from draught, until doubled in bulk, about 1 hour.

Carefully brush rolls with melted margarine. Bake in a hot oven (400°F. Mark 6) about 10 to 15 minutes, or until done. Remove from baking sheets and cool on wire racks. Makes 2 or 3 dozen rolls.

Curlicues: Divide dough into 2 or 3 equal pieces.* Roll out each piece into a 9×12-inch oblong. Brush generously with melted margarine. Cut into 12 strips (about 1 inch wide). Hold one end of each strip firmly and wind dough loosely to form coil; tuck end firmly underneath. Place on greased baking sheets, about 2 inches apart.

Pretzels: Divide dough into 2 or 3 equal pieces.* Then divide each piece into 12 pieces. Roll each into a pencil-shaped 16-inch roll. Shape into pretzels and place on greased baking sheets, about 2 inches apart.

*Divide dough into 2 pieces to make family-size rolls or divide into 3 pieces to make smaller dinner rolls.

Parkerhouse Rolls: Divide dough in half. Roll each half into a ¼-inch thick circle. Cut into rounds with a 2½-inch biscuit cutter. Crease each round with dull edge of knife to one side of centre. Brush each round to within ¼-inch of the edges with melted margarine. Fold larger side over smaller so edges just meet. Pinch well with fingers to seal. Place on greased baking sheets so rolls are almost touching.

CLOVER LEAF ROLLS

Divide Roll Dough in half. Form each half into 9-inch roll. Cut into 9 equal pieces. Form each piece into 3 small balls. Brush sides with melted margarine or butter.

Place 3 balls in each section of greased deep bun tins.

Cover. Let rise in warm place, free from draught, until doubled in bulk. (Whole Wheat, White, Refrigerator Doughs about 1 hour; Action-Quick Dough about 30 minutes.) Brush lightly with melted margarine or butter.

Bake in hot oven at 400°F. Mark 6. (Whole Wheat Rolls about 20 minutes; White Rolls about 15 minutes.) Makes 18 rolls.

Clover Leaf Rolls

HONEY PECAN ROLLS

2 ounces pecan halves or other nuts

While Roll Dough is rising prepare Honey Syrup.

Spread one-half syrup in each of two tins 8×8×2 inches. Arrange pecan halves in each tin. Divide Roll Dough in half. Form each half into 12-inch roll. Cut into 12 equal pieces. Form into balls. Place in prepared tin about ¼ inch apart. Cover. Let rise in warm place, free from draught, until doubled in bulk, about 1 hour. Bake in hot oven (400°F. Mark 6) about 25 minutes. Turn out of tins immediately. Makes 24.

Honey Syrup:
 2 ounces dark brown sugar
 8 ounces honey
 1½ ounces margarine or butter, melted
Combine ingredients.

Honey Pecan Rolls

BOWKNOTS

When Roll Dough is ready for shaping, roll dough under hand to ½-inch thickness. Cut in pieces about 6 inches long. Tie in knots. Place on greased baking sheet.

Bowknots

Fan Tans

FAN TANS

Divide Roll Dough into 3 equal pieces. Roll out each piece into an oblong about 11×9 inches. Brush lightly with melted margarine or butter.

Cut into 7 equal strips (about 1½ inches wide). Pile strips one on top of other. Cut into 6 equal pieces (about 1½ inches long). Place cut side up in greased deep bun tins.

Cover. Let rise in warm place, free from draught, until doubled in bulk. (Straight-Dough Method about 1 hour; Action-Quick Dough about 30 minutes; Refrigerator Dough about 1 hour.) Brush lightly with melted margarine or butter.

Bake in hot oven (400°F. Mark 6) about 20 minutes. Makes 18.

Bubble Loaf

BUBBLE LOAF

Divide Roll Dough in half. Form each half into a roll about 12 inches long. Cut each roll into 24 equal pieces. Form into balls.

Place a layer of balls about ½ inch apart in greased bread tin 9×5×3 inches or 9-inch tube tin. Brush lightly with melted margarine or butter.

Arrange a second layer of balls on top of first.

Cover. Let rise in warm place, free from draught, until doubled in bulk, slightly higher than edge of tin. (Straight-Dough Method about 1 hour; Action-Quick Dough about 30 minutes; Refrigerator Dough about 1 hour.)

Brush lightly with melted margarine or butter.

Bake in moderate oven (375°F. Mark 5) about 30 minutes. Makes 2 loaves.

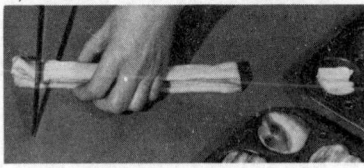

Butterflakes

BUTTERFLAKES

When Roll Dough is ready for shaping, roll out to thin rectangular sheet ⅛ inch thick. Brush dough with melted butter or margarine. Fold dough into layers about 1 inch wide and 6 or 7 layers deep. Cut pieces 1½ inches long. A pastry wheel gives the edges a crinkly effect. Set on end in greased deep bun tins.

CURLICUES

Divide Roll Dough in half. Roll out each half into an oblong about 12×9 inches. Brush generously with melted margarine or butter.

Cut into 12 equal strips (about 1 inch wide). Hold one end of strip firmly and wind closely to form coil. Tuck end firmly underneath. Place on greased baking sheets about 2 inches apart. Cover. Let rise in warm place, free from draught, until doubled in bulk. (Straight-Dough Method about 1 hour; Action-Quick Dough about 30 minutes; Refrigerator Dough about 1 hour.) Brush lightly with melted margarine or butter. Bake in hot oven at 400°F. Mark 6 about 15 minutes. Makes 24.

Curlicues

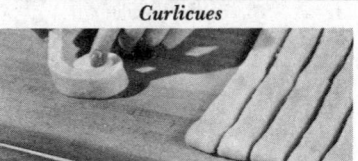

CRESCENTS

Divide Roll Dough into 3 equal pieces. Roll out each piece into a circle about 9 inches in diameter. Brush lightly with melted margarine or butter.

Cut into 8 pie-shaped pieces. Roll up tightly beginning at wide end. Seal points firmly.

Place on greased baking sheets, with points underneath, about 2 inches apart. Curve to form crescents.

Cover. Let rise in warm place, free from draught, until doubled in bulk. (Straight-Dough Method about 1 hour; Action-Quick Dough about 30 minutes; Refrigerator Dough about 1 hour.)

Brush lightly with melted margarine or butter.

Bake in hot oven (400°F. Mark 6) about 15 minutes. Makes 24.

Crescents

BUTTERFLIES

When Roll Dough is ready for shaping, roll dough into rectangular sheet ¼ inch thick and 6 inches wide. Brush with melted margarine or butter. Roll up like Swiss roll. Cut into pieces 2 inches long. Press across centre of each piece with knife handle or small rolling pin.

Butterflies

LUCKY CLOVERS

Divide Roll Dough in half. Form each half into 9-inch roll. Cut into 9 equal pieces. Form into balls.

Place in greased deep bun tins. With scissors cut each ball in half, then into quarters, cutting through almost to bottom of rolls. Brush lightly with melted margarine or butter.

Cover. Let rise in warm place, free from draught, until doubled in bulk. (Whole Wheat, White, Refrigerator Doughs about 1 hour; Action-Quick Dough about 30 minutes.)

Bake in hot oven at 400°F. Mark 6. (Whole Wheat Rolls about 20 minutes; White Rolls about 15 minutes.) Makes 18.

Lucky clovers

PARKERHOUSE ROLLS

Divide Roll Dough in half. Roll out each half into 9-inch circle. Cut into rounds with 2½-inch cutter.

Crease with dull edge of knife to one side of centre. Brush lightly with melted margarine or butter. Fold larger side over smaller so edges just meet. Seal.

Place on greased baking sheet about 1 inch apart.

Cover. Let rise in warm place, free from draught, until doubled in bulk. (Straight-Dough Method about 1 hour; Action-Quick Dough about 30 minutes; Refrigerator Dough about 1 hour.)

Brush lightly with melted margarine or butter.

Bake in hot oven at 400°F. Mark 6 about 15 minutes. Makes 24 rolls.

Parkerhouse Rolls

PAN ROLLS

Divide Roll Dough in half. Form each half into a roll about 12 inches long. Cut into 12 equal pieces. Form into smooth balls.

Place in greased shallow tins about ¼ inch apart.

Cover. Let rise in warm place, free from draught, until doubled in bulk. (Straight-Dough Method about 1 hour; Action-Quick Dough about 30 minutes; Refrigerator Dough about 1 hour.)

Brush lightly with melted margarine or butter.

Bake in moderate oven at 375°F. Mark 5 about 20 minutes. Makes 24 rolls.

Pan Rolls

ROSETTES

When Roll Dough is ready for shaping, roll dough under hand to ½-inch thickness. Cut in pieces about 6 inches long. Tie in knots, and bring one end through centre and the other over the side. Place on greased baking sheet.

Rosettes

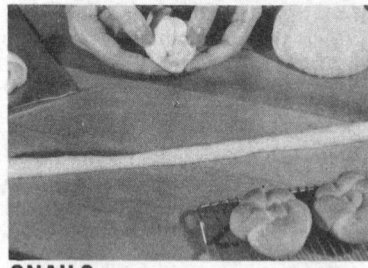

SNAILS

When Roll Dough is ready for shaping, roll dough under hand to form long pieces ½ inch in diameter. Cut into 8-inch lengths. Twist each piece by rolling ends in opposite directions. Coil to form snail. Tuck end under edge of roll to hold it in place. Place on greased baking sheet.

Snails

BUTTERMILK ROLLS

½ ounce baker's or 2 teaspoons dry yeast
3 tablespoons lukewarm water
12 fluid ounces buttermilk or sour milk
2 tablespoons fat
½ teaspoon bicarbonate of soda
2 tablespoons sugar
1 teaspoon salt
1 pound plain flour

Soften the yeast in the lukewarm (warm for dry yeast) water. Scald the buttermilk and add to it the fat, soda, sugar, salt, and 8 ounces of the flour.

Beat for several minutes, then add enough additional flour to make a light but not sticky dough. Turn out on lightly floured board and knead for 8 minutes.

Place in a greased bowl, grease the surface of the dough, cover, and allow it to rise in warm place until doubled in bulk (about 1½ hours).

Punch down and roll out on a lightly floured board. Cut into rounds and place in a deep, greased tin, close together but not touching. Allow to rise until doubled in bulk, 45 minutes. Bake in moderate oven (350°F. Mark 4) for 20 to 25 minutes.

ENGLISH MUFFINS

These are small, flat, yeast-raised cakes baked on a girdle. They may be cut from rolled-out dough or shaped by allowing balls of dough to rise in deep bun tins. English muffins are broken apart (not cut) and toasted before serving. Always store them in the refrigerator.

8 fluid ounces scalded milk
1½ ounces butter or margarine
1 teaspoon salt
2 tablespoons sugar
½ ounce baker's yeast
3 tablespoons lukewarm water
1 beaten egg
About 14 ounces plain flour
White corn meal

Pour scalded milk over butter, salt, and sugar. Soften yeast in water.

Cool milk mixture to lukewarm, then add yeast, egg, and 8 ounces flour.

Stir to blend well, then knead in remaining flour until dough is thick and elastic.

Turn batter into greased bowl. Cover and allow to rise in warm place until doubled in bulk, about 1 hour.

Sprinkle about 1 ounce white corn meal on lightly floured pastry board or cloth. Roll dough out ¼ inch thick. Cut with 3½-inch cutter.

Let cut dough rise, covered, until doubled in size. Bake on lightly greased girdle over moderate heat, about 15 minutes on first side and 7 minutes on other side. Makes about 1 dozen.

REFRIGERATOR POTATO ROLLS
(Master Recipe)

8 fluid ounces milk, scalded
7 ounces hot mashed potato
4 ounces fat
2 ounces sugar
1½ teaspoons salt
½ ounce baker's yeast
4 fluid ounces lukewarm water
2 eggs, beaten
1¼-1½ pounds sifted plain flour

Combine milk, potato, fat, sugar, and salt in a large bowl. Let stand until lukewarm.

Soften yeast in lukewarm water and add with eggs.

Add 6 ounces flour and beat well. Cover and let stand in warm place (85°F.) until full of bubbles, about 1 hour.

Stir in enough flour (about 1 pound) to make a fairly stiff dough. Knead on a lightly floured board until smooth. Return to lightly greased bowl, and grease top of dough. Cover, and chill in refrigerator.

About 1½ hours before serving time, shape desired number of rolls. Place on greased tins. Let rise until doubled in bulk, about 1 hour. Bake in hot oven (425°F. Mark 7) 15 to 20 minutes. Makes about 3 dozen rolls.

Note: Remaining dough may be kept in refrigerator several days. Punch down before placing in refrigerator.

Variations:

Butterscotch Rolls: Butter deep bun tins. Add 1 teaspoon butter, 1 teaspoon brown sugar, and 1 tablespoon chopped nuts.

Form dough into medium-sized balls. Place 1 ball in each tin. Allow to rise until doubled in bulk.

Bake in hot oven (425°F. Mark 7) 25 minutes. Turn out while hot.

Date and Walnut Rolls: Prepare recipe for refrigerator potato rolls using half white flour and half whole wheat flour.

Substitute brown sugar for white. Add 6 ounces chopped, stoned dates and 2 ounces chopped nuts.

Shape into rolls. Allow to rise until double in bulk.

Bake in hot oven (425°F. Mark 7) 20 minutes. Ice with glacé icing.

Nut and Prune Rolls: To the recipe for refrigerator potato rolls add 2 ounces chopped nuts, 6 ounces prunes, diced, and 1 teaspoon baking powder.

Shape into rolls. Allow to rise until doubled in bulk. Sprinkle with cinnamon-sugar mixture.

Bake in hot oven (425°F. Mark 7) 20 minutes.

BRIOCHE

Brioche is a yeast-raised bread rich in eggs and fat, popular in France as a breakfast roll. It may be made in many shapes and sizes, but the most familiar form is the roll made by topping one ball of dough with a smaller ball before baking to form a bun with a little hat on it.

4 fluid ounces milk
4 ounces margarine or butter
3 ounces sugar
½ teaspoon salt
3 tablespoons warm (not hot) water
½ ounce baker's or 2 teaspoons dry yeast
1 egg yolk, beaten
3 whole eggs, beaten
13 ounces flour
1 egg white
1 tablespoon sugar

Scald milk. Cool to lukewarm.

Cream margarine or butter thoroughly. Add gradually and cream together 3 ounces sugar and salt.

Measure warm water into bowl (cool to lukewarm for baker's yeast). Sprinkle or crumble in yeast and stir until dissolved. Stir in lukewarm milk and creamed mixture.

Add beaten egg yolk, beaten whole eggs, and flour. Beat 10 minutes.

Cover. Let rise in warm place, free from draught, about 2 hours or until more than doubled in bulk.

Stir down. Beat thoroughly. Cover tightly with waxed paper or aluminium foil. Store in refrigerator overnight.

Stir down and turn out soft dough on floured board.

Divide into 2 pieces, one about ¾ weight of dough and the other about ¼ weight of dough.

Cut larger piece into 16 equal pieces. Form into smooth balls. Place in well greased deep bun tins.

Cut smaller piece into 16 equal pieces. Form into smooth balls.

Make a deep indentation in centre of each large ball; dampen slightly with cold water. Press a small ball into each indentation.

Cover. Let rise in warm place, free from draught, about 1 hour or until more than doubled in bulk. Brush with mixture of 1 egg white and 1 tablespoon sugar.

Bake in moderate oven (375°F. Mark 5) about 20 minutes. Makes 16.

BATH BUNS

Shape Brioche Dough into large round buns. Place about 2 inches apart on greased baking sheet. Cover and set in warm place, free from draught. Let rise until light, about 1½ hours.

Before baking, press into the tops sliced blanched almonds, chopped citron, and chopped crystallized orange peel.

Brioche

Brush with 1 tablespoon water mixed with one egg white beaten. Bake in moderate oven (350°F. Mark 4) about 40 to 45 minutes.

CRUMPETS

These are English breakfast or tea cakes very similar to muffins except that buttered crumpet rings are always used in preparing them.

16 fluid ounces scalded milk
4 ounces butter
¾ teaspoon salt
½ ounce baker's or 2 teaspoons dry yeast
About 12 ounces sifted flour

Combine scalded milk, butter, and salt in a large mixing bowl; let cool to lukewarm.

Soften yeast in a little lukewarm water and add to the milk. Stir in ¾-1 pound flour to make a stiff dough which can be beaten with a spoon. Beat well.

Cover the dough with a towel and set in a warm place to rise until light.

Put buttered crumpet rings on a hot buttered girdle. Fill the rings half-full with the dough. Bake slowly until the crumpets are well risen and lightly browned on the under-side.

Turn, ring and all, and brown on the other side. The crumpets must be watched carefully. If they brown too quickly, lower the heat. To serve, toast the crumpets and butter generously. Makes about 1 dozen.

BAGEL

Bagel is a Jewish term for an old-time Jewish yeast-dough roll shaped (traditionally by hand) like a doughnut with a hole in the centre. It is cooked in simmering water before being baked. Its hard crust is notorious. It is often served with lox (smoked salmon) and cream cheese.

2 ounces butter
1½ tablespoons sugar
½ teaspoon salt
8 fluid ounces scalded milk
1 ounce baker's yeast
1 egg white
15 ounces plain flour

Add butter, sugar, and salt to scalded milk. When lukewarm, add yeast, well beaten egg white, and the flour.

Combine well, knead, and let rise until doubled in bulk. Cut off small pieces and roll the width of a finger and twice the length, tapering at the ends.

Shape into rings, pinching the ends together well. Let stand on a floured board only until they begin to rise.

Fill a large shallow pan half full of water. Place over heat and when very hot, but not boiling, drop the dough rings in carefully one at a time.

Cook under the boiling point until they hold their shape, then turn with a draining spoon and continue to cook. They must be light and keep their shape when handled.

Place on thin ungreased baking sheet and bake in a hot oven (400°F. Mark 6) until crisp and golden brown, first on one side, then on the other.
Note: If desired, the bagel can be sprinkled with salt and caraway seed before baking.

ONE BOWL CHEESY ONION BURGER BUNS
(No-Dissolve Method)

1½-1¾ pounds plain flour
3 tablespoons sugar
1 teaspoon salt
4 teaspoons dry yeast
1 ounce softened margarine
16 fluid ounces very hot tap water
6 ounces grated sharp Cheddar cheese
3 tablespoons finely chopped onion

In a large bowl thoroughly mix 8 ounces flour, sugar, salt, and undissolved dry yeast. Add softened margarine.

Gradually add very hot tap water to dry ingredients and beat 2 minutes at medium speed of electric mixer, scraping bowl occasionally. Add 4 ounces flour, or enough to make a thick batter. Beat at high speed 2 minutes, scraping bowl occasionally. Stir in cheese, onion, and enough additional flour to make a soft dough. Turn out onto lightly floured board; knead until smooth and elastic, about 8 to 10 minutes. Place in

greased bowl, turning to grease top. Cover; let rise in warm place, free from draught, until doubled in bulk, about 1 hour.

Punch dough down; turn out onto lightly floured board. Divide dough into 20 equal pieces. Form each piece into a smooth ball; place balls 2 inches apart on greased baking sheets. Cover; let rise in warm place, free from draught, until doubled in bulk, about 45 minutes.

Bake in hot oven (400°F. Mark 6) about 15 to 20 minutes, or until done. Remove from baking sheets and cool on wire racks. Makes 20 buns.

CROISSANTS

Croissant is the French term for crescent and refers to a particularly flaky roll of that shape.

2 teaspoons dry yeast
6 fluid ounces milk
8 ounces plain flour
½ teaspoon salt
4 ounces unsalted butter
1 egg yolk

Dissolve yeast in warm milk (110°F.). Sift together flour and salt, and add dissolved yeast. Knead until smooth and elastic.

Place in greased bowl and grease top of dough. Let rise in warm place (85°F.) until double in bulk.

Roll it out in a long strip. Dot with bits of butter and fold in thirds. Turn so an open edge is toward you. Pat and roll into another long strip. Fold in thirds. Wrap in waxed paper and chill well.

Roll out and fold ends to centre. Fold again, wrap and refrigerate.

Remove and repeat the process a fourth time. The last time, roll the dough out a little thinner but do not fold. Cut into triangles.

Brush one tip of each with beaten egg yolk mixed with a little water and roll from wide end to tip, pressing to seal.

Shape into half moons. Place on well buttered baking sheets. Cover with greaseproof paper and let rise until double in bulk.

Brush tops with beaten egg yolk. Bake in hot oven (425°F. Mark 7) 20 to 25 minutes. Serve hot. Makes 18 rolls.

BRAN REFRIGERATOR ROLLS

8 ounces fat
6 ounces sugar
4 ounces whole bran
1 teaspoon salt
8 fluid ounces boiling water
1 ounce baker's or 4 teaspoons dry yeast
8 fluid ounces water (lukewarm for yeast or warm for dry yeast)
2 well beaten eggs
1 pound 10 ounces plain flour

Measure fat, sugar, bran, and salt into large mixing bowl. Add boiling water, stirring until fat is melted. Let stand until lukewarm.

Soften yeast in lukewarm water; stir into bran mixture together with eggs. Add half of the flour and beat until smooth; add remaining flour and beat well. Cover bowl tightly and place in refrigerator overnight or until ready to use.

Shape balls of dough to fill greased deep bun tins about half full. Let rise in warm place about 2 hours or until doubled in bulk. Bake in hot oven (425°F. Mark 7) about 15 minutes. Makes 40 rolls, about 2½ inches in diameter.

ONE BOWL HARD ROLLS
(No-Dissolve Method)

1 pound to 1 pound 6 ounces plain flour
2 tablespoons sugar
2 teaspoons salt
2 teaspoons dry yeast
1½ ounces softened margarine
12 fluid ounces very hot tap water
1 egg white (at room temperature)
maize flour
4 fluid ounces water
1 teaspoon cornflour

In a large bowl thoroughly mix 5 ounces flour, sugar, salt, and undissolved dry yeast. Add softened margarine. Gradually add very hot tap water to dry ingredients and beat 2 minutes at medium speed of electric mixer, scraping bowl occasionally. Add egg white and 4 ounces flour, or enough to make a thick batter. Beat at high speed 2 minutes, scraping bowl occasionally. Stir in enough additional flour to make a soft dough. Turn out onto lightly floured board; knead until smooth and elastic, about 8 to 10 minutes. Place in greased bowl, turning to grease top. Cover; let rise in warm place, free from draught, until doubled in bulk, about 45 minutes.

Punch dough down; turn out onto lightly floured board. Cover; let rest 10 minutes. Divide in half. Form each half into a 9-inch roll. Cut into nine 1-inch pieces. Form into smooth balls. Place about 3 inches apart on greased baking sheets sprinkled with maize flour. Cover; let rise in warm place, free from draught, until doubled in bulk, about 45 minutes.

Slowly blend remaining 4 fluid ounces water into cornflour. Bring mixture to the boil. Cool slightly. When ready to bake, brush each roll with cornflour glaze. Slit tops with a sharp knife criss-cross fashion. If desired, sprinkle with sesame or poppy seeds.

Bake in a very hot oven (450°F. Mark 8) about 15 minutes, or until done. Remove from baking sheets and cool on wire racks. Makes 1½ dozen rolls.

SPEEDY PAN ROLLS

8 fluid ounces lukewarm water
5 tablespoons melted fat
1 tablespoon sugar
1½ teaspoons salt
1 ounce baker's or 4 teaspoons dry
    yeast
1 egg
14 ounces plain flour

Combine water, fat, sugar, and salt. Add yeast and mix well.

Blend in egg and add flour. Mix until dough is well blended and soft.

Roll out on well floured board and fit into greased tin (12×8 inches). Cut dough into rectangles (1×4 inches) with knife that has been dipped in melted butter.

Let rise in warm place (80° to 85°F.) until double in bulk, about 30 minutes.

Bake in hot oven (400°F. Mark 6) 20 minutes. Makes 2 dozen rolls.

BAPS
(From Scotland)

2 teaspoons dry yeast
4 fluid ounces warm water
1 pound plain flour
1 teaspoon sugar
1 teaspoon salt
2 ounces lard
4 fluid ounces undiluted evaporated
    milk

Soften yeast in warm water. Mix and sift dry ingredients; add lard, mixing well with pastry blender or palette knife.

Add yeast mixture and evaporated milk. Mix well and knead 2 minutes; put in greased bowl. Cover, let rise until double in bulk.

Knead lightly; shape into ovals about 3×2 inches.

Brush with a little additional milk, let rise until double in bulk.

Bake in hot oven (400°F. Mark 6) 15 to 20 minutes. Makes 1 dozen.

FIG-BRAN BUNS

8 fluid ounces milk, scalded
3 ounces coarsely chopped dried
    figs
2 ounces whole bran
1 teaspoon salt
3 tablespoons brown sugar
1 tablespoon fat
1 ounce baker's yeast
8 ounces flour

Pour hot milk over figs, bran, salt, sugar, and fat in mixing bowl. Cool to lukewarm, then crumble in the yeast and beat in the flour.

Drop at once by spoonfuls into greased deep bun tins, filling them half full.

Let rise in warm place until the buns fill the pans.

Bake in hot oven (400°F. Mark 6) about 20 minutes. Makes 12 good sized buns or 16 to 18 small ones.

BUTTERFLAKE ROLLS
(Master Recipe)

1 ounce baker's yeast
2 ounces sugar
12 fluid ounces milk (room tempera-
    ture)
2½ tablespoons cider or distilled
    white vinegar
2 ounces butter
2 ounces lard
1 pound 6 ounces plain flour
½ teaspoon bicarbonate of soda
1 teaspoon salt

Crumble yeast in bowl and add sugar. To the milk, slowly add vinegar stirring rapidly. Pour over yeast and sugar, then let stand 10 minutes.

Melt butter and lard; then cool. Sift together flour, bicarbonate of soda and salt.

Add the melted fat to yeast mixture. Mix well, then add sifted dry ingredients, beating until a smooth dough is formed.

Transfer dough to a well greased bowl and brush top with butter. Place bowl in warm place until dough is about tripled in bulk.

Turn out of bowl, without stirring, onto well floured board. Sprinkle top of dough lightly with flour, then roll out to desired thickness. Make into fancy shapes as desired.

Set rolls in warm place 10 to 15 minutes or until light. Bake in a hot oven (400°F. Mark 6) 15 to 20 minutes, depending upon shape and size of rolls. Remove from tin at once to cake rack, unless to be served hot.

Crisscross Rolls: Roll Butterflake dough ¼ inch thick. Brush with melted butter. Cut into long strips 1½ inches wide.

Cut strips into 2-inch lengths, then place 3 into each well greased deep bun tin in crisscross fashion, having 3rd strip in position of first. Brush tops with butter, then let rise. Bake according to directions.

Nut Rolls: Roll Butterflake Roll dough ⅛ inch thick. Brush with melted butter. Sprinkle with brown sugar and chopped nuts. Cut strips ¾ inch wide and 4 long. Roll, then place end up in greased deep bun tin. Let rise and bake according to directions.

Poppy Seed Twists: Roll Butterflake Roll dough about ⅛ inch thick. Cut into strips ¾ inch wide and 3 inches long. Place one on top of another in braid fashion. Brush tops with melted butter, then sprinkle with poppy seeds. Let rise and bake according to directions.

Butterflake Rolls

Crisscross Rolls

Poppy Seed Twists

Nut Rolls

TWISTED PLAIN OR SWEET ROLLS

Roll plain Roll Dough or Sweet Dough into long oblong shape a little less than ¾ inch thick. Spread with very soft or melted butter.

Fold ½ of dough over the other half. Trim edges to square corners.

Cut into strips ½ inch wide and 6 inches long. Use strips to make any of the following rolls:

Clothespeg Cruller Rolls: Wrap strip around greased wooden peg so edges barely touch. After baking, twist peg and pull out.

Crooked Mile Rolls: Twist and tie knot in one end of strip. Then pull longer end through centre of knot; bring it around and up through centre opening again.

Figure 8's: Hold one end of strip firmly in one hand. Twist the other end, stretching it slightly until the 2 ends when brought together will naturally form a figure 8. Seal ends well.

Twists: Make the same way as Figure 8's, but give each roll an additional twist just before placing it on baking sheet.

Sweet Dough Recipes

SWEET DOUGHS

A sweet dough is a basic yeast-flour-liquid mixture containing more sugar, shortening, and eggs than the dough for non-sweet (plain) breads and rolls. It may be a kneaded dough such as Basic Sweet Dough (Straight-Dough Method), or a stiff batter such as Rich Sweet Dough. Some breads that are considered sweet breads, such as Danish Pastry, are made from a plain dough; the sweetness comes from the filling they contain.

Many of the recipes that follow for sweet breads and rolls, coffee cakes, and tea rings call for all or part of a basic sweet dough; either the basic sweet dough or the rich sweet dough may be used.

BASIC SWEET DOUGH
(Straight-Dough Method)

An easy-to-handle kneaded dough for sweet rolls and coffee cake.
- 4 fluid ounces milk
- 4 ounces sugar
- 1 teaspoon salt
- 2 ounces fat
- 4 fluid ounces warm (not hot) water
- 1 ounce baker's or 4 teaspoons dry yeast
- 2 eggs, beaten
- 1¼ pounds plain flour

Scald milk. Stir in sugar, salt, and fat. Cool to lukewarm.

Measure into bowl 4 fluid ounces warm water (cool to lukewarm for baker's yeast). Sprinkle or crumble in yeast. Stir until dissolved. Stir in lukewarm milk mixture.

Add beaten eggs and 12 ounces flour. Beat until smooth. Stir in remaining flour.

Turn dough out on lightly floured board. Knead until smooth and elastic. Place in greased bowl; brush top with soft fat. Cover. Let rise in warm place, free from draught, until doubled in bulk, about 1 hour.

Punch down and turn out on lightly floured board. Proceed according to directions for shapes selected.

For Faster Sweet Dough (Action-Quick Dough): Use 1½ ounces baker's or 6 teaspoons dry yeast; bowl rise about 45 minutes.

Note: For ½ recipe use ½ of each ingredient.

For double the recipe use double the amount of each ingredient; bowl rise about 1 hour.

RICH SWEET DOUGH

A no-knead refrigerator dough that makes a rich, tender product.
- 6 fluid ounces milk
- 4 ounces sugar
- 1½ teaspoons salt
- 4 ounces butter or margarine
- 4 fluid ounces warm water (105°-115°F.)
- 1 ounce baker's or 4 teaspoons dry yeast
- 1 egg
- 1 pound plain flour

Scald milk; stir in sugar, salt, and butter or margarine. Cool to lukewarm.

Measure warm water into large warm bowl. Sprinkle or crumble in yeast; stir until dissolved. Stir in lukewarm milk mixture, egg, and half the flour; beat until smooth. Stir in remaining flour to make a stiff batter.

Cover tightly with greaseproof paper or aluminium foil. Refrigerate dough at least 2 hours. Dough may be kept in refrigerator 3 days. To use, cut off amount needed and shape as desired.

FROSTED SNAILS

- 1 recipe Sweet Dough
- Glacé icing
- Chopped nuts

When Sweet Dough is light, punch down. Let rest 10 minutes.

Roll into long rolls a scant ½ inch thick. Cut into pieces 9 inches long.

Coil each piece loosely to form snail, tucking end of strip under roll. Let rise until doubled, about 45 minutes.

Bake in moderate oven (350°F. Mark 4) 20 minutes.

When slightly cool, ice with glacé icing and sprinkle with chopped nuts. Makes about 3 dozen snails.

JACK HORNER ROLLS

Use 1 recipe for Sweet Dough and when it is light punch down and divide into portions for individual rolls.

Round up each portion to a smooth ball. Cover and let rest 10 minutes.

Flatten each ball to ¼ inch. Mix together 4 ounces sugar and ½ teaspoon cinnamon. Sprinkle each with ½ teaspoon of sugar and cinnamon mixture.

Place a stoned cooked prune in centre of each portion. Bring edges together, seal, and place rolls smooth side up on greased baking sheet.

Cover and let rise until doubled in bulk. Bake in moderate oven (375°F. Mark 5) 20 to 25 minutes.

When cooled, ice with glacé icing. Makes about 3½ dozen rolls.

SWEDISH TEA RING

Use ½ recipe for Sweet Dough and when it is light roll into a rectangular sheet about ½ inch thick.

Brush with melted butter and cinnamon. Nuts or raisins may be added.

Roll Swiss-roll fashion and shape into a ring on a greased baking sheet. Cut with scissors at 1-inch intervals, almost through the ring. Turn each slice slightly on its side.

Cover and let rise until doubled.

Bake in moderate oven (375°F. Mark 5) 25 to 30 minutes.

Ice while warm with glacé icing. Sprinkle thickly with chopped nuts. Makes 1 tea ring.

Swedish Tea Ring

CINNAMON BUN LOAF

Prepare as for Cinnamon Buns, cutting each long roll into 18 equal pieces (about ½-inch wide).

Place pieces ½-inch side down in greased bread tin 9×5×3 inches. Brush top generously with melted margarine or butter. If desired, top with additional sugar and cinnamon mixture.

Let rise as directed for Cinnamon Buns.

Bake in moderate oven (350°F. Mark 4) about 40 minutes. Makes 2 loaves.

Cinnamon Bun Loaf

Jack Horner Rolls

ROSEBUDS

1 recipe Sweet Dough
4 ounces raspberry, strawberry, or
    apricot jam
1 egg yolk
2 tablespoons milk

Divide Sweet Dough in half. Roll out each half into a square about 12 × 12 inches.

Spread jam evenly on each square. Roll up as for Swiss roll. Cut into 12 equal pieces (about 1 inch wide).

Place, cut side up, in greased deep bun tins 2¾ × 1¼ inches. With sharp knife or scissors cut crosses, about ½ inch deep, across tops of buns.

Cover. Let rise in warm place, free from draught, until doubled in bulk. (Straight-Dough Method about 1 hour; Action-Quick Dough about 30 minutes.)

Beat egg yolk and milk together. Brush tops of buns with egg mixture.

Bake in moderate oven (350°F. Mark 4) about 30 minutes.

Ice tops with plain icing. Makes 24.

Rosebuds

RUM ROLLS

Add 3 ounces currants to ½ recipe for Sweet Dough. When dough is light, punch down and divide into small portions for individual rolls.

Shape each portion into a smooth round ball. Place on greased baking sheet. Cover and let rise until doubled in bulk.

Bake in moderate oven (375°F. Mark 5) 15 to 20 minutes. Ice at once with glacé icing to which has been added a few drops of rum flavouring. Makes about 2 dozen small rolls.

Rum Rolls

HOT CROSS BUNS

1 recipe Sweet Dough
1 teaspoon cinnamon
¼ teaspoon mixed spice
6 ounces currants

To recipe for Sweet Dough add remaining ingredients. When dough is light, punch down. Let rest 10 minutes.

Divide into pieces the size of a walnut. Shape each piece into ball.

Place ½ inch apart in greased tins or 1½ inches apart on greased baking sheets. Let rise until doubled (about 45 minutes).

Bake in moderate oven (350°F. Mark 4) 20 to 25 minutes.

Remove at once from tins and make cross of white icing on each roll. Makes about 3½ dozen rolls.

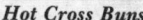

Hot Cross Buns

STOLLEN

Stollen is a German name for a rich yeast coffee cake, usually with raisins and almonds.

Use ½ recipe for Sweet Dough and when it is light add 3 ounces raisins and 3 ounces blanched chopped almonds and knead them in.

Divide dough in 2 equal portions and round them up. Cover and let rest 10 to 15 minutes.

Flatten out each ball of dough into an oval sheet. Brush ½ of each sheet with melted butter. Fold unbuttered half over buttered half.

Place on greased baking sheets. Let rise until doubled in bulk.

Bake in moderate oven (350° to 375°F. Mark 4-5) 25 to 30 minutes. Coat with glacé icing and sprinkle with chopped nuts. Makes 2 stollen.

Stollen

CINNAMON BUNS

1 recipe Sweet Dough
12 ounces sugar
2 teaspoons cinnamon
4 ounces raisins

Divide Sweet Dough in half. Roll out each half into an oblong about 14 × 9 inches. Brush lightly with melted margarine or butter.

Sprinkle each oblong with one-half mixture of sugar, cinnamon, and raisins. Roll up as for Swiss roll to make roll 9 inches long. Seal edges firmly.

Cut into 9 equal pieces. Place cut side up about 1 inch apart in greased 9-inch sandwich tin or square tin 8 × 8 × 2 inches. Cover. Let rise in warm place, free from draught, until double in bulk. (Straight-Dough Method about 1 hour; Action-Quick Dough about 30 minutes.) Bake in moderate oven (350°F. Mark 4) about 35 minutes. Ice top with plain icing. Makes 18.

Cinnamon Buns

KOLACKY

Kolacky (also spelled kolachy and kolachen) were originally Bohemian dessert breads but are now popular in other European countries and in the United States. They may be round buns topped with a fruit, cheese, or poppy-seed filling or filled square buns.

1 recipe Sweet Dough
2 tablespoons melted butter
Fruit filling
Icing sugar

When Sweet Dough is light, punch down. Let rest 10 minutes.

Divide into pieces the size of walnuts. Shape each piece into ball. Place 2 inches apart on greased baking sheets. Let rise 15 minutes.

With fingertip press down centre of each roll to make hollow. Brush with butter or margarine. Fill hollows with fruit filling. Let rise until doubled, about 30 minutes.

Bake in moderate oven (350°F. Mark 4) 20 minutes. Sprinkle with icing sugar. Makes about 4 dozen kolacky.

Fruit Filling For Kolacky:
8 ounces chopped, cooked prunes
    or apricots
4 tablespoons prune juice or apricot
    juice
4 ounces sugar
1 tablespoon lemon juice
½ teaspoon cinnamon
¼ teaspoon cloves

Combine all ingredients and mix well.

PALM LEAF ROLLS

1 recipe Sweet Dough
12 ounces sugar
2 teaspoons cinnamon
4 ounces raisins

Divide Sweet Dough in half. Roll out each half into a square about 12 × 12 inches. Brush lightly with melted margarine or butter.

Sprinkle each square with one-half mixture of sugar, cinnamon, and raisins. Roll up as for Swiss roll. Seal edges firmly.

Cut into 8 equal pieces (about 1¼ inches wide). Make two cuts through each piece, parallel to cut sides and extending to within ½ inch of other side. Turn each loaf on its side and spread the three leaves apart into fan shape. Place on greased baking sheets about 2 inches apart.

Cover. Let rise in warm place, free from draught, until doubled in bulk. (Straight-Dough Method about 1 hour; Action-Quick Dough about 30 minutes.)

Bake in moderate oven (350°F. Mark 4) about 35 minutes.

Ice tops with plain icing. Makes 16.

Palm Leaf Rolls

BOHEMIAN BRAID

Use ½ recipe for Sweet Dough and when it is light, divide into 9 portions.

Roll each portion into a long roll. Plait 4 rolls loosely and place on greased baking sheet. Then braid 3 portions and place on top of first braid. Twist last 2 portions together and place on top, tucking ends under.

Cover and let rise until doubled in bulk.

Bake in moderate oven (350° to 375°F. Mark 4-5) 40 to 45 minutes. Coat with glacé icing and sprinkle with chopped nuts. Makes 1 large braided loaf.

Bohemian Braid

BUTTERSCOTCH PECAN ROLLS

Into each deep bun tin put ½ teaspoon butter and 1 teaspoon brown sugar. Sprinkle with ½ teaspoon water. Arrange 3 or 4 pecan or walnut halves in each tin.

Use 1 recipe for Sweet Dough and when it is light punch down and let rest 10 minutes.

Roll dough out to rectangular sheet ½ inch thick and 9 inches wide. Brush lightly with melted butter and sprinkle generously with brown sugar.

Roll Swiss-roll fashion, sealing edges. Cut into 1-inch slices.

Place slices, cut side down, into prepared tins.

Cover and let rise until doubled in bulk.

Bake in moderate oven (375°F. Mark 5) 20 to 25 minutes.

Let rolls stand in tins 1 minute before turning them out. Makes about 3½ dozen rolls.

Butterscotch Pecan Rolls

HONEY ALMOND CAKE

1 recipe Sweet Dough
6 tablespoons flour
4 ounces sugar
½ teaspoon salt
16 fluid ounces milk
2 eggs, beaten
1 teaspoon vanilla
2 ounces sugar
6 ounces honey
1 ounce margarine or butter
2 tablespoons slivered, blanched
    almonds

While Sweet Dough is rising prepare Cream Filling:

Mix together in top of double saucepan flour, sugar, and salt. Gradually stir in milk. Cook over hot water, stirring constantly until thickened, about 15 minutes.

Stir slowly into beaten eggs. Return to top of double saucepan and cook over hot water for 3 minutes longer. Remove from heat. Stir in vanilla. Cool until thick enough to spread.

Divide Sweet Dough in half; form each half into smooth ball. Place in greased 8-inch sandwich tin. Cover. Let rise in warm place, free from draught, until doubled in bulk. (Straight-Dough Method about 1 hour; Action-Quick Dough about 30 minutes.)

Bring to boil in saucepan sugar, honey, and margarine or butter. Brush tops of cakes with half of honey syrup.

Sprinkle on each cake the almonds.

Bake in moderate oven (350°F. Mark 4) about 35 minutes.

Brush cakes while still hot with remaining syrup. Cool.

Slice each into 2 layers; fill with Cream Filling. Makes 2 cakes.

Honey Almond Cake

CINNAMON LOAF

Use ½ recipe for Sweet Dough and, when it is light, roll it into a rectangular sheet ½ inch thick and about 8 inches wide.

Brush with butter and spread with a mixture of 3 teaspoons cinnamon and 8 ounces sugar.

Roll Swiss-roll fashion and cut to make 2 loaves.

Place in greased bread tins, and let them rise.

Before baking, brush with milk, and sprinkle with sugar. Bake in hot oven (400°F. Mark 6) 30 to 35 minutes. Makes 2 loaves.

BABA AU RHUM

Baba is the French term for a yeast-raised cake often containing fruit or flavoured with fruit juices. It may be soaked with rum or a rum substitute before being served, and is then called baba au rhum.

½ ounce baker's yeast
4 fluid ounces scalded milk
8 ounces plain flour
4 ounces sugar
4 ounces butter
½ teaspoon salt
1 tablespoon grated lemon rind
3 eggs, well beaten

Dissolve yeast in milk, which has been cooled to lukewarm. Add 2 ounces flour and 1 tablespoon sugar. Beat until smooth.

Cover and let rise in warm place (80° to 85°F.) until doubled in bulk, about 1 hour.

Cream butter. Add remaining sugar gradually. Cream until light and fluffy. Add salt, lemon rind, and eggs and beat until smooth.

Stir in the remaining flour. Add the yeast mixture. Beat 15 minutes by hand or 5 minutes by electric mixer.

Pour in greased baba tin of 1½ pint capacity. Cover and let rise until doubled in bulk, about 1 hour.

Bake in moderate oven (350°F. Mark 4) 40 to 50 minutes.

Remove from oven. Prick top with sharp points of fork. Turn out of tin and place cake (inverted) in pie dish. Pour baba sauce over top and sides, then brush with apricot glaze.

Allow cake to stand until most of baba sauce is absorbed before serving. Makes one 9-inch cake.

Baba Sauce: Boil 8 ounces sugar and 8 fluid ounces strong clear tea 5 minutes. Cool. Add 2 teaspoons rum.

Apricot Glaze: Soak ¼ pound dried apricots overnight in just enough water to cover. Press through sieve. Measure equal parts pulp and sugar. Boil together 5 minutes, stirring constantly.

NO-KNEAD SWEET ROLLS

4 fluid ounces milk
1½ ounces fat
3 tablespoons sugar
1½ teaspoons salt
4 fluid ounces water
½ ounce baker's yeast
1 egg
12 ounces plain flour
Mixture of:
    2 tablespoons melted butter
    2 ounces sugar
    1 teaspoon cinnamon

Scald milk, and combine with fat, sugar, and salt. Cool to lukewarm with 4 fluid ounces water. Add yeast and mix well.

Blend in egg. Add flour gradually. Mix until dough is well blended and soft. Roll out dough on well floured board to form rectangle (18×12 inches).

Spread with mixture listed above. Prepared prune, apricot, or date-nut fillings may be used.

Roll as for Swiss roll and cut into 1-inch slices. Place slices, cut side down, in greased tin (12×8×2 inches) or greased deep bun tins. Let rise until light, about 1 hour. Bake in moderate oven (375°F. Mark 5) 25 to 30 minutes. Makes 18 medium-sized rolls.

ELECTION CAKE

This rich yeast cake, often called Hartford Election Cake after Hartford, Conn., where it originated in the 19th century, is sometimes made with various other crystallized fruits added to it.

½ ounce baker's yeast
4 fluid ounces lukewarm water
16 fluid ounces scalded milk
1 teaspoon salt
1½ pounds plain flour
12 ounces raisins, chopped
2 ounces sliced citron
5 ounces butter (at room temperature)
12 ounces brown sugar
1 teaspoon cinnamon
½ teaspoon nutmeg
3 large eggs or 4 medium eggs
Molasses or treacle

Soften yeast in lukewarm water. Cool milk to lukewarm and add salt and softened yeast.

Add 1½ ounces flour to chopped raisins and sliced citron. Mix well.

Add yeast mixture to remaining flour and beat with wooden spoon until well blended and "stringy". Set in warm place (80° to 90°F.) to rise until doubled in bulk.

Setting the pan of dough in water of 90° to 100°F. in temperature helps to give rapid rising, 45 to 60 minutes.

While dough is rising, cream butter, add sugar gradually and cream until fluffy. Add cinnamon and nutmeg.

Add eggs 1 at a time and mix thoroughly.

Add creamed mixture to dough and beat until no spots of white dough show. Add raisins and citron and mix. Let dough rise until doubled in bulk, 30 to 40 minutes.

Cut down dough and stir until smooth.

Turn into 3 1½-pint tins, well greased, and let rise until dough reaches tops of tins, 45 to 60 minutes.

Bake on lower shelf of moderate oven (350°F. Mark 4) 30 minutes; lower temperature to slow (325°F. Mark 3) and continue baking 30 to 35 minutes longer.

If tops brown too fast, cover after first 30 minutes with aluminium foil.

Glaze when done with molasses or treacle and return to oven for 5 minutes to set glaze. Serves 24.

BUTTER SCHNECKEN

Schnecken is the German word for snails; hence snail-shaped buns.

½ ounce baker's yeast
4 ounces sugar
6 ounces butter
4 fluid ounces milk, scalded
2 eggs
8 fluid ounces sour cream
1 pound 2 ounces plain flour
1 teaspoon salt

Crumble yeast into mixing bowl; add sugar and stir together until yeast liquefies. Let stand about 20 minutes. Meanwhile, melt butter in scalded milk. Beat eggs, add sour cream; blend well with yeast and sugar mixture. Add lukewarm milk, butter, flour, and salt all at once. Beat 8 to 10 minutes. Long beating improves the dough, which should be soft. Store in refrigerator.

The next day, let dough rise in warm place to double its original bulk, or more. Knead in 6 ounces more flour. Roll out into 2 sheets about ¼ inch thick.

Spread with mixture of 1 part pecans or walnuts to 2 parts raisins and sprinkle with mixture of ¼ teaspoon cinnamon to 2 ounces sugar. Roll lengthwise; cut like a Swiss roll into slices 1½ inches thick.

Place in buttered deep bun tins lined with mixture of 6 ounces brown sugar, 2 ounces melted butter, 2 tablespoons water, and whole pecans, using 1 tablespoon of this mixture in the bottom of each tin. Set schnecken in warm place to rise to double in bulk. Bake in hot oven (400°F. Mark 6) about 25 minutes; reduce temperature to 350°F. Mark 4, and bake 10 minutes longer.

Butter Schnecken

SOUR CREAM KOLACKY

½ ounce baker's yeast
3 tablespoons sugar
2 tablespoons lukewarm milk
3 ounces fat
5 egg yolks, well beaten
Grated rind of 1 lemon
8 fluid ounces thick sour cream
12 ounces plain flour
½ teaspoon salt
1 teaspoon bicarbonate of soda
Raisins or cherries
1 egg white, well beaten

Soften yeast and 1 tablespoon sugar in lukewarm milk. Cream fat and 2 tablespoons sugar. Add egg yolks, lemon rind, sour cream, and yeast mixture. Mix well.

Add flour sifted with salt and bicarbonate of soda and beat thoroughly. Drop from teaspoon on well-greased tins or fill greased deep bun tins half full.

Place a raisin or cherry on top of each cake. Brush with beaten egg white. Sprinkle with sugar and let rise in a warm place until light, about 2 hours.

Bake in moderate oven (375°F. Mark 5) 25 minutes. Makes about 36.

SAVARIN

A yeast-raised cake baked in a ring tin and then saturated with a syrup flavoured with rum or kirsch. The hollow centre is filled with cut-up fruit, custard, or whipped cream, or a combination of these. It is named after Jean Anthelme Brillat-Savarin, a French gastronome (1755-1826), the author of *The Physiology of Taste*, a classic work on cookery. His name has been given to several dishes.

½ ounce baker's or 2 teaspoons dry
    yeast
4 tablespoons warm water (105°-
    115°F.)
6 ounces plain flour
1 tablespoon sugar
½ teaspoon salt
2 large or 3 small eggs
4 tablespoons milk
5½ ounces butter, at room
    temperature
1 teaspoon grated lemon rind
Rum syrup (below)

Sprinkle or crumble yeast into warm water; stir until dissolved.

Combine flour, sugar, and salt in a large bowl. Stir in yeast and eggs which have been beaten slightly with the milk. Beat until the batter is smooth, about 100 strokes.

Add butter and lemon rind; beat until butter is blended into batter, about 50 strokes.

Spoon the batter into a 9-inch ring tin, filling it only half full. Cover with a cloth and let rise until the batter just fills the tin, about 1 hour.

Bake in hot oven (400°F. Mark 6) 30 to 35 minutes, or until browned.

Turn the cake out of the tin onto a serving plate. Spoon hot rum syrup over it until cake is saturated. If desired, keep warm and fill with whipped cream or a light custard just before serving. Makes 8 to 10 servings.

Rum Syrup: Combine 8 fluid ounces water, 8 ounces sugar, 2 slices lemon, 1 slice orange, 1-inch piece vanilla bean, a 2-inch stick cinnamon, and 1 clove; bring to boil, stirring until sugar is dissolved. Simmer 5 minutes; strain and add 4 fluid ounces light rum.

HOSKA

Hoska is a spectacular plaited yeast bread from old Czechoslovakia. It's light and delicately sweet. Fruit and chopped almonds throughout the tender bread provide delightful texture contrast. It is not iced, but is glazed and decorated before baking with whole almonds that toast to a beautiful brown.

8 fluid ounces milk
4 ounces fat
6 ounces sugar
½ teaspoon salt
4 tablespoons warm (not hot) water
1 ounce baker's or 4 teaspoons dry
    yeast
2 eggs, beaten
1 pound 6 ounces plain flour
1 ounce chopped citron
1½ ounces raisins
1½ ounces chopped almonds
1 egg
1 tablespoon water
1 ounce whole blanched almonds

Scald milk. Stir in fat, sugar, and salt. Cool to lukewarm.

Measure warm water into bowl (cool to lukewarm for baker's yeast). Sprinkle or crumble in yeast and stir until dissolved. Stir in lukewarm milk mixture.

Add 2 beaten eggs and 12 ounces flour. Beat until smooth.

Stir in citron, raisins, and almonds. Stir in remaining flour.

Turn out on lightly floured board. Knead until smooth and elastic. Place in greased bowl; brush with fat.

Cover. Let rise in warm place, free from draught, until doubled in bulk, about 1 hour and 15 minutes.

Punch down and turn out on lightly floured board. Divide in half. Divide one half into 3 equal pieces; roll each piece into a strip about 18 inches long. Place 3 strips on greased baking sheets. Form into braid. Brush top lightly with melted margarine or butter.

Divide ⅔ of remaining dough into 3

equal pieces. Form into a second braid about 18 inches long. Place on top of first braid. Brush top lightly with melted margarine or butter.

Form remaining dough into a third braid about 18 inches long. Place on top of second braid. If necessary, use cocktail sticks to hold braids in place.

Let rise in warm place, free from draught, until doubled in bulk, about 1 hour.

Brush with mixture of egg and water. Decorate with blanched almonds.

Bake in moderate oven (375°F. Mark 5) about 45 minutes.

Hoska

DANISH PASTRY

The flaky, flavourful pastry known to us as "Danish" actually originated in Vienna. From there it travelled to Denmark, and became so popular that we now associate it with its adopted country rather than with the country of origin. In Denmark it is still called "Vienna bread", but it's "Danish Pastry" to us.

1 ounce baker's yeast
2 tablespoons lukewarm water
6 fluid ounces milk
¾ teaspoon salt
3 tablespoons sugar
1 ounce butter
2 eggs
¼ teaspoon nutmeg
¼ teaspoon lemon essence
¼ teaspoon almond essence
About 14 ounces plain flour
4 ounces cold unsalted butter for rolling

Dissolve yeast in lukewarm water and set aside. Scald milk with salt, sugar, and butter. Cool to lukewarm and add to yeast mixture.

Beat eggs; add nutmeg and flavourings and stir mixture into the milk-yeast combination. Work in 4 ounces flour. Beat until smooth, then add enough extra flour to make a very soft dough.

Turn out onto floured board and knead until smooth. Round up, place in greased bowl, and let rise until light, about 1 hour.

Punch down, then roll out to a rectangle about 7 by 10 inches. Place ⅓ of unsalted butter, cut into tiny pieces, over ⅔ of the rectangle. Fold unbuttered third of dough towards you over the buttered part and fold last third over the first 2 to give 3 thicknesses. Press edges together and chill in refrigerator for ½ hour.

Repeat rolling, buttering, and chilling process 2 times, making 3 rollings in all.

Now divide dough into 5 pieces and while working with 1 piece, keep remainder in refrigerator.

Dough may seem hard to roll when removed from refrigerator, but the chilling produces flakiness in the finished product. Shape as indicated below.

After shaping rolls, place on ungreased baking sheets, preferably those with lips to prevent drippings of melted butter spilling on oven surface.

Cover with cloth and allow to rise until double in bulk.

Bake in moderate oven (375°F. Mark 5) 15 to 20 minutes. When rolls are cool, brush lightly with light corn syrup or golden syrup. Makes about 2 dozen.

SHAPING DANISH PASTRY

Cinnamon Fans: Combine 2 tablespoons sugar, 1 teaspoon cinnamon, and 1½ ounces finely chopped nuts.

Roll pastry into a rectangle 9 by 12 inches and sprinkle mixture over it.

Roll as for Swiss roll. Cut into 1½ inch slices. Make 2 deep gashes in each slice and separate the gashed sections and open like a fan.

Snails: Make almond filling by grinding ¼ pound unblanched almonds, and mixing with 8 ounces sugar. Gradually add 1 egg blended with 2 teaspoons cream. Mix well and spread half of it over the 9-inch half of pastry (again rolled to rectangle 9 by 12 inches).

Cut into 9 1-inch strips. Roll filled halves toward centre, turn over and spread on remaining filling. Roll this filled strip to centre. Press 2 rolls together. Turn on flat side and press down firmly with palm of hand. (Use jam as a filling if you prefer.)

Raspberry Stars: Roll dough into square, 12 by 12 inches. Cut into 3-inch squares. Moisten centre of each square with a drop of milk.

Cut each corner 1 inch toward centre. Turn every other point toward centre, pressing down firmly.

Place teaspoon of thick raspberry jam in centre of each star.

Almond Butterflies: Prepare same amount of almond filling as used for snails.

Roll well chilled dough into 10 by 12 inch rectangle. Brush with melted butter, then spread on almond filling.

Roll like Swiss roll. Cut into 1½ inch slices. Make a deep crease with handle of knife through centre of each piece parallel with cut side.

KUGELHUPF OR GUGELHUPF

Kugelhupf is a rich cake-like bread made from batter instead of a dough. In Vienna, where this cake-like bread was perhaps most famous, it is frequently served for dessert or as a special-occasion refreshment.

4 fluid ounces milk
4 ounces sugar
½ teaspoon salt
2 ounces margarine or butter
4 tablespoons warm (not hot) water
½ ounce baker's or 2 teaspoons dry yeast
2 eggs, beaten
10 ounces flour
14 to 16 whole blanched almonds
3 ounces seedless raisins
½ teaspoon grated lemon rind

Scald milk. Stir in sugar, salt, and margarine or butter. Cool to lukewarm. Measure warm water into bowl (cool to lukewarm for baker's yeast). Sprinkle or crumble in yeast and stir until dissolved. Stir in lukewarm milk mixture.

Add beaten eggs and flour. Beat vigorously, about 5 minutes.

Cover. Let rise in warm place, free from draught, until doubled in bulk, about 1 hour and 30 minutes.

Sprinkle fine breadcrumbs over sides and bottom of well greased 2½-pint tin. Arrange almonds on bottom.

Stir batter down. Beat thoroughly. Stir in raisins and grated lemon rind. Turn into prepared tin.

Let rise in warm place, free from draught, until doubled in bulk, about 1 hour.

Bake in moderate oven (350°F. Mark 4) about 50 minutes. Makes 1 cake.

VIENNESE COFFEE RING

1 ounce baker's or 4 teaspoons dry yeast
4 tablespoons lukewarm water for baker's or warm for dry yeast
8 fluid ounces milk
4 ounces sugar
1 teaspoon salt
2 ounces fat
About 13 ounces plain flour
1 egg, beaten
Topping:
5 ounces sugar
¼ teaspoon cinnamon
1½ ounces chopped nuts

Soften yeast in lukewarm water. Scald milk. Add sugar, salt, and fat. Cool to lukewarm.

Add 4 ounces flour and beat well. Add softened yeast and egg. Beat thoroughly.

Add remaining flour to make a stiff batter. Beat 3 minutes.

Pour into greased spring form tin. Mix sugar, cinnamon, and nuts for topping and sprinkle over batter. Let rise until doubled.

Bake in moderate oven (375°F. Mark 5) 35 to 40 minutes. Makes 1 coffee ring.

Viennese Coffee Ring

DATE BRAIDED CAKE

1 recipe Sweet Dough
6 ounces chopped, stoned dates
1½ ounces brown sugar
5 fluid ounces water
2 ounces chopped nuts
1 tablespoon lemon juice
1 egg yolk
2 tablespoons milk
1 ounce margarine or butter
2 tablespoons sugar
1 ounce flour
½ teaspoon cinnamon

While Sweet Dough is rising prepare Date Filling:

Combine in saucepan the dates, brown sugar, water, chopped nuts, and lemon juice. Bring to the boil over medium heat, stirring constantly, and continue boiling until mixture is thick enough to spread.

Divide Sweet Dough in half. Roll out each half into an oblong about 16×8 inches.

Spread half the Date Filling down centre third of each oblong. Cut 15 slits in dough along each side of filling, making strips about 1 inch wide.

Fold strips at an angle across filling, alternating from side to side. Place on greased baking sheet. If desired, form into a ring. Place one end in the other and seal together firmly.

Cover. Let rise in warm place, free from draught, until doubled in bulk. (Straight-Dough Method about 1 hour, Action-Quick Dough about 30 minutes.)

Combine and brush cakes with egg yolk and milk.

Sprinkle with mixture of margarine or butter, sugar, flour, and cinnamon.

Bake in moderate oven (350°F. Mark 4) about 35 minutes. Makes 2 cakes.

Date Braided Cake

BEATEN BATTER
(Master Recipe)

½ ounce baker's yeast
4 tablespoons lukewarm water
8 fluid ounces milk
2 ounces sugar
1 teaspoon salt
4 ounces fat
About 13 ounces plain flour
2 eggs
½ teaspoon vanilla, optional

Soften yeast in lukewarm water. Scald milk and add sugar, salt, and fat. Cool to lukewarm. Add 4 ounces flour and beat well.

Add softened yeast, eggs, and vanilla. Beat well.

Add remaining flour to make a thick batter. Beat thoroughly until smooth.

Cover and let rise until doubled, about 1 hour.

Use with different toppings to make coffee cakes and puff rolls. Makes 2 coffee cakes 8×8 inches or 2 9-inch cakes, or about 2½ dozen 2-inch puffs.

CRUMBLE COFFEE CAKE

½ recipe Beaten Batter
3 tablespoons milk
Crumble Topping

When beaten batter is light, stir down. Spread evenly in greased tin (8×8 inches) or 9-inch sandwich tin.

Brush with milk and sprinkle with crumble topping.

Let rise until doubled, about 45 minutes.

Bake in moderate oven (375°F. Mark 5) 30 minutes. Makes 1 coffee cake.

Crumble Topping:
2 ounces plain flour
1 ounce dry breadcrumbs
2 tablespoons sugar
½ teaspoon cinnamon
1 ounce butter

Mix flour, breadcrumbs, sugar, and cinnamon. Cut in or rub in butter until crumbly.

CRANBERRY SWIRL COFFEE CAKE

½ recipe Beaten Batter
4 ounces sweetened cranberry sauce
2 ounces sugar
¼ teaspoon cinnamon

When beaten batter is light, stir down. Spread evenly in greased 9-inch sandwich tin.

With a floured spoon make grooves in swirl design on top of batter. Fill grooves with cranberry sauce.

Mix sugar and cinnamon. Sprinkle evenly over top. Let rise until doubled, about 45 minutes.

Bake in moderate oven (375°F. Mark 5) 30 minutes. Makes 1 coffee cake.

TEA PUFFS

½ recipe Beaten Batter
1 ounce sliced almonds
2 ounces sugar
½ teaspoon cinnamon

When beaten batter is light, stir down. Drop by spoonfuls into greased deep bun tins.

Mix almonds, sugar, and cinnamon. Sprinkle over puffs.

Let rise until doubled, about 45 minutes.

Bake in moderate oven (375°F. Mark 5) 25 minutes. Makes about 16 2-inch puffs.

APPLE COFFEE CAKE

½ recipe Beaten Batter
3 to 4 medium apples
2 tablespoons melted butter
2 ounces sugar
1 teaspoon cinnamon

When beaten batter is light, stir down. Spread evenly in greased 9-inch sandwich tin.

Peel and slice apples. Arrange apple slices on top of batter, overlapping them in 2 circles.

Brush with melted butter. Mix sugar and cinnamon and sprinkle over apples.

Let rise until doubled, about 45 minutes.

Bake in moderate oven (375°F. Mark 5) 30 minutes. Makes 1 coffee cake.

SUGARPLUM LOAF

6 fluid ounces scalded milk
4 ounces fat
4 ounces sugar
2 eggs
½ ounce baker's yeast
2 tablespoons lukewarm water
1¼ pounds plain flour
1 teaspoon salt
3 ounces seedless raisins
2 ounces chopped walnuts
2 ounces chopped citron
4 ounces chopped candied cherries

Cool scalded milk to lukewarm. Cream together fat and sugar. Beat eggs and add.

Dissolve yeast in lukewarm water. Add with milk to creamed mixture. Add 4 ounces flour and mix well.

Cover and let rise in warm place until doubled in bulk.

Add salt, raisins, chopped nuts, citron, and cherries. Gradually add remaining flour and knead on lightly floured board until thoroughly mixed.

Place in greased round tin 8 inches in diameter and 3 inches high. Cover and let rise in warm place until doubled in bulk.

Bake in moderate oven (350°F. Mark 4) 1 hour and 15 minutes.

Remove from tin and cool on wire rack. If desired, spread with glacé icing. Makes 1 loaf.

Cinnamon Rolls

CINNAMON ROLLS

Use ½ recipe for Sweet Dough and when it is light roll out to long narrow sheet ¼ inch thick. Brush with 2 ounces melted butter.

Mix 8 ounces sugar and 1½ teaspoons cinnamon, and sprinkle over dough. If desired, 3 ounces raisins may be added.

Roll up Swiss-roll fashion and seal edge. Cut into 1-inch slices and place cut side down into well greased deep bun tins, ring mould, or deep cake tin.

Brush tops with milk, and sprinkle with cinnamon and sugar mixture.

Let rise until doubled in bulk. Bake in moderate oven (375°F. Mark 5) 25 minutes. Makes 3½ dozen rolls.

JULE KAGA

Jule Kaga is a Norwegian fruited sweet bread flavoured with cardamom, a favourite spice in Scandinavian countries.

- 8 fluid ounces milk
- 4 ounces sugar
- 1 teaspoon salt
- 4 ounces fat
- 3 tablespoons warm (not hot) water
- 1 ounce baker's or 4 teaspoons dry yeast
- 1 pound 2 ounces plain flour
- 1½ teaspoons ground cardamom
- 3 ounces raisins
- 1 ounce chopped citron
- 2 ounces chopped glacé cherries
- 1 ounce chopped almonds

Scald milk. Stir in sugar, salt, and fat. Cool to lukewarm.

Measure warm water into bowl (cool to lukewarm for baker's yeast). Sprinkle or crumble in yeast and stir until dissolved. Stir in lukewarm milk mixture.

Add 8 ounces flour. Beat thoroughly. Cover. Let rise in warm place, free from draught, until doubled in bulk, about 30 minutes. Stir down.

Stir in cardamom, raisins, citron, cherries, and almonds. Stir in remaining flour.

Turn out on lightly floured board. Knead until smooth and elastic. Place in greased bowl; brush with fat.

Cover. Let rise in warm place, free from draught, until doubled in bulk, about 55 minutes.

Punch down. Form into round ball and place on large greased baking sheet.

Cover. Let rise in warm place, free from draught, until doubled in bulk, about 1 hour.

Bake in hot oven (400°F. Mark 6) for 10 minutes; reduce to moderate heat (350°F. Mark 4) and continue baking for 40 minutes.

Cool. Ice with plain icing, decorate with nuts and candied fruit. Makes 1 round loaf.

BUTTER HORNS

- ½ ounce baker's or 2 teaspoons dry yeast
- 2 fluid ounces warm water for dry yeast or lukewarm for baker's yeast
- 4 fluid ounces scalded milk
- 2 ounces sugar
- ½ teaspoon salt
- 1 beaten egg
- 2 ounces soft butter
- About 11 ounces plain flour

Soften yeast in warm water about 5 minutes. Pour scalded milk over sugar and salt. Cool to lukewarm.

Add softened yeast, beaten egg, and soft butter. Blend well, then stir in 4 ounces flour, or enough to make soft batter.

Beat well, then add enough extra flour to make soft, but kneadable dough. Knead until smooth and elastic on lightly floured board.

Place in greased bowl. Grease surface lightly. Cover and set in warm place until doubled in bulk, about 1 hour.

Divide dough in half. Roll each half on lightly floured board into a circular sheet about ¼ inch thick. Cut into pie-shaped wedges, 12 to a circle for tiny rolls, or 8 to a circle for larger ones.

Spread with a little melted butter. Roll each wedge from wide end, pressing tip of dough against roll to keep it from unrolling.

Place on greased baking sheets 1 inch apart. Cover with cloth and let rise again until light, about ½ hour.

Bake in hot oven (425°F. Mark 7) 12 to 15 minutes. Makes 2 dozen.

HOLLAND CAKE

- 4 ounces butter
- 8 ounces sugar
- 8 fluid ounces strong black coffee
- 2 eggs, well beaten
- 4 tablespoons cream
- ½ ounce baker's yeast
- 2 tablespoons lukewarm water
- About 1 pound 2 ounces plain flour
- 6 ounces seeded raisins
- 2 tablespoons whole aniseed

Cream butter and sugar together until light and fluffy. Add cold coffee and the eggs and cream.

Soften yeast in lukewarm water and add to first mixture. Add flour to make soft dough. Mix well, cover and let rise until doubled in bulk, about 1½ hours.

Punch down and knead in raisins and aniseed, continuing kneading until dough is smooth and satiny. Cover and let rise until doubled in bulk, about 1 hour.

Bake in moderate oven (350°F. Mark 4) until done, about 50 minutes. When cold, ice with glacé icing. Makes one 9×15-inch loaf.

CHERRY-GO-ROUND
(No-Dissolve Method)

- 1-1¼ pounds plain flour
- 4 ounces sugar
- 1 teaspoon salt
- 2 teaspoons dry yeast
- 8 fluid ounces milk
- 4 tablespoons water
- 4 ounces margarine
- 1 egg (at room temperature)
- 2 ounces chopped pecans or walnuts
- 3 ounces light brown sugar
- 1 can (1 pound) stoned red sour cherries, well drained

In a large bowl thoroughly mix 6 ounces flour, sugar, salt, and undissolved active dry yeast.

Combine milk, water, and margarine in a saucepan. Heat over low heat until liquids are warm. (Margarine does not need to melt.) Gradually add to dry ingredients and beat 2 minutes at medium speed of electric mixer, scraping bowl occasionally. Add egg and 3 ounces flour, or enough to make a thick batter. Beat at high speed 2 minutes, scraping the bowl occasionally. Stir in enough additional flour to make a stiff batter. Cover bowl tightly with aluminium foil. Refrigerate dough at least 2 hours. (Dough may be kept in refrigerator 3 days.)

When ready to shape dough, combine 2 ounces flour, pecans, and brown sugar.

Turn dough out onto lightly floured board and divide in half. Roll ½ of the dough to a 14×7-inch rectangle. Spread with half the cherries. Sprinkle with ½ the brown sugar mixture. Roll up from long side as for Swiss roll. Seal edges. Place sealed edge down in circle on greased baking sheet. Seal ends together firmly. Cut slits ⅔ through ring at 1-inch intervals; turn each section on its side. Repeat with remaining dough, cherries, and brown sugar mixture. Cover; let rise in warm place, free from draught, until doubled in bulk, about 1 hour.

Bake in a moderate oven (375°F. Mark 5) about 20 to 25 minutes, or until done. Remove from baking sheets and cool on wire racks. Ice while warm with glacé icing. Makes 2 coffeecakes.

HAMANTASCHEN

Hamantaschen is a Jewish term for triangular yeast-raised cakes filled with a poppyseed and honey filling or other fillings and eaten at Purim, a Jewish holiday. The word is derived from the Bible character Haman, and possibly from German taschen (pockets), probably with reference to the manner in which the cakes are filled. Their shape recalls the triangular hat Haman is supposed to have worn.

Hamantaschen may be made from the basic recipes for Sweet Dough. Roll small balls of dough to ¼-inch thickness into rounds 4 to 6 inches in diameter. On each round place a mound of filling (below) and bring the edges together to form a triangle, pinching the edges together from the top down to corners.

Let the filled rolls rise in warm place until double in bulk. Brush tops with diluted egg yolk, evaporated milk, or melted fat.

Bake in moderate oven (375°F. Mark 5) until lightly browned, 20 to 25 minutes for medium-sized cakes.
Note: Similar shaped cakes may be made from a rolled sugar biscuit dough using the traditional poppyseed and honey filling.

POPPYSEED AND HONEY FILLING FOR HAMANTASCHEN

8 ounces poppyseeds
8 fluid ounces milk or water
6 ounces honey
2 ounces sugar
⅛ teaspoon salt
2 eggs, if desired

If the poppyseeds are large they should be scalded, drained well, and put through the finest blade of the mixer or pounded.

Combine the poppyseeds with milk or water, honey, sugar, and salt in a saucepan. Cook over moderate heat until thick, stirring to prevent scorching.

Let cool, then beat in the eggs. If the addition of eggs thins out the filling too much, place the mixture over moderate heat and cook 1 or 2 minutes, stirring constantly.
Variations: Chopped almonds or other nuts (1 ounce) and 1½ ounces seedless raisins or currants may be added. The filling may be flavoured with 1 tablespoon lemon juice and ½ teaspoon grated lemon rind.

SOUR CREAM FAN TAN ROLLS

2 teaspoons dry yeast
4 tablespoons warm water
6 fluid ounces scalded, cooled sour cream
⅛ teaspoon bicarbonate of soda
1 teaspoon salt
2 tablespoons sugar
About 8 ounces plain flour

Soften yeast in warm water about 5 minutes. Add cooled sour cream. Stir in bicarbonate of soda, salt, and sugar. Then gradually work in flour to make soft dough.

Round dough up and place in greased bowl. Brush top with melted fat. Cover and let rise in warm place until doubled in bulk, 1 to 1½ hours.

Turn out on lightly floured board and knead lightly 1 minute. Roll dough into rectangular sheet about ⅛ inch thick. Brush with melted butter or margarine.

Cut into strips 1½ inches wide. Pile in stacks of 6 strips. Cut in pieces 1½ inches long and place in greased deep bun tins, cut edges up.

Let rise again in warm place until doubled in size.

Bake in hot oven (425°F. Mark 7) 15 minutes or until nicely browned. Makes 1 dozen.

ORANGE ROLLS

½ ounce baker's or 2 teaspoons dry yeast
4 tablespoons water (lukewarm for baker's yeast, warm for dry yeast)
4 fluid ounces scalded milk
2 ounces fat
2 ounces sugar
1 teaspoon salt
4 fluid ounces orange juice
1 teaspoon grated orange rind
1 beaten egg
About 1 pound flour

Soften yeast in water. Pour milk over fat, sugar, and salt.

When lukewarm add orange juice, grated rind, egg, yeast, and 8 ounces flour. Beat until smooth.

Add enough flour to make dough which can be handled on board. Knead until light and elastic, about 3 minutes.

Form into ball and place in warm bowl. Grease top lightly. Cover and keep in warm place (80° to 85°F.) until doubled in bulk.

Punch down, form into rolls, and place on well greased tin. Let rise until very light and doubled in bulk.

Bake in hot oven (400°F. Mark 6) 15 to 25 minutes, depending on size. Makes about 30 rolls.
Orange Refrigerator Rolls: Follow above recipe. After placing dough in bowl, grease top. Cover and place in refrigerator.

Two hours before baking, put required amount of dough in a warm, greased bowl. Let rise in warm place about 1½ hours.

Knead and shape into rolls. Bake as directed.

CORNISH SPLITS

½ ounce baker's yeast
2 ounces sugar
1 pound plain flour

¼ teaspoon salt
3 ounces fat
6 fluid ounces lukewarm milk
2 eggs, well beaten
Melted butter
¼ pint whipped cream
2 ounces apricot jam

Combine yeast and 2 tablespoons sugar. Let stand until yeast is liquefied.

Sift flour and salt with remaining sugar. Add yeast. Cut in the fat.

Add milk to beaten eggs, and combine with the yeast mixture. Mix quickly to a soft dough. Spread with melted butter. Cover and let rise until doubled in size.

Knead and form into flat, small cakes. Place on baking sheet, brush with butter and let rise again until doubled.

Bake in hot oven (400°F. Mark 6) about 20 to 25 minutes. Cool. Split side of each and fill with the whipped cream mixed with apricot jam.

TEA CAKE

½ ounce baker's or 2 teaspoons dry yeast
4 fluid ounces scalded milk
2 ounces fat
2 ounces sugar
1 egg or 2 egg yolks, beaten
½ teaspoon salt
3 ounces currants
About 6 ounces plain flour

Topping:
2 tablespoons sugar
¼ teaspoon cinnamon
1 ounce chopped nuts

Soften yeast in milk which has been cooled to lukewarm. Add fat, sugar, egg, salt, currants, and enough flour to make a rather stiff drop batter. Beat until smooth. Let rise until doubled.

Stir down and pour into greased 8×8×2-inch tin, filling tin about ½ full. Mix sugar, cinnamon, and nuts for topping and sprinkle over the batter. Let rise until puffy and doubled. Bake in hot oven (400°F. Mark 6) 25 to 30 minutes. Makes 1 tea cake.

Tea Cake

NORWEGIAN TEA BREAD

16 fluid ounces milk
8 ounces butter
8 ounces sugar
¼ teaspoon salt
½ ounce baker's yeast
2¼ pounds plain flour
2 teaspoons ground cardamom
2 ounces finely sliced citron
3 ounces raisins

Scald milk; add butter, sugar, and salt; cool. When lukewarm, crumble yeast into milk mixture in mixing bowl. Add 1 pound sifted flour and beat until smooth.

Pour into large clean buttered bowl, cover closely, and set in warm place out of draughts until doubled in bulk, about 2½ hours.

Then stir in remaining flour, turn out on floured board, and knead thoroughly until smooth and elastic.

Knead in cardamom, citron, and raisins a little at a time. Total time given to kneading should be at least 15 minutes.

Replace in buttered bowl, cover, and again let rise to double in bulk.

Turn out onto floured board and again knead down. Divide into 3 equal portions. Shape in loaves and place in buttered loaf tins.

Cover and set in warm place until slightly more than doubled in bulk; then slash each loaf 3 times across the top and brush with melted butter.

Bake in moderate oven (375°F. Mark 5) 10 minutes; then reduce to 300°F. Mark 2 and bake 40 or 50 minutes longer.

Remove to cake racks and cool. Makes 3 loaves.

COCONUT PINEAPPLE COFFEE CAKE
(Batter Method)

1½ ounces margarine or butter
2 tablespoons dark brown sugar
2 ounces shredded coconut
2 ounces pineapple tidbits
3 fluid ounces milk
3 ounces sugar
¾ teaspoon salt
2 ounces fat
4 tablespoons warm (not hot) water
½ ounce baker's or 2 teaspoons dry yeast
1 egg, beaten
½ teaspoon vanilla
8 ounces plain flour

Melt margarine or butter in tin 8×8×2 inches. Spread evenly brown sugar and coconut. Arrange pineapple tidbits.

Scald in saucepan 3 fluid ounces milk. Stir in sugar, salt, and fat. Cool to lukewarm.

Measure into bowl 4 tablespoons warm water (cool to lukewarm for baker's yeast). Sprinkle or crumble in yeast. Stir until dissolved. Stir in lukewarm milk mixture.

Add beaten egg, vanilla, and flour. Stir until well blended, about 1 minute. Turn batter into prepared tin. Let rise in warm place, free from draught, until doubled in bulk, about 1 hour and 15 minutes.

Bake in moderate oven (375°F. Mark 5) about 35 minutes. Turn out of tin immediately. Serve warm. Makes 1 cake.

Orange Coffee Cake:
1½ ounces margarine or butter
1½ ounces dark brown sugar
2 oranges, peeled and sectioned

Melt margarine or butter in tin 8×8×2 inches. Spread brown sugar evenly. Arrange orange sections.

Proceed as for Coconut Pineapple Coffee Cake. Makes 1 cake.

HUNGARIAN FILLED BUNS

½ ounce baker's or 2 teaspoons dry yeast
2 tablespoons lukewarm water for baker's yeast or warm for dry yeast
4 ounces butter
12 ounces plain flour
6 tablespoons sour cream
3 egg yolks, beaten
2 tablespoons sugar
½ teaspoon salt
Lukewarm milk

Soften the yeast in the lukewarm water. Cut the butter into the flour with 2 knives or a pastry blender.

Add the sour cream and egg yolks and mix well. Add the sugar, salt, and the softened yeast, and enough milk to make a dough that is soft but not sticky. Allow to rise in a warm place until doubled in bulk.

Punch down and allow to rest for 10 minutes. Roll out thinly; spread lightly with softened butter; fold the sides over the centre and the ends to the centre, envelope fashion. Roll thinly and fold again. Repeat this procedure twice more.

The dough is now ready to be cut into rolls; rolled and cut into pinwheels or made into filled squares; or triangles of dough may be filled and rolled to form horns and crescents.

Brush the rolls with beaten egg white and sprinkle with aniseed or poppyseed.

Allow to rise again until doubled in bulk and bake in moderate oven (350°F. Mark 4) for 20 minutes. Makes 2 dozen rolls.

Cheese Filling: Press 1 pound cottage cheese through a sieve and mix to a

paste with 3 beaten eggs, 1 tablespoon sugar, the grated rind of 1 lemon, 3 ounces raisins, and ¼ teaspoon nutmeg.

Prune Filling: Mix together into a stiff paste 12 ounces chopped, cooked prunes, the grated rind of 1 lemon, 2 tablespoons sugar, and ½ teaspoon cinnamon.

Raisin Filling: Boil together 8 ounces sugar and 8 fluid ounces water. Add 6 ounces chopped raisins, 4 ounces chopped nuts, 1 teaspoon cinnamon, and the grated rind of 1 lemon. Cook for about 8 minutes, stirring until thick.

BABKA
(No-Dissolve Method)

This Polish Easter bread derives its name from the word meaning old woman, because the cake, which is tall and wide, looks like an old woman with wide skirts. It is also served in Czechoslovakia where young girls put love messages on Easter eggs and present them with Babka to their boyfriends.

8 ounces plain flour
2 ounces sugar
3 teaspoons dry yeast
4 fluid ounces milk
2 ounces margarine
3 eggs (at room temperature)
1 ounce mixed crystallized fruits
1½ ounces seedless raisins

In a large bowl thoroughly mix 3 ounces flour, sugar, and undissolved dry yeast.

Combine milk and margarine in a saucepan. Heat over low heat until liquid is warm. (Margarine does not need to melt.) Gradually add to dry ingredients and beat 2 minutes at medium speed of electric mixer, scraping bowl occasionally. Add eggs and 2 ounces flour, or enough to make a thick batter. Beat at high speed 2 minutes, scraping bowl occasionally. Add remaining flour and beat 2 minutes at high speed. Cover; let rise in warm place, free from draught, until bubbly, about 1 hour.

Stir in crystallized fruits and raisins. Turn into greased and floured 3-pint tube tin. Let rise, uncovered, in warm place, free from draught, for 30 minutes.

Bake in moderate oven (350°F. Mark 4) about 40 minutes, or until done.

Before removing from tin, immediately prick surface with fork. Pour Rum Syrup (below) over cake. After syrup is absorbed, remove from tin and cool on wire rack. When cool, if desired, ice with glacé icing. Makes 1 cake.

Rum Syrup: Combine 4 ounces sugar, 3 fluid ounces water, and 2 teaspoons rum extract in a saucepan; bring to the boil.

CINNAMON ORANGE CRESCENTS
(No-Dissolve Method)

1-1¼ pounds plain flour
4 ounces sugar
1½ teaspoons salt
1 tablespoon grated orange peel
4 teaspoons dry yeast
6 fluid ounces milk
4 fluid ounces water
6 ounces margarine
1 egg (at room temperature)
Melted margarine
6 ounces sugar
1 tablespoon powdered cinnamon
Glacé icing

In a large bowl thoroughly mix 6 ounces flour, 4 ounces sugar, salt, orange peel, and undissolved dry yeast.

Combine milk, water, and 4 ounces margarine in a saucepan. Heat over low heat until liquids are warm. (Margarine does not need to melt.) Gradually add to dry ingredients and beat 2 minutes at medium speed of electric mixer, scraping bowl occasionally. Add egg and 2 ounces flour, or enough to make a thick batter. Beat at high speed 2 minutes, scraping bowl occasionally. Stir in enough additional flour to make a soft dough. Turn out onto lightly floured board; knead until smooth and elastic, about 8 to 10 minutes. Place in greased bowl, turning to grease top. Cover; let rise in warm place, free from draught, until doubled in bulk, about 1 hour.

Punch dough down; turn out onto lightly floured board. Divide dough into 8 equal pieces. Roll 1 piece of dough into an 8-inch circle. Brush with melted margarine. Combine 6 ounces sugar and cinnamon. Sprinkle circle with about 1½ tablespoons cinnamon-sugar mixture. Cut into 8 pie-shaped pieces. Roll up tightly, beginning at wide end; seal points firmly. Place on greased baking sheet with points underneath. Curve to form crescents. Repeat with remaining pieces of dough and cinnamon-sugar mixture. Cover; let rise in warm place, free from draught, until doubled in bulk, about 1 hour.

Bake in moderate oven (350°F. Mark 4) about 12 minutes, or until done. Remove from baking sheets and cool on wire racks. Ice with glacé icing. Makes 64 small rolls.

LEMON DROP BALLS

1 recipe Sweet Dough
2 ounces melted butter
Lemon sugar

When Sweet Dough is light, punch down. Divide into 4 equal parts and let rest 10 minutes.

Roll each part into long rolls about ¾ inch thick. Cut into pieces ¾ inch long.

Shape each piece into ball. Dip into melted butter, then into lemon sugar. Place 3 balls in each section of greased deep bun tins. Let rise until doubled, about 45 minutes.

Bake in moderate oven (350°F. Mark 4) 25 minutes. Makes about 4 dozen rolls.

Lemon Sugar: Combine 4 ounces sugar and 2 tablespoons grated lemon rind. Mix well.

SUGAR CRISP ROLLS
(No-Dissolve Method)

8-10 ounces plain flour
10 ounces sugar
½ teaspoon salt
2 teaspoons dry yeast
4 tablespoons milk
4 tablespoons water
2 ounces margarine
1 egg (at room temperature)
3 ounces chopped pecans or walnuts
Melted margarine

In a large bowl thoroughly mix 3 ounces flour, 2 ounces sugar, salt, and undissolved dry yeast.

Combine milk, water, and 2 ounces margarine in a saucepan. Heat over low heat until liquids are warm. (Margarine does not need to melt.) Gradually add to dry ingredients and beat 2 minutes at medium speed of electric mixer, scraping bowl occasionally.

Add egg and 1 ounce flour, or enough to make a thick batter. Beat at high speed 2 minutes, scraping bowl occasionally. Stir in enough additional flour to make a soft dough.

Turn out onto lightly floured board; knead until smooth and elastic, about 8 to 10 minutes. Cover; let rise in warm place, free from draught, until doubled in bulk, about 1 hour. Punch down and let rise an additional 30 minutes.

Combine remaining 8 ounces sugar and pecans.

Punch dough down; turn out onto lightly floured board. Roll dough to a 9×18-inch rectangle. Brush with melted margarine. Sprinkle dough with half the sugar mixture. Roll up from long side as for Swiss roll; seal edges. Cut into 1-inch slices. Roll each slice of dough into a 4-inch circle using remaining sugar mixture in place of flour on board, coating both top and bottom of each circle. Place on greased baking sheets. Cover; let rise in warm place free from draught, until doubled in bulk, about 30 minutes.

Bake in a moderate oven (375°F. Mark 5) about 10 to 15 minutes, or until done. Remove from baking sheets and cool on wire racks. Makes 1½ dozen rolls.

DOUBLE-QUICK COFFEE BREADS
(Master Recipe)

2 teaspoons dry yeast
6 fluid ounces warm water (not hot—110° to 115°F.)
2 ounces sugar
1 teaspoon salt
9 ounces plain flour
1 egg
2 ounces soft butter

In mixing bowl dissolve yeast in water. Add sugar and salt, and about half the flour.

Beat thoroughly 2 minutes. Add egg and butter. Then gradually beat in remaining flour until smooth.

Drop small spoonfuls over entire bottom of greased tin. (Use 8-inch ovenproof glass dish, or 9-inch square tin or 9-inch ring mould.) Cover. Let rise in warm place (85°) until double in bulk, 50 to 60 minutes.

Bake in moderate oven (375°F. Mark 5) until brown, 30 to 35 minutes. Immediately turn out to avoid sticking. Serve warm.

Variations of Double-Quick Coffee Breads:

Jam Puffs: Fill half full 16 to 20 deep bun tins. Let rise. Bake 15 to 20 minutes. When baked, spread with thick red jam. Garnish with coconut or chopped nuts.

Cinnamon Streusel: Mix thoroughly 1 ounce butter, 3 ounces white or brown sugar, 2 tablespoons plain flour, 2 teaspoons cinnamon, 2 ounces chopped nuts. Spoon dough into tin. Sprinkle with Streusel mixture.

Tutti-Frutti: Mix into finished dough 2 ounces crystallized fruit and 1 ounce chopped nuts. Spoon into tin. When baked, ice with a mixture of 4 ounces sifted icing sugar and 1 to 2 tablespoons cream. Decorate top with crystallized fruit and nuts.

Browned Butter Almond: Melt in pan 3 ounces butter. Add 3 ounces slivered blanched almonds. Heat until butter foams up in pan and browns and almonds are light golden brown. (Almonds brown a little more while cooling.) Cool to warm. Mix in 2 tablespoons white corn syrup or golden syrup, 4 ounces sugar, ½ teaspoon almond essence. Spoon over dough.

Spicy Sugar Puffs: Fill half full 16 to 20 greased deep bun tins. Let rise. Bake 15 to 20 minutes. Immediately after baking, roll in 4 ounces melted butter, then in a mixture of 6 ounces sugar and 2 teaspoons cinnamon. Serve hot.

Things to make with Frozen Pastry

In the following recipes, shortcrust, flaky or puff pastry is used. It is wise to have a supply of these in your deep freeze for sudden emergencies and, of course, time is saved in the preparation.

The packet should be left at room temperature for ½-1 hour before rolling out the pastry.

As a general rule, flaky and puff pastry should be rolled thinly and as evenly as possible. Even rolling maintains the air structure which is the secret of successful baking. If the whole packet of pastry is not required, wrap the remainder in foil and put back into the freezer.

CHEESE PASTRY

Use either flaky or puff pastry. Roll it out on a lightly floured board to about ¼-inch in thickness. Sprinkle some grated cheese generously over half the pastry, fold over, press the edges together and roll again until about ⅛-inch thick. Repeat the folding and rolling 3 times, turning the pastry clockwise each time so that the cheese is evenly distributed.

CHEESE STRAWS

Roll the cheese pastry thinly and cut into strips about ¼-inch wide and 3 inches long. Put on to a baking sheet and bake in a moderately hot oven (400°F. Mark 5) for 10-15 minutes.

EASY CINNAMON ROLLS

1 packet flaky pastry
1½ ounces butter or margarine
8 ounces brown sugar
1 teaspoon cinnamon
2 tablespoons golden syrup

Roll pastry into an oblong shape ¼ inch thick. Brush with melted butter; sprinkle with 2 ounces brown sugar and the cinnamon. Roll as for Swiss roll; pinch edges to seal; cut in 1-inch slices.

Hot Devilled Ham Braids

Mix remaining brown sugar, the syrup, and remaining butter; heat. Spread in greased 9×9×2-inch tin. Place rolls cut-side down in mixture.

Bake in moderate oven (375°F. Mark 5) about 30 minutes. Invert to remove from tin; cool. Makes 16.

NUT TWISTS

1 packet flaky pastry
3 ounces chopped walnuts
4 ounces sugar
1 teaspoon cinnamon

Roll the pastry thinly and cut into strips about 8 inches long; roll in the mixture of nuts, sugar and cinnamon; twist into S or other shape.

Place on greased baking sheet. Sprinkle with remaining nut mixture. Bake in hot oven (400°F. Mark 6) 12 to 15 minutes. Makes 1½ dozen rolls.

ORANGE PINWHEELS

1 packet flaky or puff pastry
4 ounces sugar
2 tablespoons grated orange rind
2 tablespoons melted butter or
      margarine
2 tablespoons orange juice
2 ounces sugar

Mix 4 ounces sugar with 1 tablespoon grated orange rind, the melted butter and orange juice. Grease some large deep bun tins and put a spoonful of the mixture in each. Roll out the pastry into an oblong shape. Sprinkle with sugar and remaining orange rind and roll up. Cut into 1-inch pieces and place cut-side down in the tins.

Bake in moderate oven (375°F. Mark 5) 20 to 25 minutes. Makes 1½ dozen rolls.

HOT DEVILLED PORK BRAIDS

1 packet puff pastry
1 can pork luncheon meat (8 ounce)
1 teaspoon dry mustard
3-4 tablespoons chilli sauce
1 ounce chopped nuts

Roll pastry into rectangle about 16×10 inches.

Chop ham and mix with other ingredients. Spread in 3-inch strip down centre of dough.

On either side, perpendicular to ham strip, cut 1-inch strips of pastry just to mixture. Make braid by crossing opposite strips. Glaze with beaten egg or milk and bake in hot oven (425°F. Mark 7) 20 minutes or until golden brown. Makes about 14 servings.

HERB STICKS

½ teaspoon nutmeg
1 teaspoon leaf sage, powdered
2 teaspoons caraway seeds
1 packet shortcrust pastry

Mix the nutmeg, sage and caraway seeds. Roll the pastry thinly into an oblong shape. Sprinkle the herbs over the pastry and fold in three. Roll again into an oblong and cut into fingers.

Place on greased baking sheet, 1 inch apart.

Glaze with beaten egg or milk and bake in a hot oven (400°F. Mark 6) about 15 minutes. Makes 2 dozen sticks.

EASY PLUM KUCHEN

1 packet flaky or puff pastry
1 pound plums, cut in halves
4 ounces or more sugar
1 teaspoon cinnamon
2 egg yolks
¼ pint cream

Roll out the pastry to fit a greased deep 7×12-inch tin.

Arrange plums in parallel rows on the pastry. Mix sugar and cinnamon and sprinkle over the pastry.

Mix egg yolks with cream and drip over plums.

Bake in a hot oven (400°F. Mark 6) about 20 minutes. Makes 8 servings.

Apple or Peach Kuchen: Substitute apples or peaches for plums in the above recipe.

RED AND GREEN TWIST

1 packet shortcrust pastry
1 small can crushed pineapple
2 ounces sugar
green food colouring
4 ounces raspberry or strawberry
      jam
2 tablespoons butter or margarine
1 tablespoon golden syrup

Cook pineapple with sugar until thick; cool.

Divide pastry into 3 parts. On floured board, roll 1 part into rectangle about 10×6 inches. Spread with half of pineapple mixture; roll up from long side, Swiss roll fashion.

Repeat with second part of dough, using rest of pineapple tinted green.

Repeat with third part, using raspberry jam. On greased baking sheet, plait the 3 rolls (2 with pineapple filling, 1 with raspberry). Pinch ends to seal.

Bake in hot oven (400°F. Mark 6) 20 minutes or until done. Melt butter; mix with syrup, and brush over the pastry while still hot.

Cranberry Twist

CRANBERRY TWIST

1 packet flaky or puff pastry
1 small can cranberry sauce
2 ounces chopped nuts
2 tablespoons grated orange rind

Put the pastry on a lightly floured board and roll out to an oblong about 10 by 14 inches.

Spread cranberry sauce evenly over surface of pastry; sprinkle with nuts and grated orange rind.

Lift long edge of pastry, and roll, Swiss-roll fashion, into an even and plump roll. Seal seam by pinching along edge.

Join ends to form ring and place in well greased 11-inch pie plate, with seam side of roll down.

Mark ring in 12 equal sections. With kitchen shears cut through roll on these marks to about ½ inch from centre edge of ring. Take each cut piece and twist over on its side so that each piece rests partly on pie plate and partly on next piece with all pieces twisted in same direction.

Bake in moderate oven (375°F. Mark 4) 20 minutes or until nicely browned and top springs back when pressed. Makes 12 servings.

Mincemeat Twist: Substitute prepared moist mincemeat for cranberry sauce.

CHEESE AND CRANBERRY SLICES

1 packet flaky pastry
6 ounces grated Cheddar or
    Parmesan cheese

Filling:
4 ounces cranberry jelly
6 ounces chopped nuts
¼ teaspoon salt
2 tablespoons light brown sugar
¼ teaspoon ground cinnamon

Make Cheese Pastry (see page 101). Roll out thinly to an oblong shape and cut into two strips.

Prepare the filling by mixing all the ingredients together and spread it over one strip of pastry. Moisten the edges, cover with the second strip of pastry and press the edges well together. Cut into slices and place on a lightly floured baking sheet.

Bake in a moderately hot oven (400°F. Mark 6) for about 15 minutes.

JACK HORNER COFFEE RING

1 packet shortcrust pastry
12 small stoned cooked prunes
1 tablespoon melted butter
3 tablespoons sugar
1 teaspoon cinnamon
1½ ounces chopped almonds

Put the pastry on to a floured board and roll into rectangle about 9×12 inches. Cut into 3-inch squares.

Place a well-drained prune in centre of each square and wrap dough around it. Dip each in melted butter, then in sugar blended with spice. Then dip in almonds.

Arrange balls in greased 8-inch ring mould. Bake in moderate oven (375°F. Mark 4) about 30 minutes. Remove from pan. Sprinkle with any remaining almonds. Serve at once. Makes 8-inch ring.

BOHEMIAN FRUIT PASTRIES

1 packet puff pastry
12 stoned prunes or 12 cooked
    dried apricots
1½ ounces chopped nuts

Put the pastry on to a lightly floured board and roll to ⅛-inch thickness. Cut into rounds with 2½-inch biscuit cutter.

Place on greased baking sheet.

Press an indentation in centre of each round of pastry. Roll a prune or apricot in nuts and place in depression of each.

Bake in moderate oven (350°F. Mark 4) 20 minutes.

Drip some glacé icing over the fruit when cold. To make icing, mix 4 ounces sifted icing sugar with a little water and a few drops of vanilla. Makes 12 buns.

CREAM SLICES

1 packet puff pastry
jam
whipped cream
glacé icing

Roll the pastry out to about ⅛-inch thickness. Cut into strips 3½-inchs wide. Place on baking tray and bake in a hot oven (425°F. Mark 7) about 15 minutes. When cold, sandwich together with jam and whipped cream and top with glacé icing.

DATE MUMS

1 packet flaky or puff pastry

Date Filling:
12 ounces stoned dates
6 ounces honey
½ teaspoon nutmeg
½ teaspoon cinnamon
2 tablespoons butter or
    margarine
sugar icing

Roll pastry out on a lightly floured board. Divide into 6 equal parts. Roll each piece into an oblong shape, about ¼-inch thick.

Spread with date filling.

Roll up lengthwise as for Swiss roll. Cut each in half and form rings on greased baking sheet, pinching ends together.

Clip with kitchen shears about ¼ inch apart. Separate clips by pulling every other one to centre of ring.

Bake in moderate oven (375°F. Mark 4) 12 to 15 minutes. Drizzle with glacé icing. Makes 12 individual coffee cakes.
Date Filling: Slice dates. Combine with honey, spices, and butter, mixing well. Warm gently.

Date Mums

QUICK BREADS

Quick bread is a term used to describe any bread leavened with baking powder, bicarbonate of soda, air, or steam rather than with yeast. They include scones, muffins, coffee cakes, shallow loaves such as corn breads, deep loaves such as nut breads, spoon breads, girdlecakes, waffles, and steamed breads such as popovers. They are quick to make because they require no rising period.

Quick Breads in Loaves

Most quick breads in loaves are hard to buy so you'll have to make them if you want to serve them. Most of them taste better and slice easier if stored at least a day. Wrap the thoroughly cooled whole loaves in plastic wrap or aluminium foil or place in an airtight container. These breads may be stored in the refrigerator for short periods or in the freezer.

PINEAPPLE BRAN BREAD

5 fluid ounces pineapple syrup
2½ ounces whole bran
8 ounces plain flour
4 ounces sugar
2 teaspoons baking powder
¼ teaspoon bicarbonate of soda
1 teaspoon salt
3 ounces chopped walnuts
4 ounces drained, canned, crushed
    pineapple
1 well beaten egg
2 tablespoons melted fat

Pour pineapple syrup over bran and let stand 15 minutes.

Mix and sift flour, sugar, baking powder, bicarbonate of soda, and salt.

Add walnuts, crushed pineapple, egg, and melted fat to bran mixture and add to sifted dry ingredients. Mix until just blended.

Turn into greased loaf tin, 9×5×3 inches. Bake in slow oven (325°F. Mark 3) 1 hour and 15 minutes. Makes 1 loaf.

WHITE NUT BREAD
(Master Recipe)

8 ounces plain flour
3 teaspoons baking powder
2 ounces sugar
½ teaspoon salt
4 ounces chopped nuts
1 egg, well beaten
8 fluid ounces milk

Sift dry ingredients together. Stir in nuts.

Combine egg and milk. Pour milk mixture into dry ingredients and stir quickly to mix.

Turn into greased loaf tin, 8½×4½ inches. Bake in moderate oven (350°F. Mark 4) 45 minutes. Makes 1 loaf.

Variations:

Candied Orange Peel Bread: In master recipe substitute 4 ounces chopped candied orange peel for nuts.

Date Nut Bread: In master recipe substitute brown sugar for white, and 3 ounces chopped dates for 2 ounces nuts.

Fruit Nut Bread: In master recipe substitute 3 ounces chopped dried apricots, raisins, or currants for 2 ounces nuts.

Orange Nut Bread: In master recipe substitute 4 ounces orange marmalade for sugar. Use only 4 fluid ounces milk. Add 1 tablespoon grated orange rind.

Whole Wheat Bread: In master recipe substitute 4 ounces whole wheat flour for 4 ounces white flour and 1½ ounces brown sugar for white sugar.

BANANA TEA BREAD

7 ounces flour
2¼ teaspoons baking powder
½ teaspoon salt
3 ounces fat
5 ounces sugar
2 eggs, well beaten
2 to 3 mashed, ripe bananas

Sift together flour, baking powder, and salt. Beat fat until creamy in mixing bowl. Add sugar gradually, and continue beating until light and fluffy. Add eggs and beat well.

Add flour mixture alternately with bananas, a small amount at a time, mixing after each addition only enough to moisten dry ingredients.

Turn into a greased loaf tin (8½× 4½×2½ inches) and bake in a moderate oven (350°F. Mark 4) about 1 hour and 10 minutes or until bread is done. Makes 1 loaf.

Variations:

Banana Apricot Tea Bread: Add 6 ounces finely cut dried apricots to egg mixture.

Banana Nut Tea Bread: Add 3 ounces coarsely chopped nuts to egg mixture.

Banana Prune Tea Bread: Add 6 ounces finely cut dried prunes to egg mixture.

Banana Raisin Tea Bread: Add 6 ounces seedless raisins to egg mixture.

Holiday Banana Tea Bread: Add 4 ounces mixed, crystallized fruit, 1½ ounces raisins, and 2 ounces coarsely chopped nuts to egg mixture.

Important: If apricots or prunes are very dry, soak them in warm water until soft. Drain and dry well before using them in the bread.

A crack down the centre of a nut loaf is no mistake—it's typical.

WHOLE WHEAT NUT BREAD 2
(Master Recipe)

6 ounces plain flour
5 teaspoons baking powder
1 teaspoon salt
6 ounces sugar
6 ounces whole wheat flour
4 ounces chopped nuts
1 egg
12 fluid ounces milk
6 tablespoons melted fat

Sift white flour, baking powder, salt, and sugar together. Add whole wheat flour and nuts and mix well.

Beat egg slightly. Add milk and melted fat. Combine with dry ingredients, stirring only enough to blend.

Place in a well greased loaf tin. Bake until golden brown in moderate oven (350°F. Mark 4) for 50 to 60 minutes. Remove from tin. Cool before slicing. Makes 1 large or 2 small loaves.

Variations:

Fruit Bread: In master recipe substitute 6 ounces chopped dates, raisins, prunes, or figs for nuts.

Honey Nut Bread: In master recipe use honey instead of sugar.

Orange Nut Bread: In master recipe substitute 2 ounces chopped crystallized orange peel for 2 ounces chopped nuts.

SALLY LUNN

8 ounces plain flour
3 teaspoons baking powder
¼ teaspoon salt
3 tablespoons sugar
2 eggs, separated
4 fluid ounces milk
4 ounces melted fat

Mix and sift flour, baking powder, salt, and sugar.

Combine beaten egg yolks and milk. Add to flour mixture, stirring only enough to moisten the dry ingredients. Add the fat. Fold in stiffly beaten egg whites.

Turn into a greased square tin 8×8×2 inches. Bake in moderate oven (350°F. Mark 4) about 30 minutes. Cut into squares. Serve hot.

BRAN BREAD

12 ounces plain flour
1 teaspoon salt
2 ounces sugar
4 teaspoons baking powder
4 ounces whole bran
2 eggs
8 fluid ounces milk
2 ounces melted fat

Sift flour, salt, sugar, and baking powder together and add bran.

Beat eggs. Stir in milk and melted fat.

Pour liquid into dry ingredients all at once and stir only until dry ingredients are mixed. If desired, add 3 ounces chopped raisins.

Pour into a well greased bread tin. Bake in moderate oven (375°F. Mark 5) 50 to 60 minutes. Will keep well if wrapped in waxed paper when cool. Makes 1 loaf.

BRAN RAISIN BREAD

1 egg
8 ounces sugar
3 ounces molasses or treacle
8 fluid ounces sour milk
2 tablespoons melted fat
4 ounces whole bran
8 ounces plain flour
½ teaspoon bicarbonate of soda
3 teaspoons baking powder
1 teaspoon salt
3 ounces raisins

Beat egg slightly. Add sugar, molasses, milk, fat, and bran.

Sift flour, bicarbonate of soda, salt, and baking powder. Mix raisins with flour, and add to the first mixture. Beat well.

Bake in a well greased loaf tin in moderate oven (350°F. Mark 4) for 1¼ hours. Cool before slicing. Makes 1 large loaf.

BUTTERSCOTCH BREAD

2 eggs
12 ounces brown sugar
3 tablespoons melted butter or margarine
1 pound plain flour
1 teaspoon bicarbonate of soda
1½ teaspoons baking powder
1 teaspoon salt
16 fluid ounces sour milk or buttermilk
4 ounces chopped nuts

Beat eggs. Add sugar gradually, beating it in. Add fat.

Sift together flour, soda, baking powder, and salt. Add to egg mixture alternately with milk. Add nuts.

Pour into greased loaf tin. Bake in moderate oven (350°F. Mark 4) 45 minutes. Makes 2 1-pound loaves.

Irish Soda Bread: For a sugary topping, brush top surface of loaf with melted butter and sprinkle with sugar before baking.

APPLE BREAD

4 ounces fat
5 ounces sugar
2 eggs
6 ounces chopped unpeeled apples
8 ounces plain flour
1 teaspoon baking powder
1 teaspoon bicarbonate of soda
½ teaspoon salt
1 ounce chopped nuts

Cream fat and sugar together. Blend in beaten eggs and fruit. Include juice with the apple. Stir in mixed and sifted dry ingredients. Blend in nuts.

Pour batter into greased loaf tin (8×4 inches). Bake in moderate oven (350°F. Mark 4) 55 to 60 minutes. Makes 1 loaf.

IRISH SODA BREAD

1 pound plain flour
2 ounces granulated sugar
1 teaspoon salt
1 teaspoon baking powder
2 ounces butter or margarine
12 ounces seedless raisins
10 fluid ounces buttermilk or sour milk
1 egg
1 teaspoon bicarbonate of soda

Mix and sift flour, sugar, salt, and baking powder. Cut in butter or margarine with pastry blender or two knives until it resembles coarse corn meal. Stir in raisins.

Combine buttermilk, egg, and bicarbonate. Stir buttermilk mixture into flour mixture until just moistened.

Bake in greased 1½ pint pudding basin or casserole in moderate oven (375°F. Mark 5) 45 to 50 minutes, until golden brown.

Note: This recipe has been slightly modified. This new version adds a little butter or margarine and one egg. In its original form, Irish soda bread is known as "bannock" if baked, or "soda farls" if cooked on a girdle and cut into triangles.

Variations: The above recipe can be varied as is done in Ireland: add caraway seeds to taste; substitute 6 ounces treacle for 4 fluid ounces buttermilk (omitting sugar); use half whole wheat flour, half white.

BOSTON BAKED BREAD

6 ounces plain flour
2½ teaspoons bicarbonate of soda
1½ teaspoons salt
2 ounces sugar
8 ounces whole wheat flour
3 ounces fat
6 ounces raisins
1 well-beaten egg
16 fluid ounces sour milk or
    buttermilk
8 ounces molasses or treacle

Mix and sift flour, bicarbonate of soda, salt, and sugar. Add whole wheat flour and mix well. Cut in fat until mixture resembles coarse meal. Add raisins.

Combine egg, milk, and molasses; add to dry ingredients. Mix only until flour is dampened.

Turn into 2 greased and floured loaf tins. Bake in moderate oven (350°F. Mark 4) 45 to 50 minutes. Makes 2 loaves.

STEAMED BROWN BREAD

4 ounces plain flour
1 teaspoon baking powder
1½ teaspoons bicarbonate of soda
1 teaspoon salt
4 ounces whole wheat flour
4 ounces yellow corn meal
9 ounces seedless raisins
16 fluid ounces buttermilk or sour
    milk
8 ounces molasses or treacle

Sift white flour with baking powder, bicarbonate of soda, and salt. Add whole wheat flour, corn meal, and raisins.

Combine buttermilk or sour milk and molasses. Add dry ingredients and mix thoroughly.

Grease some pudding basins and fill ⅔ full. Cover tightly and steam about 3½ hours.

Fruit Brown Bread: Add 8 ounces chopped uncooked prunes or dates to batter in place of raisins.

CHOCOLATE TEA BREAD

12 ounces plain flour
1½ teaspoons bicarbonate of soda
1 teaspoon salt
8 ounces sugar
2 ounces cocoa
1 egg
6 tablespoons vinegar plus milk to
    make ½ pint liquid
3 ounces melted fat

Sift flour, soda, salt, sugar, and cocoa together. Beat egg, add liquid and fat, and stir all at once into flour mixture until batter is smooth.

Turn into greased 8¾×4½×2½-inch loaf tin.

Bake in moderate oven (350°F. Mark 4) 1 hour or until done. Remove from

tin and cool several hours or overnight before slicing. Makes 1 loaf.

PRUNE-OATEN BREAD

8 ounces flour
4 ounces sugar
2½ teaspoons baking powder
½ teaspoon bicarbonate of soda
1 teaspoon salt
4 ounces rolled oats, uncooked
½ pint buttermilk or sour milk
2 tablespoons melted fat
5½ ounces diced, drained, cooked
    prunes
2 ounces chopped nuts

Sift together flour, sugar, baking powder, soda, and salt. Add rolled oats and mix thoroughly.

Combine buttermilk with slightly cooled fat. (To make fresh milk sour, add 1 tablespoon of vinegar to ½ pint of fresh milk.) Add to flour mixture with prunes and nuts, stirring just enough to moisten the dry ingredients. (Batter should be lumpy.)

Put into well greased loaf tin, 9× 5×3 inches. Place extra halves of prunes and whole nuts on top.

Bake in moderate oven (350°-375°F. Mark 4-5) about 1 hour or until done. Turn out on rack to cool. Makes 1 loaf.

CHEESE NUT BREAD

8 ounces plain flour
1 tablespoon baking powder
¾ teaspoon salt
½ tablespoon sugar
4 ounces grated cheese
1 ounce chopped pecans or walnuts
1 egg
6 fluid ounces milk
1 ounce butter, melted

Mix and sift flour twice with baking powder, salt, and sugar. Add cheese and nuts and mix thoroughly.

Beat egg, add milk and melted butter and pour into dry ingredients. Stir quickly until dry ingredients are just dampened; batter should not be smooth.

Pour into buttered bread tin (8× 4×3 inches) and let stand 15 minutes at room temperature.

Bake in moderate oven (350°F. Mark 4) 1 hour or until skewer inserted in centre comes out clean. Turn loaf out onto cake rack and cool before slicing. Makes 1 loaf.

BRAZIL NUT BREAD

12 ounces whole wheat flour
6 ounces plain flour
5 teaspoons baking powder
2 teaspoons bicarbonate of soda
1½ teaspoons salt
9 ounces brown sugar
6 ounces sliced Brazil nuts
12 fluid ounces sour milk or butter-
    milk

Prune-Oaten Bread

Mix dry ingredients together. Add Brazil nuts and mix well. Add milk and stir well. Pour into 2 greased loaf tins.

Bake about 1 hour in slow oven (325°F. Mark 3). Makes 2 loaves.

LEMON NUT BREAD

2 ounces butter or margarine
10 ounces sugar
2 eggs
1½ teaspoons finely grated lemon
    rind
13 ounces plain flour
3 teaspoons baking powder
½ teaspoon salt
½ teaspoon bicarbonate of soda
¼ pint milk
4 tablespoons lemon juice
3 ounces coarsely chopped pecans
    or walnuts

Cream butter or margarine and sugar together in mixing bowl. Blend in the eggs one at a time and the lemon rind.

Stir in sifted dry ingredients alternately with liquids (milk and lemon juice). Fold in nuts.

Spoon batter into lightly greased loaf tin (9×5×2½ inches), being sure thick batter is well into corners of tin.

Bake in moderate oven (350°F. Mark 4) 1 hour or until knife inserted in centre comes out clean. Remove from tin. Cool.

Nut bread cuts more easily and flavours are more mellowed if it is cooled and wrapped for 24 hours before serving.

Note: If you prefer a nut bread without a cracked top crust, allow the batter to stand in the tin at room temperature for about 20 minutes before baking.

Make quick loaf breads the day before they are to be used, to make neat slices. Very fresh bread crumbles easily. Nut bread sandwiches call for simple fillings; soft butter or margarine, softened cream cheese, jelly, or jam.

SCOTCH OATMEAL BREAD

2 eggs
8 ounces sugar
16 fluid ounces sour milk or
    buttermilk
8 ounces molasses or treacle
12 ounces plain flour
1 teaspoon salt
1 teaspoon baking powder
2 teaspoons bicarbonate of soda
6 ounces quick or regular uncooked
    oats
2 ounces chopped nuts
9 ounces raisins

Beat eggs until light; add sugar gradually, beating until fluffy. Add sour milk and molasses, mixing well.

Sift together flour, salt, baking powder, and soda and add to creamed mixture.

Add rolled oats, nuts and raisins, stirring only enough to combine.

Bake in 2 greased paperlined bread tins (4½×8½ inches) in moderate oven (350°F. Mark 4) 1 hour.

Store in bread box one day before slicing.

ARKANSAS DATE BREAD

4 ounces flour
½ teaspoon salt
1 teaspoon bicarbonate of soda
4 ounces whole wheat flour
4 ounces whole bran
6 ounces dates
6 ounces molasses or treacle
½ pint sour milk
1½ tablespoons melted fat
1 egg, slightly beaten

Sift white flour once. Measure and sift again with salt and bicarbonate of soda. Add whole wheat flour and bran.

Cut dates in small pieces and mix through dry ingredients, with the finger tips. Add the molasses, sour milk, and fat to the egg, and stir this mixture into dry ingredients.

Pour into a well greased loaf tin. Bake in moderate oven (350°F. Mark 4) for 1½ hours. Cool before slicing. Makes 1 loaf.

PECAN BREAD

8 ounces flour
3 teaspoons baking powder
½ teaspoon salt
3 ounces brown sugar
8 fluid ounces milk
1 beaten egg
2 tablespoons melted butter
4 ounces broken pecans

Sift flour, baking powder, and salt together. Stir in brown sugar.

Combine milk and egg and add to dry ingredients, mixing until just moistened. Then add melted butter and nuts.

Spread batter into well greased loaf

tin, about 9¼×5¼×2¾ inches.

Bake in moderate oven (350°F. Mark 4) 1 hour or until lightly browned. Makes 1 loaf.

APPLE SPICE BREAD

8 ounces plain flour
1 teaspoon bicarbonate of soda
1 teaspoon salt
1 teaspoon cinnamon
½ teaspoon nutmeg
¼ teaspoon cloves
4 ounces fat
4½ ounces light brown sugar
2 eggs
1 teaspoon vanilla
6 ounces grated raw apples
2 tablespoons vinegar plus water
    to make 8 fluid ounces
2 ounces chopped nuts

Sift flour, soda, salt, and spices together. Cream fat; blend in sugar and add eggs one at a time and beat until smooth.

Add vanilla. Add flour mixture alternately with grated apple and liquid. Stir in nuts. Turn into greased 8¾× 4½×2½-inch loaf tin.

Bake in moderate oven (350°F. Mark 4) 1 hour or until done. Remove from tin and cool several hours or overnight before slicing. Makes 1 loaf.

CRANBERRY RELISH BREAD

8 ounces plain flour
1 teaspoon bicarbonate of soda
1 teaspoon salt
6 ounces sugar
1 egg
5 tablespoons orange juice
3 tablespoons white (distilled)
    vinegar plus water to make
    5 fluid ounces
1 teaspoon grated orange rind
2 ounces melted fat
4 ounces halved or coarsely
    chopped raw cranberries
4 ounces chopped nuts

Sift together flour, soda, salt, and sugar into mixing bowl.

Beat egg; add liquid, orange rind, and melted fat. Add all at once to flour mixture and stir until flour is just dampened.

Add cranberries and nuts; stir just enough to blend well.

Turn into greased 8¾×4½×2½-inch loaf tin. Bake in moderate oven (350°F. Mark 4) 60 to 70 minutes or until done.

Remove from tin and cool several hours or overnight before slicing. Makes 1 loaf.

CEREAL FLAKE ORANGE NUT BREAD

8 ounces plain flour
3 teaspoons baking powder

1 teaspoon salt
4 ounces sugar
1 tablespoon grated orange rind
2 ounces chopped nuts
1 egg, well beaten
6 fluid ounces orange juice
3 tablespoons melted fat or salad oil
2 ounces whole wheat flakes or
    cornflakes

Sift together flour, baking powder, salt, and sugar; stir in orange rind and nuts.

Combine egg, orange juice, and fat, and add to flour mixture, stirring only until well mixed. Stir in whole wheat flakes.

Turn into greased loaf tin, 8½× 4½×2½ inches, and bake in moderate oven (350°F. Mark 4) about 1 hour. Cool on rack. Makes 1 loaf.

PRUNE NUT BREAD

6 ounces prunes
12 ounces plain flour
4 teaspoons baking powder
½ teaspoon bicarbonate of soda
1 teaspoon salt
2 tablespoons sugar
2 ounces fat
2 eggs
4 fluid ounces evaporated milk
    diluted with 4 fluid ounces
    water
2 ounces chopped nuts

Rinse prunes; drain and dry on towel. If prunes are very dry, boil them 5 minutes. Remove stones, and put prunes through mincer.

Sift flour with baking powder, soda, salt, and sugar. Cut fat into flour mixture.

Beat eggs; add diluted evaporated milk and stir into flour mixture. Add prunes and nuts.

Pour into well greased loaf tin about 9×5×3 inches. Place extra halves of prunes and whole nuts on top.

Bake in moderate oven (350° to 375°F. Mark 4-5) 1 hour or until brown. Turn out on rack to cool. Makes 1 loaf.

Prune Nut Bread

MOLASSES WHOLE WHEAT NUT BREAD

2 tablespoons brown sugar
8 ounces whole wheat flour
4 ounces plain flour
¾ teaspoon bicarbonate of soda
2½ teaspoons baking powder
1 teaspoon salt
6 fluid ounces milk
6 fluid ounces water
9 ounces molasses or treacle
4 ounces chopped walnuts

Mix together sugar, whole wheat flour, white flour, bicarbonate of soda, baking powder, and salt.

Combine milk, water, and molasses; add to dry ingredients. Mix smooth. Add nuts.

Pour into 9¼×5¼×2½-inch greased loaf tin. Let stand 20 minutes.

Bake in moderate oven (350°F. Mark 4) 1½ hours.

Cool 5 minutes. Remove from tin. Cool. Bread will slice in uniformly thin slices if stored overnight.

BANANA BREAD

8 ounces plain flour
1 teaspoon bicarbonate of soda
1 teaspoon salt
4 ounces fat
8 ounces sugar
2 eggs
2 to 3 mashed ripe bananas
1 tablespoon vinegar plus milk to make 4 fluid ounces liquid

Sift together flour, soda, and salt. Cream fat, blend in sugar, add eggs one at a time, and beat until fluffy.

Add flour mixture alternately with bananas and liquid, beating well after each addition.

Turn into greased 9½×5½×2¾-inch loaf tin. Bake in moderate oven (350°F. Mark 4) 60 to 70 minutes or until done. Remove from tin and cool several hours or overnight before slicing. Makes 1 loaf.

ORANGE NUT BREAD 2

10 ounces plain flour
5 ounces sugar
1 teaspoon salt
2½ teaspoons baking powder
2 ounces chopped walnuts
1 egg
8 fluid ounces milk
1 tablespoon grated orange rind
4 tablespoons orange juice
2 tablespoons melted fat

Sift together flour, sugar, salt, and baking powder. Stir in chopped walnuts.

Beat egg and mix with milk, grated orange rind, orange juice, and melted fat. Add orange mixture to flour mixture and stir only until dry ingredients are moistened.

Pour batter into a well greased 8×6×2-inch baking dish. Bake in a moderate oven (350°F. Mark 4) for 1 hour and 15 minutes.

Slice and serve with butter, orange marmalade, and cream cheese.

BUTTERMILK NUT BREAD

12 ounces plain flour
½ teaspoon salt
¾ teaspoon bicarbonate of soda
2 teaspoons baking powder
6 ounces brown sugar
4 ounces coarsely chopped walnuts
1 egg
2 tablespoons molasses or treacle
12 fluid ounces buttermilk or sour milk
3 tablespoons melted butter

Sift together flour, salt, soda, and baking powder. Add sugar and walnuts.

Beat egg until thick and lemon-coloured. Add molasses and buttermilk. Combine with first mixture along with melted butter. Stir only to blend ingredients. Do not beat. (This will be very thick.)

Spoon mixture into well buttered loaf bread tin (9×5×3 inches) making a slight hollow in centre. Let stand 20 minutes before baking.

Bake in moderate oven (350°F. Mark 4) about 60 minutes or until a skewer thrust into centre comes out clean.

Turn out of tin onto wire rack to cool. (Breads of this type frequently crack across top during baking.) Makes 1 loaf.

Buttermilk-Fruit Bread: 3-4 ounces chopped figs, dates, or raisins may be added along with nuts.

CINNAMON RAISIN COFFEE BREAD

2 ounces butter or margarine, melted
4 ounces sugar
2 teaspoons cinnamon
10 ounces plain flour
1 teaspoon salt
1¼ teaspoons bicarbonate of soda
4 ounces sugar
2 eggs
5 tablespoons white (distilled) vinegar plus milk to make 8 fluid ounces
2 ounces melted fat
3 ounces raisins
1 ounce chopped nuts

Combine butter or margarine, 4 ounces sugar, and cinnamon. Set aside. Sift flour, salt, soda, and other 4 ounces sugar into mixing bowl.

Beat eggs, add liquid, blend well; then add fat and raisins. Pour all at once into flour mixture and stir until flour is just dampened.

Spread ½ of batter in greased 8×8×2-inch baking tin; sprinkle with ½ the cinnamon mixture. Cover with remaining batter and draw knife through batter several times to distribute filling slightly. Sprinkle top with rest of cinnamon mixture and nuts.

Bake in moderate oven (350°F. Mark 4) 45 minutes. Serve warm, cutting in squares. Makes 1 loaf.

APPLE BREAD 2

9 ounces plain flour
1 teaspoon baking powder
½ teaspoon salt
½ teaspoon nutmeg
1 teaspoon bicarbonate of soda
4 ounces sugar
2 eggs
6 ounces light corn syrup or golden syrup
1 teaspoon grated lemon rind
1 tablespoon lemon juice
6 ounces unpeeled raw red apple, finely chopped
1 ounce chopped nuts
4 ounces melted butter or margarine
Apple wedges

Sift measured flour, and resift with baking powder, salt, nutmeg, soda, and sugar into mixing bowl.

Break in eggs and add corn syrup mixed with rest of ingredients. Mix as little as possible to form dough and leave ingredients evenly distributed.

Turn into well greased loaf tin. Top with thin apple wedges dipped in butter or margarine, then in sugar.

Bake in moderate oven (350°F. Mark 4) about 1 hour. Cover tin for first 20 minutes. Makes 1 loaf, 4½×9 inches.

DATE NUT BREAD

10 ounces plain flour
1¼ teaspoons bicarbonate of soda
1 teaspoon salt
3 ounces chopped dates
2 eggs
4 tablespoons white (distilled) vinegar
6 fluid ounces milk
1½ ounces brown sugar
2 ounces melted fat
3 ounces chopped nuts

Sift flour, soda, and salt together into mixing bowl. Stir in chopped dates until all are separated.

Beat eggs, combine with vinegar and milk, and stir in brown sugar. Add melted fat and pour all at once into flour mixture. Stir only until all flour is dampened; then add nuts and mix lightly.

Turn into greased 8¾×4½×2½-inch loaf tin. Bake in moderate oven (350°F. Mark 4) 60 to 70 minutes or until done.

Remove from tin and cool several hours or overnight before slicing. Makes 1 loaf.

Corn Breads

Corn breads can justly be called a truly American dish. The best corn bread is made from the traditional "water-ground" corn meal which retains its germ and has a much-prized flavour. It is still extensively used in the South; however, it has poor keeping qualities. As true corn meal is not normally available, white or yellow maize flour can be used instead of corn meal in the following recipes.

When making corn breads use heavy metal utensils. A thin tin permits the bread to overcook on the outside before the inside is done. Grease the tins heavily and heat them well for 5 minutes before adding the batter.

CORN BREAD

    4   ounces flour
    3   teaspoons baking powder
    ½   teaspoon salt
    4   ounces sugar
    2½ ounces yellow corn meal
    8   fluid ounces milk
    1   egg, well beaten
    1   tablespoon melted fat

Mix and sift flour, baking powder, salt, and sugar, stir in corn meal.

Add milk to beaten egg and stir into first mixture. Add fat and blend.

Turn into shallow, greased 8-inch tin. Bake in hot oven (400°F. Mark 6) about 20 minutes. Cut into 6 squares. Serve hot.

Variations:

Bacon Corn Bread: Add 2 ounces diced crisp cooked bacon to sifted flour mixture.

Corn Bread Sticks: Combine ingredients as directed. Turn into hot well-greased shallow tins.

Bake in hot oven (400°F. Mark 6) 15 to 20 minutes. Makes about 12 sticks.

OLD SOUTH CORN BREAD

    1   teaspoon salt
    5   ounces white corn meal
    8   fluid ounces boiling water
    3   tablespoons vinegar
    14 fluid ounces fresh milk
    2   well beaten eggs
    2   tablespoons melted fat
    1   teaspoon bicarbonate of soda

Combine salt and corn meal. Add slowly to boiling water while stirring constantly to prevent lumping.

Combine vinegar and milk. Add 12 fluid ounces of the vinegar and milk to corn meal mixture, and mix well. Add eggs and melted fat. Stir until well blended.

Dissolve soda in remaining vinegar

and milk. Add to corn meal mixture and stir until completely blended. Turn into greased 2½ pint fireproof dish.

Bake in hot oven (400°F. Mark 6) 1 hour. Serve immediately with a spoon. Serves 5 to 6.

CRACKLING CORN BREAD

    2   ounces salt pork, chopped
    10 ounces white corn meal, pre-
        ferably stone ground
    1½ teaspoons baking powder
    ½   teaspoon bicarbonate of soda
    1   teaspoon salt
    2   beaten eggs
    About 8 fluid ounces buttermilk
        or sour milk
    Fat

Cook salt pork slowly, stirring often until lightly browned. Mix and sift corn meal, baking powder, soda, and salt.

. Mix eggs, buttermilk, and 2 tablespoons fat from cracklings. Drain off remaining fat and reserve. Add liquid ingredients to corn meal. Add cracklings and stir until corn meal is dampened.

Batter should be stiff enough almost to hold its shape when dropped from spoon.

Drop cornbread mixture from a spoon into hot fat or oil to form cakes. Brown slowly on both sides. makes about 12 corn cakes.

SOUTHERN SPOON BREAD

    1   pint scalded milk
    5   ounces sifted white corn meal
    1   teaspoon salt
    1½ tablespoons melted butter
    4   eggs, separated
    1   teaspoon baking powder

Add scalded milk to corn meal, stirring until smooth. Add salt.

Cook over hot water, stirring constantly, until thick. Stir in melted butter.

Cool slightly. Beat egg yolks and add to cooled corn meal mixture. Add baking powder and mix well.

Fold in stiffly beaten egg whites. Turn into hot, buttered fireproof dish.

Bake in moderate oven (375°F. Mark 5) until firm and brown on top. Serve from dish. Serves 8 to 10.

Bacon Spoon Bread: Add 2 ounces diced, crisp bacon to corn meal mixture with the butter. Bacon fat may be used instead of butter.

Cheese Spoon Bread: Add 3 ounces grated cheese to batter after fat has been added.

NEW ORLEANS CORN PONE

    15 ounces yellow corn meal
    1   teaspoon salt
    2   tablespoons melted fat
    12 fluid ounces boiling water
    8   fluid ounces milk

Certain meals seem to demand corn bread. Serve it piping hot with plenty of butter.

    1   well beaten egg
    2   teaspoons baking powder

Combine corn meal, salt, and fat. Add boiling water gradually, stirring until well mixed. Stir in milk and set aside for 1 hour to cool. Beat well and stir in egg and baking powder.

Pour into shallow greased tins. Bake in hot oven (400°F. Mark 6) 40 minutes or until done. Makes 2 dozen corn sticks.

SKILLET CORN BREAD

    5   ounces yellow corn meal
    6   fluid ounces boiling water
    1   tablespoon fat
    ¾   teaspoon salt
    2   tablespoons corn syrup or golden
        syrup
    1   tablespoon flour
    1   teaspoon baking powder
    2   tablespoons milk
    1   egg

Pour corn meal into boiling water. Add fat and salt; mix well. Stir in syrup, flour, baking powder, and milk. Add egg and beat well.

Spread in well greased, heavy 8-inch frying pan. Cover, and cook over low heat 10 minutes. Turn, cover, and cook about 8 minutes longer.

CORN DODGER

    5   ounces yellow corn meal
    2   ounces plain flour
    1   teaspoon salt
    1½ teaspoons baking powder
    2   teaspoons sugar
    8   fluid ounces milk
    1   egg, beaten
    2½ tablespoons hot bacon drippings

Sift the dry ingredients into a mixing bowl. Combine the milk and egg and stir into the dry ingredients. Beat well and then stir in the hot drippings.

Pour into a hot fireproof dish. Bake in a hot oven (425°F. Mark 7) for 30 minutes, or until golden brown. Serve hot in pie-shaped pieces.

Spoon bread, also called batter bread, is a moist bread, soft enough to be eaten with a spoon.

CHEESE SPOON BREAD

4 ounces corn meal
1 teaspoon salt
Dash of pepper
1 tablespoon sugar
8 fluid ounces water
2 tablespoons fat
¾ pint milk
½ pound processed cheese, sliced
3 eggs, beaten

In saucepan, mix corn meal, salt, pepper, sugar, water, fat, and ½ pint milk. Cook over medium heat until thick and boiling, stirring constantly.

Remove from heat; add sliced cheese, reserving a few slices to put on top of mixture before baking. Stir until cheese melts.

Add remaining milk and beaten eggs. Pour into greased 2½ pint shallow baking dish. Put reserved slices of cheese on top.

Bake in slow oven (325°F. Mark 3) until almost set, about 50 minutes. Serve at once from dish. Serves 4.

RICE SPOON BREAD

1¼ pints milk
3½ ounces corn meal
2 tablespoons butter, margarine, or salad oil
1 teaspoon salt
1 pound cooked rice
3 well beaten eggs

Scald 1 pint milk in saucepan. Mix remaining milk with corn meal, then stir into hot milk.

Over low heat, stir mixture until it thickens, about 5 minutes.

Remove from heat. Add butter, salt, and rice. Stir into eggs gradually.

Pour into greased 2½ pint baking dish. Bake in hot oven (425°F. Mark 7) until silver knife inserted in centre comes out clean, about 45 to 50 minutes. Serve with butter or margarine. Serves 5 to 6.

SHORT'NEN BREAD

7½ ounces corn meal
3 ounces plain flour
½ teaspoon bicarbonate of soda
¼ teaspoon salt
8 fluid ounces sour milk
4 ounces cracklings (see below)

Sift the dry ingredients together; add milk and stir in cracklings.

Pour into a greased baking tin. Bake in hot oven (425°F. Mark 7) 30 minutes, or until brown. Makes 1 loaf.

Note: Cracklings are the crisp brown bits left when lard is made. A modern version of cracklings can be made by heating fat salt pork or bacon in a frying pan. Pour off the fat until only crisp, lean bits remain. Chop fine and use in recipe.

OLD TIME MAINE TOGUS LOAF (STEAMED)

2 ounces plain flour
½ teaspoon bicarbonate of soda
1 teaspoon salt
7½ ounces yellow corn meal
12 fluid ounces fresh milk
4 fluid ounces sour milk
3 ounces molasses or treacle

Mix and sift flour, soda, and salt. Add corn meal. Mix together milk, sour milk, and molasses. Add to dry ingredients. Mix all ingredients together.

Pour into greased mould. Cover with greaseproof paper tied securely and steam 3 hours.

The batter will be very thin, but corn meal absorbs the moisture while steaming.

Serve hot with butter, or use as a base for creamed chicken. Makes 1 medium-sized loaf.

CUSTARD CORN BREAD

4 ounces yellow corn meal
2 ounces plain flour
2 tablespoons sugar
½ teaspoon salt
1 teaspoon baking powder
1 beaten egg
12 fluid ounces milk
2 tablespoons melted butter

Mix and sift corn meal, flour, sugar, salt, and baking powder.

Combine egg, 8 fluid ounces milk, and butter; add to dry ingredients and mix well. (The batter is very thin.)

Pour batter in greased tin, 8×8×2 inches. Pour remaining milk carefully over top of batter.

Bake in hot oven (400°F. Mark 6) 20 minutes. Then cut in squares and serve hot with chicken, turkey, or pork.

CORN STICKS 2

6¼ ounces corn meal
1 ounce plain flour
2 tablespoons sugar
3 teaspoons baking powder
1 teaspoon salt
9 fluid ounces milk
1 egg, beaten
4 tablespoons melted butter

Place shallow tins in the oven to heat.

Sift all the dry ingredients into a mixing bowl.

Combine the milk and egg and stir into the dry ingredients. Stir in the melted butter.

Brush the hot shallow tins with butter and fill them almost full with the mixture.

Bake in a very hot oven (450°F. Mark 8) for 10 to 12 minutes. Makes 12 sticks.

JOHNNY CAKE

10 ounces yellow corn meal
2 ounces plain flour
½ teaspoon salt
2 teaspoons baking powder
2 tablespoons sugar
1 egg, well beaten
8 fluid ounces milk
2 tablespoons melted fat

Mix and sift dry ingredients. Add well beaten egg, milk, and melted fat. Pour into greased tin, 8 inches square.

Bake in hot oven (425°F. Mark 7) until golden brown (about 25 minutes). Makes 1 loaf.

YANKEE APPLE CORN BREAD

10 ounces yellow corn meal
2 ounces sugar
1½ teaspoons salt
16 fluid ounces sour milk or buttermilk
2 tablespoons melted fat
2 well beaten eggs
1 teaspoon bicarbonate of soda
1 tablespoon cold water
6 ounces chopped raw apple

Mix corn meal, sugar, salt, milk, and fat in top part of double saucepan. Cook over hot water 10 minutes, stirring frequently. Cool.

Add eggs, soda, which has been dissolved in cold water, and apples. Bake in greased tin in hot oven (400°F. Mark 6) 20 to 25 minutes. Serves 8.

SOUR MILK CORN BREAD

15 ounces corn meal
2 teaspoons baking powder
1 teaspoon salt
1 tablespoon sugar
½ teaspoon bicarbonate of soda
16 fluid ounces sour milk or buttermilk
2 eggs, beaten
8 fluid ounces thick sour cream

Sift together the corn meal, baking powder, salt, and sugar.

Stir the soda into the buttermilk and combine with the eggs and the cream. Mix all the ingredients together and bake in a very hot oven (450°F. Mark 8) for 20 minutes.

Corn Sticks

Quick Coffee Cakes

QUICK COFFEE CAKE
(Master Recipe)
- 8   ounces plain flour
- 2   teaspoons baking powder
- ½   teaspoon salt
- 4   ounces sugar
- 3   ounces butter or margarine
- 1   egg, beaten
- 4   fluid ounces milk

Mix and sift the flour, baking powder, salt, and sugar into a mixing bowl. Cut in the fat.

Combine the egg and milk and stir into the dry ingredients until the mixture is blended.

Spread the dough evenly in a buttered 9-inch sandwich tin. Bake in a hot oven (400°F. Mark 6) for 25 to 30 minutes.

Quick Coffee Cake Variations:

Crumb Topping For Quick Coffee Cake: Spread the dough evenly in a buttered 9-inch sandwich tin.

Brush the top with 1½ tablespoons melted butter or margarine.

Mix together 4 tablespoons sugar, 1 tablespoon flour, and 1 teaspoon cinnamon and sift this mixture evenly over the top of the dough.

Bake in hot oven (400°F. Mark 6) for 30 minutes.

Cut into pie-shaped wedges while still in the tin and remove each piece to a serving dish.

Dutch Apple Coffee Cake: Spread dough in a shallow tin. Brush with melted butter.

Cover with thinly sliced tart apples in parallel rows. Sprinkle generously with sugar and cinnamon.

Bake in hot oven (400°F. Mark 6) about 30 minutes.

Iced Coffee Cake: After baking, ice cake with glacé icing, then sprinkle with chopped crystallized fruit, chopped nuts, or combination of fruits and nuts.

Nut Coffee Cake: Glaze the top of the cake before baking with a mixture of slightly beaten egg white and water, or with a mixture of 3 tablespoons sugar and 1 tablespoon water.

Sprinkle thickly with chopped nuts. Almonds are particularly good.

Currant Coffee Cake: Currants may be used in the same way as nuts, in nut coffee cake, or may be combined with them.

Prune or Plum Coffee Cake: Arrange stoned canned plums or prunes over batter.

Pour over a little of the juice. Sprinkle with cinnamon and sugar.

Bake in hot oven (400°F. Mark 6) about 30 minutes.

Upside-Down Cherry Coffee Cake: In a deep cake tin melt 2 tablespoons butter.

Sprinkle 4 tablespoons sugar over bottom of tin.

Cover with sour canned cherries (or other fruit) that have been well drained. Cover with coffee cake dough.

Bake in hot oven (400°F. Mark 6) about 20 minutes.

APPLE COFFEE CAKE
- 1   recipe Quick Coffee cake
- 3   medium apples, peeled and sliced
- 2   tablespoons melted butter or margarine
- 2   ounces sugar
- ½   teaspoon cinnamon

Spread the coffee cake batter in a buttered 9-inch sandwich tin.

Arrange the apple slices on top in circles until the entire top of the dough is covered.

Brush with the butter and sprinkle with the sugar and cinnamon. Bake in hot oven (400°F. Mark 6) for 25 minutes.

APRICOT UPSIDE-DOWN COFFEE CAKE
- 1   recipe Quick Coffee cake
- 2   ounces butter or margarine
- 1½ ounces brown sugar
- 16 cooked dried apricot halves

Melt the butter in an 8-inch square tin. Sprinkle with the brown sugar and arrange the apricot halves evenly over the butter-sugar mixture.

Cover with coffee cake batter. Bake in hot oven (400°F. Mark 6) for 25 minutes.

QUICK KUGELHUPF
- 8 ounces butter
- 8 ounces sugar
- 5 eggs
- 1 pound plain flour
- ½ teaspoon salt
- 4 teaspoons baking powder
- 8 fluid ounces milk
- 6 ounces seedless raisins
- 1 teaspoon grated lemon rind
- 1 teaspoon vanilla
- 2 ounces chopped nuts (optional)
- Icing sugar

Cream butter until soft and fluffy. Sift in sugar gradually and beat until creamy and light. Add 1 egg at a time, beating well after each addition.

Sift flour with salt and baking powder. Add sifted mixture in 3 parts to butter mixture alternating with milk in thirds. Beat smooth after each addition.

Add raisins, lemon rind, vanilla, and nuts (if desired).

Mix well and pour into greased 7-inch tube tin. Bake in moderate oven (350°F. Mark 4) about 1 hour.

When cooled, dust with icing sugar.

Orange Blossom Coffee Ring

ORANGE BLOSSOM COFFEE RING
- 4   ounces whole bran dry cereal
- 6   fluid ounces orange juice
- 1   egg
- 2   ounces soft butter
- 1   teaspoon grated orange rind
- 4   ounces plain flour
- 1½ teaspoons baking powder
- ¼   teaspoon bicarbonate of soda
- ½   teaspoon salt
- 2   ounces sugar
- 3   ounces seedless raisins

Combine whole bran cereal and orange juice; let stand until most of moisture is taken up. Add egg, butter, and orange rind; beat well.

Sift together flour, baking powder, soda, salt, and sugar. Add to first mixture together with raisins, stirring only until combined.

Fill greased 8-inch ring mould about ⅔ full. Bake in hot oven (400°F. Mark 6) about 25 minutes. Remove from ring mould; let cool. Frost with thin glacé icing and decorate with pecan or walnut halves and crystallized fruit. Makes 8 to 10 servings.

FRENCH COFFEE CAKE
- 3   ounces brown sugar
- 1   tablespoon cornflour
- ½   ounce butter
- Grated rind 1 orange
- 4   tablespoons water
- 5   tablespoons orange juice
- 1   tablespoon lemon juice
- 4   ounces plain flour
- 2   teaspoons baking powder
- 1   teaspoon salt
- 1½ ounces fat
- 5   tablespoons milk

Blend sugar, cornflour, butter, and orange rind. Reserve 2 tablespoons mixture for topping.

To remainder, add water and juices. Simmer 5 minutes. Cool.

Mix and sift flour, baking powder, and salt. Cut in fat and then add milk.

Divide dough in 3 portions. Roll to fit 8-inch square tin.

Spread layer of orange mixture in greased tin. Add layer of dough. Repeat, ending with orange mixture. Sprinkle with sugar mixture.

Bake in hot oven (425°F. Mark 7) 20 minutes. Serves 6.

Quick Coffee Ring

QUICK COFFEE RING

6 ounces seedless raisins
8 ounces plain flour
4 teaspoons baking powder
1 teaspoon salt
3 ounces fat
5 fluid ounces milk
3 tablespoons melted butter or margarine
3 ounces brown sugar
¼ teaspoon cinnamon

Rinse and drain raisins. Sift together flour, baking powder, and salt. Cut in fat. Add milk and mix well. Turn out onto lightly floured board and roll to rectangle about 10×14 inches.

Combine 2 tablespoons of the butter with brown sugar, cinnamon, and raisins. Spread over dough. Roll up as for Swiss roll.

Place sealed edge down on lightly greased baking sheet. Join ends to form ring, seal. With scissors make cuts ⅔ of way through ring at 1-inch intervals. Turn each section on its side. Brush with remaining butter.

Bake in hot oven (400°F. Mark 6) about 25 minutes, until well browned. Serve hot. Makes 1 ring.

SOUR CREAM BISCUIT CAKE

8 ounces plain flour
2 teaspoons baking powder
½ teaspoon bicarbonate of soda
Dash of salt
4 ounces sugar
2 ounces butter or margarine
8 fluid ounces sour cream
1 slightly beaten egg

Mix and sift flour, baking powder, soda, salt, and sugar. Cut in butter.

Add sour cream to beaten egg and stir lightly into dry ingredients. Turn into 8-inch square tin or oaf tin.

Bake in hot oven (400°F. Mark 6) 25 minutes for 8-inch square tin or 45 minutes in loaf tin.

If desired, sprinkle top of cake with sugar and cinnamon before baking. Makes 1 square cake or loaf.

OPEN-FACED APPLE CAKE

8 ounces plain flour
2½ teaspoons baking powder
1 teaspoon salt
3 ounces fat
About 6 fluid ounces milk
3 medium-sized apples
3 tablespoons sugar
¼ teaspoon cinnamon

Mix and sift flour, baking powder, and salt. Cut in 2 ounces fat thoroughly. Add just enough milk to hold dry ingredients together.

Turn into 2 lightly greased 8-inch sandwich tins.

Peel and slice apples thinly and arrange over dough. Dot with remaining fat. Sprinkle with sugar and cinnamon.

Bake in moderate oven (375°F. Mark 5) about 20 minutes. Serve with cream.

RAISIN COCONUT COFFEE CAKE

4½ ounces seedless raisins
5 ounces plain flour
4 ounces brown sugar
3 ounces butter or margarine
½ teaspoon baking powder
¼ teaspoon salt
¼ teaspoon cinnamon
¼ teaspoon bicarbonate of soda
1 egg
3 fluid ounces buttermilk or sour milk
3 ounces desiccated coconut

Rinse raisins and drain thoroughly. Combine flour, sugar, and fat and blend until crumbly. Set aside ½ cup of this mixture.

To remainder, add baking powder, salt, cinnamon, and soda. Stir in raisins. Beat egg lightly; add buttermilk. Stir into dry mixture and blend well.

Turn into greased 8-inch cake tin. Sprinkle reserved crumbly mixture evenly over batter and top with coconut. Bake in moderate oven (350°F. Mark 4) 30 to 40 minutes. Cut in wedges; serve warm. Serves 6.

DUTCH PEACH CAKE

Part 1:

8 ounces plain flour
½ teaspoon salt
4 teaspoons baking powder
4 ounces sugar
¼ teaspoon mace
1 egg
8 fluid ounces milk
4 tablespoons melted butter

Sift together the dry ingredients. Beat the egg until thick and lemon-coloured.

Add the milk and stir into the dry mixture along with the melted butter. Do not beat. Spread into a well buttered 9-inch square glass baking dish.

Part 2:

1 ounce butter
2 ounces sugar
2 tablespoons flour
1 teaspoon cinnamon
Peach slices, quantity depends on design

Crumble the butter into the dry ingredients. (Double the quantity if the family likes lots of topping.)

Arrange peach slices in rows or in any desired design on top of batter. Sprinkle the crumbly butter mixture over the top. Bake in a moderate oven (375°F. Mark 5) for 25 to 30 minutes. Serve hot.

Note: This is good as dessert for dinner, cut in squares and topped with whipped cream or hard sauce, or served with a jug of cream.

BLACKBERRY BUCKLE

Crumb Topping:
4 ounces sugar
3 ounces flour
½ teaspoon cinnamon
1½ ounces soft butter or margarine

Measure sugar, flour, and cinnamon into small bowl. Mix well.

Add butter or margarine and cut in with fork or pastry blender until mixture is consistency of crumbs.

Batter:
2 ounces soft butter or margarine
6 ounces sugar
1 egg
4 fluid ounces milk
6 ounces plain flour
2 teaspoons baking powder
½ teaspoon salt
1 14-ounce can blackberries or cranberries, or fresh blackcurrants, drained

Stir butter or margarine until creamy. Add sugar, gradually, mixing until creamy. Beat in egg. Add milk.

Sift together flour, baking powder, and salt. Stir into butter or margarine mixture, stirring until smooth. Gently fold in the well drained blueberries.

Spread batter into well buttered tin, 8×8 inches.

Sprinkle with crumb topping. Bake in moderate oven (375°F. Mark 5) 45 to 50 minutes.

BAVARIAN MOCK STRUDEL

8 ounces plain flour
4 ounces sugar
4 teaspoons baking powder
1 ounce non-fat dry milk solids
½ teaspoon salt
4 ounces fat
5 tablespoons water

Topping:
1 can (about 14 ounces) sweet
    cherries
2 tablespoons melted butter
1½ ounces brown sugar
2 ounces whole almonds

Sift dry ingredients together. Cut in fat. Add water and mix. Spread in greased 6 × 12-inch tin.

Arrange cherries in rows over dough. Mix other topping ingredients together and sprinkle over cherries.

Bake in hot oven (400°F. Mark 6) for 35 minutes.

Make icing with 2 ounces icing sugar, 1 teaspoon water, and few drops almond essence. Dribble over hot bread. Serve warm.

ORANGE COFFEE CAKE

Orange Crumb Topping:
4 ounces plain flour
4½ ounces brown sugar
2 tablespoons melted fat
2 tablespoons orange juice
1½ teaspoons grated orange rind
½ teaspoon cinnamon

Mix above ingredients together with a fork before mixing coffee cake.

Coffee Cake:
8 ounces plain flour
¼ teaspoon salt
4 ounces sugar
4 teaspoons baking powder
1½ teaspoons grated orange rind
2 ounces fat
1 egg
4 fluid ounces orange juice
4 fluid ounces milk

Mix and sift dry ingredients. Add orange rind and cut in fat. Blend in well beaten egg mixed with orange juice and milk.

Spread in greased and floured 8-inch square tin. Drop bits of Orange Crumb Topping over top.

Bake in moderate oven (375°F. Mark 5) 30 to 35 minutes.

HONEY COFFEE CAKE

3 ounces plain flour
2½ teaspoons baking powder
¼ teaspoon salt
4 fluid ounces milk
4 fluid ounces honey
1 egg, well beaten
3 tablespoons melted fat
3 ounces cornflakes or other cereal

Sift flour with baking powder and salt. Combine milk, honey, and egg, and add to flour mixture.

Add fat, mixing only enough to combine. Fold in cornflakes. Pour into greased tin. Sprinkle topping (see below) over batter.

Bake in hot oven (400°F. Mark 6) until done (25 minutes). Makes 1 square cake (8 × 8 × 2 inches).

Honey Coffee Cake Topping: Mix together 1½ ounces brown sugar, ½ teaspoon cinnamon, ¼ teaspoon nutmeg, 2 tablespoons melted butter, and 1 ounce cornflakes. Sprinkle over batter in tin.

POPPY SEED KUCHEN

6 ounces plain flour
4 tablespoons sugar
½ teaspoon baking powder
⅛ teaspoon salt
8 fluid ounces milk
1 egg yolk, beaten
½ pound poppy seeds
2 ounces butter
4 fluid ounces cream
1 tablespoon grated lemon rind or
    1 tablespoon grated orange
    rind

Mix and sift flour, 1 tablespoon sugar, baking powder, and salt. Blend milk with egg yolk. Add to flour mixture. Blend well and let stand ½ hour.

Grind poppy seeds well. Add remaining ingredients and mix well.

Roll dough out ½-inch thick on a floured board. Place in a cake tin. Cover with poppy seed mixture.

Bake in moderate oven (350°F. Mark 4) about 30 minutes.

DUTCH BANANA COFFEE CAKE

4 ounces plain flour
1¼ teaspoons baking powder
½ teaspoon salt
2 tablespoons sugar
2 ounces fat
1 egg, well beaten
3 tablespoons milk
3 firm bananas
2 tablespoons melted butter
2 tablespoons sugar
¼ teaspoon cinnamon
1 teaspoon grated orange rind

Mix and sift flour, baking powder, salt, and sugar. Cut in fat.

Combine egg and milk. Add to flour mixture and stir until mixture is blended.

Turn the stiff dough into a greased baking tin (8 × 10 × 2 inches), and spread evenly over bottom of tin.

Peel bananas and cut into ½-inch diagonal pieces. Cover surface of dough with overlapping pieces of bananas. Brush bananas with butter.

Mix together sugar, cinnamon, and orange rind and sprinkle over top of bananas.

Bake in moderate oven (350°F. Mark 4) about 35 minutes. Serves 6 to 8.

STAR COFFEE CAKE

1 can (13½ ounces) crushed pineapple, drained
6 fluid ounces syrup, drained from pineapple
1 recipe scone dough using 8 ounces flour
2 ounces butter or margarine, melted
3 ounces brown sugar
¼ teaspoon cinnamon
3 ounces pecans or other nuts, chopped
Glacé cherries

Drain pineapple thoroughly. Make scone dough, using pineapple syrup instead of milk. Roll out about ½ inch thick on lightly floured board, making a circle 10½ inches in diameter.

Melt butter; stir in brown sugar, cinnamon, nuts, drained pineapple.

Transfer circle of dough to greased baking sheet. Make 5 slashes from outside edge to centre. (These should be about 3 inches long and 6 inches apart at edge.)

Put 2 tablespoons pineapple mixture in each of the 5 sections.

Then, taking the corner of one section, fold it over toward centre, then overlap the other corner on top of this, making a point.

Pinch together at the tip and along double thickness to keep pineapple from oozing out.

Repeat with other 4 sections to make a 5-point star.

Spread remainder of pineapple mixture in centre area.

Brush surface of dough with melted fat. Decorate with glacé cherries.

Bake in very hot oven (450°F. Mark 8) 20 to 25 minutes. Serve hot.

Star Coffee Cake

Fig Loaf Roll

FIG LOAF ROLL

Fig Filling:

4 ounces dried figs
3 tablespoons water
2 ounces sugar
1 tablespoon flour
Dash of salt
2 tablespoons lemon juice

Cover figs with boiling water and let stand about 10 minutes; drain, clip off stems, and snip figs fine with scissors.

Add water and heat. Add sugar mixed with flour and salt, and cook gently, stirring, about 10 minutes, or until thickened.

Add lemon juice, and cool before using.

Dough For Fig Roll Loaf:

12 ounces flour
4½ teaspoons baking powder
¾ teaspoon salt
2 ounces sugar
3 ounces fat
1 egg, beaten
8 fluid ounces milk

Mix and sift flour with baking powder, salt, and sugar into mixing bowl. Cut or rub in fat until like breadcrumbs.

Add milk to beaten egg; add all at once to flour mixture and stir just until dough will hold together.

Turn out on lightly floured board, and roll or pat out about ½ inch thick. The sheet of dough should be as wide as your bread tin is long, or about 8 inches.

Spread the fig filling evenly over the dough, roll up, and cut into slices about ¾ inch thick.

Stand the slices up in their original position in a well greased 8×4×4-inch loaf tin, placing each slice tightly against the other until the tin is full.

Bake in hot oven (400°F. Mark 6) 30 to 35 minutes, until done and nicely browned. Cool slightly before cutting. Serves 6.

TOPSY-TURVY DUTCH APPLE CAKE

2 ounces margarine
4½ ounces brown sugar
1 teaspoon cinnamon
1 tablespoon milk
2 cooking apples, peeled and sliced thin
8 ounces flour
3 teaspoons baking powder
2 tablespoons sugar
½ teaspoon salt
3 ounces margarine
1 egg
6 fluid ounces milk

Melt margarine and add brown sugar, cinnamon, and 1 tablespoon milk. Pour into 9-inch sandwich tin or 9-inch square tin.

Arrange sliced apples in brown sugar mixture.

Sift together flour, baking powder, sugar, and salt. Cut in margarine.

Combine egg with milk and add to flour mixture. Stir only until flour disappears. Spread dough carefully over apples.

Bake in moderate oven (350°F. Mark 4) 45 to 50 minutes. Serve upside-down, decorated with whipped cream, if desired.

SWEDISH CHERRY RING

1 recipe scone dough
Melted butter
2 ounces sugar
1 teaspoon cinnamon
1 ounce chopped nuts
Cherry jam

Roll dough into rectangle ¼ inch thick. Spread with melted butter and sprinkle with sugar, cinnamon, and nuts.

Roll dough Swiss-roll fashion. Shape into ring on greased baking sheet. Press ends together.

From outer edge, snip almost to centre at 1-inch intervals with scissors. Pull slices apart and twist so cut surface is turned upward.

Place one teaspoon of cherry jam

in crevice of each cut. Bake in very hot oven (450°F. Mark 8) about 15 minutes, or until nicely browned.

STRAWBERRY COFFEE CAKE

8 ounces flour
2 teaspoons baking powder
6 tablespoons sugar
¾ teaspoon salt
3 ounces butter or fat
1 well beaten egg
3 fluid ounces milk
8 ounces strawberries, cleaned and hulled

Topping:

1½ ounces butter
3 tablespoons flour
2 ounces sugar

Mix and sift flour, baking powder, sugar, and salt. Cut in fat.

Combine egg and milk and add to dry ingredients, stirring with fork only to blend well.

Spread dough in well greased 8-inch square tin. Cover with strawberries, whole or cut in halves. Sprinkle with topping.

Bake in hot oven (400°F. Mark 6) 25 to 30 minutes.

Prepare topping by blending ingredients together until crumbly. Makes 1 8-inch square cake.

BLACKBERRY COFFEE CAKE

4 ounces fat
4 ounces sugar
2 eggs
7 ounces flour
3 teaspoons baking powder
½ teaspoon salt
8 fluid ounces milk
4 ounces blackberries or black-currants
1½ ounces brown sugar
½ teaspoon cinnamon

Cream fat. Add sugar and cream thoroughly. Beat eggs, and add.

Mix and sift flour, baking powder, and salt. Add alternately with milk to creamed mixture. Fold in fruit.

Turn into a greased 8-inch square tin. Sprinkle with mixture of brown sugar and cinnamon.

Bake in moderate oven (350°F. Mark 4) 50 minutes. Serve hot.

Swedish Cherry Ring

SPICE NUT COFFEE CAKE

6 ounces plain flour
5 ounces sugar
2 teaspoons baking powder
½ teaspoon salt
½ teaspoon ground cloves
½ teaspoon nutmeg
1 teaspoon cinnamon
3 ounces fat
1 egg, beaten
2 tablespoons molasses or treacle
5 fluid ounces milk
2 ounces chopped walnuts

Sift together into a bowl the flour, sugar, baking powder, salt, and spices. Cut in fat with fork or pastry blender until mixture is like coarse crumbs. Reserve some of this mixture for top of coffee cake.

To rest of crumb mixture add beaten egg, molasses, and milk. Mix lightly.

Pour into large well greased baking tin. Sprinkle top with remaining crumb mixture and the chopped walnuts.

Bake in moderate oven (350°F. Mark 4) about 45 minutes. Serves 8.

FILLED CINNAMON COFFEE CAKE

2 ounces fat
6 ounces sugar
1 well beaten egg
8 ounces plain flour
2 teaspoons baking powder
½ teaspoon salt
6 fluid ounces milk

Filling:

4 ounces sugar
3 teaspoons cinnamon
2 tablespoons flour
3 tablespoons melted butter

Cream fat and sugar together. Add egg and mix well.

Mix and sift flour, baking powder, and salt. Add sifted dry ingredients and milk alternately to creamed mixture.

Spread ½ the batter in greased tin about 7 by 11 inches.

Mix all ingredients for filling together until crumbly. Sprinkle ½ the filling over batter. Cover with remaining batter and sprinkle with remaining topping.

Bake in moderate oven (375°F. Mark 5) 30 minutes. Serves 8.

MOCK APPLE STRUDEL

8 ounces plain flour
3 teaspoons baking powder
½ teaspoon salt
2 tablespoons sugar
2 ounces fat
5-6 fluid ounces milk
1 pound chopped apple
4 ounces sugar
1 teaspoon cinnamon
Icing sugar
Vanilla

Chopped nuts

Mix and sift flour, baking powder, salt, and sugar. Cut in fat. Add milk to make a soft dough.

Turn out on floured board and knead gently. Roll out ¼-inch thick.

Brush with melted butter or margarine. Cover with chopped apple. Sprinkle sugar and cinnamon over apple.

Roll Swiss-roll fashion and form into a semicircle on a greased baking sheet.

Bake in hot oven (425°F. Mark 7) 20 to 25 minutes.

While warm, ice with glacé icing made by beating icing sugar with a little hot water until smooth, and flavoured with vanilla. Sprinkle chopped nuts over icing. Makes 12 1-inch slices.

CRANBERRY TWISTS

Cranberry Filling:

6 ounces cranberries
2 tablespoons cornflour
4 ounces sugar
2 tablespoons water
2 tablespoons margarine
Dash of nutmeg

Wash and pick over cranberries, removing stems. Mix cornflour and sugar. Add to cranberries in saucepan. Mix well. Add water.

Cook over gentle heat, stirring constantly until thickened. Sauce will be quite thick.

Remove from heat. Stir in margarine and nutmeg. Let cook while making the dough.

Dough:

8 ounces flour
3 teaspoons baking powder
¾ teaspoon salt
2 tablespoons sugar
3 ounces margarine
About 6 fluid ounces milk

Sift together flour, baking powder, salt, and sugar into mixing bowl.

Cut or rub in margarine until mixture is like coarse breadcrumbs.

Add milk and stir until dough clings together in ball.

Turn out on floured board.

Roll out to long narrow sheet a scant ½ inch thick.

Spread cranberry filling on dough, leaving a strip about ⅓ of the width of dough uncovered. Fold this strip over centre ⅓ of dough; then fold over third step. This makes 3 layers of dough and 2 layers of filling.

Cut crosswise into 1-inch slices. Twist each slice once, twisting ends in opposite directions.

Place an inch apart on greased baking sheet.

Bake in hot oven (425°F. Mark 7) 15 minutes. Serve hot.

Mock Apple Strudel

PINEAPPLE PINWHEELS

8 ounces flour
3 teaspoons baking powder
2 tablespoons granulated sugar
1 teaspoon salt
3 ounces fat
5 fluid ounces syrup drained from crushed pineapple
8 ounces drained crushed pineapple
4 ounces brown sugar
¼ teaspoon cinnamon
2 tablespoons melted butter or margarine

Sift flour, baking powder, granulated sugar, and salt together into mixing bowl. Using pastry blender or 2 knives cut in fat until finely divided. Add pineapple syrup and mix until dough holds together.

Turn out on lightly floured board and knead gently several strokes to smooth dough. Roll out to an oblong shape, about 8 × 16 inches.

Spread with following mixture: 8 ounces drained crushed pineapple, 4 ounces brown sugar, ¼ teaspoon cinnamon, and 2 tablespoons melted butter or margarine.

Starting from long side roll up as for Swiss roll; seal long edge, using fingers.

With sharp knife cut into 16 slices, 1-inch thick. Place slices, cut side down, in well greased square baking tin, 9 × 9 × 1¾ inches.

Bake in hot oven (425°F. Mark 7) 25 minutes. Makes 16 pineapple pinwheels.

Pineapple Pinwheels

Scones and Quick Rolls

BAKING POWDER SCONE HINTS

For high, light, tender, piping hot, crusty scones.

1. Turn on the oven first as correct baking temperature is important for perfect results. After assembling the ingredients and utensils, measuring dry ingredients and sifting them together into mixing bowl, measure fat into mixing bowl and cut into flour mixture with pastry blender (or 2 knives used scissors fashion) until finely blended. Mixture should look like coarse crumbs.

2. Measure the maximum amount of milk specified. Do not add all of it at first. Add almost all of it, mix it in and see if the dough seems easy to handle. Then add the rest if necessary. Too much milk makes the dough sticky and difficult to handle. Not enough milk makes the dough stiff and the finished scones tough and dry.

3. Round up on a lightly floured board. Knead very gently and quickly just to thoroughly mix ingredients and to even up texture. This means turning the dough 2 or 3 times—not more than 15 or 20 punches with flour-dusted hands. Too much handling at this point makes the scones tough.

4. Roll dough or pat it out (with floured hand) until dough is ½-inch thick.

5. Cut with pastry cutter (dipped in flour first to prevent sticking). Cut as close together as possible. (Leftover bits of dough should be fitted and pushed together, patted out and cut —not re-rolled.) Place scones close together on baking sheet for scones with soft sides—or far apart for scones with crusty sides.

BAKING POWDER SCONES (Master Recipe)

8 ounces plain flour
3 teaspoons baking powder
1 teaspoon salt
2 ounces fat
5-6 fluid ounces milk or water

Sift together dry ingredients. Cut fat into flour with 2 knives or pastry blender until consistency of breadcrumbs.

Add liquid, mixing lightly with a fork until a ball forms that separates from the sides of bowl.

Turn out on lightly floured board. Knead gently ½ minute. Roll or pat out dough ½ inch thick. Cut with floured biscuit cutter.

Bake on ungreased baking sheet in very hot oven (450°F. Mark 8) 12 to 15 minutes. Serve immediately. Makes 1½ dozen scones.

Scone Variations:

Scone Teasers: Place jam or seasoned chopped meat between 2 thin scones. Press edges together. Brush with fat or milk and bake.

Bran Scones: In master recipe substitute 4 ounces whole bran for 4 ounces white flour.

Cheese Scones: In master recipe add 1 ounce grated cheese to dry ingredients.

Chive Scones: In master recipe add 3-4 tablespoons freshly chopped chives to mixture of flour and fat.

Cream Scones: In master recipe use 6 fluid ounces double cream instead of fat and milk or water.

Drop Scones: Increase liquid in master recipe to 8 fluid ounces. Drop from teaspoon on lightly greased baking sheet or into deep bun tins.

Fried Scones: Prepare master recipe; drop spoonfuls of dough into hot greased frying pan. Turn when brown.

Fruit Scones: In master recipe add 3 ounces chopped dates, figs, prunes, or raisins to mixture of flour and fat.

Mint Scones: In master recipe add ½ ounce freshly chopped mint to mixture of flour and fat.

Nut Scones: In master recipe add 2 ounces chopped nuts to mixture of flour and fat.

Orange Scones: In master recipe add 1 tablespoon grated orange rind to mixture of flour and fat.

Orange Tea Scones: In master recipe add 1 teaspoon grated orange rind to dry ingredients. When scones have been cut, press into the top of each a small cube of sugar which has been dipped in orange juice or other fruit juice.

Peanut Scones: Substitute 3 ounces peanut butter for fat in master recipe.

Rich Shortcake Scones: To master recipe, add 1 egg and 2 tablespoons sugar. Increase fat to 3 ounces.

Savoury Scones: Add 1 teaspoon mixed herbs to dry ingredients of master recipe.

Sour Milk or Buttermilk Scones: Follow master recipe. Add ½ teaspoon bicarbonate of soda, sifting it with flour. Use sour milk or buttermilk for liquid.

Whole Wheat Scones: In master recipe substitute 4 ounces whole wheat flour for 4 ounces white flour. Use ¾ teaspoon salt instead of 1 teaspoon salt.

OLD-FASHIONED SODA SCONES

8 ounces flour
¾ teaspoon bicarbonate of soda
½ teaspoon salt
2 ounces fat
3 tablespoons distilled vinegar
4 fluid ounces fresh milk

Mix and sift flour, soda, and salt. Cut in fat. Add vinegar and milk and stir lightly.

Turn onto floured board and knead lightly.

For **Northern-style,** roll about ½ inch thick; **Southern-style,** roll about ¼ inch thick.

Cut scones and prick with fork for Southern-style. Place on greased baking sheet.

Bake in very hot oven (450°F. Mark 8) 12 to 15 minutes. Makes 16 to 18 2-inch Northern-style scones or 32 to 34 2-inch Southern-style scones.

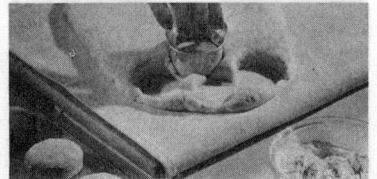

VARIETY SCONES FROM MASTER SCONES RECIPE

Banana Curls: Roll dough for baking powder scones into rectangular shape about $\frac{1}{4}$ inch thick. Brush with 2 tablespoons melted butter or margarine.

Slice 2 medium-sized ripe bananas evenly over the dough.

Mix 3 tablespoons brown sugar and $\frac{1}{2}$ teaspoon cinnamon together and sprinkle over bananas.

Roll as for Swiss roll and cut in 1-inch slices.

Place cut side up in well greased deep bun tins and brush top with melted butter. Bake in hot oven (400°F. Mark 6) 15 minutes. Makes 18 curls.

Scone Sticks: Roll or pat out dough for baking powder scones and cut into sticks $\frac{1}{2}$ inch wide and 3 inches long. Brush with melted butter.

Bake in hot oven (425°F. Mark 7).

Blackberry Scones: Prepare baking powder scone dough. Roll out $\frac{1}{4}$ inch thick. Fill as in method 1 or 2.

Bake in very hot oven (450°F. Mark 8) 12 to 15 minutes.

Method 1: Form shells by lining deep bun tins halfway up with dough. Fill the middle with sugared berries. Cover with a round of dough. Moisten edges of shells and rounds and press lightly together.

Method 2: Cut the dough into small squares or rounds. Place sugared berries between two pieces and pinch edges together.

Cheese Rosettes: To recipe for baking powder scones add 2 ounces grated Cheddar cheese before adding liquid. Substitute water for milk.

Chill slightly before using. Roll out on floured surface to $\frac{1}{4}$-inch thickness.

Cut into $\frac{1}{2}$-inch strips about 6 inches long. Tie in bowknot. After tying bring one end through centre and other end over the side and turn under.

Place on greased baking sheet, dust with paprika, and bake in hot oven (400°F. Mark 6) 10 to 15 minutes.

Cheese Squares: Roll or pat dough for baking powder scones $\frac{1}{4}$-inch thick. Sprinkle lightly with grated cheese.

With a sharp knife, cut dough into squares. Bake in hot oven (425°F. Mark 7).

Cherry Delights: Cut dough for baking powder scones into small rounds.

With a smaller cutter, remove centres from half the rounds. Brush with rich milk. Place the rings on top of the whole rounds.

Place $\frac{1}{2}$ teaspoon cherry jam in the centre of each and bake in hot oven (425°F. Mark 7) 12 to 15 minutes.

Marmalade Crescents: Prepare dough for baking powder scones. Roll out $\frac{1}{2}$ inch thick.

Brush with 2 tablespoons melted butter or other melted fat. Spread with marmalade or jam.

Cut into 3-inch squares, then cut each square diagonally in half to make triangles.

Roll each triangle Swiss-roll fashion, starting with the long edge of the triangle. Shape into a crescent.

Place on greased baking sheet and bake in a very hot oven (450°F. Mark 8) 12 to 15 minutes. Makes about 16 crescents.

Pineapple Squares: Add 2 tablespoons sugar to recipe for baking powder scones and roll out into rectangular sheet.

Cut into strips 3 inches wide and 6 inches long. Brush with melted butter.

Place 1 teaspoon crushed pineapple on $\frac{1}{2}$ of each strip and fold the other end of the strip over the fruit. Press edges together with a fork. Prick tops with fork.

Bake in hot oven (425°F. Mark 7) 25 minutes. Serve hot or cold with cream or with fruit sauce.

GIRDLE SODA SCONES
(No Fat)

1   pound plain flour
1   teaspoon bicarbonate of soda
1   teaspoon cream of tartar
1½ teaspoons salt
8   fluid ounces buttermilk or sour milk

Mix all ingredients thoroughly. Pat out on floured board to $\frac{1}{2}$-inch thickness; cut with 2½-inch cutter.

Put on hot greased girdle; cook until well-risen and light brown underneath. Turn, cook on other side until brown.

When the edges are dry, the scones are done. Makes about 15 scones.

CHEESE FAN TANS

Prepare baking powder scone dough. Shape into a smooth ball after a quick light kneading. Roll into a rectangle about $\frac{1}{8}$-inch thick and 8-inches wide.

Cut in 4 strips 2 inches wide. Spread with softened (not melted) butter. Sprinkle 3 strips with 4 ounces of grated Cheddar cheese ranging from mild to sharp as family taste suggests.

Pile the 3 strips on top of each other, covering with the fourth strip (no cheese on this). Cut across into 6 pieces. Carefully place in buttered deep bun tins, having the cut side up. Brush with melted butter.

Bake in a very hot oven (450°F. Mark 8) for 10 to 12 minutes or until cooked through with a light browning. Serve at once.

Scotch Scones

SCOTCH SCONES

A scone was originally a Scottish girdlecake made usually of oats, sometimes of barley or wheat; nowadays, it refers to a small cake resembling a baking powder scone, cut in various shapes, baked in a hot oven or on a girdle, and usually served with butter.

8   ounces plain flour
3   teaspoons baking powder
1   teaspoon salt
1   tablespoon sugar
2   ounces fat
1½ ounces currants (optional)
2   eggs
4   fluid ounces milk

Sift together flour, baking powder, salt, and sugar. Cut in fat. Add currants, if desired.

Beat together 1 whole egg and 1 egg yolk, reserving 1 white for the tops. Add milk to beaten eggs, and add all to dry ingredients. Stir only enough to make dough hold together.

Turn out on lightly floured board and knead $\frac{1}{2}$ minute. Roll out in circular shape to $\frac{1}{2}$-inch thickness.

Cut into pie-shaped wedges. Brush tops with white of egg, and sprinkle with sugar. Bake in hot oven (425°F. Mark 7) 12 to 15 minutes. Makes 10 to 12 scones.

SWEET POTATO SCONES

6   ounces plain flour
2   tablespoons baking powder
¾   teaspoon salt
4   ounces chilled fat
8   fluid ounces milk
10 ounces mashed sweet potatoes

Mix and sift flour, baking powder, and salt. Cut in fat with a pastry blender or 2 knives.

Combine milk and sweet potatoes. Add to flour-fat mixture and stir quickly.

Knead lightly on board using as little flour as possible on board. Roll $\frac{1}{2}$ inch thick. Cut with floured biscuit cutter.

Place on greased baking sheet. Bake in hot oven (425°F. Mark 7) 12 to 15 minutes. Makes about 2 dozen.

Cheese Fan Tans

HOMEMADE SCONE MIX

2 pounds plain flour
1 tablespoon salt
4 tablespoons baking powder
8 ounces fat

Mix and sift flour, salt, and baking powder into a large bowl.

Have fat at room temperature. Cut it into flour mixture with pastry blender or fork until mixture is like coarse breadcrumbs.

Store in a closely covered container. Scone mix will keep 3 to 4 weeks in a cool cupboard and much longer in the refrigerator.

Rich Homemade Scone Mix: Sift in with the flour 4 ounces dried skim milk solids.

To Make 6 Scones: Measure 6 ounces scone mix into a bowl. Stir in 2 to 3 fluid ounces milk.

To cut out and bake follow method in master recipe for Scones.

To Make 6 Muffins: Measure 6 ounces scone mix into a bowl. Add 1 tablespoon sugar, 1 well beaten egg, and about 4 fluid ounces milk.

To mix and bake follow method in master recipe for Plain Muffins.

To Make 6 Pancakes: Measure 6 ounces scone mix. Beat 1 egg well; combine with 4 fluid ounces milk and 2 tablespoons flour. Add to mix and stir only to dampen flour.

Then add more milk to make batter just thin enough to pour. To bake follow method in master recipe for Girdle Cakes.

To Make 6 Waffles: Measure 12 ounces mix; add 1 teaspoon sugar and ⅛ teaspoon salt.

Combine 2 tablespoons melted butter, 1 well beaten egg, and 12 fluid ounces fresh or sour milk. Beat liquid ingredients into scone mix.

To bake, follow method in master recipe for Waffles.

QUICK ORANGE ROLLS

1 can frozen orange juice con-
centrate
4 tablespoons water
8 ounces sugar
8 ounces plain flour
4 teaspoons baking powder
1 teaspoon salt
2 ounces fat
5-6 fluid ounces milk
6 ounces chopped dates

Combine orange juice concentrate, water, and sugar and cook to thick syrup, about 10 minutes. Cool.

Mix and sift flour, baking powder, and salt. Cut in fat with pastry blender until mixture resembles coarse breadcrumbs. Add milk to make a soft dough, while stirring quickly.

Roll out to rectangle about 8 by 16 inches. Sprinkle on the chopped dates. Roll up long way as for Swiss roll. Cut into 16 slices.

Place cut side down in deep 9-inch pie dish, placing rolls close together. Pour cooled syrup over scones.

Bake in very hot oven (450°F. Mark 8) 15 to 20 minutes. Makes about 16.

SCONE PINWHEELS

Prepare dough for standard baking powder scones. Roll into an oblong about 12 inches long and ¼ inch thick.

Spread with desired filling as directed in the following variations.

Roll lengthwise as tightly as possible, Swiss roll fashion. Pinch edge to the roll.

Cut into 1-inch slices and place cut side down in greased deep bun tins.

Bake in hot oven (400°F. Mark 6) 18 to 20 minutes. Makes about 12 pinwheels.

Butterscotch Pinwheels: Spread dough with 2 tablespoons melted fat and 3 ounces brown sugar. Roll and cut as directed above.

Cream together 3 ounces butter and 3 ounces brown sugar.

Spread thickly in each deep bun tin and place 2 or 3 pecan or walnut halves in bottom of each tin before adding pinwheels. Bake.

Cinnamon Currant Pinwheels: Spread dough with 2 tablespoons melted fat and mixture of 3 ounces sugar and 1¼ teaspoons cinnamon.

Sprinkle with 3 ounces currants. Roll, cut, and bake.

Honey or Maple Pinwheels: Brush rolled dough with melted fat. Sprinkle with brown sugar. If desired, add chopped nuts, dates, or raisins. Roll and cut as directed.

Place 1 tablespoon honey or maple syrup in bottom of each greased deep bun tin. Press cut scone into each section.

Jam Pinwheels: Spread dough with 2 tablespoons melted fat and 4 ounces jam or marmalade; roll, cut, and bake.

Peanut Butter Pinwheels: Spread dough with 2 tablespoons melted fat and 3 ounces peanut butter; roll, cut, and bake.

CORN DROP SCONES

6 ounces plain flour
2½ teaspoons baking powder
½ teaspoon salt
3½ ounces maize flour
2 ounces fat
6 fluid ounces milk

Mix and sift flour, baking powder, and salt. Blend in maize flour.

Cut in fat until mixture resembles coarse breadcrumbs. Add milk all at once and stir only until all flour is dampened.

Drop by spoonfuls onto meat and vegetable mixture in casserole. Bake in

hot oven (400°F. Mark 6) 35 to 40 minutes.

BEATEN SCONES

These are unleavened scones that depend for tenderness on long beating.

12 ounces plain flour
½ teaspoon salt
4 ounces chilled lard
5 fluid ounces milk

Mix flour and salt. Cut in fat as for pastry. Add milk and mix until dough holds together.

Turn out onto a board and beat dough vigorously with a rolling pin, or an oldfashioned wooden potato masher.

Beat until dough becomes smooth and velvety in texture. Cut tiny scones and prick each right through twice with the tines of a fork.

Bake on baking sheet in moderate oven (350°F. Mark 4) 30 minutes. Split and butter while hot. Makes 3 dozen.

PECAN ROLLS

8 ounces plain flour
3 teaspoons baking powder
½ teaspoon salt
2 ounces fat
5-6 fluid ounces milk
2 tablespoons melted butter or
margarine
3 ounces brown sugar
Pecan or walnut halves

Prepare deep bun tins by spreading thickly with a creamy mixture made by creaming together 1½ ounces butter and 6 tablespoons brown sugar. Put 2 or 3 pecan halves into each bun tin.

Sift together flour, baking powder, and salt. Cut in fat. Add milk, stirring only until dough holds together.

Turn out on slightly floured board and knead lightly for ½ minute. Roll out to ¼-inch thickness. Brush with melted butter or margarine and sprinkle with brown sugar.

Roll Swiss-roll fashion and cut into 1-inch slices. Place slices cut side down into deep bun tins.

Bake in hot oven (425°F. Mark 7) 20 to 25 minutes. Let stand in tin for a minute before turning out. Serve hot or cold. Makes 16 to 18 small rolls.

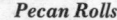
Pecan Rolls

STIR AND ROLL SCONES
(Master Recipe)

8 ounces plain flour
3 teaspoons baking powder
1 teaspoon salt
3 fluid ounces salad oil
5 fluid ounces milk

Sift flour once, measure and add baking powder and salt. Sift together into a bowl.

Pour oil and milk in 1 measuring cup but do not stir together. Then pour all at once into flour.

Stir with a fork until mixture cleans side of bowl and rounds up into a ball.

For Dropped Scones: Drop dough onto ungreased baking sheet.

For Rolled Or Patted Scones: Smooth by kneading dough about 10 times without additional flour.

With the dough on greaseproof paper, press out $\frac{1}{4}$-inch thick with hands, or roll out between greaseproof paper.

For higher scones, roll dough $\frac{1}{2}$-inch thick. Cut with unfloured biscuit cutter.

Bake on ungreased baking sheet in very hot oven (475°F. Mark 9) 10 to 12 minutes. Makes about 16.

UPSIDE-DOWN ORANGE SCONES

4 tablespoons melted butter or margarine
4 fluid ounces orange juice
6 ounces sugar
2 teaspoons grated orange rind
11 ounces flour
3 teaspoons baking powder
$\frac{3}{4}$ teaspoon salt
3 ounces butter or margarine
9 fluid ounces milk
$\frac{1}{2}$ teaspoon cinnamon

Combine melted margarine, orange juice, 4 ounces sugar, and orange rind; boil 2 minutes. Pour into greased round 9-inch baking tin.

Sift together flour, baking powder, and salt. With pastry blender cut butter or margarine into flour until coarse crumbs are formed. Add milk and stir with fork until soft dough is formed.

Knead $\frac{1}{2}$ minute on lightly floured board. Roll out to $\frac{1}{4}$ inch thickness.

Brush with a little melted butter or margarine and sprinkle with 2 ounces sugar and $\frac{1}{2}$ teaspoon cinnamon.

Roll as for a Swiss roll. Cut in 1-inch slices; place, cut side down, over orange mixture. Bake in very hot oven (450°F. Mark 8) 20 to 25 minutes. Serves 6.

Cheese Corn Meal Scone Ring

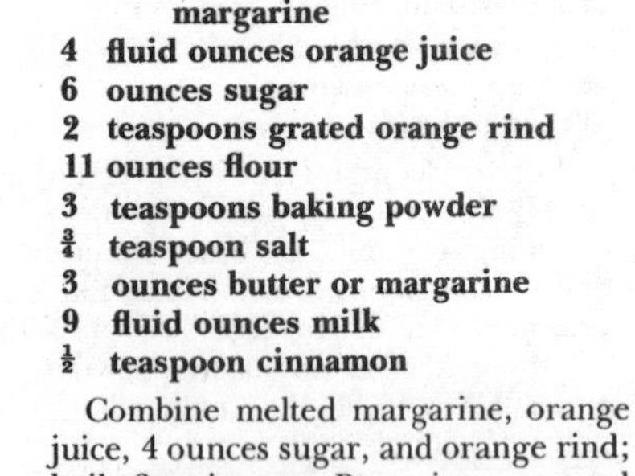

CORNFLAKE HONEY ROLLS

8 ounces plain flour
3 teaspoons baking powder
$\frac{1}{2}$ teaspoon salt
2 ounces fat
5 fluid ounces milk
3 tablespoons melted butter or margarine
6 ounces corn flakes
4 ounces seedless raisins
6 ounces honey

Sift together flour, baking powder, and salt. Cut in fat until a coarse even texture is obtained. Add milk, stirring enough to make a soft dough.

Turn onto a lightly floured board and knead about 20 seconds. Roll dough to $\frac{1}{2}$-inch thickness. Brush with melted butter.

Combine slightly crushed cornflakes, raisins, honey, and sliced maraschino cherries if you like. Spread over scone dough, roll as for a Swiss roll.

Using a knife dipped in flour, cut into 1-inch slices. Place slices on greased baking sheet.

Bake in hot oven (400°F. Mark 6) about 15 to 20 minutes. Serve at once. Makes 10 to 12 rolls.

CHEESE AND CORN SCONE RING

8 ounces plain flour
3 ounces maize flour
5 teaspoons baking powder
2 teaspoons salt
3 ounces fat
3 tablespoons chopped pimento
8 fluid ounces milk
2 ounces grated sharp cheese

Sift together flour, maize flour, baking powder, and salt. Cut in fat until mixture resembles coarse crumbs. Add pimento.

Add milk, mixing lightly only until mixture is dampened. Turn out on lightly floured board and knead gently a few seconds.

Roll out to $\frac{3}{8}$-inch thickness; brush with melted butter. Cut with floured biscuit cutter, small size.

Dip the buttered side of each scone in grated cheese.

In well greased 8-inch ring mould, stand scones on end with flat sides of scones together. Sprinkle remaining cheese over top.

Bake in hot oven (400°F. Mark 6) 20 to 25 minutes.

Let stand in ring mould 2 or 3 minutes. Invert and turn right side up. Brush with melted butter. Makes 1 8-inch ring.

Cinnamon Flake Kuchen

CINNAMON FLAKE KUCHEN

2 ounces fat
3 ounces sugar
1 egg
6 ounces plain flour
2 teaspoons baking powder
$\frac{3}{4}$ teaspoon salt
$\frac{1}{2}$ teaspoon nutmeg
5 fluid ounces milk
3 ounces brown sugar
$\frac{1}{2}$ teaspoon cinnamon
$\frac{1}{2}$ teaspoon nutmeg
1 ounce butter or margarine, melted
2 ounces cornflakes

Blend fat and sugar; add egg and beat well.

Sift together flour, baking powder, salt, and $\frac{1}{2}$ teaspoon nutmeg. Add to fat mixture alternately with milk, being careful not to overmix. Spread in greased shallow 9×9-inch baking tin.

Mix together brown sugar, spices, butter, and cornflakes; sprinkle over batter.

Bake in hot oven (400°F. Mark 6) about 25 minutes. Serve hot. Serves 12.

TRICKS WITH CHEESE AND SCONES

Cheese Turnovers: Roll scone dough $\frac{1}{4}$-inch thick. Cut in 2-inch rounds. Spread each with softened butter. Place a piece of Cheddar cheese on each. Fold it over. Press edges together. Brush tops with melted butter. Bake.

Cheese-Tomato Scone: Add 2 ounces grated dry Cheddar cheese to flour mixture; use tomato juice for the liquid.

Coral Reefs: Make up regular scone mix but use tomato juice in place of milk. Roll dough $\frac{1}{3}$-inch thick. Cut in small rounds. Put together in pairs with a round slice of Cheddar cheese between. Brush tops with melted butter. Bake as usual.

Cheese Coated Scone: Melt over hot water and mix together soft spreading Cheddar cheese (with pimento if desired) with $1\frac{1}{2}$ ounces butter. Place scones close together in tin. Top each with a spoonful of the cheese mixture. The cheese runs down, over and through the scones, as they bake.

IRISH SCONES

12 ounces plain flour
1 teaspoon salt
1 teaspoon cream of tartar
1 teaspoon baking powder
About 8 fluid ounces buttermilk
 or sour milk

Mix and sift together dry ingredients. Make a hollow in the centre and add enough buttermilk to make a soft dough.

Turn onto a floured board and knead quickly and lightly until the dough is free from cracks. Roll out to required thickness and cut in scones.

Place on a greased and floured baking sheet and bake in hot oven (400°F. Mark 6) until thoroughly baked, about 15 minutes for medium-sized scones.

BUTTERFLY CINNAMON ROLLS

8 ounces plain flour
3 teaspoons baking powder
1 teaspoon salt
4 ounces fat
1 slightly beaten egg
4 fluid ounces milk
2 tablespoons melted butter or
 margarine
3 ounces sugar
1 teaspoon cinnamon

Sift dry ingredients. Cut in fat until mixture resembles texture of coarse breadcrumbs.

Combine egg and milk and stir in dry ingredients until just blended.

Turn out on floured board. Pat out dough. Fold in half. Repeat 6 times. The last time roll to ¼-inch thickness.

Spread with melted butter, sugar, and cinnamon. Roll up and cut into 1-inch slices.

Cut slit through centre parallel to cut edges of slice down to, but not through, bottom layer of dough. Spread halves from centre out on baking sheet.

Bake in hot oven (425°F. Mark 7) until browned, 15 to 20 minutes. Makes 12 rolls.

GOLDEN CORNFLOUR STICKS

2 ounces cornflakes
5 ounces plain flour
2 ounces sugar
½ teaspoon salt
3 teaspoons baking powder
1 egg, beaten
6 fluid ounces milk
4 tablespoons melted butter or
 margarine

Combine cornflakes, flour, sugar, salt, and baking powder. Add beaten egg and milk; mix. Stir in butter.

Place in greased shallow tins or sponge finger tins. Bake in hot oven (425°-450°F. Mark 7-8) about 25 to 30 minutes. Makes 12 sticks.

DATE SURPRISES

8 ounces plain flour
3 teaspoons baking powder
1 teaspoon salt
2 teaspoons sugar
2 tablespoons melted fat
2 egg yolks
6 fluid ounces milk
1½ ounces butter
6 dates

Sift flour with baking powder, salt, and sugar.

Stir melted fat, beaten egg yolks, and milk into flour mixture. Turn out on slightly floured board; roll to ½ inch thickness and cut with biscuit cutter into circles 2½ inches in diameter.

Spread each biscuit with butter and put half a date on each. Fold biscuit over and press edges together. Place in greased sandwich tin.

Bake in moderate oven (350°F. Mark 4) 20 to 25 minutes or until browned. Makes 12 rolls.

QUICK SALT STICKS

8 ounces plain flour
1 teaspoon bicarbonate of soda
½ teaspoon salt
3 ounces fat
3 tablespoons vinegar
4 fluid ounces milk
2 ounces rice crispies
1 teaspoon salt
1½ teaspoons caraway or poppy
 seeds

Sift together flour, soda, and salt; cut in fat until mixture resembles coarse breadcrumbs. Add vinegar and milk, stirring only until combined.

Turn out on lightly floured board and knead gently a few times.

Divide into 16 equal parts. Roll each ball on board with palms of hands until it becomes a cylinder about 6 inches long. Brush with milk.

Crush rice crispies; mix in salt and caraway seeds. Roll each stick in rice crispies mixture. Place on greased baking sheets. Bake in very hot oven (450°F. Mark 8) about 15 minutes. Makes 16 sticks, 6 inches long.

BUTTERMILK SCONES

8 ounces plain flour
2 teaspoons baking powder
¾ teaspoon bicarbonate of soda
½ teaspoon salt
2 ounces fat
½ pint buttermilk or sour milk

Sift flour, measure, resift 3 times with remaining dry ingredients, the last time into a bowl.

Cut in fat with pastry blender or fork to consistency of rice grains.

Add buttermilk and mix lightly, only enough to blend ingredients.

Turn onto lightly floured board and knead lightly 5 or 6 times. Roll out ½-inch thick. Cut with 2-inch biscuit cutter. Place on ungreased baking sheet.

Bake in very hot oven (450°F. Mark 8) 15 to 18 minutes until light golden brown. Makes 1 dozen.

POTATO SCONES

4 ounces plain flour
3 teaspoons baking powder
1 teaspoon salt
1 ounce fat
7 ounces mashed potato
About 4 fluid ounces water or milk

Mix and sift flour, baking powder, and salt. Blend in fat.

Add potato and mix thoroughly. Then add enough liquid to make a soft dough.

Roll dough lightly to about ½ inch in thickness. Cut into scones. Bake in hot oven (400°F. Mark 6) 12 to 15 minutes.

CHEESE COATED SCONES 2

8 ounces plain flour
½ teaspoon salt
4 teaspoons baking powder
½ teaspoon cream of tartar
2 teaspoons sugar, if desired
4 ounces butter
5 fluid ounces milk

Sift together dry ingredients. Cut butter in using pastry blender, 2 knives, or coarse tined fork, until mixture resembles coarse crumbs. Add milk all at once and stir just until dough follows fork around the bowl.

Turn out on floured board. Knead lightly for a few seconds until smooth. Pat or roll out to ½-inch thickness. Cut with 2-inch biscuit cutter.

Place close together in shallow fireproof dish. Just before sending to the oven, spread with cheese coating.

Cheese Coating: Melt over hot water about ½ pound of grated or thinly sliced Cheddar cheese and 2 ounces butter. Whip up well before topping each biscuit with spoonful of mixture.

Bake at once in very hot oven (450°F. Mark 8) 10 to 12 minutes. Makes 16 medium biscuits.

Cheese Coated Scones 2

Muffins

MUFFIN HINTS

Perfect muffins should be light, tender, and fine in texture. Many variations can be made from a single master recipe or from a packet mix. Here are a few steps in making perfect muffins.

1. After lighting the oven and assembling the ingredients and utensils, measure the fat and put on stove to melt. Let cool while mixing batter. Grease muffin tins with any unsalted fat.

2. Sift and measure flour into the sifter. Measure other dry ingredients (baking powder, salt, etc.) and put into sifter with the flour.

3. Sift the dry ingredients together into a mixing bowl. This sifting of the flour and other dry ingredients together distributes them evenly through the flour—an aid to good texture.

4. Combine the milk, well beaten egg, and melted fat.

5. Stir the liquid into the dry ingredients just until mixed. Mix just enough to blend the ingredients, because too much mixing or beating makes tough, coarse-textured muffins.

6. Fill the greased muffin tins ⅔ full. Use a rubber scraper to push batter off the mixing spoon. Muffin tins vary in size. The surface area varies from very small to large. The depth varies from shallow to deep. This accounts for the differences in baking times. Deep bun tins or dariole tins are best to use for following recipes.

Standards for Good Muffins

Well-proportioned shape and size . . . no peaks . . . evenly browned . . . tender crust . . . even tender grain . . . no tunnels . . . good flavour.

Causes of Poor Muffins

Incorrect proportions . . . inaccurate measurements . . . overmixed batter . . . tins too full . . . incorrect baking procedure.

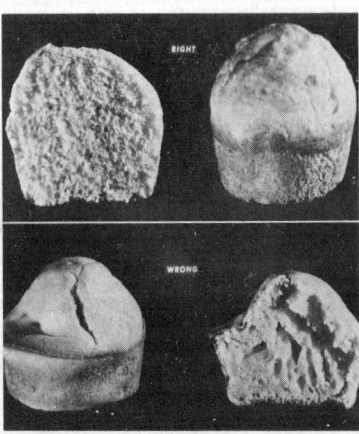

MUFFINS
(Master Recipe)

8 ounces plain flour
3 teaspoons baking powder
½ teaspoon salt
2 tablespoons sugar
1 egg, well beaten
8 fluid ounces milk
3 tablespoons melted fat

Sift together dry ingredients. Combine egg, milk, and fat. Add quickly to flour mixture, stirring only until just moistened. Do not beat.

Drop batter gently by spoonfuls into greased muffin tins, filling ⅔ full.

Bake in hot oven (425°F. Mark 7) 20 to 25 minutes, or until golden brown. Makes 1 dozen 2-inch muffins.

Muffin Variations:

Apple Muffins: In master recipe add ¼ teaspoon cinnamon and 1 ounce fat. Fold 6 ounces finely chopped apples into batter.

Bacon Muffins: In master recipe use bacon fat instead of margarine or butter. Add 1 ounce chopped, cooked bacon to sifted dry ingredients.

Berry Muffins: In master recipe add 4 ounces berries (blueberries, sweetened blackberries, sweetened strawberries) to dry ingredients.

Bran Muffins: In master recipe substitute 4 ounces whole bran for 4 ounces white flour. Soak bran in milk 5 minutes before mixing.

Cheese Muffins: In master recipe add 2 ounces grated mild cheese to dry ingredients.

Cherry Muffins: In master recipe add to muffin batter, 4 ounces drained, chopped cherries, fresh or canned.

Corn Meal Muffins: In master recipe substitute 4 ounces corn meal for 4 ounces white flour.

Cranberry Muffins: Follow master recipe; to sifted dry ingredients add 4 ounces chopped cranberries mixed with 3 tablespoons sugar.

Cream Muffins: In master recipe increase salt to ¾ teaspoon. Substitute ¼ pint double cream for milk and fat.

Dried Fruit Muffins: In master recipe add 3 ounces chopped stoned dates, figs, or raisins to dry ingredients.

Ham Muffins: In master recipe add 2½ ounces diced ham to sifted dry ingredients.

Marmalade Muffins: Follow master recipe; put ½ teaspoon butter or margarine and 1 teaspoon marmalade into each muffin tin. Drop batter for plain muffins on top.

Nut Muffins: Add 2 ounces chopped nuts to dry ingredients.

Oatmeal Muffins: In master recipe substitute 2 ounces quick-cooking oats (uncooked) for 4 ounces white flour.

Orange Muffins: In master recipe add 1 tablespoon grated orange rind to dry ingredients. Substitute orange juice for milk.

Parsley Muffins: In master recipe omit sugar. Add 2 tablespoons finely chopped parsley, stirring it into sifted dry ingredients.

Rice Muffins: Follow master recipe; to flour mixture add 3 ounces cold cooked rice and 2 well beaten eggs.

Sour Cream Muffins: Follow master recipe. Use only 1 teaspoon baking powder. Add ½ teaspoon bicarbonate of soda. Increase salt to ¾ teaspoon. Substitute 6 fluid ounces thick sour cream for milk and fat.

Sour Milk or Buttermilk Muffins: In master recipe reduce baking powder to 1 teaspoon. Add ½ teaspoon bicarbonate of soda, sifting it with flour. Use sour milk or buttermilk instead of fresh milk.

Soy Muffins: In master recipe substitute 2 ounces soy flour for 2 ounces white flour.

Whole Wheat Muffins: In master recipe substitute 4 ounces whole wheat flour for 4 ounces white flour.

WHEAT GERM MUFFINS

5 ounces plain flour
¾ teaspoon salt
3 teaspoons baking powder
2 ounces dehydrated natural wheat germ
2 tablespoons melted fat
1 beaten egg
6 fluid ounces milk
3 ounces molasses or treacle

Mix and sift flour, salt, and baking powder and mix with wheat germ.

Combine remaining ingredients and add to flour mixture. Stir only until blended. Fill greased muffin tins ⅔ full. Bake in hot oven (425°F. Mark 7) 20 minutes.

Variations:

Raisin, Date or Fig Wheat Germ Muffins: To above batter add 3 ounces raisins, diced dates, or diced figs.

Wheat Germ Muffins with Dried Milk: Sift 3 tablespoons dried skimmed milk powder with dry ingredients, and continue as directed.

Muffins keep well, so wrap leftovers in plastic wrap or aluminium foil and refrigerate or freeze to serve at another meal. Be sure to heat them before serving. Enclose muffins loosely in foil and heat about 5 minutes in preheated very hot oven (450°F. Mark 8).

BUTTER CRUST MUFFINS

4 ounces flour
½ teaspoon salt
3 teaspoons baking powder
1 tablespoon sugar
2 ounces corn meal
8 fluid ounces milk
1 beaten egg
1½ ounces peanut butter
1 tablespoon melted fat

Mix and sift flour, salt, baking powder, and sugar. Stir in corn meal.

Combine milk, egg, peanut butter, and melted fat. Add to dry ingredients and mix only until flour is moistened. Fill greased muffin tins ⅔ full. Bake in hot oven (400°F. Mark 6) about 20 minutes. Makes 12.

FRUIT BUTTERMILK MUFFINS

8 ounces plain flour
4 ounces sugar
1 teaspoon salt
¼ teaspoon bicarbonate of soda
2¼ teaspoons baking powder
2 ounces melted butter
1 slightly beaten egg
8 fluid ounces buttermilk or sour milk
4 ounces cranberries, blackberries or bilberries

Mix and sift flour, sugar, salt, soda, and baking powder.

Mix butter, egg and buttermilk together. Stir into dry ingredients, mixing just enough to moisten. Fold in fruit.

Fill greased muffin tins about ⅔ full. Bake in hot oven (425°F. Mark 7) 25 minutes. Makes 12 medium muffins.

CEREAL FLAKE MUFFINS

4 ounces plain flour
2½ teaspoons baking powder
½ teaspoon salt
2 ounces sugar
1 egg, beaten
4 fluid ounces milk
4 tablespoons melted fat
6 ounces cornflakes, slightly crushed

Sift together flour, baking powder, salt, and sugar. Combine egg, milk, and slightly cooled fat. Add to flour mixture, stirring only enough to dampen flour. Fold in cornflakes, being careful not to overmix.

Fill well greased muffin tins, 2½ inches in diameter, ⅔ full. Bake in hot oven (400°F. Mark 6) 15 to 18 minutes. Makes 12 muffins.

Nut Muffins: Add 2 ounces chopped walnuts, Brazil nuts, or pecans to sifted ingredients.

Banana Nut Muffins: Add 2 ripe mashed bananas and 2 ounces chopped nuts to egg mixture.

ORANGE PECAN MUFFINS

3 ounces fat
6 ounces sugar
3 eggs
7 ounces flour
3 teaspoons baking powder
¼ teaspoon salt
4 tablespoons orange juice
4 tablespoons milk
1 teaspoon grated orange rind
3 ounces chopped pecans or walnuts

Cream fat and sugar until light and fluffy. Add eggs and mix well.

Mix and sift dry ingredients and add alternately with orange juice, and then milk. Fold in rind and nuts.

Turn into well greased muffin tins, filling ⅔ full. Bake in moderate oven (375°F. Mark 5) 20 minutes. Makes 18 medium muffins.

PEACH MUFFINS

8 ounces plain flour
½ teaspoon salt
2½ teaspoons baking powder
2 ounces sugar
8 fluid ounces milk
1 lightly beaten egg
4 tablespoons melted fat
6 ounces sliced canned peaches, well drained
2 tablespoons sugar
1 teaspoon cinnamon
½ teaspoon nutmeg

Mix and sift flour, salt, baking powder, and sugar.

Combine milk, egg, and fat; stir into dry ingredients quickly. Fold in peaches. Turn into well greased muffin tins, filling ⅔ full.

Mix and sift 2 tablespoons sugar, cinnamon, and nutmeg and sprinkle over muffins.

Bake in hot oven (400°F. Mark 6) 25 minutes. Makes 12 medium muffins.

BANANA TEA MUFFINS

7 ounces plain flour
2 teaspoons baking powder
¾ teaspoon salt
¼ teaspoon bicarbonate of soda
2 ounces fat
3 ounces sugar
1 egg
3 ripe bananas, mashed

Mix and sift flour, baking powder, salt, and soda.

Beat fat until creamy. Add sugar gradually and continue beating until light and fluffy.

Add egg and beat well. Add flour mixture alternately with bananas, mixing until batter is smooth.

Fill well greased muffin tins ⅔ full. Bake in hot oven (400°F. Mark 6) until done, about 20 minutes. Serve hot or cold. Makes 16 small muffins.

MOLASSES MUFFINS
(Basic Recipe)

8 ounces plain flour
⅛ teaspoon bicarbonate of soda
2 teaspoons baking powder
½ teaspoon salt
3 ounces raisins, optional
1 unbeaten egg
3 ounces molasses or treacle
8 fluid ounces milk
3 tablespoons melted fat

Sift together flour, soda, baking powder, and salt. Add raisins and mix well.

Combine egg, molasses, milk and melted fat. Stir into dry ingredients, mixing only enough to blend.

Spoon mixture into well greased muffin tins about ⅔ full.

Bake in hot oven (400°F. Mark 6) 15 to 20 minutes. Makes about 10 to 12 large or 18 small muffins.

Variations:

Bran Molasses Muffins: Reduce flour to 4 ounces and add 3 ounces whole bran with raisins to sifted flour, soda, baking powder, and salt. Reduce milk to 6 fluid ounces and proceed as directed in master recipe.

Corn-Meal Molasses Muffins: Reduce flour to 4 ounces and add 4 ounces maize flour with raisins to sifted flour, soda, baking powder, and salt.

Oatmeal Molasses Muffins: Reduce flour to 4 ounces and add 4 ounces uncooked rolled oats with raisins to sifted flour, soda, baking powder, and salt. Reduce milk to 6 fluid ounces and proceed as directed in master recipe.

PINEAPPLE MUFFINS

8 ounces plain flour
4 teaspoons baking powder
½ teaspoon salt
4 ounces sugar
1 slightly beaten egg
6 ounces undrained, crushed pineapple
4 tablespoons melted fat

Mix and sift flour, baking powder, salt, and sugar. Add egg and pineapple and mix lightly. Blend in fat.

Turn into greased muffin tins, filling ⅔ full. Bake in moderate oven (375°F. Mark 5) 20 minutes. Makes 18 medium muffins.

STRAWBERRY MUFFINS

2 ounces fat
4 ounces sugar
2 eggs
8 ounces plain flour
4 teaspoons baking powder
1 teaspoon salt
5 fluid ounces milk
4 ounces strawberries

Cream fat and add sugar gradually. Beat eggs and add to mixture.

Mix and sift flour, baking powder, and salt. Add alternately with milk to first mixture.

Wash berries, hull, and cut in halves. Stir gently into batter.

Turn into greased muffin tins, filling ⅔ full. Bake in hot oven (400°F. Mark 6) 25 minutes. Makes 12 muffins.

LOUISIANA CORN MUFFINS

6 ounces flour
3 teaspoons baking powder
1 teaspoon salt
3 tablespoons sugar
3 ounces maize flour
1 well beaten egg
8 fluid ounces milk
4 ounces fat, melted
1 tablespoon chopped green pepper
1 teaspoon finely chopped onion
2 ounces grated cheese

Mix and sift flour, baking powder, salt, and sugar. Add maize flour and mix.

Combine egg, milk, and fat. Turn liquid mixture into dry ingredients and stir vigorously until all flour is dampened. Add green pepper, onion, and cheese.

Turn batter into greased muffin tins. Bake in hot oven (400°F. Mark 6) 25 to 30 minutes. Serve hot. Makes 18 muffins.

MAPLE BRAN MUFFINS

8 fluid ounces sour cream
12 ounces maple syrup
2 well beaten eggs
4 ounces plain flour
1 teaspoon bicarbonate of soda
4 ounces whole bran
1½ ounces chopped raisins
1 ounce chopped nuts

Combine cream, syrup, and eggs. Mix and sift flour and soda and mix with bran, raisins, and nuts.

Add liquid to dry ingredients and mix quickly.

Turn into greased muffin tins. Bake in hot oven (400°F. Mark 6) 25 minutes. Makes 24 medium muffins.

BANANA BRAN MUFFINS

4 ounces plain flour
¾ teaspoon bicarbonate of soda
½ teaspoon salt
2 ounces sugar
4 ounces whole bran
1 well beaten egg
2 tablespoons sour milk or buttermilk
2 tablespoons melted fat or oil
6 ounces thinly sliced ripe bananas

Mix and sift together flour, soda, salt, and sugar. Add bran and mix well.

Combine egg, milk, fat, and bananas. Add to dry ingredients, mixing only enough to dampen all flour.

Turn into well greased muffin tins. Bake in moderate oven (375°F. Mark 5) 35 minutes. Makes 6 large muffins.

OATMEAL-APPLE MUFFINS

12 fluid ounces milk
1 ounce butter or margarine
3 ounces quick cooking oats, uncooked
1 egg
6 ounces plain flour
3 ounces sugar
½ teaspoon salt
4 teaspoons baking powder
½ teaspoon cinnamon
1 apple

Scald milk. Add butter or margarine and pour over oats. Beat egg and add. Sift flour, 3 tablespoons sugar, salt, and baking powder. Add to oat mixture, stirring only enough to moisten. Fill 12 greased muffin tins ⅔ full.

Combine 2 ounces sugar and cinnamon. Peel, core, and quarter apple. Cut into thirds and dip each slice in sugar mixture, and press, curved side up, into each muffin.

Bake in hot oven (400°F. Mark 6) 20 to 25 minutes. Makes 12 muffins.

ORANGE RAISIN GEMS

8 ounces plain flour
¾ teaspoon bicarbonate of soda
½ teaspoon salt
3 ounces sugar
3 ounces raisins
1 well beaten egg
5 tablespoons orange juice
½ teaspoon grated orange rind
1⅓ tablespoons vinegar and sweet milk to make 5 fluid ounces
3 ounces fat, melted

Sift flour, soda, salt, and sugar together in mixing bowl. Add raisins.

Combine egg, orange juice and rind, vinegar and milk, and melted fat. Add to dry ingredients and stir only until dry ingredients are dampened.

Fill greased muffin tins ⅔ full. Bake in hot oven (425°F. Mark 7) 20 minutes. Remove from oven and let stand several minutes before removing from pans.

Variation: If desired, add 2 ounces nuts with raisins.

SWEETCORN MUFFINS

1 well beaten egg
½ pint milk
1½ ounces fat
8 ounces whole sweetcorn, drained
6 ounces plain flour
3½ teaspoons baking powder
1 teaspoon salt
3 tablespoons sugar
4 ounces yellow corn meal

Combine egg, milk, fat, and corn. Mix thoroughly. Mix and sift dry ingredients, add and mix quickly.

Turn into oiled muffin tins. Bake in hot oven (425°F. Mark 7) about 25 minutes. Makes 12 large muffins.

POTATO FLOUR MUFFINS

2½ ounces potato flour
1 teaspoon baking powder
½ teaspoon salt
2 teaspoons cold water
4 eggs, separated
1 tablespoon sugar

Mix and sift potato flour and baking powder. Add salt and water to egg whites and beat to a coarse foam. Sprinkle sugar over surface and beat until stiff but moist and glossy.

Beat egg yolks until thick and lemon coloured. Fold into egg whites. Fold in flour. Turn into ungreased muffin tins.

Bake in moderate oven (350°F. Mark 4) until delicately browned on top, 15 to 20 minutes. Remove by loosening from sides. Serve immediately. Makes 12 medium muffins.

OATMEAL MUFFINS

8 fluid ounces buttermilk or sour milk
4 ounces quick uncooked oats
4 ounces flour
2 ounces sugar
½ teaspoon bicarbonate of soda
2 teaspoons baking powder
½ teaspoon salt
4½ ounces seedless raisins (optional)
1 beaten egg
3 tablespoons melted fat

Pour buttermilk over rolled oats and let stand a few minutes.

Sift together dry ingredients; add to rolled oats mixture with raisins.

Add beaten egg stirring lightly; fold in melted fat.

Fill greased muffin tins ⅔ full and bake in a hot oven (425°F. Mark 7) 15 to 25 minutes, depending on size of muffins. Makes 8 large or 16 small muffins.

Variations: One cup fresh milk may be substituted for buttermilk. Omit soda and increase baking powder to 3 teaspoons.

BRAN MUFFINS

4 ounces whole bran
6 fluid ounces milk
1 egg
2 ounces soft fat
4 ounces plain flour
2½ teaspoons baking powder
½ teaspoon salt
2 ounces sugar

Combine bran and milk; let stand until most of moisture is taken up. Add egg and fat and beat well.

Sift together flour, baking powder, salt, and sugar. Add to first mixture, stirring only until combined.

Fill greased muffin tins ⅔ full. Bake in hot oven (400°F. Mark 6) about 30 minutes. Makes 9 muffins, 2½ inches in diameter.

CRUMB MUFFINS

2 ounces fat
2 ounces sugar
1 egg, beaten
4 ounces plain flour
3 teaspoons baking powder
½ teaspoon salt
4 ounces fine, dry crumbs
8 fluid ounces milk

Cream the fat. Stir in sugar, and add egg.

Sift flour, baking powder, and salt together. Add crumbs. Add to first mixture alternately with milk.

Fill greased muffin tins ⅔ full. Bake in moderate oven (375°F. Mark 5) 25 minutes. Makes 1 dozen muffins.

Berry Crumb Muffins: Add 4 ounces blackberries or cranberries.

Date Crumb Muffins: Add 4½ ounces chopped, stoned dates.

HONEY BRAN MUFFINS

8 ounces plain flour
4 teaspoons baking powder
¾ teaspoon salt
4 ounces bran flakes
3 ounces raisins
2 ounces chopped walnuts or pecans
6 ounces honey
10 fluid ounces milk
2 tablespoons melted butter or margarine
1 well beaten egg

Mix and sift flour, baking powder, and salt. Combine bran, raisins, and nuts. Add to flour mixture.

Add honey, milk, and melted butter to beaten egg and blend well.

Pour liquids into dry mixture, stirring only until dry ingredients are dampened. Fill medium-sized greased muffin tins ⅔ full.

Bake in hot oven (400°F. Mark 6) 20 to 25 minutes. Serve warm. Makes 18 medium muffins.

GINGER GEMS

2 ounces fat
4 ounces sugar
1 egg
7 ounces flour
1 teaspoon bicarbonate of soda
¼ teaspoon salt
¼ teaspoon nutmeg
¼ teaspoon ginger
¼ teaspoon cinnamon
6 ounces molasses or treacle
4 fluid ounces cold strong coffee

Cream fat and sugar until light and fluffy. Add egg and beat well.

Add sifted dry ingredients alternately with molasses and coffee in thirds, beating until smooth after each addition.

Fill greased small muffin tins about ⅔ full. Bake in moderate oven (375°F. Mark 5) 20 minutes. Makes 24 small muffins.

CORN MEAL MUFFINS

1 egg, unbeaten
8 fluid ounces milk
4 tablespoons melted fat
4 ounces plain flour
4 ounces yellow maize flour
2 tablespoons sugar
3 teaspoons baking powder
½ teaspoon salt

Place egg, milk, and melted fat in medium-sized mixing bowl. Beat with a kitchen fork until thoroughly blended (about 100 strokes).

Sift flour, maize flour, sugar, baking powder, and salt together over surface of liquid ingredients. Using gentle strokes, carefully mix until ingredients are just blended (about 25 strokes).

Bake in greased 2½ × 1¼-inch muffin tins in hot oven (425°F. Mark 7) for 20 to 25 minutes. Makes 12 muffins.

CHEESE MUFFINS

9 ounces flour
3 teaspoons baking powder
¾ teaspoon salt
3 ounces grated Cheddar cheese
1 egg
8 fluid ounces milk
4 tablespoons melted butter

Mix and sift flour, baking powder, and salt.

Add grated cheese and mix thoroughly. Beat egg, add milk and melted butter, and pour into centre of dry ingredients.

Stir quickly until dry ingredients are just dampened. Batter should not be smooth. Fill greased muffin tins about ⅔ full.

Bake in hot oven (425°F. Mark 7) 15 to 20 minutes or until golden brown. Makes 12 medium muffins.

DATE CHEESE MUFFINS

1 egg, unbeaten
8 fluid ounces milk
4 tablespoons melted fat
8 ounces plain flour
3 teaspoons baking powder
2 tablespoons sugar
½ teaspoon salt
1 ounce grated Cheddar cheese
1½ ounces chopped dates

Place egg, milk, and melted fat into medium-sized mixing bowl. Beat with a kitchen fork until thoroughly blended (about 100 strokes).

Sift flour, baking powder, sugar, and salt evenly over surface of liquid ingredients. Add cheese and dates. Using gentle strokes, carefully mix until ingredients are just blended (about 25 strokes).

Bake in greased 2½ × 1¼-inch muffin tins in hot oven (425°F. Mark 7) for 20 to 25 minutes. Makes 12 muffins.

Popovers

POPOVER HINTS

Successful popovers may be baked in deep bun tins or dariole tins. The tins should be deeper than they are wide.

The batter for popovers should be thin—about as thick as whipping cream. Do not overbeat the batter.

Good popovers really have the appearance of having tried to "pop over". They should be crisp and glazed in appearance with a thin, golden-brown crust, hollow and slightly moist inside without being wet or soggy.

When popovers won't "pop" often the difficulty lies not with the recipe or the mixing, but with the baking. Steam supplies the leavening action and since they tend to rise quickly in the oven, the mistake of removing them from the oven before they are fully baked is fairly common. They should be left in the oven for the full baking time, at the correct temperature to make sure they stay "popped".

When the popovers are punctured with a sharp fork 5 minutes before the baking is finished, the steam is allowed to escape and the insides dry a little.

POPOVERS
(Basic Recipe)

4 ounces plain flour
½ teaspoon salt
2 eggs
8 fluid ounces milk
1 tablespoon melted fat

Mix and sift flour and salt. Beat eggs with a rotary beater until light and thick.

Add flour and 5 tablespoons of the milk and continue to beat slowly until all the flour is moistened, about half a minute.

Gradually add remaining milk and melted fat, beating only until the mixture is free from lumps, 1 to 2 minutes.

Fill greased tins a little less than half full. Bake in a hot oven (425°F. Mark 7) 35 to 40 minutes or until the popovers are firm. Serve at once. Makes 6 to 8 large popovers.

Variations: To vary, add a few grains of paprika, dried sage, crushed mint, or other herbs or spices.

Stuffed Popovers: Split popovers. Fill with scrambled eggs, creamed fish, or creamed vegetables, etc.

CHEESE POPOVERS

1 egg
⅜ teaspoon salt
8 fluid ounces milk
4 ounces plain flour
4 ounces Cheddar cheese, grated

Beat egg slightly; add salt and milk and gradually stir into flour to make a smooth batter.

Beat with rotary beater until full of air bubbles.

Have tins heated and well greased.

Drop a rounded teaspoon of batter into each. Spread with a teaspoon of cheese and cover with a second teaspoon of batter.

Bake in very hot oven (450°F. Mark 8) until brown and well popped, about 20 minutes. Makes 8 or more popovers, depending on tin size.

CORN MEAL POPOVERS

12 fluid ounces milk
2½ ounces yellow maize flour
3 eggs
4 ounces plain flour
1 teaspoon salt

Scald 8 fluid ounces milk and pour over maize flour; stir well.

Combine remaining milk with eggs and beat well with a rotary beater.

Combine all ingredients and beat with rotary beater until batter is smooth and thick, about 2 minutes.

Fill well greased tins ⅓ to ½ full.

Bake in hot oven (425°F. Mark 7) 30 minutes; reduce heat to slow (325°F. Mark 3) and bake 15 to 20 minutes longer. Makes 6 to 8. Serve at once.

Scald 8 fluid ounces milk and pour over maize flour; stir well.

ORANGE POPOVERS

2 eggs
8 fluid ounces milk
8 fluid ounces orange juice
Grated rind of 1 orange
½ teaspoon salt
8 ounces plain flour

Beat eggs. Add milk, orange juice, rind, and salt. Add to flour, beating with rotary beater until smooth.

Fill preheated tins ½ full.

Bake in very hot oven (450°F. Mark 8) 25 minutes. Reduce heat to moderate (350°F. Mark 4) and bake until popovers dry out inside, 25 minutes longer. Serve hot. Makes 12 large or 18 small popovers.

Serve popovers piping hot and puffy straight out of the oven.

OATMEAL POPOVERS

3 eggs
12 fluid ounces milk
2 ounces quick rolled oats, uncooked
4 ounces plain flour
1 teaspoon salt

Combine eggs and milk; beat well. Add remaining ingredients and beat with a rotary beater until batter is smooth and thick, about 2 minutes.

Fill well greased tins ⅓ to ½ full.

Bake in hot oven (425°F. Mark 7) 30 minutes. Reduce heat to slow (325°F. Mark 3) and bake 30 minutes longer. Makes 6 to 8. Serve at once.

RYE POPOVERS

3 ounces sifted rye flour
1 ounce plain flour
¼ teaspoon salt
1 teaspoon sugar
2 eggs
8 fluid ounces milk

Mix and sift dry ingredients. Beat eggs and add milk; stir gradually into flour mixture to make a smooth batter. Beat with rotary beater until full of air bubbles.

Fill hot greased tins ⅔ full.

Bake in very hot oven (450°F. Mark 8) 20 minutes. Reduce heat to moderate (350°F. Mark 4) and bake 20 minutes or until crisp.

CHEESE COCKTAIL POPOVERS

8 fluid ounces boiling water
4 ounces butter
2 ounces plain flour
2 ounces grated Parmesan cheese
Pinch of salt
2 eggs

Put the boiling water in a saucepan and melt the butter in it. Then stir in the flour, cheese, and salt. Stir hard over low heat until mixture is smooth. Let it cool.

Half hour before ready to serve, stir in the eggs one at a time and beat well. Drop by small teaspoons on a greased, floured baking sheet.

Bake in moderate oven (350°F. Mark 4) 30 minutes. Serve immediately. Makes about 30 small popovers.

Things to Make with Scone Mix

NUT BREAD
(Basic Recipe)

    4   ounces sugar
    1   egg
    12 fluid ounces milk
    6   ounces chopped nuts
    12 ounces scone mix

Mix sugar, egg, milk, and chopped nuts. Stir in scone mix and beat hard for 30 seconds.

Pour into a well greased loaf tin $9\frac{1}{2} \times 5\frac{1}{4} \times 2\frac{3}{4}$ inches.

Bake in moderate oven (350°F. Mark 4) 45 to 50 minutes, until skewer thrust into centre comes out clean.

A slight crack in top is characteristic. Cool slightly before cutting with a bread knife.

Variations:

Fruit Nut Bread: Follow directions for Nut Bread (above) except use 6 ounces sugar and instead of milk use orange juice. Use only 3 ounces chopped nuts and add 6 ounces sultanas or other chopped dried fruit. Bake 55 to 60 minutes.

Banana Nut Bread: Follow directions for Nut Bread (above) except use 6 ounces sugar and only 4 fluid ounces milk. Use only 3 ounces chopped nuts and add 2-3 mashed bananas.

Orange Nut Bread: Follow directions for Nut Bread (above) except use 6 ounces sugar and instead of milk use orange juice plus 1 tablespoon grated orange rind. Use only 3 ounces chopped nuts. Bake 50 to 55 minutes.

CHERRY NUT BREAD

    4   ounces sugar
    1   egg
    12 fluid ounces milk
    4   ounces chopped nuts
    6   ounces chopped glacé cherries
    12 ounces mix

In large mixing bowl, stir together sugar, egg, milk, nuts, and cherries.

Cheese Tea Ring

Then add scone mix and beat briskly 30 seconds.

Turn into greased loaf tin, $10 \times 5 \times 3$ inches. Bake in moderate oven (350°F. Mark 4) 45 to 50 minutes or until done. Cool. This bread cuts best next day. Makes 1 loaf.

HEARTY PRAWN AND CHEESE SCONES

    6   ounces scone mix
    4   fluid ounces milk
    1   tablespoon finely chopped onion
    2   tablespoons finely chopped green
        pepper
    2   tablespoons chopped pimiento
    1   can prawns (4-5 ounces)
    2   ounces grated Cheddar cheese
    1   tablespoon mayonnaise
    1   teaspoon prepared mustard

Combine scone mix, milk, onion, green pepper, and pimiento. Shape into dough and knead 10 times.

Chop prawns and add cheese, mayonnaise, and mustard.

Roll dough into a rectangle 18×9 inches; cut into 3-inch squares.

Place a spoonful of prawn mixture in the middle of each square. Shape into long rolls, crescents, and square shells.

Bake in very hot oven (450°F. Mark 8) 10 to 12 minutes, or until done. Serve hot. Makes about 18 scones.

CHEESE TEA RING

    6   fluid ounces milk or single
        cream
    12 ounces scone mix
    6   ounces grated Cheddar cheese
    softened butter

Add milk to the scone mix, stirring lightly, until it can be shaped up into a ball. Turn out on floured board. Knead slightly until smooth.

Roll into a $\frac{1}{2}$ inch thick rectangle.

Spread with softened butter. Sprinkle liberally with the grated cheese.

Carefully roll up like a Swiss roll. Bring the two ends together, sealing with a little milk, to form a ring.

Place on a buttered baking sheet. Using sharp scissors, make slanting cuts through the ring almost to the centre, making slices 2 inches thick.

Turn each section cut side down on the sheet, so that the cut sides lie almost flat.

Brush lightly with melted butter.

Bake in a hot oven (400°F. Mark 6) about 25 minutes or until done and lightly browned.

Brush top again with melted butter before serving.

Serve piping hot with plenty of butter and crab apple, currant, or quince jelly. Makes 6 to 8 servings.

Hearty Prawn and Cheese Scones: A filling featuring prawn and cheese and an easy-to-make scone dough seasoned with onion make an unusual snack or party extra.

RING-O-GOLD COFFEE CAKE
Butter Crunch Mixture:

    4   ounces butter, melted
    4   ounces sugar
    2   ounces finely chopped pecans or
        walnuts
    2   ounces fine dry breadcrumbs
    grated rind of 1 orange

Coffee Cake Batter:

    3   ounces sugar
    1   egg, beaten
    3   fluid ounces milk
    4   ounces scone mix
    3   tablespoons melted fat

For the butter crunch, combine all ingredients thoroughly. Press on bottom and sides of a $1\frac{1}{2}$ pint ring mould.

For the coffee cake, add sugar to beaten egg, beating until fluffy. Add milk and scone mix, stirring lightly until combined. Lightly stir in melted fat. Pour into mould.

Bake in a moderate oven (375°F. Mark 4) 25 to 30 minutes. Let cool 5 minutes; turn out, crunch side up, on a dish. Serve warm. Makes 1 coffee cake.

APRICOT WALNUT BREAD

    8   ounces mix
    2   ounces quick-rolled oats
    6   ounces sugar
    1   teaspoon baking powder
    ¼   teaspoon salt
    3   ounces dried apricots, cut up
    4   ounces broken walnuts
    1   well beaten egg
    ½   pint milk

Stir scone mix with oats, sugar, baking powder, and salt. Add apricots and nuts. Combine egg and milk and add to dry ingredients. Beat hard 30 seconds.

Turn into greased loaf tin, $9 \times 5 \times 3$ inches. Bake in moderate oven (350°F. Mark 4) until done, about 1 hour.

Cool in tin 10 minutes and remove. Cuts best when day old. Makes 1 loaf.

ORANGE GLAZE BREAKFAST BUNS

Quick Buns:
  8 ounces scone mix
  2 ounces sugar
  1 teaspoon grated orange rind
  2 ounces fat
  1 egg, beaten
  8 fluid ounces milk
  3 ounces chopped dates

Glaze:
  3 ounces icing sugar
  1 tablespoon orange juice
  few grains salt
  chopped nuts, optional

Mix together scone mix, sugar, and grated orange rind. Cut in fat until mixture resembles coarse crumbs.

Combine beaten egg and milk; add all at once to dry ingredients, stirring only until combined. Fold in chopped dates.

Drop batter by tablespoons on to greased baking sheet. Bake in hot oven (425°F. Mark 7) about 15 minutes. Remove from baking sheet and drizzle glaze (made by combining sugar, orange juice, and salt) over hot buns. Sprinkle with nuts. Serve immediately. Makes 12 quick buns.

HIDDEN BERRY COFFEE CAKE

Batter:
  1 egg, beaten
  3 ounces sugar
  3 fluid ounces milk
  grated rind of ½ lemon
  4 ounces scone mix
  4 tablespoons melted butter or margarine
  3 ounces fresh or frozen blueberries or blackberries, drained

Topping:
  2 tablespoons brown sugar
  grated rind of ½ lemon
  1 tablespoon scone mix
  1 ounce finely chopped nuts
  1 ounce butter or margarine

For coffee cake batter, place all ingredients in bowl except blueberries; beat with rotary egg beater until fairly smooth. Do not overbeat. Stir in blueberries. Spread batter in a greased 8-inch round sandwich tin.

Combine topping ingredients; sprinkle over batter. Bake in a hot oven (400°F. Mark 6) 15 to 20 minutes. Makes 8 servings.

FIVE-MINUTE PRUNE COFFEE CAKE

  8 ounces scone mix
  3 ounces sugar
  1 egg
  4 fluid ounces milk
  8 ounces cooked prunes, stoned and halved

Combine scone mix and sugar. Beat egg, add milk and stir into dry mixture, mixing well.

Turn into greased 8-inch square tin and top with prune halves. Sprinkle on topping. Bake in moderate oven (375°F. Mark 4) about 35 minutes.

Topping: Mix 2 ounces brown sugar, 3 tablespoons scone mix, and ¼ teaspoon cinnamon.

CHERRY COFFEE CAKE

  12 ounces scone mix
  3 ounces sugar
  6 fluid ounces milk
  2 beaten eggs
  3 ounces brown sugar
  1 ounce plain flour
  2 teaspoons cinnamon
  3 tablespoons melted butter or margarine
  2 ounces chopped walnuts
  5 ounces cherry jam

Combine scone mix and sugar. Combine milk and eggs; add to scone mix, stirring just until moistened.

Spread ½ of mixture in bottom of greased 9×1½-inch sandwich tin.

Mix brown sugar, flour, cinnamon, butter, and nuts. Sprinkle over mixture in tin.

Drop remaining dough by spoonfuls around outer edge of tin.

Bake in moderate oven (350°F. Mark 4) 30 to 35 minutes. Spread with cherry jam when removed from oven. Serve warm.

Toppings and Fillings for Coffee Cakes

CINNAMON TOPPING

  3 ounces butter
  6 ounces sugar
  3 ounces plain flour
  1½ teaspoons cinnamon
  ⅛ teaspoon salt

Cream butter. Add sugar gradually, mixing well. Add remaining ingredients and stir until well mixed and crumbly.

STREUSEL TOPPING

  3 ounces butter
  3 ounces sugar
  2 ounces plain flour
  3 ounces fine cake crumbs
  1 teaspoon cinnamon

Cream butter. Add sugar gradually, mixing well. Add remaining ingredients and stir until well mixed and crumbly.

HONEY NUT TOPPING

  2 ounces butter
  2 ounces sugar
  2 ounces plain flour
  4 tablespoons honey
  2 ounces chopped nuts

Cream butter. Add sugar, mixing well. Add flour and honey and beat until well mixed. Add nuts.

RUM AND HONEY TOPPING

  4½ ounces icing sugar
  2 tablespoons honey
  1 tablespoon rum
  hot water

Blend sugar, honey, and rum. Add just enough hot water to make an icing of spreading consistency.

PINEAPPLE TOPPING

  3-4 ounces drained crushed pineapple
  3 ounces sultanas or currants
  3 ounces brown sugar
  2 ounces soft butter or margarine

Combine ingredients and spread over dough. Bake as directed.

CHEESE FILLING

  1 egg yolk
  2 ounces sugar
  8 ounces cottage cheese, sieved
  1½ tablespoons flour
  grated rind of ½ lemon
  ½ teaspoon vanilla essence

Beat egg yolk, add sugar, then the rest of ingredients. Mix well.

POPPY SEED FILLING

  6 ounces black poppy seeds
  8 fluid ounces milk
  1 ounce butter
  2 tablespoons honey
  2 ounces chopped almonds
  grated rind of ½ lemon
  1 tablespoon chopped citron
  2 ounces sugar
  1 tart apple, grated

Mince poppy seed and boil with milk, butter, honey, almonds, lemon rind, citron, and sugar until thick.

When cool, add apple. You may substitute raspberry jam for apple, if you wish.

NUT FILLING

  1 egg yolk, beaten slightly
  2 ounces sugar
  1 ounce butter
  2 ounces finely chopped walnuts
  ½ teaspoon almond essence

Mix ingredients thoroughly and use to fill any yeast or quick coffee cake. Bake as directed.

CAKES

Explore the wonderful world of cakes. You can make selections from a vast variety of forms and flavours in simple or rich layers with moist creamy fillings and luscious icings, some large and elaborate, others small and dainty, the famous torten of European cooks, the golden sponge cakes, high angel food cakes, and the traditional holiday cakes, rich in nuts and fruits.

Cakes may be divided into three basic types: (1) those made with fat (the conventional or one-bowl "quick-method" cakes), still commonly called "butter" cakes because originally butter was the fat most frequently used and now largely replaced by margarine and vegetable fat; (2) those made without fat (the angel and sponge cakes); and (3) a combination angel and fat-type cake (the chiffon cake). Although they are different in ingredients, in the way they are mixed, and in their final appearance and texture, nevertheless many rules for cake-making apply to all three.

TIPS FOR SUCCESSFUL CAKE-MAKING

1. Read the complete recipe carefully; be sure you understand it before proceeding.
2. Assemble all ingredients you will need. Have them at room temperature. This is especially important for eggs, which will not whip to full volume when cold, and for fats that are to be creamed.
3. Assemble all utensils and other tools needed.
4. Choose the size and shape of tin to fit the cake to be baked and prepare the tins for baking before mixing the batter.

5. Set the oven at the correct temperature early enough to be sure that it will be preheated to indicated temperature by the time your cake is ready to bake. (The oven thermostat should be checked frequently by utility service department or check it yourself with a portable oven thermometer.)

6. Measure ingredients accurately with scales and standard measuring spoons and use level measurements. Cake recipes are carefully balanced and careless measuring can cause inferior results.
   Flour should be sifted before measuring with a spoon. Level off with a knife or spatula. Sift the flour again with the dry ingredients as the recipe directs. Greaseproof paper is helpful in the sifting process. Use only the amount of flour called for.
   For additional hints on how to measure, see **Facts About Food and Cooking.**

7. Mix ingredients according to the directions of the specific recipe. If a recipe says stir, beat, cream, whip, or fold in, do exactly that.
   Definitions of terms used in recipes will be found in **Facts About Food and Cooking.**

8. Because the cake will rise in baking, the tins should usually not be filled more than two-thirds full. Spread the batter evenly in the tin. For layers and cupcakes be sure the batter is divided evenly among the tins.
   The following guide will be helpful in determining the size of tins for any recipes: A cake with fat containing 8 ounces flour may be baked in (a) 2 tins 9 inches in diameter or 8 inches

square, (b) 1 loaf tin 4×8 inches, (c) 12 average deep bun tins, (d) 1 tin 8×9 inches square and 2 inches deep.

The tins should usually not be filled more than two-thirds full. Spread the batter evenly in the tin. For layers and cupcakes be sure the batter is divided evenly among the tins.

9. Place tins in carefully controlled preheated oven, as near the centre of the oven as possible and away from the sides. Don't let tins touch each other or the sides of the oven. And don't place tins directly under each other. If necessary, stagger the tins on two shelves. There should be plenty of space around each tin for complete circulation of heat. Check to see that the oven temperature is accurate and correctly set.

Place tins in carefully controlled preheated oven, as near the centre as possible and away from the sides. Allow space around each tin for circulation of heat.

10. Regardless of the time given in a recipe, always test the cake near the end of the baking time given in the recipe to see if it is done, opening the oven door just enough for a quick check.

There are several tests you can apply to decide when your cake is done: (a) the surface will spring back when pressed lightly with a finger; if the impression of the finger remains, bake longer and test again, (b) a skewer or knitting needle inserted in centre will come out clean, (c) a cake will shrink slightly from the sides of the tin. Considerable shrinkage from the sides of the tin usually means the cake is over-baked.

Your cake is done when the centre surface will spring back when pressed lightly with a finger.

A cake is done when a skewer or knitting needle inserted in centre will come out clean.

11. Specific directions are given in certain recipes for removing cakes and torten from the oven, how to cool, etc. Follow these directions carefully.

The following applies to cakes with fat ("butter" cakes): Upon removing the cake from the oven, place the tin on a wire cake rack. Let it stand and cool in the tin for 5 to 10 minutes. Then carefully loosen the cake from edges of tin. Place cake rack over top of cake and invert quickly. Leave cake on rack to cool. If warm cake is placed on a board or plate, the bottom becomes soggy. If paper was used in the bottom of the tin, remove it from cake immediately.

12. Cool cake before icing. If cakes are iced while still warm, they absorb too much icing and become soggy. To ice, brush off loose crumbs and place bottom sides together with filling and icing. Cover sides first, then the top, spreading icing to edges with a light swirling motion.

Leave cake on rack to cool. If warm cake is placed on a board or plate, the bottom becomes soggy.

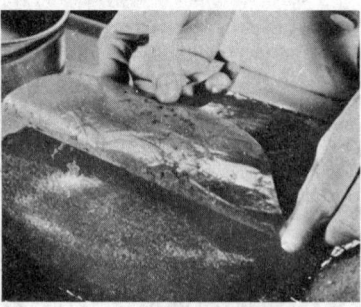

If paper was used in the bottom of the tin, remove it from the cake immediately.

Brush off loose crumbs from the cooled cake. Place bottom sides together with filling, then cover sides with icing.

Cover the top last, spreading icing to edges with a light swirling motion.

FACTS ABOUT CAKE INGREDIENTS

The finished cake can be only as good as the ingredients that go into it; therefore use only high quality ingredients.

Flour: Cake flour is obtainable in some areas. It is made from soft wheat, has a tender gluten and gives a very fine textured result. It is good for cakes with fat and for angel and sponge cakes.

Plain flour is used in the following recipes unless otherwise specified.

Self raising flour is plain flour to which baking powder has already been added.

Baking Powder: Recipes in this book call for double-acting baking powder. For an explanation of the different actions of the three different types of baking powders and how to make substitutions, see baking powder entry in index.

Sugar: Caster sugar is used in all the recipes unless otherwise indicated. Coarse sugar makes a coarse-textured cake. Caster sugar is especially important for sponge and angel cakes because there is no preliminary creaming with fat. If sugar is lumpy sift before measuring.

Brown sugar and maple sugar add flavour in addition to sweetening cake. Follow directions for using brown sugar.

Fat: Soft margarine will ensure consistently good baking results and is easy to use. Softened margarine or vegetable fat must be used in recipes for one-bowl "quick-method" cakes. In other recipes for cakes with fat, you may use vegetable fats, lard, butter, or margarine as fat. Butter may be substituted for part of the fat for the real butter flavour prized by many cake bakers.

Eggs: Use good quality fresh eggs because if they are stale the flavour of cake is affected. Fresh eggs should have thick whites and yolks that don't spread when eggs are broken. They beat to their best volume after they are three days old. Eggs should be kept refrigerated; however, they beat easier if they are at room temperature at time of beating. Therefore remove eggs at least an hour before using in cake-making.

You will note in some of our recipes that we call for measured eggs because this is the most accurate way of using eggs. When measure is not specified, use medium-sized eggs.

In separating eggs it is important that none of the yolk gets into the white. If this occurs the white will not whip to a stiff foam.

Liquid: Milk (fresh or sour, buttermilk, evaporated, and reconstituted dry milk powder) is most commonly used, but water, coffee, or fruit juices may be used.

For hints about safe substitutions in recipes, see **Facts About Food and Cooking.**

Preparing Tins: Choose the size and shape of tin to fit the type of cake to be baked. Prepare tins before mixing the batter. For cakes with fat the bottom and sides of the tin should be greased lightly. A piece of greaseproof paper cut to fit the bottom may be placed in the greased tin if desired. As an extra precaution, some like to grease the greaseproof paper too. Another method is to grease the tin lightly and then dust lightly with flour or rub with pancoat made by creaming until smooth two parts fat with one part flour.

Do not grease the tins for cakes made without fat (angel and sponge cakes) as the batter needs to cling to the sides of tins in order to reach top volume. Do not fill tins more than two-thirds full.

CAUSES OF FAULTS IN CAKES

Although you think you have followed directions very carefully for mixing and baking your cake, the cake may not turn out as expected. This is not a matter of chance but is caused by something you did or failed to do during mixing or baking. Study the following chart, note the sections that name any faults of your cake, and try to determine where you have slipped.

Cake is burned:
1. Oven heats unevenly.
2. Oven too full for good circulation of heat.
3. Oven too hot.
4. Cake placed too near side of oven.
5. Oven too hot for kind of baking tin used.

Cake is heavy:
1. Too much mixing.
2. Too much fat or liquid.
3. Not enough sugar, baking powder, or bicarbonate of soda.
4. Baking temperature not right.

Cake is not sufficiently risen:
1. Not enough baking powder or bicarbonate of soda.
2. Tin too large for amount of batter.
3. Baking temperature wrong.

Cake is tough:
1. Too little fat or sugar.
2. Too much flour.
3. Batter overmixed (in a plain cake).
4. Oven too hot.
5. Cake baked too long.

Cake ran over tin:
1. Too much batter for size of tin.
2. Oven not hot enough.
3. Too much baking powder or bicarbonate of soda.
4. Too much sugar.

Colour of crust is uneven:
1. Ingredients not well blended.
2. Oven temperature uneven.
3. Oven too crowded.
4. Cake placed too close to edge of oven.

Cake has a sticky crust:
1. Too much sugar.
2. Not baked long enough.
3. Not cooled properly.

Cake is higher on one side than other:
1. Oven shelf not level.
2. Oven temperature uneven (crust forms sooner in the hotter part of the oven, so the side of the cake on the hot side of the oven will not rise as much as on the other).
3. Batter spread unevenly in tin.
4. Dented tin used.

Cake is coarse-grained:
1. Insufficient creaming of fat and sugar.
2. Oil used instead of a hard fat (in conventional or quick-mix cakes).
3. Too much baking powder or bicarbonate of soda.
4. Oven not hot enough.

Cake falls apart while being taken from tin:
1. Too much fat, sugar, baking powder, or bicarbonate of soda.
2. Insufficient baking time.
3. Baked in too slow an oven.
4. Carelessly removed from tin.
5. Removed from tin before cooled.

Crust is soggy or doughy:
1. Cake allowed to steam while cooling.

2. Insufficient baking period.
3. Cake baked too slowly.

Cake sticks to tin, or crust comes off in balls:
1. Tin not properly greased.
2. Too much sugar.
3. Cake left in tin too long.

Cake falls:
1. Too much sugar, fat, liquid, baking powder, or bicarbonate of soda.
2. Too little flour.
3. Too short a baking period.
4. Oven not hot enough.
5. Cake tins jarred during baking before cake was firm enough to hold shape.

Crust is too light in colour:
1. Oven not hot enough, especially at last period.
2. Not enough sugar, fat, baking powder, or bicarbonate of soda.
3. Not enough batter to fill tin properly.
4. Baking temperature too low for type of baking tin used.

Top of cake is cracked or rounded too much:
(*Top of a standard loaf cake should be slightly cracked.*)
1. Too much flour.
2. Not enough liquid.
3. Batter overmixed after addition of flour.
4. Oven too hot at beginning of baking.

Cake has soggy layer at bottom:
1. Ingredients not thoroughly mixed.
2. Fat too soft.
3. Too little baking powder or bicarbonate of soda.
4. Too much liquid.
5. Lower part of oven not hot enough.
6. Egg whites not beaten sufficiently (in chiffon cakes).

Cake is dry and crumbly:
1. Too much flour, baking powder, or bicarbonate of soda.
2. Too little fat, sugar, or liquid.
3. Cornflour used with plain flour.
4. Cocoa substituted for chocolate without adding more fat.
5. Egg whites overbeaten (in conventional cakes).
6. Cake overbaked or baked too long in too slow an oven.

Cake has a tough crust:
1. Not enough fat or sugar.
2. Too much flour.
3. Baked in floured tin.
4. Baked too long.
5. Oven too hot.

Conventional Method Cakes with Fat

CONVENTIONAL MIXING METHOD

Complete mixing directions are given in each recipe; however some homemakers frequently find a step-by-step chart such as the following useful.

1. Remove butter or fat, eggs, and milk from refrigerator about an hour before making cake so ingredients will be at room temperature.

2. Sift flour once. Sift again with dry ingredients.

3. Measure essences into specified liquid or measure and add to creamed mixture later.

4. Melt chocolate if called for in recipe.

5. Cream fat and sugar until smooth and fluffy. (With electric mixer use medium speed.)

6. Beat in whole eggs or yolks. Add chocolate if called for in recipe. Beat mixture until well blended. (With mixer use medium speed.)

7. Add and stir in dry ingredients alternately with liquid in recipe. Stir flour and liquid around bowl in same direction after each addition for a cake with more even grain. (With mixer, use low speed, adding flour and liquid at the same time.) Avoid overstirring when using mixer because this will cause reduced cake volume. Stir enough to make batter smooth.

8. Add and blend in fruits, nuts, etc., if called for in recipe.

9. If stiffly beaten egg whites are specified in a recipe, fold them into cake batter lightly but quickly with a down-up-and-over motion, gradually turning bowl.

10. Turn cake batter into prepared tins.

CLASSIC BUTTER CAKE

8 ounces plain flour
3 teaspoons baking powder
½ teaspoon salt
5 ounces butter or other fat
8 ounces sugar
3 eggs, separated
5 fluid ounces milk
1 teaspoon flavouring

Sift together three times flour, baking powder, and salt.

Cream butter until soft and gradually add sugar, creaming until light and fluffy. Mix in well beaten egg yolks.

Add dry ingredients alternately with milk, stirring vigorously after each addition. Continue stirring for 2 minutes or about 300 strokes.

Fold in the stiffly beaten egg whites and flavouring. Turn into lightly greased baking tins and place in centre of preheated oven.

Bake in 2 9-inch sandwich tins in moderate oven (375°F. Mark 5) 25 to 30 minutes, or in loaf tin (8×8×2 inches) in moderate oven (350°F. Mark 4) 40 to 60 minutes.

Remove from oven, loosen edges with knife, and turn out, inverted, on cake rack. Cool and ice. If cake fails to come out immediately spread a cold damp cloth over bottom of tin for a moment or two.

Variations of Classic Butter Cake:

White Classic Cake: Omit egg yolks. Add 4 ounces fat.

Banana Nut Cake: Bake in 2 sandwich tins. Cool and fill with banana nut filling.

Coconut Cake: With stiffly beaten egg white and flavouring fold in 2 ounces desiccated coconut and 2 additional tablespoons milk.

Ice with boiled icing. Cover with coconut or with chocolate vermicelli.

Gold Cake: Omit egg whites. Substitute 4 ounces butter and 6 fluid ounces milk for butter and milk stated. Use ½ teaspoon orange essence flavouring.

Lady Baltimore Cake: Bake White Cake above in 2 9-inch sandwich tins. Fill with Lady Baltimore filling. Ice with boiled icing.

Marble Cake: Divide batter in two parts. To one part, add 1½ ounces of melted, unsweetened chocolate, stirring it in well.

Put the 2 batters into a greased loaf baking tin by alternate tablespoons. Pass a spatula through the batter to blend slightly.

Spice Cake: Sift ¾ teaspoon each of ground cloves, cinnamon, and nutmeg with the flour. Substitute brown sugar for white sugar. Ice with caramel icing.

Raisin Cake: At the last add 4 ounces seedless raisins dredged with a little of the flour. Ice with caramel icing.

SPICE CAKE

11 ounces plain flour
3 teaspoons baking powder
1 teaspoon salt
1 teaspoon cinnamon
¼ teaspoon nutmeg
¼ teaspoon mace
¼ teaspoon ground cloves
1 tablespoon boiling water
4 ounces fat
12 ounces sugar
3 eggs, unbeaten
¼ pint milk

Sift flour, measure, resift 3 times with baking powder and salt.

Measure spices into cup; add boiling water and stir to smooth paste.

Cream fat and sugar. Add eggs, one at a time, beating thoroughly. Stir in spice paste.

Add flour mixture alternately with milk in 4 or 5 portions, beginning and ending with flour and beat until smooth after each addition.

Turn batter into 2 ungreased 9-inch cake tins lined with greaseproof paper.

Bake in moderate oven (375°F. Mark 5) about 30 minutes. Remove from oven and cool on cake racks 5 minutes.

Turn out of tins, invert and cool. Remove paper and spread layers with molasses butter icing or rum nut filling and icing.

Variation: For variety, make 1 recipe creamy vanilla icing. Divide in half, add rum and nuts to ½ the icing and chocolate to the other.

Spread one layer of cake (top and sides) with one icing and the other layer with the second icing.

APPLE SAUCE FIG CAKE

4 ounces fat
8 ounces sugar
2 eggs
7 ounces plain flour
1 teaspoon salt
1 teaspoon baking powder
½ teaspoon bicarbonate of soda
½ teaspoon cinnamon
½ teaspoon nutmeg
8 ounces sweetened apple purée
1½ ounces chopped walnuts
6 ounces chopped dried figs

Cream fat; gradually add sugar, creaming until light. Add eggs; beat until fluffy.

Sift dry ingredients; add to creamed mixture alternately with apple purée, beating after each addition. Stir in nuts and figs. Pour into greased angel cake tin.

Bake in moderate oven (350°F. Mark 4) about 45 minutes. Cool in tin 10 minutes; remove. While still warm, spread top with thin icing, if desired.

Apple Sauce Fig Cake

BURNT SUGAR CAKE

12 ounces plain flour
3 teaspoons baking powder
¾ teaspoon salt
6 ounces butter or margarine
10 ounces sugar
3 eggs, separated
3 tablespoons burnt sugar syrup
    (below)
8 fluid ounces milk
1 teaspoon vanilla

Sift flour, baking powder, and salt together.

Cream butter thoroughly; add sugar gradually, creaming until light and fluffy. Add egg yolks, one at a time, beating well after each. Blend in burnt sugar syrup.

Add flour mixture alternately with milk, beating after each addition. Add vanilla.

Beat egg whites until stiff but not dry. Fold carefully into batter.

Pour into 2 well greased 8×8×2-inch square tins. Bake in moderate oven (375°F. Mark 5) 25 to 30 minutes.

Cool thoroughly on cake rack. Fill and ice layers with burnt sugar icing. Arrange salted pecans or salted peanuts around sides of cake.

Burnt Sugar Syrup: Melt 4 ounces sugar in a heavy pan, stirring constantly. When dark in colour, remove from heat and slowly add 5 tablespoons hot water, blending thoroughly.

Burnt Sugar Icing:
2 egg whites
12 ounces sugar
5 tablespoons water
1½ teaspoons light corn syrup or
    golden syrup
2 tablespoons burnt sugar syrup

Combine egg whites, sugar, water, and corn syrup in top of double pan. Beat until thoroughly blended.

Place over rapidly boiling water; beat constantly while cooking about 7 minutes, or until icing stands in peaks.

Remove from water; add burnt sugar syrup and beat until thick enough to spread on cake.

APPLE SAUCE CAKE

4 ounces fat
6 ounces brown sugar
2 well beaten eggs or 4 well beaten
    egg yolks
8 ounces plain flour
½ teaspoon salt
1 teaspoon cinnamon
½ teaspoon ground cloves
½ teaspoon nutmeg
1 teaspoon bicarbonate of soda
4 ounces chopped dates
4 ounces chopped nuts
9 ounces cold apple sauce or apple
    purée

Cream fat. Add sugar gradually, and cream together until smooth and fluffy. Mix in eggs or egg yolks.

Sift flour with salt, spices, and soda. Add dates and nuts, blend with flour. Add flour mixture alternately with apple sauce to fat-sugar-egg mixture and mix until smooth. Pour into greased tins.

Bake in moderate oven (350°F. Mark 4) 30 to 35 minutes for sandwich tins, and 45 to 50 minutes for loaf tin.

Cool in tins 5 to 10 minutes, then remove and cool on wire rack. Ice with brown sugar icing; decorate with walnut halves.

SOUR CREAM SPICE CAKE

2 ounces fat
6 ounces brown sugar
1 egg
¼ pint thick sour cream
7 ounces plain flour
¼ teaspoon bicarbonate of soda
2 teaspoons baking powder
⅛ teaspoon salt
¼ teaspoon ground cloves
2 teaspoons cinnamon

Cream fat. Add sugar gradually. Add egg and beat well. Add sour cream.

Sift flour with soda, baking powder, salt, cloves, and cinnamon.

Add 2 tablespoons of the dry ingredients to the creamed mixture. Beat thoroughly. Add dry ingredients to the first mixture, beating well.

Pour into a well greased and floured tin (8×12×2 inches). Bake in moderate oven (350°F. Mark 4) 30 minutes.

Spread glacé icing on top and sides.

FRENCH ORANGE FIG CAKE

6 ounces plain flour
2 teaspoons baking powder
½ teaspoon salt
3 ounces butter
8 ounces sugar
1 egg plus 1 egg yolk
1 teaspoon orange juice
4 fluid ounces milk

Mix and sift flour, baking powder, and salt.

Cream butter. Add sugar gradually, beating until very fluffy. Add beaten eggs combined with orange juice.

Add dry ingredients alternately with milk. Start and end with flour. Beat until well blended.

Pour into 2 greased and floured cake tins. Bake in moderate oven (350°F. Mark 4) 25 minutes.

Remove and cool. Put together with fig filling. Ice with orange icing.

DAISY PARTY CAKE

4 ounces soft fat
12 ounces sugar
4 egg whites
10 ounces plain flour
2½ teaspoons baking powder
½ teaspoon salt
8 fluid ounces milk
½ teaspoon lemon essence
½ teaspoon peppermint essence

Cream fat and sugar until fluffy; blend in each egg white.

Sift in dry ingredients alternately with milk; add flavourings.

Pour into well greased, floured oblong tin (14×9×2 inches).

Bake in moderate oven (370°F. Mark 5) 20 to 25 minutes or until top springs back when lightly touched.

Make up your favourite boiled or 7-minute icing using 2 egg whites and 12 ounces sugar.

To half the icing stir in 8 drops of yellow food colouring and ¼ teaspoon lemon essence.

Spread on sides and top half of the cake crosswise; to other half of icing, mix in 8 drops green food colouring and ¼ teaspoon peppermint essence. Spread over the rest of the cake.

Mark "yellow" cake into 16 squares; place a small daisy on each square. Mark "green" cake first into 6 diagonal strips; then divide cake crosswise into 3 strips. This marking gives 6 triangles and 6 diamonds. Place a nut dipped in yellow icing in centre of each piece —walnut halves for diamonds and almonds for triangles. Serves 12 to 14.

Daisy Party Cake

PRUNE SPICE CAKE

12 ounces plain flour
1¼ teaspoons bicarbonate of soda
1 teaspoon salt
1½ teaspoons nutmeg
1 teaspoon mixed spice
1½ teaspoons cinnamon
¾ teaspoon ground cloves
6 ounces fat
12 ounces sugar
3 eggs
12 fluid ounces sour milk or buttermilk
8 ounces, cooked, stoned and chopped prunes

Sift together dry ingredients three times.

Cream fat and sugar until light and fluffy. Beat in eggs, one at a time.

Add dry ingredients alternately with sour milk or buttermilk, beating until smooth after each addition. Add prunes and blend well. Turn into large, greased tube tin.

Bake in moderate oven (350°F. Mark 4) 1½ hours, or until done.

Cool. Spread with 7-minute icing. Decorate with grated orange rind.

MASTER BUTTER CAKE
(With 4 Eggs)

12 ounces plain flour
4 teaspoons baking powder
¼ to ½ teaspoon salt
8 ounces butter or other fat
1 pound sugar
4 eggs
8 fluid ounces milk
½ to 1 teaspoon vanilla

Sift together flour, baking powder, and salt.

Cream butter until soft and smooth. Gradually add sugar, creaming until light and fluffy. Add eggs, one at a time, beating after each addition.

Add dry ingredients alternately with milk. Add vanilla. Turn into lightly greased tins.

For sandwich cake, bake in moderate oven (375°F. Mark 5) 25 minutes. For a loaf cake, bake in slow oven (325°F. Mark 3) 40 to 45 minutes.

Cool in tins 5 to 10 minutes. Remove from tins and cool on wire rack.

Variations of 4-Egg Master Butter Cake:

Chocolate Cake: Use 7 ounces butter instead of 8 ounces and 11½ ounces flour instead of 12 ounces, and 2 ounces melted chocolate added with the vanilla.

Cupcakes: Pour into lightly greased cupcake or bun tins ⅔ full. Bake in moderate oven (375°F. Mark 5) 20 to 25 minutes.

Remove from tins and cool on wire rack. Makes 24 cupcakes.

LORD BALTIMORE CAKE

10 ounces plain flour
2½ teaspoons baking powder
¼ teaspoon salt
6 ounces butter
10 ounces sugar
8 egg yolks
6 fluid ounces milk
1 teaspoon lemon essence
1 teaspoon orange essence

Sift flour 3 times with baking powder and salt.

Cream butter thoroughly; add sugar gradually, and cream together until light and fluffy. Add egg yolks which have been beaten until very thick and lemon coloured. Beat well.

Add dry ingredients alternately with milk and flavourings, beating after each addition. Turn into 2 9-inch greased, and lined sandwich tins.

Bake in moderate oven (375°F. Mark 5) 25 minutes.

Cool. Put layers together with Lord Baltimore filling and icing. Decorate top and sides of cake with pecan or walnut halves.

HONEY CAKE

11 ounces plain flour
2 teaspoons baking powder
½ teaspoon salt
8 ounces butter
12 ounces thin honey
4 well beaten eggs
1 tablespoon lemon juice
1 teaspoon grated lemon rind
4 ounces chopped mixed peel
3 ounces chopped nuts

Mix and sift flour, baking powder, and salt.

Cream butter with honey. Blend in eggs, lemon juice, and lemon rind. Add dry ingredients. Blend smoothly. Mix in candied peel and nuts. Pour into large loaf tin lined with greased paper. Bake in oven (350°F. Mark 4) 1 hour.

BANANA LAYER CAKE

7 ounces plain flour
1 teaspoon baking powder
¼ teaspoon salt
3 ounces fat
3 ounces caster sugar
3 ounces brown sugar
2 well beaten eggs
1 teaspoon vanilla
1 teaspoon bicarbonate of soda
4 tablespoons milk
3-4 mashed bananas

Sift flour with baking powder and salt.

Cream fat until soft and smooth. Gradually add caster sugar and brown sugar, beating until fluffy. Beat in eggs and vanilla.

Dissolve soda in milk. Add with bananas to creamed mixture. Add dry ingredients, beating until smooth.

Turn into 2 greased 8-inch sandwich tins. Bake in moderate oven (350°F. Mark 4) 30 to 35 minutes. Cool 5 to 10 minutes in tins.

Remove from tins and cool on wire rack. Spread lemon filling between layers. Cover top and sides with whipped cream.

Decorate with border of fluted sliced bananas on top. Brush with lemon juice to prevent discolouring. To flute, draw lines with fork down sides of bananas, then slice.

MOLASSES ZIG-ZAG CAKE

8 ounces plain flour
2 teaspoons baking powder
¼ teaspoon salt
4 ounces fat
8 ounces sugar
2 unbeaten eggs
¼ pint milk
2 tablespoons dark molasses or black treacle
1 teaspoon mixed spice
1 ounce chopped nuts

Sift together flour, baking powder, and salt.

Blend together fat and sugar, creaming well. Add eggs. Beat 1 minute.

Add milk alternately with dry ingredients to creamed mixture, beginning and ending with dry ingredients. Blend thoroughly after each addition. (With electric mixer use low speed.)

Place ⅓ of batter in a second bowl. Add molasses and spice.

Spoon light and dark batters alternately into well greased and lightly floured 9×5×3-inch tin. Run fork through batter several times in both directions.

Bake in moderate oven (350°F. Mark 4) 70 to 75 minutes. Let cool in tin 15 minutes before turning out. Cool thoroughly; ice with cinnamon glaze. Sprinkle with chopped nuts.

Cinnamon Glaze: Combine 6 ounces sifted icing sugar, 3 tablespoons cream, 1 teaspoon vanilla, ¼ teaspoon cinnamon, and ¼ teaspoon salt. Mix thoroughly.

Molasses Zig-Zag Cake

Regal Gold Cake

REGAL GOLD CAKE

- 12 ounces plain flour
- 1½ tablespoons baking powder
- ¼ teaspoon salt
- 5 ounces butter
- 1 teaspoon vanilla
- 11 ounces sugar
- 5 egg yolks
- 4 fluid ounces evaporated milk mixed with 4 fluid ounces water

Sift flour; measure and resift with baking powder and salt.

Cream butter with vanilla; add sugar gradually and continue creaming until light and fluffy. Add egg yolks and beat well.

Add dry ingredients alternately with milk, beginning and ending with dry ingredients.

Pour into 3 9-inch sandwich tins. Bake in moderate oven (375°F. Mark 5) about 25 minutes. Ice with caramel icing. Chopped pecans or walnuts may be sprinkled over top of iced cake while icing is still soft or beaten into the icing.

LADY BALTIMORE CAKE

- 8 ounces plain flour
- 2½ teaspoons baking powder
- 1 teaspoon salt
- 4 ounces fat
- 8 ounces sugar
- 1 teaspoon vanilla
- 6 fluid ounces milk
- 3 egg whites

Sift flour, measure, resift 3 times with baking powder and salt.

Cream fat and 6 ounces sugar. Stir in vanilla.

Add flour mixture alternately with milk in 4 or 5 portions, beginning and ending with flour; beat until smooth after each addition.

Beat egg whites with rotary beater until foamy, gradually beat in remaining sugar; beat until mixture stands in soft peaks. Fold in batter lightly but thoroughly.

Turn batter into 2 ungreased 8-inch cake tins lined with greaseproof paper.

Bake in moderate oven (350°F. Mark 4) 20 to 25 minutes. Remove from oven and cool on cake racks 5 minutes. Turn out of tins. Invert and cool. Remove paper. Spread Lady Baltimore icing between layers, on top and side.

OLD-FASHIONED POUND CAKE

- 8 ounces butter
- 8 ounces sugar
- 5 well beaten eggs
- 8 ounces plain flour
- ¼ teaspoon powdered mace
- 1 tablespoon brandy or 1 teaspoon lemon essence

Cream butter thoroughly; add sugar gradually and continue beating until light and fluffy. Add well beaten eggs, then beat about 10 minutes on electric mixer at moderate speed.

Blend in flour, mace, and brandy, using low speed.

Pour into greased 9½×5½×2¾-inch loaf tin. Bake in slow oven (325°F. Mark 3) 1 hour and 15 minutes.

Note: If desired, substitute rose water for brandy or lemon essence.

FLUFFY WHITE BUTTER CAKE

- 4 ounces butter
- 12 ounces sugar
- 1 teaspoon vanilla
- 12 ounces plain flour
- 3 teaspoons baking powder
- 8 fluid ounces milk
- 4 egg whites

Let butter stand at room temperature until softened. Cream softened butter thoroughly, adding sugar gradually and continuing to cream until fluffy. Add vanilla and blend well.

Sift flour and baking powder together. Add flour mixture and milk alternately to butter-sugar mixture, beating after each addition until smooth.

Beat egg whites stiff but not dry and fold gently into cake batter.

Pour into 3 8-inch greased sandwich tins. Bake in moderate oven (375°F. Mark 5) 25 minutes.

Makes 3 layer cake.

SILVER CAKE

- 11½ ounces plain flour
- 3 teaspoons baking powder
- 1 teaspoon salt
- 5 egg whites
- 4 ounces sugar
- 5 ounces fat (at room temperature)
- 10 ounces sugar
- 8 fluid ounces milk
- 1 teaspoon vanilla or grated lemon rind

Measure sifted flour, add baking powder and salt, and sift together three times.

Beat egg whites until foamy; add 4 ounces sugar gradually, and continue beating only until meringue will hold up in soft peaks.

Cream fat; add sugar gradually, and cream together until light and fluffy. Add flour, alternately with milk, in small amounts, beating after each addition until smooth.

Add flavouring and blend. Then beat meringue into batter.

Use two round 9-inch sandwich tins, 1½ inches deep and line bottoms with paper. Pour batter into tins.

Bake in moderate oven (375°F. Mark 5) about 30 minutes.

This cake may be baked in two 9×9× 2-inch square tins or in 16×10×2-inch tin at (375°F. Mark 5) 25 to 30 minutes.

Spread with fluffy lime icing and lime fruit filling, seven minute icing or strawberry fluff.

PARTY BUTTER CAKE

- 12 ounces plain flour
- 3 teaspoons baking powder
- ½ teaspoon salt
- 6 ounces butter
- 12 ounces sugar
- 3 eggs, separated
- 1½ teaspoons vanilla
- 8 fluid ounces milk

Sift flour, measure; sift 3 times with baking powder and salt.

Cream butter thoroughly, until soft and smooth; then gradually blend in all but 2 ounces of the sugar.

Add beaten egg yolks and vanilla, and beat until fluffy. Add flour mixture and milk alternately in several portions, beginning and ending with flour and beating well after each addition.

Beat egg whites until stiff, and gradually beat in the remaining sugar. Fold into cake batter, lightly but thoroughly.

Turn batter into 3 8-inch sandwich tins, which have been lined with greaseproof paper in the bottom and buttered on the sides.

Bake in moderate oven (350°F. Mark 4) about 20 to 25 minutes, or until a skewer inserted in the centre comes out clean. Remove to cake racks to cool.

Put together with the chocolate butter icing between layers, and spread top and sides with vanilla butter icing. Decorate top with curls or shavings of chocolate. Serves 12.

Party Butter Cake

Caramel Syrup Cake

BASIC BUTTER CAKE
(With 2 Eggs)
- 4 ounces butter or other fat
- 12 ounces sugar
- 2 large eggs or 3 medium eggs
- 12 ounces plain flour
- 4 teaspoons baking powder
- 1/4 to 1/2 teaspoon salt
- 8 fluid ounces milk
- 1/4 to 1 teaspoon vanilla

Cream together butter and sugar. Add eggs, 1 at a time, beating after each.

Sift together flour, baking powder, and salt.

Add alternately with milk to creamed mixture.

Add vanilla. Pour into lightly greased tins.

For a 2-layer cake, bake in moderate oven (375°F. Mark 5) 25 minutes.

For a loaf cake, bake in slow oven (325°F. Mark 3) 40 to 45 minutes.

Cool in tins for 5 to 10 minutes. Remove from tins and cool on wire racks.

Variations of Basic 2-Egg Butter Cake:

Banana Cake: Add crushed bananas to cake filling. Ice with banana icing.

Chocolate Cake: Use 3 ounces butter instead of 4 ounces, and 11 1/2 ounces flour instead of 12 ounces.

Melt 2 ounces plain chocolate, over warm (not boiling) water, and add with vanilla.

Cocoa Cake: Reduce flour to 10 ounces. Add 5 tablespoons cocoa. Sift cocoa with dry ingredients.

Coconut Cake: Add desiccated coconut to batter. Ice with coconut icing.

Marble Layer Cake: Divide batter into 2 parts and add 1 ounce melted chocolate to one part. Put by spoonfuls into 2 greased sandwich tins, alternating light and dark mixtures. Decorate with chocolate icing.

Mocha Cake: Use 4 fluid ounces strong coffee and 4 fluid ounces water, instead of milk.

Nut Cake: Add 2 ounces chopped nuts to batter.

Orange Coconut Cake: Flavour with 1 tablespoon orange rind instead of vanilla. Substitute orange juice for milk. Mix in 2 ounces desiccated coconut with the liquid. Cover cake with orange icing and desiccated coconut.

Spice Cake: Reduce cake flour to 11 ounces and add 1 teaspoon cinnamon, 1/2 teaspoon ground cloves, and 1/2 teaspoon mixed spice or nutmeg.

White Cake: Use 4 to 6 egg whites, instead of 2 to 3 whole eggs.

Yellow Cake: Use 4 to 6 egg yolks, instead of 2 to 3 whole eggs, and add extra teaspoon of baking powder.

(1 1/2 teaspoons grated orange rind may be used instead of vanilla.)

CARAMEL SYRUP CAKE
Syrup:
- 10 ounces sugar
- 6 fluid ounces boiling water

Place 2 1/2-3 pint saucepan, containing sugar, on medium-high heat. Stir constantly with wooden spoon until sugar changes to greyish lumps (sugar masses) and then to dark brown liquid.

Slowly pour boiling water down side of pan, stirring liquid sugar as you do (it will steam and bubble). Boil 5 minutes. Keep warm. Makes about 1/2 pint.

Cake:
- 4 ounces butter or margarine
- 8 ounces sugar
- 1 teaspoon vanilla
- 2 eggs
- 8 ounces plain flour
- 2 1/2 teaspoons baking powder
- 1/2 teaspoon salt
- 1/4 pint burnt sugar syrup (above)
- 4 tablespoons milk

Cream butter or margarine and sugar together until fluffy. Stir in vanilla and each egg well.

Alternately fold in sifted dry ingredients with syrup and milk. Stir-beat vigorously for several minutes.

Pour into well greased and floured 9-inch square tin. Bake in moderate oven (350°F. Mark 4) about 35 minutes or until centre springs back when touched lightly.

Remove from pan; cool on cake rack. Ice with burnt sugar icing.

Burnt Sugar Icing:
- 4 ounces sugar
- 2 1/2 fluid ounces burnt sugar syrup
- 1 egg white

In top of double pan combine sugar, burnt sugar syrup, and egg white.

Place over boiling water, beating until icing stands in peaks when beater is drawn out (takes about 4 minutes). Makes enough for top and sides of 9-inch square cake.

LEMON PECAN CRUNCH CAKE
- 6 ounces butter or margarine
- 12 ounces sugar
- 3 well beaten eggs
- 12 ounces flour
- 3 teaspoons baking powder
- 1/2 teaspoon salt
- 8 fluid ounces milk
- Juice and grated rind of 1 lemon
- 4 ounces chopped pecans or walnuts

Cream butter until light and gradually beat in sugar, beating until light and fluffy.

Add eggs and blend well.

Sift dry ingredients together and add alternately with milk to creamed mixture, mixing until blended.

Stir in lemon juice and rind.

Generously grease 10-inch tube tin with butter or margarine and cover bottom with chopped nuts. Pour in batter.

Bake in moderate oven (375°F. Mark 5) 1 hour. Turn out on rack to cool.

WASHINGTON CREAM PIE
- 3 ounces butter
- 8 ounces sugar
- 2 eggs, unbeaten
- 7 ounces plain flour
- 2 teaspoons baking powder
- 1/4 teaspoon salt
- 4 fluid ounces milk
- 1 teaspoon vanilla

Cream butter thoroughly. Add sugar gradually. Add eggs, 1 at a time, beating after each addition.

Mix and sift dry ingredients and add alternately with milk and vanilla, beginning and ending with flour mixture.

Bake in 2 greased 9-inch sandwich tins in moderate oven (375°F. Mark 5) 20 to 25 minutes. When cool, put together with cream filling between layers and dust icing sugar over top. Makes two 9-inch sandwich cakes.

MAPLE CREAM CAKE
- 3 ounces butter
- 8 ounces sugar
- 2 eggs
- 7 ounces plain flour
- 1 teaspoon baking powder
- 1 teaspoon bicarbonate of soda
- 2 1/2 tablespoons cocoa
- 8 fluid ounces sour milk
- 1 teaspoon vanilla

Cream butter and sugar until light and fluffy. Add eggs and mix well.

Mix and sift dry ingredients and add alternately with milk and vanilla, beating smooth after each addition.

Pour into 3 greased and floured 8-inch sandwich tins. Bake in moderate oven (375°F. Mark 5) 25 minutes.

Turn out on cake racks to cool. Fill with maple cream filling. Ice with chocolate icing.

BASIC BUTTER CAKE
(With 1 Egg)

8 ounces plain flour
¼ teaspoon salt
2½ teaspoons baking powder
3 ounces butter or other fat
8 ounces sugar
1 egg
1 teaspoon vanilla
¼ pint milk

Sift together flour, salt, and baking powder.

Cream butter until soft and smooth, and gradually add sugar, beating until light and fluffy. Beat in egg and vanilla. Add dry ingredients alternately with milk.

Turn into greased tin and bake. In single square tin: moderate oven (350°F. Mark 4) 50 minutes. In 2 sandwich tins: moderate oven (375°F. Mark 5) 25 minutes. In cupcake or bun tins: moderate oven (375°F. Mark 5) 25 minutes.

Cool layers 5 to 10 minutes in tins before removing and cooling on wire rack. Remove cupcakes from tins at once and cool on wire rack.

Makes 2 8-inch layers, 1 8-inch square cake, or 1½ dozen cupcakes.

Variations of 1-Egg Butter Cake:

Boston Cream Pie: Bake in 2 layers. Spread cream filling between layers. Sift sugar over top.

Caramel Cake: Add 4 tablespoons caramel flavour with the liquid.

Chocolate Cake: Add 1 ounce melted chocolate to creamed butter.

Raisin Cake: Prepare batter. At the last, add 3 ounces chopped raisins which have been dredged with 2 tablespoons flour.

Short Cake: Bake in shallow tin. Cut in rounds. Split each round in 2 parts. Spread fruit between each part and on top. Serve with whipped cream. Decorate with fruit.

Spice Cake: Reduce cake flour to 7½ ounces and add 1 teaspoon cinnamon, ¼ teaspoon ground cloves, and ¼ teaspoon mixed spice or nutmeg.

Washington Pie: Bake in 2 layers. Spread jam or jelly between layers. Sift sugar over top.

White Cake: Use 2 egg whites in place of whole egg. Fold in stiffly beaten whites last.

Yellow Cake: Use 2 egg yolks in place of whole egg, and 1 teaspoon grated orange rind for the flavouring.

BUTTERMILK CAKE

8 ounces plain flour
¾ teaspoon bicarbonate of soda
½ teaspoon salt
5 ounces fat
8 ounces sugar
3 eggs, separated
1 teaspoon vanilla
½ teaspoon lemon essence
4 fluid ounces buttermilk or sour milk
2 tablespoons distilled vinegar

Sift flour, soda, and salt together.

Cream fat; add sugar gradually creaming until light and fluffy. Add egg yolks and beat until very light. Add vanilla and lemon essence; blend well.

Add dry ingredients alternately with combined buttermilk and vinegar. Beat until batter is smooth.

Fold in stiffly beaten egg whites. Pour into greased 7×10×2-inch loaf tin or two 8-inch sandwich tins, 1½-inches deep.

Bake loaf in moderate oven (350°F. Mark 4) 40 to 45 minutes; sandwich tins at (375°F. Mark 5) 25 to 30 minutes.

SILHOUETTE CAKE

10 ounces butter or margarine
1¼ pounds sugar
¼ teaspoon salt
1 teaspoon vanilla
4 eggs
12 ounces plain flour
4 teaspoons baking powder
8 fluid ounces milk
3 ounces plain chocolate, melted

Cream butter or margarine, sugar, salt, and vanilla until light and fluffy. Beat in eggs well.

Sift together flour and baking powder and add alternately with milk, adding flour first and last.

Pour ⅓ of batter into one 8-inch cake tin lined with greased greaseproof paper.

Add melted chocolate to remaining ⅔ batter and pour equal portions into two 8-inch sandwich tins.

Bake in moderate oven (375°F. Mark 5) about 30 minutes.

Cool and ice with boiled icing. Melt 2 ounces plain chocolate and spread lightly over top.

POUND CAKE

10 ounces butter
½ teaspoon powdered mace
Grated rind of ½ lemon
12 ounces sugar
6 eggs, separated
12 ounces plain flour
¼ to ½ teaspoon salt

Cream butter until soft. Add mace and lemon rind, then gradually add sugar, beating until mixture is light and fluffy.

Slowly add well beaten egg yolks. Fold in stiffly beaten egg whites. Add flour and salt, beating until batter is smooth.

Turn into a tube tin which has been lined with greaseproof paper. Bake in slow oven (300°-325°F. Mark 2-3) 1 to 1¼ hours.

Praline Cake

PRALINE CAKE

Cake:
2 ounces fat
6 ounces sugar
1 egg
6 ounces plain flour
¼ teaspoon salt
1½ teaspoons baking powder
¼ pint milk
1 teaspoon vanilla

Topping:
1½ ounces brown sugar
2 teaspoons flour
1 tablespoon water
2 tablespoons melted butter or margarine
2 ounces chopped pecans or walnuts

Cream fat; add sugar gradually, creaming until fluffy. Beat in egg thoroughly.

Sift together 6 ounces flour, salt, and baking powder, add to fat mixture alternately with milk, beating until smooth after each addition. Stir in vanilla.

Pour into well greased round baking dish. Bake in slow oven (325°F. Mark 3) about 40 minutes or until done. Cool slightly.

Topping: Mix together brown sugar, 2 teaspoons flour, water, melted butter, and chopped nuts; carefully spread on top of slightly cooled cake. Return to slow oven (325°F. Mark 3) and bake 10 minutes.

RICH WHITE BUTTER CAKE

8 ounces butter
1 pound sugar
1 teaspoon vanilla
12 ounces plain flour
8 fluid ounces milk
2 teaspoons baking powder
7 egg whites

Cream butter and sugar. Add vanilla. Sift flour with baking powder; add alternately with milk, beating well after each addition of flour.

Beat egg whites until stiff but not dry and fold into cake batter.

Bake in 3 greased 9-inch sandwich tins in slow oven (325°F. Mark 3) 35 minutes. Turn out on cake racks. When cool, ice with 7-minute icing.

Makes 3-layer 9-inch cake.

MARASCHINO CHERRY-NUT CAKE

6 ounces butter or margarine
12 ounces sugar
3 eggs, separated
12 ounces plain flour
3 teaspoons baking powder
½ teaspoon salt
8 fluid ounces milk
About 16 maraschino cherries, drained and chopped
2 ounces chopped pecans or walnuts
¼ teaspoon almond flavouring

Cream butter or margarine, add sugar gradually and cream well together. Add egg yolks and beat thoroughly.

Sift flour, baking powder, and salt together and add to creamed mixture alternately with milk, beginning and ending with dry ingredients.

Add well drained maraschino cherries, nuts, and almond flavouring.

Beat egg whites until stiff but not dry. With a rubber spatula or a spoon fold in the egg whites with an up and over motion.

Divide batter evenly into 2 9-inch cake tins that have been oiled on the bottom.

Bake in moderate oven (375°F. Mark 5) 20 minutes or until inserted skewer comes out clean.

Cool on racks until tins are cool enough to handle. Turn out on racks and cool before icing. Ice with 7-minute or butter icing. Decorate with red maraschino cherries.

WHOLE WHEAT NUT CAKE

4 ounces plain flour
2 teaspoons baking powder
¼ teaspoon salt
½ teaspoon cinnamon
½ teaspoon nutmeg
¼ teaspoon mixed spice
2 ounces whole wheat flour
3 ounces chopped nuts
2 ounces butter
6 ounces sugar
2 beaten eggs
½ teaspoon vanilla
¼ pint milk

Sift together plain flour, baking powder, salt, cinnamon, nutmeg, and spice. Blend in whole wheat flour and chopped nuts.

Cream butter. Add sugar gradually. Add eggs and vanilla and blend well. Add sifted dry ingredients alternately with milk, beating until smooth after each addition.

Turn into well greased loaf tin. Bake in moderate oven (350°F. Mark 4) 40 to 50 minutes. Remove from tin and cool on cake rack. Cover with orange cream cheese icing.

HONEY ORANGE CAKE

4 ounces fat
4 ounces sugar
6 ounces honey
1 egg
8 ounces plain flour
2 teaspoons baking powder
¼ teaspoon bicarbonate of soda
¼ teaspoon salt
1 ounce finely shredded orange peel
4 tablespoons orange juice
1 teaspoon grated lemon rind or 1 teaspoon lemon flavouring

Cream fat. Add sugar gradually, creaming until light and fluffy. Add honey, beating until smooth. Beat in egg.

Sift together dry ingredients three times. Add orange peel.

Combine orange juice and lemon rind or flavouring. Add dry ingredients alternately with orange juice to creamed mixture beginning and ending with flour mixture.

Spread in well greased square cake tin. The mixture is quite thick.

Bake in moderate oven (350°F. Mark 4) about 45 to 60 minutes.

Let stand 7 or 8 minutes before removing cake from tin. Serve plain, iced, or with hot fruit sauce, warm or cold. Makes 16 2-inch squares.

Honey Orange Sauce: Blend 4 fluid ounces orange juice with 3 ounces honey. Pour over the warm or cold cake or serve separately.

GOLDEN LOAF CAKE

14 ounces plain flour
3 teaspoons baking powder
1 teaspoon bicarbonate of soda
1¼ teaspoons salt
1½ teaspoons cinnamon
¾ teaspoon ground cloves
⅜ teaspoon nutmeg
¼ teaspoon powdered mace
4 ounces fat
9 ounces brown sugar
12 ounces seedless raisins
⅘ pint water
2 ounces chopped nuts

Sift flour, measure, resift 3 times with baking powder, soda, salt, and spices.

Combine fat, sugar, raisins, and water in saucepan. Boil vigorously 3 minutes. Cool. Add chopped nuts, then flour mixture in 3 or 4 portions and mix thoroughly.

Pour into ungreased loaf tin (5×9×2½ inches), lined with greaseproof paper. Bake in moderate oven (350°F. Mark 4) 1 to 1¼ hours.

Remove from oven. Cool on cake rack 5 minutes. Turn out of tin, invert and cool thoroughly. Remove paper and spread with creamy vanilla or mocha icing.

Lemon Filled Layer Cake

LEMON FILLED LAYER CAKE

8 ounces plain flour
2 teaspoons baking powder
½ teaspoon salt
4 ounces butter
8 ounces sugar
4 egg yolks
6 fluid ounces milk
1 teaspoon vanilla

Sift flour, baking powder, and salt together three times.

Cream butter thoroughly; add sugar gradually, and cream until light and fluffy.

Beat egg yolks until thick and lemon coloured; add to creamed mixture and blend well.

Add flour mixture alternately with milk and vanilla, beating after each addition until smooth.

Pour in two 8-inch, greased, lined, and again greased sandwich tins. Bake in moderate oven (375°F. Mark 5) 25 to 30 minutes.

Put layers together with lemon filling. Make design on top by laying fancy paper doily on top layer and sifting icing sugar over it. Gently remove doily. Keep cake chilled in refrigerator, especially in warm weather.

CRANBERRY SPICE CAKE

4 ounces fat
8 ounces sugar
1 beaten egg
6 ounces raisins
2 ounces chopped nuts
7 ounces plain flour
¼ teaspoon salt
1 teaspoon bicarbonate of soda
1 teaspoon baking powder
1 teaspoon cinnamon
½ teaspoon powdered cloves
8 ounces cranberry sauce, jellied or whole

Cream fat and sugar. Add egg. Stir in raisins and nuts.

Combine dry ingredients and sift; add to first mixture. Stir in cranberry sauce.

Bake in moderate oven (350°F. Mark 4) about 1 hour in greased tube tin, or for 30 to 40 minutes in greased 8-inch sandwich tins.

Ice with cranberry cream cheese icing.

Marble Cake with Creamy Chocolate Icing.

Orange Sponge Cake (above) and Almond Gâteau (below)

Layer Cake with Chocolate Cream Filling

Pineapple Meringue Cake (above) and Butterscotch Icing with Almonds (below)

SPICY MARBLE CAKE

5 ounces butter or margarine
1 pound sugar
3 well beaten eggs
12 ounces plain flour
1 teaspoon baking powder
1 teaspoon bicarbonate of soda
½ teaspoon salt
8 fluid ounces sour milk
1 tablespoon molasses or black treacle
1 ounce plain chocolate, melted
1 teaspoon cinnamon
1 teaspoon nutmeg
½ teaspoon ground cloves

Cream butter until light; gradually add sugar, creaming until very light and fluffy. Beat in eggs.

Mix and sift flour, baking powder, soda, and salt. Add to creamed mixture alternately with sour milk, blending quickly but thoroughly.

Divide batter in half. To one half add molasses, cooled melted chocolate, and spices sifted together. Blend well.

Place alternate spoonfuls of white and dark batter in well greased 10-inch tube tin. Bake in moderate oven (350°F. Mark 4) 1 hour and 10 minutes.

Turn out on cake rack and cool thoroughly. Cover top and sides with chocolate icing. Decorate outer edge of cake with walnut halves.

ALMOND MERINGUE CAKE

4 ounces butter
4 ounces sugar
4 beaten egg yolks
4 ounces plain flour
4 fluid ounces milk
1 teaspoon baking powder
¼ teaspoon salt
1 ounce plain flour

Cream butter and sugar. Add beaten egg yolks. Add alternately the 4 ounces flour and the milk.

Sift on top of mixture and fold in baking powder, salt, and 1 ounce flour.

Pour into 2 8-inch greased sandwich tins. Set in cool place while preparing meringue topping.

Meringue Topping:
4 egg whites
6 ounces sugar
1 teaspoon vanilla
3 ounces blanched almonds, chopped

Beat egg whites to a froth; add sugar gradually and continue beating until all sugar is added. Meringue stands in peaks when beaters are pulled out.

Add vanilla and spread on unbaked layers. Sprinkle with chopped almonds.

Bake in moderate oven (350°F. Mark 4) 35 minutes.

Cool and remove from tins. Meringue will shrink a little on cooling. Place 1 layer upside down on serving plate.

Cover with lemon filling and top with second layer, meringue side up.

Note: Ice cream, or whipped cream and orange marmalade blended together may be used for filling.

HUNGARIAN PLUM CAKE

4 ounces butter
8 ounces sugar
2 eggs
4 ounces plain flour
1 teaspoon baking powder
½ teaspoon salt
2 teaspoons cinnamon
½ teaspoon lemon essence
10 fresh or canned plum halves

Cream butter, add 4 ounces sugar, and cream until light and fluffy. Add eggs one at a time and beat well.

Add flour which has been sifted with baking powder, salt, and 1 teaspoon cinnamon. Add lemon essence.

Pour into a well greased tin (11×6 ×2 inches). Press the plum halves into batter. Sprinkle mixture of 4 ounces sugar and 1 teaspoon cinnamon over top.

Bake in hot oven (400°F. Mark 6) 30 minutes. Serves 5 to 6.

Variations:

Hungarian Apple Cake: Substitute 3 sliced tart apples for plums.

Hungarian Peach Cake: Substitute 10 halves of fresh or canned peaches for plums.

PINK MARBLE CAKE

8 ounces plain flour
2½ teaspoons baking powder
¾ teaspoon salt
3 egg whites
2 ounces sugar
4 ounces fat (at room temperature)
8 ounces sugar
¼ pint milk
1 teaspoon vanilla
Red food colouring

Measure sifted flour, add baking powder and salt, and sift together three times.

Beat egg whites until foamy; add 2 ounces sugar gradually and continue beating until meringue will hold up in soft peaks.

Cream fat, add 8 ounces sugar gradually, and cream together until light and fluffy. Add flour, alternately with milk, in small amounts, beating after each addition until smooth. Add vanilla and blend. Add meringue and beat thoroughly into batter.

Tint one-third of the batter pink. Use two round 8-inch sandwich tins, 1¼ inches deep; line bottoms with paper.

Put large spoonfuls of batter into tins, alternating pink and white mixtures. With a knife, cut through batter in a wide zigzag course to marble.

Bake in moderate oven (375°F. Mark 5) about 25 minutes. Spread with Hungarian chocolate icing.

LEMON BOSTON CREAM CAKE

6 ounces sugar
3 ounces butter
2 eggs
1 teaspoon concentrated frozen lemon juice
6 ounces plain flour
2 teaspoons baking powder
⅓ teaspoon salt
4 fluid ounces milk

Sift sugar. Cream butter and sugar together and beat until they are very light. Beat in eggs one at a time. Add concentrated lemon juice.

Resift flour with baking powder and salt. Add sifted dry ingredients to the batter alternately with the milk.

Line two 8-inch sandwich tins with greaseproof paper; pour batter in them and bake in moderate oven (375°F. Mark 5) about 25 minutes. Cool the layers.

Lemon Filling:
1 ounce butter or margarine
2 ounces sugar
1½ ounces plain flour
¼ teaspoon salt
6 fluid ounces milk or water
2 egg yolks
3 tablespoons concentrated frozen lemon juice

Melt butter and add sugar, flour, and salt. Stir in milk gradually, and cook over boiling water until thickened.

Add slightly beaten egg yolks, mixed with the lemon juice and cook 1 minute longer.

Cool before putting between cake layers. Put cake together and sift sugar over the top.

Lemon Boston Cream Cake

APPLE SAUCE LOAF CAKE

10 ounces plain flour
¾ teaspoon baking powder
1 teaspoon bicarbonate of soda
1 teaspoon salt
½ teaspoon cinnamon
¼ teaspoon powdered cloves
4 ounces fat
8 ounces sugar
1 teaspoon vanilla
1 egg
12 ounces unsweetened, thick,
    apple sauce or purée
6 ounces raisins
4 ounces chopped nuts

Sift flour, measure, resift 3 times with baking powder, soda, salt, and spices.

Cream fat and sugar. Stir in vanilla, then egg; beat well. Stir in apple sauce, raisins, and nuts. Fold in flour mixture thoroughly in 4 or 5 portions.

Turn into loaf tin (5¼×9¼ inches) lined with greaseproof paper. Bake in moderate oven (350°F. Mark 4) about 1½ hours.

Remove from oven, cool on cake rack 5 minutes, turn out of tin. Invert on rack and cool. Remove paper and spread with creamy vanilla icing.

WESTERN POUND CAKE

3 ounces butter
8 ounces sugar
3 eggs, unbeaten
8 fluid ounces sour milk
½ teaspoon bicarbonate of soda
8 ounces plain flour
1 teaspoon baking powder
2 teaspoons vanilla
1½ ounces each of nuts, raisins, and
    crystallized fruit

Cream butter and sugar thoroughly. Add unbeaten eggs, 1 at a time, beating after each addition.

Sift dry ingredients together. Add milk and dry ingredients alternately to creamed mixture, mixing only until well blended. Add vanilla, fruit, and nuts and mix.

Pour into a greased 5½×9½×3-inch loaf tin, or into a tube tin 8 or 9 inches in diameter.

Regal Banana Cake

Bake in moderate oven (350°F. Mark 4) 1 hour. If the loaf should be well browned after 30 minutes of baking cover with brown paper to prevent scorching.

ORANGE GOLD CAKE

8 ounces plain flour
2¼ teaspoons baking powder
1 teaspoon salt
4 ounces fat
8 ounces sugar
5 egg yolks
1 whole egg
Orange juice
4 fluid ounces milk

Sift flour, measure, resift 3 times with baking powder and salt.

Cream fat and sugar. Stir in lightly beaten egg yolks and whole egg.

Add enough orange juice to milk to make ¼ pint.

Add flour mixture alternately with liquid to the creamed mixture in 4 or 5 portions, beginning and ending with flour. Beat until smooth after each addition.

Turn into an ungreased cake tin (9×9×2 inches) lined with greaseproof paper on bottom.

Bake in slow oven (325°F. Mark 3) 50 to 60 minutes. Remove from oven, invert and cool slightly. Remove paper and spread with orange glaze while cake is still warm.

REGAL BANANA CAKE

4 ounces fat
8 ounces sugar
3 eggs, separated
6 ounces plain flour
2 teaspoons baking powder
½ teaspoon bicarbonate of soda
¾ teaspoon salt
5 ounces digestive biscuit crumbs
3-4 mashed bananas
5 tablespoons sour milk
2 ounces chopped nuts
½ pint double cream, whipped
Banana slices

Cream fat and 4 ounces sugar; beat in egg yolks.

Sift together flour, baking powder, soda, and salt. Combine with fine biscuit crumbs. Stir into creamed mixture alternately with mashed banana and milk.

Beat egg whites until almost stiff. Beat in remaining 4 ounces sugar until whites are very stiff and glossy. Fold into cake mixture along with 2 ounces chopped nuts. Pour into 3 8-inch greased and lined sandwich tins.

Bake in moderate oven (350°F. Mark 4) 35 minutes or until done. Cool 10 minutes; remove from tins.

When thoroughly cooled put layers together with whipped cream and banana slices. Decorate top with chopped nuts if desired.

SPECIAL NUT CAKE

12 ounces plain flour
2 teaspoons baking powder
¾ teaspoon salt
8 ounces butter (at room temperature)
14 ounces sugar
3 eggs, unbeaten
1 egg yolk, unbeaten
6 fluid ounces milk
1 teaspoon orange essence
1 teaspoon almond essence
3-4 ounces very finely chopped nuts

Measure sifted flour, add baking powder and salt, and sift together three times.

Cream butter, add sugar gradually, and cream together until light and fluffy. Add eggs and yolk; beat well. Then add flour, alternately with milk, in small amounts, beating after each addition until smooth. Add flavourings and nuts; mix well.

Grease and lightly flour a 9-inch tube tin. Pour batter into tin.

Bake in moderate oven (375°F. Mark 5) 1 hour, or until wire cake tester or skewer comes out clean and dry.

Cool slightly before removing from tin.

This cake may be baked in two 8×4×3-inch tins, lined on bottoms with paper, in slow oven (325°F. Mark 3) about 1 hour.

Serve un-iced to accompany fruit desserts or ice cream. Or spread with fruit icing.

BLITZKUCHEN

4½ ounces plain flour
1 teaspoon baking powder
4 ounces butter
8 ounces sugar
4 eggs, separated
1 teaspoon grated lemon rind
3 tablespoons milk
1 egg white diluted with 1 tablespoon water
¼ teaspoon salt
6 ounces sugar
2 tablespoons cinnamon
2 ounces chopped nuts

Mix and sift flour and baking powder.

Cream butter until soft and smooth. Gradually add sugar, beating until light and fluffy. Add well beaten egg yolks and lemon rind. Gradually add flour, beating well. Add milk and beat again.

Beat egg whites with salt until stiff, but not dry. Gently fold into batter.

Pour into 2 greased tins (8 × 12 inches) and spread with diluted egg white. Sprinkle liberally with combination of sugar, cinnamon, and nuts.

Bake in moderate oven (375°F. Mark 5) 20 minutes. Serve either hot or cold.

WINE CAKE

4 ounces butter
8 ounces sugar
1 teaspoon baking powder
7 ounces plain flour
6 tablespoons port, muscatel, or tokay
Juice of ½ lemon
4 egg whites
Grated rind of 1 lemon

Cream butter thoroughly, add half the sugar gradually, and beat until light and fluffy.

Sift flour and baking powder together several times and add to creamed mixture alternately with wine and lemon juice. Beat batter until light.

Beat egg whites until light and fold in the remaining sugar. Beat until sugar is dissolved and meringue will stand in peaks. Fold lightly but thoroughly into batter.

Fill greased loaf tin two-thirds full. Bake in slow oven (325°F. Mark 3) for 1 hour.

TOMATO SOUP CAKE

8 ounces plain flour
1 tablespoon baking powder
½ teaspoon bicarbonate of soda
½ teaspoon powdered cloves
½ teaspoon cinnamon or mace
½ teaspoon nutmeg
6 ounces seedless raisins
4 ounces fat
8 ounces sugar
2 well beaten eggs
1 can (about 8 ounce) condensed tomato soup

Sift together flour, baking powder, soda, and spices.

Wash and cut raisins. (Roll in a small amount of the flour mixture.)

Cream fat; add sugar gradually; then eggs, mixing thoroughly. Add flour mixture alternately with soup; stir until smooth. Fold in raisins.

Pour into 2 greased and floured 8-inch sandwich tins.

Bake in moderate oven (375°F. Mark 5) about 35 minutes, or until done. Ice as desired.

Tomato Soup Cake

MOLASSES MARBLE CAKE

4 ounces fat
8 ounces sugar
2 beaten eggs
8 ounces plain flour
2 teaspoons baking powder
¼ teaspoon salt
¼ pint milk
2 teaspoons mixed spice
3 tablespoons molasses or black treacle

Cream fat. Add sugar gradually and beat until light and fluffy. Add eggs, and cream thoroughly.

Mix and sift flour, baking powder, and salt. Add alternately with the milk to the creamed mixture. Beat after each addition.

Remove ⅔ of batter from bowl. Add spice and molasses to the remaining batter and beat well.

Drop by tablespoons into greased loaf tin, alternating light and dark mixtures.

Bake in moderate oven (350°F. Mark 4) 1 hour. Serve plain or ice as desired.

EGGLESS APPLE SAUCE CAKE

¼ teaspoon powdered cloves
½ teaspoon nutmeg
½ teaspoon cinnamon
¼ teaspoon salt
8 ounces plain flour
1 teaspoon bicarbonate of soda
3 ounces fat
9 ounces thin honey
9 ounces cold apple sauce or apple purée, slightly sweetened
6 ounces seedless raisins
1 ounce chopped nuts

Sift together dry ingredients.

Cream fat. Add honey and cream thoroughly. Add apple sauce, then sifted dry ingredients. Add raisins and nuts, mixing well.

Pour batter into a greased and floured 8-inch square cake tin. Bake in moderate oven (350°F. Mark 4) 1 hour.

HUNGARIAN APPLE SAUCE CAKE

8 ounces plain flour
1 teaspoon baking powder
½ teaspoon salt
4 ounces butter
8 ounces sugar
1 teaspoon cinnamon
Grated rind of 1 lemon
1 well beaten egg
12 ounces thick apple sauce or apple purée
1 teaspoon bicarbonate of soda
3 ounces seedless raisins
2 ounces chopped nuts

Mix and sift flour, baking powder, and salt.

Cream together butter, sugar, cinnamon, and lemon rind until soft and smooth. Add egg and beat until fluffy.

Add apple sauce, soda, raisins, and nuts. Add dry ingredients, mix well.

Turn into well greased and floured cake tin. Bake in moderate oven (350°F. Mark 4) 1½ hours.

PUMPKIN CAKE

9 ounces plain flour
3 teaspoons baking powder
½ teaspoon salt
¼ teaspoon bicarbonate of soda
1½ teaspoons cinnamon
½ teaspoon ginger
½ teaspoon mixed spice
4 ounces butter or other fat
6 ounces brown sugar
4 ounces caster sugar
1 egg and 2 egg yolks, unbeaten
6 fluid ounces buttermilk or sour milk
6 ounces canned pumpkin
2 ounces finely chopped walnuts

Measure sifted flour, add baking powder, salt, soda, and spices. Sift together 3 times.

Cream butter, add sugars gradually and cream well. Add egg and egg yolks, one at a time, beating until light. Add flour alternately with buttermilk, in small amounts, beating after each addition until smooth. Add pumpkin and nuts; mix well.

Bake in 2 round 8-inch sandwich tins, lined on bottoms with paper, in moderate oven (350°F. Mark 4) 30 to 35 minutes, or until done.

Cool and ice with fluffy icing, tinted orange. Decorate with small candied rose or violet petals.

GOLD BUTTER CAKE

8 ounces plain flour
3 teaspoons baking powder
½ teaspoon salt
4 ounces butter
8 ounces sugar
5 egg yolks
1 whole egg, beaten
¼ pint milk
1 teaspoon vanilla

Sift together flour, baking powder, and salt 3 times.

Cream butter and sugar until light and fluffy. Mix in egg yolks and whole egg. Add dry ingredients alternately with milk and vanilla, beating only until smooth after each addition.

Turn into greased 9-inch square tin. Bake in moderate oven (350°F. Mark 4) about 45 minutes.

Spread top with chocolate icing and ice sides with butterscotch nut icing.
Apricot Gold Butter Cake: Prepare half the recipe for Gold Butter Cake. Line well greased shallow tin with 8 ounces drained, cooked, sweetened dried apricots. Pour batter over.

Bake in moderate oven (350°F. Mark 4) about 35 minutes. Serve hot with apricot sauce.

Conventional Method Chocolate Cakes

STEPS IN MAKING A DELICATE CHOCOLATE CAKE

This picture story for a delicate chocolate cake gives hints that apply to other cakes with fat.

1. Assemble all ingredients and utensils needed. Have ingredients at room temperature. Measure with standard measuring spoons and scales. Prepare tins before mixing cake.

2. Cream fat and sugar until smooth and fluffy. (With electric mixer use medium speed.)

3. Add the beaten eggs, then the melted chocolate. Beat mixture until well blended. (With mixer use medium speed.)

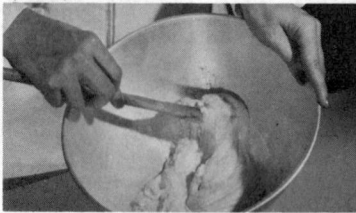

4. Stir in the dry ingredients alternately with liquid in recipe. (With mixer use low speed, adding flour and liquid at the same time.)

5. Spread the batter evenly over the prepared tins.

OLD-FASHIONED CHOCOLATE CAKE

4 ounces fat
8 ounces caster sugar
3 ounces light brown sugar
2 well beaten eggs
1 teaspoon vanilla
3 ounces chocolate
4 fluid ounces hot water
8 ounces plain flour
¼ teaspoon salt
1 teaspoon bicarbonate of soda
¼ pint buttermilk or sour milk

Cream fat; add sugars gradually and cream thoroughly.

Beat eggs well; add vanilla and add to first mixture, beating well.

Melt chocolate in hot water; blend thoroughly and cool slightly. Add to creamed mixture, blending well.

Sift flour with salt and soda; add alternately with buttermilk to creamed mixture. Mix well until smooth.

Turn into 2 9-inch greased sandwich tins. Bake in moderate oven (375°F. Mark 5) 25 to 30 minutes, or until cake springs back to touch of finger.

Cool cake in tins 5 minutes. Remove and cool thoroughly on cake racks.

Ice with mocha icing.

MASTER DEVIL'S FOOD CAKE

3 ounces cocoa
4½ ounces brown sugar
½ pint milk
4 ounces fat
8 ounces caster sugar
3 eggs
1¼ teaspoons vanilla
8 ounces plain flour
1 teaspoon baking powder
1 teaspoon salt
¾ teaspoon bicarbonate of soda

Mix cocoa with brown sugar. Scald milk over medium heat, add gradually to brown sugar mixture. Beat until smooth. Cool.

Cream fat. Add caster sugar gradually, creaming together until light and fluffy. Add eggs 1 at a time, beating after each addition. Add vanilla.

Sift together flour, baking powder, salt, and soda. Add alternately with cocoa mixture to fat-sugar-egg mixture, mixing until smooth.

Pour into greased sandwich tins. Bake in moderate oven (350°F. Mark 4) 25 to 30 minutes.

Cool in tins 5 to 10 minutes. Remove from tins and cool on wire rack. Ice with caramel icing. Sprinkle with chopped nuts.

Old-Fashioned Chocolate Cake

SOUR CREAM DEVIL'S FOOD CAKE

8 ounces plain flour
1½ teaspoons bicarbonate of soda
½ teaspoon salt
3 ounces butter or other fat (at room temperature)
10 ounces sugar
1 egg, unbeaten
3 ounces chocolate, melted
1 teaspoon vanilla
4 fluid ounces thick sour cream
8 fluid ounces milk

Measure sifted flour, add soda and salt, and sift together three times.

Cream fat; add sugar gradually, and cream together until light and fluffy. Add egg and beat well. Stir in chocolate and vanilla.

Add ¼ of the flour and blend. Then add sour cream and beat well. Add rest of flour, alternately with milk, beating after each addition until smooth.

Use 2 round 9-inch sandwich tins, 1½ inches deep; line the bottoms with paper. Pour quickly into tins.

Bake in moderate oven (350°F. Mark 4) 30 to 35 minutes. Ice with peppermint icing or easy fudge icing.

RED DEVIL'S FOOD CAKE

4 ounces fat
12 ounces sugar
2 ounces cocoa
2 eggs
8 ounces plain flour
4 fluid ounces milk
2 teaspoons bicarbonate of soda
8 fluid ounces boiling water
1 teaspoon vanilla

Cream fat and add sugar and cocoa. Cream thoroughly and then add eggs and beat well.

Add flour alternately with milk in which soda has been dissolved. Add boiling water and vanilla.

Line bottoms of 2 8-inch cake tins with waxed paper. Turn into cake tins.

Bake in moderate oven (350°F. Mark 4) 30 minutes. Ice as desired.

Feather Devil's Food Cake

FEATHER DEVIL'S FOOD CAKE

    4 ounces fat
    8 ounces caster sugar
    6 ounces light brown sugar
    2 beaten eggs
    3 ounces chocolate
    4 fluid ounces hot water
   10 ounces plain flour
    ½ teaspoon bicarbonate of soda
    2 teaspoons baking powder
    1 teaspoon salt
    ¼ pint milk
    1 teaspoon vanilla

Cream fat until soft and smooth. Gradually add sugars, beating until light and fluffy. Beat in eggs.

Melt chocolate in the hot water in top of double saucepan, stirring until thick and smooth. Cool slightly. Add to fat-sugar-egg mixture and mix well.

Sift together flour, soda, baking powder, and salt 3 times. Add alternately with milk and vanilla, beating well after each addition.

Turn into 2 greased 9-inch sandwich tins. Bake in moderate oven (350°F. Mark 4) 30 to 35 minutes.

Put layers together and cover cake with 7-minute icing. Decorate with chopped nuts or chocolate vermicelli.

FUDGE NUT CAKE

    2 ounces fat
    4 ounces sugar
    1 egg
    ½ teaspoon vanilla
    1 ounce bitter chocolate
    4 ounces plain flour
    1 teaspoon baking powder
    ½ teaspoon salt
    5 tablespoons milk

Cream fat until light; add sugar gradually and continue creaming until fluffy. Beat in egg and add vanilla.

Melt chocolate over hot water and blend with creamed mixture.

Mix and sift flour, baking powder, and salt; add alternately with milk to creamed mixture.

Pour into well greased fireproof glass baking dish. Bake in moderate oven (350°F. Mark 4) about 35 minutes

or until skewer comes out clean.

Ice with easy fudge icing and serve directly from baking dish. Serves 10 to 12.

CHOCOLATE HONEY CAKE

    3 ounces chocolate, melted
    8 ounces honey
    7 ounces plain flour
    1 teaspoon bicarbonate of soda
    ¾ teaspoon salt
    4 ounces butter or other fat
    4 ounces sugar
    1 teaspoon vanilla
    2 eggs, unbeaten
    ¼ pint water

Blend melted chocolate and honey. Sift flour once, measure, add soda and salt, and sift together 3 times.

Cream butter until soft. Add sugar gradually, creaming until light and fluffy. Add chocolate-honey mixture and vanilla. Mix well.

Add eggs, one at a time, beating thoroughly after each addition.

Add flour, alternately with water, a small amount at a time, beating after each addition until smooth.

Bake in 2 greased 8-inch sandwich tins in moderate oven (350°F. Mark 4) 30 to 35 minutes. Spread with chocolate honey icing.

POTATO CHOCOLATE CAKE

    7 ounces hot unseasoned mashed
        potatoes
    1 pound sugar
    5 ounces fat
    4 eggs, unbeaten
    1 teaspoon vanilla
    8 ounces plain flour
    2 ounces cocoa
    3 teaspoons baking powder
    1 teaspoon each cinnamon and
        nutmeg
    ½ teaspoon salt
    4 fluid ounces milk
    4 ounces chopped walnuts

Line bottoms of 2 9-inch sandwich tins or a 13×9×2-inch oblong tin with greaseproof paper cut to fit.

Prepare mashed potatoes. (Easy way: follow directions for 2 servings on packaged mashed potatoes.) Measure; set aside.

Gradually beat sugar into fat until fluffy. Add eggs 1 at a time, beating well. Add vanilla and potatoes. Add sifted dry ingredients and milk alternately, about ¼ of each at a time, beating smooth. Stir in walnuts.

Bake in moderate oven (350°F. Mark 4), layers 40 to 45 minutes, loaf about 50 minutes, or until done when tested.

Let stand 5 minutes. Turn out on racks, peel off paper. When cool, ice with butter cream, or other icing, and sprinkle thickly with walnuts.

CHOCOLATE CAKE
(Basic Recipe)

    8 ounces plain flour
    3 teaspoons baking powder
    ¼ teaspoon salt
    ½ teaspoon bicarbonate of soda
    4 ounces butter or other fat
    8 ounces sugar
    2 eggs, separated
    3 ounces melted chocolate
    ½ pint milk
    1 teaspoon vanilla

Sift flour once before measuring, then sift 3 times with baking powder, salt, and soda.

Cream butter until soft and smooth. Gradually add sugar, creaming until light and fluffy. Add beaten egg yolks. Then add melted chocolate.

Add milk alternately with dry ingredients, beating until smooth after each addition.

Continue beating for two minutes (about 300 strokes). Fold in flavouring and stiffly beaten egg whites. Turn into lightly greased tins.

Bake in 2 9-inch tins, in moderate oven (375°F. Mark 5) 30 minutes or bake in loaf tin (8×8×2 inches) in moderate oven (350°F. Mark 4) 50 to 60 minutes.

Turn out on cake rack to cool. Ice with chocolate icing.

Variations of Basic Chocolate Cake:

Chocolate Almond Cake: Prepare chocolate layers. Prepare chocolate seven-minute icing. Add chopped almonds to ⅓ of icing. Spread between layers. Decorate top with almonds.

Chocolate Cream Cake: Prepare chocolate layers. Spread cream filling between layers. Spread boiled icing on top and sides of cake.

Chocolate Maple Cake: Prepare chocolate layers. Spread maple walnut icing between layers and on top of cake. Decorate with walnut halves.

Chocolate Marshmallow Cake: Bake cake in a loaf tin (8×8×2 inches). While still warm, place over the top, marshmallows cut in half and rinsed in cold water. Let cool. Cover with chocolate butter icing.

Potato Chocolate Cake

OLD-TIME FUDGE CAKE

3 ounces chocolate, melted
4 fluid ounces milk
1 well beaten egg
5 ounces sugar
4 ounces fat
8 ounces sugar
1 teaspoon vanilla
2 eggs
8 ounces plain flour
1 teaspoon bicarbonate of soda
¼ teaspoon salt
¼ pint milk

Combine chocolate, 4 fluid ounces milk, well beaten egg, and 5 ounces sugar in saucepan; cook over low heat until thickened, stirring constantly. Cool.

Stir fat to soften. Gradually add 8 ounces sugar, and cream together until light and fluffy. Add vanilla.

Add remaining eggs, 1 at a time, beating well after each.

Sift flour, soda, and salt together 3 times.

Add flour mixture to creamed mixture alternately with ¼ pint milk, a small amount at a time.

Beat after each addition until smooth. Blend in chocolate mixture.

Bake in 2 paper-lined 9×1½-inch round tins in moderate oven (350°F. Mark 4) 25 to 30 minutes.

Ice with chocolate icing. Decorate with walnut halves.

CHOCOLATE MARASCHINO CAKE

4 ounces fat
8 ounces sugar
1 ounce chocolate, melted
1 beaten egg
7 ounces plain flour
1 teaspoon bicarbonate of soda
½ teaspoon salt
About 8 fluid ounces liquid (use juice from small bottle, 3-4 ounces, of maraschino cherries plus buttermilk or sour milk to make 8 fluid ounces)
Maraschino cherries from 3-4 ounce bottle, cut in small pieces
2 ounces chopped nuts

Cream fat. Gradually add sugar, and cream until light and fluffy. Add melted chocolate and egg. Blend well.

Mix and sift flour, soda, and salt, and add alternately with liquid. Stir in cherries and nuts.

Turn into a greased loaf tin (8×8 ×2 inches). Bake in moderate oven (350°F. Mark 4) 30 to 35 minutes. Ice with 7-minute icing.

STARLIGHT DOUBLE-DELIGHT CAKE

Chocolate Icing:
6 ounces cream cheese
4 ounces fat
½ teaspoon vanilla
½ teaspoon peppermint essence
About 1½ pounds sifted icing sugar
4 tablespoons hot water
4 ounces chocolate, melted

Cream the cream cheese, fat, vanilla, and flavouring or 2 to 3 drops oil of peppermint. Blend well. (If desired, peppermint flavouring may be omitted and vanilla increased to 1 teaspoon.)

Measure and blend half of sugar into creamed cheese mixture. Add water alternately with balance of sugar.

Blend in chocolate. Mix until smooth.

Cake:
2 ounces fat
3 eggs, unbeaten
9 ounces plain flour
1½ teaspoons bicarbonate of soda
1 teaspoon salt
6 fluid ounces milk

Combine fat and most of the chocolate icing, leaving enough to ice the top of the cake mixture; mix thoroughly.

Blend in the eggs, one at a time. Beat for 1 minute.

Sift together flour, soda, and salt. Add milk alternately with the dry ingredients to creamed mixture, beginning and ending with dry ingredients. Blend thoroughly after each addition. (With electric mixer use a low speed.)

Pour mixture into two 9-inch round sandwich tins, well greased and lightly floured on the bottoms only.

Bake in moderate oven (350°F. Mark 4) 30 to 40 minutes. Cool; ice with remaining chocolate icing.

FUDGE NUT LOAF CAKE

4 ounces fat
1 pound sugar
1¼ teaspoons salt
2 teaspoons vanilla
2 eggs
4 ounces chocolate
8 ounces plain flour
2 teaspoons baking powder
12 fluid ounces milk
4 ounces chopped nuts

Cream fat. Add sugar, salt, and vanilla. Cream until fluffy. Add eggs, one at a time, beating well after each addition.

Melt chocolate and add to creamed mixture. Beat until well combined.

Mix and sift flour and baking powder. Add alternately with milk, adding flour first and last. Add nuts, and mix until thoroughly blended.

Grease bottom of cake tin (13×9

Starlight Double-Delight Cake

×1½ inches). Dust lightly with flour. Turn batter into tin.

Bake in moderate oven (350°F. Mark 4) 40 minutes. Cool and ice with chocolate nut icing.

Fudge Nut Layer Cake: Bake in 2 8-inch sandwich tins in moderate oven (375°F. Mark 5) 25 to 30 minutes. Cool and spread a custard filling between layers. Ice as above.

CHOCOLATE PEPPERMINT CAKE

5 ounces fat
10 ounces sugar
2 eggs
1 teaspoon vanilla
8 ounces plain flour
2½ teaspoons baking powder
¼ teaspoon bicarbonate of soda
1 teaspoon salt
2 ounces cocoa
4 fluid ounces evaporated milk diluted with 4 fluid ounces water
2 drops oil of peppermint

Cream fat and sugar. Beat eggs slightly with vanilla and add.

Sift dry ingredients together. Add alternately with diluted evaporated milk to first mixture. Beat well. Add oil of peppermint.

Bake in 2 greased 8-inch cake tins in moderate oven (350°-375°F. Mark 4-5) about 30 to 40 minutes.

Ice with pink icing; decorate with crushed peppermint rock. Serves 8 to 10.

Chocolate Peppermint Cake

Gingerbreads

GINGERBREAD
(Basic Recipe)

8 ounces plain flour
1 teaspoon ground ginger
¾ teaspoon bicarbonate of soda
¾ teaspoon cinnamon
¼ teaspoon ground cloves
1 teaspoon salt
2 ounces fat
2 ounces sugar
1 egg
9 ounces molasses or black treacle
6 fluid ounces milk

Sift together dry ingredients. Cream fat. Gradually add sugar, beating until light and fluffy. Add egg and beat well. Stir molasses into the milk.

Add dry ingredients alternately with molasses mixture, beating thoroughly.

Turn into greased sandwich or loaf tins or in deep bun tins.

Bake in moderate oven (350°F. Mark 4) 30 to 40 minutes for layers, 35 to 45 minutes for loaf, and 20 to 25 minutes for cupcakes. Makes 2 8-inch layers or 1 large loaf or 1½ dozen cupcakes.

Ginger Nut or Raisin Cake: In basic recipe stir in 4 ounces of nuts or 6 ounces raisins.

Ginger Orange Cake: In basic recipe replace milk with orange juice and add 1 tablespoon grated orange rind to creamed fat and sugar.

Gingerbread Washington Pie: Prepare the recipe for Gingerbread and bake in well greased pie plate. When cool, split in two. Make half the recipe of Cornflour Pudding (see index). Cool. Spread between layers. Sprinkle top layer with caster sugar.

Gingerbread Upside-Down Cake: Melt 2 tablespoons butter in 9-inch-square cake tin. Add 3 ounces black treacle. Arrange some canned sliced peaches in decorative pattern in the tin. Pour 1 recipe of Gingerbread over fruit.

Bake in moderate oven (350°F. Mark 4) 45 minutes to 1 hour. Turn out upside-down.

WHITE HOUSE GINGERBREAD

10 ounces plain flour
1 teaspoon salt
1 teaspoon ginger
2 teaspoons cinnamon
½ teaspoon nutmeg (optional)
½ teaspoon powdered cloves
4 ounces lard
4 ounces sugar
1½ teaspoons bicarbonate of soda
12 ounces black treacle
2 eggs, unbeaten
8 fluid ounces sour milk

Mix and sift flour, salt, and spices. Cream together the lard, sugar, and soda until fluffy. Add molasses to lard-sugar mixture, then stir half of the dry ingredients into this mixture.

Add eggs, one at a time, beating well after each addition. Then add sour milk and remaining dry ingredients alternately, beating after each addition.

Pour batter into a well buttered and lightly floured tin (9 × 9 × 2 inches or 8 × 12 × 2 inches). Bake in moderate oven (350°F. Mark 4) until done, 45 minutes.

ORANGE GINGERBREAD

4 ounces butter
8 ounces orange marmalade
6 ounces molasses or black treacle
½ teaspoon salt
8 ounces plain flour
1 teaspoon ginger
1 teaspoon cinnamon
½ teaspoon nutmeg
¼ teaspoon powdered cloves
2 eggs
1 teaspoon bicarbonate of soda
1 tablespoon hot water

Cream butter; add orange marmalade and molasses. Mix well.

Sift salt, flour, and spices together and fold into first mixture. Add unbeaten eggs, one at a time.

Dissolve soda in hot water and add to all. Mix thoroughly.

Turn into well greased 8-inch square tin. Bake in moderate oven (350°F. Mark 4) 30 minutes. Serve warm.

HOT WATER GINGERBREAD

10 ounces plain flour
1 teaspoon salt
1 teaspoon baking powder
1 teaspoon ginger
2 teaspoons cinnamon
½ teaspoon powdered cloves
4 ounces fat
4 ounces sugar
¾ teaspoon bicarbonate of soda
12 ounces molasses or black treacle
2 eggs
8 fluid ounces hot water

Sift together flour, salt, baking powder, ginger, cinnamon, and cloves.

Cream fat, sugar, and soda. Add molasses. Stir in half flour mixture. Beat in eggs. Add hot water alternately with remaining flour mixture. Beat ½ minute.

Turn batter into a well greased, lightly floured 9 × 9 × 2-inch tin.

Bake in a moderate oven (350°F. Mark 4) 45 minutes.

Gingerbread is an adaptable type of cake which can be presented in many ways.

FLUFFY BRAN GINGERBREAD

3 ounces fat
3 ounces sugar
4 ounces molasses or black treacle
1 egg
2½ ounces whole bran
5 ounces plain flour
1 teaspoon baking powder
½ teaspoon bicarbonate of soda
½ teaspoon salt
¾ teaspoon ginger
½ teaspoon cinnamon
6 fluid ounces boiling water

Beat fat until creamy; add sugar slowly and beat until light and fluffy.

Stir in molasses and add unbeaten egg; beat mixture thoroughly. Add bran and let stand 5 minutes.

Sift together all dry ingredients; add to bran mixture and blend thoroughly. Add boiling water and beat until smooth.

Pour out into well greased 9-inch pie plate and bake in moderate oven (350°F. Mark 4) about 30 minutes. Serve warm. Serves 6 to 8.

MAPLE SYRUP GINGERBREAD

1 egg, beaten
12 ounces maple syrup or golden syrup
8 fluid ounces sour cream
9½ ounces plain flour
1 teaspoon bicarbonate of soda
2 teaspoons ginger
½ teaspoon salt
4 tablespoons melted butter

Combine egg, maple syrup, and sour cream. Sift together twice the flour, soda, ginger, and salt.

Stir the liquid ingredients into the sifted dry ingredients, beating well until smooth.

Add the melted butter and beat thoroughly. Pour into a buttered oblong tin.

Bake in moderate oven (350°F. Mark 4) for 30 minutes. Cool on cake rack and ice with maple icing.

One-Bowl Cakes

ONE-BOWL MIXING METHOD

Complete mixing directions are given in each recipe; however, some home-makers frequently find a step-by-step chart such as the following useful.

Use special recipes (called "easy-mix", "pastry-blend", or "quick-method") for one-bowl cakes. Attempts to adapt conventional cake recipes to the one-bowl method may bring you poor results.

1. Sift flour once. Sift together with dry ingredients into mixing bowl.

2. Softened hydrogenated vegetable fat must be used with this method. Stir the fat to soften, then add with two-thirds of the liquid in the recipe.

3. Beat at medium speed in electric mixer for 2 minutes, scraping down the batter in the bowl constantly or beat with a spoon for 2 minutes (150 strokes are equal to 1 minute of beating by mixer).

4. Add remaining liquid and un-beaten eggs (yolks or whites). Beat 2 minutes more (scraping bowl frequently in electric mixer).

5. Turn into prepared tins.

GOLDEN CAKE

    4 ounces vegetable fat
    10 ounces flour
    12 ounces sugar
    4 teaspoons baking powder
    1 teaspoon salt
    8 fluid ounces milk
    1 teaspoon vanilla
    4 egg whites, unbeaten, or 2 whole
       eggs

Place fat in bowl. Mix and sift flour, sugar, baking powder, and salt. Add to fat.

Add ¼ pint milk and the vanilla. Beat all together for 2 minutes with medium speed of electric mixer or 300 strokes by hand (150 strokes per minute).

With rubber scraper keep batter scraped from sides and bottom of mixing bowl throughout the mixing. Scrape bowl and beaters thoroughly.

Add whole eggs or egg whites and remaining milk. Beat again for 2 minutes. Scrape bowl and beaters.

Turn into 2 9-inch round tins each of which has been fitted with two circles of greaseproof paper.

Bake in moderate oven (375°F. Mark 5) about 25 minutes.

Cool on rack 5 minutes. Use end of knife to loosen sides of cake from tins. Turn out on rack to cool. Ice with golden cream icing. Top with pecans or walnuts.

BANANA LAYER CAKE

    9 ounces plain flour
    10 ounces sugar
    2½ teaspoons baking powder
    ½ teaspoon bicarbonate of soda
    ½ teaspoon salt
    4 ounces vegetable fat
    5-6 mashed ripe bananas
    2 eggs, unbeaten
    1 teaspoon vanilla

Sift together flour, sugar, baking powder, soda, and salt into large mixing bowl.

Add fat, half the bananas, and eggs. Beat 2 minutes at slow to medium speed with electric mixer or 2 minutes by hand. Scrape down bowl and beater or spoon frequently during mixing.

Add remaining bananas and vanilla. Beat 1 minute longer, scraping down bowl and beater or spoon frequently during mixing.

Turn into 2 well greased, 8-inch sandwich tins. Bake in moderate oven (375°F. Mark 5) about 25 minutes, or until done.

Ice wih your favourite icing; any flavour blends well with banana cake.

Variations:

Banana Spice Layer Cake: Sift together with the dry ingredients ⅛ teaspoon ground cloves, 1¼ teaspoons cinnamon, and ½ teaspoon nutmeg.

Banana Cupcakes: Turn batter into well greased deep bun tins. Bake in moderate oven (375°F. Mark 5) about 25 minutes or until cupcakes are done. Makes 18 to 20 cupcakes.

DEVIL'S FOOD CAKE

    8   ounces plain flour
    1   teaspoon bicarbonate of soda
    ¾   teaspoon salt
    10½ ounces sugar
    4   ounces vegetable fat
    8   fluid ounces milk
    1   teaspoon vanilla
    2   eggs, unbeaten
    3   ounces chocolate, melted

Mix and sift flour, soda, salt, and sugar.

Cream fat until soft. Add sifted dry ingredients and 6 fluid ounces milk. Mix until all flour is dampened, then beat 2 minutes with medium speed of mixer.

Add vanilla, eggs, melted chocolate, and remaining milk. Beat 1 minute longer. If mixed by hand beat the same length of time, allowing 150 strokes per minute.

Bake in moderate oven (350°F. Mark 4) 30 minutes in 2 9-inch sandwich tins or 40 minutes in 13×9×2-inch tin.

Banana Layer Cake

SPICE CAKE

    8 ounces plain flour
    3 teaspoons baking powder
    1 teaspoon salt
    1 teaspoon cinnamon
    1 teaspoon mixed spice
    ½ teaspoon powdered cloves
    ½ teaspoon nutmeg
    8 ounces sugar
    2 ounces brown sugar
    4 ounces vegetable fat
    7 tablespoons milk
    2 eggs, unbeaten
    1 teaspoon vanilla

Mix and sift flour, baking powder, salt, cinnamon, mixed spice, cloves, nutmeg, and sugar.

Add sieved brown sugar, fat, and 5 tablespoons milk. Beat for 2 minutes, 300 strokes, until batter is well blended. (With electric mixer blend at low speed, then beat at medium speed for 2 minutes.)

Add remaining 2 tablespoons milk, eggs, and vanilla. Beat for 2 minutes.

Pour batter into 2 well greased and floured 8-inch sandwich tins, at least 1¼ inches deep.

Bake in moderate oven (350°F. Mark 4) 30 to 35 minutes. Cool and ice with banana icing.

BLUEBERRY CAKE

    3 ounces vegetable fat
    8 ounces plain flour
    2 teaspoons baking powder
    ¼ teaspoon salt
    8 ounces sugar
    6 fluid ounces milk
    1 egg, unbeaten
    4 ounces blueberries, bilberries or
       blackcurrants

Stir fat to soften. Sift dry ingredients together and add. Stir in milk. Beat vigorously 2 minutes.

Add egg. Beat 1 minute. Stir in blueberries.

Turn into greased 8×8×2-inch tin. Bake in moderate oven (350°F. Mark 4) about 50 minutes. Serve warm with whipped cream.

LEMON CLOUD CAKE

8 ounces plain flour
12 ounces sugar
1½ ounces dry milk
2½ teaspoons baking powder
½ teaspoon salt
4 ounces soft butter or margarine
8 fluid ounces water
1 tablespoon grated lemon rind
3 egg whites, unbeaten
Lemon Cream Filling (below)

Sift flour, sugar, dry milk, baking powder, and salt into a large bowl. Add butter or margarine, water, and lemon rind. Beat 2 minutes at medium speed. Add egg whites and beat 2 minutes more.

Pour batter into 2 greased and floured 8-inch round tins.

Bake near centre of moderate oven (350°F. Mark 4) 30 to 40 minutes or until cake springs back when touched lightly with finger.

Cool thoroughly. Spread lemon cream filling between layers and on top to within ½-inch of edge of cake. Ice sides and top edge with seven minute icing. Sprinkle desiccated coconut over icing.

Lemon Cream Filling:

3 ounces dry milk
2 tablespoons cornflour
4 ounces sugar
½ pint water
3 egg yolks, slightly beaten
1 tablespoon grated lemon rind
4 tablespoons lemon juice
2 tablespoons soft butter or margarine

Mix cornflour, dry milk, and sugar in a 3-pint saucepan. Stir in gradually until smooth a mixture of water and egg yolks.

Cook and stir constantly over medium heat until mixture is thick and just begins to bubble. Lower heat and cook and stir 2 minutes more.

Remove from heat and stir in lemon rind, lemon juice, and butter or margarine until smooth. Cool thoroughly before spreading on Lemon Cloud Cake.

Lemon Cloud Cake

ORANGE LOAF CAKE

8 ounces plain flour
10 ounces sugar
1½ teaspoons baking powder
1 teaspoon salt
4 ounces vegetable fat
4 fluid ounces orange juice
1 tablespoon grated orange rind
3-4 eggs, unbeaten

Mix and sift flour, sugar, baking powder, and salt into mixing bowl. Add fat, orange juice, and orange rind. Beat 2 minutes at slow speed, or 300 strokes by hand.

Add eggs and again beat 2 minutes at low speed, or 300 strokes by hand.

Turn into greased loaf baking tin (5×9¼×2¾ inches). Bake in slow oven (325°F. Mark 3) 1½ hours.

WHITE LAYER CAKE
(Basic Recipe)

8 ounces plain flour
10½ ounces sugar
1 teaspoon salt
4 ounces vegetable fat
8 fluid ounces milk
1 teaspoon vanilla
3½ teaspoons baking powder
4 egg whites, unbeaten

Sift flour, sugar, and salt into mixing bowl or bowl of electric mixer.

Add fat, which is at room temperature, ⅔ of milk to which vanilla has been added.

Beat 300 strokes, scraping bowl and spoon frequently. (Or beat 2 minutes on No. 2 speed of electric mixer.) Add baking powder and beat a few seconds.

Add egg whites and remaining milk. Beat 300 strokes. (Or 2 minutes on No. 2 speed of electric mixer.)

Scrape sides of bowl and spoon frequently during beating process.

Bake in 2 well greased, floured 9-inch sandwich tins in moderate oven (350°F. Mark 4) 30 minutes.

Variations:

Cupcakes: Fill deep bun tins ½ full. Bake in moderate oven (350°F. Mark 4) 15 to 18 minutes.

Chocolate Cake: Omit 1 ounce of flour. Add 2 ounces cocoa to dry ingredients before sifting.

Orange Cake: Spread orange glacé icing between layers and on top.

Spice Cake: Omit vanilla. Add and sift with flour 1 teaspoon nutmeg, ½ teaspoon cinnamon, and ¼ teaspoon ground cloves.

Coconut Berry Cake: Spread a tart berry jelly between layers and on top. Sprinkle with desiccated coconut.

Coconut Fluff Cake

COCONUT FLUFF CAKE

9 ounces plain flour
4½ teaspoons baking powder
1½ teaspoons salt
14 ounces sugar
6 ounces vegetable fat
9 fluid ounces milk
1 teaspoon vanilla
1 teaspoon almond essence
4-5 egg whites, unbeaten

Mix and sift flour, baking powder, salt, and sugar. Add fat and milk. Beat for 2 minutes until batter is well blended and glossy.

If electric mixer is used, beat at low to medium speed for same period of time. Add vanilla, almond essence, and egg whites. Beat 2 minutes.

Pour into 2 slightly greased, floured, shallow 8-inch square tins or 9-inch round sandwich tin. Bake in moderate oven (350°F. Mark 4) 35 to 40 minutes.

Ice with fluffy white icing. Cover with desiccated coconut.

Loaf Cake: Turn batter into lightly greased, floured loaf tin. Bake in moderate oven (350°F. Mark 4) 40 to 45 minutes.

CHOCOLATE ICICLE CAKE

7 ounces plain flour
3 teaspoons baking powder
1 teaspoon salt
10 ounces sugar
2 ounces cocoa
5 ounces vegetable fat
8 fluid ounces milk
2 eggs, unbeaten
1 teaspoon vanilla

Sift together flour, baking powder, salt, sugar, and cocoa. Add fat and ¼ pint milk. Beat for 2 minutes until batter is well blended and glossy.

If electric mixer is used, beat at low to medium speed for same period of time.

Add rest of milk, eggs, and vanilla. Beat 2 minutes.

Pour into 2 lightly greased, floured, 8-inch sandwich tins. Bake in moderate oven (350°F. Mark 4) 30 to 35 minutes.

Ice cooled layers with fluffy cooked icing. Decorate edges with melted chocolate, letting the chocolate run down the sides to form "icicles."

ORANGE KISS-ME CAKE

 1 large orange
 6 ounces seedless raisins
 1½ ounces walnuts
 8 ounces plain flour
 1 teaspoon bicarbonate of soda
 1 teaspoon salt
 8 ounces sugar
 4 ounces vegetable fat
 6 fluid ounces milk
 2 eggs, unbeaten
 4 tablespoons milk

Mince together pulp and rind of orange (reserve juice for topping), raisins, and walnuts, using coarse blade of mincer.

Sift together flour, soda, salt, and sugar. Add fat and 6 fluid ounces milk. Beat for 1½ minutes, 150 strokes per minute, until batter is well blended. (With electric mixer blend at low speed, then beat at medium speed for 1½ minutes.)

Add eggs and 4 tablespoons milk. Beat for 1½ minutes. Fold orange-raisin mixture into batter.

Pour into 12×8×2 or 13×9×2-inch tin, well greased and lightly floured on the bottom only.

Bake in moderate oven (350°F. Mark 4) 40 to 50 minutes.

Note: Cake may be baked in two 8- or 9-inch sandwich tins at 350°F. Mark 4 for 35 to 40 minutes.

Orange-Nut Topping:

 5 tablespoons orange juice
 3 ounces sugar
 1 teaspoon cinnamon
 1 ounce chopped walnuts

Drip orange juice over warm cake.

Combine sugar, cinnamon, and walnuts; sprinkle over cake. Decorate with orange slices, if desired.

BALTIMORE CAKE

 7 ounces plain flour
 3 teaspoons baking powder
 1 teaspoon salt
 10 ounces sugar
 4 ounces vegetable fat
 6 fluid ounces milk
 3 egg whites, unbeaten
 1 teaspoon vanilla

Mix and sift flour, baking powder, salt, and sugar.

Add fat and 4 fluid ounces milk. Beat for 2 minutes, 300 strokes, until batter is well blended. (With electric mixer blend at low speed, then beat at medium speed for 2 minutes.)

Add remaining milk, egg whites, and vanilla. Beat for 2 minutes.

Turn batter into 2 well greased and floured 8-inch sandwich tins, at least 1¼ inches deep.

Bake in moderate oven (350°F. Mark 4) 25 to 30 minutes. Cool and ice with Lady Baltimore icing.

Orange Kiss-Me Cake

PINEAPPLE LAYER CAKE

 8 ounces plain flour
 12 ounces sugar
 3½ teaspoons baking powder
 1 teaspoon salt
 1 teaspoon grated lemon rind
 4 ounces vegetable fat
 7 fluid ounces canned pineapple
    juice
 1 teaspoon vanilla
 3 egg whites, unbeaten
 Pineapple filling
 ¼ pint whipped cream

Mix and sift flour, 10 ounces sugar, baking powder, and salt. Add lemon rind, fat, pineapple juice, and vanilla.

Beat all together 200 strokes (2 minutes by hand or with mixer at low speed). Scrape bowl and spoon or beater.

Add egg whites and beat 200 strokes (2 minutes by hand or with mixer at low speed).

Turn into 2 square greased tins (8× 8×2 inches). Bake in moderate oven (350°F. Mark 4) 25 to 30 minutes.

Chill layers and split in half. Sweeten whipped cream with 2 ounces sugar. Spread pineapple filling and sweetened whipped cream between layers. Cover top with whipped cream.

Decorate corners with pieces of pineapple. Chill cake several hours in refrigerator before serving, and keep in refrigerator until used up.

SMALL LEMON CAKE

 5 ounces plain flour
 6 ounces sugar
 2 teaspoons baking powder
 ½ teaspoon salt
 1 teaspoon grated lemon rind
 3 ounces vegetable fat
 4 fluid ounces milk
 1 teaspoon vanilla
 1 egg, unbeaten

Mix and sift flour, sugar, baking powder, and salt into mixing bowl. Add lemon rind. Drop in fat.

Add milk and vanilla and beat 150 strokes (1½ minutes by hand or on mixer at low speed). Scrape bowl and spoon or beater. Add egg and again beat 150 strokes.

Bake in 8×8×2-inch greased tin in moderate oven (375°F. Mark 5) 25 to 35 minutes. Cool. Spread with lemon icing.

ORANGE CAKE

 ¼ teaspoon grated orange rind
 4 fluid ounces orange juice
 9 ounces plain flour
 3 teaspoons baking powder
 1 teaspoon salt
 10 ounces sugar
 4 ounces vegetable fat
 4 fluid ounces milk
 2 eggs, unbeaten

Steep orange rind in orange juice for 5 minutes and strain. Discard rind.

Sift flour, measure, resift 3 times with baking powder, salt, and sugar, the last time into bowl.

Add fat and stir with spoon enough to distribute evenly. Combine orange juice and milk; add 5 ounces to flour mixture.

Beat 2 minutes in electric mixer at low speed or by hand. (While beating by hand, if necessary to rest, count beating time only.) When using electric mixer, scrape bowl frequently and scrape beaters at the end of the 2 minutes.

Add remaining milk and eggs; beat 1 minute.

Pour into 2 ungreased 8-inch sandwich tins lined with greaseproof paper on bottoms. Bake in moderate oven (375°F. Mark 5) about 25 minutes.

Remove from oven and cool 5 minutes. Turn out of tins and cool. Remove paper and spread with 7-minute or creamy vanilla icing and sprinkle with desiccated coconut.

FUDGE CAKE
- 3 ounces chocolate
- 4 tablespoons boiling water
- 8 ounces plain flour
- 1 teaspoon bicarbonate of soda
- 1 teaspoon salt
- 10 ounces sugar
- 3 ounces melted vegetable fat
- 8 fluid ounces sour cream
- 2 eggs, unbeaten
- 1 teaspoon vanilla

Melt chocolate in water, stirring until well blended and thick.

Sift together flour, soda, salt, and sugar. Add fat and sour cream. Beat for 2 minutes, or until batter is well blended and glossy.

If electric mixer is used, beat at low to medium speed for same period of time.

Add cooled chocolate mixture, eggs and vanilla. Beat for 2 minutes.

Pour into 2 lightly greased, floured, 8-inch sandwich tins. Bake in moderate oven (350°F. Mark 4) for 35 to 40 minutes.

When cool, ice with creamy chocolate icing.

Note: Fresh cream may be substituted for sour cream but add 1 tablespoon lemon juice.

EASY CHOCOLATE CAKE
- 2 ounces chocolate
- 5 ounces plain flour
- 8 ounces sugar
- 1 teaspoon bicarbonate of soda
- ½ teaspoon salt
- 2 ounces vegetable fat
- 8 fluid ounces buttermilk or sour milk
- 1 egg, unbeaten
- 1 teaspoon vanilla

Melt chocolate and cool.

Mix and sift flour and sugar. Add soda, salt, fat, buttermilk, egg, vanilla, and cooled chocolate in large bowl.

Beat with rotary beater for 3 minutes. (With electric mixer blend at low speed, then beat at medium speed for 3 minutes.)

Turn batter into greased and floured 9×9×2-inch tin. Bake in moderate oven (350°F. Mark 4) 40 to 45 minutes.

Serve warm topped with whipped cream or icing as desired.

HURRY-UP LOAF CAKE
- 9 ounces plain flour
- 2¼ teaspoons baking powder
- ½ teaspoon salt
- 8 ounces sugar
- 3 ounces softened fat
- 8 fluid ounces milk
- 1 teaspoon vanilla

Sift flour once. Measure. Add baking powder, salt, and sugar and sift together 3 times.

Add fat, milk, and vanilla. Mix only enough to dampen all flour, then beat vigorously about 1 minute.

Turn into greased, lined loaf tin (8×8×2 inches). Bake in moderate oven (375°F. Mark 5) until done, about 40 minutes.

PENUCHE LAYER CAKE
- 9 ounces plain flour
- 12 ounces sugar
- 2½ teaspoons baking powder
- 1 teaspoon salt
- 3 ounces vegetable fat
- 6 fluid ounces milk
- 1 teaspoon orange essence
- ½ teaspoon almond essence
- 3 eggs, unbeaten

Mix and sift flour, sugar, baking powder. and salt into mixing bowl. Drop in fat.

Add 4 fluid ounces milk, flavouring essences and 1 egg and beat 200 strokes (2 minutes by hand or on mixer at low speed). Scrape bowl and spoon or beater.

Add remaining milk and 2 eggs and beat 200 strokes.

Turn into 2 deep 9-inch greased sandwich tins. Bake in moderate oven (375°F. Mark 5) 25 to 30 minutes.

Spread penuche pecan icing between layers and on top and sides.

GINGER CAKE
- 8 ounces plain flour
- 1¾ teaspoons baking powder
- ¼ teaspoon bicarbonate of soda
- 1 teaspoon salt
- 8 ounces sugar
- 1½ teaspoons ginger
- 1 teaspoon cinnamon
- 4 ounces vegetable fat
- 3 ounces molasses or black treacle
- 7 fluid ounces milk
- 2 eggs, unbeaten

Sift flour, measure, resift 3 times with baking powder, soda, salt, sugar, ginger, and cinnamon, the last time into bowl. Add fat, molasses, and 4 fluid ounces milk. Stir with spoon until all flour is dampened.

Beat 2 minutes in electric mixer at low speed or by hand. (While beating by hand, if necessary to rest, count beating time only.) When using electric mixer, scrape bowl frequently, and scrape beaters at end of 2 minutes.

Add eggs and remaining milk; beat 1 minute longer.

Pour batter into 2 greased 8-inch sandwich tins lined with greaseproof paper on bottoms. Bake in moderate oven (350°F. Mark 4) about 25 to 30 minutes.

Remove from oven and cool on cake racks 5 minutes. Turn out of tins, invert and cool. Remove paper. Spread with lemon icing.

PRUNE WHIP SPICE CAKE
- 9 ounces plain flour
- 11 ounces sugar
- 2 teaspoons baking powder
- ¼ teaspoon bicarbonate of soda
- 1 teaspoon salt
- ½ teaspoon cinnamon
- ¼ teaspoon nutmeg
- ¼ teaspoon mixed spice
- 4 ounces fat
- 4 fluid ounces prune juice
- 4 fluid ounces milk
- 2 eggs, unbeaten
- 1 teaspoon vanilla

Sift together flour, sugar, baking powder, soda, salt, cinnamon, nutmeg, and mixed spice into large bowl.

Add fat, prune juice, and milk. Beat for 1½ minutes. (With electric mixer, blend at a low speed, then beat at medium speed. By hand, beat with a spoon 150 strokes per minute.)

Add eggs and vanilla. Beat for 1½ minutes.

Turn batter into tins (see sizes below), well greased and lightly floured on the bottoms only.

Bake in moderate oven (375°F. Mark 5). For two 8-inch round tins, 25 to 30 minutes; two 9-inch round tins, 20 to 25 minutes; 13×9×2-inch tin, 30 to 35 minutes; 12×8×2-inch tin, 35 to 40 minutes.

Cool and ice. (Use ½ recipe of icing for loaf cake.)

Fluffy Prune Icing: Combine 6 ounces brown sugar*, 3 ounces light corn syrup or golden syrup, 4 tablespoons prune juice*, 2 egg whites, 2 teaspoons lemon juice, and ¼ teaspoon salt in top of double saucepan.

Cook over boiling water, beating constantly with electric mixer or rotary beater, until mixture stands in peaks.

Remove from heat. Continue beating about 2 minutes. Fold in 3 ounces well drained cooked prunes, cut fine, and 2 tablespoons chopped nuts.

* Or substitute 6 ounces caster sugar and reduce prune juice to 2 tablespoons.

Prune Whip Spice Cake

Chiffon Cakes

HINTS ABOUT CHIFFON CAKES

These airy, delicate, high and luscious cakes are prepared by a method that combines some of the steps in making an angel cake and a fat-type cake. Because the method is different be sure to read the recipe very carefully before starting to mix the cake.

The mixing directions in each of the recipes are complete. As with other recipes, assemble all the ingredients and utensils, preheat the oven, and measure ingredients accurately. Use the type and size tins specified in recipe and note particularly that you do *not* grease tins unless the recipe specifically calls for it.

MOCHA MARBLE CHIFFON CAKE

- 9 ounces plain flour
- 12 ounces sugar
- 3 teaspoons baking powder
- 1 teaspoon salt
- 4 fluid ounces salad oil
- 6 egg yolks, unbeaten
- 6 fluid ounces cold water
- 2 teaspoons vanilla
- 7 egg whites
- ½ teaspoon cream of tartar
- 1 ounce chocolate, melted

Mix and sift flour, sugar, baking powder, and salt into large bowl. Make well in the centre and add oil, egg yolks, water, and vanilla. Beat with rotary beater until smooth.

Beat egg whites until foamy; add cream of tartar and beat until stiff.

Remove half the batter and to it add melted chocolate, then fold in a little beaten egg white.

Fold remaining egg white into white batter.

Alternately spoon batters into ungreased 10-inch tube tin. Bake in slow oven (325°F. Mark 3) 55 minutes.

Remove from oven. Turn upside down on cake rack. Cool for 1 minute. Loosen sides of cake and around tube. Remove from tin.

Ice with mocha icing. Decorate with browned almonds.

LEMON CHIFFON CAKE
(Basic Recipe)

- 9 ounces flour
- 12 ounces sugar
- 3 teaspoons baking powder
- 1 teaspoon salt
- 4 fluid ounces salad oil
- 5 egg yolks, unbeaten
- 6 fluid ounces cold water
- 2 teaspoons vanilla
- Grated rind of 1 lemon (optional)
- 7-8 egg whites
- ½ teaspoon cream of tartar

Mix and sift flour, sugar, baking powder, and salt. Make a well and add oil, egg yolks, water, vanilla, and (if desired) lemon rind. Beat with a spoon until smooth.

Use a very large mixing bowl in which to whip egg whites with cream of tartar until very stiff peaks are formed. Gently fold cake mixture into egg whites until well blended. Do not stir.

Pour into ungreased 10-inch tube tin (4 inches deep) immediately.

Bake in slow oven (325°F. Mark 3) 55 minutes, then at 350°F. Mark 4 10 to 15 minutes, or until top springs back when lightly touched.

Invert tin on rack until cold. To remove from tin loosen from sides and tube with spatula.

Lemon Chiffon Cake Variations:

Banana Chiffon Cake: Reduce water to 5 tablespoons. Use only 1 teaspoon vanilla or lemon rind. Add 2-3 sieved very ripe bananas to egg yolk mixture. Bake in slow oven (325°F. Mark 3) 65 to 70 minutes.

Orange Chiffon Cake: Omit vanilla and lemon rind. Add grated rind of 2 oranges (about 3 tablespoons) to egg yolk mixture. Baking time same as for lemon chiffon cake.

Walnut Chiffon Cake: Omit lemon rind. After egg mixture has been folded into egg whites, sprinkle over top of batter, gently folding in with a few strokes 4 ounces very finely chopped walnuts. Baking time same as for lemon chiffon cake.

PECAN CHIFFON CAKE

- 4 ounces plain flour
- 3 ounces brown sugar
- ¾ teaspoon salt
- 1½ teaspoons baking powder
- 4 tablespoons salad oil
- 3 egg yolks
- 6 tablespoons water
- ½ teaspoon vanilla
- ½ teaspoon almond flavouring
- 3-4 egg whites
- ¼ teaspoon cream of tartar
- 2 ounces caster sugar
- 2 ounces finely chopped pecans

Mix and sift into a mixing bowl the flour, brown sugar, salt, and baking powder. Make a hollow in centre and add salad oil. Add in order: egg yolks, water, vanilla, and almond flavouring. Beat with a spoon until smooth.

Put egg whites into a large mixing bowl. Add cream of tartar. Beat with rotary or electric beater until whites form soft peaks. Add caster sugar gradually, beating after each addition.

Beat until meringue is just stiff enough not to slide when bowl is inverted.

Pour egg yolk mixture over meringue. Gently fold yolks and pecans into meringue until well blended.

Turn into ungreased loaf tin (5×10×3 inches). Bake in a slow oven (325°F. Mark 3) 50 minutes. Ice with butter icing.

WALNUT CHIFFON CAKE 2

- 9 ounces plain flour
- 12 ounces sugar
- 3 teaspoons baking powder
- 1 teaspoon salt
- 4 fluid ounces salad oil
- 5 egg yolks, unbeaten
- 6 fluid ounces cold water
- 2 teaspoons vanilla
- 7-8 egg whites
- ½ teaspoon cream of tartar
- 4 ounces very finely chopped walnuts

Sift dry ingredients into bowl. Make a well and add oil, egg yolks, water, and vanilla. Beat with spoon until smooth or with electric mixer on medium speed 1 minute.

Measure egg whites and cream of tartar into large mixing bowl. Beat by hand until whites form very stiff peaks or with electric mixer on high speed 3 to 5 minutes. Do not underbeat. Pour egg yolk mixture gradually over beaten whites folding just until blended. Fold in chopped nuts. Pour into ungreased 10×4-inch tube tin.

Bake 55 minutes in slow oven (325°F. Mark 3), then increase to 350°F. Mark 4 and bake 10 to 15 minutes longer, or until top springs back when lightly touched.

Turn tin upside down with tube over neck of funnel or bottle. Let hang until cold.

Loosen from sides and tubes with spatula; turn tin over, hit edge sharply on table. Ice with browned butter icing (below). Then make it truly gift-gorgeous by wreathing the top with walnut halves.

Browned Butter Icing: Melt, then keep over low heat until golden brown, 2 ounces butter. Remove from heat.

Blend in about 11 ounces sifted icing sugar, 2 tablespoons cream, and 1½ teaspoons vanilla.

Stir vigorously until cool and of a consistency to spread. (If it becomes too thick to spread, stir in a little hot water.)

In High Altitudes: Adjust baking powder amounts and oven temperature as follows:

Altitudes	Baking Powder
3000-4000 ft.	2¼ tsp.
4000-6500 ft.	1½ tsp.
over 6500 ft.	¾ tsp.

Over 3500 feet, increase each oven temperature 25°.

YELLOW 2-EGG CHIFFON CAKE

2 eggs, separated
12 ounces sugar
9 ounces plain flour
3 teaspoons baking powder
1 teaspoon salt
5 tablespoons salad oil
8 fluid ounces milk
1½ teaspoons flavouring

Heat oven to 350°F. Mark 4 (moderate). Grease generously and dust with flour 2 round sandwich tins, 8 inches by at least 1½ inches deep or 9×1½ inches.

Beat egg whites until frothy. Gradually beat in 4 ounces of the sugar. Continue beating until very stiff and glossy.

Sift remaining sugar, flour, baking powder, and salt into another bowl. Pour in salad oil, half of milk, and flavouring. Beat 1 minute, medium speed on mixer or 150 vigorous strokes by hand. Scrape sides and bottom of bowl constantly. Add remaining milk, egg yolks. Beat 1 minute more, scraping bowl constantly.

Fold meringue into batter by cutting down gently through batter, across the bottom up and over, turning bowl often. Pour into prepared tins. Bake 30 to 35 minutes. Cool.

Variations of 2-Egg Chiffon Cake:
Orange-Filled Cake: Spread clear orange filling between layers. Ice with white mountain icing. Sprinkle generously with desiccated coconut.

Clear Orange Filling: Mix in saucepan 8 ounces sugar, 4 tablespoons cornflour, ½ teaspoon salt, 8 fluid ounces orange juice, 1½ tablespoons lemon juice, and 2 tablespoons butter.

Boil 1 minute, stirring constantly. Stir in 2 tablespoons grated orange rind. Chill.

White Mountain Icing: Stir until well blended in small saucepan 5 ounces sugar, 2⅔ tablespoons water, and 5 tablespoons golden syrup. Boil rapidly to 242°F. (mixture spins a 6- to 8-inch thread or a few drops form a firm ball when dropped into cold water).

When mixture begins to boil, start beating 2 large egg whites. Beat until stiff enough to hold a peak.

Pour hot syrup slowly in a thin steady stream into beaten egg whites, beating constantly with electric or rotary beater until mixture stands in very stiff peaks. Blend in 1½ teaspoons vanilla.

French Cream Cake: Split each layer into two layers. Spread cream filling, between layers and on top.

Ice sides of cake with brown beauty icing. Sprinkle top edge of cake with browned slivered almonds.

Brown Beauty Icing: Place bowl in ice water. Mix thoroughly 5½ ounces sifted icing sugar, ¼ teaspoon salt, 3 tablespoons milk, 1½ ounces soft fat, 2 ounces chocolate, melted, and ¾ teaspoon vanilla.

Add 2 or 3 egg yolks (or 1 small egg). Beat until thick enough to spread (3 to 5 minutes).

Peppermint Chocolate Chip Cake: After folding in meringue, fold in 2 ounces grated chocolate. Pour into prepared tins. Bake 30 to 35 minutes. Cool. Ice with pink peppermint icing. Trim swirls of icing with grated chocolate.

Pink Peppermint Icing: Stir until well blended in small saucepan 5 ounces sugar, 2⅔ tablespoons water, and 5 tablespoons corn or golden syrup. Boil rapidly to 242°F. (mixture spins a 6- to 8-inch thread or a few drops form a firm ball when dropped into cold water).

When mixture begins to boil, start beating 2 large egg whites. Beat until stiff enough to hold a peak.

Pour hot syrup slowly in a thin steady stream into beaten egg whites, beating constantly with electric or rotary beater until mixture stands in very stiff peaks.

Blend in ¼ teaspoon peppermint essence. Tint a delicate pink with red food colouring.

PINEAPPLE COCONUT CHIFFON CAKE

9 ounces plain flour
8 ounces sugar
3 teaspoons baking powder
1 teaspoon salt
4 fluid ounces salad oil
5 egg yolks, unbeaten
6 fluid ounces canned pineapple juice
8-9 egg whites
½ teaspoon cream of tartar
4 ounces sugar
4 ounces desiccated coconut

Mix and sift together flour, 8 ounces sugar, baking powder, and salt. Make a well in the centre and add in order: oil, egg yolks, and juice. With spoon, beat until very smooth.

With electric mixer at high speed or with egg beater, beat whites with cream of tartar until soft peaks are formed. Gradually add 4 ounces sugar, beating until very stiff peaks are formed.

Gently fold yolk mixture into whites until blended. During last few strokes fold in coconut.

Turn into ungreased 10-inch tube tin. Bake in slow oven (325°F. Mark 3) about 1 hour or until done.

Invert tin and cool. Loosen cake with spatula and invert tin. Strike edge sharply on table so cake will drop out.

Serve with whipped cream into which drained canned crushed pineapple has been folded.

CHOCOLATE CHIFFON CAKE

9 ounces plain flour
13 ounces sugar
3 teaspoons baking powder
2 teaspoons instant coffee
1 teaspoon salt
¼ teaspoon cinnamon
4 fluid ounces salad oil
6 egg yolks
6 fluid ounces water
2 teaspoons vanilla
2 ounces chocolate, melted
½ teaspoon cream of tartar
6 egg whites

Mix and sift first 6 ingredients. Make a well in the centre and add in order: oil, egg yolks, water, and vanilla. Beat with spoon until smooth. Add melted chocolate and blend well.

Add cream of tartar to egg whites. Beat until egg whites form very stiff peaks.

Gently fold first mixture into egg whites until well blended. Fold, do not stir.

Turn batter into ungreased 10-inch tube tin. Bake in slow oven (325°F. Mark 3) 70 to 75 minutes or until cake springs back when touched lightly with finger.

Immediately invert tin over funnel or bottle to cool. When cold, loosen side of cake with spatula.

Chocolate Chiffon Cake

Upside-Down Cakes

These are cakes served with the bottom side up. Fruit, sugar, butter, or whatever else is specified in the recipe as a topping is placed in the cake tin before the batter is added.

PEACH UPSIDE-DOWN CAKE

4   tablespoons melted butter
4½ ounces brown sugar
6   canned peach halves
2   ounces fat
6   ounces sugar
1   egg, unbeaten
1   teaspoon lemon juice
2   teaspoons grated lemon rind
6   ounces plain flour
2   teaspoons baking powder
½   teaspoon salt
4   fluid ounces milk

Mix butter and brown sugar together and pat into bottom of square 8-inch cake tin. Arrange peach halves over this, cut side down.

Cream fat and sugar together. Add egg, lemon juice, and rind. Beat until fluffy.

Mix and sift flour, baking powder, and salt. Add to creamed mixture alternately with milk.

Pour batter over peaches carefully. Bake in moderate oven (375°F. Mark 5) 45 minutes.

Turn out upside down. Serve plain or with whipped cream.

BANANA UPSIDE-DOWN CAKE

2   tablespoons butter
3   ounces brown sugar
3   medium bananas, cut in quarters
3   ounces raisins
Walnut halves
2   ounces fat
5   ounces caster sugar
2   beaten eggs
1   teaspoon vanilla
6   ounces plain flour
2   teaspoons baking powder
½   teaspoon salt
5   tablespoons milk

Melt butter. Add brown sugar, and stir until well blended. Pat into the bottom of a square 8-inch baking tin. Arrange bananas, raisins, and nuts over this and pat down gently.

Cream fat. Add sugar gradually and cream thoroughly. Add eggs and beat well. Add vanilla.

Mix and sift flour, baking powder, and salt.

Add flour mixture alternately with milk to creamed mixture, stirring and blending after each addition.

Beat slightly to make smooth. Pour batter carefully over bananas.

Bake in moderate oven (350°F. Mark 4) until done, about 55 minutes. Turn out upside down.

BLACKBERRY UPSIDE-DOWN CAKE

1   pound fresh blackberries, bilberries or blackcurrants
1   tablespoon lemon juice
6   ounces sugar
2   ounces fat
4   ounces sugar
1   egg
6   ounces plain flour
Dash of salt
1½ teaspoons baking powder
6   fluid ounces milk

Wash and drain blackberries. Squeeze lemon juice over top and sprinkle with 6 ounces sugar. Place in bowl and set aside.

Cream fat and 4 ounces sugar together. Add egg. Sift together flour, salt, and baking powder. Add to fat. Then add milk and beat for 2 minutes until smooth.

Plack sweetened blackberries in 8-inch square cake tin which has been well greased on sides. Arrange berries in even layer and smooth cake dough over berries.

Bake in moderate oven (350°F. Mark 4) 30 minutes. When cake is done, invert on plate. Cut in squares and serve warm with plain or whipped cream. Makes 8 to 10 servings.

PINEAPPLE UPSIDE-DOWN CAKE
(Basic Recipe)

2   ounces butter
3   ounces brown sugar
4   slices pineapple, cut in wedges
5   ounces flour
2   teaspoons baking powder
¼   teaspoon salt
6   ounces caster sugar
2   ounces butter or other fat
1   egg, unbeaten
4   fluid ounces milk
1   teaspoon vanilla

Melt butter in 8×8×2-inch square tin. Add brown sugar and blend well. Remove from heat.

Arrange pineapple wedges on sugar mixture and set aside.

Measure sifted flour, add baking powder, salt, and caster sugar, and sift together 3 times.

Cream fat. Add dry ingredients, egg, milk, and vanilla. Stir until all flour is dampened, then beat vigorously 1 minute. Pour batter over fruit mixture in tin.

Bake in moderate oven (350°F. Mark 4) about 50 minutes.

Cool cake in tin 5 minutes. Then invert on plate and let stand a minute before removing tin.

Upside-down cake is best when served warm. It may be decorated with whipped cream or a variation. It is also delicious with ice cream.

Blackberry Upside-Down Cake

Variations:

Apricot or Peach Upside-Down Cake: Use batter for plain or spiced pineapple upside-down cake.

For the topping, substitute 20 cooked dried apricot halves or 12 canned apricot halves, or well drained sliced peaches for the pineapple slices in recipe.

Arrange on sugar mixture. Cover with batter and bake as directed. Serve plain or with ice cream.

Coconut Butterscotch Upside-Down Cake: Prepare as for pineapple upside-down cake.

For the topping gently cook 1 can (4 ounces) shredded coconut in 1 tablespoon melted butter in 8×8×2-inch square tin until golden brown.

Then add 1½ ounces more butter, 3 ounces brown sugar, and 4 tablespoons water; heat until blended, stirring constantly. Serve plain or with whipped cream.

Pineapple-Spice Upside-Down Cake: Follow recipe for pineapple upside-down cake, adding 1 teaspoon cinnamon, ½ teaspoon nutmeg, and ⅛ teaspoon powdered cloves to flour mixture.

Cranberry Upside-Down Cake: Use pineapple upside-down cake batter.

For topping, melt 3 tablespoons butter in 8×8×2-inch square tin. Add 6 tablespoons sugar and 1 tablespoon grated orange rind; mix well.

Sprinkle 8 ounces fresh cranberries, coarsely cut, over sugar mixture. Cover with batter and bake as directed.

Fresh Blackberry Upside-Down Cake: Prepare as for pineapple upside-down cake.

For the topping, melt 3 tablespoons butter in 8×8×2-inch square tin.

Add 2 ounces brown sugar and mix well.

Pour 8 ounces fresh blackberries or bilberries over sugar mixture; sprinkle with ½ teaspoon grated lemon rind and 2 teaspoons lemon juice. Serve with plain whipped cream.

MINCEMEAT UPSIDE-DOWN CAKE

1½ ounces butter or margarine
2 tablespoons brown sugar
8 ounces mincemeat
4 ounces plain flour
1 teaspoon baking powder
¼ teaspoon salt
½ teaspoon cinnamon
⅛ teaspoon nutmeg
¼ teaspoon ground cloves
¼ teaspoon mixed spice
2 ounces sugar
5 tablespoons milk
6 ounces light or dark corn syrup
    or golden syrup
1 teaspoon vanilla
2 ounces fat
1 egg, unbeaten

Melt butter in an 8-inch square tin. Sprinkle with brown sugar and spread mincemeat lightly over the mixture.

Sift flour with the baking powder, salt, spices, and sugar.

Combine milk, corn syrup, and vanilla. Add fat with half of the liquid and the egg to the dry ingredients. Mix until all flour is dampened, then beat 1 minute longer (100 full strokes per minute).

Add the remaining liquid and beat 2 minutes. Pour over mincemeat and bake in a moderate oven (350°F. Mark 4) 35 minutes. Turn out immediately. Serves 6.

PEAR UPSIDE-DOWN GINGERBREAD

4 ounces plain flour
½ teaspoon bicarbonate of soda
¼ teaspoon salt
1 teaspoon cinnamon
¾ teaspoon ginger
¼ teaspoon nutmeg
1 egg, slightly beaten
5 tablespoons brown sugar
3 ounces black treacle
4 fluid ounces sour milk or
    buttermilk
2 ounces fat, melted
3 ripe pears, peeled and halved
6 walnuts
2 tablespoons chopped walnuts

Sift together all dry ingredients. Combine egg, sugar, treacle, milk, and fat; gradually add flour mixture, stirring until mixed. Beat vigorously about 1 minute until batter is smooth.

Place pear halves, cut side down, into well greased 9-inch pie plate. Place a walnut in centre of each pear.

Pour gingerbread mixture over pears. Sprinkle with chopped walnuts.

Bake in moderate oven (350°F. Mark 4) about 30 minutes. Serves 6.

FRESH PEAR UPSIDE-DOWN CAKE

1 ounce butter or margarine
2 ounces brown sugar
1 large fresh pear
⅛ teaspoon nutmeg
2 eggs, separated
12 ounces warm light corn syrup
    or golden syrup
1 teaspoon vanilla
1 tablespoon melted fat
4 ounces plain flour
1½ teaspoons baking powder
¼ teaspoon salt
2 ounces bran

Combine butter and sugar in 9-inch cake tin; cook over low heat until butter melts. Spread evenly over bottom of cake tin. Pare fruit and cut into slices lengthwise. Remove core. Arrange slices in circle in bottom of tin; sprinkle with nutmeg.

Beat egg yolks well; add corn syrup and continue beating. Add flavouring and melted fat. Stir in sifted dry ingredients and bran.

Beat egg whites until stiff but not dry; fold into batter. Spread over pears. Bake in moderate oven (350°F. Mark 4) about 45 minutes. Turn upside down on plate while hot. Serve with whipped cream or lemon sauce if desired.

CRANBERRY-ORANGE UPSIDE-DOWN CAKE

Topping:
1 ounce butter
6 ounces brown sugar
8 ounces cranberries
2 oranges, in segments

Melt butter in shallow baking tin (8 ×10 inches). Stir in sugar and spread evenly over bottom of tin.

Wash and pick over cranberries. Cut them in halves. Spread berries over sugar. Scatter orange pieces over cranberries.

Cake Batter:
6 ounces plain flour
2 teaspoons baking powder
¼ teaspoon salt
2 ounces fat
Grated rind of 1 orange
6 ounces sugar
1 egg, unbeaten
4 tablespoons evaporated milk
    mixed with 4 tablespoons
    orange juice

Sift flour with baking powder and salt.

Cream fat with orange rind. Add sugar gradually and continue creaming until light and fluffy. Add egg and beat until well blended.

Add flour mixture alternately with milk and orange juice, beginning and ending with flour.

Turn batter over cranberry mixture. Bake in moderate oven (375°F. Mark 5) 30 to 40 minutes. Serve warm.

Marbled Apple Cake

MARBLED APPLE CAKE

4-5 cooking apples, pared and sliced
8 ounces sugar
1 tablespoon flour
1 teaspoon cinnamon
1 ounce butter or margarine
2 tablespoons water
1 tablespoon lemon juice

Batter:
9 ounces plain flour
2 teaspoons baking powder
1 teaspoon ground ginger
½ teaspoon salt
4 ounces fat
8 ounces sugar
2 eggs, unbeaten
¼ pint milk
3 ounces molasses or black treacle
1 teaspoon cinnamon
¼ teaspoon powdered cloves
¼ teaspoon nutmeg
¼ teaspoon bicarbonate of soda

Combine apples, 8 ounces sugar, 1 tablespoon flour, 1 teaspoon cinnamon, butter, water, and lemon juice in saucepan.

Cook over medium heat, occasionally stirring gently, until apples are tender. Pour into well greased 13 × 9 × 2-inch tin.

Sift together 9 ounces flour, baking powder, ginger, and salt.

Blend together fat and 8 ounces sugar, creaming well. Add eggs; beat for 1 minute.

Add milk alternately with the dry ingredients to creamed mixture, beginning and ending with dry ingredients. Blend thoroughly after each addition. (With electric mixer use low speed.)

Place half of batter in second bowl. Blend in molasses, 1 teaspoon cinnamon, cloves, nutmeg and soda.

Spoon light and dark batters alternately over apples in tin.

Bake in moderate oven (350°F. Mark 4) 50 to 60 minutes.

Cool in tin 15 to 20 minutes, then invert on serving plate or on wire rack covered with waxed paper. Serve warm or cold, plain or with whipped cream.

Cheese Cakes and Pies

MASTER CHEESE CAKE

6 ounces digestive biscuit crumbs
4 ounces butter, melted
10 ounces sugar
3 eggs, separated
Grated rind and juice of 1 lemon
½ teaspoon salt
½ teaspoon grated nutmeg
¼ pint double cream, whipped stiff
1 teaspoon vanilla (optional)
2 ounces plain flour, sifted twice
1 pound cottage cheese, sieved

Combine crumbs with butter and 3 tablespoons sugar. Press half of mixture in bottom and around sides of a well-greased, deep, round baking tin or spring-form tin.

Beat egg yolks until light. Gradually add remaining sugar, beating thoroughly. Add grated rind and juice of lemon, salt, nutmeg, vanilla-flavoured whipped cream, and flour.

Mix thoroughly with the cheese and rub through a sieve to ensure absolute smoothness.

Fold in stiffly beaten egg whites. Pour carefully into the crumb case. Spread remaining crumb mixture over the top.

Bake in very slow oven (275°F. Mark 1) until firm, 1 hour, or until set. Turn off heat. Let stand in oven 1 hour, or until cooled.

Remove rim of spring-form tin, and place with tin bottom on serving plate.

Master Cheese Cake Variations:

Apricot Cheese Cake: Arrange layer of strained, cooked dried apricots in the crumb case. Cover with cheese mixture.

Pineapple Cheese Cake: Arrange a layer of well drained crushed pineapple in the crumb case. Cover with cheese mixture.

Strawberry Cheese Cake: Place a layer of well drained, mashed strawberries, which have been cooked for 5 minutes in a little sugar in the crumb case. Cover with cheese mixture.

Prune Cheese Cake: Place a layer of strained, cooked prunes in the crumb case. Cover with cheese mixture.

Petal Cheese Cake

CHEESE REFRIGERATOR CAKE

2 eggs
4 tablespoons milk
¾ pound cottage cheese
3 ounces sugar
1 ounce plain flour
¼ teaspoon salt
½ teaspoon grated lemon rind
¾ teaspoon lemon juice
¼ pint cream, whipped
3 ounces digestive biscuit crumbs, finely rolled
2 ounces sugar
¼ teaspoon cinnamon
⅛ teaspoon salt
2 tablespoons butter or margarine, melted

Beat eggs. Add milk and cottage cheese.

Combine 3 ounces sugar, flour, ¼ teaspoon salt, and lemon rind. Add to cheese mixture and cook in top of double saucepan until thick, about 10 minutes, stirring occasionally.

Remove from heat. Add lemon juice. Cool and fold in whipped cream.

Combine biscuit crumbs, 2 ounces sugar, cinnamon, ⅛ teaspoon salt, and butter.

Line a loaf tin with greaseproof paper. Arrange cheese and crumb mixtures in alternate layers. Chill in refrigerator about 5 hours, or overnight. Serves 6 to 8.

PETAL CHEESE CAKE

6 ounces digestive biscuit crumbs, finely rolled
4 ounces butter or margarine, softened
2 tablespoons sugar
1½ pounds cream cheese
3 eggs
6 ounces sugar
1 teaspoon vanilla
½ tablet strawberry jelly
½ pint boiling water
1 small can sliced peaches
3 or 4 large fresh strawberries, cut in halves

Blend biscuit crumbs, softened butter or margarine, and 2 tablespoons sugar. Press firmly against bottom and sides of a 9-inch spring-form tin.

Blend softened cream cheese, eggs, 6 ounces sugar, and vanilla. Pour into crust. Bake in moderate oven (375°F. Mark 5) 40 minutes. Cool.

Dissolve strawberry jelly in boiling water and cool until syrupy.

Arrange peach slices in a ring around edge of cake and place strawberry halves petal fashion in the centre. Spoon jelly over fruit. Chill thoroughly. Makes 10 to 12 servings.

Fresh Date Cheese Cake

FRESH DATE CHEESE CAKE

6 ounces digestive biscuit crumbs
8 ounces fresh dates
4 large eggs
8 ounces sugar
1½ pounds cream cheese, softened
1 tablespoon vanilla
¼ teaspoon salt
8 fluid ounces sour cream
1 tablespoon sugar
1 teaspoon finely grated orange rind
Halved fresh dates

Line bottom and sides of greased 9-inch spring-form tin with crumbs; press firmly into place. Cut dates into small pieces and arrange on bottom crust.

Beat eggs; gradually add 8 ounces sugar, beating until thickened. Add cream cheese gradually, beating after each addition until smooth. Stir in vanilla and salt.

Spoon mixture over dates. Bake in moderate oven (350°F. Mark 4) about 45 minutes. Cool several hours or overnight, first on wire rack and then in refrigerator.

Blend sour cream, 1 tablespoon sugar, and orange rind. Spread over cake. Decorate with halved dates.

Bake 5 minutes in very hot (475°F. Mark 8) oven. Cool before cutting. Makes 12 servings.

FLUFFY CHEESE CAKE

6 ounces digestive biscuit crumbs
10 ounces sugar
½ teaspoon cinnamon
4 ounces butter, melted
3 eggs, separated
1 ounce plain flour
1½ pounds dry cottage cheese
1 teaspoon vanilla
1 tablespoon grated lemon rind
¼ pint double cream

Combine crumbs, 2 ounces sugar, cinnamon, and melted butter. Mix thoroughly and line bottom and sides of an 8-inch spring-form tin. Chill while making filling.

Beat egg yolks until thick and lemon-coloured. Blend 8 ounces sugar and the flour together. Add to beaten yolks, mixing thoroughly.

Fluffy Cheese Cake, Continued

Rub cottage cheese through a sieve and add to yolk mixture, beating well. Stir in vanilla and lemon rind.

Whip cream until stiff. Lightly fold cream into cheese mixture, and fold in stiffly beaten egg whites. Turn cheese mixture into crumb-lined spring-form tin.

Bake in a slow oven (300°F. Mark 2) for 1¼ hours.

Cool thoroughly on cake rack before removing sides of tin. Serves 8.

CHEESE TORTE

6 ounces breadcrumbs
12 ounces sugar
1 teaspoon cinnamon
4 ounces butter, melted
4 eggs
⅛ teaspoon salt
1½ teaspoons lemon juice
1½ teaspoons grated lemon rind
¼ pint cream
1½ pounds dry cottage cheese
2 ounces flour
1 ounce chopped nuts

Combine crumbs with 4 ounces sugar, cinnamon, and butter.

Set aside some of the crumb mixture for topping.

Press remaining mixture into 9-inch tin lining bottom and sides.

Beat eggs with remaining sugar until light.

Add salt, lemon juice, lemon rind, cream, cheese, and flour.

Beat thoroughly until well blended.

Turn into lined tin, sprinkle with remaining crumbs and nuts.

Bake in moderate oven (350°F. Mark 4) about 1 hour, or until centre is set.

Turn off or reduce heat. Open oven door and let stand in oven 1 hour, or until cooled. Serves 10 to 12.

CHERRY CREAM CHEESE PIE

1 baked 9-inch pie shell
1 large can sweetened condensed milk
4 tablespoons lemon juice
3 ounces cream cheese
2 eggs, separated
1 can red cherries, well drained
¼ teaspoon cream of tartar
4 tablespoons sugar

Blend together condensed milk and lemon juice.

Cherry Cream Cheese Pie

Beat cream cheese, softened at room temperature, until smooth. Add one egg yolk at a time, beating well after each addition. Add cherries and mix thoroughly.

Fold cheese and cherry mixture into the condensed milk mixture. Put into cooled, baked pie shell.

Add cream of tartar to egg whites; beat until almost stiff enough to hold a peak. Add sugar gradually, beating until egg whites are stiff and dry.

Pile egg white mixture lightly on pie filling. Bake in slow oven (325°F. Mark 3) 15 minutes or until lightly browned. Cool.

HOLLYWOOD CHEESE CAKE

6 ounces digestive biscuit crumbs
1½ ounces butter
7 ounces sugar
1 pound cream cheese
⅛ teaspoon cinnamon
½ teaspoon vanilla
1 teaspoon grated lemon rind
1 tablespoon lemon juice
2 eggs, separated
¼ pint thick sour cream
1 tablespoon sugar
1 teaspoon vanilla

Blend biscuit crumbs with butter and 2 tablespoons sugar. Press onto the bottom of a 9-inch spring-form tin. Bake in a slow oven (300°F. Mark 2) for 5 minutes. Cool.

Blend cream cheese, softened at room temperature, with remaining sugar, cinnamon, ½ teaspoon vanilla, lemon rind, and lemon juice. Add egg yolks, one at a time, mixing well after each yolk is added.

Fold in stiffly beaten egg whites and pour the mixture on top of the crumbs.

Bake in a slow oven (300°F. Mark 2) 45 minutes.

Blend the sour cream with 1 extra tablespoon sugar and 1 teaspoon vanilla. Spread this mixture over the top of cake.

Return to oven for an additional 10 minutes. Cool before removing from tin. Do not invert.

ITALIAN RICOTTA CHEESE PIE

8 ounces flaky pastry
1½ pounds ricotta cheese
1 ounce flour
2 tablespoons grated orange rind
2 tablespoons grated lemon rind
1 tablespoon vanilla
⅛ teaspoon salt
4 eggs
8 ounces sugar

Combine ricotta cheese, flour, grated orange and lemon rinds, vanilla, and salt.

Beat eggs until foamy. Add sugar

Hollywood Cheese Cake

gradually, beating until eggs are thick and piled softly.

Stir beaten eggs into ricotta mixture until well blended and smooth. Pour ricotta filling into pastry lined 9-inch pie plate. Cover with strips of pastry to form a lattice.

Bake in moderate oven (350°F. Mark 4) about 50 to 60 minutes, until filling is firm and pastry is golden brown.

Remove from oven and place on cooling rack. Before serving, sprinkle with 2 tablespoons sifted icing sugar.

JIFFY CHEESE CAKE— BLENDER METHOD

¼ ounce gelatine
1 tablespoon lemon juice
Zest of 1 lemon
4 fluid ounces hot water or milk
3 ounces sugar
2 egg yolks
8 ounces cream cheese
6 ounces crushed ice
¼ pint sour cream
crumb crust (below)

Combine gelatine, lemon juice, lemon zest, and hot liquid in electric blender. Cover and blend at high speed 40 seconds.

Add sugar, egg yolks, and cheese; cover and blend 10 seconds. Add ice and sour cream; cover and blend 15 seconds.

Pour mixture into a spring-form tin lined with half a recipe for crumb crust. Sprinkle top with remaining crumb crust mixture. Chill until set. Serves 6.

Crumb Crust—Blender Method:
15 digestive biscuits
1 tablespoon sugar
½ teaspoon cinnamon
2 ounces butter, melted

Break 5 biscuits into quarters; place in electric blender. Blend to crumbs by flicking the motor on and off at high speed 4 times. Empty crumbs into a bowl and continue until all biscuits are crumbed.

Stir in sugar and cinnamon. Add melted butter and mix until all crumbs are moistened.

Press crumbs against sides and bottom of buttered 9-inch pie tin. Chill before adding the filling.

Pineapple Cheese Refrigerator Cake

PINEAPPLE CHEESE REFRIGERATOR CAKE

Butter-Crumb Crust:
24 digestive biscuits, crumbled
2 ounces sugar
4 ounces butter or margarine, melted

Mix all ingredients together until mixture is crumbly. Save 3-4 tablespoons for topping. Using back of spoon, press mixture against bottom and sides of 10-inch spring-form tin.

Allow crust to chill while preparing the filling.

Filling:
½ ounce gelatine
4 fluid ounces cold water
2 egg yolks
2 ounces sugar
1 teaspoon salt
4 fluid ounces milk
1 pound cottage cheese (sieved)
1 small can crushed pineapple with syrup
1 tablespoon grated lemon rind
2 to 3 tablespoons lemon juice
2 egg whites
8 fluid ounces double cream

Soften gelatine in cold water.

Beat egg yolks, add 2 ounces sugar, salt, and milk, and cook over hot water about 5 minutes or until beginning to thicken.

Remove from heat. Add softened gelatine. When cool, fold in sieved cottage cheese, pineapple, lemon juice and rind.

Beat egg whites until stiff, but not dry, and gradually fold in the remaining sugar.

Fold egg whites and whipped cream into cheese mixture. Turn into butter-crumb crust. Sprinkle remaining crumb mixture around edge. Place in refrigerator to chill.

To serve, remove sides of spring-form tin, but do not try to remove bottom. Decorate with strawberries and pineapple. Cut in wedges and top with sugared sliced strawberries and pineapple. Serves 10 to 12.

GERMAN CHEESE CAKE

Biscuit Dough Pie-crust:
4 ounces plain flour
½ teaspoon baking powder
2 ounces sugar
1 tablespoon butter
1 well beaten egg

Mix and sift flour, baking powder, and sugar. Work in butter with fingertips. Mix in egg.

Roll out ¼-inch thick on a slightly floured board and line a large pie plate with it.

Cheese Cake Filling:
6 ounces butter
8 ounces sugar
3 eggs, unbeaten
1 pound cottage cheese, sieved
1 tablespoon cornflour
Grated rind of 1 large lemon

Cream together the butter and sugar. Add unbeaten eggs one at a time, beating well.

Mix cottage cheese, cornflour, and lemon rind; beat into creamed mixture until well blended.

Spread mixture over the pastry. Bake in a very hot oven (450°F. Mark 7) 10 minutes.

Reduce to moderate (350°F. Mark 4) and bake 20 to 30 minutes or until lightly browned and done. Serve cold.

STRAWBERRY CHEESE PIE

3 ounces cream cheese
2 tablespoons milk
1 baked 9-inch pie shell
1½ pounds fresh strawberries
½ pint water
Few drops red food colouring
8 ounces sugar
3 tablespoons cornflour
8 fluid ounces double cream, whipped

Soften cheese with milk and spread over bottom of baked pie shell. Fill shell with the choicest berries, using about ½ pound.

Cook remaining berries in water until soft. Put through a sieve or mash well and add red food colouring.

Combine sugar and cornflour. Add to sieved fruit. Cook until thickened, stirring often. Pour over berries in pie shell. Chill and top with whipped cream.

PINEAPPLE COTTAGE CHEESE PIE

4 ounces short pastry
12 ounces cottage cheese
2 eggs, separated
2 ounces butter or margarine, melted
4 ounces sugar
¼ teaspoon salt
1 tablespoon flour

Grated rind of 1 lemon
2 ounces chopped nuts
4 tablespoons milk

Press cheese through a sieve twice. Combine all ingredients except egg whites, blending well.

Beat egg whites until stiff and fold into mixture.

Pour into pastry lined 9-inch pie plate.

Bake in very hot oven (450°F. Mark 7) 10 minutes. Reduce heat to moderate (350°F. Mark 4) and bake until filling is firm and pie is nicely browned, 40 minutes longer.

Spread with pineapple glaze (below) and return to oven until glaze is set. 5 minutes.

Pineapple glaze: Drain 1 small can crushed pineapple thoroughly. Combine with 4 ounces sugar and 2 tablespoons cornflour.

Add 6 fluid ounces pineapple juice and cook slowly, stirring constantly, until thick and clear. Add pineapple and cool. Spread by spoonfuls over cheese filling.

LEMON CHEESE PIE

1 baked 8-inch pie shell
8 ounces cream cheese
2 eggs
4 ounces sugar
1 teaspoon vanilla
1 teaspoon grated lemon rind
1 tablespoon lemon juice
¼ pint double cream
2 tablespoons icing sugar
1 teaspoon vanilla

Soften cream cheese; whip until fluffy. Add eggs, one at a time, beating well after each.

Blend in sugar, vanilla, lemon rind, and lemon juice. Mix well. Turn into baked pie shell.

Bake in moderate oven (350°F. Mark 4) 15 to 20 minutes, until slightly firm.

Cool. Chill at least 1 hour before serving.

Whip cream until stiff. Fold in icing sugar and vanilla. Spread over pie before serving. Decorate with grated lemon rind, if desired.

Lemon Cheese Pie

Angel Food and Sponge Cakes
HINTS ABOUT SPONGE AND ANGEL FOOD CAKES

The sponge cake family includes yellow sponge cakes made with whole eggs, and white angel cakes made with egg whites. A true sponge or angel cake contains no fat and no leavening except the air beaten into it in the mixing. Various other cakes such as thrifty sponge cake and butter sponge cake are included in this group of recipes although they are really mock sponge cakes.

Since true sponge cakes are leavened just with the air which is beaten into the eggs, particularly the egg whites, during the mixing process, the secret of getting a light, tender cake will depend on proper beating of egg whites, the lightness with which you fold in the flour and sugar mixtures to prevent the escape of air, and the temperature at which you bake the cake.

You'll find that methods vary from recipe to recipe. As for other cakes, read recipe carefully. Assemble all ingredients; use standard measuring utensils and measure accurately. Prepare tins according to directions in recipe. Do not grease tins. Some sponge cake recipes specify that tins be lined with paper. Spread mixed batter to sides of tin and fill all corners.

Angel and sponge cakes are done when the top springs back to the touch of the finger. Cool cakes in inverted tins. If the cake falls away from the tin, it may be because tin was greased or because of insufficient baking.

If you want a brown crust, remove the cake from tin just as soon as it is cool. The longer you keep cool sponge cakes in the tin, the more crust will adhere to tin. The flavour of most sponge cakes is improved by standing overnight before cutting. Store the cooled cake in a tightly covered container.

STEPS IN MAKING ANGEL FOOD CAKE

1. Assemble all utensils and ingredients. Use standard measuring utensils and measure exactly. Prepare tins according to directions in recipe. Do not grease.

2. Beat egg whites until foamy.

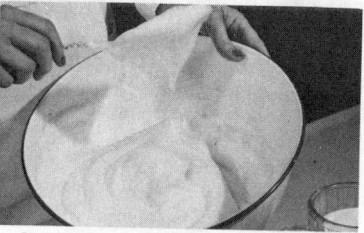

3. Add cream of tartar, continue beating until stiff but not dry. Whites should be glossy and moist, and should cling to bottom and sides of bowl.

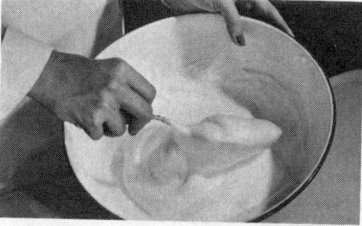

4. Using a whisk-type beater, blend in flavouring and fold in dry ingredients. Do not stir.

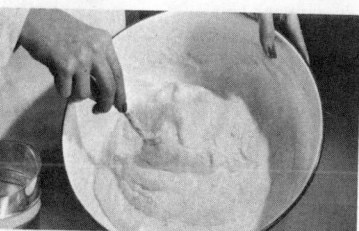

5. Turn into a dry tube tin. Cut through the batter in the tin to break any large air bubbles.

ANGEL FOOD CAKE
(Master Recipe)

- 5 ounces plain flour
- 14 ounces sugar
- ½ teaspoon salt
- 12 egg whites
- 1¼ teaspoons cream of tartar
- 1 teaspoon vanilla
- 1 teaspoon almond essence

Sift and measure flour. Sift together 5 times the flour, sugar, and salt.

Beat egg whites with a rotary beater until foamy; add cream of tartar, and continue beating until stiff but not dry. Whites should be glossy and moist, and should cling to bottom and sides of bowl.

Using a whisk-type beater, blend in flavouring and fold in dry ingredients. Do not stir.

Turn into 10-inch ungreased tube tin. Bake in slow oven (325°F. Mark 3) 1 to 1¼ hours.

Invert tin on rack until cake is cold or about 1 hour. Loosen from sides and centre with knife and remove from tin.

Angel Food Cake Variations:

Smaller Angel Food Cake: Use 4 ounces plain flour, 10 ounces sugar, ½ teaspoon salt, 1 teaspoon cream of tartar, 8 egg whites, 1 teaspoon vanilla, ½ teaspoon almond essence. Bake in 8-inch tube tin.

Chocolate Angel Food: In master recipe substitute 1 ounce cocoa for 1 ounce flour. Sift cocoa with 8 ounces of sugar. Omit almond essence.

Maraschino Angel Food: Follow master recipe. Drain and cut up about 12 maraschino cherries. Pour ¼ of batter into tin. Sprinkle cherries over batter. Add another ¼ of batter. Continue alternating batter and fruit until all used.

Marble Angel Food: In master recipe add 2 tablespoons chocolate syrup to half the batter. Omit almond essence. Alternate layers of white and chocolate batters in tin.

Orange Angel Food: Follow master recipe. Fold in 1 tablespoon grated orange rind. Substitute 1 teaspoon orange essence for almond essence. Cover with Orange Icing.

Peppermint Angel Food: In master recipe use 1 teaspoon peppermint extract or a few drops peppermint oil as flavouring. Add a few drops red or green colouring.

Pineapple Angel Food: Dice 3 ounces pineapple. Follow method for maraschino angel food above.

Spice Angel Food: In master recipe sift 1 teaspoon cinnamon, ¼ teaspoon nutmeg, ¼ teaspoon mixed spice with flour.

Angel Food Cake Variations:

Tutti-Frutti Angel Food: Follow master recipe and tint batter to a pink colour with food colouring. Fold in 6 ounces finely chopped crystallised fruits.

Yellow and White Angel Food: Prepare master recipe, omitting flavouring. Divide batter into 2 parts.

Into one part fold in 4 well beaten egg yolks, 2 tablespoons flour, and 1 teaspoon lemon essence.

Into the second part fold in 1 teaspoon vanilla.

Drop by spoonfuls into tin, alternating white and yellow batter.

Layered Angel Cake: Cut angel food cake crosswise in 2 layers. Fold toasted almonds into flavoured whipped cream for filling. Coat with whipped cream; sprinkle generously with toasted shredded almonds. Serve at once.

WHIPPED CREAM ANGEL FOOD CAKE

- 8 ounces plain flour
- 3 teaspoons baking powder
- ½ teaspoon salt
- 12 ounces sugar
- 8 fluid ounces whipping cream
- 3 egg whites
- 4 fluid ounces water
- 1 teaspoon vanilla

Sift together the flour, baking powder, salt, and sugar 3 times.

Whip cream stiff. Beat egg whites until stiff. Combine carefully. Add water and vanilla. Gradually fold in dry ingredients.

Bake in sandwich tins in moderate oven (350°F. Mark 4) until done, about 30 minutes. Spread lemon filling between layers.

ANGEL PEPPERMINT LOAF CAKE

- 2 ounces plain flour
- 6 ounces sugar
- 5 egg whites
- ⅛ teaspoon salt
- ½ teaspoon cream of tartar
- ½ teaspoon vanilla
- ¼ teaspoon almond essence
- 2 tablespoons finely crushed peppermint rock

Measure sifted flour; add 2 ounces sugar and sift 4 times.

Combine egg whites, salt, cream of tartar, and flavourings in large bowl. Beat with flat wire whip, egg beater, or at high speed of electric mixer until soft peaks are formed.

Blend in remaining sugar, 2 tablespoons at a time. Fold in flour mixture, ½ at a time. Then fold in crushed rock.

Turn batter into ungreased 10 × 5 × 3-inch loaf tin. Bake in moderate oven (375°F. Mark 5) about 25 minutes.

Cool upside down 1 hour. Serve plain or with chocolate ice cream.

MASTER SPONGE CAKE

- 4 ounces plain flour
- 5 eggs, separated
- 8 ounces sugar
- 2 tablespoons lemon juice
- 1 teaspoon grated lemon rind
- ½ teaspoon salt

Sift flour three times.

Using a rotary beater, beat egg yolks until thick and lemon-coloured. Gradually add half the sugar, beating thoroughly, and then the lemon juice and grated lemon rind. Beat until thick.

Beat egg whites with salt until stiff enough to form peaks but not dry. Fold in remaining sugar, then the yolk mixture. Fold in flour gently. Turn at once into ungreased tube tin.

Caster sugar sifted over top makes a delicate crust.

Bake in preheated slow oven (325°F. Mark 3) 50 to 60 minutes or until done.

Remove from oven and invert tin 1 hour, or until cake is cool.

Master Sponge Cake Variations:

Sponge Layer Cake: Bake master sponge cake in sandwich tins in moderate oven (350°F. Mark 4) about 30 minutes. Spread jam or jelly between layers. Sprinkle castor or icing sugar on top.

Cocoa Sponge Cake: In master sponge cake replace 4 ounces flour with 4 ounces cocoa. Replace 1 tablespoon lemon juice with 1 tablespoon water. Sift cocoa with flour.

Orange Sponge Cake: In master sponge cake add grated rind and juice of ½ orange. Grate rind before cutting orange. Omit 1 tablespoon lemon juice.

Pineapple Meringue Sponge: Bake master sponge cake in sponge sandwich tin. Spread crushed pineapple between layers and on top. Top with meringue. Place in slow oven with door ajar, until meringue is delicate brown in colour.

Swiss Roll: Omit 2 eggs from recipe for master sponge cake. Add 2 fluid ounces water and 1 teaspoon baking powder.

Line bottom of flat rectangular tin with greased paper. Spread cake evenly in thin layer. Bake in moderate oven (350°F. Mark 4) about 15 minutes.

While hot turn onto cloth sprinkled with caster sugar and remove greased paper. Trim edges. Spread with soft jelly and roll up.

MATZO SPONGE CAKE

- 8 eggs, separated
- 12 ounces sugar
- Pinch of salt
- Grated rind and juice of ½ lemon
- 4 ounces sifted matzo cake meal (If matzo meal is not obtainable use breadcrumbs)

Beat egg yolks until light; add sugar and beat again. Add salt, lemon juice and rind, then add cake meal and finally fold in the egg whites beaten until stiff but not dry.

Turn into a 10-inch spring-form tin. Bake in moderate oven (350°F. Mark 4) 45 minutes. Cool, then cut into layers.

Serve with sweetened strawberries between the layers. Spread top and side with flavoured and sweetened whipped cream.

ZUPPA INGLESE

Zuppa Inglese is an Italian term which means, literally, English soup; it is the name of a superb Italian cake with a custard filling and a topping of whipped cream.

- 4 ounces sugar
- 1 ounce plain flour
- ¼ teaspoon salt
- 16 fluid ounces milk, scalded
- 4 egg yolks
- ½ teaspoon vanilla
- 4 fluid ounces light rum
- 2 tablespoons crème de cacao
- 1 sponge sandwich
- 8 fluid ounces whipping cream
- 2 tablespoons crystallised fruits, chopped fine

Mix sugar, flour, and salt in top of a double saucepan. Gradually stir in scalded milk. Place over boiling water and cook, stirring until thickened.

Beat egg yolks until blended. Gradually add part of milk mixture to egg yolks while stirring. Slowly pour into hot mixture; cook over simmering water, stirring occasionally, until thickened. Let cool, then chill.

Divide mixture into 3 parts. Add vanilla to 1 part, 1 tablespoon rum to second, and crème de cacao to third.

Split cake layers to make 4 layers. Place 1 layer on a serving dish. Sprinkle with ¼ of remaining rum and spread with one of the three custard mixtures. Repeat with second and third layers. Cover with the fourth layer of cake and sprinkle it with remaining rum. Chill overnight in refrigerator.

At serving time, spread whipped cream over top and sides of cake; sprinkle top with crystallised fruits. Serves 8.

Sponge cakes are usually served plain or with only a light sprinkling of icing sugar.

Almond Candy Cake

ALMOND CANDY CAKE

1 large sponge or chiffon cake
Filling (below)
Almond Crisp Topping (below)
4 ounces toasted blanched almond
    halves

Split cake into 4 equal layers. Spread about half of filling between cake layers. Spread remainder over top and sides of cake. Cover cake very thickly with Almond Crisp Topping, and stick almond halves porcupine fashion over top and sides of cake. Makes 16 to 20 servings.

Filling:

16 fluid ounces whipping cream
2 tablespoons sugar
⅛ teaspoon almond essence

Whip cream with sugar and flavouring.

Almond Crisp Topping:

12 ounces sugar
3 fluid ounces water
4 tablespoons light corn syrup or
    golden syrup
1 tablespoon sifted bicarbonate of
    soda
1 teaspoon almond essence

Combine sugar, water, and corn syrup in top of double saucepan, stirring until well blended. Boil over moderate heat to hard crack stage (310°F.), until a small amount of syrup dropped into cold water will break with a brittle snap.

Remove from heat, and stir in soda and flavouring. Stir vigorously until well blended, but not enough to destroy foam made by soda.

Turn at once into ungreased shallow tin, about 9 inches square. Let stand without moving until completely cold. Knock out of pan and crush between sheets of greaseproof paper to make coarse crumbs.

SUNSHINE CAKE

5 egg yolks
4 ounces sugar
4 ounces plain flour
2 tablespoons cold water
½ teaspoon vanilla
½ teaspoon almond essence
½ teaspoon lemon essence
8 egg whites
½ teaspoon cream of tartar
½ teaspoon salt
8 ounces sugar

Beat egg yolks until thick (at least 5 minutes). Gradually beat 4 ounces sugar into egg yolks. Beat in flour alternately with cold water mixed with vanilla, almond, and lemon essence.

In another large bowl beat egg whites with cream of tartar and salt until stiff. Gradually beat remaining sugar into stiffly beaten egg whites.

Gradually and gently cut and fold egg yolk mixture into beaten egg whites.

Pour into ungreased 10-inch tube tin (4 inches deep). Bake in slow oven (325°F. Mark 3) 60 to 65 minutes.

Note: A 13×9-inch oblong tin may be used. Grease bottom of tin and bake only 35 to 40 minutes.

GENOISE

The genoise is a superb French cake. It does not contain a leavening agent other than the air that is beaten into the eggs. The name means "pertaining to Genoa" and since similar cakes are popular in Italy, it probably originated in that country.

5 eggs
8 ounces sugar
¼ teaspoon salt
1 teaspoon vanilla
5 ounces flour
Toasted slivered almonds or grated
    chocolate

Beat eggs until light and fluffy. Gradually add sugar, salt, and vanilla. Beat until thick and lemon-coloured.

Fold in flour, 8 tablespoons at a time. Fold gently but thoroughly.

Pour into 2 8-inch sandwich tins, well greased and lined with greaseproof paper on bottoms. Bake in moderate oven (350°F. Mark 4) 25 to 30 minutes.

Cool in tin. Remove layers from tins and split to form 4 layers. Spread cool crème au beurre (below) between layers and on sides of cake.

Decorate sides with toasted slivered almonds or grated chocolate. Ice top with chocolate icing (below).

Crème au Beurre: Combine 6 ounces sugar and 2 tablespoons cornflour in saucepan. Mix well. Add 3 eggs (or 6 egg yolks). Beat until light and fluffy. Stir in 12 fluid ounces milk; cook over medium heat until thick, stirring constantly.

Remove from heat; add 1 teaspoon vanilla. Cool. Blend in 4 ounces creamed butter or margarine.

Chocolate Icing: Cream 2 tablespoons butter or margarine. Blend in 5½ ounces sifted icing sugar. Add 1 small egg; beat well.

Blend in 1 ounce melted chocolate and ½ teaspoon vanilla. Beat until smooth.

BUTTER SPONGE CAKE

9 ounces plain flour
2 teaspoons baking powder
1 teaspoon salt
11 egg yolks
1 pound sugar
8 fluid ounces scalded milk
1 teaspoon vanilla
½ teaspoon lemon essence
4 ounces butter, melted

Have all ingredients at room temperature. Mix and sift flour, baking powder, and salt.

Beat egg yolks until thick, light-coloured, and fluffy. Add sugar gradually, beating thoroughly.

Combine scalded milk, vanilla, and lemon essence. Add gradually to beaten egg yolks, beating well after each addition. Gradually fold in sifted dry ingredients.

Add melted butter, blending well. Turn batter into ungreased 10-inch tube tin. Cut through batter with spatula to break large air pockets.

Bake in moderate oven (350°F. Mark 4) 50 to 60 minutes. Cool in inverted tin about 1 hour.

SUPREME SPONGE CAKE

7 ounces plain flour
½ teaspoon baking powder
½ teaspoon salt
4 fluid ounces hot water
10 slightly beaten egg yolks
8 ounces sugar
1 teaspoon lemon essence

Sift flour once. Measure and add baking powder and salt. Sift together 3 times.

Add hot water gradually to egg yolks, beating constantly. Continue beating for about 10 minutes, or until mixture is very light and has almost doubled in bulk.

Add sugar gradually, beating constantly. Add lemon essence.

Sift in dry ingredients gradually, folding gently but thoroughly.

Turn into ungreased 10-inch tube tin at once. Bake in moderate oven (350°F. Mark 4) about 1 hour.

When done, invert tin and let cool before removing.

Genoise

NORWEGIAN CROWN CAKE

6 ounces plain flour
1 teaspoon baking powder
6 egg yolks
4 fluid ounces water
8 ounces sugar
4 egg whites
½ teaspoon salt
Sliced almonds
1 can (about 1 pound) apricot halves
Peach slices, pineapple cubes, mara-
    schino cherries, fresh berries
    or grapes

Sift together flour and baking powder. Beat egg yolks with water and
4 ounces sugar until thick and ivory-
coloured. (With electric mixer beat at
high speed about 10 minutes.)

Fold in dry ingredients, ⅓ at a time,
with wire whisk.

Beat 4 egg whites with salt until
slight mounds form when beater is
raised. Add gradually remaining sugar,
beating well after each addition. Continue beating until mixture stands in
stiff, glossy peaks when beater is raised.
Fold carefully but thoroughly into
batter.

Turn into 2 well greased and lightly
floured 9-inch sandwich tins. Bake in
moderate oven (350°F. Mark 4) 25 to
30 minutes.

Remove from tins immediately; cool
thoroughly on wire racks.

Split cooled layers to form 4 layers.

Place on oven-proof plate, spreading
cream filling (below) between layers.
Spread only sides with meringue (below); decorate with sliced almonds.
Brown in moderate oven (375°F. Mark
5) 10 to 12 minutes.

Drain apricot halves well. Just before serving, arrange fruit on top of
cake to resemble jewels in a crown.
Place 4 halves in centre and remaining
halves around edge.

For additional colour, between apricots place drained, canned peach slices,
pineapple cubes, maraschino cherries,
fresh berries or grapes.

Cream Filling: Blend together 4
ounces sugar, 1 ounce flour, 2 tablespoons cornflour, and ¼ teaspoon salt
in top of double saucepan. Blend in 1
slightly beaten egg yolk and 4 fluid
ounces milk. Gradually add 16 fluid
ounces scalded milk.

Cook over boiling water, stirring constantly, until thick. Remove from heat.

Blend in 1 tablespoon butter and 2
teaspoons vanilla. Cover. Cool thoroughly.

Meringue: Beat 3 egg whites until
slight mounds form when beater is
raised. Add 6 tablespoons sugar gradually, beating well after each addition.
Continue beating until meringue stands
in stiff, glossy peaks when beater is
raised.

Norwegian Crown Cake

FEATHERY-LIGHT SPONGE CAKE

3 eggs
10 ounces sugar
½ teaspoon vanilla
½ teaspoon almond essence
5 ounces flour
1½ teaspoons baking powder
¼ teaspoon salt
4 fluid ounces hot milk

In mixing bowl beat eggs until thick
and lemon-coloured (about 5 minutes).
Gradually add sugar and flavourings.

Fold in dry ingredients, sifted together 3 times. Then, quickly stir in
hot milk.

Pour thin batter into an ungreased
loaf tin (9 × 5 × 2½ inches). Bake in
moderate oven (350°F. Mark 4) about
40 minutes or until top springs back
when touched lightly.

Remove from oven. Invert 1 hour on
cake rack to cool. Turn out on serving
plate. Ice with orange-flavoured icing;
sprinkle top with coarsely chopped
walnuts. Serves 6 to 8.

DAFFODIL CAKE

5 ounces flour
9 ounces sifted sugar
3 egg whites
¼ teaspoon salt
¾ teaspoon cream of tartar
¼ teaspoon orange essence
3 egg yolks
¼ teaspoon vanilla

Sift 3 ounces flour and 4 ounces
sugar together twice.

Beat egg whites with salt until foamy.
Sprinkle cream of tartar over egg whites
and continue beating until stiff, but
not dry.

Fold in 4 ounces additional sugar, a
small amount at a time. Sift in dry
ingredients gradually, folding in carefully.

Divide batter in half. Combine 2
tablespoons sugar, 2 tablespoons flour,
orange essence, and egg yolks, beaten
until thick and lemon-coloured. Fold
into ½ of batter.

Blend ¼ teaspoon vanilla into remaining ½ of batter.

Place by spoonfuls yellow and white
batters alternately into ungreased 9-
inch tube tin.

Bake in slow oven (325°F. Mark 3)
60 minutes. Invert pan until cake is
cold, or about 1 hour.

SPONGE LAYER CAKE

3 eggs
8 ounces sugar
Grated rind of 1 lemon
1 tablespoon melted butter
3 fluid ounces hot water
4 ounces plain flour
1½ teaspoons baking powder
¼ teaspoon salt

Beat eggs until light and lemon-
coloured. Add sugar gradually, beating
well. Add grated rind with butter and
hot water.

Mix and sift flour, baking powder,
and salt and fold into first mixture.

Pour into 2 greased and floured 8-
inch sandwich tins. Bake in moderate
oven (375°F. Mark 5) 20 to 25 minutes.

Remove cakes from tins when cool,
and ice.

Sponge Cake Roll: Bake sponge layer
cake in greased Swiss roll tin (10 × 15
inches) in moderate oven (375°F. Mark
5) 15 to 20 minutes.

Invert pan on cloth sprinkled with
icing sugar. Roll up in cloth. Place cake
seam down and cool.

Unroll gently and spread with ice
cream. Roll up and serve at once.
Serves 8 to 10.

Sponge Drop Cakes: Prepare batter for
sponge cake as above. Fill well greased
deep bun tins ⅔ full.

Bake in moderate oven (375°F. Mark
5) about 20 minutes. Remove from tins.
Cool and ice if desired.

THRIFTY SPONGE CAKE

6 ounces flour
1 teaspoon baking powder
⅛ teaspoon salt
3 eggs
8 ounces sugar
3 fluid ounces water
1 teaspoon vanilla or lemon essence

Sift flour with baking powder and
salt.

Beat eggs with rotary beater until
very light and frothy. Gradually add
sugar, beating until thick and light coloured. Then add water and vanilla or
lemon essence.

Fold in dry ingredients, blending
well. Turn into ungreased tube tin or
two 8-inch sandwich tins.

Bake in moderate oven (350°F.
Mark 4) 25 to 35 minutes.

Invert pan 1 hour, or until cold, before removing cake.

Orange Sponge Cake: In thrifty sponge
cake recipe substitute orange juice
for water and 1 tablespoon grated
orange rind for other flavouring.

Sponge Cupcakes: Fill cupcake pans
⅔ full. Bake in moderate oven (350°F.
Mark 4) about 15 minutes. Top with
lemon, orange, or pineapple icing.

MOSAIC CAKE—ITALIAN

Sponge Cake:

- 4 ounces plain flour
- 5 large or 6 medium eggs, separated
- $\frac{1}{8}$ teaspoon salt
- 8 ounces sugar
- 1 teaspoon grated lemon rind
- $4\frac{1}{2}$ teaspoons lemon juice

Sift flour, measure; sift twice again.

In large bowl, beat egg whites until frothy; sprinkle salt over top and continue beating until stiff but still moist. Beat in sugar, sprinkling in about 2 tablespoons at a time and beating after each addition until glossy.

In a small bowl beat egg yolks until thick and lemon-coloured; add lemon rind and juice, continue beating until very thick.

Gently fold egg yolk mixture into egg whites. Fold in flour, sifting in about 1 ounce at a time.

Turn into ungreased 9-inch tube tin. Bake in slow oven (325°F. Mark 3) about 1 hour or until top springs back when touched gently. Invert tin until cool, about 1 hour; remove from tin.

To Ice and Decorate: Slice cake into 3 layers; spread chocolate cheese filling between the layers. Cover top and sides with almond icing.

Decorate sides with 1 pound mixed crystallised fruits. Make circle of crystallised fruits on top around hole in centre.

Chocolate Cheese Filling: Melt 6 ounces plain chocolate and 2 tablespoons butter over hot (not boiling) water. Add 3 tablespoons hot water and blend well.

Sieve 8 ounces cottage cheese and combine with chocolate mixture. Add $\frac{1}{2}$ teaspoon almond essence and mix until well blended and creamy.

Almond Icing: Beat 1 egg white until frothy; add $5\frac{1}{2}$ ounces sifted icing sugar and beat until smooth. Add another 3 ounces sifted icing sugar and blend well.

Stir in 1 teaspoon almond essence and $\frac{1}{2}$ teaspoon lemon juice; blend until smooth.

MATZO HONEY CAKE

- 6 eggs, separated
- 4 ounces sugar
- 6 ounces honey
- 2 ounces matzo cake meal
- 2 tablespoons potato starch

Beat egg whites until they hold a peak. Gradually beat in the sugar.

Beat egg yolks until light, and beat in the honey thoroughly.

Fold the egg white mixture into the yolk mixture. Fold in the sifted dry ingredients. Bake in slow oven (325°F. Mark 3) 50 minutes in an ungreased

angel cake tin. When done leave in tin, turned upside down, until cool.

CINDERELLA SPONGE CAKE

- 4 ounces plain flour
- $\frac{1}{2}$ teaspoon salt
- 2 tablespoons lemon juice
- $1\frac{1}{2}$ teaspoons grated lemon rind
- 1 tablespoon water
- 4 egg yolks
- 8 ounces sugar
- 3 egg whites

Sift together flour and salt twice.

Combine lemon juice, lemon rind, water, and egg yolks and beat with rotary beater until very thick. Gradually add sugar, a tablespoon at a time, beating thoroughly after each addition.

Sift dry ingredients into egg mixture gradually, folding in carefully.

Beat egg whites stiff, but not dry, and fold into batter, handling gently.

Turn into ungreased 9-inch tube tin. Bake in slow oven (325°F. Mark 3) 60 to 70 minutes.

Cool in inverted tin about 1 hour. Serve plain, or cut across into 2 layers and fill with lemon filling and ice with meringue.

HOT MILK SPONGE CAKE

- 5 ounces flour
- 2 teaspoons baking powder
- $\frac{1}{4}$ teaspoon salt
- 2 eggs
- 8 ounces sugar
- 1 tablespoon lemon juice or 1 teaspoon vanilla
- 4 fluid ounces hot milk

Sift together 3 times the flour, baking powder, and salt.

Beat eggs until very thick and light, about 10 minutes. Gradually add sugar, beating constantly. Add flavouring.

Fold in dry ingredients, a small amount at a time. Add milk, mixing quickly until batter is smooth.

Turn into an ungreased 9-inch tube tin. Bake in moderate oven (350°F. Mark 4) 35 to 45 minutes.

Remove from oven. Invert tin on rack until cold before removing cake.

GOLD CAKE

- 12 ounces flour
- 2 teaspoons baking powder
- 10 egg yolks
- 1 teaspoon vanilla or lemon essence
- $\frac{1}{4}$ teaspoon salt
- 1 pound sugar
- 8 fluid ounces cold water

Sift flour with baking powder.

Beat egg yolks until thick and very light. Add flavouring and salt. Gradually beat in sugar.

Add flour alternately with water, beating after each addition until smooth.

Turn batter into ungreased 10-inch tube tin. Bake until golden brown in moderate oven (350°F. Mark 4) 50 to 60 minutes.

Invert tin on cake rack 1 hour, or until cold, before removing from tin.

ANGEL FOOD SWIRL CAKE

- 3 ounces flour
- 10 ounces sifted sugar
- 5 egg whites
- $\frac{1}{4}$ teaspoon salt
- $1\frac{1}{4}$ teaspoons cream of tartar
- 1 teaspoon vanilla
- $\frac{1}{4}$ teaspoon almond essence
- 2 tablespoons plain flour
- 4 tablespoons sugar
- 3 tablespoons cocoa

Sift together twice 3 ounces flour and 4 ounces sugar.

Beat egg whites with salt until foamy. Sprinkle $1\frac{1}{4}$ teaspoons cream of tartar over egg whites and continue beating until stiff, but not dry. Fold in 6 ounces additional sugar, a small amount at a time.

Add vanilla and almond essence. Sift in dry ingredients gradually, folding in carefully.

Divide batter in half. Sift together 2 tablespoons flour and 2 tablespoons sugar. Add to one half of batter.

Sift together 2 tablespoons sugar and 3 tablespoons cocoa and fold into remaining half of batter. Into an ungreased 9-inch tube tin, place alternate spoonfuls of light and dark batters.

Bake in slow oven (325°F. Mark 3) 60 minutes. Invert tin until cake is cold, or about 1 hour.

LEMON-ORANGE SUNSHINE CAKE

- 8 eggs, separated
- 4 tablespoons lemon juice
- 4 tablespoons orange juice
- 12 ounces sugar
- 6 ounces flour
- $1\frac{1}{2}$ teaspoons baking powder
- $\frac{1}{2}$ teaspoon salt
- 1 teaspoon grated lemon rind
- 1 teaspoon grated orange rind

Beat egg yolks until thick, light-coloured, and fluffy. Add fruit juices.

Gradually add half the sugar, beating well until sugar is dissolved. Fold in mixed and sifted flour, baking powder, and salt.

Beat egg whites until stiff but not dry; add remaining sugar and beat until well blended.

Fold egg yolk mixture into egg whites with grated lemon and orange rind.

Turn into ungreased 10-inch tube tin. Bake in moderate oven (350°F. Mark 4) 1 hour and 15 minutes.

Invert tin, but do not remove cake until thoroughly cooked. Ice with orange butter icing.

Roll Cakes

SWISS ROLL

4 ounces plain flour
2 teaspoons baking powder
¼ teaspoon salt
3 eggs
4 tablespoons cold water
8 ounces sugar
1 teaspoon vanilla
Icing sugar
Jam
Cherries and nuts for garnish

Sift flour, baking powder, and salt.

Beat eggs until thick and lemon-coloured. Add cold water and sugar, beating well. Gradually fold in sifted ingredients. Add vanilla.

Turn into well greased cake tin (10 × 15 inches) lined with greaseproof paper.

Bake in hot oven (425°F. Mark 7) 12 to 15 minutes.

Place tea towel on table, cover with greaseproof paper, sprinkle with icing sugar. Turn hot cake onto paper. Spread with jam. Hold paper and towel firmly with thumb and first finger. Lift and roll. Cool.

Unwrap. Garnish with cherries and nuts. Serves 6.

Chocolate Roll: In Swiss roll recipe, replace 1 ounce of the flour with 1 ounce cocoa before sifting. Fill with cream filling, or with whipped cream if cooled before rolling.

BRAZIL NUT CHOCOLATE ROLL

4 eggs
6 ounces sugar
3 ounces plain flour
1 teaspoon baking powder
¼ teaspoon salt
1 teaspoon vanilla
2 ounces icing sugar
3 ounces Brazil nuts

Beat eggs with rotary beater. Add sugar gradually until mixture becomes thick and light-coloured.

Strawberry Whip Roll

Sift flour with baking powder and salt, and fold into egg mixture. Add vanilla.

Pour into tin (15 × 10 inches) lined with greased paper. Bake in hot oven (400°F. Mark 6) 13 minutes.

Turn from tin at once onto grease-proof paper, covered with icing sugar and nuts. Remove paper on which cake has been baked.

Spread with chocolate Brazil nut filling and roll up. Wrap in paper and cool on rack.

YULE ROLL

4 eggs, separated
6 ounces sugar
1 teaspoon vanilla
3 ounces digestive biscuit crumbs
1 teaspoon baking powder
¼ teaspoon salt

Beat egg whites until stiff; gradually beat in 2 ounces sugar.

In separate bowl, beat egg yolks until thick and lemon-coloured; mix in vanilla. Fold egg yolks into egg whites. Combine cake crumbs, remaining sugar, baking powder, and salt. Gently fold crumb mixture into egg mixture.

Pour batter into Swiss roll tin (15½ × 10½ inches) lined with greased grease-proof paper; spread evenly. Bake in hot oven (400°F. Mark 6) 15 minutes or until done.

Loosen sides and turn out onto towel sprinkled with icing sugar. Carefully remove paper.

Fold cake over about one inch to start roll. With left hand raise towel and roll cake, guiding it with right hand. Leave in towel to cool on rack.

When thoroughly cooled, unroll and spread with chocolate cream. Roll up again.

Serve as is, or freeze for an ice cream roll.

Chocolate Cream: Pour ½ pint double cream into well chilled bowl; add 2 ounces chocolate powder. Beat with rotary egg beater until cream stands in peaks.

GINGER ROLL

5 ounces plain flour
3 ounces sugar
1¼ teaspoons bicarbonate of soda
1 teaspoon each ginger, cinnamon, nutmeg and mixed spice
3 ounces butter, melted
4 ounces molasses or black treacle
1 well beaten egg
4 fluid ounces warm water
Icing sugar
8 fluid ounces double cream, whipped

Grease a 10½ × 15½-inch Swiss roll tin; line with paper and grease paper.

Brazil Nut Chocolate Roll

Sift together twice flour, sugar, soda, and spices. Add butter, molasses, egg, and water. Stir until smooth. Spread in tin.

Bake in moderate oven (350°F. Mark 4) until cake rebounds when pressed with finger, about 15 minutes.

Cool cake briefly in tin. Cover with thin cloth, wrung out of cold water. Finish cooling in refrigerator.

Remove cloth, sprinkle cake with sugar, turn out on greaseproof paper. Remove paper adhering to under side of cake.

Spread with whipped cream, roll. Wrap in greaseproof paper.

STRAWBERRY WHIP ROLL

2 ounces flour
¾ teaspoon baking powder
¼ teaspoon salt
2 ounces sugar
3 beaten eggs
1¼ teaspoons vanilla
3 tablespoons melted butter or margarine
1 egg white
2 ounces sugar
4 ounces sliced fresh strawberries
Whole berries
Icing sugar

Sift, measure flour, and resift with baking powder and salt.

Add 2 ounces sugar to eggs gradually and beat until thick and light-coloured. Add vanilla; fold in flour mixture and add melted butter or margarine.

Pour into well greased tin (7 × 11 × 1¼ inches) lined with greaseproof paper and brushed with melted butter or margarine. Bake in hot oven (400°F. Mark 6) 10 minutes.

Turn out on damp cloth; roll cake up and cool.

Beat egg white until stiff but not dry. Gradually beat in 2 ounces sugar.

Unroll cake and spread with meringue. Top meringue with sliced strawberries.

Reroll and sprinkle top with icing sugar. Garnish with mounds of meringue topped with whole strawberries. Serves 6.

Fruit Cakes

LIGHT FRUIT CAKE

6 ounces candied orange peel
3 ounces candied lemon peel
8 ounces sliced citron
9 ounces raisins, crystallised cherries, or other dried or crystallised fruit, or a mixture of several fruits, sliced or chopped
1 teaspoon mace
½ teaspoon each cloves and mixed spice
10 fluid ounces orange or pineapple juice
12 ounces honey
8 ounces butter or margarine
8 ounces sugar
4 beaten eggs
1 teaspoon vanilla
4 tablespoons brandy or rum
4 ounces almonds—preferably blanched, shredded, and slightly toasted
1¼ pounds plain flour
1½ teaspoons salt
½ teaspoon bicarbonate of soda
3 teaspoons baking powder

Mix peels and fruits with spices, fruit juice, and honey and let stand overnight.

Cream butter with sugar; add eggs, vanilla, and brandy or rum. Blend thoroughly and mix with fruit combination and nuts.

Sift together remaining ingredients and stir into fruit mixture. Mix well.

Pour into a tube tin or 2 loaf tins that have been greased, lined with paper and greased again.

Cover with several thicknesses of greaseproof paper and tie on securely.

Place in a steamer, cover, and steam 1 large cake 3 hours or 2 small cakes 2 hours.

Remove paper covering and, if desired, glaze surface by coating it with honey and decorate with nuts and crystallised fruits.

Bake in very slow oven (250°F. Mark ½) about 2 hours. Makes about 5 pounds.

DARK FRUIT CAKE

1 pound raisins
½ pound crystallised cherries, halved
½ pound citron, thinly sliced
¼ pound figs, dates, or crystallised pineapple, sliced
3 ounces candied orange peel, sliced
3 ounces candied lemon peel, sliced
7 ounces plain flour
¼ teaspoon bicarbonate of soda
½ teaspoon each of mixed spice, cinnamon, nutmeg, and salt
3 ounces butter or margarine
4 ounces brown sugar, sifted
4 eggs, separated
4 ounces molasses or black treacle
6 tablespoons grape, apple, or pineapple juice, or rum, brandy, or sherry

If fruits are dry and hard place in a sieve and steam until soft over boiling water. Cool and prepare as indicated.

Dredge well with a little of the flour, using the hand to do this.

Sift together twice the remaining flour, soda, spices, and salt.

Cream butter, add sugar and cream until fluffy. Add well beaten egg yolks and mix thoroughly. Stir in molasses.

Add sifted dry ingredients and fruit juice or liquor alternately to creamed mixture, mixing well after each addition.

Beat egg whites until stiff and fold into batter.

Add dredged fruits and mix evenly through batter.

Line 1 large or 2 medium loaf tins with 3 thicknesses of greaseproof paper.

Press batter into tins, filling them ¾ full. If desired decorate top with crystallised cherries and citron. Cover with three thicknesses of paper and tie it on securely.

Steam for 3 hours in a steamer with a tightly fitting lid, adding more water to the pan if necessary.

Remove top paper coverings and bake in very slow oven (250°F. Mark ½) 2 hours. Remove from tins and cool.

To store, wrap in greaseproof paper or aluminium foil or a cloth saturated with brandy. Store in an airtight container in a cool place. Dampen cloth with more brandy about every 3 weeks. Makes about 5 pounds of cake.

ELEGANT WHITE FRUIT CAKE

A cake for an anniversary of great importance. May be used as an alternative to dark fruit cake as a wedding cake. Cut the candied (glacé) fruits into large uniform pieces, then when the cake is sliced for serving, the beautiful rich colours will shine against the white background.

Makes a 5½ pound cake in a springform tin with a tube centre, or a 10-inch angel food cake tin.

6 slices crystallised pineapple
4 ounces candied citron
4 ounces glacé cherries, halved
4 ounces each cut candied lemon and orange rinds
6 ounces seedless raisins
6 ounces slivered blanched almonds

Elegant White Fruit Cake

1 pound plain flour
2 teaspoons baking powder
2 teaspoons salt
6 ounces fat
2 ounces butter or margarine
1 pound sugar
6 fluid ounces milk
8 egg whites

Prepare baking tin.

Combine fruits and almonds with sifted dry ingredients.

Cream together fat, butter or margarine, and sugar until light and fluffy.

Stir in combined fruits, nuts, and sifted dry ingredients alternately with milk to make a stiff batter.

Fold in egg whites, beaten until stiff; spoon batter into prepared tin.

Bake in slow oven (300°F. Mark 2) about 2½ hours or until top is firm to light touch. (If top seems to be browning too fast, cover with heavy paper during last 45 minutes of baking.)

FRUIT CAKE WITH WHOLE NUTS

4 eggs, separated
8 ounces sugar
4 tablespoons wine
4 ounces plain flour
1 teaspoon baking powder
⅛ teaspoon salt
4 ounces crystallised pineapple
1 pound whole stoned dates
½ pound whole crystallised cherries
½ pound walnut halves
½ pound pecan halves
½ pound whole Brazil nuts

Beat egg yolks. Add sugar, and cream together thoroughly. Add wine and mix well.

Add flour sifted with baking powder and salt. Fold in stiffly beaten egg whites. Add chopped pineapple, dates, cherries, and nuts to batter. Mix well.

Grease 2 tins (4½ × 9 × 5 inches). Line with greaseproof paper and grease again. Carefully add cake mixture with a spoon.

Bake in a slow oven (325°F. Mark 3) about 1½ hours.

Cool thoroughly. Remove paper and store in an airtight container.

TO DECORATE FRUIT CAKES

A week or two before serving cake, make a glaze by combining 12 ounces sugar and 6 ounces sieved cooked, dried apricot pulp and juice. Boil to 240°F. or until sticky. Apply immediately to cake while glaze is still sticky.

Decorate tops with bits of crystallised candied fruits and blanched almonds. When first coat of glaze is dry, add another coat of hot glaze syrup.

Allow to dry, then wrap cake lightly so that some air reaches cake to keep glaze dry.

HOLIDAY STAR CAKE

4 ounces butter or margarine
4 ounces sugar
3 ounces honey
2 eggs
8 ounces plain flour
1 teaspoon baking powder
½ teaspoon salt
8 ounces mincemeat
6 ounces diced apples
3 ounces raisins
6 ounces mixed diced fruit (orange and lemon peel, citron, cherries)
2 ounces chopped nuts
1 tablespoon brandy flavouring

Cream butter or margarine, sugar, and honey together; beat in eggs one at a time.

Sift dry ingredients together and combine with egg mixture. Stir in fruit, nuts, and flavouring.

Line the bottom of a well greased 8-inch cake tin with greaseproof paper. Fill tin to within 1 to 1½ inches from the top. Bake in slow oven (325°F. Mark 3) 1½ to 2 hours.

DUNDEE CAKE

A Scotch cake often made with currants and candied peel, usually covered with almonds before baking.

9 ounces flour
1 teaspoon baking powder
½ teaspoon salt
6 ounces butter
6 ounces sugar
3 eggs
4 fluid ounces milk
6 ounces seeded raisins, chopped
3 ounces currants, washed and dried
2 ounces candied orange peel or citron, chopped
1 ounce chopped blanched almonds
12 blanched almonds, split

Mix and sift flour, baking powder and salt.

Cream butter well; add sugar and cream until fluffy. Add eggs 1 at a

time and beat after each addition until very fluffy.

Add flour mixture alternately with milk to butter mixture, stirring after each addition only until mixed. Do not beat.

Fold in raisins, currants, orange peel, and chopped almonds.

Turn into 9 × 3½-inch tin which has been lined on the bottom with greased greaseproof paper. Arrange split almonds on top.

Bake in slow oven (325°F. Mark 3) until cake begins to shrink from sides of tin, about 75 minutes. Cool about 15 minutes before removing from tin. Makes 1 cake.

NO-BAKE FESTIVE FRUIT CAKE

For 2¼ pound cake:

4 fluid ounces evaporated milk
16 finely cut marshmallows
3 tablespoons orange juice*
8 ounces digestive biscuit crumbs
¼ teaspoon cinnamon
¼ teaspoon nutmeg
⅛ teaspoon cloves
6 ounces seedless raisins
3 ounces finely cut dates
3 ounces chopped walnuts
4 ounces candied fruit**

For 4½ pound cake:

8 fluid ounces evaporated milk
32 finely cut marshmallows
6 tablespoons orange juice*
6 ounces digestive biscuit crumbs
½ teaspoon cinnamon
½ teaspoon nutmeg
¼ teaspoon cloves
12 ounces seedless raisins
6 ounces finely cut dates
6 ounces chopped walnuts
8 ounces candied fruit**

Line with greaseproof paper bottom and sides of one or two 8-inch cake tins.

Place milk, marshmallows, and orange juice into a bowl and let stand until needed.

Put biscuit crumbs into a large bowl; add cinnamon, nutmeg, cloves, raisins, dates and walnuts.

Add ready-mixed, cut-up candied fruit.

Add milk mixture. Mix with spoon, then with hands until crumbs are moistened. Press firmly into tin.

Top with fruit and nuts. Cover tightly.

Chill 2 days before slicing. Keep in cool place.

* Alcoholic flavouring can replace the orange juice if desired.

** For 2¼-pound cake you can replace the 4 ounces of ready-mixed candied fruit with: 2 ounces finely cut

crystallised pineapple, 2 ounces finely cut glacé cherries, 2 tablespoons finely cut candied orange peel.

For 4½-pound cake you can replace the 8 ounces of ready-mixed candied fruit with: 3 ounces finely cut crystallised pineapple, 3 ounces finely cut glacé cherries, and 1 ounce finely cut candied orange peel.

Butter Fruit Cake

BUTTER FRUIT CAKE

2 pounds raisins
2 pounds currants
1 pound almonds
1 pound pecans
1 pound citron
1 pound plain flour
1 teaspoon nutmeg
1 teaspoon mace
1 teaspoon cinnamon
1 pound unsalted butter
1 pound brown sugar
12 eggs
6 ounces redcurrant jelly
4 tablespoons lemon juice
4 tablespoons canned peach juice
4 fluid ounces cream

Wash and dry raisins and currants. Blanch almonds, drain and cut with pecans into quarters. Cut citron into thin slices. Place fruit in large mixing bowl.

Sift flour, measure and sift with spices and mix with fruit until well coated.

Cream butter and add sugar gradually. Add beaten eggs and jelly.

Next stir in flour, nut and fruit mixture alternately with fruit juice first, then cream.

Line tins with heavy greaseproof paper and butter lightly. Fill tins almost to top.

Bake small cakes in very slow oven (275°F. Mark 1) 3 to 3½ hours. Bake large cakes in very slow oven (250°F. Mark ½) 4 to 4½ hours. The cakes will shrink from edges when done.

Cool cakes on wire rack, without removing greaseproof paper. When cool, wrap in heavy greaseproof paper and store in tightly covered container until ready to use.

No-Bake Groom's Fruit Cake *Groom's Dark Fruit Cake*

NO-BAKE GROOM'S FRUIT CAKE

12 ounces mixed nuts (almonds, walnuts, Brazil nuts, etc.)
1 pound seedless raisins
8 ounces diced, mixed, glacé fruit
1 8-ounce jar maraschino cherries, drained
1 pound digestive biscuits
½ ounce gelatine
5 tablespoons orange juice
4 ounces sugar
8 fluid ounces molasses or black treacle
1 tablespoon grated orange rind
¼ teaspoon each: cinnamon, nutmeg, cloves
⅛ teaspoon each: mixed spice, ginger

Line a 9¼×5¼×2¾-inch loaf tin, or 2 loaf tins, 7¼×3½×2 inches, with two strips greaseproof paper, extending paper 3 inches above rim. Set aside.

Put nuts in a large mixing bowl, with raisins, glacé fruit, and maraschino cherries; mix well.

Finely crush digestive biscuits with a rolling pin; add to nut-fruit mixture.

Soften gelatine in orange juice; place over boiling water and stir until gelatine is dissolved. Add sugar; stir until dissolved.

Pour molasses into large bowl of electric mixer; add gelatine mixture, orange rind, and spices. Beat on highest speed of electric mixer 15 minutes.

Add to nut-fruit mixture; blend thoroughly with spoon or hands. Turn into prepared tins, pressing down firmly. If desired, garnish with additional maraschino cherries and sliced Brazil nuts.

Fold greaseproof paper over cake. Chill in refrigerator 6 to 8 hours. To store, wrap in aluminium foil and keep in refrigerator. Makes 4½-pound cake.

GROOM'S DARK FRUIT CAKE

6 ounces raisins
3 ounces chopped nuts
2 ounces diced citron
8 ounces plain flour
½ teaspoon bicarbonate of soda
½ teaspoon salt
1 teaspoon cinnamon
½ teaspoon mixed spice
½ teaspoon mace
¼ teaspoon cloves
4 ounces fat
4 ounces sugar
2 eggs
9 fluid ounces molasses or black treacle
4 fluid ounces milk

Combine raisins, nuts, and citron in mixing bowl.

Sift together flour, soda, salt, cinnamon, mixed spice, mace, and cloves; mix half with the fruit-nut mixture.

Cream fat; add sugar and cream well. Beat in eggs one at a time.

Combine molasses and milk; add alternately with remaining flour mixture to fat mixture. Mix in prepared fruit and nuts.

Turn into a greased and paper-lined 9¼×5¼×2¾-inch tin.

Bake in slow oven (325°F. Mark 3) 1 hour and 25 minutes.

Cool 15 minutes; remove from tin. Makes 2½ pounds fruit cake.

CALIFORNIA FRUIT CAKE

6 ounces prunes
6 ounces dried figs
1 pound seedless raisins
1 pound cherries
4 ounces crystallised lemon peel, chopped
4 ounces crystallised orange peel, chopped
8 ounces crystallised citron, chopped
1 teaspoon cloves
2 teaspoons cinnamon
2 teaspoons nutmeg
2 teaspoons mace
¼ teaspoon black pepper
8 ounces thick orange marmalade
5 tablespoons fruit juice or white wine
12 ounces butter or margarine
1 pound sugar
1 tablespoon rum flavouring
7 eggs
1¼ pounds plain flour
1 teaspoon salt
1 teaspoon bicarbonate of soda
4 ounces coarsely chopped blanched almonds
4 ounces chopped walnuts

Rinse dried fruits. Drain figs and raisins and dry thoroughly.

Cover prunes with water and boil 15 minutes. Drain and dry. Cut from stones into small pieces.

Clip stems from figs and cut figs into thin strips. Slice cherries.

Combine fruits, peels, spices, marmalade, and fruit juice and blend well. Cover and let stand overnight.

Cream butter and sugar together thoroughly. Add flavouring and well beaten eggs and beat. Add a portion of flour sifted with salt and soda and mix well. Add fruit mixture and nuts, and stir to blend. Add remainder of flour and stir until fruit is well distributed.

Pour into 10-inch tube tin which has been lined with 2 thicknesses of greased brown paper and 1 of greased greaseproof paper. (Allow paper to extend about ¾ inch above rim for safety.)

Bake in slow oven (250°F. Mark 1) about 3 hours, raise temperature to 300°F. Mark 2 and continue baking about 1½ hours.

Decorate top with whole blanched almonds and thin strips of candied citron. Baked weight about 7½ pound cake.

ORANGE FRUIT CAKE

10 ounces plain flour
1½ teaspoons bicarbonate of soda
½ teaspoon salt
1 teaspoon cinnamon
½ teaspoon cloves
¼ teaspoon mixed spice
3 ounces chopped citron
3 ounces candied pineapple, chopped
4 ounces glacé cherries, quartered
2 ounces chopped nuts
4 ounces fat
1 pound sugar
2 well beaten eggs
1 tablespoon grated orange rind
3½ tablespoons vinegar and enough sour cream to make 8 fluid ounces
6 fluid ounces orange juice

Sift flour, soda, salt, cinnamon, cloves, and mixed spice together. Add cut fruits and nuts and mix well.

Cream fat. Add 8 ounces sugar gradually and cream until fluffy.

Add eggs and grated orange rind. Beat well. Add vinegar and sour cream alternately with the flour mixture to the creamed ingredients. Mix until thoroughly blended.

Pour into well greased 9-inch tube tin. Bake in moderate heat (350°F. Mark 4) 1 hour.

Remove cake from oven, and while it is still hot, pour over it 8 ounces sugar mixed with orange juice. Let cake cool before removing from tin.

Torten and Miscellaneous Cakes

HINTS ABOUT TORTEN

The German word for tart or cake is torte (plural—torten) and the term refers to the cakes of European cooks in which minced nuts or crumbs (cake, biscuit, or bread) are usually used instead of flour. Torten are made light with eggs and generally contain no fat. There is a tendency also to apply the term to cake-like desserts, frequently differing very little from conventional cakes. The famous European torten may vary from one to twelve layers.

Many of the following recipes are baked in 9-inch spring-form tins. The spring-form tin should be greased and sprinkled lightly with flour.

The making of torten is not difficult although they sometimes require long beating. Some traditional recipes are at their best if beaten for as much as thirty minutes.

To remove torte from tin, be sure to run a spatula around the edge of torte, then release the side spring of tin. Do not remove torte from bottom of tin until thoroughly cooled unless specifically directed to do so in the recipe.

Fruit pulp or chilled jellies whipped are favourite torte fillings. Nut torten are frequently spread with whipped jelly, particularly currant jelly, and then sprinkled with blanched, browned slivered almonds.

Whipped cream flavoured with brandy, rum, essences, or coffee is the outstanding favourite for icings.

ALMOND MOCHA TORTE

4 egg yolks
8 ounces sugar
1 tablespoon melted butter or margarine
½ teaspoon vanilla
2 ounces plain flour
½ teaspoon salt
1 teaspoon baking powder
4 egg whites
6 ounces ground almonds
Toasted almonds
Glacé cherries

Beat egg yolks with sugar until thick

Almond Mocha Torte

and ivory-coloured. Beat in butter and vanilla.

Sift flour with salt and baking powder; blend into egg yolk mixture.

Beat egg whites until soft peaks form; fold in ground almonds. Combine with yolk mixture, and spread into two greased and floured 9-inch sandwich tins.

Bake in moderate oven (350°F. Mark 4) 25 minutes. Turn out on racks at once; layers get crisp as they cool. Spread with filling (below). Decorate with almond slices and glacé cherries. Let stand 12 hours in cool place before serving. Makes 1 9-inch torte.

Filling:
8 fluid ounces double cream
1 tablespoon powdered instant coffee
1 tablespoon castor sugar

Whip cream; blend in coffee and sugar.

APPLE TORTE

4 eggs, separated
6 ounces sugar
3 apples, grated
3 ounces sponge cake crumbs
Juice and grated rind of ½ lemon
1 ounce chopped almonds

Beat egg yolks and sugar until light; blend in apples, crumbs, lemon juice and rind, and then fold in the stiffly beaten whites.

Pour into a greased and floured 8-inch spring-form tin. Sprinkle with almonds, pressing them into mixture with the back of spoon.

Bake in moderate oven (350°F. Mark 4) 20 to 25 minutes. Leave torte on bottom of spring-form. Serve with cream.

NUT TORTE

5 eggs, separated
8 ounces sugar
4 ounces chopped nuts
3 ounces digestive biscuit crumbs
1 teaspoon baking powder

Beat egg yolks until light; add sugar gradually and beat until thick and lemon-coloured.

Blend in nuts and crumbs, then fold in the stiffly beaten egg whites and baking powder.

Turn into 2 round 8-inch sandwich tins. Bake in moderate oven (350°F. Mark 4) 20 minutes.

Fill the cooled layers and cover the top and sides with sweetened whipped cream flavoured with sherry. Decorate the top with pecan or walnut halves.

Imperial Waltz Torte

IMPERIAL WALTZ TORTE

12 ounces butterscotch, broken into pieces
4 ounces sugar
4 fluid ounces water
2 teaspoons vanilla
1 packet pastry mix (about 8 ounces)
8 fluid ounces double cream
4 ounces browned, chopped pecans or walnuts
Whole pecans or walnuts
Cream

In a saucepan combine butterscotch pieces, sugar, and water. Cook over low heat, stirring constantly, until smooth. Add vanilla; cool.

Blend 4 fluid ounces butterscotch sauce into pastry mix. Divide pastry into 6 equal parts.

On foil-covered baking sheets draw 7-inch circles. Place a pastry portion in centre of a circle; pat and press out dough to cover circle.

Bake in hot oven (425°F. Mark 7) 5 minutes or until done; cool. Run tip of knife under edges to loosen; lift off carefully. Repeat until six layers are made.

Fold all but 4 fluid ounces remaining butterscotch sauce into whipped cream. Spread each layer with butterscotch cream and sprinkle with about 3 tablespoons pecans or walnuts.

Stack layers; decorate top with whole pecans. Chill until serving. Thin remaining butterscotch sauce with a little cream and serve with torte.

MATZO ALMOND TORTE

5 eggs, separated
8 ounces sugar
4 ounces unblanched chopped almonds
2 ounces matzo meal or bread-crumbs
1 teaspoon baking powder
1 teaspoon cinnamon
¼ teaspoon cloves
1 tablespoon lemon juice or brandy

Beat egg yolks and sugar until light; add remaining ingredients in order given, adding the stiffly beaten whites last.

Pour into greased and floured 8-inch spring form tin. Bake in moderate oven (350°F. Mark 4) 1 hour.

SCHAUM TORTE

Schaum Torte is the German name for a meringue baked in layers or in a spring-form tin and served with fruit and whipped cream.

6 egg whites
14 ounces caster sugar
1 teaspoon vinegar
1 teaspoon almond essence
Strawberries or raspberries, crushed
Extra caster sugar
Whipped cream
Whole strawberries or raspberries

Beat egg whites until stiff. Gradually add sifted sugar, vinegar, and almond essence.

Bake in 2 loose-bottomed, buttered, 8-inch cake tins in slow oven (275°F. Mark 1) 40 minutes.

Turn off oven and leave oven door open to allow meringue to cool 30 minutes.

When cool, fill layers with strawberries or raspberries crushed with caster sugar. Also put fruit on top layer and cover with whipped cream. Decorate with whole berries. Serve immediately.

DOBOS TORTE

The Dobos Torte, created by a famous Hungarian pastry chef named Dobos, consists of a sponge type cake made in several layers with a rich chocolate filling between layers and a caramel glaze spread over the top.

Batter:
3 ounces plain flour
¼ teaspoon salt
6 eggs, separated
8 ounces sugar
1 teaspoon vanilla

Filling:
4 ounces sugar
4 large eggs
4 ounces plain chocolate
2 tablespoons boiling water
7 ounces butter
1 teaspoon vanilla

Mix and sift flour and salt 4 times.

Beat egg yolks until light and lemon-coloured. Gradually beat in sugar, and with last addition add vanilla. Gradually add flour. Beat well.

Beat egg whites until stiff, but not dry, and fold in lightly.

Grease 4 8-inch cake tins and pour in a thin layer of batter, spreading evenly. Reserve half the batter for remaining 4 layers.

Bake in moderate oven (375°F. Mark 5) 5 to 8 minutes.

Remove cake at once from tins. Grease and refill tins with remaining batter. Set layers aside to cool.

Filling: Combine in top of double saucepan sugar and eggs. Cook over boiling water, beating constantly until mixture begins to thicken. Cool slightly.

Cut chocolate into small pieces. Dissolve in boiling water and keep warm until needed.

Cream butter until light. Add melted chocolate and vanilla. Combine with egg mixture.

Spread filling between layers. Place cocktail sticks through top layers to hold layers in place until filling sets. Spread with caramel glaze (below).

Caramel Glaze: Melt and brown in a small saucepan 3 tablespoons sugar and pour over the cake. Spread with a hot knife. Let cake stand in cool place 24 hours before serving.

BREAD TORTE

The bread torte or brottorte is an old-time German cake.

5 eggs, separated
8 ounces sugar
3 ounces breadcrumbs
Juice and grated rind of ½ lemon or 2 tablespoons wine
6 ounces almonds, blanched and coarsely chopped
1½ teaspoons baking powder

Beat egg yolks and sugar until very light.

Soak breadcrumbs in lemon juice or wine. Mix all ingredients, folding in the stiffly beaten egg whites last.

Turn into 2 greased and floured 9-inch sandwich tins. Bake in moderate oven (350°F. Mark 4) 45 minutes. Fill with walnut filling.

DATE-NUT TORTE

6 ounces digestive biscuit crumbs
1 teaspoon salt
1 teaspoon baking powder
1 tablespoon sugar
3 well beaten eggs
1 pound stoned dates
3 tablespoons flour
2 ounces chopped walnuts or pecans
1 teaspoon vanilla
3 fluid ounces milk
Whipped cream

Combine crumbs, salt, baking powder, and sugar. Add eggs.

Toss dates in flour to keep them from sticking. Add floured dates, nuts, vanilla, and milk.

Pour mixture into a greased 8-inch square tin. Bake in slow oven (325°F. Mark 3) 45 minutes.

Cut into squares. Top each with whipped cream.

LINZER TORTE

A rich German cake that resembles an open-face jam pie.

6 ounces flour
2 ounces sugar
½ teaspoon baking powder
½ teaspoon salt
½ teaspoon cinnamon
3 ounces brown sugar
4 ounces butter or margarine
1 egg, unbeaten
2 ounces unblanched almonds

Sift together flour, sugar, baking powder, salt, and cinnamon. Cut in brown sugar and butter or margarine. Add egg and ground almonds. Blend with pastry blender or fork.

Reserve some of the dough for topping and chill. Press remaining dough evenly into bottom and sides of 8-inch pie plate. (Do not cover rim of plate.)

Fill with cream filling (below). Top with raspberry sauce (below).

Roll out chilled reserved dough on floured pastry board to ⅛-inch thickness. Cut into ½-inch strips with pastry wheel or knife. Arrange over filling, crisscross fashion.

Cover ends of lattice strips with another strip, circling pie but not covering rim of pie plate. Press to seal.

Bake in moderate oven (375°F. Mark 5) 30 to 35 minutes. Serve warm or cool.

Cream Filling: Beat 1 egg until fluffy, about 2 minutes. Add gradually 3 ounces sugar; beat until thick and lemon-coloured. Blend in 1 ounce plain flour and ¼ teaspoon salt.

Gradually add 12 fluid ounces milk, which has been scalded in top of double saucepan.

Return mixture to pan. Cook over boiling water, stirring constantly, until thick. Cover and continue cooking 4 to 5 minutes, stirring occasionally. Add 1 teaspoon vanilla. Cool.

Raspberry Sauce: Combine 1 packet thawed, frozen raspberries, undrained, 2 tablespoons sugar, and 2 tablespoons cornflour in saucepan. (Fresh sweetened raspberries may be substituted. Omit cornflour.)

Add 1 tablespoon lemon juice. Bring to boil and cook 5 to 10 minutes until mixture begins to thicken. Cool.

Linzer Torte

POPPY SEED TORTE

4½ ounces poppy seed
6 fluid ounces milk
6 ounces butter
12 ounces sugar
8 ounces plain flour
2 teaspoons baking powder
¼ teaspoon salt
4 stiffly-beaten egg whites
Filling (see below)

Soak poppy seed in milk overnight.

Cream butter to soften; add sugar gradually and cream together. Mix in milk and poppy seed.

Sift dry ingredients together; add to creamed mixture. Fold in egg whites.

Bake in 3 paper-lined 8 × 1¼-inch round tins in moderate oven (350°F. Mark 4) 25 to 30 minutes.

Cool 10 minutes; remove from tins.

Filling: Mix 4 ounces sugar and 1 tablespoon cornflour in double pan. Combine 12 fluid ounces milk and 4 well beaten egg yolks; gradually stir into sugar mixture and cook, stirring constantly, until thick.

Cool slightly; add 1 teaspoon vanilla and 2 ounces chopped walnuts. Cool.

Spread between cooled cake layers. For design on top, cut a daisy stencil from cardboard or heavy paper; lay it on torte. Sift icing sugar over top; lift off stencil. Centre daisy with grated orange rind.

SWEDISH APPLE CAKE

4 tablespoons butter
6 ounces digestive biscuit crumbs
Few drops lemon juice
1 tablespoon Angostura bitters
1 pound apple purée

Melt butter in saucepan, add sifted biscuit crumbs and stir until nicely brown. Add lemon juice and bitters.

Butter baking dish well and arrange crumbs and apple purée in alternating layers finishing with crumbs.

Bake in moderate oven (375°F. Mark 5) 25 to 35 minutes. Cool before unmoulding and serve with whipped cream.

Swedish Apple Cake

YAEGERTORTE
(Hunter's Cake)

½ pound whole unpeeled almonds
8 small eggs
8 ounces sugar
Grated rind of 1 lemon
1 tablespoon lemon juice
Fine breadcrumbs

Mince unpeeled almonds.

Beat 2 whole eggs and 6 yolks thoroughly for about 5 minutes. Stir in ground almonds, sugar, lemon rind, and juice. Last, fold in stiffly beaten egg whites thoroughly.

Sprinkle some fine breadcrumbs on bottom of a greased 9-inch spring-form tin. Pour in the batter.

Bake in moderate oven (375°F. Mark 5) about 1 hour. Let cool before gently removing from tin.

Ice top and sides of cake with chocolate glacé icing, and decorate with whole peeled almonds. This cake improves in flavour if kept a day or two.

Chocolate Icing: Melt 2 ounces plain chocolate with 3½ tablespoons milk and ½ ounce butter.

Cool, then add ¼ teaspoon vanilla, and work in about 9 ounces sifted icing sugar, or enough to make soft spreadable icing.

CHOCOLATE WALNUT TORTE

6 eggs, separated
8 ounces sugar
2 ounces chopped walnuts or pecans
2 tablespoons digestive biscuit crumbs
1 teaspoon vanilla
8 ounces unsalted butter
4½ ounces icing sugar
4 ounces plain chocolate
2 teaspoons sherry

Beat egg yolks, gradually adding the sugar. Add nuts and biscuit crumbs, then vanilla. Fold in stiffly beaten egg whites.

Bake in 2 greased, floured 9-inch tins in moderate oven (350°F. Mark 4) about 30 minutes. Cool.

Cream butter; add sugar and beat until fluffy.

Melt chocolate in top of double saucepan; add to sugar-butter mixture, blending well.

Spread one layer of the torte with marmalade or strawberry jam to a thickness of ¼ inch. Sprinkle with sherry.

Place on top layer and cover top and sides of cake with butter icing.

Place in refrigerator and it will keep at least two weeks, or without refrigeration for 2 to 3 days. Serves 6.

ALMOND TORTE

1 pound almonds
8 eggs, separated
8 ounces sugar
Pinch of salt
1 teaspoon baking powder
½ teaspoon almond essence
1 teaspoon vanilla

Blanch almonds, dry and mince to a fine meal.

Beat egg whites until stiff and beat into them half the sugar.

Beat egg yolks with remaining sugar until light and lemon-coloured.

Fold the yolks into whites, then carefully fold in almond meal, salt, and baking powder. Add almond essence and vanilla.

Pour into 9-inch spring-form tin. Bake in slow oven (300°F. Mark 2) 1¼ hours.

Cool and cover with whipped cream to which sugar has been added to taste.

Decorate with blanched almonds, slivered and sautéed in butter until lightly browned.

Hazelnut Torte: Substitute hazelnuts for almonds.

LEKACH
(Traditional Jewish Honey Cake)

6 eggs
8 ounces sugar
12 ounces honey
2 tablespoons salad oil or melted fat
14 ounces plain flour
1½ teaspoons baking powder
1 teaspoon bicarbonate of soda
¼ teaspoon ground cloves
½ teaspoon cinnamon
½ teaspoon mixed spice
2 ounces chopped nuts
3 ounces raisins
1 ounce finely cut citron or mixed candied fruit
2 tablespoons brandy

Beat eggs well, then gradually add sugar and beat until light and creamy. Stir in honey and fat.

Mix and sift flour, baking powder, soda, and spices; stir in the nuts and fruit, then combine with first mixture. Add brandy last.

Pour into a paper-lined and oiled rectangular tin. Sprinkle a few blanched, halved almonds on top, if desired.

Bake in a slow oven (325°F. Mark 3) about 1 hour.

Invert tin and allow cake to cool before removing. When ready to serve, cut into squares or diamond shapes.

Variation: Instead of the 6 eggs, use 4 eggs plus 4 fluid ounces coffee or tea. Dilute the honey with the hot coffee or tea before combining. The 6-egg recipe makes a cake of finer texture.

CHOCOLATE TORTE

8 eggs, separated
8 ounces sugar
2 ounces plain chocolate, grated
$1\frac{1}{2}$ ounces breadcrumbs

Beat egg yolks and sugar together until thick and lemon-coloured. Add grated chocolate and stir until mixture is well combined.

Add crumbs and then fold in stiffly beaten egg whites.

Turn into 2 buttered 8-inch sandwich tins. Bake in moderate oven (350°F. Mark 4) 40 minutes.

Remove from tins and cool on cake rack. When cool, split each layer in half, making 4 layers.

Fill between the layers and cover top and sides with following icing:

Mix together 8 ounces sugar, 8 fluid ounces milk, and 2 ounces grated plain chocolate. Cook until a soft ball is formed when dropped into cold water.

Remove from heat; then add 1 teaspoon vanilla and $\frac{1}{2}$ ounce butter, which has been creamed thoroughly with 2 egg yolks. Beat until cool enough to spread.

Whip $\frac{3}{4}$ pint double cream and fold the chocolate mixture into the cream. Add sugar to taste.

BLITZ TORTE

$4\frac{1}{2}$ ounces plain flour
$1\frac{1}{3}$ teaspoons baking powder
$\frac{1}{8}$ teaspoon salt
4 ounces fat
12 ounces sugar
4 eggs, separated
5 tablespoons milk or cream
1 teaspoon vanilla
$\frac{1}{2}$ teaspoon cinnamon
3 ounces shredded blanched almonds

Mix and sift flour, baking powder, and salt 3 times.

Cream fat. Gradually beat in 4 ounces sugar. Add egg yolks, one at a time, beating after each addition until the mixture is light and fluffy.

Alternately add dry ingredients with milk, starting and ending with flour and beating after each addition until smooth.

Add vanilla. Spread batter in two 9-inch greased tins.

Beat egg whites until stiff. Gradually beat in 8 ounces sugar and cinnamon. Spread in equal amounts on top of each layer. Sprinkle thickly with almonds.

Bake in slow oven (325°F. Mark 3) 25 minutes. Increase heat to 350°F. Mark 4 and bake 30 minutes longer.

Remove cake from tins. Cool. Put layers together with crushed sweetened fruit and whipped cream.

SACHER TORTE

A rich chocolate cake named after a famous Viennese restaurant.

4 ounces unsalted butter
$3\frac{1}{2}$ ounces icing sugar
4 ounces plain chocolate, melted
6 eggs, separated
1 tablespoon grated lemon rind
1 teaspoon cinnamon
$\frac{1}{2}$ teaspoon ground cloves
4 ounces toasted white breadcrumbs
$\frac{1}{8}$ teaspoon salt
Apricot jam

Cream butter until soft and creamy. Gradually add sugar and continue beating until well blended.

Beat in chocolate and egg yolks, one at a time, beating well after each addition. Stir in lemon rind, cinnamon, cloves, and breadcrumbs. Mix well.

Beat egg whites with salt until stiff, but not dry. Fold lightly into batter.

Bake in 2 greased 8-inch cake tins in slow oven (325°F. Mark 3) 25 minutes.

Remove from tins and cool. Spread apricot jam between layers. Ice with chocolate icing.

MERINGUE MOLASSES TORTE

Cake:
8 ounces plain flour
$\frac{1}{2}$ teaspoon salt
$\frac{3}{4}$ teaspoon baking powder
$\frac{1}{2}$ teaspoon bicarbonate of soda
3 ounces sugar
1 egg
9 fluid ounces dark molasses or black treacle
6 fluid ounces boiling water
4 ounces fat

Sift flour, salt, baking powder, soda, and sugar together. Add egg and molasses, mix well.

Pour boiling water over fat. Add to flour mixture and beat.

Bake in square cake tin in slow oven (325°F. Mark 3) for 40 minutes.

Meringue:
2 egg whites
3 ounces brown sugar
$\frac{1}{2}$ teaspoon vanilla
1 ounce chopped nuts

Beat egg whites until stiff. Beat in brown sugar gradually. Add vanilla; fold in chopped nuts.

Remove cake from oven after 40 minutes of baking; spread meringue evenly over top.

Return to slow oven (325°F. Mark 3) for 12 to 15 minutes or until meringue is browned.

FRUIT-FILLED CROWN CAKE
(French)

4 ounces butter or margarine
4 ounces plain flour
$\frac{1}{2}$ teaspoon baking powder
4 egg yolks
6 ounces sugar
2 tablespoons water
1 tablespoon rum essence or 1 teaspoon vanilla
4 egg whites
$\frac{1}{2}$ teaspoon salt
8 ounces apricot jam

Melt butter or margarine; cool. Sift together flour and baking powder.

Beat egg yolks in small mixing bowl until blended. Gradually add sugar, beating well after each addition. Continue beating thoroughly until very thick and ivory coloured. (With electric mixer beat at high speed at least 5 minutes.)

Blend in water and rum essence or vanilla. Fold in dry ingredients, $\frac{1}{3}$ at a time. Fold carefully but thoroughly until dry ingredients disappear.

Beat egg whites with salt until stiff but not dry. Fold in egg yolk and flour mixture gently. Add cooled, melted butter; fold just until blended.

Turn into well greased and lightly floured 9-inch ring mould. Fill no more than $\frac{1}{2}$ full.

Bake in moderate oven (350°F. Mark 4) 25 to 30 minutes. Cool. Spread with apricot jam. Fill centre with fruit salad just before serving.

Fruit Salad: Combine 4 oranges in segments (reserve 6 for decoration), 2 bananas, sliced, 1 apple, diced, and 4 ounces well drained pineapple.

Whip $\frac{1}{4}$ pint double cream; fold in 2 tablespoons icing sugar and 1 teaspoon vanilla. Fold $\frac{3}{4}$ of cream into fruit.

Spoon lightly into centre of cake. Decorate with remaining whipped cream and orange sections.

Fruit-Filled Crown Cake

Meringue Molasses Torte

CHESTNUT TORTE

1 pound chestnuts
3 egg yolks
6 whole eggs
3 ounces sugar
2 teaspoons vanilla
3 egg whites
Pinch of salt
¼ pint whipping cream
3 tablespoons crushed pineapple

Make a gash in each chestnut. Place chestnuts in boiling water and cook 20 minutes. Drain and remove both outer and inner shell; press through sieve.

Beat egg yolks and whole eggs; add sugar and beat together thoroughly about 5 minutes with electric mixer or 10 minutes with rotary beater.

Add chestnuts gradually and beat 15 minutes longer. Add vanilla.

Beat the 3 egg whites with salt until stiff, and fold in gently.

Bake in unbuttered torte tin in moderate oven (350°F. Mark 4) 50 minutes.

Coat with vanilla flavoured whipped cream; then fold in 3 tablespoons well drained crushed pineapple.

ORANGE TORTE

1 orange
6 ounces raisins
4 ounces plain flour
½ teaspoon bicarbonate of soda
1 teaspoon baking powder
¼ teaspoon salt
6 ounces brown sugar
4 ounces fat
1 egg
8 fluid ounces buttermilk or sour milk
4 ounces uncooked rolled oats

Squeeze orange and set juice aside. Put orange rind and raisins through medium blade of mincer.

Mix and sift flour, soda, baking powder, and salt into a bowl. Add brown sugar, fat, egg, and orange juice. Beat until smooth.

Fold in orange rind and raisin mixture, buttermilk, and rolled oats. Turn into a greased square cake tin.

Bake in a moderate oven (350°F. Mark 4) 45 to 50 minutes. Serve warm with whipped cream or hard sauce.

Fruit Cocktail Torte

HUNGARIAN TORTE

1 whole egg
6 eggs, separated
6 ounces sugar
6 ounces finely chopped walnuts
1 ounce plain chocolate, grated
1½ ounces dried cake crumbs
½ teaspoon almond essence
Currant jelly
¼ pint double cream, whipped

Beat egg yolks and whole egg until light and lemon-coloured.

Add sugar, nuts, chocolate, and cake crumbs, beating after each addition.

Add almond essence. Fold in stiffly beaten egg whites.

Bake in 2 well buttered and floured 9-inch cake tins in moderate oven (350°F. Mark 4) 15 or 20 minutes.

When cold, cut layers in half and fill with currant jelly. Cover with chocolate icing and top with whipped cream.

FRUIT COCKTAIL TORTE

4 ounces fat
10 ounces sugar
4 eggs, separated
4 ounces plain flour
1 teaspoon baking powder
⅛ teaspoon salt
3 tablespoons milk
1 teaspoon vanilla
Cream filling (below)
1 small can fruit cocktail

Cream fat; add 4 ounces sugar gradually. Cream until light and fluffy. Add well beaten egg yolks and blend.

Mix and sift flour, baking powder, and salt. Add dry ingredients to creamed mixture alternately with milk, beginning and ending with dry ingredients. Mix well. Add vanilla.

Spread batter in 2 greased 9-inch sandwich tins that have been lined with greaseproof paper.

Beat egg whites stiff, then gradually add remaining sugar while continuing to beat. Cover batter with this meringue.

Bake in moderate oven (350°F. Mark 4) about 35 minutes.

Remove from tin and cool, meringue side up on cake racks. When cake is cool, put the 2 layers together with cream filling (below). Top with drained fruit cocktail.

Cream Filling: Scald 8 fluid ounces milk. Combine 2 ounces sugar and 1 tablespoon cornflour; add to 1 beaten egg and blend well.

Add scalded milk gradually, stirring constantly. Cool. Add ½ teaspoon almond essence.

Strawberry Cream Torte

STRAWBERRY CREAM TORTE

2 ounces fat
2 ounces sugar
½ teaspoon vanilla
2 egg yolks
3 ounces plain flour
¼ teaspoon salt
1 teaspoon baking powder
4 tablespoons milk

Cream fat until fluffy. Gradually beat in sugar. Beat in vanilla and egg yolks.

Sift flour, salt, and baking powder together and add alternately with milk to egg mixture.

Pour batter into a well greased 8-inch square cake tin. Top with a meringue made of:

3 egg whites
⅛ teaspoon cream of tartar
4 ounces sugar

Beat egg whites until stiff. Add cream of tartar. Beat in sugar gradually. Spread on cake batter.

Bake in very slow oven (250°F. Mark ½) 25 minutes. Increase heat to moderate (350°F. Mark 4) and bake 20 minutes longer.

Remove from oven and cool. Top with whipped cream mixed with sliced strawberries and decorate with whole berries.

CHOCOLATE WHIPPED CREAM TORTE

7 eggs, separated
1 pound caster sugar
6 ounces plain chocolate, grated
1 teaspoon vanilla
14 ounces ground almonds
Whipped cream, almond-flavoured

Beat egg yolks with 12 ounces sugar until lemon-coloured.

Add grated chocolate, vanilla, and ground almonds. Beat thoroughly.

Beat egg whites until stiff, and fold in remaining sugar. Fold into first mixture.

Bake in 3 well buttered and floured 8-inch cake tins in a slow oven (325°F. Mark 3) about 30 minutes.

When cold, fill and cover with sweetened, almond-flavoured whipped cream.

SICILIAN STRUFOLI

About 8 ounces plain flour
¼ teaspoon salt
3 eggs
¾ pint oil for frying
6 ounces mild-flavoured honey
4 ounces sugar
Pine nuts
Smarties

Place 6 ounces flour and the salt on a board. Make a depression in the centre and add eggs. Use a spatula and mix, adding enough extra flour to make a fairly stiff dough. Knead until smooth.

Using half the dough at a time, roll on a floured board to ¼-inch thickness. Cut into ¼-inch strips. Roll each strip of dough under the hands to form a rope.

Arrange several of these ropes, side by side, and cut into ¼-inch squares. Place these separately on a floured board or tray.

Heat oil to 350°F. in a deep saucepan. Carefully lower the dough by spoonfuls into fat and fry, stirring constantly, until light brown. Remove with a perforated spoon and drain on absorbent paper. Keep warm.

Mix sugar and honey in a large saucepan. Cook over low heat, stirring constantly, to consistency of a heavy syrup, about 5 minutes.

Add fried dough and toss to coat each piece with syrup.

Shape into a mound (or other desired shape) on a serving dish and sprinkle with pine nuts and Smarties. Serves 8.

VIENNA TORTE

7 eggs, separated
10 ounces sugar
4 ounces plain flour
1 ounce cornflour
2 teaspoons baking powder
Pinch of salt

Beat egg whites until frothy. Add 4 ounces sugar gradually and beat until stiff.

Beat egg yolks until thick; then gradually beat in remaining sugar. Combine with first mixture.

Mix and sift flour with cornflour, baking powder, and salt and fold in carefully.

Turn into 4 greased 8-inch sandwich tins. Bake in moderate oven (350°F. Mark 4) about 20 minutes.

Vienna Torte Filling: Heat ½ pint milk in double saucepan. Mix 1½ ounces flour, 3 ounces sugar, and 4 tablespoons cold milk. Add to heated milk and stir until thick, then cover and cook 15 minutes. Cool.

When cool, add 8 ounces melted butter; mix well, then add 1 teaspoon vanilla and 5½ ounces icing sugar. Spread between the layers and on top and sides. Cover well with chopped nuts.

ALMOND TORTE 2

7 egg whites
8 ounces sugar
12 ounces ground almonds
½ teaspoon almond essence

Beat egg whites until stiff. Fold in sugar gradually. Fold in ground almonds. Add almond essence last.

Turn into 2 buttered and floured 9-inch cake tins. Bake in slow oven (325°F. Mark 3) about 40 minutes.

Fill and cover cooled layers with almond torte filling and icing (below).

Almond Torte Filling And Icing:
7 egg yolks
4 ounces sugar
Pinch of salt
4 ounces unsalted butter
½ teaspoon vanilla
1 teaspoon grated orange rind
Flaked almonds

Place egg yolks in top of double saucepan over hot water.

Beat yolks until creamy, gradually adding sugar and salt. Remove and cool.

Cream butter until lemon-coloured and add to first mixture. Add vanilla and orange rind.

Fill and cover layers. Sprinkle with flaked almonds.

ORANGE TORTE 2

10 ounces plain flour
1¼ teaspoons bicarbonate of soda
½ teaspoon salt
1 teaspoon cinnamon
½ teaspoon ground cloves
¼ teaspoon mixed spice
2 ounces chopped citron
2 ounces chopped crystallised pineapple
4 ounces quartered glacé cherries
2 ounces chopped nuts
4 ounces fat
8 ounces sugar
2 well beaten eggs
1 tablespoon grated orange rind
3½ teaspoons vinegar and sour-cream to make 8 fluid ounces
8 ounces sugar
6 fluid ounces orange juice

Sift flour, soda, salt, cinnamon, cloves, and spice together. Add fruit and nuts; mix well.

Cream fat. Add sugar gradually and cream until fluffy. Add eggs and grated orange rind. Beat well.

Mix vinegar and sour cream together. Add alternately with flour mixture to creamed ingredients. Mix until thoroughly blended.

Pour into well greased 9-inch tube tin. Bake in moderate oven (350°F. Mark 4) 1 hour.

After cake is removed from oven and while it is still hot, pour over it the 8 ounces sugar mixed with orange juice. Let cake cool before removing from tin.

MERINGUE CRADLE CAKE

4 egg whites
8 ounces sugar
4 ounces chopped nuts
1 ounce plain chocolate, grated
8 ounces plain flour
3 teaspoons baking powder
1 teaspoon salt
4 ounces butter or margarine
8 ounces sugar
4 egg yolks
6 fluid ounces milk
1 teaspoon vanilla

Beat egg whites until soft mounds form. Gradually add 8 ounces sugar, beating constantly until straight, glossy peaks are formed when beater is raised. Fold in nuts and chocolate.

Spread evenly over bottom and three-quarters up sides of 10-inch tube tin, well greased and lined with greaseproof paper on the bottom only.

Sift together flour, baking powder, and salt.

Cream butter. Gradually add 8 ounces sugar, creaming well. Add egg yolks; beat well.

Combine milk and vanilla. Add alternately with the dry ingredients to creamed mixture, beginning and ending with dry ingredients. Blend thoroughly after each addition. (With electric mixer use a low speed.) Pour into meringue-lined tin.

Bake in slow oven (325°F. Mark 3) 75 to 85 minutes until cake springs back completely, leaving no imprint when touched lightly in centre.

Let cool in tin 20 minutes; loosen from sides and centre tube with spatula and let cool 30 minutes longer before removing from tin.

Note: Cake may also be baked in two 9×5×3 inch bread tins for 50 to 60 minutes.

Meringue Cradle Cake

ROCOCO TORTE

- 5 eggs, separated
- 2½ ounces sugar
- 2 tablespoons fine breadcrumbs
- 1 ounce flour
- 2 ounces grated chocolate

Beat egg yolks until light and lemon-coloured. Add sugar gradually and beat well.

Blend in breadcrumbs, flour, and grated chocolate, then fold in stiffly beaten egg whites.

Turn into two 8-inch well buttered sandwich tins. Bake in a moderate oven (350°F. Mark 4) 30 minutes.

Remove from tins and cool on cake rack. When cool, fill layers and cover the top with creamy walnut icing (below).

Creamy Walnut Icing: Cream together 3 ounces butter and 2 tablespoons sugar. Combine 4 ounces ground walnuts and 4 fluid ounces single cream and stir into the butter-sugar mixture. Add teaspoon vanilla and beat until the mixture is thick and foamy.

ALMOND ANGEL TORTE

- 12 ounces almonds
- ½ pound dates
- 5 eggs, separated
- 4 ounces icing sugar
- 2 teaspoons baking powder

Blanch almonds, reserving a few to decorate the top. Mince the nuts. Stone the dates; pour boiling water over them, drain and rub to a smooth paste.

Beat egg yolks and gradually add sugar and date pulp; then lightly stir in almonds.

Fold baking powder into stiffly beaten egg whites and fold whites into the above mixture.

Turn into a well greased and floured 9-inch spring form tin. Bake in moderate oven (350°F. Mark 4) about 45 minutes.

When cool, cut in 2 layers and spread layers and top with whipped cream. Sprinkle with remaining almonds, sliced.

DATE TORTE

- 2 ounces plain flour
- ⅛ teaspoon salt
- 1 teaspoon baking powder
- 2 beaten eggs
- 4 ounces sugar
- ½ teaspoon vanilla
- ½ teaspoon almond essence
- 4 ounces chopped pecans or walnuts
- 12 ounces chopped dates
- 2 ounces chopped glacé cherries

Mix and sift flour, salt, and baking powder; add eggs beaten with sugar. Add vanilla and almond essence, nuts, and fruits.

Bake in greased 8-inch square tin in slow oven (300°F. Mark 2) 1 hour. Serve topped with whipped cream or with custard sauce. Serves 8.

LEMON ANGEL TORTE

- 1 teaspoon vanilla
- 1 teaspoon vinegar
- 1 teaspoon water
- 3 egg whites
- ½ teaspoon baking powder
- ⅛ teaspoon salt
- 8 ounces sifted sugar
- 1 beaten whole egg
- 4 beaten egg yolks
- 4 ounces sugar
- 1½ tablespoons flour
- 6 fluid ounces water
- Grated rind and juice of 1½ lemons
- ¼ pint double cream
- ½ teaspoon vanilla

Combine 1 teaspoon vanilla, vinegar, and water.

Beat egg whites, baking powder, and salt until stiff. Add 8 ounces sugar in tablespoon portions, alternating with a few drops of combined liquids. Beat until stiff and glossy.

Heap lightly into greased pie plate. Press into shape of pie shell with a spoon.

Bake in very slow oven (275°F. Mark 1) 1 hour.

Combine remaining ingredients except cream and vanilla. Cook in top of double saucepan until thick, stirring constantly. Cool.

Whip cream and flavour with ½ teaspoon vanilla.

When meringue shell is cool, spread part of whipped cream in a layer on the bottom. Pour in the cooled lemon mixture.

Decorate top of pie with remaining whipped cream. Chill several hours before serving.

CHERRY TORTE

- 1 can (about 8 ounces) drained stoned cherries
- 2½ ounces digestive biscuit crumbs
- 4 eggs, separated
- 1 pound sugar
- 4 tablespoons hot cherry juice
- 4 ounces chopped nuts
- 1 teaspoon cinnamon

Mix cherries with 1 ounce crumbs. Set aside.

Beat egg yolks and sugar until lemon-coloured. Blend in cherry juice, then add rest of crumbs and beat until smooth.

Add nuts and cinnamon, then the crumbed cherries and then fold in the stiffly beaten egg whites.

Turn into a greased 9-inch spring-form tin sprinkled with crumbs.

Bake in moderate oven (350°F. Mark 4) 40 to 50 minutes. Serve with whipped cream.

Square Dance Nut Cake

SQUARE DANCE NUT CAKE

- 7 ounces plain flour
- 2 teaspoons baking powder
- ½ teaspoon salt
- 8 ounces sugar
- 4 ounces softened butter
- ¼ pint milk
- 3 egg whites, unbeaten
- ½ teaspoon vanilla
- ¼ teaspoon lemon essence
- 2 ounces chopped walnuts

Sift together flour, baking powder, salt, and sugar. Add butter and milk.

Beat for 1½ minutes, 150 strokes per minute, until batter is well blended. (With electric mixer blend at low speed, then beat at medium speed for 1½ minutes.)

Add egg whites, vanilla, and lemon essence. Beat for 1½ minutes.

Blend in walnuts. Pour into 8×8 ×2-inch tin, well greased and lightly floured on the bottom only.

Bake in moderate oven (350°F. Mark 4) 40 to 50 minutes.

Cool. Cut cake into four squares; ice with checkerboard icing.

Checkerboard Icing: Combine 1 tablespoon warm milk, 2 tablespoons melted butter, 10 ounces sugar, 1 egg yolk, and ½ teaspoon vanilla. Beat until smooth and creamy.

Add 1 ounce plain chocolate, melted and 1 tablespoon milk to one-third of the icing.

Ice two cake squares with white icing, two with chocolate.

Arrange squares checkerboard fashion. Decorate with chopped nuts.

BREADCRUMB CAKE

- 3 eggs
- 8 ounces sugar
- 8 ounces dry crumbs
- ¼ teaspoon cinnamon
- ¼ teaspoon almond essence
- ¼ teaspoon salt
- 1 teaspoon vanilla

Beat eggs, add sugar, and stir in other ingredients. Spread mixture evenly into shallow greased tin.

Bake in slow oven (300°F. Mark 2) about 30 minutes. Cake has a texture and flavour similar to macaroons.

BISCUIT TORTE

6 ounces digestive biscuit crumbs
1¼ teaspoons baking powder
2 ounces chopped pecans or
    walnuts
2 ounces fat
6 ounces sugar
1 egg
6 fluid ounces milk
1 teaspoon vanilla

Mix biscuit crumbs with baking powder and chopped nuts.

Cream fat and sugar together; add egg, milk, and vanilla. Add to first mixture, mix well, and pour into 11×7-inch tin.

Bake in moderate oven (375°F. Mark 5) 20 minutes. Cut in squares and top with whipped cream, or put two layers together with a custard filling and ice with a butter icing. Serves 6.

DUTCH PLUM CAKE

8 ounces plain flour
4 teaspoons baking powder
½ teaspoon salt
1 tablespoon sugar
3 ounces butter
1 beaten egg
About ¼ pint milk
Plums, stoned and quartered
Sugar, cinnamon, butter

Mix and sift flour, baking powder, salt, and sugar. Cut butter into this; add egg and enough milk to make a soft dough.

Spread dough in greased baking tin; cover with a layer of plums. Sprinkle plums with sugar and a little cinnamon; dot with bits of butter.

Bake in hot oven (400°F. Mark 6) about 30 minutes. Serve with cream.

RUSSIAN STRAWBERRY TORTE

8 ounces plain flour
½ teaspoon salt
8 ounces unsalted butter
8 ounces strawberry jam
¾ pint whipped cream
⅛ teaspoon almond essence

Sift together flour and salt. Cut in butter with 2 knives or pastry blender until mixture looks like fine bread-crumbs.

Add enough cold water to hold dough together. Roll out on lightly floured board. Fold 4 times and roll out again. Separate dough into 3 parts and roll out into 3 rounds.

Prick each with a fork several times. Bake in hot oven (400°F. Mark 6) until brown, about 30 to 45 minutes.

Spread 1 round with jam and cover with whipped cream flavoured with almond essence.

Cover with another baked round, spread with jam and whipped cream, and top with third round. Spread with jam and a thick layer of whipped cream.

FRUIT TORTE

8 egg whites
1 teaspoon cream of tartar
Pinch of salt
1 pound sugar
2 teaspoons almond essence
1 pound sweetened fresh or frozen
    peaches, crushed pineapple
    or any fresh berries
¼ pint double cream, whipped

Beat egg whites until frothy and add cream of tartar and salt. Gradually beat in sugar, sprinkling 1 tablespoon at a time over top of egg whites.

Add flavouring and beat until stiff and peaked. Pour into an ungreased 9-inch spring-form tin.

Bake in very slow oven (275°F. Mark 1) 55 to 60 minutes.

Allow to cool. With a spatula or knife, loosen torte by running knife around edge of tin.

When thoroughly cool, remove sides of spring-form tin. Fill slight hollow that forms with fruit and top with flavoured whipped cream. Serves 8 to 12.

DATE AND NUT TORTE

4 ounces plain flour
1½ teaspoons baking powder
½ teaspoon salt
4 ounces fat
1 teaspoon vanilla
8 ounces sugar
2 whole eggs
2 egg yolks (reserve whites for
    meringue)
2 tablespoons water
3 ounces chopped dates
4 ounces chopped walnuts
⅛ teaspoon salt
⅛ teaspoon cream of tartar

Mix and sift flour, baking powder, and ½ teaspoon salt.

Cream fat with vanilla and gradually add 4 ounces sugar, creaming well.

Beat thoroughly 2 whole eggs plus 2 egg yolks, and 2 tablespoons water.

Add eggs and dry ingredients alternately to creamed mixture, beginning and ending with dry ingredients. Blend thoroughly after each addition. (With electric mixer use low speed.) Blend in dates and walnuts.

Turn into greased and floured 9-inch round spring-form tin (2¾ inches deep) or 8×8×2-inch tin lined with greaseproof paper.

Beat 2 egg whites until foamy. Add ⅛ teaspoon salt and cream of tartar; beat until egg whites form slight mounds when beater is raised. Gradually add remaining sugar and beat until meringue forms peaks.

Spread meringue over batter. Bake in slow oven (325°F. Mark 3) 1 hour.

BRAZIL NUT TORTE

2 ounces plain flour
2 teaspoons baking powder
6 ounces digestive biscuit crumbs
4 ounces softened fat
8 ounces sugar
3 egg yolks
3 ounces chopped Brazil nuts
1 teaspoon vanilla
Milk*
3 stiffly beaten egg whites
1 packet vanilla flavoured
    cornflour
¾ pint milk
¼ pint double cream, whipped

Line bottoms of 2 1¼-inch deep 8-inch sandwich tins with greaseproof paper.

Sift together flour and baking powder; add biscuit crumbs.

With electric mixer at medium speed, or "cream" (or with spoon), thoroughly mix fat with 8 ounces sugar, then with egg yolks, until very light and fluffy, about 4 minutes altogether. Add nuts and vanilla.

Then, at low speed, or "blend", beat in flour mixture alternately with indicated amount of milk, beating after each addition.

Quickly fold in egg whites. Turn into tins.

Bake in moderate oven (375°F. Mark 5) 30 minutes or until done. Cool in tins on wire rack.

Meanwhile, combine flavoured cornflour with ¾ pint milk and remaining sugar. Cook, stirring, over medium heat until mixture comes to boil.

Remove from heat; pour into bowl; place greaseproof paper directly on surface of pudding. Refrigerate several hours.

Beat pudding until smooth; fold in whipped cream.

Split each cake layer; spread filling between layers and on top of cake. Refrigerate at least 1 hour.

*Note: With butter, margarine, or lard, use 8 fluid ounces milk. With vegetable or any other fat, use an extra 3-4 tablespoons milk.

SAND TORTE

8 ounces butter
8 ounces sugar
6 eggs, separated
4 ounces plain flour
4½ ounces cornflour
2 teaspoons baking powder
Juice and grated rind of ½ lemon
1½ tablespoons rum or brandy

Cream butter and sugar very well; add beaten yolks.

Mix and sift flour, cornflour, and baking powder; add to creamed mixture with lemon juice and rum or brandy.

Fold in stiffly beaten whites. Turn into greased tube tin. Bake in moderate oven (350°F. Mark 4) 45 minutes.

Easter Cake

APPLE TORTE 2

6 ounces sugar
1 well beaten egg
2 ounces plain flour
½ teaspoon salt
1 teaspoon baking powder
9 ounces peeled and grated tart
    apples
1 teaspoon almond flavouring
2 ounces chopped pecans or walnuts
4 ounces chopped dates
¼ pint double cream, whipped

Beat sugar into egg gradually, using electric mixer. Add sifted dry ingredients and mix thoroughly. Stir in remaining ingredients except cream.

Turn into greased 8×8×2-inch cake tin. Bake in moderate oven (350°F. Mark 4) 30 minutes.

Cut into squares and serve warm topped with whipped cream. Serves 8.

APPLE TORTE 3

6 ounces dry digestive biscuit
    crumbs
6 ounces sugar
1½ teaspoons cinnamon
4 ounces butter, melted
3 large apples
4 tablespoons water
4 eggs, separated
1 small can condensed milk
Juice of 1 lemon
1 teaspoon vanilla
⅛ teaspoon salt

Mix breadcrumbs, sugar, cinnamon, and butter. Press ¾ of this mixture into the bottom and around the sides of a spring-form tin.

Cut the cored apples into pieces; add water and cook slowly until tender, then press through a sieve.

Beat egg yolks until light; add milk, lemon juice, vanilla, salt, and cooked apples. Fold in stiffly beaten whites.

Pour into tin and sprinkle remaining crumbs on top. Bake in moderate oven (375°F. Mark 5) 30 minutes.

CHOCOLATE NUT LOAF

10 ounces plain flour
1 teaspoon bicarbonate of soda
¾ teaspoon salt
8 ounces fat
1 pound sugar
5 eggs
4 ounces finely chopped nuts
3 ounces plain chocolate, melted
8 fluid ounces sour milk or
    buttermilk
2 teaspoons vanilla

Sift flour once, measure, add soda and salt, and sift together 3 times.

Cream fat, add sugar gradually, and cream together until light and fluffy.

Beat eggs until very thick and light; add to creamed mixture and beat well. Add nuts and chocolate and blend.

Add flour, alternately with sour milk, a small amount at a time, beating after each addition until smooth. Add vanilla.

Bake in greased tin, 13×9×2 inches, in slow oven (325°F. Mark 3) 1 hour, or until done. Spread with mocha icing.

DARK MYSTERY CAKE

8 ounces dried figs, steamed and
    chopped fine
7 ounces plain flour
1 teaspoon salt
1 teaspoon bicarbonate of soda
2 teaspoons baking powder
6 ounces fat
8 ounces sugar
3 eggs, separated
3 ounces plain chocolate, melted
½ pint milk
3 ounces sugar for egg whites

Prepare figs, snipping off stems with scissors, then chopping fine.

Measure, mix and sift dry ingredients. Reserve 4 ounces flour mixture for dredging chopped figs.

Cream fat, add sugar and cream thoroughly. Add egg yolks and beat until light, then add melted chocolate. Mix thoroughly.

Add sifted flour mixture alternately with milk, adding in thirds and beating until smooth after each addition. Add fig-flour mixture last.

Beat egg whites until light and gradually beat in 3 ounces sugar. Fold into cake mixture.

Pour into greased 9-inch cake tins. Bake in moderate oven (350°F. Mark 4) 40 minutes or bake in loaf tin at 325°F. Mark 3, 1 hour. Ice with fluffy 7-minute icing or with butter cream icing.

VANILLA TORTE

4 eggs, separated
12 ounces sugar
5 cream crackers crushed finely
1 teaspoon baking powder
1 teaspoon vanilla
½ pint double cream, whipped
2 ounces finely chopped nuts

Beat egg yolks with sugar until thick and lemon-coloured.

Blend in crumbs, baking powder, and vanilla, then fold in stiffly beaten egg whites.

Turn into 2 buttered 9-inch sandwich tins. Bake in moderate oven (350°F. Mark 4) 25 minutes.

Cool on cake rack, then put layers together with half the whipped cream. Sprinkle top with chopped nuts. Dust with icing sugar and decorate with remaining whipped cream.

EASTER CAKE

Cake
6 ounces plain flour
1½ teaspoons baking powder
¼ teaspoon salt
3 ounces fat
6 ounces sugar
1 egg
1 teaspoon vanilla
4 fluid ounces milk

Fluffy Icing:
4 tablespoons cold water
6 ounces sugar
pinch of salt
⅛ teaspoon cream of tartar
2 teaspoons light corn or golden
    syrup
1 egg white
½ teaspoon vanilla
Few drops of yellow food colouring

Sift together flour, baking powder, and ¼ teaspoon salt.

Cream fat with 6 ounces sugar until fluffy; add egg and 1 teaspoon vanilla and beat until very light.

Add sifted dry ingredients alternately with milk to creamed mixture, combining thoroughly.

Pour batter into 8-inch square Pyrex or oven glass dish. Bake in moderate oven (350°F. Mark 4) 30 to 35 minutes or until cake is done. Remove from oven and cool on rack.

Fluffy Icing: Place all icing ingredients except vanilla and colouring in top of double saucepan. Beat with rotary beater until ingredients are combined.

Place over boiling water; continue beating and cook until icing will stand in peaks. Remove from heat; add ½ teaspoon vanilla and yellow colouring and beat until thick enough to spread. Spread on cooled cake.

Decorations: Measure 2 ounces desiccated coconut into a small basin, add about 2 drops green food colouring, mixing with fork until coconut is uniformly green.

Make a nest of coconut on each corner of cake and fill with small sugar eggs.

To make a bunny, elongate a marshmallow to an oval shape with fingers. With scissors, snip long triangular cuts to make ears; push ears up and forward. Shape nose, front feet, and tail by pinching with fingers.

Using red food colouring, paint on eyes, nose, and mouth. Place a bunny on or near each nest.

Cupcakes and Other Finger Cakes

Petits Fours

PETITS FOURS

The French term petits fours may be applied to a wide variety of small cakes, pastries, fancy biscuits, and even some candied fruits; however it usually refers to very small cakes made in various shapes (squares, diamonds, rectangles, triangles, rounds, hearts, etc.) with an icing on the top and sides and delicately decorated.

8 ounces plain flour
2½ teaspoons baking powder
½ teaspoon salt
10 ounces sugar
8 fluid ounces double cream
4 egg whites, unbeaten
1 teaspoon vanilla

Sift together flour, baking powder, salt, and sugar.

Whip cream until stiff and add sifted dry ingredients, egg whites, and vanilla. Beat for 2 minutes, or until batter is well blended and glossy.

If electric mixer is used, beat at low to medium speed for same period of time.

Pour into lightly greased shallow tin lined with greaseproof paper. Bake in moderate oven (350°F. Mark 4) 20 to 25 minutes.

Turn out on cake rack while warm and remove paper. Cool.

Cut with fancy cutters or sharp knife into small squares, diamonds, triangles or any desired shape.

Ice with petits fours icing and decorate as liked with nuts, crystallised fruit, whipped cream, etc. Makes 1 cake, 15 × 10 inches.

DIGESTIVE BISCUIT PETITS FOURS

Bake cake (below) in 12½-inch rectangular baking tin. Cool thoroughly, overnight if possible.

Cut into small squares, triangles, and diamonds as desired. Place on 2 wire racks over greaseproof paper.

Digestive Biscuit Cake:
3 ounces plain flour
6 ounces sugar
2½ teaspoons baking powder
½ teaspoon salt
6 ounces digestive biscuit crumbs
4 ounces fat
6 fluid ounces milk
1 teaspoon vanilla
2 eggs

Mix and sift flour, sugar, baking powder, and salt; combine with crumbs.

Place fat in a bowl. Add dry ingredients, milk, and vanilla; mix until dry ingredients are dampened. Beat 2 minutes in electric mixer or by hand.

Add eggs and beat 1 minute.

Pour into 2 greased paper-lined 8-inch sandwich tins. Bake in moderate oven (375°F. Mark 5) about 25 minutes. Cool. Fill and ice.

Petits Fours Icing:
8 ounces granulated sugar
4 ounces butter or margarine
4 fluid ounces milk
½ teaspoon salt
1 pound icing sugar
½ teaspoon vanilla

Combine granulated sugar, butter or margarine, milk, and salt in saucepan. Bring to a boil over moderate heat; stir constantly. Boil vigorously 1 minute.

Remove from heat; stir in icing sugar and vanilla. Tint with food colouring as desired.

Cool 2 to 3 minutes or until icing is a good consistency for pouring. Pour over petits fours, covering sides with aid of spatula. Re-use surplus until all cakes are covered.

A little melted chocolate added to the surplus makes a delicious chocolate icing.

Note: Pipe or decorate as liked. Makes about 2½ dozen.

PETITS FOURS ICING HINTS

In France Fondant Icing is traditional and the small cakes are often dipped first in Apricot Glaze before the icing is applied.

To apply the glaze, insert a fork into each piece of cake and dip into glaze just to cover the top and sides. Place the pieces with uncoated side down about 1 inch apart on wire racks placed on greaseproof paper or baking sheets. Let stand until glaze sets, about 1 hour. Then cover with warm Fondant Icing. The paper or baking sheets will catch excess icing, which can be reheated and used again.

LADYFINGERS

3 eggs, separated
3 ounces icing sugar
2 ounces plain flour
⅛ teaspoon salt
½ teaspoon vanilla

Beat egg whites until stiff but not dry. Gradually beat in sugar.

Beat egg yolks until thick. Fold into egg whites. Fold in sifted flour and salt. Add vanilla.

With an icing bag and plain tube, shape into fingers (1 × 4½ inches) on baking sheet covered with ungreased heavy paper. Sprinkle with additional icing sugar.

Bake in moderate oven (350°F. Mark 4) 10 to 12 minutes.

Remove from paper with a long sharp knife. Press together in pairs. Makes about 12.

Sponge Drops: Arrange by spoonfuls on baking sheet. Bake as above. Put together in pairs with whipped cream.

MADELEINES

These small French cakes are baked in madeleine or dariole tins, or deep bun tins may be used.

2 eggs
8 ounces sugar
4 ounces plain flour
6 ounces butter, melted and cooled
1 tablespoon light rum
1 teaspoon vanilla or 1 teaspoon grated lemon rind

Combine eggs and sugar in double saucepan; heat until lukewarm, stirring constantly. Remove from heat and beat until thick, but light and creamy.

When cool, gradually add flour. Add cool, melted butter with rum and vanilla.

Pour into tins and bake in hot oven (400°F. Mark 6) about 15 minutes. Makes about 15 cakes.

PEANUT BUTTER CUPCAKES

3 ounces fat
9 ounces brown sugar
3 ounces peanut butter
2 beaten eggs
8 ounces plain flour
½ teaspoon salt
2½ teaspoons baking powder
6 fluid ounces milk
1 teaspoon vanilla

Cream fat and 6 ounces sugar well. Add peanut butter and mix well. Add eggs with remaining sugar.

Mix and sift dry ingredients and add alternately with milk and vanilla.

Fill greased bun tins ½ full. Bake in moderate oven (350°F. Mark 4) 25 minutes. Makes about 24 cupcakes.

FINGER CAKES

9 ounces flour
3¼ teaspoons baking powder
1 teaspoon salt
12 ounces sugar
4 ounces margarine
8 fluid ounces milk
4 egg whites, unbeaten
1½ teaspoons vanilla
¼ teaspoon almond essence

(Mix by hand or in electric mixer. Count only the actual beating time or strokes. Scrape bowl and spoon or beater often.)

Measure sifted flour into sifter and add baking powder, salt, and sugar.

Stir margarine just to soften. Sift in dry ingredients. Add 6 fluid ounces of the milk. Mix until all flour is dampened. Then beat 2 minutes at a low speed of electric mixer or 300 strokes by hand.

Add egg whites, remaining milk, and flavourings. Beat 1 minute longer at a low speed of electric mixer or 150 strokes by hand.

Use a 13 × 9 × 2-inch tin or two 9 × 9 × 2-inch square tins. Line bottom with paper. Pour batter into tin.

Bake in moderate oven (350°F. Mark 4) 25 to 30 minutes.

For a white layer cake, bake in two 9-inch round sandwich tins 25 to 30 minutes. Ice as desired.

When cooled, cut cake in thirds or quarters. Spread each section with icing of different tint.

Mark off "fingers" about 3 × 1 inch, scoring through icing. Decorate with tiny candies, cut citron, etc., to give an assortment. Before serving, cut through cake as marked.

LOW CALORIE CUPCAKES

4 ounces flour
1 teaspoon bicarbonate of soda
½ teaspoon salt
½ teaspoon nutmeg
1 teaspoon cinnamon
2 ounces brown sugar
1½ ounces fat
2 eggs, unbeaten
6 fluid ounces buttermilk or sour milk
4 ounces rolled oats, uncooked
1½ ounces raisins

Mix and sift flour, soda, salt, and spices into bowl.

Add sugar, fat, eggs, and about half the buttermilk. Beat until smooth, about 2 minutes.

Fold in remaining buttermilk, rolled oats, and raisins. Fill small paper baking cups or greased small bun tins ½ full.

Bake in moderate oven (375°F. Mark 5) 12 to 15 minutes. Makes 20 cupcakes, about 82 calories each.

THREE-IN-ONE CUPCAKES

8 ounces flour
3 teaspoons baking powder
¼ teaspoon salt
4 ounces butter
8 ounces sugar
2 eggs, unbeaten
6 fluid ounces milk
1 teaspoon vanilla

Sift together flour, baking powder, and salt.

Cream butter and sugar until soft and creamy. Add eggs. Beat until light and fluffy. Add dry ingredients alternately with milk, mixing thoroughly. Add vanilla.

Divide batter into 3 parts. Leave ⅓ of batter plain. Fill bun tins ⅔ full and bake in moderate oven (375°F. Mark 5) 20 to 30 minutes.

Ice plain batter cupcakes with chocolate icing and chocolate vermicelli when cool.

Prepare fruit cupcakes and spice nut cakes from remainder of batter.

Fruit Cupcakes: To ⅓ of batter add 2 ounces raisins, 2 ounces chopped citron, and 2 ounces coconut. Bake. Ice with butter icing. Decorate with fruits.

Spice Nut Cakes: To ⅓ of batter add 1 ounce grated nuts and ¼ teaspoon each of cinnamon and cloves. Serve plain or iced.

CHOCOLATE CHIP CUPCAKES

3 ounces margarine
6 ounces sugar
2 eggs, unbeaten
1 teaspoon vanilla
9 ounces flour
3 teaspoons baking powder
1 teaspoon salt
¼ pint milk
Chocolate vermicelli

Cream margarine. Add sugar gradually, creaming continually. Beat in 1 egg at a time and add vanilla.

Mix and sift flour, baking powder, and salt. Add to first mixture alternately with milk.

Place half of batter in greased deep bun tins. Sprinkle with half of chocolate vermicelli.

Add remaining batter and sprinkle with remaining chocolate vermicelli.

Bake in moderate oven (375°F. Mark 5) 20 to 25 minutes. Makes 18 cupcakes.

ORANGE CUPCAKES

4½ ounces plain flour
2 teaspoons baking powder
¼ teaspoon salt
2 ounces fat
1 teaspoon grated orange rind
6 ounces sugar
1 egg, unbeaten
4 tablespoons orange juice
4 tablespoons evaporated milk

Mix and sift flour, baking powder and salt.

Cream fat with orange rind. Add sugar gradually and cream until fluffy. Add egg and beat until well blended.

Mix the orange juice and evaporated milk. Add flour mixture alternately with juice-milk mixture, beginning and ending with flour.

Fill well greased deep bun tins ⅔ full. Bake in moderate oven (375°F. Mark 5) until golden brown, about 20 minutes. Makes about 15 medium-sized cupcakes.

COCONUT PINEAPPLE CUPCAKES

7 ounces plain flour
1½ teaspoons baking powder
¼ teaspoon salt
4 ounces fat
8 ounces sugar
2 eggs, unbeaten
2 tablespoons water
4 ounces canned crushed pineapple
1 teaspoon vanilla
4 ounces desiccated coconut

Measure sifted flour, add baking powder and salt, and sift together 3 times.

Cream fat, add sugar gradually, and cream together until light and fluffy. Add eggs, one at a time, beating well.

Combine water, crushed pineapple, and vanilla; add to egg mixture, alternately with flour, beating after each addition until smooth. Add ¼ of the coconut.

Spoon batter into paper baking cups filling each only half-full. Sprinkle batter with remaining coconut. Bake in moderate oven (375°F. Mark 5) 20 to 25 minutes. Makes 24.

LEMON MOLASSES CUPCAKES

4 ounces fat
4 ounces sugar
1 well beaten egg
6 ounces molasses or black treacle
8 ounces plain flour
2 teaspoons baking powder
½ teaspoon bicarbonate of soda
1½ teaspoons cinnamon
¼ teaspoon salt
4 fluid ounces milk
1 tablespoon grated lemon rind

Cream fat until soft and smooth. Gradually add sugar, beating until fluffy. Beat in egg, then molasses. Beat vigorously.

Mix and sift flour with baking powder, soda, cinnamon, and salt. Add alternately with milk, beating briskly after each addition. Add lemon rind.

Fill greased, floured deep bun tins ½ full. Bake in moderate oven (350°F. Mark 4) 30 minutes. Makes 15 to 20 cupcakes.

Making Use of Cake Mixes

THREE-COLOUR LAYER CAKE

Prepare cake mix as directed on packet.

Divide into 3 parts. Use ⅓ for white layer. Colour ⅓ pink with a few drops of red food colouring. Colour ⅓ yellow or other desired colour.

Pour batter into 3 prepared 8-inch sandwich tins.

Bake in moderate oven (350°F. Mark 4) about 18 minutes. Spread orange marmalade between layers. Ice top and sides with orange icing.

SURPRISE COFFEE CAKE

To dry cake mix, add 4 teaspoons instant coffee then proceed as directed on packet.

SHADOW CAKE

Prepare cake mix batter and just before turning into tin, fold in 2 ounces grated chocolate and ½ teaspoon peppermint extract.

STRAWBERRY WHIP CAKE

1 packet cake mix
½ pound fresh or frozen straw-
    berries
¼ ounce gelatine
1 tablespoon lemon juice
8 fluid ounces whipped cream

Make cake according to packet directions, baking in two 8-inch sandwich tins. Cool; split cakes in half to make 4 layers.

Soften gelatine in strawberry juice or water, dissolve over hot water. Slice strawberries, add lemon juice and dissolved gelatine.

Chill until mixture is slightly thickened. Fold whipped cream into strawberry mixture. Spread strawberry mixture between layers and ice sides and top of cake. Chill thoroughly before slicing. Makes 10 to 12 servings.

Variation: Use Strawberry Whip as a topping for slices of angel food cake, or sponge cake.

Strawberry Whip Cake

WEDDING CAKE

A ready prepared cake mixture can be used to make the beautiful cake in the picture. For a 4 tiered cake you will need 7 packets of white cake mix and 7 pounds of mixed fruit. You will need a 'very large bowl if you are making it all up at one time. All tins should be greased and lined with paper. Use 2 round tins about 13×2½ inches; 2 tins about 10×2½ inches; 3 tins about 8 inches across and 1 tin about 5, preferably with a loose bottom.

Bake all cakes in a slow oven (325°F. Mark 3). Bake the 13-inch cakes 2¼ hours or until skewer inserted in centre comes out clean, 10-inch cakes 2 hours, 8-inch cakes 1½ hours, 5-inch cake 1 hour.

Cool all cakes before removing from tins. Cakes may be baked in advance and frozen until needed.

Wedding Cake Icing:
8 ounces unsalted butter
1 teaspoon salt
about 8 pounds sifted icing sugar
10 egg whites, unbeaten
8 fluid ounces (approximately) milk
1 tablespoon rum essence or
    brandy (or desired flavour-
    ing)

Cream butter; add salt. Gradually add about 8 ounces icing sugar. Blend well. Add remaining sugar alternately with egg whites and milk; beat until thick enough to spread. Add flavouring.

Keep icing bowl covered with a damp cloth while icing cake.

Cut a circle of cardboard to fit under each tier and put two cakes of the same size together with icing. (Cardboard will keep tiers level.)

Ice entire cake with a very thin layer of icing. Allow to dry thoroughly, then put on another coat. Smooth with a spatula dipped in boiling water. Use remaining icing for decorations.

To make scallop design, as shown, mark design outline by pressing a teacup into icing around top edge of bottom tier. Use round biscuit cutters in graduated sizes to mark design on remaining tiers. Cake makes about 130 slices.

SEAFOAM CAKE SQUARES

Prepare batter from 1 packet plain cake mix. Pour into greased 13×9½× 2-inch tin. Top with mixture made by beating 6 ounces brown sugar into 2 stiffly-beaten egg whites. Sprinkle with 2 ounces chopped nuts.

Bake in moderate oven (375°F. Mark 5) until cake is done.

For the Bride: white cake mix baked in four graceful tiers and iced in pure white makes the wedding cake of her dreams. The cakes may be baked in advance and frozen until you are ready to decorate the cake.

CRANBERRY UPSIDE-DOWN CAKE

Use 1 packet white cake mix. Substitute 4 fluid ounces pineapple juice for part of liquid.

Melt 2 ounces butter or margarine in an ungreased 12×8×2inch tin. Add 3 ounces brown sugar, and stir until sugar is dissolved. Add ½ pound fresh cranberries and 6 ounces drained, crushed pineapple.

Cover with cake batter. Bake in moderate oven (375°F. Mark 5) 30 to 40 minutes.

For variations add any of the following fruits, well drained, cut side up. Use liquid specified in directions on label in preparing batter:

Apricot or Peach Upside-Down Cake: 12 apricot halves or 6 peach halves.

Pineapple Upside-Down Cake: 6 slices pineapple; fill centres with whole maraschino cherries.

PINEAPPLE CAKE

Use 1 packet white cake mix. Fold in 6 ounces drained, crushed pineapple and 1 tablespoon grated lemon rind, just before turning into tin.

Fill and ice the cake with pineapple butter icing.

CHERRY PASTEL CAKE

Prepare white cake mix batter and just before turning batter into pan, fold in 2 ounces well drained maraschino cherries and 2 ounces finely chopped toasted almonds.

LEMON PUDDING CAKE

Prepare 1 packet lemon pie filling following packet directions.

Spread filling in oblong tin (13×9½ ×2 inches). Let stand while making cake batter.

Make white cake mix batter according to directions on packet. Pour over lemon filling.

Bake in moderate oven (350°F. Mark 4) 35 to 40 minutes. Sift icing sugar over the top.

Serve warm or cold. If served cold, lemon filling will be stiffer.

BRAZIL NUT CAKE

Use 1 packet white cake mix. Fold in 2 ounces chopped, browned Brazil nuts, just before turning batter into tins. (Brown nuts by spreading them in a shallow tin; dot with 1 tablespoon butter or margarine and bake in moderate oven (350°F. Mark 4) 10 minutes.)

OLD WOMAN IN A SHOE CAKE

Prepare two 1 pound packets white cake mix according to directions on packet and bake in bread tins.

When cakes are cool, cut ⅓ from end of one loaf. Cut other end of this loaf in a rounded shape for toe of shoe.

Cut a small amount from one end of second loaf. Stand on end at the straight end of the first loaf, with bottom of cake against the other loaf and rounded side facing out.

Cut the top of the vertical loaf to make it level. Spread with a little icing and place the ⅓ cut from first cake on top.

Ice entire cake with your favourite fluffy icing.

Make shoe laces and windows from pieces of licorice ropes with shutters of sugar wafers. The door is made of sugar wafers and the chimney is pieces of marzipan. The children are small lollipops with pipe cleaner arms and faces piped in icing.

FRUIT COCKTAIL UPSIDE-DOWN CAKE

Coat bottom of buttered cake tin with 3 tablespoons brown sugar and arrange drained fruit from a small can of fruit cocktail in bottom.

Cover with cake batter made from a packet of white cake mix and bake according to directions on packet.

Serve warm with rum-flavoured whipped cream to which remaining fruit cocktail is added. Serves 8.

MOCHA DATE CAKE

Use 1 packet white cake mix. Reduce the liquid specified on packet by about ¼ pint.

Combine 3 ounces finely chopped dates with 4 fluid ounces hot strong instant coffee and allow to cool. Add coffee-date mixture with last addition of liquid.

Fill with date and nut filling; ice with coffee icing.

ALMOND PISTACHIO ANGEL FOOD CAKE

Use 1 packet angel cake mix. Add ¼ teaspoon almond essence to batter and colour with a few drops green food colouring.

Fold in 4 ounces finely sliced blanched almonds just before turning into the tin.

PINK PEPPERMINT ANGEL FOOD CAKE

Use 1 packet angel cake mix. Add 1 teaspoon peppermint flavouring to liquid and tint batter a delicate pink with red food colouring. Bake as directed on packet.

COFFEE ANGEL FOOD CAKE

Use 1 packet angel cake mix. Stir 1 tablespoon instant coffee into liquid called for on packet.

COCONUT ANGEL FOOD CAKE

Use 1 packet angel cake mix. Fold 2-3 ounces desiccated coconut into batter just before turning into the tin.

PINK ANGEL CAKE

Prepare and bake angel cake mix according to packet directions.

Split the cool cake into 2 layers. Put together and ice with fluffy icing tinted pale pink with red food colouring.
Note: For a party touch, decorate with sliced strawberries.

Old Woman in a Shoe Cake: "There was an old woman who lived in a shoe" —you remember the Old Mother Goose nursery rhyme! Well, here is the storybook shoe in edible form—made of white cake mix and biscuits—an ideal centrepiece and theme for a children's party.

BANANA SPICE CAKE

1 packet spice cake mix
1 pint double cream, whipped and sweetened
3 to 4 bananas

Use your favourite spice cake mix. Prepare according to packet directions. Bake in 2 9-inch square greased tins 25 to 30 minutes, or until skewer comes out clean and dry.

Cool, remove from tin and cover one square with some of the whipped cream.

Place 3 or 4 whole bananas on top; cover with whipped cream. Top with other cake layer; ice top and sides with remaining whipped cream.

Banana Spice Cake

ANGEL FOOD SPICE CAKE

Use 1 packet angel food cake mix. Add 1 teaspoon cinnamon, ¼ teaspoon nutmeg, and ½ teaspoon mixed spice to dry ingredients. Bake as directed on packet.

FRUIT COCONUT CAKE

1 large packet white cake mix
1 can fruit cocktail
½ pound orange marmalade
4 ounces desiccated coconut
whipped cream (optional)

Mix cake and bake according to packet directions, baking in 9×13 ×2-inch tin.

While cake is warm, drain fruit cocktail thoroughly and arrange over top of cake.

Warm marmalade gently, stir in coconut, and spread over fruit. Place under grill until lightly browned. Serve warm, plain or topped with whipped cream. Makes 12 to 15 servings.

Fruit Coconut Cake

COCONUT BUTTERSCOTCH CAKE

1 packet white cake mix
2 ounces butter or margarine
6 ounces brown sugar
2 tablespoons single cream or top of the milk
4 ounces desiccated coconut

Prepare cake according to directions on packet. Pour into greased 11×7×1½-inch tin. Bake in moderate oven (375°F. Mark 5) 25 to 30 minutes.

Cream butter and sugar. Add cream or milk, mix well and add coconut.

Remove cake from oven, while warm; spread with coconut mixture. Grill until golden brown, about 5 minutes. Cool. Cut in squares.

MARSHMALLOW CUPCAKES

Make cupcakes from a packet of cake mix. Top each baked cake with a marshmallow. Put back in oven until marshmallows melt and toast.

STRAWBERRY JELLY CREAM CAKE

Prepare 2 (8-inch) sandwich tins and make cake, using a packet mix. Let cool thoroughly, then split each layer crosswise with a sharp knife to make two thinner layers.

For filling, beat ½ pint jelly made with a tablet of strawberry jelly with a rotary or electric beater for a few seconds to make it easy to spread.

Put the four layers together with the jelly between.

Ice top and sides of cake with jelly cream icing (below).

Store cake in refrigerator until time to serve.

Jelly Cream Icing:
8 fluid ounces double cream
¼ pint strawberry jelly

Whip cream until stiff. Using the same beater, whip jelly for a few seconds. Gently fold jelly into cream. Spread on cake.

Birthday Girl Cake

CHRISTMAS WREATH CAKE

Use 1 packet white cake mix. Divide batter into two bowls.

To one half add ¼ teaspoon almond essence and add red food colouring to make batter a delicate pink.

To other half add ½ teaspoon vanilla and tint delicate green with food colouring.

Pour pink batter into prepared 9-inch ring mould; cover with green batter. Streak lightly with spatula.

Fill prepared mould half full; bake remaining batter in patty tins. Ice with a fluffy icing. Decorate with crystallized cherries and angelica.

LEMON CAKE

Prepare white cake mix batter as directed on packet. Add 2 teaspoons grated lemon rind just before turning into tin.

BIRTHDAY GIRL CAKE

Bake two layers of delicate white cake, using one of the ready-prepared packet mixes.

Cool the layers, then put them together and cover with this soft and fluffy icing.

Blushing Pink Icing:
12 ounces sugar
2½ fluid ounces warm water
2 egg whites (at room temperature)
1 teaspoon lemon juice
3 drops oil of peppermint
red food colouring

Place sugar, water, egg whites, and lemon juice in the top section of double boiler; beat with an electric or rotary beater for about 1 minute, stirring around sides and bottom with a rubber scraper. (This pre-cook beating helps to dissolve the sugar and prevent graininess in the completed icing.)

Set top section of double boiler over boiling water and continue beating until icing stiffens and holds its shape. (Be sure to use the rubber scraper occasionally during this cooking.) The beating will take about 7 minutes, a little more or less depending upon the size of the double boiler and the vigour of beating.

Turn icing out into a wide-topped bowl and add flavouring, and red colouring, a few drops at a time to get desired shade. Beat for about 2 minutes (this helps to get the icing to perfect smoothness) until icing is slightly cooled.

Ice cake between layers, around sides and top, swirling it generously. Group fat deep pink fondants on top, with pink and blue satin ribbon bows, clusters of baby roses and forget-me-nots. Place small bouquets at intervals around cake.

CRANBERRY LOAF CAKE

1 packet white cake mix
6 fluid ounces milk
2 eggs

Prepare cake mix according to packet directions using milk and eggs. Bake in a slow oven (325°F. Mark 3) 1¼ hours. Cool.

Slice cake lengthwise into three layers. Spread Cranberry Filling (below) on two layers. Stack and top with third layer. Ice with Butter Icing (below).

Cranberry Filling:
2 ounces sugar
2 tablespoons cornflour
1 can whole cranberry sauce
1 tablespoon lemon juice
2 ounces chopped walnuts

Combine sugar and cornflour. Add cranberry sauce, lemon juice, and walnuts. Cook until mixture thickens and clears. Cool.

Butter Icing:
4 ounces softened butter or margarine
1 pound sifted icing sugar
3 fluid ounces or less fruit juice

Cream butter with 6 ounces icing sugar. Add remaining sugar alternately with fruit juice. Beat until smooth and of spreading consistency. Ice top and sides of cake. Makes 8 to 10 servings.

Cranberry Loaf Cake

POLKA DOT CAKE

Use 1 packet white cake mix. Fold in 3 ounces finely grated chocolate pieces and ½ teaspoon peppermint flavouring.

Ice the baked cake with a white icing to which peppermint flavouring has been added. Decorate with polka dots.

VANILLA NUT CAKE

Flavour white cake mix batter with a few drops vanilla essence. After turning batter into tin, sprinkle with 2 ounces finely chopped nuts.

DATE CAKE

Prepare white cake mix batter and just before turning into tin, add 3 ounces finely chopped stoned dates and 1 teaspoon grated lemon rind.

EASTER LAMB CAKE

If you have a cake mould in the shape of a lamb or rabbit, this makes a good Easter party cake.

Prepare 1 packet white cake mix as directed on packet.

Pour batter into the face half of well greased mould. (Be sure some batter is placed in each ear.) Cover with back of mould and wire or tie mould together.

Place mould face down on baking sheet and bake in very hot oven (450°F. Mark 8) 10 minutes. Reduce heat to 350°F. Mark 4 and bake 35 minutes longer.

Remove mould from oven and open, removing back of mould first. Allow to cool in face of mould about 5 minutes. Loosen cake from sides of mould and remove carefully. Stand lamb cake upright on cake rack until cool.

Ice with fluffy icing (below). Cover with 1 can moist coconut. Use sultanas for eyes and nose and slice of maraschino cherry for mouth.

Fluffy Icing: Combine 1 unbeaten egg white, 6 ounces sugar, dash of salt, 3 tablespoons water, and 1 teaspoon light corn syrup or golden syrup in top of small double boiler. Beat with rotary egg beater about 1 minute, or until thoroughly mixed.

Cook over rapidly boiling water, beating constantly with rotary egg beater 4 minutes or until icing will stand in stiff peaks.

Remove from boiling water. Add ½ teaspoon vanilla and beat 1 minute or until thick enough to spread.

CHOCOLATE FLECK CAKE

Prepare white cake mix batter as directed on packet. Grate 1 or 2 ounces plain chocolate and fold into batter just before turning into tin.

RAINBOW PARTY CAKE

Prepare cake batter, using any recipe desired.

Divide into 4 portions. Tint 1 portion yellow, 1 green, and 1 red. Leave 4th portion uncoloured. Place alternate spoonfuls of each colour in buttered sandwich tins. Bake.

Put layers together with fluffy boiled icing. Serve with ice cream.

For special occasions, use a cake plate large enough so that a few flowers may be placed around the border of the dish for decoration. Green leafy sprays are also nice to use.

BANANA SPICE CAKE

Use 1 packet white cake mix. Mix in 2 teaspoons cinnamon, pinch ground cloves, ½ teaspoon nutmeg, and 1 teaspoon mixed spice.

Substitute 2 mashed bananas for 2½ fluid ounces liquid specified in directions on label. Fold in 2 ounces chopped walnuts.

Ice the baked cake with a fluffy white icing.

CHRISTMAS TREE UPSIDE-DOWN CAKE

Use 1 packet white cake mix. Fold in 2 ounces finely chopped glacé fruits, just before turning batter into tin.

Fill prepared Christmas tree mould half full. Bake remaining batter in patty tins.

ANGEL PEACH COCONUT CAKE

1 packet angel cake mix
½ tablet orange jelly
1 can sliced peaches, drained
8 fluid ounces double cream, whipped
4 ounces desiccated coconut

Prepare and bake angel cake mix in tube tin as directed on packet. Cool.

Remove from tin. Cut centre from cake to make hole 4 inches across. Place cake on flat plate.

Prepare jelly as directed on packet. Chill until partially set and fold in peaches. Fill centre of cake with this mixture. Chill until set.

Ice top and sides with whipped cream and sprinkle with coconut.

ENCORE CAKE

½ pound figs, stewed
1 packet spice cake mix
¼ pint juice from stewed figs
2 whole eggs
2 tablespoons water
moistened coconut

With scissors snip the stems off the stewed figs. Then place the figs in a mixing bowl and beat hard with electric or hand beater. The figs will be whirled into small bits.

Add the contents from the spice cake mix, plus most of the juice from the stewed figs. Beat for 2 minutes.

Add the eggs and beat 1 minute. Then add the rest of the water and beat at low speed for 1 more minute.

Place in two well-buttered 9-inch sandwich tins. Bake in moderate oven (350°F. Mark 4) about 25 minutes. Cool slightly.

Ice with your favourite vanilla flavoured seven minute icing with lots of coconut sprinkled on the icing, between the layers and on top.

PARTY TORTE

1 packet angel cake mix
1 rounded tablespoon instant coffee
3 ounces brown sugar
20 fig rolls, crumbled
8 fluid ounces milk
2 tablespoons butter
2 lightly beaten egg yolks
1 teaspoon vanilla
¾ pint double cream
2 teaspoons instant coffee
3 ounces icing sugar
1 teaspoon vanilla
2 ounces crushed toffee

Follow directions on the angel food mix packet, placing water in the mixing bowl. Then spoon out 3 tablespoons water, add the instant coffee, stir to dissolve, return to bowl.

Proceed as usual in making the cake. Bake it in two 9-inch ungreased sandwich tins. Bake in a moderate oven (375°F. Mark 5) for about 20 minutes.

Cool upside down on cake racks. When cold remove from the tins.

Meanwhile, in a saucepan combine brown sugar, rolls, milk, and butter.

Stir over low heat until the biscuits almost blend with the milk. Pour onto the egg yolks and cook for a minute more. Cool and add vanilla.

Meanwhile, stir the second measure of instant coffee into a little of the cream. Add to the cream, sugar, and vanilla and whip until very stiff.

Spread both cake layers with the fig mixture, then with the cream. Sprinkle top generously with the crushed toffee. Place in refrigerator at once. Serve very cold. Serves 8 to 10.

Party Torte

NUT CAKE

Prepare white cake mix batter as directed on packet. Add 2 ounces finely chopped nuts just before turning into the tins.

Encore Cake

MYSTERY MOCHA CAKE

1 packet cake mix (white, spice, or
  chocolate)
3 ounces brown sugar
4 ounces white sugar
4 tablespoons cocoa
8 fluid ounces cold strong coffee

Prepare cake mix as directed on
packet. Pour into greased 9-inch square
cake tin.

Combine sugars and cocoa. Sprinkle
evenly over batter. Pour coffee over
top.

Bake in moderate oven (350°F. Mark
4) 40 minutes. Serve warm.

SPICY PUMPKIN CAKE

1 packet honey spice cake mix
  (see note below)
½ teaspoon bicarbonate of soda
2 ounces chopped walnuts
8 ounces cooked or canned pumpkin
3 ounces finely-cut stoned dates

Combine cake mix and bicarbonate
of soda, then proceed according to
packet directions, substituting the
pumpkin for the last addition of liquid.
Fold in nuts and dates.

Pour batter into 2 greased and
floured 9-inch sandwich tins; bake as
directed on packet.

Fill and ice with honey whipped
cream (below). Decorate top with
mixed diced glacé fruits and candied
peel.

Honey-Whipped Cream: Whip 8 fluid
ounces double cream until fluffy; whip
in 3 tablespoons honey and ¼ teaspoon
cinnamon.

Note: Or use white cake mix with
spices added as suggested on packet,
adding soda at the same time. Add 8
ounces pumpkin instead of last addition of liquid. You can use either the
type of cake mix which calls for fresh
eggs or the type which calls for the
addition of liquid only.

QUICK MARBLE CAKE

Make up ½ packet white cake mix and
half a packet of chocolate cake mix.
Bake in paper-lined 13×9×2-inch tin.

Remove from tin; cool on rack. Cut
in half lengthwise to give two layers.
Ice between layers, on sides and top
with fudgy cream-cheese icing (below).

Fudgy Cream-Cheese Icing: Have 6
ounces cream cheese at room temperature. Blend with 2 tablespoons milk.
Gradually beat in 1¾ pounds sifted
icing sugar.

Melt and slightly cool 2 ounces plain
chocolate; blend into sugar mixture.
Stir in 1 teaspoon vanilla and dash of
salt.

COCOA MERINGUE TORTE

1 packet white cake mix
4 egg whites
⅛ teaspoon cream of tartar
dash of salt
6 ounces sugar
3 ounces finely chopped walnuts
cocoa whipped cream (below)

Prepare cake mix according to
packet directions and pour into 2
paper-lined 9×1½-inch round tins.
Beat egg whites until foamy. Add
cream of tartar and salt; continue
beating until soft peaks form. Add
sugar gradually, beating until glossy
and sugar is dissolved.

Fold in nuts. Spread mixture carefully over cake batter in both tins.

Bake in moderate oven (375°F. Mark
5) 25 to 30 minutes.

Cool cake in tins 10 minutes; then
remove from tins to finish cooling.
Ice tops and sides with cocoa whipped
cream.

Cocoa Whipped Cream: Combine ½
pint double cream. 4 ounces sugar, and
1 ounce cocoa; chill 1 hour. Beat until
stiff. Decorate cake with walnut halves.

CHOCOLATE POLKA-DOT CAKE WITH WHITE ICING

1 packet chocolate or devil's food
   cake mix
2 egg whites
12 ounces sugar
¼ teaspoon cream of tartar
2½ fluid ounces cold water
dash of salt
1 teaspoon vanilla
chocolate polka dots

Prepare chocolate cake mix and bake
in sandwich tins as directed on packet.
Cool.

Combine egg whites, sugar, cream of
tartar, water, and salt in double
boiler. Beat 1 minute with electric
mixer or rotary beater. Then cook
over boiling water, beating constantly
until icing forms peaks, about 7
minutes.

Remove from boiling water; add vanilla; beat until of spreading consistency, about 2 minutes.

Ice tops and sides of cakes, sandwich
together and decorate with polka dots.

FLAMING PEACH CAKE

Prepare a honey spice cake, see above,
from a packet of prepared mix. Let
cake cool, then fill and top with sweetened whipped cream.

Arrange well drained cling peach
halves on top, cut side up.

In the centre of each peach, place
a lump of sugar soaked in lemon
essence. Then set light to sugar lumps
and serve while flaming.

JELLY ICED LAYER CAKE

Make 2 (8-9 inch) sandwich cakes,
using a packet mix or your favourite
recipe. Let cool thoroughly, then
spread jelly fluff icing (below) between layers and over top and sides
of cake.

Jelly Fluff Icing:
½ pint wine jelly (preferably made
   with port or red table wine
   for colour)
2 egg whites
dash of salt

Place jelly in a small saucepan; stir
over medium heat until melted and
bubbling. Beat egg whites until stiff
but not dry.

Add salt, then gradually beat in the
hot jelly. Continue to beat until icing
holds its shape when the beater is
drawn through it. Spread on cake.

Wine Jelly:
Measure 1½ pounds sugar into top
of double boiler. Add ¾ pint sherry,
sauternes, burgundy, port, muscatel,
or tokay; mix well.

Place over rapidly boiling water and
heat 2 minutes, stirring constantly.

Remove from water and at once stir
in ½ bottle liquid fruit pectin. Pour
quickly into glasses. Seal at once.
Makes about 5 6-ounce glasses.

Jelly Layer Cake

MAPLE-NUT DEVIL'S FOOD CAKE

Use 1 packet devil's food cake mix.
Add a few drops maple flavouring to
batter. After turning into tin, sprinkle
with 2 ounces finely chopped nuts.

DEVIL'S FOOD NUT CAKE

Prepare devil's food cake mix batter
and fold in 2 ounces finely chopped
nuts before turning into tin.

COCONUT DEVIL'S FOOD CAKE

Prepare devil's food cake mix batter
and fold in 2-3 ounces desiccated coconut before turning into tin.

APRICOT STAR CAKE

Use 1 packet chocolate cake mix. Substitute ¼ pint apricot juice for an equal amount of the liquid. Fold in 5 ounces chopped dried apricots. Fill prepared star mould half full.

Bake remaining batter in patty tins. Ice with ornamental icing. Decorate with dragées, candied cherries, angelica.

CHERRY-NUT ANGEL FOOD CAKE

Use 1 packet angel food cake mix. Fold in 4 ounces chopped, drained maraschino cherries and 2 ounces chopped walnuts. Bake as directed on packet.

CHOCOLATE ANGEL FOOD CAKE

Use 1 packet angel food cake mix. Sift 2 tablespoons cocoa with ¼ of dry ingredients.

Fold into beaten egg white mixture. Bake as directed on packet.

GINGERBREAD WASHINGTON PIE

Bake gingerbread mix on a greased pie plate. When cool split in two. Prepare molasses cornflour pudding (below) or use desired packet pudding. Cool; spread between layers. Sprinkle top layer with caster sugar.

Molasses Cornflour Pudding:
2½ tablespoons cornflour
½ pint cold milk
1 beaten egg
⅛ teaspoon salt
3 ounces molasses or treacle
1 tablespoon butter or margarine
1 teaspoon vanilla

Mix cornflour with 4 tablespoons of the cold milk. Scald remaining milk and stir into cornflour mixture. Cook over hot water until thick and smooth.

Combine well beaten egg, salt, and molasses. Add gradually to milk, stirring all the while. Continue cooking until thick and smooth.

Remove from heat. Stir in butter or margarine. Cool slightly, then add vanilla.

Gingerbread Washington Pie

TUTTI-FRUTTI GINGERBREAD

Use 1 packet gingerbread or ginger cake mix. Fold in 4 ounces chopped fresh cranberries and 3 ounces chopped sultanas. Bake as directed on packet.

CREAM CHEESE GINGERBREAD

Prepare 1 packet gingerbread or ginger cake mix and bake as directed on packet.

Add 4 tablespoons single cream to 3 ounces cream cheese; beat until fluffy, adding additional cream if necessary. Spread over gingerbread after it has been removed from tin.

CRUNCHY-TOP GINGERBREAD

Prepare 1 packet gingerbread mix. Bake in greased 10×6×1½-inch tin in moderate oven (350°F. Mark 4) 30 minutes. Sprinkle with crunchy topping (below). Bake 10 minutes.

Crunchy Topping: Combine 1½ ounces brown sugar, 2 tablespoons plain flour, 2 tablespoons butter or margarine, dash of salt, 1 teaspoon cinnamon, and 2 ounces chopped walnuts; mix thoroughly.

SPICY APPLE SAUCE GINGERBREAD

Use 1 packet gingerbread or ginger cake mix; add 1 teaspoon cinnamon and 1 teaspoon nutmeg to dry mix.

Substitute 9 ounces canned apple sauce or ½ pint thick apple purée for 6 fluid ounces of the liquid. Bake as directed on packet.

SUGAR AND SPICE GINGER CAKE

Use 1 packet gingerbread or ginger cake mix. Pour batter into prepared tin.

Before baking, sprinkle lightly with this topping: Mix together 3 ounces brown sugar, 2 tablespoons plain flour, and 2 teaspoons cinnamon; blend in 2 tablespoons melted butter or margarine; stir in 2 ounces chopped walnuts.

CAFÉ GINGERBREAD

Use 1 packet gingerbread or ginger cake mix; add 1½ tablespoons powdered instant coffee mix. Fold in 2 ounces finely grated plain chocolate. Bake as directed on packet.

COCONUT GINGERBREAD

Use 1 packet gingerbread or ginger cake mix; fold in 4 ounces desiccated coconut. Bake as directed on packet.

CHOCOLATE SPICE CAKE

Use 1 packet chocolate cake mix. Add ½ teaspoon ground cloves, 1 teaspoon cinnamon, and ¾ teaspoon mixed spice to dry mix.

Fold into batter 1 ounce each chopped candied orange and grapefruit peel just before turning into tin. Bake as directed on packet.

PEPPERMINT DEVIL'S FOOD CAKE

Prepare devil's food cake mix batter and flavour with a few drops peppermint essence before turning into tin.

Devil's Food Cake — Fluffy White Icing

COFFEE-SPICE DEVIL'S FOOD CAKE

Use 1 packet devil's food cake mix. To dry mix add 4 teaspoons instant coffee, ¼ teaspoon nutmeg, ¼ teaspoon mixed spice, and ½ teaspoon cinnamon.

CHOCOLATE BANANA CREAM CAKE

Prepare devil's food cake mix as directed on packet. Bake as directed.

Split one of the warm layers in half crosswise to make 2 thin layers. Put layers together with sweetened whipped cream and sliced bananas in the middle. Place more whipped cream and sliced bananas on top.

Ice remaining layer as desired and save for another meal.

CHOCOLATE CRUNCH CAKE

Use 1 packet chocolate cake mix. Add 1 ounce peanut butter with liquid. Fold 2 ounces chopped peanuts into batter. Bake as directed on packet.

COCONUT CHOCOLATE CAKE

Prepare 1 packet chocolate cake mix. Add 4 ounces desiccated coconut to batter. Bake as directed on packet.

WALNUT MOCHA CAKE

Prepare 1 packet chocolate cake mix. Add 1½ tablespoons powdered instant coffee to dry mix.

Fold into batter 2 ounces chopped walnuts, just before turning into tin. Bake as directed on packet.

BLACK AND WHITE SWIRL CAKE

Use 1 packet chocolate cake mix. Prepare chocolate cake mix, substituting 4 fluid ounces orange juice for an equal quantity of the liquid; fold in 1 tablespoon grated orange rind.

Use 1 packet white cake mix. Pour white cake batter into 2 prepared 10-inch sandwich tins. Cover with chocolate batter. Swirl lightly with spatula.

Fill and ice with a chocolate icing to which 1 tablespoon grated orange rind has been added.

High-Altitude Cake Recipes

BAKING CAKES AT HIGH ALTITUDES

In a high altitude region (3,000 feet above sea level) you may find that cakes made from sea-level recipes tend to fall and give unpredictable results. For a general guide to changes in sea level recipes, see **Cooking at High Altitudes**. In addition, specific recipes for various altitudes are given in this section.

QUICK-METHOD CAKE

Preparations: Have the fat at room temperature. Line bottoms of tins with paper; grease. Use two round 8-inch sandwich tins, 1¼ inches deep. Start oven for moderate heat (375°F. Mark 5). Sift flour once before measuring.

(For 5000 feet altitude)

Measure into sifter:
8 ounces plain flour
1¾ teaspoons baking powder
¾ teaspoon salt
10 ounces sugar*

Measure into mixing bowl:
4 ounces fat (see below*)

Measure into cup:
8 fluid ounces minus 2 tablespoons milk*
1 teaspoon vanilla

Have ready:
2 eggs, unbeaten

* If the fat used is butter, margarine, or lard, decrease sugar and milk. . . . Use 8 ounces plus 2 tablespoons sugar and 4 tablespoons milk.

Mixing Method: Stir fat just to soften. Sift in dry ingredients. Add ¾ of the milk and mix until all flour is dampened. Then beat 2 minutes.
Add remaining milk and the eggs and beat 1 minute longer.
(Mix cake by hand or at low speed of electric mixer. Count only actual beating time. Or count beating strokes. Allow about 150 full strokes per minute. Scrape bowl and spoon often.)

Baking: Turn batter into tins. Bake in moderate oven (375°F. Mark 5) 25 minutes, or until done.
Or bake in a 9 × 9 × 2-inch tin or 10 × 10 × 2-inch tin in moderate oven (350°F. Mark 4) 25 to 35 minutes, or until done.

(For 3000 feet altitude)

Measure into sifter:

8 ounces plain flour
1¾ teaspoons baking powder
¾ teaspoon salt
10 ounces sugar

Measure into mixing bowl:
4 ounces fat (see below*)

Measure into cup:
6 fluid ounces plus 1 tablespoon milk*
1 teaspoon vanilla

Have ready:
2 eggs, unbeaten

*If the fat used is butter, margarine, or lard, decrease milk to 6 fluid ounces. Follow the mixture method above.

(For 7000 feet altitude)

Measure into sifter:
8 ounces plain flour
1½ teaspoons baking powder
¾ teaspoon salt
8 ounces plus 2 tablespoons sugar*

Measure into mixing bowl:
4 ounces fat (see below*)

Measure into cup:
8 fluid ounces minus 1 tablespoon milk*
1 teaspoon vanilla

Have ready:
2 eggs, unbeaten

* If the fat used is butter, margarine, or lard, decrease sugar and milk. . . . Use 8 ounces sugar and 6 fluid ounces plus 1 tablespoon milk.
Follow the mixing method above.

SILVER MOON WHITE CAKE

Preparations: Have the fat at room temperature. Line bottoms of tins with paper; grease. Use two round or square 9-inch tins, 1½ inches deep. Start oven for moderate heat (375°F. Mark 5). Sift flour once before measuring.
Prepare meringue by beating 5 egg whites with rotary egg beater (or at a high speed of electric mixer) until foamy. Add 4 ounces sugar gradually, beating only until meringue will hold up in soft peaks.

(For 5000 feet altitude)

Measure into sifter:

10 ounces plain flour
2¼ teaspoons baking powder
1 teaspoon salt
10 ounces sugar*

Measure into mixing bowl:
5 ounces fat (see below*)

Measure into small bowl:
½ pint milk*
1½ teaspoons vanilla

Have ready: meringue of
5 egg whites and 4 ounces sugar

* If butter, margarine, or lard is used, decrease sugar and milk. . . . Use 8 ounces of sugar and 8 fluid ounces plus 2 tablespoons of milk.

Mixing Method: Stir fat just to soften. Sift in dry ingredients. Add ¾ of the milk and mix until all flour is dampened. Then beat 2 minutes.
Add remaining milk, blend; then add meringue mixture and beat 1 minute longer.
(Mix cake by hand or at low speed of electric mixer. Count only actual beating time. Or count beating strokes. Allow about 150 full strokes per minute. Scrape bowl and spoon often.)

Baking: Turn batter into tins. Bake in moderate oven (375°F. Mark 5) 25 minutes, or until done.
This cake may also be baked in a 13 × 9 × 2-inch tin 35 minutes, or until done. Spread with fluffy pineapple icing.

(For 3000 feet altitude)

Measure into sifter:
10 ounces plain flour
2½ teaspoons baking powder
1 teaspoon salt
10 ounces sugar

Measure into mixing bowl:
5 ounces fat (see below*)

Measure into small bowl:
8 fluid ounces plus 2 tablespoons milk*
1½ teaspoons vanilla

Have ready: meringue of
5 egg whites and 4 ounces sugar

* If the fat used is butter, margarine, or lard, decrease milk to 8 fluid ounces.
Follow the mixing method above.

Silver Moon White Cake, Continued

(For 7000 feet altitude)
Measure into sifter:
 10 ounces plain flour
 2 teaspoons baking powder
 1 teaspoon salt
 8 ounces plus 2 tablespoons
    sugar*

Measure into mixing bowl:
 5 ounces fat (see below*)

Measure into small bowl:
 ½ pint milk*
 1½ teaspoons vanilla

Have ready: meringue of
 5 egg whites and 4 ounces sugar

 * If the fat used is butter, margarine, or lard, decrease sugar and milk. . . . Use 8 ounces sugar and 8 fluid ounces plus 2 tablespoons milk.
 Follow the mixing method above.

MIX-EASY DEVIL'S FOOD

 Preparations: Have the fat at room temperature. Line bottoms of tins with paper; grease. Use two round 9-inch sandwich tins, 1½ inches deep. Start oven for moderate heat (350°F. Mark 4). Sift flour once.

(For 5000 feet altitude)
Measure into sifter:
 8 ounces plain flour
 ½ teaspoon baking powder
 ¾ teaspoon bicarbonate of soda
 ¾ teaspoon salt
 11 ounces sugar*
 4 ounces cocoa

Measure into mixing bowl:
 5 ounces fat (see below*)

Measure into small bowl:
 ½ pint milk*
 1 teaspoon vanilla

Have ready:
 2 eggs, unbeaten

 * With butter, margarine, or lard, decrease sugar and milk to 10 ounces sugar and 8 fluid ounces plus 2 tablespoons milk.

 Mixing Method: Sift dry ingredients together twice. Stir fat just to soften. Sift in dry ingredients. Add ¾ of the milk and mix until all flour is dampened. Then beat 2 minutes.
 Add remaining milk and the eggs, and beat 1 minute longer.
 (Mix cake by hand or at low speed of electric mixer. Count only actual beating time. Or count beating strokes. Allow about 150 full strokes per minute. Scrape bowl and spoon often.)

 Baking: Turn batter into tins. Bake in moderate oven (350°F. Mark 4) 25 minutes, or until done. Spread with seven-minute icing.

 This cake may also be baked in a 13×9×2-inch tin in moderate oven (350°F. Mark 4) 30 to 35 minutes.

(For 3000 feet altitude)
Measure into sifter:
 8 ounces plain flour
 ½ teaspoon baking powder
 1 teaspoon bicarbonate of soda
 ¾ teaspoon salt
 11 ounces sugar
 4 ounces cocoa

Measure into mixing bowl:
 5 ounces fat (see below*)

Measure into small bowl:
 8 fluid ounces plus 2 tablespoons
    milk*
 1 teaspoon vanilla

Have ready:
 2 eggs, unbeaten

 * If the fat used is butter, margarine, or lard, decrease milk to 8 fluid ounces.
 Follow the mixing method above.

(For 7000 feet altitude)
Measure into sifter:
 8 ounces plain flour
 ½ teaspoon baking powder
 ¾ teaspoon bicarbonate of soda
 ¾ teaspoon salt
 10 ounces sugar*
 1½ ounces cocoa

Measure into mixing bowl:
 4 ounces fat (see below*)

Measure into small bowl:
 ½ pint milk*
 1 teaspoon vanilla

Have ready:
 2 eggs, unbeaten

 *If butter, margarine, or lard is used, decrease sugar and milk. . . . Use 8 ounces plus 2 tablespoons of sugar and 8 fluid ounces plus 2 tablespoons of milk.
 Follow the mixing method above.

SPONGE CAKE

 Preparations: Have eggs at room temperature. Start oven for moderate heat (375°F. Mark 5). Sift flour once before measuring. Use 9-inch tube tin.

(For 5000 feet altitude)
Ingredients:
 4 ounces plain flour
 8 ounces minus 1 tablespoon sifted
    sugar

 5 egg yolks
 1½ teaspoons grated lemon rind
 1½ tablespoons lemon juice
 2 tablespoons water
 5 egg whites
 ¼ teaspoon salt
 ¼ teaspoon cream of tartar

 Mixing Method: Measure sifted flour, add 2 ounces sugar, and sift together four times.
 Place egg yolks in small bowl. Add lemon rind and beat with rotary egg beater until thick and lemon-coloured. Add lemon juice and water gradually, beating until thick and light.
 Beat egg whites and salt with flat wire whisk or rotary egg beater until foamy.
 Sprinkle in cream of tartar and continue beating until egg whites are stiff enough to hold up in soft peaks but are still moist and glossy.
 Add remaining sugar in three additions, beating 50 strokes after each. Then fold in egg yolk mixture with flat wire whisk or spoon until well blended.
 Sift about ¼ of flour over mixture and fold in lightly with whisk or spoon (15 fold-over strokes), turning bowl gradually. Continue folding in flour by fourths in this way, folding well after last addition (25 strokes).

 Baking: Turn into ungreased round 9-inch tube tin. Bake in moderate oven (375°F. Mark 5) 30 minutes, or until done. Remove from oven, invert tin and let stand 1 hour, or until cake is cool.

(For 3000 feet altitude)
Ingredients:
 4 ounces plain flour
 8 ounces sifted sugar
 5 egg yolks
 1½ teaspoons grated lemon rind
 1½ tablespoons lemon juice
 2 tablespoons water
 5 egg whites
 ¼ teaspoon salt
 ¼ teaspoon cream of tartar

 Follow the mixing method given above.

(For 7000 feet altitude)
Ingredients:
 4 ounces plain flour
 8 ounces minus 2 tablespoons
    sifted sugar
 5 egg yolks
 1½ teaspoons grated lemon rind
 1½ tablespoons lemon juice
 2 tablespoons water
 5 egg whites
 ¼ teaspoon salt
 ½ teaspoon cream of tartar

 Follow the mixing method given above.

FAMILY SIZE ANGEL FOOD

Preparations: Have eggs at room temperature. Start oven for moderate heat (375°F. Mark 5). Sift flour once before measuring. Use 9-inch tube tin.

(For 5000 feet altitude)
Ingredients:
 4 ounces plain flour
 8 ounces plus 2 tablespoons sifted
    sugar
 5 egg whites
 ¼ teaspoon salt
 1 teaspoon cream of tartar
 1 teaspoon vanilla
 ¼ teaspoon almond essence

Mixing Method: Measure sifted flour, add 2 ounces sugar, and sift together four times.

Beat egg whites and salt with flat wire whisk or rotary egg beater until foamy.

Sprinkle in cream of tartar and continue beating until egg whites are stiff enough to hold up in soft peaks, but are still moist and glossy.

Sprinkle remaining sugar over egg whites, about 4 tablespoons at a time, and beat after each addition to blend (25 strokes). Beat in flavouring (10 strokes).

Sift about ¼ of flour over mixture and fold in lightly with whisk or spoon (15 fold-over strokes), turning bowl gradually. Continue folding in flour by fourths in this way, folding well after last addition (25 strokes).

Baking: Turn into ungreased round 9-inch tube tin. Bake in moderate oven (375°F. Mark 5) 30 minutes, or until done.

Remove from oven, invert tin, and let stand 1 hour, or until cake is cool. Spread with icing.

(For 3000 feet altitude)
Ingredients:
 4 ounces plain flour
 10 ounces sugar
 4 egg whites
 ¼ teaspoon salt
 1 teaspoon cream of tartar
 1 teaspoon vanilla
 ¼ teaspoon almond essence

Follow the mixing method given above.

(For 7000 feet altitude)
Ingredients:
 4 ounces plain flour
 8 ounces sugar
 5 egg whites
 ¼ teaspoon salt
 1¼ teaspoons cream of tartar
 1 teaspoon vanilla
 ¼ teaspoon almond essence

Follow the mixing method given above.

GOLD CAKE

Preparations: Have the fat at room temperature. Line bottom of 10×5×3-inch loaf tin with paper; grease. Start oven for moderate heat (350°F. Mark 4). Sift flour once before measuring.

(For 5000 feet altitude)
Measure into sifter:
 8 ounces plain flour
 1½ teaspoons baking powder
 ¾ teaspoon salt
 8 ounces sugar

Measure into mixing bowl:
 4 ounces fat (see below*)

Measure into cup:
 8 fluid ounces minus 2 tablespoons
    milk*
 1 teaspoon vanilla

Have ready:
 5 egg yolks, unbeaten

*If the fat used is butter, margarine, or lard, decrease milk to 6 fluid ounces.

Mixing Method: Stir fat just to soften. Sift in dry ingredients. Add egg yolks and 4 fluid ounces of the milk and mix until all flour is dampened. Then beat 2 minutes.

Add remaining milk and beat 1 minute longer.

(Mix cake by hand or at low speed of electric mixer. Count only actual beating time. Or count beating strokes. Allow about 150 full strokes per minute. Scrape bowl and spoon often.)

Baking: Turn batter into tin. Bake in moderate oven (350°F. Mark 4) 1 hour, or until done. Spread with butter icing.

(For 3000 feet altitude)
Measure into sifter:
 8 ounces plain flour
 1¾ teaspoons baking powder
 ¾ teaspoon salt
 8 ounces sugar

Measure into mixing bowl:
 4 ounces fat (see below*)

Measure into cup:
 6 fluid ounces milk*
 1 teaspoon vanilla

Have ready:
 5 egg yolks, unbeaten

* If the fat used is butter, margarine, or lard, decrease milk to ¼ pint.

Follow the mixing method above.

(For 7000 feet altitude)
Measure into sifter:
 8 ounces plain flour
 1½ teaspoons baking powder

 ¾ teaspoon salt
 8 ounces minus 1 tablespoon sugar*

Measure into mixing bowl:
 4 ounces fat (see below*)

Measure into cup:
 8 fluid ounces minus 2 tablespoons
    milk*
 1 teaspoon vanilla

Have ready:
 5 egg yolks, unbeaten

*If the fat used is butter, margarine, or lard, decrease sugar and milk. . . . Use 8 ounces minus 2 tablespoons sugar and 6 fluid ounces milk.
Follow the mixing method above.

Gold Cake Variations:
Sunshine Party Loaf: Omit vanilla and add 2 teaspoons grated orange rind to fat. Mix and bake as directed. Spread cake with lemon icing.

Old-Fashioned Loaf Cake: Omit vanilla in Gold Cake. Add 1½ teaspoons grated lemon rind to fat, and sift ¼ teaspoon nutmeg with dry ingredients.

MIX-EASY ONE-EGG CAKE

Preparations: Have the fat at room temperature. Line bottom of tin with paper; grease. Use 9×9×2-inch tin. Start oven for moderate heat (375°F. Mark 5).

(For 5000 feet altitude)
Measure into sifter:
 8 ounces plain flour
 1½ teaspoons baking powder
 ¾ teaspoon salt
 8 ounces sugar

Measure into mixing bowl:
 5 ounces butter or other fat

Measure into cup:
 8 fluid ounces minus 2 tablespoons
    milk
 1 teaspoon vanilla

Have ready:
 1 egg, unbeaten

Mixing Method: Stir fat just to soften. Stir in dry ingredients. Add ¾ of the milk and mix until all flour is dampened. Then beat 2 minutes.

Add remaining milk and the egg and beat 1 minute longer.

(Mix cake by hand or at low speed of electric mixer. Count only actual beating time. Or count beating strokes. Allow about 150 full strokes per minute. Scrape bowl and spoon often.)

Mix-Easy One-Egg Cake, Continued

Baking: Turn batter into tin. Bake in moderate oven (375°F. Mark 5) 30 minutes, or until done.

This cake may also be baked in two round 8-inch sandwich tins 25 minutes, or until done.

(For 3000 feet altitude)
Measure into sifter:
8 ounces plain flour
1¾ teaspoons baking powder
¾ teaspoon salt
8 ounces sugar

Measure into mixing bowl:
2½ ounces butter or other fat

Measure into cup:
6 fluid ounces milk
1 teaspoon vanilla

Have ready:
1 egg, unbeaten

Follow the mixing method above.

(For 7000 feet altitude)
Measure into sifter:
8 ounces plain flour
1¼ teaspoons baking powder
¾ teaspoon salt
8 ounces minus 1 tablespoon sugar

Measure into mixing bowl:
2½ ounces butter or other fat

Measure into cup:
8 fluid ounces minus 1 tablespoon milk
1 teaspoon vanilla

Have ready:
1 egg, unbeaten

Follow the mixing method above.

LUCKY DAY NUT LOAF

Preparations: Have the fat at room temperature. Line bottom of 10×5×3-inch loaf tin with paper; grease. Start oven for moderate heat (350°F. Mark 4). Sift flour once before measuring.

(For 5000 feet altitude)
Measure into sifter:
8 ounces plain flour
1½ teaspoons baking powder
¾ teaspoon salt
8 ounces plus 2 tablespoons sugar*

Measure into mixing bowl:
4 ounces fat (see below*)

Measure into cup:
6 fluid ounces plus 1 tablespoon milk*
1 teaspoon vanilla

Have ready:
2 eggs, unbeaten
3 ounces nuts, finely chopped

* If the fat used is butter, margarine, or lard, decrease sugar and milk. . . . Use 8 ounces sugar and ¼ pint milk.

Mixing Method: Stir fat just to soften. Sift in dry ingredients. Add ¾ of the milk and mix until all flour is dampened. Then beat 2 minutes.

Add remaining milk and the eggs and beat 1 minute longer. Add nuts. (Mix cake by hand or at low speed of electric mixer. Count only actual beating time. Or count beating strokes. Allow about 150 full strokes per minute. Scrape bowl and spoon often.)

Baking: Turn batter into tin. Bake in moderate oven (350°F. Mark 4) 1 hour and 10 minutes, or until cake is done.

(For 3000 feet altitude)
Measure into sifter:
8 ounces plain flour
1¾ teaspoons baking powder
¾ teaspoon salt
10 ounces sugar

Measure into mixing bowl:
4 ounces fat (see below*)

Measure into cup:
6 fluid ounces milk*
1 teaspoon vanilla

Have ready:
2 eggs, unbeaten
3 ounces nuts, finely chopped

*If the fat used is butter, margarine, or lard, decrease milk to ¼ pint.

Follow the mixing method above.

(For 7000 feet altitude)
Measure into sifter:
8 ounces plain flour
1½ teaspoons baking powder
¾ teaspoon salt
8 ounces sugar*

Measure into mixing bowl:
4 ounces fat (see below*)

Measure into cup:
8 fluid ounces minus 2 tablespoons milk*
1 teaspoon vanilla

Have ready:
2 eggs, unbeaten
3 ounces nuts, finely chopped

* With butter, margarine, or lard, decrease sugar and milk to 8 ounces minus 2 tablespoons sugar and 6 fluid ounces milk.

Follow the mixing method above.

Quick Cupcakes: Mix batter for Lucky Day Nut Loaf (above), omitting nuts.

Turn into deep bun tins that have been greased lightly on bottoms only, filling each only half full.

Bake in moderate oven (375°F. Mark 5) 20 minutes, or until done. Makes 18 medium or 36 small cupcakes.

Standards for a Good Layer Cake

Well-proportioned shape and size, slightly rounded top, straight sides, evenly browned, tender crust, velvety even-grained crumb, good flavour.

This Should Happen

This Should Not Happen

CAKE ICINGS, FILLINGS, AND GLAZES

The same icing that covers a cake may be used for filling between the layers, but often a different filling is preferable.

CHOOSING AN ICING

An icing should complement or enhance the flavour or colour of your cake. A rich icing should be chosen for a simple economy cake, a fluffy icing for a light moist cake, and so on. A sponge cake, angel food, or a pound cake may be served uniced or finished off with a simple icing or glaze or with a topping. Icings must be soft and manageable, yet not the least "runny."

Uncooked butter icings call for icing sugar. Coarser sugar will make them grainy. If too soft these icings can be thickened by the addition of a little more sugar. If too stiff, thin with a few drops of cream or other liquid.

Fluffy icings such as the 7-minute, boiled, and uncooked meringue types are luscious and lavish looking. Make these the day the cake is to be served. Overcooking gives these icings a sugary texture. Undercooking leaves them too soft.

Creamy cooked icings are fudge-like in consistency, creamy, and delicious. They harden more quickly than uncooked icings, so need to be spread more quickly. The bowl of icing may be placed over warm water to keep the icing soft and workable.

CAKE DECORATING WITH ICING

A plain cake is a pleasant dessert — but a decorated cake is a party. The difference is simply a skilful hand with icing. Special decorating may consist of the simple decorative touches described below, arranged in an appropriate design, or it may include more elaborate borders, rosettes, and festoons made with icing and a cake decorator. Even the elaborately decor-ated cakes which are seen in caterers' windows are not so difficult to do as might be supposed. A few simple rules and practice with cake decorating equipment will soon give you artistically decorated cakes. The equipment may consist merely of homemade paper cornucopias with a few inexpensive basic metal tubes or it may include a special cloth, rubber, or metal holder and a large variety of tubes. These may be purchased at most hardware departments and stores.

Preparing the Cake

First, ice cake as directed, but spread icing smoothly over the top and sides unless a rough surface or swirl pattern is part of the desired decorative effect.

Not all icings can be used for decorating. The icing must be stiff enough to hold its shape and yet be soft enough to pass through the small opening of a decorating tube. Butter icings are usually preferred as they keep well; an icing must be one that will not harden or dry too quickly because the decorating process often takes some time.

The icing may be tinted delicately as desired. Pastel tints are usually best but brighter colours may be used for contrast.

HINTS AND STEPS IN ICING A CAKE

1 Have the cake thoroughly cool. Brush or rub off all loose crumbs. Trim off ragged edges with scissors.

2. Choose a flat plate or tray that will "frame" the cake. A 9-inch cake looks best on a plate or tray 12 to 13 inches in diameter. This allows a border of about 2 inches all around the cake. If the plate is too large or too deep, it dwarfs the cake. If too small, it makes the cake appear clumsy and overbalanced.

3. To keep the plate clean while icing, cover the outer area of the plate with pieces of greaseproof paper extending beyond the edge of plate.

4. If your cake is quite moist, a little sugar sprinkled on the plate will keep it from sticking.

5. Place cake in position (on the papers) on the cake plate. If there is any difference in cake layers, choose the thicker layer for the bottom layer, and keep a smooth-crusted layer for the top.

6. Use a flexible spatula to spread icing.

7. For a layer cake, place some icing on the bottom layer. Spread it smoothly, almost to the edge. With a soft filling, spread to 1 inch from the edge. Then adjust the second layer so that edges are even and cake uniform in height. If top layer slides, insert a slender knitting needle through both layers. This can be removed before icing the top.

Spread icing carefully on lower layer, then fit top.

Start icing at the sides, then fill in the top.

8. To ice outside of cake, spread icing over edge and sides. Then pile remaining icing on top and spread lightly to the edges. Swirl the icing attractively as you ice.

9. Work quickly so that the icing will not crust over before you finish. Let icing set slightly, then draw out the pieces of greaseproof paper carefully from under cake.

10. For very special cakes, it pays to ice smoothly first with a thin layer of icing to hold down any crumbs and

to give an even base coat. When set or firm, the final icing may be spread more easily.

Light strokes with a spatula will vary the decorative effect.

11. For cupcakes, hold each cake, turning as you spread icing on the top. To ice the sides as well, hold cake, top and bottom, while icing sides, then place on cake rack or hold on a fork while icing the top (or the bottom).

To Ice Cupcakes Quickly: Dip the top of each cupcake into soft icing. Twirl slightly and quickly turn right side up.

SIMPLE DECORATIVE TOUCHES

Icing Sugar: (1) Sprinkle the sugar through a small sieve onto uniced cake. (2) For special designs, place a fancy paper doily or a cut-out pattern or letters on top of the cake. Then sprinkle with icing sugar. Carefully lift the pattern up and away. The design will be embossed on the cake.

Candies: Use coloured or silver balls for forming letters, festoons, or simple borders. With a cocktail stick, draw or space out the design lightly on iced cake. Then place candies carefully on design. If necessary, use tweezers to place each in position.

Chocolate: Melt chocolate over boiling water with 1 teaspoon butter for each ounce of chocolate. Use to dribble over fluffy icing from a teaspoon. Or paint the chocolate onto a smooth icing to form a design, greeting, or name.

Icing Sculpture: Ice cake with 7-minute icing. Then tint more icing with food colouring and use to form swirls or "ferns" at intervals on top and sides of cake.

Fruit and Nuts: For flower and leaf designs, coloured candies may be used with citron cut in leaf shapes. Other fruits such as raisins, glacé cherries, citron, etc. may be arranged on cakes in designs. Try cluster raisins with toasted almonds, cherry bits with strips of citron.

Pecan or walnut halves may be centred on cupcakes or cake squares. Chopped pecans, walnuts, or pistachios are attractive pressed against sides of iced cakes or around top edge in a border or scattered freely on the top.

To Toast Nuts: Place nuts in a shallow tin with a little butter (1 teaspoon butter for each 4 ounces of nuts). Heat in moderate oven (350°F. Mark 4) until lightly browned, 15 to 20 minutes. Or heat and stir in a heavy frying pan.

To Sliver Almonds: Blanch shelled almonds by covering with boiling water and letting stand until skins wrinkle, about 3 minutes. Drain and rub off brown skins. Split nuts and cut in slivers.

Coconut, Plain, Toasted, or Tinted: Sprinkle it over fluffy icings or press it against sides of cake while icing is still soft.

To Tint Coconut: Sprinkle desiccated coconut on white paper. Dilute a tiny bit of food colouring in a small amount of water; sprinkle over coconut and rub evenly through it until the coconut is evenly tinted. Or put the coconut in a glass jar, filling no more than half full. Sprinkle with a few drops of diluted colouring. Cover jar and shake until all coconut is tinted.

To Toast Coconut: Spread shredded coconut in a thin layer on a baking sheet. Toast in moderate oven (350°F. Mark 4) until golden brown, stirring it frequently to toast evenly.

Jelly: Use beaten or melted jelly for designs; for example, a red jelly heart or a green shamrock. Use a cocktail stick to mark the design on the cake, then spread the jelly inside the design.

Flowers: Dainty fresh flowers or a spray of green leaves are an especially inviting decoration on a simply iced cake. Place small flowers and feathery leaves in a small glass and insert in centre of an iced tube cake. Place matching flowers around the cake. Use tiny rosebuds or nosegays tied with ribbon for small cakes. Flowers around cakes should be grouped low enough so that the base of the cake can be seen.

Candles: Select candles and holders in the right colour and size for the cake. A single large candle or candle-flower may be used in the centre or a few medium-sized candles near the centre instead of many small candles for older people's birthdays.

HOW TO CUT CAKES

Use a long, sharp knife for cutting cakes and cut with a gently sawing motion. Do not press down. For best results with iced cakes, rinse the knife frequently in hot water. (This cannot be done at the table but it is an excellent aid when cutting cakes in kitchen for a party.)

Round sandwich cakes may be cut in wedges so that each piece has equal icing. To serve sponge cake and angel food, cut lightly with a very sharp or serrated knife, or "tear" off each piece, using two forks or a cake knife.

Here are diagrams for cutting round cakes when serving a crowd. Use the largest one for deep, single-layered cakes or try the other two for 9- or 10-inch sandwich cakes.

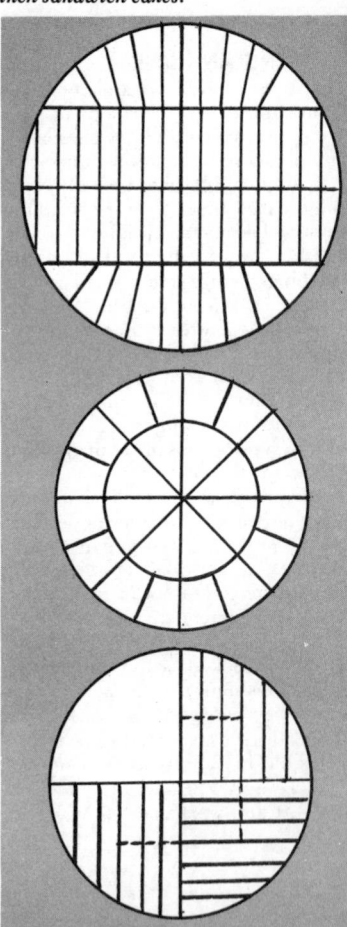

To cut a square cake 8×8×2 inches or larger.

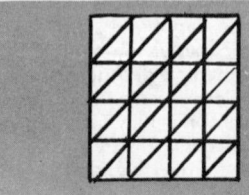

HOMEMADE CAKE DECORATOR

If you have no cake decorating set, you can make your own decorator bag for special borders and writing. For the bags, cut squares or 10×8- or 12×9-inch rectangles of sturdy greaseproof or thin parchment paper into two triangles (step 1).

Roll each triangle into a cone shape, making sure it is tightly rolled so as not to give under pressure (steps 2, 3, and 4). Fold down the top point of the cone to keep it from unfolding (step 5).

Washable bags may be shaped similarly from muslin or light canvas, then stitched.

For writing, snip off the tip of the paper cone to give a small opening. Designs can be made by cutting this tip. An inverted "v" cut will shape leaf designs or flutings; a series of tiny "y's" will form the shell designs and ridged borders.

If preferred, icing tubes may be inserted at the bottom of the canvas bag or paper cone. Cut the tip off on the dotted line and drop the icing tube in as shown in steps 6 and 7.

For best results, fill cake decorator tube, bag, or cone only half-full of icing at a time. Use one hand to guide the tip, the other to force out icing gently.

Practice on paper or an inverted tin before attempting to decorate a cake in order to make sure that the icing is of the right consistency.

If it is too soft it will not spread and the design will not be clear cut, and it will be difficult to break off the flow of icing at the right point. If it is too stiff it will be difficult to push through the tube and will tend to break or crack.

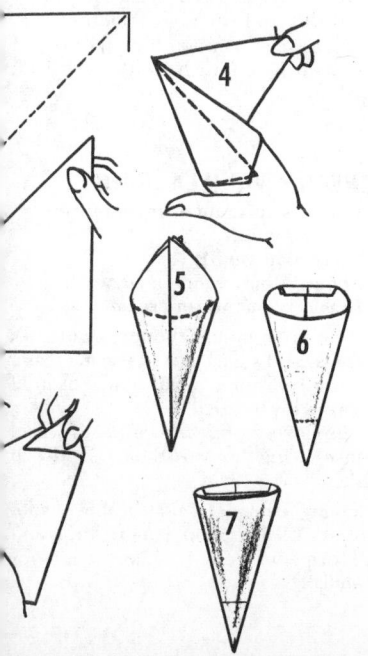

1. Begin the cutting at the lowest tier. To make the cuts even in depth, run a knife all the way round where it abuts the second lowest layer.

2. Continue this process with the next lowest tier, then with the third tier.

HOW TO CUT A WEDDING CAKE

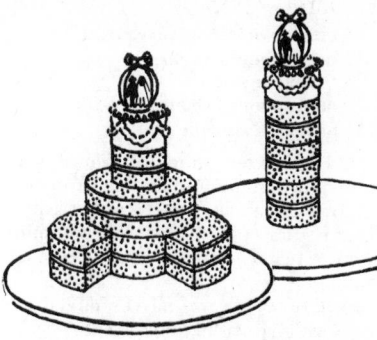

3. Then cut the lowest tier again, cutting successive slices until a single cylindrical central core remains with the ornate top in place.

4. Save the ornate top for the bride, if desired, for the first anniversary party. 5. Then finish slicing the central core beginning at the top.

Uncooked and Quick Icings

PLAIN ICING
(Master Recipe)

12 ounces icing sugar
1 ounce soft butter or margarine
1 teaspoon vanilla or almond essence
About 2 tablespoons boiling water, hot milk, hot cream, or fruit juice

Combine sugar, butter, and vanilla in a bowl. Add liquid, a little at a time, beating well with fork or spoon between additions.

Add only enough liquid to give the mixture easy spreading consistency.

Variations of Icing

Glossy Chocolate Icing: Add 1½ ounces plain chocolate melted over hot water, or 1½ ounces cocoa, sifted in with the sugar.

Coconut Icing: Just before spreading plain icing or glossy chocolate icing, add 2 ounces desiccated coconut. Decorate top of cake with more coconut.

Coffee Icing: Use strong hot coffee for the liquid.

Maple Icing: Use maple syrup or golden syrup for the liquid.

Nut Icing: Add about 2 ounces chopped nuts just before spreading. Decorate cake with nut halves or finely chopped nuts.

Raspberry Icing: Omit flavouring in plain icing and use crushed raspberries and their juice as the liquid.

Raisin Icing: Add about 3 ounces chopped raisins to plain icing just before spreading.

Rum Icing: Substitute rum or rum flavouring for other flavouring.

Strawberry Icing: Omit flavouring in plain icing and use crushed strawberries and their juice as the liquid.

Simple Lemon Icing: Substitute lemon juice for 1 tablespoon of the water. Add ½ teaspoon grated lemon rind.

Simple Orange Icing: Omit flavouring. Use orange juice for the liquid. Add 1 teaspoon grated orange rind.

BUTTER ICING
(Master Recipe)

2   ounces butter or margarine
12   ounces icing sugar
$\frac{1}{8}$ teaspoon salt
3   tablespoons cream
1   teaspoon vanilla

Cream butter until soft. Slowly stir in 6 ounces sugar and the salt. Add additional sugar alternately with cream, beating thoroughly after each addition until creamy and smooth. Beat in vanilla.

Additional cream may be added to give icing spreading consistency.

Makes icing to cover top and sides of two 8-inch sandwich cakes or 2 dozen cupcakes.

Butter Icing Variations

Almond Butter Icing: Omit vanilla in master recipe. Add 1 teaspoon almond flavouring.

Apricot Butter Icing: Omit cream in master recipe. Add 2 ounces cooked apricot pulp and 1 teaspoon lemon juice.

Chocolate Butter Icing: Melt 2 ounces plain chocolate over hot water. Blend with 2 tablespoons boiling water. Add $\frac{1}{2}$ teaspoon vanilla and salt. Substitute 2 tablespoons milk for cream.

Cinnamon Butter Icing: Substitute cinnamon for vanilla in master recipe.

Coffee Butter Icing: Substitute strong coffee for cream in master recipe.

Lemon Butter Icing: Substitute lemon juice and 1 egg yolk for the cream and vanilla in master recipe. Add $1\frac{1}{2}$ teaspoons grated lemon rind.

Maple Walnut Butter Icing: In master recipe, substitute maple flavouring for vanilla. Add 2 ounces chopped walnuts with the last of the sugar.

Mint Butter Icing: Prepare master recipe. Colour icing green. Substitute mint flavouring for vanilla.

Or melt peppermint candy and add icing for flavour and colour.

Mocha Butter Icing: In master recipe, substitute coffee for cream. Add $1\frac{1}{2}$ tablespoons cocoa with the creamed butter.

Orange Butter Icing: In master recipe, substitute 1 egg yolk and 2 tablespoons orange juice for the cream. Substitute grated orange rind for vanilla.

Pineapple Butter Icing: In master recipe, omit cream. Add about 2 ounces drained crushed pineapple. Use lemon juice for flavouring.

Pistachio Butter Icing: Prepare master recipe. Colour icing pale green. Add a few drops of almond essence.

Strawberry Butter Icing: Omit liquid in master recipe. Add about 2 ounces crushed strawberries.

Use lemon juice for flavouring. Decorate with whole strawberries.

CREAM CHEESE ICING
(Master Recipe)

3   ounces cream cheese
1   tablespoon milk
8   ounces icing sugar
1   teaspoon vanilla

Soften cheese with milk. Gradually add icing sugar and vanilla. Beat until creamy.

Variations:

Cream Cheese Chocolate Icing: Increase milk to 3 tablespoons, and icing sugar to about 1 pound. Add 2 ounces melted chocolate and $\frac{1}{8}$ teaspoon salt. Omit vanilla.

Orange Cream Cheese Icing: Substitute 2 tablespoons orange juice and 1 teaspoon grated orange rind for milk and vanilla.

FLUFFY LIME ICING

3   ounces butter or margarine
$\frac{1}{4}$ teaspoon salt
1   teaspoon vanilla
1   egg white, unbeaten
About $1\frac{1}{2}$ pounds icing sugar
$2\frac{1}{2}$ tablespoons lime juice
$2\frac{1}{2}$ teaspoons grated lemon rind

Cream together butter, salt, and vanilla. Add egg white. Then add sugar, alternately with lime juice, beating well after each addition. Add lemon rind and beat well.

Makes icing for tops and sides of two 8-inch sandwich cakes, or top and sides of a 9- or 10-inch angel food cake.

Fluffy Orange Icing: Use above recipe, substituting orange rind and juice for lemon rind and juice.

GOLDEN CREAM ICING

4   ounces butter or margarine
$\frac{1}{2}$ teaspoon salt
1   teaspoon vanilla
1   egg yolk
8-12   ounces icing sugar
1   tablespoon milk

Cream butter until soft and fluffy. Beat in salt, vanilla, and egg yolk. Add

Strawberry Meringue

sugar alternately with milk, beating constantly.

Makes icing for top and sides of two 9-inch sandwich cakes.

STRAWBERRY MERINGUE FOR SPONGE CAKE

2   egg whites
$\frac{1}{8}$ teaspoon salt
4   ounces caster sugar
1   teaspoon lemon juice
6-8   ounces sliced strawberries

Beat egg whites until stiff, but not dry. Blend in salt, sugar, and lemon juice. Continue beating until meringue stands in peaks and is well blended. Fold in strawberries.

Serve over sponge or angel food cake.

MOLASSES BUTTER ICING

2   ounces butter or margarine
$\frac{1}{4}$ teaspoon salt
3   ounces light molasses or black treacle
4   tablespoons cream
About $1\frac{1}{2}$ pounds icing sugar

Cream butter. Add salt, molasses, and cream; mix well. Add icing sugar gradually and stir until smooth.

Spread between, on top and sides of two 9-inch sandwich cakes. Use with spice cake.

CREAMY VANILLA ICING

2   ounces soft butter or margarine
$\frac{1}{8}$ teaspoon salt
1   teaspoon vanilla
About 12 ounces icing sugar
2   tablespoons warm cream

Cream 6 ounces butter. Add salt, vanilla, and sugar. Stir in warm cream.

Add remaining sugar and beat until thoroughly blended.

Spread on top and sides of cake. Makes icing for two 8-inch sandwich cakes.

Creamy Lemon Icing: In above, substitute 1 tablespoon lemon juice and $\frac{1}{4}$ teaspoon grated lemon rind for vanilla.

ORNAMENTAL ICING

Cream 1 ounce butter. Blend in 12 ounces sifted icing sugar, mixing well.

Add ½ teaspoon vanilla and 2 to 4 tablespoons hot cream, a little at a time, until icing is of right consistency to press through an icing bag.

Divide into 3 or more parts and tint each a different pastel colour by adding food colouring, a drop at a time.

Pipe cakes with the icing.

LEMON ICING
(Master Recipe)

1 egg yolk
1½ tablespoons lemon juice
1 tablespoon grated orange rind
⅛ teaspoon salt
12 ounces icing sugar

Combine egg yolk, lemon juice, orange rind, and salt. Beat until smooth.

Gradually mix in sugar and beat until of spreading consistency.

Makes icing for 2 sandwich cakes or 20 cupcakes.

Variations:

Lime Icing: Substitute lime for lemon juice and ¼ teaspoon grated lemon rind for orange rind. Tint lightly with green food colouring.

Orange Icing: Substitute 2 tablespoons orange juice for lemon juice and omit grated orange rind.

BANANA BUTTER ICING

2-3 mashed ripe bananas
½ teaspoon lemon juice
2 ounces butter or margarine
About 1½ pounds icing sugar

Mix together banana and lemon juice.

Beat butter until creamy. Add sugar and banana alternately, a small amount at a time, beating until icing is light and fluffy.

Makes enough icing for top and sides of two 9-inch sandwich cakes.

BROWNED ICING

4 ounces butter or margarine
6 ounces brown sugar
6 tablespoons cream
4 ounces desiccated coconut
4 ounces chopped nuts

Heat butter and brown sugar together until melted and well blended. Add cream, coconut, and nuts, and spread on warm cake immediately.

Place under hot grill until delicately brown, about 3 minutes.

"NO-COOK" MARSHMALLOW ICING

¼ teaspoon salt
2 egg whites
2 ounces icing sugar
9 ounces corn syrup, or golden syrup
1¼ teaspoons vanilla

Add salt to egg whites and beat with electric or rotary beater until mixture forms soft peaks.

Gradually add sugar, about 1 tablespoon at a time, beating until smooth and glossy. Continue beating and add corn syrup, a little at a time, beating thoroughly after each addition, until icing peaks. Fold in vanilla.

Makes enough to ice top and sides of two 9-inch sandwich cakes.

Variations:

Coffee Icing: Omit vanilla; add 1 tablespoon instant coffee with corn syrup.

Lemon or Orange Icing: Omit vanilla; fold in 2 teaspoons grated lemon or orange rind.

Spice Icing: Omit vanilla; add ½ teaspoon ginger, ¼ teaspoon cinnamon, and a few grains of cloves with golden syrup.

Coconut Icing: Sprinkle 4 ounces desiccated coconut over top and sides of iced cake, or fold in 4 ounces desiccated coconut with vanilla.

SUPREME CHOCOLATE NUT ICING

4 ounces butter or margarine
1 egg
2 ounces chocolate
8 ounces icing sugar
⅛ teaspoon salt
1 teaspoon vanilla
4 ounces chopped nuts

Cream butter until soft and creamy. Beat in egg.

Melt chocolate and add to butter-egg mixture. Add icing sugar, salt, and vanilla. Beat until smooth and creamy. Stir in chopped nuts.

Makes icing for 1 large loaf cake or 24 cupcakes.

FLUFFY UNCOOKED ICING

2 egg whites
1 tablespoon vinegar
1 teaspoon lemon juice
Few grains salt
2 teaspoons cornflour
About 1 pound icing sugar

Beat egg whites until stiff. Add vinegar, lemon juice, salt, and cornflour. Continue beating.

Gradually add sugar until of consistency to spread.

QUICK FUDGE ICING

6 to 8 ounces plain chocolate
2 ounces butter or margarine
About 8 ounces icing sugar
½ teaspoon cinnamon
⅛ teaspoon salt
4 fluid ounces warm milk
1 teaspoon vanilla

Melt chocolate over hot water. Blend in butter.

Combine sugar, cinnamon, and salt. Add alternately with milk to chocolate-butter mixture, beating after each addition. Add vanilla and cool.

Makes icing for 24 cupcakes or tops and sides of two 9-inch sandwich cakes.

CHOCOLATE MOCHA ICING

2 ounces butter or margarine
4 tablespoons strong coffee
About 12 ounces icing sugar
2 ounces cocoa
½ teaspoon salt
1 teaspoon vanilla

Have butter and coffee at room temperature. Sift together sugar, cocoa, and salt.

Combine all ingredients and beat until smooth and fluffy. Spread on cake.

Makes enough icing for two sandwich cakes.

FLUFFY HONEY ICING

1 egg white
Dash of salt
6 ounces honey

Beat egg white with salt until stiff enough to hold up in peaks, but not dry.

Pour honey in fine stream over egg white, beating constantly until icing holds its shape. (Beat about 2½ minutes with electric mixer, or about 4 minutes by hand.)

Makes icing to cover tops of two 8-inch sandwich cakes.

For a quick decoration, icing sugar is sprinkled through a paper doily.

MOLASSES MOCHA ICING
(Master Recipe)
About 12 ounces icing sugar
2 ounces butter or margarine
1 egg white, unbeaten
1 tablespoon cold coffee
1 tablespoon molasses or black
    treacle
1 teaspoon vanilla

Add 6 ounces sugar gradually to butter and egg white. Mix well.

Add remaining sugar alternately with coffee, molasses, and vanilla. Beat well.

Makes enough for tops and sides of two 8-inch sandwich cakes or tops of two 9-inch sandwich cakes.

Variations:

Molasses Chocolate Icing: Add 3 tablespoons cocoa or 1 ounce melted chocolate.

Molasses Orange Icing: Omit coffee and vanilla. Add 2 tablespoons orange juice, 1 teaspoon grated orange rind, and ½ teaspoon grated lemon rind.

SPICY RAISIN ICING
About 10 ounces icing sugar
1 tablespoon cocoa
½ teaspoon cinnamon
⅛ teaspoon cloves
⅛ teaspoon nutmeg
1 small can sweetened condensed
    milk
½ teaspoon vanilla
3 ounces raisins

Combine ingredients in order given. Use to ice spice cakes.

EASY CHOCOLATE ICING
1½ ounces butter or margarine
2 ounces chocolate
About 1 pound icing sugar
1 teaspoon vanilla
3 fluid ounces hot milk

Combine butter and chocolate in top of double saucepan. Cook over boiling water until chocolate is melted.

Combine sifted icing sugar with vanilla and hot milk and blend well.

Add melted chocolate and beat until smooth and thick.

To get a famous date on a cake prepare paper cutouts and put in place, then sprinkle with caster sugar.

BUTTERFLY ICING
2 tablespoons butter or margarine
About 1 pound icing sugar
1 egg white, unbeaten
About 1 tablespoon cream
⅛ teaspoon vanilla
⅛ teaspoon salt
Colouring

Cream butter; add part of sugar gradually, blending after each addition. Add remaining sugar, alternately with egg white, then with cream, until of right consistency to spread. Beat after each addition until smooth.

Add vanilla and salt. Tint delicately with colouring.

For assorted icings, divide untinted icing into four small bowls. Use one plain or flavour with ½ ounce melted plain chocolate. Tint the remaining icings to give delicate, yet decided, shades of yellow, green, and pink.

While using assorted icings, keep bowls covered to avoid crusting. If necessary, one or two drops of cream or milk may be added to keep icing of right consistency to spread. Use for decorating, if desired.

QUICK FRUIT ICING
About 1 pound 2 ounces icing sugar
3 teaspoons grated orange rind
About 4 tablespoons lemon juice
Dash of salt
2 ounces butter or other fat, melted

Combine sugar, rind, juice, and salt in small bowl. Add melted butter and beat.

Makes icing for tops and sides of two 8-inch sandwich cakes. Use half recipe for top of 8×8×2-inch square cake.

ALMOND PASTE ICING
Blanch or skin 1 pound of almonds and put through mincer, using medium blade.

Mix in 1 pound icing sugar, sifted very well.

Beat 3 egg whites slightly, then mix them in. Finally, add 1 teaspoon almond essence.

Because this makes a heavy and stiff paste, you have to place it on the cake and work it into a smooth, even layer with your hands or a rolling pin.

ALMOND ICING
Cream 2 ounces butter. Add dash of salt. Blend in about 8 ounces sifted icing sugar gradually.

Add 1 unbeaten egg yolk, ½ teaspoon almond essence, and 4 teaspoons milk. Beat until of spreading consistency.

Add few drops of yellow food colouring, if desired.

HEART'S DELIGHT CAKE

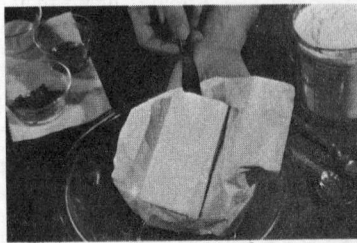

1. Soften 8 ounces cream cheese at room temperature.

2. Blend about 1½ pounds icing sugar into cream cheese. Add 2 tablespoons maraschino cherry juice and blend again.

3. Add 2 tablespoons chopped maraschino cherries, mixing them in lightly.

4. Spread icing on bottom layer of your favourite cake baked in 2 heart-shaped tins.

5. Cover with second layer of cake and spread remaining icing on sides and top of cake.

Cooked Icings

BOILED ICING
(Master Recipe)

12 ounces sugar
Dash of salt
4 fluid ounces water
3 tablespoons corn syrup or golden syrup
2 egg whites
½ teaspoon vanilla

Cook sugar, salt, water, and corn syrup to the soft ball stage (238°F.). Remove mixture from heat.

Beat egg whites quickly with a rotary beater. Pour hot syrup slowly in a fine stream over egg whites, beating constantly.

Add vanilla and continue beating until icing stands up in peaks. Quickly spread on cake.

On a rainy or humid day, boil syrup to higher temperature. If icing hardens before spreading, beat in a few drops of hot water.

Makes icing for top and sides of 2 9-inch sandwich cakes or 24 cupcakes.

Boiled Icing Variations:

Apricot Icing: Fold 4 ounces cooked apricot pulp into beaten icing.

Brown Sugar Icing: In master recipe, substitute brown sugar for white. Omit corn syrup and cook to 250°F. instead of 238°F.

Chocolate Icing: In master recipe, add 1 ounce cocoa or 2 ounces melted chocolate to sugar, and cook with sugar and water.

Coconut Icing: Sprinkle plain, tinted, or toasted desiccated coconut over icing.

Coffee Walnut Icing: In master recipe, substitute coffee for water. Omit vanilla. Add 2 ounces chopped walnuts to beaten icing.

Coloured Icing: Tint icing with food colouring as desired. Flavour as desired.

Fruit Icing: Prepare master recipe. Fold chopped crystallised cherries, chopped crystallised pineapple, or other chopped crystallised fruit into beaten icing.

Ginger Icing: In master recipe, use 1½ ounces brown sugar and 8 ounces white sugar. Fold in 4 ounces finely chopped, drained preserved ginger just before spreading.

Lady Baltimore Icing or Filling: Prepare master recipe. Chop and fold 1½ ounces each of dried figs, stoned dates, seedless raisins, and 1 ounce walnuts, and blanched almonds into beaten icing. If desired, substitute almond essence for vanilla.

Lemon Icing: Prepare master recipe. Fold into icing 2 tablespoons lemon juice and 1 teaspoon lemon rind just before spreading.

Lord Baltimore Icing or Filling: Prepare master recipe. Fold 2 ounces toasted desiccated coconut, 2 ounces chopped crystallised cherries or chopped maraschino cherries, 1 ounce chopped, blanched almonds or chopped pecans into beaten icing.

Marshmallow Icing: Prepare master recipe. Cut marshmallows into quarters. Arrange on top of cake. Spread icing over them, or fold in half-melted marshmallows just before spreading.

Molasses Icing: In master recipe, substitute 3 tablespoons molasses or black treacle for corn syrup.

Nut Icing: Sprinkle whole or chopped nuts over icing.

Peppermint Icing: Flavour master recipe with a few drops of peppermint instead of vanilla.

Strawberry Icing: Prepare master recipe and fold 4 ounces crushed strawberries into beaten icing.

SEVEN MINUTE ICING
(Master Recipe)

2 egg whites, unbeaten
12 ounces sugar
⅛ teaspoon salt
3 fluid ounces cold water
1 tablespoon light corn syrup or golden syrup
1 teaspoon vanilla

Place egg whites, sugar, salt, water, and corn syrup in top of double saucepan.

Place over boiling water and beat constantly with a large double rotary beater or electric mixer at high speed until icing will stand in peaks, about 7 minutes.

Remove from heat; beat in vanilla. Quickly spread on cake.

Makes enough icing for top and sides of 2 9-inch sandwich cakes or 2 dozen cupcakes.

Seven-Minute Icing Variations:

Chocolate Icing: Stir into beaten icing 2 ounces melted chocolate.

Coconut Icing: Sprinkle plain, tinted, or toasted coconut over icing while still soft.

Coffee Icing: In master recipe, omit vanilla. Substitute coffee for water.

Coloured Icing: Tint icing as desired with food colouring. Flavour as desired.

Fruit Icing: Prepare master recipe. Fold 2 ounces chopped crystallised cherries, chopped crystallised pineapple, or other fruit into beaten icing.

Lemon Icing: In master recipe, substitute 2 tablespoons lemon juice and grated rind of 1 lemon for 2 tablespoons water, the corn syrup, and vanilla.

Orange Icing: In master recipe, substitute 3 tablespoons orange juice and grated rind of 1 orange for 3 tablespoons water, the corn syrup, and vanilla.

Marshmallow Icing: Follow master recipe and fold in 1 dozen quartered marshmallows with flavouring.

Peppermint Rock Icing: Prepare master recipe. Fold 2 ounces crushed hard peppermint rock into beaten icing. Decorate sides of cake with additional 2 ounces of crushed hard peppermint rock.

Sea Foam Icing: Omit corn syrup in master recipe. Substitute 9 ounces brown sugar for white sugar.

PENUCHE (PANOCHA) PECAN ICING

9 ounces light brown sugar
12 ounces sugar
2 tablespoons light corn syrup or golden syrup
6 fluid ounces milk
4 ounces butter
¼ teaspoon salt
1 teaspoon orange juice
4 ounces chopped pecans or walnuts

Place both sugars, corn syrup, milk, butter, and salt in saucepan. Bring slowly to full rolling boil, stirring constantly, and boil briskly 2 minutes. Cool to lukewarm.

Add orange juice and beat until thick enough to spread. Add pecans and mix.

Makes icing to cover tops and sides of two 9-inch sandwich cakes.

Homemade icing gives a simple "bought" cake an appetizing look.

CARAMEL ICING

9 ounces brown sugar
8 fluid ounces top of milk or light
    cream
1 ounce butter or margarine
½ teaspoon vanilla
⅛ teaspoon salt

Combine sugar and milk and bring to boil, stirring constantly.

Stirring occasionally, boil to soft ball stage (236°F.).

Remove from heat and add butter, vanilla, and salt. Cool to lukewarm and beat until of spreading consistency.

Makes icing for top and sides of two 8-inch sandwich cakes or 24 cupcakes.

BUTTERSCOTCH ICING

6 ounces light brown sugar
3 ounces white sugar
2½ fluid ounces hot water
1 beaten egg white
½ teaspoon vanilla
Few grains salt

Mix together brown sugar, white sugar, and water over low heat until thoroughly dissolved. Bring to a boil and cook until syrup spins a long thread.

Pour syrup slowly over egg white, beating constantly. Add vanilla and salt.

If desired, 1 ounce chopped nuts may be added.

HONEY ALMOND ICING

2 egg whites, unbeaten
3 ounces honey
4 ounces browned, chopped
    almonds

Combine egg whites and honey in top of double saucepan, beating with rotary egg beater until thoroughly mixed.

Place over rapidly boiling water, beating constantly with rotary egg beater, and cook 7 minutes, or until icing will stand up in peaks.

Remove from boiling water. Add ½ of nuts. Spread on cake, sprinkling remaining nuts over top of cake while icing is still soft.

Makes icing to cover tops and sides of two 8- or 9-inch sandwich cakes.

MAPLE ICING

4½ ounces brown sugar
2½ tablespoons water
1 egg white
¼ teaspoon maple flavouring

Cook sugar, water, and egg white in top of double saucepan, beating constantly until mixture stands up in peaks (about 7 minutes).

Remove from heat and add maple flavouring. Beat until of spreading consistency.

FONDANT ICING

1 pound sugar
8 fluid ounces water
½ teaspoon cream of tartar or 2
    tablespoons light corn syrup
    or golden syrup

Combine the ingredients in a saucepan and stir over low heat until sugar is dissolved. Cover and bring to a rapid boil.

Uncover and continue to boil, without stirring, until a small amount of syrup forms a soft ball when dropped into cold water, or to 238°F. on a sugar thermometer. Remove from heat and allow to cool to lukewarm.

Then beat with wooden spoon until syrup becomes white and creamy. Spread quickly over cake.

If it becomes too dry for smooth spreading, add a little hot water and beat until smooth. The fondant may be delicately tinted with food colouring and flavoured as desired.

Dipping with Fondant: Make fondant icing and keep it soft over boiling water, stirring in a few drops of boiling water if mixture becomes too stiff.

Add flavouring or food colouring desired, but stir as little as possible to avoid crystallization.

Lower small cakes or biscuits into the liquid fondant on a dipping fork. Raise cake and draw the dipping fork lightly across the edge of the pan to remove any excess fondant, then invert the dipped cake onto a plate or greaseproof paper.

Work quickly so that the fondant will not become too thick. If it should thicken, however, add a few more drops of boiling water to bring it back to the right consistency.

Decorate the little cakes with a bit of candied fruit or rind, nuts, or tiny sugar flowers.

CREAMY CHOCOLATE ICING

6 ounces brown sugar
3 ounces chocolate
¼ teaspoon salt
5 tablespoons evaporated milk or
    cream
3 tablespoons butter or margarine
1 teaspoon vanilla
Icing sugar

Combine brown sugar, chocolate, salt, and milk or cream in a saucepan. Bring to boiling point. Cook on medium heat until slightly thickened, about 5 minutes. Remove from heat.

Add butter and vanilla. Cool slightly. Add enough sifted icing sugar for proper consistency to spread. Beat until smooth.

Spread between layers and on top and sides of cake.

WHITE MOUNTAIN ICING

2 egg whites
12 ounces sugar
4 fluid ounces cold water
1 tablespoon light corn syrup or
    golden syrup or ¼ teaspoon
    cream of tartar
1 teaspoon vanilla

Put the egg whites in a mixing bowl

Combine sugar, water, and corn syrup or cream of tartar in a small saucepan. Stir over low heat until the sugar has dissolved. Boil rapidly until a small amount of syrup forms a soft ball when dropped into cold water (238°F.). Remove from heat.

Beat the egg whites quickly until stiff. Continue beating while pouring the hot syrup in a fine stream over the egg whites. Add the flavouring and continue beating until the mixture is stiff enough to spread.

STRAWBERRY FLUFF

2 egg whites, unbeaten
8 ounces sugar
Dash of salt
6 ounces sliced fresh strawberries
    or use frozen sliced straw-
    berries, thawed and drained

Combine egg whites, sugar, salt, and 4 ounces strawberries in top of double saucepan. Beat about 1 minute to blend.

Place over rapidly boiling water and beat constantly with rotary egg beater or at high speed with electric mixer minutes, or until icing will stand up in stiff peaks.

Remove from boiling water and beat until cool. Fold in remaining drained berries and spread at once.

Ices tops and sides of two 9-inch sandwich cakes; top and sides of 13 × 9 × 2-inch cake. Or fills 16 × 10 × 2-inch cake roll.

Flower Garden Cake Decoration: Ice top and sides of a rectangular cake with a white icing. Spread icing evenly. Mark cake into serving-size pieces, then sprinkle with coloured sugar. Decorate with fresh garden flowers. Wrap stems with aluminium foil; place one blossom on each serving. Insert coloured cocktail sticks to form "Xs" on the top of outer edge of cake.

MOCHA ICING

About 5 tablespoons strong coffee
About 1½ pounds sifted icing sugar
4 ounces fat
⅛ teaspoon salt
1 teaspoon vanilla

To make strong coffee, add 3 tablespoons medium-ground coffee to 8 fluid ounces cold water. Heat to boiling. Remove from heat and let stand 2 minutes. Strain and cool slightly.

Combine sugar gradually with fat and add coffee as needed to make a creamy-smooth mixture. Add salt and vanilla. Spread on cooled cake.

Makes icing for tops and sides of two 9-inch sandwich cakes.

Mocha Chocolate Icing: To above recipe, add ounce melted plain chocolate. A little more coffee may be needed for good spreading consistency.

HUNGARIAN CHOCOLATE ICING

3 ounces plain chocolate
About 8 ounces sifted icing sugar
2½ tablespoons hot water
3 egg yolks
2 ounces softened butter or other fat

One whole egg may be substituted for the 3 egg yolks; use only 2 tablespoons water.

Melt chocolate. Remove from heat; add sugar and water, and blend. Add egg yolks, one at a time, beating well after each. Add butter gradually, beating well after each addition.

Makes icing for tops and sides of two 8- or 9-inch sandwich cakes, or top and sides of 8-, 9-, or 10-inch square cake, 10×5×3-inch loaf, a 9-inch 3-layer cake or 24 cupcakes.

FLUFFY COOKED ICING

12 ounces caster sugar
¼ teaspoon cream of tartar
4 fluid ounces water
3 egg whites
About 3 ounces icing sugar
½ teaspoon vanilla

Combine 8 ounces sugar, cream of tartar, and water; stir over low heat until thoroughly dissolved. Bring to a boil and cook to the medium-hard ball stage (250°F.).

Beat egg whites until stiff but not dry. Fold in remaining sugar, a tablespoon at a time, beating after each addition.

Slowly pour syrup into egg whites, beating constantly. Beat in sifted icing sugar and vanilla.

Makes icing to cover top and sides of two 9-inch sandwich cakes.

EASY FUDGE ICING

3 ounces plain chocolate
1 ounce butter or margarine
About 1 pound sifted icing sugar
7 tablespoons light cream or top of milk
Dash of salt
1 teaspoon vanilla

Melt chocolate and butter over boiling water and blend.

Add 8 ounces icing sugar, cream, and salt, all at once and beat until smooth. Cook and stir over low heat until mixture bubbles up well around edges.

Remove from heat; add vanilla and remaining sugar in thirds, beating after each addition until smooth.

Place over bowl of ice water until thick enough to spread on cake.

Ices tops and sides of two 8-inch sandwich cakes or two 8-inch square cakes.

PETITS FOURS ICING

1 pound caster sugar
8 fluid ounces water
⅛ teaspoon cream of tartar
About 8 ounces sifted icing sugar

Combine caster sugar, water, and cream of tartar. Cook over direct heat to 226°F., or a thin syrup. Stir only until sugar is dissolved. Remove from heat.

Pour into top of double saucepan and cool to somewhat above lukewarm (110°F.). Gradually add about 8 ounces sugar until icing is of proper consistency to pour.

Place a few cakes in rows on a wire rack over a baking sheet, allowing considerable space between cakes. Pour icing over cakes, covering tops and sides and allowing icing to drip onto baking sheet. Keep over hot water when not pouring.

If it becomes too thick, add a few drops of hot water. If too thin, add a little more sifted icing sugar. Scrape icing from baking sheet, reheat, and use for other cakes. Repeat the process until cakes are completely coated.

Decorate with ornamental icing, coloured sugar, candied fruit, or nuts.

SHADOW ICING

Spread cake with white mountain icing.

When the icing has set, melt 2 ounces plain chocolate in double saucepan over hot water, heating only until the chocolate is melted. Pour the chocolate over top of cake slowly and let it trickle down the sides.

For use on small tea cakes, ice the top only with the white mountain icing. Smooth the icing in the centre and make a rim around the outside edge.

Pour the chocolate in the centre to be held in place by the rim until it sets.

BOILED MARSHMALLOW ICING

1¼ pounds caster sugar
6 ounces light corn syrup or golden syrup
¼ teaspoon salt
4 fluid ounces water
2 egg whites
1 teaspoon vanilla
8 marshmallows, cut in quarters

Place sugar, corn syrup, salt, and water together in a saucepan and cook to the firm ball stage (250°F.).

Pour the hot syrup slowly into the well beaten egg whites, beating constantly.

Add vanilla and continue beating until the icing will hold its shape when tossed over the back of a spoon. Add marshmallows.

This icing recipe will stand in swirls an inch or more high.

FOUR MINUTE ICING

1 egg white, unbeaten
6 ounces sugar
Dash of salt
3 tablespoons water
1 teaspoon light corn syrup or golden syrup
½ teaspoon vanilla

Prepare as for the seven-minute icing, beating only 4 minutes.

Ices tops and sides of two 8-inch sandwich cakes (thinly) or two 8×4×3-inch loaves, or top and sides of 9 or 10-inch tube cake.

A pumpkin of orange icing tops this cake; face is painted on with chocolate.

Cake Fillings

CRÈME PÂTISSIÈRE OR PASTRY CREAM

4 beaten egg yolks
5 ounces sugar
3 ounces flour
1 teaspoon cornflour
16 fluid ounces milk, scalded
1 vanilla bean or ½ teaspoon vanilla

Cream egg yolks and sugar together until light and creamy. Blend in flour and cornflour.

Gradually add milk in which vanilla bean has been scalded. (If vanilla essence is used, add at the end.) Cook, stirring constantly, over low heat until thick and boiling.

Set pan immediately in cold water to cool it quickly or empty into a cold bowl. Stir occasionally to keep a skin from forming on top. Chill before using. Use for filling éclairs, napoleons, and other cakes.

Variations: For chocolate cream, flavour with melted chocolate; for mocha cream, flavour with coffee essence.

FRANGIPANE CREAM

A custard cream used as a pastry filling or topping. Also spelled frangipani; it is said to be named after a Marquis Frangipani, major general under Louis XIV.

To Make: Prepare Crème Pâtissière (Pastry Cream), but after removing from the heat, beat in 1 ounce butter and 1 ounce dried and rolled macaroon crumbs. If desired, flavour with lemon essence, sherry, brandy, or rum.

LORD BALTIMORE FILLING AND ICING

12 ounces sugar
½ teaspoon cream of tartar
Dash of salt
4 fluid ounces hot water
3 egg whites
½ teaspoon vanilla
2 teaspoons lemon juice
2 ounces macaroon crumbs
12 crystallised cherries, chopped
2 ounces chopped blanched almonds
1 ounce chopped pecans or walnuts

Blend sugar, cream of tartar, salt, and hot water. Cook, without stirring, to soft ball stage or 240°F. on sugar thermometer.

Beat egg whites until stiff. Pour syrup in a fine stream over beaten whites, beating constantly. Add vanilla.

Add lemon juice to crumbs. Fold crumbs, cherries, and nuts into half of the icing and use this for cake filling.

CREAM FILLING (Master Recipe)

6 ounces sugar
2½ ounces flour
¼ teaspoon salt
16 fluid ounces scalded milk
2 slightly beaten eggs
1 teaspoon vanilla

Combine sugar, flour, and salt. Slowly stir in scalded milk. Cook in double saucepan over boiling water for 15 minutes, or until thick.

Add a little of the hot mixture to egg. Stir in remaining hot mixture. Cook over simmering water for 3 minutes. Cool and add vanilla.

For a richer filling, add 2 tablespoons butter to hot cooked custard.

Makes filling for 4 large sponge cakes or 24 large cream puffs or 24 éclairs.

Cream Filling Variations:

Banana Cream Filling: In master recipe, substitute 1 teaspoon lemon juice for vanilla. Add medium-sized mashed banana to filling.

Butterscotch Cream Filling: In master recipe, substitute 4½ ounces brown sugar for white sugar. Add 2 tablespoons butter to cooked filling.

Chocolate Cream Filling: In master recipe, increase sugar to 8 ounces. Add 2 ounces plain chocolate to milk before cooking. Beat until smooth.

Coconut Cream Filling: In master recipe, add 4 ounces desiccated coconut to filling.

Coffee Cream Filling: In master recipe, substitute 4 fluid ounces strong fresh coffee for same quantity of milk. Proceed as directed.

Creamy Custard Filling: Prepare master recipe. Fold ¼ pint whipped double cream into chilled filling.

Pineapple Cream Filling: In master recipe, substitute lemon juice for vanilla. Add 4 ounces crushed, drained pineapple to filling.

DATE FILLING

1 pound chopped, stoned dates
1 tablespoon lemon juice
4 fluid ounces water
3 ounces sugar
⅛ teaspoon salt
4 ounces finely chopped nuts

Combine all ingredients except nuts and bring to boiling point, stirring constantly until thick.

Add nuts and cool. Spread between layers.

Almond Luxor Cake

ALMOND LUXOR CAKE

Make 2 8-inch sandwich cakes, put together with Luxor Custard Filling (below), ice with white icing or whipped cream, sprinkle with browned almonds, diced.

Luxor Custard Filling:
16 fluid ounces milk
5 ounces sugar
Few grains salt
1½ ounces cornflour
3 egg yolks, beaten
1 teaspoon vanilla
2 ounces browned almonds, diced

Combine 12 fluid ounces milk, sugar, and salt in top of double saucepan. Scald.

Blend remaining 4 fluid ounces milk, and beaten egg yolks; stir into hot milk, cook and stir until thick. Blend in vanilla and almonds. Cool and spread on cake.

CHOCOLATE BRAZIL NUT FILLING

2 ounces plain chocolate
6 fluid ounces milk
2 ounces flour
4 ounces sugar
½ ounce butter or margarine
½ teaspoon vanilla
2 ounces ground Brazil nuts

Add chocolate to milk in double saucepan. Beat over low heat until chocolate is melted and well blended.

Add a small amount of the chocolate mixture to the flour, which has been sifted with the sugar.

Return to double pan. Stir until smooth and cook until thickened. Add butter and vanilla.

When cool, add Brazil nuts and spread on cake.

WALNUT TORTE FILLING

2 beaten egg yolks
4 ounces sugar
6 fluid ounces milk
½ teaspoon vanilla or rum flavouring
½ pound chopped walnuts

Mix egg yolks and sugar; add milk and cook in top of double saucepan until thick.

Cool; add vanilla or rum and nuts. Spread between layer of walnut torte.

LEMON FILLING
(Master Recipe)

6 ounces sugar
2½ ounces flour
⅛ teaspoon salt
¼ pint water
1 slightly beaten egg
½ ounce butter or margarine
1 teaspoon grated lemon rind
5 tablespoons lemon juice

Combine sugar, flour, and salt in top of double saucepan. Add water and blend thoroughly. Cook over boiling water until thickened, stirring constantly.

Cover and cook additional 10 minutes, stirring occasionally.

Stir in a little of the hot mixture into slightly beaten egg. Slowly stir into the remaining hot mixture. Cook over simmering water for 2 minutes, stirring constantly.

Cool slightly. Add butter and lemon rind. Chill and add lemon juice. Makes filling for two 9-inch sandwich cakes.

Lemon Filling Variations:

Lemon Cream Filling: Fold ¼ pint whipped cream into chilled lemon filling.

Orange Filling: Proceed as for lemon filling. Decrease sugar to 4 ounces, water to 4 fluid ounces, lemon juice to 1 tablespoon, lemon rind to ½ teaspoon.

Add 1 tablespoon orange rind. When chilled, add 4 fluid ounces orange juice.

Orange Date Filling: Add 3 ounces chopped dates to orange filling.

Orange Coconut Filling: Add 2 ounces desiccated coconut to orange filling.

Orange Cream Filling: When orange filling is chilled, fold in ¼ pint whipped cream and 2 ounces plain or browned desiccated coconut.

WHIPPED CREAM FILLING
(Master Recipe)

½ teaspoon gelatine
1 tablespoon cold water
3 tablespoons icing sugar
¼ teaspoon vanilla
¼ pint double cream

Soften gelatine in cold water. Place over boiling water. Stir until dissolved. Let cool.

Mix with sugar, vanilla, and cream. Whip until stiff. Chill thoroughly before spreading. Makes filling for two 9-inch sandwich cakes.

Variations of
Whipped Cream Filling:

Applesauce Filling: Omit vanilla in master recipe. Decrease cream to ⅛ pint. Before chilling, fold in 4 ounces chilled, thick apple sauce and ½ teaspoon cinnamon.

Chocolate Filling: In master recipe, increase sugar to 4 tablespoons. Mix with 2 tablespoons cocoa before adding cream.

Coffee Filling: Substitute coffee for water in master recipe.

Pineapple Filling: Omit vanilla in master recipe. Decrease cream to 5 tablespoons. Before chilling, fold in 4 ounces drained, crushed pineapple.

BANANA FILLING

8 ounces sugar
4 tablespoons water
3 large bananas, mashed
2 lightly beaten egg yolks

Heat sugar and water until syrup spins a thread when dropped from fork or spoon (234°F.).

Combine mashed bananas with beaten egg yolk. Add syrup gradually, beating thoroughly.

Place over hot water. Heat through, beating thoroughly. Cool before spreading.

Banana Nut Filling: Add about 2 ounces chopped nuts just before spreading.

PINEAPPLE FILLING

6 ounces sugar
2½ tablespoons cornflour
⅛ teaspoon salt
Grated rind of 1 lemon
4 tablespoons lemon juice
3 slightly beaten egg yolks
4 fluid ounces canned pineapple juice
1 ounce butter or margarine

Mix sugar, cornflour, and salt in top of double saucepan. Add lemon rind and lemon juice and mix well. Add egg yolks, pineapple juice, and butter and blend.

Place over boiling water. Cook until thick and smooth, stirring constantly, about 15 minutes.

Makes filling for two 8-inch sandwich cakes.

RUM NUT FILLING AND ICING

8 ounces plain flour
6 fluid ounces milk
6 ounces butter or margarine
6 ounces caster sugar
½ teaspoon salt
½ teaspoon vanilla
3 ounces chopped nuts
3 tablespoons rum flavouring
about 1½ pounds sifted icing sugar

Measure flour into saucepan. Add milk gradually, stirring until smooth. Cook to thick paste over slow heat,

stirring constantly. Cool to lukewarm.

Cream butter, caster sugar, and salt thoroughly. Add lukewarm paste and beat with rotary beater until fluffy. Fold in vanilla and nuts.

Spread ¼ of mixture between layers of 9-inch sandwich cake.

Add rum flavouring and icing sugar to remaining mixture and stir until well blended.

Spread over top and sides of cake. Makes filling and icing for two 9-inch sandwich cakes.

LIME FRUIT FILLING

To 4 ounces of fluffy lime icing (see Index), add 2 tablespoons each of chopped raisins, nuts, candied or glacé cherries, and citron.

Spread between layers of cake. Use remaining icing to cover top and sides of cake. For a gay effect, sprinkle silver dragées or tiny coloured sweets on top of cake.

MAPLE CREAM FILLING

4 egg yolks
4½ ounces icing sugar
6 fluid ounces milk
4 ounces butter or margarine
2 teaspoons maple flavouring

Beat egg yolks until thick and lemon coloured. Add sugar and milk and cook in double saucepan, stirring constantly, until thick, about 10 minutes. Cool.

Cream butter until fluffy. Add thoroughly cold custard and maple flavouring. Beat with rotary beater until smooth.

Makes filling for 3 8-inch sponge sandwich cakes.

CARAMEL FILLING

3 ounces brown sugar
1 pound caster sugar
8 fluid ounces buttermilk or sour milk
½ teaspoon bicarbonate of soda
4 ounces butter or margarine
1 tablespoon vanilla

Combine sugars, buttermilk, soda, and butter. Cook until syrup forms a soft ball when a small amount is dropped into cold water (238°F.).

Cool. Add vanilla. Beat until creamy. Spread over cake.

SOUR CREAM FILLING

2 eggs
5 ounces sugar
8 fluid ounces sour cream
Pinch of salt
½ teaspoon vanilla

Beat eggs until thick. Gradually add sugar, beating constantly. Add sour cream and salt.

Cook over boiling water until thickened, stirring constantly, about 15 minutes.

Cool. Add vanilla. Makes filling for two 9-inch sandwich cakes.

GOLDEN CREAM FILLING

1½ tablespoons gelatine
4 tablespoons cold water
8 egg yolks
⅛ teaspoon salt
5½ ounces icing sugar
4 tablespoons strong fresh coffee
¾ pint cream, whipped

Soften gelatine in cold water.

Beat egg yolks with salt until thick. Beat sugar in gradually.

Dissolve softened gelatine in hot coffee. Add to egg-sugar mixture.

Let stand until partially set. Fold in whipped cream.

Makes filling and topping for two 9-inch sandwich cakes.

APPLE FILLING

6 ounces sugar
1 tablespoon flour
3 tablespoons lemon juice
1 tablespoon water
1 beaten egg
4 ounces grated apple

Combine all ingredients. Cook over very low heat until thick, 8 to 10 minutes. Cool.

Spread between layers. Ice cake with seven-minute icing.

Pineapple Coconut Filling: In above recipe, substitute 4 ounces drained crushed pineapple for the grated apple, and add 2 ounces desiccated coconut.

Glazes

When used on cakes, glazes are jiffy substitutes for icings. The thin coating helps to keep a cake moist but requires no particular ability to apply.

Glazes are most frequently used on angel food and chiffon cakes; however they may be used on sweet breads, fruitcakes, biscuits and small cakes such as petits fours.

A cake such as fruitcake, sweet breads, or Christmas cookies may be decorated with bits of fruit and nuts just after applying a glaze and when it dries the decorations will be held in place.

CHOCOLATE GLAZE

1 tablespoon butter or margarine
1 ounce plain chocolate
1½ tablespoons hot milk
2½-3 ounces sifted icing sugar
Dash of salt

Melt butter and chocolate together. Combine milk, sugar, and dash of salt in bowl. Blend in chocolate mixture gradually.

Pour over cake and spread with spatula. Makes enough glaze to cover cake roll or 8- or 9-inch sandwich cake.

APRICOT GLAZE

Wash and drain 3 ounces dried apricots. Put in saucepan with 1 pint water and boil uncovered 10 minutes.

Put through sieve or mincer. There should be about 1 pound apricot purée; if not, add water to make that amount.

Combine purée with 1¼ pounds sugar. Bring to a boil and boil gently 5 to 8 minutes, stirring constantly until purée is as thick as marmalade.

Cool and use for tarts, pastries, and under icings of decorated cakes to give a smooth surface over which to spread the outer icing.

To store: Keep unused glaze in covered container in refrigerator. When ready to use again, warm slightly to facilitate spreading.

APRICOT JAM GLAZE

8 ounces sugar
8 fluid ounces boiling water
6 ounces apricot jam

Stir and cook combined sugar and water in saucepan over medium heat until sugar is dissolved. Bring to boiling point, uncovered, and boil 10 minutes.

Heat apricot jam in another pan until it bubbles around the edge of pan. Remove from heat and put through a sieve into the syrup. Mix well and keep hot until ready to use, or reheat just before using to make thin enough to pour. Use for glazing petits fours, fruit pies, tarts, and coffee cakes.

LEMON GLAZE

1½ tablespoons milk
½ ounce butter or margarine
5½ ounces sifted icing sugar
1½ tablespoons lemon juice
½ teaspoon grated lemon rind

Heat milk and butter together. Measure sugar into bowl. Add liquid and stir until smooth. Then add juice and rind.

Pour over cake, letting it run down sides. Makes enough glaze to cover a 9-inch or 10-inch tube cake.

ORANGE GLAZE

1 teaspoon grated orange rind
1 tablespoon orange juice
6 ounces sifted icing sugar
About 1 tablespoon water

Combine orange rind and juice; let stand 5 minutes. Strain and discard rind.

Stir juice into sugar and add enough water to make a good spreading consistency.

Spread on slightly warm cake. Makes enough glaze for top of one 9-inch square cake.

Glazed Fruit Cake

GLAZE FOR FRUIT CAKES

About 10 ounces icing sugar
1 ounce soft butter or margarine
¼ teaspoon vanilla
1½ to 2 tablespoons milk

Combine sugar, butter, vanilla and 1½ tablespoons milk in a bowl. Beat with a spoon until smooth. If thinner glaze is desired, add remaining milk.

QUICK BLENDER GLAZE

About 10 ounces icing sugar
4 tablespoons fruit juice (lemon, lime, or orange)
1 teaspoon vanilla

Combine ingredients in blender and mix until smooth. No heating is necessary. Just spread on warm cakes or biscuits. Glaze has just the right consistency for embedding decorative fruits and nuts. Makes enough glaze for 4 square 8-inch cakes.

VANILLA GLAZE

12 ounces sifted icing sugar
⅛ teaspoon salt
3 to 4 tablespoons hot cream

Combine sugar and salt in bowl. Blend in cream until mixture has consistency of a glaze. Spread on top of cake, letting it drip down sides. Makes glaze for 9-inch tube cake.

Note: In above 2 tablespoons soft butter and 2 to 3 tablespoons milk may be substituted for cream.

Cinnamon Glaze: Combine ½ teaspoon cinnamon and ¼ teaspoon nutmeg with the sugar and salt.

COFFEE GLAZE

2½ tablespoons water
½ ounce butter or margarine
About 8 ounces sifted icing sugar
Dash of salt
2 teaspoons instant coffee

Heat water and butter together. Measure sugar, salt, and instant coffee into bowl. Add hot liquid and stir until smooth.

Pour over cake, letting it run down sides. Makes glaze to cover tube cake.

CANDIES AND CONFECTIONERY

HINTS FOR MAKING CANDIES

Before you begin making candies read the basic hints given here and follow the recipes exactly. Don't try to substitute ingredients or double the recipes.

Candies are usually classified into two general types, cream candies and hard candies. Each type has many variations. The two types are determined by the thickness of the syrup or the extent to which the sugar is caramelized in the candymaking process. The syrup becomes thick as it boils. The creamy candies, such as fondant and fudge, form crystals, which must be very small in order to avoid a coarse, grainy texture. Note that these candies are stirred only until the sugar is dissolved. The hard candies, such as butterscotch and caramels, are non-crystalline. It's important to pour and cool hard candies quickly.

EQUIPMENT FOR MAKING CANDIES

The saucepans should be sufficiently heavy to minimize scorching. Use heavy aluminium or enamel pans large enough to allow the syrup to boil vigorously without danger of boiling over.

Use a wooden spoon for stirring or beating. A medium-sized spatula is best for removing candy from the pans. Bowls should be smooth.

For cooling fondant and brittle candies a marble slab is ideal but an inverted baking sheet for brittle or a large platter for fondant make acceptable substitutes. For fudge and similar candies use shallow pans with straight sides.

Before starting to make candies assemble all ingredients and utensils so that they will be handy.

USE OF SUGAR THERMOMETER OR SACCHAROMETER

A sugar thermometer is necessary to ensure uniformity and consistency in results.

The bulb should be entirely immersed in mixture without touching pan. Have your eye on level with part of scale being tested.

The accuracy of your sugar thermometer should be checked each time you use it. Let the thermometer stand in boiling water for 10 minutes. The thermometer should register 212°F. If there is any variation, subtract or add to make the same degree of allowance in testing candy.

COLD WATER TESTS

With practice the cold water tests given below will give satisfactory results.

To make cold water test, remove pan from heat. Pour small amount of syrup from spoon into cup of cold water, not iced water. The hardness of ball formed indicates temperature of syrup.

COOKING TEMPERATURES

Soft Ball: (236°-238°F.) When dropped into cold water, syrup will form soft ball which quickly loses its shape on removal.

When using brown sugar, or on rainy or damp days, boil to higher temperature.

Firm Ball: (244°-250°F.) Syrup will form a firm but plastic ball in cold water which can be easily handled in the water and becomes soft on removal. Use for caramels.

Hard Ball: (250°-258°F.) Syrup forms firm ball in cold water but is plastic and can easily be handled in cold water.

Use higher temperature on rainy or damp days. Use for divinity, nougat, popcorn balls.

Very Hard Ball: (258°-266°F.) Syrup loses most of plastic quality in cold water. Ball will roll on buttered plate. Use for taffy.

Light Crack: (290°-300°F.) Syrup will form brittle threads in cold water. Spiral softens when removed from water. Use for butterscotch.

Hard Crack: (300°-310°F.) Syrup forms brittle threads in cold water which remain brittle on removal. Use for brittle candies.

HIGH ALTITUDE ADJUSTMENTS

For general information about effect of high altitudes on cooking temperatures, see **Cooking at High Altitudes.** When using a thermometer, adjust for temperatures as follows: If soft ball is called for at sea level at 236°F., test for soft ball at 226°F. at 3,000 feet; 223°F. at 5,000 feet; and 220°F. at 7,000 feet.

Use a sugar thermometer to ensure good results.

Quick and Uncooked Candies

UNCOOKED FONDANT
(Master Recipe)

1 egg white
½ tablespoon water
¾ teaspoon vanilla
about 1¼ pounds icing sugar

Combine egg white, water, and vanilla in a bowl. Beat until well blended.

Add sugar gradually until mixture is very stiff. Knead with hands until smooth.

Wrap in waxed or greaseproof paper. Store in refrigerator to use as desired.

Uncooked Fondant Variations

Cherry Fondant Balls: Colour fondant pink. Form into balls. Press a maraschino cherry into each.

Chocolate Fondant: Add 2 ounces plain melted chocolate to fondant. Blend thoroughly.

Chocolate Nut Cubes: Combine fondant and chopped pecans or walnuts. Cut into tiny cubes and dip in melted chocolate.

Fondant Chocolate Peppermints: Add a few drops of essence of peppermint to fondant. Mix it thoroughly.

Melt 2 ounces plain chocolate in top of double saucepan.

Form small balls of fondant. Press into round, flat patties. Dip in melted chocolate. Place on greaseproof paper to dry.

Coconut or Chocolate Fondant Balls: Form fondant balls. Roll in desiccated coconut or chocolate.

Fondant Nougats: Add chopped dates, nuts, figs, and maraschino cherries to fondant.

Spread on greaseproof paper. Cut into squares. Dip each square in caster sugar.

Fondant Nut Brown Patties: Make small balls of fondant. Roll in dry cocoa. Press flat with half a nut on each.

Pistachio Fondant Balls: Colour fondant green. Form into small balls. Press flat with a pistachio nut.

Strawberry Fondant: Coat ripe, unhulled strawberries with fondant, leaving stems uncoated. Roll in caster sugar.

Store in refrigerator until ready to serve.

UNCOOKED BUTTER FONDANT

Add 2 teaspoons butter to 3 tablespoons boiling water.

Add sifted icing sugar a little at a time until the mixture is pliable and may be moulded by hand. Use as other fondants.

MARZIPAN

Marzipan is a confection made of sweetened almond paste, usually coloured and formed into tiny fruit and vegetable shapes.

2 egg whites
1 pound ground almonds
½ teaspoon vanilla or lemon essence
6 ounces icing sugar

Beat egg whites. Mix with ground almonds. Add flavouring and enough sugar to make mixture stiff enough to handle. Allow to stand overnight.

Divide, colour, and flavour to imitate fruits or vegetables, such as pears, apples, etc. Mould into shapes.

It may also be cut into small pieces and dipped into chocolate or other coating, or used as the centre of candied cherries, dates, or prunes.

CHOCOLATE CREAM CHEESE FUDGE

3 ounces cream cheese
11 ounces icing sugar
2 ounces plain chocolate, melted
¼ teaspoon vanilla
dash of salt
2 ounces chopped pecans or walnuts

Place cream cheese in bowl and cream until soft and smooth. Slowly blend sugar into it. Add melted chocolate. Mix well.

Add vanilla, salt, and chopped pecans and mix until well blended.

Press into well greased shallow pan. Place in refrigerator until firm, about 15 minutes. Cut into squares.

Note: For slightly softer fudge blend in 1 teaspoon of cream.

MOCHA CREAMS

4 fluid ounces strong coffee
1 ounce butter
5 tablespoons cocoa
3 ounces finely chopped walnuts
½ teaspoon vanilla
1 pound 6 ounces icing sugar

Heat coffee to boiling point. Remove from heat and add butter and cocoa. Blend well. Add nuts and mix thoroughly.

Add vanilla and sugar, a little at a time, working in well and until candy is stiff enough to form into balls about size of large marbles.

Flatten balls slightly. Place on buttered plate to harden. Makes ¾ pound.

Rum Balls

RUM BALLS

12 ounces finely crushed wafer biscuits
4 ounces finely chopped walnuts
1 can sweetened condensed milk
5 tablespoons rum
icing sugar

Combine wafer crumbs and nuts. Add sweetened condensed milk and rum; blend well. Chill about 1 hour.

Dip palms of hands into icing sugar. Shape, by teaspoonful, into small balls. Roll in icing sugar. Store in covered container in refrigerator. Candies can be kept moist and fresh for several weeks.

FUDGE BALLS

Melt 2 ounces chocolate in double saucepan. Add 1 large can sweetened condensed milk.

Stir mixture over boiling water until it thickens, about 5 minutes.

Drop halves of marshmallows into mixture and lift out covered with chocolate. Roll in finely chopped nuts until well covered.

FUDGE WEDGES

1 4-ounce can flaked coconut
6 ounces plain chocolate
3 tablespoons light corn syrup or golden syrup
14 ounces icing sugar
4 ounces chopped walnuts
5 tablespoons orange juice
4 ounces finely rolled digestive biscuit crumbs

Sprinkle ⅔ of the flaked coconut over bottom of a 9-inch pie plate.

Melt chocolate over hot water. Add remaining ingredients, except flaked coconut, and mix well.

Turn into coconut-lined pie plate. Sprinkle remaining coconut over top and press down gently. Chill. Cut into thin wedges. Makes 14 to 16 wedges.

Fudge Wedges

Candied Fruits

GLAZED APRICOTS

12 ounces dried apricots
1 pound sugar
1 teaspoon cream of tartar
8 fluid ounces water

Rinse apricots. Cover with boiling water and let stand 10 minutes. Drain thoroughly.

Combine sugar, cream of tartar, and water; bring to a boil, stirring until sugar is dissolved.

Add apricots and boil slowly for 30 minutes or until fruit is transparent and syrup sheets from spoon.

Remove fruit to wire rack and drain overnight. Roll in sugar.

APRICOT COCONUT BALLS

4 ounces apricots
2 ounces nuts
3 ounces desiccated coconut
1 teaspoon grated orange rind
1 teaspoon grated lemon rind
1 tablespoon lemon juice

Put apricots, nuts, and coconut through food mincer or chop fine.

Combine with remaining ingredients, mixing well. Shape into small balls. Roll in ground nuts if desired.

CRYSTALLIZED MINT LEAVES

Remove fresh mint leaves from stems. Wipe each leaf and brush with stiffly beaten egg white.

Dip in sugar flavoured with oil of peppermint. Place on greaseproof to dry or on cake rack.

Cover with greaseproof paper. Let stand in very slow oven (250°F. Mark ½) until dry. Repeat if leaves are not thoroughly coated.

DRIED FRUIT TRAY

Steam fruits over boiling water 10 minutes or until soft. Remove stones from prunes and stuff with a piece of marshmallow, an almond, or a pecan or walnut half.

To coat prunes with chocolate, melt plain or milk chocolate over warm, not boiling, water, stirring frequently. Dip prunes, one at a time, using two forks. Drain off excess chocolate. Set on greaseproof paper to harden.

Dried Fruit Tray

CARAMEL APPLES

15 to 20 apples
2 pounds sugar
7 ounces light corn syrup or golden syrup
2 large cans evaporated milk
6 ounces chopped pecans or walnuts

Select small apples, free from blemishes. Wash and dry thoroughly and stick on wooden skewers.

Put sugar, syrup, and ½ can of the evaporated milk in a large heavy saucepan. Stir to blend well. Heat slowly until sugar is dissolved, stirring constantly. Then cook briskly to a thick syrup, stirring all the while.

Add remainder of milk slowly, keeping mixture boiling briskly, and cook to firm ball stage (242°F.), stirring constantly to prevent scorching. Remove from heat and let stand until caramel stops bubbling.

Working quickly, dip apples, one at a time, in caramel and twirl to get rid of surplus coating and make smooth.

Dip bottoms in chopped nuts. Place on aluminium foil or a well buttered baking sheet to set.

If coating becomes too hard for dipping, add a little evaporated milk and reheat, stirring to keep smooth.

The caramel should be kept quite hot so that coating will not be too heavy. Makes 15 to 20 caramel apples.

STUFFED DATES

Remove stones and stuff as suggested below. Roll in sugar or shake a few at a time in paper bag containing a little sugar.

If desired, mix 1 teaspoon cinnamon with each 2 ounces sugar.

Suggested stuffings include: marshmallows, cut in quarters; candied ginger, cut in bits; candied pineapple, cut in bits; peanut butter moistened with orange juice; salted almonds; broken nuts such as Brazil nuts, pecans, and walnuts; fondant.

Stuffed Prunes: Follow suggestions for stuffed dates. If prunes are very dry, steam until tender. Cool before stuffing.

SPANISH SWEETS (DULCES)

8 ounces walnuts
4 ounces almonds
8 ounces stoned dates
8 ounces pecans or walnuts
4 ounces cherries
4 ounces seeded raisins
icing sugar

Put all ingredients except icing sugar through food mincer, using medium blade.

On board covered with icing sugar, knead minced mixture until thick and smooth.

Caramel Apples

Shape into 1-inch balls. Wrap in greaseproof paper. Refrigerate. Makes about 5 dozen.

PEANUT BUTTER FRUIT CONFECTIONS

4 ounces stoned dates
3 ounces seedless raisins
3 ounces currants
6 ounces butter
4 tablespoons sweetened condensed milk

Put fruits through food mincer. Add peanut butter and sweetened condensed milk. Mix well.

Press into bottom of 8×8×2-inch buttered tin which has been sprinkled with icing sugar. Smooth surface of candy and sprinkle with icing sugar if desired.

Chill until firm. Cut in squares. Makes about 1⅛ pound.

CANDIED GRAPEFRUIT PEEL

Peel fruit, keeping peel in large pieces. Wash and trim out most of white from inside. Cut into strips or triangles.

Cover with cold water. Boil 5 minutes. Drain. Cover again with cold water. Boil 5 minutes. Drain. Repeat twice, or until peel is tender.

Weigh drained peel. Weigh an equal amount of honey and sugar, using half of each.

Add 5 tablespoons water for each 12 ounces honey and 8 ounces sugar. Add peel.

Simmer until peel is glazed, about 20 minutes. Drain. Roll in sugar.

Candied Orange or Lemon Peel: Simmer peel until tender without changing water, 20 to 30 minutes. Proceed as above.

Chocolate Citrus Peel: Dip candied peel in melted chocolate.

Candied Grapefruit Peel

Dipped Stuffed Figs

DIPPED STUFFED FIGS

Fillings: Nuts, e.g. walnuts, almonds, Brazils, pecans or peanuts. Preserved or candied fruits as orange or lemon peel, citron, cherries, pineapple, ginger, or marshmallows. Dipping chocolate or fondant for coating.

Rinse California dried figs, drain, wrap in towel and steam over hot water about 15 minutes, or until tender.

Remove and dry with cloth. Slit down 1 side and stuff with preferred fruit or nut filling, or fruit-nut combinations. Chill well before dipping.

Chocolate Coating: Dip stuffed figs, blossom end down, in dipping chocolate melted over warm (not hot) water. Place on greaseproof paper to harden.

Fondant Coating: Dip in fondant melted over hot water and place on greaseproof paper to harden. Malted fondant may be tinted as desired with food colouring.

Double Coating: Dip in fondant as directed, then in dipping chocolate.

APRICOT ROLL

1½ pounds sugar
8 fluid ounces evaporated milk
5½ ounces finely chopped dried
      apricots
2 ounces butter
½ teaspoon salt
2 teaspoons vanilla
2 ounces finely chopped nuts

Combine sugar, evaporated milk, apricots, butter, and salt in saucepan. Stirring constantly, bring to a boil.

Boil, stirring occasionally, to the soft ball stage, 236°F. Cool to lukewarm (120°F.).

Add vanilla and nuts and beat until stiff enough to knead.

Place on bread board and knead until smooth.

Shape into four small rolls about an inch in diameter.

Place in refrigerator to chill for several hours. Cut into small slices. Makes 80 small pieces.

Chocolate Nut Roll: Omit apricots and add 2 ounces plain chocolate

to the evaporated milk and sugar mixture.

FRUIT NUGGETS

1 pound 2 ounces light brown sugar
8 fluid ounces sour cream
½ teaspoon salt
½ ounce chocolate
1 ounce butter
3 ounces dates, cut fine
2 ounces chopped walnuts, pecans,
      or coconut

Cook sugar, cream, and salt to the soft ball stage, 234°F., stirring occasionally, wiping crystals down from side of pan.

Pour immediately into a well buttered clean pan.

Drop in chocolate and butter, and allow to stand without stirring until pan can be held comfortably on palm of hand.

Beat until mass begins to thicken and colour becomes lighter; stir in dates and nuts.

Drop by teaspoons into chopped nuts or coconut; roll until balls are coated, and place on greaseproof paper to cool.

Makes 2 pounds, or 3 dozen nuggets 1¼ inches in diameter.

FRUIT SLICES

6 ounces plumped prunes
6 ounces figs
6 ounces raisins
2 ounces nuts

Mince fruit and nuts. Mix thoroughly and shape into long, slender rolls. Roll in coconut or finely chopped nuts.

Wrap in greaseproof paper and chill. Slice off pieces as desired. Or slice off pieces and wrap in greaseproof paper.

PARISIAN SWEETS

½ pound figs
½ pound dried apricots or seedless
      raisins
½ pound nuts
icing sugar

Wash and pick over fruits. Combine with nuts. Mince through a food mincer, using medium blade.

Roll out about ½-inch thick on a board sprinkled with icing sugar.

Cut into small pieces or make balls and roll them in icing sugar. Store in a tin box or a tight jar.

FRUIT BALLS

12 ounces puffed rice or puffed
      wheat
2 ounces chopped glacé cherries
3 ounces chopped dates
2 ounces chopped nuts
9 ounces light corn syrup or
      golden syrup
3 ounces light molasses or black
      treacle
½ teaspoon salt
1 teaspoon vinegar
1 ounce fat
1 teaspoon vanilla

Crisp puffed rice in a moderate oven (350°F. Mark 4) 10 minutes; place in large greased bowl and mix with chopped fruits and nuts.

Combine syrup, molasses, salt, and vinegar in saucepan; cook until a few drops in cold water form a hard ball (255°F.).

Remove from heat; add fat and vanilla, stirring only enough to mix. Slowly pour cooked syrup over puffed rice, mixing quickly. Form into balls immediately. Makes 8 large balls.

Candied Fruit Bars: Prepare as above and pack at once into greased 7×11-inch pan. Cool and cut into bars. Makes about 30 bars.

YULE FIG BALLS

6 ounces chopped dried figs
4 ounces sugar coated rice cereal
2 ounces chopped dried apricots
8 ounces light corn syrup or golden
      syrup
3 tablespoons honey
½ teaspoon vinegar
¼ teaspoon salt
1 ounce butter or margarine
½ teaspoon grated lemon rind

Combine figs, cereal, and apricots in greased mixing bowl; set aside.

Combine syrup, honey, vinegar, and salt in small saucepan. Place over low heat and bring to boil. Cook, stirring constantly, until mixture forms a hard ball in cold water (250°F.).

Remove from heat; add butter and lemon rind. Pour over cereal mixture and mix quickly. Butter hands and shape into balls.

Yule Fig Balls

KNOW YOUR KITCHEN TOOLS AND WHAT THEY DO

When you know your tools and how to use them your job becomes so much easier. Your knowledge will also save you time besides making meal preparation fun.

POTATO MASHER
Mashes potatoes, turnips, sweet potatoes and fruits when making jams and preserves.

PASTRY BRUSH
Use for glazing, to glaze vegetables and meats, to baste meats with a sauce, brushing thin sugar icing on pastry.

SLOTTED SPOON
Ideal for skimming and lifting doughnuts, dumplings, ravioli, vegetables, etc., from boiling water.

ROLLING PIN
Rolls out dough for pies and certain pastries. Makes bread and biscuit crumbs. Crushes nuts and hard candy-like peppermint sticks for cake toppings.

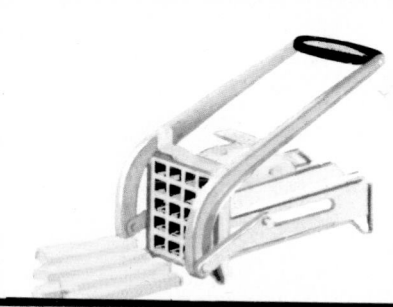

CHIP CUTTER
Cuts potatoes into chips. Cuts turnips, parsnips, cucumbers, cheese, beetroot and ham into julienne size strips.

TRIVETS
Of various shapes and sizes for cooling breads, cakes, biscuits and pastry. Holds hot pans off counter and table tops. Some shapes and sizes can be used as racks inside roaster pans to hold meats and poultry up out of juices while cooking.

SPATULA
Turns all types of fried food. Removes food from fry pans and removes biscuits and pastry from baking sheets.

DOUGH BLENDER
Blends fat into flour mixture for pies, crumb cake, biscuits and the types of yeast dough requiring this.

CHOPPER
Chops a variety of vegetables such as onions, peppers, celery. Chops fruits and nuts.

BALL CUTTER
Produces decorative balls from melons, vegetables and potatoes. Makes butter balls, cheese and ice cream balls.

COOKING FORK
Useful for coating food with flour or egg-crumb mixture; turns pan fried food, especially small pieces or cuts that might roll off a turner. Perforates pastry, scores cucumbers or other vegetables. Use as a blending fork, serving fork.

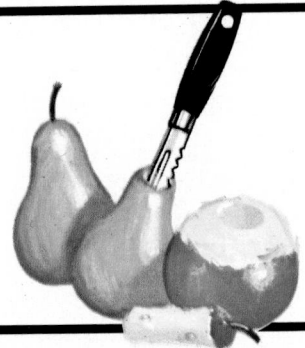

CORER
Cores apples, potatoes (prior to stuffing and baking them). Cores cucumbers and beets and zucchini for stuffing. Peels apples, potatoes, cucumbers and carrots.

MEASURING SPOON
Convenient, accurate measuring of $\frac{1}{4}$, $\frac{1}{2}$ teaspoon, 1 teaspoon and 1 tablespoon.

PIZZA ROLLER
Rolls out pizza and small quantities of dough, crushes nuts.

WIRE WHISK
Whips, blends, creams, beats eggs, whips cream, icing, fondants. Incorporates air into mixture of ingredients to expand volume.

PARING KNIFE
Pares, peels, slices fruits and vegetables. Perfect for skinning apples, pears and onions.

POTATO PEELER

Peels beets, carrots, cucumbers, potatoes, sweet potatoes, parsnips, apples, avocados, peaches, apricots, pears. Shreds cabbage, strings celery. Makes carrot curls, chocolate curls, cheese curls, bread crumbs from dried bread, flakes coconut. Scrapes rinds of citrus fruits such as limes, lemons, oranges and tangerines for flavouring.

SPATULA

Ices cakes, coffee cake, loosens large gelatin moulds, cakes and breads from tins or pans.

GRATER

Ideal for shredding vegetables and lettuce for salads. Grates cheese, chocolate and citrus fruit rind.

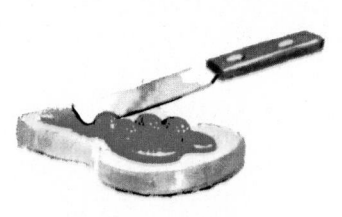

SPREADING KNIFE

Useful in spreading breads or crackers with butter, peanut butter, preserves or sandwich spreads. Spread celery with stuffings such as cream cheese.

KITCHEN SCISSORS

Cuts out core of citrus fruits, separates fish, poultry pieces, trims vegetables.

PASTRY CUTTER-CRIMPER

Cuts, trims pastry strips, edges pie and tart shells, crimps the double and single edges of pastry shells. Also cuts and scallops edges of cheese slices for appetizers and other sandwiches.

GRAPEFRUIT KNIFE

Cuts segments of grapefruit and oranges.

VEGETABLE KNIFE

Cuts, slices fruits, vegetables (both cooked and raw), pies, small meats and sausages.

SERRATED KNIFE

Cuts, slices all fruit, vegetables, cheese, small meats and sausages.

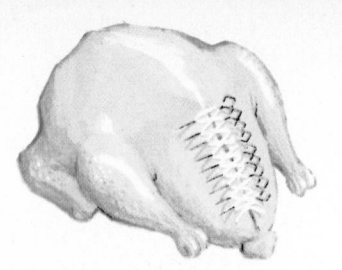

SMALL SKEWERS

Use for trussing stuffed birds or fish. Holds rolled chops, pot roasts and oven roasts. Holds top layer of cake in place while icing.

STRAINER

Rinses fruits and vegetables, ideal for crumbling hard egg yolks for sprinkling on salads.

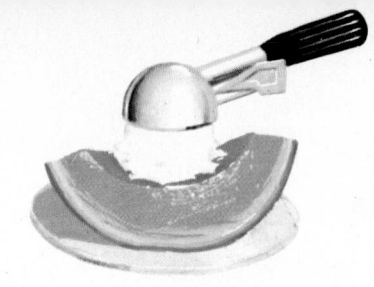

SCOOP

Serves gelatine, cottage cheese, ice cream, rice, mashed potatoes in round equal portions.

HOW TO CARE FOR YOUR TOOLS

Pegboard or wall bracket storage will keep your kitchen tools where you can locate them quickly—and keep them safely out of reach of little hands.

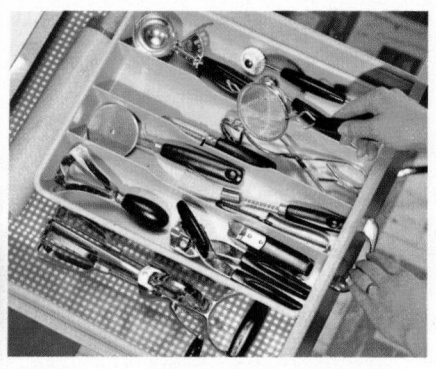

If you store them in a drawer, keep them organized—and protect points and edges by keeping only a few items in a compartment. Also, it's a good idea to keep the most used items handy in the front of the drawer.

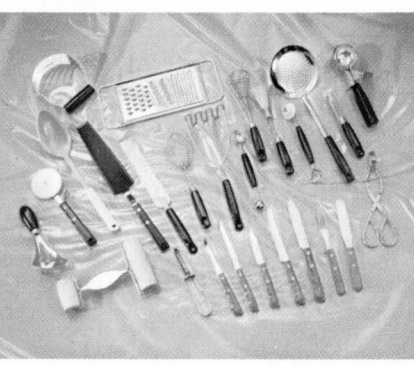

These are the kitchen tools used to create the garnishes shown in this book. With the exception of one or two of the items, it's a good basic group to have in any kitchen.

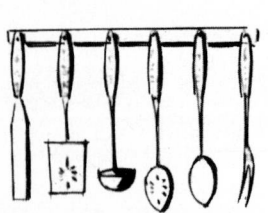

Naturally, you won't use every kitchen tool at every meal. However, you should rinse immediately any one that has been used with sticky or gummy foods. And wash *all* of them as soon as it's convenient.

Nut Treats

SUGARED ALMONDS

8 ounces sugar
4 fluid ounces water
½ pound blanched almonds
1 teaspoon vanilla
½ teaspoon cinnamon

Cook sugar and water in heavy iron pan 5 minutes. Add nuts and cook until syrup begins to appear white and slightly sugared.

Add flavourings and remove pan from heat for 10 minutes.

Replace over low heat. Stir constantly until sugar starts to melt.

Pour the whole mixture onto a cake rack which has been placed over greaseproof paper. Separate the nuts as they dry.

PEANUT CLUSTERS

Melt ½ pound plain chocolate in bowl over hot water. Remove from heat; add ½ pound roasted Spanish peanuts and stir well.

Drop from teaspoon onto waxed paper. Chill overnight in refrigerator. Keep in cool place. Makes about 36 clusters.

ALMOND PASTE

1 pound blanched almonds
1 pound sugar
8 fluid ounces water
4 fluid ounces orange juice
few drops rose water
Icing sugar

Put almonds through mincer at least 4 times, using finest blade.

Cook sugar and water just past soft ball stage (240°F.). Mix with ground almonds. Add orange juice and rose water. Stir until thoroughly blended and creamy.

Turn out on a hard surface dusted with icing sugar. Let stand until cool.

Pack in closely covered container. Store in cool, dry place and let ripen at least 1 week.

In various European countries this traditional almond paste is shaped into flat cakes or a variety of forms, decorated and served during the Christmas season. Makes 2 pounds.

CHEESE STUFFED PECANS

Choose the biggest pecan (or walnut) halves you can find; brown them lightly in a moderate oven and cool.

Put two together with highly seasoned cream cheese, Roquefort type cheese, or smoked cheese.

CURRIED NUTS

Brown nuts in the oven, and while browning sprinkle generously with curry powder and a little butter or oil.

BRAZIL NUT CHIPS

Shell Brazil nuts. Cover with cold water and bring slowly to a boil. Simmer 2 to 3 minutes. Drain and cut while damp into thin lengthwise slices, about ⅛ inch thick.

Spread out in a shallow tin. Dot with butter, allowing 1 ounce of butter for each 6 ounces of the shelled nuts. Sprinkle with salt.

Bake in moderate oven (350°F. Mark 4) 15 to 20 minutes, stirring occasionally.

Variations: Chips may also be curried or spiced. Follow above directions, and for 6 ounces shelled Brazil nuts combine 1 teaspoon curry powder with the salt. Or omit salt and substitute 1 tablespoon sugar mixed with ¼ teaspoon cinnamon.

ALMONDS IN OLIVE OIL

Blanch some almonds by pouring boiling water over the nuts, hold at simmering temperature 3 minutes, then drain and slip off the loosened skins by pressing the kernels between thumb and forefinger. Dry.

Place blanched almonds in a shallow tin; add 1 teaspoon olive oil for each 4 ounces of nuts and heat in slow oven (300°F. Mark 2) until pale brown, 25 to 30 minutes. Stir occasionally.

Salt while hot and let cool before serving.

TOASTED PUMPKIN, MARROW OR SQUASH SEEDS

Remove the fibre from unwashed seeds. To 8 ounces of seeds add 1½ tablespoons melted butter or salad oil and 1¼ teaspoons salt.

Spread the seeds in a shallow tin. Toast in a very slow oven (250°F. Mark ½) until brown and crisp, stirring occasionally.

DEVILLED ALMONDS

Sauté 8 ounces blanched almonds in 2 tablespoons salad oil until crunchy, about 5 minutes. Drain on absorbent paper.

Add ⅛ teaspoon chilli powder, 1 teaspoon salt, and ⅛ teaspoon cayenne. Toss well.

SALTED NUTS

Shell and blanch nuts, if necessary. Wash and dry thoroughly. Melt ½ teaspoon butter in a shallow tin. Add a layer of shelled nuts.

Place in moderate oven (350°F. Mark 4) about 10 minutes. Stir and turn nuts frequently.

Pour onto absorbent paper to drain off any excess butter.

Sprinkle with salt, to taste. About 1½ to 2 teaspoons salt per pound nuts is the usual amount.

SALTED SOYBEANS

Use varieties which are good for cooked dried beans. Wash and soak dried soybeans overnight. Drain and spread in a single layer and let dry at room temperature, or dry with a towel.

Fry a small handful at a time in hot deep fat (360°F.) for 8 to 10 minutes. Drain on paper towels and sprinkle with salt while still warm.

FRENCH FRIED NUTS

Fry shelled dry nuts in deep hot fat (370°F.) until lightly browned, 4 to 5 minutes.

Drain on absorbent paper. Sprinkle with salt.

GARLIC NUTS

Sprinkle nuts with garlic salt and melted butter and brown in oven until crisp.

Or, mash a garlic clove and let stand in butter ½ hour. Strain butter and use to season nuts while browning them.

LITTLE SNOWTOPS

4 ounces sugar
pinch of cream of tartar
4 tablespoons hot water
¼ teaspoon vanilla
drop or two of peppermint essence
6 ounces icing sugar
8 ounces roasted unblanched almonds

Combine sugar, cream of tartar, and hot water in small saucepan. Cook over low heat until sugar dissolves. Continue cooking to 226°F. or to a thin syrup.

Cool to lukewarm. Stir in flavourings and icing sugar.

Hold almonds 1 at a time by pointed end and dip rounded end into sugar mixture. Place on greaseproof paper to dry. Makes about 1¼ pounds.

Little Snowtops

GLACÉ NUTS

8 ounces sugar
$\frac{1}{8}$ teaspoon cream of tartar
4 fluid ounces water
nuts

Combine ingredients and heat to boiling. Stir until sugar is dissolved. Wipe all grains of sugar from sides of saucepan with a damp cloth. Boil without stirring to the light crack stage (290°F.).

Remove sugar crystals around edge of pan with wet cloth. Remove saucepan from heat. Set in pan of cold water to stop boiling immediately.

Remove from cold water and set in pan of hot water. Using a fork, dip each nut into syrup, drain, and place on greaseproof paper. If syrup becomes too thick, reheat over hot water.

BRANDIED ALMONDS OR PECANS

2 ounces butter
12 ounces icing sugar
4 tablespoons brandy or sherry
12 ounces blanched almonds or pecan halves

Cream butter and work in sugar and brandy or sherry.

Toast almonds in moderate oven (350°F. Mark 4) until golden, stirring frequently in a shallow tin.

Stir nuts into sugar mixture while hot. When nuts are well coated, spread them out on paper to cool.

ORANGE SUGARED NUTS

12 ounces sugar
4 tablespoons water
3 tablespoons orange juice
$\frac{1}{2}$ teaspoon grated orange rind
$\frac{1}{2}$ pound pecans or other nuts

Cook sugar, water, and orange juice to soft ball stage (238°F.).

Remove from heat; add rind and nuts. Stir constantly until syrup looks cloudy.

Drop onto greaseproof paper or greased surface. Separate nuts into small clusters. Makes about $\frac{3}{4}$ pound.

SPICED NUTS

2 ounces sugar
2 teaspoons cinnamon
$\frac{1}{8}$ teaspoon nutmeg
$\frac{1}{8}$ teaspoon powdered cloves
4 ounces nuts (almonds, pecans, walnuts, Brazil nuts, etc.)
1 slightly beaten egg white

Mix sugar and spices in a small bowl. Add nuts to egg white, a few at a time, in order to coat them well.

Drop into the bowl of sugar and spices. When well coated, place on buttered baking sheet and brown in slow oven (300°F. Mark 2) for 30 minutes.

CARAMEL ALMONDS

1 pound sugar
2 ounces butter
unblanched almonds

Combine sugar and butter in frying pan. Stir over low heat until sugar is melted and browned.

When mixture looks golden and slightly lumpy stir in almonds.

Coat them quickly and separate while hot on waxed paper.

RAISIN-WALNUT LOAF

12 ounces raisins
4 ounces walnuts
4 tablespoons sweetened condensed milk

Put raisins and nuts through mincer. Blend thoroughly with sweetened condensed milk.

Scrape mixture into buttered pan which has been sprinkled with icing sugar.

Smooth the top and sprinkle with more icing sugar. Cut into squares.

CHOCOLATE PEPPERMINT NUT CLUSTERS

4 ounces plain chocolate
1 ounce crushed peppermint rock
4 ounces walnuts

Melt chocolate over warm, not hot, water. Stir in peppermint rock and walnuts, mixing until nuts are coated.

Drop by teaspoons onto greaseproof paper to harden.

RAISIN PEANUT CLUSTERS—UNCOOKED

Wash 1 pound seedless raisins and dry thoroughly on a towel.

Melt $\frac{1}{2}$ pound chocolate over warm water and cool to lukewarm. Add raisins, 4 ounces shelled, roasted peanuts, and $\frac{1}{4}$ teaspoon salt. Mix well. Drop from teaspoon onto greaseproof paper or shape in paper sweet cases. Chill overnight in refrigerator. Makes about 50 small clusters.

Pulled Candies

PEPPERMINT CANES

1 pound sugar
6 ounces light corn syrup or golden syrup
4 fluid ounces water
$\frac{1}{4}$ teaspoon cream of tartar
$\frac{3}{8}$ teaspoon peppermint essence
$\frac{3}{4}$ to 1 teaspoon red food colouring

Combine sugar, corn syrup, water, and cream of tartar; stir until sugar dissolves.

Cook without stirring to hard-ball stage (265°F.). Remove from heat and add peppermint essence.

Divide in 2 portions and add colouring to 1 part.

Pour out on greased plates. When candy is cool enough to handle, pull each part separately.

Form in ropes and twist red part around white. Cut in 8-inch lengths and form in the shape of candy canes. Makes about 10.

WHITE TAFFY

1 pound sugar
5 fluid ounces water
6 ounces light corn syrup or golden syrup
2 tablespoons white (distilled) vinegar
1 tablespoon butter or margarine
$\frac{1}{8}$ teaspoon salt
$\frac{1}{2}$ teaspoon bicarbonate of soda
few drops of peppermint essence

Combine sugar, water, corn syrup, and vinegar in heavy $1\frac{1}{2}$-2 pint saucepan. Stir over low heat until sugar is dissolved. Cover and boil 3 minutes.

Uncover and boil over moderate heat without stirring until sugar thermometer registers 280°F. (soft crack stage).

Remove from heat. Blend in butter or margarine, salt, and soda. Pour onto an oiled marble slab or enamelled surface.

As candy cools, turn edges with spatula toward centre. Sprinkle essence over candy.

When cool enough to handle, gather candy into a ball and pull until white and porous. Use soft butter or margarine on fingers to prevent candy from sticking to hands.

Pull and twist into a rope about $\frac{1}{2}$ inch in diameter. Cut into $\frac{1}{2}$-inch serving pieces with scissors. Wrap each piece in waxed or cellophane paper for storing. Makes 1 pound.

CRACK TAFFY

15 ounces molasses or black treacle
1 tablespoon vinegar
6 ounces sugar
$\frac{1}{8}$ teaspoon salt
$\frac{1}{8}$ teaspoon bicarbonate of soda
1 tablespoon butter

Blend molasses, vinegar, and sugar. Boil carefully to very hard ball stage (270°F.). Remove from the heat.

Add remaining ingredients, stirring until well mixed.

Pour into greased pans. Let stand until cool. Crack with a mallet or hammer.

SALT WATER TAFFY

Mix 8 ounces sugar, 3 tablespoons cornflour, and few grains salt. Add 4 fluid ounces water and 8 ounces honey. Cook to very hard ball stage (266°F.).

Pour into greased pan. Cool. Pull until porous. Cut in 1-inch pieces.

Hard Candies and Brittles

LOLLYPOPS
(Master Recipe)

1 pound sugar
8 ounces light corn syrup or golden
    syrup
8 fluid ounces water
½ teaspoon oil of lemon
few drops yellow food colouring

Place sugar, corn syrup, and water in saucepan. Cook over low heat, stirring until sugar dissolves. Continue cooking, without stirring, to hard crack stage (310°F.).

Wrap wet cloth around a fork. While cooking, wipe crystals from sides of pan with wet cloth.

Grease lollypop moulds or flat surface.

When temperature of 310°F. is reached, add oil of lemon and colouring, stirring both in quickly.

Pour immediately into greased moulds, or drop from end of spoon onto flat greased surface.

Press end of stick into each pop as soon as each is dropped from spoon. Loosen lollypops as soon as they are firm and before they are cold.

Lollypop Variations: Vary flavouring and colouring by using oil of peppermint and pink food colouring.

To form faces, use raisins for eyes, pieces of prune for mouth, and coconut for hair. Have all decorations ready to add while lollypops are hot.

TOFFEE

8 ounces sugar
8 ounces butter or margarine
1 tablespoon light corn syrup or
    golden syrup
3 tablespoons water
3 ounces chopped almonds or pea-
    nuts
    plain chocolate

Cook sugar, butter or margarine, corn syrup, and water until a few drops tested in cold water crack (290°F. on candy thermometer).

While syrup cooks, chop nuts fine and sprinkle almost all of them over bottom of pie-plate.

Pour hot syrup over nuts, sprinkle with finely chopped chocolate and top it off with remaining almonds or peanuts. When cool, break into chunks.

NUT CRUNCH

5 ounces butter or margarine
8 ounces sugar
½ teaspoon vanilla
3 ounces chopped nuts
3 ounces plain chocolate

Melt butter, add sugar and, with constant stirring, cook slowly to 300°F.

(very brittle in ice water).

Add vanilla and half the nuts. Pour out on a smooth, greased surface (not a pan). Spread thin and cool.

Loosen candy from greased surface and mark into squares before it becomes crisp.

Melt chocolate over hot water, spread over cooled candy and sprinkle with remaining nuts.

When chocolate is cool, break crunch into squares. Makes 1¼ pound.

BUTTERSCOTCH
(Master Recipe)

12 ounces brown sugar
3 ounces light corn syrup or
    golden syrup
8 fluid ounces water
¼ teaspoon salt
2½ ounces butter
¼ teaspoon vanilla

Place sugar, corn syrup, water, and salt in saucepan. Cook over low heat, stirring until sugar dissolves.

Continue cooking without stirring until mixture reaches temperature of 290°F. Add butter, remove from heat, and add vanilla.

Pour into a buttered shallow tin. Cool slightly. Mark into squares. When cold, break into pieces. Makes about 1⅛ pounds.

Lemon Butterscotch: In master recipe substitute a few drops oil of lemon for vanilla.

Butterscotch Lollypops: In master butterscotch recipe cook sugar mixture to 290°F. Stir in butter and vanilla quickly.

Pour into greased lollypop moulds, or drop from end of teaspoon onto greased flat tin. Place stick in each pop.

PEANUT BRITTLE

6 ounces shelled peanuts
¼ teaspoon salt
8 ounces sugar
6 ounces light corn syrup or golden
    syrup
4 fluid ounces water
¾ ounce butter
½ teaspoon lemon essence

Sprinkle nuts with salt and warm in oven.

Put sugar, corn syrup, and water in pan. Stir until it boils. Wash down sides with wet pastry brush and cook to 295°F., or until mixture is very brittle when tried in cold water.

Add butter, lemon essence and nuts; pour into a shallow greased tin.

As soon as it can be handled, turn the mass over and pull and stretch it out as thin as possible. Break into irregular pieces.

Popcorn Balls

POPCORN BALLS
(Master Recipe)

½ ounce butter
8 ounces sugar
12 ounces molasses or golden syrup
½ teaspoon salt
6 pints popped corn

Melt butter. Add sugar, molasses, and salt. Boil on medium heat until very hard ball stage (260°F.).

Pour over corn. Stir corn thoroughly while pouring syrup over it.

Butter hands lightly. Shape into balls. Makes 12 to 14.

Popcorn Ball Variations

Cereal Popcorn Balls: Use half puffed cereal and half popcorn and mix before adding syrup.

Coloured Popcorn Balls: Omit molasses. Use 1 pound light corn syrup or golden syrup and add any desired food colouring and 1 teaspoon vanilla.

Nut Caramel Corn: Add 2 ounces nuts to popcorn before adding syrup. Cool slightly. Shape into balls.

Popcorn Chop Suey: Substitute 4 ounces shelled roasted peanuts and 4 ounces desiccated coconut for similar amount of popcorn. Mix before adding syrup.

Raisin Popcorn Balls: Add 3 ounces raisins to popcorn before adding syrup.

MOLASSES PEANUT CRUNCH

12 ounces molasses or black treacle
8 ounces sugar
1 ounce fat
⅛ teaspoon bicarbonate of soda
10 ounces chopped peanuts

Combine molasses, sugar, and fat; cook slowly, stirring constantly, to 252°F. (or when a small quantity dropped in cold water forms firm ball).

Remove from heat; add soda; stir until bubbling stops. Add nuts.

Pour into greased shallow tin. Cool slightly; cut in small squares or bars. Wrap in waxed paper. Makes about 1¾ pounds.

Fondants and Fudge

FONDANT
(Master Recipe)

1 pound sugar
6 fluid ounces boiling water
⅛ teaspoon cream of tartar
⅛ teaspoon salt
½ teaspoon vanilla

Place sugar, water, cream of tartar, and salt in saucepan over hot fire. Stir constantly until, but not after, sugar has dissolved. Do not splash syrup. Remove spoon. Do not use it again after syrup boils.

Remove sugar crystals around edge of pan with wet cloth.

Let syrup boil until it reaches 238°F., or until it forms soft ball in cold water. Be sure bulb of thermometer is down in syrup yet does not touch bottom of pan.

Add vanilla without stirring. Pour syrup in a thin sheet onto chilled plate to cool quickly. Do not scrape out saucepan.

When syrup is cool, work it with flat wooden spoon until it creams. When it forms a soft creamy mass, work it with palms of hands in the same way as bread dough until it is smooth.

Place fondant in an earthenware or glass dish. Cover with damp cloth. After 24 hours fondant is ready to mould. It will keep for months in a cold place if covered with moist cloth or stored in tightly covered jar.

Fondant Variations

Brown Sugar Fondant: Substitute 6 ounces brown sugar for 8 ounces white sugar.

Cherry or Nut Fondant Balls: Form ripened fondant into tiny balls. Press each between two halves of cherries or nuts or roll each in coconut, chopped nuts, cocoa, or chopped plain chocolate.

Chocolate Fondant: Knead 2 ounces melted plain chocolate and ½ teaspoon vanilla into 8 ounces ripened fondant.

Coffee Fondant: Substitute strong fresh coffee for water.

Fondant Loaves: Add fruit and nuts to fondant. Pack into loaf tin. Let stand until firm. Cut into slices.

Fondant Mints: Melt ripened fondant slowly over hot water. Colour and flavour. Drop from teaspoon onto greaseproof paper.

Fondant Nut Creams: Knead fondant, and flavour with almond or coffee essence.

Knead into it a mixture of chopped nuts or canned coconut.

Shape into balls, squares, or patties which may be dipped in melted plain chocolate.

Fruits Stuffed With Fondant: Prepare dates, figs, or prunes. Stuff with fondant.

Tutti-Frutti Fondant: Knead fondant. Add almond or maraschino essence.

Knead chopped mixture of raisins, dates, figs, glacé cherries, candied peel, or other candied fruit into ripened fondant.

Shape into a flat cake. Cut after it stands 1 hour.

Fondant Wintergreen Creams: Melt portion of fondant in top part of double saucepan until soft enough to drop from a spoon.

Add a tiny bit of red food colouring to tint delicate pink and 1 to 2 drops oil of wintergreen flavouring, stirring enough to blend.

If fondant is too thick add few drops of hot water. If too thin, let stand 5 to 10 minutes to thicken.

Drop from a teaspoon onto waxed paper or lightly buttered flat surface.

PANOCHA
(Also spelled penuchi and penuche)

1 ounce butter or margarine
6 fluid ounces half cream and half milk, or rich top milk
6 ounces brown sugar
12 ounces white sugar
1 teaspoon vanilla
2-3 ounces broken nuts

Melt butter or margarine in 2½-3 pint saucepan, using rubber spatula to bring it up around sides of pan, greasing well. Pour cream and milk into pan. Place over heat and bring to boiling point.

Add sugars and stir well to dissolve. Cover pan and bring mixture to boil slowly. Cook about 1 minute or until sugar crystals are melted down from sides of pan.

Remove cover and continue cooking gently with stirring to soft ball stage (238°F.), about 20 minutes. Remove from heat.

Allow to stand without moving, until mixture is lukewarm (110°F.) and bottom of saucepan is barely warm to the hand. This will take about 1 hour.

Add vanilla and nuts; beat with a heavy spoon. Continue beating until mixture becomes creamy and starts to lose its gloss.

Pour into a buttered 8-inch square tin. Cut into pieces while still warm. Makes about 24 pieces.

MEXICAN ORANGE FUDGE

8 ounces sugar
12 fluid ounces milk
1 pound sugar
grated rind of 2 oranges
pinch of salt
4 ounces butter
4 ounces walnuts

Melt 8 ounces sugar in a large saucepan while the milk is scalding in a double saucepan. When the sugar is melted to a rich yellow, add hot milk all at once, stirring. It will boil up quickly, so be sure to use a good-sized saucepan.

Add 1 pound sugar to this mixture, stirring until dissolved; cook until it forms an almost hard ball in water (238°F.). Just before it is done add grated orange rind, salt, butter, and nuts. Beat until creamy and pour on a buttered plate to cool.

PRALINES

8 ounces white sugar
6 ounces brown sugar
½ teaspoon bicarbonate of soda
8 fluid ounces buttermilk or sour milk
⅛ teaspoon salt
1 ounce butter or margarine
5 ounces pecan halves or walnuts
1 teaspoon vanilla

In heavy 3-4 pint saucepan combine sugars, soda, buttermilk, and salt. Stir over low heat until sugar is dissolved. Boil over moderate heat until sugar thermometer registers 230°F. (thread stage).

Remove from heat. Add butter or margarine, nuts, and vanilla.

Beat mixture until it starts to become thick and slightly sugary. Then place saucepan over low heat to prevent mixture from becoming too hard before it is dropped into patties.

Drop by tablespoons onto greaseproof paper, forming patties about 3 inches in diameter.

Cool. Remove from paper and wrap individually in waxed or cellophane paper. Makes 15.

Pralines

Chocolate and Vanilla Fudge

CHOCOLATE FUDGE
(Master Recipe)

2 ounces plain chocolate
¼ pint milk
1 pound sugar
⅛ teaspoon salt
1 ounce butter
1 teaspoon vanilla

Break chocolate into small pieces. Add to milk in saucepan. Cook over low heat, stirring constantly until mixture is smooth.

Add sugar and salt and stir until sugar is dissolved and mixture boils.

Cook slowly, without stirring, until a small quantity dropped into cold water forms a soft ball (236°F.). Remove from heat.

Add butter and vanilla without stirring. Cool to lukewarm (110°F.). Beat until fairly thick.

Pour at once into greased tin. Cool. Cut into squares. Makes about 1¼ pounds.

Chocolate Fudge Variations

Brown Sugar Fudge: In master recipe use half brown and half white sugar.

Coconut Fudge: Add 2 ounces desiccated coconut just before pouring into greased tin.

Creamy Chocolate Fudge: In master recipe add 2 tablespoons light corn syrup or golden syrup with sugar.

Fruit Fudge: Stir 3 ounces chopped dates, figs, candied fruit, dried fruit, or raisins into fudge just before pouring into pan.

Fudge Nut and Fruit Balls: Add chopped nuts and chopped cherries, dates, or figs to beaten fudge and mix until just blended.

Mould into even-sized balls with hands. Roll each in finely ground nuts.

Marshmallow Fudge: Follow master recipe. Cut 12 marshmallows into small pieces. Add to fudge just before pouring into tin.

Mocha Fudge: In master recipe decrease milk to 3 fluid ounces. Add 5 fluid ounces fresh strong coffee.

Nut Fudge: Add 2 ounces chopped nuts just before pouring into tin.

Peanut Butter Fudge: In master recipe substitute 1½ ounces peanut butter for butter and add when beating fudge after it has cooled to lukewarm (110°F.).

Panocha: In master recipe substitute brown sugar for white and water for milk.

Sour Cream Fudge: In master recipe substitute sour cream for milk. Omit butter and cook to slightly higher temperature (238°F.).

Vanilla Fudge: Omit chocolate from recipe for chocolate fudge and increase vanilla to 1½ teaspoons.

DIVINITY
(Master Recipe)

1 pound sugar
8 fluid ounces water
3 ounces corn syrup or golden syrup
⅛ teaspoon salt
2 egg whites
6 ounces chopped walnuts
1 teaspoon vanilla

Heat sugar, water, corn syrup, and salt, stirring constantly until sugar has dissolved. Continue to cook without stirring until syrup when dropped in cold water forms a hard ball (250°F.).

Beat egg whites. Pour syrup slowly into them and continue to beat until candy is stiff enough to hold its shape. Add nuts and vanilla.

Drop by spoonfuls onto greaseproof paper, or turn into buttered tin and cut in 1-inch squares when firm.

Pack in a tin box. Keep covered because it dries out quickly.

Divinity Variations

Brazil Nut Divinity: Use Brazil nuts instead of walnuts.

Brown Sugar Divinity or Sea Foam: In master recipe use half brown and half white sugar.

Cherry Divinity: Prepare master recipe. Colour delicate pink with food colouring. Add 4 ounces chopped glacé cherries.

Chocolate Divinity: Follow master recipe. After syrup and egg whites have been combined, add 2 ounces melted plain chocolate.

Coconut Divinity: Add 2 ounces browned desiccated coconut.

Fruit Divinity: Chopped dates, figs, or other dried or candied fruit may be added.

Maple Divinity: In master recipe decrease water to 4 tablespoons. Add 9 ounces maple syrup.

Neapolitan Divinity: Prepare master recipe. Divide into 3 parts. Colour 1 part with cochineal.

Add 1 ounce melted plain chocolate to second part.

Spread white, or third, part in bottom of buttered tin. Add pink part, then chocolate part. Press together. Let harden before cutting into squares.

Orange Divinity: In master recipe add 3 tablespoons coarsely grated orange rind with vanilla and nuts.

NOUGAT

6 ounces honey
1 pound sugar
4 tablespoons water
2 stiffly beaten egg whites
⅛ teaspoon salt
3 ounces chopped nuts

Combine honey, sugar, and water. Cook to hard ball stage (258°F.).

Beat egg whites with salt until stiff. Add syrup gradually, beating constantly until it stands up in peaks.

Spread in greased shallow square tin. Top with nuts. Cool and cut in rectangular pieces. Makes about 24 pieces.

MAPLE PECAN PRALINES

8 ounces sugar
6 ounces brown sugar
8 fluid ounces milk
1 tablespoon butter
6 ounces pecans or walnuts

Combine all ingredients except nuts in saucepan. Cook to soft ball stage or 240°F. on sugar thermometer. Cool to lukewarm. Beat until creamy and thick.

Place pan over hot water until mixture is soft enough to drop in flat cakes from spoon.

Arrange nuts in groups on a buttered tin. Drop mixture over them. Cool and remove pralines with spatula. Wrap in greaseproof paper.

SEA FOAM

6 ounces dark brown sugar
8 ounces caster sugar
6 fluid ounces water
3 tablespoons corn syrup or golden syrup
2 stiffly beaten egg whites
1 teaspoon vanilla
4 ounces chopped nuts

Put sugars and water into saucepan. Stir until well dissolved. Add syrup and cook to 252°F. or hard ball stage.

Pour slowly over well beaten egg whites.

Beat until mixture is light and fluffy, and piles up without spreading.

Add vanilla and nuts. Drop by spoonfuls onto greaseproof paper. Makes 3 dozen pieces.

Caramels

VANILLA CARAMELS
(Master Recipe)

1 pound sugar
small pinch of salt
1½ pounds corn syrup or golden
    syrup
4 ounces butter
1 large can evaporated milk
1 teaspoon vanilla

Combine sugar, salt, and syrup in saucepan. Cook over low heat until sugar is completely dissolved. Bring to boil. Cook until a little syrup dropped from teaspoon into cold water forms firm ball (244°F.).

Add butter and milk a little at a time so that mixture does not stop boiling. Continue cooking to 242°F.

Remove from heat. Add vanilla, stirring only to blend.

Pour into buttered tin. Mark into squares. Cut when cold. Makes about 72 pieces.

Vanilla Caramel Variations

Chocolate Caramels: In master recipe cook (4 ounces) plain chocolate with sugar, salt, and syrup.

Coconut Caramels: Add 4 ounces browned desiccated coconut after removing from heat.

Coffee Caramels: In master recipe substitute 1 teaspoon coffee essence for vanilla.

Fruit Caramels: Add 4 ounces diced figs, dates, or raisins before pouring into buttered tin.

Honey Caramels: In master recipe substitute 1½ pounds honey for corn syrup. Decrease butter to 2 ounces. Cook to firm ball stage (244°F.).

Nut Caramels: Add 4-6 ounces chopped nuts before pouring into tin.

BUTTERSCOTCH CARAMELS

⅘ pint cream
1¼ pounds light corn syrup or
    golden syrup
6 ounces sugar
4 ounces butter
chopped pecans or walnuts
½ teaspoon vanilla

Place half the cream, syrup, and sugar in pan over low heat, stirring constantly. When mixture is boiling hard, add remaining cream and butter slowly, so that mixture does not stop boiling.

Cook slowly until mixture makes a firm ball when dropped in cold water, 246° to 248°F.

Sprinkle chopped nuts on well buttered baking tin. Add vanilla to mixture and pour over nuts. Let stand several hours.

Cut in inch pieces and wrap separately in greaseproof paper. This quantity fills a 10-inch square baking tin and makes 2½ pounds of caramels.

FIVE-MINUTE FUDGE

1 small can evaporated milk
13 ounces sugar
4 ounces diced marshmallows
2 ounces chopped nuts
6 ounces chocolate drops
1 teaspoon vanilla

Place evaporated milk and sugar in large saucepan. Heat to boiling, then cook 5 minutes. Begin timing after mixture begins bubbling around edges of pan.

Remove from heat; add marshmallows, nuts, chocolate, and vanilla. Stir until marshmallows and chocolate are melted. Pour into buttered 8-inch square tin. Cool; cut in squares. Makes about 2 pounds.

Walnut Fudge: Prepare fudge as directed above, but omit chocolate drops and add 6 ounces chopped walnuts.

Five-Minute Fudge Rolls: Make Five-Minute Fudge as directed above. Spread about 4 ounces chopped nuts on heavy greaseproof paper. Pour fudge mixture over nuts. As fudge cools, form into roll. Slice.

CREAM CARAMELS

8 ounces sugar
pinch of salt
12 ounces light corn syrup or
    golden syrup
2 ounces butter
6 fluid ounces evaporated milk,
    undiluted
1 teaspoon vanilla

Stirring occasionally, boil sugar, salt, and corn syrup rapidly to 245°F. Add butter and evaporated milk gradually so that the mixture does not stop boiling at any time.

Cook rapidly to firm ball stage (242° F.). Stir constantly because the mixture sticks easily at the last. Add flavouring and pour into a buttered tin. Cool thoroughly before cutting.

Cut with a heavy sharp knife with a sawlike motion.

About 25 minutes are required for cooking. Makes 1 pound or 22 caramels (¾ × ½ inch).

NEVER-FAIL FUDGE

8 ounces plain chocolate
2 ounces butter
4 tablespoons cream
½ pound (32) marshmallows
8 ounces icing sugar
1 teaspoon vanilla
pinch of salt
4 ounces chopped nuts

Five-Minute Fudge

Place chocolate, butter, cream, and marshmallows in top of double saucepan and cook over boiling water until melted.

Stir until well blended, then add icing sugar, vanilla, and salt and stir until smooth.

Add nuts and pour into buttered tin. Cut when cool.

Allow to cool thoroughly before eating. The fudge will be somewhat soft when first cut but becomes firm overnight.

HOLIDAY CANDY SLICES

6 ounces brown sugar
8 ounces caster sugar
6 fluid ounces water
¼ teaspoon cream of tartar
1 teaspoon vanilla
4 ounces chopped almonds

Combine sugars, water, and cream of tartar; stir over low heat until sugar is dissolved. Heat to boiling, cover and boil slowly 3 or 4 minutes, to dissolve any crystals on sides of pan. Uncover, and boil without stirring to medium hard ball (242°F.).

Pour out at once onto large plate which has been rinsed in cold water. Allow to cool until barely warm. Add vanilla and stir until creamy.

Shape with hands into two rolls, 1-inch in diameter. Roll each in almonds, wrap in greaseproof paper and allow to set until firm. Cut into slices with sharp knife. Makes about 1½ pounds.

Holiday Slices

Miscellaneous Cooked Candies

COCONUT KISSES

4 fluid ounces evaporated milk, undiluted
4 ounces sugar
8 ounces desiccated coconut
¼ teaspoon almond essence

Combine ingredients. Drop from a teaspoon onto a well oiled (not buttered) baking sheet.

Bake in a slow oven (325°F. Mark 3) 15 minutes. Remove from tin while hot.

CHOCOLATE SLICES

1 pound corn flakes
6 ounces soft butter or margarine
3 ounces sugar
1 ounce cocoa
1 egg, slightly beaten
2 teaspoons vanilla
4 ounces desiccated coconut
2 ounces chopped nuts
11 ounces icing sugar
2 tablespoons milk

Crush corn flakes into fine crumbs. Combine 4 ounces butter, sugar, cocoa, and egg, in top of double saucepan. Cook over hot but not boiling water, stirring constantly until mixture is well-blended and slightly thickened. Remove from heat. Add 1 teaspoon vanilla.

Add coconut, nuts, and cornflake crumbs; mix well. Press into ungreased 8×8-inch tin. Chill.

Beat remaining butter until soft; add 1 teaspoon vanilla and sifted icing sugar gradually, stirring until well-blended. Stir in just enough milk so that mixture will spread easily. Spread over chocolate mixture. Chill.

Cover with Chocolate Glaze. Cut into squares to serve. Makes 25 1½-inch squares.

Chocolate Glaze: Melt 2 ounces plain chocolate with 1 tablespoon butter or margarine over hot but not boiling water; mix well. Spread over vanilla mixture.

Chocolate Slices

COFFEE FUDGE

8 fluid ounces water
2 teaspoons instant coffee
4 fluid ounces milk
12 ounces sugar
9 ounces brown sugar
pinch of salt
2 ounces margarine
1 teaspoon vanilla
3 ounces plain chocolate

Heat water in 2½-3-pint saucepan. Add instant coffee and stir to dissolve.

Add milk, sugars, and salt. Mix well. Bring to boil and cook to 230°F. on sugar thermometer. At this stage syrup begins to spin a thread.

Add margarine. Continue cooking over moderate heat to 235°F., or until a scant teaspoon of syrup dropped into a cup of cold water forms a soft ball.

Remove from heat and pour into large bowl. Do not scrape sides of pan. Let cool without stirring to 110-115°F. Then stir until creamy.

Add vanilla and continue stirring until mixture becomes thick and cheese-like.

Rub palms of hands lightly with margarine and knead candy in bowl until soft and creamy.

Break off bits and roll in hand to form date-shaped pieces. Or roll into long roll and cut into 1½ inch lengths.

Put pieces on margarined baking sheet or shallow tin. Cover with grease-proof paper and allow to stand 10 to 15 minutes.

Melt chocolate in small basin set into hot water. Stir until smooth. Pour in thin stream over pieces of candy. If preferred, dip ends of pieces into chocolate and then into coconut or chopped nuts.

Store in tightly closed container, or pack in greaseproof paper-lined boxes and store in freezer. Makes about 1¾ pounds or 65 pieces.

CHOCOLATE BONBONS
(Chocolate Dipping)

Melt very slowly in top part of double saucepan a good quality coating chocolate, sweetened or unsweetened. Do not heat water under chocolate above 120°F. (slightly more than lukewarm), since overheating spoils chocolate for dipping. Stir constantly while melting to keep constant temperature.

When melted, beat thoroughly. Keep heat very low while dipping.

To dip centres, use a fork or confectioners' dipper. Drop a centre into chocolate. Cover completely with chocolate. Remove with dipping fork. Drop onto greaseproof paper.

The room in which dipping is done should be cool, so that chocolate may harden quickly.

Fruit, nuts, peppermints, plain fondant, and other candies may be dipped in chocolate. One pound dipping chocolate will cover 70 to 80 assorted centres.

TURKISH DELIGHT

¾ ounce gelatine
4 fluid ounces cold water
4 fluid ounces hot water
1 pound sugar
¼ teaspoon salt
3 tablespoons lemon juice
green food colouring
peppermint flavouring
4 ounces finely chopped nuts

Soften gelatine in cold water for 5 minutes. Bring hot water and sugar to boiling point. Add salt and gelatine. Stir until gelatine has dissolved. Simmer 20 minutes.

Remove from heat and when cool add lemon juice, colouring, and peppermint flavouring. Stir in nuts.

Let mixture stand until it begins to thicken. Stir again before pouring into a pan that has been rinsed with cold water. Have the layer of paste about 1-inch thick.

Let stand overnight in cool place. Moisten sharp knife in boiling water. Cut candy into cubes. Roll in caster sugar.

FROSTED PEANUT SQUARES

6 ounces brown sugar
4 ounces peanut butter
12 ounces corn syrup or golden syrup
salted peanuts
1¼ pounds corn flakes

Combine sugar, peanut butter, and corn syrup in large saucepan. Cook and stir until mixture begins to bubble (185°F.).

Remove from heat; stir in peanuts and corn flakes. Press warm mixture evenly and firmly into buttered 15×10-inch tin. Cool; ice with fudge icing or melted chocolate and butterscotch pieces, if desired. Cut into squares when firm. Makes 60 1½-inch squares.

Frosted Peanut Squares

ORANGE CREAM BON BONS

1½ pounds sugar
4 fluid ounces evaporated milk
5 fluid ounces orange juice
4 ounces butter
1 tablespoon grated orange rind
2 ounces chopped nuts
6 ounces plain chocolate

Combine sugar, evaporated milk, orange juice, and butter in a saucepan. Stir constantly until the mixture boils. Boil, stirring occasionally, to a soft ball stage, 236°F.

Remove from heat and cool to lukewarm. Beat until thick enough to knead, then turn out onto a wooden board.

This candy may get quite hard in the pan, but it will soften up when kneaded.

Divide it in two equal parts, and into one half knead the grated orange rind and into the other the chopped nuts.

Wrap in greaseproof paper and refrigerate for several days to mellow. When ready to use, shape the candy into balls.

Melt the chocolate over low heat. Dip the balls into the chocolate until well coated, remove with a spoon, place on greaseproof paper until the chocolate hardens. Makes 4 dozen pieces.

FRENCH CHOCOLATE

2 ounces plain chocolate
1 large can condensed milk

Melt chocolate in double saucepan. Add milk and stir over boiling water 5 minutes until mixture thickens.

Finish in one of the following ways and chill 2 hours before serving. Makes about 1 pound.

Chocolate Nut Balls: Drop by teaspoons into finely chopped nuts and roll until well covered with nuts.

Chocolate Fruit Balls: Add chopped dates, raisins, nuts, or quartered marshmallows to chocolate mixture. Form in balls and roll in cocoa or cocoa and icing sugar, which have been mixed.

SOUR CREAM PANOCHA

1 pound 2 ounces light brown sugar
4 ounces caster sugar
½ pint thick sour cream
1 tablespoon butter
2 ounces coarsely chopped nuts

Combine sugars, sour cream, and butter and cook to soft ball stage (236°F.). Cool to lukewarm and beat until mixture loses its gloss.

Add nuts just before end of beating period. Pour into buttered tin. Cut when hardened.

ALMOND BRITTLE

6 ounces corn flakes
3 ounces seedless raisins
3 ounces coarsely chopped blanched
    almonds
8 ounces sugar
½ teaspoon butter
2 tablespoons vinegar
4 tablespoons water
¼ teaspoon salt

Combine corn flakes, raisins, and almonds in large basin and warm in oven.

Boil remaining ingredients to hard crack stage (300°F.).

Pour slowly over corn flake-almond mixture, blending lightly but thoroughly.

Spread in tin lined with greaseproof paper. When cool, break or cut in pieces. Makes 1 pound.

MOLASSES NUT CRUNCH

12 ounces molasses or black
    treacle
8 ounces sugar
1 tablespoon butter or margarine
¼ teaspoon bicarbonate of soda
10 ounces chopped peanuts or other
    nuts

Combine molasses, sugar, and butter or margarine in a 2½-3-pint saucepan. Place over low heat and stir until sugar is dissolved.

Cook over medium heat until syrup, when dropped in very cold water, separates into threads which are hard but not brittle, or until sugar thermometer reaches 270°F.

Remove from heat; stir in bicarbonate of soda. Add nuts. Turn into a greased 8-inch square tin; spread quickly.

When mixture is slightly cool, cut into squares. Wrap in greaseproof paper. Makes about 1¾ pounds.

QUICK BRAZIL NUT FUDGE

4 ounces plain chocolate
2 tablespoons butter
¼ teaspoon salt
1 teaspoon vanilla
1 pound sifted icing sugar
5 tablespoons milk
4 ounces chopped Brazil nuts
whole Brazil nuts

Melt chocolate and butter over low heat. Stir in salt and vanilla. Stir in sugar alternately with the milk, keeping pan over hot water.

Remove from heat and stir in chopped Brazil nuts.

Pour fudge into a 7-inch square tin. Decorate with Brazil nuts, cut in halves. Let stand several hours. Cut in squares.

CANTONESE FUDGE

1 pound brown sugar
few grains salt
1 tablespoon light corn syrup or
    golden syrup
1 tablespoon butter
6 fluid ounces evaporated milk
1 teaspoon vanilla
1½ ounces finely cut crystallised
    ginger

Mix sugar, salt, syrup, butter, and milk thoroughly in heavy saucepan.

Cook over medium heat to soft ball stage (237°F.), stirring constantly. Cool.

Stir in vanilla and ginger. Beat until crystalline.

Turn into buttered tin. Mark in squares. Makes 1⅛ pounds.

COFFEE COCOA FUDGE

1 ounce fat
5 tablespoons hot coffee
¼ teaspoon salt
1 pound sifted icing sugar
1 ounce cocoa

Place fat and the hot coffee in top of double saucepan and heat over boiling water until fat is melted.

Mix salt, sugar, and cocoa and sift together. Stir in icing sugar in 3 instalments, beating thoroughly after each addition. If necessary, add a little more hot coffee.

When mixture is well blended and smooth, remove at once from hot water, pour in greased 7×7-inch tin and cut in squares.

CHRISTMAS DIVINITY FUDGE

1 pound sugar
4 fluid ounces water
3 ounces light corn syrup or
    golden syrup
pinch of salt
2 egg whites
1 teaspoon vanilla
¼ teaspoon almond essence
few drops pink food colouring
4 ounces glacé cherries, halved
1½ ounces citron, sliced or chopped
    candied peel

Heat sugar, water, syrup, and salt, stirring until sugar is dissolved. Boil to 255°F. (firm ball in cold water).

In a large bowl beat egg whites until stiff but not dry; pour the syrup mixture slowly into them, beating with a wire whisk until mixture holds up in peaks.

Add vanilla and almond essence, pink colouring, and fruits. Pour into a greased 8-inch square tin or drop from the tip of a spoon onto waxed paper.

Remove mixture from tin before cutting. Store in airtight container. Makes about 1½ pounds.

Note: If mixture is over-beaten and becomes dry, add a small amount of water to soften it and to restore the glaze.

BOTTLING

Preservation of food, by bottling, canning, jam-making or pickling, makes use of heat and airtight containers to retain the maximum amount of flavour, texture, and food value.

Tiny organisms—moulds, yeasts, and bacteria—are normally present in fruits, vegetables, and meats, and will eventually cause fresh foods to spoil. The aim in bottling is to destroy or make inactive by heat the action of the microorganisms. Moulds, yeasts, and bacteria are always present in air, water, and soil.

In the bottling process fruits and vegetables are heated sufficiently to stop the action of these tiny organisms with the exception of some types of bacteria. There are certain heat-resistant bacteria that go through a spore phase in their life cycle, a form in which they are very difficult to kill.

In bottling foods high in acid, like fruits, tomatoes, and pickled beetroot, the spores are readily destroyed at the boiling temperature in a reasonable length of time. In all vegetables other than tomatoes it may take 15 hours or more to destroy or render inactive the spores at boiling temperature.

If cooked at 10 pounds pressure in a steam pressure cooker, these same spores are destroyed in less than 1 hour.

On the other hand the enzymes are useful to a degree in that they are responsible for the normal ripening process of fruits and vegetables. They will, however, cause decay after the normal ripening point has been reached if their action is not stopped. Extreme heat or extreme cold will inhibit and delay the action of enzymes.

DIRECTIONS FOR USING STERILIZER

This method is used for fruits and acid vegetables (tomatoes).

Any big, clean vessel will do for a sterilizer if it's deep enough to let water boil well over tops of the jars at least 2 inches, has a tight-fitting lid, and a rack to keep the jars at least ½ inch from the bottom of the vessel.

Place rack in sterilizer. Fill with boiling water. Jars must be hot when placed in the sterilizer. If necessary, heat in hot water.

Bring water to a rolling boil. If necessary, add water to keep jars covered 2 inches.

When processing time is completed open by tilting lid toward you so that steam will not come in contact with face and hands.

Remove jars one at a time. Complete seal (see directions).

DIRECTIONS FOR USING PRESSURE COOKER

Use only this method for processing all non-acid vegetables and meats.

Follow manufacturer's directions carefully for use and care of cooker.

Each time cooker is used, be sure it contains enough water to come just below the level of rack (1 to 2 inches of water).

Place jars on rack, leaving ample space between jars for free circulation of steam.

Adjust cover and fasten on securely.

Air must be exhausted by leaving valve open until a steady stream of steam escapes for 5 to 10 minutes.

Close valve. Allow pressure to rise to specified point, counting pressure time when gauge reaches desired pressure.

Maintain constant pressure by regulation of heat.

When processing time is completed remove cooker from heat.

Do not open cooker until pressure gauge registers zero. Cool slowly until zero point is registered.

Slowly open valve until all steam has escaped.

To open cover, tilt toward you, so escaping steam will not burn face or hands.

Allow jars to stand a few minutes before removing one at a time.

Complete seal (see directions).

HIGH ALTITUDE ADJUSTMENTS

Adjust cooking time or pressure to match the altitude. For water bath, add 1 minute to the processing time, if time specified is 20 minutes or less, for each 1,000 feet above sea-level. Add 2 minutes for every 1,000 feet if the time called for is more than 20 minutes. For a pressure cooker, increase pressure 1 pound for each 2,000 feet.

BOTTLING UTENSILS

Gather together tools needed before beginning to work.

Use good cooking utensils with tight-fitting lids, scales, a sieve or plenty of muslin, bowls, a colander, large spoons, a ladle, a sharp knife or two, plenty of clean towels, dishcloths, and oven gloves.

A wide-mouthed funnel, wire clamps, or tongs for removing hot jars from pressure cooker or water bath are helpful aids.

CHECKING JARS AND COVERS

Inspect jars carefully for possible defects, cracks, chips, or dents.

Have ample supply of jar tops, new rubber rings or self-sealing lids. Make sure they fit. Do not re-use rubber rings or self-sealing lids. Check to see that zinc screw lids have no loose linings. Clamp lids must be tight. If necessary, remove top clamp, bend down in centre, and bend in sides to tighten.

PREPARING JARS AND COVERS

Wash jars, lids, and rubber rings in soapy water. Rinse with clear hot water.

Sterilize by placing jars, lids, and rings in pan of hot water with a rack or cloth on the bottom of it.

Bring to the boil just before ready to fill jars.

Do not boil metal lids with self-sealing compound. Just dip in boiling water before using.

PACKING JARS

Remove 1 jar at a time from water. Pack hot jars as quickly as possible and seal immediately.

Keep jars in hot water or on cloth or several layers of paper while packing.

Don't pack food too solidly or heat will not penetrate thoroughly.

Using knife blade, work out any air bubbles formed in jar.

When packed always wipe food particles with clean damp cloth from rim of jar and from rubber ring.

COOLING JARS

Never invert jars of any type after processing—even for a moment.

Place jars on several thicknesses of cloth or newspaper.

Avoid draughts. Leave air space between jars.

Never cover jars while cooling.

LABELLING JARS

After jars have cooled for 24 hours, wipe clean, label with name, date, and with lot number, if more than one lot is prepared.

STORING JARS

Store jars upright in cool, dry, dark place. Handle as little as possible.

CHECKING JARS

Examine jars after a week or ten days for signs of spoilage.

Remove and dispose of spoiled jars of food immediately.

OPENING JARS

To open glass-top or zinc screw lids, pull out jar rubber with a pair of pliers.

To open self-sealing metal lids puncture top and lift up.

On opening bottled foods, odour should be characteristic of the product with no outrush of air or liquid.

Never taste to test for spoilage.

Before every serving, all home bottled meats and vegetables (except tomatoes) should be cooked at boiling temperature for at least 10 minutes (spinach and other leafy vegetables for 15 minutes) in a covered container, even when they are to be served cold.

HOW TO CLOSE LIDS

Metal self-sealing lids: Use only on jars with smooth, even top edges.

Put lid in place with sealing compound touching rim of jar, attach screw band, then hold your index finger on lid so it won't slip while you screw band down firmly without exerting unusual force.

Don't invert, move, or handle jars for at least 24 hours after processing.

Screw bands may be removed and reused.

Test seal by tapping lids gently with a spoon. If properly sealed, they will sound a clear, ringing note, and the lid will have a slight dip caused by the vacuum inside.

If lids bulge upward and give off a dull sound when tapped, the seal is imperfect. If seal is imperfect, open and use the food at once or immediately replace the lid with a new one and reprocess the jar for half the original time.

Glass top self-sealing lids: Use on jars with smooth, even rims free of nicks, cracks, or sharp edges.

Leave 1 inch of space in top of jar regardless of type of food being bottled.

Fit wet rubber ring round projection on under-side of glass lid.

Place lid so rubber lies between lid and top edge of jar.

Tighten bands, then loosen slightly (about ¼ turn). Bands must fit loosely during processing.

Immediately after processing, screw bands tightly to complete seal.

Remove bands 24 hours after bottling, and test seal by pulling on lid gently with the finger tips.

If screw bands are not replaced on jars, handle jars gently to prevent breaking the seal.

Do not turn filled jars upside down.

Clamp lids: Place rubber on ridge. Fasten top clamp only.

Process. Then snap down side clamp. Do not invert jars.

Zinc screw lids: Place rubber ring on sealing shoulder of jar. Screw lid down until lid and rubber ring just touch.

After processing, tighten lids the moment jars are removed.

Do not invert jars after processing.

SYRUPS FOR BOTTLING FRUITS

Thin syrup: Use 1 part sugar and 3 parts juice or water. Bring to a boil, keep hot.

Use on apples, bilberries, pears, pineapple, sweet cherries.

Medium syrup: Use 1 part sugar and 2 parts juice or water. Bring to a boil. Keep hot.

Use on apricots, blackberries, peaches, plums, raspberries, strawberries, gooseberries, sour cherries, rhubarb.

Thick or heavy syrup: Use 1 part sugar and 1 part juice or water. Bring to a boil. Keep hot.

Use on larger sour fruits.

Variations:

Honey may be used to replace as much as half the sugar required.

Golden syrup may be used to replace as much as ⅓ of the sugar required.

Do not use sweeteners that have a strong flavour, such as brown sugar or black treacle.

TIPS FOR BOTTLING

Use only the very best fresh foods for preserving. The finished product will not be any better than what went into it.

Fruits and vegetables should be bottled while they are fresh and at their best. The fresher the fruits and vegetables the higher their vitamin content and the lower the bacteria count.

Most vegetables are best before they are fully matured, so choose young, fresh vegetables.

Select fresh, firm, ripe fruits.

Remove any spots and bruises which may cause spoilage.

Sort and wash carefully, removing all traces of sand and dirt.

To keep apples, peaches, and pears from turning dark after peeling, place in a solution of 2 tablespoons each of salt and vinegar to 6 to 7 pints water.

Scald peaches and tomatoes in boiling water for 1 minute to loosen skin, then dip into cold water ½ minute and remove skin.

Bottling Vegetables in Pressure Cooker

ASPARAGUS

Select fresh, tender asparagus. Sort. Wash thoroughly, and trim off scales.

Long Pieces: Cut stalks into lengths to fit upright in container. Tie in bundles.

Place upright in cooker, with boiling water to cover lower part of stalks. Cover tightly. Boil 3 minutes.

Pack hot, removing string as asparagus slips into containers.

Add 1 teaspoon salt to each 2-pound jar. Cover with fresh boiling water.

Process at 10-pound pressure: 2-pound jars, 35 minutes.

Short Pieces: Cut stalks into 1-inch lengths. Cover with boiling water and boil 3 minutes.

Pack hot into containers. Add 1 teaspoon salt to each 2-pound jar and cover with boiling water.

Process same as above.

Allow 2 to 3 pounds for each 2-pound jar.

BEANS (Broad or Lima)

Select young, tender beans. Shell and wash. Cover with boiling water and bring to the boil.

Pack hot. Add 1 teaspoon salt to each 2-pound jar and cover with boiling water.

Process at 10-pound pressure: 2-pound jars, 60 minutes.

Beans (Lima), Continued

Allow 4 to 5 pounds beans (in pods) for each 2-pound jar.

BEANS (fresh green soya beans)

Cover shelled beans with boiling water and boil 3 or 4 minutes.

Pack hot, and add 1 teaspoon salt to each 2-pound jar. Cover with fresh boiling water.

Process at 10-pound pressure: 2-pound jars, 70 minutes.

Allow 4 to 5 pounds beans (in pods) for each 2-pound jar.

BEANS (runner or French)

Wash thoroughly, trim off ends, and remove strings if stringy. Cut into pieces (½ to 1 inch) or cut lengthwise or leave whole.

Cover with boiling water and boil 5 minutes.

Pack hot. Add 1 teaspoon salt to each 2-pound jar and cover with fresh boiling water.

Process at 10-pound pressure: 2-pound jars, 25 minutes.

Allow 1½ to 2 pounds for each 2-pound jar.

THIS IS THE WAY TO BOTTLE GREEN BEANS

1. Check jars for nicks, cracks, and sharp edges. Wash jars and caps in hot soapy water; rinse. Leave jars in hot water until ready to use. Use new lids and good bands.

2. Thoroughly wash freshly gathered beans, which are young, tender, and crisp, in several changes of water. Lift beans out of water and drain.

3. Trim ends; remove any strings; cut or break into pieces. Prepare only enough for one sterilizer load.

4. Cover beans with boiling water and boil for 5 minutes, or pack raw.

5. Stand hot jar on wood or cloth. Add 1 teaspoon salt per 2-pound jar; cover beans with boiling water, leaving 1-inch head space.

6. Wipe top and threads of jar with clean, damp cloth. Put lid on, red rubber sealing compound next to jar. Screw band down evenly and tight.

7. Put jars into steam-pressure cooker containing 2 to 3 inches of hot water, or the amount recommended by the manufacturer.

8. Place cooker over heat. Lock cover according to the manufacturer's instructions.

9. Leave valve open until steam escapes steadily for 10 minutes. Close valve. At altitudes less than 2,000 feet above sea level bring pressure to 10 pounds. Keep pressure steady for 25 minutes for 2-pound jars.

10. Remove cooker from heat. Allow pressure to fall to zero. Wait 2 minutes. Slowly open valve. Open cooker. Remove jars. Do not tighten bands.

11. Stand jars several inches apart, out of draughts, to cool for about 12 hours. Remove bands.

12. Test the seal by pressing centre of lid. If dome is down, or stays down when pressed, jar is sealed. Store without bands in dry, dark, reasonably cool place.

BEETROOTS

Select tender baby beetroots. Trim off tops, leaving 1 inch of stems. Wash thoroughly.

Cook in boiling water about 15 minutes or steam until skins slip off easily. Skin and trim. Or peel beetroots before boiling them.

Leave small beetroots whole. Cut large beetroots in sections.

Pack quickly into containers before beetroots cool. Add 1 teaspoon salt to each 2-pound jar. Cover with fresh boiling water (1 teaspoon vinegar added to each jar will help to retain the red colour).

Process at 10-pound pressure: 2-pound jars, 55 minutes.

Allow 2½ to 3 pounds fresh beetroots (without tops) for each 2-pound jar.

Note: Pickled beetroots may be processed in a sterilizer.

CARROTS

Select tender carrots. Wash thoroughly. If desired, remove skins by scraping.

Leave small carrots whole. Cut large carrots into lengthwise quarters or cubes.

Cover with boiling water. Boil 5 minutes.

Pack hot into containers. Add 1 teaspoon salt to each 2-pound jar. Cover with boiling water—the same water in which the carrots were cooked.

Process at 10-pound pressure: 2-pound jars, 25 minutes.

Allow about 2½ pounds fresh carrots (without tops) for each 2-pound jar.

CORN

Use freshly picked cobs in the milk stage. Work with small quantities at a time and complete the whole bottling process as quickly as possible. Husk and silk the corn, using a stiff brush, if necessary, to remove the silk.

Cut corn from cob so that kernels are whole. Do *not* scrape the cob.

Add ½ as much boiling water as corn. Heat to boiling point.

Pack into 2-pound jars. Add 1 teaspoon salt and ½ to 1 teaspoon sugar, if desired, to each 2-pound jar.

Process at 10-pound pressure: 2-pound jars, 85 minutes.

Allow 8 to 12 cobs for each 2-pound jar.

PEAS

Select young, tender peas. Wash pods and shell only enough to fill containers to be processed at one time.

Wash shelled peas. Cover with boiling water and bring to boiling point.

Pack hot into 2-pound jars. Add 1 teaspoon salt and 1 teaspoon sugar, if desired, to each 2-pound jar. Cover with boiling water.

Process at 10-pound pressure: 2-pound jars, 45 minutes.

Allow 2 to 2½ pounds unshelled peas for each 2-pound jar.

PUMPKIN, MARROW AND COURGETTES

Wash and peel pumpkin and marrow; do not peel courgettes. Cut into 1-inch cubes. Boil or steam until tender and press through colander. Heat to simmering (190°F.).

Pack hot. Add 1 teaspoon salt to each 2-pound jar if desired.

Process at 10-pound pressure: 2-pound jars, 80 minutes.

Allow 2 to 2½ pounds fresh pumpkin, marrow or courgettes for each 2-pound jar.

SPINACH OR OTHER GREENS

Pick over and wash greens carefully. Discard imperfect leaves and tough stems.

Heat greens in covered pan containing small amount of water until completely wilted.

Pack into 2-pound jars, being careful not to pack too solidly. Add 1 teaspoon salt to each 2-pound jar and cover greens with boiling water.

Process at 10-pound pressure: 2-pound jars, 70 minutes.

Allow 2 to 3 pounds for each 2-pound jar.

Bottling fruits and Vegetables in a Sterilizer

APPLES

Wash, peel, and cut apples into pieces of desired size.

Prepare only as many as can be processed at one time.

Boil in thin syrup 5 minutes. Pack hot into jars. Cover with boiling syrup.

There is less shrinkage by this method and the jars are better filled. Process, in sterilizer: 2-pound jars, 15 minutes.

Allow 2 to 3 pounds of apples for each 2-pound jar.

APRICOTS

Wash, cut into halves, and remove stones. (If they are to be peeled, scald in boiling water to loosen skins before cutting.)

Cold Pack: Pack apricots in glass jars. Cover with boiling syrup.

Process, in sterilizer, 2-pound jars, 30 minutes.

Hot Pack: Simmer 3 to 5 minutes in thin or medium syrup.

Pack apricots hot into containers. Cover with boiling syrup.

Process, in sterilizer, 2-pound jars, 20 minutes.

BEETROOTS, PICKLED

Select tender beetroots. Wash thoroughly.

Cook in boiling water, or steam 10 minutes or until skins slip easily. Remove skins.

Leave small beetroots whole. Cut large beetroots into sections.

Pack quickly into containers before beetroots cool.

Add 1 teaspoon salt, 2 teaspoons or more of sugar, and 6 whole cloves, if desired, to each 2-pound jar.

Cover with boiling vinegar (unless vinegar is very strong, use it full-strength).

Process, in sterilizer, 2-pound jars, 30 minutes.

CHERRIES

Wash and stone cherries.

Cold Pack: Pack into jars. Cover with boiling syrup.

Process 1-pound jars in sterilizer, 20 minutes, 2-pound jars, 25 minutes.

Hot Pack: Add 4 ounces sugar to each pound of cherries.

Bring slowly to boiling point. Boil 2 minutes.

Pack hot into glass jars. Cover with boiling syrup.

Process, in sterilizer, 1- or 2-pound jars, 15 minutes.

Allow 1½ to 2 pounds cherries for each 2-pound jar.

GOOSEBERRIES

Wash berries and remove stems.

Cold Pack: Pack into containers. Cover with boiling syrup.

Process, in boiling water bath, 1- or 2-pound jars, 20 minutes.

Hot Pack: Cover with boiling medium syrup. Boil 1 or 2 minutes. Pack into jars or cans.

Process, in sterilizer, 1- or 2-pound jars, 15 minutes.

Allow 1½ to 2 pounds fresh berries for each 2-pound jar.

THIS IS THE WAY TO BOTTLE PEACHES

1. Check jars. Be sure there are no nicks, cracks, or sharp edges. Use new lids.

2. Wash and rinse jars and lids. Leave jars in hot water until ready to use.

3. Sort, wash, and drain only enough firm-ripe peaches for one sterilizer load. Fill sterilizer half full with hot water. Put it on to heat. Prepare sugar syrup.

4. Put peaches in wire basket or muslin. Dip peaches into boiling water ½ to 1 minute to loosen skins. Dip into cold water. Drain.

5. Cut peaches into halves, stone and peel. Drop halves into salt-vinegar water (2 tablespoons each to 6½ pints cold water). Rinse before packing.

6. Stand hot jar on rubber tray, wood or cloth. Pack peaches, cavity-side down, layers overlapping. Leave ½-inch head space.

7. Cover peaches with boiling hot syrup, leaving ½-inch head space. It will take 8 to 12 fluid ounces syrup for each 2-pound jar.

8. Run rubber bottle scraper or similar non-metal utensil between fruit and jar to release air bubbles. Add more syrup, if needed.

9. Wipe top and threads of jar with clean, damp cloth. Put lid on; screw band tight . . . it must screw down evenly to hold red rubber sealing compound against top of jar.

10. As each jar is filled, stand it on rack in sterilizer. Water should be hot, but not boiling. If needed, add more water to cover jars 1 to 2 inches. Put cover on sterilizer.

11. Bring water to the boil. At altitudes less than 1,000 feet above sea level process for 25 to 30 minutes, at gentle but steady boil.

12. Remove jars from sterilizer. Allow to cool for about 12 hours. Remove bands. Test for seal by pressing centre of lid. If dome is down, or stays down when pressed, jar is sealed. Store without bands in dry, dark, reasonably cool place.

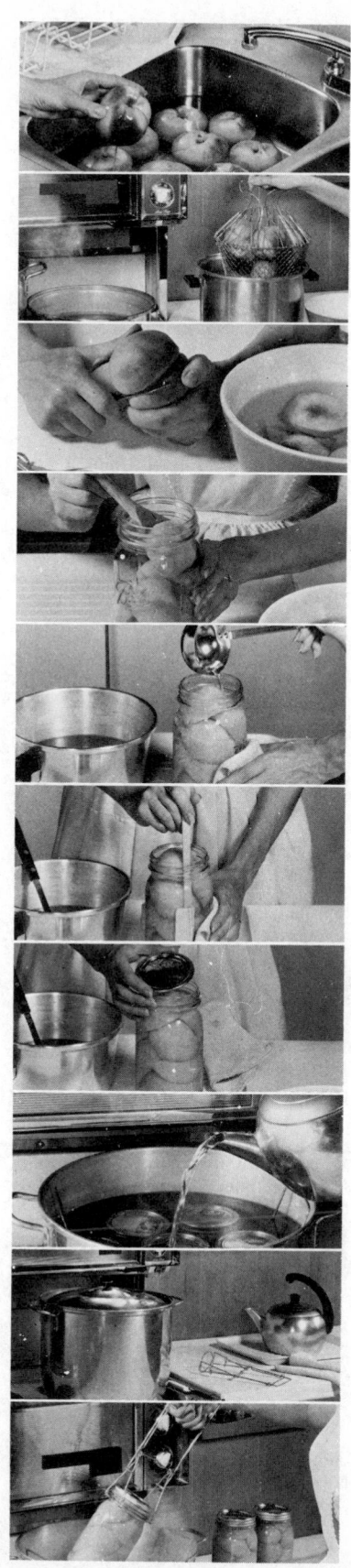

PEACHES

Select ripe, firm peaches. Plunge into boiling water to loosen skins. Remove and plunge into cold water. Peel.

Prepare only as many as can be processed at one time.

Cold Pack: Pack peaches into glass jars. Cover with boiling syrup.

Process, in sterilizer for 30 minutes.

Hot Pack: Simmer 3 to 5 minutes in syrup.

Pack peaches into containers. Cover with boiling syrup.

Process, in sterilizer, 1- or 2-pound jars, 20 minutes.

Allow 2 to 2½ pounds fresh fruit for each 2-pound jar.

PEARS

Wash, peel, cut in half, and remove core. Prepare only as many as can be processed at one time. Drain.

Boil in thin or medium syrup 4 to 8 minutes, according to size and softness.

Pack pears into containers. Cover with boiling syrup.

Process, in sterilizer, 1- or 2-pound jars, 20 minutes.

Allow 2 to 2½ pounds fresh pears for each 2-pound jar.

PINEAPPLE

Peel, core, and remove "eyes". Slice or cut in pieces.

Boil pineapple in thin syrup 5 minutes.

Pack into containers. Cover with boiling syrup.

Process, in sterilizer, 1- or 2-pound jars, 30 minutes.

Allow 1 large pineapple for each 2-pound jar.

PLUMS

Wash. Prick each plum to prevent bursting of skin.

Cold Pack: Pack plums into glass jars. Cover with boiling syrup (medium or thick).

Process 1-pound jars 20 minutes, 2-pound jars 25 minutes in sterilizer.

Hot Pack: Simmer in medium syrup 5 minutes.

Pack plums into containers. Cover with boiling syrup.

Process, in sterilizer, 1- or 2-pound jars, 15 minutes.

Allow 2 to 2½ pounds for each 2-pound jar.

RHUBARB

Select young, tender rhubarb. Wash, cut into ½-inch lengths, but do not skin.

Boil rhubarb in water or syrup until soft. Pack boiling hot into glass jars.

Process, in sterilizer, for 10 minutes.

Allow 1½ to 2 pounds for each 2-pound jar.

BLACKBERRIES

Wash carefully, remove tops, and drain.

Cold Pack: Fill glass jars, shaking or jarring against hand to make a more solid pack. Cover with boiling syrup (medium or thick).

Process, in sterilizer, for 20 minutes.

Hot Pack: Boil berries in medium syrup 2 minutes.

Pack into containers. Cover with boiling syrup.

Process, in sterilizer, 1- or 2-pound jars, 15 minutes.

Allow about 1 pound fresh berries for each 2-pound jar.

RASPBERRIES (RED)

Wash berries, being careful not to crush them. Drain.

Pack into glass jars, alternating berries and boiling red syrup until containers are filled.

Process the same as blackberries.

To prepare red syrup, use overripe or soft berries not firm enough for canning. Heat slowly to boiling point using 4 fluid ounces water to 3 ounces berries.

Extract juice by straining through fine sieve or muslin. To each 8 fluid ounces of juice add 4 ounces sugar. Bring slowly to boiling point.

Allow about 1 pound fresh berries for each 2-pound jar.

STRAWBERRIES

Wash, cap, and drain fresh, firm berries.

Heat Immediately: Add 4 ounces sugar to each pound of berries. Heat slowly to boiling point and allow to stand several hours or overnight.

Reheat slowly to boiling point. Pack berries hot into containers.

Process, in sterilizer, 1- or 2-pound jars, 15 minutes.

Heat Later: Add 4 ounces sugar to each pound of berries, alternating layers of berries and sugar. Allow to stand several hours or overnight.

Heat slowly to boiling point. Pack

berries hot into containers. Process same as above.

Allow 1½ to 2 pounds fresh berries for each 2-pound jar.

TOMATOES

Select firm, well-ripened tomatoes. Wash.

Scald, plunge in cold water to peel, and remove cores. Quarter.

Cold Pack: Pack tomatoes solidly into containers. Add 1 teaspoon salt to each 2-pound jar. When packing tomatoes in glass jars, leave ½ inch head space.

Set in boiling water and keep there until contents in centre of container are at least 160°F.

Partially seal glass jars.

Process, in sterilizer, 1-pound jars, 35 minutes; 2-pound jars, 45 minutes.

Hot Pack: Heat slowly to boiling point. Boil 2 minutes. Pack into containers.

Process, in sterilizer, 1- or 2-pound jars, 10 minutes.

Allow 2½ to 3 pounds for each 2-pound jar.

Preserving Meats

Bottle only fresh meat from healthy animals, slaughtered and handled under strictly sanitary conditions. Beef, veal, lamb, mutton, and pork may be successfully bottled at home.

Refrigerate the meat at a freezing temperature until ready for bottling. If frozen, bottle it as soon as it thaws.

Meats may be processed by either the hot pack or the raw pack method.

Raw Pack: Cut up meat as for Hot Pack (see below); add salt if desired.

Pack raw, lean strips in clean, hot jars, leaving 1-inch head space.

Place open jars in large container of warm water filled up to about 2 inches from top of containers.

Cover vessel and boil slowly until meat is medium done, about 75 minutes in glass jars. Meat thermometer should register 170°F. in centre of jar.

Add boiling stock or water to fill container.

Adjust covers; partially seal and process 2-pound jars in pressure cooker 70 minutes at 15-pound pressure.

Hot Pack: Use cuts suitable for chops, steaks, and roasts for canning large pieces; use less tender cuts and smaller pieces for stew meat.

Cut meat away from bone, remove all excess fat; use bones for soup. Cut

meat across grain ½ to 1 inch thick or cut into cubes for stews.

Precook meat slowly in covered pan until about half done with just enough water or stock added to keep meat from sticking: stir or turn occasionally.

Do not coat meat with flour or cracker crumbs.

Do not fry meats for bottling; they become hard and dry and develop an "off" flavour in processing.

Pack strips of hot meat at once in sterilized jars kept hot in boiling water. If salt is desired, add ½ teaspoon to each 1-pound jar and 1 teaspoon to each 2-pound jar.

Cover with hot broth (fat removed) or water, leaving 1-inch head space in jars. Work out air bubbles with knife.

Wipe jar rims; partially seal and process: 2-pound jars in pressure cooker, 60 minutes at 15-pound pressure.

POULTRY

Select plump stewing hens for best flavour. Joint and cut into convenient pieces; sort meaty and bony pieces; set giblets aside.

Cover bony pieces with cold water; cook for stock. Drain broth into bowl; skim off fat.

Poultry should be bled well and hung in a cool place for 6 to 12 hours before bottling.

Raw Pack: Wash thoroughly. Cut up poultry into convenient pieces; sort meaty and bony pieces; add salt if desired; pack into hot jars as directed for hot pack.

Place filled open jars in large container filled with warm water to about 2 inches from top of jars.

Cover vessel and boil slowly until meat is steaming hot and medium done, about 75 minutes for glass jars. Meat thermometer should register 170°F. for centre of jar.

Process at once at 15-pound pressure for 60 minutes.

Hot Pack: Remove excess fat from meaty pieces. Pour hot broth or water over meat to cover; cover and simmer until about half done. When cut in centre, pieces will show little or no pink colour. Stir occasionally.

Add salt, if desired, ½ teaspoon to each 1-pound jar and 1 teaspoon to each 2-pound jar.

Pack thighs and drumsticks into hot jars with skin sides next to glass; place breast pieces in centre; fit small pieces into spaces. Leave 1-inch head space in glass containers.

Cover meat with hot broth and work out air bubbles.

Partially seal and process at once for 60 minutes at 15-pound pressure.

CASSEROLES AND ONE-DISH MEALS

When you find it a problem to think of something to serve, prepare a casserole. A main dish casserole reduces the job of good menu planning to simplicity. It's the hostess's best friend and the busy housewife's helper because it is often the solution to time-saving beforehand meal preparation. Usually casseroles can be prepared hours in advance, stored in the refrigerator ready for cooking later, or can be three-fourths cooked and finished just before serving.

Modern housewives think of a casserole as a combination of protein (meat, fish, cheese, or eggs), a filler like a pasta (macaroni, spaghetti, noodles, etc.) or rice, all bound together with a sauce. A wisely chosen recipe will mean that you have used ingredients with flavours that blend well together, which offer well-balanced nutrition, and are convenient to use. Since casseroles are generally oven-to-table utensils, there's less trouble serving, less washing up to do afterwards.

Beef Casseroles

SWISS STEAK EN CASSEROLE

2 pounds topside steak
½ clove garlic
1 teaspoon salt
¼ teaspoon pepper
About 2 ounces flour
2 ounces fat
1 medium onion, chopped
4 ounces grated carrots, green pepper, and chopped celery, combined
8 ounces chopped tomatoes
8 fluid ounces boiling water
6 to 12 small potatoes, peeled

Rub steak with garlic. Pound combined salt, pepper, and flour into it.

Cook onion until tender in hot fat in heavy frying pan. Add steak and brown both sides. Transfer to casserole.

Combine vegetables and boiling water and add to browned steak.

Cover closely and cook in very slow oven (275°F. Mark 1) until tender; about 2 hours.

About 40 minutes before meat is done, brown potatoes in a little fat; add to casserole. Serves 6.

TOPSIDE OR CHUCK STEAK CASSEROLE

1 to 1½ pounds topside or chuck steak, cut ¾-inch thick
2 teaspoons salt
1 teaspoon paprika
About 2 tablespoons flour
1 ounce fat
1 medium onion, sliced
4 small potatoes, sliced
1 8-ounce can tomatoes
1 tablespoon tomato ketchup

Cut steak in to 4 pieces. Season with 1 teaspoon salt and paprika. Coat with flour. Brown in hot fat in a heavy frying pan. Transfer to casserole.

Place onion and potatoes over top. Mix tomatoes, ketchup, and remaining teaspoon salt; pour over potatoes.

Cover and bake in moderate oven (350°F. Mark 4) until tender, about 1¼ hours. If necessary, add a little water. Serves 4.

Variations: Substitute breast of lamb or lamb loin chops for beef.

FLAT RIBS—NEW ENGLAND STYLE

1 pound dried haricot beans
1 28-ounce can tomatoes
2 tablespoons prepared French mustard
6 ounces black treacle
3 tablespoons chopped onion
3 teaspoons salt
½ teaspoon black pepper
3 pounds flat ribs of beef

Soak haricot beans if necessary. Add tomatoes and seasonings. Cover and cook slowly for 1½ hours.

Brown flat ribs on all sides. Add flat ribs to beans.

Cover closely and cook slowly on top of stove or in a slow oven (300°F. Mark 2) for 2 hours. Serves 6.

HUNGARIAN GOULASH EN CASSEROLE

2 pounds beef chuck, cut in 2-inch cubes
1 large onion, chopped
3 ounces hot fat
1 tablespoon flour
1½ teaspoons salt
1 tablespoon paprika
2 bouillon cubes in ½ pint boiling water or ½ pint stock
1 8-ounce can tomato sauce
1 pound tomatoes, skinned and diced
1 clove garlic, chopped fine
1 bouquet garni (see below)

Fry beef and onions in hot fat until onions are soft and yellow.

Stir in lightly the flour, salt, and paprika; cook 5 minutes. Add remaining ingredients and heat to boiling. Turn into heated casserole.

Bake in moderate oven (350°F. Mark 4) until meat is tender, about 1½ hours. Remove bouquet garni. Serve with hot macaroni. Serves 6.

Bouquet garni: Tie in a small piece of muslin, 1 bay leaf, 2 tablespoons chopped parsley, a sprig of thyme, and a stalk of celery and leaves, chopped.

TOPSIDE WITH TOMATOES AND SWEETCORN

1½ pounds topside, cut into 1½-inch cubes
1 ounce fat
1 16-ounce can tomatoes, drained
7 ounces sweetcorn
½ teaspoon basil
Few grains nutmeg
Salt and pepper

Brown meat lightly in hot fat; transfer to casserole. Add tomatoes, sweetcorn and seasoning.

Bake in moderate oven (350°F. Mark 4) 25 to 30 minutes. Serves 4.

Prepare your casseroles in oven-to-table dishes that either harmonize with or present pleasant colour contrasts to the table dishes.

Beef Pot Pie

BEEF POT PIE

1½ pounds boneless beef (stewing,
    shin of beef, skirt)
2 tablespoons flour
1 ounce dripping
1 large onion, chopped
16 fluid ounces hot water
2 teaspoons salt
4 whole cloves
1 bay leaf
4 carrots, sliced
4 potatoes, quartered
4 ounces celery, sliced
6 ounces shortcrust pastry

Cut meat into 1-inch cubes, dust
with the flour and brown slowly and
thoroughly in the dripping. To the
browned meat add onion, water, salt,
cloves, and bay leaf. Cover and simmer
over low heat for 1½ hours.

Add vegetables. Cook for 30 minutes
more or until vegetables are tender.

To make gravy, stir in 2 tablespoons
flour mixed with 4 fluid ounces water.
When thickened, place mixture in 2½
pint casserole.

Roll pastry to a circle the same
size as casserole. Cut into 6 wedge-
shaped pieces and place on top of pie.

Cook in hot oven (425°F. Mark 7) 25
to 30 minutes or until crust is browned.
Serves 6.

BEEF STROGANOFF EN CASSEROLE

2 large mild onions, finely chopped
About 1½ ounces butter
1¼ pounds topside
Flour
8 ounces fresh mushrooms, sliced
1 can condensed tomato soup
2 fluid ounces sherry
8 fluid ounces beef bouillon or stock
Salt and pepper
Soured cream
Cooked noodles

Fry onions in butter until soft, then
transfer to casserole.

Cut steak into narrow strips, 2 inches
long. Roll meat in flour. Then brown
in hot melted butter. Transfer meat to
casserole.

Brown mushrooms in remaining butter, adding more butter if necessary.

Transfer mushrooms to casserole.

Combine soup, sherry, and bouillon
and pour over contents of casserole.
Season to taste with salt and pepper.

Cook in moderate oven (350°F.
Mark 4) until meat is tender, about 40
minutes.

Serve over hot cooked noodles, topping each portion with soured cream.
Serves 4 to 5.

BEEF AND VEGETABLE PIE

1½ pounds stewing beef, shin of
    beef or skirt, cut in 1-inch
    cubes
1 ounce fat or bacon dripping
1½ teaspoons salt
4 medium carrots, sliced
4 medium potatoes, diced
1 medium onion, sliced
Salt and pepper
6 ounces shortcrust pastry or scone
    dough

Brown meat slowly in hot fat. Add
boiling water to just cover meat. Add
salt. Cover and simmer until almost
tender, 30 to 60 minutes depending
upon meat used.

Add vegetables and more boiling
water if necessary to just cover. Simmer
until all are tender, about 20 minutes
longer.

Thicken gravy by making a paste of
2 tablespoons of flour and 2 fluid
ounces cold water, then stirring into
hot gravy and cooking 2 or 3 minutes
longer. Add salt and pepper to taste.
Bring to boil and pour into buttered
3-pint casserole.

Cover with pastry rolled thin with
several slashes cut in to allow escape of
steam or cover with scone dough rolled
out ½ inch thick.

Cook in hot oven (425°F. Mark 7)
until golden brown, about 15 minutes.
Serves 5.

Variation: Minced beef may be substituted for beef cubes. Add salt and
cover with water as above but cook only
15 to 20 minutes.

OVEN BEEF STEW

2 pounds chuck steak
4 tablespoons flour
1½ ounces hot fat
1 teaspoon salt
3 tablespoons prepared French
    mustard
1 teaspoon monosodium glutamate
1 pint tomato juice or water
6 medium potatoes, cut in halves
12 small carrots, scraped and cut in
    lengthwise quarters
12 small white onions
1 package frozen peas or sweet
    corn, thawed just enough to
    separate

Cut meat into 2-inch cubes. Sprinkle
meat with flour. Brown in hot fat and
transfer to 5-pint casserole.

Stir remaining flour and seasonings
into fat in pan. Gradually add tomato
juice or water, stirring constantly. Pour
over meat.

Cover and cook in moderate oven
(350°F. Mark 4) 1 hour.

Add potatoes, carrots, and onions;
cover and cook 45 minutes longer. Add
peas, cover and cook until vegetables
are tender, about 15 minutes longer.

Before serving, stir stew to bring
meat to top.

Note: If sweet corn is used, potatoes
may be omitted.

Oven Lamb Stew: Substitute 2 pounds
boned shoulder of lamb for beef. Have
fat trimmed off. Increase flour to 5
tablespoons.

Before serving stew, spoon off excess
surface fat.

Oven Veal Stew: Substitute 2 pounds
boned shoulder of veal for beef.

Use 8 to 12 fluid ounces white wine
instead of tomato juice or water. Increase flour to 5 tablespoons.

If desired substitute 8 ounces fresh
mushrooms for peas.

OLD FASHIONED STEAK AND KIDNEY POT PIE

1½ pounds veal kidneys
1½ pounds good quality steak
4 ounces butter or margarine
2 tablespoons flour
3 cloves garlic, crushed
1 tablespoon tomato purée
5 fluid ounces red Burgundy wine
1¾ pints beef stock or water
1 sprig parsley
1 small stalk celery
½ bay leaf
¼ teaspoon thyme
8 ounces salt pork
8 ounces pickling onions, boiled
10 fresh mushrooms
6 ounces shortcrust or suet pastry

Trim kidneys and mince. Mince
steak. Fry slowly together in 3 ounces
butter or margarine until golden
brown. Blend in flour. Add garlic,
purée, wine, and stock.

Tie in a small piece of muslin the
parsley, celery, bay leaf, and thyme.
Add with garlic to meat mixture. Add
salt and pepper to taste.

Cook in moderate oven (350°F.
Mark 4) about 40 minutes.

Remove garlic and herb bag.

Boil salt pork in water to cover until
tender. Cut into cubes and fry until
crisp. Fry mushrooms in remaining
fat. Combine ingredients and cook 15
minutes.

Spread in deep pie pan and cool.
Cover with thin pastry crust. Cut gashes
to allow steam to escape.

Cook in hot oven (425°F. Mark 7)
until crust is golden brown, about 30
minutes. Serves 6 to 8.

TEAK WITH WINE

bacon rashers
clove garlic, crushed
½ pounds steak, cut in 1-inch cubes
'lour
fluid ounces beef consommé
fluid ounces dry red wine
teaspoon salt
small onions, peeled
medium carrots, diced
whole black peppers
whole cloves
bay leaves

Cook bacon in heavy frying pan until ·own but not crisp. Remove bacon ıd add garlic to fat in pan.

Coat steak cubes with flour and ·own meat on all sides. Add con- ›mmé, wine, and salt. Heat to boiling ıd turn into large casserole. Add ıcon, cut into 1-inch pieces, and re- ıaining ingredients.

Cover and cook in slow oven (300 °F., ark 2) about 2 hours. Serves 6.

EEF CASSEROLE – UNGARIAN STYLE

2 pounds round steak, cut in ½-inch cubes
1½ ounces fat
1 large onion, chopped
1 clove garlic, chopped fine
2 tablespoons flour
Small can browned mushrooms and broth
2 ounces celery, chopped
8 ounces soured cream
8-ounce can tomato sauce
1 teaspoon salt
Pinch of black pepper
1 tablespoon Worcestershire sauce

Brown meat in hot fat. Add onion ıd garlic and cook until golden. Stir flour slowly. Add remaining ingredi- ıts and mix well.

Turn into greased 5-pint casserole. Cook, uncovered, in slow oven (325° ., Mark 3) until meat is tender, about ½ hours. Serves 6.

LAT RIBS OF BEEF 'ASSEROLE

2 pounds flat ribs of beef
1½ teaspoons salt
⅛ teaspoon black pepper
2 tablespoons flour
½ ounce dripping
4 fluid ounces water
1 tablespoon Worcestershire sauce
4 medium potatoes, peeled
4 small onions, peeled
3 medium carrots, peeled and sliced
10 ounces canned or cooked peas (optional)

Have ribs cut into serving size pieces. eason with salt and pepper. Roll in our. Brown in hot fat in frying pan.

Turn into a heated casserole with the ıt. Add water, cover, and cook in moderate oven (350 °F., Mark 4) 1 hour.

Add Worcestershire sauce, potatoes cut in halves, onions, carrots, and peas. Add up to 2 fluid ounces additional water if required.

Cover and cook until meat begins to separate from bones. Baste with sauce from casserole just before serving. Serves 4.

MEAT PIE – SOUTHERN STYLE

2 pounds braising steak
1 ounce fat
1 large onion, chopped
8 ounces celery, chopped
1½ ounces green pepper, chopped
3 8-ounce cans tomatoes and juice
3 tablespoons flour
2 teaspoons salt
¼ teaspoon black pepper
¼ teaspoon paprika
3-4 ounces canned sweetcorn, drained
Maize Flour Scone Topping (see Index)

Sear meat in hot fat until nicely browned, about 10 to 15 minutes. Remove meat from fat.

Cook onions, celery, and green pepper in the fat until tender and lightly browned. Add tomatoes gradually to flour and seasonings; add meat and vegetables. Turn into 4-pint casserole.

Cover and cook in moderate oven (350 °F., Mark 4) about 30 minutes. Top with the topping and cook as directed. Serves 8 to 10.

BEEF-PORK SAUSAGE-BEAN CASSEROLE

1 pound dried red kidney beans
½ pound small pork sausages
1 pound skirt or braising steak cut in small cubes
2 onions, chopped
2 cloves garlic, minced
½ teaspoon dried rosemary
6 fluid ounces dry red wine
2 teaspoons salt
¼ teaspoon black pepper
Dash of cayenne pepper
12 fluid ounces liquid in which beans soaked

Wash beans and bring to boil in 2½ pints water; boil 2 minutes.

Turn off heat and allow to stand 1 hour. Then simmer until almost tender.

Cut sausages in half and fry until brown. Remove from pan.

Brown steak in fat with onions and garlic.

Add rosemary, wine, salt, pepper, and cayenne. Cover and simmer 1 hour.

Combine with beans, 12 fluid ounces bean liquid, and sausages. Put in 5-pint casserole.

Cover and cook in moderate oven (350 °F., Mark 4) until beans and meat are tender, about 1½ hours. Serves 4 to 6.

STEAK AND MUSHROOM CASSEROLE

1½ pounds frying steak, cut into 4 portions
2 ounces bacon dripping
2 medium onions, sliced
1 pound mushrooms, sliced
1 10½-ounce can condensed cream of mushroom soup
5-6 fluid ounces buttermilk
2 tablespoons minced parsley
1 teaspoon salt
¼ teaspoon black pepper
¼ teaspoon mustard
4 medium potatoes, sliced

Brown steaks in dripping. Remove steaks from pan and sauté onion and mushroom slices until tender.

Drain steak, onions, and mushrooms on absorbent paper.

Combine soup, buttermilk, parsley, and seasonings. Place alternate layers of potatoes, onion, mushroom slices, and steaks in a 4-pint greased casserole. Pour a little soup mixture on each layer.

Cook uncovered in moderate oven (350°F. Mark 4) for 1 hour. Serves 4.

STEAK AND ONION PIE

1 pound braising steak, cubed
1 ounce flour
2 teaspoons salt
Pinch of black pepper
½ teaspoon paprika
Dash of ginger
Dash of allspice
2 ounces dripping
1 large onion, sliced
1 pint hot water
12 ounces diced potatoes
6 ounces shortcrust pastry

Roll meat in mixture of flour, salt, pepper, paprika, ginger, and allspice. Brown in hot fat.

Add onions and cook until light yellow. Add water. Cover and simmer until meat is tender.

Add potatoes; turn into greased shallow casserole.

Cover with plain pastry. Brush with slightly beaten egg.

Bake in very hot oven (450 °F., Mark 8) until pastry is nicely browned, about 25 minutes. Serves 6.

For variety, season scones for topping with your favourite herb and sprinkle with caraway seeds.

Minced Meat Casseroles

Mince and Potato Puffs

MINCED BEEF LAYERED CASSEROLE

- 2 pounds minced beef
- 1 ounce dripping
- 1 clove garlic
- 1 tablespoon oil
- 1½ pounds potatoes, sliced
- 1 12-ounce packet frozen green beans, thawed
- 1 12-ounce can small white onions
- 1½ teaspoons salt
- ¼ teaspoon black pepper
- ¼ teaspoon thyme
- 1 tablespoon cornflour
- 1 8-ounce can tomato sauce
- 5-6 fluid ounces beef stock
- 1 ounce grated Cheddar cheese
- 1 ounce dry breadcrumbs
- 1½ ounces melted butter

Sauté mince in dripping until browned and crumbling. Rub a 5-pint casserole with cut garlic clove and oil.

Arrange in it a layer each of half the potatoes, meat, beans, and all the onions. Finish with layers of remaining beans, meat, and finally potatoes, sprinkling salt, pepper, and thyme on each layer.

Mix cornflour to a thin paste with a little tomato sauce. Mix with remaining tomato sauce and stock. Pour over potatoes.

Top with a mixture of grated cheese and breadcrumbs. Pour butter over.

Cook uncovered in moderate oven (350°F., Mark 4) for 1¼ hours. Serves 6 to 8.

CHILLI CON CARNE CASSEROLE

- 1 pound braising steak
- 1 large onion, chopped
- 2 cloves garlic, minced
- 1½ ounces bacon dripping or fat
- 1½ teaspoons salt
- 2 tablespoons chilli seasoning
- 1 teaspoon oregano
- ¼ teaspoon cummin
- 1 bay leaf, crushed
- 1 20-ounce can tomatoes
- 1 20-ounce can red kidney beans

Have steak coarsely minced or chop it fine. Brown meat, onion, and garlic in dripping. Sprinkle with seasonings.

Combine with tomatoes and turn into a 3-pint greased casserole. Cover and cook in slow oven (325°F., Mark 3) for 1½ hours.

Remove from oven. Stir in heated beans. Replace cover and continue cooking for 20 minutes. Serves 6.

Note: The cooking may be done on the top of the cooker. Place casserole on an asbestos pad to protect it from direct heat. Cook over low heat for 2 hours. Add beans and heat through.

MINCE AND POTATO PUFFS

- 1 pound minced beef
- 1 onion, chopped
- ½ green pepper, chopped
- 1 clove garlic, minced
- ¼ teaspoon basil
- ½ teaspoon salt
- 3-ounce can sliced mushrooms
- 1 8-ounce can tomato sauce
- 1 5½-ounce packet instant mashed potatoes
- 1½ ounces grated Parmesan cheese
- 1 tablespoon chopped parsley

Brown beef, onion, green pepper, and garlic in frying pan. Add seasonings, mushrooms, and tomato sauce. Simmer 5 minutes. Turn into casserole.

Prepare mashed potatoes for 4 according to packet directions. Add Parmesan cheese and parsley to potatoes; place spoonfuls around edge of casserole on beef mixture. Cook in hot oven (400°F., Mark 6) 10 minutes or until potato puffs are lightly browned. Serves 4.

SPANISH MEAT PIE

- 1½ ounces dripping
- 1 clove garlic
- 1 pound minced beef
- 4 tablespoons flour
- 1 16-ounce can tomatoes
- 2 7-ounce cans sweetcorn
- 1 teaspoon salt
- ¼ teaspoon paprika
- ¼ teaspoon chilli seasoning

Dash of cayenne pepper

- 3 slices buttered bread

Melt dripping in frying pan. Brown garlic in hot fat. Remove garlic, and add meat. Brown well.

Blend in flour and, when well mixed, add tomatoes, sweetcorn, and seasonings. Pour into buttered 1½-pint casserole.

Cut slices of bread in half and place on top of casserole. Cook in hot oven (400°F., Mark 6) 15 minutes, or until top is browned. Serves 6.

BEEF AND NOODLE CASSEROLE

- 2 tablespoons onion, finely chopped
- 1 ounce dripping
- 1 pound minced beef
- 1½ teaspoons salt
- ⅛ teaspoon black pepper
- 8 ounces egg noodles, cooked
- 1 10½-ounce can condensed cream of tomato soup
- 2 ounces grated cheese

Fry onion in hot dripping in a heavy frying pan. Add mince and brown thoroughly.

Combine meat, seasonings, noodles, and soup in a 5-pint casserole. Top with grated cheese.

Cook in a moderate oven (350°F., Mark 4) for 30 minutes. Serves 8.

ORLEANS MEAT PIE

Filling:
- 2 ounces dripping
- 1 medium onion, chopped
- 1 pound minced beef
- 1 teaspoon salt
- 3 tablespoons tomato ketchup or chilli sauce

Scone:
- 8 ounces scone mix
- About 5-6 fluid ounces milk

Topping:
- 1 8-ounce can tomatoes, drained

Heat dripping. Fry onion slowly to golden brown. Add meat and brown well. Add salt and ketchup.

Put scone mix into mixing bowl. Pour milk quickly into dry ingredients. Stir until well blended. Turn onto lightly floured board. Knead 6 times. Roll into circular shape. Put into a 9-inch pie plate. Do not flute edges.

Fill with cooked meat. Cover with drained tomatoes. Cook in very hot oven (450°F., Mark 8) 30 minutes. Serve hot. Serves 6.

COMPANY CASSEROLE

- 1 pound minced beef
- ½ ounce butter or margarine
- 2 8-ounce cans tomato sauce
- 8 ounces noodles
- 8 ounces cottage cheese
- 8 ounces cream cheese
- 2 ounces soured cream
- 2 ounces spring onions, chopped
- 1 tablespoon chopped green pepper
- 1 ounce butter or margarine, melted

Brown mince in butter in a heavy frying pan. Stir in tomato sauce. Remove from heat.

Boil noodles in salted water 10 minutes. Drain.

Combine cottage cheese, cream cheese, soured cream, onions, and green pepper.

In a buttered 3-pint casserole spread half the noodles. Cover with cheese mixture, then cover this with remaining noodles. Pour melted butter over noodles. Pat meat sauce mixture on top.

Cook in moderate oven (350°F., Mark 4) 20 to 30 minutes. Serve hot. Makes 6 generous servings.

MOUSSAKA

This is a Greek casserole, which cooks in 4 distinct layers of aubergine and sauce with cheese topping.

1 pound minced beef
2 large onions, chopped
4 fluid ounces water
2 fluid ounces tomato ketchup
1 tablespoon chopped parsley
1 teaspoon salt
⅛ teaspoon black pepper
3 ounces dry breadcrumbs
2 slightly beaten egg whites
2 ounces butter or margarine
2 ounces plain flour
1 pint 4 fluid ounces milk
½ teaspoon salt
⅛ teaspoon nutmeg
2 egg yolks
1 large aubergine (about 2 pounds)
2 ounces lard or dripping
1 ounce grated cheese

Brown minced beef in frying pan. Add onion, water, ketchup, parsley, 1 teaspoon salt, and pepper; simmer 10 minutes.

Combine breadcrumbs with egg whites and add half of the meat mixture.

Cut aubergine into ½-inch slices, sprinkle them with salt and leave for 30 minutes.

Make a white sauce from the butter, flour, milk, ½ teaspoon salt, and nutmeg. Add a little of the white sauce to egg yolks; return to saucepan. Cook until thick.

Drain the aubergine slices, dry them and brown in hot fat.

Place half of the slices in the bottom of a buttered casserole (12×8×2 inches). Spread half the meat mixture over the aubergine. Add half the white sauce. Add second layer of aubergine, meat, and remaining white sauce.

Mix cheese with remaining breadcrumbs and egg white mixture. Sprinkle over top of mixture. Cook in a moderate oven (350°F. Mark 4) for 30 minutes. Serves 10.

HARVEST CASSEROLE

1 pound minced beef
1 large onion, chopped
2 8-ounce cans tomatoes
1 teaspoon curry powder or chilli seasoning or 1 tablespoon Worcestershire sauce
2 tablespoons salt
2 potatoes, thinly sliced
1½ ounces flour
2 7-ounce cans sweetcorn, drained
1 15-ounce can broad beans, drained
2-3 ounces sliced green pepper
6 ounces grated cheese or buttered crumbs

Combine minced beef, onions, tomatoes, one of the seasonings, and salt. Pat into a 1-inch layer in a 5-pint casserole.

Over this place, in layers, the potatoes, flour, sweetcorn, broad beans, and green pepper. Top with cheese or crumbs.

Cook in a moderate oven (350°F. Mark 4) for 1 hour. Serve hot. Serves 8 to 10.

MINCED BEEF "PIZZA"

1 pound minced beef
1½ teaspoons salt
½ teaspoon black pepper
1 8-ounce can drained tomatoes
2 ounces grated mozzarella
2 tablespoons chopped parsley
¼ teaspoon dried basil
2 tablespoons finely chopped onion

Mix minced beef with salt and pepper. Pat out in a 9-inch pie dish.

Spread tomatoes over minced beef and sprinkle with the remaining ingredients.

Cook in a moderate oven (375°F. Mark 5) 15 to 20 minutes. Cut in wedges to serve. Serves 4.

Variation: To make Sunshine Meat Pie, fill minced beef "crust" with a mixture of a 12-ounce can well drained sweetcorn, an 8-ounce can drained tomatoes, ½ teaspoon salt, and ¼ teaspoon basil. Cook as above.

MINCED BEEF CORN PONE PIE

1 pound minced beef
1 small onion, chopped
½ ounce dripping
2 teaspoons chilli seasoning
¾ teaspoon salt
1 teaspoon Worcestershire sauce
1 8-ounce can tomatoes
½ can drained red kidney beans
½ recipe for maize flour scone topping

Brown meat and onion in melted dripping. Add seasonings and tomatoes. Cover and simmer over low heat for 15 minutes. Add canned red kidney beans.

Pour into a greased casserole. Top with maize flour scone topping and cook in a hot oven (425°F. Mark 7) for 20 minutes. Serves 4.

MINCED BEEF CURRY BAKE

1 pound minced beef
1 medium onion, chopped
1 tablespoon flour
1 teaspoon salt
1 teaspoon curry powder
8 fluid ounces milk
6 ounces cornflakes, crushed
1 ounce butter or margarine

Stir and cook minced beef and onion in a heavy frying pan to brown meat. Stir in flour, salt, curry powder, and milk. Mix thoroughly.

Spoon half of this mixture over bot-

tom of a 2½-pint casserole. Sprinkle half of the cornflakes over surface. Spread remaining meat mixture on top of cornflakes. Top with layer of cornflakes.

Dot with butter and cook in a moderate oven (350°F. Mark 4) for 1 hour. Serves 4 to 6.

SWEDISH CABBAGE ROLLS

1 pound minced beef
8 ounces minced pork
12 ounces rice, cooked
1 teaspoon sugar
1 onion, chopped
1 teaspoon salt
¼ teaspoon black pepper
1 head white cabbage
½ ounce butter or margarine
8 fluid ounces hot water
1 10½-ounce can condensed cream of tomato soup

Combine the beef, pork, rice, sugar, onion, salt, and pepper.

Wilt the cabbage leaves by placing in boiling water for a few minutes.

Place about 2 ounces of the meat mixture in each cabbage leaf and roll up securely. Place rolls in a casserole. Dot each with butter.

Combine water and soup and pour over the rolls. Cook in a moderate oven (350°F. Mark 4) 1 hour. Serves 6.

SHEPHERD'S PIE

Shepherd's pie is a meat pie often made with leftovers moistened with a sauce or a gravy and cooked in a casserole, with a topping or border of mashed potatoes. This popular version contains minced beef.

1 pound minced beef
2 tablespoons chopped onion
1 ounce lard or dripping
1 teaspoon salt
12 ounces cooked diced carrots
1-1¼ pounds mashed potatoes
Parsley for garnish, if desired

Brown mince and onion lightly in melted fat in a frying pan. Add salt.

Arrange carrots in bottom of a well greased 2½-pint ovenproof glass bowl. Pour browned beef mixture over carrots. Top with mashed potato, piping some on with a forcing bag, if desired.

Cook in hot oven (400°F. Mark 6) 15 to 20 minutes or until potatoes are lightly browned and food is piping hot. Garnish with parsley and serve.

Serves 5 to 6.

Shepherd's Pie

Pork and Ham Casseroles

PORK CHOP-NOODLE CASSEROLE

6 pork chops
½ ounce dripping
2 teaspoons salt
2 tablespoons onion, grated
1 tablespoon Worcestershire sauce
1 10½-ounce can condensed tomato soup
4 fluid ounces water
8 ounces noodles, cooked

Fry chops in fat until golden brown. Season with 1 teaspoon salt.

Combine remaining salt, onion, Worcestershire sauce, tomato soup and water.

Place noodles in a casserole; add tomato soup mixture. Arrange chops overlapping round inner edge.

Cover and cook in moderate oven (350°F. Mark 4) 1½ hours. Serves 4 to 6.

PORK CHOP VEGETABLE CASSEROLE WITH RICE

6 or 8 pork chops
1 medium onion, chopped
2-3 ounces green pepper, chopped
1 10½-ounce can cream of mushroom soup
8 fluid ounces water
12 ounces rice, cooked
12 ounces cooked peas
1 teaspoon salt
⅛ teaspoon black pepper

Place pork chops in frying pan and brown on both sides. Enough fat should cook out of the pork chops so that it is not necessary to add any to the frying pan. Lift pork chops out of frying pan.

Place onion and green pepper in frying pan and cook until tender. It may be necessary to add a small amount of lard to prevent onions and peppers from sticking.

Add mushroom soup, water, rice, peas, salt, and pepper. Mix well.

Pour half the rice and pea mixture into a greased baking dish. Arrange half the chops over the rice and peas. Add the rest of the rice and peas.

Top with remaining chops and cook in a moderate oven (350°F. Mark 4) about 30 minutes.

Serves 6 or 8.

Pork Chop Vegetable Casserole with Rice

PORK CHOPS WITH POTATOES AND CABBAGE

4 pork chops, about ½-inch thick
1½ teaspoons salt
⅛ teaspoon black pepper
½ medium onion, chopped
1 10½-ounce can condensed cream of celery soup
4 fluid ounces milk
3 medium potatoes, peeled and sliced
1 pound white cabbage, shredded
1 ounce flour

Trim excess fat from pork chops. Season with salt and pepper. Grease frying pan very lightly with a piece of the fat. Brown chops on both sides over moderate heat, about 15 minutes. Remove chops. Pour off fat.

Measure 1 ounce fat into frying pan. Add onion, celery soup, and milk. Stir to blend well.

Put 2 alternating layers of potatoes and cabbage in 4-pint casserole. Sprinkle each layer with flour and pour about ¼ of celery-milk mixture over each layer. Top with chops.

Cover and cook in moderate oven (350°F. Mark 4) 1 hour and 15 minutes. Serves 4.

SPARE-RIBS AND BEANS

1 20-ounce can kidney or broad beans
2 large onions, chopped
3 pounds spare-ribs
Salt and pepper
8 fluid ounces apple juice

Place a layer of beans in a greased casserole. Season with some of the onion. Repeat layers.

Cut spare-ribs into serving pieces. Place on beans. Season with salt and pepper. Pour apple juice over all.

Cook, uncovered, in moderate oven (350°F. Mark 4) until spare-ribs are tender, about 1 hour. Serves 4.

SPARE-RIBS AND SAUERKRAUT

3 pounds spare-ribs
1 teaspoon salt
¼ teaspoon black pepper
1 large can sauerkraut
1 sharp eating apple, chopped
8 fluid ounces water
1 raw potato, grated
1 teaspoon caraway seed

Season ribs with salt and pepper. Brown in open roasting pan in extremely hot oven (500°F. Mark 10) 30 minutes. Place sauerkraut and apple on top of meat; add water and cover pan.

Reduce heat to moderate (350°F. Mark 4) and roast 1 hour longer. Stir in potato and caraway seed. Cook 30 minutes longer. Serves 6.

Pork and Vegetable Pie

PORK AND VEGETABLE PIE

1½ pounds diced hand of pork
1 medium onion, sliced
16 fluid ounces water or stock
1 teaspoon salt
¼ teaspoon black pepper
4 ounces carrots, sliced
4 ounces celery, sliced
6 ounces cooked green beans or peas
2 teaspoons Worcestershire sauce
Scone dough

Get butcher to cut pork into 1-inch cubes. Trim off fat and fry out in a heavy saucepan. Remove solid pieces and brown pork and onions in the fat.

Add water or stock and salt and pepper. Cook for 45 minutes, then add carrots and celery and cook 15 minutes. Thicken liquid with 2 tablespoons flour mixed to a smooth paste with a little water.

Add green beans or peas with Worcestershire sauce. Pour while hot into a 2½-pint casserole. Top with scone dough cut into circles or fancy shapes.

Cook in very hot oven (450°F. Mark 8) for 20 minutes or until scones are well browned. Serves 6 to 8.

HAM AND MUSHROOM RISOTTO

1 medium onion, grated
8 ounces sliced ham
3 fluid ounces olive oil
12 ounces uncooked rice
Pinch of saffron
1 pint chicken stock or canned broth
4 fluid ounces Sauternes or other white wine
4 ounces mushrooms
½ ounce chopped parsley
Grated Parmesan cheese

Sauté onion and ham gently in oil 5 minutes. Add rice and cook, stirring, for about 1 or 2 minutes.

Steep saffron in a little chicken stock, and add to rice mixture. Add remaining stock, wine, salt, and pepper to taste. Bring to boil, then pour into 3-pint casserole.

Cover and cook in moderate oven (375°F. Mark 5) 30 minutes.

Stir in mushrooms and parsley. Cover and cook 10 minutes longer. Serve with grated Parmesan cheese. Serves 6.

Ham and Rice Casserole

HAM AND RICE CASSEROLE

1 egg
2 tablespoons milk
1 teaspoon mustard
⅛ teaspoon black pepper
1½ ounces dry breadcrumbs
1 ounce grated Parmesan cheese
6 large slices ham, ⅛-inch thick
2 ounces cooking fat
12 ounces rice, cooked
8 ounces sliced Cheddar cheese
1 10½-ounce can condensed cream of tomato soup

Beat egg with a fork. Stir in milk, mustard, and pepper. Combine breadcrumbs with Parmesan cheese. Dip ham slices in egg mixture then in crumbs.

Melt cooking fat in large frying pan. Sauté ham slices in cooking fat until lightly browned on both sides.

Spoon rice into greased casserole. Arrange ham slices on rice. Top ham with cheese slices; cover with tomato soup. Cover and cook in moderate oven (375°F. Mark 5) 20 minutes. Serves 6.

HAM WITH NOODLES AND PINEAPPLE

4 ounces medium noodles
1½ ounces butter or margarine
3 tablespoons flour
8 fluid ounces milk
2 fluid ounces pineapple juice
6-8 ounces pineapple chunks
8 ounces cubed ham
1 ounce dry buttered breadcrumbs

Cook noodles in boiling, salted water until tender. Drain and rinse.

Melt butter in saucepan. Stir in flour. Gradually add milk and pineapple juice, stirring constantly until thickened. Add noodles, pineapple chunks, and cubed ham. Blend well. Pour into greased 2½-pint casserole. Sprinkle with crumbs.

Cook in moderate oven (350°F. Mark 4) 30 minutes. Serve hot. Serves 4.

HAM WITH NOODLES

4 ounces noodles, cooked
10 ounces cooked ham, minced
16 fluid ounces thin white sauce
Breadcrumbs mixed with melted butter

Place half the noodles in a greased casserole and top with half the ham. Add another layer of noodles and ham.

Pour white sauce over mixture. Top with crumbs. Cook in moderate oven (350°F. Mark 4) 20 minutes. Serves 4.

HAM, POTATOES, AND CHEESE SCALLOP

12 ounces cooked ham, thinly sliced, or 1 12-ounce can luncheon meat
1 small onion, finely chopped
4 to 6 potatoes, peeled and thinly sliced
3 tablespoons flour
½ teaspoon salt
¼ teaspoon black pepper
4 ounces grated sharp Cheddar cheese
8 fluid ounces milk
1 ounce butter or margarine
2 fluid ounces tomato ketchup

Arrange ham in greased 2½-pint casserole. Sprinkle onion over ham. Add layer of potatoes. Sprinkle with half of flour, salt, pepper, and cheese. Repeat layers.

Heat milk with butter and pour over casserole.

Cover and cook in moderate oven (350°F. Mark 4) 40 minutes. Then sprinkle with ketchup and cook uncovered until potatoes are tender, about 30 minutes longer. Serves 4 to 6.

LAYERED HAM AND VEGETABLES

1 large potato, thinly sliced
4 ounces celery, coarsely chopped
1 large onion, sliced
1 green pepper, coarsely chopped
4 slices boiled ham, cut in small pieces
1 10½-ounce can condensed cream of tomato soup
1 teaspoon salt
Dash of black pepper
1 ounce dry breadcrumbs
½ ounce melted butter or margarine

Place a layer each of potato, celery, onion, green pepper, and ham in a greased 2-pint casserole.

Season tomato soup with salt and pepper. Pour over vegetables and ham. Toss crumbs with butter and sprinkle over top.

Cook in moderate oven (350°F. Mark 4) until vegetables are tender, about 1 hour. Serves 4.

PORK CHOP-SWEETCORN CASSEROLE

5 thick pork chops
¾ ounce dripping
1½ teaspoons salt
Dash of black pepper
1 20-ounce can creamed sweetcorn
1½ ounces green pepper, diced
2 tablespoons hot water

Brown chops slowly in hot fat in frying pan. Add salt and pepper. Mix

sweetcorn and green pepper; arrange in layers with chops in greased casserole. Add hot water.

Cover and cook in moderate oven (350°F. Mark 4) 45 minutes. Remove cover and cook 15 minutes longer. Serves 5.

CRUSTY HAM AND SWEETCORN PIE

5 ounces cubed ham or luncheon meat
1 ounce butter or margarine
1 medium onion, finely diced
4 ounces celery, finely diced
1 ounce green pepper, finely diced
2 tablespoons flour
1½ teaspoons salt
¼ teaspoon black pepper
2 8-ounce cans tomatoes
½ 7-ounce can drained sweetcorn
Maize flour scone topping (below)

Brown ham in melted butter in frying pan.

Add onion, celery, and green pepper; cook until partially tender.

Blend in flour, salt, and pepper. Add tomatoes and sweetcorn. Cook until thickened.

Turn into shallow 10-inch casserole (or leave in frying pan).

Top with maize flour scone topping.

Cook in hot oven (400°F. Mark 6) about 40 minutes. Serves 6.

MAIZE FLOUR SCONE TOPPING

10 fluid ounces milk, scalded
2 ounces maize flour or polenta
8 ounces sifted plain flour
2¼ teaspoons baking powder
1 teaspoon salt
2 ounces cooking fat

Pour hot milk over maize flour and let cool completely.

Sift flour once, measure; add baking powder and salt and sift together twice. Cut in cooking fat until mixture resembles fine crumbs.

Add maize flour mixture all at once, stirring only until all flour is dampened. Drop by spoonfuls over meat mixture.

Bake in hot oven (400°F. Mark 6) 40 to 45 minutes. Serve at once.

Pastry Toppings: These lend themselves to imaginative variations in design. Use biscuit cutters to shape pastry toppings into attractive patterns.

Lamb Casseroles

LAMB CHOPS CREOLE CASSEROLE

4 best-end-of-neck lamb chops, cut
  ½- to ¾-inch thick
½ ounce dripping
1 15-ounce and 1 8-ounce can
  tomatoes
4 ounces uncooked rice
1 medium onion, cut in 4 slices
1 green pepper, cut in 4 rings
1 teaspoon salt
½ teaspoon black pepper
1 tablespoon flour

Brown chops on all sides in hot fat.
Place in casserole.

Drain tomatoes and save juice. On
each chop arrange in this order, the
following: 2 tablespoons rice, 1 slice
onion, ½ tomato, and 1 green pepper
ring. Season. Heat 4 fluid ounces
tomato juice to boiling and pour round
chops.

Cover closely. Cook in slow oven
(300°F. Mark 2) 1½ hours.

Thicken cooking liquid with flour.
Serve over chops. Serves 4.

LAMB WITH AUBERGINE AND RICE

1 medium aubergine, cut in large
  cubes
1½ pounds shoulder of lamb, cut in
  1-inch squares
1½ ounces butter or margarine
1 medium onion, diced
1 teaspoon marjoram
Pinch of thyme
Salt and black pepper
8 fluid ounces consommé or stock
8 ounces raw rice
1 15-ounce and 1 8-ounce can
  tomatoes

Soak cubes of aubergine in salted
water for 15 minutes; rinse and drain
well.

Brown lamb on all sides in hot fat.
Transfer to casserole.

Fry onion until golden. Add onion,
aubergine, seasonings, and consommé to casserole.

Brown rice in a dry frying pan; add
tomatoes with juice to rice. Pour over
casserole.

Cook in moderate oven (350°F.
Mark 4) until lamb is tender, about
1½ hours. Serves 6.

*Cook-Alongs: For efficient cooking along
with the casserole, select vegetables,
fruits, desserts, and hot breads that
require the same temperature. The same
timing is desirable, but not always
possible. To ensure top crispness in the
main dish, vegetables, fruits, and desserts which might fill the oven with
steam should be covered.*

*Plan contrast in colour. Use brightly
coloured foods to brighten up the paler
casseroles.*

LAMB WITH RICE

1½ pounds lean boneless lamb, cut
  in 1-inch cubes
2 fluid ounces wine vinegar
4 fluid ounces sweet cider or apple
  juice
2 medium onions, sliced
½ teaspoon pickling spice
2 tablespoons flour
1 teaspoon salt
⅛ teaspoon black pepper
½ teaspoon Aromat
1 ounce butter or margarine
6 ounces uncooked rice
1 pint 4 fluid ounces boiling water
3 beef stock cubes

Cover lamb with mixture of vinegar,
cider or apple juice, onions, and
pickling spice. Allow to marinate in
refrigerator overnight. Then drain
meat, reserving spiced liquid. Sprinkle
meat with flour mixed with seasonings.
Brown slightly on all sides in hot fat.

Place meat in alternating layers with
rice in a casserole. Add boiling water in
which stock cubes have been dissolved,
and the spiced liquid. Cover and cook
in moderate oven (350°F. Mark 4) 2
hours. Serves 4.

LAMB STEW CASSEROLE

1 pound lamb, cut in small chunks
Salt and Pepper
3 fluid ounces cooking oil
8 small whole onions, peeled
1 10½-ounce can condensed tomato
  soup
3 fluid ounces water
2 ounces slivered almonds

Season lamb with salt and pepper.
Brown in hot oil. Put in casserole.

Add onions. Mix soup and water in
the frying pan until it bubbles; pour
over meat. Sprinkle with almonds.

Cook in moderate oven (350°F. Mark
4) until tender, about 1 hour. Serves 4.

BAKED LAMB CHOPS

6 best-end-of-neck lamb chops
1 clove garlic
Salt and pepper
1 ounce dripping
2 medium onions, chopped
12 ounces cooked diced carrots
4 tablespoons flour
1 tablespoon chilli pickle
4 fluid ounces white wine

Rub chops with cut clove of garlic.
Season with salt and pepper. Brown on
both sides in hot fat in frying pan.
Transfer to casserole.

Sauté onions and carrots in frying
pan until onions are soft and yellow.
Stir in flour, chilli seasoning and wine.
Cook, stirring, until thickened. Place
mound of this mixture on each chop.

Cook in moderate oven (350°F.
Mark 4) 45 minutes. Serves 6.

Shank End Casserole

SHANK END CASSEROLE

6 half-legs of lamb, shank end
  (about 1 pound each)
Seasoned flour
3 tablespoons cooking oil
2 fluid ounces lemon juice
2 fluid ounces water
1 tablespoon sugar
6 bay leaves
6 medium-sized sweet potatoes,
  cooked, peeled and quartered,
  or 2 1-pound cans sweet
  potatoes, drained
1 pound cooked cut runner beans

Dredge shank ends with flour. Heat
cooking oil; add shank ends and
brown well on all sides. Place shank
ends in 6 individual casseroles; reserve
dripping.

Combine lamb dripping, lemon
juice, water, sugar, and bay leaves;
pour over shank ends. Cover and cook
in slow oven (325°F. Mark 3) about 1½
hours, or until lamb is tender.

Add sweet potatoes and beans. Cover
and cook 10 minutes, or until vegetables are thoroughly heated. Serves 6.

LAMB CUTLET CASSEROLE

3 pounds lamb loin chops
1½ teaspoons salt
1 teaspoon paprika
2 tablespoons flour
1 ounce dripping
1 small onion, sliced
4 medium potatoes, peeled and
  sliced
1 8-ounce can tomatoes
1 teaspoon salt
1 tablespoon tomato ketchup

Season chops and roll in flour to
cover evenly. Brown on all sides in
hot fat in frying pan or flameproof
casserole. Cover meat with onion and
potatoes.

Mix tomatoes, 1 teaspoon salt, and
ketchup. Pour over potatoes.

Cover and cook in moderate oven
until meat is tender, about 1¼ hours. If
necessary, add a little water. Serves 4.

Lamb Breast Casserole: Use breast
of lamb, cut into serving pieces, instead
of lamb chops.

Veal Casseroles

VEAL CUTLETS IN MUSHROOM SAUCE

6 rashers bacon
1 medium onion, finely chopped
2 pounds veal cutlets, ½-inch thick, cut into serving pieces
1 lightly beaten egg
2 tablespoons water
4 ounces sifted dry breadcrumbs
1 tablespoon Worcestershire or brown sauce
2 10½-ounce cans condensed cream of mushroom soup

Fry bacon in frying pan until crisp; remove. Cook onion in bacon fat until tender; remove.

Dip meat in egg-water mixture, then into breadcrumbs. Brown on both sides in bacon fat.

Place in flat casserole (12×8×2 inches). Sprinkle with onion and meat sauce. Top with bacon. Pour over condensed soup.

Cook in moderate oven (350°F. Mark 4) until tender, about 30 minutes. Serves 8.

VEAL SCALLOPINI CASSEROLE

2½ pounds shoulder of veal, boned
2 ounces plain flour
2 teaspoons salt
¼ teaspoon black pepper
1 medium onion, finely chopped
4 ounces dripping or cooking oil
1 15-ounce can and 1 8-ounce can tomatoes, drained
4 ounces sliced canned or fresh mushrooms
1 teaspoon sugar

Cut veal into 1¼-inch cubes. Roll in flour seasoned with ½ teaspoon salt and a dash of pepper.

Cook onions in hot fat until tender and yellow. Transfer onions to 3-pint casserole.

Brown veal in the fat on all sides and transfer to casserole. Add tomatoes, mushrooms, sugar, and remaining salt and pepper.

Cover and cook in moderate oven (350°F. Mark 4) until tender, about 1½ hours. Serve with boiled white rice or cooked spaghetti and tomato sauce. Serves 5 to 6.

VEAL CUTLETS PARMIGIANA

1½ pounds veal cutlets, cut ½-inch thick
1 teaspoon salt
⅛ teaspoon black pepper
2 slightly beaten eggs
1 ounce grated Parmesan cheese
2 ounces dry breadcrumbs
Oil for browning
8 fluid ounces tomato sauce
8 ounces mozzarella cheese

Have cutlets divided into serving pieces and flattened with mallet to ⅛-inch thickness. Season with salt and pepper.

Dip meat in eggs and then coat evenly with a mixture of Parmesan cheese and crumbs.

Brown cutlets evenly on both sides in hot oil, allowing about 3 minutes for each side.

Place in shallow casserole or individual casseroles. Put a spoonful of tomato sauce on each, then a slice of mozzarella cheese.

Cook in moderate oven (350°F. Mark 4) until cheese browns lightly, about 15 minutes. Serves 4 to 6.

VEAL CHOPS HUNGARIAN (No. 1)

6 veal chops
Salt, pepper, Aromat
Flour for coating
2 ounces dripping or oil
1 medium onion, diced
Paprika
4 fluid ounces stock or water
8 fluid ounces soured cream
½ teaspoon Aromat
Salt and pepper
Cooked noodles
Melted butter

Sprinkle chops on both sides with salt, pepper, and Aromat; coat lightly with flour.

Brown chops in the heated fat, on both sides, over moderate heat. Toward end of browning add onion and sprinkle chops generously with paprika. Add stock or water to frying pan; cover tightly. Simmer over low heat until tender, about 30 minutes.

Remove chops to hot dish. Stir soured cream, the ½ teaspoon Aromat, salt and pepper into pan gravy. Heat; correct seasoning.

Place hot cooked noodles round chops; sprinkle melted butter over noodles; shake on Aromat lightly. Pour gravy over chops. Serves 6.

VEAL PAPRIKASH CASSEROLE

4 ounces lean salt pork, cut into small pieces
3 pounds boneless stewing veal, cut in 1½-inch pieces
Flour
1 pound fresh mushrooms, sliced
1 large onion, sliced
3 beef stock cubes, dissolved in 12 fluid ounces water
1½ teaspoons salt
½ teaspoon black pepper
2 tablespoons paprika
8 fluid ounces soured cream
Chopped parsley

Fry salt pork until crisp in heavy saucepan; remove pork.

Roll veal in flour and lightly brown in pork fat. Add mushrooms and onions. Cook 15 minutes, stirring often.

Add beef stock cubes and water, salt, pepper, and paprika. Turn into 4-pint casserole.

Cover and cook in moderate oven (350°F. Mark 4) until veal is tender, 1½ to 2 hours. Just before serving, spread the soured cream on top. Sprinkle with chopped parsley. Serves 6.

Note: Topping with soured cream rather than stirring it in prevents curdling and preserves bright red colour.

SOURED CREAM VEAL AND NOODLES

1 pound veal steak
Salt and pepper
1 small onion, finely chopped
4 ounces celery, sliced
1 6-ounce can mushrooms or 4 ounces sautéed fresh mushrooms
4 fluid ounces water
8 ounces egg noodles
8 fluid ounces soured cream
Dry breadcrumbs
Butter or margarine for cooking

Cut meat into ½-inch cubes. Brown in butter. Add seasonings, onion, celery, mushrooms, and water.

Add noodles which have been cooked in boiling salted water until tender.

Add soured cream. Turn into buttered casserole. Sprinkle top with crumbs. Dot with butter. Cook uncovered in moderate oven (350°F. Mark 4) until butter melts and forms a brown crust. Cover and cook 1 hour. Serves 8 to 10.

VEAL STEW CASSEROLE

2 pounds stewing veal
1 ounce plain flour
2 teaspoons salt
¼ teaspoon black pepper
1½ ounces cooking fat or dripping
3 medium onions
1 pound fresh or canned runner beans
3 sticks celery, cut in 4-inch pieces
1 green pepper, cut in rings
1 16-ounce can and 1 8-ounce can tomatoes

Roll veal in seasoned flour. Brown slowly in hot fat. Add whole onions, runner beans, celery, green pepper rings, and tomatoes.

Cover and cook in slow oven (325°F. Mark 3) about 1½ hours or until meat is tender and vegetables are done. Serves 6 to 8.

Plan contrast in size and shape.

Frankfurter, Pork Sausage, Canned Meat Casseroles

PORK SAUSAGE WITH SWEET POTATOES AND APPLES

3 medium cooked sweet potatoes
    or 1 can sweet potatoes
3 medium apples
2 ounces brown sugar
½ teaspoon salt
8 ounces pork sausages

Peel and slice sweet potatoes and apples. Place in alternate layers in greased 1½-pint casserole. Sprinkle with brown sugar and salt.

Cover and cook in hot oven (400°F. Mark 6) 15 minutes. At the same time cook pork sausages in an open pan.

Remove cover from casserole. Top with sausages. Cook uncovered 15 minutes longer. Serves 3 to 4.

CORNED BEEF-RICE CASSEROLE

1 pound rice, cooked
12 ounces cubed cooked or canned
    corned beef
1 15-ounce can and 1 8-ounce can
    tomatoes
1 small onion, finely chopped
1 teaspoon salt
Few grains of black pepper
1 teaspoon Worcestershire sauce

Put alternate layers of rice and beef in greased casserole.

Mix tomatoes and seasonings; pour over rice-beef mixture.

Cover and cook in moderate oven (350°F. Mark 4) 30 minutes. Serves 4.

CORNED BEEF HASH CASSEROLE

1 1-pound can corned beef
½ ounce finely chopped parsley
1 ounce chopped canned pimiento
1 small clove garlic, finely chopped
1 tablespoon lemon juice
4 fluid ounces single cream
¼ teaspoon celery seed
Dash of sage
¼ teaspoon Worcestershire sauce
Dash of Tabasco sauce
¼ teaspoon salt
1 ounce crushed potato crisps

Combine corned beef, parsley, pimiento, garlic, and lemon juice. Turn into 2½-pint buttered casserole.

Mix cream, celery seed, sage, Worcestershire, Tabasco, and salt. Pour over hash mixture. Sprinkle with crisps.

Cook in moderate oven (350°F. Mark 4) 20 minutes. Serves 4.

CHILLI CON CARNE WITH MAIZE FLOUR TOPPING

Fill individual casseroles about ¾ full with canned chilli con carne. Top with Maize Flour Topping (see Index) and black olives.

Cook in moderate oven (375°F. Mark 5) 20 to 25 minutes.

FRANKFURTER AND TOMATO CASSEROLE

3 medium tomatoes, cut in 1-inch
    thick slices
Flour
6 frankfurters, cut into ½-inch pieces
1 large onion, thinly sliced
1 medium green pepper, sliced
4 ounces grated sharp Cheddar
    cheese
1 clove garlic, finely chopped
½ teaspoon salt

Sprinkle tomato slices with flour and arrange in greased 2½-pint casserole in alternate layers with frankfurter pieces, onion, green pepper, and cheese. Season each layer with garlic and salt.

Cover and cook in moderate oven (350°F. Mark 4) until cheese is bubbly. Serves 4 to 5.

Variation: Substitute 1 7-ounce can sweetcorn for cheese.

CORNED BEEF AND MACARONI

12 ounces corned beef
2 ounces butter or margarine
2 tablespoons diced green pepper
1 ounce grated sharp Cheddar
    cheese
16 fluid ounces thin white sauce
1 8-ounce packet macaroni

Cut corned beef into pieces. Fry until crisp in melted butter. Add green pepper and cook 3 minutes longer. Melt cheese in white sauce.

Cook macaroni until tender in boiling salted water. Drain.

Combine all ingredients. Turn into 3-pint buttered casserole. Set casserole in shallow pan of hot water and cook in moderate oven (350°F. Mark 4) about 30 minutes. Serves 6.

Stuffed Green Peppers: Fill parboiled green pepper shells with above mixture. Cover with buttered crumbs. Bake in moderate oven to heat and brown.

FRANKFURTERS WITH HOT POTATO SALAD

1½ pounds cooked potatoes, thinly
    sliced
3 fluid ounces cooking oil
3 tablespoons vinegar
1½ teaspoons salt
Dash of black pepper
12 ounces canned or cooked green
    beans, drained
½ medium onion, thinly sliced
4 large frankfurters, sliced

Gently mix potatoes with oil, vinegar, salt, and pepper.

Place green beans in layer in greased 2½-pint casserole. Add alternate layers of potato salad, onion, and frankfurters.

Cover and cook in hot oven (400°F. Mark 6) 30 minutes. Serves 4.

RICE AND FRANKFURTER CASSEROLE

6 ounces uncooked rice
2 medium onions, sliced
1½ ounces lard or cooking oil
2 15-ounce cans tomatoes
1 tablespoon sugar
1½ teaspoons salt
1 ounce green pepper, chopped
3 whole cloves
1 bay leaf
9 frankfurters

Cook and drain rice. Cook onions hot fat until transparent. Add remaining ingredients except frankfurters and simmer 15 minutes. Remove bay leaf and cloves. Add rice.

Arrange in alternate layers in greased casserole, using ⅓ of rice mixture first then 3 frankfurters, whole or sliced. Reserve 3 frankfurters for top layer.

Cover and cook in moderate oven (350°F. Mark 4) 50 to 60 minutes. Uncover for last 15 minutes. Serves 6.

CORNED BEEF CASSEROLE

1 10½-ounce can cream of mushroom
    soup
4 fluid ounces evaporated milk
1 12-ounce can corned beef, diced
4 ounces grated Cheddar cheese
½ medium onion, finely chopped
9 ounces broken noodles (cooked
    in unsalted water)
1 ounce crumbled potato crisps

Combine soup, evaporated milk, corned beef, cheese, onion, and noodles in a 5-pint bowl. Pour into a greased 2½-pint casserole.

Top with potato crisps. Cook in hot oven (425°F. Mark 7) 15 minutes or until bubbly hot. Serves 4.

Tuna Casserole: Use 1 7-ounce can tuna (drained) in place of corned beef.

Corned Beef Casserole

BOLOGNA OR CERVELAT SAUSAGE CASSEROLE

3 ounces grated cheese
8 fluid ounces medium white sauce
1 tablespoon onion, grated
1 teaspoon Worcestershire sauce
¼ teaspoon celery salt
¼ teaspoon garlic salt
10 ounces cooked vegetables (sweet-corn, runner beans, peas, or cabbage)
8 ounces bologna or cervelat sausage, cubed
3 ounces dry buttered breadcrumbs

Add 2 ounces cheese to white sauce and stir until melted. Add onion and seasonings.

Arrange vegetables, meat, and sauce in layers. Mix remaining 1 ounce cheese with crumbs and sprinkle over top.

Cook in moderate oven (350°F. Mark 4) until top has browned, about 20 minutes. Serves 4.

STORE CUPBOARD CASSEROLE

2 1-pound cans sweetcorn or mixed vegetables
1 1-pound can corned beef, ham or pork luncheon meat or frankfurters
4 fluid ounces water
1 10½-ounce can condensed cream of celery, tomato, chicken, or mushroom soup
1 teaspoon Worcestershire sauce
¼ teaspoon prepared mustard
2 ounces grated cheese (optional)

Spread vegetables in 3-pint shallow casserole. Cover with canned meat cut into serving portions.

Combine soup, water, and seasonings. Pour over meat. Sprinkle with cheese.

Cook in moderate oven (375°F. Mark 5) 30 to 40 minutes. Serve hot. Serves 6.

BEAN AND PORK SAUSAGE CASSEROLE

1 pound pork sausage meat
½ ounce dripping
1 pound cooked or canned lima or broad beans
12 ounces cooked or canned tomatoes
1 teaspoon salt
¼ teaspoon black pepper
1 onion, sliced
1 green pepper, sliced
3 tablespoons dry breadcrumbs

Form sausage meat into small rounds and brown slightly in dripping in frying pan.

Combine beans, tomatoes, salt, and pepper. Put layer of bean mixture in greased casserole. Add layers of onion and pepper slices, and meat.

Repeat layers until all ingredients are used. Top with breadcrumbs.

Cook in moderate oven (350°F. Mark 4) 1 hour. Serves 6 to 8.

BARBECUED SAUERKRAUT AND FRANKFURTER CASSEROLE

1 large (20- or 25-ounce) can sauerkraut
6 frankfurters
1 ounce butter or margarine
1 medium onion, chopped
2 teaspoons sugar
1 teaspoon mustard
¼ teaspoon salt
⅛ teaspoon freshly ground pepper
1 teaspoon paprika
1 teaspoon chilli sauce
2 teaspoons Worcestershire sauce
4 fluid ounces water

Open sauerkraut; drain off 3 tablespoons juice and reserve.

Cut frankfurters in halves lengthwise; cut each half into quarters.

In a saucepan, melt butter or margarine over low heat. Add onions and sauté until golden brown.

Remove from heat; add sugar, dry mustard, salt, pepper, paprika, chilli sauce, Worcestershire sauce, water, 3 tablespoons sauerkraut juice, and frankfurter pieces. Cook over low heat 10 minutes.

Turn sauerkraut into a shallow baking dish, leaving a section free in the centre. Arrange cooked frankfurter pieces in centre space and pour barbecue sauce over them. Cook in moderate oven (350°F. Mark 4) 15 minutes. Serves 6.

SURPRISE CASSEROLE

1 medium onion, chopped
1 ounce green pepper, chopped
1 ounce lard or dripping
1 12-ounce can pork-ham luncheon meat, chopped
3 ounces dry breadcrumbs
2 ounces grated Cheddar cheese
1 10½-ounce can condensed cream of mushroom soup
4 fluid ounces milk
3 lightly beaten eggs

Cook onion and green pepper in hot fat until onion is yellow. Add remaining ingredients and mix well. Pour into greased 3-pint casserole.

Cook in moderate oven (350°F. Mark 4) about 1 hour. Garnish top with green pepper rings. Serves 6 to 8.

VIENNA SAUSAGES WITH RICE

1 pound Vienna sausages
3 ounces fresh breadcrumbs or cornflakes
12 ounces cooked rice
1 8-ounce can tomatoes, sieved
1 small green pepper, chopped
1 small onion, chopped
6 black olives, chopped
Salt and pepper to taste
Butter

Leave Vienna sausages whole or cut in half as desired. Combine remaining ingredients and mix lightly.

Barbecued Sauerkraut and Frankfurter Casserole

Turn half of rice mixture into greased casserole. Spread half of sausages on rice. Add rice to fill casserole. Top with remaining sausages and dot with butter.

Cook in moderate oven (350°F. Mark 4) 25 minutes. Serves 4 to 6.

HAWAIIAN PARTY CASSEROLE

2 12-ounce cans luncheon meat, coarsely grated
1 1-pound can and 1 8-ounce can pineapple slices, drained
5 teaspoons cornflour
Juice drained from pineapple
2 ounces celery, sliced
1½ ounces green pepper, finely chopped
2 pounds potatoes, peeled and cooked

Reserve 3 slices pineapple and arrange layers of meat and remaining pineapple in 5-pint casserole.

Blend cornflour with a little pineapple juice; add remaining juice; cook until thickened, stirring constantly.

Add celery and green pepper to pineapple juice and cook until crisply tender. Pour this mixture over contents of casserole.

Season and mash potatoes; place in 5 mounds round edge of casserole. Make a depression in each. Arrange reserved pineapple slices in centre of casserole.

Cook in hot oven (400°F. Mark 6) 35 to 40 minutes. Before serving, dot potatoes with butter. Serves 6 to 8.

SAUSAGE AND RICE CASSEROLE

1 pound pork sausage meat
12 ounces rice, cooked
1 10½-ounce can condensed tomato soup

Brown sausage meat in frying pan, stirring constantly to keep separated. When lightly brown, drain off fat and add cooked rice. Put rice and sausage into casserole.

Add soup. Cook, covered, in moderate oven (350°F. Mark 4) 40 minutes. Serves 4 to 5.

Topping Tip: It's good planning to keep a packet of shortcrust pastry mix or scone mix on hand for days when time is short and you want to produce a meat pie quickly.

225

Casseroles with Offal

SPANISH LIVER

1 pound sliced calves', lambs' or
   pigs' liver
1½ tablespoons flour
1 ounce cooking fat or dripping
½ medium onion, chopped
1 ounce green pepper, chopped
½ clove garlic, chopped
1 ounce sliced mushrooms, if
   desired
1 8-ounce can tomatoes
1½ teaspoons salt
Pepper to taste
6 to 8 ounces cooked noodles or
   spaghetti
3 ounces fresh breadcrumbs

Dip liver slices in flour and cut in
cubes. Brown liver in fat; add onion,
green pepper, garlic, mushrooms, tomatoes, salt, and pepper. Cover and
simmer 10 minutes.

Place noodles or spaghetti and liver
mixture in alternate layers in greased
baking dish. Top with breadcrumbs.

Cook in moderate oven (375°F. Mark
5) until mixture is heated through and
crumbs are browned, 15 to 20 minutes.
Serves 6.

TONGUE AND RICE CASSEROLE

1 ounce melted butter
1 ounce fresh breadcrumbs
1 teaspoon finely chopped parsley
1 teaspoon finely chopped onion
1 egg yolk
1 pound cooked or canned tongue
4 ounces seasoned rice, cooked
⅛ teaspoon paprika
1 ounce grated cheese
½ ounce butter

Mix 1 ounce butter, crumbs, parsley,
onion, and egg yolk. Spread in bottom
of casserole.

Cover with layer of sliced tongue.
Top with layer of cooked rice.

Sprinkle with paprika and grated
cheese. Dot with ½ ounce butter.

Cook in moderate oven (375°F. Mark
5) 30 minutes. Serves 6.

SWISS-STYLE LIVER

1½ pounds calves' or pigs' liver
Flour
2 teaspoons salt
½ teaspoon black pepper
1 ounce lard or dripping
2 onions, sliced
1 8-ounce can tomatoes

Buy liver in one piece. Dredge with
flour mixed with salt and pepper.
Brown in hot fat.

Transfer to casserole. Add onions
and tomatoes

Cover tightly and cook in moderate
oven (350°F. Mark 4) 1½ hours.

Add water, if needed. Serves 6 to 8.

TRIPE EN CASSEROLE

1½ pounds honeycomb tripe
12 ounces celery, chopped
2 large onions, chopped
1 ounce parsley, chopped
2 ounces butter or olive oil
1 20-ounce can tomato juice
1 teaspoon salt
Black pepper
1 ounce grated Parmesan cheese
1 ounce dry breadcrumbs

Wash tripe well and cut into 2½-
inch squares.

Sauté celery, onion, and parsley in
hot oil until lightly browned. Turn
into heated casserole. Cover with tripe.

Add tomato juice, salt, and pepper
to taste.

Cover tightly and cook in slow oven
(325°F. Mark 3) until tender, about 3
hours.

Remove cover. Sprinkle with cheese
mixed with breadcrumbs. Raise oven
temperature to hot (400°F. Mark 6) and
cook until nicely browned on top, about
30 minutes. Serves 6.

LIVER-RICE CASSEROLE

12 ounces calves', lambs' or pigs'
    liver
2 ounces cooking fat or dripping
½ medium onion, chopped
1 ounce green pepper, chopped
2 ounces celery, chopped
8 ounces rice, cooked
1 8-ounce can tomatoes or tomato
   juice
1 teaspoon salt
Dash of black pepper

Cover liver with boiling water and
simmer 10 minutes. Drain and mince
or chop coarsely.

Brown liver, onion, green pepper,
and celery in hot fat. Combine with rice
and tomatoes in a casserole. Season to
taste.

Cover and cook in moderate oven
(350°F. Mark 4) ½ hour. Remove cover
and bake 10 minutes longer. Serves
5 to 6.

LIVER AND POTATO CASSEROLE

1 pound sliced liver
Flour, salt, black pepper
1½ ounces dripping
1¼ pounds thinly sliced potatoes
1 large onion, thinly sliced
12 fluid ounces medium white
    sauce

Roll liver in flour seasoned with salt
and pepper; brown in hot fat. Cut liver
in 1½-inch cubes.

Fry potatoes and onion in remaining
fat until brown and tender.

Place alternate layers of liver, potatoes, and onion in casserole. Add white
sauce.

Cook in moderate oven (350°F. Mark
4) 20 minutes. Serves 4.

OXTAILS EN CASSEROLE

2 large oxtails
1½ ounces dripping
6 small onions, peeled and
   quartered
6 small carrots, scraped and
   quartered
4 ounces celery, chopped
1 teaspoon salt
¼ teaspoon black pepper
½ teaspoon Aromat
¼ teaspoon thyme
1 garlic clove, crushed
1 pint 12 fluid ounces boiling
   water
2 beef stock cubes
3 tablespoons flour
2 tablespoons cold water

Have oxtails cut into pieces at joints.
Rinse and dry.

Fry oxtail pieces in hot fat until
lightly browned. Place half of oxtail
pieces in 4-pint casserole. Cover with
vegetables. Add seasonings. Cover with
remaining oxtail pieces.

Combine water and stock cubes in
a saucepan. Bring to boil and stir in
flour which has been blended with 2
tablespoons cold water to a smooth
paste. Bring to boil and pour into
casserole.

Cover and cook in moderate oven
(350°F. Mark 4) until tender. Serves
4 to 6.

Variation: When nearly done, add 4
fluid ounces dry red wine to casserole.

KIDNEY STEW

8 lambs' kidneys
8 ounces fresh mushrooms, sliced
6 or 8 spring onions, chopped
2 ounces butter or margarine
3 tablespoons flour
4 fluid ounces stock or beef broth
4 fluid ounces red wine (or use
   additional stock)
Salt and pepper
10 to 12 ounces potato balls, cooked
   or canned

Wash kidneys and remove outer skin.
Split in half lengthwise and remove any
membranes. Slice about ¼-inch thick.

Cook sliced kidneys, mushrooms, and
spring onions in butter about 10 minutes, then put them in greased casserole.

Add flour to butter still in frying
pan; mix well.

Add stock and wine gradually to
make a gravy; stir and cook until
thickened.

Season to taste. Add to kidneys.

Brown potatoes in a little more butter or margarine; place in casserole.

Cover and simmer in moderate oven
(350°F. Mark 4) about 25 minutes.
Serves 4.

*Plan contrast in texture. Most cas-
seroles are moist or soft in texture. As
a contrast to softness serve raw or firm
cooked vegetables or a crisp green salad.*

Poultry Casseroles

WITH COOKED OR CANNED POULTRY

CHICKEN NOODLE CASSEROLE

8 ounces noodles
8 ounces mushrooms, sliced
12 ounces diced, cooked chicken
4 ounces dry breadcrumbs
½ medium onion, finely chopped
2 sprigs parsley, chopped
1 teaspoon salt
⅛ teaspoon black pepper
16 fluid ounces hot chicken stock
1½ ounces chicken fat

Cook noodles in 3½-pints boiling salted water. Drain.

Alternate noodles, mushrooms, and chicken in a well-greased casserole.

Sprinkle each layer with breadcrumbs, chopped onion, parsley, salt, and pepper. Pour hot stock over ingredients. Top with crumbs and dot with fat.

Cook uncovered in moderate oven (350°F. Mark 4) until top layer of crumbs is golden brown, about 30 minutes. Serves 6.

CHICKEN AND ASPARAGUS AU GRATIN

12 ounces bread, cut in small cubes
4 ounces grated Cheddar cheese
4 ounces butter, melted
12 ounces cooked asparagus tips
2 ounces plain flour
2 teaspoons salt
¼ teaspoon black pepper
1 pint 4 fluid ounces milk
12 ounces diced cooked chicken

Mix bread cubes with cheese and 2 ounces melted butter. Line 3½-pint baking dish with half the cubes. Arrange asparagus tips on cubes.

Blend flour, salt, and pepper in remaining 2 ounces butter, then add milk and cook, stirring until thick and smooth. Add chicken and pour over asparagus. Sprinkle top with remaining bread cubes.

Cook in moderate oven (350°F. Mark 4) 30 minutes. Bread cubes should be golden brown before dish is removed from oven. Serves 6.

Chicken and Asparagus Au Gratin

HOT CHICKEN SALAD

1½ pounds cooked cold chicken chunks
2 tablespoons lemon juice
6 fluid ounces mayonnaise
1 teaspoon salt
½ teaspoon Aromat
8 ounces celery, chopped
4 hard-boiled eggs, sliced
6 fluid ounces cream of chicken soup
1 teaspoon onion, finely minced
2 canned pimientos, finely chopped
4 ounces grated cheese
3 ounces crushed potato crisps
3 ounces finely chopped browned almonds

Combine all except cheese, potato crisps and almonds. Place in a large rectangular dish. Top with cheese, potato crisps and almonds. Allow to stand overnight in refrigerator.

Cook in hot oven (400°F. Mark 6) 20 to 25 minutes. Serves 8.

CHICKEN JAMBALAYA CASSEROLE

8-9 ounces diced cooked chicken
4 ounces rice, cooked
12 ounces canned tomatoes
1 large onion, finely chopped
1 small green pepper, finely chopped
2 ounces celery, chopped
1 teaspoon salt
Pinch of black pepper
2 ounces dry breadcrumbs
1 ounce melted butter

Combine chicken, rice, and tomatoes. Cook 10 minutes.

Add onion, green pepper, celery, and seasonings. Turn into casserole.

Combine crumbs and melted butter. Sprinkle over casserole.

Cook in moderate oven (350°F. Mark 4) 1 hour. Serve very hot. Serves 4.

TURKEY CASHEW CASSEROLE

6 ounces chopped cooked turkey
1 10½-ounce can condensed cream of mushroom soup
6 ounces celery, coarsely chopped
4 ounces cashew nuts, coarsely chopped
1 tablespoon grated onion
Dash of black pepper
Salt, if nuts are unsalted
About 8 ounces dry breadcrumbs

Mix together first 6 ingredients. Taste; add salt if necessary.

In 2½-pint casserole layer turkey mixture and breadcrumbs ending with crumbs.

Cook in slow oven (325°F. Mark 3) 40 minutes. Serves 4.

Variations in toppings add glamour and individuality to your favourite casseroles. Consider these as topping materials: crisp cereals, crackers, or potato crisps, whole or crushed; tiny sausages, bologna or other smoked sausage in overlapping slices, grated cheese, bacon rashers, mashed potatoes, breadcrumbs, scones, and pastry.

CHICKEN-VEGETABLE-RICE CASSEROLE

6 ounces chopped cooked chicken
1 small jar chopped stuffed olives
6 ounces cooked peas
2 ounces cooked celery, chopped
1½ teaspoons salt
¼ teaspoon black pepper
1 tablespoon lemon juice
1 ounce dripping or cooking fat
2 tablespoons flour
16 fluid ounces milk
6 ounces rice, cooked
1 ounce melted butter
2 ounces dry breadcrumbs

Combine chicken, olives, peas, celery, salt, pepper, and lemon juice.

Melt fat and blend in flour; add milk gradually, stirring constantly to prevent lumping. Cook until consistency of thin white sauce. Add chicken mixture to sauce.

Spread rice in buttered 2½-pint casserole. Pour sauce mixture over rice. Toss crumbs with melted butter and sprinkle over casserole.

Cook in moderate oven (350°F. Mark 4) 25 minutes. Serves 5 to 6.

CURRIED CHICKEN CASSEROLE

4 ounces celery, finely chopped
1 ounce butter or margarine
4 ounces rice, cooked
12 ounces cooked or canned chicken, cut in chunks
1 small can (about 3 ounces) whole mushrooms
2 fluid ounces mayonnaise
2 teaspoons grated onion
About 1 teaspoon curry powder
¼ teaspoon salt
1 tablespoon lemon juice

Fry celery in butter until tender. Add remaining ingredients and mix well.

Turn into greased casserole.

Cook in moderate oven (350°F. Mark 4) until bubbly, about 20 minutes. Serves 4.

Hot Chicken Salad Pies

CHICKEN NEAPOLITAN

3 ounces butter or margarine
12 ounces fresh mushrooms, sliced
5 tablespoons flour
½ teaspoon celery salt
Pinch of white pepper
16 fluid ounces chicken stock
8 fluid ounces evaporated milk, undiluted
3 fluid ounces tomato ketchup
2 teaspoons Worcestershire sauce
Dash of Tabasco sauce
8 ounces spaghetti
1 pound coarsely diced cooked chicken
2 ounces dry breadcrumbs
1½ ounces melted butter or margarine
Grated Parmesan cheese

Fry mushrooms in melted butter in saucepan over low heat until tender; remove mushrooms.

Add flour and seasonings; blend until smooth. Gradually add chicken stock and milk. Cook, stirring constantly, until mixture thickens and comes to a boil. Cook a few minutes longer, adding ketchup, Worcestershire sauce, and Tabasco sauce.

Cook spaghetti in boiling salted water until tender; drain. Combine with half the sauce.

Fill baking dish or casserole with spaghetti, heaping it round sides of dish. Fill centre with remaining sauce, diced chicken, and mushrooms. Sprinkle with breadcrumbs, which have been moistened with melted butter, and Parmesan cheese.

Cook in moderate oven (350°F. Mark 4) until breadcrumbs are browned, about 10 minutes. Serves 6.

HOT CHICKEN SALAD PIES

1 pound shortcrust pastry
1 green pepper, finely chopped
6 ounces celery, chopped
1¼ pounds diced chicken, cooked or canned
12 fluid ounces mayonnaise
¾ teaspoon salt
Few drops Tabasco sauce
1 teaspoon Aromat
1½ teaspoons Worcestershire sauce

Make up 1 pound of shortcrust pastry. Chill.

Meanwhile combine remaining ingredients.

Roll half of pastry ⅛ inch thick on lightly floured board. Cut in 4 circles 7 inches in diameter. Fit loosely into 4 6-inch pie dishes. Trim edges.

Fill dishes with chicken salad mixture.

Roll out remaining pastry ⅛ inch thick. Cut in 4 circles 6 inches in diameter. Cut out centre of these circles with a 3-inch biscuit cutter. Scallop by hand, if wished.

Place pastry rings on pies; press edges together with floured fork. Bake in hot oven (425°F. Mark 7) 20 to 25 minutes, or until pastry is golden brown. Serve hot. Makes 4 tarts.

RICE AND CHICKEN AMANDINE

1 tablespoon finely chopped onion
2 ounces butter or chicken fat
1½ ounces flour
16 fluid ounces chicken stock
8 fluid ounces double cream
12 ounces rice, cooked
1 pound chopped, cooked chicken
2 ounces blanched, slivered, browned almonds
2 tablespoons diced canned pimiento
1 tablespoon finely chopped parsley
¼ teaspoon nutmeg
¼ teaspoon thyme
¼ teaspoon sweet marjoram
1 teaspoon salt

Sauté onion in butter. Blend in flour. Gradually add stock, stirring constantly until sauce thickens.

Simmer 10 minutes; add cream and heat thoroughly but do not boil.

Add rest of ingredients, mixing well.

Pour into buttered 3½-pint casserole. Cook in moderate oven (375°F. Mark 5) 20 to 30 minutes. Serves 6.

CHICKEN SLICES IN CHEESE SAUCE

1 pound asparagus, cooked (fresh, frozen or 1 20-ounce can)
6 slices cooked chicken
1 10½-ounce can condensed cream of chicken soup
2 ounces grated Cheddar cheese

Place asparagus in flat casserole or baking tin. Top with sliced chicken.

Stir soup and cheese together; pour over chicken.

Place under grill, or in very hot oven (450°F. Mark 8) until lightly browned. Serves 6.

CHICKEN-WINE CASSEROLE

1 10½-ounce can condensed mushroom soup
3 fluid ounces white wine
6 ounces cooked or canned chicken or turkey, chopped
3-ounce packet potato crisps, crushed
2 hard-boiled eggs, chopped
Celery salt and pepper to taste

Put soup and wine in a mixing bowl; stir until well blended. Add remaining ingredients (reserving a few potato crisp crumbs for topping) and mix well.

Turn into a greased casserole. Sprinkle with remaining potato crisp crumbs.

Cook in moderate oven (375°F. Mark 5) about 25 minutes. Serves 4.

CHICKEN-RICE GOURMET

1 5½-ounce packet quick-cooking rice
2 ounces butter or margarine
4 tablespoons flour
8 fluid ounces chicken stock
8 fluid ounces single cream or undiluted evaporated milk
2-3 fluid ounces sherry
½ teaspoon Worcestershire sauce
Salt and pepper to taste
10-12 ounces diced, cooked chicken
4 ounces canned sliced mushrooms
2 canned pimientos, finely chopped
2 tablespoons chopped parsley
Buttered dry breadcrumbs

Cook rice according to directions on packet.

Melt butter and stir in flour; add stock and cream and cook, stirring constantly, until mixture is thickened and smooth. Add sherry, Worcestershire sauce, salt, and pepper.

Combine this sauce with rice, chicken, mushrooms, pimientos, and parsley, mixing gently but thoroughly.

Turn into greased casserole, top with buttered breadcrumbs and cook in moderate oven (350°F. Mark 4) about 45 minutes. Serves 4.

Chicken-Rice Gourmet

Chicken Broccoli Casserole

CHICKEN TAMALE PIE

1 pint 4 fluid ounces chicken stock,
    or water and stock cubes
1½ teaspoons salt
7 ounces maize flour or polenta
1 large onion, grated
1 clove garlic, crushed
2 ounces chopped salt pork
2 fluid ounces cooking oil
3 7-ounce cans kernel sweetcorn,
    drained
1 8-ounce can tomatoes
2 teaspoons chilli seasoning
¼ teaspoon black pepper
½ teaspoon paprika
12 ounces chopped cooked chicken
2 beaten eggs
2 ounces grated Cheddar cheese

Heat stock or water to boiling. Add salt. Stir in maize flour slowly and cook to a thick mush.

Fry onion, garlic, and pork in hot fat until onion is light golden colour. Add sweetcorn tomatoes, and seasonings. Heat and stir until well blended.

Combine with maize flour mixture. Add sweetcorn, tomatoes, and seasonings. Heat and stir until well blended.

Cook in moderate oven (350°F. Mark 4) 50 to 60 minutes. Fifteen minutes before tamale is removed from oven sprinkle with grated cheese. Serve at once. Serves 6 to 8.

MUSHROOM CHICKEN PIE

4 small white onions, thinly sliced
1 tablespoon chopped green pepper
1 ounce cooking fat or dripping
1 10½ ounce can condensed cream
    of mushroom soup
4 fluid ounces milk or single cream
6 ounces cubed, cooked chicken
3 ounces chopped cooked carrots
    (or cooked peas)
About 6 ounces scone mix

Cook onion and green pepper until soft in dripping in frying pan.

Combine with soup, 2 fluid ounces milk, chicken, and carrots; pour into 8-inch pie dish.

Add remaining 2 fluid ounces milk to scone mix; roll dough into a circle about 9 inches in diameter. Place on top of chicken mixture; flute edge.

Cook in very hot oven (450°F. Mark 8) 15 minutes. Serves 4.

CHICKEN BROCCOLI CASSEROLE

Firmly packed white sauce mix
    (below)
16 fluid ounces warm water
4 ounces finely cubed cheese
4 chicken breasts, cooked, or 1
    pound cooked sliced chicken
1 packet frozen broccoli, cooked
Parmesan cheese

Place water in top of double boiler or heavy saucepan. Add white sauce mix and stir until smooth and thickened. Add cheese and cook until cheese has all melted, stirring occasionally.

Cook broccoli until just tender. Place broccoli in flat casserole or individual dishes. Place chicken breasts on top of broccoli. Pour cheese sauce over this.

Sprinkle with Parmesan cheese and place under grill until nicely browned. Serves 4.

White Sauce Mix: Sift 1 ounce dried milk, 1 ounce plain flour, and ½ teaspoon salt into a bowl.

Mix in 2 ounces firm butter with a pastry blender or knife, until the mixture is about the consistency of fine crumbs.

CHICKEN SUPPER CASSEROLE

1 tablespoon finely chopped onion
½ ounce butter or margarine
2 8-ounce cans tomatoes
1 teaspoon salt
¼ teaspoon thyme
12 ounces cooked or canned chicken,
    in small chunks
4 ounces rice, cooked
8 chopped stuffed green olives
4 ounces grated Cheddar cheese
Buttered dry breadcrumbs (optional)

Fry onion in butter until golden. Add 4 ounces tomatoes, salt, and thyme. Cook 5 minutes.

Add chicken, rice, olives, and cheese.

Put remaining 12 ounces tomatoes in greased casserole. Then turn chicken mixture over tomatoes.

If wished, top with buttered crumbs.

Cook in moderate oven (350°F. Mark 4) 30 to 40 minutes. Serves 4.

CHICKEN SCONE PIE

1 10½-ounce can condensed cream
    of chicken soup
2 fluid ounces water or juice from
    peas
5-6 ounces cooked chicken, cubed
3-4 ounces cooked peas
2 tablespoons chopped canned
    pimiento
Scone dough for 12 scones

Stir soup; add water slowly. Blend in chicken, peas, and pimiento. Put in greased 13×9×2-inch baking tin; top with scones.

Cook in very hot oven (425°F. Mark 7) 15 to 20 minutes. Serves 6.

CHICKEN PUFF

2 ounces butter or margarine
1 ounce plain flour
8 fluid ounces milk
¼ teaspoon basil
¾ teaspoon salt
Dash of black pepper
Dash of cayenne pepper
3 well beaten egg yolks
½ teaspoon finely chopped parsley
1 tablespoon chopped canned
    pimiento
8-9 ounces chopped cooked chicken
3 stiffly beaten egg whites

Melt butter; blend in flour. Stir milk in gradually. Add seasonings and cook until thick, stirring constantly. Remove from heat. Stir in yolks, parsley, pimiento, and chicken. Cool to lukewarm. Fold in egg whites.

Pour into 2½-pint casserole. Cook in moderate oven (350°F. Mark 4) 35 to 40 minutes, or until knife inserted comes out clean. Serves 6.

CHICKEN VEGETABLE PIE

2 ounces margarine
1 ounce plain flour
16 fluid ounces milk
½ teaspoon salt
⅛ teaspoon black pepper
5-6 ounces cubed cooked chicken
2 ounces canned mushrooms
6 ounces cooked peas
6 ounces cooked diced carrots
1 hard-boiled egg, diced
1 tablespoon Worcestershire sauce,
    if desired
1 tablespoon diced canned pimiento
Scone dough

Melt margarine in saucepan. Add flour, stirring smooth. Add milk gradually, stirring constantly until sauce comes to boil and is thickened.

Add liquid from mushrooms. Season with salt and pepper. Fold in chicken, vegetables, egg, Worcestershire sauce, and pimiento. Turn into 6 individual casseroles or a 3-pint casserole.

Top with scone rings and cook in hot oven (400°F. Mark 6) 25 minutes, or until scones are delicately browned. Serves 6.

Chicken Vegetable Pie

Mexican Chicken

MEXICAN CHICKEN

2 7-ounce cans sweetcorn
1 teaspoon salt
½ teaspoon black pepper
12 ounces cooked chicken, cut in
  large pieces
2 onions, thinly sliced
2 peppers, thinly sliced
1 small clove garlic, chopped
1 ounce chicken fat
1 tablespoon flour
2 8-ounce cans tomatoes or 5 fresh
  tomatoes, peeled and
  quartered

Place sweetcorn in bottom of well greased 3½-pint casserole. Sprinkle with half of salt and pepper; add chicken.

Cook sliced onions, peppers, and garlic in chicken fat until brown. Add remaining salt and pepper and flour; stir until well blended, add tomatoes and cook about 5 minutes or until thickened. Pour this sauce over sweetcorn and chicken.

Cook in moderate oven (350°F. Mark 4) about 30 minutes or until brown. Serves 6.

CHICKEN AND RICE, BLACKSTONE

2 ounces butter or margarine
5 tablespoons flour
8 fluid ounces gold-top milk
  or evaporated milk
4 fluid ounces chicken stock
4 fluid ounces Sauternes or other
  white wine
1 teaspoon celery salt
Salt and pepper to taste
12 ounces diced cooked or canned
  chicken
12 ounces rice, cooked
1½ ounces chopped canned pimiento
1 4-ounce can mushroom stems and
  pieces, drained
2 ounces slivered blanched almonds
Buttered dry breadcrumbs
Paprika

Melt butter and stir in flour; add milk, chicken stock, and wine. Cook, stirring constantly, until the mixture boils and thickens. Add seasoning.

Combine chicken, rice, pimiento, mushrooms, almonds, and sauce. Turn into greased casserole; sprinkle with breadcrumbs and paprika.

Cook in moderate oven (375°F. Mark 5) about 25 minutes or until bubbly and delicately browned. Serves 8.

SPICY CHICKEN "SOUFFLE"

5 slices bread
10-12 ounces cooked or canned
  chicken, cut in pieces
8 ounces grated Cheddar cheese
3 eggs
16 fluid ounces milk
½ teaspoon salt
½ teaspoon mustard
¼ teaspoon thyme
Dash of black pepper
Dash of paprika

Butter bread slices; trim off crusts and cut into ½-inch cubes.

Arrange in layers in greased 2½-pint casserole as follows: bread cubes, chicken, 6 ounces grated cheese, bread cubes, chicken, bread cubes.

Beat eggs with milk and seasonings. Pour over contents of casserole.

Place casserole in shallow pan and pour hot water into pan until 1-inch deep.

Cook in slow oven (325°F. Mark 3) 45 minutes.

Sprinkle with remaining 2 ounces cheese and cook 40 minutes longer. Serves 6 to 8.

CURRIED TURKEY AND RICE CASSEROLE

8 ounces rice
1 medium onion, chopped
2½-3 ounces butter or margarine
2 tablespoons curry powder
1 pound diced, cooked turkey meat
1 pint turkey stock
Salt

Slowly fry rice and onion in butter, stirring often until rice turns pale yellow. Blend in curry powder and cook 2 minutes.

Combine with turkey and broth, and salt to taste.

Turn into a 3½-pint greased casserole. Cook uncovered in moderate oven (350°F. Mark 4) 25 minutes or until liquid is absorbed and rice is fluffy. Serves 4.

CHICKEN-OKRA CASSEROLE

1 10½-ounce can condensed mushroom soup
2 fluid ounces milk
1 teaspoon Worcestershire sauce
5-6 ounces chopped cooked chicken
8 ounces cooked or canned sliced
  okra or ladies' fingers
Potato crisps

Combine soup, milk, and Worcestershire sauce. Add chicken and okra. Turn into casserole.

Cook in moderate oven (350°F. Mark 4) 20 minutes.

Cover with potato crisps and cook 5 minutes longer. Serves 4.

CHICKEN HINT

Here's a guide to amount to buy when you plan to make a casserole with cooked chicken.

1 3½-pound oven-ready chicken will give you about 1 pound diced cooked chicken.

2 whole chicken breasts (10 ounces each) will give you 10 to 12 ounces diced cooked chicken or 12 thin slices cooked chicken.

Note: Cook chicken breasts as for stewed chicken but cook only until tender, about 30 minutes.

CHICKEN AND BROWN RICE CASSEROLE

4 ounces celery, cut in 1-inch
  lengths plus a few chopped
  leaves
1 small onion, chopped
12 ounces cooked chicken, cut in
  1-inch chunks
1 pint chicken stock
8 ounces uncooked brown rice
1½ teaspoons salt
1 bay leaf
Dash of Tabasco sauce
1½ ounces butter or chicken fat
3 medium carrots, cut in ½-inch
  rounds
1 medium green pepper, cut in
  1-inch strips

Arrange celery, onion, and chicken evenly in greased 3½-pint casserole.

Add chicken stock, rice, salt, bay leaf (tucked to one side for easy removal), Tabasco sauce and butter.

Cover and cook in moderate oven (350°F. Mark 4) 45 minutes.

With a fork lightly mix in carrots and green pepper.

Cover and cook 45 minutes longer. Serves 6.

CHICKEN-LIMA CASSEROLE

1 packet frozen or canned lima
  or broad beans, cooked
6 ounces cooked or canned chicken,
  in large chunks
1 10½-ounce can condensed cream
  of mushroom soup
4 fluid ounces milk
3 ounces crushed potato crisps
Salt and pepper

Combine beans, chicken, soup, milk, and 2 ounces crushed potato crisps in 2½-pint casserole.

Season to taste. Sprinkle with remaining crisps.

Cook in moderate oven (350°F. Mark 4) about 30 minutes. Serves 4.

Garnish Your Casseroles: When the dish is ready to be served add a final colourful contrasting garnish such as fresh green parsley, pepper rings, watercress, pimiento strips, sliced olives, sliced carrots, slices of fruit.

Chicken pie may be topped with individual scones or a scone crust.

For a glazed scone crust, brush the topping with beaten egg yolk, mixed with equal amount of milk.

CHICKEN PIE

- 1 3-4-ounce can grilled mushrooms, sliced
- 9 ounces cooked (or 2 6-ounce cans) chicken, cut in pieces
- 6 sliced stuffed green olives
- 2 tablespoons chopped canned pimiento
- 2 chicken stock cubes
- 8 fluid ounces hot water
- 6 tablespoons flour
- ½ teaspoon salt
- Dash of black pepper
- 8 ounces scone mix

Drain mushrooms, reserving liquid. Combine mushrooms, chicken, olives, and pimiento. Place in shallow casserole or baking dish (8×8×1¾ inches).

Dissolve stock cubes in hot water. Add enough cold water to mushroom liquid to make 8 fluid ounces. Make a paste of the flour and a little of this cold liquid. Blend in remaining cold liquid and stock.

Cook until thick and smooth, stirring constantly. Add seasonings. Pour over mixture in casserole.

Prepare scone dough. Roll to fit casserole and place on top.

Cook in very hot oven (450°F. Mark 8) 15 minutes. Serves 5 to 6.

TURKEY-SWEETCORN PUDDING

- 1 tablespoon grated onion
- 1 ounce melted butter or margarine

- 1 teaspoon salt
- ¼ teaspoon black pepper
- ¼ teaspoon paprika
- 3 eggs, well beaten
- 1 large can undiluted evaporated milk
- 9-10 ounces diced cooked or canned turkey
- 1 7-ounce can sweetcorn

Combine onion, butter, and seasonings with well beaten eggs; blend thoroughly. Mix in remaining ingredients.

Pour into greased 2½-pint casserole. Set it in pan of warm water and cook in moderate oven (375°F. Mark 5) 40 minutes, or until knife inserted in centre comes out clean. Serves 6.

CHICKEN AND SWEET-CORN

- 1 ounce butter
- 1 small onion, chopped
- 1 tablespoon chopped green pepper
- 8 ounces cooked or 6-ounce can chicken, cut in small pieces
- 1 7-ounce can sweetcorn
- ½ teaspoon salt
- ⅛ teaspoon black pepper
- 2 fluid ounces milk
- 1 egg
- 1 tablespoon finely crushed dry breadcrumbs

Fry onion and green pepper in ½ ounce butter until onion is slightly brown. Add chicken, sweetcorn, salt, and pepper.

Beat milk and egg together; add to chicken and sweetcorn mixture.

Pour into small casserole.

Sprinkle with breadcrumbs. Dot with remaining ½ ounce butter.

Cook in moderate oven (375°F. Mark 5) about 40 minutes. Serves 3 to 4.

OKLAHOMA CHICKEN LOAF

- 1½ pounds diced cooked chicken, or meat of 5-pound boiling chicken
- 4 ounces rice, cooked
- 1½ ounces diced canned pimientos
- 1 tablespoon grated onion
- 8 fluid ounces milk
- 6 ounces fresh breadcrumbs (2- or 3-day-old bread)
- 16 fluid ounces rich chicken stock
- 4 beaten eggs
- 1 teaspoon salt
- 1 teaspoon black pepper

Combine all ingredients. Taste and add more seasoning if desired.

Place in shallow 3½-pint baking dish, about 2×6×12 inches.

Cook in slow oven (325°F. Mark 3) until firm, about 1 hour. Knife inserted near centre should come out clean.

Cut in squares or thick oblong slices. Loaf is nice served with chicken giblet gravy to which has been added 1 can mushroom soup. Serves 12 to 15.

CHICKEN BARLEY CASSEROLE

- 1 medium onion
- 4 leeks or spring onions
- 1 ounce margarine
- 7 ounces barley
- 1 pint 12 fluid ounces water
- 1 8-ounce can tomato sauce
- 2 chicken stock cubes
- 1 tablespoon salt
- 2 5-ounce cans boned chicken

Chop onion and leeks or spring onions coarsely and cook in melted margarine until slightly golden.

Mix in the barley and cook a few minutes longer.

Add remaining ingredients; transfer to greased casserole or baking dish. Cook in moderate oven (350°F. Mark 4) 2 hours or until barley is tender. Serves 6.

CHICKEN SAUCER PIES

- 1 pound shortcrust pastry
- 1 egg white, slightly beaten
- 2 ounces butter or margarine
- 4 tablespoons flour
- ½ teaspoon salt
- Few grains black pepper
- ½ teaspoon Aromat
- 16 fluid ounces chicken stock
- 2 tablespoons chopped chives
- ½ teaspoon Worcestershire sauce
- Few drops Tabasco sauce
- 1¼ pounds finely diced, cooked or canned chicken

Line individual pie dishes with pastry; brush with egg white.

Melt margarine; blend in flour, salt, pepper, and Aromat. Add stock; stir over low heat until smooth and thickened. Add remaining ingredients.

Fill pie dishes. Brush inside of top crusts with egg white; cover pies; press edges together; prick with prongs of fork.

Bake in very hot oven (450°F. Mark 8) 30 minutes. Makes 4 6-inch or 6 4-inch pies.

Chicken Saucer Pies make perfect lunches for work or school because they are as good cold as hot. Half a six-inch pie is enough for a small eater, but the man of the house can put away a whole one with no trouble at all.

We recommend these pies especially to housewives who pack more than one lunch every day.

Chicken Saucer Pies

Chicken and Broccoli Casserole

CHICKEN AND BROCCOLI CASSEROLE

4 ounces cornflakes
1 ounce butter or margarine, melted
2 ounces plain flour
8 fluid ounces milk
16 fluid ounces chicken stock
8 fluid ounces mayonnaise
1 teaspoon lemon juice
½ teaspoon curry powder
2 10-ounce packets frozen broccoli
1 pound cubed, cooked chicken

Crush cornflakes into fine crumbs and combine with melted butter. Reserve for topping.

Blend flour and milk to make a smooth paste; stir in chicken stock. Cook until thickened, stirring constantly. Remove from heat. Stir in mayonnaise, lemon juice, and curry powder.

Cook broccoli according to package directions only until tender. Drain well. Cut broccoli stalks in half; arrange in 3½-pint casserole. Cover broccoli with chicken; pour on sauce. Top with buttered cornflake crumbs.

Cook in moderate oven (350°F. Mark 4) about 30 minutes or until thoroughly heated and crumbs are browned. Serve immediately. Serves 6 (1 cup each).

HAM AND TURKEY BRUNCH PIE

6 ounces cheese cracker crumbs, finely rolled
2 ounces softened butter or margarine
8 ounces ham, cut in strips
8 ounces turkey, cut in strips
1 10½-ounce can condensed cream of chicken soup
2 fluid ounces milk
2 ounces grated Cheddar cheese
3 eggs, beaten
2 teaspoons French mustard
1 teaspoon Worcestershire sauce

Ham and Turkey Brunch Pie

Thoroughly blend cheese cracker crumbs and butter or margarine. Press firmly against bottom and sides of a 9-inch pie dish.

Layer ham and turkey strips in pie shell, reserving a few strips for garnish.

Combine soup, milk, and grated cheese. Heat, stirring, until cheese melts. Add beaten eggs, French mustard, and Worcestershire sauce. Pour over ham and turkey. Top with reserved strips. Cook in slow oven (300°F. Mark 2) 45 minutes or until knife inserted in centre comes out clean. Serves 4 to 6.

CHICKEN DIVAN

This dish is a simplified version of a recipe said to have originated many years ago in a French-American restaurant in New York. Turkey may be substituted for the chicken. Broccoli is sometimes used instead of asparagus.

8 stalks asparagus
½ ounce melted butter or margarine
3 tablespoons grated Parmesan cheese
4 fluid ounces sherry
4 thick slices cooked breast of chicken
2 egg yolks
8 fluid ounces white sauce.

Cook asparagus; drain well and arrange on heat-proof baking dish or in shallow casserole.

Sprinkle with butter, 1 tablespoon cheese, and 2 tablespoons sherry. Top with chicken meat.

Sprinkle with another tablespoon of cheese and 2 tablespoons sherry.

Beat egg yolks and add to white sauce; season and add remaining sherry. Pour over chicken. Top with remaining cheese.

Cook in hot oven (400°F. Mark 6) until delicately browned, about 12 minutes. Serves 2 or 3.

CHICKEN À LA KING

4 ounces butter or margarine
2 ounces flour
¾ teaspoon salt
Few grains black pepper
1½ teaspoons Aromat
1½ teaspoons paprika
1 6-ounce can grilled mushrooms
About 1¾ pints milk
1¼ to 1½ pounds diced cooked chicken
2 ounces diced canned pimiento
12 ounces cooked or canned peas
1 pound rice, cooked

Melt butter; blend in flour, salt, pepper, Aromat, and paprika.

Drain liquid from mushrooms into measuring cup; add milk to make 1 pint 12 fluid ounces; add to first mixture. Cook over low heat, stirring con-

stantly, until smooth and thickened.

Add mushrooms, chicken, pimiento, and peas.

Line oblong baking dish $12 \times 7\frac{1}{2} \times 2$ inches with rice. Fill with chicken mixture. Dot rice with butter.

Cook in slow oven (325°F. Mark 3) 15 to 20 minutes. Serves 8.

CHICKEN FONDUE

8 fluid ounces chicken stock
8 fluid ounces milk
12 ounces cooked, diced chicken
6 ounces stale bread cubes
2 tablespoons chopped canned pimiento
1½ teaspoons salt
Dash of freshly ground black pepper
4 slightly beaten egg yolks
4 stiffly beaten egg whites

Heat chicken broth and milk to boiling point.

Add chicken, bread cubes, pimiento, salt, pepper, and egg yolks.

When mixture has cooled to lukewarm, fold in egg whites beaten stiff but not dry.

Turn into greased casserole and bake in moderate oven (350°F. Mark 4) 45 to 50 minutes. Serves 6.

SUPPER PARTY TURKEY

2 ounces butter or margarine
3 ounces plain flour
1¼ teaspoons salt
16 fluid ounces milk
1 tablespoon dried onion flakes
2 tablespoons white wine, or ½ teaspoon Worcestershire sauce
12 ounces diced cooked turkey
6-7 ounces cooked or canned green peas
1½ ounces browned slivered almonds
Cooked brown rice

Melt butter; blend in flour and salt. Add milk; cook and stir until mixture boils and is thickened. Stir in onion and wine. Add turkey and peas; heat thoroughly.

Just before serving, stir in part of almonds. Sprinkle remaining almonds on top. If desired, add a few whole blanched almonds. Serve on brown rice. Serves 3 to 4.

Supper Party Turkey

Casseroles
with Fresh or Frozen Chicken

Old-Fashioned Chicken Pie

CHICKEN ALMOND CASSEROLE

1 4-pound boiling chicken
1 8-ounce packet egg noodles
1 small can mushrooms or 4 ounces
    fresh cooked mushrooms
3 ounces blanched almonds,
    browned in oil
8 fluid ounces medium white sauce
Salt and pepper
2 ounces dry breadcrumbs

Cook chicken until tender in salted water to cover. Remove meat from bones and measure out 1¼ pints skimmed broth. Cook noodles in broth until tender.

Arrange half the noodles in bottom of greased casserole. Cover with half the chicken, then add a layer of mushrooms and one of almonds. Season to taste. Repeat layers of noodles, chicken, and mushrooms.

Mix broth left from cooking noodles with white sauce and pour over all. Sprinkle with breadcrumbs and top with remaining almonds.

Cook in moderate oven (350°F. Mark 4) 1 hour. Serves 6 to 8.

CHICKEN À LA WARWICK

2 ounces uncooked rice
2 ounces lard or cooking oil
1 ounce chopped blanched almonds
1 medium onion, chopped
1 3-pound chicken, jointed
1 ounce plain flour
12 fluid ounces milk
1 teaspoon salt
1 teaspoon sugar
2 tablespoons chopped canned
    pimiento
¼ teaspoon black pepper
⅛ teaspoon cayenne pepper
¼ teaspoon thyme

Brown rice in 1 ounce hot fat or oil, stirring constantly. Add almonds and onion; cook until onion is soft. Turn into 3½-pint casserole.

Roll chicken in flour. Brown in remaining 1 ounce hot oil. Put chicken in casserole.

Combine milk and seasonings. Pour over chicken. Cook in slow oven (325°F. Mark 3) 1 hour. Serves 6 to 8.

Baked Chicken Supreme

CHICKEN GRUCCI

4 leg and thigh sections of
    roasting chickens
1 large clove garlic, crushed
Juice of 1 lime or lemon
5 tablespoons olive oil
1 tablespoon sugar
4 medium onions, cut in eighths
    and lightly browned in oil
1 green pepper, cut in strips
4 large potatoes, cut into balls
    and lightly browned in oil
2 tablespoons flour
½ teaspoon paprika
4 fluid ounces sherry
12 fluid ounces water
Salt and pepper
1 small can mushrooms
1 small can garden peas, heated
4 canned pimientos, cut in strips

Put chicken in bowl; sprinkle with garlic and lime or lemon juice. Chill at least 3 hours or overnight. Remove from marinade; dry.

Heat oil in heavy frying pan; sprinkle sugar in and quickly brown chicken. Place chicken in large casserole or individual ones; add vegetables.

Stir flour into oil left in pan; add paprika, and slowly stir in wine and water. Cook, stirring, until slightly thickened. Season with salt and pepper. Add mushrooms and pour over chicken.

Cover and cook in moderate oven (350°F. Mark 4) 30 to 50 minutes. Sprinkle on heated peas. Garnish each serving with pinwheel made of pimiento strips. Serves 4.

BAKED CHICKEN SUPREME

1 2- to 2½-pound roasting chicken,
    jointed
4 ounces dripping or cooking oil
½ to 1 clove garlic
1 teaspoon salt
1 medium onion, sliced
2 tablespoons flour
2 8-ounce cans tomatoes, drained
8 fluid ounces soured cream
1 ounce grated Parmesan cheese

Brown chicken in hot fat. Place chicken in casserole.

Prepare sauce: Slice garlic and crush with salt. Cook garlic-salt mixture and onion until onion is transparent in ½ ounce of oil left in frying pan.

Blend in flour. Add tomatoes and heat to boiling. Remove from heat.

Add soured cream gradually, stirring vigorously. Add Parmesan cheese. Mix thoroughly and pour over browned chicken.

Cover and cook in slow oven (325°F. Mark 3) until chicken is fork-tender, about 45 minutes. Serves 4 to 5.

OLD-FASHIONED CHICKEN PIE

1 chicken (4 to 5 pounds), jointed
1 bay leaf
2 teaspoons salt
Few grains black pepper
Dash of celery salt
1¾ teaspoons Aromat
Boiling water
1 pound small white onions
1 pound carrots, sliced
6 tablespoons flour
6 tablespoons cold water
1 tablespoon prepared horseradish
10-12 ounces scone mix

Place chicken in deep saucepan; add bay leaf, salt, pepper, celery, salt, and 1 teaspoon Aromat. Add enough boiling water to cover. Simmer 2 hours, or until chicken is tender.

Meanwhile, cook onions and carrots separately, adding ¼ teaspoon Aromat to each vegetable.

Remove chicken and drained vegetables to large, shallow casserole.

Strain broth in saucepan; measure 1¼ pints. Add vegetable waters to broth, to make 1¾ pints in all, adding water if necessary.

Add flour, mixed smooth with cold water; cook over low heat, stirring, until thickened; add remaining Aromat and horseradish; pour over chicken and vegetables.

Make scone dough as directed on packet of mix. Roll ½ inch thick; cut with chicken-shaped biscuit cutter. Arrange on casserole. Add bits of raisins for eyes, if desired.

Cook in hot oven (425°F. Mark 7) 25 to 30 minutes, or until biscuits are golden brown. Serves 6 to 8.

CHICKEN GIBLETS WITH RICE

2 pounds chicken giblets
2 spring onions, chopped
½ clove garlic, finely chopped
1½ ounces celery, chopped
¼ teaspoon paprika
Salt and black pepper
1 ounce butter or margarine
6 fluid ounces water
12 ounces rice, cooked

Wash fresh giblets and cut into small pieces. Place in casserole.

Add onions, garlic, celery, and paprika. Season to taste with salt and pepper. Dot with butter. Add water.

Cover and cook in slow oven (325°F. Mark 3) 2 hours. Serve with hot cooked rice. Serves 6 or more.

CHICKEN BATTER PUDDING

1 boiling chicken
Salt and pepper
1 whole onion
1 bay leaf (optional)
Finely chopped onion
Chopped parsley

Batter:
12 ounces sifted plain flour
2 teaspoons baking powder
½ teaspoon salt
4 eggs, separated
1 pint 12 fluid ounces milk
½ ounce melted butter or
    margarine

Simmer chicken until tender in water to cover. While cooking, season stock with salt, pepper, onion, and a bay leaf, if desired.

Remove chicken from stock; strain stock and cool. Remove chicken meat from bones and cut into pieces.

Make batter by mixing dry ingredients, then stirring in beaten egg yolks and milk. Add butter or margarine and fold in stiffly beaten egg whites.

Place layer of chicken in greased casserole or baking dish. Season with salt, pepper, chopped onion, and parsley, then cover with half a pint of the batter. Alternate layers of chicken and batter, having the last layer of batter.

Cook in moderate oven (350°-375°F. Mark 4-5) 1 hour.

Serve at table from casserole with gravy made by boiling down the stock and thickening it with a flour paste. Serves 6 to 8.

CHICKEN CREOLE CASSEROLE

1 roasting chicken, 3 to 3½ pounds
Flour
2½ ounces cooking fat or cooking oil
2 medium onions, thinly sliced
1 8-ounce can tomatoes
2 raw carrots, diced
½ teaspoon paprika
¼ teaspoon black pepper
1½ teaspoons salt
2 whole cloves
1¼ pints boiling water
8 ounces uncooked rice
Sliced stuffed olives

Cut chicken into frying pieces and sprinkle lightly with flour.

Fry onions in hot fat until golden; remove from fat.

Fry chicken in same fat until well browned on all sides. Place chicken in centre of 3½-pint casserole with tightly fitting cover.

Combine tomatoes, carrots, and seasonings with boiling water. Pour round chicken. Sprinkle rice and fried onion slices evenly round chicken. Cover.

Cook in moderate oven (350°F. Mark 4) until chicken is tender, rice fluffy, and water has evaporated, 1 to 1½ hours.

Remove cover for last 5 to 10 minutes. To serve, garnish with sliced stuffed olives. Serves 4 to 6.

CHICKEN WITH VEGETABLES

1 boiling chicken (4 to 5 pounds)
Salt and pepper
Flour
1 ounce butter or other fat
3 carrots, chopped
1 pound celery, chopped
1 onion, chopped
1 green pepper, chopped
8 fluid ounces hot water
8 fluid ounces milk

Cut up chicken and season with salt and pepper. Sprinkle with flour. Brown in hot fat in frying pan. Transfer the browned pieces to a casserole.

Place vegetables in frying pan to let them absorb remaining fat. Transfer to casserole. Add hot water.

Cover and cook in very slow oven (275°F. Mark 1) until chicken is tender, 3 to 4 hours. Add more water as necessary.

Just before serving, remove the pieces of chicken and skim off excess fat from the mixture of stock and vegetables.

Mix 1 ounce of this fat with 2 tablespoons flour; add with milk to contents of casserole. Cook 10 minutes longer, stirring a few times. Season to taste. Return chicken to casserole and serve. Serves 4 to 5.

CHICKEN PIE WITH BUTTER-CRISP CRUST

1 5-pound boiling chicken, cut in
    serving pieces
3¼ pints cold water
1 large onion, sliced
4 coarse stalks of celery with tops
8 sprigs parsley
1½ tablespoons salt
8 fluid ounces undiluted evaporated
    milk
3 ounces sliced Cheddar cheese
Thin flour paste
Cooked vegetables, if wished
Butter-Crisp Crust (below)

Simmer first 6 ingredients until tender. Allow chicken to cool in stock.

Then remove chicken and place in casserole. If you want to stretch the dish as well as make a whole meal of it, add cooked vegetables—carrots (cut in pieces), small white onions, peas, mushrooms, cubed potatoes, hard-boiled eggs—any or all. A few thin slices or cubes of cooked ham may be arranged in with the chicken.

For the gravy, to 1¾ pints of the strained stock, add the undiluted evaporated milk with salt and pepper to taste. Bring to a boil and stir in a thin flour paste (2 ounces flour and 8 fluid ounces water mixed smooth). Add the

Chicken Pie with Butter-Crisp Crust

sliced cheese. Simmer 5 minutes while stirring until thickened. Pour over chicken.

Top with a round of butter-crisp pastry cut a bit larger than the top of the casserole. Crimp edges and slash top here and there.

Bake in a very hot oven (450°F. Mark 8) about 30 minutes until golden brown.

Serves 8 to 10 depending upon whether vegetables have been added.

Butter-Crisp Crust:
8-9 ounces cream cheese
4 ounces butter
6 ounces sifted plain flour

Have cheese and butter at room temperature. Mix together thoroughly. Then, using a fork or pastry blender, cut this mixture into the flour and shape to form a ball. Wrap in greaseproof paper and chill in the refrigerator several hours.

When ready to use, roll the pastry to about ⅛-inch thickness. Cut slightly larger than top of casserole, following its shape. Any leftover pastry dough may be made into flan cases or used for jam turnovers.

Baked Chicken-Dumpling Casserole:
Use dumplings instead of the crust and cook them on top of the chicken combination. Be sure to use a casserole with a tightly fitting cover.

Dumplings: For the eggless dumplings, sift together 8 ounces superfine plain flour, 1 teaspoon salt, and 4 teaspoons baking powder. Add 1 tablespoon finely chopped parsley or finely cut chives. Stir in a mixture of 4 fluid ounces evaporated milk, 4 fluid ounces cold water, adding 1 ounce melted butter. Mix only until the dough holds together.

Drop by tablespoons on top of hot chicken, vegetables and gravy. Cover tightly. Cook in a hot oven (400°F. Mark 6) for 25 minutes. Do not lift the lid, no matter how curious you are!

CHICKEN WITH YELLOW RICE

2   small roasting chickens, jointed
3   fluid ounces olive oil
13-14 ounces uncooked rice
1   large onion, finely chopped
1   green pepper, finely chopped
2   or 3 cloves garlic, crushed
2   tablespoons salt
¼   teaspoon black pepper
Large pinch of saffron
8   tomatoes, cut in quarters
1   pound frozen peas, thawed
16 fluid ounces water

Fry chicken in oil in large heavy frying pan until browned. Transfer to 5-pint casserole.

In same pan fry rice until golden; add onion, green pepper, and garlic; cook a few minutes. Stir in remaining ingredients. Pour mixture over chicken.

Cover and cook in hot oven (400°F. Mark 6) 30 minutes. Remove cover and cook until chicken is tender, about 40 minutes longer. Serves 8.

PINEAPPLE CHICKEN CASSEROLE

1   roasting chicken, about 4 pounds
2   ounces plain flour
1   teaspoon salt
¼   teaspoon black pepper
2½-3 ounces margarine
1   8-ounce can sliced pineapple or pineapple chunks
1   medium-sized onion, chopped
Chicken stock

Cut chicken into serving-size pieces and coat with a mixture of flour, salt, and pepper.

Drain pineapple slices, saving juice, and brown in melted margarine. Remove from frying pan and set aside.

Sauté chopped onion in the same margarine until lightly browned and remove from pan.

Brown pieces of chicken on all sides in remaining fat.

Arrange chicken and sautéed onion in a casserole with a cover.

Measure pineapple juice and add enough stock to make 16 fluid ounces. Pour over chicken. Arrange pineapple slices (or chunks) on top. Cover.

Cook in moderate oven (350°F. Mark 4) for 1 hour and 15 minutes or until chicken is easily pierced with a fork. Serves 4 to 6.

Pineapple Chicken Casserole

CHICKEN AND RICE VALENCIA

2   fluid ounces cooking oil
3½-pound roasting chicken, jointed
12 ounces raw ham, cubed or 10 ounces cubed cooked ham
1   large onion, chopped
2   cloves garlic, finely chopped
2   4-ounce cans pimiento, in strips
2   tablespoons paprika
4   fluid ounces concentrated tomato purée
1¾ pints water
1   pound uncooked rice
12 ounces cooked peas
2   ounces coarsely chopped browned almonds or peanuts

Brown chicken well in hot oil in frying pan; set aside.

Cook ham cubes, onion, and garlic in large saucepan or flame-resistant casserole until onion is limp and lightly browned. Add pimiento, paprika, tomato purée and water; simmer 1 hour. Add rice and bring to boiling. Then add browned chicken.

Cover and cook in moderate oven (350°F. Mark 4) until rice is done and has absorbed liquid, about 45 minutes to 1 hour. About 5 minutes before serving, stir in peas and browned nuts. Serves 6.

CHICKEN BAKED IN SOURED CREAM

1 2-2½-pound roasting chicken (ready-to-cook weight)
2   ounces plain flour
1   teaspoon salt
⅛   teaspoon black pepper
2   ounces butter or margarine
1   ounce sliced mushrooms, canned or fresh
8   fluid ounces soured cream
8   fluid ounces water
¼   teaspoon thyme

Dredge chicken pieces in mixture of the flour, salt, and pepper, and brown in butter or margarine. Transfer to a casserole.

Add mushrooms and soured cream diluted with water. Sprinkle with thyme and cover closely.

Cook in slow oven (325°F. Mark 3) for 1 hour. Serve in the cream with fluffy rice or boiled potatoes. Serves 4.

LATTICE-TOPPED CHICKEN PIES

Chicken Pie Filling:
3   ounces chicken fat or lard
2   ounces sifted plain flour
1¼ pints chicken stock (or part milk)
1¼ pounds cooked chicken, cut in pieces
8   ounces cooked celery, diced
12 ounces cooked peas
10 ounces cooked potatoes, diced

Melt chicken fat or lard. Blend in flour. Add chicken stock, stirring con-

Lattice-Topped Chicken Pies

stantly until thickened. Season to taste.

Divide chicken and vegetables into 6 individual casseroles allowing 3 ounces chicken and 1½ to 2 ounces of each vegetable per casserole. Cover with hot chicken gravy. Top with lattice strips.

Lattice Topping:
6   ounces sifted plain flour
½   teaspoon salt
½   teaspoon curry powder
4   ounces lard
4   tablespoons cold water

Sift flour, salt, and curry powder together. Cut in lard with pastry blender or 2 knives until mixture resembles fine crumbs. Add water; mix only until flour is dampened. Chill dough in refrigerator for a short time.

Roll dough on floured board to ⅛- to ¼-inch thickness; cut into strips ½-inch wide. Arrange strips of dough lattice fashion over filling.

Bake in hot oven (425°F. Mark 7) 12 to 15 minutes. Serve with a cranberry relish or sauce. Serves 6.

CHICKEN SAUTERNE

1 to 2 roasting chickens, jointed (set aside neck, wings, and backs for chicken soup)
2   fluid ounces olive oil
2   ounces butter or margarine
4   ounces dried mushrooms (soaked for a few hours—save liquid)
1 to 2 stalks celery, finely chopped
1   small onion, finely chopped
4   fluid ounces tomato juice
½   teaspoon salt
¼   teaspoon black pepper
1   bay leaf
4   fluid ounces soured cream
1   packet mixed frozen vegetables, cooked, or 16- to 20-ounce can mixed vegetables
8   fluid ounces white wine

Brown chicken on all sides in hot oil in a deep pan. Cook, uncovered, over low heat 30 minutes.

Meanwhile, melt butter and add soaked and drained mushrooms, celery, onion, tomato juice, and seasonings. Cover and simmer gently 30 minutes.

Stir in soured cream 5 minutes before cooking is finished.

Pour sauce into casserole. Add chicken and any chicken liquid left in pan. Cover with hot vegetables. Add wine.

Cover casserole. Cook in moderate oven (350°F. Mark 4) 15 to 20 minutes. Serves 4.

Chicken Andalusia

CHICKEN ANDALUSIA

1 roasting chicken, 2½ to 3 pounds, quartered
2 tablespoons olive or cooking oil
1 pound new potatoes
2 teaspoons salt
¼ teaspoon black pepper
2 tablespoons tomato purée or ketchup
4 fluid ounces dry sherry
2 fluid ounces water
1 tablespoon flour
16 sliced, pimiento-stuffed olives
1 10-ounce packet frozen artichoke hearts, cooked, or 1 8-ounce can artichoke hearts

Brown chicken on all sides in hot oil in deep, flame-proof casserole; remove chicken, then brown potatoes.

Mix together salt, pepper, tomato purée, sherry, and water; slowly stir into flour. Stir flour mixture into drippings in pan.

Add chicken and olives; cover and cook over low heat 30 minutes, or until chicken and potatoes are tender. Serve with artichoke hearts. Serves 4.

CHICKEN LEGS WITH BROCCOLI CASSEROLE

8 fluid ounces soured cream
1 packet dried onion soup mix (1-pint size)
About 8 ounces dry breadcrumbs
6 chicken legs
2 packets frozen broccoli spears

Mix soured cream, onion soup mix, and breadcrumbs. Spread this mixture in bottom of a 7½ × 11¾-inch roasting pan or casserole.

Place chicken legs on soured cream mixture. Cover and cook in moderate oven (350°F. Mark 4) 1 hour or until chicken legs are almost tender.

Add broccoli spears and cook uncovered until broccoli is tender. Serves 4 to 6.

Chicken Legs with Broccoli Casserole

BARBECUED CHICKEN CASSEROLE

1 roasting chicken, jointed
1 ounce butter or margarine
1 medium onion, chopped
2 ounces celery, chopped
1 ounce green pepper, chopped
8 fluid ounces tomato ketchup
8 fluid ounces water
2 tablespoons Worcestershire sauce
2 tablespoons brown sugar
Pinch of black pepper

Coat chicken with 3 ounces flour mixed with 2 teaspoons salt and brown in 4 ounces hot lard or dripping. As pieces are browned, arrange in casserole.

Sauté onion in melted butter or margarine until clear. Add all other ingredients and bring to the boil. Pour over chicken in casserole.

Cover and cook in moderate oven (350°F. Mark 4) about 1 hour, until tender. Serves 4 to 5.

CHICKEN BIARRITZ

1 boiling chicken, jointed
Butter or other fat
2 carrots, sliced
2 small onions, diced
2 bay leaves
Salt and pepper
¾ pint water
1 dozen potato balls
1 dozen button mushrooms
2 tablespoons sherry
1 tablespoon finely chopped parsley

Brown chicken thoroughly in hot fat. Place in deep casserole. Add carrots, onions, bay leaves, seasonings, and water.

Cover tightly and cook in slow oven (325°F. Mark 3) 1½ to 2 hours.

Add the potato balls and mushrooms for the last half hour. Add sherry and parsley and cook 10 minutes longer. Serves 6.

FLORENTINE CHICKEN

1 2½-pound roasting chicken, jointed
2 ounces butter
3 cloves garlic
½ medium onion, chopped
8 fluid ounces tomato ketchup
2 fluid ounces vinegar
2 tablespoons sugar
1 teaspoon salt
2 fluid ounces Worcestershire sauce
¼ pint water

Brown chicken on all sides in butter. Place in greased 5-pint casserole.

Combine remaining ingredients and pour over chicken.

Cook, covered, in moderate oven (350°F. Mark 4) for 1 to 1½ hours. Serves 4.

TURKEY WITH WINE SAUCE

2 medium onions, sliced
1 large green pepper, sliced
1 stalk celery, diced
2 ounces butter or margarine
½ small turkey (about 3 pounds), cut in pieces
Salt and pepper
3 tablespoons brandy
6 fluid ounces white wine

Gently fry onions, green pepper, and celery in a frying pan in hot butter for 5 minutes. Remove from pan.

Sprinkle turkey with salt and pepper and brown on all sides.

Heat brandy in a small saucepan; set ablaze and pour over turkey pieces. When flames die out add white wine, onions, and pepper.

Cover tightly and simmer for 1¾ hours, or until fork tender in thickest parts. Serves 4.

SMOTHERED CHICKEN EN CASSEROLE

1 roasting chicken, cut in serving pieces
1 tablespoon flour
½ teaspoon salt
Pinch of black pepper
½ teaspoon paprika
½ stalk finely chopped celery with leaves
1 small onion, sliced
1 ounce butter or margarine
4 fluid ounces hot water
4 fluid ounces single cream

Place chicken in a casserole tin; do not overlap pieces. Combine flour, salt, pepper, and paprika; sprinkle over chicken pieces. Add celery and onion. Dot with butter.

Cook uncovered in moderate oven (375°F. Mark 5) 20 minutes. Add water, cook 20 minutes longer. Add cream, cover and cook 10 minutes. Serve with hot cooked rice. Serves 4.

Smothered Chicken En Casserole

Chicken Catalan

CHICKEN WITH RICE ORLEANS

1   large roasting chicken, jointed
4   fluid ounces olive oil
1½ teaspoons salt
½   medium onion, chopped
⅛   teaspoon ground ginger
8   ounces raw rice
1   clove garlic
Tip of bay leaf
2   1-pound cans tomatoes

Fry chicken in oil until golden brown. Place in casserole with the oil.

Sprinkle over it salt, onion, ginger, and rice, the latter washed and drained.

Bury the clove of garlic and tip of bay leaf in the ingredients. Pour tomatoes over all.

Cook, covered, in moderate oven (350°F. Mark 4) until rice is tender and fluffy and tomato juice has been absorbed, about 1 hour or slightly longer. Remove clove of garlic and bay leaf before serving.

To serve, arrange rice in a mound with chicken round it. Garnish with stuffed olives and parsley. Serves 6.

CHICKEN ALMOND PIE

1   2½-pound roasting chicken,
       jointed
¾   pint water
2   ounces chopped celery (and a
       few chopped leaves)
1   tablespoon dried onion flakes
1½ teaspoons salt
1   4-ounce can sliced mushrooms
2   ounces butter or margarine
1   ounce plain flour
½   pint single cream or milk
⅛   teaspoon black pepper
¼   teaspoon dill weed
2   ounces browned blanched
       slivered almonds
12 ounces shortcrust pastry

Chicken Almond Pie

In a pot slowly cook chicken, water, celery, onion, salt, and liquid from mushrooms about 30 minutes, or until tender. Cool chicken and remove skin and bones, leaving meat in large pieces (about 12-14 ounces).

Melt butter and stir in flour, then cream, ½ pint stock from chicken, pepper, and dill weed. Cook and stir until mixture boils and is thickened. Stir in chicken, mushrooms, and almonds.

Turn into shallow 2-pint baking dish. Top with pastry; flute and prick. Bake in hot oven (400°F. Mark 6) 25 to 30 minutes, until golden brown. Serves 5 to 6.

CHICKEN CATALAN

1   3-pound roasting chicken,
       quartered
1   clove garlic
2   tablespoons olive or cooking oil
8   small white onions
2   teaspoons salt
½   teaspoon black pepper
4   fluid ounces chicken stock or
       bouillon
4   medium tomatoes, peeled and
       diced, or 1 1-pound can
       tomatoes, drained
8   ounces fresh mushrooms, sliced
6   ounces sliced, pimiento-stuffed
       olives
4   fluid ounces dry white wine
1½ ounces plain flour
Hot cooked rice

Brown chicken with garlic in hot oil in deep, flame-proof casserole; discard garlic. Add onions, salt, pepper, stock, and tomatoes. Cover and cook in moderate oven (375°F. Mark 5) 1 hour.

Add mushrooms and olives to chicken; cook 15 minutes longer.

Remove chicken and onions. Blend white wine and flour; stir into tomato-olive sauce. Cook, stirring constantly, until thickened. Add chicken and onions. Serve with hot rice. Serves 4.

CHICKEN-NOODLE PARTY CASSEROLE

1   4-pound boiling chicken, cut up
1¾ pints water
1   tablespoon salt
2   onions, sliced
6   whole black peppers
1   clove garlic, crushed
1   carrot, cut in half
Few celery leaves
4   ounces celery, sliced
3   ounces green pepper, chopped
2   ounces flour
Stock plus water to make 1½ pints
3   chopped canned pimientos
½   teaspoon black pepper
1   pound broad noodles
8   ounces grated Cheddar cheese
       (sharp)
Paprika

Combine chicken with water, salt, onions, whole black peppers, garlic, carrot, and celery leaves. Cover and cook slowly 3 hours.

Remove meat from chicken; cut in chunks. Strain stock; cool and skim off fat.

Fry sliced celery and green pepper in chicken fat 5 minutes. Stir in flour, then add stock and water. Cook until thickened, stirring constantly. Add pimientos, pepper, and chicken.

Cook noodles in boiling salted water until tender; drain. Put in 6½-pint shallow casserole or two smaller casseroles.

Pour chicken mixture over noodles. Mix lightly with fork. Add more salt, if desired. Sprinkle with cheese and paprika.

Cook in moderate oven (375°F. Mark 5) until bubbly hot, about 40 minutes. Serves 12.

"CHICKEN IN THE CORN" PIES

1   boiling chicken, 3½ pounds
1¾ pints hot water
4   teaspoons salt
1   stalk celery
1   small onion
12 ounces cooked peas
6   tablespoons flour
4   fluid ounces cold water
1   recipe maize flour pastry
       (see below)

Cover chicken with hot water. Add salt, celery, and onion. Cover and let simmer 2 to 2½ hours or until tender.

Remove meat from bones. Cube meat and place in 6 small casseroles. Add 2 ounces peas to each.

Thicken stock with flour that has been mixed to a paste with the cold water. Fill casseroles with the gravy to ½-inch from top.

Roll out pastry to ⅛-inch thickness and cut circles 1 inch larger than casseroles. Place rounds on the pies and crimp edges. Prick tops to allow steam to escape. Bake in hot oven (425°F. Mark 7) 25 to 30 minutes or until pastry is nicely browned. Serves 6.

Maize Flour Pastry for Meat or Chicken Pies: For maize flour pastry, stir 2½ ounces maize flour or polenta into sifted flour of 9-inch 2-crust pie pastry recipe. Cut in fat and use same amount of liquid as in recipe.

"Chicken in the Corn" Pies

Chicken Casserole Fredona

CHICKEN CASSEROLE FREDONA

1 roasting chicken, 3 to 4 pounds
Salt and pepper
Flour
2 ounces butter
4 carrots, diced
2 small turnips, diced
2 onions, diced
3 medium potatoes, diced
6 medium tomatoes, sliced
½ teaspoon salt
¼ teaspoon black pepper
1 teaspoon sugar
2 chicken stock cubes
¾ pint boiling water
2 tablespoons flour
1 tablespoon aromatic bitters

Cut chicken into serving pieces. Sprinkle both sides with salt and pepper. Put a little flour in paper bag, add chicken pieces and shake.

In frying pan fry pieces in butter until golden brown. Remove chicken and in same butter brown carrots, turnips, onions, and potatoes. Add tomatoes, salt, pepper, and sugar. Remove vegetables.

Dissolve stock cubes in boiling water. Blend flour with fat in frying pan, gradually add hot stock and aromatic bitters. Cook gravy, stirring constantly, until slightly thickened.

Place vegetables in bottom of deep casserole, pour half the gravy over them, arrange chicken pieces on top and pour on remaining gravy. Cook, covered, in moderate oven (350°F. Mark 4) 45 minutes. Serves 6.

CHICKEN NEAPOLITAN

1   4-pound chicken, cut in pieces
Salt and pepper
1   teaspoon Aromat
Flour
4   fluid ounces olive or other salad oil
1   medium onion, chopped
1   clove garlic, crushed
1   small green pepper, seeded and slivered
2   ounces sliced mushrooms
1   tablespoon chopped parsley
2   tablespoons tomato purée
12 fluid ounces water
6   fluid ounces dry sherry
Cooked spaghetti or noodles
Grated Parmesan cheese

Wipe chicken pieces with damp cloth; sprinkle flesh sides with salt, pepper, and Aromat. Coat lightly with flour. Brown well in heated oil.

Arrange browned chicken in deep casserole, or leave in the frying pan if it is large enough and can be covered. Add vegetables, tomato purée, and water.

Cover; simmer until chicken is almost tender. Stir occasionally and add very little more water. Sauce should be quite thick.

About 15 to 20 minutes before serving, add sherry.

Serve with cooked spaghetti. Pass cheese round. Serves 6.

CHICKEN WITH ALMOND SAUCE

3½-pound roasting chicken, cut up
1   ounce butter
2   tablespoons olive oil
4   medium tomatoes, cut in small wedges
2   fluid ounces sherry or white wine
3   ounces salted shredded almonds
12 fluid ounces chicken stock
⅛ teaspoon rosemary
Salt and pepper to taste
8   fluid ounces soured cream
Cooked rice

Brown chicken on all sides in butter and olive oil in frying pan. Transfer to casserole. Add tomatoes, sherry, almonds, chicken stock, and seasonings.

Cover and cook in moderate oven (350°F. Mark 4) 40 minutes. Stir in cream and heat in oven about 5 minutes.

Serve with hot cooked rice. Serves 4.

POT-LUCK CHICKEN CASSEROLE

1   4- to 5-pound dressed boiling chicken, cut in pieces
1½ ounces flour
Salt and pepper
2   ounces rendered chicken or cooking fat
12 small carrots, scraped
18 small white onions, peeled
3   stalks celery, cut in 1-inch lengths
Dash of allspice
1   bay leaf
¼ teaspoon marjoram
1   teaspoon Aromat
4   fluid ounces red wine

Roll chicken pieces in flour seasoned with salt and pepper. Brown in hot fat, turning frequently to brown evenly.

Place in a large casserole. Add carrots, onions, and celery.

Pour 8 fluid ounces water into pan in which chicken was browned; add 1 teaspoon salt, pinch of black pepper, allspice, bay leaf, marjoram, and Aromat. Simmer until pan juices are loosened. Strain into casserole.

Cover and cook in slow oven (300°F. Mark 2) 1½ hours.

Add wine. Increase heat to hot oven (400°F. Mark 6) and cook covered, for 1 hour. Serves 6.

SAUCY CHICKEN WITH HERB PEACHES

2 3½-pound roasting chickens, jointed
Flour, salt, pepper, margarine
1 16-ounce can creamed sweetcorn
1 10½ ounce can condensed cream of chicken soup, undiluted
8 fluid ounces undiluted evaporated milk
4 fluid ounces water
1 ounce dried onion flakes
1 ounce green pepper, finely chopped
¾ teaspoon salt
2 1-pound cans peach halves
2 ounces melted butter
2 tablespoons lemon juice
Dried thyme

Dip chicken into flour seasoned with salt and pepper. Brown in margarine in frying pan. Transfer to large baking dish with a cover.

In a saucepan, combine sweetcorn, soup, evaporated milk, water, onion, green pepper, and ¾ teaspoon salt. Heat until bubbly, stirring occasionally; pour over chicken.

Cover and cook in moderate oven (350°F. Mark 4) 40 to 45 minutes.

Drain peaches; place cup-sides up in shallow baking dish. Combine butter and lemon juice; sprinkle over peaches. Sprinkle with thyme. Place in oven during last 10 to 15 minutes that chicken is baking. Serves 6 to 8.

Saucy Chicken with Herb Peaches

Fish and Shellfish Casseroles

WITH CANNED OR COOKED FISH

THRIFTY TUNA CASSEROLE

1   10½-ounce can condensed cream
of mushroom soup
4   fluid ounces milk
1   7-ounce can drained tuna fish
2½ ounces crushed potato crisps
1   7-ounce can green peas, drained

Empty soup into a small casserole.
Add milk and mix thoroughly.

Add tuna, 2 ounces potato crisps and
peas. Stir well. Sprinkle top with remaining potato crisps.

Cook in moderate oven (375°F. Mark
5) 25 minutes. Serves 4.

TUNA-SPAGHETTI CASSEROLE

3   ounces butter or margarine*
6   tablespoons flour
1   teaspoon salt
Few grains black pepper
12 fluid ounces evaporated milk
1   8-ounce can tomato sauce
6   fluid ounces water
¼   teaspoon thyme
¾   teaspoon Aromat
2   7-ounce cans tuna fish
8   ounces spaghetti, cooked
12 ounces cooked or canned green
peas
14 ounces well seasoned mashed
potatoes
Melted butter or margarine

Melt butter or margarine in top of
double boiler; blend in flour, salt, and
pepper.

Combine evaporated milk, tomato
sauce, and water; add all at once. Stir
over low heat until smooth and thickened. Add thyme and Aromat; cover;
set over hot water; cook 10 minutes.

Meanwhile break tuna into fairly
large pieces; combine with spaghetti
and peas. Add sauce; mix well; pour
into casserole. Top with ring of mashed
potatoes; brush with melted butter or
margarine.

Cook in hot oven (425°F. Mark 7)
about 15 minutes or until potatoes are
golden brown. Serves 6.

* Note: Or, measure oil from tuna and
add enough butter or margarine to
make 3 ounces.

Tuna-Spaghetti Casserole

CHOPSTICK TUNA

1   10½-ounce can condensed cream
of mushroom soup
2   7-ounce cans tuna fish, drained
and broken into chunks
4   ounces celery, cut in ¼-inch
diagonal pieces
4   ounces cashew nuts
2   fluid ounces evaporated milk
1   tablespoon dried onion flakes
6-8 ounces chow mein noodles
1   11-ounce can mandarin orange
sections, well drained
Few sprigs of parsley

Mix soup, tuna, celery, nuts, evaporated milk, onion, and half the chow
mein noodles in a 3-pint bowl. Put into
a greased 2½-pint deep baking dish.
Top with remaining chow mein
noodles.

Cook near centre of moderate oven
(375°F. Mark 5) about 20 minutes, or
until bubbly hot. Take from oven. Top
with mandarin orange sections and
parsley. Serve immediately. Serves 4
to 6.

MUSHROOM-TUNA-NOODLE CASSEROLE

8   ounces noodles
1   7-ounce can tuna fish
2   hard-boiled eggs, sliced
6   ounces drained, cooked or canned
peas
1   10½-ounce can condensed cream of
mushroom soup
Liquid from cooked or canned peas
1   ounce grated cheese

Cook noodles in boiling salted water
until tender. Drain well and rinse with
hot water. Drain and discard oil from
tuna fish.

Arrange layers of cooked noodles,
sliced egg, flaked tuna, and peas in
greased 2½-pint casserole, starting and
ending with noodles.

Dilute mushroom soup with equal
amount of liquid from peas or milk.
Heat to boiling point, stirring to keep
smooth.

Pour over tuna-noodle mixture in
casserole, pushing mixture aside gently
to allow soup to run down to bottom.
Sprinkle with grated cheese.

Cook in moderate oven (375°F. Mark
5) until cheese is nicely browned and
mixture is heated through, 15 to 20
minutes. Serve at once. Serves 5.
Variation: Substitute 2 ounces crumbled potato crisps for grated cheese.

TUNA COMPANY CASSEROLE

6   ounces egg noodles
1   10½-ounce can condensed cream of
mushroom soup
8   fluid ounces milk

Chopstick Tuna

4   ounces mild Cheddar cheese, sliced
2   hard-boiled eggs, chopped
1   7-ounce can tuna fish*
6   tablespoons dry breadcrumbs,
buttered

Cook noodles in boiling salted water
until tender.

Empty soup into a pan and stir well,
then add milk and heat. Add grated
cheese and stir until it melts.

Combine drained noodles, eggs, and
tuna with sauce. Turn into buttered
casserole. Sprinkle buttered breadcrumbs over top.

Cook in moderate oven (350°F. Mark
4) 25 to 30 minutes. Serves 8.

* Note: Pour half a pint of hot water
over the tuna fish just as it comes from
the can to take off the excess oil.

TUNA AND RICE CASSEROLE

1   7-ounce can tuna fish
2   tablespoons chopped green
pepper
1   10½-ounce can condensed cream
of mushroom soup
8   fluid ounces milk
12 ounces rice, cooked
Buttered dry breadcrumbs
(optional)

Pour oil from tuna into a saucepan;
add green pepper and cook over low
heat 5 minutes, stirring occasionally.

Blend in soup, stirring constantly until smooth. Add milk; heat.

Place hot rice in greased 2½-pint
casserole. Arrange tuna chunks on rice.
Pour sauce over top. If desired, sprinkle with buttered breadcrumbs.

Cook in moderate oven (350°F. Mark
4) 20 to 30 minutes. Serves 4 to 5.

JIFFY TUNA-RICE CASSEROLE

6   ounces rice, cooked
1   7-ounce can tuna fish
4   ounces grated Cheddar cheese
1   ounce parsley, chopped
2   tablespoons chopped onion
8   fluid ounces milk
2   beaten eggs
Salt and pepper
½   teaspoon Aromat

Combine all ingredients, seasoning
to taste. Turn into greased casserole.

Cook in moderate oven (350°F. Mark
4) about 1 hour. Serves 4 to 5.

TUNA CASSEROLE WITH SCONE TOPPING

1 7-ounce can tuna, flaked
2 ounces canned mushrooms
8-10 ounces frozen mixed vegetables, cooked
¾ pint medium white sauce
1 ounce sifted plain flour
5 ounces maize flour or polenta
1 teaspoon baking powder
1 tablespoon sugar
½ teaspoon salt
¼ teaspoon bicarbonate of soda
¾ cup sour milk
1½ tablespoons cooking fat or margarine, melted

Combine tuna, mushrooms, and vegetables. Season well and turn into buttered 2½-pint casserole. Pour white sauce over mixture.

Mix flour, maize flour, baking powder, sugar, salt, and soda. Add sour milk to dry ingredients. Stir in melted fat and mix until smooth. Spread lightly on top of casserole.

Cook in moderate oven (350°F. Mark 4) until corn bread is done, about 25 minutes. Remove from oven and invert on a hot serving plate, or, if desired, serve from the casserole. Serves 4 to 6.

TUNA-BROAD BEAN CASSEROLE

1 7-ounce can tuna, coarsely flaked
1 8-ounce packet frozen or canned lima or broad beans, thawed
1 10½-ounce can condensed cream of celery soup
2 fluid ounces water
3 or 4 slices toast
3 or 4 slices processed Cheddar cheese

Combine tuna, beans, soup, and water. Turn into shallow casserole.

Cover each slice of toast with a slice of cheese. Cut into triangles or other decorative pattern and arrange on top.

Cook in moderate oven (375°F. Mark 5) 45 minutes. Serves 3 or 4.

SALMON, NOODLES, AND MUSHROOMS

2 tablespoons chopped onion
2 ounces melted butter
3 tablespoons flour
1½ teaspoons salt
¼ teaspoon black pepper
¾ pint milk
2 tablespoons horseradish
¼ teaspoon Worcestershire sauce
8 ounces canned salmon, flaked
4 ounces canned mushrooms
2 tablespoons chopped canned pimiento
6 ounces cooked peas
4 ounces noodles
2 ounces dry breadcrumbs

Fry onion in 1 ounce butter until golden. Blend in flour, salt, and pepper.

Gradually add milk and cook, stirring constantly, until thickened.

Remove from heat. Add horseradish and Worcestershire sauce.

Gently combine salmon, mushrooms, pimiento, peas, and noodles with white sauce.

Turn into buttered 2½-pint casserole. Toss breadcrumbs with remaining 1 ounce butter and sprinkle over casserole.

Cook in moderate oven (350°F. Mark 4) 20 minutes. Serves 4 to 6.

TOMATO-SALMON PIE

Scone Crust:
8 ounces plain flour
3 teaspoons baking powder
½ teaspoon salt
2 ounces margarine or butter
5-6 fluid ounces milk

Sift, measure flour. Resift with baking powder and salt. Cut in margarine or butter.

Add milk and toss lightly with fork. Knead lightly on floured muslin until smooth on one side. Roll out ¼ inch thick. Fit into baking dish.

Filling:
3 tablespoons chopped onion
1 ounce chopped green pepper
2 ounces margarine or butter
3 tablespoons plain flour
1 medium and 1 small can tomatoes
¼ teaspoon salt
⅛ teaspoon black pepper
2 teaspoons sugar
1 pound canned salmon
Grated cheese

Sauté onion and green pepper in margarine or butter. Blend in flour. Add tomatoes, seasonings, and sugar and cook 15 minutes.

Spread salmon on top of scone dough. Cover with tomato sauce.

Cook in hot oven (400°F. Mark 6) 20 to 25 minutes. Sprinkle with cheese. Serves 6.

THRIFTY FISH CASSEROLE

1 onion, sliced
1 ounce diced celery and leaves
6 ounces cubed potatoes
6 ounces diced carrots
8 fluid ounces boiling water
½ teaspoon salt
¼ teaspoon black pepper
½ bay leaf
8 ounces cooked fish, flaked
1 tablespoon flour
8 fluid ounces evaporated milk
2 tablespoons dry breadcrumbs
½ ounce butter or margarine

Cook vegetables with water and seasonings until tender.

Add fish, flour, and milk, mixed together. Heat to boiling. Pour into 2½-pint casserole. Cover with crumbs. Dot with butter or margarine. Brown in moderate oven (350°F. Mark 4). Serves 4.

Tomato-Salmon Pie

SALMON CHEESE PIE

9 ounces sifted plain flour
3 teaspoons baking powder
½ teaspoon salt
3 ounces margarine or cooking fat
2 eggs
4 fluid ounces milk
1 pound canned salmon
1 tablespoon grated onion
2 tablespoons salmon juice
5-6 ounces Cheddar cheese, thinly sliced

Sift together flour, baking powder, and salt. Cut in fat until mixture resembles fine crumbs.

Combine eggs and milk; beat well. Add liquid to dry ingredients and mix only until all flour is dampened.

Roll out ⅔ of dough on well floured pastry cloth or board to 11-inch circle. Fit into 9-inch pie dish or cake pan.

Drain salmon. Flake into bowl, removing skin and bones. Add onion and salmon juice. Turn into pastry-lined pan. Cover with cheese.

Roll out remaining ⅓ of dough to 7-inch circle. Place on top of cheese.

Bake in moderate oven (375°F. Mark 5) 25 to 30 minutes. Serve hot with vegetable sauce. Serves 6.

Vegetable Sauce: Melt 2 ounces butter in saucepan. Blend in 1 ounce flour and 1 teaspoon French mustard; mix well.

Gradually add ¾ pint milk. Cook over low heat, stirring constantly, until thick. Add ½ teaspoon salt and 12 ounces any desired cooked green vegetable. Or garnish with 2 tablespoons chopped parsley.

Salmon Cheese Pie

FISH AND NOODLES

3 tablespoons chopped onion
1 ounce diced celery
½ ounce butter or margarine
½ teaspoon salt
Black pepper to taste
1 15-ounce can tomatoes
8 ounces noodles, cooked
1 pound flaked cooked fish
Breadcrumbs mixed with melted
    butter or margarine

Cook onion and celery in butter a few minutes. Add salt, pepper, and tomatoes; heat to boiling. (5 raw tomatoes, cut in pieces, may be used instead of 8 ounces cooked.)

Put alternate layers of noodles, fish, and hot tomato mixture into greased casserole. Top with crumbs.

Cook in moderate oven (350°F. Mark 4) 20 minutes or until the mixture is heated through and breadcrumbs are browned.

Variations: Use cooked spaghetti or macaroni instead of noodles. Instead of tomatoes, use cheese sauce—a thin white sauce to which 2 ounces grated sharp cheese has been added for each half pint of sauce. Sprinkle with grated cheese the last 10 minutes of cooking.

TUNA FISH-AVOCADO CASSEROLE

2 7-ounce cans tuna fish
2 ounces butter or margarine
4 tablespoons flour
2 teaspoons mustard
12 fluid ounces milk
4 fluid ounces single cream or
    top milk
Salt and pepper
1 avocado, peeled and diced
Dry breadcrumbs

Drain tuna; flake finely. Melt butter or margarine in double boiler and blend with flour and mustard.

Add milk and cream. Cook over hot water, stirring constantly, until smooth and thickened.

Add tuna. Season to taste with salt and pepper. Remove from heat. Fold in avocado.

Fill casserole with alternate layers of breadcrumbs and tuna mixture, ending with crumbs. Dot with butter or margarine.

Cook in hot oven (400°F. Mark 6) until mixture begins to bubble. Serve at once. Serves 6.

Baked Tuna in Seashells

TUNA HOLIDAY PIE

3 7-ounce cans tuna fish
1 chicken stock cube
12 fluid ounces boiling water
1 ounce butter or margarine
1½ ounces plain flour
6 fluid ounces double cream
3 medium-sized onion slices
1 ounce grated Parmesan cheese
6 ounces grated Emmenthal cheese
1 tablespoon lemon juice
5 fluid ounces chilli pickle
½ teaspoon salt
2 tablespoons chopped parsley
1 unbaked 10-inch flan case, well
    chilled

Drain tuna, reserving 3 tablespoons oil for use in cheese sauce.

Dissolve chicken stock cube in boiling water.

In a saucepan, melt butter or margarine over low heat; add tuna oil and flour and blend. Add chicken stock, cream, and onion slices. Cook over low heat until thickened, stirring constantly.

Remove onion slices; add cheese and stir until melted. Add lemon juice, chilli sauce, salt, parsley, and tuna; mix well.

Pour into unbaked flan case. Bake in hot oven (400°F. Mark 6) 30 to 35 minutes, or until pastry is done and cheese is browned and bubbly. Serves 6 to 8.

RICE AND FISH CASSEROLE

½ ounce margarine
1 tablespoon flour
Salt, pepper, paprika to taste
8 fluid ounces milk
8 ounces flaked cooked or canned
    fish
6 ounces rice, cooked

Melt margarine in saucepan. Add flour, salt, pepper, and paprika, stirring until blended and smooth. Add milk slowly, stirring constantly to avoid lumps. Cook until smooth, add fish and heat thoroughly.

Pour creamed fish over cooked rice in attractive casserole dish. Garnish with parsley, grated cheese or chopped olives. Serves 4.

BAKED TUNA IN SEASHELLS

1 7-ounce can tuna fish
1 ounce green pepper, chopped
½ medium onion, chopped
2 ounces celery, chopped
¼ teaspoon salt
Dash of black pepper
½ teaspoon Worcestershire sauce
4 fluid ounces mayonnaise
2 ounces dry buttered bread-
    crumbs

Break tuna into chunks and combine ingredients except breadcrumbs.

Place in individual seashells or casserole dishes. Sprinkle with buttered crumbs.

Cook in a moderate oven (350°F. Mark 4) about 30 minutes. Serves 4.

Tuna Holiday Pie

SCALLOPED SALMON AND BEANS

1 8-ounce can salmon
1 20-ounce can or 1 12-ounce
    packet frozen lima or butter
    beans
Milk
2 ounces butter or margarine
1 ounce plain flour
1 teaspoon salt
Few grains black pepper
½ teaspoon Aromat
8 fluid ounces milk
3 ounces buttered fresh bread-
    crumbs

Drain salmon liquid into cup.

Cook frozen beans according to directions on packet; drain; add cooking water to salmon liquid and then add milk to make up 8 fluid ounces.

Melt butter; blend in flour, seasoning and Aromat.

Add the 8 fluid ounces of liquid; stir over low heat until smooth and thickened.

Flake salmon, removing bones. Combine with beans in 2-pint casserole.

Pour sauce over all; top with buttered crumbs.

Cook in moderate oven (375°F. Mark 5) until crumbs are brown, 15 to 20 minutes. Serves 4.

TUNA-RUNNER BEAN CASSEROLE

3 to 4 slices bread
1 ounce butter or margarine, melted
1 1-pound can runner beans
1 10½-ounce can condensed cream
    of mushroom soup
1 7-ounce can tuna fish, flaked

Cut bread slices into cubes or cut into fish shapes with a biscuit cutter. Toss in melted butter.

Drain beans; add liquid to pan in which butter was melted. Cook until liquid is reduced to 4 fluid ounces.

Add soup, beans, and undrained tuna; heat. Turn into shallow casserole. Arrange cubes or "fish" on top. Cook in hot oven (400°F. Mark 6) 15 minutes. Serves 4.

Scalloped Salmon and Beans

SALMON DINNER CASSEROLE

1 pound canned salmon
2 ounces butter or other fat
2 tablespoons flour
½ teaspoon salt
Dash of black pepper
1 pint liquid (liquid from
      canned salmon plus milk to
      make volume)
4 ounces Cheddar cheese, grated
6 ounces rice, cooked
6 ounces cooked peas
1 ounce butter or other fat, melted
2 ounces dry breadcrumbs

Drain and flake salmon, saving liquid.

Melt butter, and blend in flour and seasonings. Add liquid gradually, and cook until thick and smooth, stirring constantly. Stir in cheese, and heat until melted.

Combine salmon with rice, peas, and cheese sauce. Place mixture in well greased casserole. Combine butter and crumbs; sprinkle over casserole.

Cook in moderate oven (375°F. Mark 5) until brown, 30 minutes. Serves 6.

SHERRIED TUNA FISH-CRAB CASSEROLE

1½ ounces butter or margarine
3 tablespoons flour
1¼ pints milk
4 ounces grated Cheddar cheese
3 fluid ounces sherry
3 lightly beaten eggs
1 6½-ounce can crabmeat, or 8
     ounces fresh crabmeat
1 7-ounce can tuna fish, drained
     and flaked
Salt, celery salt, onion salt, and
     black pepper to taste
2 ounces buttered dry breadcrumbs

Melt butter and stir in flour; add milk and cook, stirring constantly, until mixture is thickened and smooth. Add cheese and stir over low heat until melted.

Remove from heat. Stir in sherry, then eggs; add crabmeat and tuna; season to taste.

Pour mixture into a greased casserole (10×6×2 inches); sprinkle with buttered breadcrumbs.

Cook in a slow oven (325°F. Mark 3) for 1 hour, or until a knife inserted comes out clean. Serves 6.

Quick Salmon Macaroni Bake

MACARONI AND SALMON SURPRISE

1 pound canned salmon, drained
2 1-pound cans macaroni cheese
3 ounces sliced peeled cucumber
2 medium tomatoes, thinly sliced
1 ounce fresh breadcrumbs
1 ounce melted butter or margarine
1 ounce grated Cheddar cheese

Remove skin and bones from salmon; flake. Arrange macaroni, salmon, cucumber, and tomatoes in alternate layers in greased 3½-pint casserole.

Mix breadcrumbs, butter, and cheese; sprinkle over top.

Cook in moderate oven (375°F. Mark 5) for 45 minutes. Serves 4 to 6.

MEXICAN SALMON

1 pound canned pink salmon,
    undrained
1 egg
1 green pepper, chopped
1 small onion, chopped
1 8-ounce can tomatoes
⅛ teaspoon black pepper
2 teaspoons chilli seasoning
1 teaspoon salt
1½ ounces dry breadcrumbs
3 sprigs parsley, minced

Bone salmon and blend with egg in frying pan. Add next 7 ingredients, reserving 2 tablespoons of the crumbs. Simmer 10 minutes; add parsley.

Turn into buttered baking dish or individual casseroles. Top with balance of breadcrumbs.

Cook in hot oven (400°F. Mark 6) until crumbs are brown. Serves 6.

QUICK SALMON MACARONI BAKE

1 7- or 8-ounce can salmon
1 pound macaroni cheese
2 ounces celery, finely chopped
1 teaspoon grated onion
½ teaspoon mustard
2 tablespoons milk
Garlic bread cubes (below)

Drain and flake salmon. Combine with macaroni cheese, celery, onion, and mustard.

Spoon into 2½-pint baking dish; pour milk over top; sprinkle with garlic bread cubes.

Cook in moderate oven (350°F. Mark 4) 25 to 30 minutes, or until bubbling and browned.

To make garlic bread cubes: Melt 2 ounces butter or margarine with ½ clove garlic; sauté 5 minutes; remove garlic. Toss 1 ounce small stale bread cubes in butter. Serves 4.

Salmon Casserole

SALMON CASSEROLE

1 small onion, chopped
1 ounce green pepper, chopped
1 ounce celery, chopped
1 ounce mushrooms, sliced
2 ounces butter or margarine
3 tablespoons flour
1½ teaspoons salt
¼ teaspoon black pepper
14 fluid ounces evaporated milk
8 fluid ounces water
1 pound canned salmon, boned
    and flaked
12 ounces fresh, frozen, or canned
    peas
4 ounces crushed potato crisps

Sauté onion, green pepper, celery, and mushrooms in melted butter until lightly browned. Add flour, salt, and pepper and mix well.

Gradually stir in evaporated milk, then water and cook until smooth and thickened, stirring constantly.

Arrange layers of salmon, peas, white sauce, and potato crisps in buttered 3½-pint casserole. Top with layer of potato crisps and dot with butter.

Cover and cook in moderate oven (375°F. Mark 5) 25 minutes. Uncover and bake 10 minutes longer or until top is brown.

When using individual casseroles, cut cooking time in half. Serves 6.

THRIFTY FISH PIE WITH POTATO TOPPING

1½ ounces butter or margarine
1 ounce plain flour
1 teaspoon salt
¼ teaspoon black pepper
¾ pint milk
8 ounces cooked fish, flaked
1 small onion, grated
6 ounces cooked or canned carrots
6 ounces canned peas
14 ounces mashed potatoes

Melt butter or margarine in heavy saucepan. Add flour, salt, and pepper; mix well.

Add milk, stirring constantly, and cook over low heat until sauce is thick and smooth.

Add flaked fish, onion, carrots, and peas. Pour into 3½-pint casserole. Cover with mashed potatoes.

Cook in hot oven (425°F. Mark 7) 20 minutes. Serves 4.

CASSEROLES WITH FRESH OR FROZEN FISH

FISH AND VEGETABLE CASSEROLE

1 pound frozen fish fillets, thawed
Salt and pepper
Vegetable oil
1 1-pound can new potatoes
½ medium onion, finely chopped
3 medium tomatoes, peeled and
    thinly sliced
8 fluid ounces soured cream
1 tablespoon lemon juice
½ teaspoon dry mustard
¼ teaspoon salt
Dash of black pepper
Paprika

Cut fish into serving pieces and season with salt and pepper. Cook fish gently in hot oil until golden.

Cook potatoes and onion in hot oil until golden.

Arrange fish, potatoes, and onions in a wide shallow casserole. Cover with tomato slices. Season with salt.

Combine soured cream, lemon juice, mustard, salt, and pepper. Pour over tomato slices. Sprinkle with paprika.

Cook in moderate oven (350°F. Mark 4) 15 to 20 minutes. Serves 4.

Variations: Substitute 1½ pounds halibut or other white fish for 1 pound frozen fish fillets. Substitute (do not brown) 6-8 ounces cooked or canned green peas for potatoes.

FISH FILLETS FLORENTINE

2 ounces butter or margarine
4 tablespoons flour
½ pint rich milk
1 4-ounce can mushroom stems
    and pieces
¼ pint Sauternes, Rhine, Chablis,
    or other white wine
1 ounce grated Parmesan cheese
½ teaspoon Worcestershire sauce
Salt and pepper to taste
1 pound chopped, well drained
    cooked spinach
1½ pounds fish fillets (sole, halibut,
    salmon, or other favourite
    fish)

Melt butter or margarine and stir in flour. Add milk and liquid from mushrooms. Cook, stirring constantly, until mixture is thickened and smooth.

Add mushrooms, wine, cheese, and seasonings.

Spread spinach evenly over bottom of greased shallow casserole (large enough so that layer of spinach is not more than 1 inch deep—8×12×2 inches). Lay fillets on top of spinach. Cover with wine-cream sauce.

Cook in moderate oven (375°F. Mark 5) until fish flakes when tested with fork, about 25 minutes. Serves 4 to 5.

FISH FILLETS DIVAN

2 pounds fish fillets
1 ounce melted butter
Salt and pepper
2 packets frozen broccoli
2 ounces butter
3 tablespoons flour
12 fluid ounces milk
4 ounces Cheddar cheese, cubed
¼ teaspoon salt
½ teaspoon dry mustard
⅛ teaspoon garlic salt
½ teaspoon Worcestershire sauce

Brush fillets with melted butter; sprinkle with salt and pepper. Pre-heat grill. Grill 3 inches from source of heat for 10 to 15 minutes, or until fish flakes easily when tested with a fork.

Cook broccoli according to directions on packet.

Prepare cheese sauce as follows: melt butter in a saucepan; remove from heat, stir in flour, then milk. Return to heat and cook, stirring constantly, until thickened. Add remaining ingredients and continue cooking until cheese is melted and sauce smooth.

Arrange broccoli in casserole. Pour half of sauce over it; arrange fish fillets on top. Top with remaining sauce. Cook in moderate oven (350°F. Mark 4) for about 10 minutes to heat thoroughly. Serves 6.

FISH DINNER CASSEROLE

4 ounces butter or margarine
1 small onion, thinly sliced
1½ tablespoons flour
12 fluid ounces milk
1 packet frozen fish fillets (cod,
    haddock, or halibut) cut in
    pieces
1 small can prawns, drained, or 1
    12-ounce packet frozen
    prawns (cleaned)
1 teaspoon chopped parsley
1 small can sliced mushrooms,
    drained
3 raw potatoes, sliced

Melt butter in saucepan. Add onion and cook until soft. Remove pan from heat; stir in flour and then milk.

Return to heat. Cook, stirring constantly, until smooth and thickened.

Arrange fish and prawns in a buttered casserole. Sprinkle with parsley and mushrooms. Pour half of the sauce over fish. Top with layer of sliced potatoes and pour remaining sauce over all.

Cook in moderate oven (375°F. Mark 5) 40 minutes or until potatoes are cooked. Serves 6.

Fish Fillets Divan

SWEDISH HALIBUT

2 large mild onions
1½ ounces melted butter or
    margarine
4 tablespoons flour
1 teaspoon salt
1½ pounds (or 3 8-ounce cans)
    cooked tomatoes
2 bay leaves
2 pounds halibut steaks

Cut onions in ¼-inch slices, and place all but 2 slices in well greased casserole.

Slip the 2 slices into rings; dip into melted butter or margarine and then into seasoned flour and set aside.

Blend 3 tablespoons flour and 1 ounce butter with tomatoes and add to casserole. Place fish on it. Brush with rest of butter. Sprinkle with flour and salt. Top with onion rings.

Cook in very hot oven (450°F. Mark 8) 30 minutes. Serves 6.

FISH FILLET AND CHEESE CASSEROLE

1 pound frozen fish fillets, thawed
    (haddock, halibut, or sole)
8 fluid ounces milk
8 ounces grated sharp Cheddar
    cheese
¼ teaspoon paprika
¼ teaspoon dry mustard
¼ teaspoon Worcestershire sauce
6 ounces fresh breadcrumbs

Cut fish into serving pieces and put in shallow 2½-pint casserole.

Combine milk, cheese, and seasonings in top of double boiler. Cook over boiling water, stirring constantly, until cheese melts. Add breadcrumbs and pour over fish.

Cook in moderate oven (375°F. Mark 5) until puffy and lightly browned on top, about 25 minutes. Serves 4.

Fish Dinner Casserole

FISH NEWBURG CASSEROLE

2½ pounds haddock
8 ounces fresh mushrooms, sliced
2 ounces butter or margarine
2 tablespoons flour
½ pint milk
8 ounces Cheddar cheese,
    shredded
Salt and pepper
2 teaspoons Worcestershire sauce
2 fluid ounces sherry
2 ounces dry buttered crumbs

Simmer fish in small amount of water until tender. Remove skin and flake fish into large pieces.

Cook mushrooms gently in 1 ounce butter about 4 minutes over low heat.

Melt 1 ounce butter in a saucepan; blend in flour.

Slowly add milk and cook, stirring constantly, until sauce thickens.

Add cheese and cook, stirring constantly, until cheese is melted and blended in, about 3 minutes.

Add seasonings, sherry, fish, and mushrooms.

Turn into buttered casserole. Sprinkle with buttered crumbs.

Cook in slow oven (300°F. Mark 2) 20 minutes. Serves 6.

HADDOCK CASSEROLE

1 small onion, minced
8 ounces fresh mushrooms, sliced
2 tablespoons cooking oil
¾ pint medium white sauce
½ pint soured cream
4 ounces grated sharp cheese
1 small packet frozen peas, cooked
    and drained
2 pounds haddock fillets, cooked
    and flaked

Gently cook onions and mushrooms in cooking oil for 5 minutes. Add to hot white sauce with remaining ingredients. Turn into a casserole.

Place under grill until bubbly and delicately browned. Serves 8.

Gently cook onions and mushrooms in cooking oil for 5 minutes. Add to hot

SALMON ORIENTALE

2 pounds salmon steaks, cut 1-inch
    thick
2 teaspoons salt
Dash of black pepper
2 ounces plain flour
2 ounces melted butter or margarine
8 ounces celery, chopped
6 ounces onion rings
3 tablespoons chopped green pepper
2 7-ounce cans sweetcorn
2 tablespoons soy sauce

Sprinkle salmon on both sides with 1 teaspoon salt and dash of pepper. Roll in flour.

Brown steaks quickly in fat. Place in large, well greased casserole.

Cook celery, onion, and green pepper in remaining fat until almost tender. Add sweetcorn and soy sauce; pour over the salmon. Sprinkle with remaining salt.

Cover and cook in moderate oven (350°F. Mark 4) 25 to 30 minutes. Serves 6.

HALIBUT AND SAUERKRAUT CASSEROLE

1½ ounces butter or margarine
1½ tablespoons flour
1 medium onion, chopped
¼ teaspoon salt
⅛ teaspoon black pepper
¼ teaspoon marjoram
½ teaspoon dill seed
1 1-pound can sauerkraut
1 pound halibut
⅛ teaspoon salt
Dash of paprika

Melt butter. Blend in flour gradually, stirring constantly, until lightly browned. Add onion, salt, pepper, marjoram, dill seed, and sauerkraut. Mix thoroughly and turn into casserole. Put fish on top. Cover.

Cook in moderate oven (350°F. Mark 4) 40 to 45 minutes. Sprinkle with remaining salt and paprika. Brown under grill. Serves 4.

FISH DINNER CASSEROLE (No. 2)

4 to 6 medium potatoes
1 pound frozen fish fillets, thawed
    (cod, haddock, or sole)
2 ounces melted butter or margarine
Salt and pepper
1 ounce chopped parsley
1 pound frozen or canned peas

Boil the potatoes and allow to cool. If fish fillets are large cut them lengthwise to make 8 pieces. Lay fish skin-side up and brush with melted butter or margarine. Sprinkle with salt, pepper, and parsley.

Roll each and fasten with toothpicks. Place in centre of large shallow casserole. Cut potatoes in thin slices and stand them round inside edge of casserole so slices overlap. Leave a space between fish and potatoes for peas to be added later.

Brush potatoes and fish with remaining butter. Sprinkle fish with paprika.

Cook in hot oven (400°F. Mark 6) 30 minutes. Cook or heat peas. Drain. Season to taste. Place in space left in casserole. Remove toothpicks before serving. Serves 4.

SUNSET SCALLOP

1 8-ounce can tomatoes
¼ pint water
4 whole cloves
1 tablespoon sugar
1 teaspoon salt
1 ounce butter or margarine
2 tablespoons flour
1 ounce lard
½ medium onion, finely chopped
2 pounds fish fillets

Cook tomatoes, water, cloves, sugar, and salt for 5 minutes. Strain.

Melt butter in top of double boiler; add flour and stir until well blended. Cook 1 minute.

Slowly add the hot strained tomato mixture and stir until thickened. Cook 2 minutes longer.

Melt lard and cook onions until clear. Place cooked onions in a greased casserole.

Wipe fillets with a damp cloth and place on onions. Pour hot sauce over fish.

Cook in very hot oven (450°F. Mark 8), allowing 10 minutes per inch thickness of fish.

If frozen fillets are used, increase time to 20 minutes for each inch thickness of fish. Serves 6.

STUFFED FILLETS IN CHEESE SAUCE

2 pounds fish fillets
2 tablespoons lemon juice
Salt and pepper
2 ounces melted butter or margarine
Bread stuffing (below)
Cheese sauce (below)

Dip the fillets in melted butter. Stuff them with bread stuffing, roll up, and fasten with toothpicks.

Place in a 12-inch rectangular casserole. Pour the lemon juice over them and sprinkle with salt and pepper.

Pour the cheese sauce into the dish, and cook in slow oven (325°F. Mark 3) for 30 minutes. Serves 6.

Bread Stuffing:
4 ounces dry breadcrumbs
4 ounces melted butter or margarine
¼ teaspoon salt
⅛ teaspoon black pepper
2 tablespoons chopped parsley

Combine ingredients in the order given and mix well.

Cheese Sauce:
1 ounce butter or margarine
2 tablespoons flour
12 fluid ounces milk
8 ounces grated sharp Cheddar
    cheese
½ teaspoon salt
⅛ teaspoon paprika
½ teaspoon dry mustard

Melt butter, add flour and mix well. Slowly add milk, grated cheese, and seasonings and stir until thickened.

CASSEROLES WITH SHELLFISH, FRESH, FROZEN, AND CANNED

HOT SEAFOOD SALAD

2 ounces green pepper, chopped
1 medium onion (4 ounces), chopped
4 ounces celery, chopped
8 ounces canned or cooked crab-meat, flaked
8 ounces canned or cooked prawns, cut in pieces
½ to ¾ teaspoon salt
Dash of black pepper
1 teaspoon Worcestershire sauce
8 fluid ounces mayonnaise
3 ounces fresh breadcrumbs
1 ounce melted butter

Combine vegetables, crabmeat, salt, pepper, prawns, Worcestershire sauce, and mayonnaise.

Put mixture in greased 1½-pint casserole or 8 individual shells. Toss crumbs in butter; sprinkle over top.

Cook in moderate oven (350°F. Mark 4) until hot and crumbs are golden brown, 30 minutes. Serves 6 to 8.

SEAFOOD DINNER CASSEROLE

8 ounces cooked or canned prawns, cleaned and chopped
8 ounces clams, chopped
8 ounces flaked canned crabmeat
Salt and pepper
1 tablespoon minced celery leaves
6 fluid ounces medium white sauce
2 7-ounce cans sweetcorn
6 buttered toast triangles

Place the prawns, clams, and crabmeat in bottom of buttered casserole. Season with salt and pepper. Sprinkle with celery leaves. Pour over white sauce.

Season sweetcorn and add to casserole. Arrange toast to cover most of the top. If the sweetcorn is dry, moisten with a little milk.

Cook in moderate oven (350°F. Mark 4) about 25 minutes. Serves 6.

PRAWN CREOLE CASSEROLE

1 10- to 12-ounce can prawns
2 10½-ounce cans condensed cream of tomato soup
1 small onion, chopped
2 7-ounce cans sweetcorn
1 canned pimiento cut in strips
3 tablespoons chopped green pepper
1 teaspoon chilli seasoning
3 ounces dry buttered crumbs

Clean black veins from prawns and combine all ingredients except crumbs.

Place in casserole. Top with crumbs.

Cook in moderate oven (375°F. Mark 5) about 30 minutes. Serves 6.

PARTY PRAWN PIE

4 ounces butter or margarine
1 ounce plain flour
½ teaspoon salt
⅛ teaspoon black pepper
¼ teaspoon ground mace
¾ pint milk
1 tablespoon sherry (optional)
1 pound cooked cleaned prawns
1 tablespoon lemon juice
8 ounces sliced fresh mushrooms
2 ounces puffed rice breakfast cereal
½ ounce melted butter or margarine

Melt 2 ounces butter and stir in flour and seasonings. Add milk slowly, stirring constantly, and cook until thickened, stirring occasionally. Stir in sherry.

Sprinkle prawns with lemon juice. Cook mushrooms in remaining butter until golden brown. Reserve a few prawns and mushrooms for garnish, if desired.

Fold remaining prawns and mushrooms into sauce. Pour into buttered 2½-pint casserole.

Mix puffed rice breakfast cereal with melted butter and sprinkle over mixture. Garnish with prawns and mushrooms.

Cook in hot oven (400°F. Mark 6) about 20 minutes or until browned. Garnish with parsley, if desired. Serves 6.

PRAWN AND TOMATO CASSEROLE

1¼ pints boiling water
1 teaspoon salt
6 ounces maize flour or polenta
2 rashers streaky bacon, chopped
1 8-ounce can tomatoes
3 tablespoons finely chopped onion
3 tablespoons finely chopped green pepper
1 teaspoon salt
⅛ teaspoon black pepper
½ teaspoon Worcestershire sauce
6 ounces black olives
1 10½-ounce can prawns, cleaned
3 ounces Cheddar cheese, grated

Add 1 teaspoon salt to boiling water; gradually stir in maize flour and cook until thickened.

Fry bacon until crisp; add tomatoes, onion, green pepper, 1 teaspoon salt, pepper, and Worcestershire sauce to bacon and dripping. Cook 10 minutes.

Stone olives and cut in large pieces. Add with prawns to vegetable mixture.

Place half of maize flour in 2½-pint casserole. Cover with half of prawn-vegetable mixture and half of cheese. Repeat layers.

Cook in moderate oven (350°F. Mark 4) 30 minutes. Serves 6.

Party Prawn Pie

CLAM AND SWEETCORN CASSEROLE

2 eggs
8 fluid ounces milk
10 coarsely crumbled cream crackers
1 7-ounce can minced clams, un-drained
6 ounces frozen sweetcorn, thawed just enough to separate
1½ ounces melted butter or margarine
1 tablespoon chopped green pepper
2 tablespoons finely chopped onion
½ teaspoon Worcestershire sauce
About ¼ teaspoon salt
2 ounces grated Cheddar cheese

Beat eggs; add milk and crumbled crackers. Allow to stand a few minutes to soften.

Add remaining ingredients except cheese and gently mix together. Add more salt to taste if crackers are unsalted. Turn into 2½-pint casserole.

Cook in moderate oven (350°F. Mark 4) until firm, about 50 minutes. Sprinkle with cheese. Cook until cheese melts, about 5 minutes longer. Serves 4 to 6.

SCALLOPS NEWBURG CASSEROLE

8 scallops
1½ ounces butter
1 teaspoon lemon juice
2 teaspoons flour
¼ teaspoon salt
Dash of cayenne pepper
½ pint single cream
2 well beaten egg yolks
2 ounces dry buttered breadcrumbs

If scallops are very large cut into pieces. Cook in salted water 3 to 5 minutes. Drain and dry.

Put 1 ounce butter in a frying pan and add scallops. Heat 3 minutes and add lemon juice.

Melt remaining ½ ounce butter in saucepan. Add flour and stir until well blended.

Add salt and cayenne. Add cream gradually, stirring constantly, until mixture thickens.

Remove from heat and very slowly add to beaten egg yolks. Add scallops. Pour into 2½-pint casserole. Sprinkle with crumbs.

Brown in hot oven (425°F. Mark 7) 10 minutes. Serves 4.

CRABMEAT AND CHEESE BAKE

3 tablespoons mayonnaise or salad
    cream
1 tablespoon French mustard
¼ teaspoon salt
1 6½-ounce can crabmeat
4 ounces celery, chopped
8 thin bread slices
6 ounces Cheddar cheese, sliced
2 eggs
8 fluid ounces milk
1 teaspoon Worcestershire sauce

Combine mayonnaise, mustard, and
salt. Mix with combined crabmeat and
celery. Spread between bread slices.
Cut sandwiches in halves.

Alternate layers of sandwiches and
cheese in greased casserole. Beat eggs;
add milk and Worcestershire sauce.
Pour into casserole. Cover and cook in
slow oven (325°F. Mark 3) 45 minutes.
Serves 4.

PRAWNS IN BARBECUE SAUCE

8 ounces cleaned prawns, home-
    cooked or canned
8 ounces rice, cooked
Mexican barbecue sauce (below)
4 ounces grated cheese
Black olives (optional)

Make alternate layers of prawns and
rice in a casserole. Pour sauce over rice
and prawn layers.

Top with grated cheese and cook in
moderate oven (350°F. Mark 4) for 20
minutes. Garnish with olives. Serves 4
to 5.

Mexican Barbecue Sauce:

4 ounces butter or margarine
1 small onion, grated
1 clove garlic, crushed
1½ teaspoons mustard
2 tablespoons chilli seasoning
8 fluid ounces tomato ketchup
4 fluid ounces vinegar or lemon
    juice
4 fluid ounces water
1 tablespoon sugar
1 tablespoon Worcestershire sauce

Sauté onion and garlic in butter; add
other ingredients and boil 5 minutes or
until thick.
Note: This is a delicious sauce for
grilled or roasted meat or for adding
new flavour to leftover meats.

Prawns in Barbecue Sauce

OYSTER AND MACARONI SCALLOP

1½ ounces butter or margarine
2 ounces celery, finely chopped
1 ounce green pepper, finely
    chopped
3 tablespoons flour
⅛ teaspoon black pepper
½ teaspoon salt
¾ pint milk
1 dozen shelled oysters
8 ounces macaroni shells, cooked
2 ounces dry breadcrumbs
1 ounce butter or margarine
1 tablespoon chopped parsley

Fry celery and green pepper in 1½
ounces melted butter until tender.
Blend in flour and seasonings. Gradually add milk, stirring over low heat
until smooth and thick.

Add oysters, which have been cut in
halves if very large.

In a greased 3-pint casserole place
a layer of one-third of the cooked macaroni. Cover with half the oyster mixture.

Add a second layer of macaroni, then
a layer of oyster mixture, and top with
final layer of macaroni. Press down
slightly with a large spoon.

Brown the breadcrumbs slightly in
remaining butter or margarine. Combine with parsley and sprinkle over top
of casserole.

Cook in moderate oven (350°F. Mark
4) 30 minutes. Serves 6 to 8.

Variations:

Clam and Macaroni Scallop: Substitute a dozen shelled clams for oysters.

Ham and Macaroni Scallop: Substitute 10 ounces diced cooked or canned
ham for oysters.

**Crabmeat, Salmon, or Tuna-Macaroni
Scallop:** Substitute 2 6½ or 7 ounce cans
of other seafood for oysters. Break into
bite-size pieces before using.

LOBSTER AND MUSHROOM CASSEROLE

2 ounces butter
1½ tablespoons flour
2 tablespoons grated Parmesan or
    Romano cheese
4 fluid ounces dry white wine
4 ounces fresh mushrooms, sliced
Salt and pepper
1 slightly beaten egg
1 1-pound packet frozen lobster,
    thawed

Melt butter in saucepan. Blend in
flour and cheese. Gradually stir in wine.

Heat mushrooms in sauce. Add salt
and pepper to taste. Remove from heat.
Allow to cool, then stir in egg. Add
lobster. Turn into buttered casserole.

Cook in moderate oven (350°F. Mark
4) 30 minutes. Serves 4.

Oyster and Macaroni Scallop

CRABMEAT WITH SWEETCORN AND EGGS

8 ounces fresh-cooked or 1 6½-
    ounce can crabmeat, flaked
10 ounces canned sweetcorn,
    drained
3 hard-boiled eggs, chopped
1 tablespoon chopped parsley
2 teaspoons lemon juice
1 tablespoon finely chopped onion
2 ounces butter or margarine
2 tablespoons flour
1 teaspoon mustard
8 fluid ounces milk
½ teaspoon salt
½ teaspoon Worcestershire sauce
1½ ounces fresh breadcrumbs
1 ounce grated Parmesan cheese

Combine crabmeat, sweetcorn, eggs,
parsley, and lemon juice; turn into
2½-pint casserole.

Cook onion in 1½ ounces melted
butter in saucepan until tender, about
3 minutes. Stir in flour and mustard.
Gradually add milk and cook, stirring
constantly, until thickened. Add salt
and Worcestershire. Turn into casserole and combine with crabmeat
mixture.

Combine crumbs and cheese with ½
ounce melted butter; sprinkle over
casserole.

Cook in moderate oven (375°F.
Mark 5) until hot and browned on top,
20 to 25 minutes. Serves 6.

CLAM AND VEGETABLE PIE

4 carrots, sliced
4 onions, sliced
4 potatoes, sliced
1-2 ounces chopped celery tops
1 bay leaf
Dash of garlic salt
½ teaspoon thyme
1 teaspoon salt
⅛ teaspoon black pepper
8 fluid ounces water
1 8- to 10½-ounce can minced clams
½ ounce butter or margarine
6 ounces shortcrust pastry

Cook vegetables with seasoning in
water for 8 minutes covered. Add undrained clams.

Turn into 3-pint casserole. Dot with
butter or margarine.

Top with pastry. Bake in very hot
oven (450°F. Mark 8) 25 minutes.
Serves 4.

LOBSTER NEWBURG CASSEROLE

1 pound canned, frozen, or fresh
    cooked lobster
½ teaspoon dry mustard
3 ounces butter
4 ounces sliced fresh mushrooms
3 egg yolks
12 fluid ounces double cream
1 teaspoon salt
Dash of cayenne pepper
2 fluid ounces sherry

Separate cooked lobster meat into small pieces.

Blend mustard into melted butter in pan. Add lobster and mushrooms and sauté lightly about 5 minutes.

Mix egg yolks, cream, and seasonings together and cook in double boiler, stirring constantly, until mixture coats a spoon.

Combine with lobster and mushrooms. Heat through, then stir in sherry. Fill individual casseroles and cook in hot oven (400°F. Mark 6) until mixture is heated through, about 10 minutes. Serve at once. Serves 4.

PRAWNS, RICE, AND CHEESE DELIGHT

4 ounces fresh mushrooms, sliced
1 ounce butter or margarine
1 pound fresh cooked prawns or 2
    cans (5¾ ounces each)
6 ounces rice, cooked
6 ounces grated processed Cheddar
    cheese
4 fluid ounces single cream or
    undiluted evaporated milk
3 tablespoons tomato ketchup
½ teaspoon Worcestershire sauce
Salt and pepper

Sauté mushrooms in butter or margarine until tender, about 5 minutes. Mix lightly with prawns, rice, and cheese.

Combine cream or evaporated milk, ketchup, Worcestershire sauce, and salt and pepper to taste. Add to prawn mixture. Pour into individual casseroles. Cook in moderate oven (350°F. Mark 4) 25 minutes. Serves 5 to 6.

Variations: One pound cooked cubed chicken may be used instead of prawns. Cooked noodles or macaroni may be used instead of rice.

Crabmeat Cobbler

PRAWNS WITH RICE AND MUSHROOMS

1 pound fresh mushrooms, sliced
2 ounces butter or margarine
1 pound fresh cooked prawns,
    cleaned or 2 5¾ ounce cans
8 ounces rice, cooked
½ pound Cheddar cheese, grated
8 fluid ounces evaporated milk
    or single cream
3 fluid ounces tomato ketchup
1 teaspoon Worcestershire sauce
Salt and pepper

Sauté mushrooms in butter until tender, about 5 minutes. Add prawns, rice, and cheese.

Combine milk or cream, ketchup, Worcestershire sauce, and salt and pepper to taste. Add to first mixture. Turn into casserole.

Cook in moderate oven (350°F. Mark 4) 45 minutes. Serves 6 to 8.

CRABMEAT COBBLER

4 ounces butter or margarine
1 to 2 ounces chopped green pepper
1 medium onion, chopped
2 ounces sifted plain flour
1 teaspoon dry mustard
½ teaspoon Aromat
8 fluid ounces milk
4 ounces grated Cheddar cheese
1 6½-ounce can crabmeat, boned
1 1-pound and 1 8-ounce can
    tomatoes, drained
2 teaspoons Worcestershire sauce
½ teaspoon salt

Melt butter or margarine in top of double boiler.

Add green pepper and onion. Cook over boiling water until tender, about 10 minutes.

Blend in flour, mustard, Aromat, milk, and cheese. Cook, stirring constantly, until cheese is melted and mixture is very thick.

Add crabmeat, tomatoes, Worcestershire sauce, and salt. Blend thoroughly. Pour into 3½-pint casserole.

Cheese Scone Topping:
4 ounces sifted plain flour
2 teaspoons baking powder
½ teaspoon salt
1 ounce grated Cheddar cheese
1 ounce cooking fat or margarine
4 fluid ounces milk

Sift together flour, baking powder, and salt into mixing bowl. Add cheese.

Cut in fat thoroughly until particles are fine.

Add milk; mix only until all flour is moistened. Drop by rounded teaspoonfuls on top of hot crabmeat mixture.

Cook in very hot oven (450°F. Mark 8) 20 to 25 minutes. Serves 6 to 8.

Lobster Tails Thermidor en Casserole

LOBSTER TAILS THERMIDOR EN CASSEROLE

2 packets frozen lobster tails
    (4 tails)
½ ounce butter or margarine
1 tablespoon flour
8 fluid ounces milk
1 beaten egg
1 teaspoon dry mustard
¼ teaspoon salt
Dash of cayenne pepper
About 3 ounces dry breadcrumbs,
    coarsely crumbled

Cook lobster tails according to directions on packets. Remove meat from shell; cut into small pieces.

Melt butter or margarine; blend in flour. Gradually stir in milk; cook and stir constantly until mixture thickens and boils 2 minutes. Remove from heat.

Stir a little hot mixture into egg; combine with remaining mixture; stir in mustard, salt, cayenne, and lobster meat (and a dash of sherry if you wish). Pour into 2½-pint casserole. Sprinkle top with breadcrumbs.

Cook in moderate oven (350°F. Mark 4) 15 minutes. Before bringing to table, arrange shells on top. To serve, put shells on plates and spoon lobster into shells. Serves 4.

CRABMEAT-SPAGHETTI PARTY CASSEROLE

12 ounces thin spaghetti, broken in
    pieces
1 10½-ounce can condensed tomato
    soup
1 14-ounce can evaporated milk
1 6½-ounce can crabmeat, flaked
4 ounces grated processed Cheddar
    cheese
1 tablespoon finely chopped onion
1 ounce finely chopped green
    pepper
½ teaspoon salt
Dash of thyme
½ ounce melted butter
1½ ounces fresh breadcrumbs

Cook spaghetti in boiling salted water; drain.

Combine in 3½-pint casserole the spaghetti, soup, milk, crabmeat, cheese, onion, green pepper, salt, and thyme.

Combine melted butter and breadcrumbs; sprinkle over top.

Cook in moderate oven (350°F. Mark 4) 45 minutes. Serves 8.

CRABMEAT WITH EGGS AND MUSHROOMS

1   6½-ounce can crabmeat, flaked
3   to 4 chopped hard-boiled eggs
1   4-ounce can mushrooms
2   tablespoons chopped onion
1½ ounces melted butter
6   ounces cooked peas
4   ounces Cheddar cheese, grated
2   teaspoons lemon juice
Dash of curry powder
½   teaspoon salt
¾   pint thin white sauce
2   ounces dry breadcrumbs

Combine crabmeat, eggs, and mushrooms.

Fry onion in ½ ounce melted butter until golden; add to crabmeat mixture.

Lightly mix in peas, grated cheese, lemon juice, curry powder, and salt.

Turn into buttered 2½-pint casserole. Pour white sauce over top. Toss breadcrumbs with remaining 1 ounce melted butter and sprinkle over top of casserole.

Cook in moderate oven (350°F. Mark 4) 25 minutes. Serves 4 to 6.

TOMATO CRAB CASSEROLE

12 ounces thin spaghetti, broken
8   fluid ounces evaporated milk
1   10½-ounce can cream of tomato soup
1   6½-ounce can crabmeat, flaked
6   ounces grated sharp Cheddar cheese
1   ounce chopped green pepper
2   tablespoons grated onion
¼   teaspoon marjoram
½   teaspoon salt
⅛   teaspoon black pepper
Buttered breadcrumbs

Cook spaghetti in boiling salted water until tender, about 10 minutes. Drain.

Mix evaporated milk, tomato soup, flaked crabmeat, 4 ounces grated cheese, green pepper, onion, and seasonings. Mix in the spaghetti.

Pour into a buttered 2½-pint casserole. Top with the remaining 2 ounces grated cheese and the buttered crumbs. Cook in a moderate oven (350°F. Mark 4) 45 minutes. Serves 4 to 6.

Tomato Crab Casserole

PRAWNS WITH SPAGHETTI AND CHEESE

1   medium onion, chopped
1½ ounces butter or margarine
1   ounce chopped green pepper
1   1-pound and 1 8-ounce can tomatoes
1½ teaspoons salt
¼   teaspoon paprika
1   teaspoon Worcestershire sauce
4   ounces spaghetti, cooked and drained
½   pound fresh cooked prawns or i 7-ounce can
4   ounces grated Parmesan cheese

Sauté onion in butter until soft and yellow. Add green pepper, tomatoes, and seasonings. Simmer 10 minutes.

Add spaghetti, cleaned prawns, and 2 ounces grated cheese. Turn into casserole. Sprinkle with remaining cheese.

Cook in moderate oven (350°F. Mark 4) until cheese is melted, about 20 minutes. Serves 4.

PRAWNS WITH ARTICHOKES AND MUSHROOMS

8   to 12 cooked artichoke hearts or 1 1-pound can artichoke hearts
1   7-ounce can prawns, cleaned
8   ounces fresh mushrooms or 4 ounces drained canned mushrooms
1   ounce butter or margarine
12 fluid ounces medium white sauce
1   tablespoon Worcestershire sauce
2   fluid ounces sherry
Salt and pepper
1   ounce grated Parmesan cheese

Arrange artichoke hearts in buttered shallow casserole. Spread cleaned prawns round them.

Cook mushrooms in butter 5 minutes and add to casserole. Season white sauce with Worcestershire, sherry, and salt and pepper to taste and pour over all. Sprinkle top with cheese and paprika.

Cook in moderate oven (375°F. Mark 5) 20 minutes. Serves 4 or more.

Variation: If desired, substitute canned or fresh flaked, cooked crabmeat for prawns. Fresh cooked and cleaned prawns may also be used.

CURRIED PRAWNS IN COURGETTES

2   pounds courgettes
1½ ounces lard or dripping
1   tablespoon grated onion
1   teaspoon curry powder
½   teaspoon salt
Dash of cayenne pepper
2   tablespoons flour
2   fluid ounces undiluted evaporated milk or top milk
2   8-ounce cans prawns, cleaned
2   ounces dry breadcrumbs

Split courgettes lengthwise and cook in boiling salted water 5 minutes.

Hollow out the centres; chop the flesh and drain shells.

Melt lard; add onion, curry, salt, cayenne, flour, and milk. Stir well.

When thickened add prawns cut in small bits. Season to taste. Add chopped courgettes. Stuff shells and sprinkle with crumbs.

Brown in moderate oven (350°F. Mark 4) 15 minutes. Serves 6.

SPAGHETTI CLAM BAKE

½   small finely chopped onion
1   ounce finely chopped green pepper
1   ounce melted butter or margarine
1   7-ounce can minced clams, drained
2   fluid ounces clam liquid
½   teaspoon salt
2   1-pound cans spaghetti with tomato sauce and cheese
1½ ounces grated sharp Cheddar cheese

Sauté onion and green pepper in butter until tender. Combine with clams and next 3 ingredients; pour into 2½-pint casserole. Top spaghetti mixture with cheese.

Cook in moderate oven (375°F. Mark 5) 30 minutes or until cheese is melted and casserole is hot. Serves 4 to 6.

PRAWNS THERMIDOR EN CASSEROLE

8   ounces fresh mushrooms, sliced
2   ounces butter
Additional 3 ounces butter
2   ounces sifted plain flour
1¼ pints warm single cream
1   ounce grated Parmesan cheese
2   tablespoons dry white wine
¼   teaspoon dry mustard
Pinch of cayenne pepper
1½ pounds cooked prawns, cut in 1-inch pieces
1½ teaspoons salt
Additional grated Parmesan cheese
Additional melted butter

Cook mushrooms in 2 ounces butter until lightly browned.

Melt additional 3 ounces butter in saucepan. Stir in flour until smooth. Gradually add cream, and cook over low heat, stirring constantly, until thickened. Simmer 3 minutes.

Add 1 ounce grated cheese, wine, mustard, cayenne, cooked mushrooms, prawns, and salt. Mix well. Turn into casserole.

Sprinkle top generously with additional grated Parmesan cheese, then sprinkle with additional melted butter.

Cook in hot oven (400°F. Mark 6) 15 minutes, then place under grill to brown top. Serves 6.

Variations: Cooked lobster, crabmeat, and other shellfish may be substituted for prawns.

Sweet and Pungent Pork

Beef with Tomatoes and Green Peppers

CHINESE COOKERY

Sweet and Sour Pork

Miscellaneous Casseroles and One-Dish Meals

CHOP SUEY AND CHOW MEIN

Chop Suey is an American-Chinese dish that originated in the United States and is unknown in China. It is made of a great variety of ingredients, which may include chicken, other meats, seafood, bamboo shoots, bean sprouts, water chestnuts, mushrooms, and stock. It is served with rice. Chow Mein is a dish similar to Chop Suey but served with fried noodles instead of rice.

CHICKEN CHOP SUEY
(Basic Recipe)

2 ounces butter, margarine, cooking fat or salad oil
2 medium onions, chopped
4 outside stalks celery, finely sliced
8 ounces fresh mushrooms, sliced through stems
¼ pint boiling chicken stock or boiling bean sprout liquid
½ teaspoon salt
¼ teaspoon black pepper
12 ounces cooked chicken
1 9½-ounce can bean sprouts, drained
2 tablespoons cornflour
1 teaspoon sugar
¼ pint cold bean sprout liquid
2 tablespoons soy sauce
Hot boiled rice

Heat fat or oil over low heat in large heavy saucepan. Add onions, celery, and mushrooms. Cover and cook over low heat until celery is almost tender, about 10 minutes.

Add ¼ pint boiling stock, salt, and pepper; simmer 5 minutes.

Add chicken, cut into matchlike slivers, and drained bean sprouts.

Mix cornflour and sugar with ¼ pint cold liquid and add soy sauce.

Add ¼ pint of hot chicken mixture and mix well, then pour back into remaining chicken mixture.

Cook, stirring constantly, until mixture thickens. Serve with additional soy sauce and hot boiled rice. Serves 6.

Chow Mein

Chicken Chop Suey Variations

Lobster Chop Suey: Substitute cooked or canned lobster, cut into thin strips, for cooked chicken. Add lobster meat just before serving and heat through. Overcooking toughens lobster meat.
Crabmeat Chop Suey: Substitute flaked cooked or canned crabmeat for chicken.
Pork Chop Suey: Substitute cooked pork for chicken.
Other Variations of Chop Suey: Veal may be substituted for chicken to make Mock Chicken Chop Suey. Raw seafood or meat may be substituted for cooked or canned seafood or meat; however, it must be cut up into matchlike strips and fried in fat until delicately browned, about 5 to 10 minutes, before continuing as directed with vegetables and other ingredients in Chicken Chop Suey.
Chow Mein: Prepare Chicken Chop Suey or any variation and serve over fried noodles or canned chow mein noodles instead of boiled rice. If desired, garnish with slivered, blanched almonds.

PRAWN CHOW MEIN

8 ounces fresh or frozen prawns
1 ounce butter or groundnut oil
½ small chopped onion
½ green pepper, cut in 2-inch strips
8 fluid ounces hot water
4 ounces celery, cut in 2-inch strips
¾ teaspoon salt
Dash of black pepper
1 1-pound, 2-ounce can bean sprouts, drained
2 tablespoons cold water
2 tablespoons cornflour
2 teaspoons soy sauce
1 teaspoon sugar
Chow mein noodles
Hot boiled rice

Remove shells and black veins from prawns. Rinse in cold water and cut in half, then again in half lengthwise.

Melt butter in large frying pan over medium heat. Add onion and green pepper and cook 5 minutes.

Add hot water, celery, salt, pepper, bean sprouts, and prawns. Cover and simmer 5 minutes or until celery is tender but still slightly crisp.

Combine cold water, cornflour, soy sauce, and sugar; stir lightly into hot mixture and cook uncovered 4 minutes longer.

Serve on chow mein noodles with rice. Serves 4 to 5.
Note: You can use 1 5-ounce can prawns or 1 packet frozen cooked prawns (first thawed). Add these with cornflour mixture at the end.

CHICKEN SUBGUM CHOW MEIN

3 fluid ounces groundnut oil
1 clove garlic, crushed
8 ounces diced canned water chestnuts
8 ounces diced canned bamboo shoots
3 ounces thinly sliced runner beans
6 spring onions, chopped
8 ounces finely diced celery
8 ounces sliced Chinese cabbage
1 ounce diced fresh mushrooms
1 medium green pepper, diced
1 tablespoon salt
½ teaspoon black pepper
1½ teaspoons sugar
16 fluid ounces chicken stock or 2 chicken stock cubes and 16 fluid ounces water
3 tablespoons soy sauce
2 tablespoons cornflour
12 ounces finely shredded cooked chicken
2 ounces toasted almonds
Chow mein noodles

Heat oil in large heavy saucepan or frying pan with cover.

Add garlic, vegetables, salt, pepper, and sugar. Add stock and mix well. Cover and bring to boil. Stir well. Cover again and boil 10 minutes.

Combine soy sauce, 4 tablespoons cold water, and cornflour. Blend thoroughly and add to hot vegetable mixture. Cook, stirring, until thickened. Add chicken and cook 5 minutes longer.

Serve with chow mein noodles. Sprinkle almonds over each serving. Serves 6.
Variations: Beef, pork, veal, lamb, prawns, or lobster may be substituted for chicken.

PORK AND APPLE CHOP SUEY

1 pound fillet of pork
2 ounces lard or dripping
3 medium-sized onions
12 fluid ounces water
1 1-pound, 2-ounce can bean sprouts
½ teaspoon Aromat
8 ounces slivered celery
2 tart eating apples, thinly sliced
Soy sauce to taste
3 tablespoons cornflour

Cut pork in narrow strips about 2 inches long. Brown in hot fat; remove. Add onions; brown lightly.

Return pork to frying pan; add water, liquid from bean sprouts, and Aromat. Cover; simmer 30 minutes.

Add celery and apples; cook 10 minutes longer. Add soy sauce if desired.

Dissolve cornflour in little cold water; add, stirring constantly until thickened.

Add bean sprouts; bring to boiling point. Serve with hot cooked rice. Serves 6.

Vegetables are at their best when cooked just to "crispy-doneness" the Chinese way. Whether you cook authentically in a Chinese Wok or in a frying pan, this vegetable flavour of Cha'O Yuk will long be remembered.

VEGETABLE CHA'O YUK

- 2 tablespoons cooking oil
- ¼ pound pork fillet cut in thin strips
- 2 fluid ounces soy sauce
- 1 teaspoon sugar
- 4 stalks celery, sliced diagonally
- 1 small green pepper, cut in bite-size squares
- 4 ounces sliced cauliflower
- 1 5-ounce can bamboo shoots, diced
- 1 onion, cut in large slices
- 2 ounces mushroom slices
- 4 ounces bean sprouts (fresh or canned)
- 2 tablespoons light chicken stock
- 1 tablespoon cornflour
- 2 fluid ounces chicken broth

Heat oil in frying pan or Chinese wok on high flame for about 2 minutes. Brown pork strips quickly. When no longer pink, add soy sauce, sugar, celery, green pepper, cauliflower, bamboo shoots, and onion. Cook 1 minute.

Add mushrooms, bean sprouts, and 2 tablespoons of broth. Cook 1 minute.

Mix cornflour with 2 fluid ounces stock. Stir into vegetables. Cook 1 to 2 minutes longer or until slightly thickened. Serve over rice. Serves 4 to 6.

PINEAPPLE CHICKEN CHOW MEIN

- 2 fluid ounces salad oil
- 1 large onion, thinly sliced
- 12 ounces thinly sliced celery
- 1 1-pound 2-ounce can bean sprouts, undrained
- 1 14-ounce can pineapple chunks, drained
- 2 chicken stock cubes, dissolved in ¼ pint hot water
- 3 teaspoons salt
- ¼ teaspoon black pepper
- 2 tablespoons brown sugar
- 2 tablespoons cornflour
- 2 fluid ounces soy sauce
- 6 ounces sliced, cooked or canned chicken
- Chow mein noodles

Heat oil in deep frying pan or large heavy saucepan.

Add onions, celery, bean sprouts with liquid, drained pineapple, stock cubes dissolved in water, salt, pepper, and brown sugar. Cover and bring to boil. Blend cornflour with soy sauce and stir into vegetable mixture. Add chicken.

Cook, stirring, 3 to 5 minutes, until thickened. Serve over crisp chow mein noodles. Serves 4 to 5.

SUKIYAKI

Sukiyaki is a Japanese term which means, literally, roasted on a plough; it is a traditional Japanese dish with innumerable variations. Basically it consists of thin strips of meat (usually tender beef, sometimes chicken) with vegetables such as green pepper, celery, bamboo shoots, bean sprouts, mushrooms, spring onions, leeks, water chestnuts, and tender young spinach. Tofu (bean curd) and shirataki (gelatinous noodles) are often included. The latter resembles vermicelli or thin spaghetti and is sometimes called cellophane noodles. Tofu and shirataki are available in many Oriental grocery stores. The recipe given below is an American version without the "hard-to-find" Japanese ingredients.

Sukiyaki is prepared at the table over a hotplate or in a chafing dish, and care is taken not to overcook the vegetables, which must remain crisp.

- 2 tablespoons salad oil
- 1½ pounds sirloin steak, cut in thin diagonal slices about 2 inches long and ¼ inch wide
- 2 ounces sugar
- 6 fluid ounces soy sauce
- 2 fluid ounces water or mushroom stock
- 2 medium onions, thinly sliced
- 1 green pepper, sliced in thin strips
- 4 ounces celery, cut into diagonal 1½-inch strips
- 1 12-ounce can bamboo shoots, thinly sliced
- 1 8-ounce can mushrooms, thinly sliced
- 1 bunch spring onions, cut in 1-inch lengths with tops

Heat oil in frying pan. Add meat and brown lightly.

Mix sugar, soy sauce and water mushroom stock. Add half to meat.

Push meat to one side of pan a add onion, green pepper, and cele Cook a few minutes.

Add remaining soy sauce liqu bamboo shoots, and mushrooms. Co 3 to 5 minutes.

Add spring onions and tops. Co 1 minute longer. Stir well.

Serve at once with steamed rice a hot tea. Serves 8.

WAR MEIN

- 3 ounces butter or groundnut oil
- ¼ pound pork fillet, cut in thin strips
- ¼ pound lean veal, cut in thin strip
- 1 medium onion, finely chopped
- 2 teaspoons salt
- ⅛ teaspoon black pepper
- 8 ounces celery, finely chopped
- 8 fluid ounces hot water or stock
- 8 ounces bamboo shoots, drained and thinly sliced
- 8 ounces water chestnuts, drained and thinly sliced
- 1 can bean sprouts, drained well, or 4 ounces fresh bean sprou

Flavouring and Thickening:
- 3 tablespoons cold water
- 3 tablespoons cornflour
- 1 teaspoon Chinese brown gravy or oyster sauce
- 2 teaspoons soy sauce
- 2 teaspoons sugar

Heat oil in large frying pan; a meat and fry quickly, without brow ing. Add onions; stir and cook fi 2 minutes.

Add salt, pepper, celery, and h water. Cover and cook for 5 minut at a quick boil, stirring once.

Add well drained bamboo shoo water chestnuts, and bean sprou Mix thoroughly and bring to the bo

Add thickening and flavouring mi ture. Stir lightly and cook 2 to minutes.

Serve over hot, boiled egg noodle or vermicelli noodles. Garnish wit slices of hard-boiled eggs and th strips of spring onions. Serves 6.

Sukiyaki

Bean Bakes

BOSTON BAKED BEANS

1 pound haricot beans
2½ pints cold water
¼-½ pound salt pork
4 tablespoons black treacle
1 to 2 teaspoons salt
½ teaspoon mustard
Hot water

Wash beans. Add water, boil 2 minutes, then remove from heat, and allow to soak 1 hour. Or, add water and soak overnight in cool place.

Boil soaked beans gently in the same water for 45 minutes or until they begin to soften.

Make cuts through rind of the pork about ½ inch apart. Put half the pork in a bean pot or deep casserole. Add beans and bury rest of the pork in them, exposing only the scored rind.

Mix treacle, salt, and mustard with a little hot water. Pour over the beans, and add enough hot water to cover beans.

Cover bean pot. Cook in very slow oven (250°F. Mark ½) 6 or 7 hours; add a little hot water from time to time.

During last hour of cooking remove cover to let beans brown on top. Serves 6 to 8.

Baked Butter Beans: Substitute dried butter beans for haricot beans.

Baked Kidney Beans: Substitute dried kidney beans for haricot beans.

Baked Beans and Spareribs: Substitute 6 pork spareribs for salt pork in Boston Baked Beans.

SCALLOPED BUTTER BEANS AND PIMIENTOS

8 fluid ounces medium white sauce
2 teaspoons grated onion
¼ teaspoon celery salt
1 teaspoon salt
⅛ teaspoon black pepper
3 canned pimientos, chopped
1 1-pound can butter beans
3 ounces fresh buttered breadcrumbs

To the medium white sauce add the onion, celery salt, salt, pepper, and chopped pimientos. Add sauce mixture to the canned lima or butter beans and blend together.

Place in a greased casserole and cover the top with the fresh buttered breadcrumbs.

Cook in moderate oven (350°F. Mark 4) until crumbs are lightly browned, about 30 minutes. Serves 5.

Variations: To make a more hearty dish add to the sauce when mixing with the beans, 8 ounces canned prawns, or 8 ounces cooked or canned meat that is cubed.

ALL-AMERICAN BAKED BEANS
(Quick Recipe)

2 rashers streaky bacon
3 tablespoons grated onion
1 tablespoon black treacle
1½ tablespoons tomato ketchup
¼ teaspoon salt
¼ teaspoon dry mustard
½ teaspoon Worcestershire sauce, optional
8 ounces canned or cooked dry beans

Fry bacon, remove from pan, and cook onion for a few minutes in bacon fat. Add treacle, ketchup, salt, mustard, and Worcestershire sauce. Add beans and mix lightly.

Pour into casserole. Break bacon into bits and sprinkle over top. Cook in moderate oven (350°F. Mark 4) 20 minutes. Or heat in a saucepan on top of cooker, crumbling bacon over top before serving.

Baked Butter Beans: Use soaked butter beans and omit treacle. Place in baking dish and add other ingredients, and water to cover. Cook in moderate oven (350°F. Mark 4) until tender.

BAKED BEANS WITH MEAT
(Quick Recipe)

2 1-pound cans baked beans
½ pound canned pork loaf, chopped ham, sausages or frankfurters
2 fluid ounces tomato ketchup
1 teaspoon French mustard

Pour baked beans into 3-pint shallow, wide casserole. Cover with canned meat cut into serving pieces.

Combine ketchup and mustard; spread over meat. Cook in oven (375°F. Mark 5) 30 minutes. Serves 6.

COWBOY BEAN CASSEROLE

5 ounces diced ham
1 ounce butter or margarine
1 clove garlic, crushed
1 1-pound can baked beans
1 1-pound can red kidney beans, drained
1 1-pound can green lima or butter beans, drained
1 tablespoon brown sugar
1 tablespoon mustard with horseradish
4 fluid ounces tomato ketchup
3 tablespoons vinegar
Salt and pepper
1 medium onion, sliced

Brown ham in butter or margarine. Combine garlic, beans, ham, mustard, and seasonings.

Pour into greased casserole. Top with onion slices.

Cook in moderate oven (350°F. Mark 4) 45 to 60 minutes. Serves 6.

The idea of baking beans came from American Indians—and beans are still very popular, especially with children.

CHILLI KIDNEY BEANS WITH TOMATOES

14 ounces dry red kidney beans
1 large onion, sliced
1 large clove garlic, sliced
1 green pepper, finely chopped
2 ounces bacon fat
1½ pounds canned tomatoes
2 teaspoons salt
2 teaspoons chilli seasoning

Boil beans 2 minutes in water to cover, and soak 1 hour in the hot water. Or, boil as above and soak overnight.

Add onion, garlic, green pepper, bacon dripping, tomatoes, and salt; and simmer 2 hours in the soaking water. Add more water if needed during cooking.

Add chilli seasoning, stirring as little as possible to avoid mashing the beans.

Place in casserole or bean pot. Cover and cook in moderate oven (350°F. Mark 4) about 2 hours.

Uncover during last part of cooking if brown beans are desired. Serves 6.

Variations: If preferred, use broad or haricot beans in place of kidney beans.

TEXAS BEAN BAKE
(Quick Recipe)

5 rashers streaky bacon
1 onion, finely chopped
1 ounce chopped green pepper
2 1-pound cans red kidney beans
1 1-pound can drained tomatoes
4 ounces chopped luncheon meat
¾ teaspoon dry mustard
1 teaspoon curry powder dissolved in 1 tablespoon hot water
3 tablespoons black treacle
Salt

Dice 1 bacon rasher; fry with onion and green pepper. Mix kidney beans, tomatoes, ham, mustard, curry powder, treacle, and salt to taste. Add onion-pepper mixture.

Turn into casserole. Top with bacon rashers.

Cook in hot oven (400°F. Mark 6) until bacon is crisp, about 25 minutes. Serves 6.

BUTTER BEAN-PORK SAUSAGE CASSEROLE
(Dutch Style)

12 ounces dry butter beans
1½ pints cold water
2½ teaspoons salt
1 pound pork sausages
1 onion, thinly sliced
2 red apples, cored and sliced
1½ ounces brown sugar
1 tablespoon vinegar
4 fluid ounces tomato ketchup

Rinse butter beans and cover with the cold water. Soak 6 to 8 hours or overnight. Add 1½ teaspoons salt. Bring to boil in saucepan and simmer until beans are tender, ½ to 1 hour.

Fry sausages until half done. Remove half of them from pan. Pour off all but 1 ounce fat.

Cut sausages in pan in bite-size pieces with fork. Add onion and apples; cover and cook 5 minutes. Sprinkle with sugar, vinegar, and remaining salt.

Drain beans and reserve 6 fluid ounces liquid. Stir ketchup and reserved liquid into sausage mixture.

Turn beans into casserole. Pour sausage mixture over beans. Put whole sausages on top.

Cook in moderate oven (350°F. Mark 4) 1 hour. Serves 4.

LAST MINUTE BEAN SUPPER

1 small onion
1 ounce green pepper, chopped
2 ounces butter or margarine
3 ounces sifted plain flour
1 teaspoon salt
¾ pint milk
5 to 6 ounces cooked ham, chicken, or tuna fish pieces
2 ounces grated Cheddar cheese
3 hard-boiled eggs, quartered
10 ounces dry butter beans, cooked
1 canned, chopped pimiento

Finely chop onion and cook with green pepper in butter until soft. Blend in flour and salt. Add milk slowly, stirring constantly.

Continue cooking until smooth and thick, about 5 minutes. Add all remaining ingredients.

Last Minute Bean Supper

Keep hot on top of cooker until ready to serve. Or, turn into casserole, top with buttered crumbs, if desired, and heat in moderate oven (350°F. Mark 4) until bubbly and hot. Serves 6.

BEAN SCALLOP

2 1-pound cans tomatoes, drained and chopped
2 tablespoons chopped onion
3 ounces butter or margarine
8 ounces thinly sliced courgettes
7 ounces dry butter beans, cooked
3 tablespoons flour
1 teaspoon salt
8 fluid ounces milk
3 slices bread
2 ounces cheese spread

Cook tomatoes and onion in 2 ounces butter until softened. Add courgettes and simmer until just barely tender.

Arrange tomato mixture and beans in a 10×6×2-inch casserole.

Then measure into saucepan the remaining 1 ounce butter, flour, and salt. Blend until butter melts. Stir in milk and cook until smooth and thickened, about 5 minutes. Pour over vegetables.

Spread bread with cheese and cut into cubes. Arrange over top of casserole. Cook in moderate oven (350°F. Mark 4) 20 minutes. Serves 6.

CHILLI BEANS AND MINCED BEEF

8 ounces dry red kidney beans
Water
½ pound minced beef
1½ ounces dripping or other fat
1 medium onion, sliced
1 clove garlic, sliced
1 green pepper, finely chopped
1 1-pound can tomatoes
1 teaspoon salt
Chilli seasoning to taste

Soak beans overnight in cold water or 4 to 5 hours in lukewarm water to cover. Cook in the same water until almost tender.

Brown meat in fat. Add onion, garlic, green pepper, tomatoes, and salt, and cook a few minutes. (Raw tomatoes, cut in pieces, may be used instead of canned or cooked.) Add meat mixture and chilli seasoning to beans.

Place in casserole or bean pot. Cover and cook in moderate oven (350°F. Mark 4) about 2 hours. Uncover during the last half hour to brown the beans if desired.

Or cook the mixture slowly for about 1 hour in a covered saucepan on top of the cooker. Stir occasionally. Serves 6.

Bean Scallop

LENTIL-SAUSAGE CASSEROLE

8 ounces lentils
2¾ pints cold water
3 ounces spring onions, finely chopped
1 tablespoon finely chopped parsley
½ clove garlic, crushed
3 tablespoons finely chopped celery
2 teaspoons salt
⅛ teaspoon black pepper
½ ounce lard or dripping
1 tablespoon flour
Sliced sausages
1 tablespoon tomato purée or 2 medium tomatoes, sliced

Wash lentils and soak overnight in cold water. Drain, reserving liquid. Heat ¾ pint liquid; add lentils, onions, parsley, garlic, celery, salt, and pepper. Cook, covered, until nearly tender.

Drain; measure liquid; add enough of reserved liquid or water to make ½ pint liquid. Place lentil mixture in greased casserole.

Melt lard in saucepan; blend in flour. Slowly add reserved ½ pint liquid and cook, stirring until thickened. Pour over lentils. Fry sausage slices lightly, draining off fat. Place sausages and tomatoes (or diluted tomato purée) sprinkled with salt on top of lentils.

Cook in moderate oven (375°F. Mark 5) 20 minutes. Serve hot. Serves 4.

BEAN AND CHEESE CASSEROLE

8 ounces dry beans (peas, butter beans, red kidney beans, etc.)
1¼ pints water
1 teaspoon salt
1 ounce butter or margarine
8 fluid ounces medium white sauce
4 ounces grated strong cheese
3 ounces fresh bread cubes or crumbs

Boil beans in water 2 minutes and soak 1 hour or longer. Add salt and ½ ounce butter and boil until tender, about 2 hours. Add sauce and cheese and turn into a casserole.

Toss crumbs with remaining ½ ounce butter and sprinkle over beans.

Cook in moderate oven (350°F. Mark 4) until crumbs are brown, about 20 minutes. Serves 4.

Beans with Ham: Substitute 2 ounces finely sliced ham for cheese in above recipe.

Cook the ham until the edges curl in the butter or margarine before making the white sauce.

SUNSHINE BEAN CASSEROLE

7 ounces dry butter beans
1 teaspoon salt
½ small onion, chopped
1 ounce chopped green pepper
1 ounce butter or margarine
10 to 12 ounces canned tomatoes
1 7-ounce can creamed sweetcorn
5 ounces cubed cooked ham
Buttered crumbs, optional

Stir rinsed beans into 1¾ pints rapidly boiling water. Boil gently over low heat until tender, about 1½ to 2 hours. Season with salt before last ½ hour.

Sauté onion and green pepper lightly in heated butter. Stir in tomatoes, sweetcorn, beans and ham. Mix thoroughly and turn into greased casserole.

Top with buttered crumbs or some of ham pieces if desired.

Cook in moderate oven (350°F. Mark 4) until heated through and flavours are blended, 45 minutes to 1 hour. Serves 4 to 5.

BARBECUED BEANS

10 ounces dry butter beans
1½ pints water
1½ teaspoons salt
4 rashers streaky bacon
1 medium onion
1 clove garlic
1 10½-ounce can tomato soup
1 tablespoon vinegar
1 tablespoon French mustard
1 teaspoon chilli seasoning
1 teaspoon Worcestershire sauce

Rinse beans, add water and soak overnight or several hours. Add salt and simmer 1 to 1½ hours, or until barely tender.

Drain, reserving ¼ pint liquid. Cook bacon partially and set aside. Drain off all but ½ ounce fat. Chop onion and crush garlic. Cook onion and garlic until transparent in remaining bacon fat.

Add remaining ingredients and ¼ pint cooking liquid from beans. Heat to boiling, add drained beans and turn into 2-pint baking dish.

Top with partially cooked bacon. Cook in moderate oven (350°F. Mark 4) about 1 hour. Serves 6.

Barbecued Beans

HAWAIIAN BAKED BEANS
(Quick Recipe)

1 16-ounce can baked beans
2 slices canned pineapple, cut into pieces
1 tablespoon pineapple syrup
2 tablespoons light brown sugar
Dash of ground cloves

Combine all ingredients in 2-pint casserole.

Cook in moderate oven (375°F. Mark 5) for 30 minutes or until hot. Serves 3 to 4.

Note: This recipe may be doubled by using ⅛ teaspoon ground cloves and doubling other ingredients.

Alternate Method: Combine all ingredients in saucepan. Heat thoroughly.

BAKED BEANS WITH RED WINE

6 to 8 rashers streaky bacon
1 onion, sliced
¼ pint claret, burgundy, or any red wine
1 16-ounce can baked beans

Fry bacon until partly done, not crisp. Remove bacon. Pour off all but about 1 ounce fat. Add sliced onion and fry gently 5 minutes in hot fat. Then add wine and beans; mix thoroughly.

Pour into shallow casserole or individual casseroles. Cook in hot oven (400°F. Mark 6) until bubbly, about 20 minutes.

Top with partly cooked bacon rashers and put back in oven until bacon is crisp. Serves 4.

SAVOURY BAKED BEANS
(Quick Recipe)

2 fluid ounces black treacle
1 tablespoon vinegar
1 tablespoon French mustard
¼ teaspoon Tabasco sauce
2 1-pound cans baked beans
1 onion, sliced

Combine black treacle, vinegar, mustard, and Tabasco sauce; mix well.

Empty beans into frying pan or casserole and stir in treacle mixture.

Arrange onion slices on top of beans or layer with beans.

Simmer in frying pan on top of cooker 10 to 15 minutes, or cook in casserole in a hot oven (425°F. Mark 7) 30 minutes. Serves 4 to 5.

BAKED BEANS — WISCONSIN STYLE
(Quick Recipe)

1 16-ounce can baked beans in tomato sauce
2 tablespoons soured cream
6 ounces grated strong Cheddar cheese

Combine ingredients in casserole. Cook in moderate oven (350°F. Mark 4) 20 minutes. Serves 3.

Hawaiian Baked Beans

Economical baked bean dishes are not only budget balancers but top choices for buffet meals, picnics, and many special occasions.

SURPRISE PARTY SPECIAL

1 1-pound can baked beans
1 1-pound can red kidney beans
2 fluid ounces black treacle
1 tablespoon vinegar
1 tablespoon French mustard
1 12-ounce can luncheon meat, diced
Onion and tomato slices

Combine beans in casserole; stir in treacle, vinegar, mustard, and meat. Top with onion and tomato slices. Cook in moderate oven (375°F. Mark 5) 45 minutes. Serves 6.

BACON AND BEANS

1 3 to 4-pound joint of boiling bacon
Water
1 pound haricot beans
1 onion, sliced
2 teaspoons dry mustard
2 fluid ounces black treacle

Cover bacon joint with water. Bring to a boil, then reduce heat and simmer until bacon drops from bone, 2½ hours or longer.

Cover beans with warm water. Soak 2½ hours.

Drain. Cover with bacon broth and boil 10 minutes. Add diced bacon and sliced onion. Mix mustard and treacle with broth. Add to beans. Add broth to cover beans.

Simmer slowly or cook in slow oven (325°F. Mark 3) 1 hour. Serves 6 to 8.

Variations: If desired, pour 2 tablespoons chilli pickle or tomato ketchup over beans before baking. Black-eyed beans or red kidney beans may be substituted for haricot beans.

BACHELORS' HAM AND BEANS

1 ounce butter or margarine
4 ounces thinly sliced ham
1 10½-ounce can condensed tomato soup
¼ pint milk
1 1-pound can butter beans
1 ounce grated Cheddar cheese

Melt butter and shred ham into it. Heat through. Add soup and blend in milk. Heat to simmering.

Place drained beans in casserole. Pour sauce over them. Top with grated cheese.

Cook in moderate oven (350°F. Mark 4) about 20 minutes. Serves 4.

KIDNEY BEANS À LA CRÉOLE

4 ounces streaky bacon or bacon pieces, chopped
1 large onion, finely chopped
1 ounce diced green pepper
1 tablespoon sugar
½ teaspoon salt
½ teaspoon black pepper
1 8-ounce can tomatoes
2 1-pound cans red kidney beans

Fry bacon in frying pan until crisp. Drain off all but 1 ounce fat. Add onion and green pepper. Cook until onion is tender.

Add remaining ingredients, except beans, and simmer 10 minutes.

Put beans in 2-pint casserole; add sauce. Cover and cook in moderate oven (350°F. Mark 4) 30 minutes. Serves 4.

PINEAPPLE BAKED BEANS

2 1-pound cans baked beans
1 1-pound can pineapple chunks

Place the contents of one of the cans of beans in a 2½-pint casserole.

Drain pineapple and reserve 5 or 6 of the chunks to use to decorate the top.

Place remaining chunks in an even layer over beans and cover with second can of beans. Arrange the 5 or 6 pineapple chunks on top and cook covered in a moderate oven (350°F. Mark 4) for 20 to 30 minutes. Serves 4.

BUTTER BEANS IN CREAMY CHEESE SAUCE

2 ounces butter or margarine
4 tablespoons flour
1 pint milk
1 teaspoon salt
⅛ teaspoon black pepper
4 ounces grated Cheddar cheese
1½ pounds dried butter beans, cooked
6 ounces diced celery, cooked

Melt butter in top of double boiler, blend in flour; add milk and cook until sauce is thick. Add seasonings and cook 10 minutes.

Add cheese and cook until cheese is melted.

Add drained, cooked butter beans, and celery that has been diced or sliced in julienne strips and cooked until tender.

Pour into individual or one large casserole. Cook in moderate oven (350°F. Mark 4) 15 to 20 minutes. Serves 6.

Beans in Creamy Cheese Sauce

BOSTON BEAN CASSEROLE (Quick Recipe)

4 rashers streaky bacon
1 to 2 tablespoons finely chopped onion
1 ounce chopped green pepper
2 ounces chopped celery
2 1-pound cans baked beans

Cut 3 rashers bacon into squares and fry with onion and green pepper until bacon is crisp. Pour off excess fat and combine with celery and baked beans in a casserole. Sprinkle with 1 rasher raw bacon, finely diced. Cook in moderate oven (375°F. Mark 5) until top is browned, 40 minutes. Serves 6.

BAKED BEAN SPECIAL

4 ounces fat bacon or 6 rashers streaky bacon
1½ ounces finely chopped celery
½ small onion, chopped
1 ounce finely chopped green pepper
2 1-pound cans pork and beans or baked beans
2 fluid ounces tomato ketchup
2 tablespoons brown sugar
2 tablespoons black treacle
5 drops Tabasco sauce

Score fat bacon and brown. Cook celery, onion, and green pepper in 1 ounce bacon dripping until soft but not brown.

Combine all ingredients except bacon and pour into square (8×8×2-inch) casserole.

Put fat bacon, scored side up, in centre. Cook in moderate oven (375°F. Mark 5) 45 to 60 minutes. Serves 8.

MINCED BEEF, BEANS AND CHILLI BAKE

1 pound dried butter beans
1 teaspoon salt
½ pound minced beef
1 medium onion, cut into rings
1 clove garlic, crushed
1 tablespoon chopped chilli peppers
1 ounce fat
1 1-pound and 1 8-ounce can tomatoes, drained
1 teaspoon chilli seasoning
2 ounces grated strong Cheddar cheese

Cover butter beans with water; soak overnight. Add water if necessary and bring slowly to boiling point. Simmer uncovered 1 hour. Add salt for last half-hour of cooking. Drain and reserve ½ pint bean liquid.

Brown meat, onion rings, garlic, and chilli pepper in hot fat. Add tomatoes, chilli seasoning, butter beans, ½ pint bean liquid, and cheese.

Turn into wide shallow casserole. Cook in moderate oven (350°F. Mark 4) 1 hour. Serve topped with extra grated cheese, if desired. Serves 6 to 8.

BRAZILIAN BEANS

1 pound dried butter beans
2 teaspoons salt
1¾ pints water
5 ounces ham, minced
1 large onion, chopped
1 clove garlic, crushed
2 ounces bacon fat
½ pint tomato juice
½ pint puréed tomatoes
2 teaspoons chilli seasoning
2 teaspoons salt
2 ounces grated cheese

Soak butter beans overnight. Add beans and 2 teaspoons salt to 1¾ pints water and cook beans until tender. Drain.

Brown minced ham, onions, and garlic in bacon fat. Add tomato juice, puréed tomatoes, chilli seasoning, and 2 teaspoons salt to ham mixture; cook together for 5 minutes.

Pour cooked tomato sauce over cooked beans in 3½-pint casserole. Sprinkle top with grated cheese.

Cook in moderate oven (350°F. Mark 4) about 25 minutes or until cheese is melted. Serves 6 to 8.

BAKED BEANS DELUXE

1 pound haricot beans
2½ pints cold water
1 medium onion, chopped
¾ pint tomato pulp or 2 8-ounce cans tomato sauce
4 fluid ounces cooking oil
2 small sweet pickles, chopped
16 stuffed olives, chopped
1 small stalk celery, chopped
2 ounces grated strong cheese

Combine washed beans with cold water. Bring to boiling point and cook 1 hour, adding water if necessary; drain.

Combine onion, tomato pulp (or tomato sauce), and oil. Simmer until thick.

Add pickles, olives, and celery to beans; turn into casserole. Pour tomato mixture over bean mixture.

Cover and cook in moderate oven (350°F. Mark 4) until beans are tender, about 1½ hours.

Sprinkle with cheese and cook uncovered until cheese melts and browns. Serves 8.

BAKED BEAN RAREBIT (Quick Recipe)

Combine 1 1-pound can baked beans with 4 ounces grated Cheddar cheese, and ½ green pepper, sliced.

Pour into casserole. Cook in moderate oven (350°F. Mark 4) 45 minutes. Serves 4.

BREAKFAST CEREALS, RICE AND OTHER GRAINS

Breakfast Cereal Cookery

BASIC COOKING RULES

Quick-Cooking Oats: To 3 parts rapidly boiling salted water, gradually add 1 to 1½ parts quick-cooking oats.

Stirring constantly, cook 1 minute and leave covered for 5 minutes before serving.

Rolled Oats: To 3 parts rapidly boiling salted water, gradually add 1½ parts rolled oats.

Stirring constantly, cook 4 to 5 minutes or longer, if desired.

Wheat Cereal: To 1 pint rapidly boiling salted water or milk, gradually add 1½ ounces wheat cereal. Stir constantly until thickened. Cook slowly 5 minutes.

Cereal Cooked in Milk: Substitute scalded milk for water in the recipe. Add cereal to scalded milk. Cook, covered, over hot water until thickened and done.

Cereal Cooked with Fruit: Follow recipes given above, adding 2 ounces chopped dried apricots, stoned dates, figs, stoned prunes, raisins, or chopped nuts, a few minutes before cooking is completed.

FRIED CEREAL

Turn cooked cereal into a greased mould. Cover to prevent skin from forming. Chill until firm.

Cut into ½-inch thick slices. Dip in flour or maize flour.

Sauté in butter or vegetable oil, browning on both sides. Cook slowly, if desired dry and crisp. Serve with maple syrup, honey, or black treacle.

TEMPTING WAYS TO SERVE COOKED CEREAL

● Add dried fruits such as raisins, dates, and prunes.
● Cook cereal with milk or use part milk instead of water.
● Combine 2 or more cereals and cook together.
● Serve cereal with honey, black treacle, brown sugar, or maple syrup instead of white sugar.
● Slice cold leftover cereal and fry. Serve with butter and syrup.
● Mix leftover cereal with minced cooked meat, fish, or vegetables. Chill. Slice and fry.
● Use leftover cereal as part of stuffing for fish, meats, and poultry.
● Use leftover cereal as a stuffing for baked apples. Fill cored centres. Top with brown sugar and bake.
● Add sweetening and desired flavourings to leftover cereal. Turn into fruit cups. Chill and serve with sweet sauces.

WHITE MAIZE FLOUR MUSH

Using top of double boiler over direct heat, add 1 teaspoon salt to 1¼ pints briskly boiling water.

Gradually add 3½ ounces white maize flour. Cook, stirring constantly, until thick, about 10 minutes. Place over boiling water.

Cover and cook ½ hour longer, stirring occasionally. Serves 4 to 6.

YELLOW MAIZE FLOUR MUSH

Using top of double boiler over direct heat, add 1 teaspoon salt to 1 pint briskly boiling water.

Combine 4 ounces maize flour or polenta and ¼ pint water. Slowly add to boiling water. Cook, stirring constantly, until thick, about 5 minutes.

Place over boiling water. Cover and cook ½ hour longer, stirring occasionally. Serves 4 to 6.

HOMINY

Hominy is hulled sweetcorn (maize) coarsely broken or ground into small pieces of about the same size. When it is very coarse, hominy is sometimes called samp. Pearl hominy: whole-grain hominy with the hulls removed by machinery; lye hominy: whole grains with the hulls removed by soaking in lye water; granulated hominy: a ground form; grits: broken grains.

BOILED HOMINY GRITS

2 pints water
1½ teaspoons salt
6 ounces hominy grits

Bring water with salt to a rapid boil in the upper part of a double boiler. Add grits slowly, while stirring, and cook until thickened over direct heat.

Cover, place over lower part of double boiler and cook over boiling water, stirring occasionally, for 2 hours. Serves 6.

FRIED HOMINY GRITS

1¼ pints water
¾ teaspoon salt
6 ounces hominy grits
3 tablespoons maize flour or
    polenta
1½ ounces butter or lard

Boil 1¼ pints water; add salt. Gradually stir hominy grits into rapidly boiling water. Cook about 1 hour over hot water, stirring occasionally.

Pour hominy into greased 2-pint loaf tin. Place in refrigerator until cold.

Cut into slices about ½ inch thick and dip into maize flour.

Heat butter in pan. Cook hominy slices in hot fat until brown on each side. Serve piping hot with syrup or honey. Makes 8 slices.

Polenta

HOMINY CAKES

Mix 1 pound cooked hominy with 1 slightly beaten egg, 2 tablespoons flour, and salt and pepper to taste.

Form into small flat cakes. Brown on both sides in butter or margarine. Serve with syrup or honey.

HOMINY AND CHEESE TIMBALES

6 ounces hominy, cooked
2½ to 3 ounces grated cheese
2 beaten eggs
¾ teaspoon salt
Dash of black pepper
2 teaspoons chopped green pepper
2 teaspoons chopped canned pimiento
2 tablespoons finely chopped parsley
8 fluid ounces scalded milk

Combine all ingredients well. Turn into individual casseroles.

Place in pan of hot water and cook in moderate oven (350°F. Mark 4) ½ hour.

Unmould and serve with cheese, tomato, or Spanish sauce. Serves 6.

HOMINY WITH HAM

1 ounce butter
4 ounces thinly sliced ham
6 ounces hominy, cooked
5 fluid ounces soured cream
Dash of black pepper

Melt butter in frying pan. Chop ham and cook in butter until slightly crisp and frizzled. Add drained hominy and cook until hominy is hot.

Add soured cream and pepper. Heat briefly to serving temperature, stirring constantly. Serves 4.

Hominy with Ham

POLENTA

Polenta is an Italian dish; a porridge or mush made usually of maize flour but also of chestnut meal, barley, or semolina. It is spread thinly on a large plate and covered with tomato or meat sauce, Parmesan cheese, and sometimes sausages. Polenta al forno is cold polenta baked in the oven with sauce and cheese; originally a way of using up leftovers.

ITALIAN POLENTA

8 ounces maize flour or polenta
1¾ pints water
1 teaspoon salt
1 onion, chopped
1 clove garlic, crushed
½ pound Italian sausage, chicken livers, or other meat, shredded
2 tablespoons olive oil
1 1-pound can tomatoes
¼ teaspoon oregano or thyme
1 bay leaf
Black pepper
2 ounces or more grated Parmesan cheese

Mix maize flour with ½ pint water. Heat remaining 1¼ pint water to boiling with salt in top of a double boiler. Add maize flour and cook, stirring, until thickened.

Place over hot water in lower part of double boiler and cook, covered, stirring occasionally, 1 hour.

Brown onion, garlic, sausage, or other meat in olive oil. Add tomatoes, oregano or thyme, bay leaf, pepper, and additional salt to taste. Simmer, stirring often, until thickened.

To serve, spread half the mush on a platter. Cover with half the sauce and half the cheese. Repeat the layers. Serves 5 to 6.

Polenta Variations

Prepare corn meal mush as directed above for polenta and serve as follows:

Cheese Squares: Pour hot polenta into a pan, making it about ¾ inch thick. Cool and chill.

Cut into squares and dip in lightly beaten egg that has been mixed with 2 tablespoons water. Roll in grated cheese, place in a casserole and dot with bits of butter.

Cook in moderate oven (350°F. Mark 4) until cheese has browned lightly. Serve with tomato sauce or soured cream.

Romanian Mamaliga: Fry 4 streaky bacon rashers until crisp. Grease a casserole with bacon fat.

Arrange corn meal mush, bacon fat and bacon, and grated Emmenthal cheese in layers, using plenty of cheese and fat.

Cook in moderate oven (350°F. Mark 4) about 25 minutes. Serve with sauerkraut.

Grits Au Gratin with Creole Prawns

GRITS

Grain, especially hominy, hulled an coarsely ground. It is used as a breal fast cereal; it is also served wit gravy in place of potatoes.

GRITS AU GRATIN

4 ounces grits
1¼ pints boiling water
1 teaspoon salt
2 ounces strong cheese, grated
8 fluid ounces milk
2 ounces dry buttered breadcrumb
¼ teaspoon paprika

Slowly stir grits into boiling, salte water in top of double boiler over di rect heat. Cover, place over boilin water, and continue cooking 45 min utes, stirring occasionally.

Alternate layers of cooked grits an grated cheese in greased casserole.

Add milk and sprinkle with brea crumbs and paprika. Cook in slow ove (325°F. Mark 3) 30 minutes. Serves 6.
Note: Grits au gratin may be baked i a greased ring mould and served wit Creole prawns or creamed meat c vegetables.

TORTILLAS

Tortillas are thin, flat unleavene cakes made of pounded sweetcorn (kind of coarse maize flour) baked on hot iron plate or flat stone. They ar used throughout Mexico in place c bread and are used as a base for man dishes. The recipe given here is de signed to be used with maize flour o polenta, generally available in delicates sens and health food shops.

1¼ pounds maize flour or polenta
8 ounces sifted plain flour
3 teaspoons salt
2 ounces lard or margarine
½ pint or a little less lukewarm water

Mix maize flour, flour and salt to gether in bowl.

Cut in margarine until mixture i finely divided. Make a well in mixtur and add about 8 fluid ounces water an stir.

If necessary, add more water until a ingredients form a ball and bowl i clean.

Turn onto cloth and knead well Form dough into small balls about 1 inches in diameter. Let balls stand 1 minutes. Then flatten each ball by rol ing with rolling pin until 6 inches i diameter.

Place on ungreased frying pan o griddle and cook about 2 minutes Turn and cook about 1 minute longer Makes 18 tortillas.

ENCHILADAS

An enchilada is a tortilla rolled round a meat, chicken, or cheese mixture, served with a sauce usually containing chilli; a Mexican dish. Enchiladas may also be made by stacking the tortillas and filling like griddle-cakes.

ENCHILADAS WITH LETTUCE

12 tortillas (above)
¾ pint enchilada sauce (below)
1 small onion, finely chopped
1 pound mature Cheddar cheese, grated
1 medium head lettuce, shredded
4 fried eggs (optional)

Heat sauce in frying pan. Combine onion, cheese, and lettuce.

For each enchilada, dip a tortilla into the hot enchilada sauce and place it on a plate. Sprinkle with lettuce mixture.

Cover with another tortilla dipped into the hot sauce. Sprinkle with lettuce mixture. Repeat with a third tortilla.

Pour about 2 tablespoons of the hot sauce over the top and serve at once. If wished, place a fried egg on top of each enchilada. Serves 4.

Note: Tortillas and enchilada sauce are available at some delicatessens.

ENCHILADA SAUCE

2 fluid ounces vegetable oil
1 medium-sized onion, peeled and finely chopped
1 clove garlic, peeled and crushed
1 sprig parsley, finely chopped
1 6-ounce can tomato purée
12 fluid ounces water
1 teaspoon vinegar
½ teaspoon oregano
½ teaspoon salt
1 teaspoon sugar
⅛ teaspoon cayenne pepper
2 teaspoons chilli seasoning

Heat oil in heavy frying pan. Add onion, garlic, parsley, and tomato purée. Simmer 3 minutes.

Add water, vinegar, oregano, salt, sugar, cayenne, and chilli seasoning. Bring to boil. Simmer 15 minutes to blend flavours. Makes about ¾ pint.

TACOS

Tacos are Mexican sandwiches made of tortillas rolled or folded to enclose fillings of meat, fish, refried beans, or other food, then fried or baked, sometimes toasted.

TOSTADAS

Tostadas are tortillas fried golden and crisp and often served with starters and soups. They are sometimes served covered with spoonfuls of various mixtures including refried beans, cheese, Mexican sausage, shredded lettuce, and sauce.

TAMALE

A Mexican and Central American dish basically of minced meat and maize flour wrapped in corn husks or banana leaves, tied up, dipped in oil, and steamed. There are a number of variations, and the Mexican ones always include chilli peppers. Versions in casserole form, usually less highly seasoned, are called tamale pies.

TAMALE PIE

1 1-pound can black olives
1 pound minced steak
2 tablespoons salad oil
1 large onion, chopped
1½ ounces chopped green pepper
8 ounces sliced celery
2 1-pound cans tomatoes
2 teaspoons salt
2 teaspoons chilli seasoning
10 ounces maize flour or polenta
1½ teaspoons salt
2¾ pints boiling water
8 ounces grated Cheddar cheese

Cut olives from stones into large pieces, reserving a few whole ones.

Brown mince in oil. Add onion and pepper and cook until clear. Stir in celery, tomatoes, 2 teaspoons salt, and chilli seasoning and simmer 10 minutes.

Stir maize flour and 1½ teaspoons salt slowly into boiling water. Turn heat low and cook 10 minutes, stirring occasionally.

Stir olives into meat mixture.

In greased 5-pint casserole arrange alternate layers of maize flour, meat mixture, and cheese, topping with a few spoonfuls of maize flour and a layer of cheese over all.

Cook in moderate oven (350°F. Mark 4) 45 minutes to 1 hour. Place a whole ripe olive in each maize flour puff.

Serves 6 to 8.

KASHA OR BUCKWHEAT GROATS

Kasha is a Russian and Yiddish term for buckwheat groats. The recipe given here is an old Jewish dish.

8 ounces buckwheat groats
½ teaspoon salt
½ teaspoon paprika
1 slightly beaten egg
8 fluid ounces boiling water
½ ounce chicken fat, butter, or fat

Combine buckwheat groats, salt, paprika, and egg; blend thoroughly.

Place in a greased 2-pint casserole. Cook in moderate oven (350°F. Mark 4) for 20 minutes.

Stir in the boiling water and fat. Cover and cook 20 minutes longer.

Serve with meat and gravy, with buttered noodles and sautéed mushrooms, as a cereal, or use as a filling for blintzes and knishes, or as a stuffing for meat or poultry. Makes about 1 pound.

SCRAPPLE

Scrapple is a firm mush made by boiling cooked, shredded pork in its own spicy broth with maize flour. When cold, it is sliced and fried. A Pennsylvania-Dutch dish, it was originally made only from pig's head. Buckwheat or other flours are sometimes used in place of maize flour.

PORK SCRAPPLE

Select 3 pounds of bony pieces of pork or half a pig's head. Simmer in 5 pints water until meat drops from bone.

Strain off broth and carefully remove all pieces of bone. Chop meat finely.

There should be about 3¼ pints of broth. If necessary, add water to make this quantity. Bring broth to boiling point; slowly add 14 ounces maize flour and cook mixture until thick, stirring almost constantly.

Add chopped meat, salt, and any other seasoning desired, such as onion salt, sage, and thyme.

Pour hot scrapple into loaf tins which have been rinsed with cold water. Chill until firm.

Slice and brown in hot frying pan. If scrapple is rich in fat, additional fat is not necessary for frying.

VEGETABLE SCRAPPLE

1 medium-sized onion
1 medium-sized carrot
½ green pepper
7 ounces maize flour or polenta
1 tablespoon salt
1 pint 8 fluid ounces boiling water
1 teaspoon Aromat
4 ounces chopped peanuts
Lard or vegetable oil

Finely chop onion, carrot, and green pepper.

Add maize flour and salt to boiling water slowly, stirring constantly until thickened.

Add chopped vegetables and Aromat. Cook over hot water 1 hour.

Add peanuts. Pour into well greased loaf tin. Chill.

When cold, slice and sauté until golden brown in small amount lard or vegetable oil. Serves 4 to 6.

Vegetable Scrapple

BOURGHOL WHEAT

Bourghol wheat is a special kind of cracked wheat that since Biblical times has been a basic food of the Middle East. Because it is so delicious and so rich nutritionally, it is worth searching for. If it is not available in your local shops, you can buy it in Greek food stores or in Armenian and Syrian groceries. Bourghol is a traditional accompaniment to shish kebab. It is cooked like rice. Also spelled bulghour, boulghour, bulgor, and burghul.

BOURGHOL PILAF

4 ounces butter or margarine
1½ pounds bourghol
1 small onion, finely chopped
2½ pints broth (chicken, lamb, or beef)
Salt and pepper

Melt butter in heavy frying pan; add dry bourghol. Cook over low heat until butter begins to bubble.

Fry onion in separate pan until golden brown. Mix with bourghol; add broth, and salt and pepper to taste.

Stir well and place in moderate oven (375°F. Mark 5) for 30 minutes. Then remove from oven, stir well, and cook 30 minutes longer. Serves 8 or more.

Armenian Rice Pilaf: Omit onions, substitute rice for bourghol and proceed as directed above.

PARTY TAMALE PIE

8 ounces maize flour or polenta
1¾ pints boiling water
1 large onion, chopped
2 tablespoons salad oil
½ pound minced beef
1 small can tomato purée
16 sliced stuffed olives
1 small jar (5¼ ounces) sliced black olives
1½ ounces chopped green pepper
2 teaspoons chilli seasoning
½ pint beef stock or consommé
1 pound sweetcorn
Dash of cayenne pepper
2 teaspoons salt
4 ounces grated cheese

Stir maize flour into rapidly boiling water. Cook and stir until thick with a long-handled spoon. Remove from heat.

Brown onion in oil in a frying pan. Add minced beef. Cook and stir until redness of meat disappears. Add tomato purée, stuffed olives, black olives, green pepper, chilli seasoning, stock, sweetcorn, cayenne, and salt. Stir well. Taste to be sure there is enough salt.

Pour into a shallow casserole (12× 8×2 inches). Sprinkle grated cheese over top. Sprinkle paprika liberally over surface. Cook in a moderate oven (350°F. Mark 4) 1 hour. Serves 16.

Rice Cookery

While rice has never been to us the all important food it is in many parts of the world, nevertheless it should be remembered that it is one of the most versatile of all our foods. It can be a breakfast cereal, an alternative to potatoes, or a dessert. It makes fine casseroles with other ingredients to give flavour and colour. It is the base for many popular foreign recipes suchas sukiyaki, chop suey, the Spanish and Mexican rice dishes, Indian curries, pilafs, and other Oriental dishes.

TYPES OF RICE

Rice is marketed in a variety of ways —each kind labelled to tell you what it is and each has its special advantage.

Precooked Rice: This quick type is completely cooked and requires only to be steamed in boiling water. Follow directions on the packet.

This rice will more than double in volume as it steams.

Converted Rice: The grains of this rice are parboiled before milling by means of a special steam-pressure method which aids in the retention of much of the natural vitamins and minerals.

Specific directions for cooking are given on the packet. After cooking, the grains will be separate, plump, and fluffy. Uncooked converted rice will give about 4 times its volume when cooked.

Regular Rice: This rice is cleaned, washed, and graded in the milling process.

It is advisable to wash well before cooking to remove mill flour. Weigh, wash, and then add water and salt as suggested on the packet. Or follow directions for fluffy boiled rice given below.

Short- and Long-Grain Rice: Regular rice may be either short-grain or long-grain. Short-grain or risotto rice cooks tender and moist and the particles tend to cling together. It is generally used for croquettes, pudding, or rice rings, where you need a tender rice which will mould more readily.

Long-grain rice will be fluffy and the grains will be separate after cooking. For this reason it is usually used for serving with stews and curries and the like.

Brown Rice: This is often preferred to white rice because it is a whole-grain rice, retaining the essential food values. It has a pleasing nutty flavour. It is, however, more perishable than white rice and requires greater care in packing and storing.

Wild Rice: This is not a real rice but is actually the seed of a marsh grass. The grains are long, dark, and greenish, chewier when cooked than other rice.

It has a distinctive flavour but it is quite expensive because wild rice has to be gathered by hand. It is considered a delicacy when served with game as accompaniment or stuffing.

HOW TO COOK FLUFFY, WHITE RICE

Put 8 ounces uncooked rice, 16 fluid ounces cold water, and 1 teaspoon salt into a 3½-pint saucepan and bring to vigorous boil.

Turn the heat as low as possible. Cover the saucepan. Do not remove cover or stir rice while it is cooking. Leave saucepan over this low heat for 14 minutes.

Turn heat off. The rice is now ready to use. However, leave the cover on the saucepan to keep the rice warm if you are not ready to use it immediately. Trebles its original volume.

For Extra-Fluffy, Tender, Separate Grains: Allow the rice to steam for an additional 10 minutes—with heat off, but without removing lid.

HOW TO COOK BROWN RICE

Wash 6 ounces brown rice. Gradually add to 1¾ pints boiling water to which 1 teaspoon salt has been added. Cover and cook over low heat until all liquid is absorbed, 40 to 60 minutes.

Uncover and let stand over low heat to let rice dry out and fluff. Trebles its original volume.

Note: Meat or chicken stock may be substituted for water and salt.

HOW TO COOK WILD RICE

Combine 8 ounces washed wild rice, and 1¼ pints water or consommé (and 1 teaspoon salt if you use water).

Place in saucepan, cover, and bring to boil rapidly. Reduce heat and cook about 25 minutes, or until rice swells and absorbs water.

Uncover and allow to steam dry. Add a little butter and serve with game, or add onion and chopped giblets, and use as stuffing for poultry. Serves 4 to 6.

STEEPED WILD RICE

Wash rice thoroughly in cold water. Drain. Cover 8 ounces rice with 1¾ pints boiling water. Allow to stand about 40 minutes.

Drain and cover again with boiling water. Allow to stand 20 minutes. Repeat this twice again, using fresh boiling water each time.

Last time, add 2 teaspoons salt and then drain thoroughly. Serve with ½ ounce melted butter and season to taste.

Top O' Cooker Rice Dishes

RISOTTO

Risotto is an Italian term for various rice dishes, often for rice sautéed in oil, butter, or margarine, then cooked in stock, sometimes with chicken, meat, seafood, cheese, and other ingredients.

RISOTTO ALLA MILANESE

- 4 ounces butter or margarine
- 2 onions, chopped
- 1 pound short-grain rice
- 4 fluid ounces white wine
- 1¼ pints stock (chicken or beef, canned or cubes)
- Pinch of saffron
- Salt and pepper
- 8 ounces grated Parmesan cheese

Melt half the butter or margarine in deep frying pan, add onions and brown lightly. Add rice, stir well and cook 15 minutes.

Add wine, stock, saffron, salt and pepper to taste. Cover and simmer gently about 20 minutes, until rice is fluffy and tender. Stir occasionally while cooking.

Just before serving, melt remaining butter or margarine, and sprinkle over rice with grated cheese. Serves 4.

RICE AND CHEESE

Serve cooked rice with cheese sauce or add 6 to 8 ounces grated cheese to hot cooked rice.

PINEAPPLE RICE

Blend 1 to 1¼ pounds cooked rice with the contents of 1 1-pound can chunks or crushed pineapple, drained.

RICE MEDLEY

- 1 ounce butter or margarine
- 2 ounces diced celery
- 12 ounces cooked rice
- 1 4½-ounce can luncheon meat
- 1 egg, beaten
- ¼ teaspoon salt
- Dash of black pepper
- 2 ounces Cheddar cheese, grated
- 4 rashers streaky bacon, grilled and crumbled

Melt butter in frying pan; sauté celery until tender but not brown. Add rice, meat, egg, salt, and pepper. Heat thoroughly, stirring constantly.

Pour into buttered casserole. Top with cheese and bacon. Place under grill only until cheese is melted. Serves 4.

Rice Medley

SPANISH RICE

- 4 ounces uncooked rice
- 3 rashers finely diced streaky bacon
- 2 tablespoons chopped onion
- 2 tablespoons chopped green pepper
- 8 fluid ounces tomato juice
- 1 teaspoon salt
- ⅛ teaspoon black pepper

Cook rice uncovered in boiling salted water until tender. Drain and blanch with boiling water.

Fry bacon until crisp; remove from frying pan. Cook onion and pepper in bacon fat until golden brown and tender.

Add rice, tomato juice, salt, pepper, and bacon. Simmer 10 minutes, or until most of tomato juice has been absorbed by rice. Stir occasionally to prevent sticking. Serves 4.

CURRIED RICE

- 1 ounce lard or cooking oil
- 8 ounces uncooked rice
- 1 tablespoon chopped onion
- 1¼ pints boiling water or meat stock
- 1 to 2 tablespoons curry powder
- 2 teaspoons salt

Heat lard in a saucepan. Add rice and onion and stir until rice is golden brown.

Add boiling water or stock and seasonings. Cover and cook slowly until tender, about 30 minutes. Serves 4.

Pilaf

Pilaf, also spelled pilau, pilaff, and pilaw, is a term applied to any of a number of Near Eastern rice dishes, usually highly seasoned. The rice is often fried in butter or oil before the liquid is added; nuts, bits of meat, poultry, or fish are sometimes mixed in or served on top. The same term is often applied to other grain dishes, for example Bourghol Pilaf.

RICE PILAF

- 8 ounces uncooked rice
- 3 chicken stock cubes
- 12 fluid ounces boiling water
- 2 ounces slivered blanched almonds
- 2 ounces butter or margarine

Brown rice lightly in uncovered heavy saucepan or frying pan with tight-fitting cover. Stir occasionally to distribute heat evenly.

Dissolve stock cubes in water and add to rice. Cover and bring to boil over medium heat. Reduce heat to low and cook until rice is fluffy and done, 25 to 30 minutes.

Cook almonds in half the butter until lightly browned, stirring constantly.

Melt remaining butter with nuts, then mix with rice, tossing lightly with a fork. Serves 4 to 5.

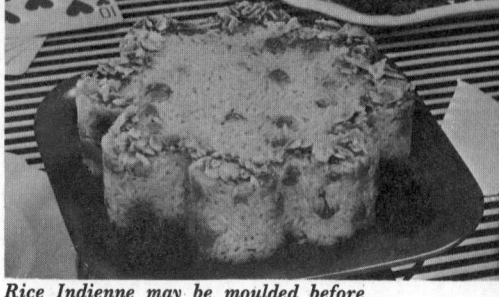

Rice Indienne may be moulded before serving.

RICE INDIENNE

- 8 ounces uncooked rice
- ¾ pint chicken stock
- 1 ounce butter or margarine
- 2 ounces sultanas
- ½ teaspoon salt
- 1 ounce browned slivered almonds

Combine rice, stock, butter, sultanas, and salt in saucepan. Bring to the boil and stir. Cover and simmer 14 minutes. Add almonds and mix lightly with a fork. Serves 4 to 6.

MEXICAN RICE

- 8 ounces rice
- ½ clove garlic, crushed
- 1 small onion, chopped
- 1 ounce margarine or lard
- 2 teaspoons salt
- ½ medium-sized green pepper, chopped
- 2 teaspoons chilli seasoning
- 1 8-ounce can tomatoes
- ¾ pint beef stock

Wash rice; sauté with garlic and onion in hot fat until browned.

Add salt, green pepper, chilli seasoning, tomatoes, and stock; cover and simmer 20 to 30 minutes, or until rice is soft. Remove cover during last 5 minutes to finish evaporation and allow mixture to dry out.

One-half pound minced beef may be cooked with rice, if desired. Serves 6.

TEXAS RICE AND RED BEANS

- 1 pound dried red kidney beans
- ¼ pound salt pork
- 3¼ pints water
- 1 small clove garlic, crushed
- 1 tablespoon chilli seasoning
- 1 teaspoon salt
- 1¼ pounds cooked rice

Cook beans with salt pork in boiling water until tender.

Add garlic, chilli seasoning, and salt to taste. Simmer until gravy is heavy. Add rice; serve. Serves 6.

Texas Rice and Red Beans

Paella Valenciana

PAELLA

Paella is a classic Spanish rice dish with many variations. The most famous is the Valencia-style, which is made of several kinds of seafood, chicken, sausage, pimiento, peas, and tomatoes, flavoured with garlic and saffron.

PAELLA VALENCIANA

2 small roasting chickens
3 fluid ounces olive oil
3½ teaspoons salt
12 ounces uncooked rice
2 cloves garlic, crushed
1 bay leaf, crumbled
Large pinch of saffron
¼ teaspoon black pepper
3 quartered tomatoes or 1 8-ounce can tomatoes
1 green pepper, sliced
1 canned pimiento or 1 sweet red pepper, sliced
Dash of cayenne pepper
1 pound fresh hot Spanish or Italian sausage or pork sausages, cut in 1-inch pieces
1 dozen shelled clams, or 1 pint mussels
1 pound cooked prawns
½ pound cooked lobster, cut up
6 ounces cooked peas

Cut chickens into 20 pieces; fry until browned in hot oil. Transfer to large casserole; season with 1 teaspoon salt.

Put rice and garlic in frying pan and cook slowly until rice browns a little. Add bay leaf, saffron, 2½ teaspoons salt, pepper, tomatoes, green pepper, pimiento, and cayenne. Bring to boil, stirring gently with fork. Pour over chicken.

Cover and cook in hot oven (425°F. Mark 7) 25 minutes. Reduce heat to moderate (375°F. Mark 5) and add sausages which have been fried until brown. Add clams or mussels, prawns, lobster, and peas. Stir lightly with fork.

Cover and cook until rice is dry and fluffy, about 15 minutes longer. Serves 8 to 10.

QUICK MEXICAN RICE

Toss cooked rice lightly with butter and chilli seasoning.

PIMIENTO RICE

To 12 ounces hot cooked rice, add 6 to 8 ounces grated cheese and 2 chopped canned pimientos.

QUICK SAFFRON RICE

2 ounces butter or margarine
½ medium onion, grated
½ teaspoon dried saffron
¾ pint canned chicken broth or 2 chicken stock cubes dissolved in ¾ pint boiling water
8 to 10 ounces packeted pre-cooked rice*

Sauté onion until golden in 1 ounce butter in frying pan.

Mix saffron with 1 tablespoon chicken broth; set aside.

Bring remaining broth to boil in saucepan. Add rice and onion; mix until all rice is moistened. Cover and remove from heat; allow to stand 13 minutes.

Lightly mix in saffron and 1 ounce butter with fork. Serve with roast chicken or chicken or seafood curry. Serves 4.

*Note: Or use 8 ounces raw, regular or processed white rice; combine with 1 pint chicken broth in saucepan; bring to boil; simmer, covered, 20 minutes; add sautéed onion, saffron, and butter.

JAMBALAYA

Jambalaya is a Creole dish of highly seasoned rice, ham, prawns or other shellfish, and tomatoes. The name is believed to come in part from the French word for ham, *jambon*.

½ ounce margarine
1 tablespoon flour
8 ounces cleaned cooked or raw prawns
1 pound chopped cooked ham
12 ounces canned or fresh tomatoes
1 onion, sliced
1 sweet red pepper, chopped
1 green pepper, chopped
1 clove garlic, crushed
Sprig of thyme (optional)
1 tablespoon chopped parsley
1 teaspoon Worcestershire sauce
1 teaspoon salt
Dash of black pepper
Paprika
1¾ pints water
8 ounces raw rice

Melt margarine; blend in flour, stirring constantly, until smooth and slightly brown.

Add prawns, ham, and tomatoes; cook 3 minutes. Add onion, red and green pepper, garlic, thyme, parsley, Worcestershire sauce, about 1 teaspoon salt, dash of pepper, a sprinkling of paprika, and water. Bring to boiling point and simmer about 12 minutes.

Add rice, cover and cook until tender, about 30 minutes.

Do not stir the mixture but lift occasionally with a fork from bottom of pot to keep rice from burning. Serves 6 or more.

RISOTTO WITH PRAWNS

1 large onion, chopped
3 ounces chopped celery
2 ounces sliced mushrooms (fresh or canned)
2 fluid ounces cooking oil
12 ounces uncooked rice, washed
1 6-ounce can tomato purée
18 fluid ounces hot water
2 teaspoons salt
1 teaspoon Worcestershire sauce
¾ teaspoon thyme
¼ teaspoon black pepper
1 clove garlic, crushed
1 pound prawns, cooked and cleaned
6 ounces cooked green peas

Cook onion, celery, and mushroom in oil until lightly browned.

Remove vegetables from pan; add rice and brown over low heat, stirring constantly.

Add remaining ingredients except prawns and peas. Cover and simmer hour, or until rice is tender.

Stir in prawns and peas. He through, about 10 minutes longe Serves 4 to 5.

CREOLE RICE PILAF WITH MUSHROOMS

1 pound mushrooms, sliced
1 medium-sized onion, chopped
1 green pepper, chopped
Few sprigs of parsley, chopped
1 8-ounce can tomatoes
1 tablespoon tomato purée
2 fluid ounces vegetable oil
½ ounce butter or margarine
Salt and pepper to taste
8 ounces uncooked rice
8 fluid ounces water

Slice mushrooms into frying pa Add onion, green pepper, parsle tomatoes, tomato purée, oil, butter margarine, salt and pepper. Place o low heat; in about 10 minutes add th rice and the water. Cook 20 minute altogether.

Add hot water, a little at a time needed, if the mixture becomes to dry; but when the rice is tender, th liquid should be completely absorbe (Watch carefully to keep from burnin If frying pan is covered during par of the cooking time, the rice cook more quickly and is less likely to stick Serves 4.

Jambalaya

Rice Oven Dishes

DOLMAS

Dolmas are combinations of meat, rice, vegetables, and spices wrapped in cabbage, fig or especially vine leaves and stewed. Variations of such dishes with or without meat are popular throughout the Near East. Originally Turkish, the word is sometimes applied to anything similarly stuffed — green peppers, tomatoes, cucumbers, courgettes, etc.

VINE LEAF ROLLS (DOLMAS)

2 medium finely chopped onions
2 fluid ounces olive oil
8 ounces uncooked rice
1 ounce pine kernels
1 tablespoon chopped parsley
Juice of ½ lemon
½ teaspoon allspice
Salt and pepper
1 can vine leaves, well drained, or
    12 fresh leaves (see note
    below)

Brown onions in oil. Add rice, pine kernels, parsley, lemon juice, allspice, salt, and pepper.

Add 8 fluid ounces warm water and cook until liquid is absorbed.

Put a spoonful of mixture on each leaf. Roll up and fasten with a toothpick.

Put the plump rolls in casserole with fluid ounces water.

Cover and cook in moderate oven (350°F. Mark 4) 45 minutes, until liquid is absorbed. Serves 4.

Note: Canned vine leaves can be bought in Greek food shops; fresh ones (12 or more large leaves for this amount of rice) may be dropped into boiling water for 1 or 2 minutes to make them pliable. Drain and use as directed.

BROWN RICE AND MUSHROOMS

4 ounces canned mushrooms
4 ounces butter or margarine
2 tablespoons flour
8 fluid ounces milk-and-mush-
    room liquid
18 ounces cooked brown rice
½ teaspoon salt
Dash of black pepper
Buttered crumbs

Brown mushrooms in melted butter. Blend in flour, then milk to make a sauce. Add rice and seasonings.

Mix and turn into greased casserole. Top with buttered crumbs. Cook in moderate oven (375°F. Mark 5) until browned. Serves 6.

RICE WITH CHEESE

Combine 1 pound cooked rice with pint cheese sauce.

Turn into casserole or individual casseroles. Cook in hot oven (400°F. Mark 6) about 15 minutes.

TURKISH RICE

1½ ounces butter or margarine
1 onion, chopped
1 green pepper, chopped
1 clove garlic, crushed
    (optional)
8 ounces fresh mushrooms, sliced
3 ounces diced celery
1 pound uncooked rice
1½ teaspoons salt
1 pound canned tomatoes
¾ pint water
Buttered crumbs
Grated cheese (optional)
2 tablespoons chopped parsley

Melt butter in saucepan; add onion, green pepper, garlic, mushrooms, and celery. Brown over low heat, then add rice, salt, tomatoes, and water. Stir to blend.

Pour mixture into large buttered casserole. Cover and cook until rice has absorbed liquid and is tender.

Uncover, stir to blend ingredients, then top with crumbs. Dot with grated cheese if desired.

Brown uncovered in moderate oven (375°F. Mark 5). Garnish with chopped parsley. Serves 6 to 8.

ORANGE RICE

2 ounces margarine
16 fluid ounces hot water
8 ounces uncooked rice
1 tablespoon chopped onion
3 ounces diced celery
2 tablespoons grated orange rind
6 fluid ounces orange juice
1½ teaspoons salt

Add 2 ounces margarine to hot water.

Mix together rice, chopped onion, diced celery, orange rind, orange juice, and salt. Add hot water to rice mixture.

Place in a 5-pint casserole dish. Cover and cook in moderate oven (350°F. Mark 4) ¾ hour. Serves 6.

RICE À LA GRUCCI

1¼ pounds cooked rice
2 ounces grated Cheddar cheese
1 chopped canned pimiento
12 fluid ounces tomato juice
1½ teaspoons salt
Dash of black pepper
4 ounces corn flakes
1 ounce melted butter or
    margarine

Combine rice, cheese, pimiento, tomato juice, and seasonings. Pour into greased 2½-pint casserole.

Crush corn flakes slightly and mix with melted butter. Sprinkle over rice mixture.

Cook in moderate oven (350°F. Mark 4) about 30 minutes, until well heated. Serve at once. Serves 6.

GREEN RICE CASSEROLE

12 ounces cooked rice
2 ounces grated strong cheese
8 fluid ounces milk
1 beaten egg
2 tablespoons grated onion
1 ounce finely chopped parsley

Combine and mix all ingredients. Add salt to taste.

Turn into greased casserole. Cook in slow oven (325°F. Mark 3) 30 minutes. Serve with creamed seafoods. Serves 6.

BROWN RICE AND MUSHROOMS

2 ounces fresh mushrooms, sliced
1 ounce butter or margarine
½ small onion, chopped
1 ounce chopped green pepper
1 teaspoon chopped canned
    pimiento
½ teaspoon salt
12 ounces cooked brown rice
3 tablespoons grated Cheddar
    cheese
8 fluid ounces hot water

Sauté mushrooms in margarine. Add onion and green pepper and cook gently 5 minutes.

Add pimiento, salt, rice, cheese, and hot water. Turn into greased casserole.

Cook in moderate oven (350°F. Mark 4) until heated through, about 30 minutes. Serves 4 to 5.

PILAF WITH SALAMI

6 ounces uncooked rice
1 ounce butter or margarine
¾ pint hot stock
1 tablespoon chopped onion
2 teaspoons Worcestershire sauce
8 ounces cubed salami

Add rice to melted butter in frying pan and fry until golden brown.

Add stock, onion, and Worcestershire sauce. Heat to boiling point. Add salami and turn into casserole.

Cook in moderate oven (375°F. Mark 5) about 40 minutes. Add more water if necessary. Serves 4.

RICE FREDONA

Fill a greased casserole with 1 to 1¼ pounds cooked rice.

Beat 2 eggs lightly with 12 to 16 fluid ounces milk and pour over rice. Season with salt and pepper. Dot with butter and sprinkle with paprika.

Cook in moderate oven (350°F. Mark 4) until browned.

Rice À La Grucci

Fried Rice and Croquettes

FRIED RICE CROQUETTES
(Master Recipe)

1½ ounces butter or margarine
3 tablespoons flour
½ teaspoon salt
8 fluid ounces milk
9 ounces cooked rice
Fine dry breadcrumbs
1 lightly beaten egg

Melt butter in a saucepan; blend in flour and salt. Add milk and cook until thickened, stirring constantly.

Add rice; mix and spread on shallow plate to cool.

Shape into 6 croquettes. Roll in crumbs, then in beaten egg and again in crumbs.

Fry in deep, hot fat (375°F.) until brown. Drain on kitchen paper.

Rice Croquette Variations

Cheese-Rice Croquettes: Prepare and chill rice as directed in master recipe.

Mix grated cheese with a few drops onion juice. If necessary, moisten with a little milk.

Shape into small balls. Coat with thick layer of rice mixture. Proceed as in master recipe.

Cranberry-Rice Croquettes: Cut chilled cranberry jelly into cubes. Coat with chilled rice mixture. Proceed as in master recipe.

Pimiento-Rice Croquettes: Add 2 tablespoons chopped canned pimiento to rice mixture of master recipe.

Rice Croquettes with Jam: Make a depression in the top of each croquette when shaping them, or form into balls, then into nests. Proceed as in master recipe.

To serve, place a spoonful of redcurrant jelly in each.

Savoury Rice Croquettes: Prepare master recipe and add ¼ teaspoon paprika and 1 tablespoon tomato ketchup to rice mixture.

Sweet Rice Croquettes: Prepare master recipe; add 2 tablespoons icing sugar and grated rind of ½ lemon before cooling mixture.

Tomato-Rice Croquettes: In master recipe, substitute tomato juice for milk. Cook 1 tablespoon grated onion with the flour.

CREOLE RICE CAKES

4 rashers streaky bacon, chopped
3 tablespoons grated onion
3 tablespoons chopped green pepper
1 teaspoon salt
½ teaspoon black pepper
1¼ pounds cooked rice
4 ounces sifted plain flour
1 teaspoon baking powder
8 to 12 ounces tomato pulp

Sauté bacon until crisp. Reserve fat.

To the bacon, add rest of ingredients and mix well. Form into small, round, flat cakes.

Brown cakes in reserved bacon fat. Serve as a vegetable. Serves 6.

CHEESE AND RICE CROQUETTES

3 fluid ounces mayonnaise
2 tablespoons flour
3 ounces plain flour
1½ teaspoons salt
⅛ teaspoon black pepper
¼ teaspoon paprika
1 teaspoon onion juice
6 ounces grated cheese
1 pound cooked rice
Dry breadcrumbs

In a saucepan, combine mayonnaise and flour. Stir in milk. Cook until thickened.

Add seasonings, onion juice, and grated cheese and cook until cheese is melted.

Cool. Add cooked rice to cheese sauce and mix thoroughly.

Shape into 12 croquettes. Roll in dry breadcrumbs. Place in refrigerator for several hours.

Place on baking sheet and cook in hot oven (400°F. Mark 6) 20 minutes, or until well browned. Serve with a tomato sauce. Serves 6.

Note: These croquettes may be made and kept in the refrigerator for 24 hours, if desired. Cook just before serving.

MUSHROOM FRIED RICE (CHINESE)

½ ounce dried mushrooms
2 tablespoons oil
1 onion, chopped
2 ounces sliced fresh mushrooms
2 tablespoons chopped spring onions
1½ pounds boiled rice, cold
2 tablespoons soy sauce
½ teaspoon sugar
2 tablespoons chopped parsley

Wash and soak dried mushrooms in hot water for ½ hour.

Heat oil and, stirring, fry onion, fresh mushrooms, and spring onions.

Shred soaked mushrooms which have been drained and add to mixture. Add rice and stir until heated.

Add soy sauce and sugar and, when all is heated, serve topped with chopped parsley. Serves 5 to 6.

Fried Rice

FRIED RICE

Fried rice is a Chinese dish of previously boiled rice sautéed in oil or bacon fat with eggs, onions, soy sauce, and bits of cooked beef, pork, chicken, ham, or shellfish.

½ pound roasted or fried ham or bacon (a can of lobster or prawns may be substituted for meat)
2 eggs, slightly beaten
1¼ pounds cooked rice
1 tablespoon chopped onion
Dash of black pepper
½ teaspoon salt
2 tablespoons soy sauce

Cut ham or bacon in small pieces and fry. It is not necessary to heat or fry cold roast meat, canned lobster or prawns; simply cut small.

Fresh prawns or lobster should be sautéed in butter 3 minutes.

Fry eggs slightly on both sides in hot, well greased frying pan. Add rice, onion, pepper, salt, meat or seafood, and mix thoroughly while cooking about 3 minutes.

Remove from heat; add soy sauce and stir. Serve while hot. Serves 4.

PRAWN SUBGUM FRIED RICE

4 tablespoons groundnut oil
2 ounces diced fresh mushrooms
1½ ounces diced, cooked green pepper
2 large onions, chopped
3 ounces diced water chestnuts, optional
1½ teaspoons Aromat, optional
Salt and pepper to taste
3 slightly beaten eggs
2¼ pounds cooked rice
8 ounces diced, cooked cleaned prawns
2 finely chopped spring onions
4 tablespoons soy sauce

Heat oil in frying pan. Add mushrooms, green pepper, onions, chestnuts, Aromat, and salt and pepper. Mix well and stir 4 minutes over moderate heat.

Add eggs and fry about 1 minute, or until firm. Add rice and prawns; mix well and stir constantly for 4 minutes.

Add spring onions and soy sauce; mix thoroughly. Serves 4 to 6.

Variations: Substitute for the prawns an equal amount of cooked lobster, chicken, roast pork, or boiled ham.

Rice Rings, Loaves, and Timbales

RICE RING
(Master Recipe)

For a 1½-to-2-pint ring mould, use 8 ounces uncooked rice and 2 ounces melted butter or margarine.

For a 3-pint ring mould, use 12 ounces uncooked rice and 3 ounces melted butter or margarine.

Cook rice and add melted butter to hot rice. Pack into well buttered ring mould. Allow to stand a minute; invert on warmed serving dish.

Fill centre with creamed ham, fish, vegetables, or chicken.

Rice-Cheese Ring: Omit butter in above. Blend 4 ounces grated cheese with cooked rice.

Mould and serve with creamed celery, eggs, or fish.

Rice-Pea Ring: Arrange layer of buttered peas in bottom of mould before adding rice.

Serve with creamed chicken, salmon, or tuna fish.

Rice-Chilli Ring: Add 1 to 2 teaspoons chilli seasoning to hot rice. Mould.

Serve with meat balls or meat sauce in centre.

RICE TIMBALES

Pack cooked rice in buttered moulds. Allow to stand in hot water about 10 minutes.

Unmould, garnish with a mushroom cap and serve with cheese sauce.

TO KEEP RICE RING HOT OR TO REHEAT

If a rice ring has been made the day before or prior to serving time, it must be reheated or kept hot until the meal is to be served.

To do this, cover the mould with foil or greaseproof paper to prevent the rice from becoming dry. Tie string just under the edge of the mould to hold the paper secure.

Put the ring in a pan of hot water and leave in a slow oven or over a low heat on top of the cooker until time to serve. No special timing is necessary. However, the ring must be left long enough for the rice to be hot when served.

To keep ring mould hot or to reheat

NUT LOAF

- 2 ounces butter or margarine
- 4 ounces chopped celery
- ½ small onion, chopped
- 1 ounce chopped green pepper
- 1 ounce plain flour
- 1½ teaspoons salt
- ⅛ teaspoon black pepper
- 12 fluid ounces milk
- 8 ounces chopped walnuts
- 12 ounces cooked rice
- 2 tablespoons chopped parsley
- 2 tablespoons canned pimiento
- 4 eggs, beaten
- 2 ounces fine dry breadcrumbs

Melt butter or margarine. Add celery, onion, and green pepper; cook slowly until soft but not brown. Blend in flour, salt, pepper, then milk; cook until thickened, stirring constantly. Add remaining ingredients; mix well.

Press into greased 9×5×3-inch loaf tin. Cook in moderate oven (375°F. Mark 5) until set, 35 to 40 minutes. Cool in tin 5 minutes, then remove from tin and allow to stand 10 minutes before slicing. Serve with Carrot Sauce (below). Serves 6.

Carrot Sauce:
- 2½ ounces butter or margarine
- 8 ounces shredded raw carrots (about 8 medium)
- 2 tablespoons chopped onion
- 1 ounce plain flour
- ¼ teaspoon salt
- ⅜ pint water
- 2 vegetable or beef stock cubes

Melt butter or margarine. Add carrots and onion; cook, stirring constantly, until carrots are almost tender. Blend in flour and salt. Add water and stock cubes. Cook, stirring constantly until thickened. Serve with Nut Loaf. Makes 1 pint sauce.

MUSHROOM RICE RING

- 8 ounces uncooked rice
- 8 ounces mushrooms, chopped
- 1 ounce butter or margarine
- 2 fluid ounces hot stock or water
- Salt and paprika

Cook rice until tender. Drain.

Sauté mushrooms in butter 3 minutes and stir in stock or water.

Combine mushroom mixture with cooked rice. Season to taste. Turn into greased 7-inch ring mould.

Set in pan of hot water. Cook in moderate oven (350°F. Mark 4) about 30 minutes.

To serve, unmould on dish. Fill centre with creamed fish, meat, or buttered vegetables. Serves 6.

Nut Loaf

RICE RING

Combine 12 ounces cooked rice with 1 ounce melted fat and 1 teaspoon salt. Turn into greased ring mould.

Place mould in pan of hot water. Cook in moderate oven (350°F. Mark 4) 25 minutes.

Unmould on dish and fill centre with creamed fish, meat, vegetable, as desired. Sprinkle with paprika. Garnish outside of ring with border of cooked peas.

CHEESE RICE RING

- 4 ounces uncooked rice
- 1 beaten egg
- 1 ounce melted butter or margarine
- 2 fluid ounces milk
- 1 to 1½ ounces grated cheese
- ⅛ teaspoon grated onion
- ¼ teaspoon salt
- 2 tablespoons chopped parsley
- 1 teaspoon Worcestershire sauce

Cook rice until tender and drain. Combine with remaining ingredients and turn into greased 7-inch ring mould.

Set in pan of hot water and cook in moderate oven (350°F. Mark 4) about 40 minutes. To serve, unmould on a dish. Serves 4.

ALMOND RICE RING WITH BEEF STEW

- 1¼ pounds cooked rice
- 2 ounces coarsely chopped browned almonds
- 2 ounces melted butter or margarine
- 2 1-pound cans beef stew

Combine rice, almonds, and butter. Put into a well greased ring mould. Set the mould in a pan of hot water and cook in moderate oven (350°F. Mark 4) about 20 minutes.

Loosen the edges with a knife and invert on a dish. Fill the centre with heated stew. Serves 4 to 6.

Almond Rice Ring with Beef Stew

CHEESE AND CHEESE DISHES

Foods come alive with flavour when cheese is a principal ingredient. Take your choice of main dish casseroles, tangy sauces and salad dressings, cool salads enriched with cheese, crusty cheese breads, tempting cheese desserts, etc. Throughout this book you'll find hundreds of recipes with new ideas in cheese uses and cheese cookery. To find everything we have published on this subject, consult the index.

CHOOSING CHEESE

Selecting and buying the right cheese is largely a matter of personal preference. Some people prefer mild cheese; others favour sharp or strong-flavoured cheeses. Children generally like mild cheeses and their elders the more pungent varieties.

Information follows on the various forms of cheese available in retail markets. These facts may enlarge your acquaintance with the cheese family and help you use cheese more interestingly and appetizingly.

CHEESE COOKERY HINTS

● Successful cheese cookery depends on brief heating at a low temperature. High temperatures and too-long cooking make cheese tough and stringy, and cause the fat to separate out. Some of the flavour is lost, too.
● Cheese blends more readily with other ingredients if you grate or dice it first.
● Soft, mature Cheddar melts and blends with other ingredients more readily than less ripened cheese, and less of it is needed because it has a more pronounced flavour. Processed cheese also melts and blends readily, but has a much milder flavour.
● Melt cheese in the top of a double boiler over simmering water, or add it to a hot mixture. When making cheese sauce, stir in the grated cheese

after the white sauce is completely cooked, and heat only enough to melt the cheese. When making a cheese omelet, add the grated cheese after the omelet is cooked — just before folding.
● Cheese can be melted under the grill, too. Open cheese sandwiches can be made this way. Grill under a medium flame just until the cheese begins to melt.
● Casserole dishes containing cheese should be cooked at low to moderate temperatures. To prevent cheese toppings from toughening or hardening during cooking, cover them with crumbs or add the cheese just before removing the food from the oven.

STORING CHEESE

Cheese keeps best in the refrigerator. How long it will keep depends on the kind of cheese and the wrapping. Soft cheeses — such as cottage, cream, and Neufchâtel — are highly perishable. Hard cheeses — Cheddar and Emmenthal, for example — keep much longer than soft cheeses if protected from drying out. Approximate storage times are given below.

Leave cheese in its original wrapper, if possible. Cover cut surfaces tightly with greaseproof paper, foil, or polythene to protect the surface from drying out, or store the cheese in a tightly covered container. If you want to store a large piece of cheese for an extended time, dip the cut surface in melted wax. Store cheese that has a strong odour, such as Gorgonzola, in a tightly covered container.

Any surface mould that develops on hard natural cheese should be trimmed off completely before the cheese is used. In mould-ripened cheeses such as Blue or Roquefort, mould is an important part of the cheese and can be

eaten. If mould penetrates the interior of cheeses, such as Cheddar and Gruyère, that are not ripened by mould, cut away the mouldy portions or discard the cheeses.

Cheese that has dried out and become hard may be grated and stored in a tightly covered jar.

Home Storage Guide for Cheese

Cottage, fresh Ricotta: Refrigerate, covered; use within 3 to 5 days.

Cream, Neufchâtel, other soft varieties: Refrigerate, covered or tightly wrapped; use within 2 weeks.

Cheddar, Emmenthal, other hard varieties: Refrigerate, tightly wrapped; will keep for several months unless mould develops.

Cheese spreads and cheese foods: Store unopened jars at room temperature; after opening, refrigerate, tightly covered; will keep for several weeks.

TO ENHANCE CHEESE FLAVOUR

Except for soft, unripened cheeses such as cottage or cream cheese, all cheeses taste better when served unchilled. This usually requires from 20 minutes to 1 hour at room temperature to bring out the distinctive flavour and texture.

TO SLICE CHEESE

You may prefer to buy a cheese slicer in order to have slices of uniform thickness. A heavy thread or fine wire can also be used to slice cheese; this works especially well with blue cheese.

GRATED CHEESE

If cheese is to be grated or shredded, the job is easier if you work with cold cheese taken directly from the refrigerator. Use ends of cheese or dry hard cheese such as Cheddar, Gruyère, Parmesan, or Romano. Grate small quantities as needed just before using.

Guide to Natural Cheeses

APPETITOST
A Danish cheese made from sour buttermilk.

ASIAGO
A cheese of Italian origin with a dark surface, cream-coloured interior, piquant flavour, and granular texture.

Use it for general table use when fresh, for grating when old and drier.

BEL PAESE
Light yellow. Mellow flavour. Soft to solid consistency.

Delicious with cream crackers or with fruit for dessert.

BLUE CHEESES
Blue, blue-mould, or blue-veined cheese is the name for cheese of the Roquefort type that is made from cow's or goat's milk, rather than ewe's milk. The French word for this type of cheese is *bleu*.

As a general term, blue is sometimes used to refer to many Roquefort-type cheeses marbled with a blue-green mould, including Stilton, Roquefort itself, Danish Blue, and Gorgonzola, etc. All have a mild-to-sharp sort of pungent salty flavour.

Use crumbled in crunchy salads, in salad dressings, for canapé spreads, and snacks. Particularly delicious with fresh pears or toasted unsalted crackers and sherry. Makes an excellent topping for grilled steaks.

BRIE
A soft, creamy French cheese with a light russet-brown crust. It has a pronounced odour and sharp flavour.

Spread it, crust and all, on biscuits, dark, whole-grain breads, on French bread, or on slices of unpeeled apple.

CACIOCAVALLO
This cheese, originally from Italy, is made in a number of unusual shapes, often tied in pairs. The surface is light brown. The cured cheese has a smooth, firm body, and preferably the interior of the cheese is white. It has a somewhat salty, smoky flavour.

Use it as a table cheese when it's fresh, that is cured not more than 2 to 4 months. When fully cured, 6 to 12 months, it is suitable for grating.

CAERPHILLY
A Welsh cheese, medium hard, white in colour, with a slight bite in the taste.

CAMEMBERT
A soft, creamy, yellowish French cheese with a thin, whitish crust. Rich, mild flavour.

To serve, soften it at room temperature. At its peak, interior will be like thick cream. Serve as for Brie.

CHEDDAR
Cheddar cheese is named after the village of Cheddar in Somerset, where it was first made probably in the latter part of the 16th century.

The colour may be light cream to orange; the flavour mild when fresh, pronounced and pleasing when cured or aged.

It is very popular and is used in sandwiches, with pies, crumbles, etc., and in cooking—casseroles, soufflés, etc. Adds zest to tossed salads.

CHESHIRE
A solid cheese, stronger in flavour than Cheddar and red in colour. More crumbly, and piquant in flavour. Blue Cheshire is a refined version of the red.

COTTAGE CHEESE
Sometimes called pot cheese and also Dutch cheese or Schmierkäse, it is a soft, uncured cheese made from skimmed milk or from reconstituted skimmed milk or non-fat dry milk solids.

Usually some cream is mixed with the cheese curd before it is marketed or consumed. If the cheese contains 4 per cent or more of fat, it is called creamed cottage cheese. Flavouring materials, such as peppers, olives, pimientos, may be added also.

Use it in salads or spreads, plain or flavoured with chives, nuts, pickle relish, diced fruit, etc.

CREAM CHEESE
Delicately flavoured, white, mild, and fresh as cream. Soft texture. Made from a mixture of cream and milk with minimum fat content of 35 per cent (usually 35 to 38 per cent).

Thin with cream to top fruit salads and desserts. Use as a sandwich filling, particularly with date and nut bread. Season and form into balls for hors d'oeuvres.

CURD CHEESE
Today, usually a commercially-made soft cheese made of skimmed milk, buttermilk or whey with salt added.

DEMI-SEL
A French cream cheese with 2 per cent salt added, and a butterfat content of at least 40 per cent.

EDAM
A round Dutch cheese with flattened ends and red coating. Usually made of skimmed milk, it is semi-soft, bland and creamy when young and less quick to melt than a young Gouda.

It is pretty to look at and the mild flavour blends well with tart apples, grapes and tangerines. Use as a bright centrepiece for a dessert or snack tray.

EMMENTHAL
The name for a true Swiss cheese which was first made, probably about the middle of the 15th century, in the Canton of Bern, in the Emmenthal Valley in Switzerland. It has a greyish brown surface, a white or slightly glossy cream interior colour. The texture is semi-hard with round, rather large holes throughout. It has a mild nut-like sweetish flavour.

Slice thin to serve on dishes with cold meats and other foods. Use with rye breads or serve in small sticks with salad plates. Adds interest to fruit and vegetable salads. Use it in fondues, etc.

ESROM
A soft, mellow cheese with numerous small holes, practically rindless. Similar to Port du Salut.

FETA, FETTA
Greek cheese, usually made mostly of goat's milk, white and flaky, kept moist by storing in brine.

GAMMELOST
A brown-coloured, strong-flavoured Norwegian cheese made of skimmed sour milk. Use for snacks and general table use.

GERVAISE
A French double-cream cheese, somewhat like a bland Camembert.

GJAETOST
A hard, dark brown, smooth-textured cheese with a full sweet flavour. It is made in Norway from goat's milk. Slice it thin and serve on biscuits or dark breads.

GORGONZOLA
A blue mould cheese made from cow's milk with a delicate, piquant flavour.

Crumble it into salads and salad dressings. Use it on cheese board and as a dessert cheese with biscuits or fruit.

GOUDA
Dutch whole-milk cheese, usually larger and richer in butterfat than Edam. Has a yellow rind and pale yellow interior. The shape is usually round but somewhat flattened on top and bottom, although some Goudas are made in other shapes. Gouda is creamy when young and becomes firmer when mature.

GRUYÈRE
A Swiss cheese with smaller holes and a taste similar to Emmenthaler, but with a higher butterfat content and a somewhat softer texture. It melts easily, and is a very popular cheese in the kitchen.

HAVARTI

A semi-hard, hole-pocked Danish cheese, mild, bland and slightly acid.

KOSHER CHEESE

Kosher cheese is made especially for Jewish consumers, to conform with Jewish dietary custom. It is made without animal rennet. Sometimes the milk is curdled by natural souring; sometimes a starter is added to the milk.

Among the kosher cheeses are soft cheeses like cream and cottage cheese, kosher gouda, and a cheese that is made by the Limburger process but, unlike Limburger, is eaten fresh. Kosher cheese bears a label by which it can be identified.

LANCASHIRE

Hard rennet-type cheese made in high and round shapes. When fresh, it is easy to spread. Also very good in cheese sauces or as an alternative to Cheddar.

LEYDEN

Dutch spiced cheese, usually made from skimmed milk, flavoured with cumin and fairly strongly salted.

LIMBURGER

Soft textured German cheese. Very characteristic odour and flavour. Despite the fact that there is so much jesting about it, Limburger is considered by many cheese fanciers to be one of the most delicious of cheeses. Actually, once you have got past the pungent smell of Limburger, you will find its taste rather mild.

Serve with toast, biscuits or rye and pumpernickel bread. The thin crust should be eaten to enjoy the flavour fully.

MOZZARELLA

A semi-soft, light, cream-coloured cheese made from buffalo's milk with a mild flavour.

It is used for the most part in cooking, especially in such dishes as aubergine or veal parmigiana and pizza. It's a "must" for real pizza.

MÜNSTER

Orange-coloured rind with light-yellow interior full of tiny holes. Often flavoured with aniseed or caraway seed. It has a semi-hard texture.

Serve with vegetable relish tray. Good with spring onions, cucumbers, carrot sticks, radishes, etc. Excellent with pumpernickel bread or date-nut bread.

MYCELLA

A Danish blue-veined cheese, similar to Gorgonzola.

MYSOST

A light brown cheese with a sweetish flavour made in the Scandinavian countries from goat's milk. Nice to slice thin and serve on biscuits or dark breads.

NEUFCHÂTEL

A cream cheese-type product of French origin with a smooth soft texture, mild flavour, white colour. Excellent for sandwiches, on crackers, in salads.

OKA

A type of Port du Salut cheese made in the Trappist monastery at Oka, Canada. It has a russet surface, creamy yellow interior with a semi-soft texture that slices well.

It is an excellent dessert cheese. The flavour goes especially well with port.

PARMESAN

Delicate yellow colour. Mild to full flavour. Texture is firm to hard—usually the latter.

Grate to serve on spaghetti, soups like minestrone and onion, on some salads and casseroles.

PETIT SUISSE

A fresh double-cream cheese of France, unsalted and made of whole milk with added cream. It is very creamy and delicate but highly perishable. Use as a dessert with honey, strawberries, sugar or jam.

PORT DU SALUT

Rennet cow's milk cheese of a type made at the Port du Salut abbey in eastern France. Delicate in flavour. It has a moderately soft interior but it slices well.

Serve with plain cream crackers or by itself. Good either way.

PROVOLONE

A smoky-tasting cheese that comes in several shapes. It's commonly seen hanging in ball shapes or long cylindrical forms in Italian provision shops.

Excellent with rye or whole wheat crackers.

RICOTTA

This soft-textured cheese is often called "Italian cottage cheese". It is made from whey with whole or skim milk added. Fresh, moist ricotta is the type usually found in our markets and it is popularly used in ravioli, lasagna, etc. Cured dry ricotta is suitable for grating.

ROMANO

An Italian cheese with a somewhat granular texture and practically no holes or eyes.

Excellent with rye bread or whole wheat crackers if it hasn't been aged more than about 8 months. More frequently it is cured for a year or more and then it is hard, very sharply piquant, and suitable for grating.

ROQUEFORT

A blue-veined and semi-soft-to-hard cheese, named after the village of Roquefort in south-eastern France, where its manufacture has been an important industry for more than two centuries. A French regulation limits use of the word Roquefort to cheese made in the Roquefort area from ewe's milk.

Other French cheese of the Roquefort type is called bleu cheese, and Roquefort-type cheese made in other countries is known as blue cheese. In addition, there are the distinctive blue-veined cheeses of England (Stilton) and Italy (Gorgonzola).

Only genuine Roquefort is allowed to have the name Roquefort. Imports are marked Roquefort-France. For uses, see above, **Blue Cheeses.**

SAMSOE

A semi-firm, whole-milk Danish cheese with holes or "eyes", mild and buttery when young, sharpening with age.

SAPSAGO

This cheese has been made in the Canton of Glarus, Switzerland, for at least 500 years and perhaps more; it is made also in Germany, where it is called Schabzeiger. It has a sharp, pungent, clover-like flavour, very hard texture suitable for grating; light green or sage green in colour. Grate it for seasoning.

SCAMORZA

A soft mild cheese of Italian origin, much like mozzarella and used in the same way. It is excellent in many Italian dishes, especially pizza. It is very tasty when toasted with bread or fried with an egg.

STILTON

Famous cheese with a ridged or wrinkled rind, creamy colour with blue or green mould interior. It has a semi-hard texture and sharp flavour.

Use it as a table cheese and for other purposes suggested for blue cheese. See **Blue Cheeses.**

TRAPPIST

Trappist cheese made in various monasteries in Europe is much the same as the Port du Salut cheese, but there are variations in the manufacturing process.

WENSLEYDALE

A whole-milk cheese, large in size, very white, slightly veined with green. Semi-creamy in texture. Made in Wensleydale, Yorkshire.

NATURAL CHEESE

Natural cheese is a product made by coagulating milk and then separating the curd, or solid part, from the whey, or watery part. Some natural cheeses are ripened (aged) to develop their characteristic flavour and texture; others are used unripened. Ripened cheeses sometimes are labelled as to the degree of ripening or ageing.

Cheddar cheese may be labelled "mild", "medium", or "mellow", "mature".

Many people prefer natural cheeses to other forms of cheese because each natural cheese has its own characteristic flavour and texture. Flavours range from bland cottage cheese to strong Blue or pungent Gorgonzola. Textures vary too — from the smooth creaminess of cream cheese to the firm elasticity of Emmenthal cheese.

The guide to natural cheeses lists cheeses likely to be found. Characteristics and suggested uses are given for each cheese.

PROCESSED CHEESES

Processed (or pasteurized processed) cheese is made by finely mincing and mixing together by heating and stirring, one or more cheeses of the same, or two or more, varieties, together with an added emulsifying agent, into a homogeneous, plastic mass. Other ingredients may be used such as small amounts of cream, water, salt, colour, and spices or flavouring materials. The cheese may be smoked, or it may be made from smoked cheese, or so-called liquid smoke or smoke "flavour" may be added.

During the manufacturing process it must be heated to pasteurizing temperature; therefore, it keeps well and does not ripen further.

Because it melts easily, it's excellent for all cheese cookery. It must be labelled "processed cheese".

CHEESE SPREADS

Cheese spreads (or pasteurized cheese spreads) are made in the same way as processed cheeses except that they contain more moisture (44 to 60 per cent) and less fat (but not less than 20 per cent) and must be "spreadable" at a temperature of 70°F. Fruits, vegetables, or meats may be added.

TO FREEZE CHEESE

Freezing is not recommended for most cheeses because they become crumbly and mealy when frozen. Small pieces (1 pound or less, not more than 1 inch thick) of the following varieties can be frozen satisfactorily: Cheddar, Edam, Gouda, Münster, Port du Salut, Emmenthal, Provolone, Mozzarella, and Camembert. You can also freeze small quantities of Danish Blue, Roquefort, and Gorgonzola for salads or salad dressings, or other uses where a crumbly texture is acceptable. Wrap cheeses tightly, freeze quickly at 0°F. or below, and store no longer than 6 months. When removed from the freezer, cheese should be thawed in the refrigerator and used as soon as possible after thawing.

Appetizing Ways with Cheese

THE CHEESE BOARD FOR SNACKS OR DESSERT

The cheese board is a simple-to-do and easy-to-serve dessert or snack. Cheese and biscuits are a favourite finish to dinner with many people and particularly with men. A perfect accompaniment to cheese is attractive pieces of fresh fruit; apples, pears, and grapes are the most popular.

Cheese arrangements may be made on any type of board or on a revolving tray. Vary the decorative effects by cutting cheeses into attractive shapes: cubes, balls, wedges, etc. Grated mature Cheddar may be moulded to look like pumpkins, pears, etc.

Recipes Featuring Cheese

WELSH RAREBIT
(Basic Recipe)

Welsh rarebit is a thick sauce traditionally of melted Cheddar cheese and ale or beer, seasoned with Worcestershire sauce, mustard, salt, sometimes pepper, and paprika. There are many variations. Milk is often substituted for the ale or beer and egg or egg yolk is sometimes added for a smoother mixture. Ideally, rarebit is made at the table in a chafing dish and accompanied by a dry white wine or beer.

1 ounce butter or margarine
2 tablespoons flour
½ teaspoon salt
Few grains cayenne pepper
8 fluid ounces milk or single cream
½ teaspoon dry mustard
4 ounces grated cheese
4 slices of toast

Prepare white sauce by melting butter, blending in flour, salt, and cayenne, and gradually adding milk. Cook over hot water, stirring constantly until thick.

Add mustard and cheese, stirring until cheese is melted and mixture smooth. Serve hot on toast. Serves 4.

Variations
Bacon Rarebit: Dice 2 or 3 rashers of crisp, drained streaky bacon and add to sauce with the cheese.

Buck Rarebit: Top each cheese-and-toast slice with an egg and put under the grill until egg is set.

English Monkey: Substitute 2 ounces dry breadcrumbs for flour in sauce. Add 1 slightly beaten egg to sauce.

Olive Rarebit: Add 16 sliced stuffed olives to sauce.

Onion Rarebit: Sprinkle grated or chopped onion over rarebit.

Oyster Rarebit: Add 6 parboiled oysters to sauce.

Roast Rarebit: Pour rarebit over toast. Cook in slow oven (325°F. Mark 3) until golden brown, about 15 minutes.

Welsh Rarebit

Rum Tum Tiddy: Add 1 teaspoon Worcestershire sauce and 1 slightly beaten egg to tomato rarebit (below).

Sardine Rarebit: Arrange 3 or 4 sardines on each slice of buttered toast. Place under hot grill 2 to 3 minutes. Pour over rarebit sauce. Serve at once.

Tomato Rarebit: Substitute 8 fluid ounces condensed tomato soup for milk. If desired, add 1 tablespoon each grated onion and chopped green pepper.

Tuna Fish Rarebit: Add 4 ounces flaked tuna fish to sauce.

WELSH RAREBIT WITH ALE OR BEER

½ ounce butter or margarine
4 fluid ounces ale or beer
1 pound grated Cheddar cheese
2 egg yolks
2 teaspoons Worcestershire sauce
1 teaspoon French mustard
Salt
2 fluid ounces milk
Paprika

Place butter and ale or beer in chafing dish or double boiler. When hot, add cheese and melt slowly, stirring continually.

When smooth, add egg yolks mixed with seasonings and milk and stir for a few minutes until thickened.

Serve on the soft side of bread toasted on one side with crusts removed. Garnish with dash of paprika. Serves 6.

EGG RAREBIT WITH ASPARAGUS SPEARS

2 to 3 ounces diced celery
½ small chopped onion
1 ounce butter
1 10½-ounce can condensed
    cream of tomato soup
½ teaspoon French mustard
Dash of Tabasco sauce, optional
4 fluid ounces milk
4 ounces grated strong or mild
    processed Cheddar cheese
6 hard-boiled eggs, coarsely chopped
2 1-pound packets frozen asparagus
    spears, cooked, or 2 1-pound
    cans asparagus spears,
    drained

Cook celery and onion, slowly, in butter until tender but not brown. Stir in soup, seasonings, and milk; heat.

Fold in cheese and eggs and allow cheese to melt and eggs to heat, stirring frequently. Pour over hot cooked drained asparagus spears. Serve plain or on toast triangles. Serves 6.

Swiss Fondue

SWISS FONDUE

This is a hot mixture of melted cheese and wine, sometimes thickened with cornflour. Traditionally Emmenthal or Gruyère cheese is used. The cheese or combination of cheeses used must be natural cheese, not the processed variety. The wine may be any light dry white wine of the Rhine, Riesling, or Chablis types. For an authentic Swiss touch kirsch is added; however you may substitute a non-sweetened fruit brandy such as applejack, slivovitz, cognac, etc., or light rum. Swiss fondue is usually made and served in a chafing dish. It is accompanied by thick cubes of crusty French bread to dip into the fondue. The bread cubes are first speared with the fork going through the soft part.

1 clove garlic
¾ pint dry white wine
1 pound Emmenthal or Gruyère
    cheese, grated
2 teaspoons cornflour
3 tablespoons kirsch, optional
Freshly-ground black pepper
1 loaf French or Italian bread

Rub the bottom and sides of an earthenware casserole or chafing dish with garlic. Add wine and heat to boiling point but do not boil.

Add cheese, stirring constantly with wooden spoon. When cheese is creamy and barely simmering, add cornflour blended with kirsch. Stir until mixture bubbles. Add pepper to taste.

Place casserole over an alcohol burner or transfer to a chafing dish or electric frying pan adjusted to low heat. Keep the fondue hot but not simmering. If it becomes too thick, add a little more wine. To serve, accompany with 1-inch cubes of bread for dipping into the fondue. Makes about 1¼ pints or about 4 servings.

Egg Rarebit with Asparagus Spears

Cheese Lunch Tart

CHEESE LUNCH TART

8 ounces shortcrust pastry
4 rashers streaky bacon, finely chopped
½ small onion, finely chopped
2 tablespoons finely chopped green pepper
12 fluid ounces milk
3 eggs
1 tablespoon canned pimiento, finely chopped
¼ teaspoon black pepper
8 ounces Cheddar cheese, grated
Sliced stuffed olives for garnish

Prepare pastry and place in pie tin. Chill.

Fry bacon until crisp. Remove from pan. Pour off all but 1 ounce fat. Cook onions and green pepper until soft but not brown.

Heat milk to scalding, then add slowly to slightly beaten eggs. Add bacon, onion-green pepper mixture, pimiento, and pepper. Add cheese.

Pour into chilled pastry crust and bake in slow oven (325°F. Mark 3) 45 minutes to 50 minutes or until set. Garnish if desired with stuffed olive slices. Serve immediately. Serves 6.

TOMATO SUPER SUPPER DISH

2 ounces soft butter or margarine
6 slices bread, toasted
10 ounces grated Cheddar cheese
3 eggs, slightly beaten
2 10½-ounce cans condensed tomato soup
¼ teaspoon salt
¼ teaspoon dry mustard

Spread butter on toasted bread; cut each slice into 6 squares.

Grease a 3½-pint casserole; place in it alternate layers of toast squares and cheese, ending with a top layer of cheese.

Combine eggs, soup, salt, and mustard; pour over bread-cheese layers.

Cook in slow oven (325°F. Mark 3) about 1 hour.

Garnish with border of finely chopped green pepper and sprigs of parsley. Serve piping hot as a hearty lunch or supper dish. Serves 6.
Variation: This dish may be made with condensed cream of mushroom soup instead of tomato for Mushroom Super Supper Dish.

BLENDER WELSH RAREBIT

12 fluid ounces milk
1 egg
1 teaspoon Worcestershire sauce
1 teaspoon salt
¼ teaspoon dry mustard
½ teaspoon paprika
1 tablespoon cornflour
8 ounces diced strong Cheddar cheese

Heat milk. Put all ingredients except milk in blender in the order given. Add hot milk gradually and blend thoroughly for about 1 minute.

Heat in double boiler over hot water until thick, about 5 minutes. Serve on hot toast. Serves 4.

GOLDEN LUNCHEON

1 ounce butter or margarine
2 teaspoons cornflour
5 fluid ounces single cream
½ teaspoon salt
½ teaspoon dry mustard
½ teaspoon Worcestershire sauce
12 ounces Cheddar cheese, cut in small pieces
1 beaten egg
Toast
6 poached eggs

Melt butter over low heat or in top of double boiler. Blend in cornflour; add cream.

Add salt, mustard, and Worcestershire sauce and cook until slightly thickened, about 2 or 3 minutes.

Add cheese and cook, stirring constantly, until cheese is melted.

Add beaten egg and stir while cooking, until very smooth.

Serve at once on toast on preheated plates. Top each serving with a poached egg. Serves 6.

CHEESE AND VEGETABLE CASSEROLE

12 fluid ounces scalded milk
3 ounces fresh breadcrumbs
2 ounces melted butter or margarine
2 canned pimientos, chopped
1 tablespoon chopped parsley
1½ tablespoons chopped onion
6 ounces grated Cheddar cheese
½ teaspoon salt
Black pepper and paprika
3 eggs, well beaten
6 ounces cooked or canned vegetables, drained

Pour scalded milk over breadcrumbs. Add butter, pimientos, parsley, onion, grated cheese, and seasoning. Add well-beaten eggs.

Put vegetables in well greased casserole and pour milk-cheese mixture over them.

Cook in slow oven (325°F. Mark 3) 1¼ hours. Serves 4 to 5.

CHEESE AND MAIZE FLOUR CASSEROLE

¾ pint boiling water
1 teaspoon salt
4 ounces maize flour or polenta
½ ounce butter or margarine
1 pound Cheddar cheese, grated

Bring water with salt to rolling boil. Gradually add maize flour, stirring constantly to prevent lumping. Cook over low heat 8 minutes, stirring occasionally.

Remove from heat and stir in butter until melted.

Cover bottom of greased shallow 9-inch casserole with cheese. Add alternate layers of maize flour and cheese until full.

Cook in moderate oven (350°F. Mark 4) 30 minutes. Serve with hot tomato sauce. Serves 4.

OLIVE CHEESE TART

20 black olives, stoned
6 rashers streaky bacon
2 tablespoons chopped onion
3 eggs
1¼ teaspoons salt
½ teaspoon French mustard
½ teaspoon Worcestershire sauce
Dash of Tabasco sauce
Dash of black pepper
8 ounces grated Cheddar cheese
¾ pint milk
8 ounces shortcrust pastry

Cut olives into large pieces. Cut bacon into ¼-inch pieces and fry until crisp. Remove bacon from pan and drain off all but ½ ounce fat.

Cook onion slowly in bacon fat until clear and yellow.

Beat eggs lightly and add seasonings. Blend in cheese, milk, olives, bacon, and onion. Turn into pastry-lined pie tin.

Bake in very hot oven (450°F. Mark 8) 15 minutes. Reduce heat to slow (300°F. Mark 2) and bake 30 to 40 minutes longer, or until set in centre.

Allow to stand 5 to 10 minutes before serving. Garnish with bacon curls and ripe olives. Serves 6 to 8.

Olive Cheese Tart

CHEESE EGG CUSTARD

12 fluid ounces milk
8 ounces cubed stale bread
6 ounces coarsely grated cheese
2 ounces butter or margarine
¼ teaspoon salt
⅛ teaspoon black pepper
Pinch of nutmeg
3 eggs, separated

Combine milk, bread, cheese, butter, and seasonings; cook over low heat until cheese is melted. Remove from heat.

Blend in egg yolks which have been beaten until lemon-coloured. Then fold in egg whites which have been beaten until stiff but not dry.

Pour into 3½-pint buttered casserole. Cook in moderate oven (350°F. Mark 4) 30 to 35 minutes. Serves 6.

CHEESE SURPRISE DUMPLINGS

8 to 9 ounces shortcrust pastry
½ large onion, chopped
1½ ounces butter or margarine
1 ounce finely chopped green pepper
4 ounces chopped celery stalks
8 ounces Cheddar cheese, grated
6 ounces (or 1 5-ounce can) cooked, shelled and cleaned prawns, cut in small pieces

Roll pastry ⅛-inch thick; cut into 8 5-inch squares.

Cook onion in butter until light golden brown. Add green pepper and celery. Cover tightly and allow to cook slowly until celery is tender, about 10 minutes, stirring occasionally.

Remove cover. Add cheese and keep over very low heat until cheese is melted, stirring constantly. Add prawns and mix well.

Place an eighth of the cheese mixture in centre of each square, moisten edges with cold water. Fold so that corners of square meet in centre over mixture and press edges firmly together to prevent leakage of filling. Prick top in several places with fork.

Bake in hot oven (400°F. Mark 6) until light golden brown, about 20 to 25 minutes.

Serve hot with horseradish or mustard sauce. Makes 8.

Cheese Surprise Dumplings

CHEDDAR CHEESE FONDUE

20 cream crackers
4 ounces grated strong Cheddar cheese
½ ounce butter or margarine
¼ teaspoon salt
½ pint milk, scalded
2 eggs, separated

Crumble cream crackers. Add cracker crumbs, cheese, butter or margarine, and salt to scalded milk.

Beat egg yolks; gradually stir in cracker mixture.

Beat egg whites stiff enough to stand in peaks, but not dry. Fold into cracker mixture.

Pour into 2-pint buttered casserole. Cook in moderate oven (375°F. Mark 5) 40 minutes or until knife inserted in centre comes out clean. Serves 4.

NUT AND CHEESE LOAF

1 tablespoon chopped onion
½ ounce butter or margarine
4 ounces grated cheese
4 ounces chopped walnuts
4 ounces dry breadcrumbs
6 fluid ounces boiling water
1 egg, beaten
Salt and black pepper, to taste

Cook onion in butter for a few minutes. Mix cheese, nuts, breadcrumbs, and water. Add melted butter, onion, egg, and salt and pepper.

Cook in a small pan in moderate oven (350°F. Mark 4) about 30 minutes. Serve with tomato sauce. Serves 4 to 6.

CHEESE, MACARONI EGG CUSTARD

2 to 3 ounces elbow macaroni
2 ounces strong cheese
8 fluid ounces milk, scalded
4 eggs, beaten
1 ounce melted butter or margarine
¾ teaspoon salt
Dash of black pepper
¼ teaspoon onion powder
2 medium tomatoes, sliced

Cook macaroni in boiling, salted water until tender. Drain, but do not rinse. Divide macaroni into 5 buttered individual casseroles.

Soften cheese in mixing bowl and add milk gradually, mixing until smooth.

Stir in beaten eggs, butter, ¾ teaspoon salt, pepper, and onion powder. Pour mixture over macaroni.

Set casseroles in pan of hot water which reaches almost to top rim of casseroles. Cook in slow oven (325°F. Mark 3) 30 minutes.

Brush tomato slices with butter and place one on top of each casserole. Continue cooking 20 minutes, then test for "doneness" (a sharp knife inserted in centre should come out clean). Serve at once. Serves 5.

Cheddar Cheese Fondue

BREAD AND CHEESE PUFF

8 slices buttered bread
8 ounces sliced processed Cheddar cheese (8 slices)
Salt and pepper
1 teaspoon Aromat
4 eggs, beaten
1¾ pints milk
½ teaspoon Worcestershire sauce
Dash of Tabasco sauce

Place 4 slices bread on bottom of shallow casserole, cutting to fit bottom.

Cover bread with half the cheese; sprinkle with salt, pepper, and ½ teaspoon Aromat. Repeat.

Combine remaining ingredients; pour over bread and cheese. Cook in moderate oven (350°F. Mark 4) 40 minutes or until top is golden brown, puffed and shiny. Serve at once. Serves 6.

CHEESE-RICE TIMBALES

1 ounce finely chopped green pepper
1 tablespoon finely chopped onion
1 ounce melted dripping
1 tablespoon flour
6 fluid ounces milk
½ teaspoon salt
½ teaspoon dry mustard
4 ounces grated cheese
2 eggs, beaten
5 to 6 ounces cooked rice

Cook green pepper and onion in dripping until tender. Blend in flour; add milk and cook, stirring constantly, until thickened. Add salt and mustard.

Remove from heat. Add cheese and stir until it is melted. If necessary, place pan over very low heat to melt cheese. Stir sauce into eggs and add rice.

Turn into greased individual casseroles. Cook in moderate oven (350°F. Mark 4) until firm, about 35 minutes.

Unmould and serve plain or with tomato sauce. Serves 4.

Bread and Cheese Puff

Tomato Cheeserole Dinner

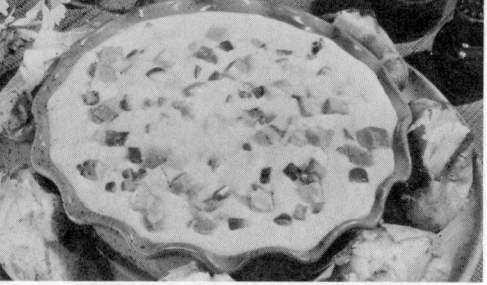

Ham and Cheese Rarebit

HAM AND CHEESE RAREBIT

4 ounces ham
4 tablespoons chopped green
    pepper
2 tablespoons chopped onion
1½ ounces butter or margarine
4 tablespoons flour
8 fluid ounces milk
½ teaspoon salt
Dash of black pepper
Dash of cayenne pepper
1 teaspoon French mustard
8 ounces grated Cheddar cheese

Cut ham into cubes and brown in frying pan. Remove ham and set aside.

Cook green pepper and onion in butter until tender, about 5 minutes. Add flour and blend.

Stir in milk gradually, and cook over low heat until thickened, stirring constantly.

Add salt, pepper, cayenne pepper, mustard, and grated cheese; stir until cheese is melted. Add ham cubes and heat.

Serve on jacket potatoes, toasted baps or split rolls, or toast. Serves 6.

QUICHE AU DIABLE

12 ounces Gruyère cheese, grated
3 eggs, beaten
¾ pint single cream
½ small onion, grated
1 teaspoon Worcestershire sauce
1 teaspoon salt
Dash of black pepper
1 8-ounce can ham or luncheon meat
1 9-inch unbaked flan shell
1 ounce grated Parmesan cheese

Combine Gruyère cheese, eggs, cream, onion, Worcestershire sauce, salt, pepper, and luncheon meat. Mix well. Pour into flan shell and sprinkle with grated Parmesan cheese.

Bake in very hot oven (450°F. Mark 8) 15 minutes. Reduce heat to 300°F. (Mark 2) and continue baking about 25 minutes or until set. Cool slightly before serving in narrow wedges. Serves 8 to 10.

Quiche Au Diable

FLUFFY TOMATO RAREBIT

1 10½-ounce can condensed tomato
    soup
8 ounces grated Cheddar cheese
½ teaspoon dry mustard
½ teaspoon Worcestershire sauce
2 eggs, separated
Toast or crackers

Heat soup slowly; add cheese and heat until melted, stirring constantly.

Add mustard and Worcestershire sauce to beaten egg yolks; stir into hot mixture.

Gently fold in beaten egg whites and heat thoroughly. Serve on hot toast or crackers. Serves 4.

WOODCHUCK

1 1-pound can tomatoes
4 ounces diced Cheddar cheese
1 beaten egg
Salt and black pepper to taste
Brown sugar to taste
Few grains cayenne pepper
Hot toast or hot toasted crackers

Cook the tomatoes until very soft (12 fluid ounces tomato purée heated may be substituted). Beat them with a wire whisk into a purée.

Stir in cheese over low heat. Cook and stir these ingredients until the cheese is melted.

Add egg; cook and stir the mixture until the egg is slightly thickened. Add salt, pepper, brown sugar, and cayenne.

Serve at once over hot toast or hot toasted crackers. Serves 4.

ONION CHEESE FLAN

Fine cracker crumbs from about 33
    cream crackers
4 ounces butter or margarine,
    melted
3 medium-sized onions, sliced thin
1 ounce butter or margarine
12 fluid ounces milk, scalded
3 eggs, slightly beaten
1 teaspoon salt
¼ teaspoon black pepper
8 ounces processed Cheddar cheese,
    grated finely

Combine cracker crumbs and melted butter. Blend thoroughly and press evenly in buttered, deep 9-inch flan dish.

Fry onions in butter until lightly browned. Place in cracker-crumb crust.

Scald milk and slowly add to eggs, stirring constantly. Add salt, pepper, and cheese. Pour over onions.

Bake in slow oven (325°F. Mark 3) 40 to 45 minutes or until silver knife inserted in centre comes out clean. Serves 4 to 6.

Quiche Lorraine

QUICHE LORRAINE

Quiche Lorraine is a rich open-faced flan, traditional in France, made of eggs, cheese and bacon. It may be served as a luncheon dish or as an hors d'oeuvre.

Pastry:
4 ounces sifted plain flour
½ teaspoon salt
3 ounces butter or margarine
3 to 4 tablespoons cold water

Sift together flour and salt. Cut in butter until particles are size of small peas. Sprinkle cold water over mixture, tossing lightly with fork until dough is moist enough to hold together. Form into a ball.

Roll out on floured pastry cloth or board to a circle 1½ inches larger than inverted 8-inch flan tin. Fit pastry loosely into tin. Fold edge to form a standing rim. Flute the edges.

Filling:
8 ounces streaky bacon
4 ounces Emmenthal or Cheddar
    cheese, grated
3 eggs
¾ pint milk or single cream
1 teaspoon salt
Dash of black pepper
Dash of cayenne pepper

Fry bacon until crisp (4 ounces cooked ham, diced, may be used instead). Crumble into pastry-lined tin.

Arrange grated cheese over bacon (3 ounces Gruyère cheese may be used instead).

Beat eggs slightly with rotary beater; add milk or cream and seasonings. Blend and pour over bacon and cheese in tin.

Bake in hot oven (400°F. Mark 6) 35 to 45 minutes. Do not overbake. Remove from oven while centre still appears soft. Cool 5 to 10 minutes before serving. Serves 6.

Onion Cheese Flan

Cheese Timbales with Tomato Sauce

CHEESE TIMBALES

1½ ounces butter or margarine
3 tablespoons flour
1 teaspoon salt
2 teaspoons mustard mixed with horseradish
Dash of cayenne pepper
1 onion, finely chopped
1¼ pint milk
8 ounces grated Cheddar cheese
5 eggs

Melt butter or margarine in top of double boiler; blend in flour and seasonings. Add onion and milk. Cook about 5 minutes, until sauce thickens.

Add grated cheese; stir constantly until cheese melts and sauce is smooth. Beat eggs slightly; gradually stir cheese mixture into eggs. Blend well.

Pour mixture into greased small individual casseroles. Place in pan of hot water. Cook in moderate oven (350°F. Mark 4) about 30 minutes or until a knife inserted in centre comes out clean.

Loosen, turn out on large plate. Serve hot with a spicy tomato sauce to which 1 ounce sliced mushrooms has been added. Garnish top of each timbale with a sprig of parsley. Serves 6.

CHEESE AND SWEETCORN PUDDING

3 ounces butter or margarine
1½ ounces plain flour
12 fluid ounces milk
1 teaspoon dry mustard
½ teaspoon salt
½ teaspoon black pepper
6 ounces cheese, coarsely grated
6 ounces cooked fresh sweetcorn, cut off the cob or 1 7-ounce can whole kernel sweetcorn, drained
3 ounces fresh breadcrumbs
5 large or 6 small eggs, separated

Melt butter, add flour, and blend; gradually add milk and cook over low heat, stirring constantly until thickened.

Add mustard, salt, pepper, and cheese. Remove from heat; add sweetcorn and breadcrumbs, and mix.

Add egg yolks, one at a time, blend-

Rice and Cheese-Stuffed Cabbage Rolls

ing each in. Fold in egg whites which have been beaten until stiff but not dry.

Pour into greased 3-pint casserole and set in a pan filled with hot water.

Cook in moderate oven (350°F. Mark 4) 1 hour. Serves 6.

OLIVE-CHEESE EGG CUSTARD

5 slices bread
1 ounce butter or margarine
Salt and pepper
16 sliced stuffed olives
4 ounces grated processed Cheddar cheese
3 eggs
¼ teaspoon dry mustard
1 pint milk

Spread both sides of bread slices with butter or margarine. Cut into cubes.

Put a layer of bread cubes in a shallow casserole. Sprinkle lightly with salt and pepper. Cover with a layer of olives, then with a layer of cheese. Repeat until all ingredients have been used.

Beat the eggs. Add mustard and milk and beat again. Pour over mixture in casserole.

Cook in slow oven (300°F. Mark 2) until set, about 40 minutes. Serves 4.

Mushroom-Cheese Egg Custard: Substitute 1 ounce sautéed sliced mushrooms for olives. If desired, mushroom stalks may be used, and the whole caps kept for other dishes.

RICE AND CHEESE-STUFFED CABBAGE ROLLS

8 large white cabbage leaves
6 ounces rice, cooked
1 ounce butter or margarine
½ teaspoon salt
Dash of black pepper
8 ounces processed Cheddar cheese, grated
2 ounces sliced celery
8 fluid ounces tomato sauce

Cook cabbage leaves in boiling water until slightly tender and transparent, about 5 minutes. Drain and cool.

Add butter, salt, pepper, cheese, and celery to rice and mix well.

Place about 3 ounces firmly packed rice-cheese mixture into each cabbage leaf. Wrap securely into a bundle and place side by side in shallow 8 × 12-inch casserole.

Pour tomato sauce over bundles.

Cook, basting occasionally, in moderate oven (350°F. Mark 4) until cabbage is tender, about 40 minutes. Serve garnished with parsley. Serves 4.

Variations: Substitute 2 ounces diced raw carrots, 16 chopped stuffed olives, or 1 ounce chopped green pepper for 2 ounces sliced celery.

CHEESE EGG CUSTARD

¾ pint milk, scalded
4 ounces grated processed Cheddar cheese
4 eggs, separated
½ teaspoon salt

Add grated cheese to scalded milk and stir carefully until cheese melts. Allow to cool.

Beat egg yolks until light; add to cooled cheese-milk mixture.

Beat egg whites with salt until stiff but not dry. Fold into cheese-milk-egg mixture.

Turn into buttered 2½-pint casserole. Place in pan of hot water and cook uncovered in moderate oven (350°F. Mark 4) until firm to the touch, 40 to 60 minutes. Serves 6.

SPANISH CHEESE FONDUE

1 medium onion, finely chopped, semi-cooked
1 ounce green pepper, finely chopped, semi-cooked
2 ounces semi-cooked mushroom caps
1 7-ounce can whole kernel sweetcorn
1 8-ounce can tomatoes
1½ ounces butter or margarine
12 fluid ounces milk
6 ounces fresh breadcrumbs
6 ounces grated Cheddar cheese
1 teaspoon salt
⅛ teaspoon paprika
Dash of black pepper
½ ounce butter, melted
3 eggs, separated

Combine vegetables and 1½ ounces butter. Heat thoroughly and divide mixture into 6 individual baking dishes or place all in large buttered casserole. Keep in warm place until cheese fondue mixture is ready for cooking.

Pour milk over breadcrumbs and allow to stand until milk is absorbed. Add cheese, seasonings, melted butter, and well beaten egg yolks, mixing lightly.

Fold in stiffly beaten egg whites. Turn into individual baking dishes or large casserole on top of vegetables.

Cook in moderate oven (350°F. Mark 4) until delicately browned and firm to the touch, 30 to 45 minutes.

Serve at once. If prepared in individual casseroles, turn out on serving plates upside down. Serves 6.

Spanish Cheese Fondue

LUNCHEON FONDUE

1½ ounces butter or margarine
3 tablespoons flour
1½ pints milk
1¾ pounds Münster or Cheddar
    cheese, grated
1 teaspoon salt
½ teaspoon black pepper
¼ teaspoon ground nutmeg
¼ teaspoon caraway seeds
French bread, cut in large cubes

Melt butter in top of double boiler. Add flour, blend well and add milk. Bring to boiling point, stirring constantly to avoid lumps.

Place over hot water; add cheese and seasonings. Cook until cheese is melted.

Serve over cubed French bread in preheated soup bowls or plates. Serves 6.

Variation: Cook in an earthenware casserole over low heat, using an asbestos mat. Then serve in the casserole, letting each person spear a cube of bread and dip into the fondue. If possible, keep the casserole hot over a spirit flame.

CHEESE-LAYERED CASSEROLE

6 to 8 thin slices bread
4 to 6 ounces Cheddar cheese,
    grated or sliced
¾ teaspoon salt
¼ teaspoon French mustard
¼ teaspoon paprika
4 beaten eggs
¾ pint milk

Arrange bread and cheese in layers in greased casserole. Have 2 or 3 layers of bread, with bread on bottom and top layers. Sprinkle seasoning between layers.

Mix beaten eggs and milk; pour over bread. Allow to stand 50 minutes.

Cook in moderate oven (350°F. Mark 4) until puffy and firm, 45 to 60 minutes. Knife inserted in centre should come out clean. Serves 6 to 8.

Bacon-Cheese Layered Casserole: Dice 4 rashers streaky bacon; fry until cooked but not crisp. Sprinkle between layers of bread and cheese. Or, cut bacon in 2-inch pieces and use as top layer.

Cheese Onion Bake

CHEESE AND EGG CASSEROLE

8 ounces cracker crumbs (use
    about 3 to 4 dozen cream
    crackers and roll)
1 pound cheese, coarsely grated
6 hard-boiled eggs, coarsely
    chopped
3 tablespoons chopped parsley
1¼ pints milk
½ teaspoon Worcestershire sauce
½ teaspoon dry mustard
Juice of 1 lemon
Salt and pepper to taste
2 eggs, well beaten

In a baking dish or casserole, arrange a layer of cracker crumbs, a layer of grated cheese, a layer of chopped eggs, and sprinkle with some of the parsley; continue until all is used up.

Heat milk to lukewarm; add Worcestershire sauce, mustard, and lemon juice and season with salt and pepper.

Add the eggs, beat, and pour the liquid over the layers in the casserole. Shake gently to distribute evenly.

Cook in moderate oven (350°F. Mark 4) 40 to 45 minutes. Serve in the casserole. Serves 6.

CHEESE AND TOMATO CASSEROLE

4 medium tomatoes, cut in ½-inch
    slices
4 ounces grated Cheddar cheese
1 small onion, thinly sliced
½ teaspoon salt
⅛ teaspoon black pepper
2 ounces crushed potato crisps

Place layer of tomato slices in grated 2½-pint casserole, using half the tomatoes.

Add alternate layers of cheese and onion. Season layers with salt and pepper. Sprinkle top with potato crisps.

Cook in moderate oven (350°F. Mark 4) until cheese is melted and bubbly, about 30 minutes. Serves 4.

CHEESE ONION BAKE

4 ounces grated Cheddar cheese
4 ounces cheese-flavoured cracker
    crumbs
1 10½-ounce can condensed cream
    of mushroom soup
¼ teaspoon pepper
2 pounds pickling onions
Paprika

Combine half grated cheese, half cracker crumbs, soup, and pepper.

Peel and cook onions in boiling water until tender. Drain well. Pour into a 2½-pint casserole.

Pour sauce over onions. Sprinkle with remaining cheese and crumbs. Sprinkle with paprika. Cook in moderate oven (350°F. Mark 4) 30 minutes. Serves 8 to 10.

Chilli-Cheese Bake

CHILLI-CHEESE BAKE

2 15½-ounce cans chilli con carne
30 or 32 crisp round cheese crackers
6 ounces strong Cheddar cheese,
    grated
1½ teaspoons dried onion flakes
3 or 4 rashers streaky bacon

Spoon ⅓ of the chilli con carne over the bottom of a 10×6×1½-inch casserole. Arrange a layer of crackers over this; sprinkle with cheese and onion. Repeat layers.

Fry or grill bacon until lightly browned. Arrange over casserole. Cook in hot oven (400°F. Mark 6) 15 to 20 minutes or until hot. Serves 6.

CHEESE-VEGETABLE TART

6 to 8 ounces shortcrust pastry
4 ounces freshly grated Cheddar
    cheese
8 fluid ounces milk, scalded
2 eggs
1½ teaspoons salt
⅛ teaspoon black pepper or paprika
1 teaspoon Worcestershire sauce
1 pound mixed, cooked vegetables
2 fresh tomatoes

Blend 2 ounces grated cheese with dry ingredients when making pastry. Roll out on floured board to ⅛-inch thickness. Line tart tin and bake blind in very hot oven (450°F. Mark 8) 10 minutes.

Meanwhile, add milk to slightly beaten eggs; add seasonings and vegetables except tomatoes.

Pour into partially baked tart shell. Cut tomatoes into eighths and arrange on top. Sprinkle top with remaining 2 ounces cheese.

Bake in moderate oven (350°F. Mark 4) about 30 minutes or until clean knife inserted in centre comes out clean. Serves 6.

Cheese-Vegetable Tart

BISCUITS AND SMALL CAKES

One of the first projects for a beginner in baking should be biscuits because modern biscuit recipes cut time and effort to a minimum and produce the maximum in goodness. Here we present a broad selection of favourite biscuits, buns and small cakes to fill or ice, and favourite recipes from around the world.

HINTS FOR BISCUIT BAKERS

As in all other baking, flour for biscuits is always sifted once before measuring.

Preheat oven to temperature given in the recipe about 15 minutes before you want to start baking.

Prepare the baking sheets and tins in advance by greasing them, unless otherwise specified, with any mild-flavoured unsalted fat. Use a pastry brush or soft paper. Only doughs containing a high proportion of fat are baked on ungreased sheets or tins.

If a baking sheet is not available, a tin with sides may be turned upside down and the biscuits baked on the bottom of the tin.

INGREDIENTS FOR BISCUITS

Individual preferences may be followed in choosing some of the ingredients.

Any mild-flavoured fat is acceptable for biscuits; however, part butter or margarine, preferably half and half, will improve flavour unless the recipe specifically calls for another fat.

The flour may be plain or self raising. Many recipes name a specific flour to be used. Where just "flour" is called for, that means plain flour.

Flavouring may be vanilla, or a combination of flavours.

Nuts may be peanuts, pecans, walnuts, Brazil nuts, or whatever kind is available.

SHAPING BISCUITS

For easy handling it is often advisable or necessary to chill the dough.

For rolled biscuits, shape the dough into medium-sized balls, roll out, and cut with cutters dipped in flour. Shake off excess flour each time. Save the scraps from each rolling, re-chill, and roll out again.

A pastry wheel may be used for cutting rectangular-, diamond-, or triangle-shaped biscuits. It saves time and makes re-rolling of dough unnecessary.

The recipes in this section give directions for a variety of biscuits and small cakes. Whichever method is followed, remember that all biscuits should be uniform in size and thickness so that they will bake evenly.

To obtain a glaze over the biscuits, brush with egg white or beaten egg yolk before baking.

When making some biscuits and cakes, chilling the dough keeps it from spreading and flattening. Allow ample space (usually at least 2 inches) between biscuits or buns.

DECORATING BISCUITS

For decorating biscuits the following materials may be used: nuts, grated or shredded chocolate, coconut, crystallised fruit such as pineapple, cherries, citron, coloured fondants and sugar, dots of marmalade and jam.

For putting biscuits together fruit fillings, softened marshmallows, and icing may be used.

HOW TO TELL WHEN BISCUITS ARE DONE

Crisp biscuits; when delicately browned. Buns; when touched lightly with finger, spring back in shape. Brownies; still moist when done, follow time given in recipe. Overbaking makes biscuits hard and dry. Watch timing carefully and test when minimum time is reached.

HINTS ABOUT BAKING SHEETS

● Baking sheets with little or no sides will let your biscuits bake evenly and quickly. The sheets should be shiny for best results.

● Do not grease a baking sheet unless the recipe calls for it because it may cause the biscuits to spread too much.

● Baking sheets should clear the sides of the oven by at least two inches for best circulation of heat and even baking.

● When re-using baking sheets, cool them before placing unbaked biscuits on them or the heat will melt the fat in the dough and cause the biscuits to spread too much during baking.

● When you bake two sheets of biscuits at one time, place one on each rack. Reverse the sheets once during baking for better browning.

TO FREEZE BISCUIT DOUGH

Most biscuit doughs freeze satisfactorily. Pack dough in freezer containers; label and freeze. To use, thaw in refrigerator until dough is easy to handle. Prepare and bake as directed in recipes.

Form refrigerator biscuit dough into rolls or use special moulds. Wrap in aluminium foil or plastic wrap; seal and label. To use, cut frozen or slightly thawed dough into slices. Bake as directed in recipes.

TO FREEZE BISCUITS

Wrap cooled biscuits in aluminium foil or plastic wrap, or place in plastic bags. Label and freeze. Fragile biscuits should be packed in freezer containers with plastic wrap or waxed paper between layers.

To serve, thaw frozen baked biscuits,

unwrapped, 15 to 30 minutes, then just before serving heat them for a moment on a baking sheet in a very slow oven (300°F. Mark 2) to restore crispness.

STORING BISCUITS

Cool biscuits thoroughly before storing. Remove from baking sheet with a spatula and place in a single layer on a wire cake rack. When cool, store different types of biscuits in separate containers. If the biscuits are very fragile, put sheets of waxed paper between layers.

Crisp Biscuits: To keep biscuits crisp, use a container with loose-fitting cover. The biscuits will remain dry and crisp except in very humid weather, and may then be dried out by placing them in a slow oven (300°F. Mark 2) for 3 to 5 minutes.

Soft Biscuits: To keep biscuits soft and chewy, use a tightly covered container. A slice of apple, orange, or bread helps keep biscuits moist. Change the fruit and bread frequently to insure freshness.

Brownies: If the brownies are to be used soon after baking, store in the tin in which they were baked. Cover tightly with foil or plastic wrap. To prolong freshness, they may be wrapped individually after cooling and cutting. Then they are ready for serving, freezing, or for packing in lunch boxes.

TO SEND BISCUITS AND CAKES BY POST

Brownies and buns will usually hold up well in shipment if packed correctly. Wrap each individually or put them into a strong plastic bag. Line a heavy cardboard box with waxed paper or aluminium foil. Bed the cakes in soft crumpled paper, stuffing the corners well. Wrap and tie securely. Attach a "fragile" sticker.

If Christmas biscuits are to be used as tree decorations, you can bake the strings for hanging right into biscuits.

Brownies

Brownies are made by spreading batter evenly and using the size tin recommended in the recipe. Cut bars and squares when they have cooled unless otherwise directed in the recipe.

BROWNIES

- 6 ounces plain flour
- 1 teaspoon baking powder
- ¼ teaspoon salt
- 6 ounces fat
- 4 ounces sugar
- 2 eggs, unbeaten
- 6 tablespoons milk
- 1 teaspoon vanilla

Sift flour once. Measure and add baking powder and salt. Sift together twice.

Cream fat and add sugar gradually, creaming until light. Add eggs, one at a time, and beat thoroughly after each addition.

Add dry ingredients alternately with combined milk and flavouring, mixing well after each addition. Beat well after last addition only.

Spread evenly in well greased tin (12×9×2 inches). Bake in moderate oven (350°F. Mark 4) until done, 20 to 25 minutes.

When cold, spread with strawberry jam or pour a lemon glacé icing in thin streams over top, or ice with chocolate icing. Cut into bars to serve.

Brownie Variations

Date-Nut Bars: Add 6 ounces chopped dates and 4 ounces chopped nuts after adding dry ingredients. Cut into squares after baking; roll in icing sugar before serving.

Tangy Spice Bars: Add 1 teaspoon cinnamon, ½ teaspoon nutmeg, ½ teaspoon mixed spice, and ¼ teaspoon cloves; sift with the dry ingredients.

Add 3 ounces molasses or treacle, 2 ounces chopped nuts, and 6 ounces chopped sultanas; blend into batter before spreading in baking tin.

Ice with Lemon Butter Icing when cold.

Chocolate Iced Bars: Add 2 ounces chocolate, melted, then blend in 2 ounces chopped nuts just before pouring into baking tin.

When cold, ice with Bittersweet Chocolate Icing.

Brownies are usually best when eaten within a day or so of baking, as the cut surfaces dry out with longer storage.

Master Brownies

MOLASSES BROWNIES

- 5 ounces butter or margarine
- 4 ounces icing sugar
- 8 ounces molasses or treacle
- 1 teaspoon vanilla
- 1 egg
- 7 ounces plain flour
- ⅛ teaspoon bicarbonate of soda
- 4 ounces chopped nuts

Cream butter and sugar until fluffy. Stir in molasses and vanilla. Beat in egg.

Add flour which has been sifted with soda. Mix well and stir in nuts.

Spread batter in 2 well greased and slightly floured 9-inch square tins. If desired, sprinkle top with chopped nuts or place a pecan half in the centre of each brownie.

Bake in moderate oven (350°F. Mark 4) 25 minutes. Makes about 3 dozen.

ORANGE AND NUT SQUARES

- 4 ounces plain flour
- 1½ teaspoons baking powder
- 1 teaspoon salt
- 3 tablespoons soft butter or margarine
- 4 ounces sugar
- 2 eggs
- 4 ounces orange marmalade
- 4 ounces whole bran cereal
- 2 ounces chopped salted almonds

Sift together flour, baking powder, and salt. Blend butter and sugar; add eggs and beat well. Stir in marmalade and whole bran cereal. Add sifted dry ingredients and almonds; mix well.

Spread in greased 9×9-inch tin. Bake in moderate oven (375°F. Mark 5) about 25 minutes. While warm, cut into squares. Roll in or sift with icing sugar when cool, if desired. Makes 25 1¾-inch squares.

Orange and Nut Squares

Golden Crunchies

GOLDEN CRUNCHIES

2 ounces butter or margarine
6 ounces sugar
2 eggs
1½ teaspoons vanilla
2 ounces dry powdered milk
½ teaspoon baking powder
¼ teaspoon salt
2 ounces sugared rice crispies
4 ounces chopped walnuts

Cream butter or margarine with sugar. Add 2 eggs and beat well. Add vanilla.

Combine dry powdered milk, baking powder, salt, and rice crispies. Add dry ingredients to butter-sugar-egg mixture and blend thoroughly. Fold in nuts.

Bake in greased 8-inch square tin in moderate oven (350°F. Mark 4) 35 to 40 minutes. Cut into squares.

BUTTERSCOTCH BROWNIES

2 ounces butter or margarine
6 ounces dark brown sugar
1 egg, unbeaten
1 teaspoon vanilla
2 ounces plain flour
1 teaspoon baking powder
½ teaspoon salt
2 ounces coarsely chopped nuts

Melt butter. Stir in brown sugar until dissolved. Cool slightly, then beat in egg and vanilla.

Mix and sift flour, baking powder, and salt. Stir in with nuts. Turn into greased 8×8-inch tin.

Bake in moderate oven (350°F. Mark 4) 25 to 30 minutes.

Cut immediately into bars. Makes 16 or more bars.

APPLE SLICES

1 pound plain flour
½ teaspoon salt
1 pound sugar
8 ounces butter or margarine
1¼ pounds peeled and sliced tart apples
1 teaspoon cinnamon

Combine flour, salt, and sugar; cut in butter until crumbly.

Divide into three portions and lightly press one third into bottom of greased tin (about 9×12 inches).

Bake in moderate oven (375°F. Mark 5) 10 minutes.

Remove from oven and spread with apple slices which have been mixed with the second third of the mixture and cinnamon. Top with remaining mixture and return to oven.

Continue baking at 375°F. Mark 5 until lightly browned, about 30 minutes. Makes about 24.

LEMON-GLAZED RAISIN BARS

8 ounces plain flour
1¼ teaspoons baking powder
½ teaspoon salt
2 eggs
8 ounces sugar
1 tablespoon soft butter
1 can raisin or other pie filling
4 ounces finely chopped pecans or walnuts

Topping:
3 tablespoons milk
2 tablespoons butter
about 11 ounces sifted icing sugar
1 teaspoon grated lemon rind
3 tablespoons lemon juice

Sift flour with baking powder and salt. Beat eggs well, gradually adding sugar. Beat in butter. Stir in pie filling, nuts, and flour mixture.

Spread mixture in 2 greased 9×9× 2-inch baking tins. Bake in slow oven (325°F. Mark 3) 30 to 35 minutes. Cool.

Topping: Combine milk, butter, and half the icing sugar; add remaining sugar, lemon rind, and juice. Blend well. Spread over cooled mixture and cut into bars. Makes about 4 dozen.

CHOCOLATE BROWNIES
(Master Recipe)

3 ounces plain flour
½ teaspoon baking powder
½ teaspoon salt
2 ounces plain chocolate
3 ounces fat
8 ounces sugar
2 eggs
2 ounces coarsely chopped nuts

Sift together flour, baking powder, and salt.

Melt chocolate with fat over hot water and beat in sugar and eggs. Add dry ingredients and mix thoroughly. Stir in nuts.

Spread in well greased square tin (8×8×2 inches). Bake in moderate oven (350°F. Mark 4) until top has dull crust, about 30 to 35 minutes. When done a slight imprint will be left when top is touched lightly with finger.

Cool and cut into squares before removing from tin. Makes 16 2-inch squares.

Chocolate Iced Brownies: Prepare Brownies and ice with Chocolate Icing before cutting into squares.
Tea Brownies: Follow master recipe, chopping nuts finely. Spread batter in 2 well greased oblong tins (9×13×2 inches). Sprinkle with 3 ounces blanched and finely sliced green pistachio nuts. Bake 7 to 8 minutes. Cut immediately into squares or diamonds. Remove from tin while warm.

PECAN TOAST

8 ounces plain flour
¼ teaspoon bicarbonate of soda
½ teaspoon salt
3 ounces fat
6 ounces sugar
¾ teaspoon anise essence or ⅛ teaspoon caraway seeds
2 eggs
1 tablespoon milk
1 tablespoon vinegar
3 ounces chopped pecans

Sift flour, soda, and salt together.

Cream fat, sugar, and anise essence together thoroughly. Beat in eggs. Stir in milk and vinegar. Blend in dry ingredients and nuts.

Spread in greased 8-inch square cake tin. Bake in moderate oven (375°F. Mark 5) about 25 minutes or until lightly browned.

Cool on cake rack. Turn out of tin. Cut into 2½×½-inch bars. Lay bars on baking sheet.

Bake in moderate oven (375°F. Mark 5) 15 to 20 minutes or until lightly toasted.

Cool on cake rack. Makes 46 2½×½-inch bars.

PRUNE RICHES

8 ounces cooked prunes
2 ounces sugar
1 teaspoon grated lemon rind
1 tablespoon lemon juice
3 ounces rolled oats, uncooked
3 ounces brown sugar
3 ounces plain flour
¼ teaspoon salt
5 ounces fat (part butter or margarine)

Chop prunes; combine with sugar, lemon rind and juice, and cook and stir over low heat until thick. Cool.

Blend rolled oats, brown sugar, flour, salt, and fat until crumbly. Put ½ of mixture in bottom of greased 8-inch square tin and pack firmly.

Spread with prune mixture and top with remaining crumb mixture. Pat lightly into filling.

Bake in moderate oven (350°F. Mark 4) 35 to 40 minutes, until lightly browned. Makes 18 bars.

Prune Riches

FLORENTINES

8 ounces plain flour
1 teaspoon baking powder
1 teaspoon salt
4 ounces fat
8 ounces sugar
2 eggs, unbeaten
1 teaspoon vanilla
3 ounces raspberry or strawberry
    jam
1 ounce chopped nuts
2 egg whites
6 ounces brown sugar
1 teaspoon vanilla

Sift flour with baking powder and salt.

Cream fat; add sugar and continue creaming. Add unbeaten eggs and vanilla and beat until fluffy. Add sifted dry ingredients. Mix thoroughly.

Spread in greased 8×12-inch tin. Spread with jam and sprinkle with nuts.

Beat egg whites until stiff. Add brown sugar and vanilla slowly. Continue beating until smooth. Spread meringue over first mixture.

Bake in moderate oven (350°F. Mark 4) 35 to 40 minutes.

When cool, cut into 2-inch squares. Makes 24 squares.

PECAN SPICE BARS

3 egg yolks
6 ounces dark brown sugar
2½ ounces plain flour
1 teaspoon baking powder
⅛ teaspoon salt
1 teaspoon cinnamon
¼ teaspoon ground cloves
1 teaspoon vanilla
3 egg whites, beaten stiff
2 ounces coarsely chopped pecans

Beat egg yolks until thick and lemon-coloured. Add sugar and beat well.

Sift flour with baking powder, salt, and spices, and add to above. Stir well. Fold in vanilla, stiffly beaten egg whites, and nuts.

Pour into greased, waxed paper-lined square tin. Bake in moderate oven (350°F. Mark 4) 25 minutes.

Cool for 5 minutes; cut into thin bars, and roll in spicy sugar (2 ounces icing sugar mixed with ¼ teaspoon ground cloves). Makes 16 bars.

Chocolate Indians

PIRATE BLOCKS

2 eggs
6 ounces brown sugar
14 digestive biscuits
1½ teaspoons baking powder
¼ teaspoon salt
3 ounces stoned chopped dates or
    raisins
2 ounces chopped nuts

Beat eggs and sugar together until light and fluffy.

Roll biscuits into fine crumbs. Mix with baking powder and salt and add to egg mixture. Add dates and nuts.

Spread in greased 8-inch square tin. Bake in slow oven (300°F. Mark 2) 25 minutes.

Cut in squares while warm. Sprinkle with icing sugar, if desired. Makes about 16.

SCOTCH TEAS

4 ounces butter or margarine
6 ounces brown sugar
4 ounces rolled oats, uncooked
¼ teaspoon salt
1 teaspoon baking powder

Melt butter and stir in sugar. When well blended add rolled oats, salt, and baking powder, mixed together. Spread in greased 8-inch square tin.

Bake in moderate oven (350°F. Mark 4) 30 minutes.

Cool about 5 minutes and cut into squares. Remove from tin as soon as biscuits are cool enough to hold together, and before entirely cooled. Makes 12 squares.

CHOCOLATE INDIANS

3 ounces plain flour
¼ teaspoon baking powder
¼ teaspoon salt
2 ounces plain chocolate
3 ounces fat
½ pound sugar
2 eggs, well beaten
1 teaspoon vanilla
3 ounces chopped walnuts or pecans

Sift together flour, baking powder, and salt twice.

Melt chocolate and fat in top of double boiler over boiling water.

Gradually add sugar to beaten eggs, beating well between additions. Add melted chocolate and blend well. Gradually stir in flour, mixing thoroughly. Add vanilla and nuts.

Bake in greased baking tin (about 8×8 inches) in moderate oven (350°F. Mark 4) about 25 minutes, or until brown and slightly shrunk from side of tin.

Remove from oven. Cut into squares in the tin while still warm. Makes 18 to 24 bars.

Norwegian Almond Bars

NORWEGIAN ALMOND BARS

8 ounces plain flour
1 teaspoon baking powder
1 teaspoon salt
6 ounces sugar
6 ounces butter or margarine
3½ ounces cold mashed potatoes
8 ounces icing sugar
8 ounces ground almonds
1 teaspoon cinnamon
¼ teaspoon cardamom
1 tablespoon water
1 egg white
1 egg yolk

Sift together flour, baking powder, salt, and sugar. Cut in butter until particles are the size of small peas.

Press ¾ of mixture into ungreased 13×9×2-inch tin. Reserve remainder for topping.

Bake in moderate oven (375°F. Mark 5) 10 minutes.

Blend together potatoes, icing sugar, almonds, cinnamon, cardamom, water, and egg white. Mix thoroughly. Spread over partially baked dough.

Combine remaining crumb mixture with egg yolk. Press together. Roll out on floured pastry board to a 10×6-inch rectangle. Cut into strips ½ inch wide. Place across filling, crisscross fashion.

Bake in moderate oven (375°F. Mark 5) 20 to 25 minutes.

Cut into bars or squares while still warm. Makes about 2 dozen bars.

TOFFEE SQUARES

8 ounces butter or margarine
6 ounces brown sugar
1 egg yolk
1 teaspoon vanilla
8 ounces plain flour
8 ounces milk chocolate
4 ounces chopped nuts

Cream butter. Add brown sugar and cream until light and fluffy. Add beaten egg yolk, vanilla, and sifted flour. Spread thinly on baking sheet.

Bake in moderate oven (350°F. Mark 4) 15 to 20 minutes.

Melt chocolate and spread over top while warm. Sprinkle with nuts. Cut into squares while warm. Makes 24 bars.

Bran Blondies

BRAN BLONDIES

    3 ounces plain flour
    ½ teaspoon baking powder
    ¼ teaspoon bicarbonate of soda
    ½ teaspoon salt
    2 ounces ready-to-eat bran
    2 ounces chopped nuts
    4 ounces butter or margarine
    6 ounces brown sugar
    1 egg, slightly beaten
    1 teaspoon vanilla
    3 ounces plain chocolate,
        coarsely chopped

Sift together flour, baking powder, soda, and salt; mix in bran and nuts.

Melt butter in saucepan. Remove from heat and stir in sugar; cool. Stir in egg and vanilla.

Add sifted dry ingredients a small amount at a time, beating well after each addition. Spread in greased 9×9-inch tin. Sprinkle with chocolate.

Bake in moderate oven (350°F. Mark 4) about 15 minutes. Makes 24 bars 2×1½ inches.

Note: Blondies are done when still soft in centre but shrunk away from sides of tin.

NUT CAKE BARS

    4 ounces plain flour
    1 teaspoon baking powder
    ½ teaspoon salt
    6 ounces fat
    8 ounces sugar
    4 eggs
    1 teaspoon vanilla
    2 teaspoons cinnamon
    2 ounces chopped nuts

Sift together flour, baking powder, and salt.

Cream together fat and sugar until light and fluffy. Add eggs, one at a time, beating well after each addition. Add vanilla. Add dry ingredients and beat thoroughly.

Spread in shallow greased tin (11×16 inches). Sprinkle cinnamon and nuts over top of batter.

Bake in moderate oven (375°F. Mark 5) 25 minutes.

Cut into bars or squares. Makes 55 bars 1×3¼ inches.

BANANA BARS

    8 ounces plain flour
    2 teaspoons baking powder
    ¼ teaspoon salt
    2 ounces fat
    8 ounces sugar
    2 eggs
    3 medium sized bananas, mashed
    ½ teaspoon lemon essence
    ½ teaspoon vanilla
    2 ounces chopped nuts
    glacé icing

Sift together flour, baking powder, and salt.

Cream together fat and sugar; add eggs, beating well. Add dry ingredients alternately with mashed bananas. Add flavouring essences and nuts and beat thoroughly.

Spread batter in greased tin (8×13 inches). Bake in moderate oven (350°F. Mark 4) 30 minutes.

While still warm, ice with thin glacé icing. When cool, cut into bars or squares.

Banana Buns: Drop dough by teaspoons on greased baking sheets and bake in moderate oven (350°F. Mark 4) 12 to 15 minutes.

Makes 32 bars 1 × 4 inches, or about 4 dozen buns.

SOUTHERN PECAN BARS

    5 ounces plain flour
    ½ teaspoon baking powder
    3 ounces butter or margarine
    3 ounces brown sugar
    2 ounces pecans, chopped finely

Sift together flour and baking powder.

Blend butter or margarine and brown sugar together, creaming well. Add dry ingredients; mix with an electric mixer or spoon until mixture resembles coarse meal.

Stir in pecans; mix well. Pat firmly into bottom of well greased 12×8×2- or 13×9×2-inch tin.

Bake in moderate oven (350°F. Mark 4) 10 minutes only.

Pecan Topping: Beat 2 eggs until foamy. Add 9 ounces dark corn syrup or treacle, 1½ ounces brown sugar, 3 tablespoons flour, ½ teaspoon salt, and 1 teaspoon vanilla. Mix well. Pour over partially baked crust.

Sprinkle with 3 ounces pecans, coarsely chopped. If desired, fold the chopped pecans into filling before pouring over crust and arrange 30 pecan halves evenly over top, one for each bar. Bake in moderate oven (350°F. Mark 4) 25 to 30 minutes. Let cool in pan; cut into bars. Store in tightly covered container. Makes about 30 bars.

COCONUT PINEAPPLE SQUARES

    1 tablespoon butter or margarine
    1 tablespoon sugar
    4 ounces plain flour
    3 teaspoons baking powder
    1 teaspoon salt
    3 eggs, well beaten
    6 ounces drained, crushed pine-
        apple
    8 ounces sugar
    1 tablespoon melted butter or mar-
        garine
    8 ounces desiccated coconut

Cream 1 tablespoon butter and 1 tablespoon sugar.

Sift flour, baking powder, and salt together. Add to creamed mixture and mix until crumbly. Add half the eggs and mix thoroughly.

Spread in 8-inch square tin. Cover with pineapple.

Mix 8 ounces sugar, melted butter, and coconut; add remaining eggs and blend well. Spread over top of pineapple.

Bake in moderate oven (350°F. Mark 4) 30 to 35 minutes. Cut into squares. Makes 24 bars.

DATE SQUARES

    7 ounces stoned dates
    8 fluid ounces boiling water
    1 teaspoon bicarbonate of soda
    ½ teaspoon salt
    4 ounces margarine
    8 ounces sugar
    1 egg
    8 ounces plain flour
    1 teaspoon vanilla
    ¼ pint double cream
    24 walnut-stuffed dates

Cut up dates. Pour boiling water over dates in bowl. Add soda and salt. Cool.

Cream margarine. Add sugar gradually, creaming until light and smooth. Add egg and beat well. Add flour and cooled date mixture alternately, mixing smooth after addition. Spread batter in greased 7×11-inch tin. Bake in moderate oven (350°F. Mark 4) 1 hour.

Cut in squares. To serve, decorate each square with whipped cream topped with nut-stuffed dates. Makes about 24 squares.

Southern Pecan Bars

GUMDROP SQUARES

4 eggs
12 ounces brown sugar
1 tablespoon water
8 ounces plain flour
⅛ teaspoon salt
1 teaspoon baking powder
1 teaspoon cinnamon
4 ounces tiny mixed gumdrops
(fresh and soft)
2 ounces nuts

Beat eggs until light. Add brown sugar gradually and water. Continue beating until blended.

Add flour, which has been sifted with salt, baking powder, and cinnamon. Stir smooth. Add gumdrops and nuts.

Spread batter ½ inch thick in greased, floured tin. Bake in moderate oven (350°F. Mark 4) 30 minutes.

Cut into squares. Makes about 18 to 24 bars.

OLD-FASHIONED RAISIN BARS

8 ounces plain flour
¼ teaspoon bicarbonate of soda
½ teaspoon salt
1 teaspoon ground cinnamon
½ teaspoon ground nutmeg
½ teaspoon mixed spice
½ teaspoon ground ginger
¼ teaspoon ground cloves
5 ounces fat
3 ounces sugar
3 ounces light molasses or golden syrup
1 egg
2 tablespoons water
1 tablespoon vinegar
8 ounces seedless raisins
3 ounces chopped nuts

Sift together flour, soda, salt, and spices.

Cream together fat and sugar thoroughly. Beat in molasses and egg. Stir in water and vinegar. Blend in dry ingredients, raisins, and nuts.

Spread in greased 15½ × 10½ × 1-inch baking tin. Bake in moderate oven (375°F. Mark 5) about 20 minutes or until lightly browned.

Cool slightly. Mark into 3 × 2-inch bars. While still warm, spread bars with thin glacé icing. Cool. Cut into bars. Makes 20 3 × 2-inch bars.

Old-Fashioned Raisin Bars

WINE FRUIT BARS

8 ounces plain flour
½ teaspoon bicarbonate of soda
½ teaspoon salt
½ teaspoon nutmeg
6 ounces raisins, chopped prunes, currants, or any dried chopped fruit
4 ounces butter or margarine
4 ounces brown sugar
1 egg
4 tablespoons port or muscatel

Mix and sift dry ingredients. Mix fruit with dry ingredients.

Cream the butter; add sugar and cream well.

Beat egg into butter-sugar mixture. Add dry ingredients to mixture alternately with wine.

Pour onto an oiled baking sheet; spread evenly.

Bake in moderate oven (375°F. Mark 5) about 12 minutes. Cut into bars while still warm. Cool and ice with wine icing (below).

Wine Icing:

1 tablespoon butter or margarine
8 ounces icing sugar
½ teaspoon nutmeg
port or muscatel

Blend butter into sugar. Add nutmeg and enough wine to give mixture a smooth spreading consistency.

FRUIT FILLED BARS

1 pound stoned dates, prunes, apricots, or figs
4 ounces sugar
3 ounces light corn syrup or golden syrup
4 tablespoons orange juice
2 teaspoons grated orange rind
¼ teaspoon salt
1 teaspoon bicarbonate of soda
10 ounces plain flour
1 teaspoon salt
8 ounces fat
6 ounces brown sugar
4 fluid ounces water
5 ounces rolled oats, uncooked

Combine fruit, sugar, syrup, orange juice, orange rind, and ¼ teaspoon salt; cook until thick. Cool.

Sift together flour, soda, and 1 teaspoon salt into bowl. Add fat, brown sugar, and water. Beat until smooth, about 2 minutes. Fold in oats.

Spread half of dough over greased 12×15-inch baking sheet. Cover with fruit filling. Roll remaining dough between 2 sheets of greaseproof paper. Chill, then remove paper and place dough over filling.

Bake in moderate oven (350°F. Mark 4) 30 to 35 minutes.

Cool and cut into bars. Makes 5 dozen bars.

Butterscotch Squares

BUTTERSCOTCH SQUARES

4 ounces butter or margarine
12 ounces brown sugar
2 eggs
1 teaspoon vanilla
6 ounces plain flour
2 teaspoons baking powder
4 ounces chopped nuts

Melt butter in heavy saucepan. Add sugar and bring to boil over low heat, stirring constantly. Cool.

Add eggs one at a time, beating thoroughly. Stir in vanilla and flour which has been sifted with baking powder. Mix in chopped nuts.

Turn into greased and floured 7×9-inch tin. Bake in moderate oven (350°F. Mark 4) 30 to 35 minutes. When cool, cut into squares. Makes 3 dozen 1½-inch squares.

COCONUT BEAUTIES

6 ounces plain flour
1 teaspoon baking powder
1 teaspoon salt
3 ounces fat
8 ounces sugar
2 eggs (reserve 1 egg white)
2 tablespoons milk
½ teaspoon vanilla
½ teaspoon lemon juice
6 ounces brown sugar
½ teaspoon vanilla
2 ounces desiccated coconut

Mix and sift flour, baking powder, and salt.

Cream fat and sugar; add eggs (reserving 1 egg white for meringue) and mix well. Add dry ingredients alternately with milk. Mix well. Add ½ teaspoon vanilla and lemon juice.

Spread ¼-inch thick in 8×12-inch greased tin.

Beat egg white until stiff. Beat in brown sugar, adding 2 ounces at a time. Add ½ teaspoon vanilla. Fold in coconut. Spread meringue over first mixture.

Bake in slow oven (325°F. Mark 3) about 30 minutes.

Cut into squares and cool. Makes 24 small bars.

JEWISH COOKERY

Knaidlach (in chicken soup),
Kreplach (right), Knishes (left)

Cheese Blintzes (rear),
Cheese Soufflé (front)

ALMOND JAM BARS

6 ounces plain flour
4 ounces sugar
½ teaspoon baking powder
½ teaspoon salt
½ teaspoon cinnamon
¼ teaspoon cloves
4 ounces fat
½ teaspoon almond essence
¼ teaspoon vanilla
1 egg, beaten
4 tablespoons milk
6 ounces jam

Sift together flour, sugar, baking powder, salt, cinnamon, and cloves.

Cream together fat and flavouring. Cut or rub fat into flour mixture.

Combine egg and milk and add to flour mixture. Mix until well blended. Spread about ⅓ of the mixture into greased tin (7×11 inches). Cover evenly with jam.

Spread remaining mixture over jam. Bake in hot oven (400°F. Mark 6) 25 to 30 minutes.

When cool, cut into bars. Makes 28 bars 1×2½ inches.

PEANUT BUTTER DATE BARS

2 ounces plain flour
1¼ teaspoons baking powder
¼ teaspoon salt
½ teaspoon nutmeg
½ teaspoon cinnamon
¼ teaspoon mixed spice
2 ounces butter or margarine
3 ounces peanut butter
8 ounces sugar
2 eggs, well beaten
4 ounces finely cut dates
½ teaspoon vanilla

Sift flour with baking powder, salt, and spices.

Cream butter and peanut butter thoroughly. Add sugar gradually to beaten eggs and beat until light and deep yellow. Stir into creamed mixture.

Add flour mixture and beat until blended. Add dates and vanilla. Turn into shallow, greased, greaseproof paper-lined tin.

Bake in moderate oven (350°F. Mark 4) 45 minutes. Turn out on rack. Remove paper.

Cool and cut into bars or squares. Makes about 24 bars.

Quick Fudge Squares

BUTTER CHEWS

6 ounces butter or margarine
3 tablespoons sugar
6 ounces plain flour
13½ ounces brown sugar
3 egg yolks, beaten
4 ounces chopped nuts
3 ounces desiccated coconut
3 egg whites, stiffly beaten
icing sugar

Cream butter; add sugar, and blend with flour. Pat in bottom of 8×12-inch greased tin.

Bake in moderate oven (375°F. Mark 5) 15 minutes.

Add brown sugar to beaten egg yolks. Add nuts and coconut. Stir in stiffly beaten egg whites and spread over first mixture. Return to oven for 25 to 30 minutes.

Dust with icing sugar. Cut any desired size. Makes 2 dozen 2-inch squares.

PEANUT BUTTER BROWNIES

2 ounces butter or margarine
1½ ounces peanut butter
8 ounces sugar
2 eggs, beaten
2 ounces plain chocolate, melted
2 ounces plain flour
½ teaspoon baking powder
⅛ teaspoon salt

Cream butter and peanut butter with sugar.

Add beaten eggs, melted chocolate, and flour which has been sifted with baking powder and salt. Spread in shallow, greaseproof paper-lined and greased tin.

Bake in moderate oven (350°F. Mark 4) about 20 minutes.

Cut in squares while still warm. Makes 16 bars.

QUICK FUDGE SQUARES

2 ounces plain chocolate
3 ounces butter or margarine
3 ounces light corn syrup or golden syrup
5 ounces sugar
½ teaspoon salt
1½ teaspoons vanilla
4 ounces uncooked oats
1 ounce chopped nuts

Melt chocolate and butter in top of double boiler over boiling water. Add remaining ingredients, blending thoroughly.

Pack firmly into greased 8-inch square tin. Sprinkle a few chopped nuts on top if desired.

Bake in hot oven (425°F. Mark 7) 12 minutes. When thoroughly cool, turn out of tin and cut in squares or bars. Store in refrigerator. Makes 36 squares or 18 bars.

Date Orange Bars

DATE ORANGE BARS

2 eggs
4 fluid ounces orange juice
2 ounces melted butter or margarine
4 ounces plain flour
1 teaspoon baking powder
½ teaspoon salt
8 ounces sugar
3 ounces coarsely chopped walnuts
3 ounces stoned, coarsely cut dates

In small mixing bowl, beat eggs until light and fluffy. Slowly add orange juice; stir in melted butter or margarine.

Sift dry ingredients into second mixing bowl; add nuts and dates; toss lightly with fork to completely coat with flour. Stir in liquid mixture thoroughly.

Pour into well greased 8-inch square tin. Bake in moderate oven (350°F. Mark 4) about 30 minutes or until centre springs back when lightly touched. Cut into bars while still warm. Makes 16 bars.

CRANBERRY SQUARES

4 ounces fat
4 ounces sugar
1 teaspoon grated lemon rind
2 egg yolks
4 ounces plain flour
½ teaspoon salt
¼ teaspoon bicarbonate of soda
1-pound can whole cranberry sauce, drained
2 egg whites
2 ounces sugar
2 ounces finely chopped walnuts

Cream fat, sugar, and lemon rind. Add egg yolks 1 at a time, beating after each addition.

Sift together flour, salt, and soda. Add to creamed mixture. Mix well.

Spread or press dough evenly into greased 12×8×2-inch tin (or one with approximate measurements). Spread cranberry sauce evenly over dough.

Beat egg whites until stiff but not dry. Gradually add sugar and continue beating until mixed. Fold in finely chopped walnuts. Spread meringue over cranberry sauce.

Bake in moderate oven (350°F. Mark 4) 45 minutes. Cool. Cut into strips or squares. Sprinkle with icing sugar.

APPLE SLICES 2

8 ounces plain flour
½ teaspoon salt
4 ounces butter or margarine
2 egg yolks
1 tablespoon lemon juice
4 fluid ounces cold water
8 apples, peeled and sliced
4 ounces sugar
¼ teaspoon salt
1 tablespoon flour
½ teaspoon cinnamon
½ teaspoon nutmeg
3 ounces sultanas

Mix and sift flour and salt; cut in fat as for pastry.

Beat together thoroughly egg yolks, lemon juice, and cold water. Add gradually to dry ingredients and stir until all flour is moistened.

Divide dough in 2 parts. Roll 1 portion as thin as pie crust and line an 8-9 inch pie plate. Fill with apple mixture made by combining remaining ingredients.

Roll second portion of dough to fit top of plate and place over apples. Press edges of dough firmly together.

Bake in moderate oven (350°F. Mark 4) until crust is nicely browned and apples are tender, about 45 minutes.

When cool, drizzle a thin glacé icing over top and cut into slices. Serves 6.

CHOCOLATE DIAMONDS

1 ounce plain chocolate
2 ounces butter or margarine
4 ounces sugar
1 unbeaten egg
1 ounce plain flour
⅛ teaspoon salt
¼ teaspoon vanilla
1½ ounces finely chopped nuts

Melt chocolate and butter over hot water. Remove from heat and add remaining ingredients except nuts.

Spread in 2 8×8×2-inch greased tins. Sprinkle with nuts. Bake in hot oven (400°F. Mark 6) about 12 minutes.

Cool slightly and mark into 1½-inch diamond shapes. When cold, remove to wire racks. Makes about 30.

EASY MOLASSES BROWNIES

1 can sweetened condensed milk
3 ounces molasses or treacle
1 egg
6 ounces digestive biscuit crumbs
¼ teaspoon cinnamon
¼ teaspoon salt
4 ounces chopped nuts

Combine condensed milk and molasses; cook over low heat, stirring constantly, until mixture thickens, about 5 minutes. Cool.

Beat egg; add molasses mixture.

Combine biscuit crumbs, cinnamon, salt, and nuts; add to molasses mixture.

Line 8×8×2-inch tin with greased greaseproof paper; pour in batter.

Bake in moderate oven (350°F. Mark 4) 40 minutes.

Remove from tin immediately, remove paper; cut in squares. If desired, sprinkle top with icing sugar.

COCONUT PEANUT BUTTER BARS

4 ounces plain flour
1 teaspoon baking powder
¼ teaspoon salt
2 ounces fat
3 ounces peanut butter
8 ounces sugar
2 eggs, well beaten
4 ounces desiccated coconut
½ teaspoon vanilla

Sift flour, baking powder, and salt several times.

Cream fat; beat in peanut butter. Gradually beat in sugar until the texture is spongy. Add eggs. Stir in dry ingredients, coconut, and vanilla.

Spread in paper-lined, greased 8×12-inch tin. Bake in moderate oven (350°F. Mark 4) until done, about 25 minutes.

Cut into strips while still warm and roll in icing sugar. Makes about 36.

ICED COFFEE BARS

6 ounces plain flour
½ teaspoon baking powder
½ teaspoon bicarbonate of soda
½ teaspoon salt
½ teaspoon cinnamon
2 ounces fat
6 ounces brown sugar
1 egg
4 fluid ounces hot coffee
3 ounces sultanas
1 ounce chopped nuts
coffee icing

Sift together flour, baking powder, soda, salt, and cinnamon.

Cream together fat and sugar. Add egg and beat well. Add coffee and gradually stir in dry ingredients. Add sultanas and nuts and beat thoroughly.

Spread in greased tin (11×16 inches). Bake in moderate oven (350°F. Mark 4) 15 to 20 minutes.

While still warm, ice with coffee icing. Cool and cut into bars. Makes 28 bars.

FIG BARS

6 ounces dried figs
6 ounces plain flour
½ teaspoon baking powder
½ bicarbonate of soda
½ teaspoon salt
2 eggs, separated

8 ounces sugar
1 teaspoon vanilla
4 fluid ounces buttermilk or sour milk
2 ounces chopped nuts

Pour boiling water over figs and let stand 10 minutes. Drain. Cut off stems. Cut figs in small pieces.

Sift together flour, baking powder, soda, and salt.

Beat egg yolks. Add sugar gradually, beating until light. Add vanilla. Add dry ingredients alternately with buttermilk or sour milk. Fold in figs and nuts. Fold in stiffly beaten egg whites.

Spread in greased tin (8×13 inches). Bake in moderate oven (375°F. Mark 5) 25 minutes.

Cut into bars. Makes 48 bars 1×2 inches.

HAZELNUT SLICES

2 large egg whites
8 ounces sugar
1 tablespoon plain flour
1 teaspoon vanilla
6 ounces coarsely chopped hazelnuts

Beat egg whites until stiff in top of double boiler. Beat in sugar gradually. Fold in flour.

Cook over boiling water, stirring constantly, 3 minutes. Remove from over hot water. Blend in vanilla and nuts.

Spread smoothly ¼ inch thick in ungreased paper-lined 13×9-inch tin. Dip fingers in warm water and moisten top by patting gently.

Bake in moderate oven (350°F. Mark 4) until top looks dull, 15 to 20 minutes.

While warm, cut into slices 2×1½ inches. Cool slightly, then turn paper over, slices and all. Dampen entire surface with cold water. Slices are easily removed when water penetrates paper. Makes 32 slices.

QUICK COCONUT BARS

2 ounces butter or margarine
6 ounces light brown sugar, sifted
1 egg
1 teaspoon vanilla or grated rind of 1 orange
2 ounces plain flour
1 teaspoon baking powder
½ teaspoon salt
4 ounces desiccated coconut

Melt butter in a 1½ pint saucepan. Add sugar and stir until very well blended. Cool slightly. Beat in egg and vanilla.

Sift the flour, baking powder, and salt together onto greaseproof paper. Add to butter mixture and stir until blended. Fold in ¾ of the coconut.

Turn into greased 8×8-inch tin. Sprinkle with remaining coconut. Bake in moderate oven (350°F. Mark 4) about 30 minutes.

When almost cool cut into bars. Makes 32 1×2-inch bars.

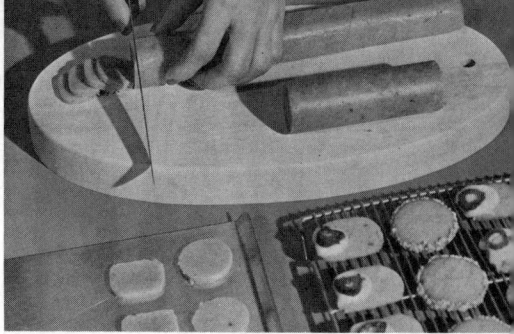

Refrigerator Biscuits

Refrigerator biscuits are made from very stiff dough which can be prepared and shaped into rolls or in special moulds and stored in the refrigerator usually up to three weeks. The advantage of refrigerator biscuits is that they can be sliced and baked as you need them.

RIBBON BISCUITS

6 ounces plain flour
1 teaspoon baking powder
¼ teaspoon salt
4 ounces fat
4 ounces sugar
½ teaspoon vanilla
1 egg, beaten
1 ounce chocolate, melted

Mix and sift flour, baking powder, and salt.

Cream together fat and sugar until light and fluffy. Add vanilla and egg. Add flour mixture to creamed mixture.

Divide dough into two parts, and add melted chocolate to one part. Wrap each portion in waxed paper and chill until firm.

Pat dough in alternate layers (chocolate, then vanilla, then chocolate) in small rectangular tin. Chill until firm. Cut into ⅛-inch slices.

Bake on ungreased baking sheet in hot oven (400°F. Mark 6) 6 to 8 minutes. Makes about 42.

PEANUT BUTTER REFRIGERATOR BISCUITS

3 ounces peanut butter
4 ounces fat
12 ounces brown sugar
1 teaspoon vanilla
2 eggs
9 ounces plain flour
2 teaspoons bicarbonate of soda
1 teaspoon salt
6 ounces chopped sultanas
8 ounces rolled oats, uncooked
2 ounces chopped nuts

Cream peanut butter and fat until well combined. Add sugar and vanilla and continue creaming until fluffy. Add eggs and beat well.

Sift together flour, soda, and salt. Add sultanas, dry ingredients, rolled oats, and nuts to peanut butter mixture, blending well.

Shape into rolls, wrapping each roll in greaseproof paper. Chill. Slice into ⅛-inch slices.

Bake on baking sheet in moderate oven (350°F. Mark 4) about 15 minutes. Store in loosely covered container to keep biscuits crisp. Makes about 90.

BUTTERSCOTCH REFRIGERATOR BISCUITS
(Master Recipe)

1 pound plain flour
1 teaspoon bicarbonate of soda
1 teaspoon cream of tartar
½ teaspoon salt
8 ounces butter or margarine
12 ounces brown sugar
2 eggs
1 teaspoon vanilla
4 ounces chopped nuts

Sift together flour, soda, cream of tartar, and salt.

Cream butter and sugar until light and fluffy. Add eggs and vanilla, beating well. Add dry ingredients and nuts and mix thoroughly.

Shape into rolls. Wrap each in grease-proof paper. Chill until very firm.

Slice thinly and bake on ungreased baking sheet in hot oven (400°F. Mark 6) 8 to 10 minutes. Makes about 6 dozen 2-inch cookies.

Butterscotch Biscuit Variations

Butterscotch Coconut Biscuits: Omit chopped nuts and add 8 ounces desiccated coconut to fat-sugar-egg mixture.

Butterscotch Date Biscuits: Omit nuts and add 12 ounces of finely chopped dates to sifted dry ingredients.

Chocolate Nut Biscuits: Add 3 ounces melted, plain chocolate to fat-sugar-egg mixture.

Coconut Orange Biscuits: Use half white and half brown sugar. Add 12 ounces desiccated coconut to sifted dry ingredients. Omit vanilla and flavour with 2 tablespoons grated orange rind and ¾ teaspoon lemon essence.

Filled Butterscotch Biscuits: Prepare dough and shape into rolls. Chill and cut into thin slices.

Put raisin filling (below) between two, pressing together with fork. Bake in moderate oven (375°F. Mark 5) 10 to 12 minutes.

Raisin Filling: Mix together 12 ounces minced seed or seedless raisins, 3 ounces brown sugar, ⅛ teaspoon salt, and 2 tablespoons cornflour. Add 8 fluid ounces water gradually, mixing well. Cook until thickened, stirring constantly. Cool before using.

DANISH DANDIES

8 hard-boiled egg yolks
8 ounces butter or margarine
6 ounces sugar
½ teaspoon salt
½ teaspoon vanilla
½ teaspoon lemon essence
7-8 ounces plain flour

Press hard-boiled egg yolks through a sieve.

Butterscotch Refrigerator Biscuits

Cream butter and sugar until light and fluffy. Add salt, flavouring essence, and egg yolks. Mix well. Add flour to make moderately stiff dough.

Shape into rolls and wrap in waxed paper. Chill. Slice ⅛-inch thick.

Bake on ungreased baking sheets in hot oven (400°F. Mark 6) 8 to 10 minutes.

Note: Dough may be formed into balls an inch in diameter. Press with fork, or with bottom of tumbler. Makes about 8½ dozen.

Spritz Biscuits: Force dough through biscuit press into various shapes.

CARROT BISCUITS

8 ounces fat
8 ounces plain flour
4 ounces sugar
½ teaspoon salt
½ teaspoon cinnamon
¼ teaspoon nutmeg
1 teaspoon vanilla
1 egg
6 ounces finely-grated raw carrots
2 ounces chopped nuts
castor sugar

Cream fat until fluffy. Sift flour, sugar, salt, and spices together. Add to fat and mix well. Add vanilla, egg, carrots, and nuts.

Form into 2 rolls 1-inch in diameter. Wrap in greaseproof paper and chill at least 2 hours.

Slice ½-inch thick and bake on ungreased baking sheet in moderate oven (375°F. Mark 5) 10 to 12 minutes. Roll in castor sugar while warm. Makes 6 dozen biscuits.

Carrot Biscuits

MASTER REFRIGERATOR BISCUITS

4 ounces fat
3 ounces brown sugar
6 ounces caster sugar
1 egg
1 teaspoon vanilla
2 ounces chopped nuts
8 ounces plain flour
2 teaspoons baking powder
½ teaspoon salt

Cream fat; add sugars and cream thoroughly. Add egg and beat well. And vanilla and nuts.

Mix and sift flour, baking powder, and salt. Add to creamed mixture and mix well.

Shape into rolls about 1½ inches in diameter. Wrap each in greaseproof paper. Chill in refrigerator several hours or overnight. Cut chilled rolls in ⅛-inch slices.

Place on greased baking sheet. Bake in hot oven (425°F. Mark 7) 8 to 10 minutes. Makes 4 dozen.

Master Refrigerator Biscuit Variations

Almond Refrigerator Biscuits: Substitute 2 ounces minced blanched almonds for chopped nuts.

Checkerboard Biscuits: Divide dough into 2 equal parts. Add 1 ounce cooled, melted chocolate to 1 part. Leave other part plain.

Line a freezing tray with greaseproof paper.

Pack half the chocolate dough into bottom and cover with uniform layer of plain dough. Add another layer of chocolate and top with final layer of plain dough.

Cover with waxed paper and chill several hours.

Turn the layered loaf out onto waxed paper. Slice with thin sharp knife into ¼-inch slices.

Place 4 slices together so that, when viewed from the end, each chocolate strip lies above a plain strip.

Slice thinly across checkerboard pattern. Bake as directed in master recipe.

Chocolate Refrigerator Biscuits: In master recipe, add 2 ounces melted chocolate or 4 tablespoons cocoa to fat-sugar-egg mixture.

Master Refrigerator Biscuits

Coconut Refrigerator Biscuits: In master recipe, substitute 2 ounces desiccated coconut for nuts.

Coconut Orange Refrigerator Biscuits: Omit vanilla and add 2 tablespoons grated orange rind to coconut cookies.

Fruit Refrigerator Biscuits: In master recipe, substitute 3 ounces currants, or any mixture of dried fruits, cut into small pieces, for nuts.

Ginger Refrigerator Biscuits: In master recipe, substitute 2 tablespoons molasses or treacle for 2 tablespoons sugar and add 2 ounces finely chopped candied ginger or 1 tablespoon ground ginger.

Pinwheel Biscuits: Divide dough of master recipe into 2 equal parts.

Add 1 ounce cooled melted chocolate to 1 part. Leave other part plain.

Roll each part ⅛-inch thick and place one sheet on top of the other.

Roll up as for Swiss roll. Wrap firmly in waxed paper and chill. Slice and bake.

Spice Refrigerator Biscuits: In master recipe, add and sift with dry ingredients 1 to 2 teaspoons mixed spices (cinnamon, ginger, and nutmeg).

RAISIN-ORANGE FILLED BISCUITS

1 teaspoon vinegar
4 fluid ounces milk
4 ounces plain flour
1 teaspoon baking powder
¼ teaspoon salt
8 ounces soft butter
6 ounces sugar
1½ pounds quick-cooking rolled oats
1 can raisin or other pie filling
4 ounces chopped candied orange peel

Stir vinegar into milk and set aside.

Sift flour with baking powder and salt. Cream butter, and sugar until light and fluffy. Blend in ½ flour mixture. Add milk and mix well. Blend in remaining flour. Stir in rolled oats. Chill at least 4 hours.

Roll to ⅛-inch thickness and cut out rounds with a 3-inch cutter. Remove a small ring from the centre of half the rounds.

Combine pie filling and orange peel. Place ½ tablespoon of filling on each round and top with the ring of dough. Seal edges with a fork.

Place on ungreased baking sheet and bake in moderate oven (350°F. Mark 4) 10 to 12 minutes. Cool. Repeat with remaining dough and filling. Makes about 2 dozen.

Chocolate Nut Slices

CHOCOLATE NUT SLICES

8 ounces plain flour
¼ teaspoon bicarbonate of soda
½ teaspoon salt
6 ounces fat
14 ounces sugar
2 teaspoons vanilla
1 egg
4 ounces plain chocolate, melted
1 tablespoon vinegar
3 ounces chopped pecans or walnuts

Sift together flour, soda, and salt.

Cream together fat, sugar, and vanilla. Beat in egg and chocolate. Stir in vinegar. Blend in dry ingredients and nuts.

Shape into 2 rolls, 2 inches in diameter. Chill several hours. Slice dough into ¼-inch slices.

Bake on baking sheet in moderate oven (375°F. Mark 5) about 10 minutes.

Cool on cake rack. Makes 7 dozen.

OATMEAL CRISPIES

3 ounces plain flour
½ teaspoon salt
½ teaspoon bicarbonate of soda
4 ounces fat
3 ounces brown sugar
4 ounces caster sugar
1 egg
½ teaspoon vanilla
6 ounces rolled oats, uncooked
1 ounce chopped nuts

Mix and sift flour, salt, and soda into bowl. Add fat, sugars, egg, and vanilla. Beat until smooth, about 2 minutes. Fold in oats and nuts.

Shape dough in 2 rolls. Wrap in greaseproof paper and chill.

Slice ¼-inch thick and place on ungreased baking sheet.

Bake in moderate oven (350°F. Mark 4) 10 to 12 minutes. Makes 3½ dozen.

Raisin-Orange Filled Biscuits
Lemon-Glazed Raisin Bars

Oatmeal Biscuits with Fig Filling

OATMEAL BISCUITS WITH FIG FILLING

8 ounces butter or margarine
9 ounces dark brown sugar
2 eggs
1 teaspoon vanilla
8 ounces plain flour
1 teaspoon baking powder
1 teaspoon salt
½ teaspoon bicarbonate of soda
10 ounces quick-cooking rolled oats

Cream butter and sugar until fluffy. Add eggs and vanilla; beat well.

Sift together flour, baking powder, salt, and soda; add to creamed mixture and beat well. Stir in rolled oats. Chill at least 1 hour.

Roll half the dough at a time on well floured pastry board to a little less than ¼ inch. Cut with round cutter. Place about 1 tablespoon filling on half the rounds. Cut small circle out of centres of remaining rounds. Place on filling; press edges to seal.

Bake on ungreased baking sheet in moderate oven (350°F. Mark 4). 12 minutes. Makes about 30 cookies.

Fig Filling:
10 dried figs, chopped
4 fluid ounces water
3 tablespoons lemon juice
1 teaspoon grated lemon peel
3 ounces sugar

Combine ingredients; simmer 10 to 5 minutes.

THREE-IN-ONE COOKIES

8 ounces plain flour
1 teaspoon baking powder
½ teaspoon salt
4 ounces fat
8 ounces sugar
1 egg
1 tablespoon milk
½ teaspoon vanilla
1 ounce chocolate, melted
1 tablespoon orange juice
1 tablespoon grated orange rind

Sift together flour, baking powder, and salt.

Fig Star Biscuits

Cream fat and sugar until light and fluffy. Add egg, milk, and vanilla; stir in dry ingredients. Mix thoroughly. Divide dough into thirds.

To one-third add melted chocolate, mixing it in thoroughly.

To another third add orange juice and rind, mixing well.

Leave remaining third plain.

Shape each third into a roll. Wrap in greaseproof paper. Chill until very firm. Slice thin and bake on greased baking sheets in hot oven (400°F. Mark 6) 10 minutes. Makes about 5 dozen biscuits.

CHRISTMAS REFRIGERATOR BISCUITS

10 ounces plain flour
1½ teaspoons baking powder
½ teaspoon salt
8 ounces butter or margarine
12 ounces sugar
1 egg, beaten
1 teaspoon vanilla
1 ounce chopped crystallised cherries
1 ounce chopped pecans or walnuts
1 ounce milk chocolate, melted

Sift flour twice with baking powder and salt.

Cream butter until soft and gradually blend in sugar. Add egg and vanilla, and beat vigorously until smooth and fluffy. Add flour mixture and mix thoroughly.

Divide dough into 3 portions. Add chopped cherries to one portion, and nuts and chocolate to the second. Roll part of each dough in greaseproof paper and chill several hours in the refrigerator.

When ready to bake, slice very thinly. Place on buttered baking sheets and bake in hot oven (400°F. Mark 6) about 10 minutes or until delicately browned.

The remaining dough may be placed in a biscuit press and pressed out into fancy shapes on greased baking sheets. Bake at the same time and same temperature as those that are sliced. Makes about 8 dozen thin cookies.

FIG STAR BISCUITS

8 ounces butter or margarine
4 ounces sugar
9 ounces corn syrup or golden syrup
¼ teaspoon maple flavouring
2 eggs, beaten
1 pound 2 ounces plain flour
1 teaspoon baking powder
½ teaspoon salt

Cream butter and sugar; beat in syrup, flavouring, and eggs. (Maple-flavoured syrup may be used in this recipe, in which case omit maple flavouring.)

Stir in flour sifted with baking powder and salt.

Shape into rolls about 2½ inches in diameter, wrap in greaseproof paper, and chill in refrigerator several hours.

Slice thin. For filled biscuits, put together in pairs, sandwich fashion, with a dot of Fig Filling No. 2 between; press edges together, and prick top with fork or mark with knife.

To Make Star Biscuits: Put a small spoonful of fig filling in the centre of each biscuit. Draw the edges up together and punch to make a star shape.

Bake filled or star cookies in hot oven (400°F. Mark 6) 8 to 10 minutes, or until delicately browned around edges. Cool on racks.

Makes about 3 dozen filled biscuits, or six dozen stars. To freshen biscuits, reheat them in the oven for a few minutes before serving, and serve warm.

DATE PINWHEEL BISCUITS

5 ounces stoned, chopped dates
3 ounces sugar
6 tablespoons water
2 teaspoons lemon juice
½ teaspoon grated lemon rind
1 ounce finely chopped nuts
8 ounces plain flour
¼ teaspoon bicarbonate of soda
¼ teaspoon salt
5 ounces butter or margarine
7½ ounces brown sugar
1½ teaspoons grated orange rind
1 egg
1 tablespoon vinegar

Combine dates, sugar, and water in heavy saucepan. Cook until thickened, about 5 minutes, stirring constantly. Remove from heat. Blend in lemon juice, ½ teaspoon lemon rind, and nuts. Cool.

Sift together flour, soda, and salt.

Cream together butter or margarine, brown sugar, and 1½ teaspoons orange rind. Beat in egg and vinegar. Blend in dry ingredients. Chill dough several hours or overnight.

Roll dough into 15×10-inch rectangle. Spread with date mixture. Starting from a long side, roll as for Swiss roll. Chill 1 hour.

Slice into ¼-inch slices. Place slices on baking sheet.

Bake in moderate oven (375°F. Mark 5) 12 to 15 minutes or until lightly browned.

Cool on cake rack. Makes 5 dozen.

Date Pinwheel Biscuits

Drop Cookies

Drop cookies are made from a soft dough and dropped from a spoon onto a baking sheet. Actually the term "drop" is a little misleading since the mixture must be stiff enough to be pushed from the spoon. Keep the cookies about two inches apart unless the recipe states otherwise. Keep them uniform in size; however the shape may be irregular since they spread on the baking sheet.

SUGAR JUMBLES
(Basic Recipe)

4½ ounces plain flour
¼ teaspoon bicarbonate of soda
½ teaspoon salt
4 ounces soft butter or margarine
4 ounces sugar
1 egg
1 teaspoon vanilla

Sift together flour, soda, and salt. Mix butter, sugar, egg, and vanilla together thoroughly. Stir in dry ingredients.

Drop rounded teaspoons about 2 inches apart onto lightly greased baking sheet.

Bake in moderate oven (375°F. Mark 5) until delicately browned (cookies should still be soft), about 8 to 10 minutes. Cool slightly, then remove from baking sheet. Makes about 3 dozen 2-inch cookies.

Variations of Sugar Jumbles

Chocolate Chip Jumbles: Add an extra 2 ounces brown sugar, 2 ounces chopped nuts and 7 ounces polka dots.

Orange Chocolate Chip Jumbles: Add 1 teaspoon grated orange rind to the fat mixture of above.

Coconut Jumbles: Add 4 ounces desiccated coconut to batter of basic recipe.

Glazed Orange Jumbles: Add 1½ teaspoons grated orange rind and 4 ounces chopped nuts to batter of master recipe. Bake.

While hot, dip tops of cookies in an orange glaze made as follows: Heat together 3 ounces sugar, 3 tablespoons orange juice, and 1 teaspoon grated orange rind.

Nut Jumbles: Add 8 ounces chopped nuts to batter of master recipe.

3-in-1 Jumbles: Divide dough of basic recipe into 3 parts. Add ½ ounce melted plain chocolate to 1 part. Drop 2 ounces whole nuts into batter, coating each nut well.

Add 2 ounces desiccated coconut to second part.

Leave third part plain and drop 14 nut-stuffed dates into batter. Coat each date well. Each coated date and nut makes a cooky.

COCONUT MACAROONS
(Basic Recipe)

1 ounce plain flour
4 ounces sugar
¼ teaspoon salt
½ teaspoon vanilla
8 ounces desiccated coconut

Mix and sift flour, salt, and sugar.

Beat egg whites until stiff and peaky but not dry. Fold whites into dry ingredients.

Add vanilla and fold in coconut.

Drop by teaspoons onto lightly greased paper-covered baking sheet. Allow space for spreading and rising.

Bake in moderate oven (350°F. Mark 4) about 20 minutes, or until golden brown and dry on surface. Makes about 20 2-inch macaroons.

Coconut Macaroon Variations

Cake Crumb Macaroons: Substitute 3 ounces cake crumbs for half the coconut.

Caramel Nut Macaroons: Substitute 3 ounces brown sugar and 4 ounces chopped nuts for caster sugar and coconut.

Cherry Coconut Macaroons: Add 2 ounces chopped crystallised cherries.

Chocolate Chip Macaroons: Substitute 4 ounces polka dots for 4 ounces coconut.

Condensed Milk Macaroons: Omit sugar and egg whites. Mix coconut, flour, salt, and vanilla with sweetened condensed milk.

Corn Flake Macaroons: Substitute 4 ounces corn flakes for coconut.

Orange Macaroons: Add 1 tablespoon grated orange rind with egg whites. Sprinkle grated orange rind over macaroons when done.

Rice Macaroons: Substitute rice crispies for coconut and add 1 ounce chopped nuts.

Blueberry Drop Cookies

BLUEBERRY DROP COOKIES

4 ounces fresh blueberries or black currants
8 ounces plain flour
2 teaspoons baking powder
¼ teaspoon salt
6 ounces margarine
8 ounces sugar
2 eggs
1½ teaspoons grated lemon rind
4 fluid ounces milk

Wash blueberries and spread on paper towel to dry thoroughly.

Sift together flour, baking powder, and salt. Cream margarine until soft and gradually beat in sugar. Add eggs and lemon rind and beat until well mixed. Add flour mixture alternately with milk, beating until smooth after each addition. Lightly fold in blueberries.

Drop by teaspoon on greased baking sheet and bake in moderate oven (375°F. Mark 5) 10 to 12 minutes. Makes about 2½ dozen cookies.

ALMOND MACAROONS

4 ounces blanched almonds
1 egg
4 ounces sugar
¼ teaspoon salt
1 tablespoon plain flour
1 tablespoon melted butter or margarine
½ teaspoon vanilla
additional almonds for decoration

Mince almonds, using fine blade of mincer. Beat egg and gradually beat in sugar, salt, and flour. Stir in butter, vanilla, and minced almonds.

Drop by teaspoon onto greased baking sheet. Top each cooky with an almond half or a few chopped almonds. Bake in moderate oven (350°F. Mark 4) 10 to 15 minutes, until lightly browned. Remove from tin at once.

Makes about 20 cookies.

Sugar Jumbles

Almond Macaroons

Banana Oatmeal Cookies

BANANA OATMEAL COOKIES

6 ounces plain flour
8 ounces sugar
½ teaspoon bicarbonate of soda
1 teaspoon salt
¼ teaspoon nutmeg
¾ teaspoon cinnamon
6 ounces fat
1 egg, well beaten
3-4 mashed ripe bananas
7 ounces rolled oats, uncooked
2 ounces chopped nuts

Sift into mixing bowl: flour, sugar, soda, salt, nutmeg, and cinnamon. Cut in fat. Add egg, bananas, rolled oats, and nuts. Beat until thoroughly blended.

Drop by teaspoons, about 1½ inches apart, onto ungreased baking sheet. Bake in hot oven (400°F. Mark 6) about 15 minutes, or until edges are browned. Remove from pan immediately and cool on rack. Makes about 3½ dozen cookies.

ALMOND PASTE MACAROONS

1 pound almond paste (see below)
   (or use ready made)
1 pound sugar
¼ teaspoon salt
4 tablespoons plain flour
4 ounces sifted icing sugar
5 egg whites, unbeaten

Soften almond paste with hands and work in sugar, salt, flour, icing sugar, and egg whites.

Drop by teaspoons 2 inches apart on ungreased greaseproof paper placed on baking sheet. Pat tops lightly with fingers dipped in cold water.

Bake in slow oven (325°F. Mark 3) until set and delicately browned, about 18 to 20 minutes.

Remove from paper. Makes about 5 dozen 2-inch macaroons.

Almond Paste for Macaroons:

Mince 8 ounces blanched almonds, thoroughly dried (not toasted), through finest blade of mincer. Then mince twice again. Mix in 8 ounces sifted icing sugar. Blend in 2 egg whites, unbeaten and 2 teaspoons almond essence. Mould into ball. Place in tightly covered container in refrigerator for at least 4 days to age. Makes 1 pound.

COFFEE AND SPICE DROPS
(Basic Recipe)

8 ounces soft fat
12 ounces brown sugar
2 eggs
4 fluid ounces cold coffee
14 ounces plain flour
1 teaspoon bicarbonate of soda
1 teaspoon salt
1 teaspoon nutmeg
1 teaspoon cinnamon

Cream fat; gradually beat in sugar and eggs and beat thoroughly. Stir in cold coffee.

Sift together flour, soda, salt, nutmeg, and cinnamon and stir in. Chill at least 1 hour.

Drop rounded teaspoons about 2 inches apart onto lightly greased baking sheet.

Bake in hot oven (400°F. Mark 6) until set (when touched lightly with finger, almost no imprint remains), about 8 to 10 minutes. Makes about 6 dozen 2½-inch cookies.

Variations of Coffee and Spice Drops

Apple sauce Drop Cookies: Include 1 teaspoon ground cloves with other spices. Add 1 pound well drained thick apple sauce, or apple purée, and 6 ounces chopped sultanas and 2 ounces coarsely chopped nuts to batter. Bake 9 to 12 minutes.

Hermits: Add 1 pound halved seedless raisins and 6 ounces chopped nuts to batter. Be careful not to overbake.

Mincemeat Drop Cookies: Add 1 pound well drained mincemeat to batter.

Spiced Prune Drops: Include ¼ teaspoon ground cloves with other spices. Add 1 pound prunes (cooked, stoned and well drained), and 4 ounces chopped nuts to batter.

PECAN DROP COOKIES

5 ounces plain flour
¼ teaspoon bicarbonate of soda
¼ teaspoon salt
3 ounces fat
7½ ounces brown sugar
1 egg
4 ounces coarsely chopped pecans

Sift flour 3 times with soda and salt.

Cream fat and sugar. Add egg and mix thoroughly.

Stir in flour mixture in 2 or 3 portions, mixing each portion until smooth. Stir in nuts.

Drop by tablespoons 2 inches apart onto lightly greased baking sheet.

Bake in moderate oven (375°F. Mark 5), 10 to 12 minutes. Cool about 4 minutes on baking sheet, then remove to cake rack. Makes about 3½ dozen 2½-inch cookies.

NO-BAKE RUM DROPS

6 ounces digestive biscuit crumbs
5½ ounces icing sugar
2 tablespoons cocoa
⅛ teaspoon salt
4 ounces finely chopped nuts or
   desiccated coconut
2 tablespoons white corn syrup or
   honey
4-5 tablespoons brandy, rum, or
   Cointreau

Roll crumbs finely. Add sugar, cocoa, salt, and nuts.

Combine liquid ingredients and slowly add to first mixture. Use just enough liquid to hold ingredients together nicely.

Shape by teaspoons into firm 1-inch balls. Roll balls in icing sugar or dry cocoa.

Store in tightly covered box at least 24 hours before using. Makes 45 to 50 1-inch balls.

CRANBERRY DROP COOKIES

4 ounces butter or margarine
8 ounces caster sugar
4½ ounces brown sugar
4 tablespoons milk
2 tablespoons orange juice
1 egg
12 ounces plain flour
1 teaspoon baking powder
¼ teaspoon bicarbonate of soda
½ teaspoon salt
4 ounces chopped nuts
10 ounces coarsely chopped cranberries

Cream butter and sugars together. Beat in milk, orange juice, and egg.

Sift together flour, baking powder, soda, and salt. Combine with creamed mixture and blend well. Stir in chopped nuts and cranberries.

Drop by teaspoons onto greased baking sheet. Bake in moderate oven (375°F. Mark 5) 10 to 15 minutes. Makes about 12 dozen tea-size cookies.

Cranberry Bar Cookies: To bake as bar cookies, spread batter on a well-greased 11×15×1-inch tin and bake in moderate oven (350°F. Mark 4) 45 minutes or until golden brown. For a sugary crust, sprinkle with granulated sugar. Makes 4 dozen 1×2-inch bars.

Cranberry Drop Cookies
Cranberry Bar Cookies

OATMEAL DROP COOKIES
(Basic Recipe)

4 ounces plain flour
1 teaspoon baking powder
½ teaspoon salt
6 ounces fat
6 ounces brown sugar
2 eggs
1 teaspoon vanilla
5 tablespoons milk
12 ounces rolled oats, uncooked

Sift together flour, baking powder, and salt into bowl. Cut in fat; add sugar, eggs, vanilla, and about half the milk. Beat until smooth, about 2 minutes.

Fold in remaining milk and the rolled oats. Drop from a teaspoon onto greased baking sheet.

Bake in moderate oven (375°F. Mark 5) 12 to 15 minutes. Makes 4 dozen.

Variations of Oatmeal Cookies

Chocolate Chip Oatmeal Cookies: Add 6-7 ounces polka dots to batter.

Coconut Oatmeal Cookies: Add 4 ounces desiccated coconut to batter.

Date Oatmeal Cookies: Add 6 ounces chopped dates to batter.

Nut Oatmeal Cookies: Add 4 ounces chopped nuts to batter.

Raisin Spice Oatmeal Cookies: Sift 1 teaspoon cinnamon and ¼ teaspoon nutmeg with dry ingredients. Omit vanilla. Add 6 ounces seeded or seedless raisins to batter.

CRISP CHOCOLATE CHIP COOKIES

4 ounces butter or margarine
2 ounces castor sugar
3 ounces brown sugar
1 egg
½ teaspoon vanilla
6 ounces plain flour
½ teaspoon bicarbonate of soda
½ teaspoon salt
3 ounces puffed rice
6 ounces polka dots

Blend butter and sugars thoroughly; add egg and vanilla and beat well.

Crisp Chocolate Chip Cookies

Sift together flour, soda, and salt. Add to first mixture and stir until combined. Stir in puffed rice and chocolate.

Drop by teaspoons onto greased baking sheets. Bake in moderate oven (375°F. Mark 5) about 12 minutes. Makes 4 dozen 1½-inch cookies.

KICHLACH

Kichlach is a Jewish term for various old-time cookies. The recipe given here has been popular for many years.

5 ounces plain flour
2 tablespoons sugar
¼ teaspoon salt
3 eggs, slightly beaten

Mix and sift flour, sugar, and salt. Make a "well" in the centre and add the eggs. Beat with a fork until formed into a smooth dough.

Drop from a teaspoon onto a slightly greased baking sheet at least an inch apart.

Bake in slow oven (325°F. Mark 3) until lightly browned at the edges and puffed, about 20 minutes. Makes about 36.

Variation: Combine as above, adding 4 fluid ounces salad oil or melted fat; beat until well blended. If desired, add 3 tablespoons fine poppy seeds to this variation.

CORNUCOPIAS

2 ounces plain flour
1 egg
3 ounces sugar
2 tablespoons water

Sift flour into a small basin. Beat egg slightly in small deep bowl; add sugar, and continue beating until very thick. Then add water gradually, beating constantly until very thick and light.

Add flour all at once and fold in with a spoon until just blended.

Grease baking sheet and dust lightly with flour, tapping sheet to remove any excess flour.

Drop cooky dough from tablespoon onto sheet, spreading each cooky with a spoon into a very thin 5-inch circle. It is best to bake only 3 cookies at a time so they may be rolled quickly when baked.) Bake in moderate oven (350°F. Mark 4) until golden brown, 10 minutes.

Remove each cooky from baking sheet with a spatula and roll at once into a cone. If necessary, place baking sheet over low heat or return to oven for a moment or two in order to remove cookies easily. Set aside to cool.

When cornucopias are cold, fill with strawberry whipped cream. Serve at once. Makes 12.

Strawberry Whipped Cream: Mix 4 ounces sugar and 8 ounces sliced strawberries. Let stand 10 minutes. Drain. Fold into 8 fluid ounces whipped cream.

Raisin Peek-a-Boo Drops

RAISIN PEEK-A-BOO DROPS

8 ounces butter or margarine
12 ounces light brown sugar
3 eggs, beaten
12 ounces plain flour
1 teaspoon bicarbonate of soda
1 teaspoon salt
1 teaspoon vanilla
rich raisin filling (below)

Cream butter and sugar together until light and fluffy; beat in eggs. Sift flour, soda, and salt together twice. Add to creamed mixture along with vanilla.

Drop dough in small mounds on ungreased baking sheet. Press a small amount of rich raisin filling in centre of each mound. Top filling with a small bit of dough.

Bake in moderate oven (350°F. Mark 4) about 10 to 15 minutes. Use a wide spatula to carefully remove cookies to wire rack to cool. Makes about 3½ dozen cookies.

Rich Raisin Filling: Measure 8 ounces seeded or seedless raisins, 4 ounces sugar blended with 1 tablespoon cornflour, and 4 fluid ounces water into a saucepan.

Cook and stir until thick, about 10 to 15 minutes; remove from heat and cool slightly.

Add 1 tablespoon each lemon juice and soft butter and 1 ounce each chopped nuts and halved crystallised cherries. Stir to blend, let stand until cold.

Cornucopias

Chocolate Peek-A-Boos

CHOCOLATE PEEK-A-BOOS

4 ounces plain flour
¼ teaspoon salt
2 ounces sugar
8 fluid ounces milk
4 ounces butter or margarine
4 eggs
1½ teaspoons vanilla
3 ounces polka dots

Sift together flour, salt, and sugar. Measure milk into saucepan. Add butter; heat just to boiling point.

Add dry ingredients, all at once, to hot liquid, stirring constantly. Cook, stirring vigorously, until mixture leaves sides of pan in smooth compact ball. Remove from heat.

Add eggs, one at a time, beating vigorously after each addition until mixture is smooth again. Blend in vanilla; mix well.

Drop dough by half teaspoons, 2 inches apart, onto ungreased baking sheet. Place 1 chocolate polka dot on each cooky. Then cover with a teaspoon of dough.

Bake in moderate oven (375°F. Mark 5) 15 to 20 minutes. Sprinkle with icing sugar, if desired. Cool. Makes about 4 dozen.

SOFT GINGER COOKIES

6 fluid ounces evaporated milk
1 tablespoon vinegar
3 ounces fat
4 ounces sugar
1 egg, unbeaten
5 ounces molasses or treacle
12 ounces plain flour
2 teaspoons bicarbonate of soda
1 teaspoon salt
1 teaspoon ginger
1 teaspoon cinnamon

Combine milk and vinegar. Cream fat and sugar thoroughly. Add unbeaten egg and molasses and beat well. Add the soured milk and blend well. Sift flour with other dry ingredients into mixture and mix well. Drop from teaspoon onto greased baking sheet.

Bake in moderate oven (375°F. Mark 5) about 15 minutes. Makes 5 dozen.

BROWN SUGAR DROPS
(Basic Recipe)

14 ounces plain flour
1 teaspoon bicarbonate of soda
1 teaspoon salt
8 ounces soft fat
12 ounces brown sugar
2 eggs
4 fluid ounces sour milk or buttermilk

Sift together flour, soda, and salt. Cream fat, gradually beat in sugar and eggs. Stir in sour milk or buttermilk. Gradually stir in flour mixture and beat thoroughly. Chill at least 1 hour.

Drop rounded teaspoons about 2 inches apart onto lightly greased baking sheet.

Bake in hot oven (400°F. Mark 6) until set (when touched lightly with finger almost no imprint remains), about 8 to 10 minutes. Makes about 6 dozen 2½-inch cookies.

Brown Sugar Drop Variations

Coconut Drops: Add 4 ounces desiccated coconut to batter.

Fruit Drop Cookies: Add 6 ounces chopped walnuts, 8 ounces crystallised cherries, cut in halves, and 12 ounces chopped dates to batter. Decorate each cooky with walnut. Make cookies slightly smaller.

Nut Drops: Add 4 ounces chopped nuts to batter.

Salted Peanut Drop Cookies: Follow recipe for Brown Sugar Drops, using 8 ounces instead of 14 ounces flour and adding 6 ounces uncooked rolled oats and 2 ounces wheat flakes cereal. Add 4 ounces coarsely chopped salted peanuts (without husks). Bake until brown, 12 to 14 minutes.

NUT CRUNCHES

6 ounces plain flour
½ teaspoon bicarbonate of soda
1 teaspoon salt
4 ounces butter or margarine
3 ounces brown sugar
2 ounces castor sugar
1 egg, beaten
½ teaspoon vanilla
2 ounces chopped nuts
3 ounces chopped sultanas

Sift together flour, soda, and salt. Cream butter and sugars together until light and fluffy. Add egg and vanilla. Beat well.

Add flour mixture to creamed mixture. Mix well. Fold in nuts and sultanas.

Drop by teaspoons onto ungreased baking sheets. Bake in moderate oven (375°F. Mark 5) 10 minutes. Makes about 5 dozen.

MARMALADE COOKIES

8 ounces plain flour
1 teaspoon baking powder
½ teaspoon salt
4 ounces butter or margarine
5 ounces sugar
1 egg, unbeaten
1 tablespoon cream or milk
2 ounces marmalade
½ teaspoon vanilla

Mix and sift flour, baking powder, and salt.

Cream butter or margarine until soft and gradually blend in sugar. Add egg and beat thoroughly, then beat in milk, marmalade, and vanilla. Add dry ingredients and mix well.

Drop from teaspoon, about 1 inch apart, onto lightly greased baking sheet.

Cover bottom of water glass with a piece of clean cloth (can be fastened on with a rubber band or string), dip in flour and press cookies flat about ⅛-inch thick.

Bake in moderate oven (375°F. Mark 5) until delicately browned, 10 to 12 minutes.

Remove to cake rack to cool. Makes about 3 dozen.

Variations: If desired, substitute other preserves such as apricot, orange, pineapple, etc., for marmalade.

LACE COOKIES

12 ounces dark molasses or black treacle
8 ounces sugar
8 ounces butter or margarine
⅛ teaspoon salt
8 ounces plain flour
1 teaspoon baking powder
½ teaspoon bicarbonate of soda

Combine molasses, sugar, and butter in saucepan. Bring mixture to boil and cook 1 minute. Remove from heat.

Add dry ingredients, sifted together, and mix well.

Place in pan of hot water to keep batter from hardening. Drop ¼ teaspoons, 3 inches apart, on greased baking sheets.

Bake in moderate oven (350°F. Mark 4) 10 minutes or until brown.

Cool slightly and quickly remove from sheet with spatula. Makes 3 dozen.

Nut Crunches

RAISIN CHERRYETTES

8 ounces cornflakes
4 ounces plain flour
½ teaspoon salt
6 ounces soft butter or margarine
6 ounces sugar
1 egg
1 teaspoon grated lemon rind
4 ounces desiccated coconut
4 ounces sultanas
2 ounces coarsely chopped
    crystallised cherries

Crush cornflakes into fine crumbs. Sift together flour and salt; mix with cornflake crumbs.

Blend butter and sugar until light and fluffy. Stir in egg and lemon rind. Add dry ingredients; mix well. Stir in coconut, sultanas, and cherries.

Drop by teaspoons onto greased baking sheets. Bake in moderate oven (350°F. Mark 4) about 15 minutes. Makes about 4 dozen cookies, 2 inches in diameter.

Raisin Cherryettes

CHOCOLATE WHEAT GERM GEMS

6 ounces plain flour
½ teaspoon baking powder
½ teaspoon salt
4 ounces butter or margarine
6 ounces brown sugar
4 fluid ounces milk
3½ ounces wheat germ
2 ounces plain chocolate, melted
2 ounces coarsely chopped nuts
1½ teaspoons vanilla

Sift together flour, baking powder, and salt. Cream butter or margarine and brown sugar together. Add dry ingredients and milk; mix well. Blend in remaining ingredients.

Drop teaspoons of batter on greased baking sheet. Bake in moderate oven (375°F. Mark 5) until done, 12 to 15 minutes. Makes about 2½ dozen cookies.

Chocolate Wheat Germ Cookies

SOUR CREAM DROP COOKIES
(Basic Recipe)

11 ounces plain flour
½ teaspoon bicarbonate of soda
½ teaspoon baking powder
½ teaspoon salt
4 ounces soft fat
12 ounces sugar
2 eggs
8 fluid ounces thick sour cream
1 teaspoon vanilla

Sift together flour, soda, baking powder, and salt.

Cream fat. Gradually beat in sugar and eggs. Stir in sour cream and vanilla. Gradually stir in dry ingredients. Chill at least 1 hour.

Drop rounded teaspoons about 2 inches apart onto lightly greased baking sheet.

Bake in hot oven (425°F. Mark 7) until delicately brown (when touched lightly with finger, almost no imprint remains), about 8 to 10 minutes. Makes about 5 dozen 2½-inch cookies.

Sour Cream Drop Variations

Chocolate Cream Drops: Add 2 ounces melted plain chocolate to fat-sugar-egg mixture. Add 4 ounces chopped nuts to batter. Ice cooled cookies with chocolate icing.

Coconut Cream Drops: Add 4 ounces desiccated coconut to batter of basic recipe.

Fruit and Nut Drops: In basic recipe, add and sift with dry ingredients 1 teaspoon cinnamon, ½ teaspoon ground cloves, and ¼ teaspoon nutmeg.

Add 6 ounces chopped dates or 6 ounces sultanas and 4 ounces chopped nuts to batter. The spices may be omitted if desired.

CHOCOLATE CHIP COOKIES

8 ounces fat
4½ ounces brown sugar
6 ounces caster sugar
2 eggs, well beaten
4 ounces chopped nuts
½ pound polka dots
1 teaspoon vanilla
10 ounces plain flour
2 teaspoons baking powder
¼ teaspoon salt

Cream fat and sugars together until light. Add eggs and blend. Add nuts, chocolate, and vanilla.

Sift flour, baking powder, and salt together and add. Mix thoroughly. Drop onto baking sheets.

Bake in slow oven (325°F. Mark 3) about 20 minutes. Makes about 4 dozen.

Display your creative talents in shaping and decorating cookies, but for best results follow the recipe for the dough.

Lemon Drops

LEMON DROPS

8 ounces plain flour
½ teaspoon bicarbonate of soda
½ teaspoon salt
4 ounces fat
8 ounces sugar
2 eggs
1 teaspoon vanilla
4 tablespoons lemon juice
1 tablespoon grated lemon rind
2 ounces lemon sugar (below)

Sift together flour, soda, and salt.

Cream together fat and sugar unt light and fluffy. Add eggs and vanilla beating well.

Add dry ingredients alternately wit lemon juice and rind, mixing well afte each addition. Drop by teaspoons on greased baking sheet. Sprinkle wit lemon sugar.

Bake in moderate oven (375°F. Mar 5) 15 minutes. Makes about 5 doze

Lemon Sugar: Mix 1 teaspoon grate lemon rind with 2 ounces caster sugar

OATMEAL ORANGE LACE COOKIES

2 ounces plain flour
½ teaspoon salt
5 ounces sugar
8 ounces fat (at room temperature)
2 eggs
½ teaspoon vanilla
1 teaspoon grated orange rind
4 ounces rolled oats, uncooked
2 ounces desiccated coconut

Sift dry ingredients together in mixing bowl. Add fat, eggs, vanill and grated orange rind; blend tho oughly. Fold in rolled oats and coc nut.

Drop from teaspoon 2 inches apa onto baking sheet. Flatten with kni which has been dipped in cold wate

Bake in moderate oven (350°F 375°F. Mark 4-5) 10 to 12 minute Remove from baking sheet immed ately. Makes 4 dozen.

Oatmeal Orange Lace Cookies

St. Patrick's Day Cookies

MOLASSES DROP COOKIES
(Basic Recipe)

- 8 ounces plain flour
- 1½ teaspoons baking powder
- ½ teaspoon salt
- ¼ teaspoon bicarbonate of soda
- 1 teaspoon ground ginger
- 1 teaspoon cinnamon
- 4 ounces fat
- 2 ounces sugar
- 1 egg
- 4 tablespoons milk
- 9 ounces molasses or treacle

Mix and sift together flour, baking powder, salt, soda, ginger, and cinnamon.

Cream fat and gradually add sugar, creaming well; add egg.

Mix milk and molasses. Add dry ingredients alternately with liquid, beating until smooth after each addition.

Drop from teaspoon onto lightly greased baking sheet.

Bake in moderate oven (350°F. Mark) about 12 minutes. Makes 4 dozen.

Variations of Molasses Cookies

Coconut Gems: Add 4 ounces desiccated coconut and 1 tablespoon milk.

Oatmeal Molasses Cookies: Use only 4 ounces plain flour and add 6 ounces uncooked rolled oats.

Raisin Molasses Cookies: Add 2 ounces nuts and 3 ounces seedless raisins to any of the variations.

Whole Wheat Molasses Cookies: Replace ½ the plain flour with whole wheat flour.

Coconut Orange Jumbos

ST. PATRICK'S DAY COOKIES

- 8 ounces plain flour
- 2 teaspoons baking powder
- 1 teaspoon cinnamon mixed spice
- ¼ teaspoon ground cloves
- ½ teaspoon nutmeg
- ½ teaspoon salt
- 3 ounces sultanas
- 1-2 ounces coarsely chopped nuts
- 4 ounces sugar
- 9 ounces corn syrup or golden syrup
- 8 ounces butter or margarine
- 8 ounces hot mashed potatoes
- 1 egg

Sift flour with baking powder, spices, and salt. Stir in sultanas and nuts.

Cream sugar, syrup, and butter or margarine and beat into mashed potatoes. Combine mixtures.

Use teaspoon-size measuring spoon and drop 3 mounds close together on lightly greased baking sheet. Arrange a piece of dough for stem. Brush with slightly beaten egg and sprinkle with sugar.

Bake in moderate oven (375°F. Mark 5) 20 minutes. Makes 2½ dozen.

COCONUT ORANGE JUMBOS

- 10 ounces plain flour
- ¼ teaspoon salt
- ½ teaspoon bicarbonate of soda
- 6 ounces fat
- 4 ounces sugar
- 6 ounces light corn syrup or golden syrup
- 2 eggs
- 8 ounces desiccated coconut
- 3 tablespoons grated orange rind
- 4 fluid ounces orange juice

Sift together flour, salt, and soda. Cream fat. Add sugar gradually and cream until light and fluffy.

Add syrup, blend thoroughly. Add eggs, one at a time, beating well after each addition. Stir in coconut and orange rind.

Add sifted dry ingredients, alternately with orange juice. Drop by teaspoons onto lightly greased baking sheet.

Bake in moderate oven (350°F. Mark 4) 15 minutes.

Cool and ice with a butter cream icing. Makes 5 dozen.

MAPLE NUT DROPS

- 8 ounces maple syrup
- 1 can sweetened condensed milk
- 8 ounces crushed digestive biscuit crumbs
- 1 teaspoon vanilla
- 4 ounces chopped nuts

Cook maple syrup and condensed milk in heavy pan until thickened, about 3 minutes. Be careful not to scorch. Cool slightly and add remaining ingredients.

Drop from teaspoon onto greased baking sheet.

Bake in moderate oven (350°F. Mark 4) 15 minutes.

Remove from tin at once. Cookies will be hard if overbaked. Store in jar to soften. Makes about 36 small cookies.

Note: Be sure to use sweetened condensed milk. Same results will not be obtained with evaporated milk.

SHERRIED BUTTER-NUT DROPS

- 12 ounces softened butter or margarine
- 8 ounces sifted icing sugar
- ¼ teaspoon salt
- 13½ ounces plain flour
- 4 fluid ounces sherry
- 4 ounces finely chopped walnuts

Cream butter and sugar thoroughly and add salt.

Add flour alternately with wine, mixing well after each addition. Stir in nuts.

Drop by teaspoons onto greased, floured baking sheets.

Bake in moderate oven (350°F. Mark 4) 20 to 25 minutes. Makes about 100.

CEREAL JUMBLES

- 3 ounces fat
- 4 ounces sugar
- 1 well beaten egg
- 1½ tablespoons milk
- 4 ounces plain flour
- ½ teaspoon baking powder
- ¼ teaspoon bicarbonate of soda
- ½ teaspoon salt
- ½ teaspoon vanilla
- 3 ounces finely chopped dates
- 2 ounces chopped nuts
- 6 ounces whole wheat flakes

Cream fat; add sugar gradually, and blend. Add egg and milk.

Sift together flour, baking powder, soda, and salt. Stir into the creamed mixture. Add vanilla, dates, and nuts.

Crush cereal flakes slightly. Drop cooky dough from teaspoon into crushed cereal flakes and roll so that balls of dough are entirely coated. Top with chopped nuts, if desired.

Place about 3 inches apart on greased heavy baking sheet.

Bake in hot oven (400°F. Mark 6) about 12 minutes. Makes 2 to 3 dozen.

Cereal Jumbles

MOLASSES PECAN COOKIES

4 ounces fat
4 ounces sugar
2 eggs
6 ounces molasses or treacle
6 ounces plain flour
¼ teaspoon bicarbonate of soda
¼ teaspoon mace
¼ teaspoon salt
4 ounces finely chopped pecans or
    walnuts

Cream together fat and sugar; add eggs one at a time, beating after each. Add molasses; mix well.

Sift together flour, soda, mace, and salt; add 2 ounces nuts; mix well.

Drop by teaspoons onto greased baking sheet 2 inches apart. Sprinkle tops with remaining nuts.

Bake in moderate oven (350°F. Mark 4) 12 minutes. Remove from tin immediately. Makes 4 dozen.

CHRISTMAS FRUIT COOKIES

9 ounces sultanas
9 ounces currants
12 ounces crystallised pineapple
12 ounces crystallised cherries
2 ounces thinly sliced citron
6 ounces chopped nuts
4 ounces butter or margarine
9 ounces brown sugar
3 eggs, separated
4 fluid ounces evaporated milk
1½ teaspoons vinegar
8 ounces plain flour
½ teaspoon bicarbonate of soda
½ teaspoon salt
1 teaspoon cinnamon
1 teaspoon ground cloves
1 teapoon allspice
dash of nutmeg

Wash sultanas and currants and dry well. Cut other fruit into small pieces.

Cream butter until smooth and creamy. Add sugar gradually and continue creaming until free from sugar granules. Beat in egg yolks.

Stir vinegar into milk and add to butter mixture.

Mix and sift flour, soda, salt, and spices. Stir into butter mixture with the fruit and nuts.

Beat egg whites until stiff but not dry. Fold into batter. Drop by teaspoons onto greased baking sheet.

Bake in slow oven (325°F. Mark 3) 20 to 25 minutes. Makes 8 to 10 dozen.

Christmas Fruit Cookies

ORANGE HONEY DROPS

12 ounces plain flour
3 teaspoons baking powder
½ teaspoon salt
4 ounces fat
4 ounces sugar
1 egg
1 teaspoon vanilla
12 ounces honey
1 ounce chopped nuts
1 ounce chopped candied orange
    peel
1 ounce chopped candied lemon
    peel

Sift together flour, baking powder, and salt.

Cream together fat and sugar until light and fluffy. Add egg and vanilla, beating well. Blend in honey.

Add dry ingredients, nuts, orange and lemon peels, mixing thoroughly. Drop by teaspoons onto greased baking sheet.

Bake in moderate oven (375°F. Mark 5) 10 minutes. Makes about 7½ dozen.

RAISIN CAKES

2 ounces butter or margarine
6 ounces sugar
1 egg
½ teaspoon bicarbonate of soda
1 tablespoon hot water
6 ounces plain flour
¼ teaspoon salt
¼ teaspoon cinnamon
¼ teaspoon nutmeg
6 ounces chopped seeded raisins

Cream the butter and sugar thoroughly. Add the beaten egg and mix well.

Dissolve soda in hot water and add alternately with a sifted mixture of the flour, salt, cinnamon, and nutmeg. Stir in the raisins.

Drop by teaspoon onto a greased baking sheet and bake in a moderate oven (375°F. Mark 5) 8 minutes. Makes 4 dozen small cookies.

BRANDY WAFERS

6 ounces molasses or black treacle
4 ounces butter or margarine
5 ounces plain flour
¼ teaspoon salt
5 ounces sugar
1 tablespoon ground ginger
3 tablespoons brandy

Heat molasses to boiling. Add butter. Add sifted dry ingredients gradually, stirring constantly. Stir in brandy.

Drop ½ teaspoons 3 inches apart on greased baking sheets.

Bake 6 cookies at a time in slow oven (300°F. Mark 2) 8 to 10 minutes. Cool 1 minute.

Remove with spatula and roll at once around handle of wooden spoon. If removed too soon, wafers will break. If not soon enough, they will not roll. Makes about 60.

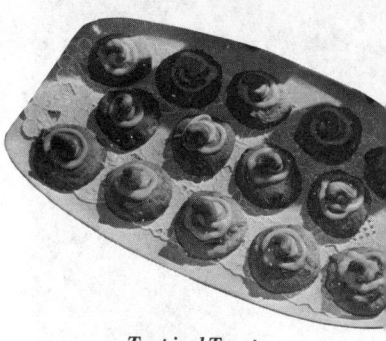

Tropical Treats

TROPICAL TREATS

4 dozen stoned dates
4 dozen halved walnuts
4 ounces margarine
1½ ounces brown sugar
4 ounces caster sugar
½ teaspoon vanilla
1 egg
7 ounces plain flour
½ teaspoon salt
1½ teaspoons baking powder
4 fluid ounces milk
creamy vanilla icing
cashew nuts or walnuts

Stuff dates with pieces of walnut. Cream margarine and sugars together until light and fluffy. Beat in vanilla and egg.

Sift together flour, salt, and baking powder. Add flour mixture alternately with milk to margarine mixture, mixing smooth after each addition.

Drop batter by teaspoons onto greased baking sheet. Press a stuffed date into each mound of batter. Cover dates with another teaspoon of batter, spreading it to cover dates completely.

Bake in moderate oven (375°F. Mark 5) 10 to 12 minutes. When cool, ice with creamy vanilla icing and decorate with cashew nut or walnut halves. Makes about 48.

BUTTERSCOTCH COFFEE WAFERS

8 ounces plain flour
2 teaspoons baking powder
½ teaspoon salt
6 ounces chopped nuts
4 ounces fat
12 ounces brown sugar
2 well beaten eggs
4 fluid ounces strong coffee

Mix and sift flour, baking powder, and salt; add nuts.

Melt fat; add sugar gradually and mix thoroughly over low heat.

Remove from heat and add well beaten eggs. Stir in flour and nut mixture, alternately with coffee.

Drop by teaspoons onto greased baking sheet. Spread with wet knife and bake in moderate oven (350°F. Mark 4) 12 to 15 minutes. Remove at once with thin knife or spatula. Makes 6 to 9 dozen, depending on size.

Fig Oatmeal Cookies

FIG OATMEAL COOKIES

5 ounces dried figs, coarsely
 chopped
8 ounces plain flour
2 teaspoons baking powder
½ teaspoon salt
1 teaspoon cinnamon
8 ounces quick-cooking oats, uncooked
2 ounces chopped nuts
6 ounces fat
6 ounces brown sugar
2 eggs
8 tablespoons water

Cover figs with hot water and allow
to stand 10 minutes. Pour off water and
reserve for liquid. Snip off stems from
figs, then chop coarsely.

Sift flour with baking powder, salt,
and cinnamon. Add oats, chopped figs,
and nuts.

Cream fat, add sugar, cream together thoroughly. Add well beaten
eggs, then add sifted dry ingredients
alternately with water to form dough.

Drop by teaspoons onto greased
baking sheet. Bake in hot oven (400°F.
Mark 6) 10 minutes. Makes 48 cookies.

SPICED FIG BALLS

3 ounces dried figs
4 ounces fat
6 ounces molasses or treacle
2 ounces sugar
¼ teaspoon ground ginger
1 egg, beaten
1 teaspoon vanilla
½ teaspoon lemon essence
1 teaspoon bicarbonate of soda
½ teaspoon cinnamon
¼ teaspoon nutmeg
¼ teaspoon salt
11 ounces plain flour

Cover figs with boiling water and let
stand 10 minutes. Drain, clip off stems,
and cut fine with scissors (if moist figs
are used softening may be eliminated).

Combine fat, molasses, and sugar.
Heat to boiling. Cool to lukewarm and
add ginger, beaten egg, vanilla, and
lemon essence.

Add sifted soda, spices, salt, and
flour. Stir in chopped figs.

Drop by teaspoons onto greased
baking sheet.

Bake in moderate oven (375°F. Mark
5) 12 minutes. Makes 3 dozen.

NEW ORLEANS DROP COOKIES

6 ounces fat
9 ounces molasses or treacle
2 eggs
9 ounces plain flour
4 teaspoons baking powder
½ teaspoon salt
1½ teaspoons cinnamon
½ teaspoon bicarbonate of soda
4 fluid ounces milk
3 ounces seedless raisins
2 ounces chopped walnuts

Slowly melt fat; cool. Add molasses
and eggs; beat well.

Sift together flour, baking powder,
salt, cinnamon, and soda; add alternately with milk to first mixture. Add
raisins and nuts.

Drop by teaspoons onto greased
baking sheet. Bake in hot oven (425°F.
Mark 7) 8 to 10 minutes. Makes 4 to 5
dozen.

PEANUT DROP COOKIES

8 ounces plain flour
2 teaspoons baking powder
½ teaspoon salt
4 ounces fat
8 ounces sugar
2 eggs
½ teaspoon vanilla
4 tablespoons milk
6 ounces chopped peanuts

Sift together flour, baking powder,
and salt.

Cream together fat and sugar until
light and fluffy. Add eggs and vanilla.
Mix well.

Add dry ingredients alternately with
milk, beating after each addition. Stir
in peanuts.

Drop by teaspoons on ungreased
baking sheets. Bake in hot oven (400°F.
Mark 6) 10 minutes. Makes about 4
dozen.

CHOCOLATE MOUNDS

8 ounces plain flour
2 teaspoons baking powder
½ teaspoon bicarbonate of soda
1 teaspoon salt
2 ounces cocoa
4 ounces fat
8 ounces sugar
2 eggs
½ teaspoon vanilla
8 fluid ounces buttermilk or sour
 milk

Sift together flour, baking powder,
soda, salt, and cocoa.

Cream together fat and sugar until
light and fluffy. Add eggs and vanilla,
beating well.

Add dry ingredients alternately with
buttermilk or sour milk. Drop by teaspoons onto ungreased baking sheet.

Bake in moderate oven (350°F. Mark
4) 12 to 15 minutes. While still warm,
ice with glacé icing. Makes 4 dozen.

POPPY SEED COOKIES

4 ounces poppy seeds
4 fluid ounces scalded milk
4 ounces butter or margarine
4 ounces sugar
2 ounces chocolate, melted
1½ ounces currants (opional)
6 ounces plain flour
1 teaspoon baking powder
⅛ teaspoon salt
½ teaspoon cinnamon
¼ teaspoon ground cloves
1½ ounces sultanas (optional)

Soak poppy seeds in hot milk for ½
hour.

Cream butter and sugar. Add remaining ingredients and mix thoroughly. Drop by teaspoons onto greased baking sheets.

Bake in moderate oven (350°F. Mark
4) 20 minutes. Makes about 30.

BRAN FLAKE CHIP COOKIES

5 ounces plain flour
1 teaspoon baking powder
¼ teaspoon salt
6 ounces butter or margarine
3 ounces brown sugar
4 ounces caster sugar
2 eggs
1 teaspoon vanilla
4 tablespoons milk
2 ounces chopped nuts
12 ounces bran flakes
6-7 ounces polka dots

Sift flour with baking powder and
salt.

Cream butter; add sugars gradually,
beating thoroughly after each addition.
Beat in eggs, one at a time; stir in
vanilla.

Add flour mixture alternately with
milk, beating until smooth after each
addition.

Stir in nuts, bran flakes, and finally
chocolate.

Drop from teaspoon onto buttered
baking sheet. Bake in moderate oven
(375°F. Mark 5) 12 minutes or until
done. Makes about 3 dozen.

Bran Flake Chip Cookies

COCONUT ISLANDS

8 ounces plain flour
½ teaspoon salt
½ teaspoon bicarbonate of soda
3 ounces plain chocolate
4 tablespoons hot strong coffee
4 ounces butter
6 ounces brown sugar
1 egg, unbeaten
¼ pint thick sour cream
1½ ounces desiccated coconut

Sift together flour, salt, and soda.

Melt chocolate in hot coffee in small saucepan over low heat. (If desired, ¼ teaspoon instant coffee and 4 tablespoons boiling water may be substituted.) Cool.

Cream butter; gradually add brown sugar, creaming well. Add unbeaten egg and the cool chocolate mixture. Beat well.

Add sour cream alternately with the dry ingredients to cream mixture. Mix until well blended. Stir in half the coconut.

Drop by heaping teaspoons onto greased baking sheets.

Bake in moderate oven (375°F. Mark 5) 12 to 15 minutes.

Ice while warm with chocolate icing (see below). Sprinkle tops with remaining coconut. Store in tightly covered container. Makes 3½ dozen.

Chocolate Icing: Heat 1½ ounces plain chocolate, 4 tablespoons sour cream, and 1 tablespoon butter in top of double boiler over hot water, stirring until chocolate melts. Immediately remove from heat.

Gradually blend in about 10 ounces sifted icing sugar, until consistency to spread. Thin with water or cream, a few drops at a time, if necessary.

NORWEGIAN AND DANISH KRINGLE (COOKIES)

8 fluid ounces sour cream
8 ounces sugar
12 ounces plain flour
1 teaspoon salt
1 teaspoon cinnamon
¾ teaspoon bicarbonate of soda
1 ounce melted plain chocolate, . optional

Combine sugar and sour cream and stir until dissolved.

Sift the flour, salt, cinnamon, and soda; add to sour cream mixture. Add the melted chocolate (this may be left out if desired).

Mix well and drop by ½ teaspoons onto greased baking sheet. Bake 20 minutes in a moderate oven (350°F. Mark 4). Makes 72 cookies.

MONKEY FACES

10 ounces plain flour
1 teaspoon bicarbonate of soda
½ teaspoon salt
½ teaspoon ground ginger
½ teaspoon cinnamon
4 ounces fat
6 ounces brown sugar
1 teaspoon vinegar
4 fluid ounces buttermilk or sour milk
6 ounces molasses or treacle
sultanas or currants for faces

Sift together flour, soda, salt, ginger, and cinnamon.

Cream together fat and sugar until light and fluffy. Add vinegar and blend well.

Combine buttermilk or sour milk with molasses. Add dry ingredients alternately with milk. Drop by teaspoons onto ungreased baking sheet. Make faces with currants or sultanas.

Bake in moderate oven (350°F. Mark 4) 10 to 15 minutes. Makes about 6 dozen.

TUTTI FRUTTI COOKIES

8 ounces fat
12 ounces molasses or black treacle
1 egg
8 ounces plain flour
1½ teaspoons bicarbonate of soda
1 teaspoon salt
1 teaspoon cinnamon
1 teaspoon nutmeg
6 ounces seedless raisins
4 ounces chopped nuts
3 ounces chopped citron, candied orange, and lemon peels

Slowly melt fat; cool. Add molasses and egg; beat well.

Sift together flour, soda, salt, cinnamon, and nutmeg; add to first mixture.

Put raisins, nuts, and fruit peels through fine-blade of mincer. Add to batter.

Drop by teaspoons 2 inches apart onto greased baking sheet.

Bake in hot oven (425°F. Mark 7) 8 to 10 minutes, until brown. Makes about 60.

COCONUT CHIP DROPS

8 ounces plain flour
¼ teaspoon bicarbonate of soda
¼ teaspoon salt
3 eggs
9 ounces brown sugar
1 teaspoon vanilla
1 tablespoon vinegar
1 tablespoon melted butter or margarine
1½ ounces plain chocolate, chopped
4 ounces chopped pecans or walnuts
4 ounces desiccated coconut

Sift together flour, soda, and salt. Beat eggs, brown sugar, and vanilla

together until thick. Stir in vinegar and melted butter or margarine. Blend in dry ingredients, chocolate, nuts, and coconut. Drop by teaspoons onto greased baking sheet. Bake in moderate oven (375°F. Mark 5) about 10 minutes or until lightly browned. Cool on cake rack. Makes 4½ dozen.

HOLIDAY OATMEAL DROPS

5 ounces butter or margarine
4½ ounces brown sugar
1 egg
1 teaspoon vanilla
8 ounces plain flour
2 teaspoons baking powder
½ teaspoon salt
4 ounces oats, uncooked
2 ounces chopped fruit, crystallised
2 ounces desiccated coconut
4 tablespoons milk
pecan or walnut halves

Cream butter or margarine and sugar until fluffy; add egg and vanilla and beat well.

Sift flour, baking powder, and salt; stir in oats, crystallised fruit, and coconut. Add oat mixture and milk to creamed mixture. Stir well.

Drop by teaspoons onto lightly greased baking sheets. Press a pecan or walnut half into each cooky.

Bake in moderate oven (375°F. Mark 5) 10 to 12 minutes. Makes 4 dozen.

COFFEE MINCEMEAT COOKIES

8 ounces mixed dried fruit
8 fluid ounces strong coffee
4 ounces fat, melted
6 ounces molasses or treacle
1 beaten egg
6 ounces flour
¾ teaspoon bicarbonate of soda
½ teaspoon salt
½ teaspoon mace

Combine mincemeat and coffee; simmer 10 minutes, or until mixture has consistency of mincemeat. Cool.

Add fat and molasses. Add egg and beat well.

Mix and sift remaining ingredients and stir in. Drop by tablespoons onto greased baking sheet about 2 inches apart.

Bake in hot oven (400°F. Mark 6) 15 minutes or until cookies are brown. Makes about 2½ dozen.

Cooky snatchers are not always the youngsters of the family. The aroma of freshly baked cookies is likely to bring everyone into the kitchen for a sample.

Rolled and Filled Biscuits

Rolled biscuits are made from a dough stiff enough to roll thin and cut with a pastry cutter, sharp knife, or a pastry wheel.

The dough should be chilled if it is too soft to be rolled out easily. If the dough is not chilled, it may be too soft to roll without adding more flour; therefore making the biscuits less tender.

Dip cutters in flour each time before cutting dough to prevent sticking.

MASTER BISCUIT RECIPE

8　ounces plain flour
1½　teaspoons baking powder
½　teaspoon salt
4　ounces butter or margarine
8　ounces sugar
1　egg, well beaten
1　teaspoon vanilla
1　tablespoon milk or cream

Sift together 6 ounces flour, baking powder, and salt.

Cream butter; add sugar gradually and cream until light and fluffy. Add egg, vanilla, and milk.

Add sifted dry ingredients, then gradually add remaining flour until dough is stiff enough to handle. Chill at least 1 hour.

Roll ⅛-inch thick on lightly floured board and shape with floured pastry cutters. Place on ungreased baking sheets. Sprinkle with sugar.

Bake in moderate oven (375°F. Mark 5) 8 to 10 minutes. Makes 50 to 60 small biscuits.

Variations of Master Recipe

Dropped Sugar Biscuits: Use only 6 ounces flour and 1 teaspoon baking powder. Drop by teaspoons 2 to 3 inches apart onto greased baking sheets.

For flat biscuits, press with knife or fork dipped in cold water or flatten with floured bottom of glass.

If mixture is too firm, shape into small balls and flatten as above.

Bake in moderate oven (375°F. Mark 5) 8 to 10 minutes.

Almond Biscuits: In master recipe, add 1 ounce chopped, blanched almonds and grated rind of ½ lemon, to flour mixture. Sift with dry ingredients ½ teaspoon each of cinnamon, ground cloves, and nutmeg.

Butterscotch Biscuits: In master recipe, substitute 6 ounces brown sugar for caster sugar.

Fruit Biscuits: In master recipe, add 2 ounces chopped crystallised cherries, and pineapple, candied orange, lemon, or grapefruit peel to flour mixture. Biscuits may also be decorated with pieces of fruit before baking.

Caraway Seed Biscuits: In master recipe, add 2 tablespoons caraway seeds.

Chocolate Biscuits: In master recipe, add 2 ounces melted plain chocolate with beaten egg. 4 ounces finely chopped nuts may be added to sifted dry ingredients.

Coconut Orange Biscuits: In master recipe, omit vanilla and add 1¼ teaspoons grated orange rind. Add 4 ounces desiccated coconut to flour mixture.

Coconut Biscuits: In master recipe, add 2 ounces desiccated coconut to flour mixture, or sprinkle coconut over biscuits before baking.

Crisp Sugar Biscuits: Follow master recipe and roll dough ¼-inch thick. Cover with sugar before baking.

Date Nut Biscuits: In master recipe, add 2 ounces each chopped dates and nuts to flour mixture.

Dried Fruit Biscuits: In master recipe, add 3 ounces of chopped apricots, prunes, dates, figs, or sultanas to flour mixture.

Ginger Biscuits: In master recipe, add 2 ounces crystallised ginger, cut finely.

Lemon Biscuits: In master recipe, substitute 1 teaspoon lemon essence and 2 teaspoons grated lemon rind for vanilla.

Maple Sugar Biscuits: In master recipe, substitute finely crushed maple sugar for caster sugar.

Molasses Biscuits: In master recipe, substitute 1½ ounces brown sugar and 3 ounces molasses or treacle for caster sugar. Omit milk. Add 1 teaspoon ground ginger and ½ teaspoon bicarbonate of soda.

Nut Biscuits: In master recipe, add 2 ounces chopped nuts to flour mixture.

Orange Biscuits: In master recipe, substitute orange juice for milk. Add grated rind of ½ orange. Use 2 egg yolks instead of whole egg.

Peanut Butter Biscuits: In master recipe, use 3 ounces peanut butter and 3 ounces brown sugar instead of butter and caster sugar. Add 1 tablespoon milk or cream.

Pinwheel Biscuits: Divide dough of master recipe into 2 equal parts. Blend 1 ounce melted chocolate into one part.

Roll each part to ⅛-inch thickness on separate pieces of floured greaseproof paper. Then place white dough on top of chocolate dough, removing paper.

Roll up as for a Swiss roll. Wrap firmly in greaseproof paper. Chill.

Slice and bake in hot oven (400°F. Mark 6) about 8 minutes.

Raisin Biscuits: In master recipe, add 3 ounces seedless or seeded raisins to butter and sugar-egg mixture.

Sand Tarts: Roll chilled dough of master recipe ¼-inch thick and cut in desired shapes.

Brush with egg white and sprinkle with mixture of 4 tablespoons sugar and 1 teaspoon cinnamon.

Decorate with blanched almond halves and crystallised fruits.

Sour Cream Biscuits: In master recipe, reduce baking powder to ½ teaspoon. Add ¼ teaspoon nutmeg and ¼ teaspoon bicarbonate of soda. Sift with flour.

Substitute ½ teaspoon lemon essence for vanilla. Use 3 fluid ounces sour cream instead of 1 tablespoon milk.

Spice Biscuits: In master recipe, omit vanilla. Sift with dry ingredients ¼ teaspoon each mixed spice, cinnamon, and ground cloves.

FILLED BISCUITS

Method No. 1: Prepare recipes for Master Biscuits and desired filling. Bake the biscuits.

When cool, spread filling on half the biscuits and cover with remaining biscuits to make "sandwiches".

Method No. 2: Prepare recipes for Master Biscuits and desired filling.

Roll out dough ⅛-inch thick. Cut out rounds with a 2½-inch plain pastry cutter.

Place 1 teaspoon filling on half the biscuits. Cover with remaining rounds, pressing edges together with fork.

Bake on ungreased baking sheet in moderate oven (375°F. Mark 5) 10 to 15 minutes. Makes about 2 dozen filled biscuits.

Method No. 3: Prepare recipe as above. Roll out and cut into squares.

Fill and fold over diagonally to make triangles with filling in pocket thus formed.

Bake in moderate oven (375°F. Mark 5) 8 to 10 minutes.

Method No. 4: Proceed as in No. 3 and fold squares or roll into cornucopias, with filling peeking out at wide end of horn.

Twist pointed end of horn to give curled effect. Bake in moderate oven (375°F. Mark 5) 8 to 10 minutes.

Orange Mincemeat Squares

ORANGE MINCEMEAT SQUARES

8 ounces plain flour
2 teaspoons baking powder
1 teaspoon salt
6 ounces sugar
4 ounces fat, melted
2 eggs
½ teaspoon orange essence
1 tablespoon shredded orange rind
6 ounces mincemeat or orange
marmalade

Sift together flour, baking powder, and salt.

Add sugar to melted fat and mix well. Add eggs, beating until mixture is smooth and well blended.

Stir in orange essence and orange rind. Gradually add flour mixture, stirring until mixture is smooth.

Cover and place in refrigerator for several hours or until dough can be easily handled.

Divide dough in half, returning one half to refrigerator. Place other half on floured board.

Roll out to 12-inch square. Cut into 16 3-inch squares. Place about 1 teaspoon mincemeat or orange marmalade in centre of each square. Bring corners of each square together in centre of square, sealing edges.

Place on baking sheet and bake in moderate oven (375°F. Mark 5) 12 to 15 minutes.

Roll out remaining half of dough and bake in same way. Makes 32 squares.

HUNGARIAN BUTTER BISCUITS

12 ounces butter or margarine
8 ounces sugar
2 eggs, separated
1 tablespoon rum
1 pound plain flour
2 ounces chopped nuts

Cream butter, gradually add sugar, creaming until fluffy.

Beat in egg yolks and rum. Work in flour to a smooth dough.

Roll out to ⅛-inch thickness. Cut into desired shapes with pastry cutters.

Beat 2 egg whites very stiff. Drop ½ teaspoon egg white on each biscuit. Sprinkle a few chopped nuts on top.

Bake in moderate oven (350°F. Mark 4) about 10 minutes or until golden brown.

PRUNE BISCUIT FILLING

6 ounces chopped cooked prunes
2 ounces sugar
2 teaspoons grated orange rind
2 ounces nuts, optional
¼ teaspoon salt
¼ teaspoon vanilla

Mix all ingredients, stirring until sugar is dissolved.

DATE RAISIN BISCUIT FILLING

3 ounces chopped seeded or seedless raisins
6 ounces chopped dates
4 ounces sugar
2 teaspoons grated lemon rind
3 teaspoons cornflour
4 tablespoons cold water
3 teaspoons lemon juice
2 ounces chopped nuts

Combine raisins, dates, sugar, and lemon rind in a saucepan.

Dissolve cornflour in cold water and add to fruit mixture. Cook over low heat, stirring constantly until thickened. Blend in lemon juice and nuts.

Use in Method No. 2, Filled Biscuits.

FIG BISCUIT FILLING

6 ounces minced figs
4 tablespoons orange juice
2 teaspoons grated orange rind
4 tablespoons water
⅛ teaspoon salt
2 ounces sugar
1 ounce chopped nuts

Mix together all ingredients except nuts.

Cook until mixture thickens, about 5 minutes, stirring constantly.

Cool and add nuts.

FIG BISCUIT FILLING 2

8 ounces dried figs
8 fluid ounces cold water
6 ounces corn syrup or golden
syrup
1 teaspoon grated lemon rind
6 tablespoons sugar
2 tablespoons flour
few grains salt
1 tablespoon lemon juice
2 ounces chopped nuts

Cover dried figs with boiling water and let stand 10 minutes; drain, clip off stems, and cut fairly fine, using scissors.

Add cold water and cook until tender, about 10 minutes. Add corn syrup and grated lemon rind, and cook a few minutes longer.

Mix sugar, flour, and salt; add all at once, and cook, stirring until thickened and clear.

Remove from heat; add lemon juice and nuts, and cool before using.

FILLED BISCUIT HINTS

Prepare Master Recipe. Roll dough to ⅛-inch in thickness and cut with a medium sized plain pastry cutter and a cutter with a scalloped edge.

Place biscuits on lightly greased baking sheet, then place in centre of each a heaping teaspoon of desired filling.

Cover plain biscuits with ones of equal size and the scalloped biscuit with ones from which centres have been removed.

Press edges of plain biscuits together with tines of a fork which has been dipped in flour.

Bake as directed and remove from tins at once onto cake rack.

Rainbow Biscuits

SPRINGERLE

Springerle are anise-flavoured German Christmas biscuits. Designs are embossed into the rolled-out dough with special rolling pins or boards.

2 eggs
10 ounces sugar
grated rind of 1 lemon
1 teaspoon anise or caraway seeds
10 ounces plain flour
½ teaspoon baking powder
½ teaspoon salt

Beat eggs until thick and lemon coloured.

Add sugar gradually, then beat with electric mixer 10 minutes or with rotary beater 20 minutes. Add flavourings and sifted dry ingredients.

Roll to ¼-inch thickness. Let stand until dry on top.

To emboss designs, press floured springerle rolling pin or board very hard on dough. Cut around designs and let dry on board overnight.

Remove to greased baking sheets. Bake in slow oven (300°F. Mark 2) 25 to 30 minutes.

Store in airtight container at least 1 week before using. Makes about 36.

BERLINER KRANZ BISCUITS

6 ounces butter or margarine
6 ounces sugar
1 teaspoon grated orange rind
1 egg
8 ounces plain flour
¼ teaspoon salt
1 egg white
green sugar*

Cream butter. Add 4 ounces sugar, orange rind, and egg, and beat until light. Add flour and salt. Chill several hours or until firm enough to roll.

Roll to ⅛-inch thickness. Cut with floured 2-inch doughnut cutter. Put on baking sheets. Beat egg white until foamy; add 2 ounces sugar gradually and beat until stiff. Brush biscuits with mixture.

Decorate with green sugar and cinnamon candies.

Bake in hot oven (400°F. Mark 6) 10 to 12 minutes.

Remove to wire racks while hot. Makes about 48.

*To make green sugar—rub a few drops of green food colouring into granulated sugar.

RAINBOW BISCUITS

8 ounces butter or margarine
1 teaspoon vanilla
5½ ounces stiff icing sugar
10 ounces plain flour

Blend together butter or margarine, vanilla, and icing sugar, creaming well. Blend in flour gradually.

Divide dough into four parts. Colour one part red, one yellow, and one green by adding 4 drops food colouring to each. Blend colour in dough thoroughly with spoon or knead in with hands. Leave fourth portion uncoloured. You will have four portions of dough, each a different colour.

Shape one-fourth of each colour dough into a long strip ½-inch thick. Place the four strips side by side on floured pastry board.

Roll out lengthwise into a long strip 2½ to 3 inches wide and ⅛-inch thick. Cut into rounds with 2½-inch cutter so that each biscuit has 4 coloured stripes.

Repeat this process three more times, using remaining dough. Reroll all extra pieces of dough together to ⅛-inch thickness and cut into rounds. Biscuits made from this dough will be marbled. Place on greased baking sheets.

Bake in moderate oven (350°F. Mark 4) 8 to 10 minutes. Do not brown. Cool.

Place biscuits together with peanut butter filling (see below) sandwich style, if desired. Or serve biscuits plain. Store in tightly covered container. Makes 2 dozen filled or 4 dozen unfilled biscuits.

Peanut Butter Filling: Combine 2 ounces brown sugar and 1 tablespoon flour in saucepan. Add 4 fluid ounces water. Cook over medium heat, stirring constantly, until thickened.

Remove from heat; add 2 ounces peanut butter. Use 1 teaspoon between each pair of biscuits.

MARMALADE RINGS

8 ounces plain flour
3 teaspoons baking powder
1 teaspoon salt
3 ounces fat
6 fluid ounces milk
marmalade

Mix and sift dry ingredients. Cut in fat thoroughly. Blend in milk to make a soft dough.

Roll out on lightly floured board to ¼-inch in thickness. Cut in 2-inch rounds. Cut centres from half the rounds.

Arrange rounds on baking sheet. Cover with those from which centres have been cut. Reroll scraps.

Bake in very hot oven (450°F. Mark 8) about 12 to 15 minutes.

Remove from oven. Fill centres with marmalade. Makes about 1½ dozen.

RAGALACH

8 ounces soft unsalted butter
½ pound soft cream cheese
¼ teaspoon salt
8 ounces plain flour
4 ounces chopped walnuts
4 ounces sugar
1 tablespoon cinnamon

Mix together the butter, cheese, and salt until creamy. Mix in flour. Form into 14 balls. Chill overnight.

Roll each ball to 6-inch circle, on lightly floured board. Cut each into quarters.

Mix nuts, sugar, and cinnamon. Drop rounded teaspoonful onto each quarter. Pinch together edges of dough and form into crescents. Place on ungreased baking sheet.

Bake in moderate oven (350°F. Mark 4) until light brown, about 12 minutes. Makes about 60.

OATMEAL SUGAR STARS

5 ounces soft fat
6 ounces sugar
1 egg
1 tablespoon milk
1 teaspoon vanilla
7 ounces plain flour
1 teaspoon baking powder
½ teaspoon salt
3 ounces quick uncooked oats
1 ounce chopped crystallised fruit

Beat fat and sugar together until creamy. Add egg, milk, and vanilla; beat until mixture is light and fluffy.

Sift flour, baking powder, and salt together; stir into fat mixture. Stir in oats. Chill dough about 30 minutes.

Roll out on lightly floured board to ⅛-inch thickness. Cut out biscuits with well-floured star-shaped biscuit cutter. Place a few pieces of crystallised fruit in centre of each star. Sprinkle with sugar. Bake on greased baking sheets in moderate oven (375°F. Mark 5) 10 to 12 minutes. Cool. Makes 3 dozen biscuits.

Oatmeal Sugar Stars

OLD-FASHIONED BUTTER BISCUITS

8 ounces butter
1 pound sugar
1 teaspoon vanilla
3 eggs, well beaten
1 pound plain flour
½ teaspoon salt

Cream butter; add sugar and vanilla and continue creaming until light. Beat eggs and add to butter mixture. Blend well.

Sift flour with salt and add to dough, using more flour if necessary to make stiff dough. Chill 20 to 30 minutes.

Roll out to ¼-inch thickness. Cut with pastry cutter and bake on lightly greased baking sheet in hot oven (400°F. Mark 6) about 10 minutes. (Biscuits may be sprinkled with sugar before baking.)

Remove from tins to cake racks to cool. Makes 5 to 6 dozen.

Filled Butter Biscuits: Roll dough to ⅛-inch thickness and cut with scalloped pastry cutter.

Place biscuits on baking sheet; place in centre of each a heaping teaspoon of date and raisin filling. Cover with biscuits of equal size with scalloped edge. Centres may be removed with small scalloped cutter.

Bake in hot oven (400°-425°F. Mark 6-7) 15 minutes. Remove from tins to cake rack.

SWEDISH TEA CAKES

8 ounces butter or margarine
3 tablespoons cream
8 ounces plain flour
1 egg white, slightly beaten
2 tablespoons finely chopped pecans or walnuts
2 tablespoons sugar
3 ounces raspberry jam

Cream butter until light and fluffy. Add cream and beat well. Add flour, mixing thoroughly.

Roll dough in greaseproof paper and chill several hours.

Divide into 2 parts. Roll 1 part about ¼-inch thick on well floured pastry board. Cut with 2½-inch doughnut cutter with centre cutter removed to make whole rounds. Place on ungreased baking sheets.

Roll and cut remaining dough in rings as for doughnuts with 2½-inch cutter. Brush rings with egg white and place egg-side down on rounds of dough.

Brush tops of cakes with egg white and sprinkle with nuts and sugar. Fill centres with jam.

Bake in hot oven (400°F. Mark 6) until delicately browned, about 12 to 15 minutes. Makes about 24.

SCOTCH SHORTBREAD
(Master Recipe)

8 ounces soft butter or margarine
6 ounces sugar
10 ounces plain flour

Cream butter and add sugar gradually, blending thoroughly. Add flour slowly and mix thoroughly to a smooth dough. Chill.

Roll out about ½-inch thick. Cut into desired shapes (small leaves, ovals, squares, etc.). Flute edges if desired by pinching between fingers as for pie crust.

Place on ungreased baking sheet. Bake in slow oven (300°F. Mark 2) about 20 to 25 minutes or until golden brown. Makes about 2 dozen 1 × 1½-inch cookies.

Scotch Shortbread Variations

Basic Shortbread Biscuits: Roll dough to ¼-inch thickness. Cut into desired shapes. Prick all over with fork. Bake about 20 minutes.

Butterscotch Shortbread: Substitute 6 ounces brown sugar for caster sugar.

Whole Wheat Shortbread: Substitute 4 ounces whole wheat flour for 4 ounces plain flour.

Honey Shortbread: Use only 4 ounces sugar and add 4 tablespoons honey.

GINGERSNAPS

8 ounces plain flour
2 ounces sugar
1 teaspoon bicarbonate of soda
½ teaspoon salt
3 teaspoons ground ginger
½ teaspoon cinnamon
2 ounces dry breadcrumbs
6 ounces molasses or treacle
4 ounces fat, melted
2 tablespoons iced water

Sift together flour, sugar, soda, salt, ginger, and cinnamon. Add crumbs, molasses, fat, and water. Mix thoroughly.

Roll ⅛-inch thick on lightly floured board. Cut into 2-inch rounds.

Bake on ungreased baking sheet in moderate oven (375°F. Mark 5) about 10 minutes. Makes about 7 dozen biscuits.

Refrigerator Gingersnaps: Dough may be shaped in roll, wrapped in greaseproof paper and stored in refrigerator. Cut chilled roll in ⅛-inch slices and bake as above.

NORWEGIAN ALMOND STICKS

14 ounces plain flour
½ teaspoon baking powder
3 eggs, well beaten
8 ounces sugar
8 ounces butter or margarine, melted
1 egg white, unbeaten
1 ounce chopped almonds

Sift together flour and baking powder.

Beat together eggs and sugar and blend in melted butter. Gradually stir in flour and mix well.

Roll out thinly on lightly floured board and cut into narrow finger-length strips.

Place on greased and lightly floured baking sheet. Brush with unbeaten egg white and dot with chopped almonds.

Bake in moderate oven (350°F. Mark 4) 8 to 10 minutes. Makes 50 to 70.

DATE-FILLED ORANGE BISCUITS

9 ounces chopped dates
4 ounces sugar
1 tablespoon grated orange rind
4 tablespoons orange juice
8 ounces butter or margarine
6 ounces light brown sugar
14 ounces plain flour
2 teaspoons baking powder
¼ teaspoon salt
4 fluid ounces water
½ teaspoon vanilla
4 ounces cornflakes, slightly crushed

Combine dates, sugar, orange rind, and juice; cook over low heat until a soft paste is formed. Let cool.

Cream fat and brown sugar well. Sift flour, baking powder, and salt together; add alternately with water and vanilla to first mixture. Stir in cornflakes. Chill.

Roll dough to ⅛-inch thickness. Cut with floured 2½- to 3-inch cutter.

Put a teaspoon of filling on one round and place a second round on top, pressing edges together.

Bake on greased baking sheet in moderate oven (375°F. Mark 5) about 15 minutes. Makes 3½ dozen.

Date-Filled Orange Biscuits

California Fig Holiday Wreaths

CALIFORNIA FIG HOLIDAY WREATHS

4 ounces butter or margarine
8 ounces sugar
3 tablespoons cream
1 teaspoon vanilla
1 egg
11 ounces plain flour
½ teaspoon salt
1½ teaspoons baking powder

Cream butter; add sugar gradually and cream thoroughly. Add milk, vanilla, and beaten egg.

Sift flour with salt and baking powder; combine with other ingredients. Chill thoroughly.

Roll out ¼-inch thick. Cut half the dough in full rounds, the remainder in doughnut shapes the same size.

Spread lower layer with Fig Filling 2; top with doughnut ring, pinch together and place on baking sheet.

Bake in moderate oven (375°F. Mark 5) 12 to 15 minutes.

LECKERLIS

8 ounces sugar
6 ounces honey
2 ounces chopped candied orange and lemon peel
1½ teaspoons ground cloves
1½ teaspoons nutmeg
1 tablespoon cinnamon
1 teaspoon bicarbonate of soda
grated rind of ½ lemon
4 ounces unblanched almonds, sliced thinly
11 ounces plain flour

Heat 4 ounces sugar and honey to boiling. Remove from heat and add peel, spices, and soda dissolved in 2 tablespoons cold water. Add remaining ingredients.

Knead until well blended. Roll dough to ½-inch thickness. Put on greased greaseproof paper on baking sheet.

Bake in slow oven (325°F. Mark 3) about 25 minutes.

Turn out on wire rack and remove paper at once. Turn right side up.

Cook remaining 4 ounces sugar and 4 tablespoons water until mixture spins a thread. Spread on Leckerlis. Cut in diamonds. Store in airtight container at least 1 week before using. Makes about 60.

GINGERBREAD BOYS

3 ounces soft fat
6 ounces brown sugar
1 pound dark molasses or dark treacle
4 fluid ounces cold water
1¾ pounds plain flour
1 teapoon salt
1 teaspoon allspice
1 teaspoon ground ginger
1 teaspoon ground cloves
1 teaspoon cinnamon
2 teaspoons bicarbonate of soda
3 tablespoons cold water

Mix fat thoroughly with sugar and molasses. Stir in 4 fluid ounces cold water.

Mix and sift flour, salt, spice, ginger, cloves, and cinnamon. Stir into first mixture.

Dissolve soda in 3 tablespoons cold water and stir in. Chill dough.

Roll out ½-inch thick. Cut with gingerbread boy cutter or cut around a greased cardboard cutout with a sharp knife.

Place carefully on greased baking sheet.

Press currants into biscuits to form eyes, nose, mouth, and shoe and cuff buttons.

Use strips of citron for tie and pieces of crystallised cherries for coat buttons.

Bake in moderate oven (350°F. Mark 4) 15 to 18 minutes. Cool slightly.

Use white icing to make outlines of collar, cuffs, belt, and shoes. Makes 1 dozen.

SWISS CINNAMON STARS

8 ounces blanched almonds
4 egg whites
grated rind and juice of ½ lemon
about 1½ pounds icing sugar
2 tablespoons cinnamon

Grate almonds.

Beat egg whites until stiff. Add rind, juice, and 8 ounces of the sugar. Continue beating until very stiff. Take out 1 breakfast cupful and set aside.

To remaining mixture, add almonds and cinnamon. Put on board generously sprinkled with icing sugar.

Sprinkle top with sugar. Roll very thin with sugar-dusted rolling pin. Cut with star-shaped cutter.

Put on brown paper on baking sheets. Spread with egg white mixture.

Bake in very slow oven (250°F. Mark ½) about 30 minutes.

Slip paper onto wet table or board. Let stand 1 minute. Loosen stars and lift to wire rack.

Store in airtight container 1 week before using. Makes about 60.

NORWEGIAN CHRISTMAS WREATHS

2 hard-boiled egg yolks
4 ounces butter or margarine
2 ounces sugar
4 ounces plain flour
½ teaspoon vanilla

Put egg yolks through sieve and cream them with butter. Add sugar gradually and continue creaming. Then add flour and vanilla.

Roll thinly and cut into doughnut-shaped biscuits. Decorate with pieces of crystallised cherry, citron, and angelica to resemble Christmas wreaths, or use red and green coloured sugar.

Bake on ungreased baking sheet in moderate oven (350°F. Mark 4) 8 to 10 minutes. Makes about 24.

VALENTINE BISCUITS

3 ounces butter or margarine
5 ounces sugar
1 egg, well beaten
½ teaspoon vanilla
8 ounces plain flour
2 teaspoons baking powder
¼ teaspoon salt
4 tablespoons milk

Cream butter or margarine and sugar. Add egg and vanilla and beat.

Sift flour, baking powder, and salt; add to creamed mixture with milk to form a dough. Chill.

Roll out to ⅛-inch thickness; cut with heart-shaped cutter.

Place half of the biscuits on a lightly greased baking sheet; brush each with water.

Cut smaller heart-shaped centres from remaining biscuits and place the heart frames on top of biscuits on baking sheet. Reroll scraps.

Bake in moderate oven (375°F. Mark 5) 10 to 12 minutes. Cool. Fill centre heart space with cherry filling. Makes 2 dozen.

Cherry Filling: Mix 2 ounces sugar, 1½ tablespoons cornflour and ¼ teaspoon salt. Add 4 fluid ounces water and 4 fluid ounces maraschino cherry juice. Cook over low heat until thickened, stirring constantly.

Remove from heat and add 18 chopped cherries and 1 tablespoon butter or margarine. Cool.

Valentine Biscuits

CITRON BISCUITS

8 ounces flour
1 teaspoon cream of tartar
½ teaspoon bicarbonate of soda
½ teaspoon salt
4 ounces butter or margarine
8 ounces sugar
2 eggs, separated
¼ teaspoon each vanilla and
      almond essence
candied citron
crystallised cherries

Sift together flour, cream of tartar, soda, and salt.

Cream butter and sugar until light and fluffy and beat in egg yolks 1 at a time, beating well after each addition.

Gradually stir in dry ingredients and mix well.

Fold in stiffly beaten egg whites flavoured with vanilla and almond. Add enough flour to make dough soft enough to roll out easily.

Roll out on floured board to ⅛-inch thickness. Cut with floured cutters. Arrange cherries and candied citron (cut into small pieces and strips) in flower designs on biscuits. Place on greased baking sheet.

Bake in hot oven (400°F. Mark 6) 8 to 10 minutes.

Store between layers of greaseproof paper in airtight container.

COFFEE JUMBLES

12 ounces plain flour
2 teaspoons baking powder
½ teaspoon salt
5 ounces fat
8 ounces sugar
2 eggs
½ teaspoon almond essence
4 tablespoons strong hot coffee
sugar
cinnamon
sultanas
almonds, halved

Mix and sift flour, baking powder, and salt.

Cream fat, stir in sugar and beat until fluffy. Stir in eggs, 1 at a time, and beat well after each addition. Stir in almond flavouring.

Add sifted flour ingredients alternately with coffee. Chill in refrigerator.

Roll part of mixture ¼-inch thick. Cut into rounds. Press edges with fork or use fancy cutter. To make bowknots, break off small pieces of dough, roll thin with fingers and knot.

Glaze jumbles with egg white diluted with a little water. Sprinkle with sugar and cinnamon, and decorate with plumped sultanas or halved blanched almonds.

Bake on ungreased sheet in hot oven (400°F. Mark 6) 10 to 12 minutes. Makes 3 to 5 dozen jumbles, depending upon size.

PINEAPPLE LEI BISCUITS

1 can drained, crushed pineapple
3 ounces sugar
1 tablespoon cornflour
1 teaspoon grated lemon rind
1 tablespoon lemon juice
8 ounces plain flour
¼ teaspoon bicarbonate of soda
½ teaspoon salt
4 ounces butter or margarine
6 ounces sugar
1 teaspoon lemon essence
1 egg
2 tablespoons pineapple juice
1 tablespoon white (distilled)
      vinegar
1 ounce desiccated coconut,
      optional

Combine pineapple, 3 ounces sugar, cornflour, and lemon rind in heavy saucepan. Cook until thickened, about 5 minutes, stirring constantly. Remove from heat. Blend in lemon juice. Cool.

Sift flour, soda, and salt together.

Cream together butter or margarine, 6 ounces sugar, and lemon essence. Beat in egg, pineapple juice, and vinegar. Blend in dry ingredients. Chill several hours.

Roll out dough ⅛-inch thick. Cut biscuits with a 2½-inch cutter. Cut a 1-inch hole in centre of half the biscuits. Place circles on baking sheet.

Drop a teaspoon of filling in centre of each circle. Top with biscuit rings. Press edges together firmly. If desired, sprinkle filling with coconut.

Bake in moderate oven (375°F. Mark 5) 15 minutes or until lightly browned. Cool on cake rack. Makes 2½ dozen.

Pineapple Lei Biscuits

CHOCOLATE HEARTS

8 ounces butter or margarine
8 ounces sugar
½ teaspoon vanilla
¼ pint sour cream
2 ounces chocolate, melted
9 ounces plain flour
¼ teaspoon salt
red food colouring

Put butter or margarine into a large bowl. Add sugar gradually and cream thoroughly. Add vanilla, sour cream, and chocolate; mix well.

Sift together flour and salt; fold into creamed mixture until thoroughly

Chocolate Hearts

blended. Chill dough in refrigerator overnight, or for several hours.

Spoon off small amount at a time; roll each to ¼-inch thickness on a lightly floured board. Cut with heart-shaped cutter.

Place 1 inch apart on lightly greased baking sheet. Bake in moderate oven (350°F. Mark 4) about 10 minutes.

Put a smaller heart-shaped cutter over each biscuit. Ice inside with glacé icing tinted pink with a few drops of red food colouring, or ice whole biscuits. Makes 3 dozen.

FANCY HOLIDAY BISCUITS

8 ounces butter or margarine
8 ounces sugar
2 eggs
1½ teaspoons vanilla
14 ounces plain flour
½ teaspoon baking powder
½ teaspoon salt
1 ounce chocolate, melted
½ teaspoon cinnamon
⅛ teaspoon ground cloves
⅛ teaspoon nutmeg
1 egg white

Cream butter or margarine and sugar; beat in eggs and vanilla.

Sift together flour, baking powder, and salt and combine with creamed mixture.

To half the mixture, add the melted chocolate and blended seasonings. Chill the doughs until firm.

Roll to ¼-inch thickness and cut into desired shapes. Bake in the upper part of moderate oven (350°F. Mark 4) 15 minutes.

Brush with egg white, decorate, and return to oven for 5 minutes. Makes 6 dozen.

Fancy Holiday Biscuits

Witch Hat Biscuits

WITCH HAT BISCUITS

    8 ounces plain flour
    1½ ounces nonfat dried milk powder
    1 teaspoon baking powder
    ¾ teaspoon salt
    4 ounces fat
    8 ounces sugar
    1 egg, unbeaten
    1 teaspoon vanilla
    2 tablespoons water
    2 ounces plain chocolate, melted

Sift together flour, nonfat milk powder, baking powder, and salt.

Cream fat. Add sugar gradually, beating until light and fluffy. Beat in egg. Stir in vanilla and water.

Add dry ingredients gradually, beating until smooth. Stir in cooled, melted chocolate.

Divide dough into 3 portions. Wrap in greaseproof paper and chill several hours.

Roll out ⅛-inch thick on lightly floured board. Cut into witch hat shape. (Make hat shape out of cardboard.)

Place on well greased baking sheet. Bake in hot oven (400°F. Mark 6) 5 minutes. Decorate cooled biscuits with children's names, using a glacé icing. Makes 38 4-inch biscuits.

POLISH HONEY CAKES

    6 ounces honey
    4 ounces sugar
    1 whole egg and 2 egg yolks
    1 pound plain flour
    1 teaspoon bicarbonate of soda
    ½ teaspoon cinnamon
    ½ teaspoon nutmeg
    ¼ teaspoon ground cloves
    ¼ teaspoon ground ginger
    blanched almonds, halved

Warm honey slightly and combine with sugar. Add eggs, reserving a small amount of egg white, and beat well.

Sift flour with soda and spices and stir thoroughly into honey mixture. Let the dough rest overnight.

Next day roll dough to a ¼-inch thickness; cut out with a pastry cutter. Brush with the reserved egg white, which has been beaten slightly. Press half a blanched almond into each biscuit and bake in moderate oven (375°F. Mark 5) for about 15 minutes.

DATE CREAM CHEESE ROLL-UPS

    8 ounces butter or margarine
    ½ pound cream cheese
    8 ounces plain flour
    ¼ teaspoon salt
    icing sugar
    stoned dates

Cream butter and cheese together. Blend in flour and salt. Chill several hours or until firm enough to roll.

Roll to ⅛-inch thickness on board sprinkled with icing sugar. Cut in 1×3-inch strips with pastry wheel. Put a date in centre of each strip and roll up. Place folded side down, on baking sheets.

Bake in moderate oven (375°F. Mark 5) about 15 minutes.

If desired, sprinkle with icing sugar. Makes about 8 dozen.

Variations: For variety, substitute nuts or crystallised cherries for dates.

ALMOND TEA BISCUITS

    8 ounces butter or margarine
    5 ounces sugar
    3 egg yolks
    10 ounces plain flour
    ½ teaspoon salt
    3 ounces ground almonds
    ½ teaspoon vanilla
    whole almonds

Cream butter and sugar together thoroughly. Blend in unbeaten egg yolks. Stir in flour, salt, ground almonds, and flavouring. Work mixture with hands until smooth.

Roll dough ⅛- to ¼-inch thick and cut into desired shapes. (Dough may be shaped into 1-inch balls and flattened with fork.) Top with half or whole almond, using the natural (unroasted) kernel, blanched or unblanched. Bake on ungreased baking sheet in hot oven (400°F. Mark 6) about 8 to 10 minutes or until a very light brown. Makes about 5 dozen.

SWEDISH GINGERSNAPS
(Pepperkakor)

    6 ounces light molasses or golden
       syrup
    3 ounces brown sugar
    4 ounces caster sugar
    4 ounces butter or margarine
    1 egg and 1 egg yolk, beaten
    2 tablespoons sour cream
    2 teaspoons cinnamon
    ½ teaspoons ground cloves
    1 teaspoon ground ginger
    ½ teaspoon bicarbonate of soda
    1 teaspoon baking powder
    10 ounces plain flour

Heat syrup to boiling and add sugars and butter. Stir until dissolved. Add beaten egg and yolk and sour cream, beating well.

Sift dry ingredients together and

add. Chill several hours or until firm enough to roll thinly.

Cut with floured cutter and decorate, if desired, with split almonds.

Bake in hot oven (400°F. Mark 6) until lightly browned, about 10 minutes. Makes about 50.

LEMON FILLED BISCUITS

    6 ounces butter or margarine
    8 ounces sugar
    1 egg, well beaten
    1½ teaspoons vanilla
    10 ounces plain flour
    ¾ teaspoon baking powder
    ¼ teaspoon salt
    lemon filling (below)

Cream butter or margarine; add sugar gradually and blend ingredients until light. Add egg and vanilla and blend thoroughly.

Sift dry ingredients together and stir into creamed mixture. Mix thoroughly and chill dough.

Roll out as thin as possible on a lightly floured board and cut with a fluted cutter. Place a spoonful of lemon filling on one round; cut two gashes in another round and cover filling. Gently lift points so filling will show. Press edges together and seal with a fork.

Place on greased baking sheet and bake in moderate oven (375°F. Mark 5) 8 to 10 minutes. Makes 40 filled biscuits.

Note: If biscuits lose crispness because of damp weather, return them to oven for 2 to 3 minutes to crisp.

Variations: These biscuits may be filled with mincemeat, preserves, or a mixture of marmalade, dates, and nuts, if desired. Or, for a single biscuit, brush the unbaked rounds with beaten egg white, sprinkle with grated almonds and sugar, and bake as directed.

Lemon Filling for Biscuits:

    4 ounces sugar
    2 tablespoons cornflour
    ¼ teaspoon salt
    4 fluid ounces orange juice
    1 tablespoon grated lemon rind
    4 tablespoons lemon juice
    1 tablespoon butter or margarine

Mix ingredients together in a saucepan. Bring to a rolling boil and boil 1 minute, stirring constantly. Chill before using.

Lemon Filled Biscuits

Miscellaneous Small Cakes and Biscuits

HINTS ABOUT MOULDED AND SHAPED BISCUITS

Moulded and shaped biscuits are more easily made if the dough is chilled first. The dough is formed into balls or sticks, sometimes with the palms of the hands. Flouring the hands will help in handling sticky doughs.

Balls are sometimes flattened with the palms of the hands or the bottom of a glass which has been greased and dipped into flour. Redip the glass for each biscuit.

ALMOND PRETZELS

8 ounces butter or margarine
8 ounces sugar
2 eggs and 2 egg yolks
8 ounces plain flour
½ pound almonds, unblanched and minced

Cream butter; add sugar and cream thoroughly.

Add eggs and egg yolks, and beat well. Add flour and minced almonds and mix.

Knead into a large roll and place in refrigerator to harden. When thoroughly cold, cut into pieces the size of a walnut. Roll out ¼-to ½-inch thick and twist into pretzel shapes.

Bake in slow oven (325°F. Mark 3) until browned, about 25 minutes.

GERMAN ALMOND CRESCENTS

5 ounces plain flour
6 ounces blanched almonds, grated
1½ ounces icing sugar
4 ounces butter or margarine, creamed

Mix flour with almonds and icing sugar. Rub in butter with the fingers as for making pastry. Knead until well blended and smooth.

Form into rolls 2 inches thick. Cut crosswise into ½-inch slices and shape into crescents.

A little beaten egg yolk may be added if dough is too crumbly to handle.

Place on greased baking sheet. Bake in slow oven (325°F. Mark 3) until crisp. They must remain almost white. Dip in Vanilla Sugar (see Index) while still hot.

Jam-Filled Dainties

CHINESE ALMOND BALLS

8 ounces plain flour
¼ teaspoon bicarbonate of soda
¼ teaspoon salt
4 ounces butter or margarine
5 ounces castor sugar
4 ounces brown sugar
½ teaspoon almond essence
1 egg, separated
2 tablespoons milk
1 tablespoon vinegar
2 ounces finely chopped blanched almonds, toasted
1½ ounces blanched almonds, split in half

Sift together flour, soda, and salt.

Cream together butter or margarine, sugars, and almond essence.

Beat in egg yolk, milk, and vinegar. Blend in dry ingredients and chopped almonds.

Shape dough into 1-inch balls. Place on baking sheet 2½ inches apart. Flatten with bottom of floured water glass.

Beat egg white slightly. Brush cookies with egg white.

Press a half almond in centre of each biscuit.

Bake in moderate oven (375°F. Mark 5) 10 to 12 minutes or until lightly browned. Cool on cake rack. Makes 4 dozen biscuits.

JAM-FILLED DAINTIES

8 ounces plain flour
½ teaspoon salt
8 ounces soft butter or margarine
3 ounces brown sugar
1 egg
½ teaspoon vanilla
4 ounces cornflakes
red currant, raspberry, or strawberry jam

Sift together flour and salt. Blend butter and sugar. Add egg and vanilla; beat well. Stir in sifted dry ingredients.

Shape dough into balls about 1 inch in diameter. Crush cornflakes into fine crumbs and roll the balls in the crumbs. Place about 2 inches apart on ungreased baking sheets. Make dent in centre of each one.

Bake in slow oven (300°F. Mark 2) 10 minutes. Remove from oven; press down dent in top of each cooky. Return to oven and bake about 10 minutes longer. Fill centres with jam when ready to serve. Makes about 4 dozen 1½ inches in diameter.

FATTIGMANDS

Fattigmands are fried biscuits of Norwegian and Swedish origin.

3 beaten eggs
3 tablespoons cream
3 tablespoons sugar

Chinese Almond Balls

1½ tablespoons melted butter or margarine
1 tablespoon lemon juice
½ teaspoon ground cardamom seed
¼ teaspoon salt
1-1¼ pounds plain flour

Mix together eggs, cream, and sugar. Stir in butter, lemon juice, cardamom, salt, and 8 ounces flour. Mix well. Stir in enough extra flour to make a stiff dough.

Wrap in waxed paper and chill at least 1 hour. Remove ¼ of the dough at a time, and roll out on a lightly floured board until paper thin.

Cut into 2-inch diamonds. Cut a slit in the centre of each and pull one corner through.

Fry in hot deep fat (350°F.) until delicately browned.

Dust with icing sugar before serving. Makes 10 dozen.

CINNAMON BALLS

8 ounces soft butter or margarine
3 ounces sugar
2 teaspoons vanilla
8 ounces plain flour
1 teaspoon cinnamon
4 ounces corn flake crumbs
4 ounces finely chopped walnuts
8 ounces icing sugar

Blend butter, sugar, and vanilla. Sift together flour and cinnamon; add with corn flake crumbs and nuts to butter mixture; mix well.

Shape into small balls; place on greased baking sheets. Bake in moderate oven (350°F. Mark 4) about 25 minutes. Roll at once in icing sugar. Makes about 4 dozen, 1½ inches in diameter.

Cinnamon Balls

ROLLED SWEDISH WAFERS

4 ounces butter or margarine
4 ounces sugar
2 slightly beaten eggs
5½ ounces plain flour
¼ teaspoon lemon essence
shredded almonds or coconut

Cream butter. Gradually add sugar and beat until smooth. Beat in eggs, flour, and lemon essence.

Drop by teaspoons onto an inverted baking tin. Spread to make very thin rounds, about 3 inches in diameter. Sprinkle with almonds or coconut.

Bake in slow oven (325°F. Mark 3) 8 to 10 minutes.

Remove from tin and roll up at once, nut side up, over handle of wooden spoon. Makes 6 dozen.

PEANUT CRUNCHIES (UNBAKED)

4 ounces butter
3 ounces peanut butter
½ pound marshmallows
2 ounces plain chocolate
6 ounces sugar-coated corn flakes

In a saucepan place butter, peanut butter, marshmallows, and chocolate; cook over low heat, stirring constantly, until ingredients are melted and well blended. Add corn flakes and mix well.

Pack into buttered 8-inch square tin and let stand until set. When cool, cut into bars. Makes 28 bars.

MARSHMALLOW-CORN FLAKE DROPS (UNBAKED)

2 ounces butter
½ pound marshmallows
6 ounces corn flakes

In a saucepan over low heat, cook butter and marshmallows, stirring constantly, until melted. Remove from heat and add corn flakes; mix well.

Moisten 2 spoons with cold water and form mixture into small balls; place on waxed paper-lined baking sheets. Let stand until firm. Makes 2 dozen drops.

Peanut Crunchies
Marshmallow-Corn Flake Drops

PEANUT BUTTER AND FIG CRUNCHIES

6 ounces butter or margarine
6 ounces caster sugar
3 ounces brown sugar
4 ounces peanut butter
1 egg, slightly beaten
1 teaspoon vanilla
7 ounces flour
½ teaspoon bicarbonate of soda
½ teaspoon salt
6 ounces chopped dried figs
additional sugar

Cream butter and sugars. Blend in peanut butter, egg, and vanilla. Add sifted flour, soda, salt, and figs; mix well.

Form into small balls; roll in sugar. Bake on ungreased baking sheets in moderate oven (375°F. Mark 5) 10 to 12 minutes. Makes about 5 dozen.

MANDELBRODT

A German and Jewish term meaning literally, almond bread. Mandelbrodt is an old-time almond-flavoured Jewish biscuit. The biscuit dough is baked in a long roll, then cut into thin diagonal slices which are browned in the oven.

3 eggs
8 ounces sugar
6 tablespoons salad oil
1 teaspoon lemon juice
grated rind of 1 lemon
¼ teaspoon almond essence
11 ounces flour
4 teaspoons baking powder
¼ teaspoon salt
2 ounces coarsely chopped
          blanched almonds

Beat eggs with sugar until light, then stir in oil, juice and grated rind of lemon, and almond essence.

Mix and sift flour, baking powder, and salt. Combine the 2 mixtures, adding nuts as dough is formed.

Knead on lightly floured surface and form into long rolls about 3 inches wide and 1 inch thick.

Bake in moderate oven (350°F. Mark 3) until light brown, 40 to 45 minutes. Transfer to a board while warm and cut into ½-inch slices.

Place slices cut side up on a baking sheet and place on top shelf of oven or under moderate grill until lightly browned. Makes 36 to 40 cookies.

Chocolate Mandelbrodt: Before shaping into rolls, remove ¼ of the dough and work into it 2 tablespoons cocoa mixed with 1 tablespoon sugar and a dash of cinnamon.

Wrap remaining rolled and flattened white dough around the chocolate roll. Shape into 2 rolls and bake as directed above.

Peanut Butter and Fig Crunchies

LEMON ANGEL HALOS

8 ounces plain flour
1 teaspoon salt
1 teaspoon bicarbonate of soda
5 ounces fat
6 ounces brown sugar
1 teaspoon vanilla
1 unbeaten egg
lemon filling (below)
meringue (below)

Sift together flour, salt, and soda.

Blend together fat and brown sugar, creaming well. Add vanilla and unbeaten egg; beat well. Blend in the dry ingredients gradually; mix thoroughly. Chill.

Prepare lemon filling and then meringue while dough is chilling.

Shape chilled dough into balls, using a level teaspoon of dough for each. Place on ungreased baking sheets. Flatten to ⅛-inch thickness.

Place a rounded teaspoon of meringue on each. Then form a hollow in the centre of each, using the back of a teaspoon dipped in cold water.

Bake in slow oven (300°F. Mark 2). 10 to 12 minutes until cream-coloured. When cool, fill hollow in top of each cooky with ½ teaspoon lemon filling. Makes about 7 dozen.

Lemon Filling: Combine 8 ounces sugar, 4 tablespoons lemon juice, 1 teaspoon grated lemon rind, and 3 slightly beaten egg yolks in saucepan. Heat to boiling, stirring constantly.

Remove from heat. Add 3 tablespoons butter; cover and cool.

Meringue: Beat 3 egg whites until slight mounds form when beater is raised. Gradually add 6 ounces caster sugar, beating well after each addition. Continue beating until mixture stands in stiff, glossy peaks when beater is raised.

Blend in 2 teaspoons lemon juice; beat until mixture again forms stiff peaks.

Lemon Angel Halos

MERINGUES (KISSES)
(Master Recipe)

4 egg whites
¼ teaspoon salt
8 ounces caster sugar
1 teaspoon vanilla

Beat egg whites with salt until stiff and dry. Beat in sugar gradually, sprinkling in 2 tablespoons at a time. Add vanilla and continue beating until mixture holds its shape.

Shape in mounds with a spoon, pastry bag, or tube on greased baking sheets covered with lightly greased heavy paper.

Bake in very slow oven (250°F. Mark ½) 50 to 60 minutes.

Remove from paper while still warm. If desired, shape in pairs. Makes about 30 large or 60 small meringues.

Meringue Variations

Coconut Kisses: In master recipe, fold in 4 ounces desiccated coconut before shaping.

Creole Kisses: In master recipe, fold in 4 ounces finely pounded nut brittle before shaping.

Date and Walnut Meringues: In master recipe, fold 4 ounces each chopped dates and nuts into meringue mixture.

Hazel Nut Kisses: In master recipe, fold 4 ounces chopped hard nuts into meringue mixture.

Marguerites: Follow master recipe and, at the last, fold in 4 ounces finely chopped nuts. Drop from a teaspoon or small chocolate or vanilla wafers.

Sprinkle with sugar. Bake in slow oven (300°F. Mark 2) 30 minutes. Makes about 48 marguerites.

Meringue Shells: Prepare basic recipe and shape in 3-inch mounds. Bake 1 to 1¼ hours. Remove from oven. Scoop out soft centre with a spoon and place in oven to dry.

To serve, fill centre with ice cream or sweetened fruit, and top with whipped cream or dessert sauce.

Meringue Shells with Pie Filling

Mushroom Meringues: Prepare master recipe. Shape with pastry bag or tube into rounds the size of mushroom caps. Sprinkle with cocoa or chocolate. Shape stems like mushroom stems. Bake, remove from paper, and place caps on stems.

Nut Meringue Shells: In master recipe, fold in 4 ounces chopped nuts (almonds, cashews, walnuts, pecans, or pistachio nuts before shaping into 3-inch mounds.

Pecan Kisses: In master recipe, substitute 6 ounces brown sugar for caster. Fold 4 ounces chopped nuts into meringue mixture.

LANGUES DE CHAT OR CAT'S TONGUES

2 ounces butter
2 ounces sugar
½ teaspoon vanilla
2 egg whites
1 ounce plain flour

Cream the butter; add sugar and vanilla and cream together until light and fluffy. Add egg whites, one at a time, mixing well after each addition. Sift flour a little at a time over the surface and fold in carefully.

On a buttered and floured baking sheet make small strips about 2 inches long and as thick as a pencil by putting the batter through a pastry bag fitted with a small plain tube.

Bake in very hot oven (450°F. Mark 8) until edges become golden brown, about 4 minutes. Remove from baking sheet and cool on absorbent paper. Makes about 20.

Variations: These may be iced or put a filling between two of the cakes using 3 parts chocolate icing and 1 part crushed nut brittle.

CHERRY BISCUITS

4 ounces fat
4 ounces sugar
1 teaspoon salt
1 teaspoon vanilla
¼ teaspoon almond essence
2 egg yolks
5½ ounces plain flour
glacé or well drained maraschino cherries, cut in quarters

Cream fat, sugar, and salt. Add flavourings and egg yolks and blend well. Stir in flour until well mixed.

Quickly roll dough into long cylinder, 1 inch in diameter and cut into ½-inch lengths. Form balls from cut pieces and place on ungreased baking sheet. Press a quarter cherry gently into centre of each.

Bake in moderate oven (375°F. Mark 5) until golden brown, 10 to 12 minutes

Remove from tin to cake rack. Makes 3½ to 4 dozen.

Snappy Turtle Biscuits

SNAPPY TURTLE BISCUITS

6 ounces plain flour
¼ teaspoon bicarbonate of soda
¼ teaspoon salt
4 ounces butter or margarine
3 ounces brown sugar
1 egg
1 egg yolk (reserve white)
¼ teaspoon vanilla
⅛ teaspoon maple or other flavouring, if desired
pecan halves

Sift together flour, soda, and salt.

Cream butter or margarine; gradually add brown sugar, creaming well. Add egg and egg yolk; beat well.

Blend in vanilla and maple flavouring, if desired. Add dry ingredients gradually; mix thoroughly. Dough will be soft. Chill, if desired.

Arrange split pecan halves in groups of three or five on greased baking sheets to resemble head and legs of a turtle.

Mould dough into balls; dip bottom into unbeaten egg white and press lightly onto nuts. Use a rounded teaspoon of dough for each, so tips of nuts will show when cooky is baked.

Bake in moderate oven (350°F. Mark 3) 10 to 12 minutes. Do not overbake.

Cool and ice tops generously with chocolate icing (see below).

Chocolate Icing: Combine 2 ounces chocolate, 4 tablespoons milk, and 1 tablespoon butter in top of double boiler. Heat over boiling water until chocolate melts; blend until smooth.

Remove from heat; add 5½ ounces sifted icing sugar. Beat until smooth and glossy. If too thin, add additional icing sugar until of desired consistency.

Press biscuits are made by forcing the dough through an icing bag and tubes to form a variety of shapes. They are usually made from a very rich dough, and it is not necessary to grease the baking sheet unless directed otherwise in the recipe.

Spritz Biscuits

SPRITZ BISCUITS

Spritz Biscuits are Scandinavian and are made in various shapes by means of an icing bag.

1 pound 2 ounces plain flour
¼ teaspoon bicarbonate of soda
1 teaspoon salt
1 pound fat
12 ounces sugar
3 eggs, beaten

Sift together flour, soda, and salt.

Cream together fat and sugar until light and fluffy. Add eggs. Add flour mixture, mixing well.

Force dough through icing bag with a 2 inch star tube onto baking sheets. Bake in moderate oven (375°F. Mark 5) 15 minutes. Makes 70 2-inch biscuits.

VIENNESE VANILLA CRESCENTS

1 pound plain flour
12 ounces butter or margarine
pinch of salt
4 tablespoons caster sugar
4 ounces unblanched almonds or hazelnuts, finely chopped

On a pastry board, work into a soft dough the flour, butter, salt, and sugar. When blended, work in the nuts. Chill the dough at least 2 hours.

Then on a lightly floured board shape the dough into little-finger-thick

rolls. Cut off pieces 2 inches long.

Bend them into crescents and bake on a lightly floured baking sheet in a moderate oven (350°F. Mark 4) for 10 to 15 minutes without allowing them to colour. While still hot remove with a broad knife and roll them carefully in Vanilla Sugar (see Index).

TEXAS STARS

Chocolate Dough:
2 tablespoons butter or margarine
6 ounces polka dots
1 can minus 2 tablespoons sweetened condensed milk (reserve remaining milk)
4 ounces plain flour
2 ounces walnuts, chopped
1 teaspoon vanilla

Melt butter or margarine with polka dots over boiling water. Remove from heat.

Blend in condensed milk; add flour and mix thoroughly. Stir in walnuts and vanilla. Mix well. Chill at least 1 hour.

White Dough:
6 ounces soft butter or margarine
4 ounces sugar
6 ounces plain flour
2 tablespoons sweetened condensed milk (reserved from chocolate dough recipe)
3 ounces crisp ready-to-eat cereal (shredded type or crumbled flakes)
4 ounces desiccated coconut
1½ ounces icing sugar

Cream the butter or margarine. Gradually add sugar, creaming well.

Blend in flour and 2 tablespoons condensed milk. Mix thoroughly. Add ½ ounce cereal; mix well. Chill 15 to 30 minutes, if desired.

Combine coconut and the additional cereal.

Roll out chilled white dough to ⅛-inch thickness on board which has been sprinkled with icing sugar. Cut into rounds with 2-inch cutter; place ½ inch apart on ungreased baking sheet.

Drop chilled chocolate dough by teaspoons into coconut-cereal mixture and roll to coat thoroughly. Mould into balls and flatten into 2-inch circles.

Place chocolate circles on top of white circles and press down to seal.

Shape into five-pointed stars by pinching white and chocolate doughs together with left thumb and index finger to form each point.

Bake in moderate oven (350°F. Mark 4) 12 to 15 minutes.

Cool and store in tightly covered container. Makes 4 dozen.

Peanut Butter Biscuits

PEANUT BUTTER BISCUITS

7½ ounces plain flour
1½ teaspoons baking powder
few grains salt
4 ounces butter or margarine
3 ounces brown sugar
6 ounces dark corn syrup or black treacle
3 ounces peanut butter
1 well beaten egg
½ teaspoon vanilla
additional peanut butter, optional*

Mix and sift together flour, baking powder, and salt.

Cream butter or margarine; gradually add sugar, and cream until light and fluffy.

Add syrup and 3 ounces peanut butter, beating until smooth and well blended. Add beaten egg and vanilla.

Add sifted dry ingredients, a little at a time, mixing well after each addition.

Shape dough into balls, about 1 inch in diameter. Place on ungreased baking sheet; flatten cookies with a fork. Place about ½ teaspoon of peanut butter on top of each cooky.

Bake in moderate oven (350°F. Mark 4) 12 to 15 minutes. Makes about 3½ dozen.

*Note: If desired, chopped peanuts may be substituted for peanut butter.

Texas Stars

PFEFFERNÜSSE

Literally, German for peppernuts; these are hard, spicy cookies the size of a large nut, sometimes containing black pepper. They are traditionally made at Christmas time.

1   pound plain flour
1   teaspoon bicarbonate of soda
½   teaspoon salt
1   tablespoon cinnamon
1   teaspoon ground cloves
1   teaspoon nutmeg
¼   teaspoon black pepper
1   tablespoon crushed cardamom seed
1   teaspoon anise or caraway seeds
¼   pound candied orange peel
½   pound citron
2   tablespoons butter or margarine
1   pound 4 ounces caster sugar
5   eggs, separated
1½ teaspoons grated lemon rind
about 4 tablespoons milk or water
5½ ounces icing sugar

Mix and sift flour, soda, salt and spices. Stir in seeds, then finely chopped orange peel and citron.

Mix together butter and sugar; add well beaten egg yolks and lemon rind and beat thoroughly. Gradually stir in flour-fruit mixture and fold in stiffly beaten egg whites. Chill 1 hour.

Shape in small balls the size of walnuts. Place on cloth and let stand, uncovered, overnight at room temperature.

In the morning brush balls with thin glacé icing made by gradually stirring milk into icing sugar.

Place on ungreased baking sheet and bake in moderate oven (350°F. Mark 4) 15 to 20 minutes. Makes about 7½ dozen.

TEIGLACH (HONEY BALLS)

Teiglach is a term for a Jewish holiday confection made of small pieces of rich dough, sometimes with nuts added, cooked in a syrup of honey, sugar, and often spices. They may be stored and served in the syrup. There is also a dry version.

Dough:
3   eggs
8   ounces plain flour
¼   teaspoon salt
½   teaspoon cinnamon or nutmeg
chopped almonds, optional

Honey Syrup:
1   pound honey
8   ounces sugar
1   teaspoon ground ginger

Beat eggs slightly in a large mixing bowl. Mix and sift flour, salt, and cinnamon or nutmeg; stir into eggs to form a stiff dough.

Turn out onto a lightly floured surface and knead 1 or 2 minutes. Pat a small ball of this dough into ½-inch thickness and cut into ¼-inch squares. Remove the cut squares to a large dish and continue with the remaining dough until all has been cut.

Or roll small pieces of dough to form long ¼-inch rolls, and then cut into ¼-inch pieces.

Combine honey, sugar, and ginger in a large saucepan and bring to a rolling boil.

Drop in the bits of dough a few at a time to prevent lowering of temperature of syrup.

After all have been dropped in, reduce heat and cook about 20 minutes, using a wooden spoon to prevent boiling over. Do not stir while cooking.

Turn out on a wet wooden board and pat with wet wooden spoon to an even thickness, about ½ inch.

If almonds are used, spread them evenly over the wet board before turning out the teiglach carefully over them without spreading the chopped nuts too far apart.

Let cool, then cut into small diamond or square shapes 1 to 1½ inches in diameter. Teiglach may be prepared well in advance of the day on which they are to be served. Store in jars or a crock after they are thoroughly cold.

Variation: If desired, individual cuts of the dough may be dropped into the boiling syrup and cooked a few at a time, skimming out as they rise to the top, about 7 or 8 minutes, then placed on a dish. When cold, store in jars.

DESSERT SHELLS

3   ounces butter or margarine
4   ounces sugar
1   egg
1   tablespoon orange juice
6   ounces plain flour
1   teaspoon baking powder
¼   teaspoon salt

Add sugar gradually to butter or margarine and cream thoroughly. Add egg and orange juice and mix well.

Sift flour, baking powder, and salt into creamed mixture. Blend well. Chill dough a few hours.

Roll dough to ⅛-inch thickness on lightly floured board; cut into large rounds. Invert some deep bun tins and grease outside of tins. Place rounds over tins; press down and pinch edges of dough at intervals to fit tins. Prick with a fork.

Bake in moderate oven (375°F. Mark 5) 6 to 8 minutes.

Cool 1 minute before removing shells. Fill with fresh strawberries, chocolate pudding, or vanilla ice cream topped with apricot marmalade or any other favourite sauce. Makes 10 to 12 shells.

Chocolate Twin Dots

CHOCOLATE TWIN DOTS

3   ounces dates
4   tablespoons water
6   ounces polka dots
6   ounces plain flour
1   teaspoon salt
½   teaspoon bicarbonate of soda
6   ounces fat
9   ounces brown sugar
1   egg, unbeaten
1   teaspoon vanilla
2   ounces quick-cooking oats, uncooked
6   ounces currants or sultanas
3   ounces icing sugar
2   ounces finely chopped nuts

Place dates, cut fine, in a saucepan with the water and simmer until soft, 2 to 3 minutes. Cool.

Melt ⅔ of the polka dots over hot water, reserving the rest for decoration.

Sift together flour, salt, and soda.

Blend together fat and brown sugar, creaming well. Add egg and vanilla and the melted chocolate. Beat well.

Blend in the dry ingredients gradually. Stir in the oats and currants or sultanas and the cool dates. Chill if necessary for easy handling.

Drop by rounded teaspoons into sifted icing sugar. Coat thoroughly and form into balls. Dip tops into chopped nuts.

Place on greased baking sheets. Press two of the reserved polka dots close together into the top of each cooky.

Bake in moderate oven (375°F. Mark 5) 10 to 12 minutes.

Cool 1 minute before removing from baking sheets. Cool thoroughly and store in tightly covered container. Makes about 5 dozen.

Dessert Shells

Sparkling Almond Rounds

SPARKLING ALMOND ROUNDS

2 ounces butter or margarine
4 ounces hydrolised fat
8 ounces sugar
¼ teaspoon almond essence
1 egg
5½ ounces flour
¼ teaspoon baking powder
¼ teaspoon each mace, cinnamon, salt
1½ ounces finely chopped un-
    blanched almonds

Brown butter or margarine in a 2½ pint saucepan; remove from heat and add fat, stirring to melt. Then blend in sugar and almond essence.

Beat in egg with spoon. (Mixture will thicken and become smooth). Mix in sifted dry ingredients and almonds.

Use teaspoon measure to take out pieces of dough; form small balls and drop into a dish of sugar; roll to coat well.

Place sugared balls about 2 inches apart on greased baking sheet. Bake in moderate oven (375°F. Mark 5) about 10 minutes or until light golden brown. Makes about 4½ dozen 2-inch rounds.

Keep crisp by storing in a canister or jar with a loose-fitting cover.

HUNGARIAN CREAM CHEESE KIPFEL

8 ounces butter or margarine
½ pound cream cheese
8 ounces plain flour
½ teaspoon salt
½ pound chopped nuts
4 tablespoons sugar
grated rind of 1 lemon
dash of cinnamon

Combine quickly with hands the butter, cheese, flour, and salt. Place in refrigerator overnight.

Roll out ⅛-inch thick on floured board. Cut into 2-inch squares.

Mix together nuts, sugar, lemon rind, and cinnamon. Place a small amount on each square, fold over, and seal edges.

Bake in moderate oven (375°F. Mark 5) 10 to 15 minutes.

Sprinkle with sugar. Makes about 80.
Variations: Kipfel may also be filled with jam or stewed dried fruit.

PRALINES

4 ounces butter or margarine
9 ounces brown sugar
1 egg, unbeaten
6 ounces plain flour
1 teaspoon vanilla
4 ounces coarsely chopped pecans or
    walnuts

Cream butter. Add sugar and egg and blend. Add flour, vanilla, and nuts. Mix well.

Shape into balls the size of a walnut. Place on greased baking sheet and flatten out to about ⅛-inch thick.

Bake in moderate oven (375°F. Mark 5) 12 minutes or until browned. Makes 3 dozen.

SWEDISH FRIED BISCUITS

3 beaten eggs
3 tablespoons cream
3 tablespoons sugar
½ teaspoon salt
flour

Combine eggs, cream, sugar, salt, and enough flour to make a very firm dough. Roll out dough very thinly. Cut in diamond shapes.

Cut a slit in centre of each diamond; draw one point of cooky through it.

Fry in hot deep fat (350°F.) ½ to 1 minute or until golden brown.

Drain on absorbent paper. Sprinkle with sugar. Makes about 36.

MAPLE RICE CRISPS

7 ounces plain flour
¾ teaspoon bicarbonade of soda
1 teaspoon salt
1 teaspoon cinnamon
4 tablespoons milk
1 egg, beaten
1 teaspoon maple flavouring
4 ounces fat
8 ounces sugar
4 ounces rice crispies
2 ounces chopped nuts
4 ounces rice crispies

Combine and sift flour, soda, salt, and cinnamon. Combine milk, egg, and flavouring.

Cream fat and sugar until light and fluffy. Add dry ingredients and liquids alternately one-half at a time. Stir only until dry ingredients are moistened. Fold in 2 ounces rice crispies and nuts carefully.

Roll rounded teaspoons of dough in additional rice crispies.

Place on greased baking sheet and bake in moderate oven (350°F. Mark 4) until done, about 15 minutes. Remove from baking sheet; cool. Makes 40 to 42 cookies.

Three-Way Banana Oatmeal Biscuits

THREE-WAY BANANA OATMEAL BISCUITS

8 ounces plain flour
1 teaspoon cinnamon
¼ teaspoon nutmeg
1½ teaspoons salt
1 teaspoon baking powder
¼ teaspoon bicarbonate of soda
8 ounces sugar
8 ounces soft fat
2 to 3 mashed bananas
2 eggs
8 ounces uncooked oats

Sift together flour, spices, salt, baking powder, soda, and sugar; add fat, mashed bananas, and eggs.

Beat until smooth, about 2 minutes; fold in rolled oats. Divide dough in three parts.

Bar Biscuits: Spread one-third of dough in a well greased 8-inch square tin. Bake in moderate oven (375°F. Mark 5) 15 to 20 minutes. Let stand 10 minutes.

Turn out of tin; cut in bars or squares; roll in icing sugar while still warm.

Drop Biscuits: Drop second portion of cooky dough by teaspoons onto well greased baking sheet. Decorate with chocolate chips, nuts, or sultanas, if desired.

Bake in moderate oven (375°F. Mark 5) 10 to 12 minutes.

Rolled Biscuits: Refrigerate third portion of dough overnight.

Sprinkle a board generously with icing sugar. Roll out cooky dough to ¼-inch thickness, sprinkling with additional sugar while rolling if necessary to prevent sticking. Cut in 2-inch circles or fancy shapes.

Bake on greased baking sheet in moderate oven (350°F. Mark 4) 8 to 10 minutes, or until brown.

Maple Rice Crisps

ROCKS

8 ounces butter or margarine
8 ounces sugar
4 eggs, separated
9 ounces plain flour
1 teaspoon cinnamon
1 teaspoon ground cloves
4 ounces walnuts
9 ounces sultanas
1 teaspoon bicarbonate of soda
1½ tablespoons boiling water

Cream butter; add sugar and beat until smooth. Beat in egg yolks one at a time.

Sift flour, cinnamon, and cloves together. Add walnuts and sultanas to flour. Stir into creamed mixture, mixing well.

Dissolve soda in boiling water; add to batter.

Beat egg whites until stiff; fold into batter.

Drop from teaspoon onto baking sheet. Bake in moderate oven (350°F. Mark 4) 15 to 20 minutes or until done. Makes about 4 dozen.

PEANUT BRITTLE

4 ounces plain flour
¼ teaspoon bicarbonate of soda
½ teaspoon cinnamon
4 ounces butter or other fat
3 ounces brown sugar
2 tablespoons beaten egg (reserve remainder)
1 teaspoon vanilla
2 ounces salted peanuts, finely chopped
1 tablespoon egg
additional salted peanuts or other nuts

Sift together flour, soda, and cinnamon.

Cream butter; gradually add sugar, creaming well. Add 2 tablespoons beaten egg and vanilla; beat well.

Blend in dry ingredients and 2 ounces chopped peanuts. Mix thoroughly.

Spread or pat dough on greased baking sheet to a 14×10-inch rectangle. Brush with remaining 1 tablespoon egg. Sprinkle with salted peanuts or other nuts.

Bake in slow oven (325°F. Mark 3) 20 to 25 minutes. Do not overbake.

Cut or break into pieces while warm. Makes about 2 dozen.

Peanut Brittle

LEBKUCHEN
(German Honey Cakes)

An iced spicy rectangular German cooky, frequently served during the Christmas season.

1 pound plain flour
¼ teaspoon bicarbonate of soda
¾ teaspoon cinnamon
⅛ teaspoon nutmeg
⅛ teaspoon ground cloves
8 ounces honey
3 ounces brown sugar
2 tablespoons water
1 egg, slightly beaten
3 ounces shredded candied orange peel
3 ounces shredded candied citron
4 ounces almonds, blanched and shredded

Mix flour, soda and spices, and sift together 3 times.

Combine honey, sugar, and water and boil 5 minutes. Cool. Add flour, egg, orange peel, citron, and nuts.

Press dough into a cake and wrap in greaseproof paper. Store in refrigerator 2 or 3 days to ripen.

Roll ¼-inch thick on lightly floured board. Cut in 1×3-inch strips.

Bake on greased baking sheet in moderate oven (350°F. Mark 4) 15 minutes.

When cool, spread with Transparent Glaze (see below). Store at least 1 day before serving. Makes about 5 dozen strips.

Transparent Glaze: Combine 11 ounces sifted icing sugar and 3 tablespoons boiling water. Add 1 teaspoon vanilla. Beat thoroughly. Spread on cookies while glaze is still warm.

Note: These cookies are characteristically hard and chewy. They develop a better flavour upon storage. Store 2 weeks or longer for best flavour.

SNICKERDOODLES

11 ounces plain flour
2 teaspoons cream of tartar
1 teaspoon bicarbonate of soda
½ teaspoon salt
8 ounces soft fat
12 ounces sugar
2 eggs

Sift together flour, cream of tartar, soda, and salt.

Cream fat; gradually beat in sugar and eggs; stir in dry ingredients. Chill dough.

Form into balls the size of small walnuts. Roll in mixture of 2 tablespoons sugar and 2 teaspoons cinnamon. Place about 2 inches apart on ungreased baking sheet.

Bake in hot oven (400°F. Mark 6) until lightly browned, but still soft, about 8 to 10 minutes.

Slice 'N Serve Cookies

These cookies puff up at first, then flatten out with crinkled tops. Makes about 5 dozen 2-inch cookies.

SLICE 'N SERVE COOKIES

5 ounces dates
3½ ounces flour
½ teaspoon baking powder
½ teaspoon salt
3 eggs
6 ounces sugar
½ teaspoon vanilla
6 ounces pecans, or walnuts, finely chopped
20 maraschino cherries
1 tablespoon icing sugar

Prepare dates by placing in a sieve and pouring boiling water over them. Cut fine with scissors or knife which has been dipped in hot water. Coat with 1 tablespoon flour.

Sift together remaining flour, baking powder, and salt.

Beat eggs until foamy. Gradually add sugar, beating constantly until thick and ivory coloured. Blend in vanilla.

Fold in the dry ingredients carefully but thoroughly. Then fold in 2 ounces pecans, finely chopped, and the cut-up dates.

Spread in 15×11-inch Swiss roll tin which has been lined with greaseproof paper, then greased generously and floured lightly.

Drain maraschino cherries. Arrange 10 cherries across each end of batter about ½ inch in from edge of tin.

Bake in slow oven (325°F. Mark 3) 30 to 35 minutes.

Turn hot cake out onto greaseproof paper which has been sprinkled with 1 tablespoon icing sugar. Remove paper, trim the edges and cut crosswise into two 11×7½-inch rectangles.

Roll each rectangle tightly, beginning with the cherry end. Wrap in greaseproof paper and chill.

Spread chilled rolls thinly with butter icing (below) and roll in chopped pecans. Chill. To serve, cut in ¼- to ½-inch slices.

Butter Icing: Cream 2 tablespoons butter or margarine. Blend in 8 ounces sifted icing sugar alternately with 3 to 4 teaspoons cream. Add ¼ teaspoon vanilla. Beat until creamy and smooth.

FRIED BOHEMIAN TWISTS

8 ounces plain flour
1 tablespoon sugar
1 teaspoon butter or margarine
½ teaspoon salt
2 egg yolks
1 whole egg
2 tablespoons cream

Mix the flour, sugar, butter, and salt together until smooth. Add the egg yolks one at a time, mixing well. Now add the whole egg and mix well. Add the cream gradually.

Turn onto a board and knead until dough does not cling to hands or board. Roll to paper thinness.

Cut dough into oblongs 4×6 inches. using pastry-wheel. Gash pieces with 5 or 6 cuts through centre lengthwise and parallel. Do not cut to edges of rectangle.

Lift with fork; poke a corner or two through the gashes, twist and drop into deep hot fat (370°F.). Fry until golden brown, turning once. Sprinkle with icing sugar. Makes 12 oblongs.

CANDY PECANS

2 ounces sugar
1 ounce pecans
5 ounces butter or margarine
1½ ounces brown sugar
6 ounces plain flour
½ teaspoon salt
1 teaspoon vanilla
icing sugar

Place 2 ounces sugar and pecans in heavy pan. Place over low heat and cook, stirring constantly, until sugar is melted and golden brown. Turn out onto buttered greaseproof paper and cool. When hard, chop finely.

Cream butter until light and fluffy. Blend in brown sugar, flour, and salt. Add vanilla and pecan candy.

Form into balls in palms of hands. Place on ungreased baking sheets. Bake in slow oven (300°F. Mark 2) 30 minutes.

Roll in icing sugar while warm. Makes about 36.

SUGAR AND SPICE BALLS

4 ounces cornflakes
8 ounces butter or margarine
3 ounces sugar
2 teaspoons vanilla
8 ounces plain flour
1 teaspoon cinnamon
4 ounces finely chopped nuts
8 ounces sifted icing sugar

Crush cornflakes into fine crumbs. Blend butter, sugar, and vanilla.

Sift together flour and cinnamon; add with cornflake crumbs and nuts to butter mixture; mix well.

Shape into small balls and place on greased baking sheets. Bake in moderate oven (350°F. Mark 4) about 30 minutes.

Roll at once in icing sugar. Makes about 4 dozen balls 1½ inches in diameter.

CRISP SWEDISH NUT CRESCENTS

2 ounces butter or margarine
6 ounces sugar
1 well beaten egg
2 tablespoons milk
1 teaspoon vanilla
5½ ounces plain flour
2 teaspoons salt
1 teaspoon baking powder
4 ounces chopped pecans or walnuts
4 ounces sugar

Cream butter and sugar together. Add egg, milk, and vanilla.

Mix and sift flour, salt, and baking powder; stir into butter mixture.

Spread dough very thin and evenly on bottom of buttered, inverted 8×8-inch tins.

Sprinkle with pecans and sugar. Mark in strips ¾×4 inches.

Bake 1 tin at a time in slow oven (325°F. Mark 3) 10 to 12 minutes.

While hot, cut into strips and shape over a rolling pin. If strips become too brittle to shape, return to oven to reheat and soften. Makes 9 dozen.

NORWEGIAN ANISE BISCUITS

11 ounces plain flour
2½ teaspoons baking powder
½ teaspoon salt
4 ounces sugar
4 ounces fat
1 teaspoon anise or caraway seeds
1 egg, beaten
5 tablespoons milk
seasame or poppy seeds

Mix and sift flour, baking powder, salt, and sugar. Cut in fat with pastry blender or 2 knives until mixture resembles breadcrumbs. Add anise seed.

Add beaten egg to milk. Make a "well" in the dry ingredients and add egg mixture. Stir until a smooth stiff dough is formed.

Pinch off balls of dough about 3 inches in diameter. Roll into strip about ¼ inch in diameter. Cut in lengths about 6 inches long.

Twist into various shapes, such as S, U, rosettes, figure 8, etc. Press gently into sesame seeds. Place seed side up, on ungreased baking sheet.

Bake in moderate oven (375°F. Mark 5) about 15 minutes.

These biscuits should be short and rich. Makes about 3 dozen.

GINGER BISCUITS

1¼ pounds plain flour
3 teaspoons bicarbonate of soda
½ teaspoon salt

3 teaspoons ground ginger
8 ounces fat
12 ounces brown sugar
2 eggs, beaten
1 teaspoon vinegar
6 ounces dark molasses or dark treacle

Mix and sift flour, soda, salt, and ginger.

Cream fat; add sugar and cream until fluffy. Add beaten eggs, vinegar, and molasses. Mix in dry ingredients.

Form into balls, using about 1 tablespoon dough for each. Place on baking sheet.

Bake in hot oven (400°F. Mark 6) 12 to 15 minutes.

The biscuits are very soft when done, but harden when cool. Makes 5 dozen.

SWEETHEARTS

2 ounces butter or margarine
6 ounces sugar
1 egg
½ teaspoon vanilla
5 ounces plain flour
1½ teaspoons baking powder
¼ teaspoon salt
5 tablespoons milk

Cream butter or margarine with sugar until light; add egg and vanilla and beat until fluffy.

Sift flour, baking powder, and salt. Add to creamed mixture with milk and stir smooth.

Brush a flat baking tin with butter or margarine; line with greaseproof paper and brush with butter or margarine again. Spread batter into tin.

Bake in moderate oven (375°F. Mark 5) 15 to 20 minutes.

Remove from tin; cool and cut out in heart shapes. Spread pink icing between hearts, sandwich fashion, and on top and sides. Decorate each with a candy heart if desired.

Pink Icing: Combine 12 ounces (approximately) sifted icing sugar, 4 tablespoons cream, ¼ teaspoon salt, and 1 teaspoon vanilla. Tint a delicate pink with red food colouring. Makes 11 double hearts or 22 single hearts.

Sweethearts

PECAN BUTTER BALLS

8 ounces plain flour
2 ounces sugar
½ teaspoon salt
8 ounces butter or margarine
2 teaspoons vanilla
12 ounces finely chopped pecans

Mix and sift flour, sugar, and salt. Work in butter and vanilla. Add 8 ounces nuts and mix well.

Shape in 1-inch balls. Roll balls in remaining nuts. Bake on baking sheets in slow oven (325°F. Mark 3) about 25 minutes. Makes about 4½ dozen.

Variations: Almonds, filberts, or walnuts can also be used. If desired, omit 4 ounces nuts and roll cookies while warm in sugar.

HEDGEHOGS

8 ounces walnuts
6 ounces dates, stoned
6 ounces brown sugar
8 ounces desiccated coconut
2 unbeaten eggs

Mince walnuts and dates in mincer. Add sugar, half the coconut, and eggs, and mix thoroughly.

Shape into rolls about 1 inch long and ½ inch in diameter. Roll each cooky in remaining coconut.

Place on greased baking sheets and bake in moderate oven (350°F. Mark 4) 15 minutes. Makes about 60.

CHILEAN LOVE KNOTS

1 egg
2 tablespoons double cream
2 tablespoons sugar
pinch of salt
1 teaspoon cinnamon
sifted flour

Beat the egg until very light. Beat in the cream, sugar, salt, and cinnamon. Beat hard, then add enough sifted flour to make a stiff paste. Roll out thinly and cut into long narrow strips. Tie each into two or three knots. Fry until golden brown in deep hot fat.

Drain and dust with caster sugar while hot. Serve with fruit sauce of any kind.

Heart-Shaped Tea Cakes

SWEDISH SPRITZBAAKEN

1 pound butter
8 ounces sugar
2 whole eggs
2 extra egg yolks
1 pound 2 ounces plain flour
vanilla

Cream sugar and butter. Add beaten eggs, then flour gradually, then vanilla to taste. Use cooky press or icing bag and tubes and form your own design.

Bake in a moderate oven (350° to 375°F. Mark 4-5) 20 minutes or until done.

Should be light in colour. These bake very quickly and need to be watched constantly. Makes 100 biscuits.

SWEDISH DREAMS (DROMMAR)

8 ounces butter
8 ounces sugar
8 ounces plain flour
1 scant teaspoon baking powder
1 teaspoon vanilla

Cream the butter; add sugar and cream thoroughly, using an electric beater if possible.

Beat in the sifted flour, baking powder, salt, and vanilla.

Put in refrigerator for a few hours, then shape into small balls and bake in a slow oven (300°F. Mark 2).

HEART-SHAPED TEA CAKES

4 ounces butter or margarine
2 ounces sugar
1 egg plus 1 egg yolk
9 ounces molasses or black treacle
6 fluid ounces milk
1 teaspoon vanilla
8 ounces plain flour
3 teaspoons baking powder
¼ teaspoon salt

Cream butter; gradually add sugar and beat until fluffy. Add whole egg and egg yolk one at a time and beat until mixture is puffy light.

Measure molasses into milk. Add vanilla. Sift together the dry ingredients. Add dry ingredients and liquid, alternately to first mixture, mixing until smooth.

Bake in well greased heart-shaped tins in moderate oven (350°F. Mark 4) 20 to 25 minutes.

Ice with glacé icing. Decorate cakes while icing is moist with chopped nuts, glacé cherries, etc.

Pecan Rolls

PECAN ROLLS

4 ounces butter or margarine
2 ounces icing sugar
¼ teaspoon vanilla
½ teaspoon almond essence
6 ounces plain flour
2 ounces chopped pecans
whole pecan halves

Cream butter thoroughly; add sugar, and beat until creamy. Stir in flavourings.

Add flour in several portions, beating after each addition. Add chopped nuts.

Shape small portions of dough into rolls about 2 inches long and ½ inch in diameter. Press a pecan half on top of each cooky.

Bake on buttered baking sheet in moderate oven (350°F. Mark 4) 10 to 15 minutes.

While hot, sprinkle lightly with icing sugar. Cool on cake racks. Makes 2½ to 3 dozen cookies, depending upon size.

MELTING MOMENTS

4 ounces butter or margarine
5 tablespoons icing sugar
1 teaspoon almond essence
¼ teaspoon salt
4 ounces plain flour
1 teaspoon baking powder

Cream butter, sugar, almond essence, and salt until light and fluffy. Add flour and baking powder and blend. Chill.

Form into balls, using a teaspoon of dough for each ball. Place on ungreased baking sheet. Flatten with fork dipped in flour.

Bake in moderate oven (350°F. Mark 4) until edges are browned, 8 to 10 minutes.

Cool before removing from pan. Makes 4 dozen.

Variations: If desired, decorate before baking.

Melting Moments
For a crisscross effect, flatten each biscuit with a floured fork.

DESSERTS

Desserts, plain or fancy, are the crowning touch to a meal. Whether you choose a traditional recipe or one that takes advantage of today's easy-to-make ingredients, you can turn out wonderful desserts that will please your family or impress guests.

The desserts presented here range from homelike simplicity to high sophistication. Included are the desserts every family depends on from day to day as well as the famous desserts of many lands. Choosing the right dessert is as much of an art as preparing it. Well-cooked and attractively served, the plain ones, too, can be exciting.

Always choose a dessert that suits your menu. If the meal has been light choose a rich dessert, or select a light one for a heavy meal. Plan to make your choise of desserts an essential part of your food planning. They can go a long way in rounding out the needs for essential nutrients—especially for the children.

Custards and Other Puddings

BAKED CUSTARD
(Basic Recipe)

2½ ounces castor sugar
¼ teaspoon salt
4 eggs, slightly beaten
1 pint, 4 fluid ounces milk, scalded
½ teaspoon vanilla essence
few grains nutmeg

Add sugar and salt to eggs. Beat until thoroughly mixed. Add milk to egg mixture, stirring constantly. Add vanilla.

Strain into buttered individual moulds and sprinkle lightly with nutmeg. Set moulds in baking dish. Pour enough hot water into dish to reach level of custard.

Bake in slow oven (325°F. Mark 3) until firm, 25 to 35 minutes, or until silver knife put into centre comes out clean. Chill. Serves 6 to 8.

Baked Custard Variations

Large Mould: Use 6 eggs; bake 1 to 1½ hours. Use silver knife test.

Bread Custard Pudding: In basic recipe, substitute 3 ounces breadcrumbs for 2 of the eggs. Add raisins, glacé fruits, or other chopped fruit. Mix and bake.

Caramel Custard: In basic recipe, add 4 fluid ounces caramelized sugar syrup to milk. Or pour 1 to 1½ tablespoons caramel syrup into each mould before pouring in custard mixture. Bake. Unmould to serve.

Chocolate Custard: In basic recipe, add 2 ounces plain chocolate to milk before scalding. Beat with wire whisk until blended.

Coconut Custard: Add 3 ounces shredded coconut to custard mixture of basic recipe.

Date or Nut Custard: Follow basic recipe; mix 4 ounces either chopped dates or nuts with custard before baking.

Fruit Custard: Place pieces of soft or soaked dried apricots or other fruit in bottom of mould before pouring in custard.

Gingerbread Custard: Prepare basic recipe. Use about 6 ounces crumbled gingerbread. Place 3 tablespoons in each mould before pouring in custard.

Golden Custard: In basic recipe, use 8 egg yolks. Omit whites.

Honey Custard: In basic recipe, substitute 6 ounces honey for sugar. Omit vanilla and nutmeg. Add dash of cinnamon.

Maple Custard: Prepare basic recipe. Pour 1 to 1½ tablespoons maple syrup into each mould. Pour in custard mixture carefully so that syrup is not disturbed. Bake. Unmould to serve.

Or substitute 4 tablespoons maple syrup or maple sugar for caster sugar in basic recipe.

Marshmallow Custard: Put 2 cut-up marshmallows into bottom of each mould. Sprinkle with shredded coconut before pouring in custard.

Rice Custard: Prepare basic recipe. Add 1 teacup cooked rice to strained custard and grated rind of ½ lemon.

Silver Custard: In basic recipe, substitute 2 egg whites for each whole egg.

MEXICAN FLAN

4 ounces caster sugar
14 ounces sweetened condensed milk
6 ounces milk
½ teaspoon vanilla essence
⅛ teaspoon salt
4 eggs, lightly beaten
2 ripe bananas, mashed
2 tablespoons lemon juice

Caramelize sugar by heating in a heavy pan. Pour into a shallow 1½-pint mould, coating the bottom and sides well.

In a saucepan combine sweetened condensed milk, milk, vanilla, salt, eggs, bananas, and lemon juice. Heat, stirring, until well blended. Pour into mould.

Set mould in pan of hot water. Bake in moderate oven (350°F. Mark 4) 65 to 70 minutes or until set. Cool. Unmould and chill until ready to serve. Garnish with mandarin orange segments and serve with shortbread biscuits. Serves 6 to 8.

SOFT CUSTARD
(Basic Recipe)

3 to 4 eggs, slightly beaten, or 4 to 6 egg yolks
3 tablespoons caster sugar
⅛ teaspoon salt
16 ounces milk, scalded
1 teaspoon vanilla

Combine beaten eggs, sugar, and salt. Slowly stir in scalded milk, stirring constantly.

Strain, then cook over simmering water 5 minutes or until mixture thickens and coats back of spoon.

Add flavouring, strain at once, and chill. Serve as sauce or pudding. Serves 4 to 6.

Soft Custard Variations

Almond Custard: Top each portion with chopped toasted almonds before serving.

Chocolate Custard: Follow basic recipe. Melt 2 ounces plain chocolate. Blend with scalded milk before adding to eggs. Add 1 tablespoon caster sugar.

Coconut Custard: Pour soft custard into baking dish. Beat 3 egg whites until stiff; fold in 2½ ounces caster sugar and 2 ounces desiccated coconut.

Spread over custard. Brown delicately in slow oven (300°F. Mark 2). Chill.

Coffee Custard: In basic recipe, substitute 8 fluid ounces strong coffee for 8 fluid ounces milk.

Cornflour Pudding: In basic recipe, substitute 3 tablespoons cornflour for eggs.

Custard Whip: Prepare basic recipe. Fold 4 fluid ounces whipped cream into cool custard.

Floating Island: Prepare soft custard with 4 egg yolks. Pour into sorbet glasses and chill.

Beat 2 egg whites, sweeten, and drop by spoonfuls on top of each serving. Garnish with a bit of maraschino cherry on top of egg white.

Fruit Custard: Prepare basic recipe. Add fresh or dried fruit to mould before pouring in custard.

Fruit Delight: Prepare soft custard. Slice fruit (peaches, oranges, strawberries, or bananas) into a bowl. Pour over the custard, or alternate layers of fruit and stale sponge cake.

Chill and serve with whipped cream.

Macaroon Pudding: Pour soft custard over macaroon or biscuit crumbs. Chill.

Orange Custard: In basic recipe, substitute 1 tablespoon grated orange rind for vanilla. Put orange segments in bottom of each mould before pouring in custard.

Or add 2 ounces candied orange peel to cool custard.

Spanish Custard Cream: Substitute 1 tablespoon unflavoured powdered gelatine for 2 eggs. Soften gelatine in 2 fluid ounces cold milk. While gelatine is softening prepare soft custard with remaining milk.

When soft custard is done, pour it slowly over soaked gelatine. Stir until dissolved. Chill.

Tapioca Custard: In basic recipe, substitute 3 tablespoons tapioca for 2 of the eggs. Cook tapioca in milk until transparent, 5 to 10 minutes. Then add to egg yolk mixture. Proceed as for soft custard.

Tipsy Custard Pudding: In basic recipe, substitute sherry for vanilla. Pour over pieces of stale sponge cake. Chill.

Yellow Custard: In basic recipe, substitute 4 egg yolks for whole eggs. Serve plain or with fruit, or use for Floating Island.

CRÈME BRÛLÉE

Brûlé is a French term meaning burnt; it is usually applied to caramelized sugar. Crème brûlée is a rich custard with a caramelized sugar coating.

1 pint, 4 fluid ounces double cream
1 vanilla pod
6 egg yolks
6 tablespoons granulated sugar
6 ounces or more brown sugar

Heat cream with vanilla pod in upper part of double saucepan.

Beat egg yolks with granulated sugar until light and creamy. Stir warm cream into egg yolks very carefully, discarding vanilla pod. Return to double saucepan.

Place over boiling water and cook, stirring constantly, until custard coats spoon. Pour into shallow glass baking dish. Place in refrigerator to set and chill thoroughly.

When ready to serve, cover top with layer of brown sugar thick enough so none of cream shows through. Set dish on layer of crushed ice or surround with ice cubes in a pan.

Place under grill until the sugar forms a bubbly brown crust. Watch it very carefully or the sugar will burn.

Serve at once or chill thoroughly and serve as is or over peaches. Serves 6.

Note: Two teaspoons vanilla may be substituted for vanilla pod. Combine with the sugar and egg yolks. Maple sugar may be substituted for brown sugar.

ZABAGLIONE OR SABAYON

This is a delicate soft custard served hot or cold alone as a dessert or as a dessert sauce. The French name is sabayon, a corruption of the Italian word zabaglione. In Italian it is also spelled zabaione. It is composed basically of beaten egg yolks, sugar, and heavy wine; however it is often varied by using various wines and combinations of favourite liqueurs. Marsala is the traditional wine in Italy. For a fluffier dessert or sauce, egg whites are sometimes beaten until stiff and folded into the custard just before serving

4 egg yolks
3 tablespoons caster sugar
4 fluid ounces sherry, Marsala, or Madeira

Beat yolks until light and thick. Add sugar. Continue beating until thoroughly blended. Slowly beat in wine.

Cook in top of double saucepan over hot, not boiling, water. Beat constantly until mixture leaves sides of pan.

Remove from heat and beat 1 minute more. Serve hot or cold in sorbet glasses as a dessert, or over chilled fruits as a sauce. Serves 4.

BAKED BLACKBERRY CUSTARD

about 4 ounces fresh blackberries
1 pint, 12 fluid ounces milk
5 eggs
5 tablespoons caster sugar
½ teaspoon salt
¼ teaspoon nutmeg
1½ teaspoons vanilla

Wash and drain blackberries, being careful not to crush or break them. Dry on paper towelling.

Scald milk. Break eggs into a bowl and beat well. Add sugar, salt, nutmeg, and vanilla. Pour in scalded milk and stir well with spoon.

Pour into individual custard or dariole moulds. Carefully arrange blackberries on top of custard (some will sink). If desired, sprinkle additional nutmeg on top.

Place moulds in pan of hot water and bake in moderate oven (350°F. Mark 4) about 15 to 20 minutes. Test with silver knife. When knife comes out clean, custard is done. Do not overcook, as custard will then turn watery. Remove custard moulds from water and cool, then chill in refrigerator. Serve icy cold. Serves 8.

Note: Other fresh fruits, in season, may be substituted for blackberries, e.g., raspberries.

Chocolat Pots De Crème

CHOCOLAT POTS DE CRÈME

2½ ounces plain or cooking
      chocolate
1 pint, 4 fluid ounces milk
4 to 6 ounces caster sugar
¼ teaspoon salt
5 egg yolks
½ teaspoon vanilla essence

Melt chocolate in a little milk in top of double saucepan, over hot water; add sugar, salt, and remaining milk; cook until chocolate is completely melted.

Remove from heat; slowly stir into beaten egg yolks. Return to double saucepan; cover and cook at simmering temperature 20 to 30 minutes or until medium thick, stirring occasionally. Remove from heat and stir in vanilla.

Pour into individual moulds or serving dishes that have been rinsed in cold water. Chill. Serve cold with cream. Serves 6.

BLACKBERRY GRUNT

A grunt is an old-fashioned American New England pudding, frequently made of blackberries although other fruits are often used.

about 6 ounces blackberries
12 fluid ounces water
6 ounces caster sugar
¼ teaspoon salt
1¾ teaspoons baking powder
5¼ ounces sifted plain flour
1 tablespoon lard
3 fluid ounces milk or more

Sort through and wash blackberries. Put in a well greased 3½-pint casserole. Add water and sugar and put into hot oven (400°F. Mark 6).

Mix and sieve salt, baking soda, and flour. Blend lard into flour mixture with a knife.

Gradually add milk to make a soft dough, handling the mixture as little as possible.

When the blackberries have been in the oven about 5 minutes, drop in spoonfuls of the dough. Cover and continue baking about 25 minutes. Serves 5 to 6.

APPLE TRIFLE

about 15 ounces sponge cake crumbs
6 fluid ounces sherry
1 3½-ounce packet blancmange
      mix
1 pint, 4 fluid ounces milk
3 rounded tablespoons black rasp-
      berry jam
½ pint apple slices
1 teaspoon grated lemon rind
1 tablespoon lemon juice
4 ounces caster sugar
8 fluid ounces double cream,
      whipped

Place sponge crumbs in dish approximately 8×12½×2-inches. Sprinkle sherry over crumbs.

Blend blancmange mix with milk; cook slowly until thickened, stirring constantly. Pour over crumbs; spoon raspberry jam over all.

Chop apples; combine with lemon rind, lemon juice, and sugar. Heat. Spoon over sponge mixture.

Chill several hours. Just before serving spoon whipped cream over apple mixture. Serves 8 to 10.

Apple Trifle

OLD-FASHIONED APPLE CRISP

6 medium cooking apples
4½ ounces fresh breadcrumbs
6 ounces caster sugar
1½ teaspoons cinnamon
about 1 ounce butter or margarine
2 tablespoons grated orange rind
3 fluid ounces water

Peel, core, and slice apples and place ½ in casserole.

Combine breadcrumbs, sugar, and cinnamon and sprinkle ½ over apples. Dot with ½ the butter.

Repeat with remaining apples, crumbs, and butter. Sprinkle with orange rind and add water.

Cover and bake in moderate oven (375°F. Mark 5) 45 minutes. Serves 6.

APPLE CUSTARD

12 fluid ounces milk
3 eggs, beaten
2½ ounces caster sugar
1 tablespoon grated orange rind
2 tablespoons orange juice
¼ teaspoon salt
9 ounces strained, sweetened
      apple sauce
⅛ teaspoon nutmeg

Add milk to beaten eggs. Mix together the sugar, grated orange rind, orange juice, salt, apple sauce, and nutmeg. Add to milk and eggs and stir until all the ingredients are blended.

Pour into 6 well-greased dariole moulds. Place moulds in a pan filled with hot water to a depth of about 1 inch.

Bake in a moderate oven (350°F. Mark 4) about 30 minutes or until the custards are firm. Serves 6.

APPLE PAN DOWDY

Apple Pan Dowdy is an old-fashioned American New England dessert of sliced apples, molasses or brown sugar, nutmeg, and cinnamon, topped with soft pastry crust and baked.

8 ounces sliced apples
3 ounces molasses, black treacle,
      or 1½ ounces brown sugar
¼ teaspoon nutmeg
¼ teaspoon cinnamon
¼ teaspoon salt
2 ounces butter or margarine
4 ounces caster sugar
1 well-beaten egg
6 ounces sifted flour
2 teaspoons baking powder
½ teaspoon salt
4 fluid ounces milk

Place apples in greased baking dish. Sprinkle with molasses, black treacle or brown sugar, spices, and salt.

Bake in moderate oven (350°F. Mark 4) until apples are soft.

Meanwhile prepare batter: Cream butter. Add sugar gradually, and egg.

Mix and sieve flour, baking soda, and salt. Add alternately with milk to first mixture. Pour over apples and continue baking. Total baking time about 35 minutes.

Serve from baking dish or turn out with apples on top. Serve with brandy butter or cream. Serves 6.

Apple Pan Dowdy

BLANC MANGE OR CORNFLOUR PUDDING
(Basic Recipe)

Old-fashioned cornflour pudding in its many variations continues to be a favourite in many homes. The name, blanc mange, is derived from the French words blanc (white) and manger (to eat).

- **3 to 4 tablespoons cornflour**
- **2 ounces caster sugar**
- **⅛ teaspoon salt**
- **2 fluid ounces cold milk**
- **14 fluid ounces scalded milk**
- **1 teaspoon vanilla essence**

Mix cornflour, sugar, and salt with cold milk. Add scalded milk slowly to cornflour mixture. Cook in top of double saucepan over simmering water until smooth and thickened throughout, about 10 minutes.

Cover and cook 10 to 15 minutes, stirring 2 or 3 times. Cool slightly. Add vanilla. Mix thoroughly.

Pour into moulds and chill. Serve plain or with fruit, nuts, and whipped cream, or sauce. Serves 6.

Blanc Mange Variations

Butterscotch Blanc Mange: In basic recipe, substitute 3 or 4 ounces brown sugar for caster sugar. Add 1 ounce butter to mixture before cooling.

Caramel Blanc Mange: In basic recipe, add 2 fluid ounces caramelized sugar syrup to milk after scalding.

Chocolate Blanc Mange: In basic recipe, add 2 ounces plain chocolate to scalded milk. Beat until chocolate and milk are smooth. Add 2 extra tablespoons caster sugar to cold milk mixture.

Or add 3 to 4 tablespoons cocoa and 2 extra tablespoons cornflour. Mix with cold milk mixture.

Chocolate Cream Blanc Mange: Fold 4 fluid ounces whipped cream or 2 beaten egg whites into chocolate pudding.

Coconut Blanc Mange: In basic recipe, add 2 ounces desiccated coconut before pouring into moulds.

Coffee Blanc Mange: In basic recipe, substitute 8 fluid ounces strong coffee for same amount of milk.

Creamy Blanc Mange: To basic recipe, add 2 egg whites, beaten stiff with ⅛ teaspoon vanilla.

Fluffy Blanc Mange: Follow basic recipe. When pudding is cooked, stir a small amount of hot mixture into 2 lightly beaten egg yolks. Stir into remaining hot mixture and cook 2 minutes, stirring constantly.

Cool slightly. Fold in 2 egg whites, beaten stiff, but not dry. Cool.

Fruit Blanc Mange: Add about ¼ pint crushed pineapple or other chopped or crushed fruits before pouring into moulds, or fill bottom of mould with fruits and pour pudding over fruit.

Layered Blanc Mange: Use food colouring; add to part of pudding before moulding. Mould in layers, alternating colours.

Moulded Blanc Mange: Increase cornflour to 4 tablespoons. Flour may be substituted for cornflour (5 to 7 tablespoons).

Nut Blanc Mange: Add 2 ounces chopped nuts to pudding.

JAPANESE PERSIMMON PUDDING

- **about 8 ounces persimmon pulp (about 3 large persimmons, or substitute Victoria plums or damsons)**
- **2 well-beaten eggs**
- **8 fluid ounces milk**
- **about 1 ounce melted butter**
- **4 ounces sieved all-purpose flour**
- **½ teaspoon bicarbonate of soda**
- **6 ounces caster sugar**
- **½ teaspoon salt**
- **¼ teaspoon cinnamon**
- **¼ teaspoon nutmeg**
- **2 ounces raisins or chopped nuts**

Mix persimmon pulp with eggs; add milk and butter.

Mix and sift flour, soda, sugar, salt, and spices. Combine with first mixture and mix to a soft batter, adding more milk if necessary. Add raisins or nuts if used.

Pour into buttered 8 × 8 × 2-inch pan. Bake in moderate oven (350°F. Mark 4) 30 to 45 minutes.

Serve with clotted double or whipped cream. Serves 6.

CHEESE-APPLE CRISP

- **1¼ pounds apple slices**
- **¾ teaspoon cinnamon**
- **8 ounces caster sugar**
- **2 fluid ounces water**
- **2 teaspoons lemon juice**
- **2½ ounces sieved plain flour**
- **⅛ teaspoon salt**
- **3 ounces butter or margarine**
- **4 ounces grated Cheddar cheese**

Arrange apple slices in a greased 9 × 9 × 2-inch pan. Combine cinnamon with 2 ounces sugar; sprinkle over apples. Add water and lemon juice.

Combine remaining sugar, flour, and salt; work in butter or margarine to form a crumbly mixture; lightly stir in grated cheese. Sprinkle flour-cheese mixture over apples.

Bake in moderate oven (350°F. Mark 4) 55 minutes, or until apples are tender, and topping is crisp and delicately browned. If desired, serve with whipped cream, ice cream, or lemon sauce. Serves 8 to 10.

Apple sauce-Rum Pudding

APPLE SAUCE-RUM PUDDING

- **about 18 ounces apple sauce**
- **6 ounces demerara sugar**
- **4 ounces broken pecans**
- **5 ounces sultanas**
- **2 ounces rum or 1½ teaspoons rum essence**
- **2 teaspoons cinnamon**
- **1 teaspoon nutmeg**
- **½ teaspoon allspice**
- **4 egg whites**
- **1 teaspoon lemon essence**
- **4 ounces caster sugar**

Combine apple sauce, brown sugar, pecans, sultanas, rum, cinnamon, nutmeg, and allspice; heat. Pour into 2½ pint casserole.

Beat egg whites stiff with rotary egg whisk, add lemon essence and gradually beat in sugar until mixture stands in peaks. Mound meringue in centre in a ring or spread over top of apple sauce mixture. Bake in slow oven (325°F. Mark 3) 15 to 20 minutes, or until meringue is delicately brown. Serve immediately. Serves 6.

Note: The apple sauce mixture can be made up the day before it is to be served, and stored in the refrigerator. The flavour is enhanced by allowing it to stand 24 hours.

Cheese-Apple Crisp

Cottage Pudding

COTTAGE PUDDING
(Basic Recipe)

The name Cottage Pudding is misleading because it is not a pudding but a simple cake served usually while still warm with a sauce.

2 ounces lard
6 ounces caster sugar
1 egg
8 ounces sieved all-purpose flour
¼ teaspoon salt
2 teaspoons baking powder
dash of nutmeg
8 fluid ounces milk

Cream shortening and sugar. Add egg and beat until light and frothy.

Sift together flour, salt, baking powder, and nutmeg. Add alternately with milk to creamed mixture, beating after each addition.

Bake in greased baking pan in moderate oven (350°F. Mark 4) about 35 minutes.

Serve warm with butterscotch, chocolate, or lemon sauce, or with sweetened fresh or tinned fruits. Serves 6.

Cottage Pudding Variations
Individual Cottage Puddings: Bake in bun tin in hot oven (400°F. Mark 6) 20 to 25 minutes.

Berry Cottage Pudding: Add 4 ounces blackberries to batter. Serve with brandy butter.

Other drained, tinned, or fresh fruits may be used the same way.

Chocolate-Chip Cottage Pudding: Add 8 ounces chocolate bits to pudding.

Fruit-Topped Cottage Pudding: Place any fruits in bottom of baking dish before adding batter. Invert to serve.

Sweet Potato Pudding with Fluffy Lemon Sauce

SWEET POTATO PUDDING
2 large mashed sweet potatoes
¼ teaspoon nutmeg
¼ teaspoon allspice
½ teaspoon salt
4 fluid ounces boiling water
4 ounces caster sugar
2 eggs, beaten
4 ounces dried milk

Boil 2 large sweet potatoes in jackets until tender, peel and mash.

Mix spices and salt; add water slowly. Add spice mixture with sugar and beaten eggs to sweet potatoes. Blend well, then add milk.

Pour into dariole moulds or baking dish. Bake in slow oven (325°F. Mark 3) until set, about 1 hour. If a deep baking-dish is used, set in a pan of hot water to bake.

Serve hot or cold with Fluffy Lemon Sauce 2. Serves 6.

GRATED SWEET POTATO PUDDING
2 eggs
7 or 8 ounces granulated or brown sugar
8 fluid ounces top of the milk
2 ounces melted butter or margarine
1 tablespoon lemon juice
½ teaspoon grated lemon rind
½ teaspoon salt
¼ teaspoon ground cloves
¼ teaspoon ginger
2 large grated raw sweet potatoes

Beat eggs until light; gradually beat in sugar. Stir in milk, butter, lemon juice, lemon rind, salt, and spices.

Mix well with sweet potatoes.

Turn into greased baking dish. Bake in moderate oven (350°F. Mark 4) about 30 minutes. Stir the pudding with a spoon and bake 15 minutes longer. Serve with cream and a tart jam. Serves 6.

Variations: This pudding has many variations. Nuts, currants, raisins are often added. Black treacle can be substituted for part of the sugar. A half teaspoon cinnamon can replace the lemon juice and rind.

Quick Fruit Trifles: Prepare instant whip mix according to directions. When the mix has set, spoon into individual sorbet or fruit dishes, making alternate layers with vanilla wafers and fruit.

Many variations may be made by combining different flavours of whip with any one or combinations of fresh or frozen fruit. Try instant vanilla whip with blackberries, peaches, strawberries, or raspberries; instant coconut whip with cherries, oranges, or pineapple; or instant chocolate whip with bananas or oranges.

INDIAN OR MAIZE PUDDING
(Basic Recipe)

Indian Pudding is an old-fashioned American baked dessert made with maize flour and molasses. Other ingredients vary widely.

1½ ounces maize flour
½ teaspoon salt
1¾ pint milk
6 ounces molasses or black treacle
½ teaspoon ginger
½ teaspoon cinnamon

Combine maize flour, salt, and 4 fluid ounces milk.

Scald remaining milk in top of double saucepan. Add maize flour mixture stirring constantly. Cook 20 minutes, or until thickened. Add molasses, ginger, and cinnamon.

Pour into a greased baking dish. Bake in slow oven (300°F. Mark 2) for 2 hours.

Serve warm with vanilla ice cream, or chill and serve with cream. Serves 6.

Apple Indian Pudding: Peel and slice 2 apples. Add to thickened mixture. Add sugar to taste.

Date or Fig Indian Pudding: Add 2 ounces chopped dates or chopped figs to thickened mixture.

INDIAN PUDDING WITH EGGS
1 pint, 12 fluid ounces milk
4 generous tablespoons maize flour
1 ounce butter
12 ounces molasses or black treacle
1 teaspoon salt
1 teaspoon cinnamon
2 well-beaten eggs
8 fluid ounces cold milk

Scald 1 pint, 12 fluid ounces milk in a double saucepan. Slowly stir in maize flour and cook over hot water 20 minutes. Add butter, molasses, salt, cinnamon, and beaten eggs.

Mix and spoon into a buttered baking-dish. Pour 8 fluid ounces cold milk over top. Bake in moderate oven (350°F. Mark 4) 1 hour. Serves 6 to 8.

Variations: Vary seasoning by using only ¾ teaspoon cinnamon and adding ¼ teaspoon nutmeg or ginger.

With Apples: Use 4 ounces sliced apples. Arrange in layer in baking dish before spooning in the pudding.

Danish Apple Cake

BROWN BETTY
(Basic Recipe)

Brown Betty is traditionally an apple pudding made with breadcrumbs, spices, and sweetening. The term Betty has been extended to similar puddings made of other fruits.

3 ounces melted butter or
    margarine
6 ounces fresh breadcrumbs
12 ounces sliced apples
4 ounces caster sugar
cinnamon or nutmeg, to taste
1 to 2 ounces chopped nuts, optional
grated rind of 1 lemon
2 tablespoons lemon juice
4 fluid ounces water

Mix butter with breadcrumbs. Arrange in a buttered baking dish, first a layer of crumbs, then a layer of apples. Sprinkle apples with some of the sugar, spice, and chopped nuts. Repeat until fruit and crumbs are used, topping dish with crumbs.

Combine lemon rind, juice, and water. Pour over top of dish.

Bake in moderate oven (350°F. Mark 4) 45 minutes. If crumbs get too brown before time is up, cover dish.

Serve with cream, lemon sauce, or brandy butter. Serves 6.

Brown Betty Variations

Apricot or Prune Betty: Substitute 12 ounces stewed apricots or prunes for apples. Use fruit juice in place of lemon juice and water.

Banana Betty: Substitute sliced bananas for apples.

Blackberry Betty: Substitute 12 ounces blackberries or other berries for apples. Sugar may be reduced to 2 ounces.

Cherry Betty: Substitute 12 ounces stoned cherries for apples.

Cornflake Betty: Substitute cornflakes for breadcrumbs. Bake in shallow dish.

Peach Betty: Substitute sliced peaches for apples.

Pineapple Betty: Substitute 12 ounces diced, canned pineapple for apples. Reduce sugar to 2 ounces.

Rhubarb Betty: Substitute 12 ounces stewed rhubarb for apples. Omit water.

DANISH APPLE CAKE

2 large or 3 medium tart apples
    (1½ pounds), peeled, cored,
    and diced
2 fluid ounces Cherry Heering
    (liqueur)
2½ ounces caster sugar
8 ounces dry breadcrumbs
2 ounces caster sugar
½ teaspoon cinnamon or nutmeg
3 ounces butter

In a saucepan combine apples, Cherry Heering, and 2½ ounces sugar. Cover and simmer for 30 minutes, or until apples are tender.

Mix breadcrumbs, 2 ounces sugar, and cinnamon or nutmeg. Melt butter in a frying pan, add crumb mixture, and stir over moderate heat until crumbs are brown. Let cool and crisp in pan.

Serve in glasses as described above, or butter a 6-inch×2 inch deep round cake pan. Put in a layer of crumbs, then a layer of apples. Alternate crumbs and apples until all ingredients are used. Bake in moderate oven (350°F. Mark 4) 30 minutes. Let cool, then turn out on serving plate. Serve with custard sauce (below). Serves 6.

CUSTARD SAUCE WITH LIQUEUR

3 egg yolks
2 tablespoons caster sugar
4 fluid ounces Cherry Heering
4 fluid ounces single cream

In top of double saucepan combine egg yolks and sugar. Heat Cherry Heering and cream until very hot, stir into egg yolk mixture and cook, stirring constantly over simmering water until sauce coats the spoon (from 10 to 15 minutes). Serve lukewarm over warm Danish Apple Cake.

NORWEGIAN PRUNE PUDDING

½ pound prunes
¾ pint cold water
8 ounces caster sugar
dash of salt
1 stick cinnamon (1 inch)
½ pint boiling water
about 1½ ounces cornflour
1 tablespoon lemon juice

Wash and soak prunes in cold water 1 hour. Boil until soft in same water. Drain and reserve juice.

Stone the prunes. Crack pips, remove insides and add to prunes. Combine prunes and juice.

Add sugar, salt, cinnamon stick, and boiling water. Simmer 10 minutes.

Mix cornflour with enough cold water to give pouring consistency. Add to prune mixture and cook 5 minutes, stirring constantly. Remove stick of cinnamon. Add lemon juice.

Turn into a mould. Chill thoroughly. Serve with cream. Serves 6.

Layer puddings are easy to make with instant whip mixes prepared according to packet directions. Use brandy glasses or any large deep stemmed glasses. Make one flavour at a time, allowing it to set about 10 minutes before adding the next flavour.

CABINET PUDDING

16 fluid ounces milk
1 ounce butter or margarine
2 tablespoons caster sugar
3 ounces bread- or cakecrumbs
2 lightly beaten eggs
¼ teaspoon salt
½ teaspoon vanilla

Combine milk, butter, and sugar in saucepan. Cook over low heat until milk reaches scalding point. Cool slightly. Add crumbs.

Combine eggs, salt, and vanilla; slowly stir into milk mixture.

Turn into greased 1½ pint casserole. Place in pan of hot water and bake in moderate oven (375°F. Mark 5) about 1 hour. Serves 6.

LEMON-FIG PUDDING

2 packets lemon pudding mix
15 fig biscuits
4 egg whites
4 ounces caster sugar

Prepare both packets of mix according to directions on the packets. Cut fig biscuits into quarters, fold into slightly cooled lemon filling. Pile into 8 individual earthenware ramekins.

Beat egg whites until foamy. Add sugar gradually, beating until mixture forms peaks. Pile on top of pudding.

Bake in hot oven (425°F. Mark 7) 5 minutes or until lightly browned. Cool. For festive occasions place ramekins in glass fruit dishes. Serve with additional fig biscuits. Serves 8.

Lemon-Fig Pudding

TAPIOCA CREAM PUDDING
(Basic Recipe)

2½ ounces quick-cooking tapioca
2½ ounces sugar
⅛ teaspoon salt
2 eggs, separated
1½ pints milk, scalded
1 teaspoon vanilla essence

Combine tapioca, sugar, salt, and egg yolks in top of double saucepan. Add milk slowly and mix thoroughly.

Cook until tapioca is transparent, stirring often. Remove from heat.

Fold into stiffly beaten egg whites. Add vanilla essence.

Serve warm or cold with cream. Serves 6.

Tapioca Cream Variations

Butterscotch Tapioca: In basic recipe, substitute demerara sugar for granulated. Add 1 ounce butter to cooked mixture before folding in egg whites. When done, fold in 2 ounces chopped nuts.

Chocolate Tapioca: Add 2 ounces plain chocolate to milk. Heat and beat with rotary whisk until blended. Increase sugar to about 5 ounces. Proceed as in basic recipe.

Coconut Tapioca: Add 2 ounces desiccated coconut to milk. Instead of folding in egg whites, pour mixture into buttered baking-dish. Fold 4 ounces sugar into stiffly beaten egg whites. Pile on top. Bake in slow oven (300°F. Mark 2) 15 minutes.

Date, Apricot or Prune Tapioca: Add 2 ounces chopped dates, prunes, or steamed apricots to mixture before folding in egg whites.

Fresh Berry Tapioca: Fold 4 ounces crushed blackberries, raspberries, or strawberries into partially cooked tapioca. Chill.

Fruit Tapioca: Arrange slices of fruit, tinned or fresh, in sorbet glasses before pouring in mixture. Chill.

Honey Tapioca: In basic recipe, substitute 4 ounces honey for sugar.

Jam Tapioca Parfait: Arrange tapioca cream pudding in alternate layers with raspberry or strawberry jam in glasses. Use enough jam to cover cream. Serve with whipped cream.

Nut Tapioca: Add 2 ounces chopped nuts before pouring into moulds.

Tapioca Gelatine Parfait: Prepare coloured gelatine. Fill half of each sorbet glass with gelatine. Fill rest of glass with tapioca cream pudding. Garnish with cubes of gelatine.

PEARL TAPIOCA PUDDING

3 ounces pearl tapioca
2 pints milk
3 to 5 eggs, separated
2 to 3 ounces sugar
grated rind of 1 lemon
juice of ½ lemon

Soak tapioca in ½ pint milk overnight in refrigerator. The next day add 1½ pints milk and cook 3 hours in a double saucepan over, not in, hot water. Let cool.

Beat egg yolks with sugar, lemon rind, and lemon juice; add to cooled tapioca mixture.

Beat egg whites until stiff but not dry.

Line a baking dish with a layer of tapioca mixture; add a layer of beaten egg whites, another layer of tapioca, and top with a layer of egg whites.

Bake in slow oven (325°F. Mark 3) about 15 minutes. Serve hot or cold with a sauce, if desired. Serves 6 to 8.

CHERRY TAPIOCA

about 12 ounces tinned sour cherries
1 pint cherry juice and water
2 teaspoons lemon juice
1 ounce melted butter or margarine
4 to 6 ounces brown sugar
¾ teaspoon salt
dash of nutmeg
2½ ounces quick-cooking tapioca

Combine ingredients in buttered casserole, mixing well.

Bake in moderate oven (375°F. Mark 5) 30 minutes, stirring every 10 minutes and again when removing from oven.

If desired, top with halved marshmallows and leave in oven just long enough to lightly brown. Serves 6.

DATE AND NUT PUDDING
(Basic Recipe)

3 ounces sifted all-purpose flour
1½ teaspoons baking powder
½ teaspoon salt
about 12 ounces chopped dates
3 ounces chopped almonds or walnuts
3 eggs
6 ounces caster sugar

Mix and sift flour, baking powder, and salt. Add dates and nuts.

Beat eggs until light. Add sugar and mix well. Add to dry ingredients.

Turn into greased, deep 9-inch pie dish. Bake in slow oven (325°F. Mark 3) 35 to 40 minutes. Cut into sections while warm.

Tear into pieces and serve in sorbet glasses topped with whipped cream or desired sauce. Serves 6.

Apricot and Nut Pudding: Substitute well-drained, soaked, dried apricots for the dates. Cut apricots in slivers.

Prune and Nut Pudding: Substitute well-drained, soaked, dried prunes for dates. Stone prunes and cut in slivers.

FRENCH WINE CUSTARD

6 eggs, separated
5 ounces caster sugar
6 fluid ounces sweet sherry
¼ teaspoon salt
cherries or strawberries

Mix egg yolks and sugar in top of 2½-pint double saucepan. Set over simmering water and beat with wire whisk until fluffy. Do not let water boil.

Add sherry gradually and continue beating until mixture resembles whipped cream. Cool quickly and chill.

Before serving, beat egg whites stiffly with salt. Fold into chilled custard. Turn into glass serving dish. Serve plain or garnish with cherries or strawberries. Serves 8.

Variations: this wine custard is especially delightful served as a sauce over canned peaches, frozen strawberries or raspberries, or most fresh fruit in season.

For jellied wine custard soften ½ tablespoon unflavoured powdered gelatine in 2 tablespoons water. Add to hot mixture while beating. Chill until syrupy. Fold in egg whites, beaten with salt.

DANISH APPLE BAKED PUDDING

1 pound, 4 ounces apple sauce
6 ounces toasted breadcrumbs
3 egg yolks, beaten
3 ounces melted butter or margarine
½ teaspoon cinnamon
2 ounces sugar
2 egg whites
3 ounces caster sugar
½ teaspoon vanilla

Combine apple sauce, breadcrumbs, egg yolks, butter, cinnamon, and 2 ounces sugar.

Bake in greased 3½ pint casserole in slow oven (325°F. Mark 3) 45 minutes. Remove from oven.

Beat egg whites until stiff. Add 3 ounces sugar gradually, continuing to beat until mixture stands in peaks. Add vanilla.

Top apple mixture with meringue and return to oven for 15 minutes, or until brown. Serves 8.

Danish Apple Baked Pudding

BREAD PUDDING
(Basic Recipe)

2 beaten eggs
about 2 ounces sugar
½ teaspoon salt
1 teaspoon vanilla
¼ teaspoon nutmeg
1 pint, 12 fluid ounces milk, scalded
2 ounces soft butter or margarine
8 ounces stale bread

Combine eggs, sugar, salt, vanilla, and nutmeg. Add scalded milk and butter; mix well. Add bread, broken in small pieces, and pour into buttered baking-dish. Set baking-dish in pan of hot water.

Bake in moderate oven (350°F. Mark 4) 45 to 50 minutes, or until a knife inserted in centre comes out clean.

Serve warm or cold with cream, plain or whipped, or lemon sauce.

Cake, gingerbread, or breadcrumbs may be substituted for bread pieces. Serves 6.

Bread Pudding Variations

Individual Bread Puddings: Pour mixture into 6 buttered individual moulds.

Bake as directed 35 to 45 minutes, or until knife inserted in centre comes out clean.

Banana Bread Pudding: Slice 1 or 2 bananas over top before baking.

Butterscotch Bread Pudding: In basic recipe, substitute 4 ounces brown sugar for granulated.

Melt butter with sugar in a frying pan, stirring until evenly brown. Slowly add to milk. Cook until blended. Proceed as directed.

Caramel Bread Pudding: In basic recipe, use 4 ounces sugar. Caramelize sugar and dissolve in milk before pouring over crumbs.

Chocolate Bread Pudding: Follow basic recipe and melt 2 ounces plain chocolate in milk. Beat until blended.

Coconut Bread Pudding: Follow basic recipe and add 2 ounces moist desiccated coconut before pouring into baking-dish.

Fruit Bread Pudding: Follow basic recipe; add 2½ ounces chopped raisins, dates, or figs just before pouring mixture into baking dish.

Honey Bread Pudding: In basic recipe, substitute 8 ounces strained honey for sugar and ¾ teaspoon lemon essence for vanilla.

Marmalade Bread Pudding: Add about 6 ounces orange marmalade to mixture of basic recipe.

Marshmallow Bread Pudding: Cover top of baked pudding with marshmallows. Return to oven until melted and slightly browned.

Mocha Bread Pudding: In basic recipe, substitute ¾ pint single cream and ¾ pint black coffee for milk.

Nut Bread Pudding: Add 2 ounces chopped nuts to chocolate or butterscotch bread pudding.

JUNKET OR RENNET PUDDING
(Basic Recipe)

2 teaspoons rennet
2 pints fresh milk
2 to 3 teaspoons caster sugar
few grains salt
½ teaspoon vanilla

Heat milk until barely lukewarm, about blood heat temperature. (Do not use evaporated, condensed, or scalded milk.) Add sugar, salt, and vanilla. Stir until sugar is completely dissolved. Check temperature and reheat slightly, if necessary.

Add rennet and stir quickly for a few seconds. Pour at once into sorbet glasses. Let stand undisturbed until set, in a warm place, about 10 minutes. Chill in refrigerator. Serves 6.

Rennet Pudding Variations

To Colour: Add a few drops of food colouring with the milk.

Chocolate Rennet: Add chocolate syrup or 2 ounces plain chocolate to the milk.

Rum Rennet: Add rum to taste.

Brown Sugar Rennet: Substitute brown sugar for caster.

Packet Rennet: Follow directions on packet of flavoured rennet.

Floating Island Bread Pudding: The "floating island" is a meringue made by beating egg whites to soft peaks, then slowly beating in sugar to make a stiff meringue. Spoon the meringue on top of each pudding. Return to oven and bake about 10 minutes or until meringue is set and nicely browned.

Fluffy Lemon-Bread Pudding

FLUFFY LEMON-BREAD PUDDIN[G]

16 fluid ounces milk, scalded
9 ounces soft ½-inch bread cubes
3 egg yolks, beaten
5 ounces caster sugar
¼ teaspoon nutmeg
1½ teaspoons grated lemon rind
¼ teaspoon lemon essence

Meringue:
3 egg whites
3 ounces caster sugar
½ teaspoon lemon essence

Pour scalded milk over bread cube[s]. Let stand until bread is soaked.

Add beaten egg yolks, sugar, nu[t]meg, lemon rind, and lemon essence and beat well with a wire whisk.

Pour into a well-greased 2½-pin[t] casserole; set in a shallow pan of h[ot] water.

Bake in a moderate oven (350°[F]. Mark 4) until an inserted knife come[s] out clean, about 1 hour. Remove fro[m] oven, leaving casserole in pan of h[ot] water.

Beat egg whites until stiff. Add suga[r] gradually, continuing to beat unt[il] mixture stands in peaks. Add lemo[n] essence.

Top pudding with meringue and re[turn] to oven for 15 minutes, or unt[il] brown. Serves 8.

MRS. TRUMAN'S APPLE DELIGHT

1 egg
6 ounces sugar
2 tablespoons flour
1¼ teaspoons baking powder
⅛ teaspoon salt
2 ounces chopped nuts
1 cooking apple, chopped
1 teaspoon vanilla essence

Beat egg. If an electric mixer is use[d] set at lowest speed and beat 1 mi[n]ute. Gradually add sugar, continuin[g] to beat until very smooth.

Mix and sift flour, baking powde[r] and salt. Add to sugar-egg mixtur[e] stirring with a spoon. Add nuts, appl[e] and vanilla. Turn into generously bu[t]tered 9-inch shallow pie dish.

Bake in moderate oven (350°F. Mar[k] 4) 35 minutes. Serve with whippe[d] cream or ice cream. Serves 4.

Apple-Rice Pudding with Butterscotch Meringue

APPLE-RICE PUDDING WITH BUTTERSCOTCH MERINGUE

- 8 ounces uncooked pudding rice
- 6 medium apples, thinly sliced
- 1 teaspoon salt
- 8 ounces sugar
- 1 teaspoon cinnamon
- 1 pint, 4 fluid ounces milk
- 2 egg yolks
- 2 egg whites
- 4 tablespoons brown sugar
- 1 teaspoon vanilla

Cook rice in saucepan with 1½ pints boiling water and 1 teaspoon salt for 10 minutes; drain.

Place half the apple slices in a buttered 3½-pint casserole. Blend together salt, sugar, and cinnamon and sprinkle ⅓ of mixture over apples.

Add ½ of the rice and remainder of apples and sprinkle with second ⅓ of sugar mixture. Top with remaining rice and sugar mixture.

Pour in milk which has been blended with beaten egg yolks.

Cover and bake in slow oven (300°F Mark 2) about 2 hours, stirring occasionally, adding extra milk, as needed. Uncover and cook 30 minutes longer to brown.

To Make Meringue: Beat egg whites until they peak; add brown sugar, 1 tablespoon at a time, beating between each addition and continue beating until very stiff. Fold in vanilla.

Spread on pudding and return to oven for 20 minutes, or until lightly browned. Cool. Serve with ice cream or single cream. Serves 6 to 8.

CREAMY RAISIN-RICE PUDDING

- 1 pint, 12 fluid ounces milk
- 4 ounces uncooked rice
- ½ teaspoon salt
- 2½ ounces raisins or sultanas
- 4 ounces sugar
- 1 teaspoon vanilla

Combine milk, rice, and salt; heat slowly to boiling. Turn into greased 2½-pint baking dish.

Bake in slow oven (300°F. Mark 2) 45 minutes, stirring 3 or 4 times.

Rinse and drain raisins. Stir raisins, sugar, and vanilla into rice, and bake 15 minutes longer. Serves 6.

Note: For extra-creamy pudding, reduce rice to 3 ounces.

OLD-TIME RICE PUDDING
(Basic Recipe)

- 6 ounces uncooked rice
- 2½ pints milk
- 6 ounces sugar
- ¼ teaspoon nutmeg
- ½ teaspoon salt
- 3½ ounces sultanas

Wash rice. Add milk, sugar, nutmeg, and salt. Place in a buttered 4-pint baking dish.

Bake in slow oven (325°F. Mark 3) 2½ hours, stirring twice during first hour. Stir brown crust into pudding several times during the remainder of baking.

Add raisins ½ hour before pudding is done. Then allow crust to form again on pudding. Serve warm or cold with cream, if desired.

To reduce baking time, cook rice 10 to 15 minutes in the milk in double saucepan before baking. Serves 6 to 8.

Variations of Old-Time Rice Pudding

Apricot-Rice Pudding: Substitute well drained, soaked apricots for raisins. Cut apricot in slivers.

Brown Rice Pudding: Substitute brown rice for white. Bake same way.

Brown Sugar-Rice Pudding: Substitute 5 ounces brown sugar for granulated. Omit raisins. Serve cold.

Chocolate-Rice Pudding: Mix 1 ounce cocoa with rice and sugar mixture. Serve with sweetened whipped cream.

Date-Rice Pudding: Substitute 4 ounces chopped dates for raisins.

Honey-Rice Pudding: Substitute 6 ounces honey for sugar.

Treacle-Rice Pudding: Substitute 6 ounces black treacle for sugar and ½ teaspoon cinnamon for nutmeg. Add scant 1 ounce butter at last stirring.

Prune-Rice Pudding: Substitute 4 ounces well-drained, stoned, soaked prunes for raisins. Cut prunes in slivers.

FRUIT-FILLED RICE RING MOULD

- 2 heaped teacups fluffy cooked rice
- ¾ pint milk
- 2 ounces sugar
- 1 ounce butter or margarine
- ½ teaspoon salt
- 3½ tablespoons cornflour
- 4 fluid ounces cold milk
- 2 teaspoons vanilla
- 3 egg whites, beaten stiff

Place the cooked rice, the ¾ pint milk, sugar, butter, and salt in a double saucepan.

Add the 4 ounces milk to the cornflour. Mix well. Pour into the double saucepan. Cook 15 minutes, or until

Fruit-Filled Rice Ring Mould

the milk has cooked into the rice, stirring occasionally. Cool.

Add vanilla. Fold in stiffly beaten egg whites.

Turn into a well-buttered ring mould. Chill at least 4 hours. Unmould on a large serving dish and fill with fresh fruit or tinned or frozen fruit. Surround the ring with extra fruit to garnish.

To unmould the ring, dip the mould quickly in hot water or cover it with a hot towel for several seconds. Place a plate over the mould, invert the plate and mould together. Shake and tap the mould until ring is released. Serves 6.

STRAWBERRY-RICE PARFAIT

- 4 generous teacups sweetened cooked rice
- 4 tablespoons sugar
- 8 fluid ounces whipping cream
- 1 to 2 drops red food colouring
- ½ teaspoon almond essence
- 1 packet frozen strawberries
- additional coloured whipping cream, if desired

To sweeten rice, add 2 tablespoons sugar to water in which rice is cooked. Chill.

Just before serving, whip the cream, fold in food colour, flavouring, and remaining 2 tablespoons sugar. Then fold into the rice. Fill fruit dishes with alternate layers of rice and strawberries. (Reserve a strawberry for the top of each serving.) Top with whipped cream. Serves 6.

Strawberry-Rice Parfait

BANANA MERINGUE PUDDING
(Basic Recipe)

1   ounce cornflour
8   ounces caster sugar
¾   teaspoon salt
1   pint, 4 fluid ounces scalded milk
3   eggs, separated
1½ teaspoons vanilla
24 small or 16 large vanilla wafers
3   large ripe bananas, sliced

Mix cornflour with 3½ ounces sugar and ½ teaspoon salt in double saucepan. Pour scalded milk over mixture. Cook over boiling water until mixture thickens, stirring almost constantly. Cover and cook 15 minutes, stirring occasionally.

Add hot mixture very slowly to beaten egg yolks, stirring constantly. Return to double saucepan and cook 2 minutes. Let cool and add vanilla.

Put alternate layers of vanilla wafers, banana slices, and pudding mixture in 2½-pint casserole, with the top layer pudding.

To Make Meringue: Beat egg whites with ¼ teaspoon salt until foamy. Gradually add 4½ ounces sugar, beating until it will stand in soft peaks. Pile lightly on pudding.

Bake in moderate oven (350°F. Mark 4) until delicately browned, about 15 minutes. Let cool, then chill in refrigerator before serving. Serves 6.

**Variations of
Banana Meringue Pudding**
Apple Meringue Pudding: Substitute 8 ounces drained tinned apples for bananas. Substitute grated lemon or orange rind for vanilla.
Coconut Meringue Pudding: Substitute 4 ounces desiccated coconut for bananas. Sprinkle 1 ounce coconut over meringue before baking. If fresh coconut is used, substitute coconut milk for an equal amount of milk.
Grapefruit Meringue Pudding: Substitute 8 ounces drained sweetened grapefruit segments for bananas. Substitute 1 tablespoon grated grapefruit rind for vanilla.
Orange Meringue Pudding: Substitute 8 ounces drained orange segments for bananas. Substitute 1 tablespoon grated orange rind for vanilla.
Chocolate Meringue Pudding: Add 2 ounces cooking chocolate to milk before scalding. Use 1 egg less and decrease sugar in meringue to 2 ounces.
Peach Meringue Pudding: Substitute 8 ounces fresh or drained canned sliced peaches for bananas. Substitute 1 tablespoon grated orange rind for vanilla.
Pineapple Meringue Pudding: Substitute 8 ounces drained canned pineapple chunks for bananas. Substitute grated lemon or orange rind for vanilla.

PORT WINE-APPLE PUDDING

4   tart apples, sliced
2   tablespoons lemon juice
5   fluid ounces port, angelica, muscatel, tokay, or any dessert wine
3   ounces butter or margarine
3   ounces sugar
2   beaten eggs
¼   teaspoon salt
¼   teaspoon nutmeg
½   teaspoon cinnamon
8   ounces dry bread pieces

Pour lemon juice and wine over sliced apples and let stand.

Cream together butter and sugar. Add beaten eggs, salt, and spices. Combine with apples and wine and bread pieces.

Turn into a baking dish; cover and bake in moderate oven (350°F. Mark 4) 35 or 40 minutes. Serve while still warm with Fluffy Wine Sauce. Serves 6.

Fluffy Wine Sauce:
Cream 1 ounce butter or margarine until light and fluffy. Blend in 4 ounces icing sugar.

Add 3 tablespoons any dessert wine and beat until mixture is smooth. Add 2 teaspoons grated lemon rind.

BLACKBERRY CRISP PUDDING

about 1 pound fresh blackberries
3   ounces granulated sugar
2   teaspoons lemon juice
2   ounces butter or margarine
3   ounces brown sugar
1½ ounces sifted all-purpose flour
about 2 ounces quick-cooking porridge oats, uncooked

Put blackberries in 2½-pint baking dish. Sprinkle with granulated sugar and lemon juice.

Cream butter or margarine; gradually add brown sugar and cream well. Blend in flour and oats with a fork. Spread topping over blackberries.

Bake in moderate oven (375°F. Mark 5) 35 to 40 minutes. Serve with plain or whipped cream. Serves 6.

Note: Canned berries may be substituted for fresh. Use two 15-ounce cans, drained, syrup-packed blackberries and 3 fluid ounces syrup. Omit granulated sugar. Bake in 1½-pint baking dish.

SWEDISH APPLE PUDDING

2   ounces butter or margarine, melted
8   ounces digestive biscuit crumbs
about 1¼ pounds sweetened apple sauce

Mix butter and crumbs. Butter baking dishes thoroughly and arrange crumbs and apple sauce in alternating layers, finishing with crumbs.

Bake in moderate oven (375°F. Mark 5) 15 minutes. Serve warm or cold with vanilla whipped cream sauce (see Index). Serves 8.

Port Wine-Apple Pudding

MAGNOLIA MANOR DESSERT

4   ounces sieved all-purpose flour
5   ounces sugar
¼   teaspoon cinnamon
⅛   teaspoon ginger
dash of ground cloves
1½ ounces butter
1½ ounces pecans or walnuts, chopped
4   fluid ounces boiling water
1   teaspoon bicarbonate of soda
3   ounces molasses or black treacle

Sift together flour, sugar, cinnamon, ginger, and cloves. Mix in butter until mixture has a coarse crumbly texture. Add chopped nuts.

Press ⅔ of crumb mixture in well-greased 8×8×2-inch pan.

Combine water and soda. Add molasses. Mix thoroughly. Pour over crumb mixture in pan. Sprinkle with remaining ⅓ crumb mixture.

Bake in moderate oven (350°F. Mark 4) 30 to 35 minutes. Serve warm topped with whipped cheese topping and warm orange sauce. Serves 6 to 8.

Whipped Cheese Topping: Soften 3 ounces cream cheese with 1 tablespoon single cream and ½ teaspoon vanilla. Blend in 3 tablespoons sieved icing sugar; cream well.

Orange Sauce: Combine 4 ounces sugar, 1 tablespoon flour, 1 tablespoon cornflour, and ⅛ teaspoon salt in saucepan. Add 6 ounces boiling water and 1 ounce butter. Cook over medium heat, stirring constantly, until thick and clear.

Remove from heat; add grated rind and juice of 1 orange and juice of 1 lemon.

Magnolia Manor Dessert

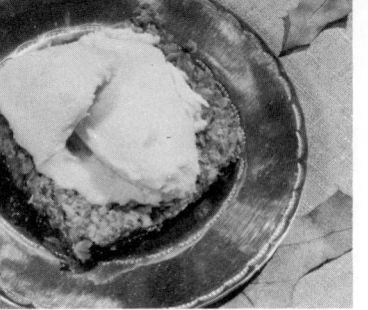

Cranberry Crunch

CRANBERRY CRUNCH

- 3 ounces uncooked porridge oats
- 2 ounces sifted flour
- 7 ounces brown sugar
- 4 ounces butter or margarine
- 1-pound can cranberry sauce (jellied or whole)
- 1½ pints vanilla ice cream

Mix oats, flour, and brown sugar. Stir in butter until crumbly.

Place half of this mixture in an 8×8-inch greased cake tin. Cover with cranberry sauce. Top with balance of mixture. Bake in moderate oven (350°F. Mark 4) 45 minutes.

Serve hot in squares topped with scoops of vanilla ice cream. Serves 6 to 8.

TIPSY PUDDING
(Basic Recipe)

- 2 stale sponge cake layers
- 4 fluid ounces sherry
- 1¼ pints milk
- 3 ounces sugar
- ¼ teaspoon salt
- 2 eggs
- 1 teaspoon vanilla
- 2 tablespoons chopped glacé cherries
- 2 tablespoons slivered, toasted almonds

Break cake into about 12 pieces and arrange in serving dish. Pour sherry over cake and chill several hours or overnight.

Scald milk in top of double saucepan. Mix together sugar, salt, and eggs. Add scalded milk very slowly, stirring constantly. Return to pan.

Cook over boiling water until mixture thickens slightly and will coat back of spoon, about 5 minutes. Cool. Add vanilla. Chill.

Pour ¾ of custard over cake. Chill several hours before serving. Pour remaining custard over pudding when ready to serve. Garnish with cherries and almonds. Serves 6.

Tipsy Pudding Variations

Layered Tipsy Pudding: Instead of breaking cake into pieces, split cake layers. Spread with jam. Put together and place in large bowl. Pour sherry over cake and proceed as directed.

Individual Tipsy Puddings: Use 6 small squares of cake. Place in individual dishes. Pour an equal amount of sherry over each. Proceed as directed.

Ladyfinger Tipsy Pudding: Use 24 ladyfingers instead of sponge cake. Split ladyfingers. Spread 12 with jelly.

Sandwich together and put 2 in bottom of each fruit dish. Stand 4 halves up around inside edge. Pour sherry and custard over each.

CHOCOLATE FUDGE BATTER PUDDING
(Basic Recipe)

- 1 ounce melted butter or margarine
- 8 ounces sugar
- 1 teaspoon vanilla
- 4 ounces sifted flour
- 8 tablespoons cocoa
- 1 teaspoon baking powder
- ¾ teaspoon salt
- 4 fluid ounces milk
- 2 ounces chopped nuts, if required
- ¾ pint boiling water

Mix butter, 4 ounces sugar, and vanilla.

Sieve flour with 3 tablespoons cocoa, baking powder, and ½ teaspoon salt. Add alternately with milk to first mixture. Mix well and stir in nuts.

Mix together 4 ounces sugar, 5 tablespoons cocoa, ¼ teaspoon salt, and boiling water. Turn into casserole (10×5×2 inches). Drop batter by tablespoons on top.

Bake in moderate oven (350°F. Mark 4) 40 to 45 minutes. Serve warm.

This pudding when baked has a chocolate sauce on bottom and cake on top. Spoon out a portion of cake and cover with sauce. If served cold, serve double or whipped cream over the thickened sauce. Serves 6.

Variations of
Chocolate Fudge Batter Pudding

Black and White Fudge Batter Pudding: Mix ½ packet white cake mix as directed on packet and substitute for chocolate batter in basic recipe. Use same sauce.

Butterscotch Batter Pudding: Follow basic recipe, omitting cocoa altogether. Substitute 10 ounces brown sugar for granulated sugar. (Use 3 ounces in batter.)

To make sauce: Mix 6 ounces brown sugar, 1 tablespoon flour, ¼ teaspoon salt, 1 ounce butter, and ¾ pint boiling water. Chopped walnuts go well with this variation.

Chocolate-Ginger Batter Pudding: Mix ½ packet gingerbread mix as directed on packet and substitute for chocolate batter in basic recipe. Use same sauce.

Spice Batter Pudding: Follow recipe for Butterscotch Batter Pudding, adding 1 teaspoon cinnamon, ½ teaspoon cloves, and ½ teaspoon nutmeg to batter. Add 2½ ounces raisins to sauce.

SYLLABUB

- ¾ pint double cream
- 2½ ounces icing sugar
- 1 teaspoon vanilla
- 2 fluid ounces Crème de Cacao, apricot brandy, sherry or Sauternes
- 12 lady fingers, split in half
- chopped almonds

Whip cream until it begins to hold shape. Then gradually beat in sugar, beating until stiff. Stir in vanilla and Crème de Cacao gradually so that mixture does not curdle. Spoon into small sorbet dishes.

Split lady fingers and place 4 halves in each glass. Sprinkle with almonds. Serve at once. Serves 6.

FRUIT BETTY

- 6 ounces stale bread cubes
- 1 ounce butter or margarine
- 6 ounces honey
- ¾ pint thinly sliced fruit (peaches, apples, raspberries)
- double cream

Brown bread cubes in butter. Add honey and fruit. Cover and cook until fruit is tender, about 8 minutes.

Serve hot or cold with cream. Serves 4.

APPLE BATTER PUDDING

- 1 pound thinly sliced apples
- 8 ounces sugar
- ⅛ teaspoon allspice
- ¼ teaspoon nutmeg
- 1 ounce lard
- 1 egg, beaten
- ½ teaspoon vanilla
- 4 ounces sifted flour
- 2 teaspoons baking powder
- ¼ teaspoon salt
- 4 fluid ounces milk

Mix sliced apples with half the sugar, the allspice, and nutmeg. Place in a well-greased 9-inch round baking dish.

Mix the lard and remaining sugar until creamy; add egg and vanilla and beat thoroughly.

Sieve together flour, baking powder, and salt; add alternately with milk to lard mixture, beating well between each addition. Pour over apples and bake in moderate oven (350°F, Mark 4) about 60 minutes. Serve hot with top of the milk. Serves 6 to 8.

Apple Batter Pudding

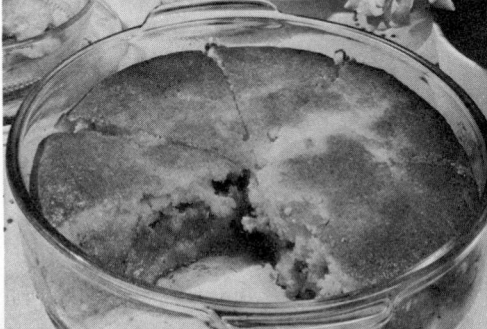

PEACH CRISP

1 pound sliced peaches
½ teaspoon cinnamon
4 fluid ounces water
1 teaspoon grated lemon rind
8 ounces sugar
4 ounces butter or margarine
¼ teaspoon salt
3 ounces flour

Arrange peaches in shallow, greased casserole (8×9 inches). Sprinkle with cinnamon. Add water and lemon rind.

Rub together sugar, butter, salt, and flour until crumbly. Spread over peaches.

Bake uncovered in moderate oven (350°F. Mark 4) until peaches are tender and top is nicely browned, 30 to 45 minutes.

Serve warm, plain or with cream. Serves 6.

Apple, Pear, Prune, Apricot Crisp: Sliced apples or pears or soaked dried fruit may be substituted for peaches.

Peach Crisp with Brown Sugar: Substitute 7 ounces brown sugar for granulated sugar.

Peach Crisp with Corn Flakes: Substitute crushed corn flakes for flour.

BAKED CRANBERRY DESSERT

4 ounces sugar
6 ounces digestive biscuit crumbs
1 teaspoon cinnamon
2 ounces chopped walnuts
3 ounces melted butter or margarine
1 tablespoon grated orange rind
1¾ pounds cranberry sauce
4 fluid ounces single cream, whipped

Mix together sugar, crumbs, cinnamon, walnuts, and melted butter or margarine. Pat ⅔ of mixture into well-greased large baking dish.

Add grated orange rind to cranberry sauce and pour on top of crumb mixture in dish. Place remaining crumb mixture on top of cranberry sauce.

Bake in moderate oven (350°F. Mark 4) 30 minutes. Cool and decorate top with whipped cream. Serves 8.

Baked Cranberry Dessert

PEACH CRUMB PUDDING
(Basic Recipe)

¾ pint milk
6 ounces soft breadcrumbs
¼ teaspoon salt
5 ounces sugar
2 eggs, beaten
1 ounce soft butter or margarine
¼ teaspoon nutmeg
½ pound sliced peaches, fresh or canned

Scald milk and pour over breadcrumbs. Cool.

Add salt, sugar, eggs, butter, and nutmeg. Mix. Fold in peaches.

Turn into buttered casserole. Bake in moderate oven (350°F. Mark 4) 1¼ hours.

Cover with meringue or serve with cream. Serves 6.

Peach Crumb Pudding Variations

Apple Crumb Pudding: Use ½ pound peeled sliced apples in place of peaches.

Blackberry Crumb Pudding: Use ½ pound blackberries or raspberries to replace peaches.

Cherry Crumb Pudding: Use ½ pound stoned halved cherries to replace peaches.

Plumb Crumb Pudding: Use ½ pound sliced stoned plums to replace peaches.

MATZO KUGEL

3 matzos
3 eggs, separated
4 ounces sugar
¼ teaspoon salt
¼ teaspoon cinnamon
1½ ounces raisins (optional)
1½ ounces lard or dripping
3 tart apples, thinly sliced
1 ounce chopped nuts
grated rind of 1 lemon or orange

Soak matzos in cold water to cover. Drain well but do not press out the water.

Beat egg yolks until light; add sugar, salt, and cinnamon. Stir in the drained matzos.

Fold in stiffly beaten egg whites and raisins.

Turn half the mixture into a well-greased and heated baking dish. Cover evenly with the sliced apples; sprinkle with nuts and grated rind.

Cover with remaining matzo mixture. Dot with remaining fat; sprinkle with additional cinnamon and sugar.

Bake in moderate oven (350°F. Mark 4) until nicely browned, about 45 to 50 minutes.

Serve with a wine or fruit sauce or with stewed berries or other fruit. Serves 6.

Sunshine Pudding with Peaches

SUNSHINE PUDDING WITH PEACHES

¾ pint milk
1 ounce cornflour
4 ounces sugar
⅛ teaspoon salt
2 eggs, separated
3 fluid ounces lemon juice
1 teaspoon grated lemon rind
1 ounce butter

Heat milk in double saucepan to scalding point.

Blend cornflour, 2 ounces sugar, and salt. Pour a little hot milk on dry ingredients while stirring; add remaining hot milk, stirring to blend. Return to double saucepan and cook 20 minutes over hot water, stirring occasionally.

Beat egg yolks, pour a little hot mixture onto yolks; return to double saucepan and cook 2 minutes longer. Remove from heat; add lemon juice, lemon rind, and butter, beating until smooth. Cool.

Beat egg whites until frothy, add remaining sugar, a tablespoon at a time, beating between each addition. Beat until stiff and fold into pudding.

Pour into individual moulds that have been rinsed in cold water. Chill. Serve in pudding dishes with sliced peaches. Serves 6.

CANADIAN FRUIT BATTER PUDDING

8 ounces sifted flour
1 teaspoon bicarbonate of soda
½ teaspoon salt
3 ounces lard
6 ounces sugar
2 eggs
2 fluid ounces white vinegar
4 fluid ounces milk
¾ pint blackberries or raspberries

Mix and sift flour, soda, and salt.

Cream lard and sugar; add eggs one at a time, beating well after each addition.

Combine vinegar and milk; add to creamed mixture alternately with sifted dry ingredients, stirring until flour is just dampened. Fold in blackberries.

Spread in greased 8×8-inch tin. Bake in moderate oven (375°F. Mark 5) about 45 minutes.

Serve warm with sauce or whipped cream. Serves 8.

Spiced Cottage Custard

BROWNIE PUDDING

2 ounces sifted flour
1 teaspoon baking powder
½ teaspoon salt
3 ounces granulated sugar
1 tablespoon cocoa
2 fluid ounces milk
1 tablespoon melted lard
½ teaspoon vanilla
1 ounce chopped nuts
4 ounces brown sugar
2 tablespoons cocoa
6 fluid ounces boiling water

Sieve flour with baking powder, salt, granulated sugar, and 1 tablespoon cocoa into bowl. Add milk, lard, and vanilla; mix only until smooth. Then add chopped nuts.

Turn into greased casserole or small baking dish.

Mix brown sugar and 2 tablespoons cocoa together and sprinkle over batter. Then pour boiling water over top of batter. This forms sauce in bottom of pan after pudding is baked.

Bake in moderate oven (350°F. Mark 4) 30 to 40 minutes. Serves 6 to 8.

DATE CRUNCH

5 or 6 ounces chopped dates
8 fluid ounces water
4 ounces granulated sugar
2 ounces chopped pecans, or walnuts
4 ounces butter or margarine
7 ounces brown sugar
4 ounces sifted flour
1 teaspoon baking powder
3 ounces uncooked quick-cooking porridge oats

Combine dates, water, and granulated sugar; cook over medium heat to consistency of soft jam. Cool and add pecans or walnuts.

Cream butter and brown sugar; add flour with baking powder. Add quick-cooking oats and mix until crumbly.

Pat ½ of crumb mixture into an 8×8-inch pan. Spread filling over crumbs. Top with remainder of crumb mixture.

Bake in slow oven (325°F. Mark 3) 45 minutes. Serve with whipped cream flavoured with vanilla and cinnamon. Serves 6 to 9.

SPICED COTTAGE CHEESE CUSTARD

¾ pint milk
3 eggs
6 tablespoons sugar
8 ounces sieved cottage cheese
¼ teaspoon salt
1 teaspoon grated lemon rind
1 teaspoon vanilla
½ teaspoon cinnamon
cooked, drained apricot halves

Heat milk in top of double saucepan.

Beat 2 whole eggs and 1 yolk, reserving extra white for meringue. Add 4 tablespoons sugar, cottage cheese, salt, lemon rind, vanilla, and cinnamon, stirring to blend. Slowly add hot milk, while stirring.

Place 2 or 3 apricot halves in each of 6 buttered individual moulds and pour cheese custard over them.

Place in pan of warm water and bake in slow oven (300°F. Mark 2) 35 to 40 minutes, until custards are almost completely set and lightly browned.

Beat egg white until stiff. Add remaining 2 tablespoons sugar, 1 at a time, beating between each addition.

Top each custard with meringue and place under grill about 3 minutes or until meringues are lightly browned. Serves 6.

CHERRY PUDDING

5 ounces sifted flour
1½ teaspoons baking powder
½ teaspoon salt
4 ounces sugar
4 fluid ounces milk
1 ounce melted lard
14 ounces drained pitted red sour cherries, fresh or canned
16 fluid ounces hot water or cherry juice and water
4 to 6 ounces sugar
1 ounce butter or margarine

Sift flour with baking powder, salt, and 4 ounces sugar into basin. Add milk and melted lard; stir only until smooth.

Spread dough evenly in greased shallow pan, about 12×8×2 inches. Arrange cherries over top.

Combine hot water or cherry juice, sugar, and butter; bring to a boil. Pour over cherries.

Bake immediately in moderate oven (375°F. Mark 5) 45 to 50 minutes. Serve warm. Serves 8.

Fig Nut Pudding: Use recipe for Cherry Pudding, omitting cherries. Add about 3 ounces chopped figs to batter and spread evenly in greased pan, about 10×6×2 inches. Sprinkle with 1 or 2 ounces chopped nuts.

Use brown sugar in the sauce mixture. Pour hot sauce over batter and bake immediately in moderate oven (350°F. Mark 4) 45 to 50 minutes. Serve warm. Serves 8.

CHOCOLATE RUM PUDDING

1 ounce plain or cooking chocolate
4 ounces sugar
¾ pint milk
⅛ teaspoon salt
5 tablespoons cornflour
1 slightly beaten egg
½ ounce butter or margarine
2 tablespoons rum flavouring
whipped cream

Place chocolate, sugar, 13 ounces scalded milk, and salt in top of double saucepan. Heat to boiling point, stirring until chocolate is melted.

Stir cornflour into remaining milk, blending well, then slowly stir into hot milk mixture. Cook over boiling water about 20 minutes, or until thickened. Add a little of hot mixture to slightly beaten egg.

Return to custard mixture and cook 5 minutes longer. Add butter and rum flavouring.

Chill in individual serving dishes. Top with whipped cream before serving. Serves 4.

APPLE SAUCE PUDDING

1¾ pounds apple sauce
8 ounces sugar
1 teaspoon grated lemon rind
1 teaspoon lemon juice
2 teaspoons vanilla
3 egg yolks
3 egg whites
⅛ teaspoon salt
9 maraschino cherries

Mix together apple sauce, ⅔ of the sugar, lemon rind, lemon juice, and 1 teaspoon vanilla.

Beat egg yolks into apple sauce mixture. Pour into 8-inch square baking dish.

Beat egg whites until fluffy. Add salt and beat until stiff but not dry. Gradually beat in remaining sugar until egg whites stand in peaks. Beat in 1 teaspoon vanilla.

Arrange meringue in 9 mounds on top of apple sauce mixture. Bake in slow oven (300°F. Mark 2) 15 minutes or until meringue is slightly browned.

Garnish with maraschino cherries. Serve either hot or cold. Serves 9.

Apple Sauce Pudding

LEMON TRIFLE

    8 fluid ounces hot scalded milk
    3 eggs, separated
    1 tablespoon sugar
    dash of salt
    1 ounce butter or margarine
    grated rind of 2 lemons
    12 ounces cakecrumbs
    juice of 2 lemons
    6 tablespoons caster sugar

Gradually stir scalded milk into slightly beaten egg yolks. Beat in 1 tablespoon sugar and dash of salt.

Cook over boiling water 5 minutes or until mixture coats a spoon, stirring constantly. Add butter; cool slightly, stirring occasionally; add lemon rind.

Put cakecrumbs into baking dish. Pour custard over; sprinkle with lemon juice.

Spread over a meringue made by beating egg whites until stiff and gradually beating in 6 tablespoons sugar.

Bake in moderate oven (350°F. Mark 4) 15 minutes or until browned.

Cool. Serves 6.

BLACKBERRY FLUMMERY

    16 fluid ounces blackberry juice,
           from canned or cooked fresh
           blackberries
    4 ounces sugar (if juice is
           unsweetened)
    3 tablespoons cornflour
    ¼ teaspoon salt
    2 tablespoons lemon juice

Heat blackberry juice in a double saucepan. Mix and sift sugar, cornflour, and salt. Add to juice and stir until mixture thickens.

Cover and cook 15 to 20 minutes. Remove from heat and add lemon juice. Beat well.

Pour into serving dish. Chill. Serve with plain or whipped cream. Serves 6.

QUEEN OF PUDDINGS

    4 ounces fine dry breadcrumbs
    16 fluid ounces milk
    1 ounce butter or margarine
    6 ounces caster sugar
    3 eggs, separated
    8 ounces strawberries or
           raspberries

Soak crumbs in milk until thickened, about 5 minutes.

Cream butter; stir in ½ cup sugar, then add well-beaten egg yolks. Stir into soaked breadcrumbs.

Pour into buttered casserole, place in pan of hot water, and bake in moderate oven (350°F. Mark 4) until firm, about 1 hour.

Place berries on top. Make a meringue of egg whites and remaining sugar; pile on top of berries and bake until golden brown, about 10 minutes. Serve either warm or thoroughly cooled. Serves 6.

MOLASSES-APPLE COTTAGE PUDDING

    1 ounce butter or margarine
    2 tart apples
    5 tablespoons molasses or black
           treacle
    3 ounces lard
    5 ounces sugar
    1 egg
    4 ounces sifted flour
    1½ teaspoons baking powder
    ¼ teaspoon salt
    4 fluid ounces milk
    ½ teaspoon vanilla

Melt butter; place in 6 greased individual moulds, dividing butter equally.

Peel apples; core; chop fine. Divide evenly in moulds; add 1 tablespoon molasses or treacle to each.

Cream together lard and sugar; add egg; beat well.

Sieve together flour, baking powder, and salt; add alternately with milk to creamed mixture. Add vanilla; mix well. Pour over apple mixture, filling moulds ¾ full.

Bake in moderate oven (350°F. Mark 4) 45 to 50 minutes. Turn upside down on serving dish. Serve immediately with any preferred sauce, or whipped cream. Serves 6.

BROWN NUTTY PUDDING

    2 ounces butter or margarine
    8 ounces sugar
    ¼ teaspoon salt
    ½ teaspoon ground cloves
    ½ teaspoon nutmeg
    1 teaspoon cinnamon
    1 egg, unbeaten
    13 fluid ounces milk
    8 ounces dry bread cubes
    about 3 ounces sultanas
    2 ounces chopped nuts
    1 teaspoon bicarbonate of soda
    2 tablespoons water

Cream butter with sugar, salt, and spices. Add egg. Beat until smooth.

Pour milk over bread cubes, raisins, and nuts. Combine with creamed mixture.

Dissolve soda in water and add to pudding. Pour into a deep 2½-pint greased casserole.

Bake in slow oven (300°F. Mark 2) 1 to 1¼ hours or until deep dark brown. Stir pudding after 30 minutes of baking. Serve warm with lemon sauce. Serves 8.

PINK MARBLE PUDDING

    about ½ pound fresh or canned stewed
           and sweetened rhubarb
    about 4 ounces fresh or frozen rasp-
           berries
    8 ounces sugar (or to taste)
    14 fig biscuits, crumbled
    8 fluid ounces double cream
    1 teaspoon vanilla
    3 tablespoons icing sugar

Molasses-Apple Cottage Pudding

Combine sweetened rhubarb and raspberries. Purée them through the food mill or a sieve. Place in a saucepan with the sugar and the fig biscuits crumbled into small bits. Heat slowly, stirring constantly until the fig biscuits are almost blended into the mixture.

When cool, place in the refrigerator to chill.

Just before serving, whip the cream with the vanilla and the sugar.

Place the fig mixture in sorbet glasses alternately with spoonfuls of the whipped cream.

Top with cream and serve very cold. Serves 6 to 8.

APPLE SAUCE FLOATING ISLAND

    16 fluid ounces milk
    2 tablespoons cornflour
    6 tablespoons caster sugar
    2 eggs
    ⅛ teaspoon salt
    1 teaspoon vanilla
    14 ounces chilled apple sauce

Scald milk in double saucepan. Add cornflour to 4 tablespoons of sugar and mix.

Separate eggs, saving whites for meringue. Beat yolks; add to sugar mixture and blend gradually; add the scalded milk, stirring to mix thoroughly. Return mixture to double saucepan and cook 5 minutes, or until thickened.

Remove from heat; add salt and vanilla. Chill.

Beat egg whites until stiff; add 2 tablespoons sugar gradually, beating thoroughly.

Fold chilled apple sauce into the chilled pudding mixture before serving. Top with spoonfuls of meringue; sprinkle with cinnamon or nutmeg. Serves 6.

Apple Sauce Floating Island

Steamed Puddings

General Directions for Steamed Puddings

Pudding mixtures may be prepared in special pudding basins or moulds, or small cylindrical tins with tight covers such as baking powder tins.

Moulds should be tightly covered with non-stick cooking paper, aluminium foil, or several layers of greaseproof paper, letting it extend at least an inch over the edge and tied in place. The mould and cover should be thoroughly greased. Mould should be only ⅔ full.

If a steamer is not available, place a trivet or wire rack in a large covered pan or roasting pan. Place the covered moulds on the trivet or rack. Add water to just below the top of trivet. Cover, let water boil slowly to form steam. Water should be boiling in pan or steamer when food is ready for cooking.

Keep water boiling, constantly refilling with boiling water as needed.

When done, remove moulds and let stand a few minutes, or set in cold water for a few seconds before unmoulding.

If desired, the batter may be poured directly into the upper part of a double saucepan and cooked over boiling water. The water should not touch the upper part. The sides and cover of the top saucepan should be well greased.

Individual Date-Nut Puddings

PLUM PUDDING—STEAMED

Plum pudding is a spicy suet pudding of English origin, traditionally served at Christmas dinners, often flaming. It contains mixed dried and candied fruits but no plums.

- 1 pound raisins
- 1 pound currants
- 1 ounce chopped nuts
- 10 ounces sifted flour
- 2 teaspoons bicarbonate of soda
- 1 teaspoon ground cloves
- 1 teaspoon allspice
- 1 teaspoon nutmeg
- 1 teaspoon cinnamon
- 2 teaspoons salt
- 4 eggs
- 8 ounces sugar
- ¾ pint molasses or black treacle
- 16 fluid ounces buttermilk
- 12 ounces finely chopped suet
- 4 fluid ounces grape juice
- 10 ounces fine dry breadcrumbs
brandy butter

Clean raisins and currants; combine with nuts. Dredge with 4 ounces flour.

Sift remaining flour, soda, cloves, allspice, nutmeg, cinnamon, and salt.

Beat eggs; add sugar, molasses, buttermilk, suet, grape juice, and crumbs. Add raisin mixture; mix well. Add flour mixture; mix well.

Pour into 2 greased 3-pound moulds. Cover; steam 3 hours.

Cool puddings, wrap in greaseproof paper; store. The puddings keep for weeks in a cool place. Resteam to heat.

Serve hot with brandy butter. Each pudding serves 12.

INDIVIDUAL DATE-NUT PUDDINGS

- 2 ounces soft butter or margarine
- 4 ounces sugar
- 1 teaspoon vanilla
- ½ teaspoon salt
- 2 eggs, beaten
- 2 fluid ounces milk
- 18 ounces soft bread cubes
- 2 teaspoons baking powder
- 5 or 6 ounces chopped, stoned dates
- 2 ounces chopped walnuts

Combine butter, sugar, vanilla, and salt; add beaten eggs and milk.

Combine bread cubes and baking powder; add to first mixture. Add dates and walnuts.

Grease 7 individual (6-ounce) fruit juice cans on inside and put 6 ounces pudding mixture into each can. Cover top of can with aluminium foil and press it down over sides of can.

Put 16 ounces water in pressure cooker; place cans on trivet in cooker. Place cover on cooker and steam pudding for 15 minutes. Close steam valve and pressure cook pudding for 30 minutes.

Let pudding cool 5 minutes before loosening with palette knife and turning it out. Serve with foamy sauce. Makes 7 individual puddings.

NEW ENGLAND PLUM PUDDING

- 4 ounces butter or margarine
- 8 ounces sugar
- 1 egg, unbeaten
- 4 ounces sifted flour
- 1 teaspoon bicarbonate of soda
- ¾ teaspoon ground cloves
- 1½ teaspoons cinnamon
- 1 teaspoon nutmeg
- 4 ounces sifted breadcrumbs
- 4 ounces broken walnuts
- 7½ ounces raisins
- 6 fluid ounces hot water

Cream butter or margarine; add sugar gradually, creaming continually. Beat in egg.

Sift dry ingredients over breadcrumbs, walnuts, and raisins; mix well. Add to first mixture alternately with hot water.

Turn into greased 3½-pint pudding basin and cover tightly.

Place on rack in very slow oven (250°F. Mark ½) and oven steam 2½ to 3 hours. Serve with foamy sauce. Serves 8.

APPLE PUDDING—STEAMED

- 6 apples
- 2 ounces sugar
- ¼ teaspoon cinnamon
- 2 fluid ounces water
- 4 ounces sifted flour
- 2½ teaspoons baking powder
- ½ teaspoon salt
- ½ ounce lard
about 3 ounces milk

Wash, peel, and quarter apples. Cut into slices about ¼-inch thick. Add sugar, cinnamon, and water. Cover and cook over low heat until tender. Stir carefully if necessary.

Mix and sift flour, baking powder, and salt. Mix in lard. Add milk, mixing quickly to make a soft dough. Pat out to fit the size of pan in which the apples are cooking. Place dough over apples. Cover pan and put in steamer.

Steam pudding about 1 hour. Turn out onto a large plate, apple side up. Serve warm with lemon sauce. Serves 6.

Plum Pudding

VANILLA PUDDING — STEAMED
(Basic Recipe)

    3 ounces lard
    8 ounces sugar
    1 teaspoon vanilla
    6 ounces sifted flour
    1½ teaspoons baking powder
    ⅛ teaspoon salt
    4 fluid ounces milk
    3 egg whites

Cream lard; add ⅔ of the sugar and vanilla. Cream until light and fluffy.

Mix and sift dry ingredients. Add in thirds to creamed mixture, alternating with milk, mixing well after each addition.

Beat egg whites until stiff but not dry. Gradually add remaining sugar, beating continuously. Carefully fold into batter.

Fill individual greased moulds ¾ full. Steam until done, about ½ hour. Serve with fruit sauce. Serves 6 to 8.

Vanilla Pudding Variations

Almond Pudding: Substitute almond essence for vanilla.

Chocolate Pudding: Melt and cool 2 ounces plain chocolate. Add with sugar-egg mixture.

Raisin-Nut Pudding: Add 2 ounces each sultanas and nuts with sugar-egg mixture.

Raisin Pudding: Add 5 ounces raisins with sugar-egg mixture.

MOLASSES PUDDING — STEAMED

    1 egg
    9 ounces molasses or black treacle
    1 ounce melted lard
    1 teaspoon vanilla
    7 ounces sifted all-purpose flour
    5 ounces raisins or 2½ ounces
        raisins and 2 ounces chopped
        nuts
    ¼ teaspoon salt
    1 teaspoon baking powder
    1 teaspoon cinnamon
    ½ teaspoon bicarbonate of soda
    4 fluid ounces cold water

Beat egg; stir in molasses or treacle, lard, and vanilla.

Sift flour and dust part of it over raisins and nuts.

Resift the rest of flour with salt, baking powder, and cinnamon.

Dissolve soda in cold water. Add sifted dry ingredients in 3 parts to molasses mixture alternately with thirds of water and soda. Beat batter well after each addition.

Pour batter into greased pudding basin. Cover closely and steam 1½ hours. Serve hot with brandy butter or whipped cream. Serves 6.

Coconut Pudding: Add 4 ounces desiccated coconut to batter.

SUET PUDDING — STEAMED

    ½ pound suet, finely chopped
    8 ounces packaged breadcrumbs
    5 ounces sultanas
    4 ounces mixed glacé fruits, or
        2 ounces nuts, chopped
    8 ounces brown sugar
    2 tablespoons molasses or black
        treacle
    4 fluid ounces milk or cider
        (liquid may be ¼ brandy)
    1 beaten egg
    ½ teaspoon each of bicarbonate of
        soda, salt, ground cloves,
        and allspice
    1 teaspoon cinnamon

Mix all ingredients except soda, salt, and spices, with your hands.

Mix soda, salt, and spices; sprinkle over batter. Blend in well.

Fill individual greased moulds about ⅔-full and cover with aluminium foil.

Set on rack in large pot or covered roasting pan. Add boiling water to depth of about 1 inch.

Cover and steam 1 hour, adding more water, if needed. Remove covers and cool thoroughly. Replace covers before storing.

To reheat: steam, covered, during first course of meal. Serve with brandy sauce or whipped cream. Serves 8.

HUNGARIAN PLUM PUDDING

    8 ounces stale breadcrumbs
    8 fluid ounces scalded milk
    4 ounces sugar
    2 eggs, separated
    6½ ounces sultanas
    6½ ounces currants
    2 ounces finely cut glacé citron
    4 ounces butter, melted
    2 fluid ounces grape juice
    ½ teaspoon nutmeg
    1 teaspoon cinnamon
    ¼ teaspoon each ground cloves
        and mace
    1½ teaspoons salt

Soak breadcrumbs in milk and cool.

Combine sugar, beaten egg yolks, raisins, currants, and citron. Add milk mixture and butter. Mix well.

Add remaining ingredients; then fold in stiffly beaten egg whites.

Pour into buttered mould. Cover and steam 5 hours. Serve hot with preferred sauce. Serves 6.

GINGER-FIG PUDDING — STEAMED

    ½ pound dried figs
    1 egg
    12 ounces molasses or black treacle
    4 ounces melted lard
    2 teaspoons ginger
    1 teaspoon bicarbonate of soda
    1 teaspoon salt
    10 ounces sifted flour
    6 fluid ounces warm water

Ginger-Fig Pudding

Cover figs with boiling water for 10 minutes; drain, reserving warm water to use in pudding; clip off stems with scissors and slice finely.

Beat egg; add molasses and lard. Sift dry ingredients together and add alternately with water.

Lastly add figs; mix well and turn into a greased pudding basin.

Set in a pan of boiling water. Put a cover over the pan and steam for 2½ hours in slow oven (325°F. Mark 3) or in conventional steamer. This will make 2 puddings and each pudding will serve 6. Keeps nicely and may be reheated. Serve with preferred sauce.

ST. PATRICK'S DAY PUDDING

    2 (7¾-ounce) packets fig biscuits
    4 fluid ounces milk
    2 ounces butter or margarine
    1 egg, well beaten
    1 teaspoon cinnamon
    ¼ teaspoon ground cloves
    ¼ teaspoon nutmeg
    1 teaspoon lemon juice
    ¼ teaspoon grated lemon rind
    1 tablespoon baking powder

Break fig biscuits into milk. Let stand 15 minutes; stir to blend.

Cream butter; add egg, cinnamon, cloves, nutmeg, lemon juice, lemon rind, and baking powder. Stir into fig mixture.

Divide into 12 small greased moulds; cover tightly with aluminium foil.

Steam 30 minutes. Cool a few minutes before unmoulding.

Garnish with preferred sauce or whipped cream.

Note: If desired, steam half the recipe in individual moulds and the remainder in a 1½-pint mould to reheat for another day.

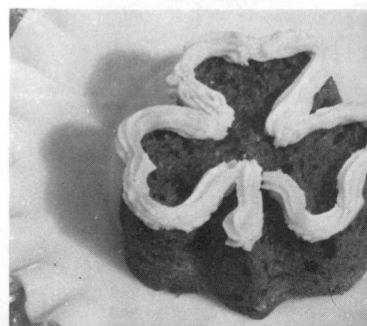

St. Patrick's Day Pudding

Dumplings, Cobblers, Shortcakes

CHERRY DUMPLINGS

Cherry Sauce:
1 ounce butter or margarine
4 ounces sugar
dash of salt
4 fluid ounces cherry juice
about 12 ounces sour stoned cherries
12 fluid ounces boiling water

Combine all ingredients in order given in heavy frying pan or large saucepan.

Bring mixture to boil, reduce heat and simmer gently about 5 minutes.

Dumplings:
4 ounces sifted flour
1½ teaspoons baking powder
dash of salt
2 ounces sugar
1 ounce butter or margarine
½ teaspoon vanilla
3 to 4 fluid ounces milk

Sift together flour, baking powder, salt, and sugar. Rub in butter or margarine until mixture is crumbly.

Add vanilla to milk. Add milk to flour mixture and stir only enough to moisten flour. Drop by spoonfuls into boiling sauce.

Cook uncovered 5 minutes. Cover and steam gently 15 minutes longer.

Serve dumplings warm with cherry sauce. Serves 4.

Cherry Dumplings

WESTERN APPLE DUMPLINGS

4 ounces sifted flour
¼ teaspoon salt
2 teaspoons baking powder
2 teaspoons sugar
2 ounces butter or margarine
1 slightly beaten egg
3 tablespoons milk
2 ounces melted butter or margarine
6 ounces finely diced, peeled, cored apples
1 ounce sultanas
1 tablespoon sugar
1 teaspoon cinnamon

Sauce:
3 ounces brown sugar
4 ounces granulated sugar
1 tablespoon cornflour
6 fluid ounces water
½ ounce butter or margarine

Mix and sift flour, salt, baking powder, and 2 teaspoons sugar. Rub in butter with pastry blender or fork until pieces are size of small peas.

Combine beaten egg with milk and stir into first mixture, forming smooth dough. Knead dough about 1 minute, then roll out in rectangle ¼-inch thick on well-floured pastry cloth. Brush with melted butter.

Mix apples and raisins and spread over dough. Combine 1 tablespoon sugar and 1 teaspoon cinnamon and sprinkle over apples and raisins.

Roll up as for Swiss roll and cut into 6 slices with sharp knife. Place rolls in individual fireproof cups or tart pans.

Cover with sauce made by mixing sugars and cornflour; add water and butter and bring mixture to boiling point.

Bake in moderate oven (375°F. Mark 5) 25 minutes. Serve warm with cream, if desired. Serves 6.

BAKED FRUIT DUMPLINGS
(Basic Recipe)

Roll scone dough ¼-inch thick. Cut into 4-inch squares.

Use 6 small apples, apricots, or peaches. Place whole fruit, peeled and cored, or pitted, in centre of each square. Sprinkle 1 tablespoon sugar and cinnamon or nutmeg mixture over fruit in each dumpling. Dot with butter.

Bring corners up over fruit. Pinch edges together. Prick with fork.

Bake in moderate oven (350°F. Mark 4) 30 minutes. Serve with preferred sauce.

One recipe for scone dough makes 6 dumplings. The amount of sugar and cinnamon or nutmeg mixture may be varied, depending upon individual taste or sweetness of fruit.

HUNGARIAN PLUM DUMPLINGS

1½ pounds boiled potatoes
2 eggs, slightly beaten
1 teaspoon salt
about 8 ounces sifted flour
12 to 15 ripe plums
1 teaspoon cinnamon
4 ounces sugar
3 ounces fresh breadcrumbs
about 2 ounces butter or margarine

Cook potatoes in jackets. Peel and mash. Add eggs and salt. Mix well. Sift in enough flour to make a smooth dough.

Roll out to ½-inch thickness on a floured board and cut into 3-inch squares.

Stone the plums; fill cavities with cinnamon and sugar. Place a plum on each square. Fold dough around plums to form balls. Cook 10 minutes, covered in boiling salted water. Drain well.

Roll dumplings in breadcrumbs which have been browned in butter. Serve hot. Serves 6 to 8.

Variations: Apricots filled with cinnamon and sugar, or sliced and sugared apples, may be substituted for plums.

OLD-FASHIONED APPLE DUMPLINGS

1 recipe plain pastry
6 medium (tart) cooking apples
3 ounces butter
1½ ounces brown sugar
1 teaspoon cinnamon
⅛ teaspoon salt

Prepare pastry and roll ⅛-inch thick on floured board. Cut into 6-inch squares.

Wash, thinly peel and core apples. Make 2 crosswise cuts through top of each apple, about ½-inch deep.

Place 1 apple on each pastry square. Put a knob of butter into each cavity. Sprinkle apple with brown sugar, cinnamon, and salt. Moisten edges of pastry squares with water. Fold corners to centre and press edges together.

Place in ungreased pan (7×11×1¼ inches). Bake in very hot oven (450°F. Mark 8) 10 minutes. Reduce to moderate heat (350°F. Mark 4) and bake 25 to 30 minutes longer or until apples are tender and crust delicately browned.

Serve hot with butterscotch sauce, or with cream. Serves 6.

Old-Fashioned Apple Dumplings

Saucy Apple Dumplings

SAUCY APPLE DUMPLINGS

8 ounces sifted flour
3 teaspoons baking powder
1 teaspoon salt
3 ounces lard
4 to 6 fluid ounces milk
4 medium-sized apples
3 ounces brown sugar

Mix and sift flour, baking powder, and salt. Rub in lard. Add milk to make a soft dough.

Turn out on lightly floured board and knead gently ½ minute. Roll into rectangular sheet about 8 inches wide and ⅛-inch thick.

Peel and core apples and chop coarsely. Spread evenly over dough.

Sprinkle with brown sugar. Roll up like a Swiss roll and seal edge. Cut into 2-inch slices. Place in greased baking tin.

Pour 8 ounces cinnamon sweet sauce (below) over slices in tin.

Bake in moderate oven (375°F. Mark 5) 40 minutes. Makes 8 dumplings.

Cinnamon Sweet Sauce: Mix 1 ounce cornflour and 3 ounces brown sugar together. Add 7 tablespoons red cinnamon sweets and 1 pint water.

Cook until clear and thickened, stirring constantly. Serve warm or cold over dumplings.

STEAMED BERRY DUMPLINGS

Stew enough gooseberries, loganberries, or blackberries to make 1½ pints. Sweeten to taste with sugar.

If desired, use canned berries, heated to boiling point.

Roll scone dough to ½-inch thickness. Cut into small circles. Drop into boiling berries.

Cover and cook 12 to 15 minutes. Serve hot with berry sauce poured over dumplings.

Steamed Apple Dumplings: Use thin apple sauce instead of berries. Proceed as directed for Steamed Berry Dumplings.

BLUSHING BEAUTY DUMPLINGS

6   tart medium-sized cooking
       apples
apple peelings
12 fluid ounces water
4   ounces sugar
¼   teaspoon red food colouring
6   ounces sifted flour
¼   teaspoon salt
4   ounces lard
1   teaspoon grated orange rind
5 to 6 tablespoons cold orange juice
2   tablespoons sugar
1   teaspoon nutmeg
1½ ounces butter

Peel and core apples. Combine apple peelings and water in saucepan. Cover; cook until tender, 5 to 10 minutes. Drain juice and to it add sugar. Cover and cook 10 minutes. Remove from heat; add red food colouring. Set aside.

Sift together flour and salt. Rub in lard and orange rind until particles are the size of small peas. Sprinkle cold orange juice over mixture, tossing lightly with fork until dough is moist enough to hold together. Form into a ball.

Roll out on floured pastry cloth or board to 18×9-inch rectangle. Cut into 9×3-inch strips.

Wrap strip around each apple, sealing tightly at bottom only.

Combine 2 tablespoons sugar and the nutmeg. Place 1 teaspoonful in centre of each apple. Top with butter (1 knob on each dumpling).

Place in 12×8-inch baking tin so dumplings do not touch one another. Pour reserved syrup around dumplings.

Bake in moderate oven (350°F. Mark 4) 50 to 60 minutes. Baste with syrup after baking 40 minutes. Serve warm, plain or with cream. Serves 6.

CARAMEL-NUT DUMPLINGS

12 ounces sugar
1   pint water
¼   teaspoon salt
1   teaspoon vanilla

Melt 6 ounces sugar over high heat, stirring constantly until amber in colour. Remove from heat and stir until liquid thickens and cools slightly.

Slowly stir in water and return to heat. Add remaining sugar, salt, and vanilla and mix well. Remove from heat.

Prepare Dumplings: Mix and sift 4 ounces sifted flour, 2 tablespoons sugar, 1¾ teaspoons baking powder, and dash of salt. Stir in 1½ ounces chopped walnuts. Add 4 fluid ounces milk and stir quickly until flour is just moistened.

Drop by teaspoons into simmering caramel sauce. Cover tightly and steam 20 minutes over low heat. Serves 6 to 8.

Blushing Beauty Dumplings

ROLLED FIG DUMPLINGS

Filling:
about 1 pound figs, chopped fine
1 tablespoon lemon juice
3 tablespoons cold water

Add lemon juice and water to figs. Heat to boiling, stir, and cool.

Syrup:
8   ounces sugar
12 fluid ounces water
grated rind and juice of 1 lemon

Mix sugar, water, lemon juice, and rind and bring to boil.

Dough:
8 ounces sifted flour
3 teaspoons baking powder
½ teaspoon salt
2 ounces lard
1 well-beaten egg
4 fluid ounces top of the milk

Sift flour, baking powder, and salt together into a basin. Add lard and rub in finely.

Beat egg well, add to milk, and blend with dry ingredients.

Knead dough lightly about ½ minute, then roll out into rectangle about ¼-inch thick. Spread with fig filling, then roll up.

Cut into 9 even slices and arrange in 8-inch baking dish, cut-side down. Pour boiling syrup over top.

Bake immediately in hot oven (400°F. Mark 6) 25 minutes. Serve hot or cold either in sauce or with cream. Makes 9.

Rolled Fig Dumplings

Master Fruit Cobbler

BLACKBERRY COBBLER

Filling:
about 6 ounces blackberries
few grains salt
sugar
1 egg, well beaten
    or 1 tablespoon quick tapioca
    or 1 tablespoon flour
butter or margarine

Batter:
2 ounces butter or margarine
4 ounces sugar
1 egg, well beaten
6 ounces sifted flour
2 teaspoons baking powder
½ teaspoon salt
4 fluid ounces milk

Filling: Add salt and sugar to taste to berries. Add egg or other thickening. Spread in buttered baking dish and dot with butter.

Batter: Cream butter. Add sugar gradually, and add egg.

Mix and sift flour, baking powder, and salt. Add alternately with milk to creamed mixture.

Cover berries with batter and bake in hot oven (425°F. Mark 7) about 30 minutes.

Serve warm with whipped cream, vanilla sauce or other preferred sauce. Serves 6.

Variations of Blackberry Cobbler

Gooseberry or Loganberry Cobbler: Use gooseberries or loganberries instead of blackberries.

Apple Cobbler: Use 8 ounces sliced fresh or canned apples instead of berries.

Peach Cobbler: Use 6 to 8 ounces fresh or canned sliced peaches instead of berries. If fresh peaches are used, put in a pip or two for especially good flavour.

Sour Cherry Cobbler: Pit cherries; cook 5 minutes in just enough water to keep from burning. Sweeten to taste and pour into baking dish.

Raspberry-Currant Cobbler: Use 4 ounces raspberries and 2½ ounces currants.

BASIC FRUIT COBBLER

Filling:
4 ounces sugar, or to taste
⅛ teaspoon salt
2 tablespoons cornflour
¾ pound sliced peaches, or other
    fruit
Pastry Crust:
4 ounces sifted flour
½ teaspoon salt
3 ounces butter or margarine
3 to 4 tablespoons cold water

Filling: Mix sugar, salt, cornflour, and fruit and pour into buttered, shallow casserole or deep oven glass cake dish, 2½ inches deep preferably.

Pastry Crust: Sift flour with salt. Rub in butter until size of wheat grains. Add water a little at a time until mixture holds together. Chill dough 15 to 20 minutes.

Roll pastry out ⅛- to ¼-inch thickness and cut into decorative pieces with pastry cutters. Place pieces of pastry at regular intervals over fruit mixture.

Bake in very hot oven (450°F. Mark 8) 20 to 25 minutes or until crust is browned. Serve hot with cream. Serves 6.

APPLE-CHEESE COBBLER

1 pound peeled and sliced apples
8 ounces sugar
1 teaspoon cinnamon
6 to 8 slices Cheddar cheese
3 ounces lard
8 ounces sifted flour
3 teaspoons baking powder
½ teaspoon salt
8 fluid ounces milk

Combine apples, sugar, and cinnamon and arrange evenly over bottom of 8×8×2-inch baking dish. Cover with slices of cheese.

Top with a drop shortcrust pastry dough made by rubbing lard into flour which has been combined with baking powder and salt. When mixture is of a coarse crumbly texture, add all of milk and stir until moisture is evenly distributed.

Bake in hot oven (400°F. Mark 6) 35 to 45 minutes, or until crust is brown and pastry topping is baked. Serve warm with cream. Serves 6 to 8.

Note: A patriotic cobbler Union Jack topping is easily made from pastry for a 1-crust pie. Roll pastry on a lightly floured surface to a 10×4-inch rectangle. Cut appropriate pastry strips and arrange on top of cobbler mixture. Be sure to leave space between strips as pastry expands when it bakes.

RHUBARB COBBLER

1¼ to 1½ pounds diced rhubarb
12 ounces sugar, to taste
½ ounce margarine
4 ounces sifted flour
1½ teaspoons baking powder
½ teaspoon salt
3 tablespoons sugar
⅛ teaspoon nutmeg
2 ounces margarine
1 egg, beaten
4 fluid ounces milk

Combine rhubard and 12 ounces sugar, mixing well. Spread into well-margarined 8×8-inch or 7×9-inch pan. Dot with margarine.

Mix and sift flour, baking powder, salt, 1 tablespoon sugar, and nutmeg into mixing bowl. Rub 2 ounces margarine into flour mixture until mixture is fine and crumbly.

Combine beaten egg and milk. Add all at one time to flour mixture and stir until well blended.

With spoon, arrange batter in lattice-effect over rhubarb in pan, or drop by spoonfuls or spread evenly over rhubarb. Sprinkle batter with 2 tablespoons sugar.

Bake in moderate oven (350°F. Mark 4) 40 to 45 minutes. Serve warm with cream or ice cream. Serves 6.

BUTTER-FRUIT COBBLER

1 pound strawberries
1 medium-sized fresh pineapple
2 tablespoons lemon juice
6 ounces sifted cake flour
¼ teaspoon salt
4 ounces butter or margarine
3 to 4 tablespoons cold water
2 tablespoons flour
4 ounces sugar

Wash strawberries thoroughly with cold water before sorting them.

Slice pineapple, peel, and cut in segments.

Combine fruits, add lemon juice, and mix together lightly. Place in refrigerator while mixing pastry crust.

Sift flour, measure 6 ounces and re-sift with the salt. Add butter and rub in with pastry blender or 2 knives until mixture has texture of rice grains. Add cold water a few drops at a time, tossing with fork until dry ingredients are just dampened.

Form into round patty and roll out on lightly floured board.

Cut with floured biscuit cutter into fancy shapes.

Butter the casserole, turn the fruit into it, and sprinkle with the 2 tablespoons flour mixed with the sugar.

Arrange the rolled pastry on top in any desired arrangement, and bake in a very hot oven (450°F. Mark 8) for 15 to 20 minutes, until crust is golden brown. Serve warm or cold. Serves 6.

EASY-TO-DO SHORTCAKES

All you have to do to make these delightful old-fashioned strawberry shortcakes is—for 6 man-sized servings—to measure into bowl 16-ounce packet scone or American biscuit mix and 2 ounces sugar.

Add about 12 fluid ounces single cream, mixing with fork. Keep dough soft but, if it is sticky, add a bit more mix. Don't over mix.

Turn out on floured board or pastry cloth. Knead 10 times to shape in ball. Pat or roll out in rectangle to ½-inch thickness. Spread with softened butter.

Fold over, keeping in rectangular shape with a bit of patting and shaping at corners.

Note: This shortcake dough can be made with milk—about 12 fluid ounces—and 3 to 4 ounces melted butter instead of cream.

Using knife dipped in flour, cut dough in 6 or 8 squares.

For round shortcakes, cut with large floured biscuit cutter but knife method is easier.

Place a little apart on baking-sheet. Spread tops with softened butter and sprinkle with sugar if desired.

Bake in very hot oven (450°F. Mark 8) about 10 minutes. These shortcakes should be baked just before serving so they'll be hot.

To serve, split shortcakes. Arrange on serving plate or plates. While hot, spread with butter.

Cover lower half with sweetened strawberries, both sliced and whole, depending on size. Use 6 to 8 ounces sugar for 1½ pints of berries, allow to stand at room temperature for a while.

Put on top crust. Cover with strawberries and juice. Serve at once, topped with plenty of slightly sweetened whipped or double cream.

Plantation Peach Shortcake

PLANTATION PEACH SHORT-CAKE

8 ounces sifted flour
3 teaspoons baking powder
½ teaspoon salt
2 ounces brown sugar
4 ounces fat
2 ounces chopped walnuts or pecans
1 well-beaten egg
5 fluid ounces single cream
sweetened, sliced peaches (fresh, frozen, or canned)
whipped or double cream

Sift together flour, baking powder, and salt into large bowl. Rub in brown sugar and lard until mixture is crumbly. Add nuts.

Combine well-beaten egg and cream; add to flour-lard mixture, mixing only until all flour is dampened.

Spread in two well-greased 8-inch round layer cake tins. (For individual shortcakes, turn out dough on well-floured board or pastry cloth; knead a few strokes. Roll to ½-inch thickness. Cut into rounds with floured 3-inch cutter. Place on ungreased baking-sheet.)

Bake in very hot oven (450°F. Mark 8) 10 to 12 minutes.

Place peaches between layers or split individual shortcakes. Top with sweetened whipped cream and peaches.

PARTY "SHORT" CAKE

Prepare white, yellow, or spice cake mix as directed on packet. Bake as directed. Allow cake to cool.

Split layer crosswise to make 2 thin layers. Spoon between layers about 12 ounces sweetened prepared fruit—fresh, frozen, or drained tinned fruit such as raspberries, peaches, bananas, etc.

Spread over top 4 fluid ounces cream, whipped. Serve at once, or keep in refrigerator until serving time.

Party "Short" Cake

RICH SHORTCAKE

8 ounces sifted flour
3 teaspoons baking powder
¾ teaspoon salt
2 tablespoons sugar, if required
4 ounces lard
about 6 fluid ounces milk

Sift flour 3 times with remaining dry ingredients, the last time into bowl. (Omit sugar for chicken, fish, or meat shortcake.)

Rub in lard with pastry blender or blending fork until mixture is consistency of rice grains. Add milk all at once and mix lightly with fork. Do not stir vigorously.

Spread to uniform thickness in lightly greased 8-inch cake tin.

Bake in very hot oven (450°F. Mark 8) 20 to 25 minutes until golden brown. Split through centre crosswise and spoon desired sweetened fruit and juice such as raspberries, peaches, or grapefruit between and over hot layers before serving.

Creamed chicken or fish may be used with unsweetened shortcake.

GRAPE PIE

plain pastry or 8 ounces packet mix
about 2 pounds stemmed washed
grapes
8 ounces sugar
1 ounce butter or margarine
1 tablespoon lemon juice
½ teaspoon cinnamon
2 tablespoons flour

Line bottom and sides of 9-inch square baking tin with pastry.

Slip grape skins away from pulp. Put pulp in saucepan. Put skins in bowl.

Cook pulp about 5 minutes, or until seeds loosen. Then put fruit through sieve to remove seeds.

Mix grape skins, grape pulp, and remaining ingredients together and turn into pastry-lined tin.

Cover with top crust, which has been slashed in several places to allow escape of steam.

Bake in very hot oven (450°F. Mark 8) 15 minutes. Reduce heat to moderate (375°F. Mark 5) and bake 30 minutes longer, or until crust is lightly browned.

Serve cooled to room temperature, plain or with cream or vanilla ice cream. Serves 6.

Peach Frying Pan Shortcake

CRANBERRY NUT PIE

16 ounces sugar
8 fluid ounces water
1 pound cranberries
2 ounces chopped walnuts
grated rind of 1 orange
1 ounce butter or margarine
4 ounces sifted flour
2 tablespoons sugar
2 teaspoons baking powder
¼ teaspoon salt
1 ounce lard
3 fluid ounces milk

Heat sugar and water to boiling point; add cranberries, walnuts, orange rind, and butter and let stand while mixing dough.

Sift dry ingredients together; blend in lard and add milk.

Roll out dough to ¼-inch thickness. Fill individual baking dishes (shallow moulds, ramekins, or vol-au-vent cases) with cranberry mixture.

Cover each with round of dough. Prick holes in top of each to allow steam to escape.

Bake in very hot oven (450°F. Mark 8) about 15 minutes.

Serve with brandy butter flavoured with 2 ounces chopped fresh cranberries and 1 tablespoon cranberry syrup from filling. Serves 6.

PEACH FRYING PAN SHORTCAKE
(With Packet Mix)

8 ounces scone or biscuit mix
2 tablespoons sugar, optional
4 fluid ounces milk
2 ounces butter or margarine, melted
1½ pounds sliced peaches, sweetened and chilled
8 ounces double cream, whipped, or 1 pint vanilla ice cream

Place a heavy frying pan on asbestos stovemat. Cover and heat slowly while mixing dough.

Combine scone mix and sugar. Add milk and melted butter or margarine and mix well with fork. Knead about 10 times. Pat or roll on board dusted with additional mix into 9-inch round.

Grease frying pan well with lard. Place round of dough in pan and cover. Be sure heat is low to prevent burning. Let bake until brown on bottom and sides and firm to touch in centre, about 20 minutes.

Turn shortcake out onto serving plate and split in half, using a plate to lift off top half. If desired, spread lower half with soft butter. Cover bottom half with ½ the peaches. Cover with top of cake, add peaches and garnish with whipped cream or ice cream. Serves 8.

Strawberry Frying Pan Shortcake: Substitute strawberries for peaches. Other fruits may be used.

BLACKBERRY COBBLER

about 9 ounces fresh blackberries, or 16 ounces canned berries and juice
sugar to taste
pinch of salt
1 tablespoon cornflour
1 ounce butter or margarine
4 ounces scone mix
3 fluid ounces single cream
1 tablespoon sugar

Heat fresh berries and 6 fluid ounces water or canned berries and juice in pan. Sweeten to taste. Add salt and cornflour blended in 2 tablespoons cold water.

Bring to boil, stirring frequently. Cook 1 minute. Dot with butter.

Mix scone mix with cream and 1 tablespoon sugar, according to directions on packet for drop-scone dough. Drop dough from tablespoon over berries in pan. Cover, and cook over very low heat for 20 minutes.

Serve hot with cream, if desired. Serves 4 to 6.

STRAWBERRY CATHERINE WHEEL SHORTCAKE

6 ounces sifted flour
1 teaspoon salt
2 teaspoons baking powder
2 tablespoons sugar
1 ounce lard
1 egg, beaten
3 fluid ounces milk
1 ounce butter or margarine
4 ounces sugar
1 tablespoon grated orange rind
12 to 16 ounces strawberries

Sift together flour, salt, baking powder, and 2 tablespoons sugar. Rub lard into flour until mixture is like coarse oatmeal. Add beaten egg and milk all at once and mix lightly.

Pat out dough on a floured board into a 9-inch square. Spread dough with melted butter or margarine. Mix together 4 ounces sugar and the grated orange rind; sprinkle on dough.

Roll as for Swiss roll; cut into 6 slices. Arrange slices, cut side up, around edge of lightly greased 10-inch pie dish. Bake in moderate oven (375°F. Mark 5) for about 25 minutes. When pastry is cool heap strawberries in centre of pie dish for serving. Serves 6.

Strawberry Catherine Wheel Shortcake

Miscellaneous Desserts

COEUR À LA CRÈME (CHEESE AND CREAM HEART)

Coeur is French for heart; coeur à la crème is a French cheese dessert moulded in individual heart-shaped moulds with perforated bottoms or in one large traditional heart-shaped wicker basket lined with moistened muslin. It is served with crushed or whole strawberries, raspberries, or other fruit.

1 pound cottage cheese
1 pound cream cheese, softened
pinch of salt
16 fluid ounces double cream
crushed fresh strawberries or
    defrosted frozen strawberries

Combine cottage cheese, cream cheese, and salt thoroughly. Gradually add cream, beating until mixture is smooth.

Turn into individual moulds or one large mould. Place on deep plate and refrigerate to drain overnight.

At serving time unmould on to chilled plates. Serve with crushed sweetened strawberries. If desired, garnish with whole strawberries and mint or parsley. Serve with French bread. Serves 6.

STRAWBERRY TRIFLES

8 ounces sifted flour
3 teaspoons baking powder
1 teaspoon salt
4 ounces lard
8 ounces sugar
2 eggs, beaten
1 teaspoon vanilla
6 fluid ounces milk

Sift together flour, baking powder, and salt.

Cream together lard and sugar until light and fluffy. Add eggs, beating well. Add vanilla. Add flour mixture to creamed mixture alternately with milk.

Fill greased 3-inch bun tins ½ full.

Bake in moderate oven (375°F. Mark 5) about 25 minutes.

Cut off tops of buns, and spread with whipped cream and halves of strawberries. Replace tops, garnish with more strawberry halves, and top with whipped cream and one whole strawberry. Makes about 14 3-inch buns.

CHERRY MERINGUE DESSERT

5 ounces sifted flour
½ teaspoon baking powder
¼ teaspoon salt
3 ounces lard
3 ounces sugar
2 egg yolks, unbeaten
1 tablespoon milk
2 ounces chopped walnuts or pecans
about 14 ounces sour red tinned
    cherries, drained (reserve
    juice)
2 tablespoons cornflour
4 ounces sugar
6 fluid ounces cherry juice
    (reserved)
¼ teaspoon almond essence
2 egg whites
2 ounces sugar

Sift together flour, baking powder, and salt.

Blend lard and sugar, creaming well. Add egg yolks and milk; beat well.

Add flour mixture all at once; stir until mixture is well blended and forms a ball. Press into bottom of well-greased and lightly floured 9-inch round layer cake tin.*

Reserve 2 tablespoons nuts for meringue. Sprinkle remainder over dough in pan.

Bake in moderate oven (375°F. Mark 5) 12 to 15 minutes until golden brown. Cool.

Transfer cooled, baked pastry circle to baking-sheet. Drop meringue (see below) by tablespoonfuls in a ring around edge on top of pastry. Sprinkle meringue with the 2 tablespoons reserved nuts.

Bake in moderate oven (350°F. Mark 4) 12 to 15 minutes, until meringue is lightly browned. Fill centre with the cooled cherry filling (see below). Serves 8 to 10.

Cherry Filling: Blend together cornflour and 4 ounces sugar in saucepan. Stir in cherry juice until sugar dissolves. Cook over medium heat, stirring constantly, until thick and clear. Remove from heat. Add almond essence and cherries. Cool.

Meringue: Beat egg whites until slight mounds form when whisk is raised. Add 2 ounces sugar gradually, beating well after each addition. Continue beating until meringue stands in stiff, glossy peaks when whisk is raised.

*Note: Dough may be rolled out to a 9-inch circle on greased baking-sheet. Bake, cool and top with meringue and cherry filling as directed.

Blackberry Dream Dessert

BLACKBERRY DREAM DESSERT

6 ounces quick porridge oats,
    uncooked
4 ounces sifted flour
7 ounces brown sugar
6 ounces butter, melted
6 ounces blackberries
1 tablespoon flour
4 ounces sugar
2 tablespoons lemon juice
⅛ teaspoon salt
6 fluid ounces water or juice from
    tinned blackberries

Mix porridge oats, 4 ounces flour, and brown sugar. Add melted butter and mix well. Line bottom of 8-inch square baking tin with mixture, reserving enough for topping.

Combine blackberries, 1 tablespoon flour, sugar, lemon juice, salt, and liquid in saucepan. Simmer about 5 minutes.

Remove from heat and pour into pastry crust. Sprinkle with remaining crumbs and bake in moderate oven (350°F. Mark 4) 45 minutes. Serve topped with whipped cream or ice cream. Serves 6 to 8.

RASPBERRY MERINGUE CAKES

For a quickly prepared dessert, serve bakery individual small rich plain cakes with a meringue into which fresh, tinned, or well-drained frozen fruit has been folded.

Slice the cakes into segments, cutting only half way through; open gently, fill with the meringue and fruit.

Raspberry Meringue Cakes

Cherry Meringue Dessert

Swedish Chocolate Dessert

SWEDISH CHOCOLATE DESSERT

9 ounces sifted flour
4 ounces sugar
1½ ounces cocoa
½ teaspoon baking powder
½ teaspoon salt
6 ounces lard
1 unbeaten egg
2 tablespoons milk

Sift together flour, sugar, cocoa, baking powder, and salt into mixing bowl. Rub in lard until particles are the size of small peas. Add egg and milk. Blend with fork or pastry blender until well combined.

Place dough on large ungreased baking-sheet, at least 15×12 inches.* Roll out on baking-sheet with floured rolling pin to 15×11-inch rectangle.

Trim edges with sharp knife or pastry wheel; divide into three 11×5-inch rectangles. Bake in moderate oven (375°F. Mark 5) for 12 to 15 minutes. Avoid over baking. Cool on baking-sheets. When cold, loosen carefully with palette knife.

Place a piece of cardboard (about 12×6 inches) on a sheet of aluminium foil or greaseproof paper (which is large enough to wrap dessert for chilling).

Stack layers on top of cardboard, spreading filling (see below) between layers but not quite to edge. Ice top (see below). If desired, decorate top with toasted slivered almonds.

Chill until icing has set. Then wrap loosely in the aluminium foil (or greaseproof paper); chill overnight. Cut into 6 or 8 rectangular-shaped pieces to serve.

*Note: If a large baking-sheet is not available, roll dough to fit the bottom of an inverted 15×10-inch shallow baking dish, then divide into 3 equal rectangles. Then use smaller baking-sheets or tins.

Vanilla Filling:

1 egg
2 ounces caster sugar
1 ounce flour
8 fluid ounces milk, scalded in top of double saucepan
1 teaspoon vanilla
4 ounces whipping cream

Whisk egg until light and fluffy. Gradually add sugar, whisking constantly until thick and light. Blend in flour. Gradually add scalded milk; return mixture to top of double saucepan.

Cook over boiling water, stirring constantly, until thick and smooth. Add vanilla; cool.

Beat whipping cream until thick and fold into cooled filling.

Chocolate Filling: Follow recipe above but combine the whipping cream with 3 tablespoons cocoa and 3 tablespoons sugar.

Chill for 30 minutes. Then beat until thick and fold into filling.

Chocolate Icing:

1 ounce butter or margarine
2 tablespoons cocoa
3 ounces sifted icing sugar
1 egg yolk
¼ teaspoon vanilla

Melt butter in saucepan. Remove from heat; blend in cocoa. Add icing sugar, egg yolk, and vanilla. Beat until smooth.

FROMAGE À LA CRÈME (FRENCH CHEESE AND CREAM)

Fromage is French for cheese; fromage à la crème is a French moulded cream cheese dessert served with fresh strawberries, or other fresh fruit or berries.

2 8-ounce packets cream cheese
2 tablespoons cream
⅛ teaspoon salt
8 fluid ounces whipped cream or
    8 ounces sour cream

Beat cream cheese with 2 tablespoons cream and the salt until soft; fold into whipped cream or sour cream. Turn into rinsed individual moulds or one large mould.

Chill thoroughly, then unmould on to chilled plates. Serve with fresh strawberries or other fresh fruit or berries. Serves 6.

CRUMBLED TORTE

2 eggs, separated
8 ounces sugar
about 5 ounces coarsely cut dates
4 ounces finely chopped nuts
1 tablespoon flour
1 teaspoon baking powder

Whisk egg yolks until frothy. Add sugar gradually, continuing to whisk until well mixed.

Add dates, nuts, flour, and baking powder. Stir until all ingredients are moistened.

Fold in stiffly beaten egg whites until mixture is blended.

Spread batter into greased 9-inch square tin. Bake in a hot oven (425°F Mark 7) 15 minutes. Let stand until cold.

Crumble torte into stemmed glasses. Top with sweetened whipped cream and cherries. Serves 4 to 6.

NORWEGIAN APPLE CAKE

8 ounces toasted breadcrumbs
½ teaspoon nutmeg
18 ounces apple sauce
butter or margarine
whipped cream
redcurrant jelly

Combine crumbs and nutmeg. Arrange alternate layers of crumbs and apple sauce in a buttered pudding basin dotting each with butter. Top with crumbs; press down well.

Bake in slow oven (325°F. Mark 3) 45 minutes. Cool, then turn out of basin. Spread with whipped cream. Dot with jelly. Serves 6.

CRANBERRY GRUNT

8 ounces cranberries
4 ounces diced apples
4 fluid ounces water
3 ounces plus 2 tablespoons sugar
3 ounces butter or margarine
¼ teaspoon powdered cloves
½ teaspoon nutmeg
6 ounces sifted flour
3 teaspoons baking powder
¼ teaspoon salt
3 fluid ounces milk

Simmer cranberries and apples in water about 10 minutes.

Blend 3 ounces sugar, 1 ounce butter, and spices with cranberries and apple. Pour mixture into a baking dish which has been brushed with butter, reserving enough to make pastry spirals.

To make dough for spirals, sift together the flour, 2 tablespoons sugar, baking powder, and salt. Rub in 2 ounces butter with pastry blender or 2 knives. Add milk, stirring until flour is just moistened.

Place on floured board, roll ½-inch thick. Brush with melted butter. Spread with remaining cranberry-apple mixture, drained. Roll as for Swiss roll. Cut into 1-inch slices. Arrange slices, cut-side down, over cranberry mixture.

Bake in a hot oven (425°F. Mark 7) about 20 minutes, or until crust is nicely browned. Serve warm, or chilled with whipped cream. Serves 6.

Cranberry Grunt

CHERRY ROLY POLY

8 ounces sifted flour
3 teaspoons baking powder
2 ounces sugar
¾ teaspoon salt
2 to 3 ounces lard
3 to 4 fluid ounces milk
about 12 ounces tinned stoned sour
    cherries
4 ounces sugar
2 tablespoons cornflour
8 fluid ounces cherry liquid

Mix and sift flour, baking powder, 2 ounces sugar, and salt.

Rub in lard until mixture has fine even crumbs. Add enough milk to make a soft dough.

Turn onto a lightly-floured surface and knead gently ½ minute. Roll into rectangle ¼ inch thick.

Drain cherries and save juice. Place cherries on dough and roll as for Swiss roll. Cut into 1-inch slices. Place cut surface down in greased 9-inch square baking-tin.

Mix sugar and cornflour. Add enough water to cherry juice to make 8 fluid ounces and add to sugar-cornflour mixture. Cook until thick and clear.

Bake rolls in hot oven (425°F. Mark 7) 15 minutes.

Pour juice over rolls and bake 10 minutes longer. Makes 8 to 10 rolls.

ALMOND GÂTEAU

4 ounces butter
3 ounces light brown sugar
2 tablespoons thick honey
6 ounces plain flour
2 eggs
4 tablespoons milk
1 teaspoon almond essence

Filling:

3 ounces butter
1½ tablespoons thick honey
4 ounces icing sugar
flaked toasted almonds

Grease and line a 7-inch round cake tin with greased paper.

Cream butter, sugar and honey together until soft and light. Gradually beat in eggs, adding a spoonful of flour between each one. Fold in sifted flour, then milk and almond essence. Turn into the prepared tin and bake in a moderate oven (350°F. Mark 4) for minutes.

Filling: Cream butter well, add honey and sugar, and beat well together. Fill and cover the top of the cake and sprinkle liberally with the almonds.

PINEAPPLE MERINGUE CAKE

2 ounces plain flour
¾ teaspoon baking powder
pinch of salt
2 eggs
6 ounces castor sugar
2 ounces butter
½ teaspoon vanilla essence
3½ tablespoons milk
    chopped blanched almonds
1 small can drained crushed
    pineapple
¼ pint double cream

Grease two 8-inch sandwich tins. Sift flour, baking powder and salt together. Beat egg yolks until thick and honey coloured. Then gradually beat in 2 ounces sugar. Add well-creamed butter and vanilla. Mix well. Then beat in flour and milk. Spread the mixture evenly between the two tins and chill.

Beat egg whites stiffly, fold in remaining sugar and spread on top of each cake. Sprinkle thickly with chopped almonds, pressing them into surface of the cakes. Bake in a low oven (300°F. Mark 2) for about 50 minutes.

When cold, sandwich layers with a little pineapple and whipped cream mixed together, and cover top with remaining pineapple and whipped cream.

SPICY APPLE SAUCE CRUNCH

16 digestive biscuits, finely rolled
    into crumbs
4 ounces butter or margarine
3 ounces brown sugar
1 teaspoon cinnamon
1 pound thick tart apple sauce

Sauté biscuit crumbs in butter or margarine until browned; mix in sugar and cinnamon.

Pour apple sauce into 8-inch round baking dish or 9-inch pie dish. Top with crumbs.

Bake in slow oven (325°F. Mark 3) 30 minutes. Serve hot garnished with whipped cream and redcurrant jelly. Serves 6.

APPLE ROLY POLY

scone, biscuit or shortcake dough
2 ounces butter or margarine
3 tablespoons sugar
½ teaspoon cinnamon
3 or 4 tart apples, diced
3 ounces brown sugar
1 tablespoon lemon juice
4 fluid ounces water

Prepare recipe for scone, biscuit or shortcake dough and pat dough into a rectangle about ½ inch thick. Brush with soft butter, sprinkle with sugar and cinnamon mixture.

Spread diced apples over this. Roll like Swiss roll. Cut into 1½-inch crosswise slices.

Place slices cut-side up in a buttered

baking dish about 2 inches deep, leaving space between.

Make a syrup of brown sugar, lemon juice, and water. Pour over pastry.

Bake in hot oven (400°F. Mark 6) 30 to 40 minutes. Serve warm, with whipped or single cream. Serves 6.

Fruit Dumplings: Follow Roly Poly recipe, patting dough to ¼-inch thickness. Cut into individual servings (squares or triangles). Fill with fruit, moisten edges with milk, pinch together. Bake in the syrup.

ANGEL FOOD SURPRISE CAKE

1½ ounces cherry-flavoured
    gelatine
8 fluid ounces hot water
about 2 to 3 ounces pitted red
    cherries
1 bakers' 13½-ounce white sponge
    cake
¼ teaspoon vanilla
6 fluid ounces double cream,
    whipped

Dissolve cherry gelatine in water and stir until dissolved. Chill until slightly thick; fold in cherries.

Slice ½ inch of cake away from inner rim of white sponge cake and cut it into ½-inch cubes; add to cherry gelatine. Refill cake centre with cherry gelatine and cake mixture.

Add vanilla to whipped cream. Cover top and sides of cake with whipped cream. Place in refrigerator until ready to serve. Serves 8.

Angel Food Surprise Cake

Gelatine Desserts

Many wonderful desserts are made from a gelatine base. These are usually called creams, whips, or snows, according to the fruit combination, such as Bavarian Cream, Lemon Snow, or Prune Whip. Other desserts may be combinations of fruit, gelatine, or cream fillings plus cake or biscuit foundation. These are often an ideal way of using the last of the biscuits, sponge, or plain cake or extending a small amount of a food to make a tempting sweet.

Snow puddings attain a characteristic light airy texture through the addition of egg whites which have been folded in when the gelatine mixture begins to set. The same holds true of Bavarian creams except that whipped cream takes the place of the egg whites.

FRUIT WHIP

1 tablespoon unflavoured gelatine
2 fluid ounces lime juice
1 teaspoon grated lime rind
6 fluid ounces syrup from tinned fruit cocktail
4 ounces sugar
¼ teaspoon salt
few drops almond essence
8 fluid ounces chilled evaporated milk
12 ounces drained tinned fruit cocktail
ladyfingers or macaroons (optional)

Soften gelatine in lime juice. Combine lime rind, syrup from fruit cocktail, sugar, and salt; heat, and dissolve softened gelatine in it. Blend in almond essence. Cool until slightly thickened.

Whip chilled evaporated milk in chilled bowl until light and fluffy. Fold in gelatine mixture. Fold in well-drained fruit cocktail. Chill a few minutes, until mixture mounds on a spoon.

Line fruit dish with ladyfingers, and spoon pudding into dish. Chill several hours, or overnight. Garnish with additional fruit cocktail, if desired. Serves 6 to 8.

Fruit Whip

FRUIT COCKTAIL MOULD

1 16-ounce can fruit cocktail
1 packet strawberry-flavoured gelatine
1 tablespoon unflavoured gelatine
2 tablespoons cold water
16 fluid ounces milk
2 eggs, separated
2 ounces sugar
¼ teaspoon salt
2 tablespoons sugar
1 teaspoon vanilla

Drain fruit cocktail thoroughly. Dissolve fruit-flavoured gelatine according to directions on packet, replacing part of water with syrup drained from fruit cocktail. Chill until slightly thickened.

Fold in fruit cocktail. Pour into bottom half of ring mould or other fancy mould. Chill until firm.

Soften unflavoured gelatine in 2 tablespoons water.

Heat milk to scalding in top of double saucepan. Beat egg yolks, sugar, and salt together until light. Slowly stir in hot milk.

Return to double saucepan. Cook, stirring constantly, until mixture coats spoon.

Remove from heat; add gelatine and stir until dissolved.

When cool and slightly thickened, fold in egg whites beaten stiff with remaining sugar and vanilla.

Pour into top half of mould. Chill until firm. Serves 6.

APPLE SAUCE BAVARIAN PIE

1 tablespoon unflavoured gelatine
2 fluid ounces cold water
1 pound, 2 ounces apple sauce
1 (15 ounces) can sweetened condensed milk
3 ounces lemon juice
2 ounces orange juice
1 tablespoon grated orange rind
2 egg yolks
1 packet chocolate biscuits (2¼-inch diameter)
4 fluid ounces double cream

Soften gelatine in water. Heat apple sauce; add gelatine. Stir until dissolved. Cool.

Combine condensed milk, lemon juice, orange juice, orange rind, and egg yolks; stir until mixture thickens. Add apple sauce; mix well.

Line bottom and sides of 9-inch pie dish with chocolate biscuits, standing biscuits around edge. Cover with ½ apple sauce mixture. Add layer of biscuits, cover with remaining apple sauce mixture. Place an overlapping circle of biscuits on top. Chill. Just before serving; whip cream stiff, use as garnish. Serves 8.

Raspberry Mould Dessert

RASPBERRY MOULD DESSERT

1 packet raspberry-flavoured gelatine
8 fluid ounces hot water
9 ounces tinned apple sauce
2 tablespoons sugar
1 teaspoon grated lemon rind
1 tablespoon lemon juice
2 to 3 ounces chopped walnuts
about 12 small marshmallows
4 fluid ounces double cream, whipped

Dissolve raspberry gelatine in hot water; add apple sauce, sugar, lemon rind and juice. Chill over iced water until slightly thickened. Fold in walnuts and marshmallows.

Pour into 1½-pint mould. Chill until firm. Unmould and serve with whipped cream. Serves 6.

SNOW PUDDING

1 tablespoon unflavoured gelatine
4 fluid ounces cold water
6 fluid ounces boiling water
6 ounces sugar
¼ teaspoon salt
2 fluid ounces lemon juice
1 teaspoon grated lemon rind
2 egg whites, stiffly beaten

Soften gelatine in cold water. Add boiling water, sugar, and salt. Stir until dissolved. Add lemon juice and rind.

Chill until mixture is slightly thicker than consistency of unbeaten egg whites. Whip until light. Add stiffly beaten egg whites.

Place bowl in iced water. Continue beating until mixture begins to hold its shape. Pour into large or individual moulds. Chill until firm.

Unmould and serve with custard sauce, chocolate sauce, or fresh crushed berries or fruit. Serves 6.

Apple Sauce Bavarian Pie

ABOUT CHARLOTTES

A true charlotte is a fruit pudding, traditionally of apples only, cooked in a mould lined with bread that has been dipped in melted butter. Today a vast variety of dishes are referred to as charlottes. They include many types of cold moulded dishes; cream fillings, jelly fillings, mixtures of nuts and fruits in various fillings, ices, etc., prepared in moulds lined with ladyfingers, sponge cake, biscuits, etc. The Charlotte Russe usually specifically refers to a cold dessert of Bavarian cream stiffened in a mould lined with savoy fingers or sometimes with cake.

COFFEE CHARLOTTE RUSSE

1   tablespoon unflavoured gelatine
4   ounces sugar
⅛   teaspoon salt
2   tablespoons instant coffee
10 fluid ounces milk
2   eggs, separated
½   teaspoon vanilla
8   fluid ounces double cream,
      whipped
savoy fingers or sponge cake

In top of double saucepan, mix gelatine, 2 ounces sugar, salt, and coffee. Stir in cold milk. Place over boiling water and scald, stirring constantly.

Beat egg yolks slightly. Slowly pour small amount of hot mixture over egg yolks. Return to double saucepan and cook, stirring constantly, until mixture coats spoon, about 3 minutes.

Remove from heat and add vanilla. Chill until mixture is slightly thicker than consistency of unbeaten egg white.

Beat egg whites until stiff and gradually beat in remaining sugar. Fold in gelatine mixture and whipped cream.

Spoon into individual serving dishes which have been lined with savoy fingers or sponge cake.

Chill until firm. Garnish with additional whipped cream, walnuts, or chocolate biscuit crumbs. Serves 10.

Coffee Charlotte Russe

LEMON JELLY
(Basic Recipe)

2 tablespoons unflavoured gelatine
4 fluid ounces cold water
1 pint boiling water
6 ounces sugar
⅛ teaspoon salt
6 fluid ounces lemon juice
1 teaspoon grated lemon rind

Soften gelatine in cold water 5 minutes. Add hot water, sugar, and salt; stir until dissolved.

Add fruit juice and grated rind. Pour into moulds and chill until firm.

Serve with plain or whipped cream, custard sauce, or fruits. Serves 6 to 8.

Lemon Jelly Variations
Fruit Bavarian Cream: When jelly begins to set, beat until foamy. Fold in 8 fluid ounces double cream which has been whipped and sweetened.

Add preferred fruit pulp. Mould and chill.

Fruit Jelly: Substitute tinned fruit juices for water. If juices are sweet, they may replace sugar as well as the liquid and flavouring.

Add fruit when jelly starts to set.

Jelly Squares: Cut firm jelly into cubes. Pile one or more colours in each glass or serve with cubed fruit.

Grape Jelly: In basic recipe substitute 1 teaspoon orange rind for lemon rind. Reduce sugar to 4 ounces and reduce lemon juice to 1 tablespoon.

Substitute 12 fluid ounces grape juice for same amount water.

Lemon Snow or Sponge Pudding: When jelly begins to set, beat with a whisk until foamy.

Beat 2 to 3 egg whites until stiff and beat into gelatine foam. Mould and chill.

Moulded Fruit Salads: Use lemon jelly to mould fruits, vegetables, fish, or meat.

Tomato juice, chicken, or meat stock may be substituted for liquid; seasonings may be varied.

For specific recipes see salads.

Orange Jelly: In basic recipe substitute 12 fluid ounces orange juice for 8 fluid ounces water. Reduce lemon juice to 2 fluid ounces. Substitute orange rind for lemon rind.

Prune Jelly: In basic recipe, substitute 12 fluid ounces prune juice for same amount liquid.

Add 2½ ounces each of raisins, cooked chopped prunes, and chopped nuts. Mould and chill.

Riced Jelly: Chill jelly until very firm. Force through potato ricer. Pile into serving dishes. Combine several colours of jelly per serving.

Whipped Jelly: When jelly is soft and quivery, beat with a whisk until light and fluffy. Mould or pile into serving dishes.

Please read about gelatine
in **Ingredients**—
How to Use Them.

LALLA ROOKH CREAM

3 eggs, separated
4 ounces sugar
4 fluid ounces single cream
1 tablespoon unflavoured gelatine
2 tablespoons cold milk
1 tablespoon rum
8 fluid ounces double cream,
      whipped

Beat yolks and add sugar and cream. Cook over hot water, stirring constantly, until mixture coats spoon.

Soften gelatine in 2 tablespoons cold milk; add to mixture and stir until dissolved.

Remove from heat. Cool, add rum, stiffly-beaten egg whites, and whipped cream.

Turn into mould. Chill until mixture holds its shape. Serve garnished with maraschino cherries and cherry juice. Serves 4.

APPLE-STRAWBERRY SNOW

1 tablespoon unflavoured gelatine
2 fluid ounces cold water
1 pound 2 ounces tinned apple
      sauce
¼ teaspoon nutmeg
pinch of salt
about 3 to 4 ounces sliced, fresh
      strawberries
1 teaspoon vanilla
2 egg whites
3 ounces sugar

Soften gelatine in cold water 5 minutes. Combine apple sauce, nutmeg, and salt; heat. Add gelatine, stirring until dissolved. Cool until slightly thickened. Add strawberries and vanilla.

Beat egg whites stiff, gradually add sugar, beating constantly. Fold into apple sauce mixture. Pour into 1½-pint mould; chill until firm. Unmould on serving dish. If desired, garnish with whipped cream and whole strawberries. Serves 6 to 8.

Apple-Strawberry Snow

Apricot Charlotte Russe

APRICOT CHARLOTTE RUSSE

1½ tablespoons unflavoured gelatine
12 fluid ounces apricot juice
2 eggs, separated
4 ounces sugar
⅛ teaspoon salt
5 fluid ounces evaporated milk
3 tablespoons lemon juice
8 fluid ounces evaporated milk,
    chilled icy cold

Soften gelatine in 4 fluid ounces of the apricot juice.

Beat egg yolks, sugar, and salt in the top of a double saucepan. Gradually add the remaining apricot juice, then the 5 fluid ounces evaporated milk.

Cook over boiling water until thickened, about 7 to 10 minutes, stirring constantly.

Add softened gelatine to the custard and stir until gelatine is dissolved. Remove from heat and cool.

When the mixture is slightly thicker than unbeaten egg white, add lemon juice. Then whip the chilled milk very stiff and fold into the apricot mixture.

Spoon into a charlotte mould that has been lined with vanilla wafers or sponge fingers.

Chill until set, about 2 to 3 hours. Makes 8 generous servings.

SHERRY JELLY

2 tablespoons unflavoured gelatine
2 fluid ounces cold water
10 fluid ounces boiling water
6 ounces sugar
¼ teaspoon salt
2 fluid ounces orange juice
2 tablespoons lemon juice
8 fluid ounces sherry

Soften gelatine in cold water 5 minutes. Add boiling water, sugar, and salt. Stir until dissolved.

Add orange and lemon juices and sherry. Mix well. Turn into moulds and chill. Serves 6.

BAVARIAN CREAM
(Basic Recipe)

1 tablespoon unflavoured gelatine
2 fluid ounces cold water
2 egg yolks
4 ounces sugar
¼ teaspoon salt
8 fluid ounces milk
8 fluid ounces double cream,
    whipped
½ teaspoon vanilla

Soften gelatine in cold water 5 minutes.

Beat egg yolks with sugar and salt. Add to milk and cook in double saucepan until thick. Add softened gelatine. Stir until dissolved.

Cool and, when mixture begins to thicken, fold in whipped cream and vanilla.

Turn into dampened mould and chill. Unmould and serve with fruit sauce. Serves 6.

Butterscotch Bavarian Cream: In basic recipe, omit granulated sugar. Cook 3½ ounces brown sugar with 1 ounce butter a few seconds, then add to hot mixture.

Maple Bavarian Cream: In basic recipe, substitute flaked maple sugar for granulated sugar. Add 2 ounces chopped pecans or walnuts.

STRAWBERRY BAVARIAN CREAM
(Basic Recipe)

1 tablespoon unflavoured gelatine
2 tablespoons cold water
½ to ¾ pound crushed strawberries
about 4 ounces sugar
⅛ teaspoon salt
1 tablespoon lemon juice
8 fluid ounces double cream,
    whipped

Soften gelatine in cold water 5 minutes. Place over hot water; stir until dissolved.

Remove from heat. Add strawberries, sugar, salt, and lemon juice. Mix well.

Cool until slightly thickened. Fold in whipped cream. Turn into mould and chill. Bottom of mould may be garnished with whole strawberries.

Unmould and serve plain, or with additional whole strawberries and whipped cream. Serves 6.

**Variations of
Strawberry Bavarian Cream**

Apricot Bavarian Cream: In basic recipe, substitute diced apricots for strawberries.

Berry-Banana Bavarian Cream: In basic recipe, substitute 3 to 4 mashed ripe bananas for half of the crushed strawberries.

Macaroon Bavarian Cream: In basic recipe, add 3 to 4 ounces crushed macaroons with whipped cream.

Nut Bavarian Cream: In basic recipe, add 3 ounces chopped nuts with whipped cream.

Peach Bavarian Cream: In basic recipe, substitute diced peaches for strawberries.

Raspberry Bavarian Cream: In basic recipe, substitute crushed raspberries for strawberries.

CHARLOTTE RUSSE

Line sorbet glasses with sponge fingers, then strips of angel food or sponge cake, or macaroons.

Fill with any Bavarian cream mixture; garnish with pieces of fruit. Chill.

CHOCOLATE SPONGE
(Basic Recipe)

1½ tablespoons unflavoured
    gelatine
2 fluid ounces cold water
1½ ounces cooking chocolate
3 ounces sugar
¼ teaspoon salt
2 fluid ounces boiling water
3 eggs, separated
1 teaspoon vanilla

Soften gelatine in cold water 5 minutes.

Melt chocolate in top of double saucepan; add sugar, salt, and boiling water. Bring to boil.

Remove from heat; add softened gelatine and stir until dissolved. Slowly add to slightly-beaten egg yolks.

Chill until mixture begins to thicken, then fold in stiffly-beaten egg whites and vanilla.

Turn into dampened mould and chill. Serve with whipped cream. Serves 6.

Variations of Chocolate Sponge

Chocolate Charlotte: Prepare chocolate sponge recipe. Line mould with sponge fingers or sponge cake before pouring into gelatine mixture.

Macaroon-Chocolate Sponge: To basic recipe, add 3 to 4 ounces crushed macaroons.

Nut-Chocolate Sponge: To basic recipe, add 3 ounces chopped nuts.

Fruit Bavarian Cream

Double-Ring Dessert

SPANISH CREAM
(Basic Recipe)

1 tablespoon unflavoured gelatine
2 fluid ounces cold water
16 fluid ounces milk, scalded
3 eggs, separated
4 ounces sugar
⅛ teaspoon salt
1 teaspoon vanilla

Soften gelatine in cold water 5 minutes; add scalded milk, stirring to dissolve gelatine.

Combine egg yolks, sugar, salt, and gelatine mixture in top of double saucepan. Cook over hot water 5 minutes, stirring constantly until sugar is dissolved.

Cool until slightly thickened. Add vanilla. Fold in stiffly beaten egg whites. Turn into moulds. Chill until firm.

Unmould and serve with chocolate sauce, whipped cream, or fruit. Serves 6.

Variations of Spanish Cream

Chocolate Spanish Cream: Follow basic recipe. Melt 2 ounces cooking chocolate in milk. Beat with whisk until blended.

Coffee Spanish Cream: In basic recipe, increase sugar to 5 ounces. Substitute 12 fluid ounces fresh hot coffee for same amount milk.

Macaroon Spanish Cream: Follow basic recipe. Fold 3 ounces crushed macaroons into egg whites.

Orange Spanish Cream: In basic recipe, omit vanilla and water. Add ½ teaspoon each grated lemon and orange rind and 1 tablespoon lemon juice. Reduce scalded milk to 12 fluid ounces. Soften gelatine in 4 fluid ounces orange juice.

Angel Cream Loaf

DOUBLE-RING DESSERT

2 packets lemon-flavoured gelatine
1 pint hot water
1½ pints vanilla ice cream
2 ounces toasted slivered almonds
3 ounces chopped maraschino cherries

Dissolve gelatine in hot water in 4½-pint saucepan. Spoon in ice cream; stir until melted.

Chill until thickened but not set (about 15 to 25 minutes); fold in almonds and cherries. Turn into 2 1½-pint ring moulds. Chill until firm.

(If only one ring mould is available, make up half the recipe, turn out of mould when set, then make other half.)

To serve, cut a section (about ⅛ from one ring, place inside second ring and line up remaining ⅞ of cut ring alongside to give entwined circles effect. Serves 12.

ANGEL CREAM LOAF

20 thin wafers
2 tablespoons sugar
¼ teaspoon salt
1 tablespoon unflavoured gelatine
1 pound, 2 ounces tinned apple sauce
3 egg yolks, beaten
½ teaspoon ground mace
1 tablespoon lemon juice
3 egg whites
2 tablespoons sugar
8 fluid ounces double cream

Line an 8½ × 4½ × 2¾-inch pan with greaseproof paper. Place 3 wafers in bottom of pan.

In top of double saucepan mix 2 tablespoons sugar, salt, and gelatine. Add apple sauce and egg yolks. Stir well. Cook over boiling water, stirring constantly, until gelatine is dissolved, about 7 minutes.

Remove from heat; stir in mace and lemon juice. Chill until mixture is the consistency of unbeaten egg white.

Beat egg whites until they hold a stiff peak. Add 2 tablespoons sugar, beating constantly. Fold into apple sauce mixture until well blended. Whip cream; fold into mixture.

Spoon ¼ of mixture on top of wafers in prepared pan. Add a layer of wafers. Repeat 3 times, ending with apple sauce mixture. Chill in refrigerator several hours or overnight. Unmould on serving dish. Peel off paper. If desired, serve with additional whipped cream. Serves 8.

RUM PUDDING

1 tablespoon unflavoured gelatine
6 fluid ounces milk
3 egg yolks
3 ounces sugar
¼ teaspoon salt
2 tablespoons rum

8 fluid ounces double cream, whipped

Soften gelatine in 2 fluid ounces milk 5 minutes. Heat remaining milk and dissolve softened gelatine in it.

Beat egg yolks and sugar until light and fluffy; add salt, rum, and dissolved gelatine. Chill.

When partially thickened, fold in whipped cream. Turn into individual moulds. Chill.

Unmould and serve with a fruit sauce. Serves 4 to 6.

FRUIT MOUSSE

12 ounces sugar
2 tablespoons grated orange rind
4 fluid ounces boiling water
2 tablespoons unflavoured gelatine
3 fluid ounces cold water
12 fluid ounces orange juice
3 fluid ounces pineapple juice
3 ounces dried milk
6 fluid ounces iced water
3 fluid ounces lemon juice
4 ounces chopped, drained maraschino cherries
4 ounces drained, crushed tinned pineapple
6 ounces chopped blanched almonds

Chill a small bowl and whisk for whipping dried milk.

Put sugar, grated orange rind, and boiling water into saucepan. Stir and boil 1 minute.

Soften gelatine in cold water. Dissolve it in the hot syrup. Add orange juice and pineapple juice.

Cool until mixture is partially set and of a jelly-like consistency. When gelatine mixture has thickened, fold in whipped dried milk.

To whip dried milk, put iced water in chilled bowl, sprinkle dried milk on top. When mixture is partially whipped, add lemon juice and beat until stiff (about 10 minutes).

After folding in whipped dried milk, fold in cherries, nuts, and pineapple.

Pour into 2½-pint mould or 2 refrigerator trays and put in refrigerator until set. Serve garnished with fresh or tinned fruit. Serves 10 to 12.

Fruit Mousse

Chilled Lemon Fluff

CHILLED LEMON FLUFF

18 to 20 large wafers, crushed
    finely
3 ounces melted butter or
    margarine
1 tablespoon unflavoured gelatine
2 fluid ounces cold water
3 eggs, separated
4 ounces sugar
¼ teaspoon salt
5 fluid ounces evaporated milk
3 fluid ounces water
1 teaspoon vanilla
8 fluid ounces evaporated milk,
    whipped
grated rind and juice of 1 lemon

Chill bowl and whisk to whip evaporated milk.

Mix wafer crumbs and butter thoroughly. Press thin layer over sides and bottom of lightly buttered 8-inch square cake tin. Set in refrigerator.

Soften gelatine in 2 fluid ounces cold water.

Mix egg yolks, sugar, salt, evaporated milk, and the 3 fluid ounces water in top of double saucepan. Cook until mixture thickens.

Add softened gelatine and stir until dissolved. Add vanilla and fold in stiffly beaten egg whites.

Chill until slightly congealed. Fold in whipped evaporated milk.

To whisk evaporated milk, first chill milk in ice-cube tray until crystals form around edge. Pour in chilled bowl. Add lemon juice after it is partially whipped and continue beating until it stands in peaks.

Fold in grated lemon rind. Pour into crust and chill until firm. Garnish with flaked milk chocolate or plain chocolate. Serves 9.

Prune Chiffon Melva

CRANBERRY WHIP

12 fluid ounces cranberry juice
1 packet lemon gelatine
4 fluid ounces evaporated milk,
    icy cold

Heat 8 fluid ounces juice. Pour over lemon gelatine. Stir until gelatine is dissolved. Add remaining juice. Set in cool place to jell.

When mixture begins to jell, beat with egg whisk until light and fluffy.

Beat cold evaporated milk in chilled bowl until very stiff. Fold into gelatine mixture. Spoon into individual moulds or 1 large mould and chill until firm. Serves 4 to 6.

STRAWBERRY GELATINE WHIP

1 teaspoon grated lemon rind
8 ounces sugar
1 tablespoon unflavoured gelatine
2 fluid ounces cold water
2 fluid ounces boiling water
3 tablespoons lemon juice
8 to 10 ounces crushed fresh straw-
    berries
4 egg whites
⅛ teaspoon salt
whipped cream

Mix lemon rind and 4 ounces sugar. Soften gelatine in cold water and dissolve in boiling water. Add sugar mixture and stir until dissolved. Add lemon juice and berries. Chill over bowl of ice cubes.

When thickened and completely chilled, whip mixture until frothy.

Beat egg whites with salt until stiff. Gradually beat in remaining 4 ounces sugar, blending well. Fold into gelatine mixture.

Spoon into fruit dishes and chill. Serve with whipped cream. Serves 8.

PRUNE CHIFFON MELVA

1 tablespoon unflavoured gelatine
4 fluid ounces cold water
2 ounces sugar
¼ teaspoon salt
2 5-ounce cans strained cooked
    prunes
3 tablespoons lemon juice
1 teaspoon Angostura bitters
8 fluid ounces double cream,
    whipped or 5 fluid ounces
    icy-cold evaporated milk,
    whipped

Sprinkle gelatine in cold water, place over boiling water in double saucepan and stir until dissolved. Add sugar and salt, stir until dissolved; remove from heat. Add prunes, lemon juice, and bitters.

Chill mixture until it is slightly thickened. Fold into whipped cream or whipped evaporated milk; pile gelatine mixture into sorbet or fruit dishes and chill until firm. Serves 4 to 6.

Cranberry Whip

PARTY DESSERT TO SERVE 25

1 1-pound 4½-ounce can pineapple
    segments
2 12-ounce packets frozen sliced
    peaches, thawed
2 10-ounce packets frozen sliced
    strawberries, thawed
2 packets strawberry-flavoured
    gelatine
3¼ pints double cream
4 ounces icing sugar
¼ teaspoon salt
1 teaspoon ginger
1 7¼-ounce packet coconut-
    covered marshmallow
    biscuits, cut in pieces

Drain fruit; combine peach and strawberry syrups and add enough water to make 1½ pints. Heat to boiling. Add strawberry gelatine, stirring until gelatine is dissolved. Cool.

Combine cream, sugar, salt, and ginger. Whip until cream holds peaks. Fold in drained fruits (cut peaches, if very large) and coconut-covered marshmallow biscuit pieces. When gelatine is firm enough to mound when dropped from a spoon, fold into cream.

Turn into 3 greased moulds in graduated sizes, 6-inch, 7-inch, and 8-inch. Freeze until firm. Unmould and stack together. Garnish with sliced fresh strawberries, whipped cream, and coconut-covered marshmallow biscuits. Serves 25.

Party Dessert to Serve 25

Pastel Snow Squares

PASTEL SNOW SQUARES

1 3-ounce packet strawberry-
     flavoured gelatine
12 fluid ounces hot water
3 egg whites
¼ teaspoon salt
about 12 digestive biscuits, crushed
Sauce:
   3 egg yolks
   3 ounces sugar
   4 ounces butter or margarine
   1 tablespoon grated lemon rind
   1 tablespoon lemon juice
   4 fluid ounces double cream,
     whipped

Dissolve gelatine in hot water. Chill
until thick and syrupy. Beat egg whites
with salt until stiff but not dry. Fold
into gelatine. Turn into a 9-inch square
tin. Chill until moulded.

Cut jelly into squares. Roll each
square in biscuit crumbs. Pile in sorbet
glasses and top with sauce.
Sauce: Beat egg yolks until thick and
lemon-coloured, gradually adding
sugar. Blend in melted butter, grated
lemon rind, and lemon juice. Fold in
whipped cream. Chill about 1 hour.
Serves 6.

Two-In-One Strawberry Charlotte

CHRISTMAS STAR MOULDS

1 tablespoon unflavoured gelatine
4 fluid ounces cold milk
2 ounces sugar
¼ teaspoon salt
about 6 to 8 ounces sliced, stoned
     dates
12 fluid ounces milk
2½ ounces sliced glacé cherries
1½ ounces slivered, blanched
     almonds
½ teaspoon vanilla
¼ teaspoon almond essence
4 fluid ounces cream, whipped

Soften gelatine in cold milk about 5
minutes.

Combine sugar, salt, dates, and milk
and heat together to scalding. Remove
from heat; add gelatine and stir to dissolve.

Chill mixture until it begins to set.
Stir in fruits and flavourings. Whip
cream and fold in.

Turn into individual star moulds or
1½-pint mould that has been rinsed in
cold water. Chill until set. Serve with
whipped cream. Serves 6.

BANANA BAVARIAN CREAM

1 packet lemon-flavoured gelatine
¾ pint hot water
¼ teaspoon salt
5 ounces sugar
4 fluid ounces heavy cream
5 bananas

Dissolve gelatine in hot water. Add
salt and sugar. Chill until cold and
syrupy.

Fold in cream, whipped only until
thick and shiny, but not stiff.

Crush bananas to pulp with silver
fork and fold at once into mixture.
Chill until slightly thickened. Turn
into mould.

Chill until firm. Unmould. Serve
with tart fruit sauce. Serves 8.

TWO-IN-ONE STRAWBERRY
CHARLOTTE

1 tablespoon unflavoured gelatine
2 tablespoons cold water
10 to 12 ounces finely crushed
     strawberries
1 tablespoon lemon juice
6 ounces sugar
⅛ teaspoon salt
8 fluid ounces heavy cream,
     whipped
sugar biscuits

Soften gelatine in cold water 5 minutes. Place over boiling water; stir
until dissolved. Blend in strawberries,
lemon juice, sugar, and salt. When
almost set, fold in whipped cream.

Line 1½-pint mould or casserole with
sugar biscuits. Spoon in strawberry
mixture. Chill several hours until
firm. Serves 6.

Christmas Star Moulds

GINGER-ORANGE
REFRIGERATOR PUDDING

1 tablespoon unflavoured gelatine
2 tablespoons cold water
16 fluid ounces milk
2 tablespoons cornflour
4 ounces sugar
2 egg yolks, beaten
8 fluid ounces orange juice
2 tablespoons grated orange rind
2 egg whites, stiffly beaten
½ pound crumbled ginger biscuits

Soften gelatine in cold water. Scald
milk in top of double saucepan.

Sift together cornflour and sugar.
Add milk. Cook 10 minutes, stirring
constantly.

Gradually add small amounts of hot
pudding to beaten egg yolks until
both are combined.

Return to double saucepan and cook
an additional 2 minutes, stirring constantly.

Remove from heat and add softened
gelatine, orange juice, and rind. Let
chill 1½ hours.

Fold stiffly beaten egg whites into
pudding.

Line pudding dishes with ginger biscuits. Fill with alternate layers of
orange pudding and biscuits, ending
with layer of biscuits.

Chill in refrigerator several hours or
overnight. Garnish edge of dishes with
biscuit halves. Serves 8.

Ginger-Orange Refrigerator Pudding

RUSSIAN CREAM WITH STRAWBERRIES

4 teaspoons unflavoured gelatine
2 fluid ounces cold water
16 fluid ounces single cream
2 ounces sugar
16 ounces sour cream
about 16 ounces fresh or frozen strawberries
double cream, whipped

Soften gelatine in cold water.

Combine cream and sugar; heat to scalding but do not boil.

Dissolve softened gelatine in hot cream and sugar mixture. Chill until it begins to thicken, stirring occasionally.

Fold in sour cream, blending until smooth. Turn mixture into an oiled 1½-pint mould. Chill until firm.

Unmould on serving dish. Top with strawberries and garnish with whipped cream. Serves 8.

APRICOT-ORANGE REFRIGERATOR DESSERT

1 tablespoon unflavoured gelatine
2 fluid ounces cold water
4 fluid ounces hot water
4 fluid ounces tinned apricot juice
4 fluid ounces orange juice
1 tablespoon lemon juice
2 ounces sugar
few grains of salt
2 egg whites
about 18 crushed macaroons
whole macaroons

Soften gelatine in cold water. Add hot water and stir until dissolved. Add fruit juices, sugar, and salt. Chill.

When thickened, beat with wire whisk until frothy. Fold in stiffly-beaten egg whites and crushed macaroons.

Line mould with additional macaroons. Fill with whipped mixture. Chill 6 hours.

Unmould and garnish top with small drained apricot halves, alternating with orange segments. Serves 6.

ANGEL FOOD GELATINE DESSERT

1 packet strawberry- or raspberry-flavoured gelatine
16 fluid ounces boiling water
8 fluid ounces double cream, whipped
about 12 ounces crumbled angel food (white sponge) cake
1 packet frozen strawberries or raspberries

Dissolve gelatine in boiling water and let stand until partially thickened.

Whip thickened gelatine until light and fluffy. Fold in whipped cream and angel food cake pieces. Chill in 3-pint mould until firm.

Unmould and garnish with thawed berries and additional whipped cream. Serves 8.

ORANGE BAVARIAN CREAM

2 tablespoons unflavoured gelatine
4 fluid ounces cold water
4 fluid ounces boiling water
8 ounces sugar
4 to 5 tablespoons lemon juice
12 fluid ounces orange juice and pulp
¼ teaspoon salt
3 egg whites
16 fluid ounces cream, whipped

Soften gelatine in cold water 5 minutes. Add boiling water and sugar; stir until dissolved. Add lemon and orange juice and pulp.

Chill until partially set, then whisk until foamy.

Add salt to egg whites and beat until stiff; fold into gelatine. Fold in whipped cream and turn into a dampened mould.

Chill until firm. Unmould on platter and garnish with orange segments. Serves 8 to 10.

Variations: Substitute other fresh fruits or cooked dried fruits for orange juice and pulp. Use drained juice instead of orange juice. Reduce sugar in accordance with sweetness of cooked fruit.

ORANGE CHARLOTTE RUSSE

Line mould with split sponge lady fingers. Fill with orange Bavarian cream mixture.

SHERRY CREAM

1 teaspoon grated lemon rind
½ pint milk
2 tablespoons sugar
few grains salt
2 slightly beaten egg yolks
1 tablespoon unflavoured gelatine
2 fluid ounces cold water
¼ teaspoon vanilla
2 tablespoons sherry
2 egg whites
8 fluid ounces cream
2½ tablespoons icing sugar

Add lemon rind to milk and scald in top of double saucepan over simmering water.

Add sugar and salt to egg yolks and blend. Pour hot milk gradually over egg yolks, stirring constantly.

Return to top of double saucepan and cook over simmering water, stirring constantly, until mixture thickens. Remove from heat.

Meanwhile soften gelatine in cold water 5 minutes. Add to hot custard and stir to dissolve completely. Add vanilla and sherry and blend well.

Whisk egg whites until stiff but not dry, then fold carefully into mixture. Chill until mixture begins to thicken.

Whisk cream until stiff, adding icing sugar gradually. Fold into custard mixture. Turn into mould.

Cover with greaseproof paper. Place in refrigerator to chill until firm.

Unmould on serving plate and cover with thawed but icy-cold frozen strawberries. Serves 6.

PEAR MINT DELIGHT

1 12-ounce jar mint jelly
2 teaspoons unflavoured gelatine
2 fluid ounces cold water
juice of 2 lemons
8 fluid ounces cream, whipped
1¼ pounds tinned large pear halves, drained
2 fluid ounces crème de menthe
6 maraschino cherries

Beat jelly with fork until broken into small pieces. Soften gelatine in cold water, then dissolve over hot water.

Add lemon juice and gelatine to jelly.

Fold in whipped cream. Spoon into sorbet dishes.

Place a pear half in each dish.

Pour 2 teaspoons crème de menthe over each pear. Garnish centres with maraschino cherries. Chill thoroughly. Serves 6.

BANANA GELATINE DESSERT

1 packet fruit-flavoured gelatine or 1 tablespoon unflavoured gelatine
2 ripe firm bananas
dessert sauce, any preferred flavour

Mix gelatine according to packet directions. Chill only until slightly thickened.

Partly fill 1 pint-sized mould with gelatine (4 to 6 individual moulds may be used in place of 1 large mould).

Peel bananas, slice and arrange on top of the gelatine. Fill mould with remaining gelatine. Chill until firm.

Unmould. Garnish with additional slices of ripe banana or other fruit, if desired.

Serve plain or topped with cream, custard sauce or fruit sauce.

Serves 4 to 6.

Banana Gelatine Salad: Serve with sour cream, mayonnaise, or a tart French-style salad dressing. Garnish with crisp lettuce.

Banana Gelatine Dessert

LIME AND GRAPEFRUIT BAVARIAN

1 large tin grapefruit segments
1 packet lime-flavoured gelatine
2 ounces sugar
¾ pint evaporated milk, chilled
    icy cold
1 ounce coarsely chopped pecans,
    toasted

Drain juice from grapefruit segments. There should be ½ pint. If not, add water to make that amount. Heat to boiling point.

Combine gelatine with the sugar. Pour hot grapefruit juice over gelatine-sugar mixture and stir until dissolved.

Chill mixture to the consistency of unbeaten egg white. Then whip chilled milk very stiff, and fold lightly but thoroughly into the gelatine mixture.

Put a grapefruit segment into the bottom of each of 8 sorbet glasses. Pile Bavarian on top and garnish each serving with grapefruit segments. Chill at least 2 hours.

Just before serving, toast pecans in a moderate oven (375°F. Mark 5) until crisp, about 5 minutes, and sprinkle over the top of each serving. Makes 8 generous servings.

BASIC CLEAR ORANGE GELATINE—FIVE WAYS

1 tablespoon unflavoured gelatine
4 fluid ounces cold orange juice
½ pint hot orange juice
3 ounces sugar
⅛ teaspoon salt

Soften gelatine in cold orange juice. Add hot orange juice, sugar, and salt; stir until dissolved.

Pour into moulds and chill until firm. Serves 4.

ORANGE SPANISH CREAM

Use recipe for orange gelatine with the following changes.

Soften gelatine in 8 fluid ounces cold milk in top of double saucepan.

Place over boiling water. Add sugar

and salt and stir until gelatine and sugar are dissolved.

Beat 2 egg yolks slightly. Pour small amount of hot mixture slowly over egg yolks. Return to double saucepan and cook over hot, not boiling water, stirring until mixture coats spoon.

Remove from heat; cool. Stir in 6 fluid ounces cold orange juice; chill until mixture is slightly thicker than unbeaten egg white consistency.

Beat 2 egg whites until stiff; fold in gelatine mixture. Turn into moulds and chill until firm.

ORANGE CHARLOTTE

Use recipe for orange gelatine with the following changes.

Reduce hot orange juice to 8 fluid ounces.

Chill mixture until slightly thicker than unbeaten egg white consistency.

Whip 8 fluid ounces double cream and fold into gelatine mixture. Turn into moulds and chill until firm. If desired, serve with chocolate sauce.

ORANGE SNOW

Use recipe for orange gelatine with the following changes.

Reduce hot orange juice to 8 fluid ounces; increase sugar to 4 ounces.

Chill until mixture is slightly thicker than unbeaten egg white consistency; beat with wire whisk until light and fluffy.

Beat 2 egg whites until stiff; add gelatine mixture. Place bowl in ice water; continue to beat until mixture begins to hold its shape. Turn into moulds and chill until firm.

ORANGE WHIP

Use recipe for orange gelatine with the following change.

Chill gelatine mixture until slightly thicker than unbeaten egg white consistency; whisk until light and fluffy. Turn into moulds and chill until firm.

RICE TIGER PARFAIT

White Layer:
1 tablespoon unflavoured gelatine
6 fluid ounces milk
1 teacup hot rice
4 ounces sugar
½ teaspoon salt
4 fluid ounces double cream,
    whipped

Dark Layer:
8 fluid ounces milk
1 teacup cooked rice
2 tablespoons cocoa
2 ounces sugar
¼ teaspoon salt
¼ teaspoon vanilla

White Layer: Soften gelatine in 6 fluid ounces cold milk until dissolved. Then add 1 teacup hot cooked rice. Add 4 ounces sugar and ½ teaspoon salt and let cool.

When cold, fold in cream which has been whipped stiff. Chill until firm.
Dark Layer: Heat 8 fluid ounces milk in double saucepan. Add 1 teacup cooked rice. Add cocoa which has been mixed with 2 ounces sugar and ¼ teaspoon salt. Cook about 35 minutes until thick, stirring occasionally. Add vanilla. Chill.
To Assemble: When both mixtures are cool, layer light and dark rice mixtures in sorbet glasses. Chill.

Serve plain or topped with sweetened whipped cream and maraschino cherries. Serves 4.

RICE STRAWBERRY BAVARIAN

4 fluid ounces cold water
1 tablespoon unflavoured gelatine
1 teacup hot cooked rice
2 ounces sugar
¼ teaspoon salt
1 teaspoon vanilla
8 fluid ounces double cream,
    whipped
3 to 4 ounces mashed strawberries

Pour cold water into saucepan and sprinkle gelatine on top of water. Let stand 5 minutes.

Place saucepan over low heat and stir until gelatine has dissolved. Add hot cooked rice, sugar, salt, and vanilla. Mix well and cool.

When mixture begins to thicken, fold in cream which has been whipped. Add mashed strawberries and mix well. (Some strawberries are sweeter than others, so taste for sweetness.)

Turn into greased mould or individual moulds or pile into individual fruit dishes.

If rice strawberry Bavarian has been moulded, chill until firm. Then unmould and serve with sliced sweetened strawberries. Serves 5.

Orange Gelatine Desserts

Refrigerator Cakes

The term refrigerator cakes covers a wide variety of chilled desserts usually of some kind of small cakes, pieces of cake, or wafers combined with a filling of whipped cream, gelatine mixtures, fruits, nuts, etc. They are made at least several hours before serving and are kept cold in the refrigerator.

MARSHMALLOW REFRIGERATOR CAKE

    2 teacups marshmallows, quartered
    6 fluid ounces double cream
    8 ounces stale cake crumbs
    3 tablespoons chopped nuts
    3 tablespoons chopped maraschino
       cherries
    1½ ounces chopped dates

Soak marshmallows in cream ½ hour. Add remaining ingredients.

Press mixture into a mould. Let stand in refrigerator overnight. Serves 6.

CHOCOLATE REFRIGERATOR TORTE

    2 ounces cooking chocolate
    4 ounces sugar
    2 fluid ounces milk
    4 beaten egg yolks
    8 ounces butter or margarine
    5½ ounces icing sugar
    4 stiffly beaten egg whites
    ¼ teaspoon salt
    lady fingers or sponge cake

Melt chocolate over hot water in top of double saucepan.

Combine sugar, milk, and beaten egg yolks. Add to chocolate and cook until thick and smooth. Cool.

Cream butter until very soft. Add icing sugar and cream thoroughly. Add chocolate mixture and mix well.

Fold in stiffly beaten egg whites to which salt has been added.

Pour into straight-sided cake or torte tin that has been lined with lady fingers.

Chill in refrigerator several hours. Serve with whipped cream to which crushed peppermint rock has been added. Serves 6.

Chocolate Refrigerator Torte

ORANGE REFRIGERATOR CAKE

    5 tablespoons lemon juice
    4 fluid ounces orange juice
    1 teaspoon grated orange rind
    ⅛ teaspoon grated lemon rind
    ¼ teaspoon vanilla
    3 tablespoons chopped, blanched
       almonds
    15 fluid ounces sweetened con-
       densed milk
    lady fingers or sponge cake

Combine fruit juices, grated rind, vanilla, almonds, and condensed milk.

Line mould with greaseproof paper. Put layer of lady fingers in bottom. Cover with fruit mixture and another layer of lady fingers, repeating until mixture is used, and topping with lady fingers.

Chill overnight. Slice. Serves 6.

ANGEL FOOD CHOCOLATE TORTE

    1 large angel food (white sponge)
       cake
    8 ounces unsalted butter or
       margarine
    14 ounces icing sugar
    1½ teaspoons vanilla
    2 ounces plain chocolate, melted
    6 tablespoons cocoa
    ⅛ teaspoon salt
    ¾ pint double cream
    2 ounces salted pistachio nuts,
       chopped

Slice cake into 3 layers.

Cream butter well. Beat 11 ounces icing sugar into the butter and cream well. Add 1 teaspoon vanilla and melted chocolate. Mix well and spread between layers.

Mix and sift remaining icing sugar, cocoa, and salt. Add to the cream and chill 2 hours or more.

Add ½ teaspoon vanilla to cream and whip until stiff. Spread on top and sides of cake. Sprinkle chopped nuts around sides of cake.

Chill thoroughly (2 hours or more) before serving. Serve 12 to 16.

MOCHA LOG

    8 fluid ounces double cream
    1½ ounces icing sugar
    1 tablespoon instant coffee
    20 chocolate wafers
    chocolate curls (see below)

Whip cream with icing sugar and instant coffee until stiff. Spread chocolate wafers with cream and put together in stacks of 4 or 5. Freeze until cream is set.

Lay stacks on edge on a plate to make one long roll. Spread remaining cream on outside of roll. Freeze.

Remove from freezer about one hour before serving and store in refrigerator. Garnish with chocolate curls. (To make chocolate curls, slightly soften, but do not melt, a large bar of milk chocolate. Use potato peeler to shave curls from the chocolate.) To serve, slice diagonally. Serves 6 to 8.

Strawberry Angel Cake

STRAWBERRY ANGEL CAKE

    1 large white sponge cake
    icing sugar
    1 10-ounce packet frozen strawberries
    juice from strawberries plus water
       to make 8 fluid ounces
    1 3-ounce packet strawberry-
       flavoured gelatine
    4 ounces melted marshmallows
    1 ounce double cream
    8 fluid ounces evaporated milk
    2 tablespoons lemon juice

Prepare cake by cutting around cake ¾-inch in from the outer edge and ½-inch in from centre edge. Cut to within 1 inch of bottom. Remove cut bits with a fork. Dust icing sugar on sides of cake.

Defrost strawberries. Drain juice. Add water to make 8 fluid ounces liquid. Heat to boiling.

Place gelatine in large bowl. Add hot liquid. Stir until dissolved. Mix melted marshmallows with 1 ounce cream and add to hot gelatine. Stir until blended. Chill until consistency of unbeaten egg white.

Chill evaporated milk in refrigerator tray until soft crystals form around edges (about 10 to 15 minutes). Whip until stiff (about 1 minute). Add lemon juice and whip until very stiff (about 2 minutes longer).

Fold strawberries and whipped evaporated milk into marshmallow mixture until well blended. Fill cake cavity and ice top with mixture. Chill until firm (about 3 hours). Slice. Garnish with strawberries. Serves 8 to 10.

Mocha Log

Chocolate Crumb Cake

CHOCOLATE CRUMB CAKE

18 large wafers
2 ounces butter or margarine, melted
pinch of salt
16 fluid ounces milk
3 tablespoons cornflour
4 ounces sugar
¼ teaspoon salt
3 eggs, separated
1 tablespoon unflavoured gelatine
3 tablespoons cold water
1½ teaspoons vanilla
2 ounces finely chopped nuts
grated chocolate

Crush wafers with rolling pin (there should be about 1½ teacups); combine thoroughly with butter and pinch of salt.

Press firmly onto sides and bottom of buttered 7½-inch charlotte mould or straight-sided baking tin; set in refrigerator to chill.

Add milk to cornflour which has been combined with ¼ sugar and the salt. Add this mixture to slightly beaten egg yolks in top of double saucepan. Cook over hot water until mixture is smooth and thickened; stir constantly.

Soften gelatine in cold water and set in pan of boiling water to melt. Add to custard.

Remove from heat and fold in egg whites, beaten stiff with remaining sugar.

Cool; add vanilla and nuts and pour into crumb-lined tin.

Grate chocolate over top and set in refrigerator 3 to 4 hours, or until firm. Serves 8.

Note: Serve cake on large plate garnished with small bunches of white or green grapes and mint leaves. And when grapes are no longer in season, maraschino cherries with stems make a pleasant colour contrast.

Malt Loaf Cream Roll

PEACH REFRIGERATOR TORTE

4 ounces finely crushed digestive biscuits
5 tablespoons granulated sugar
2 ounces melted butter or margarine
6 fluid ounces juice from tinned peaches
⅛ teaspoon salt
2 teaspoons unflavoured gelatine
2 tablespoons lemon juice
¼ teaspoon grated lemon rind
4 fluid ounces double cream, whipped
about 12 ounces peach slices

Blend crumbs, 1 tablespoon sugar, and butter. Pat into bottom and half-way up sides of sandwich loaf tin (about 7½×3½×3 inches). Chill.

Heat juice, 4 tablespoons sugar, and salt together. Soften gelatine in lemon juice and dissolve in hot syrup. Blend in rind.

Cool until mixture reaches consistency of unbeaten egg white. Fold in whipped cream and well drained peach slices. Pour into crumb-lined tin.

Chill thoroughly. Cut into slices to serve. Serves 6.

VANILLA WAFER CAKE

Arrange a layer of vanilla wafers in bottom of a sandwich loaf tin.

Spread slightly sweetened whipped cream over wafers to a depth of about ¼ inch. Then place another layer of wafers and whipped cream, repeating until pan is ¾ full and ending with wafers.

Chill in refrigerator overnight. Serve with chocolate syrup.

MALT LOAF CREAM ROLL

6 ounces cream cheese
1 8-ounce malt loaf or 8-ounce can date and nut bread
1 tablespoon single cream or orange juice
1 tablespoon finely chopped crystal-lized ginger

Allow cream cheese to soften at room temperature. Meanwhile cut loaf into round slices about ⅜ inch thick.

Cream the cheese until fluffy. Stir in cream or orange juice. Add ginger.

Spread each slice evenly with cream cheese mixture. Place one slice on top of another. Ice entire roll with remaining cream cheese mixture.

Cover carefully so that cover does not touch roll and place in refrigerator until well chilled and cheese is firm, about 2 hours.

Just before serving, cut in diagonal slices to give striped appearance. Serves 6.

Chocolate Chiffon Cake

CHOCOLATE CHIFFON CAKE

12 sponge lady fingers
1 tablespoon unflavoured gelatine
4 ounces sugar, divided in half
¼ teaspoon salt
3 eggs, separated
6 fluid ounces milk
4 to 6 ounces plain chocolate, cut in pieces
1 teaspoon vanilla
5 fluid ounces cold evaporated milk, whipped

Split lady fingers; cut off one end to stand upright and fit sides of 8-inch spring-form tin.

Mix gelatine, ½ ounce sugar, and salt in top of double saucepan.

Combine egg yolks and milk; add to gelatine mixture. Add plain chocolate pieces.

Cook over boiling water, stirring occasionally, until gelatine is dissolved and chocolate is melted. Beat with wire whisk until blended.

Remove from heat; add vanilla. Chill until mixture mounds slightly when dropped from spoon.

Beat egg whites until stiff, but not dry. Gradually add remaining sugar and beat until stiff. Fold in chocolate mixture and whipped evaporated milk.

Turn into prepared tin; chill until firm. If desired, top with additional whipped cream and chocolate bits. Serves 8 to 10.

PINEAPPLE-NUT REFRIGERATOR CAKE

4 ounces butter or margarine
8 ounces sugar
3 egg yolks
8 ounces crushed canned pineapple
2 ounces chopped nuts
14 crumbled digestive biscuits
2 fluid ounces pineapple juice
4 fluid ounces double cream, whipped

Cream together butter and sugar. Add egg yolks and continue creaming until well blended. Add pineapple and nuts.

Arrange alternate layers of crumbs and pineapple mixture in a loaf tin, having crumbs as bottom and top layer.

Moisten with juice. Refrigerate for 12 hours. Serve in slices with whipped cream. Serves 6 to 8.

MOCHA REFRIGERATOR CAKE

2 teaspoons unflavoured gelatine
2 tablespoons cold water
8 fluid ounces hot water
1 tablespoon instant coffee
2 ounces sugar
⅛ teaspoon salt
8 fluid ounces double cream, whipped
about 3 ounces chocolate biscuit crumbs

Soften gelatine in cold water 5 minutes.

Combine hot water and instant coffee. Add softened gelatine to hot coffee, stirring until dissolved. Add sugar and salt. Mix well.

Chill, stirring occasionally, until mixture becomes syrupy. Fold into whipped cream.

Turn half into a loaf or spring-form tin which has been lined with greaseproof paper. Sprinkle with ½ the biscuit crumbs. Repeat, alternating layers of mixture and crumbs.

Chill in refrigerator until firm, about 6 hours.

Unmould and cut loaf cake into slices or round cake into wedges. Garnish with whipped cream if desired. Serves 6.

PEPPERMINT ROCK CAKE

¼ pound peppermint rock
4 fluid ounces milk
1 tablespoon unflavoured gelatine
2 tablespoons cold water
12 fluid ounces double cream, whipped
12 lady fingers, split

Put rock in cloth bag and pound with hammer to crush it. Add to milk and heat in double saucepan until melted.

Soften gelatine in cold water 5 minutes. Dissolve in hot peppermint mixture.

Chill until it thickens, then whip until light. Fold in whipped cream.

Line loaf tin with greaseproof paper and cover bottom with layer of split lady fingers. Add ½ of peppermint mixture, then add another layer of lady fingers, the remaining filling, and finally, the remaining lady fingers. Chill until firm.

Garnish servings with sweet chocolate bits, if desired. Serves 6.

Moulded Swiss Roll

STRAWBERRY CREAM CAKE

1 tablespoon unflavoured gelatine
2 fluid ounces cold water
about 4 to 6 ounces crushed strawberries
1 tablespoon lemon juice
4 ounces sugar
¼ teaspoon salt
12 fluid ounces double cream, whipped
24 lady fingers

Soften gelatine in cold water and dissolve over boiling water. Add to strawberries which have been combined with lemon juice, sugar, and salt.

Cool and, when mixture begins to congeal, fold in whipped cream.

Line sides and bottom of large square tin with split lady fingers. Cover with strawberry mixture. Top with layer of lady fingers, repeating until tin is full.

Chill. Unmould on large plate. Serves 6.

ALMOND REFRIGERATOR CAKE

5 ounces butter or margarine
11 ounces icing sugar
4 eggs, separated
1 teaspoon orange essence
¼ teaspoon almond essence
2 ounces shredded almonds
lady fingers
18 macaroons

Cream butter and sugar. Add egg yolks, beating well. Add essences and almonds.

Fold in stiffly beaten egg whites.

Line mould with lady fingers. Add layer of filling, then a layer of macaroon crumbs. Repeat until 3 layers of filling are used.

Cover with macaroons and chill at least 24 hours before serving. Serves 6.

MOULDED SWISS ROLL

1 packet raspberry-flavoured gelatine
8 fluid ounces boiling water
8 fluid ounces raspberry juice
12 ounces tinned drained raspberries
12 fluid ounces heavy cream, whipped
Swiss roll with red jam
additional 8 fluid ounces double cream, whipped
fresh raspberries

Dissolve gelatine in boiling water. Add berry juice. Set aside to thicken.

Fold tinned berries into whipped cream and add to gelatine mixture.

Line a spring-form tin with ½-inch-thick slices of Swiss roll. Pour in gelatine mixture and chill 5 hours in refrigerator.

Turn out on plate; garnish with whipped cream and fresh raspberries. Serves 10 to 12.

Variations: Use strawberries, blackberries, etc., instead of raspberries.

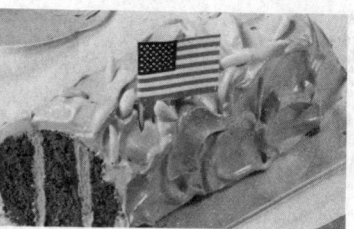

Chocolate Nut Cake

CHOCOLATE NUT CAKE

2 8-ounce chocolate cakes
4 rounded tablespoons peanut butter
8 fluid ounces double cream
1 ounce instant drinking chocolate
1 ounce slivered blanched almonds

Cut each chocolate cake into 10 round slices. Spread each slice, except one, with peanut butter. Stack slices and press together gently.

Whip heavy cream with drinking chocolate. Lay log on side; cover with whipped cream. Garnish with slivered blanched almonds. Chill.

To serve, slice on a diagonal. Serves 12 to 14.

PEACH BLOSSOM CAKE

1¾ pounds canned peach slices
1 tablespoon unflavoured gelatine
2 fluid ounces cold water
1 tablespoon lemon juice
12 ounces whipping cream
about 9 ounces crushed peanut crunch
1 8- or 9-inch bought round sponge cake
mint sprigs

Drain peach slices, saving juice. Chop peach slices; reserve a few for decorating. Heat 4 fluid ounces of the juice to boiling.

Soften gelatine in cold water; dissolve in hot peach liquid. Cool slightly and add chopped peaches and lemon juice. Chill until partially set.

Whip 4 ounces of the cream. Fold into peach mixture along with peanut crunch.

Slice cake in three layers. Fill with peach mixture; let stand in refrigerator at least 3 hours before serving.

Whip remaining cream; ice cake. Decorate with peach slices and mint sprigs. Serves 8 to 10.

Peach Blossom Cake

Yule Log

YULE LOG

21 digestive biscuits
1¼ pounds tinned apple sauce
1 teaspoon nutmeg
2 ounces finely chopped walnuts
4 fluid ounces double cream
glacé citron
red cinnamon sweets

Arrange 3 biscuits in row in loaf tin lined with greaseproof paper.

Combine apple sauce, nutmeg, and nuts. Add layer of apple sauce mixture; repeat, using 7 layers of biscuits and 6 layers of apple sauce, ending with layer of biscuits.

Chill in refrigerator several hours.

Just before serving, cover with whipped cream. Garnish with citron, cut in shape of holly leaves and red cinnamon sweets. Slice and serve. Serves 6.

Variation: Instead of whipped cream cover, a white cake icing may be used.

ALMOND-COFFEE REFRIGERATOR CAKE

8 ounces butter or margarine
about 8 ounces icing sugar
2 egg yolks, well beaten
4 fluid ounces cold extra strong coffee
⅛ teaspoon salt
1 teaspoon vanilla
2 ounces chopped toasted almonds
18 to 20 sponge lady fingers
whipped cream

Cream butter or margarine and cream in sugar gradually. Add egg yolks. Beat mixture until smooth and fluffy.

Add coffee, a little at a time, mixing enough to blend well after each addition. Add salt, vanilla, and chopped nuts.

Line loaf tin with greaseproof paper. Cover bottom of tin with split lady fingers flat-side-down.

Spread layer of coffee mixture over lady fingers. Cover with another layer of split lady fingers. Add more coffee mixture, then another layer of lady fingers.

Chill in refrigerator at least 4 hours. Turn out on small plate. Garnish with whipped cream. Serves 8.

VANILLA REFRIGERATOR CAKE PUDDING
(Basic Recipe)

6 ounces unsalted butter or margarine
8 ounces icing sugar
6 eggs, separated
about 1 teaspoon vanilla
sponge cake or lady fingers

Cream butter until light and fluffy. Add sugar. Cream well.

Beat in egg yolks, one at a time. Add vanilla or other flavouring. Fold in stiffly beaten egg whites.

Line mould with lady fingers or strips of cake. Cover with mixture. Chill in refrigerator 24 hours. Serves 6.

Variations of
Vanilla Refrigerator Cake Pudding

Chocolate: Melt 1½ ounces cooking chocolate. Add slowly to first mixture.

Fruit: Add 2 ounces each well-drained crushed pineapple and chopped maraschino cherries to mixture before folding in egg whites.

Lemon: Omit vanilla. Add juice and rind of 1 lemon to first mixture.

Macaroon: Add 3 ounces finely crushed, sifted macaroon crumbs to mixture before folding in egg whites.

LEMON REFRIGERATOR CAKE

8 ounces unsalted butter or margarine
8 ounces caster sugar
3 egg yolks, unbeaten
grated rind and juice of 1 lemon
3 egg whites
3½ dozen lady fingers

Cream butter and sugar together until very creamy. Add egg yolks and whisk until very light. Add grated lemon rind and juice and whisk.

Beat egg whites until stiff but not dry and fold into butter mixture.

Line bottom and sides of springform tin with lady fingers. Add filling and remaining lady fingers in layers, the top layer being lady fingers.

Refrigerate for 24 hours. Serve with whipped cream. Serves 8 to 10.

DIGESTIVE BISCUIT PASTRIES

4 fluid ounces double cream
2 tablespoons redcurrant jelly, whipped smooth
12 digestive biscuits

Whip cream stiff; blend in whipped jelly.

Spread cream on each biscuit and put together in stacks of 4. Ice outside of stacks with remaining cream.

Chill in refrigerator about 3 hours.

To serve, cut stacks in half. Make 6 pastries.

BANANA-RASPBERRY REFRIGERATOR CAKE

4 ounces raspberries or strawberries
5 ounces caster sugar
1 tablespoon unflavoured gelatine
2 fluid ounces cold water
¾ pint double cream
2½ dozen lady fingers
3 large ripe bananas, sliced

Pick over raspberries. Wash and drain. Add 4 tablespoons sugar and chill until ready to use.

Soften gelatine in cold water. Place over boiling water to dissolve.

Whip cream, beating in 4 tablespoons sugar gradually. Add gelatine and beat to smooth consistency.

Spread layer of whipped cream mixture over mould lined with lady fingers. Over this spread half the sugared raspberries.

Add another layer of lady fingers, then a layer of bananas, sprinkled with 2 tablespoons sugar. Add another layer of cream and finally a layer of lady fingers. Chill overnight. Serves 8.

CHOCOLATE REFRIGERATOR CAKE

4 ounces cooking chocolate
4 ounces sugar
dash of salt
2 fluid ounces hot water
4 eggs, separated
1 teaspoon vanilla
8 fluid ounces double cream, whipped
2 dozen lady fingers

Melt chocolate over hot water. Add sugar, salt, and water, stirring until sugar is dissolved and mixture is blended. Remove from boiling water.

Add egg yolks, 1 at a time, beating thoroughly after each addition.

Place over boiling water and cook 2 minutes, stirring constantly.

Remove from heat. Add vanilla and fold in beaten egg whites. Chill. Fold in whipped cream.

Line bottom and sides of a greaseproof paper-lined mould with lady fingers. Turn chocolate mixture into mould. Place remaining lady fingers on top. Chill overnight in refrigerator. Serves 8.

APRICOT REFRIGERATOR CAKE

3 ounces vanilla wafer crumbs
1 teaspoon unflavoured gelatine
2 tablespoons cold water
2 ounces butter or margarine
5½ ounces icing sugar
1 egg yolk
¼ teaspoon almond essence
12 cooked apricots, puréed
8 fluid ounces double cream

Line bottom of 8-inch-square cake pan with 2 ounces wafer crumbs.

Soften gelatine in cold water. Dissolve by placing in pan of hot water.

Cream butter or margarine and sugar until light and fluffy. Add egg yolk and almond essence and blend well. Blend in puréed apricots.

Whip cream and slowly whip in dissolved gelatine. Fold whipped cream into first mixture and spread over crumbs.

Top with remaining wafer crumbs. Chill in refrigerator overnight. Serves 8.

FRENCH REFRIGERATOR CAKE

about ½ pound vanilla wafer crumbs
4 ounces butter
5½ ounces icing sugar
2 beaten eggs
8 fluid ounces double cream, whipped
2 ounces chopped nuts
8 ounces drained, crushed pineapple

Place ½ the crumbs in ungreased, 8-inch square pan. Thoroughly cream butter and sugar; add eggs and beat well. Spread carefully over crumbs.

Combine cream, nuts, and pineapple. Spread over creamed mixture, then sprinkle with remaining crumbs. Let stand 18 to 24 hours. Cut in squares and serve on lace-paper doilies. Serves 8.

PINEAPPLE-CHERRY REFRIGERATOR TORTE

¼ pound vanilla wafer crumbs
4 ounces butter
5½ ounces icing sugar
2 beaten egg yolks
2 stiffly-beaten egg whites
1 8-ounce can crushed pineapple
1 3-ounce bottle maraschino cherries, chopped
12 fluid ounces double cream, whipped

Roll wafers to crumble; place half in 8-inch square cake tin. Thoroughly cream butter and sugar; add egg yolks and beat well. Fold in egg whites.

Spread over crumbs. Arrange pineapple, pineapple syrup, and cherries over creamed mixture.

Add cherry syrup to whipped cream; spread over fruit. Top with remaining crumbs. Chill in refrigerator overnight. Serves 8.

REFRIGERATOR FRUIT CAKE

4 ounces butter or margarine, melted
4½ ounces quick-porridge oats
1 pound chopped pecans or walnuts
1 tablespoon unflavoured gelatine
2 tablespoons water
1 teacup melted marshmallows
½ pound chopped dates
½ pound chopped figs
½ pound chopped glacé mixed fruits
½ teaspoon salt
2 teaspoons orange essence
8 fluid ounces cream, whipped
cherries
assorted glacé fruits

Combine butter or margarine, quick-porridge oats, and nuts. Toast until brown in shallow pan in hot oven (400°F. Mark 6). Turn frequently.

Soak gelatine in water 5 minutes. Dissolve over hot water. Add to melted marshmallows.

Mix ¾ of the toasted oats and nuts, marshmallows, dates, figs, mixed fruits, salt, and flavouring. Fold in whipped cream.

Sprinkle remaining toasted oats and nuts in bottom of greaseproof paper-lined 8-inch-deep charlotte mould or cake tin. Pack cake mixture into tin firmly. Cover and chill overnight.

Unmould and garnish with cherries and glacé fruit in any preferred design. Serves 8 to 10.

PEACH REFRIGERATOR CAKE

1 15-ounce can sweetened condensed milk
2 fluid ounces lemon juice
about 8 ounces sliced peaches
2 stiffly-beaten egg whites
2 dozen wafers

Blend milk and lemon juice thoroughly. Add sliced peaches. Fold in egg whites.

Line tin with greaseproof paper. Cover with fruit mixture, topping with layer of wafers. Repeat until fruit mixture is all used, topping with layer of wafers.

Chill in refrigerator 6 to 8 hours. Unmould. Remove greaseproof paper. Serves 6.

FROZEN TRIFLE

1 rich or sponge cake layer, 1-inch thick
4 fluid ounces sherry
2 ounces toasted almonds, chopped
6 ounces strawberry or raspberry jam
2 egg yolks
6 tablespoons sugar
pinch of salt
8 fluid ounces scalded milk
8 fluid ounces double heavy cream, whipped

Cut cake to fit refrigerator tray. Pour sherry over it slowly so that it will absorb the wine. Add half the nuts and cover with jam.

Beat together egg yolks, sugar, and salt. Pour scalded milk slowly over this. Cook over boiling water, stirring constantly, until the mixture coats a spoon.

Chill and add stiffly whipped cream. Pour over cake, cover with the remaining nuts, and place in freezing tray until frozen just enough to slice. Serves 6.

LEMON ANGEL REFRIGERATOR CAKE

1 tablespoon unflavoured gelatine
2 fluid ounces cold water
6 egg yolks, slightly beaten
6 ounces caster sugar
6 fluid ounces lemon juice
1½ teaspoons grated lemon rind
6 egg whites
6 ounces caster sugar
1 large white sponge or angel food cake
8 fluid ounces double cream, whipped

Soften gelatine in cold water. Combine egg yolks, 6 ounces sugar, and lemon juice and rind, and cook over hot water (not boiling) until mixture coats a spoon.

Remove from heat, add gelatine. Stir until dissolved; cool. Stir in a drop or two of yellow food colouring if you wish to deepen the colour.

Beat egg whites until stiff, and gradually add remaining sugar while beating constantly. Fold into custard.

Cut large white sponge cake into 3 layers. When filling is slightly congealed, spread between layers and very thinly over top and sides of cake.

Chill until nearly ready to serve, then ice with thin coating of whipped cream. Make about 5 flower decorations on top of cake, using pastel-coloured sugared almonds for petals.

CHOCOLATE RIBBON LOAF

1 packet chocolate blancmange mix
¾ pint milk
24 digestive biscuits
4 fluid ounces cream, whipped stiff

Prepare the blancmange mix according to directions on packet, using ¾ pint milk; cool.

Spread blancmange on digestive biscuits and put together in stacks of 4 or 5. Then lay stacks on edge on a long plate to make one long roll, with biscuits and pudding alternating. (Leave last biscuit plain.)

Spread rest of blancmange on top of loaf; ice sides and ends with whipped cream.

Chill in refrigerator about 3 hours. To serve, slice diagonally, at a 45° angle. Serves 6.

RUSSIAN TORTE

white sponge or angel food cake
2 tablespoons unflavoured gelatine
2 fluid ounces water
5½ ounces icing sugar
⅛ teaspoon salt
2 tablespoons strong liquid coffee
8 egg yolks
¾ pint double cream
1 teaspoon vanilla
2 ounces chopped almonds, roasted

Cut angel food cake in two, the bottom layer a little thicker than the top.

Soften gelatine in cold water about 5 minutes. Put over boiling water to dissolve.

Add caster sugar, salt, coffee, and set aside until it begins to jell.

In the meantime, have egg yolks well whisked, add the cream, beaten stiff, and vanilla.

Combine the two mixtures before the gelatine sets. Then beat thoroughly.

Spread between layers and over top. Sprinkle with almonds. Chill thoroughly.

CRANBERRY REFRIGERATOR CAKE

1 egg white
about 16 ounces cranberry sauce
2 ounces chopped nuts
sponge cake
4 fluid ounces cream, whipped and sweetened

Beat egg white until stiff. Combine with cranberry sauce and fold in chopped nuts.

Slice layers of sponge cake to fit a loaf tin. Alternate layers of cake and sauce until tin is full, finishing with a layer of cake.

Place weight on top. Let stand in refrigerator 8 hours.

Unmould. Garnish with whipped cream. Cut in slices to serve. Serves 6.

APPLE SAUCE REFRIGERATOR CAKE

2 teaspoons cornflour
4 ounces sugar
9 ounces apple sauce
½ ounce melted butter or margarine
4 eggs, separated
juice of 1 lemon
24 lady fingers

Combine cornflour, sugar, apple sauce, butter, and beaten egg yolks. Cook in top of double saucepan, stirring constantly, until thick.

Remove from heat. Add lemon juice and, when partially cold, fold in stiffly-beaten egg whites.

Spread layer of filling over small mould lined with split lady fingers. Cover with layer of lady fingers. Repeat until mould is filled. Chill 24 hours. Serves 6.

WALNUT PRINCESS CAKE

1 tablespoon unflavoured gelatine
3 tablespoons cold water
about 12 ounces maple syrup
pinch of salt
8 fluid ounces cream, whipped
2 ounces chopped walnuts
walnut halves
1 10-inch white sponge or angel food cake

Soften gelatine in cold water. Heat syrup and dissolve gelatine and salt in it. Cool until slightly thickened.

Fold in whipped cream and chopped walnuts. Chill a few minutes until mixture is almost set.

Spread on sides and top of large angel food cake or sponge cake. Decorate with walnut halves. Chill.

TOFFEE REFRIGERATOR CAKE

1 packet baker's sponge cake (2 layers)
1 packet butterscotch blancmange
¾ pint milk
8 fluid ounces double cream, whipped, or 1 can pressure-whipped cream

Cut sponge layers in half, crosswise, to make 4 layers.

Prepare blancmange as directed on packet, using the ¾ pint milk.

Press one of the cake layers into a medium-sized pudding basin. Add ⅓ of cooked blancmange, another cake layer, and so on, ending with the 4th cake layer. Chill several hours or overnight.

Unmould on serving plate. Swirl whipped cream on top and sides. Decorate with chocolate-tipped salted almonds (melt ½ ounce plain chocolate over the hot water, dip wide ends of almonds in chocolate). Serves 8.

FIG ROLL REFRIGERATOR CAKE

1 packet lemon-flavoured gelatine
8 fluid ounces hot water
2 packets fig rolls
1 small can evaporated milk
grated rind of ½ lemon

Dissolve gelatine in hot water. Chill until slightly thickened. Line baking tin or deep refrigerator tray with greaseproof paper; then line with fig rolls, standing them on end around sides of tin. Reserve half of the fig rolls for the top.

When gelatine is partially thick, beat it until light.

Chill evaporated milk and whip. Fold into gelatine, together with the lemon rind.

Pour half of mixture over fig rolls. Add a layer of crumbled fig rolls, then the rest of the gelatine mixture. Cover top with the rest of the whole fig rolls.

Chill until firm, then unmould, decorate with fig flowers, and serve with whipped cream. Serves 6 to 8.

Walnut Princess Cake

GINGER BISCUIT REFRIGERATOR CAKE

4 ounces soft butter or margarine
5½ ounces icing sugar
2 eggs
1 teaspoon vanilla
8 ounces pineapple, cut finely
3 bananas, cut finely
2 ounces chopped almonds
6 fluid ounces double cream, whipped
½ pound ginger biscuits, crushed

Cream butter and sugar. Beat in eggs and vanilla. Whip mixture until creamy.

Combine fruit, nuts, and whipped cream. Fold in 1 tablespoon icing sugar.

Cover bottom of a deep tin with crumbs. Pour creamed mixture over this, and sprinkle with crumb mixture.

Add layer of whipped cream mixture. Sprinkle remaining crumbs on top.

Chill in refrigerator overnight. Serves 6 to 8.

MAPLE REFRIGERATOR CAKE

about 9 ounces maple syrup
1 15-ounce can sweetened condensed milk
4 fluid ounces cream, whipped
24 vanilla wafers

Blend syrup and milk, and bring slowly to the boil in heavy saucepan. Cook gently until thickened, about 4 minutes. Cool and fold in cream.

Pour into a greaseproof paper-lined tin in a thin layer. Cover with a layer of wafers. Repeat until all of maple mixture is used. Finish with layer of wafers.

Chill in refrigerator 6 hours. Turn out onto a small plate. Remove greaseproof paper. Serves 6.

Fig Roll Refrigerator Cake

Miscellaneous Chilled Desserts

FRENCH CREAM PUDDING

½ pound vanilla wafers
4 ounces butter or margarine
5½ ounces icing sugar
2 eggs
8 fluid ounces cream, whipped
3 ounces black walnuts, finely chopped
about 5 ounces maraschino cherries, finely chopped

Crush vanilla wafers finely. Place ½ the crumbs in bottom of buttered loaf tin.

Cream together butter or margarine and sugar until light and fluffy.

Beat eggs until well blended and add to first mixture and blend well.

Fold in whipped cream, nuts, and cherries. Spread over crumbs. Top with remaining crumbs.

Chill in refrigerator 24 hours before serving. Cut in squares to serve.

Serves 6 to 8.

FRUIT FLUFFS

¾ pint double cream, whipped
about 14 ounces drained mandarin orange segments
8 ounces drained tinned pineapple titbits
about ½ pound seedless grapes
about 8 ounces sliced bananas
about 7 ounces maraschino cherries, cut in halves
1 10¼-ounce packet shortbread biscuits, crushed
½ teaspoon mace

Whip ½ the cream until stiff. Fold in ¾ of the mandarin orange segments and next four ingredients.

Line a 9-inch square tin with greaseproof paper, allowing edges to extend above tin. Spread half of the crushed shortbread mixed with mace evenly over bottom of tin; fill with fruit mixture, top with remaining crumbs. Chill overnight.

Remove from tin, cut into 10 rectangular pieces. Garnish individual pieces with reserved whipped cream and orange segments. Serves 10.

Fruit Fluffs

ALMOND-STRAWBERRY TRIFLE

1 packet vanilla blancmange mix
12 fluid ounces milk
pinch of salt
3 ounces orange juice or white wine
20 lady fingers
2 ounces toasted blanched slivered almonds
2½ ounces clear strawberry jam
8 fluid ounces whipping cream
additional almonds for garnish
fresh strawberries

Prepare blancmange as packet directs using only 12 fluid ounces milk and salt. Remove from heat and add 2 ounces orange juice. Chill.

To make trifle; arrange lady fingers over bottom and around sides of 8-inch spring-form tin or serving dish. Sprinkle with remaining orange juice and the almonds. Spoon on jam. Pour chilled blancmange over; refrigerate several hours.

Whip cream and spread over top of pudding. Garnish with additional almonds and fresh strawberries, or dollops of strawberry jam, if desired. Serves 6 to 8.

TOFFEE REFRIGERATOR DESSERT

4 ounces vanilla wafer crumbs
4 ounces butter or margarine
5½ ounces icing sugar
3 eggs, separated
1 ounce cooking chocolate, melted
½ teaspoon vanilla
2 ounces finely chopped nuts

Line bottom of 8-inch square cake tin or large freezing tray with ½ the vanilla wafer crumbs.

Cream butter or margarine and sugar together until light and fluffy. Whisk in slightly beaten egg yolks and melted chocolate.

Cool slightly and fold in stiffly beaten egg whites and vanilla. Spread over crumbs. Top with crumbs and nuts.

Place in freezing compartment of refrigerator to chill 24 hours. It will become firm but not frozen. Cut in squares and serve plain or top each serving with small scoop of ice cream.

Serves 6 to 8.

FRUIT COCKTAIL MARLOW

Cut ½ pound marshmallows into quarters and dissolve in 8 fluid ounces strong, hot coffee in the top of a double saucepan.

Cool until mixture begins to thicken. Fold in 8 fluid ounces whipped cream and 16 ounces drained canned fruit cocktail. Pour into sorbet glasses and chill. Serves 6.

Almond-Strawberry Trifle

PINEAPPLE REFRIGERATOR DESSERT

6 ounces vanilla sugar wafers
4 ounces butter or margarine
5½ ounces icing sugar
2 well-beaten eggs
4 large slices pineapple, cut up
8 fluid ounces double cream, whipped

Crush wafers. Line buttered 11×7×1½-inch cake tin with ¾ of the crumbs.

Cream butter and sugar together until light and fluffy; add eggs and blend thoroughly. Spread over crumbs.

Arrange pineapple pieces over egg mixture.

Whip cream and spread over pineapple. Sprinkle remaining crumbs over cream.

Cover with greaseproof paper. Refrigerate for 24 hours. Serves 8 to 10.

FRUIT SYLLABUB

¾ pint double cream
4 egg whites
3 ounces icing sugar
¼ teaspoon salt
2 ounces chopped blanched almonds
4 ounces glacé cherries, chopped fine
4 fluid ounces orange juice
1 teaspoon lemon juice
¼ teaspoon almond essence

Whip cream. Beat egg whites to soft-peak stage. Combine with the whipped cream. Fold in sugar and salt.

Add the almonds and cherries.

Combine juices and almond essence and fold into mixture.

Chill until very cold. Serve in sorbet or fruit dishes. Serves 10 to 12.

Fruit Cocktail Marlow

FROSTY SECRET

1 egg
6 ounces sugar
3 ounces cocoa
3 ounces margarine
4 ounces chopped pecans or
    walnuts
4 ounces vanilla wafer crumbs

Beat egg and sugar together until lemon-coloured and fluffy. Add cocoa and continue beating until well blended.

Add margarine to cocoa mixture and beat thoroughly. Add nuts and wafer crumbs.

Turn mixture into 8-inch pie dish and place in refrigerator several hours. Garnish with whipped cream.

Serves 8 to 12.

SCOTCH REFRIGERATOR DESSERT

1½ ounces butter or margarine
6 ounces brown sugar
1 ounce sifted flour
12 fluid ounces milk
2 eggs, separated
½ teaspoon vanilla
4 ounces chopped pecans or
    walnuts
1 box vanilla or ginger biscuits,
    crushed

Melt butter or margarine in top of a double saucepan over direct heat.

Mix sugar and flour; add to melted butter or margarine. Blend well.

Add milk, cook over hot water, stirring constantly, until thick and smooth. Cook 15 minutes longer.

Pour slowly over slightly beaten egg yolks, stirring constantly. Cook 2 minutes longer. Cool. Add vanilla.

Gently fold in stiffly beaten egg whites.

Cover bottom of refrigerator tray with ⅓ biscuit crumbs. Cover with ½ cooked filling; top with another layer of crumbs and chopped nuts. Continue until all are used.

Place in freezing compartment and chill several hours. To serve, cut into squares or oblong pieces. Top with whipped cream. Serves 6.

DOUBLE CHOCOLATE ROLL

8 fluid ounces double cream
2 ounces drinking chocolate
pinch of salt
23 large chocolate biscuits

Pour cream into well-chilled bowl; add chocolate and salt. Beat until cream stands in peaks.

Spread cream on chocolate biscuits and put together in stacks of 4 or 5. Then lay stacks on edge on a plate to make one long roll, with biscuits and cream alternating.

Spread remaining cream on outside of roll. Chill in refrigerator for 3 hours.

To serve, slice diagonally at a 45° angle about 1-inch thick. Serves 6.

CHEESE FREEZE

about 8 ounces chocolate biscuit
    crumbs
4 ounces soft butter or margarine
4 ounces caster sugar
4 eggs, separated
6 ounces granulated sugar
    (2 ounces in custard mix-
    ture, 4 ounces in egg whites)
1½ ounces flour
4 fluid ounces milk
2 tablespoons unflavoured gelatine
4 fluid ounces cold water
1½ pounds cottage cheese, sieved
grated rind of 2 lemons
2 tablespoons lemon juice
2 teaspoons lemon essence
1 teaspoon vanilla
8 fluid ounces double cream,
    whipped

Line a mould or tin with a mixture of chocolate biscuit crumbs, butter, and caster sugar.

Make a custard by combining egg yolks, 2 ounces sugar, and flour in top of double saucepan; gradually stir in warm milk and cook over boiling water for a few minutes.

Soften gelatine in cold water for 5 minutes; stir into custard. Let cool and add cheese, lemon rind, lemon juice, lemon essence, vanilla, and whipped cream.

Finally fold in stiffly-beaten egg whites to which 4 ounces sugar has been added. Turn into crumb-lined tin. Chill until firm. When ready to serve, garnish top with some chocolate crumbs and strawberry halves. Serves 10 to 12.

CHOCOLATE REFRIGERATOR DESSERT

4 fluid ounces milk
6 ounces sugar
5 beaten egg yolks
8 ounces butter or margarine
5½ ounces icing sugar
2½ ounces cooking chocolate,
    melted and cooled
5 egg whites
4 ounces fine vanilla wafers

Combine milk, sugar, and beaten egg yolks. Cook over low heat or over boiling water, stirring constantly, until thickened. Cool.

Cream together butter, caster sugar, and cooled chocolate; blend into cold custard mixture.

Beat egg whites stiff. Fold chocolate mixture into egg whites. Blend well.

Sprinkle half of crumbs over bottom of 8×8×2-inch tin. Pour above mixture into tin. Cover top with remaining crumbs.

Chill in refrigerator at least 12 hours. Cut into squares. Serve with whipped cream. Serves 12 to 16.

Cheese Freeze

MACAROON-MALLOW CRÈME

16 marshmallows, cut up
8 fluid ounces milk
10 almond macaroons
8 fluid ounces double cream,
    whipped
few grains salt
vanilla or almond flavouring

Dissolve marshmallows in milk over hot water. Cool.

Macaroons should not be too fresh. Break apart into coarse crumbs. (If macaroons are fresh, toast them in slow oven to dry out; then break up or crush coarsely.) Fold macaroon crumbs into whipped cream.

Fold in cooled marshmallow-milk mixture and salt. Add flavouring.

Freeze, stirring several times during freezing period, until firm. Serves 4.

CROWN ROYALE

½ pint boiling water
1 packet cherry-flavoured gelatine
¾ pint vanilla ice cream
vanilla wafers
maraschino cherries
whipped cream

Dissolve gelatine in boiling water. Stir in ice cream until well blended.

Chill until thickened, then place a small amount in bottom of 1½-pint casserole.

Carefully arrange vanilla wafers around edge of casserole; pour in remaining filling. Chill until set.

Unmould onto serving plate. Garnish with maraschino cherries, whipped cream, and a wafer in the centre, topped with a cherry. Serves 6.

Crown Royale

Frozen Desserts

TYPES OF FROZEN DESSERTS

The family of frozen desserts includes many kinds of delicacies which are divided into several types.

1. Ice Cream

a. Plain or old-fashioned ice cream: Milk or cream is sweetened, flavoured and frozen. It may or may not contain either gelatine or eggs.

b. French or cooked ice cream: Cream is folded into a custard foundation containing many egg yolks and the mixture is frozen.

c. American ice cream: Similar to French ice cream except that flour or cornflour is substituted for part or all of the egg yolks.

d. Parfait or Italian: Whipped cream and flavouring are folded into a foundation of beaten egg whites or yolks cooked with hot syrup, and the mixture is frozen.

e. Ice pudding: Actually French ice cream which has the egg whites added separately. Contains generous amounts of fruit or nuts.

2. Frozen Custard

Similar to French ice cream except that the egg whites are added separately. Usually has a lower fat content than is legal for ice creams.

3. Water-Ice

Fruit juice, sweetened with sugar, diluted with water and frozen. May or may not contain gelatine or eggs. Frappés are ices frozen to a slushy consistency.

4. Sorbet

Frozen mixture of fruit juice, sugar and milk, cream or ice cream. Usually contains a stabilizer such as gelatine.

5. Mousse

Still-frozen dessert of sweetened, flavoured whipped cream. May or may not contain fruits.

General Directions for Preparing Frozen Desserts in Refrigerator

1. Rapid freezing is important to make refrigerator ice creams that are smooth. Speed up freezing by turning temperature control to coldest point $\frac{1}{2}$ hour before preparing dessert. Allow control to remain at this point until dessert is frozen.

2. The dessert is apt to freeze more rapidly if ice cubes are not being frozen at the same time.

3. Measure sugar or any other sweetening agent carefully; excess sugar retards freezing.

4. Remove ice cubes from tray to be used and replace empty tray in refrigerator to chill while preparing dessert.

5. Pour mixture into cold tray and place tray in fastest freezing position in the unit. Usually this is the bottom of freezing unit.

6. For more rapid freezing, moisten inside bottom of freezing unit with a little water before replacing tray. This way the tray will contact the freezing unit immediately.

7. Most frozen desserts are smoother when whisked once during the freezing process. Freeze mix to consistency of mush (don't let it get too hard if you want a smooth product); empty into a chilled basin and whisk until fluffy but not melted. Return quickly to chilled tray moistened on bottom and continue to freeze.

8. When mix is frozen sufficiently, turn temperature control halfway between the coldest setting and normal.

9. When beating cream or egg whites for folding into half-frozen mixtures, beat them only until they hold a soft peak, not until stiff.

10. When beating egg whites, reserve 2 tablespoons sugar for each egg white to add gradually to the egg whites after the foamy stage is reached. This meringue-like mixture holds up better during the folding-in process than plain egg white does.

General Directions for Hand-Turned or Motor-Driven Freezers

1. A 1-quart freezer requires about 7 pounds of ice to freeze the dessert and pack it for 2 hours. A 2-quart freezer requires about 14 pounds. Allow a few extra pounds for the ice that melts while the dessert is being frozen.

2. Be sure ice is chipped from the top of the block in an ice refrigerator. Modern ice boxes are regulated so that ice must cover the bottom of the ice chamber to insure correct food compartment temperature.

3. Ice cubes from an automatic refrigerator can be used as an ice supply. 16 fluid ounces of water yield about 1 pound of ice.

4. Put pieces (or cubes) of ice into a canvas bag and crush with a mallet.

5. Finely crushed ice melts faster and hastens the freezing of ice cream.

6. Scald and cool the bucket, the cover and paddle of the freezer.

7. The ice cream mixture should be cold when it is put into the freezer. A warm mixture may result in a coarser-textured dessert.

8. Fill the bucket only two-thirds full. As the dasher turns, air is whipped into the dessert, causing it to "swell".

9. Ice cream freezes as heat from it is absorbed by the ice and salt. Ice alone is not cold enough to freeze foods; therefore, salt is added which lowers the temperature of the ice.

10. Use 7 parts ice to 2 parts freezing salt. This allows for a moderate rate of freezing so that a rather large amount of air may be incorporated. This helpes to produce a smooth ice cream. In addition, this proportion of ice to salt prevents waste of ice due to too rapid melting.

11. Churn the freezer a few times before adding the ice to be sure the freezer turns freely. Then, turn the handle while adding the ice and salt.

12. Turn the handle slowly for the first 3 minutes to chill the mixture thoroughly. Then churn rapidly to make desserts creamier.

13. When the handle becomes too difficult to turn, the dessert is frozen.

14. To improve flavour, let frozen desserts "ripen" 1 to 2 hours before serving. To do this, remove paddle, press down mixture in bucket with a spoon, place a cork in the hole of the lid and put the lid in place. Repack the freezer with a mixture of 3 parts crushed ice to 1 part freezing salt, and cover the freezer with newspapers or a heavy cloth.

15. The dessert can be ripened, also, in the tray of an automatic refrigerator. Pack the dessert firmly in tray, cover with a double layer of greaseproof paper and turn the control of the refrigerator to the coldest point. The dessert will remain smooth for several hours.

General Directions for Moulded Frozen Desserts

1. Use a regular ice cream mould, or an ordinary tin, such as a baking powder or coffee tin with a tightly fitting cover.

2. Chill mould thoroughly before filling with cold ice cream mixture.

3. Fill mould to overflowing. Cover with greaseproof paper and put on lid.

4. Seal lid edge with a piece of adhesive tape or a strip of cloth dipped in melted fat or candle wax, covering the crack completely. When fat or wax cools it hardens, making a seal to keep out the salty water.

5. Bury the mould in a mixture of 3 parts crushed ice to 1 part freezing salt. Cover ice mixture with newspaper or heavy cloth. Allow about 3 hours to freeze a quart-sized mould. Drain off water and add more ice and salt in same proportions, if necessary.

6. When frozen, remove mould, dip in warm water for a few seconds, or wrap in a cloth wrung out of hot water. Remove the strip around the lid, the cover and greaseproof paper. Invert on a serving dish.

Homemade Ice Creams

BASIC REFRIGERATOR ICE CREAM
(Uncooked Base)

2 teaspoons unflavoured gelatine
4 fluid ounces cold water
14 fluid ounces evaporated milk
4 ounces sugar
2 teaspoons vanilla
12 fluid ounces double cream, whipped

Soften gelatine in cold water. Dissolve in hot milk. Add sugar and vanilla. Cool.

Turn into freezing tray and chill until slightly thickened. Fold in whipped cream.

Return to tray and freeze to mush-like consistency. Turn into chilled bowl and beat until smooth, but not melted.

Return to cold tray and freeze. Makes about 1½ pints.

BASIC REFRIGERATOR ICE CREAM
(Cooked Base)

5 ounces sugar
1½ tablespoons cornflour
12 fluid ounces top of the milk
2 eggs, separated
2½ teaspoons vanilla
¼ teaspoon salt
8 fluid ounces single cream, whipped

Combine sugar and cornflour in top of double saucepan. Gradually stir in milk. Cook over boiling water, stirring constantly, until mixture thickens. Cover and cook 10 minutes.

Stir a little of hot mixture into beaten egg yolks. Add yolks to remaining hot mixture. Cook over hot, not boiling, water, stirring constantly for 3 minutes.

Cool. Add vanilla and salt. Fold beaten egg whites into cooled custard. Pour into refrigerator tray and freeze until firm throughout.

Remove to chilled bowl. Quickly beat with electric beater until smooth. Fold in whipped cream. Return to cold tray. Freeze. Makes 6 to 8 servings.

Variations of Refrigerator Ice Cream

Banana: Add 2 ripe mashed bananas and 1 teaspoon lemon juice with whipped cream.

Chocolate: Melt 2 ounces plain chocolate in milk; beat with wire whisk until blended. Increase sugar to 6 ounces. Use 1 teaspoon vanilla.

Cherry: Add 8 ounces chopped pitted cherries to chilled mixture just before folding in whipped cream.

Coffee: Substitute 4 fluid ounces strong coffee for same amount milk.

Frozen Pudding: Combine and add with the whipped cream, ½ teaspoon grated orange rind, 4 ounces mixed chopped glacé fruit, 2 ounces chopped maraschino cherries, and 3 tablespoons maraschino cherry juice.

Ginger: Add 2 tablespoons ginger syrup with vanilla. Add 3 tablespoons chopped preserved ginger with whipped cream.

Mint: Reduce vanilla to 1 teaspoon. Add oil of peppermint to taste (few drops) and green colouring.

Nut Crunch: Grind or crush ¼ pound nut crunch and fold in before final freezing.

Peach: Add 10 ounces mashed peaches to chilled mixture just before folding in whipped cream.

Pistachio: Use only 1 teaspoon vanilla. Add ½ teaspoon almond essence. Add green food colouring. Add 2 ounces chopped pistachio nuts with whipped cream.

Rasberry or Strawberry: Add 3 to 5 ounces crushed berries to chilled mixture just before folding in whipped cream.

BUTTER-PECAN ICE CREAM

¾ pint sweetened condensed milk
2 ounces melted butter or margarine
8 fluid ounces cold water
1 teaspoon vanilla
¾ pint double cream
4 ounces pecans or walnuts, chopped

Combine condensed milk and melted butter thoroughly. Add water and vanilla. Mix well and chill.

Whip cream until fluffy but not stiff. Fold into chilled mixture.

Pour into freezer tray and freeze to consistency of mush. Do not allow to freeze too much or ice cream will be coarse.

Remove half-frozen mixture from refrigerator. Scrape into a chilled bowl and beat until smooth but not melted.

Add nuts and blend in well. Return to freezing tray and freeze until firm. Serves 10 to 12.

PEPPERMINT ROCK ICE CREAM

2 tablespoons cornflour
8 ounces sugar
⅛ teaspoon salt
¾ pint single cream
3 well beaten egg yolks
3 egg whites, stiffly beaten
¾ pint double cream, whipped
1 teacup finely crushed peppermint rock

Mix cornflour, sugar, and salt in top of double saucepan. Add cream and cook over boiling water 10 minutes, stirring constantly.

Add small amount of hot mixture to egg yolks, and blend thoroughly. Return to double pan and cook 5 minutes longer, stirring constantly.

Cool. Fold in stiffly beaten egg whites and pour into large refrigerator tray. Freeze until mushy.

Turn into large chilled bowl and beat with electric or wire whisk until smooth. Fold in whipped cream and crushed rock. Blend thoroughly.

Return to cold refrigerator tray and freeze firm. Stir well once during first hour of freezing. Makes about 1½ pints

BUTTERSCOTCH ICE CREAM

1½ ounces butter or margarine
3 ounces brown sugar
8 fluid ounces milk
1½ tablespoons cornflour
2 tablespoons cold milk
pinch of salt
¼ teaspoon vanilla
8 fluid ounces double cream, whipped

Heat butter and sugar in top of double saucepan until butter is melted and well blended with sugar. Add 8 fluid ounces milk and heat to boiling.

Mix cornflour with 2 tablespoons cold milk; stir into butter and sugar mixture.

Add salt and cook, stirring constantly, until thickened.

Cool and add vanilla. Fold in whipped cream.

Turn into refrigerator tray. Freeze to a mush.

Remove to chilled bowl and beat quickly but thoroughly with wire whisk until smooth and fluffy. Return to tray and freeze. Serves 6.

CARAMEL ICE CREAM

3 tablespoons granulated sugar
8 fluid ounces milk
3 ounces icing sugar
⅛ teaspoon salt
1½ tablespoons flour
2 eggs, separated
16 ounces single cream
1 teaspoon vanilla

Stir granulated sugar in heavy frying pan over low heat until sugar is melted and becomes light brown in colour. Remove from heat. Gently stir in milk. Cook until sugar is dissolved.

Mix sugar, salt, and flour in top of double saucepan.

Add sugar-milk mixture. Cook over hot water until thickened, stirring constantly, about 15 minutes.

Combine with beaten egg yolks and cook 5 minutes longer, stirring constantly. Add cream and blend well.

Freeze in refrigerator tray until firm. Remove to chilled bowl.

Add vanilla and beat until mixture is light and creamy. Fold in stiffly beaten egg whites. Return to freezing tray. Freeze firm. Serves 8.

HAZELNUT ICE CREAM
16 fluid ounces milk
6 ounces sugar
1 tablespoon flour
¼ teaspoon salt
2 eggs, separated
2 teaspoons vanilla
¾ pint single cream
3 ounces chopped hazelnuts

Scald milk in top of double saucepan. Mix sugar, flour, and salt. Gradually stir into scalded milk. Cook 5 minutes over simmering water, stirring constantly.

Beat egg yolks slightly. Add about 4 fluid ounces hot milk mixture to egg yolks, blending well. Add to remaining milk and cook 2 minutes over simmering water, stirring constantly.

Chill. Add vanilla, cream, and nuts and blend well.

Beat egg whites until stiff but not dry and gently fold into mixture. Pour into 2 refrigerator trays. Freeze until nearly solid.

Turn into chilled bowl and beat until creamy. Return to trays and freeze firm. Makes about 2½ pints.

FRENCH ICE CREAM
(Freezer)
4 ounces sugar
⅛ teaspoon salt
5 slightly beaten egg yolks
16 fluid ounces scalded milk
cream
2 to 3 vanilla pods, crushed or 2 teaspoons vanilla

Mix sugar, salt, and egg yolks. Add scalded milk slowly, mixing well. Cook over hot water until mixture coats spoon, 5 to 8 minutes. Cool.

Strain and add cream and vanilla. Freeze. Makes about 2½ pints.

GELATINE ICE CREAM
(Freezer)
1 tablespoon unflavoured gelatine
2 tablespoons cold water
16 fluid ounces milk
6 ounces sugar
⅛ teaspoon salt
16 fluid ounces single cream
2 teaspoons vanilla

Soften gelatine in cold water.

Scald milk; add gelatine, sugar, and salt. Stir until dissolved. Cool.

Add cream and vanilla. Freeze. Makes about 2½ pints.

OLD-FASHIONED ICE CREAM
(Freezer)
1 pint, 12 fluid ounces single cream
8 ounces sugar
pinch of salt
2 teaspoons vanilla

Scald cream. Add sugar and stir until dissolved.

Add salt and vanilla. Cool and freeze. Makes about 2½ pints.

CUSTARD ICE CREAM
(Freezer)
16 fluid ounces milk
1 tablespoon flour
6 ounces sugar
¼ teaspoon salt
2 slightly beaten egg yolks
16 fluid ounces double cream
1 tablespoon vanilla

Scald 12 fluid ounces milk. Mix flour, sugar, and salt. Add remaining cold milk. Add scalded milk slowly.

Cook over hot water 7 minutes, stirring constantly.

Stir hot mixture slowly into egg yolks. Cook and stir 2 minutes longer. Cool.

Add cream and vanilla. Freeze. Makes about 2½ pints.

RENNET ICE CREAM
(Freezer)
2 to 3 teaspoons rennet (see directions on bottle)
1 pint, 4 fluid ounces lukewarm milk
6 ounces sugar
⅛ teaspoon salt
8 fluid ounces double cream
2 teaspoons vanilla

Mix ingredients, except rennet, and heat until lukewarm. Add rennet and mix well.

Let stand until slightly thickened. Freeze. Makes about 2½ pints.

FREEZER ICE CREAM VARIATIONS
(Use French, Gelatine, Custard, Old-Fashioned or Rennet Recipes)

Bisque: In basic recipe, substitute 2 tablespoons sherry for vanilla. Add 3 ounces chopped nuts before freezing.

Toffee Crunch: In basic recipe, add ¾ pound finely crushed toffee to mixture just before freezing.

Caramel: In basic recipe, add 2 fluid ounces caramel flavouring with cream and vanilla.

Burnt Almond: Add 4 ounces finely chopped, blanched, and toasted almonds to caramel ice cream mixture.

Chocolate: Melt 2 ounces plain chocolate. Add 2 fluid ounces hot water and blend thoroughly. Add to hot mixture in basic recipe.

Coffee: Scald 3 fluid ounces freshly-ground coffee with milk or cream. Strain before adding other ingredients. Omit vanilla in basic recipe.

Macaroon: In basic recipe, add 4 ounces crushed macaroons just before freezing. Reduce sugar to 4 ounces.

Maple: In basic recipe, substitute maple syrup or maple sugar for granulated sugar. If desired, stir in 4 ounces chopped nuts when partially frozen.

Mint: In basic recipe, substitute mint flavouring for vanilla; add green food colouring.

Peach: In basic recipe, use only 1 teaspoon vanilla; add ½ teaspoon almond essence. Just before freezing, add 16 ounces crushed peaches, sweetened to taste.

Peanut Crunch: In basic recipe, add ¾ teacup finely crushed peanut crunch to mixture just before freezing.

Peppermint: In basic recipe, add ¾ teacup finely crushed peppermint rock to mixture just before freezing.

Pineapple: In basic recipe, substitute 1 tablespoon lemon juice for vanilla. Add 16 ounces well-drained, crushed pineapple just before freezing.

Pistachio: To basic recipe, add 1 teaspoon almond essence and green food colouring. Add 3 ounces chopped pistachio nuts.

Strawberry or Raspberry: Combine 8 to 10 ounces mashed berries with 4 ounces sugar; add to basic recipe just before freezing.

Tutti-Frutti: In basic recipe, use only ½ teaspoon vanilla. Combine and add 4 teaspoons maraschino cherry juice, 4 ounces chopped maraschino cherries, 4 ounces drained crushed pineapple, and 2 ounces chopped nuts just before freezing.

AVOCADO ICE CREAM
(Freezer)
16 fluid ounces milk
4 ounces granulated sugar
¼ teaspoon salt
2 well-beaten eggs
8 fluid ounces double cream
1 teaspoon lemon essence
1 large sieved avocado

Combine milk, sugar, and salt; scald. Pour over eggs, stirring constantly. Add cream and lemon essence and cool.

Add fruit and mix thoroughly. Freeze in ice cream freezer. Makes about 1½ pints.

Since the smooth texture of this ice cream is due to the emulsified avocado oil, it is best done in a freezer.

Homemade Sorbets

REFRIGERATOR SORBET
(Basic Recipe)
2 teaspoons unflavoured gelatine
18 fluid ounces cold water
8 ounces sugar
pinch of salt
fruit and juice (see below)
2 egg whites

Soften gelatine in 2 fluid ounces cold water. Cook sugar and 16 fluid ounces water together 2 to 3 minutes. Add softened gelatine and dissolve thoroughly. Add salt and fruit juice.

Freeze in refrigerator tray to mush-like consistency.

Remove mixture to a chilled bowl and break into small pieces. Add unbeaten egg whites and beat until fluffy.

Turn into chilled trays and freeze until firm. Serves 6.

Refrigerator Sorbet Variations

Apricot Sorbet: Use 16 ounces apricot pulp and 2 tablespoons lemon juice.

Lemon or Lime Sorbet: Use 4 fluid ounces lemon or lime juice and grated rind of ½ lemon.

Orange Sorbet: Omit 8 fluid ounces water. Use 12 fluid ounces orange juice, grated rind of ½ orange, and 2 fluid ounces lemon juice.

Peach and Cherry Sorbet: Use 12 ounces peach pulp, 2 tablespoons orange juice, and 2 ounces maraschino cherries, diced finely.

Pineapple Sorbet: Use 8 ounces crushed pineapple and 1 tablespoon lemon juice.

Raspberry Sorbet: Use 8 ounces crushed fresh or canned raspberries and 2 tablespoons lemon juice.

CRANBERRY-ORANGE SORBET
1 pound cranberries
16 fluid ounces water
16 ounces sugar
2 teaspoons unflavoured gelatine
8 fluid ounces orange juice
2 teaspoons grated orange rind
3 ounces lemon juice

Cook cranberries with water until skins pop open.

Strain and add sugar and gelatine which has been softened in orange juice. Add grated rind and lemon juice.

Turn into refrigerator tray. Freeze until firm, stirring once or twice during freezing. Serves 6 to 8.

ORANGE FREEZER SORBET
(Basic Recipe)
16 fluid ounces milk and 8 fluid ounces single cream
10 ounces sugar
10 fluid ounces orange juice
2 tablespoons lemon juice
¼ teaspoon salt

Heat 8 fluid ounces milk. Add sugar and stir until dissolved. Add other ingredients.

Use freezing mixture of 2 parts salt to 7 parts ice. Turn handle of freezer slowly.

After freezing, remove dasher. Pack freezer with more ice and salt. Let sherbet stand an hour or more to ripen. Makes about 4½ pints.

Variations:

Lemon Sorbet: In basic recipe, omit orange juice. Use 8 fluid ounces lemon juice and 4 fluid ounces water.

Pineapple Sorbet: In basic recipe, substitute 8 ounces drained crushed pineapple for 4 fluid ounces orange juice.

MINT SORBET
8 ounces sugar
16 fluid ounces boiling water
4 tablespoons chopped fresh mint
1 tablespoon unflavoured gelatine
4 fluid ounces cold water
8 fluid ounces lemon juice
few drops green food colouring
2 egg whites

Add sugar to boiling water. Bring to boil again, stirring to dissolve sugar.

Add mint. Remove from heat. Cover pan and let steep 1 hour.

Soften gelatine in cold water 5 minutes and dissolve over boiling water. Stir into steeped mixture, mixing well.

Add lemon juice. Tint a pale green with food colouring.

Pour into refrigerator tray. Freeze to mush.

Beat egg whites stiff. Turn sherbet into chilled bowl. Beat quickly and fold in egg whites. Return to tray. Freeze firm.

To serve, garnish scoops of sherbet with sprigs of fresh mint. Serves 6.

LEMON-CREAM SORBET
11 ounces sugar
13 fluid ounces milk
juice and grated rind of 2 lemons
8 fluid ounces double cream

Combine sugar and milk and mix well. Add lemon juice and rind.

Whip cream until stiff and fold into lemon mixture.

Pour into freezer tray. Freeze until firm. Stir once or twice while freezing. Serves 6.

ORANGE-CREAM SORBET
6 ounces sugar
6 fluid ounces water
grated rind of 1 orange
12 fluid ounces orange juice
1 tablespoon lemon juice
4 fluid ounces single cream
2 egg whites
few grains salt

Cook sugar and water together slowly 10 minutes. Add grated rind cooking 2 minutes longer. Strain. Add syrup to fruit juices. Cool.

Pour into freezing tray. Freeze until firm.

Remove to a chilled bowl; beat quickly until light. Add cream. Fold in stiffly beaten egg whites to which the salt has been added.

Turn into tray and freeze. If mixture separates, stir occasionally. Serves 6 to 8.

WATERMELON SORBET
about ½ a diced watermelon
24 marshmallows
2 fluid ounces lemon juice
2 stiffly beaten egg whites

Press diced watermelon through sieve to extract 8 fluid ounces juice.

Heat marshmallows and watermelon juice over hot water, stirring until marshmallows are melted and smooth. Cool. Add lemon juice.

Combine marshmallow mixture with stiffly beaten egg whites. Fold gently until blended.

Pour into small refrigerator tray and freeze. When partially frozen, turn into chilled bowl. Beat quickly with wire whisk. Return to tray and freeze. Serves 5.

CANTALOUPE SORBET
12 fluid ounces water
4 ounces sugar
2 medium cantaloupes, pulp and juice
3 fluid ounces lemon juice

Boil water and sugar together for 5 minutes. Cool. Add cantaloupe and lemon juice. Pour into shallow tin and freeze until firm around the edges of the tin.

Turn into a bowl and beat until smooth. Return to tray and freeze until firm. Serves 6.

Cantaloupe Sherbet

Homemade Water-Ices

REFRIGERATOR ICE
(Basic Recipe)
5 ounces sugar
pinch of salt
12 fluid ounces water
1½ teaspoons unflavoured gelatine
3 tablespoons cold water
fruit juice (see below)

Boil sugar, salt, and water 5 minutes. Soften gelatine in 3 tablespoons cold water. Dissolve in hot syrup. Cool and add fruit juices.

Freeze in refrigerator tray to a mush-like consistency.

Remove to a chilled bowl; break into small pieces. Beat with wire whisk until fluffy (1 to 2 minutes). Return to freezing tray and freeze until firm. Serves 6.

Variations of Refrigerator Ice

Berry Ice: Follow basic recipe. Use 8-10 ounces raspberries or strawberries crushed and sieved and 1 tablespoon lemon juice.

Cherry Ice: Follow basic recipe. Use 12 ounces minced cherries and juice, 1 tablespoon lemon juice, and few grains nutmeg. Omit 4 fluid ounces water.

Cranberry Ice: Follow basic recipe. Use 12 ounces cooked strained cranberries.

Lemon or Lime Ice: Follow basic recipe. Use 3 fluid ounces lemon or lime juice.

Mint Ice: To lemon ice, add ¼ teaspoon peppermint flavouring and 2 tablespoons finely-minced mint leaves.

Orange Ice: Follow basic recipe. Add 1 tablespoon grated orange rind to hot syrup and cool. Use 12 fluid ounces orange juice and 2 tablespoons lemon juice.

PINEAPPLE-MINT ICE
1 teaspoon unflavoured gelatine
2 tablespoons cold water
12 fluid ounces pineapple juice
4 ounces sugar
⅛ teaspoon salt
1 tablespoon chopped fresh mint
8 ounces crushed pineapple
2 tablespoons lemon juice
grated rind of 1 lemon
2 egg whites

Soften gelatine in cold water 5 minutes.

Heat pineapple juice to boiling point and add softened gelatine, sugar, and salt. Stir until dissolved.

Cool. Add mint, crushed pineapple, lemon juice, and rind. Freeze to mush.

Turn into large chilled bowl. Add unbeaten egg whites and beat until light and fluffy. Return to tray and freeze, stirring several times. Serves 8.

FREEZER LEMON ICE
(Basic Recipe)
1 pint, 12 fluid ounces water
10 to 12 ounces sugar
8 fluid ounces strained lemon juice
¼ teaspoon salt
1 egg white

Boil water and sugar together 2 minutes, then put aside.

When cold, add lemon juice, salt, and unbeaten egg white. Freeze with a mixture of 2 parts salt to 7 parts ice.

Turn handle slowly until ice is firm. Remove dasher and pack freezer with more ice and salt. Let ice stand 1 hour or more to ripen.

Lemon Ice Variations

Lime Ice: In basic recipe, substitute lime juice for lemon juice. Add green food colouring.

Mint Ice: To lemon ice, add ¼ teaspoon mint flavouring and 2 tablespoons finely chopped mint leaves.

Berry Ice: Make syrup of 8 ounces sugar and 16 fluid ounces water. Mash 1 pound berries and press through sieve. Add to syrup. Cool and freeze. Raspberries, blackberries, or strawberries may be used.

Cherry Ice: Make syrup of 8 ounces sugar and 16 fluid ounces water. Mince 1 pound stoned cherries and press through sieve. Add to syrup. Cool and freeze.

Grape Ice: Make syrup of 8 ounces sugar and 16 fluid ounces water. Add 16 fluid ounces grape juice, 2 fluid ounces each of orange and lemon juice. Cool, strain, and freeze.

Orange Ice: Make syrup of 8 ounces sugar and 16 fluid ounces water. Add 16 fluid ounces orange juice and 4 tablespoons lemon juice. Cool, strain, and freeze.

AVOCADO-GRAPEFRUIT ICE
1 large sieved avocado
16 fluid ounces grapefruit juice
4 ounces sugar
¼ teaspoon salt

Cut a large avocado in halves lengthwise. Remove stone and skin, and force pulp through sieve.

Blend in grapefruit juice, sugar, and salt. Pour into refrigerator tray. Freeze firm.

Turn into chilled bowl. Beat with wire whisk until smooth and fluffy.

Return to tray and freeze to desired consistency. Makes about 1¼ pints.

Cranberry-Mint Ice

CRANBERRY-MINT ICE
1 1-pound can jellied cranberry sauce
8 fluid ounces pineapple juice
¼ teaspoon peppermint essence

Crush cranberry sauce with a fork. Add pineapple juice and peppermint essence.

Pour into freezing tray of refrigerator. Freeze.

Serve immediately. Use to top fresh fruit salad.

CRÈME DE MENTHE ICE
13 ounces sugar
1 pint, 4 fluid ounces water
4 fluid ounces lemon juice
2 fluid ounces crème de menthe

Cook sugar and water together 5 minutes.

Cool and add lemon juice and crème de menthe. Pour into small refrigerator tray.

Freeze, stirring several times during freezing. Serves 6 to 8.

GRAPEFRUIT-MINT ICE
2 teaspoons unflavoured gelatine
1 pint grapefruit juice, fresh or unsweetened
6 ounces sugar
4 fluid ounces water
few drops peppermint essence
green food colouring
2 egg whites, stiffly beaten

Soften gelatine in 2 fluid ounces cold grapefruit juice.

Boil sugar and water together 5 minutes and dissolve softened gelatine in it while hot.

Cool. Combine with remaining fruit juice. Add peppermint flavouring and a few drops of food colouring to tint pale green.

Turn into refrigerator tray. Freeze to mush.

Turn partially-frozen ice into chilled bowl. Beat until smooth. Fold in stiffly beaten egg whites. Freeze firm, stirring several times. Serves 6.

Variation: Mint flavouring and colouring may be omitted if plain grapefruit ice is desired.

Mousses

VANILLA MOUSSE
(Basic Recipe)

1 teaspoon unflavoured gelatine
8 fluid ounces single cream
6 tablespoons sugar
pinch of salt
½ teaspoon vanilla
8 fluid ounces double cream,
    whipped
2 egg whites

Soften gelatine in a little single cream or milk.

Heat remainder of single cream or milk and pour over gelatine. Add sugar and salt; stir until dissolved. Chill.

When gelatine mixture has thickened slightly, whisk to incorporate air. Add vanilla. Fold in whipped cream and well-beaten egg whites.

Mould, pack into ice and salt and freeze or turn into freezing trays and freeze until firm. Makes about 1½ pints.

Vanilla Mousse Variations

Apple Sauce Mousse: In basic recipe, omit vanilla. Add 18 ounces cinnamon-flavoured apple sauce and 2 tablespoons lemon juice with the cream.

Banana Mousse: In basic recipe, add 2 to 3 mashed ripe bananas and 2 teaspoons lemon juice with whipped cream.

Burnt Almond Mousse: Melt 8 teaspoons sugar carefully and stir in 3 ounces ground almonds. Heat until almonds are browned. Add to milk or single cream in basic recipe. Add ¼ teaspoon almond essence. Omit vanilla.

Chocolate Mousse: Add 2 ounces plain chocolate to milk or single cream in basic recipe. Add 4 ounces sugar. Heat in top of double saucepan, whisking until blended.

Coffee Mousse: In basic recipe, substitute 4 fluid ounces strong coffee for same amount of single cream.

Maple Mousse: In basic recipe, substitute 2 ounces maple syrup for sugar.

Peach Mousse: Omit vanilla in basic recipe. Add ¼ teaspoon almond essence. Add about 16 ounces peach pulp and 4 ounces sugar.

Peanut Crunch Mousse: In basic recipe, substitute ¼ pound finely ground peanut crunch for sugar.

Peppermint Mousse: In basic recipe, substitute crushed peppermint rock for sugar. Add green food colouring.

Strawberry or Raspberry Mousse: Omit vanilla in basic recipe. Add 8 to 9 ounces crushed berries and 1 to 2 tablespoons lemon juice with whipped cream.

PLUM MOUSSE

10 to 12 ounces ripe plum pulp
1 small diced orange
4 ounces diced canned pineapple
about 4 ounces caster sugar
pinch of salt
1 tablespoon lemon juice
8 fluid ounces evaporated milk,
    whipped

Select very ripe plums. Wash, dry, cut away from stone. Carefully strip off thin skin, quarter, discarding stone. Put pulp through a sieve and weigh.

Combine plum pulp, orange, pineapple, sugar, salt, and lemon juice; gently blend, not to destroy the delicate plum flavour. Fold in whipped milk.

Pour into a refrigerator tray and freeze. Serves 6.

SPUMONE

4 ounces caster sugar
about 4 ounces maraschino cherries,
    drained and cut into quarters
3 tablespoons glacé orange peel,
    cut into thin strips
1 teaspoon lemon juice
10 fluid ounces double cream,
    whipped
2 ounces chopped blanched
    almonds
about 2½ pints vanilla ice cream
¼ teaspoon almond essence

Fold sugar, cherries, orange peel, and lemon juice into whipped cream. Put into refrigerator tray to harden.

Add chopped nuts to ice cream, then flavour with almond essence. If ice cream becomes soft put in freezer to harden.

To pack mould: Line a chilled 1½-pint melon-shaped mould with ice cream to a depth of 1 inch. Leave hollow in centre but bring ice cream well up on sides of mould.

Fill mould with whipped cream mixture. Cover with greaseproof paper; fit lid on tightly. Put in freezing compartment for 24 hours.

Unmould onto chilled plate. To serve, cut into 1-inch slices. Serves 10 to 12.

Note: If preferred, use a mixture of chopped glacé angelica, citron, apricot, and lemon and orange peel instead of 3 tablespoons glacé orange peel.

MAPLE-NUT MOUSSE

4 beaten egg yolks
12 ounces maple syrup
⅛ teaspoon salt
1 teaspoon vanilla
2 ounces chopped black walnuts
¾ pint double cream, whipped

Combine beaten egg yolks, maple syrup, and salt in top of double saucepan. Cook over hot water, stirring constantly, until mixture coats spoon.

Remove immediately from heat and stir over ice cubes until cool. Add vanilla and walnuts.

Gently fold whipped cream into custard. Pour into 2 refrigerator trays. Freeze without stirring.

To serve, pile into sorbet glasses. Top with additional whipped cream. Garnish with chopped walnuts. Makes about 1½ pints.

GOLDEN MOUSSE

2 or 3 mashed ripe bananas
2 tablespoons orange juice
1 ounce desiccated coconut
3 tablespoons brown sugar
few grains salt
⅛ teaspoon grated orange rind
8 fluid ounces double cream,
    whipped

Combine and mix first 6 ingredients. Fold in stiffly-whipped cream.

Turn into freezing tray. Freeze rapidly, without stirring, until firm. Serves 6 to 8.

BISQUE MOUSSE

3 well-beaten egg yolks
8 ounces caster sugar
3 egg whites, stiffly beaten
16 fluid ounces double cream,
    whipped
½ pound dry macaroons, crumbled
2 teaspoons vanilla or brandy
    essence

Beat egg yolks and sugar until thick and lemon-coloured. Fold in remaining ingredients.

Pour into large refrigerator tray. Freeze firm. Serves 12.

MOLASSES MOUSSE

4 eggs
8 ounces molasses or black treacle
2 tablespoons orange juice
½ teaspoon cinnamon
few grains salt
16 fluid ounces double cream

Beat eggs; add molasses or black treacle. Cook over hot water, stirring constantly until slightly thickened.

Cool quickly by setting pan in iced water, stirring occasionally. Add orange juice, cinnamon, and salt.

Beat cream until slightly stiff, fold in molasses mixture.

Pour into refrigerator tray and freeze firm. Makes about 2½ pints.

Molasses Mousse

Parfaits

VANILLA PARFAIT
(Basic Recipe)

8 ounces sugar
6 fluid ounces water
2 egg whites
¼ teaspoon salt
3 teaspoons vanilla
12 fluid ounces whipping cream, whipped

Boil sugar and water to 230°F. or until it forms a thread.

Beat egg whites until frothy. Add salt and beat until stiff but not dry.

Slowly pour hot syrup over egg whites, beating constantly. Continue beating until mixture is cool and holds shape. Add vanilla and fold in whipped cream.

Turn into chilled trays and freeze until firm. Serve with additional whipped cream, fruits, and nuts. Serves 8.

Vanilla Parfait Variations

Banana Parfait: Omit vanilla in basic recipe. Add 1 teaspoon lemon juice. Fold in 2 to 3 mashed ripe bananas with whipped cream.

Chocolate Parfait: In basic recipe, add 2 ounces flaked cooking chocolate to hot syrup. Beat with wire whisk until blended before adding other ingredients.

Coffee Parfait: In basic recipe, substitute 6 fluid ounces strong coffee for water.

Maple Parfait: In basic recipe, substitute 12 ounces hot maple syrup for sugar syrup.

Maraschino Cherry Parfait: In basic recipe, substitute 2 fluid ounces maraschino cherry juice for equal amount of water in making syrup. Add 3 ounces or more diced maraschino cherries with whipped cream.

Pineapple Parfait: Omit vanilla in basic recipe. Add 8 ounces crushed drained pineapple and 1½ tablespoons lemon juice with whipped cream.

Strawberry or Raspberry Parfait: Omit vanilla in basic recipe. Add 8 to 10 ounces crushed berries and 1¼ tablespoons lemon juice with whipped cream.

Toasted Coconut Parfait: In basic recipe, add 2 ounces toasted shredded coconut with whipped cream.

BLACKBERRY AND PEACH PARFAIT

8 ounces blackberries
8 fluid ounces double cream, whipped
2 fresh peaches, peeled
3 ounces caster sugar

Fold washed blackberries into whipped cream.

Mash peaches; add sugar and fold into blackberry mixture.

Chill, but do not freeze, in refrigerator tray. Serve in sorbet glasses. Serves 6.

GOLDEN PARFAIT

4 ounces sugar
2 fluid ounces water
4 egg yolks
few grains salt
1½ teaspoons vanilla
12 fluid ounces double cream, whipped

Boil sugar and water together. Pour slowly over well-beaten egg yolks. Cook until mixture coats spoon.

Cool. Add salt and vanilla. Fold in whipped cream.

Turn into chilled tray. Freeze until firm. Serve with additional whipped cream, if desired. Serves 6.

Golden Parfait Variations

Butterscotch Parfait: In golden parfait, substitute 4 ounces brown sugar for the granulated sugar and add 1 ounce butter.

Maple-Nut Parfait: In golden parfait, substitute 6 ounces maple syrup for sugar and water. Heat syrup over low heat and proceed as directed. Add 2 ounces chopped nuts.

APPLE-LIME PARFAIT

1½ teaspoons unflavoured gelatine
2 tablespoons cold water
12 fluid ounces cold water
6 ounces sugar
2 fluid ounces lime juice
3 fluid ounces orange juice
2 tablespoons lemon juice
few grains salt
green food colouring
2 egg whites
cinnamon apple sauce (below)

Soften gelatine in 2 tablespoons cold water for 5 minutes.

Combine remaining water and sugar; boil for 2 minutes. Add gelatine; stir until dissolved. Add lime, orange, lemon juices and salt; cool. Colour light green.

Pour into freezing tray and freeze to mush.

Place in chilled bowl. Beat with wire whisk until smooth. Beat egg whites stiff and fold in. Return to tray and freeze firm. Stir several times.

Just before serving, spoon alternate layers of apple sauce and lime sherbet into glasses. If desired, garnish with green maraschino cherries and sprig of mint. Serves 4 to 6.

Cinnamon Apple Sauce:

18 ounces tinned apple sauce
1½ ounces demerara sugar
¼ teaspoon cinnamon
½ teaspoon grated lemon rind

Combine apple sauce, sugar, cinnamon, and lemon rind. Chill.

PEPPERMINT ROCK PARFAIT

4 ounces sugar
4 fluid ounces water
few grains salt
2 egg whites
13 fluid ounces evaporated milk, chilled icy cold
½ teacup finely crushed peppermint rock

Combine sugar and water and bring slowly to a boil. Boil rapidly until syrup spins a thread (230°F.).

Add salt to egg whites and beat until stiff but not dry.

Pour syrup slowly into egg whites, beating constantly.

Chill. Beat milk until very stiff. Fold in egg white mixture and rock. Pour at once into freezing trays. Freeze. Makes about 2½ pints.

PISTACHIO PARFAIT

8 ounces sugar
2 fluid ounces water
2 egg whites
green food colouring
2 ounces chopped pistachio nuts
1 teaspoon almond essence
few grains salt
¾ pint double cream

Combine sugar and water; boil to 238°F. (or when small amount dropped from tip of spoon spins long thread).

Beat egg whites stiff; gradually add syrup, beating constantly. Colour light green. Cool. Add nuts, almond essence, and salt.

Whip cream; fold in. Pour into freezing tray and freeze firm. Serves 4 to 6.

For quick parfaits layer ice cream and fruit or other sauce, then freeze until ready to serve. Create your own imaginative combinations of ice cream and sauce. Usually parfaits are served in their special glasses, but stemmed water glasses work just as well. These have been topped, just before serving, with crunchy star-shaped sugar-coated cereal instead of the usual whipped cream.

Ice Cream Specials

GOOD LUCK HORSESHOE

about 1½ pints ice cream
about 20 shortbread biscuits
8 fluid ounces double cream
2 tablespoons icing sugar
1 teaspoon vanilla
4 tablespoons chopped maraschino
   cherries

Slice ice cream about ¾-inch thick to size of biscuits. Alternate ice cream with biscuits in shape of a horseshoe, cutting the ice cream in wedges where the horseshoe curves. Freeze.

Whip cream with caster sugar and vanilla. Ice horseshoe with cream and freeze until serving time. Sprinkle with chopped maraschino cherries. Slice diagonally. Serves 6.

Good Luck Horseshoe

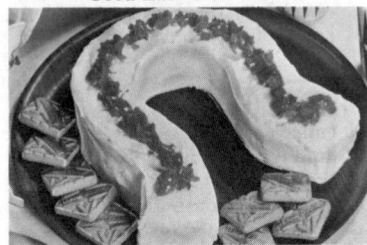

ICE CREAM CHERRY TARTS

6 individual pastry cups
1½ pints vanilla ice cream
16 ounces fresh or frozen cherries
   or tinned sweet red
   cherries

Fill cooled individual pastry cups generously with vanilla ice cream. Top with red cherries and cherry sauce (below). Serves 6.

Cherry Sauce:

8 fluid ounces cherry juice
   (sweetened juice from fresh,
   frozen, or tinned sweet red
   cherries)
2 ounces sugar
1½ teaspoons cornflour
1 teaspoon lemon juice

Blend sugar, cornflour and lemon juice. Add to cherry juice and cook, stirring until slightly thickened. Cool and serve over the ice cream. If tinned cherries are used, add more sugar to suit taste.

Frozen Trifle

RIBBON CAKE

Cut baker's rich teacake into 4 rectangular slices. Cut 1 pint strawberry ice cream into slices. Alternate cake and ice cream layers. Freeze until firm. Serve with thawed frozen strawberries or raspberries.

Ribbon Cake

REFRIGERATOR TRAY PIE

2 ounces butter or margarine
2 ounces caster sugar
6 ounces wafer crumbs
1¼ pints vanilla or coffee ice
   cream, softened

Cream butter and add crumbs and sugar. Blend together. Pack half the crumb mixture into a refrigerator tray. Chill.

Spoon ice cream over crumb mixture and pack down well. Press remaining crumbs on top of the ice cream. Spread with whipped cream, if desired. Return to refrigerator to freeze. Serves 6.

HONEYDEW-RASPBERRY DELIGHT

1 medium honeydew melon
about 1½ pints vanilla ice cream
4 ounces sweetened raspberries

Cut honeydew melon into 8 crosswise slices ¼- to ½-inch thick. Remove seeds and rind.

With a sharp knife, make diagonal slashes around edge of melon slices.

Place slices of melon on pudding plates and top each with a large scoop of ice cream. Circle scoop of ice cream with sweetened raspberries. Serves 8.

FROZEN TRIFLE

about 1½ pints vanilla ice cream
vanilla wafers
8 ounces strawberry jam
¾ pint strawberry ice cream

Pack 1 pint vanilla ice cream into bottom of 2½-pint ring mould. Add a layer of vanilla wafers; spread with ½ the strawberry jam.

Stand vanilla wafers around sides of mould. Continue layering strawberry ice cream, vanilla wafers, strawberry jam, and vanilla ice cream. Freeze until firm. Unmould on serving dish. Garnish with sliced strawberries. Serves 6 to 8.

Cut off the tops of éclair shells (home made or baker's). Fill with ice cream and put tops back on. Serve with chocolate sauce and lots of whipped cream.

STRAWBERRY ICE CREAM PIE

3 egg whites
¼ teaspoon salt
¼ teaspoon cream of tartar
6 ounces caster sugar
¾ teaspoon vanilla
about 1½ pints vanilla ice cream
about 1½ pounds strawberries
4 tablespoons caster sugar
4 fluid ounces double cream,
   whipped
½ teaspoon vanilla

Beat egg whites with salt and cream of tartar until stiff but not dry. Gradually add 6 ounces sugar and ¾ teaspoon vanilla and beat until it holds up in peaks.

Cut a circle of brown paper to fit bottom of 9-inch pie dish. Spread meringue on paper in pie dish and build up edges.

Bake in very slow oven (250°F. Mark ½) 1 hour.

Turn off heat and allow to remain in oven 1 hour longer or until dry.

Fill cooled meringue shell with ice cream. Top with sliced strawberries to which have been added 2 tablespoons caster sugar. Top with whipped cream sweetened with 2 tablespoons caster sugar and flavoured with ½ teaspoon vanilla. Decorate with a few whole strawberries. Serves 8.

Three-ring Circus: Mould 1½ pints each of vanilla, chocolate, and strawberry ice cream in 6-inch round cake tins. Decorate with animal biscuits and arrange on a tiered dish. Use a clown centrepiece and circus decorations. Dessert makes about 15 servings.

Ice Cream Snowballs

ICE CREAM SHADOW CAKE

1 bought large angel food or white
    sponge cake ring
1½ pints chocolate ice cream
¾ pint double cream, whipped and
    sweetened
chocolate sauce

Cut angel cake in 3 layers. Spread
ice cream (softened) between each
layer. Spread whipped cream on top
and sides of cake; freeze.

When ready to serve, remove from
freezer, and trickle cooled chocolate
sauce over top and sides of cake. Cut
in wedges to serve. Serves 12.

Note: If freezer isn't available, chill
cake and have cream whipped before
filling cake. Fill with ice cream; spread
with cream. Dribble sauce over top and
sides, and serve at once.

CRUNCHY CHOCOLATE SUNDAE

8 chocolate chip biscuits
1 pint vanilla ice cream

Break chocolate chip or Maryland
biscuits into coarse crumbs.

Scoop out ice cream in 4 balls; roll
in crumbs.

Serve immediately, or store in freezer
until needed. Top with chocolate sauce
and serve with additional chocolate
chip biscuits.

Variations: Use other crumbled biscuits such as coconut macaroons,
vanilla wafers or use chocolate cake
or baked meringue crumbs. Ice cream
balls or squares may be prepared in
advance by rolling in crumbs and
stored in freezing compartment of
refrigerator or freezer until time to
serve.

---

*Flaming Sundae: Pile ice cream high
in sorbet glasses, spoon on your favourite sauce or sliced fruits. Then add a
sugar cube dipped in lemon essence at
the very top of the sundae. Light the
cubes and carry your special dessert
to the table in its flaming glory.*

PARTY CLOWNS

Place a scoop of ice cream in centre
of each biscuit or cake round for
clown's head. Then make his face,
using raisins for eyes, nose, and mouth.

Place an ice cream cornet on each
scoop of ice cream for the hat. (If desired, cornets may be decorated ahead
of time with sweets. Use a little icing
sugar mixed with water to hold sweet
decoration on cornets.)

Party Clown

QUICK ICE CREAM SUNDAE SAUCES

Marshmallow Sauce: In saucepan,
combine ¼ pound (16) marshmallows
with 4 ounces honey, 3 ounces double
cream and pinch of salt.

Cook until marshmallows are almost
melted, stirring occasionally. Remove
from heat; stir until completely melted.

Chocolate-Marshmallow Sauce: Add
1½ ounces plain chocolate to marshmallows. Cook as in marshmallow
sauce (above).

Maple-Walnut Syrup: Heat some
maple syrup and chopped walnuts over
boiling water about 5 minutes. Good
hot or cold.

Honey-Almond Syrup: Heat honey
and chopped toasted almonds over
boiling water about 5 minutes. Good
hot or cold.

Coffee Coconut Syrup: Heat 12 ounces
of golden syrup with 1 tablespoon
instant coffee and 2 ounces coconut
over boiling water about 5 minutes.
Good hot or cold.

Pineapple or Grape Sauces: Slightly
thaw frozen pineapple or grape juice
concentrate.

Honey Sauce: Stir together 3 ounces
honey and 1 ounce melted butter or
margarine.

Coffee Sauce: Mix 1 to 2 tablespoons
instant coffee with 8 fluid ounces sweetened condensed milk.

ICE CREAM SNOWBALLS

Make large snowballs of vanilla ice
cream, using ice cream scoop or large
spoon.

Quickly roll each ball in chopped
pecans or walnuts. Serve plain or with
a butterscotch sauce.

ICE CREAM BUTTERFLIES

Buy or prepare 6 small rich teacakes
from instant cake mix, or use own
recipe; cool. Cut off tops of cakes; cut
tops in half.

Using 1½ pints ice cream, place a
large scoop of it on each cake; insert halves of top of cake in ice cream
to resemble butterfly wings. Serve plain
or with sauce and whipped cream.
Serves 6.

SPONGE CAKE SUNDAE

2 ounces plain chocolate
12 ounces golden syrup
¼ teaspoon vanilla
4 individual flan cases
¾ pint peppermint ice cream
hot chocolate sauce

Melt chocolate in top of double
saucepan. Add syrup, stir only until
blended, then add vanilla.

Place flan cases on plates. Top with
pink peppermint ice cream. Pass hot
chocolate sauce.

---

*Easter Sundaes: Surround a scoop of
ice cream with whipped cream. Sprinkle with coconut and jelly babies or tots.
Serve with Easter Bunnies made from
coconut-covered marshmallow cakes,
joined with toothpicks. Use sugar wafers
for ears and a marshmallow for a tail.*

Circus Party: Make round ice cream balls using a large scoop. Roll in desiccated coconut. Store in freezer. Just before serving top each with an animal biscuit.

APRICOT ICE CREAM PIE

¼ pound marshmallows
apricot jam
2 egg whites
⅛ teaspoon salt
2 ounces caster sugar
2 pints vanilla ice cream
1 9-inch baked pastry or flan case, chilled

Heat marshmallows and 2 tablespoons jam in top part of double saucepan over boiling water, until marshmallows are half melted. Remove from heat, and beat until smooth.

Beat egg whites with salt until foamy; gradually add sugar, and beat until stiff. Fold in marshmallow mixture.

Press ice cream quickly into chilled shell. Spread with jam. Cover with marshmallow meringue, spreading to cover ice cream completely.

Put under grill 1 or 2 minutes, or until lightly browned. (This meringue browns very quickly.) Cut in wedges, and garnish with spoonful of jam.

Banana Split: Peel a banana and cut in half lengthwise. Place the two halves on a shallow dish and top with 3 scoops of ice cream. Then spoon over chocolate sauce and fruit syrups and garnish with whipped cream, fruits, and nuts.

CRANBERRY ICE CREAM PIE

about 6 ounces ginger biscuit
         crumbs
2 ounces sugar
2 ounces butter or margarine
1½ pints vanilla ice cream
8 ounces canned cranberry sauce

Combine ginger biscuit crumbs, sugar, and melted butter in bowl. Mix until thoroughly blended.

Cover bottom and sides of a buttered 8-inch pie dish with crumb mixture. Pack down firmly. Chill in refrigerator.

When crust is thoroughly chilled, fill with vanilla ice cream. Top with whole cranberry sauce. Place in freezing unit and freeze until serving time.

Ice Cream Tarts

ICE CREAM TARTS

Fill baked tart shells with fresh, sliced, sweetened peaches or strawberries. Top with a scoop of vanilla ice cream.

Serve with additional fruit, to garnish.

Strawberry-Pineapple Sundae

STRAWBERRY-PINEAPPLE SUNDAE

Cut 1 large pineapple in half lengthwise, through green tops. Remove flesh with sharp knife, cutting to within ¼ inch of edges. Remove core and cut in cubes.

Wash ½ pound strawberries and remove hulls. Slice and sweeten with sugar. Combine with pineapple and chill until serving time.

Place pineapple shells on large serving tray. Fill each half with ice cream (use 1½ pints in all). Serve with pineapple-strawberry sauce. Serves 6.

Cherry-Cantaloupe Sundae

CHERRY-CANTALOUPE SUNDAE

3 small cantaloupes
2 teacups stoned dark sour cherries
8 fluid ounces cherry juice or
        water
12 ounces sugar
few grains of salt
2 tablespoons lemon juice
2 drops almond essence
1½ pints vanilla ice cream

Wash cantaloupes and cut in halves crosswise. Remove seeds and cut out inside of each to within ¼ inch of edge; dice. Chill halves. Wash and pit cherries.

Combine remaining ingredients except ice cream. Heat to boiling and cook until syrup is thick. Add diced cantaloupe and cherries and chill.

Add a little sauce to each cantaloupe half. Top with ice cream and garnish with cherries and diced cantaloupe. Serve with extra sauce. Serves 6.

RED AND WHITE SWIRL

Soften 1 quart vanilla ice cream. Swirl ¼ pint strawberry sundae topping through ice cream. Turn into refrigerator tray and freeze until firm.

ORANGE-CHOCOLATE SWIRL

Soften 1 quart chocolate ice cream. Swirl one 3-ounce can frozen orange juice concentrate through ice cream. Turn into refrigerator tray and freeze until firm.

QUICK CHOCOLATE PARFAIT

Alternate chocolate ice cream, whipped cream, and tinned crushed pineapple.

CHOCOLATE MERINGUES

Fill cooled meringue shells (see Index) with scoops of chocolate ice cream. Top with chocolate sauce.

Ice cream and meringue shells are a traditional combination in some European countries.

Baked Alaskas

BAKED ALASKA
(Basic Recipe)

Baked Alaska is an impressive dessert and not at all difficult to make. It needs last minute preparation but if everything is prepared in advance, the Alaska may be put together and finished in the oven in minutes.

- 1- to 1½-inch layer sponge or white cake
- ⅛ teaspoon salt
- 5 egg whites
- 5 ounces caster sugar
- 1½ pints firm, brick ice cream

Cover a wooden cutting board with a strip of heavy wrapping paper. If a thick wooden board is not available, a heavy baking-sheet may be used. The wood is preferred because it is an extremely slow heat conductor, an advantage when "cooking" ice cream.

Arrange cake on the paper. (The paper will help slide dessert on to plate.)

Add salt to egg whites and whisk until soft peaks form. Add sugar gradually and continue to beat until meringue holds stiff peaks.

After making meringue, centre ice cream on cake. The layer of cake should be large enough to extend ½ to 1 inch beyond edge of ice cream.

Spread meringue over entire surface of ice cream and cake edge, carefully sealing to edges of cake. Sprinkle top with granulated sugar for a snowy effect.

Bake in very hot oven (450°F. Mark 8) until golden brown, about 5 minutes.

To serve, slide from board to plate. Slice at the table in front of guests. Garnish servings with whole strawberries. Serves 6.

Baked Alaska in Pie Shells: Fill baked pie shell or individual tart shells with firm ice cream. Cover with meringue and finish as directed in Baked Alaska.

Individual Baked Alaska: Cut individual rounds or squares of sponge cake. Cover and bake as above.

Fruit Alaska: Cover cake with a layer of fresh or stewed fruit. Arrange ice cream on top. Cover with meringue. Bake as above.

Rum Alaska: Place 2 half egg shells open side up in top of meringue before baking. Bake. Fill shells with rum. Set aflame and serve.

Alaska with Nuts: Sprinkle chopped nuts over meringue.

Strawberry Alaska: Use 2 pint bricks of vanilla or strawberry ice cream.

Place 1 pint brick on the cake. Cover with a 1-inch layer of sliced and chilled strawberries; place the other pint brick on top.

Proceed as in basic recipe.

Orange Alaska: The procedure is the same as in the basic recipe but ice cream is replaced by orange water-ice.

Remove the Alaska from the oven and surround by orange segments which have been cooked in a thin syrup until glazed.

SURPRISE ALASKA

- 1 cooled 9-inch sponge cake
- 6 egg whites
- ½ teaspoon cream of tartar
- 8 ounces caster sugar
- 1½ pints vanilla or strawberry ice-cream

Place cooled cake on several thicknesses of greaseproof paper (trimmed to size of cake) on a wooden board.

Using a small plate as a guide, cut a 3½-inch circle from centre of cake, hollowing out a depression for the ice cream. Leave about a 1-inch layer of cake in the bottom of the depression.

Beat egg whites with cream of tartar until stiff. Beat in sugar a little at a time until meringue forms stiff, glossy peaks but is not dry.

Firmly pack the hollow with 1 quart ice cream; level off with top of cake.

Quickly spread meringue on sides and top of cake, covering completely.

Brown in very hot oven (450°F. Mark 8) for 4 to 5 minutes, or until meringue is lightly browned. Slip the cake from board onto a serving plate and garnish with fresh flowers or fruit. Cut into wedge-shaped pieces and serve at once with extra ice cream. Serves 8.

RASPBERRY ALASKA PIE

- about 18 to 20 digestive biscuits, finely rolled
- 2 ounces softened butter or margarine
- 2 ounces caster sugar
- 1 ounce desiccated coconut
- 2 10-ounce packets frozen raspberries
- 1 tablespoon cornflour
- 2 fluid ounces lemon juice
- 1 tablespoon grated lemon rind
- 1½ pints vanilla ice cream
- 4 egg whites
- 4 ounces sugar
- 1 ounce desiccated coconut

Mix biscuit crumbs, butter or margarine, sugar, and coconut. Blend thoroughly. Pour into a 9-inch pie dish and press firmly against bottom and sides of the pie dish. The easy way is to press crumbs into place using an 8-inch pie dish. Bake in moderate oven (375°F. Mark 5) 7 minutes. Cool and freeze.

Heat frozen raspberries with corn-

Surprise Alaska

flour, lemon juice, and rind. Simmer until juice is clear and slightly thickened. Cool.

Make very thin layers of sauce and ice cream in pie crust using about ½ of sauce (serve remaining sauce with pie). Freeze.

Whisk egg whites until foamy. Continue beating, gradually adding sugar until stiff peaks form when whisk is lifted. Spread over ice cream sealing to edges of crust. Sprinkle with coconut. Freeze until serving time.

Just before serving, pre-heat oven to 500°F. Mark 10. Place pie in oven for 2 to 4 minutes or only until meringue is lightly browned. Serve immediately. Spoon remaining sauce over individual servings. Serves 8 to 10.

Raspberry Alaska Pie

PINK LADY ALASKA

Crumb Crust:

20 digestive biscuits, finely crushed
2 ounces softened butter or margarine
2 ounces caster sugar

Blend together biscuit crumbs, butter or margarine, and sugar. Press firmly against bottom and sides of 9-inch pie dish.

If preferred, bake in moderate oven (375°F. Mark 5) 8 minutes. Chill.

(Make the crumb crust early in the day—ready to fill at serving time.)

Filling:

16 marshmallows
2 tablespoons crushed strawberries
2 stiffly-beaten egg whites
2 ounces caster sugar
¼ teaspoon salt
¾ pint vanilla ice cream, very firm
1 teacup fresh sliced strawberries

Stir and melt marshmallows and crushed strawberries over low heat until smooth. Beat sugar gradually into stiffly-beaten egg whites until they hold a peak.

Add salt. Gradually beat in cooled marshmallow mixture.

Fill crumb crust with ice cream, cover with sliced strawberries. Top with gay swirls of marshmallow meringue (be sure meringue completely covers ice cream). Brown quickly under grill; serve at once. Serves 6 to 8.

Pink Lady Alaska

PEPPERMINT ALASKA PIE

18 to 20 digestive biscuits, finely crushed
2 ounces sugar
2 ounces softened butter or margarine
4 ounces chocolate bits
1½ pints vanilla ice cream
3 ounces crushed peppermint rock
3 egg whites
6 ounces caster sugar

Thoroughly blend biscuit crumbs, sugar, softened butter or margarine, and chocolate bits. Press firmly against bottom and sides of 9-inch pie dish. (The easy way is to press crumbs into place using an 8-inch pie dish.) Bake in moderate oven (375°F. Mark 5) 8 minutes. Cool and freeze.

Soften ice cream slightly and stir in crushed peppermint rock. Pile into crust and freeze until firm.

Just before serving beat egg whites with sugar until stiff. Spread meringue over pie, sealing edges to crust. Bake in hot oven (500°F. Mark 10) 3 to 4 minutes. Serve immediately. Serves 6 to 8.

FROZEN HAWAIIAN MARLOW

12 fluid ounces milk
¼ pound marshmallows, cut in halves (about 16)
4 fluid ounces cream, whipped with 1 teaspoon vanilla
12 ounces drained crushed pineapple
2 ounces maraschino cherry halves
1 ounce chopped pecans or other nuts

Measure milk and marshmallows into top of a double saucepan. Heat over boiling water until marshmallows melt. Remove from heat and cool.

Fold vanilla-flavoured whipped cream, fruit, and nuts into cooled mixture and pour into 1½ pint refrigerator tray. Freeze. Makes about 1½ pints or 6 to 8 servings.

STRAWBERRY MARLOW

6 ounces crushed sweetened strawberries
1 tablespoon orange juice
¼ pound marshmallows (16)
2 fluid ounces water
8 fluid ounces whipping cream
½ teaspoon vanilla
few grains salt

Combine strawberries and orange juice.

Combine marshmallows and water; cook over hot water, stirring occasionally, until melted. Fold into strawberry mixture. Cool.

Whip cream slightly stiff; add vanilla and salt. Fold into strawberry mixture.

Pour into freezing tray and freeze firm. Serves 4.

Peppermint Alaska Pie

VANILLA MARLOW
(Basic Recipe)

30 marshmallows
6 fluid ounces hot milk or water
2 teaspoons vanilla
12 fluid ounces double cream, whipped

Melt marshmallows in milk or water. Cool. Add flavouring. Chill.

When mixture begins to thicken, combine with whipped cream. Pour into tray and freeze without stirring. Serves 4 to 6.

Vanilla Marlow Variations

Banana Marlow: Omit vanilla in basic recipe. Add 2 to 3 mashed ripe bananas and 1 tablespoon lemon juice to hot milk.

Chocolate Marlow: Add 2 ounces melted plain chocolate to hot milk in basic recipe.

Peach Marlow: Add 2 teacups peach pulp and 1 tablespoon lemon juice to hot milk in basic recipe. Substitute 1 teaspoon almond essence for vanilla.

BANANA- OR GRAPE-BLACKCURRANT MARLOW

10 marshmallows
3 fluid ounces grape juice or blackcurrant juice
2 tablespoons lemon juice
2 to 3 mashed ripe bananas
4 fluid ounces double cream

Combine marshmallows and 2 tablespoons grape juice. Heat slowly, folding over and over, until marshmallows are half melted.

Remove from heat and continue folding until mixture is smooth and fluffy. Fold in remaining grape juice, then fold in lemon juice and bananas.

Turn into freezing tray and chill until mixture begins to freeze. Turn into a bowl and whisk thoroughly.

Whip cream until thickened. Fold into marshmallow-banana mixture. Return to tray and freeze firm. Serves 4 to 6.

Miscellaneous Frozen Desserts

BISCUIT TORTONI

Also called Tortoni or Bisque Tortoni, this Italian dessert is sometimes flavoured with sherry or rum.

2 teaspoons unflavoured gelatine
2 fluid ounces cold water
4 ounces golden syrup
2 ounces sugar
2 egg yolks
¼ teaspoon salt
1 teaspoon vanilla
½ teaspoon almond essence
8 fluid ounces cream or evaporated milk, whipped
1 ounce chopped pistachio nuts (optional)
about 2 ounces vanilla wafer or macaroon crumbs

Soften gelatine in cold water. Heat syrup and sugar to boiling, stir until sugar is dissolved and stir into gelatine.

Beat egg yolks until very light and add syrup mixture gradually, beating constantly.

Cool thoroughly; add salt and flavourings, and fold in whipped cream or milk.

Add pistachio nuts and pour into small fluted paper cups or into a tray of the refrigerator. Dust top thickly with crumbs.

Freeze without stirring until firm. Makes enough for about 14 small cups or 6 to 8 servings.

CHOCOLATE-ORANGE VELVET

2 8-ounce packets cream cheese, softened
8 fluid ounces double cream
6 ounces plain chocolate, melted
4 ounces caster sugar
2 tablespoons grated orange rind

Whip cream cheese and double cream together. Add remaining ingredients and beat at high speed until light and fluffy. Pour into ice cube tray and freeze until firm.

Cut into pie-shaped pieces. Serve with chocolate sandwich biscuits. Serves 6 to 8.

Chocolate-Orange Velvet

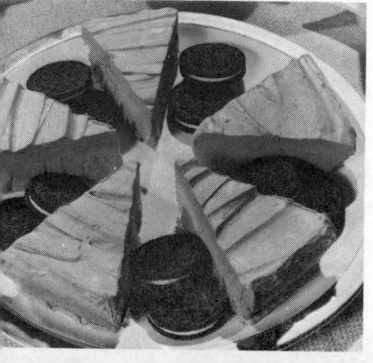

DIGESTIVE BISCUIT FREEZE
(Basic Recipe)

8 ounces digestive biscuit crumbs
10 marshmallows, quartered
4 ounces walnuts, chopped
3 ounces icing sugar
1 teaspoon vanilla
4 ounces desiccated coconut
4 fluid ounces single cream
4 fluid ounces double cream, whipped

Mix crumbs, marshmallows, walnuts, sugar, vanilla, coconut, and cream.

Pack into refrigerator tray lined with greaseproof paper. Freeze until firm.

To serve, slice with knife dipped in hot water. Top with whipped cream. Serves 8 to 10.

Digestive Biscuit Freeze Variations

Macaroon Crumb Freeze: Substitute macaroon crumbs for digestive biscuits.

Pineapple Crumb Freeze: In basic recipe, substitute 4 ounces crushed pineapple for coconut and 4 fluid ounces pineapple juice for single cream.

Prune Crumb Freeze: In basic recipe, substitute 8 ounces cooked prune pulp for single cream.

Vanilla or Chocolate Crumb Freeze: In basic recipe, substitute vanilla or chocolate biscuit crumbs for digestive biscuits.

FROZEN LEMON CHIFFON PIE

10 vanilla wafers (2-inch diameter)
2 eggs, separated
4 ounces golden syrup
pinch of salt
½ teaspoon grated lemon rind
2 fluid ounces lemon juice
2 ounces caster sugar
6 fluid ounces single cream, whipped

Roll wafers into fine crumbs. Grease a refrigerator tray with butter or margarine and coat well with crumbs. Place in freezing compartment.

Mix well in the top of a double saucepan the egg yolks, syrup, salt, lemon rind and juice. Cook over boiling water, stirring constantly until mixture is slightly thickened, and cool.

Beat egg whites until stiff, add sugar and whip until mixture stiffens again.

Whip lemon juice-egg yolk mixture into whipped cream, then fold in the blend of egg whites and sweetening.

Pour into the prepared tray and freeze quickly. To serve, cut into slices or pie-shaped wedges. To make the latter, cut across the tray diagonally from corner to corner, and then crosswise through centre. Serves 6.

Lemon Berry Frost

LEMON BERRY FROST

1 6-ounce can softened frozen lemonade concentrate
32 marshmallows, melted
13 fluid ounces undiluted evaporated milk
1 10- or 12-ounce packet frozen strawberries or raspberries

Beat lemonade concentrate and melted marshmallows together until smooth.

Chill evaporated milk in refrigerator tray until soft crystals form through milk (about 20 to 25 minutes). Whip until stiff (2 to 3 minutes). Slowly add marshmallow mixture. Whip very stiff (2 to 3 minutes longer).

Freeze in 2½-pint mould until firm (2 to 3 hours). Serve with fresh or defrosted berries. Makes about 2½ pints.

FROZEN CHOCOLATE DESSERT

8 ounces caster sugar
4 ounces butter or margarine
4 eggs
1 ounce plain chocolate, melted
4 ounces finely chopped walnuts
4 ounces vanilla wafer crumbs, finely crushed
8 fluid ounces double cream, whipped

Cream sugar and butter together thoroughly. Add eggs one at a time, beating well after each egg. Stir in chocolate and walnuts.

Line an 8½-inch loaf tin with greaseproof paper. Pour in ⅓ of the filling, add a layer of crumbs. Repeat both layers twice, freeze.

Unmould onto serving plate, ice with whipped cream. Return to freezer or serve at once. Serves 6 to 8.

Frozen Chocolate Dessert

Frozen Cranberry Loaf

FROZEN CRANBERRY LOAF

3 ounces finely ground toast crumbs
3 ounces brown sugar
1 teaspoon cinnamon
½ teaspoon nutmeg
¼ teaspoon allspice
¼ teaspoon ground cloves
¼ teaspoon ginger
1½ ounces melted butter
1 pound can jellied cranberry sauce
4 fluid ounces whipping cream
3 ounces cream cheese

Mix first seven ingredients together. Work in melted butter. Press mixture evenly against sides and bottom of an ice cube tray. Chill in freezing compartment for at least 1 hour.

Crush jellied cranberry sauce with a fork and spread over crumb crust. Whip cream. Soften cream cheese and whip with cream. Spread whipped cream-cheese mixture over cranberry sauce.

Place in freezing compartment and freeze until firm. Slice to serve. Serves 8.

Variation: Thick sour cream can be spread over cranberry sauce in place of cream cheese and whipped cream for excellent flavour.

APRICOT VELVET CREAM

1¾ pounds canned apricot halves
2 ounces caster sugar
⅛ teaspoon salt
8 fluid ounces evaporated milk, chilled for whipping

Mash apricots, reserving a few for garnish, and add sugar and salt.

Whip chilled milk until thick. Fold

Apricot Velvet Cream

in apricot mixture.

Freeze in freezing tray for 2 hours. Serves 6.

FROZEN VANILLA CUSTARD

1 egg, separated
2 ounces caster sugar
½ teaspoon vanilla
1 small can evaporated milk, chilled

Beat egg yolk. Add sugar and vanilla. Beat until sugar is dissolved.

Beat egg white stiff. Fold into yolk mixture.

Whip milk very stiff. Fold in egg mixture lightly. Pour at once into cold freezing tray. Freeze until firm. Makes ¾ pint.

Variations of Vanilla Custard

Frozen Chocolate Custard: In frozen vanilla custard, fold in 2 ounces plain chocolate, flaked or grated, after combining egg and sugar mixture with whipped milk.

Frozen Cocoa Custard: In frozen vanilla custard, omit sugar. Use in its place a syrup made by blending 2 ounces sugar, 1 ounce cocoa, and 4 fluid ounces water and boiling until thick. Chill syrup, then add to the beaten egg yolk.

Frozen Lemon Custard: Follow recipe for frozen vanilla custard and omit vanilla. Fold 3 tablespoons lemon juice and ½ teaspoon grated lemon rind into whipped milk before adding egg and sugar mixture.

Frozen Peanut Crunch Custard: In frozen vanilla custard, fold 1 bar crushed peanut crunch into egg and sugar mixture; add to whipped milk.

FROZEN ORANGE BALLS IN ORANGE CUPS

2 teaspoons unflavoured gelatine
2 fluid ounces cold water
8 fluid ounces water
6 ounces sugar
1 teaspoon grated lemon rind
1 teaspoon grated orange rind
1 can frozen orange juice concentrate, thawed, or 8 fluid ounces fresh orange juice
3 fluid ounces lemon juice
2 egg whites
⅛ teaspoon salt
8 orange peel cups

Soften gelatine in 2 fluid ounces cold water 5 minutes.

Boil 8 fluid ounces water with sugar 10 minutes. Dissolve gelatine in hot syrup. Cool.

Add lemon and orange rind and juices. Chill until it begins to thicken. Turn into chilled bowl and beat with wire whisk until fluffy.

Beat egg whites with salt until stiff. Fold gently into fruit mixture. Turn mixture into freezer tray and freeze firm.

Form balls with an ice cream scoop. Place balls in scalloped orange cups. Cut a thin slice off bottom side of cups to make them stand secure.

Serve on mustard cress in chilled serving dishes. Serves 8.

FROZEN STRAWBERRY SHORTCAKE

8 to 10 ounces strawberries
4 ounces caster sugar
1 teaspoon unflavoured gelatine
2 tablespoons cold water
sponge cake
8 fluid ounces cream, whipped

Crush strawberries and mix with sugar.

Soften gelatine in cold water. Add gelatine to strawberries and mix thoroughly.

Cover bottom of refrigerator tray with ¾-inch layer of sponge cake. Pour strawberry mixture over cake.

Chill and, when set, cover with whipped cream. Return to refrigerator and freeze. Serves 6.

LEMON VELVET

16 ounces caster sugar
16 fluid ounces gold top milk
grated rind of 2 lemons
4 fluid ounces lemon juice
¾ pint double cream

Combine sugar and milk and let stand 1 hour. Add lemon rind and juice, stirring well. Mixture will thicken slightly.

Whip cream until fairly stiff. Fold into milk mixture.

Pour into 2 refrigerator trays and freeze rapidly, 3 or 4 hours. Stir twice during freezing process to avoid separation. Serves 6 to 8.

Variation: One tall can undiluted evaporated milk may be used in place of cream. To prepare for whipping, pour into refrigerator tray and freeze until fine ice crystals form around edges. Scrape milk into chilled bowl and beat until stiff.

Frozen Orange Balls in Orange Cups

CHERRY-MACAROON FREEZE

1 16-ounce can black cherries
    drained or 1 16-ounce packet
    frozen cherries
about 4 ounces dry macaroon
    crumbs
¾ pint double cream, whipped

Stone cherries if necessary; cut in quarters. (Reserve cherry juice for cold beverage, sauce, gelatine dessert, or some other purpose.) Save enough whole cherries to use one on each serving for garnish.

Fold macaroon crumbs into whipped cream, then the cherries. Pour at once into freezing tray; freeze quickly without stirring. Serves 6 to 8.

FROZEN FIG SHORTCAKE

about 6 ounces dried figs, chopped
8 fluid ounces water
2 ounces sugar
1 teaspoon lemon juice
1 tablespoon unflavoured gelatine
1 tablespoon water
1 egg
4 tablespoons caster sugar
1 teaspoon vanilla
4 fluid ounces double cream,
    whipped
sponge, angel cake, or Swiss roll,
    1 inch thick, or fig biscuits

Simmer chopped figs and water with 2 ounces sugar 15 minutes; add lemon juice. Dissolve gelatine in cold water, then dissolve in the fig mixture. Cool.

Beat egg with 4 tablespoons sugar until light; add vanilla and fold in whipped cream.

Line deep refrigerator tray with greaseproof paper; place inch-thick slice or layer of cake on bottom. Spread cooled fig mixture over cake, then top with the cream.

Freeze several hours or overnight. Garnish with fig flowers and whipped cream. Serves 6 to 8.

Frozen Fig Shortcake

STRAWBERRY BOMBE

Digestive Biscuit Crust:
2 ounces butter or margarine
2 ounces sugar
20 digestive biscuits, finely crushed

Let butter or margarine stand at room temperature until softened. Blend all ingredients well with pastry fork or hands.

Pour crumb mixture into 2½-pint pudding basin. Set a smaller basin on top of crumbs, and press them firmly into an even layer against bottom and sides of pudding basin.

Strawberry Bombe Filling:
2 eggs, separated
1 15-ounce can sweetened condensed
    milk
2 fluid ounces lemon juice
1 pound strawberries, sliced
few drops red food colouring

Beat egg yolks until thick and lemon-coloured; mix in condensed milk. Add lemon juice; mix until thick. Beat in half the strawberries.

Beat egg whites stiff; fold in egg yolk mixture and remaining berries. Tint pink with a few drops of red colouring.

Pour into biscuit crumb crust in basin. Freeze for at least 6 hours.

To unmould, run a palette knife around sides of basin. Put serving plate upside down on basin and invert. Serve garnished with whipped cream and strawberry halves. Serves 8.

FROZEN LIME CREAM CUPS

2 eggs
4 ounces caster sugar
6 ounces golden syrup
8 fluid ounces single cream
8 fluid ounces milk
3 fluid ounces lime juice
1 teaspoon grated lime rind
green food colouring
whipped cream

Beat eggs until lemon-coloured. Slowly add sugar to eggs, beating until mixture is thick and custard-like.

Add syrup, cream, milk, lime juice, and grated lime rind, blending well. Tint a delicate green with food colouring.

Turn into refrigerator tray and freeze. When frozen, remove to chilled bowl and whisk until light and creamy.

Line tart tins with pastel-coloured fluted paper cups or use standard ice cream cups. Spoon mixture into them, filling almost to top. Freeze firm.

To serve, pipe whipped cream over tops. Decorate with thin slivers of lime. Serves 12.

Strawberry Bombe

FROZEN LEMON CREAM

grated rind of 2 large lemons
strained juice of 4 large lemons
8 ounces caster sugar
4 tablespoons water
4 eggs, separated
¾ pint double cream, whipped

Put lemon rind, lemon juice, ¾ of the sugar, and water together in top of double saucepan, over direct heat. Stir to dissolve sugar.

Beat egg yolks until thick and foamy; stir in hot mixture gradually; return mixture to saucepan over hot water. Stir and cook until mixture is thickened and smooth. Remove from hot water; cool completely; then chill.

Whisk egg whites until foamy; gradually beat in remaining sugar, as for meringue. Fold mixture into cooled lemon custard. Fold in whipped cream.

Freeze in one large or 2 small trays, stirring gently once or twice during freezing period. Freeze until firm. Serves 6 to 8.

FROZEN PEACH MALLOW

20 marshmallows, cut small
8 fluid ounces milk
8 ounces sugar
1 pound fresh peaches or 1
    packet (16-ounce) frozen
    peaches
few drops almond essence
¾ pint whipped cream

Put marshmallows and milk in top of double saucepan over hot water. Stir occasionally until marshmallows are dissolved. Stir in sugar. Set aside to cool completely.

Crush peaches to pulp, but do not strain; stir in flavouring. Combine cooled marshmallow mixture and peaches; fold in whipped cream.

Freeze until crystals begin to form around edge of tray.

Turn into chilled bowl and whip until smooth and light; return to freezing tray or, if mixture is not whipped, stir several times during freezing. (Stir from outer edges toward centre.) Freeze until firm. Serves 4 to 5.

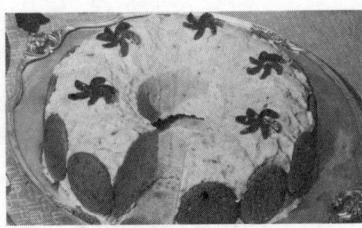

Holiday Mousse

HOLIDAY MOUSSE

1 large 20-ounce can crushed pine-
    apple
3 bananas
4 ounces caster sugar
6 ounces finely rolled ginger bis-
    cuit crumbs
8 fluid ounces evaporated milk,
    chilled icy cold
1 tablespoon lemon juice
8 fluid ounces double cream
whole ginger biscuits

Combine fruit with sugar and ginger biscuit crumbs. Add lemon juice
to evaporated milk; whip until stiff.

Whip cream stiff. Combine whipped
mixtures; fold in fruit mixture.

Line a 3½-pint mould with whole
ginger biscuits; pour in mousse. Freeze
overnight. To serve, unmould on to a
plate. Serves 12.

FROZEN MINT PUDDING

1½ teaspoons unflavoured gelatine
2 tablespoons water
2 ounces crushed white pepper-
    mint rock
2 ounces milk
2 eggs, separated
6 drops green food colouring
¼ teaspoon salt
6 tablespoon caster sugar
8 fluid ounces double cream
12 plain chocolate biscuits, crushed

Sprinkle gelatine on the water and
soak a few minutes.

Dissolve rock in milk over boiling
water.

Beat egg yolks well. Pour a little of
the hot liquid into them. Add to the
rest of the hot mixture, and cook until
thick, stirring constantly. Stir in the
colouring.

Add gelatine to the cooked mixture
and stir until dissolved. Cool until
thick but not set.

Add salt to egg whites, beat until
stiff but not dry. Gradually add sugar,
beating constantly. Combine the beaten
egg whites and gelatine mixture.

Whip the cream and fold it in.

Put half the crumbs into two freezing trays. Pour in prepared mixture,
and cover with rest of crumbs.

Freeze without stirring, at the coldest refrigerator temperature, 3 to 4
hours. Serves 8.

SHERRY PEACH DELIGHT

8 fluid ounces single cream or
    evaporated milk, chilled
4 peaches, finely sliced
4 fluid ounces sherry
1 teaspoon unflavoured gelatine
2 tablespoons cold water
2 eggs
3 ounces sugar
½ teaspoon salt
¾ pint milk
1 teaspoon almond essence

Pour single cream into freezing tray,
allowing about 1 hour for the cream
to begin to freeze. When crystals have
formed throughout, it is ready to whip.

Slice peaches and marinate in sherry.
Soften gelatine in cold water.

Whisk eggs with sugar and salt; stir
in milk. Cook over boiling water, stirring constantly, until mixture coats the
spoon. Do not overcook. Remove from
heat. Stir in softened gelatine. Cool.

Add peaches and sherry. Add almond essence.

Whip the frozen cream (or evaporated milk) and fold into peach-custard.
Turn into tray and freeze partially.
Whip with electric rotary beater. Freeze
until firm. Makes about 1½ pints.

FROZEN PLUM PUDDING

4 ounces sugar
2 ounces plain chocolate
4 fluid ounces milk
¾ pint double cream
1 teaspoon vanilla
2 ounces chopped nuts
2 ounces chopped maraschino
    cherries
5 ounces chopped raisins
2 ounces chopped dates

Add sugar and grated chocolate to
milk in a saucepan and cook until
chocolate is melted and mixture is
slightly thick. Chill.

Whip the cream until thick but not
stiff; add chocolate mixture, vanilla,
nuts, cherries, and the raisins and dates
which have been "plumped" by cooking in a small amount of water which
is allowed to evaporate.

Freeze at coldest temperature for 1½
hours, then reduce cold for remainder
of freezing period. Serves 8.

EASY STRAWBERRY FROZEN
CREAM

8 ounces strawberry jam
3 tablespoons lemon juice
2 drops almond flavouring
8 fluid ounces double cream

Stir jam, lemon juice, and flavouring together; fold into whipped cream.

Pour into freezing tray and freeze
until firm, stirring several times during
freezing period. Serves 4.

FRUIT SHERBET TARTS

20 digestive biscuits, finely
    crushed
2 ounces softened butter or mar-
    garine
2 ounces caster sugar
1 large banana
2 fluid ounces orange juice
2 tablespoons lime juice
6 ounces sugar
½ pint milk
1 egg white

Thoroughly blend together biscuit
crumbs, butter, and sugar.

Divide mixture into 8 fluted paper
cups set in tart tins. Press crumbs firmly
against bottom and sides of paper cups
with a spoon or a straight-sided glass.
Place in freezing compartment of refrigerator.

Mash banana with a fork; add orange
juice, lime juice, and sugar. Stir in
milk. Freeze 1 hour.

Beat mixture with a wire whisk. Beat
egg white until stiff but not dry and
fold into sherbet mixture.

Spoon sherbet into tart shells. Place
in freezing compartment of refrigerator and freeze 3 to 4 hours. Remove
fluted paper cups before serving.
Makes 8 tarts.

COCONUT MOUSSE

4 ounces hazelnuts
6 ounces sugar
2 fluid ounces water
6 egg yolks, stiffly beaten
2 teaspoons vanilla
½ teaspoon salt
¾ pint double cream
coconut biscuits, rectangular

Cook hazelnuts in water to cover 15
minutes; drain and chop.

Combine sugar and water; bring to
boiling, stirring constantly; boil 5 minutes without stirring. Pour in a fine
stream over egg yolks, beating constantly. Mix in vanilla and salt; beat
until cool.

Whip cream stiff; fold cream and
hazelnuts into egg yolk mixture. Stand
coconut biscuits around sides of 8-inch
square cake tin. Set a glass in centre
of tin. Pour hazelnut mixture around
glass. Freeze until firm.

To serve, remove glass, unmould
mousse on serving plate. Replace glass
in centre and fill with flowers. Decorate mousse with whipped cream and
nut slices. Serves 9.

Coconut Mousse

DESSERT SAUCES

Almost everybody loves desserts, but everyone, without exception, loves desserts dressed up with a delicious sauce. The right sauce makes your dessert even better. Choose your sauce with flavour and eye appeal in mind.

LEMON SAUCE
(Basic Recipe)

4 ounces sugar
1 tablespoon cornflour
⅛ teaspoon salt
8 fluid ounces boiling water
juice of ½ lemon
grated rind of ½ lemon
⅛ teaspoon nutmeg, optional
½ ounce butter or margarine

Mix together sugar, cornflour, and salt. Gradually add boiling water; bring to boil. Cook over low heat until thickened and clear, about 15 minutes.

Stir in lemon juice and rind. Add nutmeg and butter. Serve hot over puddings and other desserts. Makes about ½ pint.

Lemon Sauce Variations

Fluffy Lemon Sauce: Just before removing from heat, quickly stir in 1 slightly-beaten egg yolk and cook 1 minute, stirring constantly.

Remove from heat and fold in 1 stiffly-beaten egg white.

Orange Lemon Sauce: Substitute fresh or tinned orange juice for water.

Pineapple-Lemon Sauce: Substitute pineapple juice for water.

Lime Sauce: Omit nutmeg; substitute juice and rind of 1 lime for lemon.

Whipped Cream Lemon Sauce: Fold together equal parts of lemon sauce and whipped cream.

Golden Lemon Sauce: Substitute 9 ounces golden syrup for sugar. Use only 4 fluid ounces water.

CHOCOLATE SAUCE
(Basic Recipe)

6 ounces golden syrup
8 ounces sugar
8 fluid ounces water
3 ounces plain or cooking chocolate
1 teaspoon vanilla
8 fluid ounces evaporated milk

Cook syrup, sugar, and water to soft ball stage (236°F.). Remove from heat.

Add chocolate and stir until melted. Add vanilla. Slowly add evaporated milk, stirring constantly. Cool.

Serve hot or cold. Store in covered jar in refrigerator. Makes about 1¼ pints.

Chocolate Sauce Variations

Hot Fudge: Reheat chocolate sauce in top part of double saucepan.

Chocolate-Whipped Cream Sauce: Fold into chocolate sauce an equal quantity of whipped cream.

Mint-Chocolate Sauce: Substitute 2 drops oil of peppermint for vanilla.

Mocha Sauce: Substitute strong, fresh coffee for all or part of water.

Orange-Chocolate Sauce: Substitute orange juice for half or all of water; add grated rind of 1 orange.

Rum- or Brandy-Chocolate Sauce: Add 1 tablespoon rum or brandy.

HOT FUDGE SAUCE

1 ounce cooking or Meunière chocolate
8 ounces sugar
2 tablespoons golden syrup
⅛ teaspoon salt
3 fluid ounces water
½ ounce butter or margarine
½ teaspoon vanilla

Combine chocolate, sugar, syrup, salt, and water in saucepan. Heat slowly until chocolate is melted and sugar is dissolved.

Boil, stirring constantly, until a small amount forms a soft ball in cold water (230°F.). Add butter and vanilla.

Serve hot over ice cream, puddings, or plain cake. Makes about ½ pint.

CHERRY SAUCE

16 ounces sweet cherries, fresh or tinned, drained
1 tablespoon sugar
2 fluid ounces orange juice
2 fluid ounces water or cherry juice

If fresh cherries are used, cook in water until tender. Press through a sieve.

Add sugar and juices to puréed or whole fruit mixture and serve cold.

More sugar may be added for tart fruit. Makes 1 pint.

Variations: Pineapple, strawberries, raspberries, peaches, apricots, etc., may be treated in a similar fashion.

BUTTERSCOTCH SAUCE

10 ounces brown sugar
8 ounces golden syrup
4 fluid ounces water
4 fluid ounces evaporated milk

Boil sugar, syrup, and water to soft ball stage (235°F.).

Cool. Stir in milk. Makes ¾ pint.

QUICK BUTTERSCOTCH SAUCE

Melt 30 small vanilla-caramel sweets in 8 fluid ounces water over hot water.

CLEAR JAM SAUCE

Stir a jar of clear jam into 2 fluid ounces hot water. Add 1 tablespoon butter and cook in a double saucepan for a few minutes.

Thicken slightly with cornflour smoothly blended with a little water, then add to mixture in saucepan.

HARD OR BUTTER SAUCE
(Basic Recipe)

A cold, firm sauce of butter, sugar, and flavouring. It is most commonly used in the form known as Brandy Butts (see below).

3 ounces unsalted butter or margarine
5½ ounces icing sugar
½ teaspoon vanilla
1 tablespoon boiling water

Cream butter until soft. Gradually add sugar, creaming well.

Mix in vanilla and water a few drops at a time, beating until fluffy.

Pile lightly in serving dish. Chill until cold, but not hard. Makes about 6 ounces (4 to 6 servings).

Hard Sauce Variations

Apricot Hard Sauce: Omit vanilla. Whisk in 4½ ounces strained apricot pulp with the sugar. Add 1 teaspoon apricot brandy.

Banana Hard Sauce: Omit vanilla. Beat in ½ to 1 mashed banana.

Berry Hard Sauce: Omit vanilla. Beat in 2 to 3 ounces crushed berries.

Brandy or Rum Butter: Substitute 2 tablespoons brandy or rum for vanilla.

Brown Sugar Hard Sauce: Substitute brown sugar for icing sugar. Flavour as desired.

Butterscotch Hard Sauce: Substitute 3½ ounces brown sugar for icing sugar. Add 1 teaspoon vanilla and 1 tablespoon single cream.

Cherry Hard Sauce: Substitute 2 tablespoons cherry syrup for vanilla. Add 4 ounces drained chopped cherries.

Cocoa Hard Sauce: Add 2 tablespoons cocoa with the icing sugar. Rum, brandy, or orange juice and rind may be used for the flavouring instead of vanilla.

Cream Hard Sauce: Add 2 fluid ounces cream. Beat in thoroughly.

Date and Ginger Hard Sauce: Omit vanilla. Add 2 ounces chopped dates and ⅛ teaspoon ginger.

Fluffy Hard Sauce: Fold in 1 stiffly-beaten egg white. Add vanilla to taste.

Ginger Hard Sauce: Omit vanilla. Add 4 tablespoons chopped preserved ginger.

Lemon Hard Sauce: Substitute 1 teaspoon grated lemon rind and 1 teaspoon lemon juice for vanilla.

Liqueur Hard Sauce: Omit vanilla. Add 2 tablespoons preferred liqueur or fruit-flavoured cordial.

Orange Hard Sauce: Substitute 2 teaspoons grated orange rind and 1 tablespoon orange juice for vanilla.

Orange Marmalade Hard Sauce: While beating, work in 2 tablespoons orange marmalade.

Peach Hard Sauce: Omit vanilla and hot water. Beat into sauce 4 ounces mashed peaches.

Spicy Hard Sauce: Add ⅛ teaspoon each of powdered cinnamon and ginger and a slight grating of nutmeg to hard sauce.

Walnut Hard Sauce: Add 2 tablespoons chopped walnuts or other nuts.

Whipped Cream Hard Sauce: Fold in 2 fluid ounces double cream, whipped.

Wine Hard Sauce: Add 1 to 3 tablespoons sherry, Madeira, or port to hard sauce.

Yellow Hard Sauce: Add 1 beaten egg yolk. Use any preferred flavouring.

LOW CALORIE WHIPPED TOPPING
(Use Instead of Whipped Cream)

4 fluid ounces iced water
1 tablespoon lemon juice
1 teaspoon vanilla
2 ounces dried milk
3 tablespoons caster sugar

Put water, lemon juice, and vanilla in a bowl. Sprinkle dry milk on top. Beat until stiff with electric whisk or wire whisk, about 10 minutes.

Beat in sugar; continue beating until stiff enough to hold soft peaks, about 5 minutes longer.

Coffee Topping: Add 1 teaspoon instant coffee with vanilla.

WHIPPED CLEAR JAM SAUCE

Add 5 ounces tart clear jam to 1 unbeaten egg white. Beat with wire whisk until fluffy and light.

Serve on angel food cake, sponge cake, or pudding.

VANILLA WHIPPED CREAM SAUCE

1 slightly-beaten egg
2 tablespoons sugar
4 fluid ounces cream, heated
1 teaspoon vanilla
4 fluid ounces double cream, whipped

Mix egg and sugar in top of double saucepan. Add heated cream and cook until thick, stirring constantly.

Remove from heat. Add vanilla and cool, beating occasionally.

When cold, fold in whipped cream carefully.

Bread pudding in its many variations becomes a party dessert when garnished with a whipped topping.

VANILLA SAUCE
(Basic Recipe)

4 ounces sugar
1 tablespoon cornflour
⅛ teaspoon salt
8 fluid ounces boiling water
1 egg yolk
2 teaspoons vanilla
1 ounce butter or margarine
1 egg white

Mix sugar, cornflour, and salt. Gradually add hot water. Cook over moderate heat in saucepan until thick, stirring constantly, 6 to 7 minutes.

Add egg yolk. Cook 1 to 2 minutes, then add flavouring and butter.

Cool slightly. Fold in beaten egg white. Makes about 12 fluid ounces sauce.

Vanilla Sauce Variations

Chocolate Sauce: Add 1 ounce grated chocolate with hot water.

Lemon Sauce: Add 2 tablespoons lemon juice and 1 teaspoon grated lemon rind to sauce. Omit vanilla.

Marshmallow Sauce: Cut up 6 marshmallows. Fold in last, leaving sauce somewhat lumpy.

Nutmeg Sauce: Add ½ to ¾ teaspoon grated nutmeg to sauce.

Raisin-Nut Sauce: Add 2 ounces mixed raisins and nuts, diced, and 1 teaspoon grated orange rind to sauce.

FRUIT JUICE SAUCE

1 tablespoon cornflour
8 ounces sugar
4 fluid ounces boiling water
2 tablespoons lemon juice
8 fluid ounces fruit juice, fresh or canned

Mix cornflour and sugar. Add boiling water and boil 5 minutes. Cool and add fruit juice.

If sweetened juices are used, the sugar may be reduced as desired. Makes about 1 pint.

Variations: Any type of juice (strawberry, raspberry, pineapple, blackcurrant, peach, rhubarb, etc.) may be used.

Everybody loves desserts with straw-berries. Plain cake makes a delicious dessert when topped with whipped cream and served with Rhubarb-Straw-berry Sauce.

RHUBARB-STRAWBERRY SAUCE

12 ounces finely diced fresh rhubarb
2 tablespoons water
6 ounces sugar
½ ounce margarine
4 ounces sliced strawberries

Cook rhubarb in the water in a covered saucepan over low heat. Add sugar and margarine. Cool.

Fold in strawberries. Serve over squares of whipped cream-topped cottage pudding. Garnish with whole strawberries. This makes enough sauce for 8 servings.

ALL-PURPOSE FRUIT DESSERT SAUCE

This recipe is called "all-purpose" because it has so many uses. It may be used by itself or combined with whipped cream and served over waffles, ice cream, puddings, custards, etc., and its ingredients are available at any season of the year.

11 ounces dried apricots
½ pint water
12 ounces sugar
2½ pounds tinned crushed pine-apple

Cook apricots in water in a wide-bottomed pan until the fruit is pulpy and disintegrates readily when stirred with a wire whisk.

Add sugar and stir until dissolved, then add crushed pineapple. Bring to a boil. Pour into jars and cover. Store in refrigerator. Makes about 3¼ pints.

FLUFFY LEMON SAUCE

1 knob butter or margarine
3 ounces icing sugar
4 fluid ounces evaporated milk, chilled
1 tablespoon lemon juice
grated rind of 1 lemon

Cream butter. Add sugar, a little at a time, mixing well.

Whip milk until stiff. Add lemon juice and whip to blend.

Fold sugar mixture and lemon rind into whipped milk. Serves 6.

BRANDY CREAM SAUCE

3 ounces butter
5½ ounces icing sugar
3 tablespoons brandy
2 egg yolks
4 fluid ounces single cream

Place the butter in top of double saucepan over (not in) hot water; whisk until soft. Gradually add sugar and beat until creamy. Slowly beat in brandy, then beat in egg yolks, 1 at a time. Add cream and cook until slightly thickened. Serve over cottage pudding or gingerbread. Makes about 12 fluid ounces.

With Liqueurs: Substitute any favourite liqueur for the brandy.

ALMOND-HONEY SAUCE

4 ounces almonds
½ ounce butter or margarine
¾ pint strained honey
few grains salt

Blanch almonds by covering with boiling water and letting stand a few minutes until skins are wrinkled. Drain and rub between fingers to remove skins; dry on paper towelling.

Melt butter in pie dish in moderate oven (350°F. Mark 4). Spread blanched almonds over melted butter. Bake until nuts are lightly browned, stirring occasionally, about 15 minutes.

Cool and slice or cut nuts in halves. Stir nuts into honey. Add salt.

Serve with ice cream or other desserts. Serves 6.

HOT SPICED CHERRY SAUCE

1 large can pitted sour red cherries
4 ounces sugar
2 2-inch sticks cinnamon
16 whole cloves
2 teaspoons cornflour

Drain cherries and reserve syrup. Measure syrup and add enough water to make 8 fluid ounces. Add sugar and spices and bring to boiling point. Cook 10 minutes. Strain out spices.

Blend a little hot syrup with cornflour. Add to hot mixture. Cook until slightly thickened, about 10 minutes. Add cherries and heat.

Serve hot. Serves 4.

GOOSEBERRY SAUCE

1 pound gooseberries
4 fluid ounces water
12 ounces sugar

Pick over berries and rinse well. Drain. Add water and sugar. Bring slowly to boiling point.

Reduce heat and cook slowly uncovered for 10 minutes.

Serve with meat or as sauce for pudding. Makes about 1¼ pints.

SPECIAL FUDGE SAUCE

5 ounces cocoa
6 ounces sugar
½ teaspoon salt
1 tablespoon cornflour
6 ounces golden syrup
4 fluid ounces milk
1 ounce butter or margarine
2 tablespoons vanilla

Mix dry ingredients; add syrup and milk and mix thoroughly. Cook 15 minutes over hot water, stirring until thickened. Add butter.

Cool and add vanilla. Makes about 1¼ pints.

FLUFFY MAPLE SAUCE

9 ounces treacle
2 ounces brown sugar
2 tablespoons water
⅛ teaspoon salt
1 egg white
¼ teaspoon maple flavouring

Mix treacle, sugar, and water in saucepan. Cook until it forms very soft ball when dropped into cold water (236°F.).

Pour syrup slowly over egg white beaten stiff with salt added. Add flavouring and beat until mixture holds peaks. Serve with hot pudding. Makes about ¾ pint.

MELBA SAUCE

5 ounces redcurrant jelly
4 ounces sugar
4 ounces pulp and juice of raspberries
½ tablespoon cornflour
1 tablespoon cold water

Add jelly and sugar to raspberries. Bring to boiling point. Add cornflour mixed with cold water.

Cook, stirring constantly until mixture becomes thick and clear. Cool and strain. Makes about ¾ pint.

Note: A packet of thawed frozen raspberries may be used.

Peach Melba: Place a tinned peach half, cut-side up, in each of 6 individual fruit dishes. Top each with a scoop of ice cream and pour the cooled sauce over the top.

Peach Melba

SWEETENED WHIPPED CREAM OR CREME CHANTILLY

Whip 8 fluid ounces double cream until stiff. Then fold in 1 to 3 tablespoons sifted icing sugar and ½ teaspoon vanilla. Serve with cold puddings or frozen desserts, or use as a filling for cakes.

Variations: The sweetened whipped cream may be varied in innumerable ways. Here are a few examples: (1) To the whipped cream above add 4 to 5 ounces jam or orange marmalade; (2) add 2 ounces blanched, toasted, slivered almonds or other nuts; (3) add 2 ounces crushed peppermint rock; (4) add 2 ounces lightly toasted coconut and 1 tablespoon light rum.

BANANA SAUCE

½ ounce butter or margarine
1 tablespoon flour
2 ounces sugar
4 fluid ounces milk, scalded
1 egg yolk
1 banana, well mashed
4 fluid ounces double cream, whipped with a few grains salt

Cream the butter and add flour. Blend thoroughly; add sugar gradually.

Combine with scalded milk. Cook until thickened, stirring constantly. Add egg yolk, slightly beaten. Cook 3 minutes.

Remove from heat. Add bananas. Chill. Fold in whipped cream. Makes about 12 fluid ounces.

Variations: Substitute strawberries and other fresh or canned fruits for banana.

LIQUEUR SAUCES

Allow for each serving about 1½ tablespoons of your favourite liqueur. Crème de menthe and kirsch are especially popular. Pour over ice cream, ices, or light-sugared fruits. Garnish with maraschino cherries.

MAPLE NUT SAUCE

1½ ounces broken pecans or walnuts
2 ounces butter or margarine
4 tablespoons brown sugar
9 ounces golden syrup
1 tablespoon cold water
2 tablespoons flour
4 fluid ounces boiling water
½ teaspoon maple flavouring or vanilla

Sauté nuts in butter or margarine to delicate brown and combine with sugar and syrup.

Mix cold water with flour in saucepan. Add boiling water and cook until thick. Add sugar mixture and bring to the boil. Add flavouring. Serve hot. Makes about 12 fluid ounces.

CARAMEL SAUCE

2 ounces butter or margarine, melted
6 ounces brown sugar
1 tablespoon cornflour
8 fluid ounces cold water
2 teaspoons vanilla

Combine butter, sugar, and cornflour dissolved in water in top of double saucepan. Bring slowly to boiling point, stirring to blend.

Remove from heat. Add vanilla. Cover until ready to serve.

Should mixture congeal, place over low flame, heat slowly, then thin to desired consistency with hot water, beat with spoon until smooth. Makes about ¾ pint.

Brandy, Rum or Lemon Caramel Sauce: Vary caramel sauce by substituting 2 tablespoons of any of these flavourings for vanilla.

CARAMEL SAUCE 2

Melt 8 ounces sugar in heavy frying pan over low heat until light brown in colour.

Remove from heat and slowly add 8 fluid ounces boiling water. Boil 10 minutes or until caramel is dissolved. Makes about 8 fluid ounces.

WHIPPED FRUIT SAUCE

4 ounces fresh berries
4 to 8 ounces sugar
few grains salt
1 teaspoon lemon juice

Amount of sugar depends upon the sweetness of berries.

Combine ingredients in a deep bowl and beat until fluffy. Serve on cake or pudding.

COFFEE SAUCE

3 fluid ounces freshly ground coffee
6 fluid ounces boiling water
3 ounces sugar
1 tablespoon cornflour
⅛ teaspoon salt
1 egg yolk
1 tablespoon butter
½ teaspoon vanilla
3 fluid ounces top of the milk cream

Place coffee in saucepan, add boiling water, heat to boiling. Cover, turn off heat, steep 5 minutes; strain through double thickness of muslin.

Combine sugar, cornflour, and salt in top of double saucepan. Add egg yolk; mix thoroughly. Stir in coffee gradually.

Place mixture over hot water; cook 8 to 10 minutes until thickened, stirring frequently. Remove from hot water, stir in butter and vanilla.

Set in cold water to cool, stirring frequently. Stir in cream gradually. Chill; serve over ice cream. Makes about ¼ pint sauce.

SOUR CREAM SAUCE

3 ounces butter or margarine
5½ ounces icing sugar
¼ teaspoon lemon juice
¼ teaspoon vanilla
2 to 4 fluid ounces sour cream, plain or whipped

Cream butter. Add sugar slowly and beat well. Add lemon juice and vanilla.

Beat in enough sour cream to make sauce light and fluffy.

Serve on fruit brown betty, hot baked apples or dumplings, steamed or baked puddings. Makes about 8 fluid ounces.

RUM SAUCE

2 ounces butter or margarine
7 ounces brown sugar
2 egg yolks, well beaten
4 fluid ounces single cream
⅛ teaspoon salt
3 tablespoons rum

Cream together butter and sugar. Add egg yolks, cream, and salt.

Cook over boiling water until creamy and thickened.

Remove from heat. Cool, add rum. Makes 8 fluid ounces.

HOT BROWN SUGAR SAUCE

6 ounces treacle
4 ounces brown sugar
4 teaspoons flour
¼ teaspoon salt
8 fluid ounces water
½ ounce butter or margarine
1 teaspoon vanilla

Combine treacle, brown sugar, flour, salt, water, and butter in small saucepan.

Boil 10 minutes, stirring occasionally. Add vanilla. Makes 8 fluid ounces.

STRAWBERRY SAUCE

3 ounces butter or margarine
8 ounces caster sugar
1 egg white
1 teacup strawberries

Cream butter; add sugar gradually, then egg white with strawberries.

Stir until fruit is mashed. Makes about 12 fluid ounces.

Variations: Almost any variety of fresh fruit may be substituted.

RUM TOFFEE SAUCE

6 ounces demerara sugar
1 fluid ounce top of the milk
1 ounce butter or margarine
4 teaspoons rum

Combine sugar, cream, and butter. Bring to the boil and simmer 5 minutes. Cool to lukewarm and add rum.

Serve warm on vanilla ice cream or cottage pudding. Makes about ½ pint.

PINEAPPLE SAUCE

16 ounces crushed pineapple
2 ounces sugar
1 tablespoon cornflour
½ ounce butter or margarine
¼ teaspoon salt

Drain juice from crushed pineapple. Mix cornflour and sugar. Add to juice. Cook over direct heat until sauce thickens, stirring constantly.

Add drained fruit, butter, and salt. Cook a few minutes longer.

Serve hot or cold over cottage pudding or plain cake. Makes about 16 fluid ounces.

MARSHMALLOW-MINT SAUCE

8 ounces sugar
4 fluid ounces water
16 marshmallows, cut finely
few grains salt
1 egg white
1 or 2 drops oil of peppermint
green food colouring

Combine sugar and water in saucepan.

Simmer 5 minutes, stirring occasionally. Add marshmallows, stirring to blend.

Add salt to egg white; beat until stiff. Gradually fold marshmallow mixture into egg white.

Add oil of peppermint and green colouring to tint delicately. Serve hot or cold on ice cream. Serves 6.

Marshmallow Sauce: For plain marshmallow sauce, omit oil of peppermint and green food colouring. The egg white may also be omitted.

FOAMY EGG SAUCE

3 to 4 ounces butter or margarine
5½ ounces icing sugar
1 well-beaten egg
2 tablespoons hot water
1 teaspoon vanilla

Cream butter and add sugar gradually. Beat in egg and hot water.

Heat over hot water, beating constantly, until mixture thickens. Add vanilla.

Serve hot or cold. Makes 1 teacup.

HOT BRANDY SAUCE

3 ounces sugar
½ tablespoon cornflour
⅛ teaspoon salt
8 fluid ounces hot water
½ ounce butter or margarine
2 tablespoons brandy

Combine sugar, cornflour, and salt in a saucepan. Add hot water slowly. Cook until clear, stirring constantly. Add butter and flavouring.

Serve hot over mincemeat pie or steamed pudding. Makes 8 fluid ounces.

PEPPERMINT SAUCE

1½ ounces butter or margarine
10 ounces sugar
8 ounces golden syrup
6 fluid ounces undiluted
**   evaporated milk**
green food colouring
few drops of peppermint oil

Combine butter, sugar, and syrup; bring to boil. Cook to soft ball stage (235°F.). Cool slightly; add milk and stir until mixed.

Add green food colouring to produce desired light green colour. Add peppermint oil to taste. Serve over vanilla ice cream. Makes 16 fluid ounces.

MADEIRA SAUCE

8 ounces sugar
2½ tablespoons flour
⅛ teaspoon salt
16 fluid ounces boiling water
1½ tablespoons lime juice
4 fluid ounces Madeira wine
1 ounce melted butter

Mix sugar, flour, and salt. Stir gradually into boiling water. Cook until thickened, 5 to 10 minutes, stirring constantly.

Add lime juice, Madeira wine, and butter. Stir well. Do not boil. Remove from heat. Makes 16 fluid ounces.

MOLASSES OR BLACK TREACLE SAUCE

12 ounces molasses or black treacle
1 tablespoon lemon juice
1 ounce butter or margarine
⅛ teaspoon salt
1 egg, well beaten

Simmer molasses or treacle 15 minutes or until quite thick. Add lemon juice, butter, and salt; pour mixture over well-beaten egg, whisking while pouring.

Then cook 3 minutes in top of double saucepan, stirring constantly. Makes about 12 fluid ounces.

HONEY-WINE FRUIT SAUCE

6 ounces honey
4 fluid ounces water
3 cardamom seeds, peeled and
**   crushed finely**
½ teaspoon salt
6 or 8 mint leaves, crushed
1 tablespoon lemon juice
4 fluid ounces sherry, Madeira, or
**   port**
chilled fruit as desired

Mix honey, water, and crushed cardamom seeds; simmer 5 minutes. Add salt and mint leaves. Cool and strain. Add lemon juice and wine.

Pour over chilled fruit and serve. Makes about ½ pint.

Note: Cantaloupe balls, honeydew melon balls, and blackberries make a delicious combination. The sauce is excellent, too, on grapefruit segments.

SHERRY SAUCE

2 eggs, separated
8 ounces caster sugar
3 tablespoons sherry

Whisk yolks until thick. Gradually beat in half the sugar. Beat egg whites until stiff; add ½ the caster sugar gradually, beating until sugar disappears. Fold into yolk mixture. Flavour with sherry. Makes about 12 fluid ounces.

FOAMY ORANGE SAUCE

3 ounces butter or margarine
8 ounces caster sugar
1 egg, separated
2 fluid ounces orange juice

Cream butter until soft, whisk in sugar gradually, then egg yolk and orange juice.

Just before serving, fold in stiffly beaten egg white.

Variations: Flavour with 1 tablespoon brandy, or substitute sherry for orange juice. Whipped cream may also be folded into the mixture. Makes about 12 fluid ounces.

HONEY SAUCE

2 teaspoons cornflour
1 ounce melted butter or margarine
6 ounces honey

Add cornflour to melted butter and stir until smooth.

Add honey and cook 6 minutes. Makes about 6 fluid ounces.

LEMONADE HARD OR BUTTER SAUCE

2 ounces soft butter or margarine
8 ounces caster sugar, sifted
1 tablespoon plus 1 teaspoon
**   frozen concentrate for**
**   lemonade (undiluted)**

Cream butter; add caster sugar, creaming and beating until light and fluffy. Add concentrate for lemonade and beat well again.

Chill slightly and mould in small balls or drop from a teaspoon on to greaseproof paper. Top with a clove, slices of maraschino and a clove, or nuts.

Chill and serve with hot steamed pudding.

Lemonade Hard or Butter Sauce

DATE PECAN SAUCE

about 4 ounces sliced, stoned dates
2 fluid ounces water
2 ounces brown sugar
6 ounces golden syrup
⅛ teaspoon salt
½ teaspoon vanilla
2 ounces chopped pecans

Combine dates, water, sugar, syrup, and salt. Bring to boil; cook 1 minute, stirring constantly.

Remove from heat. Add vanilla and nuts. Let cool. Serve over vanilla ice cream. Serves 6.

HONEY AND ORANGE SAUCE

12 ounces honey
1½ to 2 ounces chopped orange peel
4 fluid ounces orange juice
pinch of salt

Combine all ingredients. Let stand over hot, not boiling, water about 30 minutes to blend flavours.

Serve on gingerbread, steamed puddings, or ice cream. Makes 12 fluid ounces.

HOT BUTTER SAUCE

4 ounces butter or margarine
8 ounces sugar
4 fluid ounces single cream
1 teaspoon vanilla

Melt butter or margarine. Blend in sugar and cream. Heat. Add vanilla.

Serve hot over puddings. Serves 6.

PLUM PUDDING SAUCE

2 ounces butter or margarine
5½ ounces icing sugar
2 tablespoons cider
2 eggs, separated
4 fluid ounces evaporated milk

Cream butter and icing sugar. Add cider.

Beat egg yolks until lemon coloured and add. When well mixed, stir in evaporated milk.

Cook in double saucepan until sauce is thick as custard. Remove from heat.

Beat egg whites until stiff. Gradually add hot mixture, beating constantly until blended. Makes 8 fluid ounces.

PEANUT BUTTER-FRUIT SAUCE

4 ounces sugar
6 ounces treacle
3 fluid ounces water
½ teaspoon salt
2 ounces peanut butter
1½ ounces raisins or chopped glacé fruit

Mix sugar, treacle, water, and salt. Simmer 10 minutes; cool.

Stir treacle slowly into the peanut butter and raisins or glacé fruit.

Serve on ice cream or steamed puddings. Makes about 8 fluid ounces.

SWEET LEMON SAUCE

4 ounces butter or margarine
8 ounces sugar
1 egg, beaten
3 tablespoons boiling water
1 lemon, grated rind and juice

Cream butter. Add sugar and continue creaming. Stir in egg and mix well. Add water gradually.

Cook over low heat or in top of double saucepan, stirring constantly, until mixture thickens. Add lemon juice and rind. Blend well. Serves 6.

HOT BURNT SUGAR SAUCE

14 ounces sugar
8 fluid ounces hot water
1¼ tablespoons cornflour
¼ teaspoon salt
about ¾ ounce butter or margarine

Melt 2 ounces sugar in heavy frying pan, stirring occasionally. When lightly browned, stir in hot water.

Let simmer until caramel is melted.

Mix remaining sugar with cornflour and salt and add to hot mixture. Cook, stirring constantly, until thickened and clear. Add butter and serve hot. Serves 8 to 12.

FOAMY LEMON SAUCE

3 ounces butter or margarine
¼ teaspoon salt
11 ounces sifted icing sugar
1 egg yolk
1 teaspoon grated lemon rind
2 fluid ounces lemon juice

Cream butter with salt. Add 8 ounces sugar gradually. Beat in egg yolk. Blend in lemon rind and juice.

Add remaining sugar and blend. Makes ½ pint.

HOT SPICY SAUCE

1 tablespoon cornflour
1 pound sugar
¼ teaspoon cinnamon
¼ teaspoon nutmeg
¾ pint water
2 ounces butter or margarine

Combine cornflour, sugar, cinnamon, and nutmeg. Add water gradually, stirring to mix well. Add butter.

Heat to boiling, stirring constantly, and cook 5 minutes. Serve hot with puddings. Serves 6.

FOAMY BRANDY SAUCE

2 egg yolks
5½ ounces icing sugar
few grains salt
2 tablespoons brandy or 1 teaspoon vanilla
8 fluid ounces double cream, whipped

Beat egg yolks very light, gradually adding sugar and salt. Add brandy or vanilla. Fold in whipped cream. Makes ¾ pint.

FOAMY SAUCE

⅛ teaspoon salt
1 egg white
1½ ounces brown sugar
¼ teaspoon vanilla
1 egg yolk
2 fluid ounces double cream, whipped

Add salt to egg white and beat until foamy.

Sift brown sugar and gradually add 2 tablespoons sugar to the egg white, beating until well blended and egg white is stiff.

Add remaining sugar and vanilla to egg yolk and beat until fluffy. Combine both mixtures and fold in whipped cream. Makes 12 fluid ounces.

Note: Sauce should not stand more than 2 hours before serving.

HOT WALNUT SAUCE

4 ounces margarine
2 tablespoons cornflour
3 to 4 ounces brown sugar
½ pint boiling water
about 1½ ounces chopped walnuts
1 tablespoon lemon juice

Melt margarine in top of a double saucepan.

Combine cornflour and brown sugar; blend with margarine. Add water and cook until thick, stirring constantly. Add walnuts and lemon juice. Serve hot. Serves 12.

BUTTERSCOTCH SAUCE 2

4 ounces butter or margarine
1 pound brown sugar
1 tablespoon lemon juice
4 fluid ounces double cream

Combine all ingredients. Cook in double saucepan 1 hour, stirring occasionally.

Add toasted almonds to sauce if desired. Makes about 1¼ pints.

HONEY HARD SAUCE

Cream 3 ounces butter and gradually beat in 9 ounces honey. Add 1 teaspoon lemon juice. Chill until cold, but not hard.

Place several sauces and balls of ice cream on the table for a "make-your-own" ice cream sundae.

DOUGHNUTS

A doughnut is defined as a small cake of sweetened leavened dough, usually ring-shaped, fried in deep, hot fat. The names friedcakes and crullers are often applied to the same product; however usage differs as to the names.

The name doughnut may be derived from the fact that early doughnuts were balls or "nuts" of dough. Crullers derived their name from the Dutch word krullen, meaning curled, and they differed from doughnuts mainly in shape, being twisted, curled, or gashed across. Bismarcks are variations of the doughnut in which the dough is filled with jam, jelly, or marmalade before or, more often, after being fried in deep fat. In some places a distinction is made between a doughnut and a fried cake. The former being made with yeast and the latter a baking powder dough.

DOUGHNUT MAKING HINTS

Mixing and Cutting: The dough for quick doughnuts (made with baking powder or bicarbonate of soda) should be as soft as can be handled. Chill the dough for at least an hour to make rolling out easy.

Roll and cut a little of the dough at a time, keeping the remaining dough in the refrigerator. Use a floured cutter to cut doughnuts. For variety, cut dough into strips 1 inch wide and 3 inches long to make "Long Johns." Quick doughnuts should be allowed to stand about 15 minutes before frying.

Yeast-raised doughnuts should be handled in much the same way as other yeast breads. The doughnuts should rise in a warm place until almost double in bulk before frying.

Frying: Fry in deep hot fat (375°F.). The pan should be about half full or have at least 3 inches of fat. The temperature of the fat is very important because if the fat is too cold, the doughnuts will absorb fat; if too hot, the doughnuts will brown before they are cooked through.

Fry only a few doughnuts at a time or the fat will cool too rapidly. Turn the doughnuts when they are brown on the underside—usually when they rise to the top of the fat. Drain on absorbent paper.

To Sugar Doughnuts: When cool, put a few at a time in a paper bag with icing or caster sugar and shake well.

To Glaze Doughnuts: Gradually add about 5 tablespoons boiling water to 5½ ounces icing sugar and mix well. Dip warm doughnuts into glaze.

PLAIN DOUGHNUTS

3 tablespoons butter
8 ounces sugar
2 beaten eggs
15 ounces sifted plain flour
4 teaspoons baking powder
½ teaspoon salt
6 fluid ounces milk
1 teaspoon vanilla essence

Cream the butter; add sugar gradually and cream until light. Stir in beaten eggs.

Mix and sift flour, baking powder, and salt; add to creamed mixture alternately with the milk. Stir in vanilla essence. Chill thoroughly.

Roll out ⅓ inch thick on lightly floured surface. Cut with floured cutter. Fry in deep hot fat (375°F.) until brown, turning once. Drain. Makes about 3 dozen.

Variations of Plain Doughnuts

Plain Crullers: Increase fat in Plain Doughnuts to 2 ounces. Roll out ½ inch thick and cut into strips. Twist or form in knots. Fry in deep hot fat (375°F.). Drain on absorbent paper.

Bismarcks: Make Plain Doughnut dough and roll out ¼ inch thick. Leave the rolled dough for 5 minutes and then cut into rounds with a lightly floured pastry cutter. Again leave the dough for 5 minutes.

Put 1 teaspoon jam or marmalade in the centre of half the rounds. Sandwich with a second round of dough and seal the entire edge by pressing between your fingers. Fry in deep hot fat (375°F.) and drain.

Chocolate Doughnuts: Increase the sugar in Plain Doughnuts to 10 ounces and add 1½ ounces unsweetened chocolate, melted, to the egg-sugar mixture. If you like, chopped nuts may also be added.

Drop Doughnuts: Drop dough from a spoon into the hot fat. For drop doughnuts the dough may be slightly softer than for rolled doughnuts.

Fruit Doughnuts: To the dry ingredients add 3 ounces fruit such as raisins or chopped candied peel.

Sour Milk or Buttermilk Doughnuts: Reduce baking powder to 2 teaspoons and add ½ teaspoon bicarbonate of soda. Use sour milk or buttermilk instead of milk. Flavour with ¾ teaspoon grated nutmeg, if you like.

Spice Doughnuts: Add ½ teaspoon grated nutmeg and ¼ teaspoon ground mace to the dry ingredients.

Nut Doughnuts: Add 2 ounces chopped pecans or walnuts to the dough.

Orange Doughnuts: Add 1 teaspoon ground mace to dry ingredients and stir in 1 teaspoon grated orange rind.

RAISED DOUGHNUTS
(Basic Recipe)

about ¾ pint scalded milk
2 teaspoons dry yeast
6 ounces sugar
1 pound 2 ounces sifted plain flour
3 tablespoons butter
1 egg, well beaten
1½ teaspoons grated nutmeg
1 teaspoon salt

Cool milk to lukewarm. Add the yeast and 1 tablespoon sugar. Stir until dissolved. Add 12 ounces of flour and beat well. Cover and leave to rise in a warm place about 1 hour.

Cream butter until fluffy. Add sugar, and cream together until light. Add egg, nutmeg, and salt, and stir into yeast mixture. Add remaining dough flour, knead lightly, and place dough in a greased bowl.

Brush dough with salad oil, cover with a towel, and leave to rise until double in bulk, about 1½ hours.

Roll on a floured board to ½-inch thickness. Cut with floured doughnut cutter. Leave to rise until double in bulk, about 1 hour.

Fry in deep hot fat (370°F.) until brown, turning once. Drain on absorbent paper. Makes about 2½ dozen.

Raised Doughnut Variations

Bismarcks: Roll dough ½ inch thick. Cut rounds with a 3-inch pastry cutter. Fry as for raised doughnuts.

When cool, cut a short slit in side of each to the centre. Put a teaspoon of jam in centre. Close tightly. Roll in sugar.

Crullers: 1. Roll dough ½ inch thick. Cut into strips ¾ inches long. Shape into twists or figure 8's. Fry as for raised doughnuts.

2. Roll dough ¼ inch thick. Cut into 2-inch squares. Make four slits in each. Then lift by picking up alternate strips between fingers and thumb. Fry same way.

RICH CRULLERS

1 pound 2 ounces sifted plain flour
1¼ teaspoons bicarbonate of soda
2½ teaspoons cream of tartar
½ teaspoon salt
1 teaspoon grated nutmeg
3 eggs
8 ounces sugar
8 fluid ounces double cream

Mix and sift the dry ingredients. Beat the eggs until thick and lemon-coloured; gradually beat in the sugar, then stir in the cream.

Gradually stir in the flour mixture, blending until almost smooth.

Turn out on floured board and roll out ¼ inch thick. Cut with floured doughnut cutter and fry in deep hot fat (370°F.) until golden brown.

POTATO DOUGHNUTS

1 pound sifted plain flour
4 teaspoons baking powder
1 teaspoon salt
1 teaspoon bicarbonate of soda
1 teaspoon grated nutmeg
2 eggs, well beaten
8 ounces sugar
2 tablespoons salad oil
7 ounces mashed potato
8 fluid ounces sour milk or butter-milk

Mix and sift flour, baking powder, salt, bicarbonate of soda, and nutmeg.

Beat eggs and sugar until light. Add oil, potato, and milk, beating until smooth. Stir in flour mixture. Chill thoroughly.

Roll on a floured board to ½-inch thickness. Cut with doughnut cutter. Fry in deep hot fat (370°F.). Drain on absorbent paper. Makes about 3 dozen.

FRENCH CRULLERS

2 ounces sugar
½ teaspoon salt
2 ounces fat
8 fluid ounces water
4 ounces sifted plain flour
3 eggs
1 teaspoon vanilla essence

Mix together sugar, salt, fat, and water in heavy saucepan and heat. When briskly boiling, add flour all at once, stirring vigorously with a wooden spoon.

Beat until mixture forms a smooth ball which pulls away cleanly from sides of pan.

Place in a bowl. Beat in thoroughly one egg at a time then continue beating until mixture is smooth and shiny and breaks off when spoon is raised. Add vanilla essence. Chill.

Pipe mixture, using a pastry bag, in the shape of rings onto strips of oiled greaseproof paper.

Carefully turn the paper upside-down so that the crullers will drop gently into deep hot fat.

Fry at 380°F. until golden brown on all sides. Drain. Cool. Brush with a little glacé icing. Makes 10 crullers.

RICE CRULLERS OR FRITTERS
(Calas)

12 ounces cooked rice
3 beaten eggs
¼ teaspoon vanilla essence
½ teaspoon grated nutmeg or grated lemon rind
6 tablespoons flour
4 ounces sugar
½ teaspoon salt
3 teaspoons baking powder

Mix together the rice, eggs, vanill essence, and nutmeg. Mix and si flour, sugar, salt, and baking powde Mix thoroughly with rice-egg mixtur

Drop the mixture, a spoonful a time, in deep hot fat (365°F.) and f until golden brown. Drain on absorbe paper.

Sprinkle with icing sugar. Ser very hot with tart jam. Makes abou 1½ dozen.

YEAST-RAISED RICE CRULLERS OR FRITTERS

9 ounces cooked rice, very soft
1 teaspoon dry yeast
4 fluid ounces warm, not hot, wate
3 eggs, beaten
5 ounces sifted flour
2 ounces sugar
½ teaspoon salt
¼ teaspoon grated nutmeg

Mash rice and cool to lukewar Soften yeast in warm water and st in lukewarm rice. Mix well. Cover a leave to rise overnight.

The next morning, add eggs, flou sugar, salt, and nutmeg. Beat un smooth. Leave in a warm place f 30 minutes.

Drop the mixture, a spoonful a time, in deep hot fat (360°F.) and f until golden brown, about 3 minute Serve sprinkled with caster sugar sugar mixed with ground cinnamo These are excellent served with fr or maple syrup. Makes 2 dozen.

Yeast-Raised Rice Crullers

BANANA DOUGHNUTS

- 1¼ pounds sifted plain flour
- 4 teaspoons baking powder
- 1 teaspoon bicarbonate of soda
- 2 teaspoons salt
- 1 teaspoon grated nutmeg
- 2 ounces fat
- 8 ounces sugar
- 3 eggs, well beaten
- 1½-2 mashed bananas
- 4 fluid ounces sour milk or buttermilk
- 1½ teaspoons vanilla essence
- 2 ounces flour for rolling
- melted fat or oil

Sift together flour, baking powder, bicarbonate of soda, salt, and nutmeg.

Beat fat until creamy. Add sugar gradually and continue beating until light and fluffy. Add eggs and beat well.

Mix together the bananas, milk, and vanilla essence. Add this mixture to creamed mixture and blend. Add flour mixture and mix until smooth.

Turn a small amount of dough onto a floured board. Knead very lightly. Roll out to ⅜-inch thickness. Cut with floured 2½-inch doughnut cutter.

Heat fat to 375°F. or until a 1-inch cube of bread will turn golden brown in about 40 seconds. Slip doughnuts into fat with fish slice. Fry about 3 minutes, or until golden brown, turning them frequently.

Drain on absorbent paper. Makes 3½ dozen. Sugar the doughnuts, if you like.

BLACK TREACLE DOUGHNUTS

- 6 ounces black treacle
- 4 ounces granulated sugar
- 2 eggs
- 1½ tablespoons melted butter
- 1¼ pounds sifted plain flour
- 1 teaspoon bicarbonate of soda
- 1 teaspoon salt
- ½ teaspoon ground ginger or 1 teaspoon grated nutmeg
- 8 fluid ounces sour milk or buttermilk

Beat the treacle, sugar, and eggs until smooth. Add butter.

Mix and sift 8 ounces flour with the soda, salt, and ginger or nutmeg. Add alternately with the sour milk or buttermilk to the first mixture.

Add sifted flour to make a dough that can be handled easily. Chill in refrigerator.

Roll dough a little at a time. Shape with small doughnut cutter. Fry in deep hot fat (370°F.). Drain on absorbent paper. Makes about 4 dozen.

RUM OR BRANDY CRULLERS

- 5 egg yolks
- 2 whole eggs
- 6 ounces sugar
- 2 tablespoons sour cream
- 2 tablespoons rum or brandy
- 2 teaspoons vanilla essence
- about 14 ounces sifted plain flour

Beat egg yolks and whole eggs until thick and lemon-coloured. Add sugar gradually, beating well. Blend in sour cream, rum, and vanilla essence.

Add flour gradually until dough becomes too hard to handle in the bowl.

Toss on floured tea cloth and knead dough until smooth and elastic.

Roll out portion of dough on floured cloth until paper-thin; cut into 1-inch by 3-inch strips. Slit centre of each strip and take one end and pull it through slit on other side.

Fry in deep fat (375°F.) first on one, then on the other side, until pale, golden brown, about 2 minutes on the first and 1 minute on other side. Drain on absorbent paper; sprinkle with icing sugar. Makes 3 to 4 dozen.

BROWN SUGAR DOUGHNUTS

- 2 eggs
- 9 ounces brown sugar
- 4 tablespoons melted butter
- 8 fluid ounces milk
- 1 pound sifted plain flour
- 4 teaspoons baking powder
- ½ teaspoon ground cinnamon
- ½ teaspoon salt

Beat eggs until they are light and stir into sugar. Stir butter and milk into egg mixture.

Add baking powder, cinnamon, and salt to flour and sift again. Add to egg-butter mixture, stirring only enough to get ingredients thoroughly blended.

Chill in refrigerator at least 24 hours if possible. This prevents the doughnuts from soaking up the fat when fried.

Roll out a little of the dough at a time on floured board; cut with floured doughnut cutter.

Fry in hot deep fat (365°F.) until brown on one side. Turn and brown the other side. Drain and roll in caster sugar.

This dough may be kept at least a week in a covered container in the refrigerator. Break off and cook only enough of the dough needed at a time, as freshly cooked doughnuts are better than those left standing overnight. Makes about 35.

QUICK DOUGHNUTS
(With Prepared Mix)

- 1 packet crumpet mix
- 1 tablespoon sugar
- 1½ teaspoons ground cinnamon
- 1 teaspoon grated nutmeg
- about 6 fluid ounces water

Mix the crumpet mix, sugar, and spices together. Add water and knead dough 30 seconds on lightly floured board. Roll out dough to ½-inch thickness. Cut with doughnut cutter.

Fry in deep hot fat (375°F.) 3 minutes, turning once. Drain on absorbent paper. Makes 1 dozen.

RAISED ORANGE CRULLERS

- 2 teaspoons dry yeast
- 4 tablespoons warm water
- about 1 pound sifted plain flour
- 8 fluid ounces milk, scalded and cooled
- 2 ounces butter or margarine
- 8 ounces sugar
- 1 egg
- 1 teaspoon salt
- 1 tablespoon grated orange rind

Dissolve yeast in water and leave for 5 minutes.

Add 4 ounces flour to milk and beat until smooth, using electric mixer if possible. Add yeast and leave for 30 minutes.

Cream butter and sugar until light and fluffy. Add egg and salt and beat well. Add to flour mixture. Add remaining flour gradually. Knead dough until smooth and elastic.

Place dough in a greased bowl, cover, and leave until double in bulk.

Turn out on floured teacloth and cut into 24 equal pieces. Roll each piece until smooth and about ¾ inch in diameter and 12 inches long.

Fold in half and pinch end together; twist lightly. Cover and leave to rise until light, about 45 minutes.

Fry in deep fat (350°F.) until crullers are golden brown. Drain on absorbent paper. Roll in mixture of granulated sugar and orange rind. Makes 2 dozen.

BAKING POWDER CRULLERS

- 1 pound sifted plain flour
- 3½ teaspoons baking powder
- ½ teaspoon salt
- ½ teaspoon grated nutmeg
- 8 ounces sugar
- 2 tablespoons fat
- 2 well-beaten eggs
- 8 fluid ounces cream

Mix and sift flour, baking powder, salt, and nutmeg.

Cream sugar and fat together thoroughly; add eggs and beat well. Add sifted flour mixture alternately with cream to creamed mixture and mix thoroughly.

Roll out on floured board to ½-inch thickness. Cut into strips 6×1 inches. Twist strips, pressing ends together.

Fry in deep fat (370°F.) until brown, about 3 minutes. Drain on absorbent paper. When slightly cooled, sprinkle with icing sugar. Makes about 24.

PIED PIPER DOUGHNUTS

2 eggs
10 ounces sugar
7 ounces mashed potatoes
5 tablespoons fat, melted
1¼ pounds sifted plain flour
5 teaspoons baking powder
1 teaspoon bicarbonate of soda
1 tablespoon ground cinnamon
½ teaspoon grated nutmeg
½ teaspoon ground cloves
1 can (10 ounces) condensed tomato
      soup
fat for frying

Beat eggs and sugar until fluffy; add potatoes and melted fat.

Sift flour with baking powder, soda and spices; add to egg-sugar mixture alternately with soup; mix well after each addition.

Roll dough on floured board until about ½-inch thick. Cut with doughnut cutter. Fry in 3- to 4-inch deep fat (380°F.) until brown, about 2 minutes.

Drain on absorbent paper. Dust while hot with a mixture of 1 teaspoon ground cinnamon and 4 ounces of sugar. Makes about 40 doughnuts.

OLD-TIME DOUGHNUTS

8 ounces sifted flour
½ teaspoon bicarbonate of soda
⅛ teaspoon grated nutmeg
¼ teaspoon salt
2 tablespoons fat
4 ounces sugar
1 egg
½ teaspoon vanilla
2 tablespoons vinegar and milk
      to make 4 fluid ounces

Mix and sift flour, soda, nutmeg, and salt.

Cream the fat; add sugar gradually and continue creaming. Add egg and beat well. Add vanilla. Add vinegar and milk mixture alternately with dry ingredients and stir only until well blended.

Roll small quantities of dough at a time, about ⅓-inch thick. Cut doughnuts with a 2½-inch cutter and leave about 10 minutes. Fry in deep hot fat (365°F.) to delicate brown. Turn once. (Fry only 4 or 5 doughnuts at a time so fat will not cool too much.) Drain on absorbent paper. Makes 1½ dozen.

ONE BOWL FAST NIGHT CAKES (FASTNACHTSKUCHEN)
(Non-Dissolving Method)

In Germany, and in America, persons of German ancestry serve Fastnachts on Shrove Tuesday. The delicious little holeless doughnuts are part of a lavish feast the night before the Lenten fasting begins, just as pancakes are eaten here and Shrovetide buns in Scandinavia.

1-1¼ pounds unsifted flour
3 ounces sugar
½ teaspoon salt
2 teaspoons dry yeast
2 ounces softened margarine
8 fluid ounces very hot tap water
1 egg (at room temperature)
peanut oil

In a large bowl thoroughly mix 5 ounces flour, sugar, salt, and the dry yeast. Add softened margarine.

Gradually add very hot tap water to dry ingredients and beat 2 minutes at medium speed of electric mixer, scraping bowl occasionally. Add egg and 2 ounces flour, or enough flour to make a thick batter. Beat at high speed 2 minutes, scraping bowl occasionally. Stir in enough extra flour to make a soft dough. Cover; leave to rise in warm place, free from draught, until double in bulk, about 1 hour.

Turn dough out onto lightly floured board; knead until smooth and elastic, about 8 to 10 minutes. Roll out into an 8×16-inch rectangle. Cut into 2-inch squares. Cut a slit about ¼-inch deep in the top of each square. Place on ungreased baking sheets. Cover; leave to rise in a warm place, free from draught, until double in bulk, about 45 minutes.

Fry in deep hot (375°F.) peanut oil until golden brown on both sides. Drain on paper towels. If you like, dip warm doughnuts in cinnamon sugar. Makes 32 doughnuts.

ORANGE TEA DOUGHNUTS

1 pound fat
1 egg, beaten
4 fluid ounces milk
1 teaspoon vanilla
2 teaspoons grated orange rind
3 ounces sugar
5¼ ounces sifted flour
2 teaspoons baking powder
¼ teaspoon salt
1 tablespoon extra cooled melted
      fat

Place the fat in a small, deep pan or saucepan. Depth of melted fat should be at least 2 inches. Heat slowly to 350°F. when dough is ready for frying.

Mix together egg, milk, vanilla, and orange rind. Sift together sugar, flour, baking powder, and salt. Mix dry with liquid ingredients. Do not beat. Stir in 1 tablespoon cooled, melted fat.

Dip teaspoon into hot fat, then spoon a little of the batter. Quickly immerse spoon into hot fat and drop off the batter. Turn doughnut balls when they come to surface. Do not crowd pan; fry only 4 or 5 doughnuts at a time. Fry for 3 to 5 minutes or until delicately browned.

Drain doughnuts over the pan, then on absorbent paper. When cool, roll in icing sugar or coat with Orange Butter icing. Makes 14 medium or 18 small doughnuts.

MAIZE FLOUR DOUGHNUT DROPS

2 ounces maize flour
8 fluid ounces boiling water
2 ounces margarine
1 teaspoon salt
4 ounces sugar
2 teaspoons dry yeast
extra 4 tablespoons warm water
about 12 ounces sifted flour
3 tablespoons instant milk powder
2 eggs
1 teaspoon grated lemon rind,
      optional
fat for frying
sugar

Measure maize flour into a large mixing bowl. Pour boiling water over the flour, stirring until smooth. Add margarine, salt, and sugar. Stir to melt margarine. Leave 15 minutes.

Meanwhile, sprinkle yeast over warm water in cup. Leave 5 minutes.

To maize flour mixture, add 4 ounces flour and instant milk. Mix well.

Stir yeast and mix into batter. Add eggs and beat hard. Add lemon rind, if using, and enough flour to make a thick batter. Beat smooth.

Batter should just drop from a spoon and hold its shape. Scrape down sides of the bowl. Cover and stand bowl in a warm place for dough to rise until double (about 1 hour).

Heat deep fat for frying to 365°F. Dip a tablespoon into hot fat; then drop the mixture, a spoonful at a time, in hot fat. Fry until golden brown on one side and turn doughnuts to brown the other side. Turn doughnuts several times until done, 6 to 8 minutes all together.

Remove from fat and drain on paper towels or brown paper.

Fry only as many doughnuts at one time as will float easily and without crowding the pan.

When all doughnuts are fried, roll in granulated sugar or dust with icing sugar. Makes about 3 dozen.

Maize Flour Doughnut Drops

Cocktails and other alcoholic drinks are countless in the variations of mixtures and the names by which they are designated.

The wide selection in this section includes the most popular drinks as well as the correct names by which they should be designated. Some standard drink recipes may not be mixed precisely the way you like your particular drink, but they are the proportions most generally followed by professional bartenders, to please most tastes. In addition to the standard cocktails and long drinks, we have included a variety of quantity party punches for special occasions as well as guidance about serving wines with meals.

HINTS FOR MIXING COCKTAILS AND OTHER DRINKS

Most of the cocktail recipes in this book are given for one drink. Amounts may be increased proportionately. The drinks are based on the table of measurements given below. By using these measurements, it's easy to compute the requirements for greater quantities.

The term "part" is equivalent to a measure which may mean more or less than a jigger, depending upon individual taste.

A silver or glass cocktail shaker or a large tumbler is ideal for shaking or mixing drinks. There is no inflexible rule about mixing drinks; some are shaken, some stirred. If shaking is called for, add the ice and shake vigorously. Strain and serve promptly.

Usually cocktails containing wine as a principal ingredient are stirred, but there are exceptions to the rule.

Never stir or shake carbonated water vigorously because this releases the gas and leaves the drink flat.

DRINKS

SHOPPING GUIDE FOR THE HOME BAR

Watch a professional mixer in a large bar, and you'll see that he uses only a few gadgets; his basic tools are functional. Fancy pouring devices and trick shakers are all very well but they take up space. The basic utensils and tools are listed below. Most of them may be bought in hardware or hotel supply shops; for long service, buy the best.

2 mixing glasses and 1 metal top which may be combined with a glass for a shaker.

Glass cocktail shaker for special events.

Long-handled bar spoon for stirring.

Measuring spoon.

Cocktail strainer (rounded and perforated, or flat with flexible spring round the edge).

2 squeezers (regular one for lemons and oranges; pincer-type for limes and lemon sections).

Sharp small-bladed knife (stainless steel).

Corkscrew.

Ice pick or crusher.

Canvas bag and mallet for pounding ice.

Paper towels and dish cloths.

1 insulated ice bucket—to eliminate frequent trips to the kitchen.

1 hard-wood muddler—a round-based wooden stick used for mashing various ingredients.

1-ounce measuring glass with lip (the type used by chemists).

1 bottle opener.

STANDARD BAR MEASUREMENTS

1 dash	3 drops
1 teaspoon	$\frac{1}{8}$ fluid ounce (approx.)
3 teaspoons.....................................	1 tablespoon ($\frac{1}{2}$ fluid ounce)
1 pony..	1 fluid ounce
1 jigger..	1$\frac{1}{2}$ fluid ounces
1 large jigger..................................	2 fluid ounces
1 wine glass (aver.)	4 fluid ounces
1 gill or quartern	5 fluid ounces
1 pint	20 fluid ounces
A fifth ($\frac{4}{5}$ American quart)..................	25·6 fluid ounces
1 quart...	40 fluid ounces
1 gallon	160 fluid ounces
$\frac{1}{2}$ bottle wine	12 fluid ounces
1 bottle wine (aver.).........................	24 fluid ounces
Magnum (2 bottles)...........................	52 fluid ounces
Jeroboam (4 bottles)	104 fluid ounces
Rehoboam (6 bottles)........................	156 fluid ounces
A twist or curl of lemon	A thin slice of outer peel cut with curved knife

Note: The generally accepted size of a jigger is 1$\frac{1}{2}$ fluid ounces. However, there has been an attempt to standardize the size at 2 fluid ounces instead. If you use a jigger, test it and find out how much it really holds.

TO FROST RIMS OF GLASSES

Put lemon juice into shallow dish. Sift some caster or icing sugar on to plate about ¼ inch deep.

Invert each glass in lemon juice. Lift out of juice on to sugar for a minute.

Lift carefully out of sugar so as not to jar the sugar coating which has formed on rim. Place in refrigerator until "set".

Fill glasses, being careful not to disturb frost.

GLASSES—SELECTION AND USE

Most cocktails are served in 2½-, 4-, or 5-fluid ounce glasses. Get the large ones—not measuring less than 3 fluid ounces. The average cocktail measures about 2½ to 3 fluid ounces, but the glass should never be filled to the brim. Cocktail glasses should preferably have stems because a drink is warmed by the hand, and a cocktail should remain cold.

Whisky is traditionally served in broad, almost straight tumblers measuring 6 fluid ounces.

Long drinks are served in tumblers measuring 9 to 12 fluid ounces.

Collins and Rickeys are served in 10-12-, or 14-fluid ounce tumblers.

Get the larger sizes of tumblers if you want to keep the number to a minimum and make them do for long drinks, collins, and juleps.

Liqueurs are traditionally served in tiny liqueur glasses, primarily because fine liqueur is expensive. If you want to dispense with the necessity of acquiring this extra set of glasses, you need only remember that a little in a larger glass will taste just as good and, in addition, you will get the pleasure of the aroma which is a part of the pleasure of sipping a fine liqueur from a large glass. That's why fine old brandies are traditionally served in 18-fluid ounce balloon glasses or "Napoleons".

Selections of glasses may always be made so that various glasses may serve several purposes—but, above all, let your glasses be made of *glass*. They may be either expensive cut glass or the Woolworth variety, but be sure they are *glass*. Metal, even gold-plated silver drinking cups and goblets may be beautiful to look at but most drinks do not taste right out of them.

For most cocktails and wines, we recommend the all-purpose tulip-shaped wine glass which may be obtained in any well-stocked shop.

SIMPLE BAR SYRUP

Sugar and water boiled together to use when sugar alone might be hard to dissolve, as in cold drinks.

2½ pounds sugar
½ pint water

Combine sugar and water and place over heat. Stir until sugar is dissolved; reduce heat so mixture is simmering. Simmer until liquid is clear.

The mixture may be bottled and kept either in the refrigerator or in an air-tight container.
Note: If you wish to clarify syrup further, add 1 well-beaten egg white. Skim until perfectly clear.

Brandy Cocktails
ABOUT BRANDY

When no specific qualification is added, the term brandy means an alcoholic spirit distilled from grape wine or from marc, the residue of the grape press. Since the fermented juice of apples, apricots, cherries, peaches, pears, and other fruits can also be distilled, brandies made from fruits other than grapes must be referred to by the name of the fruit—for example, apple brandy, apricot brandy, cherry brandy.

The difference between a brandy and a liqueur or cordial is in the distillation. Brandy is made by distilling the fermented juice of the fruit itself, whereas liqueurs or cordials are the result of infusing fruits or other flavouring material in grain alcohol or other liquors (chiefly brandy).

One of the most famous brandies is Cognac, which is distilled from grapes grown in a prescribed region around the French city of Cognac. Cognac labels often carry various initials and symbols supposed to denote quality, but these have no recognized authority.

Armagnac is another famous French brandy, less well known than Cognac but scarcely less fine. A little darker and heavier-flavoured than Cognac, it is produced in a legally delimited area in southwest France.

Good brandies are produced also in Italy, Spain, Portugal, Germany, the Balkan countries, North Africa, and the United States (chiefly California).

Brandies should not be bottled at less than 40° Gay Lussac (40 per cent alcohol). They are frequently allowed to age for many years. If a brandy is less than 2 years old, a statement showing the age must appear on the bottle. In extremely rare cases brandies have been allowed to age up to 60 years, but fine brandies are at their best after 25 to 40 years. It should be noted that most of the good Cognacs on the market are between 5 and 10 years old.

Brandy is left to age in oak barrels, which give it colour. For additional colour caramel is added when the brandy is bottled.

APPLEJACK OLD-FASHIONED

1½ fluid ounces applejack
1 lump sugar
2 dashes Angostura bitters
dash of soda water

Use a whisky tumbler. Muddle sugar in a little soda water until dissolved. Add 2 dashes Angostura bitters and a good-sized ice cube. Pour in applejack. Stir.

Decorate with fruit or twist of lemon peel. Serve with stirring rod.

APPLE CAR COCKTAIL
2 fluid ounces applejack
1 fluid ounce Cointreau
juice of ½ lemon
 Shake with ice. Serve in 4-fluid-ounce cocktail glass.

BETWEEN-THE-SHEETS
1 fluid ounce brandy
1 fluid ounce rum
1 fluid ounce Cointreau
juice of ½ lemon
 Shake with ice. Serve in 4-fluid-ounce cocktail glass.

BRANDY ALEXANDER
(Panama Cocktail)
1½ fluid ounces brandy
¾ fluid ounce crème de cacao
½ fluid ounce double cream
 Shake vigorously with ice. Serve in 4-fluid-ounce wine glass.

BRANDY COCKTAIL
1½ fluid ounces brandy
½ fluid ounce curaçao
1 teaspoon simple bar syrup
 Stir with ice. Strain into cocktail glass. Add twist of lemon peel. Serve.

BRANDY EGG SOUR
1 fluid ounce brandy
1 fluid ounce curaçao
1 egg
1 teaspoon icing sugar
2 dashes lemon juice
 Shake with ice. Strain into small wine glass.

COFFEE COCKTAIL
1 fluid ounce brandy
1 fluid ounce port
1 teaspoon sugar
yolk of egg
 Pour brandy and port into mixing glass. Add ice. Then drop egg and sugar on top of ice. Shake well and serve in wine glass.

CUBAN COCKTAIL
1½ fluid ounces brandy
½ fluid ounce apricot brandy
juice of ½ lime
 Shake well with ice. Serve in cocktail glass.

STINGER
2 fluid ounces brandy
1 fluid ounce crème de menthe
 Shake with ice. Serve in 4-fluid-ounce cocktail glass.

STAR COCKTAIL
1½ fluid ounces applejack
1½ fluid ounces Italian vermouth
 Stir with ice. Strain into cocktail glass. Decorate with maraschino cherry.

SIDECAR COCKTAIL
1 fluid ounce brandy
1 fluid ounce Cointreau
1 fluid ounce lemon juice
 Shake with ice. Serve in 4-fluid-ounce cocktail glass.

JACK ROSE COCKTAIL
1½ fluid ounces applejack
juice of ½ lemon
2 dashes grenadine
 Shake with ice. Serve in 4-fluid-ounce cocktail glass.

ABOUT GIN
 Gin may be regarded as the simplest of spirits, consisting as it does merely of neutral spirits (a pure grade of alcohol), water, and flavouring. The name is derived from genièvre, the French word for juniper, which was corrupted in English to geneva and then to gin.
 Most British gins are of the type known as London Dry. They are neutral spirits redistilled over juniper berries and other aromatics such as angelica root, coriander, cardamom, and cassia bark, so as to absorb the flavours. Gins are never left to age.
 Holland was the first country to produce gin, and present-day Dutch gin is a distinctive type, more aromatic and heavier in body than others. It is usually drunk straight with bitters and has too much flavour to be used in mixed drinks.
 Plymouth gin has a distinctive flavour, owing to the water that is used in making it, which is soft and runs through the moors of Devon.
 Sloe gin, made from sweetened dry gin flavoured with sloes (small, acid blue-black plums), is drunk as a liqueur.

ADMIRAL COCKTAIL
1½ fluid ounces dry gin
1 fluid ounce cherry cordial
juice of ½ lime
 Shake with ice. Strain into 4-fluid-ounce cocktail glass.

ALEXANDER COCKTAIL
1½ ounces gin
¾ fluid ounce crème de cacao
½ fluid ounce double cream
 Shake vigorously with ice. Serve in 4-fluid-ounce wine glass.

ARMY COCKTAIL
2 fluid ounces dry gin
1 fluid ounce Italian vermouth
2 dashes grenadine
slice of orange
 Shake with ice. Strain into 4-fluid-ounce cocktail glass. Add slice of orange.

AVIATION COCKTAIL
2 fluid ounces dry gin
juice of ½ lemon
4 dashes maraschino
 Shake with ice. Strain into 4-fluid-ounce cocktail glass.

BERMUDA COCKTAIL
1¾ fluid ounces dry gin
¾ fluid ounce peach brandy
2 dashes grenadine
2 dashes orange juice.
 Shake with ice. Strain into 4-fluid-ounce cocktail glass.

BLACKOUT COCKTAIL
1¾ fluid ounces dry gin
¾ fluid ounce blackberry brandy
juice of ½ lime
 Shake with ice. Strain into 4-fluid-ounce cocktail glass.

BRONX COCKTAIL
2 fluid ounces dry gin
1 fluid ounce Italian vermouth
2 half slices of orange
 Add orange to ingredients and ice in mixing glass and shake vigorously. Strain into 4-fluid-ounce cocktail glass.

CAFÉ DE PARIS COCKTAIL
1½ fluid ounces dry gin
½ fluid ounce anisette
½ fluid ounce double cream
1 egg white
 Shake well with ice. Serve in 4-fluid-ounce wine glass.

CLOVER CLUB COCKTAIL
1½ fluid ounces dry gin
4 dashes grenadine
juice of ½ lemon
1 egg white
 Shake well with ice. Serve in 4-fluid-ounce wine glass.

CLOVER LEAF COCKTAIL
1½ fluid ounces dry gin
juice of ½ lemon
4 dashes grenadine
1 egg white
4 or 5 mint leaves
 Shake well with ice. Serve in 4-fluid-ounce wine glass. Decorate with one mint leaf on top.

COOPERSTOWN COCKTAIL
2 fluid ounces dry gin
1 fluid ounce French vermouth
1 fluid ounce Italian vermouth
2 sprigs mint
 Shake well with ice. Strain into 6-fluid-ounce cocktail glass.

LONE TREE COCKTAIL
3 fluid ounces dry gin
1 fluid ounce Italian vermouth
 Stir with ice. Strain into 6-fluid-ounce cocktail glass. Twist orange peel on top.

FOURTH ESTATE COCKTAIL
1 fluid ounce dry gin
1 fluid ounce French vermouth
1 fluid ounce Italian vermouth
3 dashes absinthe
Shake with ice. Strain into 4-fluid-ounce cocktail glass.

GIBSON COCKTAIL
1 fluid ounce gin
¼ fluid ounce Italian vermouth
¼ fluid ounce French vermouth
Stir with crushed ice. Strain into cocktail glass. Serve with pickled onion. Twist lemon peel over drink.

GIMLET
1 teaspoon caster sugar
juice of ½ lime
1½ fluid ounces dry gin
Dissolve sugar in the lime juice in a 6-fluid-ounce glass. Add gin, and ice if desired. Fill with chilled soda water. Stir slightly.
Note: Vodka has become a popular substitute for gin in this drink.

HAWAII COCKTAIL
1½ fluid ounces dry gin
1 fluid ounce pineapple juice
1 dash of orange bitters
1 egg white
Shake well with ice. Serve in 4-fluid-ounce wine glass.

MARTINI COCKTAIL
2 fluid ounces dry gin
1 fluid ounce French vermouth
Stir with ice. Strain into cocktail glass. Decorate with olive. (Do not wash the brine off the olive.)

DRY MARTINI COCKTAIL
3 fluid ounces dry gin
1 fluid ounce French vermouth
Stir with ice. Strain into cocktail glass. Decorate with olive.

SWEET MARTINI COCKTAIL (Gin and It)
2 fluid ounces dry gin
1 fluid ounce Italian vermouth
Stir with ice. Strain into cocktail glass. Decorate with maraschino cherry.

NAPOLEON COCKTAIL
1½ ounces dry gin
½ fluid ounce Dubonnet
2 dashes Fernet Branca
2 dashes curaçao
Stir with ice. Add twist of lemon peel.

ORANGE BLOSSOM COCKTAIL
2 fluid ounces dry gin
2 fluid ounces orange juice
Shake with ice. Strain into cocktail glass.

PARADISE COCKTAIL
2 fluid ounces dry gin
1 fluid ounce apricot brandy
1 fluid ounce orange juice
Shake with ice. Strain into 6-fluid-ounce cocktail glass.

PERFECT COCKTAIL
1 fluid ounce dry gin
1 fluid ounce French vermouth
1 fluid ounce Italian vermouth
Stir with ice. Strain into cocktail glass. Add twist of lemon peel.

PARISIAN COCKTAIL
2 fluid ounces dry gin
1 fluid ounce French vermouth
3 dashes crème de cassis
Shake with ice. Strain into 4-fluid-ounce cocktail glass.

PINK LADY
1½ fluid ounces dry gin
½ fluid ounce applejack
4 dashes grenadine
1 egg white
Shake well with ice. Serve in 4-fluid-ounce wine glass.

RED LION COCKTAIL
1½ fluid ounces dry gin
¾ fluid ounce Grand Marnier
¼ fluid ounce lemon juice
3 dashes grenadine
Shake with ice. Strain into 4-fluid-ounce cocktail glass.

ROYAL SMILE COCKTAIL
2 fluid ounces dry gin
1 fluid ounce applejack
4 dashes grenadine
juice of ½ lime
Stir with ice. Serve in cocktail glass.

SOCIETY COCKTAIL
3 fluid ounces dry gin
1 fluid ounce French vermouth
4 dashes grenadine
Shake with ice. Strain into 6-fluid-ounce cocktail glass.

GIN TODDY
1½ fluid ounces dry gin
1 lump of sugar
dash of Angostura bitters
Muddle sugar and bitters in a whisky tumbler. Add gin, cube of ice, and a little water. Serve with stirring rod.

TURF COCKTAIL
2 fluid ounces dry gin
1 fluid ounce French vermouth
1 fluid ounce Italian vermouth
dash of Angostura bitters
dash of absinthe
Stir with ice. Strain into 6-fluid-ounce cocktail glass.

TORPEDO COCKTAIL
2 fluid ounces dry gin
1 fluid ounce French vermouth
dash of Pernod
Stir with ice. Strain into 4-fluid-ounce cocktail glass.

WHITE LADY
2 fluid ounces dry gin
1 fluid ounce Cointreau
juice of ½ lemon
1 egg white
Shake well with ice. Serve in 4-fluid-ounce wine glass.

Rum Cocktails
ABOUT RUM
Rum is an alcoholic beverage distilled from fermented sugar-cane juice, fermented black treacle, or mixtures of these. It may range in flavour from almost characterless to extremely full-bodied, in colour from white to very dark. As a rule of thumb, the lighter the colour, the lighter the flavour. Actually, however, colour has nothing to do with either the flavour or the alcoholic content, since it comes chiefly from added caramel. The real differences are due to variations in ingredients, in methods of fermentation and distillation, and in subsequent maturing.

Rum is made in most of the islands of the West Indies and on the eastern seaboard of the United States (primarily New England and Philadelphia). Most of the light rums come from Puerto Rico; the heavy ones from Jamaica, Barbados, Demerara, and Martinique. A good illustration of the range is that, whereas a tablespoonful of Jamaica rum will give a cup of strong coffee a marked rum flavour, a tablespoonful of strong coffee will give a cup of white rum a predominantly coffee flavour. It is therefore important to know which kind to use. While there are no hard-and-fast rules, the following classifications should be kept in mind.

Navy Rum: A light-bodied, light-coloured rum with a delicate flavour and aroma. It is marketed at 43° Gay Lussac (43 per cent alcohol). Use it in delicate cocktails such as Bacardis and Daiquiris.

Jamaica Rum: A darker-coloured rum with a stronger flavour and aroma but about the same alcoholic content. Use it in cooking and in such drinks as Cuba Libres, Collinses, and Rum Manhattans.

Demerara Rum: A very dark rum with a pungent flavour and aroma. Use it in cooking and in punches. It is also often drunk "neat".

BACARDI COCKTAIL

1½ fluid ounces Bacardi rum
juice of ½ lime
1 teaspoon sugar or 2 dashes
         grenadine

Shake well with ice. Strain into cocktail glass.

DAIQUIRI (Standard)

1½ fluid ounces navy rum
juice of ½ lime
1 teaspoon sugar

Shake well with ice. Strain into cocktail glass.

DAIQUIRI (Frozen)

2 fluid ounces navy rum
juice of ½ lime
1 teaspoon sugar
dash of maraschino

Pre-chill container of electric blender. Put in ingredients. Then add a heaped champagne glass of crushed ice. Blend briefly. Serve unstrained in a chilled champagne glass with short straws.

JAMAICA RUM COCKTAIL

1½ fluid ounces Jamaica rum
juice of ½ lime
1 teaspoon sugar

Shake with ice and strain into cocktail glass.

LATIN MANHATTAN COCKTAIL

2 fluid ounces rum
2 fluid ounces Italian vermouth

Stir with ice. Serve in 6-fluid-ounce cocktail glass. Decorate with maraschino cherry.

PRESIDENTE COCKTAIL

1½ fluid ounces navy rum
¾ fluid ounce French vermouth
1 dash grenadine
twist of orange peel

Stir with ice. Serve in cocktail glass.

Vodka Cocktails and Other Drinks

ABOUT VODKA

Vodka is the national drink of Russia, now made in other countries as well. The best vodka is distilled from rye and barley malt; however, cheaper maize and potatoes are commonly used. In Russia it is drunk neat, with food. In Britain, however, it is usually mixed. It can be used in almost any drink calling for gin and it is often substituted for whisky in some mixed drinks. Since vodka is colourless, nearly tasteless going down, and almost odourless afterwards, it can be a deceptively strong drink when mixed. It may not be legally sold at less than 40° Gay Lussac (40 per cent alcohol) and ranges up to 60° Gay Lussac.

BLOODY MARY

3 fluid ounces vodka
6 fluid ounces tomato juice
2 dashes Angostura bitters
juice of ½ lemon

Shake well with ice. Strain into 12-fluid-ounce glass.

MOSCOW MULE

2 fluid ounces vodka
juice of 1 lime
ginger beer

Fill a glass or pewter mug with crushed ice. Squeeze in lime juice. Add vodka. Fill with ginger beer. Stir.

SCREWDRIVER

1½ fluid ounces vodka
orange juice

Pour the vodka over crushed ice in a long tumbler. Add fresh orange juice to fill the glass and stir briskly.

TWISTER

Pour 2 fluid ounces vodka into a rather small tumbler. Add ice and fill with ginger ale. Garnish with a slice of lemon.

VODKA DAIQUIRI

2 fluid ounces vodka
1 teaspoon sugar
juice of ½ lemon

Shake in crushed ice. Strain into a cocktail glass.

VODKA COLLINS

2 fluid ounces vodka
1½ teaspoons icing sugar
1 fluid ounce lemon juice

Shake well with crushed ice. Pour into 12-fluid-ounce serving glass.

Fill with soda water; garnish with a cherry and a slice of lemon.

VODKA FIZZ

2 fluid ounces vodka
1 teaspoon icing sugar
3 fluid ounces pineapple juice

Shake well with crushed ice and pour into an 8-fluid-ounce glass. Fill with soda water.

VODKA MARTINI

4 fluid ounces vodka
1 fluid ounce dry vermouth

Pour into stirring glass filled with crushed ice. Add a couple of strips of lemon peel. Stir until frosty.

Strain into cocktail glass and serve with a garnish of lemon peel.

VODKA COOLERS

Pour 2 fluid ounces vodka into a medium-sized straight-sided tumbler. Add ice and fill with cola, ginger ale, grape juice, ginger beer or grapefruit juice. No garnish is used.

Whisky Cocktails

ABOUT WHISKY

All whisky, whether Scotch, Irish, rye, bourbon, or Canadian, is a spirit distilled from a fermented grain mash. The grain may be maize, rye, oats, barley, or any other. Good whisky is matured for a number of years before it is bottled—Scotch and Irish in sherry casks, American whisky in charred oak barrels. Once it is bottled the maturing process stops.

There are two kinds of Scotch whisky. Malt whisky is made from malted barley only. It is full of flavour and body. Grain whisky is made from maize, oats, rye, and a proportion of malted barley. It is a more neutral spirit, with less flavour.

Bourbon, which is made from at least 51 per cent maize, is usually bottled straight. Most of the whiskys called rye are a blend of whisky and neutral spirits.

Purely as a matter of custom, the Irish and U.S. products are called whiskey, with an e; the Scotch and Canadian, whisky.

ABOUT ALCOHOLIC STRENGTH

Since the United Kingdom joined the European Economic Community on 1 January 1973 it has adopted the Gay Lussac measurement of alcoholic strengths. In this system, the strength of spirits is denoted simply by the amount of alcohol it contains. Hence, Scotch whisky, which contains 60 per cent water and 40 per cent alcohol, is now known as being 40° Gay Lussac, instead of, as previously, 70° proof.

MANHATTAN COCKTAIL

2 fluid ounces rye whisky
1 fluid ounce Italian vermouth
dash of Angostura bitters

Stir with ice. Decorate with maraschino cherry.

DRY MANHATTAN COCKTAIL

2 fluid ounces rye whisky
1 fluid ounce French vermouth
dash of Angostura bitters

Stir with ice. Add twist of lemon peel.

ROB ROY COCKTAIL

2 fluid ounces Scotch whisky
1 fluid ounce Italian vermouth
dash of Angostura bitters

Stir with ice. Serve in cocktail glass. Add twist of lemon peel.

WARD EIGHT

1½ fluid ounces rye whisky
juice of ½ lemon
3 dashes grenadine

Shake with ice and serve in tumbler with finely crushed ice.

Decorate with fruit. Serve with straws.

OLD-FASHIONED COCKTAIL

1½ fluid ounces rye whisky
1 lump sugar
dash of soda water
2 dashes Angostura bitters

Use a whisky tumbler. Muddle sugar in a little soda water until dissolved. Add two dashes Angostura bitters and a good-sized ice cube. Pour in whisky. Stir. Decorate with fruit or twist of lemon peel. Serve with stirring rod.

ZAZERAC COCKTAIL

1½ fluid ounces bourbon
1 dash Pernod
1 lump sugar
1 teaspoon water
2 dashes Peychaud bitters

Use two whisky tumblers. Muddle the sugar and water and bitters in one glass and add bourbon. Stir thoroughly.

Rinse other glass with 2 or 3 drops of Pernod and rub edge of glass with wet cork from anisette bottle. Add lump of ice.

Pour contents of first glass into this one and serve with twist of lemon peel.

BLARNEY COCKTAIL

1½ fluid ounces Irish whiskey
1 fluid ounce Italian vermouth
2 dashes green crème de menthe

Shake well with ice. Strain into small cocktail glass. Serve with green cherry.

SHAMROCK COCKTAIL

1 fluid ounce Irish whiskey
1 fluid ounce French vermouth
3 dashes green crème de menthe
3 dashes green chartreuse

Stir with ice. Serve in cocktail glass.

BOURBON SOCIETY COCKTAIL

Serve 1 fluid ounce bourbon in whisky tumbler over tiny ice cubes. Add twist of lemon peel.

SCOTCH MIST

Fill whisky tumbler ¾ full of crushed ice. Pour in 1½ fluid ounces Scotch whisky. Add twist of lemon peel. Serve with straws.

SANTA ANITA

Shake 1½ fluid ounces Scotch whisky with crushed ice and serve unstrained in whisky tumbler. Add twist of lemon peel.

BLACKTHORN COCKTAIL

1½ fluid ounces Irish whiskey
1 fluid ounce French vermouth
dash of anisette

Stir with ice. Serve in cocktail glass.

Wine and Liqueur Cocktails

ABOUT LIQUEURS AND CORDIALS

A liqueur is any combination of potable spirit with sugar syrup and flavouring. The terms liqueur and cordial are interchangeable, but cordial tends to be restricted to fruit-flavoured liqueurs.

Unlike whisky and brandy, which are made by fermentation and subsequent distillation, liqueurs are made by adding the flavouring (herbs, spices, fruits, flowers) to already distilled grain alcohol or other spirits, chiefly brandy. Some are then redistilled.

The alcoholic content of liqueurs varies a great deal. Most are sweet, but even some of these have a dry aftertaste. Certain liqueurs are fairly standard, with very similar ones produced by a number of manufacturers. Examples are fruit liqueurs such as apricot, blackberry, and peach, or non-fruit liqueurs such as menthe (white or green), triple sec or curaçao (orange) kümmel (caraway), anisette (anise), and cacao (cocoa). Others are proprietary, with distinctive flavours achieved by formulas that are closely guarded by the makers. Examples are Bénédictine, Forbidden Fruit, Drambuie, Chartreuse, Cordon Rouge, Cordial Médoc, and Grand Marnier.

Serve liqueurs at the end of the meal. Many drinkers, particularly men, express a decided aversion to the sweeter ones and prefer those that have a dry aftertaste, such as Drambuie, Bénédictine, or B and B. Non-drinkers usually like the sweet fruit liqueurs.

CHAMPAGNE COCKTAIL

pre-chilled champagne
1 lump sugar
dash Angostura bitters

Chill a wide-top champagne glass. Put in sugar. Add a dash of sugar to the bitters. Add small ice cube.

Fill with champagne and top with twist of lemon peel.

ARMOUR COCKTAIL

1½ fluid ounces dry sherry
1 fluid ounce Italian vermouth

Stir with ice and strain into cocktail glass. Serve with twist of lemon peel.

DUBONNET COCKTAIL

2 fluid ounces dry gin
2 fluid ounces Dubonnet

Stir with ice. Add twist of lemon peel.

CORONATION COCKTAIL

1½ fluid ounces dry sherry
1 fluid ounce Italian vermouth
2 dashes maraschino
2 dashes orange bitters

Stir with ice and strain into cocktail glass.

DOCTOR COCKTAIL

2 fluid ounces aquavit
1 fluid ounce Swedish punch
juice of 1 lime

Shake with ice and strain into 4-fluid-ounce cocktail glass.

MERRY WIDOW COCKTAIL

2 fluid ounces French vermouth
2 fluid ounces Dubonnet

Stir with ice. Add twist of lemon peel.

SUISSESSE COCKTAIL

1½ fluid ounces absinthe
½ fluid ounce anisette
white of egg

Shake well with ice and strain into wine glass.

ANISETTE COCKTAIL

1 fluid ounce anisette
½ teaspoon Benedictine
2 drops Angostura bitters

Shake with crushed ice. Strain into frosted cocktail glass; drip water through ice to fill glass.

VERMOUTH COCKTAIL 1

1½ fluid ounces Italian vermouth
1 dash Angostura bitters

Stir with crushed ice. Strain into chilled cocktail glass. Serve with pickled onion.

VERMOUTH COCKTAIL 2

1½ fluid ounces French vermouth
1 dash Pernod

Shake with crushed ice. Strain into chilled cocktail glass.

Long Drinks, Coolers, and Juleps

BAHAMAS HIGHBALL

1½ fluid ounces dry gin
1 fluid ounce French vermouth
1 slice lemon
tonic water

Serve with ice in 10-fluid-ounce tumbler. Stir.

BLACK VELVET

5 fluid ounces Guinness
5 fluid ounces champagne

Pre-chill wine and stout and pour into tall glass.

CLARET PUNCH

3 fluid ounces claret
2 dashes curaçao
juice of ½ lemon
1 teaspoon icing sugar

Fill goblet with crushed ice. Add all ingredients. Stir. Garnish with fruit.

JOHN COLLINS

2 fluid ounces Dutch gin
juice of medium-sized lemon
1 teaspoon sugar

Shake well. Strain into tall tumbler in which ice cubes have been placed. Add soda water to fill.

ORANGE BLOSSOM COLLINS

2 fluid ounces dry gin
juice of small orange
1 teaspoon sugar

Shake well. Strain into tall tumbler in which ice cubes have been placed. Add soda water to fill.

RUM COLLINS

1½ fluid ounces rum
juice of small lemon
1 teaspoon sugar

Shake well and strain into tall tumbler with 2 ice cubes. Fill glass with soda water.

SALTY DOG COLLINS

1½ fluid ounces dry gin
pinch of salt
juice of 1 lime

Shake well. Strain into tall tumbler in which ice cubes have been placed. Add soda water to fill.

RAMOS FIZZ

2 fluid ounces navy gin
juice of ½ lemon
juice of ½ lime
2 dashes orange flower water
1 fluid ounce double cream
1 egg white
1 teaspoon sugar

Shake vigorously with ice. Strain into 10-fluid-ounce tumbler. Add soda water to fill.

TOM COLLINS

2 fluid ounces dry gin
juice of medium-sized lemon
1 teaspoon sugar

Shake well. Strain into tall tumbler in which ice cubes have been placed. Add soda water to fill.

WHISKY COLLINS

2 fluid ounces rye whisky
juice of medium-sized lemon
1 teaspoon sugar

Shake well. Strain into tall tumbler in which ice cubes have been placed. Add soda water to fill.

COBBLERS

Cobblers are tall drinks made with finely crushed ice, fruit, and wine or spirits. Berries and fresh fruits used for garnish make them particularly attractive.

Fill goblet with finely crushed ice. Add 1 teaspoon sugar. Add 3 fluid ounces of burgundy, claret, Sauternes, sherry, port, or Rhine wine, brandy, or whisky.

Stir well and garnish with slices of orange or slivers of pineapple, and a sprig of mint.

RUM COBBLER

1½ fluid ounces rum
½ fluid ounce curaçao
juice of ½ lemon

Stir and strain into goblet of crushed ice. Decorate with fruit and sprig of mint.

GIN FIZZ

1½ fluid ounces dry gin
juice of small lemon
1 teaspoon sugar

Shake with ice. Strain into 10-fluid-ounce tumbler. Add soda water.

Golden Fizz: Add 1 egg yolk to Gin Fizz.

Royal Fizz: Add 1 whole egg to Gin Fizz.

Silver Fizz: Add 1 egg white to Gin Fizz.

Southside Fizz: Garnish Gin Fizz with mint leaves.

SLOE GIN FIZZ

1½ fluid ounces sloe gin
juice of ½ lemon
1 teaspoon sugar

Shake well with ice. Strain into tall tumbler and add soda water.

STRAWBERRY FIZZ

1½ fluid ounces dry gin
dash of single cream
1 teaspoon sugar
4 ripe strawberries
juice of ½ lemon

Shake well with ice. Strain into 10-fluid-ounce tumbler. Add soda water to fill.

MINT JULEP

2 fluid ounces bourbon
1 teaspoon icing sugar
4 sprigs mint

Strip leaves from stem and drop into a 12-fluid-ounce tumbler or pewter mug. Add sugar and dash of water.

Mash these ingredients with a muddler until sugar is dissolved.

Add whisky and fill with crushed ice.

Stir until outside of tumbler is frosted.

Decorate with a bouquet of mint. Sprinkle with icing sugar.

PLANTER'S PUNCH

2 fluid ounces Jamaica rum
juice of 1 lime
1 teaspoon caster sugar

Shake well and strain into tall glass filled with crushed ice. Decorate with thin slice of lime and long stick of fresh pineapple.

HIGHBALLS

All highballs should be served in 8- or 10-fluid-ounce tumblers. To prepare any highball, place an ice cube in the glass, add 1½ fluid ounces of the spirit desired, and top up the glass with soda water or ginger ale.

Serve with a small bar spoon in glass and a twist of lemon peel, if desired.

The following spirits may be used in preparing highballs: Applejack, bitters, bourbon, Cognac, gin, rye, rum, Scotch whisky, and liqueurs.

REMSEN COOLER

2 fluid ounces dry gin
lemon rind

Insert spiral of lemon rind in tall glass. Add ice cubes, gin, and soda water to fill. Stir and serve.

WINE COOLER

Pour half a glass (or more) of your favourite wine over ice cubes in a tall glass. Vermouth, red or white table wine or dessert wine may be used.

Add soda water or a carbonated table water to fill, stir slightly and serve.

Wine Coolers

ALABAMA FIZZ

1½ fluid ounces dry gin
1 teaspoon brown sugar
juice of ½ lemon

Stir with ice. Add soda water. Garnish with mint sprigs. Serve in 10-fluid-ounce tumbler.

CUBA LIBRE

1½ fluid ounces rum
cola
juice and rind of ½ lime

Squeeze lime juice into 12-fluid-ounce glass. Drop in rind. Add ice cubes and cola and stir.

GIN AND TONIC

1½ fluid ounces gin
slice of lemon
tonic water

Serve in tall glass containing ice cubes.

GIN BUCK

1½ fluid ounces dry gin
juice of ½ lemon
ginger ale

Serve in tall tumbler with ice cubes. Fill with ginger ale. Stir.

GIN RICKEY

1½ fluid ounces dry gin
juice of ½ lime

Squeeze juice of lime into tall tumbler. Drop in rind and cube of ice. Add gin. Top with soda water. Stir.

GIN SLING

1½ fluid ounces dry gin
1 teaspoon sugar

Place ice cubes in 10-fluid-ounce tall glass. Add twist of lemon peel. Add soda water. Stir.

RUM SLING

1½ fluid ounces Jamaica rum
2 dashes Angostura bitters

Serve in tall glass with crushed ice. Fill with soda water. Add twist of lemon peel. Stir.

SINGAPORE GIN SLING

2 fluid ounces dry gin
⅔ fluid ounce cherry brandy
juice of 1 lemon
dash of Benedictine

Shake. Strain into tall glass containing ice cubes. Garnish with slice of orange and sprig of mint. Add soda water. Top with dash of Benedictine.

VERMOUTH CASSIS

3 fluid ounces French vermouth
1 fluid ounce crème de cassis

Pour into tall glass with ice cubes. Fill with soda water. Stir. Add twist of lemon peel.

NEW ORLEANS FIZZ

2 fluid ounces dry gin
juice of ½ lemon
1 fluid ounce double cream
2 dashes of orange flower water
1 egg white
1 teaspoon sugar

Shake vigorously with ice. Strain into 10-fluid-ounce tumbler. Add soda water.

ZOMBIE

1 fluid ounce golden rum
1 fluid ounce light rum
1 fluid ounce Jamaica rum
½ fluid ounce cherry brandy
½ fluid ounce apricot brandy
juice of half lime
1 dash papaya or pineapple juice
¼ fluid ounce 75° Gay Lussac Jamaica rum

Fill a 14-fluid-ounce tumbler half full of finely crushed ice. Put in ingredients and stir. Top with the rum. Decorate with a sprig of mint. Serve with straws.

SPRITZER

3 fluid ounces Rhine wine, Chablis, or dry Sauternes
soda water

Put one cube of ice in tumbler. Add wine. Fill with soda water and stir.

RUM PUNCH

1½ fluid ounces rum
juice of ½ lemon
orange juice equal to amount of lemon juice
pineapple juice equal to amount of lemon juice
1 teaspoon caster sugar
dash of brandy

Shake well and strain into goblet half full of crushed ice. Top with dash of brandy. Decorate with fruit.

MAMIE TAYLOR

2 fluid ounces Scotch whisky
slice of lemon
6 fluid ounces ginger ale

Serve with two cubes of ice in a tall glass.

BRANDY COBBLER

½ teaspoon sugar
1 teaspoon curaçao
2 fluid ounces brandy

Add to goblet ¾ filled with crushed ice; stir and decorate with fruit. Serve with straws and a spoon.

GIN FIX

¾ fluid ounce dry gin
¾ fluid ounce cherry brandy
1 teaspoon sugar
juice of 1 lemon

Dissolve sugar in a little water. Add lemon juice, gin, and brandy. Fill tall tumbler with crushed ice. Stir slowly.

Egg Nogs and Milk Punches

BRANDY EGG NOG

1 egg
1 tablespoon sugar
2 fluid ounces brandy
6 to 8 fluid ounces milk

Shake well with crushed ice. Strain Serve with nutmeg on top.
Variations: Substitute port, rum sherry, or whisky for brandy.

MILK PUNCH

1½ fluid ounces rye whisky
8 fluid ounces milk
1 teaspoon sugar

Shake, strain, and serve in 12-fluid-ounce glass. Sprinkle nutmeg on top.

BALTIMORE EGG NOG

1 fluid ounce brandy
1½ fluid ounces Madeira wine
2 teaspoons sugar syrup
½ fluid ounce rum
1 whole egg
4 fluid ounces fresh milk

Shake vigorously with crushed ice. Strain into 12-fluid-ounce glass, adding cold milk to fill glass. Stir gently and sprinkle with nutmeg.

HOLIDAY EGG NOG

6 eggs, separated
6 ounces sugar
¾ pint milk, chilled
½ pint Cognac or Lotus brandy
2 fluid ounces rum
¾ pint double cream, chilled
nutmeg

Beat egg whites until almost stiff enough to hold a peak. Add sugar gradually, beating until stiff but not dry.

Beat egg yolks until thick; stir in milk, Cognac, and rum, blending well.

Whip cream until stiff and fold into egg-milk mixture. Fold in beaten egg whites.

Keep cold until ready to serve. Pour into punch bowl. Sprinkle each serving with nutmeg, if desired. Makes about 5 pints.

Holiday Egg Nog

After Dinner Drinks

ABSINTHE FRAPPÉ

1½ fluid ounces absinthe*
¾ fluid ounce water
1 teaspoon sugar

Shake well with ice and strain into wine glass.

*Note: Genuine absinthe contains a toxic drug (Artemisia or wormwood); hence its manufacture and sale are now illegal in many countries. Absinthe substitutes include Pernod, Oxygénée, Herbsaint, and others. These do not include the harmful wormwood content, are sweeter and less strong, though very similar in taste. To serve plain, add about ⅔ water just before serving.

BRANDY AND BENEDICTINE (B AND B)

½ fluid ounce Benedictine
½ fluid ounce brandy

Pour Benedictine into a liqueur glass, then float brandy on top, so that the liqueurs are separate.

CAFÉ AU KIRSCH

1½ fluid ounces kirsch
1½ fluid ounces black coffee
1 teaspoon sugar
white of egg

Shake with ice and strain into wine glass.

CRÈME DE MENTHE FRAPPÉ

Fill brandy glass with crushed ice. Pour in crème de menthe until glass is almost full. Serve with short straws. (This is sometimes served with brandy on top; it may then be called—incorrectly—a Brandy Float.)

GRASSHOPPER

1 fluid ounce white crème de cacao
1 fluid ounce green crème de menthe
1 fluid ounce double cream

Shake vigorously with ice and serve in a 4-fluid-ounce wine glass.

POUSSE CAFÉ

½ teaspoon grenadine (red)
½ teaspoon crème de cacao (brown)
½ teaspoon maraschino (white)
½ teaspoon green crème de menthe
½ teaspoon crème Yvette (violet)
½ teaspoon brandy (amber)

Pour, in the order named, very carefully and slowly into a liqueur glass. This may be best accomplished by pouring the different liqueurs from a small measuring glass with a lip.

FRAPPÉS

Pack a brandy goblet with crushed ice and fill with preferred cordial or liqueur. Serve with short straws.

Hot Drinks

BLUE BLAZER

1 wine glass Scotch whisky
1 wine glass boiling water
1 teaspoon icing sugar

Use two small pans with long handles. Put the whisky into one pan and the boiling water in the other.

Set the whisky alight, and while it blazes mix the ingredients by pouring them four or five times from one mug to the other. If this is properly done it will have the appearance of a continued stream of liquid fire.

Pour into an 8-fluid-ounce tumbler in which a silver teaspoon has been placed. Add icing sugar. Stir. Serve with twist of lemon peel.

HOT BUTTERED RUM

1½ fluid ounces Jamaica rum
4 cloves
1 lump sugar or 1 tablespoon honey
½ ounce butter

Scald whisky tumbler or mug. Put in rum, cloves, and sugar or honey. Fill glass with boiling water. Top with butter. Stir. Serve with a small silver spoon.

HOT RUM TODDY

1½ fluid ounces Jamaica rum
slice of lemon
1 teaspoon sugar
3 cloves
stick of cinnamon

Scald a whisky tumbler. Put ingredients in and fill with boiling water. Sprinkle ground cinnamon on top. Stir. Serve with a silver spoon.

HOT WHISKY TODDY

1½ fluid ounces rye whisky
juice of ½ lemon
1 teaspoon sugar

Scald a whisky tumbler. When glass has been thoroughly heated, pour water out.

Muddle sugar and lemon juice until sugar is dissolved. Add whisky and fill with boiling water. Stir. Serve with a small silver spoon.

TOM AND JERRY

1½ fluid ounces Jamaica rum
1 teaspoon sugar
1 egg
dash of brandy
pinch of allspice

Separate yolk and white of egg and beat yolk.

Beat egg white until fairly stiff, then add sugar, and beat to a stiff froth.

Combine yolk and white and add allspice. Put the mixture into a scalded mug. Add rum, then fill with boiling water. Stir well. Top with the brandy.

SWEDISH GLOGG

6 ounces granulated sugar
2 fluid ounces Angostura bitters
¾ pint claret
¾ pint sherry
8 fluid ounces brandy

Combine ingredients and heat in saucepan until piping hot, but do not boil.

Preheat whisky tumbler with boiling water and place in the bottom of it 1 large raisin and 1 unsalted almond.

Place spoon in glass to prevent breaking and fill ⅔ full with hot wine mixture.

MULLED WINE (Gluehwein)

4 fluid ounces water
1 lemon, sliced
1 stick cinnamon
1 tablespoon cloves
3 ounces sugar
1 bottle claret
16 fluid ounces pineapple juice
8 fluid ounces orange juice

Boil water with lemon slices, cinnamon, cloves, and sugar for 5 minutes. Strain and mix with wine and fruit juices. Serve hot. Serves 8.

JERSEY LIGHTHOUSE

2 lumps sugar
2 dashes Angostura bitters
4 whole cloves
1 spiral lemon peel
3 fluid ounces applejack

Mix in preheated mug. Fill with boiling water. Add float of applejack; set alight and serve blazing.

TOM AND JERRY (To Serve 6)

6 eggs, separated
4 ounces sugar
8 fluid ounces rum
8 fluid ounces brandy
½ teaspoon cinnamon
½ teaspoon nutmeg
1¼ pints boiling water

Beat egg whites until stiff. Beat yolks until thick with the sugar.

Blend whites and yolks together lightly and add rum and brandy.

Add spices and gradually add the boiling water, stirring the mixture until well mixed. Serve in earthenware mugs with a dash of nutmeg.

Miscellaneous Cocktails and Other Drinks

GROG

Grog originally referred to rum diluted with water, and was named after Old Grog, nickname of Admiral Vernon (1684-1757), a British naval officer who introduced the drink about 1745. He was so called because he wore a *grogram* cloak. The following is a popular version of the drink.

1 teaspoon simple bar syrup
1 tablespoon strained lemon juice
2 fluid ounces dark rum

Stir together in an 8-fluid-ounce mug and fill with very hot water or tea. Garnish with twist of lemon peel.

Variation: Substitute black treacle for bar syrup. Sprinkle with ground nutmeg or cinnamon.

HORSE'S NECK

rind of lemon peeled in a spiral
ginger ale

Arrange spiral of lemon rind so that one end curls over edge of glass. Add ice cubes. Fill with ginger ale.

With a Spike: Add 1½ fluid ounces rye whisky. Serve with stirring rod.

PRAIRIE OYSTER

yolk of egg
1 dash Worcestershire sauce
cayenne pepper and salt to taste
1½ fluid ounces brandy or Madeira

Mix well and serve in whisky tumbler. Add dash of vinegar on top.

WHISKY SOUR

1½ fluid ounces rye or Scotch whisky
juice of ½ lemon
1 teaspoon sugar

Shake with ice and strain into a wine glass.

Decorate with half slice of orange and maraschino cherry.

GIN SMASH

1 lump sugar
mint leaves
1½ fluid ounces dry gin

Muddle sugar and mint leaves that have been splashed with soda water in a whisky tumbler. Add gin and 1 ice cube. Stir. Top with soda water. Decorate with small sprig of mint.

PORT OR SHERRY FLIP

2 fluid ounces port or sherry
1 teaspoon sugar
1 whole egg

Shake well with ice in mixing glass. Strain into wine glass; then pour back and forth until smooth. Sprinkle with nutmeg.

BRANDY FLOAT

Place whisky tumbler upsidedown tightly over jigger measure filled with brandy. Holding jigger in place, reverse whisky tumbler and pour half full of soda water. Lift jigger along edge of larger glass to leave brandy floating on top of soda water.

DAISIES

1½ fluid ounces dry gin
3 dashes grenadine
juice of ½ lemon

Stir into a goblet half filled with finely crushed ice. Add a squirt of plain soda water. Garnish with fruit and a sprig of mint.

Variations: Brandy, applejack, rum, or whisky may be used instead of gin.

MAJOR BAILEY

mint leaves
juice of ½ lemon
1 teaspoon sugar
2 fluid ounces dry gin

Bruise mint leaves in the lemon juice and sugar with muddler. Fill tall glass with crushed ice. Add gin.

Stir until all ingredients are thoroughly combined and outside of glass is frosted. Do not touch glass with hands while performing this rite.

Decorate with sprigs of mint. Serve with straws.

RUM SCOUNDREL

1½ fluid ounces rum
juice of ½ lime
1 teaspoon sugar
dash of Angostura bitters

Serve in whisky tumbler with ice, slices of lemon and orange. Rub the rim of the glass with a cut lemon and dip it in sugar to coat it.

RUM CRUSTAS

1½ fluid ounces rum
½ fluid ounce maraschino
juice of 1 lime
2 dashes of Angostura bitters
½ teaspoon sugar
Spiral of orange peel

Frost the rim of a tall tumbler and fill with crushed ice. Cut a large circle of orange peel from circumference of large orange; fit in glass so that it is even with edge. Shake ingredients and strain into glass. Add soda water.

WINE LEMONADE

Prepare lemonade in the usual manner with ice. For each glass, add 2 to 4 fluid ounces any red or white table wine. Sweeten to taste.

FRENCH SEVENTY-FIVE

2 fluid ounces dry gin
1 teaspoon sugar
juice of ½ lemon
champagne

Shake well with ice. Strain into tall glass in which ice cubes have been placed. Top with champagne.

ABOUT BEER AND ALE

Beer is an alcoholic beverage—one of the oldest—made by brewing and fermenting cereals, particularly malted barley, to which hops are usually added as a flavouring agent and stabilizer. Modern beers usually contain from 3 to 6 per cent alcohol. Although the beers of Britain, continental Europe and the United States differ notably in flavour and content, the brewing processes are similar.

Malt, produced from barley, is first crushed and then mixed with water to make a "mash". This is allowed to stand until the starch in the malt is converted by enzymes into sugars. To the resultant liquid, or "wort", hops and sugar are added, and the mixture is then thoroughly boiled. The hops are then strained off and the rest of the mixture is passed into fermenting vessels, where yeast is added to convert the sugars into alcohol and carbon dioxide. When fermentation is complete, surplus yeast is removed and the beer is either run off into casks (for draught beer) or passed through further processes for bottling or kegging.

Draught beer—mild ale, bitter and stout. Mild ales and stouts are first primed with a sugar solution.

Bottled Beers

Lager is a beer that has been stored to mature it. The slow fermentation at low temperatures and the long maturing process give it a very long shelf life. It *must* be served cold.

Stout is brewed from malts that have been well roasted, which accounts for its dark colour. Some stouts are quite sweet, while others are drier.

Pale Ale (also called "light" or "light ale")—the "light" refers to alcoholic strength, not colour.

Brown Ale is so called because of its colour, but alcoholicly it is a light beer.

India Pale Ale is a pale bitter beer sold both in bottles and on draught, so called because it used to be shipped to the East India Company.

Export is another term for a full-bodied brew that, because of its higher alcoholic content, was supposed to be better able to withstand a sea voyage.

Natural Beers are allowed to mature in the bottle, which gives the beer its sparkle through fermentation. The sediment should be disturbed as little as possible when pouring.

Punch Bowl and Cup Drinks

Punch bowl and cup drinks are very similar. The former are usually mixed in a bowl to be served buffet style, while the latter are served in garnished pitchers at the table.

CLARET CUP

½ fluid ounce maraschino liqueur
1 fluid ounce orange curaçao
3 tablespoons caster sugar
1½ bottles claret

Mix liqueurs with sugar in large pitcher. Add crushed ice and stir thoroughly. Stir in chilled claret and garnish with fruit and berries. Serve in wine glasses.

WHITE WINE CUP

1 fluid ounce maraschino liqueur
½ fluid ounce curaçao
½ fluid ounce simple bar syrup
1½ bottles dry white wine

Mix liqueurs and syrup in large pitcher. Add crushed ice and pour in wine. Stir and serve in wine glasses.

FISHERMAN'S PUNCH

1¾ pints rye whisky
¾ pint sweet vermouth
¾ pint sherry
8 fluid ounces Jamaica rum
4 fluid ounces lemon juice
4 teaspoons orange bitters
4 teaspoons grenadine
¾ pint soda water

Mix all ingredients except soda water and place in refrigerator for at least 2 hours, preferably overnight.

Add soda water and ice just before serving. Makes about 30 servings.

WINE PUNCH

1 bottle port or claret
¾ lemon juice
8 fluid ounces grenadine, grape juice, or pineapple juice
¾ pint orange juice
1 24-ounce bottle soda water
16 fluid ounces ginger ale
sugar syrup (8 fluid ounces or more)

Combine ingredients, adding enough sugar syrup to sweeten, and pour into punch bowl in which a block of ice has been placed. Garnish with sliced oranges. Serves 30.

CHAMPAGNE PUNCH

2 bottles champagne
2 bottles soda water
½ bottle or 12 fluid ounces each curaçao, brandy, maraschino
6 fluid ounces grenadine or sugar to taste

2 bottles Sauternes
fruit to garnish, if desired

Chill champagne and soda water thoroughly. Place large block of ice in punch bowl. Slice fruit over it, if used.

Add liqueurs and Sauternes. Pour in champagne slowly and add soda water last. Stir gently, not vigorously. Serves 50.

WEDDING BELL LEMONADE PUNCH

4 6-ounce cans frozen lemon juice
4 6-ounce cans frozen pineapple juice
8 cans water (about 2½ pints)
3¾ pints ginger ale
1¾ pints soda water
1¾ pints dry champagne
ice cubes (or block of ice)

Combine the juices and water to keep chilled.

When ready to use, add ginger ale and soda water and pour over ice cubes (or block of ice) in a large punch bowl.

Then pour the well chilled champagne as evenly as possible over the punch and stir it gently through the punch. Makes approximately 50 4-ounce servings.

WASSAIL

The term wassail was formerly used as a salutation given in drinking the health of a person on festive occasions. By association it came to mean any alcohol in which healths are drunk, especially old English punches of spiced beer, ale, or wine. Such punches are served hot from a big bowl (Wassail Bowl) at Christmas time. The Wine Wassail given below is a modern version of such a punch.

WINE WASSAIL

2 pints apple juice
2 pints orange juice
8 ounces sugar
4 ounces slivered blanched almonds
5 ounces raisins
2 sticks cinnamon
28 whole cloves
4 pints Burgundy

Combine apple juice with next 4 ingredients. Tie cinnamon sticks and cloves in a muslin bag. Add to apple juice mixture. Boil 5 minutes.

Remove bag. Add burgundy. Heat very slowly. Do not boil. Strain if desired. Serve hot. For garnish, float notched orange slices in punch bowl. Makes 8 pints.

MAY WINE

3½ pints Sauternes, Rhine wine or Chablis
3 ounces sugar
½ pint orange juice
4 to 5 ounces strawberries, sliced
2 oranges, sliced

Chill wine. Dissolve sugar in orange juice in chilled punch bowl. Add wine, sliced strawberries, and orange slices.

Float a few flowers (orange blossoms are good) on surface of punch just before serving. Serves 12 to 15.

FROSTY NEW YEAR'S PUNCH

3 pints orange water ice or sorbet
3 bottles Sauternes or other white wine, chilled
2 6-ounce cans frozen orange juice
sugar to taste
1 large bottle champagne, well chilled

Place sorbet in punch bowl. Pour in Sauternes and frozen juice, diluted with water according to directions on can. Stir until no lumps of sorbet remain.

Add sugar, if desired, and stir until dissolved. Add champagne. Makes about 75 3-fluid-ounce servings.

ANNIVERSARY PUNCH

1 12-ounce packet frozen strawberries
2 teaspoons grated lime rind
juice of 1 lime
1 bottle sparkling burgundy
1 bottle dry champagne
1 bottle Sauternes
block of ice for punch bowl

Combine strawberries, lime rind, and lime juice in saucepan. Simmer together 10 minutes; put through vegetable mill or sieve. Cool.

Pour fruit mixture over ice in punch bowl. Add wines just before serving.

Garnish with whole strawberries and lime slices, if desired. Makes about 25 servings.

Variation: Instead of the frozen berries, use 8 ounces fresh, sliced strawberries, 1 tablespoon water, and 2 ounces sugar.

Anniversary Punch

Wines and Serving Wine

Wine may be simply defined as the fermented juice of sound, ripe grapes which have been crushed after harvesting. If we crush a handful of grapes and leave it in a cup, it will turn into wine. The alcohol in wine is simply Nature's way of preserving the juice of the grape.

Wine production, however, cannot be so simply presented inasmuch as there are actually hundreds of varieties of wines. Many of them may be made according to special formulas and processes which will give them the qualities particular vineyards are attempting to achieve.

The quality of really fine wines is contingent upon a number of factors, each of which can very greatly influence the finished product. When one of these factors changes, the wine will also change.

The extremely wide variations among wines arise primarily from the differences in the soil and climate in which the grapes are grown. As a matter of fact, the influence of these two factors is so great that if a vine is transplanted a very short distance from its original site a very different wine may be obtained from the grapes grown on the transplanted vine. For example, there are areas in France where certain exceptional wines come from grapes grown on the hillsides of one side of a valley and a quite different wine of ordinary quality will result from similar vines growing on hillsides on the opposite side of that same valley. Then again, a variety of grapes grown in a volcanic soil will produce a different wine from the same variety of grapes grown in a gravel or clay soil.

A good wine is one which is satisfactory in taste, bouquet, and in appearance. It must be made naturally, without the aid of chemicals, or excess sugar, and there must be no secondary fermentation of the alcohol into vinegar.

WINE NAMES

There are hundreds of different names for wines. This need not be confusing as long as we remember that virtually all wines fit into one of these five groups:

(1) apéritif wines, (2) white table wines, (3) red table wines, (4) sweet dessert wines, and (5) sparkling wines.

THE TWELVE PRINCIPAL WINE TYPES

In the above-named five groups and among the hundreds of wine names, there are 12 distinct known wine types of wine "families." If you can recognize by sight, taste, and smell these 12 well-known wine types,

you may consider yourself as well informed about wines as the average wine merchant.

These 12 distinct wines types are:

Sherry and Vermouth (apéritif wines).

Claret and Burgundy (red table wines).

Sauternes and Rhine Wine (white table wines).

Port, Madeira, Marsala, and White Port (dessert wines).

Champagne and Sparkling Burgundy (sparkling wines).

Practically all other wines fall into these "families" but, because of various minor differences in the grapes used, in the blending methods, or even in trade names applied by vintners, they may be known by other names to indicate varying shades of colour, flavour, and richness.

Don't expect to be able to recognize all the minor differences of the wines bearing other names than these 12. Not even a professional wine taster knows them all.

For those who want to delve more deeply into wine lore, the information that follows will be helpful.

RED AND WHITE WINES

All wines are classified as either red or white wines, although the variation in hues from true red to true white is endless. If a wine, however, has any tinge of red in it, that wine is a red wine and if a wine has no trace of red in it, that wine is a white wine. Hence, white wines vary in shade from a very pale straw colour to an almost deep dark brown, and reds from almost deep purple to the palest rosé.

"DRY" AND SWEET WINES

Wines may also be classified by taste or by alcoholic content. The term "dry" is applied to wines having a low sugar content (usually less than 1%). The term therefore means the opposite of sweet—and at no time does it mean sour. Sour wines taste of vinegar and are spoiled through secondary fermentation.

Most red wines are dry. The exceptions are port and port-style wines.

White wines vary in sweetness from the very dry Manzanilla sherry to the extremely sweet Sauternes.

The dry wines are generally used for table wines, i.e., drunk with meals. Dry wines are usually produced in areas where the summers are relatively short, and the grapes when they are ripe are not too sweet.

Sweet wines are made from extremely sweet, sometimes overripe, grapes. Their sugar content may go as high as 10%.

NATURAL AND FORTIFIED WINES

Wines may be additionally classified as either "natural" or "fortified," depending upon their alcoholic content. A natural wine contains 10% to 14% alcohol, which is the maximum normally obtainable through natural fermentation.

The alcoholic content of fortified wines ranges from 17% to 21%. This high alcoholic content is obtainable by the addition of brandy to the wine at some stage in the fermentation. If the brandy is added early in the fermentation process, the fortified wine will be sweet since little of the natural grape sugar will have been transformed into alcohol. If the brandy is added at the end, the wine may be quite dry.

In any case, after the addition of the brandy the high alcoholic concentration prevents the further natural fermentation which in time causes wine to spoil when exposed to air.

The two fortified wines of outstanding importance are sherry, imported from Spain, and port, imported from Portugal. Other fortified wines that are popular are Madeira and Marsala.

As a general rule, most fortified wines are too heavy and too sweet for consumption during meals, are known as dessert wines, and are usually served at the end of the meal as are desserts. The most usual exceptions are some sherries which are served slightly chilled before the meal.

The popular dry wines (red and white Burgundy, red Bordeaux, Moselle, and Rhine) are all natural wines and are used as table wines.

Some semi-sweet wines such as the Sauternes are also used for the same purpose.

OTHER PLANT AND FRUIT WINES

The term "wine" is also applied to alcoholic beverages made from plants and fruit other than grape. Examples of these are blackberry, elderberry, and dandelion wine.

VERMOUTHS AND OTHER APPETIZER WINES

Apéritif wines are so called because they are favoured for cocktail use and before-meal drinking. They include dry sherry, vermouth, Dubonnet, Byrrh (red), St. Raphael (white), and other brand name apéritif wines served chilled.

Apéritif wines (with the exception of sherry) are not true wines but have been modified by the addition of herbs, roots, seed, flowers, or other flavouring materials which were steeped in the wine for periods ranging from a few weeks to several years. Many of them are made from sweet wines but the various flavouring ingredients used in blending them give them a dry after-taste.

There are two types of vermouth — French and Italian. The French type is made of a relatively dry white wine and it is used in cocktail recipes in this book which call for "dry" vermouth. The alcoholic content is 19%. Italian-type vermouth has as its base a much sweeter wine as well as a different assortment of flavouring constituents. The alcoholic content is 17%. Recipes in this book calling for "sweet" vermouth refer to the Italian type.

In France and Italy both vermouths are drunk neat. Elsewhere their use is confined for the most part to the preparation of cocktails, although an increasing number of people are gradually learning to drink the vermouths in the "continental" manner.

European Wines

Europe has for centuries been a centre both for the production and the consumption of wine. The principal producing countries have been France, Germany and Italy, and French and German wines are probably still the most popular wines drunk in Britain. However, increasing demand from all over the world is leading to higher prices for French and German wines and so more of the excellent wines from Spain and Italy are finding their way to the British dining table.

The best-known French wines are Claret, Burgundy and Champagne. Each is made from grapes grown in an area strictly delimited by French law and only wine coming from such an area may carry the inscription "Appellation Contrôlée". Claret is the red wine from the Bordeaux region, and within that region particular areas (such as Médoc and Graves) produce their own distinctive wines. It is the biggest wine producing area in France. In 1855 the then existing vineyards or châteaux were classified into five categories or "growths" based on the prices received by the vineyards for their wines in the preceding 100 years. The five châteaux comprised in the first growth were Lafitte, Latour, Mouton-Rothschild, Margaux and Haut-Brion. Although it is now often criticized as being out of date, the 1855 classification is still a good, if not infallible, guide to quality. As well as producing claret, which in the nineteenth century was the most widely drunk table wine in England, the area produces white wine and now in fact the production of white wine has surpassed that of red. Most of the white wine comes from the south eastern part of the Bordeaux region, from Graves and Entre-deux-Mers (so called because it is situated in the area between the Garonne and the Dordogne rivers before they both merge into the Gironde estuary). Many of the white wines of Bordeaux are sweet and make excellent dessert wines. The best known of these is probably Château d'Yquem, which in the 1855 classification was placed in a unique category as a First Great Growth.

Wines from the province of Burgundy come from six principal areas, Chablis, Côte de Nuits, Côte de Beaune, Côte Chalonnaise, Maconnais and Beaujolais. With the exception of Chablis, which is to the north west of Dijon, these areas stretch between Dijon in the North and Lyon in the South. About three quarters of the wine produced in Burgundy is red wine, and nearly half of all the wine produced is exported. Red wine in Burgundy is made from grapes grown from the Pinot Noir vine, and white wine from the Chardonnay vine. The red wines from Burgundy tend to be full and robust, often giving the impression of being heavier and richer than claret from Bordeaux. It has, however, recently become common to drink red Burgundy, and particularly Beaujolais, when it is young, and "Beaujolais de l'année" (as Beaujolais drunk in the year it is produced is known) can be a refreshing and light wine. White Burgundy is usually a drier wine than white Bordeaux, but, once acquired, a taste for the many and varied white wines of the region will never be lost.

But perhaps the wine most commonly associated with France is Champagne. Everything about it is distinctive, its bottle, its sparkle, and its taste. This wine produced from vines grown in the region between Epernay and Reims, north east of Paris, is still the hallmark of a special occasion. Despite its ever-increasing price, it will remain popular and in demand, because the many sparkling white wines which are sold in competition with it simply do not taste the same. Champagne as we know it has evolved through the skills of many people, such as Dom Perignon in the seventeenth century, and the widow Clicquot in the nineteenth century, whose names remain famous through their association with the wine. Champagne is made by bottling the wine early so that it continues to ferment in the bottle. The bottles are stored face downwards, so that the sediment collects in the neck and eventually adheres to the base of the cork. The cork is then extracted to remove the sediment and at this point, before re-corking the wine, it may be sweetened to the degree of sweetness eventually required. The whole process will take a number of years and is labour intensive, hence the rising price of the wine.

Apart from these well-known regions of France, many other regions produce good wine, although until recently little of it was exported. The wines of the Loire Valley, particularly the white wines of Vouvray and Sancerre, together with Muscadet from the Nantes area, are becoming better known in Britain, although their red wines such as Bourgueil and Chinon are still difficult to find. Equally, the red wines of the Rhône Valley such as the well-known Châteauneuf-du-Pape, are gaining in popularity. As the Dordogne region becomes more exploited by English and other tourists, so their wines such as the well-rounded red wines from Cahors and the sweet white wine of Montbazillac may become more frequently obtainable in Britain.

Just as the demand for wines from France shows no sign of diminishing nor does that for wines from Germany. Germany in fact produces about one tenth of the amount of wine which is produced in France and nearly eighty-five per cent of the wine produced in Germany is white. Germany's vineyards lie along the Rhine, its tributary the Nahe, and along the Mosel. The French system of describing wine according to the geographical situation of the vines is not followed in Germany, but laws passed in 1971 regulate the quality of the wines by prescribing certain standards before a wine can carry certain descriptions. The majority of the wine produced derives from the Riesling vine, the other popular vine being the Sylvaner, which in fact produces twice as much wine per plant as the Riesling. Most Rhine and Mosel wines can be drunk young and their well-known fragrance and delicacy make them particularly attractive as luncheon wines or for summer drinking.

A number of the wines, however, can and should be allowed to mature, and are best drunk on their own on some special, and preferably contemplative, occasion. These are the wines described as Spätlese, Auslese or Beerenauslese. Spätlese is wine made from grapes harvested late and which are therefore riper, and Auslese or Beerenauslese are refinements on Spätlese. The ultimate refinement is Trockenbeerenauslese which is made from the finest grapes which have been left to the latest possible time for gathering.

In addition to France and Germany, however, other European countries are important winegrowers and of these the most important is Italy. Italy is the biggest wine producing country in the world and although most British people equate Italian wine with bulbous straw-covered bottles from Chianti, a number of regions of Italy, other than the Chianti growing area south of Florence, are devoted to the production of good red and white wines. The practice of restricting names to wine made from vines in a particular area was not introduced until 1963 when the Italian government imposed a system of "Denominazione di Origine Controllata" similar to the French system of "Appellation Contrôlée". Although Chianti remains the best-known Italian wine, wine from Piedmont in the north west, from Brescia and Verona in the east, and from Orvieto further south, are well known and will become more popular.

Spain, as well as being the producer of sherry, is also becoming increasingly well known as a country which produces very palatable red and white table wines. By far the best-known red wines are those of Rioja, produced from vines on the river Ebro, northeast of Madrid, although this also produces some white wine, but the area with the greatest output of red wine is La Mancha, to the south-east of Madrid, which produces the majority of the cheaper Spanish table wines which are now consumed in large quantities in Britain.

In addition, the wines of other countries are being drunk in greater profusion. The white Yugoslav Rieslings have been popular for some years, and a number of pleasant table wines, both red and white, are now available from Portugal, Austria, Morocco, and as far afield as Australia and Chile.

Serving Wines

The amount of misinformation regarding wines is so tremendous and the number of "dos" and "don'ts" about wine service that have been enumerated by so-called connoisseurs are so great in number that the average host or hostess has frequently hesitated to serve wines.

Yet for hundreds and even thousands of years before this long list of rules was elaborated wine added much pleasure to dining and entertaining.

It certainly is not necessary then to memorize these numerous and complex rules before serving wine.

In fact serving wine need be no more complex than serving good coffee or tea. Many of us enjoy our "cup of tea"

without making a study of the almost infinite variations of tea grown in the tea-growing areas of the world. There is no doubt, of course, that this study as well as the pastime of testing and knowing wines may be entertaining.

The few simple suggestions that follow are based on the assumption that one drinks and serves wines for enjoyment. They are based on the preferences of the vast majority of wine drinkers who do abide by certain preferences in order to get the maximum enjoyment from drinking wine.

In addition a chart is offered for the benefit of those people who would like to know the rules laid down for "formal" dinners where a variety of wines may be served, and specific types of wines chosen for each course.

Basic Hints for Serving Wines

● Remember that really "fine" wines are rare treats for special occasions. The important consideration when choosing a table wine for ordinary occasions is that the wine should be sound—and that does not mean high-priced.

● Your guests will be more impressed, if they know anything about wines, with a sound wine rather than one that has a fancy label.

● If they are uninformed you may enjoy the pleasure of starting their education.

● Unless you have the necessary cool wine cellar, buy only enough wine to fill immediate needs. Wine may deteriorate rapidly in a warm cupboard.

● Buy from a well-informed, reputable merchant who may be a storehouse of reliable information in guiding you and helping you avoid impressive names that would just cause you to waste money.

● It is quite proper to serve only one wine with a meal. For this purpose select a plain sound wine such as a Rhine wine or Claret.

● One good wine is far simpler and more palatable than half a dozen of doubtful quality.

● For formal occasions champagne or another sparkling wine is often served throughout a meal.

● Red or white light wines may be served with almost any dishes.

● Avoid however serving dry wines with sweet dishes or foods that have sweet sauces and avoid serving red wines with fish.

● This last is one of the few basic rules that have come down to us that seems to make sense. For some inexplicable reason fish seem to have a property that makes red wine taste unpleasantly metallic to some people. If it doesn't have that effect on you then there is no reason why you shouldn't forget about it insofar as your own preferences are concerned but remember that may not be the case with your guests.

● Your own experience will tell you that a dry wine would not necessarily go well with sweet dishes nor would a very sweet wine go well with the usual foods in a meal for the same reason why you wouldn't serve syrup with roast beef.

● Most people like white wines slightly colder than red wines but this, too, is a matter of personal preference.

● The ideal temperature for white wines is 45° to 50°F.

● Sparkling wines should always be well-chilled. Champagne, for example, is at its best when served at a temperature of 40°F. or slightly less.

● To chill wine thoroughly place the bottle in a refrigerator for an hour or two and then in a wine cooler (a bucket of ice) for 20 to 30 minutes.

● If you plan to serve a wine at room temperature allow it to stand in the room where it is to be served for several hours.

● Never warm wine artificially or it will spoil.

● A few customs have entrenched themselves so well that they have become almost traditional. They include the service of white wines with hors d'oeuvres, fish, and white meats, and serving red wines with cheeses, salads, and dark meats—and serving white wines before red wines, and dry wines before sweet wines. The reasons for some of these are obvious, as explained above.

● Others have grown out of the fact that white wines are not generally as full flavoured as the reds and as a result may be a happier choice with the more delicately flavoured dishes, and red wines which are usually more fully flavoured may make a better accompaniment for the more highly flavoured and seasoned dishes.

GUIDE TO FORMAL WINE SERVICE

Food	Kind of Wine	How to Serve
Apéritif When wine is served alone as an apéritif	Champagne or sparkling wines Dubonnet or Byrrh Sherry (dry), or Vermouth	Chilled 35°-40°F. Chilled 40°-50°F.
Appetizers (canapés, hors d'oeuvres, etc.)	Dry white wines such as: dry Sherry Chablis (white Burgundy) Graves (white Bordeaux) Rhine or Moselle Champagne or sparkling wines	All chilled 40°-50°F. Chilled 35°-40°F.
Soups	Dry Sherry (with clear soups) Other dry white wines such as: dry Sauternes, dry Madeira, Moselle, Rhine, Chablis Champagne or sparkling wines	Chilled 50°-60°F. or room temperature (70°F.) All chilled 45°-50°F. Chilled 35°-40°F.
Fish or Seafood	Any white table wines such as: Rhine, Moselle, Chablis, Graves, or dry Sauternes Dry Champagne or sparkling wines	All chilled 50°F. Chilled 35°-40°F.
Poultry or other white meat	Any dry white table wine as suggested for fish or seafood Dry Champagne or sparkling wines	All chilled 45°-50°F. Chilled 35°-40°F.
Wild fowl, game, and red meat	Red table wines such as: red Burgundy, Claret, Chianti, etc.	All at cellar 55°-60°F. or room temperature 70°F.
Cheese	Red table wines such as: Claret, Burgundy, Madeira, or Port	All at room temperature 70°F.
Dessert	Sweet wines such as: Marsala, Madeira, and Port Sweet Sauternes Sweet Champagne or sweet sparkling wines	All at room temperature 70°F. Chilled 50°F. Chilled 35°-40°F.
Coffee	Vintage Port or Madeira Recommended instead of wines, however, are brandy and liqueurs.	All at room temperature 70°F.

How to Keep Wines

QUANTITY WINE STORAGE FOR LONG PERIODS

To keep all wines in quantity the ideal storage place is a dark, dry cellar which maintains a uniform temperature of about 55°F. It should be well-aired but free of draughts. It must also be free of vibrations and that includes slight ones caused by street traffic.

Shelves should be away from furnaces or electric wiring or heating pipes of any kind.

Such really ideal conditions for the storage of wines in quantity are found only in deep underground cellars.

The chief problem for most of us in keeping a small stock of wines is the change in temperature in the average cellar or cupboard in a flat. If it is gradual and doesn't go above 70° or 75° or below 40°F. no serious damage will be done. Freezing temperatures or temperatures above 75°F. will be very harmful.

In addition proper racks should be installed in a cupboard so that one bottle may be removed at a time without disturbing the others.

NATURAL AND FORTIFIED WINES

In caring for wines, you must distinguish between natural wines and fortified wines.

Natural (unfortified) wines continue to change after being bottled. They have to be kept tightly sealed to keep out all air. If these wines are allowed to stand up for any length of time the corks will dry up enough to allow air to come in and permit additional fermentation which, in time, will cause the wine to turn sour.

For this reason, it is necessary to store all wines which have an alcoholic content of 14% or less on their side with the cork slightly down so that it will be kept moist by the wine.

Fortified wines have had sufficient alcohol added to them to prevent further fermentation.

They should be kept standing in such a way that you may remove one bottle at a time without disturbing the others.

When bottles of corked table wines and sparkling wines must be kept upright for display or sales purposes, old stock should be moved to the front of shelves every time new stock is added.

WHEN WINE IS LEFT OVER

Natural Wines (Table Wines): Because of their low alcoholic content, these are perishable after opening of their corks brings them into contact with air. If table wines are left in a partly empty bottle they will "go off" (spoil) even though corked.

Actual spoilage begins within a few days or a few weeks, depending upon the individual wine and the weather. Storage in the refrigerator slows but does not prevent spoilage.

What to Do: If there is an unfinished bottle of wine, cork it tightly, place in refrigerator, and use in a day or two.

If it must be kept longer, pour into clean smaller bottles, close with a cornical cork from a chemist, and place in refrigerator. Plan to use it within a week.

If it's a large flagon, pour what is left into clean smaller bottles. Cork tightly, store in refrigerator, and plan to use within a week.

If you plan to use leftover wine for cooking, it need not be refrigerated if you add enough olive oil to form a thin film on the wine. Such wines should be used in fish and meat cookery, not in desserts or with fruit.

Fortified Wines (apéritif and Dessert Wines): On opening, there is no danger from further fermentation; they will keep well for many weeks unless they are exposed to air for long periods.

DUMPLINGS

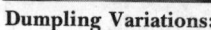

There is something very Middle-or Eastern-European about dumplings and in some European countries the way of a woman with dumplings is as important as her charm and beauty. A good old-fashioned dumpling gives a hearty and tasty touch to soups and stews.

SOME HINTS ABOUT MAKING DUMPLINGS FOR SOUPS AND STEWS

● Use a wide-topped cooking vessel and never crowd it.
● Use ample liquid and give each dumpling room to expand.
● Cook in *gently* boiling liquid, close to a simmer.
● Cover the vessel as soon as instructed in the recipe so the steam can begin functioning.
● Resist temptation and do not lift the cover until the dumplings are done. You can see the dumplings swell without lifting the lid if you use a tight-fitting, heat-resistant glass cover or pie dish.
● Test for "doneness" when the dumplings look fluffy by inserting a cocktail stick. If it comes out clean, the dumplings are done.

BAKING POWDER DUMPLINGS (Master Recipe)

8 ounces sifted plain flour
1 teaspoon salt
4 teaspoons baking powder
1 ounce lard or margarine
6 to 8 fluid ounces milk or water

Sift together the flour, the salt, and baking powder. Cut in margarine with pastry blender or 2 knives.

Add liquid until a thick drop batter is obtained.

Drop by tablespoonfuls into boiling soup or stew; cover tightly. Cook 12 minutes. Serves 5.

Dumpling Variations:

Parsley Dumplings: In master recipe add 1 ounce finely chopped parsley to flour mixture.

Meat Dumplings: Add leftover cooked meat or crackling to master recipe just before dropping dumplings into boiling soup or stew.

Puffy Cheese Dumplings: In master recipe reduce margarine to ½ ounce and add 2 ounces grated strong Cheddar cheese to flour mixture.

MAIZE FLOUR DUMPLINGS

7 ounces maize flour or polenta
1 teaspoon salt
½ pint boiling water
1 teaspoon chopped parsley
2 slightly beaten eggs
½ teaspoon grated onion
1 to 2 ounces plain flour

Combine maize flour and salt and gradually add to boiling water, stirring constantly.

Remove from heat and stir until smooth. Cool.

Add remaining ingredients except flour. Mix thoroughly.

Drop by spoonfuls onto greaseproof paper heavily sprinkled with flour. Roll round in flour to form balls.

Drop into boiling meat or chicken stew. Cover tightly. Cook 10 minutes. Serves 6.

GERMAN LIVER DUMPLINGS OR LEBERKLOESSE

5 ounces chopped, cooked liver
8 fluid ounces water
3 ounces fresh breadcrumbs
1 teaspoon salt
⅛ teaspoon black pepper
½ teaspoon grated onion
1 slightly beaten egg
Grated lemon rind (optional)

Chicken, goose, ox or calves' liver may be used.

Cook water and breadcrumbs to a paste, stirring to prevent burning.

Cool. Add remaining ingredients. Mix well.

Form into balls the size of walnuts. Drop into rapidly boiling salted water or boiling soup. Cook 5 to 10 minutes. Serves 6.

Liver Dumpling Variations:

Fried Liver Dumplings: Roll cooked liver dumplings in dry breadcrumbs and fry in hot fat.

Chicken Gizzard Dumplings: In liver dumplings use cooked heart and tender part of gizzards with or without chopped liver.

Marrow Dumplings: In liver dumplings substitute cooked or uncooked beef marrow for chopped liver and proceed as directed.

NOCKERLN

Nockerln is a German term for light dumplings made in several different ways. The recipe that follows is one of the most popular types. Egg Foam Dumplings are another type of nockerln.

2 ounces butter or margarine
1 egg
4 ounces plain flour
Pinch of salt
6 tablespoons milk

Cream together the butter and egg.

Stir in flour and a pinch of salt. Moisten to form a stiff batter by adding milk gradually.

Cut out the batter with a teaspoon to form small balls or Nockerln.

Drop them into boiling soup stock; cover the pan, and cook for 10 minutes.

MATZO MEAL DUMPLINGS
(Knaidlach)

Knaidlach or knaidel are Yiddish terms for dumplings. These light matzo meal dumplings are traditionally served at Passover.

2 eggs, separated
2 ounces matzo meal
½ teaspoon salt

Beat egg yolks and whites in separate bowls, then combine and add matzo meal and salt gradually while stirring until smooth.

Chill in refrigerator for 30 minutes or longer before shaping into small balls with a teaspoon or by rolling in the palms of hands.

Drop one at a time into boiling clear soup; cover and simmer for 20 minutes. Serves 4.

Variations of Matzo Meal Dumplings:

1. Add 1 tablespoon cooked or uncooked beef marrow to the mixture with or without 2 tablespoons chopped parsley.

2. Add 2 tablespoons chopped liver to the mixture just before shaping into balls.

3. Add 1 tablespoon finely chopped nuts to the mixture; season with a dash of cinnamon or ginger.

4. Season mixture with a dash of ginger; if desired, add 2 tablespoons chopped parsley.

GRATED RAW POTATO DUMPLINGS

12 ounces grated raw potatoes
Scant 3 ounces plain flour
1 egg
½ teaspoon salt
½ teaspoon grated onion
2 tablespoons breadcrumbs

Drain grated potatoes well. Combine all ingredients to form a batter thick enough to shape into balls the size of a walnut.

Drop into rapidly boiling soup or salted water; cook 20 minutes.

When done, the dumplings will rise on top. If cooked in salted water, remove with a slotted spoon. Drain. Serve with gravy or soup. Serves 6.

LITTLE DROP DUMPLINGS

3 eggs, separated
Milk
½ ounce butter or margarine
4 ounces sifted plain flour
¼ teaspoon salt
Dash of black pepper

Combine egg whites with enough milk to make 8 fluid ounces liquid. Pour into hot buttered pan.

Add flour and stir constantly until mixture leaves side of pan. Cool.

Add egg yolks 1 at a time, stirring well. Season. Drop by teaspoonful into boiling soup. Cook 10 minutes.

GNOCCHI

Gnocchi is an Italian dish, one that cannot be described in a word. Perhaps the closest approximation is dumpling. Gnocchi may be made of flour, mashed potatoes, or farola.

GNOCCHI WITH POTATOES

2 medium-sized potatoes
4 fluid ounces milk
2½ ounces butter
4 ounces plain flour
2 eggs
1 teaspoon salt
¼ teaspoon paprika
3 tablespoons grated Parmesan cheese, optional

For gnocchi, use a dry mealy type of potato. Boil the potatoes in their jackets, peel and mash.

Heat combined milk and butter to boiling point. Stir in flour until dough forms a ball. Remove from heat, then beat in eggs, salt, paprika, and the mashed potatoes.

Sprinkle the dough with a little flour to prevent sticking. Cut into 5 pieces and shape each into a long roll about ½-inch thick. Cut into pieces about 1 inch long.

Drop about a third of the gnocchi at a time in large pan of boiling salted water and cook gently, uncovered, for 3 to 5 minutes. Remove to a heated bowl and keep warm. Repeat until all the gnocchi have been cooked. Serve with melted butter and grated Parmesan cheese. Serves 6.

Variation: The gnocchi may be served with 12 fluid ounces canned or homemade Italian-style tomato sauce and 4 ounces grated Parmesan cheese. Toss the cooked gnocchi with 8 fluid ounces sauce and 2 ounces cheese. Turn onto serving plate and pour remaining sauce over it. Then sprinkle with remaining grated cheese.

GNOCCHI WITH FLOUR

1 ounce butter
2 tablespoons flour
2 tablespoons cornflour
½ teaspoon salt
8 fluid ounces milk, scalded
1 egg yolk
2 ounces grated cheese, optional

Melt butter in frying pan. Mix the flour, cornflour, and salt; blend into melted butter and stir until smooth.

Stir in scalded milk; lower heat, add egg yolk and, if desired, the grated cheese. Beat the batter until egg has thickened and cheese has melted.

Pour into shallow greased pan. Allow to cool, then cut into narrow pieces

about 2 inches long. Drop the pieces into gently boiling water and cook about 2 minutes. Drain and serve with melted butter. Serves 4.

Variation: If desired, do not boil the gnocchi. Place the pieces in a pan; pour additional melted butter over them, and sprinkle with additional grated cheese. Heat through in moderate oven, then serve.

GNOCCHI WITH FAROLA

2 ounces farola
½ ounce butter or margarine
½ teaspoon salt
¾ pint hot milk
1 beaten egg
½ pound strong cheese, grated
½ small onion, chopped
1 ounce chopped green pepper
1 ounce dripping
2 8-ounce cans tomatoes
1 teaspoon salt
⅛ teaspoon black pepper
Pinch of cayenne pepper

Stir farola, butter, and salt into hot milk and cook in top of double boiler 15 minutes.

Add egg and cheese. Reserve 2 ounces grated cheese.

Pour into shallow, greased pan. Chill, then cut into 12 squares and place in large, flat casserole.

Brown chopped onion and green pepper in hot fat. Add other ingredients and cook 10 minutes. Pour sauce over farola squares. Sprinkle with remaining cheese.

Cook in slow oven (325°F. Mark 3) until cheese is melted, about 15 minutes. Serves 4.

MARROW BALLS FOR SOUP

1 ounce fresh beef marrow
1 ounce butter or margarine
3 eggs
¼ teaspoon salt
⅛ teaspoon paprika
2 tablespoons chopped parsley
breadcrumbs

Combine marrow and butter and beat until creamy.

Add eggs, salt, paprika, parsley, and just enough breadcrumbs to make the right consistency to shape into balls.

Cook in simmering soup 15 minutes.

Gnocchi with Farola

SPATZEN OR SPAETZEL

A German term for tiny dumplings, sometimes called German egg dumplings.

10 ounces plain flour
½ teaspoon salt
¼ teaspoon baking powder
Dash of nutmeg, optional
2 eggs, lightly beaten
4 fluid ounces milk
4 fluid ounces water
4 ounces melted butter

Combine flour, salt, baking powder, and nutmeg in a bowl. Mix together the eggs, milk, and water; gradually stir into the flour mixture.

The consistency of the dough depends upon the method of shaping to be used. The dough may be made softer by the addition of a small amount of water or stiffer by adding more flour. The softer the dough, the lighter the dumplings; however, it must be firm enough to retain its shape. Spatzen should be light and delicate; try out a sample and if it is too heavy, add a little water to the dough.

Cut or break off small bits (about ¼ × 1-inch) of the dough with a spoon, and drop into 5 to 6 pints rapidly boiling salted water. Cook 1 or 2 minutes. Or place the dough on a plate and cut shreds with a knife from the side of the plate into the water. Or the dough may be forced through a metal colander into the boiling water.

When done, remove them with a slotted ladle to kitchen towels to remove excess water. Toss with melted butter. Serves 6.

Variations: (1) Cook spatzen in clear soup just before serving; serve with the soup; (2) Place drained spatzen in a dish and cover with 1 ounce breadcrumbs which have been sautéed in 2 ounces butter; (3) Toss spatzen with 6 fluid ounces warm soured cream and a little butter; (4) Toss with butter and 1 ounce crumbled crisp bacon bits; (5) Toss with 2 ounces grated sharp Cheddar cheese and butter.

There's plenty of flavour and nourishment in an old-time stew with dumplings.

MASHED POTATO DUMPLINGS
(Kartoffel Kloesse)

3 ounces ¼-inch bread cubes
Dripping
14 ounces mashed potatoes
1 tablespoon grated onion
1 slightly beaten egg
3 ounces sifted plain flour
1½ teaspoons salt
½ teaspoon black pepper

Fry bread cubes in hot dripping. Add ½ ounce dripping to hot mashed potatoes. Cool.

Add onion and egg; mix well with fork. Sift in flour, salt, and pepper. Mix well.

Shape into 12 balls, forming each round 4 to 5 fried bread cubes. Cook, covered, in boiling salted water 10 to 12 minutes.

If desired, brown in melted dripping before serving. Serves 6.

Variations of Mashed Potato Dumplings

Savoury Potato Dumplings: Add 1 teaspoon nutmeg and marjoram to dry ingredients.

Potato Meat Dumplings: Add leftover cooked meat to potato dumplings just before shaping into balls.

Potato Dumplings with Farola: Omit bread cubes; add 2 ounces farola to flour and proceed as for potato dumplings.

Potato Dumplings with Matzo Meal: Omit bread cubes; use 3 ounces matzo meal in place of flour in dumplings.

EGG FOAM DUMPLINGS

3 eggs, separated
Dash of salt
3 tablespoons plain flour

Beat egg whites with salt until stiff. Add egg yolks one at a time, beating slightly after each addition.

Fold in flour and pour into clear, boiling soup. Cook 5 minutes.

Lift out of soup; cut into ovals with the side of a tablespoon. Serve with hot soup.

LIVER SAUSAGE DUMPLINGS

4 ounces liver sausage
½ egg or 1 egg white or yolk
2 ounces cream cracker crumbs, or more if the egg is large
1 tablespoon chopped parsley or chives
1 tablespoon tomato ketchup

Combine sausage, egg, cracker crumbs, parsley or chives, and ketchup.

Shape the mixture into 1-inch balls. Cook gently for about 2 minutes in soup stock. Makes about 20 1-inch balls.

KNISHES

Knishes is a Yiddish term for any of several types of patties or dumplings, baked or fried and frequently served with soup. A popular type is made of thinly rolled or stretched dough, filled with seasoned chopped meat, cottage cheese, mashed potatoes, or kasha (cooked buckwheat groats). It is an old-time Jewish dish.

8 ounces sifted plain flour
1 teaspoon baking powder
¼ teaspoon salt
2 eggs, well beaten
4 fluid ounces vegetable oil
Cheese or meat filling (see below)

Mix and sift flour, baking powder, and salt. Mix beaten eggs and oil and combine with flour mixture; mix to a smooth dough.

Roll out on a floured board to ⅛-inch thickness. Fold in three and roll out again to ⅛-inch thickness. Repeat the folding and rolling.

Cut into 2½-inch squares. Place a spoonful of filling in the centre of each square. Bring the dough up over the filling and press dough firmly together.

Place on a baking tin and bake in moderate oven (375°F. Mark 5) until golden brown, about 25 minutes. Serve hot. Makes about 30.

Note: These may be made in advance, wrapped in aluminium foil and stored in the refrigerator. To serve, heat in slow oven (325°F. Mark 3) for 15 minutes.

MEAT FILLING FOR KNISHES

10 to 12 ounces minced cooked meat, chicken, or turkey
2 tablespoons finely chopped celery
2 tablespoons finely chopped onion
½ ounce chicken fat
1½ teaspoons salt
¼ teaspoon black pepper
1 egg, well beaten
Gravy or soup stock to moisten

Remove all fat and gristle from meat before mincing. Lightly brown the celery and onion in fat, about 5 minutes.

Mix all ingredients until well blended, using just enough gravy or soup stock to make a stiff paste. Makes about 12 ounces.

CHEESE FILLING FOR KNISHES

1 pound dry cottage cheese
1 egg, slightly beaten
1 tablespoon sugar
¼ teaspoon cinnamon
¼ teaspoon salt
1 ounce seedless raisins, optional

Mix all ingredients until well blended. Makes about a pound.

KISHKE

Kishke, often called stuffed derma, is a Yiddish term for the intestine of beef stuffed with any of various savoury fillings, then roasted; an old-time Jewish dish. The most common filling is made of flour and dripping seasoned with onions, salt, and pepper. Nowadays it is sold already prepared and quick frozen, ready for cooking. It is usually served with meat or poultry.

Beef casings for stuffing may be purchased from your butcher, usually requiring additional cleaning at home. Wash the casings in cold water and scrape free of any fat. As a final cleansing, use lukewarm water and turn the casings inside out. (They should be cut into short lengths—about 12 inches—to make it easy to do this.)

Sew up one end of each piece and stuff with kishke filling.

Kishke Filling for Each 12-Inch Piece:

 4 ounces sifted plain flour
 2 ounces chopped beef suet (fat from casings may be used)
 1 small onion, grated
 2 tablespoons dry bread or biscuit crumbs
 ⅛ teaspoon salt
 Dash of black pepper

Combine in the order given and mix well in a shallow bowl.

Place the sewn end of the casing in the centre of the mixture and begin stuffing by turning in the end with the mixture as you fill the entire length of the casing.

Do not stuff too tightly because the filling expands and the casing shrinks during cooking.

Sew or tie the open end and rinse the outer surface free of any filling mixture.

Drop into boiling water for 1 minute to shrink the casing. To cook, place in roasting pan with poultry. Or it may be roasted separately on a bed of sliced onions to which rendered poultry fat has been added. Cook until lightly browned in moderate oven (350°F. Mark 4), about 1½ to 2 hours.

CHEESE DUMPLINGS

 4 ounces plain flour
 1½ teaspoons baking powder
 ½ teaspoon salt
 ½ ounce lard or dripping
 4 ounces grated Cheddar cheese
 4 fluid ounces water

Mix and sift flour, baking powder, and salt. Cut in lard with pastry blender or 2 knives. Add cheese. Gradually add water and mix smooth.

Drop by tablespoonfuls into boiling soup. Cover tightly. Cook 12 minutes without removing cover. Serves 5.

PIROSHKI

Piroshki is the Russian and Yiddish name for little cases of raised dough (baking powder or yeast) or pastry with various fillings, which are baked or fried. They are served with soup, as canapés, or—filled with fruit—as sweets. In Poland, similar little pies are called pirogi or pirogen; they are sometimes simmered or steamed like dumplings.

Filling:

 12 ounces cooked beef
 2 grilled chicken livers
 1 onion, sliced and fried
 1 egg
 Salt, pepper, cinnamon

Dough:

 6 ounces sifted plain flour
 1½ teaspoons baking powder
 1 slightly beaten egg
 2 ounces chicken fat or lard
 Pinch of salt
 About 2 fluid ounces water

Put the cooked beef, chicken livers, and onion through vegetable mill. Add the egg; season to taste and mix well.

Combine the dough ingredients, adding just enough water to make a soft dough.

Roll out about ⅛-inch thick and cut in 3½-inch rounds.

Fill each round with 1 tablespoon meat mixture. Shape in half moons by folding the edges together over the filling. Pinch the edges together securely.

Bake on a greased baking tin in hot oven (400°F. Mark 6) until nicely browned, 25 to 30 minutes. Serve with clear soups.

Variations: These old-time European baked dumplings or turnovers may also be made with a yeast dough or shortcrust pastry.

If a yeast dough is used, allow the filled pirogen to rise 1 to 1½ hours on the greased baking tin, then brush with chicken fat, melted lard, or egg yolk diluted with equal amount of water.

Bake in moderate oven (375°F. Mark 5) until nicely browned, 20 to 25 minutes.

Other well seasoned fillings such as cooked liver, poultry, or kasha (cooked buckwheat groats) may be used.

SPONGE DUMPLINGS

 6 tablespoons milk
 2 eggs, separated
 2 ounces soft butter or margarine
 3 ounces sifted plain flour
 ¼ teaspoon salt

Combine milk, egg whites, butter, flour, and salt in a small pan. Cook over low heat, stirring constantly.

When thick, remove pan from heat. Beat in egg yolks.

When cool, drop by spoon into simmering soup. Simmer 5 minutes and serve. Serves 6.

FLUFFY CHEESE DUMPLINGS

 1 pound dry cottage cheese
 2 eggs
 4 ounces sifted plain flour
 1 teaspoon salt
 5 pints boiling water
 1½ ounces butter or margarine
 8 fluid ounces soured cream

Mash cheese; add eggs and mix well. Stir in sifted dry ingredients.

Drop by tablespoonfuls into rapidly boiling salted water. Cover and boil 15 minutes.

Drain and pour melted butter or margarine over dumplings. Serve with soured cream. Serves 4.

MATZO BALLS FOR SOUP

 1½ ounces melted chicken fat
 2 eggs, separated
 3 to scant 4 ounces matzo meal
 4 fluid ounces hot water
 Salt
 ⅛ teaspoon ground ginger (optional)

Place chicken fat and egg yolks in a large bowl; beat until well blended.

Add 3 ounces matzo meal alternately with hot water (3 additions of each).

Taste and add up to 1 teaspoon salt; stir in ground ginger.

Form a trial ball, about 1 inch in diameter. Drop into a pan of simmering water. Cover and cook 5 minutes. It should hold its shape. If it crumbles, add a little more matzo meal (1 to 3 tablespoonfuls) and make another trial ball.

When consistency is satisfactory, chill mixture from 1 to 3 hours.

Then form into small balls and simmer 15 to 20 minutes in hot water or hot soup. For larger balls, allow a longer period of time, up to 25 minutes. Serves 6.

Matzo Balls for Soup

EGGS

In most homes in this country, eggs are a staple food that housewives find indispensable in planning and preparing family meals. Eggs can be served in so many ways and are an ingredient in so many types of recipes that they are likely to appear in some form at every meal.

And, in addition to their versatility as a food, eggs make a worthwhile contribution to the nutrient content of diets. They are highly valued as a source of protein, iron, vitamin A, and riboflavin, and are one of the few foods that contain vitamin D. Because of the amount and quality of their proteins, eggs make a good substitute for meat.

Nutrition experts usually suggest that a person eat from 4 to 7 eggs a week, including those used in cooking. If you are counting calories, you can allow for a large egg having 80 calories, 60 of which come from the yolk.

BUYING EGGS

When you shop for eggs, you may find several grades, two or more sizes within one grade, and considerable range in price per dozen.

To be sure of getting good quality eggs, buy classified eggs at a shop that keeps them in refrigerated shelves. The classification mark gives assurance that the eggs were of a specific quality at the time of testing. If they have been properly handled since testing, there will be little loss of quality.

CLASSES AND SIZES OF EGGS

The European Economic Community has developed standards used since 1 February 1973 throughout the U.K. to classify eggs into three grades: Class A, or "fresh" eggs; Class B, or "second quality or preserved eggs", and Class C, or "non-graded eggs intended for the manufacture of food stuffs for human consumption".

Cartons of graded eggs are marked to show quality and size. The mark certifies that each egg has been graded for quality and sorted for size.

Lower quality eggs are sometimes satisfactory for scrambling, for making omelets, and for combining with other ingredients, in cooked dishes.

The class of the egg does not affect its food value; lower grades are as high in nutrients as top grades. Shell colour is determined by the breed of hen and does not affect the nutritive value or quality of an egg.

The size classifications of eggs are based on weight. Size is independent of quality; eggs of any size may be included in each quality grade.

Common sizes and minimum weight are:

Large—$2\frac{3}{16}$ ounces
Standard—$1\frac{7}{8}$ ounces
Medium—$1\frac{5}{8}$ ounces
Small—$1\frac{1}{2}$ ounces
Extra Small—less than $1\frac{1}{2}$ ounces

Since 1 February 1973 eggs may now also be classified by weight under the E.E.C. regulations, which comprise seven grades, as follows: Grade 1, 70 grams or over per egg; Grade 2, 65—70g; Grade 3, 60—65g; Grade 4, 55—60g; Grade 5, 50—55g; Grade 6, 45—50g; Grade 7, under 45g. This new grading is not yet obligatory, however.

COMPARE PRICES

When small and medium eggs are plentiful in the late summer or autumn, they are often more economical as a source of protein than larger sizes. To find which size is the most economical, compare prices within a quality grade.

Medium eggs are as good a buy as large eggs when they cost one-eighth less. Small eggs are as good a buy when they cost one sixth less than medium or a quarter less than large eggs.

STORING EGGS

To store eggs properly, keep them clean, cold, and covered.

Most graded eggs sold in retail stores are clean. Eggs should not be washed before storing because washing removes the thin protective film or "bloom" that seals the pores, retains moisture, and keeps out bacteria, mould, and odours.

Covering eggs retards moisture loss and helps prevent absorption of odours. The paper carton in which eggs are sold makes an excellent storage container. See that eggs are large end up in the carton to help keep the yolk centred.

Put eggs in a cool place promptly after purchase—they cannot be expected to maintain their quality if kept in a hot car or kitchen.

For best flavour and cooking quality, use eggs within a week. They may still be usable after a few weeks' storage in a home refrigerator. With prolonged storage, however, eggs are likely to develop off-flavours and lose some thickening and leavening power.

Cover leftover yolks with cold water and store in the refrigerator in a tightly closed container. Extra egg whites should also be refrigerated in a tightly covered container. Use leftover yolks and whites within a day or two.

HINTS ABOUT USING EGGS

Everyone can cook eggs so that they retain their flavour, tenderness, and attractiveness if a few simple rules are followed.

Moderate to low temperature cookery is important. Cook eggs at low to moderate temperature to assure uniformly tender, attractive eggs and egg dishes. High temperature and overcooking toughen eggs.

In dishes thickened with eggs such as egg custards and sauces, high temperature and overcooking cause curdling or watering.

Eggs, Separated: It is easier to separate eggs when they are still chilled, just after being taken from the refrigerator.

Crack each egg by striking it at middle against edge of bowl or with cutting edge of knife. Then, holding egg over bowl, insert thumb in crack and pull shell apart. The yolk will settle to bottom half and most of the white will flow out. Carefully turn yolk into other half of shell, letting remaining white drop into bowl; repeat if necessary. Drop yolk into second bowl.

Eggs, Beaten: Whole eggs, whipped until whites and yolks are well blended, are used principally to give light texture to batters and dough, and also as a binder in these products and in salad dressings.

Eggs, Slightly Beaten: Whole eggs beaten just enough to blend yolks and whites. This is enough beating when you are using them to thicken foods like egg custard. If you're using eggs with crumbs to coat foods before deep-frying, beat them only slightly.

Eggs, Well Beaten: Whole eggs beaten until whites and yolks are well blended and look light and frothy. They are beaten to this stage for use in many baked products.

Egg Yolks, Well Beaten: Egg yolks beaten until thick and lemon-coloured. This is important in producing fine texture in sponge cakes.

Egg Whites, Beaten Stiff: Egg whites beaten until they stand in peaks when beater is lifted from surface, with points of peaks drooping over a bit and surface still moist and glossy. In this stage, they hold air which expands when heated.

If you don't beat the egg whites enough, they won't hold enough air; if you beat them too stiff, the foam will break down when the other ingredients are added.

When you add sugar to beaten egg whites in small amounts, the air-holding property of the egg whites is increased.

Angel cake is leavened by the expansion of air held in the egg whites and by steam during baking.

Egg Whites, Beaten Very Stiff: Egg whites beaten until points of peaks stand upright, without drooping, when beater is lifted from surface. Surface should look dry.

SOFT-BOILED EGGS
Cold Water Method: Cover eggs in pan with water to come at least 1 inch above the eggs. Bring rapidly to the boil. Turn off heat and, if necessary, take pan off ring to prevent further boiling. Cover and allow to stand 2 to 4 minutes, depending on individual taste.

Cool eggs promptly in cold water for several seconds to prevent further cooking and to make them easy to handle.

Boiling Water Method: Bring water in pan to rapid boil, using enough to cover eggs as above. Meanwhile warm very cold eggs slightly in warm water to avoid cracked shells. Transfer eggs to water with spoon, and allow to simmer for 3 to 4 minutes according to taste. Cool as above.

Cooking More Than 4 Eggs: Use either method. Do not turn off but reduce heat to keep water below simmering. Leave 4 to 6 minutes. Cool as above.

Coddled Eggs: See Boiling Water Method above.

HARD-BOILED EGGS
Cold Water Method: Follow directions for Soft-Boiled Eggs—Cold Water Method. Allow to stand 15 minutes. Cool promptly and thoroughly in cold water—this makes the shells easier to remove and helps prevent dark surface on yolks.

Boiling Water Method: Follow directions for Soft-Boiled Eggs—Boiling Water Method, and allow to simmer gently for about 6 to 8 minutes. Cool as above.

To Remove the Shell: Crackle the shell: roll egg between hands to loosen shell, then start the peeling at the large end of the egg. Dipping in a bowl of water helps to ease the shell off.

FRIED EGGS
Method No. 1: Heat ½ to 1 ounce fat in a frying pan just hot enough to sizzle a drop of water. Break and slip eggs into pan—from a saucer if preferred. Reduce heat immediately. Cook slowly for 3 to 4 minutes.

Baste with fat during cooking. Instead of basting, frying pan may be covered, or eggs be turned over.

Egg whites won't whip up if there is any moisture, egg yolk, or other food on the egg beater.

Method No. 2: Use just enough fat to grease frying pan. Proceed as above. Cook over low heat until edges turn white, about 1 minute. Add ½ teaspoon water for one egg, decreasing proportion slightly for each additional egg.

Cover frying pan tightly to hold in steam which bastes the egg. Cook until done.

FRIED EGGS AU BEURRE NOIR
(With Black Butter)
Fry eggs and transfer to hot plate. Sprinkle with grated onion or chopped chives if desired. Add ½ ounce butter to frying pan. Cook until brown. Add 1 tablespoon lemon juice or vinegar. Heat and pour over eggs.

FRENCH OMELET
(Master Recipe)
6 eggs
3 fluid ounces milk
¾ teaspoon salt
⅛ teaspoon black pepper
1 ounce butter or margarine

Beat eggs until whites and yolks are well mixed. Add milk, salt, and pepper.

Melt butter in frying pan. Pour in mixture and place over moderate heat.

While cooking, lift edges and tip frying pan so uncooked mixture flows under cooked portion. When bottom is browned, fold over. Serves 3 to 4.

French Omelet Variations
Bacon or Ham Omelet: Add 2 ounces diced crisp bacon or chopped cooked ham to egg mixture.

Cheese Omelet: Sprinkle omelet with 1 ounce grated Cheddar cheese before folding.

Mushroom Omelet: Sauté 1 to 2 ounces chopped mushrooms in butter for 3 or 4 minutes. Add egg mixture and cook as directed.

Crouton Omelet: Sauté 3 ounces small bread cubes in butter. Add to mixture.

Rum Omelet: Omit milk and decrease salt to ⅛ teaspoon. Add 2 tablespoons water, 2 teaspoons icing sugar and 2 tablespoons rum to beaten eggs. Cook as directed.

After turning omelet onto hot dish pour 3 to 4 tablespoons rum round it. Ignite rum and serve at once. Sprinkle omelet with additional sugar if desired.

Vegetable Omelet: Sauté 2 tablespoons grated onion in butter. Add 3 to 6 ounces canned or cooked peas, broad beans, or mixture of vegetables.

Season to taste and heat. Pour over omelet before folding or add to white sauce and pour over folded omelet.

Sweet Omelet Omit pepper. Add 1½ tablespoons icing sugar and ½ teaspoon vanilla. Serve sprinkled with icing sugar.

PUFFY ("SOUFFLÉ") OMELET
(Master Recipe)

    4 eggs, separated
    ½ teaspoon salt
    pinch of black pepper
    4 tablespoons milk
    ½ ounce butter or margarine

Beat egg yolks until thick. Add salt, pepper, and milk.

Beat egg whites until they form peaks. Fold whites into yolks.

Pour into well buttered hot frying pan, spreading mixture evenly and cooking slowly until omelet puffs up and is firm on the bottom.

Cook in moderate oven (350°F. Mark 4) until top is slightly dry and springs back when pressed lightly with fingertip, about 5 minutes.

Cut about halfway through omelet at the centre, fold over with a spatula.

Serve immediately on hot dish. Serves 2 or 3.

Puffy ("Soufflé") Omelet Variations

Puffy Bacon or Ham Omelet: Add 2 ounces chopped cooked ham or diced crisp bacon to egg yolk mixture, or sprinkle over omelet before folding.

Puffy Cheese Omelet: Add 2 tablespoons grated cheese to egg yolk mixture.

Puffy Omelet with Chicken: Sprinkle 6 ounces diced cooked chicken over omelet just before folding.

Puffy Omelet with Chicken Livers: Dice 2 ounces chicken livers and sauté in butter. Season with salt and pepper and Worcestershire sauce. Pour over omelet just before serving.

Puffy Omelet with Seafood: Sauté canned or cooked whole prawns, chunks of canned or cooked crabmeat or lobster in butter and serve round omelet. Garnish with lemon wedges.

Or, pour creamed seafood over omelet before folding.

Jam Omelet: Spread jam on omelet before folding.

Puffy Omelet with Kidney: Sprinkle 2 ounces cooked and chopped kidney (see index) over omelet before folding.

Puffy Onion Omelet: Sauté grated onion in butter. Fold in before cooking omelet.

Puffy Parsley Omelet: Add 2 tablespoons chopped parsley when folding in egg whites.

Puffy Potato Omelet: Add 3 ounces seasoned mashed potatoes to egg yolk mixture.

Puffy Omelet with Sauce: Pour cheese, tomato, or mushroom sauce over omelet after folding.

Puffy Rice Omelet: Add 2 ounces cooked rice and ½ teaspoon tomato ketchup to egg yolk mixture.

Puffy Spanish Omelet No. 1: Serve Spanish Sauce (see index) in fold and round omelet.

PUFFY ("SOUFFLÉ") OMELET HINTS

Cook on top of cooker slowly until omelet puffs up and is firm on the bottom.

Cook in moderate oven until top is slightly dry, then cut halfway through the omelet at centre.

Fold omelet over with a spatula.

Serve immediately on a hot dish, attractively garnished.

Puffy Spanish Omelet No. 2: Sauté 1 tablespoon each finely chopped onion and green pepper in 1 ounce butter until tender.

Add 1 8-ounce can tomatoes and cook until moisture is almost evaporated.

Add 1 to 2 tablespoons sliced mushrooms, about ¼ teaspoon salt, a few grains cayenne pepper, and 2 teaspoons capers. Serve in fold and around omelet.

Puffy Tomato Omelet: Cover half of omelet with slices of grilled tomato before folding, or serve omelet with hot tomato sauce.

NOODLE OMELET

    4 ounces noodles
    1½ ounces butter or margarine
    2 tablespoons chopped onion
    3 eggs
    2 tablespoons milk or water
    ½ teaspoon salt
    ⅛ teaspoon black pepper

Cook noodles according to packet directions. Drain well. Cook onion in the butter until softened but not browned. Add noodles and blend.

Meanwhile, blend eggs, milk, salt and pepper with a fork. Mix well but do not beat frothy, and pour over noodles.

Cook rapidly, lifting mixture with fork, at the same time tipping frying pan to let uncooked egg mixture flow to bottom of pan. Keep mixture as level as possible. Shake frying pan while cooking to be sure mixture is not sticking at any point.

When mixture no longer flows, reduce heat for a minute or two to completely "set" the omelet and brown the bottom. Loosen edges if necessary and slide spatula underneath to be sure omelet is free. Fold in half. Serve promptly. Serves 4.

MATZO BRIE OR FRIED MATZO

    2 eggs
    4 fluid ounces milk or water
    ¼ teaspoon salt
    dash of cinnamon
    2 matzos
    1½ ounces butter or fat

Beat eggs; add milk or water, salt, and cinnamon. Break matzos into this mixture.

Melt butter in frying pan; pour in matzo mixture. Cover and cook over moderate heat about 10 minutes or until browned on under side. Turn and cook, uncovered, until browned, about 3 minutes.

Serve hot, plain or with a sprinkling of sugar and cinnamon, honey, or apple sauce. Serves 2.

KAISER SCHMARREN

Kaiser Schmarren is a German name for sweet omelets sometimes called Emperor's Omelets. It is an Austrian dish that is made in various ways in other Central European countries.

4 eggs, separated
2½ tablespoons sugar
7 fluid ounces milk
4 ounces sifted plain flour
⅛ teaspoon salt
1½ ounces butter or margarine
vanilla sugar
additional ½ ounce butter or
    margarine
3 tablespoons raisins
icing sugar

Combine egg yolks with 2½ table-spoons sugar, milk, flour, and salt to make a smooth paste.

Beat egg whites until stiff and carefully fold into first mixture.

In a large frying pan melt ¼ of the 1½ ounces butter. Pour in ¼ of mixture. It should be thinner than ¼ inch.

Cook gently and allow to puff. Turn and brown lightly on other side. Do not cook too long or it will become dry.

With 2 forks, tear bits of the schmarren off, about the size of a 10p piece, until all is torn to pieces.

Put torn schmarren onto a plate sprinkled with icing sugar in which a bit of vanilla pod has been kept, and leave until 3 more omelets have been cooked and torn.

Then put ½ ounce butter into frying pan; add all torn schmarren with 3 tablespoons raisins washed and dried; sprinkle with icing sugar, and stir in the pan until heated, or about 5 minutes.

Serve on warmed plates with a fine tart fruit compote (sour cherries, cranberries, or stewed plums). Serves 4.

Spanish Rice Omelet

PENNSYLVANIA-DUTCH SMOKEHOUSE EGGS

1 to 2 ounces cooked ham and bacon
    (4 parts ham to 1 of bacon)
handful of watercress
6 eggs
2 fluid ounces thick buttermilk (or
    double cream)

Dice the cooked ham and bacon. While this is browning lightly over medium heat, take scissors and snip up the watercress.

Beat eggs and add the thick buttermilk or cream. Pour into well buttered pan on low heat. When bottom has just set, toss in the browned chopped ham, bacon and cress. With fork, gently fold these in and stir egg only enough to work into inch-long flakes—not whipped and frizzled into fine, overcooked crumbs. Cook only until set throughout. Serves 4 to 6.

SPANISH RICE OMELET

6 eggs, beaten
4 fluid ounces milk
½ teaspoon salt
dash of black pepper
½ ounce butter or margarine
rice filling (below)
3 slices Mozzarella cheese

Combine eggs, milk, salt, and pepper. Mix well. Melt butter in a 10-inch frying pan. Add egg mixture and cook over medium heat. As the eggs begin to set, draw the edges toward centre with a spatula, tilting pan to hasten flow of uncooked eggs on bottom.

When eggs have set, spoon half of the Spanish rice filling over the eggs and arrange Mozzarella cheese slices on top. Place under grill until cheese is melted. Cut in wedges and serve. Serves 6.

Rice Filling:
1½ ounces butter or margarine
10 spring onions, chopped fine
1½ ounces green pepper, chopped
pinch of garlic salt
1 1-pound can tomatoes
½ bay leaf
½ teaspoon sugar
1 teaspoon salt
⅛ teaspoon black pepper
⅛ teaspoon cinnamon
16 sliced black olives
1 pound cooked rice

Melt butter in saucepan. Add onions, green pepper, and garlic salt; sauté until tender.

Stir in tomatoes, seasonings, and black olives. Simmer about 15 minutes. Stir in cooked rice.

Note: Use leftover rice filling as a vegetable for a future lunch or dinner or freeze for later use.

CREAMED EGGS
(Master Recipe)

Blend 1 ounce flour thoroughly with 2 ounces melted butter or margarine. Gradually add ¾ pint milk.

Cook over hot water, stirring constantly, until thick.

Quarter 6 hard-boiled eggs and add to sauce. Season with salt and pepper, and heat. Serve on hot toast. Serves 4.

Optional: About 2 teaspoons Worcestershire sauce or grated onion may be added.

Creamed Egg Variations

Creamed Eggs with Fish, Meat, or Poultry: Make a thin white sauce by reducing flour to 2 tablespoons and butter to 1 ounce.

Use fewer eggs, if desired, and add 8 to 16 ounces flaked cooked fish, prawns, diced meat or poultry.

Creamed Eggs with Bacon: Add diced crisp bacon to creamed mixture or place rashers of crisp bacon over hot buttered toast. Pour over creamed mixture.

Creamed Eggs with Peas or Asparagus Tips: Cut eggs into slices or chop finely. Add 6 ounces cooked or canned peas or asparagus tips.

Creamed Eggs with Tomatoes: Sauté or grill 1-inch-thick slices of tomatoes. Arrange tomato slices on toast. Cover with creamed eggs.

Curried Creamed Eggs: Season sauce with curry powder.

Eggs à La King: Add 1 to 2 ounces sliced cooked mushrooms, 6 ounces cooked peas, and 1 canned pimiento sliced in thin strips, to creamed mixture. Heat thoroughly.

Grill thick slices of tomato for 5 minutes. Place one slice on each serving of buttered hot toast, and pour over creamed mixture.

Eggs Goldenrod: Separate whites and yolks. Chop or slice whites and add to sauce.

Press yolks through sieve and then sprinkle over each serving. Sprinkle with paprika.

Creamed Eggs with Asparagus

EGG FOO YONG
(Master Recipe)

Egg Foo Yong is a Chinese omelet made with additions of vegetables and almost any cooked meat or seafood. It is served with a sauce of thickened chicken stock seasoned with soy sauce. The name is spelled in various ways.

5 ounces chopped cooked ham or roast pork
1 medium onion, chopped
1 8-ounce can bean sprouts, drained
3 tablespoons chopped spring onion tops
1 tablespoon soy sauce
1 teaspoon salt
3 eggs
oil for deep frying

Put meat, onion, bean sprouts, spring onion tops, soy sauce, and salt in a bowl; mix well.

Stir the eggs lightly into the mixture.

Use a soup ladle to spoon out the mixture and lower into the hot oil. Tip the ladle at once to release the omelets.

Let them fry until they rise to the top. Turn each to brown the other side.

Lift out with a large slotted spoon. Serve on a hot dish covered with a little sauce (below). Serve additional soy sauce separately. Serves 4.

Egg Foo Yong Variations

Chicken Foo Yong: Use cooked chicken or turkey instead of ham or pork.

Crabmeat Foo Yong: Use canned or cooked crabmeat instead of ham or pork.

Lobster Foo Yong: Use canned or cooked lobster meat instead of ham or pork.

Prawns Foo Yong: Use canned or cooked prawns instead of ham or pork.

Vegetable Foo Yong: Omit meat; use 6 to 8 ounces chopped green pepper, celery, onion, and canned bean sprouts combined. Season with an additional 1 teaspoon salt.

Subgum Foo Yong: To the master

recipe or any variation, add 2 ounces diced mushrooms, 2 ounces diced green beans, and 2 ounces diced canned bamboo shoots. Mix and cook as directed.

Sauce for Egg Foo Yong:

12 fluid ounces chicken stock
1 teaspoon black treacle
1 teaspoon soy sauce
1 teaspoon cornflour
2 tablespoons cold water

Heat stock with treacle and soy sauce. Combine cornflour with cold water; stir in until smooth. Bring to boiling point and cook until thickened.

ARTICHOKE OMELET

1 8-ounce can or packet frozen artichoke hearts
2 fluid ounces olive oil
1 clove garlic, crushed
2 to 4 tablespoons parsley
1 onion, thinly sliced
4 eggs
salt and pepper

Cut artichoke hearts into $\frac{1}{4}$ to $\frac{1}{2}$ inch lengthwise slices. Heat oil; add artichokes, garlic, and parsley; cook, stirring frequently, until lightly browned. Add onion and cook a little longer.

Slightly beat eggs seasoned with salt and pepper; pour over artichoke mixture. Cook very slowly until browned on bottom; turn out on large frying pan lid, then slide back into pan and brown on the other side. Cut into wedges. Serves 6.

Artichoke Omelet

SWEDISH OMELETS

10 eggs
6 fluid ounces milk
1 teaspoon salt
2 ounces butter or margarine
6 slices sautéed ham
parsley

Beat eggs; add milk and salt. Pour a portion of the mixture into a small frying pan in which butter or margarine has been melted. Cook over low heat until set; lift occasionally from the bottom of pan with spatula while cooking.

Place a piece of sautéed ham on each omelet and roll omelet round ham.

Prepare omelets individually, or make two large ones. Serves 6.

ITALIAN COURGETTE OMELET
(Frittata di Zucchini)

6 tablespoons olive oil
1 ounce butter or margarine
10 to 12 ounces sliced or chopped courgettes
4 eggs
3 tablespoons chopped parsley
$\frac{1}{4}$ teaspoon salt
dash of black pepper
1 tablespoon grated Parmesan cheese

Heat 2 tablespoons oil and $\frac{1}{2}$ ounce butter in a frying pan. Add courgettes and cook slowly, stirring often, until vegetable is soft and lightly browned, or about 5 minutes. Cool thoroughly.

Beat eggs until fluffy. Add parsley, salt, pepper, cheese, and cooled courgettes.

Heat remaining oil and butter in a clean pan. Add egg-courgette mixture and cook over a moderately high heat, lifting mixture around edge, until only centre remains uncooked.

Grill under a very low heat until centre is firm. Turn out on a dish and cut into pie-shaped wedges to serve. Serves 2.

SWISS OMELET

2 eggs
2 tablespoons milk or water
$\frac{1}{2}$ teaspoon salt
few grains black pepper
2 ounces creamed chicken, meat, or fish
1 ounce Gruyère cheese

Prepare each omelet separately as follows: Mix eggs, milk, salt, and pepper thoroughly. Avoid foaminess.

Heat fat in frying pan (6- to 7-inch) just hot enough to sizzle a drop of water. Pour in egg mixture. Reduce heat.

As the mixture at the edge begins to thicken, draw the cooked portion with the fork toward the centre so that the uncooked portions flow to the bottom. Tilt pan as it is necessary to hasten flow of uncooked eggs.

Do not stir and keep mixture as level as possible. Shake frying pan occasionally to be sure omelet is not sticking. When eggs no longer flow and surface is still moist, increase heat to brown bottom quickly. Loosen edge.

Place creamed chicken, meat or fish in centre of omelet. Fold in half or roll.

Set omelet on heatproof serving dish or baking tin until required number of omelets are cooked. Then top with the cheese cut in strips.

Grill, or place in hot oven several minutes until cheese begins to melt. Serve promptly.

For pleasing texture, flavour and colour contrast, serve with cranberry sauce. Makes 1 omelet.

Egg Foo Yong

SHIRRED EGGS
(Master Recipe)

Place 1 tablespoon cream in each individual buttered ramekin.

Break an egg into each; season with salt and pepper.

Place ramekins on a baking tin and cook in slow oven (325°F. Mark 3) until eggs are firm, 8 to 10 minutes.

Note: Watch the timing carefully but do not try to hurry shirred eggs by increasing the heat. They must be cooked by gentle oven heat. Care must be taken not to overcook the eggs as the whites can become quite hard and rubbery. The centres should be soft and the whites just set. Note that ramekins will retain heat and continue cooking the eggs after they are removed from the oven. Many cooks prefer to set the ramekins in a pan of hot water deep enough to reach within ½ inch of the top of them.

Shirred Egg Variations

Shirred Eggs in Bacon Rings: Cook bacon slightly and line each cup with a rasher of bacon while still soft.

Break egg into each ramekin. Cook in slow oven (325°F. Mark 3) until eggs are set.

Shirred Eggs in Ham Cups: Line each ramekin with slice of boiled ham large enough to form cup.

Break an egg into each and cook in slow oven (325°F. Mark 3) until eggs are set.

Shirred Eggs in Noodle Cups: Make nest of seasoned cooked noodles in each ramekin.

Break an egg in each and cook until set.

Shirred Eggs in Potato Cups: Make nest of seasoned mashed potatoes. Break egg in each and cook.

For additional flavouring add finely chopped chives.

Shirred Eggs in Rice Cups: Line ramekins with cooked rice. Break an egg into each.

Cook in slow oven (325°F. Mark 3)

Eggs Florentine may be prepared in single servings as given in variations of Shirred Eggs or it may be prepared as a family size casserole dish.

until eggs are set, 15 to 20 minutes. Serve with hot cheese sauce.

Shirred Eggs in Toast Cups: Cut crust from slices of bread and gently press bread into greased ramekins. The four corners will extend up to the top rims, forming a cup.

Break an egg into each cup. Season with salt and pepper. Dot with butter or add 1 tablespoon cream for each egg.

Cook for 15 minutes in moderate oven (350°F. Mark 4).

Shirred Eggs in Tomatoes: Cut a slice from stem end of each tomato. Remove enough pulp so that an egg may be placed in each. Season with salt and pepper. Cover with buttered breadcrumbs.

Arrange in baking tin or casserole. Cook in slow oven (325°F. Mark 3) until crumbs are brown and eggs are set, about 25 minutes.

Shirred Eggs with Cheese: Sprinkle grated cheese over each egg or mix grated cheese with breadcrumbs and sprinkle over eggs.

Shirred Eggs with Crumbs: Dot eggs with butter. Sprinkle with seasoned fine, dry breadcrumbs.

Cook until eggs are set and crumbs lightly browned.

Eggs Florentine: Place 3 or 4 tablespoons chopped, cooked spinach in each casserole. Season with salt and pepper. Dot with butter. Drop an egg in each and sprinkle with fine breadcrumbs.

Cook 10 minutes in slow oven (325°F. Mark 3), then sprinkle with grated cheese and cook additional 10 minutes.

SCOTCH WOODCOCK

Scotch Woodcock may be scrambled eggs or creamed chopped eggs served on toast spread with anchovy butter or paste, then garnished with capers and anchovy fillets. Or it may be the special version given below.

2 slices toast
6 anchovy fillets
4 egg yolks
4 fluid ounces double cream
1½ ounces butter or margarine
Black pepper
Parsley, chopped

Butter toast generously and cut into finger lengths. Keep hot.

Wash anchovy fillets and pound to a paste. Spread on the toast.

Beat together lightly the egg yolks and the cream. Put this mixture into a saucepan over boiling water with the butter and a little freshly ground pepper. Stir with a wooden spoon until the eggs yolks and cream are like a creamy sauce.

Strain over the prepared toast and garnish with parsley. Serves 2.

SPANISH EGGS

4 tablespoons chopped onion
4 tablespoons chopped green pepper
2 ounces butter or margarine
8 to 10 eggs
2 ounces day-old breadcrumbs
3 ounces grated Cheddar cheese
8 fluid ounces beer
Paprika

Sauté onion and green pepper in butter until tender. Pour into shallow casserole. Carefully break eggs into dish without breaking yolks. Mix breadcrumbs with cheese and sprinkle over eggs. Spoon beer over eggs; sprinkle with paprika.

Cook in moderate oven (350°F. Mark 4) until eggs are set as you like them, about 12 to 15 minutes. Serves 4 to 5.

Spanish Eggs make a filling winter supper dish that is sophisticated enough for guests. Serve with a hearty vegetable such as broad beans or brussels sprouts and beer or ale.

EGGS MORNAY

½ teaspoon paprika
1½ ounces grated cheese
¾ pint thin white sauce
2 egg yolks
4 to 6 whole eggs

Add paprika and cheese (reserve about 2 tablespoons cheese for top) to hot, well seasoned sauce. Beat in the 2 egg yolks.

Pour layer of sauce into well greased casserole or individual ramekins. Slip eggs into sauce, one at a time.

Pour remaining sauce round edge, leaving yolks partially exposed.

Sprinkle with remaining cheese.

Cook in moderate oven (375°F. Mark 5) 15 to 20 minutes, depending upon how well done you like your eggs. Serves 2 to 3.

Eggs Mornay

SCRAMBLED EGGS
(Master Recipe)

5 eggs
4 fluid ounces milk or cream
½ teaspoon salt
⅛ teaspoon black pepper
1 ounce butter or margarine

Beat eggs, milk, and seasoning lightly.

Melt butter in frying pan or top of double boiler. Pour in eggs and cook until soft and creamy, stirring and scraping mixture from bottom and sides of pan occasionally.

Serve at once on warm dish. Garnish with parsley and dash of paprika. Serves 3 to 4.

Scrambled Egg Variations

Scrambled Eggs with Bacon: Use 2 rashers of diced cooked streaky bacon. Omit butter, using bacon fat for cooking eggs.

Scrambled Eggs with Cheese: Place scrambled eggs on toast. Cover with grated cheese and brown in oven.

Cream Cheese Rarebit: Use 6 fluid ounces milk. When almost done, crumble and stir in 3 ounces cream cheese. Serve on toast.

Scrambled Eggs with Fish: Add 3 ounces cooked, flaked fish.

Scrambled Eggs with Green Peppers: Remove seeds and membranes from 2 medium green peppers. Parboil 5 minutes. Chop finely. Add when eggs begin to thicken.

Scrambled Eggs with Meat or Poultry: Add 2 to 3 ounces chopped cooked beef, cooked ham, sausage, chicken, or other left-over meat.

Scrambled Eggs with Mushrooms: Drain and chop canned mushrooms. Add to egg mixture before cooking. If fresh mushrooms are used, chop and sauté in butter before adding egg mixture.

Savoury Scrambled Eggs: Add 1 tablespoon chopped parsley, ½ teaspoon grated onion, and ½ tablespoon chopped chives.

Scrambled eggs and their many variations are good chafing dish "starters" for the newcomer in this form of cookery.

Scrambled Eggs with Brains: Add 6 ounces chopped parboiled brains.

Scrambled Eggs with Cottage Cheese: Reduce milk to 2 fluid ounces. Add 4 to 6 ounces cottage cheese and 1 tablespoon chopped chives or parsley when eggs are almost done.

Scrambled Eggs with Soured Cream: Substitute soured cream for milk. Add chopped spring onions, if desired.

Scrambled Eggs with Toast Cubes: Sauté 3 ounces toast cubes until golden brown before adding egg mixture.

Scrambled Eggs with Spinach: Add 2 ounces well drained, finely chopped cooked spinach.

Scrambled Eggs with Sweetbreads: Add 4 ounces diced parboiled sweetbreads.

Scrambled Eggs with Tomatoes: Add 4 ounces cooked tomatoes.

Scrambled Eggs with Leftover Vegetables: Add 2 to 3 ounces chopped cooked vegetables.

POACHED EGGS
(Master Recipe)

Fill heavy shallow pan ⅔ full of water to which ⅛ teaspoon salt has been added. Bring to boiling point.

Break eggs into a saucer and slip into gently boiling, salted water. Allow to simmer gently for 2 to 3 minutes, or until eggs are as firm as you want them.

Remove eggs carefully with a slotted spoon and serve on toast. Add salt and pepper to taste.

Egg poachers may be used to help keep the shape of the egg.

Two teaspoons of vinegar may be added to each pint of water to help set the white of egg.

Poached Egg Variations

Poached Eggs and Corned Beef Hash: Serve poached eggs on cakes of corned beef hash. Garnish with parsley.

Poached Eggs Au Gratin: Arrange poached eggs in shallow, buttered casserole. Pour over medium white sauce. Sprinkle with grated cheese. Brown in slow oven (325°F. Mark 3).

Poached Eggs in Cheese Sauce: Pour ¾ pint cheese sauce into shallow pan. Poach eggs in sauce. Serve on buttered toast.

Poached Eggs in Milk: Substitute milk for water in poaching eggs. Pour milk over toast.

Poached Eggs on Creamed Toast: Pour hot white sauce over toast. Place poached egg on each slice. Sprinkle with chopped parsley.

Poached Eggs on Tomatoes: Sauté thick tomato slices in olive oil. Season to taste with salt and pepper and, if desired, a pinch of basil. Place on warmed plates. Top with poached eggs.

Poached Egg Oriental: Mix cooked rice with white sauce. Season with grated onion and chopped celery. Top each serving with poached egg.

POACHED EGG HINTS

1. Slide the egg into the bubbling water very gently. Poach as many eggs at a time as will fit into the pan without running together.

2. Test to see if done by gently pressing back of fork against yolk.

3. Remove with slotted spoon and drain well by holding spoon on a piece of paper towelling for a few seconds.

4. Serve immediately on hot buttered toast, rusks, or toasted scones.

EGGS GOLDILOCKS

Cut 4 hard-boiled eggs in half lengthwise. Remove the yolks, mash and combine with 4 tablespoons mayonnaise. Season to taste with salt and pepper. Fill the whites.

Remove the crusts from 4 slices of bread. Cut in half diagonally and toast. Arrange the toast triangles on a large plate and top each with a stuffed egg half.

Melt 8 ounces of processed cheese in the top of a double boiler.

Gradually add 3 fluid ounces milk, stirring constantly until the sauce is smooth.

Pour the cheese sauce over the eggs.

Garnish with parsley and serve at once.

MUSHROOMS AND EGGS IN TOMATO-CHEESE SAUCE

5½ ounces margarine
8 fluid ounces milk
12 ounces grated strong cheese
2 ounces sliced, cooked mushrooms, fresh or canned
2 10½-ounce cans condensed tomato soup
1 teaspoon Worcestershire sauce
¼ teaspoon black pepper
8 hard-boiled eggs, cut in quarters

Combine all ingredients except eggs in saucepan. Cook over medium heat, stirring constantly, until mixture comes to the boil.

Add and stir in hard-boiled eggs. Serves 8.

CURRIED EGGS

1 ounce butter or margarine
¼ teaspoon curry powder
1½ teaspoons salt
½ teaspoon sugar
½ teaspoon French mustard
dash of cayenne pepper
1 medium onion, chopped
1 ounce chopped green pepper
1 clove garlic, crushed
1 1-pound and 1 8-ounce can tomatoes
4 fluid ounces water
4 hard-boiled eggs, cut in quarters

Melt butter in a saucepan; add curry, salt, sugar, mustard, and pepper; blend well. Add onion, green pepper, and garlic; cook until green pepper and onion are soft, about 5 minutes.

Add tomatoes and water; cook until thickened, about 15 minutes.

Arrange eggs in a buttered 2½-pint casserole. Pour sauce over eggs.

Heat in moderate oven (350°F. Mark 4) 10 minutes. Serves 4.

SCALLOPED EGGS AND CHEESE

1 ounce butter or margarine
1½ tablespoons flour
¼ teaspoon salt
⅛ teaspoon black pepper
⅛ teaspoon paprika
1 teaspoon Worcestershire sauce
8 fluid ounces milk
3 ounces fresh breadcrumbs
6 hard-boiled eggs, sliced
2 ounces grated strong cheese
1½ ounces butter or margarine

Melt 1 ounce butter in saucepan; blend in flour and seasonings. Slowly add milk and cook over low heat, stirring constantly, until thick.

Arrange in greased casserole in layers: half the crumbs, eggs, cheese, and sauce. Top with remaining crumbs mixed with 1½ ounces butter.

Cook in moderate oven (375°F. Mark 5) until sauce is bubbly and top nicely browned, about 40 minutes. Serve plain, or with tomato sauce. Serves 4.

Egg Cutlets

EGG CROQUETTES OR CUTLETS

2 ounces butter or margarine
4 tablespoons flour
8 fluid ounces milk, scalded
8 hard-boiled eggs, chopped
¾ teaspoon salt
⅛ teaspoon black pepper
¼ teaspoon paprika
1 tablespoon finely chopped parsley
pinch of cayenne pepper
2 eggs, beaten with 2 tablespoons water
dry breadcrumbs

Melt butter in the top of a double boiler. Blend in flour and gradually add milk. Stir and cook until thickened; then add chopped eggs, salt, pepper, paprika, parsley, and cayenne. Mix well and chill thoroughly.

Shape into croquettes or patties, as desired. Roll in egg beaten with water, then in breadcrumbs, coating completely and evenly.

Deep fry in hot fat (350°F.) for 1 minute. Drain on absorbent paper. Serve with tomato sauce. Serves 6.

EGG AND CHEESE CAKES

4 eggs, beaten
1 tablespoon grated onion
1 ounce plain flour
½ teaspoon salt
⅛ teaspoon black pepper
1 teaspoon baking powder
5½ ounces strong cheese
3 ounces lard for frying

Combine eggs with onion, flour, salt, pepper, and baking powder. Add cheese, cut in ¼-inch cubes.

Heat fat in frying pan until a drop of water sizzles. Drop a large spoonful of mixture into hot fat.

Brown well on both sides, turning once. Serve promptly with marmalade or jam. Makes 12 cakes.

Scalloped Eggs and Cheese

FRIED EGGS IN RINGS

1 slice bread
½ ounce butter or margarine
1 egg
salt and pepper

Remove centre from bread with biscuit cutter.

Brown in butter on one side in the frying pan, then turn. Slip egg into ring. Cook egg to desired firmness. Season to taste.

Fried Eggs in Rings

EGGS BENEDICT

Split and toast soft rolls or scones, allowing two halves for each serving, or cut slices of bread into 3-inch rounds and toast.

Cover each half roll or toast round with a slice of grilled or sautéed ham or back bacon and top with a poached egg.

Pour over 1 tablespoon Hollandaise sauce and serve hot.

Eggs Benedict

MUSHROOM EGGS BENEDICT

4 thin slices ham, fried
4 slices toast, buttered
4 eggs, poached
1 10½-ounce can condensed cream
   of mushroom soup
3 fluid ounces milk
1 tablespoon chopped parsley

Place fried ham on buttered toast; top each with a poached egg.

Blend soup and milk; heat and pour over ham and eggs. Sprinkle with chopped parsley. Serves 4.

MOCK EGGS BENEDICT

Fry thin slices of luncheon meat or ham in butter or margarine until lightly browned on both sides.

Meanwhile, poach number of eggs desired.

Arrange luncheon meat or ham on toast. Top with eggs and spoonful of slightly heated mayonnaise or white sauce.

EGGS CARLTON

Cook bacon rashers until crisp.

Season tomato slices with salt and pepper. Roll in flour and sauté in bacon fat. Sprinkle each tomato slice with chopped bacon. Serve topped with a poached egg.

Pour Hollandaise sauce over the eggs.

SMOKED SALMON AND EGGS ON TOAST

thin slices of smoked salmon
buttered toast
poached or fried eggs

Dip salmon into boiling water. Drain and place on toast.

Cover with poached or fried eggs.

GRILLED EGGS

Heat just enough fat to grease a shallow frying pan or flame-proof casserole. When fat is just hot enough to sizzle a drop of water, break eggs and slip into frying pan—from a saucer if preferred. Cook on top of oven just until edges turn white, about 1 minute.

Place frying pan under heated grill and grill eggs under moderate flame until done, 2 to 4 minutes.

Variations: (1) Pour 1 tablespoon of cream per egg into frying pan when edges are white and before placing under grill. (2) Sprinkle over eggs 1 teaspoon grated cheese or buttered crumbs before placing under grill.

Grilled Eggs

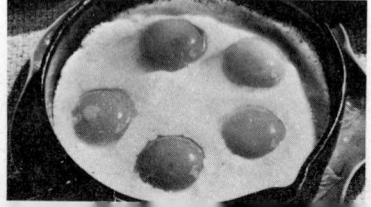

American Fondue

AMERICAN FONDUE
(Master Recipe)

½ pint milk
4 ounces soft bread, broken or
   cubed
½ ounce margarine
¾ teaspoon salt
⅛ teaspoon black pepper
3 or 4 eggs, separated

Scald milk in double boiler. Add pieces of bread, margarine and seasonings. Cool, then add well beaten egg yolks. Fold in stiffly beaten egg whites.

Place in greased casserole or in individual moulds which have been greased on bottom only. Set in pan of hot water and cook in moderate oven (350°F. Mark 4) until firm to gentle touch, 50 to 60 minutes.

A knife inserted in centre should come out clean. Serves 4 to 6.

American Fondue Variations

Cheese Fondue: Add 4 ounces grated cheese to milk mixture. Stir until cheese is melted. Cool and follow master recipe.

Fish Fondue: Follow master recipe, adding 6 to 8 ounces shredded cooked cod, salmon, lobster, or fresh fish just before folding in egg whites. Serve with any fish sauce. Reduce salt if seafood is salty.

Ham Fondue: Follow master recipe, adding 6 to 8 ounces minced ham just before folding in egg whites. Reduce salt accordingly.

Vegetable Fondue: Follow master recipe, adding 6 to 8 ounces sweetcorn, chopped spinach, or other vegetable just before folding in egg whites. Reduce salt if necessary. Serve with vegetable or Hollandaise sauce.

PICKLED EGGS—CANADIAN STYLE

¾ pint malt vinegar
1 teaspoon mixed pickling spice
1 medium-sized lemon, peeled and
   sliced
2 tablespoons sugar
1 teaspoon salt
12 hard-boiled eggs, shelled

Combine first 5 ingredients and simmer 8 minutes. Place the shelled eggs in a large wide-mouthed jar. Strain in the hot vinegar.

Cover and chill in refrigerator for several hours before using. The eggs will keep in the pickling solution for several weeks.

Devilled Eggs En Casserole

Ham and Egg Surprise

DEVILLED EGGS EN CASSEROLE

Devilled Eggs:
8 hard-boiled eggs, shelled
½ ounce butter or margarine
¼ teaspoon salt
few grains black pepper
1 teaspoon French mustard
1 tablespoon mayonnaise

Cut eggs in half lengthwise; remove yolks and mash until smooth with remaining ingredients.

Refill whites with devilled mixture. Level off filling; put together in pairs, reserving a few halves for garnish.

Cheese Sauce:
1½ ounces butter or margarine
2 tablespoons grated onion
3 tablespoons flour
½ teaspoon salt
⅛ teaspoon black pepper
¾ pint milk
5 ounces grated Cheddar cheese
fluffy mashed potatoes

Melt butter over low heat, add onion and simmer until tender. Add flour and seasonings; blend.

Gradually add milk and cook until mixture boils and thickens, stirring constantly. Stir in cheese until smooth.

Arrange whole devilled eggs in buttered casserole; pour cheese sauce over them.

Mash 5 or 6 medium-cooked potatoes, season with butter, salt, and pepper. Beat in about ¼ pint of milk until potatoes are fluffy. Make a border of mashed potatoes round edge of casserole.

Lightly brown potatoes under grill, under medium flame. Serves 6.

POACHED EGGS NEW ORLEANS

1½ ounces butter or margarine
2 tablespoons flour
8 fluid ounces milk
4 ounces chopped cooked prawns
½ teaspoon salt
⅛ teaspoon black pepper
1 tablespoon pickles
4 poached eggs
4 slices buttered toast

Melt butter or margarine in a saucepan over low heat. Blend in flour. Add milk and cook over low heat until the mixture boils and thickens, stirring constantly.

Add cooked prawns, salt, pepper, and pickles. Cook for 2 minutes, stirring occasionally.

Place poached eggs on buttered toast; cover with hot sauce. Serves 4.

EGGS CREOLE

4 tablespoons oil
1 medium onion, chopped
¼ clove garlic, crushed
1½ ounces chopped green pepper
8 ounces canned or fresh tomatoes, skinned and quartered
8 ounces rice, cooked
salt and pepper to taste
tomato juice, if needed
6 eggs
2 ounces grated cheese
2 ounces melted butter or margarine

Heat oil; add onion and garlic, and cook over low heat for 10 minutes. Add green peppers and cook 5 minutes longer. Add tomatoes and cooked rice and season to taste. The mixture should be well moistened, so, if fresh tomatoes were not very ripe and juicy, add some tomato juice.

Divide the mixture between 6 individual ramekins. Make a depression in the middle and break an egg into each. Sprinkle with grated cheese and melted butter.

Cook in a moderate oven (350°F. Mark 4) 15 to 25 minutes, depending on whether the eggs are to be cooked soft or well done. Serve in the dishes. Serves 6.

CREAMED EGG CASSEROLE

2 ounces butter or margarine
4 tablespoons flour
1 teaspoon salt
⅛ teaspoon black pepper
¾ pint milk
2 tablespoons grated onion
4 ounces grated Cheddar cheese
6 shelled, hard-boiled eggs
4 ounces cooked diced celery
16 sliced olives (green or stuffed)
1½ ounces buttered breadcrumbs

Melt butter; add flour and seasonings and blend. Gradually add milk and cook over low heat until smooth and thickened, stirring constantly.

Add grated onion and grated cheese and stir until cheese is melted.

Cut hard-boiled eggs in quarters lengthwise. Place half the egg slices, half of celery and olive slices in bottom of buttered 2½-pint casserole. Top with half the sauce. Repeat, sprinkling buttered crumbs on top.

Cook in slow oven (325°F. Mark 3) for 20 minutes, until lightly browned. Serves 6.

HAM AND EGG SURPRISE

1½ ounces fresh breadcrumbs
4 fluid ounces milk
5 ounces minced baked ham or luncheon meat
½ teaspoon French mustard
¼ teaspoon black pepper
1 beaten egg
6 hard-boiled eggs, shelled

Mix crumbs and milk in saucepan. Heat slowly. Stir into a paste. Add meat, mustard, pepper, and beaten egg. Mix well.

Cover each hard-boiled egg completely with mixture.

Deep fry in hot fat (375°F.) until lightly browned, 3 to 4 minutes. Drain on absorbent paper.

Serve hot with medium tomato sauce. Serves 6.

EGG-CHEESE-TOMATO CASSEROLE

1 10½-ounce can condensed tomato soup
6 tablespoons mayonnaise
2 fluid ounces soured cream
4 fluid ounces milk
2 tablespoons chopped parsley
¼ teaspoon salt
6 hard-boiled eggs, sliced
4 ounces Cheddar cheese

Combine all ingredients but eggs and cheese. Heat thoroughly. Cut cheese in small thin slices.

In a greased shallow casserole, place an egg slice, overlap with a slice of cheese, then another egg slice and continue until bottom of casserole is covered and all slices have been used. Pour tomato sauce over egg and cheese.

Cook in moderate oven (375°F. Mark 5) 15 minutes. Serves 4.

Creamed Egg Casserole

HOW TO CONVERT DRIED EGGS

Dried Whole Egg: Use 2 tablespoons powdered whole egg plus 2½ tablespoons lukewarm water to equal each fresh whole egg. Add a little water to dried egg. Stir to blend into a medium thick paste with no lumps of egg powder. Gradually add remainder of water and stir or beat until smooth.

Dried Egg Yolk: Use 1½ tablespoons powdered egg yolk plus 1 tablespoon lukewarm water to equal each fresh egg yolk. Follow directions for Dried Whole Egg.

Dried Egg Whites: Use 1 tablespoon powdered egg white plus 2 tablespoons lukewarm water to equal each fresh egg white. Sprinkle egg powder onto water. Allow to stand 15 minutes or more to dissolve, stirring occasionally.

MEXICAN EGGS

    2 green peppers, chopped
    1 large Spanish onion, chopped
    1 clove garlic, crushed, optional
    12 ounces luncheon meat or salami
       sausage, diced
    1 ounce butter or margarine
    1 teaspoon salt
    3 large tomatoes, peeled and diced
    1 teaspoon chilli seasoning,
       optional
    9 eggs
    melted butter or margarine
    watercress

Cut 6 slices from small end of peppers and chop the rest after removing seeds.

Peel and slice onion; reserve 6 small slices and chop the rest.

Add chopped vegetables, garlic, and luncheon meat or sausage to butter melted in frying pan. Sauté until light brown and add salt and tomatoes. Cook 5 minutes. Add chilli seasoning.

Beat eggs until frothy and add tomato mixture to them.

Grease generously the bottom of deep 9-inch cake tin. Pour in egg mixture.

Cook in moderate oven (350°F. Mark 4) 25 to 30 minutes or until set. Cut in wedges, decorate with reserved slices of pepper and onion and serve at once garnished with watercress. Serves 6.

Mexican Eggs

EGG AND CHEESE TIMBALES

    2 ounces butter or margarine
    1 tablespoon flour
    12 fluid ounces milk
    5½ ounces strong cheese, grated
    ½ teaspoon salt
    ⅛ teaspoon black pepper
    1½ teaspoons Worcestershire sauce
    ½ teaspoon mustard, scant
    1½ teaspoons chopped canned
       pimiento
    3 eggs, beaten

Melt butter. Add flour and blend well. Add milk and cook over low heat, stirring constantly until thickened. Add cheese and stir until blended.

Remove from heat and add seasonings and pimiento. Pour slowly into beaten eggs, stirring constantly. Pour into well-greased individual ramekins.

Set ramekins in pan of hot water and cook in slow oven (325°F. Mark 3) until firm, about 45 minutes, or until knife inserted in centre comes out clean.

Unmould to serve. Chopped pickles, chilli pickle or whole cranberry sauce are good accompaniments. Serves 4.

EGGS BARCELONA

    2 tablespoons olive oil
    ½ cup grated onion
    1 pound canned tomatoes
    ½ teaspoon salt
    1 teaspoon chilli seasoning (or less)
    2 ounces mushrooms, finely chopped
    4 tablespoons chopped cooked ham
    6 eggs
    buttered toast

Heat olive oil in frying pan; add onions and cook until light brown.

Add tomatoes, salt, chilli seasoning, mushrooms, and ham. Stir and cook 3 minutes.

Add whole raw eggs, keeping them unbroken. Cook until eggs are set.

Remove with slotted spoon and place on slices of buttered toast on a hot platter. Pour sauce round; serve hot. Serves 6.

SWISS PUFF

    6 slices buttered toast, cubed
    8 ounces grated Emmenthal cheese
    3 eggs, slightly beaten
    ¾ pint milk
    1 teaspoon salt
    ¼ teaspoon black pepper
    ½ teaspoon dry mustard
    1 teaspoon Worcestershire sauce

Butter a 3-pint casserole and fill with alternate layers of toast cubes and cheese.

Combine eggs, milk, and seasonings; pour over toast-cheese mixture.

Cook in moderate oven (350°F. Mark 4) 35 minutes, or until a knife inserted in centre comes out clean. Serves 4.

Egg Potato Pie

EGG POTATO PIE

    1 ounce dripping or lard
    1 tablespoon flour
    2 fluid ounces milk
    1 ounce grated strong cheese
    ½ teaspoon salt
    dash of black pepper
    6 medium potatoes, cooked and
       mashed
    5 hard-boiled eggs, sliced
    2 tablespoons chopped parsley

Melt dripping, add flour, blend well and cook over low heat until bubbly.

Add cold milk all at once and cook, stirring constantly, until thickened. Stir in grated cheese. Add salt and pepper.

Line bottom and sides of a greased 8- or 9-inch pie dish or shallow casserole with half of the well seasoned mashed potatoes. Arrange the sliced eggs in potato shell. Top with parsley, cheese sauce, salt and pepper. Cover with remaining mashed potatoes. Brush top with milk.

Bake in moderate oven (350°F. Mark 4) until nicely browned and thoroughly heated, about 30 minutes. If desired, garnish top with slices of hard-boiled egg. Serves 5.

EGGS TETRAZZINI

    1 ounce sliced fresh mushrooms
    2 ounces diced celery
    1 tablespoon grated onion
    2 tablespoons chopped green
       pepper
    4 ounces butter or margarine
    1 ounce plain flour
    ¾ pint milk
    1 teaspoon Worcestershire sauce
    ½ teaspoon salt
    dash of black pepper
    4 hard-boiled eggs
    4 ounces spaghetti, cooked

Cook mushrooms, celery, onion, and green pepper in 2 ounces butter until lightly browned.

Prepare sauce: blend flour into remaining 2 ounces butter, then gradually add milk. Cook over low heat, stirring constantly, until smooth and thickened. Blend in seasonings and sautéed vegetables.

Chop 3 of the eggs coarsely and blend into mixture. Pile hot cooked spaghetti in centre of warm serving dish. Pour sauce over it. Garnish with slices of remaining hard-boiled egg. Serves 4.

OMELET MAISON

3 ounces mature Cheddar cheese
2 fluid ounces milk
4 fluid ounces double cream, whipped
2 large mushrooms
2 ounces butter or margarine
⅛ teaspoon chopped chives
⅛ teaspoon chopped parsley
¼ teaspoon salt
⅛ teaspoon black pepper
2 eggs, separated
8 stalks or tips of canned or cooked asparagus

Heat together over hot water the cheese and milk. Stir until smooth. Chill and add 2 fluid ounces whipped cream. Reserve.

Peel mushrooms, wash, and slice. Sauté in 1 ounce butter and add chives, parsley, salt, pepper, and remaining whipped cream.

Beat egg whites stiff and fold in beaten egg yolks. Add mushroom mixture and fold in.

Melt remaining 1 ounce butter in small frying pan. Add egg mixture, cover and cook over very low heat until top is dry and bottom a golden brown.

Fold, turn out on serving dish and surround with asparagus. Pour reserved cheese sauce over all and grill quickly until surface is golden brown. Serves 2.

SPICY BAKED EGGS

3 fluid ounces salad dressing or mayonnaise
¼ teaspoon salt
⅛ teaspoon black pepper
½ teaspoon paprika
½ teaspoon Worcestershire sauce
4 fluid ounces milk
4 ounces grated strong cheese
8 eggs

Combine salad dressing and seasoning. Gradually add milk, stirring after each addition until smooth. Add cheese and cook over low heat until cheese is melted, about 5 minutes.

Pour 2 tablespoons of the sauce into each of 4 individual greased ramekins. Break 2 eggs into each dish and top with remaining sauce. Place in pan of hot water.

Cook in moderate oven (350°F. Mark 4) until eggs are desired consistency, 12 to 15 minutes. Serves 4.

TOMATO-DEVILLED EGGS

4 hard-boiled eggs
2 fluid ounces mayonnaise
1 tablespoon chopped parsley
1 teaspoon grated onion
1 10½-ounce can condensed tomato soup
2 teaspoons French mustard
1 teaspoon lemon juice or vinegar

Split eggs lengthwise; scoop out yolks and combine with mayonnaise, parsley, and onion. Fill egg whites with this mixture.

Place eggs in a shallow casserole and cover with a sauce made by combining soup, mustard, and lemon juice. Cook in a moderate oven (350°F. Mark 4) about 15 minutes. Serves 4.

PEACH OMELET WITH MINT CHEESE SPREAD

½ ounce butter or margarine
6 eggs, slightly beaten
6 tablespoons single cream
¼ teaspoon salt
1 ounce melted butter or margarine
8 ounces sliced, cooked peaches
2 ounces sugar
1 tablespoon lemon juice

Melt butter in frying pan. Combine beaten eggs, cream, salt, and butter. Pour egg mixture into frying pan. As mixture cooks on the bottom and sides, prick with a fork so that the uncooked egg mixture will flow to the bottom of the frying pan.

Just before it is ready to be folded, place the sliced peaches on half of the omelet. Fold, and sprinkle with sugar and lemon juice.

Place pan under a preheated medium grill for a few minutes. Turn out on a hot serving dish and serve immediately. Serve with toast spread with Mint Cheese Spread. Serves 6.

Mint Cheese Spread:
3 ounces cream cheese
1 tablespoon chopped mint leaves
1 tablespoon cream

Combine cream cheese, mint, and cream. Makes 4 fluid ounces.

SHERRIED SCRAMBLED EGGS WITH MUSHROOMS

1 ounce butter or margarine
2 ounces sliced mushrooms
8 eggs, beaten
2 fluid ounces single cream
2 fluid ounces sherry
2 teaspoons salt
¼ teaspoon black pepper
¼ teaspoon paprika

Melt butter or margarine in saucepan or chafing dish. Add mushrooms and cook slowly 5 minutes.

Add beaten eggs to which cream, sherry, salt, pepper, and paprika have been added.

Cook over hot water (or over very low heat), stirring constantly as mixture begins to thicken. Cook until creamy and to the desired degree of firmness. Serve at once. Serves 4 or more.

Eggs à La King on Sweetcorn Rings

EGGS À LA KING ON SWEET-CORN RINGS

½ ounce butter or dripping
1 tablespoon grated onion
3 tablespoons flour
¾ pint milk
1 teaspoon salt
⅛ teaspoon black pepper
½ teaspoon Worcestershire sauce
1 ounce chopped green pepper
6 hard-boiled eggs, sliced
6 slices fried maize flour mush

Melt butter in top of double boiler over direct heat. Add grated onion and cook until tender.

Stir in flour and add milk, seasonings, Worcestershire sauce, and green pepper.

Cook over hot water, stirring until smooth and thickened. Add hard-boiled egg slices.

Serve on rounds of fried maize flour mush. Serves 6.

Maize Flour Mush: Pour cooked maize flour or polenta into a round can or mould that has been rinsed in cold water. Cover, and chill until firm.

Cut into ½-inch slices; dip in flour and sauté in dripping until crisp and brown.

HOLLANDAISE SARDINE-EGG NESTS

2 soft rolls or scones
4 eggs
2 3¼-ounce cans sardines
1 cup Hollandaise sauce

Cut scones in half and toast. Poach eggs.

Place sardines on scones; add a poached egg to each serving and top with sauce. Serves 4.

Hollandaise Sardine-Egg Nests

STUFFED EGG AND SPINACH CASSEROLE

8 ounces cooked spinach
1½ ounces melted butter or margarine
1 small onion, chopped
1 ounce plain flour
8 fluid ounces milk
4 fluid ounces spinach liquid
1 teaspoon salt
dash of black pepper
½ teaspoon prepared horseradish
½ teaspoon French mustard
6 hard-boiled eggs

Drain spinach (reserve liquid) and finely chop. Melt butter in top of double boiler over boiling water. Add onion and cook until tender. Stir in flour until well blended.

Add milk and spinach liquid and cook, stirring constantly, until mixture thickens. Season with salt and pepper. Add horseradish and mustard. Fold in chopped spinach and reheat. Pour into greased casserole.

Top with stuffed eggs made as follows: Cut hard boiled eggs in halves lengthwise. Remove yolks and mash with 2 tablespoons grated onion, ¼ teaspoon French mustard, 3 tablespoons salad dressing, ¼ teaspoon salt, and a dash of pepper.

Refill whites with mixture. Place stuffed eggs on top of spinach.

Cover and cook in moderate oven (375°F. Mark 5) 15 minutes. Serves 6.

OMELET WITH MUSHROOMS IN WINE

2 ounces butter or margarine
juice of 1 lemon
salt and pepper
4 fluid ounces Rhine or Sauternes wine
½ pound fresh mushrooms, sliced
6 eggs, separated
6 tablespoons milk

Heat 1 ounce butter or margarine in frying pan. Add lemon juice, ½ teaspoon salt, dash of pepper, and the wine. Simmer mushrooms in this mixture until cooked.

Prepare omelet as follows: Add milk, ½ teaspoon salt, and dash of pepper to the egg yolks which have been beaten until light.

Fold into stiffly beaten egg whites. Melt remaining 1 ounce butter or margarine in omelet pan and heat well.

Pour omelet mixture into hot frying pan, and cook over low heat for 3 to 5 minutes.

Then place omelet in a moderate oven (350°F. Mark 4), and cook for about 15 minutes. The omelet is done when it springs back when indented with the fingertip.

Crease omelet through the centre and place half the mushrooms on one side of the omelet, folding the other half of omelet over mushrooms. Serve on hot dish topped with remaining mushrooms. Serves 6.

STUFFED EGGS ON RICE WITH CURRY SAUCE

2 ounces margarine
1 ounce flour
¾ pint milk
½ teaspoon salt
½ teaspoon curry powder
dash of black pepper
1½ pounds fluffy cooked rice
1 ounce margarine
3 hard-boiled eggs
3 tablespoons chopped cooked prawns
¼ teaspoon salt
¼ teaspoon dry mustard
1 tablespoon mayonnaise
1 pound cooked prawns

Melt 2 ounces margarine in a saucepan. Blend in flour. Remove from heat and stir in milk. Cook until it is medium thick, stirring constantly.

Add salt, curry powder, and pepper. Spoon 2 tablespoons of the sauce into each individual ramekin.

Mix rice with 1 ounce margarine and place 4 ounces in each ramekin over the sauce.

Stuff egg whites with egg yolks mixed with chopped prawns, salt, mustard, and mayonnaise. Place over the rice.

Place 5 to 6 whole prawns round each egg. Brush with melted margarine.

Heat in moderate oven (350°F. Mark 4) 15 to 20 minutes. Serve with hot curry sauce. Serves 6.

CREOLE SCRAMBLED EGGS IN BREAD BASKETS

6 eggs, unbeaten
2 fluid ounces cream
½ teaspoon salt
dash of black pepper
½ teaspoon onion juice
2 to 3 ounces chopped, cooked bacon
2 tablespoons finely chopped canned pimiento or green pepper
1 ounce butter or margarine

Break eggs into a mixing bowl; add cream, salt, pepper, onion juice, bacon, and pimiento. Beat slightly.

Melt butter in frying pan over low heat. Pour egg mixture into pan and cook slowly without stirring until eggs are partially cooked. Then stir with fork, loosening sides and scraping bottom of pan so liquid portion can run down.

Continue cooking until eggs are set to firmness desired. Spoon egg mixture into bread baskets. Serves 6.

Eggs de Jonghe

EGGS DE JONGHE

8 poached eggs
6 ounces fresh breadcrumbs
2 ounces butter or margarine, melted
½ teaspoon garlic salt
½ teaspoon pepper
6 slices luncheon meat, halved
paprika

Poach eggs for 2 or 3 minutes only. If necessary, keep eggs hot until all are poached by holding them in a shallow pan of warm water.

Combine crumbs with melted butter or margarine and seasonings. Put a thin layer in the bottom of 4 preheated shallow individual ramekins.

Place 2 poached eggs in each dish with 3 half slices of luncheon meat on the side. Top with remaining crumbs.

Place under grill or in a very hot oven (450°F. Mark 8) until crumbs are browned, 3 to 8 minutes. (If placed under grill, watch carefully!) Add a dash of paprika before serving. Serves 4.

Note: A crushed garlic clove and salt may be used instead of garlic salt for seasoning.

EGGS ON TOAST WITH SHERRY CREAM SAUCE

1 ounce butter or margarine
2 tablespoons chopped green pepper
2 tablespoons flour
6 fluid ounces milk
2 fluid ounces sherry
½ teaspoon salt
¼ teaspoon black pepper
½ teaspoon Worcestershire sauce
1 teaspoon sugar
2 fluid ounces chilli pickle, optional
6 slices buttered toast
6 hard-boiled eggs

Melt butter or margarine; add green pepper and cook 3 minutes.

Shake flour and milk in a covered container until the mixture is smooth. Add to butter and green pepper and cook, stirring constantly, until thickened and smooth.

Add sherry, salt, pepper, Worcestershire sauce, and sugar. Add chilli pickle if desired.

Slice eggs and arrange 1 sliced egg on each slice of toast. Pour sauce over the eggs on toast. Serve hot. Serves 6.

Creative Garnishing

To put a wholesome, well balanced meal on a dinner table, or prepare the dishes for a buffet supper party is not difficult today. Convenience foods and pre-cut, prepacked meats abound in our stores. However, the trick is to take inexpensive foods and to give them a look of originality, variety and luxury.

for appetizers and buffet suppers

A Garnishes can be delicious treats as well as being decorative—as demonstrated by this party buffet. Nor do they require a lot of time or money to prepare. Here is a complete buffet meal—or appetizers for a main meal.

B Stuffed green peppers—or tomatoes, if you prefer—can be filled with your favourite dip and topped with a cherry tomato flower, pimento strips or egg yolk.

C First, the top is sliced off. Then the inside is hollowed out with a grapefruit knife. The hollow is filled with dip, using a spatula. For the final garnish, hard-boiled egg yolk is forced through a strainer with the back of a spoon to decorate the top.

D Meat and fruit kebabs offer attractive combinations of colours and tastes as the skewers are stuck conveniently into grapefruit or pineapple foundations. Make up combinations of meats, pickles and olives for the meat kebabs. And use small whole fruits and melon balls for tangy fruit kebabs.

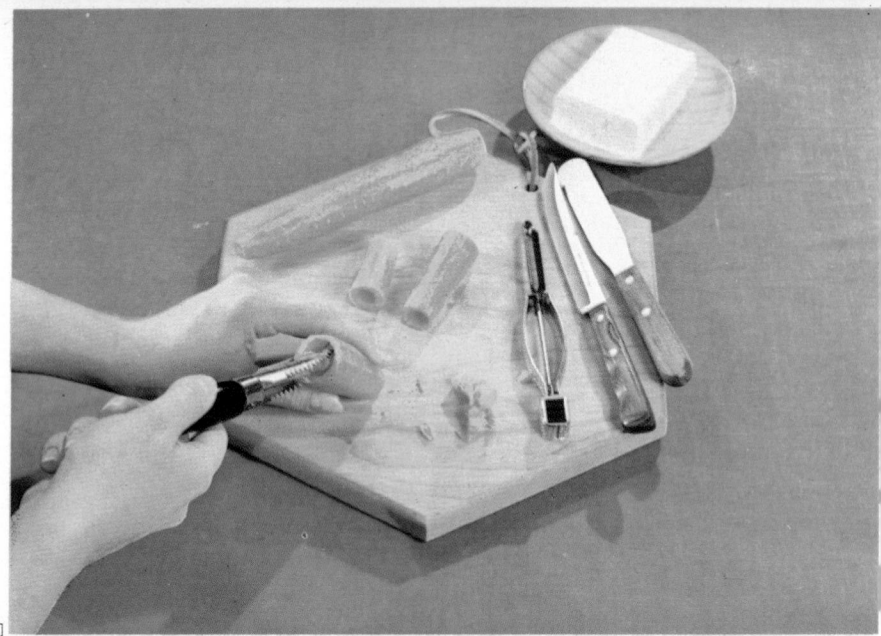

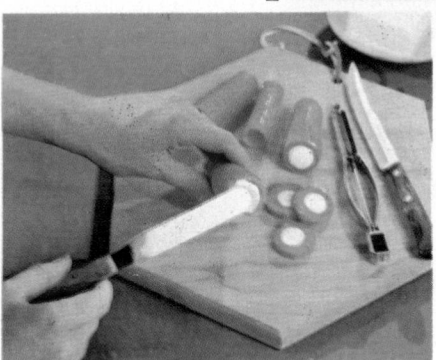

E To make stuffed carrots, you start with large carrots at room temperature and, after peeling, cut the top portions into two or two and a half inch lengths. Then the centre portion is hollowed out with an apple corer. When you have a smaller diameter carrot use a peeler.

F The hollows are then filled with cream cheese—or any hard spread—and put into the refrigerator for thorough chilling. Then they can be cut into bite size pieces and arranged for the buffet board. Cucumbers can also be hollowed out and filled with pimento cheese.

G To make lunch meat roll-ups, the meat slices are spread with softened cream cheese, rolled and held together with a small skewer or toothpick. After chilling, they are cut into bite size portions. Roll-ups may be made also with bread, or lettuce or cabbage leaves replacing the meat.

H Using a ball cutter, you can form little balls of cream cheese or processed cheese. These are then rolled in crushed nuts, crumbs or chopped prepared meat. Add pretzel stick handles—and presto!—another treat for early or late snack times.

I Casseroles are often part of the buffet meal—or even form the main dish of a dinner. Most are inexpensive, but you can make them look more luxurious, like this sea food casserole with a lemon topknot to set it off.

J Cut a lemon in half *lengthways*, and then slice one of the halves into five wedges. Put an olive on one end of a cocktail stick—and push the other end down through a lemon wedge to attach it to the skin side of the remaining half of lemon. The wedges are then used for the individual servings from the casserole. Other garnishes of citrus fruits are also appropriate for many casseroles.

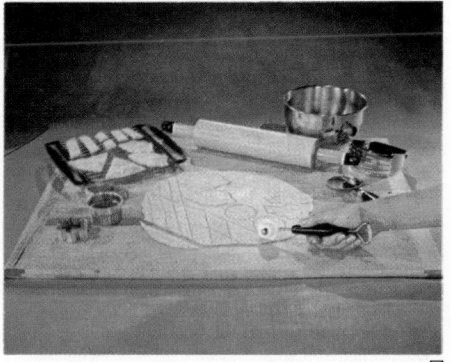

K Some casseroles may be garnished with grated cheese and cheese balls. If an additional touch of colour is desired, add some strips or a round of green pepper.

L Pastry cut-outs go well with many types of casseroles. Fancy shapes are cut with a sharp knife or pastry cutter—or use a biscuit cutter. Brush the top of the crust with egg white or milk —and bake the pastry shapes right with the casserole. Cut-outs from cheese slices can be added after cooking or ten minutes before you finish baking. Similar cut-outs can be used with some desserts.

M Crunchy, zesty casserole garnishes that are very quick and inexpensive are made simply from crumbs which are sprinkled over the top. Make them from flavoured cocktail crackers —or from cereal—or from toasted rye or pumpernickel bread. For vegetable casseroles, the garnishes also enhance the flavour.

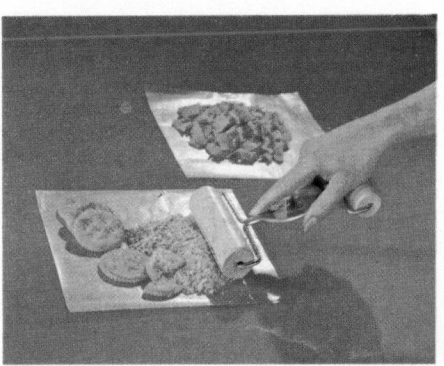

Garnishes for family dinners and supper parties

A Vegetables can be glamorous as well as nutritious. Who could resist a potato flower like this? When you have the right tools, it's no trouble at all to prepare.

B The flowers are made from new potatoes, peeled and with eyes and one slice from one end removed. They are then put partway through a French Fry Cutter—to within about three-eighths inch from the end . . . then pushed back through the cutting blades with the pusher plate. Of course, a knife may be used to cut the potato in a similar pattern. The potato flowers are then cooked in the oven with the roast.

C Another appealing combination is hollowed beets filled with peas. Cone shaped hollows are made with an apple corer, and after the beets are filled, the combination is warmed in the oven. Green pepper stuffed with corn is also colourful and tasty.

D Meat, being the main course of a meal, receives particular attention from the diners, and should receive special attention from the cook, as

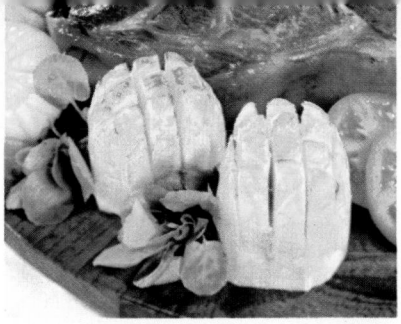

A

B

C

D

well. The added touch of a garnish is evidence of that attention — such as this onion chrysanthemum.

E To make the chrysanthemum, you make a series of radial slices in the onion — from the centre out — and to within a half to a quarter inch from the bottom, slicing first in quarters, then in eighths, and so on. It is then placed in coloured water to slightly colour it. If you wish a fuller flower — place cocktail sticks between your radial cuts to hold the blossom open. Remove cocktail sticks before serving.

E

F Tomatoes with a mashed potato garnish are another attractive and appetizing way of serving vegetables. The top of the tomato is sliced off. Then, after the tomato has been cut down slightly to form an outside ridge, the depression is filled with mashed potatoes. The combination is warmed in an oven.

G Lemon basket garnishes can be made quickly by cutting away wedges to leave a handle—and then removing the pulp with a grapefruit knife. Fill the baskets with chutney for beef—or cranberry sauce for turkey or poultry.

H For lamb roasts, the lemon baskets are usually filled with mint jelly and arranged around the roast.

I To garnish ham, make pineapple flowers with petals cut from pineapple slices. The leaves and stems are cut from green peppers, with cherries forming the centres.

A

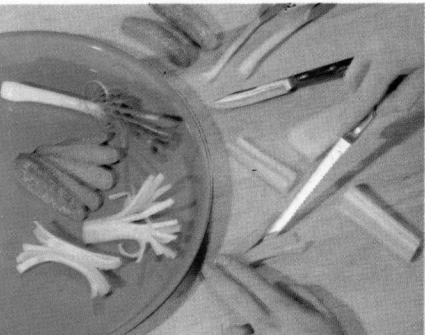

B

C

Garnishes
for delectable salads

D

A *Any* dish can be garnished. Even salads—with all their usual variety—will be much more tempting if you give them a little special decoration.

B Just look what you can do with pickle slices—celery—and green onions—fans, flutes, curls, ruffles. The celery and green onion garnishes are chilled thoroughly in iced water after cutting.

C Or start with carrots, radishes or turnips—and a sharp knife and a parer and grater. You can make all sorts of flowers, curls and feathers. Again, chill in iced water after cutting. Also, colourful carrots can be shredded and sprinkled on top of a tossed salad.

D A Chip Cutter is extremely useful for preparing a julienne salad—producing the fine strips of crisp vegetables. Use a knife to cut the julienne strips of meat or cheese you may include in the salad.

E Citrus fruits are another great source of colour and flavour. Make them into curls, crosses, wedges, flowers . . . and use them singly, or combine them in designs. Or cut a continuous strip of peeling and let it coil. Any of these are also good for fish and soup garnishes.

F You can make two kinds of tomato roses. Cut a tomato half way down in sixths or eighths. Then peel down the outer skin about a quarter of the way with a serrated knife. Or, pare the skin of a tomato off in one length and coil it to form a rose.

G Many garnishes can be enhanced by using food products as they come from the containers or store—such as fruit sections or cherries. Or add olives, capers, nuts and bits of parsley to "garnish the garnishes"

E

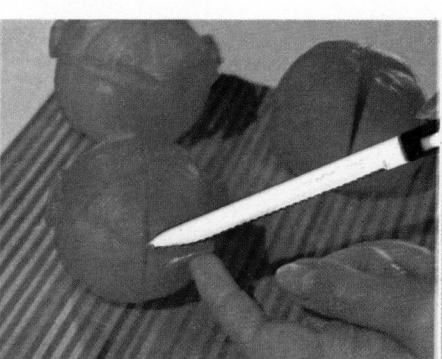

F

G

Garnishes
for soups and sandwiches

A Don't forget lunch time, either. Soup and sandwich time doesn't need to be dull—not when a tempting garnish is so quick and easy to add.

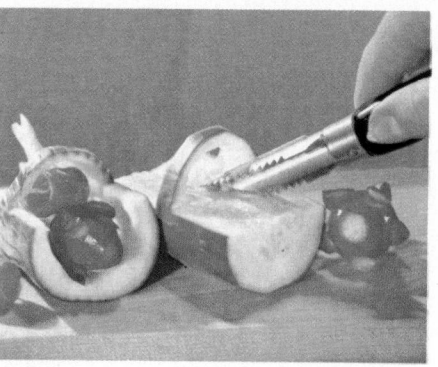

B Soups can be garnished in many ways—according to the kind of soup. Pictured here are some suggestions for cold and cream soups. Cold soups can be topped with sour cream, sliced cucumber, hard-boiled egg, sliced lemon.

Cream soups are garnished with croutons, frankfurter slices, sour cream, and grated cheese or shredded carrots. To clear soups add lemon slices, chopped parsley, chives or green pepper.

C A cucumber basket is made by hollowing out a two inch length of pared cucumber—and then filling it with an olive, celery and carrot curls. The cucumber could have been scored with a fork, rather than pared. Or, it might have been sliced lengthwise to form a "boat" for filling. Radish roses make an interesting garnish. Slice the radish petals and chill the radish in iced water to obtain fullness.

Desserts, too, become more appetizing as you add your own art of garnishing.

Garnishes

for taste-tempting desserts

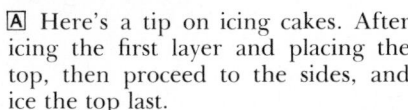

A Here's a tip on icing cakes. After icing the first layer and placing the top, then proceed to the sides, and ice the top last.

B Fluffy icing can be swirled in "esses" or circle with the spatula. Or, the spatula can be lifted from contact with the icing to form fluffy peaks.

C Then add a little garnish to the icing—grated orange or lemon peel—crushed or whole nuts—or chocolate curls shaved with a parer. For additional garnishes, use small sweets or whole nuts arranged in attractive designs.

D For pies, lattice tops are especially attractive. The dough strips may be either plain or twisted—and note how the alternate strips in one direction are folded back for placing the crossing strips.

E Any kind of pie can be improved in appearance—and in flavour, too—with an appropriate garnish. Here are some suggestions for refrigerator or pudding pies—top with fresh fruit or berries, chocolate biscuit crumbs, crushed peppermint, candy, gum drops, candied cherries, nonpareils. One-crust fruit pies can be topped with whipped cream, half nuts, tinted coconut, crushed toffee candy.

Two-crust pies can be garnished with cheese cut-outs, pastry cut-outs, fancy slits, brandy butter balls.

Appetizing, Nutritious!

You'll find that garnishes not only make a meal look better, but they add nutrition, too — helping to assure a balanced meal with a full share of each of the four basic food groups — and helping to assure that everyone *eats* what he needs!

FACTS ABOUT FOOD AND COOKING

Guides to Better Cooking

SUCCESS WITH RECIPES

1. Read the recipe carefully.

2. Check your supplies to see that you have the necessary ingredients.

3. Assemble the ingredients and equipment needed for measuring, mixing, cooking, or baking — spoons, scales, bowl, pans, etc.

4. Light the oven if a preheated oven is necessary.

5. Use level measurements; measure the ingredients accurately.

6. Follow the procedure given for combining ingredients.

7. Follow directions given for cooking and baking. Use as nearly as possible the size pan indicated. Follow cooking time or baking time and temperatures given; also test for doneness by physical means since oven heat varies. Use thermometers for baking, deep fat frying, and sweet making.

8. Handle finished product as indicated. Follow directions for removing from pan, moulding, chilling, etc.

9. In making substitutions in a recipe, follow the rules for substitution and equivalents carefully.

10. To reduce a recipe choose a recipe in which the ingredients may be divided easily. Measure smaller quantities carefully. It is not practical to reduce successfully certain recipes such as boiled icing, steamed puddings, etc.

11. To increase a recipe, it is best not to exceed doubling the quantities of ingredients at one time. When the recipe is doubled, the cooking time is not necessarily increased since the larger quantity may be baked in two pans or a larger pan of no greater depth.

CORRECT MEASURING METHODS

Use British standard measuring spoons. Measure dry ingredients before measuring liquids to save extra dish.

For small quantities use $\frac{1}{2}$ and $\frac{1}{4}$ teaspoons for greater accuracy.

White sugar: If lumpy, sift before measuring. Do not pack down into measuring spoon. Level off with spatula or straight knife.

Brown sugar: Pack firmly into spoon, so that when turned out it will hold shape of spoon. If lumpy, roll and sift before measuring.

Syrup and treacle: Rinse spoon in cold water before measuring.

Solid fats: When fat comes in 1-pound or $\frac{1}{2}$-pound rectangular form, it can be divided into required fractions. Or measure by weighing or packing firmly into measuring spoon and levelling off top with spatula or straight knife.

White flour: Sift once. Lift lightly onto scales. If using a measuring spoon level off top with spatula or straight knife.

Other flours, fine meals, fine crumbs, dried eggs, dry milk: Stir instead of sifting. Measure like flour.

Baking powder, cornflour, cream of tartar, spices: Stir to loosen. Dip measuring spoon into can, bring up heaping full, level with spatula or knife.

Liquids: Place standard glass measuring jug on a flat surface. Bend down so that you can read the measure at eye level. A safety rim above the full mark is provided so that you can get accurate measurements without spilling a drop.

Oil or melted fat: When it's necessary to measure by spoon, pour oil into a cup. Dip measuring spoon into the oil. Lift out carefully; the spoon should be so full it won't hold another drop.

OVEN TEMPERATURES

At least once a year have your oven regulator tested for accuracy by the gas or electricity board that serves your area, because even the best cooker becomes inaccurate occasionally and requires expert attention to re-set it.

Very slow oven	250°-275°F.	Mark $\frac{1}{2}$-1
Slow oven	300°-325°F.	Mark 2-3
Moderate oven	350°-375°F.	Mark 4-5
Hot oven	400°-425°F.	Mark 6-7
Very hot oven	450°-475°F.	Mark 8-9
Extremely hot oven	500°-525°F.	Mark 10

For accurate measuring use standard utensils, not table cups and spoons.

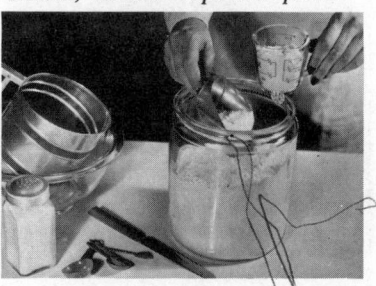

409

HANDY EQUIVALENTS

		Volume Measure
Breadcrumbs, dry	2 ounces	4 heaped tablespoons
Breadcrumbs, soft	1 slice bread = 1 ounce	1 heaped tablespoon
Butter or margarine	2 ounces	1 level tablespoon
Cheese, Cheddar	2 ounces	8 heaped tablespoons
Chocolate	1 ounce	1 square
Coconut – desiccated	2 ounces	2 heaped tablespoons
Cottage cheese	2 ounces	1 heaped tablespoon
Digestive biscuits	2 biscuits = 2 ounces	3 heaped tablespoons coarsely or finely crumbled
Cream Crackers	2 biscuits = 1 ounce	2 heaped tablespoons fine crumbs
Crackers, soda	20 to 22 small squares	1 cup fine crumbs
Cream cheese	3 ounces	7 heaped tablespoons
Currants	2 ounces	2 heaped tablespoons
Flour:		
Plain	2 ounces	4 level teaspoons, unsifted
Whole wheat	2 ounces	4 level tablespoons
Lemon juice	1 aver. lemon	3 to 4 tablespoons
Lemon rind	1 aver. lemon	1½ teaspoons grated rind
Marshmallows	¼ pound	16 marshmallows
Nuts, chopped	2 ounces	3 heaped tablespoons
Orange juice	1 aver. orange	6 to 8 tablespoons juice
Orange rind	1 aver. orange	1 tablespoon grated rind
Raisins	2 ounces	2 heaped tablespoons
Rice	2 ounces	2 tablespoons, un-cooked; about 4 tablespoons, cooked
Sugar:		
Brown	2 ounces	2 heaped tablespoons
Icing	2 ounces	4 heaped tablespoons
Granulated or Caster	1 pound	2 cups
Treacle or Honey	2¼ ounces	3 tablespoons
Whipping cream	8 fluid ounces	2 cups when whipped
Zwieback or Rusk	2 ounces crumbs	4 heaped tablespoons

WEIGHTS AND MEASURES

Measurements in all recipes are based on British standard weights old measures. Cutlery spoons do not necessarily correspond accurately with the capacity of measuring spoons.

dash, pinch	= Less than ⅛ teaspoon
3 teaspoons	= 1 tablespoon
1 tablespoon	= ½ fluid oz.
2 tablespoons	= 1 oz. liquid or fat
4 tablespoons	= 2 fluid oz.
6 tablespoons	= 3 fluid oz.
8 tablespoons	= 4 fluid oz.
10 tablespoons	= 5 fluid oz.
12 tablespoons	= 6 fluid oz.
18 tablespoons	= ½ Imperial pint or 10 fluid oz.
4 gills	= 1 Imperial pint
20 fluid oz.	= 1 Imperial pint
1 pint	= 1 pound liquid or fat
2 pints	= 1 quart or 32 fluid oz.
4 quarts (liquid)	= 1 gallon

1 wine glass = 4 oz = 8 tablespoons. (This is a claret glass and is most commonly used in the average home.)

1 sherry glass = 3 fluid oz. = 6 tablespoons

1 port glass = 2 fluid oz. = 4 tablespoons.

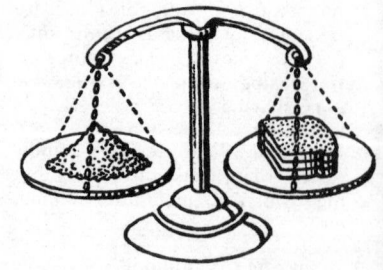

HOW MUCH TO BUY

How much meat to buy for dinner? How many servings will come from a pound of fish or chicken? The food shopper with an eye to thrift and good management learns to buy carefully just what she can use.

The figures below can help you decide how much to buy and, when reading market ads, you can use these figures to help decide what are real bargains.

The amount of meat, poultry, and fish per serving varies with the amount of bone and fat. It also varies with the amount of extenders—such as stuffing, potatoes, rice—used with the meat.

Size of serving for each fruit and vegetable is given for whichever way it is most commonly served—cooked or uncooked. Size of serving for dry beans and peas and for cereals and cereal products—except flaked and puffed—is given for the cooked form.

MEAT
Amount to buy per serving

Much bone or gristle	½ to 1 pound
Medium amounts of bone	⅓ to ½ pound
Little bone	¼ to ⅓ pound
No bone	⅕ to ¼ pound

POULTRY
(Dressed weight*)

Chicken:
Grilling	¼ to ½ bird
*Frying and roasting	¾ to 1 pound
Stewing	⅓ to ¾ pound
Ducks	1 to 1¼ pounds
Geese	¾ to 1 pound
Turkeys	⅔ to ¾ pound

POULTRY
(Ready-to-cook weight*)

Chicken:
Grilling	¼ to ½ bird
Frying and roasting	⅔ to ¾ pound
Stewing	¼ to ⅔ pound
Ducks	¾ to 1 pound
Geese	⅔ to ¾ pound
Turkeys	About ½ pound

* Number of servings depends on kind, weight, age, sex, grade and way prepared.

FISH

Whole or round	1 pound
Dressed, large	½ pound
Steaks, fillets	¼ pound

METRIC CONVERSION

English	Metric	English	Metric
1 oz.	28 gm.	1 lb. (16 oz.)	454 gm.
2 oz.	57 gm.	2 lb.	908 gm.
3 oz.	85 gm.	3 lb.	1.36 kg.
4 oz. (¼ lb.)	114 gm.	4 lb.	1.82 kg.
5 oz.	142 gm.	5 lb.	2.27 kg.
6 oz.	171 gm.	6 lb.	2.73 kg.
7 oz.	199 gm.	7 lb.	3.18 kg.
8 oz.	227 gm.	8 lb.	3.64 kg.
9 oz.	252 gm.	9 lb.	4.09 kg.
10 oz.	280 gm.	10 lb.	4.54 kg.
11 oz.	312 gm.	11 lb.	5.00 kg.
12 oz. (¾ lb.)	340 gm.	12 lb.	5.46 kg.
14 oz.	397 gm.	14 lb.	6.37 kg.
3.5 oz.	100 gm.	0.17 pint	100 cl.
7.0 oz.	200 gm.	0.35 pint	200 cl.
10.5 oz.	300 gm.	0.53 pint	300 cl.
1 lb. 13.4 oz.	500 gm.	0.88 pint	500 cl.
2.2 lb.	1000 gm.	1.76 pint	1 litre
1 pint	568 cl.		
½ pint	284 cl.		
¼ pint	142 cl.		

EMERGENCY SUBSTITUTIONS

For these	You may use these
1 whole egg, for thickening or baking	2 egg yolks. Or 2 tablespoons dried whole egg plus 2½ tablespoons water.
8 ounces butter or margarine for fat	7 ounces lard, or rendered fat, with ½ teaspoon salt. Or 8 ounces cooking fat sold under brand name, with ½ teaspoon salt.
1 square (ounce) chocolate	3 or 4 tablespoons cocoa plus ½ tablespoon fat.
1 teaspoon double-acting baking powder	1½ teaspoons phosphate baking powder. Or 2 teaspoons tartrate baking powder.
Fresh milk and baking powder, for baking	Equal amount of sour milk plus ½ teaspoon bicarbonate of soda per 8 fluid ounces. (Each half teaspoon soda with 8 fluid ounces sour milk takes the place of 2 teaspoons baking powder and 8 fluid ounces fresh milk.)
8 fluid ounces sour milk, for baking	8 fluid ounces fresh milk mixed with one of the following: 1 tablespoon vinegar. Or 1 tablespoon lemon juice. Or 1¾ teaspoons cream of tartar.
8 fluid ounces whole milk	4 fluid ounces evaporated milk plus 4 fluid ounces water. Or 4 tablespoons whole milk plus 8 fluid ounces water. Or 4 tablespoons nonfat dried milk plus 2 teaspoons table fat and 8 fluid ounces water.
8 fluid ounces skim milk	4 tablespoons skim milk plus 8 fluid ounces water.
1 tablespoon flour, for thickening	½ tablespoon cornflour, potato starch, rice starch, or arrowroot starch. Or 1 tablespoon granulated tapioca.

Terms Used in Recipes

Certain terms which might require further explanation recur in recipes; also some words which are occasionally found in recipes are not generally familiar. If any of the cookery methods and terms are new to you, read below and you'll find precise definitions.

AGE

A term sometimes applied to the maturing and tenderizing of game and other meats by allowing them to hang for a time in a cool place. Cheese, wine, and other food products are similarly allowed to age in order to develop their flavour fully.

ASPIC

A jelly made from meat, poultry, or fish stock that has been boiled down sufficiently to become firm when cold. Also fish or vegetable stock or tomato juice that has been thickened with gelatine. It is used to make moulded salads or to give a shiny, transparent coat to meats and other foods. In classical cookery the term is applied only to the entire dish, not to the jelly itself.

BAKE

To cook by dry heat, usually in an oven or ovenlike appliance. As modern recipes use it, "bake" simply means to cook in the oven. When applied to meat in uncovered containers, it's generally called roasting.

A recipe should tell you the kind and size of tin; whether the dish should be baked with or without a cover; the temperature, and baking time or similar way to determine when the dish is done. See also **Roast.**

BARBECUE

A term of Latin American origin. Originally an American outdoor social gathering at which an ox or a pig was roasted whole over an open fire. It has become a popular form of outdoor cooking in many parts of the world, and any sort of food is now cooked on the barbecue.

To barbecue: to cook with direct heat under a grill, over coals, or in the oven, basting frequently with a highly seasoned sauce. The word may also mean any food, especially sliced or chopped meat, that is cooked or served in such a sauce.

BARD

To cover lean meat, poultry, or fish with a layer of fat before cooking it, in order to prevent it from drying out. See **Lard.**

BASTE

To moisten foods during cooking with dripping, water, or special sauce, to prevent drying, or to add flavour.

BATTER

A flour and liquid mixture usually containing eggs, sugar, and leavening, soft enough to be stirred or mixed with a spoon, as opposed to dough, a similar mixture which is so stiff that it must be mixed with the hands or rolled on a board or cloth and cut. Usually you speak of cake or pancake batter, biscuit or bread dough.

BEAT

To make a mixture smooth, or add air by using a brisk whipping or stirring motion with a spoon, an electric mixer, or a hand rotary beater.

If you use a spoon, mix vigorously with a rapid over-and-over rotary motion. If you are doing your beating with an electric mixer or a hand rotary beater, use medium-to-fast speed.

BIND

To thicken with a binder, i.e., ingredients such as flour, starch, eggs, cream; to mix chopped meat, vegetables, etc., with a sauce.

BIRD

This is a general term applied to poultry and game birds.

It also refers to "meat birds", a dish made in various ways but usually consisting of stuffed thin oblong pieces of beef or veal, rolled, and tied or skewered. They are then coated with flour, browned, and cooked in a small amount of liquid.

BLANCH

To preheat in boiling water or steam. Used to aid in removal of skins from nuts, fruits, and some vegetables. Also used to deactivate enzymes and shrink food in preparation for canning, freezing, and drying. Vegetables are blanched in boiling water or steam; fruits in boiling water, syrup, fruit juice, or steam.

Blanch—Pour hot water over foods to blanch them. Soak for a few minutes.

BLEND

To combine (mix) two or more ingredients together to bring about a change of colour, texture, or flavour. It's done by stirring or creaming, or by a combination of the two techniques. When you're adding or blending a thin liquid into a thick mixture in an electric mixer, low is not only the best speed but the least likely to be splashy.

BOIL

To boil means to cook in liquid at boiling temperature (212°F. at sea level). When this point is reached, adjust heat to maintain it.

The term "boiling" is so frequently misunderstood by cooks that it requires elaboration. For example, many a cook mistakenly thinks that the harder a food boils, the quicker it is done. And the term is often incorrectly applied to such foods as "boiled" beef. Actually most foods are simmered, not boiled, as water below the boiling point is kinder to food proteins. Eggs, meat, poultry, fish, are or should be simmered. Jams and vegetables are boiled.

Here we explain everyday recipe phrases for boiling.

Bring to Boiling Point or Bring to the Boil: This signifies the step before cooking. You'll know that water or any liquid is reaching that point when bubbles appear at the bottom, rise to the top, then break. When a vapour appears and all liquid is in motion, it's come to the boil.

Boil Rapidly: This follows boiling. The liquid goes into rapid motion; the surface breaks into small lumpy waves.

A rapid boil won't cook food faster, but for some uses it's better; to cook cereals (keeps particles separated), to evaporate soup or jam, to concentrate syrup.

Full Rolling Boil: This is the point at which the liquid rises in the pan, then tumbles into great waves that can't be stirred down. It happens only in heavy sugar mixtures like syrup or icing, and in jam-making when jam is almost done or when liquid pectin is about to be added.

See also: **Simmer: Parboil: Scald: Steam: Blanch: Poach: Steep.**

BONE (In meat cookery)

To bone meat is to remove the bone from it. This is usually done to make carving easier or to allow for stuffing.

BOUILLON

Clear, seasoned stock or broth usually made from browned beef, For many purposes, a quick substitute is 1 meat stock cube or ½ teaspoon concentrated meat extract dissolved in 8 fluid ounces hot water.

Bouillon or Stock Cube: A small cube of concentrated chicken meat, or vegetable stock used with boiling water as a substitute for fresh stock.

BRAISE

To cook slowly in a small amount of liquid in a tightly covered utensil on top of range or in the oven. The food may or may not be browned (usually it is browned) in a small amount of fat before braising. It's a highly recommended method for the less tender cuts of meat or poultry.

BREAD

To coat with fine breadcrumbs alone, or to coat with breadcrumbs, then with slightly diluted beaten egg or milk, and again with breadcrumbs.

HINTS FOR COOKING BREADED FOODS

● Breaded foods have a tendency to stick to the pan and to lose their coating when they are fried in shallow fat. The best way to prevent this is to bread the foods ahead of time and let them stand on greaseproof paper at least 20 minutes, turning them over several times.

● When cooking these foods in shallow fat, turn them carefully with a spatula or palette knife.

● If breaded meats are to be braised in gravy after frying, keep the temperature just at simmering. Boiling loosens the delicate coating more than simmering.

● In deep frying the breading may have a tendency to break off if the surface of the foods is not completely covered with egg and crumbs or the foods are fried too soon after they are crumbed.

Breading

BREW

To cook or steep in hot liquid until the flavour is extracted, as with tea.

BRINE

A solution of salt to which other preservatives may be added; used for preserving meats, vegetables, etc.

BRITTLE

A test used in sugar cookery; it has the same meaning as crack; also a very hard, brittle sweet, as peanut brittle.

BROTH

Soup, obtained by simmering meat, poultry, game, fish, or shellfish, in water, generally with the addition of vegetables or herbs, then removing fat and straining. Sometimes rice and vegetables are added to the strained broth.

BROWN

To make food brown either by cooking it in a small amount of fat on top of the cooker or by exposing it to dry heat in the oven.

BRUSH

To spread with butter or margarine, egg, etc., thinly with a brush or small piece of paper or cloth.

BURNT SUGAR

See **Caramel**.

BUTTERSCOTCH

A term applied to various foods flavoured with a large proportion of brown sugar and butter.

CANDY

To cook in sugar or syrup when applied to sweet potatoes and carrots. When applied to fruit, fruit peel, or ginger, to cook in heavy syrup until plump and transparent, then drain and dry.

CARAMEL

Burnt sugar, made by slowly melting the sugar and heating it until it is golden brown—a process called caramelizing. The browning of the sugar produces a distinctive flavour. When cooked until all its sweetness has disappeared, caramel is used to colour brown sauces. The term caramel also means a chewy sweet made from sugar, milk or cream, and golden syrup.

TO CARAMELIZE SUGAR

Rub a heavy frying pan lightly with butter. Pour in sugar, not more than 4 ounces at a time, and set frying pan over moderate heat. Stir constantly until the sugar melts. Add more sugar, 4 ounces at a time, and stir as before until you have as much clear brown syrup as desired.

CARAMEL SYRUP

Caramelize 8 ounces sugar as above, and add 4 fluid ounces boiling water very slowly so that the mixture will not boil over. Simmer 10 minutes.

CARAMEL COLOURING FOR GRAVIES

Caramelize sugar and continue cooking it until it is almost black. Then add boiling water very slowly and let simmer until the sugar dissolves. Store in a covered container and use as needed to colour gravy. No sweet flavour remains.

CASING

A covering into which sausage meat is packed. Formerly cleaned animal intestine was always used; nowadays various synthetic substitutes are common.

CHILL

To allow to become thoroughly cold but not frozen.

CHOP (The food)

A small cut of meat, usually from the rib or loin; the name is derived from the fact that the piece is chopped off.

CHOP (The cooking term)

To cut food into smaller pieces with a scissors, a knife and cutting board, chopping knife and bowl, or some type of mechanical cutter. When a large knife and cutting board are used, one hand holds the knife tip on board; the other moves blade up and down through food. For a quick job, cut a whole bunch of celery, onions, or rhubarb at one time.

Chop—A heavy knife and hardwood board do a quick chopping job.

CHOWDER

A thick unstrained soup, especially one made of fish, clams, etc., cooked with vegetables, often in milk.

CLARIFY

To clear a liquid, such as consommé, by adding slightly beaten egg white and egg shells. The beaten egg coagulates in the hot liquid and the particles which cause cloudiness adhere to it. The mixture is then strained.

CLOVE

A segment of a bulb, as of garlic. Also the name of a herb.

COAT

To cover the surface with fine crumbs, batter, or seasoned flour, sugar, etc. To do this, use dredger or sifter to sprinkle with flour, sugar, etc. Or roll in these until coated. Or shake with flour, breadcrumbs, etc., in paper bag until coated.

COAT SPOON

A term used with reference to mixtures, such as custards, that thicken when cooked. It indicates the point at which a thin, even film adheres to a spoon that is dipped into the mixture and then allowed to drip.

CODDLE

To cook gently, as an egg, by heating in water just below boiling point.

COLANDER

A bowl-shaped, footed sieve or perforated container for draining liquids.

COMPOTE

A mixture of stewed fruit, often dried, but whole or halved with special attention given to retaining their shape.

Compote

CONDIMENT

A seasoning or relish for food, as pepper, mustard, sauces, etc.

CONFECTIONERY

A synonym for sweetmeats, but it is often used to include a wide range of sweet foods.

CONNECTIVE TISSUE

A tissue in meats, usually of white elastic fibre that binds together and supports outside tissue.

CONSOMMÉ

A clear, concentrated stock or broth usually made from a combination of two or more kinds of meat, such as beef, veal, and poultry plus some vegetables for seasoning. It is well seasoned, strained, and clarified.

For many purposes, a quick substitute is 1 chicken bouillon cube dissolved in 8 fluid ounces hot water.

CORN

To preserve or pickle in brine, as in corned beef.

CORNUCOPIAS

Cone-shaped paper containers for nuts, sweets, etc.; pastry rolls filled with whipped cream or meringue with nuts; cone-shaped slices of bread, meats, fish, etc., with various fillings served as hors d'oeuvres.

CRACKLING

The crisp, crunchy morsels left after rendering pork or poultry fat. In earlier days, when families butchered their own pigs, it was much used in corn bread and for nibbling.

CREAM (The cookery term)

To cream means to rub, stir, or beat with spoon or electric mixer until the mixture is soft, smooth and creamy.

If you use a spoon, a wooden one is preferred, and you cream with the back of the spoon, working or pressing one ingredient or more against the side of the bowl continuously until soft and creamy.

If you use an electric mixer, set the speed at low.

The word "cream" is often used instead of "blend" in instructions for combining a fat with sugar.

CREOLE

(French): Pertaining to the Creoles. The Creoles in the United States are descendants of French or Spanish settlers of Louisiana.

The term is applied to soups, garnishes, sauces, etc., prepared in a manner characteristic of the Creoles. Tomatoes, peppers, okra, onions, filé powder and other seasonings are usually characteristic of these dishes.

CRISP

To make firm or brittle in cold water, as vegetables, or in moderate dry heat, as bread.

CROQUETTE

A term derived from the French croquer, to crunch. It is usually a small, rounded or cone-shaped mass of chopped meat, fish, or vegetables, fried or baked to obtain a crisp coat.

Hints for Making Croquettes

Although croquettes are sometimes made with freshly cooked ingredients (finely chopped or minced chicken, oysters, meat, lobster, etc.) more frequently they are a means of utilizing leftover food. Specific directions are given with various croquette recipes throughout this book.

In general, however, to make croquettes prepare thick white sauce (see index) and combine with cooked chicken, meat, fish, or vegetables. Use 6 to 8 fluid ounces thick white sauce to 1 pound minced or finely chopped solids. The solids should always be very well drained, not watery. Add just enough of the sauce to the solid ingredients so that they are well bound but still of a rather stiff consistency. The amount of sauce used with the solids may vary provided that after chilling the mixture can be handled easily.

Spread the combined mixture in a greased pan and chill thoroughly in the refrigerator. If desired, the top may be brushed lightly with butter to avoid forming a crust. When well chilled, form into desired shapes.

To egg and crumb: Beat an egg just enough to blend evenly, and stir in 2 tablespoons water. Coat the prepared food thoroughly with fine dry bread or cream cracker crumbs. Then dip in the egg mixture carefully covering the entire surface. Roll again in crumbs. Set on a rack or piece of greaseproof paper. If convenient, it's better to prepare these an hour before frying so that you have time to chill them. The coating is less likely to slip off during frying.

CROUTONS

Small cubes of toasted or fried bread often used as garnish for soups or salads.

To prepare croutons: Butter bread slices (add a bit of garlic if desired). Toast in a little hot fat in frying pan or in slow oven (300°F. Mark 2). Trim, then cut into small squares.

Or cut bread slices into ½-inch squares; toss in melted butter or margarine. Toast under grill.

Croutons

CRYSTALLIZED

Candied. See **Candy.**

CUBE

To cube is just what it sounds like — to cut a solid into little cubes anywhere from ½ to 1 inch. Use a very sharp knife and a cutting board. Special cubing gadgets are sold. To dice is exactly the same process but the cubes are made smaller — less than ½ inch.

CURE

To preserve by salting, smoking, pickling, or other means.

CUSTARD

A mixture of milk and eggs, cooked until it thickens. Sweetened and flavoured custards, often baked, make up a large class of desserts. Whatever the method, a custard must always be cooked at a low-to-moderate temperature or it will curdle. Those cooked on top of the heat must be stirred constantly.

CUT IN

To "cut in" means to mix fat with dry ingredients by using a pastry blender, two knives, or a fork. This is the method that cuts a solid fat into fine particles and mixes them with dry ingredients. It's the initial step, and an important one, when you're making biscuits or pastry.

Cutting In

CUTLET

A small slice of meat from the ribs or leg, for frying or grilling, often served breaded. Also a small, flat croquette of chopped meat, fish, etc.

CUTTING TERMINOLOGY

See **Chop; Cube; Dice; Flake; Grate; Grind; Julienne; Mince; Shred; Sliver.**

Cut food with scissors when you need small pieces.

DECANT

To pour off a liquid gently without stirring up the sediment.

DEEP FRY

See **Fry.**

DEGLAZE

A term that describes the incorporation in the cooking liquid of the flavourful cooking juices and tidbits that remain in the roasting pan or frying pan after meat or poultry has been roasted or browned. To do this, first the pan is degreased (excess fat is removed), then a small amount of liquid required in the recipe is added to the pan. The mixture is returned to the heat, simmered and stirred while scraping in the coagulated cooking juices. It is then blended with the remaining ingredients. This is an important step in the preparation of meat sauces and gravies because in that way some of the flavour of the meat or poultry is incorporated in the sauce.

DEGREASE

To remove excess fat from the surface of hot liquids such as sauces, soups, stocks; from stews, from a roasting pan, or a pan in which meats or poultry have been browned.

DEVILLED

Highly seasoned food. Usually refers to food seasoned to make it hot, as with mustard, red pepper, Tabasco sauce, and the like.

DICE

To cut into very small cubes of less than ½ inch. Use a very sharp knife and cutting board.

DOT

To scatter small particles, usually butter, over food.

DOUBLE SAUCEPAN OR BOILER

Fill bottom part of double saucepan with about 2 inches water; bring to the boil. Put double saucepan top, containing food, in place. Then cook over hot or boiling water as directed in recipe.

DOUGH

A mixture of flour, liquid, etc., worked into a soft thick mass too stiff to stir; it must, therefore, be kneaded, cut with a knife, or rolled. Doughs may be either soft or stiff, depending upon the amount of flour used. A soft dough is sticky, while a stiff dough is firm to the touch.

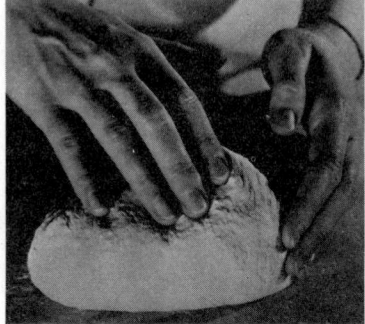

A cook soon learns from experience the "feel" of a pouring batter, a soft dough, and a stiff dough.

DRAIN

See in entry for **Strain.**

DREDGE

To sprinkle or coat food with flour, fine crumbs, cereal, or other fine substance. Dredging is very often a preliminary step to frying.

DRESS

To prepare for cooking, as by cleaning or trimming.

DRESSING

A sauce added to salads and other dishes.

DRIPPING

This may refer to the combined fat and juices that drip from meat or poultry while roasting (used for gravy ordinarily), or to just the fats rendered in the process of cooking fat meats such as bacon, salt pork, etc.

DRY

When applied to a beverage, usually wine, this term means low in sugar. Though the opposite of sweet, it never implies sourness.

DRY HEAT

A term applied to roasting, grilling, or pan-grilling. As the name implies, it is a method of cooking in which no water is used. Only tender cuts of meat should be cooked in this manner.

DRY INGREDIENTS

When used in recipe instructions, this term refers to flour, baking powder, bicarbonate of soda, salt and spices.

DUMPLINGS

These may be small pieces of dough, ball-shaped bits of batter or other foods steamed or boiled and served with meat or soup. When served with soups, meat stews, or as the main dish for luncheon, dumplings are usually cooked by steaming on top of the meat and vegetables in a tightly closed saucepan. When used as a dessert, dumplings are crusts of dough filled or combined with fruit, and they may be steamed, boiled, or baked.

DUST

To cover lightly with a sprinkling of flour, sugar, or some other powder.

DUTCH OVEN

A deep, heavy casserole with a close-fitting lid. It is sometimes equipped with a trivet or rack, and may be with or without a bail or side handles. It is used for stewing meats or cooking food that requires time and low heat. Any iron casserole with a close-fitting lid can be used as a Dutch oven.

Dutch Oven

DUXELLES

A French term for a flavouring used in preparing brown sauces and gravies consisting of finely chopped fresh mushrooms sautéed in butter with shallots or onions and seasoned with chopped parsley, salt, and sometimes various herbs. Duxelles may be prepared in advance, stored in the refrigerator, and used not only in brown sauces and gravies but also may be used as a basis for soup or added to stews, stuffings, and vegetables, or wherever a mushroom flavour is wanted. Some cooks like to add a bit of Madeira wine or brandy for additional flavouring. It is named after a famous French gourmet, the Marquis d'Uxelles, and the word is often spelled in this fashion.

How to Prepare Duxelles: Chop ½ pound mushrooms very fine or, if you are using the tops in another way, chop the stems only. Cook 1 ounce chopped onion in 2 tablespoons butter until golden. Add the mushrooms and sauté until the moisture is absorbed. Season delicately to taste with nutmeg and other herbs as desired, and salt and pepper.

ESCALLOP

See **Scallop**.

FELL

A thin paper-like covering over the outside of the lamb carcass. It does not affect the flavour unless the lamb has been hung for some time, and it may be left on or removed from roasts. Normally, it should not be removed from the leg, since this cut keeps its shape better and is juicier if it is left on. Chops, however, are better without it.

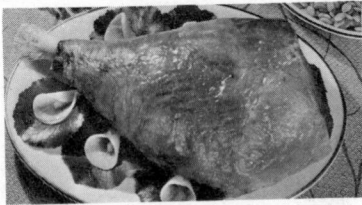

The fell keeps the roast leg of lamb in shape.

FILET

See **Fillet**. Filet mignon: a very small round cut of fillet of beef, which is grilled or sautéed.

FILLET

A boneless lean piece of meat or fish. The French spelling filet and the corresponding pronunciation are often used—though never by fishmongers. With animals, the term always refers to the cut from the loin or under-cut from the loin. With poultry and game birds, it is applied to the meat cut from the breast.

FLAKE

To break or pull apart a food like cooked or canned fish or chicken that divides naturally. All you do is follow these divisions, pulling at them gently with one or two forks. Or if you prefer, you can flake with your fingers.

FLORENTINE

In cookery this term usually denotes a dish prepared with spinach, as eggs Florentine, poached eggs served on a bed of spinach and dressed with a cream or cheese sauce.

FLOUR (The recipe term)

To coat food or tins with a thin film of flour. "Dust with flour" refers to this coating of cake tins, and to meats before browning.

FLUTE

To make rounded indentations, as around the edge of a pie crust.

FOLD IN

To combine ingredients with a large spoon, a whisk, fork, or spatula.

The folding-in motion goes gently down, across, up and over, that is, you cut down through the mixture, the tool slides across the bottom of the bowl, and you bring it up and over the top close to the surface.

The advantage of this easy action is that you prevent the loss of air when you are adding ingredients to a delicate food or mixture, or you are putting light ingredients like whipped cream or egg whites into heavier ones.

FORCEMEAT

Also called stuffing or dressing; a mixture of minced meat and seasonings used as a stuffing.

FORCING BAG

A cone-shaped bag of firm textile material into which metal pipes of different shapes and sizes may be fitted at the small end.

FORK-TENDER

Softened by cooking until fork pierces easily.

FORM INTO A BALL

This is a step that's important in pastry. Pick up dough with both hands and press (don't pat) firmly together. Turn as you press until you have a ball-shaped mass that holds together with no crumbs.

FOWL

A general term for any of the larger birds used as food, such as chicken, duck, or goose. In modern recipes it is being replaced by the specific name of the bird called for. Nowadays, if it is still used, it means a full-grown older hen used for stewing, as distinguished from a grilling or a frying bird.

FRENCHED

A term referring to cutlets or roasts from which some of the fat has been removed to expose the end of the bone.

FRICASSÉE

When applied to the dish itself, fricassée usually refers to poultry, veal, or lamb, cut up, stewed, and served in a sauce of its own gravy.

To fricassée is to prepare meat by this method. See **Stew or Fricassée.**

FRIZZLE

To cook in a small amount of fat until the edges are crisp and curled; a term often applied to dried beef.

FRY

Fry means to cook in hot fat or oil in a pan over direct heat; however we must make a distinction among the several methods of frying.

Pan-Fry: (Also called sauté.) This means to brown food lightly in a little hot cooking fat or oil. It is often the first step in braising or stewing. It provides the brown basis you need for most gravies.

Shallow-Fat Frying: This means to cook food in a medium amount of cooking fat or oil, about enough to half cover the food. Frying this way in semi-deep fat is sometimes used for foods like fritters, and for chicken when you want it a deep crisp brown but don't want to make gravy.

Deep Frying: This means to cook foods in a lot of hot cooking fat or oil, enough to more than cover them. Deep frying is the method used for such foods as potatoes, doughnuts, and most batter-coated foods.

Deep Fryer: An uncovered cooking utensil with a perforated, meshed, or sieve-like insert basket with one handle; also an electric deep fat fryer.

HINTS FOR DEEP FRYING

The selection of fat and the care given it is important in deep fat frying. Cooking fats, ground-nut oil and cereal and vegetable oils are used for deep frying since they can be heated to a high temperature without smoking or burning.

If particles of flour or crumbs remain in the fat it will smoke at a lower temperature than normal. The absorption of fat in the fried food increases as the smoking point is lowered. It is therefore important to avoid heating fat to the smoking point, and to clarify fat after it has been used.

To reclaim fat, cooked sliced raw potatoes in it to absorb flavours and strain through a cheesecloth or fine sieve to remove any particles.

A deep heavy saucepan is best to use. A frying basket is convenient to lower the food into the fat and lift it out. A slotted spoon may be used.

A thermometer is an aid although the bread cube test is practical for temperature determinations.

Drop a 1-inch cube of stale bread into the hot fat. If bread browns in 60 to 70 seconds the temperature is satisfactory for uncooked mixtures (360°-370°F.); if it browns in 40 to 50 seconds, it is right for cooked mixtures (375°-385°F.); and if it browns in 20 to 30 seconds, it is hot enough for most cold foods (380°-390°F.).

For automatically controlled heat use an electric fryer.

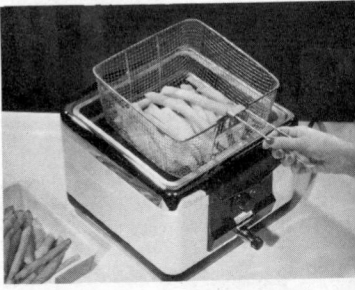

DEEP FRYING TIME-TABLE

FRIED FOODS	TEMPERATURE	MINUTES
Croquettes of cooked food	375°-385°F.	2-4
of uncooked food	370°F.	5-6
Doughnuts	370°-380°F.	2-3
Fritters	365°-375°F.	2-5
Chipped potatoes	370°F.	5-7
then	390°F.	1-1½
Vegetable rings	365°-375°F.	2-5
Oysters	375°F.	1-2
Small fish	375°-385°F.	2-5
Prawns	375°F.	2-5

DEEP FRYING PROCEDURE

Fill heavy saucepan about ⅔ full of melted fat. Heat to desired temperature. Drain food on absorbent paper and lower gently into the hot fat, a few pieces at a time.

Do not fry too much at one time because the temperature of the fat may be lowered too greatly, which would increase the cooking time and also cause the food to absorb more fat.

As soon as food rises to surface of the fat, turn it several times for even browning.

Do not crowd the pieces. When golden brown, lift food out with wire basket or slotted spoon, allowing fat to drain over the saucepan.

Transfer to pan lined with absorbent paper so that excess fat will be absorbed.

The length of time required for frying depends upon the kind of food, size of pieces, and temperature of the fat.

Fat which is reclaimed each time after using may be used over and over again. Keep fat in a cool place away from light. When fat smokes it has been overheated and changed, and is no longer as good for deep frying.

Hints for Batter-Coated Fried Foods

In deep frying, some batters may have a tendency to peel off. To avoid this, check these hints:
● If batter is too thick, add more liquid.
● If batter is too thin, add more flour.
● If batter is too rich in fat, reduce amount of fat in batter.
● Check temperature of fat; if too low, increase temperature.
● Add less food at a time to deep fat; too much food added at one time reduces temperature too quickly.

GARNISH

To decorate or ornament food, usually with something edible.

GIRDLE

A heavy, flat metal plate or pan for cooking pancakes, etc.

GLACÉ

(French): 1. Having a smooth, glossy surface; 2. Covered with icing or sugar, as candied fruits; 3. Frozen or iced. See **Glaze.**

GLAZE

(1) To coat with a thin sugar syrup cooked to crack stage. (2) To give vegetables a brown coating (glazed vegetables) produced by cooking in sugar and fat. (3) To coat meats with a sauce made from brown stock evaporated until thick.

GRATE

To rub on a grater so as to tear off coarse-to-fine particles of food. The degrees of fineness in grating vary from coarse shreds of cheese to powder-fine nutmeg. You can use either one of the hand graters or get a mechanical gadget to do your grating for you.

GRATIN

A French term for the thin crust that forms on the surface of certain foods when they are browned in the oven or under the grill; hence, any of a number of creamed dishes sprinkled with a topping of crumbs and butter or cheese and browned. Au gratin: having such a crust.

GRAVY

The juice given off by meat in cooking; a sauce made from the fat or stock in which meat has been cooked.

GRAVY BOAT

A dish for serving gravy; so called from its shape.

GREASE

To rub a thin film of cooking fat or oil over surface of frying pan, cake tin, girdle, etc., before it is used.

GRILL

To cook by exposing to direct heat usually under a grill, or over coals. The recommended method is to use constant moderate temperatures.

Also refers to the framework of metal wires or bars used to grill food.

GRISTLE

A cartilage; an elastic but very tough tissue, like soft bone.

HARD-BOILED

Used of eggs, although this is a bad term, because the proper way to cook them is in water just below boiling point.

HASH

A chopped mixture of cooked meat and vegetables, usually baked or pan-fried. Also, to chop meat and vegetables into small pieces for cooking.

INFUSION

A method of extracting flavour from a substance by pouring hot liquid over it and allowing it to stand; also, the resulting flavoured liquid. Tea and coconut milk are infusions.

JELL

To become or cause to become jelly.

JULIENNE

(French): Match-like strips of meat, vegetables or cheese; also, a clear soup with such vegetables; named after the French chef Jean Julien, who liked to garnish his clear soup with vegetable strips.

KETTLE

A covered or uncovered metal cooking utensil with a bail handle. The capacity is stated in liquid measurement.

KNEAD

Kneading is a process of mixing, in the home usually done by hand. You knead to ensure complete mixing, to make some doughs or mixtures smooth and elastic.

To knead yeast dough, shape it first into a ball. Then, using both hands press down with the heels of palms and push dough away from you. Do this twice with quick, even pressure. Give dough a quarter turn and repeat the pushing process. Keep turning and pushing until dough is smooth and satiny.

In sweet-making, the mixture is worked into a mass, then pushed and pressed the same way until it's smooth and combined.

LARD

A term not only used to describe the rendered fat of the pig, but also to indicate the process of inserting strips of fat (salt pork, for example) through lean meat with what is known as a larding needle. These strips are called lardoons. It also refers to the placing of fat on top of uncooked lean meat or fish for flavour, or to prevent dryness.

A more correct term for the latter is bard.

LEAVE, OR ALLOW, TO RISE

This applies to yeast dough. Put dough in a warm place (about 85°F.) so yeast can "grow" and cause dough to expand and get "light." It has risen enough if the dent remains when you press the surface lightly with your fingers.

LIAISON

(French): The process of thickening; a term applied to soups and sauces. The usual agents for producing a liaison are flour, cornflour, cold butter, egg yolks, and cream, sometimes combined.

MACERATE

To marinate (which see); a term applied to fruits in a syrup or alcoholic liquid.

MARBLING (in meats)

A term used to describe the fat intermingled in the lean of meat. It gives the meat a mottled or streaked appearance. It is not to be confused with the white connective tissue which replaces it when the animal grows past the peak-of-flavour age. Marbling is a definite mark of fine-quality meat.

MARINADE

A liquid in which food is steeped for added flavour and tenderness. It usually includes oil, an acid (wine, vinegar, or lemon juice), and spices and herbs.

MARINATE

To let stand in a marinade (which see). The length of time depends on the food in question.

MARROW

The soft, fatty tissue that fills the cavities of long bones. It is very tasty by itself and is also used in sauces, as a garnish, and in dumplings for soup.

MASK

To cover completely; usually applied to the use of mayonnaise or other thick sauce but may refer to jam.

MATIGNON

A French term for preparation of seasoned chopped vegetables sometimes spread over or under meat or poultry being braised or pot-roasted to flavour them during cooking. It is similar to mirepoix (which see). The term mirepoix is applied when the vegetables are coarsely diced, matignon when the vegetables are finely chopped.

MEAT EXTRACT PASTE

Extract of meat, concentrated to a paste, with seasoning added.

MEAT GLAZE

Stock boiled down to jelly stage. Commercial products are available.

MEAT JUICE

The liquid contained in the meat fibres. It is expressed from slightly heated meat. It is high in flavour and contains some food value.

MEAT TENDERIZERS

These are commercial preparations containing papain, the dried juice of the papaya (a melon-like fruit). This substance, which is harmless to the human digestive system, tenderizes meats by the action of the enzymes it contains.

They should be used in accordance with directions on the labels to improve the tenderness and palatability of less-tender cuts of meat such as chuck steaks or shoulder chops. Such relatively inexpensive cuts of meat are as nutritious as the more expensive cuts and often just as flavourful. The meat tenderizers are well worth trying on them.

MELTED FAT

Fat heated in small saucepan over low heat until melted. Cooking oil may be used in recipes that call for melted fat.

MEUNIÈRE

(French): A method of cooking fish. The fish is sautéed in butter, then this or other browned butter is poured over it, and it is sprinkled with a little lemon juice and with chopped parsley.

MINCE

To reduce to particles by cutting, crushing, or mincing. Food mincers have two or more blades. Use a blade with smaller holes to mince foods finely; one with larger holes for coarser chopping, as of meat for a juicy meat loaf.

MIREPOIX

A French term for a mixture of vegetables (diced carrots, onions, and celery) and herbs which can be made with or without meat (diced bacon, ham, or salt pork) and used as a layer over or under meat, poultry, or shellfish dishes to give flavour to the dishes. It is often used with meat or poultry being braised or pot-roasted. Mirepoix may be used in making soups, stews, and sauces, especially the brown sauces.

To Make Mirepoix: Dice 1 or 2 small carrots, 1 onion, about 2 ounces celery heart, 1 tablespoon chopped bacon, ham, or salt pork, and add ½ crushed bay leaf and a sprig of thyme. These may be used raw as a base under the meat. Or heat 1 tablespoon butter in heavy frying pan and sauté these ingredients until vegetables are soft, and use on top of meat as a seasoning. If desired, rinse the frying pan with a bit of Madeira or sherry and pour over the mirepoix.

MIXED GRILL

A dish of several grilled foods served together; the composition varies.

MOIST HEAT

A method of cooking less tender meat by the application of steam or the addition of liquid.

MULL

To heat, sweeten, and flavour with spices; a term used for beverages such as cider, wine, and beer.

Mixing Terms You Should Know

To mix means to combine ingredients, usually by stirring. A good cook, however, knows that mixing or combining casually may mean many a cooking failure; foods just can't be thrown together just any old way.

When you come right down to it, cooking is putting ingredients together, fusing them into one and a number of words are used in recipes for ways to mix and combine.

The cook striving for perfection should see the following:

Stir; Cream; Blend; Fold In; Cut In; Toss; Beat; and Whip.

In the first six of these methods, mixing or combining is the one and only purpose; in the other two methods, beat and whip, one thing more is done—air is incorporated.

ONION JUICE

Juice scraped with teaspoon from centre of halved onion.

PAN-GRILL

To cook uncovered over direct heat on a hot surface, such as a frying pan or girdle. Use no fat at all or very little —just enough to keep food from sticking to surface. Fat is poured off as it accumulates.

PAN-FRY

See **Fry.**

PARBOIL

To cook food in a boiling liquid until partially done. This is usually a preliminary step to further cooking. Beans and ham, for instance, are parboiled, later baked.

PARCH

To cook in dry heat until the outside is dry and sometimes slightly browned.

PASTE

(1) Dough; specifically a term applied either to certain pastry doughs containing a high proportion of fat or to the

shaped and dried doughs usually called pasta or macaroni products. (2) A creamy-textured food made by mincing or pounding, such as almond or meat paste. (3) A jelly-like candy.

PASTEURIZE

To preserve food by heating sufficiently to destroy certain microorganisms and arrest fermentation. Generally applied to liquids, such as milk and fruit juices. The temperature varies with the food but commonly ranges from 140° to 180°F.

PASTRY

Any dough made with fat and used for the crust of tarts or pies. Sometimes, by extension, fancy breads or cakes as well.

PASTRY BLENDER

This is a hand-gadget for cutting fat into flour for pastry. It consists

Pastry Patty Shell

of several wires looped to a handle. It is used with a chopping motion. See **Cutting In.**

PASTRY JAGGER OR WHEEL

A metal wheel used to make a fancy edge on a pie or other form of pastry.

PATTY

A pastry case filled with a creamed mixture of food. The term is also used for a small, flat cake of minced meat, fish, etc., usually fried.

PEEL

The outer covering of a fruit or vegetable; also, to remove this covering.

PICKLE

To preserve or flavour by steeping in brine or vinegar, often with spices. Also any food so preserved.

PLANK

A specially made board, usually of kiln-dried oak, on which meat or fish is sometimes grilled and served; also to prepare and serve food on such a board, usually with an elaborate garnish of vegetables, often inside a deco-

rative border of mashed potatoes or other puréed vegetables. The planks often have a tree design cut down their length to drain juices into a shallow depression toward the end.

If all the cooking is done on the plank, it will char rapidly. Steaks are therefore usually grilled on an oven grill fully on one side and partially on the other before being placed on the plank.

New planks should be seasoned by brushing with oil and placing in a

Planked Whole Fish

very slow oven (225°F. Mark ¼) for at least one hour. To protect it while cooking, oil well any exposed part or cover with a decoration of mashed potatoes.

POACH

To cook covered by liquid at or below simmering (not boiling) using precautions to retain shape. Eggs cooked in a so-called poacher over hot water are actually steamed, not poached.

POTPIE (OR HOT POT)

A stew of meat or poultry, usually with potatoes and other vegetables, baked in a casserole with a topping of pastry or suet crust. Also, sometimes, a meat stew with dumplings.

Potpies

POT ROAST

Any large cut of beef, or occasionally other meat, that is cooked by braising. Examples are chuck, brisket, and topside, all of which tend to be tough unless cooked with moist heat. See **Braise.**

POUNDING

A method of making meat more tender or thinner. A meat hammer, the

edge of a heavy saucer, or a wooden potato masher may be used to break down the connective tissues.

PRECOOK

To cook partially in a liquid below the boiling point, before preparing in final form.

PRE-HEAT OVEN

To bring the oven to the desired temperature before putting in the food. Almost all oven-cooked dishes require the pre-heating of the oven.

PULLED BREAD

Fresh unsliced bread, with the crust removed, that is torn or pulled into pieces and toasted in the oven.

PUNGENT

A term implying agreeably sharp or acrid, when applied to taste or smell.

PURÉE

(French): A creamy pulp made by cooking solid food until it is soft and then putting it through a sieve, a colander, or a vegetable mill or crushing it in a mortar or an electric blender; a term also applied to a soup thickened with such a pulp. Also, to make into a purée.

RAMEKIN

Also spelled ramequin; an individual baking dish; also, any food baked in such a dish.

REDUCE

To decrease the quantity of a liquid by continuing cooking, thus concentrating its flavour and sometimes thickening it. A concentrated sauce or stock is made this way, the final product often being a half or a third, etc., of the original quantity. Naturally, reducing applies only to sauces without or before the addition of egg. Those sauces which have a flour base have to be watched carefully and stirred frequently to avoid scorching.

RELISH

A highly flavoured food, such as pickles, olives, or chutney, served as a condiment or to stimulate the appetite.

RENDER

To melt fat trimmed from meats and poultry by heating it slowly at a low temperature, in order to obtain only the portion that will liquefy.

RICE

To press potatoes or other food through a container perforated in such a way that the food emerges in rice-like particles.

RIND

A hard or firm outer layer or coating, as the rind of citrus fruits (lemons, oranges, etc.), of cheese, of a side of bacon, and the like.

ROAST

To cook by dry heat in the oven; also, to cook over or in coals. The method is the same as the one called baking, but the two terms are usually applied to different foods. The word roast originally meant to cook by direct exposure to an open fire and is still used for foods that were prepared in that way, such as meats and poultry; the word bake has always meant to cook in the oven and is used for the same old oven-cooked foods, such as bread and pastry. An unsolved mystery, however, is why ham and fish and spare-ribs are said to be baked while chestnuts are described as being roasted.

ROASTER

A special tin, oven, or apparatus for roasting meat. Tins especially designed for roasting, with or without covers or racks, are made in various sizes designated by the weight of the poultry they will hold. The term is also applied to a young chicken or other animal suitable for roasting, especially whole.

ROLLING BOIL

See **Boil.**

ROLL OUT

Doughs for pastry, breads, or biscuits are rolled out.

For a pastry circle, flatten out a ball of dough to about ½ to 1-inch thick. Then roll with a rolling pin in a press-and-spread motion from centre to edge, pressing less near the edge. Continue rolling from centre to edge as though following spokes in a wheel, until the dough reaches proper thickness.

ROUX

(French): A mixture of fat and flour to which liquid is added to make gravy or sauce. It is the commonest way to thicken a sauce; butter is the preferred fat. The roux may be blanc (white), blond (golden), or brun (brown). The longer it is cooked, the darker it will be and as a result the darker the sauce in which it is used.

To make a roux, melt the butter and blend in the flour, then cook them together over very low heat, stirring constantly. It may be made in advance and stored in the refrigerator, then reheated in the top of a double boiler.

SALT (The cookery term)

To add salt, or to rub with salt. Also to cure or season with salt.

SAUTÉ

To pan-fry. See **Fry.**

SCALD

To heat (milk or other liquid) to just below boiling point; tiny bubbles will appear at the edge of the pan. The term is also used in the same sense as blanch (which see).

SCALLOP

The shell of the scallop or a similarly shaped baking dish. Hence, also, to bake in a style suitable for such a container, usually in a sauce or other liquid and very often with crumbs; actually, a casserole is most commonly used for the purpose. Sweet corn, potatoes, tomatoes, and oysters are frequently scalloped.

SCORE

To cut narrow grooves or gashes part way through the outer surface of food. For example, solid fat like the top of ham is scored to release melting fat and to decorate; tough meats like stewing steaks are scored to make them tender.

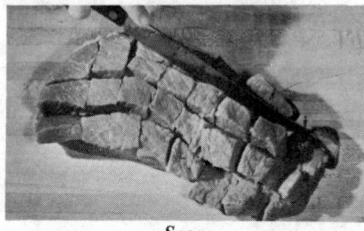

Score

SCRAMBLE

To prepare eggs or mixture containing eggs by stirring while cooking until mixture sets.

SEAR

To cook at a very high temperature for a short time in order to quickly form a brown crust on the outer surface of meat. This method increases shrinkage, but develops flavour, improves appearance.

SHRED

To cut or tear into small, long narrow pieces. The fineness varies—recipes will often say that foods should be "finely" or "coarsely" shredded. A knife may be used or a hand or mechanical shredder. Crisp vegetables, like cabbage may be cut to shreds with a sharp knife on a cutting board.

Shred—make an easy job of shredding with a razor-sharp cutter.

SHUCK

A shuck is the shell of such shellfis as oysters and clams. Recipes will some times call for "shucked" oysters o clams, meaning shellfish which hav been removed from their shells.

The term shuck is also applied the outer husk of corn (maize).

SIFT

To put one or more dry ingredien like flour or sugar through a sifter o fine sieve to separate particles; to flu those that tend to pack; to mix severa kinds uniformly.

SIMMER

To cook gently in a liquid just belo boiling point at temperatures of 185 to 210°F. Adjust the heat to maintai this stage.

In simmering, the food cooks s slowly that the surface moves onl slightly; no bubbles show because the form slowly and collapse below th surface. See **Boil.**

SINGE (POULTRY)

Hold over flame to burn off feather

SKEWER

To fasten or hold food to keep it i position while it cooks, with metal o wooden pins (skewers).

"Skewer" may also mean assembling cooking, and serving kebab-style o skewers.

SKILLET

Originally a three-legged, long-hand led stewing pot to cook food in a fire place, sometimes called "spider" be cause of its resemblance to same.

Nowadays the word is sometime used for a frying pan.

SLIVER

To cut or split into long, thin strip with a knife on a cutting board. Fo example, the term is applied to al monds and to pimento pieces used fo decoration. See also **Julienne.**

SMOTHER

To cook in a covered dish or in close mass, as smothered onions; als to cover completely, as with a sauce o gravy.

SNIP

To cut into small pieces, as wit kitchen shears.

SPATULA

A wide, flat, flexible knife-like utensi used for spreading creamy mixtures o for lifting solid foods. Also, a similarly shaped implement of wood or rubbe used for folding or stirring.

SPIT

A thin, pointed rod or bar on which food is placed and held to be grilled or roasted over a fire.

SPONGE

A very light sweet cake made with flour, milk, eggs, and sugar.

SPRING-FORM TIN

A cake tin with removable sides held in place by a clamp.

STEAM

To cook by steam in a closed container. Dumplings and puddings are examples. Or you can cook by steam under pressure in less time by using a special pressure saucepan.

STEAM-BAKE

To cook in the oven in a pan set over a container of hot water.

STEAM COOKER

A covered saucepan or sauce pot having one or more perforated insert pans equipped with a handle or handles.

STEEP

To let a food stand in hot liquid, below boiling, to extract flavour, colour, or both, as in tea.

STERILIZE

To free from living micro-organisms by application of intense heat.

STEW OR FRICASSÉE

To stew or fricassée means to simmer or cook food slowly in a small amount of liquid in a covered pan. The meat may or may not be browned first. "Stew" usually means meat; "fricassée" most often refers to chicken. Whatever the method is called, it is a fine way to cook tougher cuts of meat.

STIR

When a recipe tells you "to stir" without other specific instructions, it usually means to stir with a spoon, wielding it in a round-and-round motion that follows the outline of the bowl or pan you're using. Keep stirring until you get a smooth, uniform consistency, or according to the directions given in your recipe.

If you're stirring with an electric mixer, set it for slow or medium to get the equivalent speed.

Use a long-handled spoon for hot foods.

STIR-FRYING

A method used in Chinese cooking which results in the tender, crisp, and nicely coloured vegetables so typical of Chinese-style dishes. Traditionally, stir-frying is done in a big open conical pan called a *wok* held erect by a ring stand over very high heat. This method of cooking requires only 3 to 4 minutes of cooking time; however preparation time is the slow part since the vegetables must be carefully cut into uniform pieces.

A small amount of cooking oil, usually groundnut oil, is added to a pre-heated pan, then the vegetables are added one at a time. Those that require the longest cooking time go in first. The vegetables are stirred rapidly to make sure they are well coated with hot oil, then stirred constantly over high heat until just tender.

When making combination dishes of meat and vegetables, thin slivers of meat are cooked first, then removed and kept warm. The meat is added to the crisply tender vegetables just before serving.

Chinese Wok

STOCK

The richly flavoured liquid in which fish, meat, poultry, or vegetables have been cooked. Used in soups, sauces, and general cooking.

Stock Cube: See **Bouillon.**

STRAIN

To separate a liquid from solid pieces of food through a coarse sieve or colander. The term "drain" is used when the separation need not be exact.

To strain soup stock, pour it through a piece of cheesecloth fastened over a large bowl.

TART

This term means sharp in taste, sour, acid. In pastry-making, the term was originally used in Europe, and it referred to any open-faced fruit pie. As used nowadays in England it means any shallow open-faced pastry case with a filling usually of fruit or jam.

TENDERIZE

To make meat tender by pounding, marinating, or using a commercial product. See **Meat Tenderizer; Pounding; Marinate.**

THICKEN

See **Thickening Agents,** in Ingredients—How to Use Them.

TIMBALE

A highly flavoured mixture of meat, chicken, fish, shellfish, or vegetables baked with a creamy sauce in a mould.

Timbale

TIMBALE MOULD

Refers to any shape of mould in which delicate creamed mixtures are baked.

TOAST (The cookery term)

To brown by direct heat in a toaster, under a grill, or by using any other direct heat source.

Sometimes when recipes call for dried bread, you may be told to "toast" the bread in a slow oven.

TOSS

To mix ingredients lightly by tumbling them lightly with a lifting motion.

To prevent crushing and to do a thorough job, use two implements: two forks or a fork and a spoon.

The most usual use is mixing greens and other salad ingredients, coating them with dressing. "Tossed" now describes a salad on many menus.

TRIM

To cut away ragged or unsightly parts of food before or after cooking, to improve its appearance.

TRIVET

A short-legged metal stand for holding hot dishes on a table; also a similar type of metal stand used in a frying pan, casserole, roasting tin, or saucepan to prevent excessive cooking and scorching of food at the bottom. A trivet is sometimes used when meats are braised or simmered in liquids.

TRUSS

To tie meat or fowl with string or fasten it with metal or wooden pins (skewers) so it keeps its shape during cooking. Chicken, duck, and turkey, for example, are usually trussed before roasting.

TRUSSING NEEDLE

A special needle designed for trussing poultry. It is used to pass string through the bird's body.

TRY OUT

To render fat. An old term not much used any more.

TURK'S HEAD TIN

A round cake tin with spiral-shaped indentations in the walls, and a tube in the centre like an angel food tin.

UNMOULD

See **Gelatine**, in **Ingredients—How to Use Them.**

UNTIL DONE

The phrase "until done" is usually qualified in recipes to indicate precisely what it means in reference to the specific finished product: cake, pie, vegetable, etc. When the unqualified phrase is used, it means, for fish, cook until the flesh is whitely opaque and flakes readily; for meat, until the meat is quite tender and browned; for poultry, until it is so tender that the joints move easily; for vegetables, cook until just tender.

Cakes are done when they begin to shrink slightly from the sides of the pan, when the centre surface will spring back when lightly pressed with a finger, and when a wire tester or cocktail stick inserted into the centre comes out clean.

UNTIL SET

Until a liquid has become firm, usually applied to a gelatine mixture.

WHIP

To beat rapidly with a rotary beater, an electric mixer set on fast speed, or a wire whisk, to incorporate air and produce expansion.

You'll find the term used most often in instructions about egg whites, whipping cream, gelatine, and other foods like them that expand when whipped and become very light and frothy. Here, in other words, the introduction of air is the main idea; the mixing is only secondary.

WHISK

A device usually made of wire used to beat or stir liquids.

WHITE STOCK

A richly flavoured, light-coloured liquid in which poultry or white meats have been cooked.

ZESTS

Zests are fine gratings of the coloured outermost coatings of oranges, tangerines, limes, or lemons called for in many recipes. Use a small hand grater when grating these and avoid the inclusion of any of the white part beneath the coloured parts because the white is bitter. The outer coloured portions of the rinds provide a stronger flavour than the citrus juices because of a heavy concentration of oil in them. Some cooks like to grate coloured coatings coarsely and to squeeze them through a piece of cheesecloth onto sugar. They let the sugar stand at least 15 minutes before using it.

Buckwheat Flour: A meal or flour ground from buckwheat kernels. It is especially tasty in pancakes or waffles.

Rice Flour: A fine white flour ground from rice kernels. It is used in cookies and in some quick breads and cakes but has too little gluten to make satisfactory bread.

Rye Flour: A flour produced generally from the whole grain, from either winter or spring varieties. It is used in baking rye and pumpernickel breads and for rolls. Rye meal is simply coarsely ground whole rye flour.

Whole Wheat or Wholemeal Flour: This is made of the entire grain of wheat, including a large part of the bran; it may be finely or coarsely ground. The term is really a misnomer because usually part of the bran has been removed, and sometimes the wheat germ. It is used in bread, rolls and cookies.

Brown or Wheatmeal Flour: Usually contains 80-90% of the cleaned wheatgrain.

Seasoned Flour: Flour mixed with seasonings; commonly used proportions are 1 ounce flour to $\frac{3}{4}$ teaspoon salt plus $\frac{1}{4}$ teaspoon each of pepper and paprika.

Other Flours: Barley, corn, cottonseed, lima-bean, groundnut, and soy flours are available for special purposes. These as well as rye, buckwheat, rice, and potato flours are usually used in combination with wheat flour because, with the exception of rye, they lack gluten-forming proteins. Rye flour produces gluten of low elasticity. Bread and pastry flours are used principally by commercial bakers.

Ingredients—How to Use Them

FACTS ABOUT FLOURS AND MEALS

Flour is a product produced by grinding and sifting cleaned grain, especially wheat. Flour should be bought according to the purpose for which it is to be used and should be stored in a dry place.

Plain Flour: There are different qualities of plain white flour available. Top grade "Patent" flour gives the best cooking results. Strong flours with a high protein content produce recipes with a large volume and light open texture and should be used for recipes with yeast, puff and flaky pastries. Soft flour with lower protein content is better for biscuits, shortcrust pastry and cakes.

Self-Raising Flour: This is an all-purpose flour to which a leavening agent and salt have been added. Using it for home baking saves time, but recipes have to be changed to omit salt and baking powder called for in them. For best results, follow the manufacturer's directions.

Pre-sifted Flour: Flour to be used in batters and doughs should be sifted before measuring. Nowadays some flours have been sifted for you. We suggest you follow the directions on the containers of such flour.

Potato Flour: This is produced from potatoes that have been cooked, dried, and ground. Potato flour makes an especially desirable thickening agent. It cooks quickly and smoothly in a liquid and leaves no raw taste. Use $\frac{1}{2}$ the amount of flour called for in the recipe.

MEAL

Any edible grain, or the edible part of any grain, coarsely ground.

BRAN

The skin or husk of a cereal grain such as wheat, rye, oats, or corn, which is separated from the flour or meal by sifting or bolting.

CORN MEAL

A meal produced from white or yellow corn (maize), and ground to varying degrees from coarse to fine. It is particularly good for making corn breads, or as a cereal. The coarse ground variety is not normally available, but fine corn meal is now more widely obtainable in the form of white or yellow maize flour.

DURUM

A variety of hard wheat; flour made from it is used in macaroni and other pasta products.

FARINA

Strictly, meal made from any grain. In common usage, the term refers to a particular wheat cereal used as a breakfast food and for puddings. It is similar to but finer than semolina and is sometimes used instead of it.

GROATS

Hulled, or hulled and coarsely cracked grain, especially wheat or oats.

MAIZE FLOUR

See **Corn Meal (on p. 422)**

MILLET

Millet is a cereal grass with a small grain used for food in Europe and Asia. This plant has been cultivated from very ancient times.

OATMEAL

While this name does mean oats crushed into meal or flakes as well as rolled or ground oats, for the sake of clarity the term "oats" is used in recipes when uncooked rolled oats are called for. Oatmeal is used to refer to cooked oats.

SEMOLINA

Coarsely ground wheat, a by-product in the manufacture of fine flour. It is used in making pastas and in puddings and other dishes.

WHEAT GERM

The embryo of a grain of wheat; it is nutritionally rich and has a pleasant nut-like flavour and texture. Wheat germ may be sprinkled over breakfast cereals and other foods, or it may be added to meat loaf and especially to breads, pancakes, waffles, or muffins.

FACTS ABOUT BUTTER, MARGARINE, OILS, LARD, AND OTHER FATS

Butter: Butter is the solidified fat of milk, made by churning cream. Its average composition should be not less than 81·5% milk fat, 15·9% water, up to 2·5% salt and up to 2·0% milk protein and other residues. It is illegal to use preservatives or additives except salt, which is optional. There are two sorts of butter available: "sweet cream" is a mild-flavoured, firm and waxy-textured butter. "Lactic" butter has a full flavour and a very fine texture.

Unsalted or sweet butter: this is a "lactic" butter with a pleasing aroma and delicate sweet flavour preferred by some people for table use and in some sorts of cooking. It is made from "cream" butter with a saltier flavour It keeps longer than unsalted butter.

Salted butter: this is a "sweet cream" butter with a saltier flavour. It keeps longer than unsalted butter.

The following table gives the food values of one ounce of butter:

Calories	211
Protein	0·1g
Fat	23·4g
Calcium	4mg
Iron	Trace
Vitamin A	850 I.U.
Vitamin D	17 I.U.

To Store Butter

Store butter in the coldest part of the food compartment of your refrigerator in its original wrapper. Any portion which has been partially used should be kept in a covered dish to protect its delicate flavour. If your refrigerator has a special butter compartment, keep butter in it only for immediate use.

Homemade Whipped Butter

This whipped butter mixture is sometimes used by dieters. Soften 4 tablespoons gelatine in 1 pint milk and heat over hot water until dissolved.

Cut 1 pound butter in pieces and place in a bowl over hot water. Whip the gelatine mixture gradually into the butter. Season with salt to taste. If milk bubbles appear, continue beating until they disappear. Pour the butter into moulds and chill well before using.

SHAPING BUTTER FOR SERVING

Butter Pats: To cut neatly, cover knife blade with a fold of greaseproof paper or non-stick paper in which the butter has been wrapped. Dip a fork in hot water and draw scores across squares of butter diagonally. Garnish with small sprigs of parsley.

Butter Balls: Scald, then chill a pair of wooden butter paddles. Measure butter by teaspoonfuls for uniformity. Roll lightly between paddles to form a ball. To shape rolls, flatten balls into cylinders between paddles. Drop butter balls onto chilled plate, cracked ice, or into ice water.

Butter Curls: Use butter curler. Dip it in hot water each time. Beginning at the far side of a pound of butter, draw curler lightly and rapidly toward you, making a thin shaving of butter which curls up.

Butter Moulds: Scald and chill fancy butter moulds. Pack solidly with butter and level off with knife. Press out and chill.

Margarine: Most of today's margarine is made from refined food fats other than butter fat (primarily ground-nut and soya bean oils). Like butter, it is 80 per cent fat. Skim milk used in the manufacturing process is largely responsible for its appetizing flavour.

Since margarine is fortified with vitamin A, it is nutritionally comparable to butter and is uniform in food value throughout the year. It makes a fine table spread, and is also used extensively in cooking and baking.

In many recipes it is suggested that margarine may be substituted for butter, weight for weight or measure for measure; however this is usually an economy measure. It should be noted that margarines lack the desirable butter flavour and usually produce textures somewhat different from butter in both cooking and baking. For added butter flavour, some margarines have added dairy fat. To determine this read the label.

To Store Margarine

Margarine should be kept refrigerated in the store in which you buy, and at home should be carefully wrapped or covered and stored in the refrigerator.

Hydrogenated All-Vegetable Cooking Fat: The fats, which are sold under various trade names, are made of vegetable oils refined and chemically treated with hydrogen to make them solid fats. They may also be treated in various other ways such as by homogenization or with emulsifying agents.

Although especially adapted for use in quick-method cakes, as most labels indicate, they are used with equal success in other types of cakes, baking, frying, deep fat cookery.

Combination Meat Fat and Vegetable Fat: These fats are similar in appearance to all-vegetable types and are used in exactly the same ways.

They are packed in cans and require no refrigeration.

Lard: Lard is the rendered fat of pigs. Most lard is steam rendered.

Leaf lard, of which only a small amount is made, is saucepan rendered. It has a characteristic flavour which some people prefer.

Dry rendering is a third method of preparing lard.

Lard may be stabilized by the addition of an anti-oxidant, by hydrogenation or treated by other methods to give it improved flavour and cooking and keeping qualities.

Lard has excellent shortening qualities. It is also used for pan-frying, shallow and deep frying, baking breads, etc.

Keep lard, covered, in refrigerator.

Poultry Fat: This is the rendered fat from chicken, duck, goose, or turkey. It is sold in speciality shops in jars or cans but mainly rendered at home. Used in cooking, baking, frying.

Suet: This is the rather stiff white fat stripped from beef. Sold by the pound from butcher's. Used for larding lean meat and also as an ingredient in steamed puddings and to make suet crust pastry.

To Render Suet

Place chopped suet in saucepan over medium heat. As it melts, pour into bowl. Don't overheat melted suet or it will turn dark and have a strong flavour.

Store in a cool place until ready to use.

Dripping: This is fat usually rendered in the process of cooking fat meats, such as bacon, salt pork, ham, beef, or lamb. Dripping is sometimes home-rendered from meat scraps.

Oils: Cooking oils are made from cottonseed, corn, groundnuts, and soya, or from olives. Some may be a blend of two or more oils.

Cooking oils are purchased for salad dressing bases, for frying (pan-frying, deep, or shallow frying), for preparing dishes calling for melted fat, and are now used frequently (except olive oil) in pastry, cakes and quick breads.

You'll find cooking oils (except olive oil) ideal for deep frying because they can be heated to a high temperature without smoking and can be used over and over again.

Olive oil, with its unique flavour, is popular for salad dressings, in Italian-style dishes, etc; however it is too unstable for deep frying.

Fats used for deep frying should be strained when cool and stored in a covered container. Slices of potato may be cooked in the fat to remove strong flavours.

To Store Oils

After pouring what you need from a bottle of cooking or olive oil, before screwing cap back on again, be sure to wipe off neck of bottle and inside of cap with a paper towel.

Cooking oils should be stored in a cool dark place; most do not require refrigeration. Check the labels.

FACTS ABOUT MILK AND CREAM

Everyone needs milk every day, so never skimp on that daily quota. Pregnant and nursing mothers need more than other adults. Milk products whose value is equivalent to fresh whole milk can be used for part or all of the requirement.

Grades of Milk Available:
The system of grading milk for retail sale differs from dairy to dairy so it is best to check what you want to buy with your milkman. All milk must be designated as either Pasteurised or Sterilised, or Untreated. It is safest to buy treated milk.

Pasteurised Milk: This is treated in a special way by heating to destroy harmful bacteria and improve keeping quality.

Sterilised Milk: This is homogenised milk which has been bottled and heat-treated at a high temperature; it has good keeping qualities.

Homogenised Milk: This is pasteurized whole fluid milk treated in such a way that the cream is permanently mixed through and it can't rise to the top.

Whole Milk: Contains not less than 8·5% milk solids, not less than 3·25% butterfat. When left standing, it shows a collar of cream at top of bottle.

Skim Milk: This is milk with the cream removed—that is, most of the

butterfat removed. Contains half the energy value of whole milk. Used in reducing and low fat diets.

Top of the Milk: Top cream layer removed from bottle of whole, non-homogenized milk.

Buttermilk: Strictly speaking, this is the liquid remaining after milk or cream has been churned into butter. The usually available beverage is actually cultured buttermilk made from fresh fluid skim milk. A specially prepared culture of bacteria is added to the milk to produce the desirable acidity, body, flavour, and aroma so characteristic of buttermilk. Salt is usually added. The yellow flecks in some buttermilk are bits of real butter added for extra flavour. Because it is relatively low in calories it is popular in reducing diets.

To Make Sour Milk
If you have an old-fashioned recipe calling for sour milk, substitute the same amount of buttermilk. If you want to make your own sour milk for cooking, pour 1 tablespoon of lemon juice or vinegar into measuring jug and add milk to make 8 fluid ounces. Some old-fashioned recipes called for whole or skim milk allowed to sour naturally. Since the milk supply sold in Britain is generally a pasteurized and homogenized product, it will not sour naturally, but merely spoil.

Frozen Milk
It is not recommended that milk be frozen, but if it does freeze it can be used after thawing. You will notice only a slight change in the appearance.

Chocolate Milks: When buying these flavoured milks, note that there is a distinction among the types available. *Chocolate milk* is whole milk to which has been added chocolate syrup. If it is made with skim milk or partially skimmed milk, it is called *chocolate milk drink* or *chocolate milk beverage*. When made from whole milk and cocoa, it is called *chocolate-flavoured milk*. When made from skim milk and cocoa, it is called *chocolate-flavoured drink*.

Malted Milk: This is a soluble powder from whole dried milk and dried malted cereals. It's an easily digested concentrated food because the starch is predigested. To serve, the food value may be increased by preparing it with hot or cold milk.

Dried or Powdered Milk: This is milk with the water removed. Whole dried milk, seldom sold in groceries, has the nutritive content of fresh whole milk.

Dried skim milk is made by removing virtually all butterfat and water from fresh whole milk. The remaining portion is a nonfat or skim milk powder which contains all of the important nutrients of fresh whole milk except vitamins A and D and, of course, the butterfat.

Instant dried skim milk products differ from non-instant dried skim milk products only in ease of reconstitution into liquid milk.

Dried milks, especially the skim types, are finding more and more uses in home cooking. They are economical buys. Even if you have a pronounced distaste for the flavour of skim milk, you can still enjoy the economy of the product by using it in cooking. Simply mix in the powder with the other dry ingredients and add water at the point where the recipe calls for milk. Or reconstitute it as directed on the label and use in the recipe in place of fresh milk.

In many recipes you can step up the food value of a dish by adding some dried skim milk without adding water; for example, in meat loaves.

Whole fresh milk may be fortified by the addition of 1 tablespoon powdered milk for each glass of liquid milk, and many children prefer the flavour of this enriched milk.

To Whip Instant Dried Skim Milk

Equal parts of instant dried skim milk and water or juices may be whipped. While it is possible to whip with cold liquids, more volume and stability of foam are produced if all ingredients are at room temperature. Lemon juice (2 tablespoons for each 2 ounces instant dried skim milk) is often added to the whipped topping after soft peaks are formed. This stabilizes the whip and accents the flavour, especially when bland fruit juices are used. Sugar and flavourings to suit the taste may be added after the stiff peaks form.

Evaporated Milk: This is whole milk from which a little more than half of the water has been removed—that is, concentrated to double richness. It is homogenised and pasteurised before it is put in the can, then sterilised after the can is sealed. It is fortified with a large amount of vitamin D. When it is mixed half-and-half with water, it may be used as whole milk and has the same nutritive value. It can be used as it comes from the can in place of cream, or, when it has been thoroughly chilled, it can be whipped.

Keep evaporated milk in the can after opening. Cover the top with a food cover or a piece of foil pressed close against top edge. Refrigerate when not in use.

Condensed Milk: This is a mixture of whole milk and sugar from which about 60 per cent of the water has been removed before the mixture is canned. It is used to sweeten coffee and for special cooking purposes. It is rarely used with sugar.

Note that canned sweetened condensed milk is not the same as evaporated milk.

TO WHIP EVAPORATED MILK

- Pour 8 fluid ounces undiluted evaporated milk into a refrigerator tray and put in the ice cube section of the refrigerator to chill.
- When very cold, the milk will have soft crystals throughout (That will take about 20 to 30 minutes).
- Pour the chilled milk into a medium-sized bowl.
- Whip it with an egg beater until it is beginning to get stiff, about 1 minute.
- Add 3 tablespoons lemon juice.
- Whip until very stiff. If you are using the whipped milk for a topping, sweeten to taste. The milk triples in volume.

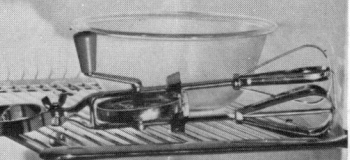

CREAM

Cream is a part of milk containing a high percentage of butter fat.

Single Cream: Cream containing not less than 18 per cent butter fat.

Half Cream: A mixture of milk and cream which contains 12% milk fat.

Whipping Cream: Cream sufficiently heavy to thicken and hold its shape when beaten, containing not less than 35% butter fat. It should be very cold at time of beating; chill the bowl and beater, too. Use a rotary, or electric beater; beat with continuous motion.

Double Cream: The best cream of all, containing not less than 48% butterfat.

Cream in Aerosol Cans: A cream packed under pressure in an aerosol container to cause whipping of the product. It may also contain sugar, flavouring, and a stabilizer. Since there are many whipped toppings in this form, be sure to check the label before purchasing if you want real cream.

How to Whip Cream

Keep it cold! The bowl and beaters as well as the cream should all be chilled in the refrigerator for at least 2 hours before whipping. Use a deep bowl with straight sides. Whip rapidly; stop whipping in time, before churning starts and butter begins to form. If the cream really threatens to turn into butter, whip in 2 or more tablespoons evaporated milk or cream and continue to beat. If you are using an electric beater, use medium high speed until the chilled cream begins to thicken, then lower the speed and watch carefully. It is not advisable to try to whip cream in a blender.

To Store Milk and Cream

Milk and cream should be kept covered in the refrigerator, since both pick up flavours from other food.

Milk from different bottles should not be mixed and unused liquid should not be poured back into the original container if there is other milk in it. This will cause either milk or cream to sour faster. If either does sour, it can be used in cooking.

Nonfat dry, evaporated, or condensed milk can be kept in the cupboard until opened or reconstituted. Then they must be treated like fresh milk.

SOUR CREAM

Cream especially soured for cooking purposes and table use is generally available, often labelled cultured sour cream. It is a single cream of custard-like consistency with a characteristic sour flavour produced by the addition of a culture or lactic acid starter. It is made from fresh sweet cream (with approximately 18 to 20% milk fat content) which is pasteurised and homogenised. After the culture has been added the cream is allowed to ripen until the desired flavour and consistency have been reached. Modern recipes calling for sour cream mean dairy sour cream—not to be confused with the old-fashioned homemade soured cream. As a safety measure it is always advisable to use only sour cream and milk that have been pasteurised and cultured.

To Store Dairy Sour Cream

Keep it clean, cold, and covered. Store in original container in the coldest part of the refrigerator. Dairy sour cream should not be frozen. Some prepared dishes made with sour cream may be frozen successfully.

Sour Cream Cookery Hints

When cooking with dairy sour cream, handle it with care. Heat gently, but do not boil. Add to other ingredients just before serving. If it does happen to curdle, only the appearance is affected not the taste. Always fold sour cream into other ingredients carefully, as over-stirring may thin it.

Most dairy sour cream can be whipped. Follow general directions for whipping cream. It will take about 5 minutes. The sour cream will thin out at the beinning of the whipping process, will never become as thick as whipped cream. It will double in volume.

When dairy sour cream is used in dressings or sauces along with vinegar, lemon juice, or comparable acid foods, the sour cream may become thin when stirred to mix. Upon storing the product in the refrigerator it will return to its original consistency.

When dairy sour cream is added to condensed canned soups or if flour is added to the sauce made with sour cream, the cream will not separate or curdle. Sour cream will enhance the flavour of either soup or sauce.

SOUR CREAM SUBSTITUTES

These are lower calorie substitutes for sour cream and are to be used only for garnish or in uncooked dressings.

Blender Cream: Combine 8 ounces cottage cheese, 2½ fluid ounces buttermilk, and 1 tablespoon lemon or lime juice. Blend for 2 or 3 seconds.

Evaporated Milk: Use 8 fluid ounces evaporated milk at room temperature (70 °F.); mix with 1 tablespoon vinegar. Let stand until it clabbers and thickens.

DEVONSHIRE CREAM (CLOTTED CREAM)

This is cream prepared in clotted form used as a topping for berries or other desserts or as a spread for bread. It is mainly produced in Devon and Cornwall and has a characteristic sweet flavour.

To make Devonshire cream, pour 2 gallons rich fresh milk (not homogenised) into a large shallow pan. Let it stand until the cream rises, about 6 hours.

Move it very gently onto the cooker and heat it very slowly until bubbles begin to appear around the edges. This should take about an hour and the milk must never be allowed to boil or the richness and texture of the cream will spoil.

Remove from heat and let it cool for a full 24 hours, then skim off the cream. It will be thick and clotted.

TO MAKE SOUR CREAM

Place 8 fluid ounces of 20 per cent pasteurised cream in a quart glass jar. The cream may be heavier, and the heavier the cream, the better the end product.

Add 5 teaspoons buttermilk. The commercial type which has 1 per cent acid and has carefully controlled bacteria is easier to use than the less-acid and less-controlled home product.

Cover the jar and shake these ingredients vigorously.

Then stir in an additional 8 fluid ounces of 20 per cent pasteurised cream.

Cover the jar and allow this mixture to stand at 80°F. for 24 hours. The sour cream may then be used at once although storage in the refrigerator for another 24 hours makes a finer product.

YOGURT

Yogurt (also spelled yoghurt, yoghourt) is a thick, custard-like, smooth textured dairy product with a sour flavour. It is a cultured milk product that has been prepared with a mixed culture of lactic bacteria. It is usually made with fresh, partially skimmed milk that has been enriched by the addition of dried skim milk. The milk is pasteurised and homogenised before the culture is added. The nutritive value of yogurt is the same as the milk from which it is made. In addition to the plain yogurt, you may find flavours such as strawberry, coffee, vanilla, orange, lime, prune, or pineapple.

About Serving Yogurt

Yogurt is most popular in dips, toppings, and salad dressings. It can also be served as a dessert, spooned right from the container onto fruit, or eaten with sugar and honey.

Since it was originally a Bulgarian fermented milk, a great many Near Eastern recipes call for yogurt. When using yogurt in cooking, stir or fold it into the other ingredients. The custard-like texture or body of the yogurt will be broken down by any vigorous beating, so treat it gently. When cooked, yogurt thins out even more than sour cream. However, it is stabilized by flour or cornflour and water.

To Store Yogurt

To retain the fresh flavour and smooth texture of yogurt, store it in the refrigerator but do not freeze.

To prepare Yogurt: Let 4 tablespoons prepared yogurt stand at room temperature for about 3 hours.

Bring 2 pints milk to boiling point in top part of double saucepan. Let it cool to temperature of 120 °F. Combine with the 4 tablespoons prepared yogurt and set over hot water.

Keep at a temperature of 100°F. to 105°F. about 3 hours, or until mixture has the consistency of thick custard. Pour into 5 or 6 custard glasses.

Chill thoroughly in the refrigerator. Always reserve 4 tablespoons of this batch to use as "starter" for the next quart.

SOYA BEAN "MILK"

A liquid somewhat similar to milk can be made from soya beans. In the Orient it has been used for hundreds of years as milk for babies. This "vegetable milk" is not equal to cow's milk in food value but it contains most of the food elements in slightly smaller amounts.

It can be used in making custards, soups, breads, cakes, sauces, and drinks such as cocoa, and it can be drunk as a beverage with a little sugar and salt to season it.

The two methods that follow have been used for centuries in the Orient.
Method 1: Wash dry soya beans and soak them overnight. Remove the skins by rubbing them in the water; they will float to the surface and can be discarded.

Mince the beans fine in a mincer. Put the minced beans in a cheesecloth bag and immerse it in a bowl of lukewarm water, using 5 pints of water to a pound of dry beans. Work thoroughly with the hands for 5 to 10 minutes, then wring the bag until it is dry.

Boil the creamy white liquid over low heat for 30 minutes, stirring frequently to prevent scorching. Add sugar and salt to taste. Keep in refrigerator.

Method 2: Wash soya beans. Dry them thoroughly, then crack them by crushing coarsely in a mincer. The skins then can be easily removed. Grind fine in the mincer. To each pound add 5 pints of water and soak for 2 hours.

Boil for 20 minutes, stirring constantly, then strain through cheesecloth. Add sugar and salt to taste. Keep in refrigerator.

FACTS ABOUT LEAVENING AGENTS

To leaven means "to make dough rise". Leavening agents are substances that form bubbles of gas (carbon dioxide) which expand when a batter or dough is heated. They make a batter or dough rise, increase in volume or bulk, and become light and porous during preparation and subsequent baking. Three common sources of carbon dioxide gas are yeast, baking powder, and bicarbonate of soda plus food acid.

Physical leavenings such as steam and air also make products rise. Steam is formed in any batter or dough as it is heated. It is the principal leavening agent in products such as popovers and cream puffs. Air is beaten or folded into mixtures or introduced into ingredients by beating, creaming, and sifting. Air leavens by expansion during heating.

Bacteria of certain species, under suitable conditions of temperature and moisture, grow rapidly and produce gases from sugar. Salt-rising bread is made from dough leavened in this manner.

Leavening Changes at High Altitudes

For guidance about amounts of leavening to use in your sea-level recipes, see **Cooking at High Altitudes.** For specific recipes for various altitudes, see **Cakes at High Altitudes.**

BAKING POWDERS

Baking powders are classified according to the acid ingredients they contain. There are three available types: tartrate, phosphate, and SAS-phosphate (usually referred to as double-acting). These terms refer to the chemicals that react with the bicarbonate of soda in the powder, when liquid is added, to release carbon dioxide gas, the leavening agent. The various brands clearly indicate the type on the labels.

Tartrate Baking Powder: This type reacts rapidly, almost entirely at room temperature when the liquid is added to the dry ingredients. The gas formed then expands when the batter or dough is heated.

Phosphate Baking Powder: This type releases most of its gas at room temperature when combined with liquid, but retains some until the batter or dough is heated.

SAS-Phosphate Baking Powder: This type, often called double-acting or double-action, releases only a small amount of its gas when combined with liquid, then the major portion is given off during baking.

The advantages of a "double-acting" baking powder is that it allows a little more latitude in the mixing and a longer time interval between preparing the batter or dough and putting it into the oven.

Recipes in this book are based on double-acting (SAS-phosphate) baking powder. In general, if you use a single-acting baking powder (tartrate) as a substitute for double-acting baking powder, use 1½ times the amount specified in the recipe.

Because different brands differ in both activity and bulk, the cook who changes from one brand to another, particularly if it is a different type, may find that her usually successful cake recipe doesn't come out just right. A little more baking powder if the cake doesn't rise properly—a little less if it is too porous—will usually take care of the problem. Many cooks prefer to adjust their recipes to a brand and then stick to that brand.

BAKING SODA

Baking soda (also known as sodium bicarbonate or bicarbonate of soda) is used alone or with baking powder to leaven cakes and other products made with buttermilk, sour milk, chocolate, treacle, vinegar, lemon juice and other fruit juices, etc. Acid from these ingredients reacts with bicarbonate of soda to release a leavening gas. When using bicarbonate of soda, don't delay mixing or baking.

One-half teaspoon bicarbonate of soda plus 8 fluid ounces sour milk or treacle is equivalent in leavening power to 1 teaspoon double-acting baking powder. You can make sour milk from sweet milk by adding vinegar or lemon juice.

YEAST

Yeast in compressed or dry form is a microscopic living plant that produces a gas (carbon dioxide) from sugar when temperature and moisture are favourable for its growth.

Compressed yeast is a perishable moist mixture of yeast and starch which must be kept in the refrigerator. To use, soften compressed yeast in lukewarm water or milk (85-95°F.) for 5 to 10 minutes.

Dry yeast is similar to compressed yeast except that the yeast-and-filler mixture has been dried and is then packed in granular form. Before you use dry yeast, soften it in warm water (105-110°F) for 5 to 10 minutes.

CREAM OF TARTAR

Cream of tartar is an acid substance used extensively before baking powders became common, It seems to be an essential ingredient in angel food cake. Without cream of tartar this cake has a tendency to shrink excessively and is less tender. It also gives very desirable results in sponge cakes and in recipes calling for a large amount of egg whites.

HARTSHORN

A baking ammonia, used in some old-time recipes, and still occasionally used by bakers in sponge cakes and cream puffs. It may be purchased in drug stores in coarse crystals, and should be completely dissolved in a liquid before it is added to a dough or batter. Hartshorn is a powerful leavening agent and should be used cautiously.

FACTS ABOUT THICKENING AGENTS

Flour: Unsifted flour is the most commonly used thickener, especially in sauces. The new easy-blending flour is excellent for saucemaking. Flour must be thoroughly blended with fat over very low heat before the liquid is added. Frequent stirring keeps the sauce smooth as it cooks.

Note: The mixture of flour and fat is called a roux. White roux is made without browning. Brown roux for dark sauces is made by browning the fat and flour before adding the liquid.

Or flour may be blended with a cold liquid before combining with the hot mixture. For example, to thicken a hot mixture such as a stew, measure liquid to be thickened. For each 8 fluid ounces, mix 1½ tablespoons flour with 3 tablespoons cold water until smooth. Stir into hot liquid; cook until thickened. Flour requires at least 5 minutes cooking time.

In sweet mixtures, flour may be combined with the sugar before the hot liquid is added.

Cornflour: This is an especially useful thickener in clear sauces, in some Chinese sauces, and in dessert sauces. Cornflour should be mixed with a little cold water before being added to the hot liquid. One tablespoon cornflour will thicken 12 to 16 fluid ounces of liquid. To substitute cornflour for flour in thickening, use 1½ teaspoons cornflour for 1 tablespoon flour. Since there are several types of cornflour on the market, it is best to follow the manufacturer's directions for length of cooking time. In general, it is usually advisable to thicken dessert sauces with cornflour in the top of a double saucepan over (not in) hot water until the raw taste of the cornflour disappears. Other sauces, particularly the clear Chinese types, are usually thickened over direct heat.

Other Starches: See **Table of Substitutions** for use of other starches in place of flour.

Eggs: Egg yolks not only thicken but enrich a dish. When used for thickening, eggs are slightly beaten and are never added directly to a hot liquid.

To add them to a hot mixture, first stir a small amount of the hot mixture into the eggs, then stir the egg mixture into the remaining hot mixture. If additional cooking is required, use low heat and stir constantly.

TAPIOCA

A starch obtained from cassava root, used to thicken soups and puddings. It is marketed chiefly in pearl and quick-cooking forms. Besides taking longer to cook, pearl tapioca must first be soaked for some time.

SAGO

A starch made from the pith of an East Indian palm tree, used chiefly to thicken puddings and fillings.

ARROWROOT

An easily digestible starch made from the roots of a tropical plant. Clear and almost tasteless when cooked, it is used to thicken sauces and puddings and also in baking.

FACTS ABOUT GELATINE

Gelatine is a tasteless, odourless, brittle substance extracted by boiling bones, hoofs, and animal tissues; also, a somewhat similar product made chiefly from seaweeds (vegetable gelatine). Gelatine dissolves in hot water and forms jelly when cool. When the term gelatine is used in a recipe without further description, it means granulated, unsweetened, and unflavoured gelatine.

To use, first soften it in a small amount of cold liquid for about 5 minutes, then dissolve it in a hot liquid or over hot water. To hasten setting, part of the added liquid may be cold, once the gelatine has dissolved. One envelope of gelatine is equivalent to 3 level teaspoons and is enough to set 1 pint of liquid firmly. Remember to count the cold liquid used for softening as part of the total.

Packed gelatine desserts called jellies are mixtures of plain gelatine, sugar, fruit acids, flavourings, and colourings. Dissolve them in hot liquid, according to instructions.

Hints About Unmoulding Jelly

Before the mixture is poured in, the mould should be dipped in cold water or (for salads) brushed with cooking oil, so that the set jelly will come out easily.

To unmould, loosen the edge of the mould with a spatula or a small knife dipped in warm water. Then quickly immerse the mould just to the top in lukewarm water (hot water will melt the jelly). Shake the mould. Place an inverted serving dish on top, turn dish and mould over, and lift the mould off carefully. If the mould is large, moisten the jelly surface and

the plate; this makes it easy to centre the mould. Remove excess moisture with a towel.

Surround large moulds with salad after turning them out; they may break if unmoulded on crisp lettuce.

Caution About Fresh or Frozen Pineapple

Gelatine will not jell with fresh or frozen pineapple. Always bring fresh or frozen pineapple to the boil, or use canned pineapple. Fresh pineapple contains an enzyme (bromelin) that inhibits jelling. Canned pineapple presents no problem.

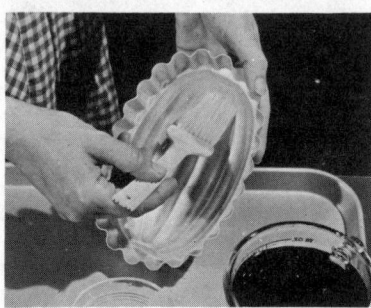

For salads, brush cooking oil in mould so the set jelly will unmould easily.

Shake the set moulded salad lightly and turn onto serving plate.

FACTS ABOUT SUGARS, SYRUPS, AND SYNTHETIC SWEETENERS

As used in recipes, the term sugar refers to beet or cane granulated sugar. When another sugar is called for it will be specifically named as: brown sugar or icing sugar.

White sugar can be made from either sugar cane or beet sugar; the two products are identical and either kind can be used interchangeably in all cookery.

Granulated Sugar: This is the main product of the normal refining process. It is pure, white, and free-flowing. It is the cheapest sugar and is good for all general sweetening purposes, especially for recipes in which liquid content and cooking time allow the crystals to dissolve completely.

Caster Sugar: Has finer crystals than granulated. It is good for sifting over fruit, etc., for all cakes made by the creaming method, and for giving meringues the right texture.

Cube Sugar: These pressed or cut lumps of sugar are handy for sweetening hot drinks. They are sold in handy 1- and 2-pound boxes.

Icing Sugar: This is made by pulverising sugar crystals to a very fine powder. It is quite different from the granulated and caster sugars which are both boiled to a given size of crystal. Because it is a powdered sugar and dissolves very quickly it is useful for cold drinks, whipped cream, fruit fools and purées, icings, butter-cream, and uncooked sweets like trifles.

Brown Sugars: These sugars have varying amounts of molasses in them which gives them their colour. They may be variously named as "golden brown", "light brown", and "dark brown". "Demerara" is coarse crystal brown sugar.

The molasses flavour increases with colour. The light brown sugars have more delicate flavours and are desirable for general cookery. The darker brown sugars impart more colour and flavour, and are desirable for such foods as baked beans, baked hams, and other cookery where more intensity of treacle flavour is preferred.

FLAVOURED SUGARS

Cinnamon Sugar: Blend 2 tablespoons cinnamon with 8 ounces sugar. Use with toast and coffeecake toppings.

Citrus Flavoured Sugars: Scrub and rinse thoroughly the desired citrus fruit (lemon, orange, or tangerine). Grate the coloured outermost part of the rind very fine. Combine 1 to 2 teaspoons grated rind to 8 ounces sugar. Store covered in a cool place. Use with custards and other desserts.

Vanilla Sugar: Make this by keeping a whole vanilla bean in a closed container of sugar. Or crush the bean with a few tablespoons of sugar before adding it to the stored sugar. Then, strain the sugar and replace it with new sugar until the bean has lost its flavouring power.

TO STORE SUGARS

Store sugars in the original or other covered containers. Icing, and sometimes granulated, sugar have a tendency to cake because they pick up moisture much the same as salt does. These usually can be broken up with a spoon or by putting the sugar through a sieve.

Modern brown sugar packets are designed to retain the sugar's moisture longer and thus to keep it soft and fresh. After each use, close the packet or bag well. Storing it in the refrigerator keeps it best because there it obtains the small amount of moisture from the air that it needs to keep it soft.

If brown sugar should lump, place it in a jar with a damp piece of cheesecloth over the top of the jar or put a slice or two of very fresh white bread or apple in the jar. Replace cover and sugar should be soft within a few hours.

SUGAR SUBSTITUTES (SYNTHETIC SWEETENERS)

These are produced under many trade names; however they may be divided into two main types. One is saccharin or saccharin based, the other is based on cyclamate sodium. They have approximately equal sweetening power. The saccharin types should not be used in cooking since they produce a bitter flavour. The cyclamate sodium types can usually be used in cooking and baking since they retain their sweetness when heated. Some types actually increase their sweetening power with some cooked foods. Many recipes that call for sugar to add sweetness, *not bulk,* can be adapted to these sweeteners. Baked goods, however, in which sugar produces volume, as in creaming it with fat or beating it with eggs, are still off-limits for these sugar substitutes. Hence, the cyclamate sodium substitutes should be used only in baking recipes especially developed for them.

Note: Because of the ban on cyclamates consult your doctor before using them.

BLACK TREACLE OR MOLASSES

Black treacle is a by-product of cane sugar, an important source of iron and should be used often. It is excellent for all cooking in which many spices are present, as in gingerbreads, Indian pudding, etc.

Blackstrap molasses tastes bitter, but contains more iron and calcium than higher grades. It is what's left after the economic exhaustion of crystalline sugar, and is generally regarded as unfit for human consumption except by certain food faddists. It is used for cattle feeding and industrial purposes, and is sold at "health stores" and some groceries.

MAPLE SUGAR AND SYRUP

These are made from the sap of hard maple trees. Maple sugar is sold as maple cream, which has the consistency of peanut butter, as stirred sugar, which is similar to brown sugar, and as soft and hard maple sugar. Maple candies are a fondant made of pure maple frosted with a crystal of pure maple sugar.

Maple sugar is made by concentrating maple sap or by solution of maple sugar. Syrups which are not pure maple are less expensive than the pure syrups. The composition of blended syrups is stated on the label.

GOLDEN SYRUP

A purified syrup made from the thick concentrated juice obtained from the cane or beet, during crystallisation. It is easy to digest and is an excellent energy food.

HONEY

Honey is a natural sugar manufactured by the honey bee. Its flavour and colour depend on the flowers from whose nectar it was made. Dandelion, heather, white clover, and buckwheat are examples.

Comb Honey: Honey sold in the comb. It is sometimes cut into small pieces, packaged, and sold as *cut comb honey.*

Chunk Honey: Consists of pieces of comb placed in glass jars with enough extracted honey added to fill.

Extracted Honey: Liquid honey which has been removed from the comb.

Granulated and solidly crystallized honey are also available.

To Store Honey

It should be stored at room temperature. If it crystallizes, the container can be placed in a bowl of lukewarm water until the crystals are melted.

FACTS ABOUT CHOCOLATE AND COCOA

Chocolate and cocoa are products of the bean of the cacao tree, which is native to tropical America. The word cocoa is a corruption of cacao (the Spanish version of the Aztec word cacahuatl), which is now used in the trade to refer to the raw beans.

Chocolate is the manufactured product when it appears in solidified form such as bars. Cocoa is a powder made from the beans with part of the cocoa butter removed. Breakfast cocoa contains at least 22 per cent cocoa butter.

Dutch Process Cocoa: This is made by a chemical treatment that produces a cocoa of a darker colour and somewhat different flavour from other products. The method originated in Holland, but also is used domestically.

Instant Cocoas and Ready-to-Serve Cocoas: These require only the addition of hot or cold water or milk to be served as a beverage.

Unsweetened Chocolate: This is made from carefully selected beans, with no cocoa butter removed.

Semisweet Chocolate: This has just enough flavouring sweetening added to give a pleasing, half-sweet flavour. Some cocoa butter is removed.

To Melt Chocolate

Place chocolate in small bowl or top half of a double saucepan (or foil or non-stick paper); set over hot, not boiling, water until melted. Or melt in original wrapping, on piece of foil, placed in oven while oven is heating or cooling off. Remove chocolate as soon as it is melted. Never melt chocolate over direct heat. Cool slightly before using.

FACTS ABOUT SALT

Salt is sodium chloride, a white crystalline substance used for seasoning and preserving food and essential to the diet. It is mined from natural beds or obtained by evaporation from sea water.

Table Salt: Finely ground salt, used at table or in cooking.

Iodized Salt: Table salt to which iodine has been added. This is done to prevent goitre.

Coarse or Sea Salt: Salt in large crystals, used in cooking and as a garnish on such baked goods as rolls and pretzels.

Rock Salt: A non-edible unrefined type of salt used in freezing ice cream and sometimes as a base for baking oysters and potatoes.

Seasoned Salts: Various commercial mixtures of table salt and ground herbs or spices. The commonest are celery, garlic, and onion salts.

Salt substitutes: Various substances resembling table salt in appearance and taste but containing no sodium.

FOOD COLOURING

Food colours have to comply with specified purity standards. They are available in liquid and paste forms and in a variety of colours. Follow the directions on the containers for using them. In general, however, food colour should be added a drop at a time either with an eye-dropper or with the tip of a wooden pick. Blend in until desired colour is reached.

FACTS ABOUT EXTRACTS

An extract is a preparation containing a food or flavouring in concentrated form, solid or liquid.

Flavouring extracts are essential oils in solution, usually with an alcohol added. When a recipe refers simply to vanilla, it means the extract; with other extracts such as almond, lemon, and orange, the word is always included.

Flavouring extracts should be purchased in small quantities and kept tightly closed because their flavours deteriorate quickly when exposed to air.

Pure vanilla extract is an extract of the vanilla pod, conforming to required standards. The pod is the fruit of a climbing vine of the orchid family native to Mexico and Central America. Vanilla flavouring has been popular since pre-Columbian times, when the Aztecs used it in chocolate.

Imitation vanilla extract is a solution of synthetic flavourings that yield a product simulating pure vanilla extract.

In using vanilla or other flavouring extracts, try to add them to cooled ingredients only. Because they have an alcohol base, much of the flavour evaporates when they are cooked or added to hot substances.

The vanilla pod is far more flavoursome than the extract made from it. To use it, steep a small piece in whatever hot liquid you are using—about a ½-inch piece for 1 pint liquid. It may be taken out or finely crushed and left in; if taken out it can be washed, dried, and used to make vanilla sugar. To flavour an uncooked dessert, split the piece of pod, scrape it well, and add the pulp to the other ingredients.

Beef extract is a beef preparation used for flavouring. It lacks food value because the fat and protein are almost entirely removed from the concentrated beef broth from which it is made. It is often used as a quick and easy substitute for beef broth or consommé in sauces and other dishes.

FACTS ABOUT COCONUT

Coconut is the fruit of the coco palm, having a thick, fibrous brown oval husk under which is a thin, hard shell enclosing a layer of edible white meat. When it is fresh, its hollow centre is filled with a sweet whitish fluid. Coconut is packed shredded or flaked in several ways.

How to Tint Coconut: Blend 1 teaspoon milk or water with a drop or so of desired food colour. Add grated coconut, also a little almond, peppermint, or vanilla extract if desired. Toss with fork until blended.

To Open and Prepare Fresh Coconut: With a long nail or ice pick,

puncture the indentations ("eyes") at the end of the coconut. Drain off the coconut water inside (sometimes called the "milk", but to Hawaiian cooks, coconut "milk" means a liquid extracted from the grated meat).

Then bake the whole coconut in a shallow pan in a moderate oven (350°F. Mark 4); cool it for half an hour, then tap with a hammer to crack the shell. Pry out the meat in as large pieces as possible. Remove the brown outer skin with a sharp knife or vegetable peeler.

Then grate the meat on a vegetable grater. A medium-sized coconut usually yields about 12 ounces grated coconut.

To Make Coconut Milk: To make coconut milk to be used in curry sauce, pudding, or pie filling, pour 8 to 16 fluid ounces boiling water or coconut water over 12 ounces shredded coconut; let stand 15 minutes, then strain or squeeze through doubled thickness of cheesecloth. After the milk has been extracted, the drained coconut still retains enough flavour to be usable in making sweets or macaroons.

For a thick coconut milk, or "cream", to serve over puddings or cereals, use only 4 to 6 fluid ounces boiling water or coconut water.

For coconut cream pie filling, part of the shredded coconut is sometimes scalded with the milk, then strained out before making the filling. Fresh coconut is often sprinkled over the pie before serving.

BOUGHT SAUCES IN RECIPES

All of them should be used discreetly; amounts are specified in the recipes.

Worcestershire sauce: A pungent, dark-coloured condiment containing soy sauce, vinegar, onion juice, lime juice, chilli, and spices. It originated in Worcester. The composition may vary.

Soy Sauce: A salty brown condiment made from soya beans that have been fermented and steeped in brine. It is essential to Chinese and Japanese cooking. Since the various brands differ in strength and in monosodium glutamate content, be sure to taste the dish you are cooking before using all the soy sauce called for in a recipe.

Tabasco Sauce: A very pungent proprietary condiment sauce made of cayenne peppers. It's used in small quantities for seasoning many foods.

Bottled Sauce for Gravy: Any of a number of commercial preparations used to give rich brown colour and flavour to gravies and sauces.

Bottled Meat Sauce: Any of a number of commercial preparations for, not made of, meat, such as A.1., Heinz Beefsteak Sauce, etc., of a rather thick consistency.

Shoyu: Japanese name for soy sauce (which see).

FACTS ABOUT NUTS

ALMONDS

The edible nut-like seed of a fruit closely resembling the peach, except that the fruit is fleshless. The "nuts" of sweet almond varieties are eaten raw or roasted and are pressed to obtain almond oil. When called for in recipes in this book, the dry sweet form is the type to be used. Bitter almond varieties also yield oil from which the poisonous prussic acid is removed in the extraction process. The bitter almond is sometimes specified in small quantities in certain recipes for flavouring, for example in Orgeat syrup. Almond oil is used in soaps, and cosmetics and medicinally as a demulcent. It is sometimes used for flavouring; however it is dangerous to use in excess.

ALMOND PASTE

A preparation made from finely ground blanched almonds, used as a base for macaroons, sweets, and pastry fillings. It is the main ingredient of marzipan (which see).

BEECHNUTS

Edible three-cornered nuts of a number of related trees with smooth, grey bark, hard wood, and dark-green leaves. Beechnuts have a sweet flavour but are now seldom eaten except in the poorer areas of Europe.

BRAZIL NUTS

The edible, oily, three-sided, hard-shelled seed, or nut, of the Brazilnut tree, a very tall tree of tropical America. The nuts grow clumped together in large, round, woody and extremely hard seed pods. The meat of the seed (the "nut") is very rich in oil.

Brazil nut chips may be used to decorate cakes and biscuits or toasted and salted for delicious nibbling.

BUTTERNUT

The hard-shelled nut of the North American white walnut tree used mostly in the manufacture of sweetmeats to which it lends a pleasant, buttery flavour. Butternuts are sweet, oily, and nutritious.

CASHEW

A kidney-shaped nut that grows on the outside of the cashew apple, the fruit of a tropical American tree. In the West Indies, the cashew apple, which is white, yellow, or red, juicy and slightly acid, is eaten or fermented to make wine.

CHESTNUTS

These are the smooth-skinned, sweet, edible nuts of any of a group of trees of the beech family. They contain more starch and less fat than most other nuts. Home-grown chestnuts are very small and chestnuts on the market are imported, usually from Italy and France. Chestnuts are eaten cooked—roasted or boiled. They are particularly delicious with Brussels sprouts. Puréed boiled chestnuts are good accompaniments for game, pork, and turkey and often used in stuffings.

Freshly roasted chestnuts are relished as a dessert. The French word marron, which actually refers to a particular type of chestnut, is used for chestnuts preserved in syrup, candied, or dried. Do not confuse these chestnuts with water chestnuts which are usually available in canned form and often called for in various Chinese-style recipes.

Preparation: Wash chestnuts; cut a gash on the flat side of each chestnut.

Place the nuts in a heavy pan; add 1 teaspoon of cooking oil for 4 ounces of nuts. Shake until coated with oil.

Set pan in moderate oven (350°F. Mark 4) and heat until shells and skins can be removed easily.

Remove shells and skins with a sharp knife; cover with boiling salted water and cook gently until tender when tested with a cocktail stick, 15 to 20 minutes.

Drain, mash or rice, and season with salt, pepper, and butter or margarine. Serve with medium white sauce or use in stuffing.

Savoury Puréed Chestnuts: Prepare as above but add (for 1 pound chestnuts) to the cooking water 1 tablespoon vinegar, 3 stalks of celery, and 1 small peeled onion.

Season the mashed cooked chestnuts with 2 tablespoons butter or margarine, $\frac{1}{4}$ teaspoon pepper, 2 or more tablespoons hot cream, and salt to taste.

SAUTÉED CHESTNUTS

Sauté drained cooked chestnuts in butter and serve as garnish for turkey, ham, or as a vegetable.

CREAMED CHESTNUTS

Reheat cooked (sliced or whole) chestnuts in small amount of double cream.

ROAST CHESTNUTS

With a sharp knife, make two crosswise slashes on the flat side of each chestnut.

Melt some butter or oil in a saucepan (about 1 teaspoon for 4 ounces of nuts). Drop in the nuts and keep shaking in the pan over a hot flame until all nuts are coated with fat.

Then bake them in a moderate oven (350°F. Mark 4) until tender and the shells and inner skins can be removed easily, about 30 minutes.

FILBERT

The cultivated variety of the Hazelnut; these small round nuts are sweet-tasting and increasing in popularity. They are much used in cooking, especially for biscuits and sweets.

LITCHI

Also spelled lichee; the fruit (nut) of a small Chinese evergreen tree now being cultivated to a limited extent in Hawaii and California. Litchi nuts as usually purchased consist of dried raisin-like pulp enclosed in a fragile shell. They are available in Chinese stores. The litchi is also available canned in syrup.

MACADAMIA NUT

A rich, crunchy nut grown in Hawaii, somewhat similar to a hazelnut when shelled and roasted. It is served as a cocktail tidbit.

PARADISE NUT

A South American hard-shelled nut resembling the Brazil nut.

PEANUT

Peanut is the name of a vine of the pea family with yellow flowers as well as brittle pods ripening underground. The seeds—peanuts—are eaten fresh or roasted and are used in cookery and confectionery. Other names for the peanut are goober, pinder, earthnut, groundnut, and ground pea. Peanuts have a high protein content and make an economical contribution to the diet.

Peanuts may be roasted at home; however the commercial method yields a superior product. To roast at home, keep the oven at a low temperature (300°F. Mark 2) and roast in the shell for 30 to 45 minutes, or 20 to 30 minutes if shelled. Turn them constantly to avoid scorching. Check for doneness by removing skins. The inner brown skins are nutritious and have a pleasant flavour.

BLENDER PEANUT BUTTER

Use fresh roast or salted peanuts and a bland oil such as vegetable or sunflower oil. Combine in blender, allowing $1\frac{1}{2}$ to 3 tablespoons oil per 4 ounces of nuts. Blend to desired consistency. If nuts are unsalted, add salt to taste.

PECANS

These are olive-shaped nuts with a thin, smooth shell and the kernels are similar to walnuts. The tree they grow on is related to the hickory, and is one of the most important nut trees of the United States. A rich food (containing 70% or more of fat) the pecan is the most popular American nut after the peanut. Cultivated American varieties with unusually thin shells (called papershelled pecans) have been developed but wild pecans are gathered in quantities and sold and are exported to Britain.

PINE NUT OR INDIAN NUT

The pine nut is a tiny, thin-shelled nut found in the cones of certain pines and removed by roasting. It has a sweet, delicate flavour, and is much used in Italian and Near Eastern cooking and baking. Also known by the Italian name pignolia, the Spanish piñón, and the French pignon.

PISTACHIO

The greenish seed of a tree native to Asia Minor and now grown also in the Mediterranean regions and to a limited extent in California. Valued for its delicate flavour and colour, it is used especially in confections, ice creams, and pastries. It is served salted in the shell as a dessert nut.

WALNUT

A roundish or oval nut with a two-lobed seed; either the strong, distinctively flavoured black walnut, or the pale tan, mild-flavoured English (or California) walnut. Recipes calling for walnuts refer to the latter, unless specifying the former.

WATER CHESTNUT

The water chestnut is a crunchy nut-like fruit of any of a number of related water plants with floating leaves and small white flowers. It is widely used in Chinese and other Oriental cooking and can be bought canned.

TO STORE SHELLED NUTS

Nuts are rich in oil, and shelled nuts will become rancid if stored in a warm place for any length of time.

Store them in a tightly covered container in refrigerator, preferably for not more than a few months.

To Recrisp Nuts

Spread on a baking sheet and place in a slow oven (300°F. Mark 2) for about 10 minutes. Let cool and use as desired.

FACTS ABOUT VINEGARS

Vinegar is a sour liquid containing acetic acid, made by bacterial action from various diluted alcoholic liquids. The sourness, richness, or mellowness of vinegars make quite a difference in various dishes, hence recipes often specify the type of vinegar or dilution if required.

Cider: A vinegar made from fermented apple juice; it is an all-purpose standby for salads and salad dressings.

Malt: A vinegar made from fermented malt; its rich flavour goes well with many fish and meat sauces, salad dressings, and various seafoods.

Wine: Vinegars made from red or white wines; they are preferred by many people for salad dressings, sauces, and many other dishes.

Distilled or white: Clear, colourless vinegar made from plain alcohol; it is ideal for pickling and preserving.

Any of the above may be flavoured with various herbs. Recipes for home-made flavoured vinegars have been included in this book; however nowadays you can buy a large variety of delightfully flavoured vinegars to use in cooking. Here are a few examples:

Tarragon: A herb fragrance that is often preferred in salads, salad dressings, sauces, and pot roasts.

Garlic Wine: Often used instead of garlic in salads, sauces, stews, and hamburgers.

Basil, Mixed Herb, Mixed Herb and Spice: Any of these should be used lightly with cooked greens, cole slaws, salad dressings, sauces, and other dishes.

GARLIC VINEGAR

Mash 6 garlic cloves through a garlic press into just slightly less than a pint of cider vinegar in a scalded pint jar.

Put uncovered jar in shallow pan of water. Bring water to boil and remove from heat. Let stand 45 minutes.

Remove from water to cool. Cover tightly. Let stand a week, shaking jar occasionally. Strain, bottle, and label.

TARRAGON VINEGAR

Put several sprigs of fresh tarragon or 2 tablespoons dried tarragon in vinegar. Proceed as directed for garlic vinegar.

MIXED HERB VINEGAR

Add a pinch each of basil, chopped chives, dill, oregano, parsley, tarragon, and thyme to 1 pint cider vinegar.

Place uncovered jar in pan of water. Bring to boil. Remove from heat and let stand 45 minutes.

Remove from water to cool. When cool, add 1 small onion which has been pierced many times with a fork. Let stand 1 week, then strain, bottle, and label.

QUICK HERB VINEGAR

8 fluid ounces wine or cider vinegar
1 teaspoon dried crushed herbs
   (basil, tarragon, etc.)
2 tablespoons chopped parsley
1 tablespoon chopped chives

Combine vinegar and herbs. You may use this at once with olive or cooking oil.

You may add ½ clove of garlic and remove it later. Shortly before you serve it, add parsley and chives.

Food Terms You'll Want to Know

Included here are well-known—and not so well-known—dishes and terms of foreign lands and infrequently used utensils and foods.

ACIDOPHILUS MILK

A form of milk fermented with cultures of Lactobacillus acidophilus. It is tart and buttermilk-like and is sometimes prescribed in cases of intestinal disorder.

ADOBO

A Philippine national dish that takes many forms. It is a type of stew, usually with a base of pork, chicken, or fish or some combination of these. Also spelled adobe.

AGAR-AGAR

Also called agar. A gelatinous substance made from several kinds of seaweed, it is used in some Oriental cooking and in preparing various jellied dishes. Although most agar comes from the Far East, California is also a source of supply. It is marketed in the form of dried flakes.

Agar is often prescribed as a laxative in chronic constipation. It may be taken alone, cut into small pieces and eaten as a cereal with cream and sugar, or combined with a drug such as cascara sagrada to increase the cathartic action.

AGNEAU

(French): Lamb.

AGUACATE

(Spanish): Avocado. The name is probably derived from the Aztec name: ahucatl. See **Avocado.**

AIGUILLETTE

(French): A diminutive of aiguille (needle), referring to a manner of carving; a small, narrow strip or slice of cooked meat from a meat animal, fish, or breast of fowl.

À LA

(French): After, or according to, the style of; in the manner of. This phrase (with its variants à l', au, aux) is used to describe different ways of preparing or serving food. Sometimes the style is said to be that of a country—à l'allemande: German; à la russe: Russian. Sometimes the names are more descriptive of the dish and sometimes fanciful—à la printanière: made with spring vegetables; à l'estragon: served or cooked with tarragon; au vert pré: coloured green with vegetables or served with a green garnish; aux champignons: served with or containing mushrooms.

AL, ALLA

The Italian equivalents of the French terms (see preceding entry) are also used in cookery—al burro: cooked with butter; alla cacciatore: sautéed with a sauce of tomatoes, mushrooms, and peppers; al forno: roasted or baked.

ALBACORE

Strictly speaking, albacore is a fish of the tuna family; commonly, any of several related fishes, including the bonito. See **Tuna.**

ALLUMETTE

(French): Match; a term sometimes applied to foods cut in matchlike strips. Pommes allumettes: straw potatoes; allumettes au fromage: cheese straws.

AMANDINE

(French): Garnish with or containing almonds. Fish such as fillet of sole or trout are sometimes covered with a butter sauce to which slivered almonds have been added. Vegetables may also be served this way.

AMÉRICAINE

(French): American; à la Américaine: "in American style".

ANANAS

(French): Pineapple.

ANCHOVY

The anchovy is a small, slender, salt-water fish of the herring family. In the Mediterranean countries where they are caught, anchovies are often eaten fresh; they are also available salted, spiced, and canned in oil or made into a paste. They are used as appetizers and to flavour other food, particularly salads and sauces. For recipes see index.

ANDALOUSE

(French): A term indicating that the dish to which it is applied contains tomatoes and sweet pimientos.

ANGLAISE

(French): English; in English style: à l'Anglaise.

ANTIPASTO

(Italian): The first, or starter, course of a meal. It consists of cold or spicy hors d'oeuvres such as anchovy, salami, hot peppers, olives, celery, and pickled relishes. Prepared jars of antipasto are available in many food stores. They are a convenience to have on hand. Just chill and prepare colourful appetizing arrangements on individual plates.

APÉRITIF

(French): A drink of moderate alcoholic content taken before meals to stimulate the appetite.

APFEL

(German): Apple; apfel kuchen: apple cake or tart; apfel strudel: a delicate pastry made of paper-thin dough covered with an apple filling, then rolled and baked.

APPLE SNOW

A whipped dessert consisting of apple pulp and stiffly beaten egg whites, usually flavoured with lemon and vanilla.

ARTICHAUT

(French): Artichoke.

ASPERGES

(French): Asparagus.

AU, AUX

See in À **La.**

BAIN-MARIE

(French): A utensil for cooking or keeping hot certain delicate foods that should not be exposed to a direct flame. The vessel containing the food is placed in or over another pan, in which water is kept at or below the boiling point. The double boiler is a type of bain-marie.

BALLOTTINE

(French): A piece of meat, poultry, or game; boned, stuffed, and rolled up—usually served hot.

BANNOCK

In Scotland and northern England, a thick, round flattened cake made of oat, rye, or barley meal, usually unleavened and baked on a griddle. Also, a type of Irish soda bread.

BAR-LE-DUC

A jam of seeded whole red (or sometimes white) currants, named after the French town in which it is said to have originated. Nowadays, the term is also applied to similar jams made with gooseberries and other berries.

BARLEY

A cereal grass whose seed or grain is used in making liquors and beers and also in soups. Barley as the source of strong alcoholic liquor, especially whiskey, is humorously personified in the United States as John Barleycorn—a term also applied to the liquor itself.

BARLEY SUGAR

A confection made by heating sugar until it begins to melt and caramelize, forming coarse grains. This clear, hard sweetmeat was formerly made with a barley extract—hence the name.

BARQUETTE

(French): A small oval or boat-shaped pastry case. Barquettes may be filled with various mixtures for hot or cold hors d'oeuvres, or with fruit, custards, etc., for desserts.

BAVAROISE

(French): Moulded dessert of Bavarian cream; à la Bavaroise: Bavarian style.

BEEF À LA MODE

A well-larded piece of beef slowly cooked in a little water or wine with vegetables; a form of braised beef.

BEIGNET

(French): A fritter.

BEURRE

(French): Butter. Au beurre noir: with black butter. The butter is not really black but browned in a pan. With lemon added, this makes a nice sauce for fish and vegetables. Beurre fondue: melted butter; beurre manié: butter and flour kneaded together and gradually added to a sauce to thicken it.

BIRD'S NEST SOUP

A Chinese soup thickened with the mucilaginous substance used by a certain species of birds (swifts) to hold their nests together.

BISCUIT

A thin, flat cake with basic ingredients of flour and water (or milk) without any leaven.

BISMARCK HERRING

The fillets of herring are pickled with their roe in a mixture of white wine and vinegar, seasoned with onions, salt, and whole black peppers. They are served as a starter.

BISQUE

A thick, rich cream soup made from shellfish or, formerly, from game; hence, also, various thick vegetable soups.

BITOCHKY SMETANA

(Russian): Russian meatballs in a sour-cream sauce.

BITTERS

An infusion of bark, herbs, roots, and other aromatic materials used to flavour cocktails and other drinks and some foods. There are a number of trademarked brands, whose formulas are usually secret. Abbott's, Angostura, Fernet Branca, and Peychaud's are among the most popular brands. Angostura bitters have been used in a number of the food recipes in this book calling for aromatic bitters.

BLANQUETTE

(French): A stew of white meat (chicken, veal, or lamb) made with white sauce.

BLOATER

A specially selected fat herring or mackerel that has been cured (bloated), salted and smoked, in a special way.

BOEUF

(French): Beef; boeuf rôti: roast beef; boeuf à la mode: well larded, sometimes marinated, beef, braised with vegetables; boeuf salé: salt beef; boeuf braisé: braised beef.

BOLOGNA

(Italian): Also called Bologna sausage; a mildly seasoned smoked sausage, usually made of beef, pork, and veal.

BOMBAY DUCK

A strong-flavoured dried fish served in India and elsewhere with curries.

BOMBE

(French): A dessert made by freezing two or more ices, ice creams, or sherbets of contrasting colours and flavours in concentric layers in a round or melon-shaped mould.

BONBON

(French): A confection or sweetmeat that has a fondant centre or is dipped in fondant.

BONNE FEMME, À LA

(French): Literally, in the manner of a good woman; hence, originally, cooked in a plain, home style. The term now refers to a garnish of vegetables cooked with meat or of mushrooms cooked with fish.

BOUCHÉE

(French): Literally "mouthful." A small patty of light pastry usually filled with a savoury creamed fish or meat mixture.

BOURGEOISE, À LA

(French): In simple family style; a kind of garnish consisting of vegetables such as onions and carrots.

BOURGUIGNONNE

(French): À la bourguignonne: in the style of Burgundy, a region of France noted for its food and wine. Escargots à la bourguignonne: snails in a garlic-flavoured butter sauce; sauce bourguignonne: a red-wine sauce with many variations — depending on whether it is intended to accompany meat, poultry, fish, or eggs — but usually containing shallots or onions, butter, and mushrooms.

BRAID

A fancy bread in which the dough is cut into strips which are braided, either three or four strands being used. The braids are wider at the centre than at the ends.

Braid

BRATWURST

(German): Small, highly seasoned pork link sausages, served hot.

BRAUNSCHWEIGER

(German): Soft liver sausage.

BREWER'S YEAST

This is obtained as a by-product in the brewing of beer. It does not have leavening power. Brewer's yeast is a concentrated source of high-quality protein and of many of the B vitamins. Because it is also a good source of the minerals iron and phosphorus, it sometimes is prescribed for patients needing dietary supplements.

BRILLAT-SAVARIN, JEAN ANTHELME

A French gastronome (1755-1826), the author of *The Physiology of Taste*, a classic work on cookery. His name has been given to various dishes.

BROCHETTE

(French): A small skewer. En brochette: Grilled or served on a skewer.

BROWN STEW

Stew in which the meat is browned in fat before liquid is added.

BRÛLÉ

(French): Burnt; a term usually applied to caramelized sugar. Crème brûlée: a rich custard with a caramelized sugar coating.

BRUNOISE

(French): The cutting of vegetables into shreds or into tiny rounds, cubes, or other uniform shapes. The term also describes a mixture of vegetables slowly cooked in butter or some other fat and used for making soups, sauces, or other dishes.

BUBBLE AND SQUEAK

A traditional dish of beef and cabbage, so named because of the sound it makes while cooking.

BUCK RAREBIT

Welsh rarebit topped with a poached egg.

BUN

A large round roll, made of yeast dough usually somewhat sweetened and often spiced or enriched with raisins, etc.

BUNDKUCHEN

(German): A circular-shaped cake.

BURRO

(Italian): Butter.

CABINET PUDDING

A cold, moulded dessert of layers of jelly, thickened custard, and cake or fruit.

CAFFEINE

An alkaloid present in coffee, tea (in which it is known as theine), and cola drinks and, in small amounts, in cocoa. When taken in moderation, caffeine is a mild stimulant; taken to excess, it can have a harmful effect on the heart and nervous system.

CALF'S-FOOT JELLY

A jelly made from the gelatine extract from calf's feet by long, gentle cooking; an old-time Jewish dish known in Yiddish as pitcha or sülze.

CANARD

(French): Duck.

CANNELON

(French): When used alone, the word usually refers to a small roll or "stick" of pastry, stuffed with minced meat or sweets, baked or fried. When applied to meat, as "cannelon of beef," it means a stuffed roll of beef, cooked usually by braising.

CANNOLI

(Italian): A Sicilian pastry made of thin dough shaped into a cylinder and fried in deep fat, then filled with ricotta cheese, pudding, whipped cream, or ice cream.

CAPONETTE OR CAPETTE

A hormone treated chicken of either sex, usually marketed at an earlier age than a capon. It is usually lighter in weight but retains all the advantages of a capon.

CARBOHYDRATE

The class of foodstuffs that includes starches and sugars (the two other main food classes are proteins and fats). Carbohydrate foods are used by the body essentially for immediate energy; when eaten in excess of need, they are converted rapidly into stores of fat.

CARNATZLACH

(Yiddish): A highly seasoned minced meat dish of Rumanian origin. The meat is formed into small sausage-like shapes and grilled.

CAROB

An evergreen tree native to the Mediterranean area with long, fleshy, edible pods which have been used as food for animal and man since prehistoric times. The pods have numerous names including locust pod, St. John's bread, and bokser. The pods are eaten fresh or dried. The carob pod is often found in Italian food shops.

A powder made from the carob pod is sometimes available and is used in baking to add flavour to wheat flour; a lower oven temperature (not over 350°F. Mark 4) must be used because carob powder scorches easily. About 1 ounce carob powder may be substituted in each 4 ounces wheat flour, and a similar amount of wheat flour must be deducted from the recipe.

CARTE, À LA

(French): Literally, from the bill of fare. This term refers to the practice of listing dishes on a menu item by item, with a separate price for each, as opposed to table d'hôte, in which a price is fixed for the entire meal.

CASSAVA

Any of a number of related tropical plants with edible starchy roots; also called manioc. Bitter cassava, the kind most commonly used, contains hydrocyanic acid and is deadly poisonous until it is cooked. In South America cassava is cooked like sweet potatoes, ground into a flour used for bread, and fermented to make an intoxicating beverage; elsewhere it is known chiefly as the source of tapioca.

CASSOLETTE

(French): Individual heatproof dish; food cooked and served in such a dish. In English this is usually called an individual casserole. Not to be confused with *cassoulet*, see over.

Cassolette

CASSOULET

(French): A complex stew made in many versions with a large variety of ingredients; however white beans and pork are basic ingredients in most recipes.

CECI

(Italian): Chick-peas.

CELLULOSE

The substance (chemically, a carbohydrate) that makes up the cell walls or woody parts of plants. Since it is not digested by human beings, vegetables such as cabbage that contain a high proportion of it form a residue (bulk) in the bowel.

CERVELAT

A sausage made of beef and pork.

CHAMPIGNONS

(French): Mushrooms.

CHANTILLY

(French): A term applied to a great many dishes made or served with whipped cream.

CHAPON

(French): A crust or cube of bread usually rubbed with garlic and tossed with salad to give it flavour. Caesar salad is made with chapons. Also the French term for capon.

CHAROSES OR KHAROSES

(Yiddish): A mixture of nuts, apples, and wine served by Jewish people at dinner on the eve of the first two days of their Passover holiday. It symbolizes the mortar used by the Israelites when they were slaves in ancient Egypt.

CHICKEN-FRIED STEAK

Steak dredged in flour and seasonings, fried, and served smothered in gravy.

CHIFFONADE

(French): Literally, "rags." Refers to a garnish of finely shredded vegetables used for soups and salads.

Chiffonade dressing is a salad dressing (usually French dressing) with chopped or shredded vegetables in it.

CHOP (The food)

A cut of meat; the name is derived from the fact that the piece is chopped off.

CHOU

(French): Cabbage.

CHOU-FLEUR

(French): Cauliflower.

CHOUX DE BRUXELLES

(French): Brussels sprouts.

CHOWCHOW

Chopped vegetable pickle in a highly seasoned mustard sauce. Also, chopped preserved fruits.

CIVET

(French): A highly seasoned stew of rabbit or other game. The animal's blood is always used in the sauce of a true civet.

CLABBER

Milk that has soured to the stage where a firm custard has been formed but not to the point of separation of the whey.

COBBLER

A deep-dish pie of sweetened fruit topped sometimes with suet crust rather than piecrust. Also, a type of alcoholic beverage served over crushed ice.

Cobbler

COCKTAIL

An appetizer—either a short, mixed alcoholic beverage or liquid or solid food (fruit or vegetable juice, chilled mixed fruits, seafood).

COCOTTE

(French): An earthenware or porcelain-covered casserole. Small cocottes are generally used for such dishes as shirred (baked) eggs. Larger sizes are used for chicken and other entrées. Foods so cooked (which are described as being en cocotte) should be served from the dish.

Cocotte

COLCANNON

Irish dish of potatoes, salt pork, cabbage. It is similar in character to the English dish called, "Bubble and Squeak."

COLLOP

A small piece or slice, especially a thin, boneless piece of meat, dipped into eggs and crumbs and sautéed.

CON CARNE

(Spanish): With meat.

CONDÉ

(French): Stewed fruit served with rice. Also a French almond-paste cake.

CONFITURE

(French): Jam.

COQUILLE

(French): Literally, shell; usually that of the scallop. Hence, a similarly shaped cooking vessel or food prepared in one. En coquille: served in a shell.

En Coquille

CORAL

The ovaries of the female lobster. Considered a delicacy.

CORBEILLE

(French): Literally, basket; used on menus to mean a basket of fruit.

CORDON BLEU

(French): Literally, blue ribbon; the name of a famous French cooking school. Often used loosely to denote any exceptionally fine cook.

CÔTELETTE

(French): Cutlet, a small boneless slice of meat.

COUPES

(French): Fruit sundaes, i.e., a combination of ice creams with various flavours usually served in stemmed glasses. Although sundaes are common throughout the world, the idea is of French origin. **Coupe Jacques:** vanilla ice cream served with mixed fruit. **Coupe Melba:** Vanilla ice cream topped with a peach half with sweetened puréed raspberries spooned over it, and garnished with whipped cream and slivered almonds.

COUSCOUS

A dish that takes many forms throughout the various North African countries. It commonly refers to a coarse ground grain or meal (wheat semolina, cracked millet, cracked wheat, or buckwheat) steamed in beef, chicken, or mutton stock served separately with the meat or poultry used for the stock. Or couscous may be a complex all-in-one dish of chicken, lamb or mutton, or beef cooked with a variety of vegetables and served with one of the grains mentioned above.

CRÈME

(French): Cream; frequently used in the names of liqueurs. Crème d'ananas: flavoured with pineapple; crème de bananes: flavoured with bananas; crème de cacao: made from cacao and vanilla beans; crème de café: flavoured with coffee; crème de Cassis: mildly alcoholic, made from black currants; crème de menthe: green or colourless, flavoured chiefly with peppermint; crème de moka: flavoured with coffee; crème de rose: flavoured with rose-petal oil and vanilla; crème de thé: flavoured with tea; crème de vanilla: flavoured with vanilla bean: crème de violette: made from vanilla and cacao, perfumed with oil of violets; crème Yvette: lavender-coloured, similar to crème de violette. À la crème: with cream.

CRESSON

(French): Watercress.

CREVETTE

(French): Prawns.

CROQUEMBOUCHE

(French): A spectacular pyramid-like dessert made from about 100 walnut-size cream puff shells filled with French pastry cream or other filling. After filling, these are dipped in caramelized sugar syrup which serves both as a glaze and adherent to keep the cream puffs in place in row upon row to form the pyramid around some suitably shaped dish.

CROUSTADE

(French): A hollowed-out chunk of fried or toasted bread, or a pastry case, made to hold creamed or other soft food. Croustades are made in various shapes.

Croustades

CROÛTE

(French): A bread crust, pastry crust, or crust formed on anything. En croûte: baked in a crust, or covered with a crust.

CUISINE

(French): Kitchen, cookery, or a particular style of cooking.

DAGWOOD

A huge sandwich containing many different fillings, named for the comic strip character addicted to them.

DAMPFNUDELN

(German): Steamed noodles.

DAMSON

A variety of small, purple plum.

DARIOLE

(French): (1) A small cup-shaped mould filled with various savoury mixtures and baked or steamed. (2) A small cream-filled tart.

DAUBE

(French): A style of braised meat, poultry, or game; usually beef braised in a wine stock. Also, a Creole-style pot roast.

DÉJEUNER

(French): Lunch. Petit déjeuner: breakfast; the French breakfast usually consists of hot rolls and coffee.

DELMONICO

Delmonico steak: a rib steak: Potatoes Delmonico: sliced cooked potatoes baked with white sauce, crumbs, and cheese. Both are named after a famous New York restaurant of the 19th century.

Delmonico Steaks

DEMI-TASSE

(French): Literally, half-cup. After-dinner coffee, served in small cups, usually black, although cream and sugar may be added if desired.

DENTE, AL

(Italian): Literally, to the tooth; a term describing pasta products cooked only until they are barely tender. When they are to be served plain or with a sauce, this is how they should be.

DENVER OR "WESTERN" SANDWICH

A sandwich made of scrambled egg with bits of ham and sometimes green pepper and onion in it.

DIABLE, À LA

(French): Devilled, or seasoned with spicy condiments.

DIVINITY

A kind of sweetmeat; soft, light, and creamy.

DRIED BEEF

A form of preserved beef cured by salting, smoking, and drying.

DUCHESS

Duchess Potatoes: potatoes whipped very light with seasonings and beaten egg yolk, usually piped through a pastry tube as a border for grilled or planked meats; also called Potatoes Duchesse. Duchess apples: an early cooking variety.

DUCK, PRESSED

An epicurean dish of roasted duck that is squeezed in a special press at the diner's table and is served with a sauce prepared in a chafing dish. Called Canard à la Presse in French, this dish is served only in the most elaborate restaurants.

Pressed Duck

DUFF

An old-fashioned thick flour pudding boiled or steamed in a cloth bag. Also, a fruit dumpling.

DU JOUR

(French): A term used on menus to indicate feature of the day, as soupe du jour (soup).

DULSE

Any of several edible seaweeds with large, red, wedge-shaped fronds.

DUTCH APPLE CAKE

A form of sweet bread, usually a biscuit or shortcake dough, baked in a flat sheet with tart, wedge-shaped slices of apple arranged in regular rows on the top and spread with sugar and cinnamon.

ÉCREVISSE

(French): The fresh-water crayfish.

ENTRÉE

(French): Correctly used, this term means a small dish served between the main courses at a formal dinner. However, it is often used for the main course of a meal, the one preceded by a starter and followed by dessert.

ENTREMETS
(French): Literally, between dishes. In earlier centuries, this term referred to a variety of sweet or vegetable side dishes served between the many courses of the elaborate French meals then in fashion. Nowadays it means dessert.

ESCALOPE
(French): A small thin slice of meat or fish.

ESCARGOTS
(French): Snails.

ESCOFFIER
A French chef (1847-1935), one of the great names in French cookery.

ESPAGNOLE
(French): Spanish. Espagnole sauce: a brown sauce.

FARCE
(French): A forcemeat; a mixture of minced meat and seasonings used as stuffing for meats and poultry.

FARCI
(French): Stuffed with forcemeat or some other filling, as cabbage stuffed with sausage meat.

FARFEL
(Yiddish): Noodle dough chopped into fine grains and boiled, usually in soups.

FECULA
Any form of starch, used for thickening, often produced from potatoes, manioc (cassava), or other food plants rather than from a cereal grain. Potato flour (which see) is a good example.

FLAMBÉ
(French): Literally, flamed; a term applied to food that has a liquor, usually brandy, poured over it and ignited.

FLAN
(French): An open-faced tart. Also, a baked custard.

FLANNEL CAKE
A thin, tender pancake, often one made with yeast.

FLEISHIGS
(Yiddish): Meat or meat derivatives, or dishes made with these. See **Kosher.**

FLOUNDER
A bony, flat fish common to English shores. Its flesh is sweet and good when fresh. It should not be confused with plaice though in parts of England it is so called.

FLUFF
A dessert of stiffly beaten egg whites or whipped cream, sugar, and fruit pulp, cooked or uncooked; also called whip, snow, foam, syllabub, and soufflé.

Orange Fluff

FLUMMERY
A dessert made of rice or oatmeal with milk and flavourings; also, a type of custard dessert.

FOIE
(French): Liver. Foie gras: fat goose liver; foie de veau: calf's liver. See also **Pâté,** for pâté de foie gras.

FONDANT
Mixture used as centres for bon bons and chocolates, coating for nuts, as base for mints and puddings. There are two kinds, one a cooked mixture of sugar and water, the other uncooked icing sugar, butter, and milk or water.

FONDUE
(French): Swiss fondue (which see); also, a baked soufflé made with eggs, cheese, milk, and crumbs. In French, the term is used in addition for various vegetable preparations cooked to a pulp. Fondue à la bourguignonne: chunks of beef cooked individually in a chafing dish by the diners, who then choose a sauce for them from among a variety set out.

FOOL
A dessert of chilled stewed strained fruits and sweet cream.

FOUR
(French): Oven.

FRAISE
(French): A strawberry; also, a French brandy made from strawberries.

FRAMBOISE
(French): A raspberry; also, a French brandy made from raspberries.

FRANÇAISE, À LA
(French): In the French manner: a term applied to various dishes with no specific meaning.

FRAPPÉ
(French): Fruit juice sweetened with sugar, diluted with water, and frozen to a slushy consistency. Also a beverage poured over crushed ice.

FRENCH DOUGHNUT
A doughnut made of puff pastry.

FRENCH PASTRY
Individual pastries, most frequently made of puff pastry with various fillings.

FRENCH ROLL
A hard, crisp roll; also called Vienna roll.

FRICANDEAU
(French): Larded meat, usually veal, in a sauce.

FRITTO MISTO
(Italian): A fried or sometimes pan-grilled mixture of delicate meats and vegetables or fish.

FROMAGE
(French): Cheese.

FRUITS DE MER
(French): Seafood.

FUMÉ
(French): Smoked; saumon fumé: smoked salmon.

FUMET
(French): The concentrated stock or broth of meat, fish, or vegetables.

FUNNY CAKE
A Pennsylvania-Dutch dish. A cake batter and sauce, baked in a pie case. The sauce forms a layer between cake and pie case.

GALANTINE
(French): Boned poultry, game, or meat stuffed and roasted, simmered, or braised, then pressed into a symmetrical shape and cut into slices or moulded in aspic.

GALUPTZE
(Russian): Minced meat rolled in cabbage leaves.

GÂTEAU
(French): Cake; petits gâteaux: small cakes; gâteaux assortis: assorted cakes.

GAUFRE
(French): A waffle of the French type, made of a very light, sweetened dough or batter.

GELÉE
(French): Jelly or jellied.

GEM
A term variously used; often applied to muffins or cupcakes.

GHEE
A clarified butter which is one of the commonest articles of diet in India, and is used extensively in all forms of cooking.

GHERKIN
A small, knobby variety of cucumber, or the immature fruit of the common cucumber, used for pickling.

GOLDEN BUCK
Welsh Rarebit topped with a poached egg.

GOOBER
A peanut. The term is a corruption of an African (Bantu) word.

GOURMAND

Originally, a glutton; now a person who likes and is a judge of fine foods. In the latter sense it has the same meaning as epicure and gourmet, but the implication is still one of heartiness rather than delicacy.

GOURMET

An epicure; a person who likes and is a judge of fine foods and drinks. In French, the term originally referred to a winetaster.

GROUNDNUT

Any of several plants with edible tubers or tuber-like parts; specifically, a term for peanut.

GRUEL

A thin porridge.

HACHÉ

(French): Minced or chopped.

HACHIS

(French): Mincemeat or hash.

HAGGIS

Considered the national dish of Scotland, it is a sort of meat pudding made of liver, lungs, and other parts of mutton mixed with oatmeal, onion, suet, and herbs, and cooked in a sheep's stomach. Since the stomach is tripe, the whole pudding is considered edible.

HALKE

(Yiddish): A potato or flour dumpling. Also called knaidel.

HALVAH OR HALVA

A confection consisting of a paste made with ground sesame seeds and nuts mixed with honey and other ingredients. It is a great delicacy in Turkey and other countries of the Near East.

HANGTOWN FRY

Usually a combination of scrambled eggs and fried oysters.

HARD TACK

Unsalted, hard, dry biscuit; the name given by sailors in early days to the ship's biscuit or bread.

HARICOT

(French): Bean. Haricots verts: green beans. Also a stew, usually of mutton; this term has nothing to do with the word for bean but comes from halicoter, to chop.

HARLEQUIN

See Neapolitan.

HASTY PUDDING

In New England, corn-meal mush; in Great Britain, a flour or oat porridge.

HOTCHPOTCH

Also called hodgepodge; a thick Scottish stew of meat (usually mutton) and various vegetables in a very little brown stock. It needs stirring because it may stick to the bottom of the pot.

HOMARD

(French): Lobster.

HONGROISE, À LA

(French): Hungarian style. It usually refers to a paprika sauce, pink or red, depending upon the amount of paprika used, with chopped onion and sour cream. Served hot with fish, lamb, veal and poultry.

HOOTSLA

A Pennsylvania-Dutch dish consisting of bread cubes which are first browned in butter, then a mixture of beaten eggs, milk, and seasoning is poured over and fried until brown.

HOT POT

An English meat stew with many variations.

HUILE

(French): Oil.

HUÎTRES

(French): Oysters.

HYSON

A variety of Chinese green tea; the early crop is called young hyson, and the inferior leaves are called hyson skin.

IMBOTTITO

(Italian): Stuffed. The plural forms are imbottiti and imbottite.

INDIENNE, À L'

(French): In the Indian manner: generally, with curry or similar East Indian seasonings.

IRISH MOSS

An edible seaweed (carrageen) dried and bleached for use in medicine and as a thickening agent, particularly in milk desserts. Also, blancmange, which is sometimes made with it.

IRRADIATE

To treat with ultra-violet light in order to increase the vitamin D content. Milk is commonly irradiated.

JAMBON

(French): Ham.

JARDINIÈRE À LA

(French): Literally, gardener's style; garnished with diced mixed vegetables.

JERKED BEEF

Beef preserved by slicing it into strips and drying these in the sun or over a fire.

JOHNNYCAKE

A type of corn bread. The name comes from the term journey cake—that is, one that would keep well on a journey.

JUGGED HARE

A rabbit stew in a wine sauce.

JULEP

A cold beverage with a distinctive flavour, often of herbs; specifically, a mint julep.

JUMBLES

Name used for several kinds of English biscuits.

JUNKET

A sweetened, flavoured milk dessert curdled or jellied by rennet (which see).

JUS

(French): Juice or gravy; au jus: served in the natural juice or gravy.

KARTOFFEL

(German): Potato. Kartoffel klösse: potato dumplings.

KÄSE

(German): Cheese.

KEBAB

Also spelled kabob or cabob; highly seasoned meat or other foods cooked on skewers. The word is derived from shish kebab.

KEBI

Also spelled kibbie; a Syrian national dish made primarily of minced lamb and other meats, bulgur (cracked wheat), and pine nuts.

KING, À LA

Usually applies to a method of preparing chicken, served in a rich cream sauce usually containing mushrooms, pimientos, and green peppers; sometimes flavoured with sherry.

KLÖSSE

(German): Dumplings.

KOCH KÄSE

(German): Boiled cheese.

KOSHER

(Yiddish): A term designating foods selected and prepared in accordance with Jewish dietary law; derived from a Hebrew word meaning fit, right, proper. Kashruth, as the dietary law is called, makes demands both difficult and subtle. At Passover, for instance, when leavened foods (see Matzo) are prohibited, Orthodox Jews must not use gaseous drinks containing food colouring with an alcoholic base, since this is often made from leavened grain. The Old Testament prohibition against cooking a kid (a young goat) in its mother's milk is extended to keeping separate dishes for meat and dairy products, some pareve (neutral) dishes, and additional sets used only during Passover.

One reason kosher meat is more expensive is that it must be ritually examined before and after slaughter under rabbinical supervision.

Kosher products, often indicated by the letter U, are put out under many national brand names. Kosher cheeses are also made, without animal rennet; they are identified by a label and come in cream, cottage, Gouda, Limburger, and other types.

KRANZKUCHEN
(German): A sweet cake in the form of a braid.

KUCHEN
(German): A cake, often a coffee cake.

KUMISS
Fermented or distilled mare's or camel's milk, drunk by Tatar nomads of Asia. Imitations made of cow's milk are used in certain special diets. Also spelled koumis, koumiss, koumyss.

LACHS
(German): Salmon.

LAIT
(French): Milk. Au lait: made or served with milk.

LANGOUSTE
(French): A sea crayfish or spiny lobster.

LANGUE
(French): Tongue. Langue de veau: veal tongue; langue de chat: cat's tongue, a flat, narrow chocolate or a similarly shaped biscuit.

LEGUME
The term, legume, refers to any plant of the pea family; also, the edible pod of any of these including beans, peas, peanuts, carob, lentils, and soya beans. In French the word is used to mean any vegetable. Legumes provide valuable and nutritive foods because the food stored for the embryo in the seed (the pea) is rich in protein. In many areas of the world, especially where meat is scarce or expensive, legumes are staples of the diet. See index for recipes for beans, peas, lentils, etc.

LEMON OIL
An oil obtained from the rind of lemons.

LINGUINE
(Italian): A narrow, flat noodle about ⅛ inch wide, meaning literally "little tongues".

LINSEN
(German): Lentils.

LIVER SAUSAGE OR LIVER-WURST
A sausage made from pork livers and trimmings, seasoned, and packed in casings of various sizes.

LOX
(Yiddish): Smoked salmon.

LUTFISK
Lutfisk is often called Swedish Christmas Fish for this fish is usually served only during the holiday season. It is a type of dried salt cod which is soaked in lye water or bicarbonate of soda water for several days to a week, then in fresh water, before it is cooked. It is used almost exclusively by Scandinavians and it can be bought in Scandinavian delicatessen stores ready to cook, especially at Christmastime.

LYONNAISE
Prepared with finely sliced, fried onions: said especially of potatoes sautéed with onions.

MACÉDOINE
(French): A mixture usually of fruits or vegetables, cut into small, uniform pieces.

MADRILÈNE
(French): A clear, tomato-flavoured consommé, served hot or jellied.

MAÎTRE D'HÔTEL
(French): The man in charge of hotel catering or restaurant food service. Also, a term implying the use of chopped parsley. Maître d'hôtel butter: creamed, seasoned butter mixed with minced parsley and lemon juice, served on grilled meats, grilled or poached fish, and certain vegetables; maître d'hôtel sauce: béchamel sauce with chopped parsley, butter, and lemon juice added.

MANDELTORTE
(German): Almond Torte.

MARGUERITE
(1) An unsweetened cracker spread with boiled icing, sprinkled with coconut, nuts, or chocolate pieces, and baked until golden. (2) a cracker with a melted marshmallow on it. (3) a spongecake batter baked in small shapes.

MARMITE
(French): A stock pot used for cooking soups or stews. Petite Marmite: A French soup served in small earthenware casseroles.

MASA
(Spanish): Dough; a term sometimes used specifically to mean the dough for tortillas, which is made of corn kernels soaked in lime water and then ground fine.

MATÉ
Also known as Paraguay tea and yerba maté; a kind of tea made from the dried leaves of a South American evergreen tree of the holly family. It is a popular beverage in some parts of South America. In Spanish the word is spelled without the accent, which is used in English so that the second syllable will be pronounced.

MATELOTE
(French): A stew of fish with wine, mushrooms, onions, and garlic, properly made only with fresh-water fish; also, a sauce for fish with similar ingredients.

MATZO
(Hebrew): A Jewish unleavened bread made of flour and water. It is thin and cracker-like, pricked in a pattern that resembles stitching. As a reminder of the Biblical Israelites, who departed so hastily from their slavery in Egypt that they took with them dough that was still unleavened, religious Jews eat no other bread during the week of Passover. The plural of the word is matzoth.

MATZOON
(Armenian): Yogurt.

MEAT BIRDS (PAUPIETTES)
Meat birds, or in French, paupiettes, is a dish made in various ways but usually consisting of thin, oblong pieces of beef or veal that are stuffed, rolled, and tied or skewered. They are then coated with flour, browned, and cooked in a small amount of liquid.

MELBA
The name of a famous Australian operatic star who died in 1931, Dame Nellie Melba, who gave her name to many dishes. The most famous is Peach Melba, originally made in her honour by the great French chef Escoffier. This dish consists of halves of peaches on a layer of ice cream covered with a raspberry sauce. Nowadays almost any fruit is served in the same way.

MERINGUE
(French): Stiffly beaten egg whites sweetened and flavoured if desired and baked to a delicate brown. It is used on pastry, puddings, cakes, and other desserts, and as small cakes. It is also made in the form of shells which are filled with ice cream.

MIGNON
(French): Dainty. Filet mignon: a small choice fillet of beef tenderloin or occasionally some other meat.

MILANAISE, À LA
(French): In the style of Milan. Applied to meats, this term usually indicates a coating of breadcrumbs mixed with Parmesan cheese; with other dishes it most frequently implies the use of macaroni, cheese, chopped cooked meat, and a tomato sauce.

MILLE-FEUILLES
(French): Literally, a thousand leaves; a delicate pastry made of many thin leaves of puff pastry, with a cream filling.

MILT

The reproductive glands of male fishes, especially when filled with germ cells, and the milky fluid containing them. It is cooked like fish roe and is considered a delicacy by some people. Also called soft roe. Milter: a male fish in breeding time.

MINESTRA

(Italian): Pottage, soup, broth.

MIROTON

(French): Cooked, sliced leftover meat heated in various ways, usually in a brown gravy to which onions and pickles are often added.

MOCHA

A variety of coffee originally exported from Mocha, a port on the Red Sea, and noted for its quality: hence, a term often applied to foods flavoured with coffee or with coffee and chocolate.

MOCK CHICKEN LEG

Meat, usually seasoned minced veal or pork or a combination, formed around a wooden skewer in the shape of a chicken leg. It is usually coated with crumbs before cooking.

MOCK DUCK

A meat prepared in a duck-like shape. Leg of lamb is commonly used.

MOCK TURTLE SOUP

A soup made from calf's head with a variety of seasonings.

MODE, À LA

(French): Literally, fashionable or according to a particular custom; a term applied to a method of braising beef and also, with no specific significance, to various other ways of cooking or serving food.

MOLLET

(French): Soft. Oeufs mollets: soft-boiled eggs.

MONGOLE

(French): Literally, Mongolian style. Purée mongole: a split-pea soup containing tomatoes, garnished with julienne vegetables.

MORTADELLA

(Italian): A large smoked sausage.

MOSTACCIOLI

(Italian): A tubular pasta about ½-inch in diameter, cut obliquely about 2½ inches long.

MOUSSAKA

Also spelled mousaka or mussaca, a Near Eastern casserole dish made in many variations, often of lamb and vegetables, frequently including aubergine.

MOUSSE

(French): Literally, froth. A frozen dessert of sweetened, flavoured whipped cream, with or without fruits; also, a chilled dessert of whipped cream or beaten egg whites, variously flavoured. The term is also applied to a number of moulded dishes of minced fish, meat, or poultry prepared with beaten egg white or with gelatine.

MOUSSELINE

(French): A term applied to a number of preparations made with whipped cream; also, any of several very light cakes. Sauce mousseline: usually Hollandaise sauce with whipped cream, sometimes mayonnaise with whipped cream.

MULLIGAN STEW

A stew made of odds and ends of meat and vegetables; a slang term originating with American hoboes.

MUTTON

The meat of a sheep one or more years of age.

NATUREL

(French): Natural; au naturel: in plain or simple style.

NAVARIN

(French): A mutton or lamb stew with turnips, onions, and potatoes and a rich gravy.

NEAPOLITAN

Brick ice cream layered in different flavours; also, sometimes, a jelly arranged in layers of different colours. Also called harlequin.

NOISETTE

(French): Hazelnut. Hence, also, small round pieces of lean meat or browned potato balls.

NORMANDE, À LA

(French): In the style of Normandy, a region of northern France; a term often implying the presence of cream, cider, or apples or a combination of these. Normande sauce: a rich cream sauce containing fish or shellfish stock and mushrooms or mushroom stock, served with seafood.

NOUGAT

(French): Any of several varieties of sweetmeat; usually, a paste containing chopped nuts, such as pistachios or almonds.

NOUVEAU

(French): New. Applies to peas, potatoes, etc.

NÜSSE

(German): Nuts; also, small nut-sized or nut-shaped cakes.

OATEN

Of or made of oats or oatmeal.

O'BRIEN POTATOES

Cooked, diced potatoes pan-fried with chopped onions and green pepper, pimientos, or both.

OEUF

(French): Egg. Oeuf brouillé: scrambled egg; oeuf dur: hard-boiled egg; oeuf en cocotte: baked or shirred egg; oeuf frit or oeuf sur le plat: fried egg; oeuf farci: stuffed egg; oeuf mollet: soft-boiled egg; oeuf poché: poached egg.

OLEOMARGARINE

Margarine. This name, which dates from the time when the product was made with beef fat (oleo), is falling into disuse now that most margarine consists of vegetable oils.

OLLA PODRIDA

(Spanish): A rich stew of sausages, poultry, beans, beef, cabbage, and other ingredients baked slowly in an earthenware pot, from which it takes its name. The term is no longer used much in Spain; such a stew is usually now called a cocido.

OMELETTE

(French): Omelet; omelette au fromage: cheese omelet; omelette au jambon: ham omelet; omelette au rhum: omelet flavoured with rum; omelette parmentier: omelet with potatoes; omelette aux fines herbes: omelet with finely chopped herbs.

OOLONG TEA

A type of Chinese and Japanese tea that is only partly fermented before being dried. It therefore differs both in colour and in flavour from virtually all the other teas, which are black or fully fermented. Oolong makes a lighter coloured beverage with a slightly astringent taste.

ORANGE PEKOE

A black tea grown in Ceylon and India, made from the small leaves at the tips of the stem. The term denotes the size of the leaf, not the quality of the tea.

ORETIKA

(Greek): Hors d'oeuvres or appetizers.

PAIN

(French): Bread. Pain rôti or pain grillé: toast; pain perdu (literally, lost bread): French toast, or, in Creole cookery, a kind of fritter.

PAN BREAD

A quick loaf baked in a covered saucepan on top of the range.

PAN FISH

A general term for small fish for cooking whole in a small amount of fat.

PANADA

Originally, any dish containing soaked breadcrumbs (the name comes from the Spanish word for breaded); hence, a simple French soup made of stale crusts of bread gently cooked in water or milk to the consistency of gruel, then enriched with butter and egg and seasoned with salt and pepper. Also, and more commonly, a paste of bread, flour, or cereal cooked with milk or stock to form the foundation for forcemeat or stuffing or to be used in thickening sauces.

PANÉ

(French): Prepared with or coated with breadcrumbs.

PANOCHA

A sweetmeat made of brown sugar, milk, butter, and nuts. Also a coarse sugar made in Mexico. Also spelled penuche or penuchi.

PAPILLOTE, EN

(French): Cooked in parchment or in a paper bag. Nowadays, aluminium foil is usually substituted for the paper.

Aluminium foil cookery is a modern version of "en papillote".

PAREVE

(Yiddish): A term applied to food that is neither a dairy (milchig) nor a meat (fleishig) product and can therefore, according to the dietary laws, be eaten with either by Orthodox Jews. Also spelled parve. See **Kosher.**

PARFAIT

A frozen dessert made of whipped cream and flavouring folded into a foundation of beaten egg yolks cooked with hot syrup. Also, a dessert of several layers of ice cream, fruit or syrup, and whipped cream served in a tall glass called a parfait glass.

Parfaits

PARMENTIER

(French): A name applied to dishes containing potatoes; from Antoine-Auguste Parmentier (1737-1817), who popularized the potato in France and invented many ways of cooking it.

PASTRAMI

A type of highly seasoned, peppery, cured smoked beef, usually rib, of Rumanian origin. Available either uncooked or cooked and ready to eat, it is good for sandwiches or for hors d'oeuvres.

PÂTE

(French): Any pastry dough or batter.

PÂTÉ

(French): Any pie with both top and bottom crusts. Also, by extension, any of a number of minced- or chopped-meat mixtures originally prepared in pie form. The most famous of these is pâté de foie gras (literally, fat livers), which is made from the oversized white livers of geese that have been fattened by being confined to pens and stuffed with food; they are cooked with Madeira, seasonings, and usually truffles.

PÂTE À CHOUX

(French): Cream-puff paste.

PÂTISSERIE

(French): Pastry; pastry shop; pastry-making.

PAUPIETTE

(French): A meat bird. See **Bird.**

PAYSANNE, À LA

(French): Cooked plainly or peasant-style; specifically, a term applied to braised meats or poultry served with root vegetables and celery.

PÊCHE

(French): Peach.

PEMMICAN

Also spelled pemican, pressed lean venison or buffalo (bison) meat pounded to a paste with fat and berries and pressed into cakes, made by American Indians as a travel food. It keeps a long time; therefore, a similar preparation made of dried beef, raisins or other dried fruits, and suet is used as a concentrated food for explorers and hunters.

PEPERONI

(Italian): A highly peppered sausage of the salami type.

PÉRIGOURDINE, À LA

(French): In the style of Périgord, a region of western France; a term always implying the presence of truffles and sometimes of pâté de foie gras, two specialities of the region.

PERSILLADE

(French): Prepared with parsley, as potatoes persillade.

PETIT, PETITE

(French): Small.

PETITS POIS

(French): Very small green peas.

PIÈCE DE RÉSISTANCE

(French): The main course or dish of a meal.

PIGS IN BLANKETS

Small sausages wrapped in dough and baked. The term is sometimes applied also to angels on horseback: oysters rolled in bacon and grilled or cooked in a small amount of fat.

PILCHARD

A small fish of the herring family, common along the European coast. Its young is the sardine.

PIQUANT

Agreeably pungent or stimulating to the taste; pleasantly sharp or biting.

PIZZAIOLA

(Italian): In the style of a pizza; a term applied to dishes, usually meat, with a highly seasoned topping of tomatoes and sometimes cheese.

PLOMBIÈRES

(French): A frozen dessert of ice cream and candied fruit, with whipped cream. Also, an almond-flavoured ice cream with a custard base.

POIS

(French): Peas. Petits pois: very small peas; pois cassés: split peas.

POIVRADE

(French): Pepper sauce.

POIVRE

(French): Pepper; au poivre: cooked or heavily seasoned with pepper.

POLLO

Chicken in Italian and Spanish.

POLONAISE, À LA

(French): In the Polish style. When applied to meat dishes, this term generally indicates the use of red cabbage, beets, horseradish, or sour cream; applied to vegetables (mainly asparagus, cauliflower, and broccoli), it refers to a sauce of melted butter, breadcrumbs, and chopped egg yolk.

POMME

(French): Apple; pomme bonne femme: baked apple.

POMME DE TERRE

(French): Apple of the earth or potato.

POMODORO

(Italian): Tomato.

PORRIDGE

Cereal or meal boiled in water or milk until thick, usually made of oatmeal.

PORTERHOUSE

A choice cut of beef from the centre of the short loin. Its name is said to come from its having been a speciality of a famous New York porterhouse or tavern. The porterhouses were so-called because they served the dark ale known as porter, which in turn got its name from its popularity with porters — that is, load-carriers.

PORTUGAISE SAUCE

(French): A type of tomato sauce.

POTAGE

(French): Soup.

POULET, POULARDE, POULE, POUSSIN

(French): Types of chicken. Poulet: chicken in general, but commonly a bird no larger than about $3\frac{1}{2}$ pounds; poularde: a specially fattened hen or a large roaster; poule: a stewing chicken; poussin: a very young chicken, a squab chicken.

PRESSED MEAT

Jellied meat, often made of chopped, cooked meat mixed with concentrated, well-seasoned stock with a high gelatine content. This is poured into a mould and allowed to stand several hours. In the mould, it may be pressed by use of weights.

Pressed Meat

PRINTANIER

(French): Literally, springlike; a term applied to dishes made or garnished with mixed fresh vegetables. The form à la printanière is also used. Consommé printanier; a chicken consommé containing a variety of vegetables. Printanière sauce: a white sauce coloured with green vegetables.

PROVENÇALE, À LA

(French): In the style of Provence, a region of southern France. Dishes in this style always contain garlic (usually a great deal of it) and often tomatoes.

PULLET

A female chicken of 3 to 6 pounds ready-to-cook weight (depending upon the breed), that is in the first six months of egg production. It is usually plump and juicy, and generally fine. Pullets can be fried or roasted, but usually are stewed, fricasséed, or used in chicken pie, creamed chicken, etc.

PUNCH

A sweetened, variously flavoured, sometimes spiced beverage often made with a distilled liquor or with wine. The name is derived from the Hindu word for five, which refers to the original number of ingredients.

QUENELLE

(French): A dumpling made of pounded or finely minced meat or fish. Small quenelles are used as a garnish for soups or other dishes; larger ones are served with a sauce as a first course or a luncheon dish.

QUICHE

(French): A quiche may be an individual tart or a pie served as an appetizer or a main luncheon dish. There are many versions; however the most famous is Quiche Lorraine, a rich savoury custard pie.

Quiche

RAGOÛT

(French): Stew; as used in English, one that is highly seasoned and thick.

RASHER

A thin slice of bacon.

RASSOLNIK

(Russian): A soup made of pickled cucumbers, various other vegetables, chicken giblets and other meats (often veal kidneys), and sour cream.

RAVIGOTE SAUCE

(French): Any of several sauces flavoured with vinegar: a French dressing with chopped onion, capers, tarragon, sometimes hard-boiled egg, and other seasonings; a hot white sauce with herbs; a highly seasoned mayonnaise containing anchovy paste.

RÉCHAUFFÉ

(French): Reheated or warmed over in sauce. Refers especially to meats.

REINE, À LA

(French): Literally, in queenly style; a term applied to various dishes made with a purée of chicken.

RELEVÉ

French term for meat, fish, or poultry served after hors d'oeuvres, before the roast. Much the same as the French entrées, though there used to be more of a distinction.

RENNET

Rennet is any substance containing the digestive enzyme rennin, which has the property of curdling milk; specifically, an extract prepared from the stomachs of calves. It is used in making cheese and milk puddings. Rennet is available in tablet, powder, and liquid forms under various trade names.

RIBBON CAKE

A cake made from batter that is divided into equal parts, variously coloured and put into a tin in even layers to produce a striped effect. Sometimes the different colours are baked as separate layers and put together with fillings.

RIJSTTAFEL

An Indonesian term which means literally, rice table, and refers to a meal consisting of boiled rice and a wide variety of curried dishes and/or various other hot spicy dishes and the accompanying relishes.

RILLETTES

(French): A highly seasoned pâté of minced or mashed pork, served as an appetizer or starter.

RIS

(French): Sweetbread. Ris d'agneau: sweetbread of lamb; ris de veau: sweetbread of veal.

RISI E BISI

(Italian): A soup of rice and peas.

RISSOLES

(French): Savoury minced or chopped mixtures, usually meat.

Rissoles

RIZ

(French): Rice.

ROCK CANDY

Large, hard, clear crystals of sugar, made by pouring a sugar syrup cooked to a certain density into deep pans that have been laced with heavy thread on which the crystals deposit while being formed.

ROE

Fish eggs, especially when still massed in the ovarian membrane, a film-like skin. Those chiefly used are from the sturgeon, shad, carp, cod, salmon, white-fish, and mullet. Caviar is the salted roe, particularly of sturgeon.

ROGNONS

(French): Kidneys.

ROLLMOP

A small herring fillet rolled around a tiny gherkin, marinated, and usually served as an appetizer.

ROLY POLY

A fruit dessert consisting of a sheet of suet crust dough spread with sugar, spice, and fruit or jam and rolled like a Swiss roll. It is then steamed, boiled or baked.

Roly Poly

RÔTI

(French): Roast; roasted.

RÔTIE

(French): Toast. Rôtie au beurre: buttered toast.

RÔTISSERIE

An oven, oven-like device, or grill equipped with an automatically rotating spit. Also, a restaurant specializing in grilled and roasted meats or a part of the kitchen reserved for grilling meats.

ROULADE

(French): A rolled, sometimes stuffed piece of meat.

ROYALE

(French): A thick, unsweetened custard cut into various shapes and used as a garnish for soup. À la royale: garnished with custard shapes; also, a

term applied to various dishes coated with a thick cream sauce.

RUM TUM TIDDY

Also known as rink tum tiddy, a tomato-flavoured variation of Welsh Rabbit, sometimes made with onion and egg.

RUSK

A slice of light bread, cake, or slightly sweetened biscuit dried and toasted in an oven.

RUSSEL

(Yiddish): A soured beet juice, used especially by Jewish people to make borsht (beet soup) during the Passover holiday.

RUSSIAN DRESSING

Mayonnaise plus chilli sauce and a variety of other seasonings, if desired. Very similar to Thousand Island dressing, but usually with a smaller variety of added ingredients.

SADDLE

A cut of lamb or mutton from an unsplit carcass, including part of the backbone and the two loins. Long saddle: loin and rump; short saddle: loin only.

ST. GERMAIN

(French): A term applied to many dishes made or garnished with green peas. St Germain Soup: a green pea soup.

ST. JOHN'S BREAD

See **Carob.**

SALAMI

A highly spiced, salted sausage, originally Italian.

SALMAGUNDI

Any mixture or medley, especially a dish of chopped meat, eggs, etc. flavoured with onions, anchovies, pepper, vinegar, and oil.

SALMIS

(French): Also spelled salmi; a type of stew made of game birds. They are first roasted until about two-thirds done, then cut up, trimmed, and stewed in a rich sauce that usually contains wine, truffles, and mushrooms. The final stages, or at least the finishing touches, are often performed at the table in a chafing dish.

SALPICON

(French): Any kind of mixture (fish, meat, poultry, or vegetables) chopped up or cut into very small pieces and bound with a sauce. Salpicons are used as stuffings, made into croquettes, or put into various pastry or bread cases.

SALT FISH

Fish preserved by salting, either with a dry salt or brine.

SALT PORK

Pork cured in salt, usually in brine, especially the fatty parts from the back, side, or belly of a pig, and used most frequently as a seasoning in various dishes.

SAMOVAR

(Russian): A metal urn for heating water to make tea. It is heated by charcoal placed in an internal tube and has a spigot for drawing off the water.

SARDINE

Any of a variety of young fish preserved in various sauces in tightly packed tins. The true sardine is the pilchard, but sprats and herrings are also commonly used.

SARMA

A Balkan and Near Eastern dish of wilted grape leaves or cabbage leaves stuffed with a well-seasoned mixture of minced meat and often rice, then rolled and cooked in a sauce, most commonly a tomato sauce.

SAUCISSON

(French): Sausage; saucisse: very small sausage.

SAUMON

(French): Salmon.

SAUSAGE

Minced, highly seasoned meat, often combined with other ingredients and usually stuffed into a casing made of animal intestine or other membranous tissue. More than a hundred distinct varieties are known, some of them very ancient. One of the earliest is said to have been made of mixed shellfish. The common sausage is made of beef or potato flour, water, and seasonings—a very simple product by sausage standards. Sausages are classified as wet or dry, depending on whether the ingredients are fresh or cooked.

SAVOURY

This name is applied not only to the herb (which see) but also to a piquantly flavoured dish served at the end of dinner.

SCHMALTZ

This Yiddish term derived from German for melted fat refers to rendered chicken or goose fat. It has become a slang expression for anything very sentimental and unctuous, as certain music, literature, etc., that is, unctuous sentimentalism.

SCHNITZEL

Schnitzel is German for a cutlet of meat, usually veal. Wiener schnitzel (Vienna schnitzel): a thin slice of veal, breaded and fried, then often served with anchovies and capers; schnitzel Holstein: veal cutlet with a fried egg on top, garnished with anchovies.

SHASHLIK

(Russian): Lamb on skewers.

SHORTCAKE

A light, rich biscuit; often, specifically, a biscuit of this kind served with fruit (commonly strawberries) and plain or whipped cream. The term is sometimes applied to a similar dessert made with sponge cake.

SHREWSBURY BISCUITS

A rich rolled biscuit, often cut in star shape.

SILVER CAKE

A delicate, rich, white cake.

SILVER DRAGÉES

Tiny ball-shaped, silver-coloured sweets.

SIMNEL CAKE

Rich fruit cake with an almond paste layer, baked in position, not put in later, traditional in England for the fourth Sunday of Lent, or "Mothering Sunday," a holiday for servant girls by old custom, so that they could visit their mothers. The name "Simnel" is derived from the Latin word simila which means "the finest wheat flour."

Those who prefer a more far-fetched explanation may like to know of a theory that the name of the cake arose out of a squabble, between a husband and wife called Simon and Nellie, as to how a cake should be cooked, whether boiled or baked. In the end, they compromised by boiling it first and then baking it; and in some old recipes Simnel Cake is boiled first and then baked.

SKATE

A flat fish of the ray family, ugly but edible.

SMÖRGÅSBORD

(Swedish): Literally, bread-and-butter table; a buffet intended for appetizers or for a light lunch or supper. In fact one can often make a dinner of it. It may contain as many as 50 different dishes, including several types of bread; many kinds of fish, cheese, and cold meats; a variety of salads and relishes; and a number of hot foods.

SOLE

Sole is a sea flatfish highly valued as food. It has white flesh, close-grained but delicate. There are several varieties, the best is Dover or black sole. Next in quality is the lemon sole, and there are also inferior Torbay or witches sole which are very bony.

SORBET

(French): Another name for water ice.

SORGHUM

Any of a number of related tropical cereal grasses. Some are grown chiefly as fodder, others for the sweet juice extracted from their stalks. Also, the syrup made from the juice, which is similar to black treacle.

SOUPÇON

(French): Literally, a suspicion: hence, a very small amount, especially of a given seasoning or flavour.

SOUVLAKIA

(Greek): Lamb on skewers.

SPUMONE

(Italian): A moulded frozen dessert often made of 2 or more colours, flavours, and textures of ice cream, often with candied fruit scone, nuts, and rum flavouring.

SPUN SUGAR

Sugar syrup which has been boiled to the long-thread stage, then drawn out into threads over bars; it is often coloured.

STOCKFISH

Fish, usually cod, dried hard in the open air. The best known is a heavily salted Norwegian cod that must be soaked for at least 3 days before it is cooked. It is widely used in northern Europe and—despite a good deal of locally produced dried salt cod—on the Mediterranean coast of France.

STREUSEL

(German): A crumb-like topping for cakes, usually made of butter, flour, sugar, and cinnamon. Fine bread or cake crumbs and chopped nuts, such as almonds, are sometimes included.

STURGEON

Any of several large food fishes with rows of spiny plates along the body and a projecting snout. The largest species is the Russian or beluga of the Caspian and Black Seas and the Sea of Azov; it reaches a length of 13 feet and a weight of up to a ton. Although the meat is coarse, smoked sturgeon is considered a delicacy in many areas. Sturgeon eggs are the source of better grades of caviar. See **Caviar** in index.

SUBGUM

(Chinese): With mixed vegetables.

SUISSE, À LA

(French): Swiss style.

SÜLZE

German for "in aspic"—that is, jellied; also the name of an old-time Jewish dish, a calves foot jelly also known as "pitcha."

SUNDAE

Ice cream topped with a sauce or syrup. Nuts or fruit and whipped cream may be added.

SUPRÊME

(French): A delicate and tender portion of boneless meat, poultry, or fish; also a term applied to various elaborate desserts. Suprême de volaille: boned chicken breast; suprême sauce: a cream sauce made with reduced chicken stock, served with poultry, eggs, and vegetables.

SYLLABUB

A form of eggnog made of sweetened milk or cream mixed with wine, cider, or brandy and beaten to a froth; sometimes whipped cream is added. When combined with gelatine it becomes a chilled dessert.

TABLE D'HÔTE

(French): Literally, table of the host; a complete meal of a definite number of courses for which an all-inclusive price is specified on the menu.

TAGLIARINI

(Italian): A ribbon-shaped pasta.

TARTELETTE

(French): A little tart.

TASSE

(French): Cup. Demitasse: literally, half a cup; a small cup used for black coffee.

TAVOUK DOLMA

(Armenian): Chicken stuffed with rice.

TERRINE
(French): An earthenware pot resembling a casserole. Also, a cold jellied dish of chopped or diced meat cooked in such a pot.

THURINGER
(German): A mildly seasoned sausage of beef and pork, usually in an edible casing.

TOAD-IN-THE-HOLE
Sausages cooked in batter.

TOFFEE
A chewy sweetmeat made by cooking a sugar solution with butter until it melts; as it cools it hardens. It may be flavoured or coated in various ways.

TOFU
(Chinese and Japanese): Soya bean curd. It has a cheese-like consistency and is used in many Oriental dishes. It is available in Chinese and Japanese grocery stores.

TOMALLEY
The liver of the lobster, which turns green when cooked and is considered a delicacy.

TORTCHEN
(German): A small pastry or tart.

TOURTIÈRE
A French-Canadian two-crust pie, usually of minced pork seasoned with nutmeg, mace, garlic, salt, and pepper. It is generally served hot.

TRIFLE
A dessert, usually of sponge cake sliced and soaked in wine or fruit juice, then spread with jam, and served with custard or whipped cream.

TUNA
The tuna (also called tunny) is a large game fish of the mackerel family, which inhabits warm waters in the Atlantic, the Pacific, and the Mediterranean. Its weight averages 60 to 200 pounds and has been known to reach 1,500. In Europe and in certain coastal areas of the United States it is eaten fresh, but it is also bought canned. The related albacore and bonito taste much the same when canned and are often confused with tuna.
Fresh tuna fish may be braised or roasted in the same way as veal. For canned tuna recipes, see index.

TURBAN
A rolled fillet, usually of fish. Also, a ring or border of food.

TURBOT
Turbot is a large European flatfish, highly regarded as food. It may weigh up to 40 pounds. It is particularly choice when small and is then called chicken turbot in English, turbotin in French. The name is also applied to a number of other similar flatfish.

TURKISH DELIGHT
Also called Turkish paste; a soft jelly-like sweetmeat made of a fruit flavoured syrup, cut into cubes or rectangles and dusted with sugar.

TUTTI-FRUTTI
(Italian): Literally, all fruits; a mixture of preserved or candied fruits, usually cut small. Also, as used in English, a confection of mixed fruits with ice cream.

TZIMMES
(Yiddish): A traditional stew with many variations. It usually contains carrots, potatoes, and sweet potatoes and may or may not include meat. The word has become a Jewish colloquialism meaning fuss.

UOVA
(Italian): Eggs; uova fritte: fried eggs; uova affogate: poached eggs; uova con funghi: eggs with mushrooms; uova con pomodoro: eggs with tomatoes; uova strapazzate: scrambled eggs; uova sodo: hard-boiled eggs.

UVA
(Italian): Grapes.

VANILLIN
The fragrant component of vanilla, a white crystalline substance produced from the vanilla bean or made synthetically.

VEAU
(French): Veal.

VERMICELLI
(Italian): Literally, little worms; very thin spaghetti.

VÉRONIQUE
(French): A garnish of seedless white grapes, used chiefly with chicken.

VERT, VERTE
(French): Green. Vert-pré: literally, a green meadow; a term applied either to a garnish of shoestring potatoes and watercress or to chicken or fish coated with a green sauce of mayonnaise mixed with chopped spinach and herbs.

VIANDE
(French): Meat.

VIENNA COFFEE
Coffee served with single cream and garnished with whipped cream.

VIENNA SAUSAGE
A slender sausage 3 to 3½ inches long, often made of a mildly seasoned mixture of lean beef and pork in a soft, edible casing. Also called wienerwurst.

VITELLO
(Italian): Veal.

VOLAILLE
(French): Poultry.

VORSPEISEN
(German): Appetizers.

WAFER
A very thin, crisp biscuit.

WASHINGTON PIE
Traditionally, sponge cake layers put together with jelly or jam, sprinkled on top with icing sugar; however, the name is often applied to cake layers put together with custard, chocolate, and the like.

WHEY
The thin, watery part of milk which separates from the thicker part (curds) after coagulation, as in cheesemaking. It has considerable food value as well as a refreshing quality.

WURST
(German): Sausage.

YANKEE POT ROAST
Braised beef served in its own thickened gravy with fresh vegetables and corn fritters.

YERBA MATÉ
See **Maté**.

ZAKUSKI
(Russian): Appetizers.

ZWIEBACK
(German): Literally, twice-baked; a type of rusk (which see). Also called Brussels biscuit.

FISH AND SHELLFISH

Guides for Buying and Preparing Fish

Fish is frequently less costly than meat and, like meat, it is a primary source of protein and the essential vitamins and minerals. Fish dishes, very often, are time-savers for the busy housewife, in as much as the cooking time for most fish is short. Fish, then, should always be kept in mind as an alternative, not a substitute, for meat in the daily menu. The flavour of fish is delicate. When properly cooked and skilfully combined with other foods it soon becomes a favourite dish several times a week.

Variety is one of the keys to successful meal planning. Very few people realize how many varieties of fish are available. Modern refrigeration, quick-freezing, and rapid transportation make it possible for people inland as well as those living on the shores to enjoy the great variety of fish all the year round.

HOW TO BUY FRESH FISH

Most varieties of fish, like many other types of food products, are particularly abundant fresh in season during the year. Local fishmongers will gladly give you information concerning seasonal offerings, and indicate those varieties that can be used to the best advantage, including the less familiar varieties. If you want to save time in preparation and cooking, fish should be bought as fillets, steaks, or dressed.

When buying whole fish, the following points are a guide to freshness:

Eyes: Bright, clear, full, and bulging.

Gills: Reddish-pink, free from slime or odour.

Scales Adhering tightly to the skin, bright coloured with characteristic sheen.

Flesh: Firm and elastic, springing back when pressed, not separating from the bones.

Odour: Fresh, free from objectionable odours.

Quantity to Buy

Servings of fish are generally based on $\frac{1}{3}$ to $\frac{1}{2}$ pound of the edible flesh per person. When serving steaks or fillets, allow $\frac{1}{3}$ pound per person or 2 pounds for 6 people. For dressed fish, allow $\frac{1}{2}$ pound per person or 3 pounds for 6 people. For whole fish, allow about 1 pound per person or 5 pounds for 6 people.

STORING FRESH FISH

Fish, like many other food products, will spoil easily if not handled with care. It should be wrapped in foil or placed in a tightly covered dish and stored immediately in the refrigerator. Stored in this manner, the odour of fish will not penetrate other foods. If fish cannot be thoroughly refrigerated, it should be cooked at once and reheated for serving.

HOW TO BUY FROZEN FISH

In recent years a considerable trade has developed in frozen fish, so that now most varieties are available throughout the year. Frozen fish may be used interchangeably with fresh fish.

Quantity to Buy: In buying frozen fish, the serving for each person is the same as for fresh fish: $\frac{1}{3}$ to $\frac{1}{2}$ pound of the edible flesh per person.

CARE AND STORAGE OF FROZEN FISH

When frozen fish which is wrapped in parchment paper or cellophane is to be used shortly after buying, it should have another wrapping of paper put round it before being placed in the refrigerator. The additional wrapping prevents the absorption of odours by other foods as the fish thaws. Packaged frozen fish should remain in the unopened package until time to use.

If you wish to keep the fish frozen for several days, place the unopened package in the freezing unit or frozen foods compartment of your refrigerator. Fish will keep as long as it remains solidly frozen, but once it thaws it should be used immediately. Never refreeze fish after it thaws.

THAWING FROZEN FISH

Fillets, steaks, and dressed fish may be cooked as if they were in the unfrozen form; however, additional cooking must be allowed. When fish are to be rolled in bread- or golden crumbs or stuffed, it is more convenient to thaw them first to permit easier handling. Thawing is necessary for the cleaning and dressing of whole or drawn fish.

Thawing fish in the refrigerator at a temperature of 37° to 40° has become the accepted practice. The fish should be held at this temperature only long enough to make preparation easy. Whole or drawn fish may be thawed more readily by holding them under cold running water. Thawing at room temperature, although sometimes practised, is not recommended since a considerable amount of water usually results.

BASIC FISH COOKERY HINTS

Although the flavour, texture, appearance, and size vary according to the type, the fundamental rules for cooking most fish are few and easy to follow. For this reason, the use of basic recipes, such as frying, grilling, boiling, and steaming, are emphasized through this section.

The principal difference in types of fish, as related to fish cooking, is the variation in fat content.

As a rule, oily fish, such as salmon or shad, are best for baking and grilling because their fat content will keep them from becoming dry.

White fish, such as cod and haddock, are preferred by some for boiling and steaming as their flesh is firm, and will not easily fall apart during cooking. Both oily and white fish are suitable for frying.

There are, however, so many exceptions to these rules that actually all fish may be cooked by any of the basic methods with excellent results if allowances are made for the fat content. For example, white fish, such as halibut, may be grilled or baked if basted frequently with melted fat; otherwise they will have a tendency to become dry.

Most Important Cookery Rule: The most important thing to remember when cooking fish is that it is too often overcooked. Just enough cooking for the flesh to be flaked easily from the bones will leave the fish moist and tender and bring out its delicate flavour.

TYPES OF FRESH AND FROZEN FISH

Fish is sold in various ways for different uses. Knowing these "cuts" is important when buying fish. The best known types of fish are given below.

Whole or Round Fish

Whole or round fish are those sold just as they come from the water. Before cooking, they must have the scales and entrails removed. The head, tail, and fins may be removed if you

like, and the fish either split or cut into portions, except in fish intended for baking. Some small fish, like smelt, are frequently cooked with only the entrails removed.

Drawn Fish

Drawn fish are sold with only the entrails removed. In preparation for cooking, they are generally scaled. Head, tail, and fins are removed, if you like, and the fish split or cut into portions. Small drawn fish, or larger sizes intended for baking, may be cooked as bought after having the scales removed.

Dressed Fish

Dressed fish have scales and entrails removed, usually with the heads, tails, and fins removed. The smaller sizes are ready for cooking as bought. The larger sizes of dressed fish may be baked as bought but frequently they are cut into steaks or portions.

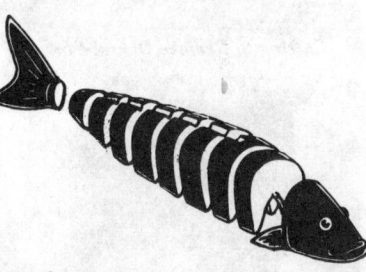

Steaks

Steaks are cross-section slices of the larger sizes of dressed fish. They are ready to cook as bought, except for dividing the very largest into portions. A cross-section of the backbone is usually the only bone in the steak.

Fillets

The sides of the fish, cut lengthways away from the backbone, are called fillets. They are practically boneless and require no preparation for cooking. Sometimes the skin, with the scales removed, is left on the fillets; others are skinned. A fillet cut from one side of a fish is called a single fillet. This is the type of fillet usually sold.

Butterfly Fillets

Butterfly fillets are the two sides of the fish corresponding to two single fillets held together by uncut flesh and the skin.

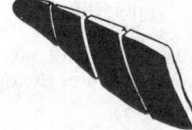

Fingers

Fingers are pieces of fish cut lengthways or across from fillets or steaks into portions of uniform width and length.

CLEANING AND DRESSING FISH

Today the cook can obtain almost any variety of fish—fresh or frozen—already cleaned and dressed, filleted or cut in steaks. Therefore, most of the time, there will be no need for cleaning and dressing fish for cooking.

However, freshly caught fish may be available at times, so information on cleaning and preparing fish for cooking is given here.

Scaling: Lay the fish on the table and with one hand hold the fish firmly by the head. Holding a knife almost vertical, scrape off the scales, working from the tail towards the head. Since scales are more easily removed from a wet fish, it is advisable to soak the fish in cold water for a few minutes before you start. Take care to remove all the scales near the base of the fins and head.

Cleaning: Remove the entrails after cutting the entire length of the belly from the vent (anal opening) to the head. Cut around the pelvic fins and remove them. Remove the head, including the pectoral fins, by cutting above the collar bone. If the backbone is large, cut down to it on each side of the fish, and then snap the backbone by bending it over the edge of the cutting board or table. Cut any remaining flesh which holds the head attached to the body. Cut off the tail.

Fish Fins: Remove the dorsal or large back fin by cutting the flesh along both sides of the fin. Then, giving a quick pull forward towards the head of the fish, remove the fin with the root bones attached. Remove the other fins in the same way. Never trim the fins off with scissors or a knife since the bones at the base will be left in the fish. Wash the fish under cold running water, removing the blood, any remaining slime, and membranes. The fish is now dressed and ready for cooking. Large fish may be cut into steaks.

Filleting: With a sharp knife, cut through the flesh along the back from the tail to just behind the head. Then cut down to the backbone just above the collar bone. Turn the knife flat and cut the flesh along the backbone to the tail, keeping the knife close to the rib bones. Lift off the entire side or fillet of the fish in one piece. Turn the fish over and repeat the operation on the other side.

Skinning: If you wish, you may skin the fillets. Lay the fillets flat on the cutting board or table, skin side down. Hold the tail end with your fingers, and with a knife cut through the flesh to the skin about one-half inch from the end of the fillet. Flatten the knife on the skin and cut the flesh away from the skin by pushing the knife forward while holding the free end of the skin firmly between your fingers.

Fish Fins

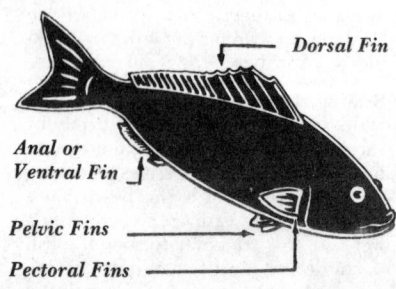

Removing Scales

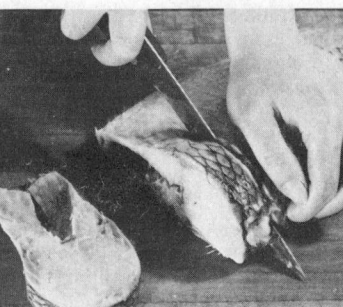

Cutting a Steak

Removing Head

Cutting Fillet from Tail to Head

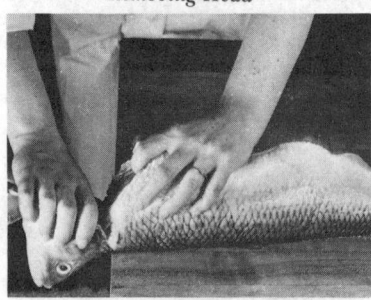

Breaking Backbone

Cutting Along Backbone to Remove Fillets

Cutting to Remove Dorsal Fin

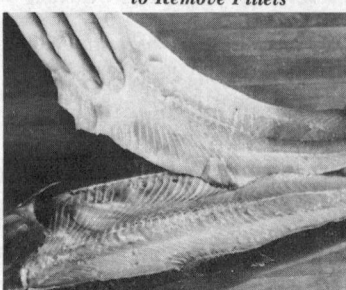

Freeing Fillet at the Tail

Removing Dorsal Fin

Skinning a Fillet

USUAL TYPES

AND

SIZES OF FISH SOLD

Type	Oily or White	Usual weight of whole fish	Usual way sold
SALT-WATER FISH			
Bream	White	2 to 3 pounds	Whole
Brill	White	2 to 6 pounds	Whole, drawn, and filleted
Cod	White	3 to 20 pounds	Drawn, dressed, steaks, and fillets
Coley or Saithe	White	2 to 8 pounds	Whole or fillets
Dab	White	$\frac{1}{4}$ to $\frac{3}{4}$ pound	Whole
Eel	Oily	2 to 4 pounds	Alive
Gurnard	White	1 to 5 pounds	Whole or fillets
Haddock	White	$1\frac{1}{2}$ to 7 pounds	Drawn and fillets
Hake	White	2 to 5 pounds	Whole, drawn, dressed and fillets
Halibut	White	8 to 75 pounds	Dressed and steaks
Herring, John Dory	Oily	$\frac{1}{4}$ to 1 pound	Whole
Mackerel	Oily	$\frac{3}{4}$ to 3 pounds	Whole, drawn, and fillets
Mullet, Grey	White	2 to 3 pounds	Whole, dressed (optional)
Mullet, Red	White	6 to 12 ounces	Whole
Pilchard	Oily	$1\frac{1}{2}$ to 2 ounces	Whole, canned
Plaice	White	$\frac{1}{2}$ to 5 pounds	Whole, dressed, and filleted
Salmon	Oily	3 to 30 pounds	Whole or steaks
Sardine	Oily	Bought by the pound	Whole, drawn
Sea bass	White	$\frac{1}{4}$ to 4 pounds	Whole, dressed, and fillets
Sea or salmon trout	White	1 to 6 pounds	Whole, drawn, dressed, and fillets
Skate	White	$1\frac{1}{2}$ to $2\frac{1}{2}$ pounds	Pieces only known as "wings"
Sole, Dover	White	$\frac{1}{2}$ to $1\frac{1}{2}$ pounds	Whole, dressed, and fillets
Sole, Lemon	White	1 to 2 pounds	Whole, dressed, and fillets
Sprats	Oily	Bought by the pound	Whole, drawn
Tuna or Tunny Fish	Oily	5 to 100 pounds	
Turbot	White	4 to 6 pounds	Whole, dressed, filleted and steaks
Whitebait	White	Bought by the pound	Whole, drawn, dressed, and fillets
Whiting	White	$\frac{1}{2}$ to 2 pounds	Whole
FRESH-WATER FISH			
Bass	White	$\frac{3}{4}$ to 1 pound	Whole and drawn, also reserved as game fishes
Bream	White	2 to 3 pounds	Whole
Carp	White	2 to 8 pounds	Whole and fillets
Catfish or Rock Salmon	White	1 to 10 pounds	Whole, dressed, and skinned
Smelt	White	2 ounces	Whole
Trout	White	1 to 2 pounds	Whole, drawn
Perch	White	$\frac{1}{2}$ to 1 pound	Whole and fillets
Pike	White	$1\frac{1}{2}$ to 10 pounds	Whole, dressed, and fillets

Baked Fish

BAKED STUFFED WHOLE FISH

3 or 4 pound fish, dressed
1½ teaspoons salt
bread stuffing (see below)
4 tablespoons butter or other fat,
    melted
3 rashers of bacon (optional)

Clean, wash, and dry fish. Sprinkle inside and out with salt.

Stuff fish loosely, and sew opening with needle and string, or close with skewers.

Place fish in greased baking dish. Brush with melted fat. Lay the rashers of bacon, if using, over top. Bake in moderate oven (350°F. Mark 4) 40 to 60 minutes or until fish flakes easily when tested with a fork. If fish seems dry during baking, baste it occasionally with pan juices or melted fat.

Remove string or skewers and serve fish immediately on a hot dish, plain or with a sauce. Serves 6.

BAKED STUFFED FISH FILLETS OR STEAKS

2 fillets or steaks, about 1 pound
    each
1 teaspoon salt
⅛ teaspoon pepper
bread stuffing (½ recipe, below)
4 tablespoons butter or other fat,
    melted
3 rashers of bacon (optional)

Skin the fillets if this has not been done. Sprinkle both sides of the fillets or steaks with salt and pepper.

Place one fillet or steak in a well greased baking dish. Place stuffing on the fish and cover with remaining fillet or steak. Fasten together with toothpicks or skewers. Brush top with melted fat and lay rashers of bacon, if using, on top.

Bake in moderate oven (350°F. Mark 4) 30 to 40 minutes or until fish flakes easily when tested with a fork. Transfer fillets or steaks carefully to a hot platter, remove the toothpicks or skewers, garnish and serve hot with a sauce. Serves 6.

BREAD STUFFING FOR FISH

3 tablespoons chopped onions
3 ounces chopped celery
6 tablespoons butter or other fat,
    melted
1 teaspoon salt
⅛ teaspoon pepper
1 teaspoon thyme, sage, or savory
    seasoning
1 pound dry breadcrumbs

Cook celery and onions in melted fat for about 10 minutes, or until tender. Add cooked vegetables and seasonings to breadcrumbs; mix thoroughly.

If dressing seems very dry, add 2 tablespoons water, milk, or fish stock to moisten.

BAKED WHOLE FISH

3 or 4 pound fish, dressed
1½ teaspoons salt
⅛ teaspoon pepper
4 tablespoons butter or other fat
seasoned mashed potatoes
seasoned cooked vegetables (peas,
    carrots, cauliflower, toma-
    toes, or onions)

Clean, wash, and dry fish. Sprinkle inside and out with salt and pepper. Brush with melted fat.

Place fish on a greased ovenproof glass or metal platter. Bake in a hot oven (400°F. Mark 6) 35 to 45 minutes or until fish flakes easily when tested with a fork.

Remove from oven and quickly arrange a border of hot mashed potatoes around fish. Place under preheated grill until potatoes are slightly browned, about 5 minutes.

Remove and arrange two or more hot vegetables around fish. Garnish with parsley and lemon or tomato wedges. Serve immediately. Serves 6.

BAKED FISH FILLETS OR STEAKS

2 pounds fish fillets or steaks
1 teaspoon salt
⅛ teaspoon pepper
2 tablespoons lemon juice
1 teaspoon finely chopped onion
4 tablespoons butter or other fat,
    melted
paprika

Cut fish into portions. Sprinkle both sides with salt and pepper. Add lemon juice and onion to melted fat.

Dip each piece of fish into this mixture and place in a greased baking dish. Pour rest of fat over fish.

Bake in moderate oven (350°F. Mark 4) 25 to 30 minutes or until fish flakes easily when tested with a fork. Sprinkle with paprika. Serve immediately on a hot dish. Serves 6.

A whole fish, stuffed and baked, is one of the most attractive ways to serve fish.

BAKED HALIBUT WITH CHEESE SAUCE

2 1-pound halibut steaks
6 tablespoons butter
paprika
2 tablespoons lemon juice
4 tablespoons flour
16 fluid ounces milk
1 teaspoon salt
⅛ teaspoon pepper
4 ounces grated Cheddar cheese
3 tablespoons grated Parmesan
    cheese
2 hard-boiled eggs, sieved

Place halibut steaks in grill pan. Dot with 2 tablespoons butter and sprinkle with paprika. Grill about 15 minutes, or until fish flakes when tested with a fork. Place in a shallow buttered dish and sprinkle with lemon juice.

While the fish is grilling, melt the 4 tablespoons of butter in a saucepan. Add flour, mixing to a smooth paste. Cook over medium heat for about 1 minute. Remove from heat. Add half of the milk, salt and pepper, stirring until it is blended.

Return pan to heat and stir constantly until the mixture begins to thicken. Add remaining milk. Heat until the sauce is simmering. Cook about 5 minutes. Blend in Cheddar cheese slowly, stirring until it is melted. Pour sauce over fish and top with Parmesan cheese.

Bake in moderate oven (350°F. Mark 4) 20 minutes. Sprinkle with sieved hard-boiled eggs and serve at once. Serves 4 to 5.

Baked Halibut with Cheese Sauce

WHOLE FISH COOKED IN FOIL

Use small or medium fish such as bass, red mullet, trout, and perch.

Clean and wash fish; remove heads and tails, if you like. Wipe dry and sprinkle inside and out with salt and pepper.

Cut sheets of foil large enough to wrap each fish separately. Spread the centre of each sheet with 1 tablespoon butter or margarine. Wrap up fish and fold over foil to seal edges.

To Cook Indoors: Put wrapped fish on baking sheet. Bake in moderate oven (375°F. Mark 5) about 30 minutes.

To Cook Outdoors: Put wrapped fish directly on hot coals and cover with more coals. Cook 10 to 15 minutes, depending on size of fish.

HERRING

Herring is notorious for its many bones. The roe is as highly valued as the flesh and is served with it or alone, usually the soft roes, as in soft roes on toast. Both may be baked or grilled; the roe is often parboiled first.

BAKED HERRING

Clean and split the herring. Place skin side down in a greased shallow baking dish.

Sprinkle with salt and pepper. Brush with melted butter.

Bake in hot oven (400°F. Mark 6) 20 to 25 minutes, basting frequently with melted butter. Garnish with parsley. Serve at once.

With Creamed Roe: After baking, spread creamed roe (below) over fish. Sprinkle with 2 ounces dry bread-crumbs mixed with a little melted butter. Brown under grill.

Creamed Roe:
 1 herring roe, parboiled
 2 tablespoons butter or margarine
 1 teaspoon finely chopped onion
 2 tablespoons flour
 4 fluid ounces single cream
 2 egg yolks, slightly beaten
 1 tablespoon lemon juice

Remove the outer membrane of the roe. Mash the roe. Melt butter in a saucepan.

Add onion and blend in flour. Slowly stir in cream and cook over low heat until it thickens, about 5 minutes. Slowly add to beaten egg yolks, stirring constantly. Add lemon juice and roe. Season to taste with salt and pepper.

RED MULLET

This esteemed fish has delicate white flesh and a bright pink skin. The liver is considered to be a delicacy and is usually left in the fish, the remaining entrails being removed through the gills. It is most often cooked "en papillote" with 2-3 tablespoons lemon juice, butter, salt and pepper added inside the paper envelope. Red mullet can also be fried or grilled whole.

BASS

Bass is a round silvery fish with a firm, crisp flesh. Small bass can be grilled or fried but the larger fish are best stuffed and baked "en papillotte".

BASS EN PAPILLOTTE
 6 medium-sized bass
24 fluid ounces water
 1 chopped shallot or 2 tablespoons
      chopped onion
 6 tablespoons butter or margarine
18 fluid ounces white wine
 4 ounces crabmeat, flaked
 1 8-ounce can prawns diced
 ½ clove garlic, chopped
 1¼ large onions, chopped
Pinch of thyme
 1 bay leaf
16 fluid ounces fish stock
 2 tablespoons flour
 2 egg yolks
Salt and pepper

Clean the bass and cut into 6 fillets, removing heads and backbones.

Put the fish heads, bones, and water in a pan and simmer until there is 1 pint stock.

Sauté shallot and fillets in 2 table-spoons butter. Add ½ pint wine; cover and simmer gently until fillets are tender, 5 to 8 minutes.

Sauté crabmeat, prawns, and ¼ clove garlic in 1 tablespoon butter. Add onions and remaining garlic and cook 10 minutes. Add thyme, bay leaf, and 14 fluid ounces fish stock; simmer 10 minutes.

Blend together 2 tablespoons butter and flour and gradually add remaining fish stock. Add to crabmeat mixture with stock drained from fillets. Cook, stirring constantly, until the sauce thickens.

Beat egg yolks and add hot sauce and remaining wine. Mix thoroughly. Place in refrigerator to chill until firm.

Cut 6 heart-shaped pieces of grease-proof paper 8 inches long and 12 inches wide. Grease them well and place spoonfuls of sauce on the side of each heart. Lay poached fillet on sauce and fold over. Crimp or staple the edges.

Lay the parcels on a greased baking sheet. Bake in very hot oven (450°F. Mark 8) 15 minutes, or until paper parcels are browned. Serve at once in the paper parcels. Serves 6.

BAKED TROUT

Wipe the cleaned trout and wrap each one in a rasher of bacon. Place in baking dish.

Bake in moderate oven (350°F. Mark 4) 20 minutes without turning.

Haddock Bake with Sour Cream Topping

HADDOCK BAKE WITH SOUR CREAM TOPPING
 1 pound frozen haddock fillets
 1 ounce flour
 1 teaspoon salt
 ¼ teaspoon ground black pepper
 4 fluid ounces milk
 2-3 cracker biscuits, crushed
 2 tablespoons butter or margarine,
      melted
 4 fluid ounces sour cream

Cut fish into pieces. Coat them with a mixture of the flour, salt, and pepper. Arrange them in a single layer in a baking dish. Pour milk over fish.

Bake in moderate oven (350°F. Mark 4) 45 minutes. Brown the biscuit crumbs lightly in melted butter or margarine. Spoon sour cream over fish. Sprinkle with the crumbs. Bake 10 minutes longer. Serves 4.

FISH FILLETS BAKED IN WINE-MUSHROOM SAUCE
 3 tablespoons butter or margarine
 3 tablespoons flour
 1 10½-ounce can condensed cream
      of mushroom soup
 4 fluid ounces dry white wine
 2 tablespoons grated Parmesan
      cheese
 2 tablespoons chopped parsley
 1 to 1½ pounds fish fillets (sole,
      halibut, etc.)

Melt butter and stir in flour; add soup and wine and cook, stirring constantly, until the mixture boils and thickens; add Parmesan cheese and parsley.

Arrange fillets in a single layer in a greased shallow baking dish, or in 3 or 4 shallow individual ramekins. Pour sauce over fish.

Bake in moderate oven (375°F. Mark 5) about 25 minutes, or until fish flakes easily. Serves 3 or 4.

Fish Fillets Baked in Wine-Mushroom Sauce

HADDOCK

This large, round fish has firm white flakes of flesh. It has a dark line down each side and a black "finger" mark behind each gill, known as St. Peter's mark. Small fillets are often sold as block fillets.

HADDOCK WITH TOMATO SAUCE

1 3-pound haddock (or other large fish), dressed
seasoned flour
6 tablespoons butter or margarine
½ large onion, chopped
8 ounces chopped celery
1-2 tablespoons chopped green pepper
1 20-ounce can tomatoes
1 tablespoon Worcestershire sauce
1 tablespoon tomato ketchup
1 teaspoon chilli powder (optional)
½ lemon, finely sliced
2 bay leaves
1 clove garlic, chopped
1 teaspoon salt
small pinch of cayenne pepper

Sprinkle fish inside and out with seasoned flour. Place in baking dish lined with buttered greaseproof paper.

Melt butter; add onion, celery, and green pepper; simmer 15 minutes.

Add tomatoes, Worcestershire sauce, ketchup, chilli powder, if used, lemon, bay leaves, garlic, salt, and cayenne pepper. Simmer until celery is very tender, then put the mixture through a potato ricer or sieve.

Pour the sauce around fish.

Bake in slow oven (325°F. Mark 3) about 45 minutes.

Baste frequently with sauce. Serves 6.

FISH STEAKS OR FILLETS IN WHITE WINE

3 thick fish steaks or fillets
8 fluid ounces dry white wine
3 carrots
1 onion, sliced
3 tablespoons butter or margarine
2 tablespoons flour
1 bouillon cube
slices of lemon

Marinate the fish steaks or fillets in wine for several hours in refrigerator.

An hour before dinner, cut carrots in strips, parboil 8 minutes in ½ pint of boiling salted water; pour into shallow baking dish without draining. Add

Fish Piquant

onion. Drain fish from marinade and place on top of vegetables. Reserve marinade.

For sauce, melt butter or margarine, add flour; stir in bouillon cube and reserved marinade. Pour over fish. Season with salt and pepper; top with slices of lemon.

Bake uncovered in hot oven (450°F. Mark 8) 25 minutes, or until tender. Pile hot string beans around fish. Serves 6.

FILLET OF FISH MARGUERY

3 tablespoons butter or margarine
1 onion, chopped
6 cooked or canned prawns
½ pint hot white sauce
2 egg yolks
4 fluid ounces cream
1 tablespoon chopped parsley
small pinch of grated nutmeg
juice of ½ lemon
2-3 tablespoons sherry
2 pounds fish fillets

Sauté onion and prawns about 5 minutes in 2 tablespoons melted butter.

Beat egg yolks with cream and slowly pour hot white sauce into egg-cream mixture, stirring constantly. Return to heat and cook 1 minute. Add remaining butter, parsley, nutmeg, and lemon juice; mix well. Remove from heat and add wine.

Place fish fillets in greased casserole. Arrange sautéed onion and seafood on fillets. Cover with sauce.

Bake in moderate oven (350°F. Mark 4) about 20 minutes. Serves 6.

Note: Oysters and mushrooms may be added to prawns.

FISH STEAKS FRANCISCO

Marinate 4 fish steaks in 8 fluid ounces dry white wine for 3 or 4 hours in refrigerator. Place fish and wine in shallow baking dish. Sprinkle with salt and pepper.

Bake in moderate oven (375°F. Mark 5) about 25 minutes, or until fish flakes when tested with fork. Drain off liquid.

Before serving, pour melted butter or margarine over it and top with slices of lemon. Pile hot string beans and carrots around the fish steaks. Serves 4.

Note: Halibut, salmon or any favourite firm white fish may be used in this recipe.

FISH PIQUANT

4 onions, sliced
2 pounds fish fillets—cod, sole, haddock, or perch
4 fluid ounces mayonnaise
2 teaspoons Worcestershire sauce

Baked Haddock

2 tablespoons lemon juice
1 ounce grated Parmesan cheese
2 tablespoons chopped parsley

Cover sliced onions with water and cook until tender but still crisp. Spread drained onions in a shallow, well greased baking dish.

Cut fish into portions. Place fish pieces on the onions. Mix the remaining ingredients well. Spread mixture on fish pieces.

Bake in moderate oven (350°F. Mark 4) 30 to 40 minutes or until fish flakes easily when tested with a fork. Serves 6.

BAKED HADDOCK

Place 6 medium haddock fillets in a glass baking dish. Season with salt and pepper.

Melt ¼ pound butter and stir in 6 ounces of crushed cracker biscuits. Cover fillets with butter-crumb mixture. Sprinkle with chopped parsley, if you like.

Bake in moderate oven (350°F. Mark 4) 30 minutes or until fish is tender and the crumbs are browned.

Serve with pickled onions and baby beetroots, if you like. Serves 6.

BAKED FISH IN SOUR CREAM

3 pounds frozen fish fillets
½ teaspoon salt
⅛ teaspoon pepper
1½ teaspoons Aromat
onion rings
8 fluid ounces thick sour cream

Thaw fish; place in buttered or oiled flat baking dish. Sprinkle both sides of fillets with salt, pepper, and Aromat, and set aside for 10 minutes.

Cover fish with onion rings (slice onions thinly and push out into rings); pour or spoon sour cream over onions.

Bake uncovered in moderate oven (350°F. Mark 4) until fish flakes easily when tested with a fork, about 30 to 35 minutes.

Baste fish occasionally with the cream and if liquid evaporates too fast, or fish seems dry, add a tablespoon or two of hot water.

Serve from baking dish, adding watercress for garnish, at the last moment just before serving. Serves 6.

Baked Stuffed Salmon

BAKED STUFFED SALMON

Remove head, tail, and fins from 8- to 10-pound fresh or frozen whole salmon.

Sprinkle Aromat lightly inside cavity; fill with stuffing (below), being careful to stuff it loosely.

Skewer or truss fish to close the opening. Brush with oil; place on a strip of foil (for easy removal later) in shallow roasting pan.

Bake in moderate oven (350°F. Mark 4), allowing 12 minutes per pound.

Garnish with sprigs of parsley and lemon twists. Slice and serve with egg sauce accompanied by boiled new potatoes and peas.

Savoury Stuffing for Salmon:
¼ large onion, finely chopped
2 tablespoons butter or margarine
¼ teaspoon dried savory, crumbled
¼ teaspoon dried marjoram
⅛ teaspoon dried thyme
1 teaspoon finely chopped parsley
1 teaspoon finely grated lemon rind
1 teaspoon salt
⅛ teaspoon pepper
1 teaspoon Aromat
6 ounces fresh breadcrumbs, browned
1 egg, slightly beaten

Brown onion lightly in butter or margarine. Add herbs, lemon rind, salt, pepper, and Aromat. Mix well. Lightly stir in breadcrumbs and egg.

Fill cavity of fish; skewer or truss to close the opening.

Makes enough for 8- to 10-pound dressed fish.

BAKED FISH PARMIGIANA

4 fish fillets or steaks
salt and pepper
½ pint tomato sauce
2 ounces grated Parmesan cheese
2 tablespoons melted butter or margarine (optional)

Place fish (thawed, if frozen) in shallow baking dish. Season lightly with salt and pepper.

Spread tomato sauce over each fillet; sprinkle with cheese. For a more attractive appearance, sprinkle with melted butter or margarine.

Bake in hot oven (425°F. Mark 7) until fish flakes easily, 15 to 20 minutes. Serves 4.

FISH CREOLE

1½ pounds fish fillets
2 tablespoons butter or margarine
1 large onion, chopped
2-3 tablespoons chopped green pepper
1½ teaspoons salt
¼ teaspoon pepper
¼ teaspoon paprika
2 8-ounce cans tomatoes, drained

Haddock, cod, halibut, turbot and pike may be used. If you like, 2 pounds whole fish may be used.

Arrange fish in greased shallow baking dish or casserole.

Sauté onion and green pepper in butter. Add seasonings and tomatoes. Pour over fish.

Bake in moderate oven (375°F. Mark 5) 30 minutes. Serves 4 to 5.

COD OR HADDOCK— ITALIAN STYLE

1 pound cod or haddock
½ teaspoon salt
½ pint tomato sauce
1 tablespoon lemon juice
1 ounce grated Parmesan cheese
2 tablespoons butter or margarine

Cut fish into 3 pieces and sprinkle with salt. Place in greased pie dish.

Pour tomato sauce (the better its flavour the better the dish) and lemon juice over fish. Sprinkle with cheese and dot with bits of butter.

Bake in hot oven (400°F. Mark 6) until fish flakes easily when tested with a fork and cheese has browned lightly, about 25 minutes. Serves 3.

HADDOCK À LA CREOLE

1 3-pound haddock
½ teaspoon salt
small pinch of pepper
1 large onion, chopped
1 bay leaf, crumbled
3 sprigs parsley, chopped
1 sprig thyme, chopped
8 fluid ounces white wine
3 tablespoons butter or margarine
2 tablespoons flour
2 ounces chopped mushrooms
6 tomatoes, finely chopped
1½ ounces crushed cracker biscuits

Clean and wash fish. Season with salt and pepper.

Mix onion, bay leaf, parsley, and thyme. Spread evenly over bottom of baking dish and put in fish. Pour wine over fish.

Bake in moderate oven (350°F. Mark 4) 20 minutes.

Melt 2 tablespoons butter in a saucepan. Sprinkle in flour, and when browned add mushrooms and tomatoes. Simmer 10 minutes. Pour over fish. Cover with crumbs. Dot with remaining butter. Bake 10 minutes longer. Serves 6.

BAKED HADDOCK AU GRATIN

1 whole or filleted haddock, about 3 pounds
1 large can (about 20 ounces) tomatoes
1 clove garlic, finely chopped
4 tablespoons Parmesan cheese, cut in bits
salt and pepper, to taste
1 tablespoon chopped thyme

Place fillets in greased baking dish. Add remaining ingredients.

Bake in moderate oven (350°F. Mark 4) until fish flakes easily when tested with fork, about 1 hour. Serves 6.

Note: Cod fillets may be substituted for haddock. Cut down baking time to 35 minutes.

BAKED FISH FILLETS IN SWEET-SOUR PINEAPPLE

1 green pepper, cut in strips
1 coarsely chopped, medium-sized onion
2 tablespoons salad oil
1 teaspoon ground ginger
1 tablespoon brown sugar
1 tablespoon cornflour
1 tablespoon soy sauce
1-2 tablespoons vinegar
1 16-ounce can pineapple tidbits, not drained
1 to 1½ pounds thawed frozen or fresh fish fillets, or 2 pounds fish steaks, 1-inch thick (cod, haddock, whitefish, halibut)

Sauté green pepper and onion in salad oil in a frying pan for 5 minutes; add ginger and remaining ingredients except for the fish. Cook, stirring, until the mixture thickens.

Arrange fillets in shallow baking dish; sprinkle with salt and pepper; pour on sauce.

Bake in moderate oven (350°F. Mark 4) 30 minutes. Serves 4 to 6.

Baked Fish Fillets in Sweet-Sour Pineapple

Grilled Fish

GRILLED FISH FILLETS OR STEAKS

2 pounds fillets or steaks
1 teaspoon salt
$\frac{1}{8}$ teaspoon pepper
4 tablespoons butter or other fat, melted

Cut fish into portions. Sprinkle both sides with salt and pepper.

Place fish in a preheated greased grill pan about 2 inches from the heat, skin side up, if skin has not been removed from fillets.

Brush fish with melted fat. Grill for 5 to 8 minutes or until slightly browned, baste fish with melted fat, and turn carefully. Brush other side with melted fat and cook 5 to 8 minutes or until fish flakes easily when tested with a fork.

Remove carefully to a hot dish, garnish, and serve immediately plain or with a sauce. Serves 6.

GRILLED TROUT
(Or Other Small, Fresh-Water Fish)

Line grill pan with aluminium foil, or grease it thoroughly.

Brush whole, cleaned fish inside and out with melted fat. Sprinkle inside and out with salt, pepper, and Aromat. Place on foil.

Grill, with surface of fish 3 inches away from the heat for 5 minutes. Turn; grill 4 to 5 minutes longer. Brush with melted butter or margarine several times during grilling. Serve with cucumber sauce.

CRUMBLE TOP FISH FILLETS

1 pound frozen fish fillets (cod or haddock)
2 ounces butter, melted
1$\frac{1}{2}$ ounces fresh breadcrumbs
2$\frac{1}{4}$ ounces grated Gruyère cheese
1 tablespoon chopped onion
$\frac{1}{2}$ teaspoon salt
$\frac{1}{8}$ teaspoon pepper
small pinch of paprika pepper

Put the frozen fillets to thaw on bottom shelf of refrigerator or at room

Low-Calorie Grilled Fish

temperature until they can be pulled apart. Put them in the grill pan. Brush with a little melted butter. Grill about 3 inches from the heat 10 to 15 minutes or until fish flakes easily when tested with a fork.

Meanwhile mix remaining butter with remaining ingredients. Remove fillets from heat and turn them with a fish slice. Spread with breadcrumb mixture. Grill 2 to 3 minutes or until crumbs are brown. If you like, garnish with slices of lemon and parsley. Serves 3 to 4.

LOW-CALORIE GRILLED FISH

Choose a white fish such as haddock, halibut, plaice or cod. Have the fish cut thin if it isn't already cut.

The pan in which the fish is cooked need not be greased (calories saved); the moisture from the fish keeps it from sticking. Preheat grill pan and arrange fish in it when hot. Cover with any of the following low-calorie toppings and grill 2 to 3 inches from the heat—4 minutes if fish is thin; 8 minutes, turning once, if fish is thicker than plaice, for example. Fish is cooked when it flakes easily with a fork.

The toppings given below are created to give flavour and appeal to the fish by adding the fewest calories possible. Normally, the browned and colourful finish is achieved with butter and paprika. Not an ounce of butter or margarine is used here.

1. Brush with a thin layer of Worcestershire sauce, sprinkle with paprika pepper.

2. Cover fish during the last 3 minutes of cooking with a mixture of finely chopped cucumber, pimiento, onion, and salt and pepper.

3. Sprinkle during last 3 minutes of cooking with fish herb mixture (or your own favourite combination) and a little grated fresh carrot for colour.

4. Spread with a thin layer of tomato ketchup or chilli sauce (fewer calories than butter).

GRILLED HALIBUT STEAKS

2 halibut steaks about 1-inch thick (2 pounds)
1 teaspoon Aromat
Salt and pepper
Melted butter or margarine

Sprinkle surface of fish with Aromat, following the rule of $\frac{1}{2}$ teaspoon per pound. Set it aside for 5 minutes.

Crumble Top Fish Fillets

Sprinkle with salt and pepper. Brush with melted butter or margarine. Place on greased rack in grill pan, with surface of fish about 3 inches from the heat.

Grill about 8 minutes on each side, brushing frequently with melted butter or margarine. Serves 6.

HALIBUT STEAKS WITH PIMIENTO SAUCE

Plan on one half halibut steak for each person. If steaks are frozen, put them to thaw on refrigerator shelf or at room temperature. Brush with melted butter, sprinkle with salt and pepper. Grill them 2 or 3 inches from the heat, 5 to 8 minutes.

Turn steaks carefully. Season again and brush with melted butter and grill 5 to 8 minutes, or until fish flakes easily when tested with a fork. Serve in a hot dish. Pour pimiento sauce (below) over fish and arrange a border of cooked vegetables around the fish. Garnish with lemon wedges.

Pimiento Sauce: For 3 halibut steak halves, melt 3 tablespoons butter, add the juice of half a lemon, season with half teaspoon of salt and a dash of pepper. Slice 1 pimiento into thin strips and add to sauce.

Halibut Steaks with Pimiento Sauce

GRILLED MACKEREL WITH ONION SLICES

4 1-pound mackerel or other small
    whole fish
3 onions, sliced
2 tablespoons butter

Rub inside of fish with salt. Make several slits on each side of the fish. Slip a piece of onion and a dot of butter in each slit on the top side, pushing the slice of onion well into the slit.

Place fish under grill. Fish should be about 6 inches from the heat. Grill for 3 minutes, turn fish and insert onion slices and dots of butter into slits on other side. Grill 6 minutes or until fish flakes easily when tested with a fork. Serves 4 to 6.

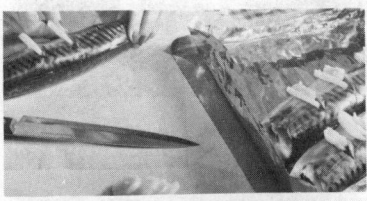

Grilled Mackerel with Onion Slices

GRILLED SALMON STEAKS WITH MAYONNAISE SAUCE

4 salmon steaks, about ¾-inch thick
4 fluid ounces mayonnaise
2 tablespoons chopped parsley
2 tablespoons chilli sauce

Preheat hot grill for 10 minutes.

Arrange salmon steaks in greased grill pan. Place under grill and grill about 8 minutes or until lightly browned.

Mix the mayonnaise, parsley, and chilli sauce together. Spread the salmon steaks generously with the mayonnaise mixture. Grill salmon 2 to 3 minutes longer or until sauce is delicately browned.

Put steaks on individual lettuce leaves on a large platter. Garnish with slices of tomato and cucumber. Serves 4.

*Grilled Salmon Steaks
with Mayonnaise Sauce*

GRILLED STUFFED FISH FILLETS

1   medium onion
6   plaice or sole fillets (about 2 pounds)
1   teaspoon salt
⅛   teaspoon pepper
2   teaspoons Aromat
2   ounces finely chopped celery
2¼ ounces melted butter or margarine
1   teaspoon savory
12 ounces fresh breadcrumbs
Creole sauce

Grate onion over surface of fish fillets; sprinkle with salt, pepper, and Aromat.

Mix the celery, melted butter, savory and breadcrumbs together; spread over fillets. Roll up and tie or fasten with wooden cocktail sticks.

Grill with surface of fish 4 inches from the heat for 15 to 20 minutes. Do not turn. Serve with Creole sauce. Serves 6.

GRILLED EEL

Skin and clean eel, remove backbone and cut in pieces. Rub with salt and set aside for 10 minutes.

Wipe the pieces to remove salt, brush them with melted butter or oil, and place in greased grill pan 4 inches from heat.

Grill for 10 minutes, or until golden brown. The flesh should flake easily when tested with a fork.

Sprinkle with salt and pepper and chopped parsley. Serve with maître d'hôtel butter or lemon juice.

TROUT GRILLED WITH BACON

Have trout cleaned and ready for the pan. Wrap each trout in a rasher of bacon, fastening bacon with a wooden cocktail stick.

Lay them flat in the grill pan and cook under moderate heat until the bacon is crisp on side next to heat. Turn and crisp the other side.

BARBECUED FISH STEAKS

Cut 3 pounds ¾-inch thick salmon or halibut steaks into pieces. Place in shallow dish. Cover with a mixture of juice of 1 lemon and 2-3 tablespoons salad oil. Chill ½ hour, turning once.

Arrange fish in large squares of foil; brush well with hot barbecue sauce. Cook close to coals until golden brown, about 3 minutes. (Cook fish quickly to prevent its drying.)

Brush with sauce, turn, cook other side and brush with sauce. Serves 8.

Variations: Place the fish steaks in shallow dish. Cover with Texas barbecue sauce or lemon barbecue sauce (see Sauces) and set aside for 1 hour. Cook as above.

Grilled Stuffed Fish Fillets

GRILLED SMELTS

Clean as for deep fried smelts. Dip in olive oil, then in breadcrumbs. Dust with paprika pepper.

Grill quickly until golden brown. Put on hot dish. Sprinkle with melted butter.

GRILLED FISH CALIFORNIA

2 to 4 small whole fish
2-3 tablespoons lemon juice
½ teaspoon Aromat
½ teaspoon salt
small pinch of pepper
melted butter or margarine

Remove heads from fish and clean; do not split. Rub inside with lemon juice, Aromat, salt, and pepper.

Place on rack of grill pan, brush with melted butter. Grill, with surface of fish 3 to 4 inches from heat 8 minutes; turn; brush with melted butter; grill 5 to 8 minutes longer, depending on size of fish, or until fish flakes easily when tested with a fork.

Serve with California sauce (below); garnish with lemon wedges and fresh mint. Serves 4.

California Sauce:
2   tablespoons butter or margarine
2   tablespoons flour
½   teaspoon salt
½   teaspoon Aromat
4   tablespoons brown sugar
4   fluid ounces lemon juice
4   fluid ounces water
2½ ounces golden seedless raisins

Melt butter or margarine; blend in flour, salt, Aromat, and brown sugar.

Mix the lemon juice and water together; add and stir over low heat until smooth and thickened. Add raisins; simmer 5 minutes. Makes about 1 pint.

Grilled Fish California

Fried Fish

PAN-FRIED FISH

2 pounds fillets or steaks fish
1 teaspoon salt
⅛ teaspoon pepper
1 egg
1 tablespoon milk or water
4 ounces dry breadcrumbs, golden
    crumbs or flour

Cut fish into portions. Sprinkle both sides with salt and pepper.

Beat egg slightly, and mix in the milk. Dip fish in the egg and roll in crumbs.

Place fish in a heavy frying pan which contains about ⅛ inch melted fat, hot but not smoking. Fry at a moderate heat. When fish is brown on one side, turn carefully and brown the other side. Cooking time about 10 minutes, depending on the thickness of the fish. Drain on absorbent paper.

Serve immediately on a hot platter, plain or with a sauce. Serves 6.

Pan-Fried Fish Fillets: If frozen fish is used for frying, it is better to partially thaw it in refrigerator for even cooking throughout.

OVEN-FRIED FISH FILLETS

2 pounds fish fillets
1 teaspoon salt
1 tablespoon paprika
¼ teaspoon pepper
8 fluid ounces milk
4 ounces dry breadcrumbs
4 tablespoons butter or other fat

Cut fillets into pieces. Season with salt, pepper, and paprika. (If frozen fillets are used, thaw them before cutting.)

Dip the fish in milk and roll in crumbs. Place in a well greased baking dish. Pour melted fat over the fish.

Place the dish on shelf near the top of a very hot oven (500°F. Mark 10) and bake 10 to 12 minutes, or until fish flakes easily when tested with a fork. Serve at once on a hot platter, plain or with a sauce. Serves 6.

FRIED FISH IN BATTER

2 pounds fish fillets
½ teaspoon salt

Batter No. 1:
6 ounces plain flour
3 teaspoons baking powder
1 teaspoon salt
2 eggs
8 fluid ounces milk

Season fish and cut in pieces. If the pieces of fish are more than half an inch thick but not thick enough to slice easily, make three or four slits in the sides. The fish will cook more evenly and quickly.

To make batter, mix and sift dry ingredients. Beat eggs well and stir milk into eggs. Pour liquid into dry ingredients and beat until smooth.

Dip pieces of fish into batter and fry in deep fat (375°F.) until golden brown, turning once. This will take about 7 minutes. Drain on absorbent paper. Serves 6.

Batter No. 2: Beat 1 egg and add ½ pint water. Stir in flour just until dampened. Batter will be lumpy.

Note: As a general rule, a batter made with water will be crisp while a batter made with milk will be soft.

SAUTÉED TROUT

Wipe the cleaned trout. Sprinkle with salt. Roll in flour. Sauté in butter until delicately brown. Remove trout to a hot dish.

To the juices in pan add additional butter, salt, and lemon juice. Brown it slightly and pour over fish. Sprinkle with chopped parsley.

For Trout Amandine, sprinkle sautéed trout with slivered almonds which have been sautéed with extra butter in the pan drippings.

FISH FILLETS IN WINE, PORTUGUESE STYLE

Crush or chop 3 cloves garlic. Add 1 teaspoon salt, ¼ teaspoon red pepper, ½ pint wine vinegar, and 12 fluid ounces water.

Pour over 2 pounds fish fillets and leave overnight. Drain fillets from liquid, fry in deep fat, or sauté until delicately browned. Serves 6.

Batter-dipped Fried Fish: Sprinkle prepared fillets with salt and dip in batter.

Fry batter-dipped fish in hot fat at 375°F. until golden brown. Drain on absorbent paper.

DEEP-FRIED SMELTS

Remove small scales with a sharp knife. Slit fish along the underside and remove entrails. Then remove silver lining from stomach by grasping with thumb and index finger. Rinse and dry.

Dip fish in egg beaten with a little milk. Roll in flour or crumbs or use a mixture of corn meal and cracker crumbs.

Fry in hot deep fat (370°F.) until golden brown, 3 to 5 minutes. Drain on absorbent paper. Sprinkle with salt, pepper, and lemon juice. Serve with tartar sauce or tomato ketchup and lemon wedges.

Note: Smelts may be fried whole and the bones eaten.

PAN-FRIED OR SAUTÉED SMELTS

Clean as for deep fried smelts. For best results use a half inch of bacon fat in a heavy frying pan. Brown until crisp on one side. Turn and brown other side.

Smelts may also be sautéed in butter until brown on both sides.

Smelts Meunière: Sauté smelts in butter. Remove to a hot dish. Sprinkle with chopped parsley. Melt extra butter in pan. Pour over smelts. Serve with lemon wedges.

Smelts Amandine: Sauté smelts in olive oil. To serve, sprinkle with slivered almonds sautéed in oil.

Smelts Au Beurre Noir (With Black Butter): Serve sautéed smelts with black butter (See Index) poured over fish.

Frozen breaded fish portions just seem to be made for busy days. Since they were dipped in batter and seasoned breadcrumbs before being packed and frozen, all you need do is follow directions on the packet for deep-fat frying or for pan-frying. Serve them with a well-seasoned sauce.

FISH FILLETS MEUNIÈRE

Season and dredge fish fillets with flour. Fry in butter. When cooked, remove from pan.

Place a little unsalted butter in the same pan and cook it until nut-brown in colour. Pour over the fish. Sprinkle with chopped parsley and a little lemon juice.

With Almonds: Sprinkle fish fillets meunière with slivered almonds, sautéed in butter.

TROUT SUPRÊME

Sprinkle cleaned and dressed trout inside and out with lemon juice, salt, and pepper. Dip in egg beaten with 2 tablespoons milk, then in dry breadcrumbs or golden crumbs.

Melt enough butter or margarine in a frying pan just to cover the bottom. Add fish and sauté until golden brown on both sides, about 3 to 4 minutes, or until fish flakes easily when tested with fork.

Remove to a hot platter and serve with mushroom-butter sauce (below).

Mushroom-Butter Sauce:
2 ounces butter
1 small can (3 ounces) sliced mushrooms, drained
1 tablespoon lemon juice
½ teaspoon salt

Melt butter. Add mushrooms, lemon juice, and salt. Serve hot with trout. Makes enough for 3 to 4 small trout.

Trout Suprême

DEEP FAT-FRIED FISH

Prepare 2 pounds fish as for pan-fried fish.

Use a deep pan with a frying basket and enough fat to cover the fish, but do not have the pan more than half full of fat. Heat the fat to 375°F.

Place a layer of fish in the frying basket and cook to an even golden brown, about 3 to 5 minutes. Lift out the basket, remove fish, and drain on absorbent paper.

Serve immediately on a hot platter, plain or with a sauce. Serves 6.

EELS

Eels should be alive when bought and will be skinned, cut up, and cleaned on request.

To prepare at home, cut off the head and slit the skin lengthwise. Peel off, cut open and remove entrails. Wash in salt water and cut into convenient lengths.

FRIED EEL

Cut eel in 2-inch lengths. Wash and dry thoroughly. Season with salt and pepper.

Dip in crumbs, then in egg, and again in crumbs. Brown quickly in a small amount of fat. Cover, reduce heat, and cook slowly until tender.

Serve with tomato sauce or other chosen sauce.

Poached or "Boiled" Fish

LIQUIDS USED FOR BOILING FISH

Boiled fish may be improved in flavour by cooking in one of the following liquids: **Acid Water, Fish Stock,** or **Court Bouillon.**

ACID WATER

To each quart of water add 1½ tablespoons of salt and 3 tablespoons of lemon juice or vinegar.

FISH STOCK

3 pounds fish bones
2 tablespoons butter
3 quarts water
2 stalks celery with leaves
2 large carrots, cut in pieces
2 onions, cut in pieces
½ leek, chopped
3 bay leaves
2 or 3 cloves garlic
8 peppercorns
2 teaspoons salt
1 teaspoon thyme

Wash fish bones in several changes of water. Melt butter in a large pan; add fish bones and water and cook, stirring about 5 minutes.

Add remaining ingredients and bring to the boil. Reduce heat and simmer ½ hour. Strain and store in refrigerator for a week or longer. Makes about 3 quarts.

Note: This stock may be frozen and used as needed.

COURT BOUILLON

Court bouillon is a well-seasoned liquid in which fish is poached. It is usually made of water, carrots, onion, celery, wine or vinegar, and various herbs and spices.

1-2 tablespoons diced carrots
1-2 tablespoons chopped onion
1-2 tablespoons chopped celery
2 sprigs parsley
2 tablespoons butter or other fat, melted
3 pints water
6 whole black peppercorns
2 whole cloves
1 bay leaf
2 tablespoons salt
2 tablespoons vinegar

Cook the vegetables in fat about 5 minutes to brown slightly.

Add water, spices (tied in muslin), and vinegar; simmer 30 minutes. Strain.

Court Bouillon with Wine: Omit vinegar in Court Bouillon recipe, and add about ¼-½ bottle dry white or red wine.

Fish Stock with Court Bouillon: Cover fish bones and scraps with Court Bouillon. Simmer 30 minutes or longer and strain. Use as liquid in making sauces to serve with fish or in fish soups.

POACHED OR "BOILED" FISH

2 pounds fillets
3 pints water
3 tablespoons salt

Cut fillets into portions.

Place fish in a wire basket or on a plate. The plate if used should be tied in a piece of muslin. Lower the fish into the salted, boiling water and simmer (never boil), about 10 minutes or until fish flakes easily when tested with a fork.

Remove fish carefully to a hot platter. Garnish and serve hot with a rich, bright coloured sauce. Serves 6

GEFILTE FISH
(Traditional Jewish Stuffed Fish)

Gefilte fish means literally, stuffed fish in Jewish. It is an old-time Jewish dish of chopped fish mixed with other ingredients, highly seasoned. It is stuffed into the fish skin or into pieces of it, or shaped into balls, then cooked. Some variation of it was prepared in every country of Central and Eastern Europe. Serve it with prepared horse-radish.

3 pounds fish (see below)
2 onions
1 egg
2 tablespoons breadcrumbs or matzo meal
about 1 teaspoon salt
about ⅛ teaspoon pepper
small pinch of ground cinnamon
about 4 fluid ounces water
1 carrot, sliced
1 potato, sliced (optional)
1 stalk celery, sliced

Use any firm-fleshed fish, preferably pike or carp, or a combination of these.

Clean and wash fish thoroughly; sprinkle with salt and place in refrigerator until ready to prepare.

Either leave fish whole or cut it into 2-inch slices. If the fish is left whole, do not remove head or tail. In either case, fillet the fish by removing flesh with bones leaving the skin intact.

Remove the flesh from bones; put the filleted parts or flesh and 1 onion through a mincer, then place in wooden chopping bowl.

Add egg, breadcrumbs, or matzo meal, seasoning, and enough water to make a soft light mixture. Chop until thoroughly mixed and smooth.

Wet your hands with cold water and fill the skin with this mixture. If the fish has been sliced form the mixture into oval cakes and fit them into bands of skin.

Place the bones, 1 sliced onion, carrot, potato, and celery in a deep pan. Season with salt, pepper, and cinnamon.

Place fish pieces neatly on top; add cold water to cover. Put the lid on the pan and bring quickly to the boil. Take off the lid, turn down heat, and keep fish at a slow boil 1½ to 2 hours.

The liquid should be reduced by half. When cool, remove to a platter carefully to retain shape of each piece of fish. Strain liquid over fish or into a separate bowl.

Chill thoroughly before serving, using carrot for garnish.

The jellied sauce may be chopped and served separately or as an additional garnish. Serves 4 to 6.

Gefilte Fish Balls: Place bones, head, and skin removed in the process of filleting fish on bottom of a deep pan. Arrange several stalks of celery on top.

Form the fish mixture into balls and place on top of celery to make removal easier when cooked.

The bones and skin add flavour to the fish sauce; discard after removing fish and straining sauce.

SQUID

Squid is a long, slender sea creature with ten arms, two of which are much longer than the others. It is a mollusc, but its shell is very small and is on the inside. Small squid are used as food and for fish bait. They have a sweet, rich flavour and are used in many Mediterranean and Oriental dishes. In coastal areas they are available fresh, but usually they are frozen and shipped inland. They are sometimes available canned.

SQUID À LA GRUCCI

1½ pounds squid
1 medium onion, chopped
3 tablespoons olive oil
1 tablespoon chopped parsley
1 clove garlic
½ teaspoon rosemary
¼ pound mushrooms, sliced
2 tablespoons tomato sauce
4 fluid ounces water

Clean squid and remove skin; cut meat into small pieces.

Brown onion in hot olive oil. Add parsley, garlic, rosemary, and mushrooms; cook 5 minutes.

Add tomato sauce, water, and squid; cover pan and cook gently about 40 minutes, or until squid is tender. Cooking time will depend on size of squid. Serves 4.

BLUE TROUT OR TRUITE AU BLEU

This is a method of cooking fresh-water fish very quickly by plunging it into boiling court bouillon. It is used especially for trout. With this method it is essential that the fish be not only fresh but actually alive when brought to the kitchen. The fish is stunned, cleaned quickly, plunged into the court bouillon, and removed the instant it is done, usually in 10 to 12 minutes. It is then served with melted butter, plain boiled potatoes, and chopped parsley. The name comes from the vinegar in the court bouillon, which turns the fish slightly blue.

CIOPPINO
(San Francisco Fish Stew)

Cioppino is a fish or fish-and-shellfish stew simmered in highly seasoned tomato sauce, often with wine added. The name is Italian, but the dish as usually prepared originated in San Francisco, California.

2-3 tablespoons salad or olive oil
2 cloves garlic, chopped
½ large onion, chopped
1 small green pepper, chopped
1 large can (20 ounces) tomatoes
1 7-ounce can Napolitana sauce
1 bay leaf
⅛ teaspoon oregano
salt and pepper to taste
16 fluid ounces dry white wine
1 pound frozen lobster meat
1 pound frozen cod fillets
10 ounces frozen prawns
1 8-ounce can minced clams

Heat oil in large heavy frying pan over medium heat; add garlic, onion, and green pepper; cook until lightly browned, 8 to 10 minutes.

Add tomatoes, tomato sauce, bay leaf, oregano, salt and pepper.

Cover and cook slowly, stirring frequently, about 1 hour, adding wine during last 10 minutes.

Add lobster meat and cod, simmer about 10 minutes. Add prawns and clams and simmer until tender, about 10 minutes. Serves 6 to 8.

STEAMED FISH FILLETS

2 pounds fillets
1½ teaspoons salt

Salt fish on both sides. Place fish in a well greased steamer, and cook over boiling water for 10 to 12 minutes or until fish flakes easily when tested with a fork.

Remove fish carefully to a hot platter, and serve hot with a rich brightly coloured sauce. Serves 6.

Cioppino

Fish Fillets Duglaré

FISH FILLETS DUGLERÉ

1 pound frozen fish fillets
2 tablespoons butter or margarine
1 medium onion, chopped
1 clove garlic, minced
1 large can (20 ounces) tomatoes
4 tablespoons white wine or lemon juice
1 tablespoon chopped parsley
1 tablespoon flour
¼ teaspoon oregano
2 tablespoons double cream

Put fish fillets to thaw on the bottom shelf of the refrigerator or at room temperature. Cut fillets in pieces.

Melt 1 tablespoon butter or margarine in a frying pan; add onion and garlic. Place fish on top; cover with tomatoes, wine or lemon juice, and parsley. Bring to the boil; lower heat; cover the pan and cook 10 to 15 minutes.

Remove fish to a chafing dish to keep warm. Cream remaining butter with flour and stir into sauce. Add oregano. Cook, stirring occasionally, for about 5 minutes. Blend in the cream. Garnish with extra parsley. Serves 4.

Fish Cooked In Water

Wipe fish and sprinkle with salt

Tie neck of paper enclosing fish and onion and celery mixture

BUTTER BARBECUED FISH FILLETS

4 ounces butter or margarine
1 small onion, chopped
2 tablespoons chopped green pepper
1 tablespoon Worcestershire sauce
2 tablespoons tomato ketchup
2 teaspoons vinegar
2 slices lemon
1 teaspoon prepared mustard
2 pounds frozen fish fillets

Sauté onion and green pepper in butter in a large frying pan. Add Worcestershire sauce, ketchup, vinegar, lemon slices, and prepared mustard and simmer for 5 minutes.

Cut fish fillets into 4 equal pieces and place in the frying pan. Cover and simmer for 10 minutes. Turn.

Simmer 10 to 15 minutes more or until the fish flakes easily when tested with a fork. Serves 4 to 6.

"BOILED" HADDOCK OR COD, NEW ENGLAND STYLE

Split a 3- to 4-pound haddock or cod. Clean and rub inside well with salt. Leave for 3 hours.

Rinse fish and wrap in muslin, leaving long ends of the cloth for handles. Simmer the fish in boiling salted water 25 to 35 minutes or until fish flakes easily when tested with fork.

Put the fish on a hot platter. Garnish with crisply fried pieces of salt pork, and surround with boiled potatoes and slices of boiled buttered beetroot. Serve with parsley sauce or egg sauce. Serves 4 to 6.

FISH COOKED IN WATER (Flavour-saving Method)

Portions of whole fish or fillets which are to be used for salads, casseroles, fish cakes, or creamed fish dishes may be cooked in water.

Wipe fish with a damp cloth. Sprinkle fish with salt and place on a sheet of dampened greaseproof paper or a piece of greased aluminium foil. Measure thickness of fish.

Add 1 tablespoon each of chopped onion and celery. Wrap securely. Gather together corners of the paper, like a pouch, and tie with string. Or fold foil over fish closing the open edges with double folds to make the parcel watertight.

Place the parcel in rapidly boiling water and cover. When water returns to the boil, time the cooking period. Boil 10 minutes per inch thickness for fresh fish and about 20 minutes per inch thickness for frozen fish.

When removing fish from the parcel, save the juices which can be substituted for liquid in sauces or casseroles.

Fish Fillets with Brazil Nut Sauce

FISH FILLETS WITH BRAZIL NUT SAUCE

Thaw 1 pound fish fillets until they can be separated. Place in a frying pan. Add 2-3 tablespoons water and 1 tablespoon lemon juice. Cover pan and simmer 8 to 10 minutes or until fish flakes easily when tested with a fork.

Place the fillets on a warm dish and pour Brazil Nut Sauce (below) over fish. Serves 3.

Brown Butter Sauce with Brazil Nuts: Put 3 tablespoons butter in a heavy saucepan; melt and cook very slowly until it is hazelnut brown. Serve over fish fillets garnished with browned Brazil nuts.

To Prepare Brazil Nuts: Cover shelled Brazil nuts with cold water. Bring water slowly to the boil and simmer 3 to 4 minutes. Drain. Slice nuts. Brush slices of nuts with melted butter, place on a baking sheet or in baking dish. Place in moderate oven (350°F. Mark 4) 10 or 15 minutes until golden brown. Turn the slices occasionally.

FISH COOKED IN MILK

2 pounds fish fillets
2 pints water
1 tablespoon salt
24 fluid ounces hot milk

Wipe the fish with a damp cloth, and cut in pieces. Soak 5 minutes in the water to which 1 tablespoon salt has been added. Drain.

Place fish pieces in the hot milk, and simmer until fish flakes easily when tested with a fork, allowing about 15 minutes per inch thickness of fish. Make a white sauce, using the milk in which the fish was cooked. Serves 6.

"Boiled" Haddock, New England Style

COD PROVENÇAL

4 thick slices cod
salt and pepper
1 medium onion, finely chopped
1 clove garlic, crushed
2 tablespoons chopped parsley
pinch of thyme
2 medium tomatoes, peeled and
    chopped
4 ounces thinly sliced mushrooms,
    sautéed in butter or mar-
    garine
½ bottle white wine
1 tablespoon butter or margarine

Season fish with salt and pepper. Place in well greased shallow baking dish. Sprinkle with onion, garlic, parsley, and thyme. Add tomatoes, sautéed mushrooms, and wine.

Place over low heat and simmer gently until fish is tender and flakes easily when tested with a fork, 15 to 20 minutes.

Transfer fish to a heated dish and keep warm while sauce is reduced by half. Add butter and pour sauce over fish. Serve at once. Serves 4.

Note: Haddock fillets may be substituted for cod.

CURRIED FISH

1½ to 2 pounds fish
2 tablespoons fat
1 tablespoon chopped green pepper
1 small onion, chopped
1 ounce chopped celery
2 tablespoons flour
8 fluid ounces liquid from sim-
    mered fish
¼ to 1 teaspoon curry powder
salt to taste
1-1½ pounds cooked rice
3 tablespoons chopped parsley

Simmer fish about 10 minutes in a small quantity of water in a shallow pan. Drain and save liquid.

Melt fat. Cook green pepper, onion, and celery in fat a few minutes. Stir in flour, then add fish liquid with milk or water to bring the quantity to ½ pint. Cook until it thickens, stirring constantly.

Add curry powder and salt, to taste. Remove skin and bones from cooked fish. Arrange on a hot platter with a border of rice. Pour sauce over fish and sprinkle with chopped parsley. Serves 6.

CREOLE BOUILLABAISSE

2 pounds fish fillets
¼ pound mushrooms
1 tablespoon margarine or butter
1 large onion, chopped
1 clove garlic, crushed
1 tablespoon flour
2 8-ounce cans tomatoes, crushed
    to a pulp

8 fluid ounces water
1½ bay leaves
¾ teaspoon curry powder
4 tablespoons sherry
dash of Tabasco sauce
½ teaspoon salt
4 whole cloves

For best results, use 2 kinds of white fish such as cod and haddock.

Poach fish in boiling water for 15 minutes.

Slice mushrooms very thinly and sauté in fat with onion, garlic, and flour. When golden brown, add remaining ingredients and simmer for 30 minutes.

Add this sauce to drained fish and cook about 5 minutes. Place pieces of fish on buttered toast, cover with the sauce and serve. Serves 6 to 8.

POACHED SALMON WITH HERB SALAD DRESSING

Choose salmon steaks of even thickness, buying 1 large steak for 2 portions.

Place piece of aluminium foil in bottom of frying basket. Place 1 steak on foil, top with another piece of foil; continue until all the steaks are added.

Place basket in a deep pan; add 1 or 2 slices of onion, 3 slices of lemon, 3 or 4 whole black peppercorns, a piece of bay leaf, 1 to 2 teaspoons salt, and ½ teaspoon Aromat per pound of fish.

Add enough boiling water to cover fish. Set over low heat; simmer 15 to 20 minutes depending on amount of fish.

Lift out basket. Remove steaks by lifting foil under each. Cool; then chill.

To serve, top with chilled cooked asparagus and herb salad dressing. Garnish with cucumber slices, watercress, and capers.

Herb Salad Dressing:
1½ tablespoons sugar
1 teaspoon salt
¼ teaspoon Aromat
2 teaspoons prepared mustard
¼ teaspoon rosemary
⅛ teaspoon thyme
¼ teaspoon savory
2 tablespoons flour
1 egg, slightly beaten
6 fluid ounces milk
4 tablespoons lemon juice
1 tablespoon butter or margarine

In the top of a double boiler put the sugar, salt, Aromat, mustard, herbs, and flour. Add egg and mix well.

Add milk slowly, blended well. Add lemon juice.

Cook over hot water, stirring constantly, until it thickens. Add butter or margarine; stir until melted. Cool, then chill.

Add 2 to 4 fluid ounces single cream if you want a thinner dressing. Makes about ½ pint dressing.

French Rolled Fish Fillets

FRENCH ROLLED FISH FILLETS

1 tablespoon butter or margarine
2 tablespoons finely chopped onion
1½ pounds fish fillets
1½ teaspoons salt
small pinch of pepper
4 peeled, quartered small tomatoes
¼ pound mushrooms, sliced
4 fluid ounces dry white wine
4 fluid ounces cold water

Grease a large frying pan with butter. Scatter the onion over it.

Roll each fillet like a Swiss roll, place in frying pan, seam side down. Sprinkle salt and pepper over fillets.

Arrange tomatoes round and place mushrooms on top. Pour over wine and water. Cover and simmer 10 minutes, or until fish is tender, and flakes easily when tested with a fork.

Remove fish to a hot platter and keep warm while preparing sauce.

Sauce: To prepare sauce cook liquid left in frying pan until about ½ pint remains. Cream 3 tablespoons softened butter. Add 3 tablespoons flour. Add to the liquid and simmer until it thickens. Sprinkle fish with parsley. Pour sauce over fish. Grill until browned on top.

If you like, small cooked potato balls may be placed round fish before pouring over sauce and grilling. Serves 4.

Poached Salmon with Herb Salad Dressing

Dried, Smoked, and Salt-Cured Fish

COD BALLS
(Basic Recipe)
10 ounces flaked salt cod
4-6 medium potatoes, peeled and diced
2 slightly beaten eggs
2 tablespoons butter or margarine
4 tablespoons milk
⅛ teaspoon pepper
pinch of celery salt
paprika pepper

Break the fish into small flakes and place in a saucepan. Cover with cold water. Heat slowly to boiling point. Drain. Repeat, using fresh water if fish is hard and salty.

Mix with the diced potatoes and cook, covered, in about 16 fluid ounces boiling water, until potatoes are tender. Drain well and mash thoroughly. Add remaining ingredients. Beat with spoon until light and fluffy. Chill.

Shape into balls or drop by spoonfuls into hot deep fat (375°F.). Fry until browned. Drain on absorbent paper.

Serve with tomato sauce, ketchup, egg sauce, or chilli sauce. Serves 6.

Variations of Cod Balls

Cod Hash: Spread mixture evenly in a large, hot, well greased frying pan. Cook slowly until a brown crust forms on bottom. Fold like an omelet.

Cod Patties: shape into patties. Brown on both sides in hot fat.

Curried Cod Balls: Add 1 teaspoon curry powder to mixture.

CREAMED COD
10 ounces flaked salt cod
4 tablespoons butter or margarine
4 tablespoons flour
16 fluid ounces milk
⅛ teaspoon pepper

Cover cod with water. Heat slowly to boiling point. Repeat once or twice if fish is hard and very salty. Drain well.

Heat butter. Add cod and cook over low heat about 2 minutes. Blend in flour. Slowly add milk. Cook until thickened, stirring constantly. Add pepper.

Serve on toast or baked potatoes. Serves 6.

COD CAKES
5 ounces flaked salt cod
7 ounces hot mashed potatoes
20 salted biscuits, finely crushed
1 egg
1 tablespoon chopped onion
small pinch of pepper
golden crumbs

Place fish in muslin or fine sieve and run cold water through it for 1 minute before using.

Mix together fish, potatoes, bread crumbs, egg, onion, and pepper.

Shape into 8 patties; roll in golden crumbs. Sauté until golden brown. Serve with tomato sauce. Serves 4.

FINNAN HADDIE
Finnan haddie is smoked haddock. The name is a corruption of Findon haddock, Findon being a fishing port on the coast of Scotland famous for its cured haddock.

CREAMED FINNAN HADDIE
2 pounds finnan haddie
2 tablespoons butter or margarine
4 fluid ounces cream or top of the milk

Cover fish with water and simmer 10 minutes. Drain.

Place on a hot platter; dot with butter and add hot milk or cream before serving. Garnish with parsley. Serves 6.

STEAMED FINNAN HADDIE
Steam over boiling water until tender, 15 to 20 minutes. Each piece should be exposed to steam. Do not pile on top of each other. Serve with butter sauce.

FINNAN HADDIE RABBIT
In a double boiler, heat ½ pound mature Cheddar cheese, cut small, with 8 fluid ounces double cream and about 8 ounces flaked steamed finnan haddie. When well blended, stir in 1 beaten egg and serve on toast. Serves 6.

FINNAN HADDIE BAKED IN MILK
2 pounds finnan haddie
2 tablespoons butter or margarine
8 fluid ounces milk

Cover fish with boiling water; simmer 10 minutes. Drain.

Add milk and butter to fish. Bake in moderate oven (350°F. Mark 4) 15 minutes. Serves 6.

KIPPERS
To kipper means to preserve fish by splitting, salting, and smoking it. A fish cured by this method, usually a herring, is often referred to as a kipper. A bloater is a large, specially selected herring or mackerel that has been cured (bloated) by salting and smoking.

GRILLED KIPPERS
Remove head and tail from fish, and wipe with a damp cloth.

Place skin side up, in grill pan 4 inches from heat and grill 3 minutes.

Turn fish, dot with butter, grill 3 minutes longer. Serve with lemon.

BAKED KIPPERS
4 kippers
½ green pepper, chopped
2-3 tablespoons chopped onion
1 tablespoon butter or margarine
12 fluid ounces tomato juice
¼ teaspoon pepper

Remove head and tail from kipper and wipe with a damp cloth. Place in a greased baking dish.

Sauté chopped green pepper and onion in butter; spread over fish. Pour tomato juice over fish; sprinkle with pepper.

Bake in hot oven (425°F. Mark 7) 15 minutes. Serves 4.

SAUTÉED KIPPERS
Soak the kippers in boiling water to cover for 10 minutes. Drain.

Sauté the kippers in hot oil or butter in a frying pan for about 5 minutes, turning once. Serve with butter sauce.

CANNED KIPPERS
Place kippers in a shallow baking dish. Brush them with melted butter and lemon juice. Sprinkle with pepper. Pour over juice from can.

Heat in hot oven (425°F. Mark 7) for 5-8 minutes. Garnish with lemon wedges and chopped parsley.

SALT COD PORTUGUESE
1½ pounds fillet of salt cod
1-2 tablespoons olive oil
1 Spanish onion, chopped
2 cloves garlic, crushed
½ pound tomatoes, peeled and chopped
1 red sweet pepper, chopped
bouquet garni
4 tablespoons white wine
½ pint fish stock or water
1 tablespoon tomato purée
salt, pepper
chopped parsley

Cut the cod into 4-5 pieces, put into a pan, cover with cold water and poach for 10 minutes. Drain well.

Heat the oil in a saucepan, add the vegetables and sauté for a few minutes. Add bouquet garni, wine and stock. Cover, and simmer until the vegetables are tender, then remove the bouquet garni and rub the vegetables through a sieve. Add tomato purée and seasoning as required. Cover the bottom of a casserole with some of the purée, arrange the fish on top and cover with the remaining purée. Cover, and bake in a moderate oven (375°F. Mark 5) about 20 minutes. Sprinkle with parsley and serve with plainly boiled potatoes or boiled rice.

MARINATED (PICKLED) HERRING

12 milter herring
2 lemons, sliced very thin
4 large onions, sliced
12 bay leaves
2 tablespoons mustard seed
2 tablespoons black peppercorns
16 fluid ounces vinegar
8 fluid ounces water
3 tablespoons sugar

Soak herring in cold water to cover for 3 hours, changing water twice. (Or soak in cold water to cover overnight.)

Drain. Cut off heads and tails. Split the herring. Remove and reserve the milt. If you like, skin and bone the herring. Remove the skin by running a knife from head to tail. Leave fillets whole or cut into 3-inch pieces.

Place herring in a crock or large earthenware bowl in alternating layers with sliced lemon, sliced onions, a few pieces of bay leaf, and a sprinkling of mustard seed and black peppercorns.

Bring the combined vinegar, water, and sugar to the boil; cool. Mash the milt with a fork; add a little of the cooled vinegar mixture to thin it. Put through a sieve, then mix with remaining vinegar mixture. Pour over herring to cover.

Cover crock or dish and put in a cool place. The herring are ready to be served in 4 to 6 days.

Note: If you like, 1 large apple, grated, may be added with the vinegar mixture.

JIFFY HERRING IN WINE WITH SOUR CREAM

1 2-pound jar herring in wine
8 fluid ounces sour cream
1 tablespoon chopped onion
2 tablespoons chopped chives
1 tablespoon chopped basil

Drain the sauce from the herring and add to it the remaining ingredients. Pour this mixture over the herring. Serve chilled as an appetizer on lettuce. Serves 6.

Pickled herring appetizers are quick and easy to prepare with the ready-made varieties available in most stores. For a savoury to accompany drinks serve herring in a bowl with small slices of pumpernickel and rye breads.

MARINATED HERRING WITH CREAM

6 milter herring
4 tablespoons vinegar
1 lemon, very thinly sliced
1 onion, thinly sliced
2½ tablespoons mixed pickling spices
8 fluid ounces sour cream

Soak, clean, and fillet herring as for marinated herring recipe. Cut fillets into 1½-inch pieces.

Mash ½ the milt; combine with vinegar. (Dilute the vinegar with a little water if it is very strong.)

Place remaining milt and herring in a crock or large earthenware dish in alternate layers with the lemon, onion, and a sprinkling of pickling spices.

Pour vinegar mixture over herring. Add sour cream. Keep in a cool place. Serve it after 48 hours.

FINNAN HADDIE CASSEROLE

¾ pound finnan haddie
3 tablespoons butter or margarine
3 tablespoons flour
12 fluid ounces milk
½ teaspoon salt
⅛ teaspoon pepper
2 cooked potatoes, diced
1 hard-boiled egg, sliced
2 slices bread
2 tablespoons butter

Wash finnan haddie. Soak 30 minutes in half milk and half water to cover. Bring to the boil in same liquid and simmer gently 20 minutes. Drain; remove any skin and bones and flake fish.

Melt butter; blend in flour. Slowly add milk, salt, and pepper and cook, stirring constantly, until thickened. Add flaked fish, potatoes, and egg. Pour into individual ramekins or heat-proof dishes.

Remove crusts from bread; cut into small cubes, and brown carefully in 2 tablespoons melted butter. Top the dishes with brown cubes.

Bake in moderate oven (350°F. Mark 4) 30 minutes. Serves 4.

Roe and Milt

Roe are the eggs of fish which are removed intact. They are commonly found in fish in the spring. Roe may be bought by the pound or in cans.

Milt are the spermatic glands of the male fish. It is prepared like roe.

Canned roe may be used in place of parboiled roe. Herring roe is considered a great delicacy and it is the most expensive; however, roe, is commonly obtained from cod, haddock and mackerel, as well as herring. Salt herring usually contains roe or milt.

Roe should be parboiled before using in recipes. Follow the method for parboiled herring roe, but cut the time for roe from smaller fish. Five to

10 minutes is usually enough, depending upon size of roe. The roe is sufficiently done when it blanches (whitens).

A pair of roe from 1 herring will serve 2. For other roe or milt, allow about 1 pound to serve 4 to 5, depending upon how it is served.

PARBOILED HERRING ROE

Handle roe carefully in pairs with the membrane intact. Cover with boiling water and for each quart of water add 1 tablespoon vinegar or lemon juice, ½ teaspoon salt, and, if you like, ½ teaspoon pickling spice.

Lower heat and simmer until white and firm, 5 to 20 minutes, depending on size of roe. Drain, cover with cold water, cool, and drain again. Remove membrane or not as desired.

Note: Roe of very small herring do not have to be parboiled or at the most parboil for 2 minutes.

GRILLED HERRING ROE

Brush the dried parboiled roe with melted butter or margarine seasoned with salt and pepper, and a little lemon juice if desired.

Place in the greased grill pan and broil about 2 inches from the heat until golden brown. Turn and broil other side.

Baste several times with melted butter or margarine. The roe should be firm but not dry or hard. Serve with lemon wedges.

HERRING ROE MEUNIÈRE

Cook parboiled herring roe in butter or oil. Add lemon juice, salt, and pepper to taste. Sprinkle with chopped parsley. Cover with melted browned butter.

Herring Roe Amandine: Follow recipe for Herring Roe Meunière, and garnish with chopped almonds which have been browned in the oven.

BAKED HERRING ROE

Place the drained parboiled roe in a greased baking dish. Cover with tomato sauce.

Bake in hot oven (400°F. Mark 6) about 20 minutes, basting 5 times with sauce in pan. Serve with additional tomato sauce.

FRIED OR SAUTÉED HERRING ROE

Season the drained, parboiled roe with salt and pepper. Sprinkle with lemon juice if you like.

Dip in dry breadcrumbs, then in beaten egg, diluted with 1 tablespoon milk or water, and again in crumbs.

Sauté in butter or margarine until cooked through and lightly browned or fry in hot deep fat (390°F.).

Serve with lemon wedges or tartar sauce.

Dishes with Canned or Cooked Fish

BUYING CANNED FISH

In using canned fish, the more attractive high grades are better for salads or serving plain. For such dishes as casseroles or fish cakes, lower grades will do. They are just as nutritious and full of flavour as top quality.

The oil or salty liquid from canned fish adds flavour and food value to seafood dishes. Use the oil, for instance, as fat in the white sauce in making creamed tuna fish. Brine may be part of the liquid in jellied fish salad.

SALMON-MACARONI LOAF WITH TOMATO SAUCE

4 ounces elbow macaroni
1 can (1 pound) salmon, drained
      and flaked
5 ounces grated Cheddar cheese
7 ounces corn flakes
8 fluid ounces milk
2 eggs, slightly beaten
2-3 tablespoons chopped pimiento
1 tablespoon chopped parsley
½ teaspoon finely chopped garlic
1 teaspoon salt
½ teaspoon pepper
1 tablespoon butter, melted
¼ teaspoon paprika

Cook macaroni in plenty of boiling salted water only until tender. Drain, rinse, and drain again. Mix with salmon, 4 ounces cheese, 3 ounces corn flakes, milk, eggs, pimiento, parsley, garlic, salt, and pepper. Spread evenly in greased 10×6 inch baking dish.

Crush the remaining corn flakes into fine crumbs. Mix them with the remaining cheese, butter, and paprika. Sprinkle over salmon mixture.

Bake in moderate oven (350°F. Mark 4) about 40 minutes. Cut into 3×2½-inch pieces and serve, accompanied with hot tomato sauce. Serves 8.

Tomato Sauce. Sauté ½ large onion, chopped, and ½ green pepper, chopped, in 2 tablespoons butter. Then stir in salt, pepper, and chilli powder to taste and a can of condensed tomato soup. Serve hot.

*Salmon-Macaroni Loaf with
Tomato Sauce*

CREAMED FISH
(Basic Recipe)

Mix together about 12 ounces flaked fish (cooked or canned) and 12 fluid ounces medium white sauce. Heat in a double boiler over hot water.

Season to taste with salt and pepper. Serve on toast, or rusks. Serves 4 to 6.

Note: Tomato or Creole sauce may be substituted for white sauce.

Creamed Fish Variations

Creamed Fish with Eggs: In basic recipe use about 8 ounces flaked fish and 2 or 3 hard-boiled eggs, sliced.

Creamed Fish with Vegetables: In basic recipe increase white sauce to 16 fluid ounces and add about ½ pound diced cooked vegetables.

Fish Au Gratin: Put creamed fish in a greased baking dish and cover with 2 ounces buttered breadcrumbs mixed with 1 ounce grated cheese.

Bake in hot oven (400°F. Mark 6) until sauce is bubbly and the top is well browned, 20 to 30 minutes.

Creamed Fish in Noodle Ring: Prepare noodle ring. Place on hot serving plate. Place creamed fish in centre. Garnish.

SCALLOPED FISH
(Basic Recipe)

1   pound flaked, cooked fish
2   teaspoons grated onion
1   teaspoon lemon juice
12 fluid ounces medium white sauce
4   ounces buttered breadcrumbs

Arrange fish in a greased casserole or individual ramekins. Sprinkle with onion and lemon juice. Add white sauce. Cover with buttered breadcrumbs.

Bake in moderate oven (375°F. Mark 5) until crumbs are brown, 20 to 25 minutes. Serves 6.

Scalloped Fish Variations

Scalloped Fish Mushroom Casserole: In basic recipe, substitute canned cream of mushroom soup for white sauce. If necessary, dilute soup with a little milk.

Scalloped Fish with Potato Border: In basic recipe, substitute mashed potatoes for buttered crumbs.

Scalloped Fish and Eggs: In basic recipe, increase white sauce to 16 fluid ounces. Arrange fish, 3 sliced hard-boiled eggs, and sauce in alternate layers in casserole, sprinkling each layer with onion and lemon juice.

SALMON DIABLE

6 fluid ounces sour cream
4 tablespoons sherry
1 tablespoon lemon juice
1 teaspoon Worcestershire sauce
½ teaspoon dry mustard
2 eggs, slightly beaten
1 can (1 pound) salmon, drained
      and flaked
1 ounce golden crumbs
4 tablespoons chopped parsley
1 tablespoon chopped onion
salt and pepper
6 thin lemon slices
paprika pepper

Mix sour cream, wine, lemon juice, Worcestershire sauce, mustard, and eggs. Stir in the salmon, crumbs, parsley, and onion. Add salt and pepper.

Spoon mixture into 6 greased scallop shells or individual heatproof dishes. Top each one with a lemon slice and sprinkle with paprika. Bake in oven (350°F. Mark 4) 30 minutes. Serves 6.

Salmon Diable

TUNA IN MUSHROOM SAUCE

2 cans (about 7 ounces each) tuna
      fish in vegetable oil
1 can (10½ ounces) condensed cream
      of mushroom soup
1 can (3 ounces) mushrooms, sliced
4 fluid ounces sour cream
1 tablespoon chopped parsley, op-
      tional

Mix the tuna, undiluted mushroom soup, and mushrooms with liquid from can in a frying pan or saucepan. Bring to the boil; simmer gently 5 minutes.

Remove from heat; stir in sour cream. Sprinkle with chopped parsley and serve with hot boiled noodles or rice. Serves 4.

Tuna in Mushroom Sauce

SALMON CROQUETTES

1 can (1 pound) salmon or about 1
    pound fresh cooked salmon
½ teaspoon salt
pinch of cayenne pepper
1 teaspoon chopped parsley
½ tablespoon chopped onion
about 1 ounce golden crumbs or
    fine breadcrumbs
1 well beaten egg

Flake fish, removing any skin or bones. Mix well with remaining ingredients. Shape into croquettes. Roll in extra golden crumbs or breadcrumbs.

Beat 1 additional egg lightly with 1 tablespoon water. Dip croquettes in egg-water mixture, then again in crumbs. Let stand in refrigerator at least 30 minutes.

Fry in deep hot fat (375°F.) until golden brown. Drain on absorbent paper. Serve with tartar sauce.

KEDGEREE

Kedgeree is a hash of flaked fish with rice. The name comes from India, where it is applied to various more or less similar spiced rice dishes.

1 pound cooked fish (see below)
12 ounces hot cooked rice
4 hard-boiled eggs, cut in quarters
    or chopped
⅛ teaspoon pepper
3 tablespoons chopped parsley
4 fluid ounces single cream
1 tablespoon butter or margarine
1 teaspoon salt

Use cod fillets, sole, flounder, or haddock. Flake fish; place in top part of a double boiler with remaining ingredients. Heat thoroughly over boiling water. A pinch of curry powder may be added, if you like. Serves 4.

BAKED SALMON CUTLETS

16 fluid ounces thick white sauce
2 teaspoons Worcestershire sauce
2 teaspoons lemon juice
1 tablespoon finely chopped onion
⅛ teaspoon celery salt
about 1 pound cooked or canned
    salmon

Make the thick white sauce. Add Worcestershire sauce, lemon juice, finely chopped onion, and celery salt. Mix well.

Salmon Loaf

Flake salmon, removing skin but using soft bones and oil, and add fish to sauce. Chill well.

Shape into cutlets and roll them in finely sifted dry breadcrumbs. Place on greased pan. Bake in hot oven (400°F. Mark 6) 20 minutes.

Serve with lemon wedges, chilli, or tartar sauce. Serves 6.

TUNA FISH AND CORN CASSEROLE

2-3 tablespoons chopped onion
3 tablespoons chopped green
    pepper
2 tablespoons butter or margarine
1 tablespoon flour
1 teaspoon salt
⅛ teaspoon white pepper
1 teaspoon paprika
12 fluid ounces milk
1 small can (about 8 ounces) corn
1 7-ounce can tuna
about 1½ ounces fresh white
    breadcrumbs
2 tablespoons melted butter

Sauté onion and green pepper in 2 tablespoons melted butter or margarine until tender.

Blend in flour, salt, pepper, and paprika. Gradually add milk, and cook, stirring constantly, until mixture is smooth and thickened. Add corn and flaked tuna fish. Mix thoroughly.

Turn into 4 individual greased heatproof dishes or 1 large casserole. Bake in slow oven (325°F. Mark 3) 20 minutes.

Toss the breadcrumbs with 2 tablespoons melted butter and sprinkle over the tuna fish just a few minutes before serving. Serves 4.

SALMON LOAF

3 ounces fresh white breadcrumbs
4 fluid ounces evaporated milk
    diluted with 4 fluid ounces
    water
1 can (about 9 ounces) salmon,
    drained and flaked
1 teaspoon salt
1 tablespoon butter or margarine
1 tablespoon finely chopped onion
1 teaspoon lemon juice
2 beaten egg yolks
2 egg whites, stiffly beaten
4 hard-boiled eggs

Soak breadcrumbs in diluted milk for 10 minutes. Add salmon, salt, butter, onion, lemon juice, and egg yolks. Blend.

Fold in stiffly beaten egg whites.

Fill well greased loaf pan (8½×4½×2½ inches) half full; top with a row of 4 hard-boiled eggs. Pack rest of mixture firmly around and over eggs.

Bake in moderate oven (350°F. Mark 4) about 45 minutes.

Unmould the loaf on a platter. Serve with Creole or tomato sauce. Serves 6.

Devilled Tuna

DEVILLED TUNA

1 tablespoon chopped onion
1 can (3 ounces) mushrooms,
    sliced and drained
2 ounces butter or margarine
1 ounce flour
½ teaspoon salt
½ teaspoon dry mustard
¼ teaspoon paprika
⅛ teaspoon black pepper
pinch of cayenne pepper
12 fluid ounces milk
½ teaspoon Worcestershire sauce
1 teaspoon lemon juice
2 hard-boiled eggs, sliced
1 can (7 ounces) tuna fish, drained
    and flaked

Sauté onion and mushrooms in butter or margarine. Stir in next 6 ingredients. Add milk, Worcestershire sauce, and lemon juice.

Cook, stirring constantly until the sauce thickens. Add sliced eggs and tuna fish. Heat and serve on toast. Serves 4 to 6.

FISH PATTIES

about 12 ounces flaked, cooked or
    canned fish
½ teaspoon salt
1 egg
about 10 ounces mashed potatoes
1 tablespoon finely chopped onion
⅛ teaspoon pepper
flour and fat

Mix together all ingredients except flour and fat. Shape mixture into patties and roll in flour. Brown in shallow fat. Serve with creamed peas. Serves 4.

Fish Potato Puffs: In fish patties recipe, add 2 egg yolks instead of a whole egg to the mixture of fish and potato. Add seasonings and fold in stiffly beaten egg whites.

Put mixture into greased custard cups and bake in a moderate oven (350°F. Mark 4) 30 minutes. Serves 4.

Fish Patties with Creamed Peas

*Cheese Salmon Ring with
Creamed Vegetables*

CHEESE SALMON RING WITH CREAMED VEGETABLES

4 tablespoons butter or margarine
½ large onion, diced
½ large green pepper, diced
4 tablespoons flour
1½ teaspoons salt
¼ teaspoon pepper
1 pint milk
2 eggs, separated
2 tablespoons lemon juice
4 ounces grated Cheddar cheese
4 ounces dry breadcrumbs
4 ounces diced cooked celery
1 can (1 pound) salmon, flaked

Cook onion and green pepper in butter until tender. Add flour and seasonings and blend. Stir in milk and cook until the sauce boils and thickens, stirring constantly.

Pour a little hot mixture into slightly beaten egg yolks. Return this liaison to the sauce. Add remaining ingredients and stir well. Fold in stiffly beaten egg whites.

Turn mixture into a buttered 1½-quart ring mould.

Bake in a moderate oven (350°F. Mark 4) for about 40 to 45 minutes. Unmould on hot serving plate. Fill centre of the ring with creamed peas and garnish with lemon wedges and watercress, if you like. Serves 6.

FISH LOAF

3 tablespoons butter or margarine
4 tablespoons chopped onion
1½ tablespoons flour
12 fluid ounces tomato juice
1 tablespoon lemon juice
¼ teaspoon marjoram
about 12 ounces cooked fish, flaked (leftover or canned)
4½ ounces fresh white breadcrumbs
2 lightly beaten eggs
oil and breadcrumbs for loaf pan

Fish Loaf

Cook onion in melted butter 5 minutes. Blend in flour; add tomato juice gradually. Cook a few minutes, stirring to avoid lumps.

Add lemon juice and marjoram; cook a few minutes longer. Remove from heat.

Add fish and breadcrumbs; mix, then add beaten eggs. Blend well and turn into a large loaf pan (9×5×3 inches), well oiled and dusted with breadcrumbs.

Bake in moderate oven (350°F. Mark 4) 35 to 40 minutes.

Let it stand 5 minutes before turning out. Serves 6.

TUNA FISH AND CELERY-NOODLE BAKE

1 packet (6 ounces) egg noodles
1 can (10½ ounces) condensed celery soup
4 fluid ounces milk
1 can (about 7 ounces) tuna fish, flaked
2 ounces buttered golden crumbs
2 ounces grated Cheddar cheese

Cook noodles in plenty of boiling, salted water until tender. Drain. Mix the soup and milk together.

Alternate layers of noodles and tuna fish in a greased 1½-quart casserole. Pour soup mixture over tuna fish and noodles. Top with buttered crumbs and grated cheese. Bake in moderate oven (350°F. Mark 4) 20 minutes.

Garnish with slices of stuffed olive and parsley. Serves 6.

CREOLE TUNA

2 tablespoons butter or margarine
2 tablespoons chopped green pepper
1 small tomato, peeled and cut in eighths
2 tablespoons flour
12 fluid ounces milk
salt and pepper
1 can (about 7 ounces) tuna fish, flaked

Melt butter in a saucepan. Add green pepper and tomato; cook 3 minutes. Blend in flour. Gradually add milk and cook, stirring until smooth.

Season with salt and pepper to taste. Add tuna fish and cook for about 10 minutes. Serve on toast. Serves 6.

TUNA FISH AND MUSHROOM LOAF

1 can (3 ounces) button mushrooms, sliced
1 can (about 7 ounces) tuna fish
1 can (10½ ounces) condensed cream of mushroom soup
4½ ounces fresh white breadcrumbs
1 tablespoon chopped pimiento
1 tablespoon dried parsley
¼ teaspoon salt
2 beaten eggs

Arrange 2 rows of mushroom slices on bottom of greased loaf pan (9×5×3

inches). Add remaining mushrooms to rest of ingredients. Mix well.

Put mixture in pan. Bake in moderate oven (375°F. Mark 5) 45 minutes, until firm. Serves 6.

TUNA CHEESE RABBIT

2 ounces butter or margarine
3 tablespoons flour
12 fluid ounces milk
½ pound grated processed Cheddar cheese
½ teaspoon salt
¼ teaspoon dry mustard
¼ teaspoon paprika pepper
small pinch of cayenne pepper
1 tablespoon grated onion
1 teaspoon Worcestershire sauce
½ 8-ounce can tomatoes
1 can (7 ounces) tuna fish

In a saucepan, melt butter or margarine over low heat; add flour and blend. Add milk and cook until thickened, stirring constantly.

Add cheese, salt, mustard, paprika, pepper, onion, Worcestershire sauce, and tomatoes. Stir until cheese is melted.

Add undrained tuna fish; mix lightly wih a fork, breaking the fish into large chunks.

Serve on toasted bread or rolls. Serves 6.

BAKED SEAFOOD NEWBURG

16 fluid ounces medium cream sauce
1 tablespoon dried onion flakes
½ teaspoon dry mustard
1 teaspoon dried parsley
1 teaspoon Worcestershire sauce
1 tablespoon lemon juice
3 tablespoons dry sherry
2-3 tablespoons pimiento strips
1 can (7 ounces) tuna fish
1 can (4½ to 6½ ounces) prawns
1 can (5 to 6 ounces) crabmeat
about 1¼ ounces crushed cornflakes
3 tablespoons butter or margarine

Mix the cream sauce, seasonings, lemon juice, and sherry together well. Add pimiento, oil from tuna fish, and fish broken into chunks, and drained prawns and crabmeat; mix lightly. Put in baking dish.

Mix cornflake crumbs and melted butter; make a border on top of the mixture. Bake in hot oven (425°F. Mark 7) about 20 minutes, until heated through. Serves 6.

Baked Seafood Newburg

SALMON, RICE, AND TOMATOES

10 medium tomatoes, cut in pieces
  or 1 can (about 16 ounces)
  with juice
2-3 tablespoons diced onion
2-3 tablespoons diced green pepper
2 tablespoons bacon fat
12 fluid ounces boiling water
salt and pepper
about 2¼ ounces raw rice
8 chopped olives, optional
about 1 pound flaked canned or
  cooked salmon

Mix together the tomatoes, onion, green pepper, fat, water, salt, and pepper in a large saucepan. Bring to the boil.

Add rice and simmer until rice is tender (20 to 25 minutes), adding more water if needed.

Add olives and fish and cook 2 or 3 minutes longer to blend flavours. Serves 6.

Variations: Other cooked fish may be used in place of salmon.

Six ounces cooked rice may be used instead of the uncooked rice. Omit boiling water. Add the rice, olives, and fish as soon as the vegetables are tender and cook 5 to 10 minutes longer.

Celery may be used instead of green pepper.

CREAMED MUSHROOMS AND FLAKED FISH

2 ounces mushrooms, sliced
2 tablespoons butter or margarine
4 tablespoons flour
½ teaspoon salt
small pinch of pepper
16 fluid ounces milk
about 1 pound cooked or 1 can (1
  pound) fish, flaked
1 tablespoon chopped parsley

Sauté mushrooms in butter or margarine; blend in flour, salt, and pepper. Gradually add milk.

Cook over hot water, stirring constantly, until the mixture is thick. Add fish and parsley; heat. Serve on toast, or in a ring of boiled rice. Serves 4.

Creamed Mushrooms and Flaked Fish in a Rice Ring

SALMON SHORTCAKE AU GRATIN

24 fluid ounces medium white sauce
4 ounces freshly grated cheese
about 12 ounces flaked salmon
6 ounces cooked peas
1 tablespoon lemon juice
baking powder scone dough

Make the medium white sauce. Add cheese, salmon, peas, and lemon juice. Heat thoroughly.

Make baking powder scone dough and bake in a round cake pan. Split and serve hot salmon mixture as a filling and topping for scone shortcake. Serves 6.

CREAMED SALMON AND CORN

2 tablespoons butter or margarine
4 tablespoons flour
¾ teaspoon salt
small pinch of pepper
1 teaspoon sugar
16 fluid ounces milk
about 12 ounces cooked salmon
1 medium can (about 10 ounces)
  sweetcorn
1 tablespoon chopped pimiento

Melt butter or margarine; blend in flour, salt, pepper, and sugar. Gradually add milk.

Cook over hot water, stirring constantly, until thick. Add salmon, corn, and pimiento. Serve on toast. Serves 4.

CELERY SALMON LOAF

1 can (1 pound) salmon, flaked,
  with juice
6 ounces dry breadcrumbs
½ large green pepper, finely chopped
2 slightly beaten eggs
1 can (10½ ounces) condensed cream
  of celery soup

Mix all the ingredients together well. Pack lightly into a greased loaf pan (9×5×3 inches).

Bake in a moderate oven (350°F. Mark 4) about 1 hour or until cooked. Pour off extra juice and turn out on a warm platter. Serve with celery sauce. Serves 6.

FISH SHORTCAKE

2 to 3 tablespoons chopped onion
4 tablespoons fat
4 tablespoons flour
16 fluid ounces milk
about 2 ounces grated cheese
about 12 ounces flaked cooked fish
salt and pepper to taste

Cook onion slowly in fat until tender. Blend in flour. Add milk slowly, stirring constantly, and cook until sauce is thickened.

Add cheese and fish. Season with salt and pepper. Heat mixture through, stirring occasionally. Serve on toast. Serves 4.

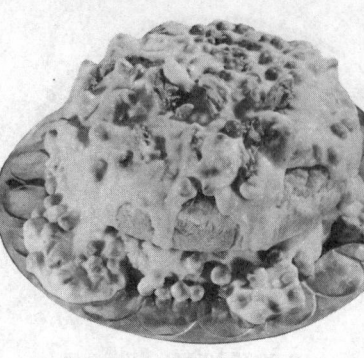

Salmon Shortcake Au Gratin

Salmon Potpie: Prepare fish mixture as above, using cooked or canned salmon. Turn it into a greased baking dish, top with rounds of bread, and bake in hot oven (425°F. Mark 7).

SALMON VEGETABLE PIE

Cheese Scones:

4 ounces grated Cheddar cheese
1 pound packet scone mix
6 fluid ounces milk

Combine cheese and scone mix; add milk and stir to make a soft dough.

Turn out onto lightly floured board; knead 30 seconds. Roll or pat out to ½- to ¾-inch thickness.

Cut with a floured pastry cutter and place on top of salmon pie.

Salmon Vegetable Pie:

3 tablespoons butter
4 tablespoons diced onion
5 tablespoons flour
1½ teaspoons salt
⅛ teaspoon pepper
1 teaspoon Worcestershire sauce
1 pint milk
about 12 ounces cooked celery,
  diced
½ pound cooked, sliced mushrooms
about 12 ounces flaked, boned
  salmon
2 tablespoons finely chopped
  parsley

Melt butter, add onions and cook over low heat until tender. Add flour, seasonings, and Worcestershire sauce; mix together.

Gradually stir in milk and cook until thick and smooth, stirring constantly.

Add celery, mushrooms, salmon, and parsley, stirring well.

Turn into a 2½ pint buttered casserole; top with cheese scones and bake in a very hot oven (450°F. Mark 8), 15 minutes, or until lightly browned. Serves 6.

Salmon Vegetable Pie

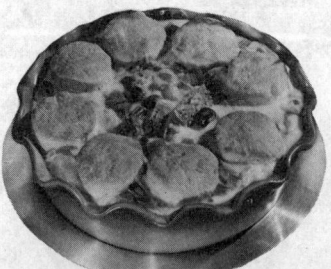

Tuna Fish Piquant

TUNA FISH PIQUANT

3 tablespoons butter or margarine
½ large green pepper, finely
    chopped
3 tablespoons flour
½ pint milk
4-5 tablespoons chilli sauce
4-5 tablespoons sherry
2 cans (7 ounces each) tuna fish,
    flaked
salt to taste

Melt butter in a saucepan; add green pepper and cook gently for 5 minutes.

Blend in flour; add milk, chilli sauce, and sherry; cook, stirring constantly, until mixture is thickened and smooth.

Add tuna and salt; heat gently for 5 minutes or so before serving.

Serve in scallop shells or in 1 large dish, on toast or with boiled rice. Serves 6.

Note: The above sauce may curdle when the liquids are added but will become smooth when the mixture boils and thickens.

SALMON CASSEROLE

1 can (1 pound) salmon
½ large onion, finely chopped
½ large green pepper, chopped
½ teaspoon salt
⅛ teaspoon pepper
small pinch of chilli powder
1 beaten egg
8 fluid ounces tomato purée
3 ounces fresh white breadcrumbs
1 small can (about 5 ounces) con-
    densed mushroom soup
2 tablespoons chopped parsley
2 tablespoons lemon juice
2 tablespoons melted butter

Mix the salmon, onion, green pepper, salt, pepper, chilli powder, egg, tomato purée, and 1½ ounces breadcrumbs in a saucepan.

Simmer 5 minutes. Then add mushroom soup, parsley, and lemon juice. Simmer 5 minutes longer.

Turn into buttered 2-quart casserole. Toss remaining breadcrumbs with melted butter; sprinkle on top of casserole. Bake in moderate oven (350°F. Mark 4) 20 minutes. Serves 6.

TUNA FISH OR SALMON PIE

4 tablespoons butter
2 ounces flour
about 1¾ pints hot milk and
    vegetable stock
2 teaspoons salt
⅛ teaspoon pepper
1 tablespoon finely chopped onion
12 ounces cooked peas
12 ounces cooked carrots
2 7-ounce cans tuna fish or salmon
cheese pastry strips (see Index)

Melt butter in the top of a double boiler. Add flour and blend. Add liquid gradually, stirring until smooth.

Add salt, pepper, and onion and continue cooking, stirring occasionally, until the mixture thickens.

Add peas, carrots, and fish and turn into large rectangular or square casserole.

Arrange cheese pastry strips on top of casserole in crisscross or lattice pattern.

Bake in moderate oven (375°F. Mark 5) 30 minutes, or until crust is baked. Serves 6 to 8.

FISH TURNOVERS

shortcrust pastry made with 1 pound
    flour or prepared shortcrust
    pastry
12 ounces cooked fish, flaked (or
    use canned tuna or salmon)
1 small can (about 5 ounces) con-
    densed mushroom soup or
    4 fluid ounces medium white
    sauce
1 slightly beaten egg
½ tablespoon chopped parsley
1 teaspoon lemon juice
1 hard-boiled egg, chopped
salt and pepper to taste
1 beaten egg yolk, for brushing
    turnover tops

Roll out pastry dough about ⅛-inch thick and cut into 12 equal squares.

Mix the fish, mushroom soup or white sauce, beaten egg, parsley, lemon juice, and hard-boiled egg together well. Taste for seasoning.

Put a tablespoon of this mixture on each square. Brush edges with water and fold over. Press edges with a floured fork to seal them.

Brush with beaten egg yolk and prick with a fork. Set the turnovers on greased baking sheet.

Bake in moderate oven (375°F. Mark 5) 20 minutes. Serve with green salad. Serves 6.

CREAMED FISH CASSEROLE

2 tablespoons butter or margarine
7 ounces mashed potatoes
about 1½ pounds cooked fish in
    lumps, salmon or tuna fish
    (leftover or canned), well
    drained

8 fluid ounces sour cream
1 egg
salt and pepper to taste
about 4 tablespoons grated cheese
1 tablespoon butter or margarine

Butter a baking dish or deep pie plate very well. Line bottom and sides with a thin layer of mashed potatoes. If potatoes are too dry, add milk and beat in. Put fish into potato shell.

Beat sour cream; add egg and seasonings and beat again; add 2 tablespoons grated cheese.

Pour mixture over fish pieces. Dot with 1 tablespoon butter.

Bake in moderate oven (350°F. Mark 4) 30 minutes, until browned. Sprinkle top with more grated cheese before serving. Serves 6.

TUNA FISH TREAT

1 large can (28 ounces) cling peach
    halves
4 fluid ounces water
6 whole cloves
½ teaspoon cinnamon
¼ teaspoon nutmeg
4 tablespoons vinegar
1 can (3 ounces) mushrooms, sliced
1 tablespoon cornflour
5 ounces quick-cooking rice,
    cooked according to packet
    directions
2 cans (7 ounces each) tuna fish,
    drained
½ teaspoon salt
pepper to taste

Drain peaches and reserve syrup. Mix together the peach syrup, water, cloves, cinnamon, nutmeg, and vinegar; bring to boiling point over medium heat.

Drain mushrooms and reserve liquid. Blend the mushroom liquid with the cornflour.

Gradually add cornflour mixture to hot syrup and continue cooking until thickened and clear, stirring occasionally. Add mushrooms and cooked rice.

Break tuna into large pieces with a fork and add to rice mixture.

Arrange alternate layers of tuna mixture and peach halves in a 2-quart casserole.

Cover and bake in moderate oven (350°F. Mark 4) 30 minutes. Serve piping hot. Serves 6.

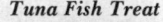

Tuna Fish Treat

Shellfish

Shellfish include any aquatic animal with a shell; the most important are abalone, clams, cockles, crabs, crawfish, lobsters, mussels, oysters, prawns, scallops, shrimps, whelks and winkles. Snails, though land animals, are often classified as shellfish in cook-books; so are inkfish or squid, frog legs and turtles, which are zoologically unrelated.

Clams

There are three varieties of clams generally used—the hard-shell, the soft-shell, and the razor clam.

The hard-shell is the one that is most usually available. It has a stronger flavour than the soft-shell and is the one used in chowders.

Clams bought in the shell must be tightly closed, thereby proving that they are alive. They will usually be opened on request by the fishmonger. To prepare them at home, scrub thoroughly, rinse and steam open or force open with a special heavy knife.

For clam chowder, buy whole or chopped clams in bulk by the pint or quart. Whole or chopped canned clams are also available.

CLAMS CASINO

Open clams carefully to retain the juice. Remove upper shell, leaving clams in the deeper half.

Sprinkle each one with few drops of lemon juice, a bit of finely chopped green pepper, and chopped onion. Season with salt and pepper. Put 3 bits of bacon on each.

Put in the grill pan and grill, or bake in very hot oven (450°F. Mark 8) until the bacon crisps.

Clams Casino: Piping hot stuffed clams may be served as hors d'oeuvre or for an informal lunch or supper.

FRIED CLAMS

Clean and dry clams. Roll clams in seasoned flour or roll in fine maize flour and shake off excess by placing in a sieve.

Fry in hot deep fat (375°F.) until browned. Drain on absorbent paper.

GRILLED CLAMS

Arrange small clams on half-shells. Sprinkle with breadcrumbs. Dot with bits of butter. Grill 5 to 7 minutes. Serve very hot.

ROAST CLAMS

Scrub clams well with a brush and wash thoroughly. Place them in a flat layer in a pan over a layer of rock salt, if you like. Bake in hot oven (425°F. Mark 7) until shells open.

Remove upper shells carefully to avoid spilling the liquor. Serve with seasonings, melted butter, and lemon wedges.

STEAMED CLAMS

Allow 10 to 15 per person. Soft-shell clams are best for steaming. Tightly closed shells indicate that the clams are fresh. Scrub thoroughly and wash in running water to remove all sand. Steam in covered pan with 4 fluid ounces water per 4 quarts of clams, over moderate heat until shells partially open, 15 to 20 minutes. Do not overcook.

Transfer clams to hot platters. Strain the clam broth left in the pan into small glasses. Serve with clams together with small individual dishes of melted butter seasoned with lemon juice, salt, and pepper.

To eat steamed clams, remove from shells by the neck, and dip in clam broth, then in butter. Eat all but the hard black skin of the neck.

CLAMBAKE CLAMS

The traditional clambake calls for a deep pit and a variety of seafood. For the most simple type, make a wood fire and preheat a bed of stones. After the fire dies down, cover the hot stones with a very thin layer of seaweed.

Have the clams thoroughly scrubbed with seawater and place them on this. Cover with seaweed and a piece of sail cloth to keep in the steam. Let the clams steam until they open.

CLAM FRITTERS

Drain 1 pint clams. Chop very fine and add to fritter batter. Fry in hot deep fat (375°F.) 3 to 5 minutes. Drain on absorbent paper. Serve with tomato or Creole sauce.

Serves 4 to 6.

Devilled Clams

DEVILLED CLAMS

2 cans (8 ounces each) minced clams, drained
4 fluid ounces clam liquor from cans
2 tablespoons chopped onion
2 tablespoons each chopped green pepper and celery leaves
1 ounce chopped celery
4 tablespoons butter or margarine
$\frac{1}{8}$ teaspoon pepper
$\frac{1}{2}$ teaspoon prepared mustard
3 ounces dry breadcrumbs or golden crumbs

Cook onion, green pepper, celery leaves, and celery in melted butter until tender. Mix with remaining ingredients.

Mix with the clams and add only enough of their liquor to bind the mixture. Fill greased scallop shells or custard cups.

Bake in moderate oven (350°F. Mark 4) 20 minutes. Serves 4 to 6.
Variation: Lemon juice may be substituted for the onion or green pepper.

NEW ENGLAND CLAM PIE

1 can (8 ounces) minced clams
6 fluid ounces milk
2 tablespoons clam liquor from the can
$\frac{1}{2}$ teaspoon dry mustard
1 beaten egg
1 teaspoon chopped parsley
1 tablespoon butter or margarine
pinch of salt
pastry made with 8 ounces flour or pastry mix

Mix all ingredients except pastry, adding salt to taste.

Roll pastry for bottom crust. Fit into an 8-inch pie dish. Trim edges. Fill with clam mixture.

Roll pastry for top. Slash the top to allow escape of steam. Place pastry on pie. Seal well.

Bake in hot oven (425°F. Mark 7) until crust is brown, about 25 minutes. Serves 4.

Crabs

A crab is a shellfish (crustacean) with short, broad covering shell and five pairs of legs, the first pair bearing claws or pincers.

Blue Crab: This is the common crab of the Atlantic coast much used as food. It is sold as a soft-shell crab if it is caught after it has shed its shell and before the new shell has hardened. Because the entire soft-shell crab, including the shell, is edible these are usually grilled, sautéed (pan-fried), or deep-fat fried.

Dungeness Crab: This is a Pacific coast crab and is best in the 2½ to 3 pound weight. It is sold alive, as frozen cooked meat, or canned.

King Crab: This is the largest (up to 15 pounds) of the edible crabs found in the North Pacific. It is sold canned or frozen.

Rock Crab: A delicate-meated crab from the Atlantic coast. It is usually available frozen or canned elsewhere.

HOW TO PREPARE SOFT-SHELL CRABS

Stick a knifepoint into the body between the eyes. Lift the pointed ends of the top shell and scrape off the spongy white substance between the shell and body on each side.

Place the crab on its back and, with a small sharp knife, remove the "apron" or small loose shell which comes to a point at about the middle of the undershell. Wash the crabs and cook at once.

FRIED SOFT-SHELL CRABS

Prepare as above. Dry and sprinkle with salt and pepper. Dip in slightly beaten egg and roll in crumbs. Fry in hot deep fat (365° to 375°F.) until well browned, 3 to 5 minutes. Being very light, the crabs will rise to the top and should be turned 2 or 3 times while frying. Drain on absorbent paper.

Serve at once with tartar sauce and lemon wedges. The entire crab, including the shell, is edible.

SAUTÉED SOFT-SHELLED CRABS

Sauté, cleaned prepared crabs in butter or other fat over moderate heat. Transfer to a hot platter. Pour the pan juices over them.

GRILLED SOFT-SHELL CRABS

Sprinkle the cleaned, dried soft-shell crabs with salt, pepper, and lemon juice. Brush with melted butter.

Grill about 2 inches from heat. Cook until brown on both sides, about 5 minutes for each side or a total of 10 minutes in all.

Serve with tartar sauce and lemon wedges.

BOILED HARD-SHELL CRABS

Plunge live crabs head first into boiling salted water, using 1 teaspoon salt per quart water. Boil in a covered pan until the shell is red and meat white, 20 to 25 minutes.

Fold back tapering points on each side of back shell and remove spongy material underneath. Remove apron, the small pointed piece at lower part of shell.

Serve in the shell or remove the meat for other dishes. The edible crabmeat is in the inner top of the back and in the claws. Crack claws with nutcracker.

Allow 1 hard-shell crab or 4 ounces meat per serving.

DEVILLED FRESH CRABS

8 hard-shell crabs, boiled
4 slices bread, crumbled
2 ounces butter
1 tablespoon Worcestershire sauce
salt and pepper
milk
dash of Tabasco sauce
buttered crumbs

Remove meat from crab shells and wash shells carefully.

Mix together the crab meat, crumbled bread, butter, Worcestershire sauce, with salt and pepper to taste. Moisten with a little milk seasoned with Tabasco sauce. The mixture should be soft.

Pack loosely into shells. Top with buttered crumbs. Bake in moderate oven (350°F. Mark 4) until delicately browned.

CREAMED CRABMEAT

Heat 8 ounces crabmeat in 8 fluid ounces medium white sauce or cream sauce. Serve on toast or in patty shells. Serves 4.

Variations of Creamed Crabmeat

Crabmeat À La King: To above, add 1 tablespoon finely chopped red and green pepper and 2 ounces cooked or canned sliced mushrooms. Season to taste with sherry.

Crabmeat Creamed with Mushrooms: Combine the white sauce with 8 ounces crabmeat, 2 ounces sliced mushrooms, and 1 diced pimiento.

Cook in top of a double boiler over hot water for 10 minutes.

Crabmeat Au Gratin: Pour creamed crabmeat in casserole or ramekins. Top with a mixture of 2-3 tablespoons buttered crumbs and 1 ounce grated cheese.

Bake in moderate oven (350°F. Mark 4) until crumbs are lightly browned.

Devilled Crabmeat

DEVILLED CANNED CRABMEAT

1 can (10½ ounces) condensed cream of celery soup
1 7-ounce can crabmeat
2 tablespoons chopped green pepper
2 teaspoons chopped onion
2 teaspoons lemon juice
½ teaspoon prepared mustard
2 tablespoons fresh white bread-crumbs
2 tablespoons melted butter

Mix the soup, crabmeat, green pepper, onion, lemon juice, and mustard together. Place in 1 large casserole or 6 small buttered heatproof dishes.

Mix together breadcrumbs and butter; sprinkle over crab mixture. Bake in moderate oven (350°F. Mark 4) about 20 minutes or until lightly browned. Serves 6.

CRABMEAT CREOLE

1 can (about 7 ounces) crabmeat
1 large can (28 ounces) tomatoes
1 clove garlic, crushed
2 large onions, chopped
2 teaspoons paprika
2-3 tablespoons ketchup
4 tablespoons chopped parsley
1 chopped green pepper
4 ounces thinly sliced celery
½ teaspoon filé powder
5 ounces quick-cooking rice

Remove hard membrane from crabmeat, leave in large chunks, set aside.

Put all other ingredients, except rice and filé powder in a heavy frying pan. Stir well. Cook over low heat, covered, until vegetables are tender. Season with salt and pepper to taste. Stir in filé powder. Combine with crabmeat and reheat. Serve with rice. Serves 3 to 4.

Crabmeat Creole

CRABMEAT SUPRÊME

1 pound flaked crabmeat
2 ounces grated cheese
2 well beaten eggs
16 fluid ounces milk
golden crumbs
2 tablespoons melted butter or
    margarine
juice of 1 lemon

Mix together the crabmeat and cheese. Add beaten eggs and milk. Pour into buttered casserole.

Cover with the crumbs mixed with melted butter. Pour over the lemon juice. Cover and stand casserole in a pan of warm water.

Bake in moderate oven (350°F. Mark 4) about 30 minutes. Serves 6 to 8.
Salmon or Lobster Supreme: Use 1 pound canned salmon or 1 pound canned lobster instead of crabmeat.

DEVILLED CRAB IN AVOCADO

about 2 ounces slivered blanched
    almonds
2 tablespoons butter
2½ tablespoons sifted flour
½ teaspoon salt
8 fluid ounces milk
1 teaspoon prepared mustard
½ teaspoon Worcestershire sauce
2 teaspoons lemon juice
1 pound cooked crabmeat
3 to 4 medium-sized avocado pear
    halves
fresh lime or lemon juice

Toast almond slivers in slow oven (300°F. Mark 2) 10 to 15 minutes, until lightly browned.

Melt butter, blend in flour and salt; stir in milk. Cook and stir until mixture boils and thickens. Add mustard, Worcestershire sauce, and lemon juice. Add crab and half of almonds; heat but do not boil.

Cut avocado pears in half, lengthways; remove seed but do not skin. Squeeze a little lime or lemon juice over cut surface of avocados to prevent darkening. Spoon hot crab mixture into avocado halves and sprinkle with remaining almonds. Serve at once. Serves 3 to 4.
Note: Avocado pears should be at room temperature, not chilled. Recipe may be doubled, if you like.

Devilled Crab in Avocado Pear Halves

CRABMEAT CASSEROLE

6 slices bread, crusts trimmed
12-14 ounces cooked crabmeat
½ pound Cheddar cheese, grated
4 eggs
16 fluid ounces milk
about 1 teaspoon salt
small pinch of pepper
small pinch of cayenne

Arrange slices of bread in bottom of greased casserole. Cover with flaked crabmeat. Sprinkle with cheese.

Beat eggs; add milk and season to taste. Pour over cheese.

Bake in slow oven (325°F. Mark 3) until set, 45 to 50 minutes. Serves 6 to 8.

CRABMEAT AND CRISPS CASSEROLE

2 ounces butter or margarine
2 ounces flour
small pinch of celery salt
16 fluid ounces milk
2-2½ tablespoons mayonnaise
1 can (about 7 ounces) crabmeat,
    flaked
6 ounces crushed potato crisps
2 ounces grated Cheddar cheese
⅛ teaspoon paprika

Melt butter in saucepan over low heat. Stir in flour and celery salt.

Add milk gradually; stir until thickened and smooth. Stir in mayonnaise.

Put alternate layers of flaked crabmeat, sauce, and crushed potato crisps in greased 1½-quart casserole. Sprinkle cheese and paprika over top.

Bake in moderate oven (350°F. Mark 4) 20 to 30 minutes. Serves 6.

SPANISH CRABMEAT

2 tablespoons butter or margarine
1 green pepper, finely sliced
2 tablespoons flour
½ teaspoon salt
¼ teaspoon mustard or ⅛ teaspoon
    paprika
6 fluid ounces scalded milk
1 beaten egg
4 ounces grated cheese
1 can (10½ ounces) condensed
    tomato soup
1 can (7 ounces) crabmeat, flaked

Melt butter or margarine in a saucepan over low heat. Add green pepper and sauté gently without browning.

Mix together the flour, salt, and mustard or paprika, and stir into the saucepan, cooking and stirring over low heat until the mixture is smooth and well blended. Gradually add scalded milk, stirring constantly until mixture thickens.

Remove from heat and add a little of hot mixture to beaten egg. Stir well and add egg mixture to first mixture, blending well. Stir in cheese.

Heat the soup in another saucep and, when just at the boiling poi add to the thickened mixture with t crabmeat.

Place over heat just long enough heat through. Do not boil.

Serve at once on toast. Serves 6 to

CURRIED CRABMEAT

3 tablespoons butter or margarine
1½ teaspoons finely chopped onion
4 tablespoons flour
¾ teaspoon salt
1 tablespoon curry powder
12 fluid ounces chicken stock
12 ounces cooked or canned crab-
    meat
1 tablespoon lemon juice

Heat butter in saucepan. Add onic cook until clear and limp.

Add flour, salt, and curry powd Stir until smooth. Blend in chick stock.

When thickened and smooth, a crabmeat and lemon juice. He through and serve with hot boil rice. Serves 6.

CHAFING DISH CRAB NEWBURG

2 7¾-ounce cans crabmeat
2 ounces butter
4 fluid ounces sherry
4 egg yolks
about 12 fluid ounces double crear
½ teaspoon salt
paprika

Remove cartilage from crabmea keeping chunks whole. Place crab, bu ter, and sherry in chafing dish ov direct heat and reduce the sherry about one-half.

Place egg yolks in measuring cu and add enough cream to make fluid ounces. Beat until smooth a add salt. Stir cream mixture into cr mixture and place bowl over a pan hot water. Cook, stirring, until mi ture thickens. Sprinkle with paprik Serve with boiled rice. Serves 6.

Chafing Dish Crab Newburg

CRABMEAT DELIGHT

In a chafing dish, or in the top of a double boiler melt 1 pound of processed cheese. Add 4 fluid ounces milk gradually, stirring constantly until the sauce is smooth.

Add one 6¼-ounce can crabmeat, boned and flaked.

Serve on crisp fresh toast triangles. This is an easy recipe for Sunday night supper.

CRABMEAT ALASKA

12 ounces flaked crabmeat, canned or fresh
4 fluid ounces cream
1 egg yolk
1 teaspoon salt
small pinch of pepper
¼ teaspoon Worcestershire sauce
6 slices white bread
4 tablespoons butter or margarine
6 large oysters
about 1¼ ounces buttered fresh white breadcrumbs

Mix together the crabmeat, cream, egg yolk, and seasonings.

Remove crusts from bread; fry slices in butter until golden brown. Spread each slice with crab mixture; top with an oyster and sprinkle with buttered breadcrumbs.

Arrange slices on a baking sheet; place in hot oven (400°F. Mark 6) for about 10 minutes or until delicately browned. Serve hot. Serves 6.

CRABMEAT OR LOBSTER CUTLETS

2½ tablespoons butter or margarine
about 1¼ ounces flour
8 fluid ounces warm milk
1 egg yolk
½ teaspoon salt
¼ teaspoon pepper
1½ tablespoons lemon juice
1 pound cooked or canned crabmeat or lobster

Melt butter. Blend in flour. Gradually add milk, stirring until the sauce boils. Add egg yolk, seasonings, lemon juice, and seafood.

Spread the mixture on a plate to cool. When cold, shape into cutlets. Dip in fine, dry breadcrumbs, then in beaten egg and again in crumbs.

Fry 1 minute in deep, hot fat (375°F.). Serve with green peas.

Serves 6.

HOT CRABMEAT SALAD

8 ounces crabmeat, flaked
3 ounces fresh white breadcrumbs
8 fluid ounces single cream or top of the milk
12 fluid ounces mayonnaise
6 hard-boiled eggs, diced
1 tablespoon chopped parsley
1 teaspoon finely chopped onion
½ teaspoon salt
⅛ teaspoon pepper
small pinch of cayenne pepper
1½ ounces buttered crumbs

Mix together all ingredients except buttered crumbs. Place in greased ramekins or shells; sprinkle with buttered crumbs.

Bake in moderate oven (350°F. Mark 4) until crumbs are golden brown, about 20 minutes. Serves 8.

CRAB DELICIOUS

8 fluid ounces single cream
6 ounces boiled rice
salt and paprika pepper, to taste
8 ounces flaked crabmeat
2 tablespoons melted butter or margarine
3 tablespoons ketchup
patty shells or toast

Heat cream and cooked rice together in top of a double boiler over hot water. Season to taste, adding celery or parsley salt, if preferred to paprika.

When well heated and blended, stir in crabmeat and butter. Heat through and, just before serving, stir in ketchup.

Serve at once in patty shells or on crisp toast. Serves 4.

CRABMEAT COQUILLES

1 can (about 3 ounces) mushrooms, sliced
3 tablespoons butter or margarine
3 tablespoons flour
milk

½ teaspoon salt
small pinch of pepper
2 tablespoons chopped green pepper
1 6-ounce can crabmeat
2 tablespoons fresh white breadcrumbs

Drain mushrooms and reserve liquid.

Melt butter. Add flour and blend thoroughly.

Add milk to mushroom liquid to make 16 fluid ounces and add to butter and flour mixture. Cook until thickened, stirring constantly.

Add mushrooms, salt, pepper, and green pepper.

Remove hard fibre from crabmeat. Flake, and add to cream sauce. Pour into individual shells or medium sized baking dish. Top with breadcrumbs.

Bake in moderate oven (375°F. Mark 5) 20 minutes. Serves 4 or 5.

ASPARAGUS-TOPPED CRABMEAT IMPERIAL

1 pound crabmeat
4 tablespoons butter or margarine
4 tablespoons flour
14 fluid ounces milk
1 teaspoon salt
½ teaspoon Aromat
½ teaspoon dry mustard
2 teaspoons lemon juice
2 teaspoons chopped green pepper
½ teaspoon Worcestershire sauce
1 teaspoon finely chopped onion
pinch of mace
2 beaten eggs
18 asparagus tips, canned or freshly cooked
1 ounce grated Parmesan cheese

Melt butter and stir in flour; cook until smooth. Add milk; cook until thick, stirring constantly.

Add remaining ingredients except eggs. Remove from heat; quickly stir in eggs. Blend carefully so as not to break up the crabmeat.

Fill scallop shells or ramekins; top with asparagus tips and cheese.

Bake in hot oven (400°F. Mark 6) until golden brown. Serves 6 to 8.

Asparagus-Topped Crabmeat Imperial

Lobsters and Spiny Lobster Tails

LOBSTER

Any of a group of edible sea crustaceans* distinguished by huge claws or pincers, which constitute the first of five pairs of legs. When the true lobster is boiled or grilled as soon as it is taken from the sea, it has a juicy, tender taste that defies description. The meat of the claws is especially succulent.

Lobsters may be bought alive or already cooked. Live lobsters should be active and mottled blue-green in colour. Cooked lobster is red. Test it to make sure it was alive when it was cooked: the tail will spring back into position when straightened, and it will be heavy for its size.

Chicken lobsters weigh $\frac{3}{4}$ to 1 pound, medium lobsters up to $1\frac{1}{4}$ pounds, and large or select lobsters $1\frac{1}{2}$ to 2 pounds. Cooked lobster meat may also be bought canned or frozen. Three pounds of cooked lobster in the shell gives about 6 ounces of meat.
*Note: Crustacean: Any of various types of shellfish with jointed shells. Lobsters, shrimps, and crabs are examples

LOBSTER TAIL

Lobster tail comes from the crawfish, which is not closely related to the true lobster, though often confused with it. The tail sections are marketed, usually frozen, under the name crawfish or spiny lobster to distinguish them from the true lobster.

The meat of the spiny lobster tail, although not quite as fine-textured, tastes very much like the true lobster and can be prepared in any of the same ways.

BOILED LOBSTER

Pick up the lobster from behind the head and plunge it into boiling salted water (1 tablespoon of salt to 2 quarts of water).

Boil 7 to 10 minutes, depending upon size of lobster. If lobster weighs less than 2 pounds, 7 minutes is sufficient.

When the lobster is cool, split it from end to end, starting at the head. Remove the stomach and the intestinal vein. Do not remove the green meat (also called tomalley or liver) found in the head section. Crack the claws. Extract the meat.

GRILLED BOILED LOBSTER

Boil and clean as above. Flatten halves. Season with salt and pepper. Brush with melted butter.

Grill under moderate heat until lightly browned, about 5 minutes. Serve with hot melted butter.

HOW TO SPLIT A LIVE LOBSTER FOR GRILLING

Place the lobster on its front. Holding a cloth over the back and tail to counteract the reflex jump, with one hand, insert the point of a sharp knife through the centre of the slightly indented cross lying in the centre of the main shell. This kills the lobster quickly by piercing the spinal cord. Split the shell open from head to tail, cutting through the back shell.

Remove the stomach and the intestinal vein that runs the length of the tail section close to the back.

Do not remove the juices, or the greyish-green looking meat found in the body cavity.
To Grill: Place split lobster in preheated grill pan. Brush with butter. Grill 15 to 20 minutes, never longer. Have the pan far enough from the heat so the lobster will not scorch. Serve with melted butter and lemon wedges.

BAKED STUFFED LOBSTER

Split the live lobsters as for grilling. Fill the cavity in the head with dressing (below).

Pour melted butter over lobster and bake in very hot oven (450°F. Mark 8) 20 minutes. Serve with melted butter.
Dressing: Mix together 3 ounces crushed cream cracker and $\frac{1}{2}$ teaspoon salt. Moisten with 2 tablespoons Worcestershire sauce and 4 tablespoons butter. Makes enough stuffing for 4 lobsters.

TO BOIL LOBSTER TAILS

Place lobster tails, either thawed or frozen, in a large pan of boiling salted water (1 teaspoon salt for each quart of water). When water reboils, lower heat and boil tails gently 1 minute longer than their individual weight in ounces. (Boil 6-ounce tails, 7 minutes; 8-ounce tails, 9 minutes.) If tails are frozen, add 2 minutes more. Drain off hot water; drench tails with cold water.

To remove meat from shell, use scissors and cut lengthways through centre of membrane covering meat. Insert fingers under meat at open end and pull meat out. Use meat in recipes calling for cooked lobster meat.

GRILLED LOBSTER TAILS

Thaw the lobster tails and preheat the grill. Using scissors, cut length-

Remove the stomach and intestinal vein

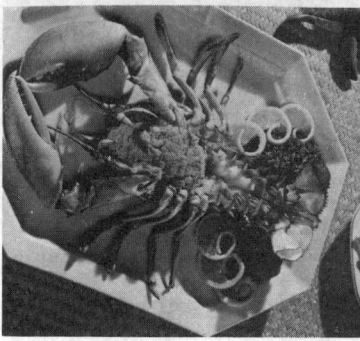

Baked Stuffed Lobster

ways down sides of membrane covering flesh, and remove membrane Grasp tail in both hands and bend backwards toward shell side to crack and prevent it from curling. Arrange tails shell side up, in preheated grill pan. Turn heat to medium and grill 5 minutes 5 inches from heat. Turn flesh side up, spread with butter and grill about 8 or 9 minutes on the flesh side, until the meat is opaque. Serve with cups of melted butter and lemon wedges.

LOBSTER TAILS WITH CLARIFIED BUTTER

Cook 6 lobster tails in boiling salted water (as above) or in accordance with packet directions.

Drain, cut along each edge, and remove the thin top covering. Flatten with your hand and insert a skewer into the tail to keep tail flat.
Clarified Butter Sauce: Melt $\frac{1}{2}$ pound butter over low heat and set aside for 15 minutes.

Carefully pour off the liquid fat, leaving the solids. Add lemon juice to taste, 1 teaspoon salt, and $\frac{1}{4}$ teaspoon white pepper. Reheat and serve hot. If any sauce remains, it may be refrigerated and used later.

Brush lobster meat with clarified butter; sprinkle lightly with salt and pepper. Grill 3 inches from heat about 5 minutes or until sufficiently brown. Serve remaining sauce with lobster. Serves 6.

LOBSTER NEWBURG
(Basic Recipe)

Newburg sauce is a rich cream sauce made with egg yolks and sherry. Although it is usually lobster that is served this way, almost any kind of reheated food may have a Newburg sauce.

Lobster Newburg, a creation of Delmonico's Restaurant in New York, is believed to have been named for Delmonico's friend and customer, Gus Wenburg, a fruit importer. When the two friends had a disagreement, Delmonico, the story goes, reversed two letters in the name. Originally light rum, not sherry, was used in the sauce.

6 ounces diced cooked lobster
2 tablespoons butter or margarine
½ tablespoon flour
4 fluid ounces single cream
2 tablespoons sherry
2 slightly beaten egg yolks
½ teaspoon salt
small pinch of cayenne pepper

Cook lobster in melted butter over low heat 5 minutes.

Sprinkle in flour. Add cream slowly, stirring constantly, until the sauce boils.

Stir in sherry and egg yolks. Cook 1 minute. Remove from heat.

Overcooking will curdle the sauce. Season with salt and cayenne. Serve on crisp toast or in the halved lobster shells. Serves 4 to 5.

Variations of Lobster Newburg

Clam Newburg: Drain liquid from 1 pint clams.

Chop hard parts finely. Leave soft parts whole. Use in place of lobster. Canned clams may also be used.

Crab Newburg: Use 6 ounces flaked crabmeat instead of lobster.

Prawns Newburg: Use 6 ounces cooked or frozen prawns instead of lobster.

Scallops Newburg: Cook 1 pint of scallops in their own liquid for 3 minutes. Drain and substitute for lobster.

For elegant serving, save the shells of the cooked lobsters and serve Lobster Newburg in them.

LOBSTER THERMIDOR

Cooked lobster meat is cut up and mixed with a cream sauce, then returned to the shell, sprinkled with cheese and sometimes crumbs, and browned in the oven or under the grill.

2 live lobsters, weighing about 2 pounds each
3 tablespoons butter or margarine
2 ounces sliced mushrooms
1 teaspoon grated onion
3 tablespoons flour
12 fluid ounces single cream (may be part milk)
2 slightly beaten egg yolks
1 teaspoon salt
½ to ¾ teaspoon mustard
small pinch of cayenne pepper
about 1¼ ounces grated Parmesan cheese or 4 ounces grated Cheddar cheese
2 to 3 tablespoons sherry (optional)
1 tablespoon lemon juice

Plunge lobsters headfirst into boiling salted water to cover. Boil 8 minutes after water returns to the boil.

Remove lobsters and cool. Split lengthways from head to tail and remove meat, discarding hard sac near head and dark intestinal vein. Twist off big claws, crack and remove the meat.

Dice meat from body and claws. Wash shells and reserve.

Heat butter, add mushrooms and onion. Cook slowly until tender but not browned.

Add flour and blend well. Add all but 2 tablespoons of cream. Cook, stirring, until mixture thickens.

Add egg yolks, while stirring briskly, and then cook, stirring, until thickened again.

Add salt, mustard, cayenne, and about ⅔ of cheese. When cheese has melted, add sherry and lemon juice. Add lobster meat.

Fill the reserved lobster shells with the lobster in the thickened sauce.

Spread the surface with remaining 2 tablespoons cream. Sprinkle with remaining cheese.

Slide the stuffed lobsters under the preheated grill. Grill until the surfaces are brown and bubbling. Good accompaniment is rice pilaf. Serves 4.

LOBSTER TAILS THERMIDOR

4 to 6 (6- to 8-ounce) lobster tails
about 2½ ounces butter or margarine
1 teaspoon finely chopped onion
3 tablespoons flour
½ teaspoon salt
¼ teaspoon white pepper
1 tablespoon lemon juice
4-5 tablespoons dry vermouth
16 fluid ounces single cream
3 egg yolks

Lobster Tails Thermidor

Cook and remove meat from lobster tails as directed in Boiled Lobster Tails. Save lobster shells. Dice meat and chill.

Melt butter or margarine in a saucepan. Add onion and cook until onion is soft. Remove pan from heat. Stir in flour, salt, and pepper. Mix lemon juice with vermouth. Gradually add to flour mixture, stirring to blend. Stir in the cream. Return pan to heat and cook over low heat, stirring constantly, until thickened.

Add a little of the hot mixture to beaten egg yolks, then stir egg yolks into sauce. Add lobster meat and continue cooking until lobster is heated. Do not let sauce boil. Spoon into lobster shells. Serve immediately. Serves 4 to 6.

LOBSTER TAILS, CHINESE STYLE

6 (4-ounce) lobster tails
1 clove garlic, crushed
2 tablespoons vegetable oil
¼ teaspoon salt
8 fluid ounces water
1 tablespoon cornflour
1 tablespoon soy sauce
2 large spring onions sliced
1 egg, beaten
about 1¼ pounds cooked white rice
sharp mustard sauce

Parboil frozen lobster tails by dropping into a pan of boiling salted water. When water reboils, drain immediately, drench with cold water and cut away the thin underside membrane. Remove meat from shells and cut it into small pieces.

In a heavy frying pan, lightly sauté garlic in oil. Add lobster meat, salt, and water. Mix cornflour with soy sauce and add to mixture. Stir gently until sauce thickens. Add sliced spring onions.

Just before serving, stir in beaten egg. Serve with bowls of fluffy white rice and a sharp mustard sauce. Serves 6.

Lobster Tails, Chinese Style

LOBSTER À L'AMÉRICAINE

French and American chefs have argued for years about the origin of this truly de luxe dish for special occasions. American chefs claim it was created by an American chef and French chefs claim it as a French creation. Américaine is French for "in the American manner". It sometimes appears incorrectly as "à l'Armoricaine", the latter meaning "in the manner of Brittany" from the old Roman name for that part of France, Armorica.

2 live lobsters, 1½ to 2 pounds each
4 tablespoons olive oil
1 tablespoon butter or margarine
1 bay leaf
pinch of thyme
2 tablespoons chopped shallot or onion
pinch of cayenne pepper
2 fluid ounces tomato purée or tomato sauce
1 clove garlic, crushed (optional)
about 4 fluid ounces dry white wine

Remove and crack claws of lobsters. Remove tail sections from the bodies and cut into 3 or 4 slices. Split lobsters in half, lengthways. Discard veins and sacs. Remove and save green meat and corals. Season lobsters with salt.

Heat oil and butter in a large heavy frying pan. Add bay leaf, thyme, and shallot or onion. Add lobster. Sprinkle with cayenne. Add tomato purée. Add garlic, if you like.

Cover and cook very gently until shells are red and lobster tender, 10 to 15 minutes.

Take lobster meat from shells. Strain sauce. Add green meat and corals to strained sauce. Cook, stirring constantly, 3 to 4 minutes, or until thickened. Add wine to taste. Add lobster meat and reheat, without cooking. Serves 4.

LOBSTER TAIL AMBASSADOR

4 4- to 6-ounce lobster tails
6 ounces cream cheese
8 fluid ounces sour cream
vinegar to taste
4½-ounce jar pimiento-stuffed olives, chopped
red hot sauce to taste
salt

Lobster Tail Ambassador

Cook lobster tails as directed on packet, or see index. Drench with cold water, cut down both sides of undershell with scissors. Remove from shell in one piece by inserting thumb between meat and shell and gently pulling meat away from shell. Chill. Slice chilled lobster into medallions (thin round slices).

Cream the cheese; beat in sour cream and add 1 tablespoon vinegar. Add additional vinegar to taste, and to thin dressing to desired consistency. Add olives, season with hot sauce and salt to taste. On a flat plate arrange lobster medallions in overlapping circles around generous heap of dressing. Garnish with olive slices.

Serve this dish either as an appetizer with cocktail sticks so your guests can pick and dip, or as a main coarse with a crisp green salad and cool drink any warm day.

LOBSTER AND MUSHROOM CASSEROLE

6 tablespoons butter or margarine
½ pound mushrooms, sliced
3 stalks celery, diced
½ small onion, finely chopped
½ green pepper, finely chopped
⅛ teaspoon basil
1 pound lobster meat
16 fluid ounces medium white sauce
2 ounces golden crumbs
1 ounce grated Cheddar cheese

Melt 4 tablespoons butter in a large saucepan over moderate heat. Add mushrooms, celery, onion, green pepper, and basil; simmer gently until mushrooms and celery are tender, but not soft, about 10 minutes.

Add lobster to mushroom mixture. Mix well and heat 5 minutes. Add white sauce and mix thoroughly.

Turn into casserole. Cover with layer of golden crumbs, then with layer of grated cheese. Dot with remaining butter.

Bake in moderate oven (350°F. Mark 4) until golden brown, about 25 minutes.

Serve very hot from casserole. Serves 4.

Variations: Raw oysters, clams, or scallops may be substituted for lobster. Clams or oysters are heated only 2 minutes and baking time is reduced to 15 to 20 minutes.

HOT LOBSTER MOUSSE

8 ounces lobster meat, minced very fine
4 fluid ounces medium white sauce
2 beaten eggs
salt, pepper, and paprika pepper
2 tablespoons sherry

Use cooked or canned lobster. Mix the very finely minced lobster with white sauce, eggs, seasonings, and sherry. Turn into a buttered casserole or individual moulds. Stand in a pan of hot water. Cover with greased paper.

Bake in moderate oven (350°F. Mark 4) 35 to 40 minutes for casserole, about 20 minutes for small moulds.

Turn out and serve with mushroom sauce. Serves 4.

Hot Crab or Prawn Mousse: Substitute cooked or canned prawns or crabmeat for lobster in above recipe.

LOBSTER CANTONESE

2 tablespoons fat or salad oil
1½ teaspoons salt
pepper
½ pound lean pork, coarsely minced
1 tablespoon finely diced carrot
1 tablespoon finely chopped celery
1 tablespoon chopped spring onion
2 live baby lobsters or 1 10-ounce can cooked lobster
8 fluid ounces chicken stock
1 egg, slightly beaten
2 tablespoons cornflour
2 teaspoons soy sauce
4 tablespoons water

In a preheated, heavy 10-inch frying pan place fat or salad oil, 1 teaspoon salt, and dash of pepper.

Put the minced pork in a mixing bowl with carrot, celery, and spring onion. Add ½ teaspoon salt and dash of pepper and mix thoroughly.

Cook lobsters in boiling water 5 minutes. Take out of water, remove and crack claws, cut edible portion of belly in several pieces with heavy knife or cleaver.

Place pork mixture and lobster in frying pan. Add chicken stock. Cover pan tightly and cook over moderate heat about 10 minutes.

Add slightly beaten egg. Cook over high heat 2 minutes, stirring constantly.

Blend together and add cornflour, soy sauce, and water. Cook a few more minutes, stirring constantly, until juice thickens and mixture is very hot. Serve immediately with hot boiled rice. Serves 4.

STEAMED LOBSTER

Place live lobsters in a steamer and cover tightly. Keep water in steamer boiling rapidly and steam 20 to 40 minutes, depending upon size of lobsters.

BUTTERED LOBSTER

Use cooked or canned lobster meat or the meat from lobster tails. Sauté in hot melted butter until heated through. Season with salt, pepper, and lemon juice.

SCALLOPED LOBSTER
3 tablespoons butter or margarine
3 tablespoons flour
½ teaspoon celery seed
1 teaspoon salt
½ teaspoon paprika pepper
16 fluid ounces milk
4 ounces cooked lobster meat
6 ounces cooked green peas
2 hard-boiled eggs, sliced
2½ ounces bread cubes

Melt 2 tablespoons butter or margarine. Add flour, celery seed, salt, and paprika, stirring until all ingredients are well blended.

Add milk and cook over low heat, stirring constantly, until thickened.

Cut lobster into pieces about 1 inch in size, reserving about 4 fairly large pieces for garnishing. Add lobster to cream sauce.

Pour half of creamed lobster into well greased 2-pint baking dish. Cover with cooked peas and with layer of sliced eggs. Place remaining creamed lobster over ingredients in dish. Top with bread cubes and large pieces of lobster. Pour the remaining butter, melted, over bread cubes and large pieces of lobster.

Bake in moderate oven (350°F. Mark 4) about 30 minutes. Garnish with parsley. Serves 6.

STUFFED LOBSTER TAILS
4 6-ounce lobster tails
1 tablespoon butter
6 fluid ounces milk
3 ounces fresh white breadcrumbs
1 egg
¼ teaspoon salt
1 tablespoon made mustard
1 teaspoon aromatic bitters

Cook and remove meat from lobster tails as directed in Boiled Lobster Tails. Flake the meat.

Melt butter in saucepan, add milk and breadcrumbs. Simmer 2 minutes.

Remove from heat. Add egg, salt, mustard, bitters, and flaked lobster meat. Mix well. Pack in shells loosely. Reheat in hot oven (400°F. Mark 6) 5 minutes. Serves 4.

Stuffed Lobster Tails

LOBSTER FARCI
2 hard-boiled egg yolks
4 ounces cooked lobster meat
1 tablespoon chopped parsley
8 fluid ounces medium white sauce
3 tablespoons sherry
salt to taste
small pinch of white pepper
2 ounces buttered dry breadcrumbs

Rub egg yolks through a fine sieve. Mix with lobster, parsley, sauce, sherry, and salt and pepper to taste.

Mix well and use to fill split lobster shells or place in buttered casserole. Top with crumbs.

Bake in moderate oven (375°F. Mark 5) until brown, about 15 minutes. Serves 2.

Note: Canned lobster meat may be used and the mixture may be baked in scallop shells or individual ramekins.

DEVILLED LOBSTER TAILS
4 lobster tails (½ pound each)
2 ounces butter or margarine
½ teaspoon dry mustard
1 small onion, finely chopped
1 teaspoon Worcestershire sauce
16 fluid ounces medium white sauce
salt and pepper
grated Parmesan cheese
butter or margarine

Steam or simmer lobster tails 8 to 10 minutes. Cool and split. Remove and dice meat.

Melt the butter; add mustard, onion, and Worcestershire sauce. Simmer 5 minutes.

Add white sauce and lobster meat. Season with salt and pepper.

Fill shells. Sprinkle with Parmesan cheese and dot with butter. Grill until browned. Serves 4.

LOBSTER AND CRABMEAT SOUR CREAM RAMEKINS
½ pound lobster meat
½ pound crabmeat
8 fluid ounces sour cream
⅛ teaspoon salt
small pinch of cayenne pepper
4 sprigs tarragon, chopped

Use freshly cooked lobster and crabmeat. Remove bony particles from crabmeat.

Mix the seafood and place in 4 individual ramekins. Mix sour cream with salt, cayenne, and tarragon. Pour over seafood.

Bake in moderate oven (350°F. Mark 4) until thoroughly heated and bubbly. Serve at once. Serves 4.

Variations: If you like, substitute cooked prawns for lobster.

CURRIED LOBSTER TAILS
5 pints boiling water
3 teaspoons salt
6 frozen lobster tails
1½ teaspoons Aromat
4 tablespoons butter or margarine
4 tablespoons flour
1 teaspoon salt
½ teaspoon paprika pepper
⅛ teaspoon nutmeg
1½ teaspoons curry powder
16 fluid ounces milk
2½ tablespoons lemon juice

Bring water to the boil in a large pan. Add salt, lobster tails and 1 teaspoon Aromat.

When water returns to the boil, lower heat and cook length of time indicated in packet directions.

Drain; drench with cold water; remove meat from shells; chill, then dice.

Melt butter or margarine; blend in flour, salt, paprika, ½ teaspoon Aromat, nutmeg, and curry powder. Add milk; stir over low heat until smooth and thickened.

Add lemon juice and diced lobster meat. Heat thoroughly; refill shells. Serves 6.

LOBSTER TAILS BAKED IN ALUMINIUM FOIL
Thaw and cut undershell around edge and remove. Fold each tail securely into a piece of foil cut 4 inches longer than length of tail.

Place on baking sheet. Bake in very hot oven (450°F. Mark 8) 25 minutes for tails weighing 4 to 8 ounces, 30 minutes for tails weighing 9 to 12 ounces, and 35 minutes for tails weighing 13 to 16 ounces.

LOBSTER TAILS IN SAUCE
½ pound butter or margarine
1 teaspoon flour
1 teaspoon tomato sauce
2 teaspoons Worcestershire sauce
1 teaspoon paprika pepper
2 drops Tabasco sauce
3 tablespoons ketchup
1 teaspoon salt
½ teaspoon pepper
juice of 1 lemon
4 lobster tails, cooked and removed from shell

Melt butter in a chafing dish or sauté pan, stirring with wooden spoon constantly. Stir in the flour and blend until smooth.

Add tomato and Worcestershire sauce, paprika, Tabasco, ketchup, salt, pepper, and lemon juice. Stir until thickened and smooth. Simmer for about 10 minutes longer.

Cut cooked lobster into serving pieces. Add pieces to the hot sauce and coat well with mixture. Serve immediately on toast. Serves 4.

Mussels

Mussels include any of various bivalve molluscs. If you buy them fresh, make sure the shells are tightly closed. They are also available canned or in a brine solution in jars.

HOW TO PREPARE MUSSELS

Mussels must be carefully cleaned to remove sand from inside; they help to do the job themselves if soaked in a colander in cold running water for a couple of hours. Scrub and rinse them. Steam them open or force the shells with a knife; remove and discard the hairy beard. Mussels are called for in many recipes and may also be prepared like oysters or clams.

MUSSEL STEW

Clean the mussels and remove the beard. Steam, strain, and reserve the liquid. Follow recipe for Oyster Stew, substituting mussels for oysters.

ROASTED MUSSELS

Scrub and rinse mussels. Spread in flat layer in a pan. Bake in very hot oven (450°F. Mark 8) until shells open.

Remove upper shells and bearded parts carefully to avoid spilling juice. Serve with seasonings, melted butter and cups of hot broth.

MUSSELS MARINIÈRE

4 to 5 dozen mussels
8 fluid ounces dry white wine
1 tablespoon finely chopped shallots or onion
2 tablespoons chopped parsley
small pinch of cayenne pepper
½ bay leaf
2 tablespoons butter or margarine

Scrub mussels thoroughly, scraping shells with a knife and changing the water several times.

Place in a saucepan with the wine, shallots, 1 tablespoon parsley, cayenne, bay leaf, and butter. Cover tightly and cook over low heat until shells open, 5 to 10 minutes, shaking the pan from time to time.

Remove the mussels. Drain and reserve the liquid. Remove the beards. Loosen mussels from shells and place in half shells on hot serving dishes.

Pour reserved liquid into saucepan, being careful not to mix in any sediment. Reduce by boiling to 6 fluid ounces.

Add additional butter and seasonings if necessary. Pour over mussels. Sprinkle with extra parsley. Serve very hot. Serves about 6.

Oysters

Oysters include any of a group of bivalve molluscs that live in the coastal waters of most temperate regions. In many places they are in season only from September to April; this is done to protect the beds from depletion, not because the oysters are unsafe to eat during the summer.

Oysters may be bought live in the shell, fresh or frozen shelled, and canned.

Oysters in the shell are generally sold by the dozen and must be alive when bought. The shells must be tightly closed.

Shelled oysters are sold by the pint or quart. They should be plump and have a natural creamy colour, with clear liquid and free from particles.

Canned oysters are sold in a variety of can sizes.

The quantity to buy depends to a large extent on how the oysters are to be served. In general, for 6 servings allow 3 dozen shell oysters, 2 pints shelled oysters, 2 9-ounce cans, or 2 packets frozen oysters.

OPENING OYSTERS

Wash and rinse the oysters thoroughly in cold water. Open an oyster by placing it on a table, flat shell up, and holding it with the left hand. With the right hand, force an oyster knife between the shells at or near the thin end.

To make it easier to insert the knife, the thin end or "bill" may be broken off with a hammer—a method preferred by some cooks.

Now cut the large adductor muscle close to the flat upper shell in which it is attached and remove the shell.

Cut the lower end of the same muscle, which is attached to the deep half of the shell, and leave the oyster loose in the shell if it is to be served on the half shell, or drop it into a container.

After opening, examine the oysters for bits of shell, paying particular attention to the muscle to which pieces of shell sometimes adhere.

Oysters on the Half Shell

OYSTERS ON THE HALF SHELL

Open oysters. Loosen oysters from the deeper half shells but leave them in the shells. Discard the other half shells.

Serve on a bed of crushed ice in shallow bowls or soup plates. Place 6 half-shell oysters on the ice, with a small container of cocktail sauce in the centre. Garnish with lemon wedges.

FRIED OYSTERS

Drain oysters. Dry carefully between towels. Roll in flour, seasoned with salt and pepper, then in beaten egg diluted with 1 tablespoon water. Roll in dry breadcrumbs or golden crumbs.

Fry in deep fat (365°-375°F.) until golden brown. Drain on absorbent paper. Serve with tartar sauce.

Fried Oysters 2: Dip dried oysters in batter and fry as above.

Fried Oysters 3: Dip dried oysters in fine dry breadcrumbs, then in mayonnaise, and again in crumbs. Fry as above.

Sautéed Oysters: Prepare as in Fried Oysters 1 or 2 and sauté in a single layer in butter.

OVEN-FRIED OYSTERS

Prepare oysters as in Fried Oysters 1. After coating with crumbs, dip in olive oil. Arrange in shallow baking dish.

Bake in hot oven (400°F. Mark 6) until browned, about 15 minutes.

GRILLED OYSTERS

Roll fresh oysters in a mixture of half bread and half golden crumbs. Press flat with hands. Grill 2 minutes on each side.

Salt lightly and brush with melted butter. Serve on buttered hot toast.

Cutting Muscle

Cutting Oyster from Shell

CREAMED OYSTERS

1 pint oysters
2 tablespoons butter or margarine
2 tablespoons flour
milk, cream, or stock
about ¾ teaspoon salt
about ⅛ teaspoon pepper
½ teaspoon Worcestershire sauce or
1 teaspoon sherry

Drain oysters, reserving liquid.

Melt butter in saucepan. Slowly blend in flour. Gradually add oyster liquid with enough milk, cream, or stock to make 8 fluid ounces.

Cook over low heat, stirring constantly, until smooth. When boiling, add drained oysters. Heat thoroughly but do not boil.

Season with salt, pepper, and Worcestershire sauce or sherry. Serve on toast or in scallop shells. Serves 4.

Variation: For a richer dish, blend a little of the creamed mixture with 2 egg yolks, beating constantly. Return to remaining mixture and cook, stirring constantly, for 1 minute to thicken slightly. Season to taste.

QUICK SCALLOPED OYSTERS

1 pint oysters
1 can (10½ ounces) condensed
  asparagus, celery or mush-
  room soup
4 ounces dry breadcrumbs
3 tablespoons melted butter or
  margarine
1 tablespoon finely chopped parsley
about ¼ teaspoon salt

Drain oysters, reserving liquid. Mix together the soup and oyster liquid and heat to boiling point. Add oysters and cook until the edges curl.

Toss crumbs with melted butter, parsley, and salt.

Line bottom of heated flameproof casserole with half the crumb mixture. Add oyster-soup mixture and top with remaining crumbs.

Brown under a moderate grill. Serves 6.

OYSTERS CASINO

1 pint oysters
1½ ounces finely chopped green
  pepper
1½ ounces finely chopped bacon
1 tablespoon lemon juice
pepper to taste

Drain oysters and arrange on a greased ovenproof dish. Sprinkle with green pepper, bacon, lemon juice, and pepper.

Bake in very hot oven (450°F. Mark 8) about 10 minutes. Serves 6.

OYSTERS MEUNIÈRE

Dip drained oysters in flour. Brown quickly but gently in butter. Serve on toast, with melted butter and lemon juice poured over each portion.

OYSTERS ROCKEFELLER

This is a famous New Orleans dish of oysters on the half shell topped with a purée of spinach and herbs, and buttered crumbs. The prepared oysters in half shells are then embedded in pans of rock salt and baked until plump. It's also a good way to use bulk oysters in separately bought shells.

36 oysters in shell
1½ pounds cooked spinach
4 tablespoons chopped onion
2 bay leaves
1 tablespoon parsley
½ teaspoon celery salt
½ teaspoon salt
6 drops Tabasco sauce
6 tablespoons butter or margarine
1½ ounces fresh white breadcrumbs

Open shells and drain oysters; place them on deep half of shells.

Put spinach, onion, bay leaves, and parsley through a sieve. Add seasonings to mixture, and cook in butter for 5 minutes. Add breadcrumbs and mix well. Spread mixture over oysters.

Bake in hot oven (400°F. Mark 6) about 10 minutes. Garnish with lemon slices. Serves 6.

Note: If shell oysters are not available, 1½ pints shelled oysters may be used. Drain oysters and arrange on shallow buttered baking dish. Spread with seasonings and cook as above.

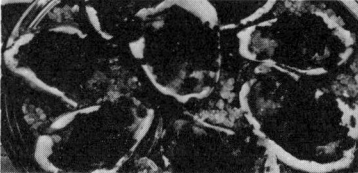

Oysters Rockefeller

DEVILLED OYSTERS

1½ pints oysters
2 tablespoons finely chopped onion
2 tablespoons butter or margarine
4 tablespoons flour
12 fluid ounces milk
1 teaspoon salt
¼ teaspoon nutmeg
small pinch of cayenne pepper
1 teaspoon prepared mustard
1 tablespoon Worcestershire sauce
1 teaspoon chopped parsley
1 beaten egg
2 ounces dry breadcrumbs
2 tablespoons butter or margarine

Chop oysters. Cook onion in butter until tender. Blend in flour. Add milk and cook until thick, stirring constantly.

Add seasonings, beaten egg, and oysters, and heat.

Spoon mixture into buttered ramekins. Cover with crumbs tossed with 2 tablespoons butter or margarine.

Bake in hot oven (400°F. Mark 6) 10 minutes, or until brown. Serves 6.

OYSTER FRITTERS

Prepare fritter batter (see Index). Add 1 pint drained and chopped oysters. Fry in hot deep fat (365°-375°F.). Drain on absorbent paper. Serves 4 to 6.

OYSTER LUNCHEON LOAF

1 large loaf unsliced bread
melted butter or margarine
12 oysters
evaporated milk
1 8-ounce can tomato sauce
6 tablespoons butter or margarine
1 green pepper, diced
4 tablespoons flour
1 teaspoon salt
small pinch of pepper
½ teaspoon Aromat
¼ teaspoon rosemary
¼ teaspoon savory
6 hard-boiled eggs

Remove top of loaf of bread in one thin slice; do not remove crusts on sides and ends. With a sharp knife, remove centre of loaf in one piece, leaving a shell about ¾-inch thick.

Cut centre into cubes and toast golden brown in moderate oven (350°F. Mark 4). With a star-shaped pastry cutter, cut 4 stars from top slice. Brush shell and stars with melted butter or margarine and toast in moderate oven (350°F. Mark 4).

Measure oyster liquid; add enough evaporated milk to make 16 fluid ounces; add tomato sauce.

Melt 6 tablespoons butter or margarine; cook green pepper in this until soft; blend in flour, salt, pepper, and Aromat. Add evaporated milk mixture; stir over low heat until smooth and thickened.

Add oysters, rosemary, and savory; cover and cook over a pan of hot water 15 minutes. Add toasted bread cubes.

Place toasted bread shell on platter; surround with halves of hard-boiled eggs. Fill case with oyster mixture; cover eggs with remaining oyster mixture. Place stars on top. Serve at once. Serves 6.

Oyster Luncheon Loaf

OYSTER NOODLE CASSEROLE

1 pint oysters
3 tablespoons butter or margarine
3 tablespoons flour
12 fluid ounces milk
12 ounces cooked noodles
2 tablespoons finely chopped green pepper
½ teaspoon salt
⅛ teaspoon pepper
2 ounces dry breadcrumbs
2 tablespoons butter or margarine

Drain oysters. Melt butter in top of a double saucepan. Blend in flour. Add milk and cook until thickened, stirring constantly.

Place layer of noodles in buttered casserole. Cover with layer of oysters. Sprinkle with green pepper, salt, and pepper. Repeat with alternate layers. Pour sauce over all. Cover with buttered crumbs. Bake in moderate oven (350°F. Mark 4) 30 minutes or until brown. Serves 6.

OYSTERS LOUISIANA

coarse rock salt
large oysters on half shell
salt, black pepper, paprika pepper
1½ teaspoons finely chopped green pepper
½ teaspoon finely chopped pimiento
chopped bacon

Fill shallow roasting pans with coarse rock salt and heat to smoking hot in oven. Remove from oven.

Lay on the hot salt large oysters on the half shell. Season them with salt, black pepper, paprika, green pepper, and pimiento. Sprinkle with chopped bacon.

Put the shells under hot grill; cook at high heat 5 to 6 minutes. When bacon is crisp and oysters cooked, serve them at once in shells, with the dishes of hot salt on heatproof plates.

OYSTER PIE

1 pint oysters
4 ounces diced celery
1½ ounces diced green pepper
4 tablespoons butter or margarine
5 tablespoons flour
16 fluid ounces milk
1 teaspoon salt
⅛ teaspoon pepper
2 tablespoons pimiento, chopped
shortcrust pastry

Cook oysters in their liquid about 5 minutes or until the edges begin to curl. Drain.

Cook celery and green pepper in butter until tender. Stir in flour. Add milk and cook until thickened, stirring constantly. Add oysters and seasonings. Heat thoroughly. Pour into pie dish. Top with pastry.

Bake in hot oven (425°F. Mark 7) 15 minutes or until pastry is brown. Serves 6.

GRILLED OYSTERS ON HALF SHELL

36 oysters in shell
½ teaspoon salt
⅛ teaspoon pepper
2 ounces dry breadcrumbs
2 tablespoons butter or margarine

Open shells and drain oysters. Place on deep half of shells.

Sprinkle with salt, pepper, and buttered breadcrumbs.

Place in preheated grill pan about 3 inches from heat. Grill until brown, 5 minutes. Serves 6.

OYSTERS À LA CREOLE

1 small onion, chopped
2 tablespoons butter or margarine, melted
1½ tablespoons flour
1 small can (8 fluid ounces) tomato juice
2 dozen raw oysters, drained
2 tablespoons chopped parsley
½ teaspoon Tabasco sauce
¾ teaspoon salt

Sauté onion in butter in saucepan until tender. Blend in flour; then add tomato juice, and cook, stirring, until thickened.

Add oysters, parsley, Tabasco sauce, and salt, and heat until the edges of oysters curl. Serve on buttered toast. Serves 4 to 6.

CREAMED OYSTERS AND MUSHROOMS

3 tablespoons fat
5 tablespoons flour
1 teaspoon salt
¼ teaspoon pepper
12 fluid ounces milk
2 ounces chopped mushrooms
1 pint oysters

Heat fat in top of a double saucepan. Add flour, salt, and pepper. Mix until smooth. Add milk gradually, stirring constantly. Cook over hot water 8 minutes.

Fry mushrooms in a little fat until tender.

Drain oysters, clean and trim. Heat in oyster liquid until the edges curl. Add to white sauce with mushrooms.

Serve on hot toast or in scallop shells. Serves 6.

BAKED OYSTERS ON THE HALF SHELL

36 oysters in shell
½ teaspoon salt
⅛ teaspoon pepper
2 tablespoons finely chopped onion
4 tablespoons butter or margarine

Remove shells and drain oysters. Place them on deep half of shells.

Sprinkle with salt, pepper, and onion. Dot with butter.

Place oysters in baking dish. Bake in hot oven (400°F. Mark 6) until the edges begin to curl, about 10 minutes. Serves 6.

SCALLOPED OYSTERS

1 pint oysters
6 ounces fresh white breadcrumbs
½ teaspoon salt
⅛ teaspoon pepper
4 ounces butter or margarine, melted
¼ teaspoon Worcestershire sauce
8 fluid ounces milk

Drain oysters. Mix the breadcrumbs, salt, pepper, and butter; sprinkle one-third in a buttered casserole. Cover with a layer of oysters. Repeat layer.

Add Worcestershire sauce to milk, and pour over contents of casserole. Sprinkle remaining crumbs on top.

Bake in moderate oven (350°F. Mark 4) until brown, 30 minutes. Serves 6.

PAN-FRIED OYSTERS

1 pint oysters
4 tablespoons butter or margarine
2 tablespoons lemon juice
salt and pepper
lemon slices

Drain oysters. Place them in a frying pan and cook over low heat until the edges curl.

Add butter, lemon juice, and pepper and salt, to taste. Bring to the boil. Add a dash of Worcestershire sauce, if you like.

Serve on hot toast and garnish with lemon slices. Serves 4 to 6.

OYSTERS AU GRATIN

6 slices buttered toast
2 beaten eggs
1 teaspoon salt
1 teaspoon made mustard
½ teaspoon paprika pepper
4 fluid ounces milk
1 pint oysters
4 ounces grated cheese

Trim crusts from bread. Cut each slice into quarters.

Mix together the beaten eggs, seasonings, and milk.

Arrange layer of bread in buttered casserole. Cover with layer of oysters. Sprinkle with grated cheese. Repeat layer.

Pour milk mixture over contents of the casserole. Cover with grated cheese.

Place casserole in a pan of hot water and bake in moderate oven (350°F. Mark 4) until brown, 30 minutes. Serves 6.

Oysters Au Gratin

Prawns, Shrimps and Scampi

Any of a number of small, slender, long-tailed crustaceans with ten jointed legs. There is no basic difference between a shrimp and a prawn; the latter differs from the true shrimp in having a toothed beak (rostrum) projecting from its head. They may grow as long as 7 inches, but most are smaller. The small ones are good for sauces, and the large ones, like the Mediterranean and Pacific prawns, are best used for hors d'oeuvre, main dishes and garnishes.

There are two kinds of shrimp, the brown and the pink. The brown are true shrimps and the colour only applies to the outer shell. The pink shrimp is often a young prawn. Colour does not indicate the flavour or the quality. The cellophane-like shell turns pink when cooked. Prawns and shrimps in the shell may be bought raw, cooked, or frozen. Peeled prawns and shrimps are available cooked, canned, or frozen.

Scampi are really Mediterranean prawns, but any large prawn, like Pacific or Dublin Bay, may be used as scampi. Dublin Bay prawns are a different variety, with a hard shell, and look rather like a baby crawfish.

TO SHELL PRAWNS AND SHRIMPS

Raw prawns and shrimps (fresh or frozen) may be shelled either before or after boiling. Some people think it is easier to remove the small vein when the shrimp is raw, while others prefer to cook the shrimp before shelling. The smell of cooking them will not be as strong if they are shelled before cooking.

Wash the prawns or shrimps. Stand frozen ones in cold water about 15 minutes.

To clean prawns or shrimps, hold tail end in left hand, slip thumb under shell, between feelers, and lift off 2 or 3 segments in one movement. Then, still holding firmly to tail, pull out the meat from remaining shell section and tail.

With a knife, cut along outside curvature and lift out the black vein, if you like. The vein is harmless, but some

Removing shell from raw prawn

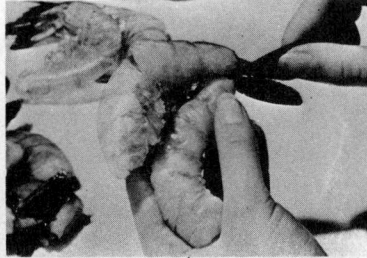

people object to the appearance of the black line. Then, rinse with cold water.

BOILED PRAWNS

Add 1 tablespoon salt to 1 quart water. Bring to the boil.

Add 1 pound prawns and bring to boil again. Turn heat down so that water just simmers. Cover saucepan and cook 2 to 5 minutes, never longer. Drain the prawns.

PRAWNS COOKED IN COURT BOUILLON

1 quart water
½ stalk celery
1 carrot, sliced
1 small white onion, sliced
juice of ½ lemon
1 teaspoon salt
½ teaspoon pepper
1 pound raw prawns, fresh or frozen

Put water in saucepan. Add all ingredients except for the prawns. Bring water to the boil.

Add the prawns and let water come to boil again. Turn heat down so water just simmers. Cover saucepan and cook prawns 2 to 5 minutes, never longer. Drain prawns.

FRIED FRESH PRAWNS

1½ pounds raw prawns
8 fluid ounces milk
⅛ teaspoon paprika
¼ teaspoon salt
maize flour

Shell and remove black vein from prawns.

Mix together milk, paprika, and salt.

Soak prawns in seasoned milk 30 minutes. Season with additional salt and roll in maize flour.

Fry in deep fat (375°F.) until golden brown. Drain on absorbent paper. Serve with tartar sauce. Serves 4 to 5.

Fried Cooked or Canned Prawns: Season cleaned prawns with salt and pepper. Dip in milk and roll in maize flour. Fry as above.

BUTTERFLY PRAWNS

1½ pounds very large prawns
2 eggs
3 tablespoons flour
½ teaspoon salt
pinch of pepper

Remove shells from prawns but leave tails on. Split along the back and remove black vein but do not cut all the way through. Wash and dry with towel.

Mix the eggs, flour, salt, and pepper in bowl to a smooth batter.

Drop in prawns and coat thoroughly. Lift out prawns one at a time with a fork and drop into deep hot fat (375°F.) and fry until golden brown, 2 to 5 minutes. Serve hot. Serves 4 to 5.

SAUTÉED PRAWNS

Sauté cooked or canned cleaned prawns in melted butter lightly. Place on hot serving dish. Pour butter over the prawns. Sprinkle with chopped parsley.

Serve on wooden cocktail sticks as an hors d'oeuvre. Serve with melted butter flavoured with lemon juice and freshly ground pepper.

FRIED PRAWNS—BATTER COATED

2 ounces sifted flour
½ teaspoon baking powder
½ teaspoon salt
¼ teaspoon black pepper
1 egg, slightly beaten
4-5 tablespoons milk
2-3 drops Tabasco sauce
2 pounds peeled cleaned prawns

Sift flour with baking powder, salt, and pepper. Mix egg and milk. Add to dry ingredients and beat until smooth. Add Tabasco sauce.

Dip prawns in batter and fry in hot deep fat (375°F.) until golden.

Serve hot, with a sauce for dipping.

SCAMPI IN GARLIC BUTTER

Scampi is the Italian word for prawns.

2 pounds scampi, fresh or frozen
¼ pound butter or margarine
1 clove garlic, finely chopped
salt to taste
pepper to taste

Remove shells from scampi, except portion which covers tail. Cut down centre of back and remove the vein.

Melt butter and add garlic. Simmer 3 minutes.

Place scampi on individual flame-proof dishes, or in a large grill pan. Pour garlic butter over them. Sprinkle with salt and pepper.

Place under preheated grill 3 inches from heat and grill 5 to 7 minutes or until browned and tender.

Serves 4 to 5.

Scampi in Garlic Butter

PRAWN TEMPURA

Tempura is a Japanese term for any food dipped in an egg batter and deep-fried in oil. Fish, shellfish, and vegetables are commonly prepared in this way. Tempura is served with a soy sauce dip and small bowls of grated radish, horseradish, and ginger.

1 pound prawns
oil for frying
4 ounces sifted flour
½ teaspoon salt
1 beaten egg
6 fluid ounces milk

Shell prawns, leaving tail shell on. Slash the backs. Heat oil for deep frying.

Mix the flour and salt. Add egg and milk; beat together.

Dip prawns in batter; add to hot oil (375°F.). Fry 2 to 3 minutes, until golden, turning once. Drain.

Serves 6 to 8 as appetizer or 4 as a main dish, with a spicy dip.

Sauce: Mix together 4-5 tablespoons sherry, 2 tablespoons soy sauce, 1 teaspoon sugar, and pinch of ground ginger.

SEAFOOD À LA KING

2 tablespoons butter or margarine
1 green pepper, diced
2 tablespoons sliced pimiento
4 ounces sliced mushrooms
1 tablespoon flour
½ teaspoon salt
⅛ teaspoon pepper
¼ teaspoon paprika pepper
8 fluid ounces single cream
4 ounces cooked peeled prawns
4 ounces cooked flaked fish
3 egg yolks
4 tablespoons sherry

Melt butter or margarine in a chafing dish; add green pepper, pimiento, and mushrooms. Cook and stir for 3 minutes, or until pepper is soft.

Stir in flour, salt, pepper, and paprika and gradually add cream, stirring constantly. Add prawns and flaked fish.

Beat egg yolks lightly; add sherry and stir into à la King mixture. Cook, stirring constantly, until mixture thickens. Serve on toast. Serves 4.

Seafood à la King

PRAWNS DE JONGHE

1 clove garlic
6 ounces butter or margarine
1 teaspoon salt
4 ounces dry white breadcrumbs
4 fluid ounces dry sherry
2½ to 3 pounds cooked prawns
chopped parsley

Crush garlic clove until it is almost a paste.

Cream together the garlic, butter, and salt until well blended. Add crumbs and sherry. Blend well.

Place alternate layers of cooked cleaned prawns and crumb mixture in 6 individual ovenproof dishes, ending with crumbs. Sprinkle chopped parsley over top of each.

Bake in hot oven (400°F. Mark 6) 20 to 25 minutes. Serve at once. Serves 6.

PRAWNS ARNAUD— APPETIZER

2 tablespoons tarragon or cider vinegar
4-5 tablespoons olive oil
1 tablespoon paprika pepper
2 tablespoons strong made mustard (Creole mustard preferred)
about 1 teaspoon salt (more or less to suit taste)
4 ounces very finely chopped celery
4-6 very finely chopped spring onions
4 tablespoons finely chopped parsley
2 pounds prawns, cooked, peeled, and cleaned

Mix together all ingredients except prawns in a bowl.

Pour enough sauce over the prawns to moisten them and mix well. Cover and stand in refrigerator 30 minutes to 2 hours before using so the sauce flavour penetrates the prawns.

Pour remaining sauce over prawns just before serving. Serves 4-5.

GRILLED FRESH PRAWNS

Remove shells, leaving on last segment and tail. Remove black veins. Dip raw prawns in melted butter or salad oil.

Grill under moderate heat 4 to 6 minutes, depending upon size of prawns. Season to taste with salt and pepper. Serve with a butter sauce.

CREAMED PRAWNS

Heat cleaned, cooked or canned prawns in medium white sauce or cream sauce. Season to taste with salt and pepper.

If you like, additional seasonings may be added as given in variations of white sauce (see Index).

For colour, add chopped pimiento or chopped parsley. Serve on toast. Sprinkle with paprika pepper.

SWEET AND SOUR PRAWNS

1 pound prawns, fresh or frozen
1 can (about 8 ounces) sliced pineapple
3 ounces brown sugar
4 fluid ounces vinegar
2 tablespoons soy sauce
½ pint water
3 tablespoons cornflour
1 green pepper, cut in strips
1 tomato, cut into wedges

Clean and cook prawns. Drain syrup from pineapple into a saucepan. Cut pineapple slices in half and reserve. Add brown sugar, vinegar, soy sauce, and 8 fluid ounces water to pineapple syrup. Bring to the boil.

Blend the cornflour with remaining water. Add to sugar mixture. Cook, stirring constantly, until thickened. Add green pepper, pineapple, and tomato wedges. Cook 2 minutes. Add prawns and cook to heat them through. Serve immediately. Serves 4.

Sweet and Sour Prawns

PRAWNS CREOLE

4 tablespoons butter or margarine
1 large onion, chopped
½ large green pepper, finely chopped
1 clove garlic, chopped
1 teaspoon salt
pinch of pepper
⅛ teaspoon paprika pepper
⅛ teaspoon dried rosemary (optional)
1 large can (about 16 ounces) tomatoes
1 pound cooked prawns
12-18 ounces cooked rice

Melt butter in saucepan; add onion, green pepper, and garlic. Sauté 10 minutes or until tender.

Add salt, pepper, paprika, rosemary, and tomatoes. Bring to the boil; cover, reduce heat. Simmer 15 minutes.

Add prawns and heat thoroughly. Serve on boiled rice. Serves 4.

Prawn Creole

PRAWNS WITH LOBSTER STYLE SAUCE (CHINESE)

½ pound minced pork
1 tablespoon chopped spring onion
1 tablespoon chopped carrot
1 tablespoon chopped celery
salt and pepper
2 tablespoons salad oil
2 pounds raw peeled prawns
8 fluid ounces chicken stock
1 beaten egg
2 tablespoons cornflour
2 tablespoons cold water
1 tablespoon soy sauce

Mix pork, vegetables, and seasonings in pan with hot oil and cook about 5 minutes.

Add cleaned and washed prawns and stir-fry until they turn pink.

Add stock and cook, covered, for 10 minutes.

Add egg and stir for 2 minutes and then add remaining ingredients which have been well blended. Stir until thickened. Serve with boiled rice.

Serves 4 to 6.

PRAWNS AU GRATIN

½ pound cooked peeled prawns
2 tablespoons butter
2 tablespoons flour
about 5 fluid ounces evaporated
    milk
2-3 tablespoons water
1 teaspoon paprika pepper
4 ounces diced Cheddar cheese
3 slices white bread, diced
2 tablespoons butter, melted
grated Parmesan cheese

Arrange prawns in 4 individual casseroles or in the bottom of a buttered ¾-pint casserole.

Melt butter in a saucepan. Add flour, then blend in evaporated milk and water. Stir until smooth and thickened. Add paprika and diced cheese and stir until cheese is melted.

Pour over prawns and top with bread cubes which have been tossed with the last 2 tablespoons of butter.

Sprinkle with grated Parmesan cheese and bake in a hot oven (400°F. Mark 6) for 20 minutes. Serves 4.

Prawns au Gratin

PRAWN SOUFFLÉ CASSEROLE

6 slices buttered bread
dry mustard
2 8-ounce cans prawns
½ pound Cheddar cheese, grated
3 eggs
16 fluid ounces milk
salt and pepper

Spread bread lightly with dry mustard. Remove crusts and cut into ½-inch cubes.

Put alternate layers of bread cubes, prawns, and cheese in a greased casserole.

Beat eggs and mix with milk. Season with salt and pepper. Pour over other ingredients.

Stand in pan of hot water and bake in moderate oven (350°F. Mark 4) 1¼ hours, or until silver knife inserted in centre comes out clean. Serves 6 to 8.

QUICK PRAWN CASSEROLE

3 ounces thin noodles
1 can (about 9 ounces) prawns
1 12-ounce can whole kernel corn
1 4-ounce can mushrooms
2 tablespoons butter or margarine
2½ tablespoons flour
8 fluid ounces milk
¼ pound Cheddar cheese,
    shredded
salt and pepper

Cook noodles until tender in boiling salted water. Drain and place in casserole.

Clean black veins from prawns. Arrange corn, prawns, and sliced mushrooms over noodles. (Save liquid from mushrooms and prawns.)

Melt butter in saucepan. Blend in flour. Add mixture of milk and liquid from prawns and mushrooms gradually; cook over low heat, stirring constantly, until thickened and smooth.

Add half the cheese, salt and pepper to taste; stir over low heat until cheese is melted. Pour sauce over other ingredients. Mix gently. Sprinkle with remaining cheese.

Bake in hot oven (400°F. Mark 6) until heated through, about 30 minutes. Serves 6.

Variations: Substitute peas for corn. Substitute clams or oysters for prawns.

MEXICAN PRAWNS IN SAUCE

1 onion, finely chopped
2 ounces butter or margarine
1 teaspoon chilli powder
1 ounce flour
8 fluid ounces milk
2 tablespoons chopped parsley
2 level tablespoons ketchup
8 ounces cooked peeled or canned
    prawns

Sauté onion in butter until lightly browned. Stir in chilli powder and

flour. Slowly add milk.

Cook, stirring over low heat, for 10 minutes.

Add parsley, ketchup, and prawns; bring to the boil. Serve immediately. Serves 4.

CURRIED PRAWNS À LA CEYLON

2 tablespoons butter or margarine
½ large onion, chopped
½ large green pepper, chopped
2 ounces chopped celery
2 tablespoons flour
2 teaspoons curry powder (more if
    you like)
3 teaspoons soy sauce
8 fluid ounces water
1 can (16 ounces) tomatoes
8 ounces uncooked white rice
1 teaspoon salt
1 pound frozen thawed prawns or 2
    5-ounce cans prawns

Melt butter or margarine in a frying pan or saucepan. Add onion, green pepper, and celery. Cook, stirring occasionally, until the onion is yellow.

Blend in flour. Stir in curry powder and soy sauce. Stir in 8 fluid ounces water and the tomatoes. Cover and simmer 20 minutes.

While the sauce cooks, put rice, salt, and remaining water in a 3-pint saucepan. Bring to vigorous boil. Turn the heat as low as possible. Leave on this low heat 14 minutes.

Remove saucepan from heat but leave lid on until ready to serve rice or at least 10 minutes.

While rice cooks, peel frozen thawed prawns. Remove the vein easily by running knife along back from head to tail.

Wash in water. Place prawns in boiling salted water. Cover and return to boiling point. Turn heat down and simmer 5 minutes. Drain.

After sauce cooks, stir in cooked, frozen thawed or canned prawns. Heat 5 minutes.

Arrange cooked rice on a hot dish. Pour prawns and sauce over rice. Serves 6.

Curried Prawns à la Ceylon

INDIVIDUAL PRAWN-VEGETABLE CASSEROLES

12 fluid ounces medium white sauce
⅛ teaspoon dry mustard
¼ teaspoon Worcestershire sauce
2 drops Tabasco sauce
1 can (about 8 ounces) whole
    kernel corn, drained
12 ounces cooked or canned peas,
    drained
4 ounces cooked peeled prawns
fresh white breadcrumbs and butter
    or margarine

Mix together sauce and seasonings. Add corn and peas.

Place in individual heatproof dishes or scallop shells. Top with prawns. Sprinkle with crumbs. Dot with butter.

Bake in hot oven (400°F. Mark 6) 20 minutes. Serves 4.

PRAWNS WITH RICE IN WINE SAUCE

6 tablespoons butter or margarine
1 large onion, finely chopped
12 ounces uncooked rice, washed
    and drained
½ teaspoon salt
½ teaspoon pepper
2 large mushrooms, sliced
4 fluid ounces dry white wine
1 pint hot stock or water
2 tablespoons chopped parsley
½ teaspoon dried thyme
2 teaspoons lemon juice
2 pounds uncooked peeled prawns

Melt butter over medium heat in a heavy saucepan or electric frying pan and add onion, rice, salt, and pepper. Stir frequently until rice is golden. Add mushrooms and wine. Cook until wine is reduced, about 4 minutes.

Add stock, parsley, thyme, lemon juice, and prawns. Cover pan and simmer until rice is tender, about 10 minutes. Remove the lid and fluff rice. Serves 4 to 6.

Prawns with Rice in Wine Sauce

LICHEE GARDENS PRAWNS

2½ pounds or 30 large prawns
3-4 finely chopped spring onions
3 ounces finely chopped mush-
    rooms
1 ounce finely chopped almonds
2 tablespoons butter or margarine
salt and pepper
¼ teaspoon Aromat

If prawns are frozen, thaw. Shell and remove veins.

Mix spring onions, mushrooms, and almonds; sauté in butter until tender; sprinkle with salt, pepper, and Aromat.

Make a slit or pocket in prawns at thickest part. Fill with about 1 teaspoon sautéed mixture. Place on perforated spoon; dip in batter and drain.

Lower into deep hot fat (375°F.) 2 minutes or until golden brown. Serves 5 to 6.

Batter For Lichee Gardens Prawns:

2 eggs
6 fluid ounces milk
6½ ounces flour
1½ teaspoons salt
½ teaspoon Aromat
1½ tablespoons butter or margarine,
    softened

Beat eggs until thick and lemon coloured; add milk. Sift in flour, salt, and Aromat; add butter. Mix until just smooth.

PRAWNS TERIYAKI

4 fluid ounces pineapple juice
2 to 4 tablespoons soy sauce
5 fluid ounces vegetable or peanut
    oil
1 pound peeled prawns

Mix together pineapple juice, soy sauce, and oil. Pour over prawns and leave them to marinate about 15 minutes.

Drain and grill prawns under grill or on barbecue about 4 inches from heat source for 3 or 4 minutes on each side. Serve with boiled rice. Serves 3.

NEAPOLITAN PRAWNS

1 pound prawns, fresh or frozen
1 clove garlic, finely chopped
5 fluid ounces olive or other salad
    oil
3 anchovy fillets (optional)
1 can (20 ounces) Italian
    tomatoes
¼ teaspoon dried oregano
small pinch of crushed chilli
    pepper
1 tablespoon chopped parsley

Remove shells from prawns. Make a slash along back of prawns, cutting deeply but not all the way through. Wash away vein. Drain prawns on absorbent paper.

Heat olive oil in large frying pan. Add garlic and prawns, placing them

Lichee Gardens Prawns

in the pan with backs down. Fr[y] prawns about 5 minutes, turning t[o] sides to finish cooking. Remove prawn[s] and place on backs in a chafing dish.

Add remaining ingredients to pa[n]. Mix thoroughly, breaking up tomatoe[s]. Cook slowly at least 15 minutes.

Pour sauce round prawns in chafin[g] dish. Serve with slices of fried Frenc[h] bread. Serves 3 to 4.

PRAWN WIGGLE WITH TOMATO SAUCE

1 pound prawns
8 fluid ounces water
2 whole black peppercorns
1 teaspoon salt
1 small bay leaf
½ stalk celery
1 teaspoon Aromat
1 large onion, sliced
3 tablespoons butter or margarine
2 8-ounce cans tomato sauce
2 tablespoons cornflour
2 tablespoons cold water
salt and pepper

Wash prawns under cold runnin[g] water. Bring water to the boil; ad[d] whole black peppercorns, salt, ba[y] leaf, celery, and the ½ teaspoon Aroma[t].

Add prawns, cover; simmer 5 mi[n]utes; drain; shell; remove the veins.

Sauté onions in butter or margarin[e] until golden brown. Add tomato sauc[e]. Simmer 5 minutes.

Blend cornflour with the cold wate[r]; add; stir until thickened. Add remai[n]ing Aromat and prawns, heat thor[o]ughly. Season to taste. Garnish wit[h] small triangles of toast. Serves 4.

Neapolitan Prawns

PRAWNS AND LOBSTER IN RICE RING

12 ounces uncooked rice
3 tablespoons butter or margarine
3 tablespoons flour
12 fluid ounces liquid (juice from canned lobsters and prawns, milk to make up difference)
1 teaspoon salt
½ teaspoon paprika pepper
1 9-ounce can lobster, flaked
1 7-ounce can prawns

Cook rice in plenty of boiling salted water until tender, about 30 minutes. Drain and rinse with hot water. Place over hot water or in low oven to dry out.

Pack rice in buttered ring mould. Keep hot while making lobster and prawn mixture.

Melt butter in saucepan over low heat. Remove from heat and blend in flour until smooth. Gradually add liquid. Return to heat, cook, stirring constantly until thick.

Add seasonings, flaked lobster, and prawns. Heat thoroughly.

For serving, turn rice ring onto a hot serving dish and fill centre with lobster and prawn mixture. Serves 6.

PRAWN AND GREEN PEPPERS (Chinese Style)

1 pound fresh prawns
1 pound green peppers
1 clove garlic, chopped
5 fluid ounces salad oil
about 1¼ teaspoons salt
¼ teaspoon pepper
⅓ teaspoon dried rosemary
1½ tablespoons cornflour
6 fluid ounces stock or 1 bouillon cube and water
1 teaspoon gravy colouring

Remove shells and veins from prawns. If they are very large, cut in half, lengthways.

Cut cleaned peppers into strips about 1 inch wide.

Heat oil in heavy frying pan; add green peppers and garlic. Cook until peppers are soft, about 3 to 4 minutes.

Add prawns. Add salt, pepper, and rosemary. Gently mix and turn peppers and prawns to cook evenly on all sides. Cover and cook over low heat about 7 minutes.

Blend the cornflour with the stock or bouillon and add to green pepper and prawns mixture. Add gravy colouring.

Serve with boiled rice or with cooked macaroni or noodles. Serves 4 to 6.

CREAMED SEAFOOD IN SHELLS

2 tablespoons flour
8 fluid ounces water
8 fluid ounces evaporated milk
½ teaspoon salt
pinch of pepper

Prawns and Lobster in Rice Ring

4 ounces lobster meat or crabmeat, cooked or canned
4 ounces peeled prawns
about 14 ounces mashed potatoes
cheese (optional)

Stir water slowly into flour to keep smooth. Bring mixture to the boil, stirring constantly to prevent lumps from forming.

Add milk and seasonings and continue cooking over a pan of hot water until thickened, about 10 minutes. Add lobster meat or crabmeat and prawns, and pour into individual baking dishes.

Garnish with mashed potatoes. Sprinkle with grated cheese, if you like.

Brown in very hot oven (450°F. Mark 8). Serves 6.

PRAWN CURRY—HAWAIIAN

4 large onions, chopped
3 large cloves garlic, chopped
4 tablespoons butter or margarine
24 fluid ounces water or coconut milk
3 large tomatoes, peeled and chopped
2 large apples, chopped
4 ounces chopped celery
1 tablespoon desiccated coconut
1 piece fresh ginger root or ¾ teaspoon ground ginger
1 tablespoon sugar
1½ tablespoons curry powder
1½ tablespoons flour
1½ teaspoons salt
¼ teaspoon pepper
1½ pounds raw peeled prawns

Sauté onions and garlic in butter until lightly browned. Add water, bring to the boil.

Add tomatoes, apples, celery, coconut, and fresh ginger root if available.

If ground ginger is used, blend it with sugar, curry powder, flour, salt, and pepper. Add cold water to moisten to a paste and add, stirring, to boiling mixture. Simmer, stirring occasionally, until vegetables are very tender, or about 40 minutes.

Add prawns and cook 5 minutes. Serve on boiled rice. Makes about 12 or more servings.

PRAWNS LOUISIANA

2 ounces butter or 2 fluid ounces oil
2 medium onions, finely chopped
2 green peppers, finely chopped
4 fluid ounces prawn stock, chicken bouillon, or water
16 fluid ounces tomato sauce
12 ounces cooked rice
2 pounds cooked peeled prawns
salt, celery salt, Tabasco sauce
4 egg yolks
16 fluid ounces cream

Melt butter in a chafing dish over direct heat. Add chopped onions and peppers, and cook until soft but not brown.

Add prawn stock, chicken bouillon, or water, and simmer until vegetables are tender.

Add tomato sauce, rice, and prawns. Season with salt, celery salt, and a dash of Tabasco.

Beat egg yolks, add to cream, and stir into hot prawn mixture a few minutes before serving. This sauce should not boil. Serves 6 to 8.

PRAWNS AND PEPPERS

1 pound uncooked peeled prawns*
6 tablespoons flour
2 tablespoons grated Parmesan cheese
1 teaspoon salt
1 clove garlic
6 medium peppers
4 fluid ounces olive or salad oil
4 tablespoons dry white wine
¾ teaspoon salt
pinch of pepper

To coat the prawns: mix flour, cheese, and salt in a paper bag, add prawns and give bag a good shake.

Crush or chop garlic; remove seeds and stems from peppers and cut peppers in inch-wide strips.

Heat oil in a large frying pan, toss in the prawns and garlic and cook about 5 minutes or until prawns are golden.

Now scoop prawns from pan and set aside. Put pepper strips in the pan, cover tightly and cook over a medium heat for 10 to 15 minutes or until tender but still slightly crisp.

Add prawns, wine, salt, pepper and heat through. Serves 4.

*Note: 2 8-ounce cans prawns or 2 10-ounce packets frozen prawns may be substituted.

PRAWNS WITH EGG (CHINESE)

6 ounces finely chopped lean pork
1 clove garlic, chopped or crushed
4 water chestnuts, crushed
2 tablespoons salad oil
8 ounces peeled raw prawns
1 tablespoon soy sauce

1 tablespoon cornflour
4 fluid ounces water
2 tablespoons chopped spring onion
  tops
1 egg
salt

Sauté pork, garlic, and chestnuts in oil until lightly browned. Add prawns and cook, stirring often, 3 to 5 minutes. Add soy sauce.

Blend cornflour with water and add to mixture. Cook, stirring, until thickened. Simmer 2 minutes.

Add chopped onions and egg, stirring constantly, and cook slowly until egg resembles a soft jelly. Add salt to taste. Serve with boiled rice. Serves 2 to 3.

SWEET AND SOUR PRAWNS (CHINESE)

Sauce Ingredients:
3 large green peppers
2 large tomatoes
8 fluid ounces vinegar
8 fluid ounces water
¾ teaspoon salt
pinch of pepper
1 can (20 ounces) pineapple
  chunks
8 ounces sugar
1½ teaspoons Aromat, optional
3 tablespoons cornflour
3 tablespoons ketchup
2 tablespoons salad oil

Cut each large cleaned green pepper diagonally into 8 pieces. Cut each large tomato into 8 wedges. Set aside.

Batter Ingredients:
2 slightly beaten eggs
3 ounces flour
½ teaspoon salt
2 tablespoons cold water
1½ pounds very large peeled prawns

Mix the eggs, flour, salt, and cold water well.

Remove shells from prawns. Split down the back but do not cut all the way through. Remove black vein, wash, and drain.

Sherried Prawns Creole

Dip prepared prawns in batter, coating well. Fry prawns in deep hot oil (375°F.) until golden brown, 2 to 5 minutes.

Mix together all sauce ingredients except tomatoes in a saucepan. Mix well and bring to the boil.

Add prawns and tomatoes. Mix thoroughly and cook 3 minutes. Serves 4.

SHERRIED PRAWNS CREOLE

2 pounds fresh prawns, or 1 pound
  cooked, peeled prawns
2 ounces butter or margarine
2 tablespoons finely chopped onion
2 large tomatoes, cut in pieces
1 bay leaf
½ teaspoon salt
½ teaspoon dried thyme
pinch of cayenne pepper
1 teaspoon sugar
1 can (10½ ounces) condensed mushroom soup
4-5 tablespoons sherry
2 pimientos, cut in strips

Wash prawns in cold water. Drop into boiling salted water and cook 6 to 8 minutes. Drain. Cover with cold water. Remove shells, and dark vein along back of each prawn.

Melt butter or margarine. Cook onion in butter or margarine until it turns yellow. Add tomatoes, bay leaf, salt, thyme, cayenne, and sugar.

Dilute mushroom soup with sherry; add to tomato mixture. Finally add prawns and pimientos. Cook 5 minutes. Serve with hot boiled rice. Serves 6.

PRAWN WIGGLE IN TOAST CUPS

4 ounces cooked peeled prawns
4 tablespoons butter
4 tablespoons flour
16 fluid ounces milk
1 teaspoon salt
4 ounces cooked peeled prawns
pepper
6 ounces cooked peas

Melt butter in a saucepan. Remove pan from heat. Stir in flour until blended. Gradually add milk, stirring until smooth.

Return pan to heat and cook, stirring constantly, until thickened. Add salt and pepper, prawns, and peas.

Continue cooking until prawns and peas are heated through. Serve in toast cups. Makes 8 toast cups, enough to serve 4.

To Make Toast Cups: Trim crusts from slices of white bread. (Sandwich sliced bread works best.) Butter both sides of bread slices.

Press each slice into a bun tin so that corners turn up. Toast in moderate oven (375°F. Mark 5) until golden brown.

Toast cups can be made in advance and heated just before serving.

Scallops (Coquilles Saint-Jacques)

Scallops include any of a number of bivalve molluscs with deeply grooved shells. They are in season from October to March, and should be bought alive. The fishmonger will open and clean them for you.

Scallops should be cream coloured, not white, and odourless. The bright orange part is the roe or coral and is particularly delicate.

Allow about 1½ to 2 pounds or 1½ to 2 pints for serving 6 to 8. Buy the smaller quantities if the scallops are to be served in a scalloped dish or in a sauce, the larger quantities if they are to be served sautéed or fried.

GRILLED SCALLOPS

Drain and wash scallops. Dip in milk and roll in breadcrumbs. Place in single layer in greased shallow flameproof dish. Dot with butter.

Grill, turning frequently, until browned on all sides, about 3 minutes. Serve with melted butter and lemon juice.

SAUTÉED SCALLOPS

Prepared as for grilled scallops. Fry in a well greased frying pan, turning frequently, until brown on all sides, about 3 minutes.

SCALLOPS SAUTÉ PROVENÇAL

1½ pounds scallops
seasoned flour
6 tablespoons olive or salad oil
1 or 2 garlic cloves, crushed
salt and pepper to taste
1 ounce chopped parsley

Dust the scallops with seasoned flour.

Heat oil; add scallops and garlic; cook quickly, tossing to brown evenly. Add salt and pepper to taste.

Remove from heat; add parsley; toss to coat scallops evenly. Serves 4.

Scallops Sauté Provençal

SCALLOPS IN GARLIC SAUCE

1 pound scallops
¼ pound butter or margarine,
    melted
1½ teaspoons chopped chives
1½ teaspoons dried parsley
¼ teaspoon dried tarragon
    (optional)
¼ teaspoon garlic salt
½ teaspoon onion salt
pinch of black pepper
breadcrumbs

Mix butter and seasonings. If large scallops are used, cut into small pieces.

Arrange 18 clam shells on a baking sheet. Place some of the butter mixture in the bottom of each shell.

Put about 4 pieces of scallop in each shell and top with remaining butter mixture. Sprinkle with breadcrumbs.

Bake in moderate oven (350°F. Mark 4) for 5 minutes. Serve as an hors d'oeuvre. Serves 6.

Note: If clam shells are not available, scallops may be prepared in shallow baking dish and served on small plates, or in individual ramekins.

FRENCH FRIED SCALLOPS

Method 1: Wipe scallops with damp cloth. Dip in batter and fry in hot deep fat (375°F.) 3 to 4 minutes, or until golden brown. Serve with a tartar sauce.

Method 2: Wipe scallops with damp cloth. Roll in flour, dip in beaten egg, and roll in dry breadcrumbs. Fry in hot deep fat (375°F) 3 to 4 minutes, or until golden brown. Serve with tartar, chilli, or tomato sauce.

SCALLOPS ORIENTAL

2 pounds scallops
3 ounces honey
2 tablespoons mustard
2 teaspoons curry powder
1 teaspoon lemon juice

Line grill pan with aluminium foil. Arrange scallops in bottom of pan.

Mix the remaining ingredients together well. Brush scallops generously with curry mixture. Place grill pan in lowest position under source of heat. Grill slowly 10 minutes.

Turn scallops; brush with curry mixture; grill 10 minutes longer or until nicely browned. Serves 4.

Scallops Oriental

SCALLOPS BAKED IN SHELLS

2 pounds scallops
16 fluid ounces dry white wine
8 fluid ounces water
1 teaspoon salt
few celery tops
few sprigs parsley
1 bay leaf
1 small onion
½ pound mushrooms
6 tablespoons butter or
    margarine
1 teaspoon lemon juice
1 ounce flour
2 egg yolks
4 fluid ounces double cream
4 tablespoons dry breadcrumbs

Cook scallops, wine, water, salt, celery tops, several sprigs parsley, and bay leaf together over low heat for about 10 minutes or until scallops are tender.

Scoop out the greenery and save liquid to use later on. Chop scallops into little chunks.

Chop onion, mushrooms, and several more parsley sprigs rather fine. Cook in 2 tablespoons melted butter or margarine and lemon juice for about 10 minutes, then mix with cooked scallops.

Make the sauce by melting remaining butter or margarine, stir in flour smoothly and gradually add liquid in which scallops were cooked. Cook, stirring constantly, until sauce thickens. Takes about 5 minutes.

Beat egg yolks slightly, add cream, stir in a little hot sauce slowly, then blend all the sauce with egg yolks (no curdling this way). Cook over low heat, still stirring, for 5 minutes longer or until thick.

Mix vegetable-scallop mixture, spoon into 6 or 8 scallop shells. Sprinkle with crumbs. Dot with butter, brown under grill. Serves 6.

SCALLOPED SCALLOPS

1½ pounds scallops
2 ounces butter or margarine
12 ounces fresh white breadcrumbs
1¼ teaspoons salt
1 teaspoon finely chopped onion
1 teaspoon chopped parsley
1 teaspoon chopped chives
1 tablespoon lemon juice

If large scallops are used, quarter or slice them.

Melt butter and add all the ingredients except scallops; toss together until well mixed.

Place in alternate layers with scallops in a well greased baking dish, with crumb mixture for top layer.

Bake in hot oven (400°F. Mark 6) until crumbs are brown, about 20 minutes. Serves 6.

Scallops Baked in Shells

SCALLOPS AU GRATIN

3 tablespoons butter or margarine
3 tablespoons flour
12 fluid ounces milk
2 ounces grated Cheddar cheese
1 pound scallops, sliced
celery salt to taste
juice of ½ lemon
golden crumbs

Melt butter or margarine. Add flour and mix to a smooth paste. Add milk gradually, stirring over low heat until mixture is smooth and thick.

Add cheese and continue stirring until cheese is melted.

Place a layer of scallop slices in the bottom of a greased casserole.

Add celery salt, lemon juice, and a layer of cheese sauce. Repeat until all ingredients are used up. Sprinkle with the crumbs.

Bake in moderate oven (375°F. Mark 5) until crumbs are browned and scallops tender, about 30 minutes. Serves 4 to 6.

SCALLOPS IN WINE SAUCE

2 ounces butter or margarine
1 teaspoon Worcestershire sauce
2-3 tablespoons finely chopped onion
1 pint scallops
4 tablespoons dry white wine

Melt butter in small frying pan with Worcestershire sauce. Add onion and cook until golden.

Pick over and rinse scallops. Divide into 4 large scallop shells or individual heatproof dishes.

Divide butter-onion mixture evenly and sprinkle over scallops. Add 1 tablespoon wine to each.

Bake in very hot oven (500°F. Mark 10) 10 minutes. Serve at once. Serves 4.

Scallops Side-By-Side: Here you see scallops, side-by-side, showing the entire mollusc before the muscle (that marshmallow-shaped part) is removed. The crescent-shaped part that encircles the muscle is the roe, coral coloured in the female. The roe is considered a delicacy.

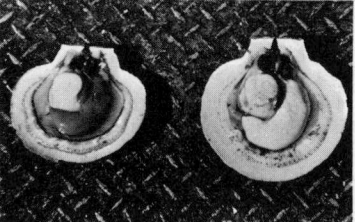

Miscellaneous Shellfish

ABALONE

An abalone is a very large sea mollusc with an oval, somewhat spiral shell perforated along the rim and lined with mother-of-pearl. The edible part is the central muscle, which resembles a giant scallop. It is usually only available from Chinese food shops, in cans. The fresh meat is tough if not pounded before cooking.

It is best chopped and served in chowders or fish soups; however, it is also served fried (though this method runs the risk of overcooking it) or creamed or used in canapé or sandwich spreads. Simmer abalone in water until tender. Chop it fine and use it in recipes for chowder or fish soup.

FRIED ABALONE

Pound the raw slices with a wooden mallet. Wipe dry. Roll in seasoned crumbs, then in beaten egg diluted with water, and again in crumbs. Sauté in oil or butter 1 to 1½ minutes on each side. Take care not to overcook because it toughens.

CREAMED ABALONE

Add 1 can diced raw abalone to about 14 fluid ounces medium white sauce. Season to taste and simmer 2 minutes. Stir in 1 slightly beaten egg yolk. Serve on hot toast. Garnish with chopped hard-boiled egg. Serves 4.

COCKLES

A marine bivalve mollusc with shells of equal size marked by radial ribs which fan out from the base. They are eaten in the same way as oysters or clams.

CRAYFISH

These delicate-tasting fresh-water crustaceans look like baby lobsters. To cook, wash live crayfish thoroughly and drop them into boiling salted water or court bouillon for 5 minutes. Let them cool in the water. Scandinavians frequently add fresh dill to the boiling water. To serve, pull out the tail fin and the intestinal vein with it. Crayfish are usually served in their bright-red shells.

CONCH AND WHELK

The conch is a shellfish (a marine mollusc) probably best known for its attractive shell. Some varieties are edible. The conch is sometimes confused with the whelk, another species of marine mollusc with similar types of shells found in temperate waters. The latter is very popular in Britain where it is sold shelled and ready-cooked. They are usually eaten well sprinkled with vinegar.

PERIWINKLES

Periwinkles are various types of tiny salt-water snails. Many people consider them a delicacy.

They are sold cooked, and are eaten sprinkled with vinegar. To remove from shell: using a sterilized pin, lift off dark cap, pierce the winkle and twist gently as you pull it out of the shell.

BAKED PERIWINKLES

    6 dozen periwinkles
    4 ounces softened butter
    4-5 tablespoons finely chopped
        parsley
    2 cloves garlic, finely chopped
    salt
    24 large snail shells (see Snails)

Cover the periwinkles with warm water and soak long enough to break the membranes that seal them in their shells. Discard any that do not emerge from the shells.

Drain, then cover the periwinkles with salted water; bring to the boil. The periwinkles will recede into their shells because of the heat. Drain.

Remove the periwinkles from their shells as described above. Rinse several times in cold water.

Cream together the butter, parsley, garlic, and salt to taste. Grease the inside of 24 large snail shells; insert 3 periwinkles in each, and fill the shells with creamed butter mixture.

Arrange shells, butter side up, in baking dish and set aside for 2 hours. Then bake in very hot oven (450°F. Mark 8) 10 minutes. Serves 4.

SHELLFISH SALAD

    8-10 mussels
    8-10 shelled cooked prawns
    5-6 ounces crab or lobster meat,
        flaked
    1 tablespoon white wine vinegar
    little made mustard
    3 tablespoons olive oil
    1 tablespoon chopped green pepper
    2-3 tablespoons mayonnaise (see
        page 831)
    lettuce
    chopped parsley
    paprika

Served in deep scallop shells this salad looks very attractive.

Prepare the mussels as described on page 476 and dry them on a cloth. Put the mussels into a bowl with the prawns and crab meat. Make a dressing with the vinegar, mustard, salt, pepper and oil and pour over the fish. Leave to stand about 1 hour. Add the green pepper and bind altogether with the mayonnaise.

When required, make a bed of chopped lettuce in 4-5 deep scallop shells. Divide the fish mixture between them. Garnish with alternate lines of chopped parsley and paprika. Serves 4-5.

SHELLFISH AND RICE MOULD

    6 ounces long grained rice
    3 ounces butter or margarine
    1 shallot, chopped
    6 tablespoons dry white wine
    6 tablespoons water
    6 ounces frozen scampi
    4 scallops
    6 ounces shelled cooked prawns
    1 tablespoon flour
    salt, cayenne pepper, lemon juice
    1 egg yolk
    4 tablespoons cream

Cook the rice in plenty of boiling salted water for 12 minutes. (If quick cooking rice is used, follow the directions on the packet.) Drain well, add about 2 ounces butter and leave it to melt through.

Press the rice into a greased or oiled ring mould, cover with buttered paper and keep hot.

Put the shallot into a small pan with the wine and water and simmer until it is translucent. Add the scampi and simmer a few minutes longer until the scampi looks opaque. Remove the scampi and keep warm.

Wash the scallops and remove the black intestinal line. Trim off any hard edges and cut the white part into thin slices, keeping the tongues intact. Add the sliced scallops and tongues to the liquid in the pan and simmer about 4 minutes. Remove and put with the scampi. Warm the prawns in the liquid, then put with the rest of the shellfish. Melt the remaining butter in a pan, stir in the flour and mix well. Gradually add the strained stock and a few drops of lemon juice. Stir until boiling, then simmer for a few minutes. The sauce should be fairly thin so add a little water if necessary.

Add the prepared shellfish and season with salt and cayenne pepper. Draw away from the heat and carefully stir in the egg yolk and cream mixed together.

Unmould the rice ring on to a heated serving dish. Remove the scallop tongues carefully from the sauce. Pour the sauce into the centre of the rice ring and garnish with the scallop tongues.

Variation

1. Add a little paprika to the sauce to give it a pink colour.
2. Add some strips of cooked green pepper.
3. Add 2 ounces button mushrooms cooked in a little butter.

Turtles, Snails & Frogs' Legs

TURTLE AND TERRAPIN

A considerable variety of turtles are used for food in various localities. The name terrapin is commonly applied to fresh water turtles and the name tortoise to land species. The marine green turtle is the usual source of turtle soup and canned turtle meat.

TURTLE BALTIMORE

Combine ⅓ pint chicken stock and turtle meat. Simmer very gently until stock is reduced by half its original volume.

Add the liver, cut into small pieces, 2 tablespoons butter, salt and black pepper to taste, and 2 well beaten egg yolks, stirring constantly while adding (If desired, omit the egg yolks and increase the butter to, adding the butter bit by bit.)

Before serving, season with 1½ to 2 tablespoons sherry.

TURTLE WASHINGTON

Melt 1½ tablespoons butter. Blend in 1½ tablespoons flour until smooth. Add ½ pint cream and bring to boiling point, stirring constantly.

Add the cooked turtle meat with the liver cut into small pieces, chopped small intestines, ½ cup sautéed sliced mushrooms, and 1 hard-boiled egg, coarsly chopped. Simmer gently 3 to 5 minutes.

Just before serving, stir in 2 slightly beaten egg yolks. Season to taste with salt and pepper. If desired, add 1½ to 2 tablespoons sherry. Serve very hot.

TURTLE STEW

4-5 ounces sliced fresh or canned mushrooms
2 tablespoons butter or margarine
1 can condensed cream of mushroom soup
8 fluid ounces milk
about ½ teaspoon salt
about 1 pound chopped, cooked turtle meat
2 fluid ounces dry white wine

Fry the mushrooms in butter 5 minutes.

Add soup and milk; taste and add more salt if necessary. Then add cooked meat and heat 1 or 2 minutes.

Add wine and heat through, about 1 minute.

Serve hot on buttered toast. Serves 4 to 6.

SNAILS (ESCARGOTS)

A land variety of edible mollusc, with a short, thick, wormlike body and a protective spiral shell. Large quantities of snails are eaten in France, but the consumption is gradually declining. The best type is known as the Burgundy large white. Most snails are gathered in vineyards; some are raised on special farms. They are available in cans.

While snails are becoming increasingly popular in this country, nevertheless the preparation is tiresome.

To serve 5 to 6, use 1 pound fresh snails (2 to 2½ dozen). Soak in heavily salted water 3 to 4 hours, then wash in several waters and simmer 30 minutes.

Remove snails from shells and cook in court bouillon (see Index) about 3 to 4 hours.

Meanwhile wash shells and dry thoroughly. Replace cooked snails in shells and pack with butter mixture (below). (It may be necessary to use 2 cooked snails in each shell.)

Place in shallow baking dish and, if you like sprinkle with fine breadcrumbs. Bake in hot oven (400°F. Mark 6) until heated through, about 20 minutes. Serve with special snail tongs and fork, or wooden toothpicks.

BUTTER MIXTURE FOR SNAILS

4 ounces butter or margarine
4 tablespoons finely chopped parsley
1 teaspoon chopped onion or shallot
1 clove crushed garlic
about ½ teaspoon salt
pinch of freshly ground pepper

Cream butter or margarine until soft and work in remaining ingredients.

Leftover butter mixture may be used as sauce for fish or vegetables.

CANNED SNAILS

Canned snails are sold in special containers, with the prepared snails in one container and the cleaned shells in another.

To serve, place snails in shells, pack with butter mixture and serve as for fresh snails.

If you like, canned snails may be heated in a little white wine seasoned with chopped onion or shallot before placing in shells.

Another favourite stuffing frequently used instead of the butter mixture is a mixture of equal parts butter and ground hazelnuts which have been creamed together in a bowl which was rubbed slightly with a cut clove of garlic.

SNAILS IN WHITE WINE

16 fluid ounces dry white wine
1 tablespoon chopped shallot
48 canned snails and shells
parsley butter (below)

Boil wine with chopped shallot until the wine is reduced to 6 fluid ounces. Strain through a fine sieve.

Pour 1 scant teaspoon of the reduced wine into each shell. Put snails in shells and seal with parsley butter.

Put prepared snails on a baking sheet or in a shallow roasting pan and place in hot oven (400°F. Mark 6) until heated through, about 10 minutes. Serves 6.

Parsley Butter: Cream together ½ pound butter, 8 tablespoons finely chopped parsley, and a few drops lemon juice.

FROGS' LEGS

The hind legs of the frog are the only ones used. If bought fresh, they will be skinned, cleaned, and ready for use.

Allow 4 to 6 large legs or ½ pound (8 to 10) small legs per portion.

FROGS' LEGS PROVENÇAL

12 frogs' legs
flour
6 tablespoons butter or margarine
3 cloves garlic, crushed
1 tablespoon lemon juice
3 tablespoons chopped chives
2 tablespoons chopped tarragon
1½ tablespoons chopped parsley
salt and pepper
2 tablespoons brandy
4 tablespoons dry white wine

Dry cleaned frogs' legs and roll in flour.

Melt butter in a frying pan; add garlic and lemon juice. Blend well.

Add frogs' legs and shake the pan gently occasionally to prevent them from sticking.

Slowly brown well on all sides, 6 to 8 minutes.

Add chives, tarragon, parsley, and salt and pepper to taste. Cook 1 to 2 minutes, then heat brandy and flame, and add with the wine. Cook 1 minute longer. Serve at once. Serves 2 or 3.

FRIED FROGS' LEGS

Season legs with salt, pepper, and lemon juice. Dip in sifted breadcrumbs, then in beaten egg mixed with 2 tablespoons water, and again in crumbs. Chill 1 hour.

Fry in hot deep fat (375°F.) 3 minutes, or sauté in butter until brown. Serve with tartar sauce.

FRITTERS

Banana Fritters

The term fritter, which is derived from the Latin *frigere* meaning to fry, is applied to several kinds of fried food. Some fritters are small batter cakes belonging, like doughnuts, to the bread family and are always deep-fat fried. Other fritters are combinations of small pieces of fruit, vegetables, meat, fish, etc., and batter which are usually deep-fat fried; however, some types are pan-fried (sautéed).

Sometimes the term is also applied to such fried items as timbale cases and rosettes which are intended to hold other foods.

Correct frying procedure is perhaps the most important step in making good fritters. See deep fat frying hints in **Facts About Food and Cooking.**

For a complete list of the frittered foods in this book, consult the index.

BASIC FRITTER BATTER

  7 ounces sifted plain flour
  3 teaspoons baking powder
  1 tablespoon sugar
  ½ teaspoon salt
  2 eggs, slightly beaten
  8 fluid ounces milk
  1 tablespoon melted fat

Sift dry ingredients. Omit sugar unless batter is to be used for fruit.

Mix together eggs, milk, and fat. Mix liquid and dry ingredients and stir until smooth.

Add 6 to 12 ounces chopped vegetables, cooked or canned, or chopped fruit, well drained, or 6 to 12 ounces drained corn.

Drop gently from a tablespoon into deep hot fat (365°F. to 370°F.). Turn as soon as fritter comes to surface. Remove from fat when well browned on both sides. Drain on absorbent paper. Serves 6.

BASIC FRITTER BATTER FOR COATING

  1 egg, slightly beaten
  8 fluid ounces milk or 8 fluid ounces water or fruit juice
  1 tablespoon melted fat
  4 ounces sifted plain flour
  ½ teaspoon sugar
  ¼ teaspoon salt

Mix together egg, milk, water, or fruit juice and fat. Add gradually to dry ingredients. Mix until smooth.

Dip fruit into the batter and fry in deep fat, heated to 365°F.-370°F. Remove when light brown on both sides. Drain on absorbent paper.

This batter may be used for apple, banana, or pineapple slices or for orange segments. Serve fruit fritters sprinkled with icing sugar.

Variation 1: For a thicker batter decrease milk to 5 fluid ounces and add 1 teaspoon baking powder to flour with sugar and salt. Use with berries or very juicy fruits.

Variation 2: Vary by adding ¼ teaspoon cinnamon, grated nutmeg, or grated rind of lemon or orange.

ORANGE FRITTERS

  3 oranges
  8 ounces sugar
16 fluid ounces water
  4 tablespoons brandy
     fritter batter for coating

Peel oranges, separate the segments, and carefully remove the seeds and pith.

Make a sugar syrup by dissolving sugar slowly in water and brandy, then boiling. Reduce heat to simmer; add orange segments, and simmer gently 10 minutes. Drain orange segments well and let them cool.

Just before serving, pour fritter batter over segments and let fruit and batter stand 10 minutes.

Fry in hot deep fat (375°F.) a few at a time, until they are delicately browned all over, turning them with a wooden spoon. Drain fritters on absorbent paper; dust with icing sugar. Serves 5 to 6.

BANANA FRITTERS

  4 ounces sifted plain flour
  2 ounces sugar
  2 teaspoons baking powder
  1¼ teaspoons salt
  1 beaten egg
4-5 tablespoons milk
  2 teaspoons melted fat
  3 medium green-tipped bananas, cut diagonally in 3 pieces
    extra 2 to 3 tablespoons plain flour
    fat
    fluffy hard sauce (below)

Sift together flour, sugar, baking powder, and salt.

Mix together egg, milk, and melted fat; add to dry ingredients; mix until smooth.

Roll banana pieces in 2 to 3 tablespoons flour; spread with batter, making sure they are well coated. (This batter is stiff—do not thin.)

Fry in deep hot fat (370°F.) until golden brown, about 1 to 2 minutes. (Fritters stay crisp 15 to 20 minutes.)

Serve with fluffy hard sauce. Serves 4.

Fluffy Hard Sauce: Cream 2 ounces butter or margarine well with 5½ ounces sifted icing sugar in an electric mixer; add ½ teaspoon vanilla essence. Chill before serving, if you like.

Variations: Vary flavour with lemon or orange juice and grated rind. Sprinkle with grated nutmeg, if you like. Makes about 6 fluid ounces.

FRITTER BATTER FOR HORS D'OEUVRES

2 ounces plain flour
¼ teaspoon salt
1 whole egg
1 tablespoon melted butter
4 fluid ounces flat beer
1 stiffly beaten egg white

Sift flour with salt. Beat egg; add butter and mix with flour. Add beer and stir only until the mixture is smooth.

Let batter stand at room temperature until light and foamy, about 1 to 2 hours. Then fold in stiffly beaten egg white.

FRITTERS FOR HORS D'OEUVRES

Prepare fritter batter for hors d'oeuvres (above). To the fritter batter add one of the following mixtures. Drop by tablespoons into deep hot fat (375°F.) and fry until golden brown. Drain and serve hot with or without a sauce for dipping.

Ham Fritters: Mix together 8 ounces minced ham, 1 tablespoon chopped parsley, and freshly ground black pepper to taste.

Chicken or Turkey Fritters: Mix together 8 ounces minced cooked chicken or turkey, 1 tablespoon finely chopped chives or spring onion, and salt, pepper, and ground nutmeg to taste.

Tuna Fritters: Mix together 1 can (about 7 ounces) finely chopped tuna fish, 2 tablespoons finely chopped celery, and lemon juice and salt and pepper to taste.

ROSETTES

Rosettes are a type of fried cake made from a thin batter fried in fancy shapes by means of a special rosette iron. They are usually used as a base for creamed foods such as creamed chicken or for desserts topped with a fruit sauce.

2 eggs
1 tablespoon sugar (see below)
¼ teaspoon salt
4 ounces sifted plain flour
8 fluid ounces milk
2 tablespoons melted butter

Beat eggs until blended, then beat in sugar and salt. Stir in flour alternately with milk and butter, mixed together.

To fry, dip iron in deep hot fat (375°F.), then into batter. Do not let batter cover top of iron or it will be difficult to remove rosette. Dip the batter-coated iron into the hot fat for 20 to 35 seconds. Remove rosette with a fork. Repeat process, alternately dipping iron into hot fat and then into batter and frying. Drain on absorbent paper. Makes about 3 dozen.

Variations: If rosettes are not to be used as a dessert, omit sugar from above recipe. If served as a dessert, sprinkle the fried rosettes with icing sugar.

"HUSH PUPPIES"

A hush puppy is a maize flour fritter served with fried fish and traditionally fried in the same deep fat used for the fish. It is a traditional dish from southern America. The name is said to have originated at outdoor fish fries, at which bits of the frying batter would be cooked and thrown to the dogs to keep them quiet.

8 ounces maize flour
1 tablespoon plain flour
1 teaspoon baking powder
½ teaspoon baking soda
1 teaspoon salt
3 tablespoons finely chopped onion
1 egg, well beaten
8 fluid ounces buttermilk

Mix and sift dry ingredients. Add onion, well beaten egg, and buttermilk.

Drop a spoonful at a time into deep hot fat (375°F.). Fry until golden brown. Drain on absorbent paper. Serves 6 to 8.

FRENCH FRITTERS (BEIGNETS)

Prepare Choux Pastry Dough (see index) but instead of baking, drop a teaspoon at a time into deep, hot fat (370°F.) and cook until delicately brown. As soon as they are cooked enough on one side, they will turn themselves over. Remove when browned on both sides. Drain and sprinkle lightly with icing sugar.

Queen Fritters: Cook as above, but cut a slit in each one and fill with jam or marmalade, or with chocolate pastry cream filling. Sprinkle with icing sugar.

BLACKBERRY FRITTERS

4 ounces sifted plain flour
1 teaspoon baking powder
½ teaspoon salt
2 tablespoons sugar
2 eggs, separated
2 to 3 tablespoons water
3 ounces blackberries

Mix and sift dry ingredients. Mix egg yolks with water and stir into dry ingredients, mixing only until smooth.

Fold in stiffly beaten egg whites, then mix in the blackberries.

Drop a spoonful at a time into hot deep fat (365°F.) and fry until lightly browned.

Drain on absorbent paper and serve with icing sugar or fruit sauce.

Variations: Other fruits, such as diced peaches, apples, or bananas, or other berries, may be used. If cranberries are used, they must first be cooked in 4 fluid ounces water and 4 ounces sugar until the skins burst, then drained and cooled.

APPLE FRITTERS

1 egg, separated
1 teaspoon water
1 tablespoon oil
⅛ teaspoon salt
3½ ounces sifted plain flour
2 medium apples

Beat egg yolk with water, oil, and salt. Add flour; beat well until thick and smooth. Set it aside to "rest" at room temperature for about 2 hours.

Peel 2 apples; core and cut them into ¼-inch wedges.

Just before frying, beat egg white very stiffly. Blend carefully into first mixture.

Dip slices of apple into batter; fry in deep fat (375°F.) until golden brown. Drain. Before serving, sprinkle with icing sugar. Serves 4 to 6.

SWEDISH TIMBALE CASES

These are pastry shells of fried batter, made with a special iron, in which creamy foods are served. Most people find the fluted irons easier to handle than the plain ones.

4 fluid ounces milk
2 egg yolks, beaten
3 ounces sifted plain flour
½ teaspoon salt

Add milk to egg yolks. Gradually stir in flour sifted with salt.

Mix well, cover, and set aside 1 hour.

Heat deep fat to 370°F. and heat timbale iron in it for 2 to 3 minutes.

Drain and dip into batter to within ¾ inch of top. Immediately return to hot fat and hold there until case is crisp and lightly browned.

If batter slips off, the iron is too cold. If it sticks to iron, it is too hot. Makes 24 timbale cases.

ANDALUSIAN HONEY FRITTERS

1 tablespoon creamed butter or margarine
4 ounces sugar
4 eggs, well beaten
1 teaspoon grated orange rind
1 tablespoon sherry
¼ teaspoon salt
6 ounces sifted plain flour
1½ teaspoons baking powder

Cream together the butter and sugar. Beat in eggs, orange rind, sherry, and salt. Beat to a smooth cream.

Sift together flour and baking powder. Stir this slowly into first mixture until well mixed.

Set aside 15 minutes, then roll out thin on slightly floured board. Cut into pieces 1 × 4 inches and fry in deep hot fat (360°F. to 370°F.). Drain; serve hot with honey or maple syrup. Serves 6.

FRESH FRUIT FRITTERS

4 ounces sifted plain flour
¼ teaspoon salt
2 eggs
5 fluid ounces milk
1 teaspoon salad oil
salad oil or fat for deep frying
apples, peaches, or bananas

Sift flour with salt into bowl.

Beat eggs, stir in milk and teaspoon of salad oil or fat. Add dry ingredients and beat to a smooth batter. Cover and chill several hours.

To Prepare Fruit: Apples: core, peel and slice in rings ½ inch thick. Peaches: peel, and quarter. Bananas: peel, slice once lengthways, and then in half.

Dip into batter and drain off excess batter. Deep-fry in hot deep oil or fat heated to 370°F. until golden brown, 3 to 4 minutes. Drain on absorbent paper.

Serve with meat, or sprinkle with icing sugar and serve with lemon sauce as a dessert. Serves 6 to 8.

CHERRY FRITTERS

1 can (about 8 ounces) well drained
    Morello cherries, stoned
2 tablespoons sugar
1 tablespoon brandy, kirsch, or rum
    (optional)
4 ounces sifted plain flour
¼ teaspoon salt
1 teaspoon baking powder
1 beaten egg
about 4 fluid ounces milk
1 tablespoon melted butter or
    margarine

Mix cherries, sugar, and alcohol.

Sift together flour, salt, and baking powder.

Mix egg, 4 fluid ounces milk, and butter. Add milk mixture to dry ingredients and stir only until smooth. Add and fold in cherry mixture. Add additional milk if batter is too thick.

Drop a tablespoon at a time into hot deep fat (365°F. to 375°F.) and fry until browned, turning as fritters rise to the surface.

Drain on absorbent paper. Sprinkle with icing sugar and, if you like, serve with cherry sauce that has been flavoured with the same alcohol that was used in batter. Serves 4.

SWISS FRIED CAKES

8 fluid ounces single cream
2 beaten eggs
1 teaspoon salt
8 ounces sifted plain flour
4 ounces butter

Mix together well cream, eggs, and salt. Add flour to make a soft dough

and turn out onto a floured board.

Dot dough with butter and with the hands work it into the dough. The butter should be firm but not hard.

Chill dough in refrigerator 1 hour, then roll out ⅛-inch thick.

Cut in any desired shape, making a ½-inch gash through the centre of each. Fry in deep hot fat (370°F.).

Drain on absorbent paper and roll in icing sugar while still hot. Makes about 36.

OB'L PUFFERS

4 ounces sifted plain flour
2 tablespoons sugar
1½ teaspoons baking powder
¼ teaspoon salt
1 beaten egg
4 fluid ounces milk
2 medium apples, peeled, cut in
    ⅛-inch rings or wedges

Sift together dry ingredients.

Add milk to egg and blend with dry ingredients. Add the cut apples to batter.

Dip a long-handled spoon or tongs in the hot fat, then lift a batter-covered piece of apple with it and slide into deep hot fat (375°F.).

Re-dip the spoon about every fourth or fifth "puffer". (This process makes it easier and less messy in handling the food in the batter stage.)

Brown completely on one side and then turn for cooking the other side. Drain on absorbent paper and sprinkle with icing sugar.

Serve piping hot. Makes 12 to 16 "puffers".

HAM AND CORN FRITTERS

6 ounces cooked ham
1 can (about 8 ounces) whole kernel
    corn (liquid reserved)
1 tablespoon chopped onion
3½ ounces plain flour
1½ teaspoons baking powder
4 tablespoons milk or corn liquid

Drop ham and corn fritter mixture into hot deep fat a teaspoon at a time.

Mix minced ham, corn, and onion

Sift dry ingredients together. Add to corn mixture. Add liquid and mix well

Drop a teaspoon at a time into deep hot fat (365°F.). Be careful as the corn may burst as it cooks. Fry until golden brown. Drain. Serves 4.

APRICOT FRITTERS WITH RUM SAUCE

1 teaspoon sugar
5 ounces sifted plain flour
⅓ teaspoon baking powder
pinch of salt
2 eggs
4-5 tablespoons milk
½ tablespoon butter
apricots

Mix and sift dry ingredients. Beat eggs well; add eggs, milk, and butter to dry ingredients. Mix to a stiff batter.

Remove stones from apricots and cut into quarters. Dust with flour and dip each apricot into batter. Drop into hot deep fat (370°F.). Fry until brown Serve with Rum Sauce.

Rum Sauce:
8 fluid ounces mixed fruit juice
6 ounces sugar
¼ teaspoon red food colouring
2 tablespoons rum essence

Mix all ingredients and cook slowly for 1 hour. Stir occasionally.

CHEESE FRITTERS

5 ounces sifted plain flour
¼ teaspoon salt
2 teaspoons baking powder
5 fluid ounces milk
1 egg, well beaten
3 ounces grated Cheddar cheese

Mix and sift flour, salt, and baking powder. Mix together the milk and egg. Combine the two mixtures.

Add grated cheese and beat hard for 3 minutes or until smooth.

Drop a tablespoon at a time into hot deep fat (360°F. to 370°F.). Fry until brown. Drain on absorbent paper Serve hot. Serves 6.

Ham and Corn Fritters

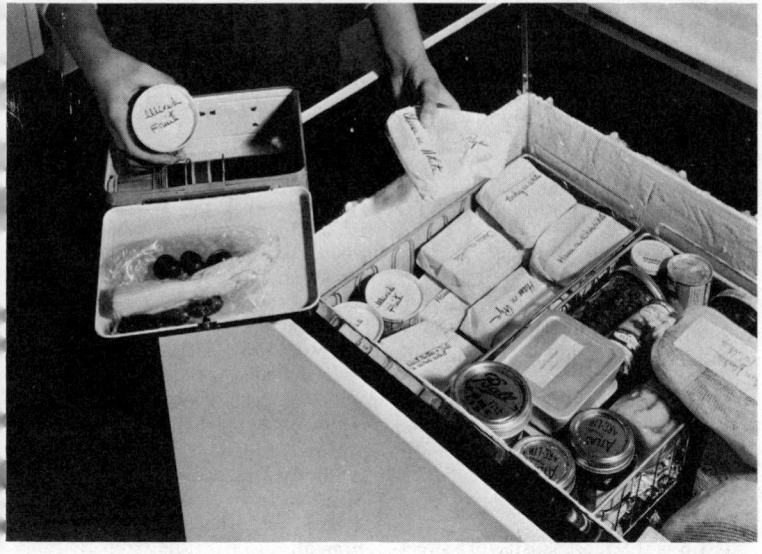

FROZEN FOODS

Having a freezer and making proper use of it can be like having an extra pair of hands in the kitchen or like having an extra day in every week. Begin by thinking of your freezer as more than just a place for food storage. Think of it as part of your daily cooking equipment, plan round it, and rely on it every day to help you.

However to enjoy the advantages of a freezer to the fullest, you'll find it wise in the very beginning to take a little time to learn the facts about freezing—how to prepare, pack, freeze, store, and cook frozen foods.

BASIC PRINCIPLES OF SUCCESSFUL FREEZING

Frozen foods are attractive, full of flavour, and high in nutritive value when carefully prepared with strict attention to basic principles of freezing. There is a great difference, however, between frozen foods of quality and foods that are merely safe to eat because they have been frozen. Carelessness in any of the basic steps may easily produce foods that are entirely safe, yet whose quality is so diminished that you will have little pleasure in eating them.

1. Choose high quality foods. The frozen product will be no better than the food in its original state. Freezing does not improve the flavour or quality of any food.

2. Process foods carefully. Follow instructions about blanching vegetables, cutting and trimming meat and poultry, cooking and chilling prepared foods. Speed in handling is essential at all stages.

3. Wrap foods properly. Choose only freezer packing materials which will protect food from air. If using special thick polythene bags, wrap tightly and seal with freezer tape.

When air reaches food during storage, the result is loss of moisture accompanied by a change in flavour. This is the condition known as "freezer burn".

4. Label all foods accurately. Label each container with date, name of product, weight (if meat) and number of pieces or servings. It is helpful to add an "expiration date" to the label—the maximum storage time. All foods should be used before their expiration date.

5. Freeze at 0°F. or lower. Foods should always be frozen as rapidly as possible. Put unfrozen foods in the fastest freezing area or in direct contact with freezer walls or shelves and away from already frozen foods. Place packages so air can circulate between them.

6. Do not overload freezer with unfrozen foods. Put in only as much food as your freezer will freeze without unduly raising the temperature of foods already stored there. Overloading also keeps the new items from freezing quickly enough for optimum quality. Follow the directions with your freezer to determine how much food may be frozen at one time.

7. Store foods at 0°F. Keep a thermometer in the storage compartment, and make sure the temperature remains at zero or below. Foods stored at temperatures above zero lose flavour and nutritive value rapidly. Ice or snow inside the container usually indicates fluctuation of temperatures above zero.

8. Avoid long storage. No food remains at top quality indefinitely even though frozen. Freezing retards bacterial and enzymatic action greatly but cannot stop it entirely, and it is best to plan on normal seasonal turnover of foods. Foods frozen first should always be used first.

How to Freeze Fruits

Fruits are especially easy to freeze, so allow ample space in your freezer for a complete variety. Most fruits have a high sugar content and, for best results, should be frozen quickly.

Which Fruits to Select

Most fruits, berries and melons can be frozen satisfactorily, but some freeze better than others. In the same way, certain varieties of each fruit freeze better than others. Directions for freezing specific fruits give a rating as to suitability for freezing. If in doubt about freezing certain fruits, consult the general enquiries department of your local office of the Ministry of Agriculture and Fisheries.

Whole citrus fruits should not be frozen, but serving slices, sections and juices are delicious and easy to freeze. Raspberries are delicious when frozen.

When to Pick or Buy Fruit

The ideal time to freeze most fruits is at the height of maturity. It is best to allow most fruit to reach this stage on the vine, bush, or tree. However, fruits like peaches, plums, and figs are apt to become soft on the plant and are easily bruised in handling. Pick such fruits in the "firm ripe" stage and store overnight; this ensures more even ripening and, with peaches, they are easier to peel.

Pick fruit in early morning. Sun-heated fruit may bruise excessively from handling and result in an inferior frozen product. Pick no more fruit than can be quickly prepared, packaged, and frozen at one time.

While speed of handling is not so critical with fruit as with vegetables, the shorter the holding time after picking for most fruits, the better the frozen fruit will be.

Wash Fruit Thoroughly

This is one of the most important steps in preparing fruits for freezing. Low-growing fruits and all wild fruits should be washed twice or more to remove sand and dust.

Wash no more than one pound of small fruit (berries or cherries) at one time. This can be done in a colander, using a spray when possible. Never allow fruit to stand in water more than one minute as water-soaked fruit will not freeze successfully.

After washing, drain fruit thoroughly. Spread fruit carefully on a tray or in a large utility dish on which several thicknesses of absorbent paper towels have been placed. If possible, set tray in refrigerator about one hour to cool and firm the fruit.

Stem Fruits Carefully

Never squeeze the stems off berries. The stems of raspberries, loganberries, and gooseberries may be lifted off with the fingers. Use a sharp knife to stem strawberries.

Peel Fruits Rapidly

Apples, apricots, peaches, nectarines, and pears oxidize and discolour rapidly after the skin is removed.

To prevent this, peel and slice fruit directly into a solution of 3 tablespoons lemon juice (or 3 tablespoons salt OR 4½ teaspoons citric acid) to each gallon of cold water.

Don't allow fruit to remain in solution longer than one minute, so do no more than one container at a time.

Rinse in cold water and drain befor packing. Then continue to peel, slice, and pack until all fruit has been prepared.

Remove Stones Carefully

Fruits with stones (plums, damsons, peaches, apricots, and nectarines) must have the stone removed before freezing. Avoid bruising fruit.

Purée

Fruit to be puréed may be cooked before forcing through a sieve or mixing in a blender. Such fruits as strawberries, grapes, raspberries, peaches, and plums may be forced through a sieve or mixed in a blender without cooking.

Sweeten Fruits Properly

Many fruits retain better flavour if sweetened before freezing. There are two methods of sweetening fruit: dry sugar method and syrup method.

DRY SUGAR METHOD

Method 1: After the fruit has been washed, drained, and cooled, carefully transfer fruit to a bowl. Sprinkle sugar over fruit. Sweeten one pound at a time to avoid bruising.

A clean flour sifter will give more even distribution of sugar.

To mix sugar through fruit, use a perforated spoon and gently lift fruit through sugar. Pack at once.

Method 2: Wash, cool, and drain fruit. Fill container about ¼ full. Sprinkle in ¼ of sugar, about one or two tablespoons. Continue filling container in this way.

The container may be shaken occasionally to distribute sugar, but avoid pressure on it. Seal at once.

SYRUP METHOD

Syrup is the most satisfactory sweetening agent if fruit is to be used for sauce. Syrup is preferable for apricots, pears, and figs.

The simplest way to add the syrup to the fruit is to first fill the container with fruit and then add syrup to cover. Seal at once.

The syrup must always be cold before using; a good idea is to make the syrup a day in advance and store it in a covered container in the refrigerator.

SUGAR SYRUP

Add sugar to boiling water and cook until sugar is thoroughly dissolved.

The degree of sweetness in the frozen fruit should govern the syrup to be used. See specific directions for recommended syrup with each particular fruit.

Very Thin: 8 ounces sugar to 32 fluid ounces boiling water.

Thin: 8 ounces sugar to 24 fluid ounces boiling water.

Medium: 8 ounces sugar to 16 fluid ounces boiling water.

Heavy: 8 ounces sugar to 8 fluid ounces boiling water.

Pack Fruits Carefully

Polythene bags are excellent, but care should be taken when sealing and handling the bag before the fruit is frozen. Rigid cartons, tin cans (if lacquered inside), and special glass freezing jars may be used.

Containers must be moisture and vapourproof because air leakage causes destruction of vitamins and minerals and also spoils the appearance of the fruit.

Pack According to Use

Decide how the frozen fruit is to be used and then pack the fresh fruit accordingly. For instance, fruits to be used for pies or jams need not be sweetened before freezing, with the exception of apricots and peaches which sometimes discolour unless sugar or syrup is added.

As a sauce, a pint carton of fruit will serve 3 or 4. A pint will make a skimpy 8-inch pie but a quart will make four generous individual shortcakes. But if used as a topping for ice cream, a pint of strawberries will serve 5 or 6.

Choose container sizes that adequately take care of a meal, with no leftovers. Frozen fruits lose their flavour if left standing several hours after thawing. *Never refreeze fruit.*

Allow for Expansion and Seal Carefully

Pack fruit firmly but do not use pressure or crush the fruit. If using a rigid container, there should be sufficient air space to allow for some expansion. Fill container to within ½ inch of top for dry sugar packs and ½ to ¾ inch for syrup packs. Make container airtight.

Label Clearly and Freeze at Once

After sugar or syrup has been added to fruit in container, it should be sealed, labelled clearly, and placed immediately in quick-freeze compartment with the sealed side up to prevent leakage. If this is not practical, place containers in freezer compartment of refrigerator until ready to load the freezer.

A Hint for Mothers of Small Children

When sorting fruits for freezing, use only those which are firm and ripe. Those which are overripe but still usable can be puréed for the baby and young children. Peaches, apples, apricots, plums, and pineapples are easy to purée and will save both time and money in the preparation of the children's meals.

How It's Done: Peel (or pare) the fruit and then cook thoroughly; be careful not to overcook. You may want to add a bit of sugar as the fruit cooks. Then force it through a sieve or mix it in a blender. Cool thoroughly.

After the fruit is cool, pour into refrigerator ice cube tray with the dividers in place. Freeze. When cubes are firmly frozen, remove them from the tray and wrap one or two cubes, enough for an individual serving, in small polythene bags.

To serve: Stand the cubes at room temperature until suitable for serving

How to Prepare Fruits for Freezing

APPLES FOR SAUCE

Rating for freezing: good — 1¼ pounds yield approximately 1 pound.

Peel and core the apples. Cut into eighths. Place in saucepan and add only enough water to start the apples cooking. Bring to a quick boil. Reduce heat to simmering and cook about 10 minutes until apples are mushy. Add sugar to taste and stir.

Some apples cook to a fine mush without sieving, but if sieving is necessary, force the sauce through a fine sieve. Cool thoroughly. Pack in polythene bags. Freeze.

APPLES FOR PIE

Rating for freezing: good — any high-acid variety. 1 pound yields about ¾ pound.

Freeze enough in one container for a pie; a 1½-pint container holds apples for a 9-inch pie. *Do not freeze apples which have turned brown on the inside or have started to turn bad.*

Peel and core the apples. Cut into slices for pie. Apples discolour rapidly after the skin has been removed, so slice apples immediately into a solution of 3 tablespoons lemon juice (or 3 tablespoons salt OR 4½ teaspoons citric acid) to 1 gallon cold water. Never allow apples to remain in solution more than one minute. Rinse in cold water before draining.

Place slices on a tray covered with several thicknesses of absorbent paper towels. Place tray in refrigerator and allow to drain. Thorough draining before packing makes slices easier to separate for making pies.

Immediately after draining, pack into polythene bags and freeze. Add sugar, if you like, in the proportion of 1 part sugar to 4 parts apples.

APRICOTS

Rating for freezing: good — any tree-ripened variety. ¾ to 1 pound yields approximately ¾ pound.

With skins: Choose firm, fully ripened fruit of bright apricot colour, with no traces of green. Wash thoroughly. Remove stem. Cut in half and remove the stone.

Dip apricot halves in a solution of 1 tablespoon lemon juice and 1½ pints water. Drain by placing cut side down on a tray covered with several thicknesses of absorbent paper towels.

Put in polythene bags or rigid containers. Cover with cold, medium syrup. Seal. Freeze at once.

Without skins (Preferred): Place about 20 apricots in a wire basket. Plunge into boiling water to cover for 1 minute. Remove and plunge into cold water to cover for 1 minute, or until cool.

Remove skin. Cut in half and remove stone. Dip halves in a solution of 1 tablespoon lemon juice to 1 quart water. Drain by placing cut side down on a tray covered with several thicknesses of absorbent paper towels.

Put in polythene bags or rigid containers. Cover with cold, medium syrup. Seal. Freeze at once.

BLACKBERRIES

Rating for freezing: fair — 2 pounds berries yield about 2 pounds frozen fruit.

Choose firm, fully matured fruit. Unripe blackberries, even though a good black in colour, turn reddish black when frozen.

Wash carefully in cold water, never more than 1 pound of berries at a time. Gently move the berries through the water by hand, then lift them to a tray covered with several thicknesses of absorbent paper towels. Spread them only one layer thick.

Place immediately in refrigerator to cool before packing. If you wish to add sugar to berries, use the same method as for raspberries. Wrap in polythene bags, seal and freeze.

For use as a sauce, pack berries in polythene bags or rigid containers and cover with a thin or medium syrup. Seal and freeze immediately.

BLUEBERRIES

Rating for freezing: excellent — any small-seeded variety. 1 pound berries yields approximately 1 pound frozen fruit.

Carefully remove leaves, foreign matter and immature berries. Wash thoroughly. Remove stems. Drain on absorbent paper towels. Place in bowl. Add sugar in proportion of 2 tablespoons sugar to 4 ounces berries. Stir gently to avoid bruising the fruit.

Pack in polythene bags or rigid containers. Seal. Freeze.

CHERRIES, SOUR

Rating for freezing: excellent — Montmorency, 2 pounds cherries yield about 1 pound frozen fruit.

Wash thoroughly and quickly. Remove from water at once. Remove stems. Place on tray covered with several thicknesses of absorbent paper towels.

Before freezing cherries, remove the stones with a fork.

Put tray in refrigerator until cherries are firm again.

Then remove stones. Gently press prong of a fork into stem end and lift out the stone. Squeezing the stone out bruises the fruit. Work with only 1 pound at a time because juice accumulates and the cherries may have to be drained again.

Add 2 tablespoons sugar to 6 ounces cherries and pack in polythene bags. Freeze.

Cherries for pies may be frozen without sugar.

CHERRIES, SWEET

Rating for freezing: fair — 2 pounds cherries yield about 1 pound frozen fruit.

Choose fully ripened cherries. Proceed as for sour cherries. A medium syrup may be used if the sweet cherries are to be used as a sauce.

Pack in polythene bags or rigid containers. Seal and freeze at once.

CRANBERRIES

Rating for freezing: excellent — ½ pound yields approximately ½ pound.

Sort berries carefully. Remove stems and all spongy or poorly formed cranberries. Wash berries carefully. Drain.

Pack in polythene bags. Freeze. Cranberries do not need sugar for successful freezing.

CURRANTS

Rating for freezing: good — any large variety. ¾ pound yields about ¾ pound.

Wash and drain currants before removing from stems. Then remove stems and place currants in a bowl. Mix with sugar in proportion of 1 part sugar to 4 parts currants.

Put in polythene bags. If currants are to be used as a sauce, put in rigid containers and cover with a medium syrup. Seal and freeze.

FIGS

Rating for freezing: excellent.

Use figs that are completely ripe but not bruised or softened. Figs may be frozen with or without skin.

Peeled Figs: Wash thoroughly. Remove stems. Using a sharp knife, peel very thin. Packet according to size of family, allowing 4 or 5 figs per serving. Freeze.

Put figs in polythene bags. When bag is ¼ filled, sprinkle sugar over figs. Continue alternating figs and sugar. Use 1 part sugar to 4 parts figs. Seal and freeze. Prepared this way, figs are delicious served with cream.

Or fill container. Cover figs with a medium syrup. Seal and freeze.

If figs are to be used as a topping for ice cream, use a heavy syrup.

Unpeeled Figs: Sprinkle 12 pounds of figs with 4 ounce baking powder. Pour 5 quarts boiling water over them. Set aside for 10 minutes. Rinse in cold water. Drain thoroughly on absorbent paper towels on a tray. Put tray in refrigerator to chill.

Put in polythene bags. Add medium syrup. Seal and freeze.

GOOSEBERRIES

Rating for freezing: excellent — any large-sized variety. 1 pound fresh berries yields approximately 1 pound frozen fruit.

Frozen gooseberries are excellent for pie. Choose fully matured green gooseberries. Wash thoroughly. Remove stem and blossom end. Drain. Place berries in bowl. Add sugar, if you like, in proportion of 2 tablespoons sugar to 6 ounces gooseberries. Put in polythene bags and freeze.

GRAPEFRUIT AND ORANGE SEGMENTS

Chill fruit thoroughly. Then, peel and divide the fruit in segments, making sure all skin and membrane are removed. Drain on absorbent paper towels. Prepare only enough for 3 or 4 packets at one time as a protection against vitamin loss.

Put in polythene bags with sheets of polythene between layers. Seal and freeze. Sugar may be added to grapefruit segments, if you like.

MELON

Rating for freezing: good — any fully ripened, deep yellow variety. 1 melon yields approximately 3 pounds.

Good for fruit cups or salads during the winter months. Choose firm, fully ripened melon. Cut in half and remove seeds. A scoop is ideal for scooping out the flesh. If one is not available, remove rind, cut melon in slices and cube. Drain before packing.

Put in polythene bags. Seal and freeze. Once thawed, melon must be used immediately.

NECTARINES

Practically all varieties suitable for freezing.

Same procedure as for peaches.

PEACHES

Rating for freezing: Yellow, excellent. White, excellent — 1 to 1½ pounds yield approximately 1 pound.

Choose tree-ripened peaches. Peel, rather than scald peaches, doing only a few at a time.

Slice peaches directly into the polythene bag in which they are to be frozen.

Add sugar alternately with the peaches in proportion of 2 tablespoons sugar to 6 ounces peaches. Seal and freeze. This method helps to retard browning or oxidation of peaches.

Or, you may peel and slice about one quart at one time. Place in a bowl and sprinkle 1 tablespoon lemon juice over them to retard discolouring.

Add sugar in proportion of 2 tablespoons sugar to 6 ounces peaches. Turn peaches over and over in bowl with wooden spoon.

Handle gently. If you like, peaches may be packed in medium syrup in polythene bags or rigid containers.

Note: Sometimes, due to growing season and the variety of peaches selected for freezing, the peaches may discolour in spite of anything that can be done.

PEARS

(Not especially recommended for freezing.)

Rating for freezing: fair — 1 to 1¼ pounds yield approximately 1 pound.

Choose tree-ripened fruit. Wash, peel and cut to size wanted. Place peeled and cored fruit in a solution of 1 tablespoon lemon juice (or 1 tablespoon salt OR 1 teaspoon citric acid) to 1 quart of cold water. Drain on tray covered with several thicknesses of absorbent paper towels. Put tray in refrigerator to chill pears.

Put in polythene bags or rigid containers. Add medium syrup to cover pears completely. Seal and freeze.

PINEAPPLE

Rating for freezing: excellent. 1 pineapple yields approximately 12 to 14 slices.

An easy way to peel pineapple is to lay the fruit, on its side, on a good chopping board. Grasp the stem end with one hand. With a sharp knife, cut bottom end off pineapple. Place pineapple upright on the board and, while holding by stem, remove peel

by slicing downwards. When peel is removed, turn the pineapple onto its side and cut in ½-inch slices. Discard stem when last piece is sliced. Remove any "eyes" remaining in each slice. Cut out core.

These slices may be frozen whole. Place in freezer foil or in polythene bags. Pineapple may be grated and 2 tablespoons of sugar added to every 8 ounces. Or, a thin syrup may be used. Place in polythene bags or rigid containers. Seal. Freeze.

Note: If frozen pineapple is to be used in gelatine dessert, it must be brought to the boil and cooked a minute or two before using, otherwise gelatine will not set.

PLUMS

Rating for freezing: Plums, very good — Damsons, very good — 1¼ pounds yield approximately 1 pound.

Choose fully ripened fruit, not yet brown around the stone. Wash, sort, stem and cut in half, removing the stone. Drain on tray with several thicknesses of absorbent paper towels. Put tray in refrigerator to chill fruit.

Place fruit in bowl. Add sugar in proportion of 8 ounces sugar to 30 ounces fruit or use medium syrup. Put in polythene bags. Freeze.

RASPBERRIES

Rating for freezing: excellent. 1 pound fresh berries yields approximately 1 pound frozen ones.

Raspberries are exceptionally fragile. Great care should be used in washing them, as they bruise easily.

If possible, wash raspberries in water which has been cooled, with ice, to about 40°F. Wash only a few berries at a time and do not allow them to remain in the water more than 30 seconds.

Use the same procedure as strawberries (see below). Drain thoroughly. Then place berries on tray covered with several thicknesses of absorbent paper towels.

Put tray in refrigerator to cool and firm the fruit; takes about one hour.

Put raspberries in polythene bags or rigid containers. When container is ¼ filled with berries, add ¼ of the sugar (use proportion of 2 tablespoons sugar to 2 ounces raspberries). Continue alternately adding berries and sugar until container is filled. Seal. Freeze immediately.

Raspberries, continued

Raspberries make their own syrup when sugar is added. A pound of raspberries gives 4 portions.

RHUBARB

Rating for freezing: excellent. 1¼ pounds yield approximately 1 pound.

Freeze rhubarb as early in the spring as possible, before the rhubarb becomes tough and stringy.

Wash under running water. Remove stem and leaf end.

Cut in 1-inch pieces (cuts much easier with scissors). Drain. Put in polythene bags. Seal and freeze.

Rhubarb keeps beautifully without sugar or syrup. A quart makes one 9-inch pie.

STRAWBERRIES

Rating for freezing: excellent. 1¼ pounds yield approximately 1 pound.

Do not remove stem from fruit until after berries are washed. Sort and place in colander. Wash strawberries with a fine spray, if possible. If not, dip colander in large container filled with very cold water. Gently lift colander up and down in water two or three times. Drain thoroughly.

To remove stem, use a sharp paring knife. Do not squeeze stem off with fingers. Slip knife directly under the stem, taking care not to cut through into the centre of the fruit. Lever the stem off.

Place fruit on tray covered with several thicknesses of absorbent paper towels and put tray in refrigerator to chill the strawberries. Strawberries may be frozen in syrup or by adding sugar.

Add sugar in proportion of 2 tablespoons sugar to 8 ounces strawberries. The drained and cooled strawberries may be placed in a bowl and the sugar sprinkled over them, or they may be sweetened in container in which they are to be frozen. When container is ¼ full, add ¼ of the sugar, repeating until container is filled.

Put in polythene bags or rigid containers. Seal and freeze at once.

WATERMELON

Rating for freezing: any variety is fair for freezing if thoroughly ripened. Centres of melons are best to use.

Same as for melon.

Note: The freezer is an ideal place for quickly cooling a watermelon for picnics. Place whole melon in freezer for 3 or 4 hours.

Wash fruit in cold running water or use a gentle spray.

Use a sharp knife and gently remove strawberry stem.

Drain fruit on tray with absorbent paper towels.

Fruit may be sweetened by mixing with sugar before packing.

Sugar may be added alternately with fruit as it is packed.

Seal tightly by twisting polythene. Fasten with acetate bands.

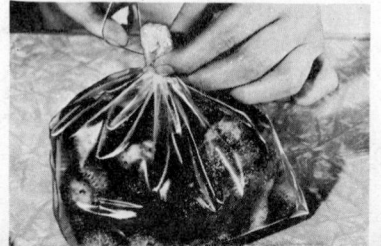

HOW TO PREPARE FROZEN FRUITS FOR SERVING

Always thaw fruit in the container or packet in which it was frozen. This usually requires about 2 to 3 hours at room temperature.

Do not open the container or packet until the fruit is nearly thawed since frozen fruit, once thawed, collapses quickly.

Remove from freezer only the quantity of fruit you plan to use at one time.

Frozen fruit cannot satisfactorily be refrozen once it is thawed.

How to Freeze Fresh Vegetables

When to Pick or Buy Vegetables

Choose only those which are in prime condition for freezing. As a rule, young vegetables have not fully developed all their sweetness and flavour. Old vegetables will neither taste good nor keep satisfactorily. The best time to pick vegetables is in the early morning when the dew is gone. Never pick vegetables at night and keep them in the refrigerator until the next day; they lose that garden-fresh flavour.

If you do not grow your own vegetables, buy freshly picked ones from local gardens or nearby markets. The vegetables you buy are satisfactory for freezing only if you *arrange to get them within an hour or two after picking*. Vegetables which have stood longer will not be as tender, nutritive or well-flavoured as garden-fresh ones. Freezing captures and preserves the flavour and goodness but it cannot improve them. Frozen foods come from the freezer only as good as when they were frozen.

Speed Is Essential

Use only as many vegetables as can be completely processed and placed in the freezer within two hours. The *"2 hours from vine to freezer"* rule is an excellent one to remember.

Wash, sort, scald, chill, drain, pack and freeze without wasting any time between steps.

Having all your supplies and materials ready before you begin is a big step towards accomplishing this "2-hour" rule.

Learn these steps, follow them closely and results will be excellent. Have all packing materials ready before you start freezing. It saves valuable time.

1. Pick vegetables in early morning, choosing the choice grades and only quantities that can be handled speedily.

2. Wash and sort vegetables carefully.

3. Scald according to directions for each vegetable.
4. Cool and drain quickly.
5. Pack in airtight containers.
6. Freeze at once.
7. Enter item in your freezer inventory file.

Which Vegetables to Choose

Most vegetables can be frozen satisfactorily. Exceptions: salad greens, celery, radishes, and whole tomatoes. Certain varieties of vegetables freeze better than others. Directions for freezing specific vegetables give a rating as to suitability for freezing. For success of freezing other varieties, consult the general enquiries department of your local office of the Ministry of Agriculture and Fisheries.

Wash and Sort Vegetables Carefully

Vegetables are prepared for freezing in much the same manner as for cooking. Wash carefully and thoroughly. While washing, sort for size and discard all inferior vegetables. For the best frozen vegetables, freeze only the choice fresh vegetables. Size-sorting of many vegetables (peas, beans, etc.) is important because you can obtain better uniformity.

Scald Vegetables Properly

Scalding is a must, never to be omitted! It retards enzymatic action, thus holding back the "growing process". Scalding "locks in" colour, preserves flavour and saves vitamins so that, when served, the vegetable is as fresh as it was when taken from the garden.

Scald only one pound of any vegetable at a time. Steam cannot penetrate evenly through large amounts. Too many vegetables scalded at once may cause an inferior product.

Steam Scalding

This is the best method.

Necessary Equipment: Any large utensil with a tight-fitting lid, a trivet or rack, and a fine-mesh wire basket. If a wire basket is not available, a metal colander with small perforations may be used. It must not interfere with the lid's tight fit. If neither basket nor colander is available, loosely tie the vegetables in muslin.

Procedure: Place rack in utensil. Add sufficient water to keep the utensil from boiling dry during scalding, but not enough to touch the vegetables.

Keep this water boiling vigorously throughout the entire scalding period.

Place vegetables in basket. When water is boiling violently, set basket in utensil and cover at once. Start counting scalding time when the lid is replaced.

Bain Marie Scalding

Necessary Equipment: Large utensil with tight-fitting lid, fine-mesh wire basket or muslin.

Procedure: Boil at least a gallon of water in the utensil. The water must boil briskly so that temperature will not drop when vegetables are added.

Place vegetables in wire basket or tie loosely in muslin. Lower into rapidly boiling water and cover immediately.

Start counting scalding time from the moment vegetables are placed in the boiling water.

Cool and Drain Quickly

Quick, effective cooling makes better frozen products. Draining is also most important. Moisture clinging to the vegetables when they are packed will form ice crystals and make it difficult to separate frozen vegetables when ready to cook.

Necessary Equipment: Large pan or sink filled with iced water, clean tea towels or absorbent paper towels.

Procedure: Immediately after scalding, cool vegetables quickly in iced water.

With small vegetables (peas, beans, etc.) leave vegetables in container used during scalding and immerse it in iced water. Move basket back and forth to speed the cooling.

Drain thoroughly by placing several thicknesses of absorbent paper towels on a tray. Carefully spread the vegetables on this. Shake tray slightly to bring all sides of vegetables in contact with paper.

Pack in Convenient Quantities

Determine the size containers that will best suit your family's needs. For instance, a pint carton of vegetables will usually give 3 large or 4 small portions. A quart carton will give from 6 to 8 portions. Containers larger than pints and quarts are not recommended for average-sized families because they waste valuable freezer space. Also food not eaten at one meal may be wasted as it is never advisable to refreeze thawed vegetables.

If freezing for a family of two, freeze in one polythene bag just enough to serve two persons and enclose several of these bags in a larger one. Mark number of smaller bags on outside of larger one.

Never Skimp on Packing

Buy only packing materials that are both moistureproof and vapourproof.

Glass freezing jars and outer cardboard cartons and foil dishes may be used over and over again.

Thick polythene bags may be washed and reused providing they are free from pricks and holes.

Plain tin cans, which can be sealed airtight, may also be used except for asparagus and spinach, which must be frozen in enamel or lacquer-lined cans.

Freezing always results in expansion of the food; therefore it is necessary to leave space at the top to allow for this expansion.

Pint cartons: $\frac{1}{2}$-inch space.
2-pint cartons: $\frac{3}{4}$-inch space.
Glass jars: 1- to $1\frac{1}{2}$-inch space.
Tin cans: 1-inch space.

Seal Carefully

Be sure all containers are airtight! To close polythene bags: Put food in bag. Then, starting at the bottom, *gently* press all the air out of the bag. When the top of the food is reached, twist the bag tightly several times. Loop the top of the bag over and secure tightly with either a piece of string, plastic-coated wire ties, or freezer tape. Rubber bands do not hold at low temperatures.

Freeze at Once

When containers are filled, sealed and labelled, place them immediately in the quick-freezing compartment of the freezer. If this is not practical, place them in freezer compartment of refrigerator until you are ready to load the freezer.

Never allow filled containers to stand at room temperature.

A Hint for Mothers of Small Children

When sorting vegetables such as green beans, peas, carrots, or beets, you will find some that are too old for freezing. Set these aside until after you have frozen the rest. These can be cooked, puréed, frozen, and used later for the baby and young children.

Here's how it's done: Steam the vegetable until it is well cooked—not overcooked. Purée in a blender or by forcing through a sieve. Thoroughly cool the puréed vegetable.

After vegetable is cool, pour into refrigerator ice cube tray with the dividers in place. Freeze. When cubes are firmly frozen, remove them from the tray and wrap one or two cubes, enough for an individual portion, in small polythene bags.

To serve: Heat cubes in a covered saucepan. Start with low heat until food is thawed.

How to Prepare Vegetables for Freezing

ASPARAGUS

(Do not use iron utensil, as it will discolour asparagus.)

Rating for freezing: excellent—1½ pounds yield approximately 1 pound.

Scalding time:

Small Spears
By steam, 5 minutes.
By boiling water, 3 minutes.

Large Spears
By steam, 6 minutes.
By boiling water, 4 minutes.

Wash thoroughly. Discard all woody portions. Sort by size of root end.

Cut stalks correct length to fit polythene bag—usually about 5 inches for -pint-sized bag.

If you are planning to wrap asparagus in freezer foil, it is not necessary o cut all stalks a specific length.

Remove all scales by slipping sharp nife under scale and snipping off. and collects under these scales. Also, weetness of frozen product is much mproved if scales are removed. Do ot bruise stem.

When scalding, stand asparagus with ps up. Cool and drain. Pack stalks arallel in polythene bags or freezer oil. placing heads in opposite directions. Freeze at once.

AUBERGINE

Rating for freezing: good—1½ to 2 ounds yield approximately 1 pound.

calding time:

By steam, 5 minutes.
By boiling water, 4 minutes.

Choose ripe aubergines. Peel and ut into about ½-inch slices.

If boiling water method of scalding s used, add 4½ teaspoons pure citric cid to 1 gallon of water.

If steam method is used, add same mount of citric acid, or 3 tablespoons emon juice, to cooling water.

Put through another cold water inse. Drain.

Place polythene between each slice. ack in polythene bags or freezer foil. reeze.

BEANS, BROAD

Rating for freezing: excellent—2 to 2½ pounds in pods yield approximately 1 pound.

Scalding time:

Baby Broad Beans
By steam, 5 minutes.
By boiling water, 3 minutes.

Large Broad Beans
By steam, 6 minutes.
By boiling water, 4 minutes.

Wash pods, shell beans. Sort for size. Old beans are not recommended for freezing. Scald, cool and drain. Pack in polythene bags. Freeze.

Beans still in their pods may be scalded in boiling water for 1 minute longer than shelled beans. Then cool, shell, drain, sort and pack in polythene bags. Freeze.

BEANS, GREEN

(Do not use iron utensil as it will discolour beans.)

Rating for freezing: excellent—⅔ to 1 pound yields approximately ¾ pound.

Scalding time:

By steam, 5 minutes.
By boiling water, 3 minutes.

Wash thoroughly. Sort for size. Remove the stem end. Leave blossom end on; it is particularly rich in vitamins and minerals.

For quick preparation, grasp as many beans as can be easily held in one hand. With small, sharp knife held in other hand, snip off stem ends. Cut in 1-inch pieces.

Do not scald small and large beans together. Cool, drain, pack and freeze. Pack in polythene bags.

BEETROOT

Rating for freezing: good—1¼ pounds, without tops, yield approximately 1 pound.

Scalding time:

Young tender beetroots, up to 1½ inches in diameter, 3 minutes submerged in boiling water. **All other beetroots,** cook until tender.

Wash thoroughly before scalding or cooking. Immediately after scalding, cool beetroot and remove skin.

Small beetroot may be frozen whole. Large beetroots may be sliced, diced or quartered.

Cool, drain on absorbent paper towels, pack in polythene bags. Freeze.

BROCCOLI

Rating for freezing: excellent—2 pounds yield approximately 1 pound.

Scald not more than one pound of any vegetable at one time.

Cool vegetable quickly by immersing in iced water.

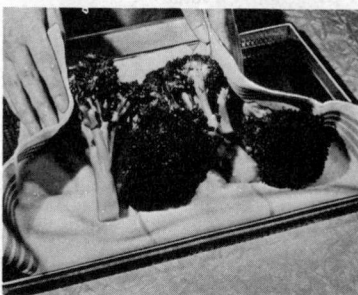
Drain vegetable thoroughly on absorbent paper towels.

Pack in polythene bag and gently force out any air pockets. Seal securely. Freeze immediately.

Scalding time:

Medium-Sized Pieces
By steam, 5 minutes.
By boiling water, 3 minutes.

Large Pieces
By steam, 6 minutes.
By boiling water, 5 minutes.

Choose compact heads of uniform colour. Immerse broccoli for ½ hour in a solution of salt water to remove any insects. Use 8 ounces salt to 1 gallon of water. Wash carefully.

Remove woody portions. Separate heads in convenient size for packing.

Scald, cool and drain. Pack in freezer foil or polythene bags. Freeze.

BRUSSELS SPROUTS

Rating for freezing: excellent — $1\frac{1}{2}$ pounds yields approximately 1 pound.

Scalding time:

By steam, 5 minutes.
By boiling water, 4 minutes.

Sprouts should be firm and dark green in colour.

Immerse in salt water as for broccoli. Remove stem. If wilted, remove the outer leaves.

Scald, cool, drain, pack in polythene bags. Freeze. Allow 5 to 6 sprouts per portion.

CARROTS

Rating for freezing: excellent — $1\frac{1}{4}$ to $1\frac{1}{2}$ pounds yield approximately 1 pound.

Scalding time:

Sliced
By steam, 4 minutes.
By boiling water, 2 minutes.

Whole
By steam, 5 minutes.
By boiling water, 3 minutes.

Choose only young, small carrots. Never attempt to freeze carrots which have grown to full maturity.

Wash and scrape. Sort for size. Scald, cool, drain and pack in polythene bags.

Alternate top and tip of whole carrots when packing. Seal and freeze.

CAULIFLOWER

Rating for freezing: good — 1 pound yields approximately 1 pound.

Scalding time

By steam, 4 minutes.
By boiling water, 3 minutes.

Choose compact, tender white heads. Trim and cut in pieces about 1 inch thick, or break small flowerets in medium-sized pieces.

Sometimes it is necessary to immerse cauliflower in a salt solution (as for broccoli) to remove insects.

Allow 5 to 6 medium pieces for each serving.

Scald, cool, drain and pack in polythene bags. Remove as much air as possible from the packet. Freeze.

Corn on the cob frozen at the peak of summertime perfection is undeniably a treat on a winter menu. The prepared corn may be wrapped individually in freezer wrap, and taped securely.

CORN ON THE COB

(Follow directions and corn will be just like fresh-picked.)
Rating for freezing: excellent.

Scalding time:

By boiling water — ears $1\frac{1}{2}$ to 2 inches at base, 8 minutes.
Larger ears require 11 minutes.

Choose corn with kernels well formed, while milk is thin and sweet.

With a sharp knife, cut a section about $\frac{1}{2}$ inch wide from both ends. Husks will come off easier. Remove the husk corn and silk (fine whispy strands).

If necessary, wash corn. Sort for size.

Scald for length of time indicated and cool in iced water the same length of time. Drain.

Pack in freezer foil or polythene bags according to your family's serving needs, with not more than 6 ears to a packet. Freeze.

CORN, WHOLE KERNEL

Rating for freezing: Same as corn on the cob. 6 ears yield approximately 1 pound when cut from cob.

Scalding time:
Same as for corn on the cob.

Scald corn. Cool. To remove kernels from cob: Impale base end of cob on large nail driven through a small square of wood.

Place the wood in flat dish or on two thicknesses of greaseproof paper.

Cut corn from cob, holding knife not flat but at a sharp angle.

Examine kernels carefully, removing any bits of silk. Pack in polythene bags. Freeze.

GREENS
(Spinach, Kale, Chard and Other Greens)

Rating for freezing: Spinach, good. Kale, excellent. Chard, excellent. 1 to $1\frac{1}{2}$ pounds yield approximately 1 pound.

Spinach, Kale, Chard
Scalding time:

By steam, $2\frac{1}{2}$ minutes. Best metho Use wire basket, if possible.
By boiling water, 2 minutes.

Use 2 gallons of water for ea pound of greens.

Choose young, tender greens. Di card all bruised leaves and cut o stems before washing.

Wash several times in water. L leaves from one pan of water to th other; don't pour off water — it ma leave sand on the leaves.

Scald only a small amount of greer at one time; use a wire basket if po sible, particularly for spinach. Drai

Complete draining of spinach is in possible, some water will remain o the leaves.

If these recommendations are fo lowed, there will be little matting greens. Do not use pressure whe packing. Polythene bags are excelle for greens of all kinds. Freeze.

MUSHROOMS

Scalding time:

Button Size — Steam 3 minutes.

Medium Size — Steam 4 minutes.

Sliced — Steam 3 minutes.

Warning: Unless you are complete familiar with wild mushrooms and ca accurately identify edible ones, neve attempt to freeze them.

Mushrooms must be handled quick to prevent blackening.

Wash thoroughly. Remove toug portion of stem. Scald, cool quick and drain.

Pack in polythene bags. Start free ing immediately to avoid darkening.

OKRA

Rating for freezing: good — $1\frac{1}{2}$ pound yield approximately 1 pound.

Scalding time:

Small to Medium Pods — Steam minutes. This is the only metho recommended for okra.

Choose young, tender pods. Scru thoroughly. Rinse.

Remove stem end but do not cu into seed section. Care in cutting pre vents the sticky juice from oozing ou

Scald, cool and drain. Pack tightl in polythene bags, alternating top an tip ends. Freeze.

PEAS, GREEN

Rating for freezing: excellent — $1\frac{1}{2}$ t 2 pounds yield approximately 1 poun

Peas, continued
Scalding time:
By steam, 3 minutes.
By boiling water, 1 minute.

Choose peas that are tender and are not fully grown.

Wash pods before shelling. Discard all tiny and wrinkled peas while shelling. If pods are very full and difficult to shell, plunge pods in boiling water for 1 minute, then cool at once in ice water.

Scalding the pods does not take the place of scalding the peas. Scald, cool, drain and pack in polythene bags. Freeze at once.

PEPPERS, GREEN

Rating for freezing: very good.
Sliced or Diced: Do not scald! Wash carefully, remove stem end and seeds.

Slice or dice and pack in small polythene bags in amounts you will use at one time. Several small bags may be packed in a pound or 2-pound carton. Freeze at once.

Halved for Stuffing: Cut green pepper in half, lengthways. Remove stem end and seeds.

Scald in boiling water 2 minutes. Cool in ice water, drain well.

When packing, separate halves with polythene, place in polythene bags. Freeze immediately.

SQUASH, COURGETTES AND MARROW

Rating for freezing: excellent—1 pound yields approximately 1 pound.
Scalding time:
By steam, 3 minutes.
Select squash or marrow not fully ripe. Outer skin should be easily punctured with fingernail.

Wash thoroughly. Use a vegetable brush to remove dirt lodged in crevices.

Remove stem end. Do not peel. Cut in ½- to 1-inch slices. Do not remove seeds.

Scald. Cool 1½ to 2 minutes. To avoid longer soaking, use quantities of ice in the water.

Drain carefully. Pack in polythene bags. Freeze.

SUCCOTASH

Prepare sweetcorn and broad beans as given under directions for each. Use baby beans only.

Steam corn first, and while it is cooling and being cut from cob, scald and cool the beans.

Mix together in equal portions. Pack in polythene bags. Freeze.

HOW TO PREPARE FROZEN VEGETABLES FOR SERVING

All vegetables—*except* corn on the cob and aubergine—are best cooked from the frozen state.

Break frozen vegetables into 3 or 4 chunks before placing in pan. Add about 4 tablespoons water. Salt to taste.

Cook about ⅓ to ½ of the time recommended for fresh vegetables. Frozen vegetables are scalded before freezing, so need less cooking time.

Corn on the cob and aubergine should be thawed before cooking. Thaw at room temperature. Thawing requires about 20 minutes for aubergine; 2 hours for corn on the cob.

Cook corn in boiling water 4 to 5 minutes.

Prepare aubergine according to your favourite method.

Caution: Do not overcook vegetables, either frozen or fresh. Overcooking causes loss of colour and flavour, as well as vitamins.

How to Freeze Meats, Poultry and Game

Freezing meat is quite easy. Only a few simple rules must be followed to assure a delicious product.

Which Meats to Choose

When choosing meats for freezing, choose joints which will produce the weight and quality of cuts preferred by the family.

Excessive fatness is unnecessary, but an ample fat covering is desirable and protects the lean from drying out during frozen storage. This does not apply to veal since it rarely has surplus fat.

Whenever possible choose good quality meat, as this will be less affected by the process of freezing than inferior cuts and joints. If in doubt, ask your butcher's advice before deciding.

Proper Wrapping of Meat Is Important

The quality of frozen meat is partly determined by the proper selection of wrapping material and the method of wrapping.

Improper wrapping results in "drying out" of meat and game which affects both the appearance and flavour. This condition is called "freezer burn".

It is unwise to attempt to economize on wrapping materials. Ordinary greaseproof paper, or grocery bags must never be used.

Polythene bags secured with freezer tape is best. Aluminium foil or freezer paper is also satisfactory.

If a bone protrudes, use a double thickness of polythene as "padding" over the bone, then wrap the whole piece of meat in freezer foil. Be sure to work as much air as possible out of the packets before sealing.

Wrapping of meat is simple, yet requires care. Wrappings for meats must be moistureproof, easy to handle, tough enough to resist tearing and easy to label.

Keep meat cool both during and immediately after wrapping.

When wrapping, the polythene or foil must be pulled tightly around the meat to eliminate all possible air. The finished packet should be smooth and firmly packed to conserve storage space.

Place two sheets of polythene between chops, steaks, or hamburgers (if they are to be wrapped together) to facilitate separating them when ready to use. This also makes it easier to grill or fry meat from the frozen state.

As a rule, each packet should contain the meat needed for a single meal for the family.

Chill Meat Thoroughly

Meat should be chilled as soon as the carcass has been prepared. Chilling removes body heat and arrests the destructive growth of bacteria, moulds and yeasts which multiply rapidly at temperatures about 70°F., but slowly at temperatures between 30°F. and 40°F. Improper chilling may ruin the flavour of the meat or even make it unfit for use.

Cut Meat to Family Preferences

Again, this is no job for the novice. Most butchers or suppliers have expert meat cutters. Specify the cuts your family enjoys most and have the meat cut in family-sized portions. This eliminates waste.

Boning meat is recommended because less storage space is required and the danger of bones puncturing the wrapping is eliminated.

Label Clearly

After the meat is packed, the next important step is proper labelling. Write on the packet the kind of meat enclosed, the approximate number of servings and the date of the packing. If meat is to be used with a definite recipe, label accordingly.

Start Freezing Immediately

Just as soon as the meat is packed and labelled, it should be placed in the freezer. If this is not practical, place the packets in the freezer compartment of your refrigerator until ready to load the freezer. Do not allow packed meat to remain at room temperature any longer than is absolutely necessary.

Do Not Refreeze
Thawed Uncooked Meat

Never refreeze thawed uncooked meat! The meat will still be good but some of the flavour will be lost. Uncooked meat, that you wish to refreeze, must be cooked first.

A Guide to Remember: Meat may be frozen successfully once when raw and once after it has been cooked.

Preparing a Carcass

For high quality meat it is imperative that the carcass be properly prepared and chilled. Few people, except skilled butchers, know how to do this correctly.

If weather is not cold enough to do a proper job of chilling, make advance arrangements to have the cleaned and dressed carcass removed immediately to a chilling room. The temperature of slaughtered meat is about 100°F. and body temperature of the carcass must be reduced to between 33°F. and 40°F. within 24 hours after slaughtering.

BEEF

Beef should be aged, but that is a job for the expert. Ageing or ripening tenderizes and improves the flavour of the beef. Prime beef with a one-inch coating of fat all over should be aged a little longer than the poorer qualities of beef.

If the beef carcass is from a reasonably young, well-bred and well-fed animal, the sirloin and rump can be cut into satisfactory steaks and the first cuts of the rib and shoulder are usually sufficiently tender to be cooked as oven roasts.

If the animal was old and thin, even the rump steaks may not be sufficiently tender for grilling or frying, but should be cut for braising.

If there is any doubt as to the suitability of the meat for various cuts and methods of cooking, it is advisable to ask your butcher or supplier, who will help you.

Roasts are usually boned and rolled to save space. Also the bone may be removed from the rump.

Less-tender cuts such as shin, shank, brisket, neck and flank are most often boned, then minced, or cut into one-inch cubes without gristle or too much fat, and packed in suitable amounts for stews and casserole dishes.

Mince is not salted before freezing. If it is to be grilled or fried, make into patties before wrapping. A pound of meat makes 6 generous-sized hamburgers. If this is done before freezing, it is not necessary to thaw the hamburgers before cooking.

The liver may be sliced before freezing. The heart and tongue may be cleaned and frozen whole.

Packing and wrapping beef is same as for all meats. Freeze at once.

LAMB

Lamb may have a fat covering which is comparable to beef. Since it comes from an animal which is less than a year old, any longer than a five-day holding or ageing period would result in excessive shrinkage.

The weight of the dressed carcass is usually about half that of the live animal.

As with all other meat, rapid chilling is extremely important. Since the lamb is small, the temperature of the carcass should reach between 33°F. and 40°F. in 24 hours or less. Longer first chilling is apt to destroy the fine flavour of the meat.

Lamb is packed as other meats. Label and freeze at once.

VEAL

The calf should weigh from 110 to 200 pounds. As with beef, it is desirable to cut veal to suit the immediate needs of the family.

The veal carcass will yield about 80 to 90 pounds of roasts, chops, stew and mince.

The hindquarter of the veal is cut into rump, loin, buttock and flank.

The forequarter is cut into shank, shoulder, and breast. The loin may be cut into chops.

The rump, shoulder and breast may be boned, rolled and tied for roasting.

Approximate Yield of Beef Carcass

Live weight			750 lbs.
Whole carcass			420 lbs.

Trimmed cuts from whole carcass:	Live Weight	Carcass Weight	
Steaks and oven roasts	23%	40%	172 lbs.
Pot roasts	11%	20%	83 lbs.
Stews and minced meat	11%	20%	83 lbs.
	45%	80%	338 lbs.*

Forequarters will yield:			
Steaks and oven roasts		25%	55 lbs.
Pot roasts		32%	70 lbs.
Stews and minced meat		27%	59 lbs.
		84%	184 lbs.

Hindquarters will yield:			
Steaks, oven roasts and pot roasts		58%	117 lbs.
Stews and minced meat		18%	37 lbs.
		76%	154 lbs.

*The loss of 82 pounds between the actual yield of finished product and the dressed carcass is due to bones which are removed before packaging, plus normal shrinkage, fat and meat trimming, and the liver, tongue and heart. To conserve freezer space, it is advisable to remove as much bone as possible as well as unnecessary fat.

The flanks and shanks are usually minced.

Veal is slaughtered and prepared as for beef. However, because veal has little or no fat, it is packed immediately after the chilling period is finished, and does not go through any ageing process.

Veal must be chilled to 33°F. to 40°F. within 24 hours after slaughtering.

Veal should be packed or wrapped immediately after chilling. Freeze at once.

PORK

Pork is a highly perishable meat, and great care must be exercised in preparing the carcass after the pig is slaughtered.

Pork may sour in 12 hours if hung in warm air temperatures; therefore, *rapid chilling is essential*. The carcass must cool to between 33F. and 40°F. in a maximum of 24 hours.

Immediately after the chilling, the carcass should be cut, wrapped and frozen.

Pork does not require ageing; on the contrary, the speedier pork can be frozen after chilling, the better the quality of the frozen meat.

When to Butcher Pork

On the farm, butchering should be done when the weather is as favourable as possible. Temperatures between 33°F. and 40°F. are best.

Should the weather be extremely cold, hang the carcass in a shed and protect it from freezing by wrapping in a sheet.

If the pig is butchered in warm weather, and chilling facilities are not available at home, arrangements should be made with your local butcher or meat market to hang the carcass in their chilling rooms immediately after the carcass is cut and cleaned. These arrangements should be made in advance.

Approximate Yield of Pork Carcass

		Live Weight	Carcass Weight	
Live weight				225 lbs.
Whole carcass				176 lbs.
Trimmed cuts:				
Hams, legs, loins, shoulders, and fillet		40%	50%	90 lbs.
Belly, spare ribs, trotters and sausages		15%	20%	34 lbs.
		55%	70%	124 lbs.
Lard, rendered		12%	15%	27 lbs.

Cutting the Pork

As with beef, pork should be cut in family-sized pieces.

Chops should be cut to the right size for frying.

The legs are usually cured, but the shoulders may be sliced ready for frying, or cut into roasts.

Spare ribs consume considerable room in a storage compartment due to their bony structure. However, frozen spare ribs are excellent and keep as satisfactorily as any other portion of the pig.

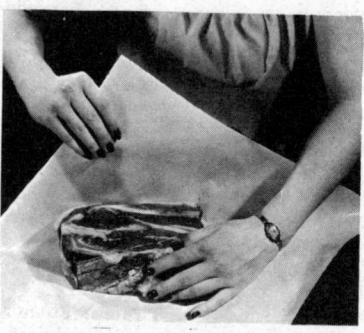

If you cannot use polythene bags to wrap meat for the freezer, use a suitable wrapping and make certain the meat is well wrapped and sealed. Fasten the loose ends securely with freezer tape. Label with date, kind of meat, cut, and number of servings or weight. Freeze quickly, and store at 0°F. or lower.

Such meats as pork chops and lamb chops will retain their natural flavour and moisture content longer if cut thick for freezing.

Store meats in small packets wherever possible. They freeze more quickly and thus retain more of their original quality.

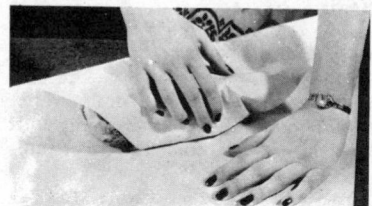

Quality meat properly wrapped, frozen, and stored should come out of the freezer juicy, full of flavour, and bright in colour.

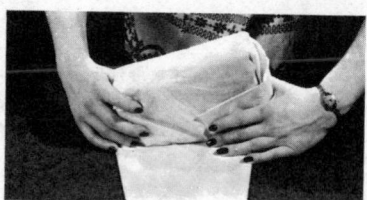

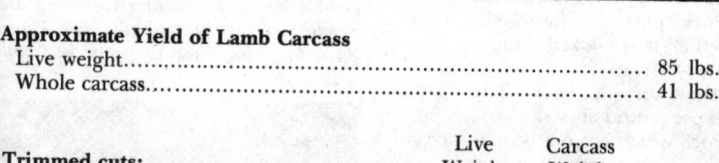

Approximate Yield of Lamb Carcass

	Live Weight	Carcass Weight	
Live weight			85 lbs.
Whole carcass			41 lbs.
Trimmed cuts:			
Legs, chops, shoulders	37%	75%	31 lbs.
Breast and neck	8%	15%	7 lbs.
	45%	90%	38 lbs.

SAUSAGE, CURED HAMS, BACON

These pork products do not freeze well and should not be kept over 3 weeks. The salt used as a seasoning and preservative activates oxidation which, in turn, results in rancidity.

Sausage

Freezing seasoned sausage is a controversial subject. Many authorities state that sausage is the only meat which may be seasoned before freezing. Seasoning includes the addition of salt, black pepper, red pepper, sage, smoking or the addition of cereals. Some authorities believe smoking improves flavour, stabilizes colour, partially sterilizes the meat, improves appearance, increases tenderness, prevents rancidity and drives off up to 20% of the water.

Cured Hams and Bacon

Cured hams may be frozen either sliced or whole. Bacon also may be frozen, but does not adapt itself as well to freezing as ham.

If the bacon is sliced before freezing, dehydration may occur.

If the supply of bacon is greater than can be used within a limited time, it may be desirable to freeze a portion of it.

It is advisable to cut the smoked bacon into 1- or 2-pound slabs, wrap, freeze, take out packets as needed and slice after thawing.

RABBITS

Freeze rabbits in much the same way as poultry.

Immediately after killing, skin, cut off head and remove entrails. The carcass should then be thoroughly and carefully washed, chilled and cut into pieces for cooking.

Pack as for chicken fricassée.

VENISON

Prepare, pack and freeze the same way as beef or veal.

How Long May Meat Be Kept at 0°F.?

This also is a controversial subject and depends upon many factors, such as proper slaughtering, chilling, ageing, wrapping and the speed with which the meat starts on its way to being frozen, after wrapping. However, the following times are recommended at 0°F.:

Product	Storage Period
Mince	1 to 3 months
Fresh pork and fish	3 to 6 months
Lamb and veal	6 to 9 months
Beef and poultry	6 to 12 months

HOW TO COOK FROZEN MEATS

There are two satisfactory methods of cooking frozen meats: (1) remove from frozen storage, unwrap and cook from the frozen state or (2) thaw before cooking the meat.

Cooking meats from the frozen state is better as there is a minimum loss of weight and juices, resulting in better flavour and a more tender piece of meat, but it is necessary to add extra minutes to the cooking time.

Roasting: A five-pound roast thaws completely in about 24 hours at room temperature.

If placed in the food compartment of a refrigerator, it requires from 36 to 48 hours to thaw.

If roasts are thawed, and if there is any doubt of the complete thawing of the meat, allow longer roasting time than for fresh meat.

In roasting meat from the frozen state, add an additional 15 to 20 minutes per pound of meat.

The ideal method is to place the meat in the oven immediately after removing from the freezer.

When the meat is completely thawed, place a meat thermometer through the thickest part and cook by temperature. The meat thermometer is the most accurate method of cooking meat whether it is frozen or fresh.

Grilling: Grilling steaks from the frozen state requires an additional 10 to 15 minutes per side, depending on how well cooked you want them.

From tests which we have conducted, we have found grilling from the frozen state gives a juicier and better-flavoured steak.

Caution About Cooking Pork

Pork must be thoroughly cooked whether it is cooked from the frozen or thawed state.

Allow an additional 15 to 20 minutes per pound of pork.

Pork which has not been thoroughly cooked can cause an infection called trichinosis. There is some belief that freezing kills trichinae, but until that fact is definitely proved, frozen pork should be given the same thorough cooking as fresh pork.

WRAPPING HAMBURGERS WIT POLYTHENE

1. Separate hamburgers with sma pieces of Pliofilm, turn stack on its side and place diagonally on the large oute piece of Pliofilm. Smooth the back corne of Pliofilm forward across the ham burgers as closely as possible.

2. Fold in each side in turn, pressing snugly to the meat to eliminate as much air as possible. Be sure to use enough Pliofilm to allow for a sufficien overlap as each corner is folded into place.

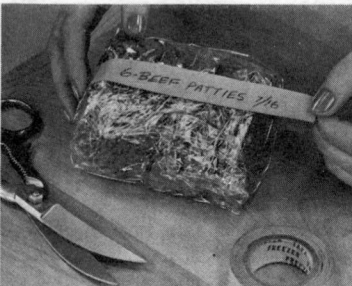

3. After sides are folded in, bring up the remaining corner, pulling it up tightly. Seal with freezer tape and label. Wrapping in this way makes individual hamburgers easy to remove if you do not need them all at one time.

Time-saver hint: When making meat loaf for a family dinner, prepare a double or triple quantity. Freeze the remainder as individual meat loaves in a bun tin. Pack singly or in family size units.

The same basic guides for success in freezing meat also apply to the freezing of poultry. All kinds of poultry may be frozen, but freeze only birds of high quality.

POULTRY

Wrap Poultry Carefully

Poultry must be protected so that it will not lose moisture or flavour during freezing or storage.

Poorly wrapped birds dry out and are tough and dry when cooked. This condition is often referred to as "freezer burn."

Birds may also become rancid or take on foreign flavours if not properly wrapped.

Aluminium Foil (recommended) — Can be smoothed to conform to the shape of the bird, thus eliminating air pockets. Use outer wrap for extra protection.

Polythene (recommended) — Wrap polythene sheets or bags carefully round the bird and force out any air pockets which might form during wrapping. Secure tightly. Use outer wrap of waxed or plastic-lined bags for extra protection.

Cut-Up Poultry

Cut-up poultry can be packed in aluminium foil and polythene bags to form a neat, compact packet.

To Freeze Giblets

Clean giblets thoroughly and package in polythene bags for freezing.

Seal Securely

Inner wrappings should be securely sealed with freezer tape or wire ties.

Protective sheet wrappings should also be sealed with freezer tape.

Aluminium foil is sealed securely if edges are tightly folded and pressed firmly against bird. No further sealing is necessary.

Label Clearly

With china marking pencil or waterproof ink, indicate kind of poultry, how prepared, weight and date of freezing.

Thaw Poultry Before Stuffing

Frozen poultry must be thawed completely before stuffing.

It may be thawed in one of three ways: (1) at room temperature, (2) in the refrigerator for slow defrosting, or (3) in a 300°F. Mark 2 oven for quickest defrosting.

Do not soak frozen poultry in water to speed thawing.

A whole chicken requires 6 to 8 hours to thaw at room temperature or 3 to 5 hours per pound if thawed in the main food compartment of refrigerator.

An average-sized turkey requires 24 to 36 hours to thaw at room temperature. This same turkey will thaw in about 2 hours in a 300°F. Mark 2 oven.

Caution When Freezing Poultry

Warning: Poultry (chicken, duck, turkey, and other birds) should never be stuffed before it is frozen!

Extensive research has shown that three different organisms which are frequently found in poultry can cause extreme illness—even death. While it is true that a sufficiently high oven temperature will destroy most of these organisms, the thawing time of a frozen stuffed bird is so slow that it makes a perfect "breeding ground" for these bacteria.

Therefore, you are advised that all poultry be frozen without stuffing—and then, after thawing, the bird may be stuffed just before it is placed in the oven for roasting.

It is also advisable to use a dry stuffing in preference to a moist one.

The stuffing may be made the evening before it is to be used, and stored in the refrigerator overnight.

The frozen bird, if kept at room temperature overnight, will be thawed sufficiently by morning for easy stuffing. In this way, the bird may be stuffed quickly on the morning it is to be roasted.

Note: Commercially frozen stuffed turkeys are frozen under carefully controlled conditions which cannot be duplicated in the home and hence are safe to use. Follow the cooking directions on the wrapper. *Do not thaw commercially frozen stuffed poultry before cooking.*

HOW TO COOK FROZEN POULTRY

For Frying or Fricassée: Frozen pieces of chicken or young turkey may be rolled in seasoned flour and fried immediately without any preliminary thawing. Or, pieces may be thawed and fried the same as unfrozen chicken.

For Stewing: Remove wrapping and place frozen chicken in a large pan. Cover with boiling water and cook as unfrozen chicken.

For Grilling: Grill without any preliminary thawing. Put grill pan at least 5 inches away from heat.

Allow 20 to 30 additional minutes for each half chicken.

Otherwise, thaw chickens overnight and cook as unfrozen chickens.

WRAPPING POULTRY FOR FREEZING

1. Wrap giblets separately and place in centre of polythene. Arrange legs and wings round them.

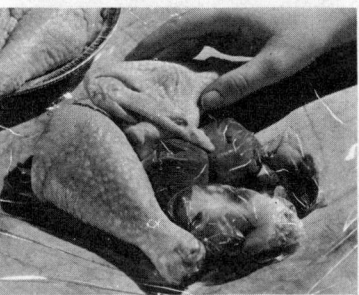

2. Fit thighs, breast, and back pieces neatly together on top. Fold the polythene down tightly.

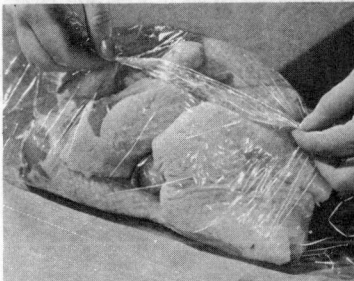

3. Fold in ends of polythene and seal with freezer tape. Label with type of poultry and date.

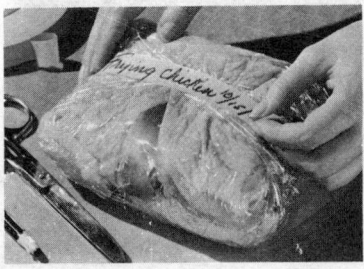

How to Freeze Fish and Shellfish

Fish is an exceptionally perishable food. Contamination by bacteria from the air and water begins within a few hours after it is caught.

Chilling fish with ice or placing in the household refrigerator retards bacterial action but does not prevent it. Organisms which attack fish normally live at lower temperatures than those which attack meats. Speed in preparing and freezing fish is, therefore, essential.

The storage period for frozen fish is relatively short. One to three months usually is considered the maximum.

Selection for Freezing

Fish that contain a high fat content, such as salmon, mackerel, carp, and herring, do not keep as long or as satisfactorily as the non-oily varieties, such as halibut, haddock, and trout.

Preparation for Freezing

Fish to be frozen should be prepared for freezing immediately after catching. Or, in case of delay, it should be promptly packed in quantities of ice.

Prepare as for cooking. Remove fins, tails, entrails, and scales, if any. Fillet large fish. Rinse or dip in salt water, about 8 ounces pickling salt to 1 gallon of water.

Individual portions of fish are more convenient to use if first wrapped in polythene or aluminium foil.

To prevent any possible exchange of odours with other foods during storage, the individually wrapped packets should be wrapped in a second layer of aluminium foil, or polythene bags.

Two pieces of polythene between the individual fillets or slices of fish will not only aid the retention of the original quality, but facilitate handling when preparing for cooking.

Place two sheets of polythene between fish fillets so they will be easy to separate when frozen.

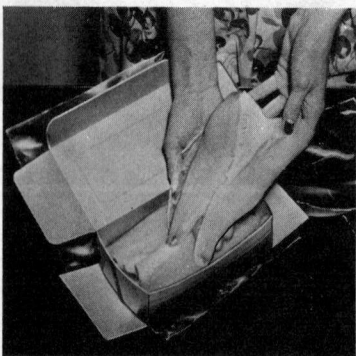

HOW TO FREEZE CRABS AND LOBSTERS

In parts of the country where crabs and lobsters are available, it is often desirable to freeze their meat. Frozen meat is excellent and makes delicious salads.

Lobsters are handled the same way as crabs.

1. Use only live crabs.
2. Remove back shell. (Note: Iced or chilled crabs will be less active than those fresh out of the water.)
3. Eviscerate and wash. Be sure to remove the jelly-like substance which is the newly forming shell.
4. Break crabs in half. Pre-cook by placing in a pressure cooker, a steamer or a large pan containing an inch of vigorously boiling water.

When using a pressure cooker, let out steam from petcock 7 to 10 minutes, then tighten the petcock and raise the pressure to 2 pounds. Cook for 12 to 15 minutes.

When using a steamer or large pan, count the time from when steam flutters the lid or escapes rapidly. Steam the crabs 20 to 22 minutes.

5. Remove meat. A small amount of cold water may be used to cool down a few crabs to start with, but it is better if the meat does not come in contact with water at this point. Keep leg and body meat separate to facilitate packing.
6. Pack meat for freezing in rigid containers or polythene-lined containers.
7. Cover meat with a salt brine (1 level tablespoon of salt to 1½ pints of water), leaving space at the top for expansion. Seal.
8. Freeze immediately.

Optional Method for Killing and Cooking

Live crabs may be killed and cooked by dropping into a large amount of vigorously boiling salted water and boiling 20 to 25 minutes.

The method outlined above, however (killing and cleaning before cooking), is preferred, since it produces a better-tasting meat.

HOW TO FREEZE CLAMS

1. Rinse off external sand, if necessary, by washing under cold running water.
2. Place clams in cold water to which salt has been added in the proportion of 3 ounces (about 4 tablespoons) to each gallon of water. Allow to stand for about an hour so that the clams

will clean themselves of most of the sand held within the body.

3. Open the clams as follows in order of preference:

  a. Remove shells from raw clams, saving liquid.

  b. Steam open, keeping the pan steaming until majority of shells open.

  c. Immerse in boiling water for 2 to 3 minutes to open shells.

4. Wash clams well under running water, having slit the neck lengthways to remove any dirt, sand and stomach contents. Drain off excess water.
5. If you like, the necks may be cut off, minced and packed separately for use in chowder.
6. Pack body, whole or minced, in glass freezing jars, waxed tubs or polythene-lined cartons.

Cover with clam liquid. A salt solution (1 level tablespoon to a quart of water) may be substituted for the clam liquid.

The clam meat should be thoroughly covered with the liquid or brine to prevent "freezer burn" and off-flavour development during storage. Leave space at the top for expansion. Seal well.

7. Freeze.

Note: If there is any question about "mussel poisoning" or "clam poisoning" during the late spring or summer months, consult the nearest local or county health officer.

HOW TO FREEZE OYSTERS

Oysters are more susceptible to various types of spoilage than are some of the other seafoods. They must be handled with care and *as rapidly as possible.*

Assemble everything needed before starting.

1. Use only live oysters.
2. Wash under cold running water to remove external debris from shell.
3. Open them raw in usual way, saving oyster liquid.
4. Wash thoroughly in salt brine (1 level tablespoon salt to 1½ pints of water).

Leave oysters in brine for one hour but no longer.

5. Drain off excess water or brine.
6. Package in polythene carton, waxed tubs or glass jars.
7. Cover surface with oyster liquid to prevent exposure to air. Leave space at the top for expansion.
8. Seal and freeze.

HOW TO COOK FROZEN FISH AND SHELLFISH

Fish is best when cooked from the frozen state. Cook just as you would unfrozen fish but allow a little extra time.

For stews, chowders and soups, seafood is cooked from the frozen state.

For use in hors d'oeuvre and salads, or for frying, seafood is thawed in food compartment of the refrigerator. Thaw in sealed freezing container in which seafood was frozen.

How to Freeze Dairy Products

HOW TO FREEZE EGGS

Eggs are among the most satisfactory of all foods to freeze. They keep well for 6 to 8 months and, when used, it is impossible to tell them from fresh eggs.

The volume of the frozen egg white is equal to fresh egg whites and, if frozen properly, they continue to keep their fresh taste.

There is one important fact to remember when freezing eggs. They must be strictly fresh, for the frozen product is only as good as the fresh or original product.

However, we do not recommend freezing quantities of eggs in one container, unless that full amount will be used at once when the eggs are removed from the freezer.

Eggs do not last long after they have thawed and there may be considerable waste of the frozen product if more eggs are frozen in one container than will be used at one time.

It is advisable to freeze in one container only the amount of whole eggs, egg yolks, or egg whites that will be used at one time.

For example, if you make 3-egg cakes frequently, pack three eggs to a container. Then when you want to make a cake, lift out one container.

Freeze egg whites for angel cake the same way.

For omelets, separate the egg whites and yolks, put them in separate polythene bags, then pack several of them together. Then when you want to make an omelet, take out one packet containing the proper assortment of whites and yolks.

WHOLE EGGS

Beat eggs slightly with a fork, just enough to mix yolk and white.

Add ¼ teaspoon salt for every 3 eggs. Pour into small polythene bags, seal in rigid carton and freeze.

EGG WHITES

Measure out the amount needed in a specific recipe which you prepare often.

Pour into polythene bag, seal in rigid carton and freeze. Egg whites do not need any mixing before freezing.

EGG YOLKS

Egg yolks should be slightly beaten, but not enough to make them fluffy or lemon coloured.

To every 3 egg yolks, add ¼ teaspoon salt. The addition of salt prevents coagulation of the yolk during storage. Pack in polythene bags, seal in rigid carton and freeze.

COTTAGE CHEESE

Cottage cheese may be frozen and kept in rigid containers for 2 to 3 months.

It should be of good quality and made from pasteurized milk, the curd washed and salted but not creamed.

In packaging, be sure to leave space at the top for expansion.

Thawing cottage cheese takes 3½ to 4 hours at room temperature.

How to Thaw Frozen Eggs and Cottage Cheese

Place sealed container of eggs in a bowl of cold water. They will defrost in about 30 minutes. Or, they can be left in the sealed container at room temperature which requires about 2 hours to thaw.

Cottage cheese should be thawed slowly in the refrigerator. If thawed at room temperature, it will take 3½ to 4 hours. When thawed, add cream and use immediately.

CREAM

Fresh cream is not, as a rule, recommended for freezing. Pasteurized cream may be frozen and kept for 2 to 3 months. Unpasteurized cream does not keep satisfactorily for more than 2 to 3 weeks.

When cream is frozen, the water and milk solids separate so, after thawing, do not mix to their original form.

Cream may be frozen in polythene bags or rigid containers. Leave 1-inch space at top for expansion.

CREAM, WHIPPED

Whip, season and flavour cream as usual.

Spoon out or pipe rosettes in portions, onto a baking sheet that has been

Serve whipped cream while still frozen as it will thaw quickly.

covered with greaseproof paper.

Put baking sheet in freezer. When whipped cream is frozen solid, remove cream with a spatula and pack in polythene bags. Seal and freeze immediately.

BUTTER

Butter may be frozen satisfactorily. Recommended storage period is approximately 3 months.

Butter for freezing should be made from freshly pasteurized cream, well salted and thoroughly worked to remove all traces of buttermilk.

Butter made from unpasteurized cream will turn rancid rapidly and should *never* be frozen.

Wrap butter in double thickness of aluminium foil to prevent transfer of odour.

It is not advisable to freeze more than two pounds of butter in any one packet.

To keep ice cream at its best, place a piece of Pliofilm on the remaining ice cream each time some of it is eaten to prevent the formation of ice crystals. Overwrap the outer container, and use within a short time.

Note: Freezing Garnishes: Individual ingredients of various dishes or garnishes may sometimes be advantageously frozen. Nuts freeze well; so do whipped cream rosettes. Candied fruits and grated cheese stored in the freezer are a convenience, too.

How to Freeze Ready-Cooked Foods

Freezing ready-cooked foods in advance of their need saves time. Cook more than is needed at one meal, for instance, and freeze what is left to use at some future date. Much of the food for holiday meals or dinner parties can be prepared, cooked, and frozen a week, a month or even more in advance, thus eliminating last-minute confusion and clutter in the kitchen. Frozen food need only be reheated when wanted.

Practically every cooked food that is commonly used has been tested for freezing. Some frozen cooked foods are far more satisfactory than others. In this book, we are giving instructions for freezing only those cooked foods which retain a high quality of flavour, texture, and general appearance after freezing and which represent a substantial saving in time for the housewife when cooked and frozen in advance.

Three Important Things to Remember

1. The quality of food to be frozen should be top notch. Freezing may slightly improve the flavour of some foods, but it never makes a high-quality product out of inferior food. Don't waste valuable freezer space on ready-cooked foods that do not freeze well or are below standard quality.

2. Ready-cooked foods must be packed properly. Like all other foods to be frozen, ready-cooked foods must be stored in moisture-vapour-proof containers or wrapping materials. Particular care must be taken so moisture will not evaporate, causing the foods to lose flavour and texture.

3. Follow reheating or refreshing procedures given in the chart. This is most important in retaining original flavour and texture of food.

How to Freeze Bread

Breads which are most satisfactory for freezing are:
Yeast Breads—white and whole-wheat
Yeast Rolls
Baking Powder Nut Bread
Steamed Brown Bread
Danish Tea Ring

All these are baked before freezing, except brown bread which is steamed. All bread must be cooled to room temperature before freezing.

Danish tea ring, pancakes, and waffles are particularly nice for breakfast and will reheat while the rest of the breakfast is being prepared.

If the family is small, yet enjoys homemade bread, a four-loaf recipe may be made and two or three loaves frozen. When reheated, it tastes exactly like freshly-baked bread.

Frozen rolls always make a hit with the family or guests because two or three kinds may be frozen in a single bag or carton, which provides a nice variety for the meal. It is impossible to tell them from freshly-baked rolls.

Use your favourite recipe for any of these breads. Nut bread is excellent for sandwiches or slicing for any occasion.

The chart will guide you as to packing, freezing, and reheating.

Homemade breads, yeast rolls, pecan rolls, coffee cakes, and other leavened baked goods should be baked before freezing. Always cool to room temperature before wrapping, then wrap, seal securely, and label.

PACKING, STORING AND REHEATING BREADS AND ROLLS

FOOD	SIZE OF PACKET	HOW PACKED	STORAGE TIME	HOW TO REHEAT
Yeast Bread	One loaf	Freezer foil is ideal for packing all breads and rolls. Can be placed directly in oven for heating without removing wrapping.	Not to exceed six months	Thaw at room temperature for 1 hour, then warm in preheated 300°F. Mark 2. oven 10 to 15 minutes. OR, remove from wrappings, reheat, unthawed bread in preheated 300°F. Mark 2 oven 25 to 30 minutes.
Steamed Brown Bread	According to size of family		Not to exceed six months	Thaw at room temperature for 1 hour or longer, then reheat in oven in wrappings for 15 to 20 minutes at 300°F. Mark 2.
Baking Powder Biscuits	As desired		Not over six months	In foil for 30 to 40 minutes in 375°F. Mark 5 oven.
Danish Tea Ring	One, usually. If two are wrapped together, separate with sheet of polythene or Pliofilm.		Not to exceed four months	Unwrap. 30 minutes on baking sheet in 350°F. Mark 4 oven.
Yeast Rolls	One or two dozen, assorted		Not to exceed six months	In foil for 30 to 40 minutes in 375°F. Mark 5 oven.
Nut Bread	One loaf		Not to exceed four months	Thaw at room temperature for 3 hours.
Pancakes Waffles	According to size of family	Separate by Pliofilm	Not over two months	Remove wrapping. Reheat in automatic toaster set at "light". Put through toasting twice to heat thoroughly.

How to Freeze Cakes

Cakes may be frozen either frosted or unfrosted, as preferred. Both are satisfactory. While the uncooked mixture may be successfully frozen, we prefer to freeze the cake after it has been baked. Saves considerable time when the cake is needed.

Also does not tie up the cake tins, because a piece of cardboard covered with polythene or aluminium foil can be used to support the cake.

It is often a good idea to freeze cakes in portions as well as whole. If the family is small, a half cake or even a quarter may be better suited to its needs.

Angel Cakes, and any of the other air-leavened cakes such as lemon sponge, freeze beautifully. There is little, if any, change in texture of the cakes after freezing.

Butter Cakes also freeze well, though the texture may become a little finer and the cake more firm.

Fruit Cakes definitely improve with freezing. May be made well in advance. Fruit cakes which have been frozen do not crumble when sliced after they are thawed.

Iced Cakes should be frozen before wrapping to prevent damaging the soft icing.

Bake cake, ice it, put in freezing compartment for a couple of hours, then wrap. This is particularly advisable for special birthday cakes with ornamental decorations.

Iced cakes must be unwrapped immediately after removing from freezer to prevent icing from sticking to wrapping.

Plain Layer Cakes should be separated by a round of polythene between each layer before wrapping and freezing. Or, layers may be wrapped separately.

How to Freeze Pies

You may freeze pies before or after baking. When properly thawed, pies frozen *after* baking are almost impossible to tell from freshly baked pies.

Not all pies freeze well. Mince pies and pies made of fruit or berries are most satisfactory. Double-crust pies freeze best. It is not worth the effort or storage space to attempt to freeze pies with meringue.

In making berry pies, it is essential to add extra thickening, since freezing develops more juice in the fruit. Otherwise, the pies will be too "runny". See recipes for fillings.

Such fruits as apples, peaches, and apricots do not generally require a great deal of thickening. However, especially in the case of apples, it is necessary to judge whether the fruit is juicy or dry and to add thickening accordingly. Even with the juiciest fruits, 4 tablespoons of flour or cornflour are sufficient.

If frozen fruit is used for a pie, add same amount of thickening recommended for fresh fruit pie to be frozen.

How to Wrap: Pies may be wrapped in polythene and aluminium foil; or in special foil dishes.

Recommended Storage Time: Unbaked fruit or berry pies may be stored for 2 months—unbaked mince pies for 4 months. Baked fruit or berry pies may be stored for 4 months—baked mince pies for 4 months.

How to Thaw: All *baked* frozen pies

PACKING, STORING AND THAWING CAKES AND BISCUITS

FOOD	HOW PACKED	STORAGE TIME	HOW TO THAW
Plain Layer Cake, Iced		Not to exceed four months	Remove wrappings, let stand at room temperature 2 hours.
Chocolate cake, Iced	Aluminium foil, or polythene bags are excellent for all packing of cakes and biscuits.	Not to exceed four months	Remove wrappings, let stand at room temperature 2 hours.
Angel and Sponge Cake		Six to eight months	Remove wrappings, let stand at room temperature 2 hours.
Fruit Cake		One year	Thaw in wrappings. Requires about 2 hours for 2 pounds of cake.
Biscuits		Two months	Remove wrappings, let stand at room temperature for ½ hour.

are thawed by placing them unwrapped in a preheated 375°F. Mark 5 oven for 45 minutes.

Thaw *unbaked* pies, unwrapped, in preheated 375°F. Mark 5 oven for 1 hour.

To keep top crust from becoming too brown, place a piece of aluminium foil or butter paper over pie the last 20 minutes of baking.

How to Make Pie Fillings from Frozen Fruit: Place frozen fruit in a saucepan. Break gently with a fork. Start over low heat.

Mix sugar and flour (cornflour, if used) together. When fruit begins to melt, add sugar mixture. Stir with fork to avoid breaking fruit. Cook until thickened.

Be sure to cool fruit before filling the pie shell. Bake pie the usual length of time. Serve pie hot or cold.

Do not freeze pie baked with frozen fruit filling . . . the second freezing will cause additional loss of flavour and juice.

> **Recipes for Fillings Using Fresh or Frozen Fruit**

APPLE PIE FILLING
about 1 pound apples, sliced
10 ounces sugar
4 tablespoons flour (maximum)

BLUEBERRY PIE FILLING
12 ounces berries
5-6 ounces sugar
2 tablespoons flour and
    2 tablespoons cornflour OR
    4 tablespoons flour

CHERRY PIE FILLING
1½ pounds stoned fresh cherries
5-6 ounces sugar
2 tablespoons flour and
    2 tablespoons cornflour OR
    4 tablespoons flour

Caution: Not even best wraps nor the most careful packing will prevent dehydration of foods if storage temperature rises above zero frequently.

GOOSEBERRY PIE FILLING
1½ pounds gooseberries
4 tablespoons cornflour (or flour)
1½ cups sugar
2 tablespoons water

MINCE PIE FILLING
Follow your usual recipe. No extra thickening is required.

PEACH PIE FILLING
1¼ pounds peaches
6 ounces sugar
4 tablespoons flour (maximum)

RHUBARB PIE FILLING
1½ pounds rhubarb
12 ounces sugar
2 tablespoons flour and
    2 tablespoons cornflour OR
    4 tablespoons flour

As a rule, pies may be frozen baked or unbaked. You'll find fruit, mince, and chiffon pies especially good to freeze. Custard or cream-filled pies, however, tend to become grainy, and are not good for freezing. Meringues toughen during freezing and should not be used.

How to Freeze Ready-Cooked Meat and Poultry

Meat which requires long, slow cooking, such as stews and meat sauces, can be frozen satisfactorily. However, cool all meat dishes before freezing. Partially cool in the pan in which it was cooked and finish cooling mixture in the refrigerator.

HINTS ABOUT INGREDIENTS IN MAIN DISHES

● As a rule, fried foods do not freeze successfully. French-fried potatoes and French-fried onion rings are the exceptions.
● Crumb or cheese toppings should be added when the food is reheated for serving.
● Rice is a good binder in casseroles and freezes well.
● Add unblanched or thawed uncooked peas to casseroles, stews, and soups to be frozen. The peas will cook during the reheating time.
● Do not include potatoes in stews and other dishes unless the product is to be eaten in a very short time. Potatoes tend to become soft and have a poor flavour when frozen. Add during reheating.
● Sauces containing a large amount of milk frequently separate during freezing and thawing but often may be stirred or beaten smooth again.
● Meat pies and turnovers are best frozen uncooked.

EFFECT OF FREEZING ON SPICES AND SEASONINGS

Pepper, cloves, and vanilla essence have a tendency to get strong and bitter. Onion also intensifies tremendously under freezing, and many commercial firms use dried onions to combat this. Celery seasonings also become strong, and curry sometimes develops a musty off-flavour. Salt loses flavour and may tend to increase rancidity of any item containing fat.

Consequently, it is best to season foods very lightly before freezing, and add flavouring as needed during the reheating.

MAIN DISHES WHICH FREEZE WELL

Meat loaves; pot roast beef with vegetables; beef or veal stew; hash; stuffed peppers; meat balls in sauce; veal fricassée; veal birds; ham loaf; ham or chicken turnovers; chicken loaf with sauce; roast turkey or chicken slices packed in gravy; creamed chicken; chicken or turkey à la king; chicken gumbo; stewed chicken; creamed fish; fish loaves; prawns à la king; prawns Creole; Lobster Newburg; chilli con carne; Spanish rice; chop suey; Mexican rice; Hungarian goulash; lasagna.

How to Freeze Soups

Soups with a milk base do not freeze satisfactorily. Vegetable, chicken, lentil and other dried legume soups are excellent when frozen. When making any of these soups which require long, slow cooking, make an extra amount and freeze whatever is not used immediately. Be sure to cool soups before starting to freeze them.

Clear broths (chicken, turkey, or beef) freeze satisfactorily. Do not add noodles or rice when planning to freeze these broths; add when broth is reheating.

How to Pack: When cool, soups may be poured into ice cube trays, frozen and cubes removed and packed in polythene bags.

Or, pack in glass jars suitable for freezing, polythene bags, or rigid cartons.

Storage Time: Not over 4 months.

How to Reheat: Remove from packet. Heat in covered saucepan on low heat for 45 minutes to one hour.

Hint: Three of the frozen cubes will make one serving of soup when heated.

Caution: When packing soups, sauces, or other liquids, leave at least one inch of space at top of the container to allow for expansion during freezing.

GENERAL POINTS ABOUT FREEZING

PARTY FARE FROM YOUR FREEZER

When you are planning a party or buffet and have space available, freezing most or all the food to be served is worthwhile. You can be as elaborate as you like with your most imaginative canapés and sandwiches when you prepare them at your leisure before the party. Canapés or open sandwiches should be frozen first and wrapped as soon as filling or topping is firm. Canapés may be stored in freezer containers in layers with a sheet of freezer wrap between each layer and then overwrapped. Separate the layers when thawing so that fillings will not be damaged as they thaw.

POWER CUTS

Keep the freezer tightly closed. If the freezer is full when the power goes off, food will stay frozen at least 48 hours; if half full, about 24 hours. Manufacturers will tell you in their instruction booklets how long power can be cut off without food damage.

Check with the local electricity board to see when service will be restored. If the interruption is to be more than a reasonable length of time, you have two alternatives: (1) put dry ice into the freezer, or (2) transfer the food to another freezer or commercial plant which has standby power.

To avoid the risk of losing the contents of your freezer, you can insure the contents against loss due to accidental power failure. The cost is usually about 5% for every pound sterling's worth of food. Most reliable insurance brokers will advise you about this.

SHOULD THAWED FOODS BE REFROZEN?

As a rule, frozen foods which have been thawed should not be refrozen. Frozen meat which has been thawed may be kept in the refrigerator for a limited time, or it may be cooked and frozen again. This is not actually refreezing.

If you suspect a food has been thawed too long, do not take a chance.

HINTS ABOUT COMMERCIALLY FROZEN FOODS

Correct handling of commercially frozen foods is equally as important as handling home-processed frozen foods if quality is to be maintained.

The greatest threat to quality lies in letting the temperature rise above zero. This is most likely to occur from the time foods are bought at the supermarket until placed in the freezer at home. These precautions will help you prevent excessive temperature changes:

1. Make frozen foods the final items bought.
2. Avoid allowing frozen foods to stand for long periods in a heated car or one parked in summer sun.
3. Do not let frozen foods stand in the kitchen unnecessarily before being put in the freezer.

The higher the temperature to which a packet of frozen food is allowed to rise, the greater the speed with which unfavourable changes in quality take place. Even products stored for a full year at 0°F. without fluctuations will be of considerably better quality than those which rise as high as 25°F. for only one day due to careless handling.

Squeezing a packet of frozen foods is not a reliable way to find out if the food is cold enough. Many packets feel frozen hard at temperatures as high as 15 or 20°F.

El Patio Fruit Platter

FRUIT

In this section are suggestions about choosing, storing, and preparing all the well-known—and many not so well-known—fruits. The recipes included here may be varied in innumerable ways by making different combinations of fruits, varying the flavours with wine, brandy, rum, or a bit of lemon juice, or by substituting one sweetening for another such as brown sugar, maple sugar, honey, and flavoured syrups instead of white sugar.

Fruit in some form is a good addition to any meal and is an especially desirable dessert to finish a heavy meal. Fruits are not only high in essential nutrients but they also have a wide appeal, are simple to prepare, and are low in calories compared with cakes, puddings, pies, and most other desserts. To find all the recipes containing fruit that are included in this book, consult the index.

HINTS ABOUT FRUIT

Wash All Fruit: All fruit should be washed carefully before using, because the sprays used on some fruit trees may be harmful. This also applies to wrapped fruit because there is always a possibility of traces of the spray lingering on the fruit even though it is usually washed before packing.

To Prevent Darkening of Peeled Fruit: Many fruits darken when peeled. This is harmless but detracts from the appearance, and can be avoided if the fruit is dipped immediately into citrus or pineapple juice.

Dried Fruits: The dried fruits (prunes, apricots, dates, raisins, peaches, apples, currants, figs, and pears) are among the magic fruits of the kitchen. They are popular either stewed as a breakfast fruit or in preparing tempting, tasty desserts.

To Stew Dried Fruits: Modern processing methods have removed the necessity of long soaking of most types of dried fruits. Always check the packet directions. Or use the directions given below.

Wash fruit quickly in several waters or until the water is clear. Drain, put in a pan, cover with water, bring to the boil, then simmer until tender. Add more water if needed. Unless otherwise specified, add sugar to taste 5 minutes before removing from heat. Specific recipes for various dried fruits are given throughout this book.

STEWED UNPEELED FRUIT

2 pounds unpeeled, unpared fruit
16 fluid ounces boiling water
4 to 8 ounces sugar

Add unpeeled fruit to boiling water. Simmer until nearly tender.

Add sugar; cook until fruit is tender. This method keeps the skin soft.

STEWED PEELED FRUIT

16 fluid ounces water
4 to 8 ounces sugar
1/8 teaspoon salt
2 pounds prepared fruit

Boil the water, sugar, and salt 3 minutes.

Drop prepared fruit into the boiling syrup. Cook gently until tender.

FRUIT WHIP OR SNOW

8 ounces fruit, dried or sliced
sugar to taste
1 teaspoon lemon juice
2 egg whites

Use soft, fresh fruit or any stewed fruit (apples, prunes, bananas, peaches, or apricots). If very juicy fruits are used, the juice should be drained thoroughly before rubbing through a sieve. Sour, raw apples may be grated.

Sweeten fruit pulp to taste and add lemon juice.

Beat egg whites until stiff, then beat in sweetened fruit pulp and continue beating until the mixture is very fluffy.

Pile lightly in individual serving dishes and chill thoroughly. Serve with cream or custard. Decorate with jam, if you like. Serves 4 to 6.

EL PATIO FRUIT PLATTER

1 can (28 ounces) peach halves
8 ounces strawberries
lettuce leaves
1 avocado pear
lemon juice
salt
1 large grapefruit
10 large cooked prunes
1 3-ounce packet cream cheese
2 tablespoons peach syrup or prune liquid
1 banana
mint sprigs

Drain peaches and arrange in a ring around strawberries on crisp lettuce leaves.

Cut avocado pear into half and remove stone and skin. Cut across in slices and sprinkle with lemon juice and salt.

Pare and break grapefruit into segments. Drain and stone the prunes.

Soften cheese with a fork and blend in peach syrup. Fill the prunes with cheese. Cut banana into thick slices.

Alternate grapefruit segments and avocado pear slices between peaches. Circle with banana slices and stuffed prunes.

Decorate with mint sprigs. Serve with lemon-honey dressing. Serves 5 to 7.

STEWED MIXED DRIED FRUIT

Wash fruit; remove cores from apples and pears. Cover generously with water; boil 35 to 45 minutes. Add 2 ounces sugar for each 8 ounces fruit about 5 minutes before removing from heat.

DRIED FRUIT PURÉES

Cook the fruit slightly longer than when it is to be served whole. Put the cooked fruit through a sieve, colander, or ricer.

For some recipes such as whips and sauces, the cooked fruit may be beaten to a pulp instead of being puréed. 8 ounces of uncooked fruit yields about 8 fluid ounces purée.

BAKED FRESH FRUIT COMPOTE

Mix together several kinds of fresh fruit in a baking dish. Add syrup made of 1 part water to 1 part sugar.

Cover and bake in a moderate oven (350°F. Mark 4) until tender, 15 to 20 minutes.

FRUIT WITH YOGURT

Sweeten yogurt with sugar and vanilla essence to taste. Sprinkle the top with ground cinnamon. Serve well chilled with crushed fresh or frozen strawberries, apricots or peaches, or with stewed cherries.

Fruit with Cottage or Cream Cheese: Prepare and serve either in the same way as yogurt (above).

FRUIT SALAD COMPOTE

pineapple cubes, fresh, frozen, or
    canned
mandarin orange segments, canned
peach slices, fresh, frozen, or
    canned
strawberries, fresh or frozen
cherries, fresh or canned
12 fluid ounces fruit juice and water
sugar
2 teaspoons aromatic bitters
2 teaspoons poppy seeds

Prepare fruit and chill. Mix the juice from fruit with enough water to make 12 fluid ounces. Put it in small saucepan. Add sugar to taste and stir over low heat until sugar is dissolved. Cover and cook 3 minutes. Chill.

Fruit Salad Compote

Add bitters and poppy seeds. Arrange fruit in a glass bowl and pour syrup over.

WINE FRUIT COMPOTES

1. Sprinkle melon balls (water-melon, honeydew, cantaloupe) with caster sugar; add port, angelica, or sweet white wine to about half-cover the balls, and chill thoroughly, stirring once or twice.

2. Arrange drained canned pear halves and black sweet cherries in a shallow bowl.

Heat enough port almost to cover the fruit, add 2 or 3 thin strips each of lemon and orange peel, and a little sugar; heat just to boiling point.

Cool slightly, pour over fruit, chill thoroughly.

3. Pour port or white wine over lightly sugared strawberries in coupe glasses. Serve for dessert.

SPICY DRIED FRUIT COMPOTE

1 11-ounce packet mixed dried
    fruits
4 ounces brown sugar
2 tablespoons lemon juice
1 teaspoon whole cloves
1 1-inch stick cinnamon

Mix the ingredients in 1½-quart casserole. Add water to cover, about 16 fluid ounces.

Cover and bake in moderate oven (350°F. Mark 4) 1½ hours. Serves 6.

FRUIT BAKED IN WINE

4 pears, apples, or peaches or 12
    plums
2 tablespoons lemon juice (optional)
4 fluid ounces Marsala, Madeira,
    or port
about 4 tablespoons water
1 tablespoon or more brandy
    (optional)

Peel pears, apples, or peaches. Cut fruit in half and remove cores and stones. Arrange in baking dish, with cut-sides up.

Fill fruit cavities with sugar and add lemon juice and wine. Pour water round fruit.

Cover and bake in moderate oven (350°F. Mark 4) until fruit is tender, basting several times with juice in pan.

Soft fruits will need 20 to 30 minutes, hard pears about 1 hour. Add water as needed. Add brandy to juice in pan and pour over fruit. Serve warm or cold, plain or with cream. Serves 4.

Chocolate Minted Pears: Bake pears as above but omit lemon juice and wine. When tender, place a plain or chocolate mint cream or 2 in each cavity. Reheat, uncovered, until chocolate melts to form a sauce.

Fresh Fruit Dessert Cups

FRUIT WITH SOUR CREAM

Serve chilled canned or almost defrosted frozen fruits, such as apricots, peaches, and raspberries with sour cream and a sprinkling of grated nutmeg.

FRESH FRUIT DESSERT CUPS

1¼ ounces brown sugar
2 tablespoons cornflour
16 fluid ounces orange juice
1 teaspoon grated lemon rind
3 tablespoons lemon juice
pinch of grated nutmeg
6 whole cloves
1 3-inch stick cinnamon
1¼ pounds sliced fresh nectarines
1 pound stoned cherries, halved
1 pound melon balls
½ pint sour cream (optional)

Mix the sugar and cornflour in a small saucepan. Gradually blend in orange juice until smooth. Add lemon rind and juice, nutmeg, cloves, and cinnamon. Cook, stirring constantly, until thickened and clear. Cool.

Pour over nectarines, cherries, and melon balls. Chill 2 to 3 hours. Serve plain or topped with sour cream. Serves 10 to 12.

HOW TO GLAZE CANNED FRUIT FOR DESSERTS

Soften 1½ packets gelatine in 4½ tablespoons cold water 5 minutes. Add 12 fluid ounces boiling water and stir to dissolve gelatine. Tint a delicate yellow with a drop or two of yellow food colouring.

Arrange chilled canned fruit on a cake rack which has been placed over a baking sheet. When glaze is slightly set, pour small amounts over fruit. The excess that falls onto the baking sheet may be spooned up, stirred, and used over again.

If glaze becomes too thick while being used, place over a pan of lukewarm water, stir until smooth, and chill over iced water to proper consistency.

Glazing may be done a day before fruit is to be served. Remove fruit from cake rack with a palette knife and store in refrigerator.

To add colour to a pale fruit such as pears before glazing, add a few drops of yellow food colouring to the syrup of the canned fruit and leave the fruit in the syrup until delicately coloured.

To add a "blush" to fruits after glazing, brush lightly with red food colouring.

Apples

Historians tell us that the apple was known to ancient cavemen and to the early Greeks and Romans—perhaps not in the succulent form in which expert horticulturists give it to you today, but nevertheless with many of the desirable eating qualities which make it known as the "King of Fruits".

Today, apples are a "standby" for cooks—for pies, sauces, baking individually or for scores of appetizing new dishes. Too many housewives, however, buy apples without regard to variety and consequently fail to get the best available. There is no such thing as the typical apple flavour, as each variety has its own distinctive taste—sweet, mellow, or tart, as the case may be. Some apples are better suited for baking, some for eating fresh, while others make better sauce because of their flavour characteristics.

HINTS ABOUT BUYING APPLES

Here are a few points to bear in mind when buying apples. Those that measure 2½ inches or more in diameter are ideal for general use. The large sizes (3 inches and up) of the baking varieties are best for that purpose. This does not mean that those smaller should be neglected entirely for often they are priced so as to be more economical for cooking than the larger ones.

In choosing apples, try to get those that have good colour for their variety and are firm to the touch. This latter point is particularly important when buying the large sizes. Big apples tend to ripen more rapidly than the smaller ones and, when soft, usually have a mushy texture with an over-ripe flavour too mellow for real taste enjoyment.

Warm temperatures hasten the ripening process and cause apples to lose very rapidly their crispness and tangy flavour. If you keep reserve supplies in the refrigerator or some equally cool spot, they will be at their best when you are ready to use them.

COMMONLY USED APPLE VARIETIES

Belfort: Bright red, sweet apple. This is a popular dessert apple on the Continent, and is imported to Britain mainly towards the end of the season.

Bramley's Seedling: The best and most popular all-purpose cooking apple. Large green fruit, sometimes flushed with red. Stores well for winter use.

Cox's Orange Pippin: Considered the very best British dessert apple. Dull red with russet skin; its flesh is firm and juicy, the flavour is particularly sweet and distinctive. Stores well, usually until Christmastime.

Delicious: Striped red to solid red over yellow skin; excellent for eating raw and in salads. Mildly sweet, crisp, juicy.

Golden Delicious: Same shape as ordinary Delicious but light yellow; marvellous eating, one of best salad apples grown.

Red Delicious: Luscious taste; in all ways like the Delicious, but darker red. Same eating qualities.

Golden Noble: A cooking apple with clear yellow, slightly rough skin; yellow, soft flesh.

Granny Smith: This is a hard green dessert apple with a good crisp flesh. Imported from Australia and New Zealand.

James Grieve: A very early apple, liable to bruise. Pale yellow with red streaks, rather soft texture.

Jonathan: Rich red, overlaying a straw-coloured background; excellent for all purposes.

Laxton's Fortune: An early dessert apple, yellow with red flush; crisp and juicy. Often mistaken for Cox's but has an inferior flavour.

Newton Wonder: A late cooker, which is also good to eat. Large yellow-green fruits with crimson flush and stripe.

Rome Beauty: The ideal baker; large yellow or green mottled with bright red and striped with carmine.

Worcester Pearmain: Golden-yellow, heavily suffused and streaked with scarlet-crimson; flesh crisp and juicy, with a pleasant sweet flavour.

Yellow Newtown: Yellow or yellowish-green, excellent for all uses; delicious as a dessert apple or where quality is desired. Medium to large, uniform in colour.

PREVENTING DISCOLORATION OF APPLES

Place slices as they are peeled in a pan of cold water to which a pinch of salt has been added for each whole apple peeled.

APPLE COMPOTE
(Basic Recipe)

1½ to 2 pounds cooking apples
12 fluid ounces water
6 ounces sugar
few grains salt
slice of lemon (optional)
candied orange peel (optional)

Wash, pare, and quarter ripe apples. Drop into cold water to prevent discoloration.

Bring to the boil the water, sugar, salt, lemon, and orange peel. Drop apple quarters, a few pieces at a time, into the syrup.

Cover pan and simmer gently until fruit is transparent and tender, turning apples when half done.

Serve hot or cold. If fruit is very hard, pre-cook before adding to syrup. Serves 6.

Apple Compote Variations

Apple-Raisin Compote: In basic recipe, add 1¼ ounces seedless raisins. Cook with apples.

Apple Slices: Follow basic recipe. Cut apples across into circles. Add to syrup and simmer until tender.

Cinnamon Apple Rings: Cut apples in rings. Add a good pinch of cinnamon to sugar and water in basic recipe.

Glazed Apples: Core apples. Cook whole, unpeeled, in coloured syrup. Score the skin in small squares before cooking to keep fruit from bursting.

Minted Apples: Colour syrup pale green. When apples are done, flavour syrup with oil of peppermint.

SNOW-CAPPED APPLE SLICES

Core red apples; cut across in ½-inch slices. Spread generously with whipped dessert topping. Sprinkle with toasted desiccated coconut.

Variation: Spread apple slices with tart redcurrant jelly before adding topping.

Snow-Capped Apple Slices

BAKED APPLES
(Basic Recipe)

Wash baking apples. Core ⅔ of the way down from top of apples. Do not break through blossom end of skins. Put them in baking dish.

Fill each cavity with sugar, cinnamon, and nutmeg. Allow ¼ teaspoon ground cinnamon or nutmeg to 8 apples. If nutmeg is used, add to each apple a few drops of lemon juice and a few gratings of lemon rind.

Cover dish with boiling water ¼ inch in depth. Cover and bake in moderate oven (375°F. Mark 5) about 40 minutes, or until apples are soft.

Remove the lid, bake 10 minutes longer. If baked uncovered, baste occasionally with syrup in pan.

Remove apples. Boil syrup until thick and pour over apples. Serve hot or cold with cream.

Baked Apple Variations

Honey Baked Apples: In basic recipe, substitute honey for sugar.

Maple or Brown Sugar Baked Apples: In basic recipe, substitute maple or brown sugar for granulated.

Rosy Cinnamon Apples: In basic recipe, add a good pinch of cinnamon to water before baking.

Baked Apple Rings: Cut apples crossways in rings and place in casserole. Add sugar, water, and lemon juice as for baked apples. Bake until tender.

Praline Apples: Bake apples as in basic recipe, adding only the sugar and cinnamon.

Cool them and place in ice cream or dessert dishes.

Place 4½ ounces granulated sugar and 2 ounces blanched and flaked almonds in a saucepan over medium heat. Heat until sugar is caramelized golden brown. Spoon quickly over apples. Cool. Serve with whipped cream.

Stuffed Baked Apples: Follow basic recipe. Before baking, stuff cavities with mincemeat, chopped dates and nuts, sliced bananas, or bananas and cranberries combined, marmalade, jelly, crushed pineapple, etc.

Baked apples become a surprise dish with the many variations in sauces and stuffings given in the basic recipe.

Marshmallow Baked Apples: Follow basic recipe. Stuff cavities with any suggested stuffings. When baked, top with marshmallow and return to oven to brown, about 5 minutes.

Cranberries in Baked Stuffed Apples: Fill the cavity in the centre of each apple with cranberry sauce or jelly. Add sugar to water in pan if filling is not sufficiently sweet. Bake.

BAKED APPLE SAUCE
(Basic Recipe)

6 to 8 tart apples
ground cinnamon to taste, or 2 thin slices lemon
4¼ fluid ounces water
about 6 ounces sugar

Wash apples (do not peel), remove bruised spots, and cut in quarters.

Place in a baking dish. Add ground cinnamon or lemon and water.

Cover and bake in moderate oven (375°F. Mark 5) until tender, 20 to 30 minutes.

Put through a sieve. Add sugar and mix. Serve hot or cold.

Serves 6 to 8.

Baked Apple Sauce Variations

Creamed Apple Sauce: Substitute 4 fluid ounces single cream for water. Add ½ teaspoon ground cinnamon and ¼ teaspoon grated nutmeg with sugar.

Honey Apple Sauce: Substitute honey for sugar. Add 1 tablespoon grated lemon rind.

Maple Apple Sauce: Substitute 12 ounces maple syrup for sugar and water.

Orange Apple Sauce: Add 2 tablespoons grated orange rind while cooking.

APPLE SAUCE
(Basic Recipe)

Wash, pare, and core 8 cooking apples. Add about 4 fluid ounces water and ⅛ teaspoon salt. Cook in covered pot until soft.

Add about 4 ounces sugar while hot. Simmer just long enough to melt sugar. Amount of sugar and water varies with sweetness and juiciness of apples.

For additional flavouring, add with sugar, grated nutmeg, ground cinnamon, grated lemon rind or juice, or a combination of spices. Serves 8.

Apple Sauce Variations

Honey Apple Sauce: In basic recipe, substitute 6 ounces honey for sugar. Add 1 to 2 teaspoons grated lemon rind.

Minted Apple Sauce: In basic recipe, add ½ ounce chopped mint with sugar.

Orange Apple Sauce: In basic recipe, add 2 to 3 teaspoons grated orange rind with sugar.

Spiced Apple Sauce: In basic recipe substitute 2 ounces firmly packed brown sugar for granulated sugar. Add ¼ teaspoon ground cinnamon and 1 teaspoon grated lemon rind.

Strained Apple Sauce: Do not pare apples. Remove any bruised spots. Cut into quarters and cook until soft. Work through a coarse sieve. Add sugar and flavouring. Simmer to dissolve sugar.

SPICED APPLES TO SERVE WITH MEAT

4 pounds sweet apples
whole cloves
8 fluid ounces cider vinegar
2 fluid ounces water
9 ounces brown sugar
1 tablespoon ginger root
2 tablespoons mixed pickling spice
1 tablespoon lemon juice
1 teaspoon grated lemon rind

Wash apples; stick each apple with 4 whole cloves.

Make a syrup of vinegar, water, and brown sugar. Add spices, tied in a muslin bag, lemon juice, and rind. Simmer 5 minutes.

Add apples; cook slowly until tender, spooning liquid over them occasionally.

Lift out on a plate and chill. Serve around the meat.

BRANDIED FRIED APPLES

Peel and core small, soft, sweet apples. Cut in thin rounds.

Soak in a mixture of equal parts brandy, lemon juice, and sugar. Drain and dust with flour.

Sauté in butter until light brown, turning carefully.

Sprinkle with a mixture of icing sugar and ground cinnamon. Serve very hot.

FRIED APPLES

Wash, quarter, and core firm apples. Slice in medium thin pieces. Sauté in small amount of hot butter until brown. If tart, sprinkle with a little brown sugar or honey while cooking.

BROWNED APPLES

Core and slice firm apples about ½ inch thick. Arrange in pan. Sprinkle with brown sugar and butter if tart.

Bake in hot oven (375°F. Mark 5) or grill until brown and tender.

CRAB-APPLES

Crab-apples are mostly used for making jellies, jams, and preserves. They are small in size (about 1½ inches in diameter), with a sour taste that makes them unsuitable for eating raw. Choose them in the same way as you would apples.

Apricots

Fresh apricots, which date back to the days of the ancient Persians, have a flavour (between a peach and a plum) entirely different from that of the dried variety.

Buying Hints: Golden-yellow colour, plumpness, and firmness are indications of quality in apricots. Since they are an extremely delicate fruit, you should avoid buying those that are soft to the touch or have a wilted or shrivelled look about them. Such fruit decays quickly and lacks a good flavour.

Fresh apricots may be used in most dishes that call for peaches; cooked and puréed apricots may be used in any dish that calls for apple sauce.

To Peel Apricots: Drop raw apricots into boiling water. Remove from heat and let stand ½ minute. Remove apricots and plunge into cold water. The skin will pull off easily.

APRICOT SAUCE

Follow method in basic recipe for apple sauce or any of its variations.

ORANGE APRICOT PORCUPINES

32 whole firm apricots
1 ounce blanched almonds slivered
1 pound sugar
4 fluid ounces white vinegar
4 fluid ounces orange juice
½ teaspoon salt
½ teaspoon almond essence

Scald apricots 1 minute in boiling water; plunge into cold water; drain and peel. Press about 3 pieces of almond into each apricot.

Mix together sugar, vinegar, orange juice, salt, and almond essence in a 1½-quart saucepan; bring to the boil on high heat.

Lower apricots, studded with almonds, carefully into hot syrup; cook on high heat about 3 minutes. Remove from heat.

Lift apricots into hot sterilized, wide-mouthed jam jars, using a slotted spoon. Pour on syrup, working out bubbles by running a palette knife down sides of the jars. Seal. Makes about 4 pounds.

Orange Apricot Porcupines

STEWED DRIED APRICOTS

Wash and drain apricots. Cover with water; boil until tender, 30 to 40 minutes. Add 2 to 4 ounces sugar for each 8 ounces fruit for the last 5 minutes of cooking.

PICKLED CANNED APRICOTS

1 can (28-ounce) whole peeled apricots
4-5 tablespoons vinegar
2 sticks cinnamon
2 or 3 pieces ginger root
2 whole cloves

Drain apricots. Mix together the apricot juice, vinegar, cinnamon, ginger root, and cloves; simmer 10 minutes.

Add apricots; simmer 10 minutes longer. Chill before serving.

Serves 4 to 6.

APRICOT APPLE SAUCE

¼ pound dried apricots
16 fluid ounces water
5 cooking apples
5-6 ounces sugar

Wash apricots in cold water; cover with water and soak 4 hours.

Drain; add the water and cook 10 minutes.

Wash, pare, core, and slice apples very thin; add to apricots and cook 10 minutes.

Add sugar, stir to mix thoroughly, and cook 1 or 2 minutes longer. Serve, or work through a coarse sieve, if you like. Serves 4 to 6.

ARMENIAN APRICOT DESSERT

1 pound dried apricots
¼ pound prunes
¼ pound seedless raisins
sugar to taste
almonds

Cover apricots and prunes with cold water and soak 4 hours. Put fruits in a saucepan with the same water.

Add raisins and enough extra water to cover. Bring to the boil and cook gently, adding sugar to taste.

When tender, remove from heat and cool. Serve cold with 6 or 7 blanched almonds on each portion. Serves 6 to 8.

APRICOTS SUPREME

1 teaspoon cinnamon
½ teaspoon ground cloves
2 level tablespoons mayonnaise
16 peeled apricots, halved and stoned

Mix together the cinnamon and cloves. Sprinkle this mixture on halved apricots. Spoon mayonnaise in the centre of half the apricots. Sandwich with remaining halves.

Place on baking sheet or in grill pan and bake in hot oven (375°F. Mark 5) or grill about 5 minutes or until apricots begin to brown. Serve with baked ham.

Avocado Pears

The avocado pear (also called alligator pear) is a pear-shaped tropical fruit native to Mexico and northern South America and now grown in other countries. It is yellowish-green to purplish-black and has a single large stone embedded in a firm, buttery yellowish flesh. It varies greatly in size and weight and contains from 10 to 20 per cent fat.

Buying Hints: This rich, mild-flavoured fruit is best when fully ripe. (The flesh of a ripe avocado pear will give slightly under light pressure.)

It is usually eaten raw with salt, pepper, and lemon juice or with a salad dressing. Allow half a medium-sized avocado pear per serving for a main-dish salad. Allow 3 to 4 servings per avocado pear if it is puréed, seasoned with a French or other dressing, and used in salads. Because of its mildness, the avocado pear mixes well with other fruit or with vegetables.

Note: Avocado pear flesh rapidly discolours when exposed to air. To prevent discoloration sprinkle with citrus or pineapple juice. If using only part of an avocado pear, keep the unused part unpeeled, preferably with the stone embedded in it; wrap in foil and store in the refrigerator. When mixing with cooked foods, add at the last moment, and away from heat.

AVOCADO PEAR AND BACON

Mash the pulp of 1 avocado pear with a fork. Season with lemon juice, salt, and onion juice. Heap in small mounds on 2 plates.

Garnish with rashers of fried bacon, chopped parsley, and paprika pepper. Serves 2.

AVOCADO PEAR DESSERT

Peel ripe avocado pears and put the pulp through a fine sieve. Flavour with lemon juice, caster sugar, and, if you like, a pinch of ground cloves.

Beat mixture with a rotary beater until fluffy. Chill thoroughly.

Avocado pear may be cut into interesting shapes to use as attractive edible garnishes.

BAKED AVOCADO PEAR

3 ripe avocado pears
3 tablespoons lemon juice
¼ teaspoon salt
5½ ounces icing sugar

Scoop avocado pulp from shells. Mash and put through a sieve. Mix it with lemon juice, salt, and sugar in a buttered baking dish.

Bake in moderate oven (350°F. Mark 4) for 30 minutes, or until a brown crust forms on top. Serves 6.

AVOCADO PEARS STUFFED WITH CHEESE

Peel medium-sized avocado pears. Cut lengthways and remove the stones. Stuff halves with any cream cheese.

Dip in beaten egg, then in crumbs. Sauté in butter until brown or fry in deep hot fat in basket.

Cover with your favourite tomato sauce and heat through in a moderate oven (375°F. Mark 5). Serve as a vegetable.

FRUIT-FILLED AVOCADO PEAR

2 medium-sized avocado pears
salt
1½-2 grapefruits, split in segments
1½ dozen stuffed olives
French dressing

Cut avocado pears in half and remove the stones. Scoop out flesh, leaving a thin layer to hold shells in shape. Cut the portion removed into cubes and sprinkle with salt.

Cut grapefruit segments into cubes. Cut olives into rounds.

Toss fruit together lightly and refill shells. Add dressing and chill. Serves 4.

AVOCADO PEAR AND SOUR CREAM DIP FOR PRAWNS

2 ripe avocado pears, stones removed
8 fluid ounces sour cream
½ teaspoon Aromat
¼ teaspoon salt
2 tablespoons made horseradish
1 small onion, grated

Mash avocado pears to a smooth pulp with a wooden spoon or in electric blender. Whip in remaining ingredients. Serve with chilled prawns.

For a buffet lunch: avocado pear halves ready for serving with creamed chicken or Creole prawns for filling.

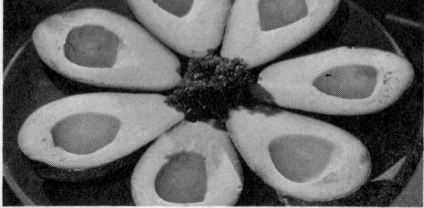

Bananas

Buying guide: The colour and condition of the peel are good indications of the use of bananas. When the skin is all yellow, the banana is firm enough to cook and serve as a vegetable and ripe enough to be eaten uncooked. If the peel is yellow but flecked with brown, the banana is fully ripe and ideal for serving fresh with cereals, in fruit cups, salads, and desserts. Fruit with a mouldy skin that has turned black is of poor quality, although some bananas with a dark skin are very ripe and still good for eating.

For proper ripening and best flavour, leave bananas to ripen at room temperature.

Don't keep bananas in refrigerator —except ones already fully ripe and flecked with brown.

To whip or mash 3 or more bananas: Break in pieces; beat with electric mixer or blender. For 1 or 2 bananas: Slice into a bowl and mash with a fork, or use a mixer or blender.

BAKED BANANAS

6 firm bananas
2 tablespoons melted butter or margarine
salt

Peel bananas. Put them in a well-buttered baking dish. Brush well with butter and sprinkle with salt.

Bake in moderate oven (375°F. Mark 5) 15 to 18 minutes, or until bananas are tender, easily pierced with a fork.

If you like, bake until almost cooked, then place under grill until tender and browned. Serves 6.

Serve hot as a vegetable or as a dessert with cream or a hot fruit sauce.

Baked Banana Variations

Bananas Baked with Black Treacle: Just before baking, brush bananas with lemon juice. Pour 8 to 12 ounces black treacle over bananas. Bake as above.

Serve hot with beef or ham, or decorate with chopped toasted almonds and serve as a hot dessert. Maple syrup may be substituted.

Bananas Baked with Brown Sugar: Just before baking, sprinkle bananas lightly with brown sugar. Bake as above.

Serve hot with beef, ham, lamb, or chicken.

Bananas Baked with Curry Sauce: Pour 16 fluid ounces of your favourite curry sauce over bananas. Bake as above.

Serve hot with rice, pork, lamb, chicken, duck, or prawns.

Baked Bananas Served with Sour Cream: To serve as a vegetable, top each hot banana with about 4 tablespoons sour cream. Sprinkle with paprika pepper, if you like.

To serve as a hot dessert, top each banana with about 4 tablespoons sour cream. Sprinkle with sugar, grated nutmeg, or ground cinnamon, if you like.

Bananas Baked with Cranberries: Pour 8 fluid ounces hot cranberry sauce over bananas. Bake as above. Serve hot with beef, chicken, or turkey. Tart jams, jellies or marmalades may be used in place of cranberry sauce.

Baked Bananas with Apple Sauce or Apple Cheese: Spread bananas evenly from tip to tip with apple sauce or apple cheese. Use about 4 tablespoons for each banana. Bake as above. Serve as a hot dessert.

Honey Baked Bananas: Sprinkle honey over bananas with the butter. Add a sprinkling of lemon juice, if you like.

Baked Bananas with Sherry or Rum: Pour a little sherry or rum over bananas while baking.

FRIED BANANAS

Peel and cut firm bananas in half lengthways. Fry bananas slowly in butter until tender and golden brown, turning them to brown evenly. Serve hot as a vegetable.

Fried Banana Variations

Glazed for Dessert: Brush well with lemon juice before frying and sprinkle with brown sugar while frying.

Banana Newburg: Sprinkle fried bananas with brown sugar while cooking. Add a little sherry and let them simmer a few minutes.

Fried Bananas with Rum: Pour some rum into the pan when fried bananas are done. Light it. Baste bananas with flaming syrup. Serve immediately.

RUM-FLAMED BANANAS

4 bananas
4 tablespoons butter
2 tablespoons icing sugar
2 tablespoons brown sugar
4-5 tablespoons rum

Peel bananas, cut in half crossways.

Melt butter in chafing dish over direct heat or in a sauté pan.

Place bananas in hot butter; sprinkle with mixed sugar and cook until browned lightly on all sides, about 4 to 6 minutes.

Pour the rum over the bananas; flame the rum, and serve on dessert plates. Serves 4.

Banana Scallops

BANANA SCALLOPS

1   egg
1½ teaspoons salt
6   firm bananas
3   ounces golden crumbs or dry
        white breadcrumbs

Beat egg slightly and add salt. Slice peeled bananas crossways into 1-inch thick pieces. Dip into egg and roll in crumbs.

Fry in hot deep fat (375°F. Mark 5) 1½ to 2 minutes or until brown and tender. Drain and serve immediately. Serves 6.

Note: Bananas may be prepared for frying several hours in advance.

BANANAS IN BLANKETS

Peel and cut firm ripe bananas into quarters crossways. Dip in lemon juice and sprinkle very lightly with sugar.

Roll in very thin rashers of bacon or boiled ham.

Fasten bacon with cocktail sticks. Sauté bananas in a frying pan or bake in moderate oven (350°F. Mark 4) until bacon is crisp. When using ham, grease the pan lightly.

GRILLED BANANAS

Peel firm, ripe bananas. Put in grill pan. Brush bananas well with melted butter or margarine and sprinkle lightly with salt.

Grill under moderate heat for about 5 minutes on each side or until bananas are browned and tender and easily pierced with fork. Serve hot as a vegetable.

Grilled Banana Variations

Grilled Bananas with Curry Sauce: To serve as a hot vegetable, top grilled bananas with hot curry sauce.

Grilled Bananas with Apple Sauce: For a delicious new flavour, cover each banana with about 4 tablespoons apple sauce or apple cheese. Top with plain, whipped or sour cream.

Grilled Bananas with Cream: To serve as a vegetable, top each banana with about 4 tablespoons sour cream. Sprinkle with paprika pepper, if you like. To serve as a hot dessert, top each banana with plain, whipped or sour cream. Sprinkle with sugar, grated nutmeg, or ground cinnamon, if you like.

Berries

Here are two good tips to remember about berries. First, remember that only the popular strawberry is privileged to wear a cap as a sign of ripeness. Second, for best quality and taste, choose berries that are firm, plump, and full coloured for the variety.

TO SERVE FRESH BERRIES

Spread berries on a tray; remove soft or mouldy berries. Chill until ready to serve. Then wash in a colander; drain thoroughly.

Sprinkle with sugar if you like and chill a little longer. If fruit is too tart, sprinkle with sugar and leave 1 to 2 hours. A sprinkling of lemon juice will neutralize excessive tartness.

BARBERRIES

Barberry is the name of a family of perennial herbs and shrubs. The bright red berries of several species of the shrubs often used for landscaping are edible but are seldom eaten raw; however they are sometimes used for making preserves. They have a tart, pleasant flavour.

CRANBERRIES

The cranberry is a firm, sour, red berry, the fruit of a trailing evergreen shrub that grows in bogs or marshes. These berries are a good source of vitamin C. The commercially cultivated varieties are native to North America, where the serving of cranberry sauce with turkey is traditional.

Colour is no indication of ripeness in cranberries, as they vary from a bright red to a dark, blackish red according to variety.

CRANBERRY SAUCE
(Basic Recipe)

1   pound cranberries
12 ounces sugar
16 fluid ounces water

Wash, pick over, and drain cranberries.

Put berries, sugar, and water in a saucepan. Bring slowly to the boil. Cover and cook slowly about 10 minutes, or until skins burst. Skim and cool. Makes about 1½ pints.

Cranberry Sauce Variations

Moulded Cranberry Jelly: Increase sugar to 1 pound. Cook until a thin syrup is formed, about 20 minutes. Pour into mould; chill.

Glazed Cranberries: Prepare as in basic recipe. Do not drain thoroughly.

Measure and mix equal parts sugar and berries in the top of a steamer or basin.

Cook over hot water until sugar forms thick syrup, about 1 hour, and berries are glazed. Stir carefully a few times at the start.

Minted Cranberry Sauce: In basic recipe, stir in 1 teaspoon chopped fresh mint.

BAKED CRANBERRY SAUCE

Wash and pick over berries. Place in a baking dish. Add 14 ounces sugar and 8 fluid ounces water for every 2 pounds of berries.

Cover and bake in slow oven (325°F. Mark 3) 30 minutes, or until berries are tender.

CRANBERRY STRAWBERRY COMPOTE

Cook 1 pound cranberries, in water to cover, in covered pan about 5 minutes.

Add 8 ounces sugar and 1 pound hulled strawberries. Cook 5 to 8 minutes. Serve cold.

FROSTED CRANBERRIES

1   egg white
½ teaspoon water
4   ounces fresh cranberries
8   ounces granulated sugar

Lightly beat egg white and water together just until blended. Dip cranberries in mixture until completely coated. Roll in sugar. Leave to dry at room temperature or in refrigerator.

This treatment is also very successful with redcurrants.

Frosted cranberries keep well in the refrigerator. Use them as nibblers or as decorations on ice cream.

CURRENTS

Two different fruit are described by the term currant. One is the dried fruit of a small, seedless grape grown in the Mediterranean region, used in cooking; however, the name usually refers to the small, sour, red, white, or black berry of a large group of hardy shrubs. They are used for jellies and jams. Choose firm, ripe currants for jelly-making. Over-ripe fruit does not "jell" so well.

TO SERVE FRESH CURRANTS

Wash, drain, and remove stems from chilled red or white currants. Sprinkle liberally with sugar, since these berries are very sharp. They are particularly good when mixed with other sweeter berries.

If served with cream, serve the cream separately because the acid may turn the cream.

Ripe black currants are decorative but do not have as much flavour as the red or white.

ELDERBERRIES

These are the small black berries of the elder bush, principally used in jelly and wine-making.

GOOSEBERRIES

The gooseberry is a small, sour berry resembling a currant but larger. Ripe gooseberries are soft and have a light amber colour—the large ones usually being the best. Gooseberries are usually cooked with sugar for 10 or 15 minutes before they are eaten. Their chief use is in preserves and pies.

GOOSEBERRY FOOL

This dessert is sometimes made with other chilled stewed fruits.

1 pound ripe gooseberries
6 fluid ounces water
6 ounces sugar
1 tablespoon butter or
        margarine
⅛ teaspoon salt
2 eggs, separated

Stem berries; wash in cold water and drain. Put into saucepan with water.

Cover the pan and boil gently until the berries are soft, 8 to 10 minutes.

Put through a sieve, taking care to push through all pulp or purée in a blender. Return purée to saucepan; add 4 ounces sugar, butter, and salt; stir to mix.

Beat egg yolks well; stir into purée.

Beat egg whites until stiff; gradually add remaining sugar and beat until stiff and shiny.

Place purée over heat; stir constantly until mixture bubbles and thickens. Quickly pour hot berry mixture over egg whites; cut and fold in until

thoroughly blended. Cover; chill in refrigerator.

Serve in chilled dessert cups with a topping of whipped cream, a sliced strawberry, or finely chopped nuts. Serves 4.

HUCKLEBERRIES, WHORTLEBERRIES OR BILBERRIES

These are all dark-blue berries, the fruit of any of a number of related shrubs.

The berries commonly sold are really a development through horticultural research of the wild huckleberry. Large berries are better than smaller ones, as they have a better flavour.

STEWED BILBERRIES

Cook bilberries in very little water. When they are nearly tender, add a few grains salt and sugar to taste. Cook a minute longer.

BILBERRY SLUMP

2   pounds bilberries
12 ounces sugar
4   tablespoons arrowroot or corn-
        flour
juice of 1 lemon
4   tablespoons butter or margarine
¼   teaspoon salt
1   egg
4   fluid ounces milk
6   ounces sifted flour
2   teaspoons baking powder

Wash berries and drain. Mix 8 ounces sugar with the arrowroot; add to berries. Place in greased casserole; sprinkle with lemon juice.

Cream together butter and remaining sugar. Add salt. Beat egg and add to creamed mixture. Add milk and mix well. Stir in flour and baking powder quickly and spoon over berries.

Bake in hot oven (425°F. Mark 7) 20 to 25 minutes. Serve warm with vanilla ice cream. Serves 8.

BILBERRY FLUMMERY

1   pound bilberries
about ¾ pint water
4   ounces sugar
3½ tablespoons cornflour
pinch of salt
juice of 1 lemon

Simmer berries in just over ⅔ of the water until very tender. Put through a sieve, pressing through as much pulp and skin as possible.

Add sugar to juice and sieved pulp; bring to the boil.

Blend the cornflour with the remaining cold water, and add with salt to hot mixture. Cook, stirring constantly, until mixture thickens.

Remove from heat; stir in lemon juice. Cool, then pour into serving dish, and chill. Serve with sugar and cream, if you like. Serves 4.

JUNIPER BERRIES

The juniper berry is the fruit of the juniper shrub or tree. It is often used to flavour stuffings and sauces for meat and game, and is the dominant flavouring in gin.

LOGANBERRIES

The loganberry is a red berry of uncertain origin. It is either a variety of dewberry or a cross between the dewberry and the raspberry. These sweet berries are used like raspberries.

MULBERRIES

Mulberries are very sweet and may be eaten raw, usually served with lemon juice or cream. In recipes they are prepared in the same way as raspberries.

STRAWBERRIES

Large strawberries are the choicest for eating, as they usually have the sweetest taste. For bottling and preserving, medium size, tart-flavoured berries are best.

STRAWBERRY APPLE SAUCE

½ pound fresh strawberries or 1
        packet frozen strawberries
¾ pint apple sauce, chilled

Wash fresh strawberries; hull and halve. Mix with apple sauce. Sweeten to taste. Place in serving dish. Top with whipped cream, if you like. Serves 4 to 6.

Strawberry Apple Sauce Delight

STRAWBERRIES ROMANOFF

4 pounds strawberries
sugar
1 large block vanilla ice cream
8 fluid ounces double cream,
    whipped
juice of 1 lemon
4 tablespoons Cointreau or Curaçao
2 tablespoons rum

Clean and hull strawberries. Sweeten with sugar.

Whip ice cream slightly and fold in whipped cream. Add lemon juice, Cointreau or Curaçao, and rum. Pour over berries. Spoon into chilled coupe glasses to serve. Serves 8.

Note: To blend flavours correctly, prepare the topping several hours before serving and store in refrigerator tray with temperature control at normal.

DIPPED STRAWBERRIES

Wash fresh, ripe strawberries. Drain, but do not remove stems and hulls.

Pile whipped sweet or heavy sour cream in centre of individual serving dishes.

Arrange fruit around cream, so guests may, using the stems to hold them, dip the berries into the cream.

If you like, 4 ounces desiccated coconut may be folded into 8 fluid ounces heavy cream, which has been whipped and sweetened with a couple of teaspoons of sugar and a drop of vanilla essence.

STRAWBERRIES WITH KIRSCH CREAM

2 pounds ripe strawberries
2¾ ounces icing sugar
8 fluid ounces double cream
3 tablespoons kirsch

Wash berries. Reserve 12 unhulled berries. Remove hulls and cut remaining berries into halves. Sprinkle with icing sugar and leave for 10 minutes.

Whip cream until stiff; flavour with kirsch.

Fold berries into cream and serve in coupe glasses decorated with the whole berries. Serves 6.

STEWED RASPBERRIES

2 pounds raspberries
8 fluid ounces water
4 to 8 ounces sugar
1 tablespoon lemon juice

Wash, drain, and hull raspberries. Heat water with sugar in a saucepan.

When the water-sugar mixture simmers, add berries, cover and simmer 10 minutes.

Add lemon juice and chill. Serves 4 to 6 as a sauce with ice cream, cake, and puddings.

BRAZILIAN STRAWBERRY COMPOTE

2 pounds ripe strawberries
caster sugar, to taste
grated rind of 1 orange
about 4 to 8 tablespoons Cointreau
    or Triple Sec
1 tablespoon kirsch

Stem and wash strawberries. Dust them with icing sugar.

Grate in the orange rind. Moisten with Cointreau or Triple Sec, and add kirsch. Toss well; chill for at least 4 hours.

Serve each portion with 1 tablespoon well chilled rose-tinted whipped cream on top, sprinkled with slivers of blanched almonds. Serves 4 to 6.

STRAWBERRY AND COTTAGE CHEESE PARFAIT

8 ounces cottage cheese
1 egg white
2 tablespoons caster sugar
½ teaspoon salt
8 fluid ounces double cream
½ teaspoon almond essence
1 packet frozen strawberries,
    defrosted, or 1 pound fresh
    strawberries, crushed and
    sweetened

Beat cottage cheese until smooth.

Beat egg white until frothy, then beat until stiff, adding sugar and salt. Fold into cottage cheese.

Whip cream, adding almond essence. Fold into mixture. Spoon cottage cheese mixture and fruit alternately into individual serving dishes. Serves 6.

STRAWBERRIES AND SOUR CREAM

1 pint sour cream
8 ounces cottage cheese
1 tablespoon caster sugar
1 pound strawberries, washed,
    drained dry and hulled

Mix together cream, cottage cheese, and sugar. Beat with a spoon until blended.

Just before serving, stir in berries. Serve with split hot scones. Makes about 1½ pints.

BLACKBERRY WHIP

2 egg whites
pinch of salt
2 ounces caster sugar
1 tablespoon lemon juice
grated rind of 1 lemon
1 pound fresh blackberries

Beat egg whites with salt until stiff, then gradually beat in sugar, 1 tablespoon at a time.

Fold in lemon juice, rind, and washed, well drained blackberries. Chill. Serve plain or with custard. Serves 4.

QUICK STRAWBERRY FLUFF

1 packet strawberry instant whip
1 packet (10 ounces) frozen straw-
    berries, defrosted
3 egg whites
single cream

Sprinkle dry pudding mix over strawberries and work only until mixed together. Leave for 5 minutes.

Beat egg whites until stiff but not dry. Fold into strawberries. Serve with single cream. Serves 4.

Cherries

High quality in cherries is denoted by plumpness with a bright appearance, firmness, and good colour. You'll need a quick handy tool for stoning them if you're going to make full use of this delicious fruit for pies, jams, fruit salads, or cups. Special cherry-stoners can be bought or use a clean strong hair pin.

STEWED MORELLO CHERRIES

2 pounds Morello cherries
8 fluid ounces water
8 ounces sugar

Wash the cherries and remove stones and stems.

Mix the water and sugar together; stir over low heat until sugar is dissolved. Bring to the boil and boil for 5 minutes.

Add cherries and boil gently 5 to 10 minutes or until cherries are tender.

MARASCHINO CHERRIES

Originally, these were cherries preserved in maraschino, a very sweet, colourless liqueur. Most of those so called nowadays are in an artificially coloured and flavoured sugar syrup.

CHERRIES JUBILEE

Cherries Jubilee always involves the use of a liqueur or brandy. If you do not wish to flame the brandy, it may be added to the cherries well in advance so they can absorb the flavour.

1 can (20 ounces) cherries, stoned
1 teaspoon cornflour
4 fluid ounces Cognac or kirsch
2 pints vanilla ice cream

Drain juice from canned cherries. Reduce 8 fluid ounces juice to 6 fluid ounces by boiling hard.

Blend the cornflour with 2 tablespoons of remaining cherry juice. Add to hot juice and cook, stirring until thick and clear. Remove from heat.

Add cherries. Pour into metal pan, heat-resistant casserole, or chafing dish.

Carefully pour Cognac or kirsch on top. Set alight and spoon flaming cherries over individual portions of ice cream. Serve immediately. Serves 8.

Citrus Fruits

GRAPEFRUIT

How this name originated is still a moot question, but it is generally attributed to the fact that the fruit grows in clusters like grapes.

Buying Hints: You may find that two grapefruit of the same size will often vary in taste and juiciness. The one will be heavy, firm, and smoothly textured, with a well-rounded shape—a good indication of fine, juicy grapefruit. The other will be coarse, puffy, and rough—indicative of lack of juice, as well as taste. Since grapefruit is, on the average, over three-quarters liquid, heaviness is a good indication of juice content.

Do not rely solely on colour as a guide to flavour, as good grapefruit can range from pale yellow to russet or bronze. Brightly coloured fruit is naturally more appealing—yet a russeted fruit may often be tastier and juicier. Minor surface blemishes do not affect the eating quality although the presence of a bad bruise may indicate some internal breakdown which is not apparent on the outside. The pink-fleshed grapefruit is a cross-bred creation, and many people consider the "pink flesh" somewhat sweeter than others.

GRILLED OR BAKED GRAPEFRUIT

Wash grapefruit and cut in halves. Remove seeds, core, and loosen segments. Sprinkle each half with 1 tablespoon brown sugar, then pour 1 tablespoon sherry or brandy over each.

Put under the grill until the sugar melts, or bake in moderate oven (350°F. Mark 4). Serve at once as a dessert.

Grilled Honeyed Grapefruit: Prepare grapefruit as above. Spread with honey and sprinkle with ground cinnamon and mace instead of other ingredients. Brown lightly under moderate grill.

Grapefruit with French Dressing: Use French dressing instead of above ingredients. Spoon 2 tablespoons over each prepared grapefruit half, making sure it covers them completely. Bake or grill as above. Serve hot as a first course.

GRAPEFRUIT COCKTAIL

Cut chilled grapefruit in halves. Loosen the pulp from the peel with a very sharp knife. Remove the pips and cut out the tough fibrous centre with a grapefruit knife or scissors.

Five minutes before serving sprinkle the grapefruit with icing sugar. Just before serving add 1 tablespoon sherry to each half.

For a party touch, notch the edge of the grapefruit and put a maraschino cherry in the centre.

TO PEEL AND SEGMENT GRAPEFRUIT

Chill whole fruit thoroughly. With a straight-sided sharp knife cut a slice from the top, then cut off peel in strips from top to bottom. Or cut off peel round and round in one long spiral. Always cut deep enough to remove white membrane.

Go over fruit again removing any remaining white membrane.

Cut along membrane of each section from outside to the core. Tip knife outwards and roll the whole segment out one at a time. Cut fruit segments over a bowl to catch the juice.

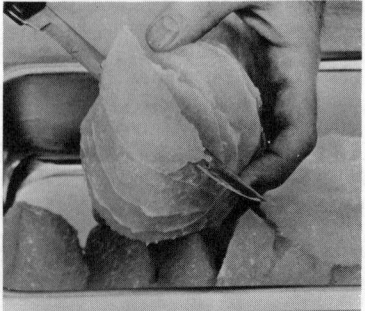

BAKED GRAPEFRUIT

4 ounces crushed cornflakes
3 ounces brown sugar
½ teaspoon ground cinnamon
2 ounces melted butter or margarine
2 grapefruit, halved and cored

Mix together cornflakes, sugar, cinnamon, and butter. Fill and top the halves of grapefruit in which the segments have been loosened.

Bake in hot oven (400°F. Mark 6) about 10 to 12 minutes. Serve at once. Serves 4.

KUMQUATS

The kumquat is a citrus fruit of Chinese origin. It is about the size of a small plum, orange in colour, with an acid pulp partway between that of an orange and a lemon in flavour. It has a thin, sweet, aromatic rind. The entire fruit, rind and all, is edible if it is fully ripe; however, kumquats are used mainly in preserves and jelly or candied. They may be sliced very thin and used in salads; remove the large seeds.

Stuffed Kumquats: Slice in half. Remove the large seeds. Stuff the fruit with cream cheese or chopped nuts and use to garnish salads.

BOILED KUMQUATS

Wash 1 pound kumquats. Cover with cold water; bring to the boil, then cover and simmer 30 minutes.

Add 1 pound sugar and, if you like, ¼ teaspoon ground cinnamon, and boil 5 minutes.

The kumquats may be served whole or they may be cut in half, in which case remove the large seeds. Chill thoroughly and use as a garnish for a meat platter or in salads.

Note: Kumquats may also be cooked in water to cover (without sugar) until the skin is clear and tender, about 20 to 30 minutes.

CITRON

The citron is a yellow, thick-skinned fruit resembling a lime or lemon but larger and less acid. It is cultivated for its thick, spongy rind, which is candied or glacéed for use as a sweet or in fruit cakes.

CALAMONDIN

The calamondin is a citrus fruit that looks like a small tangerine but is more like a lime in flavour and acidity.

LEMONS

Lemons should be fine textured, heavy for their size and moderately firm. These points are indicative of juiciness. Avoid green-tinted fruit, as generally this has not been fully "cured". Of all the members of the citrus family, lemons are the most versatile. Many uses for juice and rind are given in individual recipes throughout this book.

LIMES

The lime is a small, almost round, greenish-yellow citrus fruit. The juice is aromatic, refreshing, sour, and rich in vitamin C. The characteristic flavour of limes makes them especially useful for cold drinks or for squeezing over melon or fruit compote. They are at their best when their skins are bright green. Limes should be kept in the refrigerator.

GLORIFIED GRAPEFRUIT

3 medium-size grapefruit
1 can (1 pound, 1 ounce) fruit
   cocktail
2 tablespoons maraschino cherry
   syrup
2 to 3 tablespoons brown sugar

Cut grapefruit in half. With curved grapefruit knife, remove fruit in one piece, leaving shell intact. Segment fruit, removing membranes.

Drain fruit cocktail thoroughly and add to grapefruit, together with maraschino cherry syrup. Mix lightly and spoon into grapefruit shells. Sprinkle with brown sugar.

Place in grill pan under moderate heat and grill until thoroughly heated and tinged with brown. Serve warm. Serves 6.

Glorified Grapefruit: The sweet fruits of canned fruit cocktail combine with fresh grapefruit to make a delicious breakfast treat.

ORANGES

China is placed as the original home of this citrus fruit, with Columbus being given credit for introducing them to the New World.
Buying Hints: As in any other member of the citrus family, the weight of an orange is indicative of its juice content. Also bear this point in mind: make sure the fruit is firm and has a skin that is not too rough. Colour is not a sure guide to quality.

POACHED ORANGES

6 seedless oranges
1 pound sugar
16 fluid ounces water

Cut oranges in half crossways. Cover with water; bring to the boil. Pour off and discard water.

Mix the sugar with the water; bring to the boil. Add oranges; cook gently until skins can be easily pierced with wooden cocktail stick (20 to 30 minutes). Chill.

ORANGE COMPOTE

2 seedless oranges
8 fluid ounces water
6 ounces sugar
⅛ teaspoon salt
3 extra oranges
1 tablespoon rum or liqueur
   (optional)

Cut yellow rind off 2 oranges. Cut rind into thin slices and add water, sugar, and salt. Boil 20 minutes.

Skin and remove membrane from the 2 oranges and from 3 extra oranges. Place the segments in a serving bowl. Pour the hot syrup and rind over them. Chill the compote. If you like, add rum or liqueur before serving. Serves 4.

ORANGE BANANA AMBROSIA

Ambrosia is a versatile old favourite dish consisting usually of sliced oranges, bananas, and desiccated coconut; however it is often varied by the addition of honeydew and cantaloupe melon balls and sometimes sprinkled with lime juice.

2 medium-sized oranges
2 ripe firm bananas
2 tablespoons caster sugar
2 to 3 ounces desiccated coconut

Peel oranges and cut crossways in thin slices, removing pips and fibrous portions. Peel bananas and slice about ¼-inch thick.

Arrange alternate layers of orange and banana slices in large shallow dish, sprinkling each layer with sugar.

Use orange slices for bottom and top layers. Sprinkle top generously with coconut. Chill about 1 hour before serving.

Just before serving, decorate with additional ripe banana and orange slices, if you like. Serves 4 to 6.

TANGERINES AND SATSUMAS

Tangerines are small, slightly flattened oranges with easily removed skins and loosely adhering segments. They are also called mandarin oranges. This fruit is best when it is deep orange in colour and firm in texture, rather than puffy. Satsumas are similar to tangerines.

TANGERINES IN KIRSCH

Peel the tangerines and separate the segments. Arrange in glass serving dish and sprinkle with icing sugar.

Sprinkle with kirsch and refrigerate 2 hours before serving.

TANGERINE SURPRISE

8 medium tangerines
12 fluid ounces water
4 ounces sugar
5 2-inch cinnamon sticks
6 whole cloves
2 tablespoons lemon juice

Wash, peel, and segment tangerines, placing rind from 3 tangerines in saucepan. Remove all white membrane from fruit; add membrane to rind, along with water, sugar, spices, and lemon juice. Bring to a rolling boil; boil, uncovered, 10 minutes.

Remove rind, add tangerine segments and bring to the boil again. Boil 1 minute, then cool. Refrigerate. Serve with cream cheese and cracker biscuits. Serves 4.

A jumbo brandy balloon makes a dramatic serving dish for ambrosia as well as other fruit combinations.

Dates

DATES

Fresh dates, when fully ripe, have a golden brown colour and are slightly moist. Their origin may be traced back to ancient Africa where the appearance of date palms usually heralded the location of a water-hole or spring in the midst of a desert.

To serve fresh dates, wash carefully, remove stems, and serve as part of a fruit salad or platter.

SPICED FRESH DATES

3 **pounds fresh dates**
shelled walnuts or almonds
2 **pounds sugar**
12 **fluid ounces vinegar**
4 **fluid ounces water**
½ **teaspoon salt**
few drops oil of cinnamon and
cloves

Remove stones from dates and stuff with large pieces of nut; the almonds may be blanched or not, as preferred.

Pack into small jars, standing dates on end.

Make a syrup of remaining ingredients, simmer for 5 minutes, and pour over dates in jars. Seal while hot.

Figs

The fresh fig is a great favourite of epicures. Best known to the Oriental people, this fruit is fairly abundant in hot, tropical areas. Varieties include Mission, large dark purple; Calimyrna, large white; Adriatic, white; Kadota, smaller and white. Figs are highly perishable; ripeness can be ascertained by the degree of softness to the touch, while over-ripeness is detectable by a sour odour which is due to fermentation of the juice.

Serve sliced fresh figs with cream, or with lemon or orange juice. If they are

Gold Dessert Compote

thoroughly ripe, they need no sweetening.

Use them in practically any other way, as for other fresh fruits—in fruit cups, salads, etc.

STEWED DRIED FIGS

Rinse figs; cover with water and boil 20 to 30 minutes. For each 8 ounces fruit add 1 tablespoon sugar for the last 15 minutes of cooking.

Stewed Figs with Oranges: Cook as above, adding ½ slice orange for each 6 figs for the last 5 minutes of cooking. Serve lukewarm. Sugar may be added if you like.

SPICED CANNED FIGS

1½-2 **pounds bottled or canned figs**
in syrup
4 **ounces sugar**
4 **tablespoons cider vinegar**
⅛ **teaspoon salt**
1 **stick cinnamon**
¼ **teaspoon whole allspice**
whole cloves

Drain fruit. Mix together syrup, sugar, vinegar, salt, and cinnamon. Add allspice tied in a muslin bag. Bring to a rolling boil and boil 2 minutes.

Stick 2 cloves in each fig and add to hot syrup. Simmer 10 minutes. Do not boil.

Remove spice bag. Cover. Chill 24 hours before serving.

SPICED DRIED FIGS

1 **pound dried figs**
16 **fluid ounces cold water**
sliced lemon peel
1 **1-inch piece ginger root**
4 **ounces sugar**
2 **tablespoons lemon juice**

Wash figs and remove tough stems. Mix with water, lemon peel, and ginger root in a saucepan. Simmer until figs are tender, about 30 minutes.

Add sugar and simmer 10 minutes. Remove from heat and add lemon juice. Stir and chill. Serves 6 to 8.

GOLD DESSERT COMPOTE

12 **dried figs**
4 **ounces desiccated coconut**
2 **oranges, peeled and sliced**
6 **thin slivers candied ginger**
3 **ounces honey**
4-5 **tablespoons orange juice**
1 **tablespoon grated orange rind**

Arrange figs, coconut, oranges, and ginger in a decorative bowl.

Mix together honey, orange juice, and rind; pour over fruits. Chill for an hour before serving. Serves 6.

Melons

Melons are fruits of the gourd family, one that includes many trailing or climbing plants such as the marrow and pumpkin. There are many varieties of melon; the watermelon, cantaloupe or muskmelon, honeydew, and charentais are perhaps the best known.

Hints on Buying Melons

Melons of all types are at their best when fully ripe. Ripeness in almost all kinds of melon is indicated by the softening at the part of the fruit which surrounds the "eye" or stem end and should yield to pressure of the finger. In some melons a change of colour to a more or less yellowish or orange tinge is also a sign of ripeness. Usually the fragrant aroma that most melons diffuse becomes stronger and is most perceptible when a melon is fully ripe. No one indication is infallible. Sometimes one, and sometimes a combination of indications must serve as a guide. If melons have soft spots on them, they are overripe and may not taste or look right.

Watermelon is tested for ripeness by thumping with the knuckle; if ripe, it gives a resonant, hollow sound.

Unripe melons should never be chilled, because they do not then fully ripen. In quantity, melons are stored at a temperature of 70°F. until ripe, and then chilled just before serving. An unripe melon will ripen in 1 or 2 days on a sunny window ledge.

A cut melon should always be wrapped in greaseproof paper or the cut section covered with moistened greaseproof paper before placing in refrigerator to prevent its smell permeating other foods.

To Serve Melons

Melons should be washed and chilled thoroughly before serving fresh in the shell or cut into various shapes and served in fruit cups, salads, etc. Lemon or lime wedges may be served with melons in the shell such as cantaloupe, honeydew, casaba because the citrus juice emphasizes the melon's flavour. If you like, melon may be served on ice, but the cavity should never be filled with ice because that injures the fruit and dilutes the flavour.

FRUITED MELON

Top melon wedges with canned fruit cocktail and bit of grated orange rind. Or serve a pitcher of lime, lemon, or orange juice.

LACED WATERMELON

To impregnate a watermelon with rum or other spirit, remove a small plug of watermelon, add the spirit slowly. Replace plug and leave for about 8 hours.

MELON LACED WITH PORT

Cut a plug in the upperside of the melon. Dig out the seeds with a long handled spoon. Pour in 6 to 8 fluid ounces port. Chill melon in bowl of ice in the refrigerator. Slice and serve with rind removed. Use the marinating port as a dressing.

STUFFED MELON SLICES

Peel cantaloupe or honeydew mellons. Cut off enough of one end so you can remove the seeds. Fill the cavity with a fruit jelly mixture. Allow it to set. Cut the melon in slices and serve on crisp lettuce leaves. If you like, garnish with sour cream or yogurt.

MELON SLICES WITH RASP-BERRIES OR STRAWBERRIES

Cut chilled cantaloupe or honeydew melon into 1- to 2-inch crossways slices, allowing one slice for each serving.

Remove the seeds and place slices on individual serving dishes. Fill the centres with chilled, sugared raspberries or strawberries. Serve with lemon or lime wedges.

WATERMELON BOWL

Cut a watermelon in half; scoop out flesh from both halves with a ball cutter. Prepare cantaloupe and honeydew balls in same way.

Mix melon balls with any other fresh fruits—pineapple, grapes, sliced peaches, figs. Pour enough wine (sherry, port, or sweet white) over fruit to cover; chill for several hours.

Just before serving, drain fruit thoroughly and heap into one half of the scooped-out watermelon shell. Set filled shell on a platter for serving.

Fruit Pinwheel: Melon balls topped with shimmering grapefruit segments either chilled, canned, or frozen, make a tempting summer dessert.

Cantaloupe Seafood Appetizer: Cut cantaloupes in half with a zigzag cut. Trace zigzag line around middle, then make deep thrust with knife into centre one way, then the other way, all the way around. Remove seeds. Fill cavity with tomato cocktail sauce and set each half shell in shallow bowl of crushed ice. Arrange prawns around cantaloupe on ice. Garnish with lime or lemon wedges. Serve with a cocktail fork and a teaspoon.

BAKED CANTALOUPE MELON

2 cantaloupe melons
1½ pounds sliced peaches
4 ounces sugar
pinch of ground mace
mint sprigs

Halve the melons; remove seeds. Mix together peaches, sugar, and mace. Fill cantaloupes with peaches, arranging slices in a decorative pattern on top.

Bake in hot oven (425°F. Mark 7) 15 minutes. Garnish with mint. Serve at once. Serves 4.

Peaches and Nectarines

PEACHES

Buying Hints: When buying peaches, the best thing to remember is that they must look good to be good. Size and colour should play an important part in your choice. Make sure they are plump, smooth skinned, and well filled out. The colour on the underside of a peach should be creamy white or yellow, blushed with red. Over-ripeness is generally indicated by the deeper reddish-brown colour and a softness of the fruit. Peaches in this stage are suitable for immediate use, but cannot be kept for any length of time.

Either the white or yellow-fleshed varieties of peaches are suitable for any number of delicious dishes—the white varieties being just as sweet and tasty as the yellow. But remember to select fruit that is not too deeply green tinged, for such fruit is unripe and will not ripen properly at home.

NECTARINES

The nectarine is a smooth-skinned variety of peach, often mistakenly believed to be a cross between a peach and a plum. Peach trees occasionally produce nectarines and nectarine trees may produce peaches. The nectarine can be served in exactly the same way as the peach and substituted for it in recipes.

GRILLED PEACHES

Place fresh or canned peach halves,

cut-side up, in a buttered shallow pan. Place 1 teaspoon butter in each cavity. Sprinkle with brown sugar.

Grill under moderate heat until lightly browned.

Curried Peaches: To above, add a small pinch of curry powder.

GLACIER PEACHES

1 can (1 pound, 13 ounces) cling
    peach halves
1½ ounces brown sugar
2 or 3 tablespoons wine vinegar
1 teaspoon onion flakes
¼ teaspoon seasoned salt
Glacier Topping:
1 packet (8 ounce) cream cheese
2 tablespoons spiced syrup from
    peaches
2 tablespoons mayonnaise or sour
    cream
2 or 3 drops Tabasco sauce
¼ teaspoon seasoned salt
2 tablespoons sweet pickle relish,
    drained (or 1 tablespoon
    each chopped green pepper
    and pimiento)

Drain peaches, saving syrup. Mix 8 fluid ounces peach syrup with sugar, vinegar, onion, and salt. Bring to the boil; pour over drained peaches and chill thoroughly 4 or 5 hours or overnight.

When ready to serve, drain peaches and fill each one with a snowy cap of Glacier Topping. Serve with sandwiches, salad, or with barbecued or other meats or turkey.

Glacier Topping: Soften cheese; beat in syrup and mayonnaise until smooth. Add all remaining ingredients; chill until ready to serve. Serves 5 or 6.

BAKED PEACHES

Peel, cut in halves, and remove stones from firm juicy peaches. Place in baking dish.

Fill each hollow with ½ teaspoon butter, 1 teaspoon sugar, a sprinkling of lemon juice, and a dusting of grated nutmeg or ground cinnamon.

Place 2 tablespoons water in the bottom of dish. Bake in moderate oven (350°F. Mark 4) 20 minutes.

Glacier Peaches

FRUIT BAKED IN WINE

4 peaches, apples, or pears
¼ pint red wine
5½ ounces sugar
½ stick cinnamon
4 whole cloves
⅛ teaspoon salt
½ thinly sliced lemon, pips
    removed

Peel peaches, apples, or pears; place in a baking dish.

Mix together wine, sugar, cinnamon, cloves, salt, and lemon. Heat but do not boil and stir; pour over fruit.

Cover and bake in moderate oven (350°F. Mark 4) until tender when tested with fork. Baste it every 10 minutes. Turn it so that it will cook evenly. Serves 4.

FLAMING FRESH PEACHES

6 large fresh peach halves, peeled
6 tablespoons brown sugar
1 ounce butter or margarine
6 maraschino cherries
4-5 tablespoons brandy

Place peach halves in baking dish. Sprinkle hollows with brown sugar and dot with butter. Grill until sugar forms a crust, about 3 minutes.

Place cherry in each peach hollow. Pour brandy over all. Set alight and serve while flaming. Serve with whipped cream or chilled custard. Serves 6.

PEACHES WITH BRANDIED CREAM

4 fluid ounces double cream
1 tablespoon brandy
small pinch of salt
3 tablespoons caster sugar
small pinch of ground mace
8 fresh peaches

Whip cream slightly. Add salt, 1 tablespoon sugar, and mace. Whip until cream is thickened.

Peel and slice peaches. Add remaining sugar and mix well. Arrange in serving dishes and top with cream. Serves 4.

SPICED PEACHES

1 can (28 ounces) peach halves
1 tablespoon vinegar
1 to 2 sticks cinnamon
1 teaspoon whole cloves

Mix the ingredients in saucepan and bring to the boil. Simmer 5 minutes. Chill.

Drain before serving. Stud peaches with whole cloves.

STEWED DRIED PEACHES

Rinse peaches; cover with water and boil 5 minutes. Drain and remove skins.

Cover with fresh water and boil 35 to 45 minutes. Allow 4 ounces sugar for each 6 ounces peaches and add for last 5 minutes of cooking.

Pears

There are about 800 known varieties of pears, but only a few of these are grown commercially today. Behind the cultivation of such a large number of varieties lies a story about the landed gentry who lived in France about 1850. At that time it was the fashion, just as dog or horse breeding is today, to see who could produce the finest species of pears. As a result, scores of new types came into being very quickly, and almost all of them were just as quickly forgotten once the fad was dropped. From this French "horticultural spree" came many of the pears found today, such as d'Anjou, Du Comice, Bosc, and Nelis.

Buying Hints: When buying pears, don't be misled by a scar or minor surface blemish, as this in no way affects the fruit's inner delicacy. As a matter of fact, many of the most delectable pears have a highly russeted skin.

Pears are packed and shipped green because it is characteristic that they develop a finer flavour and smoother texture when ripened off the tree. Remember that they should be fully ripe for "fresh" use, such as eating raw, in salads, or shortcakes. If they are hard and unyielding to the touch when you buy them, allow them to stand at ordinary room temperature until the flesh responds readily to a gentle pressure of the hand just as a ripe peach does. They are then in prime condition for eating. However, for baking and cooking purposes, pears are best when they are still firm and slightly under-ripe.

Bartletts are the summer pears. They're creamy yellow when ripe, with an attractive red blush. The Seckel, a late summer pear, is small, sweet, and luscious, richly russeted and excellent for eating. D'Anjou pears are usually medium to large in size with a smooth, thin, light green or creamy yellow skin when ripe. The Bosc, with its long tapering neck, ripens to a rich golden cinnamon, with brownish mottles running to almost solid russet at the blossom end. Another russet pear, very sweet in flavour, is the Winter Nelis, while probably the most luscious of all is the Du Comice.

FLAMING PEARS

Allow 1 ripe pear per serving. Cut unchilled pears in half. Remove core and place pears on an ovenproof plate.

Prick them with a fork and sprinkle with icing sugar. Pour over each pear half a tablespoon brandy. Flame the brandy at the table.

Baked Pears with Lemon Cream Sauce

BAKED PEARS WITH LEMON CREAM SAUCE

6 large fresh pears
3 tablespoons lemon juice
4 ounces sugar
2 ounces melted butter or margarine
5 ounces cornflakes
Sauce:
2 ounces icing sugar
8 fluid ounces sour cream
2 tablespoons lemon juice

Peel, halve, and core pears. Dip at once into lemon juice in which sugar has been dissolved.

Dip in melted butter. Roll in crushed cornflakes. Arrange pears, cut-side up, in a shallow baking dish.

Bake in moderate oven (350°F.-375°F. Mark 4-5) for 20 to 25 minutes or until pears are tender but not soft.

To make lemon cream sauce, beat icing sugar into sour cream and flavour with lemon juice. Serves 6.

PEARS BAKED IN PINEAPPLE JUICE

4 pears
1 teaspoon grated orange rind
juice of 1 lemon
4 fluid ounces canned pineapple
    juice
4 ounces sugar

Cut pears in half, peel, and core. Put in 1½-quart casserole. Mix remaining ingredients and pour over pears.

Cover and bake in hot oven (400°F. Mark 6) for 45 minutes, or until pears are tender. Baste pears every 15 minutes with some of the syrup in bottom of casserole. Chill. Serves 4.

STEWED FRESH GINGER PEARS

3 pears
3 ounces brown sugar
2 to 4 ounces granulated sugar
grated rind and juice ½ lemon
pinch of salt
1 teaspoon ground ginger
⅛ teaspoon ground cinnamon
4 fluid ounces water

Peel, core, and dice pears.

Mix the remaining ingredients in saucepan; bring to the boil. Add pears. Simmer, covered, for 20 minutes, or until pears are tender. Serves 4.

For an easy fruit dish, brush halved and cored Bartlett pears with pineapple juice to prevent them from darkening. Separate grapes into small bunches. Peel bananas and flute by lightly pressing fork prongs down sides. Cut into chunks and dip in pineapple juice. Arrange on fresh garden leaves with pineapple slices.

SOUTHERN BAKED PEARS

6 canned pear halves, drained
6 whole cloves
4 ounces light brown sugar
3 tablespoons pear juice
2 teaspoons lemon juice
3 tablespoons orange juice
¼ teaspoon grated orange rind
1 tablespoon butter or margarine
2 tablespoons chopped nuts

Arrange pear halves, with cored side up, in greased baking dish. Stick a clove in each pear.

Mix light brown sugar, fruit juices, orange rind, and butter in a saucepan. Bring to the boil and boil for 10 minutes, stirring occasionally.

Add nuts. Pour syrup over pears. Bake in moderate oven (350°F. Mark 4) about 30 minutes. Serve hot with meat course or use as a dessert. Or serve cold with whipped cream.

SPICED PEARS

1 can (28 ounces) Bartlett pears
1 stick cinnamon
8 to 12 whole cloves
4 tablespoons vinegar or lemon
    juice

Drain syrup from pears. Heat it with cinnamon stick and cloves for 5 minutes.

Remove from heat and add vinegar or lemon juice. Pour back over pears and leave overnight in refrigerator.

PEARS IN PORT

3 large fresh pears
8 fluid ounces water
3 ounces brown sugar
16 fluid ounces port

Stew pears, halved, peeled and cored, in the water and brown sugar, until tender, taking care not to break them. Drain; add port. Chill in refrigerator when cool. Serve cold.

Pineapple

Buying Hints: Fully ripe pineapples are slightly soft to the touch, golden yellow in colour, and have a "piney" aroma. Size has little to do with quality but you should avoid fruit that appears too green, as it may not ripen well. In fact, the exquisite flavour is only fully appreciated when it is eaten where the fruit is field-ripened because it does not increase in sweetness if picked green. If field-ripened, even the core is tender and can be eaten. Over-ripeness, on the other hand, is most frequently shown by slight decay at the base or on the sides in dark, soft, watery spots.

Fresh pineapples bruise easily, so they should be handled as carefully as possible. Store at 70°F. and away from sunlight. Rounded, plump pineapples have more flesh than the tapering ones. The aroma of ripeness is noticeable at the leafy end when one or two leaves are pulled out. A pineapple weighing 2 pounds gives about 1½ pounds of fruit.

PREPARATION OF FRESH PINEAPPLE

Wash pineapple. Cut off leafy end and a slice from stem end. Stand pineapple upright and cut off skin in strips from top to bottom. Remove eyes with pointed knife or special pineapple knife.

Prepare as below. Sprinkle with sugar and chill. Sugar will dissolve as it stands.

Shredded Pineapple: Cut very thin slices. Shred with a fork.
Pineapple Rings: Cut into thin serving slices. Cut out round core.
Pineapple Spears: Cut prepared pineapple into wedges with core removed. Cut into strips.
Pineapple Wedges or Cubes: Cut slices into wedges or cubes after core is removed.
Pineapple Ambrosia: Cut prepared pineapple into slices or cubes. Add 6 ounces each of orange and grapefruit segments and 2 ounces desiccated coconut. Chill 1 hour or more before serving.

PINEAPPLE TRIFLE

1 can (8 ounces) crushed pineapple, drained
10 marshmallows, cut in pieces
3 ounces macaroon crumbs
6 ounces chopped dates
6 fluid ounces heavy cream,
    whipped

Mix the pineapple, marshmallows, macaroon crumbs, and dates in a bowl. Fold whipped cream into above ingredients. Chill. Serves 6 to 8.

GLAZED PINEAPPLE

Method 1: Drain canned pineapple slices or spears; dip in brown sugar. Brown by cooking in hot bacon fat, or butter.
Method 2: Drain canned pineapple slices. Place in shallow buttered baking dish. Do not let the slices overlap.

Dot with butter or margarine. Bake in slow oven (325°F. Mark 3) 1 hour. Serve with a maraschino cherry in each slice.
Method 3: Sprinkle drained canned pineapple slices or spears with grated cheese. Season with a few grains red pepper. Grill or bake in moderate oven (350°F. Mark 4) to melt cheese.

PINEAPPLE IN SPICED WINE

8 fluid ounces port or Madeira
8 ounces sugar
18 whole cloves or 1 4-inch stick
    cinnamon
12 slices fresh or canned pineapple

Simmer wine, sugar, and cloves or cinnamon in a saucepan for 5 minutes.

Add pineapple slices and simmer 5 minutes. Turn the slices several times. Serve as a dessert. Serves 6.

CANDIED PINEAPPLE

1 can (1 pound, 4 ounces) sliced
    pineapple
14 ounces granulated sugar
icing sugar

Drain syrup from pineapple thoroughly. (Allow to drain in a colander several minutes.)

Put half of granulated sugar in the bottom of a large pan; then pineapple, and cover with remaining sugar. Store, covered, about 24 hours at room temperature.

Empty into large frying pan and boil 5 minutes. Reduce heat and gently simmer 15 minutes. Turn occasionally during the cooking, taking care that it does not scorch or turn brown. Remove slices to a cake rack to dry about 24 hours.

Pat sides and edges of slices heavily with sifted icing sugar. A crusty glaze will form after standing on the cake rack overnight.

SPICED PINEAPPLE CHUNKS

4 tablespoons vinegar
12 ounces sugar
8 whole cloves
small piece whole ginger
grated rind of 1 lemon
½ large, ripe pineapple, cut in
    small chunks

Mix the vinegar, sugar, spices, and lemon rind in saucepan. Bring to the boil.

Add pineapple and boil until transparent, about 15 minutes. Serve as accompaniment to meat.

Plums

Buying Hints: When shopping for fresh plums you will find the best quality ripe fruit is plump, full coloured for the variety, and soft enough to yield to slight pressure.

Plums vary in colour, according to variety, from a greenish-yellow to the familiar deep bluish-purple. The softness of the flesh is a fairly reliable guide to ripeness—the softer ones being more ripe. Overripe fruit, of course, is very mushy to the touch and, unless used quickly, is a poor buy.

Prunes are actually a variety of plum particularly suitable for drying, as a fresh ripe prune can be separated from the stone like a freestone peach. They are blue-black, oval, firm-fleshed, and represent the late plum crop.

COMMONLY USED PLUMS

Czar: A rounded plum, dull red when ripe with a waxy blue bloom. It is a good cooking plum with golden flesh and red juice.

Kirke's: A purple-black plum with a blue bloom and good flavour. It is one of the finest dessert plums.

Victoria: A bright red plum with dark speckling, sometimes flushed yellow. It is excellent for open plum pie, for bottling and jam-making, and also has a pleasant flavour for dessert use.

Switzers: A dark cooking plum imported mainly from Yugoslavia. It has an excellent flavour and keeps its purple-black colour when cooked.

DAMSONS

These belong to the same family as plums and are particularly good for cooking and jam-making. They are smaller than plums and tapered at both ends. The best variety is the Merryweather, a large black fine-flavoured fruit which is excellent for pies and purées, as well as for bottling. You can use damsons in any recipe that calls for plums.

PLUMCOTS

A cross between the plum and apricot, plumcots have a red flesh and a purple skin. Choose them as you would apricots. Plumcots are not very widely known.

SLOE

A small, acid blue-black plum that grows on the blackthorn tree. It is used chiefly to flavour sloe gin.

PLUM SLICES

4 slices day-old sandwich bread
1 pound ripe plums, stoned

Butter bread and place on a greased baking sheet. Put three plum halves on each slice and sprinkle sugar round them to cover the bread completely. Bake near the top of a moderate oven, 330°F. Mark 3.

STEWED PLUMS

1 pound plums
12 fluid ounces boiling water
4 to 8 ounces sugar

Cut in half and remove stones from plums, or use whole plums.

Drop into boiling water. When they are nearly tender, add sugar. Cook a few minutes longer.

PLUM-FIG AMANDINE

1 can (1 pound, 13 ounces) purple plums
1 can (1 pound) figs
4 tablespoons orange juice
1 ounce slivered toasted almonds

Add 8 fluid ounces syrup from plums and figs to orange juice. Pour over drained fruits and chill. Add almonds just before serving. Serves 6 to 8.

Remove lid from jar; set lid aside. Drain liquid from prunes; save liquid.

Place wine, prune liquid, sugar, and spices in saucepan. Cook, stirring occasionally, until mixture comes to the boil. Reduce heat and cook gently 5 minutes.

Remove from heat and cool slightly before pouring over prunes. Put lid back on jar and seal tightly. Store in refrigerator until ready to use.

SPICED OR PICKLED PRUNES

1 pound prunes
whole cloves
1¼ pints water
6 ounces dark brown sugar
8 fluid ounces vinegar
4 3-inch sticks cinnamon

Wash prunes. Stick 2 cloves in each prune. Soak in water for 2 hours.

Add sugar, vinegar, and cinnamon. Bring to the boil. Simmer 30 minutes. Chill overnight in syrup. Makes 2 pounds.

PRUNE WHIP

about 1½ pounds unsweetened cooked prune pulp
3 to 4 ounces sugar
grated rind and juice of ½ lemon
⅛ teaspoon salt
2 egg whites

Drain the cooked prunes before stoning so that the pulp is not too moist.

Place all ingredients in a deep bowl and beat until mixture is thick and holds its shape. Electric mixer may be used. Place in serving dishes. Chill. Serve with cream or custard sauce. Serves 4 to 5.

Variation: Fold in 1 ounce chopped nuts or desiccated coconut after mixture is beaten until stiff.

Plum-Fig Amandine

Prunes and Raisins

CLARET PRUNES

1 jar (about 1 pound) stewed prunes
¼ pint red wine
4-5 tablespoons prune liquid
1½ ounces brown sugar
¼ teaspoon ground cinnamon
⅛ teaspoon ground allspice
6 whole cloves

Prune Whip

PRUNE PURÉE

1 pound prunes
16 fluid ounces water
4¼ ounces sugar

Wash prunes; cover with water and soak 2 to 3 hours. Then cover pan and cook in the same water until tender, about 35 minutes.

Add sugar for the last 5 minutes of cooking. Drain off liquid and put prunes through a sieve. Makes about 1 pound purée.

STEWED PRUNES
(Basic Recipe)

½ pound dried prunes
1¼ pints hot water
1 to 2 tablespoons sugar
slice of orange or lemon

Wash prunes and soak in hot water 1 to 2 hours. Simmer in same water until tender, about 30 minutes.

Add sugar and lemon or orange slice for last 5 minutes of cooking.

If syrup is very thin, remove prunes and boil down syrup. Serve hot or cold.

Variations:

Stewed Prunes and Apricots: Use ¼ pound each of dried prunes and dried apricots. Double the amount of sugar.

Stewed Prunes and Peaches or Pears: Use ¼ pound each of dried prunes and dried peaches or pears. Increase sugar slightly.

PRUNE PUDDING

To 1½ pounds stoned stewed prune pulp and juice add a mixture of about 1 ounce cornflour, ¼ teaspoon cinnamon, and 4-5 tablespoons cold water.

Cook until clear and thick, stirring constantly. Chill. Serves 4 to 5.

RAISINS

Seeded raisins sometimes called for in recipes are the large variety from which the seeds have been removed. The sweetness released when they were slit open makes them sticky.

Seedless raisins are the small variety; both light and dark are dried from seedless grapes. Cut or chop them to get the full sweetness and flavour.

PLUMPED RAISINS

Wash raisins, cover with boiling water and leave for about 15 minutes or until cool. Drain, cover again with boiling water and soak 15 minutes. Drain and use in recipes.

STEWED RAISINS

Wash raisins. Add 8 fluid ounces water for every 6 ounces of raisins. Cover and simmer 10 minutes. Add ½ tablespoon sugar for every 6 ounces of raisins and cook 5 minutes longer.

Rhubarb

The rhubarb plant, sometimes referred to as pie plant, is classified as a herb and sometimes as a vegetable; however for cookery it is classed with fruits.

Buying Hints: Fresh garden or hothouse rhubarb is available. When making your choice, get fresh, large, crisp, and straight stalks of red or cherry colour. Condition of the leaves is a reliable guide in judging freshness.

STEWED RHUBARB

Wash 2 pounds rhubarb. Cut off leaves and root ends. Peel only if stalks are tough.

Cut into 1-inch pieces. Add 4 fluid ounces hot water. Simmer, covered, 10 minutes.

Add 6 ounces sugar and simmer 5 minutes longer, or until tender.

The amount of sugar necessary may vary with the tartness of the rhubarb. Add pinch of cinnamon, if you like. Serves 6 to 8.

Steamed Rhubarb: Prepare as above and cook in top of a steamer until tender, about ½ hour.

STEWED RHUBARB AND PINEAPPLE

Mix equal parts diced washed rhubarb and diced fresh pineapple. Sweeten to taste. Set aside for 1 hour or more.

Heat slowly until sugar dissolves. Simmer until rhubarb is tender.

BAKED RHUBARB

Arrange alternate layers of cleaned diced rhubarb and sugar in baking dish. Sprinkle top with sugar.

Bake in slow oven (300°F. Mark 2) until rhubarb is deep red in colour, about 1 hour.

RHUBARB WHIP

Whip 1 pint of double cream until stiff. Sweeten. Fold into 8 ounces stewed rhubarb.

Place each serving in a coupe glass which has been lined with lady fingers or pineapple spears. Chill. Serves 6.

RHUBARB BANANA DESSERT

Cook fresh rhubarb and sweeten to taste. While rhubarb is still warm, add sliced bananas (3 bananas to 2 pounds cooked rhubarb). Chill. Serve with cream if you like.

Miscellaneous Fruit

BREADFRUIT

The breadfruit is a large, round fruit with a starchy whitish pulp, breadlike when baked. It grows on a tree found in the South Pacific. It is sometimes available fresh in specialist shops.

CUSTARD APPLE

This is a tropical fruit otherwise known as a Cherimoya. Although it is normally tree-ripened, it must be allowed to stand for several days before it becomes soft and edible.

The flesh is creamy and smooth in texture, and has a flavour suggesting a mixture of strawberry and pineapple. To serve, chill the soft fruit thoroughly and cut in halves if small, quarters or wedges if large.

The fruit can either be served on plates to be eaten with spoons or can be peeled and sieved to be used in icecreams or custards. It is especially good combined with bananas.

GUAVA

The guava is a tropical pear-like fruit, somewhat like a peach in texture. It is grown in Florida and California and is seldom seen fresh except where grown. The fruit is red to yellow in colour. Some guavas are sweet, some sour. The sweeter types are best for using fresh in salads and desserts, and for cooking; the sour ones are best for making jellies and jams. The peel is not eaten. They are available in cans.

GRAPES

When you buy grapes, choose bunches that are well formed and good looking. You will find colour is a good guide to ripeness. The darker varieties should be free of a green tinge, while white grapes should have a decided amber colouring when completely ripe. Fully ripened grapes are fairly soft to the touch and delicate in taste. When ripe for eating, grapes are highly perishable and should be stored in the refrigerator.

Britain imports many varieties of dessert grapes, depending on the time of year. Among these are the Alphonso and Waltham Cross grapes imported from South Africa in the winter months. American Red Emperor grapes are also available from December. Belgian Royals are good high quality dessert grapes from Europe, and Spain and France both produce varieties of the sweet Alicante grapes popular in England. White Muscat grapes are another plentiful and delicious sweet variety available in the Autumn.

VINE LEAVES

Large, tender leaves can be used for making dolma (see Index). Pickled vine leaves in cans or jars may be bought in some delicatessens and supermarkets.

CRYSTALLIZED GRAPES

Choose perfect red or purple grapes. Wash and drain well. Cut into small clusters.

For each pound of grapes, use 4 fluid ounces water and 8 ounces sugar. Mix water and sugar and boil 5 minutes.

Dip each cluster of grapes separately into hot syrup. Let excess syrup drain off. Sprinkle grapes at once with granulated sugar.

Place on cake rack to harden and place rack in refrigerator.

FROSTED GRAPES

Choose perfect red or purple grapes. Wash and dry well. Cut into small clusters.

Beat egg white until slightly frothy. Sprinkle it over the grapes. Dust with granulated sugar. Leave to dry.

JUJUBE

This is the date-like fruit of a number of trees and shrubs of the buckthorn family, growing in warm climates. It varies considerably in size, is shaped somewhat like a plum and is brown or reddish-brown in colour.

It can be eaten fresh, or the dried fruit can be chopped and added to breads, cakes or cooked cereals. The fresh fruit is sometimes skinned and pickled.

LOQUAT

The loquat is a delicious plum-like fruit of an ornamental fruiting tree. Fruits of the better varieties grow as large as eggs.

Fresh ones are sometimes available, and loquats may be used as table fruits, in preserves, pickled, or in pies. For loquat pie, follow ordinary fruit pie recipes, allowing 1 to 1½ pounds stoned loquats for a pie.

MANGO

The mango is a yellowish-red oblong tropical fruit with a thick rind, a somewhat acid and juicy orange pulp, and a hard stone. It tastes like a combination of peach, pineapple, and cantaloupe melon. It is good raw; stewed like any other fruit; in puddings, water ices or ice cream; or made into preserves, jelly or sweet pickles (mango is an important ingredient in chutney). Raw mangoes may be chilled but are delicious at room temperature. Halve them, remove the stone, and eat the soft pulp with a spoon. Or peel and slice the flesh and eat it with a fork, with or without cream and sugar. A sprig of mint and a half lime make a pleasant garnish.

OLIVE

The small oval fruit of an evergreen tree with leathery leaves and yellow flowers. Fresh olives are eaten green or black (ripe ones) or are pressed to extract olive oil. Olive trees have been grown since prehistoric times in Asia Minor, and their cultivation spread very early to all Mediterranean countries.

Green olives are picked when full grown but unripe. They may be cured and packed in a simple brine, or the brine may be spiced or the olives later pickled in vinegar. Green olives are often stoned and stuffed with pimiento, anchovies, onions, or nuts.

Black olives may be salted or pickled in many ways, often in oil.

PAWPAWS

Pawpaws (also spelled papaw) are often confused with papayas but these two fruits are different botanically. Pawpaws can grow in colder climates than papayas and the fruit is entirely different. Pawpaws are about 6 inches in length, with a width of about 3 inches and an average weight of ¾ pound. The flesh is yellow, creamy in texture, and has a pungent smell. They often are not enjoyed at first, a taste for them having to be acquired.

There is another variety of the pawpaw tree whose fruit is shaped like a banana but is dark brown in colour and flat in appearance. This is sometimes called St. John's bread. The common name for the species of trees on which the pawpaw grows is custard-apple.

PAPAYA

The papaya is a large, yellowish-orange tropical fruit that resembles a melon. It has a soft flesh ranging in colour from yellow to deep salmon pink.

The papaya is ripe when it is soft enough to yield to slight pressure with the thumb. It is eaten raw. Small papayas may be served at room temperature, with a fruit knife; large ones are chilled and served in any of the ways suitable for melon. They mix well with other fruit in cocktails or salads. They may be made into jam, pickles, or ketchup or into ices and other desserts. In Hawaii, green papayas are steamed or baked and served as a vegetable.

PASSION FRUIT (GRANADILLA)

Passion fruit, sometimes called the granadilla, grows extensively in South America and Australia and is also cultivated in California in increasing quantities. The fruit is the size and shape of an egg and has a tough, purple skin. The meat is yellow with many black seeds, and is usually eaten in the fresh stage with a spoon; otherwise it is used in making jelly and as a base for fruit punch.

The passion fruit is said to derive its name from the fact that early Christian missionaries to South America, noticing it for the first time, saw in its flower formation symbols of the Crucifixion—the crown of thorns, nails, etc.

PERSIMMONS

The persimmon is the fruit of any of several trees of the ebony family. They are about the size and texture of tomatoes and range in colour from rosy orange or salmon pink to yellow. They should be tested for ripeness in the same way as tomatoes; an unripe persimmon is inedibly acid-tasting.

Persimmons are most commonly used as a dessert fruit. They should be thoroughly chilled. To serve, set the persimmon stem-end down on a plate and cut off a bit of the top, so that the pulp may be spooned out. Or quarter it from the top, cutting not quite through the stem end, and spread out the segments petal-fashion.

Persimmons ripen best in a cool, dark place. This fruit is extremely delicate and should receive no unnecessary handling. It is ready to eat when soft, but when storing it temporarily you should be sure it is kept dry.

PLANTAIN

The plantain is a type of banana, starchier and less sweet than the common species. It is a staple food of the tropics; it is picked green and cooked as a vegetable. It is good sliced thinly and fried in deep fat like a potato crisp and sprinkled with salt. The slices should be very crisp even when cold. **Note:** The name is also applied to any of a number of related weeds with ribbed leaves. Some are cooked and eaten as a vegetable when young and tender.

POMEGRANATE

The pomegranate is a tropical fruit, the berry of a somewhat thorny shrub or small tree. It is about the size of a large orange, and its leathery skin varies in colour from light yellow to deep purplish red. Those with a thin skin of bright colour and fresh appearance are best. The enclosed seeds and crimson juice are used in salads, cocktails, and punches. To serve pomegranates as a dessert, mix the scooped-out seeds with powdered sugar or honey and chill them. The fruit may also be eaten as it is. Pomegranate juice is the basis of grenadine syrup. In the Far East it is made into wine.

QUINCE

The quince is an autumn fruit which is generally grown locally for use in jelly-making and preserving. It may also be stewed, baked, or used in pies or tarts. Good-quality quinces are firm, free from blemishes and are a pale yellow colour when fully ripe. They bruise very easily and must be handled carefully, although they may be kept for a period of time in a dry, cool place.

Quinces resemble a yellow apple a great deal, although their flesh is more acid-bitter with numerous hard seeds throughout.

BAKED QUINCES

  6 **medium quinces**
12 **fluid ounces water**
  8 **ounces sugar**

Peel, core, and slice the quinces into a casserole. Add water and sugar. Cover and bake very slowly until the fruit is tender and deep red in colour.

If the water evaporates, add a little from time to time to ensure enough syrup to surround the fruit when it is served.

TAMARIND

The tamarind is a tropical fruit with a brown pod 3 to 8 inches long, which contains a juicy, acid pulp used in chutneys and preserves, especially in guava jellies. A drink is made by adding sugar and water to the pulp. The tamarind is grown in the East and West Indies and also in Florida.

A marmalade can be made from tamarind as follows: Wash 2 pounds tamarinds; drain and mix with 12 fluid ounces water. Bring to the boil, reduce heat and simmer until soft. Put through a sieve to remove fibres and seeds. Heat the pulp and add 8 ounces sugar for every 8 ounces pulp. Simmer, stirring constantly, until the mixture thickens. Seal and store as for other preserves (see Index).

Fruit Soups

Fruit soups are especially popular in the Scandinavian countries and in Israel. Colourful, tart, and appetizing, they are particularly delightful for summer meals.

When served cold, they should be thoroughly chilled. Serve hot fruit soups when the remainder of the menu consists of cold food.

CHILLED FRUIT SOUP
(Basic Recipe)

2 **tablespoons tapioca**
12 **fluid ounces water**
1 **tablespoon sugar**
pinch of salt
4 **fluid ounces quick-frozen concentrated orange juice**
1½ **pounds diced fresh fruit (peaches, cherries, apples, bananas, etc.)**

Put tapioca and water in saucepan. Bring to the boil, stirring constantly. Remove from heat.

Add sugar, salt, and concentrated orange juice; blend. Cool, stirring once after 15 to 20 minutes. Cover and chill.

Before serving, add fruit. If thinner soup is wanted, add more juice or less fruit.

Decorate bowl with fruit such as halved strawberries, orange segments, cherries, bananas.

Serves 5 to 6.

SWEDISH FRUIT SOUP

½ **pound mixed dried fruits (prunes, peaches, apricots)**
4 **ounces dried apples**
1¼ **ounces currants**
1¼ **ounces seedless raisins**
4 **pints cold water**
2 **ounces sago or tapioca**
1-inch stick cinnamon
⅛ **teaspoon salt**
2 **tablespoons sugar**
1 **tablespoon grated lemon rind**
16 **fluid ounces raspberry juice**

Wash dried fruits thoroughly. Cover with cold water; leave overnight.

In the morning add sago or tapioca and cinnamon. Bring to the boil; cover, reduce heat and simmer 1¼ hours. Add remaining ingredients.

Chill soup. Serve very cold as dessert, sprinkled with finely sliced almonds. Serves 6.

BERRY SOUP

1 **pound bilberries, raspberries, or other berries**
about 1½ pints water
16 **fluid ounces apple juice**
¼ **teaspoon salt**
⅛ **teaspoon grated nutmeg**
sugar to taste
2 **tablespoons cornflour**
4 **tablespoons lemon juice**

Mix berries and water in a saucepan; bring to the boil. Cover and cook 20 minutes or until soft; put through sieve.

Add apple juice, salt, nutmeg, and sugar to taste. Add cornflour blended with 2 tablespoons cold water. Cook until clear, stirring constantly. Chill and add lemon juice.

Top each serving with a spoonful of whipped cream if you like. Sprinkle with chopped mint. Serves 6.

Berry Cream Soup: After chilling add 8 fluid ounces thick sour cream.

Chilled Fruit Soup

HERBS, SPICES, AND CONDIMENTS

Everyday cooking becomes a culinary triumph with just a little addition of the right herb or spice.

Herbs are spices, but in practice a distinction is made between the two. A spice may be the roots, bark, stems, leaves, seeds, or fruits of a plant, and many of the seasonings that are called spices come from the tropics; herbs are the leaves of soft-stemmed or grassy plants, usually from the temperate zone.

The drums, jars or packets of herbs and spices in stores are dried. Besides the unmixed varieties, many blends are sold—poultry seasoning, chilli powder, curry powder, mixed spice, and others.

The word condiment can be applied to any herb or spice and also to salt and monosodium glutamate (which are chemicals, not spices) and to bottled seasonings like ketchup or made mustard.

HINTS FOR COOKING WITH HERBS

● Since experience is obviously the best teacher, use herbs sparingly until you become acquainted with them.
● The important thing to remember is that herbs should never dominate the foods with which they are used. Herbs are meant to season, to add flavour, to bring out natural flavours.
● Use $\frac{1}{4}$ teaspoon of dried herbs for a dish serving four unless you are sure you like more. Do not use over $\frac{1}{2}$ teaspoon of mixed herbs in a dish serving four.
● Do not use herbs in several dishes at the same meal—use them for variety and accent only.
● Remember that there is a difference in the strength of fresh and dried herbs.
● Dried herb leaves are four times stronger than the same measure of fresh leaves.

● Since dried herbs tend to lose their fragrance, soaking them in a few drops of water or lemon juice for 15 minutes before using helps to bring out the flavour.
● Fresh herbs from the garden can be used just as successfully in cooking as freshly dried herbs, but you always use less of the dried than the fresh.
● Always cut, crush, or chop fresh herbs before using to bring out the volatile oils and true flavours. For some purposes, pound them in a mortar. The more the cut surface is exposed the more completely the aromatic oil can be absorbed.
● Blending or heating herbs with butter or other fats is a good way to draw out and extend the flavour of aromatic oils.
● Remember that the strength of the flavour herbs give food is increased by the length of time they cook, by a lid on the pot, the freshness of the herb.
● Herbs left too long in soups or gravies will impart unpleasantly strong flavours. They are best added a short time before the cooking is finished.
● For soups or gravies add a bouquet garni (sprigs of fresh herbs tied in tiny bunches) or use dried herbs in muslin bags and remove them after they have served their purpose.
● In uncooked foods, like tomato cocktail, herbs must stand overnight to release their full flavour.

HERBS AND SPICES IN SALT-FREE DIETS

Pure herbs and spices (not blended mixes or sauces) are often allowed in salt-free diets to add interest and zest to bland foods. Many different flavours resulting from a variety of combinations of herbs and spices help cover up the lack of salt in most dishes.

Note that celery and parsley flakes may contain too much sodium for inclusion in these diets.

HOW TO START A HERB AND SPICE SHELF

Don't buy everything at once. The beginner would be wise to buy the most used and most versatile herbs and spices first and learn to enjoy them. When you are an expert in the use of these, add others to your seasoning shelf.

It pays to buy only small quantities of quality brands for full natural flavour. Among the herbs basil, marjoram, savory, tarragon, thyme, and rosemary are especially versatile. Less versatile but very popular is sage.

TO FREEZE FRESH GARDEN HERBS

Choose young sprays of parsley, mint, or whatever herbs you have, or make bouquets garnis. Wash, then blanch them in boiling water 10 seconds. Chill in iced water 1 minute and pat dry.

Seal enough herbs for a single use in a small freezer bag or foil. Clip or staple all bags of the same herb to a piece of cardboard and label. To use: While still frosty, snip the herbs into soup, casserole, butter, etc.

CARE OF HERBS AND SPICES

Since spices are subtle perfume oils trapped within the cell walls of various plants, they must be carefully guarded lest their exotic fragrances evaporate. Observe these simple rules to keep your spices in top condition.

1. Always keep your spice jars tightly covered. If jars are left open, dust and airborne bacteria promote deterioration. Likewise, evaporation causes loss of spice oils and strength of flavour.

2. Keep spices in a clean, dry, cool place, preferably in the dark. Do not keep near a stove, radiator, or any other warm place, since heat hastens evaporation and loss of flavour. Do not keep in a humid place. Dampness encourages "caking" and the growth of mould resulting in a musty smell and flavour.

3. Keep your spices dry. Do not dip a wet spoon into a jar of spices. Any moisture introduced into the spice itself may cause deterioration.

4. If spices lose their delicate aroma, replace them with fresh ones.

> ## TO DRY FRESH HERBS
> *When fresh herbs begin to flower, pick off tops and perfect leaves.*
> *Wash and spread on muslin on a tray. Dry in warm, sunny spot, turning occasionally, 2 to 3 days. Then crush leaves (no stems) and store in jars.*

THE NAMES, DESCRIPTIONS, HINTS FOR USING THEM
ALLSPICE
Dried fruit of a West Indian tree. Sometimes called pimento and Jamaica pepper. Flavour resembles a blend of cinnamon, nutmeg, and cloves—hence the name.

Uses: Whole in pickling, gravies, meats, fish dishes; ground in or on cakes, puddings, relishes, tomato sauce, preserves, pot roast, steak.

ANGELICA
An aromatic plant of the carrot family, native to the Northern Hemisphere and New Zealand. The young leafstalks and stems are candied and used as a decoration for desserts and cakes. A herb tea is brewed from the leaves.

ANISE
A plant of the carrot family, native to the Mediterranean region but long cultivated elsewhere for its aromatic and medicinal qualities. It has clusters of small white or yellow flowers and a greenish-brown oval seed (aniseed) similar in appearance to caraway.

Uses: The seeds have a pungent, liquorice flavour, and are used for sweets, pastry, anisette, and herb tea and in some cheese dishes. Try some on sweet rolls.

AROMAT
A trade name for monosodium glutamate.

BASIL
Leaf of a plant of the mint family, native to India and Persia. It has a fragrant, spicy flavour.

Uses: Italians use it in tomato paste. The French flavour soups, meat pies, stews. Add some to peas, string beans. Sprinkle over lamb chops before grilling. Wonderful in spaghetti sauces, tomato dishes, on fish, cheese and egg dishes, especially omelets.

BAY LEAVES
Aromatic shiny green leaf of evergreen laurel tree, native to Mediterranean area. Used by Greeks to crown heroes. Do not confuse with ordinary laurel leaves which are poisonous.

Uses: For pickling, stews, pot roasts, sauerbraten, sauces for prawns and fish, gravies, soups, spiced vinegars, tomato mixtures, and bouquet garni.

BEE BALM
This name is applied to several herbs, especially *Melissa officinalis*, a perennial of the mint family. It is sometimes cultivated for its lemon-like smell and flavour. The leaves and the oil distilled from them (known as melissa or balm) are used for seasonings and beverages.

BERGAMOT
(1) A perennial herb of the mint family, used to make a kind of tea. (2) A type of citrus fruit, grown chiefly in Italy, whose thin yellow rind yields an oil used in some perfumes. (3) A variety of pear.

BORAGE
A herb with large, hairy leaves and blue flowers, used in salads and with green vegetables and to flavour soups and stews. It is also used to flavour a wine or fruit cup.

BOUQUET GARNI
Bunches of herbs and sometimes spices tied together or enclosed in a piece of muslin and removed and discarded after cooking.

A usual combination consists of bay leaf, parsley, and a sprig of thyme. Various combinations are used for soups and stews. For example, parsley, thyme, and clove are often used for lamb stew.

BURNET
A herb of the rose family, with lacy leaves. It is used in salads (especially with cucumbers) and sometimes for herb teas and vinegars.

CAMOMILE OR CHAMOMILE
The name of several herbs of the *Anthemis nobilis*. It has an apple-like aroma and is used for "camomile tea", which is made from the dried flower heads.

CAPER
The flower bud of a southern European shrub, which is pickled and used as a garnish or for sauces. Excellent with prawn salad, fish in black butter, pizza topping, or with boiled lamb or mutton.

CAPSICUM
This is the family name of all peppers and chillies; they are vegetables and are not related to ordinary peppercorns.

There are many varieties which include the sweet green and red bell pepper (also called pimento and pimiento), red bonnet peppers and pimientos, and hot chilli peppers. Dried and ground, certain varieties become paprika pepper, cayenne pepper and chilli powder.

Sweet peppers are usually bought fresh as they do not dry well; they are also available in cans, usually under the name pimiento.

See also **Cayenne pepper; Chilli peppers and powder; Paprika pepper.**

CARAWAY
Dried fruit of plant of parsley family, grown in Northern Europe.

Uses: In rye bread and rolls. Add to sauerkraut, cabbage, noodles, asparagus, French fried potatoes, soft cheese spread, biscuits. Sprinkle on liver and kidneys before cooking.

CARDAMOM
Tiny brown seeds in a small pod, these are the fruit of the cardamom plant from India and Guatemala.

Uses: To flavour Danish pastry, coffee cake, buns, stewed fruit, grape jelly, and curries. It also has medicinal uses. Sprinkle ground cardamom on iced melon.

In the Orient people chew the seeds to sweeten the breath.

Seeds may be steeped in hot water or milk, strained and the flavoured liquid used for the recipe.

CASSIA
Dried bark of evergreen tree of laurel family, native to China and Malaysia. Ground cassia resembles cinnamon in flavour. Most people can't tell the difference between genuine cinnamon and cassia.

CASSIA BUDS
Cassia "buds" are dried unripe or ripe buds of tree from which cassia bark is obtained. Has rich flavour and high oil content.
Uses: In pickling.

CAYENNE PEPPER (RED PEPPER)
Cayenne is a ground spice made of the hottest of chilli pods. Red pepper is milder, but brighter in colour.

Uses: Cayenne is used in Tabasco sauce, chilli powder, curry, and in moderation peps up many a soup, fish dish, barbecue sauce, cheese mixture.

Red pepper goes into commercial ginger ales, and is an excellent seasoning for meat and fish dishes.

Cayenne pepper must be used moderately, since it is fiery-hot.

CELERY SALT
A combination of ground celery seed and salt.

Uses: Add to tomato juice, soups, potato salad, salad dressings, bouillon, oyster stew, clam juice, croquettes. Try it on boiled or fried eggs.

CELERY SEED

It is not the seed of the common celery but the tiny seed-like brown fruit of parsley, the family which tastes like celery. Grown in many countries, especially India and France.

Uses: For pickling, salads, salad dressings, sauces. Add it to pastry when baked to be used as a salad accompaniment. Try it with vegetables, stews, and hamburgers.

CHERVIL

Leaf of herb grown in many countries in the temperate zone. Resembles parsley in flavour but is sweeter and more aromatic.

Uses: It may be used in any way that parsley is used. Include it in mixed herb preparations for salads. Good in soups, egg and cheese dishes, and with fish.

Try it chopped fine and sprinkled over grilled fish just a couple of minutes before removing from grill.

CHIVES

A hardy plant of the onion family with small, slender, hollow green leaves which have a delicate onion flavour. To use, snip fine or chop and add to cheese and egg dishes, meat and poultry dishes, stews, salads, soups, and vegetables, etc.

CHILLI PEPPERS

Some sixty varieties are grown, most of them red; the pods may be mild or hot.

Uses: Mexican varieties go into chilli powder. Whole chillies are most frequently used in pickling or curries. Mixed pickling spices contain them. Break up one or two for soups and stews.

CHILLI POWDER

A mixture of chilli pepper and other spices which may be bought either mild or hot. Oregano and cumin seeds and sometimes garlic go into it.

Uses: Used in cocktail sauces, barbecue sauces, casseroles, bean dishes, chilli con carne, in some spaghetti sauces, soups, stews. Try it with hamburger, meat loaf.

CINNAMON

Aromatic bark of cinnamon tree. Most people can't tell the difference between true cinnamon and cassia "cinnamon". The former is lighter in colour and milder in flavour than cassia. Stick cinnamon is the dried bark of the tree. Ground cinnamon is made from stick cinnamon.

Uses: It is used in many types of cooking and baking.

Sticks are often used in pickling, for spiced coffee, cider, chocolate, and wine.

Pumpkin pie, puddings, rolls, spice cake, and the popular cinnamon toast are just a few ways of using it ground.

CLOVES

Nail-shaped dried brown buds of evergreen clove tree, grown in East and West Indies.

Uses: Whole, for baked ham, pickling, special syrups, apple dishes.

Ground, for chocolate pudding, sweets, cake.

Stud a small onion with 3 whole cloves; add to meat stew.

Do not confuse with a clove or segment of a garlic bulb.

CORIANDER

Dried fruit of small plant of parsley family. Flavour resembles combination of lemon peel and sage. Grown in North Africa and Argentina.

Uses: Whole, in mixed pickles, gingerbread, biscuits, cakes, poultry stuffings, curries, mixed green salads.

Rub ground coriander on pork before roasting.

CRESS

Also known as garden or mustard cress, a small, peppery-flavoured plant; it is usually sold in small punnets but can easily be grown in small seed boxes.

Uses: In salads and sandwiches; as garnish.

CUMIN

Aromatic seed of a caraway type herb which it resembles in shape. It comes from Mediterranean islands, Mexico, Syria, Iran, India, and other places. It is one of the oldest known spices.

Uses: It is a favourite in Mexican and South American cooking. Used in Germany to flavour bread, in Holland for cheese, and in Norway for anchovies. It's an ingredient in sausage, pickles, chilli, and curry powder.

If you want to try it, add a little to stews or boil the seed briefly and pound it. Then use it in cheese, stuffed eggs, pies, soups, and in some canapé spreads.

CURRY POWDER

It is a blend of spices (about 16 ingredients) which include cumin and other seed, several varieties of red peppers, ginger, and turmeric.

Uses: It is basic in the cookery of India and Pakistan where curried dishes include fish, meats, poultry, and rice.

It's good with eggs, in cheese spreads, and in fish chowders. Try it in tomato soup, French dressing, and in scalloped tomatoes.

Because of the yellow turmeric which it contains, curry powder colours as well as flavours the foods in which it is used.

DILL

This is a herb of the parsley family, resembling fennel in appearance.

Uses: Dill should be used more often to flavour potatoes; it's good with sauerkraut, fish, and in salad dressings and stews.

Try it with cabbage, turnips, and cauliflower.

FAGGOT

A bouquet garni tied into a bundle.

FENNEL

This small seed-like fruit of a plant of the parsley family has a flavour similar to liquorice.

Uses: The seed is used in sweet pickles, fish dishes, sweets, pastry, and liqueurs. Italian bakers use the seed on rolls and breads. Try a dash of the seed in apple pie.

Note: The vegetable fennel resembles celery but smells and tastes more like anise. The bulbous white root may be eaten raw and sliced in a salad, or cooked like celery and eaten as a vegetable. Also known as finocchio or Florence fennel.

FENUGREEK

Hard seed, strong and pleasant aroma.

Uses: It is not particularly useful to the housewife. It is used in curry powder, in mango pickle and green mango chutney recipes.

FILÉ POWDER

This is an aromatic powder of dried sassafrass leaves. It is used in many Creole dishes, especially the gumbos.

It is usually added to a dish shortly before serving because the powder becomes sticky on cooking. In some cases, okra may be substituted as it gives the same gelatinous texture.

FINES HERBES

A French term for mixed herbs. These are combinations of several herbs which are used in stews, soups, fish sauces, fish and meat stuffings, and other recipes.

The herbs are finely chopped, and added to food just before serving. For example, in pork dishes 1 tablespoon each of sage, basil, and savory are sometimes used this way.

GARLIC

Garlic is the strong-flavoured bulb of a plant of the lily family, made up of small sections called cloves. It is an indispensable seasoning in much of the world's cooking.

Good quality garlic is thoroughly dry, with firm and well-shaped bulbs. White and red varieties are obtainable but there is little difference in flavour between the two.

Unless garlic is kept in a closed jar, its strong, pungent odour penetrates all food close to it. Because of this, many grocers sell fresh garlic from which the tops have been removed, handily packed in small cellophane bags containing 4 to 5 bulbs.

To Use Garlic: A peeled clove may be added whole or halved to a dish; if a cocktail stick is inserted in clove it is easy to remove after cooking. Or it may be crushed in a garlic press. Or clove may be sprinkled with a little salt and crushed to a paste with the back of a spoon. Or rub a cut garlic clove on inside of salad bowl or other bowl used for mixing ingredients.

GARLIC SALT

Ground garlic cloves mixed with salt.

Uses: It's a convenient way to get the tangy garlic flavour and aroma. Use it in addition to or in place of plain salt in many dishes.

Add it to tomato juice, salad dressings, salads, meat, vegetable, spaghetti dishes, and on steaks just before grilling.

GERANIUM

Some varieties of this common garden flower have leaves with aromas which make them popular for culinary use—especially the rose, apple, lemon, nutmeg, and orange scented geranium leaves. Among the dishes in which they are used are baked apples, fruit compote, custards, jellies, and sometimes just as a garnish in fruit drinks.

GINGER

This is the pungent-flavoured root of a plant grown in Jamaica, China, Japan.

Uses: Preserved in syrup or candied, ginger is a pepper-upper of many a sauce and pudding.

The fresh root is sometimes available, and grated, it is often used in curry.

Gingerbread, ginger biscuits, and like baked products make use of the ground dried spice.

Try chopped candied ginger in sauce for ham or chicken, or add it to a meringue or whipped cream topping

for pumpkin pie. Add a pinch of ground ginger to hot cider or wine.

HORSERADISH

The potent-flavoured root of a plant of the mustard family. Ground or grated and mixed with vinegar and salt, it is a favourite seasoner for beef, corned beef, ham, or other meats, and an ingredient in many sauces.

LAVENDER

The dried flowers, leaves, and stalks of this plant of the mint family are usually used to fill sachets and to perfume drawers or wardrobes. Some people, however, use minute quantities of the flowers and leaves as a seasoner in salads, beverages, jellies, and desserts.

LEMON BALM

A herb related to mint. The fragrant leaves are prized for herb teas and for flavouring other beverages, soups, stuffings, salads, and sauces. See **Bee Balm.**

LEMON VERBENA

An aromatic herb from a shrub of the verbena or vervain family, with a delicate flavour similar to that of lime or lemon. The fresh leaves are used to flavour fruit salads, fruit cups, jellies, and cold drinks. A herb tea may be made from them.

LIQUORICE

A small plant of the pea family, native to Europe. A juice obtained from the root is used in flavouring sweets and drinks and for medicines. Also spelled licorice.

LOVAGE

A European herb of the carrot family, formerly cultivated for use as a medicine. The stalks may be eaten like celery. The roots yield an oil used to flavour tobaccos and perfumes. The seeds and leaves are used to season meats and salads. Like lavender, lovage is often used to fill sachets.

MACE

Fleshy orange-red skin covering nutmeg, the fruit of an evergreen tree. Native to Molucca (Spice) Islands. Has a softer flavour than nutmeg itself.

Uses: Ground or in blades, in sauces, meat stuffings.

Add a teaspoon to 1 pint whipped cream to increase delicacy.

The whole mace (called blade mace) is used most often in pickling and sauces.

Try a chopped blade in stewed cherries or gingerbread mixture.

MARIGOLD

Flower petals of the hardy annual

plant have been used in cooking for hundreds of years. Fresh petals are used as a garnish for salads. A yellow colouring has been made from it as a substitute for saffron. It is used for colouring butter, cheese, cakes, biscuits, as well as for making such unusual specialties as marigold buns. The petals give a rather exotic flavour for shellfish dishes, chowders, stews.

MARJORAM

Dried leaf of grey-green herb of mint family.

Uses: It has a thousand uses—stews, gravies, roasts, fish, omelets, poultry seasonings, in the manufacture of sausage. May be used as a herb salad.

Sprinkle dried marjoram leaves into lamb dishes; or over lima beans, peas, green beans.

When used moderately, the mint relationship of marjoram can be capitalized upon for fruit salads.

MINT

Any of various aromatic plants whose leaves are used for flavouring. Spearmint or peppermint makes the dried product, which is used whole, crushed, or pulverized to flavour soup, stews, meat, fish, sauces, and jelly.

Other mints are the scented ones: apple, eau-de-cologne, and pineapple. The last two are especially good in fruit or wine cups, or made into tea. Apple mint is a good substitute for sage in a savoury stuffing, and for flavouring apple jelly.

MONOSODIUM GLUTAMATE (MSG)

A white crystalline substance derived from a vegetable protein, which emphasizes natural food flavours without adding any flavour, colour, or aroma of its own. It has long been a standard ingredient in Chinese and Japanese cooking. It may be used as a basic seasoning, like salt and pepper, in practically all cooked dishes.

Monosodium glutamate is sold under various trade names; however, one type, Aromat, is so widely distributed that the name is now frequently used in recipes. Also called MSG.

MUSTARD

Small seed of annual plant of mustard family. Black, brown, white, or yellow varieties.

Uses: This seed may be bought whole for pickling, ground for sauces and salad dressings or ready-made in tubes or jars. There are various kinds available, ranging from English to French and German.

Devilled eggs and potato salad need mustard as much as a "hot dog".

White sauce flavoured with mustard makes an excellent dressing for fish, meat, or vegetables.

NASTURTIUM

A rather common flower, the leaves of which are sometimes used in salads or to flavour jelly or sauces. The seeds are pickled and used as a substitute for capers.

NUTMEG

It is really the seed of the fruit of the nutmeg tree which grows in the East and West Indies. The whole fruit consists of an outer husk, the mace (see **Mace**), an inner shell around which the mace curls, and the nutmeg or kernel. May be bought whole or ground. The ground spice is more popular. The whole nutmeg is ground as needed and retains its flavour longer.

Uses: The ground spice is used in cakes, pies, many different puddings, and other desserts. Very good with such vegetables as asparagus, cauliflower, and spinach. Excellent with fruit salad.

It's almost a "must" for eggnog and custards and a pinch certainly improves lemon sauce for puddings. Rice puddings and apple sauce are improved with it.

Try it sprinkled on fried bananas or on bananas and berries with cream.

ONION SALT

Mixture of ground dehydrated onions and salt.

Uses: Use for any dish where onions are used.

OREGANO

Dried leaf of mint family herb. Grown in Mexico and Italy. Has strong aromatic flavour. Also called common or wild marjoram.

Uses: Flavours pork, beef stew, meat sauces, omelets, boiled eggs, chilli con carne.

Use it in tomato dishes, especially Italian spaghetti sauce, in mixed green salads with or without tomatoes.

PAPRIKA PEPPER

Mildest of the capsicums, paprika pepper is made by grinding dried large red peppers of mild flavour. Hungarian and Spanish paprika are best.

Uses: The bright colour makes it a popular garnish for such white foods as fish, potatoes, cottage cheese, cauliflower.

Used in salad dressings, ketchups, chilli sauces, in large amounts in such dishes as Hungarian goulash or chicken paprika.

PARSLEY

One of the most common herbs, and used in bouquet garni.

Uses: Fresh parsley is a garnish for almost anything up to dessert.

The dried parsley is worth keeping on hand for times when the fresh green is unavailable. Dried parsley is especially nice for soups and stews, in dumplings for flavour and colour.

PEPPER, WHITE OR BLACK

Totally unrelated to the capsicums (cayenne pepper, paprika pepper, red pepper, etc.) these peppers are the small dried berries (peppercorns) of a vine-like plant. World's most popular spice, they are native to the East Indies.

Black pepper is ground from the whole peppercorn before it is ripe. White pepper is made from the same peppercorn when it is ripe, with the outer hull removed. White pepper is milder and liked especially in light foods where the black specks might be unattractive.

Grind your peppercorns in your own pepper mill for the freshest and most pungent flavour.

PICKLING SPICE

This is generally a mixture of a dozen or more whole spices.

Uses: Used for pickling and preserving relishes, meats, and vegetables. Sometimes used when boiling beetroots and cabbage.

Try a little muslin bag of spice in a stew but remove it as soon as the stew is flavoured to your liking.

PIMENTO, PIMIENTO

This refers to the capsicum sweet red bell pepper, the kind which is available both fresh and canned.

Pimento is also the name for the allspice tree, its berry and the spice made from it.

See **Allspice; Capsicum; Paprika.**

POPPY SEED

Seed of a non-narcotic plant of poppy family, native to Asia; however, Holland is the home of the best of these tiny blue-black seeds used so much by bakers. They have a nut-like flavour.

Uses: Whole seed used as topping for rolls, bread, cakes. Good in salads, with noodles, with cottage cheese.

POTHERB

Any plant whose leaves or stems are used in cooking.

POULTRY SEASONING

Mixture of herbs and spices, often o sage, thyme, marjoram, savory, rose mary. A "must" for seasoning poultry

Uses: For poultry, veal, pork, fish stuffings. Use in meat loaf.

Add ⅛ teaspoon to batter for French fried onions.

ROSEMARY

The herb "for remembrance" is a native of Mediterranean regions. It is a sweet, fresh-tasting herb resembling curved pine needles in appearance.

Uses: Good with roast beef, lamb beef and lamb stews.

Try it in green salads, with fish, in soups. Delicious with green beans potatoes, turnips, cauliflower.

Used commercially in meat packing and in pickles and perfumes.

Dried rosemary needs to steep in liquid before its flavour is fully developed. Add it to the dressing for salad instead of to the salad itself, or steep it in the vinegar for a few minutes.

ROSE HIPS

The fleshy red berries of some rose plants, especially wild roses, which have been found to contain considerable vitamin C. They are sometimes used to flavour jellies and preserves.

ROSELLE

A plant of the mallow family that resembles okra. It is grown for its bright-red buds which taste a little like sorrel. It is used to flavour soups and stews.

RUE

A strong-scented herb with yellow flowers and bitter-tasting leaves that were formerly much used in medicine. It is sometimes used as a seasoning. The leaves are mainly used for making bitters.

SAFFLOWER

A thistle-like herb long cultivated in various parts of the world for food, medicine, and as a substitute for the costly saffron. An edible oil is also produced from the plant.

SAFFRON

The dried stamens of a plant of the crocus family. It is the world's most expensive spice, because the stamens of at least 64,000 flowers are needed to make a pound. It is yellow and has a pleasantly bitter flavour. It was introduced into Europe by the Arabs.

Uses: Because of its cost, saffron is often used in such small quantities that its delicate flavour is lost and only its colour is apparent; this has made possible the ancient practice of substituting other yellow colouring agents. Saffron is used a great deal in Mediterranean and Latin American cooking, especially in rice dishes. In France it appears in chicken fricassée and is essential to bouillabaisse. The English make saffron breads and cakes.

For a golden colour and an Oriental flavour, add a dash to water in which rice is to be boiled.

SAGE

Fresh or dried leaf of a herb of the mint family.

Uses: It's an old-time favourite for stuffings, sausages, and cheese.

Use with poultry, baked fish, and in salad. Goes well with pork and poultry.

SARSAPARILLA

Any of a number of related tropical American plants with large, fragrant roots and heart-shaped leaves. An extract of the dried root is used as a tonic and especially as a flavouring for carbonated drinks.

SASSAFRAS

The fragrant dried bark and root of the sassafras tree, used for making a tea and root beer. The dried leaves are used for making filé powder.

SAUSAGE SEASONING

Blend of herbs and spices including white pepper, coriander, and nutmeg.

Uses: Excellent ready-mixed seasoning if you make your own sausages.

Used also in meat loaf, veal birds, etc.

SAVORY

Fresh or dried leaf of widely grown herb of the mint family. There are two kinds: winter and summer savory.

Uses: Good in stuffings, stews, egg dishes, meat sauces, gravies, and casseroles which include meat.

Savory is sometimes called the "bean herb" because it dresses up so many kinds of beans including all fresh and dried beans as well as peas.

SESAME SEED

The small seed of a herb native to Asia and widely grown throughout the tropics. There are black and white varieties; the white, or honey-coloured, is the one found in most stores.

Uses: It has a pleasant nut-like flavour and is used in baking and in various sweets; it is the basic ingredient of halva, the Middle Eastern sweetmeat. Try it on breads, and biscuits. The seed also yields a distinctively flavoured oil that is widely used in

Middle Eastern and Oriental cooking.

Benne is a grass grown chiefly for its seeds from which an oil is obtained, sometimes called oil of sesame.

SHALLOTS

Shallots, which belong to the green onion family, are generally red in colour with purplish-white cloves beneath the outer skin. Shallots have a mild, faintly garlicky flavour. They are called for in many recipes throughout this book.

When shallots are sautéed, they should not be browned as they become bitter. Three or four shallots may be substituted for one medium-sized onion.

SORREL

A green herb, whose leaves have a sharp, vinegary taste. Much used on the Continent.

Uses: In a purée to serve with eggs, veal—it is the classic accompaniment to fricandeau.

SWEET CICELY

The name of several plants (European, Asiatic, and American herbs) all closely related and all of the parsley family. They are fragrant perennials with aromatic, liquorice-flavoured roots, once considered medicinal. The seeds and leaves are sometimes used as a garnish for salads and cold vegetables. Dried seeds are sometimes used in cakes, sweets, and liqueurs.

TANSY

Any of a number of plants of the aster family, especially one species with bitter leaves that are used sometimes for seasoning and herbal teas, but more frequently as a medicine.

TARRAGON

The leaves and tops of a perennial green herb; it has a mild liquorice flavour.

Uses: Flavouring for tarragon vinegar, sauces, tomato and chicken dishes.

Try it in tomato juice cocktail, any salad made with tomatoes, with green beans. Sprinkle over steaks or chops.

Tarragon vinegar is available in most large stores or you can make it at home by steeping the leaves in vinegar. Use tarragon vinegar in sauces for fish and shellfish, especially lobster. Use it to flavour mayonnaise for any fish salad.

THYME

Leaves and stems of widely grown mint family plant. Strong, distinctive flavour, and forms part of a bouquet garni.

Uses: Stews, soups, stuffings are better for that "pinch of thyme". Italians use it in some of their special dishes. Greeks use it in green salads.

Excellent in clam chowder, clam juice, poultry, meat loaf.

Try it in onion soup, chicken fricassée, on baked or grilled fish.

Thyme is particularly nice with lamb in almost any form. Good also with carrots, peas, or creamed onions.

TURMERIC

Aromatic root of ginger family and native to Asia. It is bright yellow in colour and at one time was used as a dye. It is only available ground.

Uses: For turmeric pickles, chow chow, relishes. Used in curry powder. Often used to replace saffron as colouring agent.

VANILLA

The vanilla plant is a climbing orchid native to tropical America, Mexico and parts of the East and West Indies.

The dried bean or pod is about 5 inches long and dark brown in colour. It is full of tiny seeds which are aromatic; vanilla essence is extracted from the bean.

Uses: The bean can be used for infusing milk, cream and custards. After infusion, if the bean is rinsed and dried, it can be used several times. Vanilla sugar is made by keeping a bean in a jar of sugar for flavouring. The essence is stronger than the bean but can be substituted for it in most cases.

VERBENA

See **Lemon Verbena.**

WATERCRESS

A pungent plant of the mustard family that grows in wet soil or slow-running water. It has a pleasant peppery taste; choose bunches with a fresh, deep green colour and crispness rather than with long stems. The leaves are used chiefly in salads, soups, and sandwiches, or as a garnish, but may also be cooked as a vegetable.

To Keep Watercress: Cut off about $\frac{1}{2}$ inch of the stem end. If bought in a bunch, loosen it and put it, stems first, in a large jar or other container which does not press on the sides or top. Fill the container with about 1 inch of cold water, cover, and store in refrigerator.

WINTERGREEN

An evergreen shrub with red berries, white bell-shaped flowers, and egg-shaped leaves. An oil made from the leaves is used in medicine and as a flavouring for sweets and chewing gum.

WOODRUFF

An aromatic herb used especially to flavour the German punch called May wine. It is sometimes used in other fruit punches; however it should not be left in more than half an hour.

JELLIES, JAMS, AND PRESERVES

Jam, jelly, conserves, marmalade, preserves—any of these fruit products can add zest to meals. Most of them also provide a good way to use fruit not at its best for canning or freezing—the largest or smallest fruits and berries and those that are imperfect or are irregularly shaped.

Basically these products are much alike; all of them are fruit preserved by means of sugar, and usually all are jellied to some extent. Their individual characteristics depend on the kind of fruit used and the way it is prepared, the proportions of different ingredients used in the mixture, and the method of cooking.

The following definitions will help the housewife to understand recipes for these fruit products preserved by cooking with sugar.

Jelly: Made by cooking extracted fruit juices only with sugar. A transparent, quivery product which holds its shape; delicately tender but not syrupy.

Jams: Made from crushed fruits cooked with sugar until the mixture is homogeneous and thick.

Preserves: Contain whole fruits or large pieces of fruit preserved in a heavy sugar syrup.

Conserves: Made of 2 or more fruits, one of them usually a citrus fruit, with nuts, raisins or both added.

Marmalades: Made from pulpy fruits, usually one or more citrus fruits are used and cut into comparatively large pieces and cooked so they hold their shape in a thick jellied transparent syrup.

Fruit Cheeses: Made from strained fruit purée cooked with sugar and spice to a thick, smooth consistency.

The pulp of some fruits from which the juice has been extracted for jelly is often used if it has enough flavour and pectin.

SEALING JELLIES, JAMS, AND PRESERVES

All jars must be sterilized, dry and warmed before filling.

With jam jars, leave about ¼-inch space at the top when filling jars. Cover immediately with wax paper disc and seal tightly with transparent film or parchment jam pot covers; tie down with elastic bands or string. Or cover immediately with about ⅛-inch layer of hot paraffin. Prick any air bubbles that appear. These cause holes to form in paraffin as it hardens and make a poor seal. (Melt paraffin and

keep it hot in a basin over a pan of hot water.)

Allow jellies and jams to stand, undisturbed, overnight or until cool. Cover glasses or jars with lids.

If bottling jars and lids are used, the paraffin may be omitted. Prepare jars according to manufacturers' directions. Fill hot, sterilized jars with very hot jelly or jam. Wipe top and threads of jar with clean, damp cloth. Put lid on, the rubber sealing compound next to jar. Screw band down evenly and tight.

Invert jar for about 30 seconds so hot jam or jelly can destroy mould or yeast which may have settled on lid. Then stand upright to cool. When jars are cold, test for seal by pressing centre of lid. If dome is down, or stays down when pressed, jar is sealed. If the product was not hot enough to produce a vacuum seal, the bands must be left on to keep the jars tightly closed; otherwise the bands are not needed after jars are sealed.

ESSENTIALS IN MAKING JELLY AND JAM

In order to "jell", a fruit must contain the right amount of pectin and acid. Pectin is a natural, gum-like substance found in most fruit, and the amount and quality of pectin in fruits varies according to the stages of ripeness.

A combination of fruits low in pectin and one rich in pectin will often bring about satisfactory results, or a commercial pectin (tartaric acid or citric acid, which can be bought in powder or liquid form) may be added. Carefully follow the manufacturer's directions given with these products.

Fruits Rich in Pectin: Sour apples, crab apples, unripe grapes, all citrus fruit, blackberries, currants, cranberries, gooseberries, plums, and quinces.

Fruits Low in Pectin: Sweet apples, cherries, peaches, pears, pineapples, rhubarb, strawberries, and some others. With these, added pectin is required or combination with a fruit rich in pectin.

To Test for Pectin: To 1 teaspoon cooked juice, add 1 teaspoon grain alcohol and stir slowly. Warning: Wood or denatured alcohol may be used, but do not taste, as these are poison.

A large mass (solid) indicates a large amount of pectin. If moderately rich, there will be a few pieces of jelly, and, if poor in pectin, only a small flaky sediment.

To Test Jelly or Jam for Setting: Remove pan from the heat, put a little of the jelly or jam on a cold plate and cool it quickly. Run your little finger through the centre and, if it is ready, the jelly or jam will crinkle slightly and remain in two separate portions. It will also form a firm drop on your finger.

With a thermometer, cook syrup until it registers between 216° and 220°F.

Jellies

APPLE OR CRAB APPLE JELLY

Wash 15 pounds tart apples and quarter without peeling.

Place in preserving pan, just cover with cold water, and simmer gently until soft and tender.

Drain through jelly bag. Shift pulp gently occasionally to keep juice flowing; do not force juice through as this will make the jelly cloudy.

Measure 32 fluid ounces juice into 12-quart pan and boil 5 minutes.

Add 1½ pounds sugar and boil 5 to 8 minutes longer, or until a drop jells on a cold plate.

Pour into hot clean jars and seal.

Continue cooking 32 fluid ounces at a time until all juice is used. Use pulp for apple cheese.

Mint Apple Jelly: Cook a few sprigs of fresh mint with apples when preparing to extract juice. (1 or 2 drops of mint sauce may be used if fresh mint is not available.)

Add a few drops green food colouring and mint sauce just before pouring into the jars. Avoid adding too much flavouring and colouring.

Spiced Apple Jelly: Tie a few whole cloves in a piece of muslin. Drop into juice at the beginning of cooking and only remove when jelly is poured into the jars.

BERRY JELLY

Blackberries, raspberries, and loganberries are but a few of the many which may be used for jelly.

Choose firm fruit, using a mixture of ripe and slightly underripe fruit. Pectin is most abundant in slightly underripe fruits. Ripened fruits give the best flavour.

Wash and stem the berries. Drain, then mash to release some of the juice.

To every pound of berries, add 2½ tablespoons water. If the berries are very juicy, do not add any water.

Boil gently from 10 to 15 minutes, pour into a jelly bag and drain.

Measure juice. Place in large preserving pan and boil for 5 minutes.

Add 6 ounces sugar for each 8 fluid ounces juice. Stir until sugar dissolves, then boil rapidly without stirring or skimming until jelly sets when tested.

Skim and pour into hot, clean jars and seal.

REDCURRANT AND RASPBERRY JELLY

4 pounds redcurrants
6 pounds raspberries
sugar, as method

Wash currants, place in preserving pan, and mash. Add washed, well-drained, and mashed raspberries. Stir.

Cover and simmer gently 40 minutes. This must not boil.

Put in jelly bag to drain. Do not squeeze bag.

Measure 32 fluid ounces juice into 12-quart preserving pan. Bring to boiling point, and boil hard 5 minutes.

Add 1½ pounds sugar, bring to a rolling boil, and boil 3 minutes. Test for setting.

Pour into hot, dry jars and seal.

Continue cooking 32 fluid ounces juice with 1½ pounds sugar until all juice is used.

REDCURRANT JELLY

Pick over currants. Do not remove stems. Wash and drain. Place in preserving pan. Mash with potato masher.

Add 5 fluid ounces water to about 4 pounds fruit. Bring to the boil, simmer until currants appear white.

Strain through jelly bag. Measure juice.

Add 9 ounces honey and 6 ounces sugar for every 16 fluid ounces juice.

Cook only 32 fluid ounces juice at a time. Stir until sugar dissolves.

Cook until a drop sets on a cold plate.

Pour into hot, dry jars and seal.

GRAPE JELLY

Pick over and wash 4 pounds green grapes. Crush and boil together with 1 pint water for 20 minutes.

Drain through a jelly bag.

Use 6-8 ounces sugar for each 8 fluid ounces of grape juice. Bring grape juice to the boil. Add sugar and stir until sugar is dissolved.

Continue boiling until jelly sets when tested. Remove from heat and skim.

Pour into hot, dry jars and seal.

For grape jelly at its best, use canned unsweetened juice. Fresh grape juice contains tartaric acid crystals which form readily in jelly. Canned unsweetened grape juice has much of the acid in crystal form removed.

WINE JELLY

Measure 1½ pounds sugar into a large basin. Add 16 fluid ounces wine (sherry, port, red or white); mix well.

Place over a pan of rapidly boiling water and heat 2 minutes, stirring constantly.

Remove from heat and at once stir in ½ bottle neat liquid pectin. Test for setting, then pour at once into hot, dry jars and seal. Makes about four ½-pound jars.

Jams

STRAWBERRY JAM

2 pounds strawberries
2½ pounds sugar
5 fluid ounces unstrained lemon juice

Wash, drain, and hull berries. Weigh 2 pounds. Crush berries in large pan.

Place in layers in 12-quart preserving pan, covering each layer with sugar. Set aside for 4 hours.

Bring slowly to a rolling boil and boil vigorously 8 minutes.

Add lemon juice and again bring to a rolling boil. Then boil 2 minutes longer.

Skim, test for setting, then turn into hot, dry jars, filling to ½ inch of top, and seal at once. Makes 3½ pints.

GRAPE JAM

Wash and pick over 4 pounds green grapes. Separate pulp from skins, putting into separate pans.

Bring pulp slowly to boiling point, stirring continually until pips separate from pulp.

Force pulp through sieve to remove pips. Add skins to pulp, stir thoroughly, and measure.

Add 6 ounces sugar for each 8 ounces fruit. Stir well and cook about 15 minutes, or until thick. Test for setting.

Pour into hot, dry jars to ½ inch of top and seal at once. Makes 6 ½-pint jars.

DAMSON PLUM JAM

8 pounds plums
2 pints water
sugar

Wash and drain plums. Cut in half. Add water, bring to boiling point, and simmer 15 minutes.

Cool slightly. Remove the stones.

Measure pulp and juice and add 6 ounces sugar for each 8 ounces. Stir until thoroughly mixed.

Bring slowly to the boil and boil gently until clear and thick, about 20 minutes, stirring constantly to prevent it from burning. Test for setting.

Pour into hot, dry jars, filling to ½ inch of top. Seal at once.

RASPBERRY JAM

Wash raspberries, crush, and measure. If berries are sour, add equal measure of sugar. If sweet, use ¾ as much sugar as berry mixture.

Cook in own juice until thickened, stirring to prevent it from burning. Boil rapidly because long cooking tends to darken the fruit. Test for setting.

Pour while boiling hot into hot, dry jars and seal immediately.

APRICOT-PINEAPPLE JAM

Stone 5 pounds apricots. Cut into pieces. Mix with 2½ pounds chopped pineapple and 3¾ pounds sugar.

Simmer until thick and clear, stirring frequently to prevent scorching. Test for setting.

Pour into hot, dry glasses. Seal when cool.

QUINCE JAM

Wash, peel, and remove core from 4 pounds quinces. Chop into very small pieces.

Add 4 pounds sugar, ¼ pound chopped crystallized ginger and juice, and grated rind of 2 lemons.

Cook until thick and clear. Test for setting. Pour into hot, dry jars. Seal.

CHERRY JAM

2 pounds cherries
4 fluid ounces lemon juice
2 pounds sugar

Wash and drain cherries. Remove stems and stones. Chop cherries or work in a blender until roughly chopped.

Measure 32 fluid ounces cherries and juice into 10- or 12-quart preserving pan. Add sugar. Leave 4 hours.

Bring slowly to a rolling boil and boil hard for 12 minutes, stirring occasionally.

Add lemon juice and again bring to a rolling boil, then boil 2 minutes longer.

Skim, and test for setting. Pour into hot, dry jars, filling to $\frac{1}{2}$ inch from top, and seal at once. Makes 1 to $1\frac{1}{2}$ pints.

NEW METHOD UNCOOKED JAMS

This method saves time and effort; however, because the jams are not sterilized by cooking they must be kept in the refrigerator or freezer. They keep well in the refrigerator for several weeks and, of course, much longer in the freezer.

UNCOOKED CHERRY OR STRAWBERRY JAM

16 fluid ounces puréed Morello
      cherries or finely mashed or
      sieved strawberries
2   pounds sugar
$\frac{1}{2}$ bottle liquid pectin

Mix together the fruit and sugar. Leave for about 20 minutes, stirring occasionally. The cherry purée should be as nearly uniform as possible.

Put fruit in a blender and mix. Add fruit-sugar mixture to liquid pectin and stir about 2 minutes.

Pour into dry jelly jars. Stand at room temperature 48 hours, or until jelled. Seal with paraffin. Store in refrigerator or freezer. Makes 6 jars.
Note: Powdered pectin may be substituted for liquid pectin. Use 1 packet. Mix with 8 fluid ounces water.

Heat to boiling point and boil rapidly for 1 minute, stirring constantly.

Remove from heat and add fruit-sugar mixture, which has stood for 20 minutes. Proceed as above.
Uncooked Red Raspberry Jam: Use 24 fluid ounces finely mashed or sieved red raspberries and 3 pounds sugar.

Proceed as above but set it aside after jam has been poured into jars, only 24 hours. Makes 9 jars.

Preserves

STRAWBERRY PRESERVES

● Wash and hull ripe, firm strawberries. Measure a good 1 pound after draining the berries thoroughly. Add 1 pound sugar and start over low heat. When juice begins to flow from berries, shake the pan to mix juice, berries, and sugar.
● When sugar is dissolved, increase heat and bring to a good rolling boil as soon as possible. Then start counting cooking time. Boil rapidly for 10 minutes, shaking pan instead of stirring preserves.
● Remove pan from heat and allow to cool. Add another good 1 pound of berries and another 1 pound of sugar. Bring slowly to a good rolling boil. Shake pan frequently and boil another 10 minutes.
● Pour the hot preserves into shallow trays or baking dishes and skim. Shake pan occasionally while cooling. Stand overnight for berries to swell.
● Pack the cold preserves into sterilized, dry jars—the half-pints are nice for small families—fill jars to within $\frac{1}{4}$ inch of top.
● Clean inside neck of jar above surface of the preserves. Cover preserves with a thin layer of smoking hot paraffin. Rotate the jar so the paraffin will stick to glass above surface of preserves. Put self-sealing cap on and screw the band tight. This keeps out dust and insects. Store in cool, dry place.

SWEET CHERRY PRESERVES

4   pounds dark sweet cherries
4   tablespoons strained lemon juice
1   packet powdered pectin
$3\frac{1}{4}$ pounds sugar

Wash, stone, and halve cherries. Place in preserving pan. Sprinkle with lemon juice and place over medium heat.

Add pectin and blend thoroughly. Bring to the boil. As soon as mixture boils rapidly, gradually add sugar. Blend well.

Bring to a rolling boil and continue boiling for 2 minutes.

Remove from heat and skim. Pour into hot, dry glasses and seal. Makes 8 $\frac{1}{2}$-pints.

PEACH PRESERVES

2   pounds peaches
$1\frac{1}{2}$ pounds sugar

Scald peaches. Dip into cold water and peel. Remove stones. Cut into half, quarters, or thick slices.

Make a heavy syrup of sugar and water. Cook peaches in syrup until mixture is thick and clear.

Pour into hot, dry jars and seal.

EASY RED RASPBERRY PRESERVES

1 12-ounce packet frozen raspberries
1 pound sugar

Let berries thaw with sugar, in saucepan.

Place over low heat, bring to the boil slowly. (Use larger saucepan than ingredients would indicate as mixture tends to boil over in too small a pan.) Skim off any froth as it forms.

Cook until mixture is thick and translucent.

Test for setting as for jelly or jam.

Remove from heat; cover and leave it overnight.

The next day pour preserve into hot, dry jars to within $\frac{1}{2}$ inch of top. Seal. Makes about 6 6-ounce jars.

RASPBERRY PRESERVES

Mix thoroughly equal amounts of raspberries and sugar.

Cook slowly and stir until mixture boils. Boil gently for 6 minutes. Test for setting.

Pour into hot, dry jars. Seal at once.

TOMATO PRESERVES

2½ to 3 pounds tomatoes
3 lemons
2 pounds sugar

Scald tomatoes and peel. Cut into small pieces and drain in colander or sieve. (Use juice for soup, sauce, or bottle for future use.)

Measure 2 pounds pulp. Place in preserving pan with thinly sliced lemons.

Cook gently uncovered 40 minutes or until lemon skins are tender.

Add sugar, continue cooking 15 minutes, stirring occasionally. Test for setting.

Pour into hot, dry jars and seal at once.

Conserves

GRAPE CONSERVE

3 pounds grapes, weighed after removing stems
16 fluid ounces water
3 pounds sugar
juice of 3 oranges
½ pound seedless raisins
¼ pound walnuts, chopped

Remove pulp from grapes. Save skins. Add water to pulp and cook until seeds settle. Sieve to remove seeds.

Mix the pulp with skins and remaining ingredients, except walnuts. Cook until it tests for setting as for jelly or jam.

Add nuts. Pour into hot, dry jars. Seal.

Cranberry or Plum Conserve: Follow above recipe, substituting cranberries or plums for grapes and adding juice of 3 lemons.

PLUM CONSERVE

16 fluid ounces plum pulp
8 to 12 ounces sugar
juice and grated rind of ½ lemon
juice and grated rind of ½ orange
6 ounces seedless raisins
2 ounces chopped nuts

Mix ingredients, except the nuts. Cook mixture in a preserving pan until thick and clear.

Add nuts. Test for setting. Pour into hot, dry jars. Seal.

GOOSEBERRY AND PINEAPPLE CONSERVE

3 pounds gooseberries
1 pound chopped pineapple
4 pounds sugar
1 pound raisins, finely chopped
12 ounces chopped walnuts

Wash gooseberries and boil in small amount of water until they burst.

Add sugar, pineapple, and raisins. Boil mixture slowly until thick. Add walnuts. Test for setting.

Pour into hot, dry jars. Seal.

FIG CONSERVE

2 pounds figs (any kind)
8-ounce can diced pineapple
sugar
3 ounces roughly chopped almonds or walnuts

Prepare the figs as you ordinarily do for cooking, slicing them if you wish. Add the pineapple, with its juice, to the figs. Weigh or measure and add an equal amount of sugar.

Place pan on asbestos mat and boil, stirring occasionally, until thick but still runny.

Add the nuts just before taking the conserve from the heat. Test for setting. Pour into hot, dry jars and seal. Makes about 2 pints.

PEACH CONSERVE—QUICK METHOD

1. Peel and slice fresh, ripe peaches. Place in pressure cooker with thinly sliced oranges and peel of one orange, thinly sliced peeled lemon including 1 teaspoon grated lemon rind, and water.

4. Add sugar (12 ounces to each pound of fresh peaches) and remaining ingredients (raisins, blanched flaked almonds or walnuts) and cook. Test conserve for setting.

2. Place lid on pressure cooker.

5. Pour preserve into hot, dry jars when cool. Cover with melted paraffin and seal.

3. When steam escapes, put indicator weight on lid and cook 5 minutes at 15-pounds pressure. Quick cool. Remove lid.

6. Supply of beautiful yellow glossy peach conserve.

STRAWBERRY AND RHUBARB CONSERVE

Cut 1 quart rhubarb into ½-inch pieces, being careful not to peel.

Mix together 1 quart hulled strawberries, the rhubarb, and 3 pounds sugar.

Cook mixture slowly until it is thick and clear. Test for setting. Pour into hot, dry jars. Seal.

Miscellaneous Preserves

ORANGE MARMALADE

8 oranges
2 lemons
water
sugar

Wash and dry fruit. Cut unpeeled oranges and lemons into quarters lengthways. Slice very thin crossways.

Measure sliced fruit. Add twice as much water as fruit and juice. Set aside overnight.

Next morning, cover preserving pan, bring to the boil, and cook 1 hour. Then set aside for 24 hours.

Stir well and measure out 16 fluid ounces juice and fruit. Put into a 4- or 6-quart preserving pan.

Add 1 pound sugar. Bring to a rolling boil and boil 9 minutes only, or to temperature of 220°F. Test for setting. Pour into hot, dry jars. When cold, seal.

Continue cooking 16 fluid ounces fruit and juice with 1 pound sugar, as given above, until all fruit is cooked. Makes approximately 10 6-ounce jars.

Amber Marmalade: Follow method for Orange Marmalade, using 1 grapefruit, 1 orange, 1 lemon, sugar, and water.

PEAR AND PINEAPPLE MARMALADE

Peel fresh pears. Slice and cover with sugar, using 6 ounces sugar to every 8 ounces fruit. Set aside until it forms a syrup.

Boil slowly until thick.

When fruit is partly cooked, add 10-ounce can chopped pineapple for every 4 pounds pears. Test for setting. Pour into hot, dry jars. Seal.

PINEAPPLE MARMALADE

1 pineapple
1½ pounds sugar
3 lemons
12 ounces raisins

Peel pineapple, saving all juice. Cut into small cubes.

Add sugar and grated rind and juice of lemons and pineapple.

Cook 30 minutes or until thick. Add raisins. Cook 5 minutes longer. Test for setting.

Pour into hot, dry jars. Seal. Makes about 6 ½-pint jars.

PLUM CHEESE

Wash fruit. Place in preserving pan. Add 16 fluid ounces water to 4 pounds of plums.

Cook slowly until pulp separates from stones. Work pulp through sieve. Measure.

If pulp is thin, cook until thick enough to mound on spoon.

Add sugar, allowing 6 ounces sugar to every 8 fluid ounces of pulp.

Cook rapidly, stirring constantly to prevent scorching. Test for setting by drawing a wooden spoon through the centre; if it leaves the mixture separated and shows the bottom of the pan, it is done. Pour into hot, dry jars. Seal.

PEACH CHEESE

4 pounds peaches
16 fluid ounces water
sugar
2 teaspoons ground cinnamon
1 teaspoon cloves

Peel peaches. Remove stones and spots. Place in pan with water and cook until tender. Work through sieve and measure.

Allow 6 ounces sugar for every 8 fluid ounces of pulp. Add spices. Cook until thick, stirring frequently. Test as for plum cheese.

Pour into hot, dry jars. Seal.

APPLE CHEESE

10 pounds cooking apples
1¼ pints water
32 fluid ounces sweet cider
4 pounds sugar
1½ teaspoons ground cloves
3 teaspoons ground cinnamon
1½ teaspoons grated nutmeg
1½ teaspoons ground allspice

Wash and core apples. Cook in water until soft and work through sieve.

Boil cider down to 16 fluid ounces.

Mix the cider, apples, sugar, and spices in preserving pan and cook slowly until it is ready for setting as jelly or jam. Stir about 3 or 4 times.

Pour into hot, dry jars. Seal.

Sterilize 10 minutes in pan of boiling water. Makes 4 pints.

PINEAPPLE HONEY

16 fluid ounces water
2 pounds sugar

1 pound fresh pineapple, coarsely grated

Boil sugar and water together for 5 minutes. Add pineapple, and boil until translucent, about 10 minutes.

Pour into hot, dry jars, filled to overflowing. Seal.

QUINCE HONEY

1 pound fresh quince, coarsely grated
1 pint water
2 pounds sugar

Boil sugar and water together 5 minutes. Add quince, and boil until translucent, about 10 minutes.

Pour into hot, dry jars, filled to overflowing. Seal.

GRAPE CHEESE

Use 1 pound sugar to 4 pounds grapes.

Wash and stem grapes. Cook in a small amount of water until skins are soft. Work pulp through a sieve to remove seeds and skins.

Add sugar and cook until thick and clear. Test as for plum cheese.

Pour into hot, dry jars. Cool and seal.

APPLE AND PLUM CHEESE

4½ pounds apples
3 pounds plums
16 fluid ounces water
3 pounds sugar
1 teaspoon ground cinnamon

Wash and cut apples and plums in half, removing peel and cores.

Add water and cook until fruit is tender. Work through a sieve.

Add sugar and cinnamon to purée. Cook until thick and clear. Stir occasionally to prevent it from sticking. Test as for plum cheese.

Pour into hot, dry jars. Seal. Makes 6 jars.

CALIFORNIA BAR-LE-DUC

5 pounds fresh apricots or 3 pounds dried apricots
16 fluid ounces water
1½ pounds raisins, chopped
juice of 2 lemons
3 pounds sugar

Cut fresh apricots in half and remove stones. Add water. Cook slowly until tender.

Work through a coarse sieve. Add raisins, lemon juice, and sugar to purée.

Cook slowly until a rich, heavy syrup is formed. Pour into hot, dry jars and seal.

If dried apricots are used, wash and soak overnight in water to cover. Cook in same water until soft and work through a coarse sieve.

MEAT AND GAME MEAT

Meat makes the meal—if it's cooked properly! The fame of each cut of meat depends upon the way you cook it. For instance, a prime porterhouse steak would be quite tasteless if it were *braised* and a piece of top-side would be unchewable if it were *grilled*. The illustrations of each meat cut with the guidance offered for the best way to cook them will help you treat each cut correctly.

CHOICE OF MEAT

At one time, meat was bought according to the season, e.g. pork was plentiful and at its best when there was an 'R' in the month, so pork was seasonable from September to April. Today, with modern methods of transport and cold storage, there is always a wide choice of meat. Most butchers sell home-killed meat as well as chilled or frozen imported meat, and if the frozen meat is carefully thawed and cooked there is little difference—except perhaps in the price.

The parts of the animal which are most active in its life, such as leg and neck, have more connective tissue and are therefore less tender and need longer, slower cooking than cuts from the less active portions of its anatomy. Meat which has been too recently killed and insufficiently hung also tends to be tough. It can be marinated in oil and vinegar, flavoured with spices and herbs, or one of the good proprietary meat tenderisers on the market can be used.

Generally, it is best to select meat which has not got an undue amount of fat, and what fat there is should be firm and free from dark marks or discolouration. Lean meat should be finely grained, firm and slightly elastic.

Beef should be bright red in colour, the fat firm and white and the flesh firm to the touch.

Mutton should be a dull red colour, firm and with a fine grain, the fat, white and hard.

Lamb should be more pink in colour with firm white fat.

Veal should be a pinkish white colour, not so firm as beef and lamb, but not flabby, and the fat slightly pink.

Pork varies in colour according to the age of the animal. In a young pig it is practically white, while in an older one it is pink. The fat should be white and the flesh finely grained and firm to the touch.

BUYING MEAT

The amount of bone and fat must be considered in figuring the cost of meat—beef, pork, lamb, or veal. For example, beef short ribs may cost less per pound than the best minced beef but will yield only $\frac{1}{3}$ to $\frac{1}{2}$ as many servings.

In buying beef when you plan to have grilled steaks or roasts, select the best cuts, but when you want pot roasts, you may do just as well to buy cheaper cuts. These are also more economical to use for stews and dishes made with minced meat. How much meat to buy per serving is found in **Facts About Food and Cooking.**

HOW TO STORE MEAT

It's important to keep it cold, so store in refrigerator at 36°F. to 40°F. Unsmoked meat such as roasts, chops, and steaks must be allowed some air. Loosen any tight transparent coverings. Cover again loosely and use within a few days.

Minced fresh meat and all kinds of offal, especially liver and brains, spoil more quickly than others. Store loosely wrapped, and cook within 2 days for best flavour.

Smoked meats, such as ham, frankfurters, bacon, etc., may be kept tightly wrapped during storage. They keep longer than unsmoked meats, although bacon is likely to change flavour.

Keep cooked meat as well as broths and gravies covered and in the refrigerator. Use within a few days.

HOUSEHOLD REFRIGERATOR MEAT STORAGE CHART

A chart giving time limits meat may be held for maximum flavour and eating pleasure can only be a general guide.

Many factors influence storage limits, including the quality and the age of meat when bought, the method of preparation and handling, and the conditions in the home refrigerator.

	Storage Limit at
Beef:	36° to 40°F.
Brisket of Beef	7 days
Topside	5 to 6 days
Ribs	5 to 8 days
Steak	3 to 5 days
Stewing	2 days
Minced	2 days
Lamb:	
Leg or shoulder	5 days
Chops	3 days
Stewing	2 days
Pork:	
Leg or loin	5 to 6 days
Chops	3 days
Sausage	2 to 3 days
Spareribs	3 days
Bacon	7 days
Whole Ham	2 weeks
Half Ham	7 days
Veal:	
Chops and Steaks	4 days
Roasting	5 to 6 days
Stewing	2 days
Offal:	
Liver (sliced)	2 days
Heart	2 days
Other	1 day
Cooked Meat:	
Home-Cooked Meat	4 days
Frankfurters	4 to 5 days
Luncheon Meat (sliced)	3 days
Liver Sausage (sliced)	2 to 3 days
Liver Sausage (uncut)	4 to 6 days
Continental Sausage (uncut)	2 to 3 weeks

Beef Cuts and How to Cook Them

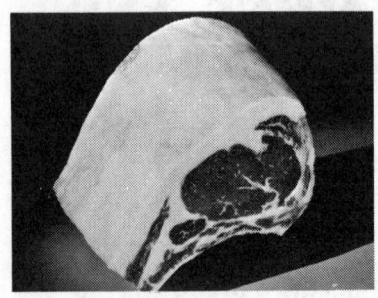

Standing Rib
Roast

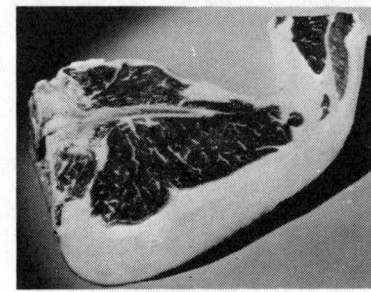

T-Bone Steak
Grill or fry

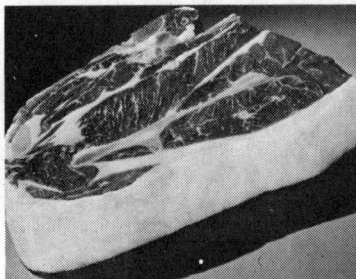

Blade Bone
Braise

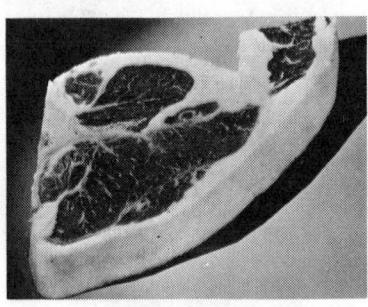

Porterhouse Steak
Fry or grill

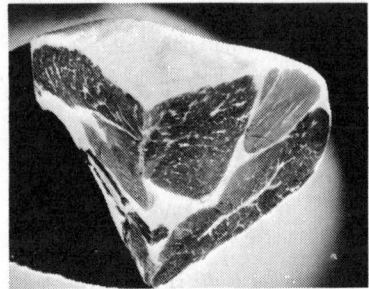

Aitch bone
Braise, Roast

Shank Cross Cuts
Braise, Cook in Liquid

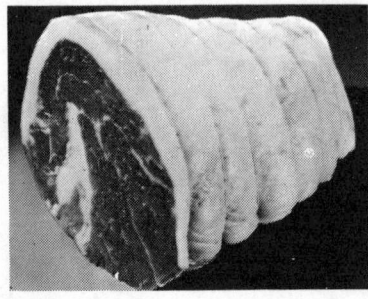

Rolled Rump
Braise, Roast

Flank
Braise

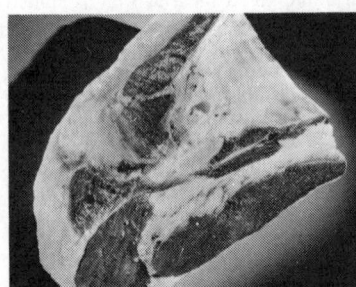

Brisket (Bone In)
Braise, Cook in Liquid

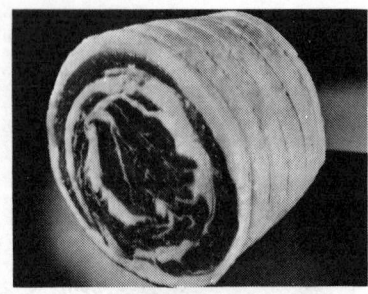

Rolled Rib
Roast

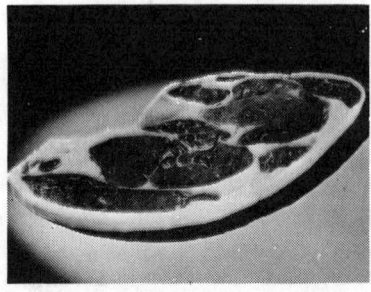

Sirloin Steak
Grill or fry

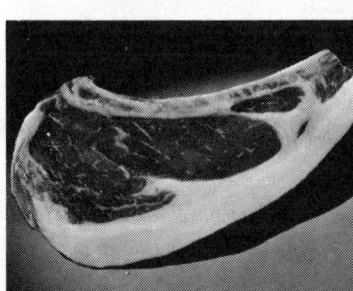

Rib Steak
Grill or fry

BEEF CHART

RETAIL CUTS OF BEEF—WHERE THEY COME FROM AND HOW TO COOK THEM

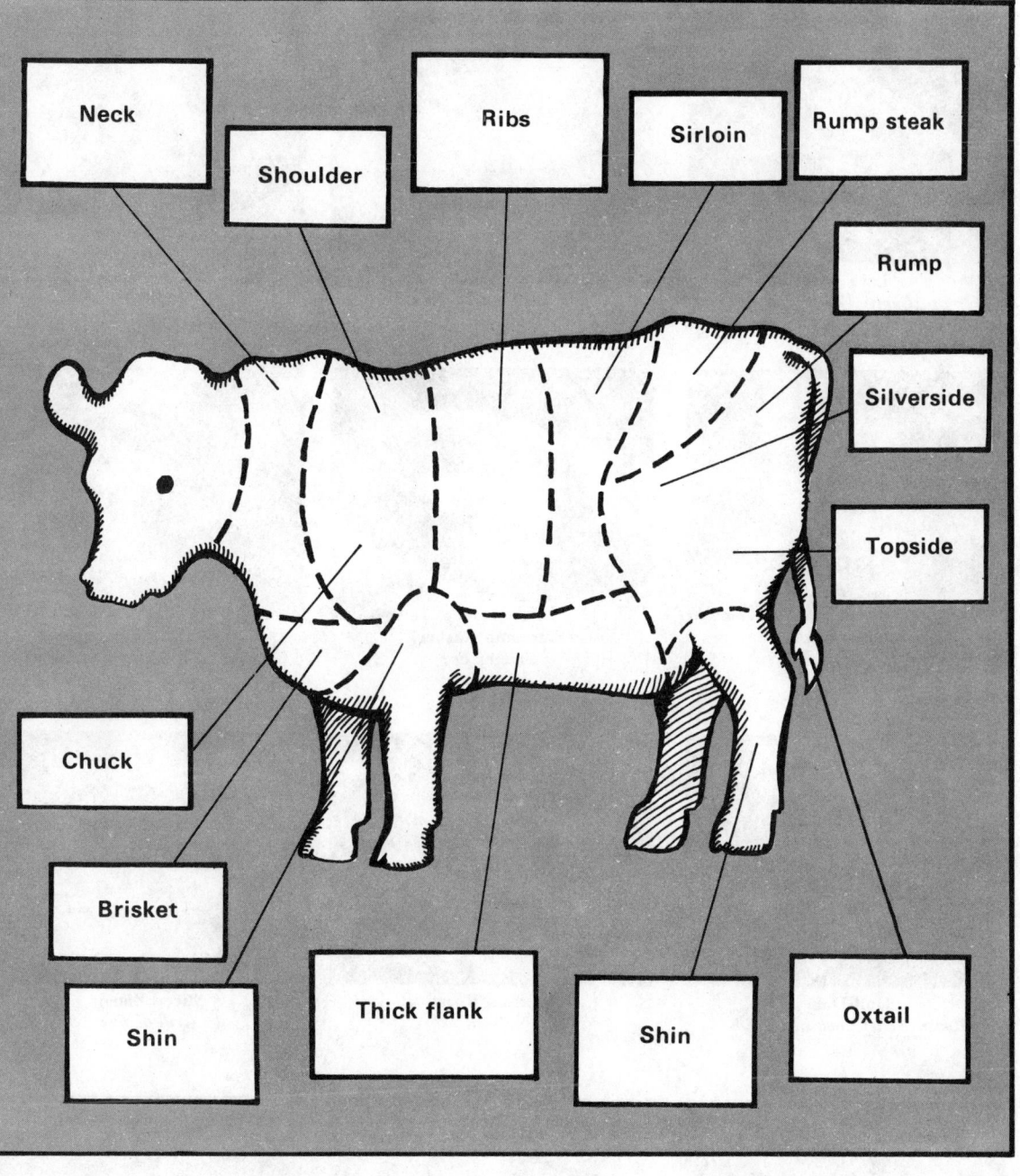

Neck

Shoulder

Ribs

Sirloin

Rump steak

Rump

Silverside

Topside

Chuck

Brisket

Shin

Thick flank

Shin

Oxtail

Pork Cuts and How to Cook Them

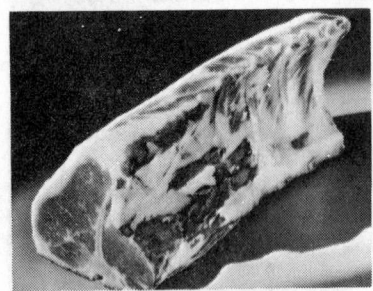

Loin Roast
(Centre Cut) Roast

Spare ribs—*Roast,*
Braise, Cook in Liquid

Loin Chops
Grill or Fry

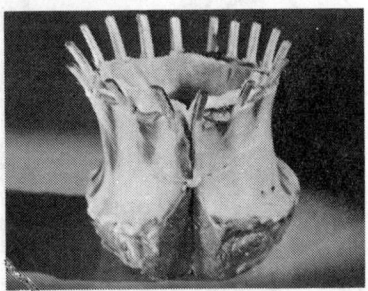

Crown Roast
Roast

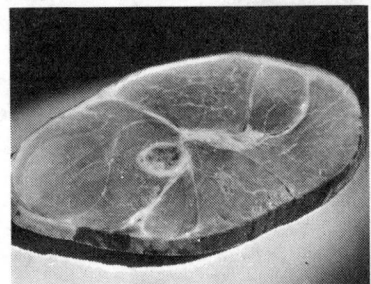

Gammon Rasher
Grill or Fry

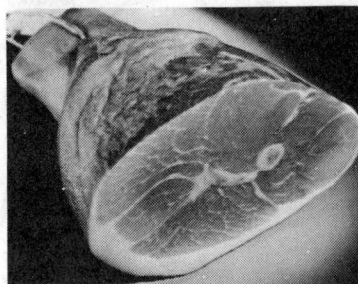

Half Ham (Shank End)
Roast (Bake), Cook in Liquid

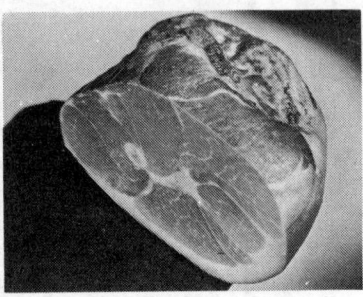

Half Ham
Roast (Bake), Cook in Liquid

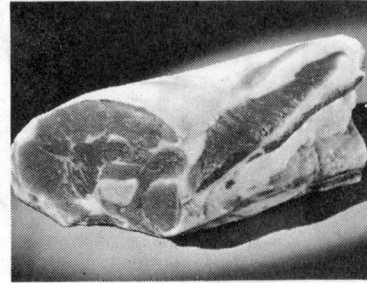

Sirloin Roast
Roast

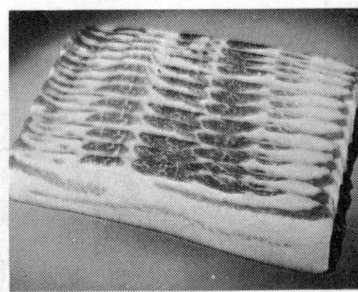

Sliced Bacon
Grill or Fry

Blade Bone
Roast

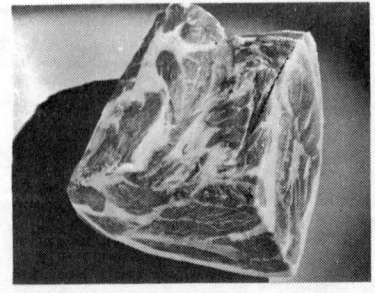

Butt
Roast

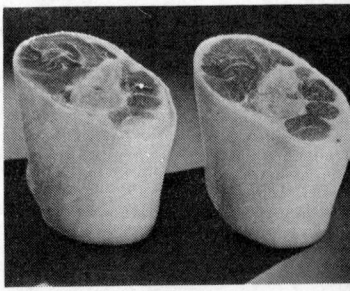

Hocks
Braise, Cook in Liquid

RETAIL CUTS OF PORK—WHERE THEY COME FROM AND HOW TO COOK THEM

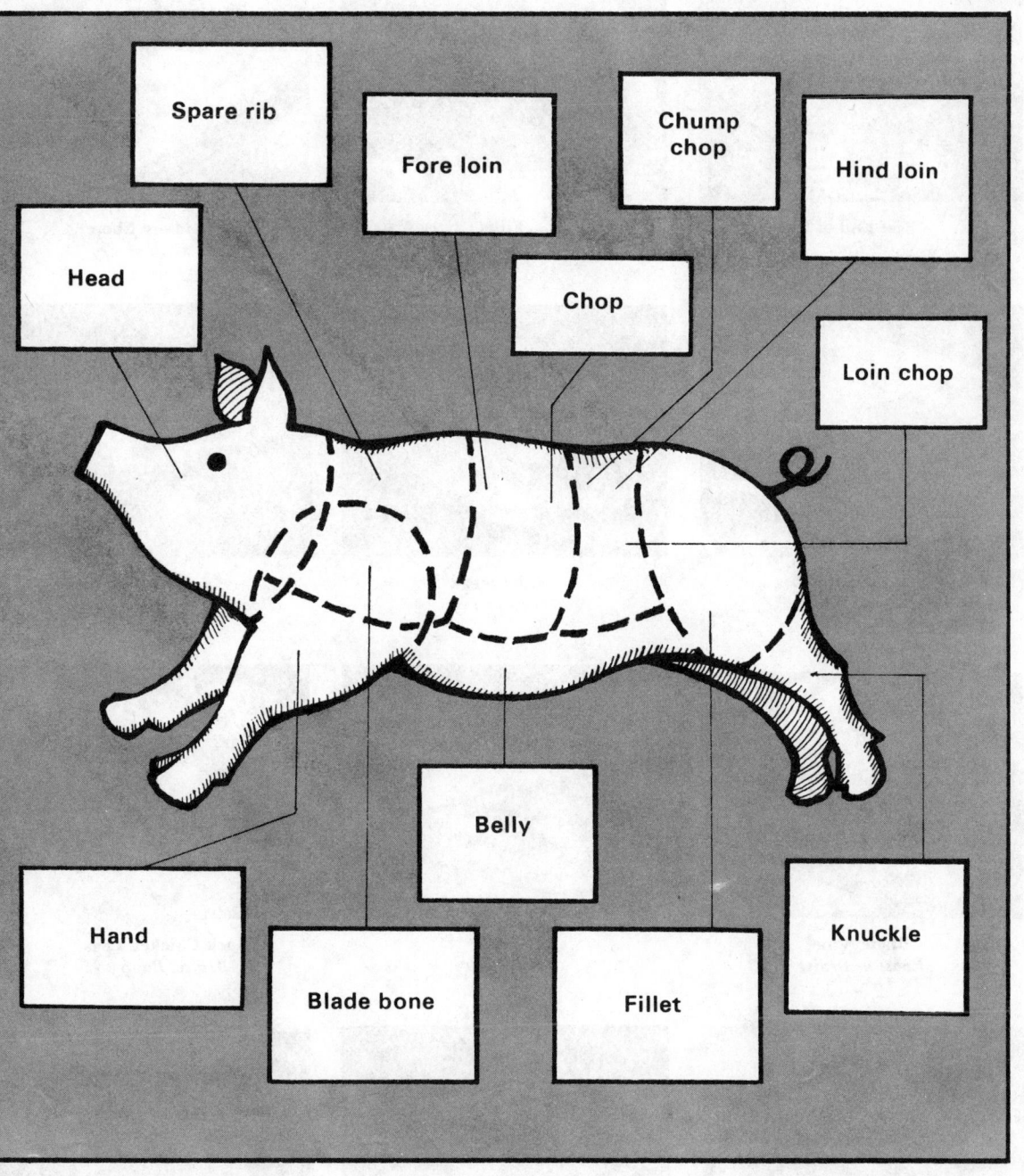

Veal Cuts and How to Cook Them

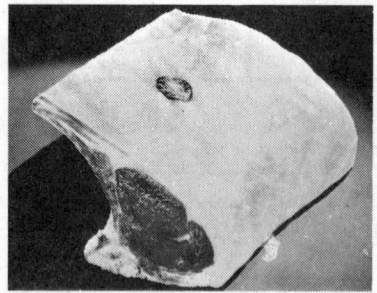

Best End of Neck
Roast

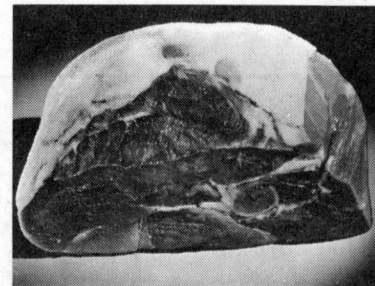

Fillet
Roast, Braise

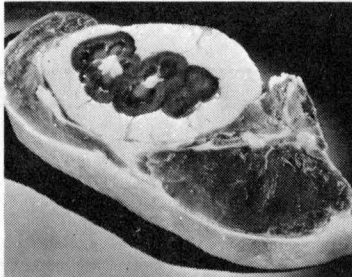

Kidney Chop
Grill or Fry

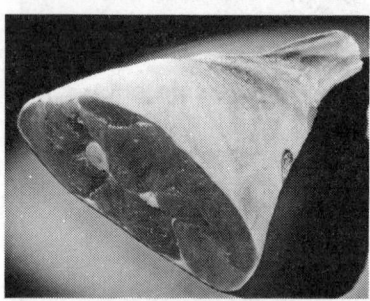

Shank Half of Leg
Roast, Braise

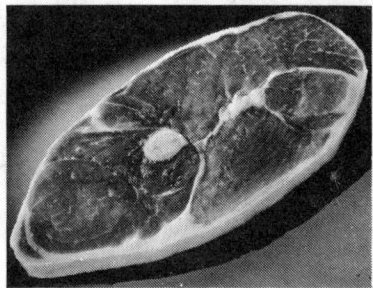

Fillet Steak
Grill or Fry

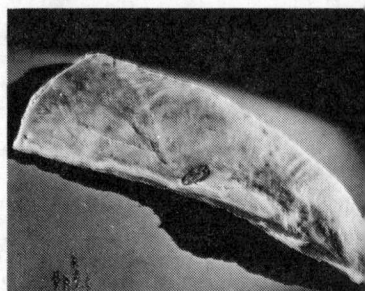

Breast
Roast, Braise, Cook in Liquid

Blade Bone
Roast or Braise

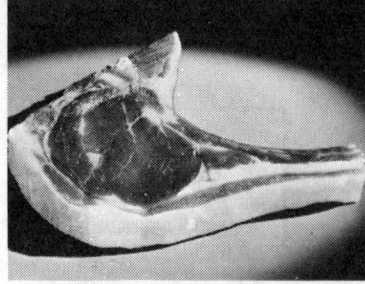

Cutlet
Grill or Fry

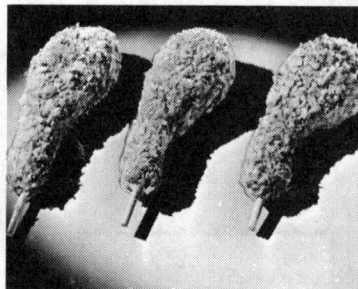

Mock Chicken Legs
Braise, Panfry

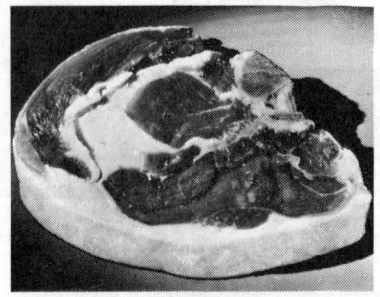

Loin Chop
Grill or Fry

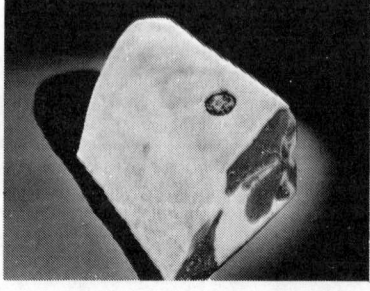

Loin
Roast, Braise

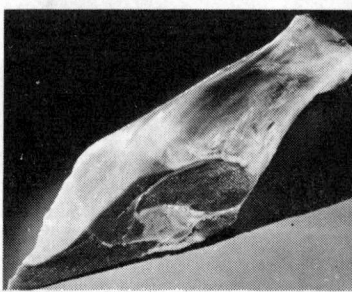

Knuckle
Braise, Cook in Liquid

VEAL CHART

RETAIL CUTS OF VEAL—WHERE THEY COME FROM AND HOW TO COOK THEM

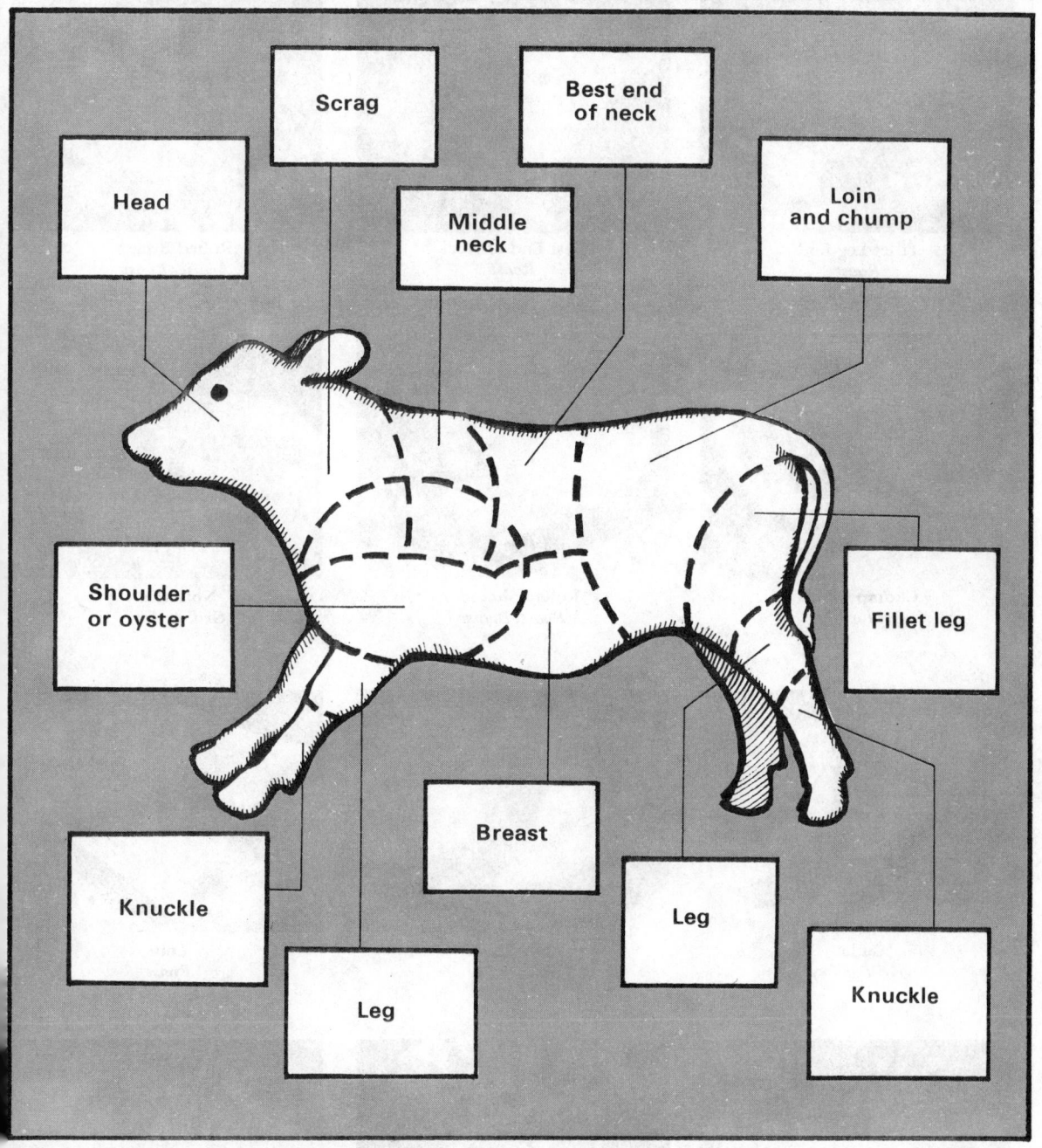

Scrag

Best end of neck

Head

Middle neck

Loin and chump

Shoulder or oyster

Fillet leg

Breast

Knuckle

Leg

Leg

Knuckle

Lamb Cuts and How to Cook Them

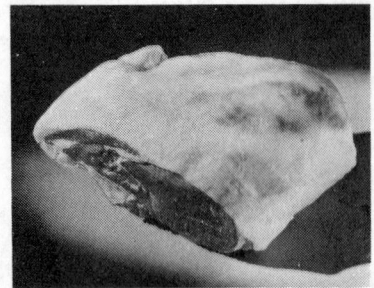

Fillet Leg End
Roast

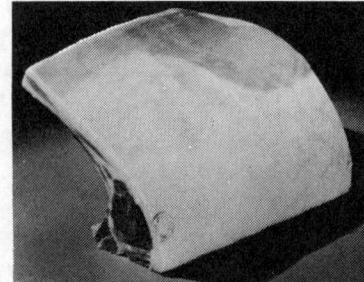

Best End of Neck
Roast

Rolled Breast
Braise, Roast

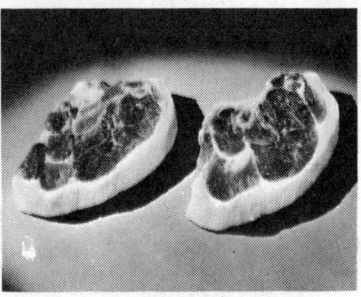

Chump Chops
Grill or Fry

Rolled Shoulder
Roast, Braise

Noisettes
Grill or Fry

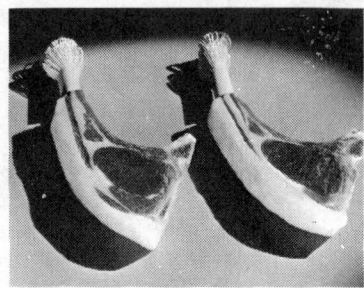

Cutlets
Grill or Fry

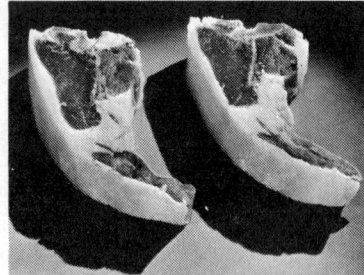

Loin Chops
Grill or Fry

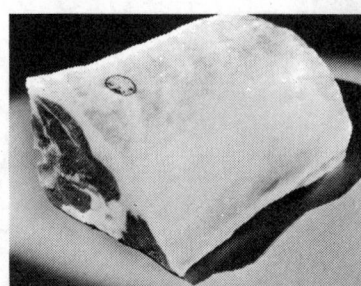

Loin
Roast

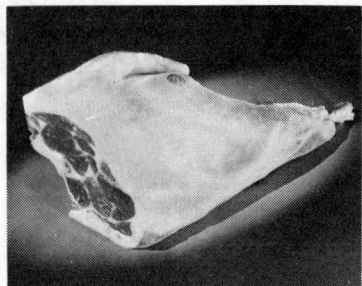

Leg Knuckle End
Roast

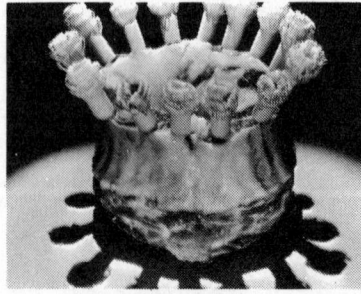

Crown Roast
Roast

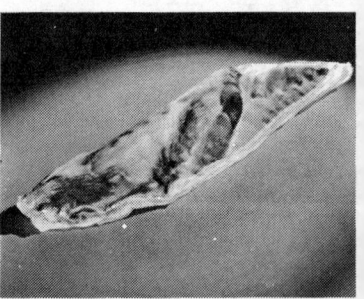

Breast
Braise, Roast

RETAIL CUTS OF LAMB—WHERE THEY COME FROM AND HOW TO COOK THEM

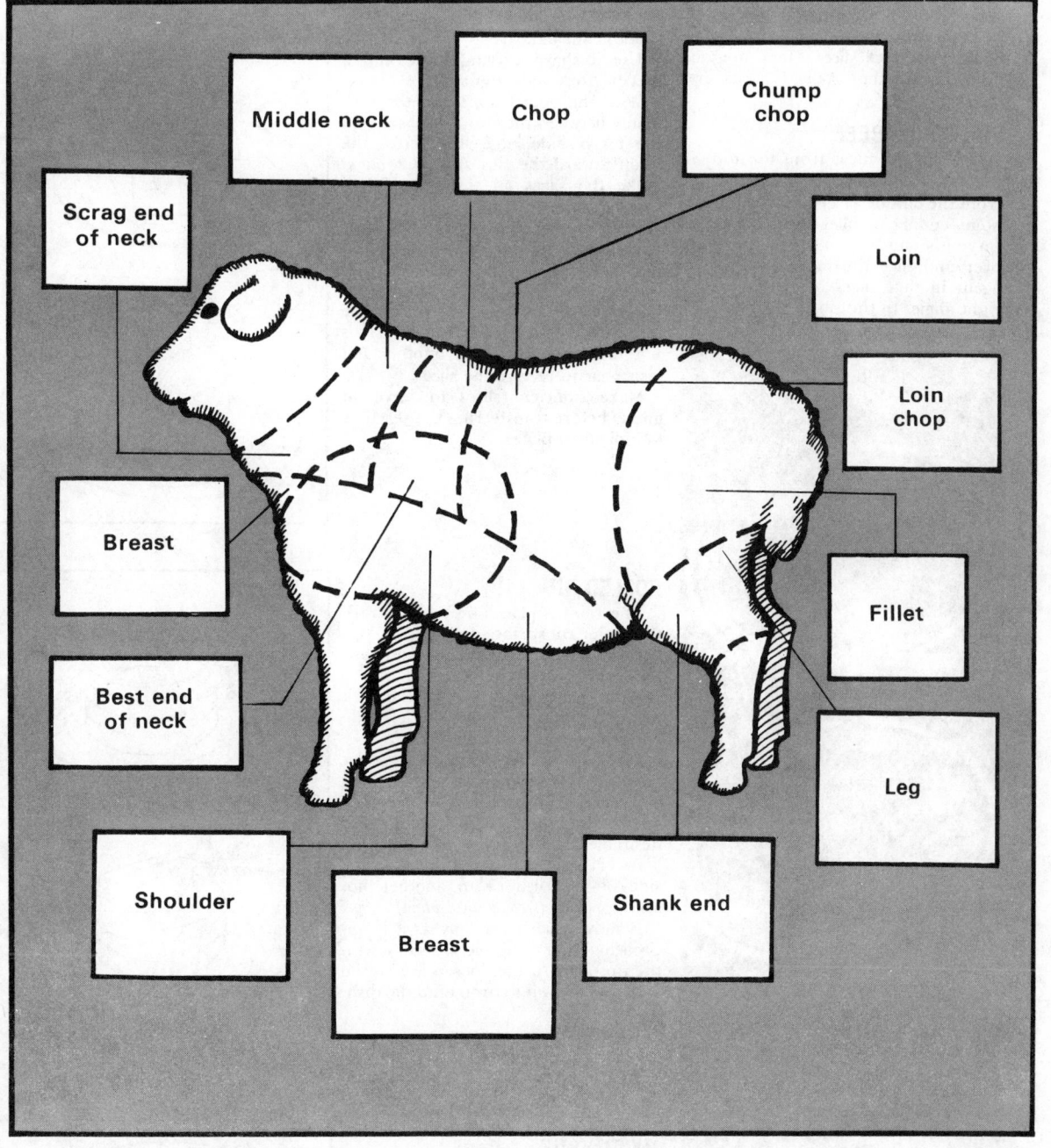

How to Carve Meat

Meat is cut across the grain as a general rule. It is therefore necessary to understand the structure of the joint and where the fat and lean are to be found so that they can be distributed evenly or according to individual preference. Generally, beef is sliced very thinly, mutton and lamb in fairly thick slices, and pork or veal in medium thick slices. Ham, tongue, brawn, and other cooked meats are sliced thinly.

SIRLOIN OF BEEF

First cut the meat from the top of the joint in thin slices downwards from the outside layer of fat to the rib bone, cutting parallel to the bone. To carve the under cut, turn the joint over and slice the meat downwards, again in thin slices but this time at right angles to the rib bone.

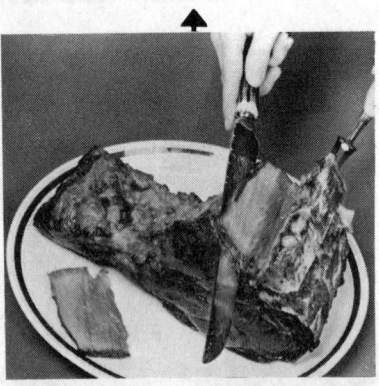

RIB OF BEEF

When a rib of beef is purchased, the butcher will, on request, remove the short ribs and separate the backbone from the ribs. The backbone can then be removed in the kitchen after roasting. This makes the carving much easier, as only the rib bones remain.

The roast is placed on the dish with the small cut surface up and the rib side to your left.

Use a sharp carving knife and a carving fork with a guard.

With the guard up, insert the fork firmly between the two top ribs. From the far outside edge slice across the grain toward the ribs. *(first illustration)* Make the slices an eighth to three-eighths of an inch thick.

Release each slice by cutting close along the rib with the knife tip. *(second illustration)*

After each cut, lift the slice on the blade of the knife to the side of the dish. *(third illustration)* If the dish is not large enough, have another hot dish near to receive the slices.

Make sufficient slices to serve all guests before transferring the servings to individual plates.

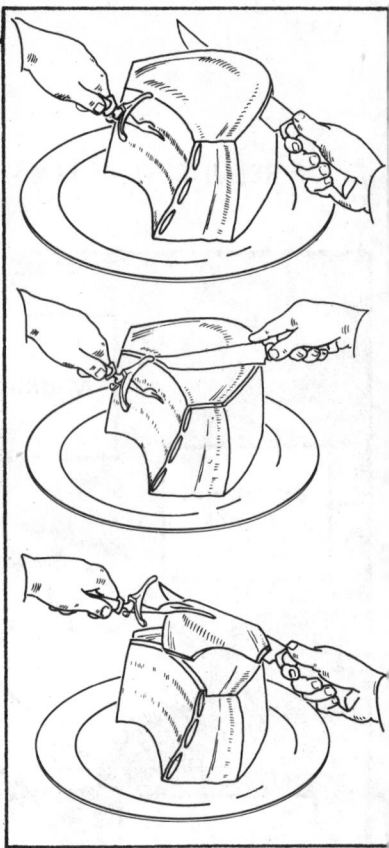

ROLLED RIB

The roast is placed on the dish with the larger cut surface down.

Use a sharp carving knife and fork as above.

With the guard up, push the fork firmly into the roast on the left side an inch or two from the top.

Slice across the grain toward the fork from the far right side. *(first illustration)* Uniform slices of an eighth to three-eighths of an inch thick make desirable servings.

As each slice is carved, lift it to the side of the dish or to another hot serving dish. *(second illustration)*

Remove each cord only as it is approached in making slices. Sever it with the tip of the blade, loosen it with the fork and allow it to drop onto the dish.

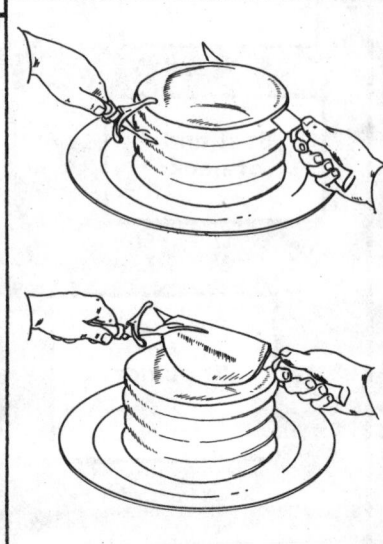

OX TONGUE

Slice off excess tissue and cartilage from the large end of the tongue. Continue making thin, even and parallel slices. This gives lengthwise slices from the small end of the tongue, as in diagram.

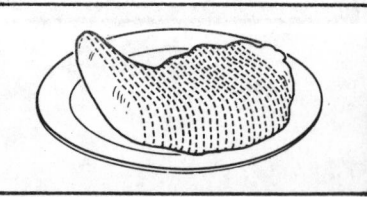

SHOULDER OF MUTTON OR LAMB

Place the joint so that the blade-bone points away from the carver. Insert the fork securely in the meat, and with the aid of the fork, raise the far side of the joint slightly, then make a vertical cut through the centre of the meat up to the bone. This will cause the joint to open out slightly, making it appear that a slice has already been removed. Cut thick slices from each side of this gap as far as the blade-bone on the one side and the knuckle on the other. Next turn the joint so that the blade-bone faces the carver and carve the meat on top of the blade-bone downwards in strips, parallel with the central "fin" of the bone. Finally, turn the joint upside down and carve the meat from the underside horizontally in slices.

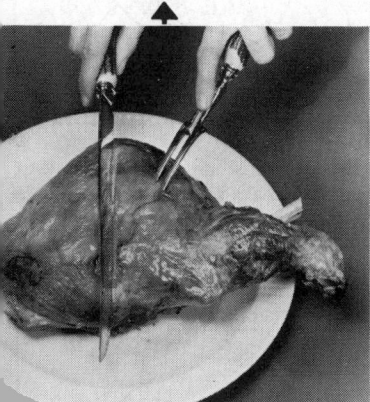

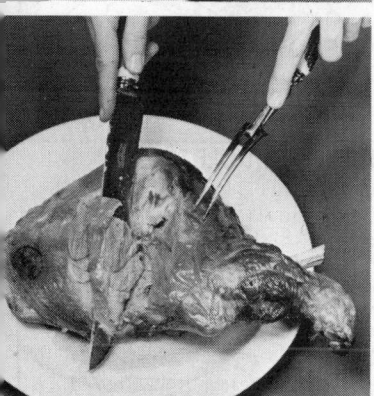

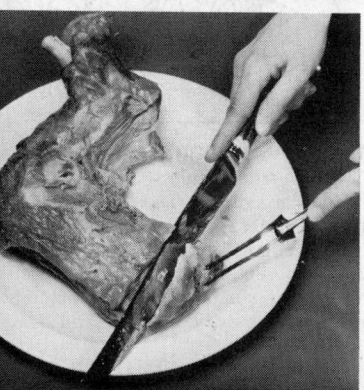

ROAST LEG OF LAMB

The leg of lamb should be placed before the carver so that the shank bone is to his right and the thick meaty section, or cushion, is on the far side of the dish. Different roasts will not always have the same surface uppermost because of the difference in right and left legs. However, this does not effect the method of carving. The illustrations show a right leg of lamb resting on the large smooth side.

Use a sharp carving knife and a fork with a guard.

Insert the fork firmly in the large end of the leg and carve two or three lengthwise slices from the near thin side. (*first illustration*)

Turn the roast so that it rests on the surface just cut. The shank bone now points up from the dish.

Insert the fork in the left of the roast. Starting at the shank end slice down to the leg bone. Parallel slices may be made until the aitch bone is reached. (*second illustration*) One-quarter to three-eighths of an inch is a desirable thickness.

With the fork still in place, run the knife along the leg bone releasing all the slices. (*third illustration*)

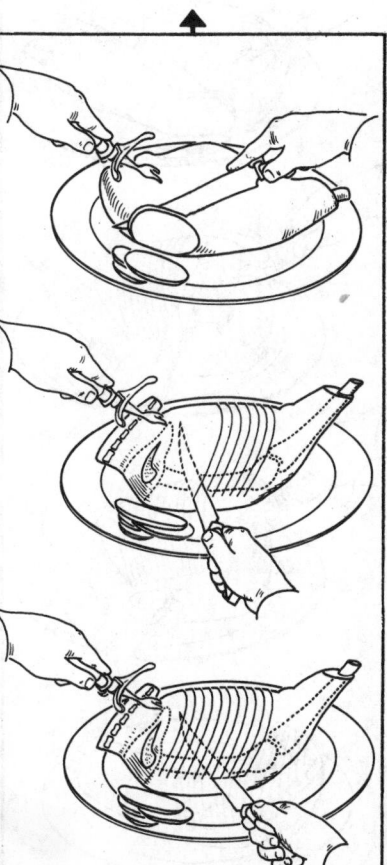

LAMB CROWN ROAST

A lamb crown roast is made from the rack or rib section of the lamb. A pork crown is made from the rib sections of two or more loins of pork. Either cut is carved in a method similar to that of pork loin.

Move to the side of the dish any garnish in the centre which may interfere with carving. Stuffing can be cut and served along with the slices.

Steady the roast by placing the fork firmly between the ribs.

Cut down between the ribs, allowing one rib to each slice. (*first illustration*)

Lift the slice on the knife blade, using the fork to steady it. (*second illustration*)

Crown Roast

For a party or special occasion a crown roast adds a festive touch. Frills may be put on rib ends and attractive garnishes are easy to arrange. If stuffing is used to fill the centre it should be of a consistency that can be sliced with the chops. If cauliflower is the centre garnish ample dish space will be needed so that the carver may place the cauliflower out of his way.

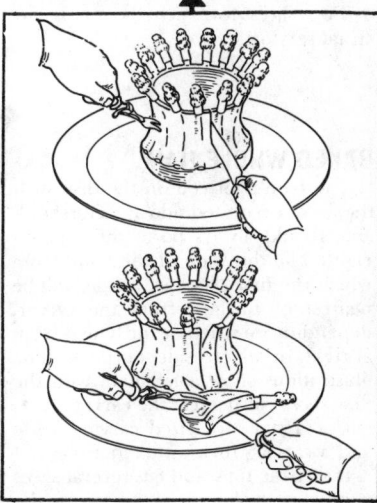

BEEF BRISKET

Place on the dish with the round side away from you. Trim off excess fat. Make slices in rotation from three sides as shown in illustration. Slices should be thin and at a slight angle. Carving in this way makes all cuts across the grain.

ROAST LOIN OF PORK

It is much easier to carve a loin of pork if the backbone is separated from the ribs. This is done at the market by sawing across the ribs close to the backbone. The backbone becomes loosened during roasting; note in the first illustration that it has fallen away from the ribs.

If you have a choice, select a fairly small carving knife.

Before the roast is brought to the table remove the backbone by cutting between it and the rib ends (second illustration).

The roast is placed on the dish so that the rib side faces you. This makes it easy to follow the rib bones, which are the guides for slicing. Make sure of the slant of the ribs before you carve, as all the ribs are not perpendicular to the dish.

Insert the fork firmly in the top of the roast. Cut close against both sides of each rib. You alternately make one slice with a bone and one without. Roast pork is more tempting when sliced fairly thin. In a small loin each slice may contain a rib; if the loin is large it is possible to cut two boneless slices between ribs.

Two slices for each person is the usual serving.

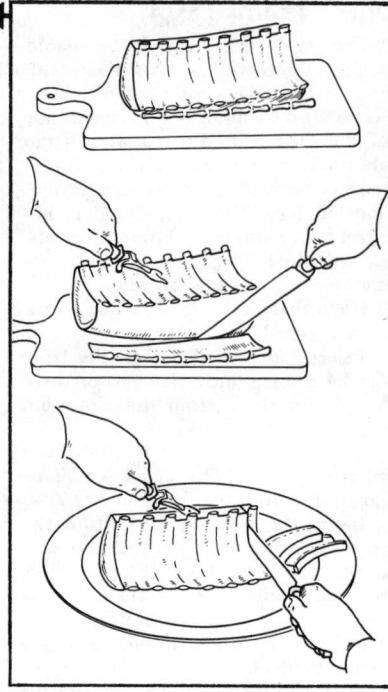

BAKED WHOLE HAM

The ham is placed on the dish with the fat or decorated side up. The shank end should always be to the carver's right. The thin side of the ham, from which the first slices are made, will be nearest or farthest from the carver, depending on whether the ham is from a right or a left side of pork. The illustrations show a left ham with the first slices cut nearest the carver.

Use a standard sized carving knife and a carving fork with a guard.

Insert the fork and cut several slices parallel to the length of the ham on the nearest side (first illustration).

Turn the ham so that it rests on the surface just cut. Hold the ham firmly with the fork and cut a small wedge from the shank end (second illustration). By removing this wedge the succeeding slices are easier to cut and to release from the bone.

Keep the fork in place to steady the ham and cut thin slices down to the leg bone (second illustration).

Release slices by cutting along bone at right angles to slices (third illustration).

For more servings turn the ham back to its original position and slice at right angles to the bone (fourth illustration).

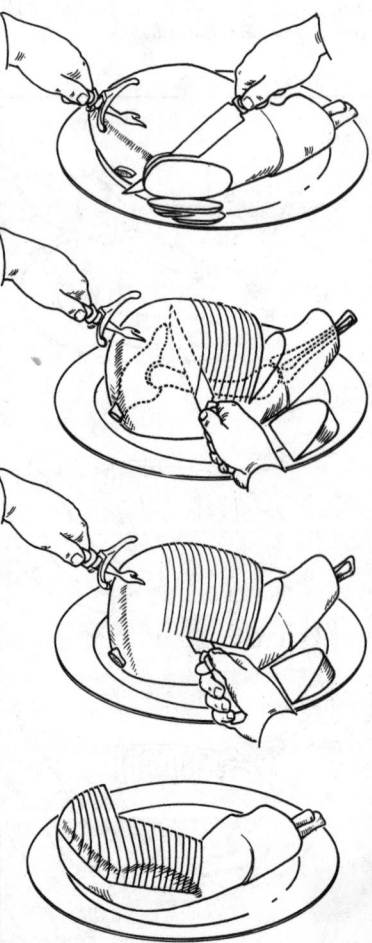

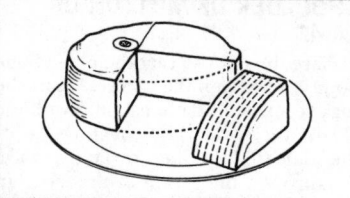

CENTRE OF GAMMON

Divide into thirds and turn one of the sections on its side as shown in illustration. Make slices the desired thickness across the grain. Carve other sections in the same way. The bone must be removed from the last section before slicing.

PORK LEG

Procedure is almost identical with that of the baked ham. Cut a few slices from the smaller meaty side to make a flat surface. Turn the shoulder to stand on this surface. Slice to bone starting at shank end. Release slices by cutting along bone.

ROLLED SHOULDER OF LAMB

This cut is boneless and easy to carve. Cut slices about three-eighths of an inch thick through the meat and dressing.

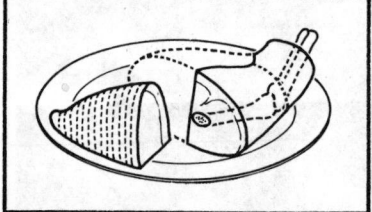

HALF HAM (Shank End)

Remove the cushion section, turn it on the cut side, as shown in the illustration, and make slices beginning at the large end. For further servings from the remaining section, separate it from the shank by cutting through the joint. Remove bone, turn and slice.

Meat Cookery—Basic Methods

The most important guide to follow in all meat cookery is to use a *low* cooking temperature. This keeps the juice and flavour in the meat, cuts down shrinkage, keeps the meat more tender and palatable, and prevents burnt fat drippings.

General rules for the basic methods for cooking meat are described below; however more specific instructions are given in each recipe throughout this book. These methods fall into two basic groups: with dry heat or moist heat, depending on whether liquid is used.

Dry Heat Methods	Moist Heat Methods
Roasting	Braising
Grilling	Cooking in Liquid:
Dry-frying	Soup-Making
Frying	Stewing
Rotisserie cooking	Pressure cooking

Note: For pressure cooking, soup-making, and rotisserie cooking, see separate sections or consult index for specific recipes.

For hints about cooking frozen meat, see **Frozen Food** section.

TIME AND TEMPERATURE CHARTS FOR COOKING MEAT

Specific times are given in each recipe. In addition, you will find time and temperature charts for cooking meat preceding major subdivisions of this section; for example, preceding the beef, pork, veal, and lamb sections. The times given are necessarily only approximate. This is particularly true in roasting meat. The quality of the meat, size, and shape of joint, and its temperature at the start, all affect the time required.

The use of a meat thermometer is recommended. If you use one, insert it so the bulb is at the centre of thickest part of meat and does not touch fat or bone. Where a range of times is given, use lower figure for larger joints.

Grilling

HOW TO SLOW ROAST

The modern method of roasting meats at low temperature does away with spattered ovens, cuts down shrinkage, and gives more and juicier servings per pound. ("Baking" is the term usually applied to roasting smoked hams and picnic hams.)

1. Sprinkle meat with salt and pepper.
2. Place fat-side-up on rack in roasting tin. (For lean meat, such as veal, ask your butcher for a piece of pork or beef fat to lay over the top, or use a few strips of bacon or salt pork.)
3. If you have a meat thermometer, insert through the outside fat into thickest part of muscle so point does not rest on fat or bone.
4. Roast in slow oven (300°F. Mark 2) to 350°F. Mark 4). Use this same temperature throughout cooking period.
5. Remove from oven when meat thermometer registers desired degree, or follow the time schedule given in time and temperature chart or recipe.

HOW TO FRY

"Frying" is a term applied to cooking meats in a small amount of fat in a frying pan.

Frying rather than dry frying is necessary when meat has very little fat or when meat is breaded or floured.

Procedure is the same as for dry frying except that fat is added first.

HOW TO GRILL

To grill is to cook in a direct heat, either under a grill or over a hot coal or charcoal fire. It is a quick method of cooking, and only tender and juicy cuts of meat are suitable.

The grill should always be preheated and the meat brushed with oil or melted fat on both sides. The grid should also be brushed with fat. Place the meat under the grill and cook quickly so that the surface juices coagulate, keeping in the flavour and goodness. Allow about 2 minutes. Then turn and cook on the other side. Turn once or twice during the cooking using tongs or two spoons, taking care not to pierce the flesh or else the juice will run out.

When the meat is cooked, remove from the grill and serve at once with maître d'hôtel butter and garnish with watercress and grilled tomatoes or mushrooms.

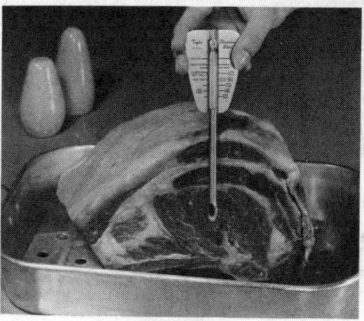

Roasting

HOW TO DRY-FRY

1. Preheat a heavy frying pan. Do not add fat except with minced meat rissoles. If you believe the meat will stick, rub pan with a piece of suet or grease lightly with other fat.
2. When pan is very hot, put in meat, brown quickly on both sides. Do not cover pan.
3. Reduce heat and cook slowly until done. If fat collects in pan, pour it off. Season before serving.

Dry-Frying

HOW TO MAKE A STEW

"Stewing" is the term applied to the braising method when enough liquid is used to cover the meat.

1. Cut beef, veal, or lamb into uniform pieces, 1 to 2 inches square. Season with salt and pepper. Flour the meat if you want a deep brown colour.
2. Brown on all sides in hot cooking fat. If desired, brown chopped onions along with the meat.
3. Barely cover meat with hot water, stock, or other liquid. (To make a quick meat stock, dissolve a bouillon cube or 1 teaspoon beef extract in ½ pint hot water or liquid from cooked vegetables.)
4. Cover pan closely and cook slowly until meat is tender. Simmer, do not boil. Add extra liquid if necessary.
5. Add vegetables just long enough before meat is tender to be done but not over-cooked.
6. Thicken gravy with flour and water, using a little flour and enough water to make a smooth paste.

Braising

HOW TO BRAISE

"Pot roasting" is a popular term applied to braising large cuts.

Braising is a method of moist-heat cookery in which the meat is browned in a little hot fat, then cooked slowly in a covered utensil, usually with a small amount of added liquid. Examples are pot roast and braised steak.

1. Season meat with salt and pepper. For a richer brown, sprinkle with flour.

2. Brown meat slowly on all sides in a little hot fat.

3. Add small amount of liquid. As liquid cooks away, a little more may be added.

4. Cover tightly. Cook over low heat at simmering temperature on top of stove or in moderately slow oven (325°F. Mark 3) until meat is tender, 2 to 3 hours for a pot roast, 1 to 2 hours for braised steak.

5. Vegetables may be added 30 to 45 minutes before meat is done. Continue cooking until meat and vegetables are tender.

HOW TO COOK MEAT IN WATER

"Boiling" is the popular term used for cooking meat in water. Tests prove that this meat is more tender if cooked at a *simmering* rather than a *boiling* temperature.

This is a method often used for cooking cuts such as salt beef, fresh brisket, hocks, ham shank, and smoked tongue.

1. Cover meat with hot water.

2. Season with salt and pepper unless cooking cured or smoked meats such as salt beef, ham, or smoked tongue. Add a peeled onion and herbs and spices, if desired.

3. Cover and cook over low heat at simmering temperature (just below the boiling point) until done. Allow 40 to 50 minutes per pound for fresh or salt beef, 35 to 40 minutes per pound for smoked pork, and 50 minutes per pound for tongue.

4. If vegetables are to be cooked with the meat, add them 30 to 45 minutes before meat is done.

Beef Recipes

HINTS FOR COOKING BEEF

The different cuts of beef vary in tenderness. It is necessary, therefore, to determine the cooking method to be followed and to select the cuts of meat best suited to that method.

For cooking by dry heat—roasting, grilling, and dry-frying—select tender cuts with small amounts of connective tissue.

For cooking by moist heat—braising, stewing, and soup-making—select the less-tender cuts. The less-tender cuts are more economical and are equal in food value to the tender cuts.

All cuts of meat may be made equally tender and tasty through the selection of the proper cooking method. Other means for making meat tender are mincing, pounding, and marinating. Mincing cuts up the connective tissue and the meat may then be cooked like any other tender meat. Pounding tenderizes by cutting through the connective tissue. Marinating, which is accomplished by letting the meat stand in an oil-acid mixture like French dressing, softens the connective tissue.

ROAST RIB OF BEEF

When you buy the joint have the chine bone removed to make carving easier. Season with salt and pepper.

A meat thermometer will assure you of a perfect roast. It registers the internal temperature of meat. The bulb should not touch bone or rest on fat.

Place meat fat-side-up on a rack in a roasting tin.

Roast in a slow oven (300°-325°F. Mark 2-3). Allow 18 to 20 minutes per pound for cooking a rare roast, 22 to 25 minutes per pound for medium, and 27 to 30 minutes per pound for a well-done roast.

With meat thermometer, there will be no overcooking or undercooking. Thermometer will read 140° for rare, 160° for medium, and 170° for well-done.

Serve on a heated dish, attractively garnished. Allow 2 to 3 servings per pound.

ROLLED RIB OF BEEF

Select a 3-rib boned and rolled roast. Season with salt and pepper.

Place roast fat-side-up on rack in roasting tin. Insert meat thermometer in thickest part of meat.

If roast hasn't a generous fat covering, place suet or other fat over top.

Proceed as for rib of beef, increasing roasting time 10 to 15 minutes per pound. Allow 3 to 4 servings per pound.

BEEF ROASTING CHART		
Roasted at 325°F. Mark 3 Oven Temperature		
Cut	Meat Thermometer Reading	Minutes Per Lb.
Rib of Beef (rare)	140°F.	18-20
Rib of Beef (medium)	160°F.	22-25
Rib of Beef (well done)	170°F.	27-30
Rolled Ribs	Same as above	Add 10-15 per lb.
Blade Bone (high quality only)	150°-170°F.	25-30
Topside (high quality only)	150°-170°F.	25-30
Fillet	140°-170°F.	20-25

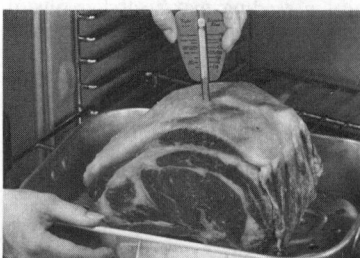

Roast Rib of Beef

Rolled Rib of Beef

552

YORKSHIRE PUDDING
(Accompaniment to Roast Beef)

This batter pudding is served with roast beef. Traditionally, Yorkshire pudding was baked in the pan with the roast or under the roast, letting the drippings fall upon it. Now it is generally cooked in a Yorkshire pudding tin or fireproof dish or in deep patty tins.

4 ounces plain flour
½ teaspoon salt
1 egg
½ pint milk
1-2 ounces dripping or other fat

Sift flour and salt into a basin, make a well in the centre, drop in the egg. Add half the milk and beat till smooth. Stir in remaining milk. Leave to chill in the refrigerator. Heat a little fat in the tins, half fill with the batter and bake in a moderate oven (375°F. Mark 4) allowing 35 to 40 minutes for a large pudding, 15 to 20 minutes if cooked in patty tins.

ROAST FILLET OF BEEF

Sprinkle fillet with salt and pepper. Place on rack in open roasting pan. Lay 4 or 5 bacon slices or slices of salt pork over meat.

Roast in slow oven (325°F. Mark 3) until done, 22 minutes per pound for rare and 25 minutes per pound for medium.

Because of the lack of fat in this meat cut, it is not advisable to roast until well done.

STUFFED FILLET OF BEEF

3- to 3½-pound fillet of beef
2 ounces butter or margarine
1 very small onion, chopped
1 can (4 ounces) mushrooms
4½ ounces soft breadcrumbs
3-4 stalks celery diced
hot water
salt and pepper
4 or 5 slices bacon

Get butcher to split and flatten fillet.

Brown onion and mushrooms lightly in butter or margarine. Add breadcrumbs, celery, and hot water to moisten.

Season and spread over half the meat. Bring second half over top and fasten edges together with wooden skewers or use trussing needle and string.

Season with salt and pepper. Lay bacon slices over top.

Roast uncovered in moderate oven (350°F. Mark 4) 1 hour. Serves 6 to 8.

RUMP ROAST
(using meat thermometer)

If a rump roast is of top quality, it may be oven roasted (cooked like a rib roast). If it's from the lower grades, braising (pot roasting) is the better method to use. Allow 3 to 4 servings per pound.

Sprinkle meat with salt and pepper. Place fat-side-up on rack in open roasting pan.

Insert meat thermometer through outside fat into thickest part of muscle so point does not rest on fat or bone.

Do not add water, do not cover, do not baste.

Roast in slow oven (325°F. Mark 3). For rare, roast 22 to 26 minutes per pound or until meat thermometer registers 140°F.; for medium, roast 26 to 30 minutes per pound or until meat thermometer registers 160°F.; for well done, roast 33 to 35 minutes per pound or until meat thermometer registers 170°F.

BRAISED RUMP

Season meat with salt and pepper. Sprinkle with flour for a richer brown.

Brown meat slowly on all sides in a little hot fat.

Add small amount liquid. As liquid cooks away, a little more may be added.

Cover tightly. Simmer over low heat on top of range, or in slow oven (325°F. Mark 3) until meat is tender, 2 to 3 hours for a pot roast.

BEEF À LA MODE

4 pounds topside of beef
½ pound salt pork, cut in thin strips
2 teaspoons salt
⅛ teaspoon pepper
2 ounces flour
4 ounces fat
4 ounces shelled peas
2 ounces diced carrots
3-4 stalks celery, diced
1 small onion, diced

Lard beef with salt pork, using a larding needle to insert ¼-inch strips of salt pork into meat.

Season with salt and pepper. Coat with flour and brown in fat.

Add about ½ pint of hot water, cover and cook slowly about 2½ to 3 hours or until meat is tender.

Add peas, carrots, celery, and onions ½ hour before meat is done, adding more water if necessary to cover the vegetables.

When meat is done, place on hot dish with vegetables arranged round it and serve with brown gravy.

Serves 6 to 8.

Rump Roast

SAUERBRATEN

Sauerbraten is a German term meaning, literally, sour roast; it is a pot of beef that has been marinated for several days in spiced vinegar and is then braised in the marinade.

4- to 5-pound topside of beef
¾ pint water
¾ pint vinegar
1 tablespoon salt
½ teaspoon pepper
2 tablespoons white or brown sugar
2 medium onions, sliced
1 clove garlic
6 cloves
2 bay leaves
3 or 4 celery tops
12 gingersnaps

Place meat in large earthenware or glass bowl.

Heat vinegar and water; dissolve salt, pepper, and sugar in it. Top meat with sliced onions; pour vinegar mixture over.

Add remaining ingredients except gingersnaps to vinegar around meat. Cover and refrigerate 3 to 4 days, turning meat daily.

Remove meat and drain well. Strain liquid and save.

Dredge meat with flour; brown in hot fat in heavy pan. Add 4 fluid ounces of the strained liquid, cover and cook over low heat until meat is tender (3 to 4 hours). Add more liquid as needed.

Remove meat and keep hot. To make gravy, add more strained vinegar mixture to juice in the pan to make about 1¼ pints liquid. Bring to boil and stir to dissolve all brown drippings. Add 12 gingersnaps, simmer and stir until gravy is thickened and smooth. Serves 8 to 10.

Sauerbraten

BEEF POT ROAST WITH PRUNES AND OLIVES

3½-4 pounds topside beef
salt and pepper
⅛ teaspoon ground ginger
2 cloves garlic
3 onions, sliced
4 fluid ounces oil
⅘ pint water
2 ounces dried mushrooms
8 ounces prunes
4 ounces black olives

Rub meat with salt, pepper, and ground ginger.

Chop garlic fine, slice onions, and cook in oil. Add meat and brown on all sides; then add 4 fluid ounces water. Cover tightly and simmer for 1½ hours. Turn frequently.

While the meat is cooking, soak dried mushrooms and prunes in water.

Add prunes, mushrooms, soaking water, and black olives to meat, and continue cooking another hour, or until tender.

Remove meat to dish and surround with olives and prunes. The sauce may be thickened if desired. Serves 6 to 8.

POT ROAST WITH VEGETABLES

2 ounces flour
⅛ teaspoon salt
⅛ teaspoon pepper
½ teaspoon Aromat
about 3 pounds blade bone or chuck
2 tablespoons fat
water
12 small carrots
12 small onions
1 ounce flour
½ teaspoon salt, or to taste
½ teaspoon pepper
½ teaspoon Aromat

Combine first 4 ingredients; coat meat with this mixture.

Heat fat in a heavy pan and brown meat slowly on each side. Pour off excess fat. Add water.

Slip a low rack under meat; cover pan; simmer 2½ hours, adding more water if necessary, to keep at least ½ inch in bottom of pan.

Pot Roast with Vegetables

Add vegetables; cook 45 minutes longer, or until meat and vegetables are fork-tender.

Arrange meat and vegetables on hot dish; keep warm.

Add ¾ pint water to liquid in pan. Combine last 4 ingredients; blend to smooth paste with 4 fluid ounces cold water; add to liquid in pan; stir over low heat until smooth and thickened. Serve with pot roast. Serves 6.

FLEMISH POT ROAST

3 to 4 pounds topside of beef
½ pound salt pork
2 teaspoons salt
dash of pepper
2 tablespoons dry mustard
4 ounces fat
4 large onions, sliced thin
8 fluid ounces (or more) beef stock
3 medium tomatoes, peeled
2 tablespoons red wine vinegar

Lard beef, using thin strips of salt pork in larding needle. Combine salt, pepper, and mustard, and rub into meat on both sides.

Melt fat in a heavy pan with a lid. Brown meat on both sides; remove from pan.

Add onions to pan and cook until golden brown. Then put meat on bed of onions and add beef stock.

Cook covered 2½ to 3 hours in slow oven (325°F. Mark 3). During last half hour of cooking, add tomatoes cut in half and red wine vinegar. Continue cooking until meat is tender.

Serve on dish, surrounded by onions. Garnish with parsley or watercress. Serves 6 to 8.

BAVARIAN POT ROAST

4 pounds topside beef
2 teaspoons salt
¼ teaspoon pepper
8 fluid ounces sour cream
1 tablespoon flour
6 fluid ounces dry red cooking wine
1 medium onion, finely chopped
6 carrots, peeled and halved

Sprinkle beef with salt and pepper. Brown well on all sides in hot fat in heavy pan about 15 to 20 minutes. Combine sour cream and flour in bowl; pour over beef. Add wine and onion.

Cover pan; simmer slowly about 2½ to 3 hours, or until meat is almost fork-tender, turning occasionally or basting with the liquid.

Then add carrots; cook 30 minutes, or until tender.

On heated dish, arrange roast and carrots, and boiled potatoes or rice if desired. Serve gravy separately. Serves 6.

Creole Pot Roast

CREOLE POT ROAST

4- to 5-pound chuck or blade bone
salt and pepper
1 bottle stuffed olives (5-5½ ounces)
4 tablespoons water
1 small can condensed tomato soup
1 medium onion, chopped

Flour the meat and brown slowly in a little hot fat. Sprinkle with salt and pepper.

Mix together 4 tablespoons liquid from bottled olives, 4 tablespoons water, and the condensed tomato soup. Pour half of this over and around meat.

Top meat with 1 ounce thinly sliced stuffed olives and chopped onion.

Cover the meat and place in slow oven (325°F. Mark 3). Cook for 2½ to 3 hours, or until the meat is tender.

If preferred simmer in a heavy pan for 2½-3 hours.

As the liquid cooks away (after about the first hour), add rest of liquid.

Thicken gravy with flour, adding more water to make of the desired consistency. Serve gravy over rice or noodles. Serves 8.

HERB BEEF POT ROAST

4- to 5-pound chuck or blade bone
flour, salt, pepper, and lard
2 celery stalks with leaves
2 medium onions
½ teaspoon basil
½ teaspoon marjoram
½ teaspoon rosemary

Dredge meat with flour and brown slowly in a little hot lard in a large, heavy pan. Sprinkle with salt and pepper.

Place meat on a rack and top with sliced celery and onions. Add herbs to 4 fluid ounces of water or bouillon, add seasonings and pour over and around meat.

Cover and cook over low heat until tender, 2½ to 3 hours, adding more liquid as needed. Make gravy from drippings. Serves 8.

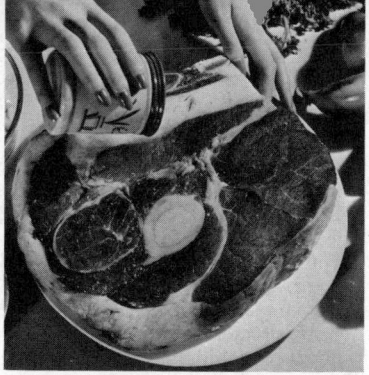

1. For a beef pot roast use the less tender cuts. Season meat with salt and pepper. Sprinkle with flour (optional).

2. Brown meat on all sides in hot fat.

3. Add a small amount of liquid. Cover closely; simmer until tender (2½ to 3 hours). Add whole vegetables just long enough before serving time for them to be cooked tender but not over-cooked.

4. Serve on a heated dish attractively garnished.

BEEF POT ROAST
(Master Recipe)

2 onions, sliced
2 tablespoons fat or salad oil
3 to 5 pounds beef (chuck or topside
flour
salt and pepper
8 fluid ounces boiling water or stock
2 bay leaves (optional)

Brown onions in hot fat. Sprinkle meat with flour; brown on all sides; season with salt and pepper. Add water or stock and bay leaves.

Cover tightly; simmer slowly until meat is tender, 2½ to 3 hours. Add more water or stock if necessary.

Serves 6 to 8.

Beef Pot Roast Variations

Pot Roast with Chilli Sauce: Add chilli sauce to taste when meat has been simmering 1½ hours. Continue cooking another 1½ hours.

Pot Roast with Olives: Before browning, cut slits in meat and insert stuffed olives. Continue as in master recipe.

Pot Roast with Potatoes: Boil peeled potatoes for 15 minutes. Drain and add to pot roast during last 45 minutes of cooking.

Pot Roast with Tomato Juice: Substitute tomato juice or stewed tomatoes for water.

Pot Roast with Vegetables: Add whole carrots, onions, and potatoes during last 45 minutes of cooking time.

Other Pot Roast Variations: Use these miscellaneous seasoning suggestions, chilli powder, curry powder, oregano, dill seed or chopped dill pickles, liquid from sweet pickles, caraway seed, horseradish, and vinegar.

Oven Pot Roast: After seasoning meat, lay pieces of suet over the top. Put meat on rack in roasting tin.

Cover closely and cook until tender in moderate oven (375°F. Mark 5) about 1½ to 2½ hours.

About 45 minutes before meat is done, place six peeled medium potatoes in tin around meat. Turn potatoes in dripping and sprinkle with salt.

Cover and cook until meat and potatoes are tender. Before serving, remove lid to allow potatoes to brown.

BEEF POT ROAST WITH BARBECUE SAUCE

3 pounds blade bone
2 teaspoons salt
¼ teaspoon pepper
3 tablespoons fat
4 fluid ounces water
1 8-ounce can tomato sauce
3 medium onions, sliced
2 cloves garlic, crushed
2 tablespoons brown sugar
½ teaspoon dry mustard
4 tablespoons lemon juice
4 tablespoons ketchup
4 tablespoons vinegar
1 tablespoon Worcestershire sauce

Season meat with salt and pepper. Brown in hot fat. Add water, tomato sauce, onions, and garlic. Cover and cook over low heat 1½ hours.

Combine remaining ingredients and pour over meat. Cover and cook until tender, about 1 hour. Remove meat to hot dish.

Skim most of fat from gravy. Dilute gravy with water to suit taste, then thicken with 2 tablespoons flour mixed to a smooth paste with a little water. Serves 6.

SWEDISH POT ROAST

3 tablespoons fat
2 medium onions, sliced
1 clove garlic, crushed
3 to 3½ pounds topside beef
1 tablespoon salt
8 fluid ounces thick sour cream
8 fluid ounces water
4 or 5 ounces noodles

In a heavy pan, lightly brown onion and garlic in hot fat. Push to one side of pan. Rub meat with salt and brown well.

Combine sour cream with water and pour over meat. Top with browned onions, cover and cook over low heat (or in 325°F. Mark 3 oven) for 2½ hours, or until tender.

Cook noodles in boiling salted water.

Remove roast from pan and make gravy from drippings, adding to it the sour cream and onion mixture from top of roast. Season to taste with salt, pepper, and paprika.

Serve noodles and meat topped with gravy. Serves 6 or more.

CRANBERRY POT ROAST

3- to 4-pound rolled chuck or topside
flour
3 tablespoons fat
salt and pepper
8 fluid ounces unsweetened cranberry sauce
8 fluid ounces hot water

Coat meat with flour. Brown in hot fat. Season with salt and pepper. Pour cranberry sauce and water over meat.

Cover and cook in slow oven (325°F. Mark 3) until tender, about 3 hours, adding water from time to time if necessary.

Remove to hot dish when done and thicken liquid in pan for gravy. Serves 6 to 8.

QUICK SAUERBRATEN WITH RAISINS

3 to 4 pounds beef chuck
salt
2 tablespoons lard
2 medium onions, sliced
1 bay leaf
4 tablespoons water
4 tablespoons vinegar
1 tablespoon brown sugar
$\frac{1}{8}$ teaspoon cinnamon
$\frac{1}{4}$ teaspoon allspice
$\frac{1}{8}$ teaspoon ground cloves
3 ounces raisins

Sprinkle meat with salt. Brown in hot lard in a large, heavy pan. Top with sliced onions and bay leaf.

Combine water and vinegar. Add sugar and stir until dissolved. Add remaining seasonings and pour over meat. Cover and cook over low heat until almost tender, about 2 hours, adding more water as needed.

Turn meat and top with raisins. Cover and continue cooking until meat is tender, $\frac{1}{2}$ to 1 hour.

Remove meat to serving dish. Spoon off most of fat. Dilute liquid with water, if necessary, and thicken with a flour-and-water paste. Season to taste. Serves 6 to 8.

DUTCH POT ROAST OF BEEF CHUCK WITH VEGETABLES

4- to 5-pound beef chuck, boned
        and rolled
salt and pepper
flour
3 tablespoons salt pork or bacon fat
8 fluid ounces boiling water
4 ounces sliced carrots
1 large onion, chopped
3-4 stalks celery, diced
4 ounces diced turnips
$\frac{1}{4}$ clove garlic, crushed
2 tablespoons finely chopped parsley
8 fluid ounces red wine or grape
        juice

Season meat with salt and pepper. Roll in flour until thickly covered. Heat fat in heavy pan and brown meat all over.

Add boiling water and cover tightly. Simmer 4 hours, turning 3 times during cooking and adding water as necessary to maintain level.

Add remaining ingredients. Cover and simmer until vegetables are tender, about $\frac{1}{2}$ hour.

Remove meat to hot dish and mask with vegetables; keep warm.

Strain gravy and return it to pan. Reduce to $\frac{3}{4}$ pint by rapid boiling and stir in a smooth paste of 1 to 2 tablespoons each of butter and flour, depending on thickness of reduced liquid. Serve gravy in separate dish. Serves 10.

BRAISED BEEF IN WINE MARINADE

3 to 4 pounds topside
$\frac{3}{4}$ pint red wine
$\frac{1}{2}$ teaspoon garlic salt or onion salt
        or 1 tablespoon minced onion
$\frac{1}{8}$ teaspoon thyme
1 bay leaf
3 to 4 thin slices onion
drippings or margarine
4 fluid ounces boiling water

Mix wine and remaining ingredients. Pour over the meat and allow to stand in cool place overnight.

Remove from marinade. Rub with salt.

Place in roasting tin. Dot top well with drippings or margarine.

Place, uncovered, in moderate oven (350°F. Mark 4) until meat begins to brown; then add marinating sauce and boiling water.

Cover. Continue to cook 3 to 4 hours, basting occasionally, until meat is tender. Serves 6 to 8.

BEEF POT ROAST WITH HORSERADISH SAUCE

3 pounds topside beef
2 tablespoons melted fat
1 teaspoon garlic salt
1 5-6 ounce bottle horseradish
6 onions, peeled
3 tablespoons plain flour
2 tablespoons water

Brown meat in fat in deep casserole. Sprinkle with garlic salt. Add enough water to horseradish to make 8 fluid ounces; pour over meat.

Cover and cook over low heat for 2 hours. Add onions and cook, covered, for 30 minutes or until onions are tender. Remove meat and onions.

Add enough water to sauce to make $\frac{4}{5}$ pint. Blend flour and 2 tablespoons water until smooth. Add thickening to sauce and cook over low heat, stirring constantly, until thickened. Serves 6.

SPICED BEEF WITH RED WINE

$\frac{3}{4}$ pint water
4 fluid ounces vinegar
1 teaspoon whole black peppers
$\frac{1}{2}$ teaspoon mace
2 onions, sliced
3 ounces brown sugar
2 teaspoons mixed pickling spices
$\frac{1}{2}$ pint red wine
3 to 4 pounds topside beef
4 teaspoons salt
carrots
flour to thicken gravy

Combine water, vinegar, whole black peppers, mace, sliced onions, brown

sugar, and pickling spices. Bring to boiling point. Add wine; pour over the meat. Store in refrigerator overnight.

Rub meat with salt; brown on all sides in a little hot fat.

Pour half the sauce over meat and simmer, covered, for about 2 hours.

Add remaining spice sauce and the carrots; simmer 1 hour longer.

Measure liquid in bottom of pan. Thicken with flour, allowing 2 tablespoons flour for each 8 fluid ounces of liquid. Serve with noodles or dumplings.

Serves 6 to 8.

CALIFORNIA POT ROAST

3 to 4 pounds beef chuck, or blade
        bone
8 fluid ounces sour cream
1 teaspoons salt
$\frac{1}{2}$ teaspoon paprika
$\frac{1}{2}$ teaspoon pepper
1 clove garlic
1 large carrot
1 large onion
8 fluid ounces burgundy or other
        red wine
3 tablespoons flour
4 fluid ounces water
1 tablespoon lemon juice or vinegar

Buy the meat boned, rolled and larded. Remove sour cream from refrigerator so it's at room temperature.

Mix salt, paprika, and pepper, and rub thoroughly over meat. Brown on all sides in a heavy pan over high heat, about 10 to 15 minutes.

Meanwhile, crush garlic, peel and slice carrot, peel and cut onion into rings. Add to meat in pan and cook until onions are golden, about 3 or 4 minutes.

Heat wine and add to meat along with sour cream. Turn down heat, cover tightly and cook over very low heat so mixture barely simmers until meat is tender, about $2\frac{1}{2}$ hours.

Remove meat to hot dish while making gravy. Skim any excess fat.

Blend flour and water to a smooth paste and stir into hot liquid. Cook and stir about 5 minutes.

Add a little more water if gravy is too thick. Add lemon juice and serve at once. Serves 6 to 8.

California Pot Roast

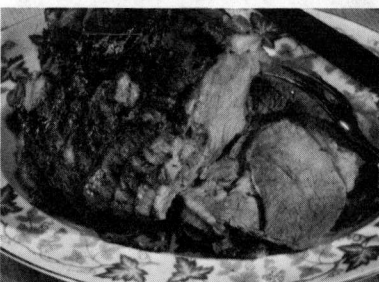

Swiss or Braised Steaks

SWISS STEAK
(Master Recipe)

Swiss steak is a thick cut of topside or sometimes chuck or rump, that has been coated with flour and then pounded, in order to tenderize it, then braised with or without vegetables.

2 pounds beef, 1 inch thick
salt and pepper, to taste
1 ounce flour
1 can tomatoes (16 ounce)

Season meat with salt and pepper. Sprinkle with flour. Pounding helps make meat tender.

Cut meat into serving pieces and brown in fat. Add tomatoes or juice. Cover and simmer gently until tender, 2 to 2½ hours. Serves 6.

Swiss Steak Variations

Swiss Steak with Brown Gravy: Use water instead of tomatoes. When done, remove meat. Add water if needed to make ¾ pint total liquid, and if necessary, thicken with flour blended with cold water.

Swiss Steak with Onion Gravy: Add 2 thinly sliced large onions to Swiss Steak with Brown Gravy during last ½ hour of cooking.

SPANISH STEAK

Follow master recipe for Swiss Steak, using 1½ pounds of meat.

Brown 1 medium sized chopped onion and 4 ounces chopped green pepper in fat.

Cook 6 ounces macaroni in boiling salted water. Mix macaroni, onions, and pepper with tomato sauce. Serve over meat. Serves 6.

SWISS STEAK SUPREME

2 pounds topside, 1 inch thick
3 ounces flour
2 large onions, sliced
1 ounce fat
1 teaspoon dry mustard
2 teaspoons salt
¼ teaspoon pepper
1 clove garlic, finely chopped
4 fluid ounces water
chilli sauce to taste or 3-4 cooked tomatoes

Pound flour into steak with a meat mallet or edge of heavy saucer.

Fry onions in hot fat in a sauté pan. Remove from pan.

Brown steak on both sides. Cover with onions. Add mustard, salt, pepper, garlic, water, and chilli sauce or cooked tomatoes.

Cover and cook over low heat or bake in moderate oven (350°F. Mark 4) about 1½ hours. Serves 6.

SWISS STEAK 2

2 pounds topside or chuck steak, 1 to 2 inches thick
flour, salt, pepper, garlic salt, and fat
1 large can (16 ounces) tomatoes
2 medium onions, sliced
1 stalk celery
1 bay leaf
2 teaspoons Worcestershire sauce

Sprinkle steak well with flour and pound it thoroughly into meat with edge of a heavy saucer or a meat mallet.

Brown steak slowly in hot fat in a heavy pan. Drain off excess fat and sprinkle steak with salt, pepper, and garlic salt.

Pour tomatoes over and around meat; top with sliced onions and celery; add bay leaf and sprinkle with Worcestershire sauce.

Cover and cook over low heat or in slow oven (325°F. Mark 3) until tender, 1½ to 2 hours, depending on thickness of steak. Serve steak with the tomato gravy spooned over it. Serves 4 to 6.

SWISS STEAK IN SOUR CREAM

3 pounds topside, 1 inch thick
salt, pepper
Aromat
1 teaspoon paprika
flour
1 small onion, chopped
¼ pint sour cream
boiling water

Wipe steak with damp cloth; rub in seasonings; pound with meat mallet or heavy knife until meat fibres are well broken, adding a little flour at a time and pounding it well into the steak.

Brown meat on both sides in hot fat along with onion, tossing onion around and over top of steak.

Pour off excess fat; add sour cream and enough boiling water to barely cover steak. Cover and simmer until tender, about 2½ hours. Serves 6 to 8.

SWISS STEAK IN RED WINE

2 ounces flour
1½ teaspoons salt
½ teaspoon pepper
2 pounds topside, cut ¾ to 1 inch thick
3 tablespoons bacon dripping or other fat
8 fluid ounces cooking burgundy, claret, or other red wine
1 small can mushrooms
1 onion, thinly sliced
6 medium-sized carrots, cut crosswise in halves and lengthwise in quarters

Mix flour, salt, and pepper. Place meat on a board and pound flour mixture into it with a meat mallet or the edge of a heavy plate. Cut meat into serving-size pieces.

Heat bacon dripping in large, heavy pan; add meat and sauté until well browned on both sides. Place on trivet in pressure cooker. Add wine and liquid from mushrooms.

If any flour remains on board, sprinkle it over the meat. Close cooker and bring to 15-pound pressure. Cook for 18 minutes. Reduce pressure according to manufacturer's directions.

Add vegetables and again bring to pressure. Cook for 3 minutes. Reduce pressure.

Before serving, taste and add additional salt and pepper, if necessary. Buttered noodles and a tossed green salad are excellent accompaniments to this dish. Serves 6.

Note: If you do not have a pressure cooker, flour and brown meat as directed; add all remaining ingredients (including mushroom liquid and any flour remaining on board.) Cover pan and simmer, stirring occasionally, for 1½ to 2 hours, or until meat is very tender.

Swiss Steak in Red Wine

Beef Steaks

GRILLED STEAK

Buy a tender porterhouse, or sirloin steak cut 1 to 2 inches thick. Slash the fatty edge of the steak but do not cut into the meat or you'll lose good meat juice.

The grill may be preheated or not, as desired. With some grills, thick steaks may be cooked without preheating the grill.

Place steak on rack of grill pan 2 to 3 inches from the heat. Steaks 1½ to 2 inches thick should be at least 3 inches from the heat; those 1 inch or less in thickness, about 2 inches. Grill until top side is brown. The steak should be approximately half done by the time it is browned on top.

Season the top side with salt and pepper. Steaks brown better if browned before salting. Turn and brown the other side. For determining accurately the degree of doneness of a thick steak, a meat thermometer may be used. Season and serve at once. To keep grilled steak hot, the dish should be heated. For 1-inch steak, allow about 8-10 minutes. For 1½-inch steak, allow about 10-12 minutes. For 2-inch steaks, allow about 15 minutes.

GRILLED STEAK-SEARING METHOD

Preheat grill until very hot. Brush with melted butter or oil. Place steak under heat so that top of steak is 2 to 3 inches from source of heat. Sear or brown on each side, turning only once, allowing 5 minutes for each.

Reduce heat or place steak 6 to 7 inches from source of heat and finish cooking.

When half done, season top side, turn and finish cooking. Season other side and serve.

Allow the same time as for even temperature method, including searing in total time. The searing method produces a steak with surface nicely browned while interior may be rare or medium.

PLANKED STEAK

Grill steak, cutting time for top side by 5 minutes. Place less-done side up on a greased wooden platter. Season.

Arrange border of mashed potatoes round edge of platter. Place one or more cooked vegetables between steak and potatoes. Brush all with melted fat.

Place under grill 3 inches from heat and brown potatoes. Garnish with parsley, watercress, tomato wedges or slices.

STEAK CUTS	GRILLING TIMES IN MINUTES
Rump (1½-pound slice, 1 inch thick, serves 3-4). Is improved if brushed with oil 1-2 hours before grilling.	Rare: 6-7 Medium: 8-10 Well done: 14-16
Sirloin or *entrecôte* (¾-1 inch thick, serves 1). Cut from the top part of the sirloin.	Rare: 5 Medium: 6-7 Well done: 9-10
Minute (½ inch thick, serves 1). Then slice of entrecôte, should be cooked quickly.	Rare: 1-1½ Medium: 2-3
T. Bone (1½-2 inches thick, serves 2-3). A whole slice cut from the sirloin with bone.	Rare: 7-8 Medium: 8-10
Porterhouse (1½-2 inches thick, serves 1-2). A slice cut from the wing rib, taken off the bone.	Rare: 7-8 Medium: 8-10
Fillet (1-1½ inches thick, serves 1). The most expensive and most tender steak. The fillet lies under the sirloin, whole piece weighs 5-6 pounds.	Rare: 6 Medium: 7 Well done: 8
Tournedos (1-1½ inches thick, serves 1). These are cut from the centre 'eye' of the fillet.	Rare: 6 Medium: 7-8
Châteaubriand (3-4 inches thick, serves 2). A thick cut from the heart of the fillet. When cooked is sliced downwards for serving.	Rare to Medium rare: 15-18

STEAK WITH MUSHROOMS

After grilling steak, top with mushroom caps which have been browned in butter.

STEAK WITH ROQUEFORT TOPPING

Blend 1 ounce Roquefort or other blue cheese with 2 tablespoons cream. Season with a few drops Worcestershire sauce and spread over hot grilled steak.

STEAK WITH OYSTERS

Grill beef steak until nearly done. Place it in a pan. Cover with drained oysters. Season oysters lightly with salt and pepper and dot with butter. Bake in moderate oven (375°F. Mark 5) until oysters are plump. Serve with lemon butter. Garnish with chopped parsley.

FRIED STEAK

Use tender steak ¾ to 1 inch thick. Trim off excess fat.

Heat heavy sauté pan moderately and grease very lightly. Place steak in it. Brown quickly on both sides.

Reduce heat. Cook slowly until done, pouring off fat as it accumulates. To test, cut near bone. Season with salt and pepper and serve.

FILET MIGNON

Have a fillet cut ¾ to 1½ inches thick.

Shape each cut into a nice round shape and wrap a rasher of bacon round the edge. Fasten in place with a cocktail stick.

Grill until cooked, 7-10 minutes, turning frequently. Serve rare but not raw.

FRIED RUMP STEAK

1½ to 2 pounds rump steak, ½ inch thick
2 tablespoons milk
2 beaten eggs
3-4 ounces breadcrumbs
2 ounces fat
salt and pepper

Pound steak thoroughly with meat mallet or edge of heavy saucer.

Mix milk and eggs; dip steak in mixture, then in crumbs. Brown on both sides in hot fat in frying pan. Season.

Cover and cook over very low heat for about 30 minutes. Serves 6.

SAUTÉED RUMP STEAK

Use rump steak about ⅓ inch thick. Cut into serving-size pieces. Dip in flour.

Sauté until brown in hot fat over moderately high heat. Reduce heat to low. Cover and cook until steak is tender.

GARLIC SEASONED STEAK

Rub grilled steak with cut garlic clove.

Planked Steak

Fillet Steak with Red Wine Sauce

FILLET STEAK WITH RED WINE SAUCE

8 to 10 small fillet steaks about ½-inch thick
2 ounces butter
½ pound mushrooms
3 tablespoons flour
6 fluid ounces red table wine
8 fluid ounces beef stock

Sauté fillets in about ½ ounce butter, about 3 minutes per side. Remember the meat is very tender, so do not overcook.

While meat is browning, melt remaining butter in another pan, slice mushrooms and sauté until lightly browned. Blend in flour. Add wine and beef stock and cook until the mixture comes to the boil. Simmer 5 minutes.

Just before serving, add fillets with any pan juice to gravy and cook until heated through. Serves 4 to 5.

PEPPERED STEAK (STEAK AU POIVRE)

A generous amount of fresh coarsley crushed or ground black pepper is the secret to success of this very popular dish.

6 fillet or mignon steaks
2 tablespoons black pepper, coarsely ground
salt
2 tablespoons butter
Worcestershire sauce
Tabasco sauce
lemon juice
2 fluid ounces cognac, optional
chopped parsley, optional
chopped chives, optional

Sprinkle both sides of each steak with pepper and work it into the meat with the heel of the hand or with the flat side of a cleaver. Let stand 30 minutes.

Sprinkle a light layer of salt (about 2 teaspoons) over the bottom of a heavy frying pan. Place over high heat and when the salt begins to brown, add the steaks. Cook uncovered over high heat until browned on one side.

Lower the heat to moderate, turn the steaks, and cook to desired degree of rareness.

Place a teaspoon of butter on each steak and add Worcestershire, Tabas-co, and lemon juice to taste. Reduce the heat to low; flame the steaks with the cognac and transfer to a heated serving dish. Pour the sauce in the pan over the steaks and, if desired, sprinkle with parsley and chives. Serves 6.

CHÂTEAUBRIAND

Chateaubriand is a French term for a steak cut from the thickest part of the fillet of beef, weighing usually 1 to 2 pounds. It is grilled or sautéed rare and served with any of the sauces suggested for steak. Inasmuch as the steak is always thick, care must be taken to avoid charring the outside while the inside remains raw.

STEAK DIANE

1 to 1½ tablespoons butter or margarine
¼ teaspoon salt
freshly ground black pepper to taste
½ to 1 teaspoon each finely chopped chives and parsley
1 teaspoon Worcestershire sauce
individual steak of any thickness, 8 to 10 ounces

Mix all ingredients except meat in heavy frying pan and, when very hot, place steak in pan.

Cook at very high heat until done. Serve immediately, pouring residue of sauce over meat. Serves 1.

FLANK FINGER STEAKS

about 2 pounds flank of beef
flour
2 ounces fat
1 teaspoon salt
½ teaspoon pepper
8 fluid ounces beef stock
2 tablespoons minced parsley
2 tablespoons ketchup
1 tablespoon prepared mustard
1 tablespoon vinegar
2 tablespoons minced onion
1 can mushrooms (about 4 ounces)

Cut meat into 6 portions. Dredge with flour and brown in fat.

Remove from pan. Add and mix remaining ingredients with fat.

Return steak to pan. Cover tightly and bring to boil. Reduce heat and simmer 1¼ hours. Serves 6.

PAN-BARBECUED STEAK

2 pounds steak (topside or flank, 1½ to 2 inches thick)
½ teaspoon salt
½ teaspoon pepper
3 tablespoons fat
½ onion, finely chopped
2 stalks celery, chopped
½ clove garlic, crushed
1 can condensed tomato soup
2 tablespoons brown sugar
2 tablespoons Worcestershire sauce

2 tablespoons lemon juice
2 teaspoons prepared mustard
dash of Tabasco sauce

Sprinkle steak with salt and pepper; pound thoroughly.

Melt fat in heavy saucepan. Brown steak, onion, celery, and garlic in hot fat.

Add remaining ingredients. Stir well and cover. Cook in moderate oven (350°F. Mark 4) or on top of range for about 1½ hours or until tender.

Double all the sauce ingredients for additional barbecue sauce to serve over fluffy rice or mashed potatoes. Serves 6.

COUNTRY FRIED STEAK

1. Select a piece of topside, ½ to ¾-inch thick. Cut into individual servings. Pound seasoned flour into each side of individual steaks. Melt 2 to 4 tablespoons fat in sauté pan.

2. Brown steaks slowly on both sides. Cover and cook at a low temperature 45 minutes to 1 hour.

3. Remove steaks from pan, stir 1 ounce flour into the fat. Add ¾ pint stock stirring constantly until thickened. Serve gravy over or with steaks.

CONTINENTAL BEEF

4 ounces fat
2 onions, sliced thin
2 pounds chuck or blade bone
1 teaspoon salt
⅛ teaspoon pepper
1 clove garlic, crushed
½ pound fresh mushrooms, sliced
1 green pepper, sliced thin
1 8-ounce can tomato sauce
8 fluid ounces water

Melt fat in a sauté pan. Add onions and cook until golden brown: remove onions.

Rub meat with salt, pepper, and garlic; place in hot pan and sear quickly on both sides. Add browned onions, sliced mushrooms, green pepper, and tomato sauce.

Cook 15 minutes, then add water. Cover, and simmer over slow heat about 1½ hours or until meat is tender and sauce has thickened.

Remove to hot dish. Serve hot with parsley buttered potato balls. Serves 5 to 6.

STUFFED FLANK

about 2½ pounds beef flank
salt and pepper
2 tablespoons butter or margarine
1 small finely chopped onion
6 ounces soft breadcrumbs
¼ teaspoon caraway seed
½ teaspoon celery salt
8 fluid ounces tomato juice

Get butcher to score meat. Sprinkle with salt and pepper. Melt fat and in it lightly cook onion. Mix with breadcrumbs, caraway seed, celery salt, salt and pepper to taste.

Spread stuffing on unscored side of meat and roll parallel to its length. Tie in 3 or 4 places with string or fasten with short metal skewers and lace with string.

Brown meat in sauté pan in a little hot fat. Add tomato juice, cover and cook over low heat or in moderate oven (350° F. Mark 4) 2 hours, or until tender. Serves 4 to 6.

Savoury Beef Flank

BRAISED STEAK AND ONIONS

¾ to 1 pound rump or topside
    cut 1 inch thick
salt, pepper, flour
fat
water
1 or 2 large onions, sliced

Season meat with salt and pepper; sprinkle with flour.

Pound on both sides with meat mallet or the edge of a heavy saucer to help make meat tender.

Cut meat into serving pieces and brown in a little fat in a fry pan.

Add water to ½-inch depth. Cover pan and cook slowly until meat is very tender, about 2 hours, adding onions during last half hour.

To serve, place meat on hot dish and cover with onions. Make gravy with the fat left in the pan. Serves 4.

TOPSIDE BRAISED WITH OLIVES

1½   pounds topside, ¾-inch thick
2   tablespoons fat
1   medium onion, chopped
1   small green pepper, chopped
1   bottle (3½ ounces) pimiento
       stuffed olives, sliced
1 can (10½ ounces) cream of
       tomato soup

Cut meat into serving pieces. Brown with onion and green pepper in hot fat in heavy pan or flame-resistant casserole. Add olives and olive brine. Add tomato soup. Cover tightly and bake in moderate oven (350°F. Mark 4) or cook over low heat until tender, about 1½ hours. Serves 4 to 5.

SAVOURY BEEF FLANK

about 2½ pounds beef flank, well
    scored
salt and pepper
2 tablespoons chopped parsley
1 clove garlic, crushed
1 ounce grated Parmesan cheese
2 tablespoons fat
2 cans condensed cream of tomato
    soup, diluted with an equal
    quantity of water
1 teaspoon cider or wine vinegar
1 teaspoon oregano

Sprinkle one side of flank with salt, pepper, parsley, garlic, and cheese.

Roll steak up tightly, Swiss-roll fashion, and secure with string. Brown on all sides in fat in large sauté pan.

Combine soup, water, vinegar, and oregano; pour over meat. Simmer, covered, 3½ to 4 hours, or until tender.

Serve with noodles or spaghetti. Serves 4 to 6.

Dilly Beef Flank

DILLY BEEF FLANK

4 tablespoons wine vinegar
4 tablespoons oil
6 fluid ounces water
1 teaspoon onion flakes
¼ teaspoon dried dill
⅛ teaspoon garlic powder
½ teaspoon salt
⅛ teaspoon pepper
about 1½-2 pounds beef flank
1 tablespoon cornflour
1½ teaspoons sugar

Combine vinegar, oil, 4 tablespoons water, onion, dill, garlic powder, salt, and pepper. Place meat in shallow glass dish. Pour vinegar-oil mixture over steak. Cover and let stand 2 to 3 hours.

Drain steak and remove to grill pan, reserving marinade. Grill about 5 minutes on first side, 4 minutes on second side for rare. Remove to heated serving dish.

Combine cornflour, sugar, and remaining water with reserved marinade. Add to fat in grill pan. Cook, stirring constantly, until mixture boils and is thickened.

To serve, slice meat thinly, diagonally to the grain, and top with sauce. Serves 6 to 8.

BEEF SKIRT

Beef skirt is a cut from the diaphragm, so called because it skirts the ribs. When properly trimmed, it is all lean meat. Its long, tough fibres may be tenderized by marinating or light scoring with a knife. It is usually an economical and convenient cut for grilling or sautéing. It is often rolled into pinwheels before being cut into individual portions. Sometimes erroneously called fillet, a term properly applied to a long strip on either side of the backbone.

BRAISED BEEF FLANK

Have the meat scored. Dip into flour, season with salt and pepper.

Brown in hot fat. Add 4 fluid ounces hot water. Cover and cook over low heat or in moderate oven (350°F. Mark 4) until tender, about 1½ hours.

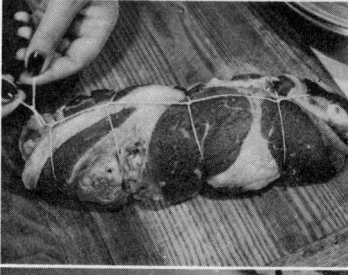

Rolled Stuffed Topside

TOURNEDOS

Tournedos is a French term for a small, uniform slice cut from the heart of the fillet of beef then usually encased in a thin layer of fat and securely tied. They are so cut for quick cooking. These are most often sautéed in butter or olive oil or in a mixture of the two. They may also be grilled but are generally considered better if sautéed and served with a sauce.

COUNTRY FRIED TOPSIDE

1 pound topside, cut ½-inch thick
1 teaspoon salt
dash of pepper
1 ounce flour
1 tablespoon fat
2 tablespoons water

Cut meat into serving pieces. Season with salt and pepper. Roll in flour. Brown on both sides in hot fat.

Add water; cover and simmer until meat is tender, 15 to 20 minutes. Serve with gravy from the pan poured over meat. Serves 4.

Variation: If desired, the flour may be seasoned with the salt and pepper and pounded into steak before browning.

With Milk Gravy: Make milk gravy by adding enough milk to liquid in the pan to make ⅜ pint liquid. Combine 3 tablespoons flour with 4 fluid ounces of the milk and add slowly to the boiling liquid in pan. Stir and boil 5 minutes. Add more salt if necessary.

ROLLED STUFFED TOPSIDE

9 ounces soft breadcrumbs
½ small onion, chopped
2-3 stalks celery, chopped
1 tablespoon chopped parsley
½ teaspoon powdered sage
½ teaspoon salt
pepper
3 fluid ounces stock or hot water
2-2½ pounds topside, cut ½-inch thick
3 tablespoons fat
4 tablespoons water

Combine breadcrumbs, onion, celery, parsley, seasonings, and enough stock or water to moisten.

Spread stuffing on meat and roll like a Swiss roll. Tie in several places or fasten with skewers.

Brown roll on all sides in fat. Add water. Cover closely and cook slowly about 1½ hours, or until meat is tender.

Remove to hot dish and make gravy with the liquid in the pan.

Serves 6 to 8.

MARINATED SIRLOIN STEAKS WITH FRIED ONIONS

sirloin steaks, 1½ inches thick
4 fluid ounces olive oil
Worcestershire sauce
salt and pepper
2 tablespoons lemon juice
3 large Spanish onions, sliced
4 fluid ounces evaporated milk
flour

Rub steaks with cut clove of garlic, if desired.

Season olive oil to taste with Worcestershire sauce, salt, and pepper. Add lemon juice and pour mixture over steak in a shallow pan. Let stand 2 hours.

Grill steaks under moderate heat. About 15 to 20 minutes will be required for medium well-done steak, or 8 to 10 minutes on a side.

Break onion slices into rings and dip in milk, then in flour. Drop into hot fat and cook until delicately browned. Serve over steaks.

TOPSIDE MARINATED IN WINE

about 2 pounds topside, cut ½- to ¾-inch thick
salt and pepper
4 tablespoons dry red wine
1 small clove garlic, crushed
1 small onion, sliced
flour, fat

Cut meat into serving pieces and mix with other ingredients except flour and fat. Refrigerate at least 1 hour.

Remove meat from marinade. Dry. Coat lightly with flour and brown in fat. Add marinade. Cover and simmer until tender, about 1½ to 2 hours. Serve with liquor from the pan. Serves 4.

DEVILLED BEEF FLANK

1½ pounds beef flank
1 ounce flour
1 ounce butter or margarine
1 teaspoon chopped onion
1 teaspoon salt
½ teaspoon pepper
1 teaspoon mustard
⅛ teaspoon paprika
1 tablespoon vinegar
⅘ pint water

Cut meat into small pieces and coat with flour.

Brown onion in melted butter in sauté pan. Remove onion and brown meat in butter. Remove meat from pan.

Add salt, pepper, mustard, paprika, and remaining flour to butter in pan, blending well.

Add vinegar and water slowly. Bring to boil, stirring to prevent lumping. Add meat and onion.

Cover tightly and simmer gently until meat is tender, about 2 hours. Serve with the pan gravy. Serves 6.

FLANK PINWHEELS

Roll boned flank as roll and fasten with wooden skewers at approximately 1-inch intervals.

Brown rolls on both sides in 3 tablespoons hot fat. Season with salt and pepper.

Add 4 tablespoons water. Cover and cook slowly for 1 hour or until tender. Serves 4.

Flank Pinwheels

BACHELORS' STEAK
(Beef with Beer)

1 thick porterhouse steak
vinegar and olive oil
salt and pepper
2 ounces butter or margarine
1 pound fresh or canned mush-
    rooms
2 tablespoons flour
¾ pint beer

Rub steak with oil and vinegar, season on both sides and let stand in refrigerator.

For a 2-inch steak, grill 7-8 minutes
for rare. 8-10 minutes for medium rare.

A few minutes before the steak is
done, fry sliced mushrooms in butter,
season with salt and pepper, add flour,
then steak juice from grill pan and
beer. Stir well while cooking, let come
to the boil, pour over steak and serve.

SPANISH RUMP STEAK

1½ teaspoons salt
⅛ teaspoon pepper
1 ounce flour
2 pounds rump steak, cut 1 inch
    thick
3 tablespoons fat
1 large onion, sliced
1 green pepper, chopped
1 can (10-12 ounces) tomatoes

Mix salt, pepper, and flour. Coat
steak with seasoned flour and brown
in fat. Add onion, green pepper, and
tomatoes.

Cover and cook slowly on top of
stove or in slow oven (300°F. Mark 2)
1½ hours or until tender.

Thicken cooking liquid for gravy, if
desired. Serves 4-5.

STEAK À LA DRAKE

1 8-10 ounce sirloin steak, well
    trimmed
1½ tablespoons butter or margarine
1 tablespoon brandy
2 tablespoons sherry
1 tablespoon butter creamed with
    1 teaspoon chopped chives

Pound meat very thin with mallet or
steak hammer.

*Ginger Steak Strips: Marinate a less
tender cut of beef for marvellous flavour
development — use the marinade to make
a zippy sauce.*

Heat butter in a frying pan. Fry the
steak quickly in the butter, turning it
once.

Add brandy. Flame. Add sherry and
butter creamed with chives.

Place steak on a warm plate and
pour gravy over it. Serves 1.

CHUCK STEAK-SPANISH STYLE

1½ to 2 pounds chuck steak
2 tablespoons melted meat drip-
    ping
2 tablespoons vinegar
1½ teaspoons salt
¼ teaspoon pepper
1 onion, chopped
1 tablespoon chopped parsley
1 tablespoon chopped celery leaves
1 small green pepper, chopped
¾ pint tomato sauce

Score steak on both sides. Cover with
a marinade dressing made of fat, vinegar, onion, and other seasonings. Soak
for 1 hour or longer.

Sear meat, using extra fat if needed.
Then place in a shallow baking dish or
casserole.

Add what is left of the marinade
dressing and the tomato sauce. Bake in
slow oven (325°F. Mark 3) until meat is
tender, about 2 hours. Serves 4.

GINGER STEAK STRIPS

2 tablespoons prepared mustard
1 tablespoon salt
1 teaspoon ground black pepper
1 teaspoon chilli powder
1 teaspoon sugar
1 tablespoon lemon juice
3 fluid ounces salad oil
1 clove garlic, sliced
1 onion, sliced
¾ pint water
½ pint cider vinegar
2 pounds topside of beef
16 to 18 small white onions, peeled
3 green peppers, cut in strips
about 15 ginger snaps
4 fluid ounces water

Mix first 11 ingredients in a large
bowl. Add beef, cut in strips about
½×1×2 inches. Marinate 5 to 6 hours.

Boil onions and green peppers together 10 minutes.

Remove meat from marinade. Drain.

Place strips of meat in a casserole
with onions and green peppers and
cook in a moderate oven (375°F. Mark
4) about 20-25 minutes or until tender.
Measure out ¾ pint of the marinade and
strain into a pan with the crushed
gingersnaps and water. Stir till boiling,
then boil quickly to reduce a little.
Check the seasoning and pour over the
meat. Serves 4 to 6.

Chuck Steak—Spanish Style

BEEF ROLLS—BORDELAISE SAUCE

3 pounds topside, sliced thinly
3 hard-boiled eggs, chopped finely
1 large onion, thinly sliced
2 teaspoons salt
dash of pepper
¼ teaspoon nutmeg
3-4 tablespoons finely chopped
    parsley
3 anchovies, chopped
2 tablespoons chopped suet
2 ounces fat

Cut meat into 12 pieces. Combine
remaining ingredients except the fat,
and mix well.

Spread over the pieces of meat and
roll each carefully and tightly. Fasten
with skewers or string. Dust with flour.

Brown well on all sides in fat. Add
4 fluid ounces water. Cover and simmer
gently until tender, about 2 hours.

Thicken the liquid left in the pan
to make gravy. Serve over beef rolls.
Serves 6.

TOPSIDE SPECIAL

1½-2 pounds topside, ½ inch thick
salt, pepper, flour, fat
1 large onion, sliced
2 8-ounce cans tomato sauce
2 tablespoons soy sauce
1 tablespoon sugar
1 bay leaf
½ teaspoon herbs (thyme, basil,
    marjoram, or oregano)

Sprinkle meat with salt, pepper, and
flour. Pound on both sides with meat
pounder or edge of heavy saucer.

In a large, heavy pan, brown meat
well in a few tablespoons hot fat. Top
with sliced onions.

Combine tomato sauce with rest of
ingredients and pour over meat.

Cover and cook over low heat until
tender, about 1½ hours. Watch carefully to prevent sticking. Add water as
tomato sauce cooks away.

Remove steak to serving dish. Skim
fat from sauce and pour over meat.
Serves 4.

Topside Special

Beef Brisket and Salt Beef

Brisket is the breast of the animal, usually cooked by braising. It is also a popular cut for salt beef.

"BOILED" BEEF WITH HORSERADISH SAUCE

4 pounds fresh brisket of beef
salted water
3 or 4 whole black peppers
1 bay leaf
1 onion
1 stalk celery
1 tablespoon butter or margarine
1 tablespoon flour
8 fluid ounces milk
1 tablespoon lemon juice
salt and pepper
2-3 tablespoons prepared horse-
radish

Place brisket in pan with salted water to cover. Add whole black peppers, bay leaf, onion, and celery. Cover and simmer until meat is tender, about 3 hours.

If desired, cook potatoes in the stock.

To make sauce, blend flour into melted butter over low heat. Add milk gradually, stirring constantly, until smooth and thickened. Season sauce with salt, pepper, lemon juice and horseradish. Serves 8 or more.

BEEF BRISKET WITH SAUERKRAUT

3 pounds beef brisket
3 tablespoons bacon or other fat
1 small onion, chopped
2 pounds sauerkraut
⅘ pint boiling water

Tie beef brisket into a compact shape.

Melt fat in a deep pan; add and brown onions lightly.

Add meat and cover with sauerkraut. Add boiling water and simmer until meat is tender, about 2½ hours.

Season to taste with salt and pepper and, if desired, caraway seed and dry white wine.

Slice meat and serve with boiled potatoes covered with sour cream and sprinkled with chopped parsley. Serves 6.

PICKLING BRINE FOR SALT BEEF

about 3 pints water
4 ounces salt
3 tablespoons sugar
1 bay leaf
6 peppercorns
1 clove garlic, crushed
2 teaspoons mixed pickling spices

Combine ingredients in a stoneware crock and stir well.

Add 5 or 6 pounds beef (brisket or rump). Cover with a plate and place a heavy weight on it. (A tightly sealed jar filled with water or a heavy weight will serve as the weight to keep the meat well under the solution.)

Leave the meat in the brine for 36 hours.

PICKLING BRINE FOR SALT BEEF (KOSHER STYLE)

8 ounces coarse salt
about 6 pints water
1 teaspoon saltpetre
2 ounces sugar
1 tablespoon mixed whole spices
1 teaspoon paprika
12 to 15 bay leaves
4 to 5 cloves garlic

Dissolve salt in water. Combine with remaining ingredients except garlic and boil for 5 minutes. Cool.

Place beef in a stoneware crock. Add 4 to 5 cloves of sliced garlic and pour over the brine.

Cover with a large heavy plate and weight it down with a tightly sealed jar filled with water or a heavy weight to keep the meat well under the solution.

Cover with two thicknesses of heavy muslin tied securely around crock.

Store the covered crock in a cool place 2 to 3 weeks, turning meat once a week.

The crock cover may be adjusted; however, see that it is propped up so that air circulates between it and the muslin cover.

This amount will pickle up to 10 pounds of beef or tongue. If the brine is not salty enough, more salt may be added during the pickling process.

NEW ENGLAND "BOILED" DINNER

4 pounds salt beef
6 whole small carrots
6 turnips, diced
6 whole small potatoes, peeled
6 whole small onions
1 head cabbage, cut in wedges

Cover beef with cold water. Bring to boiling. Simmer slowly 40 to 50 minutes per pound, about 3½ hours.

Add carrots, turnips, potatoes, and onions 45 minutes before beef is done.

Add cabbage for last 15 minutes. Serves 6 to 8.

Salt Beef Hash: Combine equal parts chopped cooked salt beef and chopped boiled potatoes. Shape into patties and brown in hot fat.

Thrifty Salt Beef Hash: Chop all leftovers from New England Boiled Dinner. Form into patties and brown in hot fat.

HOW TO "BOIL" SALT BEEF

Cover salt beef with water. Bring to boil. Reduce heat so that water just simmers. Keep kettle tightly covered.

A 2- to 3-pound piece of salt beef will cook tender in 2½ to 3 hours. A whole brisket (10 to 12 pounds) will take about 6 hours.

No seasonings are needed in the cooking water but you may add a few whole black pappers, an onion, and a stalk of celery or a carrot.

To Cook Kosher-Style Salt Beef: Cook as above, but add 1 clove garlic to the water for each pound salt beef. Let cool in the water.

To serve hot, drain and sprinkle heavily with paprika. Heat in moderate oven (350°F. Mark 4) ½ hour.

SALT BEEF AND CABBAGE

Cook salt beef as directed above. No seasoning is needed in water. About 20 minutes before meat is tender, remove enough stock to cook cabbage.

Skim off excess fat. Add cabbage cut in small wedges. Boil, uncovered, until cabbage is just tender, 15 to 20 minutes.

Place meat on hot dish. Drain cabbage and arrange around meat. Sprinkle with salt and paprika.

ROAST BRISKET OF BEEF

Beef brisket is a cut that usually should be braised (pot-roasted) or cooked in water; however the method given here for oven roasting in a pan with a tight-fitting cover is successful and has been a favourite dish with Jewish housewives for many years.

3 pounds lean beef brisket
1 teaspoon salt
½ teaspoon pepper
¼ teaspoon ground ginger
⅛ teaspoon garlic powder
2 tablespoons fat
3 large onions, peeled

Choose a piece of beef brisket with as little fat as possible. Rub the salt, pepper, ginger, and garlic powder into the meat; let stand about 1 hour.

Melt the fat (or use oil) in a roasting pan with a tight-fitting cover. Slice onions and mix with the fat in a pan. Place meat over onions; cover pan tightly and cook in moderate oven (350°F. Mark 4) until the meat is very tender, about 3 hours. Timing will vary with the quality of the meat.

To serve, slice the meat across the grain, arrange on a heated dish and garnish with the onions. Serve the pan gravy separately. Sliced brisket is also delicious served cold. Serves 6.

With Potatoes: Small, boiled and peeled potatoes may be placed around the meat during the last half hour of cooking.

*Glazed Salt Beef with
Noodles and Peas*

GLAZED SALT BEEF BRISKET

Remove the hot "boiled" brisket from cooking liquid.

Score fat covering of brisket into diagonal strips, then score into diamond shapes.

Spread lightly with prepared mustard. Sprinkle lightly with sifted brown sugar. Stud each centre of diamonds with a whole clove.

Place meat in shallow pan. Bake in hot oven (400°F. Mark 6) to melt sugar and glaze surface of brisket, about 20 minutes.

CHOLENT

Like the Puritans who baked beans on Saturday so that they would not have to cook on Sunday, Orthodox Jewish housewives traditionally prepared cholent for the Sabbath because of a similar religious prohibition. There are many versions of the dish, which is basically a mixture of lima or pea beans, potatoes, beef, and onions. It owes its distinctive savour to very slow overnight cooking; in some places the local baker's brick oven was used by the entire community. Some scholars believe that the Yiddish term, cholent, is a corruption of schul ende, referring to the fact that the dish would be ready when the synagogue service was over on Saturday morning; by others it is believed to be derived from the French chaud (hot).

2 large onions, diced
2 tablespoons chicken or other fat
½ pound dried lima beans, soaked overnight in cold water
8 to 10 medium potatoes, pared and cut in quarters
3 ounces medium barley
2 pounds brisket of beef, in one piece
2 tablespoons flour
salt, pepper, and paprika to taste

Sauté onions in fat in large pan.

When onions are light brown, add presoaked beans, potatoes, and barley. Sink the beef in centre.

Mix flour with seasonings and sprinkle over top. Add boiling water to cover.

Adjust lid and cook on top of range over very low heat (a low simmer) 5 hours. Serves 6.

Beef Thick Ribs

"BOILED" BEEF THICK RIBS

Use beef thick ribs and follow method for New England "Boiled" Dinner. Simmer until meat is tender. Add vegetables, and salt and pepper to taste.

BRAISED THICK RIBS OF BEEF

4 pounds thick ribs
flour
2 teaspoons salt
dash of pepper
2 tablespoons salad oil or melted fat
8 fluid ounces boiling water
8 ounces cooked or canned tomatoes
1 clove garlic
6 medium potatoes
12 small onions
6 medium carrots

Roll thick ribs in flour seasoned with salt and pepper. Brown on all sides in hot oil or fat.

Place in heavy pan and add water, tomatoes, and garlic. Cover and simmer over low heat 1½ hours.

Add peeled vegetables. Cook until vegetables and meat are tender, ½ to 1 hour.

Arrange meat and vegetables on dish. Thicken gravy with 1½ tablespoons flour and 2 tablespoons water for each 8 fluid ounces liquid. Serve over meat. Serves 6.

THICK RIBS — SAUERBRATEN STYLE

3 pounds thick ribs, cut into serving pieces
8 fluid ounces water
8 fluid ounces ketchup
1 tablespoon vinegar
1 tablespoon Worcestershire sauce
1 tablespoon horseradish
1 tablespoon sugar
1 tablespoon dry mustard
¼ teaspoon pepper
1 teaspoon salt
2 onions, sliced
1 bay leaf
flour
3 tablespoons fat

Place meat in a bowl. Mix remaining ingredients together except flour and fat and pour over ribs. Cover. Place in refrigerator overnight.

Remove ribs; drain and roll in flour. Brown floured ribs in hot fat, then add liquid in which ribs were soaked.

Cover and cook slowly until meat is tender, about 1½ hours. Serves 4 to 5.

BARBECUED THICK RIBS

3 pounds thick ribs beef
1 medium sized onion, chopped
2 tablespoons fat
4 fluid ounces water
4 tablespoons vinegar
8 fluid ounces ketchup
3-4 stalks celery, sliced
2 tablespoons sugar
2 teaspoons salt
3 tablespoons Worcestershire sauce
1 teaspoon prepared mustard

Cut meat into serving pieces. Brown with onions in hot fat. Add remaining ingredients.

Cover and bake in moderate oven (350°F. Mark 4) until tender, or cook over very low heat 1½ to 2 hours. Serves 4 to 5.

SWEET-SOUR THICK RIBS

2½ to 3 pounds thick ribs
salt, pepper, flour, and lard
1 large onion, sliced
1 clove garlic
12 fluid ounces hot water
1 small bay leaf
3 tablespoons brown sugar
4-5 tablespoons ketchup
4 tablespoons vinegar

Cut meat into individual servings. Trim off excess fat. Sprinkle with salt and pepper and roll in flour.

Brown well on all sides in large pan in several tablespoons hot lard. Remove to another pan.

Add onions and sliced garlic to fat in pan and cook until lightly browned; add to meat.

Combine remaining ingredients with ½ teaspoon salt and pour over meat. Cover and cook over low heat until tender, 2½ to 3 hours. Remove meat to serving dish and keep in warm place.

Pour off most of fat from gravy, stir in 2 tablespoons flour and enough water to dilute to strength desired. Cook until thickened.

Serve meat on hot buttered noodles topped with sauce. Serves 4.

Sweet-Sour Thick Ribs

Beef Stews

BROWN BEEF STEW WITH POTATO FRILL

1 to 1½ pounds boneless beef chuck, neck, flank, or shank meat or similar cuts from loin or rib of beef, cut in 1½-inch cubes
2 tablespoons flour
2 tablespoons fat or dripping
1 onion, chopped
2 teaspoons salt
½ teaspoon pepper
1 bay leaf
4 whole cloves
¾ pint boiling water
4 carrots, sliced
3 small potatoes, quartered
4 ounces peas, frozen or canned

Roll meat in flour and brown slowly and thoroughly in hot fat 15 to 20 minutes. Brown onion at same time.

To browned meat and onion add salt, pepper, bay leaf, cloves, and boiling water.

Turn the heat very low, then cover pan and simmer gently 2 to 3 hours.

Add sliced carrots, potatoes, and peas. Add another 8 fluid ounces of water and 1 more teaspoon salt (for vegetables); cover and cook 45 minutes or until vegetables are tender. Serves 4 to 6.

To Thicken Gravy: Remove meat and vegetables to a casserole.

Mix 1 tablespoon flour with 3 tablespoons cold water, and stir into gravy of the stew to thicken it. Pour over meat and vegetables.

Surround with frill of seasoned mashed potatoes. Heat in oven or under grill until potato peaks are browned.

Variations: Stew may omit frill of mashed potatoes and, instead, small scones may be used for topping. Different combinations of vegetables, also dumplings, help make stews interesting.

Beef stew becomes a party dish when served from a chafing dish accompanied by crisply fried corn fritters.

BEEF STEW WITH WINE OR BOEUF BOURGUIGNONNE

5 medium-sized onions, sliced or 12 whole small white onions
2 tablespoons bacon fat or 2 ounces salt pork or suet
2 pounds lean beef
2 tablespoons flour
salt, pepper, marjoram, and thyme
8 fluid ounces stock
8 fluid ounces dry red wine
½ to 1 pound sliced fresh mushrooms
12 small new potatoes (optional)

Fry onions in bacon fat in a heavy deep pan until brown.

Remove onions and set aside. Add beef cut into 1-inch cubes and brown well, adding a little more fat if necessary.

Sprinkle with flour and seasonings, about a pinch each of salt, pepper, marjoram, and thyme. Add stock and wine. Stir slightly.

Cover and simmer as slowly as possible, 3½ hours. Or, place in a casserole in extremely slow oven (250°F. Mark ½).

Add onions, mushrooms, and, if desired, potatoes and cook until vegetables are tender, about 45 minutes longer. Adjust seasoning to taste.

HUNGARIAN BEEF STEW WITH SAUERKRAUT

2 pounds boneless beef chuck cut into 1-inch cubes
1 ounce flour
4 tablespoons oil or 2 ounces fat
1 small onion, chopped
1 teaspoon salt
¼ teaspoon pepper
1 teaspoon caraway seed
½ teaspoon paprika
⅘ pint water
1 can or about 1½-2 pounds sauerkraut
2 teaspoons sugar
¼ pint sour cream

Roll meat in flour to coat evenly or shake in paper bag with flour.

Heat oil or fat in a heavy pan over medium heat; put in meat and brown well on all sides.

Add onion, salt, pepper, caraway seed, paprika, and water. Reduce heat, cover and cook slowly until meat is almost tender, about 1¼ hours.

Add sauerkraut and sugar; cook an additional 30 minutes or until meat is tender.

Just before serving, add sour cream; leave over low heat 2 to 3 minutes. Serves 6 to 8.

Beef Stew with Potato Frill

BEEF GOULASH

Goulash is a dish of Hungarian origin, and its name is a corruption of gulyás. It is a thick stew of beef or veal and vegetables seasoned with paprika. Some variations contain sauerkraut, sour cream, or both.

1 pound stewing beef meat
1 clove garlic
2 medium onions
2 teaspoons paprika
1 teaspoon salt
⅛ teaspoon pepper
2 beef stock cubes
⅘ pint boiling water
12 ounces raw diced potatoes

Cut meat into 1-inch cubes and brown in a little hot fat.

Add crushed garlic, sliced onions, seasonings, and stock cubes dissolved in hot water. Cover and simmer 2½ hours.

Add 8 fluid ounces hot water and potatoes cut in ¾-inch cubes. Cook 20 minutes longer, or until potatoes are tender. Season to taste and thicken, if necessary. Serves 4.

FRENCH CANADIAN BRAISED BEEF

2 pounds stewing beef
1½ ounces cornflour
2 teaspoons salt
dash of pepper
1 ounce fat
1 medium onion, finely chopped
12 fluid ounces water
4 ounces carrots, diced
4 ounces green beans (cut in 1-inch lengths)
12 new potatoes
1 can condensed cream of mushroom soup

Cut meat in serving pieces. With meat mallet or edge of a saucer, pound in as much cornflour as it will take. Sprinkle with salt and pepper.

Heat fat in heavy sauté pan; add chopped onion; cook until golden brown.

Turn in beef; sear on all sides. Cover with water. Simmer gently until almost tender.

Add carrots, beans, and new potatoes; add mushroom soup. Simmer until vegetables are tender. Serves 6.

HOLLAND STEW

¾ pound stewing beef
½ pound fresh pork
½ pound ox liver
about 3 pints boiling water
2 small onions, sliced
1 teaspoon salt
¼ teaspoon pepper
1 ounce flour
4 tablespoons cold water
1 recipe plain dumplings, see
    below

Cut meat in small pieces; add water, cover, and simmer 2 hours, adding onions and seasonings the last half hour of cooking.

Thicken with flour and cold water mixed to a smooth paste.

Drop dumplings by spoonfuls into hot stew and cook, covered, 15 minutes. Serve at once. Serves 6.

BEEF POT POI
(Pennsylvania-Dutch)

2 pounds stewing beef
2½-3 pints boiling water
2 teaspoons salt
1 teaspoon chopped onion
1 teaspoon chopped parsley
1 egg
3 tablespoons milk
8 ounces plain flour
8 medium-sized potatoes, cubed

Simmer meat in salted water until tender. Remove meat from broth.

Add onion and parsley to broth and bring broth to boiling point.

To make pot pie dough, beat egg and add milk. Add flour to make a stiff dough. Roll out thin and cut into 2-inch squares.

With broth at boiling point (this is important), add alternate layers of cubed potatoes and squares of dough. Cover and cook 20 minutes, add more water if needed.

Add meat and stir through pot pie. Serves 8.

HODGEPODGE
(Dutch Vegetable Beef Stew)

1½ pounds chuck steak
1½ pints water
1 tablespoon salt
4 carrots, sliced
4 potatoes, quartered
4 onions, chopped

Put meat in large stewpan with water and salt. Cover and simmer for 2 hours.

Add vegetables, cook another half hour. More water may be added during cooking period, if necessary, but all the water should be cooked away when dish is ready to serve.

Remove meat from pan, put on serving dish, keep hot.

Mash together all the vegetables in pan with potato masher. Serve with sliced meat. Serves 4.

BEEF STEW WITH WINE AND HERBS

2 pounds stewing beef, cut into
    2-inch cubes
8 fluid ounces red wine
1. large bay leaf
1 clove garlic, sliced
1 teaspoon salt
½ teaspoon freshly ground black
    pepper
2 tablespoons dripping or other fat
12 fluid ounces beef stock
1 stalk celery (diced) with leaves
1 onion, sliced
few sprigs parsley
¼ teaspoon thyme
8 cloves
1 piece ginger root

Place meat in a deep bowl. Add wine, bay leaf, garlic, salt, and pepper; refrigerate several hours, turning frequently.

Drain meat, reserving marinade, and brown meat thoroughly in dripping.

Simmer together for 10 minutes reserved marinade, stock, and remaining ingredients, tied in a muslin bag.

Add meat, cover, and simmer until tender, about 2½ to 3 hours. Add water if necessary.

If desired, when meat is just tender, vegetables such as peas, carrots and onion may be added. Cook until vegetables are tender.

Discard herb bag and remove meat to a hot dish.

Thicken gravy with cornflour mixed with a little cold water, using ½ tablespoon cornflour per 8 fluid ounces of broth. Boil, stirring, 2 minutes. Serve sauce over meat with vegetables, if used, arranged attractively around it. Serves 4 to 5.

BEEF STEW WITH DUMPLINGS

1½ pounds stewing beef, cut into
    2-inch cubes
salt
bacon dripping or fat
8 fluid ounces water
6 large carrots, diced
6 potatoes, diced
8 small white onions, diced
8 ounces plain flour
4 teaspoons baking powder
1 teaspoon salt
1 ounce fat
8 fluid ounces milk

Season cubed meat with salt; brown well in small amount of bacon dripping or fat in deep sauté pan.

Add water; cover and cook 1 hour on low heat which allows liquid just to bubble.

Add vegetables to meat. If necessary, add more water. Cover and continue cooking until vegetables are tender, about ½ hour longer.

To Make Dumplings: Sift together flour, baking powder, and salt. Cut in fat as for pastry.

Stir in milk, blending to form soft dough.

Have at least 8 fluid ounces of boiling broth in stew pan before dropping in dumplings.

Dip a tablespoon into broth, scoop up a spoonful of batter and slip it on top of vegetables in pan. Work quickly; arrange dumplings so that steam circulates round all sides.

Cover pan tightly and steam 10 minutes. As soon as dumplings are tender, arrange them with vegetables and meat on large dish. Serve immediately.

Thicken liquid in pan if necessary and serve gravy with stew. Serves 6 to 8.

OLD-FASHIONED BEEF STEW

4 tablespoons fat
2 pounds topside of beef, cut into
    1½-inch cubes
Bouquet garni (see below)
about 1½ pints beef stock
1 pound small potatoes
1 bunch carrots, cubed
8 to 10 small onions
2 tomatoes, chopped
3 tablespoons flour
3 tablespoons water

Heat fat. Add cubed beef and brown. Add bouquet garni and stock. Cover; simmer 1 hour.

Add potatoes, carrots, onions, and tomatoes. Simmer, uncovered, 40 minutes, or until vegetables are tender.

Remove spices. Combine flour and water with 3 tablespoons stew stock; blend, add to stew, stirring well. Simmer until slightly thickened. Serves 6.

Bouquet Garni: Use 2 whole peppercorns, 1 bay leaf, 3 cloves, ½ teaspoon thyme, pinch cayenne, and 1 garlic clove, halved. Tie in a muslin bag.

Stew with Dumplings

Ragoût with Chicory

DANISH BEEF STEW

1½ pounds stewing steak, cut in
    cubes
flour
2 ounces butter or margarine
1 small onion, sliced
salt and pepper
½ teaspoon sugar
juice of 1 lemon
hot water
1½ pounds diced raw potatoes

Roll meat in flour and brown in hot melted butter. Add onion and brown lightly. Season to taste with salt and pepper.

Mix sugar and lemon juice and stir in. Simmer gently 3 or 4 minutes.

Add hot water to just cover meat. Cover tightly and simmer until meat is tender.

Turn into heated casserole. Add potatoes, cover and bake in moderate oven (375°F. Mark 5) 30 minutes. Serves 6.

BAVARIAN STYLE STEW WITH RED CABBAGE

2 pounds stewing beef
2 medium-sized onions
3 tablespoons fat
1¼ pints hot water
1 bay leaf
3 teaspoons salt
¼ teaspoon black pepper
1½ teaspoons caraway seed
4 tablespoons vinegar
1 medium-sized red cabbage
7-8 gingersnaps

Cut meat into 2-inch cubes. Brown meat and sliced onions in hot fat in heavy saucepan.

Add water, bay leaf, salt, pepper, and caraway seed. Cover tightly and cook slowly 1½ hours.

Then add vinegar and place cabbage wedges on top. Cover and cook about 45 minutes to 1 hour more, or until tender.

Meanwhile, soak gingersnaps in 4 tablespoons warm water.

Lift out cabbage and meat. Add gingersnaps to liquid and bring to boil, stirring to make smooth gravy.

Add meat to gravy. Reheat and serve in cheese noodle ring or on bed of plain boiled noodles. Surround with red cabbage wedges. Serves 6.

RAGOÛT WITH CHICORY

4 large (or 8 small) heads chicory
4 tablespoons cooking oil
1 onion, thinly sliced
1 pound lean boneless beef
½ pound lean boneless pork
8 fluid ounces beef stock
salt to taste
1 tablespoon paprika
½ teaspoon marjoram
4 ounces wide noodles, cooked
1 teaspoon caraway seeds
1 tablespoon cornflour
2 tablespoons cold water
¼ pint sour cream

If large heads of chicory are used cut in half lengthwise beginning at root end.

Heat oil in large heavy pan over moderate heat. Add onions and cook until transparent. Add meat cut into 1-inch cubes and brown on all sides, stirring frequently. Add stock and salt, if needed. Simmer, tightly covered, over low heat until meat is very tender, about 1 hour. Add water if necessary to replace liquid lost by evaporation.

When meat is tender be sure the liquid is ½-inch deep in pan. Stir in paprika and marjoram. Then carefully place the chicory on the meat, cut side up, cover tightly and simmer gently until tender and transparent, but not overcooked, 10 to 15 minutes.

Place noodles which have been cooked according to packet directions on serving dish. Arrange chicory on noodles around edge of dish. Sprinkle with caraway seeds, and keep in warm place.

Into liquid in pan pour cornflour and water which have been blended together. Cook, stirring gently, until thickened. Stir in sour cream which has been allowed to stand at room temperature and stirred to soften. Heat gently, but do not allow to boil. Spoon meat mixture over dish, being careful not to cover points of chicory. Serve immediately. Serves 4.

BEEF STEW WITH WINE

1 pound chuck beef, cut in cubes
1 ounce flour
1½ teaspoons salt
¼ teaspoon pepper
8 fluid ounces cold water
4 fluid ounces claret or burgundy
4 onions
4 small potatoes
8 small carrots

Roll beef in mixture of flour, salt, and pepper.

Sauté in hot fat until browned on all sides. Add water and wine; simmer very slowly about 1 hour.

Add onions, potatoes, and carrots; cook for 25 to 30 minutes longer. Serves 4.

TOMATO BEEF STEW

2 tablespoons flour
2 teaspoons salt
¼ teaspoon pepper
2 pounds stewing beef, cubed
2 tablespoons fat
1¼ pints water
1 can condensed tomato soup
6 small onions
6 small carrots
3 potatoes, quartered

Combine flour, salt, and pepper; roll meat in this mixture.

Brown meat in fat in a heavy saucepan. Add water; cover and simmer 1½ hours, stirring occasionally.

Add soup, onions, carrots, and potatoes; cook until vegetables are tender, about ½ hour. Serves 6.

RAGOÛT OF BEEF

1 pound stewing beef, cut in cubes
salt, pepper, flour
2 to 3 tablespoons fat
1 small onion, chopped
½ small green pepper, chopped
3 to 4 stalks celery, chopped
2 tablespoons chopped parsley
paprika
hot water

Sprinkle beef with salt, pepper, and flour. Brown well in fat in heavy pan. While meat is browning, add chopped vegetables.

Sprinkle with paprika and add hot water to cover. Cover pan. Cook slowly 2½ to 3 hours.

If gravy is not thick enough, blend 1 to 2 tablespoons flour with a little cold water and stir into the stew. Cook 3 to 5 minutes.

Season to taste with salt and pepper. If additional seasoning is desired, add ketchup, chilli sauce, or grated horseradish. Serves 4.

BELGIAN BEEF STEW

2 tablespoons butter or margarine
3 onions, sliced
1 pound stewing beef, cut in cubes
1 bay leaf
8 fluid ounces water
salt and pepper

Melt butter in saucepan and cook sliced onions until brown.

Add meat, bay leaf, and water. Cover and simmer slowly until meat is tender, adding more water as needed.

One-half hour before serving, season with salt and pepper to taste. Serve with boiled potatoes. Serves 4.

Miscellaneous Beef Recipes

BEEF STROGANOFF

1½ pounds lean stewing beef
salt and pepper
1½ ounces butter or margarine
½ pound fresh mushrooms, sliced
2 medium-sized onions, sliced
2 tablespoons flour
¾ pint beef stock
2 tablespoons tomato paste
1 teaspoon dry mustard
3 tablespoons sherry
¼ pint sour cream

Cut meat into strips about 2 inches long and the width of a pencil. Sprinkle with salt and pepper and let stand in cool place for 2 hours.

Melt 1 ounce butter in a heavy pan. Sauté mushrooms until tender, about 15 minutes. Remove mushrooms and set aside.

Sauté onions until browned. Remove and set aside.

Melt remaining butter. Brown meat on all sides but leave it rare. Remove meat and set aside.

Blend flour into butter remaining in pan. Gradually add stock, stirring constantly, until smooth and slightly thickened. Add tomato paste, dry mustard, and sherry and blend thoroughly.

Combine sauce with meat, mushrooms and onions and cook slowly over a very low heat for 20 minutes.

Blend in sour cream about 5 minutes before serving and heat thoroughly.

Serve with riced potatoes, potato balls, or boiled rice. Serves 4 to 5.

CREOLE GRILLADES

2 pounds stewing steak or veal
2 ounces butter or margarine
1 tablespoon salt
1 teaspoon Aromat
¼ teaspoon pepper
1 tablespoon butter or margarine
1 tablespoon flour
1 medium-sized onion, chopped
4 fluid ounces water or tomato
    juice
1 clove garlic, crushed
boiled rice

Cut meat into serving pieces, removing and discarding any bone.

Heat 2 ounces butter or margarine in large, heavy pan over low heat. Add meat and brown well on one side.

Turn and sprinkle with one-half of a mixture of salt, Aromat, and pepper. Brown well on second side and sprinkle with remaining seasoning mixture. Remove meat from pan.

Heat 1 tablespoon butter or margarine in the pan over low heat. Blend in flour. Heat until mixture bubbles, stirring constantly.

Stir in onion and cook, stirring constantly, until mixture is lightly browned.

Remove from heat and blend in water or tomato juice. Return pan to heat.

Add meat and garlic. Cover tightly and cook slowly over low heat about 1 hour, or until meat is tender. Turn meat occasionally. Add more liquid if necessary.

While meat is cooking, prepare boiled rice. Serve meat on hot rice, with sauce spooned over meat. Serves 4 to 6.

MEAT BIRDS (PAUPIETTES)
(Master Recipe)

1½ to 2 pounds stewing beef, cut ¼
    to ½ inch thick
3-4 ounces veal stuffing
salt and pepper
flour
2 tablespoons fat or salad oil
8 fluid ounces tomato juice or meat
    stock

Cut meat into pieces about 3×5 inches. Pound to any desired thinness.

Put mound of stuffing in centre of each piece; roll and fasten with cocktail sticks or tie with string.

Sprinkle with salt and pepper, roll in flour, and brown on all sides in hot fat.

Add about 4 fluid ounces liquid. Cover tightly and simmer until tender, about 1 hour. Add liquid in small quantities as required.

Remove sticks or string before serving. Gravy may be thickened. Serves 6.

Variations: Lamb or veal may be substituted for beef.

Meat Bird Casserole: Prepare birds as above. Brush with 2 tablespoons fat and place in greased casserole.

Bake in slow oven (325°F. Mark 3), basting occasionally with fat and hot water. Remove cover for last 10 minutes to brown birds.

BEEF KEBABS (BEEF ON SKEWERS)

Use tender steak and cut into 1½-inch cubes. Alternate cubes on skewers with wedges of slightly underripe tomatoes, small mushrooms, slices of raw or par-boiled onion, pieces of bacon, etc.

Brush the filled skewers with melted butter. Place under hot grill.

While grilling, brush with more melted butter. Turn to cook evenly on all sides. Season to taste when done.

Note: If desired, kebabs may be breaded before grilling.

Meat Birds or paupiettes may be varied by using any of your favourite stuffings.

OVEN-BAKED CHUCK STEAK

1¾ pounds chuck steak, at least
    1-inch thick
4 tablespoons olive oil or butter
1 clove garlic, crushed
1 can (6 ounces) tomato paste
stock or water
pinch of rosemary
salt and pepper
8 to 10 small potatoes, peeled

Sprinkle meat lightly with flour.

Brown garlic in hot oil or butter. Remove garlic; add meat and brown on both sides in hot fat. Transfer to casserole.

Combine tomato paste with enough stock or water to make ¾ pint liquid; season to taste. Pour into casserole with meat.

Cover and bake in moderate oven (350°F. Mark 4) until tender, about 1 hour. About 20 minutes before meat is done, add potatoes. Serves 4 to 6.

BEEF WITH TOMATOES AND GREEN PEPPERS

2 tablespoons fat or salad oil
1 pound topside or flank steak, cut
    into ⅛-inch thick slices
1 teaspoon salt
dash of pepper
2 tablespoons chopped onion
1 clove garlic, crushed
8 fluid ounces beef stock
2 green peppers, diced
4 small tomatoes, quartered
2 tablespoons cornflour
2 tablespoons soy sauce
4 tablespoons water
boiled rice

Heat fat in heavy pan. Add meat, salt, pepper, onion, and garlic. Cook over moderately hot heat, stirring constantly, until meat is brown.

Add stock and green peppers. Cover closely and cook over low heat 10 minutes. Add tomatoes and cook 1 minute longer.

Blend together cornflour, soy sauce, and water. Add to pan and cook 3 or 4 minutes longer, stirring constantly, until mixture is hot and sauce is thickened.

Serve at once with hot boiled rice. Serves 4.

BEEF WITH PEA PODS (Chinese)

4 tablespoons peanut oil
½ teaspoon salt
½ pound beef fillet, sliced about
    ¼ inch thick and 2 inches
    square
¼ pound Chinese pea pods or sugar
    peas* cut in 2 pieces diagon-
    ally
1 can (4-ounce) button mushrooms,
    cut in halves if large
4-5 canned water chestnuts, sliced
    crosswise in thin slices
1 tablespoon cornflour
½ teaspoon black treacle
1 teaspoon soy sauce
1 teaspoon salt
½ teaspoon Aromat
¼ teaspoon black pepper
¼ pint chicken stock

Heat oil with ½ teaspoon salt in a heavy saucepan; add beef and cook gently until lightly browned but not dry, about 2 minutes on each side.

Add pea pods, mushrooms, and water chestnuts; cook, turning often, over moderate heat for about 5 minutes.

Blend cornflour and seasonings with chicken stock; add to vegetable-beef mixture. Cover and cook over low heat until mixture is thick and glazy, about 5 minutes, turning a few times. Serve with fried rice. Serves 2 to 3.
Note: For additional colour, add about 2 tablespoons pimiento (cut in 1-inch squares) with the other vegetables.
*Very young pods in which peas are just beginning to form.

PEPPER CHUCK STEAK

4 tablespoons melted fat or salad oil
3 pounds beef chuck, in 2 cuts
6 green peppers, seeded
salt and pepper
3 large onions, sliced thin
1 can (about 16 ounces) tomatoes
6 fluid ounces tomato sauce
¼ pint beef stock or water
2 bay leaves
2 sprigs green celery leaves
1 sprig thyme
8 sprigs fresh parsley

Brown beef well on both sides in hot fat. Place 1 steak in roasting tin. Cover steak with 3 green peppers, cut in strips. Season with salt and pepper.

Over this, place other steak and cover with remaining green peppers cut in strips and mixed with onions.

Combine tomatoes and sauce and pour over all. Season with salt and pepper. Pour beef stock or water over this. Add a bouquet garni made up of bay leaves, celery leaves, thyme, and parsley tied with thread. Bring to the boil.

Cover and cook in moderate oven (350°F. Mark 4) 2 to 2½ hours. Baste several times with gravy. Remove bouquet garni. Serve steak on hot dish. Serves 6.

STEAK AND SPANISH SAUCE

1 pound topside
1 tablespoon vinegar
1 teaspoon salt
¼ teaspoon pepper
2 tablespoons chopped onion
1 tablespoon chopped parsley
2 tablespoons chopped celery leaves
3 tablespoons chopped green pepper
1 can (about 16 ounces) or 1 pound
    fresh tomatoes, peeled and
    diced
2 tablespoons fat

Pound steak on both sides. Cover with mixture of remaining ingredients except fat. Let stand 1 hour, turning once or twice so that meat is thoroughly seasoned.

Brown meat slowly on both sides in hot fat. Place in shallow casserole. Pour over mixture in which meat was soaked.

Cover and cook in slow oven (325°F. Mark 3) until meat is tender, about 2 hours. Serve at once. Serves 4.

BEEF WITH MUSHROOMS—CHINESE STYLE

2 tablespoons oil or fat
1 teaspoon salt
dash of pepper
1 pound beef flank
2 tablespoons finely chopped onion
1 clove garlic, crushed
¼ pint beef stock
1 pound fresh mushrooms, sliced
2 tablespoons cornflour
2 teaspoons soy sauce
4 tablespoons water

Place oil or fat, salt, and pepper in a pre-heated, heavy 10-inch frying pan.

Cut meat into ⅛-inch-thick slices, and add with onion and garlic.

Cook over moderately hot heat, stirring constantly, until meat is brown.

Add stock and mushrooms. Cover pan tightly and cook over low heat for 10 minutes.

Blend together cornflour, soy sauce, and water and add. Cook a few minutes more, stirring constantly, until the juice thickens and the mixture is very hot.

Serve immediately with hot, boiled rice. Serves 4.

PAPRIKA BEEF

2 pounds topside, cut ½-inch thick
1 teaspoon salt
⅛ teaspoon paprika
1 clove garlic, peeled
2 tablespoons fat
8 fluid ounces water
2 tablespoons Worcestershire sauce
¼ pint sour cream
1 teaspoon paprika
1 ounce flour

Rub meat with salt and ⅛ teaspoon

paprika. Brown garlic in hot fat. Remove garlic. Add meat and brown it well.

Add water and Worcestershire sauce. Cover and cook slowly about 2 hours.

Add sour cream and 1 teaspoon paprika. Cook slowly 15 minutes longer.

Remove steak to hot dish. Thicken broth with flour mixed with 4 fluid ounces cold water. Stir and boil 5 minutes. Serve gravy over meat. Serves 6.

QUEBEC BOILED DINNER

1 pound lean beef
¼ pound lean pork
½ pound breast of lamb
1 tablespoon fat
2½-3 pints hot water
2 whole cloves
1 large onion
¼ turnip, cut in 4 or 6 pieces
6 carrots
1 small cabbage
1 pound green beans tied in
    bunches
6 potatoes quartered
salt and pepper

Cut the meat in pieces. Sear in hot fat in a heavy pan. Or do not sear the meat and add the boiling water.

Stick the cloves in the onion. Add to the meat and cook gently until the meat is almost tender.

Add the vegetables and continue to cook until done. Season to taste with salt and pepper. (One pound salt pork can be added, if desired.) Serves 6.

STEAK NEW ORLEANS

1½ pounds topside, 1-inch thick
seasoned flour
3 tablespoons fat
2 medium-sized onions, thinly
    sliced
1 can (about 16 ounces) tomatoes
8 fluid ounces tomato juice
1 tablespoon grated Parmesan
    cheese
1 green pepper, cut into rings
4 medium-sized sweet potatoes,
    peeled and sliced ¾-inch
    thick
salt and pepper to taste

Dredge meat in flour seasoned with salt and pepper.

Melt fat over low heat; add onion slices and cook until golden brown. Remove.

Brown meat well on both sides. Add tomatoes, tomato juice, cheese, and green pepper rings. Top with onion rings.

Cover; cook over low heat until meat is tender (about 1 hour). Add sweet potato slices.

Cover; continue cooking until potatoes are tender, about 15 minutes. Season to taste with salt and pepper.

Serves 4 to 6.

TZIMMES

A traditional Jewish dish with many variations, usually a combination of meat, carrots, potatoes, and sweet potatoes; sometimes made of a combination of meat, prunes, and potatoes; frequently it is a meatless dish made of carrots, potatoes, and sweet potatoes, with a large dumpling (knaidle) tucked into its centre.

The word Tzimmes has gone into the foodlore and folklore of the Jewish people, and has come to mean "making a fuss over someone or something, or some event," in a favourable and friendly sort of way.

The traditional method of making tzimmes of carrots, potatoes, and sweet potatoes is the slow cooking procedure given below.

6 medium-sized carrots
6 medium-sized whole potatoes
3 medium-sized sweet potatoes
2½ to 3 pounds fresh beef brisket
1 teaspoon salt
4 ounces sugar or 6 ounces honey
cold water to cover
1 small onion (optional)
2 tablespoons chicken fat or vegetable fat
1 ounce flour

Scrape and slice or dice carrots. Peel and cut potatoes and sweet potatoes into 1-inch rounds.

Sear meat in a large heavy pan.

When meat is browned on all sides, add prepared vegetables, salt, and sugar or honey. Cover with cold water (about 1 inch overall). Bring to boil over moderate heat.

Remove cover and skim. Reduce heat and simmer, uncovered, 2½ to 3 hours or until meat is very tender. Do not stir.

To prevent sticking, shake pan occasionally. Boiling water may be added if required a little at a time.

If onion is used, it should be peeled and cut into thick wedges to permit flow of juice and added after boiling begins. (The onion should not be permitted to fall apart but lifted out before it disintegrates.)

When the liquid has been reduced by half and meat is tender, brown flour in melted fat in a pan.

Stir in about 4 fluid ounces of liquid from pan to make a smooth paste. Add this paste to tzimmes and shake pan slightly to distribute evenly.

Turn into casserole and cook in moderate oven (350°F. Mark 4) 30 minutes or until brown on top. Serves 6 to 8.

Pressure Cooker Method: Sear meat in cooker first, then let cool.

Add prepared vegetables, salt, sugar, and onion (if used). Add 8-12 fluid ounces cold water.

Cook according to directions for cooker (at 15 pounds pressure for 20 minutes).

Cool cooker quickly as directed by manufacturer before turning contents into casserole for cooking as above.

Thickening may be added just before placing in oven.

OVEN BEEF STEW No. 2

1 pound stewing beef
salt, pepper, flour
3 tablespoons lard
2 medium onions, chopped
¾ pint water
1 can condensed tomato soup
1 small bay leaf
2 whole cloves
1 stalk celery, sliced
4 carrots, sliced
3 medium potatoes
1 8-ounce packet frozen peas

Cut meat into 1-inch cubes; sprinkle with salt and pepper and dredge with flour. Melt lard in a frying pan and in it brown meat thoroughly. Transfer meat to a 3 pint casserole.

Lightly brown chopped onion in the hot lard; add to meat. Heat water with tomato soup and pour over meat. Add seasonings and sliced celery.

Cover and bake in a slow oven (325°F. Mark 3) for 1½ hours, or until meat is nearly tender.

Add sliced carrots, potatoes cut in eighths, and peas; sprinkle with salt and pepper and mix in with beef and gravy. Cover and continue baking for 45 minutes. Serves 4.

THICK RIBS OF BEEF EN CASSEROLE

2 pounds thick ribs of beef
1 teaspoon dry mustard
1 teaspoon salt
¼ teaspoon pepper
½ teaspoon Aromat
2 tablespoons vinegar
1 large onion, sliced
⅘ pint water
2 beef bouillon cubes
6 potatoes, peeled and quartered

Cut ribs into serving-size pieces. Trim off excess fat. Brush meat with mixture of mustard, salt, pepper, Aromat, and vinegar. Place meat in 4-4½-pint casserole.

Add onion, water, and bouillon cubes.

Cover and cook in moderate oven (350°F. Mark 4) 1¾ hours.

Place potatoes around meat and cook until potatoes and meat are tender, about 35 minutes longer. Uncover to brown. Serves 4.

BRAISED STEAK WITH HERBS

1 ounce flour
2 teaspoons salt
1 teaspoon pepper
1 clove garlic, crushed
1 teaspoon dill seed
¼ teaspoon dried marjoram
¼ teaspoon dried tarragon
2 pounds topside, cut 1-inch thick
4 ounces fat
1 small onion, sliced
16 fluid ounces hot water
4 fluid ounces white wine (optional)

Combine flour, salt, pepper, garlic, dill, marjoram, and tarragon. Spread half over meat; pound with a meat hammer or edge of a heavy saucer until seasoned flour is worked into the meat.

Turn; sprinkle with remaining flour mixture, and pound into meat.

Brown meat on both sides in hot fat. Add onion; pour in water.

Cover and simmer or cook in moderate oven (350°F. Mark 4) until tender, 1½ to 2 hours. Add more water if necessary to keep the meat moist.

Before serving, pour wine over meat and heat through, about 2 minutes. Serves 6.

Variation: Omit dill. Add 4 tablespoons ketchup, 1 teaspoon oregano, and 1 tablespoon paprika to the water.

GERMAN BEEF ROLLS

4 very thin slices of topside
salt and pepper
4 rashers bacon
1 large onion, chopped
2 tablespoons chopped sweet pickle
4 fluid ounces water
1 8-ounce can tomato sauce
1 teaspoon meat glaze

Flatten slices of meat and season with salt and pepper.

Grill bacon and save fat. Brown onion in fat.

Crumble crisp bacon and mix it with browned, drained onions and pickle. Place spoonful of mixture in centre of each slice of beef. Roll beef and tie ends.

Brown rolls in bacon fat. Add tomato sauce and meat glaze. Simmer gently until tender. Season to taste.

Serve hot. Serves 4.

BEEF THICK RIB CROWN

Sew ends of two sections of thick ribs together or tie with cord to form crown. Season with salt and pepper. Place in roasting tin. Fill centre with bread stuffing.

Roast, uncovered, in moderate oven 1 hour.

Add about ½ pint hot water. Cover tightly and cook 2 hours longer. Serves 6 to 8.

BEEF IN SOUR CREAM
2½-3 pounds topside
flour
2 tablespoons bacon fat
½ pint sour cream
water
1 large onion, sliced
1 small bay leaf
¾ teaspoon salt
⅛ teaspoon black pepper
1 sweet pepper, finely chopped

Pound flour into meat, as much as it will take, using meat mallet.

Melt bacon fat in heavy deep pan. Add meat; brown all over.

Then add sour cream, enough water to come up to level of meat, onion, bay leaf, salt, black pepper, and sweet pepper.

Set pan in another containing hot water. Let cook, covered, until tender.

Remove steak to hot dish. Pour over gravy; serve hot. Serves 6.

STUFFED FLANK STEAK
2- to 3-pound beef flank
1 teaspoon meat tenderizer
6 large mushrooms, thinly sliced
1 small onion, thinly sliced
1 tablespoon butter or margarine
½ teaspoon rosemary
½ teaspoon salt
dash of pepper
4 fluid ounces red wine

Get the butcher to cut a sizable pocket in meat. Treat it with meat tenderizer according to directions on label of container.

Cook mushrooms and onion in melted butter or margarine for several minutes. Season with rosemary, salt (if you use seasoned tenderizer, omit salt), pepper, and wine.

Cook a few more minutes or until onions are tender.

Drain vegetables (save liquid to use later on) and stuff into pocket of flank.

Sprinkle meat with additional salt and grill 8 to 10 minutes on each side. Baste occasionally with liquid from vegetables. Carve in thin bias slices. Serves 6.

DUTCH BRISKET OF BEEF WITH SAUERKRAUT
2 tablespoons flour
1 tablespoon brown sugar
1 tart apple, grated
1 small onion, chopped
1½ pints or 1½ pounds sauerkraut
2½ to 3 pounds beef brisket
salt and pepper

Add flour, sugar, apple, and onion to sauerkraut and place half in heavy pan with tightly fitting lid.

Season meat well with salt and pepper and lay on top. Top with remaining sauerkraut. Cover with water.

Cover tightly and simmer very slowly 3 hours. Serves 8.

BEEF SCALOPPINE
1 ounce flour
1 teaspoon salt
⅛ teaspoon pepper
1 teaspoon paprika
2 pounds beef, cut for scaloppine*
4 tablespoons salad oil or fat
1 clove garlic
1 bay leaf
8 fluid ounces red cooking wine
2-3 ounces black olives, cut in quarters
1 beef bouillon cube

Combine flour, salt, pepper, and paprika on a piece of waxed paper; dip pieces of beef into it to coat lightly.

In heavy pan, heat oil or fat; add beef, cook over medium heat until browned on both sides.

Add garlic (on a cocktail stick so it will be easy to remove), bay leaf, wine, olives, and bouillon cube.

Cover, bring to the boil; reduce heat and simmer for 30 minutes, stirring occasionally.

Remove garlic and bay leaf before serving. Serves 6 to 8.

*Note: Buy topside beef sliced about ¼ inch thick; cut in strips about 2×5 inches; flatten by pounding with meat mallet or rolling pin.

BEEF STROGANOFF
1½ pounds fillet beef, cut in shoestring strips
salt and pepper
1 tablespoon flour
2 tablespoons butter or margarine
16 fluid ounces beef stock
1 tablespoon tomato paste
½ pound mushrooms, cut not too fine
1 tablespoon chopped onion
2 tablespoons sour cream

Season meat well with salt and pepper; let stand 2 hours.

Brown flour in melted butter; work to a smooth paste, then gradually stir in stock. Bring to the boil.

Stir in tomato paste. Add mushrooms.

Sear meat in butter with chopped onion. When the meat is brown, add meat and onions to sauce and simmer 5 minutes.

Add sour cream, heat through and serve at once. Serves 6.

BEEF WELLINGTON
(Whole Loin of Beef Baked in Pastry)
Pastry:
1 pound plain flour

1 teaspoon salt
4 ounces butter
4 ounces margarine
1 egg, lightly beaten
about 4 fluid ounces iced water

Combine flour, salt, butter, and margarine in a large bowl; blend with pastry blender or tips of fingers until a crumbly mass has been obtained. Add egg and just enough water to make a dough. Form into a ball; wrap in waxed paper and chill thoroughly.

Filling:
1 whole beef fillet, about 3 pounds
2 tablespoons brandy
salt and pepper
6 rashers bacon
5 to 8 ounces canned pâté de foie gras or pâté of chicken livers (see Index)
3 or 4 truffles, optional
1 egg for brushing pastry

Get outside membrane and excess fat removed from meat. Rub beef all over with brandy and season with salt and freshly-ground pepper.

Place bacon over top and fasten with string if necessary. Place on rack in roasting tin; roast, uncovered, in preheated very hot oven (450°F. Mark 8) 15 minutes for rare, 20 to 25 minutes for medium.

Remove from oven and remove bacon; cool to room temperature before continuing. Spread pâté all over top and sides of cooled meat.

Roll out the well chilled pastry into a rectangular shape about 18×12 inches and ¼ inch thick, large enough to envelop the meat.

Cut truffles into halves and arrange in a row in centre of pastry so that the pieces will be covered by the meat. Place meat in centre with that side down which you want eventually to be up.

Fold pastry over meat, trimming ends if necessary, and seal seams and ends with water or beaten egg.

Place seam side down, on buttered baking sheet and brush top and sides with one egg well beaten and mixed with a little water or cream. Prick pastry thoroughly with fork in criss-cross design, to allow escape of steam.

If desired, decorative shapes may be cut from pastry trimmings and the pieces arranged down the centre of the pastry. Brush the shapes with remaining egg mixture.

Bake in preheated hot oven (425°F. Mark 7) 30 minutes, until pastry is cooked.

Serve hot with Madeira Sauce (see Index). Serves 4 to 8.

Note: Puff pastry may be used but be sure to roll it very thinly.

Recipes with Leftover Beef

RED FLANNEL HASH

A New England dish of salt-beef hash with chopped beets in it.

8 ounces chopped leftover salt beef
¾-1 pound chopped cooked
      potatoes
½ raw onion, finely chopped
about 8 ounces cooked leftover
      vegetables, chopped (carrots
      or other)
6 ounces chopped cooked beets
salt and pepper
stock or gravy

Combine ingredients with enough stock to moisten.

Spread in hot, greased frying pan, cover, reduce heat, and cook until well browned on bottom. Then fold over like an omelet and serve. Serves 6.

ROAST BEEF HASH

1½ pounds cooked beef
3 medium carrots
3 medium potatoes, peeled
3-4 stalks celery, chopped
2 small onions
8 fluid ounces milk
8 fluid ounces tomato soup
¾ teaspoon salt
½ teaspoon pepper
buttered breadcrumbs

Mince meat and vegetables with coarse blade of mincer. Add remaining ingredients except breadcrumbs.

Place in well greased casserole; cover top with buttered crumbs. Bake in moderate oven (350°F. Mark 4) 1 hour. Serves 6.

MEAT CROQUETTES—FRIED

1 pound minced cooked meat (beef,
      veal, lamb, pork, or ham)
about ½ pint thick white sauce
2 teaspoons grated onion
1½ teaspoons Worcestershire sauce
½ teaspoon dry mustard
1 egg
fine dry breadcrumbs

Combine sauce with rest of ingredients, except egg and crumbs. Add salt and pepper to taste. Chill several hours or overnight.

Divide chilled mixture into 8 portions and shape into croquettes, or balls. Chill again ½ hour.

Dip in beaten egg mixed with 1 tablespoon water, then roll in breadcrumbs.

Fry croquettes, a few at a time, in deep fat, which has been heated to a temperature of 365°F. Turn occasionally to brown evenly; fry 2 to 5 minutes, or until golden brown. Makes 8.
Note: To make thick white sauce, use 2 ounces each of fat and flour, ½ pint milk, and ½ teaspoon salt.

BEEF MIROTON

2 onions, finely chopped
3 tablespoons fat
1 tablespoon flour
½-¾ pint stock
1 tablespoon vinegar
¾ pound cooked beef
salt and pepper to taste
pinch of thyme
¾ pound sliced, cooked potatoes
2 gherkins, sliced
1 teaspoon finely chopped parsley
1 ounce breadcrumbs

Cook onions in hot fat until golden brown. Stir in flour and add liquid slowly. When well combined, add vinegar. Boil 8 to 10 minutes.

Pour some of the sauce in bottom of greased casserole. Add slices of beef. Season with salt, pepper, and thyme.

Put potatoes in border round beef. Pour in remaining sauce. Arrange sliced gherkins and chopped parsley over top. Sprinkle with crumbs. Dot with fat.

Brown in moderate oven (375°F. Mark 5) 20 to 25 minutes. Serves 6.

OVEN MEAT CROQUETTES

1 pound minced cooked beef, veal,
      lamb, or pork
4 ounces grated raw carrots
3 ounces soft breadcrumbs
½ small onion, grated
1 beaten egg
1 teaspoon salt
⅛ teaspoon pepper
bacon fat, butter, or margarine
dry breadcrumbs

Combine minced meat, carrots, breadcrumbs, onion, egg, and seasonings. Mix well.

Divide mixture into 6 parts and shape into croquettes.

Roll in melted bacon fat, butter, or margarine; then in dry breadcrumbs.

Place on baking sheet and bake in moderate oven (350°F. Mark 4) 40 minutes. Serve with mustard or mushroom sauce. Serves 4 to 6.

JELLIED MEAT LOAF

¼ ounce gelatine
4 tablespoons cold water
6 fluid ounces boiling water
4 tablespoons vinegar
½ teaspoon salt
1 stalk celery, diced
1 chopped pimiento
½ chopped green pepper
2 tablespoons finely chopped onion
4 fluid ounces mayonnaise or
      boiled dressing
1 pound finely diced cooked meat
2 hard-boiled eggs, sliced

Soak gelatine in cold water, then dissolve in boiling water. Add vinegar and salt. Cool.

When mixture begins to thicken, mix in all other ingredients except eggs.

Rinse mould or loaf tin in cold water and arrange egg slices on bottom and sides. Pour in meat mixture.

Chill until very firm. Serve on a bed of shredded lettuce. Serves 6.

LEFTOVER STEAK WITH ONIONS

Slice onions thin. Place in sauté pan with a little fat and season with salt and pepper. Cover and brown slightly and put onions to one side.

Place leftover steak in the pan, smother with onions, cover tightly, and cook over low heat until steak is heated through. When ready to serve, spread onions on top.

MEAT CAKES

Combine 8 ounces minced cooked meat with 1 slice of bread (crumbled), 1 tablespoon milk, and ½ teaspoon prepared mustard.

Beat 1 egg slightly. Combine half of egg with meat mixture and form into 2 ½-inch patties.

Dip patties into remaining egg mixed with a tablespoon of water or milk. Roll patties in flour, brown on both sides in a little fat in a frying pan.

Serve with ketchup, chilli sauce, or mustard. Makes 2 large cakes.

Oven Meat Croquettes

Meat Pie with Scone Topping

MEAT PIE WITH SCONE TOPPING

2 tablespoons fat, or salad oil
1 pound cooked meat, cut in ¾-inch cubes
2 tablespoons plain flour
½ teaspoon salt
16 fluid ounces thin leftover gravy
½ teaspoon dried rosemary
4 ounces cooked carrots, cut in 1-inch strips
4 ounces cooked peas
8 very small cooked onions
4 ounces plain flour
1½ teaspoons baking powder
½ teaspoon salt
2 tablespoons fat
1 ounce grated sharp processed cheese
1 tablespoon finely chopped pimiento
6 tablespoons milk

Heat fat in large sauté pan on high heat. Turn to medium heat; add meat and brown slightly. Add 2 tablespoons flour and ½ teaspoon salt and blend.

Add gravy and rosemary to pan, and stir constantly until mixture begins to thicken.

Reduce heat. Add carrots, peas, and onions to first mixture. Cover and heat thoroughly while making scone topping.

Sift flour, baking powder, and ½ teaspoon salt together into a small mixing bowl. Cut in fat with pastry blender or 2 knives until mixture resembles fine breadcrumbs.

Add cheese and pimiento and mix. Add milk to flour mixture and mix with a fork to make a soft dough.

Turn onto a lightly floured pastry board and knead dough lightly. Roll dough into rectangle 9×7 inches and ¼ inch thick. Using a 2-inch round biscuit cutter, cut 12 scones.

Pour hot meat mixture into a 10×6×2-inch baking dish, and arrange scones on top. Bake in very hot oven (450°F. Mark 8) for 10 to 15 minutes. Serves 4 to 6.

SALT BEEF HASH

1 onion, chopped
2 green peppers, chopped finely
2 celery stalks, chopped finely
1 clove garlic, crushed
3 tablespoons butter or margarine
2 pounds cooked salt beef coarsely chopped
5 medium potatoes, cooked and diced
1 tablespoon chopped parsley
1 tablespoon Worcestershire sauce
4 fluid ounces beef stock

Sauté onion, peppers, celery, and garlic in butter until onions are golden. Add beef, potatoes, and parsley; sprinkle with Worcestershire sauce.

Heat mixture over medium heat, adding beef stock a little at a time. Stir constantly as mixture cooks until well blended.

Transfer hash to buttered frying pan and brown on both sides, turning once. May be served with poached eggs. Serves 6.

BUBBLE AND SQUEAK

about 1 pound cooked cabbage, finely chopped
1 onion, sliced
2 ounces butter or margarine
½ teaspoon salt
pepper
4 servings thinly sliced cooked beef (roast, pot roast, or boiled)

Sauté the cabbage and the onion in half the fat until onion is tender. Season with salt and pepper to taste.

In another frying pan, sauté beef gently in the remaining fat until very hot. Place on dish and top with cabbage. Serves 4.

BEEF PARMIGIANA

4 servings sliced cooked beef (about 1 pound)
1 beaten egg
2 tablespoons milk
1 teaspoon salt
¼ teaspoon pepper
1 teaspoon dry mustard
2 ounces fine breadcrumbs
2 ounces grated Parmesan cheese
4 ounces fat
1 8-ounce can tomato sauce

Combine egg, milk, salt, pepper, and mustard. Melt fat in heavy frying pan.

Dip pieces of beef into egg mixture, then into breadcrumbs and last into cheese.

Fry in hot fat until browned on both sides. Serve with hot tomato sauce. Serves 4.

BRUNSWICK STEW

1 pound cold roast meat, beef or lamb cut into 2-inch cubes
1¼ pints water
1½ teaspoons salt
¼ teaspoon pepper
2 teaspoons Worcestershire sauce
4 ounces diced green beans
4 ounces butter beans
8 small new potatoes
8 small white onions, peeled
4 ounces green peas
6 ounces young carrots, peeled and sliced

Place meat, water, salt, pepper, and Worcestershire sauce in 4-4½ pint casserole.

Add vegetables and bake about 1¼ hours in a moderate oven (350°F. Mark 4) or until vegetables are tender and gravy is somewhat thickened. Serves 8.

YORKSHIRE BEEF PUFF

Using leftover roast or pot roast, cut 1 pound of meat into small thin pieces and arrange over the bottom of a 9×9-inch glass baking dish that contains about ⅛-inch fat.

Sift 4 ounces flour with ¼ teaspoon salt. Add 2 eggs and 6 fluid ounces milk. Stir till smooth, then beat for 2 minutes and pour over meat.

Bake in very hot oven (450°F. Mark 8) about 30 minutes. Serve with leftover gravy or mushroom sauce. Serves 4.

CREOLE BEEF WITH RICE OR MACARONI

½ pound chopped cooked beef
2 tablespoons fat
1 tablespoon chopped onion
1-2 stalks celery, chopped
1 tablespoon flour
8 ounces cooked tomatoes
¼ teaspoon chilli powder
½ teaspoon salt
1 teaspoon Worcestershire sauce
4 fluid ounces water
8 ounces cooked rice, spaghetti, or macaroni

Stir and brown meat in fat in a sauté pan. Add onion and celery and brown lightly.

Sprinkle flour over meat and vegetables, then add tomatoes, seasonings, and water. Stir and simmer about 10 minutes to blend flavours. Taste and season more if necessary.

Serve over hot cooked rice, spaghetti, or macaroni. Serves 2 to 3.

Minced Meat

HOW TO BUY MINCED BEEF

Minced beef varies in quality of beef and the proportion of fat and lean meat. The ready-minced beef sold by a reliable butcher is good fresh beef.

When beef is minced to order as topside steak, shoulder (chuck), flank, etc., check the leanness of the meat and if very lean ask for 2 ounces suet to be minced with each pound of meat. This is particularly necessary with minced topside steak.

Ask for the meat to be minced twice for most uses. Twice-minced meat is more compact. For extra juicy, tender patties it should be minced only once. Freshly minced beef is bright red in colour.

HANDLING MINCED BEEF

The less handling minced beef gets, the more juicy and tender it will be. When mixing meat loaves, toss together lightly.

Pat patties loosely into shape. When you cook, don't pack them down with the spatula.

HOW TO STORE MINCED BEEF

Wrap the mound of beef loosely in greaseproof paper with ends slightly open. Or, if desired, shape at once into patties and place between squares of greaseproof paper and cover. Store at once in refrigerator. Use within two days.

Frozen minced beef should be kept frozen until ready to use, or thawed in refrigerator just before cooking. Frozen minced beef should be used within 2 to 3 months.

Meat Balls

TO SHAPE MEAT BALLS

For easier handling rinse hands with cold water before shaping meat balls.

SWEDISH MEAT BALLS —FAMILY STYLE

3 tablespoons chopped onion
2 tablespoons fat
¼ pound finely minced beef
¼ pound finely minced veal
¼ pound finely minced pork
3 slices fresh white bread, crusts removed
4 fluid ounces milk or water
1 egg
1 teaspoon salt
⅛ teaspoon freshly ground black pepper

Brown the onion in 1 tablespoon fat. Mix together the browned onion, meats, bread, milk, egg, salt, and pepper. Mix with the hands until thoroughly blended. Form into 12 balls.

Brown the meat balls in the same pan, using the remaining fat. Shake pan to keep balls round. When cooked, remove balls to a hot dish and keep hot.

For gravy, add to 2 tablespoons of fat in the pan 2 tablespoons of flour. Brown the flour, stirring, over low heat. Add 8 fluid ounces of milk, stirring, and cook, stirring, until mixture boils. Season to taste and, if desired, add 3-4 tablespoons cream. Serves 4.

Note: For appetizers, to be served on sticks with cocktails, make the meat balls marble size, cook as indicated above, but omit gravy. The same size balls may be served in clear or vegetable soup.

TOMATO MEAT BALLS

1 pound minced beef
1 egg
1 medium onion, finely chopped
2 tablespoons finely chopped parsley
1 teaspoon salt
¼ teaspoon basil, if desired
⅛ teaspoon pepper
dash of cayenne
2 ounces raw rice
1 pint canned tomato juice
4-5 stalks celery, thinly sliced
½ teaspoon chilli powder
¼ teaspoon salt
4 tablespoons water

Place minced beef, egg, onion, parsley, salt, basil, pepper, and cayenne in medium-size bowl; toss together lightly with a fork.

Shape into 12 small balls; pat rice on balls.

Combine tomato juice, celery, chilli powder, salt, and water in large frying pan; bring to the boil; add meat balls. Simmer, covered, 35 to 40 minutes, or until rice is cooked. Serves 4.

KOENIGSBERGER KLOPS (German Meat Balls)

½ pound minced beef
¼ pound minced veal
¼ pound minced pork
1 tablespoon finely chopped onion
1 ounce breadcrumbs
1 teaspoon salt
1 egg, slightly beaten
flour
½ pint clear beef stock
8 fluid ounces water
½ lemon, sliced

Combine meat, onion, crumbs, salt, and egg. Shape into 1-inch balls. Roll balls in flour.

Heat stock and 4 fluid ounces water in saucepan. Add floured balls. Simmer 15 to 20 minutes.

Mix 2 tablespoons flour with 4 tablespoons cold water. Add to beef stock and cook, stirring constantly, until thickened. Serve with lemon slices. Serves 4.

MEAT BALLS STROGANOFF

1 pound minced beef
¾ pound minced pork
4 ounces breadcrumbs
2 teaspoons salt
dash of pepper
dash of thyme
dash of oregano
4 fluid ounces milk
2 eggs
2 tablespoons fat
¾ pint sour cream
1 small can mushrooms

Combine meats, crumbs, seasonings, milk, and eggs. Mix well and form into 1½-inch balls. Brown in hot fat.

Drain off excess fat. Add ½ pint sour cream. Cover and simmer 1 hour.

Remove meat balls to warm serving dish. Stir remaining sour cream into mixture in the frying pan. Add mushrooms. Heat to boiling point. Pour over meat balls. Serves 6 to 8.

MINCED BEEF KEBABS

about ¼ pint undiluted evaporated milk
1½ pounds minced beef
2 ounces breadcrumbs
1 egg
1 small onion, chopped
1 teaspoon garlic salt
½ teaspoon salt
1 tablespoon prepared mustard
small tomatoes
thick onion slices

Combine evaporated milk, beef, breadcrumbs, egg, onion, garlic salt, salt, and mustard in large mixing bowl. Mix thoroughly. Shape meat mixture into 12 balls. Add a little more milk if mixture is too stiff.

Alternate meat balls with small tomatoes and thick onion slices on 6 skewers. Grill about 5 minutes on each side, or to taste. Serves 6.

Minced Beef Kebabs

Meat Balls with Celery Sauce and Noodles

MEAT BALLS WITH CELERY SAUCE AND NOODLES

½ pound minced beef
½ pound minced pork
4 ounces fine dry breadcrumbs
1 tablespoon minced onion
¼ teaspoon nutmeg
1 teaspoon salt
¼ teaspoon pepper
about ½ pint evaporated milk
1 slightly beaten egg
1 ounce fat
1 can condensed cream of celery soup
½ ounce finely chopped parsley
8 ounces broad noodles

Mix meat with crumbs, onion, nutmeg, salt, and pepper. Stir in 8 fluid ounces milk and egg, and blend well.

Shape mixture into balls, using about 1 tablespoon of the mixture for each.

Melt fat in large frying pan. Add meat balls and cook over low heat, cooking and turning until balls are browned on all sides. Remove meat balls and discard any drippings in pan.

Empty contents of can of celery soup into pan. Gradually stir in the remaining milk, keeping mixture smooth. Add parsley and meat balls.

Cover and let simmer gently, stirring occasionally, until heated through, about 15 minutes.

While meat balls are simmering in sauce, drop noodles into about 4 pints boiling water to which 1 tablespoon salt has been added. Cook until tender.

Drain well, then toss in bowl with about 1 tablespoon butter. Shape into border on heated dish. Fill centre with meat balls and sauce.

Serves 4 to 6.

BARBECUED MEAT BALLS AND BAKED BEANS

1 pound minced beef
1 teaspoon salt
¼ teaspoon pepper
1 ounce fine, dry breadcrumbs
4 tablespoons ketchup
2 tablespoons brown sugar
2 tablespoons vinegar
2 teaspoons Worcestershire sauce
1 teaspoon prepared mustard
ans beans with pork
readcrumbs,

and 6 fluid ounces water. Form in small balls about 1½ inches in diameter; brown over medium heat. Pour off fat.

Add remaining ingredients, except beans; simmer 5 minutes. Add beans; put in 2-2½-pint casserole.

Bake in moderate oven (350°F. Mark 4) 25 minutes, or until hot and bubbly. Serves 4.

MEAT BALLS WITH RICH WINE SAUCE

1 pound chuck or topside beef, minced
1 large apple, peeled and shredded
1 slightly beaten egg
1¼ teaspoons salt
⅛ teaspoon pepper
1 ounce flour
2 tablespoons fat or salad oil
½ small onion, chopped
¼ pint burgundy
4 tablespoons water
2 8-ounce cans tomato sauce
½ teaspoon basil
¼ teaspoon rosemary
¼ teaspoon sugar

Combine minced beef, apple, egg, salt, and pepper; shape into balls about 1 inch in diameter; roll in flour.

Heat fat or salad oil in a sauté pan; add meat balls and onion; cook over medium heat about 10 minutes, until lightly browned on all sides.

Combine wine, water, tomato sauce, basil, rosemary, and sugar. Pour over meat balls; cover and simmer 15 minutes. Serve over hot cooked spaghetti. Serves 4 to 6.

MEXICAN MEAT BALLS

1 pound minced beef
1 ounce white corn meal or flour
1 egg
1 clove garlic, crushed
1 small onion, finely chopped
1¼ teaspoons coriander seed, pounded (optional)
1¼ teaspoons salt
½ teaspoon pepper
chilli tomato sauce (below)

Mix beef, corn meal, egg, garlic, onion, and seasonings. Shape in tiny balls about ½ inch in diameter.

Drop into boiling chilli tomato sauce; cover, and simmer 5 minutes. Serves 4.

Chilli Tomato Sauce:

1 tablespoon fat
1 small onion, chopped
1 clove garlic, crushed
2 to 3 tablespoons chilli powder
1¼ pints tomato juice
salt

Melt fat in large saucepan. Add onion and garlic, and cook slowly until lightly browned. Add chilli powder, tomato juice, and salt to taste; cook 10 minutes.

ZESTY MEAT BALLS ON NOODLES

1 pound minced beef
1 teaspoon salt
6 ounces noodles, cooked
2 fluid ounces chilli sauce
8 fluid ounces tomato juice
1 teaspoon Worcestershire sauce
1 teaspoon prepared mustard

Combine meat and salt. Form into 6 balls. Spread noodles in a lightly buttered baking dish. Top with meat balls.

Combine chilli sauce, tomato juice, Worcestershire sauce, and mustard. Pour over noodles. Bake in moderate oven (350°F. Mark 4) 25 minutes. Serves 6.

SWEET AND SOUR MEAT BALLS

1 pound topside beef, minced
1 egg, slightly beaten
2 tablespoons flour
salt and pepper
4 fluid ounces peanut oil
8 fluid ounces chicken stock
2 large green peppers, cut in small pieces
4 slices canned pineapple, cut in small pieces
3 tablespoons cornflour
1 tablespoon soy sauce
½ teaspoon Aromat
4 fluid ounces vinegar
4 fluid ounces pineapple juice
4 ounces sugar

Form meat into 16 small balls.

Combine egg, flour, salt and pepper to taste to form a smooth batter.

Heat oil in a sauté pan. Dip meat balls in batter. Fry in hot oil until brown on all sides. Remove meat balls and keep warm.

Pour all but 1 tablespoon fat from pan. Add 4 fluid ounces stock, green pepper, and pineapple. Cover and cook over medium heat 10 minutes.

Blend remaining ingredients and add to pan. Cook, stirring constantly, until mixture comes to the boil and is thickened.

Return meat balls to sauce and heat through. Serve with hot, fluffy boiled rice. Serves 4.

Sweet and Sour Meat Balls

SWEDISH MEAT BALLS —PARTY STYLE

1 pound minced beef
½ pound lean pork
1 pound veal
4 slices bread
6 fluid ounces milk
1 onion, finely chopped
2 teaspoons salt
⅛ teaspoon nutmeg
⅛ teaspoon allspice
1 clove garlic, crushed
¼ teaspoon pepper
2 lightly beaten eggs
fat for frying
¾ pint beef stock

Ask for the beef, pork, and veal to be minced together 2 or 3 times.

Crumble bread and add milk. Stir to blend until it is of paste-like consistency. Combine with meat in a mixing bowl. Add seasonings and eggs. Beat and stir with wooden spoon until the mixture is stiff.

Spoon out rounded teaspoonfuls and roll between hands into 1-inch balls. Place on greaseproof paper about half an hour to dry a bit.

Heat enough fat in a large frying pan to make it ½ inch deep. Brown meat balls in this hot fat.

Put meat balls in a single layer in a large shallow baking tin. Add hot stock.

Cook in moderate oven (350°F. Mark 4) about 30 minutes, or until the stock is absorbed. Serve the balls without gravy or sauce. Makes 80 1-inch meat balls.

Variation: Remove browned balls from pan. Pour off all but 3 tablespoons of fat. Stir in 4 tablespoons flour. Add enough water to make desired consistency of gravy. Boil 3 minutes. Put in top of double boiler. Add meat balls. Keep warm until served.

MEAT BALLS WITH BURGUNDY

¾ pound minced beef
1 ounce fine dry breadcrumbs
½ small onion, finely chopped
¾ teaspoon cornflour
⅛ teaspoon allspice
1 egg, slightly beaten
6 fluid ounces milk
½ teaspoon pepper
¾ teaspoon salt
2 ounces fat
3 tablespoons flour
¾ pint water
8 fluid ounces Burgundy wine
2 beef bouillon cubes
¼ teaspoon salt

Combine beef, breadcrumbs, onion, cornflour, allspice, egg, milk, salt, and pepper.

Shape into about 30 small balls and brown balls in melted fat. Remove balls from pan and add flour and blend.

Stir in water, Burgundy, bouillon cubes, and ¼ teaspoon salt. Cook, stirring constantly, until smooth.

Place balls in sauce; cover, and simmer 30 minutes. Transfer to chafing dish and keep hot on buffet table. Serve with rice or noodles. Serves 6.

SWEET AND SOUR MEAT BALLS

3 large green peppers
1 pound minced beef
1 beaten egg
2 tablespoons flour
1½ teaspoons salt
few grains pepper
4 tablespoons salad oil
8 fluid ounces chicken bouillon or stock
4 slices canned pineapple, diced
12 maraschino cherries
3 tablespoons cornflour
2 teaspoons soy sauce
4 fluid ounces vinegar
6 ounces light corn syrup or golden syrup

Cut green peppers in sixths. Form seasoned beef into 16 small balls.

Combine egg, flour, ½ teaspoon salt, and pepper; dip meat balls in this batter.

Heat salad oil; add remaining salt. Fry meat balls in hot oil, turning to brown on all sides.

Remove meat balls; drain off all but 1 tablespoon of oil. Add 3 fluid ounces bouillon, diced pineapple, cherries, and green peppers; simmer 10 minutes.

Blend cornflour, soy sauce, vinegar, corn syrup, and remaining bouillon. Add to pineapple mixture. Cook slowly, stirring until thickened. Pour over meat. Serve with fluffy boiled rice. Serves 4.

CHINESE MEAT BALLS

3 tablespoons fat
1 teaspoon salt
½ pound minced beef
½ small onion, diced
3-4 stalks celery, diced
8 ounces sliced carrots
8 ounces cooked lima beans
8 fluid ounces beef stock
2 tablespoons cornflour
1 tablespoon soy sauce
4 tablespoons water

Melt fat. Add salt to meat and shape into small balls. Cook in fat with onion until tender.

Add celery, carrots, lima beans, and stock. Cover and cook 15 minutes.

Blend cornflour, soy sauce, and water. Add to hot mixture and cook, stirring until thick. Serve with fluffy rice. Serves 6.

MEAT BALLS IN SOUR CREAM SAUCE

1 slightly beaten egg
8 fluid ounces milk
1 teaspoon salt
¼ teaspoon pepper
4 ounces fine dry breadcrumbs
1 teaspoon grated onion
1½ pounds minced lean beef
2 tablespoons bacon fat
1 medium onion, chopped
2 tablespoons flour
2 8-ounce cans tomato sauce
8 fluid ounces sour cream
4 ounces coarsely chopped black olives

Prepare the meat balls in advance. Beat egg with milk, salt, pepper, crumbs, and grated onion. Allow to stand for a few minutes.

Add minced beef; mix lightly with a fork and shape into 2-inch balls.

Cover with greaseproof paper or foil; keep in refrigerator until ready to use.

Heat fat in chafing dish over direct heat. Sauté meat balls until uniformly browned. This may have to be done in two or three batches, depending on the size of your pan.

Remove from pan. Sauté onion in pan juices for 5 minutes.

Blend in flour; then add tomato sauce and meat balls.

Place over hot water. Cover and simmer 30 minutes.

Add sour cream and mix gently with a wooden spoon until meat balls are coated with cream. Scatter olives over all. Heat through and serve.

Serves 8 to 10.

LILLIPUT MEAT BALLS

1 pound minced beef
1½ ounces soft breadcrumbs
4 tablespoons milk
1 tablespoon finely chopped onion
2 tablespoons butter or margarine
4 fluid ounces sherry
4 fluid ounces ketchup
¼ teaspoon oregano (optional)

Mix beef, breadcrumbs, milk, onion, and 1 teaspoon salt. Shape mixture into little balls, using 1 teaspoon per ball.

Melt butter in a large sauté pan; brown balls nicely on all sides. Pour off most of fat from pan.

Mix wine, ketchup, and oregano; pour over balls; add salt to taste. Cover and simmer gently about 20 minutes, shaking pan gently from time to time to cook balls evenly.

Serve in a chafing dish or in a pottery casserole set over a candle warmer, and provide cocktail sticks or fondue forks for spearing the balls. Makes about 60 tiny balls.

Hamburger Sandwiches and Patties

HINTS ABOUT PREPARING HAMBURGERS

1. It is not necessary to use top-side beef for hamburgers, as the less expensive minced chuck or flank is just as satisfactory. In fact, many people prefer chuck to top-side because it contains more fat and makes a juicier hamburger. High quality, ready-minced meat also may be used.

2. Use 1 teaspoon salt and ⅛ teaspoon pepper for each pound of minced beef.

3. For extra-juicy hamburgers, add 4 tablespoons water or evaporated milk per pound of meat.

4. Add some finely chopped onion, if desired, also one or several of the following seasonings: Worcestershire sauce, mustard, ketchup, thyme, poultry seasoning, caraway seed, horseradish. Or add 1 ounce finely chopped nuts or 1 tablespoon parsley to each pound of meat.

5. A good variation in preparing hamburgers is to put two thin hamburger patties together with well-seasoned bread dressing. Pinch edges together before cooking.

6. Frying is the easiest method for cooking hamburgers. However, they may be grilled if the patties are not too thin.

GRILLED DEVILLED HAMBURGERS

1 pound minced beef
4 tablespoons ketchup
1½ teaspoons Worcestershire sauce
1 teaspoon salt
dash of pepper
6 soft bread rolls, split

Combine all ingredients except rolls. Toast uncut surfaces of rolls under grill and spread with meat mixture.

Grill about 6 minutes, with meat surface about 3 inches from the heat. Serves 3.

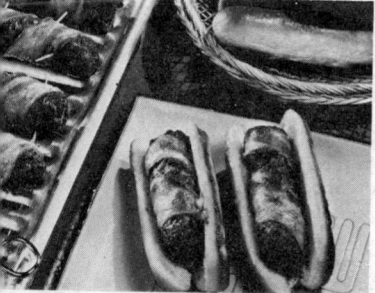

Frankburgers with Bacon

STANDARD AMERICAN HAMBURGER

1 pound minced beef
1 teaspoon salt
2 tablespoons chopped onion, optional
1 teaspoon fat

Combine meat, salt, and onion thoroughly.

Shape into 4 thick or 8 thin patties. Brown on one side in hot fat. Do not press the patties. Do not overcook. Turn to brown other side.

Serve hot for dinner or as sandwich filling. Serves 4.

With Sauce: When patties are done, remove from pan.

Add to pan 2 tablespoons flour, 1 tablespoon Worcestershire sauce or ketchup. Stir and pour over hamburgers.

GRILLED DE LUXE HAMBURGERS

Shape Standard American Hamburgers into 2 thick patties. Place in a roasting tin.

Grill 3 inches from heat 5 to 10 minutes, turning once.

To serve, spread with a mixture of one of the following:

1. Two tablespoons butter mixed with 2 tablespoons Worcestershire sauce.

2. Two tablespoons butter mixed with 1 tablespoon prepared mustard.

3. Two tablespoons butter mixed with 2 tablespoons ketchup, 1 teaspoon prepared mustard or chilli powder.

4. Two tablespoons butter mixed with 2 tablespoons chopped chives.

5. Two tablespoons butter mixed with 2 tablespoons blue cheese.

GRILLED DELUXE CHEESEBURGERS

Prepare Grilled Deluxe Hamburgers. Before removing from grill, top each with a slice of cheese. Grill until cheese melts, about 2 minutes.

FRANKBURGERS WITH BACON

4 ounces cornflakes
4 fluid ounces milk
1 teaspoon salt
⅛ teaspoon pepper
2 tablespoons finely chopped onions
1 pound lean minced beef
8 rashers bacon
8 oblong soft bread rolls

Crush cornflakes slightly; combine with milk. Let stand a few minutes until soft. Add salt, pepper, onions, and minced beef; mix well. Shape meat mixture into 8 frankfurter shaped portions. Wrap each spirally with a bacon rasher, fastening with cocktail stick.

Grill until meat is brown and bacon is crisp, about 6 minutes per side. Serve in warm rolls. Makes 8.

Big Boy Cheeseburgers

BIG BOY CHEESEBURGERS

4 ounces cornflakes
1 pound lean minced beef
1 teaspoon salt
¼ teaspoon pepper
1 tablespoon Worcestershire sauce
4 tablespoons ketchup or chilli sauce to taste
½ small onion, finely chopped
4-5 tablespoons evaporated milk
French bread
3 ounces sharp Cheddar cheese, grated

Crush cornflakes finely. Combine beef, salt, pepper, Worcestershire sauce, ketchup, onions, cornflake crumbs, and evaporated milk in 2-2½-pint bowl; mix lightly but thoroughly.

Cut unbaked bread in half lengthwise. On cut side of each half-loaf bread spread a quarter of meat mixture, covering to edges. Place on baking sheets crust side down.

Bake in hot oven (400°F. Mark 6) about 25 minutes or until beef is done. Top with grated cheese or cheese strips during last 5 minutes of baking. Remove from oven; serve immediately. Makes 4-6 servings.

BARBECUED HAMBURGERS

1 pound minced beef
½ small onion, finely chopped
1 teaspoon salt
¼ teaspoon pepper
1 tablespoon fat
8 fluid ounces ketchup
1 onion, sliced
4 tablespoons vinegar
1 tablespoon sugar
½ teaspoon dry mustard

Mix together meat, onion, salt, and pepper. Shape into 4 large patties.

Fry in hot fat to brown on both sides. Combine remaining ingredients. Pour over hamburgers. Cover and simmer 20 minutes more. Serve with hot, fluffy rice. Serves 4.

Note: Store leftover barbecue sauce in refrigerator. Use for barbecued frankfurters or with cooked rice or macaroni for a quick casserole.

SALISBURY STEAKS
(Master Recipe)

Salisbury steak is another name for hamburger, however as used on menus it usually means a fancy form, often with cream added, and sometimes coated with fresh breadcrumbs. It is formed in a fairly thick patty, grilled or pan-fried, and served with a sauce. Popular versions are given below.

Patty:
1 pound minced beef
¼ teaspoon pepper
1 teaspoon salt
2 tablespoons fat

Combine meat, pepper, and salt. Shape into patties about 2 inches in diameter.

Pan-fry in hot fat in a heavy frying pan. Serves 4.

Bacon Salisbury Steaks: Chop 4 slices cooked bacon and add to above recipe. Form into 6 patties.

Pan-fry in hot fat in a heavy frying pan.

Salisbury Steaks with Curry Sauce:
1 recipe master Salisbury steaks
½ ounce sliced mushrooms
    (optional)
2 tablespoons flour
8 fluid ounces water
1 beef bouillon cube
½ teaspoon curry powder

Remove patties to a warm plate. Pan-fry mushrooms. Add flour to fat left in the pan. Stir. Add water, bouillon cube, and curry powder.

Cook until mixture boils, cube is dissolved, and sauce is thickened. Pour over patties.

Salisbury Steaks with Sour Cream Sauce:
1 recipe master Salisbury steaks
2 tablespoons flour
4 fluid ounces water
¼ pint sour cream
1 teaspoon horseradish
¼ teaspoon thyme

Remove patties to a warm place. Stir flour into fat left in pan. Add remaining ingredients. Bring to boiling point. Pour over patties.

Open-Face Cheeseburgers

CHEESE HAMBURGER

1 pound minced beef
4 ounces shredded Cheddar cheese
1 teaspoon salt
⅛ teaspoon pepper
4 tablespoons water
1 tablespoon fat

Thoroughly combine meat, cheese, salt, pepper, and water. Form into 5 large, flat patties.

Slowly brown patties on each side in hot fat in a heavy frying pan. Cook slowly until meat is cooked as desired. Serves 5.

WINE HAMBURGERS

¼ pint claret, Burgundy, or any red wine
6 ounces dry breadcrumbs
1 medium onion, finely chopped
1 beaten egg
1 pound minced beef
1½ teaspoons salt
¼ teaspoon pepper

Pour wine over breadcrumbs. Add minced onion. When bread is soft, add beaten egg, minced beef, salt and pepper. Mix well. Form into 8 patties.

Brown in hot fat in frying pan. Serve on rolls if desired. Serves 4 to 6.

OPEN-FACE CHEESEBURGERS

Place on baking sheet the lower halves of large rolls which have been spread liberally with butter, mixed with prepared mustard if desired.

Toast under grill until golden brown. Keep hot in oven until needed.

In the meantime, quickly grill seasoned hamburger patties or roll.

Arrange on each half-roll a crisp lettuce leaf, onion rings or thin slices, thinly sliced tomato, a spoonful of hot baked beans—any one or all as fancy and taste dictate.

Top each with a hot hamburger patty.

Place on each:

(1) A slice of Cheddar cheese, or—

(2) A mixture of blue cheese, 2 ounces, mixed with 2 ounces butter, 2 teaspoons Worcestershire sauce, or—

(3) 2 ounces sharp Cheddar cheese spread mixed with 2 teaspoons Worcestershire sauce.

Place low under grill until the cheese is bubbly, browned, and melted. Serve at once.

Have the hot buttered toasted roll tops handy to clap on the sandwich, if you like, but this creation is more easily eaten with a fork than as a portable meal!

Barbecued Hamburger Stacks

BARBECUED HAMBURGER STACKS

1 pound minced beef
½ teaspoon salt
⅛ teaspoon pepper
5 bread stuffing patties (see below)

Combine minced beef, salt, and pepper. Shape into 10 meat balls.

Place 3 inches apart on sheet of greaseproof paper. Cover with another sheet of greaseproof paper.

Flatten meat balls into patties about 3 inches in diameter.

Bread Stuffing Patties:
4 slices bread cut in ½-inch cubes
4 tablespoons hot milk
1 beaten egg
4 tablespoons melted fat
¼ teaspoon salt
⅛ teaspoon pepper
2 tablespoons chopped onion

Combine soft bread cubes, hot milk, beaten egg, fat, salt, pepper, and onion.

Shape into 5 bread patties about 3 inches in diameter.

Barbecue Sauce:
2 ounces fat or dripping
2 tablespoons chopped onion
1-2 sticks celery, chopped
4 tablespoons vinegar
4 tablespoons tomato purée or
    tomato paste
1 tablespoon Worcestershire sauce
½ teaspoon garlic salt
2 tablespoons sugar
4 fluid ounces water
¼ teaspoon pepper
½ teaspoon salt

Melt fat in a frying pan. Add onion and celery and sauté until tender.

Add vinegar, tomato purée. Worcestershire sauce, garlic salt, sugar, water, pepper, and salt. Simmer 10 minutes.

To Make Hamburger Stacks: Place 5 meat patties in shallow baking dish. Top each with bread patty.

Finish by placing a meat patty on top of each bread patty. Pour barbecue sauce over hamburger stacks.

Cook in moderate oven (375°F. Mark 5) 30 minutes, occasionally basting stacks with barbecue sauce. Serves 5.

*Hamburger Tuck-Ins
Cheese-Cross Burgers*

SPECIAL HAMBURGER DINNER PATTIES

2 pounds minced beef
2 teaspoons salt
2 tablespoons chopped onion
1 ounce chopped mushrooms
 (optional)
1 tablespoon fat
1 ounce butter or margarine
1 tablespoon lemon juice

Put the meat into a basin; sprinkle with salt. (Add ¼ teaspoon pepper, if desired.) Brown onion and mushrooms lightly in fat and add to beef.

Use hand to combine ingredients thoroughly. Shape into 4 giant patties 1½-inches thick.

Grill about 10 minutes on each side or until crispy brown on both sides and rare inside.

Mix together butter and lemon juice (add 1 tablespoon parsley if liked). Spread over hamburgers. Serves 4.

Variations: (1) Spread top of grilled beef patties with crumbled blue cheese or blue cheese spread.

(2) Brush top of beef patties with French-dressing or thin barbecue sauce before and after grilling each side.

(3) Add chopped spring onions to butter topping for patties.

(4) Make 8 1-inch patties of the beef mixture. Melt a tablespoon of fat in heavy frying pan and fry, turning 2 or 3 times to cook and brown evenly, about 15 minutes.

HAMBURGER MUSHROOM STEAK ON TOAST

¼ pound mushrooms, sliced
butter or margarine
1 pound minced beef
1 teaspoon onion juice
1 teaspoon salt
¼ teaspoon pepper
4 slices bread, toasted on one side

Cook mushrooms in 1 tablespoon butter until lightly browned. Mix with beef, onion juice, and seasonings.

Butter untoasted side of bread; spread with meat mixture, and dot with butter. Put under grill until browned. Serves 4.

HAMBURGER TUCK-INS

1 pound minced beef
1 teaspoon salt
⅛ teaspoon pepper
2 teaspoons Worcestershire sauce
4 tablespoons finely chopped onion

Mix minced beef with salt and pepper. Shape into 8 thin patties.

Combine Worcestershire sauce and onion. On each of 4 patties, place 1 tablespoon chopped onion.

Top with a second patty and pinch edges together well.

Pan-fry or grill about 15 minutes, turning once. Serves 4.

CHEESE-CROSS BURGERS

Combine 1 pound minced beef with 4 tablespoons water, 1 teaspoon salt, and ⅛ teaspoon pepper.

Shape into 4 or 5 patties and pan-fry or grill until well browned. The last few minutes of the cooking time, top each patty with 2 strips of processed cheese, arranged criss-cross.

Continue cooking until cheese begins to melt. Garnish each with a slice of stuffed olive. Serves 4 or 5.

HAMBURGER PARMIGIANA

1 pound minced beef
¾ teaspoon salt
1 beaten egg
2 tablespoons milk
1 teaspoon dry mustard
¼ teaspoon pepper
1 ounce fine dry breadcrumbs
1 ounce grated Parmesan cheese
1 ounce butter or margarine
1 8-ounce can tomato sauce

Mix beef and salt; shape in 8 rectangular patties about ½-inch thick.

Mix egg, milk, and seasonings. Dip patties in mixture, then in crumbs, then in cheese.

Fry in butter over medium heat until browned on both sides. Serve with heated tomato sauce. Serves 4.

SCOTCH-POCKET HAMBURGERS

1 pound minced beef
1 teaspoon salt
⅛ teaspoon pepper
2 teaspoons Worcestershire sauce
4 tablespoons finely chopped onion
4 thin slices tomato (medium size)

Mix minced beef with salt and pepper. Flatten beef into a large square. Divide into 8 equal parts and make a thin patty of each.

Mix together the Worcestershire sauce and onion. On half the patties place a slice of tomato and a tablespoon of chopped onions. Top with a second patty and pinch edges together.

Grill about 15 minutes, turning once. Serves 4.

BEEF À LA LINDSTROM
(Swedish Meat Cakes)

3 small potatoes, cooked
2 medium beetroots, cooked
2 small onions
4 fluid ounces water
½ teaspoon salt
1 pound finely minced beef
4 egg yolks
5 tablespoons single cream
1 tablespoon finely chopped capers
1 teaspoon salt
¼ teaspoon white pepper
2 ounces butter or margarine
8 fluid ounces beef consommé

Chop cooked potatoes and beetroots into tiny cubes.

Finely chop onions; add water and ½ teaspoon salt. Cook, uncovered, until water has evaporated, about 3 minutes.

Pound meat with potato masher. Mix egg yolks and cream and add gradually to meat, mashing thoroughly. Add potatoes, beetroots, onions, capers, and seasonings.

Shape into flat cakes ½-inch thick. Fry quickly in butter, 1½ minutes on each side. Remove to warm dish.

Add consommé to pan. Bring to boil and pour over meat. Makes 12 cakes.

SLOPPY JOES

1 pound minced beef
1 large onion, finely chopped
1 green pepper finely chopped
1 tablespoon sugar
2 tablespoons prepared mustard
1 tablespoon vinegar
1 teaspoon salt
8 fluid ounces tomato sauce
½ teaspoon finely chopped olives
4 to 6 soft bread rolls

Brown meat slowly until crumbly but not hard. Combine remaining ingredients and add to meat.

Cover and simmer about 30 minutes. Serve on split rolls. Serve 4 to 6.

TEXASBURGERS

1 pound minced beef
1 small onion, chopped
1 teaspoon salt
¼ teaspoon pepper
2 tablespoons fine, dry breadcrumbs
2½-3 fluid ounces milk
6 soft bread rolls, split and toasted
2 large tomatoes, sliced
6 ounces coleslaw
pickle relish

Mix beef, onion, salt, pepper, breadcrumbs, and milk; form in 6 patties. Grill until browned on both sides.

Put patties on bottom halves of rolls. Top with sliced tomato, spoonful coleslaw, and a little pickle relish.

Cover with top halves of rolls. Serve at once. Serves 6.

HAMBURGER SANDWICH BAKE

1 ounce butter or margarine
8 slices bread
½ pound minced beef
a little chopped onion
1 stalk celery, chopped
1 teaspoon prepared mustard
4 ounces shredded cheese
3 eggs, beaten
¾ pint milk
¾ teaspoon salt
⅛ teaspoon pepper

Butter 4 slices bread, and put, butter side up, in baking tin; brown lightly in moderate oven (350°F. Mark 4).

Meanwhile, brown beef with onion and celery, stirring with fork. Add mustard.

Spread meat mixture on toasted bread; sprinkle cheese on top; cover with remaining bread slices.

Combine eggs, milk, salt, and pepper; pour over sandwiches. Bake in moderate oven (350°F. Mark 4) about 45 minutes. Serves 4.

HAWAIIAN HAMBURGERS

1 pound minced beef
1 medium onion, finely chopped
1 clove garlic, crushed
4 fluid ounces soy sauce
¼ teaspoon ground ginger

Mix beef and onion. Shape in 8 patties. Put in shallow dish.

Combine remaining ingredients, and pour over patties. Let stand 30 minutes, turning once.

Drain, and grill or pan-fry. Serve with spiced pineapple. Serves 4.

HAMBURGER SCONES

1 pound minced beef
2 teaspoons prepared mustard
1 teaspoon salt
¼ teaspoon savory or mixed herbs
½ pound scone mix. See recipe page 573 and use 8 ounces plain flour
about 4 fluid ounces milk
ketchup or tomato sauce

Combine meat, mustard, salt, and savory. Shape into 6 patties.

Make up scone mix and roll out ¼ inch thick on a lightly floured pastry board. Cut 12 circles the size of the patties.

Place 2 scones together. Place patties and scones on a baking sheet.

Bake in a hot oven (400°F. Mark 6) for 15 minutes. Serves patties between scones with ketchup or tomato sauce. Serves 6.

WIENERBURGERS ON ROLLS

2 pounds minced beef
1 tablespoon chopped onion
2 tablespoons cream
1 teaspoon Worcestershire sauce
1 teaspoon salt
¼ teaspoon pepper
3 gherkins
12 oblong bread rolls, split and toasted

Mix beef, onion, cream, Worcestershire, salt, and pepper.

Cut gherkins in quarters, lengthwise.

Shape meat mixture round pieces of gherkin to form wiener shape.

Bake in hot oven (425°F. Mark 7) about 15 minutes. Serve on rolls. Makes 12.

"ORIENTAL" HAMBURGER SANDWICH

1 tablespoon finely chopped fresh ginger root (or 2 teaspoons powdered ginger)
2 cloves garlic, crushed
1 small onion, chopped finely
2 tablespoons sugar
4 fluid ounces soy sauce
4 tablespoons water
1 pound minced beef

Make sauce from ginger root, garlic, onion, sugar, soy sauce, and water. Pour over meat. Let stand 1 to 2 hours in refrigerator.

Split 6 soft bread rolls, spread with the meat mixture and grill for about 5 minutes. Serves 6.

HAMBURGER WESTERN SANDWICHES

¼ pound minced beef
1 small onion, chopped
½ medium green pepper, chopped
salt and pepper
4 eggs, slightly beaten
butter or margarine
8 slices bread or toast

Cook beef, onion, and green pepper, stirring with fork, until meat loses its red colour. Sprinkle with salt and pepper.

Pour eggs over mixture. Reduce heat to medium, and cook until eggs are set; do not stir.

Cut in quarters; turn, and brown on other side. Serve hot between buttered bread or toast. Serves 4.

CREOLE HAMBURGER ON ROLLS

1 pound minced beef
2 medium onions, chopped
1 medium green pepper, chopped
1 teaspoon salt
¼ teaspoon pepper
1 8-ounce can tomato sauce
1 ounce cornflakes
6 oblong bread rolls, split and toasted

Cook beef, stirring with fork, until it loses its red colour. Add onions, green pepper, salt, and pepper.

Blend 4 fluid ounces water with tomato sauce. Add sauce and cornflakes to first mixture; bring to the boil, and simmer 15 minutes. Serve on rolls. Serves 6.

GRILLED DEVILLED HAMBURGERS

1 pound minced beef
4 tablespoons ketchup
1½ teaspoons prepared mustard
2 teaspoons horseradish
2 teaspoons minced onion
1½ teaspoons Worcestershire sauce
1 teaspoon salt
dash of pepper

Combine all ingredients. Split 6 soft bread rolls and toast uncut surfaces under the grill. Spread cut sides with the meat mixture.

Return to the grill and grill about 6 minutes. (Rolls may be used untoasted, but toasting makes them crisper.) Serves 4.

HURRY-UP BURGERS

1 pound minced beef
4-5 sticks celery, diced
1 teaspoon salt
1 tablespoon fat
1 tablespoon Worcestershire sauce
4 soft bread rolls split and buttered

Brown and cook meat, celery, and salt in fat in a heavy frying pan.

Add Worcestershire sauce. Heap meat mixture on halves of large round rolls. Serves 6.

Cheese Hurry-Ups: Follow the above recipe. After heaping each roll with meat mixture, top with a slice of cheese. Grill until cheese melts. Serve hot.

HERB HAMBURGERS

1 pound minced beef
½ small onion, chopped
1 tablespoon fat
pinch of celery seed
¼ teaspoon garlic salt
1 teaspoon dried parsley
⅛ teaspoon marjoram
⅛ teaspoon thyme
½ teaspoon salt

Thoroughly combine all ingredients. Shape into patties ¾ inch thick.

Grill or fry about 5 minutes on each side.

Spread each while piping hot with a little butter or margarine. Serves 4.

With Lemon Butter: Combine 1 tablespoon lemon juice with 2 ounces softened butter or margarine; spread on the cooked hamburgers.

With Cheese: Sprinkle shredded cheese over the hot hamburgers.

OLIVE CHEESEBURGERS

6 ounces breadcrumbs
3 tablespoons liquor from a jar of olives
3 tablespoons water
¾ teaspoon Aromat
⅛ teaspoon pepper
1½ pounds minced lean beef
prepared mustard
12 large stuffed olives
8 slices process Swiss cheese

Combine crumbs, liquor from olives, water, Aromat, and pepper; mix well; add to minced beef.

Form into 8 large patties; grill on 1 side about 7 minutes.

Turn; spread with mustard; cover with sliced olives; top each with slice of cheese.

Grill 5 minutes longer, or until cheese melts and is delicately browned. Serves 8.

TOASTED DEVILLED HAMBURGERS

1 pound minced beef
2 tablespoons chilli sauce
1½ teaspoons prepared mustard
1½ teaspoons prepared horseradish
1 teaspoon finely chopped onion
1½ teaspoons Worcestershire sauce
1 teaspoon salt
¼ teaspoon pepper
8 slices of bread

Combine ingredients and spread on bread. Grill for about 8 minutes at moderate heat and serve immediately. Serves 8.

TABASCO HAMBURGERS

3 pounds minced beef
1 large onion, chopped
1 medium green pepper, chopped
4 fluid ounces special hot barbecue sauce (see sauces)

Combine ingredients; shape into 12 patties.

Grill 5 to 8 minutes. Baste and serve with additional special hot barbecue sauce. Makes 12 servings.

BOHEMIAN BEEF PATTIES

1 pound minced beef
3 tablespoons finely chopped onion
3 tablespoons chopped gherkin
1 small pickled beetroot, chopped
6 ounces cooked diced potatoes
4 tablespoons milk
½ teaspoon salt
2 tablespoons fat

Mix all ingredients except fat. Shape into 8 patties 1 inch thick.

Pan-fry in hot fat in heavy frying pan about 15 minutes or until well done and browned on both sides. Makes 8 patties.

PEPPERBURGERS

1½ pounds minced beef
1 teaspoon salt
¼ teaspoon pepper
4 green peppers, halved
8 soft bread rolls

Mix minced beef with salt and pepper. Shape into 8 patties. Grill or cook in hot, greased frying pan.

Fry or boil green peppers until tender. Place on top of patties. Serve between split, heated rolls. Makes 8.

BLUE CHEESE BURGERS

2 pounds minced beef
3 tomatoes
onion salt
salt and pepper
1½ ounces blue cheese
2 tablespoons chopped green pepper

Shape meat into 6 oblong steaks 1 inch thick. Grill until half cooked. Turn, and make a shallow, lengthwise slit down centres.

Sprinkle tomato halves with a pinch of garlic salt, and grill with meat until meat is almost cooked. Sprinkle with salt and pepper.

Press a spoonful of cheese into slit in each hamburger. Top tomatoes with green pepper. Return to grill until cheese is melted. Serves 6.

MINT MEAT PATTIES

1 pound minced beef
½ ounce chopped fresh mint
1 teaspoon salt
pinch of pepper and nutmeg
2 slices white bread, crusts removed
¼ pint sour cream
4 tablespoons bacon fat

Combine meat, mint, salt, pepper, and nutmeg. Soften bread in sour cream 10 minutes. Blend with meat mixture. Shape into small patties and brown in bacon fat. Makes about 12 patties.

POTATO BURGERS

½ pound minced beef
6 ounces grated raw potatoes
2 tablespoons finely chopped onion
⅛ teaspoon pepper
1 teaspoon salt
3 tablespoons fat or salad oil
½ teaspoon dry mustard
1 tablespoon chopped parsley

Mix together beef, potato, onion, pepper, and salt. Shape into 8 patties.

Sauté in hot fat in frying pan until crisp, and brown; then remove from pan and keep warm.

Add mustard and parsley to fat remaining in pan; heat; pour over patties. Serves 4.

HAMBURGER ROLLS

3 pounds minced beef
2 10½-ounce cans tomato soup
2-3 tablespoons piccalilli
1 tablespoon salt
½ teaspoon pepper
24 soft-bread rolls, split and heated

Cook beef until browned, stirring with fork.

Add soup, piccalilli, salt, and pepper; simmer about 15 minutes. Serve on rolls. Makes 24.

BEEF AND MUSHROOMS ON TOAST

1 pound minced beef
1 medium onion, finely chopped
2-3 stalks celery, diced
½ medium green pepper, finely chopped
2 ounces sliced mushrooms
1½ teaspoons salt
⅛ teaspoon pepper
dash of cayenne
2 tablespoons quick-cooking tapioca
8 slices toast

Brown beef, stirring with fork. Add onion, celery, green pepper, mushrooms, seasonings, and about ¾ pint water.

Cover, and simmer 25 minutes. Add tapioca, and cook until gravy thickens slightly and tapioca is clear. Serve on toast. Serves 4.

BARBECUED SPOONBURGERS

3 tablespoons fat
1 onion, chopped
1 green pepper, chopped
1 pound minced beef
8 fluid ounces tomato ketchup
1 teaspoon salt
¼ teaspoon pepper
8 soft bread rolls

Melt fat in heavy frying pan. Add onion and green pepper and fry about 5 minutes. Add meat and continue cooking and stirring until pink colour of meat has disappeared.

Add tomato sauce, salt, and pepper and cook slowly until flavours are blended, about 15 minutes. (Add some red pepper if a "hotter" mixture is desired.) Serve in hot split buttered rolls. Serves 8.

Note: Make this barbecue mixture in advance; then heat for serving.

STUFFED HAMBURGER PATTIES

Press seasoned minced beef into thin patties between greaseproof paper.

Put 2 patties together with a filling made of chopped raw onion mixed with bottled sauce or ketchup, crimping the edges of the patties firmly together.

Grill and serve in hot buttered rolls.

With Cheese: Substitute cheese slices for onion in above.

Minced Meat Loaves

MASTER MEAT LOAF

1 pound minced beef
½ pound minced pork
2 slightly beaten eggs
2 ounces soft breadcrumbs
8 fluid ounces milk
½ small onion, finely chopped
2 teaspoons salt
⅛ teaspoon pepper
½ teaspoon sage

Combine all ingredients and pack lightly into meat loaf tin.

Bake in moderate oven (350°F. Mark 4) 1 hour. Serve with tomato sauce, mushroom sauce, or white sauce with vegetables added. Serves 4 to 6.

Master Meat Loaf Variations

1. Meat: In place of pork, use pork sausage meat or ½ pound chopped bologna sausage; or use ¼ pound pork and ¼ pound veal.

2. Liquids: In place of milk, use meat stock or bouillon, tomato juice, diluted canned soups, or half tomato sauce or chilli sauce and half water.

3. Seasonings: Worcestershire sauce, mustard, horseradish, garlic salt, celery salt, poultry seasoning, thyme, parsley, chilli powder, savory.

4. Picnic Meat Loaf: Place a row of hard-boiled eggs in centre of loaf before baking.

5. Glazed Loaf: Invert baked loaf on a baking sheet and brush with a mixture of mustard and ketchup. Return to hot oven 10 minutes.

6. Meat Ring: Pack meat loaf mixture into a ring mould and bake 45 minutes. Let stand in a warm place for a few minutes before serving.

Then invert on a round or square dish and fill centre with a buttered vegetable.

7. Midget Loaves: Bake meat loaf mixture in deep patty tins or dariole tins. Bake 30 minutes.

8. White-Capped Loaf: Thirty minutes before loaf is done, cover top with a row of overlapping onion slices. Continue baking.

Picnic Meat Loaf

9. Blue Cheese Meat Loaf: Shape half the mixture in loaf tin or on a shallow pan.

Spread with filling made by crumbling ¼ pound blue cheese and combining with 2 ounces soft margarine, 2 teaspoons Worcestershire sauce, and ½ teaspoon dry mustard. Shape rest of meat mixture on top; bake.

PORCUPINE MEAT LOAF

1½ pounds minced beef
4 ounces uncooked rice
1 large onion, finely chopped
1½ teaspoons salt
¼ teaspoon pepper
1½ teaspoons poultry seasoning
1 teaspoon Worcestershire sauce
2 beef bouillon cubes
1 ounce flour

Mix meat, rice, onion, 4 fluid ounces water, salt, pepper, poultry seasoning, and Worcestershire sauce. Shape into a round loaf and put in 1½-2 pint casserole.

Dissolve bouillon cubes in ¾ pint hot water and pour round loaf.

Cover; bake in moderate oven (350°F. Mark 4) for 2 hours. Remove loaf to hot dish.

Thicken liquid remaining in casserole with a paste of the flour and 4-5 tablespoons cold water. Season to taste. Serve hot with the gravy and glazed apple rings, if desired. Serves 6.

PENNY-PINCHER'S PLANKED STEAK

1 pound minced beef
1 teaspoon garlic salt
1 tablespoon Worcestershire sauce
1 egg
4 tomatoes
2 tablespoons chopped green pepper
2 ounces grated Cheddar cheese

Combine beef, garlic salt, Worcestershire sauce, and egg; shape into patty.

Grill 3 inches from the heat 7 to 8 minutes.

Remove stem ends of tomatoes. Combine green pepper and cheese. Top tomatoes with cheese mixture.

Turn meat. Arrange tomatoes on grill and cook 6 to 8 minutes. Serve with butter pats topped with chopped chives, if desired.

Arrange steak and tomatoes on a board or heat-proof dish. Whip up fluffy mashed potatoes and make a border around edge of plank. Serves 4.

Variation: This devilled steak is a delicious change: Add 1 small finely chopped onion, ½ small green pepper chopped to basic meat mixture; when patty is turned, spread the top with ¼ cup chilli sauce.

Crusty Meat Loaf

CRUSTY MEAT LOAF

8 ounces cornflakes
2 slightly beaten eggs
8 fluid ounces milk
2 teaspoons salt
⅛ teaspoon pepper
1 teaspoon Worcestershire sauce
½ ounce chopped parsley
1 tablespoon chopped onion
1¼ pounds minced beef
¼ pound minced pork

Crush cornflakes slightly; combine with remaining ingredients and mix thoroughly. Spread in greased 9½× 5½-inch loaf tin.

Bake in moderate oven (350°F. Mark 4) about 1 hour. Unmould loaf and place on greased baking sheet or ovenproof dish.

Topping:

1½ pounds seasoned mashed potatoes
2 ounces cornflakes
1 tablespoon melted butter or margarine

Coat loaf with mashed potatoes. Crush cornflakes into fine crumbs; mix with melted butter. Sprinkle over mashed potatoes.

Bake in moderate oven (350°F. Mark 4) about 20 minutes longer. Serves 8.

KETCHUP MEAT LOAF

1½ pounds minced beef
3 ounces soft breadcrumbs
1 slightly beaten egg
5 tablespoons tomato ketchup
1½ teaspoons salt
¼ teaspoon pepper
1 small onion, chopped

Combine all ingredients. Mix lightly but well. Shape into a loaf in shallow baking tin.

Bake in moderate oven (350°F. Mark 4) 1 hour. Serves 6 to 8.

Penny-Pincher's Planked Steak

Upside-Down Meat Loaf

UPSIDE-DOWN MEAT LOAF

1   packet veal stuffing
4   fluid ounces milk
3-4 tablespoons tomato ketchup
1   medium onion, chopped
1½ pounds minced beef
¾   teaspoon salt
few grains pepper
¾   teaspoon Aromat
few drops Tabasco sauce
½   teaspoon Worcestershire sauce
3 to 4 canned cling peach halves

Empty stuffing into large bowl. Combine milk and ketchup; pour over stuffing; let stand 15 minutes or until stuffing is soft.

Add remaining ingredients, except peaches; mix thoroughly until all ingredients are well blended.

Arrange peach halves, cut side down, in greased loaf tin; cover with meat mixture.

Bake in moderate oven (350°F. Mark 4) 1 hour. Unmould on serving dish. Fill centres of peach halves with redcurrant jelly. Serves 6.

PICKLE BEEF PINWHEELS

1   pound minced beef
1   unbeaten egg
2   tablespoons sweet pickle
1   tablespoon grated onion
1½ teaspoons salt
⅛   teaspoon pepper
7   ounces seasoned mashed potatoes

Combine beef, egg, sweet pickle, onion, salt, and pepper. Mix thoroughly.

Place on greaseproof paper and pat out to a rectangle, about 8 × 10 inches.

Spread mashed potatoes over meat. Carefully roll up like Swiss roll.

Cut into slices and grill, 10 to 15 minutes, or until done. Serves 4 to 6.

Pickle Beef Pinwheels

TOMATO MEAT LOAF

2   cans condensed tomato soup
     (save 8 fluid ounces for the
     sauce)
1   pound minced beef
½   pound minced pork
4½ ounces soft bread cubes
½   ounce chopped parsley
1   slightly beaten egg
1   tablespoon Worcestershire sauce
1   teaspoon salt
¼   teaspoon pepper
1   small onion, chopped
For Sauce:
8   fluid ounces soup (saved from
     meat loaf)
dash of allspice
4   tablespoons fat or dripping

Combine 4 fluid ounces soup with other loaf ingredients (save rest of soup for sauce).

Shape meat mixture into a loaf or pack tightly into a greased loaf tin.

Bake in moderate oven (350°F. Mark 4) about 1 hour or until cooked through.

Remove loaf from tin and combine ingredients for sauce. Heat for 5 minutes. Serve hot sauce with loaf. Serves 6.

Tomato Meat Loaf Variations

Mushroom Meat Loaf: Follow recipe for tomato meat loaf but use condensed cream of mushroom soup instead of condensed tomato soup.

For sauce: Leave out allspice; instead, add 2-3 tablespoons chopped pimento.

Celery Meat Loaf: Follow recipe for tomato meat loaf but use condensed cream of celery soup instead of condensed tomato soup.

For sauce: Leave out allspice; instead, add 2 tablespoons chopped parsley.

HAMBURGER-SCONE PINWHEELS

Baking Powder Scone Dough:
8 ounces plain flour
3 teaspoons baking powder
1 teaspoon salt
2 ounces fat
Filling:
1 small onion, chopped
2 tablespoons fat
1 pound minced beef
½ teaspoon salt
¼ teaspoon pepper
3 tablespoons tomato ketchup

Fry onion in fat until golden brown. Add meat and brown. Season with salt, pepper, and ketchup. Cool.

Make scone dough—see page 573 and roll into a rectangle about ⅛ inch thick.

Spread with filling. Roll as for Swiss roll.

Cut into 1-inch thick slices. Place on ungreased baking sheet. Bake in

very hot oven (450°F. Mark 8) about 15 minutes. Serve hot with mushroom sauce. Serves 6.

15-MINUTE MEAT LOAF WITH TOMATO SAUCE

1½ pounds minced beef
1½ teaspoons salt
⅛ teaspoon pepper
2   tablespoons chopped green
     pepper (optional)
2   tablespoons chopped onion
2   8-ounce cans tomato sauce
2   tablespoons sugar
2   teaspoons Worcestershire
     sauce

Combine beef, salt, pepper, onion, green pepper, and ½ can tomato sauce. Press into greased 9×12×2-inch baking dish.

Bake on lowest shelf in very hot oven (450°F. Mark 8) for 10 minutes. Grill 5 minutes longer.

While meat is cooking, combine remaining tomato sauce, sugar, and Worcestershire sauce. Bring to the boil. Boil about 3 minutes.

Cut meat in half crosswise. Arrange sandwich fashion on dish, pouring tomato sauce between and on top of meat. Serves 6.

TAMALE LOAF

1 onion, chopped
1 small clove garlic, crushed
5 tablespoons olive oil
¾ pound minced beef
2 teaspoons salt
1 pound tomatoes, skinned and
     mashed
2 teaspoons chilli powder
dash of cayenne or Tabasco sauce
3 ounces corn meal
6 fluid ounces milk
1 small can creamed sweetcorn
2 ounces pitted black olives

Cook onion and garlic in olive oil for 5 minutes. Put in the meat and, stirring often, cook until meat begins to brown. Add salt, tomatoes, chilli powder, and cayenne. Cook 15 minutes.

Mix corn meal with milk, and add mixture to meat. Stir and cook another 15 minutes. Then add corn and olives, and when all is well mixed pour into a greased 8×12-inch tin. Spread olive oil lightly over top and bake in moderate oven (350°F. Mark 4) for 1 hour. Serves 8.

Hamburger-Scone Pinwheels

MEAT LOAF — MEXICAN STYLE

1 pound minced beef
1 pound minced pork
1 egg
2 ounces corn meal
1 small onion, chopped
½ small green pepper chopped
1 can (about 12 ounces) tomatoes
2 teaspoons salt
¼ teaspoon pepper
½ teaspoon sage
¼ teaspoon chilli powder

Mix all ingredients thoroughly. Put into 9½×5½×3-inch loaf tin.

Bake in moderate oven (350°F. Mark 4) 1½ hours. Garnish with ketchup and serve with hot, buttered whole kernel corn. Serves 8 to 10.

SAVOURY MEAT LOAF

2 pounds minced beef
½ pound minced pork
2 ounces fine dry breadcrumbs
2 tablespoons milk
1 tablespoon lemon juice
2 tablespoons chopped onion
2 teaspoons salt
¼ teaspoon pepper
4 hard-boiled eggs

Combine all ingredients except hard-boiled eggs. Pack half the meat mixture into a 5×9-inch loaf tin.

Arrange shelled hard-boiled eggs in a lengthwise row through centre of loaf. Pack remaining meat mixture over eggs.

Bake in moderate oven (350°F. Mark 4) until done, about 1½ hours. Serve hot or cold. Serves 8.

SWEET AND SOUR MEAT LOAF

1 8-ounce can tomato sauce
1½ ounces brown sugar
4 tablespoons vinegar
1 teaspoon prepared mustard
1 egg
1 small onion, finely chopped
1 ounce dry breadcrumbs
2 pounds minced beef
1½ teaspoons salt
¼ teaspoon pepper

Mix tomato sauce with sugar, vinegar, and mustard until sugar is dissolved.

Beat egg slightly; add onion, breadcrumbs, beef, salt, pepper, and 4 fluid ounces tomato sauce mixture; combine lightly but thoroughly.

Shape meat into oval loaf in a bowl; turn into shallow baking dish, keeping loaf shape. Pour on rest of tomato sauce mixture.

Bake in hot oven (400°F. Mark 6) 45 minutes, basting occasionally. With 2 broad spatulas, lift onto dish. Pass round juices, after spooning off as much fat as possible. Serves 8.

GOLDEN MEAT LOAF

8 ounces cornflakes
1¼ pounds minced beef
¼ pound minced pork
2 slightly beaten eggs
8 fluid ounces milk
2 teaspoons salt
⅛ teaspoon pepper
1 teaspoon Worcestershire sauce
½ small onion, chopped
4 ounces grated raw carrots
½ ounce chopped parsley

Crush cornflakes slightly. Combine with remaining ingredients and mix well.

Spread in greased 9½×5¼-inch loaf tin. Bake in moderate oven (350°F. Mark 4) about 1¼ hours. Serves 8.

MEAT LOAF WITH MUSHROOM SAUCE

1 10½-ounce can cream of mushroom soup
1½ pounds minced beef
4½ ounces soft breadcrumbs
1 medium onion, chopped
½ ounce chopped parsley
1 egg
1 tablespoon Worcestershire sauce
1 teaspoon salt
¼ teaspoon pepper
4 tablespoons milk
1 pimento, chopped

Combine 4 fluid ounces soup with remaining ingredients, except milk and pimento. Pack into 9×5×3-inch loaf tin.

Bake in moderate oven (350°F. Mark 4) 1¼ hours. Pour off liquid; turn loaf out on hot dish.

Heat remaining soup with milk. Add pimento and pour over loaf. Serves 6.

WESTERN RANCH MEAT LOAF

1 small onion, chopped
2-3 stalks celery, diced
2 ounces fat
½ small green pepper diced (optional)
1 tablespoon salt
2 eggs
9 ounces soft breadcrumbs
4 fluid ounces water
2 pounds minced beef
4 fluid ounces tomato juice
2 tablespoons butter or margarine, melted

Brown onion and celery in the fat. Combine with green pepper, salt, eggs, breadcrumbs, and water to make a stuffing.

Add half of the stuffing to the meat, mixing well. Pat out half the meat mixture in a 2-2½ pint loaf tin. Cover with remaining stuffing, then top with remaining meat mixture.

Bake in a moderate oven (350°F. Mark 4) 1¼ hours. Baste twice with tomato juice and melted butter to keep loaf moist. Serves 10 to 12.

Golden Meat Loaf

QUICK HAMBURGER LOAVES

1 pound minced beef
½ small onion, finely chopped
1 teaspoon salt
½ teaspoon Aromat
1½ ounces fresh breadcrumbs
1 can condensed vegetable soup, undiluted

With fork, mix meat lightly but thoroughly with rest of ingredients.

Spoon into deep patty tins or dariole cups. Bake in very hot oven (450°F. Mark 8) 15 minutes. Serves 6.

BACON-LATTICED MEAT LOAF

1½ pounds minced lean beef
2 ounces chopped parsley
1 large onion, chopped
1½ teaspoons salt
¼ teaspoon pepper
¾ teaspoon Aromat
1½ teaspoons Worcestershire sauce
2 ounces fine dry breadcrumbs
8 fluid ounces water
6 rashers bacon, partially cooked

Combine all ingredients except bacon; blend well. Pack into 8×4×3-inch loaf tin. Bake in slow oven (325°F. Mark 3) 45 to 50 minutes.

Arrange half-cooked bacon lattice fashion over top of meat loaf. Continue baking 10 to 15 minutes longer or place under grill until bacon is crisp.

If desired, garnish loaf on its dish with scoops of potato (seasoned with salt, pepper, and Aromat) arranged on fried pineapple slices and topped with sprinkling of coconut. Serves 6.

Bacon-Latticed Meat Loaf

MINCED BEEF STEAK SUPREME

1 pound minced beef
1 ounce fine dry breadcrumbs
1 beaten egg
1 teaspoon salt
$\frac{1}{8}$ teaspoon pepper
3 tablespoons finely chopped onion
1-2 stalks celery, finely chopped
1 can condensed mushroom soup
4 fluid ounces water

Mix all ingredients except mushroom soup and water. Shape into an oval about 1-inch thick.

Brown in a sauté pan in hot fat; carefully turn and brown other side.

Pour the mushroom soup which has been diluted with the water over the meat. Cook slowly in covered pan 25 minutes.

Serve mushroom gravy over boiled or mashed potatoes. Serves 5 to 6.

ORANGE-GLAZED HAMBURGER LOAVES

6 tablespoons brown sugar
$\frac{1}{2}$ teaspoon dry mustard
6 unpeeled slices small orange
1$\frac{1}{2}$ pounds minced beef
6 ounces soft breadcrumbs
1 egg
1 medium onion, finely chopped
1 medium green pepper, finely chopped
$\frac{1}{4}$ teaspoon pepper
1 teaspoon salt
4 fluid ounces orange juice
juice of 1 lemon

Put brown sugar in 6 greased, small baking dishes. Sprinkle with mustard, and top each with a slice of orange.

Combine remaining ingredients; mix well. Press into baking dishes.

Bake in moderate oven (350°F. Mark 4) 1 hour. Let stand a few minutes before turning upside down on dish. Serves 6.

PLANKED MINCED STEAK

1 small onion, chopped
2 tablespoons margarine
2 eggs
1$\frac{1}{2}$ pounds minced beef
$\frac{1}{2}$ pound minced pork
8 fluid ounces milk
2 teaspoons salt
$\frac{1}{8}$ teaspoon pepper
1 teaspoon Worcestershire sauce
$\frac{1}{2}$ ounce chopped parsley
1$\frac{1}{2}$ ounces oats, uncooked
1$\frac{1}{4}$ pounds mashed potatoes
6 parboiled onion cups filled with cooked, seasoned peas

Sauté onion in margarine for a few minutes.

Beat eggs and add to meat with milk, onion, seasonings, and oats. Mix thoroughly.

Form into a flat loaf on a greased plank, shallow baking tin or oven-proof dish; score in diamond shapes across top.

Bake in hot oven (425°F. Mark 7) 40 minutes. Arrange mashed potatoes along the two long sides of loaf and filled onion cups at ends. Brown in hot oven. Serves 6.

HERBAL MEAT LOAF

1 pound minced beef
$\frac{1}{2}$ pound minced pork
1 ounce dry breadcrumbs
2 medium onions, chopped
1 clove garlic, crushed
1 tablespoon olive oil
$\frac{1}{4}$ teaspoon marjoram
$\frac{1}{4}$ teaspoon savory
$\frac{1}{2}$ teaspoon salt
$\frac{1}{8}$ teaspoon pepper

Basting Sauce:
1 tablespoon bacon fat
1 tablespoon olive oil
1 teaspoon dry red wine
1 tablespoon ketchup
salt and pepper

Herbal Meat Loaf: Combine all ingredients; mix well. Pack in greased loaf tin.

Bake in moderate oven (375°F. Mark 5) 1 hour. Baste every 15 minutes with hot basting sauce.

Basting Sauce: Combine all ingredients; heat. Serves 6.

GRILLED BEEF PINWHEELS

1 pound minced beef
1$\frac{1}{2}$ teaspoons salt
$\frac{1}{8}$ teaspoon pepper
1 egg
2 tablespoons melted fat
6 tablespoons breadcrumbs
2 tablespoons tomato juice or milk
10 ounces mashed potatoes, seasoned
6 ounces mashed peas, seasoned
butter or margarine, melted

Mix together all but the last 3 ingredients. Pat out on waxed paper to form rectangular sheet $\frac{1}{2}$-inch thick.

Spread mashed potatoes on crosswise half of meat. Spread other half with mashed peas. Roll meat firmly, Swiss roll fashion, starting with the end covered with peas.

Wrap in greaseproof paper and chill several hours. When ready to cook, cut with sharp knife into six 1-inch slices.

Place on preheated grill 3 to 4 inches below source of heat. Brush with melted butter and grill slowly about 5 minutes. Turn and brush again with melted butter and finish grilling. Serves 6.

Baked Pinwheels: Place 2-inch slices on a greased baking tin. Brush surface with melted butter. Bake in a hot oven (400°F. Mark 6) 30 minutes.

BRAISED MEAT LOAVES

1$\frac{1}{2}$ pounds minced beef
1 egg
1$\frac{3}{4}$ teaspoons salt
$\frac{1}{8}$ teaspoon pepper
1$\frac{1}{2}$ ounces soft breadcrumbs
3 fluid ounces milk
flour
2 tablespoons fat

Mix beef, eggs, 1$\frac{1}{4}$ teaspoons salt, pepper, crumbs, and milk. Shape in 4 individual meat loaves. Dredge with flour.

Brown on all sides in fat in a sauté pan. Drain off fat. Add 4 fluid ounces water and remaining $\frac{1}{2}$ teaspoon salt. Cover, and simmer 30 minutes, or until done. Serve with potato pancakes. Serves 4.

BURGUNDY MEAT LOAF

$\frac{3}{4}$ pound minced beef, lamb, or veal
3 ounces rolled oats
4 fluid ounces burgundy or claret wine
3 tablespoons chopped onion
1$\frac{1}{4}$ teaspoons salt
$\frac{1}{4}$ teaspoon pepper
$\frac{1}{8}$ teaspoon mixed herbs
1 beaten egg
2 tablespoons melted fat or dripping

Combine ingredients in order given. Pack into greased small loaf tin. Bake in moderate oven (350°F. Mark 4) 1 hour or until done. Serves 4 or 5.

VELVET-SMOOTH MEAT LOAF

1 pound fresh minced beef
1 egg
1$\frac{1}{2}$ teaspoons salt
1 small onion, finely chopped
1 large can evaporated milk, undiluted
6 ounces soft breadcrumbs

Combine all ingredients, mixing thoroughly.

Pack into a greased loaf tin and bake in moderate oven (350°-375°F. Mark 4-5) about 1 hour. Slice and serve hot or cold. Serves 6.

CHEESE MEAT CUPS

1$\frac{1}{2}$ pounds minced beef
2 ounces dry breadcrumbs
$\frac{1}{2}$ small onion, finely chopped
2 tablespoons finely chopped green pepper
4 tablespoons chilli sauce
2 to 3 drops Tabasco sauce
5 fluid ounces milk
2 eggs
$\frac{3}{4}$ teaspoon salt
dash of pepper

Mix ingredients thoroughly. Fill greased deep bun tins.

Bake in moderate oven (350°F. Mark 4) 45 minutes. Makes about 10 "cups". Or bake in 8$\frac{1}{2}$ × 4$\frac{1}{2}$ × 2$\frac{1}{2}$-inch loaf tin about 1 hour. Serves 6 to 8.

JUICY MEAT LOAF

1 pound minced beef
2 ounces quick oats
1 beaten egg
½ small onion, finely chopped
1½ teaspoons salt
¼ teaspoon pepper
5 fluid ounces tomato juice

Combine all ingredients thoroughly; pack firmly into a loaf tin.

Bake in moderate oven (350°F. Mark 4) 45 to 50 minutes. Let stand 5 minutes before slicing. Serves 6.

Variations:

Dinner Hamburgers: Use meat loaf recipe above, omitting beaten egg. Combine ingredients thoroughly. Shape into 6 dinner hamburgers; chill.

Pan-fry in hot fat and serve sizzling hot.

Meat Balls: Use meat loaf recipe above, omitting beaten egg. Shape combined ingredients into 12 meat balls; roll in flour; then brown in hot fat.

Add tomato sauce; simmer 20 to 25 minutes.

Mock Drumsticks: Use meat loaf recipe above, omitting beaten egg. Shape combined ingredients into 6 drumsticks; chill.

Roll in breadcrumbs. Brown on all sides in hot fat; cover and cook slowly 10 minutes longer.

SOYA MEAT LOAF

¾ pound minced meat
12 fluid ounces vegetable stock, tomato juice, or milk
2 ounces salt pork, diced
2 tablespoons chopped onion
2-3 stalks celery, chopped
3 ounces soya flour
2 tablespoons chopped parsley
2 teaspoons salt
2 ounces soft breadcrumbs
⅛ teaspoon pepper

Select one kind of meat or a mixture of two or more kinds.

Blend vegetable stock, tomato juice, or milk with the meat.

Fry salt pork until crisp and remove from fat. Cook onion and celery in the fat for a few minutes.

Add all the ingredients to the meat and mix well. Pack mixture into a loaf tin or mould it into a loaf and place in an uncovered baking tin.

Bake loaf in a moderate oven (350°F. Mark 4) until well done and brown, about 1 hour. Serves 6 to 8.

Variation: To vary the flavour, serve the loaf with brown gravy or tomato sauce.

LOUISIANA BEEF ROLL

1½ pounds minced beef
1 slightly beaten egg
2 ounces soft breadcrumbs
2 tablespoons finely chopped onion
1½ teaspoons salt
¼ teaspoon pepper
1 tablespoon horseradish
¼ teaspoon dry mustard
1 small can sweet potatoes, drained and mashed
2 tablespoons chopped parsley
2 tablespoons chopped onion
salt
3 rashers lean bacon

Combine beef, egg, crumbs, onion, salt, pepper, horseradish and mustard. Mix well.

Spread meat mixture on a piece of heavy waxed paper to make a rectangle about 8 × 10 inches.

Combine sweet potatoes, onion, and salt to taste. Mix well, and spread evenly over beef. Roll like a Swiss roll.

Place in shallow baking tin and top with bacon. Bake in moderate oven (350°F. Mark 4) 45 minutes to 1 hour. Serve with tomato sauce. Serves 6.

INDIVIDUAL BEEF FILLED RICE LOAVES

8 ounces uncooked rice
2 ounces margarine
1 pound minced beef
2 tablespoons chopped onion
½ teaspoon salt
¼ teaspoon pepper
6 tablespoons tomato ketchup

Cook rice in boiling salted water until tender and fluffy.

Melt 2 tablespoons margarine in frying pan. Add minced beef and cook over medium heat until red colour disappears, stirring constantly with fork. Add onion, salt, and pepper. Mix well.

Into well greased individual baking dishes put ½ the hot rice, pressing down firmly.

On top of rice arrange layer of beef. Over meat spread 1 tablespoon ketchup in each dish.

Cover meat with remaining rice, pressing down firmly. Dot with remaining 2 tablespoons margarine.

Set baking dishes on baking sheet. Bake in moderate oven (350°F. Mark 4) 25 to 30 minutes.

Unmould on hot plates. Serve hot with creamed peas or creamed asparagus. Serves 6.

Note: May also be baked in well greased 8 × 8 × 2-inch tin.

Put layer of rice into tin, then layer of meat. Spread with ketchup and cover with rice.

Dot with margarine and bake as directed. Cut in squares to serve.

STANDARD MEAT LOAF
(Master Recipe)

1 beaten egg
4 ounces rolled oats, uncooked
1½ pounds minced beef
½ small onion, chopped
2 teaspoons salt
¼ teaspoon pepper
1 tablespoon Worcestershire sauce
8 fluid ounces water or milk

Mix all ingredients together thoroughly. Pack into 9 × 5 × 3-inch greased loaf tin.

Bake in moderate oven (350°-375°F. Mark 4-5) 1 hour. Serves 8.

Variations:

Party Meat Loaf: Add ½ teaspoon powdered sage to master recipe.

Combine 3 tablespoons brown sugar, 4 tablespoons tomato ketchup, ¼ teaspoon nutmeg, and 1 teaspoon dry mustard and spread over loaf before baking.

Filled Cheeseburgers: Shape meat mixture into 20 very thin patties.

Combine 2½ ounces Roquefort cheese, 2 tablespoons mayonnaise, and 1 teaspoon prepared mustard.

Spoon this mixture on 10 patties. Top with remaining patties, and press edges together.

Grill slowly 12 minutes on first side, and 8 minutes on other side.

SPICY MEAT LOAF

1½ pounds minced beef
½ pound sausage meat
1 medium onion, grated
1 egg
3 ounces soft breadcrumbs
4 fluid ounces milk
1 teaspoon salt
¼ teaspoon pepper
½ teaspoon nutmeg
½ teaspoon allspice
⅛ teaspoon ginger

Combine all ingredients, mixing lightly but thoroughly. Shape in a loaf.

Bake in moderate oven (350°F. Mark 4) about 1¼ hours. Serves 8.

MOCK PORTERHOUSE

1½ pounds minced beef
1½ teaspoons salt
2 ounces quick-cooking rolled oats
½ small onion, chopped
4 fluid ounces top of the milk or single cream
butter or margarine

Mix together the meat, salt, rolled oats, onion, and milk. Pat this mixture into a mound about 2 inches thick.

Grill slowly about 20 minutes. Dot surface with butter and serve on a hot dish. Serves 6.

Top-of-Range Dishes

CREAMED MINCED BEEF
(Master Recipe)
1 pound minced beef
1 small onion, chopped
1 tablespoon fat
4 ounces shredded carrots
　　　(optional)
2 teaspoons salt
1 ounce flour
¾ pint water

Brown meat and onion in hot fat in a large frying pan. Add carrots and salt. Cook and stir 15 minutes.

Sprinkle flour over meat and stir until blended. Add water. Cook until thickened.

Add seasonings to taste, such as Worcestershire sauce, dry mustard, or pepper. Serve hot over toast, baked or mashed potatoes, or rice. Serves 8.

Creamed Hamburger and Corn: Add 1 small can whole sweetcorn to master recipe.

EASY HAMBURGER
1 pound minced beef
1 teaspoon Worcestershire sauce
½ 10½-ounce can condensed cream
　　　of celery soup
1 ounce shredded cheese

Brown meat lightly in a frying pan. Stir in Worcestershire sauce. Spread soup over all.

Top with shredded cheese. Cover. Cook slowly for 10 minutes. Serves 4.

STUFFED CABBAGE—SWEET AND SOUR
10 to 12 large cabbage leaves
1 pound minced beef
4 ounces cooked rice
1 egg
1 teaspoon salt
⅛ teaspoon pepper
3 ounces sultanas
1 onion, sliced thinly
juice of 1 lemon
about 1½ ounces brown sugar
1 can (16 ounce) tomatoes
8 fluid ounces water

Use large, whole, outside leaves of cabbage. Place in boiling water for 5 minutes to soften.

Combine meat, rice, egg, salt, pepper, and half the sultanas. Put a generous amount on each leaf. Fold in sides. Roll up and fasten with wooden cocktail sticks.

Shred the heart of cabbage. Line bottom of a saucepan with shredded cabbage. Put stuffed cabbage on top, close together.

Add remaining shredded cabbage, onion, sultanas, lemon juice, sugar, tomatoes, and water. Simmer gently 2½ to 3 hours. Serves 6.

SQUAW RICE
1 pound minced beef
1 pound cooked rice
2 teaspoons salt
⅛ teaspoon pepper
1 small can whole kernel corn,
　　　drained
1 medium onion, sliced
½ can tomatoes, drained
8 fluid ounces tomato juice

Lightly brown beef, rice, salt, and pepper.

Add remaining ingredients; cover and simmer about 30 minutes. Serves 8.

MINCED BEEF CHOP SUEY
½ pound minced beef
1 large onion, sliced
3-4 stalks celery, cut into strips
2 tablespoons salad oil
1 can bean sprouts, drained
12 fluid ounces beef consommé or
　　　bouillon
1 ounce sliced mushrooms
1 tablespoon cornflour
1 tablespoon salt
4 tablespoons soy sauce
hot cooked rice

Pan-fry meat, onion, and celery in oil in a heavy saucepan. Add bean sprouts, consommé, and mushrooms.

Mix cornflour with 4 tablespoons water and add. Cook and stir 10 minutes. Season to taste with salt and soy sauce. Serve on hot cooked rice with additional soy sauce. Serves 6.

Minced Beef Chow Mein: Prepare minced beef chop suey and serve on chow mein noodles.

STUFFED WHOLE CABBAGE
1½ pounds minced beef
2 teaspoons salt
¼ teaspoon pepper
2 ounces fine dry breadcrumbs
1 medium onion, chopped
1 medium head cabbage
2 beef bouillon cubes

Combine all ingredients, except cabbage and bouillon, with 8 fluid ounces water.

Remove core from cabbage; cook cabbage in boiling salted water about 5 minutes; drain. Separate leaves.

Line colander with large piece of several thicknesses of muslin. Form cabbage head again by lining muslin with cabbage leaves, then a layer of beef mixture, continuing until all meat and cabbage are used, making 4 or 5 layers of each. Pull cloth tightly around cabbage head; tie top firmly with string.

Put in large saucepan, and almost cover with boiling water. Add bouillon cubes; cover, and simmer about

1½ hours. Remove from liquid; drain, and untie. Put on plate; remove muslin; cut in large wedges. Serve with ketchup or horseradish. Serves 6.

CHILI CON CARNE
Chili or Chile Con Carne is Spanish for peppers with meat. It is a dish of Mexican origin now popular in most places in various versions. Its chief ingredients are beef, tomato sauce, beans, and chilli peppers. Chilli powder is usually substituted for the crushed chilli peppers.

8-12 ounces pinto beans (red beans)
salt and pepper
1 pound minced beef
2 tablespoons fat
2 large onions, chopped finely
2 cloves garlic, crushed
2 small cans tomato concentrate
1 to 4 tablespoons chilli powder

Wash and soak beans overnight. Simmer until tender (about 2 hours). Season with salt and pepper.

Brown minced beef in large, heavy frying pan, turning frequently to keep from sticking.

Melt fat in small frying pan and brown onion and garlic.

Combine onion, garlic, tomato paste, and chilli powder with browned meat. Simmer about 20 minutes.

Add chilli mixture to cooked, seasoned beans and simmer over low heat about 1 hour, stirring often to prevent sticking. Serves 6.

QUICK CHILI CON CARNE
1 pound minced beef
2 medium onions, chopped
2 tablespoons fat
1 teaspoon salt
1 teaspoon chilli powder
¼ teaspoon pepper
1 pound tomatoes, cooked
8 ounces small haricot beans,
　　　cooked

Brown meat and onions in hot fat. Season meat well. Add tomatoes and haricot beans. Cook over low heat 20 to 30 minutes. Serves 6 to 8.

Steaming bowls of chili con carne and a green salad are all that's needed for a simple but satisfying supper.

LIMA BEAN CHILI

1 medium onion, chopped
1 pound minced beef
2 or 3 teaspoons chilli powder
1¼ teaspoons salt
1 packet frozen lima beans
1 large can tomatoes

Cook onion and beef in large saucepan, stirring with fork, until meat loses its red colour.

Add remaining ingredients; bring to boil; cover, and simmer about 30 minutes, stirring occasionally. Serves 4.

TROPICAL HAMBURGER

4 ounces desiccated coconut
½ pound minced beef
¼ teaspoon nutmeg
1 teaspoon salt
8 fluid ounces pineapple juice
2 tablespoons lemon juice
4 fluid ounces water
2 tablespoons cornflour
fried noodles

Brown coconut in sauté pan until crispy. Stir in meat and cook until lightly browned. Add nutmeg and salt.

Combine pineapple juice, lemon juice, and water with cornflour. Stir into meat mixture. Stir and heat 5 to 10 minutes.

Serve on fried noodles, garnished with salted, slivered almonds. Serves 4.

RICE AND BEEF HAMBURGER

1 pound minced beef
1 pound cooked rice
1 teaspoon salt
⅛ teaspoon pepper
1 small can whole kernel corn, drained
1 large onion, sliced
1 teaspoon salt
1 8-ounce can tomatoes, drained
8 fluid ounces tomato juice

In a large saucepan, mix together minced beef, rice, salt, and pepper. Fry, stirring frequently, until beef is browned.

Stir in corn, onions, salt, tomatoes, and tomato juice. Cover and cook over low heat 30 minutes. Serves 10.

BARBECUED BEEFBURGERS WITH RICE

1 pound minced beef
1 egg
⅛ teaspoon pepper
1 teaspoon salt
3 tablespoons fat
1 large onion, chopped
2 tablespoons Worcestershire sauce
1 tablespoon vinegar
2 tablespoons sugar
2 8-ounce cans tomato sauce
2¼ pounds hot cooked rice

Mix together the beef, egg, salt, and pepper. Shape into 6 flat cakes.

Melt 1 tablespoon fat in a sauté pan and brown cakes, first on one side, then on other.

While cakes are browning, melt remaining 2 tablespoons fat in saucepan. Add onions and cook in fat until tender.

Add Worcestershire sauce, vinegar, sugar, and tomato sauce and mix well. Pour this sauce over cakes.

Cover pan and simmer 15 minutes. To serve, arrange hot rice on a dish. Place beef cakes over rice and pour sauce over beef cakes and rice. Serves 6.

Barbecued Beefburgers with Rice

Master Freezer Sauce

From one frozen "starter" recipe in the freezer you can quickly prepare a variety of dishes. The master Italian meat sauce "starter" is excellent on rice, potatoes, or frankfurters as well as for preparing the dishes given here.

ITALIAN MEAT SAUCE
"Starter"

8 fluid ounces oil or 8 ounces cooking fat
3 cloves garlic, crushed
3 green peppers, chopped
3 large onions, sliced finely
3 pounds minced beef
3 6-ounce cans tomato paste
3 8-ounce cans tomato sauce
1¼ pints boiling water
1 tablespoon salt
1 tablespoon paprika
1 teaspoon celery salt
1 teaspoon garlic salt
1 teaspoon chilli powder
2 tablespoons Worcestershire sauce
3 tablespoons any meat sauce
3 tablespoons chilli sauce

Heat oil in large heavy saucepan. Add crushed garlic, green pepper, and onions. Cook over low heat 5 minutes.

Add meat; mix well and cook on high heat until lightly browned.

Add tomato paste, tomato sauce, and water. Cook over low heat for 2 hours. Add seasonings.

Cool quickly. Package and freeze in pint containers. Makes 8 pints.
To Thaw: Put container under hot water and let hot water run long enough so that contents can be slipped out.

Or remove from freezer and let stand at room temperature several hours before using.

Or remove from freezer the night before using and keep in refrigerator.

MEAT SAUCE AND SPAGHETTI

1½ pints Meat Sauce Starter
4 fluid ounces tomato juice
8 ounces spaghetti
1 tablespoon salt
grated Parmesan cheese

Thaw meat sauce with tomato juice. Cook spaghetti in boiling salted water until tender. Drain. Serve with meat sauce and cheese.

TAMALE PIE

1½ pints Meat Sauce Starter, thawed
Corn Meal Scone Topping (See Index)

Pour meat sauce into a 3-3½-pint casserole. Prepare topping, spread over the sauce mixture and bake for about 45 minutes in a hot oven (425°F. Mark 7) reducing the heat after 35 minutes if the topping is getting too brown.

MEAT SAUCE WITH RED KIDNEY BEANS

¾ pint Meat Sauce Starter
2 cans red kidney beans, drained
3 fluid ounces red wine

Combine all ingredients in a 2½-3-pint casserole. Bake in moderate oven (350°F. Mark 4) for 1 hour.

EGGPLANT or AUBERGINE WITH MEAT SAUCE

1 eggplant
¾ pint Meat Sauce Starter, thawed
2 tablespoons grated Parmesan cheese

Peel and slice eggplant in ½-inch slices.

Alternate slices of eggplant with meat sauce and cheese in a 2½-3-pint casserole. Bake in moderate oven (350°F. Mark 4) for 1 hour.

Cabbage Rolls

CABBAGE ROLLS

8 large cabbage leaves
½ pound minced beef
4 ounces cooked rice
1 egg
1 teaspoon salt
¼ teaspoon pepper
2 tablespoons chopped onion
2 tablespoons fat
2-3 cooked tomatoes
½ small onion, chopped
1 bay leaf (optional)
4 whole cloves (optional)

Cook cabbage leaves in salted water for 5 minutes.

Combine meat, rice, egg, salt, pepper, and onion. Brown lightly in hot fat.

Place a spoonful of meat mixture in each leaf and roll up. Secure with a cocktail stick. Place in sauté pan.

Add tomatoes, onion, bay leaf, and cloves. Cover and simmer 45 minutes. Serve with parsleyed rice. Serves 4.

BEEF AND GREEN BEANS
(Chinese)

1 large onion, very finely chopped
1 small clove garlic, crushed
1 tablespoon fat
¾ pound minced beef
1¼ pints water
3 tablespoons soy sauce
1 pound green beans, diced
2½ tablespoons cornflour
hot cooked rice

Brown onion and garlic lightly in fat in heavy saucepan. Add meat and cook 3 minutes, stirring to break up meat.

Add water and soy sauce and heat to boiling. Add beans and cook 10 minutes.

Blend cornflour with a little cold water. Add to mixture and cook until thickened, stirring constantly. Serve with hot rice. Serves 4.

HAMBURGER PILAF

6 ounces rice
1 pound minced beef
1 large onion, chopped
1 6-ounce can tomato concentrate
2 teaspoons salt
¼ teaspoon pepper

Cook rice, beef, and onion, stirring with fork, until lightly browned.

Add remaining ingredients and ¾

pint water; stir and bring to boil.

Cover and simmer 35 to 40 minutes, or until rice is tender. Stir gently with a fork once during cooking.

Serves 4 to 6.

HAMBURGER-SPAGHETTI SUPPER

1 16-ounce can tomatoes
½ clove garlic, crushed
1 bay leaf
1 pound minced beef
1 medium onion, chopped
½ medium green pepper, chopped
2 tablespoons flour
1 teaspoon sugar
1 teaspoon salt
⅛ teaspoon pepper
hot cooked spaghetti or noodles

Put tomatoes, garlic, and bay leaf in saucepan; bring to boil, and simmer, uncovered, 10 minutes. Rub through a sieve.

Cook beef, onion, and green pepper in sauté pan, stirring with fork, until beef is browned.

Blend in flour, sugar, and seasonings. Add sieved tomato mixture, and cook until thickened, stirring constantly. Serve on spaghetti or noodles. Serves 4.

BEEF AND LIMA BEANS

1 pound minced beef
1 small onion, chopped
1 clove garlic, crushed
2 stalks celery, sliced
8 ounces or 1 can cooked lima beans
6 fluid ounces bean liquid
1 teaspoon Worcestershire sauce
½ teaspoon chilli powder
salt and pepper to taste
3 ounces shredded sharp Cheddar cheese

Cook beef, onion, garlic, and celery, stirring with fork, until meat loses its red colour.

Add remaining ingredients, except cheese. Bring to boil; cover, and simmer 10 minutes, stirring occasionally. Add cheese. Serves 4.

CREAMED HAMBURG-CABBAGE

¾ pound minced beef
1 small onion, chopped
3 tablespoons fat
1 pound coarsely chopped cabbage
1 ounce flour
1½ teaspoons salt
¼ teaspoon paprika
½ teaspoon celery seed
¾ pint milk

Brown meat and onion in hot fat. Add cabbage. Fry lightly with onion and meat. Add flour and seasonings. Blend into mixture.

Pour milk over all. Cover. Simmer 15 to 20 minutes, or until cabbage is tender. Serves 6.

BEEF WITH SPANISH RICE

2 tablespoons fat
6 ounces rice
2 tablespoons chopped onion
3 tablespoons chopped celery
1 pound minced beef
1 tablespoon salt
1 large can tomatoes
8 fluid ounces bouillon or stock
1 teaspoon soy sauce
1 teaspoon sugar

Brown rice slowly in hot fat in a sauté pan, stirring constantly.

Add onion, celery, and meat, and continue browning.

Add remaining ingredients. Cover and simmer 45 minutes. Serves 4.

BEEF DINNER-IN-A-FRYING PAN

½ pound minced beef
1 slightly beaten egg
4 tablespoons milk
1 ounce fine dry breadcrumbs
1½ tablespoons chopped onion
½ teaspoon salt
¼ teaspoon dry mustard
few grains pepper
1 ounce flour
4 tablespoons salad oil
1 10½-ounce can condensed soup (tomato or mushroom)
6 fluid ounces milk
¾-1 pound cooked vegetables
½ teaspoon salt

Combine first 8 ingredients. Shape into 12 small meat balls, using about 1 tablespoon meat mixture for each. Roll in flour.

Heat salad oil in frying pan over medium heat about 3 minutes. Add meat balls and fry about 10 minutes. When brown, arrange meat balls round the side.

Gradually pour condensed soup and milk which have been mixed together in centre of pan.

Place vegetables over soup; add salt. Cover and simmer about 10 minutes. Serves 4.

Note: 1-2 packets frozen mixed vegetables may be substituted for the cooked vegetables. Allow an additional 15 minutes for cooking.

Beef Dinner-in-a-Frying Pan

Miscellaneous Minced Beef Recipes

CORNISH PASTIES

A pasty is a small pie or turnover of meat wrapped in pastry. Some are baked; others are fried. The most famous is the Cornish pasty; its filling is beef, potatoes, onions, and sometimes carrots.

Pastry:
12 ounces plain flour
1 teaspoon salt
8 ounces fat
about 4 fluid ounces water
Filling:
1 pound minced beef
1 tablespoon fat
6 ounces cubed potatoes
4 ounces cubed carrots
1 small onion, chopped
1½ teaspoons salt

Prepare pastry from flour, salt, fat, and water. Roll out into 6-inch circles.

Brown meat in hot fat in a heavy frying pan. Add potatoes, carrots, onion, and salt. Cook 5 minutes.

Place equal portions of filling on half of each pastry circle. Moisten edges with water. Fold over half of circle and seal with a fork. Place on baking sheet.

Bake in very hot oven (450°F. Mark 8) 15 minutes. Reduce heat to moderate (350°F. Mark 4) and bake 30 minutes longer.

Serve hot with ketchup, hot gravy, or mushroom sauce. Makes 6 pasties.

STUFFED HAMBURGER PIE

1 pound minced beef
1 teaspoon salt
4 tablespoons milk
6 ounces soft bread cubes
2 ounces grated raw carrot
1-2 stalks celery, chopped
1 tablespoon finely chopped onion
1 teaspoon salt
½ teaspoon mixed herbs

Mix meat, salt, and milk. Make a stuffing of remaining ingredients.

Place half of meat mixture in an 8-inch pie plate. Place stuffing on top of meat. Top with remaining meat, packing firmly.

Twin Beef Turnovers

Bake in a hot oven (400°F. Mark 6) for 25 minutes. Serves 4.
Note: Vegetables will be crisp. If a softer texture is desired, precook carrots and celery 5 minutes before adding to stuffing.

MINCED BEEF PARTY CASSEROLE

1 pound minced beef
1 tablespoon butter or margarine
2 8-ounce cans tomato sauce
8 ounces noodles
8 ounces cottage cheese
8 ounces cream cheese
4 tablespoons thick sour cream
3-4 chopped spring onions
1 tablespoon chopped green pepper
2 tablespoons melted butter or margarine

Brown meat in 1 tablespoon butter in heavy frying pan. Stir in tomato sauce. Remove from heat.

Cook noodles in boiling salted water 10 minutes. Drain.

Combine cottage cheese, cream cheese, sour cream, onions, and green pepper.

Spread half the noodles in a buttered 3-3½-pint casserole. Cover with cheese mixture, then cover with remaining noodles. Pour the melted butter over noodles. Pat the beef-tomato sauce mixture over top. Bake in moderate oven (350°F. Mark 4) 20 to 30 minutes. Serves 6.

TWIN BEEF TURNOVERS

2 ounces butter or margarine
½ small onion, chopped
½ small green pepper, chopped
1 pound minced beef
1 packet (8 ounces) frozen peas
2 ounces shredded carrot
1 teaspoon salt
¼ teaspoon pepper
1½ ounces flour
pastry made with 10 ounces flour

Melt butter or margarine in a frying pan; add onion, green pepper, and beef; brown lightly.

Add peas and carrots and sprinkle with salt, pepper, and flour. Stir well.

Prepare pastry dough and divide in half. Roll each into a 12-inch circle on floured pastry board. Remove to baking sheet.

Pile filling on half of each circle. Moisten edges of dough with water. Fold pastry over filling like a giant turnover and press edges together to seal. Cut open design for escape of steam.

Bake in very hot oven (450°F. Mark 8) 15 minutes. Reduce heat to moderate (375°F. Mark 5) and continue baking for 20 minutes. Serves 6.

HAMBURGER-VEGETABLE PIE

1 pound minced beef
1 teaspoon onion salt
salt and pepper
2 teaspoons prepared mustard
2 teaspoons Worcestershire sauce
2 tablespoons fat
8 fluid ounces beef stock
1 8-ounce can tomato sauce
1 packet (8 ounces) frozen peas
1 small jar cocktail onions

Combine meat, onion salt, salt, pepper, mustard, and Worcestershire sauce; form into 8 patties; brown in fat.

Remove patties; add gravy and tomato sauce to pan; heat.

Arrange patties, peas, and onions in casserole. Add stock.

Make scone topping. See page 573, and arrange scones on top.

Bake in very hot oven (450°F. Mark 8) 20 minutes. Serves 4.

MINCED BEEF AND MACARONI (Italian Style)

¾ pound macaroni or spaghetti
1 can (6 ounces) tomato paste
12 fluid ounces water
¼ teaspoon bicarbonate of soda
½ pound bacon, cut in small pieces
1 pound minced beef
½ pound sliced fresh mushrooms
½ green pepper, finely sliced
1 small onion, chopped
1½ teaspoons salt
⅛ teaspoon oregano
1 medium clove garlic, crushed fine
¼ ounce chopped parsley
3 ounces grated Parmesan cheese

Cook macaroni in boiling salted water until tender; rinse with cold water.

Combine tomato paste, water, and bicarbonate of soda.

Fry bacon in a saucepan until almost cooked, then add minced beef, stirring constantly, about 5 minutes.

In another saucepan, fry mushrooms and green pepper in 2 tablespoons butter about 5 minutes. Add all vegetables, seasonings, and half of tomato mixture to meat. Cover pan and cook about 7 minutes.

Place half of the cooked macaroni in well greased casserole (8×12×1½ inches). Sprinkle with half the Parmesan cheese. Cover with all of the meat and vegetable mixture. Then cover with remaining macaroni mixture. Sprinkle with remaining Parmesan cheese. Finally, top with remaining half of tomato mixture. Cover casserole tightly. Bake in moderate oven (375°F. Mark 5) 30 minutes. Serves 8.

HAMBURGER PIE WITH GREEN BEANS

1 pound minced beef
1 large onion, chopped
1 tablespoon fat
1 10½-ounce can condensed cream of tomato soup
1½ teaspoons salt
8 ounces cooked green beans
1 egg
2 tablespoons butter or margarine
1¼ pounds mashed potatoes

Cook meat and onion in melted fat in heavy frying pan. Stir and cook until they are browned.

Mix in soup, 1 teaspoon salt, and green beans. Place in a 2½-3-pint casserole.

Mix egg, butter, and ½ teaspoon salt with mashed potatoes. Place potatoes on top of meat-and-bean mixture in casserole. Bake in moderate oven (350°F. Mark 4) 30 minutes. Serves 4 to 6.

HAMBURGER SWEET POTATO PIE

2 ounces cornflakes
1½ ounces soft breadcrumbs
1 ounce butter or margarine
¾ pound minced beef
1 egg
1 teaspoon salt
⅛ teaspoon pepper
⅛ teaspoon thyme
⅛ teaspoon sage
1 bay leaf, crumbled
1 small onion, chopped
1-1½ pounds hot, seasoned mashed sweet potato
paprika

Crumble cornflakes with crumbs, and spread on bottom and sides of greased, deep 8-inch pie dish. Dot with butter, and put in oven until butter melts.

Mix beef, egg, seasonings, and onion; spread in crumbed dish, and bake in moderate oven (350°F. Mark 4) 10 minutes.

Whip potatoes until light. Arrange around edge of pie dish; sprinkle with paprika. Return to oven 10 minutes, or until lightly browned. Serves 4.

CHILLI MINCE

4 pounds coarsely minced beef
1 large onion, chopped
2 cloves garlic, crushed
1 teaspoon ground oregano
1 teaspoon cummin seed
6 teaspoons chilli powder (more if needed)
1 can whole tomatoes
few drops Tabasco sauce
salt to taste
¾ pint hot water

Place meat, onion, and garlic in large heavy frying pan. Cook until light-coloured.

Add oregano, cummin seed, chilli powder, tomatoes, Tabasco, salt, and hot water. Bring to the boil, lower heat, and simmer about 1 hour. Skim off fat during cooking. Serves 8 to 10.

MINCED BEEF PARTY CASSEROLE

1 pound minced beef
1 large onion, chopped
1 pound tomatoes, cooked or 1 can
1 teaspoon chilli powder or curry powder, or 1 tablespoon Worcestershire sauce
2 teaspoons salt
2 potatoes, sliced thinly
1½ ounces flour
2 small cans drained whole kernel corn
2 small cans lima beans
1 small green pepper, sliced
6 ounces shredded cheese or buttered crumbs

Combine beef, onions, tomatoes, chilli powder, and salt. Pat into 1-inch layer in 4½-pint casserole.

Over this place layers of potatoes, flour, corn, lima beans, and green pepper. Top with cheese or crumbs.

Bake in moderate oven (350°F. Mark 4) 1 hour. Serves 8 to 10.

SCALLOPED BEEF AND EGG-PLANT or AUBERGINE

1½ pounds minced chuck beef
1 teaspoon onion salt
¼ teaspoon pepper
2 tablespoons salad oil
1 medium eggplant
1½ ounces flour
½ teaspoon salt
⅛ teaspoon pepper
4 tablespoons salad oil
2 8-ounce cans tomato sauce
4 ounces grated sharp Cheddar cheese
¼ teaspoon oregano

Mix minced beef, onion salt, and ¼ teaspoon pepper; lightly form into 8 patties. Sauté patties in 2 tablespoons hot salad oil until brown on both sides but rare inside. Remove from pan.

Cut washed eggplant into 8 ½-inch thick slices. Sprinkle with mixture of flour, salt, and ⅛ teaspoon pepper. Sauté in 4 tablespoons hot salad oil until golden on both sides.

Arrange half the eggplant slices with half of the patties in greased casserole (12×8×2-inches). Spread with half the tomato sauce. Sprinkle with half of cheese and oregano. Repeat layers.

Bake uncovered in moderate oven (350°F. Mark 4) until cheese is bubbly, about 30 minutes. Serves 4.

MINCED BEEF À LA GRUCCI

1 green pepper, chopped finely
1 pound minced beef
2 tablespoons olive oil
½ pound sharp cheese, grated
1 small onion, grated
1 clove garlic, crushed
2 ounces sliced stuffed olives
2 ounces sliced black olives
4 tablespoons olive liquid
¼ pound noodles, cooked
1 can whole kernel corn
1 can (16 ounces) tomatoes
½ teaspoon salt
¼ teaspoon pepper

Blend green pepper with meat and brown in olive oil. Add remaining ingredients and blend thoroughly. Pour into greased casserole. Bake in moderate oven (350°F. Mark 4) 45 to 60 minutes. Serves 8.

CREOLE MEAT SCONES

Meat Sauce:

½ pound minced beef
2 tablespoons chopped onion
3-4 stalks celery, finely chopped
1 ounce fat
1 ounce flour
8 fluid ounces boiling water
½ teaspoon chilli powder
1 teaspoon salt
½ teaspoon Worcestershire sauce
1 pound cooked tomatoes
1 tablespoon chopped green pepper

Scones:

Scone Topping (see page 573)

Brown the meat, onion, and celery in fat. Stir in flour. Add water to make a sauce. Add seasonings, tomatoes, and green pepper. Cook slowly 1 hour.

Make up scone topping. Roll or pat to ½-inch thickness. Cut 6 scones with 3-inch cutter.

Place on baking sheet and bake in a very hot oven (450°F. Mark 8) 15 minutes.

Serve hot with meat sauce, between and over top of each split scone. Serves 6.

CREAMED HAMBURGER AND EGGS

½ pound minced beef
1 10½-ounce can condensed cream of celery soup
8 fluid ounces milk
4 hard-boiled eggs, sliced
4 slices hot buttered toast

Stir and cook meat until red colour disappears. Stir in celery soup and milk. Heat.

Stir in sliced eggs carefully. Serve hot on hot toast or in pastry cases. Serves 4.

Miscellaneous Minced Meat — Pork, Ham, Lamb, and Veal

GRILLED LAMB PATTIES

Use minced lamb shoulder or breast, allowing ¼ pound per person.

Season with salt and pepper; shape into patties 1-inch thick and 3-inches in diameter.

If desired, wrap a rasher of streaky bacon round each patty; fasten with cocktail stick.

Grill, turning when ½ total cooking time is completed.

For medium patties, allow 18 minutes; for well done, allow 20 to 24 minutes.

Pan-Grilled Lamb Patties: Prepare patties as above. Rub heavy frying pan with small amount of fat or salad oil. Brown patties on both sides.

Cook slowly, turning frequently, about 10 to 12 minutes, or until done, pouring off any fat which accumulates.

SAVOY CABBAGE, STUFFED WHOLE

1 Savoy cabbage
1 pound minced veal
¾ pound minced cooked ham
1 medium onion, chopped
1 garlic clove, crushed
1½ teaspoons salt
few grains pepper
1 teaspoon Aromat
2 chicken bouillon cubes
8 fluid ounces boiling water
1 bay leaf, crumbled
¼ teaspoon thyme

Hold cabbage under running hot water and gently separate leaves without removing them, being careful not to tear them. Drain thoroughly.

Combine minced meats, onion, garlic, salt, pepper, and Aromat. Stuff meat mixture between cabbage leaves. Tie firmly with string.

Place cabbage in deep saucepan slightly larger than the cabbage in diameter.

Dissolve bouillon cubes in the boiling water. Pour over cabbage; add bay leaf and thyme.

Cover saucepan tightly. Simmer 1½ hours or until tender. Remove string. Serves 6.

Savoy Cabbage, Stuffed Whole

Lamb Patties

TOURTIERE (CANADIAN PORK PIE)

1 teaspoon salt
¼ teaspoon pepper
¼ teaspoon nutmeg
1 clove garlic, whole
⅛ teaspoon mace
few grains cayenne pepper
   (optional)
½ tablespoon cornflour
8 fluid ounces water
1 pound minced lean pork
   (shoulder or leg)
6 ounces pastry

Add seasonings, cornflour, and water to pork, and simmer covered in a saucepan 30 minutes.

Uncover and cook 10 minutes more. Remove garlic.

Pour mixture into pastry-lined 8-inch pie plate. Cover with pastry lid which has been pricked in several places to allow steam to escape during baking. Fold upper crust over bottom crust at edge and press together firmly.

Bake in hot oven (425°F. Mark 7) about 10 minutes. Then reduce heat to moderate (350°F. Mark 4) and continue baking 30 minutes more. Serve hot. Makes 1 8-inch pie or 6 servings.

Here are two famous Mexican dishes, so easy to prepare. Empanadas: light pastry surrounding a chilli, pork, and tomato filling which is also served as a sauce. For dessert, try a Mexican Flan: banana flavoured caramel custard garnished with mandarin orange sections, rich but so good.

PORK EMPANADAS

Empanadas are turnovers made with a pie crust (often spicy) and with a vast variety of fillings, either sweet or spicy. Mince makes a very desirable filling. They may be baked or fried, served hot or cold, and served as an appetizer, main dish, or dessert. If served as an hors d'oeuvre, they should be made very small. The version given below should be served hot as a main dish.

8 ounces plain flour
1 teaspoon salt
6 ounces fat
4 to 5 tablespoons iced water
2 medium onions, chopped
1 ounce butter or margarine
1½ pounds minced pork
1 6-ounce can tomato paste
1 ounce chopped pimiento
1 ounce chopped stoned olives
2 hard-boiled eggs, chopped
3 to 4 tablespoons tomato ketchup
3 tablespoons chilli powder
1 teaspoon salt
⅛ teaspoon ground black pepper
¼ teaspoon ground cumin
about ½ pint chicken stock

Sift flour and salt. Rub in the fat until mixture resembles breadcrumbs. Add water. Toss lightly until dough forms a ball. Chill until ready to use.

In a frying pan sauté onion in butter or margarine, add pork and sauté until cooked. Drain off excess fat. Add tomato paste, pimiento, olives, hard-boiled eggs, ketchup, chilli powder, salt, pepper, and cummin. Mix well.

Roll dough out on a floured board to 1/10-inch thickness. Cut into circles about 5 inches in diameter. Makes 12.

Place 1 tablespoon of pork mixture on one half of the dough. Brush edges with water. Fold over and seal edges.

Place on an ungreased baking sheet. Bake in hot oven (425°F. Mark 7) 15 to 20 minutes or until golden brown. Add chicken stock to remaining meat mixture to make a sauce consistency. Pour over empanadas.

Veal and Ham Loaf

VEAL AND HAM LOAF

2 pounds veal shoulder, minced
½ pound ham, minced
3 tablespoons chopped parsley
2 tablespoons grated onion
4½ ounces soft breadcrumbs
4 fluid ounces evaporated milk
1 unbeaten egg
1 teaspoon salt
⅛ teaspoon pepper
1½ teaspoons Aromat
¼ teaspoon Tabasco sauce
canned pineapple slices
1½ ounces brown sugar

Combine veal, ham, parsley, onion, crumbs, evaporated milk, egg, and seasonings; mix well.

Arrange pineapple slices in a design in bottom of greased loaf tin (9×5×3 inches). Sprinkle with brown sugar.

Pack meat mixture in loaf tin. Cover with aluminium foil.

Bake in moderate oven (350°F. Mark 4) ½ hour; remove foil. Continue baking 1 hour longer. Serves 8.

STUFFED CABBAGE ROLLS

¾ pound minced beef
½ pound minced pork
1½ teaspoons salt
½ teaspoon pepper
1 small raw onion, grated
4 ounces raw rice
1 head cabbage

Combine all ingredients except cabbage. Remove core from cabbage and place in boiling water for a few minutes to wilt leaves.

Shape meat and rice mixture into loose rolls and wrap each meat roll in a cabbage leaf. Fasten with a wooden cocktail stick. Place in baking tin.

Cover with water. Cover and cook in moderate oven (350°F. Mark 4) for 1½ hours, or until rice is done. Serves 6.

Stuffed Cabbage Rolls

HAM-PINEAPPLE LOAF

1 pound minced ham
½ pound minced pork
6 fluid ounces milk
2 ounces breadcrumbs
pepper
1 can pineapple pie filling
3 ounces seedless raisins
2 tablespoons prepared mustard
½ teaspoon horseradish

Combine ham, pork, milk, breadcrumbs, and pepper. Pat out to a 15×10 inch rectangle on waxed paper.

Combine pie filling, raisins, mustard, and horseradish; spoon half the mixture down centre of meat rectangle. Spread to cover meat but do not bring to the edges. Lifting waxed paper, roll Swiss roll fashion starting at the short end. Pat ends to seal.

Wrap loaf in waxed paper and refrigerate about 2 hours. Place in a 7×11×2-inch fireproof baking dish. Bake in moderate oven (350°F. Mark 4) 1 hour; spoon remaining pineapple sauce over loaf and bake 15 to 20 minutes longer. Serves 6 to 8.

Ham-Pineapple Loaf

INDIVIDUAL HAM LOAVES

¾ pound smoked ham, minced
    finely
¾ pound lean pork, minced finely
½ teaspoon salt
dash of pepper
3 tablespoons finely chopped onion
1½ ounces fine breadcrumbs
1 egg, beaten
6 fluid ounces milk

Combine ingredients and mix well. Pack lightly in large deep bun tins.

Bake in moderate oven (350°F. Mark 4) 45 minutes. Serve with horseradish sauce or mustard sauce.

The mixture may be baked in a loaf tin, 9½×5¼×2¾ inches, if desired. Serves 6 to 8.

ORANGE UPSIDE-DOWN HAM LOAVES

6 tablespoons brown sugar
½ teaspoon dry mustard
6 thin unpeeled orange slices
1 pound minced, cooked ham
1 pound pork-sausage meat
1 small onion, finely chopped

1½ ounces fresh breadcrumbs
1 egg
4 fluid ounces orange juice
½ teaspoon paprika
½ teaspoon Worcestershire sauce
½ teaspoon dry mustard
pinch of ground cloves

In each of 6 individual casseroles (about 3½ inches in diameter) place 1 tablespoon brown sugar; sprinkle with a little of the mustard; top with orange slice.

Combine ham and remaining ingredients; pack lightly into the casseroles.

Bake in moderate oven (350°F. Mark 4) 45 minutes; let stand 5 minutes. Drain; then invert onto serving plate. Serves 6.

Note: This may also be baked in 9×5×3-inch loaf tin, 1¼ hours, using 3 or 4 orange slices.

BEEF AND PORK PARTY LOAF

1½ pounds minced beef
½ pound minced pork
½ small onion, finely chopped
2 teaspoons salt
¼ teaspoon pepper
¼ teaspoon sage
¼ teaspoon mixed herbs
1 tablespoon Worcestershire sauce
2 eggs
8 fluid ounces tomato juice
4 slices bread

Combine meat with onions and seasonings.

Beat eggs and add to tomato juice. Cube bread and soak in liquid mixture. Beat well. Add to meat and mix lightly.

Pack into a 5×9-inch meat loaf tin and bake in moderate oven (350°F. Mark 4) 1¼ hours.

Let loaf stand 10 minutes, then drain off liquid and turn out of pan. Spread with ketchup or hot tomato sauce. Serves 6 to 8.

Variation: If desired, the loaf may be spread with 3-4 tablespoons tomato ketchup before baking. This adds moisture and interesting flavour.

Beef and Pork Party Loaf

PINEAPPLE UPSIDE-DOWN HAM LOAF

Topping:
1 tablespoon butter or margarine
2 tablespoons molasses or treacle
1 tablespoon sugar
3 slices pineapple
3 maraschino cherries

Ham Loaf:
1 pound cooked, minced ham
1 pound uncooked, minced pork
2 ounces crushed cornflakes
½ teaspoon salt
¼ teaspoon pepper
1 teaspoon dry mustard
2 beaten eggs
4 tablespoons milk

Melt butter or margarine in 4×9×3-inch loaf tin, measured across bottom. Stir in molasses and sugar; spread uniformly over bottom of tin.

Arrange pineapple and cherries over molasses-butter mixture.

Mix all ingredients for ham loaf in order given.

Spread mixture in tin over pineapple; press down. Bake in moderate oven (350°F. Mark 4) 1 hour.

Turn out on hot dish with pineapple and cherries on top. Makes 16 slices, ½-inch thick.

KEBI (Syrian National Dish)

1 pound minced lamb
1 pound fine Bulgar wheat (cracked wheat)
3 onions, chopped
1 pound cooked meat, chopped
4 ounces pine nuts (pignolia) or walnuts

Mix together the lamb and Bulgar wheat and knead thoroughly, adding a small amount of water.

Sear onions in a little hot fat; combine with cooked meat and pine nuts. Season with salt and pepper.

Place a layer of half the lamb mixture in a baking dish. Add a layer of the second mixture (cooked meat). Cover with a layer of the first mixture (lamb).

Cut into diamond-shaped pieces and lightly cover with butter or olive oil. Bake in moderate oven (350°F. Mark 4) 1 hour. Serves 8.

Note: Bulgar (cracked wheat) can be bought in Armenian, Syrian, and Greek stores and in Health Food Shops.

LEMON PORK LOAF

2 pounds minced pork
½ pound breadcrumbs
1 beaten egg
2 teaspoons salt

grated rind of 3 lemons
6 rashers bacon
8 fluid ounces sour cream or 2-3 chopped tomatoes
paprika

Combine minced pork, breadcrumbs, egg, seasonings, and grated lemon rind; shape into loaf.

Place in baking dish and add water to cover bottom of dish. Cover with bacon.

Bake covered in moderate oven (350°F. Mark 4) 1 hour. Remove cover and pour over sour cream or tomatoes. Sprinkle with paprika. Bake 30 minutes longer. Serves 8 to 10.

LAMB AND BACON WHIRLS

½ pound rashers of bacon
1½ pounds minced lamb shoulder
1 teaspoon salt
⅛ teaspoon pepper
¼ teaspoon marjoram
1 tablespoon Worcestershire sauce
2 ounces crushed cornflakes
3 tablespoons water

Place bacon on waxed paper on a chopping board so that the lean edge overlaps the preceding strip about 1 inch.

Combine remaining ingredients and mix well. Spread out in an even layer over the bacon.

Roll up like a Swiss roll and fasten with skewers.

Slice in serving-size rounds, and grill or fry, allowing about 8 to 10 minutes on each side. Serves 8.

STUFFED CABBAGE CASSEROLE

1 small cabbage
1 medium onion, minced
1 ounce butter or margarine
1 pound lamb shoulder, minced
1 pound cooked rice
1 teaspoon salt
few grains pepper
1 teaspoon Aromat
½ teaspoon paprika
4 fluid ounces tomato ketchup
1 tablespoon lemon juice
1 teaspoon sugar
1 teaspoon dried mint leaves

Cook cabbage in boiling salted water to cover 15 minutes. Cool. Strip off leaves.

Cook onion in butter or margarine until soft but not brown; combine with remaining ingredients.

Line shallow baking dish with large cabbage leaves.

Make 6 "cups" of smaller cabbage leaves; fill cups with meat mixture. Cover with remaining large leaves.

Bake in moderate oven (350°F. Mark 4) 1 hour. Serve with a tomato sauce. Serves 6.

Lamb and Bacon Whirls

CURRIED LAMB PATTIES

1½ pounds minced lean lamb
1 large onion, finely chopped
2 tablespoons quick-cooking tapioca
12 fluid ounces milk
2 teaspoons salt
¼ teaspoon pepper
1 teaspoon Aromat
1 teaspoon curry powder

Place all ingredients in bowl; blend lightly but thoroughly.

Form into small patties. Roll in flour and brown well in hot oil or fat.

Pour off excess fat; add enough hot water to cover meat. Cover and cook over low heat until meat is tender, about 30 minutes.

As the gravy reduces, add a few spoons hot water. Thicken gravy. Turn meat and gravy out on hot dish; surround with a border of hot buttered rice or noodles. Serves 6.

Stuffed Cabbage Casserole

CHOPPED LAMB PILAF (Armenian)

1 pound chopped or minced shoulder of lamb
1 onion, chopped
1 can tomatoes
2 teaspoons allspice
½ teaspoon cinnamon
1 teaspoon marjoram
salt to taste
4 fluid ounces sherry
8 ounces quick-cooking rice
2 tablespoons butter or olive oil

Sauté lamb in a large sauté pan until lightly browned, pouring off excess fat.

Add onion and cook slowly for 5 minutes. Then stir in chopped tomatoes and juice and cook for about 15 minutes. Add seasonings and wine.

Cook raw rice in butter or olive oil until rice turns light golden colour.

Form a hollow in centre of lamb mixture; fill with rice. Liquid should cover both meat and rice, so add water, if necessary, to supplement tomatoes. Bring to the boil, cover, and cook slowly for about 15 minutes.

Turn heat off and, with cover still on pan, let rice steam until fluffy for about 10 minutes longer.

To serve, fill warm casserole dish and garnish with chopped fresh parsley, spring onions, and tomatoes. Serves 4.

LAMB LOAF

2 pounds minced lamb
2 teaspoons salt
¼ teaspoon black pepper
½ clove garlic, crushed (optional)
2 tablespoons finely chopped onion
1 green pepper, finely chopped
2 tablespoons chopped parsley
1 beaten egg
8 fluid ounces milk
4 ounces crumbs

Mix ingredients thoroughly. Pack into greased loaf tin or ring mould.

Bake in slow oven (325°F. Mark 3) 1 hour and 20 minutes. If desired, serve with an olive sauce. Serves 8.

Olive Sauce: Blend 2 ounces butter and 1 ounce flour. Add ¾ pint milk gradually and stir over moderate heat until thickened.

Add 3-4 tablespoons sliced or chopped stuffed olives and salt and pepper to taste.

SWEDISH HAM BALLS IN SWEET-SOUR SAUCE

1½ pounds fresh boneless pork, minced
1 pound minced cooked ham
6 ounces breadcrumbs
2 well-beaten eggs
8 fluid ounces milk
salt and Aromat

Combine pork, ham, crumbs, beaten eggs, milk, and seasonings; mix well. Form into small round balls about the size of a walnut. Place in shallow 9-inch baking dish.

Bake in moderate oven (350°F. Mark 4), basting frequently with sweet-sour sauce (below) until meat is tender, about 50 minutes.

Sweet-Sour Sauce:
6 ounces brown sugar
1 teaspoon dry mustard
4 fluid ounces vinegar
4 fluid ounces hot water
1½ ounces sultanas

Combine ingredients, stirring to dissolve sugar. Pour over ham balls after they have begun to cook, about 10 minutes after placing in oven.

VEAL LOAF

2 pounds minced veal
½ pound minced pork
¼ pound chopped suet
½ pound sliced mushrooms
1 ounce butter
2 teaspoons salt
½ teaspoon pepper
1 teaspoon marjoram
1 teaspoon chopped parsley
2 beaten eggs
1 10½-ounce can tomato soup, undiluted

Mix veal and pork together. Cook mushrooms in butter for 5 minutes. Add to meat with suet, seasonings, herbs, eggs, and soup. Shape into loaf,

Bake in moderate oven (350°F. Mark 4) for 1 hour. Bacon may be placed on top of loaf before baking. Serves 10.

BITOCHKY SMETANA (Russian Meat Balls)

1½ pounds minced veal
4 medium-sized potatoes, cooked and chopped
1½ small onions, grated
1½ teaspoons salt
⅛ teaspoon pepper
1 egg, beaten
2 ounces butter or margarine
½ pint sour cream

Mix together veal, potatoes, onions, seasonings, and egg. Shape in round balls and fry in butter until well browned.

Add half the sour cream and simmer, covered, 15 minutes.

Just before serving, add remaining cream and bring to the boil. Makes 12 balls (6 servings).

LAMB PATTIES WITH BURGUNDY

1 onion, finely chopped
6 ounces dry breadcrumbs
6 fluid ounces burgundy
1 well-beaten egg
1 pound minced lamb
1½ teaspoons salt
¼ teaspoon pepper

Mix onion and breadcrumbs together; add wine and egg. Mix well. Combine with meat and seasonings.

Shape into 8 small patties or loaves. Pan-fry slowly in hot fat. Serves 4.

BAKED PORK LOAF WITH MUSHROOM GRAVY

2 pounds fresh, lean shoulder of pork
½ pound cooked ham
6 ounces cornflakes, crushed
2 eggs, beaten
1 (11-ounce) can condensed tomato soup
1 teaspoon salt
few grains pepper
1 teaspoon Aromat
1 (11-ounce) can condensed mushroom soup
4 fluid ounces water

Mince the pork and ham together. Place meat in bowl; add cornflakes, eggs, tomato soup, salt, pepper, and Aromat. Mix lightly but thoroughly.

Pack into loaf tin. Bake in moderate oven (375°F. Mark 5) about 1½ hours. Pour off fat after loaf is baked.

Heat mushroom soup and water together to make gravy. Serves 6.

ORIENTAL LAMBURGERS

2 pounds minced shoulder of lamb
1 clove garlic, crushed
1½ teaspoons salt
1 teaspoon pepper
3 tablespoons shelled pine nuts or chopped walnuts
½ ounce chopped parsley
1 egg
8 rashers bacon

Mix the lamb with garlic, salt, pepper, nuts, and parsley. Add egg, slightly beaten, and mix well. Form into round patties.

Wrap a rasher of bacon round each patty and secure with a small skewer.

Grill slowly and turn so that lamb is browned on both sides and cooked through but with a tinge of pink in the middle.

Serve lamburgers with English mustard or with your favourite barbecue sauce. Makes 8 patties.

SAVOURY HAM AND PORK BALLS

1 pound minced ham
¾ pound minced pork
1 beaten egg
4 tablespoons milk
⅛ teaspoon pepper

Mix all ingredients and shape into 2½-inch balls. Brown slowly in a shallow pan with a small amount of fat.

Add enough water to just cover the bottom of the pan. Cover tightly and simmer gently for 45 minutes. Serve with chilli sauce. Makes 8 balls.

Pork Recipes

HINTS FOR COOKING PORK

Some cuts of pork are in demand as fresh pork, while others are in greatest demand when smoked, as ham. Many pork cuts are sold both fresh and smoked.

All cuts of pork are tender, therefore all large or chunky cuts, both fresh and smoked, may be cooked by roasting. Roasting of cured (smoked) cuts is usually referred to as "baking". Roasting and baking, however, so far as meat is concerned, are synonymous.

Fresh pork is usually roasted at 350°F. Mark 4, and ham at 300°F. Mark 2, or 325°F. Mark 3. Slow cooking helps retain much of the flavour of pork. The use of a meat thermometer is desirable. Specific times are given in each recipe. Pork should always be well cooked. The cooked lean of fresh pork should be greyish white without even a tinge of pink.

ROAST PORK
(Master Recipe)

If loin is selected, get butcher to separate backbone from ribs i.e. chived —to make carving easy.

Season with salt and pepper. If desired, rub with cut clove of garlic and dredge with flour.

Place in shallow pan, fat side up. Roast in preheated moderate oven (350°F. Mark 4).

For centre loin cut weighing 4 to 5 pounds, allow 35 to 40 minutes per pound.

For end cuts weighing 4 to 5 pounds, allow 45 to 50 minutes per pound.

Do not cover. Do not add water.

If meat thermometer is used, insert so that bulb is in centre of the thickest part.

Roast until well done or thermometer registers 185°F.

Loin may be boned, stuffed, rolled, and cooked in same manner. With boned and rolled pork joints, add 10 to 15 minutes per pound to cooking time.

CROWN ROAST OF PORK

Ask butcher to prepare crown of 10 or 12 ribs. Season with salt and pepper. Tie strips of salt pork or bacon round end of each rib to keep bones from charring, or cover with foil.

Put in roasting tin bone-ends-up. Fill centre with favourite stuffing.

Roast in moderate oven (350°F. Mark 4), allowing 30 to 35 minutes per pound.

To serve, place paper frills over bone

Crown Roast of Pork

ends. If stuffing isn't used, do not cover bones and cook roast upside down.

Fill centre with vegetables when serving. Serves 10 to 12.

ROLLED SHOULDER OF PORK

Buy the shoulder boned and rolled. Prepare meat as suggested under Roast Pork. Place on rack in shallow tin. Put the removed bones in the tin.

Roast in moderate oven (350°F. Mark 4), allowing 45 minutes per pound. Turn every 30 minutes. Prepare gravy from fat left in the tin.

BAKED STUFFED FILLET ROLL

But 2 fillets split and flattened. Season with salt and pepper.

Spread bread, mushroom, or potato stuffing over one. Lay the other on top. Roll and tie securely.

Sprinkle outside with salt and pepper. Put 4 or 5 rashers of bacon over top.

Place on rack in open roasting tin. Roast in slow-to-moderate oven (325°F. or 350°F. Mark 3-4) until tender, 1 to 1½ hours.

ROAST LEG OF PORK

A leg of pork is prepared like loin of pork.

Roast it on rack in uncovered tin in slow oven (325°F. Mark 3) 35 to 40 minutes per pound for whole ham, 45 to 50 minutes per pound for half leg of pork.

Leg of Pork with Mexican Corn Stuffing

PORK COOKING CHART

Cut	Method of Cooking
LOIN The best and most expensive cut	Roasted whole or boned and stuffed or divided into chops for grilling or frying. Chump chops also suitable for pot-roasting or casseroling.
LEG	Roasted whole or boned and stuffed. Strips from the top can be used in pies or sautéed.
SPARE RIB Taken from the top of the neck	Roasted or divided for stewing or can be grilled or barbecued.
FILLET One of the best cuts lying under the loin	Can be split, stuffed and roasted or cut into pieces for frying or grilling.
HAND AND SPRING This is the foreleg	Can be boned or cut into small joints for roasting, pot roasting or boiling.
BLADEBONE Cut from the top of the foreleg	Roasted.
BELLY	Generally salted and boiled or can be cut in slices and fried or grilled.
TROTTERS	Used for stews and brawn.
HEAD	Boiled for brawn.

Roast Hand of Pork with Almond-Rice Stuffing

LEG OF PORK WITH MEXICAN CORN STUFFING

Order an 8- to 12-pound leg of pork, boned and scored. Sprinkle inside cavity of leg generously with Aromat; let stand 30 minutes.

Fill cavity with Mexican Corn Stuffing (below). Truss to hold shape during roasting.

Place in open roasting tin. Bake in moderate oven (350°F. Mark 4), allowing 35 to 40 minutes per pound or until meat reaches an internal temperature of 185°F.

Mexican Corn Stuffing:
6 rashers bacon, chopped
3 tablespoons bacon fat
3-4 stalks celery, chopped
1 large onion, chopped
3 ounces soft breadcrumbs
2 cans (10½ ounces) Mexican corn, drained
½ teaspoon powdered sage
1 teaspoon salt
½ teaspoon pepper
1½ teaspoons Aromat

Fry bacon until crisp; drain on absorbent paper.

Measure fat into frying pan. Cook celery and onions in hot fat until tender. Add breadcrumbs; toss lightly over high heat until golden.

Add remaining ingredients; mix well; remove from heat.

Fill cavity; bake as directed above. Garnish with poached oranges (see index). Serves 10 to 12 generously.

ROAST HAND OF PORK WITH ALMOND-RICE STUFFING

1 medium onion, chopped finely
3 ounces butter or margarine
1 teaspoon salt
few grains pepper
¼ teaspoon Aromat
1 teaspoon mixed herbs
1½ pounds cooked rice
1½ ounces browned chopped almonds
1 boned hand of pork

Cook onion in butter until soft. Add seasonings, rice, almonds. Mix well and stuff meat. Secure with a skewer.

Place on rack in roasting tin. Bake in moderate oven (350°F. Mark 4), calculating 40 minutes per pound of weight before stuffing. Serves 6 to 8.

Gravy: Pour off all but 4 tablespoons of fat from tin, leaving brown sediment.

Put the tin over low heat; stir in 1 ounce flour, ¼ teaspoon Aromat, 1 teaspoon salt, few grains pepper.

Slowly add 1 pint water, blending after each addition. Cook and stir until gravy is smooth and thickened. Add more salt and pepper if necessary. Makes about 1 pint gravy.

BOILED PIGS' TROTTERS

Wash, scrape, and rinse pigs' trotters. Put in a large pot with ½ sliced onion, 1 bay leaf, and ½ teaspoon salt.

Cover with cold water. Bring to boiling point and simmer 4 to 6 hours. Store in stock until used.

Serve cold or hot with vinegar. Use one per serving. Serve with sauerkraut and mashed potatoes.

Grilled Pigs' Trotters: Boil as above and drain. Sprinkle with salt and pepper.

Place on greased grill and grill 5 minutes on each side. Serve with vinegar, lemon juice, or Maître d'Hôtel butter.

Fried Pigs' Trotters: Boil as above and drain. Dip in a batter of flour, salt, and water. Fry in deep fat (385°F.) until brown. Serve with Maître d'Hôtel butter.

Pickled Pigs' Trotters: Boil as above and drain. Pour hot vinegar over the trotters and leave in the liquid for several days. Serve cold.

STEWED PORK HOCKS

Cover pork hocks with seasoned boiling water. Cover and simmer until tender, 1½ to 3 hours.

To cook vegetables with the hocks, add potatoes for the last ½ hour of cooking or cabbage or greens for the last 15 minutes of cooking.

JELLIED PIGS' TROTTERS

6 pigs' trotters, split into halves
1 cut clove of garlic
1 large onion, sliced
1 lemon, sliced
2 bay leaves
6 whole cloves
4 whole black peppers
white vinegar or dry wine
salt, if necessary

Cover the washed trotters with water. Bring to boiling point, cover pan, reduce heat and simmer for 3 hours.

Add remaining ingredients except salt and vinegar or wine. Add boiling water if necessary.

Cover and simmer 1 hour longer.

Strain the stock through a sieve. Remove skin and bones from trotters. Return the meat to the stock and season with salt if necessary and a little vinegar or dry wine.

Pour into mould and chill until firm. If desired, 1 chopped pimiento may be added to the mould before chilling. Serves 6.

FRUITED PORK CHOPS

4 chump chops
flour, salt, paprika
2 cooking apples
sultanas, brown sugar

Trim excess fat from the chops and render it down in a large frying pan. Remove pieces.

Flour pork chops and brown on both sides in the hot fat. Sprinkle each side with salt and paprika. Pour off excess fat.

Core apples, but do not peel; cut into thick slices. Top each chop with 1 or 2 apple slices and fill centres with sultanas. Sprinkle apples with brown sugar.

Pour 4 tablespoons water round chops. Cover and cook over low heat about 35 minutes or until chops are tender. Baste once or twice during cooking with liquid in pan. Add more water, if needed.

(If desired, pork chops may be baked with the fruit in a large covered baking dish in moderate oven (350°F. Mark 4) 45 minutes.) Serves 4.

Fruited Pork Chops

PORK BIRDS

2 pounds pork cut very thinly from
  the blade bone
2 teaspoons lemon juice
½ teaspoon salt
¼ teaspoon pepper
¼ teaspoon Aromat
  (optional)
8 ounces dry breadcrumbs
3 ounces seedless raisins, cut into
  halves
¼ pint cream or evaporated milk
2 tablespoons flour
2 tablespoons fat
8 fluid ounces boiling stock or
  water

Pound the meat to a thickness of ¼
inch. Cut into 6 oblong pieces. Season
by rubbing with a mixture of lemon
juice, ½ teaspoon salt, pepper, and
Aromat.

Combine breadcrumbs, raisins, cream
or milk, and 1 teaspoon salt. Spread
the meat with breadcrumb mixture.
Roll up and fasten with small skewers
or tie with string.

Sprinkle the rolls with flour and
brown in hot fat. Add boiling water
or stock.

Cover pan and simmer about 20
minutes. Serve with the juices in pan.
Serves 6.

PORK BUTT COOKED WITH VEGETABLES

3-4 pounds butt or blade bone
4 large carrots, cut lengthwise
4 large parsnips, cut lengthwise
1 small cabbage, quartered
½ teaspoon salt
⅓ teaspoon pepper

Simmer pork butt in water to cover
1½ hours.

One hour before serving, add vegetables and seasonings. Cook until tender.

Cut pork in slices. Arrange in centre
of dish, with vegetables around meat.
Serves 6 to 8.

BRAISED PORK FILLET PATTIES

Cut meat into serving pieces, coat
with flour and brown in a little fat;
then add seasonings and a small
amount of liquid. Cover the pan tightly,

Braised Pork Fillet Patties

and cook slowly until tender, 35 to 45
minutes.

Herbs, spices, or seasonings, such as
Worcestershire and Tabasco sauce,
added to the liquid during braising,
gives the meat an interesting flavour.

SWEET AND SOUR PORK

1 pound lean pork
fat, salt, pepper
8 fluid ounces bouillon or stock
2 medium green peppers
3 tablespoons chopped onion
4 slices canned pineapple
3 tablespoons cornflour
2 ounces sugar
4 tablespoons vinegar
2 teaspoons soy sauce
4 fluid ounces pineapple juice
1½ pounds boiled rice

Cut pork into ½-inch cubes, and
brown well in a little hot fat. Sprinkle
well with salt and pepper.

Add bouillon and cook, covered,
over low heat 20 minutes. Cut green
peppers into 1-inch strips and add.
Add onion and pineapple slices cut
into eighths. Cook another 10 minutes.

Blend cornflour with sugar, vinegar,
soy sauce, and pineapple juice, and add
to mixture. Stir constantly until thickened. Cook 5 minutes longer.

Add more salt and pepper if necessary. Serve in individual rice rings or
nests of boiled rice. Serves 4.

BRAISED PORK

Buy lean pork sliced 1½ inches
thick. Place in baking dish. Sprinkle
with salt, pepper, and flour.

Add 4 fluid ounces consommé or
bouillon, and arrange half slices of
pineapple or thick slices of tomato
over pork.

Cover and bake in moderate oven
(350°F. Mark 4) until tender, about 1
hour. Allow 1¼ pounds pork to serve 4.

ROAST PORK SHOULDER BUTT

Rub roast with salt, pepper, and a
little sage, if desired. Place on rack in
shallow roasting tin and roast in slow
oven (325°F. Mark 3) 40 minutes per
pound.

Place roast on a dish and surround
with a ring of fried apple wedges. To
prepare apple wedges, heat a little butter or margarine in a frying pan, add
apples, sprinkle with brown sugar,
cover and cook until tender.

PORK FILLET, BAKED IN SOUR CREAM

1½ pounds pork fillet
½ teaspoon salt

Sweet and Sour Pork

⅛ teaspoon pepper
½ teaspoon Aromat
flour, fat
8 fluid ounces sour cream

Wipe meat with damp cloth. Sprinkle with salt, pepper, and Aromat; cut
into 1¼-inch slices.

Roll slices in flour; brown quickly in
hot fat.

Place in a shallow baking dish; cover
with sour cream. Bake in moderate
oven (350°F. Mark 4) about 30 minutes.

When tender, pour off liquid and
thicken for the gravy. Strain gravy
over meat; return to oven until sauce
is hot and bubbly. Serves 6.

CASSEROLE OF PORK PATTIES

For the patties:
1 pound lean pork
2 ounces stale bread
1 shallot or small onion
1 teaspoon salt
¼ teaspoon pepper
pinch each of nutmeg, ginger,
  cloves and mace
milk to moisten
oil or lard for frying
For the sauce:
1 onion finely chopped
2 stalks celery, thinly sliced
2 tomatoes, peeled and chopped
1 ounce flour
½ pint stock
2 tablespoons white wine or wine
  vinegar
1 teaspoon salt
¼ teaspoon pepper

Put the pork, bread and peeled
shallot twice through the mincer.
Add salt, pepper and enough milk to
moisten. Divide into eight portions
and pat each into a flat cake ½-1 inch
thick.

Melt enough oil or lard to cover the
bottom of a pan or casserole large
enough to take a single layer of
patties. Fry until brown on both sides.
Remove to a casserole. Fry the onion,
celery and tomatoes in the remaining
fat. Add the flour and mix well. Add
the stock, wine and seasoning, stir
until boiling. Pour over the meat,
cover and cook in a moderate oven,
(375°F. Mark 5) for about 45 minutes.
Serves 4.

Roast Loin of Pork with Stuffing

ROAST LOIN OF PORK WITH STUFFING

Spread a 4- to 5-pound loin of pork with 3-4 tablespoons prepared mustard. Place on rack in open roasting pan with fat side up and roast in slow oven (325°F. Mark 3).

During the last hour of roasting, place stuffing (below) under meat and peeled potatoes round roast. Baste occasionally. Continue baking until potatoes are cooked and nicely browned. Serves 6 to 8.

Stuffing:

3-4 stalks celery, diced
1 tablespoon crushed onion flakes
4 fluid ounces water
3 ounces butter or margarine
1 teaspoon salt
¼ teaspoon pepper
½ teaspoon sage
12 ounces stale breadcrumbs

Simmer celery and onion flakes in water for 5 minutes. Mix in remaining ingredients. Arrange in mound on foil or dish.

Place roast over stuffing during last hour of cooking.

FILLET PATTIES WITH VEGETABLES

1 pork fillet, about 1¼ pounds
1 tablespoon fat or dripping
1 teaspoon salt
1 medium onion, chopped
2-3 stalks celery, chopped
4 ounces finely cut carrots
2 ounces cooked peas
8 fluid ounces bouillon or meat stock
1 ounce flour
4 tablespoons water

Cut meat crosswise in 2-inch pieces. Flatten slightly with meat mallet and brown in fat. Season with salt.

Add vegetables to pan. Add bouillon. Cover and cook slowly about 45 minutes, either in moderate oven (350°F. Mark 4) or on top of stove.

Remove meat from pan. Blend flour with water and add to vegetables. Cook until thickened. Serve vegetables with meat. Serves 5.

ROAST PORK CANTONESE STYLE

½ teaspoon salt
5 tablespoons soy sauce
3 tablespoons lemon juice
2 ounces sugar
⅛ teaspoon cochineal
1 pound lean pork
1 small onion, sliced
4 spring onions, cut in 1-inch lengths
3 pieces fresh ginger, crushed, or ¼ teaspoon ground ginger
6 cloves garlic, crushed
4 fluid ounces chicken stock or canned consommé

Combine salt, soy sauce, lemon juice, sugar, and cochineal. Rub onto pork. Add onion, spring onion, ginger, and garlic. Allow to stand ½ hour.

Place in roasting tin. Add 4 fluid ounces chicken stock. Cook in slow oven (325°F. Mark 3) 1 hour. Slice in ¼-inch slices. Serve hot with rice. Serves 3 to 4.

SWEET AND SOUR PORK (Chinese)

1 pound lean pork, cut into 1-inch cubes
2 tablespoons sherry or 1 teaspoon soy sauce
1 egg, slightly beaten
2 ounces flour
½ teaspoon salt
4 tablespoons water
oil for frying
4 ounces fresh pineapple cubes
8 fluid ounces water
1 green pepper, cut into 1-inch strips
4 tablespoons vinegar
1½-2 ounces brown sugar
1 tablespoon molasses or treacle
1 tomato, cut into wedges
2 tablespoons cornflour

Toss meat in sherry, or soy sauce, and let stand 20 minutes, turning once or twice.

Mix egg, flour, salt, and water until smooth. Add pork and turn to coat each cube with batter.

Fry pork in deep hot oil (350°F.) until brown. Place on absorbent paper and keep warm.

To prepare sauce, cook pineapple in water, covered, until just tender. Add pepper strips, vinegar, brown sugar, molasses, and tomatoes. Boil 2 minutes.

Mix cornflour with enough water to give a thin mixture. Add to boiling sauce, stirring, and cook, stirring, until thickened.

Add pork and serve at once with rice. Serves 4.

PORK CHOPS WITH GARLIC SAUCE

1 small onion, coarsely chopped
1 small carrot, coarsely chopped
2 ounces butter or margarine
1 ounce flour
2-3 tomatoes, peeled and chopped
6 fluid ounces beef bouillon
2 cloves garlic, crushed
½ teaspoon salt
½ teaspoon sugar
freshly ground black pepper
bouquet garni (see below)
6 loin pork chops.

Sauté onion and carrot in butter until soft but not brown.

Add flour, stirring until smooth. Add tomatoes, bouillon, garlic, salt, sugar, pepper, and bouquet garni tied in muslin. Cook and stir until mixture thickens. Cover and simmer 1 hour.

Strain. While sauce is cooking, season chops with salt and pepper.

Brown both sides of chops and sauté over low heat until tender, about 20 minutes. Serve garlic sauce hot over steak. Serves 6.

Bouquet Garni: Use 1 small bay leaf, pinch of thyme, 4 sprigs of parsley, 1 sprig of celery leaves, and 1 whole clove. Tie in piece of muslin.

PORK AND GREEN NOODLE CASSEROLE

8 fluid ounces water
1 can (6 ounces) tomato paste
1½ pounds pork, cut in ½-inch pieces
about 4 ounces butter or margarine
1 small onion, chopped
3-4 stalks celery, sliced in ¼-inch strips
3 teaspoons salt
¼ teaspoon pepper
½ teaspoon thyme
½ teaspoon Aromat
½ pound green noodles
½ can (5½ ounces) mushroom soup, undiluted
1 packet frozen peas, cooked
2 ounces grated Cheddar or Parmesan cheese

Combine water and tomato paste.

In a saucepan, fry pork in hot fat, then add onions and fry until light brown, about 3 minutes.

Add celery, 2 teaspoons salt, pepper, thyme, Aromat, and tomato paste-water mixture.

Cover pan and simmer over low heat until meat is tender, about 30 minutes. Every 10 minutes, stir all ingredients well.

Cook noodles in 3½ pints boiling salted water until tender, about 8 minutes. Drain, and add 2 ounces butter and 1 teaspoon salt, blending well.

Combine noodles with cooked meat mixture. Add mushroom soup and cooked peas. Blend all ingredients and turn into a greased 3½ pint casserole. Sprinkle top with cheese.

Bake in moderate oven (375°F. Mark 5) 30 minutes. Serves 6 to 8.

PORK PIE WITH SAGE SCONES

1½ to 2 pounds boneless pork, cut in 1½-inch cubes
1 ounce flour
1½ to 2 teaspoons salt
¼ teaspoon pepper
2 tablespoons lard
4-5 stalks celery, chopped
1 small onion, chopped
2 chicken bouillon cubes
¾ pint hot water
8 ounces cooked peas

Dredge meat in flour combined with seasonings and brown on all sides in hot lard. Add celery, onion, and bouillon cubes dissolved in hot water. Cover and simmer for 1½ hours.

Thicken with a paste made of a little flour and cold water. Add peas, reserving 2-3 tablespoons for a garnish, and season to taste. Place mixture in casserole. Top with sage scone rings. (Add ½ teaspoon powdered sage to 8 ounces flour in standard recipe.)

Bake in hot oven (425°F. Mark 7) 15 to 20 minutes. Fill centres of rings with remaining hot buttered peas. Serves 6 to 8.

PORK WITH ALMONDS AND VEGETABLES — CANTONESE

2 ounces chopped blanched almonds
4 tablespoons oil
1 pound lean pork, cut in ½-inch cubes
4 fluid ounces chicken stock or canned consommé
1 teaspoon salt
4 ounces cooked carrots diced
8 ounces cooked peas
4-5 stalks celery diced
2 tablespoons cornflour
2 teaspoons soy sauce
3 fluid ounces cold water

Brown almonds in 1 tablespoon of the oil.

Put remainder of oil in a sauté pan; add pork and cook until golden brown.

Add chicken stock and salt and cook about 30 minutes or until pork is tender.

Add carrots, peas, and celery; cook 10 to 15 minutes longer.

Blend cornflour, soy sauce, and water. Add to meat mixture and cook until liquid thickens. Turn into serving dish. Garnish with almonds.

Serve immediately with hot boiled rice. Add additional soy sauce, if desired. Serves 6 to 8.

CUSHION STYLE HAND AND SPRING

Buy meat boned and sewn on 2 sides. This leaves 1 side open for inserting stuffing. Season inside and out with salt and pepper.

Fill cavity with bread stuffing (see Index). Sew or skewer edges together. Place fat-side-up on rack in open pan.

Roast in moderate oven (350°F. Mark 4) until done. Allow 40 to 45 minutes per pound.

PORK AND NOODLES — HAWAIIAN

1½ pounds lean pork, cut in 1-inch cubes
2 tablespoons fat
4 medium onions, coarsely chopped
3 carrots, sliced
1½ pints water
1 tablespoon salt
1 small can pineapple chunks
2 tablespoons lemon juice
1 tablespoon soy sauce
4 tablespoons cornflour
4 tablespoons brown sugar
4 ounces medium noodles, cooked and drained
2 green peppers, cut into pieces

Brown pork on all sides in hot fat in heavy sauté pan. Add vegetables and brown very lightly. Add water and salt. Simmer very gently until meat is almost tender, about 40 minutes.

Make a smooth paste of pineapple juice from canned pineapple, lemon juice, soy sauce, cornflour and brown sugar. Pour over pork and cook, stirring occasionally, until sauce thickens.

Carefully mix in noodles, green peppers, and pineapple. Pour into casserole.

Bake in moderate oven (350°F. Mark 4) 15 to 20 minutes. Serves 6.

VEAL AND PORK PARTY CASSEROLE

1 pound diced veal
1 pound diced pork
2 ounces sliced fresh mushrooms
3 tablespoons fat
½ pound noodles
1 small can pimento, chopped
2 tablespoons grated onion
½ pound Cheddar cheese, grated
1 small can (about 7-8 ounces) cream-style corn
1 can condensed chicken soup
2 teaspoons salt
½ teaspoon pepper
2 ounces buttered crumbs

Brown meat and mushrooms in hot fat.

Cook noodles in boiling salted water. Drain and rinse.

Combine meat, mushrooms, noodles, chopped pimento, grated onion, grated cheese, corn, soup, salt, and pepper. Pour into casserole.

Bake in moderate oven (350°F. Mark 4) 45 minutes.

Remove cover, sprinkle with crumbs and cook uncovered 15 minutes longer. Serves 10 to 12.

CHINESE ROAST PORK

4 teaspoons sugar
1 teaspoon salt
4 teaspoons honey
3 teaspoons soy sauce
3 tablespoons chicken bouillon
2 pounds pork butt or blade bone

Place all ingredients except meat in bowl. Mix well.

Cut meat lengthwise in 3 pieces and add. Marinade pork for ¾ of an hour, turning occasionally.

Remove from bowl and place on rack in a roasting pan, adding a few tablespoons of water to prevent smoking.

Roast in moderate oven (350°F. Mark 4) for about 1 hour and 15 minutes turning occasionally. Slice pork and serve immediately with English mustard. Serves 6.

PINEAPPLE PORK (CHINESE)

Part No. 1:
8 ounces lean pork, sliced in ½-inch pieces
1 small egg, well beaten
¼ teaspoon salt
½ teaspoon Aromat
2 ounces flour
fat, for deep frying

Coat pork pieces by dipping in egg; transfer to paper bag containing mixture of salt, Aromat and flour. Shake until meat is well and evenly coated. Remove pork; dust off excess flour.

Deep-fry pork in hot fat or oil (360°F.) 6 to 8 minutes or until tender.

Remove pork to absorbent paper to drain. Keep warm.

Part No. 2:
1 tablespoon cooking oil
3 fluid ounces clear chicken stock (free from fat)
2 ounces canned pineapple chunks
1 medium green pepper, cut in ½-inch pieces
½ small onion, coarsely chopped
1 teaspoon cornflour
1 teaspoon soy sauce
2 tablespoons sugar, brown or white
3 fluid ounces pineapple juice
1 teaspoon tomato ketchup

Lightly toss together in hot oil in the stock, pineapple, green pepper, and onion. When mixed, cover and cook 2 minutes.

Add fried pork pieces; cook uncovered 2 minutes longer.

Combine remaining ingredients; blend smooth. Add to pork mixture; toss lightly and continuously until juice has thickened.

Turn out and pile up on hot serving dish. Serves 2.

Leftover Pork

CHINESE PORK AND RICE

2 tablespoons butter or margarine
5 ounces uncooked long grain rice
1 teaspoon salt
1 large onion, cut in thin slices
12 fluid ounces boiling water
1 bouillon cube
1 green pepper, cut in thin strips
2 stalks celery, cut in thin strips
5 ounces cooked, cubed pork
2 teaspoons soy sauce

Melt butter in sauté pan. Add uncooked rice. Season with salt and cook until rice grains turn golden, stirring occasionally.

Add onion to rice and cook several minutes, then pour in boiling water in which bouillon cube has been dissolved. Cover tightly and cook until rice is tender, about 15 minutes.

Add pepper, celery, and pork. Cover tightly and place over very low heat about 10 minutes more or until vegetables are tender but still slightly crisp.

Just before serving, stir in soy sauce. Serves 4.

CREOLE PORK

1 large onion, sliced
10 ounces diced cooked pork
2 tablespoons oil
1 can (about 14 ounces) tomatoes
½ small green pepper, diced
1-2 stalks celery, diced
½ teaspoon chilli powder
1 teaspoon sugar
1½ teaspoons salt
freshly ground black pepper
1 tablespoon flour

Sauté onion and pork in oil until onion is golden brown.

Add tomatoes, green pepper, celery, chilli powder, sugar, salt, and pepper. Cover and simmer 45 minutes.

Combine flour and 2 tablespoons water and stir into tomato mixture. Cook and stir 5 minutes. Serves 6.

PORK SUPPER

1 tablespoon chopped onion
1 tablespoon fat
4 tablespoons vinegar
6 fluid ounces water
1 tablespoon cornflour
2 tablespoons brown or white sugar
1 teaspoon salt
5 ounces minced cooked pork
6 ounces cooked green beans
6 ounces cooked, diced carrots

Brown onion in fat in a sauté pan. Combine vinegar, water, cornflour, sugar, and salt. Stir into onions. Heat.

Add pork and cook 10 minutes. Add drained beans and carrots. Heat slowly 25 to 30 minutes. Serve hot. Serves 4.

FRUITED PORK LOAF

4 ounces dry noodles
½ pint sweetened apple purée
1 tablespoon lemon juice
4 fluid ounces orange juice
1 tablespoon grated orange rind
¼ teaspoon salt
⅛ teaspoon dry mustard
⅛ teaspoon ground cloves
1 tablespoon brown sugar
5 ounces cubed cooked pork

Cook noodles in boiling salted water until tender, about 6 minutes. Drain and rinse.

Combine with remaining ingredients and mix well. Turn into greased loaf tin.

Cover and bake in moderate oven (350°F. Mark 4) 25 minutes. Serves 6.

SCALLOPED PORK AND POTATO CASSEROLE

1 pound chopped cooked pork
12 ounces thinly sliced potatoes
2 tablespoons finely chopped green pepper
2 tablespoons finely chopped onion
1 can (about 10½ ounces) condensed cream of celery soup
4 fluid ounces milk
1 teaspoon salt
⅛ teaspoon pepper
⅛ teaspoon savory
2 ounces shredded cheese (optional)

Combine all ingredients except cheese in a 1½-2-pint casserole.

Bake in moderate oven (350°F. Mark 4) 30 minutes. Remove from oven. Sprinkle cheese on top.

Return to oven and continue baking for 30 minutes or until potatoes are done. Serves 4 to 5.

SAVOURY PORK IN SWEET POTATO NESTS

1 pound mashed sweet potatoes
milk
1 tablespoon melted butter or margarine
12 ounces finely chopped cooked pork
4 ounces cooked peas
4 fluid ounces gravy
½ teaspoon salt
⅛ teaspoon thyme

To the mashed sweet potatoes add enough milk to make mixture smooth and easy to shape. Divide in 4 mounds on a baking sheet. Make a well in the centre of each mound with the back of a spoon. Brush with melted butter.

Combine pork, peas, gravy, and seasonings in a baking dish and cook, together with potato nests in a moderate oven (350°F. Mark 4) 15 to 20 minutes. Spoon pork into sweet potato nests. Serve hot. Serves 4.

Fruited Pork Loaf

BARBECUED PORK BAPS

2 ounces fat or dripping
1 medium onion, chopped
2-3 stalks celery, finely chopped
1 or 2 cloves garlic, crushed
4 fluid ounces water
4 tablespoons vinegar
5 tablespoons Worcestershire sauce
2-3 tablespoons chilli sauce
1 teaspoon salt
¼ teaspoon pepper
¾ teaspoon Aromat
¾ teaspoon chilli powder
2 tablespoons brown sugar
thinly sliced roast pork (for 6)
6 baps

Heat fat in saucepan; add onion, celery, garlic; sauté 2 to 3 minutes.

Add all remaining ingredients except meat and baps. Cover; simmer 5 minutes.

Add sliced pork (trim off surplus fat); cover and simmer 5 to 10 minutes longer.

Split the baps, toast them and arrange hot slices of meat on top. Pour sauce on top. Garnish as desired. Serves 6.

PORK AND MUSHROOM RING

1 tablespoon finely chopped onion
5 tablespoons melted butter or margarine
2 ounces flour
½ teaspoon salt
¾ pint scalded milk
2 egg yolks, beaten
2 ounces sliced mushrooms
12 ounces diced cooked pork

Sauté onion in 4 tablespoons butter until golden brown.

Add flour, salt and blend. Add hot milk gradually, stirring constantly. Simmer 10 minutes; stir occasionally.

Strain and add gradually to egg yolks, stirring constantly. Heat but do not boil.

Sauté mushrooms in remaining butter. Add mushrooms and pork to sauce; heat thoroughly.

Pour in centre of mashed potato ring. Serve immediately. Serves 6.

U

Pork Chops

FRIED PORK CHOPS

Rub pork chops with garlic or rosemary, or other desired seasoning.

Brown on both sides in a heavy sauté pan in just enough fat to keep them from sticking. Reduce heat. Season with salt and pepper. Cover pan closely.

Cook on top of stove or in a slow oven (325°F. Mark 3) until chops are tender, 30-45 minutes, depending upon thickness of chops.

Pour off excess fat as they cook. Use drippings in the pan to prepare gravy.

BRAISED PORK CHOPS

Use 1-inch-thick loin chops. Trim off a little fat and heat in a sauté pan.

Brown chops slowly on both sides, about 10 minutes. Add 2 to 4 tablespoons water, depending upon size of pan. Cover and cook slowly over low heat or in moderate oven (350°F. Mark 4) until well done and tender, about 30 minutes.

Season chops after cooking. If desired, dredge chops with flour before browning. Make gravy from the drippings in the pan.

Thin chops do not need the added water, but use cover and very low heat to keep chops moist.

Variations: Instead of water, use barbecue sauce, tomato juice, canned tomatoes, consommé or bouillon, orange juice, pineapple juice, or diluted lemon juice.

Chops may be rubbed with a cut clove of garlic before braising or with a little dry mustard, sage, or soy sauce.

BAKED PORK CHOPS

4 pork chops
fat
2 6-8-ounce cans tomato sauce
4 fluid ounces water
1-2 stalks celery, finely diced
2 tablespoons brown sugar
juice of ½ lemon
½ teaspoon salt
½ teaspoon dry mustard
⅛ teaspoon pepper

Brown chops in fat. Place in shallow greased baking dish.

Combine tomato sauce, water, celery, brown sugar, lemon juice, and seasonings. Pour over chops.

Cover and bake in moderate oven (350°F. Mark 4) about 45 minutes or until chops are tender. Serves 4.

TO BROWN EDGES ON PORK CHOPS

Place chops side by side, bone edge up, in small amount of hot fat. Hold in position with spatula and fork. Rock chops back and forth to brown evenly.

CHICKEN-FRIED PORK CHOPS

6 pork chops, ¾-inch thick
2 beaten eggs
2 tablespoons milk
4 ounces fine dry breadcrumbs
2 ounces fat
½ teaspoon salt
dash of pepper
4 tablespoons water

Pound chops thoroughly with meat mallet to ½-inch thick. Mix eggs and milk. Dip meat into mixture, then into crumbs.

Brown on both sides in hot fat. Season with salt and pepper. Add water. Cover and cook over low heat 35-40 minutes. Lift chops occasionally to prevent sticking.

For crisp coating, remove cover the last 15 minutes. Garnish as liked. Serves 6.

PORK CHOPS IN SOUR CREAM

4 thick pork chops
salt and pepper
4 slices each lemon and onion
4 rings green pepper
2 ounces brown sugar, honey, molasses or treacle
¼ pint sour cream
3-4 tablespoons chilli sauce

Brown pork chops on both sides in a sauté pan. Season with salt and pepper.

Put a slice each of lemon and onion, and a green pepper ring on each chop. Top each with 1 tablespoon brown sugar, honey, molasses, or treacle.

Mix sour cream and chilli sauce and pour over all. Cover tightly. Cook gently until chops are tender, about 35-40 minutes, depending upon thickness of chops. Serves 4.

PORK CHOPS WITH RED BEANS

4 pork chops
½ small onion, chopped
4 ounces quick cooking rice
1 can (15 to 16 ounces) red or kidney beans, drained
¾ teaspoon salt
pepper, cayenne, and garlic seasoning, to suit taste
¾ pint water

Brown pork chops in sauté pan; if thick cover and leave for a few minutes to partially cook. Lift out chops and drain off the fat in the pan.

Add remaining ingredients and place chops on top. Bring to the boil. Stir, cover, and lower heat. Cook 20 to 25 minutes or until rice is tender, most of liquid is absorbed, and chops are done. Serves 4.

Stuffed Pork Chops: Pockets may be cut in double thick chops to hold the stuffing.

STUFFED PORK CHOPS—BAKED

2 tablespoons melted butter or margarine
6 ounces soft breadcrumbs
1-2 stalks celery, diced
2 tablespoons chopped onion
2 tablespoons chopped parsley
salt and pepper
8 pork chops, cut thinly
4 tablespoons tomato juice

Mix butter, crumbs, celery, onion, parsley, and salt and pepper to taste.

Wipe chops with damp cloth. Season with salt and pepper. Place chops together with stuffing between (sandwich style). Put in greased baking dish. Add tomato juice.

Bake in moderate oven (350°F. Mark 4) until tender, about 45 minutes. Serves 4.

Variations: Pockets may be cut in double-thick chops and filled with stuffing. Sliced tart apples or half slices of pineapple may be used instead of bread stuffing.

BREADED PORK CHOPS

Wipe meat with a damp cloth. Roll in seasoned breadcrumbs. Dip in slightly beaten egg diluted with 2 tablespoons water and roll again in crumbs.

Brown slowly in minimum of hot fat. Pour off excess fat and cook until done.

Serve with a highly seasoned sauce made by thickening the drippings in the pan with flour.

Or, after browning chops, remove from pan. Add chopped green pepper, chopped onion, and canned tomato to drippings. Place chops in sauce. Cover and simmer about 40 minutes.

Pork Chops with Red Beans

Pork Chops with Tomato Sauce

PORK CHOPS WITH TOMATO SAUCE

6 pork chops
1 tablespoon fat
dash of black pepper
6 slices onion
6 rings green pepper
1 can condensed tomato soup

Brown chops in fat in a sauté pan; sprinkle with pepper.

Place an onion slice and a ring of green pepper on each chop; pour soup over all. Cover and simmer about 40 minutes. Serves 6.

PORK CHOP—PINEAPPLE BAKE

Sear 6 chops in hot bacon fat in frying pan. Place in casserole. Brown 6 slices pineapple lightly in fat and put on chops. Add 6 fluid ounces pineapple juice.

Cover and bake in moderate oven (350°F. Mark 4) until done, about 35 minutes. Baste often. Thicken juice with flour. Serves 6.

PORK CHOPS WITH SWEET POTATOES

2 tablespoons salad oil
6 loin chops
6 medium sweet potatoes, peeled and thinly sliced
1 large onion, thinly sliced
1 medium green pepper, cut into rings
salt and pepper
¼ teaspoon crushed thyme
¼ teaspoon crushed marjoram
1 can (16 ounce) tomatoes

Heat oil in a sauté pan and brown chops on both sides.

Arrange sweet potato slices, onion slices, and green pepper rings over pork chops. Sprinkle with salt and pepper, thyme, and marjoram. Pour tomatoes over all. Cover and cook over low heat, about 45 minutes, or until meat and sweet potatoes are tender. Serves 6.

Pork Chops with Sweet Potatoes

PORK CHOPS WITH APRICOT STUFFING

1 small onion, chopped
1-2 stalks celery, chopped
3 tablespoons butter or margarine
6 ounces fine dry breadcrumbs
3 ounces dried apricots, chopped
1 teaspoon salt
⅛ teaspoon pepper
8 thin loin pork chops

Sauté onion and celery in butter or margarine until golden. Combine with breadcrumbs, dried apricots, salt and pepper; toss lightly.

Divide stuffing onto 4 pork chops. Top each with another chop; fasten together with cocktail sticks or skewers.

Bake in moderate oven (350°F. Mark 4) about 1 hour or until chops are tender and browned. Serves 4.

Pork Chops with Apricot Stuffing

DEVILLED PORK CHOPS

4 pork chops, cut 1-inch thick
3-4 tablespoons chilli sauce
1 tablespoon lemon juice
1 small onion, chopped
¼ teaspoon dry mustard
½ teaspoon salt
dash of pepper
1 teaspoon Worcestershire sauce
4 fluid ounces water

Marinate chops in a mixture made by combining all the ingredients (except meat of course) for an hour or longer.

Drain, reserving marinade, and dry chops with paper towels.

Sauté in bacon or other fat until browned. Add reserved liquid and cook, covered, until tender or about 40 minutes.

Remove chops to dish and cover with sauce in pan. Serves 4.

PORK CHOPS À LA CREOLE

4 loin pork chops
3 tablespoons flour
1 teaspoon salt
¼ teaspoon pepper
¼ teaspoon garlic salt
¼ teaspoon thyme
4 slices of onion
4 ounces uncooked rice
1 can (16 ounce) tomatoes

Dip chops in flour seasoned with half the salt, pepper, garlic salt, and thyme. Brown chops in a little fat. Place chops in bottom of casserole.

Top with onion slices and rice. Season with remaining salt, pepper, garlic salt, and thyme. Pour tomatoes over rice and chops.

Cover and bake in moderate oven (350°F. Mark 4) 30 minutes. Remove cover and bake 20-30 minutes longer, basting occasionally. Serves 4.

CRANBERRY PORK CHOPS

6 pork chops
½ teaspoon salt
1 pound cranberries, chopped
6 ounces honey
½ teaspoon ground cloves

Brown chops quickly on both sides in hot frying pan. Sprinkle with salt. Place 3 chops in greased casserole.

Combine cranberries, honey, and cloves. Spread half over chops in casserole. Place remaining chops on top. Cover with remaining cranberry mixture.

Cover. Bake in moderate oven (350°F. Mark 4) about 45 minutes. Serves 6.

PORK CHOPS WITH VEGETABLES

4 pork chops
1 pound sliced potatoes
1 small green pepper, diced
4-5 sticks celery, diced
1 large onion, sliced
2 teaspoons salt
⅛ teaspoon pepper
1 can condensed tomato soup
4 fluid ounces water
¼ teaspoon Tabasco sauce

Brown pork chops in a deep sauté pan; remove from pan.

Starting with potatoes, put vegetables in layers in the pan. (Reserve about ⅓ of green pepper, celery, and onion.) Sprinkle each layer with part of the salt and pepper.

Place browned pork chops on top of vegetables. Top with remaining green pepper, celery, and onion. Sprinkle with remaining salt and pepper.

Mix together tomato soup, water, and Tabasco; pour over meat.

Cover and cook on top of stove over low heat about 1 hour. Serves 4.

Pork Chops with Vegetables

Pork Chops with Corn and Apple Rings

PORK CHOPS WITH CORN AND APPLE RINGS

4 loin pork chops
1 teaspoon Aromat
salt and pepper
4 tablespoons water
2 cans (12-ounces each) Mexican-style kernel corn
4 thick, unpeeled apple rings
cinnamon-sugar

Sprinkle chops with ½ teaspoon Aromat, salt, and pepper. Brown slowly in their own fat in a sauté pan, turning to brown both sides. Add the water to pan; cover; simmer 30 minutes. Remove from pan.

Pour corn into pan without draining. Season to taste with salt, pepper, and remaining ½ teaspoon Aromat.

Place chops on corn. Top each chop with apple ring dusted with cinnamon-sugar. Cover; cook 10 minutes or until apple rings are tender. Serves 4.

SPANISH PORK CHOPS

1 large onion
1 tablespoon fat
4 pork chops
salt and pepper
1 large can (16-ounce) tomatoes
1 small green pepper, chopped
½ teaspoon chilli powder

Cut onion into ½-inch-thick slices. Brown in fat in sauté pan. Remove onion and reserve.

Season pork chops with salt and pepper and brown in same pan. Top the chops with onion, tomatoes, green pepper, and chilli powder.

Cover and cook slowly about 45 minutes or until chops are fork-tender. Serves 4.

Pork Chops with Rice

PORK CHOPS WITH VEGETABLES

4 pork chops
1 tablespoon fat
4 fluid ounces water
4 large potatoes, quartered
8 small onions, halved
8 small carrots
1 small can lima beans
1½ teaspoons salt
⅛ teaspoon pepper

Brown chops in fat in large sauté pan with tight-fitting lid. Add water, cover, and simmer 30 minutes.

Add vegetables and seasonings. Cover, and simmer 30 minutes, or until vegetables are tender. Serves 4.
Variation: Lamb chops may be substituted for pork.

PORK CHOPS WITH MACARONI AND CORN

4 ounces elbow macaroni
4 loin pork chops, ½-inch thick
2 teaspoons salt
¼ teaspoon pepper
2 tablespoons finely chopped onion
½ small green pepper, finely chopped
1 ounce flour
4 fluid ounces water
4-5 tablespoons chilli sauce
1 tablespoon brown sugar
1 tablespoon vinegar
1 can (8-ounce) creamed sweetcorn

Cook macaroni until tender in boiling salted water; drain.

Season chops with 2 teaspoons salt and the pepper. Brown chops on both sides in a large sauté pan. Remove chops and brown onion and pepper lightly.

Blend in flour, then add water, chilli sauce, sugar, and vinegar. Cook, stirring constantly, until thickened.

Mix in macaroni and corn. Turn into 3-3½-pint casserole. Arrange chops on top.

Cover and bake in moderate oven (350°F. Mark 4) until chops are tender, about 1 hour. Serves 4.

PORK CHOPS WITH RICE

6 pork chops
4 ounces uncooked rice
8 fluid ounces water
2 teaspoons salt
1 small onion, chopped
1 can (1 pound) tomatoes, broken up
1 can (8-ounce) whole kernel yellow corn
¼ teaspoon black pepper

Trim some fat from pork chops. Render down in a fairly large sauté pan. Add chops and brown very slowly on both sides. Lift out. Pour off excess fat.

Spread rice over bottom of pan. Add water. Sprinkle with 1 teaspoon salt. Arrange chops over rice. Sprinkle

with the other 1 teaspoon salt. Add onion and tomatoes. Spoon on the corn. Sprinkle with black pepper. Bring to the boil.

Turn heat down low. Cover and simmer 25 to 35 minutes or until the rice is tender. Add a small amount of water, should mixture cook dry. Serve at the table from one of the colourful, casseroles. Serves 6.

PORK CHOPS ON SPAGHETTI WITH APPLE SAUCE

4 loin pork chops
salt and pepper
2 tablespoons fat
4 tablespoons water
3 ounces butter or margarine
3 ounces plain flour
¾ pint apple juice
salt and pepper to taste
dash celery salt
8 ounces spaghetti, cooked

Season pork chops with salt and pepper. Melt fat over low heat in a sauté pan; add chops and brown well on both sides.

Add water and cover. Cook over low heat until tender, 25-30 minutes.

Meanwhile, melt butter or margarine over low heat; add flour and blend. Cook over low heat until flour mixture is golden brown, stirring constantly.

Gradually stir in apple juice and continue cooking until thickened, stirring constantly. Add salt, pepper, and celery salt.

Serve pork chops and apple sauce with cooked spaghetti. Serves 4.

PORK CHOPS NEAPOLITAN

2 tablespoons olive oil
1 clove garlic, crushed
6 loin pork chops, cut about ¾- to 1-inch thick
1 teaspoon salt
½ teaspoon Aromat
¼ teaspoon pepper
1 pound mushrooms, sliced
2 green peppers, chopped
4 ounces canned tomatoes, sieved
3 tablespoons dry white wine

Heat olive oil in large sauté pan having a tight-fitting lid. Add garlic and cook until lightly browned.

Meanwhile, wipe pork chops with a clean, damp cloth. Season with a mixture of salt, Aromat and pepper. Place into pan, and slowly brown chops on both sides.

When chops are browned, add mushrooms and peppers. Stir in slowly a mixture of tomatoes and wine.

Cover pan and cook over low heat 50-60 minutes, depending on thickness of chops. Add small amounts of water as needed.

Test by cutting meat near bone; no part of meat should be pink in colour. Serves 6.

Spareribs

OVEN-BARBECUED SPARE-RIBS

3 to 4 pounds spareribs, cut in
    pieces
1 lemon, sliced with peel
1 large onion, thinly sliced
8 fluid ounces tomato ketchup
¾ pint water
2-3 tablespoons Worcestershire
    sauce
1 teaspoon chilli powder
2 or 3 dashes of Tabasco sauce
1 teaspoon salt

Place spareribs, fat sides up, in a
shallow roasting tin. Put a thin slice
each of lemon and onion on each piece
of sparerib.

Roast in very hot oven (450°F. Mark
8) ½ hour.

Combine remaining ingredients in
a saucepan. Bring to the boil and pour
over ribs.

Reduce heat to moderate (350°F.
Mark 4) and roast until tender, about
30 minutes. Baste ribs every 15 minutes with the sauce in pan, adding a
little more water if needed. Serves 4.

BAKED SPARERIBS WITH SAUERKRAUT

2 sides spareribs
salt, pepper, paprika
1 can sauerkraut (about 1
    pound)
1 small onion, chopped
1 apple, chopped
3 cloves
½ teaspoon caraway seed
3 tablespoons brown sugar

Buy spareribs cut into serving-size
pieces. Put a layer of ribs in bottom
of a large roasting pan. Sprinkle with
salt and pepper.

Combine kraut with chopped onion,
chopped apple, cloves, caraway seed,
and brown sugar.

Cover ribs with kraut mixture, then
top with rest of ribs. Sprinkle with salt,
pepper, and paprika. Add a little water
if sauerkraut seems dry.

Cover pan and bake in slow oven
(325°F. Mark 3) 1 hour. Uncover and
cook another half-hour. Serves 4.

Baked Spareribs with Sauerkraut

SWEET AND SOUR SPARERIBS

2 sides well-fleshed spareribs
1 tablespoon fat or salad oil
½ teaspoon salt
1 small garlic clove
1 can sliced pineapple (about 16
    ounce)
2 medium green peppers
2 tablespoons cornflour
1 teaspoon soy sauce
1 teaspoon Aromat
4 fluid ounces wine vinegar
2 ounces sugar
8 fluid ounces water
maraschino cherries

Buy spareribs cut in serving-size
pieces. Place on rack in roasting tin.
Roast in slow oven (325°F. Mark 3) 1½
hours.

Meanwhile heat fat or salad oil; add
salt and garlic; cook over low heat 10
minutes; remove garlic.

Add syrup from pineapple. Cut
green peppers in 1-inch pieces; add;
cook over low heat 10 minutes.

Blend remaining ingredients, except
cherries; add. Cook, stirring constantly
until thickened and clear. Add pineapple slices and cherries; heat. Pour
sauce over spareribs. Serves 6.

BAKED STUFFED SPARERIBS

Select a whole sparerib piece or part
of two, so that one part can be laid
over the other. Have the breast bone
cracked so that you can cut between
the ribs when cooked.

Rub with 1 teaspoon salt and ¼ teaspoon pepper to each pound. Spread
prune or apple stuffing (see Index)
over larger piece. Cover with other
part. Fasten with small skewers.

Bake in moderate oven (350°F. Mark
4) 1½ hours. Allow ¾ to 1 pound ribs
per person.

If necessary, to prevent burning,
pour 4 tablespoons water in pan.

Baked Without Stuffing: Allow about
1 hour for a whole sparerib. If desired,
sprinkle ribs with flour after seasoning.

CHINESE BARBECUED SPARE-RIBS

2 tablespoons sugar
3 tablespoons honey
8 fluid ounces chicken stock
½ teaspoon salt
dash of pepper
2 tablespoons soy sauce
3 pounds spareribs

Mix sauce ingredients together and
marinate ribs in mixture for 1 hour,
turning frequently.

Remove ribs to rack of roasting tin.
Place small amount of water in tin.

Roast in moderate oven for about 1
hour, turning from time to time.

Serves 4.

Sweet and Sour Spareribs

GLAZED SPARERIBS

Three pounds of spareribs will serve
3 or 4 persons.

Place ribs on rack in a roasting tin.

Bake in slow oven (325°F. Mark 3)
1½ hours, basting frequently with this
mixture: 8 fluid ounces stock or bouillon, 3-4 tablespoons honey or molasses,
1 teaspoon salt, and 2 tablespoons
vinegar.

WINE-BAKED SPARERIBS

3 pounds spareribs
½ pint claret, burgundy or any
    red wine
salt, pepper and mustard
6 ounces brown sugar

Buy the spareribs cracked through
centre. Wipe ribs with damp cloth.

Arrange meat in a shallow baking
tin. Sprinkle surface with salt and
pepper. Rub with dry mustard.

Bake in moderately slow oven (325°F.
to 350°F. Mark 3-4) about 1 hour,
basting at intervals with red wine.

After 1 hour of baking, remove from
oven and rub brown sugar over surface of spareribs. Return to oven and
bake ½ hour longer, basting occasionally with wine and fat from bottom
of tin. Serves 4 to 5.

HAWAIIAN SPARERIBS

2 sides spareribs
3 tablespoons brown sugar
2 tablespoons cornflour
½ teaspoon salt
4 tablespoons vinegar
4 fluid ounces tomato ketchup
1 small can crushed pineapple
1 tablespoon soy sauce

Buy ribs cut into serving pieces.

Combine sugar, cornflour, and salt;
stir in vinegar, ketchup, pineapple and
juice, and soy sauce. Cook until slightly
thickened, about 5 minutes, stirring
constantly.

Arrange a layer of spareribs in roasting pan. Cover with part of pineapple
mixture. Add another layer of ribs and
top with remaining sauce.

Cover tightly. Bake in moderate oven
(350°F. Mark 4) about 1½ hours. Serves
4.

Pork Sausage

ABOUT HOMEMADE SAUSAGE

The recipes for homemade sausage are old-time favourites that have been in use for many years and have wide appeal. Tastes for various seasonings, however, differ and the strength of spices is variable. Adjustment of seasonings to personal taste is recommended but uncooked pork cannot be tasted. We suggest, therefore, that you mix a small sample of any desired recipe and cook it in the form of patties for taste-testing before you season the entire recipe.

OLD-TIME COUNTRY SAUSAGE MEAT

9 pounds fresh lean pork
2 tablespoons thyme or sage
1 teaspoon red pepper
2 tablespoons black pepper
1 ounce salt

Cut pork in small pieces and put through mincer, using medium blade. Mix thoroughly with the seasonings.

Pack tightly into cotton bags 3 inches wide and 12 inches long. Tie the bags at one end.

When ready to use, turn back the end of a bag, and cut meat into ½-inch slices. To cook, start slices in a cold ungreased frying pan over moderate heat and cook until medium brown on both sides and done throughout. This sausage will keep for several weeks in the refrigerator. Makes 9 pounds.

CREOLE PORK SAUSAGE

This Creole sausage is often called chaurice, a name that was probably derived from the Spanish chorizo, a Spanish and Mexican sausage which is sometimes similarly seasoned.

4 pounds lean pork
2 pounds pork fat
2 large onions, finely chopped
1 clove garlic, crushed
3 teaspoons salt
2 teaspoons black pepper
1 teaspoon chilli pepper
1 teaspoon paprika
½ teaspoon cayenne
2 tablespoons finely chopped parsley
¼ teaspoon thyme
½ teaspoon allspice
2 bay leaves, finely chopped
5 yards sausage casing

Put pork and pork fat through the mincer, using medium blade. Place the minced meat in a large bowl; add remaining ingredients and mix until thoroughly blended.

Remove the cutting blade from the mincer and attach the sausage stuffer. Using a yard of casing at a time, work all but a few inches of casing onto the sausage stuffer. Tie a knot at the end of the casing. Refeed the meat through the mincer and into the casing. Twist into links. Keep the sausages in the refrigerator. Makes about 6 pounds.

ITALIAN HOT SAUSAGE

4½ pounds fresh lean pork
1½ pounds fresh fat pork
1 medium onion, chopped
1 large clove garlic, crushed
3 tablespoons salt
1½ tablespoons black pepper, freshly ground
1½ teaspoons paprika
2 tablespoons crushed dried red peppers
2 teaspoons fennel seeds
½ teaspoon crushed bay leaf
¼ teaspoon thyme
pinch of coriander
¼ pint red wine or water
2½ yards sausage casing

Cut the meats into small pieces and put through the mincer with the onion and garlic, using the fine blade. Sprinkle the seasonings and wine over the minced mixture and mix thoroughly.

Remove the cutting blade from the mincer and attach sausage stuffer. Work about half the sausage casing onto the stuffer, leaving a few inches off and tie a knot at the end of the casing.

Put the seasoned minced meat through the mincer and into the casing twisting into desired links. Store the filled sausage in the refrigerator; it is perishable. Makes about 6 pounds.

SPICED PORK SAUSAGES

9 pounds fresh lean pork
3 tablespoons salt
¾ teaspoon red pepper
1½ tablespoons black pepper, freshly ground
1½ tablespoons crushed sage
6 yards sausage casing

Cut the pork into small pieces and put through the mincer, using the fine blade. Sprinkle the seasonings over the minced meat and mix thoroughly.

Remove the cutting blade from the mincer and attach the sausage stuffer. Use a yard of sausage casing at a time, and work all but a few inches of the casing on to the stuffer. Tie a knot at the end of the casing.

Put the minced meat through the mincer and into the case, twisting into desired links. Store the filled sausage in the refrigerator; it is perishable. Makes about 9 pounds.

SPANISH AND MEXICAN HOT SAUSAGE (CHORIZO)

2 pounds lean pork
½ teaspoon crushed hot pepper or 2 small hot red peppers, finely chopped
2 teaspoons salt
3 cloves garlic, crushed
2 tablespoons chilli powder
1 teaspoon black pepper, freshly ground
1 teaspoon oregano
¼ teaspoon ground cummin
4 tablespoons vinegar
1 yard sausage casing

Cut the pork into small pieces and put through the mincer, using the coarse blade. Add remaining ingredients and mix well.

Remove cutting blade from mincer and attach sausage stuffer. Work all but a few inches of casing onto stuffer; tie a knot at the end of casing. Put meat mixture through the mincer and into casing, twisting into desired links. If desired, hang the sausage in cool place to dry. The dried sausage may be kept for a few weeks. Cook as for fresh sausage. Makes about 2 pounds.

CAPE COD SAUSAGE CAKES

½ teaspoon Aromat
1 pound pork sausage meat
8 ounces sugar
8 fluid ounces water
8 ounces fresh cranberries

Add Aromat to sausage meat; mix well. Form into 6 cakes. Fry until well browned; drain on absorbent paper.

Combine sugar and water in saucepan; cook, stirring, until sugar dissolves; simmer 5 minutes.

Pour cranberries into shallow baking dish; add hot syrup. Arrange sausage cakes in pan.

Bake in hot oven (400°F. Mark 6) 30 minutes, or until cranberries have popped open. Serves 6.

Cape Cod Sausage Cakes

PORK SAUSAGES

Method No. 1: Separate the sausages and put in a cold frying pan. Cook over low heat 12 to 15 minutes, pouring off fat as it accumulates.

Method No. 2: Separate the sausages and put in a frying pan with 2 tablespoons water. Cover and steam 5 minutes.

Drain off water and cook sausages over low heat, turning frequently, until well browned.

Do not puncture skins during cooking.

FRIED PORK SAUSAGE PATTIES

Shape bulk sausage meat into thin patties. Place in cold frying pan.

Cook slowly, turning occasionally, until centre has lost pink colour. Drain off fat as it accumulates.

SAUSAGE WITH GLAZED APPLES

2 firm tart apples
4 ounces sugar
4 fluid ounces water
1 teaspoon butter or margarine
4 sausage patties (½ pound) or sausages
1 tablespoon flour
¼ teaspoon sugar

Core and cut apples into ½-inch slices. Combine sugar and water and boil 5 minutes. Add butter.

Drop apple rings into syrup and cook slowly until nearly tender, about 5 minutes. Drain.

If sausage meat is used, form into patties, roll in mixture of flour and ¼ teaspoon sugar. Grill under moderate heat about 8 minutes. If sausages are used, cook as directed in preceding recipe. Serves 4.

PORK SAUSAGE-SWEET POTATO-APPLE CASSEROLE

3 medium sweet potatoes
3 medium tart apples
3 ounces brown sugar
½ teaspoon salt
⅛ teaspoon allspice
1 pound pork sausages
2 tablespoons dripping or fat
4 tablespoons boiling water

Boil sweet potatoes until tender; peel and cut in thick slices. Lay half the slices in greased casserole.

Core unpeeled apples and cut across into ⅛-inch slices. Put half the slices on top of potato slices.

Sprinkle with brown sugar mixed with allspice and salt. Add remaining potatoes and apples.

Fry sausages 10 minutes and place in casserole.

Mix water with a little of the fat; pour over all. Bake in moderate oven (375°F. Mark 5) about 30 minutes. Serves 4.

SAUSAGE SURPRISES

8 ounces plain flour
3 teaspoons baking powder
1 teaspoon salt
2 ounces fat
milk to mix
10 pork chipolatas, cooked

Make scone dough as Master Recipe. Page 115.

Roll out to a scant ¼-inch thickness. Cut twenty circles of dough, using a floured biscuit cutter (about 3-inch size).

Place a cooked sausage on ten of the circles. Place a second circle on top of each, sealing edges with the tines of a fork. Cut a slit about an inch long in the centre of each.

Place on an ungreased baking sheet. Bake in hot oven (425°F. Mark 7) 12 to 15 minutes. Serve plain as an appetizer or with warm applesauce or sausage gravy for a main dish. Makes 10 surprises.

BAKED PORK SAUSAGE PATTIES

Break 1 slice of bread into small pieces. Combine with 1 pound pork sausage meat, 1 egg, 1 small apple grated, and 1 teaspoon salt.

Mix well. Shape into 6 uniform patties ¾-inch thick.

Place on rack in open roasting tin. Bake in moderate oven (350°F. Mark 4) about 40 minutes. Serves 6.

BAKED SAUSAGES

Place sausages on a rack in a roasting tin. Cook in moderate oven (350°F. Mark 4) until done.

SAUSAGES IN WHITE WINE

1 tablespoon butter or margarine
1 onion, finely chopped
12 large pork sausages
8 fluid ounces consommé
8 fluid ounces white wine
2 tablespoons tomato purée
buttered toast
beurre manié (1½ tablespoons flour kneaded with 2 tablespoons butter)

Melt butter in a sauté pan; add onion and pork sausages, pricked with a fork. Cook until the onions and sausages are lightly browned.

Add consommé, white wine, and tomato purée. Simmer, covered, for 10 to 15 minutes.

Place sausages over slices of buttered toast on a heated dish and keep them warm.

Continue to cook the sauce until it is reduced to about 8 fluid ounces and thicken it with bits of beurre manié. Stir well until the sauce is smooth and thick. Taste for seasoning and pour the sauce over the sausages. Serves 6.

Sausage Surprises

SOUTHERN SAUSAGE LOAF

1 pound sausage meat
1 pound lean minced beef
2 ounces fine breadcrumbs
¼ teaspoon pepper
1 teaspoon sage
1 teaspoon salt
2 well beaten eggs
4 tablespoons single cream

Mix all ingredients thoroughly. Form into loaf and bake in moderate oven (350°F. Mark 4) 1 hour, or until done.

This is delicious served with a cream sauce. Serves 6.

HUNGARIAN PORK SAUSAGE LOAF

Combine 2 pounds pork sausage meat with 12 ounces breadcrumbs, 1 slightly beaten egg, and 8 fluid ounces sour cream. Season with paprika.

Pack firmly into loaf tin. Bake in moderate oven (350°F. Mark 4) about 1½ hours. Serves 5 to 6.

RICE AND SAUSAGE CASSEROLE

½ pound pork sausage meat
1 can condensed vegetable soup (without meat)
8 ounces cooked rice
4 tablespoons water

Fry sausage meat (loose, not formed into patties) until brown. Drain off fat to save or discard.

Combine sausage meat, soup, rice, and water. Mix well.

Bake in greased casserole or in individual casseroles in moderate oven (350°F. Mark 4) 20 minutes.

For a decorative touch, fry some sausage meat in small balls and use these with some cooked peas and carrots as a garnish. Add this garnish during final minutes of cooking period. Serves 6.

Rice and Sausage Casserole

Bacon and Gammon

To produce bacon, the flesh of a bacon pig is dry salted or brined and smoked. Green bacon is brine cured but not smoked.

Gammon is the hind leg of a bacon pig, cut square off the side of the bacon and not rounded like ham. The average weight of a whole gammon is 12-16 pounds and is a good lean joint with a rim of fat. The lean should be firm and of a deep pink or bright red colour without any yellow or greenish stains. A dark dry appearance on the cut surface indicates that the joint has been cut for some time and exposed to the air. The fat should be white and firm. Poor quality bacon fat is soft and oily. The rind should be thin, smooth and elastic, but the colour will depend on the method of curing and smoking.

Bacon is usually soaked in cold water before cooking to remove excess salt. The time varies between 2 and 24 hours according to the size of the joint and whether it is smoked or unsmoked.

After soaking large joints, remove the "rust" from the rind and underside by scraping with the back of a knife. Most small joints are sold boned.

All boiling joints should be skinned before serving. If the joint is to be served cold, allow it to get cold in the liquid, then remove and peel off the skin. If it is to be served hot, skin in the same way. When the skin peels off easily it is an indication that the meat is well cooked.

Various parts of the bacon are used as joints for boiling. Gammon joints are usually cooked and served as ham and can be cut into four pieces.

Corner Gammon: A good lean joint generally weighing 4-4½ pounds. It is best boiled and can be served hot or cold. Gammon rashers are cut from this joint.

Middle Gammon: Average weight 5-6 pounds but can be divided into smaller joints which are more convenient for a small family. Serve hot or cold. Good lean rashers suitable for grilling or frying with eggs are cut from this joint.

Gammon Hock: Average weight 5-6 pounds. This is very suitable for partial cooking by boiling and then glazing and baking. See Glazes. Compared with other gammon joints, hock has less cut surface and more outside fat so the flesh is less inclined to be dry.

Gammon Slipper: A small lean boiling joint weighing about 1½ pounds. Suitable for a small family.

Fore Leg or **Fore Hock** can also be cooked whole or divided into three. The whole joint weighs about 8 pounds.

Butt: Leanest cut, weighing about 3-4 pounds, and is best boiled.

Fore Slipper: Like the gammon slipper but fatter and the meat is generally coarser. The average weight is 1-1½ pounds, and is best boiled.

Small Hock: The average weight is 3 pounds. It has a high proportion of bone and is generally used boned and minced for pâté, mousse, etc.

Collar: This is a good boiling joint weighing about 5-6 pounds, but can also be partially boiled and finished in the oven. It is evenly streaked with fat and less expensive than gammon.

BACON RASHERS

These are cut from the back of the pig. Sometimes the pieces are boiled whole but more often sliced and used as rashers.

Back Rashers: Good for frying or grilling. Usually have about equal amounts of fat and lean.

Short Back: Similar to the above but cut into short rashers.

Long Back: Long rashers, good for frying, generally leaner than back rashers

Topback: Usually cut fairly thick like gammon rashers—often served with pineapple.

Streaky: These rashers vary in width. The flavour is good and they are best to serve with liver and kidneys.

Flank: A narrow rasher with a high proportion of fat—very good to use for lining dishes for pâté and to serve with liver.

Rashers are sliced in varying thicknesses depending on personal taste. Slicing machines have numbers, the lowest, e.g. 4, is a thin cut and gives a crisp rasher when fried.

Decorated Baked Ham: Cut stems for flowers from green peppers or cucumber rind. Make blossoms by cutting canned pineapple into small rings, and maraschino cherries in half. Arrange on ham to form gay bouquet, holding in place with cocktail sticks. Brush with a little additional glaze and return to oven until fruit and ham are glazed to perfection. Remove cocktail sticks before serving.

TO COOK A BUTT JOINT

Use a joint of about 3 pounds. Place in deep saucepan and cover with cold water. Bring just to boiling; reduce heat and simmer (*do not boil*) 30 minutes per pound, or until tender. Remove from water.

Place in roasting tin. Spread butt with prepared mustard. Stud with whole cloves. Sprinkle with brown sugar. Bake in moderate oven (350°F. Mark 4) until glazed, about 30 minutes. Serves 8.

GLAZES FOR BAKED HAM

General Directions: Thirty minutes before end of baking time, remove the ham from oven, score fat (cut shallow crisscross gashes), stick with cloves, spread with a glaze and return to oven.

Brown Sugar-Orange Glaze: Mix together 6 ounces brown sugar, 1 teaspoon dry mustard, and enough orange juice to moisten.

Brown Sugar-Pineapple Glaze: Mix 4½ ounces brown sugar with 4 ounces crushed pineapple.

Molasses Glaze: Mix dark molasses or treacle with a very little vinegar from sweet pickles. Spread sparingly on ham. Sprinkle with fine breadcrumbs.

Maple-Cider Glaze: Mix 6 ounces maple or golden syrup, 4 fluid ounces cider, and 2 tablespoons dry mustard.

Spiced Honey Glaze: Mix 12 ounces honey with 2 tablespoons mustard. Spread over ham. Sprinkle with fine dry breadcrumbs.

Jelly Glaze: Mix 8 ounces red currant jelly with 4 tablespoons horseradish.

Cranberry Glaze: Mix 1 can whole or jellied cranberry sauce, mashed with a fork, with 6 ounces light corn syrup or golden syrup. Or, use cranberry sauce alone.

ROTISSERIE-ROASTED HAM

Use a boned and cooked ham. Centre ham lengthwise on spit and tie with cord if necessary. Place on rotisserie. Roast about 10 minutes per pound or until meat thermometer reads 130°F. During the last 30 minutes glaze by occasionally spooning orange marmalade over the turning ham.

BAKED BACON WITH CIDER

3-4 pounds gammon
black treacle
cloves
½ pint dry cider

Soak the bacon in cold water for at least 4-5 hours or overnight. Scrape to remove any "rust", then put into clean cold water and bring to boiling point. Remove any scum which rises then cover and simmer for half the required cooking time. (Allow 30 minutes per pound.) Alternatively, this part of the cooking can be done in a pressure cooker. (See page 941.)

Remove the bacon from the liquid and cut off the rind.

Using a sharp knife, score the fat in crisscross fashion, making a diamond pattern. Press a clove into the fat in each diamond. Place the meat in a roasting tin and trickle some black treacle all over the surface. Pour the cider round the meat and finish the cooking in a moderately hot oven (400°F. Mark 6) basting frequently with the cider mixture. Serve the cider with the meat as an unthickened gravy. Suitable accompaniments are creamed potatoes, and peas, green beans, broad beans, spinach or red cabbage.

The remainder is delicious served cold with potato salad, green salad or tomato salad and your favourite relish.

SPICED COTTAGE ROLL (BONED BUTT)

Place ham (about 3 pounds) in a large saucepan. Cover with water. Add 6 whole cloves, ½ bay leaf, 1 stick cinnamon, ½ teaspoon celery seed, 1 sliced onion, and 4 fluid ounces vinegar.

Cover tightly. Let simmer until done. Allow 30 minutes per pound.

"BOILED" HAM

Place smoked ham in saucepan with water to cover. Bring to boiling point. Reduce heat until water just simmers but does not bubble. Cover closely and simmer until tender.

For a very large ham (12 to 16 pounds), allow 25 minutes per pound; for a 10- to 12-pound ham, allow 30 minutes per pound; for a half ham, allow 35 minutes per pound.

If ham is not to be served hot, let it cool in the water in which it was cooked.

If ham is to be baked, remove from liquid, remove rind, score and glaze ham as in baked ham.

Bake in moderate oven (350°F. Mark 4) about 30 minutes.

PROSCIUTTO

This Italian-style ham is becoming increasingly popular and generally available everywhere. It is a pepper-covered and air-dried ready-to-eat ham which may be served hot or cold. It is most commonly used on an hors d'oeuvres tray.

It should be sliced very thin. It goes very well with potato salad and makes an excellent wrap-round for tiny pickles.

A classic hors d'oeuvre is prosciutto served with fresh figs or slices of melon.

CAPOCOLLO

Capocollo is an Italian term for cooked, boneless pork butt that has been rolled in spices and pepper. It is served in thin slices as an appetizer.

GLAZED SMOKED PORK BUTT WITH CHERRIES

1 2½-3 pound butt joint
6 whole cloves
1 bay leaf
2 tablespoons brown sugar
1 teaspoon dry mustard
1 small can cherries, drained

Cover pork butt with water. Add cloves and bay leaf and simmer until tender, about 2 hours. Remove and place in shallow roasting tin. (Save broth for cooking vegetables such as beans or cabbage.)

Mix sugar and mustard and sprinkle over pork. Pour sherry juice into tin.

Bake in moderate oven (350°F. Mark 4), basting often with juice in tin, about 25 minutes or until well glazed.

Heat cherries in roasting tin and serve with pork. Serves 6 to 8.

Ham en Croûte

HAM EN CROÛTE

4 ounces dry breadcrumbs
1 teaspoon onion flakes
4 ounces plain flour
4 ounces fat
4 tablespoons cold water
1 (1½ to 2 pounds) canned ham

Mix breadcrumbs, onion flakes and flour. Cut in fat. Stir in cold water to form a very stiff dough. Turn out on to a floured board and roll into a rectangle about 8 × 12 inches.

Remove jelly and excess fat from ham. Place ham in centre of pastry and fold over the ham. Invert on shallow baking tin.

Flute edges of crust, and prick with a fork along top and sides. Bake in hot oven (400°F. Mark 6) 50 minutes or until brown. Serve hot or cold. Serves 4.

SLICED BUFFET HAM

Slice some cooked ham and arrange neatly in a baking dish. Spread with orange marmalade and bake for 10-15 minutes in a slow oven (325°F. Mark 3).

BAKED ORANGE HAM

Place smoked ham in slow oven (325°F. Mark 3), allowing 30 minutes per pound.

Half an hour before end of baking period, remove ham from oven. With sharp knife, cut fat into crisscross gashes.

Mix 4½ ounces brown sugar with grated rind and juice of 1 small orange; spread over fat.

Using whole cloves, stick a few half orange slices and maraschino cherries onto fat.

Return to oven to brown. The last 10 minutes, increase oven heat to 400°F. Mark 6.

Baked Orange Ham

Quick Ways with Cooked Ham

CREAMED HAM
(Master Recipe)

¾ pint medium white sauce
12 ounces diced cooked ham
¼ teaspoon dry mustard

Combine all ingredients in top of double boiler. Heat thoroughly.

Adjust seasoning to taste with additional mustard or a few drops Tabasco sauce.

Serve on toast, scones, split squares of buttered corn bread, in pastry cases, croustades, with mashed potatoes, or with croquettes. Serves 6.

Ham à La King: Add 1 canned pimiento, chopped, 3 tablespoons chopped green pepper, and, if desired, ½ pound sliced and sautéed mushrooms.

Other Variations of Creamed Ham: Add any of the following to creamed ham: 2 ounces cooked sweet corn, canned whole kernels, 4 ounces cooked or canned green peas, 1 tablespoon chopped black olives, or 3 tablespoons chilli sauce.

Ham with Cheese Sauce: Substitute cheese sauce for medium white sauce in master recipe.

CREAMED HAM, CELERY, AND WALNUTS

½ small head celery, sliced
8 fluid ounces water
milk, as needed
3 ounces butter or margarine
1½ ounces flour
few grains pepper
½ teaspoon Aromat
1 tablespoon cut chives
1 pound diced, leftover ham
3 ounces coarsely broken walnuts
salt to taste

Cook sliced celery in water until tender. Drain; measure water; add enough milk to make 1¼ pints.

Melt butter or margarine; blend in flour, pepper, and Aromat. Add milk mixture; cook over low heat until smooth and thickened.

Add chives, ham, walnuts, and cooked celery. Salt to taste. Serve with hot toasted garlic bread. Serves 6.

Creamed Ham, Celery, and Walnuts

HAM WITH PINEAPPLE AND SWEET POTATOES

3 tablespoons chopped onion
2 ounces butter or margarine
2 tablespoons flour
4 fluid ounces pineapple juice
2 ounces pineapple pieces
2 ounces brown sugar
1½ pounds chopped cooked ham
6 sliced cooked sweet potatoes

Pan-fry onion in butter in chafing dish or sauté pan. Blend in flour.

Add pineapple juice and cook until thickened.

Stir in pineapple pieces, brown sugar, and ham.

Arrange sweet potatoes on top. Cover and simmer for 10 minutes. Serve hot. Serves 4 to 6.

HAM AND MUSHROOM CASSEROLE

6 ounces uncooked noodles
¾ pint medium white sauce
2 ounces grated Cheddar cheese
½ teaspoon onion powder or 1 tablespoon grated onion
2 stalks celery
1 4-ounce can mushrooms
1 pound diced leftover ham
salt and pepper
buttered crumbs

Cook noodles in boiling, slightly salted water.

Make white sauce and melt cheese in hot sauce. Add onion, sliced celery, and mushrooms, which have been browned in a little hot fat.

Add noodles, ham, and salt and pepper to taste.

Turn into greased baking dish; cover with fine buttered crumbs and bake in moderate oven (375°F. Mark 5) 30 minutes, or until crumbs are brown. Serves 4.

SHERRIED HAM-CHEESE PUFF

6 slices bread, buttered and cubed
6 ounces grated Cheddar cheese
8 ounces finely diced baked or boiled ham
2 slightly beaten eggs
8 fluid ounces milk
3 fluid ounces sherry
½ teaspoon Worcestershire sauce
salt and pepper to taste

Arrange alternate layers of bread cubes, cheese, and ham in a greased baking dish, ending with a layer of bread cubes on top.

Mix remaining ingredients; pour over contents of baking dish. Bake in a slow oven (325°F. Mark 3) for 1 hour. Serves 4.

Ham with Pineapple and Sweet Potatoes

HAM AND CORN CUSTARD

2 tablespoons finely chopped onion
2 tablespoons bacon fat
3 beaten eggs
8 fluid ounces milk
4 ounces whole kernel corn
8 ounces diced cooked ham
1 tablespoon finely chopped parsley
salt and pepper

Sauté onions in fat until tender. Beat eggs; add milk, corn, ham, parsley, and salt and pepper to taste. Stir in onions.

Pour into oiled casserole and bake in moderate oven (350°F. Mark 4) 30 to 40 minutes or until custard is firm.

This makes a good luncheon or supper dish and may be served with a tomato or mushroom sauce. Serves 4 to 6.

SOUTHERN CREAMED HAM

1 can (10½ ounces) condensed cream of mushroom soup
4 tablespoons milk
8 ounces cubed cooked ham
2 tablespoons diced pimiento
corn bread

Blend soup, milk, ham, and pimiento in saucepan; heat thoroughly.

Pour over corn bread or waffles. Serves 4.

HAM AND SWEET POTATO PATTIES

1 pound cooked ham, chopped finely
4 cooked and mashed sweet potatoes
½ teaspoon salt
4 tablespoons milk
1 tablespoon butter or margarine
1 egg
⅛ teaspoon nutmeg
⅛ teaspoon cinnamon
2 ounces pineapple, chopped finely
4 ounces crushed cornflakes
2 to 4 tablespoons fat

Combine all ingredients except cornflakes and fat. Shape into 8 patties. Dip in cornflakes.

Melt 2 tablespoons fat in frying pan. Brown patties slowly, adding more fat as necessary. Fry on both sides until crisp and well browned. Serves 4.

Ham Ring with Creamed Peas

AM LOAF OR RING

4 slices slightly stale bread
3 fluid ounces milk
1 egg
1 pound minced cooked ham
½ pound minced beef
1 small onion, chopped
salt and pepper

Crumble bread into fine crumbs and oak in milk about 5 minutes. Beat egg ightly and add with meats and onion o crumbs. Season to taste with salt nd pepper.

Put in greased loaf tin or ring mould. ake in moderate oven (375°F. Mark 1 hour. To serve, fill centre with reamed peas. Serves 6.

ariation: Use 6 fluid ounces milk and tablespoons tomato ketchup in place f 8 fluid ounces milk.

PSIDE-DOWN HAM LOAF

1 ounce butter
1½ ounces brown sugar
8 to 12 canned pineapple slices
whole cloves
2 pounds minced cooked ham
2 tablespoons grated onion
½ teaspoon dry mustard
4 ounces breadcrumbs
4 fluid ounces pineapple juice
2 slightly beaten eggs
dash of cayenne

Melt butter in bottom of greased loaf in or casserole; sprinkle with brown ugar. Stud pineapple slices with whole loves and arrange on top of sugar.

Combine ham and remaining in-redients; pack into tin or casserole n top of pineapple slices.

Bake, covered in moderate oven 375°F. Mark 4) about 30 minutes.

Turn out upside-down on hot dish. erves 6 to 8.

Golden Ham Casserole

HAM AND CORN AU GRATIN

1 pound diced cooked ham
10 ounces canned or cooked whole
    kernel corn
2 tablespoons grated onion
½ small finely chopped green
    pepper
12 fluid ounces medium white sauce
½ teaspoon dry mustard
2 ounces grated cheese
2 ounces buttered crumbs

Arrange ham, corn, onion, and green pepper in layers in greased casserole.

Mix mustard with white sauce; pour into casserole. Top with grated cheese and buttered crumbs, mixed. Sprinkle with paprika.

Bake in moderate oven (375°F. Mark 4) about 25 minutes or until browned. Serves 6.

HAM AND RICE ROUNDUP

5 ounces quick-cooking rice
1 can (10½ ounces) condensed
    cream of mushroom soup
5 fluid ounces milk
2 tablespoons grated onion
8 ounces cubed cooked ham
2 tablespoons chopped parsley
2 tablespoons chopped pimiento
¼ ounce cornflakes

Cook rice according to directions on packet.

Combine soup, milk, and grated onion in 2½-pint casserole; mix well.

Add cooked rice, ham, parsley, and pimiento; sprinkle cornflakes over top.

Bake in moderate oven (375°F. Mark 4) about 25 minutes, or until hot. Serves 6.

GOLDEN HAM CASSEROLE

1 tablespoon vinegar or lemon
    juice
8 fluid ounces milk
¾-1 pound diced cooked ham
2 eggs, slightly beaten
salt and pepper
4 ounces grated cheese
10 ounces uncooked noodles
1 tablespoon grated onion
sliced, stuffed olives, sliced celery,
    fried mushrooms, or cooked
    peas as liked

Stir vinegar or lemon juice into milk and let stand a few minutes.

Combine ham, milk, eggs, ½ tea-spoon salt, ⅛ teaspoon pepper, cheese, and noodles which have been cooked in boiling salted water until barely tender, then rinsed in warm water.

Add onion, olives, celery, mush-rooms, or cooked peas (or use more than one of these if desired). Pour mixture into greased casserole.

Top with buttered breadcrumbs or crushed cereal flakes. Bake in moder-ate oven (375°F. Mark 4) 35 minutes.

Serves 5 to 6.

HAM TREAT

1 ounce butter or margarine
1 ounce flour
12 fluid ounces milk
12 ounces leftover chopped ham (or
    any leftover meat)
3 eggs, separated
2 tablespoons grated onion
1 teaspoon salt
¼ teaspoon pepper
1 teaspoon Worcestershire sauce
4 ounces fine dry breadcrumbs

Melt the butter in the top of a double pan, blend in flour and gradually stir in milk. When sauce thickens, add chopped ham, slightly beaten egg yolks, grated onion, seasonings and Worces-tershire sauce. Cool.

Mix in breadcrumbs and then fold in egg whites, which have been beaten stiffly.

Pour into greased casserole; bake in moderate oven (350°F. Mark 4) 1 hour. Serves 4 to 6.

HAM LOAF

1½ pounds minced cooked ham
1 tablespoon brown sugar
1 tablespoon vinegar
8 ounces soft breadcrumbs
½ small onion, finely chopped
2 tablespoons finely chopped
    parsley
¼ teaspoon pepper
½ pint milk
2 beaten eggs

Combine ingredients and fill greased loaf tin.

Place in a pan of hot water. Bake in moderate oven (350°F. Mark 4) 1 hour. Serves 6.

HAM AND PINEAPPLE FRITTERS

3½ ounces plain flour
1 teaspoon baking powder
3 fluid ounces milk
2 eggs
1 tablespoon Angostura bitters
1 pound minced, cooked ham
2 ounces crushed, drained pine-
    apple
fat for deep frying

In mixing bowl, sift flour with baking powder. Add milk, eggs, and bitters; mix until smooth. Fold in ham and well-drained pineapple.

Drop by teaspoonful into deep hot fat (350°F.) and fry until golden brown. Drain on paper towels. Makes 20 to 30 small fritters.

Ham and Pineapple Fritters

HAM, GREEN BEAN, AND MUSHROOM CASSEROLE

1 pound green beans, cut in 2-inch pieces
1 pound fresh mushrooms
2 ounces butter
1½ ounces plain flour
¾ pint milk
8 fluid ounces cream
1 teaspoon salt
dash of white pepper
1½ pounds cooked ham, cut in strips
1 small pimiento, cut in strips
grated cheese for top

Cook beans until tender. Cut mushrooms lengthwise and in quarters and sauté in butter 5 minutes.

Sauté a few mushrooms whole for top garnish and set them aside. Blend in sifted flour gradually to butter and mushrooms; add milk, cream, salt, and pepper and cook until thickened.

Add ham, beans and pimiento to above sauce; mix and place in a 3-pint casserole. Top with whole mushrooms. Sprinkle with grated cheese.

Bake in moderate oven (350°F. Mark 4) for 20 minutes. Serves 6 to 8.

HAM WITH ORANGE CURRIED RICE

1 ounce butter or margarine
2 tablespoons chopped green pepper
1 tablespoon chopped onion
2 tablespoons brown sugar
1 pound cooked ham, cut into small pieces
1 teaspoon salt
⅛ teaspoon curry powder
4 fluid ounces orange juice
1 tablespoon grated orange peel
8 ounces cooked rice

Pan-fry green pepper and onion in butter for 5 minutes. Add brown sugar and ham. Stir and continue cooking for 5 minutes.

Add remaining ingredients. Mix well. Cover and cook for 10 minutes. Serves 4.

HAM AND SWEET POTATO CASSEROLE

12 ounces diced cooked ham
1 tablespoon butter or bacon fat
1½ pounds sweet potatoes, cooked and mashed (or use canned)
2 beaten eggs
4 fluid ounces milk
1½ tablespoons lemon juice
about ½ teaspoon salt

Brown ham slightly in hot fat.

Whip potatoes until smooth and mix with beaten eggs, milk, lemon juice, and salt to taste. Whip again.

Mix with browned ham and fat from the pan. Turn into greased 1½-2-pint casserole.

Bake, uncovered, in moderate oven (350°F. Mark 4) 45 minutes. Serves 4 to 5.

BACON AND HAM STACKS

Mix 1 pound minced leftover ham with a beaten egg. Make into 5 patties.

Cross two rashers of bacon; lay on them one slice of pineapple, one patty of mashed seasoned sweet potato, and one patty of minced ham.

Fold over ends of bacon and fasten with a cocktail stick. Place in baking dish and bake in moderate oven (350°F. Mark 4) for 1 hour. Serves 5.

BAKED HAM TIMBALES

4 eggs
1 pound minced cooked ham
12 fluid ounces milk
½ teaspoon salt
½ teaspoon paprika
¼ teaspoon celery salt
1 teaspoon chopped onion
1 tablespoon chopped parsley

Beat eggs and add to other ingredients. Mix well. Pour into buttered dariole tins.

Place tins in pan of water. Place in slow oven (325°F. Mark 3) 1 hour. Remove from tins to serve. Serves 6.

HAM BALLS IN SOUR CREAM GRAVY

½ small onion, chopped
2 ounces fat
1 pound minced cooked ham
¼ teaspoon pepper
1 egg
1 ounce flour
4 fluid ounces water
8 fluid ounces sour cream

Pan-fry onion in fat in a frying pan. Remove and combine with ham, pepper, and egg.

Shape mixture into 2-inch balls and brown in hot fat. When evenly browned remove from pan onto a dish.

Combine flour with remaining fat in frying pan. Add water and sour cream and cook until thickened. Pour over ham balls and serve. Serves 4 to 5.

GLAZED HAM PATTIES

1 pound minced cooked ham
1 ounce dry breadcrumbs
1 beaten egg
¼ pint evaporated milk
dash of pepper
pinch of thyme
½ small onion, chopped finely
3 ounces brown sugar
1½ tablespoons vinegar
½ teaspoon dry mustard

Use medium blade for mincing ham. Mix thoroughly with breadcrumbs,

Bacon and Ham Stacks

egg, milk, pepper, thyme, and chopped onion.

For baking patties, use 12 large deep bun tins. Grease them lightly and pack in ham mixture lightly, filling about ⅔-full. Bake in moderate oven (350°F. Mark 4) 10 minutes.

Meanwhile, blend brown sugar, vinegar, and dry mustard in saucepan. Boil syrup 1 minute, stirring occasionally.

After 10 minutes of baking, remove patties from oven and spoon syrup over each. Return to oven and bake 10 minutes longer to glaze patties. Makes 12 patties (6 servings).

HAM CONES, HAWAIIAN

1 pound minced cooked ham
1 tablespoon grated onion
1 tablespoon chopped parsley
1 tablespoon prepared mustard
2 tablespoons pineapple syrup
1 slightly beaten egg
4 ounces crushed cornflakes
10 drained pineapple slices

Mix first 6 ingredients together thoroughly. Shape into 10 cone-shaped patties.

Roll cones carefully in crushed cornflakes and place on drained pineapple slices in shallow baking dish.

Bake in moderate oven (375°F. Mark 4) about 25 minutes. Serve with creamy sauce (below). Makes 10 cones.

Creamy Sauce: Melt ½ ounce butter. Blend in ½ ounce flour.

Add ¼ teaspoon salt, dash of black pepper, dash of Ac'cent or Aromat, and 6 fluid ounces milk, stirring constantly to keep mixture smooth while cooking until slightly thickened, about 5 minutes.

Glazed Ham Patties

HAM AND SWEET POTATOES – HAWAIIAN

6 medium sweet potatoes
1½ ounces butter or margarine
½ teaspoon salt
⅛ teaspoon pepper
pinch of nutmeg
milk
1 pound diced cooked ham
1 small can pineapple chunks, drained
1 small green pepper, cut into strips
2 tablespoons brown sugar
1 tablespoon cornflour
6 fluid ounces juice, drained from pineapple
2 tablespoons vinegar

Cook and mash sweet potatoes, then add ½ ounce butter, salt, pepper, nutmeg, and enough milk to whip potatoes.

Pan-fry ham in remaining butter until golden. Add pineapple and green pepper; cook 3 minutes. Mix sugar and cornflour. Then blend in pineapple juice and vinegar.

Cook, stirring constantly, until clear and thickened. Pour mixture into a shallow casserole. Drop spoonfuls of whipped sweet potato on top.

Bake in hot oven (400°F. Mark 6) until thoroughly heated, about 20 minutes.

Serves 4 to 5.

HAM PUFF

8 ounces chopped cooked ham
7 ounces mashed potatoes
¼ teaspoon salt
1 egg, separated
2 ounces grated Cheddar cheese
buttered julienne carrots

Mix ham, potatoes, and salt. Add egg yolk and fold in beaten egg white.

Pile mixture in centre of a buttered pan or shallow glass baking dish and sprinkle with cheese.

Bake in moderate oven (350°F. Mark 4) 30 minutes. Serve with a border of hot buttered julienne carrots. Serves 4.

HAM WITH SWEET POTATOES AND PEAS

1 pound diced, cooked ham
8 ounces cooked peas
1 can condensed cream of mushroom soup
4 hot cooked medium sweet potatoes
1 ounce butter or margarine
¼ teaspoon salt
½ teaspoon cinnamon

Combine ham, peas, and soup in greased 2½-pint casserole.

Mash sweet potatoes; add butter, salt, and cinnamon. Place in 6 mounds on top of mixture in casserole.

Bake in moderate oven (350°F. Mark 4) 30 minutes. Serves 6.

BARBECUED PORKIES

1 small onion, chopped
1 ounce butter or margarine
1½ ounces light brown sugar
1 teaspoon salt
3-4 tablespoons chilli sauce
8 fluid ounces tomato juice
2 tablespoons Worcestershire sauce
6 tablespoons cider or salad vinegar
2 pounds cooked boneless ham

Sauté onion in butter in sauté pan until lightly browned.

Add remaining ingredients except meat; simmer, uncovered, 20 minutes, stirring occasionally.

Slice meat ⅛ to ¼ inch thick; place in barbecue sauce. Simmer, covered, 20 minutes.

Skim off any excess fat. Serve in heated soft bread rolls or baps. Makes 10 to 12 Porkies.

HAM WITH MACARONI AND SPINACH

8 ounces elbow macaroni
¾ pint milk
½ pound process cheese, cubed
2 teaspoons prepared mustard
8 ounces cubed cooked ham
8 ounces chopped cooked spinach
1 tomato, cut in wedges

Cook macaroni in boiling salted water until tender; drain.

Combine milk, cheese, mustard, and ham. Add to drained macaroni and mix lightly.

Place spinach in bottom of greased shallow casserole. Pour macaroni mixture over spinach.

Arrange tomato wedges in a ring on top of macaroni mixture, pressing gently into macaroni. Dot with butter, if desired.

Bake in moderate oven (375°F. Mark 5) 20 to 30 minutes. Serve at once. Serves 4 to 6.

HAM BURGERS

1 pound canned or cooked sweet potatoes, mashed
12 ounces minced cooked ham
4½ ounces brown sugar
1 teaspoon dry mustard
3 tablespoons milk
1 teaspoon salt
¼ teaspoon pepper
crushed cereal flakes

Mix all ingredients, except cereal flakes, thoroughly.

Form into flat patties. Coat with cereal flakes.

Brown slowly on both sides in small amount of bacon fat. Serves 6.

HAM AND POTATOES IN SOUR CREAM SAUCE

¾ pint sour cream
1 tablespoon melted butter
1 tablespoon flour
1 lightly beaten egg
pinch of salt
pinch of nutmeg
breadcrumbs
½ pound ham, thinly sliced
1 pound cooked potatoes, sliced
grated cheese
1 tablespoon butter

Blend together sour cream, 1 tablespoon melted butter, and flour. Gradually stir in egg, keeping mixture smooth. Add salt and nutmeg. Cook over medium heat, stirring constantly, until smooth and thickened. Remove from heat at once and let cool.

Sprinkle a well buttered 1½-2-pint casserole liberally with breadcrumbs.

Arrange ham in casserole. Put layer of potatoes on ham. Cover with layer of sour cream mixture. Repeat until all ingredients are used up.

Sprinkle top with grated cheese. Dot with butter. Bake in slow oven (300°F. Mark 2) 1 hour. Serves 3 to 4.

SCALLOPED HAM AND EGGPLANT (AUBERGINE)

1 medium eggplant, peeled and sliced
1 large onion, chopped
2 ounces butter or margarine
pint apple purée
1 pound diced cooked ham
½ teaspoon sage
¼ teaspoon salt
3 ounces soft buttered breadcrumbs

Cook eggplant until tender in boiling salted water; drain and chop.

Pan-fry onion in butter and add to eggplant with apple purée, ham, and seasonings. Turn into 2½-pint casserole. Top with crumbs.

Bake in moderate oven (375°F. Mark 5) 25 minutes. Serves 4 to 6.

CRANBERRY HAM ROLLS

1 pound minced cooked ham
2 ounces fine breadcrumbs
1 slightly beaten egg
2 tablespoons milk
¼ teaspoon allspice
⅛ teaspoon pepper
¼ teaspoon ground cloves
1 ounce butter or margarine
1 can jellied cranberry sauce
1 teaspoon vinegar

Combine all ingredients except butter, cranberry sauce, and vinegar. Form into 6 balls. Brown on all sides in butter in a frying pan.

Heat cranberry sauce and vinegar in a small saucepan until melted. Pour over balls. Cover pan and cook slowly for 20 minutes. Serves 6.

Quick Ways with Gammon Rashers

BARBECUED GAMMON RASHER

1 gammon rasher, cut 1-inch thick
2 tablespoons dry mustard
2 tablespoons brown sugar
3 drops Tabasco sauce
5 tablespoons vinegar
few grains cayenne
½ teaspoon paprika
2 tablespoons hot water
3 tablespoons red currant jelly

Parboil gammon for 5 minutes in water to just cover. Drain. Sear on both sides under grill.

Place in greased casserole which, if liked, may be first rubbed with cut clove of garlic.

Combine remaining ingredients and spread over meat. Add 2 tablespoons water or stock.

Cover closely. Bake in moderate oven (350°F. Mark 4) 35 to 40 minutes. Serves 4.

FRIED GAMMON RASHER

Trim rind from gammon rasher. Heat frying pan and rub with lard. Brown slice on both sides.

Cover and cook over low heat slowly until tender, turning several times.

Allow about 10 minutes for ¼-inch-thick slice and about 15 minutes for ½-inch thick slice.

GAMMON RASHER HAWAIIAN

1 small can crushed pineapple
1 1-inch thick slice of gammon
3 ounces brown sugar

Drain pineapple; reserve syrup. Place gammon on rack in shallow baking tin. Pour pineapple syrup over it. Bake in slow oven (325°F. Mark 3) 1 hour.

Combine pineapple with brown sugar. Spread over top of meat. Bake in hot oven (400°F. Mark 6) an additional 15 minutes.

Garnish with canned whole beets which have been hollowed out a bit and filled with horseradish sauce (below). Serves 4 to 6.

Horseradish Sauce: Combine ¼ pint whipped cream with 3 tablespoons drained, prepared horseradish and ¼ teaspoon salt.

Gammon Rasher Hawaiian

GRILLED GAMMON RASHER

Preheat the grill and grease rack with a piece of ham fat.

Gash fat edge on the gammon in several places to prevent curling during cooking.

Place meat on rack. Brush with a little oil or melted butter and grill under moderate heat for about 10 minutes each side.

Gammon Rasher with Peaches: When the gammon is turned, arrange well drained peach halves on the grill rack.

Brush the peaches with melted margarine or butter and grill until heated through and slightly browned.

Grilled Gammon Meal: The cooked dinner vegetables may be heated at the same time as the gammon is being grilled, by placing them in the lower part of the grill pan to catch the fat which drips from the meat and take on added flavour.

GAMMON RASHER WITH SWEET POTATOES

¾ to 1 pound slice of gammon
2 medium-sized sweet potatoes, peeled
2 tablespoons brown sugar
8 fluid ounces hot water

Cut gammon in serving pieces and brown in a frying pan, then place in a baking dish.

Slice sweet potatoes over it and sprinkle with sugar. Add water to fat left in the pan, and pour over sweet potatoes.

Bake in moderate oven (350°F. Mark 4) about 45 minutes, basting occasionally with the liquid. Remove cover for last 15 minutes. Serves 4.

BAKED GAMMON RASHER COUNTRY STYLE

1 gammon rasher, cut 1-inch thick
pepper to taste
pinch of thyme
1 can tomatoes
4 sprigs parsley, chopped
¼ pound grated Cheddar cheese,
½ small onion, chopped
1 bay leaf

Put gammon in greased casserole or baking dish with a tight-fitting lid.

Sprinkle with pepper and thyme. Cover with remaining ingredients which have been well mixed.

Cover tightly and bake in moderate oven (350°F. Mark 4) about 45 minutes, turning once during the cooking. Serves 4.

Baked Stuffed Gammon Rashers

BAKED STUFFED GAMMON RASHERS

12 ounces soft breadcrumbs
3 ounces sultanas
1½ ounces brown sugar
1 teaspoon dry mustard
2 ounces melted butter
2 slices (2 pounds) gammon ½ inch thick
9 slices pineapple
30 whole cloves
parsley

Mix breadcrumbs, sultanas, sugar, and mustard together. Pour butter evenly over mixture.

Place 1 slice of gammon in 4½-5 pint shallow baking dish. Spread dressing lightly over slice. Top with second slice of gammon. Stick cloves in fat around edge.

Cut 1 pineapple slice into wedges to make flower petals for top of meat. Place 2 pineapple slices, 1 on top of the other, in each corner of the dish.

Bake in slow oven (325°F. Mark 3) 1 hour. Garnish with parsley and serve. Serves 6 to 8.

SAVOURY GAMMON RASHER IN CREAM GRAVY

2 tablespoons dry mustard
2 tablespoons water
1 slice gammon, about 1½ inches thick (weight about 2 pounds)
8 fluid ounces milk

Make a paste of the mustard and water. Spread on both sides of gammon.

Place gammon in a shallow baking dish. Add milk and bake in slow oven (325°F. Mark 3) until tender and nicely browned. Serves 6.

SPICY BAKED GAMMON

½ teaspoon each of caraway seeds, chervil, garlic salt, nutmeg, and oregano
1 teaspoon each of chopped parsley and tarragon
8 fluid ounces water
8 fluid ounces wine vinegar
1 2-inch thick slice of gammon

Combine herbs and spices with water and vinegar; heat through and pour over gammon.

Bake in moderate oven (350°F. Mark 4) 2 hours. Spoon sauce over the meat once or twice while baking. Serves 6.

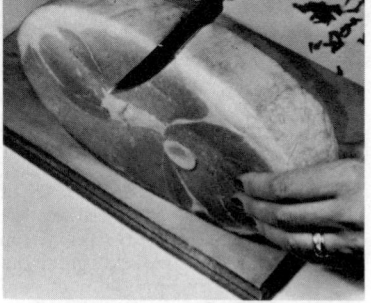

Slash edges of fat about 2 inches apart.

Add brown sugar and bake.

Holiday Baked Gammon.

GRILLED GAMMON WITH ASPARAGUS

slice of gammon (to serve 4)
cooked asparagus spears
4 thick slices jellied cranberry
    sauce
4 thick slices Cheddar cheese,
    halved

Cut gammon into four portions, grill and place in a shallow fireproof serving dish. Place 2 or 3 spears of cooked asparagus on top of each serving. Then place a slice of cranberry sauce and slices of cheese (in opposite directions

Grilled Gammon with Asparagus

so that the cranberry sauce shows).

Place under grill until cheese melts. Serve immediately. Serves 4.

HOLIDAY BAKED GAMMON

A baked slice of gammon makes a good holiday dish. The slice can be from 1 to 2 inches thick, and the same method could be used for ham.

A centre-cut slice is best for a party meal, but any other cut could be used. Horseshoe slices make handsome individual roasts which require no at-the-table carving.

First, slash the edges of the fat about 2 inches apart. These slashes will keep the slice from curling as the meat heats. Stud the fat with whole cloves and place the slice in a shallow baking tin.

Pour 12 fluid ounces of fruit juice over and around the slice. Use pineapple juice or the syrup from canned pears or spiced peaches. If pear syrup is used, add a piece of stick cinnamon or a few pieces of chopped ginger root or candied ginger.

Now, cover the surface of the gammon with brown sugar. This is done most evenly by rubbing the sugar through a sieve.

Bake in slow oven (325°F. Mark 3). Gammon will require 1½ hours for a 2-inch slice. Allow about 45 minutes for heating a cooked slice of ham of the same thickness.

Spoon the syrup over the slice once or twice during baking.

CRANBERRY GLAZED GAMMON RASHERS

2 slices gammon, cut 1 inch thick
1 can cranberry sauce
6 ounces light corn syrup or golden
    syrup
2 tablespoons whole cloves

Gash fat several places around edge of the rashers. Place 1 slice in greased baking dish.

Cover with mixture of cranberry sauce and corn syrup. Cover with a second rasher.

Cover with remaining cranberry sauce-syrup mixture.

Stick whole cloves in fat around edge.

Bake, uncovered, in slow oven (325°F. Mark 3) 1½ hours, basting occasionally. Serves 6.

BAKED GAMMON RASHER WITH ORANGE GLAZE

2 tablespoons fat
1 slice gammon, 1½-inches thick
2 oranges, thinly sliced
2 tablespoons brown sugar
½ teaspoon cinnamon

Heat fat in a heavy frying pan; sear meat well on both sides.

Remove from heat; cover with thinly

sliced oranges. Sprinkle with a mixture of sugar and cinnamon. Cover closely.

Bake in moderate oven (350°F. Mark 4) until gammon is tender, about 1 hour. Uncover for last 10 minutes of baking. Serves 5.

BAKED GAMMON RASHER WITH RICE AND CHEESE

1 gammon rasher cut 1-inch thick
3 ounces molasses or treacle
4 tablespoons water
8 ounces cooked rice
1 ounce grated Cheddar cheese

Slash fat edge of gammon in several places. Place in baking dish.

Add molasses and let stand 15 minutes.

Add 4 tablespoons water. Cover and bake in moderate oven (350°F. Mark 4) until tender, 40 minutes.

Cover with rice. Sprinkle with cheese. Grill until cheese melts and browns. Serves 6.

GAMMON RASHER FRANÇOIS

1 1-inch slice of gammon
8 ounces apricot jam
8 fluid ounces sauterne or other
    white wine

Trim rind from gammon. Slice and slash fat on edge in several places to prevent curling.

Place meat in shallow baking tin. Combine jam and wine. Pour over meat.

Bake in moderate oven (350°F. Mark 4) 1 hour. Baste frequently. Serves 4 to 6.

GAMMON RASHER WITH APRICOT GLAZE

2 1-inch thick slices of gammon
1 can apricot juice
2 teaspoons Worcestershire sauce
2 tablespoons brown sugar

Score fat edges of gammon to prevent curling. Place side by side in a lightly greased shallow baking tin. Combine remaining ingredients and blend well. Spoon ½ of the mixture evenly over the rashers.

Place in moderate oven (350°F. Mark 4) and bake uncovered 45 minutes. During cooking period baste meat every few minutes with some of the remaining sauce. Cut into serving pieces and serve with some of the juices left in the pan. Serves 6.

Gammon Rasher with Apricot Glaze

Bacon and Salt Pork

HOW TO COOK BACON

Fried Bacon: Arrange rashers in a cold frying pan so that the lean of one rasher is on top of the fat of another. This prevents the bacon becoming hard and dry during cooking. Allow 3-5 minutes for thin rashers.

Do not let the fat smoke or bacon will have a burnt flavour.

Pour off fat as it accumulates during cooking.

Grilled Bacon: Place rashers on the rack under a pre-heated grill and grill at moderate temperature 2½ to 3 minutes per side, turning only once.

This bacon needs no draining.

Oven-Cooked Bacon: Lay rashers on a wire rack in a shallow pan.

Bake in a moderately hot oven (375°F. Mark 5) about 10 minutes, or until the desired crispness.

This bacon needs no draining and browns evenly from end to end without curling. This method is recommended when cooking large quantities because bacon requires less watching and needs no turning at all.

BACON AND BANANAS

Cut bananas in half. Roll rashers round and fasten with cocktail sticks.

Grill or bake in moderate oven (350°F. Mark 4) until bananas are tender and bacon is crisp. Turn frequently.

FRIED SALT PORK AND MILK GRAVY

Cut salt pork into thin slices, about ⅛ inch thick. Gash each rind in 3 or 4 places.

Fry in heavy frying pan over moderate heat until crisp and brown, turning often and removing fat as it accumulates.

Drain on absorbent paper and keep hot. Serve with medium white sauce made with milk and pork fat instead of other fat.

Variations: If desired, dip pork slices in flour and corn meal before frying. Add cubed boiled potatoes to the white sauce. Serve on hot plates with sauce and potatoes in centre surrounded by pork slices. Garnish with chopped parsley.

Allow 1 pound salt pork, ½ pint sauce, and 8 ounces cubed boiled potatoes to serve 4.

FRIED BACON

Place bacon rashers in cold frying pan.

Turn bacon frequently while cooking over low heat. Pour off excess fat.

Drain bacon on absorbent paper before serving.

BACON AND PINEAPPLE RINGS

Fry bacon. Drain.

Dip canned pineapple slices in seasoned flour and sauté in bacon fat until brown. Serve with crisp bacon.

BACON AND LIMA BEANS

¾ pound bacon, sliced thin
1 can green lima beans

Fry bacon quickly in frying pan. Remove from pan, and keep hot.

Add undrained beans to fat in the pan and heat thoroughly. Pour into serving dish and top with bacon. Serves 4.

BOILED PICKLED PORK OR BACON

Allow 6-8 ounces blade or belly of pork for each person. These are the cuts usually pickled. Top streaky, top and short back, middle gammon, corner gammon, gammon hock and prime collar are all suitable for boiling.

For small pieces, soak for about 1 hour in enough cold water to cover. Large pieces should be soaked for 4-5 hours or longer if they are very salty.

Put the meat into cold water to cover. Bring slowly to boiling point and remove any scum which has risen. Add 1 onion, peeled and stuck with 4-5 cloves, 1 bay leaf and 6 peppercorns. Cover and simmer.

For pieces weighing under 1 pound, allow 45 minutes. Pieces 1-2 pounds, allow 1-1½ hours and for a joint weighing over 3 pounds allow 30 minutes per pound.

Vegetables can be added for the last ¾-1 hour of cooking. Leave them in large pieces and use carrots, parsnips, turnips, onions, celery or potatoes as you wish.

Before serving remove the rind from the bacon and use the vegetables as garnish.

Pickled pork can be cooked in a pressure cooker. Allow 12 minutes per pound and ½ pint water or half water and half cider for every 15 minutes of cooking time. Place the meat on a trivet in the bottom of the pan with the fat side upwards. Add 3-4 cloves and 1 tablespoon brown sugar and cook at 15 pounds pressure. Allow the pressure to drop slowly before removing the meat. If vegetables are not cooked with the pickled pork, serve with potatoes and cabbage cooked separately — or green beans or broad beans with parsley sauce.

If the meat is to be served cold, leave it to cool in the cooking liquid. Remove the rind and sprinkle with browned crumbs. Serve with potato salad or beetroot and chicory salad and pickles or chutney.

GLAZED CANADIAN BACON

Remove the skin from a 3½-4 pound piece of cooked bacon. Place in a large roasting tin, and score the fat into squares or diamonds with a sharp knife. Cover with one of the suggested glazes and bake for 45 minutes in a moderate oven (350°F.).

Serve with pineapple rings and glacé cherries arranged round the bacon and secured with cocktail sticks, and sprinkle with brown sugar.

Veal Recipes

Veal is the flesh of a calf usually weighing from 110 to 200 pounds. The carcass yields 80 to 90 pounds of veal. The lighter the colour the better the meat; the most desirable is that from a milk-fed calf, but this is not always available. Older and darker veal may be improved by soaking overnight in milk in the refrigerator or by blanching briefly, starting in cold water.

HINTS FOR COOKING VEAL

Because veal comes from immature animals it lacks fat and, although it is tender, it has considerable connective tissue which means that it requires long, slow cooking.

Veal is delicate in colour and becomes lighter when cooked. It also has a fine delicate flavour. Cooking methods which intensify colour and make the flavour more pronounced should be used.

The best methods of cooking veal are roasting, frying, and braising. Veal is also cooked in liquid for stews. Veal chops, steaks, and cutlets are best if fried or braised.

Rich colourful sauces and gravies are delicious with veal because it combines so well with many flavours. Veal frequently appears in many interesting Italian and French dishes.

For grilling or frying, only loin chops and cutlets from high-quality heavy or more-mature veal should be used, and a lower temperature than that for beef and lamb is advisable. Always cook veal to the well-done stage.

ROAST VEAL

Select roast from leg, loin, rib, or shoulder. Bacon or salt pork strips or suet placed over roast improve the flavour. More seasoning is required for veal than for other meats. An onion added while roasting helps.

Dredge meat with flour before placing in pan. Add sliced onion. Season with salt and pepper.

Place fat-side-up on rack in roasting tin. Roast in slow oven (300°F. Mark 2), allowing 25 minutes per pound for leg, 30 to 35 minutes per pound for loin. If roast is rolled, allow additional 10 to 15 minutes per pound.

Serve with brown gravy made from fat in pan.

If meat thermometer is used, it will register 170° when veal is well done.

SPICED POT ROAST OF VEAL

5	pound piece veal rump
1	tablespoon dry mustard
2	tablespoons flour
1	tablespoon brown sugar
1	tablespoon salt
1	teaspoon mixed herbs
$\frac{1}{8}$	teaspoon black pepper
3	tablespoons fat or salad oil
2	tablespoons vinegar
1	large onion, chopped
1	tablespoon parsley
1	teaspoon celery seed
12	small carrots

Roll meat in mixture of mustard, flour, sugar, salt, and seasonings.

Brown well on all sides in a little fat or salad oil in a sauté pan with a tight lid.

Add vinegar, onion, parsley, and celery seed. Cover and simmer for 2 to 2¼ hours or until tender.

During last half hour of cooking, small whole carrots may be added. Make gravy from juices left in the pan. Serves 8.

BRAISED VEAL SHOULDER

Brown rolled shoulder in hot fat. Season with salt and pepper.

Place on rack in roasting tin. Add small amount of water. Cook in slow oven (300°F. Mark 2) until tender, about 35 to 40 minutes per pound.

Add vegetables for last 45 minutes of cooking. Make gravy with fat and sediment left in the pan.

ROLLED STUFFED SHOULDER OF VEAL

veal shoulder
3 tablespoons bacon fat
½ small onion, chopped
½ small green pepper, chopped
1-2 stalks celery, chopped
3 pints day-old bread cubes
1 teaspoon salt
¼ teaspoon pepper
¼ teaspoon marjoram
5 tablespoons milk

Have bones removed from veal shoulder.

Melt bacon fat; add onion, green pepper, and celery and cook until soft, but not brown.

Add mixture to bread cubes. Add seasonings and milk and mix well.

Spread veal open, spread with stuffing and roll like a Swiss roll. Tie roast firmly with string (about 7 strings around the roast will hold it firm).

Place roast on rack in shallow tin and bake in slow oven (300°-325°F. Mark 2-3) until meat thermometer registers 170°F., or about 35 to 40 minutes per pound.

Serve with gravy made from fat and drippings in pan. Serves 12 to 14.

Rolled Stuffed Shoulder of Veal

VEAL COOKING CHART

Cuts	Method of Cooking
Breast	Roast or boil
Chops from loin or cutlets	Grill or fry
Chump end of loin	Roast
Feet	Boil for stock or soup
Fillet	Roast, grill or fry, stew or braise
Leg: whole thin slices	Roast Grill or fry
Loin	Roast
Neck: best end chops from best end middle and scrag end	Roast Grill or fry Stew or braise
Head	Boil or use for brawn

Stuffed breast of Veal

STUFFED BREAST OF VEAL

1   medium onion, chopped
4   large stalks of celery, chopped
4   ounces butter or margarine
12 ounces fine dry breadcrumbs
2   tablespoons chopped parsley
½ teaspoon sage
¼ teaspoon pepper
¾ pint white stock
3   to 4 pounds breast of veal

Sauté onion and celery in butter or margarine until onions are golden. Combine with crumbs, parsley, sage, pepper, and half the stock.

Cut breast of veal in half widthwise. Spread stuffing evenly over one section; cover with remaining section. Skewer evenly on all sides with cocktail sticks or poultry pins; lace with cotton thread.

Place on low rack in baking tin. Spread top with thin layer of fat. Pour in remaining stock, cover.

Bake in moderate oven (350°F. Mark 4) 2 hours. Uncover and bake 30 minutes longer. Serve with gravy (below). Serves 6 to 8.

Note: For mushroom and sour cream gravy, dissolve 1 tablespoon flour in a little water. Add to fat and sediment left in the tin with 1 tablespoon grated onion and the contents of a small can of mushroom slices. Cook until mixture boils and thickens.

Spoon in ⅓ pint sour cream. Season to taste with salt, pepper and a dash of nutmeg. Bring to the boil, correct the seasoning and serve with creamed potatoes, leeks or any other green vegetable.

BRAISED VEAL WITH WINE

Use a shoulder of veal. Coat with flour, seasoned with salt and pepper.

Brown in hot fat. Add 2 onions, sliced and 8 fluid ounces water or stock. Cover closely and simmer until tender, about 3 hours.

Add 4 fluid ounces dry white wine and finish cooking. Remove meat and thicken liquid for gravy.

Veal Chops, Cutlets, Steaks

VEAL SCALOPPINE OR ESCALOPES ALLA MARSALA

Scaloppine or escalope is the Italian term for small, thin slices of meat, generally veal. They are prepared in a number of styles. The basic method is usually to sauté them until brown, then cook them in wine or a sauce until they are tender.

1½ pounds boned veal, cut into very thin, even slices
flour
salt and pepper
2   ounces butter
5   tablespoons Marsala wine
3   tablespoons canned concentrated bouillon

Pound the veal lightly until very thin. Dip in flour seasoned with salt and pepper.

Heat butter in a heavy frying pan; add the veal and brown on both sides. Add wine and cook 1 minute longer over moderately high heat.

Remove meat to warm serving dish. Add bouillon to fat left in the pan. Scrape all brown particles loose and bring to the boil. Pour over meat. Serves 4.

Veal Scaloppine with Mushrooms: Fry ½ pound sliced fresh mushrooms in 1 ounce butter. Transfer mushrooms to warm serving dish. Proceed as for Veal Scaloppine Alla Marsala. Serve veal and sauce on the same serving dish with the mushrooms.

VEAL CHOPS FLAMENCO

6 loin veal chops
salt and pepper
flour
4 tablespoons olive oil
1 can (10 ounces) condensed beef consommé
2 teaspoons grated lemon rind
1 tablespoon Worcestershire sauce
1 small green pepper, chopped
1 small onion, chopped
6-8 whole pitted black olives
3-4 tablespoons chopped pimento
2 tablespoons capers
1 tablespoon cornflour
4 tablespoons cold water

Sprinkle veal chops with salt and pepper. Roll in flour, and brown on all sides in hot olive oil.

Add consommé, lemon rind, Worcestershire sauce, green pepper, olives, onion, pimento, and capers. Cover pan tightly. Cook over low heat, turning chops occasionally until meat is tender, about 40 to 45 minutes. Add water occasionally to keep up the level of the liquid.

Thicken the sauce with a mixture of 1 tablespoon cornflour mixed with 4 tablespoons cold water. Serve with buttered noodles. Serves 6.

VEAL PARMIGIANA

Parmigiana, or alla parmigiana, i an Italian term applied to a numbe of dishes containing Parmesan cheese often in combination with tomato sauce.

4 veal cutlets
1 teaspoon salt
¼ teaspoon pepper
2 eggs
3 ounces fine breadcrumbs
3 tablespoons grated Parmesan cheese
6 tablespoons olive oil
1 can (8 ounces) tomato sauce
½ pound Mozzarella cheese, sliced

Pound the cutlets with a mea mallet.

Add salt and pepper to eggs and beat well.

Mix crumbs with Parmesan cheese Dip cutlets in egg, then in crumbs.

Heat oil in a flame-proof casserole. Add cutlets and sauté until golden brown, about 5 minutes on each side.

Pour tomato sauce over cutlets. Top with slices of Mozzarella cheese.

Bake in slow oven (325°F. Mark 3) until cheese is melted and delicately browned, about 15 minutes. Serves 4.

VEAL MARENGO CASSEROLE

1½ pounds fillet of veal, cut into serving pieces
1 clove garlic, crushed
2 tablespoons olive or salad oil
2 tablespoons flour
12 fluid ounces white stock or canned bouillon
salt and pepper
4 medium tomatoes, peeled and cut in thin slices
2 ounces sliced fresh mushrooms

Dredge meat with flour and brown with garlic in hot oil. Remove to greased casserole.

Add flour to pan; stir until browned then add stock, salt, and pepper. Cook, stirring constantly, until slightly thickened and smooth. Lay tomatoes on meat. Pour in sauce.

Cover and bake in moderate oven (350°F. Mark 4) at least 1½ hours. Add mushrooms during last hour of cooking. Serves 6.

Veal Chops Flamenco

VEAL SCALOPPINE

1½ pounds fillet of veal, cut ½-inch thick
1 teaspoon salt
1 teaspoon paprika
4 fluid ounces salad oil
4 tablespoons lemon juice
1 clove garlic
1 teaspoon prepared mustard
¼ teaspoon nutmeg
½ teaspoon sugar
1 ounce flour
2 ounces fat
1 medium onion, sliced thinly
1 green pepper, cut in strips
1 10½-ounce can chicken bouillon
¼ pound mushrooms
1 tablespoon butter or margarine
6 stuffed olives, sliced

Cut veal into serving pieces.

Make sauce by combining salt, paprika, oil, lemon juice, garlic, mustard, nutmeg, and sugar. Beat well, or shake in bottle to combine thoroughly.

Lay veal flat in baking tin. Pour sauce over veal. Turn pieces of veal to coat with sauce. Let stand 15 minutes.

Remove garlic. Lift veal from sauce. Dip into flour. Brown well in heated fat in a sauté pan.

Add onion and green pepper. Combine chicken bouillon with remaining sauce and pour over veal. Cover and cook slowly until veal is tender, about 40 minutes.

Clean and slice mushrooms. Brown lightly in butter. Add mushrooms and olives to veal. Stir and pour sauce over veal. Cook about 5 minutes more. Serve veal with sauce poured over it. Serves 6.

BREADED VEAL CHOPS

about 2 ounces flour
1 teaspoon salt
pepper
4 veal chops, cut ¾-inch thick
1 slightly beaten egg
2 tablespoons water
2 ounces dry crumbs
4 ounces fat
¾ pint water
2 tablespoons chopped parsley
1 teaspoon Worcestershire sauce

Mix flour, salt, and pepper to taste and coat chops with mixture.

Mix egg with water and dip chops first in egg and then in crumbs.

Sauté chops in fat until well browned and remove to a dish.

If necessary, add more fat to that in pan to make 4 tablespoons. Add 4 tablespoons flour (use any left over from flour mixture, adding enough to make 4 tablespoons). Brown well.

Add water and cook, stirring until thickened. Return chops to gravy and season with parsley, Worcestershire sauce, and additional salt and pepper. Simmer, covered, until tender, about 40 minutes. Serves 4.

VEAL STEAKS – MEXICAN STYLE

1 clove garlic, crushed
1 medium onion, finely chopped
2 ounces fat
4 veal steaks (about 6 ounces each) cut ½ inch thick from fillet or leg
1 ounce flour
1 teaspoon salt
¼ teaspoon pepper
1 can tomatoes (about 16 ounces)
4 tablespoons tomato paste
½ teaspoon salt
1 teaspoon brown sugar
1 teaspoon curry powder
½ teaspoon thyme
1 teaspoon soy sauce
3-4 tablespoons chopped pimento

Cook garlic and onion in hot fat until golden brown. Remove from pan.

Dredge veal in flour sifted with 1 teaspoon salt and ¼ teaspoon pepper. Brown in the fat. Add remaining ingredients. Cover tightly. Simmer slowly until tender, about 45 minutes. Serves 4.

CALIFORNIA VEAL CHOPS

4 ¾-inch veal loin chops or cutlets
salt and pepper
4 slices pineapple
4 prunes
8 medium carrots
4 fluid ounces hot water

Brown chops in hot fat. Season with salt and pepper.

Place pineapple on each chop with prune in centre. Add carrots. Add water. Cover and cook slowly 1½ hours. Serves 4.

ITALIAN-STYLE VEAL WITH TOMATO SAUCE AND CHEESE

¾-pound fillet of veal, thinly sliced
salt and pepper
breadcrumbs
1 beaten egg
3 tablespoons hot melted fat or salad oil
1 8-ounce can tomato sauce, heated
¼ pound Mozzarella cheese, thinly sliced

Buy veal cut into servings and pounded thinly. Season with salt and pepper. Dip in crumbs, then in beaten egg, and again in crumbs.

Brown meat quickly on both sides in hot fat.

Place browned cutlets in flameproof dish and pour hot tomato sauce over them. Top with cheese.

Grill until cheese melts, bubbles, and browns. Serves 2.

Note: If Mozzarella cheese is not available, other cheese may be substituted.

VEAL BIRDS – FRENCH STYLE

about 2 pounds fillet or leg of veal
2 ounces fine breadcrumbs
4 tablespoons milk
½ pound pork sausage meat
½ small onion, chopped
½ clove garlic, crushed
2 rashers of bacon, cooked and diced
1 tablespoon chopped parsley
1 egg yolk
2 tablespoons fat
¾ pint veal stock or canned consommé
1 tablespoon flour

Pound veal until it is ¼ inch thick.

Combine crumbs with milk, then mix with sausage, onion, garlic, bacon, parsley, and egg yolk.

Put 1 tablespoon of filling across centre of each piece of meat. Roll up and fasten with a wooden pick.

Cook over low heat in hot fat in a sauté pan until brown on all sides.

Add hot stock and simmer until done, 45 minutes to 1 hour.

Thicken the sauce with a paste made of the 1 tablespoon flour and a little cold water.

To serve, place birds on a heated dish and pour sauce over them. Garnish with parsley and slices of lemon. Serves 6.

VEAL CHOP AND POTATO BAKE

4 veal loin chops or cutlets, cut ¾-inch thick
2 tablespoons lard or dripping
4 potatoes, peeled and sliced
salt and pepper
1 ounce flour
¾ pint milk
1 ounce grated cheese

Brown chops on both sides in lard or dripping. Season.

Place half the sliced potatoes in greased casserole. Season with salt and pepper. Sprinkle with flour. Add remaining potatoes and flour. Pour milk over all.

Place browned chops on top of potatoes. Sprinkle with grated cheese.

Cover and cook in slow oven (300°F. Mark 2) until tender, about 1½ hours.

Italian-Style Veal

PAPRIKA VEAL STEAK

Chop 1 bunch spring onions, including part of tops (or use 4-5 tablespoons chopped white onions) and brown lightly in hot fat. Remove onions.

Coat veal with flour and brown in hot fat. When browned, sprinkle each side well with salt, pepper, and enough paprika to make meat quite red. Scatter onions over steak.

Dilute ¼ pint sour cream with 2 tablespoons milk. Pour over veal.

Cover pan, and cook slowly 35 to 40 minutes or until very tender.

During cooking, turn veal and spoon sour cream over top.

Remove meat from pan, and make gravy from sour cream and fat left in the pan, adding a little flour blended with cold water.

WIENER SCHNITZEL
(Breaded Veal Cutlet)

This is one of the classic, traditional Sunday dishes in Vienna—served with cucumber salad and boiled potatoes, or with mixed fruit compote and rice.

1½ pounds fillet of veal
flour
2 well-beaten eggs
1 tablespoon milk
salt and pepper to taste
finely sifted breadcrumbs (dry)
lemon slices
parsley sprigs
fat for deep frying

Buy the meat cut into very thin slices and pounded flat. Meat must be paper-thin.

Wash and dry meat. Slash corners if necessary, and pound again if necessary. Dredge meat with flour.

Blend eggs, milk, and seasonings with wire whisk. Dip meat into egg mixture, letting excess drip off.

Cover with breadcrumbs. Shake off excess crumbs.

Fry schnitzel in deep hot fat (375°F.) 5 to 6 minutes or until golden brown.

Drain on absorbent paper. Garnish with lemon slices and parsley sprigs.

The lemon slices are part of the dish; sprinkle schnitzel with a few drops of lemon juice before serving. Serves 5 to 6.

Wiener Schnitzel

STUFFED VEAL ROLLS

1¼ pounds veal, ½-inch thick cut
    from fillet or leg (4 pieces)
1 small onion, chopped
2 ounces butter or margarine
6-8 gherkins coarsely chopped
about 4 ounces dry breadcrumbs
4 fluid ounces liquid from
    gherkins
¼ teaspoon pepper
2 eggs, beaten

Get butcher to flatten veal ¼-inch thick. Sauté onion in butter or margarine. Stir in remaining ingredients. Place large spoonful of stuffing on each piece of veal. Roll and secure with cocktail sticks if necessary.

Place in covered baking dish and bake in moderate oven (350°F. Mark 4) 1½ hours. Serve with your favourite cheese sauce. Serves 4.

VEAL CUTLETS IN WINE SAUCE

2 pounds fillet or leg of veal cut
    into 6 portions
salt and pepper
2 tablespoons olive oil or salad oil
½ small onion, chopped
2 ounces sliced mushrooms
1 tablespoon chopped parsley
2 tablespoons flour
12 fluid ounces stock or water
4 tablespoons white wine
2 tablespoons lemon juice

Sprinkle veal with salt and pepper; fry in fat until browned on both sides. Place meat in a casserole.

To fat in frying pan, add onions, mushrooms, and parsley and cook for a few minutes.

Stir in and brown the flour. Add remaining ingredients.

Cook until smooth and thick, stirring constantly. Pour over meat. Bake in slow oven (325°F. Mark 3) 1 hour. Serves 6.

BAKED VEAL CHOPS

4 shoulder veal chops (2 pounds)
salt and pepper
1 egg, beaten
breadcrumbs
1 medium onion, sliced
1 can (10½ ounces) condensed
    tomato soup
½ soup can water
1½ tablespoons Angostura bitters
1 teaspoon oregano
salt and pepper to taste

Sprinkle chops with salt and pepper. Dip each chop first in egg and then in breadcrumbs. Brown slowly on both sides in frying pan.

Put chops in baking dish and place onion slices on top. Mix tomato soup with water and heat until blended. Add bitters, oregano, and salt and pepper to taste. Pour sauce over chops. Bake in moderate oven (350°F. Mark 4) 30 minutes. Serves 4.

Stuffed Veal Rolls

VEAL CHOPS GENOVESE

1 clove garlic
6 loin veal chops, ¾ inch thick
flour
1 teaspoon salt
¼ teaspoon pepper
3 tablespoons fat
1 pound cooked tomatoes
2 medium onions, sliced thinly
4 fluid ounces sherry
½ pound mushrooms, sliced
3 tablespoons butter or margarine
8 black olives, sliced

Cut gashes in peeled garlic clove; rub over sauté pan; discard. Coat veal chops with flour and seasonings.

Brown in hot fat. Add tomatoes, onion, and sherry. Simmer 1 hour and 15 minutes. Sauté mushrooms in butter; add with olives. Simmer 15 minutes longer. Serves 6.

VEAL VEGETABLE BUNDLES

2 pounds veal, cut ¼-inch thick
    from fillet or leg
6 small carrots
1 onion, sliced
salt and pepper
1 egg plus 2 tablespoons water
sifted crumbs
2 ounces fat
8 fluid ounces water or chicken broth

Cut steaks into servings about 2 by 3 inches.

Wrap a clean whole carrot and a slice of onion in each piece of veal. Season and fasten with wooden cocktail sticks.

Dip in diluted egg, then in crumbs. Brown in hot fat, turning to brown all sides.

Add water or broth. Cover and cook slowly until carrots and veal are done, about 1 hour.

For sauce thicken liquid in pan with a blend of flour and cold water (2 tablespoons flour for each 8 fluid ounces of gravy). Serves 6.

Baked Veal Chops

FRENCH VEAL CASSEROLE

1½ pounds fillet veal, ½-inch thick
flour, salt, and pepper
4 ounces fat
1 small onion, chopped
1 clove garlic, crushed
4 tablespoons flour
12 fluid ounces beef stock or
canned bouillon
4 medium tomatoes
½ pound fresh mushrooms

Cut the veal into 6 pieces. Dip in flour seasoned with salt and pepper. Heat fat in frying pan; add onion and garlic and cook until golden brown; remove from fat.

Brown meat in flavoured fat; remove from pan.

Add 4 tablespoons flour to fat and stir until browned. Add stock to make brown sauce, cooking until smooth. Season well and add onion and garlic.

Peel and slice tomatoes and arrange in greased 2-2½-pint casserole. Lay meat on layer of tomatoes and pour brown sauce over meat.

Cover and bake in moderate oven (350°F. Mark 4) 45 to 50 minutes. During the last 15 minutes of cooking add mushrooms, and finish cooking with cover off. Serves 6.

HUNGARIAN VEAL BIRDS

2 pounds fillet of veal
salt, pepper, paprika, and thyme
6 ounces soft breadcrumbs
1 tablespoon each chopped parsley,
onion, and mushrooms
2 ounces fat
1 tablespoon chopped gherkins
1 tablespoon chopped olives
flour
melted fat
clove of garlic
6 fluid ounces boiling water or stock

Cut veal into 6 servings ¼-inch thick. Season with salt, pepper, paprika, and thyme.

Combine breadcrumbs with parsley, onion, and mushrooms. Brown this mixture lightly in hot fat for 2 to 3 minutes, stirring constantly.

Remove from heat. Stir in gherkins and olives. Season with salt and pepper. Divide this mixture evenly among the 6 portions of veal. Roll up and tie with string.

Brush with melted fat. Roll in flour and brown in 2 or 3 tablespoons fat. Rub a casserole with garlic clove and grease it. Place meat birds in casserole. Add boiling water or stock.

Bake, covered, in moderate oven (375°F. Mark 4) 45 minutes. Turn birds once during baking process. Serves 6.

STUFFED VEAL CHOPS CHABLIS

4 veal chops, about 1¼ inches thick
4½ ounces soft breadcrumbs
4 ounces chopped cooked ham
1 tablespoon chopped onion
3 tablespoons melted butter or
margarine
salt and pepper to taste
flour
3 tablespoons bacon fat or other fat
8 fluid ounces chablis, sauterne, or
other white wine
1 can condensed cream of mushroom soup

Have each chop slit from fat side to bone to form pocket.

Mix breadcrumbs, ham, onion, and butter; season with salt and pepper. Stuff chops with mixture. Fasten openings securely with skewers or wooden cocktail sticks.

Coat chops with flour seasoned with salt and pepper. Heat bacon fat in large sauté pan and brown chops nicely on both sides.

Add wine; cover and simmer gently about 45 minutes, or until chops are very tender. Place chops on heated dish.

Measure 8 fluid ounces of the juices in the pan, adding water if necessary to make that amount. Combine with mushroom soup and heat to boiling. Season to taste with salt and pepper. Pour gravy over chops or serve separately. Serves 4.

VEAL AND NOODLES BAKED IN WINE SAUCE

1 pound fillet of veal, cut in
¾-inch cubes
1 medium onion, sliced
3 tablespoons fat
6 fluid ounces sauterne, Rhine, or
other white wine
1 bouillon cube dissolved in 6
fluid ounces of water
1 can condensed mushroom soup
1 can (4 ounces) sliced mushrooms
and liquid
1 teaspoon Worcestershire sauce
salt and pepper
½ pound fine noodles
grated Parmesan cheese

Sauté veal and onion in fat until meat loses its red colour.

Add wine, consommé, mushroom soup, mushrooms and liquid, Worcestershire sauce, and salt and pepper to taste.

Mix well and bring to boil, then add noodles. Cook and stir until noodles are limp and well mixed with other ingredients, about 5 minutes. Turn into greased casserole.

Cover and bake in moderate oven (350°F. Mark 4) 1 hour. Serve with grated Parmesan cheese. Serves 4 to 5.

VEAL WITH SAUSAGES, TOMATOES, AND RICE

4 pork sausages
1 slice fillet or leg of veal (about ¾
pound), pounded very thinly
3 tablespoons flour
1 teaspoon salt
¼ teaspoon pepper
1 medium onion, sliced
6 ounces raw rice
3-4 stalks celery, thinly sliced
1 can tomatoes (about 16 ounces)
1 teaspoon salt
⅛ teaspoon pepper
1 tablespoon Worcestershire sauce

Brown sausages in a large sauté pan; reserve the fat.

Cut veal in 4 pieces; wrap each around 1 sausage and secure with a wooden cocktail stick.

Coat the rolls with flour seasoned with 1 teaspoon salt and ¼ teaspoon pepper.

Brown the veal-sausage rolls in sausage fat in the pan; remove rolls.

Add onion and rice to fat in the pan and cook, stirring, 5 minutes. Add veal rolls, celery, tomatoes, 1 teaspoon salt, ⅛ teaspoon pepper, and Worcestershire sauce.

Cover and simmer, stirring occasionally, until veal rolls and rice are tender and the liquid has been absorbed, about 40 minutes. Serve sprinkled with chopped parsley. Serves 4 to 5.

VEAL FILLETS FRENCH STYLE

6 or 8 fillets of veal
3 tablespoons butter or margarine
8 fluid ounces stock
2 teaspoons chopped parsley
1 teaspoon chopped onion
salt and pepper to taste
2 tablespoons white wine

The veal should be cut about a half-inch thick. Get the butcher to pound them thin or do so at home by wrapping the meat in waxed paper and flattening it with a heavy plate.

Heat butter in a frying pan until it is very hot. Cook fillets 3 minutes on each side.

Add remaining ingredients except wine. Cover. Simmer 20 minutes.

Remove veal to hot platter and keep hot.

Add wine to dripping in pan. Heat, simmer briefly and pour over meat.

Serve with rice, noodles, or riced potatoes. Serves 4.

Note: If desired, serve tomato sauce in place of sauce indicated.

Miscellaneous Veal Dishes

SAVOURY VEAL STEW

2 pounds stewing veal, cut in
    1-inch cubes
1½ ounces flour
2 teaspoons salt
½ onion, chopped
3 ounces fat
¾ pint water
4-5 stalks celery, sliced
6-8 small whole carrots
1 tablespoon Worcestershire sauce

Dip veal cubes in seasoned flour. Brown veal and onion in fat in a sauté pan.

When well browned, add water, cover, and cook over low heat until veal is tender, about 40 minutes.

Add celery, carrots, and Worcestershire sauce, and continue cooking until vegetables are tender, about 20 minutes. Serve in rice ring if desired.

Serves 4 to 6.

VEAL AND PEPPERS— ITALIAN STYLE

1½ pounds boneless lean veal
3 tablespoons salad oil
2 medium green peppers, cut in
    eighths
1 small can sliced mushrooms,
    undrained
pinch of crushed red pepper
2 8-ounce cans tomato sauce
salt and pepper

Cut meat in bite-size pieces. Brown meat on all sides in hot oil in a sauté pan.

Add peppers. Cover and reduce heat. Cook 10 minutes, stirring occasionally.

Add mushrooms and liquid, red pepper, and sauce. Cover and simmer until tender, 30 minutes longer.

Season to taste. Serve on hot cooked rice, macaroni, or spaghetti. Serves 4.

HUNGARIAN VEAL PAPRIKA

1 pound boneless veal, cut into
    1-inch cubes
2 tablespoons bacon fat
1 large Spanish onion, sliced thinly
1 can beef bouillon
1 teaspoon salt
1 tablespoon paprika
8 fluid ounces sour cream
1 tablespoon flour
8 ounces noodles, cooked

Brown meat well in bacon fat in a sauté pan.

Add onion and stir and cook until onion is lightly browned.

Add beef bouillon diluted with 1 can water, salt, and paprika.

Cover. Cook slowly on top of the stove or in moderate oven (350°F. Mark 4) about 1 hour or until veal is tender.

Combine sour cream and flour and stir into broth around veal. Cook to thicken. Serve on hot noodles. Serves 4.

VEAL AND SAUERKRAUT GOULASH

2½ pounds lean veal
3 tablespoons fat
½ onion, chopped
2 tablespoons diced green pepper
1 teaspoon salt
1 teaspoon paprika
¼ teaspoon pepper
½ teaspoon marjoram
1 teaspoon caraway seeds
½ 16-ounce can tomatoes
4 ounces diced carrots
1 pound sauerkraut

Cut meat into 1-inch cubes. Heat fat in sauté pan; add meat and brown.

Add onion and green pepper; sauté 5 minutes.

Add seasonings, caraway, and tomatoes. Cover, simmer 40 to 45 minutes or until meat is tender.

Add carrots and sauerkraut. Cook 20 minutes longer. Add a little water if necessary. Serves 6.

VEAL WITH MUSHROOMS IN SOUR CREAM

3 pounds stewing veal
1 teaspoon sugar
2 tablespoons butter or margarine
2 tablespoons finely chopped onion
2 tablespoons flour
1½ teaspoons salt
⅛ teaspoon pepper
¼ teaspoon Aromat
grated rind of ¼ lemon
1¾ pints boiling water
½ pound fresh mushrooms, sliced
¼ pint sour cream

Remove any bone and gristle and cut meat into bite-size pieces.

Melt sugar in a sauté pan; add butter or margarine and onion. Stir until onion is coated.

Add veal and stir until it slightly changes colour. Add flour, salt, pepper, Aromat, and lemon rind.

Pour in boiling water, then transfer to casserole. Cover and bake in moderate oven (350°F. Mark 4) 1 hour.

Stir in mushrooms, cover, and bake an additional hour. Stir in sour cream, heat through, and serve garnished with parsley. Serves 4.

VEAL ESCALOPES À LA PROVENÇALE

1½ to 2 pounds veal escalopes
flour
4 tablespoons olive oil
½ pound fresh mushrooms, sliced

2 cloves garlic, crushed
4 fluid ounces dry white wine
4 medium tomatoes, peeled and
    chopped
salt and pepper
chopped parsley

Pound the veal thinly, coat with flour and brown in olive oil in chafing dish or sauté pan over direct heat.

Push veal to side of pan; add mushrooms and cook, stirring often, 2 or 3 minutes.

Arrange mushrooms on veal; add garlic, wine, tomatoes, and salt and pepper to taste. Simmer about 10 minutes. Serve sprinkled with parsley. Serves 6 to 8.

SUPREME OF VEAL WITH RHINE WINE

4 tablespoons butter or margarine
½ pound mushrooms, sliced
½ small green pepper, diced
1 ounce flour
¼ pint single cream or evaporated
    milk
8 fluid ounces veal stock or chicken
    bouillon*
salt and pepper to taste
1 pound diced, cooked veal
2 tablespoons chopped pimiento
¼ teaspoon oregano or marjoram
¼ pint Rhine wine

Melt butter in a chafing dish or electric frying pan. Add mushrooms and green pepper; cook about 5 minutes, or until mushrooms are golden brown and tender.

Sprinkle with flour, stir and mix. Add cream or milk and stock or bouillon. Stir until thickened. Add salt and pepper if needed. Add veal, pimiento, oregano or marjoram, and Rhine wine. Cook 5 minutes longer.

Serve on parslied, freshly cooked macaroni. Serves 6.

*1 chicken bouillon cube dissolved in ½ pint hot water.

Supreme of Veal with Rhine Wine

Veal à La Suisse

VEAL À LA SUISSE (SWISS VEAL)

1½ pounds leg of veal, cut in thin
    strips about one-half inch
    wide
1 medium onion, chopped
2 large mushrooms, sliced
3 ounces butter or margarine
¼ pint single cream
1 tablespoon sifted flour
8 fluid ounces dry white wine
1 tablespoon chopped parsley
salt and pepper, to taste

In Electric Frying Pan: Preheat uncovered electric frying pan on high
(7) for 3 minutes. Meantime, mix veal
with onion and mushrooms. Turn heat
to 5½ setting and melt butter. Add meat
mixture and stir until slightly browned
(8 to 10 minutes).

Blend cream with flour. Add to meat
and stir until food comes to the boil
(about ½ minute). Turn to 4 setting;
cover pan and allow to cook for 5 or
6 minutes or until veal is tender.

Mix wine with parsley. Add to meat
and allow to boil once, stirring constantly. Turn heat to 1½ setting; cover
pan and simmer for 2 minutes. Serve
immediately. Serves 6.

In an ordinary Frying Pan: Heat a
heavy frying pan over high heat; add
butter and reduce heat to moderately
high. Mix veal, onion, and mushrooms, sauté in butter, stirring often,
until slightly browned, 8 to 10 minutes.

Blend cream with flour; add to meat
and cook, stirring, until mixture boils.
Turn heat to low; cover and simmer
until veal is tender, 5 to 6 minutes.

Mix wine and parsley; add to meat
and let mixture boil up once, stirring
constantly. Turn heat to very low,
cover and let simmer 2 minutes.

JELLIED VEAL LOAF

2 pounds shoulder of veal
2 knuckles of veal
2 whole black peppers
1 bay leaf
2 tablespoons vinegar
2 teaspoons salt
1 green pepper, chopped
2 stalks celery, chopped
2 hard-boiled eggs, diced
4 ounces cooked peas
¼ ounce gelatine
4 tablespoons cold water

Cover veal and knuckles with warm
water. Add seasonings and simmer

until meat is tender.

Strain stock; there should be about
1½ pints.

Dice meat; add green pepper, celery,
eggs, and peas. Place in oiled ring or
other mould.

Soften gelatine in cold water; dissolve in hot meat stock. Pour into
mould. Chill until firm.

To serve, unmould and serve with
cucumber sauce (see Index). Serves 8.

VEAL SUPREME WITH RICE

1 pound boneless veal
2 teaspoons salt
1 onion
few celery leaves
6 whole black peppers
2 ounces flour
⅛ teaspoon mace
dash of cayenne
salt to taste
3 hard-boiled eggs
2 tablespoons sherry (optional)

Cover veal with ¾ pint water. Add
salt, onion, celery leaves, and whole
peppers. Simmer covered until meat
is tender.

Remove celery leaves and whole peppers. Cut meat into short strips.

Thicken broth with flour and stir in
meat. Add mace, cayenne, and salt to
taste.

Press egg yolks through fine sieve,
cut egg whites lengthwise and add to
meat.

Cook until thickened; add sherry, if
desired. Serve on steamed rice. Serves
5.

VEAL AND POTATO CAS-SEROLE

1 pound boneless veal, cut in 1½-
    inch cubes
4 to 5 tablespoons butter or
    margarine
3 to 4 medium potatoes, peeled and
    cut into 1-inch cubes
3 to 4 medium onions, peeled and
    cut into 1-inch cubes
1 small clove garlic, crushed
2 teaspoons salt
½ teaspoon pepper
½ teaspoon oregano
2 tablespoons chopped parsley
1 16-ounce can tomatoes
2 tablespoons cornflour

Brown meat well on all sides in hot
fat. Add potatoes, onions, and garlic
and cook until vegetables are lightly
browned. Add seasonings, parsley, and
tomatoes.

Blend cornflour with 2 tablespoons
cold water or tomato juice; add and
simmer about 5 minutes. Turn mixture
into casserole.

Cover and bake in slow oven (325°F.
Mark 3) until meat and vegetables are
tender, about 40 to 45 minutes. Serves
4 to 6.

VEAL RAGOUT (Ragout De Veau)

2 rashers of bacon
1 large onion, sliced
3 spring onions, chopped
3 tablespoons butter or margarine
2 pounds boneless veal, cut in
    1½-inch cubes
2 tablespoons flour
1½ teaspoons salt
¼ teaspoon pepper
⅛ teaspoon oregano
4 fluid ounces water
¼ pint sour cream
chopped parsley or chives

Cut bacon into 1-inch pieces. Stir and
cook in sauté pan until lightly cooked
but not brown.

Add onions and butter. Stir and cook
until onions are partially cooked but
not brown.

Roll veal in flour seasoned with salt,
pepper, and oregano. Add to pan and
brown. Stir and mix to brown veal.

Add 4 fluid ounces water. Cover and
simmer about 1 hour. Do not scorch.

When veal is tender, push to one
side of pan. Stir sour cream into fat
left in the pan. Stir all together.

Cover and heat about 15 minutes
over very low heat to blend flavours.
Serve garnished with chopped parsley
or chives. Serves 6.

GREEN BEAN AND VEAL STEW (GERMAN)

1 pound stewing veal
1¼ pints cold water
2 teaspoons Aromat
2 pounds green beans
1½ ounces butter or margarine
1½ ounces flour
1 tablespoon sugar
1 teaspoon salt
2 tablespoons vinegar
¼ teaspoon summer savory
1 tablespoon chopped parsley
⅛ teaspoon pepper

Cut veal into ½-inch pieces. Add cold
water and 1 teaspoon of the Aromat.
Bring slowly to the boil; lower heat;
simmer 1 hour.

Wash beans; break off tips; remove
strings, if any. Break into 1-inch pieces;
add to veal; cover; cook 25 minutes,
or until tender.

Melt butter or margarine; blend in
flour, sugar, salt and remaining Aromat.

Measure liquid from green beans
mixture; add enough water to make 1½
pints; add to flour mixture with vinegar. Cook, stirring, until smooth and
thickened; return to green bean mixture.

Add savory, parsley, and pepper.
Cook, uncovered, over low heat 15
minutes. Top each serving with generous mound of mashed potatoes. Serves
6.

Leftover Veal

VEAL CROQUETTES

1 ounce butter or margarine
2 ounces flour
8 fluid ounces milk
1 pound minced cooked veal
1 teaspoon salt
2 tablespoons chopped onion
fine breadcrumbs

Make a white sauce of butter, flour, and milk. Add veal, salt, and onion. Cool.

Shape into 6 croquettes. Roll in breadcrumbs.

Fry croquettes in deep hot fat until well browned. Drain on absorbent paper.

Serve with hot spicy beets or other tart relish. Serves 6.

Note: One can creamed chicken soup may be substituted for white sauce.

Variations: Add one of these to veal mixture: 1 ounce shredded cheese, $\frac{1}{2}$ clove garlic, crushed, 1 tablespoon ketchup, or 1 tablespoon chopped parsley.

VEAL À LA KING

8 ounces diced cooked veal
1 10$\frac{1}{2}$-ounce can cream of chicken soup
$\frac{1}{4}$ pint single cream or top of the milk
4-5 sliced black olives or canned mushrooms
1 tablespoon butter or margarine
$\frac{1}{8}$ teaspoon nutmeg
1 tablespoon pickle relish or chopped green pepper
4 slices toast, buttered

Heat soup and milk in saucepan. Add remaining ingredients except toast. Stir and heat slowly.

Taste and season. Serve hot on hot toast. Serves 4.

CURRIED VEAL OR LAMB PIE

1 ounce butter or margarine
4 fluid ounces hot milk
salt and pepper to taste
1$\frac{1}{4}$ pounds mashed potatoes
1 well beaten egg
1$\frac{1}{2}$ pounds minced cooked veal or lamb
1 medium onion, chopped
$\frac{3}{4}$ pint curry white sauce (see Index)

Melt butter in hot milk; add salt and pepper. Beat into mashed potatoes. Add well beaten egg and beat until light.

Fill a greased 2$\frac{1}{2}$-pint casserole with part of potato mixture.

Combine meat, onion, and curry sauce; turn into casserole and top with remaining potato mixture.

Bake in hot oven (425°F. Mark 7) about 30 minutes or until heated through and lightly browned. Serves 6.

VEAL TERRAPIN

$\frac{1}{2}$ pint thin white sauce
1$\frac{1}{2}$ pounds chopped cooked veal
3 hard-boiled eggs, chopped
1 teaspoon lemon juice
1 tablespoon Worcestershire sauce
1$\frac{1}{4}$ pounds cooked rice

Prepare white sauce with thin cream or evaporated milk; add veal and egg and heat thoroughly.

Just before serving, add lemon juice and Worcestershire sauce; serve with a border of rice. Serves 6.

PINEAPPLE-VEAL PATTIES

1 pound minced leftover roast veal
1 ounce fine, dry breadcrumbs
4 tablespoons tomato ketchup
$\frac{1}{2}$ small onion, finely chopped
$\frac{1}{2}$ teaspoon salt
$\frac{1}{8}$ teaspoon pepper
$\frac{1}{8}$ teaspoon thyme
1 slightly beaten egg
4 or 5 slices canned pineapple
1$\frac{1}{2}$ ounces butter or margarine
2 ounces brown sugar
4 fluid ounces pineapple syrup

Combine meat, crumbs, ketchup, onion, seasonings, and egg; mix well.

Shape into 4 or 5 large patties. Place on pineapple slices in greased shallow casserole. Combine remaining ingredients and spoon over patties. Cover.

Bake in moderate oven (350°F. Mark 4) 30 minutes. Uncover and bake 10 minutes; baste occasionally. Serves 4 to 5.

VEAL TIMBALES

1 ounce fat
1 ounce flour
8 fluid ounces meat broth or thin gravy
2 well beaten eggs
salt and pepper to taste
lemon juice to taste
1 pound minced cooked veal
1 tablespoon chopped parsley

Make a sauce of fat, flour, and liquid.

Add eggs, seasoning, and meat. Mix thoroughly.

Pour into greased timbale moulds or dariole tins. Place tins in pan of water.

Bake in moderate oven (350°F. Mark 4) about $\frac{1}{2}$ hour, until set in centre.

Turn timbales out and serve hot sprinkled with parsley. Serves 6.

Variations: Chicken, lamb, or other leftover meat may be used instead of veal.

VEAL IN SOUR CREAM

Place cooked, sliced veal in a shallow oven-proof dish. Cover lightly with sour cream and sprinkle with a little nutmeg.

Bake in moderate oven (350°F. Mark 4) until well heated.

Creamed Veal and Vegetables in Parsley Noodle Ring

CREAMED VEAL AND VEGE-TABLES IN PARSLEY NOODLE RING

3 ounces butter or margarine
1 ounce flour
$\frac{3}{4}$ pint milk
1 teaspoon salt
few grains of pepper
1 pound diced cooked veal
6 ounces diced cooked celery
4 ounces cooked peas
$\frac{1}{8}$ teaspoon thyme (optional)
$\frac{1}{2}$ ounce finely chopped parsley
1 pound cooked noodles

Melt 2 ounces butter in a saucepan; blend in flour; gradually add milk. Cook over low heat, stirring constantly, until thick.

Add salt and pepper. Cook 5 minutes, stirring occasionally. Add veal, celery and peas. Season more if necessary.

Combine remaining butter, thyme and parsley; add to hot noodles; mix well. Press into oiled ring mould.

Unmould on hot serving dish; fill centre with veal mixture. Garnish with parsley. Serves 8.

VEAL AND OKRA CASSEROLE

4 tablespoons milk
1 can condensed mushroom soup
1 teaspoon grated onion
$\frac{1}{2}$ pound chopped cooked veal

Mix all ingredients. Pour into greased casserole.

Bake in moderate oven (350°F. Mark 4) 20 minutes. Top with potato crisps and bake 5 more minutes. Serves 4.

CELERY VEAL RING

1 pound diced cooked veal (pork or lamb also may be used)
$\frac{1}{2}$ small head of celery, chopped
3 slices white bread, cubed
1 teaspoon salt
3 beaten eggs
dash of curry powder
2 tablespoons finely chopped onion
1 tablespoon melted butter or margarine
$\frac{3}{4}$ pint hot gravy or milk

Combine veal, celery, bread cubes, salt, eggs, curry powder, onion, and butter. Add gravy and mix well.

Bake in greased 9-inch ring mould or loaf tin in moderate oven (350°F. Mark 4) 1 hour. Serve with tomato sauce. Serves 6.

Lamb and Mutton Recipes

COOKING HINTS FOR LAMB AND MUTTON

The thin paper-like covering over the outside of the lamb carcass is known as the "fell". It does not affect the flavour unless the lamb has been kept for some time, and it may be left on or removed from joints. Under normal conditions, the fell should not be removed from the leg, since this cut keeps its shape better and is juicier if the fell is left on. This parchment-like membrane is often removed from cuts other than the leg before it reaches the retail market.

Most cuts of high-quality lamb are tender, therefore roasting, grilling, and frying are the cooking methods most used.

Lamb and mutton contain a very small amount of fat and very little moisture. If cooked too long or at too high a temperature the meat will dry and harden.

The neck, shank and breast may be prepared for braising or cut into small pieces for stew, which is cooked in liquid. The meat from these cuts also may be minced for patties or meat loaves, then cooked by dry heat. Most cuts of the lower quality lamb are best if cooked by moist heat.

Lamb is cooked medium or well done. If cooked so that it is still slightly pink on the inside, there will be less shrinkage and the meat will be juicy and delicious. Mutton requires a little longer cooking.

Always serve lamb and mutton very hot or cold. It should never be served lukewarm.

Roast Leg of Lamb is one of the easiest meats to prepare for Sunday dinner or any festive occasion. Lamb calls mint to mind. But lamb is companionable with lemon, orange, and pineapple flavours, too. A subdued tomato barbecue sauce is favoured on lamb by some, but use it sparingly to avoid overpowering the delicate flavour of the meat.

LAMB AND MUTTON COOKING CHART

Cuts	Method of Cooking
Breast:	Roast, stew, braise or boil
Chops:	Grill or fry
Cutlets:	Grill or fry
Head:	Soup or stock
Leg:	Roast, stew, braise or boil
Neck:	
Best end	Roast
Middle	Stew, braise or boil
Scrag end	Boil, soup or stock
Loin:	Roast
Saddle: (a double loin)	Roast
Shoulder:	Roast, stew or braise
Trotters:	Soup or stock

ROAST LEG OF LAMB

Do not remove fell or thick skin. If desired, gash meat and tuck in slivers of garlic. Rub surface with salt and pepper.

If a meat thermometer is used, insert it in the centre of the meatiest part so it does not touch the bone.

Roast in a fairly slow oven (325°F. Mark 3) 30 to 35 minutes per pound or until the meat thermometer registers 175°F. for medium, 180°F. for well done.

Serve with gravy, mint sauce, or jelly.
Roasted Lamb with Minted Pineapple: Rub a 5- to 6-pound leg of lamb with about 2½ to 3 teaspoons Ac'cent (pure monosodium glutamate) or Aromat and roast as above.

Half an hour before roast is done, heat 5 or 6 slices canned pineapple in 4-5 tablespoons mint jelly. Place on roast; return to oven and finish roasting. Baste lamb occasionally with remaining jelly. To serve, drain off fat and make gravy from fat left in the pan. Serves 6 to 8.

STUFFED SHOULDER OF LAMB

Use 3- to 4-pound shoulder of lamb. Have bones removed from side to form pocket.

Fill cavity with celery or other stuffing. See page 626. Fasten edges together by sewing or with skewers.

Place fat-side-up on rack in roasting tin. Roast, without basting and without adding water, in slow oven (300°F. Mark 2) until done. Allow 35 to 40 minutes per pound, or until meat thermometer registers 180°F.

Crown Roast of Lamb filled with your favourite stuffing, garnished with hot chutney-filled pear halves. Cooked small white onions cover the rib ends.

CROWN ROAST OF LAMB

Have crown of 10 to 16 ribs prepared by the butcher. Season with salt and pepper.

Wrap rib ends with salt pork or bacon or aluminium foil to prevent charing. Fill centre with stuffing of your choice.

Place roast on rack in roasting pan. Roast in a fairly slow oven (325°F. Mark 3), allowing 30 to 35 minutes per pound or until meat thermometer inserted in thickest part of roast registers 175°F. to 180°F.

Remove salt pork, bacon, or foil and replace with paper frills. Serve with gravy.

If stuffing isn't used, place roast upside down in roasting tin so fat from roast will baste rib ends. Fill centre with cooked peas, tiny carrots, or cooked cauliflower at serving time.

ROAST SHOULDER OF LAMB WITH PINEAPPLE GLAZE

1 4- to 5-pound shoulder of lamb
2 teaspoons salt
½ teaspoon pepper
1 tablespoon curry powder
1 can (13-14 ounces) crushed pineapple

Place lamb on rack in roasting tin. Sprinkle with salt and pepper. Bake in fairly slow oven (325°F. Mark 3) 2½ hours.

Combine curry powder and pineapple and add to lamb. Cook 15 minutes, turning occasionally. Garnish with pineapple and cherries. Serves 4 to 6.

Roast Shoulder of Lamb with Pineapple Glaze

Rolled Shoulder of Lamb

ROLLED SHOULDER OF LAMB

Season 5- to 6-pound rolled shoulder of lamb with salt and pepper. Place on rack in roasting pan. Insert meat thermometer if used so that bulb reaches centre of thickest part. Do not add water.

Roast in slow oven (300°F. Mark 2), basting every half hour with French dressing. For medium-done lamb, meat thermometer should register 175°F., and 180°F. for well-done lamb. Allow 30 to 35 minutes to pound. Serves 10 to 12.

BRAISED STUFFED BREAST OF LAMB

1   breast of lamb
salt and pepper
3   tablespoons chopped celery
1½ tablespoons chopped onion
2   tablespoons fat
6   ounces fine breadcrumbs
1   ounce chopped mint
¾ teaspoon salt
¼ teaspoon pepper
6   tablespoons salad oil

Get a pocket cut into breast of lamb from the large end. Sprinkle inside and out with salt and pepper.

To make the stuffing, brown the celery and onion in hot fat. Add breadcrumbs, mint, and seasoning. Mix well.

Stuff pocket of roast. Fasten edges together with skewers.

Brown breast on all sides in hot fat. Add 4 fluid ounces hot water and cover tightly. Cook slowly until done, about 1½ to 2 hours. Serves 4 to 6.

Braised Stuffed Breast of Lamb

BRAISED SHOULDER OF LAMB

Rub meat with cut clove of garlic, then with salt. Brown well on all sides in a little fat in a heavy saucepan.

Add 4 tablespoons water, 1-2 stalks celery, 1 small chopped onion, 8 ounces canned tomatoes, and a bay leaf.

Cover and cook over very low heat or in moderate oven until tender. A 4-pound shoulder will take about 2½ hours.

BRAISED BREAST OF LAMB

Get butcher to bone breast of lamb. Spread with sausage or favourite stuffing, then roll up tightly. Hold together with skewers or tie with string.

Brown in small amount of hot fat. Add 4 tablespoons water to pan. Cover and simmer gently until meat is tender, about 2 hours. Add water as necessary. Remove skewers or string before serving.

Variations: Use a can of tomato juice instead of water. Or, use condensed cream of mushroom soup diluted with half as much water, and, if desired, add a little sour cream.

JELLY GLAZED ROAST LEG OR SHOULDER OF LAMB

Select a leg or a boned and rolled shoulder of lamb. Rub with chopped mint leaves. Season with salt and pepper.

Roast as directed for Roast Leg of Lamb. During last 30 minutes, baste often with red currant jelly diluted with a little hot water.

Make gravy from the juices left in the pan thickened with a little flour and water paste.

BREAST OF LAMB WITH RICE AND NUT STUFFING

1 breast of lamb
1 clove garlic, cut
6 ounces rice, brown or white
1 ounce chopped nuts
1 teaspoon salt
2 tablespoons chopped parsley
1 ounce flour or fine breadcrumbs
4 tablespoons melted fat or salad oil
¾ pint boiling soup stock or water

Cut a deep pocket in the lamb for the stuffing.

Pre-cook rice in boiling salted water for 14 minutes; drain.

Rub the lamb inside and out with cut clove of garlic. Trim off bits of fat and chop or cut fine; combine with drained rice, nuts, salt, and parsley.

Stuff the breast and fasten opening with skewers. Coat all over with flour or sifted fine breadcrumbs.

Heat fat or oil in roasting tin; place stuffed breast in it and spoon some of the oil over meat.

Add stock or water and cook, 1½ to 2 hours in slow oven (300°F. Mark 2) or 30 to 35 minutes per pound of meat. Baste occasionally with fat in the tin. Serves 4 to 6.

BARBECUED LEG OF LAMB

1 5-pound leg of lamb
salt and pepper
flour
2 tablespoons Worcestershire sauce
2 tablespoons sugar
½ teaspoon dry mustard
4 tablespoons vinegar
8 fluid ounces water
3-4 tablespoons tomato ketchup
2 medium onions, chopped

Sprinkle meat with salt and pepper and rub with flour. Place in roasting tin.

Combine remaining ingredients; mix well and pour over meat.

Cover pan and roast in slow oven (325°F. Mark 3) until tender, 30 to 35 minutes per pound. Baste occasionally with sauce in the tin.

Remove cover 30 minutes before meat is done to let it brown. Serve with the sauce. Serves 6 to 8.

BARBECUED BREAST OF LAMB

2 pounds breast of lamb, cut into 4 pieces
2 teaspoons salt
2 tablespoons fat
1 medium onion, sliced
3-4 tablespoons chilli sauce
¼ teaspoon cayenne pepper
1 tablespoon vinegar
8 fluid ounces water

Season lamb with salt. Brown in hot fat in a saucepan or casserole.

Add onion, chilli sauce, cayenne, vinegar, and water.

Cover and simmer or bake in moderate oven (350°F. Mark 4) about 1½ hours.

Uncover and cook until the sauce is almost absorbed, about 20 minutes. Serves 4.

CELERY STUFFING

3 ounces soft breadcrumbs
3-4 stalks celery, chopped
½ medium onion, chopped
1 ounce fat
1 teaspoon salt
¼ teaspoon pepper
1 teaspoon dried sage or savory
1 egg

Melt fat and sauté the celery and onion for a few minutes. Add all the other ingredients and enough water to bind.

Leftover Lamb

~~RE~~ED NOODLES AND LAMB

1 pound diced, roast lamb
2 tablespoons fat
2 cloves garlic, crushed
1 6-ounce can tomato paste
1½ pints water
1½ teaspoons salt
⅛ teaspoon pepper
2 teaspoons paprika
8 ounces broad noodles
grated Parmesan cheese

Brown lamb lightly in fat. Add garlic, tomato paste, water, and seasonings. Bring to boil; cover, and simmer about 5 minutes.

Add noodles, and continue cooking until noodles are tender, stirring occasionally to prevent sticking. Add more water, if necessary.

Sprinkle with cheese just before serving. Serves 4.

~~L~~AMB CASSEROLE

1½ pounds cooked lamb, cut in pieces
1 tablespoon fat
4 ounces cooked carrots, cut in cubes
4 ounces cooked potato balls
8 cooked small onions
about ½ pint leftover gravy

Brown lamb in fat. Place in baking dish.

Add carrots, potato balls, and onions. Add gravy and enough hot water to moisten. Season with salt and pepper if necessary.

Cover and bake in moderate oven (350°F. Mark 4) 20 to 25 minutes or until thoroughly heated. Serves 6.

~~L~~AMB WITH EGGPLANT OR AUBERGINE, BALKAN STYLE

4 tablespoons oil
1 small onion; cut into thin slices
1 small eggplant, cut into 1½-inch chunks
1 can (about 16 ounces) tomatoes
1 tablespoon chopped dill or parsley
1 teaspoon salt
¼ teaspoon pepper
1 slightly beaten egg
1 tablespoon water
1 tablespoon lemon juice
2 pounds cooked lamb, cut into 1½-inch chunks

Heat oil in chafing dish or sauté pan over direct heat. Brown onion and eggplant, then push to one side.

Add tomatoes, dill or parsley, salt and pepper to chafing dish. Cover and cook until eggplant is tender.

Place pan over hot water. Combine egg, water, and lemon juice, then stir in 2 tablespoons of hot sauce from chafing dish. Spoon back into chafing dish. Add lamb. Heat but do not boil, stirring occasionally. Serves 6 to 8.

QUICK LAMB CURRY

2 ounces sliced mushrooms
4 ounces diced apple
½ small onion, finely chopped
3 tablespoons butter or margarine
2 cans condensed cream of celery soup
2 teaspoons curry powder
1½ pounds cubed cooked lamb
6 ounces rice, cooked
desiccated coconut

Cook mushrooms, apple, and onion until soft in butter. Add soup, curry powder, and lamb; simmer about 20 minutes.

Heap curried lamb on hot rice; top with coconut. Serves 6.

LEFTOVER LAMB KEBABS

Lamb kebabs are usually made with uncooked lamb, but the leftover roast may be used in this way, too.

The trick is to cut the lamb into fairly uniform 1½- to 2-inch cubes. To assure even browning, dip lamb cubes into French dressing, garlic, or lemon-flavoured melted butter, or a tart barbecue sauce before grilling. Then brush with sauce during cooking.

Pineapple chunks, mushrooms, sliced bacon, tomato sections, and small boiled onions may be threaded alternately on the skewers to make interesting combinations.

Since the lamb is cooked, grill fairly quickly and turn to brown evenly.

LAMB PUFFS

1 pound chopped, cooked lamb
1 well beaten egg
¾ pound hot mashed potatoes
salt and pepper to taste
⅛ teaspoon paprika
flour

Add enough leftover gravy to seasoned lamb to make it spreadable.

Blend egg, seasoned potatoes, and enough flour to make a mixture stiff enough to roll out on floured board. Roll ¼ inch thick and cut with a large biscuit cutter.

Drop a spoonful of lamb mixture into centre of each round. Bring up edges to form a three-cornered puff. Press edges together and brush with melted butter or margarine.

Place puffs on greased baking sheet and bake in hot oven (400°F. Mark 6) 10 to 15 minutes, or until hot and browned. Serve with lamb gravy or tomato sauce. Serves 6.

Variation: Pastry can be used in place of potato, if desired.

Quick Lamb Curry

LAMB STEW

1 pound cubed cooked lamb
2 tablespoons fat or salad oil
1½ pints water
2 teaspoons salt
1 teaspoon Worcestershire sauce
8 small white onions
4 ounces sliced carrots
4 ounces cooked or canned peas
flour
hot cooked rice

Brown lamb in fat or salad oil. Add water, salt, and Worcestershire sauce; simmer 5 minutes.

Add onions and carrots; cook 20 minutes. Add peas; heat. Drain off liquid in pan.

Blend a little flour to smooth paste with water; add to liquid. Cook slowly, stirring constantly, until thickened. Add to lamb and vegetable mixture.

Arrange lamb mixture on dish with rice. Serves 4.

SPANISH LAMB AND RICE

8 ounces uncooked rice
2 ounces bacon fat or butter
1 medium onion, chopped
4-5 stalks celery, diced
1 can (about 16 ounces) tomatoes
8 fluid ounces water or lamb broth
1 teaspoon salt
¼ teaspoon pepper
1 pound cubed or slivered cooked lamb

Brown rice lightly in bacon fat or butter, stirring often. Add onion and celery and brown a few minutes longer.

Add tomatoes, lamb broth or water, salt, and pepper. Cook, covered, over low heat, stirring occasionally, until rice is tender, about 25 minutes.

Add lamb, reheat and adjust seasonings. Serves 4.

LEFTOVER LAMB AND EGGPLANT OR AUBERGINE

Sauté 1 large chopped onion and 1 crushed clove garlic, in 2 tablespoons olive oil until yellow.

Add 3-4 chopped tomatoes, 1 medium eggplant, peeled and cubed, 1 bay leaf, and ½ teaspoon salt. Cook until eggplant is just tender, stirring often.

Add 1 pound diced or minced cooked lamb and heat to simmering. Adjust seasonings.

Serve on rice. Serves 4 to 5.

Lamb or Mutton Chops and Steaks

FRIED LAMB OR MUTTON CHOPS

Cutlets, or loin or chump chops may be used. Place chops in heavy greased frying pan and brown on both sides.

Reduce heat and cook until well done or to taste. Add no extra fat or water. Do not cover pan.

Pour off excess fat as it collects in pan. Turn the chops frequently to cook uniformly. Sprinkle with salt. Serve at once on hot dish.

BRAISED LAMB CHUMP CHOPS

4 chump chops, cut ½-inch thick
1 teaspoon salt
¼ teaspoon black pepper
garlic or garlic salt
1 teaspoon paprika
1 tablespoon lemon juice
2 tablespoons water

Brown chops thoroughly on both sides in a greased sauté pan.

Combine seasonings, lemon juice, and water and pour over chops. (If garlic clove is used, rub cut clove over chops.)

Cover and simmer 25 to 30 minutes, turning once during cooking. Serves 4.

CHUMP CHOPS, HUNTER STYLE

2 tablespoons butter or margarine
4 chump chops, about 1½ inches thick
½ onion, sliced
2 cloves garlic, crushed
1 can (about 16 ounces) tomatoes
½ pound mushrooms, sliced
½ teaspoon oregano
salt and pepper to taste
4 fluid ounces dry red wine
1 pound spaghetti

Melt butter or margarine; add chops and cook until lightly browned on both sides.

Add onion, garlic, tomatoes, mushrooms, oregano, salt, and pepper. Cook covered over low heat about 30 minutes or until lamb is tender. Add wine. Cook 15 minutes.

Meanwhile, cook spaghetti in boiling salted water. Drain in colander. Serve with chops. Serves 4.

Chump Chops, Hunter Style

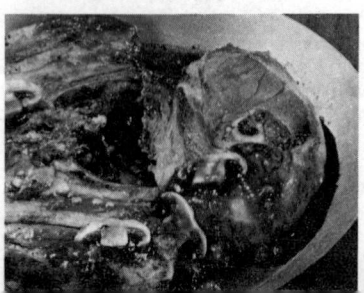

BAKED CHUMP CHOPS

6 chump chops
1 clove garlic
salt and pepper
1 ounce fat
2 medium onions, chopped
8 ounces cooked carrots, diced
2 ounces flour
4 tablespoons chilli sauce
4 fluid ounces Sauternes or Rhine wine

Rub chops with cut clove of garlic; sprinkle with salt and pepper. Brown on both sides in hot fat in frying pan. Remove to baking dish.

Sauté onions and carrots in pan until onions are soft. Add flour, chilli sauce, and wine; cook until thickened.

Place a mound of carrot mixture on top of each chop. Bake in moderate oven (350°F. Mark 4) for 45 minutes. Serves 6.

STUFFED LAMB CHOPS

8 thick lamb chops
flour seasoned with salt
6 large mushrooms, finely chopped
1 clove garlic, crushed
1 teaspoon finely chopped parsley
2 tablespoons breadcrumbs
1 tablespoon cream
salt and pepper to taste
1 egg yolk
2 tablespoons melted butter or margarine
4 fluid ounces boiling water

Using a sharp knife cut a pocket in each chop and roll them in seasoned flour. Mix remaining ingredients except butter and water. Stuff chops.

Brown in butter. Place in roasting tin. Add butter in which chops were browned. Add water. Cover and cook in slow oven (325°F. Mark 3) about 45 minutes.
Serves 8.

LAMB GRILLING CHART

Cut	Time in Minutes
Cutlets ¾-1 inch	7-8
Loin chops 1-1½ inches	8-9
Chump chops 2 inches	10-12

Chops should be brushed with fat or oil before grilling and turned once or twice during the cooking. Serve with a pat of parsley butter.

Grilled Lamb Steaks with Mint Glaze

GRILLED LAMB STEAKS WITH MINT GLAZE

4 slices lamb, about 1 to 1½ inches thick, cut from fillet end of leg
4 fluid ounces mint jelly
salt and pepper
3 tablespoons chopped parsley

Grill lamb 7 to 8 minutes, or until lightly browned. Turn. Spread with jelly; sprinkle with remaining ingredients. Grill a further 8 minutes or until tender.

Serve with escalloped potatoes, seasoned peas, and fresh vegetable salad. Serves 4.

GRILLED LAMB OR MUTTON CHOPS

Have cutlets, loin or chump chops cut ¾ to 1 inch thick. See chart. Brush with fat or oil and place under pre-heated grill.

When brown, season; turn and brown other side. See chart for cooking time. Allow 2 to 3 minutes longer for mutton chops. Serve on a heated dish attractively garnished with vegetables.

LAMB HOT-POT

6 loin mutton or lamb chops
1 lamb kidney
4 mushrooms, chopped
¼ teaspoon salt
¼ teaspoon pepper
2 teaspoons Worcestershire sauce
potatoes, sliced
parsnips, sliced
2 tablespoons melted butter or margarine

Cut the kidney in 12 slices and place 2 slices on each chop.

Sprinkle the chopped mushrooms, salt, pepper, and Worcestershire sauce over all. Barely cover all this with stock.

Fill dish with equal parts of sliced potatoes and parsnips. Pour in melted butter.

Cover tightly and bake in slow oven (300°F. Mark 2) 2 hours. Serve with cranberry jelly. Serves 6.

PLANKED LAMB STEAK DINNER

2 slices lamb from fillet end of leg
3 tomatoes, halved
canned asparagus tips
2 tablespoons butter or margarine
3 egg yolks
salt and pepper
¾-1 pound hot riced potatoes

Have slices from leg of lamb cut 1 to 2 inches thick.

Brown on one side in hot pan. Season and transfer, with brown side down to a flat fireproof dish.

Place tomato halves around steaks. Arrange asparagus tips tied in bundles in dish; dot with butter.

Add 2 tablespoons butter, egg yolks, and seasonings to potatoes and beat. Make border around other foods with potatoes.

Place in hot oven (400°F. Mark 6) or under grill, to brown and finish cooking lamb and to heat vegetables. Serves

LAMB CHOPS VIENNESE

Have cutlet or loin chops cut 1 inch thick. With a sharp knife, cut a pocket in each chop, to the bone.

Insert a thin rasher fried bacon in each pocket. Fasten cut edges with cocktail sticks. Grill chops about 4-5 minutes each side. Season with salt and pepper and serve.

Paper frills may be slipped over the cutlet ends. Cutlets are small, so allow two to a person. One loin chop should satisfy a normal appetite.

MUTTON CHOPS, COUNTRY STYLE

6 mutton chops, 2 inches thick
olive oil
salt and pepper
3 beaten egg yolks
3 tablespoons cream
salt
freshly ground black pepper
dry breadcrumbs
grated cheese
melted butter or margarine

Trim chops and flatten slightly with broad side of cleaver. Brush chops with olive oil and grill on 1 side 4 minutes. Remove from grill.

Season lightly with salt and pepper and spread over grilled side a mixture of egg yolks, cream, salt and pepper to taste. Coat with equal parts breadcrumbs and grated cheese.

Place chops in greased shallow tin. Brush with melted butter. Bake in hot oven (400°F. Mark 6) 15 minutes. Serves 6.

MUTTON CHOPS, MAÎTRE D'HÔTEL

6 mutton chops, 2 inches thick
salt and pepper
2 ounces creamed butter or margarine
½ teaspoon lemon juice
1 tablespoon chopped parsley
crisp bacon
parsley

Trim excess fat from chops and flatten slightly with flat side of cleaver or meat mallet.

Grill about 5 to 6 minutes on each side. Season with salt and pepper.

Just before serving, place 1 teaspoon maître d'hôtel butter on each.

Garnish with crisp bacon and parsley.

Prepare butter by adding lemon juice, finely chopped parsley, a sprinkle of salt and pepper to creamed butter. Serves 6.

BAKED LAMB CHOPS

4 ounces bacon fat
2 ounces fine dry breadcrumbs
2 teaspoons finely chopped onion
1 teaspoon salt
¼ teaspoon pepper
1 teaspoon Worcestershire sauce
2 hard-boiled eggs (optional)
4 lamb chops, cut thick

Put fat in a frying pan and brown crumbs, onion, and seasonings in it. Add Worcestershire sauce.

Chop whites of eggs, force yolks through a sieve and add to crumb mixture.

Wipe chops with damp cloth and coat with crumb mixture. Place in baking tin. Bake, covered, in slow oven (325°F. Mark 3) about 40 minutes. Serves 4.

LAMB CHOPS WITH MUSHROOMS

6 lamb chops
½ pound large mushrooms
1 egg, slightly beaten
fine breadcrumbs
1½ ounces butter or margarine
buttered hot toast
parsley

Grill or fry chops, allowing 8-10 minutes.

While chops are grilling, wash mushrooms, dry and cut in halves lengthwise through caps and stems.

Dip each half in egg, roll in crumbs, and fry slowly in butter in heavy frying pan about 5 minutes, or until golden brown, turning frequently; remove and keep hot.

Serve grilled chops on buttered toast, placing mushrooms over each chop so as to completely cover it. Garnish with parsley. Serves 6.

QUICK AND EASY GRILL

Trim the chops and arrange on grill rack. Brush with butter or oil. Place cooked green beans and sliced carrots in grill pan. Season vegetables with salt and pepper.

Place grill rack over vegetables and place under the preheated grill. Grill on one side until chops are browned, about 4-5 minutes.
Season, turn and grill on the second side until brown. Season only when turning is necessary. The vegetables will heat while meat is cooking.
Serve chops on a heated dish accompanied with green beans and carrots. Pour a little fat from the grill pan over the chops.

Miscellaneous Lamb Dishes

OVEN SHISH KEBABS

3 pounds boneless shoulder of
    lamb, cut in 1½-inch cubes
1 large onion, thinly sliced
1 clove garlic, cut in half
2 green peppers, cut in 1-inch
    squares
1 teaspoon salt
½ teaspoon coarse black pepper
¾ teaspoon oregano
4 tablespoons salad oil
6 fluid ounces sherry

Put meat, onion, garlic, and green peppers in a bowl; add seasonings, oil, and wine; mix well. Let stand in refrigerator several hours or overnight, stirring occasionally.

An hour or so before serving time, remove from refrigerator and string meat cubes on metal skewers alternately with pieces of green pepper.

Lay filled skewers on a rack in a shallow baking tin.

Bake in very hot oven (450°F. Mark 8) for about 20 minutes. Serve on the skewers. Serves 6.

BAKED LAMB (OR VEAL) STEW

2 pounds shoulder of lamb or veal
1 ounce fat
1 sliced onion
salt to taste
6 ounces sliced raw carrots
½ small head celery diced
6 ounces raw peas
½ ounce chopped parsley

Brown 1-inch cubes of meat in hot fat. Add onion and brown slightly.

Add salt and vegetables, except parsley. Barely cover with water and bring to boiling point.

Thicken with 2 tablespoons flour stirred to smooth paste with water. Pour into casserole.

Cover and bake in slow oven (325°F. Mark 3) until meat is tender, 45-60 minutes. Garnish with chopped parsley. Serves 4.

Sweet and Sour Lamb

LAMB (OR VEAL) CURRY

1½ pounds lamb or veal
1 small onion, chopped
1 tart apple
1½ teaspoons salt
⅛ teaspoon pepper
1 teaspoon curry powder
½ teaspoon ginger
1 teaspoon sugar
¾ pint bouillon or water
1½ ounces sultanas (optional)
hot boiled rice

Brown meat cubes in a little hot fat or oil.

Add onions, apple, seasonings, and liquid. Cover and cook gently 1 hour.

Thicken, if desired, with a flour-water paste. Add sultanas and cook 15 minutes longer.

Serve over hot boiled rice. If desired, sprinkle with chopped nuts or coconut. Serves 4 or 5.

SWEET AND SOUR LAMB

2 pounds best end neck of lamb
1 teaspoon salt
1½ pints boiling water
1 tablespoon peanut or vegetable
    oil
½ small onion, diced
4 ounces carrots, thinly sliced
4 ounces pineapple tidbits or
    chunks
1 green pepper, cut in 1-inch
    squares
6 small sweet pickles, sliced
Sweet and Sour Sauce:
1 clove garlic crushed with ½
    teaspoon salt
1 teaspoon monosodium glutamate
    (Ac'cent or Aromat)
2 tablespoons cornflour
2 tablespoons brown sugar
2 tablespoons soy sauce
4 tablespoons vinegar
4 fluid ounces cold water
8 fluid ounces pineapple juice
1 bouillon cube (chicken or beef)
    dissolved in 4 tablespoons
    boiling water

Have your butcher separate the cutlets and chop them in halves. Add salt and lamb to boiling water in a saucepan, cover and simmer until tender. Drain, saving liquid for soup or sauces. Brown the lamb pieces slowly in the oil.

Mix together all of the sauce ingredients. Add to the browned lamb, and cook, stirring constantly, until sauce is transparent. Add onion, carrots, pineapple, green pepper, and sweet pickles. Simmer mixture, covered, until vegetables are tender, but still a little crisp. Serve with steamed rice and/or fried noodles. Serve with dishes of mustard, pickle relish, a tart jelly, and a raw vegetable salad. Serves 4.

Lamb Curry is a perfect buffet dish. Serve on plain rice, rice pilaff, or rice into which sultanas and slivered almonds have been stirred. Include a variety of accompaniments such as chutney, fine coconut, chopped hard-boiled egg white and bacon, pineapple cubes, etc.

IRISH STEW

2 pounds lamb or mutton
about 1½ pints boiling water
3 medium-sized carrots, cut into
    ½-inch slices
1 small raw turnip diced
1 medium-sized onion, sliced
3 tablespoons chopped parsley
2 teaspoons salt
¼ teaspoon pepper
1 bay leaf

Select meat from shank, neck, shoulder, breast or flank. Cut into 2-inch pieces. Place in a saucepan and cover with water. Cover and simmer about 1 hour.

Add vegetables and seasonings and cook about ½ hour longer.

Thicken liquid with 2 tablespoons flour mixed smooth with 4 tablespoons cold water. Serves 6.

With Dumplings: Mix and sift 4 ounces plain flour, 1½ teaspoons baking powder, and ½ teaspoon salt. Add 4 fluid ounces milk and 2 tablespoons melted fat or salad oil to make a soft dough.

Bring the stew to the boil, then drop in dumplings from a spoon. Cover tightly and steam, without lifting cover, 12 to 15 minutes.

Irish stew may be made of lamb or mutton. The meat is not browned before it is stewed.

Serve hot braised lamb shanks on a bed of rice and sautéed mushrooms. Pass the gravy separately.

BRAISED LAMB SHANKS

4 large lamb shanks
salt and pepper
2 tablespoons fat
¾ pint hot water
6 ounces raw potatoes, diced
6 ounces raw carrots, diced
3 ounces celery, diced
1 medium-sized onion, chopped

Season shanks with salt and pepper. Brown on all sides in hot fat.

Add water. Cover and bake in moderate oven (350°F. Mark 4) about 1 hour.

If necessary, add more water to prevent shanks from burning.

Add potatoes, carrots, celery, and onion. Cook until vegetables are tender, about 30 minutes longer. Serves 4.

Note: If preferred, the shanks may be cooked on top of the stove over a very low heat.

BARBECUED LAMB SHANKS

4 lamb shanks, about 1½ pounds each
2 tablespoons fat
2 onions, sliced
¼ pint tomato ketchup
8 fluid ounces water
2 teaspoons salt
2 tablespoons Worcestershire sauce
4 fluid ounces vinegar
1½ ounces brown sugar
2 teaspoons dry mustard

Brown shanks in hot fat in heavy saucepan or casserole. Combine remaining ingredients and pour over shanks.

Cover and simmer on top of stove or bake in moderate oven (350°F. Mark 4) until meat is tender, about 1½ hours. Spoon sauce over shanks 2 or 3 times during cooking period.

Uncover and cook 15 minutes longer. Serves 4.

LAMB STEW WITH SOUR CREAM

2 pounds shoulder or breast of lamb
2 tablespoons flour
2 tablespoons fat
2 small onions, sliced
1 pound tomatoes or 1 can tomato soup
2 tablespoons chopped parsley
salt, pepper, paprika
dill seed, if desired
¼ pint thick sour cream

Have meat boned and cut into cubes. Roll in flour and brown in fat. Brown onions with meat. Add tomatoes, parsley, and seasonings. Cook slowly about 1½ hours. Add sour cream just before serving and blend it well with the tomato sauce. Serves 4.

EAST INDIAN CURRY

1½ pounds lean lamb, cut in 1-inch square pieces
1 ounce butter or margarine
3 small onions, chopped finely
1 clove garlic, crushed
1 tablespoon curry powder (more or less)
1 apple, peeled, cored and cut in pieces
3 tomatoes, peeled and cut in pieces
¾ pint water or stock
1 teaspoon salt
⅛ teaspoon pepper
1½ ounces flour

Brown lamb lightly in butter with onions and garlic. Add curry, apple and tomatoes.

Add water, salt, and pepper. Stir well; simmer, covered, until lamb is tender, about 1 to 1½ hours. Remove lamb.

Strain sauce and thicken with flour mixed to smooth paste with little cold water. Return meat to sauce, and heat through.

Serve with plain boiled rice or rice pilaff. Serves 4.

BARBECUED LAMB

2½-3 pounds neck of lamb
salt and pepper
2 onions, sliced
4-5 tablespoons tomato ketchup
4 fluid ounces water
2 tablespoons vinegar
1 tablespoon sugar
2 teaspoons Worcestershire sauce
dash of Tabasco sauce
1 teaspoon dry mustard
clove of garlic, crushed

Cut up the meat and brown slowly and thoroughly in a sauté pan. Drain off the fat. Sprinkle the meat with salt, and pepper.

Add sliced onions. Combine remaining ingredients and pour over the meat and onions.

Cover and cook slowly until fork-tender, about 1 hour. Stir occasionally while cooking. Serves 4.

Lamb Stew with Mashed Potato Topping

LAMB STEW WITH MASHED POTATO TOPPING

2 pounds breast, shank, or neck of lamb
flour
3 tablespoons lard
salt and pepper
rosemary or thyme, to taste
8 fluid ounces water
6 carrots
6 small onions
hot mashed potatoes

Cut meat into 1½-inch cubes. Dredge with a few tablespoons flour and brown well on all sides in hot lard.

Season with salt and pepper, rosemary or thyme; add 8 fluid ounces water and simmer about 1 hour.

Cut up carrots and add with onions. Season. Cover and continue cooking until vegetables are tender.

Pour into casserole and top with hot mashed potatoes.

Bake in very hot oven (450°F. Mark 8) until potatoes are brown. Serves 4 to 6.

BAKED VEGETABLES WITH LAMB (BULGARIAN)

3 onions, sliced
1 pound lamb, cut into cubes
2 green peppers, cut into small pieces
salt and paprika
2 potatoes, peeled and quartered
4 ounces runner beans
4 ounces canned or fresh peas
4 ounces canned or fresh tomatoes

Brown onions in a little fat in a flameproof casserole. Add lamb and peppers. Season with salt and paprika.

Bake in moderate oven (350°F. Mark 4) until meat is tender, about 45 minutes. Add potatoes, runner beans, peas, and tomatoes. Bake about 20 minutes longer. If fresh vegetables are used, bake about ½ hour longer. Serves 4 to 5.

Barbecued Lamb

LAMB PILAFF

1 pound shoulder of lamb, cut into
    small pieces
6 ounces butter or margarine
juice of ½ lemon
salt
water
8 ounces rice
tomatoes or yogurt

Sauté lamb slowly in 2 ounces butter until brown.

Add lemon juice, salt to taste, and a few drops of water.

Simmer until lamb is tender, adding water a little at a time as needed to prevent sticking.

While lamb is cooking, prepare rice. Place remaining butter in a heavy saucepan. Add rice and cook, stirring often, until golden brown.

Add ½ teaspoon salt and ¾ pint water. Cover and cook without stirring over very low heat until rice is tender and grains are separate.

If desired, rice may be flavoured with tomatoes or it may be left plain and the final dish served with yogurt.

If tomatoes are used peel and chop them and add when rice is half tender.

Add hot lamb to hot rice. Serves 4.

NECK OF LAMB
AND VEGETABLES

2-2½ pounds neck of lamb
1 ounce lard, melted
salt and pepper
4 fluid ounces water
2 carrots, diced
2 potatoes, diced
1 large onion, diced
1 green pepper, diced

Cut the meat into pieces and brown well on all sides in melted lard. Spoon off fat.

Season with salt and pepper. Add water. Cover and simmer 1 hour.

Add carrots, potatoes, onion, and green pepper. Cover and simmer ½ hour longer.

Thicken gravy and serve with meat and vegetables. Serves 4.

Neck of Lamb and Vegetables

ITALIAN STYLE LAMB

1 large onion, sliced thinly
1 clove garlic, crushed
4 tablespoons olive oil
2 ounces flour
1½ teaspoons salt
½ teaspoon pepper
1 teaspoon paprika
2 pounds cubed, lean stewing lamb
1 can (6 ounces) tomato paste
¾ pint warm water
cooked rice

Cook onion and garlic slowly in hot oil until light yellow. Remove from oil.

Roll lamb cubes in flour seasoned with salt, pepper, and paprika. Brown meat on all sides in hot oil.

Return onion and garlic to pan. Pour tomato paste and water over all.

Cover tightly and cook slowly until tender, 1 hour. Serve over cooked rice. Serves 6.

LAMB-APPLE CASSEROLE

1 pound shoulder of lamb, diced
salt and pepper
1 tablespoon fat
2-3 sliced tart apples
1 teaspoon grated lemon rind
3 whole cloves
2 tablespoons water
1 ounce dry breadcrumbs
1½ ounces brown sugar

Season meat with salt and pepper. Brown on all sides in hot fat. Transfer meat to shallow casserole.

Add apples, lemon rind, cloves, and water. Sprinkle with crumbs, then with brown sugar.

Cover and bake in moderate oven (350°F. Mark 4) ½ hour. Uncover and bake until nicely browned on top, about 15 minutes longer. Serves 4.

PERSIAN PILAFF

1 pound shoulder of lamb
1 medium onion, chopped
2-3 chopped fresh tomatoes
1 pound uncooked rice
2 tablespoons butter or margarine
8 fluid ounces stock or water
salt and pepper

Cut lamb in 1-inch cubes and brown well.

Add chopped onions and brown lightly. Add tomatoes and cook 15 minutes.

Meanwhile soak rice in heavily salted water. Wash well in cold water and put over the top of meat.

Top with butter; add stock or water around the edges of meat. Season to taste.

Bake in moderate oven (350°F. Mark 4) 1 hour. Turn out on dish and serve immediately. Serves 4.

Mexican Chilli

MEXICAN CHILLI

4 tablespoons oil or melted fat
2 pounds lean lamb, beef, or pork,
    cubed
2 tablespoons flour
2 tablespoons chilli powder
1 medium onion, chopped
2 cloves garlic, crushed
¾ pint stock or water
2 teaspoons salt
1 teaspoon Aromat

Heat oil in sauté pan; add meat; brown lightly over moderate heat. Push meat to one side.

Mix flour with chilli powder; add to pan with onion and garlic. Continue cooking until onions are lightly browned.

Add stock or water, salt, and Aromat. Cover tightly; simmer over low heat until meat is very tender, about 1½ hours.

Serve over hot cooked rice. Serves 6.
Variations: In place of chilli powder use 6 to 8 chillies (seeds removed), 1 teaspoon oregano, ¼ teaspoon cummin seed, and 2 tiny hot red peppers. Remove stems and seeds from the chilli pods; cut in very thin strips with scissors. Add after adding stock or water; continue as directed.

LAMB AND VEGETABLE
CASSEROLE

2½ pounds shoulder or neck of lamb
2 tablespoons flour
1½ ounces butter or margarine
4 carrots, scraped and diced
4-5 stalks celery, diced
6 ounces diced, peeled marrow
1 can tomatoes (about 16 ounces)
1½ teaspoons salt
1 teaspoon Aromat
¼ teaspoon powdered mint
4 small mild onions, cut in halves

Remove excess fat from meat. Cut in small cubes and roll in flour. Brown in butter; transfer to casserole.

Cover with carrots, celery, marrow, and tomatoes mixed with seasonings. Put onions on top. Cover and bake in moderate oven (350°F. Mark 4) until lamb is tender about 1½ hours. To serve, sprinkle with chopped parsley. Serves 4.

SPANISH LAMB STEW

2 pounds breast of lamb
1 ounce fat
3 pints hot water
1 large onion, chopped
1 green pepper, chopped
4 ounces rice
1 teaspoon salt
¼ teaspoon pepper
1 can tomatoes (about 16 ounces)
4 ounces canned peas
1 beaten egg
1 teaspoon olive oil
½ teaspoon vinegar

Cut lamb in small pieces. Brown lightly in fat; add hot water and simmer, covered, about 1 hour.

Add onion, green pepper, rice, and seasonings and simmer ½ hour longer, or until vegetables and rice are done, adding tomatoes and peas the last 10 minutes of cooking.

Combine egg, olive oil and vinegar; add to stew, stirring until thickened; serve at once. Serves 6.

BLANQUETTE OF LAMB

4 pound boneless breast or shoulder of lamb
1 ounce fat
1 teaspoon salt
dash of pepper
1 pound small white onions
2½ ounces butter or margarine
¼ pound mushrooms, sliced
1 ounce flour
8 fluid ounces milk
4 tablespoons sherry or white wine
¼ pint double cream

Cut lamb into small chunks, brown in melted fat for about 10 minutes.

Season with salt and pepper; cook slowly for 15 minutes longer.

Peel onions and cook whole in 1½ ounces melted butter until barely tender. Add mushrooms; cook 5 minutes more.

To make sauce: Melt remaining butter in a separate saucepan; stir in flour smoothly, add milk gradually and cook slowly, stirring constantly, until sauce bubbles.

Add lamb to onion-mushroom mixture.

Rinse lamb pan with wine and add to meat mixture. Stir in sauce and cream, cover and cook slowly for 35 minutes. Serves 6.

MEAT AND POTATO CASSEROLE

1 ounce fat
2 onions, chopped
1 clove garlic, crushed
¼ teaspoon salt
¼ teaspoon freshly ground pepper
1 teaspoon marjoram
2 tomatoes, cut in quarters
1 tablespoon chopped parsley
2 pounds lamb or veal (neck or shoulder)
8 fluid ounces water
1 pound diced potato or potato balls

Melt fat and sauté onion and garlic. Add seasonings, tomatoes, and parsley. Turn into casserole. Add meat cut in large cubes.

Cover closely and cook slowly for 30 minutes.

Add water and potatoes. Cover and cook 1½ hours longer. Serves 6.

LAMB SHANKS WITH POTATOES AND CARROTS

4 lamb shanks
1 or 2 cloves garlic, cut in slivers
1 ounce flour
¼ teaspoon salt
2 tablespoons fat
½ pint tomato juice
1 small onion, sliced
½ teaspoon salt
dash of pepper
⅛ teaspoon oregano
4 fluid ounces sherry
4 to 6 medium potatoes, peeled
4 to 8 medium carrots, scraped

Get butcher to crack shank bones. Slit skin of each shank in several places and insert garlic slivers. Coat shanks with flour seasoned with ¼ teaspoon salt. Brown shanks on all sides in hot fat in heavy frying pan. Transfer to large casserole.

Combine tomato juice, onion, salt, pepper, oregano, and sherry in a saucepan. Heat to boiling point and pour over shanks.

Cover and cook in moderate oven (350°F. Mark 4) until fat begins to pull away from bone, about 1½ to 2 hours. Skim off excess fat. Add potatoes and carrots. Cook until tender, about 30 minutes longer. Serves 4.

LAMB AND EGGPLANT OR AUBERGINE SUPREME

2 large eggplants
1 pound breast or shoulder of lamb, cut in 1-inch squares
1 small onion, chopped
1 teaspoon salt
dash of pepper
2 tablespoons tomato purée
8 fluid ounces water or meat stock
½ pint medium white sauce
1 ounce grated Cheddar or Parmesan cheese

Bake whole eggplants in moderate oven (350°F. Mark 4) while preparing meat.

Sauté lamb and onion in small amount of butter or oil until browned. Add salt, pepper, tomato purée, and stock. Cover and cook very gently 1 hour.

When eggplants have baked soft, remove skins and mash pulp. Place in top of double boiler. Add well seasoned white sauce and grated cheese. Beat until very fluffy.

Serve hot, with lamb and its sauce topping the portions of eggplant. Serves 6.

LAMB STEW WITH DUMPLINGS

2 pounds lamb, cubed
1 tablespoon fat
2 teaspoons salt
½ teaspoon pepper
1½ pints water
6 medium carrots
6 small whole onions
½ pound green beans
1 tablespoon melted butter or margarine
1½ tablespoons flour

Brown meat in hot fat, then simmer in covered pan with salt, pepper, and water for about 1 hour.

Add carrots, onions, and beans and cook ½ hour more.

Mix melted butter and flour into a paste and stir into stew. Cook until slightly thickened.

Dumplings: Sift together 6 ounces plain flour, 2 teaspoons baking powder, and 1 teaspoon salt.

Beat 1 egg and mix with 6 fluid ounces milk. Add to dry ingredients, stirring only enough to moisten flour.

Drop by tablespoons into hot stew. Cook covered for 5 minutes.

Remove lid and cook 15 minutes more. Serves 8.

LAMB STEW À LA MASI

butter or margarine
12 spring onions
6 medium turnips, halved and cooked
12 young carrots, cooked
1 pound green beans, cooked
12 small new potatoes, cooked
1 packet frozen or 1 can lima beans, cooked
1 can consommé
4 tablespoons dry wine
1 teaspoon sugar
salt and pepper
2 pounds shoulder of lamb, diced

Prepare vegetables first. Sauté spring onions in butter, other vegetables in water, separately, except the potatoes. Cook these in canned consommé. Combine vegetables, adding the consommé from the potatoes and the wine and sugar. Season to taste with salt and pepper.

Now cook the lamb in butter for 5 minutes, or until done. Season.

Add vegetables and liquid and shake the pan over moderate heat until meat and vegetables have become permeated with the sauce. Serve in small casserole. Serves 6.

Offal

The culinary reputations of many noted chefs have been made with the cooking of liver, tongue, sweetbreads, and other offal, including hearts, brains, kidneys, oxtails, and tripe.

This delicate art is worth perpetuating, for such dishes are well flavoured, highly nutritious, and usually quite inexpensive.

When including any of these types of meat in your menus, take our tips on buying, storing, and serving. They'll prove a handy guide to the skilful preparation of some delicious main dishes.

BRAINS

Brains of calf, lamb, and pig may be used. Although there is very little difference in the tenderness or flavour, calf brains are the most popular and highest priced.

Brains may be used in most recipes calling for sweetbreads or may be combined with sweetbreads. Brains combine well with other food and need only a little pep in flavour (Worcestershire sauce, sherry, etc.) to make them very good.

Allow 1 pound to make 4 servings. Calf brains weigh about ½ pound, lamb and pig's brains about ¼ pound each.

Brains are a very delicate and perishable food and should be cooked within 24 hours after purchase. Keep covered in refrigerator.

HOW TO COOK BRAINS

Soak brains in cold salted water (1 tablespoon salt per 1½ pints water) for 15 minutes.

Drop into boiling water; adding 1 tablespoon vinegar or lemon juice to 1½ pints.

Cover, reduce heat and simmer (do not boil) 15 minutes. Drain, cover with cold water, then drain well.

Use at once or cover and store in refrigerator. If brains are to be kept in the refrigerator, leave the membrane on until ready to use, then remove it with the tip of a paring knife.

Brains
From Left to Right, Ox, Calves, Pigs, Lamb – Grill, Braise, Cook in Liquid. Ox brains are seldom used in the recipes given here.

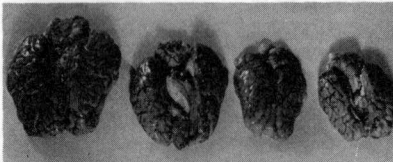

Note: Brains are sometimes used without precooking, particularly when scrambled with eggs. They may also be steamed before using in recipes, instead of being precooked as above.

FRIED BRAINS

Cut precooked brains into pieces. Season with salt and pepper. Roll in dry crumbs; dip in beaten egg diluted with 1 tablespoon water, then roll again in crumbs.

Fry in shallow fat or salad oil or in deep hot fat (370°F.) until brown. Drain on absorbent paper. Serve with mushroom sauce.

GRILLED BRAINS

Brush cooked brains with oil or melted butter. Sprinkle with paprika.

Grill under moderate heat until done, turning to brown both sides, 10 to 12 minutes. Baste occasionally with melted butter. Serve garnished with chopped parsley and lemon wedges.

BRAINS AND BACON

Cut each precooked brain into several pieces. Wrap each piece with a strip of bacon. Fasten with a wooden cocktail stick.

Place in an oiled pan. Sprinkle with paprika. Dot with butter.

Bake in moderate oven (350°F. Mark 4) until brains and bacon are done, about 20 minutes.

BRAINS À LA KING

1 pound cooked brains
2 chopped green peppers
2 teaspoons grated onion
3-4 sticks celery, diced
2 tablespoons fat
¾ pint medium white sauce
2 tablespoons chopped pimento
½ teaspoon salt
⅛ teaspoon pepper
6 slices toast

Separate cooked brains into small cubes.

Sauté green peppers, onion, and celery in fat. Add white sauce with pimento, salt, and pepper.

Add brains and heat thoroughly. Serve on toast. Serves 6 to 8.

STEAMED BRAINS

Wash 1 pair of brains under cold running water; remove membrane with the tip of a paring knife.

Place in a saucepan and add 3 tablespoons water and 1 tablespoon vinegar. Cover tightly and simmer 15 minutes. Chill thoroughly.

SCRAMBLED BRAINS WITH EGGS

½ pound cooked brains
4 eggs
2 tablespoons tomato ketchup

Grilled Brains

¼ teaspoon salt
dash of Worcestershire sauce
4 tablespoons fat
4 slices toast
2 tablespoons finely chopped parsley

Cut cooked brains in ½-inch pieces. Beat eggs slightly and add seasoning and brains.

Heat fat in frying pan. Pour in brain egg mixture. Cook slowly, stirring enough to scramble. Serve on hot toast garnished with parsley. Serves 6.

FRITTO MISTO
(Italian Fritters)

Batter:
8 ounces flour
1 teaspoon salt
¼ teaspoon pepper
12 fluid ounces milk
3 well-beaten eggs
2 tablespoons melted fat

Meat and Vegetables:
½ pound liver, sliced thick, cut into small pieces, and seasoned with salt, pepper, and Aromat
½ pound brains, precooked and cut into small pieces
6 artichoke hearts (canned in water) drained
2 courgettes, cut crosswise into 1-inch slices
3 sticks celery, cut into 3-inch pieces

Note: This is an excellent way to use leftover vegetables such as cauliflower, string beans, strips of onion, carrots, and marrow or courgettes as well as cold cooked chicken or veal.

To prepare batter, mix and sift flour, salt, and pepper.

Combine milk, eggs, and fat; gradually add sifted flour mixture beating until smooth.

Drop each vegetable and piece of meat into batter. Lift the batter-coated pieces with a teaspoon and drop in deep hot fat (365°-375°F.).

Cook until golden brown, 4 to 5 minutes. Turn the pieces occasionally during frying.

Do not fry too many pieces at one time. Fry only as many pieces as will float uncrowded one layer deep in the fat. Drain on absorbent paper and serve on warm dish. Serves 6.

HOW TO COOK HEART

Use ox, calf, sheep, or pig's heart. Calves' heart is the most tender and delicate in flavour. All hearts require moist cooking over low heat.

Remove large arteries and veins at top and inside of heart. Wash in cold water.

Cover heart with water. Add ½ teaspoon salt per pound of heart. Cover and simmer until tender.

Ox and pigs' heart take about 2 hours. Sheep and calves' heart 1 to 1½ hours.

When done, slice crosswise, mince or chop and use in meat pies or casserole dishes calling for cooked meat, or serve sliced heart with gravy made from stock, or serve chopped heart on buttered toast.

An ox heart weighing 3 to 3½ pounds will serve 8 to 10, pigs' hearts weigh about ½ pound and will serve 2, sheeps' hearts weigh about ¼ pound and will serve one, calves' hearts weigh about ⅜ pound and will serve 2 to 3.

HEART IN SWEET AND SOUR SAUCE

1 ox heart or 2 calves' hearts
fat or salad oil
1 can tomatoes (about 16 ounces)
4 tablespoons water
4 fluid ounces vinegar
1¼ ounces brown sugar
1 ounce flour
1 teaspoon salt
⅛ teaspoon paprika

Trim heart and cut into small cubes.

Heat 3 to 4 tablespoons fat or oil in heavy saucepan. Add heart and sauté over moderate heat 10 minutes.

Add tomatoes, water, vinegar, and sugar. Cover and simmer until heart is tender, 35 to 40 minutes.

Add flour to 2 tablespoons fat melted in a frying pan. Stir in 4 tablespoons sauce from hearts. Cook, stirring constantly, until smooth. Combine with hearts.

Add more salt, if necessary, and paprika. Cook 5 minutes longer.

Serves 6 to 8.

Hearts
From Left to Right, ox, calves', pigs', sheeps' — braise, cook in liquid.

Glazed Stuffed Ox Heart

GLAZED STUFFED OX HEART

1 ox heart (about 3-3½ pounds)
parsley stuffing (below)
1 onion, sliced
3 tablespoons fat
2½ pints boiling water
2 teaspoons salt
¼ teaspoon pepper
1 teaspoon Aromat
1 teaspoon celery salt
1 teaspoon leaf marjoram
4 ounces red currant jelly
1 tablespoon water
2 teaspoons lemon juice
3 ounces flour
4 fluid ounces cold water

Remove fat, veins, and arteries from ox heart. Stuff with parsley stuffing.

Cook onions in fat in a large saucepan until lightly browned; push to one side; brown heart on all sides.

Add boiling water, salt, pepper, Aromat, and celery salt. Simmer, covered, 2½ to 3 hours, or until meat is tender.

Add marjoram about 15 minutes before end of cooking time.

Remove heart from liquid.

Break up jelly with fork, add 1 tablespoon water; melt over low heat; brush over heart to glaze.

Strain liquid; measure 1¼ pints back into saucepan. Add lemon juice. Thicken with flour mixed to smooth paste with cold water. Serve gravy separately.

Parsley Stuffing:
12 ounces soft breadcrumbs
½ teaspoon salt
few grains pepper
¼ teaspoon Aromat
1 teaspoon mixed herbs
1 tablespoon finely chopped parsley
2 ounces butter or margarine
½ small onion, finely chopped

Combine crumbs, salt, pepper, Aromat, herbs, and parsley.

Melt butter or margarine; add onion; simmer until onion is soft but not brown. Stir in crumb mixture; blend well.

Makes enough stuffing for 3-3½-pound ox heart.

KIDNEYS

Kidneys cooked alone or attached to veal and lamb chops and sold as kidney chops are prized highly by many people. Like all offal, they are highly nutritious.

Ox, pigs', sheeps', and calves' kidneys can all be used to good advantage.

Calves' and sheeps' kidneys require very little cooking. Ox kidney is most often well cooked and served in beef and kidney pie.

All kidneys should be used within 24 hours. Keep loosely wrapped in the refrigerator.

HOW TO COOK KIDNEYS

To cook ox and pigs' kidneys, remove outer membrane. Split in half. Trim off all fat and white veins. Rinse well in cold water.

Simmer in water about 30 minutes, or brown in fat and then cook slowly in a little water.

To cook sheeps' or calves' kidneys, remove outer membrane. Trim white veins and fat. Grill or pan fry.

BAKED CALVES' KIDNEYS

Place kidneys in a pan, fat-side up. Bake uncovered in slow oven (300°F. Mark 2) until tender, about 45 minutes.

One calf's kidney weighing 8 to 12 ounces makes a nice small roast for 1 person.

GRILLED KIDNEYS

Use sheeps' or calves' kidneys. Get butcher to leave about ¼-inch fat on kidneys.

Split and place under the grill with fat-side up.

Grill with kidneys about 3 inches from source of heat until fat is brown and crisp.

Season with salt and pepper and turn. Continue grilling until done. Total grilling time about 10 minutes.

Grill butter-brushed mushroom caps or 1-inch thick slices of tomato and slices of bacon with the kidneys, if desired. Serve as a mixed grill.

Kidneys
From Left To Right, Calves', Ox, Sheeps', Pigs'. Ox And Pigs' — Braise, Cook In Liquid. Calves' And Sheeps' — Grill, Fry, Braise, Cook In Liquid.

BEEFSTEAK AND KIDNEY PIE

¾ pound boneless stewing beef
¾ pound ox kidney, trimmed
1½ ounces flour
1½ tablespoons fat
½ small onion, chopped
about 1 pint hot water
1½ teaspoons salt
⅛ teaspoon pepper
3 whole cloves
½ teaspoon mixed herbs
pastry

Cut beef and kidney in 1-inch cubes and dredge with flour.

Melt fat, add onion and sauté until lightly brown. Remove onion, add meat and brown well. Remove meat.

Add water to the pan, stirring until smooth. Return onion and meat to pan, add salt and pepper, cloves, and herbs. If necessary, add more water to cover meat.

Cover tightly and simmer 1½ to 2 hours or until meat is tender. Remove cloves.

Place meat in pie dish. Cover with pastry and bake in hot oven (400°F. Mark 6) 25 to 30 minutes, until crust is cooked. Serves 6.

If Using Pressure Cooker: Reduce water to 12 fluid ounces and cook 20 minutes at 15 pounds pressure. Cool cooker slowly. Then place meat in casserole and finish as above.

KIDNEY SPOON CAKES

1 pound kidney
1 teaspoon salt
⅛ teaspoon pepper
2 eggs
sausage or bacon fat

Use ox, pigs', lamb, or calves' kidneys. Wash kidneys and put through mincer. Add seasonings and eggs and beat until well mixed.

Drop into hot fat by tablespoons. Brown second side until crisp. Serve hot with creamed onions. Serves 6.

Kidneys and mushrooms on toast are nice for a Sunday buffet-brunch.

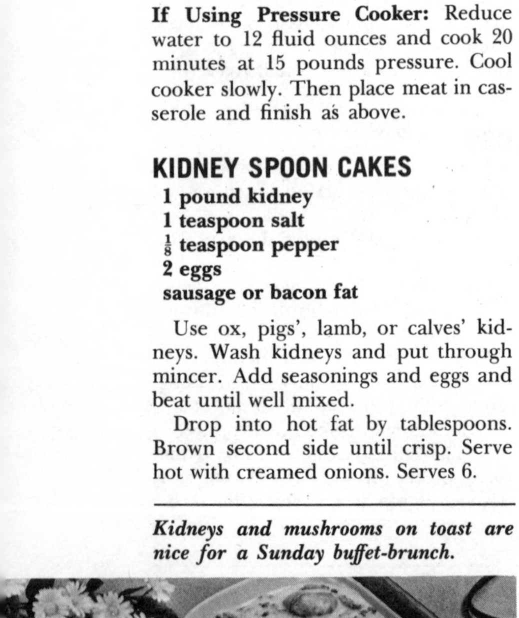

BAKED KIDNEYS WITH BACON

4 lamb kidneys
1 slightly beaten egg
3 teaspoons Worcestershire sauce
½ teaspoon salt
fine breadcrumbs
4 rashers bacon

Cut kidneys in half. Wash and remove tubes.

Mix egg, Worcestershire sauce, and salt. Dip kidneys in sauce, then in crumbs.

Wrap each in a rasher of bacon. Secure with cocktail stick. Place in shallow baking tin.

Bake in moderately hot oven (375°F. Mark 5) until bacon is crisp and kidneys are browned, about 15 minutes. Serves 4.

SAVOURY SAUTÉED KIDNEYS

1 pound calves' or lamb kidney
garlic
2 ounces butter or margarine
1 medium onion, sliced
salt and paprika
1 tablespoon lemon juice or 4 tablespoons sherry or dry red wine

Remove some of the fat from the kidneys. Cut them crosswise into slices. Cut away all the white tissue.

Rub a frying pan with a cut clove of garlic. Melt the butter and pan fry the onions until very lightly browned.

Add the kidneys and pan fry until tender, about 5 minutes.

Season with salt, paprika, and the lemon juice or wine. Serves 4.

KIDNEYS AND MUSHROOMS ON TOAST

8 lamb kidneys
2 tablespoons flour
1 medium onion, finely chopped
2 ounces butter or margarine
1 beef bouillon cube
6 fluid ounces water
1 small can sliced mushrooms with liquid
½ teaspoon salt
⅛ teaspoon pepper
2 tablespoons sherry
hot toast

Wash kidneys, cut in quarters, and remove tubes and fat. Sprinkle kidneys with flour.

Cook onion in half the butter or margarine. Remove onion and set aside.

Put remaining butter or margarine in frying pan and brown kidneys on all sides, stirring frequently.

Add onion and remaining ingredients except sherry and toast. Bring to the boil, cover, and simmer 15 to 20 minutes. Add sherry and serve on toast.

Serves 4.

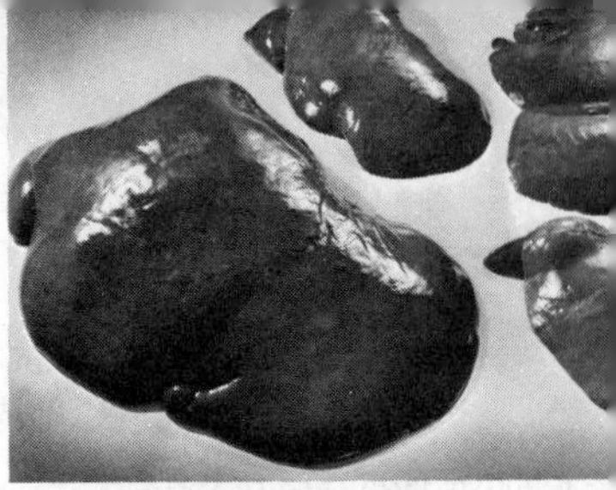

Liver
Ox: Lower Left—Roast, Braise, Fry
Calves': Upper Left—Grill, Fry
Pigs': Upper Right—Roast, Braise, Fry
Lamb: Lower Right—Grill fry, Fry

LIVER

Ox livers are plump and easy to distinguish because of the one large and one small lobe, or section. Pigs', calves', and lamb livers are smaller in size. Calves' and lamb livers are particularly mild in flavour. Ordinarily butchers carry the one or two types for which demand is greatest in their neighbourhoods.

Allow 1 pound for 4 servings.

Preparation and Refrigeration: Do not soak or scald liver. Precook liver only when it is to be minced. Refrigerate and use soon after purchase.

FRIED (SAUTÉED) LIVER

Remove outer membrane (skin) from ¼- to ½-inch slices of liver. Veins are easily removed with kitchen scissors.

Dip slices in well seasoned flour. Brown quickly in very little hot bacon fat or melted butter over moderate heat, a matter of 2 or 3 minutes. The liver will be done when the second side is brown. Don't overcook—liver toughens easily.

Variations: If desired, rub the pan with a cut clove of garlic before frying the liver, or flavour the liver when cooked with grated lemon rind and juice.

Liver with Wine Sauce: After frying liver as above, rinse the frying pan with a few tablespoons dry red wine and use for sauce.

Liver with Sautéed Onions: Slice onions crosswise; sauté them in a small amount of bacon fat. Brown evenly, season, and keep them hot while frying liver.

Cook liver on one side as directed above, turn it, pile the onions on the cooked side and continue to cook the liver until done.

Liver and Bacon: Cook the bacon first; keep it hot while preparing the liver as above. Liver, bacon, and onion are a good combination.

FRENCH-FRIED LIVER

Cut pigs' liver in ½-inch strips. Let stand in French dressing ½ hour; drain. Dip in beaten egg; roll in breadcrumbs. Fry in deep, hot fat (360°F.) until browned. Drain on paper towels.

GRILLED SLICED LIVER

Use calves' or lamb liver sliced ⅛ to inch thick.

Brush the slices with oil or melted butter and cook under a hot grill for minutes on each side. Reduce the heat and continue to grill until tender – about 8 minutes altogether. Then, season to taste.

Serve with bacon and sliced onions, previously fried. Garnish with lemon wedges and parsley.

BRAISED LIVER

Dip slices of ox or pigs' liver in flour. Season with salt and pepper. Brown quickly on both sides in a little hot fat. Reduce heat. Add 1 bouillon cube dissolved in ¼ pint hot water, and thinly sliced onions. Cook until tender, about 20 minutes.

HOW TO "BOIL" LIVER

Wash liver thoroughly. Place in water to cover. Cover pan and simmer gently until tender, adding ½ teaspoon salt per pound when half done.

Very thin slices will take 5 to 15 minutes. Allow a little longer for thicker slices.

Drain, mince, and use in salads, sandwich fillings, creamed dishes, etc.

BRAISED LIVER IN WHITE WINE

1½ pounds ox or pigs' liver, sliced thinly
8 fluid ounces Sauternes, Rhine, Chablis or other white wine
flour, salt, pepper
2 ounces bacon fat
pinch of thyme
4 fluid ounces water

Wash liver. Let stand in wine for an hour.

Pour off wine, reserving it for later use. Coat liver with seasoned flour. Brown on both sides in hot fat in chafing dish over direct heat.

Add wine and thyme. Cover and simmer 10 minutes.

Add water and continue simmering for 20 minutes, or until tender. Serves 5.

Liver and Bacon Patties

LIVER LOAF

3 sticks celery
1 medium-sized onion, chopped
8 fluid ounces water
1 pound sliced liver
2 rashers bacon
1 or 2 beaten eggs
¾ teaspoon salt
⅛ teaspoon pepper
4 ounces dry breadcrumbs
½ teaspoon thyme or marjoram
8 fluid ounces liquid (liver stock, tomato juice, milk, or bouillon)
3-4 tablespoons tomato ketchup

Boil the water with celery and onion for 5 minutes; add liver and simmer 3 minutes. Drain, reserving liquid.

Put liver, vegetables, and bacon through mincer. Add remaining ingredients except the ketchup; blend well.

Pour the ketchup in a greased loaf tin. Pack the liver mixture into the tin. Bake in moderate oven (350°F. Mark 4) about 40 minutes. Serves 6 to 8.

LIVER CREOLE

2 rashers bacon
½ pound liver (¼-inch thick)
2 tablespoons flour
1 can condensed tomato soup
2-3 tablespoons chopped green pepper
¼ teaspoon chilli powder

Cut bacon into small pieces; fry until crisp in a frying pan, then remove from pan.

Dust liver with flour; brown in bacon fat. Add bacon and remaining ingredients. Cover; simmer 45 minutes. Serves 4.

LIVER AND BACON PATTIES

1 pound pigs' liver
2 tablespoons tomato ketchup
¼ teaspoon salt
1 large onion
4 rashers bacon

Simmer liver in water until firm. Then mince or chop.

Combine with ketchup and salt. Shape into 4 large patties.

Cut onion in ½-inch slices. Place a patty on an onion slice. Wrap bacon around patty and onion. Fasten with a wooden cocktail stick.

Bake in hot oven (400°F. Mark 6) until bacon is crisply brown, about 30 minutes. Serves 4.

FRIED LIVER CUBES

1 pound liver, cut in 1-inch cubes
¼ pint French dressing
1 ounce flour
12 grilled rashers of bacon

Marinate liver cubes in French dressing 1 hour, drain.

Dredge cubes in flour and fry in hot deep fat (375°F.) 2 minutes or until well browned. Serve with rashers of bacon. Serves 4.

CALVES' LIVER-BURGUNDY CASSEROLE

4 rashers of bacon
1 pound calves' liver, cut in 4 slices
flour
1 pound cooked rice
½ eggplant (aubergine), peeled and cut in 1-inch cubes
4 raw tomatoes, cut in quarters
1 medium onion, sliced
salt, pepper, paprika
¼ pint Burgundy wine
1 tablespoon butter

Cook bacon until crisp and brown. Remove from pan.

Dust liver with flour and brown lightly on both sides.

Line a greased casserole with half the cooked rice. Add half the eggplant, 2 tomatoes, onions, and seasonings to taste, liver, and bacon, crumbled into pieces.

Cover with rest of rice, eggplant, and tomatoes. Add wine to moisten. Dot top with bits of butter.

Cover and cook in moderate oven (350°F. Mark 4) 30 minutes. Remove cover and cook 10 minutes. Serves 4.

MEXICAN BRAISED LIVER

1½ pounds liver, sliced
8 tablespoons bacon fat
6 carrots
2 green peppers
6 small onions
salt and pepper to taste
¼ pint water
cooked rice

Dredge liver with flour. Brown in bacon fat.

Prepare and dice the carrots, green peppers, and the onions. Arrange in mounds on pieces of liver. Season with salt and pepper and add water; cover.

Simmer gently for about 45 minutes or until vegetables are tender, adding more water if necessary.

Serve on a bed of fluffy rice. Serves 6.

Mexican Braised Liver

SWEETBREADS

These are the pancreas and thymus glands from the calf or lamb. Ox sweetbreads are less often used and need slow, careful cooking to make them tender. Sweetbreads should be bought when fresh and used up quickly, but they have a delicate flavour and are easily digested. They are generally sold by the pound and usually 1 pound is sufficient for 3-4 portions.

Preparation And Refrigeration: Wash and precook in simmering water to cover for about 20 minutes. If sweetbreads are frozen, increase cooking time 10 minutes. Many cooks prefer to add 1 tablespoon vinegar or lemon juice and 1 teaspoon salt per 1½ pints of cooking water.

Drain, cover with cold water, and let stand until cool enough to handle. Remove membrane and tubes. Refrigerate or grill, sauté, or prepare as desired.

GRILLED SWEETBREADS

Method 1: Cut precooked sweetbreads in half crosswise. Sprinkle with salt and pepper. Brush with melted butter or margarine.

Place under a pre-heated grill and grill about 10 minutes, turning once.

Method 2: Break precooked sweetbreads into large pieces. Dry well and roll in seasoned flour.

Wrap in bacon and secure with wooden cocktail sticks. Dot well with butter and grill, basting frequently with the juices that drip from them and if they are rather dry baste with additional butter.

Season the fat with lemon juice or sherry and serve with the sweetbreads.

DEEP FAT-FRIED SWEETBREADS

Prepare as for pan-fried sweetbreads. Fry in deep hot fat (360°F.) until golden brown, 7 to 10 minutes.

Sweetbreads
*From Left to Right, Ox, Calf, Lamb —
Grill, Fry, Braise, Cook in Liquid*

PAN-FRIED SWEETBREADS

Cut precooked sweetbreads in half. Dry thoroughly. Dip them in seasoned very fine breadcrumbs. Then dip in 1 slightly beaten egg diluted with 2 tablespoons water. Dip again in crumbs.

Pan-fry them in hot butter until they are a rich brown. Serve with a well seasoned white or tomato sauce or a creamed vegetable.

BRAISED SWEETBREADS

Use calf or lamb sweetbreads, allowing 1 pair per serving.

Cover with cold water; let stand 30 minutes. Drain and remove membrane. Dip sweetbreads in seasoned flour and pan-fry in a small amount butter or salad oil, turning to brown on all sides. Cover and cook slowly 20 minutes.

Blend together a little flour and water; add to fat in pan. Cook, stirring constantly, until thickened. Serve on sweetbreads.

If desired the fat may be seasoned with a little sherry.

CREAMED SWEETBREADS
(Basic Recipe)

1 pound cooked sweetbreads, cubed
¾ pint medium white sauce
6 ounces cooked or canned peas
seasoning to taste

Add cubed sweetbreads to white sauce. Heat thoroughly, stirring gently. Add peas. Season to taste.

Serve hot on toast, or in patty cases. If desired, stir in 1 slightly beaten egg yolk before serving. Serves 4 to 6.

Creamed Sweetbread Variations
Creamed Sweetbreads and Mushrooms; Substitute 6 ounces cooked or canned mushrooms for peas.
With Almonds: Add 1 ounce slivered toasted almonds to Creamed Sweetbreads with Mushrooms.
With Asparagus Tips: Substitute cooked or canned asparagus tips for peas.
With Oysters: Substitute oysters for peas. Heat oysters in their own liquor until edges curl before adding.
With Other Meats: Substitute diced cooked chicken, ham, or veal for peas.
Quick Creamed Sweetbreads: Substitute 1 can (10½ ounces) condensed cream of mushroom soup diluted with ½ can milk for medium white sauce.

SWEETBREADS WITH PINEAPPLE

Slice 3 pairs precooked calf or lamb sweetbreads and brown in hot fat. Brown 3 pineapple slices in the fat.

Add water to 1 can condensed cream of mushroom soup; heat and pour over sweetbreads and pineapple.

Sweetbreads Melba

SWEETBREADS MELBA

3 pairs sweetbreads
juice of 2 lemons
1 teaspoon salt
1½ teaspoons Aromat
¾ pint beef stock or bouillon
2 celery sticks and leaves, chopped
several sprigs parsley
¼ teaspoon thyme
¼ teaspoon mace
⅛ teaspoon allspice
3 ounces butter or margarine
2 tablespoons prepared mustard
few grains pepper
1 tablespoon lemon juice
Melba toast

Cover sweetbreads with cold water soak 1 hour, changing water severa times.

Cover with fresh cold water, add juice of 2 lemons, salt, and ½ teaspoon Aromat. Bring slowly to the boil simmer 15 minutes.

Plunge into cold water. Carefully remove tubes and membranes; place in saucepan with stock, celery, parsley thyme, and spices; bring to boil; simmer ½ hour. Drain, saving broth.

Melt butter or margarine; blend in mustard, pepper, Aromat, and 1 table spoon lemon juice. Add ½ pint strained broth.

Slice sweetbreads; add to sauce; re heat. Serve on Melba toast. Serves 6.

TONGUE

Available fresh, smoked, pickled Pork and lamb tongues being small are mostly canned whole. The larger size of beef and veal tongues makes them better for home use.

Preparation and Refrigeration: Wipe with a damp cloth. Refrigerate or use at once.

To Cook Fresh Tongue: Cover with cold water; add 1½ teaspoons salt to each 1½ pints of water; bring to the boil Fresh tongues are better when spice and seasonings are added to cooking water. Simmer slowly until tender.

Allow 2½ to 3 hours for ox tongue weighing about 4 pounds. About 1 hour for calf or pork tongue. Remove the outer skin and the roots.

To Cook Pickled Tongue: Cover with cold water, bring to boil. Reduce heat and simmer 2½ to 3 hours, or until

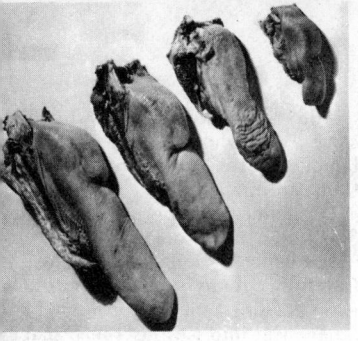

Tongues
*From Left To Right, Ox, Calves', Pigs',
Lamb—Cook In Liquid*

tender. Remove the outer skin and
roots.

To Cook Smoked Tongue: Cover with
water and simmer 50 minutes per
pound or until tender. Remove the
outer skin and roots.

"BOILED" SEASONED BEEF TONGUE

1 beef tongue
6 whole black peppers
4 whole cloves
1 tablespoon vinegar

Fresh, or smoked tongues may be
used. A 4-pound tongue serves 8 to
10.

Smoked tongues are improved by
soaking in cold water for several hours
before cooking.

Scrub tongue under running water.
Place in deep saucepan. Add seasonings and boiling water to cover. Boil
10 minutes, then lower heat and simmer until a fork will penetrate easily
to the centre, 2½ to 3 hours.

Let tongue remain in water until cool
enough to handle. Peel off outer skin.
Cut out membranous portions of roots.

Press into shape for serving. Serve
hot with horseradish or raisin sauce,
use in other recipes, or slice and serve
cold.

Variations of "Boiled" Seasoned Beef Tongue

Tongue with Cranberries: Place sliced
cooked tongue in a pan.

Combine 4 fluid ounces water or tongue liquid, 2 ounces stewed cranberries, 1½ ounces brown sugar, 2 table-
poons melted fat, and 3 slices lemon.

Add to tongue. Simmer until heated
through. Serve hot.

Baked Fresh Tongue: After peeling
fresh cooked tongue, place in a shallow
roasting tin. Rub with hot fat.

Bake in moderate oven (350°F. Mark
4) about 50 to 60 minutes.

Beef Tongue Piquant: After peeling
cooked fresh tongue, dust with flour
seasoned with salt and pepper. Brown
in hot fat.

Combine 6 ounces tart jelly and 8

fluid ounces hot water. Mix thoroughly.
Pour over tongue. Simmer about 40
minutes.

Jellied Tongue: Peel and trim cooked
fresh tongue. Place in a mould or
basin.

Strain tongue liquid. Measure enough
to fill mould.

Soften ½ ounce gelatine in 4 fluid
ounces cold tongue liquid and add to
measured liquid.

Bring to boiling point and pour over
tongue. Chill until firm.

TONGUE—SWEET AND SOUR

1 cooked beef tongue
1 large onion, chopped
1 tablespoon fat
1 tablespoon flour
¾ pint hot tongue liquid
½ teaspoon salt
1 tablespoon finely chopped
    almonds
1 stick cinnamon (½ inch)
4 cloves
2 ounces sultanas
1½ ounces brown sugar
1 tablespoon molasses or treacle
juice of 1 lemon

Peel and slice cooked tongue.

Brown onion slightly in hot fat. Remove onion and set aside.

Stir flour into hot fat and cook 3
minutes. Gradually add hot tongue
liquid and salt and simmer gently until
smooth and thickened, about 5 minutes.

Add browned onions, almonds, cinnamon, cloves, and sultanas. Mix well.

Blend together the brown sugar,
molasses, and lemon juice and stir into
the mixture. Simmer about 10 minutes,
stirring constantly.

If desired, add more salt, sugar, and
lemon juice to taste. Add sliced tongue
and simmer until heated through.
Serve hot with sauce.

SUGAR-GLAZED TONGUE

1 fresh smoked beef tongue, about
    4 pounds
3 fluid ounces cider vinegar
1½ teaspoons salt
8 whole cloves
3 tablespoons brown sugar
1 tablespoon lemon juice

Cover tongue with cold water; bring
to boiling point and drain.

Again cover with water; add vinegar
and salt; simmer until tender. Let cool
in the liquid.

Remove skin, small bones, and cartilage. Stud with cloves and place in a
shallow baking tin.

Mix together the brown sugar and
lemon juice; brush over the tongue.

Bake in moderate oven (350°F. Mark
4) ½ hour, basting frequently. Slice and
serve hot. Serves 6.

OXTAILS

Oxtails are usually sold jointed or
the butcher will joint them when
purchased. The meat is fine flavoured
and oxtails make excellent soup. The
proportion of bone is large so allow 1
pound for 2 servings.

HOW TO COOK OXTAILS

Wash thoroughly in cold water.
Cover with water. Add salt.

Simmer until meat is tender, about
2 hours. Serve in a hot tomato sauce
or other desired spicy sauce.

BRAISED OXTAILS WITH VEGETABLES

4 tablespoons butter or beef
    dripping
1 large onion, chopped
2 oxtails, jointed
flour
2 teaspoons salt
¼ teaspoon pepper
1 tablespoon vinegar
1 pint water
4 carrots, sliced
4-5 sticks celery, diced
1 large green pepper, chopped
4 medium-sized potatoes, cut in
    half

Heat fat in a saucepan; add onion.
Roll oxtail in flour and brown in the
hot fat with onion.

Add salt, pepper, vinegar, and water.
Cover tightly and simmer 3 hours. Add
more water as necessary to prevent
burning.

Add carrots, celery, green pepper,
and potatoes. Cover; increase heat to
start vegetables cooking, then reduce
heat and simmer 45 minutes.

Remove vegetables to a hot dish.
Thicken the broth for gravy with a
little flour-water paste. Serves 5 to 6.

TRIPE

Tripe is the inner lining of the
stomach of meat animals. It can be
prepared in many delicious ways, but
requires careful preparation.

Two forms of tripe are commonly
sold, one plain, one honeycomb. Plain
is the lining of the first stomach of
the animal, honeycomb (the more delicate of the two) is the lining of the
second stomach. Either may be purchased fresh or pickled.

Fresh tripe is usually partially cooked
before selling. Further cooking in water
is preliminary to all ways of serving.
The cooking time varies but at least
two hours' cooking at a simmering
temperature is required to make it
tender. Allow 6-8 ounces per portion.

Pickled tripe is usually thoroughly
cooked but requires soaking before
using.

HOW TO COOK "FRESH" TRIPE

Wash tripe well in several waters. Cover with water. Cover, heat to boiling, then reduce heat and simmer until fork tender, 2 hours or more. Add ½ teaspoon salt per pound when half-done.

Use for various dishes.

Note: If fresh tripe has not been partially cooked (as it usually is before being sold) where tripe calls for 4 hours' or more simmering; if it is cut into strips you may allow 2 hours or more.

FRIED TRIPE

Dip boiled tripe in egg diluted with 2 tablespoons cold water. Roll in fine breadcrumbs.

Repeat and fry in a little hot fat until brown on both sides.

TRIPE À LA MODE DE CAEN

A classic French dish from Normandy.

3 pounds fresh honeycomb tripe
2 calf's feet, split
2 pounds onions, sliced
¼ pound beef suet, cut in small cubes
1 onion, stuck with 3 cloves
1 bay leaf
bouquet garni (see below)
4 tablespoons calvados or other apple brandy
cider or water
thick paste made of flour and water
salt and freshly ground pepper

Wash the tripe carefully in several changes of water. Drain and slice the tripe into pieces two inches square. In two separate pans, cover the tripe with cold water and the calf's feet with cold water. Bring each to the boil. Immediately add two cups cold water to each pan to stop the cooking, then drain well.

Line the bottom of a large earthenware casserole with a layer of onions, then a layer of tripe and a sprinkling of beef suet. Build successive layers, topping with the split calf's feet, the onion stuck with whole cloves, bay leaf, and bouquet garni.

Add the calvados or other apple brandy and enough cider or water to cover all ingredients. Bring to boiling point on top of stove. Remove from heat. Cover the casserole with a lid and seal the cover with a thick paste made of flour and water.

Bake in very slow oven (250°F. Mark 1) at least 12 hours.

At serving time, break and discard the pastry seal. Remove the bouquet garni, the whole onion, and bay leaf. Skim the fat from the liquid and season to taste with salt and pepper.

Pick the meat from the calf's feet and discard the bones. Return the meat to the casserole. Heat through and serve in individual heated casseroles with hot boiled potatoes on the side. Serves 8.

Note: For bouquet garni use 1 bay leaf, 1 clove, 2 sprigs parsley, 1 clove garlic, 1 teaspoon thyme, and 10 peppercorns, all tied securely in a muslin bag.

TRIPE À LA CREOLE

1 pound tripe
water
1½ ounces butter or dripping
3 tablespoons chopped green pepper
3 tablespoons chopped onion
3 tablespoons flour
½ pound tomatoes, peeled and chopped
1 teaspoon salt
¼ teaspoon pepper

Cover tripe with water and simmer 2 hours, or until the cut surface has a clear, jelly-like appearance. Drain and cut into 2-inch pieces.

Melt fat and cook green pepper and onion in it until tender. Add flour; stir until smooth, then add tomatoes, stirring constantly until thickened. Season and add tripe. Simmer 10 minutes. Serves 6.

BRAWN

This is a jellied loaf made from the head of a pig or calf, with the trimmings and sometimes the feet included. It is highly seasoned and is moulded in its natural aspic.

1 pig's or calf's head with ears, tongue, and brain
water
1 large onion
4 whole cloves
salt
10 whole black peppers
bouquet garni of mixed herbs
nutmeg, sage, cayenne pepper

Get the butcher to scrape and clean the head, split it, remove the eyes, brain, and tongue. Scrub the tongue well. Rinse all thoroughly.

Place head and tongue in a deep saucepan. Cover with cold water. (Half water and half white wine may be used.)

Add the onion stuck with whole cloves, salt, whole black peppers, and bouquet garni. Bring to boiling and skim carefully.

Let simmer until meat is very tender, 3 to 4 hours. Let cool in stock.

If tongue is done early remove it. Carefully cut any rind from head. Cut ears into small slices. Cut tongue and other meat into various 1-inch shapes.

Parboil the brains in a little of the cooking liquid.

Combine all meat and season to taste with nutmeg, sage, and cayenne. If wine was not used, add ¼ pint vinegar. If vinegar is used, add ¼ pint of the cooking liquid. Toss to mix thoroughly.

Press the mixture firmly into a bread tin or other mould. Cover and press down with a heavy weight.

Chill 2 to 3 days, in the refrigerator. Serve cold in thin slices with salads.

To serve hot, dip slices in slightly beaten egg, roll in fine crumbs, and fry in a little fat.

CHITTERLINGS

Chitterlings are the intestines (usually the small ones) of pigs prepared in various ways. Usually they are boiled, well seasoned, then dipped in batter of flour and milk, and fried in deep fat. A common pronunciation is "chittlin's" without an "e", "r", and "g".

5 pounds chitterlings
2 cloves garlic, crushed
1 lemon, quartered
2 medium onions, sliced
4 tablespoons vinegar
2 bay leaves
several sprigs of parsley
1 teaspoon salt
1 teaspoon pepper
1 tablespoon thyme
1 teaspoon whole cloves
1 teaspoon mace
1 teaspoon allspice
1 tablespoon marjoram
3-4 tablespoons tomato ketchup or tomato sauce

Soak chitterlings overnight. Wash through 4 or 5 waters. Turn inside out, remove excess fat but leave a small amount for seasoning.

Put chitterlings in a saucepan. Add remaining ingredients except ketchup or tomato sauce.

Cover with water; bring to boiling point, lower heat and simmer until tender. Cut into small pieces.

During last 30 minutes of cooking, add the ketchup or tomato sauce and hot pepper to taste.

FRIED CHITTERLINGS

Prepare chitterlings as in above recipe. Omit vinegar and ketchup or tomato sauce. When tender, drain well.

Cut into 2-inch squares. Dip in fritter batter and fry in deep hot fat. Drain on absorbent paper.

Tripe À La Creole

GAME MEAT

Venison

Venison actually means the flesh of any antlered game animal such as deer, moose, elk, caribou or reindeer, but in popular usage it generally refers to deer when used as food.

The flesh of venison should be dark and finely grained and the fat firm, clear and white. It should be well hung for at least 2 weeks before using in order to acquire the characteristic "gamy" flavour. The flesh of the fallow deer is considered to be the best and the buck is superior in quality to the doe.

Buck venison is in season from June until the end of September. Doe venison is in season from October until the end of December.

Venison is cooked in much the same way as other meats but some of the joints are very lean and need to be well larded or marinated. Recipes for marinades are given below.

The best joint for roasting is the haunch, and the loin and neck are also good cooked this way. The shoulder and breast are generally braised or used for a ragoût. Chops are cut from the loin or neck, and steaks from the leg. The more tender parts — steaks, chops and saddle — may be cooked without marinating.

MARINADES

A simple marinade of oil and vinegar can be used for small pieces of venison, e.g. cuts from the loin or chops and steaks cut ½-1½ inches thick. Leave the meat in the marinade for at least 1 hour.

A cooked marinade is more often used for larger joints and any of the liquid left can be re-boiled and saved for future use.

COOKED MARINADE

1 bottle of white wine or draught cider
¼ pint wine vinegar
2 onions, roughly chopped
2 carrots, roughly chopped
2-3 shallots, roughly chopped
5-6 peppercorns
5-6 juniper berries
1 bay leaf

Boil all the ingredients together for 30 minutes. Leave to get quite cold. Then stir in 3 tablespoons oil. Allow the meat to remain in this for at least 12 hours, basting and turning from time to time.

MARINADE FOR VENISON, HARE, etc.

¼ pint red wine
3 tablespoons salad oil
1 shallot, sliced
2 bay leaves
black pepper
5-6 juniper berries, crushed

Put all ingredients together in a saucepan, bring to boiling point, remove from the heat and leave to cool then pour over the meat, cover and leave for 20-24 hours, turning the meat over at intervals.

ROAST VENISON

Use thick loin or upper leg cuts from young venison. Rub with butter. Sprinkle with salt and pepper.

Place in roasting tin. Cover with strips of fat salt pork. If desired, stick a few cloves of garlic deep into flesh.

Roast in moderate oven (350°F. Mark 4) until done, allowing about 25 minutes per pound. Baste frequently throughout roasting period with melted butter.

Make brown gravy from the fat left in the tin. Serve with a tart jelly.

HUNTERS STEW

3 pounds venison
flour
2-3 onions, peeled and chopped
butter or margarine
8 ounces green bacon, cut in one
    piece
2-3 cloves garlic
3 cloves
1 teaspoon mixed herbs
½ bottle red wine
3 carrots, peeled and quartered
3 medium sized potatoes, peeled
    and quartered

Trim the meat, removing any bone or sinew, and cut into 2 inch pieces. Toss in flour to which a little salt and pepper has been added. Sauté the onions in the butter in a large casserole. When soft, but not coloured, remove from the pan. Add the bacon, cut into dice, fry until golden; then remove.

Brown the venison in the remaining fat. Then return the onion and bacon to the casserole. Add garlic, cloves and herbs, cover and put into a slow oven (275°F. Mark 1) for 2 hours.

Reduce the wine over high heat to half the original quantity, add to the stew with carrots and potatoes, and cooked a further 1 hour. Serves 6.

CASSEROLE OF VENISON

2-3 pounds venison

4 ounces bacon, cut in one piece
flour
¾ pint stock or water
1 large onion, peeled and chopped
2 tablespoons red currant jelly
bouquet garni
2 tablespoons lemon juice
salt, pepper
forcemeat balls

Wipe and trim the meat, and cut into 1 inch square pieces. Trim bacon and cut into strips. Put it into a frying pan and fry for a few minutes, until the fat begins to run and the bacon pieces begin to get crisp. Remove the bacon to a casserole.

Coat the venison with flour and brown well in the bacon fat. Then put with the bacon.

Add stock to the frying pan and stir over high heat, scraping all the crusty bits from the sides and the bottom of the pan into the stock. Strain over the venison. Add onion, redcurrant jelly, bouquet garni and lemon juice. Season to taste with salt and black pepper.

Cover and cook in a slow oven for 2-2½ hours (300°F. Mark 2). About 20 minutes before serving add some forcemeat balls.

Forcemeat Balls. Mix 8 ounces sausage meat with 1 teaspoon mixed herbs, and bind with beaten egg. Shape into small balls.

VENISON IN PORT WINE

¼ pint oil
4 ounces butter or margarine
2 carrots, peeled and sliced
1 onion, peeled and sliced
2 cloves garlic, crushed
1 sprig thyme
1 bay leaf
6-7 pound saddle of venison
salt, pepper
½ pint port wine
beurre manié
1 tablespoon redcurrant jelly
garnish of button mushrooms,
    sautéd in butter and fried
    croutons

Heat the oil and butter in a large sauté pan, add carrots, onion, garlic, thyme and bay leaf. Place venison on top and sprinkle with salt and pepper. Cover, and cook in a moderate oven (375°F. Mark 5) until the meat begins to brown. Pour the wine over and continue to cook, basting frequently until the meat is tender. Remove to a serving dish and keep warm.

Skim surplus fat from the juices left in the pan and strain into a small saucepan. Reduce by boiling until the liquid is reduced by half. Thicken with a little beurre manié and add the redcurrant jelly. Correct the seasoning and strain the sauce over the meat.

Garnish with button mushrooms and fried croutons. Serves 8-10.

RABBIT AND HARE

Rabbit and hare resemble chicken in texture but are less fat and have a slightly "gamy" flavour.

The female rabbit is generally more tender than the male, and wild rabbits have a better flavour than tame ones. The flesh of the tame rabbit, however, is whiter and more delicate.

Many famous continental dishes are based on rabbit or hare, and some recipes are given below.

A rabbit will serve 3-4 people. A hare is sufficient for 6-8. When a hare is required for roasting, choose a leveret, i.e. a young hare under one year of age, as it is more tender. Older animals are better for jugged hare or soup.

HOW TO SKIN A RABBIT OR HARE

Hang up by hind legs in cool place for several days. To skin it, leave it hanging. Carefully cut up the front from tail to throat with a sharp knife. Take out entrails. Cut out bile sack from liver, saving liver and heart. Discard other parts.

Cut fur around each of the 4 ankles, pulling legs through. Cut off ears.

Strip the fur skin, separated from the inner skin, from the hind legs down and over the head.

Cut off the head, throat, and paws and discard these parts together with the skin from the belly. Remove small waxy kernels directly between body and forelegs.

Wipe thoroughly inside and out with a cloth dipped in a mixture of ½ pint water and 2 tablespoons vinegar.

TO JOINT A RABBIT OR HARE

Cut off the legs by the joint, leaving forelegs whole but cut hind legs into 2 pieces, chopping through the bone. Cut the body across into 4-5 pieces and divide the breast in half so that it becomes flatter. Trim off any loose skin. The liver, heart and kidneys can be cooked and served or used for soup.

RABBIT WITH OLIVES

    4   joints of rabbit
    3   tablespoons oil
    4   onions, peeled and sliced
    1   ounce flour
    ¼   pint dry white wine
    ½   teaspoon rosemary
    1½ ounces stoned black olives
        salt, pepper
        chopped parsley

Heat the oil in a sauté pan, add the rabbit and brown well on all sides. Add the onions and sprinkle with the flour. Continue to cook until the onions and flour are lightly browned. Stir in the wine, add salt, pepper and rose-mary. Cover and cook gently until the rabbit is tender, about ¾-1 hour.

Halfway through the cooking, add the olives. Serve very hot, sprinkled with chopped parsley.

RABBIT WITH MUSTARD SAUCE

    1   rabbit
    2   tablespoons flour
        salt, pepper
    2   tablespoons oil
    2   tablespoons butter
    4   ounces fat bacon, diced
    4   shallots, peeled and chopped
        bouquet garni
    ¼   pint dry white wine
    ¼   pint chicken stock
    1   teaspoon Dijon mustard
    1   teaspoon made English mustard
    ½   pint double cream

Cut the rabbit into serving pieces, coat with flour to which some salt and pepper has been added.

Heat the oil and butter in a sauce-pan, add the diced bacon and rabbit and sauté until the rabbit has browned. Add shallots, bouquet garni, white wine and stock, cover and simmer gently until rabbit is tender—about ¾-1 hour. Remove the pieces of rabbit on to a serving dish and keep warm. Skim excess fat from the stock, blend the mustards with the cream and stir into the stock. Correct the seasoning, add-ing more mustard as required. Return the rabbit to the sauce and heat through.

BLANQUETTE OF RABBIT

    1   rabbit
        juice of 1 lemon
    2   pints chicken or veal stock
    1   large onion, peeled and stuck
        with 2 cloves
    4   carrots, peeled and
        quartered
        bouquet garni
    2   ounces rice
        pinch of powdered saffron
    2   tablespoons butter
    2   tablespoons flour
    2   egg yolks
    ¼   pint double cream

Cut rabbit into serving pieces, cover with cold water, add the juice of ½ lemon and leave overnight.

Rinse well. Then put into clean water and bring slowly to boiling point. Skim carefully and drain off the water. Cover with the stock, add onion, car-rots and bouquet garni and bring to boiling point. Skim if necessary, cover and simmer for 30 minutes. Add the rice and saffron and continue to sim-mer until the rabbit is tender.

Melt the butter in a saucepan, stir in the flour and mix well. Add 1 pint of stock from the rabbit, stir until boiling and simmer for 10 minutes, stirring frequently. Remove from the heat, stir in the egg yolks and cream blended together and the remaining lemon juice. Check the seasoning.

To serve, arrange the pieces of rabbit in a deep serving dish and strain the sauce over. Garnish with triangles of toast.

JUGGED HARE

    1   jointed hare with the liver and
        blood
    1½ pints water
        salt, pepper
    1   tablespoon vinegar
    1   large onion, sliced
    1   large carrot, sliced
    2   ounces dripping or fat
    2   ounces flour
    ¼   pint port wine
    2   tablespoons redcurrant jelly.

Cook the liver in the seasoned water for 30 minutes. Strain off the stock and add enough extra water to make 1½ pints again. Mash or sieve the liver. Soak the hare in cold water with the vinegar for 1-2 hours. Lift out the pieces of hare and pat dry.

Fry the onion and carrot in the hot dripping for 5-6 minutes, stir in the flour and mix well. Then gradually stir in the stock, the blood from the hare, wine, redcurrant jelly and mashed liver. Stir until boiling and correct the seasoning.

Put the hare into a casserole and cover with the sauce. Cover and cook in a very moderate oven (325°F. Mark 3) for 3½-4 hours.

Serve with fried bread, cut into fancy shapes, redcurrant jelly and forcemeat balls (see Index).

HARE À LA GALOPADE

    1   large hare
    4   ounces butter or margarine
    2   tablespoons flour
    1½ pints hot red wine
        bouquet garni
    20 button onions
    8   ounces button mushrooms
        salt, pepper

When the hare is dressed, reserve the blood. Tenderize the hare by pounding it with the flat side of a cleaver. Then cut into serving pieces.

Heat 3 ounces of butter in a large pan and brown the hare well on all sides. Sprinkle with flour and mix in well. Then add the hot wine. Add the blood of the hare, bouquet garni, and a little salt and pepper. Cook over fairly high heat for 30 minutes.

Meanwhile, sauté the onions in the rest of the butter, trim and wipe the caps of the mushrooms. Add these to the pan when the hare has cooked for the 30 minutes. Correct the seasoning and cook for another 30 minutes.

Serve with fried croutons and boiled potatoes. Serves 8.

ROAST RABBIT
1 large rabbit, cleaned and dressed
Stuffing:
4 ounces breadcrumbs
2 ounces suet, finely chopped
2 teaspoons chopped parsley
1 teaspoon thyme
1 teaspoon lemon juice
salt, pepper
beaten egg or milk to bind

Rub inside of cleaned, dressed rabbit with salt.

Fill with stuffing. Sew up and truss. Brush with melted fat or bacon dripping. Sprinkle with salt and pepper. Place on side in roasting tin.

Roast in slow oven (325°F. Mark 3) until tender, about 1½ hours. Turn at least once while cooking. Baste frequently with melted fat.

RABBIT STEW
4 ounces small haricot beans
1 small rabbit, dressed and cut in serving-size pieces
boiling water
2 teaspoons salt
⅛ teaspoon pepper
1 teaspoon Aromat
1 bay leaf
1 medium-sized onion, sliced
3-4 carrots, sliced
2 large green peppers
2 tablespoons butter or margarine

Soak beans overnight in cold water; drain.

Wash rabbit; place in large saucepan with drained beans; cover with boiling water; add salt, pepper, Aromat, bay leaf, and onion; simmer ½ hour.

Add carrots; cook 1 hour longer or until rabbit is tender. Add more boiling water as needed.

Cut seeded green peppers in rings; add during last 15 minutes, with butter or margarine. Thicken gravy if desired. Serves 6.

HASENPFEFFER
A German dish of rabbit marinated, seasoned, and braised.
4 fluid ounces vinegar
¾ pint water
2 teaspoons salt
¼ teaspoon pepper
½ teaspoon whole cloves
2 teaspoons sugar
4 bay leaves
1 medium onion, sliced
small rabbit (about 2½ pounds ready-to-cook) cut in serving pieces
flour
3 tablespoons fat
2 teaspoons Worcestershire sauce
3 tablespoons flour

Make pickling mixture by combining the vinegar, water, salt, pepper, cloves, sugar, bay leaves, and onion in a glass or enamelled-ware bowl.

Add pieces of rabbit and sliced giblets and cover the bowl. Allow to stand in refrigerator 8 to 12 hours, turning the pieces occasionally so that they will absorb the flavour evenly.

Remove the rabbit pieces. Save liquid and onions but discard bay leaves and cloves.

Roll the rabbit in flour. Heat fat or oil in a heavy pan and brown the rabbit in it, turning to brown all sides.

Pour the pickling mixture over the rabbit. Cover pan and cook over low heat about 1 hour, or until rabbit is tender.

Take rabbit from pan and keep it hot. Add Worcestershire sauce to the liquid. Mix the 3 tablespoons flour with a little cold water, add a few tablespoons of hot liquid to it, and pour the mixture back into the pan. Stir and cook until the sauce is thick and smooth, then cook a little longer.

Pour sauce over rabbit. Serves 4.

To use a hare (about 4 to 5 pounds ready-to-cook), double the amounts of ingredients for the pickling mixture.

It is important to have enough to flavour all of the meat.

Use 3 ounces fat to brown the hare and 1½ ounces flour to thicken the sauce. It may be necessary to skim off part of the fat before thickening the sauce. Serves 8 to 10.

RABBIT OR HARE FRICASSEE WITH VEGETABLES
rabbit (about 3 pounds ready-to-cook) cut in serving pieces
flour, salt, pepper
3 ounces cooking fat or 6 tablespoons oil
¾ pint hot water
1 pound raw vegetables (peas and coarsely chopped carrots, onions, and celery)
1 teaspoon salt
1 ounce flour

Roll rabbit in mixture of flour, salt, and pepper.

Heat fat or oil and brown the rabbit slowly, turning often. Add water and cover pan.

Cook slowly on top of stove about 1 hour, or until rabbit is almost tender. Add water if needed during cooking. Add vegetables and salt and cook about 20 minutes longer, or until vegetables are done.

Or, after browning, bake the rabbit in slow oven (325°F. Mark 3) about 1 hour, add vegetables, and bake about 30 minutes longer.

Mix the flour with a little cold water, add a few tablespoons of hot liquid from the pan, and stir the mixture into the liquid in pan. Cook 15 minutes longer, or until sauce is smooth and thick. Serves 8.

To fricassee a smaller rabbit (about 2 pounds ready-to-cook), use 2 ounces fat or 4 tablespoons oil for browning, and half the quantity of the other ingredients in the recipe above. Cooking time on top of stove before adding vegetables is about 30 minutes; in oven, about 45 minutes. Serves 4.

RABBIT IN CASSEROLE
1 rabbit, cut up
3 tablespoons flour
1 teaspoon salt
½ teaspoon pepper
1 ounce butter or margarine
2 tablespoons cooking oil
8 fluid ounces claret or burgundy
2-3 diced fresh tomatoes
2-3 sticks celery, diced
3 tablespoons sugar

Shake rabbit pieces in paper bag with flour, salt, and pepper. Brown in butter and oil in frying pan. Remove to casserole.

Pour wine into the pan; stir well, then pour over rabbit.

Add remaining ingredients; cover and bake in slow oven (325°F. Mark 3) 1 hour. Serves 6.

Rabbit Stew

NUTRITION AND WEIGHT CONTROL

In building the human body, the best foods in the correct proportions are needed.

The ABC of Nutrition

Nutrition is the science that deals with food at work—food on the job for you.

Modern knowledge of food at work brings a new kind of mastery over life. When you—and your family—eat the right food, it does far more than just keep you alive and going.

The right food helps you to be at your best in health and vitality. It can even help you to stay younger longer, postponing old age. An individual well fed from babyhood has a better chance to enjoy a long prime of life. But, at any age, you are better off when you are better fed.

Food's Three Big Jobs

1. Food provides materials for the body's building and repair. Protein and minerals (and water) are what tissue and bone are chiefly made of. Children must have these food materials for growth; and all life long the body continues to require supplies for upkeep.
2. Food provides regulators that enable the body to use other materials and to run smoothly. Vitamins do important work in this line, so do minerals and protein.
3. Food provides fuel for the body's energy and warmth. There's some fuel in every food.

Body's Needs, A to Z

From vitamin A to the mineral zinc, a list of nutrients—chemical substances that the body is known to require from food—would total more than 40. And there may be some not yet detected.

You can put nutrition knowledge to use without being introduced to all of the body's A-to-Z needs. When daily meals provide sufficiently for the following key nutrients, you can be reasonably sure of getting the rest.

PROTEIN

Protein was named from a Greek word meaning "first". Nearly a hundred years ago, it was recognized as the main substance in all of the body's muscles and organs, skin, hair, and other tissues. No simple substance could build and renew such different tissues, and protein has proved to be complex and varied.

Protein in different foods is made up of varying combinations of 22 simpler materials called amino acids. If need be, the body can make its own supply of more than half of these amino acids. But the remaining amino acids must come ready-made from food. And to get the best use from these special ones, the body needs them all together, either in one food or in some combination of foods.

The best quality proteins have all of these especially important amino acids, and worthwhile amounts of each.

You get top-rating proteins in foods from animal sources, as in meat, poultry, fish, eggs, milk, cheese. Some of these protein foods are needed each day; and it is an advantage to include some in each meal.

Next best for proteins are soya beans and nuts and dried beans and peas. When these are featured in main dishes, try to combine them with a little top-rating protein food, if you can.

The rest of the protein required will then come from cereals, bread, vegetables, and fruits. Many American-style dishes, such as meat and vegetable stew, egg sandwiches, macaroni and cheese, cereal and milk, are highly nourishing combinations. For in the body's remarkable chemistry, the high-grade proteins team with the less complete proteins in many companion foods and make the latter more useful than if eaten alone.

CALCIUM

Calcium is one of the chief mineral materials in bones and teeth. About 99 per cent of all the calcium in the body is used for framework. Small but important, the other 1 per cent remains in body fluids, such as the blood. Without this calcium, muscles can't contract and relax and nerves can't carry their messages.

For calcium to be used properly, other substances are needed, too, in appropriate quantities; vitamin D and phosphorus, for example.

Many people go through life with bones that are calcium-poor. If a child gets too little calcium in his food or if his bones fail to deposit the calcium properly, then the bones will be smaller than they should be, or malformed as when legs are bent in rickets. Older people who are calcium-poor may have brittle bones that break easily and mend slowly. Whether you are young or old, it's a good thing for the diet to be calcium-rich.

The outstanding food for calcium is milk. You can hardly get enough calcium without using a good deal of milk in some form. Next-best foods for calcium are some of the leafy green vegetables—notably turnip tops and kale.

These foods build, repair and regulate.

IRON

One of the essential materials for red blood cells is iron. Without its iron supply, the blood could not carry oxygen from the lungs to each body cell.

When meals are varied, you get some iron from many different foods. Liver is outstanding for iron. And one good reason for eating leafy green vegetables is their iron content.

Some of the other foods that add iron are egg yolks, meat in general, peas, and beans of all kinds, dried fruits, black treacle, bread and other cereal foods made from the whole grain or enriched.

IODINE

Your body must have small but steady amounts of iodine to help the thyroid gland to work properly. The most familiar bad effect of getting too little iodine is a swelling of the thyroid gland, called goitre.

Along the sea coast, and in some other parts of the country, iodine is contained in the drinking water and vegetables and fruits grown in local soil.

It is well to plan to include iodine in the diet, particularly if you live inland. Eating salt-water fish or other food from the sea at least once a week will help.

VITAMINS

Nearly 20 vitamins that are known or believed to be important to human well-being have so far been discovered. A few more vitamins are known to be important to such creatures as fish, chickens, or insects, but not to people.

When you eat a variety of food you are sure of getting a well-rounded assortment of the vitamins you need —except perhaps vitamin D. And you

may also be getting other vitamins still undetected in food, but serving you just the same.

Separate doses of one or more selected vitamins are best taken under doctors' orders. For research is showing more and more instances in which a vitamin or other nutrient seeks a different nutrient in a meal as a special partner to assist in its work. When a vitamin pill brings in a mass army, the right partners may not be ready to use so much specialized help.

The following vitamins are of practical importance in planning family meals.

The B-Vitamin Family

There was once supposed to be just one vitamin B. Then, vitamin B was found to be complex and it has in time been separated into about a dozen vitamins, each with particular functions and importance. Most of them are now called by names that tell something about their chemical nature.

Thiamine, riboflavin, and niacin are the most generally known and best understood B's. Getting enough of these in food helps with steady nerves, normal appetite, good digestion, good morale, healthy skin. When these B's are seriously wanting in diet, malnutrition such as beri-beri and pellagra follow. But far more common in this country are borderline cases. The chronic nagger, the lazy-bones, the nervous man, the housewife with vague complaints, may be showing effects of food providing too little of these important B's.

Recently identified B's are folic acid and vitamin B_{12}, both important for healthy state of the blood. Folic acid and B_{12} are being used medically with success in treating two hard-to-cure diseases—pernicious anaemia and sprue.

Few foods contain a real wealth of B vitamins, but in a varied diet many foods contribute some and so build an adequate supply.

One way to make sure of raising your B level is to use regularly bread and flour that have been made from whole grain or that have been enriched so as to restore important B vitamins.

Getting ample milk in the diet is important for B's, too, and for riboflavin in particular.

B vitamins play a part in converting fuel in foods into energy. It follows that any one who eats large quantities of starches and sugars also requires more food containing B vitamins.

Vitamin A

Vitamin A is important to the young

for growth. And at all ages it is important for normal vision, especially in dim light.

In one way or another, many vitamins help protect the body against infection, and vitamin A's guard duty is to help keep the skin and the linings of nose, mouth, and inner organs in good condition. If these surfaces are weakened, bacteria can invade more easily.

You can get vitamin A from some animal foods. Good sources are liver, egg yolks, butter, whole milk and cream, and cheese made from whole milk or cream. Fish-liver oils which children take for vitamin D are rich in vitamin A besides.

From many vegetable foods you can get carotenes, which are yellow-orange substances that the body converts into vitamin A. Green, yellow, and some red vegetables are good sources of carotene. One good reason for including a vegetable from the "leafy, green, and yellow group" every day is to keep stocked with this vitamin. Margarine, a vegetable fat, is nearly always fortified with vitamin A or carotene.

Some vitamin A can be stored in the body. So it is to your advantage to eat heartily of foods that provide for it, such as the green and yellow vegetables. A savings account of vitamin A in your system may be drawn upon, if in any emergency this vitamin is wanting in the diet.

Vitamin C

The first vitamin distinguished in food was vitamin C, now also called ascorbic acid. Tissues throughout the body cannot keep in good condition without vitamin C.

When diet is very low in this vitamin, gums are tender and bleed easily,

Concentrated sources of energy

joints swell and hurt, and muscles weaken. In advanced stages, the disease called scurvy results. This misery used to attack sailors on long voyages when they got no fresh food. In time, they found they could fight scurvy with lemon, lime, or orange juice added to rations. Much later, vitamin C, the scurvy-fighter itself, was discovered.

Scurvy is now rare in this country. But many people get too little vitamin C for their best state of health.

You need some food rich in vitamin C daily, because the body can't store much of this vitamin.

All of the familiar citrus fruits are bountiful sources of vitamin C. Half a glass (4 ounces) of orange or grapefruit juice, fresh or canned, goes far toward meeting a day's needs. The same is true of half a grapefruit, a whole orange, or a couple of tangerines.

Other good sources of vitamin C include tomatoes and tomato juice, canned or fresh; fresh strawberries and melon; also raw green food, such as cabbage, green pepper, and green lettuce. The potato's many values include some vitamin C.

Vitamin D

Vitamin D is especially important to the young, because it works with minerals to form straight, strong bones, and sound teeth. Babies with bowlegs may have too little vitamin D. An individual should get some of this vitamin regularly, at least through the growing stage. It is also important for pregnant women and nursing mothers.

"Sunshine vitamin" is vitamin D's nickname, because the sun's rays striking the skin have power to change certain substances in the skin into vitamin D.

From baby days on, children can make good use of sunshine. But they should be protected well against sunburn or sunstroke.

Children can't get much vitamin D from the sun when they must wear thick warm clothes for cold weather, or when sunlight is cut off by clouds, smoke, fog, dust, or ordinary window glass.

A few foods, such as egg yolk, butter,

Vegetables and fruits are regulators and protectors of the body.

salmon, tuna fish, and sardines, help out with vitamin D, and some milk, both fresh and evaporated, has vitamin D added. But to supplement sunshine and food, babies and young children usually need to take a special vitamin D preparation or one of the fish-liver oils regularly. These oils from halibut, shark, and cod are the richest natural sources of this vitamin known.

FUEL

For the body's energy in work and play, fuel must come from food. The value of foods for this purpose is calculated in calories. Main sources are starches and sugars, and fats, but all foods furnish calories—some many, some few, in a certain portion.

Your needs for food as fuel depend mainly on two things—the size of your body and how active you are. An average-size man who is a desk worker with no strenuous sport or hobby needs about 2,400 calories from daily food. A fast-growing, lively teen-ager, boy or girl, may need more calories than this grown man.

If body weight stays about right for your health and build it's a sign that fuel intake from food matches your needs. The calories are taking care of themselves.

But suppose you are overweight . . . what then?

When the body gets more energy food than it can use, it stores up the excess as fat. Accumulation of too much fat is sometimes termed the most frequent malnutrition problem among adults in the West. To put it more plainly, many adults eat too much.

Up to 35 years of age, if you can't be just right in weight, it is better to be plump than skinny. Beyond 35, excess fat becomes a greater health liability than thinness. Ills such as high blood pressure and heart and kidney ailments are more common among overweights. Underweights tend to tire readily and may be an easy prey to infections.

FINDING OUT WHAT'S IN FOODS

Taking foods apart chemically, scientists are learning more exactly, nutrient by nutrient, what each familiar food can provide for the body's needs.

The table on a following page gives a rough idea of how well different kinds of foods in this country's diet can provide for the body's various needs.

You can judge from this table that no one food has a wealth of all nutrients —not even milk, "the most nearly perfect food". Most foods contain more than one nutrient, and so help in more ways than one.

SERVING BY SERVING
Foods Provide for Daily Needs

Stars in the chart that follows give a rough idea of how servings from groups of familiar foods contribute toward dietary needs.

A serving that rates 5 stars provides more than 50 per cent of the day's need for a nutrient. A 4-star serving provides about 40 per cent; 3-star serving, 30 per cent; 2-star serving, 20 per cent; 1-star serving, 10 per cent. Smaller amounts of nutrients are not shown.

These ratings are based on daily allowances of nutrients for a moderately active man.

Some foods within a group have more of a nutrient, some less; but in a varied diet, which is common in this country, a group is likely to average as shown.

It's Up to You

● To get all the nutrients needed, it's wise to choose a variety of foods. It is also important to get enough of the different nutrients from food. A food plan worked out by nutritionists, such as the one that follows, is a handy guide.

● You will be off to a good start nutritionally if you plan meals by some orderly plan, so that daily food includes needed quantities of protein, minerals, and other nutrients.

● You are following through effectively when you cook by up-to-date methods that keep delicate vitamins and minerals from being wasted.

● And, rounding out a family nutrition programme, you can make mealtime interesting and food associations pleasant. For, after all, food must be eaten to count for good nutrition. You can, for example . . .

● Select nutritious recipes that the whole family enjoys, and use them reasonably often.

● When re-using one of these favourites, vary the meal with different food combinations.

● If an inexpensive dish seems dull, vary flavour with seasonings, or combine with other foods in different ways.

● Use contrast in food colours, flavours, textures. Some bright-coloured food, something crisp, for example, can heighten the visual appeal and appetite appeal of a meal.

● Give children small servings, remembering that big amounts may be discouraging. It's better for a child to form the habit of emptying his plate and asking for a second helping, if wanted.

● Introduce a new food to a young child in sample quantities, and at the start of a meal when he is hungry . . . and if he doesn't like it at first, try it another day.

Kind of food	Size of Serving	Protein	Calcium	Iron	Vitamin A value	B-vitamins			Vitamin C (ascorbic acid)	Food energy (in calories)
						Thiamine	Riboflavin	Niacin		
Leafy, green yellow vegetables.	½ cup			★	★★★★				★★	30
Tomatoes, tomato products.	½ cup			★	★★★			★	★★★	35
Potatoes	1 medium			★		★			★	105
Other vegetables	½ cup	·							★	40
Citrus fruits	½ cup								★★★★★	55
Other fruits	½ cup				★				★	70
Milk, cheese, ice cream.	1 cup milk	★	★★★		★	★	★★			170
Meat, poultry, fish	4 ounces	★★		★★	★	★★	★	★★★		225
Eggs	1 egg	★		★	★		★			80
Dry beans and peas, nuts.	½ cup beans cooked	★★	★	★★★		★★	★	★★		215
Baked goods, flour, cereals.	2 slices bread	★		★		★	★	★		130
Butter, fortified margarine	1 pat				★					50
Other fats (includes bacon, salt pork).	2 tablespoons									230
Sugar, all kinds	2 teaspoons									35
Molasses, syrups, preserves.	2 tablespoons			★						115

★★★★★ More than 50 per cent of daily need.
★★★★ About 40 per cent of daily need.
★★★ About 30 per cent of daily need.
★★ About 20 per cent of daily need.
★ About 10 per cent of daily need.

Have a Food Plan

To see that your family is well fed, it is wise to plan their diet. This way you can be sure to provide each important kind of food—and enough of it.

A food fact worth knowing is: When families are poorly fed, the foods they neglect are most often milk and milk products, and vegetables and fruits—especially the leafy, green, and yellow vegetables and citrus fruits. Watch for these when planning family meals.

A Ready-Made Food Plan

A helpful guide for weekly shopping and meal planning is a food plan worked out by nutritionists. Such a plan is given on a following page. Other plans could be made that would provide good nutrition. Any plan that does this must bring into the kitchen foods that offer recommended amounts of protein, minerals and vitamins, and food energy.

In the plan given, foods are in groups according to their major contributions of nutrients, as well as their place in the meal. Amounts to provide for adequate diets are shown in pounds and pints of food for a week.

More information about planning by food groups, and the way they work out in servings, is also given on the following pages. You can see that there is ample choice within groups to allow for varied meals from day to day wherever you live. The groups allow, too, for including family favourites among the foods.

In the pages on food groups, the "plan to use" headings are intended as a guide so that you may work out a food plan of your own to suit your family.

Ways to Use This Plan

You can make use of the food plan for good nutrition in several ways. It can serve as a shopping guide, as it stands, to show the approximate amount of food needed for each member of the family. Or you can compare it to kinds and quantities of food you regularly use, just to make sure that you are not short of any important kind.

If you have a garden or store food for the winter, the food plan can help as a general guide to amounts of foods that the family will use.

To Figure Your Family's Needs

To use the food plan, calculate weekly amounts of the food groups that will be required by your family.

The rows of figures in the plan are arranged to show food quantities according to age, sex, and how active the individual is. Where a range is given: For children, the first quantity is for the youngest age. For adults, the first quantity is for the less active. The most active adults do really heavy work or take strenuous exercise.

For pregnant and nursing women, the first quantity is for pregnant and the second for nursing women.

No figures are given for children under 1 year because they are often breast-fed or have milk or other food prepared especially for them.

Guided by these ranges, you can estimate the quantity needed for each person in the family. Use your own judgment in doing this. If a child is having a spurt of growing, he may need the amount of food usually suggested for children a year or two older.

As you add up the amount of each kind of food your family members need in a week, write the figure in the column provided at right of the food plan sheet. This is your shopping guide, to use as it stands or to compare with amounts you've been buying.

YOUR FOOD AND YOUR MONEY

Quantities in the food plan can be bought for about the same amount of money that the average family spends on food. This assumes that you will choose moderately priced foods, or mix some cheaper foods with more expensive ones.

If you have more money to spend, you can choose now and again the more expensive items, such as luxury foods and those out of season. On the other hand, if you want to cut down food costs, reduce somewhat—perhaps by about one-third—the quantities of meat, poultry and fish in the plan, and also the group described as "other vegetables and fruits". To take their place, increase potatoes and cereals by about one-fourth.

In either case, try not to change very much the quantities given in the plan for milk and milk products, leafy, green, and yellow vegetables, and tomatoes and citrus fruits.

A FOOD PLAN FOR GOOD NUTRITION (Quantities for One Week)

Kinds of food	For children 1 to 6 years	For children 7 to 12 years	For girls 13 to 20 years	For boys 13 to 20 years	For women — All activities	For women — Pregnant and nursing	For men, all activities	Total suggested for your family
Leafy, green, and yellow vegetables	2-2½ lbs.	2½-3 lbs.	3½ lbs.	3½-4 lbs.	3½-4 lbs.	4 lbs.	3½-4 lbs.	
Citrus fruits, tomatoes	2-2½ lbs.	2½-3 lbs.	3 lbs.	3-3½ lbs.	2½-3 lbs.	3½-4½ lbs.	2½-3½ lbs.	
Potatoes	½-1 lb.	1½-2 lbs.	2½ lbs.	3½-4½ lbs.	2-3 lbs.	2-3 lbs.	3-5 lbs.	
Other vegetables and fruits	2 lbs.	2½ lbs.	3½ lbs.	3½ lbs.	3-4 lbs.	3-3½ lbs.	3-4 lbs.	
Milk[1], cheese	9 pts.	11 pts.	10 pts.	11 pts.	8 pts.	12-16 pts.	8 pts.	
Meat, poultry, fish[3] Eggs Dry beans and peas, nuts	1-1¼ lbs. 6-7 eggs 1 oz.	2 lbs. 7 eggs 2 ozs.	2½-3 lbs. 7 eggs 2 ozs.	3 lbs. 7 eggs 4-6 ozs.	2½-3 lbs. 6-7 eggs 2-4 ozs.	3 lbs. 7 eggs 2 ozs.	3-3½ lbs. 6-7 eggs 4 ozs.	
Baked goods, flour, cereals[1] Wholegrain, enriched or restored	1-1½ lbs.	2-3 lbs.	2½-3 lbs.[2]	4-5 lbs.	2-4 lbs.	2-2½ lbs.	3-7 lbs.	
Fats, oils	¼ lb.	½-1 lb.	¾ lb.	1-1½ lbs.	¾-1 lb.	¾ lb.	1-2 lbs.	
Sugar, syrups, preserves	¼-½ lb.	¾ lb.	1 lb.	1-1½ lbs.	¾-1 lb.	¾ lb.	1-1½ lbs.	

[1] For explanation of milk-equivalent and flour-equivalent foods see What's In Each Food Group.

[2] Larger quantities are for the younger girls.

[3] To meet the iron allowance needed by children 1 to 6 years, girls 13 to 20, and pregnant and nursing women, include weekly 1 large or 2 small servings of liver or other offal.

What's in Each Food Group

Here are common foods grouped as in The Food Plan for Good Nutrition. Foods in each group can be used similarly in meals, so within the group there is room for variety. Foods in each group provide about the same nutrients but some are better providers than others.

Leafy, Green, and Yellow Vegetables

Leafy, green, and yellow vegetables are rich in vitamin A value, especially the dark green leafy kinds, and carrots. They also provide worthwhile amounts of riboflavin, iron, and some calcium; and cabbage, broccoli, Brussels sprouts, and greens offer vitamin C.

Plan to use: 1 or more servings daily. The food plan provides: 10 to 12 servings per week.

All kinds of greens—kale, turnip greens, spinach, and many others, cultivated and wild; carrots, peas, green beans, okra, green asparagus, broccoli, Brussels sprouts, green lima beans, pumpkin, green cabbage.

Citrus Fruits, Tomatoes

Citrus fruits and tomatoes are mainstay sources of vitamin C.

Plan to use: 1 or more servings daily. The food plan provides: 7 to 10 servings a week.

Oranges, grapefruit, tangerines, other citrus fruit, tomatoes.

The following foods are also good sources of vitamin C and may be used as alternates:

If eaten raw—cabbage, salad greens, green peppers, turnips, strawberries, pineapple, melon. If cooked briefly, in very little water—cabbage, broccoli, Brussels sprouts, greens.

Potatoes

Potatoes contain a number of nutrients. Because of the quantities in which they are eaten, potatoes can become quite important as a source of vitamin C.

Plan to use: 1 or more servings daily. The food plan provides: 7 to 9 servings a week.

Other Vegetables and Fruits

These vegetables and fruits help toward a good diet with vitamins and minerals.

Plan to use: 1 or more servings daily. The food plan provides: 10 to 12 servings a week.

Beetroot, cauliflower, sweetcorn, cucumbers, onions, sauerkraut, turnips, white cabbage, apples, peaches, bananas, berries, rhubarb, dried fruit —all vegetables and fruits not included in other groups.

Milk and Cheese

Milk—whole, skim, evaporated, condensed, dried, buttermilk—is our leading source of calcium. Milk also provides high-quality protein, riboflavin, vitamin A, and many other vitamins and minerals.

Plan to use, as the food plan provides, the following amounts of milk daily.

Include milk used for drinking as well as cooking:

Children and adolescents: 1½-1¾ pints.
Adults: 1 to 1¼ pints.
Pregnant women: 1¾-2 pints.
Nursing mothers: 2⅝ pints.

On the basis of calcium they contain, the following may be used as alternates for 1 cup of milk: Cheddar cheese, 1½ ounces; cream cheese, 15 ounces; cottage cheese, 11 ounces.

Meat, Poultry, Fish

Meat, poultry, and fish are important primarily for high-quality protein. Foods in this group also provide iron, thiamine, riboflavin, niacin, vitamin A.

Plan to use: 1 serving daily, if possible.

The food plan provides: 7 to 8 servings a week.

All kinds, including liver, heart, and other offal.

Count bacon and salt pork in with fats.

Eggs

Eggs are a source of high-quality protein, iron, vitamin A, riboflavin, vitamin D, and provide some calcium and thiamine.

Plan to use: 4 or more a week.

The food plan provides: 6 or 7 a week.

Dried Beans and Peas, Nuts

Dried beans and peas and nuts contain good protein, also some calcium, iron, thiamine, riboflavin, and niacin.

Plan to use: 1 or more servings a week.

The food plan provides: 1 to 2 servings a week.

Dried beans of all kinds, dried peas, lentils; soya beans, soya products; peanuts, other nuts; peanut butter.

Baked Goods, Flour, Cereals

Wholegrain cereals, or those with added vitamins and minerals or restored to wholegrain value, provide significant amounts of iron, thiamine, riboflavin, niacin. Foods in this group also help out with protein and calories.

Plan to use as the food plan provides: Some every day.

Flour or meal made from wheat, corn, oats, buckwheat, rye; cooked and ready-to-eat cereals; rice, barley, noodles, macaroni; breads, other baked goods.

Quantities suggested in the food plan are in terms of pounds of flour and cereal. Bread and other baked goods average two-thirds flour by weight. Therefore, count 1½ pounds of bread and other baked goods as 1 pound of flour.

Fat, Oils

Butter and fortified margarine are rich in vitamin-A value. Like all fats, they furnish many calories.

Plan to use as the food plan provides: Some butter or margarine daily; other fats as needed in cooking.

Butter, margarine, salad oil, shortening, bacon, salt pork, lard, suet, drippings.

Sugar, Syrups, Preserves

Sugar, syrups, preserves are useful mainly for the calories they provide for bodily energy.

The food plan includes for the average person about a pound a week.

Any kind of sugar—granulated (beet or cane), icing, brown, and maple; treacle or any kind of syrup or honey; jams and jellies; sweets and chocolates.

CONTROLLING WEIGHT

If you are under 20 years of age, don't try to reduce except under a physician's guidance. This is also advisable if you are a young mother or have anything wrong with heart or other organs. If you are not in these groups, and need to reduce, take it slowly. A pound or two off a week is plenty.

To reduce calories without starving your body of its other needs:

Eat three meals a day, but don't be tempted by between-meal snacks.

Avoid high-calorie foods like the fat on meat, cooking fat, salad oil, fried foods, gravies and rich sauces, nuts, pastries, cakes, cookies, rich desserts, candies, jellies, and jams. Eat small-size servings of bread or cereal.

Don't skimp on fruits and vegetables. Eat a variety—yes, potatoes, too. A medium-sized potato has no more calories than a big orange or a big apple. But take fruits and vegetables straight—vegetables without cream, sauce, or fat, fruit without sugar and cream. Don't skimp on protein-rich foods, for you need plenty of lean meat, milk and eggs.

If you are underweight you need to turn the tables to put some fat on your bones. You need three balanced meals, as overweights do. To these meals, you can freely add the extras shunned by the weight reducers—such as rich gravies and desserts, salad dressings, and jams. And you can well take some extra food as between-meal snacks.

Calorie Counter's Guide

A calorie is a unit of heat, or energy, generated in the body by food, used to measure the amount of heat, or energy, required by the body at different ages and under various conditions.

If you eat more in total calories for the day than the body needs, it is stored as fat. By counting calories, dieters can and should eat well balanced meals—and still lose or gain weight.

Calorie values can seldom be exact, especially for "manufactured" foods. For example, two dishes of ice cream, even of the same flavour, can vary considerably in calorie value because the ingredients vary. One may have more sugar than another, or be made with richer cream. One might have more chocolate or fruit in its composition. But even approximate calorie values can be very helpful to one who is dieting for one reason or another.

The data given here are in quantities that can be readily adjusted to servings of different sizes.

Values for prepared foods and food mixtures have been calculated from typical recipes.

Values for cooked vegetables are without added fat.

HOW TO ESTIMATE YOUR CALORIE NEEDS

Dieters should know the number of calories the body needs just to keep in top physical condition.

1. Estimate your "ideal" weight for height and build. Weight charts are usually for the average person. Large-boned people may top this average by 10 to 20 percent; slender-boned people fall under it.

2. Multiply your "ideal" weight by 15. Your body needs 15 to 20 calories per pound per day.

3. In order to lose weight, reduce the answer above by one-third. In order to gain, in most cases add one-third. The result is your calorie quota for one day.

4. Divide your total for your three meals.

CALORIE COUNTER GUIDE

As explained previously, it is not always possible to give the exact calorific content of every kind of food and the following is given as an approximate guide.

BEVERAGES	QUAN-TITY	CALO-RIES
Beer mild	½ pt	130
pale ale	½ pt	150
stout	½ pt	140
Cider dry	½ pt	140
Chocolate made with milk	½ pt	300
Cocoa made with milk	½ pt	275
made with half milk	½ pt	110
Ginger ale	½ pt	95
Grapefruit juice—canned unsweetened	½ pt	112
Orange juice fresh	½ pt	140
Spirits brandy	1 fl oz	80
whisky	1 fl oz	85
gin	1 fl oz	80
rum	1 fl oz	150
Tea—with milk, no sugar	½ pt	20
Wines dry	4 fl oz	80
sweet	4 fl oz	95
Champagne	4 fl oz	120
Port	2 fl oz	110
Sherry dry	2 fl oz	70
sweet	2 fl oz	100

BISCUITS, BREAD	QUANTITY	CALORIES
Plain	1 oz	110-115
Sweet	1 oz	134-145
Bread white	1 oz	74
brown	1 oz	68
Crispbread	1 slice	28

CAKES	QUANTITY	CALORIES
Plain sponge	2 oz	150
With icing	2 oz	210
Light fruit	2 oz	180

CEREALS	QUANTITY	CALORIES
Arrowroot	1 oz	110
Barley pearl	1 oz	95
Cornflour	1 oz	110
Cornflakes and similar breakfast cereal	1 oz	100-110
Flour white	1 oz	100
Lentils dried	1 oz	165
Macaroni uncooked	1 oz	80-100
Oatmeal	1 oz	110
Rice uncooked	1 oz	95
Sago uncooked	1 oz	50
Soya flour whole	1 oz	120
low fat	1 oz	90
Spaghetti uncooked	1 oz	80
Shredded wheat	1 oz	100
Tapioca uncooked	1 oz	50
Weetabix	1 oz	100

DAIRY PRODUCTS	QUANTITY	CALORIES
Butter	½ oz	120
Cheese Cheddar	1 oz	120
cottage	1 oz	45
cream	1 oz	145
Dutch	1 oz	90
processed	1 oz	110
Cream single	1 oz	60
double	1 oz	100
Eggs raw or boiled	2 oz av	80
fried	2 oz av	120-140 depending on amount of fat used
white	av egg	11
yolk	av egg	69
lard	½ oz	130
Margarine	½ oz	110

MILK	QUANTITY	CALORIES
Whole	½ pt	170-180
Skimmed	½ pt	70
Condensed	1 oz	100
Evaporated	1 oz	45
Yoghourt	¼ pt	100

FISH	QUANTITY	CALORIES
Cod cooked fillets	4 oz	95
Crab edible part	2 oz	70 app
Haddock fresh cooked	4 oz	115
smoked	4 oz	120

FISH contd.	QUANTITY	CALORIES
Hake cooked (not fried)	4 oz	90
Halibut cooked (not fried)	4 oz	140
Herring	3 oz	145
Kipper (not fried)	3 oz	150
Lobster	4 oz	65
Mackerel	4 oz	90-100
Oysters	6 med	65
Plaice steamed	4 oz	90
Salmon fresh boiled	4 oz	155
canned	4 oz	190
smoked	2 oz	175
Sardines	2 oz	160
Shrimps shelled	4 oz	55
Sole	4 oz	90-120 according to method of cooking
Sprats cooked without fat	4 oz	170
Turbot boiled	4 oz	85
Whiting	4 oz	82

FRUIT Fresh	QUANTITY	CALORIES
Apple	4 oz app	45
Apricots		30
Avocado pear	½ pear	275
Banana	1 av	75-90
Blackberries	4 oz	30
Blackcurrants	4 oz	32
Cherries	4 oz	45
Figs raw green	2 oz	26
Gooseberries	4 oz	40
Grapes	4 oz	70
Grapefruit	½ med size	60
Lemon	3 oz	30
Loganberries	4 oz	20
Melon	4 oz	16-20
Olives green	1 large	20
black	1 large	25
Orange	6 oz	
Peach	3 oz	35
Pear	6 oz	55
Pineapple	about 6 oz slice	65
Plums	4 oz	30
Raspberries	4 oz	25
Rhubarb	4 oz	5
Strawberries	4 oz	30
Canned		
Apricots	4 oz	60
Blackberries	4 oz	15
Cherries	4 oz	95
Peaches	4 oz	65
Pears	2 halves	75
Pineapple	4 oz	80
Plums	4 oz	80
Dried		
Apricots	2 oz	100

FRUIT, Dried—contd.	QUANTITY	CALORIES
Dates	2 oz	175
Figs	2 oz	115
Prunes	2 oz	75
Raisins	2 oz	125
Sultanas	2 oz	140

MEAT	QUANTITY	CALORIES
Bacon rashers lean	2 oz	175
rashers with fat	2 oz	250 app
Beef roast lean	4 oz	210
roast with fat	4 oz	up to 300
corned	4 oz	475
Ham cooked lean		265
with fat	4 oz	375 app
Heart	4 oz	265
Kidney	4 oz	145
Lamb roast lean	4 oz	230
with fat	4 oz	375 app
Liver	4 oz	160
Pork roast lean	4 oz	270
with fat	4 oz	up to 450
Rabbit stewed	4 oz	180
Sausages beef	4 oz	240 app
pork	4 oz	290 app
Steak lean	4 oz	300
Sweetbreads	4 oz	250
Tongue cooked	4 oz	290
Veal roast lean	4 oz	145

NUTS	QUANTITY	CALORIES
Almonds	1 oz	165
salted	12	100
Brazil nuts	1 oz	172
Chestnuts	1 oz	165
Peanuts	1 oz	165
Pecans	1 oz	180
Walnuts	1 oz	175

POULTRY	QUANTITY	CALORIES
Chicken	4 oz	165
Duck	4 oz	190
Goose	4 oz	355
Turkey	4 oz	185

VEGETABLES	QUANTITY	CALORIES
Asparagus	4 oz	20
Beans canned baked	4 oz	100
broad	4 oz	60
haricot dried	2 oz	140
runner	4 oz	15
Beetroot boiled	2 oz	15
Broccoli	4 oz	15
Brussels sprouts	4 oz	20
Cabbage	4 oz	20
Carrots	4 oz	
Cauliflower	4 oz	20
Celery raw	2 oz	5
Cucumber	2 oz	10
Leeks	4 oz	15
Lettuce	2 oz	negligible

VEGETABLES contd.	QUAN-TITY	CALO-RIES
Mushrooms	2 oz	negli-gible
Marrow or squash	2 oz	11
Onions boiled	4 oz	25
Parsnips boiled or baked	4 oz	55
Peas fresh	4 oz	75
canned	4 oz	25
dried	1 oz	85
Peppers green or red	2 oz	20
Pimento canned	1 med size	10
Potatoes boiled	4 oz	95
fried	4 oz	270
Spinach	4 oz	25
Sweetcorn boiled	1 ear	85 app
Tomatoes fresh	4 oz	20
Turnips	4 oz	40

SUGARS AND SWEETS

Boiled sweets	1 oz	120 app
Chocolate plain	1 oz	140
milk	1 oz	160
Honey	1 oz	90
Ice cream	2 oz	115-130
Jam	1 oz	70-100
Marmalade	1 oz	70
Sugar white	1 oz	110
brown	1 oz	100
	1 lrg lump	20
Syrup golden	1 oz	90

MISCELLANEOUS

Cocoa	¼ oz	25
Coconut fresh grated	1 oz	170
desiccated	1 oz	180
Gelatine	¼ oz	25
Mayonnaise	1 tbsn	90
Salad oil	1 tbsn	125
Yeast dried	½ oz	20
compressed	1 oz	25

Low Calorie Menus

Suggestions are given here for well-balanced low calorie meals. On Sunday, when most members of the family are home together the main meal is generally served midday. For the rest of the week the main meal is generally taken in the evening and the following menus are worked out accordingly, but you can change them round to suit your own particular habits.

A low calorie meal does not necessarily mean you must forgo all desserts and puddings. Fresh fruit is of course, ideal to finish a meal, but you will find in several of the menus a sweet or pudding is included and small quantities of these are quite permissible if the meal is properly planned.

Sugar substitutes. There are several on the market and these can be used for sweetening beverages and also in cooking.

Fortified sugar is a mixture of sugar and saccharine. Sift 8 ounces of castor sugar with 24 crushed saccharine tablets and store in a jar with a tightly fitting lid. When using this in cakes and puddings use only *half* the given weight, e.g. if your recipe calls for 4 ounces sugar, use 2 ounces of fortified sugar. When using it for sweetening fruit add the fortified sugar after the fruit has been cooked.

Other sweeteners are available in tablet or liquid form, and instructions on the packet should be followed.

A little extra flavouring in cakes and puddings will mask any slightly unusual flavour or bitterness.

Recipes are given for some of the dishes in the menus and you will find good use has been made of artificial sweeteners.

It is not wise to do without breakfast altogether. Have half a grapefruit or fresh fruit juice which can be followed if you wish with a breakfast cereal. However, a protein dish—such as a boiled or poached egg or a grilled rasher of bacon and tomato is to be preferred. One thin crisp piece of toast or crispbread or a starch reduced roll with some sugarless marmalade can round off the meal. Take your coffee or tea without sugar. In the menus which follow, a breakfast of this kind has been taken into consideration.

LOW CALORIE WINTER MENUS

SUNDAY

Midday meal
Creole Tomato Soup
Roast Beef
   green vegetable
   parsnips
Apple Fluff

Evening meal
Tuna Salad
Baked Peaches

MONDAY

Midday meal
Stuffed Aubergine
Cheese and Fresh Fruit

Evening meal
Quick French Onion Soup
Curried Beef—Rice
Baked Apples

TUESDAY

Midday Meal
Easy Herbed Tomato Soup
Baked Stuffed Fish
   braised celery
Orange Sponge Pudding
   orange sauce

Evening Meal
Hungarian Goulash en Casserole
   cabbage and carrot salad
Omelette Soufflé

WEDNESDAY

Midday Meal
Cauliflower a la Creole
Devon pears

Evening Meal
Beef Bourbon
   green vegetable
Banana Custard

THURSDAY

Midday Meal
Baked Kidneys with Bacon
   chicory salad
Cheese and Biscuits

Evening Meal
Onion Soup Italienne
Grilled chops
Upside-down pudding

FRIDAY

Midday Meal
Stuffed Egg and Spinach Casserole
   salad
Coffee Whip

Evening Meal
Blender Borsht
Roast Chicken
   pineapple and celery salad
Cheese and Biscuits

SATURDAY

Midday Meal
Devilled Chicken
   boiled rice and chutney
Spiced Pears

Evening Meal
Cottage Cheese Soup
Navarin of lamb
   green vegetable
Apple Soufflé

LOW CALORIE SUMMER MENUS

SUNDAY

Midday Meal
Tomato Juice cocktail
Roast lamb—mint sauce
   green vegetable—roast potatoes
Orange cups

Evening Meal
Jellied Madrilene
Prawn salad
Cheese and Biscuits

MONDAY
Midday Meal
Cold lamb
   aubergine salad
Fresh Fruit

Evening Meal
Almond Soup
Casserole of Pigeons
Apple Baskets
Orange Snow

TUESDAY
Midday Meal
Pear and Cream Cheese Salad
Honeycomb Mould

Evening Meal
Cold Yoghourt Soup
Liver and bacon kebabs
   green salad
Gooseberry Fool

WEDNESDAY
Midday Meal
Haddock Stroganoff
   carrots
Cheese and Biscuits

Evening Meal
Grilled gammon and pineapple
   spinach
Orange Ring Mould

THURSDAY
Midday Meal
Cottage Cheese and Vegetable Salad
Blackcurrant Whip

Evening Meal
Mushrooms à la Greque
Veal and Ham Mould
   tossed salad
Fresh Fruit

FRIDAY
Midday Meal
Cod Provençal
   salad
Lemon Jelly

Evening Meal
Grilled pork chops
   cabbage—apple salad
Raspberry Sherbet

SATURDAY
Midday Meal
Tongue and Vegetable Salad
Stewed rhubarb

Evening Meal
Grapefruit and orange
   cocktail
Swedish Cabbage Rolls
   tossed salad
Cheese and Biscuits

Low Calorie Recipes

APPLE FLUFF
1 pound cooking apples
1 tablespoon honey
**1-2 saccharine tablets or sugar
   substitute**
¼ pint yoghurt
grated rind and juice of 1 lemon
2-3 egg whites

Peal and core the apples and cook with a very little water. Beat to a purée then whisk in the honey and crushed saccharines.

Add yoghurt and grated rind and juice of the lemon.

Beat the egg whites until they hold in peaks, fold into the apple mixture. Pile into a serving dish or individual glasses and decorate with a little toasted or coloured coconut if liked.
Note: Desiccated coconut can be coloured by rubbing in a few drops of food colouring.

ORANGE SPONGE PUDDING
3 eggs
1 ounce sugar
**grated rind and juice of 1 large
   orange**
4 ounces flour
½ teaspoon baking powder
**8 saccharine tablets or sugar
   substitute**

Separate the eggs and whisk the whites until stiff. Whisk in the sugar, egg yolks, and grated orange rind and continue to whisk until the mixture is thick and creamy.

Fold in the flour and baking powder sifted together and then the saccharine dissolved in the orange juice.

Turn into a well-greased and floured ring mould and bake in a moderate oven (375°F. Mark 5) for about 20-25 minutes.

Turn out onto a hot serving dish and serve with:

ORANGE SAUCE
grated rind and juice of 2 oranges
6 tablespoons water
2 teaspoons arrowroot
**2 saccharine tablets or sugar
   substitute**

Simmer the grated orange rind in the water for about 10 minutes. Blend the arrowroot smoothly with the orange juice, stir into the pan and cook until thick and clear. Add saccharine or sugar substitute.

OMELETTE SOUFFLÉ
2 eggs
**few drops of liquid sweetener or a
   little sugar**
grated lemon rind

**1 tablespoon jam (low calorie if
   possible)**

Separate the eggs, put the yolks into a basin with the lemon rind or other flavouring and mix well with a wooden spoon until of a pale creamy consistency.

Whip the egg whites with a pinch of salt until they stand in peaks, then fold into the egg yolks.

Put the mixture into a buttered omelette pan and cook in a hot oven (425°F. Mark 6) for 7-10 minutes or until well risen and golden brown. Slide out onto a hot dish, put the jam in the centre and fold over. Serve at once.

DEVON PEARS
2 large dessert pears
lemon juice
4 cloves
1 tablespoon arrowroot
¼ pint cider
4 saccharine tablets
cochineal

Peel and halve the pears, remove the cores.

Arrange on a serving dish and sprinkle with lemon juice. Insert a clove at the base of each half pear.

Mix the arrowroot smoothly with the cider and put into a pan with ¼ pint water and the saccharine.

Heat until the sauce becomes thick and clear. Add a few drops of cochineal to give a pale pink colour.

Coat the pears with the sauce and, if liked, place a small piece of angelica in the stem end of each half pear.

BEEF BOURBON
1½ pounds stewing steak
1 ounce fat
1 clove garlic, crushed
1 onion, sliced
8 ounces tomatoes
½ pint red wine
salt
black pepper
2 carrots
2 sticks celery
1 leek
8 ounces potatoes
chopped parsley

Trim and dice the meat, removing any excess fat.

Heat the fat in a frying pan, add the meat and brown on all sides, then remove to a casserole.

Add the garlic and onion to the fat remaining in the pan and sauté for a few minutes. Add the tomatoes, peeled and chopped, wine, salt, pepper, and 2 tablespoons water. Bring to boiling point, cover and simmer for

20 minutes.

Prepare the carrots, celery, and leek, slice very thinly and scatter over the meat in the casserole. Pour the tomato mixture on top.

Peel and cut the potatoes into ¼-inch slices and arrange on top of the vegetables. Cover and cook in a slow oven (300°F. Mark 2) about 1½ hours.

Remove the lid, brush the potatoes lightly with a little melted fat and sprinkle with salt.

Return to the oven, increase the heat to 350°F. Mark 4, and cook until the potatoes are browned. Sprinkle with parsley before serving.

ORANGE CUPS

½ ounce gelatine
2 tablespoons warm water
juice of 2 oranges
juice of 1 lemon
6 tablets saccharine
2-3 teaspoons grated orange rind
¼ pint double cream
2 tablespoons top of the milk
angelica

Dissolve the gelatine in the water, mix with the orange and lemon juice, crushed saccharine and grated orange peel, stir to mix well and set aside to cool. Whip the cream and milk together and fold into the orange mixture when it begins to set.

Pour the mixture into the orange cases or into individual glasses. Decorate with angelica.

COFFEE WHIP

½ ounce powdered gelatine
¼ pint strong black coffee
½ pint milk
2-3 saccharine tablets or sugar substitute
2 egg whites
1 tablespoon single cream or top of the milk
few almonds

Dissolve the gelatine in the coffee.

Warm the milk and add the crushed saccharine or sugar substitute. Add dissolved gelatine.

Leave to get cold and when beginning to set whisk in the stiffly beaten egg whites and cream.

Chill and serve sprinkled with chopped or slivered almonds.

UPSIDE-DOWN PUDDING

1 pound cooking apples
liquid sugar substitute
2 eggs
6 saccharine tablets
2 tablespoons water
¾ ounce sugar
3 ounces flour
¼ teaspoon baking powder

Peel the apples, slice them very thinly and arrange in the bottom of a buttered dish. Dissolve the sugar substitute in water and pour over the fruit.

Separate the eggs and whisk the whites until stiff. Whisk in the sugar and then the egg yolks. When thick and creamy fold in the flour and baking powder sifted together and the saccharine tablets dissolved in the water. Spread over the fruit.

Bake in the centre of a moderate oven (375°F. Mark 5) for 30-35 minutes. Turn upside down onto a hot serving dish.

HADDOCK STROGANOFF

1 lemon
1½ pounds fresh haddock fillet
salt
pepper
paprika
1 carton sour cream or yoghurt
cress for garnish

Peel the lemon, remove all the white pith and cut into very thin slices. Arrange these in the bottom of a shallow baking dish. Remove any skin from the fish, cut into neat pieces and put on top of the lemon. Sprinkle lightly with salt and pepper. Cover and bake in a moderate oven (375°F. Mark 5) for about 20 minutes or until the fish can be easily flaked with a fork.

Uncover and spread lightly with the cream or yoghurt. Sprinkle with a little salt and paprika and brown lightly under a hot grill. Garnish with cress.

CASSEROLE OF PIGEONS

2 pigeons
2 ounces butter or margarine
½ pint dry cider
¼ pint stock or water
8 ounces tomatoes
salt
black pepper
chopped parsley

Split the pigeons in half through the back. Heat the butter in a saucepan, put in the pigeons and brown on all sides. Remove to a casserole. Pour the cider and stock into the pan in which the pigeons were browned and bring to boiling point. Add the chopped tomatoes and seasoning and simmer for 10 minutes. Rub through a sieve and pour over the pigeons. Put the lid on the casserole and cook in a slow oven (325°F. Mark 3) for 1½-2 hours.

Sprinkle with parsley before serving.

ORANGE RING MOULD

1 pint milk
2 oranges
½ ounce gelatine
2 tablespoons water
6 tablets saccharine
4 ounces fresh cherries
cherries or grapes to decorate

Put the milk with the thinly peeled orange rind into a double saucepan and leave over very low heat for about 30 minutes to extract the flavour.

Dissolve the gelatine in the warm water.

Remove the orange rind from the milk and add the gelatine and crushed saccharine.

Strain into a wetted ring mould and leave to set.

Turn out, fill the centre with fruit and decorate with orange slices and more cherries or grapes.

BLACKCURRANT WHIP

1 pound blackcurrants
1 pound cooking apples, peeled and sliced
¼ ounce gelatine
saccharine

Cook the blackcurrants in a little water and strain off the juice. Cook the apples with a very little water and when quite soft, sieve or mash to a purée. Measure the quantity—there should be about ½ pint.

Dissolve the gelatine in 2 tablespoons warm water, add to the fruit juice and sweeten to taste with saccharine. Add to the apple purée, mix in well and pour the mixture into a large basin.

When cool and just beginning to set, whisk thoroughly until the mixture is light and fluffy. Fold in the blackcurrants.

To serve, pile in tall individual glasses.

HONEYCOMB MOULD

2 eggs
½ pint milk
1 tablet saccharine
¼ ounce gelatine
1 tablespoon warm water
vanilla or other flavouring essence

Separate the eggs and make a custard with the yolks, milk and saccharine.

Dissolve the gelatine in the warm water and add to the custard with the flavouring.

Beat the egg whites until they stand in peaks, then fold lightly into the custard. Pour into a wetted mould and leave in a cool place to set.

Turn out and decorate as liked.

Serves 2.

OVEN MEALS

Oven meals can be our best time and labour savers on busy days. Usually the main dish, vegetables, bread and/or dessert can be cooked at the same time. If your cooker has an automatic clock, the food can even be placed in the oven several hours before cooking begins. Set the clock for the time you want your oven heat to turn on—and the food cooks quietly out of sight while you go about your other business.

Oven meals can also save a lot of dishwashing too, if the food is cooked in the casserole in which it will be served. Then you can sit down to dinner with a clean orderly kitchen. This helps to make cooking a pleasure.

Here's How to Plan an Oven Meal

The magic key to time-saving oven meals is to plan ahead and plan wisely.

The Main Dish: Plan this first. It might be a meat loaf, one-dish casserole, oven brown stew, baked pork chops, Swiss steak, or pot roast. What oven temperature does this dish take? Most meat, cheese, milk, and egg dishes require slow to moderate oven (325° to 350°F. Mark 3-4).

This temperature should be used for the rest of the meal and will determine what other foods to combine with the main dish. Then choose vegetables and dessert that can be cooked at the same temperature for about the same time.

You can still make the most of oven heat even if you select vegetables and dessert that require less time than the main dish. Put in the main dish, then with the aid of a minute timer, you slide each dish into the oven at its correct time.

Remember—if you have a roast or bread or other dishes which need to be browned, do not plan foods that make

steam—unless of course, you can brown the dessert or casserole dish at the end when the "steamy" foods are out of the oven.

Vegetables: Many vegetables can be cooked in the oven in a tightly covered pan. Place just enough water on the vegetables to form steam, usually not more than 2 to 4 tablespoons. Add seasonings and cover tightly.

If the oven meal is to cook for an hour, cut the vegetables into strips, thin slices, or small cubes. If the meal takes longer to cook, leave the vegetables in larger pieces or even whole.

Vegetables which may be cooked by this method are potatoes, carrots, parsnips, corn, turnips, onions, sauerkraut, beetroot, dried beans, and tomatoes. Peas, green beans, and asparagus may be cooked by this method. Frozen asparagus requires about 30 minutes and peas require 14 minutes at 350°F. Mark 4.

It is usually better to omit the green vegetables since they keep their colour and vitamins best if they are cooked on top of the cooker.

If your meal is to cook for a short time, give your potatoes a head start by placing them in boiling water for 15 minutes before putting them in the oven.

Desserts: Fruit puddings, fruit cobblers, custards, stewed dried fruits, whole baked apples or pears, gingerbread, and upside-down cakes bake well with oven meals. Cakes and pies usually do not brown well if there are a lot of "steaming" foods in the oven—unless they can be removed during the last 15 minutes of baking.

Breads: When the oven is in use, the wise homemaker usually likes to give her family a special treat with a hot bread. Yeast rolls and quick breads such as corn bread, muffins, coffee cakes, rolls, and nut breads can be baked with oven meals. They may need to be baked alone for the last 15 minutes in order to brown. These can be made from your own recipe or from a prepared mix.

If you want to cut preparation time still more, heat bakery rolls or French bread. Garlic bread or herb French bread are good with oven meals.

Make the Most of Oven Heat with these Oven Meal suggestions

FOR HOT OVEN (400°F. Mark 6) TIME: 25 TO 30 MINUTES

Main Dishes:
Meat or Chicken Pie (Leftover Meat —scone top)
Meat Scone Roll-ups
Baked Canned Luncheon Meat
Baked Canned Salmon or Tuna

Vegetables:
Scalloped Corn
Scalloped Onions
Scalloped Tomatoes

Breads:
Corn Bread
Muffins
Coffee Cake—quick or yeast
Plain Yeast Rolls

Desserts:
Baked Apples (precooked in syrup
5 minutes)
Apple Dumplings
Fruit Cobblers
Fruit Roll-ups
Shortcake

**FOR MODERATE OVEN
(350°F. Mark 4)
TIME: 45 TO 60 MINUTES**

Main Dishes:
Casseroles
Individual Meat Loaves
Mock Chicken Legs
Shepherd's Pie
Spanish Rice
Stuffed Peppers
Baked Fish

Vegetables:
Baked Potatoes (medium)
Baked Sweet Potatoes (medium)
Steamed Carrots (strips)
Stuffed Onions
Quick Baked Beans

Breads:
Sweet Rolls
Yeast Coffee Cakes

Desserts:
Baked Apples or Pears
Apple Dumplings
Brown Betty
Apple Crisp
Upside-Down Cake
Cottage Pudding
Gingerbread

**FOR MODERATE OVEN
(350°F. Mark 4)
TIME: 1 TO 1½ HOURS**

Main Dishes:
Meat Loaf
Pork Chops
Sausage Patties
Spareribs
Scalloped Potatoes and Ham
Ham Shanks
Meat Balls in Sauce
Ham Slice
Oven-Fried Chicken
Scalloped Chicken
Scalloped Oysters
Salmon or Cheese Soufflés
Macaroni and Cheese
Braised Lamb

Vegetables:
Baked Potatoes (large)
Baked Sweet Potatoes (large)
Scalloped Potatoes
Apple and Sweet Potato Scallop
Steamed Carrots (quarters, halves)

Breads:
Nut and Fruit Breads
Spoon Breads

Desserts:
Bread Pudding
Date Pudding
Dried Fruits (presoaked/covered
with water)
Baked Apples (large)

**45-MINUTE OVEN DINNER
FOR 6**

**Meat Loaf with Tomato Sauce
Baked Frozen Green Peas
Baked Marrow or Courgettes
Brown Betty**

Hints: Entire meal goes into moderate oven (375°F. Mark 5) at the same time, and is cooked for 45 minutes.

Frozen green peas are cooked in covered baking dish with 2 tablespoons butter or margarine, no water.

MEAT LOAF WITH TOMATO SAUCE

**3 slices bread, cubed
2 pounds minced beef
3 teaspoons salt
¼ teaspoon pepper
1 medium onion, grated
2 eggs, slightly beaten
4 fluid ounces milk
8 fluid ounces canned or fresh
    tomato sauce
½ teaspoon Worcestershire sauce
3 drops Tabasco sauce
1 teaspoon sugar**

Blend bread into minced beef mixed with 2 teaspoons salt and ¼ teaspoon pepper.

Reserve 2 tablespoons grated onion; add remainder to meat mixture with the eggs and milk.

Shape meat into loaf tin or on centre of lightly greased shallow baking tin.

Prepare sauce by mixing together tomato sauce, remaining grated onion, Worcestershire sauce, Tabasco sauce, 1 teaspoon salt and sugar.

Pour sauce over meat loaf and bake, uncovered, in moderate oven (375°F. Mark 5) about 45 minutes. Serves 6 to 8.

BAKED MARROW

Peel a medium-sized marrow lengthways; if the marrow is very young, the peel may be left on. Cut across into slices about 1½-2 inches thick and remove the seeds from each slice. Place the marrow rings in a greased baking dish, season and dot with butter. Cover with buttered greaseproof paper and then a lid. Cook in the coolest part of a moderate oven (375°F. Mark 5) for about 45 minutes, until tender.

To serve, fill the marrow rings with cooked green peas.

BAKED COURGETTES

Cut the bends off 2 pounds courgettes and blanch them by broiling them for 2 minutes. Drain them and cut into slices ½-¾ inch thick. Place them in a buttered ovenproof dish, sprinkle them with lemon juice, season and dot with butter. If wished, chopped fresh herbs may be added.

Cover the dish and cook in the coolest part of a moderate oven (375°F. Mark 5) for about 30 minutes.

If wished, combine the courgettes and peas before serving.

BROWN BETTY

**12 digestive biscuits (about 6
    ounces)
1½ ounces butter or margarine,
    melted
3 ounces brown sugar
4-5 large crisp eating apples or
    cooking apples, peeled,
    cored and sliced
1 tablespoon lemon juice
½ teaspoon finely grated lemon
    rind
2¾ fluid ounces water**

Place the biscuits between two sheets of greaseproof paper and crush them with a rolling pin to make fine crumbs. Mix the crumbs with the melted butter or margarine and the sugar.

Place one-third of the crumb mixture in a greased ovenproof dish (about 2-pint capacity). Place half the apple slices over the crumbs. If using cooking apples, sprinkle them with extra sugar according to taste. Sprinkle with half the lemon juice and grated rind. Add another layer of crumbs (one-third), then remaining apples, lemon juice and rind, and sugar if necessary.

Cover with the remaining crumbs and pour the water over. Cook in moderate oven (375°F. Mark 5) 45 minutes. Serves 6.

1-HOUR OVEN DINNER NO. 1 FOR 6

**Savoury Stuffed Pork Chops
Candied Tomato Sauce
Sweetcorn and Lima Beans
Apple Dumplings**

Hints: Set oven for moderate (350°F. Mark 4). Put all foods in the oven and cook for 1 hour.

SAVOURY STUFFED PORK CHOPS

9 ounces fresh white breadcrumbs
5 ounces finely chopped, cooked
    ham
¼ teaspoon salt
pinch of pepper
¼ teaspoon nutmeg
1 beef stock cube
2 fluid ounces boiling water
6 1-inch thick rib pork chops, cut
    with pockets
2 ounces plain flour
¾ teaspoon salt
pepper to taste
pinch of ground sage
pinch of thyme
4 fluid ounces water

To make stuffing, combine crumbs, ham, salt, pepper, and nutmeg. Dissolve stock cube in boiling water; pour over mixture and toss lightly.

Stuff pork chops and fasten with wooden cocktail sticks. Coat chops with mixture of flour, salt, pepper, sage, and thyme.

Brown chops in hot fat in a frying pan on top of cooker. Arrange in baking dish, add water; cover with aluminium foil. Cook on lower oven rack of moderate oven (350°F. Mark 4) 1 hour. Serves 6.

CANDIED TOMATO SAUCE

½ pint freshly made tomato purée, or
    canned tomato sauce
8 ounces sugar
2 tablespoons lemon juice

Combine tomato purée, sugar, and lemon juice in saucepan and cook for 5 minutes. Pour into a 1-pint greased casserole.

Cover and cook on lower oven rack in moderate oven (350°F. Mark 4) 1 hour. Serve over pork chops. Serves 6.

SWEETCORN AND LIMA BEANS

Partially break up 1 10-ounce packet of frozen sweetcorn and 1 12-ounce packet of frozen lima beans. Place in buttered 2-pint casserole; add 1 ounce butter or margarine, salt and pepper to taste, and 2 tablespoons single cream.

Cover and cook on top oven rack in moderate oven (350°F. Mark 4) 1 hour. Serves 6.

APPLE DUMPLINGS

1 pound sugar
8 fluid ounces water
2 ounces butter or margarine
6 apples
1 tablespoon lemon juice
¼ teaspoon nutmeg
¼ teaspoon cinnamon
8 ounces plain flour
1 teaspoon salt
1 tablespoon baking powder
6 ounces lard, margarine or butter
4 fluid ounces milk

Make a syrup with 8 ounces sugar and the water. Add butter or margarine; set aside.

Peel, core, and slice apples. Sprinkle with lemon juice, 8 ounces sugar, nutmeg, and cinnamon.

Sift flour with salt and baking powder into bowl; cut in the 6 ounces fat. Add milk; stir until moistened. Roll out in a sheet about 18 by 12 inches. Cut into 6 6-inch squares.

Put mound of apples on each square of pastry. Moisten edges of squares with water; bring four corners up over apples; pinch sides together.

Place in individual greased baking dishes; pour syrup around dumplings. Bake on upper rack in moderate oven (350°F. Mark 4) 1 hour. Serves 6.

1-HOUR OVEN DINNER NO. 2 FOR 6

**Spicy Topside
Oven-Browned Potatoes
Green Bean Casserole
Lemon-Coconut Pudding**

Hints: Put all foods in the oven and cook for 1 hour at moderate heat (350°F. Mark 4).

SPICY TOPSIDE

1 ounce plain flour
1 teaspoon salt
¼ teaspoon pepper
2 pounds topside, ½-inch thick
1½ ounces fat
8 fluid ounces tomato ketchup
4 fluid ounces water
1 medium onion, thinly sliced
1 lemon, thinly sliced
1 green pepper, sliced
5 whole cloves

Combine flour, salt, and pepper; pound into steak.

Melt fat in a frying pan and brown steak. Place in baking dish.

Blend ketchup and water; pour around steak. Add onion, lemon, green pepper, and cloves.

Cover with aluminium foil; place on lower oven rack. Cook in moderate oven (350°F. Mark 4) 1 hour. Serves 6.

OVEN-BROWNED POTATOES

Peel 12 small potatoes and dip in melted fat. Cook uncovered in shallow baking tin on top rack in moderate oven (350°F. Mark 4). Serves 6.

GREEN BEAN CASSEROLE

Partially thaw 1¼ pounds packet frozen French beans. Arrange in alternate layers with condensed mushroom soup (1 10¾-ounce can) in buttered 2-pint baking dish.

Sprinkle top with 2 tablespoons grated Parmesan or Cheddar cheese and 2 tablespoons toasted breadcrumbs.

Cover; place on lower oven rack in moderate oven (350°F. Mark 4). Serves 6.

LEMON COCONUT PUDDING

1 ounce butter or margarine
8 ounces sugar
4 eggs, separated
2¾ fluid ounces lemon juice
1 tablespoon finely grated lemon
    rind
¼ teaspoon salt
5 ounces desiccated coconut
2 tablespoons plain flour
8 fluid ounces milk
2 tablespoons redcurrant jelly

Cream butter or margarine, adding sugar gradually. Add egg yolks to butter-sugar mixture and beat well.

Add lemon juice, grated lemon rind, and salt; blend thoroughly.

Fold in 3 ounces of the coconut and the flour. Stir in milk.

Beat egg whites until stiff but not dry. Fold into lemon mixture.

Pour into 2-pint baking dish. Set in a baking tin containing ½-inch hot water. Bake on upper oven rack in moderate oven (350°F. Mark 4) 1 hour.

Before serving, toast rest of coconut in oven; use as decoration with jelly. Serves 6.

1¼-HOUR OVEN DINNER FOR 4

**Savoury Pork Chops
Crusty Baked Potatoes
Creamy Carrots and Onions
Baked Apples Connecticut**

Hints: Set oven for moderate (350°F. Mark 4). Put all the foods in the oven and bake for 1¼ hours. Scrub the potatoes before baking on oven rack.

SAVOURY PORK CHOPS
4 pork chops, ¾-inch thick
1 teaspoon salt
¼ teaspoon pepper
¼ teaspoon sage

Arrange chops in single layer in roasting tin.
Sprinkle with salt, pepper, and sage. Bake in moderate oven (350°F. Mark 4) 1¼ hours. Serves 4.

CREAMY CARROTS AND ONIONS
½ pound carrots, sliced
1 bunch chopped spring onions
½ teaspoon salt
½ teaspoon sugar
2 fluid ounces water
8 fluid ounces single cream

Place all ingredients except cream in a baking dish. Cover. Cook, covered, in moderate oven (350°F. Mark 4) 1¼ hours.
To serve, heat cream and pour over baked carrots and onions. Serves 4.

BAKED APPLES CONNECTICUT
4 cooking apples, cored
lemon juice
6 ounces sugar
¼ teaspoon nutmeg
1 ounce butter or margarine
2 fluid ounces water

Dip cut ends of apples in lemon juice, place in baking dish.
Combine sugar and nutmeg, fill centres of apples with sugar mixture. Dot apple tops with butter.
Pour water into bottom of baking dish. Cover. Bake in moderate oven (350°F. Mark 4) 1¼ hours. Serves 4.

1-HOUR OVEN DINNER 1 FOR 4

Honeyed-Orange Ham Slice
French Beans Amandine
Cherry Crumb Dessert

Hints: Put all foods in the oven and cook for 1 hour at slow heat (325°F. Mark 3).

1-Hour Oven Dinner 1 for 4

HONEYED-ORANGE HAM SLICE
1 pound ham slice, 1-inch thick
6 ounces honey
1 tablespoon grated orange rind

Place ham in shallow baking tin. Combine honey and orange rind; spread over ham.
Bake in slow oven (325°F. Mark 3) 1 hour. Serves 4.

FRENCH BEANS AMANDINE
Place 1 packet frozen French beans, 2 fluid ounces boiling water, 1 ounce butter or margarine, and 1 ounce slivered blanched almonds in greased baking dish. Cover.
Bake in slow oven (325°F. Mark 3) 1 hour. Serves 4.

CHERRY CRUMB DESSERT
20 ounces canned cherries
¼ teaspoon almond extract
2 ounces flour, sifted
3 ounces brown sugar
½ teaspoon allspice
¼ teaspoon nutmeg
2 ounces butter or margarine

Combine cherries and almond extract. Turn into 8×8-inch baking dish.
Rub butter into flour and stir in sugar and spices; sprinkle over cherries.
Bake in slow oven (325°F. Mark 3) 1 hour. Serves 4.

1-HOUR OVEN DINNER 2 FOR 4

Veal Chops Hungarian
Continental Green Beans
Sweet Potato and Apple Bake
Fruit and Bread Scallop

Hints: Put veal and green beans on lower rack and sweet potatoes and fruit scallop on upper rack of oven. Set oven control at moderate (375°F. Mark 5) and bake for 1 hour.

VEAL CHOPS HUNGARIAN 2
1 ounce flour
⅛ teaspoon salt
pinch of pepper
4 veal chops
2 tablespoons fat
½ pint soured cream

Mix flour, salt, and pepper; coat chops with seasoned flour.
Brown chops on all sides in hot fat, then arrange in greased 3½-pint casserole.
Pour over soured cream. Cover tightly and bake in moderate oven (375°F. Mark 5) for 1 hour. Serves 4.

CONTINENTAL GREEN BEANS
1 small onion, chopped
3 ounces diced bacon
2 tablespoons flour
1 pound cooked or canned tomatoes
1 pound cooked or canned green beans
½ teaspoon salt
¼ teaspoon pepper
¼ teaspoon paprika
1 bay leaf
3 ounces coarse digestive biscuit crumbs
1 ounce butter or margarine, melted

Brown onion with bacon in a large saucepan, then blend in flour.
Add tomatoes, green beans, salt, pepper, paprika, and bay leaf. Mix together, then turn into greased 2-pint baking dish.
Combine cracker crumbs with melted butter. Sprinkle over top.
Bake in moderate oven (375°F. Mark 5) 1 hour. Serves 4 to 6.

SWEET POTATO-APPLE BAKE
1 28-ounce can sweet potatoes
1 ounce butter or margarine
2 tablespoons cream
1 teaspoon salt
pinch of pepper
2 firm cooking apples
8 marshmallows

Heat sweet potatoes and mash, blending in butter, cream, salt, and pepper.
Spread mashed sweet potatoes in 8-inch square baking dish.
Wash and core apples; cut in half but do not peel.
Arrange apples on sweet potato layer. Decorate top with marshmallows.
Bake in moderate oven (375°F. Mark 5) 1 hour. Serves 4.

FRUIT AND BREAD SCALLOP
2 ounces butter or margarine
9 ounces fresh white breadcrumbs
6 ounces brown sugar
½ teaspoon cinnamon
¼ teaspoon nutmeg
1 pound rhubarb, cut in 1-inch pieces
9 ounces apple purée or canned apple sauce
2 firm bananas, sliced
1 tablespoon lemon juice
3 tablespoons golden syrup

Melt butter and brown the crumbs in it. Mix the sugar, cinnamon, and nutmeg.
Use a large greased loaf tin; arrange alternate layers of breadcrumbs, sugar mixture, rhubarb, apple sauce, and bananas, starting and ending with breadcrumbs.
Sprinkle the top with a mixture of lemon juice and syrup.
Bake in moderate oven (375°F. Mark 5) for 1 hour. Serves 4 to 6.

1-HOUR OVEN DINNER 3 FOR 6

Ham Loaf and Gravy
Baked Frozen Sweetcorn
Baked Potatoes
Cherry Crumb Pie

Hints: Set oven control for hot oven (400°F. Mark 6) and preheat oven. Toward the back of lower rack place the ham loaf and frozen sweetcorn, and in front of these 6 medium-sized potatoes.

The two pies go on the front section of the upper rack. They may be put in at the start of the oven meal baking period or after 20 minutes, since they require 20 minutes less baking time.

When the meal is done, turn the oven off. Invert the ham loaf on an ovenproof dish and return to the warm oven.

Cut a cross on the top side of the potatoes and gently press the potatoes to soften and to push some of the potato up through the opening. After putting one tablespoon of butter or margarine on top of each potato, place them in a 12¼×8×2-inch baking dish and place them back in the oven.

Make gravy and serve the meal hot from the oven.

HAM LOAF AND GRAVY

3 ounces brown sugar
about 9 ounces canned sliced pineapple
6 whole maraschino cherries, drained
1 pound ham, minced
½ pound fresh pork, minced
3 ounces fresh white breadcrumbs
1 egg, unbeaten
8 fluid ounces milk
1 small onion, finely chopped
1 stick celery, finely chopped
½ teaspoon salt
¼ teaspoon pepper
juice from pineapple, meat liquid, and water to make 8 fluid ounces
⅛ teaspoon bottled brown sauce
8 fluid ounces water
3 tablespoons flour

Spread brown sugar in bottom of greased 9½×5¼×2¾-inch loaf tin.

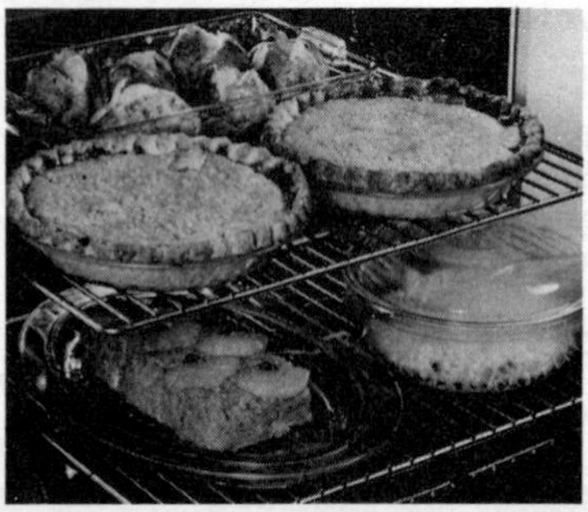

Remove and drain 2 slices of pineapple, reserving remainder for making gravy. Cut each pineapple slice in 3 pieces. Arrange pineapple and cherries on brown sugar so that some of each can be served with each portion of meat.

Mix ham, pork, breadcrumbs, egg, milk, onion, celery, salt, and pepper. Pack meat mixture firmly in loaf tin over pineapple and cherries.

Bake in hot oven (400°F. Mark 6) for 1 hour. Remove from oven; pour juice from pan and reserve for gravy.

Invert meat loaf onto overproof serving dish and keep warm in oven while making gravy.

Put pineapple juice, meat liquid, brown sauce, water, and remainder of pineapple, diced, in a 2-pint saucepan.

Shake water and flour vigorously in covered jar until thoroughly blended. Add to liquid in saucepan.

Bring to boil on a high heat, stirring constantly. Switch to a low heat and boil 1 minute. Serves 6.

BAKED FROZEN CORN

1 pound frozen sweetcorn
2 fluid ounces water
½ teaspoon salt
1 ounce butter or margarine

Place sweetcorn, water, salt, butter in a 3½-pint casserole. Cover.

Bake in hot oven (400°F. Mark 6) for 1 hour. Serves 6.

CHERRY CRUMB PIES

1 recipe pastry for two-crust pie
about 2½ pounds canned cherries, drained
16 fluid ounces cherry juice and water
1 pound sugar
4 tablespoons quick-cooking tapioca
1½ teaspoons salt
½ teaspoon almond extract
½ ounce butter or margarine, melted
4 drops red food colouring
6 ounces sifted flour
4 ounces butter or margarine

Line two 9-inch pie plates with pastry, making high fluted edges.

Combine cherries, juice and water, 12 ounces sugar, tapioca, ½ teaspoon salt, almond extract, butter or margarine, and food colouring. Divide evenly into the two pie shells.

Combine flour, 1 teaspoon salt, and 4 ounces sugar in small mixing bowl. Cut in butter or margarine with pastry blender or knife until mixture resembles fine breadcrumbs. Sprinkle one half of crumb mixture evenly over each pie.

Bake in hot oven (400°F. Mark 6) for 40 to 50 minutes. Makes 6 to 8 servings for each pie.

Make the Most of Oven Heat

Ready to serve hot from the oven is this meal of ham loaf, baked potatoes, and baked frozen sweetcorn with two cherry crumb pies baked at the same time—the extra pie to freeze for future use.

1½-HOUR OVEN DINNER FOR 6

Chicken Casserole
Tomato Rice
Cherry Scallop

Hints: Preheat moderate oven (350° F. Mark 4). Place chicken casserole and tomato rice on lower rack, cherry scallop on upper rack. Cook for 1½ hours. Serve with a bowl of pre-crisped green salad.

BAKED CHICKEN

4 pounds jointed chicken
milk, flour, salt, and pepper
4 ounces fat
½ pound fresh mushrooms
1 tablespoon finely chopped onion
16 fluid ounces creamy milk, heated

Dip pieces of chicken in milk, then in seasoned flour. Fry in fat until nicely browned. Place in casserole.

Fry mushrooms and onion in pan about 2 or 3 minutes. Sprinkle over chicken. Pour hot milk over all.

Cook on the lower rack of moderate oven (350°F. Mark 4) for 1½ hours. Serves 6.

TOMATO RICE

2 pounds canned tomatoes, strained
8 fluid ounces water
1½ teaspoons salt
1 tablespoon sugar
1 ounce butter or margarine
12 ounces uncooked rice, washed

Combine first five ingredients and boil for five minutes.

Place washed rice in buttered casserole. Pour tomato mixture over rice. Cover.

Cook on lower rack of moderate oven (350°F. Mark 4) for 1½ hours. Serves 6.

CHERRY SCALLOP

6 slices bread
2 15-ounce cans cherries
8 ounces sugar
½ teaspoon nutmeg
2 ounces butter or margarine

Toast bread lightly and cut in cubes.

Place alternate layers of bread, cherries, sugar and nutmeg in buttered casserole.

Pour cherry juice over top layer. Dot with butter. Cover.

Bake on upper rack of moderate oven (350°F. Mark 4) 1½ hours. Serves 6.

1-Hour Oven Dinner 3 for 4

1-HOUR OVEN DINNER 3 FOR 4

Ham Slice with Crushed Pineapple
Baked Sweet Potatoes
French Style Green Beans
Date-Nut Pudding with
Whipped Cream

Hints: On the lower rack, place sweet potatoes and ham slice. On upper rack, put metal casserole with string beans, place custard cups in baking tin and pour warm water around them to depth of one inch. Set your oven at moderate (350°F. Mark 4) for 1 hour.

Either whip the cream while waiting for coffee, or do it early, and place in the refrigerator until you need it for dessert.

HAM SLICE WITH CRUSHED PINEAPPLE

2 pound, 1-inch thick ham slice
8 whole cloves
2 tablespoons brown sugar
8 ounces crushed pineapple with juice
1 tablespoon cherry juice
1 ounce frozen, canned, or maraschino cherries

Place ham slice in greased 5 × 8-inch baking dish; press cloves into fat, which you have slit to prevent curling.

Cover ham with brown sugar and crushed pineapple, the fruit juices, and use the cherries for decoration.

Cook on lower rack of moderate oven (350°F. Mark 4) for 1 hour. Serves 4.

FRENCH STYLE GREEN BEANS

1 packet frozen French cut green beans
1 ounce butter or margarine
4 fluid ounces water

Place ingredients in saucepan, cover tightly. Cook on upper rack of moderate oven (350°F. Mark 4) for 1 hour. Serves 4.

DATE-NUT PUDDING

3 eggs
8 ounces sugar
½ teaspoon vanilla
1 ounce flour
¼ teaspoon salt
1 teaspoon baking powder
½ teaspoon nutmeg
7 ounces chopped dates
4 ounces chopped nuts
8 fluid ounces double cream, whipped

Beat the eggs, gradually add sugar and vanilla.

Sift flour, salt, baking powder and nutmeg together and stir into egg mixture.

Fold in dates and nuts. Blend well and pour batter into 4 greased ovenproof dishes.

Place the dishes in a baking tin and pour warm water round them to a depth of 1 inch. Cook on upper rack of moderate oven (350°F. Mark 4) 1 hour.

When cooked, unmould and cover with whipped cream. Serves 4.

35-MINUTE OVEN DINNER FOR 4

Salmon Casserole
Buttered Broccoli
Potatoes Au Gratin
Apricot Cobbler

Hints: Preheat moderate oven (375° F. Mark 5). Put broccoli and potatoes on lower shelf. Place salmon casserole and apricot cobbler on upper shelf. Bake for 35 minutes.

SALMON CASSEROLE

2 teaspoons finely chopped onion
2 ounces butter or margarine
4½ ounces fresh white breadcrumbs
1 1-pound can salmon
milk
1 beaten egg
1 tablespoon chopped parsley
¼ teaspoon grated lemon rind
1 teaspoon lemon juice
½ teaspoon salt
pinch of pepper

Lightly brown onion in melted butter. Add crumbs and toss to mix the butter with crumbs. Then brown the crumbs slightly.

Drain liquid from salmon and add milk to make ½ pint liquid. Remove bones and skin, then flake salmon.

Combine all ingredients; mix well and turn into greased 2-pint casserole.

Bake in moderate oven (375°F. Mark 5) 35 minutes. Serves 4.

BUTTERED FROZEN BROCCOLI

1 packet frozen broccoli
4 fluid ounces water
¼ teaspoon salt
1 ounce butter or margarine, melted

Place broccoli, water, and salt in oven dish. Cover tightly. Cook in oven with dinner. To serve, drain and season with melted butter. Serves 4.

POTATOES AU GRATIN

2 ounces butter or margarine
1 ounce flour
½ teaspoon salt
pinch of pepper
¼ teaspoon dry mustard
16 fluid ounces milk
1½ tablespoons prepared horseradish
1½ pounds potatoes, cooked and diced
2 ounces grated Cheddar cheese

Melt butter in a saucepan; blend in flour, salt, pepper, and mustard until smooth.

Gradually add milk, stirring constantly. Cook until thickened, then add horseradish.

Mix sauce with diced cooked potatoes.

Turn into greased 2-pint baking dish.

Sprinkle cheese over the top.

Bake in moderate oven (375°F. Mark 5) for 35 minutes. Serves 4.

APRICOT COBBLER

6 ounces dried apricots, soaked overnight in ½ pint water
6 fluid ounces hot apricot juice
2 ounces butter or margarine, melted
1 teaspoon grated orange rind
5 tablespoons granulated sugar
3 ounces brown sugar
1 packet scone mix
1 ounce lard or margarine
5 fluid ounces milk
1 well-beaten egg

Cook apricots in the water in which they are soaked. Drain them and place in greased 9-inch square baking dish.

Combine the hot apricot juice with butter, orange rind, 3 tablespoons granulated sugar, and 3 ounces brown sugar; carefully pour over apricots.

With a pastry blender, or knife, cut fat into scone mix.

Blend in 2 tablespoons granulated sugar, milk, and well-beaten egg.

Spoon dough onto hot apricot mixture.

Bake in moderate oven (375°F. Mark 5) 35 minutes. Serves 4.

PANCAKES AND WAFFLES

With crisp bacon or tasty sausages, pancakes and waffles are hearty enough for lunch. Waffles are a welcome dessert after a simple main course.

A pancake is a thin, fried cake, made with a special batter. Pancakes may have sweet or savoury fillings, and the basic batter can be adapted in many ways for different types of pancake.

Whether they are called pancakes, griddlecakes, hotcakes, flapjacks, wheatcakes, or flannel cakes, they are among the most popular foods—and in one form or another are included in the cookery of all nations.

PANCAKES
(Basic Recipe)

1 or 2 eggs, well beaten
about 12 fluid ounces milk
2 tablespoons melted fat
8 ounces sifted flour
3 teaspoons baking powder
½ teaspoon salt
1 tablespoon sugar

Mix together the egg, milk, fat. Add to sifted dry ingredients. Beat only until smooth. Pour the batter, a spoonful at a time, into a shallow, greased heavy frying pan. The batter should just cover the bottom of the pan.

Cook until the pancake is brown underneath—a few minutes. Free the edge of the pancake with a palette knife and toss or turn over and brown the other side. Slide the pancake onto a plate. Makes about 15 medium-sized pancakes.

Variations of Pancakes

Apple Pancakes: Add 4 ounces finely chopped tart apple to batter.

Banana Pancakes: Add 1 thinly sliced banana to batter.

Blueberry Pancakes: Add 4 ounces fresh, or drained canned blueberries to batter.

Buckwheat Pancakes: Substitute 4 ounces buckwheat for 4 ounces white flour.

Cherry or Peach Pancakes: Add to batter 6 ounces drained, chopped cherries or peaches, fresh or canned. Serve hot with butter and a syrup of sugar and cherry juice or sugar and peach juice.

Chocolate Pancakes: Increase sugar to 4-5 tablespoons. Add 1 ounce melted, unsweetened chocolate to liquid ingredients. Serve as dessert with sweetened, flavoured whipped cream.

Maize Flour Pancakes: Substitute 3 ounces maize meal for 3 ounces white flour and 1 tablespoon black treacle for 1 tablespoon sugar.

Meat Pancakes: Add 4 ounces any chopped cooked meat to batter.

Nut Pancakes: Add 1 ounce chopped pecans or walnuts to dry ingredients.

Pancake Sandwich: Place a thin slice of cooked ham or sausage over first pancake, cover with batter, brown and turn.

Pineapple Pancakes: Add 8 ounces drained, crushed pineapple to batter.

Rice Pancakes: Substitute 6 ounces cooked rice for 4 ounces flour. Reduce milk to 8 fluid ounces. Add rice to egg-milk mixture.

Sour Milk Pancakes: Substitute scant 16 fluid ounces sour milk or buttermilk for milk. Use only 2 teaspoons baking powder and add 1 teaspoon bicarbonate of soda.

Soy Pancakes: Substitute 1½ ounces soy flour for 1½ ounces white flour.

Wholewheat Pancakes: Substitute 4 ounces wholewheat flour for 4 ounces white flour.

PANCAKE MAKING HINTS

Prepare pancake batter by one of the following recipes. Stir the batter only until blended. Do not over-mix. The stiffer the batter, the less mixing is required.

To Cook Pancakes on a Griddle

Heat a heavy griddle and grease it with a bit of bacon. If 2 or more tablespoons fat are used for every 8 fluid ounces liquid, griddle need not be greased.

Test griddle by letting a few drops of cold water fall on it. If the water bounces and splutters ("dances on surface") the griddle is ready.

Pour a good spoonful of the batter from spoon onto the hot griddle. To get a round cake pour it from the tip of the spoon. Cook until bubbles appear on the surface and begin to burst, then lift the pancake with a spatula or palette knife to see if it is well browned underneath before turning. Usually 2 to 3 minutes is sufficient baking before turning. Turn only once.

The batter may be thinned or thickened as you like. After making a small test pancake, thin with a tablespoon milk or thicken with a tablespoon flour.

Pancakes should be served as soon as possible. If they cannot be served at once, stack them on top of each other, with a layer of grease-proof paper in between, and wrap them in a clean tea towel. To reheat, place pancakes, overlapping, on a greased baking sheet, brush with a little melted butter, and heat in a hot oven (400°F Mark 6) for about 7 to 8 minutes.

Egg Roll

EGG ROLL

Egg roll is a Chinese dish; a very thin pancake (called egg roll skins) made of a batter of flour, cornflour, eggs, water, and salt and filled with various mixtures; among the possible ingredients are finely chopped or grated raw carrot, celery, spring onion, water chestnut, cooked pork, and cooked prawns. The completed egg rolls are fried in deep fat and are usually served with an apricot sauce and a mustard sauce.

Filling:
about 10 ounces finely chopped
    cooked pork
about 7 ounces finely chopped
    cooked prawns or lobster
8 ounces finely chopped celery
6-8 finely chopped spring onions
8 ounces finely chopped water
    chestnuts
1 tablespoon Aromat
1 tablespoon soy sauce
2 teaspoons sugar
1 teaspoon salt
1 small egg
2 ounces melted fat

Egg Roll Skins:
  about 5¼ ounces sifted flour
  3 ounces cornflour
  ½ teaspoon salt
  2 unbeaten eggs
  12 fluid ounces water

For filling, mix first 5 ingredients in a large bowl. Blend in next 6 ingredients and mix thoroughly; refrigerate.

Next make egg-roll skins. Sift together flour, cornflour, and salt.

Blend together with a fork the eggs and 4 fluid ounces water. Add gradually to dry ingredients, blending thoroughly with spoon or rotary beater. Gradually add remaining water and beat until smooth.

Reserve about 2¼ fluid ounces batter for sealing edges of egg rolls.

Brush a heavy 7-inch frying pan lightly with fat; place over medium heat.

Holding it at a slight angle, pour about 2 tablespoons batter into the pan. Tip quickly in all directions to make a thin pancake.

Cook until mixture looks dry and begins to curl around edges. Remove from heat.

Repeat with remaining batter, stacking egg rolls until all are fried.

Place about 4 ounces filling in centre of each egg roll, then fold 2 sides over filling.

Brush edges with reserved batter. Beginning at one open end, roll up egg roll, pressing edges *gently* to seal.

Fry immediately or store in refrigerator several hours before frying.

Fry in deep, hot fat (360°F.) until crisp and golden brown, about 5 to 8 minutes; turn only once. Serve hot with apricot sauce, hot mustard sauce or both. Makes 24 egg rolls.

For Apricot Sauce: Mix together 1 pound apricot jam, ¾ ounce finely chopped pimiento, and 2 tablespoons vinegar in saucepan. Bring to the boil and simmer for 2 minutes, stirring occasionally. Cool.

For Hot Mustard Sauce: Blend together dry mustard and water to form a paste.

JIFFY ORANGE PANCAKES

1 beaten egg
8 fluid ounces single cream
1 6-ounce can frozen concentrated
    orange juice
1 packet pancake mix
orange syrup (below)

Mix together the egg, cream, and 4 tablespoons of the concentrated orange juice (reserve remainder). Add 8 ounces pancake mix, stirring to remove most of lumps.

Bake in hot greased pan, turning once. Serve with warm orange syrup. Makes about 18 pancakes.

Orange Syrup: Mix together 4 ounces butter or margarine, 8 ounces sugar, and reserved concentrated orange juice. Bring just to the boil, stirring occasionally. Makes about 12 fluid ounces.

SWEDISH PANCAKES

8 ounces sifted flour.
½ teaspoon salt
1 tablespoon sugar
3 eggs
16 fluid ounces milk

Mix and sift flour, salt, and sugar. Beat eggs well and mix with milk. Gradually add flour mixture, beating until smooth.

Use a special Swedish griddle containing several small moulds or fry quickly in a greased, heavy, hot frying pan, making one large pancake at a time.

Spread with jam. Roll large pancakes and dust with caster sugar. Stack small pancakes. Reheat and serve. Makes 14 to 16 large pancakes or 24 to 30 small pancakes.

LATKES OR GRATED POTATO PANCAKES

Latke is a Jewish term for pancakes, especially those made of grated raw potatoes as in the following recipe. The Jewish term kugel is applied to a potato pie made of similar ingredients. They are traditional Jewish dishes.

6 medium raw potatoes
1 small onion
2 slightly beaten eggs
3 tablespoons flour
pinch of pepper
1 teaspoon salt
½ teaspoon baking powder
    (optional)

Peel and grate raw potatoes and onion. Leave for 10 minutes so that liquid runs from them.

Remove liquid. Stir in eggs. Add other ingredients and blend together.

Drop the batter, a spoonful at a time, into a hot well-greased heavy frying pan. Brown pancake on both sides over moderate heat. Drain on absorbent paper.

Serve hot with apple sauce, sugar, or sour cream. Serves 6.

Potato Pancake Variations

Potato Cakes with Meat: Add about 3 ounces diced, cooked meat. Substitute fine dry breadcrumbs for flour. Fry as above.

Potato Cupcakes: Bake potato pancake mixture in well-greased custard cups in moderate oven (350°F. Mark 4) until brown, about 40 minutes. Serve hot.

Potato Pie (Kugel): Prepare potato pancake mixture and bake in a shallow greased casserole in a moderate oven (350°F. Mark 4) until brown, about 40 minutes. Serve hot.

SWISS-APPLE CINNAMON PANCAKE

4 ounces sifted flour
½ teaspoon baking powder
pinch of salt
2 beaten eggs
4 fluid ounces milk
1 teaspoon melted butter
3 large apples
sugar and cinnamon

Mix and sift flour, baking powder, and salt. Mix with eggs, milk, and melted butter. Beat until batter is smooth.

Peel and slice apples. Sauté in a little butter in 9- or 10-inch frying pan until apples are turning soft. Sprinkle lightly with cinnamon and sugar.

Pour batter over apples, smoothing it to edges of pan. Bake in hot oven (400°F. Mark 6) until golden brown. Serve very hot, sprinkled liberally with sugar and cinnamon. Serves 4.

BLINTZES

Blintzes is a Jewish term for a dish of very thin pancakes filled with a cottage cheese mixture or sometimes with berries or other fruit, rolled up, then browned in butter or baked. Blintzes are usually served with sour cream.

Batter:

4 ounces sifted flour
1 teaspoon salt
4 eggs, well beaten
8 fluid ounces milk, or water

Cheese Filling:

1½ pounds dry cottage cheese
1 or 2 egg yolks, beaten
1 tablespoon melted butter
salt
sugar and cinnamon to taste

Pancakes: Sift flour and salt. Mix eggs with liquid. Stir in flour. Mix until smooth to form thin batter.

Pour into a hot lightly greased 6-inch frying pan enough batter to form a very thin pancake, tilting the pan from side to side so that batter spreads evenly.

Cook over a low heat on one side only until the top of cake is dry and blistered. Turn out on clean tea towel, cooked side up. Allow to cool. Repeat until all batter is used.

Filling: Mix cheese with egg yolks and butter and with salt, sugar, and cinnamon to taste. Place a tablespoon of mixture in centre of each pancake. Fold edges over to form envelope.

Blintzes may be prepared and filled in advance and kept in refrigerator until ready to fry. Just before serving, fry in butter until brown on both sides, or bake in a moderate oven (350°F. Mark 4).

Serve hot with sour cream, or with sugar and cinnamon mixture. Makes about 10 blintzes.

Variations of Blintzes:

Apple Blintzes: Mix 8 ounces peeled and cored chopped apples, 1½ table-spoons ground almonds, 1 egg white, caster sugar, and cinnamon to taste. Proceed as for cheese blintzes. Serve with sugar and cinnamon mixture.

Blintzes may be made very small, filled with a fruit filling such as cherries, and served as a dessert with a light main course.

Cherry Blintzes: Mix 6 ounces drained, stoned canned cherries, small pinch of cinnamon, 1 tablespoon flour, and sugar to taste. Proceed as for cheese blintzes. Serve with sour cream or with cinnamon and sugar.

Blueberry Blintzes: Substitute blueberries for cherries and proceed as instructed above.

CRÊPES SUZETTE

Crêpes Suzette is a French term for very thin pancakes (crêpes) rolled up and served with a flaming brandy sauce. This is an ideal recipe for making in a chafing dish.

Batter:

3 ounces sifted flour
2 teaspoons sugar
½ teaspoon salt
6 fluid ounces milk
3 eggs, slightly beaten

Sauce:

4 ounces unsalted butter
4 ounces caster sugar
1 orange, juice and grated rind
4 tablespoons Curaçao or brandy

Mix flour, sugar, and salt. Add milk alternately with eggs. Beat until smooth.

Grease bottom of a heavy frying pan when very hot. Cover bottom of pan with thin layer of batter and quickly tilt pan so that the pancake is evenly paper-thin. Brown on both sides.

Successful making of crêpes depends upon the thinness of the batter. If made ahead of time, pancakes may be reheated in oven. Roll each one and serve with following sauce.

Crêpe Suzette Sauce: Cream butter (do not melt). Add caster sugar, grated rind and juice of orange, and Curaçao or brandy.

Arrange pancakes in a row on a hot dish. Pour over some of the sauce, sprinkle with Curaçao or brandy, and flame just before serving. Makes 10 to 12 5-inch pancakes.

FRENCH PANCAKES WITH PINEAPPLE

Prepare batter as for Crêpes Suzette. Drain canned pineapple rings; slice each piece into 3 parts to make 3 very thin rings, and dry the rings on a towel.

Heat and butter a very small frying pan, the bottom of which is only slightly larger than the pineapple rings.

Pour in a little batter to cover the bottom and when it is set and brown on the underside, place a ring of pineapple on it.

Pour another very thin layer of batter over it, turn and brown the pancake on the other side.

Place the pancakes on a hot serving dish and sprinkle with icing sugar.

Crêpes Suzette: Special pans are often used by restaurants specializing in these famous pancakes; however you can make them at the table in a chafing dish or electric frying pan. Otherwise, make them in advance in the kitchen, put them on a warmed serving dish and pour sauce over them. At serving time, sprinkle with warmed brandy and light with a match.

FRENCH PANCAKES WITH KIRSCH

Prepare batter as for Crêpes Suzette and make small pancakes about 5 to 6 inches in diameter.

Spread them with a little butter that has been creamed with sugar and flavoured with a little kirsch.

Roll the pancakes and place them in a shallow baking dish. Sprinkle with granulated sugar and glaze them very quickly under the grill.

NORWEGIAN PANCAKES

Use same batter and fry as for Crêpes Suzette, but do not roll the pancakes. Pile several flat pancakes on serving plate.

Spread jelly or butter and maple sugar between them and over the top. Serve hot, cut in pie-shaped wedges.

OATMEAL PANCAKES

6 ounces quick-cooking oats, uncooked
1¼ ounces sifted plain flour
2½ teaspoons baking powder
1 teaspoon salt
2 eggs, separated
2¼ ounces melted fat

Heat milk and pour over oats. Allow to cool. Sift together flour, baking powder, and salt. Beat egg yolks and add to oat mixture. Add melted fat and stir in dry ingredients. Fold in stiffly beaten egg whites.

Drop batter, a spoonful at a time, into a hot greased heavy frying pan. When surface is covered with bubbles, turn and brown on other side. Oatmeal pancakes take longer to brown than plain pancakes. They can also be cooked on a griddle.

Apple oatmeal Pancakes: Add ¼ teaspoon ground cinnamon, 2 tablespoons brown sugar, and 4 ounces finely chopped, peeled apples to batter before adding egg whites. Cook as for oatmeal pancakes.

SWEDISH DESSERT PANCAKES (Plättar)

    3 eggs
    ½ teaspoon salt
    2 ounces sugar
    4 ounces sifted plain flour
    16 fluid ounces milk
    1 teaspoon vanilla essence
    3 tablespoons melted butter or
       margarine

Beat eggs well with hand beater; gradually add salt, sugar, flour, milk, and vanilla essence, beating well after each addition. Stir in butter.

Grease frying pan lightly. Make little thin pancakes. Spread each pancake with filling of your choice: whipped cream, lingonberries, preserves, apple sauce, cottage cheese, or sour cream.

Stack in groups of six; or roll up each pancake. Or, as each pancake comes from pan, roll it up; sprinkle lightly with sugar; served with whipped cream, lingonberries, etc. Serves 4 to 6.

BUTTERMILK GRIDDLECAKES

    3 well beaten egg yolks
    ½ pint buttermilk or sour milk
    2 ounces melted butter
    6 ounces sifted plain flour
    ½ teaspoon salt
    1 teaspoon baking powder
    1 teaspoon bicarbonate of soda
    1 teaspoon sugar
    3 egg whites, stiffly beaten

Mix egg yolks, buttermilk or sour milk, and melted butter. Stir in sifted dry ingredients and beat until smooth. Fold in egg whites. Pour batter onto hot, lightly greased griddle.

Cook on one side until bubbles appear on surface, then turn and cook on other side until lightly browned. Makes about 24 small griddlecakes.

COTTAGE CHEESE PANCAKES

    2 eggs
    4 ounces sieved cottage cheese
    6 fluid ounces sour cream
    3 ounces sifted plain flour
    ½ teaspoon bicarbonate of soda
    1 teaspoon salt

Beat eggs, and blend with cottage cheese; stir in sour cream.

Sift flour with bicarbonate of soda and salt. Add to egg mixture and beat thoroughly.

Leave a few minutes before using. Cook pancakes as for basic recipe, turning once.

Serve hot with butter and apple sauce. Makes 10 to 12 pancakes 3½ to 4 inches in diameter.

RHODE ISLAND JOHNNY CAKES

    4 ounces maize flour
    1 tablespoon flour
    1 teaspoon sugar
    ½ teaspoon salt
    8 fluid ounces boiling water
    4 fluid ounces milk

Mix together the dry ingredients. Pour the boiling water over them and stir in. Add the milk.

Cook on a griddle generously greased with bacon fat. Makes 10 to 12 pancakes.

BUTTERMILK BUCKWHEAT PANCAKES

    2 ounces sifted plain flour
    ½ teaspoon baking powder
    ½ teaspoon salt
    2 teaspoons sugar
    1 teaspoon bicarbonate of soda
    6 ounces buckwheat flour
    1¼ pints buttermilk or sour milk
    2 tablespoons melted butter

Mix and sift flour, baking powder, salt, sugar, and bicarbonate of soda.

Add buckwheat flour and mix well. Stir in milk and melted butter and beat only until batter is blended. Cook as in basic recipe.

MASHED POTATO PANCAKES

    7 ounces mashed potatoes
    8 ounces sifted plain flour
    1 teaspoon salt
    3 teaspoons baking powder
    2 eggs, beaten
    8 fluid ounces milk
    4 tablespoons golden syrup
    1 teaspoon grated nutmeg

Mix together potatoes, sifted flour, salt, and baking powder.

Mix together the eggs and milk and stir lightly into the potato-flour mixture. Add golden syrup and nutmeg and beat well.

Bake on a greased griddle until pancakes are brown on both sides. Makes 12.

MATZO MEAL PANCAKES

    2 ounces matzo meal
    1 teaspoon salt
    1 tablespoon sugar
    2 eggs, separated
    8 fluid ounces milk or water

Mix matzo meal, salt, and sugar. Beat egg yolks; add milk and blend with dry ingredients. Leave mixture for ½ hour, then fold in stiffly beaten egg whites.

Bake on hot greased griddle until bubbly on top and brown underneath, then turn and brown the other side. Serve with syrup or sprinkled with sugar.

PINEAPPLE PANCAKES

    ½ teaspoon salt
    1 tablespoon caster sugar
    2 ounces sifted flour
    2 eggs, beaten
    1 tablespoon melted butter
    ¼ pint milk
    ½ teaspoon grated orange rind
    tidbit sauce (below)

Add salt and sugar to flour. Mix remaining ingredients; add to flour, beating until smooth.

Heat 5-inch frying pan, butter lightly. Fry each pancake separately, dropping 1 tablespoon batter into pan and tilting pan so batter covers bottom. Fry about 1 minute on each side.

Spoon 1 tablespoon tidbits (from sauce) on each pancake. Roll. Place pancakes in shallow baking dish or chafing dish, pour over remaining sauce. Heat in chafing dish or in moderate oven (350°F. Mark 4) about 10 minutes. Makes 16 pancakes.

Tidbit Sauce:
    4 fluid ounces pineapple syrup
      (drained from tidbits)
    1 orange, grated rind and juice
    2 ounces granulated sugar
    3 tablespoons butter
    1 can (20 ounces) drained pine-
      apple tidbits

Mix together all ingredients except tidbits; simmer 10 minutes. Add tidbits and heat.

Pineapple Pancakes

LACY BISCUIT PANCAKES

2   ounces sifted plain flour
6   ounces sugar
1   teaspoon bicarbonate of soda
1½ teaspoons baking powder
1   teaspoon salt
3   ounces coarsely crushed
        digestive biscuits
4   eggs, beaten
8   fluid ounces sour cream
about 3 tablespoons water

Mix and sift flour, sugar, bicarbonate of soda, baking powder, and salt.

Add biscuit crumbs and fold in the eggs, which have been beaten until they are thick and lemon-coloured. Then stir in the sour cream and the water.

The batter should be just thin enough so that the pancakes will run a little at the edges, when dropped on a hot griddle.

The griddle should be completely covered with a thin layer of fat. Try using half butter and half bacon fat. The cakes should be dark brown in colour, with a crisp, lacy surface texture and uneven edges.

If they are almost impossible to turn, the batter is the right consistency. Serve hot with butter and syrup, or with caster sugar and jam.

DOWN EAST PANCAKES

8   ounces sifted plain flour
1   teaspoon bicarbonate of soda
3   tablespoons sugar
¾   teaspoon salt
2   well beaten eggs
4   tablespoons vinegar
about ¾ pint milk
2   ounces fat

Mix and sift flour, soda, sugar, and salt. Mix together well eggs, vinegar, milk, and fat. Add to dry ingredients and stir only until smooth.

Pour batter from tip of large spoon or from pitcher onto a large greased frying pan or griddle. When underside is browned and before bubbles burst on top, turn and brown the other side. Makes about 20 medium pancakes.

Variations: For apple pancakes add 4 ounces grated raw apples. For blueberry pancakes add 2 ounces well-drained blueberries.

PANCAKES WITH KIRSCH

3   eggs, separated
2   tablespoons sugar
¼   teaspoon salt
4   ounces melted butter
8   fluid ounces milk
2   ounces sifted plain flour
2¾ ounces sugar
4   fluid ounces kirsch

Beat egg yolks well; add 2 tablespoons sugar, salt, and 2 tablespoons melted butter. Add milk and flour; beat until smooth.

Beat egg whites until stiff and fold into first mixture until well blended.

Spoon small portions of the batter into a greased 6-inch frying pan. When slightly browned underneath, turn and brown other side.

Roll and place over heat in chafing dish. When 4 or 5 pancakes are made, sprinkle generously with icing sugar, melted butter, and kirsch. Flame the liqueur and burn until it goes out.

Add other pancakes as they are cooked and repeat additions of sugar, butter, and kirsch, serving as needed. Serves about 6.

BUTTER PANCAKES

12 ounces sifted plain flour
3   teaspoons baking powder
1   teaspoon salt
2   tablespoons sugar
3   eggs, separated
24 fluid ounces milk
4   ounces butter, melted

Sift flour twice with baking powder, salt, and sugar.

Beat egg yolks, add milk and melted butter. Add the flour; beat until batter is smooth.

Beat egg whites until stiff and fold into batter thoroughly.

Cook on a moderately hot, buttered griddle, using a scant 4 tablespoons for each pancake. Cook until golden brown underneath; then turn and cook until browned on other side. Turn only once.

Serve hot with butter and sprinkle with a mixture of brown sugar and chopped pecans or walnuts. Makes 3 dozen 4-inch pancakes.

GERMAN APPLE PANCAKE

4   ounces sifted plain flour
½   teaspoon baking powder
pinch of salt
8   fluid ounces milk
5   eggs
2   tablespoons melted butter
thinly sliced apples sautéed in butter, or hot apple sauce

Mix and sift dry ingredients. Stir in milk. Add unbeaten eggs one at a time, beating each separately into batter. Add melted butter.

Pour into hot greased frying pan. Put on direct heat for 1 minute, then bake in hot oven (425°F. Mark 7) until browned, puffed, and curled up at edges, 20 to 25 minutes.

Sprinkle with caster sugar and lemon juice, if you like. Serve at once with hot thin slices of apple which have been sautéed in butter or with hot apple sauce. Serves 4 to 6.

RUMANIAN PANCAKES

4   ounces sifted plain flour
8   fluid ounces milk
1   egg, beaten
¼   teaspoon salt
1   tablespoon sugar
pinch of ground cinnamon, optional
canned cherries
caster sugar

Add flour to milk and beat until well blended. Add egg, salt, sugar, and cinnamon. Mix thoroughly.

Cook in a greased frying pan as for basic recipe until brown on one side. Turn and brown other side.

Spread cherries over pancakes while hot. Roll up and sprinkle with caster sugar.

Serve hot as dessert. Serves 4.

ICELANDIC PANCAKES

4   ounces sifted plain flour
2   eggs
about 4 fluid ounces milk
2 to 3 tablespoons melted butter or margarine
2   teaspoons vanilla essence

Sift flour into a bowl. Beat eggs and add half the milk.

Stir egg-milk mixture, melted butter, and vanilla essence into flour.

Add enough extra milk to make a batter of the thickness of whipping cream.

Use a small 5- to 6-inch frying pan. Cover bottom of lightly buttered hot pan with a thin layer of batter by tilting the pan slightly.

Brown pancake lightly on both sides. When cooked, spread 1 teaspoon of jam and a tablespoon of whipped cream over pancake. Fold twice and place on warm serving plate. Serves 6.

A tasty way to make leftovers into a hearty lunch is to serve pancakes with such dishes as creamed chicken, mushrooms, tuna fish, or ham. If you like, sandwich the pancakes together, using the creamed mixtures as fillings. Serve immediately or keep the pancakes warm in a very slow oven.

OLDEN EGG PANCAKE

2 eggs
¼ teaspoon salt
1 tablespoon sugar
1½ ounces sifted flour
4 fluid ounces milk
1 teaspoon fat

Beat eggs, salt, and sugar together. .dd flour and milk to eggs. Beat until mooth.

Heat fat in deep 10- to 12-inch frying an until drop of water in pan sizzles. our in all of batter. Cook 2 minutes.

Place in very hot oven (450°F. Mark and bake 15 minutes or until surface brown. Leave in pan until ready to rve.

Dot with butter and sweetened fruit r marmalade, syrup, or honey. Roll r fold from opposite sides to centre, naking 3 layers. Turn out on warm late. Sprinkle with icing sugar. erves 1 to 2.

'ariations of Egg Pancake

Place one of the following over the atter just before placing it in the oven.

pple: 1 layer of thinly sliced apples.

acon: 3 to 4 rashers crisply cooked acon, diced. Reduce salt to ¼ teaspoon.

lam: 1¼ ounces finely diced cooked am. Reduce salt to ¼ teaspoon.

LINI

Blini is a Russian term for very small east-raised pancakes, often made with uckwheat flour. They are served as a ule with caviar, sour cream, cheese, r melted butter. The name is someimes also applied to small pancakes nade with baking powder.

24 fluid ounces warm milk
2 teaspoons dry yeast
8 ounces fine buckwheat flour
4 eggs, separated
½ teaspoon salt
1 tablespoon sugar
2 teaspoons melted butter

Pour 12 fluid ounces warm milk over e yeast. Stir to dissolve and add nough flour to make a thick spongy nixture. Cover with a warm cloth. Set n a warm place (80 to 85°F.) for about ½ hours.

Beat egg yolks with salt and sugar nd stir in remaining warm milk. Add utter and stir into the yeast mixture. old in remaining flour and stiffly eaten egg whites. Cover again and ave to rise for at least 20 minutes.

Bake small pancakes (about 3 inches cross and not more than ¼ inch thick) n a hot, greased griddle. Brown lightly n both sides, turning only once. Serve ith caviar or with melted butter and ur cream. Makes about 30 pancakes.

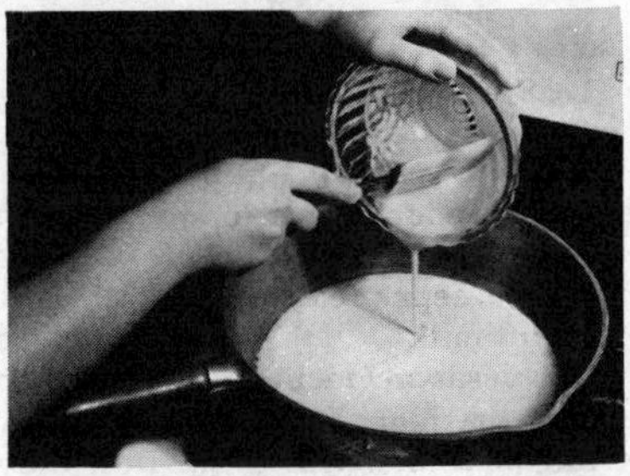

1. Pour batter into a 10- or 12-inch hot greased frying pan.

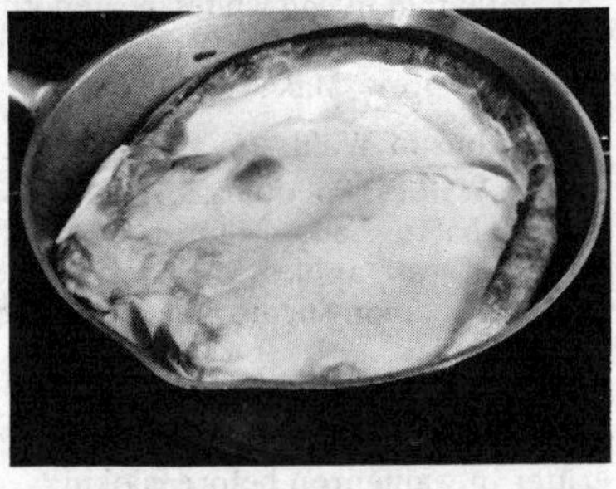

2. Cook on top of stove over moderate heat 2 minutes, then bake in very hot oven (450°F. Mark 8) until surface is browned, about 15 minutes.

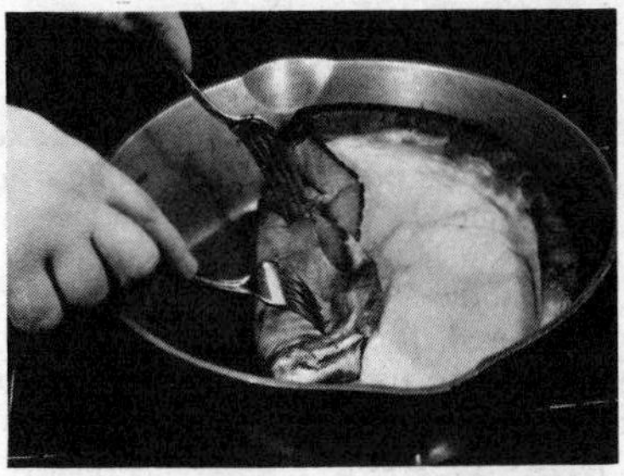

3. Roll or fold from opposite sides to centre making three layers.

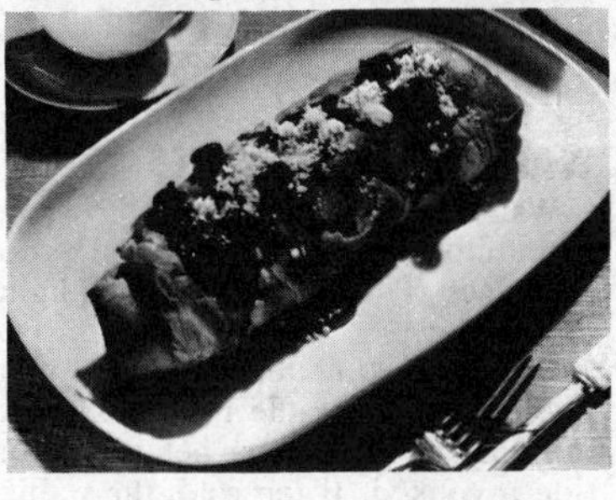

4. Turn out on a warm dish and serve with sweetened fruit or marmalade, syrup, or honey. Sprinkle with icing sugar.

GERMAN PANCAKES

6 eggs, separated
2 ounces sifted flour
1 teaspoon baking powder
pinch of salt
4 fluid ounces milk

Beat the egg yolks until thick and lemon-coloured.

Mix and sift flour, baking powder, and salt; add to the egg yolks alternately with the milk.

When all ingredients are blended, fold in stiffly beaten egg whites.

Melt a little butter in a frying pan and pour in a tablespoon of the batter. Tip pan so that batter will cover bottom of it in a thin layer. When brown on one side, turn and brown the other.

Serve pancakes very hot with sugar and wedges of lemon.

HUNGARIAN PANCAKES
(Palascinta)

1 egg
3 ounces flour
16 fluid ounces milk
⅛ teaspoon salt
1 teaspoon sugar

Mix all ingredients together well with rotary beater or electric mixer. Leave the batter about 30 minutes.

Put enough butter in small frying pan to coat bottom of pan lightly. Heat until pan is hot.

Pour in just enough batter to make a very thin layer on the bottom of pan, tipping pan when batter is added so entire bottom of pan is covered.

Fry pancake over low heat until browned on one side. Transfer to heated dish.

Spread a thin layer of jelly on half the pancake, then roll up.

Sprinkle caster sugar over top. Serve at once. Makes about 10 pancakes.

RAISED BUCKWHEAT CAKES

18 fluid ounces boiling water
1 teaspoon dried yeast
2 tablespoons lukewarm water
6 ounces buckwheat flour
1 teaspoon salt
4 teaspoons sugar
2 ounces sifted flour
¼ teaspoon bicarbonate of soda

Boil 16 fluid ounces water, cool to lukewarm. While it is cooling, dissolve yeast in 2 tablespoons lukewarm water.

Reserve bicarbonate of soda and 3 teaspoons sugar. Add remaining ingredients and dissolved yeast to the 16 fluid ounces lukewarm water. Cover and leave in a fairly warm place 12 hours or overnight.

Add the other 2 fluid ounces water, cooled to lukewarm, with bicarbonate of soda and 3 teaspoons sugar dissolved in it. Mix well and cook on griddle.

Four fluid ounces of batter may be reserved as "seed". Use "seed" in place of yeast after first day. "Seed" should be stored in cool place. Makes about 12 pancakes.

Waffles

A waffle is a sort of crisp pancake cooked in a utensil called a waffle iron —two metal plates studded on the inside, which are hinged together and then shut. Waffle batter is similar to that used for pancakes, but richer. Waffles are usually served with butter and syrup but may also be accompanied by fresh or stewed fruit, preserves, ice cream, or creamed chicken.

WAFFLE BAKING HINTS

Waffles should be evenly browned and uniform in shape, well filled out to the edges. They should be crisp, light, and tender.

Correct baking temperature is important. If the waffle iron is too hot, the outside will brown before the inside is cooked. If too cold, the waffles will stick or appear spotted.

If the waffle iron is not thermostatically controlled, the iron may be tested by throwing drops of water upon it. The iron is ready to use when the drops form into balls and "skid" across.

Pour the batter from a pitcher around the centre of the grid, filling the iron only two-thirds full to prevent the batter from overflowing. Cook until steaming stops. It takes 3 to 5 minutes to cook the average waffle, a little longer for a thin batter. Lift waffle off the iron with a fork.

Store leftover batter in the refrigerator; it will keep for about 3 days in a covered container.

CARE OF WAFFLE IRONS

Modern waffle irons usually require no greasing and some do not require tempering. The manufacturer's directions should be followed regarding tempering of the grids, use of heat control and indicator, and cleaning after use.

If manufacturer's directions are not available, the following general cleaning hints may usually be followed. Wash off the outside with a damp cloth wrung out in hot soapy water, then polish the iron with a dry cloth. Remove excess batter from the grids with slightly dampened steel wool. Then brush the grids with an even film of melted unsalted fat. Close the iron, turn on the current, and heat for 2 minutes. Wipe off excess fat with paper towels.

WAFFLES
(Basic Recipe)
8 ounces sifted flour
3 teaspoons baking powder
2 tablespoons sugar (optional)
1 teaspoon salt
3 eggs, separated
½ pint milk
4 tablespoons melted fat

Sift dry ingredients. Beat egg yolks. Add milk and melted fat. Beat thoroughly. Add to dry ingredients. Mix together quickly.

Gently fold in egg whites, beaten stiff but not dry. Cook 3 or 4 minutes in a hot waffle iron. Makes 5 to 6 waffles.

Variations of Waffles:

Apple Waffles: Follow basic recipe. Just before baking, add 4 ounces of ½-inch cubes of raw apples to batter. Serve with cinnamon-sugar mixture, and butter.

Bacon Waffles: Follow basic recipe. Sprinkle cooked, diced bacon over batter in waffle iron before cooking.

Blueberry Waffles: Follow basic recipe. Mix 4 ounces blueberries with 2 tablespoons sugar, and add to batter just before cooking. Serve with caster sugar.

Cheese Waffles: In basic recipe add 4 ounces grated Cheddar cheese to batter before folding in beaten egg whites.

Coconut Waffles: Follow basic recipe. Before closing iron, sprinkle coconut over each waffle or add 4 ounces desiccated coconut to batter.

Maize Flour Waffles: In basic recipe substitute 2 ounces maize flour for 2 ounces white flour.

Date or Fig Waffles: Follow basic recipe; add 5 ounces chopped dates or dried figs to batter just before cooking. Serve with caster sugar.

Ginger Waffles: In basic recipe add 4 tablespoons black treacle and 1½ teaspoons ground ginger. Omit 4 tablespoons milk.

Ham Waffles: Prepare basic recipe. Sprinkle 2 tablespoons finely diced, cooked ham over batter of each waffle before closing iron.

Orange Waffles: Follow basic recipe. Add 2 teaspoons grated orange rind to the egg yolk and milk mixture. If you like, substitute 4 fluid ounces orange juice for 4 fluid ounces milk.

Walnut Waffles: In basic recipe add 4 ounces chopped walnuts to batter or sprinkle over batter of each waffle before closing iron.

Sour Cream Waffles: In basic recipe use only 1 teaspoon baking powder. Add ½ teaspoon bicarbonate of soda. Substitute ½ pint thick sour cream for milk and fat.

Sour Milk or Buttermilk Waffles: basic recipe substitute 12 fluid oun sour milk or 12 fluid ounces butt milk for milk. Add ¾ teaspoon bicarb ate of soda and use only 2¼ teaspoo baking powder.

Wholewheat Waffles: In basic rec substitute 2 ounces wholewheat flo for 2 ounces white flour.

SPONGE CAKE WAFFLES
4 ounces sifted flour
1 teaspoon baking powder
¼ teaspoon salt
3 eggs, well beaten
8 ounces sugar
1½ ounces melted butter
4 tablespoons cold water
1 teaspoon vanilla

Sift together the flour, baking po der, and salt.

Mix together well-beaten eggs a sugar. Add sifted dry ingredien melted butter, water, and vani beating until smooth.

Cook in a hot waffle iron until de cately browned, about 2 minutes.

May be served as a shortcake. Spr kle with caster sugar, and serve w berries and whipped cream or cream. Makes 6 waffles.

SWEET POTATO WAFFLES
4 tablespoons fat
1 tablespoon sugar
1 egg, separated
8 fluid ounces milk
salt
cayenne pepper
grated nutmeg
3 ounces sifted flour
7 ounces mashed sweet potatoes
2 teaspoons baking powder

Cream the fat and sugar un smooth. Add well-beaten egg yo milk, and seasoning, and continue beat until smooth.

Beat in the flour, sweet potatoes, a baking powder. Fold in the stiffly beat egg white.

Cook in a heated waffle iron un golden brown. Serve sprinkled wi sugar and cinnamon. Serves 5 to 6.

Waffle ice cream sandwiches are alwe popular with the youngsters

RENCH TOAST WAFFLES

1 beaten egg
4 tablespoons milk
1 ounce melted butter
⅛ teaspoon salt
sliced bread

Mix together the egg, milk, butter nd salt.

Cut sliced bread into pieces to fit waffle iron, then coat bread well in ie batter. Toast in a hot waffle iron.

REAM DESSERT WAFFLES

4 ounces sifted flour
2 teaspoons baking powder
¼ teaspoon salt
2 eggs, separated
8 fluid ounces double cream

Mix and sift the dry ingredients; iix to a smooth batter with beaten gg yolks and cream.

Fold in stiffly beaten egg whites. Cook in a hot waffle iron. Makes 4 vaffles.

'ariations:

:hocolate Waffles: Stir into the bater 2 ounces melted unsweetened chocolate and 6 tablespoons sugar.

piced Chocolate Waffles: Add to hocolate waffle batter ¼ teaspoon round cinnamon, ¼ teaspoon ground utmeg, and 1 teaspoon vanilla essence.

UTTERMILK WAFFLES

7 ounces sifted flour
2 teaspoons baking powder
1 teaspoon bicarbonate of soda
½ teaspoon salt
3 eggs separated
12 fluid ounces buttermilk or sour milk
4 ounces melted butter

Mix and sift dry ingredients. Mix to light batter with the egg yolks, which ave been well beaten, and the butterilk or sour milk.

Stir in melted butter. Fold in egg vhites which have been stiffly beaten. Cook in hot waffle iron. Makes 8 waffles.

'ariations:

ogurt Waffles: Use 16 fluid ounces ogurt in place of buttermilk in above ecipe.

our Cream Waffles: Use 16 fluid unces sour cream in place of butterilk and stir in only 2 tablespoons nelted butter.

SOUR CREAM WAFFLES 2

2 eggs, separated
16 fluid ounces sour cream
8 ounces sifted flour
1 tablespoon maize flour
1 teaspoon bicarbonate of soda
½ teaspoon salt

Beat whites and yolks of eggs sep-rately.

Mix with the beaten yolks, the sour ream, flour, maize flour, bicarbonate f soda, and salt.

Finally fold in the stiffly beaten egg whites. Cook at once in a hot iron. Makes 6 waffles.

WHOLEWHEAT WAFFLES
(Yeast-Raised)

12 fluid ounces milk
6 ounces honey
1½ teaspoons salt
2 tablespoons fat
4 fluid ounces warm (not hot) water
2 teaspoons dry yeast
2 eggs, beaten
12 ounces wholewheat flour

Scald milk. Stir in honey, salt, and fat. Cool to lukewarm.

Measure 4 fluid ounces warm water into bowl. Sprinkle in yeast. Stir until dissolved. Stir in lukewarm milk mixture.

Add beaten eggs and flour. Beat until smooth. Cover. Leave to rise in a warm place, free from draught, until doubled in bulk, about 40 minutes.

Stir batter down.

Cook in waffle iron at medium heat until golden brown, about 8 minutes.

Serve with butter and hot syrup. Makes 5 large waffles.

BROWNIE WAFFLES

6 ounces sifted flour
½ teaspoon salt
6 ounces fat
4½ ounces sugar
2 egg yolks
6 fluid ounces milk
2 ounces unsweetened chocolate, melted
2 ounces chopped nuts
2 egg whites, stiffly beaten

Sift together flour and salt. Cream fat and add sugar gradually. Beat until light and fluffy. Add egg yolks and mix well.

Add milk to creamed mixture alternately with flour. Fold in remaining ingredients.

Cook in moderately hot waffle iron about 5 minutes. Serve with a scoop of vanilla ice cream or whipped cream topped with chocolate sauce.

GINGERBREAD WAFFLES

2 eggs
2 ounces sugar
6 ounces black treacle
8 fluid ounces sour milk
6 ounces sifted flour
1 teaspoon ground ginger
¼ teaspoon salt
1 teaspoon bicarbonate of soda
1 teaspoon baking powder
2¼ ounces melted fat

Beat eggs until light. Add sugar, black treacle, sour milk, and remaining dry ingredients sifted together. Beat until smooth and add fat. Ground cinnamon and clove may be added if you like.

Cook in a hot waffle iron. Serve with whipped cream, ice cream, or cold apple sauce. Makes about 5 waffles.

OLD-FASHIONED WAFFLES

8 ounces sifted flour
1 teaspoon bicarbonate of soda
1 tablespoon sugar
½ teaspoon salt
2 eggs, separated
4 tablespoons vinegar
14 fluid ounces milk
2¼ ounces melted fat

Mix and sift flour, soda, sugar, and salt. Beat egg yolks, vinegar, and milk together. Add dry ingredients and melted fat. Stir until batter is smooth.

Beat egg whites until stiff but not dry and fold into batter.

Pour batter on heated waffle iron to about 1-inch from edge. Cook 3 to 4 minutes or until waffles stop steaming.

Serve with butter and syrup. Or, serve with creamed meat, poultry, or fish spooned over for a lunch or supper dish. Makes 6 to 7 waffles.

Walnut or Pecan Waffles: Add 3 ounces chopped walnuts or pecans.

CHOCOLATE WAFFLES 2

8 ounces sifted flour
4 teaspoons baking powder
½ teaspoon salt
2 ounces sugar
2 ounces cocoa
2 eggs, separated
14 fluid ounces milk
4 ounces melted butter or margarine

Mix and sift flour, baking powder, salt, sugar, and cocoa.

Mix together the egg yolks, milk, and melted butter or margarine and add to dry ingredients. Beat slightly.

Beat egg whites until stiff but not dry and fold into batter. Cook in hot waffle iron. Serve with chocolate sauce. Makes 8 waffles.

For a heartier dish, serve waffles with creamed eggs, chicken, or mushrooms, or with sausages, bacon, or fried chicken.

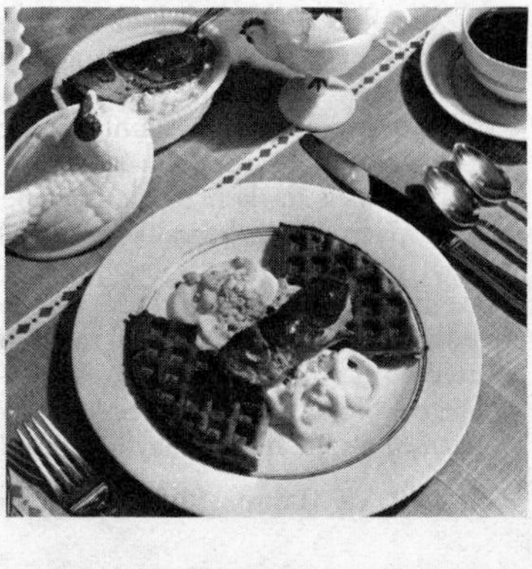

PICKLES AND RELISHES

Although food shops today offer a wide variety of pickles and relishes, many housewives like to make their own pickle products when garden vegetables and fresh fruits are in abundant supply. This section gives specific directions for a wide variety of old-fashioned recipes as well as some quickly prepared modern recipes.

PICKLING HINTS

Use only fresh, good quality fruits and vegetables. Cucumbers and green tomatoes are best pickled within 24 hours of picking. Fruits may be slightly underripe.

Use a good, clear standard vinegar—free from sediment—one with 4 to 5 per cent of acetic acid. Use white vinegar (barley malt, corn, rye) if the pickles are light in colour; cider (apple) or wine vinegar for all others.

Use pure granulated salt. A medium coarse salt is preferable to table salt because the carbonates, or bicarbonates of sodium, calcium, or magnesium added to table salt to prevent lumping may not give you as good results.

Use soft water for best results.

Use fresh, whole spices for longer lasting flavour.

Store pickles in jars with glass tops or in well-sealed crocks to avoid corrosion.

For a Bright-Coloured Pickle: Use glass or pottery for soaking pickles. Enamel is preferred for heating acid pickling liquids; however brightly scoured aluminium, or stainless steel saucepans may be used.

Iron utensils darken pickles, copper ones impart an undesirable greenish hue.

A stronger vinegar than recommended may give a darker colour than desired.

To give pickles a fresh, green colour, spinach or grape leaves may be added.

Hollow or Limp Pickles: These result from overripe or imperfect vegetables or when vegetables have been standing too long before pickling.

Cloudy Pickles: These are caused by a weak brine and a weak vinegar solution.

Soft Pickles: These may result from too weak a brine solution or from neglecting to cover pickles completely in the brine.

Tough or Shrivelled Pickles: May be caused by excessive salt, or sugar, or excessively strong vinegar.

If very sour or very sweet pickles are desired it is best to put them in a weak solution at first and increase the strength later. Hurrying the processes of cooking or brining may cause shrivelling.

CUCUMBER OIL PICKLES

- **8 pounds small, sliced cucumbers**
- **6 ounces salt**
- **2 quarts water**
- **12 fluid ounces cider vinegar**
- **4 ounces sugar**
- **2 ounces mustard seed**
- **1 teaspoon celery seed**
- **1 teaspoon whole black peppers**
- **4 fluid ounces olive oil or cooking oil**

Place cucumbers in a bowl. Dissolve salt in water and pour over cucumbers. Add more water if needed to cover cucumbers. Let stand overnight.

Drain cucumbers, cover with fresh water, heat to boiling and drain again. Pack into hot sterilized jars.

Heat vinegar, sugar, spice, and oil to boiling point, stirring until sugar is dissolved. Pour over pickles, filling jars almost to rim. Seal immediately. Makes about 6 pints.

SWEET GHERKINS

Use cucumbers no larger than 2 inches in length. Leave ¼ inch or more of the stem on each. Wash and place in stone jars. Salt, using 12 ounces of salt to 4 pounds of the cucumbers.

Pour boiling water over them and let stand 24 to 36 hours.

Remove pickles from the brine and drop them into a solution of equal parts vinegar and water. Heat to boiling point and remove pickles to clean jars.

Add a teaspoonful of mixed pickling spices to each quart, and also a fairly long strip of horseradish root, if it is available.

Pour over the pickles the hot vinegar and water to which 8 ounces of sugar per quart has been added. Seal.

EASY KOSHER DILL PICKLES

- **2 pounds cucumbers**
- **4 fluid ounces lemon juice**
- **2 tablespoons salt**
- **spray of dill**
- **water**
- **clove of garlic**

Sterilize jars and pack with firm clean cucumbers.

Add lemon juice and salt. Fill to the neck of the jar with clear, cold water.

Put the spray of dill and clove of garlic on top and seal loosely.

This pickle is not ready for use for six weeks. Complete seal at that time. Makes 2 pounds.

ICICLE PICKLES

Cut large cucumbers into 4 to pieces lengthwise. Let stand in ice water 8 hours or overnight.

Pack into hot sterilized jars. Fill centre of each jar with 2 pieces of celery and 6 pickling onions.

Combine 1 quart cider vinegar, ounces medium-coarse salt, and ounces sugar; heat to a boil. Fill jars and seal.

In these recipes "hot sterile jars" mean containers and lids that have been scrubbed in hot sudsy water, rinsed and then boiled 15 to 20 minutes just before use.

[MI]XED MUSTARD PICKLES

[ ] pounds sliced cucumbers
[ ] pound quartered, small, green tomatoes
[ ] pound cauliflower flowerets
[ ] pound string beans, cut in 1-inch pieces
[ ] small whole onions or 2 large onions, sliced
[ ] ounces sliced young tender carrots
[ ] sweet red peppers, cut in small pieces
[ ] sweet green peppers, cut in small pieces
[Sal]t

Cover vegetables with a brine made [wit]h 6 ounces salt to 1 quart water. Let [sta]nd overnight.

[D]rain, rinse in fresh water; drain [aga]in and cover mixture with equal [pa]rts of strong white vinegar and water [ab]out 1½ pints each, water and vine[ga]r). Let stand 1 hour.

[H]eat to a rapid boil. Drain, add [mu]stard dressing. Simmer 5 minutes. [P]ack into hot, sterilized jars and seal [t]ight. Makes about 5 pints.

Make Mustard Dressing:
[ ] tablespoons flour
[ ] tablespoons dry mustard
[ ] teaspoons turmeric
[ ] teaspoons celery seed
[ ] quart strong white vinegar
[1]0 ounces black treacle or sugar

Mix flour with spices. Slowly add [vin]egar. Mix thoroughly and stir in [bla]ck treacle or sugar.

Cook until thick, stirring constantly.

[E]ASY DILL PICKLES

[C]ucumbers of even size
[ ] head dill for each jar
[ ] quarts water
[ ] pints cider vinegar
[ ]2 ounces salt

Scrub small, firm cucumbers thor[ou]ghly and rinse. Pack closely into [qu]art jars. Place a head of dill in the [top] of each jar.

Mix water, vinegar, and salt; bring [to] a boil, and pour at once over cucum[be]rs.

Seal jars and store in a cool, dark [pla]ce for at least six weeks before open[ing]. During this period the cure is [com]pleted. Pickles canned this way are [be]st eaten within a period of 6 or 8 [mo]nths.

[O]LD VINEGAR PICKLES

[ ]Wash and dry small cucumbers. Pack [clo]sely into sterilized jars.

[T]o each quart, add 1 tablespoon [wa]shed rock salt, 2 tablespoons sugar, [1 ta]blespoon mixed pickling spices.

[F]ill jar with cold vinegar, seal, and

store in a cool place.

A few slices of onion may be added to each jar, if desired.

SWEET SPICED CUCUMBERS

4 pounds sliced cucumbers
6 ounces salt
1 quart vinegar
12 to 16 ounces white granulated sugar or tightly packed brown sugar
1 teaspoon whole allspice
2 sticks whole cinnamon, broken
1 teaspoon whole cloves
1 tablespoon white mustard seed

Arrange cucumbers and salt in a bowl or stone crock and let stand 3 hours.

As soon as cucumbers have been prepared, boil, covered, for 10 minutes the vinegar, sugar, and spices (spices should first be put in a square of cheese cloth and tied together in a bag). Let mixture stand, covered.

After 3 hours drain cucumbers and press to remove excess moisture. Remove spice bag from vinegar mixture and add cucumbers to it. Bring to a simmering point. Do not boil.

Pack in hot, clean jars, seal or partially seal, according to type of closure. Process in a boiling water bath 10 minutes. Makes about 5 pints.

BREAD AND BUTTER PICKLES

25 medium cucumbers, sliced
12 onions, sliced
6 ounces salt
1 pound sugar
2 teaspoons turmeric
2 teaspoons cassia buds (optional)
1 quart vinegar
2 teaspoons mustard seed
2 teaspoons celery seed

Soak cucumbers and onions in ice water with salt for 3 hours.

Combine remaining ingredients and heat to boiling.

Add cucumbers and onion and heat for 2 minutes. Do not allow to boil. Fill clean jars. Seal at once.

MILD DILL PICKLES

4½ pounds cucumbers
6 tablespoons salt
1½ tablespoons yellow mustard seed
1½ pints distilled white vinegar
1½ pints water
5 ounces dill seed
6 bay leaves
6 peeled cloves garlic

Wash cucumbers and halve crosswise. Quarter each half lengthwise.

Pack in clean pint jars that have been rinsed in hot water.

Combine salt, mustard seed, vinegar,

and water. Heat to boiling.

Pour liquid over cucumbers in jars, covering them. Add to each pint 2 tablespoons dill seed, a bay leaf, and a clove of garlic. Be sure jars are filled to not more than a half-inch from top.

Seal jars according to type of closure used and process immediately in a boiling water bath for 10 minutes. Makes 6 pints.

Note: Garlic may be omitted.

DILL PICKLES IN A CROCK

12 pounds cucumbers
4 tablespoons whole mixed pickling spice
grape or cherry leaves
dill
2 gallons soft water
1½ pounds cooking salt
1 pint vinegar

Wash and scald 4 or 5 gallon crock and cover the bottom with a layer of well washed grape or cherry leaves.

Add a layer of dill. Sprinkle a third of the spice over dill.

Wash the cucumbers well and pack half of them into the crock.

Add another layer of grape or cherry leaves, dill, and a sprinkling of spices.

Pack in remaining cucumbers and top with a third layer of leaves, dill, and spices.

Boil water, salt, vinegar together for 5 minutes and cool. Pour over cucumbers and place a cover or plate with a weight on it, over them so the cucumbers will be kept below the brine during fermentation.

Place a clean cloth over the top of the crock and leave crock in a fairly warm place, between 80-85 degrees to ferment. Active fermentation will begin in a few days and will be completed after 2 or 3 weeks, possibly a little longer.

Remove scum from top of pickles two or three times a week, for if scum remains it will cause spoilage. If brine evaporates, add more made in the same proportion. When fermentation ceases, no more scum will form.

Draw off the brine, pack pickles into clean jars with a sprig of dill in each jar.

Bring brine to boiling point, pour over pickles and seal. Store in a cool place. Pickles will be ready for use after 4 to 6 weeks.

Kosher Dill Pickles: Make these in the same way as above, but add when canning, 1 clove garlic, 2 bay leaves, 1 teaspoon mustard seed, 2 ounces sugar, a strip of hot red pepper, and 8 fluid ounces vinegar for every 1½ pints brine. Boil 2 minutes, pour over packed pickles and seal at once.

SAUERKRAUT
(Glass-Jar Method)
20 to 25 pounds cabbage
¼ pound salt

Remove the outer leaves and wash cabbage; drain. Cut in halves or quarters; remove the core. Shred about 5 pounds of cabbage at a time and, using the hands, mix thoroughly with 3½ tablespoons salt. Measure accurately—oversalting prevents proper fermentation.

Pack into clean glass jars, pressing down firmly and evenly. Fill with cabbage to shoulder of jar (1½ to 2 inches from top) and be sure juice completely covers cabbage. A quart jar takes about 2 pounds of cabbage.

Wipe off top of jar. Cover cabbage with two or three layers of thin, clean white cloth, and tuck edges down against inside of jar. Crisscross two dry, clean wood strips (ice cream spoons or wooden garden labels cut to right size are suitable) over cloth to keep cabbage pressed under brine. Put lid on jar; don't seal tightly.

Set jars on a tray or pan to catch juice that leaks out. Keep at room temperature, about 70°F. is best. Every few days, remove scum if it forms. Add a little weak brine to keep cabbage covered (1½ tablespoons salt to 1 quart water). Let ferment about 10 days, or until liquid settles and bubbles no longer rise to surface.

If you are planning to use the kraut in a few weeks, it isn't necessary to process in a boiling-water bath. Seal the jars tightly and keep in a cool place.

To Store: Remove lids and set jars in a kettle, with cold water to shoulders of jars. Cover kettle. Bring water to boiling and boil 10 minutes.

Remove jars. Add boiling-hot brine if needed to fill jars to ½ inch of top (1½ tablespoons salt to 1 quart water). Wipe off jar rims and adjust lids. Boil jars in boiling-water bath—25 minutes for pints, 30 minutes for quarts—making sure that water covers jars. Remove jars; complete seals. Makes 8 to 10 quarts.

KOSHER STYLE GREEN TOMATO DILLS

Choose small, firm, green tomatoes. Wash thoroughly, and pack into clean jars.

To each quart jar add a garlic clove, a stalk of celery, and a quarter of a green pepper.

Make a solution in the following proportions: 2 quarts water, 1 quart vinegar, and 12 ounces salt. Add 1 head of dill for each jar and boil solution 5 minutes.

Pour over green tomatoes in jars, placing dill in each. Seal and store 6 weeks. Pickles will not be thoroughly cured before that time.

GREEN TOMATO PICKLE
4 pounds green tomatoes
6 medium onions, sliced
6 ounces salt
1 to 2 green peppers, chopped
1 pound sugar
1 pint vinegar
2 tablespoons each celery and mustard seed
1 tablespoon whole cloves
1 teaspoon whole black peppers
2 3-inch sticks cinnamon

Slice tomatoes ¼ inch thick. Place layers of tomatoes and onions in a large bowl, sprinkling each with salt; let stand overnight.

Drain and rinse in cold water.

Place in saucepan and add green peppers, sugar, vinegar, celery, and mustard seed. Tie cloves, whole black peppers, and cinnamon in cheesecloth and add to mixture.

Bring to a rapid boil, stirring, and cook, stirring often, until thickened, about 20 minutes. Remove spice bag, pour into hot sterile jars and seal. Makes about 3½ pints.

PICKLED ONIONS
4 quarts small pickling onions (silver-skins)
boiling water
cold water
12 ounces salt
1½ ounces mixed pickle spice
2 quarts vinegar
1 pound sugar

Cover onions with boiling water; let stand 5 minutes. Drain; cover with cold water. Peel onions; place in bowl or enamel pan. Add salt; cover with fresh cold water; let stand overnight.

Next day, drain onions; rinse with cold water; drain again.

Tie spices in muslin or cheesecloth bag; boil with vinegar and sugar 5 minutes.

Remove spice bag. Add onions to boiling liquid; boil 2 to 3 minutes.

Pour into clean hot jars; fill to overflowing with liquid. Seal at once. Store at least 1 week before serving. Makes 6 or 7 pints.

BEETROOT PICKLES
4½ pounds cooked beetroot
2 teaspoons each mustard seed and celery seed
4 teaspoons salt
1 teaspoon whole cloves
2 sticks cinnamon
1 quart strong vinegar
8 ounces sugar
5 small onions, sliced (optional)

Peel beetroots. If small, leave who If large, slice or quarter them.

Tie spices in cheesecloth bag. spices and remaining ingredients, cept the onions and beetroots, in large pan and bring to a boil.

Add beetroot and onions, and heat to boiling. Remove spice bag.

Pack in hot, sterilized jars. Pour t hot liquid over beetroot and seal a tight. Makes 6 pints.

PICKLED PEPPERS
6 red peppers
6 green peppers
1 pint vinegar
1 pint water
4 ounces sugar
2 teaspoons salt
1 teaspoon mustard seed
1 teaspoon whole allspice

Remove tops and seeds from pe pers. Cut in quarters lengthwise.

Combine vinegar, water, and suga heat to boiling. Add peppers; h through slowly.

Pack in hot, sterilized jars. To ea pint add ½ teaspoon salt, ¼ teaspo mustard seed, and ¼ teaspoon who allspice. Cover with hot vinegar liqui Seal. Makes 4 pints.

PICKLED CAULIFLOWER
3 medium heads cauliflower
2 pounds small white onions
12 ounces salt
1 tablespoon mustard seed
1 tablespoon celery seed
1 teaspoon whole cloves
2 sticks cinnamon, broken
2 quarts white vinegar
1½ pounds sugar

Separate cauliflower into flowere Peel onions. Place in large bowl crock and cover with water in whi salt has been dissolved. Let stand ov night.

Drain vegetables, rinse in cold wa and drain.

Tie spices in square of cheesecло Boil with vinegar and sugar 5 minut

Add vegetables and boil 3 minut Remove spice bag.

Pack vegetables in hot sterile ja Cover with boiling syrup. Seal tight Makes about 8 pints.

PICKLED GREEN BEANS
4 to 6 pounds fresh green beans
salt
12 ounces sugar
1 pint vinegar
1 pint water
2 fluid ounces lemon juice

Cook whole beans in salted wat until tender.

Drain and pack in hot, sterilized ja

Combine remaining ingredients; h to boiling, simmer 5 minutes. Po over beans. Seal.

Spiced and Pickled Fruits

SPICED FRUIT
(Basic Recipe)

8 pounds fruit
whole cloves
2½ pints vinegar
3 pounds brown sugar
1 ounce stick cinnamon

Use peaches, pears, crabapples, or apples. Select fine, firm fruit.

Remove skin from peaches or pears, leaving the fruit whole.

With crabapples, the skin and stem should be left on but the fruit carefully washed and cleaned.

Remove skin from apples. Cut into quarters or eighths, depending on size of apples.

If using more than one variety of fruit do not combine. Pickle each kind separately.

Place 3 or 4 cloves in each piece of fruit. To help retain shape of fruit, cook until tender a few pieces at a time in vinegar, sugar, and cinnamon syrup.

Place in sterilized jars. Fill with syrup. Seal.

WATERMELON PICKLES

4 pounds prepared watermelon
**   rind**
limewater
2 tablespoons whole allspice
2 tablespoons whole cloves
10 2-inch pieces stick cinnamon
1½ quarts white vinegar
1 lemon, sliced thin
1 quart water
4½ pounds sugar

To prepare melon, peel skin and pink flesh. Cut into 1½ to 2-inch squares.

Soak for 2½ hours in limewater made with 2 quarts cold water and 2 tablespoons lime of calcium oxide, purchased from the chemist.

Drain, cover with fresh water, and cook until tender, about 1½ hours, adding more water as needed. Let stand several hours or overnight. Drain.

Put spices in cheesecloth bag, tying loosely. Bring to boil spices, vinegar, lemon, water, and sugar.

Add rind and boil slowly for 2 hours, or until syrup is fairly thick.

Remove spice bag. Pack pickles in clean, hot jars; fill with boiling syrup, and seal.

WHOLE PICKLED GRAPES

Select bunches of grapes of the same size and ripeness. Any type of grape may be used, but they should not be overripe.

Leave grapes on stems and, after washing and drying, pack the bunches closely into clean glass jars. To avoid bruising, do not pack tightly.

Prepare syrup of 12 ounces sugar to each ½ pint white vinegar. Boil 5 minutes. Pour over grapes to fill jars. Seal.

PICKLED PEACHES

8 pounds small or medium-sized
**   peaches**
2 tablespoons whole cloves
8 2-inch pieces stick cinnamon
2 pounds sugar
1 quart vinegar

Wash and peel peaches; stick 2 cloves in each peach. Or put cloves and cinnamon loosely in a clean, thin white cloth and tie top tightly. Cook together spices, sugar, and vinegar for 10 minutes. Add peaches; cook slowly until tender, but not broken. Let stand overnight.

In the morning, remove spices if they have been cooked in a bag. Drain syrup from peaches; boil syrup rapidly until thickened.

Pack peaches in clean, hot, sterile jars. Pour hot syrup over peaches, filling jars to top. Seal tightly.

Keep in a cool place several weeks before serving to blend flavour. Makes about 6 pints.

BRANDIED CHERRIES

Select ripe, large white or red cherries. Wash and drain. Cut stems short. Pack into wide-mouthed quart bottles.

To each quart container, allow 2 ounces granulated sugar, alternating layers of cherries and sugar until the jars are ¾ full.

Fill to brim with brandy, using about 8 fluid ounces for each quart. Seal securely.

Turn jars upside down, and turn them end for end again every hour for 4 consecutive hours, so as to mix sugar and brandy.

Then store in a cool, dry, dark place at least 3 months before using.

PICKLED SWEET CHERRIES

Fill clean fruit jars with large sweet cherries, leaving the stems on. Pack the fruit as closely as possible.

Mix together 1 tablespoon salt and 8 fluid ounces vinegar for each quart of cherries and pour over fruit.

Fill each jar with cold water and seal. Allow the cherries to stand in this brine for at least 2 weeks before opening any of the jars.

Pickled cherries are an excellent garnish and accompaniment for meats.

SPICED CRANBERRIES

1 pound sugar
4 fluid ounces vinegar
¾ teaspoon whole cloves
3 inches stick cinnamon
1 pound cranberries

Combine sugar, vinegar, and spices. Bring to boiling point.

Add cranberries and cook slowly, without stirring, until skins pop open. Pack in clean, hot jars. Fill with syrup. Seal.

PICKLED CRABAPPLES OR PEARS

7 pounds crabapples or small
**   pears**
1 quart white vinegar
4 pounds sugar
2 ounces whole cloves
1 stick cinnamon
1½ teaspoons whole ginger

Wash and remove blossom ends from fruit. Prick each piece several times.

Heat vinegar and sugar to boiling. Add spices tied loosely in a cheesecloth bag. Add fruit and boil gently until tender but not broken. Remove spice bag.

Quickly pack one hot sterilized jar at a time. Fill to ⅛ inch from top. Be sure vinegar solution covers the fruit. Seal each jar at once. Makes 6 pints.

Relishes

SWEET CORN RELISH

2 ounces flour
1 tablespoon turmeric
1 ounce dry mustard
3 pounds sweet corn, cut from cob
2 red peppers, chopped
8 ounces chopped cabbage
4 onions, chopped
1 quart vinegar
2 tablespoons salt
1 pound sugar
1½ tablespoons celery seed

Blend flour, turmeric, and mustard to a paste with a little of the vinegar.

Mix all ingredients and simmer for 45 minutes, stirring frequently to prevent scorching. Seal in clean, hot jars.

INDIA RELISH

12 large green tomatoes
1 red pepper
1 green pepper
4 large onions
1 tablespoon salt
12 ounces golden syrup
8 fluid ounces vinegar
1 tablespoon mustard seed
1 tablespoon celery seed

Put the tomatoes, peppers, and onions through vegetable mill, using coarse knife.

Drain well, reserving juice for soup or beverage.

Add remaining ingredients and mix well. Cook gently until vegetables are tender and mixture is thick, about 15 minutes.

Turn into hot, sterilized jars, filling to ½ inch from top. Seal at once. Makes 3 pints.

CHUTNEY

Chutney is a highly seasoned relish made in many different ways. It originated in India and is served with curries. It is often based on mangoes, but homemade chutneys include tomatoes, peppers, apples, pears, peaches, and other fruits. The following is a popular version.

12 green tomatoes, peeled
6 sweet red peppers, chopped
1 hot red pepper, chopped (optional)
1 large chopped onion
2 ounces chopped celery
2 tablespoons salt
1 pint vinegar
1 pound white or brown sugar
3 tablespoons whole mixed pickling spice
1 tablespoon ginger root
6 sour apples, peeled and chopped
½ pound seedless raisins (optional)

Mix vegetables with salt and let stand overnight.

Add remaining ingredients and cook, stirring often, until mixture is thick and clear.

Pour into sterile, hot jars and seal. Makes about 3 pints.

CHILLI SAUCE

7 pounds ripe tomatoes, cored and peeled
½ pound sweet green peppers
½ pound sweet red peppers
1 large chopped onion
1 tablespoon salt
1 bay leaf
1 tablespoon celery seed
½ teaspoon whole cloves
½ teaspoon whole allspice
1 teaspoon mustard seed
4 ounces sugar
12 fluid ounces vinegar

Chop all vegetables. Add salt and spices that have been tied in a piece of cheesecloth.

Simmer until mixture begins to thicken, stirring occasionally.

Add sugar and vinegar and cook, stirring often, until mixture is a thick sauce. Remove spice bag.

Pack into hot, sterile jars and seal. Makes about 3 pints.

PEPPER-ONION RELISH

2 pounds finely chopped onion
6 ounces finely chopped sweet red pepper
6 ounces finely chopped green pepper
8 ounces sugar
1 quart vinegar
4 teaspoons salt

Combine all ingredients and bring slowly to boil. Cook until slightly thickened.

Pour into clean, hot, sterile jars. Fill jars to top; seal tightly.

TOMATO KETCHUP

9 pounds sliced red tomatoes
4 red peppers
5 large onions
1 stalk celery
8 fluid ounces cider vinegar
12 ounces sugar
2 tablespoons salt
2 ounces whole mixed pickling spices

Simmer sliced tomatoes until soft, about ½ hour. Place in sieve or colander. Drain off juice.

Put peppers, onions, and celery through vegetable mill. Add to tomato pulp.

Simmer 1 hour and press through fine sieve.

Add vinegar, sugar, salt and spices tied in a cheesecloth bag. Simmer 1½ to 2 hours, or until thick.

Turn into hot, sterilized jars. Seal at once. Makes about 2 pints.

Note: Use drained juice for beverage or bottle for future use.

PEACH CHUTNEY

4 pounds sliced peaches
1 pint vinegar
6 ounces brown sugar
6 ounces sultanas
1 medium onion, chopped
1 green pepper, chopped
1 clove garlic, chopped (optional)
1 tablespoon chopped candied ginger
2 teaspoons salt
⅛ teaspoon cayenne pepper

Combine ingredients. Simmer until thick, stirring frequently.

Seal in sterilized jars. Makes 2 pints.

PICCALILLI

Originally from India, hence piccalilli is often called Indian pickle.

2 pounds chopped green tomatoes
2 medium-sized sweet red peppers, chopped
2 medium-sized sweet green peppers, chopped
2 large mild onions, chopped
1 small head cabbage, chopped
4 ounces salt
1½ pints vinegar
1 pound brown sugar
1 teaspoon mustard, or 2 tablespoons mixed pickle spices, tied in cheesecloth bag

Combine the vegetables, cover with salt and let stand overnight.

Drain and press in a clean, thin white cloth to remove all the liquid possible.

Add the vinegar, sugar, and spices and simmer until clear.

Discard spice bag and pack into clean, hot, sterile jars. Fill jars to top, seal tightly. Makes about 3 pints.

SWEET CHUTNEY

2 pounds cooking apples
1 pound sugar
1 pound seedless raisins
1 ounce red chillies
1 ounce garlic, crushed
1 ounce ginger, chopped
½ tablespoon salt
½ pint vinegar

Peel and core apples and chop coarsely.

Combine all ingredients in a pan, simmer gently and stir occasionally until the chutney thickens. Put into jars and, when cold, cover tightly.

CRANBERRY GRAPE RELISH

With fork, break up contents of 1-pound can whole cranberry sauce, chilled. Add 1 teaspoon grated orange rind and 4 ounces seedless grapes, cut in half.

CRANBERRY ORANGE RELISH

1 pound fresh cranberries
2 oranges, quartered and seeded
1 pound sugar

Put cranberries and oranges (including the rind) through the vegetable mill (coarse blade). Stir in the sugar and chill. Makes 1 pound. Keeps well for weeks stored in the refrigerator.

Note: 4 tablespoons sucaryl solution may be substituted for sugar if desired.

Variations: (1) To ½ pound basic relish add 1 ounce desiccated coconut; (2) To ½ pound basic relish add 1 teaspoon lemon juice and 2 ounces thinly sliced celery; (3) To ½ pound basic relish add 2 tablespoons raisins and 1 ounce chopped walnuts; (4) To ½ pound basic relish add ¼ teaspoon ginger and 1 tablespoon slivered lemon or orange rind.

For Family Meals from the Freezer: Simple garnishes and relishes add an interesting touch to family meals. Cranberry relishes, for example, can be frozen in cubes for a quick garnish any time.

PIES AND PASTRY

Whether you serve a fruit pie warm from the oven or a party pie from the refrigerator or freezer, you'll find pies an appetizing dessert which can be easily prepared in advance.

PIE-PASTRY HINTS

Plain flour is generally used; it should be very dry and for pastry-making it should be sifted.

Use chilled water and be very sparing with it.

Don't overmix. Handle dough as little as possible and as lightly as possible.

Chill after mixing.

Plain pastry, made by the standard method, is tender and flaky. Hot water pastry is tender but has a tendency to crumble. It is somewhat difficult to handle, although some cooks consider it easier to make.

ABOUT EQUIPMENT

A board, rolling pin, a wire pastry blender or blending fork, a measuring cup, knife, and spoon are all that are necessary.

If a pastry blender is not available, use two knives.

A pastry cloth (medium-weight cotton canvas) for the board and stockinette for the rolling pin reduces flour needed to roll dough and makes handling of pastry easier, especially in hot weather.

ABOUT PIE DISHES

A standard pie dish with a slanting rim is best.

Pastry will brown more readily on the bottom in a glass baking dish or enamel pan, or in a tin that has grown dark from use than in a new tin or aluminium pan. Glass has the advantage that you can inspect the bottom to see if the crust is thoroughly baked, and it does make a more attractive serving dish.

PIE MAKING AT HIGH ALTITUDES

For general information about high altitude cooking, see **Cooking at High Altitudes.** Pie crust is usually not affected by altitude except for the faster rate of evaporation. Therefore, you may get better results if you add a little more liquid.

PIE FAULTS— HOW TO OVERCOME THEM

Although you think you have followed directions very carefully for making your pie, it may not turn out as expected. This is not a matter of chance but is caused by something you did or failed to do during the preparation or baking. Study the following chart, note the sections that name any faults of your pie, and try to determine where you have slipped.

Pastry has shrunk:

a. Pastry should be allowed to rest about 10 minutes before trimming and baking.

b. Not letting upper crust extend over rim of dish so that it can be moulded into rim with lower crust.

c. Pastry should not be stretched to fit into dish. Fit it loosely and press gently into shape of dish.

Pastry crumbles:

a. Flour and fat over-mixed.

Pastry is tough:

a. Too much water added to flour-fat mixture.

b. Too little fat in proportion to flour.

c. Too much handling and rolling.

d. Too much flour on board. It works into pastry.

e. Pastry over-mixed.

Bumps and bubbles on baked pie cases:

a. Air trapped under pastry when fitted into or over dish.

b. Bottom and sides of crust not pricked with prongs of fork before baking.

Pies do not brown:

a. With fruit or custard pies use a glass pie dish or an enamel plate. Try baking such pies at a constant temperature of 400°F. to 425°F., Mark 6 to 7.

Bottom crust of filled pie is soggy:

a. Too low a temperature was used.

b. Pastry too damp to begin with.

Fruit pie filling has bubbled over:

a. Not enough thickening with watery fruit.

b. Use a pie funnel to form a vent so juice can bubble up but not over, or bind edge of juicy fruit pies with pie tape, strip of gauze, or cloth dipped in cold water. Remove after pie is baked.

c. Make lower crust large enough to fold over edge of fruit.

d. Oven was too hot.

Cream pie filling is runny although the same recipe was used which gave good results at another time:

a. Eggs not as fresh or smaller than usual.

b. Filling may not have been cooked long enough after eggs were added.

c. Occasionally when starch is used for thickening, it is affected by very acid ingredients. This may particularly occur with brown sugar, chocolate, or lemon fillings.

Meringue is tough, shrinks, or "weeps":

a. Oven too slow.

b. Meringue was not spread well out on the edge of outer crust all round.

c. Too much sugar was used or sugar is too coarse.

d. Egg whites may have been under-beaten.

e. Sugar may not have been thoroughly blended into egg whites.

Why butter and margarine are generally not recommended for pastry:

a. Butter and margarine scorch at lower temperature.

b. They contain water and milk solids which do not give as tender crusts as pure fats.

Pastries for Pies

PASTRY FOR DOUBLE-CRUST PIE

For 8-inch 2-crust pie:
  6 ounces sifted flour
  ¾ teaspoon salt
  4 ounces fat
  3 to 4 tablespoons iced water

For 9-inch 2-crust pie:
  8 ounces sifted flour
  1 teaspoon salt
  5 ounces fat
  4 to 6 tablespoons iced water

Step 1: Sift together the flour and salt. Cut in the fat with a pastry blender or blending fork (or two knives used scissors fashion) until pieces are size of small peas.

To make pastry extra tender and flaky, divide fat in half. Cut in first half until mixture looks like fine breadcrumbs. Then cut in remaining half until pieces are the size of peas.

Step 2: Sprinkle water, a tablespoon at a time, over part of mixture. Gently mix with a fork and push to one side of bowl. Sprinkle next tablespoon water over dry part; mix lightly and push to moistened part at side. Repeat until all is moistened. Be sparing with water because too much makes pastry tough.

Step 3: Use just enough water to make it possible to gather dough together with the fingers so it cleans the bowl. Chill about ½ hour, if time permits.

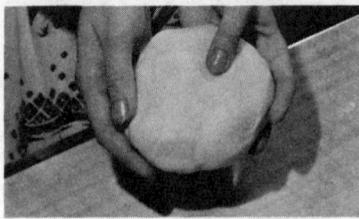

Step 4: Divide dough about in half. Use a little more than half for under crust. Use fingers rather than the palm of hand to shape the portion that is to be rolled into a ball. Press lightly and evenly all over to make a smooth circle of dough, round and somewhat flat in shape.

Step 5: Roll dough for bottom crust on lightly floured board or pastry cloth, using a stockinet-covered rolling pin. Roll lightly, but evenly, from centre to edges. If edges split, pinch together. Keep it in a circle ⅛ inch thick and large enough to extend ½ inch over edge of pie dish. (Estimate by holding dish over the dough.)

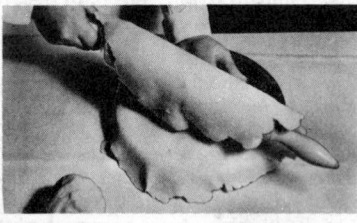

Step 6: Transfer to pie dish folding dough in half for easy transfer to pie dish, or roll it on rolling pin unrolling it into pie dish. Do not stretch pastry but pat and fit it loosely down into dish. It should cover rim of dish well.

Step 7: Trim off overhanging edges with scissors.

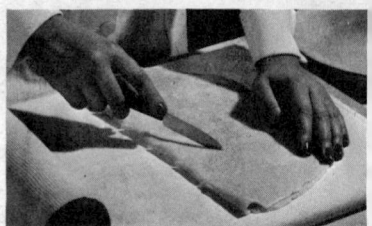

Step 8: Roll second ball of dough as described above. Make several gashes in a design to allow escape of steam. Place filling in pie according to pie recipe used.

Step 9: Place top crust over filling, by rolling it over the rolling pin, transferring to pie dish, and unrolling into place. Crust will not break if this method is used.

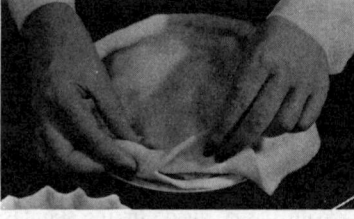

Step 10: Moisten the edge of the lower crust. With scissors, trim the upper crust half an inch beyond edge and tuck it under the edge of the lower crust. Then crimp edges together with fork, spoon, or fingers. Bake according to directions given in recipe for pie.

TO CUT A PIE BEFORE BAKING

1. Outline wedges of pie before baking. For a 2-crust pie, cut slits into top crust using cocktail sticks and a string as a guide.
2. For a single-crust pie, cut ½-inch strips of pastry. Outline wedges with the pastry instead of making regular lattice top.

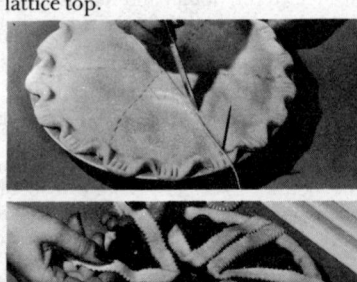

TO MAKE THREE EASY EDGES ON A DOUBLE-CRUST PIE

1. To put a high fluted edge on a pie crust, cut dough off ½ inch beyond rim of dish. Fold under. Then crimp dough between knuckle of left forefinger and thumb and forefinger of right hand.

2. Press edges together with the prongs of a fork.

3. For a pretty scalloped edge, press edges together with the tip of a teaspoon.

FLAKY HOT WATER PASTRY

2 fluid ounces boiling water
4 ounces lard or vegetable fat
6 ounces sifted flour
½ teaspoon baking powder
¼ teaspoon salt
1 teaspoon sugar

Pour boiling water over fat in mixing bowl; stir until smooth and well blended; cool.

Combine remaining dry ingredients in sifter; sift over cooled fat; stir only enough to mix well. Chill before rolling. Makes 1 8-inch two-crust pie.

EGG PASTRY

8 ounces sifted flour
1 teaspoon salt
5 ounces fat
1 slightly beaten egg
2 tablespoons water
2 teaspoons lemon juice

Mix and sift flour with salt into mixing bowl. Cut in fat with a pastry blender or 2 knives until particles are the size of small peas.

Combine egg, water, and lemon juice; sprinkle over flour mixture while tossing and stirring lightly with fork until dough is just moist enough to hold together. If necessary add a few more drops water.

Divide in half and form into balls. Roll out one ball on floured surface to a circle 1½ inches larger than inverted 8- or 9-inch pie dish. Fit loosely into dish. Fill with desired filling.

Roll out remaining dough. Cut slits for escape of steam. Place top crust over filling. Bake according to recipe for filling. Makes 2-crust 8- or 9-inch pie.

QUICK OIL PIE CRUST

8 ounces sifted flour
½ teaspoon salt
¼ teaspoon baking powder
4 fluid ounces vegetable oil
2 fluid ounces water

Sift dry ingredients together.

Combine oil and water and stir lightly.

Toss dry ingredients with a fork while adding liquid ingredients in a small steady stream; work rapidly.

Press dough together; divide into 2 balls and place ball of dough on lightly floured board. Cover with greaseproof paper to prevent dough from sticking to rolling pin and roll immediately.

Pie Case: Bake 15 minutes in a hot oven (425°F. Mark 7).

Two-crust Fruit Pie: Bake 10 minutes in very hot oven (450°F. Mark 8), then reduce heat to moderate (350°F. Mark 4) and bake until fruit is tender, usually 25 to 35 minutes.

Makes 2 9-inch pastry cases or pastry for 1 9-inch 2-crust pie.

CHEESE PASTRY

To recipe for shortcrust pastry (9-inch double-crust) add 1 tablespoon more fat.

Combine flour, salt, and shortening with pastry blender, then stir in 1 ounce grated sharp cheese.

Then add iced water and continue as directed in shortcrust pastry.

This is excellent for apple pies, and it is sometimes used for cherry pies.

SPICED PASTRY

Sift ½ teaspoon cinnamon, ¼ teaspoon ginger, and ¼ teaspoon ground cloves with the flour and salt in recipe for 2-crust 9-inch shortcrust pastry. Good for apple pie.

BUTTER-CRUST PASTRY

4 ounces butter
2 tablespoons sugar
4 ounces sifted flour

Combine butter, sugar, and flour in small mixing bowl. Using low speed of mixer, mix just until dough forms.

Place 1 to 2 ounces of mixture in small pan. With well-floured fingers press remaining mixture evenly over bottom and sides of 9-inch pie dish.

Bake in moderate oven (375°F. Mark 5) until golden brown, 12 to 15 minutes. Bake the crumbs 10 to 12 minutes.

Cool, then fill with desired filling. Sprinkle top with crumb mixture. Makes a 9-inch pie crust.

Variations: Stir in 2 ounces chopped nuts or desiccated coconut before pressing into pie dish.

TO MAKE A LATTICE TOP FOR A FRUIT PIE

Using recipe for 2-crust pie, fit lower crust into dish, cut off pastry to allow ½-inch overhang. With knife or pastry-wheel, cut strips ½ inch wide. Cover pie with half of the strips. Starting at centre, fold back every other strip and weave additional strips diagonally across pie, under and over until top is covered. Press ends of strips to rim, fold the overhanging crust up and over and crimp edge. Pastry strips may be woven into lattice on greaseproof paper. Whole lattice may be flipped over onto filling and greaseproof paper peeled off.

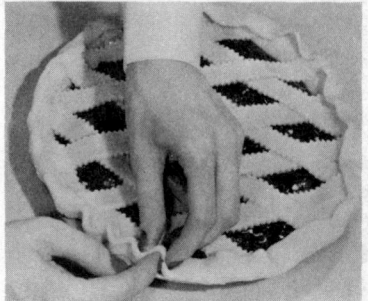

PASTRY FOR SINGLE-CRUST PIE

(Makes 8- or 9-inch pastry case)

4 ounces sifted flour
½ teaspoon salt
3 ounces fat
2 to 3 tablespoons iced water

Step 1: Mix and sift flour and salt.

Step 2: Cut in fat with a pastry blender.

Step 3: Sprinkle with cold water. Gather dough together and press firmly into a ball.

Step 4: Roll out into a circle 1 inch larger than dish, all around.

Step 5: Fit loosely into dish. Avoid stretching to prevent shrinkage.

(**Note:** For precise instructions regarding above steps, see shortcrust pastry for 2-crust pie.)

Step 6: Let pastry rest a few minutes, then fold extra pastry back and under, and build up a high fluted edge even with dish rim.

Step 7: Prick bottom of unfilled pastry case with fork to keep pastry from puffing up and warping during baking. Bake in very hot oven (450°F. Mark 8) until delicately browned, 12 to 15 minutes. (After 5 minutes of baking look at pastry case and quickly collapse any bubbles by pricking.)

Step 8: Cool pastry case in the dish on a cake rack out of draughts before adding filling.

Step 9: Or, if filling and pastry are baked together do not prick the crust. Bake according to recipe directions for the pie.

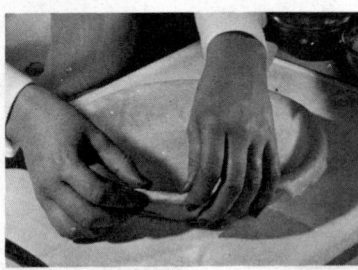

After letting pastry in dish rest a few minutes, fold extra pastry back and under.

Build up a high fluted edge to hold a generous amount of filling.

TO KEEP CRUST FROM SHRINKING

1. Fit pastry loosely into dish and shape without stretching. Build up fluted edge, then prick all over to prevent puffing up and warping during baking. Let cool, then fill.

2. Pie crusts hold to shape and shrink less when baked on the back of the pie dish. Let dough fall loosely over dish and shape without stretching. Crimp edges and prick all over to prevent blistering.

3. Pie crusts may be baked between 2 dishes of equal size. Fit dough into dish without stretching, trim and press down edges with prongs of fork and prick all over. Place second dish on top of dough. After 8 minutes of baking time, remove top dish to allow crust to brown.

CRISPER UNDERCRUSTS

For crisper undercrusts in pumpkin or custard pies freeze unbaked pie crusts before you fill them. Brush pastry with a little beaten egg, then place pie crust in freezing compartment or in food freezer. Before baking, fill frozen pie crusts and place in oven without defrosting.

NUT PASTRY CASE

Follow recipe for shortcrust pastry for 1-crust pie, adding 1 ounce chopped nuts to the flour. This is most frequently used for cream pies.

ORANGE PASTRY CASE

Follow recipe for shortcrust pastry for 1-crust pie, substituting orange juice for the water, and adding ½ teaspoon grated orange rind. This is used with orange and lemon pies, and sometimes for other pies.

CHOCOLATE PASTRY

6 ounces sifted flour
2½ tablespoons cocoa
2 teaspoons sugar
½ teaspoon salt
4 ounces lard or vegetable fat
about 6 tablespoons cold water

Mix and sift flour, cocoa, sugar, and salt.

Cut in lard until mixture is of a coarse consistency.

Add only enough water to hold ingredients together.

Pat pastry into a ball. Chill 1 hour, if time allows.

Roll out and fit into pie dish. Prick with prongs of fork to prevent bubbles.

Bake in hot oven (400°F. Mark 6) about 12 minutes. Makes 1 9-inch pie case.

MUERBETEIG
(Rich Egg Pastry)

4 ounces flour
1 egg yolk
1 tablespoon sugar
4 ounces butter or margarine
grated rind of 1 lemon
pinch of salt

Sift flour onto a pastry board or into a bowl.

Make a well in the centre of the flour and put into it the egg yolk, sugar, butter, lemon rind, and salt.

Mix these centre ingredients into a smooth paste and then quickly work in the flour, adding a very little iced water to moisten the dough, if necessary.

Press the dough, with the fingers, into a 9-inch pie plate, or chill it for 1 hour in the refrigerator and roll it out ¼ inch thick to fit a sandwich tin.

This paste or dough is used for many types of kuchens, fruit pies, and desserts.

Chill the lined pie plate or sandwich tin for 30 minutes before covering it with fruit, sugar, and spices. Bake as directed in recipe.

HOW TO USE LEFTOVER PASTRY

Roll out trimmings from pie crusts. Sprinkle with grated cheese, or sugar and cinnamon. Cut in fancy shapes, and bake. Serve with hors d'oeuvres, salads.

Crumb Pie Shells

DIGESTIVE BISCUIT PIE SHELL
(Basic Recipe)

**6 ounces digestive biscuit crumbs
(16 or 18 biscuits)
3 ounces soft butter or margarine
3 tablespoons sugar**

Use only fresh biscuits. Roll into fine crumbs on greaseproof paper or in plastic bag. Or crush crumbs in vegetable mill or blender.

Combine and mix dry ingredients, then add butter softened at room temperature. (Don't melt; the softened fat mixes more easily and evenly.)

Blend all ingredients well with pastry blender, blending fork, or your hands.

Turn mixture into a 9-inch pie dish. Using a flat-bottomed glass mould, press firmly, making the bottom slightly thicker than the sides. Use the back of a tablespoon to pack crumbs firmly into angles of dish and firmly against sides of dish. Use hands to finish moulding crust firmly around rim; make it slightly rounded and at least ¼ inch thick for easier cutting and serving of pie.

Chill thoroughly before using. This shell may be baked in preheated moderate oven (350°F. Mark 4) for 8 to 10 minutes, which gives a firmer shell and is desirable if a cooked filling rather than an instant pudding or a gelatine filling is used. Chill the baked shell before filling.

Or for a pie to be covered with meringue, pour cold filling into the freshly shaped shell, spread on meringue in usual way, then bake in moderate oven (350°F. Mark 4) 12 to 15 minutes to brown meringue.

Chocolate Digestive Biscuit Shell: Follow method for digestive biscuit shell, using chocolate digestive biscuit crumbs.

CRUMB SHELLS—QUICK WAY

Empty crumb mixture into a 9-inch pie dish and spread evenly across the bottom.

Place an 8-inch pie dish, which has been greased on the outside, on the crumb mixture, and press mixture firmly into an even layer against the bottom and sides.

Remove greased pie dish and chill or bake, as desired.

Use only fresh biscuits. Roll into fine crumbs.

To the mixed dry ingredients, add butter softened at room temperature.

Pack crumbs firmly into angles of pan and firmly against sides of pan.

OTHER CRUMB SHELLS

Chocolate Biscuit Shell: Use 6 ounces chocolate biscuit crumbs and 3 ounces soft butter or margarine. Follow method for digestive biscuit shell.

Corn Flake Shell: Use 6 ounces finely crushed corn flakes (or other ready-to-eat cereal), 3 ounces sugar, and 3 ounces soft butter or margarine. Follow method for digestive biscuit shell.

Ginger Biscuit Shell: Use 6 ounces ginger biscuit crumbs, 3 ounces soft butter or margarine, and a dash of salt. Follow method for digestive biscuit shell.

Barmouth Biscuit Shell: Use 6 ounces Barmouth biscuit crumbs and 2 ounces soft butter or margarine. Follow method for digestive biscuit shell.

Other Variations: Almost any crisp biscuits may be used in the same way. Some people prefer to use melted butter; in that case grease the pie dish well before spreading the crumb mixture.

If desired, spread only the bottom of the pie dish with biscuit crumbs and line sides of dish with whole biscuits, cut in halves.

Meringues

MERINGUE TOPPING

This meringue may be used for other desserts as well as pies.

For 9-inch Pie:
**3 egg whites
¼ teaspoon salt
6 tablespoons sugar
½ teaspoon flavouring (optional)**

For 8-inch Pie:
**2 egg whites
¼ teaspoon salt
4 tablespoons sugar
¼ teaspoon flavouring (optional)**

Beat egg whites with salt until frothy. (Whites will whip fluffier if they are at room temperature.)

Then beat in sugar, 1 tablespoon at a time. Beat until meringue is stiff and glossy. The meringue is ready for the pie when the sugar has dissolved and the meringue is stiff enough to hold a point, yet still looks moist.

Add ½ teaspoon flavouring, if desired. Beat only enough to blend.

Swirl meringue lightly on pie, sealing to edge of crust to prevent shrinking.

Bake in moderate oven (350°F. Mark 4) 12 to 15 minutes, until delicately browned.

Always pile meringue thick and high.

Swirl meringue lightly on pie, sealing to edge of shell to prevent shrinkage.

Meringue may be spooned onto filling to make a wreath. Leave in peaks.

MERINGUE CASES

4 egg whites
1 teaspoon cream of tartar
½ teaspoon salt
½ teaspoon vanilla
½ pound sifted granulated sugar

(Note: Egg whites should be at room temperature to whip up extra fluffy, but eggs should be separated while cold.)

To Mix: Add cream of tartar, salt and vanilla to egg whites in large bowl. Using rotary egg beater or electric mixer, beat egg whites until stiff (mixture holds a peak) but not dry. The stiff peaks are still glossy.

Add sugar gradually, 1 tablespoon at a time. Beat after each addition until well blended and sugar is dissolved. If you taste a little, there should be no sugar crystals.

To Shape and Bake: Line baking sheet with non-stick paper, cut to fit. Trace a heart on it, or other desired shape, using a cardboard pattern or heart-shaped cake tin.

Using a full recipe of meringue, smooth out to edge of pattern with back of tablespoon and build up rim.

Bake meringue heart in very slow oven (250°F. Mark ½) for 1¼ hours. The heart will be tinged with golden brown. The outside will be crisp, the inside tender and a little moist.

To Serve: Just before serving, fill cooled meringue with ice cream, lemon pie filling, or other desired filling.

Individual Meringues: These may be heart-shaped or round. Drop by spoonfuls on small heart pattern drawn on liner paper or heap in a circle. Hollow out with back of spoon.

Bake individual meringues in slow oven (275°F. Mark 1) for 50 minutes.

To Freeze Meringues: Place in freezer or freezing compartment of refrigerator. When frozen, wrap in freezer paper and seal.

To serve, remove from freezer and allow to stand at room temperature 30 to 45 minutes.

Heart-Shaped Meringue

Fruit Pies

APPLE PIE
(Basic Recipe)

pastry for 9-inch 2-crust pie
7 to 8 medium-sized tart, juicy
apples (2¼ pounds)
1 tablespoon flour
dash of salt
5 to 6 ounces sugar (larger
amount for very tart apples)
1 tablespoon butter or margarine
1 tablespoon lemon juice (optional)
¼ teaspoon cinnamon or nutmeg

Prepare pastry. Roll out bottom crust; line pie dish and trim off even with dish rim.

Roll out top crust; cut design in centre for escape of steam. Cover pastry with greaseproof paper while preparing filling.

Wash apples, peel, quarter, remove cores, and cut quarters lengthwise into 3 or 4 slices. There should be a full 2 pounds of sliced apples, firmly packed.

Blend flour, salt, and sugar; sprinkle ¼ of mixture over bottom of pastry lined pie dish.

Stir the remaining mixture lightly through apples; turn into dish, placing them close together and piling them higher than the rim of the pie dish. Fruit should be slightly rounded in centre.

Dot with butter. Sprinkle with lemon juice, then with cinnamon.

Moisten the edge of lower pastry with a little cold water. Then carefully place the pastry for top crust evenly on top of the filling, allowing it to fall loosely in place. Press down gently around edge to seal.

Trim off any extra edges with scissors, but leave ½ inch overhanging edge of pie dish.

Fold the extra edge of top pastry under edge of lower pastry so fold is even with pie dish rim.

Again press down gently all around edge and flute with the fingers or crimp with the prongs of a fork.

Bake in very hot oven (450°F. Mark 8) 15 minutes, then reduce heat to slow (325°F. Mark 3) and bake until apples are tender and juice boils out of vents, about 35 minutes. Remove to cake rack to cool.

To make 8-Inch Pie: Use pastry for 2-crust 8-inch pie, 1½ pounds medium-sized tart juicy apples, 2 teaspoons flour, pinch of salt, 7 tablespoons to 4 ounces sugar, 1 teaspoon butter or margarine, 2 teaspoons lemon juice, and a scant ¼ teaspoon cinnamon.

Deep-Dish Apple Pie: Bake ingredients for apple pie above in pastry lined 6½ × 10½-inch oblong baking dish.

Cheese Crumble Apple Pie

CHEESE CRUMBLE APPLE PIE

8 ounces shortcrust pastry mix
4 ounces sugar
3 ounces brown sugar
¾ teaspoon cinnamon
3 tablespoons butter
8 ounces grated Cheddar cheese
3 pounds cooking apples, peeled
and sliced
1 tablespoon flour

For crumble topping: Measure 4 ounces of shortcrust mix and combine with sugars and cinnamon. Cut in butter thoroughly. Set aside.

Mix 4 ounces Cheddar cheese into remaining shortcrust mix. Blend with 2 to 2½ tablespoons water. Roll dough and line pie dish.

Place apples in pastry-lined 9-inch pie plate. Sprinkle with flour and nutmeg and cover with half of crumble mixture.

Sprinkle remaining 4 ounces Cheddar cheese over all. Top with remaining crumble mixture. Bake in moderate oven (375°F. Mark 5) about 40 minutes or until apples are tender.

TO KEEP JUICE FROM BOILING OVER WHEN MAKING FRUIT PIES

1. Cut off lower crust at edge of dish. With scissors, cut off top crust ½ inch beyond edge. Tuck this under the lower crust before crimping. This seals in the juices of the pie.

2. Place 1½-inch pieces of uncooked macaroni or straws in top. The juice boils up into these little "chimneys" instead of boiling over the sides. May be used with a lattice or 2-crust pie.

3. Cut a circular piece of pastry the size of the inside top of the pie dish. When this is placed over the filling, it leaves a narrow opening around the edge and permits the steam to escape.

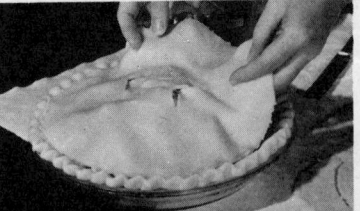

CANNED APPLE PIE

1½ tablespoons quick-cooking
    tapioca
6 ounces sugar
⅛ teaspoon salt
¾ teaspoon cinnamon
¼ teaspoon nutmeg
1 pound sliced apples
pastry for 8-inch double-crust pie
2 tablespoons butter or margarine

Mix tapioca, sugar, salt, cinnamon, nutmeg, and apples.

Line pie dish with pastry rolled ⅛-inch thick.

Fill with apple mixture; dot with butter. Moisten edge of pastry.

Cut slits in top crust to permit escape of steam and adjust, opening slits with knife. Bake in hot oven (425°F. Mark 7) 55 minutes or until syrup boils with heavy bubbles that do not burst.

CANNED PINEAPPLE PIE

1 large can (1¼ pounds. pineapple
    slices or titbits
4 fluid ounces pineapple juice
3 tablespoons cornflour
6 ounces sugar
grated rind and juice of 1 lemon
3 tablespoons butter
pastry for 2-crust 9-inch pie

Drain pineapple and cut into pieces. Heat juice. Blend cornflour with sugar and add to hot juice. Cook over low heat until mixture is clear and thickened, stirring constantly. Add lemon juice and rind, butter, and pineapple. Let cool while making pie crust.

Fit lower crust into 9-inch pie dish and fill. Fit on top crust, trim and crimp edges. Cut gashes to allow steam to escape. Bake in hot oven (425°F. Mark 7) 25 to 30 minutes or until crust is browned.

FRESH PINEAPPLE PIE

2 eggs
12 ounces sugar
1 tablespoon lemon juice
1¼ pounds shredded fresh pineapple
pastry for 9-inch double crust

Beat eggs slightly and combine with sugar, lemon juice, and pineapple.

Line 9-inch pie dish with pastry; pour in filling. Cover with pastry.

Bake in very hot oven (450°F. Mark 8) 10 minutes. Reduce heat to moderate (350°F. Mark 4) and bake 30 minutes, or until crust is nicely browned and pineapple is tender.

Pineapple and Strawberry Pie: Use 12 ounces shredded fresh pineapple and 12 ounces sliced strawberries.

GUAVA PIE

pastry for 9-inch double crust
2½ pounds ripe or 1 pound canned
    guavas
scant 8 ounces sugar
1 tablespoon butter or margarine
dash of nutmeg

Peel fresh guavas thinly and scoop out seedy part in centre. Rub through food mill and discard seeds.

Cut the fleshy guava shells into thin slices and combine with purée. (There should be 1½ pounds purée and slices.)

Stir sugar into fruit and turn into pastry lined pie dish. Spread evenly and dot with butter. Sprinkle with nutmeg.

Fit top pastry over filling, sealing well. Bake in very hot oven (450°F. Mark 8) 15 minutes. Reduce heat to slow oven (325°F. Mark 3) and bake 30 minutes, or until pastry is lightly browned and fruit is tender. Let cool on rack before cutting.

GRAPE PIE

2 pounds grapes
5 to 6 ounces sugar
1 ounce flour or 1 tablespoon quick-
    cooking tapioca
⅛ teaspoon salt
grated rind and juice of ½ lemon
pastry for 9-inch 2-crust pie

Slip pulp out of grape skins. Reserve skins. Cook pulp until seeds loosen and press through colander or vegetable mill.

Mix sugar, flour, or tapioca, salt, lemon rind, and juice. Add grape juice and skins.

If tapioca has been used, let mixture stand 15 minutes.

Turn into pastry lined 9-inch pie dish and cover with pastry.

Bake on lower rack of very hot oven (450°F. Mark 8) 15 minutes. Lower heat to moderate (350°F. Mark 4) and bake about 20 minutes longer.

FRUIT FLAN

Use 1½ pounds fruit such as apples, apricots, peaches, and plums. Fresh fruit or cooked or canned fruit may be used.

Line flan ring or pie dish with Flan Pastry (below). Fill with fruit. Sprinkle with sugar to taste.

Bake in hot oven (425°F. Mark 7) about 25 minutes.

FLAN PASTRY

This sweet, rich pastry, very similar to Muerbeteig, is generally used in France and other European countries for open fruit pies.

4 ounces sifted flour
½ teaspoon salt
1 tablespoon sugar
6 tablespoons butter or margarine
1 egg yolk
1 tablespoon water
1½ tablespoons lemon juice or
    1½ tablespoons rum

Mix and sift flour, salt, and sugar. Cut in butter with pastry blender or 2 knives.

Beat egg yolk with water and lemon juice and work into dough with the fingers. Chill thoroughly.

Roll or pat ¼-inch thick to fit 9-inch pie dish or flan ring or roll ⅛-inch thick to fit 9 × 12-inch dish.

Fill and bake as in Fruit Flan.

There are many versions of this classic pastry. Yeast coffee cake dough is often used. After the last rising, pat it out very thin, and make a rim by pinching the edges of the dough all the way around. Fill with the fruit and cover with a streusel topping (see Index). Bake as directed for the coffee cake dough.

FRENCH FRUIT TART

about 8 ounces Barmouth biscuit
    crumbs, finely rolled
2 ounces butter or margarine, melted
1 tablespoon instant coffee
5 egg yolks
6 ounces sugar
3 tablespoons flour
1 pint milk
1 teaspoon vanilla
fresh peaches, peeled and sliced
fresh strawberries, hulled and
    washed
fresh blueberries
5 ounces red currant jelly

Combine Barmouth biscuit crumbs and melted butter into which the instant coffee has been stirred. Pour crumb mixture into a 9-inch pie dish, pressing crumbs firmly against bottom and sides using an 8-inch pie dish. Bake in moderate oven (375°F. Mark 5) 8 minutes. Cool.

Beat egg yolks and sugar until thick and lemon-coloured. Slowly beat in flour until well blended.

Scald milk with vanilla and stir into egg mixture. Return custard to saucepan and cook over medium heat, stirring constantly until custard thickens and boils. Boil for 1 minute.

Cool in a bowl, covering the surface of the custard with greaseproof paper to prevent a skin forming. Spoon into pie case. Top custard with the fresh fruit in any pattern you wish.

Melt red currant jelly in a saucepan and brush over the fruit to glaze. Refrigerate until ready to serve. Makes 8 servings.

French Fruit Tart

FRESH SOFT FRUIT PIE
(Basic Recipe)

pastry for 2-crust 9-inch pie
2 pounds soft fruit
7 to 8 ounces sugar
4 tablespoons flour
2 teaspoons quick-cooking tapioca
½ teaspoon cinnamon
1 tablespoon butter or margarine

Use fresh ripe fruit (strawberries, raspberries, bilberries, blackberries, or loganberries, etc.). Wash them, pick over, and remove stems and hulls.

Drain and increase or decrease sugar in accordance with sweetness of fruit (up to 12 ounces sugar for 2 pounds berries).

Fill pastry lined 9-inch dish with fruit, sprinkling them with the sugar-flour mixture. Sprinkle tapioca over when half the fruit is in the dish and again towards top.

Sprinkle with cinnamon and dot with butter. If fruit is dry, sprinkle with 1 to 2 tablespoons water. Cover with top crust.

Bake in very hot oven (450°F. Mark 8) 10 minutes, then in moderate oven (350°F. Mark 4) about 30 minutes, until crust is nicely browned and berries are cooked through. Serve slightly warm, not hot.

CANNED SOFT FRUIT PIE
(Basic Recipe)

pastry for 9-inch double crust
2 pounds canned soft fruit
4 to 6 ounces sugar
4 tablespoons flour
½ teaspoon cinnamon (optional)
1 tablespoon butter or margarine
4 fluid ounces juice from fruit

Drain fruit well. Taste juice and use minimum amount of sugar.

Mix sugar and flour; sprinkle ½ of it over chilled pastry in 9-inch dish.

Add fruit, sprinkling remaining flour and sugar through them. Sprinkle with cinnamon. Dot with butter. Add juice. Quickly cover with top crust.

Bake in very hot oven (450°F. Mark 8) 15 minutes, then about 20 minutes in moderate oven (350°F. Mark 4) until nicely browned. Serve slightly warm, not hot.

Deep Dish Strawberry Pie

FROZEN SOFT FRUIT PIE
(Basic Recipe)

pastry for 9-inch double crust
2 pounds sugar packed soft fruit, thawed
4 tablespoons flour
1 ounce butter or margarine

Line a 9-inch pie dish with pastry.

Fruit should be thawed enough to separate easily.

Sprinkle 1 tablespoon flour over bottom of pastry case.

Blend remaining flour with some of the fruit juice, making a smooth paste. Stir into remaining fruit and juice.

Fill pastry lined dish. Dot with butter. Cover with top crust.

Bake in very hot oven (450°F. Mark 8) 15 minutes. Reduce heat to moderate (375°F. Mark 5) and bake 20 minutes longer.

Note: If unsweetened fruit is used, add 4 to 8 ounces sugar as in basic recipe.

If syrup-packed fruit is used, pour off syrup after thawing, measure 3 fluid ounces syrup and add to 2 pounds drained fruit. Add no sugar.

STRAWBERRY GLAZE PIE

1 9-inch baked pie case
2 pounds fresh hulled strawberries
6 ounces sugar
2 tablespoons cornflour
¼ teaspoon salt
½ pint water

Line baked pastry case with strawberries.

Combine sugar, cornflour, salt, and water. Cook over low heat slowly until thickened and clear, about 10 to 15 minutes.

Pour glaze over strawberries. Chill. Just before serving, garnish with whipped cream and whole berries.

Peach or Raspberry Glaze Pie: Fresh sliced peaches or whole raspberries may be substituted for strawberries, if desired.

DEEP DISH STRAWBERRY PIE

4 to 8 ounces sugar (depending on sweetness of fruit)
1 ounce flour
⅛ teaspoon salt
2½ pounds washed and hulled strawberries
2 tablespoons butter
pastry for 2-crust 9-inch pie

Mix sugar with flour and salt. Toss lightly with the berries. Fill a 2-pint baking dish with the fruit mixture and dot with butter.

Top with the pastry which has been rolled out on pastry cloth to size 1 inch larger all around than top of baking dish. Fold edges of pastry under and press firmly to rim of dish. Flute edges and cut gashes in pastry to allow steam to escape.

Bake in hot oven (425°F. Mark 7) 25 minutes or until crust is browned. Serve slightly warm with plain or whipped cream.

FRESH CHERRY PIE

pastry for double crust 9-inch pie
2 pounds cherries, stoned
8 ounces sugar (10 ounces for very sour cherries)
¼ teaspoon salt
2 tablespoons cornflour or 2½ tablespoons tapioca
2 tablespoons butter or margarine

Combine sugar, salt, and cornflour. Add to the stoned cherries. Place fruit in pastry lined pie plate. Dot with butter.

Cover with top crust, slashed toward the centre to allow for escape of steam. Press the edges of the two crusts together tightly, so that the juices will not run out.

If a glaze is wanted, brush the top pastry with milk or cream.

Bake in very hot oven (450°F. Mark 8) 15 minutes, then reduce heat to 350°F. Mark 4 and bake about 30 minutes longer.

CANNED CHERRY PIE

pastry for 9-inch double crust
1¾ pounds unsweetened cherries
4 tablespoons cornflour
4 fluid ounces cherry juice
8 ounces sugar
1 tablespoon butter or margarine
¼ teaspoon salt
½ teaspoon almond flavouring

Prepare pastry as directed for 2 crusts.

Drain cherries. Combine cornflour and cherry juice and bring to boil. Cook, stirring constantly, until thick and clear. Add sugar.

Remove from heat and add butter or margarine, salt, cherries, and almond flavouring, stirring carefully to prevent crushing cherries. Cool.

Fill pie case. Place top crust over filling. Trim pastry and seal as directed for double-crust pie. Bake in hot oven (425°F. Mark 7) 35 minutes.

The Liberty Bell topping on this fruit pie was made from leftover bits of pastry baked on a baking sheet.

FROZEN CHERRY PIE

2 pounds frozen cherries
plain pastry for 9-inch double crust
3 tablespoons flour
4 teaspoons cornflour
⅛ teaspoon salt
6 ounces sugar
6 fluid ounces cherry juice, drained
    from cherries
1 tablespoon butter or margarine
few drops red food colouring
    (optional)

Thaw cherries and drain; there should be 10 to 12 fluid ounces juice and 1¼ pounds drained cherries.

Make pastry; roll out ½ of it and line 9-inch pie dish.

Blend flour, cornflour, salt, and sugar in 3-quart saucepan. Stir in cherry juice gradually until smooth. (Thicken leftover juice and serve over pie.) Cook and stir until thickened.

Remove from heat; stir in butter, colouring, and cherries. Cool thoroughly, then turn into pastry lined dish, spreading level. Cover with top crust.

Bake in very hot oven (450°F. Mark 8) 15 minutes, then reduce heat to moderate (350°F. Mark 4) and bake 25 minutes longer, or until nicely browned. Remove to cake rack to cool.

LATTICE CANNED CHERRY PIE

plain pastry using 8 ounces flour
2 pounds canned red cherries,
    drained
4 fluid ounces juice
4 tablespoons cornflour
8 ounces sugar
¼ teaspoon salt
1 tablespoon butter or margarine

Mix cherries, juice, cornflour, sugar, salt, and dots of butter. Pour into lined 9-inch pie dish or plate.

Roll out remainder of dough and cut into strips. Make a lattice work across top of pie.

Bake in hot oven (425°F. Mark 7) 10 minutes; continue baking 40 to 45 minutes at 350°F. Mark 4. Cool and serve. Serves 6 to 8.

FRESH APRICOT PIE

1½ pounds fresh apricots, halved
3 tablespoons flour
6 to 8 ounces sugar
½ teaspoon nutmeg
1 tablespoon lemon juice
1 tablespoon butter or margarine
pastry for 9-inch double crust

Line a pie plate with pastry. Arrange fresh ripe apricots close together.

Combine flour, sugar, and nutmeg. Sprinkle over fruit. Add sprinklings of lemon juice. Dot with butter.

Cover with top crust, perforated to allow steam to escape.

Bake in hot oven (400°F. Mark 6) 50 to 60 minutes. May be sprinkled with cinnamon if desired.

DRIED APRICOT PIE

½ pound dried apricots
1 pint cold water
8 ounces sugar
water or canned peach syrup
1½ tablespoons cornflour
⅛ teaspoon salt
1 tablespoon butter or margarine
pastry using 10 ounces flour

Wash apricots quickly but thoroughly with cold water.

Place in saucepan with water. Cover and let soak at least 2 hours.

Then add 4 ounces sugar; place over heat, cover and simmer gently about 20 minutes, or until fruit is tender. Drain off and measure juice; add enough water or peach syrup to make ½ pint.

Blend 4 ounces sugar with cornflour and salt; sprinkle 2 tablespoons of mixture over bottom of pastry lined 9-inch dish.

Stir remainder gently into apricots and turn into lined dish. Dot with butter. Cover with lattice top.

Bake in hot oven (425°F. Mark 7) about 30 minutes, or until crust is nicely browned and juice bubbles up through lattice. Remove to cake rack to cool. Makes 1 9-inch pie.

FRESH PEACH PIE

pastry for 9-inch double crust
1½ pounds sliced fresh peaches
8 ounces granulated sugar or 4
    ounces brown sugar and 4
    ounces granulated sugar
¼ teaspoon salt
1 tablespoon flour
2 tablespoons butter or margarine

Fill pastry lined 9-inch pie dish with sliced peaches and cover with mixture of sugar, salt, and flour. Dot with butter. Top with gashed upper crust or lattice strips.

Bake in very hot oven (450°F. Mark 8) 10 minutes. Reduce heat to moderate (350°F. Mark 4) and bake about 30 minutes longer.

CANNED PEACH PIE

3½ pounds canned peaches, well
    drained
6 ounces granulated sugar
¼ teaspoon salt
⅛ teaspoon nutmeg
¼ teaspoon cinnamon
1 tablespoon flour
1 tablespoon melted butter or
    margarine
1 tablespoon lemon juice
pastry for 9-inch double crust

Thoroughly drain peaches in colander, then slice them. Mix sugar, salt, spices, and flour. Lightly combine with peaches.

Fill pastry lined 9-inch pie dish;

sprinkle melted butter and lemon juice over top.

Roll remaining pastry thin and cut about 7 2-inch circles. Arrange them on top of fruit.

Bake in very hot oven (450°F. Mark 8) 10 minutes; reduce heat to 350°F. Mark 4 and bake about 30 minutes longer, or until crust is nicely browned. Cool before slicing.

(If you wish, bake pastry circles on a baking sheet in hot oven 5 to 10 minutes, then set them on top the baked pie to avoid overbrowning.)

PERSIMMON PIE

1 8-inch baked pie case
1 pint persimmon pulp
4 ounces sugar
½ teaspoon mace
1 teaspoon grated lemon rind
2 teaspoons butter or margarine
2 beaten egg yolks
2 stiffly beaten egg whites
4 tablespoons sugar

Press enough ripe or canned persimmons through a colander to make 1 pint pulp free from seed and skin.

Add sugar mixed with mace and lemon rind and place over low heat. Add butter and beaten egg yolks.

Cook and stir until mixture is slightly thickened. Pour into baked pie case. Cool.

Cover with meringue made from egg whites and 4 tablespoons sugar. Brown lightly in moderate oven (350°F. Mark 4).

RAISIN PIE

10 ounces seedless raisins
1 pint bottled grape juice
3 tablespoons vinegar
4 ounces sugar
3 tablespoons cornflour
¼ teaspoon salt
3 fluid ounces water
2 tablespoons butter or margarine
pastry for single (9-inch) crust

Combine raisins, grape juice, and vinegar. Heat to boiling, lower heat and simmer 5 minutes. Stir in sugar blended with cornflour, salt, and water. Add butter. Cook, stirring, until mixture boils and becomes clear and thickened.

Cool slightly. Pour into pastry lined pie dish. Bake in very hot oven (450°F. Mark 8) 25 to 30 minutes until crust is golden brown.

Serve warm or cold, either plain or with whipped cream. Makes 1 9-inch pie.

Note: Single crust pie may be decorated with a few baked pastry cut-outs, if desired. To make a double crust pie, cover filling with top crust, flute rim and cut a few slits in top.

PRUNE PIE

1 pound cooked dried prunes
1 orange
3 ounces brown sugar
¼ teaspoon salt
2 tablespoons cornflour
½ pint liquid from prunes
2 tablespoons butter or margarine
1 9-inch baked pastry case
2 egg whites
2 ounces granulated sugar

Stone prunes and cut in halves. Peel orange and remove inner white peel. Dice the orange.

Combine sugar, salt, and cornflour. Add prune liquid. Bring to boil and cook, stirring constantly, until thickened.

Add prunes, orange, and butter and cook 10 minutes longer, stirring frequently.

Cool slightly and pour into baked pie case.

Cover with meringue made by whipping egg whites until stiff and gradually folding in the sugar. Brown in moderate oven (350°F. Mark 4) about 12 to 15 minutes.

SOUR CREAM PRUNE PIE

2 whole eggs
1 egg yolk
3 ounces brown sugar, firmly packed
2 ounces granulated sugar
½ pint sour cream
8 ounces soaked, chopped prunes
3 fluid ounces prune juice (water in which prunes were soaked)
1 9-inch baked pastry case

Beat eggs and yolk lightly; stir in sugars and sour cream. Combine with prunes and prune juice in saucepan. Place over medium heat and cook until thickened, about 10 minutes, stirring constantly.

Remove from heat, cool slightly. Pour into baked pastry case. Cool and top with wreath of meringue.

Meringue: Beat 1 egg white until slightly stiff; gradually add 2 tablespoons brown sugar, beating until stiff. Spoon in wreath around edge of pie. Brown lightly in hot oven (400°F. Mark 6) 6 minutes.

Sour Cream Prune Pie

CRANBERRY ORANGE PIE

1 pound sugar
6 fluid ounces water
1 pound fresh cranberries
1¼ ounces cornflour
⅛ teaspoon salt
2 tablespoons butter
8 ounces orange sections or slices
recipe for 9-inch 2-crust pie

Combine sugar and water; bring to boil. Add cranberries and cook over low heat until cranberries begin to pop.

Mix cornflour to a smooth paste with a little cold water. Add to cranberries and cook over low heat until thickened, stirring constantly. Add salt and butter and allow to cool. Fold in orange.

Fit lower crust in 9-inch pie dish and fill. Cut circle from centre of top crust and cover filling. Trim and crimp edges. Bake in hot oven (425°F. Mark 7) 25 to 30 minutes or until crust is browned.

From leftover pastry, cut leaves and bake on baking sheet until lightly browned. Just before serving, place leaves on top crust with whole berries for garnish.

CRANBERRY PIE

1¼ pounds sugar
6 fluid ounces water
1¼ pounds cranberries
2 ounces quick-cooking tapioca
¼ teaspoon salt
2 tablespoons butter or margarine
1 9-inch unbaked pastry case
pastry strips for top

Boil sugar and water 5 minutes; add cranberries and boil until all berries have popped. Cool.

Add tapioca, salt, and butter; let stand 15 minutes.

Fill pastry lined pie dish with cranberry mixture. Adjust lattice strips on top.

Bake in very hot oven (450°F. Mark 8) 15 minutes. Reduce heat to moderate (350°F. Mark 4) and bake 25 minutes longer.

CRANBERRY APPLE PIE

1 pound can cranberry sauce (whole berries)
8 ounces chopped apple
4 ounces sugar
¼ teaspoon salt
1 teaspoon tapioca
pastry for 9-inch double crust

Mix ingredients together in a bowl, then put mixture in a chilled pastry lined pie plate or dish.

Dot with butter, sprinkle with 2 teaspoons grated orange rind and cover with top crust.

Bake in hot oven (400°F. Mark 6) 30 to 40 minutes, or until done.

Cranberry Orange Pie

RHUBARB PIE

pastry for 9-inch case and strips for top
2 well beaten eggs
14 ounces sugar (about)
1 ounce flour
¼ teaspoon salt
1 pound sliced rhubarb
butter or margarine

Combine eggs, sugar, flour, and salt. Add rhubarb and mix well.

Arrange in pie case. Dot with butter or margarine.

Top with pastry strips to form a star design.

Bake in very hot oven (450°F. Mark 8) 15 minutes. Reduce heat to moderate oven (350°F. Mark 4) and bake 30 minutes longer.

RHUBARB-STRAWBERRY PIE

pastry for 9-inch case and top strips
12 ounces pink rhubarb, cut in ½-inch pieces
8 ounces large whole fresh strawberries
3 tablespoons butter or margarine
2 well beaten eggs
1¼ pounds sugar
4 tablespoons cornflour

Wash rhubarb; do not peel. Wash and drain strawberries; remove hulls.

Cream butter until soft; add beaten eggs; stir until smooth.

Combine sugar and cornflour; add to butter-egg mixture; mix well.

Put fruits together in pastry-lined dish; pour egg mixture over.

Adjust crisscross pastry strips for top. Moisten rim with cold water

Bake at once in very hot oven (450°F. Mark 8) 10 minutes; reduce heat to (325°F. Mark 3) and bake until filling has thickened and top is nicely browned, about 25 to 30 minutes.

Cool completely before serving. Serve soon after making. This is a pie which should be eaten immediately.

Rhubarb-Strawberry Pie

AVOCADO PIE

digestive biscuit crust for 9- or
   10-inch pie
2 large avocados, sieved
6 fluid ounces lemon juice
½ pint sweetened condensed milk

Prepare crust and chill while mixing filling.

Choose fully ripe avocados, cut in halves, remove seeds,· and peel.

Mash to fine pulp or put through sieve. Mix with lemon juice and the sweetened condensed milk.

Fill digestive biscuit case and bake in moderate oven (350°F. Mark 4) 20 minutes. Chill before serving.

CANNED GOOSEBERRY PIE

pastry for 8-inch double crust
1 tablespoon flour
3 to 4 ounces sugar
1 large can (1 pound) gooseberries
   in heavy syrup
1 tablespoon butter or margarine

Blend flour and sugar in a bowl; turn berries into bowl and stir gently to mix well.

Turn berries into pastry lined 8-inch dish. Dot with butter. Cover with top crust.

Bake in very hot oven (450°F. Mark 8) 15 minutes; reduce heat to moderate (350°F. Mark 4) and bake 25 to 30 minutes longer or until nicely browned. Remove to cake rack to cool to lukewarm before serving.

REDCURRANT PIE

pastry for 9-inch double crust
2 pounds redcurrants
8 ounces sugar
2 tablespoons cornflour
1 tablespoon butter or margarine
   (optional)

Wash currants carefully through 2 or 3 cold waters. Drain in colander, then strip fruit from stems. There should be about 1¾ pounds stemmed fruit. Chill thoroughly in refrigerator.

Blend sugar and cornflour; sprinkle 3 tablespoons of mixture over bottom of pastry lined 9-inch dish.

Turn in chilled currants, levelling surface. Sprinkle rest of sugar mixture over top. Dot with butter. Cover with top crust.

Bake in very hot oven (450°F. Mark 8) 12 minutes; reduce heat to moderate (350°F. Mark 4) and bake 25 to 30 minutes longer or until nicely browned and juice bubbles up through vents.

DUTCH APPLE PIE

7 or 8 juicy tart cooking apples
3 tablespoons butter or margarine
6 ounces sugar
½ teaspoon cinnamon, if desired
unbaked 8-inch pie case
Streusel Topping:
3   ounces flour
¼   teaspoon cinnamon
2   ounces demerara sugar, firmly
      packed
2½ ounces butter or margarine

Peel apples; quarter and remove core. Cut each quarter into 4 slices lengthwise.

Melt butter in saucepan; add apples and toss about until each slice is well coated.

Add sugar which may be mixed with cinnamon, and again toss about to distribute through apples.

Arrange apples compactly in pastry lined dish. They should be slightly heaped in centre.

Make streusel by mixing flour thoroughly with cinnamon. Stir in brown sugar.

Cream butter until soft and smooth and work in the flour-cinnamon-sugar mixture until well blended. Sprinkle this crumbly mixture over top of pie.

Bake in very hot oven (450°F. Mark 8) about 20 minutes, or until crust is well browned. Reduce heat to slow oven (325°F. Mark 3) and continue baking about 30 minutes more, or until apples are translucent and tender. Cool.

VERMONT APPLE PIE

pastry for 2-crust 9-inch pie
1 pound peeled, sliced apples
4 fluid ounces maple syrup
2 ounces sugar
¼ teaspoon salt
3 tablespoons flour
1 tablespoon butter or margarine

Combine all ingredients except butter and let stand while preparing pastry.

Fill unbaked pie case with fruit mixture. Dot with butter. Slightly moisten edge of bottom crust with cold water.

Roll out top crust, cut slits to let out steam and place it over filling, folding top crust over, then under edge of bottom crust.

Press the two crusts into fluting to make a "crinkle edge". Press lightly so as not to tear pastry.

Bake in moderate oven (375°F. Mark 5) about 60 minutes, until crust is a light brown. Cool.

NEW ENGLAND BLUEBERRY PIE

5 ounces blueberries or bilberries
8 ounces sugar
6 fluid ounces water
2 tablespoons flour
2 fluid ounces water
1 pound blueberries
1 baked 9-inch pastry case
½ pint double cream, whipped, or 1
   pint vanilla ice cream

Cook 5 ounces blueberries with sugar and 6 fluid ounces water until berries are soft. Put through sieve.

Mix flour and 2 fluid ounces water to a paste and add to sieved blueberry mixture. Cook slowly until thickened. Cool.

Then add to 1 pound uncooked blueberries.

Pour into pastry case and chill several hours. Serve topped with whipped cream or ice cream.

FROSTED STRAWBERRY PIE

1 8-inch crumb shell
1 egg white
8 ounces sugar
2 fluid ounces water
pinch of salt
½ teaspoon cream of tartar
1 teaspoon vanilla
1 pound drained, sliced strawberries

Place unbeaten egg white, sugar, water, salt, and cream of tartar in double boiler.

Cook over boiling water, beating constantly, until mixture thickens and forms peaks, about 7 minutes.

Remove from heat, add vanilla, and continue beating until cool.

Arrange sliced strawberries in crumb shell. Pour filling over fruit. Garnish with whole berries. Chill 1 hour before serving. Serves 6.

Frosted Strawberry Pie

Miscellaneous Pies

PUMPKIN PIE

For 8-Inch Pie:

3 ounces brown sugar
2 teaspoons flour
¼ teaspoon salt
1½ teaspoons pumpkin pie spice
8 ounces cooked or canned
    pumpkin
½ pint evaporated milk
1 slightly beaten egg
4 teaspoons black treacle

For 9-Inch Pie:

5 ounces brown sugar
1 tablespoon flour
½ teaspoon salt
2¼ teaspoons pumpkin pie spice
12 ounces cooked or canned
    pumpkin
12 fluid ounces evaporated milk
1 slightly beaten egg
2 tablespoons black treacle

Mix in a bowl the sugar, flour, salt, and spice. Add pumpkin, evaporated milk, egg, and black treacle; stir until smooth.

Pour into pie dish lined with un-baked pastry made with pastry mix or from pastry recipe.

Bake on centre rack in moderate oven (375°F. Mark 5) about 40 to 45 minutes, until firm.

For a More Mildly Spiced Pumpkin Pie: Omit black treacle and pumpkin pie spice. For 8-inch pie, use ¾ tea-spoon cinnamon, ¼ teaspoon each of nutmeg and ginger and add 2 tea-spoons lemon juice.

For 9-inch pie, use 1 teaspoon cin-namon, ½ teaspoon each of nutmeg and ginger, and add 1 tablespoon lemon juice. Bake as directed above.

Sweet Potato Pie: Omit black treacle and substitute sieved, cooked or can-ned sweet potatoes for pumpkin.

. Reduce sugar for 8-inch pie to 2½ ounces and add 2 teaspoons melted fat; use 4 ounces sugar and 2 table-spoons melted fat for 9-inch pie.

PECAN PIE

1 9-inch unbaked pie case
14 fluid ounces golden syrup
6 ounces brown sugar
2 ounces butter or margarine
¼ teaspoon salt
2 eggs
4 ounces pecans or walnuts

Cook golden syrup and brown sugar together until mixture begins to boil.

Remove from heat; stir in butter or margarine. Add ¼ teaspoon salt. Cool.

Beat eggs and add to syrup mixture.

Pour filling into 9-inch unbaked pastry case. Sprinkle pecans or walnuts on top of filling.

Bake in moderate oven (350°F. Mark 4) about 50 minutes or until done.

MINCEMEAT PIE

1½ to 2 pounds mincemeat (home
    made or bought)
2 ounces chopped apple, if desired
1 to 2 tablespoons orange juice or
    brandy
pastry for 9-inch double crust

Mix mincemeat, apple, and orange juice or brandy. Fill pastry-lined pie dish. Cover with top crust.

Bake in very hot oven (450°F. Mark 8) about 30 minutes.

TRADITIONAL MINCEMEAT

1 pound stewing beef (optional)
¾ pint boiling water
1 teaspoon salt
1 pound chopped apples
1 pound seedless raisins
2 ounces minced orange peel
8 ounces chopped mixed peel
½ pound chopped suet
8 fluid ounces black treacle
8 ounces sugar
¾ pint strong fresh coffee
½ pint cider or fruit juice
1 teaspoon each cinnamon and
    nutmeg
½ teaspoon each cloves and allspice

Simmer beef with boiling water and salt until very tender. Drain, reserve stock and chop meat.

Combine in heavy saucepan meat with remaining ingredients and ½ pint of the meat stock. Stir over heat until thoroughly mixed.

Continue cooking over low heat about 2 hours, or until most of the liquid is absorbed. Stir occasionally during cooking and often as mixture thickens.

Pour into hot sterilized jars and seal completely. Makes about 5½ pints.

GREEN TOMATO MINCEMEAT

5½ pounds firm green tomatoes
1 pound chopped tart apples
4 ounces chopped mixed peel
4 fluid ounces orange juice
4 fluid ounces vinegar
3 ounces finely minced suet
1 pound brown sugar
1 teaspoon salt
1 teaspoon whole allspice
1 teaspoon whole cloves
1 teaspoon powdered cinnamon
1 pound dark seedless raisins

Wash tomatoes; remove stems; cut in pieces; put through vegetable mill.

Put all ingredients except raisins in heavy saucepan tying spices in muslin or cheese-cloth bag.

Cook over low heat, stirring fre-quently, 1 hour.

Add raisins; continue cooking until mixture is thick.

Remove spice bag and discard. Fi hot sterilized jars. Seal at once. Make about 5½ pints.

WALNUT PIE

4 ounces soft butter or margarine
3 ounces firmly packed brown suga
6 ounces granulated sugar
4 well beaten eggs
¼ teaspoon salt
3 ounces thin golden syrup
4 fluid ounces double cream
6 ounces chopped walnuts
1 teaspoon vanilla
1 9-inch unbaked pie case, chilled

Combine butter or margarine wit both sugars in top of large doubl boiler. Cream until fluffy.

Stir in eggs, salt, golden syrup, an cream. Place over boiling water an cook 5 minutes, stirring constantl Add walnuts and vanilla.

Pour into pastry lined pie dish. Bak in moderate oven (350°F. Mark 4) hour.

Cool. Top with ring of whippe cream studded with walnut halves.

LEMON SPONGE PIE

2 ounces melted butter or
    margarine
8 ounces sugar
3 tablespoons flour
3 slightly beaten egg yolks
juice and grated rind of 1 lemon
12 fluid ounces milk
3 stiffly beaten egg whites
plain pastry for 9-inch pie case

Blend butter with sugar and flou add egg yolks, lemon juice and rin and milk.

Fold in egg whites and pour into inch pastry lined pie dish.

Bake in very hot oven (450°F. Mar 8) 8 minutes. Reduce heat to slow ove (325°F. Mark 3) and bake 25 minutes.

To make the stars in this mincemea pie, cut through the top crust with star pastry cutter after placing th crust in place, but do not remove th stars. This will allow steam to escape

Lemon Angel Pie

LEMON ANGEL PIE

4 egg yolks
6 ounces sugar
2 fluid ounces fresh lemon juice
1 tablespoon butter or margarine
2 egg whites, stiffly beaten
1 8-inch baked pie case

Cream egg yolks and sugar together thoroughly. Add lemon juice and cook in double boiler until thickened (about 10 minutes), stirring often. Add butter.

Remove from heat and fold in beaten egg whites. Pour into an 8-inch baked pie case.

Top with lemon-flavoured meringue made with 2 remaining egg whites. Brown in slow oven (325°F. Mark 3) for 15 minutes.

Lemon Meringue: Add 4 tablespoons sugar gradually to 2 egg whites which have been beaten until frothy, and continue beating until egg holds its shape in peaks. Fold in 1 teaspoon lemon juice.

LEMON MERINGUE PIE 2

6 tablespoons cornflour
¼ teaspoon salt
8 ounces sugar
¾ pint water
3 egg yolks
2 tablespoons butter or margarine
1½ teaspoons grated lemon rind
5 tablespoons lemon juice
3 egg whites
¼ teaspoon cream of tartar
6 tablespoons sugar
1 baked 9-inch pie case

Combine cornflour, salt, and 4 ounces sugar in top of double boiler; gradually add water.

Place over boiling water and cook, stirring constantly, until mixture thickens. Cover and cook 10 minutes, stirring occasionally.

Stir small amount of hot mixture into egg yolks which have been mixed with remaining 4 ounces sugar. Immediately pour back into remaining hot mixture over boiling water. Blend thoroughly and cook 2 minutes longer, stirring constantly.

Remove from heat; add butter, lemon juice, and rind. Cool to room temperature without stirring. Pour into pie case.

Add cream of tartar to egg whites and beat until frothy. Gradually beat in sugar and continue beating until mixture is stiff and glossy.

Spread meringue lightly on filling, sealing edges to crust. Bake in hot oven (400°F. Mark 6) until delicately browned, 8 to 10 minutes.

KEY LIME PIE

4 eggs, separated
1 large can (15-ounce) sweetened condensed milk
2½ fluid ounces lime juice
1 teaspoon grated lime rind
1 baked 9-inch pie case

Beat 4 egg yolks and 1 egg white together until light coloured and thick.

Add milk and beat thoroughly. Add lime juice and rind and stir until mixture thickens.

Fold in remaining egg whites which have been beaten stiff. Turn into baked pie case.

Bake in slow oven (325°F. Mark 3) about 15 to 20 minutes or until set.

Decorate edge of pie with chocolate drops, if desired.

ICE CREAM PARFAIT PIES
(Basic Recipe)

10 fluid ounces hot fruit juice or water
1 tablet fruit jelly
8 to 12 ounces drained soft fruit (optional)
1 baked 8- or 9-inch pie case

Prepare 8- or 9-inch pie case with pastry mix or shortcrust pastry. Bake and cool.

Heat liquid to boiling in 2-quart saucepan. Remove from heat. Add jelly; stir until dissolved.

Add ice cream, cut into pieces, to hot liquid; immediately stir until melted. Chill until mixture is thickened but not set, 10 to 35 minutes.

Fold in drained fruit, if desired. Turn into cooled, baked pastry case. Chill until set, 10 to 30 minutes.

STRAWBERRY PARFAIT PIE

Follow basic recipe. Prepare 12 ounces sliced fresh strawberries; sweeten if desired. Drain well; reserve juice. (12 ounces frozen strawberries, thawed and drained, may be substituted.)

Fold the fruit into parfait made with 10 fluid ounces liquid (reserved strawberry juice plus water), 1 tablet lemon-flavoured jelly, and 1 pint vanilla ice cream.

PEACH PARFAIT PIE

Follow basic recipe, using an 8-inch baked pastry case, 1 tablet strawberry jelly, 10 fluid ounces hot water, 1 pint vanilla ice cream, and ½ pound thoroughly drained, sweetened sliced peaches, fresh or frozen. Garnish pie

with whipped cream and additional peaches, if desired.

SHOO-FLY PIE

A Pennsylvania Dutch single-crust pie with a cake-like filling, topped with crumble made of flour, sugar, and fat.

1 ounce sifted flour
4 ounces sugar
⅛ teaspoon salt
3 tablespoons fat
1 egg
4 ounces black treacle
2 tablespoons boiling water
½ teaspoon bicarbonate of soda
1 unbaked 9-inch pie case

Mix flour, sugar, salt, and fat together until crumbs are formed.

Beat egg until light and fluffy. Add egg to black treacle, boiling water, and bicarbonate of soda, and beat until bicarbonate of soda is dissolved.

Add all but 1 ounce crumb mixture to black treacle mixture and stir until well blended. Pour into pastry lined dish. Sprinkle top with reserved crumbs.

Bake in moderate oven (375°F. Mark 5) 35 minutes.

LIME ANGEL PIE

3 eggs, separated
¼ teaspoon cream of tartar
12 ounces sugar
⅛ teaspoon salt
4 fluid ounces lime juice
1 teaspoon grated lime rind
½ pint double cream

Beat egg whites until frothy; add cream of tartar and 8 ounces sugar gradually, beating constantly. Continue beating until stiff.

Spread egg white mixture evenly over bottom and sides of greased 9-inch pie dish. Bake in very slow oven (275°F. Mark 1) for 1 hour. Cool thoroughly.

Beat egg yolks slightly; add 4 ounces sugar, salt, lime juice, and lime rind. Cook over medium heat, stirring constantly, until thickened. Cool thoroughly.

Beat cream until stiff. Fold into lime mixture. Cool thoroughly. Pour into meringue case and chill until firm.

Strawberry Parfait Pie

GREEN TOMATO PIE

pastry for 9-inch lower crust and
    narrow strips for top
2 pounds sliced green tomatoes
boiling water
10 ounces sugar
¼ teaspoon salt
3 tablespoons flour
¼ teaspoon ground nutmeg
small pinch ground cloves
grated rind and juice of 1 medium
    lemon
2 tablespoons water
2 tablespoons butter or margarine

Line deep pie dish with pastry. Cut strips for lattice top.

Wash tomatoes; do not peel. Slice ⅛ inch thick into bowl. Pour on boiling water to cover; let stand 5 minutes. Drain.

Stir sugar, salt, flour, and spices until well mixed. Combine lemon rind, lemon juice, and water.

Fill pastry lined dish with layers of tomato slices, sprinkling each layer with sugar mixture and dotting each layer with butter.

When dish is filled, pour lemon mixture over top. Arrange pastry strips to make a lattice top over filling. Moisten rim of pastry with cold water.

Bake in very hot oven (450°F. Mark 8) 8 to 10 minutes to set crust; reduce heat to moderate (375°F. Mark 5) and bake until tomatoes are tender, about 40 minutes. Or, bake at (425°F. Mark 7) about 50 minutes. Cool pie completely before serving.

PINEAPPLE SPONGE PIE

3 eggs, separated
1 teaspoon grated lemon rind
3 tablespoons lemon juice
8 ounces sugar
3 tablespoons flour
½ teaspoon salt
8 ounces pineapple chunks
½ pint hot milk
⅛ teaspoon salt
18 pineapple chunks
6 maraschino cherries
plain pastry for 10-inch pie case

Add grated lemon rind and lemon juice to egg yolks and beat until light.

Sift sugar, 3 tablespoons flour, and ½ teaspoon salt together and stir into egg mixture.

Cut pineapple chunks into smaller pieces and add to egg mixture. Stir in hot milk.

Add ⅛ teaspoon salt to egg whites and beat until stiff. Carefully fold egg whites into rest of mixture. Pour into 10-inch unbaked crust.

Bake in hot oven (425°F. Mark 7) 10 minutes. Lower temperature to (350°F. Mark 4) and continue baking about 35 minutes longer.

Cool pie before serving and garnish with pineapple chunks and maraschino cherries.

CHOCOLATE BROWNIE PIE

pastry for 1 9-inch pie crust
2 squares (2 ounces) unsweetened
    chocolate
2 tablespoons butter or margarine
3 large eggs
4 ounces sugar
10 ounces golden syrup
3 ounces pecan or walnut halves

Melt together over hot water the unsweetened chocolate and butter.

Beat eggs, sugar, chocolate mixture, and golden syrup thoroughly with rotary beater.

Mix in pecan or walnut halves. Pour into pastry lined dish.

Bake in moderate oven (375°F. Mark 5) 45 to 50 minutes, just until set.

Serve slightly warm or cold garnished with ice cream or whipped cream.

Note: To use cocoa, omit chocolate and sift 2 ounces cocoa with sugar. Then add 2 ounces melted butter to egg and sugar mixture.

MAGIC LEMON PIE

1 crumb or baked pastry 8-inch
    pie case
1 large can (15-ounce) sweetened
    condensed milk
4 fluid ounces lemon juice
1 teaspoon grated lemon rind or
    ¼ teaspoon lemon extract
2 eggs, separated
¼ teaspoon cream of tartar, if
    desired
4 tablespoons sugar

Put condensed milk, lemon juice, lemon rind or extract, and egg yolks into mixing bowl; stir until mixture thickens. Pour into chilled crumb crust or cooled pastry case.

Add cream of tartar to egg whites; beat until almost stiff enough to hold a peak. Add sugar gradually, beating until stiff and glossy but not dry. Pile lightly on pie filling.

Bake in slow oven (325°F. Mark 3) until lightly browned, about 15 minutes. Cool.

GRAPEFRUIT PIE

1 large can (15-ounce) sweetened
    condensed milk
2 fluid ounces lemon juice
1 teaspoon grated grapefruit rind
8 ounces grapefruit segments
1 8-inch baked pastry case
2 egg whites, beaten stiff with
2 ounces sugar
2 ounces desiccated coconut, if
    desired

Stir together condensed milk, lemon juice, and grapefruit rind. Filling will thicken as though cooked. Add grapefruit.

Pour into the baked pastry case. Cover with meringue made from the egg whites and sugar. Sprinkle with coconut, if desired. Brown in oven. Chill and serve.

BLACK TREACLE PIE

plain pastry for 8-inch pie case
2 ounces broken pecans or walnuts
3 eggs
1 tablespoon flour
8 ounces sugar
12 ounces black treacle
2 tablespoons melted butter or
    margarine
pinch of salt

Sprinkle nuts on the bottom of pastry lined 8-inch dish.

Beat eggs, flour, and sugar together until well combined. Add black treacle, melted butter, and salt; mix thoroughly. Pour over nuts in dish.

Bake in very hot oven (450°F. Mark 8) 10 minutes. Reduce heat to slow oven (300°F. Mark 2) and bake 30 minutes.

Cool and top with whipped cream, if desired.

ALOHA PIE

1 9-inch baked pastry case
1 large can pineapple chunks
5 ounces sugar
2 tablespoons cornflour
¼ teaspoon salt
2 eggs
½ pint milk
2 tablespoons butter or margarine
½ teaspoon vanilla
3 drops green food colouring

Drain pineapple chunks, reserving syrup.

Combine in saucepan the sugar, cornflour, salt, and eggs; stir in milk and 3 fluid ounces of pineapple syrup. Cook over medium heat 5 minutes, stirring constantly, until mixture thickens.

Remove from heat and add butter or margarine, vanilla, and food colouring. Beat with electric or rotary beater to smooth. Cool completely.

Pour into baked pastry case. Spoon glazed pineapple chunks (below) around edge. Wreath with whipped cream. Chill about 2 hours.

Glazed Pineapple Chunks: Combine in saucepan 3 ounces sugar, 3 tablespoons cornflour, and 6 fluid ounces pineapple syrup.

Cook on medium heat for 5 minutes or until thickened and clear.

Remove from heat, stir in 2 drops yellow food colour. Fold in 12 ounces pineapple chunks. Cool.

Aloha Pie

SWEET POTATO PIE 2

14 ounces mashed, hot sweet pota-
    toes
3 tablespoons melted butter or
    margarine
1 teaspoon cinnamon
½ teaspoon nutmeg
½ teaspoon ginger
1¼ teaspoons salt
6 ounces black treacle
2 fluid ounces orange juice
1 tablespoon grated orange rind
3 well beaten eggs
½ pint milk
plain pastry for 9-inch pie case

Mix together ingredients in order given. Turn into unbaked pie case.

Bake in very hot oven (450°F. Mark 8) 10 minutes, then reduce heat to moderate (350°F. Mark 4). Bake until set, about 40 minutes.

Cool. Serve with whipped cream flavoured with a dash of cinnamon.

PUMPKIN PIE 2

4 ounces brown sugar, firmly
    packed
8 to 10 ounces cooked or canned
    pumpkin
½ teaspoon salt
2 unbeaten eggs
12 fluid ounces evaporated milk
2 teaspoons cinnamon
½ teaspoon ginger
¼ teaspoon mace
¼ teaspoon nutmeg
3 fluid ounces boiling water
1 9-inch unbaked pastry case

Combine brown sugar, pumpkin, salt, and eggs. Mix well. Gradually add evaporated milk.

Mix spices together and add boiling water. Stir this into pumpkin mixture and blend well.

Pour into a 9-inch unbaked pastry case.

Bake in hot oven (400°F. Mark 6) 35 to 40 minutes. If a glass pie dish is used, bake at 375°F. Mark 5 approximately 55 minutes.

OLD SOUTH SUGAR PIE

1 unbaked 9-inch pastry case
3 eggs
1¼ pounds moist light brown sugar
4 fluid ounces milk
⅛ teaspoon salt
1 teaspoon vanilla
4 ounces melted butter

Beat eggs; then beat in brown sugar. Add milk, salt, vanilla, and melted butter.

Pour into pastry lined dish. Bake in very hot oven (450°F. Mark 8) 10 minutes. Reduce heat to slow oven (325°F. Mark 3) and bake 25 minutes.

With Pecans: Add 2 ounces halved pecans or walnuts before baking.

PECAN PUMPKIN PIE

plain pastry for 1-crust 9-inch pie
3 slightly beaten eggs
4 ounces granulated sugar
3 ounces firmly packed brown
    sugar
2 tablespoons flour
½ teaspoon salt
1 teaspoon cinnamon
½ teaspoon nutmeg
½ teaspoon allspice
12 ounces pumpkin, cooked or
    canned
12 fluid ounces single cream, heated
1 tablespoon butter or margarine
2 tablespoons brown sugar
3 ounces pecan or walnut halves

Combine eggs, granulated sugar, brown sugar, flour, salt, cinnamon, nutmeg, and allspice. Add pumpkin; mix well.

Gradually add heated cream; mix well. Turn into pastry lined dish.

Bake in very hot oven (450°F. Mark 8) 10 minutes, then at 350°F. Mark 4 20 minutes.

Melt butter and 2 tablespoons brown sugar together. Add pecan or walnut halves and stir until nuts are thoroughly coated.

Remove pie from oven and immediately cover with pecan mixture.

Bake in moderate oven (350°F. Mark 4) 20 to 30 minutes, until a knife inserted about half way between centre and edge of filling comes out clean.

TEXAS PECAN PIE

1 unbaked 9-inch pastry crust
2 ounces butter or margarine
4 ounces granulated sugar
3 eggs, unbeaten
10 ounces black treacle
juice of 1 lemon
3 ounces broken pecans or walnuts
1 ounce pecan or walnut halves

Line a 9-inch pie dish with pastry. Cream butter and sugar; add eggs, black treacle, and lemon juice. Beat with rotary beater.

Add broken pecans or walnuts and pour into pastry lined pie dish. Place halves around the edges of the crust.

Bake in very hot oven (450°F. Mark 8) 10 minutes. Then decrease heat to moderate (350°F. Mark 4) and bake 30 minutes longer.

OATMEAL CRUST FRUIT PIE

2 ounces sifted flour
4½ ounces uncooked rolled oats
5 ounces brown sugar
1 teaspoon salt
1 teaspoon cinnamon
4 ounces melted fat
1¼ pounds sweetened fruit (sliced
    peaches, apples, or apricots
    either raw or cooked)

Combine dry ingredients; add melted fat, mixing thoroughly.

Pack all but 8 ounces of this mixture firmly in bottom and on sides of a pie plate.

Arrange sliced fruit on top; cover with remaining crumb mixture.

Bake in moderate oven (375°F. Mark 5) 30 minutes, or until brown. Serve hot or cold, plain or with cream. Serves 6.

PEAR-MINCEMEAT PIE

2 large pears
1 pound homemade or canned
    mincemeat
pastry for 9-inch double crust

To mincemeat, add pears which have been washed, cored, and diced. Pour into pastry case and cover with lattice crust.

Bake in hot oven (425°F. Mark 7) for 35 to 45 minutes. Serve warm or cold.

QUANTITY PASTRY MIX

1½ pounds sifted flour
1 tablespoon salt
1 pound fat

Sift flour with salt. With a pastry blender, or 2 knives, cut in fat until the mixture is the consistency of small peas.

Store in covered container in a cool place.

For a 9-inch single-crust pie, use 7 ounces pastry mix with 1 to 3 tablespoons water.

For a double-crust pie use 1 pound with 4 to 6 tablespoons water.

Follow directions for handling pastry given in the recipe for shortcrust pastry.

TO KEEP BOTTOM CRUST FROM SOAKING

1. When making custard or pumpkin pie, take a little of the beaten egg and spread over the unbaked crust with pastry brush or back of spoon. Place in refrigerator to let egg dry while making filling.

2. When making fruit pies, combine flour with sugar, salt, and spices. Sprinkle some of this mixture over bottom crust before filling pie. Combine rest of mixture with fruit and toss lightly, so that all fruit is coated.

Cream and Custard Pies

CUSTARD PIE
(Basic Recipe)

shortcrust pastry for one 9-inch pie
    case
4 eggs (or 2 eggs and 4 yolks),
    slightly beaten
4 ounces sugar
¼ teaspoon salt
½ teaspoon vanilla
½ teaspoon almond extract
1 pint scalded milk
nutmeg (optional)

Line 9-inch pie dish with pastry. Be sure there are no bubbles under pastry and no holes in pastry. For best results have pastry slightly thicker than usual. Place in refrigerator while preparing filling.

Blend eggs with sugar, salt, and flavourings.

Slowly pour scalded milk into egg mixture, stirring constantly.

Pour custard mixture into pastry lined 9-inch pie dish. To avoid custard spilling over edges while transferring pie to oven pour in last lot of filling after pie is in position for baking.

Bake in hot oven (400°F. Mark 6) until knife inserted halfway between outside and centre of custard comes out clean, 25 to 30 minutes.

Remove promptly to cooling rack. Do not cut pie until just before serving. If desired, sprinkle surface with nutmeg.

Avoid spills by pouring the last lot of custard pie filling after pie is in position for baking. This is a good trick with cup custards, too.

Test custard pie by inserting knife halfway between outside and centre of custard. When done, knife comes out clean.

Custard Pie Variations

Almond Custard Pie: Brown 4 ounces chopped blanched almonds in 2 tablespoons of butter in the oven. Sprinkle over bottom of pastry.

Butter Custard Pie: Add 2 tablespoons butter to milk before scalding. Makes a nicely browned top on finished pie.

Coconut Custard Pie: Sprinkle 4 ounces desiccated coconut in unbaked pastry case. Pour custard over coconut. Bake the same as plain custard pie.

Digestive Biscuit Pastry: Roll out regular pastry. Sprinkle with 1 ounce fine digestive biscuit crumbs. Roll crumbs lightly into crust. Place pastry in pie dish—crumb side down. Bake as directed above.

Slip-Slide Custard Pie: A sure way to keep the crust crisp under a delicate custard pie is to bake the custard in a separate pie dish the same size as the baked pie case.

SLIP-SLIDE CUSTARD PIE

1 baked 9-inch pastry case
4 eggs
4 ounces sugar
¼ teaspoon salt
1¼ pints milk
teaspoon grated nutmeg

Cool the pie case in dish in which it was baked. Butter a second dish of the same size.

Beat eggs slightly; add sugar and salt. Add milk. Strain mixture into the buttered dish. Grate nutmeg over top.

Set pie dish in a larger dish in which you have about ½ inch of water.

Bake in very hot oven (450°F. Mark 8) 10 minutes. Then reduce heat to slow oven (325°F. Mark 3) and bake until a knife blade inserted in centre comes out clean, about 25 to 30 minutes.

Remove from oven. Let custard cool, having loosened the edges after taking from the oven.

Slide the baked custard into the baked pie case. It works if you have courage, a deft hand, and a firm custard.

Grilled Pineapple Custard Pie

GRILLED PINEAPPLE CUSTARD PIE

4 eggs
4 ounces sugar
¼ teaspoon salt
¼ teaspoon nutmeg
1 teaspoon vanilla
¾ pint single cream
4 fluid ounces pineapple syrup
1 unbaked 9-inch pastry case
Topping:
2 ounces desiccated coconut
3 tablespoons brown sugar
1 tablespoon melted butter
5 pineapple slices

Beat eggs lightly, then beat in sugar, salt, nutmeg, and vanilla. Add cream and pineapple syrup.

Turn mixture into pastry lined pie dish. Bake on lower shelf in hot oven (425°F. Mark 7) until filling is barely set in centre, about 30 minutes.

Remove pie from oven and let stand 5 to 10 minutes. (Heat contained in pie will continue cooking so centre will set.)

Topping: Combine coconut, brown sugar, and butter. Arrange drained pineapple slices on top of pie; sprinkle with topping.

Cover edge of crust with foil to prevent excessive browning. Place pie under grill a minute or two until topping is bubbly. Remove from oven and cool.

FRUIT-SPICE PIE

4 ounces butter or margarine
12 ounces light brown sugar
4 egg yolks
2 tablespoons sifted flour
1 teaspoon cinnamon
1 teaspoon freshly grated nutmeg
½ teaspoon allspice
½ pint cream
3 ounces chopped dates
3 ounces raisins
2 ounces broken pecans or walnuts
1 9-inch baked pastry case
meringue

Cream butter and sugar together. Beat in egg yolks.

Mix and sift flour, cinnamon, nutmeg, and allspice. Add to first mixture.

Add cream, dates, raisins, and pecans or walnuts.

Turn into baked pie case and bake in moderate oven (375°F. Mark 5) 35 to 40 minutes, until set.

When cool, cover with meringue and bake as directed in recipe for meringue.

Chocolate-Topped Cream Pie: Fill baked pie case with vanilla cream filling. Melt six ounces semi-sweet chocolate over hot water and blend in three tablespoons single cream or top milk. Spread over cream filling. Top with unsweetened whipped cream at serving time.

BASIC CREAM PIE
(Vanilla Cream Pie)

8 ounces sugar
2 ounces flour
½ teaspoon salt
¾ pint scalded milk
3 eggs, separated
2 tablespoons butter or margarine
1 teaspoon vanilla
1 9-inch baked pastry case

Mix 6 ounces sugar, flour, and salt. Gradually stir in milk and set over hot water. Stir until thoroughly thickened.

Cover, and cook 10 minutes, stirring a few times to keep smooth.

Blend a small amount of hot mixture into slightly beaten egg yolks. Combine with mixture in double boiler.

Cook about 2 minutes, stirring constantly. Add butter and vanilla.

Cool slightly. Pour into cooled, baked pastry case.

Cover with meringue made by gradually beating 3 ounces sugar into stiffly beaten egg whites.

Bake in moderate oven (350°F. Mark 4) until lightly browned, about 15 minutes. Chill.

Note: Meringue may be omitted and pie served with whipped cream. If pie is made with only 2 eggs, reduce sugar to 6 ounces.

Variations of Basic Cream Pie

Almond Cream Pie: In basic cream pie, substitute ⅛ teaspoon almond extract for vanilla.

Add toasted slivered almonds to cooled filling just before pouring into pastry case.

Top with whipped cream. Garnish with toasted slivered almonds.

Banana Cream Pie: Prepare basic cream pie filling. Alternate layers of sliced bananas and cream filling or add 7 ounces mashed bananas to cooked filling.

Butterscotch Cream Pie: In basic cream pie, substitute 3 ounces firmly packed brown sugar for granulated sugar.

Increase butter to 3 tablespoons.

Chocolate Cream Pie: Add 2 ounces (2 squares) chocolate to milk in recipe for basic cream pie. When melted, beat until smooth.

Reduce flour to 6 tablespoons. Proceed as for basic cream pie.

Chocolate Sponge Pie: Prepare Chocolate Cream Pie Filling.

Fold meringue into filling. Bake as for basic cream pie. Chill. Serve with whipped cream.

Coconut Cream Pie: Stir 2 ounces desiccated coconut into basic cream pie filling.

Cover with meringue and sprinkle with coconut before or after browning.

Fruit Cream Pie: Lightly stir 8 ounces fresh berries, 4 ounces well drained crushed pineapple, 6 ounces chopped dates, or 6 ounces raisins into cooked basic cream pie filling just before turning into baked pastry case.

Cover with meringue and brown.

VINEGAR PIE

1 9-inch baked pastry case
1 ounce sifted flour
4 ounces sugar
½ pint water
additional 4 ounces sugar
3 beaten egg yolks
⅛ teaspoon salt
1 tablespoon butter or margarine
¼ teaspoon lemon extract
3 tablespoons vinegar

Line a 9-inch pie dish with flan pastry and bake as usual.

Mix together the flour and 4 ounces sugar in top of double boiler. Add water gradually and cook over hot water 15 minutes or until thickened, stirring constantly.

In a bowl combine additional 4 ounces sugar with beaten egg yolks and salt. Beat until sugar is dissolved.

Pour first (hot) mixture into this gradually, beating vigorously until blended well.

Return to double boiler; cook over hot water 3 minutes longer or until thick and smooth. Add butter, lemon extract, vinegar. Blend well and cool.

Pour into baked pastry case; top with meringue; bake in slow oven (325°F. Mark 3) 15 minutes, or until delicately brown. Serve hot.

STRAWBERRY CREAM PIE

8 ounces sugar
6 tablespoons cornflour
½ teaspoon salt
1 pint milk, scalded
2 slightly beaten eggs
3 tablespoons butter or margarine
½ teaspoon vanilla
1 9-inch baked pastry case
1 pound strawberries, sliced
½ pint double cream, whipped

Mix sugar, cornflour, and salt; gradually add milk and cook in double boiler until thick.

Add small amount of hot mixture to eggs; stir into remaining hot mixture. Cook until thick, stirring constantly.

Remove from heat; add butter and vanilla. Chill.

Pour into cooled baked pastry case. Cover with strawberries. Chill.

Spread with sweetened whipped cream just before serving. Garnish with halved berries.

ORANGE MERINGUE CREAM PIE

1 baked 9-inch pastry or crumb case
8 ounces sugar
5 tablespoons cornflour
¼ teaspoon salt
¾ pint strained orange juice
4 egg yolks
2 tablespoons butter or margarine
3 fluid ounces lemon juice
1 tablespoon grated orange rind
4 egg whites

In top of double boiler, stir together 6 ounces sugar, the cornflour, and salt until well mixed.

Stir in orange juice, keeping mixture smooth.

Place over hot water. Cook, stirring constantly, until mixture thickens and is clear.

Beat egg yolks; add little of hot mixture and stir together. Return to cooked mixture in double boiler; stir and cook until egg yolks thicken, 3 to 5 minutes.

Remove from heat. Stir in butter. Gradually stir in lemon juice and grated orange rind. Cool.

Beat egg whites until stiff but not dry; gradually beat in remaining sugar to make stiff meringue. Fold lightly and carefully into cooled orange filling.

Pour into pie case; chill until firm.

Whipped cream, lightly sweetened, may be served over top of pie; or, a thin spread of orange marmalade. If marmalade is very thick, thin it down with a little water or fruit juice. Drained fresh orange sections are also a pretty garnish.

Garnish Strawberry Cream Pie with whole or halved berries.

Garnish Banana Chocolate Cream Pie with additional banana slices just before serving.

BANANA CHOCOLATE CREAM PIE

1½ squares (1½ ounces) un-
     sweetened chocolate)
1 pint milk
6 ounces sugar
5 tablespoons flour
½ teaspoon salt
2 egg yolks, slightly beaten
1 tablespoon butter or margarine
½ teaspoon vanilla
1 baked 9-inch pie case or 6
     3½-inch tart cases
3 ripe bananas

Melt chocolate in milk in top of double boiler over rapidly boiling water, beating until blended.

Mix sugar, flour, and salt. Stir into chocolate mixture. Keep stirring and cook until well thickened.

Cook 10 minutes longer, stirring occasionally.

Stir hot mixture into egg yolks. Cook 1 minute. Add butter or margarine and vanilla.

Cool thoroughly. Cover bottom of pie case with small amount of filling.

Peel bananas and slice into pie case. Cover with remaining filling.

Top with meringue or sweetened whipped cream, if desired. Makes 1 pie or 6 tarts.

With Instant Whips: Packets of bought instant whips of any flavour may be used as filling for this pie. Prepare according to directions on packet. Then cool thoroughly and follow the above recipe directions for placing filling and bananas into pie case.

French Silk Chocolate Pie

CHOCOLATE CAKE PIE

plain pastry for 1 9-inch pie short-
     crust case
8 ounces sugar
2 tablespoons flour
pinch of salt
3 eggs, separated
2 ounces (2 squares) unsweetened
     chocolate, melted
½ pint rich milk

Sift together sugar, flour, and salt.

Beat egg yolks until light and fluffy; stir in sifted dry ingredients. Stir in melted chocolate and milk.

Beat egg whites until stiff; fold into chocolate-egg yolk mixture.

Pour into pastry lined 9-inch dish. Bake in very hot oven (450°F. Mark 8) 15 minutes. Reduce heat to moderate oven (350°F. Mark 4) and bake 30 minutes.

Variations:

Pineapple Cake Pie: Omit chocolate and add 1 teaspoon grated lemon rind, 2 tablespoons lemon juice, and 4 ounces drained crushed pineapple.

Strawberry Cake Pie: Omit chocolate and add 1 tablespoon lemon juice and 4 fluid ounces strawberry purée.

EGGNOG PIE

3 beaten egg yolks
4 ounces sugar
1 pint single cream
⅛ teaspoon salt
⅛ teaspoon nutmeg
½ teaspoon vanilla
3 stiffly beaten egg whites
plain pastry for 9-inch pie case

Beat egg yolks, sugar, and cream. Add salt, nutmeg, and vanilla. Fold in egg whites.

Pour into 9-inch pastry lined pie dish.

Bake in very hot oven (450°F. Mark 8) 10 minutes. Reduce heat to slow oven (325°F. Mark 3) and bake until firm, about 25 minutes.

Variations: Sherry or rum to taste may be substituted for vanilla.

FRENCH SILK CHOCOLATE PIE

1 8-inch baked pie case
4 ounces butter
6 ounces sugar
2 squares (2 ounces) unsweetened
     chocolate, melted
1 teaspoon vanilla
2 eggs

Cream butter; gradually add sugar, creaming well.

Blend in melted and thoroughly cooled chocolate and vanilla.

Add eggs, one at a time, beating 5 minutes after each addition. (With electric mixer use medium speed.)

Turn into cooled, baked pie case. Chill at least 2 hours.

Before serving top with whipped cream and walnuts, if desired.

PUMPKIN CREAM PIE

pastry for 9-inch pie case
1 pound strained, cooked pumpkin,
     fresh, frozen, or canned
2 teaspoons cinnamon
5 ounces brown sugar
½ teaspoon ginger
½ teaspoon salt
12 fluid ounces milk
2 well beaten eggs
4 fluid ounces double cream

Combine pumpkin, cinnamon, sugar, ginger, and salt.

Slowly add milk and beat with rotary beater until thoroughly blended. (If you have a blender, use it instead of the rotary beater to blend the mixture.) Stir in eggs and cream.

Pour pumpkin mixture into pastry lined 9-inch dish. Sprinkle top with cinnamon.

Bake in slow oven (325°F. Mark 3) 50 minutes. Serve warm with whipped cream, if desired.

ONTARIO MAPLE SYRUP PIE

2 tablespoons cornflour
pinch of salt
½ pint milk
¾ pint maple syrup
2 egg yolks
1 9-inch baked pie case
2 egg whites
2 tablespoons granulated sugar

Blend cornflour and salt with a little of the milk.

Heat rest of milk with maple syrup to boiling point. Add cornflour mixture and cook 5 minutes in double boiler, stirring constantly.

Pour some of the mixture over beaten egg yolks, return to double boiler and cook 5 minutes longer, stirring continually.

Pour into baked pie case. Top with meringue made from well beaten egg whites and sugar.

PEACHES AND CREAM PIE

1 unbaked 9-inch pastry case
about 8 large ripe peaches
few grains salt
3 tablespoons flour
4 ounces sugar
½ pint single cream
2 drops almond flavouring

Peel peaches; cut each in half; remove stone. Arrange peach halves, hollow side up, in pastry lined dish, without crowding. Fill in between peach halves with few peach slices.

Stir salt, flour, and sugar together until well mixed; stir in cream and flavouring. Pour over peaches.

Bake in moderate oven (350°F. Mark 4) on low rack, until peaches are tender (test with a fork). Cool pie on wire rack. Serve soon after cooling.

Gelatine Pies

FRESH FRUIT CHIFFON PIE
(Basic Recipe)

1 pound any fresh fruit
10 ounces sugar
2 tablespoons arrowroot or corn-flour
water
2 teaspoons gelatine
4 egg whites
1 baked 9-inch pastry case
4 fluid ounces double cream, whipped
dash of liqueur or ½ teaspoon vanilla

Peel, stone, or prepare fruit according to variety chosen. Crush and add 4 ounces sugar. Cook until tender and purée if desired.

Heat to boiling; add arrowroot or cornflour, which has been blended with small amount of cold water. Cook, stirring, until thickened. Boil, stirring, 2 minutes.

Soften gelatine in 2 tablespoons cold water; add to hot fruit mixture and stir until dissolved.

Beat egg whites until almost stiff; add remaining 6 ounces sugar gradually and beat until stiff. Fold into fruit mixture.

Pour into baked pie case and chill until set. Flavour whipped cream with liqueur or vanilla and spread over pie.

ORANGE CHIFFON PIE

2 fluid ounces cold water
1 tablespoon gelatine
4 eggs, separated
8 ounces sugar
½ teaspoon salt
4 fluid ounces orange juice
1 teaspoon lemon juice
1 teaspoon finely grated orange rind
1 9-inch pie case, baked and cooled
4 fluid ounces double cream (optional)

Sprinkle gelatine over cold water, stir slightly, and set aside.

Place egg yolks in small mixing bowl and beat until light and lemon coloured. Add 4 ounces sugar and the salt and blend thoroughly. Add juices gradually and blend.

Pour mixture into 1-quart saucepan

Orange Chiffon Pie

and cook on medium heat, stirring constantly, until mixture just begins to thicken (about 2 minutes).

Switch to low heat, and continue cooking, stirring constantly, until mixture resembles consistency of a soft custard (about 4 minutes). Remove from heat.

Add orange rind and gelatine mixture to hot egg yolk mixture and stir until gelatine is dissolved.

Chill in refrigerator until mixture is very thick, but not stiff.

Place egg whites in large-sized mixing bowl. With clean beater, beat until stiff but not dry. Add remaining 4 ounces sugar, 1 tablespoon at a time, while beating until very stiff.

Add egg yolk mixture and fold in until completely blended.

Pour mixture into baked pie case and spread evenly. Chill in refrigerator until firm (about 1 hour).

Just before serving, spread whipped cream over filling.

NESSELRODE PIE

Originally, the name Nesselrode was applied to a frozen pudding made with chestnuts, fruit, and cream, invented by the chef of an early-19th-century Russian statesman of German descent, Count Karl Robert Nesselrode. The name is also applied nowadays to various other desserts and dessert sauces, and especially to a pie flavoured with rum, containing preserved fruits, and often topped with flaked chocolate.

2 teaspoons light rum
2 ounces chopped candied fruit
2 tablespoons gelatine
2 ounces sugar
½ teaspoon salt
1 pint cold milk
3 eggs, separated
additional 3 ounces sugar
½ pint double cream, whipped
baked 9-inch pie case
flaked chocolate or candied fruit, optional

Sprinkle rum over candied fruit and set aside. Combine gelatine, 2 ounces sugar, and salt in top part of double boiler. Gradually stir in milk and cook over hot water, stirring until gelatine has dissolved.

Beat egg yolks in a bowl, then gradually stir milk mixture into egg yolks. Return to double boiler and cook, stirring constantly, until mixture is slightly thickened and coats a spoon. Let cool, then add candied fruit.

Beat egg whites until stiff, then gradually beat in 3 ounces sugar. Gently fold into gelatine mixture. Fold in whipped cream. Turn into the baked pie case; chill until firm. If desired, garnish with flaked chocolate or candied fruit.

PEPPERMINT CHIFFON PIE

1 tablespoon gelatine
2 fluid ounces cold water
3 egg whites
3 ounces sugar
½ pint double cream, whipped
few drops oil of peppermint
4 ounces crushed peppermints
1 9-inch chocolate digestive biscuit crumb shell

Soften gelatine in cold water and dissolve over boiling water. Cool.

Beat egg whites until stiff and beat in sugar gradually.

Add dissolved gelatine to egg whites and fold in whipped cream, flavouring, and crushed peppermints.

Turn into crumb shell and chill.

CHOCOLATE CHIFFON PIE

1 tablespoon gelatine
2 fluid ounces water
2 ounces (2 squares) unsweetened chocolate
4 fluid ounces water
3 eggs, separated
¼ teaspoon salt
1 teaspoon vanilla
¼ teaspoon cream of tartar
4 ounces sugar
1 9-inch digestive biscuit pie case

Soften gelatine in 2 fluid ounces water.

Meanwhile melt chocolate in remaining 4 fluid ounces water in top of double boiler. Stir into egg yolks.

Return to double boiler; cook and stir until creamy. Stir in gelatine until dissolved. Blend in salt and vanilla; cool.

Beat egg whites and cream of tartar until almost stiff. Gradually beat in sugar until very stiff and glossy. Fold in slightly thickened chocolate mixture.

Spoon into crumb shell. Garnish with lattice of whipped cream for that extra special touch.

Chocolate Chiffon Pie

LEMON CHIFFON PIE

1 9-inch digestive biscuit crumb
    shell
1 tablespoon gelatine
2 fluid ounces cold water
3 eggs, separated
6 ounces sugar
½ teaspoon salt
4 fluid ounces lemon juice
1 teaspoon grated lemon rind
chopped nuts for garnish

Soften gelatine in cold water at least 5 minutes.

Beat egg yolks; add 4 ounces sugar, salt, and lemon juice. Cook over boiling water, stirring constantly, until of custard consistency.

Add lemon rind and gelatine, stir until gelatine dissolves. Cool until slightly thickened.

Beat egg whites until they form soft peaks. Gradually add remaining sugar; beat until stiff. Fold into custard mixture. Pour into digestive biscuit crumb shell.

Chill to set. Before serving, garnish with chopped nuts.

Note: For a quick and easy method, substitute 4 fluid ounces bottled lemon juice for 4 fluid ounces fresh lemon juice and lemon rind.

RASPBERRY CHIFFON PIE

1 tablet raspberry jelly
½ pint boiling water and juice from
    berries
3 ounces sugar
dash of salt
2 tablespoons lemon juice
4 fluid ounces cold water and juice
    from berries
3 fluid ounces iced water
3 ounces dried milk
8 ounces frozen raspberries, thawed
    and drained or fresh rasp-
    berries plus 3 tablespoons
    sugar
1 baked 9-inch pie case

Thaw raspberries in strainer over bowl and reserve juice.

Dissolve raspberry jelly in boiling water. When thoroughly dissolved, add sugar and salt. Stir until dissolved.

Add cold juice and lemon juice and

Raspberry Chiffon Pie

allow to chill until almost set.

When ready, place iced water into the small bowl of mixer, add dried milk and beat until stiff. Remove to smaller bowl.

Beat partially set jelly until thick and fluffy. Fold in drained berries and whipped milk.

Turn into baked pie case and chill until firm. Decorate with whipped cream and fresh berries.

PINEAPPLE CHIFFON PIE

1 9-inch digestive biscuit crumb
    shell
1 tablespoon gelatine
2 fluid ounces cold water
8 ounces undrained crushed pine-
    apple
2 ounces sugar
3 eggs, separated
1 tablespoon butter or margarine
¼ teaspoon salt
4 ounces sugar
4 fluid ounces double cream
    (optional)

Soften gelatine in cold water.

Combine pineapple, 2 ounces sugar, and egg yolks. Cook over low heat until mixture coats a metal spoon, stirring frequently.

Blend in margarine. Stir in softened gelatine. Chill until mixture begins to thicken.

Add salt to egg whites and beat until they stand in soft peaks.

Gradually beat in 4 ounces sugar, one tablespoon at a time. Fold into pineapple mixture.

Pour into cold digestive biscuit pie shell.

Chill until ready to serve. If desired, top with whipped cream.

COFFEE CHIFFON PIE

1 tablespoon gelatine
2 fluid ounces cold water
2 tablespoons instant coffee
6 fluid ounces hot water
¼ teaspoon salt
4 ounces sugar, divided
3 eggs, separated
1 9-inch chocolate biscuit crumb
    shell

Soften gelatine in cold water.

Dissolve coffee in hot water in top of double boiler. Add salt and 2 ounces sugar. Cook over direct heat until sugar is dissolved.

Beat egg yolks slightly. Slowly add hot liquid, stirring constantly. Return to top of double boiler and cook over hot water, stirring constantly, until mixture is slightly thickened.

Remove from heat and add softened gelatine, and stir until dissolved.

Chill until consistency of unbeaten egg whites.

Beat egg whites until stiff, gradually beat in remaining 2 ounces sugar. Fold in chilled coffee mixture.

Turn into 9-inch chocolate biscuit crumb shell and chill until firm. If desired, garnish with whipped cream and flaked chocolate.

Coffee Chiffon Pie

EGGNOG CHIFFON PIE

2 tablespoons gelatine
2 pints bottled eggnog
2 ounces sugar
¼ teaspoon nutmeg (optional)
4 teaspoons rum flavouring
    (optional)
½ pint double cream, whipped
1 10-inch baked pie case

Sprinkle gelatine in ½ pint of cold eggnog in top of double boiler to soften.

Place over boiling water. Add sugar and stir until gelatine and sugar are dissolved. Add remaining eggnog.

If additional flavouring is desired, add nutmeg and flavouring. Chill until consistency of unbeaten egg white.

Whip gelatine mixture until light and fluffy; fold into whipped cream. Turn into pie case; chill until firm.

Garnish with additional whipped cream, flaked chocolate, chopped maraschino cherries, orange peel, and angelica.

Variation: To make Nesselrode Pie, fold in 4 ounces chopped maraschino cherries and 2 ounces chopped nuts just before turning into pie case.

Eggnog Chiffon Pie

Pumpkin Chiffon Pie

PUMPKIN CHIFFON PIE

1 9-inch crumb shell
3 egg yolks
5 ounces brown sugar
12 ounces cooked or canned
     pumpkin
4 fluid ounces milk
½ teaspoon salt
½ teaspoon ginger
1 teaspoon cinnamon
½ teaspoon nutmeg
1 tablespoon gelatine
2 fluid ounces cold water
3 egg whites
6 tablespoons granulated sugar

Beat egg yolks and brown sugar until thick; add pumpkin, milk, salt, and spices; cook in double boiler until thick.

Add gelatine softened in cold water; stir until gelatine dissolves. Cool mixture until it begins to set.

Beat egg whites until fluffy. Gradually add granulated sugar, beating well after each addition, until stiff. Fold egg whites into pumpkin mixture. Pour into baked shell and chill.

If desired, top with whipped cream and sprinkle with cornflake crumbs.

APRICOT CLOUD PIE

1 tablespoon gelatine
2 fluid ounces cold water
2 eggs, separated
4 ounces sugar
¼ teaspoon salt
½ pint apricot pulp and juice
2 tablespoons lemon juice
3 fluid ounces iced water
1½ ounces dried milk
2 ounces sugar
3 tablespoons apricot brandy
1 9-inch baked pie case

Soften gelatine in cold water.

Beat egg yolks in top of double boiler. Add 4 ounces sugar, salt, apricot pulp and juice, and lemon juice. Cook over hot water until mixture coats spoon.

Add gelatine. Stir until dissolved. Cool until slightly set.

Place egg whites and iced water in small bowl of electric mixer. Add dried milk. Beat at low speed until smooth. Beat at high speed until it forms stiff peaks. Add 2 ounces sugar gradually. Fold this and brandy into gelatine mixture. Turn into crust. Chill until firm.

Variations of Apricot Cloud Pie
Lemon Cloud Pie: Omit apricot pulp, juice and brandy. Increase lemon juice to 4 fluid ounces. Add 1½ teaspoons grated lemon rind.

Or, use 1 6-ounce can frozen lemonade concentrate and omit sugar, lemon juice and rind.

Orange Cloud Pie: Reduce lemon juice to 1 tablespoon. Add 3 fluid ounces undiluted frozen orange concentrate.

Cranberry Cloud Pie: Omit lemon juice and rind. Use ½ pint strained cranberry pulp, 4 fluid ounces frozen orange concentrate and 1 teaspoon grated orange rind.

BRAZIL NUT BLACK BOTTOM PIE

1 tablespoon gelatine
2 fluid ounces cold water
6 ounces sugar
1 tablespoon cornflour
4 eggs, separated
¾ pint milk, scalded
12 ounces semi-sweet chocolate
     pieces
1 teaspoon vanilla
¼ teaspoon salt
1 10-inch Brazil nut pie case

Soften gelatine in cold water.

Combine ⅓ cup sugar and cornflour.

Beat egg yolks slightly; slowly add scalded milk. Stir in sugar mixture. Cook in double boiler, stirring constantly, until mixture is slightly thickened.

To ½ pint custard, add semi-sweet chocolate pieces. Stir until chocolate is melted; set aside.

To remaining custard, add softened gelatine. Stir until gelatine is dissolved; add vanilla. Chill until consistency of unbeaten egg white.

Beat egg whites until stiff; gradually beat in salt and remaining 3 ounces sugar. Fold in custard-gelatine mixture.

Stir chocolate mixture; turn into pie case. Spoon gelatine mixture over chocolate layer and chill until firm.

Garnish with whipped cream, maraschino cherries, and Brazil nut slices.

BRAZIL NUT PIE SHELL

10 ounces finely chopped Brazil
     nuts (¾ pound unshelled
     nuts)
3 tablespoons sugar

Mix Brazil nuts with sugar in a 10-inch pie plate. Press this mixture with back of tablespoon against bottom and sides, up to rim of pie plate.

If a toasted flavour is desired, bake in hot oven (400°F. Mark 6) 8 minutes, or until lightly browned. Cool. Makes 1 10-inch shell.

PEACH CHIFFON PIE

1 9-inch crumb or baked pastry
     case
2 teaspoons gelatine
2 fluid ounces cold water
3 eggs, separated
½ teaspoon salt
2 teaspoons lemon juice
6 ounces sugar
1 pound fresh peaches, crushed or
     sieved

Soften gelatine in cold water.

Beat egg yolks slightly and add salt, lemon juice, and about 2 ounces sugar. Cook over hot, not boiling, water until thickened, stirring constantly.

Stir softened gelatine into hot mixture until dissolved.

Remove from hot water. Add peaches and chill until mixture begins to thicken.

Beat egg whites until stiff but not dry; gradually beat in remaining sugar. Fold into peach mixture.

Pile lightly into crumb case and chill until firm. Top with whipped cream and garnish with sliced peaches.

SHERRY CHIFFON PIE

1 baked 9-inch pie case
1 tablespoon gelatine
3 fluid ounces cold water
4 eggs, separated
8 ounces sugar, divided
6 fluid ounces sherry
⅛ teaspoon salt
4 fluid ounces whipping cream
     (optional)

Soften gelatine in cold water 5 minutes.

Beat egg yolks light; add gradually 4 ounces sugar while continuing to beat. Add sherry.

Cook over hot water, stirring constantly, until mixture is the consistency of soft custard. Add gelatine; stir until dissolved and let cool.

Beat egg whites stiff; beat in remaining 4 ounces sugar and salt. Combine with the custard. Spoon into pastry case. Chill until firm, about 3 hours.

When ready to serve, garnish with whipped cream and a dash of nutmeg, if desired.

Sherry Chiffon Pie

BUTTERSCOTCH CHIFFON PIE

1 tablespoon gelatine
2 fluid ounces cold water
3 well beaten egg yolks
6 ounces firmly packed brown sugar
¼ teaspoon salt
½ pint scalded milk
1 teaspoon vanilla
3 egg whites, beaten stiff
½ pint double cream, whipped
1 9-inch baked pastry or crumb
shell

Soften gelatine in cold water.

Mix egg yolks, sugar, salt, and milk. Cook over boiling water, stirring constantly, until mixture is slightly thickened.

Add gelatine and stir until dissolved. Chill until mixture is thick. Fold in vanilla, egg whites, and cream.

Turn into pie case and chill several hours or overnight.

Half of the whipped cream could be reserved and used as topping for pie.

STRAWBERRY-ORANGE CHIFFON PIE

2 egg yolks
2 ounces sugar
¼ teaspoon salt
2 tablespoons cornflour
⅛ teaspoon nutmeg
½ pint orange juice
10 fluid ounces milk
1 tablespoon gelatine
2 fluid ounces cold water
½ teaspoon vanilla
8 ounces strawberries, sliced
2 egg whites
2 ounces sugar
½ pint double cream, whipped
1 9-inch cornflake shell

Combine egg yolks, 2 ounces sugar, salt, cornflour, and nutmeg. Add orange juice and milk gradually. Cook over low heat, stirring constantly, until thickened.

Soften gelatine in cold water. Add gelatine to custard, stirring until gelatine is dissolved.

Cool custard until thickened. Add vanilla. Add strawberries.

Beat egg whites until peaks begin to form. Gradually add sugar and continue beating until a soft meringue is formed.

Fold meringue into custard mixture. Turn into shell and chill 2 hours or more before serving.

Serve with cream which has been whipped, and sweetened if desired.

Raspberry or Peach-Orange Chiffon Pie: Substitute raspberries or very ripe fresh peaches for strawberries.

BITTERSWEET MINT PIE

1 9-inch baked digestive biscuit
crumb shell
1 tablespoon gelatine
4 fluid ounces cold milk
8 fluid ounces milk, scalded
6 ounces sugar
3 eggs, separated
2 ounces (2 squares) unsweetened
chocolate, melted
4 fluid ounces double cream
2 fluid ounces crème de menthe

Soften gelatine in cold milk.

Pour a little scalded milk into sugar and slightly beaten egg yolks; combine with remaining milk. Cook over hot water, stirring constantly, until mixture coats spoon.

Stir in gelatine; divide in half.

To one half, add melted chocolate. Chill both mixtures until partially set.

Whip cream stiff; fold into chocolate mixture. Pour into digestive biscuit crumb shell; chill.

Beat egg whites stiff; fold into remaining custard with crème de menthe. Pour over chocolate mixture. Chill until firm.

RHUBARB AND STRAWBERRY BAVARIAN PIE

1 baked 9-inch pie case
8 ounces sugar
1 pound rhubarb, cut in 1-inch
pieces
2 tablespoons gelatine
2 fluid ounces cold water
8 ounces mashed strawberries
½ pint cream, whipped
2 egg whites, stiffly beaten

Sprinkle 6 ounces sugar over rhubarb and let stand to extract juice while making pie case.

Soften gelatine in cold water.

Heat rhubarb to boiling; lower heat and simmer until just tender, 5 minutes or longer. Stir gently or shake pan to prevent sticking.

Add softened gelatine and stir gently until dissolved. If desired, remove the most perfect pieces of rhubarb for garnishing, and put a spoonful of syrup over them. Set them aside, but do not chill.

Add strawberries to rhubarb mixture and more sugar if desired. Cool and then chill until beginning to set.

Fold in half the whipped cream and the meringue made by beating remaining sugar into beaten egg whites. Turn into pie case and chill until set.

At serving time, garnish with reserved whipped cream, reserved pieces of rhubarb, and additional whole strawberries.

SWEET POTATO CHIFFON PIE

Crumb Shell:
20 digestive biscuits finely rolled
(7 ounces crumbs)
2 ounces softened butter or
margarine
2 ounces sugar
¼ teaspoon cinnamon

Thoroughly blend together crumbs, softened butter or margarine, sugar, and cinnamon.

Pour mixture into 9-inch pie plate; firmly press against bottom and sides of plate.

Bake in moderate oven (375°F. Mark 5) 8 minutes. Cool.

Filling:
1 tablespoon gelatine
10 fluid ounces milk
3 eggs, separated
6 ounces sugar
½ teaspoon cinnamon
7 ounces mashed, cooked sweet
potato

Soften gelatine in 2 fluid ounces milk. In top of double boiler, beat egg yolks; stir in remaining ½ pint milk, 3 ounces sugar, cinnamon, and sweet potato. Cook over hot water, stirring constantly, until thickened.

Stir in gelatine until dissolved; chill until slightly thickened.

Beat egg whites until fairly stiff; gradually beat in remaining 3 ounces sugar until stiff peaks form. Fold in custard mixture. Heap into crumb shell. Chill.

Before serving, garnish with a wreath of whipped cream and sprinkling of sultanas.

RHUBARB CHIFFON PIE

8 ounces finely chopped fresh
rhubarb
6 ounces sugar
2 fluid ounces hot water
1 tablespoon gelatine
2 fluid ounces cold water
2 egg whites
4 fluid ounces double cream,
whipped
1 tablespoon grated orange rind
1 baked 9-inch pie case

Cook rhubarb with 4 ounces sugar and hot water until tender. Force through coarse sieve.

Soften gelatine in cold water and add to hot rhubarb mixture. Chill until almost firm.

Beat egg whites until frothy and add remaining sugar gradually, beating until stiff. Fold into cold rhubarb mixture which has been beaten until fluffy.

Fold grated orange rind into whipped cream and fold into mixture. Turn into pie case. Chill until firm.

Turnovers and Tarts or Miniature Pies

TURNOVERS

This is an excellent way to use left-over pastry trimmings. Roll pastry ⅛-inch thick. Cut into 3- to 4-inch circles or squares.

Place a teaspoon of fruit filling or preserves on half of each pastry. Moisten the edge of half of each pastry. Fold over to form half a circle or a triangle, and seal the edges by pressing together with the prongs of a fork.

Prick the tops to form small steam vents. Bake in hot oven (425°F. Mark 7) about 15 minutes.

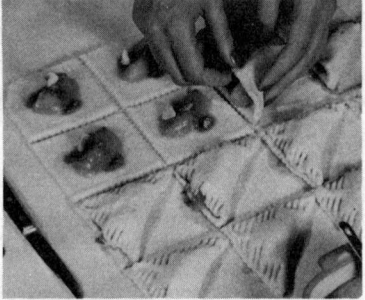

Place filling on half of each square; fold pastry to form triangle. Seal.

PEACH TURNOVERS
(Basic Recipe)

8 ounces sifted flour
3 teaspoons baking powder
½ teaspoon salt
2 ounces fat
5-6 fluid ounces milk
8 ounces sliced peaches
2 tablespoons butter or margarine
2 tablespoons brown sugar

Sift together flour, baking powder, and salt. Cut or rub in fat until mixture is crumbly. Add milk to make a soft dough.

Turn out on lightly floured board or pastry cloth and knead gently 30 seconds.

Roll out into rectangular sheet about ¼ inch thick. Cut into 8 rectangles 6×3 inches.

Place peach slices on half of each rectangle. Dot with butter or margarine and sugar. Fold over and seal.

Bake in hot oven (425°F. Mark 7) 15 to 18 minutes. Makes 8 turnovers.

Variations: Other fruits may be substituted for peaches.

BANBURY TARTS

These small triangular turnovers are named after the town noted for its pastry.

pastry for 9-inch double crust pie
4 ounces sugar
1 tablespoon flour
1 egg
6 ounces seedless raisins
1 ounce chopped nuts
1 tablespoon lemon juice
2 teaspoons grated lemon rind

Roll pastry ⅛ inch thick; cut 4-inch squares.

Combine sugar and flour and stir into slightly beaten egg. Combine with remaining ingredients.

Place filling on half of each square; fold pastry to form triangle. Seal edges and flute with fingers or a fork. Cut or prick small steam vents.

Bake in hot oven (425°F. Mark 7) about 15 minutes. Makes 12.

CHEESE APRICOT TURNOVERS

9 ounces cream cheese
3 ounces butter or margarine
8 ounces sifted flour
1 teaspoon salt
½ pound dried apricots, cooked and puréed
4 ounces sugar

Blend together cream cheese and butter. Gradually cut in mixed and sifted dry ingredients; chill.

Roll out very thin on a lightly floured board. Cut into 4-inch squares.

Combine apricots and sugar. Place 1 tablespoon of apricot mixture on each square of pastry. Fold squares into triangles and seal edges with a fork. Prick tops with a fork.

Place on a baking sheet. Bake in moderate oven (375°F. Mark 5) 20 to 25 minutes. Makes 18 to 20 turnovers.

OLD-FASHIONED FRIED PIES

8 ounces sifted flour
1 teaspoon salt
3 ounces fat
iced water
filling (below)
fat for frying

Sift flour and salt together. Cut in fat until crumbs are the size of small peas. Gradually add water (about 3 fluid ounces) to make a soft dough.

Roll out to ⅛-inch thickness on lightly floured pastry cloth. Cut in 5-inch rounds (use a sharp-pointed knife and a cardboard cut-out or the top of a coffee can).

Put 1½ tablespoons filling on half of each circle, keeping it ½ inch from the edge.

Moisten edge of pastry with water and fold the empty half over the filling to make a half circle. Seal the edges by pressing together with the prongs of a fork. Prick the tops 2 or 3 times with a fork.

With a palette knife, slide 3 or 4 at a time into deep, hot fat (360°F.) and fry until golden brown on the underside, 2 to 3 minutes. Turn and brown other side.

Lift out and drain on absorbent paper. Serve warm or cold. Sprinkle with icing sugar, if desired. Makes 10 to 12 pies.

Dried Apricot Filling:
1 pound stewed dried apricots, drained
2 ounces sugar
2 tablespoons melted butter or margarine

Cook the apricots; stir in sugar and butter.

Dried Apple Filling:
1 pound stewed dried apples, drained
2 ounces sugar
2 tablespoons melted butter or margarine
¼ teaspoon nutmeg or cloves

Cook apples; stir in sugar, butter, and spice.

Apple Sauce Filling:
½ pint apple sauce
1 ounce firmly packed brown sugar
1 ounce seedless raisins
¼ teaspoon allspice
1½ teaspoons lemon juice
1 tablespoon melted butter or margarine

Mix ingredients thoroughly.

Old-Fashioned Fried Pies

CHESS TARTS

6 ounces seedless raisins
4 ounces butter or margarine
5 ounces firmly packed brown sugar
3 unbeaten eggs
4 ounces broken walnuts
1 tablespoon brandy extract
6 4-inch tart cases

Rinse and drain raisins. With electric mixer at medium speed, or "cream" (or with spoon), thoroughly mix butter with sugar.

Add eggs, one at a time, beating well after each addition. Stir in nuts, brandy, and raisins. Spoon into cases.

Bake in hot oven (425°F. Mark 7) 10 minutes. Reduce heat to moderate (350°F. Mark 4) and bake 25 minutes longer. Cool. Serve with whipped cream.

Assorted Fruit Tarts: Make patty tin tart cases. Just before serving, fill baked cases with fresh fruit in season. Picture shows bilberries, sliced peaches, and strawberries. Serve with sweetened whipped cream.

TART CASES

Roll out pastry ⅛ inch thick as directed in recipe for shortcrust pastry. (The 9-inch double-crust recipe will make 8 medium-sized tart cases.)

Cut into circles, using a sharp-pointed knife to cut around cardboard pattern or a can.

Line tart tins with pastry circles and press into the flutings on sides of cups with back of a knife.

Press pastry overhang against sharp pan edges to cut off neatly.

Prick pastry with prongs of fork or not, according to recipe directions for filling.

Bake filled tart cases according to directions given in recipe for tarts.

To prevent puffing, prick unfilled tart cases thoroughly all over with prongs of fork and bake in very hot oven (450°F. Mark 8) until delicately browned, 10 to 15 minutes. Cool thoroughly before filling.

DOUBLE CRUST TARTS

Line tart tins, being careful not to stretch the dough. Trim off pastry with scissors ¼ inch beyond cup rim.

Cut design in centre of circles for top crusts to make steam vents.

After filling tarts, moisten edge of trimmed lower crust, cover with top crust and press gently around edge to seal.

Trim with scissors ¼ inch beyond rim of tin. Turn overhang under lower crust so fold is even with edge of tin.

Flute or crimp as for full-sized double-crust pie.

Note: Fruit tarts may also be covered with lattice top if desired.

PATTY TIN TART CASES

Use patty tins with cups 3 to 3½ inches in diameter. Cut 5-inch pastry circles, using a sharp-pointed knife and a cardboard pattern or the top of a coffee can.

Fit the circles over the backs of patty cups. Pinch edges together 6 or 7 times to fit dough to cup. Prick liberally with prongs of fork over "tops" of cups and "down" sides.

Bake in very hot oven (450°F. Mark 8) until lightly browned, about 10 minutes.

Cool before removing tart cases from patty cups.

PETAL TART CASES

Roll out shortcrust pastry. Cut 5 circles the same size as the bottom of the patty tin cup.

Lay one circle in bottom of cup; press 4 circles to sides and bottom of cup so that they overlap.

Prick well and bake in very hot oven (450°F. Mark 8) 10 to 15 minutes, or until golden brown.

Cool and lift out carefully. Fill with preferred filling and top with whipped cream if desired.

BISCUIT TART CASES

    3 ounces butter or margarine
    4 ounces sugar
    1 egg
    1 tablespoon orange juice
    6 ounces sifted flour
    1 teaspoon baking powder
    ¼ teaspoon salt

Cream butter or margarine; add sugar gradually and mix well. Add egg and orange juice; mix well.

Sift flour, baking powder, and salt together. Add to creamed mixture and blend well. Chill dough.

Roll dough on a lightly floured board to ⅛-inch thickness, cut into rounds.

Invert patty tins and grease outside of cups. Place rounds over cups, press down and pinch edges of dough at intervals to fit cups. Prick with a fork.

Bake in moderate oven (375°F. Mark 5) 6 to 8 minutes.

Cool one minute before removing cases. Fill with soft fruit, yoghurt, or ice cream for serving. Makes 10 or 12 tart cases.

PATTY CASES

Roll out shortcrust pastry ¼ inch thick. Cut with round, floured cutter. Remove centres from ½ these circles with a small cutter.

Wet edges of the whole circles. Place the rings on them.

Brush tops carefully with an egg slightly beaten with 1 tablespoon water. Take care not to moisten sides. Chill until stiff.

Bake in very hot oven (450°F. Mark

8) 10 to 20 minutes. Bake small centres 10 minutes and use as tops after cases are filled.

GLAZED STRAWBERRY CREAM CHEESE TARTS

    3 ounces cream cheese
    2 tablespoons cream
    6 baked tart cases
    1½ pounds strawberries
    glaze No. 1 or No. 2 (see following
        recipes)
    4 fluid ounces cream, whipped

Blend cheese and cream. Spread in bottom of tart cases.

Fill shells with strawberries that have been washed, hulled, and drained.

Cover fruit with glaze and chill. Garnish with whipped cream, sweetened if desired.

GLAZE FOR TARTS 1

    1 pound strawberries
    4 fluid ounces water
    ½ pint sugar
    2½ tablespoons cornflour
    1 tablespoon butter or margarine
    red food colouring

Crush berries. Add water, sugar, and cornflour. Cook, stirring, until thickened and clear.

Add butter and enough colouring to give a bright red. Strain. Makes enough for 6 tarts.

GLAZE FOR TARTS 2

Melt any good fruit jelly (currant, quince, apple, crab apple, etc.) in top of double boiler. Pour over fruit. One cup of jelly is enough for 6 tarts.

MINCEMEAT PIE FACES

Make up recipe for a 2-crust pie. Cut 8 circles from rolled out dough. With sharp knife, cut "faces" in four of the circles.

Place 2 ounces of mincemeat in centre of the 4 remaining circles. Moisten edge of dough with water. Top with "faces" and press crusts together with prongs of fork. Bake on baking sheet in hot oven (400°F. Mark 6) about 15 minutes.

Mincemeat Pie Faces

VIENNESE CREAM CHEESE TARTS

- 4 ounces butter or margarine
- 3 ounces cream cheese
- 2 ounces sifted flour
- 4 ounces redcurrant, raspberry, strawberry, or grape jelly
- 1 egg yolk
- 2 tablespoons milk
- 2 ounces finely chopped nuts
- icing sugar

Work butter or margarine and cream cheese together until soft, then stir in flour thoroughly. Chill in refrigerator or about an hour or until manageable.

Roll dough about ⅛ inch thick on lightly floured board and cut into -inch squares.

Spoon a bit of jelly (¼ teaspoonful or more) near centre of square.

Fold a corner of dough over jelly to form a triangle and pinch edges to seal.

Pull 2 corners of the triangle around to shape a crescent and dip into a mixture of egg yolk and milk.

Roll crescents in chopped nuts.

Place on an ungreased baking sheet and bake in hot oven (400°F. Mark 6) to 10 minutes. Sprinkle with icing sugar and cool. Makes 2 dozen.

GLAZED GRAPE TARTS

- 2 pounds grapes
- 6 ounces sugar
- 1 tablespoon cornflour
- 1 to 2 tablespoons lemon juice
- 5 to 6 unbaked tart cases
- 8 ounces redcurrant or apple jelly

Slip pulp out of skins. Reserve skins. Cook pulp until seeds loosen; put through sieve to remove seeds.

Mix sugar and cornflour. Add to pulp. Add skins and lemon juice; pour into tart cases.

Bake in very hot oven (450°F. Mark) 10 minutes. Lower heat to moderate (350°F. Mark 4) and bake 20 minutes longer.

Heat jelly with 1 to 2 teaspoons water, stirring until thin and smooth. Pour over grapes to glaze. Cool. Serve with whipped cream.

Cherry Cream Tarts

PINEAPPLE LIME TARTS

- 1½ pounds sliced pineapple
- ¾ tablet lime jelly
- 6 fluid ounces whipping cream
- 6 baked and cooled pastry cases

Drain pineapple; cover and refrigerate.

Add enough water to syrup to make 12 fluid ounces liquid. Heat and dissolve jelly in it. Chill until slightly thickened.

Whip cream until stiff and fold into jelly. Fill tart cases. Chill.

Just before serving, top with a pineapple slice and garnish with a maraschino cherry.

Pineapple Lime Tarts

WALNUT TARTS

- 4 ounces walnuts, coarsely chopped
- 3 fluid ounces hot milk
- 6 tablespoons sugar
- 2 teaspoons rum
- 4 unbaked 3-inch tart cases

Mix all ingredients well. Pour into tart cases.

Bake in hot oven (425°F. Mark 7) 15 to 20 minutes.

CHERRY CREAM TARTS

- 6 baked tart cases
- 3 ounces cream cheese
- 2 tablespoons sugar
- ¼ teaspoon lemon juice
- ½ teaspoon grated lemon rind
- 3 ounces double cream, whipped
- 1¼ pounds sour, red, stoned cherries, well drained
- 3 tablespoons sugar
- 1 tablespoon cornflour
- 6 fluid ounces cherry juice

Soften cream cheese at room temperature; cream until smooth. Gradually add sugar while stirring; beat with spoon until fluffy.

Add lemon juice and lemon rind. Fold in whipped cream.

Put 2½ tablespoons cream cheese mixture into each baked tart case. Chill in refrigerator 1 hour.

Combine 3 tablespoons sugar and cornflour in saucepan. Gradually stir in cherry juice. Cook over medium heat until thick and clear. Cool slightly.

Spoon cherries over cream cheese mixture. Cover with cherry-cornflour mixture. Makes 6 3¾-inch tarts.

Biscuit Tarts

BISCUIT TARTS

Cut out rounds of pie dough with scalloped biscuit cutter. Cut centres from half of these rounds. Bake on baking sheet in hot oven (425°F. Mark 7) 10 minutes. Spread whole rounds with preserves and top with circles.

RASPBERRY TARTS

- 2 tablespoons sugar
- 1 tablespoon cornflour
- ⅛ teaspoon salt
- 6 fluid ounces fruit juice
- 1 teaspoon lemon juice
- 4 to 6 baked tart cases
- 1 pint fresh raspberries

Blend together the sugar, cornflour, and salt in a saucepan.

Stir in fruit juice and cook over low heat until thick and clear. Cool. Add lemon juice.

Fill tart cases with raspberries. Pour fruit sauce over berries. Chill. Top with whipped cream, if desired.

PUMPKIN CHIFFON TARTS

- 3 slightly beaten egg yolks
- 4 ounces sugar
- 12 ounces canned pumpkin
- 4 fluid ounces milk
- ½ teaspoon salt
- 1 teaspoon ginger
- ½ teaspoon nutmeg
- ½ teaspoon cinnamon
- 1 tablespoon gelatine
- 2 fluid ounces cold water
- 4 ounces sugar
- 3 stiffly-beaten egg whites
- 8 baked pastry tart cases

Combine egg yolks, 4 ounces sugar, pumpkin, milk, salt, and spices; cook in double boiler until thick. Add gelatine which has been softened in cold water. Mix thoroughly and cool.

Add remaining 4 ounces sugar to egg whites; fold into pumpkin mixture. Pour into baked tart cases and chill. Garnish with whipped cream.

COTTAGE CHEESE AND CHERRY TARTS

Heat canned red cherries; add sugar to taste, and thicken to desired consistency with cornflour. Cool.

Fill cooled, baked tart cases with creamed cottage cheese and top each with the cooked and sweetened cherries.

Any pie may be made in the form of individual tarts for festive desserts and they make service simple when the party is large.

CALIFORNIA CHESS TARTS

4 ounces butter or margarine
8 ounces sugar
¼ teaspoon salt
¼ teaspoon cinnamon
¼ teaspoon nutmeg
¼ teaspoon cloves
4 egg yolks, unbeaten
5 ounces seedless raisins
4 ounces chopped walnuts or
    pecans
4 fluid ounces sherry
8 unbaked tart cases

Cream 4 ounces butter or margarine and 8 ounces sugar together until light and fluffy.

Add salt, cinnamon, nutmeg, and cloves.

Add unbeaten egg yolks, one at a time, beating well after each addition.

Add raisins (rinsed with boiling water and drained well), walnuts or pecans, and sherry; blend thoroughly.

Spoon mixture into unbaked tart cases. Bake in moderate oven (350°F. Mark 4) about 40 minutes, or until firm.

Serve warm or cold, topped with either whipped cream or vanilla ice cream. Serves 8.

CRANBERRY TARTS

1 pound chopped cranberries
1 teaspoon grated orange rind
2 oranges, peeled and chopped
1 pound sugar
3 tablespoons quick-cooking tapioca
1 tablespoon butter or margarine,
    melted
½ teaspoon salt
1 orange, sectioned
6 unbaked tart cases

Combine cranberries, orange rind, oranges, sugar, tapioca, butter, and salt.

Pour into tart cases. Arrange orange sections on top of filling.

Bake in very hot oven (450°F. Mark 8) 10 minutes; reduce temperature to moderate (350°F. Mark 4) and bake 25 to 30 minutes.

QUICK LEMON MERINGUE TARTS

1 packet lemon pudding or pie
    mix
4 ounces sugar
1¼ pints water
2 eggs, separated
6 large or 12 small baked tart cases
2 ounces sugar

Combine lemon pudding, sugar, and water in a saucepan.

Beat yolks slightly and add to mixture. Cook over medium heat, stirring constantly, until mixture thickens and comes to the boil.

Cool slightly. Pour into baked tart cases.

Beat egg whites until stiff but not dry; gradually beat in sugar until mixture stands in peaks. Pile lightly on tarts.

Bake in hot oven (425°F. Mark 7) about 5 minutes, until lightly browned. Makes 6 large or 12 small tarts.

BRUNSWICK MINCEMEAT TARTS

Prepare pastry, using 1 pound short-crust pastry mix and following directions on packet.

Roll out thin and cut in rounds with a 4-inch cutter. Line the inside of tiny (2-inch) patty tins with these rounds. Prick pastry.

Bake cases in a very hot oven (450°F. Mark 8) 12 minutes. Cool. (Leave cases right in the patty tins.)

Fill cases with mincemeat filling (below). Bake in a moderate oven (350°F. Mark 4) for 45 minutes.

Remove from cups while still warm. Serve warm or cold, plain or topped with a bit of sherry-flavoured hard sauce. Makes 24 miniature tarts.

Mincemeat Filling:

4 ounces softened butter or
    margarine
6 ounces firmly packed brown
    sugar
1½ tablespoons flour
4 egg yolks
12 ounces mincemeat
2 ounces chopped walnuts
3 fluid ounces sherry
¼ teaspoon each cinnamon and
    nutmeg
¼ teaspoon salt

Cream butter, sugar, and flour together until thoroughly blended. Beat in egg yolks, one at a time.

Add remaining ingredients; mix well. Spoon into tart cases as directed above.

GLAZED WALNUT MINCE TARTS

Spoon moist mincemeat into baked tart cases; top with coarsely broken walnut kernels.

Sprinkle a little honey over the nuts; place under grill a few minutes to glaze.

MAPLE SYRUP BUTTER TARTS

2 eggs
6 ounces brown sugar
¼ teaspoon salt
2 teaspoons vinegar
4 fluid ounces maple syrup
6 tablespoons melted butter
3 ounces chopped nuts
pastry

Beat eggs only until yolks and white are well blended.

Beat in sugar and salt and add vinegar and maple syrup. Mix well and add melted butter and nuts.

Line patty cups with pastry, and fi ½ to ⅔ full.

Bake in very hot oven (450°F. Mar 8) 10 minutes, then reduce heat t moderate (350°F. Mark 4) and bake 2 to 25 minutes more, or until filling firm.

DEEP DISH APPLE PIE

pastry for 6 individual pies with
    lattice strips (basis 6 ounces
    flour)
12 ounces sliced apples
6 ounces sugar
½ teaspoon salt
½ teaspoon cinnamon
⅛ teaspoon nutmeg
2 tablespoons flour
2 tablespoons butter or margarine
2 tablespoons lemon juice
6 fluid ounces sweet dessert wine

Arrange a layer of sliced apples i each individual deep dish pie case.

Mix sugar, salt, spices, and flou Sprinkle half the dry ingredients ove layers of apples.

Add remaining apples and remain ing dry ingredients in succeedin layers.

Dot with butter or margarine Sprinkle with lemon juice. Add tw tablespoons wine to each pie. Top wit lattice pastry.

Bake in very hot oven (450°F. Mar 8) 10 minutes, then reduce heat t moderate (350°F. Mark 4) and bak 30 to 35 minutes longer until apple are done and crust is browned.

Deep Dish Apple Pie

Choux Pastry (Pâte à Choux)

Far from being an item reserved for special desserts, choux pastry can become something to be served at almost any point in the meal. For example, thimble-sized puffs can be made for hors d'oeuvre, stuffed with thirst-provoking mixtures and served with cocktails. Larger shells may be fried in deep fat, producing a crisp surface that is a good contrast for creamed fish or poultry.

Or after forcing the batter through a pastry bag, éclairs can be made with a rich homemade filling which are far more tasty than bought éclairs.

CHOUX PASTRY
(Basic Recipe)

½ pint water
4 ounces butter or 2 ounces butter,
    2 ounces vegetable fat
¼ teaspoon salt
4 ounces sifted flour
4 eggs

Heat water, fat, and salt to boiling. Simmer until fat has melted.

Reduce heat as much as possible without eliminating it altogether. Add flour all at once. Stir briskly until mixture forms a ball that leaves the sides of the saucepan, but no longer.

Remove from heat. Add eggs one at a time, beating after each addition until mixture is stiff and glossy.

The batter having been prepared, the next step is to shape it. The size and form chosen depend on the method of presentation — very small for hors d'oeuvre shells, larger for main course and dessert purposes.

To make cream puff shells, scrape a tablespoonful of batter per puff onto a lightly greased baking sheet. Bake in a hot oven until puffy, light, delicately brown.
For éclair shells, the choux pastry may be forced from a pastry bag or dropped from a spoon. Make éclairs an inch wide, four inches long.

When choux pastry is baked or deep-fat fried, it expands to many times its original size and a mass of air occurs in the centre.

SHAPING CHOUX PASTRY

Cocktail Puff Shells: Use about ¾ teaspoon of pastry. Scrape off end of spoon onto lightly greased surface, arranging shells about 2 inches apart.

Bake only until brown and dry, or about 30 minutes in a hot oven (425°F. Mark 7). The basic recipe yields 4 dozen cocktail shells

Fried Puff Shells (for main dish salads, creamed mixtures): Scrape mixture from spoon into deep, hot fat (370°F.). Use one rounded tablespoon per puff. Turn often. Fry about 12 minutes. Drain on greaseproof paper. Yield of basic recipe: 12 large puffs.

Cream Puff Shells (for dessert): Scrape rounded tablespoonfuls of pastry onto lightly greased baking sheet about 2 inches apart. Bake in hot oven (425°F. Mark 7) about 50 minutes or until brown and no bubbles show on surface. Yield of basic recipe: 12 large puffs.

Éclair Shells (for dessert): Force choux pastry through pastry bag, using largest plain tip or no tip at all if set includes only the small type. Make éclairs about an inch wide and four inches long. Bake as for cream puffs. The basic recipe yields 12 to 18 shells.

CREAM PUFF SWANS

To make the swan neck and head, pipe choux pastry through a large pastry bag, using a large star tip, onto a buttered baking sheet into the shape of an "S".

For the tail, pipe a comma-shaped piece separately.

After filling cream puffs, insert a "head" and a "tail" in each to make a swan, cutting holes if necessary.

The cream puff tops that have been cut off to admit the filling may be cut in two and replaced to simulate lifted wings.

HINTS FOR FILLING AND FINISHING CHOUX PASTRY SHELLS

Fill choux pastry shells as near serving time as possible.

Cut a hole in the side and use a pastry bag and tip to insert the stuffing.

Or cut off a portion of the top and fill with a spoon.

Cream puffs and éclairs are best finished off with a sifting of icing sugar. If you like very sweet desserts, an icing or whipped cream are tasty, or use any dessert sauce that would harmonize with the filling.

Cream puff shells may be prepared in advance of serving and stored in foil or covered container. After filling, cream puffs should be refrigerated unless served promptly.

CREAM FILLING FOR CREAM PUFFS AND ÉCLAIRS

1½ pints milk
2 ounces flour
¼ teaspoon salt
6 ounces sugar
3 eggs or 6 yolks, slightly beaten
1½ teaspoons vanilla
3 tablespoons butter or margarine
    or 4 to 8 fluid ounces double cream, whipped

Scald milk in top of a double boiler.

Mix flour, salt, and sugar. Add milk while stirring.

Return to top of double boiler and cook, stirring, until thickened. Leave in double boiler, cover and cook 5 minutes.

While stirring, add mixture gradually to beaten eggs. Return to double boiler and cook, stirring until thickened, or about 2 minutes.

Add vanilla and butter. Chill. Whipped cream gives a richer, lighter textured filling. If used, add it just before filling shells. Makes enough for 12 large cream puffs.

Variations of Cream Filling

Butterscotch: Substitute 6 ounces dark brown sugar for granulated and cook butter in the mixture.

Chocolate: Increase sugar to 8 ounces. Add 3 to 4 ounces (squares) chocolate, shredded or grated, to mixture before cooking.

Coffee: Substitute 6 fluid ounces very strong coffee for that same amount of milk.

Fruit: Fold into mixture just before filling shells 8 ounces sliced or chopped fruit, well drained. Strawberries, bananas, and pineapple are recommended.

Ginger: Add 2 ounces finely chopped preserved ginger to vanilla or butterscotch filling.

Maple: Substitute maple sugar for granulated.

Nut or Coconut: Add 3 ounces chopped nuts or coconut to vanilla, chocolate, coffee, or maple filling.

Rum or Sherry: Omit vanilla and add 2 tablespoons or more rum or sherry to the cream filling.

Profiteroles is a French term for wal-nut-size puff shells, which may be filled with custard or cream to make a dessert or with meat or other savoury fillings to be served as an appetizer or with soup.

PROFITEROLES

Bake small cream puffs. Cool and fill with Crème Pâtissière à la Vanille (below), whipped cream, or ice cream.

Serve with hot chocolate or other dessert sauce.

Crème Pâtissière à la Vanille:
- 4 ounces sugar
- 2 ounces flour
- 2 tablespoons cornflour
- ¼ teaspoon salt
- 1 egg yolk
- 4 fluid ounces milk
- 1 pint hot milk
- 1 tablespoon butter
- 2 teaspoons vanilla

Combine sugar, flour, cornflour, and salt in top of double boiler.

Beat egg yolk slightly. Add cold milk. Blend in dry ingredients and stir until smooth.

Blend in hot milk. Cook over boiling water, stirring constantly, until thick. Cover and cook for 5 minutes.

Remove from heat. Add butter and vanilla. Cover and cool.

Miscellaneous Pastries

STRUDEL

Strudel is a German term for a Central European pastry of stretched paper-thin dough rolled up with a filling of fruit, nuts, poppy seeds, cottage cheese, vegetables, or meat and baked. It is superlatively fragile and delicious. People tend to be afraid of trying to make the stretched dough, but once they have done so, many agree that it is no more difficult than making a good pie crust.

STRUDEL DOUGH
- 12 ounces sifted flour
- ½ teaspoon salt
- 1 tablespoon vegetable oil
- 1 beaten egg
- ½ pint lukewarm water

To Mix and Knead Dough: Sift flour and salt into a large bowl. Make a well in the centre of the flour; place oil and egg in the depression.

Work flour gently into oil and egg and gradually add water to make a soft dough. (The dough will be sticky.)

Turn dough out onto a lightly floured pastry board. Hold dough high above board and crash it down against the board. Repeat this about 100 to 125 times or until the dough is smooth and elastic and leaves the board clean. (After 15 or 20 times it will no longer stick.)

Knead slightly and pat it into a round. Lightly brush surface of dough with oil (not olive oil).

Cover dough with an inverted warmed bowl and allow to rest from 30 minutes to 1 hour.

To Stretch Dough: Spread a large table (about 3×5 feet) with a clean cloth, allowing cloth to hang down.

Sprinkle cloth lightly but thoroughly with about 2 ounces flour.

Place dough in centre of cloth and roll it into a large oblong, turning it several times to prevent it sticking to the cloth, and rolling the outer edges as thinly as possible.

With a soft brush, lightly brush the dough with cooking oil (not olive oil); the oil aids in preventing the formation of holes during stretching.

Now reach under the dough and start stretching (do not pull) gently from the centre to the outer edge.

Some people work with the backs of the hands. They turn the palms downward and stretch with slightly raised knuckles only. Others prefer to keep the palms up with the fingers straight out, working with a circular motion under the dough. You will soon learn which method is most convenient for you.

Work around the table until the evenly stretched dough is as thin as paper and drapes over the edges of the table on all sides.

As you stretch, keep the dough close to the table. The dough should not have any torn spots. If some should appear, do not try to patch them.

With kitchen scissors, trim off the thick outer edges that overhang the table.

Allow the stretched dough to dry a little, about 10 minutes. It should lose its stickiness but avoid drying too long because it becomes brittle.

To Fill and Roll: Brush the entire surface with cooled melted butter. Sprinkle with breadcrumbs as directed in recipe for filling. Cover from a half to two-thirds of the surface with remaining ingredients for the filling.

Fold over the overhanging flaps on three sides over the filling. Butter the turned-up edges, and then with the aid of the table cloth start to roll the dough over, pulling the cloth and dough to-ward you with both hands. Roll fairly loosely to give room for expansion.

With the last roll slide the strudel on a well buttered baking sheet, bending it into a horseshoe shape.

Or cut the strudel in halves, and lifting each half on cloth, gently roll onto the baking sheet.

To Bake: Brush the surface with melted butter and bake in moderate oven (350°F., Mark 4) until golden brown, 35 to 45 minutes. Baste and brush with melted butter several times during baking.

When strudel makes a crackly sound on touching it is done. (Strudel should not be smooth.)

To Serve: Remove to cooling rack; cool slightly. Sift icing sugar generously over it. Remove to a cutting board and cut into 2-inch slices. Serve warm with unsweetened whipped cream. Makes 12 to 15 servings.

Note: The trimmings of dough may be kneaded with a little flour, rolled out, and when dry, cut into broad noodles.

APPLE STRUDEL
- 1 recipe strudel dough
- 4 ounces butter, melted and cooled
- 2 ounces fine breadcrumbs
- 1½ pounds tart apples, peeled, cored, and finely sliced (4 to 6 apples)
- 4 to 6 ounces sugar (depending on tartness of apples)
- 1 teaspoon cinnamon
- 5 ounces raisins
- 4 ounces chopped walnuts or almonds, if desired

Make and stretch strudel dough. Brush dough with some of the melted butter. Sprinkle two-thirds of the surface with breadcrumbs and apples.

Sprinkle over this the sugar, cinnamon, raisins, and nuts. Roll, place on buttered baking sheet. Brush with butter.

Bake in moderate oven (350°F. Mark 4) 35 to 45 minutes, basting frequently with melted butter.

Variations:

Sour Cherry Strudel: Use 2 pounds sour cherries, stoned, in place of apples. Omit raisins.

Sweet Cherry Strudel: Use 2 pounds sweet black cherries, stoned, in place of apples. Use only 4 ounces sugar. Omit cinnamon and raisins.

Fresh Peach Strudel: Use sliced peaches in place of apples.

Plum Strudel: Use sliced stoned plums in place of apples.

CABBAGE STRUDEL

1 recipe strudel dough
1 head (about 3 pounds) cabbage
    (about 3 quarts, shredded)
2 tablespoons salt
2 ounces butter
¾ to 1 teaspoon pepper
2 fluid ounces thick sour cream
1 ounce fine, dry breadcrumbs

Remove and discard wilted outer leaves of cabbage. Rinse; cut into quarters (discarding core) and finely shred.

Place cabbage in a large bowl and mix with salt. Let stand ½ hour, mixing occasionally.

Melt butter in a 3-quart saucepan. Squeeze cabbage, a small amount at a time, discarding juice; put cabbage into saucepan. Cook, uncovered, over medium heat, stirring frequently, 10 to 15 minutes, or until just tender.

Remove cabbage from heat and mix in pepper. Set cabbage aside.

After strudel dough is stretched and slightly dried, spoon sour cream over entire surface in small mounds. Carefully spread mounds of cream with spatula.

Sprinkle breadcrumbs over the sour cream. Spoon cabbage in small mounds over breadcrumbs. With spatula spread mounds carefully.

Roll, bake and slice as directed in strudel dough recipe. Do not sprinkle with icing sugar. Serve warm. Makes 12 slices.

POPPY SEED STRUDEL

1 recipe strudel dough
½ pound freshly ground poppy seeds
8 ounces sugar
2 ounces raisins
2 teaspoons grated lemon rind
4 ounces butter, melted and cooled

Mix poppy seeds, sugar, raisins, and lemon rind together. Set aside.

After strudel dough is stretched and lightly dried, sprinkle cooled, melted butter over it. Spoon poppy seed mixture over the butter.

Roll and bake as directed in recipe for strudel dough.

Viennese Tarts

CANNOLI

A Sicilian fried pastry usually filled with a ricotta cheese filling, as given below; however pudding, whipped cream, and ice cream fillings are often used.

1 pound sifted flour
¼ teaspoon cinnamon
1 tablespoon powdered instant
    coffee
grated rind of ½ lemon
2 ounces sugar
1 egg, slightly beaten
1 egg yolk, slightly beaten
2 tablespoons cooking oil
about ½ pint Sauternes or other
    semi-sweet white wine
additional 2 egg yolks, slightly
    beaten

Mix and sift flour, cinnamon, and coffee into a bowl. Stir in lemon rind, sugar, egg and egg yolk, and oil.

Mix with your hands, adding just enough wine to hold ingredients together to form a dough. Turn out on a floured board and knead until smooth and elastic, about 10 minutes. Chill dough several hours.

Cut off pieces of dough about the size of a walnut, and roll out very thin on a well-floured board. Using a 5-inch cutter or a saucer cut into 5-inch rounds. Wrap each around a cannoli tube (a metal tube about 1-inch in diameter) or use pieces of clean broomstick handle about 5 inches long. Seal dough by brushing with remaining egg yolks.

Fry 2 or 3 at a time by dropping wrapped tubes into deep hot fat (375°F. Mark 5) until lightly browned, about 1 minute. Drain on absorbent paper; let cool slightly then push moulds out one end.

Just before serving fill cannoli, garnish ends with chopped nuts and sprinkle cannoli with icing sugar. Makes about 30.

Ricotta Cheese Filling: Combine 2 pounds ricotta cheese, 12 ounces sugar, 4 ounces semi-sweet chocolate, 1 ounce finely chopped angelica, and 1 teaspoon vanilla.

VIENNESE TARTS

4 ounces sifted flour
¼ teaspoon salt
3 ounces shortening
4 ounces cottage cheese
marmalade or jam

Sift together flour and salt. Cut or rub in fat. Add cottage cheese and mix well.

Form into smooth ball. Chill 30 minutes or longer.

Roll out on lightly floured board or pastry cloth. Cut into 3-inch squares.

Put a teaspoon of tart marmalade or jam in centre of each square. Pinch all edges together to hold filling. Place on ungreased baking sheet.

Bake in hot oven (425°F. Mark 7) about 10 minutes or until browned. Makes about 2 dozen 1½-inch tarts.

BAKLAVA

A sweet, rich Near Eastern dessert made of many paper-thin layers of pastry dough that are filled with a mixture of butter and nuts and covered with syrup. It can be bought from shops which sell fresh or Syrian specialities.

Pastry:
8 ounces sifted flour
4 ounces fat
1 teaspoon salt
1 egg and water to make 4 fluid
    ounces

Cut fat into flour and salt until mixture looks like fine breadcrumbs.

With a fork, blend the egg and water. Add to dry ingredients, mixing until all dry ingredients are thoroughly dampened.

Turn onto greaseproof paper. Knead 8 times. Roll into ball and let rest ½ hour.

Filling:
8 ounces slivered almonds
3 ounces brown sugar, firmly
    packed
4 ounces melted butter or
    margarine
1 teaspoon cinnamon
½ teaspoon nutmeg

Mix together all ingredients for filling.

Divide pastry into 4 portions. Roll out 1 portion very thin on a lightly floured pastry cloth into a rectangle 8×16 inches.

Cut rectangle in half to form 2 8-inch squares.

Place 1 square in bottom of 8×8×2-inch baking dish. Spread 2 tablespoons of the filling over this pastry.

Place second layer of pastry on top of filling.

Roll out another portion of pastry as above. Continue making layers of pastry and filling.

Spread no filling on the top layer of pastry.

Syrup:
½ pint water
8 ounces sugar
grated rind of 1 orange
grated rind of 1 lemon

Mix ingredients for syrup in saucepan. Boil 5 minutes.

Cut baklava into 8 servings. Pour 3 tablespoons of syrup over baklava.

Bake in moderate oven (350°F. Mark 4) 35 to 40 minutes.

Serve remaining sauce (cooled) over the hot baklava. Serves 8.

PUFF PASTRY
(Basic Recipe)

Puff pastry is a flaky, air-filled butter-rich pastry with infinite uses.

1 pound unsalted butter
1 pound flour
1 teaspoon salt
8 to 10 fluid ounces iced water

Wash the butter by putting it in a bowl of iced water and kneading and squeezing it with the hands until it is smooth, waxy, and as pliable as putty.

Remove it from the water. Place it in a clean cloth and press out any water that may have been trapped in it.

Set aside 2 tablespoons butter. Shape the remaining butter into a flat, square cake about ½ inch thick. Wrap in greaseproof paper and chill in coldest part of the refrigerator.

Sift flour with salt into a large mixing bowl or in a mound on a board.

Add the 2 tablespoons washed butter to the flour and, with the fingertips, work it into flour.

Add iced water gradually and, again using the fingertips, mix quickly and lightly to make a dough with about the consistency of the washed butter. The dough should be firm but not hard.

Place the dough on a lightly floured board and roll it out in a rectangle ½ inch thick.

Place the ½-inch-thick square cake of butter in the centre of the dough.

Fold the upper flap of dough down to cover the butter. Fold the lower flap of dough up over the upper flap, making 3 layers and completely covering the butter.

Press the side edges of the dough firmly together to enclose as much air as possible. Chill the paste in the refrigerator for 20 minutes.

Place the chilled dough on a board with either side facing you.

Gently roll the paste away from you to make a long rectangle about ½ inch thick and about 20 inches long. The dough should be rolled without letting the butter break through the surface of the dough. This is one of the secrets of making puff pastry. If you let the butter break through, it means enclosed air is being lost, and it is this enclosed air that will make the pastry puff.

Fold the rectangle of dough into thirds as you did the first time and turn it so one of the edges faces you. This rolling, folding, and turning is called a "turn."

Make another turn and again chill the dough in the refrigerator for 20 minutes.

Then make 2 more turns and chill again in the refrigerator for 20 minutes.

Then make 2 more turns (this makes six turns in all) and chill for 15 min-

utes before rolling and cutting the dough for baking.

If the paste is not used at once, wrap it in greaseproof paper and store in the refrigerator; it may be kept several days before using.

When ready to use, roll ¼ to ⅓ inch thick, cut as desired and place on baking sheet rinsed with cold water and drained thoroughly. Prick shapes and chill it again before baking. The pastry should be ice cold when placed in the oven.

Bake in very hot oven (450°F. Mark 8) about 8 minutes, or until pastry has risen its full height; then reduce heat to moderate (350°F. Mark 4) and bake 10 to 20 minutes, or until delicately browned. This amount of dough will make 2½ to 4 dozen fancy pastries.

CREAM HORNS

Use a small amount of puff pastry at a time, leaving remaining pastry in refrigerator until needed.

Roll puff pastry on a pastry cloth ⅛ inch thick, keeping shape rectangular.

With a sharp knife, cut it into long strips ½ to ¾ inch wide.

Roll these strips around metal cream horn forms, overlapping edges slightly. Or use cornucopias made out of stiff brown paper, one for each strip of pastry. Place on cold dampened baking sheet and bake in very hot oven (450°F. Mark 8) until well puffed and lightly browned, about 20 minutes. Quickly remove from oven; quickly brush with egg white wash (1 slightly beaten egg white combined with 1 teaspoon water) and return to oven to finish baking, about 5 minutes.

Remove from metal horns or paper cornucopias and cool on cake rack. When cool, fill with vanilla-flavoured whipped cream or cream filling.

NAPOLEONS

Roll puff pastry on pastry cloth that has practically no flour on it, into a rectangle about ⅛ inch thick.

Cut into strips 2½ inches wide. Prick all over with a fork. Place on a baking sheet that has had cold water run over it and excess shaken off. Chill until dough is very stiff.

Bake in very hot oven (450°F. Mark 8) about 8 minutes, or until pastry has risen its full height. Then reduce heat to moderate (350°F. Mark 4) and bake until dry and delicately browned, 10 to 20 minutes.

Cool thoroughly and cut into 3-inch bars. Sandwich two bars together with whipped cream or a rich cream filling.

BOUCHÉES

Roll puff pastry about ⅛ inch thick. Shape in the same way as small vol-au-vent cases, making them much smaller (1½ to 2 inches in diameter).

VOL-AU-VENT

This is a large puff pastry case usually 6 to 8 inches in diameter, to be filled with meat, poultry, or game mixtures. A vol-au-vent may be shaped on the back of a deep dish or may be fashioned in the same manner as individual patty cases.

Roll puff pastry about ⅓ inch thick. Cut 2 large ovals or rounds, using floured mould or sharp-pointed knife (cutting around a cardboard pattern).

Brush outer edge of one with cold water. Cut off a ¾-inch-wide band around edge of remaining oval and place this ring on plain oval, pressing lightly.

Then press in very lightly the inside edge of ring to prevent uneven rising.

Prick several places with a fork and chill thoroughly.

Roll the remaining cut-out piece ⅛ inch thick and cut shape for cover.

Bake in very hot oven (450°F. Mark 8) about 8 minutes. Then reduce heat to moderate (350°F. Mark 4) and bake 20 to 30 minutes, until delicately browned. Cover with paper if pastry browns too quickly.

PUFF PASTRY PATTY CASES

Use a small amount of the pastry at a time, leaving the rest in the refrigerator until needed.

Roll the pastry out on a pastry cloth that has practically no flour on it to a thickness of ¼ inch.

Cut into 3-inch rounds with a lightly floured cutter. Cut out centres from half the rounds with a small cutter.

Moisten underside of each ring with cold water and place on remaining plain rounds, pressing down lightly. Then press in lightly the inside edge of ring to prevent uneven rising.

Brush the surface with beaten egg or with milk mixed with beaten egg. Chill thoroughly.

Bake in very hot oven (450°F. Mark 8) 8 minutes, or until pastry has risen its full height; then reduce heat to moderate (350°F. Mark 4) and bake 10 to 20 minutes, or until delicately browned.

The small rounds cut out from the circles may be baked separately for caps.

Baked patty shells are sold ready-to-serve in many bakeries; frozen patty shells are available in groceries.

PIZZA

Pizza is the Italian word for pie; specifically a pie of Neapolitan origin with a crust of bread dough that is spread with tomatoes or tomato sauce, cheese (usually Mozzarella), oregano, and sometimes various other toppings. It is eaten hot.

PIZZA 1

(For two 12-inch round pies)

Dough:

½ pint warm (not hot) water
½ ounce fresh yeast or 2 teaspoons dried yeast
1 teaspoon sugar
1 teaspoon salt
2 tablespoons olive or vegetable oil
8 ounces sifted flour
additional 6 ounces sifted flour (about)

Topping:

6 ounces tomato purée
4 fluid ounces water
1 teaspoon salt
1 teaspoon crushed oregano
dash of pepper
½ pound Mozzarella cheese, sliced about ⅛ inch thick
4 tablespoons olive or vegetable oil
4 tablespoons grated Parmesan cheese

Sprinkle or crumble yeast into the 1 cup water and stir until dissolved. Stir in 1 teaspoon sugar, 1 teaspoon salt, and 2 tablespoons oil.

Add 8 ounces flour and beat until smooth, then gradually stir in the additional 6 ounces flour. Dough should be as soft as biscuit dough. Turn out on lightly floured board and knead until smooth and elastic.

Place in greased bowl; brush top with soft fat. Cover and let rise in warm place (85°F.), free from draughts, until doubled in bulk, about 45 minutes.

Mix together the tomato purée, 4 fluid ounces water, 1 teaspoon salt, 1 teaspoon oregano, and dash of pepper.

When dough is doubled in bulk, punch down and divide in half. Form each half into a ball and place on greased baking sheet. Press out with palms of hands into circles about 12 inches in diameter, making edges slightly thick.

On each circle of dough arrange half of the Mozzarella cheese. Spread evenly half of the tomato mixture; sprinkle evenly 2 tablespoons oil and 2 tablespoons grated Parmesan cheese.

Bake in hot oven (400°F. Mark 6) about 25 minutes. Serve hot. Makes 2 12-inch pies.

PIZZA 2

(For an 11 × 15-inch pan)

½ ounce fresh yeast or 2 teaspoons dried yeast
6 fluid ounces warm (not hot) water
1½ tablespoons olive or vegetable oil
¼ teaspoon salt
12 ounces sifted flour
¼ pound salami
12 ounces solid part Italian plum tomatoes
2 tablespoons olive oil
1 teaspoon crushed oregano
½ to 1 teaspoon crushed basil
freshly ground pepper
¾ pound Mozzarella cheese, sliced about ⅛-inch thick
4 ounces anchovies in oil

Add yeast to water and stir until dissolved. Add the oil, salt, and flour and mix well. Dough should be as soft as biscuit dough. Add a bit more flour if necessary.

Turn onto a floured board and knead until very smooth and elastic. Place in a greased bowl; grease surface and let stand in a warm place (85°F.), free from draught, until doubled in bulk. On cool days bowl of dough may be put in pan of warm water.

Turn dough out of bowl and shape into a smooth ball. Place in a greased shallow dish, about 11 × 15 inches, and press until the dough fits dish.

Cover with pieces of tomato and sprinkle with oil. Sprinkle with oregano, basil, and pepper.

Cover two-thirds of dough with Mozzarella, leaving uncovered the third adjacent to a lengthwise rim.

Arrange anchovies on outer half of cheese-covered dough. Put salami on dough that has no cheese on it. This leaves centre part with only cheese on it.

Bake in very hot oven (450°F. Mark 8) 15 to 20 minutes or until brown. Cut into strips or squares and serve piping hot. Makes 30 to 36 strips.

Early Preparation Methods for Pizza

(1) Prepare the yeast dough several hours before serving time and chill it in the refrigerator.

About 2 hours before time to bake the pizza, spread the dough in the dish, apply the topping and cover with greaseproof paper or aluminium foil. Return to the refrigerator.

Remove to a warm place for 20 minutes or while heating the oven and bake as directed, using the lower shelf of the oven.

(2) Bake the pizza until half done or until the dough is set. Cool the pizza, cover well and let stand at room temperature. Complete the baking just before serving.

The first method gives a fresher topping, but requires more judgment, for it is difficult to estimate the rate of rising in the refrigerator. Partial baking gives a very acceptable product.

PIZZA WITH SHORTCRUST PASTRY MIX BASE

1 pound shortcrust pastry mix
2 ounces chopped onion
1 tablespoon olive oil
8 ounces tomato sauce
6 ounces tomato purée
1 teaspoon salt
¼ teaspoon oregano
⅛ teaspoon garlic salt
⅛ teaspoon pepper
olive oil or vegetable oil
½ pound Bel Paese or Mozzarella
    cheese
1 ounce finely-cut parsley
2 to 3 tablespoons grated Parmesan
    cheese, if desired

Prepare dough and let rise as directed in basic recipe on pastry mix packet.

Sauté 2 ounces chopped onion in 1 tablespoon olive oil until golden brown.

Combine and add tomato sauce, tomato purée, salt, oregano, garlic salt and pepper.

Divide dough into 4 parts. Flatten each piece and pat into bottoms of 4 9 or 10-inch pie-dishes. (If desired, dough may be divided in half, rolled to 2 12×8×2-inch rectangles and placed on ungreased baking sheets.)

Brush with olive oil or vegetable oil.

Slice thin or grate ½ pound Bel Paese or Mozzarella cheese. Arrange half of cheese on dough. Cover with the tomato sauce. Top with remaining cheese and additional topping as desired. See suggestions below.

Sprinkle with 1 ounce finely-cut parsley and 2 to 3 tablespoons grated Parmesan cheese, if desired.

Bake immediately in very hot oven (450°F. Mark 8) 15 to 20 minutes. Serve hot.

Pizza Variations:
Mushroom Pizza: Place 2 ounces mushrooms, chopped or sliced, over dough.

Anchovy Pizza: Place 12 to 14 anchovies (whole or pieces) over dough.

Italian Salami Pizza: Arrange 8 ounces salami or other Italian sausage, diced or sliced thin, over dough.

Pork Sausage Pizza: Place 8 ounces cooked pork sausage over dough.

QUICK PIZZA CRACKER SNACKS

1 can (10 ounces) condensed
    tomato soup
1 small clove garlic, chopped
¼ teaspoon oregano
¾ pound sharp Cheddar cheese,
    sliced
50 cream crackers

Combine soup, garlic, and oregano. Let stand for at least 20 minutes. Top each cream cracker with a bit of tomato sauce and a slice of cheese.

Sprinkle with additional oregano if desired.

Bake on baking sheet in hot oven (400°F. Mark 6) until cheese melts, about 3 to 5 minutes. Makes about 50.

PIZZA WITH BISCUIT BASE

1¼ pounds cooked tomatoes
1 ounce chopped green pepper
1 clove garlic, chopped
1 teaspoon salt
½ teaspoon oregano, optional
dash of pepper
8 ounces sifted flour
3 teaspoons baking powder
1 teaspoon salt
2 ounces fat shortening
5 to 6 fluid ounces milk
melted butter or margarine
8 ounces grated Bel Paese or sharp
    Cheddar cheese

Combine tomatoes, green pepper, garlic, salt, oregano, and pepper. Mix well and let stand while preparing biscuit dough.

Sift together flour, baking powder, and salt. Cut or rub in fat until mixture is crumbly. Add milk to make a soft dough. Mix well.

Divide dough in 4 equal portions. Pat each portion out on greased baking sheet to circle about 7 inches in diameter, making a slight ridge around the edge. Brush lightly with butter or margarine.

Sprinkle 1 ounce cheese over each biscuit round. Spoon tomato mixture over cheese. Top with remaining cheese.

Bake in hot oven (425°F. Mark 7) 15 minutes. Reduce heat and bake in moderate oven (350°F. Mark 4) 15 minutes longer.

Cut into pie-shaped pieces and serve hot. Makes 4 individual pizza-style pies.

PIZZA-STYLE SNACKS WITH BAPS

6 baps
3 ripe tomatoes or 10 ounces
    drained stewed tomatoes
24 anchovy fillets or dash of rose-
    mary
12 thin slices of cheese
olive oil
salt and pepper

Break baps apart; toast until slightly crispy.

Thinly slice tomatoes and place 1 slice or 2 tablespoons stewed tomatoes on each bap half.

Add either 2 anchovy fillets or dash of rosemary. Add another layer of fresh tomato or stewed tomatoes and top with slice of cheese.

Sprinkle with olive oil, salt, and pepper. Place under grill and grill until cheese melts. Serves 6.

PIZZA-STYLE SNACKS

8 ounces sifted flour
3 teaspoons baking powder
1 teaspoon salt
3 fluid ounces vegetable oil
6 fluid ounces milk
vegetable oil
Tomato Topping (below)
½ pound process cheese

Sift flour, baking powder, and salt into bowl. Pour 3 fluid ounces oil into bowl; add milk and pour all at once into dry ingredients. Stir with fork until mixture rounds up into a ball. Knead about 10 times without flour.

Roll dough between greaseproof paper to ¼ inch thickness. Cut into 3½-inch rounds. Place on ungreased baking sheet. Brush top of each round with oil. Spread with Tomato Topping.

Bake in hot oven (400°F. Mark 6) 1 minutes or until edges are lightly browned.

Remove from oven and arrange strips of cheese in spoke fashion on top. Bake 5 minutes more, or until cheese is melted. Makes 6 individual snacks.

Tomato Topping:
8 ounces canned drained tomatoes
2 ounces chopped stuffed olives
2 tablespoons finely chopped spring
    onions
¼ teaspoon oregano
½ teaspoon salt
⅛ teaspoon pepper

Break up tomatoes and combine with olives, onions, and seasonings. Drain well just before placing on rounds of dough.

PIZZA-STYLE SNACKS WITH BAPS No. 2

Split 6 large baps in half. Remove centres, reserving crumbs for casserole dishes.

Brush each half with butter and add filling as given above. Grill until filling is bubbly and hot and cheese melts. Serves 6.

Pizza-Style Snacks

POULTRY AND GAME BIRDS

MODERN POULTRY

The biggest differences between modern poultry and the chickens, turkeys, and ducks our mothers were able to buy are in tenderness, amount of available meat per pound, and constancy of supply. Modern poultry raising is such a streamlined process that a steady supply of tender meaty poultry comes to our markets throughout the year, maintaining a fairly constant quality and price.

All modern poultry is fed a carefully balanced diet, designed to produce a high percentage of meat, compared to total weight, at a very early age. As a result chickens and turkeys have more breast meat and larger drumsticks; ducklings have a minimum amount of excess fat. The younger marketing ages mean lower prices for the consumer, too.

CHICKEN SELECTION HINTS

Chicken is available in different types; size, age, and sex of the chicken determine the type. Age influences tenderness which, in turn, determines the cooking method.

The common types are: Spring Chicken, Roaster and Boiler. Capon is another type found in some markets.

Age and sex cannot easily be determined. However, it is unnecessary for the consumer to judge them because there are easy guides for selection:

(1) Quality (in reference to the general appearance, the meatiness and the finish—that is, the amount and distribution of fat); (2) characteristics which identify each type and quality of chicken.

Guides for quality selection are sometimes to be found on a label or on the wrapping.

When this labelling information is not present, there are identifying characteristics which are helpful in selecting chicken: the size; the texture and thickness of the skin; the firmness of the flesh; the amount and distribution of fat; and the flexibility of the breastbone. These characteristics are described in the following definition of each type:

Spring Chicken: A young chicken (either sex, usually 10 to 16 weeks of age) with smooth, thin, soft skin; tender-meated, soft flesh; small amount of fat underneath skin along backbone, over drumsticks and thighs and along the sides of breast; and flexible-tipped (cartilaginous) breast-bone.

Roaster: A young chicken (either sex, usually under 8 months of age) having the same characteristics as a spring chicken. There is usually slightly more fat, the chicken is larger, and the breastbone is slightly less flexible.

Capon: A young chicken (unsexed male, usually under 10 months of age) having the same characteristics as the roaster, but with exceptionally good finish, flavour, and tenderness caused by emasculation. It has a large proportion of white meat.

Boiler: A mature chicken (female, usually more than 10 months of age). It has less-tender, firm flesh; thick, firm skin; well developed connective tissue; a layer of fat underneath the skin, giving the chicken a full, well rounded appearance; and a non-flexible breastbone.

PREPARATION OF POULTRY FOR COOKING

Fresh Poultry: Oven-ready birds should need no preparation before cooking. But you may have to remove a few pinfeathers. Wash and dry bird.

If poultry is purchased "dressed", it should be drawn promptly, and refrigerated at 36-40°F. loosely wrapped. If whole, use it within 2 to 3 days; if cut up, within 1 or 2 days. Wash the bird in cold water and pat dry just before cooking.

How to Clean Poultry: Dry-plucked poultry is preferred or it may be dipped into hot, not boiling, water until water penetrates to skin.

Grasp feathers close to skin and pull in direction they grow, not against it. ("Dressed" birds have been bled and plucked but the head and feet and internal organs have not been removed.)

Singe off hairs by holding dry bird over direct flame, turning to expose all parts of the body. Remove pinfeathers with dull edge of knife or tweezers. Cut off head and feet and wing tip, if desired.

Cut out the oil sac on top of tail. Cut circle around vent below tail, leaving it free to be removed with internal organs. Make a crosscut, large enough for drawing, between the two cuts.

Insert hand and carefully loosen entrails from back and sides; draw out internal organs, making sure lungs are removed. Save heart, liver, and gizzard.

Slit skin lengthwise at back of neck, leaving skin on bird. Slip skin down and remove crop and windpipe. Cut neck off short and save.

How to Clean Giblets: Giblets include the gizzard, heart, and liver. The giblets and neck are usually included when a whole bird is purchased.

To clean giblets from a "dressed" bird, cut blood vessels from heart and carefully cut away green gall bladder from liver. Be careful not to break the gall bladder. Gall is bitter and will spoil the flavour of any meat it touches.

Cut through one side of gizzard to inner lining, remove lining and throw away.

When the giblets are included with the oven-ready poultry they should also be cleaned promptly.

Any blood vessels in the heart and any gall stain on the liver should be cut away. Be sure the gizzard has been split open and the inner bag removed. Scrape the lining of the gizzard with a knife.

Giblets may be kept 1 or 2 days, wrapped and placed close to the freezing compartment. If quick-frozen, cook promptly after defrosting.

DEFROSTING FROZEN POULTRY

Follow directions on packet or defrost poultry by one or a combination of these methods:

1. Leave bird in its original wrapping. Place on shelf in refrigerator. A chicken will defrost in the refrigerator overnight; a turkey may take from 2 to 4 days.

2. Place bird, still in its original wrapping, under running cold water, 2 to 4 hours for chicken and up to 6 hours for turkey.

Prompt cooking after defrosting is preferable. Do not refreeze. A defrosted, oven-ready or a fresh-drawn bird can be kept for two or three days in a refrigerator at 38°F. or less. Wrap bird loosely in aluminium foil or greaseproof paper.

In whole birds, be sure to remove the giblets and neck, which are wrapped separately and placed in either the body cavity or wishbone area.

Rinse the bird, giblets, and neck in cold water and pat dry before cooking.

Poultry may be put on to cook when partly defrosted; that is, when whole birds are pliable enough to remove giblets, and cut-up poultry is pliable enough to separate the parts. Allow additional cooking time.

CARE OF COOKED POULTRY

Refrigerate cooked poultry immediately after the meal. If poultry has been cooked several hours, or a day or two in advance, cool it rapidly and refrigerate at once. Cover or wrap it well to prevent drying out or loss of flavour.

If roast poultry has been stuffed, remove any stuffing from the cavities and store it separately, well covered.

Do not allow the poultry, the stuffing, or the gravy to stand in the kitchen after the meal.

Use leftover stuffing within a day or two and heat very thoroughly before serving.

For the best flavour, use poultry meat within 2 or 3 days after cooking and stock within 1 or 2 days.

GIBLET COOKERY

The neck is usually included with the giblets when whole birds are purchased fresh or frozen.

Moist heat is required to soften the gizzard, heart, and neck. When they are added to gravy, sauces, or stuffing or served with broiled and fried chicken, the giblets and neck must be precooked by simmering in seasoned water until the gizzard is tender when pierced with a fork.

When poultry is braised or stewed, the giblets and the neck may be cooked with the bird.

Liver is very tender and requires only 10 to 15 minutes' cooking at low temperature. It is so tender that it may be grilled or fried without the preliminary cooking required for gizzard, heart, and neck.

HOW TO RENDER CHICKEN OR GOOSE FAT

If a chicken is to be used for soup, or if goose has excess fat, it is advisable to remove the excess fat and render it. The rendered fat and the crackling are used in a number of recipes given in this and other sections of the book.

Cut the excess fat from the bird and, if crackling is wanted, also remove the fatty parts of skin. Cut them into small (1-inch-square) pieces.

Place in a heavy frying pan. Add cold water to cover. Cover and bring to the boil. Cook about 20 minutes.

Uncover and cook over low heat until all water has evaporated and only the melted fat and crackling remain.

Add 1 diced onion and continue cooking until the skin is crisp and well browned and the onion brown but not burned.

Strain off the fat. Chill and use in cooking. Serve the crackling with rye bread and savoury biscuits.

Recipes with Chicken Breasts

HOW TO BONE CHICKEN BREASTS

Boneless chicken breasts are the basis of many elegant dishes and are called for in a number of recipes in this book. Breast of chicken when it is removed raw from one side of the bird in a skinless, boneless piece is called a suprême. Some butchers will bone the breasts for you, but it is not difficult to do yourself, and with a little practice you can easily master the technique.

Cut the chicken breasts in half. Place the breasts on a flat surface and, using your fingers, pull off the skin. Then with a sharp paring knife, cut against the ridge of the breastbone to loosen the flesh. Continue cutting along the rib cage, pulling flesh from bone as you cut until meat from one side of the breast separates from the bone in one piece. Be careful not to tear the meat. Cut and pull out the white tendon that runs about two-thirds down underneath the meat. Flatten the suprêmes lightly with the side of a heavy knife.

LEMON CHICKEN ROLLS

½ pound fresh mushrooms, sliced
1 ounce butter
½ teaspoon dill seed
½ teaspoon salt
⅛ teaspoon ground black pepper
1 tablespoon chopped chives
2 teaspoons grated lemon rind
About 4 ounces biscuit crumbs, finely crushed
4 chicken breasts, boned and split
1 ounce butter, melted

Sauté mushroom in butter with dill seed. Stir in salt, pepper, chives, lemon rind, and biscuit crumbs. Mix lightly but well.

Place chicken breasts between 2 pieces of greaseproof paper. Flatten to about ⅛-inch thick with a rolling pin. Place ⅛ of the stuffing on each chicken breast. Roll up and secure with toothpicks.

Place on an ungreased baking sheet. Brush with melted butter. Sprinkle with paprika, if you like. Bake in moderate oven (350°F. Mark 4) 25 to 30 minutes. Serves 8.

CHICKEN BREASTS WITH BACON

2 whole chicken breasts, split
4 rashers of bacon
2¾ ounces butter
1 tablespoon Worcestershire sauce
1 tablespoon chopped chives

Split chicken breasts. Make 2 cuts across each half of chicken breast. Put ½ rasher of bacon into each cut.

Lemon Chicken Rolls

Chicken Breasts with Bacon

Cream butter. Beat in Worcestershire sauce and chopped chives. Spread mixture over chicken breasts and put them in a roasting dish.

Bake in moderate oven (375°F.) 40 minutes, or until breasts are tender and brown. Brush chicken breasts with the juices in the dish 4 to 5 times during cooking. Serve with cooking juices, noodles Romanoff and green beans. Serves 2.

CHICKEN À LA KIEV

A classic recipe created during the Czarist days in Russia. It is rolled, boneless breast of chicken stuffed with butter, often seasoned with chives. The butter should spurt out when cut with a knife.

3 whole breasts of chicken or
    6 fresh or frozen halves
4 ounces chilled unsalted butter
Salt and pepper
1 tablespoon chopped chives
Flour for dusting
2 eggs, lightly beaten
4 ounces very fine dry breadcrumbs
Fat for deep frying

Cut the breasts in half. Remove the bone from the breasts of chicken. Place them between sheets of greaseproof paper and pound flat and very thin with a mallet. Do not split the flesh. Remove the greaseproof paper.

Cut the butter into six finger-shaped pieces. Place a piece in the middle of each breast and sprinkle with salt, pepper, and chives. Roll the chicken round it and fold the flaps like an envelope, completely enclosing the butter. Secure with cocktail stick if necessary. Dust lightly with flour. Brush with beaten egg. Roll in dry breadcrumbs. Refrigerate one hour or more so the crumbs will adhere.

Fill a deep frying pan with enough fat to completely cover the breasts. Heat the fat until hot (360°F.). Add chicken gradually and fry until golden brown on all sides. Drain on absorbent paper. One half breast makes a portion. Serves 6.

CHICKEN BREASTS EN PAPILLOTE

En papillote is a French term meaning cooked in non-stick cooking paper or in a paper bag. Nowadays, aluminium foil is usually substituted for the paper.

3 chicken breasts, halved
Chicken broth or lightly salted water
2 ounces butter
2 ounces flour
2 fluid ounces milk
4 fluid ounces dry white wine
1 lightly beaten egg yolk
Salt and pepper
Pinch of cayenne pepper
Pinch of nutmeg or mace
Pinch of ground cloves
½ ounce finely chopped mushrooms
1 teaspoon chopped onions or chives

Place chicken breasts in small saucepan and barely cover with broth or water. Bring to the boil, reduce heat, cover and simmer gently until tender, 20 to 40 minutes, depending upon the size of the breasts.

Remove chicken from liquid and let cool. Then carefully remove skin and bones from the meat.

Cut 6 pieces of aluminium foil large enough to make an envelope for each breast half. Spread the foil with half the butter.

Melt remaining butter in a saucepan; add the flour and stir until blended. In another pan, bring milk, wine, and 4 fluid ounces of the cooking liquid to the boil; add all at once to the butter-flour mixture, stirring vigorously until sauce is smooth and thick.

Pour a little of the hot sauce onto the beaten egg yolk, then combine with remaining sauce, and stir gently until thick. Do not boil. Add seasonings; stir in mushrooms and onions or chives.

Place a half chicken breast in centre of each square of foil; spoon some sauce over top. Fold the foil to make a secure package, crimping the edges to seal tightly. Arrange on baking sheet and bake in hot oven (400°F. Mark 6) 10 minutes. Serve in the foil. Serves 6.

CHICKEN AND GRAPES

3 ounces crumbs, finely crushed
½ teaspoon salt
¼ teaspoon ground black pepper
¼ teaspoon basil leaves
¼ teaspoon tarragon leaves
3 chicken breasts, split
3½ ounces butter
¼ medium onion, finely chopped
4 fluid ounces water
12 fluid ounces white wine
1 chicken bouillon cube
½ pound fresh mushrooms, sliced
½ pound seedless grapes or
    Muscat grapes, seeded

Mix crumbs, salt, pepper, basil, and tarragon. Remove skin from chicken breasts. Coat chicken in the crumbs. Heat 2 ounces butter in large frying pan and brown chicken on all sides.

Place chicken in single layer in large baking dish. Add minced onion to butter in frying pan and cook until soft. Pour in water and wine. Add chicken bouillon cube, crumbled. Bring liquid to the boil, stirring to dissolve bouillon cube and pour around chicken. Cook, uncovered, in moderate oven (375°F.) 40 minutes.

Meanwhile, sauté mushrooms in remaining butter. At end of 40 minutes' cooking add mushrooms and grapes to chicken. Continue to cook 8 to 10 minutes. Serves 6.
Note: Another part of the chicken may be used, if desired.

Chicken and Grapes

CHICKEN SUPRÊME, FOIL-BAKED

6 chicken breasts
1½ teaspoons salt
Pinch of pepper
1 tablespoon finely chopped spring onion
1 tablespoon finely chopped parsley
1 clove garlic, finely chopped
½ teaspoon dried tarragon
Pinch of thyme
1 10½ ounce can condensed cream of mushroom soup

Sprinkle chicken with salt and pepper. Combine remaining ingredients; spread on surface and in cavity of chicken breasts.

Place each piece of chicken on square of aluminium foil; bring edges together and seal by crimping the edges and folding corners under.

Place on baking sheet. Bake in very hot oven (450°F. Mark 8) 20 to 25 minutes; turn packages over; bake 20 minutes. Serve in foil. Serves 6.

Chicken Suprême, Foil-baked

How to Carve Poultry

1. Cut off tip and first joint of wing. (The one next to the platter must be cut off in advance.) This may be done in advance of placing bird on platter in the kitchen.

2. Insert fork, just below the thigh, to steady the bird while slicing. Cut thin slices of leg meat, away from carver, parallel to the bone until thigh bone and joints are exposed. Arrange slices of meat in neat overlapping style around platter's edge.

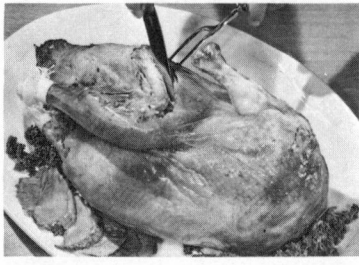

3. With point of knife cut around the thigh bone, loosening meat and skin adjacent to the bone.

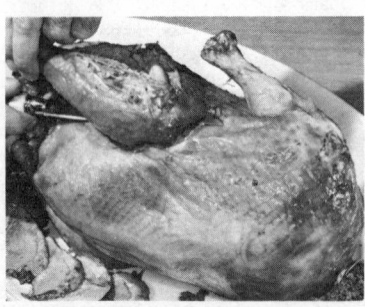

4. Cut skin underneath the leg to free it from the body.

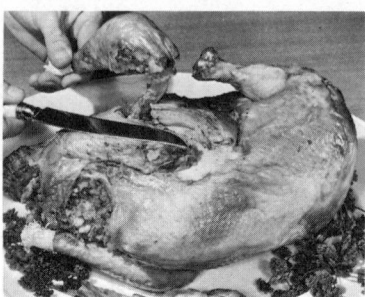

5. Lift drumstick up taking thigh bone with it—in one piece. If the bird is properly cooked, the joint holding the leg to the body should give easily. Place this piece behind the bird at the back of the platter. If drumstick meat is to be served, cut joint separating leg into drumstick and thigh bone. Transfer drumstick to side plate or platter.

6. Hold drumstick upright, or at a convenient angle to the plate. Slice meat turning drumstick to obtain uniform slices. Avoid cutting into tendons that may be present.

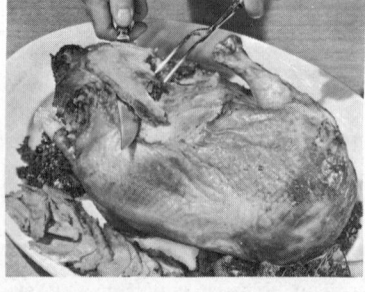

7. Slice remaining thigh meat down to the body. If possible, include some of the "oyster" meat with each slice.

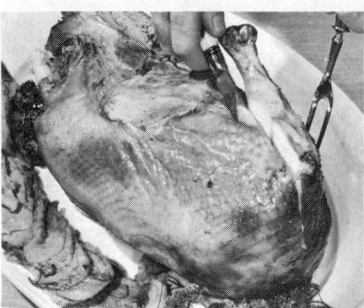

8. Insert fork into the body, just below the wing joint. Make a cut in front of and parallel to the wing joint, cutting into the breast meat down to the bone.

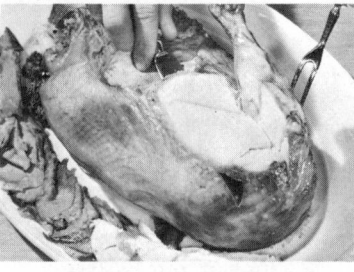

9. Keeping fork in the same position and holding knife parallel to the platter, cut slices of white meat until enough slices are obtained or until breast bone is exposed. Arrange slices as they are carved, around the edge of the platter.

10. Unless stuffing is exposed, cut an opening, large enough to insert a serving spoon. Remove stuffing with spoon and place serving portions on dinner plates.

11. For each serving, lay slices of dark and white meat over the hot stuffing.

Roast Chicken

ROAST CHICKEN
(Basic Recipe)

All sizes of tender chicken may be roasted. Plumpness is a desirable quality.

Stuffing: Rub cavity of prepared bird with ½ to 1 teaspoon salt. If desired, stuff. *Do not stuff bird in advance, but just before roasting.* Stuffing prepared in advance must be refrigerated. Stuff body and wishbone cavities lightly.

Trussing (or Shaping): This assures compactness to give even cooking and browning. The chicken is more attractive and easier to carve.

To truss: Fasten neck skin to the back with skewers. Shape wings "akimbo" style and bring wing tips onto the back.

Close abdominal opening with skewers and string.

Tie drumsticks to tail. A skewer above the tail on the back helps to hold this string in place.

If there is a bridge of skin at abdominal opening, push drumsticks underneath this bridge. It will hold them down without skewers and string.

Roasting: Brush skin thoroughly with fat.

Place trussed bird breast up or down, as desired, on a rack at least ½ inch high in shallow open pan.

Cover top of chicken with fat-moistened thin scalded muslin. Do not wrap bird in the muslin.

The muslin helps in uniform browning and makes basting unnecessary.

Roast at a constant low temperature. See timetable below.

Do not sear. Do not add water. Do not cover.

If muslin dries during cooking, moisten muslin with fat from drippings in the pan.

If bird was started breast down, turn breast up when about ¾ done.

To test, press the thickest part of the drumstick between the fingers—meat should be very soft. Protect the fingers with paper or cloth.

Another test is to move the drumsticks up and down; leg joints should move readily or break.

A low roasting temperature assures excellent meat juices, rich in colour and flavour for the gravy, not burned or dried in the pan.

Remove skewers and any string. Place on warm platter while preparing gravy with the juices in the roasting pan.

Do not partly roast stuffed poultry on one day and complete roasting the following day.

STUFFING AND TRUSSING POULTRY FOR ROASTING
How to get a chicken or turkey ready to go into the oven.

Fill neck cavity with stuffing.

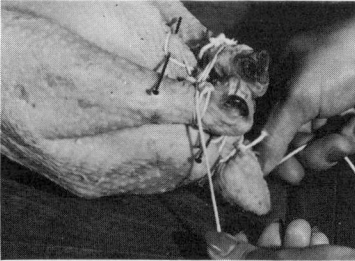
Tie drumsticks to tail, or push them under bridge of skin if it is present.

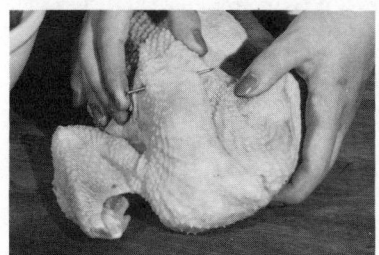
Skewer neck skin to back.

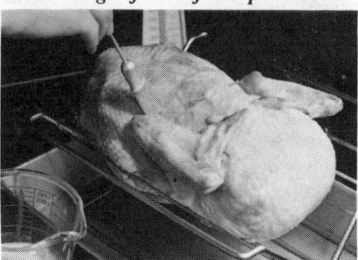
Brush skin with fat.

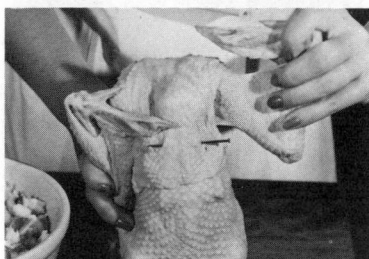
Lift wing up and out forcing the tip back until it rests flat against neck skin.

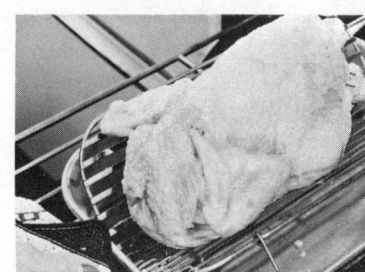
Roast at a low temperature.

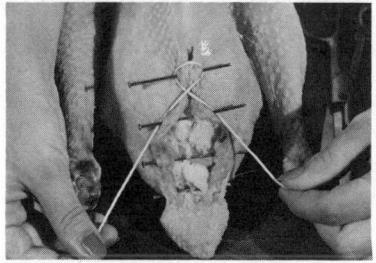
Lace abdominal opening to hold stuffing.

Test if bird is cooked.

TIMETABLE FOR ROASTING CHICKEN

Dressed Weight	Ready-to-Cook Weight	Oven Temperature	Approximate Roasting Time
2 to 3½ lbs.	1⅓ to 2½ lbs.	350°F. Mark 4	1¼ to 2 hrs.
3½ to 4½ lbs.	2½ to 3½ lbs.	350°F. Mark 4	2 to 3 hrs.
4½ to 6 lbs.	3½ to 4¾ lbs.	325°F. Mark 3	3 to 3½ hrs.
6 lbs. and up	4¾ lbs. and up	325°F. Mark 3	3½ to 3¾ hrs.

JELLY GLAZED ROAST CHICKEN

Whip 4 ounces redcurrant jelly. Spread over roast chicken for last 30 minutes of cooking. Complete roasting uncovered. Baste frequently with jelly and pan juices.

CHICKEN ROASTED IN NON-STICK PAPER

Prepare chicken as directed in Roast Chicken. Omit fat-moistened muslin.

Wrap in non-stick cooking paper (or greaseproof paper), doubling the paper over breast. Secure with poultry pins.

Roast in slow oven (325°F. Mark 3), allowing 30 to 40 minutes per pound, depending upon size. Unwrap for last half hour to let bird brown.

CHICKEN COOKED IN ALUMINIUM FOIL

Have the chicken at room temperature. Prepare for roasting and wrap completely in aluminium foil.

Roast in hot oven (400°F. Mark 6) for 20 minutes. Reduce heat to moderate (350°F. Mark 4) and roast from then on at 25 minutes per pound.

Open the foil about 30 minutes before roasting time is up to let chicken brown. Baste frequently during this period with pan juices.

SAVOURY CHICKEN LEGS

6 tablespoons golden crumbs
½ teaspoon onion salt
½ teaspoon garlic salt
¼ teaspoon pepper
¼ teaspoon dried savory
¼ teaspoon curry powder
¼ teaspoon monosodium glutamate
8 to 10 chicken legs with thigh removed (about 2 pounds)
4 fluid ounces evaporated milk
8 fluid ounces mayonnaise

Combine golden crumbs and seasonings. Dip chicken legs in evaporated milk, then coat generously with seasoned golden crumbs. Place in foil-lined shallow baking tin. Do not crowd. Bake in hot oven (400°F. Mark 6) about 15 minutes to set crumbs.

Spoon mayonnaise generously on top of chicken legs. Reduce heat to slow oven (300°F. Mark 2) and cook about 1 hour until tender but not dry. Hot buttered rolls and honey complement this dish. Serves 4 to 6.

Savoury Chicken Legs

COUNTRY STYLE ROAST CHICKEN

Place chicken in an uncovered pan in very hot oven (450°F. Mark 8) and sear for 20 minutes, or until chicken is brown on all sides.

Reduce heat to slow oven (275°F. to 300°F. Mark 1 to Mark 2). Pour 2 fluid ounces boiling water into pan. Cover pan and roast until bird is tender, allowing 25 to 30 minutes per pound.

Do not baste. For a crisp skin, uncover during last 30 minutes. Prepare gravy from pan juices.

ROAST CHICKEN WITH POTATO-BREAD STUFFING

1 4-pound roasting chicken
15 ounces stale bread cubes
2 ounces instant potato powder
2 teaspoons finely chopped sage
2 teaspoons salt
¼ teaspoon pepper
½ teaspoon celery salt
1 medium onion, finely chopped
12 fluid ounces milk
2 ounces butter or margarine
½ teaspoon paprika

Prepare dressing, combining bread cubes, instant potato powder, sage, salt, pepper, celery salt, and onion. Heat milk and butter over low flame until butter is melted; add to bread mixture; mix thoroughly.

Clean chicken. Sprinkle cavity with 1 teaspoon salt and a pinch of pepper. Stuff and truss chicken.

Place on rack in roasting pan. Rub with 1 ounce butter or margarine; sprinkle with a mixture of 1 teaspoon salt, pinch of pepper, and ½ teaspoon paprika.

Roast in moderate oven (350°F. Mark 4), calculating 25 minutes per pound weight before stuffing. Serves 5 to 6.

ROAST CHICKEN WITH SAUSAGE-BREAD STUFFING

1 4- to 5-pound roasting chicken
¼ pound sausage meat
1 chicken liver, finely chopped
1 ounce mushrooms, finely chopped
½ medium-sized onion, finely chopped
10 ounces small dry bread cubes
1 teaspoon salt
½ teaspoon chicken seasoning
Pinch of dried thyme
½ teaspoon Aromat

Rinse chicken and pat dry. Mix remaining ingredients for stuffing, blending lightly but thoroughly. Fill cavity of chicken with stuffing; truss.

Roast in slow oven (325°F. Mark 3) until tender, allowing 35 minutes per pound stuffed weight of chicken.

Baste with following mixture:

4 fluid ounces white wine
¾ teaspoon Aromat
2 ounces butter or margarine

Heat ingredients together in saucepan and keep warm. Baste chicken frequently while roasting. Use up all the mixture. Serve chicken with unthickened pan juices. Serves 6.

OVEN CRUSTY CHICKEN

This easy oven method that requires no attention while cooking chicken until golden has become a popular way of preparing chicken. Quantities can easily be increased for a pleasing party dish.

1 2½ to 3-pound spring chicken, cut up
2 to 2¾ ounces butter or margarine, melted
1 teaspoon salt
½ teaspoon pepper
4 ounces golden crumbs

Wash chicken pieces and dry thoroughly. Mix melted butter or margarine with salt and pepper. Dip chicken pieces in seasoned butter, then roll in golden crumbs until well coated. Place skin side up in shallow baking tin lined with aluminium foil; do not crowd pieces.

Cook in moderate oven (350°F. Mark 4) about 1 hour or until tender. Do not cover pan or turn chicken while cooking. Serves 4 to 5.

Note: For **Corn-Crisped Chicken,** add salt and pepper to golden crumbs; substitute evaporated milk for butter.

Variations of Oven Crusty Chicken:

Barbecued Crusty Chicken: Use about ¼ pint barbecue sauce in place of seasoned butter.

California Crusty Chicken: Mix 2 to 3 tablespoons lemon juice with the seasoned butter.

Gourmet Crusty Chicken: Omit pepper. Combine ¼ teaspoon thyme, ¼ teaspoon paprika, and ¼ teaspoon curry powder with golden crumbs.

Italian Crusty Chicken: Combine ¼ teaspoon crushed oregano, ¼ teaspoon garlic salt, and ½ teaspoon paprika with golden crumbs.

Parmesan Crusty Chicken: Combine 2 ounces grated Parmesan cheese with golden crumbs.

Sesame Crusty Chicken: 2 tablespoons sesame seeds may be added to golden crumbs with salt and pepper.

Oven Crusty Chicken

POUISSIN is a baby chicken killed when 4-6 weeks old and usually weighs about 1-1¼ pounds.

Generally, 1 poussin is allowed per person.

POUSSIN MAPIE

4 poussin
6 ounces butter
Fine breadcrumbs
2 shallots
4 teaspoons flour
½ pint dry white wine
1 large tomato
1 tablespoon cognac
½ teaspoon French mustard
2 tablespoons chopped herbs
(parsley, tarragon, chervil)
Salt, pepper

Split the chicken and flatten them. Brush with half the melted butter and grill for 6-10 minutes on both sides, brushing the under side with butter when turning. Remove from the heat, roll each piece in breadcrumbs and sprinkle with butter. Return to the grill for a further 5 minutes. For the sauce—heat the remaining butter in a pan and sauté the finely chopped shallots until brown then stir in the flour. Boil the wine down to half the quantity, add to the flour mixture and stir until smooth. Chop the tomato, rub through a fine sieve and add 2½ tablespoons of the juice to the sauce.

Add cognac, mustard and the drippings from the grill pan. Add herbs and seasoning to taste and simmer for 10 minutes.

POUSSIN FARCI

4 poussin
2 ounces rice
4 teaspoons turmeric
5 tablespoons oil
3 ounces butter
Salt, pepper

Prepare the poussin for stuffing.

Cook the rice in boiling salted water to which the turmeric has been added. When the rice is just tender, drain and rinse. Add the oil, salt and pepper. Stuff the birds and secure the opening with small skewers.

Heat the butter in a sauté pan and brown the birds on both sides. Sprinkle with salt, cover the pan and cook over low heat for about 15 minutes.

Baked Chicken Quarters with Raisin-nut Stuffing

GRILLED POUSSIN WITH TARRAGON BUTTER

4 poussin
4 ounces butter
3-4 sprigs fresh tarragon
Salt, pepper

Clean and split the birds.

Melt the butter in a small pan, add tarragon and leave in a warm place until required.

Brush the birds on both sides with the tarragon butter, sprinkle with salt and pepper and place skin side down on the grill pan. Grill for about 10 minutes, brushing frequently with the butter.

Turn, brush again and grill a further 8-10 minutes or until tender and golden brown. Arrange on a serving dish, sprinkle with a little chopped tarragon and strain the remaining tarragon butter over the top.

Serve with small new potatoes and buttered green peas or baby onions.

BAKED CHICKEN QUARTERS WITH RAISIN-NUT STUFFING

2 spring chickens, quartered
Aromat, salt, and pepper
12 ounces day-old breadcrumbs
5½ ounces melted butter or
margarine
5 ounces light seedless raisins
4 ounces chopped walnuts
2 teaspoons salt
½ teaspoon Aromat
¼ teaspoon pepper
½ teaspoon oregano
½ teaspoon chicken seasoning or
mixed herbs

Have broilers quartered by the butcher, with necks and backbones removed. (Save them for soup or stock.)

Sprinkle chicken pieces inside and out with Aromat, salt, and pepper; leave bird to stand while preparing stuffing.

Combine remaining ingredients; toss lightly with fork to mix. Place in open roasting tin.

Arrange chicken quarters over stuffing. Brush with additional melted butter or margarine.

Roast in moderate oven (350°F. Mark 4) 1½ hours, or until chicken is golden brown and tender. Brush occasionally with melted butter or margarine during cooking. Serves 8.

ROAST CHICKEN STUFFED WITH PARSLEY (DANISH STYLE)

1 ready-to-cook young chicken, 2 to
3 pounds
Salt
1 bunch parsley
8 ounces butter, melted
4 fluid ounces cream
Stock or water

Rub chicken inside thoroughly with salt. Stuff with parsley mixed with butter.

Grease skin thoroughly and place on rack in shallow pan. Roast in moderate oven (350°F. Mark 4) until tender, 1½ to 2 hours.

If you like, baste occasionally during roasting with melted butter and juices from bottom of pan.

About ½ hour before done, pour the cream over chicken. Place chicken on warm serving platter while preparing gravy. Serves 4.

Gravy: For about ¾ pint gravy, use the pan drippings, 3 tablespoons flour, and about ¾ pint chicken stock, previously prepared by cooking giblets and neck in water with seasoning and root vegetables.

CHICKEN AND SCONE OVEN DINNER

1 2½ to 3-pound spring chicken,
cut up
2 ounces flour
2 ounces wheat germ
1½ teaspoons paprika
2 teaspoons salt
2 ounces butter or margarine

Dip chicken pieces in mixture of flour, wheat germ, paprika, and salt. Coat well.

Melt butter or margarine in shallow baking tin (9×13×2 inches) in hot oven (425°F. Mark 7). Remove baking tin from oven and place chicken skin side down in a single layer. Roast in hot oven (425°F. Mark 7) 45 minutes. Turn chicken.

Now prepare your favourite scone mix according to directions on packet. Enrich by adding 1½ tablespoons wheat germ to dry mix. Add milk called for in directions plus 1 extra tablespoon. Roll dough; cut out scones. Place in one end of roasting pan, pushing chicken to other end. Be sure both chicken and scones remain in single layer.

Cook another 15 minutes or until scones are lightly browned. Serves 4.

Chicken and Scone Oven Dinner

ROAST CHICKEN—SOUTHERN STYLE

1 4½-pound ready-to-cook roasting chicken
Salt
1¼ pounds southern stuffing (below)
½ lemon
½ ounce butter or margarine, melted
1 tablespoon finely chopped celery leaves
¼ teaspoon tarragon
1 tablespoon chopped chives
2 tablespoons cream
3 oranges

Rinse chicken and wipe dry; rub cavity with salt and stuff with dressing (do not pack). Skewer or sew opening.

Truss chicken and rub with lemon and butter. Sprinkle with celery leaves, tarragon, and chives. Wrap loosely in aluminium foil.

Roast on rack in an open, shallow pan in hot oven (400°F. Mark 6) for 1½ hours.

Open foil; brush with cream and continue roasting at 350°F. Mark 4 until brown and tender, about 45 minutes.

Meanwhile, cook whole oranges in boiling water for 15 minutes; drain, cut in half and roast cut side up for the last 20 minutes. Arrange around chicken on platter before serving. Serves 6.

Southern Stuffing:

4 ounces sausage meat
1 small onion, chopped
½ teaspoon paprika
½ teaspoon salt
1 ounce diced carrots
1 ounce chopped celery
9 ounces fresh breadcrumbs
2 tablespoons parsley
2 tablespoons milk

Cook sausage meat and onion, stirring frequently until lightly browned.

Combine with remaining ingredients and mix well. Makes about 12 ounces stuffing.

Roast Chicken—Southern Style

ROAST MARYLAND CHICKEN

Use 2 spring chickens weighing about 2½ pounds each; disjoint, cut in pieces for serving, and wash and dry.

Roll in seasoned flour; dip in egg, beaten slightly with 2 tablespoons water, and roll in coarse breadcrumbs. Place close together in well greased pan or casserole.

Bake, uncovered, in moderate oven (375°F. Mark 5) 45 to 60 minutes, or until tender. Baste frequently with hot mixture of 2¾ ounces butter, 2 tablespoons water, and 1 teaspoon lemon juice.

Serve with gravy made from giblet stock and cream. The crusty crumb covering serves as a dressing. Serves 6.

SAVOURY FLORIDA ROAST CHICKEN

2 spring chickens, halved·
Seasoned flour
4 tablespoons fat or salad oil
½ pint water
2 whole cloves
1 bay leaf
Pinch of thyme
Pinch of marjoram
Few grains of mace
6 fluid ounces orange juice
Orange slices

Shake chicken in paper bag containing flour seasoned with salt and pepper. Brown on both sides in hot fat or salad oil in frying pan.

Remove to large roasting tin. Pour water into frying pan in which chicken was browned. Add herbs and mace. Simmer 10 minutes and strain over chicken in roasting tin.

Cover and roast in moderate oven (350°F. Mark 4) 1 hour.

Add orange juice. Roast ½ hour longer, or until chicken is tender. Thicken gravy if you like. Garnish with orange slices. Serves 4.

CANADIAN ROAST CHICKEN

1 roasting chicken (5 to 5½ pounds)
10 rashers of bacon
Whole cloves
1½ ounces brown sugar
1 teaspoon salt
Pinch of pepper
1 tablespoon cornflour
1 ounce fat
5 fluid ounces hot water

Have the chicken cut in serving pieces.

Roll each piece in a rasher of bacon and fasten with wooden toothpicks.

Stick 3 whole cloves in each section; place in roasting tin. Sprinkle with a mixture of sugar, salt, pepper, and cornflour; add fat and hot water.

Cover tightly and roast in hot oven (400°F. Mark 6) 1 hour, or until tender. Serve with mashed potatoes. Serves 6.

Chicken International

CHICKEN INTERNATIONAL

2 ready-to-cook young chickens, 2½ pounds
Stuffing:
1 pound cooked rice
1 ounce butter or margarine, melted
12 ounces drained, canned tomatoes
½ large onion, chopped
1½ ounces chopped green peppers
2 ounces chopped celery
2 chicken livers, chopped
1¼ teaspoons salt
½ teaspoon curry powder
¼ teaspoon pepper
1 teaspoon Aromat
1 egg
Sauce:
2 tablespoons cornflour
½ pint chicken stock
½ pint vinegar
2 ounces sugar
1 teaspoon salt
½ teaspoon Aromat
2 tablespoons soy sauce
1 clove garlic, whole or chopped
1½ ounces chopped green pepper
1 16-ounce can pineapple chunks, drained
3 tablespoons grated orange rind
2 pimientos, sliced

Stuffing: Put rice into mixing bowl; add butter or margarine; blend. Add remaining stuffing ingredients; mix well.

Stuff body and wishbone cavities of chickens lightly. Truss.

Place birds breast-side-down on rack in shallow open tin. Roast in moderate oven (350°F. Mark 4) 1½ to 2 hours, until tender. Turn breast-up when about ¾ done.

Sauce: Blend cornflour with 4 tablespoons of the stock. Combine with remaining sauce ingredients except pimientos in saucepan.

Cook, stirring constantly, until thickened and clear.

Pour sauce over chickens 20 minutes before they are done. Baste several times.

Add pimientos to sauce about 5 minutes before serving. (For added colour and crispness, garnish with slices of red apples.) Serves 8.

ROAST CHICKEN HAWAIIAN

2 3-pound plump chickens
Salt
1½ pounds rice and orange stuffing
   (below)
1½ ounces butter or margarine,
   melted
1 tablespoon cornflour
½ pint chicken stock
4 fluid ounces vinegar
6 ounces sugar
½ teaspoon Aromat
2 tablespoons soy sauce
1 clove garlic, chopped
1½ ounces chopped green pepper
1 16 ounce can pineapple chunks,
   drained
3 tablespoons grated orange rind

Rub birds inside and out with salt; stuff bodies and wishbone cavities lightly with stuffing, and truss. Brush with melted butter.

Place birds breast-side-down on rack in shallow open pan. Roast in slow oven (325°F. Mark 3) about 2 to 2½ hours, or until tender. Turn breast up, when about ⅔ done.

Meanwhile, blend cornflour with 4 tablespoons broth. Mix with remaining ingredients and cook over low heat, stirring constantly until thickened and clear. Pour over chickens 20 minutes before they are done. Baste every 8 minutes. Serves 8.

Rice and Orange Stuffing:
½ pound raw rice
1 small onion, finely chopped
2 tablespoons cooking fat or chicken
   fat
1 large orange
2 tablespoons seedless raisins
½ teaspoon salt
⅛ teaspoon pepper
½ teaspoon celery salt

Cook rice in boiling lightly salted water until barely tender. Drain thoroughly.

Sauté onion in fat until golden. Grate rind of orange; peel and remove membrane and seeds; chop orange flesh coarsely. Place rind, chopped orange, rice, onion, and raisins in a bowl. Add combined seasonings and mix well.

Makes about 1 pound of stuffing, enough for a 5- to 6-pound bird. Use for duck, turkey, chicken, or goose.

ROAST SPRING CHICKENS

Cut cleaned chicken into quarters. Brown on all sides in melted butter or margarine in frying pan.

Place in baking tin. Pour over 4 fluid ounces hot chicken stock or milk. Season to taste with salt and pepper.

Cover and roast in slow oven (325°F. Mark 3) about 1 hour.

To serve, remove chicken from tin and thicken gravy with flour-water

paste. Season to taste. Additional stock, cream, or milk may be used to increase amount of gravy.

ROAST CHICKEN KUCERA

1 3-pound ready-to-cook roasting or
   spring chicken
½ lemon
2 ounces sausage meat
2 ounces butter or margarine
3 tablespoons chopped onion
½ teaspoon paprika
¾ teaspoon salt
1 ounce chopped celery
1 tablespoon chopped parsley
12 ounces fresh breadcrumbs
Milk
1 tablespoon chicken or sausage fat
2 tablespoons chopped celery leaves
½ teaspoon rosemary
4 fluid ounces cream

Rub skin of chicken with cut lemon and set aside.

Cook sausage meat over low heat until golden, breaking it into small pieces as it cooks. Add butter and 2 tablespoons chopped onion. Continue cooking until the onion has softened but not browned.

Remove from heat and add paprika, salt, celery, parsley, and breadcrumbs. Add just enough milk to bind the mixture.

Stuff body and neck cavities lightly; then truss. Rub skin with chicken fat, and sprinkle with celery leaves, rosemary, and remaining 1 tablespoon onion.

Wrap loosely in aluminium foil. Place on rack in open shallow pan. Roast in slow oven (325°F. Mark 3) 1 hour.

Open foil and pull it back to expose chicken so it will brown. Brush with cream and continue to cook until nicely browned and tender, about 45 minutes. Serves 4.

ROAST STUFFED CHICKEN (IRANIAN STYLE)

1 ounce cracked wheat or Bulgar
   Wheat
½ teaspoon salt
1 tablespoon butter
½ pint water
8 ounces canned chick-peas
4 ounces chopped, toasted almonds
1 ready-to-cook young chicken, 3 to
   3½ pounds
Salt and pepper
Butter or margarine
4 fluid ounces chicken stock or water
2¾ ounces butter or margarine

Cook cracked wheat, salt, 1 tablespoon butter, and water over simmering water until wheat is tender, 1½ to 2 hours. Water should be absorbed by this time.

For stuffing, combine cereal with chick-peas and almonds.

Add black pepper and additional salt to taste.

Meanwhile rub salt, pepper, and softened butter on inside of chicken. Stuff and truss bird as usual. Grease outside skin.

Place on rack in shallow baking tin and roast in moderate oven (350°F. Mark 4) until tender and nicely browned, 2½ to 3 hours. Baste during roasting, with stock and butter mixed together.

Serves 5 to 6.

ROAST CAPON WITH CHESTNUT STUFFING

1 6-pound ready-to-cook capon
Salt
1½ pounds chestnut stuffing (below)
3 rashers of bacon
4 fluid ounces hot chicken stock
3 tablespoons butter or margarine

Rinse capon, pat dry and rub inside and out with salt.

Stuff with chestnut stuffing (do not pack). Close opening with skewers and truss.

Place on rack in baking tin breast up. Lay bacon over breast. Roast uncovered in moderate oven (375°F. Mark 5) 30 minutes.

Reduce heat to slow oven (325°F. Mark 3) and roast for 1¾ hours or until the capon's leg joints move easily. Baste often during roasting with hot broth mixed with butter.

Transfer bird to a warm platter. Prepare gravy from pan juices.

Serves 6 to 8.

Chestnut Stuffing:
½ pound chestnuts
8 ounces lightly packed dry breadcrumbs
3 tablespoons melted butter or
   margarine
1 teaspoon salt
1 teaspoon dried sage
⅛ teaspoon pepper
1 well beaten egg
4 fluid ounces cream or top milk

Wash chestnuts and make a gash in each shell. Bake in extremely hot oven (500°F. Mark 10) 15 minutes.

Cool and remove shells and skins. Cook in boiling salted water for 20 minutes. Drain and chop fine.

Add remaining ingredients and mix well. Makes about 1 pound stuffing.

The meat thermometer tells when a bird is done. For greater accuracy, insert it between thigh and lowest rib to centre of stuffing.

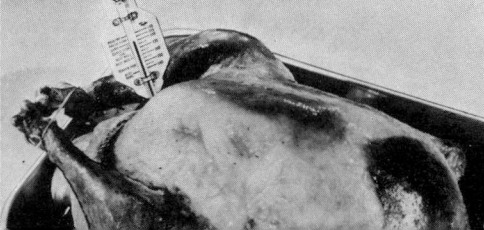

Turkeys

TURKEY SELECTION

Turkeys are sold fresh or frozen, dressed or ready-to-cook.

Top quality frozen ready-to-cook turkeys have the tendons removed from the drumsticks to make carving easier. If a dressed turkey is bought, get the butcher or poultry dealer to pull out the tendons and clean the bird so it is ready to cook.

The smallest turkeys may be as little as 2 pounds ready-to-cook weight (roasting-fryers) to more than 25 pounds ready-to-cook weight for the largest turkeys.

Buy a hen turkey if you want an 8- to 15-pound bird. Hen turkeys mature faster and are usually better finished than cocks of the same weight. Buy a cock if you want a 16- to 25-pound bird.

WHAT SIZE BIRD TO BUY

When buying medium or heavy birds, 12 pounds or over, allow $\frac{1}{2}$ to $\frac{3}{4}$ pound (ready-to-cook weight) per serving. When buying turkeys under 12 pounds, allow $\frac{3}{4}$ to 1 pound per serving. The table below gives the approximate number of servings.

Ready-to-cook Turkey (pounds)	Number of Servings
6 to 8	6 to 10
8 to 12	10 to 20
12 to 16	20 to 32
16 to 20	32 to 40
20 to 24	40 to 50

The actual number of servings depends on the quality of the turkey, correct cooking and carving skill.

ROAST TURKEY

Stuffing: A turkey may or may not be stuffed for roasting. The stuffing may be cooked separately in a casserole or suitable baking tin—loaf or muffin size.

When birds are stuffed, these directions should be followed: *mix ingredients just before stuffing bird.*

Dry ingredients may be measured and prepared in advance. Liquid or moist ingredients may be measured but must be kept in the refrigerator until they are to be mixed with the dry ingredients. Meats, if one of the ingredients, such as minced beef, giblets, liver, oysters, or sausage must be thoroughly cooked before combining them with other ingredients.

Stuff the turkey just before it is placed in the oven.

Allow 4 ounces stuffing per pound of turkey, ready-to-cook weight.

To Stuff Turkey: Rub $\frac{1}{2}$ to $1\frac{1}{2}$ teaspoons salt, depending upon turkey size, into the cavity. Stuff body and wishbone cavities lightly to avoid a soggy, compact stuffing.

To Cook Stuffing Separately: Prepare stuffing in the usual way. Pile lightly into roasting pan from which pan juices have been removed, greased casserole, or loaf tin.

Cover, if a moist stuffing is desired. Bake in moderate oven (350°F. Mark 4) 30 to 50 minutes, depending upon shape and depth of stuffing.

If covered, remove cover the last 10 minutes to brown top.

To Truss Turkey: Fasten the neck skin to the back with 1 or 2 skewers.

Shape wings "akimbo" style and bring wing tips onto the back.

Close abdominal opening with skewers and string.

Tie drumsticks to tail. A skewer above or through the tail helps to hold this string in place.

If there is a bridge of skin at abdominal opening, push drumsticks underneath this bridge. It will hold them down without skewers and string.

To Roast Turkey: Brush skin of bird thoroughly with fat.

Place bird, breast up, on a rack at least $\frac{1}{2}$ inch high in shallow baking tin. If a meat thermometer is used, insert it so that the bulb rests in the centre of the inside thigh muscle adjoining the body cavity. If a V-rack is used, place turkey breast-down.

Take a piece of aluminium foil 4 to 5 inches longer than the turkey. Lay it over bird. Pinch the foil at the drumstick and breast ends, pressing it lightly at those ends to anchor it. Leave the cap loose over the top and at the sides.

Or, the turkey may be covered with fat-moistened scalded muslin, large enough to cover the top and drape down on all sides. Do not wrap bird in the muslin. Aluminium foil or muslin helps in uniform browning. Basting is unnecessary.

Place in preheated slow oven (325°F. Mark 3). Do not brown. Do not add water. Do not cover. If muslin dries during cooking, moisten with cooking juices in the bottom of the pan.

When the turkey is about $\frac{2}{3}$ done according to the timetable, cut the string or the band of skin, holding the drumstick ends to the tail, to release the legs. This allows the heat to reach the inside thigh to assure thorough cooking.

About 20 minutes before the turkey is done according to the approximate total time given in the timetable, or if a meat thermometer is used it should register 190°F., try these physical tests to see if bird is cooked:

(a) Press the fleshy part of the drumstick between the fingers, protected with paper or cloth. Meat should feel very soft.

(b) Move the drumstick up and down; the drumstick should move readily or twist out of the joint.

When turkey is done, remove from oven. Keep hot while preparing gravy with cooking juices in roasting pan.

HOW TO COOK SMOKED TURKEY

Wash bird thoroughly. Soak overnight in enough cold water to cover. Wipe dry throughout.

Stuff bird if you like, but omit salt in stuffing.

Truss bird and place on V-shaped rack breast-side up in a slow oven (250°F. Mark $\frac{1}{2}$).

Turn the bird for even cooking. Do not baste with pan juices as they are likely to be too strong. Use a mixture of brown sugar and vinegar, flavoured with a dash of ground cloves and mustard.

At this temperature, a young 10-pound turkey will require about $4\frac{1}{2}$ hours. If the bird is an older smoked turkey, wash thoroughly and simmer in water (do not boil), whole or in pieces.

A sliced onion and several sticks of celery may be added to the liquid.

Cooking time will range from 4 to 5 hours. Cool bird in the liquid. Serve roast or boiled smoked turkey in thin slices, hot or cold.

TIMETABLE FOR ROASTING WHOLE TURKEY

Ready-to-cook Weight*	Oven Temperature	Total Approximate Roasting Time (Stuffed Bird)
4 to 8 lbs.	325°F. Mark 3	$3\frac{3}{4}$ to $4\frac{1}{2}$ hrs.
8 to 12 lbs.	325°F. Mark 3	4 to 5 hrs.
12 to 16 lbs.	325°F. Mark 3	5 to 6 hrs.
16 to 20 lbs.	325°F. Mark 3	6 to $7\frac{1}{2}$ hrs.
20 to 24 lbs.	325°F. Mark 3	$7\frac{1}{2}$ to 9 hrs.

* If you buy a dressed turkey, subtract 15 to 20% of the dressed weight to obtain the approximate ready-to-cook weight.

TURKEY COOKED IN ALUMINIUM FOIL

The method given here is based on unstuffed turkeys weighing 8 to 24 pounds, ready-to-cook weight. Two distinct advantages are the shortened cooking time and the fact that spattering of the oven is prevented – important factors for the cook.

The skin of turkeys cooked in foil may be less brown (the colour may be spotty), have a light colour, and be very soft. The 15- to 20-minute cooking with the foil folded back gives it the desired golden brown appearance.

Although cooking results in tests were the same irrespective of the foil weight, medium weight of aluminium foil ("heavy duty") is preferred. Thin foil tears easily during wrapping and heavy foil tends to be too stiff. An 18-inch foil is a good width.

To Wrap the Turkey in Aluminium Foil: Tie drumsticks to tail. Press wings to body, with wing tips flat against sides of breast.

Place the bird in the centre of the aluminium foil. The foil should be wide enough to have 5 to 6 inches extending beyond the leg and breast ends of the bird. If it is not wide enough, join two pieces tightly together on a flat surface by crimping the edges to prevent leakage of the juices.

Bring one side of the foil strip snugly up and over the breast. Then bring the opposite side up and over, using a simple pleat. These ends should overlap 2 to 3 inches.

Fold the foil down snugly at each end of the bird, breast and legs. Then bring ends up. The top of these ends should be high enough to prevent the juices from escaping from the top and into the pan. If the juices escape into the pan, they brown quickly and cause sharp odours and smoke.

To Cook the Turkey: Place the aluminium foil-wrapped turkey, breast up, in the bottom – not on a rack – of shallow pan.

Place pan with turkey in a preheated very hot oven (450°F. Mark 8) and cook to within 15 or 20 minutes of the total cooking time given in the timetable.

Remove from oven. Quickly fold foil back away from the bird to the edges of the pan. If a meat thermometer is used to test if bird is cooked, insert it now. Insert it so the bulb reaches the centre of the inside thigh muscle – the side next to the body cavity.

Return to the very hot oven (450°F. Mark 8) and continue cooking according to the timetable. Apply the physical tests (given in recipe for whole Roast Turkey) and meat thermometer reading to tell if the bird is cooked.

TIMETABLE FOR COOKING TURKEY IN ALUMINIUM FOIL

Ready-to-cook Weight (Pounds – Unstuffed)	*Oven Temperature* (A Very Hot Oven)	*Total Cooking Time* (Hours – Approximate)	*Interior Temperature*
8–10	450°F. Mark 8	2¼ to 2½	185–190°F.
10–12	450°F. Mark 8	2¾ to 3	185–190°F.
14–16	450°F. Mark 8	3 to 3¼	185–190°F.
18–20	450°F. Mark 8	3¼ to 3½	185–190°F.
22–24	450°F. Mark 8	3¼ to 3¾	185–190°F.

Lift turkey from the foil onto a warm serving platter. Keep hot.

Pour the juices into a saucepan. If desired, concentrate the juices by boiling to reduce them and to intensify the colour.

Prepare gravy with these juices as directed for gravy (see Index). If you like, add additional colour.

ROAST HALF OR QUARTER TURKEY

Rub cavity (cut side) with salt. Skewer skin to meat along cut edges to prevent shrinking from meat during roasting.

Tie leg to tail. Lay wing flat over white meat and tie string round breast end to hold wing down.

Place turkey skin-side-down on a rack in a shallow pan. Grease with cooking fat and cover with aluminium foil or fat-moistened scalded muslin.

Place in preheated slow oven (325°F. Mark 3). Do not brown. Do not add water. Do not cover. (When the turkey is about ⅔ done, according to the timetable, cut the string holding the drumstick end to the tail, to release the leg. This allows the heat to reach the inside thigh to assure thorough cooking.)

If muslin dries during cooking, moisten with juices in the bottom of the pan. Turn skin-side-up when about ¾ done.

Test as for whole turkey, above. If the breast quarter is roasted, the meat in the thickest area should be soft.

Stuffing the Half or Quarter Turkey: Prepare stuffing, allowing about 2¼ ounces per serving. Press lightly into greased pan or casserole or place in aluminium foil. Cover or not as you like. Bake with turkey the last 1 to 1½ hours of turkey roasting time.

Or, when half or quarter turkey is ¾ done, remove from pan. Arrange stuffing on a piece of foil or non-stick cooking paper to fit area of turkey cavity. Replace turkey skin-side-up on stuffing. Continue roasting until turkey is done.

TURKEY-BY-THE-PIECE WITH WHOLEWHEAT WALNUT STUFFING

Place turkey pieces or quarters round mound of stuffing. Lay fat-moistened muslin over all.

Roast in moderate oven (350°F. Mark 4) 1½ to 2 hours for cut-up pieces or 50 minutes per pound for quarters.

Wholewheat Walnut Stuffing:

2 medium onions
4 ounces butter or margarine
1½ pounds fresh wholewheat breadcrumbs
4 ounces walnuts
3 ounces seedless raisins
4 ounces diced celery
1½ teaspoons salt
Few grains pepper
1½ teaspoons Aromat
1 tablespoon mixed herbs
Hot water

Grate onions with coarse grater; cook in butter or margarine until soft but not browned; add to crumbs.

Add remaining ingredients with enough hot water to make fairly moist.

Makes enough stuffing for 8- to 10-pound turkey.

BONELESS TURKEY ROAST (ROLL)

Place on a rack in an open pan. Roast in a slow oven (325°F. Mark 3) until a meat thermometer inserted in the centre registers 170° to 175°F. Or, follow cooking directions printed on the packet.

TIMETABLE FOR ROASTING HALF OR QUARTER TURKEY

Ready-to-cook Weight	*Oven Temperature*	*Approximate Roasting Time*
3½ to 5 lbs.	325°F. Mark 3	3 to 3½ hrs.
5 to 8 lbs.	325°F. Mark 3	3½ to 4 hrs.
8 to 12 lbs.	325°F. Mark 3	4 to 5 hrs.

OVEN-BARBECUED SMALL TURKEY

1 5- to 6-pound turkey, cut into serving pieces

Herb Barbecue Sauce:
½ pint tomato juice
1 10½-ounce can condensed consommé
½ pint water
4 fluid ounces salad oil
4 tablespoons wine vinegar
½ teaspoon salt
⅛ teaspoon cayenne
¼ teaspoon dried tarragon
¼ teaspoon dried thyme
¼ teaspoon freshly ground black pepper
4 whole cloves
2 cloves garlic, crushed
2 tablespoons brown sugar
¼ large onion, finely chopped
1½ tablespoons finely chopped green pepper
1 tablespoon dried parsley
4 fluid ounces sherry

Combine all sauce ingredients except sherry; simmer 30 minutes.

Spread turkey pieces flat in a baking dish. Pour barbecue sauce over turkey.

Cook in slow oven (300°F. Mark 2) for 3 hours. Spoon the sauce over turkey 2 or 3 times during cooking. Add water to the sauce if necessary to keep turkey moist.

Before serving, pour the sherry over the turkey and heat through about 15 minutes. Serve the sauce with turkey. Serves 6.

Variations: Add to the sauce before serving about 3 ounces lightly browned sliced mushrooms, 16 sliced black olives, and about 2 ounces slivered toasted almonds.

WESTERN BARBECUED TURKEY

1 turkey (4 to 6 pounds, ready-to-cook weight), cut in pieces for serving
8 fluid ounces tomato ketchup
10 fluid ounces water
4 fluid ounces burgundy or other red wine
1 tablespoon wine vinegar
4 ounces butter, margarine, or oil
½ large onion, finely chopped
Grated garlic or garlic powder to taste
2 teaspoons Worcestershire sauce
1 tablespoon sugar
2 teaspoons paprika
½ teaspoon salt (or to taste)

Place turkey skin-side-down in a roasting tin.

Combine remaining ingredients; heat to boiling; pour over turkey. Cover and cook in a moderate oven (375°F. Mark 5) 1 hour, basting occasionally.

Remove cover and turn turkey skin-side-up. Continue roasting, uncovered, about ¾ to 1¼ hours, or until turkey is tender, basting and turning turkey occasionally. (Thin sauce with more wine if necessary.) Serves 4 to 6.

QUARTER TURKEY WITH CIDER

1 4- to 5-pound turkey breast or hind quarter
2 teaspoons salt
½ teaspoon pepper
1 teaspoon allspice
2 ounces butter or margarine
2 medium onions, thinly sliced
2 carrots, finely diced
½ pint cider

Sprinkle turkey quarter with salt, pepper, and allspice. Brown in a heavy frying pan in moderately hot butter, turning frequently for about 30 minutes. Remove from pan.

Arrange a bed of onions and carrots in the pan with turkey on top. Pour cider over.

Cover and cook over low heat for about 2½ hours or until tender when pierced with a fork in the thickest parts.

Baste occasionally and add more cider if necessary.

Transfer turkey to a warm serving dish.

Strain pan juices, mashing the vegetables through a sieve to make a rich gravy. Season to taste.

Garnish platter with garlic croutons and halves of canned fruit filled with seedless raisins. Serves 6.

TURKEY WITH CRANBERRY STUFFING

1 16-pound ready-to-cook turkey
2 teaspoons Aromat
1 pound fresh or frozen cranberries
½ pound sugar
3 pounds small bread cubes
½ pound melted butter or margarine
10 ounces raisins
1 tablespoon salt
1 teaspoon cinnamon
2 teaspoons lemon rind
½ pint turkey stock

Prepare turkey for roasting and dust cavity with Aromat.

Chop cranberries and place in a saucepan with sugar. Bring to the boil and remove from heat.

Moisten bread cubes with melted butter and combine with cranberries, raisins, seasonings, lemon rind, and broth; mix well.

Stuff and truss turkey. Roast according to chart. Serves 18.

*** Note:** Prepare the turkey stock by cooking the turkey giblets.

Roast Chicken or Turkey with Wine

Prepare chicken or turkey for roasting in the usual way (see Index). Mix 6 fluid ounces of warm table wine with 2 ounces melted butter or margarine and spoon it over the bird while it roasts. For chicken, use a white table wine like Sauternes, Chablis or Rhine wine. For turkey, use a red table wine like burgundy or claret.

ROAST SMALL TURKEY

1 turkey, 6 to 8 pounds
Aromat, salt, pepper
2 ounces diced celery
½ medium onion, finely chopped
2 tablespoons butter or margarine
8 ounces crumbled corn bread
6 to 9 ounces fresh breadcrumbs
2 teaspoons chicken seasoning or mixed herbs
1 teaspoon Aromat
2½ ounces seedless raisins
2 ounces melted butter or margarine
2 beaten eggs
Salt and pepper to taste

Sprinkle body and neck cavities of turkey with Aromat, salt, and pepper. Set aside while preparing stuffing.

Cook celery and onion in 2 tablespoons butter or margarine until onion is soft but not browned; combine with corn bread and breadcrumbs. Add chicken seasoning or mixed herbs, Aromat, raisins, and the melted butter or margarine. Toss to mix well. Stir in eggs.

Stuff turkey lightly with this mixture; do not pack. (Any extra stuffing may be dotted with butter and baked in separate pan.) Truss turkey.

Sprinkle lightly with Aromat, place breast-side-down on rack in open, shallow roasting tin. Lay fat-moistened scalded muslin over turkey.

Roast in slow oven (325°F. Mark 3) 3½ to 4 hours. Turn turkey breast-up when about ¾ done. If muslin dries out, moisten with juices in pan. Serve hot or cold. Makes about 8 servings.

Note: For turkeys weighing 4 to 6 pounds, the approximate cooking time in a slow oven (325°F. Mark 3) is 3 to 3½ hours. Roasting time will vary with individual birds.

Grilled and Barbecued Poultry

POULTRY FOR GRILLING

Because younger marketing ages have resulted from the scientific mass production of all poultry, you can grill chicken, ducklings, and even small turkeys, or half turkeys, with every assurance that the cooked meat will be tender and delicious. The recipes for grilling poultry include the basic timing and technique for cooking modern poultry in this modern way.

GRILLED CHICKEN
(Basic Recipe)

All sizes of tender, small chicken may be grilled, but the preference is usually a 1½- to 2½-pound bird, ready-to-cook weight. This gives a meaty, tasty chicken and the grilling time is relatively short.

The chicken is split in half, lengthwise, with the backbone, neck and breast-bone removed. Larger sizes may be cut crosswise after grilling to give quarters.

Steps in Grilling

Place chicken halves in bottom of grill pan—not on the rack—so that chicken is kept moist in the juices. Bring wing tip onto back under the shoulder joint.

Season with ¼ to ½ teaspoon salt and ⅛ teaspoon pepper for each half.

Brush well with butter, margarine, or any other fat. Flatten halves skin side down in pan.

Place pan under grill so that surface of chicken is 7 to 9 inches from the heat. Grill slowly, regulating heat or pan position so that browning begins after 10 to 15 minutes of cooking.

Turn every 15 minutes, brushing with additional fat each time.

Grill until tender, nicely browned and crisp on the outside. Chicken is done when the drumstick and wing joints yield easily to fork pressure. The grilling time for a 2- to 2½-pound chicken is 50 to 60 minutes.

The liver (uncooked) and the precooked gizzard, heart, and neck (see Giblet Cookery) may be brushed with fat and placed in grill pan the last 15 minutes, or long enough to heat and brown.

Serve on warm platter skin side up. Pour the pan juices over the chicken.

Variations: Herbs may be rubbed into the chicken before grilling or the chicken may be marinated in French dressing 1 to 3 hours.

Lemon juice may be sprinkled over the chicken during the grilling.

GRILLING FROZEN CHICKEN

See packet directions or hints given under Defrosting Frozen Chicken.

Sprinkle with seasoning.

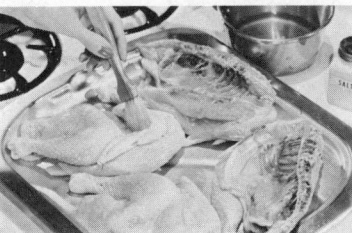

Brush halves with fat.

Test if cooked when golden.

Serve attractively garnished.

GRILLED-PARBOILED CHICKEN

Large chickens may be parboiled about 10 to 15 minutes before grilling.

GRILLED-STEAMED CHICKEN

Place bird on rack in shallow pan. Add enough water to reach just below bird.

Cover and steam in moderate oven (350°F. Mark 4) 30 minutes.

Brush bird with melted fat. Sprinkle with salt. Cook under hot grill.

BARBECUED CHICKEN

Grill chicken and baste with barbecue sauce during the grilling. Thick sauces should be diluted with water.

Chicken may also be marinated in barbecue sauce before grilling.

Still another method is to serve barbecue sauce with grilled chicken for individual use at the table.

ROAST-GRILLED CHICKEN

Bake bird in an open pan in moderate oven (350°F. Mark 4) 15 minutes. Sprinkle with salt. Brush with melted fat. Grill until evenly browned.

GRILLED SMALL TURKEY

Choose a young turkey about 3 to 4 pounds. Have turkey split in half lengthwise for grilling. Snap drumstick, hip and wing joints to keep bird flat during grilling.

Flatten halves and skewer leg to body. Fold wing tip back under wing. Skewer wing flat against cut edge of backbone.

Season each half turkey with about ¼ teaspoon salt and a sprinkling of pepper.

Place turkey in grill pan (not on rack). Brush with melted fat and then place skin-side-down.

Grill Slowly: Place under grill 7 to 10 inches from heat. Regulate heat or pan position so that turkey just begins to brown lightly in 15 minutes. Cook slowly.

Turn and brush with fat. Baste frequently during grilling to brown and cook evenly. Total cooking time, about 60 minutes for 4-pound ready-to-cook turkey.

Test if Cooked: The turkey is cooked when meat on the thickest part of the drumstick cuts easily and there is no pink colour visible.

Serve on warm platter, with pan juices poured over turkey.

If giblets are served with grilled turkey, coat the liver and precooked heart and gizzard with fat, season and grill just long enough to brown.

FRYING PAN CHICKEN BARBECUE

1 3-pound ready-to-cook chicken, cut up for frying
2 ounces cooking fat
½ small onion thinly sliced
1½ tablespoons chopped green pepper
1 small clove garlic, crushed
1 10½-ounce can condensed tomato soup
2 tablespoons brown sugar
2 tablespoons Worcestershire sauce
2 tablespoons lemon juice or vinegar
2 teaspoons prepared mustard
Dash of Tabasco sauce

Brown chicken on all sides in hot fat in a heavy frying pan.

Remove chicken and gently fry onion, green pepper, and garlic for 5 minutes.

Mix in remaining ingredients and simmer until thoroughly blended.

Return chicken to pan, and spoon over sauce. Cover and simmer about 30 minutes, or until chicken is done, turning occasionally. Serves 4.

OVEN BARBECUED CHICKEN OR TURKEY

You may want to use plump grilling-spring chickens, cut in half, or young roasting turkeys (4 to 7 pounds, ready-to-cook) halved or quartered. Or, cut-up poultry, fresh or frozen.

Place halves or quarters, skin side up, in roasting or grill pans and pour barbecue sauce over them ½ to 1 inch deep.

Roast uncovered in slow oven (325°F. Mark 3). Turn occasionally and baste each time, leaving sauce in the rib cages when the halves are turned up.

As the birds cook, the sauce will thicken into rich gravy. If the sauce becomes too thick, add a little hot water.

Chickens will be cooked in from 1½ to 2¼ hours, depending on size. Young turkeys will require ½ hour or more extra time. To test if legs are cooked, do as in grill barbecuing.

For rich crustiness, place cooked birds skin side up, baste and turn up heat to 500°F. Mark 10 or place under grill. Watch carefully! Two or three minutes may be plenty.

Serve the birds, with thick sauce poured over them, on warm plates or platter. Or, serve sauce separately.

LEMON BARBECUED SMALL TURKEY

Have a young turkey about 3 to 4 pounds prepared for grilling. Place turkey halves in grill pan.

Barbecue Mixture: Rub both sides of turkey with cut lemon, squeezing lemon to obtain plenty of juice. Brush with melted fat.

Sprinkle with a mixture of 1 teaspoon each of salt and sugar, ¼ teaspoon paprika, and ⅛ teaspoon freshly ground black pepper for each half. Place skin-side-down in grill pan (not on rack).

To Grill: Follow directions for grilling.

FIESTA GRILLED CHICKEN

2 2½- to 3-pound ready-to-cook chickens, split
2 teaspoons salt
2½ ounces apple jelly
4 ounces butter or margarine
2 fluid ounces white wine

Wipe chicken, sprinkle with salt and place in grill pan skin-side-down.

Combine apple jelly, butter, and wine; bring to the boil and brush mixture over chicken with pastry brush.

Place under grill for 20 minutes. Turn chicken to brown evenly, baste again and continue to cook for 30 minutes. Serve with hot rolls and apple jelly. Serves 6.

Fried Poultry

FRIED CHICKEN
(Basic Recipe)

Select young chickens. Joint them and cut up for cooking.

Mix ¼ teaspoon pepper, 1½ teaspoons salt, and 1½ tablespoons paprika with 4 ounces flour for every 3 pounds of meat. Rub flour into pieces. Save leftover flour for gravy.

Melt fat in a heavy frying pan to depth of ½ to ¾ inch. Brown meaty pieces first in the hot fat, slipping less meaty pieces in between as chicken browns. Avoid crowding, use two pans if necessary.

As soon as chicken begins to brown, about 10 minutes, reduce heat, and cook slowly until tender, 30 to 60 minutes, depending upon size of pieces. Cover tightly as soon as it is a light, uniform tan.

Add 1 to 2 tablespoons water before covering if pan cannot be covered tightly or if bird is heavier than 3 pounds.

Uncover last 15 minutes to brown. Turn several times to brown evenly.

To Test: Cut thickest part of any piece to the bone. If done, the meat should cut easily and no pink colour be visible.

To Fry Giblets: Simmer gizzard until tender. Drain well and rub seasoned flour into giblets. Fry until browned, about 10 minutes.

MARYLAND FRIED CHICKEN

1 young chicken (3 pounds)
Salt and pepper
4 ounces flour
2 eggs, slightly beaten
4 tablespoons water
4 ounces dry breadcrumbs
2 ounces butter or margarine
2 ounces lard

Cut chicken in pieces for serving, wash and dry. Season with salt and pepper, roll in flour, dip in slightly beaten eggs, diluted with water, and roll in crumbs.

Sauté in butter and pork fat in heavy frying pan until browned on all sides; cover and place in slow oven (300°F. Mark 2) ½ to ¾ hour, or until tender.

If chicken weighs more than 3 pounds, add 4 fluid ounces hot water to pan in oven.

Serve with cream gravy made from cooking juices in pan. Serves 6.

Chicken Cream Gravy: To 4 tablespoons of cooking juices add 4 tablespoons of flour. Stir until blended.

Slowly add 1 to 1½ pints of milk or half milk and half cream. Heat slowly over low heat, stirring constantly until thick and smooth. Season to taste.

Use young chicken, cut-up, for frying. Coat chicken with seasoned flour.

Brown in shallow fat. Start the larger pieces first.

Add a little water; cover and cook slowly.

Test if cooked.

FRENCH-FRIED CHICKEN

2 1¾-pound ready-to-cook spring chickens, halved
1 tablespoon salt
¾ teaspoon pepper
4 ounces flour
Fat for frying

Coat each chicken half with seasoned flour.

Heat deep fat to 370°F. on frying thermometer, or until a 1-inch bread cube browns in 1 minute.

Put chicken in frying basket, 1 or 2 pieces at a time; lower carefully into hot fat. Fry chicken 12 to 15 minutes, or until golden brown and tender.

Drain on absorbent paper. Keep hot in heated oven until all pieces are fried. Serves 6.

Variations: If you like, use 1 large spring chicken—2¾ pounds ready-to-cook—quartered. To vary flavour, add 1 teaspoon ground ginger to the flour.

CHICKEN SAUTÉ SEC

1 roaster (about 3½ pounds), cut
    in pieces for serving
Flour
Salt and pepper
4 tablespoons butter or margarine
2 shallots or green onions, finely
    chopped
2 tablespoons chopped parsley
Sprinkling of thyme and basil
4 fluid ounces Sauternes or other
    dry white wine
2 ounces canned mushrooms, sliced

Dust pieces of chicken with flour seasoned with salt and pepper. Melt butter in a large, heavy frying pan; add chicken and sauté until golden brown, turning the pieces frequently and adding more butter, if necessary.

Add shallots, parsley, thyme, basil, and wine; cover tightly and simmer gently for 30 minutes.

Drain mushrooms and add; continue cooking for 15 minutes, or until chicken is tender and no liquid remains in the pan. Serves 3 or 4.

CANTONESE FRIED CHICKEN

1 2½ to 3½-pound roaster, cut up
2 tablespoons Chinese brown gravy
    sauce or any rich brown sauce
1 teaspoon salt
¼ teaspoon pepper
1 teaspoon sugar
¼ teaspoon monosodium glutamate
    (optional)
3 tablespoons butter
3 tablespoons cooking fat
6 canned water chestnuts, sliced
4 ounces sliced fresh mushrooms
½ pint chicken stock
1 tablespoon soy sauce
½ teaspoon salt
½ teaspoon sugar
1 tablespoon cornflour
1 tablespoon water
Spring onions

Place chicken in enough boiling water to cover. Add brown gravy sauce, salt, pepper, sugar, and monosodium glutamate. Cook slowly for 15 minutes. Drain and pat dry.

Brown chicken in mixture of hot butter and fat until a golden brown. Cover and cook slowly for 20 minutes.

Remove and place on a serving dish. Pour off all but 3 tablespoons fat; add

Cantonese Fried Chicken

water, chestnuts, mushrooms, stock, soy sauce, salt, and sugar. Cover and simmer about 5 minutes.

Blend cornflour and water; pour into vegetable mixture. Cook until thickened. Pour sauce over chicken and serve garnished with spring onions. Serves 4 to 6.

OVEN-FRIED CHICKEN

Prepare chicken as in basic recipe for fried chicken. When pieces are uniformly and delicately browned, transfer to covered roasting dish, or casserole. Add a little water if you like. Bake in slow oven (325°F. Mark 3) until tender, 1 to 1½ hours. To crisp, remove lid the last 5 to 10 minutes of cooking.

MANDARIN CHICKEN

1 young chicken, 2 to 2½ pounds
    ready-to-cook weight, cut up
2 ounces flour
2 teaspoons salt
1 teaspoon paprika
¼ teaspoon ground pepper
4 ounces fat for frying
¼ teaspoon ground cloves
¼ teaspoon ground nutmeg
1 tablespoon water
1 ounce flour
4 tablespoons water
½ pint pineapple juice
½ pint orange juice (2 to 3 medium
    oranges or frozen juice)
About 6 ounces pineapple cubes
2 small oranges or tangerines, cut
    in segments
2 ounces salted almonds, slivered
1½ pounds cooked rice, hot

Blend 2 ounces flour, salt, paprika, and pepper in plastic or sturdy paper bag.

Drop chicken, 2 or 3 pieces at a time, into bag and shake to coat evenly.

Heat fat in heavy frying pan until drop of water just sizzles.

Start browning meaty pieces first, slipping less meaty pieces in between as chicken browns. Turn as necessary to brown evenly, 15 to 20 minutes. Sprinkle with cloves and nutmeg.

Add 1 tablespoon water. Cover tightly and cook over low heat until thickest pieces are tender when pierced with a fork, 25 to 30 minutes. Turn pieces as necessary to cook evenly.

Meanwhile, blend 2 ounces flour and 4 tablespoons water until free of lumps. Blend with pineapple and orange juices. Cook in saucepan until thickened throughout, stirring constantly.

Add pineapple cubes, orange segments, and almonds. (Some of almonds may be reserved for garnishing rice.)

Pour over chicken and cook over low heat, uncovered, about 10 minutes to blend flavours. Serve with rice. Serves 4 to 5.

CHICKEN SAUTÉ CHASSEUR

Chasseur is a French term meaning hunter; it often appears on menus as "à la chasseur," meaning hunter's style and it is applied to various ways of cooking chicken, meat, and game. Usually popular versions of this dish, as given below, contain tomatoes.

3 tablespoons butter or margarine
1 ounce flour
2 teaspoons salt
¼ teaspoon pepper
¼ teaspoon thyme
2- to 2½-pound roasting chicken
    (cut in pieces)*
4 spring onions, chopped
4 ounces mushrooms, cut into
    quarters
2 tablespoons lemon juice
1 teaspoon sugar
1 teaspoon salt
2½ fluid ounces apple juice
2 medium tomatoes, diced (or 2
    whole canned tomatoes,
    drained and diced)
2 tablespoons chopped parsley and
    chives

Heat butter in heavy frying pan.

Mix flour, salt, pepper, and thyme in a paper bag. Shake pieces of chicken in seasoned flour mixture and brown thoroughly in butter in pan.

Add onions and mushrooms. Cover and simmer 3 minutes.

Mix lemon juice, sugar, salt, and apple juice and pour over chicken. Cover and simmer 5 minutes. Add tomatoes.

Cook slowly over low heat about 1 hour or until chicken is tender when pierced with a fork. Sprinkle with parsley and chives. Serve hot. Serves 4 to 5.

* Note: If an older chicken is used, cook slowly for 2 hours.

WINE-FRIED CHICKEN

Joint a good-size spring chicken; season but do not flour.

Heat 2 tablespoons butter and 1 tablespoon oil in a frying pan. Add chicken and brown thoroughly on all sides. Then add 6 fluid ounces white wine; cover tightly and simmer 20 minutes or until tender.

Add 4 fluid ounces cream (sweet or sour), heat again and serve with the wine and cream gravy poured over the chicken. Serves 4.

Mandarin Chicken

PAN-FRIED SMALL TURKEY

A young turkey weighing 4 to 5 pounds (ready-to-cook weight) is suitable for frying. It is usually jointed and cut up.

Coating: For each pound of turkey, blend 1 ounce flour, 1 teaspoon paprika, ¾ teaspoon salt, and ⅛ teaspoon pepper in a paper bag.

Shake turkey, 2 or 3 pieces at a time, in bag to coat evenly. Save any left-over flour for gravy.

Preliminary Browning: Heat ½ inch of vegetable oil or fat in a frying pan until a drop of water just sizzles. Start browning meaty pieces first, slipping less meaty pieces in between as turkey browns.

To brown evenly, turn as necessary with kitchen tongs or two spoons. This browning takes 15 to 20 minutes.

Slow Cooking: Reduce heat, cover tightly and cook slowly until tender, 45 minutes for 4-pounds ready-to-cook weight, 50 to 60 minutes for 5-pound ready-to-cook weight.

If pan cannot be covered tightly, add 1 to 2 tablespoons water and cover.

The liver and precooked heart, gizzard, and neck may be floured and browned with turkey the last 15 minutes.

Remove lid last 10 minutes to recrisp skin.

To Test if Cooked: The turkey is cooked when meat on the thickest part of the drumstick cuts easily and there is no pink colour visible.

Lift turkey onto a warm platter. If you like, make gravy with pan juices.

SAVOURY PAN-FRIED TURKEY

Use butter or margarine in place of oil or fat. Add one or more additional seasonings to coating flour such as Aromat, garlic powder, or thyme.

OVEN-FRIED SMALL TURKEY

This method is excellent when two or more turkeys are being fried.

Coating and Browning: Coat the cut-up turkey with seasoned flour. See Pan-Fried Small Turkey.

Brown in at least ½-inch layer of fat in a heavy frying pan. If a large quantity of turkey is prepared, it may be deep-fat browned. Place golden-browned turkey, one layer deep, in a shallow baking dish.

Slow Oven Cooking: For each 2 pounds of turkey, spoon a mixture of 2 tablespoons of melted butter and 2 tablespoons of stock or milk over the turkey.

Continue the cooking in a moderate oven (350°F. Mark 4) until turkey is tender, 50 to 60 minutes. Turn once to crisp evenly. During the cooking, broth or milk may be sprinkled over turkey if it appears dry.

Test if bird is cooked in the same way as for pan-fried turkey.

SPANISH FRIED CHICKEN

1 chopped onion
4 tablespoons fat
1 roaster, cut up
Seasoned flour
1 chopped green pepper
2 medium tomatoes, chopped
½ tablespoon chilli powder
4 ounces uncooked rice
½ pint milk or 4 fluid ounces evaporated milk diluted with 4 fluid ounces water

Cook onion in hot fat for a few minutes.

Roll chicken in flour and brown on both sides. Arrange in casserole. Add other ingredients and enough water to cook rice. Cook slowly, covered, in moderate oven (350°F. Mark 4) until chicken is tender.

If necessary add more milk, but only enough to cook rice, as it must be quite dry when served. Serves 4 to 6.

SMOTHERED-FRIED CHICKEN

1 2¼-pound ready-to-cook spring chicken
1½ teaspoons salt
¾ teaspoon pepper
2 ounces flour
4 ounces fat
1 pint water

Cut chicken in frying pieces and coat with seasoned flour.

Brown quickly on all sides in hot fat in large frying pan.

Pour off fat. Add water. Cover and simmer until chicken is tender, about 30 minutes. Add more seasoning if necessary. Serves 4.

Variations: Substitute ½ pint white wine for ½ pint water or, if you like, milk or half milk and half water may be substituted for all the water.

Vary seasoning by adding 1 to 2 teaspoons ground marjoram, or sage to the flour.

NORTH-WEST FRIED CHICKEN

Prepare young chickens, 1½ to 2½ pounds, for frying. Cut into half, quarters or pieces, whichever way is preferred.

Heat in iron or heavy aluminium frying pan enough fat, oil, or half butter and half fat, to cover half the depth of the chicken.

Dip chicken in 6 fluid ounces cream or evaporated milk. Dredge in a well-blended mixture of 2 ounces flour, ½ teaspoon salt, ½ teaspoon pepper, and ¼ teaspoon paprika.

Fry slowly until golden brown; turn and brown other side until same colour and until done, 25 to 30 minutes.

Place on platter with sprigs of parsley and serve hot.

GARLIC CHICKEN

4 ounces butter or margarine
1 young chicken, about 3½ pounds, cut up
1 teaspoon salt
8 cloves garlic
1 ounce chopped parsley.

Melt half of butter in heavy frying pan. Place chicken in frying pan and brown on all sides over low to medium heat. Sprinkle with salt.

Mash garlic with fork or put through garlic press. Mix with remaining butter, chopped parsley, and cream all ingredients well. Add to chicken.

Cover and cook over low heat until tender, about 30 to 40 minutes. During cooking turn chicken occasionally and spoon sauce over it. Serve sauce with chicken. Serves 4.

CHICKEN SUBLIME

1 tablespoon aromatic bitters
1 tablespoon lemon juice
4 tablespoons water
1 2 to 2½-pound roaster or spring chicken, cut in serving pieces
1 tablespoon salt
2 teaspoons monosodium glutamate
1 teaspoon garlic salt
2 eggs, well beaten
12 ounces cornflakes
2 ounces flour
½ pint vegetable oil

Mix bitters, lemon juice, and water in small saucepan. Heat to boiling.

Season chicken pieces with salt, monosodium glutamate, and garlic salt, mixed together. Place chicken pieces in shallow pan. Pour hot sauce over chicken. Set aside at room temperature 1 hour, turning pieces frequently. Drain, saving leftover sauce; combine with eggs.

Crush the cornflakes into fine crumbs. Coat chicken pieces first with flour, then dip in egg mixture and then in cornflakes. Fry in 1 inch of oil until golden brown on both sides, about 15 minutes per side. Serves 4.

Chicken Sublime

Oven-fried Chicken with Tropical Fruit Sauce

OVEN-FRIED CHICKEN WITH TROPICAL FRUIT SAUCE

2 ounces wheat germ
4 ounces dry breadcrumbs
½ teaspoon salt
½ teaspoon onion salt
¼ teaspoon garlic salt
½ teaspoon savory
½ teaspoon curry powder
⅛ teaspoon pepper
1 3-pound spring chicken, cleaned and cut into serving pieces
2 ounces melted butter or margarine

Combine wheat germ, breadcrumbs, salt, onion salt, garlic salt, summer savory, curry powder, and pepper. Brush chicken pieces with melted butter or margarine, then dip in crumb mixture to coat outer surface.

Place skin side up in shallow baking dish. Sprinkle with any remaining butter or margarine. Bake in hot oven (400°F. Mark 6) until tender, 50 to 60 minutes. For a lightly browned chicken, cover dish with aluminium foil during last 15 minutes of cooking.

Serve with Tropical Fruit Sauce. If preferred, sauce may be poured over chicken during last 5 to 10 minutes cooking time. Serves 4.

Tropical Fruit Sauce:
1 15¼-ounce can pineapple chunks
½ green pepper, optional
4 fluid ounces orange juice
2 tablespoons lemon juice
1 tablespoon cornflour
2 ounces sugar
1 tablespoon chopped preserved ginger, optional
1 teaspoon grated orange rind

Drain pineapple chunks; save syrup. Remove stem and seeds of green pepper; wash and cut into strips or 1-inch cubes.

Combine pineapple syrup, orange and lemon juice, cornflour, and sugar; stir until blended. Cook, stirring constantly, until clear and thickened.

Stir in ginger, orange rind, pineapple chunks, and peppers; heat thoroughly. Serve over or with Oven-fried Chicken. Makes about 1 pint sauce.

CHICKEN SAUTÉED CREOLE STYLE

2 frying chickens
1 ounce butter or margarine
2 large onions, sliced
2 tablespoons flour
6 tomatoes, sliced
3 green peppers or pimentos, chopped
1 clove garlic, finely chopped
1 sprig thyme
1 sprig parsley, chopped
1 bay leaf
1 pint chicken consommé or stock
Salt and pepper
Cooked rice

Cut up the chickens into frying pieces. Season well with salt and pepper.

Melt butter in a large saucepan; add chicken and brown on all sides.

Add onions and brown lightly, then sprinkle with flour and mix well.

Add tomatoes, peppers or pimentos, garlic, and herbs. Simmer for 20 minutes, then add the hot consommé which has been highly seasoned with salt and pepper. Simmer for 45 minutes.

To serve, put pieces of chicken on a hot platter and cover with sauce. Serve with boiled rice. Serves 6.

CHICKEN MARSALA

2½- to 3-pound ready-to-cook roaster (cut for frying)
Flour
4 tablespoons butter or margarine
1 medium onion, chopped
1 green pepper, chopped
1 canned pimento, sliced
½ 7½-ounce can button mushrooms
1 to 2 tablespoons chopped parsley
1 clove garlic, crushed or finely cut
1 teaspoon salt
¼ teaspoon pepper
½ pint stock or water
4 fluid ounces water
2 fluid ounces marsala
4 fluid ounces light cream and 4 fluid ounces water if sauce is wanted

Have the chicken cut either in 4 pieces; or in 2 drumsticks, 2 thighs, 2 wings and centre breast.

Melt butter and heat in a heavy frying pan or electric frying pan. Brown meaty pieces of chicken first, slip less meaty ones in between. Brown chicken evenly on all sides about 10 minutes.

Meanwhile blend all vegetables with seasonings and stock; add to chicken. Cover and cook over moderate heat for 10 minutes.

Turn chicken pieces with spatula; add water and wine. Cover pan and cook until chicken is tender, about 30 minutes if chicken is cut into 4 pieces, and 20 to 25 minutes if chicken is cut into smaller pieces as indicated above. Turn chicken once or twice during cooking.

If you want gravy, remove chicken to heated platter, add cream and water to gravy in pan. Cook over moderate heat for 3 to 5 minutes until gravy is smooth and well blended, stirring constantly.

Add chicken and serve directly from pan. Serves 4 to 6.

Note: Serve with fluffy rice, cranberry sauce, and bowl of salad, if you like.

SPICY FRIED CHICKEN

1 young chicken, 2 to 2½ pounds, ready-to-cook weight, cut up
Grated rind and juice of 2 medium oranges
1 tablespoon grated onion
½ teaspoon salt
½ teaspoon dry mustard
⅛ teaspoon pepper
Dash of Tabasco sauce
3 ounces flour
1½ teaspoons salt
1 teaspoon paprika
⅛ teaspoon pepper
About 4 ounces fat
About 1 tablespoon water

Place chicken one layer deep in shallow dish. Mix the orange rind, orange juice, onion, salt, dry mustard, pepper, and Tabasco. Pour mixture over chicken. Marinate 1 to 3 hours.

Drain, reserving marinade for gravy.

Mix the flour, salt, paprika, and pepper and coat chicken thoroughly with this mixture. Save any leftover flour mixture for gravy.

Brown chicken in heavy frying pan containing ½ inch hot fat. Turn occasionally to brown evenly.

When chicken is lightly browned, 15 to 20 minutes, add the water and cover pan tightly. Cook slowly until thickest pieces are tender when pierced with a fork, 20 to 30 minutes. Turn chicken as necessary to brown and cook evenly.

Remove lid and continue cooking slowly to crisp coating, about 5 minutes. Remove chicken to warm dish and prepare gravy, using marinade mixture as part of liquid. Serves 4 to 5.

Chicken Marsala

OVEN-FRIED HERB CHICKEN

1 young chicken, 3 to 3½ pounds
    ready-to-cook weight,
    jointed
½ teaspoon thyme
½ teaspoon marjoram
Flour
Fat
½ teaspoon rosemary
2 tablespoons chopped parsley
1 teaspoon salt
¼ teaspoon pepper
4 fluid ounces hot water

Sprinkle the chicken with thyme and marjoram; let stand ½ to 1 hour.

Roll in flour and fry in ¼-inch hot fat just long enough to brown on both sides.

Remove each piece as it browns, and place in shallow baking dish. Sprinkle with rosemary, parsley, salt, and pepper.

Pour the hot water into a frying pan; stir thoroughly. Pour the hot liquid over chicken.

Cook uncovered in moderate oven (375°F. Mark 5) about 45 minutes. Serves 6.

SAUTÉED CHICKEN BREASTS

Remove breasts from 2 cleaned, dressed chickens. Wash and dry them and cut each in 2 pieces. Sprinkle each with salt and pepper.

Dip in light cream or evaporated milk; roll in flour and sauté in butter or margarine until golden brown.

Arrange sautéed chicken breasts in a baking dish. Dot with 2 tablespoons butter or margarine. Cover with non-stick cooking paper and bake in moderate oven (375°F. Mark 5) 20 minutes. Serves 4.

CHICKEN SAXONY

1 2½- to 3-pound roaster, cut in
    serving pieces
Salt and pepper
1 small garlic clove
4 tablespoons salad oil
4 fluid ounces lemon juice
2 tablespoons grated onion
½ teaspoon thyme
4 ounces butter or margarine

Season chicken with salt and pepper. Keep in covered dish in the refrigerator until thoroughly chilled.

Mix the garlic, oil, lemon juice, onion and thyme together, season with a little salt and pepper. Leave for 30 minutes or longer, then remove garlic.

Melt butter or margarine in chafing dish pan over direct heat. Brown chicken on all sides. Turn the pieces skin-side up and pour the garlic mixture over.

Cover pan; cook gently until chicken is tender, about 40 minutes. Serves 4.

WESTERN FRIED CHICKEN

½ teaspoon onion salt
1 teaspoon paprika
Pinch of garlic salt
½ teaspoon pepper
4 ounces flour
1 tablespoon salt
2 3-pound broilers, cut in pieces
½ pound fat
4 ounces butter or margarine
4 tablespoons water
Parsley and vegetables for garnish

Combine dry ingredients in a paper bag. Place chicken pieces, a few at a time, in bag and shake well.

Place pieces in hot fat and butter in a heavy frying pan. Cover and cook for 20 minutes.

Turn chicken and continue to cook for 20 minutes or until golden brown.

Sprinkle with the water. Cover again and cook for 5 minutes. Remove from pan and drain on absorbent paper. Garnish with parsley and fresh vegetables. Serves 6 to 8.

CALIFORNIA CHICKEN DINNER

2 broilers, cut in serving pieces
1 teaspoon salt
¼ teaspoon pepper
8 tablespoons olive or peanut oil
1 garlic clove, finely chopped
6 spring onions, whole
1 pint (2 8-ounce cans) tomato sauce
1½ pint chicken bouillon or broth
8 tablespoons mushroom ketchup
2 ounces button mushrooms

Season chicken well with salt and pepper. Heat oil in chafing dish over direct heat and sauté chicken until well browned on all sides.

Add garlic and onions. Pour tomato sauce and bouillon over chicken. Add mushroom ketchup.

Cover pan and cook about 30 minutes, or until chicken is tender and the sauce around it is reduced.

Add mushrooms about 10 minutes before serving. Serves 4 to 6.

SOUTHERN FRIED CHICKEN

2 spring chickens or 1 young
    roasting chicken
2 ounces sifted flour
½ teaspoon salt
⅛ teaspoon pepper
1 egg, slightly beaten
2½ fluid ounces milk
1 pound salt pork

Rinse the cleaned and dressed chickens, wipe dry and cut in serving pieces.

Sift the flour with the salt and pepper; mix the beaten egg and milk and stir into the dry ingredients; mix thoroughly. Dip the pieces of chicken into this batter.

Cut the salt pork in small cubes and heat in a heavy frying pan to make fat 1-inch deep. Remove bits of pork.

When fat is hot, lay the pieces of chicken in, brown quickly, then cover the pan and cook slowly until tender, 35 to 60 minutes. Serve with cream gravy. Serves 4 to 6.

CHICKEN SAUTÉ BURGUNDY WITH MUSHROOM SAUCE

1 spring chicken (about 3½ pounds),
    cut in pieces for serving
Flour
Salt and pepper to taste
2 tablespoons butter or margarine
2 tablespoons salad oil
4 tablespoons burgundy or other
    red wine

Dust chicken with flour seasoned with salt and pepper.

Heat butter and oil in large, heavy frying pan with a tight-fitting lid. Add chicken and sauté until nicely browned on all sides.

Add the red wine. Cover and cook over low heat 45 minutes, or until chicken is tender.

Meantime, prepare sauce as follows:

2 ounces diced celery
2 tablespoons diced onion
4 tablespoons butter or margarine
3 tablespoons flour
10 fluid ounces chicken stock (can-
    ned or bouillon cube broth
    may be used)
4 fluid ounces burgundy or other
    red wine
4 ounces canned mushrooms,
    roughly chopped
Pinch of thyme
Pinch of marjoram
Pinch of paprika
Salt and pepper to taste
2 tablespoons chopped parsley

Sauté celery and onion gently in butter 5 minutes. Blend in flour; add stock; cook, stirring constantly, until mixture boils and thickens.

Add wine, mushrooms (undrained), and seasonings; bring to the boil, then simmer 5 minutes, stirring frequently.

Just before serving, add parsley. Pour sauce over chicken, or serve separately. Serves 3 to 4.

*Southern Fried Chicken
with Cream Gravy*

Rock Cornish Hen

Also known as Cornish game hen and is sometimes dealt with under the category of game birds.

It is a small-boned, all white meat bird of fine flavour developed by cross-breeding of the Cornish hen with other breeds of chicken. It is generally used when 5-8 weeks old and the ready-to-cook weight is seldom more than one pound.

Rock Cornish Hens generally come frozen and need to be defrosted before cooking. Although they are usually cooked whole—in the oven, grilled or barbecued—they may also be split then grilled or fried.

Guinea fowl, which is similar to Rock Cornish Hen, is dealt with in the section on Game, but all the recipes given for Rock Cornish Hen can be used for Guinea fowl.

ROAST ROCK CORNISH HEN

Place defrosted hens on baking sheet or shallow pan breast-side-up. Brush entire bird with melted butter, margarine, or cooking fat. Season to taste.

Roast in hot oven (425°F. Mark 7) 20 minutes. Reduce heat to moderate oven (350°F. Mark 4) and roast 25 minutes more, then turn bird breast down and continue to roast until golden brown, about 15 minutes.

Baste during cooking, adding hot water or consommé to pan juices to make a gravy.

GRILLED ROCK CORNISH HENS

Split the birds; sprinkle with salt and pepper and rub with melted butter, margarine, or cooking fat and a few drops of Worcestershire sauce.

Place flesh-side-down 3 to 5 inches from moderate heat for 15 to 20 minutes.

Turn; add ½ pint of white wine to grill pan and baste frequently until done, 15 to 20 minutes.

Candlelight dinner for two features roast Rock Cornish game hens with a stuffing of crumbs, prunes, and walnuts.

ROCK CORNISH HENS WITH CHINESE GLAZE

4 Rock Cornish hens, about 14 ounces each
1 teaspoon salt
¼ teaspoon pepper
1 large onion, cut in large pieces
2 sticks of celery, cut in 1-inch pieces
4 medium carrots, cut in ½-inch pieces
1 ounce butter or margarine, melted

Rub hens inside and out with salt and pepper. Stuff with vegetables.

Place breast-side-up on rack in shallow pan; brush with butter or margarine. Roast, uncovered, in moderate oven (350°F. Mark 4) for 30 minutes.

Remove from oven; brush with glaze. Return to oven; roast another 30 minutes, or until tender; baste occasionally. Serves 4.

Chinese Glaze: Use a prepared Chinese duck sauce or make your own as follows: Cook 2¾ ounces dried apricots as directed on packet, drain.

Press through wire sieve or vegetable mill. Add 1½ teaspoons grated orange rind, 4 tablespoons orange juice, 1 tablespoon golden syrup, 1 tablespoon vinegar, 1½ teaspoons soy sauce, and pinch of ground ginger. Bring slowly to boil, stirring often.

STUFFED CORNISH GAME HENS

About 2 ounces shredded wheat crumbs
2 tablespoons butter or margarine
2 ounces chopped walnuts
1 tablespoon grated lemon rind
About 2½ ounces chopped prunes
½ teaspoon salt
1 teaspoon ground allspice
1 teaspoon ground marjoram
4 tablespoons juice from 8-ounce can cranberries
1 teaspoon ground ginger
2 frozen Rock Cornish game hens, thawed

Mix crumbs with remaining ingredients except hens. Stuff hens. Truss.

Place on rack in a shallow baking dish and roast in moderate oven (350°F. Mark 4) about 1 hour. Brush with melted butter or margarine and baste occasionally while cooking. Serves 2.

ROCK CORNISH HENS GRUCCI

4 whole Cornish hens
Salt and pepper
6 ounces cooked wild rice
About 2 tablespoons diced ham
2 tablespoons chopped mushrooms
2 shallots, chopped
4 fluid ounces sherry
4 tablespoons brandy
2 ounces butter
4 tablespoons broth or consommé

Season hens inside and out with salt and pepper.

Mix the rice, bacon, mushrooms, and shallots; moisten with 4 tablespoons sherry and the brandy. Stuff loosely into cavities. Skewer openings and truss birds.

Place breast-side-up in baking dish. Dot with butter. Roast in moderate oven (350°F. Mark 4) until nicely browned and cooked through, about 45 minutes.

Remove hens to a warm dish. Add remaining sherry and broth to juices in pan. Stir up brown bits and thicken sauce with 1 teaspoon flour, if you like. Pour over hens. Serves 4.

CORNISH HEN APPLE CASSOULET

2 teaspoons dried onion flakes
2 tablespoons water
2 tablespoons salad oil
½ pound boiling sausages
2 Rock Cornish hens, split in half
½ teaspoon salt
3 tart apples, peeled and sliced
1 green pepper, cut in rings
2½ 8-ounce cans butter beans or white haricot beans
¼ teaspoon Tabasco sauce
1 teaspoon Worcestershire sauce

Combine onion and water; leave until water is absorbed.

Heat salad oil in large frying pan. Cut sausages in chunks; brown in oil; remove. Rub hens with salt; brown in same pan; remove.

Add apples and green pepper rings to pan; cook 5 minutes. Add beans, Tobasco, Worcestershire sauce, and onions; mix well. Spoon bean mixture into 4 individual casseroles; place hens on top; cover.

Bake in moderate oven (350°F. Mark 4) 45 to 60 minutes, or until hens are cooked. Serves 4.

Cornish Hen Apple Cassoulet

Boiled Chicken

CHICKEN STEW WITH HERB DUMPLINGS

2 medium-sized onions, finely chopped
1 green pepper, finely chopped
1 garlic clove, finely chopped
2 tablespoons fat
1 3- to 3½-pound chicken, jointed
1 8-ounce can tomato sauce
4 fluid ounces water
1½ teaspoons salt
⅛ teaspoon pepper
1 teaspoon Aromat
1 teaspoon poultry seasoning
About 1½ pints boiling water
About 12 ounces cooked fresh or canned green peas

In deep flameproof casserole cook onions, green pepper, and garlic in hot fat until soft but not brown. Add chicken.

Combine tomato sauce, 4 fluid ounces water, and seasonings; pour over chicken.

Add enough boiling water to cover; simmer 1½ hours, adding more water if necessary.

Add peas; drop in dumpling batter; cover; boil 12 minutes longer. Serves 6.
Herb Dumplings: Use favourite recipe, or follow directions on packet of prepared dumpling mix, adding 1 teaspoon oregano or marjoram to dry ingredients.

SMOTHERED CHICKEN WITH CREAM GRAVY

1 4½-pound dressed roasting chicken, cut for frying
2 ounces flour
2 teaspoons paprika
2 teaspoons salt
¼ teaspoon pepper
3 ounces chicken fat or cooking fat
2 10½-ounce cans condensed cream of mushroom soup

Shake chicken in a paper bag with flour, paprika, salt, and pepper.

Brown it on all sides in fat in a flameproof casserole.

Pour soup over chicken. Cover and simmer over low heat about 1 hour, or until tender. Spoon sauce over chicken occasionally. Serves 6.

Mediterranean Chicken

Chicken Stew with Herb Dumplings

MEDITERRANEAN CHICKEN

1 spring chicken (3 pounds)
2 ounces butter or margarine
2 pounds (about 16) small new potatoes
2 teaspoons tomato paste
Salt and pepper
2 cans (4½-ounce) stoned black olives
1 14-ounce can artichoke hearts
¼ pint sherry

Have chicken cut into quarters. Wash with cold water and dry with absorbent paper. Brown slowly in 2 tablespoons butter in a flameproof casserole, uncovered.

Wash potatoes, scraping them, if you like, and brown lightly in remaining butter.

After chicken has cooked 30 minutes, stir tomato paste into juices in bottom of pan; then add potatoes. Season with salt and pepper. Cook, covered, over low heat until potatoes and chicken are tender, about 20 minutes.

Add drained olives and artichoke hearts; cook 5 minutes longer. Remove the chicken and the potato mixture to a serving dish and rinse out pan with sherry, scraping well. Spoon this over chicken and serve. Serves 4.
Note: Chicken isn't salted at beginning because it makes butter too brown.

COQ AU VIN

Coq au Vin is French for chicken with wine and there are many versions; however, the name is usually applied to cut-up chicken browned in butter, transferred to a casserole, and braised in red wine as in the following recipe. Any good red wine may be used in preparing it.

2 roasters, about 2½ pounds each, halved
2 onions, diced
2 carrots, diced
3 bay leaves
2 sticks celery, cut in 1-inch pieces
Salt and pepper
Burgundy or other dry red wine to cover
Flour
2 ounces butter

Mix the chicken, onions, carrots, bay leaves, and celery together in a bowl; add a sprinkling of salt and a dash of pepper and cover with wine. Set it aside for 2 to 4 days in the refrigerator.

At cooking time, remove the chicken from the marinade and dry it thoroughly with a towel. Sprinkle the bird all over with flour.

Heat butter in a heavy frying pan; add chicken and brown on all sides. Transfer chicken to a flameproof casserole with a lid.

Add the marinade and the vegetables to the pot and cook over very low heat until the chicken is tender and the marinade has been reduced to a rich brown sauce. The lid should be lifted slightly off-centre to allow the escape of steam. Transfer the chicken to a hot dish; strain the sauce and pour over it. Serves 4.

BRAISED CHICKEN MONTE CARLO

3 tablespoons butter or margarine
3 tablespoons olive or salad oil
2 2½-pound ready-to-cook roasters, quartered
1 teaspoon salt
¼ teaspoon white pepper
1 teaspoon Aromat
1 medium onion, thinly sliced
4 fluid ounces white wine
½ pint single cream
1 small can (3 ounces) button mushrooms
6 radishes, sliced

Heat butter and oil in a flameproof casserole. Brown chicken pieces on all sides. Sprinkle with salt, pepper, and Aromat.

Add onions and cook until onions are soft.

Pour wine over. Cover and simmer gently for 20 minutes.

Stir in cream and drained mushrooms. Heat through and serve at once garnished with radish slices. Serves 8.

BOILING A CHICKEN

Cut chicken into pieces or leave whole. Add water and seasonings.

Simmer chicken, covered, until tender. Test if cooked, with a fork.

As a variation, brown chicken before boiling.

Prepare gravy from the broth.

Boiled Chicken with Dumplings.

BOILED CHICKEN
(Basic Recipe)

Choose a 3½- to 5-pound chicken. Place the chicken, whole or cut up, in a flameproof casserole. Choose one with a tight-fitting lid.

Add 4 fluid ounces water and ½ teaspoon salt for each pound of chicken ready-to-cook including giblets and neck. If the chicken is to be served with gravy and dumplings, or mashed potatoes, increase the water to 8 fluid ounces and the salt to a scant ¾ teaspoon per pound of chicken, ready-to-cook weight.

For additional flavour, 1 small carrot, 1 small onion, 2 or 3 sticks of celery, a clove, and 2 or 3 whole black peppercorns may be added.

Bring water to a rapid boil. Skim any froth from the surface, reduce heat to simmering. Cook the chicken gently until the thickest pieces are tender when pierced with a fork, 2½ to 4 hours.

Remove chicken, strain broth, and cool meat and broth at once. Cover and refrigerate unless it is served immediately.

Steps in Preparing Gravy for Boiled Chicken

Remove chicken from broth.

Skim fat from the surface of the broth. Set this fat aside. Some will be used for the gravy.

If necessary, strain the broth and then measure it. For gravy allow about 4 fluid ounces broth per serving. Add milk or water to broth if necessary to make up the necessary amount.

For each ½ pint gravy, mix 1½ tablespoons each of flour and chicken fat and 4 tablespoons water until smooth.

Pour the flour mixture slowly into the simmering broth, stirring constantly until it is smooth and thickened throughout. Cover and simmer 5 to 10 minutes depending upon the amount of gravy.

Replace chicken in gravy. Season gravy well to taste. Serve very hot.

Variations: Sometimes boiled chicken with gravy is referred to as a White Stew.

To prepare White Stew follow directions for cooking the chicken. Add 8 fluid ounces milk to the broth before preparing the gravy.

BRAISED CHICKEN
(Basic Recipe)

Any size mature chicken may be cooked by braising.

Coat the cut-up chicken, giblets, and neck with seasoning and flour. For each 1 pound of chicken use 2 tablespoons flour, ½ teaspoon salt, ¼ teaspoon paprika, and ⅛ teaspoon pepper.

Use a heavy flameproof casserole with a well-fitting lid. Brown chicken

pieces slowly in a thin layer of moderately hot fat, turning with tongs or 2 spoons. About ½ hour is required to brown 4 pounds of chicken.

Remove pan from heat while adding 2 to 4 fluid ounces of water. Cover tightly.

Replace the pan over very *low* heat or place in slow oven (325°F. Mark 3) and cook slowly until the thickest pieces are tender when pierced with a fork, 2½ to 3½ hours. Should the liquid be used up before chicken is tender, add more water 2 to 4 fluid ounces at a time.

Lift chicken onto a warm serving dish.

Prepare gravy with the cooking juices.

Variations: Milk, plain or sour cream, fruit or vegetable juices, cider, or wine may be used instead of water. When chicken is braised in the oven, ketchup, chilli or barbecue sauce, tomatoes or creamed soups give flavour and variety. Seasonings in addition to salt and pepper may be chosen to taste.

BRAISING A CHICKEN

To braise a chicken, first flour and brown the chicken pieces.

Add the liquid, cover tightly and cook on top of the stove or in the oven.

Serve braised chicken with boiled rice or vegetables.

CHICKEN FRICASSÉE

Cut up chicken and cook as for Boiled Chicken.

Roll cooked pieces in well seasoned flour and sauté in chicken fat in a heavy pan until browned.

Thicken 12 fluid ounces of the stock with 2 tablespoons flour blended into 2 tablespoons chicken or other fat.

Or, mash the vegetables and use to thicken stock. Serve with boiled rice, spaghetti, or noodles.

CHICKEN CACCIATORE

Cacciatore, or as it often appears on menus, "alla cacciatore", is an Italian term meaning hunter's style. It is a method of cooking chicken and sometimes veal in a well-seasoned sauce of tomatoes and wine. Mushrooms and peppers are often included in various versions of chicken cacciatore.

1 ready-to-cook chicken, 2½ to 3
**   pounds, jointed**
About 4 fluid ounces olive oil
1 teaspoon paprika
1 finely sliced onion
1 large can (28 ounces) tomatoes
**   or 8 medium tomatoes**
1 clove garlic
1 teaspoon salt
¼ teaspoon pepper
4 fluid ounces white wine
**   (optional)**

Dry chicken. Cook gently in hot olive oil in a flameproof casserole until well browned. Sprinkle with paprika to aid browning. Turn occasionally to brown evenly.

Spoon off 2 or 3 tablespoons oil. Add onions, tomatoes, garlic, salt, and pepper. Cover tightly and simmer until chicken is tender, about ¾ hour.

If sauce is watery, remove chicken and simmer sauce for several minutes to thicken it.

Return chicken to sauce. Add wine and heat. Remove garlic before serving. Serves 5.

Note: Flour, brown, and cook giblets and neck with chicken. If you like, before serving, cut neck in 3 pieces and slice gizzard, heart, and liver meat into thin slices and serve them in the sauce.

EASY CHICKEN PAPRIKA

1 3-pound chicken, cut into pieces
Flour
2 ounces cooking fat
2 tablespoons finely chopped onion
4 ounces mushrooms, sliced
1 10½-ounce can condensed tomato
**   soup**
8 fluid ounces sour cream
1 bay leaf
½ teaspoon salt
¼ teaspoon pepper
2 teaspoons paprika

Dust chicken with flour; brown on both sides in hot melted fat in a heavy frying pan.

Add onion and mushrooms and cook until lightly browned.

Blend in remaining ingredients; cover and simmer slowly, stirring occasionally, for 45 minutes, or until tender.

Remove bay leaf before serving. Serves 6.

CHICKEN BRUNSWICK STEW

Brunswick stew is a name for a popular American dish which may be made of chicken, rabbit, squirrel, or pork and may include such vegetables as corn, green lima beans, okra, and tomatoes. A popular version is given below.

1 5-pound ready-to-cook boiling
**   chicken**
3½ pints water
1 tablespoon salt
1 medium onion, diced
2 8-ounce cans tomatoes
1 16-ounce can lima beans
½ 8-ounce can creamed corn
4 ounces okra or ladyfingers, wiped
**   and stem end removed**
1 teaspoon salt
½ teaspoon ground black pepper
⅛ teaspoon thyme
1 bay leaf

Wash the chicken inside and out. Cut into pieces or leave whole. Put into a deep flameproof pan. Add water, salt, and onion. Cover and simmer about 3 hours or until the chicken is tender.

Remove chicken from the broth and strip the meat from the bones. Cut the

Easy Chicken Paprika

meat into bite-sized pieces.

Use a big spoon to skim off most of the fat from the broth. Return the chicken meat to the broth. Add all the vegetables and remaining seasoning. Simmer 1 hour.

Taste and season if necessary. Remove bay leaf before serving.

Serves 6 to 8.

Note: This is a one-dish meal. It should be fairly thick and served in soup bowls for eating with a spoon. Serve with crusty rolls or French bread.

CHICKEN CREOLE

1 frying chicken, 3½ pounds
1 teaspoon salt
Small pinch of black pepper, freshly
**   ground**
2 fluid ounces olive oil
2 tablespoons butter or margarine
1 tablespoon flour
½ large onion, finely chopped or 6
**   chopped shallots**
5 tablespoons chopped green pepper
1 large can (20 ounces) tomatoes
Small pinch of cayenne
1 sprig thyme or ¼ teaspoon dried
**   thyme**
1 tablespoon chopped parsley
1 bay leaf
2 cloves garlic, chopped
4 fluid ounces white wine

Cut chicken into frying pieces. Sprinkle with salt and pepper. Brown on all sides in olive oil.

In another pan, melt the butter, blend in flour, and cook until brown. Add onion or shallots and green pepper and brown slightly.

Add tomatoes, cayenne, thyme, parsley, bay leaf, and garlic. Cook over low heat until sauce is thickened, about 15 minutes.

Add chicken, cover and simmer over low heat until chicken is perfectly tender, about 45 minutes.

Add wine 15 minutes before cooking time is up. Serve on a bed of cooked rice. Garnish with parsley and avocado slices, if you like. Serves 4 to 6.

Chicken Cacciatore

Olive Chicketti

OLIVE CHICKETTI

1 5-pound boiling chicken
2 fluid ounces oil
2½ pints hot water
1 tablespoon salt
2 tablespoons chopped onion
2 tablespoons diced green sweet
    pepper
4 ounces sliced celery
About 4 tablespoons diced pimiento
1 pound spaghetti
4 to 6 ounces ripe olives
½ pound grated Cheddar cheese

Joint the chicken and brown in hot oil in a flameproof casserole. Add hot water and salt, cover and cook slowly until tender. Cool sufficiently to handle.

Skim off excess fat. Remove skin and bones from chicken, leaving meat in large pieces.

Cook onion, pepper, and celery in a little of the chicken fat until soft and almost transparent. Stir into chicken and broth, add pimiento and heat to boiling.

Add broken spaghetti. Boil until spaghetti is tender, adding more water if needed.

Cut some of olives into large pieces and leave some whole.

Just before serving, stir olives and cheese into chicken mixture and heat slowly until cheese is melted.

Serves 8 to 10.

ARROZ CON POLLO
(Latin American Chicken with Rice)

This dish takes its name from the word arroz, the Spanish term for rice.

1 young 3½-pound chicken
4 fluid ounces olive oil
3-4 tablespoons diced onion
1½ teaspoons salt
Pepper to taste
1 large can (20 ounces) tomatoes
1 clove garlic
1 bay leaf
1 cup uncooked rice

Cut up and fry chicken in a heavy pan in oil gently until evenly browned. Remove chicken.

Cook onions lightly. Replace chicken. Add salt and pepper.

Add tomatoes heated to boiling. Drop garlic and bay leaf on top. Add rice. Cook gently over low heat (or in

moderate oven, 350°F. Mark 4) until rice is tender and fluffy, about 1 hour.

Lift and stir once after first 15 minutes.

Remove garlic and bay leaf. Serve the chicken on a warm dish, garnished with slivers of olives and green pepper rings.

Serves 5 to 6.

Arroz De Franzo: In Portugal, white wine is added.

Spanish Arroz Con Pollo: In Spain, saffron and cummin seed are added.

CHICKEN ROMANO

1 2½-pound ready-to-cook chicken,
    cut in pieces
1 ounce flour
1 teaspoon salt
¼ teaspoon pepper
2 fluid ounces olive or salad oil
1 8-ounce can small white onions
1 medium-sized green pepper, cut
    in strips
1 small can (3 ounces) mushrooms,
    drained
1 small clove garlic, crushed
1 10½-ounce can condensed tomato
    soup
4 fluid ounces water
2 tablespoons vinegar or lemon
    juice
1 tablespoon Worcestershire sauce
½ teaspoon oregano

Wash chicken pieces and pat dry. Roll in flour seasoned with salt and pepper. Brown chicken in olive oil in a large flameproof casserole; remove chicken.

Sauté onions, green pepper, mushrooms, and garlic in the same pan; blend in remaining ingredients.

Add chicken; cover and simmer about 30 minutes, or until chicken is done. Stir occasionally. Serve on a bed of cooked spaghetti. Serves 4.

CHICKEN IN RED WINE

4 tablespoons fat
1 boiling chicken (4 to 5 pounds),
    cut in pieces for serving
8 fluid ounces chicken broth (made
    with a bouillon cube)
1 8-ounce can tomato sauce
4 fluid ounces Burgundy or other
    red wine
1 medium onion, thinly sliced
2 sticks of celery, chopped
2 tablespoons chopped parsley
Salt and pepper to taste
6 medium carrots, scraped and
    sliced
8 ounces fresh or 1 packet frozen
    peas, cooked
1⅓ ounces flour
2 tablespoons sherry

Heat fat in a heavy flameproof casserole; add chicken and fry gently until nicely browned on all sides.

Add chicken broth, tomato sauce, wine, onion, celery, parsley, and salt

and pepper. Bring to the boil, then cover and simmer gently for 2 to 2½ hours (or longer, if necessary), until chicken is almost tender.

Add carrots; continue cooking for ½ hour, or until chicken and carrots are tender.

Remove chicken and vegetables from liquid. Pour liquid into a measuring jug or bowl; skim off excess fat and add water to make 1¼ pints. Return to the casserole and heat to boiling.

Mix flour with 4 fluid ounces of water to a smooth paste. Add slowly to the boiling liquid, stirring constantly. Simmer about 5 minutes. Season to taste with salt and pepper. Add sherry.

Return chicken and vegetables to gravy. Add peas. Heat thoroughly before serving. Serves 5 or 6.

CHICKEN ALMOND CURRY

1 chicken (3½ to 4 pounds), jointed
2 teaspoons salt
Small pinch of pepper
1½ teaspoons Aromat
1 medium onion, sliced
Boiling water
1 tart apple, diced
6 tablespoons butter or margarine
6 tablespoons flour
1 tablespoon curry powder, or to
    taste
Salt and pepper
2 ounces chopped, toasted almonds

Place chicken in deep flameproof casserole. Add salt, pepper, 1 teaspoon Aromat, and onion. Cover with boiling water. Simmer 1½ hours, or until chicken is tender. Add apple during last half hour.

Strain broth and measure 1¼ pints.

Bone chicken, leaving meat in as large pieces as possible.

Melt butter or margarine; blend in flour, remaining Aromat, and curry powder. Add broth; stir over low heat until thickened; add chicken and heat thoroughly.

Season to taste with additional salt and pepper. Pour into serving dish and top with almonds.

Serve with whole, sautéed bananas and curry accompaniments, such as chutney, coconut, and golden raisins. Serves 6.

Chicken Almond Curry

Miscellaneous Dishes with Fresh or Frozen Chicken

CHICKEN MOLÉ

Molé is a highly seasoned Mexican sauce for poultry containing a small amount of chocolate. In Mexico the word is spelled without the accent, which is added in English so that the second syllable is pronounced.

1 ready-to-cook chicken, 3 pounds
3 dried sweet red peppers, broken into small pieces
2 dried hot red peppers, broken into small pieces
1 teaspoon salt
4 fluid ounces water
1 slice white bread, cubed
2 tablespoons sesame seed
4 fluid ounces olive oil
2 tablespoons flour
8 fluid ounces chicken stock
1 teaspoon salt
2 whole cloves
½ ounce unsweetened chocolate

Joint and cut up chicken. Simmer in seasoned water to cover with giblets and neck until tender, 2½ to 3 hours.

Prepare sauce: Remove stems and seeds from peppers; break into cold salted water and soak 20 minutes.

Drain. Brown drained peppers, bread cubes, and sesame seed in olive oil. Add remaining ingredients and chocolate. Cook slowly until chocolate is melted, about 10 minutes.

Force the sauce through a fine sieve. Serve sauce poured over hot chicken. Serves 5 to 6.

CHICKEN BARCELONA

1 roasting chicken (3 pounds), quartered
2 teaspoons salt
1 teaspoon paprika
2 fluid ounces olive or salad oil
1 teaspoon rosemary
½ teaspoon thyme
1 clove garlic, sliced
1 pint water
¼ teaspoon saffron
8 ounces uncooked rice
2 bay leaves
1 12-ounce packet frozen green peas
10 sliced pimiento-stuffed olives

Chicken Barcelona

Sprinkle chicken with 1 teaspoon salt and paprika. Brown on all sides in hot oil in a frying pan.

Meanwhile, mix together remaining 1 teaspoon salt, rosemary, thyme, garlic, and water in saucepan; bring to the boil; add chicken neck and giblets. Simmer 25 minutes; strain and reserve 16 fluid ounces stock.

Remove chicken from pan; drain off all but 3 tablespoons fat. Stir saffron and rice into pan. Cook 15 minutes or until rice is golden, stirring occasionally. Add bay leaves, peas, reserved stock, and olives; mix well.

Add chicken; cover and cook over low heat 30 minutes or until chicken and rice are tender; stir occasionally. Serves 4.

CHICKEN TETRAZZINI

Tetrazzini is a term applied to a casserole of chicken baked with mushrooms and spaghetti in a rich wine-flavoured sauce. The original dish was named after the Italian opera soprano Luisa Tetrazzini (1874-1940). Turkey, lobster, and veal are often prepared in much the same manner. Although Luisa Tetrazzini was distinctly Italian, the dishes named after her are usually distinctly American.

1 4-pound chicken
1 teaspoon salt
2 ounces fresh mushrooms, sliced
6 tablespoons butter or margarine
½ pound spaghetti
3 tablespoons flour
16 fluid ounces chicken stock
8 fluid ounces double cream
2 tablespoons sherry
Grated Parmesan cheese

Cover cleaned chicken with hot water. Add salt and simmer until tender.

Cool in the liquid, then shred chicken and put back the skin and bones. Reduce liquid to little more than ¾ pint, so that when strained there will be ¾ pint.

Sauté mushrooms in 3 tablespoons butter 2 to 3 minutes.

Cook spaghetti in plenty of boiling salted water.

Make sauce: Melt 3 tablespoons butter, blend in flour, and add the stock, stirring and cooking over low heat until smooth and thickened. Add cream and sherry.

Divide sauce and add chicken to one half and spaghetti and mushrooms to other part. Put spaghetti in a large baking dish, making a well in the centre for the chicken mixture.

Sprinkle over grated cheese. Bake in moderate oven (350°F. Mark 4) until lightly browned. Serve at once. Serves 8.

CHICKEN MILANO

1 frying chicken (2½ to 3 pounds)
2 tablespoons olive or cooking oil
2 tablespoons butter or margarine
Salt and pepper
1 clove garlic, sliced
1 onion, chopped
½ 8-ounce can or 3 diced fresh peeled tomatoes
4 fluid ounces water
Juice of 1 lemon
1 tablespoon chopped parsley

Cut chicken as for fricassee. Wipe pieces dry, then sauté slowly until brown in oil and butter. Sprinkle with salt and pepper while cooking.

When well browned, add garlic and onion. Cook slowly until onion is soft, then add tomato, water, and lemon. Cover and cook slowly for 30 minutes longer.

Sprinkle with parsley before serving. Any juice left in the pan should be spooned over the chicken. Serves 4.

CHICKEN MARENGO

According to legend Chicken Marengo is supposed to have been invented for Napoleon at Marengo, Italy, after one of his most important victories. Traditionally, the dish contained mushrooms, tomatoes, wine, garlic, and was garnished with crayfish and fried eggs. Nowadays there are many versions of this dish and the name is also applied to veal dishes.

1 3- to 4-pound chicken, jointed
Cooking fat or oil
Salt and pepper
Thyme
6 spring onions, chopped
10 fluid ounces chicken stock
6 fluid ounces white wine or Rhine wine
2 tablespoons tomato paste
1 tablespoon flour

Heat 1 inch melted cooking fat in a frying pan. Dry chicken pieces, and fry until golden brown on both sides.

Season with salt, pepper, and thyme. Transfer to a baking dish.

Sprinkle with chopped onions. Add 4 fluid ounces chicken stock, and cook, uncovered, in moderate oven (325°F. Mark 3) 30 minutes.

Add 4 fluid ounces wine and the tomato paste. Cover, and cook, 20 minutes longer.

Remove lid, and cook, 10 minutes. Transfer the chicken to a hot dish.

Add remaining stock and wine to the juices in pan. Mix the flour with 4 tablespoons cold water and add to gravy. Cook until slightly thickened. Serve sauce poured over chicken. Serves 4.

POULTRY

Chicken Mexicana

CHICKEN POACHED IN LEMON BUTTER

4 ounces butter or margarine
2 tablespoons lemon juice
1 teaspoon salt
1 clove garlic, peeled
$\frac{1}{8}$ teaspoon pepper
$\frac{1}{2}$ teaspoon paprika
1 spring chicken, cut up

Put all ingredients except chicken in a deep frying pan and bring to boil.

Arrange chicken in the pan; bring again to boil. Cover and simmer for 30 minutes, or until chicken is tender, turning several times. Serves 4.

REGAL CHICKEN

1 can (about 8 ounces) creamed sweetcorn
8 ounces dry breadcrumbs
$\frac{1}{2}$ teaspoon salt
$\frac{1}{4}$ teaspoon poultry seasoning
4 whole chicken breasts
4 ounces butter or margarine, melted
8 fluid ounces sour cream

Put the creamed corn into medium-sized bowl. Add breadcrumbs, salt, and poultry seasoning; toss lightly.

Fill cavity of each chicken breast with stuffing. Skewer with cocktail sticks. Place in shallow baking dish in melted butter or margarine; turn once to coat both sides. Bake in slow oven (325°F. Mark 3) 45 minutes.

Turn chicken and bake an additional 45 minutes or until tender. Transfer to a warm dish or serving plates.

Stir sour cream into cooled pan juices. Heat over low heat several minutes. Do not boil. Spoon over chicken. Serves 4 to 6.

CHICKEN MEXICANA

1 4-pound chicken, jointed
16 fluid ounces boiling water
2 tablespoons chilli powder

Regal Chicken

$\frac{1}{4}$ teaspoon pepper
$\frac{1}{4}$ teaspoon cinnamon
2 tablespoons chopped onion
1 teaspoon Aromat
1 teaspoon salt
2 ounces fat or dripping
1 pint pineapple juice
1 16-ounce can pineapple chunks
1 teaspoon sugar
2 bananas, sliced lengthways
1 ripe avocado pear, stone removed, and sliced
$\frac{1}{2}$ pound white grapes

Place chicken in deep flameproof casserole; add boiling water, chilli powder, pepper, cinnamon, onion, Aromat, and salt. Cover; simmer 1 hour.

Drain chicken; brown pieces on all sides in hot fat or dripping; arrange in baking dish.

Add pineapple juice to liquid in which chicken was cooked; heat and pour over chicken.

Arrange pineapple chunks over chicken; sprinkle with sugar.

Bake in moderate oven (375°F. Mark 5) 30 minutes.

Remove chicken and fruit to serving dish; garnish with the slices of banana, avocado slices, and grapes. Serve gravy separately. Serves 6.

CHICKEN-RICE DINNER

1 5-pound chicken
1 onion, chopped
Fat for browning
8 ounces uncooked rice
1 teaspoon salt
$\frac{1}{8}$ teaspoon white pepper
1 $7\frac{1}{2}$-ounce can mushrooms or 2 carrots, chopped
16 fluid ounces stock or 4-5 medium tomatoes

Cut chicken in pieces. Brown them in a pan with onion in a small amount of fat.

Add boiling water almost to cover. Add uncooked rice, salt, pepper, mushrooms or chopped carrots, and stock or tomatoes.

Simmer on top of the stove or in moderate oven (350°F. Mark 4) until chicken is almost, but not quite, falling off the bones. The time depends on the tenderness of the chicken, but do allow about $1\frac{1}{2}$ hours.

Serve a generous amount of rice with the pieces of chicken. Serves 4 to 6.

CHICKEN GUMBO WITH RICE

1 large boiling chicken
2 tablespoons fat
1 slice ham, diced
2 teaspoons salt
$\frac{1}{4}$ teaspoon pepper
$\frac{1}{2}$ large onion, chopped
3 ounces chopped green pepper
$\frac{1}{4}$ teaspoon thyme
1 large can (20 ounces) tomatoes
1 quart water
12 ounces sliced okra
24 ounces hot cooked rice

Cut chicken into pieces. Wash thoroughly in cold water. Pat dry.

Heat fat in a deep flameproof casserole. Add chicken and ham. Cover and cook 15 minutes.

Add salt, pepper, onion, green pepper, thyme, and tomatoes. Add water. Cover and allow to simmer 2 hours, or until chicken is tender.

Add okra. Cover and cook 20 minutes, or until okra is tender. If you like, remove chicken meat from bones.

Serve the gumbo in a soup tureen, if you like. Place hot rice in soup bowls and pour gumbo over rice. Be certain the gumbo is steaming hot when it is served. Serves 8.

CREAMY SMOTHERED CHICKEN AND MUSHROOMS

$3\frac{1}{2}$- to 4-pound chicken
2 ounces flour
2 ounces fat
12 fluid ounces hot water
Milk
$\frac{1}{2}$ pound mushrooms
Cooked rice or noodles

Wash chicken, dry and joint it.

Mix 1 ounce flour, 1 teaspoon salt, and a small pinch of pepper; use to dredge over the chicken.

Brown chicken in fat. Add hot water, cover and simmer until chicken is tender, about 40 minutes. There should be about 4 tablespoons stock in pan. Add milk to make 16 fluid ounces.

Blend remaining flour to a smooth paste with cold water; add to stock and milk in pan and cook slowly, stirring constantly until thick.

Sauté mushrooms in butter. Arrange hot cooked rice or noodles, chicken, and mushrooms in a serving dish. Pour a little of the gravy over chicken. Hand round the remaining gravy. If you like, serve chutney in green pepper rings. Serves 6.

Chicken Gumbo with Rice

CHICKEN PAPRIKASH (HUNGARIAN)

1 ready-to-cook chicken about 2½ pounds
1 ounce flour
¾ teaspoon salt
⅛ teaspoon pepper
4 ounces fat for frying
½ large onion, finely chopped
2 to 3 tablespoons water
1 tablespoon paprika to taste
3 tablespoons flour
8 fluid ounces sour cream
½ pint water
Grated rind of 1 lemon
1-2 tablespoons lemon juice

Joint the chicken and coat with the flour, salt, and pepper, mixed together.

Brown chicken in hot fat in a flame-proof casserole. Add onion and water. Sprinkle chicken generously with paprika.

Cover pan tightly and cook gently over low heat or in moderate oven (350°F. Mark 4) until chicken is tender when pierced with a fork, 40 to 50 minutes. If necessary, add more water a tablespoon at a time to prevent sticking.

Transfer chicken to serving dish and keep hot.

Prepare gravy: Add flour to juices in pan and mix thoroughly. Cook over low heat until bubbly. Add sour cream and water and cook, stirring constantly, until thickened throughout.

Cover and simmer about 5 minutes. Add lemon rind and juice. Season well to taste. Serve gravy spooned around chicken or separately. Serves 4 to 5.

Note: Unless some other use is planned, flour, brown, and cook giblets and neck with chicken. To serve, cut neck into 3 pieces and gizzard, heart, and liver into slices. Add all to gravy.

DEVILLED CHICKEN

2 2½- to 3-pound ready-to-cook roasting chickens, split in half
6 tablespoons butter or margarine
1 teaspoon salt
1 tablespoon vinegar
1 tablespoon Worcestershire sauce
4 ounces dry breadcrumbs

Place halves of chicken skin-side-down in shallow pan and grill 6 inches from heat about 5 minutes on each side. Turn the chickens.

Mix 4 tablespoons butter with the rest of ingredients, except crumbs, and spread over the chicken. Melt rest of butter, stir in crumbs, and spread over chicken.

Bake uncovered in a moderate oven (350°F. Mark 4) until chicken is tender and crumbs are browned (about 50 to 60 minutes). Potatoes may be pan-roasted with chicken if you like. Serves 4.

BAKED CHICKEN WITH MUSHROOMS

1 roasting chicken, 3½ to 4 pounds
Milk
Flour
Salt and pepper
4 ounces fat
½ pound fresh mushrooms
1 small onion, thinly sliced
16 fluid ounces hot cream or top of milk

Cut chicken into pieces; dip them in milk, then in seasoned flour.

Fry the pieces in hot fat until nicely browned. Put in 1½-quart casserole.

Clean mushrooms and cut caps and stems into pieces. Fry mushrooms in fat about 2 or 3 minutes. Add mushrooms and onion to the chicken, and add hot cream or top milk.

Bake in moderate oven (350°F. Mark 4) 1½ to 2 hours, or until chicken is tender and cream is a thick sauce. Serve on a hot plate. Serves 6.

Note: If cream is used, it may curdle slightly. A little water can be added to it and stirred until sauce is smooth.

LEMON BARBECUED CHICKEN

1 roasting chicken
Salt and pepper
6 tablespoons butter or margarine
6 fluid ounces lemon sauce (below)

Have chicken drawn and cut into pieces, or, if quick-frozen, thaw according to directions on the package. Rinse in cold water and dry. Season with salt and pepper.

Melt butter in a heavy aluminium or stainless steel frying pan and brown chicken, skin side down. Turn and brown.

Pour lemon sauce over chicken pieces. Cover and cook slowly until tender, about 30 to 40 minutes.

Arrange chicken pieces on a dish and pour the sauce over them. Serves 4.

Lemon Sauce:
1 small clove garlic
½ teaspoon salt
4 tablespoons salad oil
4 fluid ounces lemon juice
2 tablespoons chopped onion
½ teaspoon celery salt
½ teaspoon black pepper
½ teaspoon dried thyme

Crush the garlic clove with salt in a bowl. Add remaining ingredients and mix together.

If possible, allow sauce to stand overnight to blend the flavours before using. Makes 6 fluid ounces.

IMPERIAL CHICKEN

1 2½- to 3-pound roasting chicken, cut up
6 to 8 ounces Shredded Wheat
3 ounces grated Parmesan cheese
2 teaspoons salt
⅛ teaspoon pepper
1 clove garlic, crushed
3 to 4 tablespoons chopped parsley
4 to 5 ounces butter or margarine, melted

Wash chicken pieces and dry thoroughly. Crush the Shredded Wheat into medium-fine crumbs; mix them with grated cheese, salt, pepper, garlic, and parsley. Dip chicken pieces in melted butter, then roll in cereal crumbs until well coated.

Place chicken pieces skin side up in shallow baking dish lined with aluminium foil; do not crowd the pieces. Bake in moderate oven (350°F. Mark 4) about 1 hour or until tender. Do not cover dish or turn chicken while cooking. Serves 4 to 5.

GUMBO FILÉ (CREOLE)

1 3-pound chicken
1½ teaspoons salt
¼ teaspoon black pepper
2 tablespoons fat
2 tablespoons flour
1 small onion, finely chopped
1 tomato, sliced
3¼ pints hot water
½ teaspoon thyme
Dash of cayenne pepper
2 ounces chopped celery
2 3¾-ounce cans oysters
2 tablespoons chopped parsley
2 tablespoons filé powder
Boiled rice

Remove chicken from bones. Cut meat in small pieces and mix with salt and pepper and brown lightly in fat in a frying pan.

Remove chicken and add flour, stirring constantly until brown and smooth. Add onion and cook until yellow; add tomato and cook a few minutes.

Put in chicken, hot water, thyme, cayenne, and celery. Simmer until meat is tender, 1½ to 2 hours.

Add oysters and parsley and cook until the edges of the oysters curl.

Remove from heat and stir in filé powder. Do *not* cook after adding filé powder. Serve with a spoonful of rice in each soup plate. Serves 8.

Imperial Chicken

CHICKEN PIE (ENGLISH STYLE)

1 boiler chicken, 3 to 6 pounds,
  cut up, giblets and neck
4 tablespoons chicken fat
2 ounces flour
1¼ pints chicken stock
8 fluid ounces top of milk or
  single cream
½ teaspoon ginger
¾ teaspoon pepper
2 to 4 hard-boiled eggs, sliced
4 to 6 ounces shortcrust pastry

Cook chicken several hours or a day in advance, simmering chicken, giblets, and neck until tender in seasoned water to cover, 2½ to 3 hours. Refrigerate until pie is prepared.

Melt fat over low heat. Add flour and mix thoroughly. Add stock and milk together. Cook, stirring constantly, until the mixture thickens. Add seasonings.

Meanwhile, trim giblets and cut into thin slices. Remove meat from neck or cut neck into 2 or 3 sections. Add all to gravy.

Arrange chicken in 2-quart shallow casserole, cutting the larger pieces in half. If bones are left in, alternate meaty and less-meaty pieces. Add eggs and hot gravy.

Cover with pastry dough rolled ¼-inch thick. Brush top with milk. Bake in hot oven (425°F. Mark 7) until top is nicely browned and sauce is bubbly, 20 to 25 minutes. Serves 6 from 3-pound chicken.

If the larger-sized chicken is cooked, gravy and pastry dough may be increased. For pastry topping, use favourite shortcrust pastry recipe made with 8 ounces flour or 1 7½-ounce packet frozen pastry.

SAUCY MUSHROOM CHICKEN WITH BROCCOLI

2½ pounds frozen chicken pieces,
  thawed
2 tablespoons butter or margarine
¼ large onion, chopped
1 10½-ounce can condensed cream
  of mushroom soup
8 fluid ounces chicken stock
1 teaspoon salt
1 head of broccoli, cut into florets

Brown chicken in butter. Add onion, soup, stock, and salt. Cover and cook over low heat 40 minutes.

Arrange broccoli over chicken. Cover and cook 10 minutes.

If you like, serve with lemon slices. Serves 4.

Fried Herb Chicken: For a gourmet trick, substitute 4 fluid ounces white wine for soup. Reduce chicken stock to 4 fluid ounces. Make a bouquet garni of 1 bay leaf, 3 whole black peppercorns, 3 sprigs parsley, and 1 clove garlic. Add bouquet garni with onion, wine, stock, and salt.

CHICKEN PUFF CASSEROLE

1 3-pound chicken
3 tablespoons flour
1 teaspoon salt
¼ teaspoon pepper
4 tablespoons fat
4 ounces maize flour
16 fluid ounces boiling water
1 tablespoon butter or margarine
1½ teaspoons salt
2 ounces sifted flour
1 tablespoon sugar
3 teaspoons baking powder
4 eggs, separated
4 fluid ounces milk

Cut the chicken into pieces. Coat with flour seasoned with 1 teaspoon salt and ¼ teaspoon pepper. Melt fat in a frying pan and fry chicken until well browned on all sides. Remove chicken to a large casserole. Save the juices left to make gravy.

Slowly stir maize flour into boiling water. Add butter and 1½ teaspoons salt. Cook over low heat, stirring frequently, until mixture thickens, about 5 minutes. Pour into a large bowl.

Mix and sift flour, sugar, and baking powder. Beat egg yolks well until thick; stir them into maize flour mixture with milk. Stir in sifted dry ingredients.

Beat egg whites until stiff and gently fold into mixture. Pour over chicken.

Bake in moderate oven (350°F. Mark 4) until the topping is set and lightly browned, about 1 hour.

Make milk gravy from reserved chicken juices. Serve chicken at once with milk gravy. Serves 4.

CHICKEN PILAF CREOLE

2 roasting chickens, jointed
4 ounces butter or margarine
1 small onion, chopped
1 large can (20 ounces) tomatoes
2 ounces chopped celery
4 chicken bouillon cubes
1½ pints boiling water
12 ounces uncooked rice
1 teaspoon salt
⅛ teaspoon pepper
¼ teaspoon nutmeg

Roll each piece of chicken in flour seasoned with salt and pepper.

Melt butter or margarine in a deep frying pan over low heat. Put in pieces of chicken. Add onion. Turn chicken frequently until each piece is well browned.

Add tomatoes and celery and continue cooking 5 minutes.

Dissolve bouillon cubes in boiling water. In a large flameproof casserole, cook rice in bouillon 10 minutes.

Lay chicken pieces on top of rice and pour tomato mixture over. Season with salt, pepper, and nutmeg.

Cover closely and continue cooking slowly over low heat until the rice and chicken are done, about 30 minutes. If necessary, add more water with bouillon cube dissolved in it.

When cooked, spoon the rice and tomatoes down the centre of a large serving dish and arrange the chicken pieces along both sides. Serves 6.

CHICKEN BREASTS AND OYSTERS BIARRITZ

4 chicken breasts, boned
4 ounces butter or margarine
½ pound fresh mushrooms, sliced
1 pint oysters and liquid
16 fluid ounces chicken stock
3 tablespoons flour
2 tablespoons cream
½ teaspoon salt
Small pinch of cayenne pepper
½ teaspoon fresh dill (optional)
4-5 ounces toasted bread cubes

Gently fry chicken breasts in 2 ounces butter until lightly browned on both sides; remove from pan.

Cook mushrooms in the same pan for 3 or 4 minutes.

Arrange in 3-quart casserole a layer each of chicken, mushrooms, and drained oysters.

Mix the chicken stock with oyster liquid; thicken with flour mixed to a paste with a little cold water. Add cream and seasonings. Pour over chicken.

Top with bread cubes and sprinkle over the remaining butter, melted.

Bake, uncovered, in moderate oven (375°F. Mark 5) 30 minutes. Serves 4.

PUERTO RICAN ARROZ CON POLLO

1 4-pound chicken
Salt and pepper
Lard for browning
1 dozen olives
1 tablespoon capers
1 onion, sliced
½ large red bell pepper
2 medium-sized tomatoes, cut in
  pieces
1 pound uncooked rice
1¼ pints boiling water
1 can peas
Pimientos

Cut chicken in pieces; rub them with salt and pepper and brown in melted lard in a frying pan.

Add olives, capers, onion, red pepper, and tomatoes.

Cover and cook slowly, stirring occasionally, until tender.

When tender, add rice and boiling water. Cover and cook until rice is cooked, stirring occasionally, about 10-12 minutes.

Heat peas separately.

To serve, surround a mound of rice with chicken pieces. Cover with peas and garnish with pimientos. Serves 6.

UNITED NATIONS CHICKEN

1 ready-to-cook young chicken,
    2½ pounds, jointed
2 ounces flour
¾ teaspoon salt
¼ teaspoon ginger
⅛ teaspoon pepper
1 garlic clove
4 ounces fat for frying
1 pound uncooked rice
1½ teaspoons salt
¼ teaspoon oregano
¼ teaspoon curry powder
12 tiny white onions, cooked
6 small carrots, cooked
Paprika
3 to 4 tablespoons finely chopped
    chives
16 fluid ounces chicken gravy
    (below)

Coat the chicken pieces with flour, salt, ginger, and pepper, mixed together. Include giblets and neck. Add garlic clove to fat and fry chicken until nicely browned and tender when tested with a fork, about 40 minutes.

Meanwhile boil the rice, adding salt, oregano, and curry for seasoning.

Mound rice in shallow 5-pint casserole. Arrange chicken, onions, and carrots, whole or cut in uniform pieces, in rows with chicken at edge of casserole. Sprinkle chicken generously with paprika.

Reheat in moderate oven (350°F. Mark 4) 15 to 20 minutes. Then sprinkle rice with chives. Serve with chicken gravy. Serves 5 to 6.

Prepare gravy: Use 2 tablespoons fat from frying and 3 tablespoons flour. Mix and add chicken stock, stirring constantly until the gravy thickens. Season to taste.

Variations: A boiler may also be used. Cook chicken in seasoned water 2½ to 3 hours until tender when tested with a fork. Drain, cut into pieces. Coat with seasoned flour and seasoning given in recipe. Brown and proceed as above.

BAKED CHICKEN AND CORN

1 3¾-pound ready-to-cook chicken,
    cut up
2 tablespoons butter or margarine
1 11-ounce can whole kernel corn
Milk
2 ounces fine dry breadcrumbs
2 lightly beaten eggs
½ teaspoon salt

Season chicken pieces with salt and pepper. Brown on all sides in melted butter in a large frying pan over medium heat.

Drain corn. Measure liquid and add enough milk to make 12 fluid ounces.

Mix the corn, crumbs, eggs, and salt together. Slowly stir in milk mixture. Spread evenly in 2-quart greased shallow casserole. Arrange chicken pieces on top. Pour over the juices left in the frying pan.

Bake uncovered in moderate oven (350°F. Mark 4) until chicken is tender, about 1 hour. Serves 4.

COUNTRY-STYLE BAKED CHICKEN

2 eggs
2 teaspoons Worcestershire sauce
1 teaspoon onion juice
2 3-pound ready-to-cook roasting
    chickens, cut in pieces
8 ounces fine dry breadcrumbs
1 teaspoon sage
½ teaspoon paprika
Pinch of garlic salt
½ teaspoon salt
⅛ teaspoon pepper
4 tablespoons vegetable oil
4 rashers of bacon
4-5 tablespoons milk

Beat eggs, Worcestershire sauce, and onion juice until thoroughly mixed.

Dip chicken pieces in this mixture, then roll in a mixture of breadcrumbs and seasonings.

Pour oil in a flat baking dish. Arrange chicken in dish, with bacon rashers spread over it.

Bake in moderate oven (350°F. Mark 4) 1 hour. Add milk. Cover with a lid or foil and continue to bake for 15 to 20 minutes. Serves 6.

BAKED CHICKEN WITH OYSTERS

1 chicken, cut up (2½ to 3½ pounds)
4-5 ounces golden crumbs
½ teaspoon salt
Pinch of pepper (optional)
8 ounces butter or margarine
½ pint oysters, shelled or 1¾-ounce
    can oysters, drained
¾ pint top of the milk or single cream

Roll chicken pieces in crumbs seasoned with salt and pepper. Brown in half the butter and place in a deep casserole.

Roll oysters in crumbs and fit into spaces between chicken.

Heat milk and melt remaining butter in it. Pour over the chicken pieces. Sprinkle over the remaining crumbs.

Cover and bake in moderate oven (350°F. Mark 4) until chicken is tender, about 1 hour.

Remove the lid during last 15 minutes to let the top brown. Add more milk during baking if mixture gets dry. Serves 4 to 6.

CHICKEN RAMEKINS— NORMANDY

1 chicken (3½ pounds)
Salt and pepper
2 ounces flour
3 ounces butter
10 fluid ounces cider
10 fluid ounces bouillon
1 small can (3 ounces) mushrooms
6 medium potatoes
4 tablespoons hot milk
2 eggs

Cut chicken into pieces. Dredge them in well seasoned flour. Fry in 4 tablespoons butter until lightly browned and almost tender. Remove from heat. When cool enough to handle, remove meat from bones and cut into pieces.

Place chicken in 6 ramekins. Sprinkle with flour, then add 2 tablespoons cider and 2 tablespoons bouillon to each ramekin.

Bake in moderate oven (350°F. Mark 4) 15 minutes. Then add mushrooms and additional liquid if chicken is cooking dry and bake 10 minutes longer, or until chicken is tender.

Meanwhile boil the potatoes, drain and mash. Add 2 tablespoons butter to them, 1 teaspoon salt, small pinch of pepper, and hot milk. Then beat in the eggs.

The potatoes will be soft and yellow. Cover each ramekin with potato-egg mixture, allowing room at the edges for expansion. Brown under grill. Serves

CHICKEN FRICASSÉE CASSEROLE

1 4-pound chicken
About 2½ ounces flour
1 teaspoon salt
Small pinch of pepper
3 tablespoons fat
2 ounces chopped celery
2 to 3 tablespoons chopped onion
2 pimientos, chopped
1 10½-ounce can condensed mush-
    room soup
10 fluid ounces water

Cut chicken into pieces. Rub them with seasoned flour. Brown in hot fat. Remove chicken to casserole.

Cook celery and onion in fat until golden. Drain off excess fat and add to chicken.

Add pimientos, soup, and water. Stir lightly to blend.

Cover and bake in slow oven (325°F. Mark 3) until tender, 1½ to 2 hours. Serve from the casserole or around a mound of hot boiled rice on a platter. Serves 6.

Chicken Fricassée Casserole

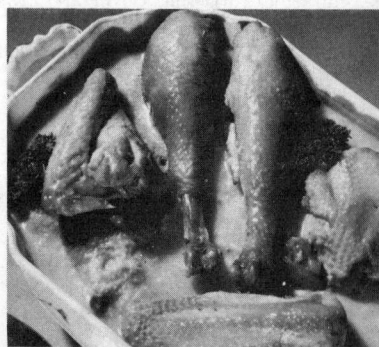

FRICASSÉED CHICKEN (GERMAN STYLE)

1 ready-to-cook chicken, about 3 pounds, cut up
1 medium onion
4 whole black peppercorns
2 cloves
½ bay leaf
1 tablespoon salt
3 tablespoons chicken fat
7 tablespoons flour
1¼ pints chicken stock
½ teaspoon grated lemon rind
¼ teaspoon black pepper
2 to 3 tablespoons white wine
1 egg yolk
4 tablespoons cream

Place chicken pieces in a flameproof casserole and just cover with boiling water. Add onion, whole peppercorns, cloves, bay leaf, and salt. Cook gently until meat is tender, 2½ to 3 hours.

Lift out chicken and strain broth.

Prepare fricassée gravy: Mix chicken fat and flour in saucepan. Add the stock and place over heat. Cook, stirring constantly, until it thickens.

Add lemon rind and pepper. Add wine. Taste for additional seasoning. Simmer about 5 minutes.

Place chicken in gravy to heat.

Blend egg yolk and cream in a small bowl or cup. To it add, while stirring, some of the hot gravy. Then pour back into chicken and gravy mixture and cook 2 or 3 minutes, stirring constantly. Serve at once. Serves 5 to 6.

GRILLED CHICKEN (PAKISTAN STYLE)

1 ready-to-cook roasting chicken, not over 2½ pounds
2 tablespoons melted fat
½ large onion, finely chopped
½ garlic clove, chopped
2 green chillies (canned), finely chopped
¼ teaspoon each ground ginger, black pepper, cloves, cardamom, and cumin seeds
½ teaspoon salt
Juice from chillies

Split chicken in half lengthways. Break drumstick, hip, and wing joints to keep bird flat during grilling. Skewer wing and leg to body to make a compact flat piece of chicken.

Brush with melted fat and then rub with a paste made from the seasonings and chilli juice.

Place chicken pieces skin-side-down in grill pan (not on rack). Place the pan at least 7 inches from the heat. Chicken should be grilled slowly. When rib cage is browned, 10 to 15 minutes, turn chicken over. Grill 15 minutes. Brush with melted fat as needed. Total grilling time is about 45 minutes. Serves 2.

CHICKEN WITH RICE (GREEK)

1 ready-to-cook young chicken, 2½ to 3 pounds, jointed
6 ounces butter or margarine
1 medium onion, chopped
1 teaspoon salt
¼ teaspoon black pepper
1 5-ounce can tomato paste
½ teaspoon sugar
1¼ pints boiling water
8 ounces uncooked rice

Brown chicken pieces in a flameproof casserole in 4 ounces butter, turning to brown evenly.

Add onion, salt, pepper, tomato paste, sugar, and 2 or 3 tablespoons water. Cover and cook gently until chicken is barely tender.

Add boiling water. Sprinkle rice over top. Cover and cook until rice is tender, about 40 minutes.

Arrange chicken and rice on serving dish. Melt remaining butter and pour over rice and chicken. Serves 4 to 5.

CHICKEN BELVEDERE

1 clove garlic, halved
4 tablespoons salad oil
1 young chicken, 2½ pounds ready-to-cook weight, jointed
1½ teaspoons salt
½ teaspoon pepper
½ teaspoon oregano
1 clove garlic, chopped
½ 7½-ounce can mushrooms
2 ounces sliced celery
1 5-ounce can tomato paste

Brown halved garlic clove in hot oil; remove garlic.

Season chicken with salt, pepper, oregano, and chopped garlic. Fry chicken in hot oil in a frying pan 10 to 12 minutes, or until golden brown.

Drain mushrooms, reserving liquid. Mix together mushroom liquid and water to make 10 fluid ounces, celery, and tomato paste; add to chicken.

Cover; simmer 30 minutes; add mushrooms; simmer 15 minutes.

Serves 4.

FRICASSÉE OF CHICKEN POPUCH

1 3-pound roasting chicken, jointed
1½ tablespoons flour
4 ounces butter or margarine
6 fresh mushrooms
1 tablespoon salt
¼ teaspoon pepper
16 fluid ounces double cream
4 tablespoons brandy

Roll the chicken pieces in flour. Heat butter in frying pan; add chicken and slowly cook, covered, until golden brown, about 20 minutes.

Peel mushrooms, quarter, and add to chicken. Cook, covered, 5 minutes longer. Add salt, pepper, and cream and cook, covered, slowly 20 minutes. Add the brandy just before serving. Serves 3.

KOREAN CHICKEN AND PORK

1 roasting chicken, 2½ to 3 pounds, jointed
½ pound pork, cut in 1-inch cubes
4 fluid ounces vinegar
2 cloves garlic, crushed
3 bay leaves
3 tablespoons soy sauce
1½ teaspoons salt
⅛ teaspoon pepper
2 ounces fat or 2 to 3 tablespoons oil

Put chicken pieces and pork into 5-pint saucepan.

Add vinegar, garlic, bay leaves, soy sauce, and seasonings; set aside for 1 hour. Then add enough boiling water just to cover the meat.

Simmer over low heat until meat is tender. Remove garlic, bay leaves, and any excess liquid. Add fat; fry pork and chicken, one piece at a time, so that each piece is nicely browned.

After the meat has been removed from the pan, add 4 fluid ounces of the meat stock and stir to remove any bits of chicken or pork from the bottom of the pan. Simmer for about 5 minutes and pour over chicken and pork. Serve hot with boiled rice. Serves 4.

QUICK CURRIED CHICKEN (HAWAIIAN)

1 roasting chicken, 3 to 4 pounds
3 tablespoons salad oil
1 clove garlic, crushed
6 to 8 spring onions, including green stems, cut in 1 inch lengths
Salt and pepper
4 fluid ounces hot water
About ½ pint creamy milk
3 tablespoons flour
1 to 2 tablespoons curry powder

Ask the butcher to chop the legs, thighs, wings, breast, wishbone, and back of chicken crossways, right through the bone and meat, into pieces about an inch long. At home, cut the thickest pieces of meat into smaller chunks. (There will be about 50 chunks of chicken altogether.)

Add crushed garlic to oil in a large frying pan and heat slowly 5 minutes. Remove garlic.

Put in chicken pieces and cook over medium heat about 15 minutes, turning occasionally, until lightly browned.

Sprinkle with salt and pepper, add chopped onions and hot water, cover tightly and simmer about 20 minutes, until chicken is tender.

Mix the milk, flour, and curry powder together in a pint jar or bottle. Put on lid and shake until smooth, then add this liquid to chicken and cook, stirring gently, until the gravy thickens smoothly.

Serve on a bed of hot boiled rice. Serves 6 to 8.

CHICKEN BREASTS EPICUREAN

2 whole chicken breasts
1 slightly beaten egg
4 ounces fine dry breadcrumbs
1 teaspoon salt
¼ teaspoon thyme
¼ teaspoon marjoram
¼ teaspoon paprika
Fat for frying
8 fluid ounces pineapple juice
2 tablespoons lemon juice
1 tablespoon cornflour
¼ teaspoon curry powder
1 tablespoon sugar
2 tablespoons sherry
4 slices hot toast
Slivered almonds

Split breasts in half. Remove bones but keep meat in one piece.

Dip chicken in beaten egg. Roll in crumbs mixed with salt, thyme, marjoram, and paprika.

Fry chicken in ¼-inch of hot fat in a frying pan until brown on both sides.

Drain fat from pan. Mix the juices, cornflour, curry, and sugar. Pour over chicken.

Cover and cook slowly 25 minutes. Then stir in sherry. Serve chicken breasts on hot toast. Top with slivered almonds. Serves 4.

CHICKEN IN WINE-CHERRY SAUCE

2½ to 3½ pounds chicken, cut up
    for frying
1¼ 17-ounce cans dark sweet
    cherries
½ bottle port or Burgundy
3 tablespoons lemon juice
2 cloves garlic, chopped
¼ teaspoon ginger
½ teaspoon oregano
2 ounces flour
2 teaspoons salt
Pinch of pepper
2 ounces cooking fat or 2-3 table-
    spoons salad oil
1 chicken bouillon cube

Wash chicken; dry. Drain cherries; make marinade by mixing ½ pint of the cherry syrup with wine, lemon juice, garlic, ginger, and oregano. Pour over chicken and set aside for several hours or overnight. Then remove chicken; wipe dry, reserving the marinade.

Mix the flour, salt, and pepper together; coat each piece of chicken with flour mixture.

Heat the fat or salad oil in a large frying pan; add chicken and cook over medium heat until brown on all sides.

Strain garlic from marinade; pour over chicken. Bring to the boil; add bouillon cube and stir to dissolve.

Reduce heat and simmer about 30 minutes. Add cherries; cook about 15 minutes longer. Serves 4 to 6.

EASY CHICKEN BREASTS SUPREME

1 10½-ounce can condensed cream of
    mushroom soup
1 teaspoon poultry seasoning
¼ teaspoon salt
4 fluid ounces milk
4-6 large frozen chicken breasts
1 ounce grated Cheddar cheese

In a large frying pan or flameproof casserole with a lid, mix soup, poultry seasoning, salt, and milk together well. Bring to boil over low heat.

Add frozen chicken breasts. Cover and cook over low heat 15 minutes.

Remove the lid; with the help of forks, carefully separate chicken pieces.

Place breasts, with meaty sides down, in sauce. Cook, covered, 20 to 25 minutes longer, or until tender.

Sprinkle with cheese; put under grill long enough to melt and lightly brown cheese. Serves 4 to 6.

TARRAGON CHICKEN

1 3½-pound dressed roasting
    chicken, cut in pieces
Salt
½ lemon
½ teaspoon celery salt
1 teaspoon Aromat
¼ teaspoon pepper
4 ounces butter or margarine
1 teaspoon dried or 3 teaspoons
    fresh tarragon

Soak chicken in heavily salted cold water for 30 minutes. Drain and pat dry.

Rub thoroughly with lemon. Sprinkle with mixture of ½ teaspoon salt, celery salt, Aromat, and pepper.

Place in a shallow pan skin-side-down. Dot with 2 tablespoons of butter. Preheat grill and brown chicken pieces lightly on both sides.

Meanwhile, melt remaining butter with tarragon and cook over low heat for 10 minutes.

Pour butter evenly over chicken and continue to grill 5 minutes on each side under medium heat.

Then transfer chicken pieces to a baking dish and bake in moderate oven (350°F. Mark 4) 25 minutes, basting twice with sauce. Serve with cranberry sauce. Serves 4.

SWEDISH CHICKEN

1 roasting chicken, cut up
3 ounces flour
2 teaspoons salt
16 fluid ounces evaporated milk
    or single cream

Coat chicken with flour and place in a heavy frying pan.

Mix salt with milk or cream and pour over chicken. Cover tightly and simmer over low heat 45 minutes.

As chicken cooks, the milk will thicken and the chicken will brown lightly. Serves 4 to 5.

HAWAIIAN CHICKEN LUAU

1 2½-pound chicken, cut-up for
    frying
Flour
4 ounces butter or margarine
1 teaspoon salt
About 8 fluid ounces water
8 fluid ounces hot milk
4 ounces desiccated coconut
2 pounds fresh spinach
2 tablespoons finely chopped onion
½ teaspoon salt

Dip pieces of chicken in flour.

Melt butter in a heavy frying pan. Add chicken and fry until lightly brown. Add salt and ½ pint water. Cover and simmer until chicken is tender (about 30 minutes).

Pour hot milk over the coconut and leave for 15 minutes; then simmer 10 minutes.

Wash spinach, remove stems. Lay bunches of leaves on a chopping board and cut into 2-inch strips. Boil with onion in salted water about 5 minutes. Drain.

Add spinach and coconut with milk to chicken. Simmer 3 minutes. Serve hot. Serves 6.

BUFFET CHICKEN CURRY

5-pound chicken, cut in pieces
About 2½ ounces butter or margarine
    (part chicken fat may be used)
¼ large onion, chopped
1 to 2 tablespoons curry powder
About 2 ounces flour
12 fluid ounces milk
16 fluid ounces chicken stock
¼ teaspoon sugar
Salt
2 tablespoons sherry

Poach chicken in a pan or cook in a pressure cooker until tender.

Melt butter and sauté onion until soft and golden. Blend in curry powder and flour.

Gradually add milk and strained chicken stock; cook, stirring constantly, until mixture is thick and smooth.

Transfer to a double boiler. Add sugar and salt to taste.

Remove cooked chicken meat from bones, cut in fairly good-sized pieces and add to sauce. Cover and cook over gently boiling water for 30 minutes. Just before serving add sherry. Serve with boiled rice and a selection of curry accompaniments. Serves 6 to 8.

Curried Lamb: Substitute cooked lamb for chicken in above.

Duck or Duckling

Duck producers aim to have young ducks ready for sale at 7 or 8 weeks of age. About 90 per cent of the ducks on the retail market are frozen, and ready to cook. Most ducks are sold as ducklings or young ducks and usually weigh 4 to 6 pounds.

Small ducks can be cut up and fried or grilled. Larger whole ducks can be put on a spit and cooked over a barbecue or on a rôtisserie.

When buying, allow at least 1 pound ready-to-cook weight per person.

Thawing time in the refrigerator for frozen ducks weighing 3 to 5 pounds is 1 to 1½ days.

ROAST DUCKLING

Ducklings today are prepared for roasting just like chickens. Place duckling breast-side-up on a rack in a shallow open pan in slow oven (325°F. Mark 3).

If roasted for 1½ to 2 hours or until meat thermometer inserted in stuffing records an internal temperature of 165°F., the duckling will be moderately well done but juicy and delicious. Allow 18 minutes per pound for dressed weight (5 to 7 pounds).

For very well done duckling, the internal temperature should read about 185°F. Allow 22 to 25 minutes per pound.

For ducklings with drawn (ready-to-cook) weight of 3½ to 5 pounds, allow 25 minutes per pound for medium well done, 30 to 35 minutes per pound for very well done.

When well done, the thick flesh on the drumstick feels soft when pressed, and leg joint moves easily.

Roast Fat Duckling: If a duck has excess fat, prick the skin over back and round tail to let fat drain off in cooking. Roast as above, but pour off fat as it accumulates in the pan to keep the pan juices light-coloured and delicately flavoured. Allow at least 30 minutes per pound, then test if the bird is cooked. No basting is needed.

Stuffing Hints for Duckling: Tart, well seasoned stuffings (especially fruits) combine well with rich duck meat. Some cooks just put a whole orange or a whole, cored apple inside; others fill small birds with chopped onion and celery, or chopped onion and quartered apple. A stuffing of rice and apricot or other dried fruit is another favourite.

Glazed Roast Duckling: Roast as directed in Roast Duckling. Remove from oven just before duck is done. Raise oven temperature to very hot (450°F. Mark 8).

Mix together well: 8 ounces apricot preserves, 3-4 tablespoons clover honey, 1 tablespoon Cointreau or other orange-flavoured liqueur, and 1 tablespoon brandy. Coat the duck with this thick glaze and return to oven until the glaze caramelizes, 10 to 15 minutes.

ROAST DUCK BIGARADE

Bigarade is the French term for the bitter or Seville orange, which should be used in preparing this dish.

Prepare duck for roasting. Do not stuff. Season with salt and pepper. If you like, fill cavity with orange slices.

Roast, uncovered, on rack in slow oven (325°F. Mark 3), allowing 20 to 25 minutes per pound.

Do not baste. Prick skin several times and turn to brown all over.

Skim fat from pan juices and prepare gravy, using 4 fluid ounces orange juice and 4 fluid ounces water.

Boil whole peel of 1 orange in water to cover for 5 minutes. Drain, scrape out white pulp and discard. Cut peel into thin julienne strips and add to gravy. Season to taste.

If you like, a little lemon juice, white wine, or Curaçao may be added.

GRILLED DUCKLING

Ask your butcher to prepare the duckling by removing the backbone and keel from breastbone.

Place duck skin-side-down on ungreased pan under preheated moderate grill.

Grill for a total of 20 to 25 minutes on each side, turning pieces when golden brown. Baste if you like. (For more detailed directions, see Grilled Chicken.)

With Honey Glaze: Just before serving, brush duckling with a mixture of 2 tablespoons honey and 1 teaspoon mixed herbs. Return to grill for 2 minutes. Serve immediately.

DUCK EN CASSEROLE

1   duck, 4 to 5 pounds
2½ ounces flour
1½ teaspoons salt
¼   teaspoon pepper
½   teaspoon Aromat

2½ ounces butter or margarine
1   small onion, finely chopped
1   teaspoon powdered mint
1¼ pints boiling water
3   chicken bouillon cubes
1   20-ounce can peas, drained

Clean duck well, removing pin feathers. Dry and cut in sections as for fricassée. Dip duck pieces in mixture of flour, salt, pepper, and Aromat. Fry in hot fat in a frying pan until lightly browned on all sides.

Transfer to 2-quart casserole. Add onion and mint. Pour in water in which the bouillon cubes have been dissolved.

Cover and bake in moderate oven (350°F. Mark 4) until tender, about 1¼ hours. Add drained peas about 10 minutes before duck is done. Serves 4.

DUCKLING AU VIN

2   tablespoons corn oil
2   3-pound ducklings, quartered
2   teaspoons salt
1   tablespoon Worcestershire sauce
4   ounces sliced celery
1   large onion, sliced
16 fluid ounces white wine
Chicken stock (optional)
2   tablespoons butter
2   tablespoons flour
1   7½-ounce can button
      mushrooms, drained
2   16-ounce cans white onions,
      drained

Heat oil in a frying pan. Brown ducklings well on all sides. Drain off excess fat.

Sprinkle duckling with salt and Worcestershire sauce. Add celery, onion, and white wine. Cover tightly. Cook over a medium heat, turning occasionally, for 1 hour or until duckling is tender. Add chicken stock if necessary during cooking if liquid starts to evaporate.

When duckling is tender, transfer pieces to an ovenproof dish and keep warm.

Cream butter. Stir in flour to form a paste. Skim excess fat from the stock in the pan. Add paste to the hot stock. Cook over a low heat stirring constantly until smooth and thick. Add mushrooms and onions. Reheat and pour hot sauce over duckling. Serve with wild rice and peas cooked with white grapes. Serves 6 to 8.

Duckling Au Vin

FRIED DUCKLING

1 duckling, 3½ to 4 pounds
4 ounces flour
2 teaspoons salt
¼ teaspoon pepper
2 teaspoons paprika
2 ounces butter or margarine
2 ounces fat
4 tablespoons water

Cut duckling into pieces, or, if quick-frozen, thaw according to directions on the packet. Rinse in cold water, and drain.

Mix flour, salt, pepper, and paprika in a paper bag. Shake 2 or 3 pieces of duckling at a time in the bag in order to coat thoroughly with flour.

Heat butter and enough of the fat in a heavy frying pan to make a layer of fat ¼ inch deep. With kitchen tongs, place duckling in hot fat skin-side-down. Brown and turn.

Add water and cover tightly. Reduce heat and cook slowly about 1½ hours, or until duckling is tender. To crisp the crust, remove the lid during last 10 minutes. Serves 4 to 5.

Oven-Fried Duckling: Prepare as above; after adding water, bake, covered, in moderate oven (350°F. Mark 4) about 1 hour. Remove lid and bake about 30 minutes longer.

DUCKLING QUARTERS, BAKED IN FOIL

1 4½-pound ready-to-cook duckling, quartered
1 clove garlic
½ teaspoon salt
¼ teaspoon pepper
1 teaspoon Aromat
8 small white onions
1 large juicy grapefruit, peeled and cut in sections
4 fluid ounces giblet stock
2 teaspoons cornflour
4 fluid ounces white wine

Rub the cleaned duckling with garlic. Sprinkle with a mixture of salt, pepper, and Aromat.

Arrange skin-side-down in a roasting pan lined with heavy foil. Brown in hot oven (425°F. Mark 7), turning several times so both sides are browned. Pour off fat.

Arrange onions and grapefruit segments over and around duckling. Crimp another piece of foil over pan to fit snugly.

Bake in moderate oven (350°F. Mark 4) for 1 hour, or until tender.

Discard grapefruit segments. Transfer duck and onions to a warm platter.

Skim excess fat from pan juices. Add the stock. Bring to a boil and thicken gravy with cornflour mixed with wine. Season to taste and serve in a separate dish. Serves 4.

DEVILLED DUCKLING

1 4-pound ready-to-cook duckling
1½ tablespoons soy sauce
2 small onions
2 celery tops
1 teaspoon dry mustard
½ teaspoon powdered ginger
¼ teaspoon pepper

Clean and rinse duckling; pat dry. Brush inside and out with soy sauce.

Insert onions and celery tops into cavity. Pin neck skin to back with skewers.

Stir mustard, ginger, and pepper until well mixed; sprinkle a good coating over the soy sauce-moistened duck.

Place on a rack in a roasting pan. Roast in a preheated hot oven (400°F. Mark 6) ½ hour. By now a nice crust should be formed.

Reduce heat to slow oven (325°F. Mark 3) and continue to roast for 1 hour, or until duckling is tender. The crisp skin is so spicy and delicious that the duckling is equally good served hot or cold. Serves 4.

ROAST DUCK WITH ORANGE-WINE SAUCE (FRENCH)

1 duck
8 fluid ounces orange juice
4 fluid ounces port
1 teaspoon salt
1 whole orange, preferably seedless

Rinse the duck inside and outside with clear water. Dry well with a paper towel. Truss and place on a rack in a roasting pan breast-side-up.

Roast in slow oven (325°F. Mark 3) for 35 minutes per pound. Baste every 10 minutes with a mixture of the orange juice, port, and salt.

Cut the whole orange (with skin) in thin slices. Arrange slices around the duck and on rack in the roasting pan (not in the sauce) about 10 minutes before the end of the cooking time. Garnish the duck with the orange slices for serving.

Allow 1 pound dressed weight per person when estimating number of servings.

HOW TO SKIN DUCKLING

With a sharp-pointed knife, cut the skin from the neck to the vent, first along breast of duck, then along backbone.

Loosen the skin by running knife underneath, close to flesh of duck. Peel skin back as it is loosened, cutting the skin where necessary but keeping the flesh intact.

It is really easy and simple to remove the skin since there is a solid layer of fat between the skin and flesh, but, if you prefer, ask your butcher to skin the duck for you.

BRAISED DUCKLING
(Basic Recipe)

Cut the cleaned duckling into quarters. Place skin-side-up on rack in shallow roasting pan. Roast in slow oven (325°F. Mark 3) for 1 hour.

Meanwhile, cook giblets and prepare your chosen sauce, using duck stock (from cooking giblets) or fruit juice.

Transfer duck to a flameproof casserole. Pour sauce over duck and cover tightly. Continue braising in sauce until duck is tender, about 30 minutes longer.

For a brown finish, brush duck with 1 teaspoon mixed herbs and 2 tablespoons of honey before cooking in sauce.

ROAST DUCK WITH WINE SAUCE

1 4- to 5-pound duck
1 bottle claret or other red wine
4-5 tablespoons brandy
¼ medium onion, chopped
2 tablespoons chopped parsley
¾ teaspoon salt
¼ teaspoon pepper
½ pound sliced mushrooms
2 tablespoons flour
4 tablespoons cold water

Cut duck in quarters. Arrange pieces on rack in shallow roasting pan. Brown in hot oven (400°F. Mark 6) for 30 minutes. Pour off all fat except 4 tablespoons. Remove rack from pan and place duck in bottom.

Add wine and brandy to chopped onion, parsley, salt, pepper, and mushrooms. Pour over duck. Return to oven; reduce heat to moderate (375°F. Mark 5). Roast 1½ hours, or until duck is tender; baste frequently with sauce. Remove from pan and keep hot while preparing gravy.

Blend flour in cold water until smooth. Add to liquid in pan. Cook, stirring constantly, until it thickens. Add salt and pepper to taste.

Place duck on hot dish and serve sauce in a bowl; or place duck on a dish and spoon over the wine sauce. Serves 4.

ROAST DUCK—CHINESE STYLE

4 teaspoons sugar
1 teaspoon salt
4 teaspoons honey
3 teaspoons soy sauce
3 tablespoons chicken bouillon
1 4-pound duckling, cleaned

Place all ingredients except duckling in a large mixing bowl. Mix well.

Add the duckling to the marinade. Soak duckling for 40 minutes, turning occasionally.

Remove duckling from bowl and place on rack in a roasting pan, adding a few tablespoons of water to prevent smoking.

Roast in slow oven (325°F. Mark 3) until tender, turning occasionally, about 1¾ hours. Serve immediately. Serves 4.

Duckling Italienne

DUCKLING ITALIENNE

1 duckling, 4 to 5 pounds,
 ready-to-cook weight
2 tablespoons fat
½ medium onion, finely chopped
1 ounce finely diced celery
½ pint tomato sauce
1 teaspoon mixed herbs
1½ teaspoons sugar
1½ teaspoons salt
⅛ teaspoon oregano
12 ounces spaghetti, cooked

Wash duckling in cold water and dry
carefully. Cut off wing tips. Cut duckling in pieces. Melt fat in a deep frying
pan. Add pieces of duckling and brown
on all sides over moderate heat. Add
onion and celery and cook for about 5
minutes longer.

Mix the tomato sauce, mixed herbs,
sugar, salt, and oregano together.
Pour over duckling. Cover tightly and
bring to boil. Cook until the duckling
is tender, about 45 minutes.

Meanwhile, cook giblets and neck in
boiling salted water until tender. Cook
spaghetti.

When ready to serve, remove pieces
of duckling from sauce. Pour off fat.
Chop giblets and add to tomato sauce
if you like. Drain spaghetti then pour
sauce over spaghetti and mix well.
Arrange spaghetti on serving dish. Top
with pieces of duckling and serve immediately with a tossed green salad.
Serves 6.

PINEAPPLE DUCK

1 4-pound duckling, quartered
2½ pints cold water
2 teaspoons salt
2 tablespoons salad oil or fat
12 fluid ounces duck stock
1 16-ounce can pineapple chunks,
 drained and juice reserved
¼ teaspoon ground ginger
1 medium green pepper, cut in
 small pieces
2 tablespoons cornflour
1 tablespoon soy sauce
⅛ teaspoon pepper
6 tablespoons pineapple juice

Place quartered duckling in saucepan. Add cold water and salt. Bring
to boil over high heat. Reduce heat,
cover, and simmer gently 45 minutes.

Remove duckling and drain thoroughly. Reserve stock.

Heat oil or fat in a large frying pan.
Add drained duckling and cook gently,
turning frequently, until golden brown,
about 15 minutes.

Add the duck stock, pineapple
chunks, ginger, and green pepper.
Cover and cook over moderate heat 15
minutes. Remove duck and keep warm.

Blend the cornflour with soy sauce,
pepper, and pineapple juice; stir into
the stock and pineapple mixture in the
frying pan. Stir until it thickens.

Return duck to sauce. Cover and
heat thoroughly, about 10 minutes.
Serve with hot boiled rice. Serves 4 to 5.

BRAISED DUCK IN BLACK CHERRY SAUCE

1 5- to 6-pound duckling, quartered
2 ounces fat
1 tablespoon duck fat
1 tablespoon chopped onion
12 fluid ounces duck stock
½ teaspoon salt
1 bay leaf
⅛ teaspoon marjoram
1 large can (17-20 ounces) black
 cherries
2 tablespoons cornflour

Brown duck quarters in fat in a
heavy saucepan; roast uncovered in
slow oven (325°F. Mark 3).

Meanwhile, cook giblets. Drain off
liquid. Allow fat to rise to top and
pour it off.

Place 1 tablespoon fat in saucepan.
Add onion. Cook over low heat about
3 minutes. Add duck stock, salt, bay
leaf and marjoram.

Drain cherries. Combine 4 fluid
ounces cherry juice and cornflour. Stir
into hot stock. Cook, stirring constantly, until sauce thickens and boils.
Remove bay leaf.

Add cherries and heat thoroughly.
Serve hot over braised duck quarters.

If you like, substitute 4 fluid ounces
red wine for 4 fluid ounces stock.
Serves 4.

CANTONESE DUCK

5- to 6-pound duckling, dressed
 weight
4 tablespoons sherry
2 tablespoons honey
Salt and pepper

With a sharp pointed knife, cut
through duck skin along centre of
breast from neck to vent. Loosen skin
by pulling away from flesh and at the
same time running knife underneath.

Cut skin where necessary, but keep
flesh intact. Discard skin.

Cut skinned duck into pieces and
place in a bowl.

Mix remaining ingredients together
and pour over duck meat. Cover and
let marinate in cool place 3 hours,
turning occasionally.

Place duck and marinade in large
covered frying pan and cook over low
heat until tender, about 45 minutes to
1 hour.

Serve immediately or, if a crisp
brown crust is desired, place pieces of
duck in uncovered baking dish and
heat in moderate oven (350°F. Mark 4)
at least 15 minutes. Serve hot or cold.
Serves 4.

BRAISED DUCKLING, BURGUNDY

1 duckling, 5 to 6 pounds, cut in
 pieces
½ garlic clove, minced
2 tablespoons flour
1 bottle Burgundy or other red
 wine
1 7½-ounce can mushrooms
1 small bay leaf
¼ teaspoon rosemary
1 teaspoon salt
1 teaspoon Aromat

Remove skin and fat from the duckling pieces.

Cook skin and fat with giblets and
neck; drain off liquid. Chill until fat
rises to top; pour off.

Put 2 tablespoons of this fat into a
heavy frying pan. Heat; brown duckling in hot fat; remove to casserole
with cooked giblets.

Add garlic to fat; cook 1 minute.
Stir in flour. Add wine, mushrooms,
bay leaf, rosemary, salt, and Aromat.
Cook over low heat, stirring, until
sauce thickens; pour into casserole and
cover.

Bake in moderate oven (350°F. Mark
4) 1½ hours, or until duckling is well
done and tender. Serves 4.

Braised Duckling, Burgundy

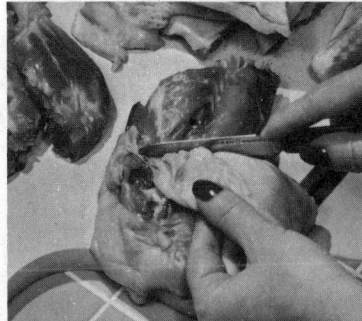

Pigeon

Pigeons are best at the age of 4 to 5 weeks and at a weight of 12 to 14 ounces. The flesh is very tender. Very young pigeons are sometimes called squabs.

GRILLED PIGEON ON TOAST

Split the cleaned dressed birds down the back and spread open. Rub the meat with lemon juice, brush with melted butter, margarine, or bacon fat and sprinkle with salt and pepper.

Place on greased rack in grill pan and grill under moderate heat 15 to 20 minutes. Turn to brown both sides.

Serve on hot buttered toast and spread with pigeon giblet paste. Allow 1 whole small pigeon, or ½ of a large pigeon per person.

Pigeon Giblet Paste: Simmer giblets of 3 pigeons in water to cover for 15 minutes, or until tender. Mash, season to taste with salt and paprika and add 1 tablespoon Worcestershire sauce and 2 tablespoons of any tart jelly.

ROAST PIGEON

Rub the inside of cleaned pigeon with salt. Stuff lightly with wild rice or mushroom stuffing.

Place on rack in roasting pan. Spread with melted butter, margarine, or bacon fat. Sprinkle with salt and dust with flour.

Roast, uncovered, in slow oven (325°F. Mark 3) 45 minutes, or until tender. Baste frequently with a mixture of about 2½ ounces butter or margarine, about 4½ tablespoons boiling water, and 4 ounces redcurrant jelly stirred in. Remove the roasted birds to a hot serving dish.

Thicken the pan juices with 1 tablespoon flour mixed with a little water to make a smooth paste; bring to boiling point, cook 2 minutes and serve with the birds. Allow 1 small or ½ large pigeon per person.

CASSEROLE OF PIGEONS

4 pigeons
Salt and pepper
12 ounces uncooked rice
½ pound whole mushrooms, washed
1 packet frozen peas, thawed just enough to separate
8 small peeled white onions
2 small dills, chopped
Chopped pigeon livers
8 fluid ounces chicken stock
½ bottle dry white wine

Ask the butcher to clean the pigeons but do not split them. Keep the livers and add to casserole. Season pigeons well inside and out.

Brown rice in a dry frying pan over low heat. Place in layer in a deep casserole. Place pigeons on rice. Put mushrooms, peas, onions, dills, and livers around the birds.

Heat stock and wine but do not boil; add to casserole.

Cover and cook in moderate oven (350°F. Mark 4) until pigeons are tender, about 1 hour. Serves 4.

PIGEONS IN WINE SAUCE WITH WHITE GRAPES

4 pigeons, cleaned
2 ounces softened butter or margarine
1 teaspoon salt
4-5 tablespoons chicken consommé
4-5 tablespoons white wine
¾ pound seedless white grapes

Rub pigeons with butter. Sprinkle cavities with salt. Place in a buttered casserole; cover and bake in moderate oven (375°F. Mark 5) for 10 minutes.

Add consommé and wine. Cover again and continue to bake in slow oven (325°F. Mark 3) 45 minutes, or until tender. Five minutes before pigeons are done, add grapes. Serves 4.

Geese

Geese generally are sold young because weight gained after the first 11 weeks is mostly in the form of fat.

Chilled or frozen ready-to-cook young geese (goslings) usually weigh from 6 to 12 pounds. Young geese have tender, flavourful meat that makes a delicious roast. Small geese braise well cut up. Thawing time in the refrigerator for frozen geese weighing 4 to 14 pounds is 1 to 2 days.

ROAST GOOSE

When buying goose, allow 1 to 1¼ pounds per person. Goose is cleaned, stuffed, trussed, and roasted like chicken. If very fat, prick the skin lightly in several places with a sharp-pointed fork after the goose has baked for an hour. This allows some of the fat to drain out.

Roast on a rack in slow oven (325°F. Mark 3) allowing 25 to 30 minutes per pound for total roasting. A 10- to 12-pound goose will require 3½ to 4½ hours. Test if cooked the same as for chicken.

Make gravy for goose, using 4 tablespoons each of pan juices and flour and 1 pint stock prepared by cooking the giblets in seasoned water.

BOHEMIAN ROAST GOOSE-POTATO STUFFING

5 large potatoes
1-2 tablespoons chopped onion
1 tablespoon chopped parsley
1 teaspoon caraway seed
1 egg

1 tablespoon melted poultry fat
1 roasting goose
Salt and pepper to taste

Wash potatoes. Boil with skins on. When done, peel, mash and add onion, parsley, caraway seed, egg, and fat. Mix well and season to taste.

Wash and dry goose. Remove excess fat. Stuff and truss.

Melt down excess fat in pan on top of the stove. Rub melted fat into goose. Sprinkle with flour, salt and pepper.

Place on rack in roasting pan. Do not add water. Prick skin several times to let fat run out.

Roast, uncovered, in slow oven (325°F. Mark 3) 20 to 25 minutes per pound. Baste every 15 minutes. Serves 6 to 8.

Gravy: Remove all but 2 tablespoons fat from roasting pan. Sift into pan 3 tablespoons flour. Blend smoothly with fat. Add 1¼ pints water.

Place pan over low heat and stir constantly until gravy thickens, blending in brown juice from bottom of pan. Season with salt and pepper.

FRICASSÉE OF GOOSE (GAENSEKLEIN)

Back, wings, neck, gizzard, and heart of goose
Ginger, salt and pepper
1 clove garlic, chopped
½ onion, sliced
2 sticks of celery, diced
2 tablespoons fat
2 tablespoons flour
½ pint goose stock
1 teaspoon chopped parsley

Season meat well with salt, pepper, ginger, and garlic. Set aside for about 12 hours or overnight.

Cover goose pieces with boiling water; add onion and celery. Simmer gently until meat is tender, about 2 hours.

When done, remove meat from the cooking liquid. Heat fat; blend in flour, then gradually add the hot goose liquid. Cook until thickened, stirring constantly. Add parsley; simmer for several minutes and serve the sauce spooned over the cooked meat. Serve with dumplings. Serves 4.

Roast Goose

Game Birds

In general, before being cooked it is necessary to hang many freshly killed wild birds to tenderize and improve the flavour. The actual length of time to allow game birds to hang is best determined by preference and experience. For example, some people like their birds "high" and let them hang for 10 days or longer in a cool place. Two days is usually sufficient ripening time for most birds. Ducks must never be allowed to hang "until high".

The most commonly used wild birds are grouse, pheasant, quail, and wild duck. When bought, they are dressed, drawn, and if you like, cut up ready for use. Like other game, birds are lean and require generous use of extra fat during cooking to prevent drying out. The light-meated birds such as partridge and quail should always be cooked until well done. Dark-meated birds may be served rare.

Any of the stuffings used for domestic poultry may be used for game; however, wild rice stuffing is the favourite for game birds. The addition of tart apple or orange to bread stuffing is an improvement in strong-flavoured birds.

Cooking juices are made into gravy with a little wine frequently added, or a wine sauce may be made from the pan drippings. A tart jelly is a good accompaniment for roasted or grilled birds. The latter are generally served on toast.

HOW TO DRESS BIRDS

Ducks, geese and grouse are usually dry plucked. To do this, hang the bird up by one leg. Pluck the pinion and tail feathers first, then the small feathers from shanks and inside of thighs. Then pluck the remaining body feathers.

To pluck and avoid tearing the skin, grasp only a few feathers at a time and pull downward in the direction the feathers grow.

Game birds are drawn (entrails removed) in the same way as with domestic fowl.

FISH-EATING GAME BIRDS

The flavour of birds depends upon the type of food they eat. Birds that eat fish have a "fishy" flavour which some people find objectionable. This flavour may be eliminated by parboiling the birds for 10 to 20 minutes, depending upon size of birds.

Add to enough water to cover 2 birds 1 teaspoon baking soda and 1 teaspoon black pepper, then parboil.

Drain well and rub with salt and pepper. Tie a piece of bacon over breast. Brown the birds in melted butter in heavy flameproof casserole. Cover tightly and cook over low heat until tender, about 1½ hours. Add giblet stock during last part of cooking. Serve with gravy.

ROAST WILD DUCK OR WILD GOOSE

Cut off tail, removing oil sack. Draw and wipe with damp cloth. Rub inside with salt and pepper.

Fill with savoury stuffing or wild rice stuffing or omit stuffing and put a small stick of celery, or a whole apple or a whole onion in the cavity. If you like, add 1 tablespoon wine and 1 tablespoon melted butter. Close openings with small skewers. Truss wings to body.

Cover breast side with strips of fat salt pork or rashers of bacon, or rub skin with butter or oil. Sprinkle with salt and pepper.

Bake, uncovered, breast-side-up in slow oven (300°F. Mark 2) until cooked. Allow 15 to 20 minutes per pound or ½ to 1 hour, depending upon size of bird. Duck should be served rare; therefore take care to avoid overcooking. Baste frequently with juices from pan. Serve with gravy made from pan juices and giblet stock.

GRILLED WILD DUCK

Use young mallards. Cut off tail, removing oil sack. Split down the back. Draw and wipe well with a damp cloth. Do not wash.

Rub with salt and pepper and then with melted butter or oil, or spread with rashers of bacon.

Spread open and lay skin-side down on rack of grill pan. Grill under moderate heat until tender, 15 to 20 minutes, turning at least once. Take care to avoid overcooking.

Serve with melted butter seasoned with a little lemon juice and chopped parsley. A tart jelly is a natural accompaniment.

Pheasant Muscatel with Nutted Rice in Fluted Orange Cups.

PHEASANT MUSCATEL

3 1½-pound pheasants, dressed, split in half
½ lemon
Salt and pepper
About 2½ ounces butter or margarine
Juice of 3 oranges (save peel)
6 ounces white raisins
1 teaspoon grated lemon rind
4-5 tablespoons muscatel wine
½ pint chicken stock

Rinse pheasants inside and outside with warm water. Drain well.

Rub pheasants inside with lemon. Season with salt and pepper. Place in a roasting dish, breast-side-up. Spread with butter. Add orange juice, raisins, lemon rind, wine, and chicken stock.

Bake in moderate oven (350°F. Mark 4) 45 minutes, basting about every 10 minutes. Serve with Nutted Rice in Fluted Orange Cups (below). Serves 6.

Nutted Rice in Fluted Orange Cups: In a saucepan, combine 16 fluid ounces chicken stock and 8 ounces uncooked rice. Bring to the boil, stir, cover and cook over low heat 14 minutes. Remove from heat. Stir in 2 tablespoons butter or margarine, 2½ ounces chopped pecans or walnuts, and 2 tablespoons chopped parsley. Season to taste with salt. Flute orange peel cups and spoon the rice into shells.

ROAST PHEASANT

Use young hens weighing about 3 pounds each when dressed. Draw and truss as for chicken.

Rub inside with butter or oil. Sprinkle with salt. Fill lightly with a bread or wild rice stuffing. Cover with rashers of bacon or pieces of fat salt pork or rub skin with butter or oil.

Roast, uncovered, in slow oven (325°F. Mark 3) until tender, about 1 hour. Baste often with butter or pan juices. Serve with gravy made from pan juices.

PHEASANT BAKED IN SOUR CREAM

Cut bird into pieces. Roll them in flour and sprinkle with salt and pepper. Brown in melted butter in a heavy pan. Add 8 fluid ounces single cream.

Cover and bake in moderate oven (350°F. Mark 4) 30 minutes. Turn occasionally. Serve with gravy made from cream in pan.

WOODCOCK AND SNIPE

Woodcock and snipe are small, highly esteemed game birds. Dark-fleshed and strong-flavoured, they are cooked whole and are often eaten entrails and all; indeed, this is considered the most delicate part. The entrails (called the trail) shrivel in cooking and are easily removed at the table. The squeamish may remove the lower end before cooking the birds.

Woodcock may be wrapped in thin rashers of bacon or strips of salt pork, roasted in 10 to 15 minutes, and served on toast with a gravy of the pan juices; snipe roasts in even less time. Allowing for the difference in size, either of these birds may be substituted in recipes for quail, grouse, or partridge. Unlike quail and grouse, however, they must first be hung for 3 to 4 days.

PARTRIDGE

True partridges of several varieties are only found in England and Europe. Partridge, grouse, and quail can be treated alike in cookery. Some people like it to hang for at least four days so that its delicate, fragile flavour can develop.

ROAST PARTRIDGE

Wipe cleaned birds with a damp cloth. Rub with melted butter or oil. Sprinkle inside and out with salt and pepper.

Cook in roasting tin in slow oven (325°F. Mark 3) until tender, 30 to 40 minutes.

ROAST GROUSE

Wipe inside and out with damp cloth. Rub inside and out with salt.

Fill with bread or wild rice stuffing, or if preferred, put a rasher of bacon or strip of salt pork inside. Do not fasten opening.

Cover breast with rashers of bacon or strips of salt pork. Cook in slow oven (325°F. Mark 3) until tender, about 30 minutes.

GRILLED WOODCOCK

Woodcock is not drawn. The entrails shrivel up when cooked and are easily removed at the table. If one is finicky about this, the lower end of the trail (intestines) may be removed.

Clean birds and wipe with damp cloth. Rub with butter. Wrap completely in rashers of bacon or thin strips of fat salt pork. Grill under very moderate heat about 15 minutes, turning frequently.

GRILLED PARTRIDGE, PHEASANT, QUAIL, OR GROUSE

Clean birds and split them down back. Sprinkle with salt and pepper. Dust with flour to keep juices in.

Grill on wire rack, laying the inside first toward the heat. Length of grilling time will depend upon size of bird and how well done you like the meat. Allow 10 to 15 minutes for quail, 15 to 20 minutes for grouse, and 20 to 30 minutes for young partridge and pheasant.

When cooked, place bird on warm serving dish and butter or oil well on both sides. If the breasts are quite thick, use very moderate heat.

ROAST QUAIL

Wipe the cleaned bird with a damp cloth. Brush inside and out with butter. Rub with salt. Place a large mushroom inside the bird.

Place in a roasting pan. Cover with buttered non-stick aluminium foil. Roast, uncovered, in slow oven (325°F. Mark 3) 25 to 30 minutes. Remove paper after first 20 minutes.

SPIT-ROASTED WILD DUCKS

2 wild ducks
1 apple or orange
1 teaspoon salt
¼ teaspoon pepper
3 tablespoons oil
4 tablespoons melted butter or margarine
4 tablespoons orange juice
1 tablespoon chopped parsley

Stuff ducks with pieces of apple or orange. Sprinkle with salt and pepper; rub with oil. Truss well.

Place on the spit. Turn frequently and baste with oil. Cook about 20 minutes, or until blood will not run when meat is pricked. Wild duck should not be overcooked. It has a much finer flavour if served rare.

Remove fruit. Pour melted butter mixed with orange juice and parsley over ducks. Serves 4.

PTARMIGAN

A game bird of the grouse family. Most species live in arctic or sub-arctic regions. They have feathered legs and feet, and their plumage changes colour with the season. To cook, follow recipes for grouse or quail.

WILD DUCKS À LA PABLO MASI

2 wild ducks, cleaned and drawn
Salt and pepper
2 ounces butter or margarine
4 rashers of bacon
1 14-ounce can sauerkraut, drained
2 apples, peeled, cored and chopped
4 fluid ounces white wine
1 teaspoon cornflour

Season ducks lightly with salt and pepper. Brown on all sides in hot butter. Cover with rashers of bacon and place in a casserole.

Arrange sauerkraut and apple round birds; pour wine over.

Cover and bake in moderate oven (350°F. Mark 4) 1½ hours or until birds are tender. Transfer them to a warm serving dish.

Stir cornflour, mixed to a thin paste with 4 tablespoons cool water, into the sauerkraut. Cook until it thickens slightly. Serve separately. Serves 4.

ROAST GUINEA HEN

A guinea hen or fowl is a small domestic bird with a slightly gamy flavour. It has a rounded body and dark feathers spotted with white. It is so called because it was originally imported from Guinea.

Young guinea fowl weigh ¾ to 1¼ pounds; guinea chickens weigh 1½ to 2¼ pounds, guinea hens weigh 2½ to 3 pounds. Allow ¾ to 1 pound per person.

Clean the bird, following directions for poultry.

Rub inside with butter. Season cavity with salt and pepper. Put 1 medium-sized quartered onion in cavity or stuff with well seasoned stuffing.

Place breast-side-down on rack in roasting pan. Arrange thin strips of salt pork over back.

Roast, uncovered, in slow oven (325°F. Mark 3) 30 minutes.

Turn breast-side-up. Season with salt and pepper. Transfer salt pork to breast. Roast about 30 minutes longer. Allow 35 to 45 minutes per pound for total roasting. If onion was used, remove from cavity before serving.

Serve with giblet gravy made from pan juices and giblet stock, with minced or chopped giblets and 4 tablespoons currant jelly added to gravy. Allow about 1 pound per portion.

FRIED GUINEA BREASTS

Use breasts from young guinea chickens. Sprinkle with salt and pepper and fry very slowly in butter or bacon fat in a heavy frying pan about 20 minutes, or until browned and tender.

Place on hot dish and serve with buttered mushroom caps and sauce made from pan juices and cream. Allow 1 breast per person.

Recipes for Using Cooked or Canned Poultry

Quick Creamed Chicken and Mushrooms

CREAMED CHICKEN OR TURKEY
(Basic Recipe)

Chicken, turkey, or veal may be used interchangeably in the basic recipe or any of its variations. You should feel free to follow any creative urge in creating your own variations in proportions, seasonings, etc., provided that good combinations are used.

- 3 tablespoons butter or margarine
- 4 tablespoons flour
- 8 fluid ounces chicken or turkey stock
- 8 fluid ounces milk
- ½ teaspoon salt
- ½ teaspoon paprika
- ⅛ teaspoon pepper
- 1 teaspoon finely chopped onion
- 12 ounces diced cooked turkey
- 2 tablespoons sherry (optional)

Melt butter, add flour and stir over low heat until blended. Add cold stock and milk. Cook, stirring constantly, until it is thick.

Then set pan over hot water. Add seasonings and turkey and heat thoroughly.

Add more seasoning if you like. Blend in sherry just before serving, if using.

Serve on toast, plain or fried noodles or rice. Serves 6.

Note: If creamed mixture is thicker than you want, thin with hot milk or water. All recipes below serve 6.

Variations of Creamed Chicken or Turkey

Turkey À La King: Cook 1-2 tablespoons finely chopped green pepper in the butter for a few minutes before adding flour. Proceed as for Creamed Turkey.

Add 1 chopped pimiento and a small can (3 ounces) well drained mushrooms with seasonings.

Turkey Terrapin: Prepare Creamed Turkey, reducing the turkey meat to 8 ounces.

Just before serving, add 4 chopped hard-boiled eggs and 8 chopped black olives.

Turkey Curry: Prepare Creamed Turkey. To above seasonings add ½ to 1½ teaspoons curry powder and ¼ cup grated fresh or desiccated coconut. Serve on a bed of boiled rice.

Turkey Curry, Hawaiian Style: Prepare Turkey Curry. Serve in coconut shells which have been sawed in half crossways to make 6 serving shells. Remove some of coconut meat and use in preparation of curry.

Prepare 1-1½ pounds cooked rice. Grease inside of shells. Line shells with ½-inch layer of rice, reserving enough to cover top. Pour in turkey curry. Top with rice.

Bake in a hot oven (400°F. Mark 6) about 20 minutes.

Creamed Turkey and Pineapple: Prepare Creamed Turkey. Just before serving, add 3-4 tablespoons canned chopped well drained pineapple or 3-4 tablespoons finely diced fresh pineapple and 1 ounce slivered almonds.

This may be served in hollowed-out fresh pineapple shells cut lengthways and with stem still on.

Top with Parmesan cheese and place under grill as far as possible from heat. Grill until top is lightly browned.

Turkey, Rarebit Style: Prepare Creamed Turkey, reducing turkey meat to 8 ounces. Add half a well drained 7½-ounce can of mushrooms.

Just before serving, stir in 2 ounces grated Cheddar cheese and 1 chopped canned pimiento.

Serve on toast or rusks. For variation, top each portion with a slice of pineapple heated in its own juice or sautéed in a small amount of butter.

Creamed Turkey and Ham: Prepare Creamed Turkey, substituting 4 ounces diced cooked ham for 4 ounces turkey.

Creamed Turkey and Prawns: Prepare Creamed Turkey, substituting 4 ounces cooked or canned prawns for 4 ounces of turkey.

Creamed Turkey with Vegetables: Prepare Creamed Turkey, substituting 2-3 ounces cooked vegetables (peas, corn or mixed vegetables) for 2-3 ounces of turkey.

QUICK CREAMED CHICKEN AND MUSHROOMS

- 2 tablespoons butter or margarine
- 12 ounces diced cooked chicken
- 3 tablespoons flour
- 1 10½-ounce can condensed cream of mushroom soup
- 4 hard-boiled eggs
- salt and pepper

Melt butter and brown chicken in it slightly. Add flour and blend well.

Add soup and cook until thick, stirring constantly. Add sliced egg whites and allow them to heat through. Season to taste.

Serve on squares of hot buttered toast or in toast cups and sprinkle with sieved egg yolks. Garnish with watercress. Serves 4.

EASY CHICKEN À LA KING

- 1-2 tablespoons chopped green pepper
- 2 tablespoons diced celery
- 2 tablespoons butter or margarine
- 1 tablespoon flour
- 1 10½-ounce can condensed cream of chicken soup
- 1 7½-ounce can mushrooms, sliced
- 8 ounces cooked chicken, diced
- 1-2 tablespoons chopped pimiento
- ¼ teaspoon Aromat
- Salt and pepper

Cook green pepper and celery in butter until tender. Blend in flour. Gradually add soup. Add mushrooms and liquid. Cook until thick, stirring constantly.

Add chicken, pimiento, and seasonings; heat thoroughly. Serve on toast triangles. Serves 4 to 6.

CHICKEN SQUARES

- 1½ pounds diced or sliced cooked chicken
- 8 ounces cooked rice
- 1½ tablespoons chopped parsley
- 1½ tablespoons chopped pimiento
- 1 teaspoon salt
- ⅛ teaspoon pepper
- 3 eggs, slightly beaten
- 12 fluid ounces hot chicken stock
- 2 ounces cornflakes, crushed
- 1 tablespoon melted butter or margarine

Mix the chicken, rice, parsley, pimiento, salt, pepper, and eggs together. Stir in hot chicken stock. Pour into greased 8 × 8-inch square cake pan.

Mix the cornflakes and melted butter together; sprinkle over chicken mixture. Set in pan of hot water. Bake in moderate oven (350°F. Mark 4) about 40 minutes, or until set. Makes 9 2½-inch squares.

Chicken Squares

PARTY CHICKEN LOAF
Filling:
- 1 3½-4-pound chicken, cooked and diced
- 2 ounces chopped celery
- 1 egg, unbeaten
- 2 tablespoons chopped pimiento
- 1 to 1½ teaspoons salt
- ½ teaspoon Worcestershire sauce
- ⅛ teaspoon pepper
- 2 ounces chicken fat or butter
- 1 ounce flour
- About 6 fluid ounces chicken stock

Mix the cooked chicken, celery, egg, pimiento, salt, Worcestershire sauce, and pepper together.

Melt chicken fat or butter in saucepan; blend in flour. Mix until smooth.

Gradually add chicken stock; cook over medium heat, stirring constantly until very thick. Blend thoroughly with chicken mixture. Refrigerate while preparing pastry.

Pastry:
- 8 ounces sifted plain flour
- 1 teaspoon salt
- 6 ounces fat
- 6 to 7 tablespoons cold water

Sift flour and salt together into a mixing bowl. Cut in the fat until pieces are the size of small peas.

Sprinkle cold water gradually over mixture while tossing and stirring lightly with fork. Add water to driest particles, pushing lumps to side, until dough is just moist enough to hold together.

Divide into two portions, one twice as large as the other. Form into balls. Flatten to about ½-inch thickness; smooth dough at edges.

Roll out larger portion on floured board to 15×10-inch rectangle. Fit loosely into a loaf tin, approximately 9×5×3 inches. Fill with chicken mixture.

Roll out remaining dough to 10× 6-inch rectangle. Cut several slits for escape of steam. Moisten rim of bottom crust. Place top crust over filling; fold edge over bottom crust. Crimp the edge against inside of tin. Brush top with milk.

Bake in hot oven (425°F. Mark 7) 30 to 40 minutes until golden brown. Cool

Party Chicken Loaf

in pan 5 minutes. Gently turn out on wire rack; then place right side up on serving plate. Cut into 2½-inch slices; serve hot with mushroom sauce (below).

For Individual Tarts: Divide dough into two portions, one slightly larger. Form into balls as above. Roll out larger portion to ⅛-inch thickness. Cut out six 6-inch circles; fit loosely into six 4-inch tart tins. Fill each with about 2-3 ounces chicken filling.

Roll out remaining dough to ⅛-inch thickness; cut six 5-inch circles (dough will need to be re-rolled). Cut two or three slits in the centre of each for escape of steam. Moisten rims of bottom crusts. Place a top crust over filling of each tart; fold edge under bottom crust. Press to seal; crimp edge. Bake in hot oven (425°F. Mark 7) for 20 to 25 minutes.

Mushroom Sauce: Melt 3 tablespoons chicken fat or butter in saucepan over medium heat. Blend in 3 tablespoons flour. Gradually add 12 fluid ounces chicken stock, stirring constantly. Continue cooking and stirring until it thickens. Add ½ 7½-ounce can mushrooms and ¼ to ½ teaspoon salt.

Turkey Loaf-Gourmet

TURKEY LOAF-GOURMET
- 1 pound cooked turkey
- 6 ounces soft breadcrumbs
- 1-2 tablespoons celery, chopped very fine
- 3 egg yolks
- About 4-5 tablespoons sherry
- 2 tablespoons cream
- 1 teaspoon salt
- 1 teaspoon finely chopped onion

Cut turkey into very small pieces. Add breadcrumbs and chopped celery.

Beat egg yolks. Add wine and cream to egg yolks. Add salt and chopped onion. Mix all together lightly.

Pack into greased loaf pan (8×4×3 inches). Bake in moderate oven (350°F. Mark 4) about 40 minutes.

Serve with giblet gravy, mushroom, or cheese sauce. Serves 4 to 5.

CHICKEN-IN-A-RING
- 12 ounces uncooked rice
- 1 medium green pepper, diced
- 2 ounces butter, margarine, or chicken fat
- 1 ounce flour

- 1 pint chicken stock
- ½ teaspoon salt
- Pinch of pepper
- 2 teaspoons lemon juice
- 1½ pounds diced cooked chicken
- 1 small can (3 ounces) mushrooms
- 1-2 tablespoons chopped pimiento
- 1 egg, slightly beaten

Cook rice, keep hot. Cook green pepper in butter until soft; mix in flour. Add chicken stock, stirring until thickened. Add remaining ingredients except rice.

Heat thoroughly, stirring constantly. Pile hot rice in ring around serving dish or mould in a ring. Place chicken in centre. Serves 6 to 7.

CHICKEN SPIRAL LOAF
Chicken Filling:
- 6 ounces diced cooked chicken
- 4 ounces chopped celery
- 1-2 tablespoons chopped green pepper (optional)
- 1 tablespoon chopped onion
- 3 sliced hard-boiled eggs
- ½ teaspoon salt

Pastry:
- 12 ounces sifted plain flour
- 2 ounces maize flour
- 1 teaspoon baking powder
- 1 teaspoon salt
- 4 ounces fat
- 4 fluid ounces milk

For chicken filling, mix all the ingredients well.

For pastry, sift together dry ingredients. Cut in the fat until mixture resembles coarse crumbs. Add milk, tossing lightly with a fork until mixture will just hold together.

Knead gently a few seconds on a lightly floured board. Roll dough out to form a 10×12-inch rectangle. Transfer dough to baking sheet.

Spoon chicken filling onto dough, spreading mixture evenly over the dough. Roll up, beginning on the long side, as for a Swiss roll.

Place roll with pastry seam underneath on baking sheet. Seal ends by pressing dough together.

Bake in hot oven (425°F. Mark 7) 20 to 25 minutes. Slice and serve with a cheese sauce. Serves 6.

Chicken Spiral Loaf

Pimiento Chicken

PIMIENTO CHICKEN

4   onions, thinly sliced
2   ounces butter or margarine
1   ounce flour
1   tablespoon curry powder (or to taste)
16 fluid ounces chicken stock
12 ounces cut-up cooked chicken
1   teaspoon salt
¼   teaspoon pepper
1   whole pimiento, chopped

Sauté onions in butter or margarine. Stir in flour and curry powder. Add chicken stock and chicken. Simmer 30 minutes.

Add salt, pepper, and pimiento. Keep hot and serve on rice. Serves 4.

CRUNCHY CHICKEN WITH RICE

8   ounces rice
2   tablespoons butter or margarine
1   medium onion, sliced
1   medium green pepper, cut into strips
12 ounces sliced celery
10 fluid ounces chicken stock
1   tablespoon soy sauce
6   ounces cooked chicken
1   small can (3 ounces) mushrooms, drained
2   tablespoons cornflour
3   tablespoons mushroom liquid
2   ounces walnuts or slivered almonds

Cook rice in plenty of boiling salted water, drain and keep hot.

Cook onion in butter until tender. Stir in green pepper, celery, chicken stock, and soy sauce; simmer 10 minutes. Add chicken and mushrooms.

Blend cornflour with mushroom liquid to a smooth paste; stir into chicken mixture. Bring to the boil; add nuts and serve on a bed of boiled rice. Serves 6.

Crunchy Chicken with Rice

CHICKEN OR TURKEY HASH

2   ounces butter or margarine
2   tablespoons chopped onion
2   ounces fresh mushrooms, sliced
About 12 ounces diced, boiled potatoes
6   ounces diced, cooked chicken
6-8 fluid ounces milk or cream
Salt and pepper to taste
Paprika to taste

Cook onions and mushrooms in fat until onions are lightly browned.

Add potatoes, chicken, and enough milk or cream to moisten well. Cook slowly over low heat until thickened.

Add salt, pepper, and paprika to taste. Serves 4.

Baked Chicken or Turkey Hash: Turn into a casserole. Top with buttered golden crumbs. Bake in moderate oven (375°F. Mark 5) about 30 minutes, until hot and top is browned.

CHICKEN CROQUETTES

6   ounces chopped cooked chicken
½   pint thick white sauce
2   teaspoons chopped parsley
Salt and pepper
2   eggs, beaten
2   tablespoons water
Dry breadcrumbs

Mix the chicken, sauce, and parsley together; season with salt and pepper.

Pack into greased square cake tin and chill thoroughly. Form mixture into croquettes.

Beat eggs; add water. Roll croquettes in crumbs; dip in egg; roll in crumbs. Fry in shallow fat or deep hot fat (375°F.) 5 minutes, or until brown. Drain on absorbent paper. Serves 4.

Chicken Croquettes

CHICKEN WITH PINEAPPLE

2   tablespoons peanut oil
1   small can (3 ounces) sliced water chestnuts
1   can (about 7 ounces) bamboo shoots
2   ounces finely diced celery
4   ounces finely chopped spinach
1   teaspoon sugar
1   teaspoon Aromat
1   tablespoon soy sauce
8   fluid ounces chicken stock
1½ tablespoons cornflour

3   tablespoons water
1   cooked breast of chicken, thinly sliced
2-3 tablespoons pineapple tidbits, drained

Cook vegetables in oil 3 to 5 minutes. Add seasonings and stock and bring to boil.

Blend cornflour and water until smooth. Add slowly to simmering liquid, stirring constantly until thickened throughout.

Add chicken and pineapple and heat for about 5-10 minutes. Serve hot with boiled rice. Serves 4.

CHICKEN AND VEGETABLE LOAF

6   ounces diced cooked chicken
12 ounces cooked or 1 medium can peas or peas and carrots
3   ounces fresh breadcrumbs
1   ounce chopped celery
4   fluid ounces chicken stock or milk
2   slightly beaten eggs
1½ teaspoons salt
1   tablespoon chopped onion
1   tablespoon chopped pimiento

Mix the ingredients together and pack lightly into a greased tin.

Bake in moderate oven (350°F. Mark 4) about 40 minutes.

Turn out into serving dish. Serve with chicken gravy or mushroom sauce. Condensed cream of mushroom soup may be thinned slightly with milk for a sauce. Serves 6.

ALMOND-PINEAPPLE CHICKEN

2   tablespoons butter or margarine
2-3 tablespoons crushed pineapple
4   fluid ounces pineapple juice
1½ tablespoons cornflour
16 fluid ounces chicken stock
6   ounces diced cooked chicken
2   ounces slivered toasted almonds
2   ounces sliced celery
1½ teaspoons salt
Chow mein noodles

Let pineapple sauté in butter 5 minutes. Add pineapple juice mixed with cornflour.

Add chicken stock and stir over low heat until thickened. Add diced chicken, almonds, celery, and salt. Heat through.

Serve with chow mein noodles. Serves 6 to 8.

Almond-Pineapple Chicken

Chicken Almond with Rice

CHICKEN ALMOND WITH RICE

2 ounces blanched almonds
3 tablespoons salad oil
1 teaspoon salt
1 clove garlic, crushed
3-4 ounces diced cooked chicken
1 can (about 8 ounces) cubed bamboo shoots
1 small can (3 ounces) or 2 ounces fresh mushrooms, sliced
2 tablespoons liquid (use 1 tablespoon each from bamboo shoots and water chestnuts cans)
1 small can (3 ounces) thinly sliced water chestnuts
1½-2 ounces thinly sliced celery
2 teaspoons cornflour
½ teaspoon sugar
4 tablespoons water
4 teaspoons soy sauce
3-4 sliced spring onions

Brown almonds in 1 tablespoon oil. Set aside.

Mix the salt, crushed garlic, and 1 tablespoon oil in a frying pan with a tight-fitting lid. Heat and add the chicken and brown lightly.

Add 1 tablespoon oil, bamboo shoots, and mushrooms. Brown lightly.

Add 2 tablespoons liquid. Cover and cook over low heat 5 minutes.

Add water chestnuts, celery, and half the almonds. Heat through. Celery and chestnuts should stay crisp.

Blend cornflour, sugar, water, and soy sauce; stir into hot mixture. Cook until it is thick and smooth.

Serve on a bed of boiled rice, sprinkling remaining almonds and spring onions over top. Serves 4.

HOT TURKEY AND HAM MOUSSE

3 tablespoons butter or margarine
3 tablespoons flour
16 fluid ounces milk
Salt and pepper
8 ounces minced leftover turkey
3 ounces minced cooked ham
1½ ounces fresh breadcrumbs
2 eggs

Melt butter or margarine; blend in flour. Gradually add milk; cook over hot water, stirring constantly, until thick. Season with salt and pepper.

Cool slightly; add turkey, ham, and crumbs. Beat eggs; add.

Pour into individual greased moulds. Stand them in a pan of warm water.

Bake in moderate oven (350°F. Mark 4) 45 minutes, or until a knife inserted down the side comes out clean. Serves 4.

CHICKEN FINALE

2 tablespoons finely chopped green pepper
1 tablespoon butter or margarine
1 10½-ounce can condensed cream of chicken soup

1 pound cooked noodles
2-4 ounces diced cooked chicken

Cook green pepper until tender in butter in saucepan.

Add soup, noodles, and chicken. Mix well. Cook over low heat about 10 minutes.

Serve on warm dish. Garnish with green pepper rings and additional slivers of cooked chicken if you like. Serves 4.

CHICKEN CUSTARD LOAF

10 ounces coarsely minced cooked chicken
4 ounces fresh breadcrumbs
6 fluid ounces chicken stock
2 ounces chopped celery
1 tablespoon chopped parsley
1 teaspoon grated onion
1 teaspoon salt
⅛ teaspoon pepper
¾ teaspoon Aromat
2 teaspoons lemon juice
2 beaten eggs
4 fluid ounces evaporated milk

Combine ingredients in order given, mixing lightly and thoroughly. Fill them into a well greased large loaf pan; set in pan of hot water.

Bake in moderate oven (350°F. Mark 4) until loaf is firm and top delicately browned, about 1 hour.

Remove from hot water; let stand 5 to 10 minutes before unmoulding. Slice and serve with thin gravy, either chicken-mushroom or plain chicken gravy. Serves 6.

Note: If the chicken was cooked originally with Aromat, or if it was used in the broth, then only ½ teaspoon Aromat is needed in the recipe.

CHICKEN À LA BORDELAISE

2 tablespoons butter
2 tablespoons flour
8 fluid ounces chicken stock
1 teaspoon Worcestershire sauce
1 clove garlic, crushed
Salt and pepper to taste
12 large mushroom caps
4 tablespoons sherry or Madeira
6 ounces cooked chicken, diced
4 tablespoons double cream

Heat butter in the top pan of a chafing dish placed directly over a low flame, and when melted, stir in flour

and chicken stock. Continue to stir until it is thick and smooth.

Add Worcestershire sauce, garlic, salt and pepper to taste.

Add mushrooms and sherry or Madeira and simmer for 5 minutes.

Add diced chicken, heat, and stir in double cream. Serves 6.

CHICKEN-SPAGHETTI LOAF WITH MUSHROOM SAUCE

24 strands of spaghetti, broken
4 ounces diced cooked chicken
4 ounces dry breadcrumbs
4 ounces grated cheese
12 fluid ounces warm milk
2 ounces melted butter or margarine
1-2 tablespoons chopped green pepper
2 tablespoons chopped pimiento
1 teaspoon salt
3 slightly beaten eggs

Cook spaghetti in boiling, salted water. Drain; add remaining ingredients.

Bake in large shallow greased baking dish in moderate oven (350°F. Mark 4) 1 hour. Serve with mushroom sauce. Serves 6.

Mushroom Sauce: Stir 4 tablespoons milk into 1 10½-ounce can condensed cream of mushroom soup. Heat.

With a freezer, leftover turkey can be packaged for various uses as turkey sandwich slices, turkey bits, or turkey pieces as required for your recipes.

HAWAIIAN CURRY

16 fluid ounces hot milk
4 ounces desiccated coconut
2 cloves garlic, chopped
2 teaspoons ground ginger
3 spring onions, chopped
1 to 2 tablespoons curry powder
4 ounces butter or margarine, softened
1¼ ounces flour
½ teaspoon salt
4 fluid ounces cream
1½ pounds cooked, boned chicken meat

Pour hot milk over coconut and set aside for 30 minutes. Add garlic, ginger and onion to coconut (in milk).

Mix the curry powder and 2 tablespoons of butter in the top of a double boiler. Stir in coconut milk mixture and cook over hot water for about 2 hours, stirring frequently. Strain through double thickness of muslin.

Blend flour and remaining butter in top of double boiler. Add strained coconut milk. Stir and cook over hot water until the sauce is thick and smooth.

Stir in salt and cream. Add chicken and cook slowly to prevent curdling, about 20 minutes. Serve hot on a bed of hot boiled rice. Serves 6.

Serve with an assortment of six of the following accompaniments:

Chopped crisply fried bacon
Chutney
Chopped spring onions
Chopped hard-boiled egg yolks
Finely chopped parsley
Chopped peanuts
Desiccated coconut
Chopped hard-boiled egg whites

CREAMED CHICKEN (CHINESE STYLE)

3 tablespoons cornflour
16 fluid ounces milk
1 10½-ounce can condensed cream of mushroom soup, undiluted
1 pound diced, cooked or canned chicken
1 small can (3 ounces) chopped mushrooms, undrained
1 small can (5 ounces) water chestnuts, drained, sliced
⅛ teaspoon each salt, pepper, dried marjoram, and Aromat
½ teaspoon paprika
1 tablespoon sherry
Chow mein noodles

Blend cornflour in a saucepan with some of the milk to form a smooth paste, then mix in remaining milk and soup.

Add remaining ingredients except noodles. Cook over low heat until bubbling hot. Cook the noodles in plenty of boiling salted water until just tender. Drain.

Arrange cooked noodles on a large warm platter; cover with chicken mixture. Serves 6.

CHICKEN À LA REINE

3 ounces butter or margarine
6 tablespoons flour
24 fluid ounces chicken stock
Salt and pepper
¾ teaspoon Aromat
⅛ teaspoon ground nutmeg
2 beaten egg yolks
2 to 3 tablespoons dry sherry (optional)
1 to 1½ pounds diced cooked or canned chicken
1½ pounds potatoes, boiled, mashed and well seasoned

Melt butter or margarine; blend in flour until smooth. Add chicken stock; cook over low heat, stirring until it is smooth and thick. Season with salt and pepper to taste. Add Aromat and nutmeg.

Add slowly to beaten egg yolks; stir and cook 2 minutes over low heat.

Remove from heat; add sherry and chicken. Turn into 6 individual ramekins.

Make a border of mashed potato around each ramekin. Brown under a hot grill. Serves 6.

TURKEY CHEESE TURNOVERS

Cheese pastry (see below)
2 ounces butter
2 tablespoons chopped onion
2 ounces finely diced celery
3 tablespoons flour
1 teaspoon salt
⅛ teaspoon pepper
8 fluid ounces milk
1 pound diced, cooked turkey
2 tablespoons chopped parsley

Make your favourite pastry with 9 ounces flour, reducing fat in recipe to 4 ounces; blend in 4 ounces grated cheese when cutting in fat.

Roll out to ⅛-inch thickness on a floured board and cut in 6-inch squares or 4-inch circles.

To make filling: Melt butter; add onion and celery; cook over low heat until tender.

Blend in flour and seasonings; gradually stir in milk and cook until mixture boils and thickens, stirring constantly. Add turkey and parsley; remove from heat.

Pile turkey filling on each piece of pastry; fold pastry to make triangle or half-circle. Press edges together with fork. Prick tops to let steam escape.

Bake in very hot oven (450°F. Mark 8) for 10 minutes; reduce heat to hot (400°F. Mark 6), and bake 15 minutes longer, until lightly browned. Serve hot with mushroom sauce. Serves 6.

ORIENTAL CHICKEN PILAF

4 ounces butter or margarine
1 pound cooked chicken, cut into strips about 1½ inches long
2-3 tablespoons chopped onion
2 teaspoons salt
⅛ teaspoon pepper
½ teaspoon oregano or thyme
8 ounces uncooked white rice
1 pint chicken stock or 1 pint water and 3 chicken bouillon cubes
1 large tomato, chopped or ½ 8-ounce can tomatoes, drained and chopped
2 ounces chopped walnuts

Melt butter or margarine in a large saucepan. Add chicken and onion and cook until chicken browns. Add salt, pepper, and oregano or thyme.

Add rice and cook, stirring occasionally, for 5 minutes.

Slowly add chicken stock or water and bouillon cubes. Add tomatoes and walnuts. Bring to the boil.

Cover and simmer 20 minutes or until rice is tender. Do not stir. Serve hot. Serves 8.

HOT CHICKEN MOUSSE

3 ounces butter or margarine
3 ounces dry breadcrumbs
16 fluid ounces single cream or evaporated milk
⅛ teaspoon salt
¼ teaspoon nutmeg
1½ pounds chopped cooked chicken
6 slightly beaten eggs
4-5 tablespoons sherry
3 large avocado pears
12 fluid ounces mayonnaise

Melt butter in the top of a double boiler. Add crumbs, cream, salt, and nutmeg; cook 10 minutes, stirring frequently.

Mix together chicken, eggs, and sherry; add hot cream sauce.

Pour into well greased ring mould. Place mould in a pan of water and cover with sheet of greaseproof paper.

Bake in moderate oven (350°F. Mark 4) 45 to 60 minutes, or until firm. A ring mould will take about 30 to 35 minutes.

Remove stones and peel avocado pears and cut the flesh into cubes; mix with mayonnaise and pour around mousse or fill the centre of a ring mould. Serves 6.

Turkey Cheese Turnovers

CHICKEN ROYALE

1   4½-pound chicken, cooked
6   ounces fresh breadcrumbs
8   ounces cooked rice
1   teaspoon salt
½   teaspoon paprika
3   ounces milk powder
1-2 tablespoons chopped pimiento
4   well beaten eggs
24 fluid ounces chicken broth
2   ounces butter or chicken fat

Joint the bird, cook it in water to cover until tender; cool, remove meat from bones and dice.

Combine ingredients in order given and mix well. Turn into buttered 10-inch ring mould or 13½×8½-inch baking dish and place in pan of hot water.

Bake in moderate oven (350°F. Mark 4) 1 hour.

Allow to stand for 10 minutes before unmoulding onto a hot dish. Fill centre with mushroom sauce and garnish with parsley. Serves 8.

Mushroom Sauce:
4   ounces butter
1   pound fresh mushrooms, sliced
2   ounces flour
4   ounces milk powder
1¾ pints chicken stock
2   well beaten egg yolks
4   fluid ounces cream
½   teapoon salt
    Paprika
1   tablespoon chopped parsley
1   tablespoon lemon juice

Melt butter in a heavy frying pan; add sliced mushrooms and cook gently 5 minutes.

Remove mushrooms from butter and keep hot.

Transfer butter from the pan to a double boiler; add flour and milk powder and mix well; gradually stir in chicken stock, place over hot water and cook until thick, stirring until smooth.

Stir in egg yolks mixed with cream; add seasoning, lemon juice, and mushrooms. Serve hot in the chicken ring.

TURKEY SUPPER RING

2   ounces butter or margarine
4   tablespoons flour
16 fluid ounces milk
3   chicken bouillon cubes
2   well beaten eggs
½   pint mayonnaise
½-1 pound diced cooked turkey
2   ounces slivered blanched
        almonds
1   can Chinese fried noodles

Melt butter; blend in flour; add milk and chicken cubes; stir over low heat until it is smooth and thick. Cool slightly.

Add to eggs. Stir in mayonnaise.

Fold in turkey, almonds, and noodles.

Bake in well greased ring mould in moderate oven (350°F. Mark 4) 50 to 60 minutes or until set.

Let stand 5 minutes. Unmould. Fill centre with mushroom sauce.

Serves 4 to 6.

Mushroom Sauce: Slice ½ pound mushrooms; cook in 1½ ounces butter until golden brown.

Blend in 3 tablespoons flour and ½ teaspoon salt. Combine 1 10½-ounce can condensed cream of celery soup and 2-3 tablespoons cream; add; stir smooth over low heat.

CHICKEN AND MUSHROOM DELIGHT

2   ounces butter or margarine
1   tablespoon cornflour
2   tablespoons flour
12 fluid ounces chicken stock
12 fluid ounces single cream
    Salt and pepper
1   pound cold, cooked chicken, cut
        in large pieces or diced
About 2 ounces grilled fresh
        mushrooms
2-3 tablespoons sliced pimiento
1   truffle (optional)
1   ounce thinly sliced celery,
        cooked 10 minutes
2   slightly beaten egg yolks

Melt butter in saucepan. Mix cornflour and flour; add to butter and stir until blended.

Add chicken stock and cream. Add seasonings, and heat to boiling point, stirring constantly.

Add chicken, mushrooms, pimiento, grated truffle, if possible, and celery. Heat until boiling.

Remove from heat; add yolks, stirring constantly. Serves 4 to 6.

CHICKEN TERRAPIN

1½ ounces butter or margarine
3   hard-boiled eggs
5   tablespoons flour
¾   teaspoon dry mustard
1   teaspoon salt
¼   teaspoon white pepper
1   pint milk or milk and stock
12 ounces diced, cooked chicken
1   pimiento, chopped
1   tablespoon chopped green
        pepper
4   black olives, coarsely chopped
1   tablespoon lemon juice

Melt butter or margarine. Blend in mashed egg yolks, flour, and seasonings. Add liquid and cook until thickened.

Add chopped egg whites and remaining ingredients except lemon juice. Heat thoroughly.

Taste and add more seasoning if needed. Add lemon juice last. Serve on toast. Serves 4 to 6.

BUFFET CHICKEN PIE

5   tablespoons flour
1   teaspoon salt
⅛   teaspoon pepper
½   pint cold water
16 fluid ounces hot chicken stock
9   small onions
4   ounces chopped celery
12 ounces cooked peas
12 ounces cooked carrot slices
1½ pounds cooked chicken

Crust:
6   ounces sifted plain flour
¼   teaspoon baking powder
½   teaspoon salt
4   ounces butter or margarine
5 to 6 tablespoons iced water

Mix together the flour, salt, pepper, and ½ pint cold water. Add to the hot chicken stock and cook until thick and no starchy taste remains; stir constantly.

Parboil onions about 10 minutes. Add to the thickened chicken stock the onions, celery, cooked peas, cooked carrots, and chicken. Pour into 2½-quart baking dish.

Crust: Sift together the flour, baking powder, and salt. Cut in the butter or margarine until it is the size of peas.

Add iced water a little at a time, mixing only enough to bind the ingredients together.

Place dough on lightly floured board and roll to about ⅛-inch thickness. Cut dough into strips and arrange in lattice work effect across top of pie.

Bake in preheated hot oven (400°F. Mark 6) about 25 minutes or until crust is browned. Serve with a tomato and cucumber salad in individual ramekins. Serves 9.

CHICKEN À LA KING 2

2½-3 ounces butter
6   tablespoons flour
½   teaspoon salt
16 fluid ounces milk
12 ounces cooked chicken in 1½-
        inch or larger pieces
2   ounces diced cooked celery
3   tablespoons diced cooked green
        pepper
2   tablespoons chopped pimiento
2   beaten egg yolks
1   tablespoon Worcestershire sauce

Melt butter, blend in flour and salt, add milk and cook, stirring constantly over low heat or in a chafing dish until the sauce is thick and bubbly.

Add chicken, celery, green pepper, and pimiento and heat through.

Beat eggs with the Worcestershire sauce, add a small amount of the creamed mixture, stir well, and add to the rest of the creamed mixture.

Stir in well, away from heat, and serve at once on slices of toast or cooked noodle squares. Serves 8.

Party Creamed Chicken

PARTY CREAMED CHICKEN

2   ounces butter or margarine
2   ounces chicken fat
¾   teaspoon salt
½   teaspoon garlic salt
7   tablespoons plain flour
24 fluid ounces milk or 12 fluid
      ounces each milk and
      chicken stock
1½-1¾ pounds cooked seasoned large
      chicken pieces
9   ounces cooked seasoned frozen
      peas

Melt butter and chicken fat. Mix the seasonings and flour together. Add to fat and stir until free of lumps. Remove from heat.

Add milk and stir until thoroughly mixed.

Return to low heat. Cook, stirring constantly, until sauce has thickened. Add chicken and peas.

Pour into heated casserole. Garnish with hot buttered Shreddies (below). Serves 6.

Hot Buttered Shreddies:
2-3 ounces melted butter or margarine
4   ounces Shreddies
¾   teaspoon salt

Pour melted butter or margarine over the shredded wheat. Sprinkle with salt. Mix carefully. Turn into a flat baking dish.

Heat in moderate oven (375°F. Mark 5) 20 minutes, stirring gently after 10 minutes. Serves 6.

CURRIED CREAMED CHICKEN WITH NOODLES

3   ounces butter or margarine
1-2 tablespoons chopped onion
1½ ounces chopped celery
6   tablespoons flour
1   tablespoon curry powder
24 fluid ounces chicken stock or
      bouillon
Salt
1   pound diced, cooked chicken or
      turkey
8   ounces noodles
1¼ ounces chopped peanuts

Melt butter or margarine in the top of a double boiler; add onion and celery and cook until tender.

Place over boiling water; add flour and curry powder and stir until well blended.

Gradually add chicken stock or bouillon and cook, stirring constantly, until the mixture thickens. Season to taste with salt. Add chicken and reheat.

Cook noodles in boiling, salted water until tender. Drain, rinse with boiling water and place in warm buttered casserole.

Pour curried chicken in the centre of noodles. Sprinkle with chopped peanuts and serve. Serves 6.

SPAGHETTI AND TURKEY CASSEROLE

½   pound spaghetti, broken in 2-inch
      pieces
1   pound coarsely diced cooked
      turkey
3   ounces butter or margarine
½   pound mushrooms, sliced
3   teaspoons flour
½   teaspoon salt
⅛   teaspoon white pepper
16 fluid ounces chicken bouillon or
      stock
8   fluid ounces evaporated milk
8   ounces dry breadcrumbs

Cook spaghetti in boiling salted water until tender. Drain and combine with diced turkey.

Melt 4 tablespoons butter in saucepan and fry the mushrooms 5 minutes. Push to one side and blend flour and seasonings in the pan juices. Add bouillon or stock slowly and cook over low heat until thickened, stirring constantly. Stir in evaporated milk.

In a greased baking dish, arrange alternate layers of turkey mixture and sauce. Mix the breadcrumbs with the remaining butter or margarine, melted, and sprinkle over spaghetti and turkey. Bake in very hot oven (450°F. Mark 8) until brown and bubbling, 20 to 25 minutes. Serves 6.

TURKEY (OR CHICKEN) BUDGET PIE

12 ounces cooked, chopped turkey
2-3 medium potatoes, cooked and
      diced
2   ounces diced carrots or celery
2   tablespoons finely chopped onion
2   ounces grated cheese
½   pint white sauce or 1 10-ounce
      can condensed creamed soup
Salt and pepper
Shortcrust pastry

Mix the turkey, potatoes, carrots, and onion together. Add cheese and sauce.

Season to taste with salt and pepper. Place in shallow baking dish.

Roll out pastry and cut it slightly larger than baking dish.

Cover dish with pastry, pressing firmly just below edge of dish.

Cut "turkeys" from scraps of dough left over, and arrange the shapes on top of the pastry. Cut slits in the pastry for steam to escape.

Bake in preheated hot oven (400°F. Mark 6) until pastry is nicely browned and filling begins to bubble. Serve very hot. Serves 4 to 5.

CHICKEN AND MUSHROOM CROQUETTES

2   ounces butter or margarine
5   tablespoons flour
1   teaspoon salt
¼   teaspoon pepper
8   fluid ounces liquid (milk, canned
      chicken soup, or mushroom
      liquid)
1   pound cooked chicken, finely
      chopped or minced
1   small can (3 ounces) mushrooms,
      drained and chopped
Dry breadcrumbs or golden crumbs
1   egg, slightly beaten with 1 table-
      spoon water

Melt the butter or margarine in saucepan. Add flour, salt, and pepper and blend. Add liquid and cook until smooth and thick, stirring constantly. Add chicken and mushrooms and blend well.

Spread mixture in a shallow pan, 7×11 inches, and chill until stiff.

Cut the mixture into rounds with a pastry cutter. Coat with crumbs, then dip in egg, and again in crumbs.

Fry in deep hot fat (375°F.), about 1½ inches deep, until the croquettes are brown. Drain them on absorbent paper. Serve with mushroom sauce. Serves 6.

CREAMED CHICKEN IN A RICE RING

Creamed Chicken:
1   ounce butter or margarine
2   tablespoons flour
8   fluid ounces chicken stock
8   fluid ounces evaporated milk,
      undiluted
½   teaspoon salt
1   pound diced cooked chicken

Make a sauce of the butter or margarine, flour, stock, evaporated milk, and salt. Add diced chicken and heat in a double boiler.

Pour creamed chicken into the centre of a rice ring. Garnish with parsley. Serves 8.

Rice Ring:
1   egg
½   teaspoon salt
1   teaspoon finely chopped onion
8   fluid ounces evaporated milk,
      undiluted
4   fluid ounces chicken stock
1½ pounds cooked rice

Beat egg. Add remaining ingredients. Pour the rice mixture into a well buttered ring mould. Set over a pan of hot water.

Bake in moderate oven (350°-375°F. Mark 4-5) until set, about 45 minutes. Serves 6 to 8.

CHICKEN OR TURKEY TETRAZZINI AU VIN BLANC

½ pound spaghetti
2 ounces sliced mushrooms
1½ ounces butter or margarine
3 tablespoons flour
6 fluid ounces consommé
6 fluid ounces white wine
4 fluid ounces evaporated milk
8 ounces leftover turkey or
    chicken, diced
Buttered breadcrumbs
Grated Parmesan cheese

Cook spaghetti in boiling salted water until tender; drain and rinse with hot water.

Cook mushrooms in butter or margarine for 5 minutes. Sprinkle with flour, stir, add consommé and wine; cook, stirring until smooth. Add evaporated milk; season to taste.

In a greased baking dish, put a layer of spaghetti, then a layer of turkey, and a layer of mushroom sauce. Repeat, ending with a top layer of spaghetti.

Sprinkle top generously with buttered breadcrumbs mixed with grated Parmesan cheese.

Bake in hot oven (450°F. Mark 8) until lightly browned and bubbling. Serves 5 to 6.

TURKEY RICE CASSEROLE

8 ounces uncooked rice
2-2½ tablespoons chopped onion
2 ounces chopped celery
2 pints turkey stock or water and
    4 chicken bouillon cubes
1-2 tablespoons chopped green
    pepper
1-2 tablespoons chopped pimiento
¾ teaspoon Worcestershire sauce
1½ teaspoons salt
1 pound diced cooked turkey or
    chicken
1 ounce dry breadcrumbs mixed
    with 1 tablespoon melted
    butter

Cook rice, onion, and celery in stock until all but about 8 fluid ounces stock is absorbed by the rice.

Then add green pepper, pimiento, Worcestershire sauce, salt, and diced turkey or chicken.

Place in casserole and top with buttered breadcrumbs. Bake in moderate oven (350°F. Mark 4) 1 hour. Serves 6.

DEVILLED MOCK DRUMSTICKS

2 eggs
½ pint thick white sauce
1 teaspoon Worcestershire sauce
2 tablespoons chopped parsley
2 tablespoons chopped onion
½ teaspoon salt
Few drops Tabasco sauce
8 ounces minced cooked turkey
2 tablespoons water
Dry breadcrumbs

Beat 1 egg; add to sauce. Add Worcestershire sauce, parsley, onion,

salt, Tabasco, and turkey; mix well. Chill. Shape the mixture like drumsticks.

Beat remaining egg; add water. Roll drumsticks in crumbs; dip in egg; roll in crumbs.

Fry in deep fat or salad oil heated to 375°F. 5 to 7 minutes, or until brown. Drain on absorbent paper. Insert wooden skewers into the mock drumsticks and place paper chop frills on skewers. Serves 4.

CHICKEN-RICE TIMBALES

12 ounces cooked rice
8 ounces diced cooked chicken
1 tablespoon finely chopped onion
2 beaten eggs
8 fluid ounces milk
5 tablespoons chicken stock or milk
½ teaspoon salt
Pepper

Mix all ingredients together. Divide mixture among custard cups or individual baking dishes.

Place cups in a pan of very hot water and bake in moderate oven (350°F. Mark 4) about 30 minutes, or until a knife inserted in centre of the cups or dishes (timbales) comes out clean. Serves 5 to 6.

Variations: Cooked ham, pork, turkey, fish, or rabbit may be used in place of chicken.

If you have less than the 12 ounces of chicken (or other meat) the recipe calls for, stretch meat with sliced hard-boiled eggs and cooked peas; or you can add mushrooms, fresh or canned.

TURKEY-MACARONI LOAF

12 fluid ounces hot milk
2 ounces fat
4 well beaten eggs
3 ounces fresh breadcrumbs
4 ounces grated cheese
12 ounces diced cooked turkey
6 ounces cooked macaroni or
    noodles
2 tablespoons chopped parsley
1 small onion, finely chopped
1 tablespoon chopped pimiento
1 teaspoon salt
⅛ teaspoon pepper
½ teaspoon Aromat (optional)

Melt fat in hot milk. Mix the remaining ingredients together. Pour milk and fat over mixture, stirring constantly.

Pour into a medium loaf pan or heatproof dish. Set in a pan of hot water. Bake in moderate oven (350°F. Mark 4) until a knife inserted half-way between centre and outside edge comes out clean, 50 to 60 minutes.

Leave the loaf pan in pan about 5 minutes before inverting on a plate. Slice or cut the loaf in squares. Serve plain or with mushroom sauce. Serves 8 to 10.

CHICKEN VALENCIA

1 medium onion, chopped
3 cloves garlic, crushed
3 tablespoons fat
1 large can (20 ounces) tomatoes
1 small can (7½ ounces) frank-
    furters
8 ounces diced cooked chicken
½ pound ham, diced
1½ pints chicken stock
1 pound uncooked rice
1 teaspoon salt
6 ounces cooked peas
2-3 tablespoons diced pimiento
3 hard-boiled eggs, quartered

Sauté the onion and garlic in hot fat until lightly browned. Add tomatoes, sausage, chicken, and ham. Cook for 10 minutes and then add chicken stock, rice, and salt.

Cook until rice is done. Add peas and pimiento.

Turn out onto a dish and garnish with hard-boiled eggs. Serves 8 to 10.

CHICKEN DINNER-IN-A-DISH

4 ounces celery, cut in 1-inch
    lengths, plus a few chopped
    leaves
1 small onion, chopped
12 ounces cooked chicken, cut in
    1-inch squares
1 pint chicken stock
8 ounces uncooked brown rice
1½ teaspoons salt
1 bay leaf
Dash of Tabasco sauce
1 ounce butter or chicken fat
3 medium carrots, cut in ½-inch
    rounds
1 medium green pepper, cut in
    1-inch strips

In a greased 2-quart casserole arrange celery, onion, and chicken evenly. Add chicken stock, rice, salt, bay leaf (tuck it to one side for easy removal), Tabasco sauce, and butter.

Cover and bake in moderate oven (350°F. Mark 4) for 45 minutes.

With a fork, lightly mix in the carrots and green pepper; cover and bake 45 minutes longer. Serves 6.

Or cook all ingredients, covered, except carrots and green pepper in a heavy saucepan or flameproof casserole over low heat on top of the stove for 35 minutes. Add carrots and green pepper; cook 40 minutes longer.

Chicken Dinner-in-a-Dish

This section is for working wives and mothers, career girls and bachelors, many of whom live in flats and cook for themselves, and any other busy people who love to entertain and serve good food but find time scarce for preparing elaborate meals. It is possible to wine and dine guests lavishly without stirring, simmering, watching, and garnishing for hours. Many gastronomic concoctions can be made quickly and the quality of the food need not be sacrificed. In every section of this book you'll find many good quick and easy recipes. Here, however, we have assembled recipes and tips designed to put you on an easy route to good simple cookery—even gourmet cookery—and guaranteed to save you many hours in the kitchen. Your helpers in many of these quick and easy recipes are packaged, tinned or frozen foods.

Quick and Easy Meat Recipes

BARBECUED PORK LOAF

1 tablespoon butter or margarine
1 medium raw onion, minced
1 teaspoon paprika
¼ teaspoon pepper
3 tablespoons lemon juice or vinegar
1½ tablespoons sugar
1 teaspoon dry mustard
1 tablespoon Worcestershire sauce
1 rounded tablespoon ketchup
12 ounces tinned pork loaf

Cook onion in melted butter until tender.

Add remaining ingredients except meat.

Cut meat into 8 slices. Bake in the sauce in moderate oven (350°F. Mark 4) 30 minutes. Serve between toasted hamburger rolls. Serves 4.

GOLDEN ROUND-UP

8 ounces rice, uncooked
1 pint chicken broth
1 teaspoon salt
½ teaspoon Aromat
1 medium raw minced onion
1 pound canned whole tomatoes
12 ounces tinned luncheon meat, cut in finger-lengths (½ inch by 2 inches)
4 ounces grated sharp Cheddar cheese

Place rice, broth, salt, Aromat, and onion in 3½-pint casserole. Stir well.

Cover and bake in moderate oven (350°F. Mark 4) 45 minutes or until rice is barely done.

Remove casserole from oven. Drain tomatoes and place down in rice. Place meat on top of rice; sprinkle cheese over meat.

Cover; return casserole to oven. Bake 20 to 30 minutes longer or until cheese is melted. Serves 6.

QUICK HASH WITH BROWN PEAR CRUST

12 ounces tinned luncheon meat, finely chopped
9 ounces cooked diced potatoes
1 large raw chopped onion
2 ounces diced celery
1 ounce diced green pepper
1 teaspoon Aromat
½ pint broth
1 16-ounce can pear halves, drained
butter, softened
brown sugar

Lightly toss together all ingredients except pears, brown sugar, and butter.

Blend well; turn into buttered 2½-pint shallow casserole. Bake in hot oven (400°F. Mark 6) 30 minutes.

Remove from oven; arrange pears on top. Lightly butter pears; sprinkle with brown sugar.

Return to oven; bake 15 minutes longer. Lightly brown under the grill, if desired. Serves 4 to 6.

GRILLED PINEAPPLE TOP HATS

12 ounces canned luncheon meat, finely chopped
2 ounces oats, quick or old fashioned, uncooked
4 tablespoons pineapple juice
2 tablespoons ketchup
1 teaspoon English mustard
6 slices pineapple, drained

Combine luncheon meat, rolled oats, pineapple juice, ketchup, and mustard. Shape into 6 patties. (Chill if desired.)

Arrange pineapple slices on grill pan; place a patty on each. Grill under medium heat until meat is lightly browned, 7 or 8 minutes. Serves 6.

LUNCHEON MEAT GRILL

Arrange slices of tinned luncheon meat, parboiled potato slices, and thick tomato slices in grill pan. Brush with melted fat or cooking oil.

Cook in preheated grill on one side only, until hot and lightly browned.

Variations: Another good combination for the grill: tinned luncheon meat slices, parboiled swedes cut in thick slices, and sliced pineapple or apple dotted with brown sugar and butter.

Quick Hash with Brown Pear Crust

BAKED CANNED CORNED BEEF

Remove corned beef whole from 1-pound can. Stud it with whole cloves.

Make a paste by stirring a little water into 1½ ounces brown sugar and 1 teaspoon chilli powder.

Add 2 tablespoons chopped gherkins to it and spread over the beef.

Bake in moderate oven (350°F. Mark 4) 10 minutes. Serves 4.

CANNED CORNED BEEF HASH PATTIES

3 tablespoons chopped onion
1 ounce butter or margarine
2 tablespoons horseradish
½ teaspoon thyme
1 1-pound can corned beef
3 medium potatoes, parboiled and finely diced

Brown onion lightly in melted butter. Add remaining ingredients, mix well. Form into patties and brown lightly on both sides.

Serve with slices of firm tomato which have been fried in dripping, and then seasoned with brown sugar and salt and pepper. Serves 4.

LUNCHEON MEAT RICE BAKE

1 pint tomato juice
1 rounded tablespoon ketchup
1 packet boil-in-the-bag rice
1 medium onion, chopped
2 ounces chopped celery
½ green pepper, chopped
½ teaspoon sugar
½ teaspoon salt
⅛ teaspoon pepper
⅛ teaspoon marjoram or oregano
Small bay leaf
1 12-ounce tin luncheon meat
½ lemon, thinly sliced

Combine tomato juice, ketchup, rice, onion, celery, green pepper, and seasonings (sugar, salt, pepper, marjoram or oregano, and bay leaf) in 3½-pint baking dish.

Cut luncheon meat in eight slices. Place the meat on top of rice mixture, overlapping slices slightly.

Insert lemon slices between meat slices.

Bake, covered, in moderate oven (375°F. Mark 5) 30 to 35 minutes, or until rice is tender. Serves 4.

Luncheon Meat Rice Bake

SPICY BAKED HAM LOAF

Score top of 10-ounce tinned ham loaf. Stick in 10 cloves. Bake in moderate oven (350°F. Mark 4) 10 minutes.

Combine 2 ounces brown sugar, ½ teaspoon cinnamon, 1 teaspoon English mustard, ¼ teaspoon vinegar, and 1 teaspoon water; spread over top. Bake additional 15 minutes. Serves 3.

CORNED BEEF HASH SUGGESTIONS

Mix 1 1-pound can corned beef with 3 finely diced parboiled potatoes. Brown lightly in 2 ounces of butter. Then serve:

With Fried Eggs: Top hash with lightly fried eggs.

With Macaroni Casserole: Place hash browned side up on top of cooked macaroni in a casserole. Pour cheese sauce over all.

Bake in moderate oven (375°F. Mark 5) until heated through.

With Scrambled Eggs: Brown corned beef hash until crisp in butter. Then scramble eggs with the mixture.

With Cabbage: Heat 1 ounce butter in large pan. Add 2 pounds shredded cabbage. Cover and cook 8 to 10 minutes, stirring frequently.

Add flaked corned beef hash and heat thoroughly. Season to taste.

Patties with Sauce: Add 2 well-beaten egg yolks to ¾ pint (14 to 16 ounces) flaked corned beef hash. Fold in 2 stiffly beaten egg whites.

Drop by spoonfuls on greased baking-sheet.

Brown under grill. Serve with well seasoned tomato sauce.

RING-AROUND-ROSY BEEF

1 can (10 ounces) condensed tomato soup
¼ pint water
1 teaspoon chopped parsley
1 10-ounce can corned beef, broken into chunks
8 ounces rice, cooked

Combine soup, water, parsley; heat. Add corned beef chunks; stir gently. Serve in a ring of rice. Serves 6.

EGGS IN CORNED BEEF HASH

Prepare corned beef hash from basic recipe above; divide into 4 parts.

Press each portion into a buttered ovenproof ramekin. Make a depression in each and put 1 egg in the centre.

Sprinkle tops with grated Cheddar cheese and paprika.

Bake in moderate oven (375°F. Mark 5) until the eggs are set. Garnish with chopped parsley. Serves 4.

Easy Chop Suey

EASY CHOP SUEY

1 pound pork, cut in 1-inch cubes
1 ounce cooking fat
1 large onion, chopped
1 can (approx. 10½ ounces) condensed cream of celery soup
1 small can (approx. 4 to 5 ounces) mushrooms (save juice)
¼ pint water
2 teaspoons Worcestershire sauce
8 ounces rice, cooked

Brown pork cubes in cooking fat in heavy saucepan. Add onion and cook until soft.

Blend in soup, mushrooms and juice, water, and Worcestershire sauce.

Cover; simmer 30 minutes. Remove cover; cook until pork is tender. Serve over hot rice. Serves 6.

HAM DINNER

1 1½-pound tin baked ham
2 medium swedes or parsnips, cooked and halved
4 spiced peach halves, reserve juice from can
1 large packet frozen peas

Slice ham into four; arrange in centre of oven-proof dish.

Arrange swedes or parsnips and spiced peach halves around ham. Spread with mixture of 3 ounces brown sugar, ½ teaspoon dry mustard, and 8 tablespoons spiced peach juice.

Grill about 7 minutes. Brush with 1 ounce melted butter; turn and grill 7 minutes.

Cook peas until tender; drain. Arrange food on serving dish or individual plates. Serve at once. Serves 4.

Corned Beef Hash Topped with Eggs

Creamed Dried Beef

CREAMED DRIED BEEF
(Basic Recipe)

1 ounce butter or margarine
2 tablespoons flour
¾ pint milk or single cream
½ pound dried beef, shredded and
    scalded
¼ teaspoon pepper

Melt butter. Stir in flour until smooth. Gradually add milk, stirring constantly until mixture boils and thickens.

Add beef, pepper, and salt if required. Serve on toast. Serves 6.

Creamed Dried Beef Variations

Frizzled Dried Beef: Sauté beef in butter until it curls. Proceed as above, adding flour and cream to butter in pan.

Creole Dried Beef: Prepare Frizzled Dried Beef. At the last, add 4 tablespoons chilli or sweet chutney sauce.

Dried Beef Curry on Rice: Prepare Frizzled Dried Beef. Season sauce with ¼ teaspoon curry powder. Serve on freshly boiled rice.

DRIED BEEF IN SOUP

1 ounce butter or margarine
1 small onion, chopped
4 ounces dried beef, cut in strips
1 can (10½ ounces) condensed cream
    of celery soup
4 fluid ounces milk
1 pound asparagus, cooked (fresh,
    canned or frozen)

Melt butter in saucepan; add onion and cook until golden.

Add dried beef, soup, and milk; heat thoroughly. Serve over hot asparagus. Serves 4.

Sweet-Sour Pork Orientale

GAMMON STEAKS WITH FRUIT

2 1-inch thick gammon steaks
3 ounces brown sugar
½ teaspoon dry mustard
1 14-ounce can fruit cocktail

Place one gammon steak in a shallow baking dish. Mix brown sugar and mustard together and sprinkle half over ham. Pour over ½ can of the fruit cocktail.

Cover with remaining gammon steak and top with remaining mixture and fruit cocktail.

Bake in moderate oven (350°F. Mark 4) 25 to 35 minutes or until done, basting with juice in pan. Serve with glazed carrots.

Cover slices of gammon with cold water, bring to a simmer and cook, covered, 20 minutes. Then drain and proceed as above. Serves 4 to 6.

MUSHROOM-SMOTHERED VEAL

4 veal cutlets
1 egg
2 tablespoons water
2 ounces fine dry breadcrumbs
2 ounces margarine or cooking fat
2 cans (1½ pints) condensed cream
    of mushroom soup

Wipe cutlets dry. Combine egg and water; beat lightly. Dip pieces of meat first in egg mixture, then in breadcrumbs.

Brown cutlets on both sides in margarine in a heavy frying pan. Pour soup over cutlets; cover and cook slowly for about 30 minutes or until done. Serve on a hot dish. Serves 4.

SWEET-SOUR PORK ORIENTALE

1 ounce butter or margarine
½ green pepper, cut in thin strips
1 12-ounce can luncheon meat,
    diced
1 13½-ounce can pineapple chunks
1 1-pound can bean sprouts, well
    drained
4 fluid ounces vinegar
2 ounces brown sugar
1½ tablespoons soy sauce
2½ tablespoons cornflour
4 teacups hot cooked rice

Melt butter or margarine in large frying pan; add green pepper and luncheon meat; cook 5 minutes, stirring occasionally.

Add pineapple and pineapple juice, bean sprouts, vinegar, brown sugar, and soy sauce; heat thoroughly.

Blend cornflour to smooth paste with 3 tablespoons water; stir into hot mixture. Bring to boiling, stirring constantly; cook until slightly thick.

Serve with hot, fluffy rice; pass extra soy sauce. Serves 4.

QUICK LAMB PIE

Heat 2 1-pound cans lamb stew; turn into 1½-pint baking dish. Cover with crust made from 1 8-ounce packet of short crust pastry. Mix following directions.

Bake in hot oven (425°F. Mark 7) about 20 minutes, or until crust is baked and browned. Serves 4.

Steak and Kidney Pie: Follow recipe for Shepherd's Pie, substituting 2 10-ounce cans steak and kidneys in gravy for lamb stew.

BEEF STEW WITH PASTRY TOPPING

Pour a can of beef stew in a shallow casserole. Cover with a thin layer of short crust pastry (8 ounces) to which grated onion has been added.

Bake in hot oven (425°F. Mark 7) until pastry is done and stew is heated through.

FRONTIER BEEF STEW

1 large onion, coarsely chopped
4 ounces uncooked long-grained rice
1 teaspoon salt
¼ teaspoon black pepper
½ pint liquid from peas and carrots,
    plus water
1 1-pound can tomatoes and juice
2 teaspoons Worcestershire sauce
1 1-pound can meatballs and gravy
    (use 2 cans for more meat)
1 1-pound can peas and carrots,
    drained

Put the onion, rice, salt, pepper, and ½ pint liquid from peas and carrots (including added water) in a 3½-pint saucepan. Bring to a vigorous boil. Turn heat down. Cover and simmer 14 minutes.

Stir in tomatoes. Break into small pieces. Add Worcestershire sauce, meatballs in gravy, and peas and carrots.

Cover and simmer about 15 minutes. Add water if a thinner mixture is desired. Add salt and pepper to taste. Serves 5 to 6.

Frontier Beef Stew

BAKED BEANS WITH HAM

Pour canned baked beans into a shallow casserole. Cover with small slices cooked ham or lightly grilled rashers of back bacon. Spread with chilli sauce or drizzle honey over top. Bake in moderate oven (375°F. Mark 5) 20 to 30 minutes.

LUNCHEON HAM ROLLS

2 ounces butter or margarine
1 small finely chopped onion
2 sticks chopped celery
16 ounces cooked rice
Salt and pepper
8 slices ($\frac{1}{8}$-inch slices) boned boiled ham
Cranberry glaze (below)

Melt butter in small saucepan. Add onion and celery. Cook until soft.

Remove from heat. Add rice and seasoning. Spread on each ham slice. Roll up. Fasten with cocktail stick. Place in greased shallow baking tin.

Make cranberry glaze. Spoon over ham rolls. Bake in moderate oven (350°F. Mark 4) 15 to 20 minutes. Makes 8.

Cranberry Glaze: Crush contents of 1 8$\frac{1}{2}$-ounce can whole cranberries. Mix together with 10 ounces melted red-currant jelly and 3 ounces brown sugar.

FRITOQUE

This is an easily prepared and very flavourful dish from the Mexican border. Alternate in a casserole layers of canned chilli con carne (either plain or with beans), cheese, onions, and corn crisps.

Heat in a moderate oven until cheese is thoroughly melted.

TAMALE-CHILLI DINNER

Small chopped onion
1 ounce dripping or lard
1 10$\frac{1}{2}$- ounce can tamales
1 10$\frac{1}{2}$-ounce can chilli
2 ounces grated Cheshire or Gruyère cheese

Cook onion until golden.

Remove shucks from tamales. Add tamales and chilli to onion. Cover. Heat thoroughly.

Arrange in serving dish. Top with additional hot tamales if desired. Sprinkle with grated cheese. Serves 4 to 6.

Tamale-Chilli Dinner

CHILLI BEAN BAKE

1 small can chilli con carne without beans
5 ounces approx. canned red kidney beans
1 small tin cocktail sausages, drained and sliced
Coarsely crushed corn crisps or potato crisps

Combine chilli con carne, kidney beans and sausage.

Turn into 1$\frac{1}{2}$-pint baking dish; top with corn or potato crisps. Bake in moderate oven (375°F. Mark 5) until bubbling hot, about 25 minutes. Serves 2.

Note: Stir in additional chilli powder, if you like extra hot chilli.

VEAL BIRDS

2 thin large slices veal
Salt and pepper
dash of Worcestershire sauce
2 hard-boiled eggs, shelled
1 ounce butter
1 10$\frac{1}{2}$-ounce tin condensed cream of chicken soup
1 teaspoon Worcestershire sauce
2 tablespoons pimiento
2 tablespoons chopped parsley

Pound veal until very thin. Sprinkle with salt, pepper, and dash of Worcestershire sauce. Place 1 hard-boiled egg on each piece of veal. Wrap veal around egg. Fasten with a cocktail stick.

Melt butter. Brown veal birds on all sides. Add soup mixed with 1 teaspoon Worcestershire sauce. Add pimiento and parsley. Cover and cook about 20 to 25 minutes, or until veal is tender. Serves 2.

Veal Birds

EASY LUNCHEON HAM DISH

4 $\frac{1}{4}$-inch slices cooked ham
4 slices canned pineapple
$\frac{3}{4}$ pint mashed swede
5 ounces orange or apricot marmalade

Place slices of ham in baking dish. Top each slice with slice of pineapple. Divide swede in 4 portions and place in a mound on each slice of pineapple. Spread mounds with marmalade.

Bake in hot oven (400°F. Mark 6) about 20 minutes to heat and brown. Serves 4.

Note: Plain mashed potatoes can be substituted for swedes.

Chilli Bean Bake

HAM PIE WITH CHEESE PASTRY TOP

3 tablespoons minced onion
4 tablespoons chopped green pepper
2 ounces butter or margarine
6 tablespoons flour
1 10$\frac{1}{2}$-ounce can condensed chicken soup
$\frac{1}{2}$ pint milk
7 ounces diced ham
1 tablespoon lemon juice

Cook onion and green pepper in butter or margarine until soft but not browned. Add flour and stir until frothy.

Add soup and milk and cook until thick and smooth. Add ham and lemon juice; pour into buttered casserole.

Cheese Pastry Top:
8 ounces shortcrust pastry mix
8 ounces grated cheese
6 tablespoons milk

Mix pastry mix and cheese together and stir in milk to make a medium soft dough.

Roll out on a floured board and cut with a round pastry cutter.

Arrange pastry on top of ham pie and bake in very hot oven (450°F. Mark 8) 20 minutes, or until pastry is golden brown. Serves 4 to 6.

EASY BEEF PIE WITH CHEESE

2 9-ounce tins beef stew
1 teaspoon Worcestershire sauce
Buttered white bread triangles
2 ounces grated Cheddar cheese

Add Worcestershire to beef stew and heat. Place in a shallow baking dish.

Arrange bread triangles around edge and sprinkle top with cheese. Brown under grill. Serves 4.

Easy Beef Pie with Cheese

Ham Loaf with Piccalilli Stuffing

HAM LOAF WITH PICCALILLI STUFFING

1 1-pound can luncheon meat
4 ounces fine dry breadcrumbs
⅛ teaspoon black pepper
⅛ teaspoon thyme
1 small finely chopped onion
1 egg
4 ounces dried milk

Stuffing:
1 teaspoon prepared English mustard
1 ounce dried milk
2 ounces fine dry breadcrumbs
4-5 ounces Piccalilli

Empty can of luncheon meat into large mixing bowl. Shred meat into bits by running tines of fork over the meat.

Add the breadcrumbs, seasonings and onion, and mix thoroughly. Beat in egg and 4 ounces of dried milk.

Divide meat mixture in half. Pack one half in bottom of a well greased, loaf pan, about 2¼×8½×4¾ inches.

Stir mustard into the 1 ounce dried milk. Add the 2 ounces of crumbs and Piccalilli and blend thoroughly. Spread Piccalilli stuffing evenly and firmly on top of meat.

Pack remaining half of meat mixture over Piccalilli layer.

Bake in moderate oven (375°F. Mark 5) 45 minutes. Makes 6 generous servings.

Note: 1 pound lightly packed minced leftover cooked or baked ham can be used in place of luncheon meat.

If ham is used, reduce amount of fine dry breadcrumbs used in meat mixture by one-half.

PORK LOAF O'BRIEN

1 1-pound can pork loaf
2 ounces bacon drippings
8 ounces diced cooked potatoes
1 large chopped onion
1½ ounces chopped green pepper
1 teaspoon salt

Cut 5 thin slices from loaf. Dice the rest.

Brown potatoes and onion in hot fat. Add diced meat, green pepper, and salt when potatoes are beginning to brown.

Brown slices of meat and serve with potato mixture. Serves 5.

DEVILLED HAM CASSEROLE

1 small can devilled ham or 2½ ounces ground cooked ham
1 teaspoon finely chopped onion
2 tablespoons chilli sauce
1 teaspoon horseradish
1 teaspoon prepared English mustard
1 teaspoon Worcestershire sauce
4 slices slightly stale bread
1 ounce grated sharp process Cheddar cheese
1 ounce butter or margarine
3 beaten eggs
¾ pint milk
½ teaspoon salt

Combine ham, onion, chilli sauce, horseradish, mustard, and Worcestershire sauce. Spread bread slices with mixture and cut slices into ½-inch cubes.

In 2½-pint buttered casserole, alternate layers of cubes and cheese, ending with bread cubes. Dot with butter. Combine eggs, milk, and salt; pour over all.

Place casserole in pan of hot water and bake in moderate oven (350°F. Mark 4) 1¼ hours. Serves 6.

SPANISH KIDNEY BEANS

4 rashers streaky bacon
1 onion, chopped
½ green pepper, minced
1 pound minced beef
1 can tomato purée (2¼ ounces)
¼ teaspoon each salt and pepper
1 can red kidney beans (10 ounces)
Buttered breadcrumbs

Fry bacon in heavy pan. When lightly browned, add onion and green pepper and sauté 3 to 5 minutes. Add meat and cook until meat loses its red colour. Add tomato purée, salt, and pepper. Add kidney beans and their liquid.

Place in casserole. Top with crumbs. Heat and brown top in 350°F. Mark 4 oven. Serves 4.

CHILLI STUFFED PEPPERS

6 green peppers
½ pint boiling water
½ pound minced meat
1 large can chilli con carne (plain or with beans) drained (save liquid)
1 medium onion, chopped
1½ teaspoons salt
1 raw or canned tomato, chopped

Remove stems and seeds from pepper. Parboil in boiling water for 5 minutes.

Combine meat, chilli con carne, onion, salt, and tomato.

Stuff peppers and arrange in shallow baking dish or casserole. Pour liquid from chilli con carne plus ½ pint water over peppers. Bake in moderate oven (350°F. Mark 4) for 45 minutes. Serves 6.

LAMB CHOP GRILLED MEAL

4 medium courgettes
8 cutlets or loin chops, or 4 chump chops, cut ¾-inch thick
Salt and pepper
2 large tomatoes, cut in half
4 large mushrooms
2 ounces butter or margarine, melted

Wash courgettes, slice, and simmer until tender.

Place chops on rack in grill pan. Grill under medium heat. When one side is browned, season and turn.

Place tomatoes cut-side up in grill pan, on rack. Top with a mushroom button. Arrange courgette slices on rack.

Brush tomatoes, mushrooms, and courgettes with melted butter.

Continue grilling until chops are done and vegetables lightly browned. Serves 4.

10-MINUTE CORNED BEEF AND CABBAGE

1 small head of cabbage
1 1-pound can corned beef, sliced
Butter or margarine
1 tablespoon lemon juice
Salt and pepper

Cut cabbage into thick wedges and place in large pan with small amount of boiling, salted water.

Place corned beef in a strainer, suspended over top of cooking pan but not touching the water. Cook 8 to 10 minutes. The steam from the cabbage will heat the corned beef.

Season cabbage with melted dripping, lemon juice, salt, and pepper. Serve on warm dish with corned beef slices. Serves 4.

ORANGE HAM LOAF WITH RAISIN SAUCE

1 1-pound can pork-ham luncheon meat
2 large oranges

Slice meat crosswise in ¼-inch slices to within 1 inch of bottom. Place loaf in shallow baking dish.

Peel and section oranges. Place orange sections between meat slices to form fan-shaped loaf.

Pour raisin sauce over loaf.

Bake in moderate oven (375°F. Mark 5) 20 minutes. Baste occasionally during baking. Serves 4.

Raisin Sauce: Combine 3 ounces brown sugar, 1 tablespoon flour, 1 teaspoon dry mustard, 1 teaspoon grated lemon rind, 1½ tablespoons lemon juice, 1½ tablespoons vinegar, and 2 ounces seedless raisins in saucepan. Heat to boiling point and cook over low heat 1 minute, stirring constantly.

Frankfurters

BARBECUED GRILLED OR ROASTED FRANKFURTERS

Grill frankfurters or cook on a rack in roasting pan. During cooking baste them frequently with barbecue sauce.

SAUTÉED FRANKFURTERS

Cover frankfurters with boiling water. Allow to stand 7 to 8 minutes.

Slice lengthwise and sauté in a little dripping or cooking oil. Turn to brown both sides.

BOILED FRANKFURTERS

Cover frankfurters with boiling water. Simmer gently 7 to 8 minutes.

GRILLED FRANKFURTERS

Cover frankfurters with boiling water. Allow to stand for 7 to 8 minutes.

Slice lengthwise and brush with dripping or cooking oil.

Place skin-side-down on grill rack under medium heat. Grill until brown.

FRANKFURTER KEBABS

2 to 3 ounces tomato chutney
1 ounce brown sugar
3 tablespoons vinegar
3 drops Tabasco sauce
3 slices onion
12 frankfurters
8 rashers of streaky bacon

Combine chutney, brown sugar, vinegar, Tabasco sauce, and onion in saucepan. Simmer 5 minutes.

Cut each frankfurter into quarters and each rasher of bacon into 6 pieces. Arrange alternately on skewers.

Place on baking-sheet and spread with half the sauce. Grill 5 minutes under moderate heat. Turn, spread with remaining sauce, and grill 5 minutes longer. Serves 6.

FRANKFURTER FRITTERS

Slice frankfurters lengthwise and spread inside with English mustard. Press together.

Dip into fritter cover batter (see Index) and fry in deep hot oil (365°F.) until browned. Serve two per portion.

Frankly delicious! Top pork and beans, broad beans, or kidney beans (the three are good together) with grilled or fried frankfurters. Pour on ketchup or chilli sauce.

BAKED OR GRILLED STUFFED FRANKFURTERS

7½ ounces fresh breadcrumbs
¼ teaspoon salt
⅛ teaspoon pepper
1 teaspoon each sage and thyme
1 small onion, finely chopped
3 ounces melted butter or margarine
10 frankfurters
10 rashers of streaky bacon

Combine crumbs, seasonings, onion, and butter or margarine. Blend well.

Slice frankfurters lengthwise and fill with stuffing. Wrap each with a bacon rasher. Fasten with cocktail sticks.

Grill 10 minutes or bake in moderate oven (350°F. Mark 4) 30 minutes. Serves 5 or more.

Variations:

Apple-Stuffed Frankfurters: Use chopped apple instead of stuffing.

Cheese-Stuffed Frankfurters: Use slice of Cheddar or Gloucester cheese instead of stuffing. Grill or bake until cheese melts and bacon is browned.

Piccalilli-Stuffed Frankfurters: Combine 2 to 3 ounces Piccalilli and 2 tablespoons English mustard. Use instead of stuffing.

FRANKFURTERS STUFFED WITH SAUERKRAUT

Slice frankfurters lengthwise; spread the outside with mustard and fill the centre with sauerkraut.

Wrap each stuffed frankfurter with a rasher of bacon; fasten with a wooden cocktail stick.

Grill or bake in hot oven (400°F. Mark 6) until bacon is crisp and frankfurters are well cooked.

Variation: Substitute sour pickles for sauerkraut.

BARBECUED FRANKFURTERS

12 ounces canned tomatoes
4 fluid ounces red wine or water
2 cloves garlic, mashed
1 onion, finely chopped
1 carrot, minced
2 tablespoons chilli powder
1 teaspoon curry powder
½ teaspoon dry mustard
1½ teaspoons Worcestershire sauce
Salt to taste
1 ounce bacon dripping
1 dozen frankfurters

Simmer together for 30 minutes the tomatoes, wine, garlic, onion, carrot, chilli powder, curry powder, mustard, Worcestershire sauce, and salt.

When sauce has almost finished cooking, melt the bacon fat in a frying pan, add frankfurters and sauté. Then pour the finished sauce over frankfurters, cover and cook over low heat about 10 minutes. Serves 6.

Frankfurters with Sweet and Pungent Sauce

FRANKFURTERS WITH SWEET AND PUNGENT SAUCE

2 ounces butter or margarine
1 clove garlic, crushed
1 ounce chopped green pepper
2 tablespoons brown sugar
¼ teaspoon ground ginger
1 pound frankfurters, sliced crosswise
2½ ounces raisins
9 ounces of pineapple, crushed, drain liquid
8 fluid ounces apple juice
4 fluid ounces wine vinegar
½ teaspoon salt
1 tablespoon cornflour
2 fluid ounces cold water

Melt butter or margarine and sauté garlic and green pepper. Stir in brown sugar and ginger.

Add frankfurters and cook until tender, about 10 minutes. Add raisins, pineapple, apple juice, vinegar, and salt. Mix well.

Stir cornflour into cold water. Add to frankfurter mixture. Simmer, stirring occasionally, 15 minutes or until raisins are soft. Serve on cream crackers.

CREOLE FRANKFURTERS

4 frankfurters
1½ tablespoons finely chopped onion
1 tablespoon finely chopped green pepper
1 ounce lard
1 rounded tablespoon ketchup
2 fluid ounces water
¼ teaspoon malt or wine vinegar
2 teacups cooked rice
2 tablespoons chopped parsley

Lightly brown frankfurters, onion, and green pepper in lard in frying pan. Stir in ketchup and remaining ingredients; cook over low heat 5 minutes. Serves 2.

Creole Frankfurters

*Onion Frankfurters
with Spiced Sauerkraut*

ONION FRANKFURTERS WITH SPICED SAUERKRAUT

1¾ pounds sauerkraut
1 teaspoon celery seed
pinch celery salt
½ teaspoon dry mustard
6 frankfurters
3 small onions
2 ounces butter or margarine, melted

In a basin, combine sauerkraut, celery seed, celery salt, and mustard; toss lightly but thoroughly.

Slit each frankfurter diagonally in four places. Peel onions and cut each into 8 thin slices. Insert an onion slice into each slit in frankfurters.

Arrange half of sauerkraut mixture in bottom of 2½ pint casserole. Place 3 frankfurters on top of sauerkraut mixture in casserole. Top with remaining sauerkraut mixture.

Place remaining 3 frankfurters side by side on top of casserole. Pour melted butter or margarine over all.

Bake in moderate oven (350°F. Mark 4) 25 minutes. Serves 4 to 6.

GRILLED CHEESE AND FRANK-FURTER SPECIAL

8 frankfurters
¾ pound processed Cheddar cheese
8 bread slices

Parboil 8 frankfurters and split lengthwise. Place cheese in thin slices on 8 bread slices, reserving several strips for garnish.

Grill until cheese is melted and slightly browned.

Top each slice with split frankfurter and remaining cheese. Grill until cheese strips are slightly melted.

Arrange on serving dish. Garnish with olives, pickles, and celery leaves. Serve with English mustard. Serves 4 to 8.

Grilled Cheese and Frankfurter Special

FRANKFURTER PUFFS

Pour boiling water over 6 frankfurters; cover; let stand 8 minutes. Slit frankfurters lengthwise. Spread with mustard.

Combine 14 ounces well seasoned mashed potatoes, 1 small chopped onion, 1 to 2 tablespoons chopped pimiento, and small bunch chopped parsley.

Spread over frankfurters. Brown under grill or in oven. Serves 6.

FRANKFURTERS IN BLANKET

Lay a frankfurter on a slice of bread. Spread frankfurter with mustard, chilli sauce or Piccalilli.

Wrap bread around frankfurter and secure with small metal skewers.

Brush bread with melted butter. Place on baking-sheet or pie-dish. Bake in hot oven (425°F. Mark 7) about 15 minutes.

CHEESE AND FRANKFURTERS

1 pound frankfurters
4 ounces grated Cheddar cheese
2 to 3 ounces chopped peanuts
2 tablespoons salad dressing
long rolls

Cut a long slit in each frankfurter. Combine cheese, peanuts, and salad dressing. Fill each frankfurter with cheese mixture.

Place frankfurters on baking-sheet. Bake in slow oven (325°F. Mark 3) 10 minutes or until cheese is melted and frankfurters are heated through. Serve in warmed buns.

STUFFED FRANKFURTER CASSEROLE

4 ounces uncooked macaroni
8 fluid ounces milk
2 tablespoons minced pimiento
1½ teaspoons salt
1½ teaspoons Worcestershire sauce
4 ounces grated cheese
1 ounce Piccalilli or Branston pickle
1 small minced onion
8 frankfurters

Cook macaroni in boiling salted water until tender. Drain.

Combine macaroni, milk, pimiento, salt, Worcestershire sauce, and ¾ of the cheese. Pour into greased, shallow casserole.

Combine Piccalilli and chopped onion. Slit frankfurters lengthwise but do not cut all the way through. Fill frankfurters with Piccalilli and onion top with remaining cheese and place on macaroni.

Bake in moderate oven (350°F. Mark 4) 25 minutes. Serves 6 to 8.

FRANKFURTER, APPLE AND CHEESE PIE

8 frankfurters
3 tart apples, peeled and thinly sliced
2 ounces granulated or brown sugar
2 ounces grated Cheddar cheese

Put the frankfurters in a layer in baking dish. Spread lightly with mustard.

Cover with apple slices. Sprinkle with sugar and bake in moderate oven (350°F. Mark 4) about 20 minutes.

Sprinkle with cheese and bake or grill until cheese melts. Serves 4.

FRYING-PAN FRANKFURTERS

1 pound frankfurters
1 ounce butter or margarine
1 rounded tablespoon ketchup
1 tablespoon English mustard
9 to 10 long rolls

Fry frankfurters in butter in heavy frying pan until browned.

Combine ketchup and mustard and pour over frankfurters. Turn to coat well with sauce. Heat 2 or 3 minutes. Serve in a split roll. Serves 6 to 8.

FRANKFURTERS IN TOMATO PASTRY ROLLS

1 8-ounce packet short crust pastry mix
tomato juice
2 ounces grated Parmesan cheese
1 tablespoon chopped p:
12 frankfurters
2 tablespoons melted bu. .. r margarine

Prepare pastry mix according to directions on packet, substituting tomato juice for liquid required.

Roll into 12-inch circle; sprinkle with grated cheese and chopped parsley.

Cut into 12 pie-shaped pieces and roll a frankfurter in each piece, rolling from wide edge of dough.

Brush with melted butter or margarine and bake in hot oven (400°F. Mark 6) for 15 to 20 minutes. Serves 12.

Frankfurters in Tomato Pastry Rolls

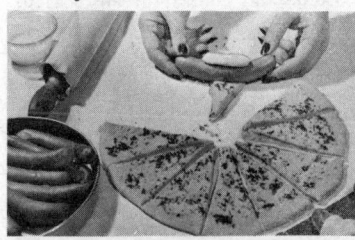

Quick and Easy Poultry Recipes

CHICKEN CASSEROLE

1 packet frozen chicken and mush-
    room casserole
4 fluid ounces single cream
1 ounce butter or margarine
3 tablespoons sherry
¼ pound processed Cheddar cheese,
    sliced

In saucepan over low heat, heat frozen chicken casserole with cream 20 minutes, stirring often to prevent sticking.

Add sherry to chicken.

Pour into 10×7½×2-inch baking dish; top with cheese; grill a few seconds under a heated grill. Serve on toast triangles. Serves 4.

BAKED CHICKEN PUFF

1 can (10½ ounces) condensed
    cream of mushroom soup
3 ounces milk
6 ounces cooked chicken
14 ounces cooked green beans,
    drained
4 eggs, separated
1 ounce grated Cheddar cheese

Combine soup and milk in 2½ pint casserole; add chicken and beans. Bake in moderate oven (375°F. Mark 5) 10 minutes.

Meanwhile, beat egg yolks well; add cheese. Beat egg whites until stiff and fold into egg-cheese mixture.

Pile fluffy egg topping on hot chicken; continue baking 30 minutes. Serves 6.

Baked Beef Puff: Follow recipe for Baked Chicken Puff, but use 1 can of condensed cream of celery soup instead of mushroom, cooked beef instead of chicken, and cooked, diced carrots (about 12 ounces) instead of green beans.

Baker Tuna Puff: Follow recipe for Baked Chicken Puff, but use 1 7-ounce can of tuna fish instead of chicken, and cooked green peas instead of beans.

CHICKEN-IN-CREAM POTATO PIE

1 tablespoon butter or margarine
1¼ pounds thick seasoned mashed
    potato
¾ pound creamed chicken, or 1 can
    chicken suprême
Salt, pepper to taste

Spread butter over inside of 8-inch pie dish or pan. Spread ⅔ of the mashed potato over bottom and sides of pan. Build up edge slightly.

Season creamed chicken mixture with salt, pepper to taste.

Pour into potato-lined dish. Put remaining potato through forcing bag to make a fluted edge and to decorate top.

Place in moderate oven (375°F. Mark 5) 25 to 30 minutes until heated through and bubbly hot. Serves 4 to 6.

CHICKEN TETRAZZINI

¼ pound narrow noodles
¼ pound sliced mushrooms
1½ ounces butter or margarine
1 14- or 16-ounce can pre-cooked
    chicken
1 tablespoon sherry
3 tablespoons grated Parmesan
    cheese

Cook noodles in boiling salted water until tender; drain.

Meanwhile, sauté mushrooms in butter until tender. Add chicken; heat quickly; don't simmer or stir. Stir in sherry.

Place drained noodles in 10×7½×2-inch baking dish. Pour mixture into centre. Sprinkle with Parmesan cheese; grill until golden under medium heat. Serves 2 to 3.

CHICKEN ALMONDINE

1 14- or 16-ounce can pre-cooked
    chicken
1 ounce slivered almonds
⅛ teaspoon salt

Heat chicken quickly; don't simmer or stir. Stir in almonds and salt with a fork. Serves 2 or 3.

Chicken-in-Cream Potato Pie

CHICKEN PAPRIKA

1 sliced onion
2 tablespoons butter or margarine
1 14- or 16-ounce can pre-cooked
    chicken
4 ounces sour cream
½ teaspoon paprika

Sauté onion in butter until tender. Add chicken. Heat quickly; don't simmer or stir.

With fork, stir in sour cream and paprika. Heat. Serves 2 or 3.

SPAGHETTI-POULTRY CASSEROLE

Top a casserole of plain cooked spaghetti with a tin of sliced turkey or chicken.

Cover with a can of cream of mushroom soup and bake in a moderate oven (350°F. Mark 4) 25 minutes.

BAKED CHICKEN SALAD

1 pound (approx.) tinned boned
    chicken, coarsely cut up
6 ounces sliced celery
2 ounces chopped walnuts
½ teaspoon salt
dash of pepper
2 teaspoons minced onion
2 tablespoons lemon juice
4 tablespoons mayonnaise
2 ounces crushed potato crisps

Combine all ingredients except potato crisps; toss lightly.

Pile into 4 individual baking dishes or 9-inch deep pie dish. Crush potato crisps; sprinkle over all.

Bake in very hot oven (450°F. Mark 8) 15 minutes, or until lightly browned. Serves 4.

CHICKEN CURRY

1 large chopped onion
1 ounce minced green pepper
2 tablespoons lemon juice
2 rounded tablespoons tomato
    ketchup
1 clove garlic, crushed
1 1-pound tin boneless pre-cooked
    chicken
¼ teaspoon curry powder

Mince onion and green pepper. Add lemon juice, ketchup and crushed garlic clove. Simmer together until sauce has cooked down almost dry.

Cut chicken into fork-size pieces. Add chicken and gravy to sauce. Season with curry and heat thoroughly. Serves 4.

For whole meal sandwiches in casseroles: place ½ inch thick, oblong slices of whole wheat bread on a baking-sheet in moderate oven (350°F. Mark 4) and bake until crisp and toasted. Then place a slice of toast in a shallow casserole, cover with slice of cooked turkey, then a crisp, cooked bacon rasher. Cover all with thick, well seasoned cheese sauce. Bake in moderate oven (350°F. Mark 4) until cheese is bubbly, 15 to 20 minutes. Serve at once.

Chicken Fricassée
in Green Bean and Rice Ring

CHICKEN FRICASSÉE IN GREEN BEAN AND RICE RING

8 ounces uncooked rice
1 pint water
1 teaspoon salt
¼ teaspoon Aromat
1 pound tinned cut green beans
¼ teaspoon Aromat
2 7¼-ounce cans pre-cooked chicken suprème
¼ teaspoon Aromat
Salt to taste

Cook rice with water, salt, and ¼ teaspoon Aromat until tender and all water is absorbed. Spoon a layer of rice into bottom of well oiled 8-inch ring mould.

Heat beans in their liquid with Aromat. Use remaining rice and hot green beans alternately to fill mould level full.

Place in moderate oven (350°F. Mark 4) to heat through.

Heat chicken in saucepan. Turn mould out upside-down on hot plate. Fill centre with hot chicken mixture. Serves 4 to 5.

CHICKEN CURRY FREDONA

1 can (10½ ounces) condensed cream of chicken soup
6 fluid ounces condensed milk
4 fluid ounces chicken broth
1 teaspoon curry powder
1½ pound tinned boned chicken or turkey, cut into large pieces
½ teaspoon chopped ginger
6 ounces mushrooms
4 ounces shredded coconut
6 ounces chow mein noodles

Combine soup, milk, broth, and curry powder.

Heat combined liquids in saucepan over low heat, stirring until blended.

Add chicken, ginger, mushrooms and coconut. Heat through.

Serve over heated noodles with chopped peanuts, pickled peaches and shredded coconut.

Serves 6.

CHICKEN À LA SHERMAN

1 7¼-ounce can chicken suprème or 14-ounce packet frozen chicken and mushroom casserole
2½ ounces cooked ham
lightly cooked asparagus tips
butter or margarine
breadcrumbs

To the can of chicken suprème or packet of frozen chicken casserole (defrosted), add ham cut into small squares. Heat.

Place in a shallow casserole or heat-proof glass pie dish. Top with lightly cooked asparagus tips. Dot with butter. Sprinkle with breadcrumbs and set under the grill just long enough to brown crumbs.

Serve bubbling hot from the casserole. This same combination may also be placed on buttered toast. Serves 4.

CRUNCHY CHICKEN CASSEROLE

1 10½-ounce can condensed cream of chicken soup
4 fluid ounces milk
5 ounces cubed cooked chicken
2 ounces cornflakes
scant ½ pound unsalted cooked lima or small white haricot beans, drained

Empty soup into a small casserole. Add milk and mix thoroughly.

Add chicken, 2 ounces cornflakes, and beans. Stir well.

Sprinkle top with remaining cornflakes.

Bake in moderate oven (375°F. Mark 5) 25 minutes. Serves 4.

CHICKEN CASSEROLE

Turn 1 can of chicken suprème into greased casserole. Top with 1 packet frozen spinach or broccoli, cooked and seasoned, and grated Parmesan cheese.

Bake in moderate oven (375°F. Mark 5) 15 to 20 minutes. Serves 2 to 3.

QUICK CHICKEN CHOW MEIN

2 cans (1 pound each) chicken chop suey
1 tablespoon brown sugar
1 tablespoon vinegar
1 can (4-, 5-, or 6-ounce) boned chicken, cut in strips
6 ounces cooked chow mein noodles
soy sauce

Carefully combine chop suey, brown sugar, vinegar, and chicken in medium-sized saucepan, reserving a few strips of chicken for garnish. Heat, stirring gently.

Place chow mein noodles in shallow baking dish; heat in moderate oven (375°F. Mark 5) 5 minutes.

Serve piping hot over heated chow mein noodles; pass round soy sauce. Serves 4 to 5 generously.

CHICKEN RAREBIT

1 packet frozen broccoli
1 12-ounce can Welsh rarebit
12 ounces hot chicken broth
1 12-ounce can chicken or turkey
4 ounces cooked, chopped celery

Cook broccoli according to the directions on the packet. Drain and reserve liquid for soup.

Arrange broccoli in a greased baking dish. Place the Welsh rarebit in a basin and stand in a pan of boiling water. Add the chicken broth and stir until the mixture is well blended.

Cut chicken into 1-inch pieces and add with the celery to the rarebit. Place broccoli in a casserole; pour rarebit mixture over top and bake in a moderate oven (350°F. Mark 4) about 15 minutes or until thoroughly heated. Serves 4.

CHICKEN SUPRÊME ON WAFFLES

1 packet frozen waffles (see note below)
1 12-ounce can whole kernel sweetcorn, chopped
2 packets frozen chicken and mushroom casserole or two cans chicken suprème
1 can, 10½ ounces peas

Prepare waffles according to the directions on packet.

Heat chicken mixture in the top of a double boiler; add peas and sweetcorn and serve over the hot waffles. Serves 6.

Note: Scone or pancake mix may be used. In that case, mix sweetcorn into batter and bake as directed.

CORN AND CHICKEN BAKE

12 ounces diced cooked or tinned chicken
1½ ounces crushed potato crisps
1 10½-ounce can cream-style sweet-corn
12 ounces milk
few grains pepper
¾ teaspoon Aromat
2 beaten eggs

Combine all ingredients; pour into casserole; top with additional crushed potato crisps if desired.

Set casserole in pan of warm water. Bake in slow oven (325°F. Mark 3) until knife inserted comes out clean, about 1 hour. Serves 6.

Quick Chicken Chow Mein

Chicken Livers and Giblets

CREAMED CHICKEN LIVERS

Drop chicken livers into boiling chicken stock to cover; reduce heat and simmer until tender, about 6 to 8 minutes.

Drain and add them to medium white sauce made with part rich milk or cream and part chicken stock. Use about half as much sauce as there are livers.

Season with about 1 tablespoon sherry and salt and pepper to taste. Serve with scrambled eggs, rice, or on buttered toast.

GIBLETS AND NOODLES

1 pound chicken giblets
1 teaspoon salt
1½ pints water
1 packet chicken-noodle soup mix
2 teacups uncooked egg noodles

Simmer giblets in salted water until tender. Cool; remove meat, and slice.

Measure giblet stock to 1½ pints, add water, if necessary. Add soup mix and noodles; cook 10 minutes. Add giblets; simmer few minutes. Serves 4 to 6.

CHICKEN LIVER SAUTÉ

1 pound fresh or thawed frozen chicken livers
2 ounces butter or margarine
1 minced small onion (optional)
2 ounces flour
¾ pint water
1 teaspoon salt
sherry to taste, or 2 teaspoons Marmite

Cut livers in half. In frying pan, sauté livers and onion in butter over low heat, turning often, about 5 minutes. Remove livers.

Stir flour into fat; gradually stir in water; cook, stirring, until thickened. Add salt, sherry, and livers. Serve on toast or toasted hamburger rolls. Serves 4.

Liver-Mushroom Sauté: Sauté a few sliced mushrooms with livers.

Curried Liver Sauté: Substitute curry powder to taste for sherry.

Chicken Liver Sauté with Rice

FRICASSÉED GIBLETS

Chicken giblets including livers
1 ounce chopped green pepper
1 ounce chopped celery
1 ounce butter or margarine
1 ounce flour
8 fluid ounces chicken stock
salt and pepper

Simmer the giblets in slightly salted water to cover until tender. Add the chicken livers, green pepper, and celery for the last 15 minutes.

When cooked, drain and reserve the stock.

Melt butter or margarine and stir in flour, mixing until smooth. Gradually pour in the stock; stir until mixture boils and thickens, then cook about 3 minutes longer, stirring occasionally. Season to taste.

Add the giblets and reheat. Serve on toast. Serves 2 or 3.

CHICKEN LIVERS SUPRÊME

1 teacup uncooked rice
1 ounce butter or margarine
1 pound chicken livers, fresh or frozen
1 small can mushroom slices
1 10½-ounce can mushroom soup
3 fluid ounces milk
dash of pepper
few sprigs parsley
2 tablespoons white wine
1 ounce chopped toasted almonds

Cook rice until tender according to packet directions. Drain off any excess liquid.

Melt butter or margarine in frying pan; toss in chicken livers and brown quickly.

Add mushrooms and mushroom liquid, mushroom soup, milk, pepper, chopped parsley, and wine. Cook until hot and smooth, then mix with rice.

Pour into 3½-pint casserole; top with almonds and bake in moderate oven (350°F. Mark 4) 30 minutes. Serves 4 to 6.

CHICKEN LIVERS WITH OLIVES IN WINE SAUCE

1 pound chicken livers
2 ounces butter or margarine
3 tablespoons flour
8 fluid ounces chicken broth or bouillon
3 fluid ounces sherry
½ teaspoon salt
⅛ teaspoon pepper
10 sliced stuffed olives

Rinse chicken livers; cut off black or green spots, drain and dry.

Sauté livers in hot butter in saucepan over direct heat until nicely browned, turning frequently; remove from pan.

Blend in flour. Gradually add broth, sherry, and seasonings. Cook and stir until thickened and smooth.

Add livers and olives to sauce. Heat to piping hot. Serve at once on hot cooked noodles or rice. Serves 4.

CHICKEN LIVERS WITH PINE-APPLE AND PEPPERS

4 slices canned or fresh pineapple
2 medium green peppers, slivered
2 tablespoons oil or dripping
1 pound chicken livers
½ teaspoon salt
dash of pepper
8 fluid ounces chicken broth or bouillon
2 tablespoons cornflour
2 teaspoons soy sauce
4 fluid ounces wine vinegar
4 ounces sugar, granulated

Sauté pineapple (cut each slice in 6 pieces) and peppers in oil until peppers are slightly soft. Don't allow them to brown.

Remove from pan and add livers with salt and pepper. When livers are lightly browned and tender, remove to hot plate.

Mix cornflour to paste with a little of broth; add remaining broth, soy sauce, vinegar, and sugar.

Add to frying pan in which livers were browned. Cook and stir until sauce thickens and is clear.

Add peppers and pineapple. Heat thoroughly and pour over livers. Serve with rice. Serves 4.

CHICKEN LIVERS EN CASSEROLE

1 pound chicken livers
2 ounces butter or margarine
¼ teaspoon ground black pepper
1 large bay leaf, crumbled
1 tablespoon dried sliced onion
1 small can button mushrooms, drained
1 pound stewed tomatoes, slightly drained
1 10-ounce packet frozen mixed vegetables
2½ ounces (approx.) chicken- or bacon-flavoured crisps, finely crushed

Sauté chicken livers in butter or margarine. Add remaining ingredients, reserving 2 tablespoons of crisps for topping. Mix well.

Cook over medium heat 5 minutes, stirring constantly. Pour into a 2½-pint casserole. Bake in moderate oven (350°F. Mark 4) 1 hour. Serves 4.

Chicken Livers en Casserole

Curried Chicken Livers

CURRIED CHICKEN LIVERS

1 pound fresh or thawed frozen
    chicken livers
2 ounces butter or margarine
1 small minced onion
1 teaspoon salt
¼ teaspoon pepper
1 tablespoon curry powder
6 fluid ounces lager or ale
4 teacups hot cooked rice

Cut chicken livers in halves. Melt butter in frying pan or chafing dish. Add livers and onion and sauté 5 to 8 minutes, turning often, until livers are cooked.

Add salt, pepper, curry powder, and lager and bring to a simmer; continue cooking over low heat 3 minutes longer. Serve over rice. Serves 4.

SAVOURY CHICKEN LIVERS WITH RICE

1½ ounces butter or margarine
1 pound chicken livers
Salt and pepper to taste
⅛ teaspoon rosemary
4 fluid ounces white wine
4 teacups fluffy cooked rice

Melt butter; when bubbling, add chicken livers and season with salt, pepper, and rosemary. Cook until well browned, stirring occasionally.

Add wine and simmer 10 minutes. Serve over rice. Serves 4.

CHICKEN LIVERS WITH MIXED HERBS (Starter)

1 pound chicken livers
1 tablespoon minced onion
1 tablespoon chopped parsley
½ teaspoon salt
dash of pepper
¼ teaspoon celery salt
½ teaspoon crushed oregano
2 tablespoons olive oil
Flour as needed
Fat, oil, or butter as needed
minced parsley as needed

Remove black or green spots; wash livers; drain well.

Combine all ingredients; pour over livers. Let stand ½ hour to marinate.

Drain livers; roll in flour. Sauté lightly in fat 5 minutes. Place each liver on cocktail stick on plate; sprinkle with celery salt and parsley just before serving. Yield: 1 pound (16 individual servings).

CHICKEN LIVERS AND MUSH-ROOMS IN WINE SAUCE

1 pound chicken livers cut in
    halves
16 to 20 mushroom caps, depending
    on size
melted butter
1 more ounce butter
1½ ounces flour
12 fluid ounces chicken stock, made
    with cube
4 fluid ounces dry white wine
Salt and paprika

Brush chicken livers and mushroom caps with melted butter and put under grill briefly. The chicken livers will take 5 to 8 minutes, including both sides, and the mushroom caps 3 to 5 minutes.

Arrange 4 or 5 mushroom caps in each of 4 individual ramekins. Put 1 piece of chicken liver on each mushroom cap.

Cover with sauce as follows: Melt 1 ounce butter; blend in flour and add chicken stock slowly, stirring until thick and smooth. Add the white wine, salt, and paprika and cook until smooth.

Pour over mushrooms and chicken livers and place in moderate oven (350°F. Mark 4) 10 to 15 minutes, or until hot and bubbly. Serves 4.

CHICKEN LIVERS IN MADEIRA SAUCE

1 pound chicken livers, cut in
    large pieces
1½ fluid ounces olive oil
1 tablespoon tarragon vinegar
Salt and pepper
1 clove garlic
4 fluid ounces Madeira wine
pinch of sugar
1 ounce butter or margarine
scant 1 ounce flour
7 fluid ounces chicken stock
finely shredded or grated rind of 1
    orange

Cover livers with a mixture of olive oil, vinegar, salt, pepper, garlic, 2 fluid ounces Madeira, and sugar. Set in refrigerator overnight.

Drain livers on paper towels. Sauté in butter; transfer livers to a warm plate.

Thicken juices in pan by adding flour mixed with enough water to make a thin paste. Then add chicken stock and 2 ounces Madeira, stirring constantly until smooth and thickened.

Finally, add shredded orange rind. The shredding may be done rather simply by peeling a whole orange with a potato peeler and then chopping it very fine, or it may be grated the usual way.

Serve on freshly buttered toast. Serves 4.

CHICKEN LIVERS FLORENTINE

6 ounces long spaghetti
2 ounces butter or margarine
3 or 4 chopped spring onions
1 small clove garlic, chopped
½ pound chicken livers, diced
1½ ounces flour
½ teaspoon salt
pinch freshly ground pepper
⅛ teaspoon oregano
pinch sweet basil
7 ounces beef stock, made with
    cube
4 fluid ounces dry red wine

Cook spaghetti in boiling salted water until tender (about 15 minutes). Drain and rinse.

While spaghetti is cooking, melt butter or margarine in frying pan. Add onions, chopped with some of the green stems, and garlic; brown lightly.

Add chicken livers which have been diced and brown well.

Stir in flour and seasonings. Add beef stock and wine and cook until thickened, stirring constantly.

Arrange spaghetti on hot dish and top with chicken liver sauce. Sprinkle with chopped parsley. Serves 4 to 5.

CRUSTY CHICKEN LIVERS AND MUSHROOMS ON TOAST

12 chicken livers
1 egg, well beaten
2 teaspoons Worcestershire sauce
½ packet (4 ounces) shortcrust
    pastry mix
2 ounces butter or margarine
1 small can mushrooms
½ pint brown gravy
2 tablespoons sherry
6 slices toast
6 rashers grilled streaky bacon

Cut chicken livers in half. Beat egg with 1 teaspoon Worcestershire sauce. Dip chicken livers into egg mixture. Roll livers in pastry mix, coating generously.

Melt butter or margarine in frying pan. Fry livers until golden brown and crisp.

Heat mushrooms in gravy to boiling point. Add 1 teaspoon Worcestershire sauce and sherry. Place chicken livers on toast. Spoon gravy over all. Serve with crisp streaky bacon and hot applesauce. Serves 6.

Crusty Chicken Livers and Mushrooms on Toast

Quick and Easy Fish and Shellfish Recipes

QUICK PRAWN NEWBURG

Blend 1 ounce flour with 3 ounces cream of prawn soup (from 1 13-ounce can). Add remaining soup and 2 egg yolks, beaten; cook until thickened, stirring often.

Add 1 5-ounce can prawns, drained and deveined; heat thoroughly.

Just before serving, add 2 tablespoons sherry; serve in pastry cases, on toast or over hot, seasoned rice.

Serves 3 or 4.

Lobster or Crab Newburg: Use 1 7-7½-ounce can lobster or crab meat in place of prawns.

SALMON-RICE CASSEROLE

1 packet boil-in-the-bag rice
4 fluid ounces milk
½ pound processed Cheddar cheese, grated
¾ teaspoon salt
dash of pepper
7½ ounces canned salmon, flaked
8 chopped stuffed green olives

Cook rice as directed on packet.

Combine milk, cheese, salt, and pepper in a double saucepan. Heat and stir occasionally until well blended and smooth.

Place in 2½-pint casserole alternate layers of rice, salmon, olives, and cheese sauce, having a top layer of cheese sauce. Bake in moderate oven (350°F. Mark 4) 30 minutes. Serves 6.

Tuna-Rice Casserole: Substitute 7½ ounces tuna fish, flaked, for salmon.

PRAWN CHOP SUEY

2 1-pound cans meatless chop suey
1 5- or 7-ounce can prawns, drained and deveined
1 3- or 4-ounce can sliced mushrooms
1 tablespoon soy sauce

Carefully combine all ingredients in medium-sized saucepan. Heat, stirring gently.

Serve with hot rice; pass extra soy sauce. Serves 4.

Creamed Seafood with Wine

SALMON AND POTATO BAKE

2 ounces butter or margarine
1 ounce cornflour
1¾ pints milk
1 medium onion, chopped fine
1 teaspoon salt
¼ teaspoon pepper
1 tablespoon minced green pepper
1½ pounds thinly sliced raw potatoes
2 cans (14 ounces) salmon, flaked
2 or 3 ounces crushed potato crisps

Melt butter and blend in cornflour. Add milk, onion, salt, pepper, and green pepper. Cook, stirring constantly, until thickened.

Place alternate layers of potatoes, salmon with liquid from can, and sauce in greased casserole.

Cover, and bake in moderate oven (350°F. Mark 4) about 20 minutes. Remove cover and sprinkle with potato crisps. Bake until potatoes are tender, about 25 minutes. Serves 6.

QUICK LOBSTER THERMIDOR

1 can (10½ ounces) condensed cream of mushroom soup
¼ can white wine or soup water
1 tablespoon lemon juice
4 tablespoons grated Parmesan cheese
pinch of dry mustard or ½ teaspoon prepared English mustard
4 to 8 ounces cooked or canned lobster meat

To a can of condensed cream of mushroom soup, add white wine or water, lemon juice, grated cheese, and mustard.

Heat in top of double saucepan and add lobster meat, cut into good-sized cubes.

Place in shallow buttered casserole or in lobster shells. Sprinkle with cheese and bake in very hot oven (450°F. Mark 8) 15 minutes or set under the grill about 5 minutes until cheese melts and slightly browns.

Serve bubbling hot from shells or making dish. Serves 4 to 6.

CREAMED SEAFOOD WITH WINE

2 ounces single cream
1 can (7½-ounces) of tuna, salmon, prawns, or crab
1 can (10 ounces) condensed cream of mushroom soup
2 tablespoons sherry

Add cream and coarsely flaked seafood to soup and heat gently over direct heat or over hot water.

Add wine, reheat and serve on hot buttered toast. Serves 4.

PRAWN JAMBALAYA

1 ounce butter, margarine, or lard
4 ounces chopped celery
1 medium minced onion
1 small chopped green pepper
2 tablespoons wholemeal flour
2¼-ounce can tomato purée
1¾ pints water
1 teaspoon salt
dash of pepper
2 7-ounce cans prawns
3 to 4 teacups cooked rice

Melt butter in frying pan; add celery, onion, and green pepper and cook until tender.

Stir in flour and gradually pour in tomato purée and water mixed together. Add seasoning and cook 5 minutes longer, stirring constantly.

Add prawns and heat thoroughly. Serve over rice. Serves 6.

PRAWN AND CRAB MEAT CASSEROLE

1 medium green pepper, chopped
1 medium onion, chopped
4 ounces chopped celery
1 6½-ounce can crab meat, flaked
1 7-ounce can prawns, cleaned
½ teaspoon salt
⅛ teaspoon pepper
1 teaspoon Worcestershire sauce
4 rounded tablespoons mayonnaise
3 ounces fresh breadcrumbs

Combine all ingredients except crumbs. Turn into buttered casserole or individual ramekins.

Sprinkle with crumbs. Bake in moderate oven (350°F. Mark 4) 30 minutes. Serves 6 to 8.

NOODLE PRAWN CURRY

8 ounces medium egg noodles
1 can (10½ ounces) condensed cream of celery soup
3 tablespoons tomato ketchup
½ teaspoon paprika
1 teaspoon curry powder
⅛ teaspoon ginger
1 pound fresh or frozen prawns (cooked and cleaned)

Cook noodles in 4½ pints boiling salted water (1 tablespoon salt). Drain in colander.

Combine soup, ketchup, paprika, curry powder, and ginger; mix thoroughly. Cook over low heat 5 minutes, stirring occasionally. Add prawns; heat thoroughly.

Turn cooked noodles into heated serving dish; top with prawn curry.

Serve with accompaniments such as pickled onions, chutney, sieved or chopped hard-boiled eggs, chopped or whole peanuts, grated fresh coconut, or crumbled crisp streaky bacon. Serves 4.

uick and Easy Rice and Pasta Recipes

EASY MACARONI AND CHEESE

1. Melt ½ pound of natural Cheddar cheese in top of double saucepan.

2. When cheese is melted, slowly add a large can (13 fluid ounces) of evaporated milk, stirring constantly.

Add 1 teaspoon salt and ⅛ teaspoon pepper to cheese sauce.

3. Place 8 ounces quick macaroni (which has been cooked until tender in boiling salted water, and drained) in 2½ pint casserole.

Pour cheese sauce over macaroni and mix lightly.

Mix 4½ ounces coarse fresh breadcrumbs, lightly packed with ½ ounce melted margarine or butter, and sprinkle over top of macaroni.

4. Bake in moderate oven (350°F. Mark 4) 25 minutes. Serve at once. Serves 6.

NOODLE-SAUSAGE MEAL

8 ounces egg noodles
1 pound chipolata sausages
6 ounces cooked peas, canned or frozen
12 fluid ounces canned tomato juice
1 teaspoon salt
¼ teaspoon pepper

Cook noodles in boiling, salted water until tender. Drain.

Brown sausages over low heat; pour off any excess fat.

Add noodles, peas, tomato juice, and seasonings. Simmer, uncovered, 15 minutes, stirring occasionally. Serves 6.

TOMATO CHEESE MACARONI

1 can (10½ ounces) condensed tomato soup
4 fluid ounces milk
8 ounces grated sharp Cheddar cheese
1 bunch finely chopped parsley
1 pound cooked macaroni (½ pound uncooked)
2 tablespoons buttered breadcrumbs, if desired

Heat soup, milk, and 6 ounces cheese over low heat; when cheese melts, add parsley. Blend with macaroni; pour into a buttered 3½-pint casserole.

Top with remaining cheese and buttered breadcrumbs. Bake in hot oven (400°F. Mark 6) 20 minutes. Serves 6.

CHILLI RICE MEXICALI

1 ounce butter or margarine
1 teaspoon chilli powder
1 packet boil-in-the-bag rice
12 fluid ounces cold water
1 ounce lard
1 medium onion, sliced
1 green pepper, diced
1 can (8¾ ounces) kidney beans
2 tomatoes, diced
1 can (12 ounces) whole kernel sweetcorn
2 tablespoons chilli powder
salt and pepper to taste
1 teaspoon Aromat
½ pound sharp Cheddar cheese, grated

Melt butter or margarine; blend in 1 teaspoon chilli powder. Add rice and cold water. Bring to a full boil, fluffing rice occasionally with fork. Boil 2 minutes. Remove from heat; cover, let stand 10 minutes.

Meanwhile melt lard; cook onion and green pepper in lard until soft but not brown.

Add beans, tomatoes, sweetcorn, and seasonings; mix well. Add cheese; stir over low heat until cheese melts.

Pack hot rice into ring mould; invert on serving plate. Fill centre with bean mixture. Garnish with fried banana quarters. Serves 6.

MACARONI AND CHILLI DE LUXE

1 tablespoon salt
4½ pints boiling water
8 ounces quick macaroni
1½ ounces butter or margarine
1½ ounces diced green pepper
2 medium-sized onions, thinly sliced
1 large can chilli con carne with beans
7 fluid ounces tomato juice

Add 1 tablespoon salt to rapidly boiling water. Gradually add macaroni so that water continues to boil. Cook uncovered, stirring occasionally, until tender. Drain in colander.

Melt butter or margarine over medium heat; add green pepper and onions and sauté until tender.

Add macaroni, chilli, and tomato juice; mix well. Cook over low heat until thoroughly heated, stirring occasionally. Serves 4 to 6.

SPAGHETTI CASSEROLE DE LUXE

2 ounces butter or margarine
3 tablespoons flour
1 teaspoon salt
⅛ teaspoon pepper
8 fluid ounces milk
8 fluid ounces chicken or vegetable stock
1 pound cooked spaghetti
½ pound fresh mushrooms, sliced
5 ounces diced, cooked chicken
2 ounces grated Parmesan cheese

Melt butter in saucepan. Stir in flour and seasonings. Add milk and stock gradually, stirring constantly to prevent lumping. Allow to boil and cook 3 minutes.

Place spaghetti in buttered casserole. Scatter mushrooms and chicken over it. Pour sauce over all. Sprinkle cheese on top.

Bake in slow oven (325°F. Mark 3) until mushrooms are tender (about 30 minutes). Serves 6.

Variations: Veal or tuna fish may be substituted for chicken.

If canned mushrooms are used, bake just until cheese is melted and mixture heated through.

If stock is not available, use ½ chicken stock cube with 8 fluid ounces hot water.

Chilli Rice Mexicali

Quick and Easy Cheese Recipes

EASY SWISS FONDUE

1 pound Swiss cheese
6 fluid ounces white wine
hot toast or French bread

Cut the cheese in small pieces. Place in top of double saucepan or in a fondue dish over hot water.

Add wine; heat and stir until cheese melts and the mixture is smooth.

Serve with hot toast, or thick slices of French bread. Serves 4.

Variation: Omit wine. Use 2 ounces butter or margarine; season with ½ teaspoon salt and ⅛ teaspoon white pepper.

MONTEREY JACK

4 slices streaky bacon, diced
1 medium onion, sliced
1 green pepper, diced
2 cans (17½ ounces) red kidney
    beans
3 tomatoes, diced
2 tablespoons chilli powder
½ teaspoon salt
few grains pepper
1 teaspoon Aromat
½ pound sharp Cheddar cheese,
    grated

Fry bacon until crisp; drain on absorbent paper.

Cook onion and green pepper in 1 ounce of the bacon fat until soft but not brown.

Add kidney beans, tomatoes, bacon, seasonings, and cheese. Stir over low heat until cheese melts. Serves 8.

Note: One pound dried kidney beans soaked overnight and cooked until tender may be used instead of canned beans.

GRILLED TOMATOES AND CHEESE TOAST

4 large tomatoes
½ teaspoon salt
1 teaspoon sugar
½ ounce butter or margarine
4 slices bread
¼ to ½ pound Cheddar cheese, sliced
    thin
12 gherkin slices

Cut tomatoes in half and sprinkle with salt and sugar; dot with butter or margarine.

Remove grill pan and preheat grill for 5 minutes. Place tomatoes on rack of grill pan. Grill slowly for 6 minutes; place slices of bread on grill and toast on one side.

Turn bread over and top with cheese slices. Continue grilling tomatoes and cheese toast for 3 to 5 minutes until tomatoes are tender and cheese melts.

Remove from grill; cut cheese toast diagonally into quarters. Serve all on plate, with 4 of the tomato halves placed on the cheese toast and topped with pickle slices. Serves 4.

CHEESE FONDUE

12 fluid ounces scalded milk
4½ ounces bread cubes
¼ pound Cheddar cheese, diced
½ ounce butter or margarine
½ teaspoon salt
¼ teaspoon mustard
2 eggs, separated

Mix scalded milk with bread cubes, cheese, butter, salt, and mustard.

Beat egg yolks until lemon coloured; blend cheese mixture into egg yolks.

Beat egg whites until stiff and fold into first mixture.

Pour into an oiled pie-dish, 9 inches in diameter. Bake in moderate oven (350°F. Mark 4) 20 to 30 minutes, or until set. Serve immediately. Serves 4 to 5.

SPIEDANO ROMANO

1 loaf unsliced white bread
4 ounces margarine or butter
1 small finely grated onion
1 rounded tablespoon prepared
    mustard
1 tablespoon poppy seeds
½ pound sliced processed cheese
½ teaspoon Aromat
2 or 3 slices streaky bacon, cut in
    half

Spiedano Romano

Remove all crusts from bread. Make regular diagonal cuts about 1½ inches apart, but do not cut completely through loaf.

Soften margarine or butter; blend in onion, mustard, and poppy seeds. Spread all but 1 ounce of mixture between cuts.

Fill cuts with cheese, sprinkling each cheese slice with Aromat. Press loaf together. Spread outside and over top with reserved mixture. Arrange bacon on top.

Place in greased shallow baking dish. Bake in moderate oven (350°F. Mark 4) until cheese is melted and loaf is browned, about 15 minutes. Serve at once.

Serves 4 to 6.

Note: If the loaf of bread is sliced, trim off and discard crusts and spread some of the butter mixture on each slice. Top with cheese; sprinkle with Aromat.

As you go along, press slices together in buttered bread pan to make a bread-loaf shape. Put bacon or anchovy butter on top, as you prefer; bake as directed.

BACON AND CREAM CHEESE ROLL

Trim the crusts from a fresh loaf of white bread and cut ¼-inch lengthwise slices. Spread each slice with cream cheese which has softened at room temperature.

Roll up each slice like a Swiss roll.

Cut each roll in half crosswise, and wrap a slice of streaky bacon around each roll, fastening it with a cocktail stick.

Place the rolls on the grill rack, and toast them under moderate grill heat, turning often until the bacon is cooked.

Arrange the rolls on a plate or dish and serve with stuffed olives.

Bacon and Cream Cheese Rolls

Pressure-Cooked Recipes

SPAGHETTI MEAT SAUCE

1 ounce cooking oil
1 pound minced beef
4 or 5 medium onions, sliced
3 or 4 cloves garlic, chopped
1 can (8 ounces) tomato sauce
2 cans (6 ounces) tomato paste
½ teaspoon red pepper
1 tablespoon chilli powder
1 teaspoon salt
dash of pepper
16 fluid ounces water

Combine all ingredients in pressure cooker. Adjust cover. Exhaust air from cooker. Cook at 15-pound pressure 20 minutes.

Reduce pressure quickly. Serve over cooked spaghetti (8 ounces long spaghetti). Top with grated Parmesan cheese. Serves 6.

CHICKEN FRICASSÉE

1 2- to 3-pound ready-to-cook
    chicken, cut in pieces, or 2
    1-pound packets frozen
    chicken pieces
2 ounces lard
8 fluid ounces water
2 small onions, sliced
2 bay leaves
½ ounce chopped celery leaves
2 teaspoons salt
dash of pepper
milk
3 ounces plain flour
½ teaspoon salt
¼ teaspoon mixed herbs

Roll chicken in seasoned flour (2 teaspoons salt and 2 teaspoons paprika to 4 ounces flour). Brown in hot fat in pressure cooker.

Add water, onions, bay leaves, celery leaves, 2 teaspoons salt, and pepper. Cook at 15-pound pressure 35 minutes.

Allow pressure to go down normally. Remove chicken. Strain broth; add milk to make 1¼ pints.

Mix ½ pint of the liquid with flour until blended. Add remaining liquid. Return to pressure cooker. Cook, stirring constantly, until gravy is thick.

Add ½ teaspoon salt and mixed herbs. Pour over chicken.

Serves 4 to 6.

Chicken Fricassée

QUICK SAUERBRATEN

3 pounds rump of beef or stewing
    steak
3 ounces grape jelly
2 large onions, cut in ¼-inch slices
6 whole black peppers
2 bay leaves, crushed
2 teaspoons salt
½ teaspoon allspice
½ teaspoon ginger
¼ teaspoon pepper
3 fluid ounces vinegar
2 fluid ounces water
1 teaspoon mixed herbs

Trim excess fat from meat and fry the fat lightly in pressure cooker.

Brown meat slowly on all sides in the hot fat. Allow 10 to 20 minutes for browning.

Spread with grape jelly; top with onion slices and sprinkle with seasonings.

Combine vinegar, water, and mixed herbs; pour over meat.

Cook at 15-pound pressure 40 to 45 minutes. Allow pressure to go down normally. Serves 6 to 8.

MEAT HEDGEHOGS

1½ pounds minced beef
4 ounces rice
1 teaspoon salt
½ teaspoon pepper
1 tablespoon chopped onion
1 can (10½ ounces) condensed
    tomato soup
4 fluid ounces water

Combine meat, rice, salt, pepper, and onion. Form into small balls.

Blend soup and water; heat in pressure cooker until mixture begins to simmer.

Add meat balls. Cook at 15-pound pressure 10 minutes.

Allow the pressure to go down normally. Serves 4 to 6.

TEXAS CHILLI CON CARNE

1 pound minced beef
2 cans (20 ounces) tomatoes
1 can (1 pound cooked) chilli or
    kidney beans
1 large chopped onion
3 ounces chopped green pepper
1 clove garlic, minced
2 bay leaves
1 tablespoon flour
1 tablespoon chilli powder
1 tablespoon brown sugar
1 teaspoon salt
1 teaspoon ground oregano
½ teaspoon basil
dash of cayenne

Combine all ingredients. Cook at 15-pound pressure 15 minutes. Let pressure go down normally. Serves 6 to 8.

LAMB CUTLETS IN WINE SAUCE

4 lamb leg cutlets
flour
salt and pepper
3 tablespoons cooking oil
1 clove garlic, cut in half
1 carrot quartered
1 onion, chopped
1 stalk celery and leaves, chopped
3 tablespoons chopped parsley
1 bay leaf
8 fluid ounces red wine
6 fluid ounces water

Flour the cutlets lightly; season with salt and pepper. Brown on all sides in hot oil.

Add remaining ingredients plus 6 fluid ounces of water.

Cover and cook at 15-pound pressure for 30 minutes. Reduce pressure immediately.

Thicken gravy with 1 tablespoon flour blended with 2 tablespoons cold water. Serves 4.

Hint: This recipe goes specially well with an accompaniment of 1 packet of savoury rice or 1 packet boil-in-the-bag rice. Place cutlets on bed of rice in hot serving dish, pour over gravy and garnish with orange slices.

CHICKEN VESUVIO

1 ounce butter or margarine
2 medium onions, minced
1 green pepper, chopped
1 clove garlic, minced
1 tablespoon chopped parsley
2 rounded tablespoons tomato
    purée
8 fluid ounces dry white wine
1 teaspoon salt
3- to 4-pound chicken
1½ ounces sultanas

Brown vegetables in butter in pressure cooker. Add tomato purée, wine, and salt.

Cut chicken into serving pieces; place in sauce and cook 40 minutes at 15-pound pressure.

Reduce pressure at once and remove chicken bones, leaving the meat in the sauce.

Add raisins and cook 5 minutes more at 15-pound pressure. Serve with cooked spaghetti or rice. Serves 6.

Texas Chilli Con Carne

NEW ENGLAND BOILED DINNER

1½ pounds gammon
8 fluid ounces water
4 small potatoes, halved
4 small onions
1 small turnip, sliced
4 medium carrots
1 small cabbage, quartered
⅛ teaspoon pepper

Place gammon and water in pressure cooker. Adjust cover and exhaust all air according to directions for cooker. Cook 20 minutes at 15-pound pressure. Reduce pressure rapidly.

Open cooker, add vegetables and pepper. Do not fill cooker over ⅔ full.

Return cooker to stove. Adjust cover and exhaust all air from cooker. Cook at 15-pound pressure 5 to 8 minutes, depending on size of vegetables. Cool cooker at once. Serves 4.

PORK FILLETS IN SOUR CREAM

2 pork fillets (3 to 4 pounds)
1 ounce butter or margarine
1 small onion, minced
16 ounces sour cream

Cut fillets in 4 pieces each; flatten by pounding.

Brown in butter in pressure cooker, frying onion slightly towards end of browning period.

Pour in sour cream. Cover and cook 25 minutes at 15-pound pressure.

Serves 4 to 6.

LAMB OR VEAL CURRY

1½ pounds veal or lamb
4 tablespoons flour, seasoned
2 ounces lard or cooking oil
1 large onion, sliced
1½ teaspoons curry powder
2 tablespoons lemon juice
16 fluid ounces tomato juice
1 tablespoon cornflour
2 fluid ounces water

Cut veal into serving pieces and roll in seasoned flour.

Heat cooker and add fat. Brown meat. Add onions and cook until limp. Add curry powder, lemon juice, and tomato juice. Mix well.

Adjust cover and exhaust all air from

Lamb or Veal Curry

cooker. Cook 15 minutes at 15-pound pressure. Cool cooker gradually.

Thicken with a paste made from cornflour and water. Serve on a bed of rice. Serves 4 to 6.

HAWAIIAN CHICKEN

2 fluid ounces cooking oil
1 onion, minced
2 ounces thinly sliced celery
1 ounce sliced fresh or canned mushrooms (drain liquid)
6 to 7 ounces diced cooked chicken
1 small can (about 3 ounces) water chestnuts (optional)
4 ounces drained bean sprouts
4 fluid ounces strong chicken stock
4 tablespoons soy sauce
¼ teaspoon sugar
2 teaspoons cornflour
2 ounces blanched almonds

Heat pan and add 1½ ounces oil. Lightly brown onion, celery, mushrooms, chicken, and water chestnuts.

Add bean sprouts, chicken stock, soy sauce, and sugar. Cook at 15-pound pressure 1 minute.

Reduce pressure. Remove cover and thicken with a paste made of cornflour and 2 tablespoons water.

Add blanched almonds which have been browned in remaining cooking oil. Serve with steamed rice or fried noodles. Serves 4 to 5.

CHICKEN CURRY

1 chicken (about 3½ pounds), cut up
12 fluid ounces water
1 large sweet onion, minced
1 large tart apple, minced
3 sticks celery, chopped
2 fluid ounces olive oil
2 tablespoons flour
1 teaspoon salt
2 tablespoons curry powder
½ teaspoon ginger
4 drops Tabasco sauce
2 teaspoons Worcestershire sauce
2 egg yolks, beaten
8 ounces single cream
3 teacups cooked rice or noodles

Place chicken on rack in pressure cooker; add water and cook 35 minutes at 15-pound pressure.

Cool quickly; remove chicken pieces; pour off and reserve the liquid.

Remove meat from bones and cut into small pieces, using scissors.

Brown onion, apple and celery in hot oil in pressure cooker. Stir in flour; add seasonings and chicken stock, adding enough water to make 16 fluid ounces.

Return chicken meat to mixture. Bring to the boil uncovered, then set aside to cool.

If time permits, cool 3 hours for seasoning to permeate the meat

thoroughly. Just before serving reheat and stir in mixed egg and cream. Serve on boiled rice or noodles. Serves 6.

SPANISH POT ROAST

5 pounds rump steak
1 ounce olive oil
10 rashers streaky bacon, cut in halves
10 cloves garlic, cut in halves
allspice
1 pint 12 fluid ounces tomato juice
6 carrots, diced
2-3 sticks celery, chopped
6 onions, chopped
4 fluid ounces vinegar
1 bay leaf, crushed
2 teaspoons salt
¼ teaspoon pepper

Brush meat with olive oil.

Sprinkle bacon with allspice, and roll bacon half slices around the half cloves of garlic.

Roll rump steak and secure with twine. With a sharp-pointed knife, make deep gashes in steak. Push bacon and garlic rolls into the gashes at uniform distances over entire surface.

Brown roast on all sides in cooker. Lift and put rack in place.

Add tomato juice and sprinkle remaining ingredients over roast. Adjust cover and cook 1 hour at 15-pound pressure, opening to add potatoes towards end of cooking period, if desired.

Serve, using the tomato and vegetable mixture as a sauce. Serves 6 to 8.

SCOTCH LAMB STEW

1½ ounces barley
4½ fluid ounces warm water
2 pounds lamb, cut in pieces ½-inch thick
½ ounce lard
4 fluid ounces water
3 or 4 potatoes
6 small onions
3 carrots, cut in half
3 or 4 sticks celery, cut in 3-inch pieces
2 teaspoons flour
2 teaspoons salt
½ teaspoon pepper
2 tablespoons boiling water

Soak barley in 4½ fluid ounces warm water overnight.

Flour the meat; brown in hot fat, then drain. Add 4 fluid ounces water, potatoes, onions, carrots, and celery to browned meat. Sprinkle with 2 teaspoons flour, salt, and pepper.

Drain barley; turn into 12-inch square of aluminium foil shaped to form a pocket; add 2 tablespoons boiling water to the pouch. Pinch corners of foil together; don't tie. Add to pressure cooker.

Cook at 15-pound pressure 8 minutes. Let pressure return to normal. Serves 4.

Spareribs with Barbecue Sauce

SPARERIBS WITH BARBECUE SAUCE

about 4 pounds pork spareribs
salt, pepper, paprika
1 ounce lard or dripping
1 large onion
1 rounded tablespoon ketchup
2 tablespoons water
2 tablespoons vinegar
1 teaspoon sugar
1 teaspoon Worcestershire sauce
¼ teaspoon chilli powder
¼ teaspoon celery salt

Have spareribs cut into serving pieces; sprinkle with salt, pepper and paprika.

Melt lard in pressure cooker, and brown spareribs a few at a time until all are well browned.

Slice onion; mix ketchup with remaining ingredients.

Put half the spareribs in the pressure cooker; cover with half the sliced onions and half the barbecue sauce. Repeat with remaining spareribs etc.

Place cover on pressure cooker and cook for 15 minutes at 15-pound pressure. Reduce pressure slowly. Serves 4.

SPARERIBS AND SAUERKRAUT

2 pounds pork spareribs
½ ounce lard or dripping
salt and pepper
2 pounds sauerkraut
1 tablespoon brown sugar

Cut ribs into serving pieces. Heat pressure cooker and add fat. Brown ribs on both sides.

Season with salt and pepper. Place sauerkraut over ribs and sprinkle with brown sugar. Do not fill cooker over ⅔ full.

Cook 15 minutes at 15-pound pressure. Cool cooker at once. Serves 4 to 6.

HUNGARIAN VEAL GOULASH WITH NOODLES

2 ounces lard
1½ pounds onions, sliced
1½ pounds shoulder veal, cut in 1½-inch pieces
2 tablespoons paprika
½ bay leaf
1 clove garlic, chopped fine
1 pint 12 fluid ounces chicken or vegetable stock
1 medium tomato, peeled and chopped fine
salt and pepper to taste

Heat cooker and add lard. Cook onions until yellow. Add veal and brown.

Mix in paprika, bay leaf, garlic, stock, tomato, and salt and pepper to taste.

Pressure cook 35 minutes at 15-pound pressure. Remove bay leaf and serve with hot buttered noodles—a green salad on the side. Serves 4 to 5.

POT ROAST WITH VEGETABLES

½ ounce lard or dripping
3 to 4 pounds stewing beef or rump steak
salt and pepper
4 fluid ounces water
4 to 6 small potatoes
4 to 6 medium onions
4 to 6 medium carrots

Heat pressure cooker; add fat. Brown meat on all sides.

Season. Add water. Adjust the cover; exhaust air from cooker.

Cook roast at 15-pound pressure 30 to 35 minutes.

Let pressure return to normal. Open cooker. Place potatoes, onions, and carrots on top. Season.

Adjust cover; exhaust air from cooker. Cook at 15-pound pressure 10 minutes.

Reduce pressure rapidly; serve vegetables on hot dish with meat. Serves 4 to 6.

FRESH TONGUE

3 pounds tongue
16 fluid ounces water in cooker with rack
1 tablespoon salt
2 bay leaves
6 whole black peppers
6 cloves
1 onion, quartered

Wash tongue. Place on rack with water and other ingredients in cooker. Adjust cover and exhaust all air from cooker.

Cook 45 minutes at 15-pound pressure. Then cool cooker.

Remove skin; strain liquid. Keep tongue in liquid until ready to serve.

Tongue may be served with cucumber or raisin sauce. (See Index.)

Serves 6 to 8.

BRISKET OF BEEF WITH SAUERKRAUT

1 ounce lard or beef dripping
3 pounds of beef brisket
2 tablespoons flour
2 teaspoons salt
⅛ teaspoon pepper
2 pounds sauerkraut
1 tablespoon sugar
6 ounces grated raw potato
1 teaspoon caraway seed
1 small grated onion

Heat lard in cooker. Rub flour and seasonings over the brisket and brown on all sides.

Lift meat from cooker; put rack in place and place sauerkraut on rack.

Return meat to cooker and sprinkle with remaining ingredients. Cook 1 hour at 15-pound pressure.

Serve with boiled potatoes which may be put in cooker, round meat, for last 15 minutes of cooking period.

Serves 6 to 8.

BRAISED RIBS OF BEEF

4 pounds ribs of beef
1 tablespoon salt
¼ teaspoon pepper
1 onion, chopped
1 clove garlic, minced
1 bay leaf
4 fluid ounces water

Get butcher to cut meat into individual servings. Season meat with salt and pepper. Place fat-side-down in pressure cooker or frying pan and brown well, turning to brown all sides.

Place in pressure cooker on a rack with bone side down. Add onion, garlic, bay leaf, and water.

Cook in pressure cooker at 15-pound pressure for 25 minutes.

Remove meat to hot dish and make gravy from liquid in pan.

Serves 6 to 8.

BEEF STEW

1 to 1½ pounds shin, leg or brisket of beef, cut in 1-inch cubes
1 ounce lard or dripping
salt and pepper
8 fluid ounces water
1½ pounds potatoes, cut in 1-inch cubes
8 ounces carrots, cut in 1-inch pieces
4 to 5 small onions, halved
3 ounces fresh or frozen peas
3 ounces broad beans, tinned

Heat pressure cooker, add lard and brown meat well.

Season with salt and pepper. Add water. Cook 12 minutes at 15-pound pressure. Cool cooker at once.

Add potatoes, carrots, onions, peas, and broad beans. Mix well. Cook 5 minutes at 15-pound pressure. Cool cooker at once. Serves 4 to 5.

BURGUNDY DUCK

1 duck (about 5½ pounds), cut up
1 onion, cut in quarters
1 leek, washed and quartered
3 sticks celery, cut in pieces
1 lemon, cut into wedges
8 fluid ounces Burgundy
salt and pepper
12 small white whole onions, peeled,
   or 1 can or jar onions
4 apples, cored and quartered
1 jar (12 ounces) cranberry jelly,
   or redcurrant jelly

Flour duck lightly and fry gently in a little olive or cooking oil until golden brown.

Put duck in pressure cooker with onion, leek, celery, lemon, Burgundy, and salt and pepper. Cook at 15-pound pressure for 30 minutes.

Reduce pressure gradually.

Meanwhile, boil onions, unless you are using canned onions. Add onions, apples, and cranberry jelly, broken up a bit with a fork, and cook without pressure on top of range until the jelly is melted. Serve in a deep dish with juices from duck and the jelly mixture. Serves 4.

SAVOURY DUCKLING WITH SOUR CREAM

1 duckling (about 4 pounds), cut
   up
2 cloves garlic, halved
1 medium onion, quartered
1 small bunch finely chopped
   parsley
1 teaspoon rosemary
½ teaspoon marjoram
1 can (6 fluid ounces) frozen
   orange juice, diluted with
   1 can water
1 lemon, sliced thin
salt and pepper
16 fluid ounces sour cream

Flour the duck lightly and fry gently with garlic until golden brown.

Drain off excess fat; remove garlic, and put duck in the pressure cooker with onion, seasonings, diluted orange juice, lemon, salt, and pepper.

Almond Chicken Gizzards in Burgundy

Cover; cook at 15-pound pressure for 30 minutes. Reduce pressure gradually.

Skim off fat and add sour cream, stirring it well into the juices. Serves 4.

LOUISIANA CHICKEN SUPPER

1 3½-pound frying chicken, cut in
   serving pieces
about 3 ounces maize flour
1½ ounces flour
2 teaspoons salt
½ teaspoon celery salt
¼ teaspoon pepper
1½ ounces lard
4 medium-sized swedes, peeled
4 slices pineapple
⅛ teaspoon allspice
½ teaspoon cinnamon
1½ ounces brown sugar
1 ounce melted butter or
   margarine
1 tablespoon lemon juice
parsley

Shake chicken pieces in paper bag containing mixture of maize flour, 1 teaspoon salt, celery salt, and pepper.

Heat lard in pressure cooker over medium heat and fry chicken to an even golden brown.

Place swedes on an 18-inch square of aluminium foil. Arrange pineapple slices over them. Sprinkle with spices, sugar, and remaining teaspoon salt; dot with melted butter.

Pull edges of aluminium foil up and twist together making a tightly sealed packet.

Put rack under chicken; sprinkle with lemon juice and add 4 fluid ounces water and foil packet. Cover and cook at 15-pound pressure for 15 minutes. Reduce pressure gradually. Serves 4.

ALMOND CHICKEN GIZZARDS IN BURGUNDY

16 fluid ounces chicken stock or 2
   chicken stock cubes, dissolved in 16 fluid ounces hot
   water
1 pound chicken gizzards (about 10
   or 12)
2 tablespoons finely chopped
   parsley
cornflour
½ teaspoon salt
¼ teaspoon pepper
4 fluid ounces Burgundy
slivered toasted almonds

Place chicken stock, parsley, and gizzards in the cooker. Place cover on cooker. Release all air from cooker. Cook 30 minutes at 15-pound pressure. Quick cool.

Remove gizzards from stock and slice thinly.

Thicken stock with cornflour. Add seasonings, sliced gizzards, and wine. Reheat. Serve on toast triangles with slivered almonds sprinkled over.

Serves 4 to 6.

CHICKEN AND BEEF BRUNSWICK STEW

1 4-pound boiling chicken, cut up
16 fluid ounces water
1 pound brisket of beef, cut in
   cubes
2 teaspoons salt
1 teaspoon paprika
4 rashers streaky bacon, cut in
   small pieces
1 medium onion, minced
12 ounces broad beans
1 can (14 ounces) whole kernel
   sweetcorn
16 ounces cooked tomatoes
3 large potatoes, diced

Cook chicken with 16 fluid ounces water in cooker 35 minutes at 15-pound pressure.

While chicken cooks, sprinkle beef with salt and paprika and let stand until ready to use.

Remove chicken from liquid; pour off remaining liquid and reserve.

Fry bacon in pan until crisp; add onion and fry to light brown.

Add beef and brown, while removing chicken meat from bones. Cut chicken to desired size, add, and brown slightly.

Now add liquid in which chicken was cooked, adding enough to nearly cover the meat. Cover and cook 30 minutes at 15-pound pressure.

Reduce pressure at once; add vegetables and cook 10 minutes at 15-pound pressure. Serves 8.

STEWED CHICKEN WITH DUMPLINGS

1 3½-pound chicken, cut in pieces
1 small sliced onion
1 pint 12 fluid ounces hot water
1 bay leaf
salt and pepper

Dumplings:
4 ounces sifted plain flour
2 teaspoons baking powder
1 teaspoon salt
1½ ounces lard or suet
4 fluid ounces milk

Cook the chicken, onion, and seasonings in the hot water for 22 minutes at 15-pound pressure.

Reduce pressure immediately and transfer chicken to a hot deep dish, leaving the juices in the pan. Keep chicken hot.

While chicken is cooking, make dumplings. Sieve dry ingredients into a basin. Rub in the lard until the dough is firm and flaky. Add milk.

Drop dumplings into the liquid in cooker from a tablespoon which has been dipped in the hot liquid. Cover and steam without pressure for 8 minutes. Add dumplings to chicken and serve. Serves 4 to 6.

Quick and Easy Salads

QUICK TOMATO ASPIC

Heat 8 fluid ounces tomato juice or vegetable juice cocktail; add to 1 packet lemon-flavoured gelatine and stir until thoroughly blended. Add 8 more fluid ounces of juice.

Pour into lightly oiled mould or moulds and chill. Serves 4.

TOMATO TOP HATTERS

Wash 3 tomatoes and slice in half. Season cottage cheese with salt, pepper, finely chopped shallot, carrot, and cucumber. Pile spoonfuls of cheese on tomato halves.

SWEETCORN AND BEANS

1 can (about 10 ounces) whole kernel sweetcorn
1 can (about 10 ounces) cut green beans
10 to 12 sliced radishes
2 rounded tablespoons mayonnaise
2 tablespoons chilli sauce

Drain sweetcorn and beans, then mix together. Add radishes.

Blend mayonnaise with chilli sauce. Add to vegetables and toss lightly. Serve on lettuce. Serves 6.

TOSSED SALAD, GOURMET

Cut or break up leaves of lettuce or other greens into bowl. Add segments of pink or white grapefruit and slices of avocado pear.

Sprinkle a few capers over top and toss with French dressing.

AVOCADO-CRANBERRY SALAD

Arrange avocado pear halves or quarters on lettuce. Heap with tinned cranberry sauce, mixed with diced celery. Serve with French dressing.

AVOCADO PEAR WITH CHIVE COTTAGE CHEESE

Peel avocados; cut each in half lengthwise and remove the stones.

For each serving place half an avocado on endive. Fill the centre with creamed chive cottage cheese. Serve with French dressing.

The richness of avocado pear is set off by the filling of chive cottage cheese.

FLOWER GARDEN SALADS

Flower garden salads make an attractive luncheon dish—or, in a smaller size, a dinner salad.

First, arrange a bed of lettuce or greens. Next, place cottage cheese on top of this. Then arrange sliced peaches or peach halves in flower formation on or around cottage cheese.

A slice of green pepper can be the stem, and bits of cut green pepper the leaves. Maraschino cherry adds a colourful centre.

PINEAPPLE FRUIT COCKTAIL

Arrange drained canned pineapple slices on lettuce. Fill centres with drained tinned fruit cocktail.

PEAR SALAD

Use tinned or fresh pears, placing one half, hollow side up, on a bed of lettuce. Fill with chopped nuts and maraschino cherries.

APRICOT 'N' CREAM CHEESE

Place drained halves of tinned apricots cut-side-up on lettuce. Top with softened cream cheese and chopped dates.

Apricot 'n' Cream Cheese

PINEAPPLE CUCUMBER SALAD

Arrange drained tinned pineapple slices on lettuce. Score a cucumber with a fork, leaving skin on. Cut in thin slices.

Overlap 3 cucumber slices on each pineapple slice. Place a mound of cream cheese in centre. Decorate with pimiento slices.

APPLE AND ORANGE TOSS

Dice a tart apple into a basin.

Grate the rind of an orange over apple, then peel the orange and dice it into basin with the apple.

Add a sprinkling of chopped walnuts. Toss with salad dressing, and serve on lettuce. Serves 2 to 3.

MELON RING SALAD

Place ring of honeydew melon on lettuce leaf. Centre with scoop of raspberry water ice.

Arrange fresh peach and pear slices, dipped in lemon juice, around sides.

Serve with honey-lime dressing made by combining 2 parts honey and 1 part lime juice.

Flower Garden Salads

MINTED PEACH SALAD

Place peach halves on bed of lettuce. Sprinkle with lemon juice and chopped mint. Serve with whipped cream dressing.

PEACH CREAM CHEESE SALAD

Arrange drained tinned peach halves, cut-side-up, on lettuce.

Fill centres with cream cheese which has been softened with a small amount of peach syrup. Top with chopped nuts.

CORONATION SALAD

Drain tinned pear halves well. Put two halves together with cream cheese which has been softened with a small amount of the pear syrup. Sprinkle paprika on one side to form a blush.

Place a small strip of green pepper or a twiglet on top of pear for a stem. Arrange upright on lettuce.

AVOCADO AND ORANGE SALAD

Alternate sections of oranges with slices of peeled avocado pear.

Serve with lemon wedges and French dressing.

GRATED CARROT SALAD

Wash young, tender carrots. Grate on fine grater. Using a fork, gently combine with French dressing.

Place on lettuce leaves. Serve at once. A bit of cheese may be grated with carrots.

Easy Salad with Fruit: Line serving plate with crisp Cos or Webb's Wonder lettuce. Arrange drained chilled tinned fruits on top. Garnish with watercress and sprinkle with chopped nuts. Serve with fruit salad dressing. Fruit combinations to use: pear halves and light sweet cherries; apricot halves and purple plums; fruit cocktail and dark sweet cherries; citrus segments and pineapple cubes.

Quick and Easy Breads and Rolls

Ready-to-Bake bread rolls can be used as the base for some quick and easy 'goodies' for serving with coffee or at tea time.

BUTTERSCOTCH ROLLS

Combine 2 ounces soft butter, 3 ounces brown sugar, and ¼ teaspoon nutmeg.

Spread butter mixture over rolls. Bake in a moderate oven (375°F. Mark 5) about 15 minutes.

COCONUT COFFEE CAKES

2 ounces butter or margarine
1½ ounces brown sugar
5 tablespoons dark corn syrup or treacle
2 ounces desiccated coconut
6 Ready-to-Bake rolls
melted butter or margarine

Cook butter, sugar, and syrup together until butter melts and mixture is syrupy.

Pour into 6 deep bun tins. Sprinkle part of coconut in each, then add rolls. Brush rolls with melted butter.

Bake in moderate oven (375°F. Mark 5) until lightly browned, about 15 minutes.

CRANBERRY GLAZED ROLLS

1 ounce chopped nuts
4 ounces jellied cranberry sauce
1½ ounces brown sugar
6 Ready-to-Bake rolls

Grease deep bun tins or daride cups. Sprinkle a few chopped nuts into each.

Combine cranberry sauce that has been crushed with a fork and brown sugar. Put a tablespoon of the mixture in each tin.

Turn rolls upside down and press into each tin. Bake in hot oven (400°F. Mark 6) for 12 to 15 minutes. Let cool for 4 to 5 minutes. Invert tins and gently remove rolls.

Cranberry Glazed Rolls

ALMOND RING

Cut some Ready-to-Bake rolls in half and arrange in a ring on a lightly floured baking sheet, slightly overlapping and with cut side downwards.

Bake in moderate oven (375°F. Mark 5) for 15 to 20 minutes until golden brown. Spread with glacé icing and sprinkle with slivered almonds. If desired, garnish with maraschino cherries. Serve warm.

CARAMEL PECAN ROLLS

2 ounces butter or margarine
1½ ounces brown sugar
5 tablespoons dark corn syrup or treacle
pecans or walnuts
6 Ready-to-Bake rolls

Melt butter; blend in brown sugar and syrup. Boil 1 minute.

Pour into 6 deep bun tins. Add a few pecan halves to each, then add rolls.

Bake in moderate oven (375°F. Mark 5) until lightly browned, about 15 minutes.

HONEY NUT ROLLS

2 tablespoons honey
2 tablespoons sugar
1 ounce soft butter or margarine
1 ounce flour
6 Ready-to-Bake rolls
1 ounce chopped walnuts

Combine honey, sugar, butter, and flour. Spread on top of rolls. Sprinkle with walnuts.

Place on greased baking sheet; bake in moderate oven (375°F. Mark 5) until lightly browned, about 15 minutes.

ORANGE-NUT CAKE

8 ounces scone mix
2 ounces sugar
¼ pint milk
2 well-beaten eggs
2 ounces chopped walnuts

Combine scone mix and sugar. Add alternately with milk to well beaten eggs. Stir in nuts.

Spread batter in greased 8×1½-inch round tin. Bake in hot oven (400°F. Mark 6) about 25 minutes.

Orange Topping: Melt 3 ounces butter or margarine; mix with 4 ounces brown sugar. Spread over warm cake; sprinkle with grated orange rind and walnuts.

Pour 4 fluid ounces orange juice over mixture and place cake under grill until bubbly. Serve warm.

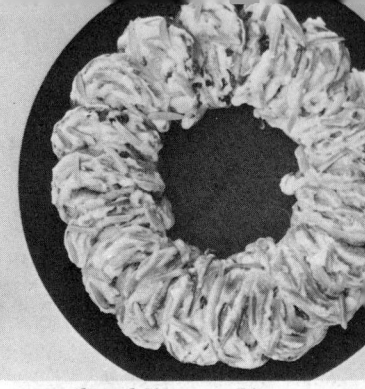

Almond Cinnamon Ring

ORANGE BLOSSOM BUNS

Place 1 teaspoon melted butter and 1 tablespoon orange marmalade in bottom of deep bun tins.

Arrange a roll, topside down in each tin and bake.

HERB-BUTTERED ROLLS

Combine 3 ounces softened butter, 1 tablespoon lemon juice, ¼ teaspoon garlic salt, 2 tablespoons finely chopped parsley, and ½ teaspoon thyme.

Top Ready-to-Bake rolls with butter mixture and bake in a moderate oven (375°F. Mark 5) for about 15-20 minutes.

ROUND-THE-CLOCK COFFEE LOAF

1 packet scone mix
6 ounces sugar
¾ teaspoon cinnamon
1 ounce chopped walnuts
2 ounces butter or margarine, melted
1 ounce cream cheese
4 ounces icing sugar
1 teaspoon milk
¼ teaspoon vanilla essence

Make up the scone mix, roll out and cut into rounds with a 2-2½ inch cutter. Mix the sugar, cinnamon and nuts together. Dip the scones first in melted butter then in the sugar mixture.

Cover the bottom of a Swiss roll tin with some of the scones and arrange the rest on top, overlapping slightly.

Bake in a hot oven (425°F. Mark 7) until golden brown, 20-25 minutes. Mix the cream cheese, icing sugar, milk and vanilla and beat well together. Spread over the loaf while it is still warm and sprinkle the remaining sugar mixture on top.

Round-the-Clock Coffee Loaf

Quick and Easy Sweets

APPLE PAN DOWDY
7 to 8 ounces cooked apples,
    drained
1½ ounces brown sugar
¼ teaspoon nutmeg
¼ teaspoon cinnamon
¼ teaspoon salt
1 packet white cake mix

In the bottom of a buttered baking dish, arrange apples. Sprinkle with brown sugar, nutmeg, cinnamon, and salt.

Make up white cake mix according to directions. Pour batter over apples.

Bake in moderate oven (350°F. Mark 4) 20 to 25 minutes or until cake is done.

At serving time, bring to the table in its own baking dish. Cut into squares and serve with sweetened whipped cream. Serves 6.

QUICK CHOCOLATE MOUSSE
6 ounces plain or cooking chocolate
3 eggs, separated
1 teaspoon vanilla

Melt chocolate over hot water. Remove from heat and beat in egg yolks one at a time. Add vanilla.

Beat egg whites until stiff, but not dry; gently fold into chocolate mixture.

Spoon into glasses, and chill. Serve garnished with double cream or soft vanilla ice cream. Serves 4.

BLACKBERRY DELIGHT
4 ounces caster sugar
3 tablespoons cornflour
¼ teaspoon salt
about 10 ounces blackberries,
    slightly crushed
juice and grated rind of 1 lemon
18 shortbread biscuits, coarsely
    crumbled

Mix together sugar, cornflour, and salt in saucepan.

Combine blackberries, lemon juice, and rind; stir into sugar mixture, blending well. Cook over low heat, stirring constantly, until thick and clear; cool.

Alternate layers of blackberry mixture and shortbread crumbs in 6 sorbet glasses. Top with whipped cream. Serves 6.

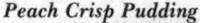
Peach Crisp Pudding

BRAZILIAN CREAM
1 tablespoon instant coffee
1 packet vanilla pudding mix
16 fluid ounces milk
8 ounces single cream, whipped

Combine coffee and pudding powder in a saucepan. Add milk gradually, blending well. Cook and stir over medium heat until mixture comes to the boil, and is thickened. Turn into basin, cover, and chill well.

Then beat slowly with rotary whisk and fold in whipped cream. Turn into sorbet glasses. Garnish with sponge fingers, coconut, and maraschino cherries with stems. Serves 5.

GEORGIA CRUNCH
1 (10½ ounces) can sliced peaches
4 ounces butter or margarine
1½ ounces wheat cereal flakes
3 ounces brown sugar
½ teaspoon cinnamon
½ teaspoon nutmeg
4 ounces chopped walnuts

Drain peaches well. Arrange in the bottom of a shallow baking dish.

Rub cereal flakes and brown sugar into butter. Add cinnamon and nutmeg. Sprinkle evenly over peach slices. Top with chopped walnuts.

Bake in moderate oven (375°F. Mark 5) 10 minutes. Serves 6.

FRENCH CHOCOLATE-CREAM PUDDING
1 packet chocolate pudding mix
8 fluid ounces cold milk
2 ounces plain or cooking
    chocolate
½ teaspoon vanilla
8 fluid ounces double cream

Empty contents of chocolate pudding mix into a heavy saucepan. Stir in milk gradually and keep stirring until mixture is absolutely smooth.

Add chocolate and cook very slowly, stirring constantly, until chocolate has melted and the pudding is as thick as mayonnaise.

Remove from cooker and allow pudding to cool. Add vanilla to cream and beat until thick.

Mix or fold the whipped cream into cooled chocolate pudding. Pour into small custard moulds. Serves 6.

PEACH CRISP PUDDING
Cream 2 ounces butter and 4 ounces sugar together. Combine with 12 ounces soft ½-inch bread cubes and 1 large can sliced peaches.

Bake in buttered 2½-pint casserole in moderate oven (375°F. Mark 5) for 30 minutes. Serve with whipped cream. Serves 8.

A variety of cold party puddings can be quickly prepared with packaged puddings mixes. Alternate the chilled puddings with sweetened, flavoured whipped cream in sorbet glasses.

LEMON CHIFFON PUDDING
2 eggs, separated
3 to 4 ounces lemon curd pie filling
dash of salt
4 tablespoons caster sugar

With egg yolks, cook lemon pie filling as directed on packet; cool about 10 minutes.

Add salt to egg whites; beat until foamy and just stiff enough to hold a peak; gradually beat in sugar until smooth and glossy. Fold into lemon mixture. Spoon into tall glasses and chill. Serves 4 to 6.

CHOCOLATE PUFF
3 ounces plain or cooking
    chocolate
8 fluid ounces milk
3 tablespoons caster sugar
dash of salt
1 teaspoon vanilla
3 eggs

Melt chocolate pieces in milk over hot water; beat with egg whisk until smooth. Add sugar, salt, vanilla, and eggs.

Beat with egg whisk one minute. Cover and cook over boiling water for 20 minutes without lifting the cover. Remove from heat and serve immediately with cream. Serves 6.

FIG-BROWNIE PUDDING
24 fig biscuits (about)
8 fluid ounces sweetened condensed
    milk
4 fluid ounces water
1½ teaspoons baking powder
1 ounce plain or cooking chocolate,
    melted
1 small packet chocolate bits
1 teaspoon vanilla
2 ounces chopped walnuts

Crumble the fig biscuits into the milk, add the remaining ingredients and stir together.

Place in a generously buttered baking dish. Bake in moderate oven (350°F. Mark 4) for about 25 minutes or until a little puffy. Serve in fruit dishes while warm, with whipped cream, double cream, or clotted cream.

Serves 5 to 6.

"DIFFERENT" PASTRY CASES

Prepare 1 packet rich short-crust or flaky pastry mix according to label directions:

Coffee Pecan Case (perfect for a chocolate chiffon pie): Substitute coffee for liquid in recipe. Add 2 ounces ground pecans.

Spiced Case (for ice cream pie): Add 1½ teaspoons cinnamon, ½ teaspoon nutmeg, ¼ teaspoon allspice, and 2 ounces caster sugar.

Cheddar Case (for apple pie): Add 2 ounces caster sugar.

"DIFFERENT" TART FILLINGS

Prepare 1 packet vanilla blancmange mix according to directions on label.

Rich Coffee Pecan: Substitute 8 fluid ounces strong coffee for 8 ounces liquid.

Fold in 4 ounces double cream, whipped, and 2 ounces chopped pecans just before turning into pie-dish.

Brazil Nut: Fold 2 ounces slivered toasted Brazil nuts into filling before turning into pie-dish.

Fudge-Coated Orange: Combine orange blancmange mix, 2 teaspoons grated orange rind, and 12 fluid ounces milk. Cook according to label directions.

Remove from heat and add 4 fluid ounces orange juice.

Melt 3 ounces semi-sweet chocolate pieces over low heat.

Spread melted chocolate over bottom of pastry case. Pour cooked filling over chocolate. Chill.

Banana: Arrange sliced bananas on pastry before adding filling.

Top with whipped cream and slivered chocolate before serving.

BLACKBERRY CREAM CHEESE TARTLETS

Start with a packet of pastry mix. Makes 6 tartlets. If time is really at a premium, buy individual flan cases.

Beat a packet of cream cheese until smooth. Add ripe, plump blackberries, a bit of sour cream, and sugar.

At serving time, fill the cooled tartlets or flan cases with chilled cheese mixture.

Strawberry Cream Tart

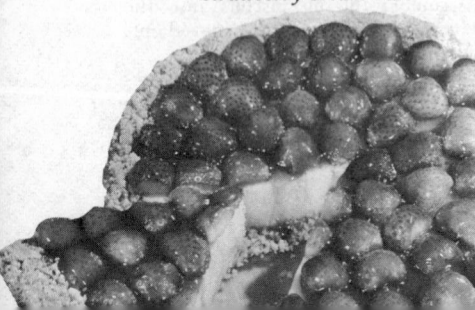

PEACHES AND COCONUT CREAM TART

Make your favourite cream pie filling, or prepare a packet of vanilla blancmange, according to the directions.

Cool slightly, then fold in 4 ounces toasted coconut. Pour into a baked and cooled pastry case. Chill.

Just before serving, top with well drained and chilled canned peach halves. Garnish centres with more toasted coconut. Nice, too, made in individual tart cases. Serve with sweetened whipped cream, if desired.

To toast coconut: Spread in a shallow pan and bake in moderate oven (350°F. Mark 4) about 10 minutes.

Peaches and Coconut Cream Tart

PECAN TREACLE TART

Combine 1 ounce melted butter and 2 ounces brown sugar. Add 2 ounces chopped pecans.

Spread mixture over top of bought treacle tart.

Bake under a preheated grill (350°F. Mark 4) for 10 minutes. Serve while hot.

CHOCOLATE BANANA TARTS

Line 5 cooled tart or flan cases with sliced bananas. Add chocolate pudding made from a prepared mix. Chill.

Top with additional banana slices and whipped cream just before serving.

STRAWBERRY CREAM TART

Filling: Prepare vanilla-flavoured blancmange according to directions on packet.

Pour into well chilled cereal crumb shell (see Index). Cover with fresh strawberries, sliced in half.

Melt ½ jar redcurrant jelly over low heat, beating until smooth. When cool but still syrupy, pour over strawberry topping. Chill again before serving. Other fruits of the season may be used.

Note: If using a blancmange mix that requires cooking or a standard recipe for cream pie filling, it is better to bake the cereal crumb shell in moderate oven (350°F. Mark 4) 7 to 10 minutes.

Chill thoroughly before adding filling. Shell will harden while it cools.

Lazy Girl Fig Tart

LAZY GIRL FIG TART

Bake a 10-inch pastry case; cool.

Meanwhile, crumble about 14 fig biscuits into 16 fluid ounces milk. Add 1 packet vanilla-flavoured blancmange. Stir over heat until pudding bubbles.

Remove from heat and stir in 6 ounces treacle, 1 teaspoon cinnamon, and ½ teaspoon allspice. Add 1 teaspoon vanilla and ½ teaspoon salt. Cool.

Then place in pastry case. Top with sweetened, vanilla-flavoured whipped cream. Serves 6 to 8.

MAGIC APPLE TART

1 packet frozen puff pastry, defrosted
15 ounces sweetened condensed milk
3 fluid ounces lemon juice
1¼ pounds cooked, sliced apples
1 teaspoon cinnamon

Remove pastry from packet. Flatten to ¼-inch thickness.

Press into buttered baking dish (8×10×2-inch) to cover bottom; arrange remaining pastry around sides of pie-dish, and flute with a fork.

Brush pastry with about 4 to 5 tablespoons sweetened condensed milk, covering bottom and sides completely.

Bake in hot oven (400°F. Mark 6) about 20 minutes or according to packet directions.

Add lemon juice to remaining sweetened condensed milk, stirring until mixture thickens. Fold in apples and cinnamon. Pour mixture into baked pastry crust. Chill. Garnish with whipped cream. Serves 6.

CHOCOLATE-MINT BROWNIES

Prepare fudge brownies as directed on packet of brownie mix. When done, remove from oven and place 16 after-dinner chocolate mints on top.

Return to oven 5 minutes or until chocolate mints soften.

Using palette knife spread chocolate evenly over top of brownies. Cool, then cut into 16 squares.

BERRY SPONGE SANDWICHES

Split 2 sponge cakes to form 4 layers. Fill with sweetened berries.

Cut into pie slices; top with ice cream, whipped cream, or custard sauce.

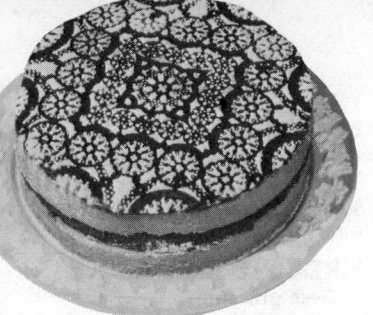

Ten-Minute Boston Cream Cake

TIPSY PARSON

2 sponge cake layers
redcurrant, grape, or apple jelly
slivered almonds

Place between the sponge cake layers, redcurrant, grape, or apple jelly. Sprinkle liberally with shredded almonds. Place top layer over jelly.

Spread top of cake with a thin layer of jelly and sprinkle with almonds.

Tipsy Sauce: Prepare the sauce from a packet of vanilla-flavoured blancmange by using 1½ times as much liquid as required for a regular pudding. Cook according to packet directions. Add 4 fluid ounces sherry or Madeira. Stir and chill.

At serving time, cut cake into regular servings and pass chilled sauce in a separate bowl. Serves 6 to 8.

RIBBON ICE CREAM CAKE

1 6-inch round white sponge cake
½ pint chocolate ice cream
½ pint peppermint ice cream
8 fluid ounces double cream, whipped and sweetened
2 ounces shredded coconut, lightly toasted

Split cake crosswise into 3 layers. Slightly soften ice creams and spread chocolate ice cream on bottom layer. Put middle layer of cake into place and spread this with peppermint ice cream. Replace top of cake.

Cover entire cake with whipped cream and sprinkle with toasted coconut. Place in freezing compartment 20 minutes or longer. Serves 6 to 8.

Variations: Any two flavours of ice cream that taste well together may be used.

Quick Cranberry Refrigerator Cake

TEN-MINUTE BOSTON CREAM CAKE

6 ounces semi-sweet chocolate pieces
6 fluid ounces evaporated milk
2 8-inch sponge cake layers
icing sugar

Put semi-sweet chocolate and evaporated milk in saucepan; place over low heat. Cook, stirring occasionally, until mixture is blended.

Bring to the boil and cook, stirring constantly, until mixture thickens, about 3 to 5 minutes. Cool.

Spread icing between layers, reserving about 2 tablespoons to thinly spread over top layer.

Sprinkle with icing sugar or, if attractive design is desired, place paper doily on top of cake and sprinkle with icing sugar. Remove doily. Makes 8 servings.

PINEAPPLE-CREAM CAKE

1 8-inch sponge cake
about 9 ounces pineapple marmalade
12 ounces double cream, whipped

Slice cake and put on individual serving plates. Fold marmalade into cream and use to top cake slices.

ORANGE SPONGE CAKE

Sprinkle 2 sponge cake layers with 2 fluid ounces orange juice. Fill with whipped cream. Top with grated orange rind and chopped walnuts.

COCONUT BARS

Butter slices of sandwich cake; cut into bars and sprinkle with coconut, then grill until lightly browned.

PEACH SPONGE LAYER CAKE

Fill 2 sponge cake layers with slightly thawed frozen peaches; top with whipped cream.

QUICK CRANBERRY REFRIGERATOR CAKE

1 egg white, stiffly beaten
1 jar cranberry sauce
1 8-ounce sponge cake
6 fluid ounces double cream, whipped

Fold stiffly beaten egg white into cranberry sauce.

Slice sponge cake into 3 horizontal sections. Alternate layers of diced sponge cake and sauce in a shallow dish, with cake as both top and bottom layer.

Cover the top and sides of cake with whipped cream. Refrigerate until ready to serve. Serves 8.

COCONUT HONEY BARS

Slice sponge sandwich ½ inch thick. Cut each slice in 4 strips.

Spread 3 sides with butter and honey; roll in coconut and place on greased baking sheet. Toast a delicate brown in moderate oven (375°F. Mark 5) 5 to 10 minutes.

BUTTERSCOTCH SANDWICH LOAF PUDDING

1 packet butterscotch pudding
1 (14 ounce) sponge sandwich

Prepare butterscotch pudding according to directions on packet.

Cut cake in half lengthwise. Cut each lengthwise strip into 3 circles.

Arrange cake circles in pudding plates. Pour butterscotch pudding over each cake circle. Serves 6.

QUICK SHORTCAKE

Make shortcake from scone mix according to directions on the packet, or buy tart cases from bakery.

Fill and top with fresh, or thawed frozen strawberries, raspberries, or sliced peaches and whipped cream.

SPONGE SQUARES

1 8-ounce sponge sandwich
8 ounces butter icing
½ ounce cooking chocolate, melted
1 teaspoon hot water
1 tablespoon grated orange rind
½ teaspoon orange essence (Cointreau can be substituted)

Slice cake horizontally into 3 equal-size layers. Even off cake top if it is rounded.

Spread ⅓ of the butter icing on bottom layer and cover with middle layer.

Add melted chocolate and hot water to ⅓ of the icing and spread over middle layer.

Place top layer over chocolate icing. Add orange rind and juice to remaining butter icing.

Spread orange butter icing over top of cake, leaving sides un-iced. After icing has set, cut cake into 8 small squares.

Sponge Squares

BERRIES JUBILEE WITH ICE CREAM

peel from 1 lemon
2 tablespoons frozen orange juice, undiluted
1 pint fresh or frozen whole strawberries
2 fluid ounces brandy

Cut the peel from 1 lemon and leave it curled cork-screw style. Place in a shallow oven-proof serving dish if convenient. Add orange juice. Heat gently about 3 minutes, pressing the peel to get all the flavour.

Add strawberries and toss berries around in the hot juice. Pour on brandy. Warm and light with a match.

At serving time, do all this at the table if you can and serve the flaming berries over vanilla ice cream, lemon or orange water ice. Serves 4 to 6.

Raspberries Jubilee: Raspberries can be used in the same fashion.

PEACH DELIGHT

1 large can peach halves, drained
2 ounces vanilla biscuit crumbs
8 fluid ounces double cream, whipped
walnut halves

Roll peach halves in vanilla biscuit crumbs until well coated. Place halves, cut-side-down, in sorbet glasses.

Top each with spoonful of whipped cream and a walnut half. Serves 6.

SPICED FRUIT COMPOTE

1 large can fruits for salad or canned fruits of your choice
1 tablespoon vinegar
6 inches stick cinnamon
1 teaspoon whole cloves

Combine fruits (with their syrup), vinegar, cinnamon, and cloves in saucepan; heat to boiling. Simmer 5 minutes.

Garnish with a few spiced crabapples if desired. Keep hot in serving dish. Serves 6 to 8.

BANANAS JUBILEE

Cut bananas into thin slices. Arrange on top of white sponge cake slices. Serve with warm spiced cherry sauce.

Drain syrup from 1 can (about 1 pound) dark sweet cherries; add water, if needed, to make 8 fluid ounces.

Place 1 tablespoon cornflour and a dash each of salt and ground cloves in small saucepan; stir in syrup. Cook and stir until sauce thickens and boil 1 minute; add cherries; heat through.

ORANGE FLUFF CAKES

Whip 8 fluid ounces double cream; mix with 4 ounces coconut, 2 tablespoons orange juice, 1 teaspoon grated orange rind; use to top sponge cake wedges.

CHOCOLATE BAKED ALASKA CAKE

4 egg whites
6 tablespoons caster sugar
½ teaspoon vanilla
1 8-inch layer cake
1½ pints firm chocolate ice cream

Beat egg whites until stiff, but not dry. Blend in sugar and vanilla. Continue beating until meringue stands in peaks and is well blended.

Place cake on a sheet of brown paper on a baking sheet. Pile ice cream on cake, leaving about ½ inch around edge of cake uncovered.

Cover ice cream and cake with meringue, making sure that ice cream is well covered by the meringue.

Brown quickly in very hot oven (450°F. Mark 8) for about 5 minutes. Serve immediately. Serves 6 to 8.

BLUE CHEESE PEARS WITH WINE SAUCE

about 3 ounces crumbled blue cheese
1 tablespoon milk
8 canned pear halves
6 fluid ounces pear juice
2 tablespoons sherry

Combine cheese and milk; mix until well blended. Fill pear halves with cheese mixture.

Place in shallow baking-dish and bake in hot oven (400°F. Mark 6) about 10 minutes, or until cheese is melted and pears are heated through.

Meanwhile, combine pear juice and sherry; heat to boiling point.

Place 2 pear halves in each serving dish and cover with wine sauce. Serve hot. Serves 4.

QUICK CHEESE CAKE

1 8-ounce sponge sandwich
1 tablespoon lemon juice
½ pound cottage cheese
¼ teaspoon cinnamon
3 tablespoons granulated sugar
¾ pint sour cream
1 can (about 10½ ounces) sliced peaches
3 tablespoons brown sugar
½ teaspoon vanilla

Cut sandwich cake into thin slices. Line a 9×9-inch baking-dish with slices and sprinkle the lemon juice over cake.

Combine cottage cheese, cinnamon, granulated sugar, and ¼ pint sour cream.

Drain peaches and finely chop half of them. Mix chopped peaches with cheese mixture; pour over cake slices.

Combine remaining sour cream with brown sugar and vanilla; spread over cheese mixture.

Arrange remaining peach slices on top. Bake in hot oven (400°F. Mark 6) 15 minutes. Serves 6 to 8.

APRICOT CREAM TORTE

Crush 1 large can drained apricots. Stir in 2 tablespoons caster sugar. Spoon onto 1 sponge cake layer. Circle with whipped cream.

PINEAPPLE FLUFF

1 fresh pineapple
2 ounces caster sugar
½ pound marshmallows, cut in small pieces
8 ounces double cream, whipped
sliced maraschino cherries

Pare and cut pineapple into fine pieces. Place in basin in layers, sprinkling each layer with sugar and marshmallow pieces. Cover and let stand several hours.

To serve, fold in whipped cream and spoon into serving dishes. Garnish with maraschino cherries. Serves 8.

STEWED FIGS À LA GLACE

canned figs, thoroughly chilled
vanilla ice cream
rum or brandy (optional)

Place a scoop of vanilla ice cream into individual fruit dishes, sorbet glasses, or champagne glasses of the saucer type. On top of the ice cream, carefully place 2 or 3 figs together with a little of the syrup.

Add a teaspoonful of rum or brandy to each serving.

QUICK CHOCOLATE TORTE

1 large white sponge cake
8 ounces butter or margarine
11 ounces icing sugar
1 teaspoon vanilla
2 ounces cooking chocolate, melted
2½ to 3 ounces icing sugar
6 tablespoons cocoa
⅛ teaspoon salt
16 fluid ounces whipping cream
2 ounces chopped salted pistachio nuts

Slice cake into 3 layers, using long, thin, sharp-bladed knife.

Cream butter well. Beat 11 ounces icing sugar into butter; cream well. Add vanilla and melted chocolate. Mix well, then spread between layers of cake.

Sift together remaining icing sugar, cocoa, and salt. Add to unwhipped cream. Chill 2 hours or more.

Add vanilla to cream and whip until stiff. Spread on top and sides of cake. Sprinkle chopped nuts around sides of cake. Chill several hours before serving. Makes 16 servings.

BANANAS ON HALF SHELL

Halve each banana crosswise. Remove half of peel lengthwise, without removing fruit; cut fruit crosswise (not through peel) into ½-inch slices. Top with whipped cream and sprinkle with nutmeg.

Quick and Easy Timed Menus with Recipes

50-MINUTE SUNDAY SPECIAL MENU

Serves 4
Chilled Vichyssoise with Chives
Glazed Baked Ham
Hot Spiced Cherries
Browned Potatoes
Parsley-Butter Carrots
Garden Salad Bowl
Pineapple-Peppermint Delight
Coffee   Milk

Bake the ham first—

GLAZED BAKED HAM

Remove one 3- to 4-pound ham from can. Place ham, fat side up, on rack in shallow baking dish. Stud top with cloves; drizzle with 6 ounces honey.

Bake in slow oven (325°F. Mark 3) 45 minutes, basting often with additional honey. (Use remaining ham for another meal.)

Chill the soup next—

VICHYSSOISE WITH CHIVES

Place 2 cans ready-to-serve vichyssoise, in freezing compartment; chill, but do not freeze.

Just before serving, beat with wire whisk; sprinkle with chopped chives.

Now for the creamy-rich sweet—

PINEAPPLE-PEPPERMINT DELIGHT

Drain well 1 can (about 8¼-ounce) crushed pineapple. (Pineapple juice may be added to cherry sauce.)

Whip ½ pint double cream, beating in 2 tablespoons sugar. Fold in pineapple and 8 tablespoons coarsely crushed peppermint rock; spoon into sorbet glasses; chill.

Then the cherries—

HOT SPICED CHERRIES

Combine 1½ tablespoons cornflour, 2 ounces sugar, ¼ teaspoon each allspice and ground cloves in saucepan.

Gradually stir in juice drained from 1 can (about 1 pound, 4 ounces) red sour stoned cherries and juice drained from crushed pineapple, if desired.

Cook until thick and clear, stirring constantly; blend in few drops red food colouring and cherries. Serve hot with baked ham.

Hints: There's time to brown 1 can (about 1 pounds, 4 ounces) whole white potatoes in 1 ounce butter or margarine, and to heat and season 1 (1 pound) can carrots.

Prepare the salad and coffee, and set the table. Dinner will be ready in about 50 minutes.

20 MINUTE TAKE-IT-EASY DINNER

Serves 4
Chicken à la King
Chow Mein Noodles
French Beans
Whole-Kernel Sweetcorn
Tomato Aspic Salad
Hot Spiced Apple Sauce Sundaes
Coffee   Milk

First the—

CHICKEN À LA KING

Combine 1 10½-ounce can creamed chicken, 1 can condensed cream of mushroom soup, 1 6-ounce can boned chicken, and 2 fluid ounces milk in saucepan; add 1 teaspoon chopped green pepper; 1 teaspoon chopped pimiento; heat thoroughly.

Serve hot over 3¾ ounces chow mein noodles heated according to directions on can.

Then the sweet—

HOT SPICED APPLE SAUCE SUNDAES

Combine 1 can (1 pound) apple sauce, 2 tablespoons sugar, ¼ teaspoon cinnamon, and dash each of allspice and cloves in small saucepan.

To serve, heat well and spoon over individual dishes of vanilla ice cream. (Keep apple sauce hot in a double saucepan, while eating main course.)

Hints: For the vegetables, heat separately 1 can (1 pound) whole-kernel sweetcorn and 1 can (1 pound) French beans. Drain and season each with butter or margarine, salt and pepper.

Slice prepared tomato aspic (See Index); serve on watercress with French dressing.

After you've made coffee and set the table, this meal is ready in about 20 minutes.

45-MINUTE MENU WHEN GUESTS ARRIVE

Serves 4
Grapefruit-Cranberry Cocktail
Chicken 'n' Dumplings
Pimiento Asparagus   Pickled Peaches
Lettuce Wedges
with Blue Cheese Dressing
Grilled Pineapple-Topped Spicecake
Coffee   Milk

The sweet comes first—

GRILLED PINEAPPLE-TOPPED SPICECAKE

Prepare 1 packet spicecake mix according to directions, using 9×9×2-inch or 11×7×1½-inch baking dish.

When cake is baked, remove from oven and arrange 1 can (about 1 pound, 4 ounces) sliced pineapple, well drained, over top of cake, reserving juice for first course.

Sprinkle cake with 3 ounces brown sugar and ¼ teaspoon ground ginger; dot with 2 tablespoons butter or margarine.

Grill 1 to 2 minutes, or until topping browns. Cool on wire cake rack; cut in squares.

Note: Have topping ingredients ready to put on as soon as cake is baked. Sliced peaches, drained, may be substituted.

Next, the starter—

GRAPEFRUIT-CRANBERRY COCKTAIL

Divide 1 can (about 1 pound, 4 ounces) grapefruit sections among 4 sorbet glasses; add reserved pineapple juice.

Top each with several small cubes of jellied cranberry sauce, or a few whole cooked cranberries. Chill.

Then the salad dressing—

BLUE CHEESE DRESSING

Blend 2 rounded tablespoons mayonnaise or salad cream with 2 tablespoons crumbled blue cheese.

Sharpen with lemon juice or red wine vinegar, if desired. Spoon over crisp Cos lettuce wedges.

Now for the main course—

CHICKEN 'N' DUMPLINGS

Heat 2 cans (about 1 pound each) creamed chicken in large saucepan with tight-fitting cover.

When hot and bubbling, open 1 packet puff pastry, defrosted; cut in circles and place on chicken. Simmer, tightly covered, 15 minutes.

Hints: While chicken simmers, you've time to heat and season 1 can (1 pound, 4 ounces) asparagus; garnish with 1 pimiento, diced.

Spoon 1 can (1 pound, 4 ounces) spiced peaches into serving dish, make coffee and set the table. You're ready to serve in 45 minutes.

Chicken 'n' Dumplings

30-MINUTE SUPPER FROM THE SHELF
Serves 4
Chilled Pineapple Juice
Tuna 'n' Noodle Bake
Buttered Peas and Whole Onions
Tomato-Cucumber-Chive Salad
Plum Shortcake
Coffee   Milk

First the casserole —

TUNA 'N' NOODLE BAKE
Combine 2 15-ounce cans tuna and noodle dinner, 1 can condensed cream of mushroom soup, 4 fluid ounces milk and about 12 black olives sliced from stones.

Turn into 1½ pint baking-dish; sprinkle with crushed potato chips.

Bake in very hot oven (450°F. Mark 8) 20 minutes, or until bubbling hot.

Note: Substitute 1 can cooked noodles and 1 7½-ounce tin tuna or beef for tuna and noodle dinner.

Next the sweet —

PLUM SHORTCAKE
Combine 2 ounces sugar, 1½ tablespoons cornflour, and dash of salt in medium-sized saucepan.

Gradually stir in juice drained from 1 can (1 pound, 15 ounces) halved, stoned purple plums; cook until thick and clear, stirring constantly.

Add ¼ teaspoon almond essence and plums.

Serve warm over plain tea scones reserving extra scones and sauce for another meal.

Garnish with whipped cream, if desired.

Hints: Heat together 1 can (1 pound) peas and 1 can (1 pound, 4 ounces) whole onions, drained; season with butter or margarine, salt and pepper.

For salad, arrange tomato and cucumber slices on crisp lettuce; serve with salad dressing and a sprinkling of chopped chives.

Pour pineapple juice over crushed ice. After coffee is made and the table set, you'll have a hearty meal ready to serve in less than 30 minutes!

Old-Fashioned Beef Stew

25-MINUTE HOT AND HEARTY SUPPER
Serves 4
Tomato and Sauerkraut Blend
Old-Fashioned Beef Stew
Hot Scones   Cherry Jam
Apple Betty
Coffee   Milk

First the sweet —

APPLE BETTY
Combine 1 pound, 4 ounces unsweetened sliced apples, 1½ ounces brown sugar, ½ teaspoon cinnamon, and ⅛ teaspoon salt in 1½ pint baking dish. Top with 3 slices bread, cut in cubes; drizzle with 3 ounces honey.

Bake in hot oven (400°F. Mark 6) 20 minutes, or until bubbling. Serve warm with cream or whipped cream.

Then the first course —

TOMATO AND SAUER-KRAUT BLEND
Blend 1 pint tomato juice, chilled, with 4 ounces tinned sauerkraut juice; season with juice of ½ lemon and few drops Tabasco sauce; chill until serving time.

Next the stew —

OLD-FASHIONED BEEF STEW
Combine in large saucepan 1 1-pound can beef and gravy, 1 can condensed cream of celery soup, 1 8-ounce can whole onions (drained), 1 8-ounce can peas and carrots, and 2 rounded tablespoons chilli sauce or ketchup. Heat thoroughly; serve in soup bowls.

OR, to vary the main dish, serve —

QUICK BRUNSWICK STEW
Combine in large saucepan 1 can (about 1½ pounds) beef stew, 1 can (about 1 pound) chicken stew, 1 can (1 pound) lima or broad beans, 1 6-ounce can tomato paste, ½ teaspoon Worcestershire sauce, and 2 dashes of Tabasco sauce; heat thoroughly.

Serve in soup bowls. (Chilled pineapple juice makes a good first course with this stew.)

Hints: Buy plain scones at the bakery and pop in oven with Apple Betty for about 5 minutes to warm.

With coffee made and table set, dinner's ready in about 25 minutes.

35-MINUTE SUNDAY DINNER
Serves 4
Hot Madrilene with Lemon Slices
Turkey and Mushroom Casserole
Potatoes with Cheese
Peas and Carrots
Pineapple-Cranberry-Cress Salad
Steamed Fig Pudding
with Orange Sauce
Coffee   Milk

First the casserole —

TURKEY AND MUSHROOM CASSEROLE
Combine 1 can condensed cream of chicken soup, 1 4- or 6-ounce can sliced mushrooms, and ¼ teaspoon Worcestershire sauce in 1½ pint baking dish.

Add 1 6-ounce can boned turkey or chicken, diced. Sprinkle with 2 ounces packed sage and onion stuffing.

Bake in moderate oven (375°F. Mark 5) 25 minutes, or until bubbling hot. (Or bake in 4 individual baking dishes 20 minutes.)

Next —

POTATOES WITH CHEESE
Place 1 can (1 pound, 4 ounces) whole white potatoes, drained, in 8-inch pie-dish. Sprinkle with 2 ounces shredded Cheddar cheese and 3 tablespoons milk.

Place in oven with turkey casserole to heat thoroughly. (Bake at 375°F. Mark 5, 20 minutes.)

Then pudding —

STEAMED FIG PUDDING WITH ORANGE SAUCE
To heat pudding, open 1 12-ounce can fig pudding; place in double saucepan over boiling water; heat, covered, about 20 minutes.

To make sauce, gradually stir syrup drained from 1 can (1 pound, 4 ounces) orange segments into 1 tablespoon cornflour in small saucepan. Cook, stirring constantly, until thick and clear.

Add orange segments; serve hot over pudding. (Add 2 tablespoons of rum or brandy to sauce, if desired.)

Hints: There's still time to combine, season and heat 1 can (1 pound) peas with 1 8-ounce can julienne carrots — a bit of fresh mint does wonders here.

Make coffee and arrange 4 slices drained canned pineapple (8¼-ounce can) with spoonfuls of whole or jellied cranberry sauce on crisp watercress; serve with French dressing.

Heat 2 cans madrilene and serve with thin slices of lemon. When you have the table set, dinner is ready in about 35 minutes.

45-MINUTE FESTIVE FARE
Serves 4
Orange-Grapefruit Cocktail
Ham Parisienne
Aspic and Artichoke Salad
Peach Cream Cake
Coffee   Milk

Begin with the sweet—

PEACH CREAM CAKE

Whip ½ pint double cream; sweeten with 2 tablespoons sugar. Spread thin layer of cream over top of one 8-inch sponge flan case.

Drain well 1 large can (1 pound, 13 ounces) sliced peaches; arrange half of peaches over flan case; top with second flan case.

Spread remaining cream over top and sides of cake. Arrange remaining peaches over top of cake. Put 2½ ounces chopped toasted almonds on sides of cake; refrigerate until ready to serve.
Note: Refrigerate left-over cake for another meal.

Now for the main dish—

HAM PARISIENNE

Prepare corn bread (see Index) the day before; or cut 4 thick slices of wholemeal bread, trim off crusts and toast lightly.

Cut 8 slices ham (½ of 3-pound tinned ham; use remaining ham for another meal). Heat ham in covered frying pan with 2 tablespoons gelatine from ham can or water; keep hot until serving time.

Heat 1 large can (1 pound, 4 ounces) asparagus spears; drain well; keep warm.

Combine 1 can condensed cream of mushroom soup, 1 4- or 6-ounce can sliced mushrooms including liquid and 1 pimiento, diced; heat thoroughly; add 1 tablespoon sherry, if desired.

To serve, cut corn bread into 4 squares. Split and place squares on large dish. Arrange ham, then asparagus on corn bread; spoon hot mushroom sauce over top.
Hints: To make salad, slice chilled tomato aspic and arrange with 1 8-ounce can artichoke hearts, chilled and drained, on lettuce; serve with tart French dressing.

For first course, blend 1 6-ounce can frozen concentrated orange and grapefruit juice with water according to directions; serve over ice. Use ½ of orange and ½ of grapefruit juice, if mixture is not available.

Make coffee, set the table, and you're ready to serve in about 45 minutes.

30 MINUTE SATURDAY NIGHT FAVOURITE
Serves 4
Frying-Pan Corned Beef and Cabbage
with Mustard Sauce
Buttered Potatoes
Tomatoes with Pickles
Celery
Grilled Ginger Pear Halves
Vanilla Cream Wafers
Coffee   Milk

Start with—

FRYING-PAN CORNED BEEF AND CABBAGE

Brown in large frying pan 1 can (about 12 ounces) corned beef in 1 ounce butter or margarine, breaking up meat with fork.

Wash, core and coarsely chop 1 medium-sized head cabbage (about 1½ pounds). Add cabbage to corned beef with 1 teaspoon salt and dash of pepper; toss lightly.

Simmer, tightly covered, 10 minutes, or until cabbage is just tender, stirring often.

Then the—

MUSTARD SAUCE

Prepare 1 packet white sauce according to directions, blending in 2½ tablespoons prepared English mustard. (Or combine 1 can condensed cream of celery soup with 1 to 2 tablespoons mustard; heat thoroughly.)

Serve hot as a sauce with the corned beef and cabbage.

Next the—

TOMATOES WITH PICKLES

Combine 1 large can (1 pound, 4 ounces) tomatoes, 1½ ounces sweet gherkins (coarsely chopped), 2 teaspoons sugar, ½ teaspoon salt, and dash of pepper; heat thoroughly.

The sweet last—

GRILLED GINGER PEAR HALVES

Arrange 1 large can (1 pound, 13 ounces) pear halves with syrup in shallow baking dish.

Fill each pear centre with honey; sprinkle lightly with ground ginger or thinly sliced crystallised ginger.

Place under grill until bubbling hot; serve at once.
Hints: Heat 1 can (1 pound, 4 ounces) whole new potatoes; drain and season with butter or margarine, salt, and pepper.

Have pears ready to pop into hot grill while you're clearing the table.

You've still time to prepare celery, make coffee, set the table. You'll be serving dinner in about 30 minutes.

25-MINUTE MENU FOR CRISP AUTUMN DAYS
Serves 4
Frankfurters 'n' Sauerkraut
Stewed Tomatoes
Green-Gold Salad
Hot Doughnuts à la Mode
Coffee   Milk

Main dish first—

FRANKFURTERS 'N' SAUERKRAUT

Combine in large saucepan 1 pound, 13 ounces cooked sauerkraut, 1 pound, 4 ounces sliced apples, 1 12-ounce can frankfurters, 1 tablespoon sugar, and 1 teaspoon caraway seeds.

Toss lightly with fork; simmer, covered, 15 minutes, or until thoroughly heated.

Next—

STEWED TOMATOES

Combine in medium-sized saucepan 1 can (about 14 ounces) tomatoes, 2 slices bread (cut in cubes), 1 tablespoon sugar, 1 ounce butter or margarine, ½ teaspoon each salt and onion salt and dash of pepper. Heat thoroughly.

Then the salad—

GREEN-GOLD SALAD

Drain 1 can (1 pound) peas, reserving liquid for soup or gravy.

Toss peas lightly with 2 ounces each sliced celery and cubed processed Cheddar cheese, ½ teaspoon salt, and 2 tablespoons mayonnaise or salad dressing blended with a bit of lemon juice or red wine vinegar. Spoon onto lettuce leaves.

For the sweet—

HOT DOUGHNUTS À LA MODE

Put 4 doughnuts in double saucepan over boiling water to heat while you sit down to dinner.

Before serving heat 1 small can chocolate syrup in small saucepan.

Arrange doughnuts in individual serving dishes; top each with scoop of vanilla ice cream, hot chocolate syrup and a sprinkling of chopped mixed nuts.
Note: Sponge cake or leftover cake may be substituted for doughnuts.
Hints: With coffee made and table set, you're serving in 25 minutes.

30-MINUTE DOWN-EAST DINNER

Serves 4
Quick Baked Beans
Codfish Cakes   Tomato Sauce
Coleslaw   Malt Bread
Indian Pudding
Coffee   Milk

Begin with the beans—

QUICK BAKED BEANS

Combine in medium-sized saucepan 2 1-pound cans baked beans in tomato sauce with 1 rounded tablespoon ketchup or chilli sauce, 1 tablespoon prepared English mustard, and ½ teaspoon Worcestershire sauce. Heat thoroughly.

Then—

CODFISH CAKES

Defrost 1 packet frozen codfish cakes (4). Dust lightly with flour; brown on both sides in 1 ounce butter or margarine in frying pan.

Heat 1 8-ounce can tomato sauce; serve with hot codfish cakes.

Hints: Because it takes time to heat, slice 1 loaf of malt bread and heat in top of double saucepan over boiling water after preparing the baked beans. Serve malt bread hot.

Use top of same double saucepan to reheat Indian pudding (see Index) prepared the day before.

Before serving, top hot pudding with cream, brandy butter or vanilla ice cream. (For a light fruit sweet, substitute canned purple plums.)

Make your favourite coleslaw, adding 1 small can crushed pineapple, well drained, if desired. Then set the table and make coffee. Your dinner—New England style—is ready in about 30 minutes.

15-MINUTE MENU

Serves 4
Quick Spaghetti and Meat Balls
Swiss Spinach
Celery and Black Olives
Crusty Bread   Butter
Fruited Sandwich Loaf
Coffee   Milk

First—

QUICK SPAGHETTI AND MEAT BALLS

Combine 2 1-pound cans spaghetti in tomato sauce and 1 15-ounce can meat balls with gravy. Simmer, covered, 10 minutes, or until thoroughly heated, stirring carefully.

Serve with sprinkling of Parmesan cheese; pass round extra cheese.

Note: Or use 1 15-ounce can minced beef in gravy.

Then—

SWISS SPINACH

Heat 1 large can (1 pound, 4 ounces) chopped spinach in medium-sized saucepan; drain thoroughly.

Return to saucepan; toss lightly with 2 ounces top of the milk, cream, or evaporated milk, ½ teaspoon onion salt and ¼ teaspoon nutmeg. Heat well, but do not boil.

Sweet next—

FRUITED SPONGE SANDWICH

Have ingredients ready to put together after you've cleared the main course.

Place 4 slices sponge sandwich on baking sheet ready to toast on both sides under grill. Open 1 1-pound can fruit salad.

At serving-time, put 1 slice toasted sponge sandwich on each serving plate; spoon fruit over cake and top with whipped cream, if desired. (A little crème de menthe sprinkled over the fruit adds interest, colour and flavour.)

Hints: While the spaghetti and spinach heat, prepare a plate of the raw vegetables, make coffee and set the table. A good meal in 15 minutes.

30-MINUTE HOT-OFF-THE GIRDLE SUPPER

Serves 4
Corn Pancakes and Sausages
Hot Syrup
Celery Sticks
Grapefruit Surprise
Coffee   Milk

The sweet first—

GRAPEFRUIT SURPRISE

Spoon 1 large can (1 pound, 4 ounces) grapefruit segments into 4 individual fruit dishes.

Top with 1 packet frozen strawberries, partially thawed. Chill until time to serve.

Pancakes last—

CORN PANCAKES AND SAUSAGES

Combine and sift together 4 ounces sieved plain flour, 1½ teaspoons baking powder and ½ teaspoon salt.

Combine 1 well beaten egg, 1 can (8 ounces) creamed sweetcorn, and 8 fluid ounces milk; stir into dry ingredients with 1 ounce melted butter.

Bake on lightly greased girdle or in frying pan until golden brown, turning once. Put pancakes in warm oven to keep hot until all are baked.

Serve hot with heated, tinned maple syrup or dark treacle; and pass round a plate of chipolata sausages, kept warm in oven after frying.

Note: Or you may use rashers of bacon in place of sausages for a quick variation.

Hints: Corn pancakes are best when they're hot off the girdle, so have the table set, celery sticks cut and coffee made before you start baking them. This supper or lunch is ready in less than 30 minutes.

40-MINUTE MENU FOR WINTRY DAYS

Serves 4
Chilli-Topped Corned Beef Hash
'n' Eggs
Buttered Green Beans
French-Fried Onion Rings
Cabbage and Tomato Slaw
Hot Rolls
Cherry Puff Dumplings
Coffee   Milk

Baked dish first—

CHILLI-TOPPED CORNED BEEF HASH 'N' EGGS

Spread 1-pound can corned beef hash in 9-inch pie dish. Top hash with 1 can (about 1 pound) whole-kernel sweetcorn, drained; make 4 depressions in corn and break 1 egg into each; top with 1 tablespoon chilli sauce.

Bake in hot oven (400°F. Mark 6) 20 minutes, or until eggs are set.

Then pudding—

CHERRY PUFF DUMPLINGS

Combine 2½ ounces sugar and 1½ tablespoons cornflour in medium-sized frying pan with tight-fitted cover.

Gradually add juice drained from 1 can (1 pound, 4 ounces) red sour stoned cherries and few drops red food colouring.

Cook until thick and clear, stirring constantly. Add cherries; heat to bubbling hot.

Open 1 packet puff pastry, thawed; prepare according to directions. Divide in half, and then cut 4 circles from pastry and place on cherries. Simmer tightly covered, 15 minutes, or until pastry is done.

Keep cherry puff warm; serve with cream or top with vanilla ice cream.

Hints: While you're waiting for hash to bake and pudding to cook, drop 1 large sliced onion, separated into rings and coated with golden crumbs into hot oil, and fry until crisp.

Heat 1 can (1 pound) French style green beans; season with butter or margarine, salt and pepper.

Then make coffee and coleslaw, and heat bakery rolls. Here's a 40-minute meal.

Quick Eggs Benedict

30-MINUTE SAVE-A-PENNY SUPPER

Serves 4
Tomato Cocktail
Quick Eggs Benedict
Chick Peas and Bean Sprouts Marinade
Cherry Crunch Pudding
Coffee   Milk

Salad first—

CHICK PEAS AND BEAN SPROUTS MARINADE

Drain and combine 1 can (1 pound, 4 ounces) chick peas and 1 can (1 pound, 4 ounces) bean sprouts, reserving liquid for first course.

Toss lightly with 2 tablespoons French dressing, 1 tablespoon soy sauce, and ½ teaspoon salt; chill.

When ready to serve, spoon onto lettuce leaves; top with sliced olives.

First course next—

TOMATO COCKTAIL

Combine liquid reserved from chick peas and bean sprouts and 1 pint tomato juice.

Season with 1 teaspoon lemon juice and a few drops Tabasco sauce. Chill until serving time, or serve over ice.

Then pudding—

CHERRY CRUNCH PUDDING

Prepare 1 packet vanilla blancmange mix according to directions.

Fold in 1 8-ounce can dark sweet cherries, well drained, and 10 digestive biscuits, broken into bite-sized pieces. Chill until serving time.

Note: Canned crushed pineapple, apple sauce, fruit cocktail, or strained fruits for babies may be used in place of cherries.

Now for—

QUICK EGGS BENEDICT

Heat 1 8½- or 9-ounce can cheese rarebit in top of double saucepan over boiling water.

Split and toast 4 baps; spread with 3 ounces devilled ham.

Just before serving, top each bap half with 1 hot poached egg; spoon hot rarebit over eggs. Serve at once, two halves per person.

Note: Or use 8 ounces of packet cheese sauce in place of rarebit.

Hints: Make coffee and set table for a 30-minute meal.

30-MINUTE MENU FOR MAN-SIZED APPETITES

Serves 4
Hamburgers and Gravy on Rice
Buttered Green Beans
4-Fruit Salad
French Bread
Chocolate Crunch Pudding
Coffee   Milk

First the—

HAMBURGERS AND GRAVY ON RICE

Combine 10 ounces beef gravy and 1 15-ounce can hamburgers and gravy in saucepan; simmer, covered, 10 minutes, or until hamburgers are thoroughly heated.

Serve over 1 packet boil-in-the-bag rice, prepared according to directions.

Note: Tinned beef stew or tinned beef with gravy may be substituted for hamburgers and gravy.

Then sweet—

CHOCOLATE CRUNCH PUDDING

Prepare 1 packet chocolate blancmange mix according to packet directions.

Fold in 2 ounces coarsely crushed peanut brittle or chopped unsalted peanuts. A good substitute is 1 bar of toffee and 1 ounce peanuts, mixed.

Chill until serving time. If you have any leftover cake, fold in 1 or 2 slices cut in bite-sized pieces.

Now the salad—

4-FRUIT SALAD

Drain syrup from 1 8-ounce can each of sliced peaches, white cherries, pear halves, and crushed pineapple. (Reserve syrup for fruit drinks.)

Arrange fruit on crisp lettuce; top each salad with spoonful of sweet or

sour cream and a generous sprinkling of nutmeg.

Hints: There's time to heat and season 1 can (1 pound) green beans, adding 2 tablespoons each tartar sauce and chilli sauce.

Make coffee and set the table for another 30-minute meal.

40-MINUTE MENU FOR EASY ENTERTAINING

Serves 4
Onion Soup
Chicken and Prawn Curry
on parsley rice
Raisins — Pineapple —
                    Chutney — Coconut
Buttered Peas   Julienne Beetroot
Garden Salad   French Dressing
Choco-Mint Cake
Coffee   Milk

It's sweet first—

CHOCO-MINT CAKE

Prepare and bake 1 packet white cake mix according to packet directions, using 13 × 9 × 2-inch baking tin.

When cake is baked, remove from oven; arrange 8½ ounces chocolate after-dinner mints over top of cake. Return cake to oven for 3 minutes, or until chocolate is melted.

Score top lightly with fork; sprinkle with 2 ounces coarsely chopped peanuts, walnuts or almonds. Cool on wire cake rack. Cut in squares.

While cake bakes—

CHICKEN AND PRAWN CURRY ON PARSLEY RICE

Blend 1 can condensed cream of chicken soup with 2 fluid ounces milk. Add 1 to 2 teaspoons curry powder (real curry fans will like the larger amount); 1 6-ounce can boned chicken and 1 5-ounce can prawns, drained and deveined. Heat thoroughly.

Serve over 1 packet boil-in-the-bag white or 1 packet savoury rice, tossed with 2 tablespoons chopped parsley, 1 tablespoon butter or margarine, and ¼ teaspoon salt. (Wild rice, obtainable from health food shops, is a special treat.)

Hints: Next heat and season vegetables, using 1 can (1 pound) petits pois and 1 can (1 pound) julienne beetroot.

Fill small dishes with raisins, pineapple cubes (1 large can: 1 pound), chutney and coconut.

Then heat 2 cans ready-to-serve onion soup, arrange lettuce, make coffee and set table—all done in about 40 minutes.

Chilli and Tamales

25-MINUTE DOWN MEXICO WAY MENU

Serves 4
Chilli and Tamales
Crisp Cream Crackers   French Bread
Mixed Salad
Hot Spiced Apricots
Coffee   Milk

First—

CHILLI AND TAMALES

Combine 2 cans (about 1 pound, 10 ounces) chilli con carne with beans and 1 can (about 15 to 16 ounces) red kidney beans, drained, in medium-sized saucepan; heat.

Place 1 can (about 15 ounces) tamales over chilli; heat thoroughly.

The sweet next—

HOT SPICED APRICOTS

Drain into saucepan syrup from 1 can (1 pound, 13 ounces) apricot halves or whole apricots.

Add 3 lemon slices, 8 whole cloves, and ⅛ teaspoon allspice; simmer 5 minutes. Add apricots; heat thoroughly and serve hot.

Note: Peaches, pears, pineapple, or sweet cherries may be substituted.

Hints: Make your favourite mixed salad, adding a little crumbled blue cheese. Make coffee; set the table.

Heat the French bread and crackers. You're ready to serve this hearty meal in less than 25 minutes.

35-MINUTE FRIDAY DINNER

Serves 4
Vegetable Juice Cocktail
Salmon Scallop
Herb Peas
Lettuce Wedges   French Dressing
Bread or Grissini Sticks
Prune-Peach Whip
Coffee   Milk

The casserole first—

SALMON SCALLOP

Drain and flake 1 7-ounce can salmon.

Combine 8 ounces coarsely crushed salted cream cracker crumbs, 3 ounces melted butter or margarine, 1 table-spoon minced parsley, 1 teaspoon grated onion and dash of pepper.

Spread 4 ounces crumb mixture in 8-inch pie pan. Cover with salmon; sprinkle with remaining crumb mixture. Pour 8 fluid ounces milk or undiluted evaporated milk over crumbs.

Bake in hot oven (400°F. Mark 6) 20 minutes, or until crumbs brown and casserole is thoroughly heated.

Note: Or use 1 6-ounce can lobster or crabmeat in place of salmon.

Pudding next—

PRUNE-PEACH WHIP

Whip 8 ounces double cream, beating in 2 teaspoons sugar. Carefully fold in 1 can (4¾ ounces) strained prunes and 1 can (4¾ ounces) strained peaches—baby-food jars.

Arrange sponge fingers around sides of dishes; pile prune-peach mixture in centre. Chill until serving time.

For the vegetable—

HERB PEAS

Drain liquid from 1 can (1 pound) peas into saucepan; boil quickly to reduce to about 3 ounces.

Add peas, ½ ounce butter or margarine, ½ teaspoon salt, and ⅛ teaspoon mixed herbs; toss lightly; heat well.

Hints: While scallop bakes, prepare the salad, make coffee, set the table and pour the chilled juice or serve over ice (12-ounce can mixed vegetable juices to serve 4). Dinner's ready in 35 to 40 minutes.

25-MINUTE SOUP TUREEN SUPPER

Serves 4
Quick Lobster Chowder
Mixed Salad   Parmesan Dressing
Potato Crisps   Bakery Rolls
Orange Sponge Pudding
                 Whipped Cream
Coffee   Milk

Soup first—

QUICK LOBSTER CHOWDER

Blend 1 can condensed cream of mushroom soup, 1 can condensed cream of tomato soup, 1 soup can milk and 8 ounces single cream; heat, but do not boil.

Drain 1 6-ounce can lobster; pick over meat, discarding any hard fibre; flake meat. Add to soup; heat well.

Note: As a substitute for the lobster, any one of the following may be used (5 to 7 ounces): 1 can crabmeat, 1 can prawns, 1 can tuna fish, 1 can salmon, or 1 can minced clams.

Hints: Next, open 1 can Orange Sponge Pudding (about 8 ounces) and place in top of double saucepan; heat, covered, over boiling water about 20 minutes. (For party flavour, add 2 to 3 tablespoons of sherry while heating.)

At serving-time, slice pudding and top with whipped cream, or serve with double cream.

Toss salad lightly with French dressing and 1 tablespoon grated Parmesan cheese.

Heat bakery rolls in a brown paper bag, first sprinkling with water, in moderate oven. Now there's time to make coffee and set the table.

For extra crisp potato crisps, pop them in oven with rolls just to heat. In about 25 minutes the meal's ready—wonderful enough for easy party food, filling enough for a hungry family.

30-MINUTE SUPPER

Serves 4
Macaroni and Cheese-Stuffed Peppers
Stewed Tomatoes   Curried Carrots
Celery Sticks
Strawberry and Pineapple Compote
Coffee   Milk

First—

MACARONI AND CHEESE-STUFFED PEPPERS

Cut 2 large, or 4 small, green peppers in half lengthwise; remove all seeds and veins; wash. Steam, covered, in simmering water 10 minutes, or until just tender; drain well.

Meanwhile, heat 2 cans (about 1 pound each) macaroni with cheese sauce.

Place hot drained peppers in shallow baking dish; fill with hot macaroni and cheese. Top with shredded Cheddar cheese (about 1 tablespoon for each pepper) and sprinkle with paprika.

Just before serving, put under grill until cheese topping melts.

Note: You may use 2 cans (about 1 pint, 10 ounces) Spanish rice in place of macaroni and cheese.

Then—

CURRIED CARROTS

Heat 1 can (1 pound) diced carrots; drain and season with butter or margarine, salt, pepper, and ½ to ¾ teaspoon curry powder; toss lightly.

Hints: Heat 1 can (1 pound) stewed tomatoes; cut celery sticks; make coffee and set the table.

Open 1 packet frozen pineapple cubes and 1 packet frozen strawberries; let thaw while you're serving main course.

At serving-time, spoon fruits into fruit dishes; sprinkle a teaspoon of Cointreau over each, if desired.

779

The salad-conscious housewife will choose salads to fit the meal. If they accompany the main course of the dinner, she will choose a light salad. If served as a first course, the salad will be made up of tart fruits or seafood. A frozen salad or a fruit salad will be chosen for the dessert course.

If a salad is chosen as the main course of the meal, it should have some protein-rich food such as meat, poultry, fish, eggs, or cheese as the main ingredient.

Garnishes for Salads

Suitable garnishings for meat and vegetable salads are: sliced cucumbers, quartered and sliced tomatoes, canned beetroots cut into cubes, sticks, or slices, sliced or quartered hard-boiled eggs, green and red pepper, canned pimiento, stuffed olives, carrot sticks, sliced or diced pickles, cheese sticks, cubes, or slices, and other suggested garnishes.

Fruit salads may be garnished with maraschino cherries, melon balls, mint leaves, herbs, strawberries, dark fruits, black olives, nuts, coconut, chopped dates, figs, and stoned prunes.

ASPARAGUS TIPS

Marinate small canned asparagus tips in French dressing. Sprinkle ends with paprika.

TO MAKE CARROT FLOWERS

Scrape tender carrots. Make lengthwise cuts ⅛ inch deep into carrots. Cut crosswise into paper-thin slices. Keep slices in iced water an hour or so to curl "petals".

CARROT STRIPS

Wash and scrape young, tender carrots. Cut into thin strips lengthwise. Chill in iced water.

CARROT CURLS

Slice carrot paper-thin lengthwise. Roll up each slice and fasten with cocktail stick. Crisp in iced water. Remove stick.

CARROT STICK BUNDLES

Slice carrot lengthwise into small strips.

Remove stones from large olives. Push 3 or 4 strips through openings in olives.

CUCUMBER BALLS

Cut large cucumbers into balls with melon baller. Marinate in dressing. Sprinkle with paprika.

FLUTED CUCUMBERS

Cucumbers may be left unpeeled or peeled. Run a fork down the length of cucumber, repeating completely round the cucumber. Slice.

CUCUMBER RADISH FANS

Cut ends of 2 unpeeled cucumbers. Quarter lengthwise. Cut each quarter in ⅛-inch slices. Do not cut all the way through.

Cut 8 large radishes crosswise into thin slices. Insert radishes between cucumber slices.

RADISH ROSES

Cut thin strips of the red peel of radishes almost through to stems to form petals.

Place radishes in iced water. As they chill the peel will curl back like petals.

CALLA LILIES

Peel a white turnip. Cut into thin lengthwise slices. Chill in iced water until they curl and resemble calla lilies. Form stems from carrot strips.

STUFFED GHERKINS

Core large gherkins. Fill with cream cheese. Chill thoroughly and slice.

SALADS

CUCUMBER BOATS

Cut a cucumber in half lengthwise. Remove seeds and pulp. Fill with cream cheese.

Chill well and slice again, if desired.

Beetroots and carrots may be cooked until just done and then filled with cottage cheese.

LETTUCE CUPS

For lettuce leaves to lie flat on the plate, cut each leaf up from the stem end about 2 or 3 inches.

Fit 2 leaves together on each plate, interlocking the slits.

GREEN OR RED PEPPER RINGS

Cut off tops. Remove seeds and centres. Cut crosswise into thin slices.

Crisp in iced water. Dry before using.

SPRING ONIONS (Scallions)

Trim washed green stalks, leaving about 3 inches. Trim onion if skin is loose or shrivelled. Chill in iced water.

ONION RINGS

Cut large Spanish onion into thin slices. Crisp in iced water, then loosen rings and drain well.

RADISH FANS

Select firm and rather long radishes. With a thin, very sharp knife, cut thin slices crosswise almost through radish.

Chill in iced water. The slices spread fan-shaped as they chill.

TO MAKE CELERY CURLS

Cut small stalks or short pieces of celery lengthwise into thin shreds, cutting to within ½ inch of the leaves or end of piece. Place in iced water to curl.

HINTS FOR MAKING SALADS

● Buy the freshest lettuce possible, wash it, dry thoroughly, and store in refrigerator in the vegetable compartment or polythene bag or in a damp towel until ready to serve. Fresh, clean, crisp lettuce is the basis of a good green salad.

● All ingredients should be well drained before they are combined with salad dressing, to avoid giving the dressing a watery consistency. Dry greens thoroughly by patting with a towel or kitchen paper.

● Use a variety of greens. Try shredded cabbage, chicory, watercress, and cos lettuce as a change from round or leaf lettuce. Tear lettuce into bite-size pieces instead of cutting. Outer leaves of lettuce should be discarded only when they are bruised.

● When mixing salads, toss ingredients gently until mixed. Don't stir vigorously.

● Add the dressing to salads at serving time to avoid wilting the lettuce, or, better still, serve the dressing from a separate bowl. People differ in the amount of dressing they prefer.

● Use leftover vegetables in salads.

● The flavour of some salads, especially those containing cooked vegetables or meats, is improved by marinating the ingredients in French dressing. To do this, allow foods to stand in the dressing in a cool place until they are well seasoned. Drain before serving.

● Wooden salad bowls should not be washed. Wipe clean with a cold damp cloth. Before using, season with warm salad oil, then rub the bowl with a cut clove of garlic.

● Use a variety of dressings. It is not necessary to make a fresh dressing each time. Most dressings keep well in the refrigerator.

● Avoid too much garnish. Depend upon the natural colour and flavour of foods for an attractive appetizing salad. Arrange salads lightly and attractively.

Grapefruit Starter

First Course Starter Salads

Starter salads are usually miniature salads served as a first course for luncheon or dinner. Almost any favourite salad could be used for this purpose if arranged attractively on a small bed of lettuce on an individual plate, and accompanied with a tart dressing. Naturally the type of salad depends somewhat on the courses that are to follow, but the variety is endless. Because salads have become so popular and can be made so tasty and attractive it's the wise housewife who turns to them as a curtain raiser.

ITALIAN STARTER SALAD 1 (Antipasto)

Lettuce
Thick tomato slices
Thin Italian salami slices
Cole slaw
Anchovies
Olives

Arrange lettuce leaves on individual salad plates. Cover with tomato and salami slices.

Pile well-seasoned cole slaw into a cone on top of this. Cross the top with 2 anchovies. Garnish with black and stuffed olives.

Serve olive oil and wine vinegar in cruets to accompany the salad.

ITALIAN STARTER SALAD 2

On each serving dish arrange thin, unpeeled apple slices, strips of green pepper, a mound of cole slaw, a canned pimiento, one or two sardines, stuffed pickled onions, black olives and stuffed olives.

Serve olive oil and wine vinegar in cruets to accompany the salad.

BARBECUED AUBERGINE SALAD

Grill 2 medium aubergines until rather burned and very soft.

Peel aubergines carefully.

Then chop and add 1 medium onion, finely chopped, 1 ounce chopped parsley, 2 fluid ounces each vinegar and salad or olive oil, and 1½ teaspoons salt and ¼ teaspoon pepper. Chill well. Serves 8 to 10.

STARTER TOMATO-CHEESE

For each serving arrange 2 slices of tomato, a ball of cream cheese and chives, and 2 radish roses on a lettuce leaf. Serve with mayonnaise.

GRAPEFRUIT STARTER

For each serving arrange grapefruit sections alternately with strips of green pepper on a lettuce leaf.

Serve with Thousand Island dressing made by blending ½ pint mayonnaise with 4 fluid ounces chilli pickle.

HONEYDEW WITH PROSCIUTTO

1 large honeydew melon
½ pound prosciutto ham

Have the ham sliced paper-thin. Cut the melon into 8 wedges and arrange a wedge of melon with 2 or 3 slices of ham on an individual plate for each person. Serve with a small knife and fork.

TOMATO AND EGG STARTERS

Lettuce
Slices of large tomatoes
Slices of hard boiled eggs
Stuffed olive slices
3 ounces cream cheese
1½ tablespoons French dressing

Arrange tomato slices on lettuce leaves on individual dishes. On each slice of tomato arrange 3 slices of hard-boiled egg topped with olive slices.

Moisten cheese with French dressing. Press mixture through pastry tube round edge of tomatoes.

Variations: Omit cream cheese and French dressing. Spread tomatoes with French mustard before topping with egg slices. Sprinkle egg slices with cayenne pepper or paprika.

PACIFIC COAST STARTER

Hollow out chilled, fresh tomatoes, reserving the pulp and juice for Close-To-The-Border Sauce (below).

Fill tomato cups with your favourite seafood cocktail, and serve on chilled, crisp Webb's Wonder lettuce.

Close-To-The-Border Sauce: A tasty, uncooked sauce to serve with meat, fish, and other first course foods.

Combine ¾ pint fresh tomato pulp and juice with 2 tablespoons each chopped green pepper, celery, and cucumber. Add 1 tablespoon of wine vinegar and salt and pepper to taste.

A bit of chilli seasoning will add "heat" for those who want it. This sauce is especially good on enchiladas, tamales, and other Mexican foods.

Pacific Coast Starter

DICED CUCUMBER COCKTAIL

1 large cucumber
2 fluid ounces tomato ketchup
2 fluid ounces chilli pickle
1 teaspoon Worcestershire sauce
Juice of ½ lemon
1 teaspoon prepared horseradish
Dash of Tabasco sauce or cayenne
    pepper
4 lettuce leaves

Chill cucumber. Combine remaining ingredients except lettuce to make sauce and chill.

Just before serving, peel cucumber; make lengthwise parallel grooves with tines of fork. Chop in ¼ inch pieces. Place on lettuce leaves in fruit cups. Top with sauce. Serves 4.

AVOCADO-TOMATO COCKTAIL

1 avocado
2 tomatoes
Small lettuce leaves
4 fluid ounces chilli pickle
1 tablespoon horseradish
Juice of ½ lemon
½ teaspoon salt
⅛ teaspoon black pepper

Peel and dice chilled avocado and tomatoes. Put on lettuce in fruit cups.

Mix remaining ingredients, and serve as sauce. Serves 4.

CAULIFLOWER COCKTAIL

1 head of cauliflower
4 fluid ounces mayonnaise
3 tablespoons chopped sweet pickle
1 tablespoon capers
½ teaspoon French mustard
1 tablespoon lemon juice
Few grains of salt

Cook the cauliflower until just tender. Chill thoroughly and separate into flowerets.

Serve in fruit cups on lettuce topped with a dressing made of the remaining ingredients.

AVOCADO-OLIVE STARTER

1 large, ripe avocado
8 fluid ounces highly seasoned
    French dressing
9 chopped stuffed olives

Peel avocado. Cut in two and remove stone. Cut in ¼ inch lengthwise slices. Cover with French dressing and allow to stand in refrigerator 30 minutes.

Drain and reserve dressing for future salads. Sprinkle with olives. Serves 4.

FROZEN TOMATO AND CUCUMBER COCKTAIL

4 large tomatoes, diced
1 large cucumber, diced
4 fluid ounces chilli pickle
2 teaspoons horseradish
1 teaspoon Worcestershire sauce
1 tablespoon lemon juice

Put tomatoes in refrigerator tray and partially freeze. Spoon into fruit cups, filling each about half full. Fill with cucumber.

Mix remaining ingredients and use for topping cocktail. Serves 6 to 8.

TOMATO-CAVIAR-PRAWN STARTERS

Lettuce leaves
Caviar
Chopped hard-boiled egg yolks
Few drops of lemon juice
Thin slices of tomato
Chopped hard-boiled egg whites
Marinated cooked or canned prawns

Arrange lettuce leaves on individual plates. Combine caviar and chopped egg yolks; season with lemon juice. Spread this mixture on tomato slices. Garnish with chopped egg whites.

Place in centres of lettuce leaves. Garnish the centres with prawns.

CHICORY STARTER

6 chicory leaves
2 tablespoons caviar
2 lemon wedges
3 ounces cream cheese
Seasonings
Mayonnaise

Fill chicory leaves with caviar and arrange 3 leaves on each plate, meeting at the centre on a lemon wedge.

Season cheese highly and moisten with mayonnaise; shape in balls and arrange 3 on each plate between chicory leaves. Serves 2.

EGG-SARDINE STARTER

Cut hard-boiled eggs in halves, lengthwise. Season with salt, pepper, and paprika.

Place a small well-drained sardine or rolled fillet of anchovy over each egg half.

Arrange on a crisp lettuce leaf. Garnish with a bit of lemon.

GARLIC SAUSAGE AND TOMATO STARTERS

3 ounces garlic sausage spread
3 tablespoons mayonnaise
½ teaspoon grated onion
4 large tomatoes
Parsley

Combine sausage, mayonnaise, and onion. Wash, dry, core, and cut each tomato into 4 ¼-inch crosswise slices.

Spread garlic sausage mixture on half the tomato slices and top each with a second tomato slice to make sandwiches.

Arrange on lettuce on individual dishes. Garnish with mayonnaise and a sprig of parsley. Serves 8.

EGG AND TOMATO STARTER

4 eggs
¼ teaspoon salt
¼ teaspoon paprika
3 large, firm tomatoes

Hard-boil eggs and chop 3 of them while still warm. Add salt, paprika, and a few drops of onion juice.

Pack tightly into small buttered moulds; chill 4 to 5 hours.

Remove from moulds and cut into ½-inch slices. Place thick slices of tomato on lettuce; add egg slices. Cover with desired dressing.

SARDINE STARTER

2 large cans boneless, skinless
    sardines
4 ounces butter, creamed
Lemon juice
Paprika
8 ounces pimiento-stuffed olives,
    sliced

Mash sardines with fork; add creamed butter. Mix and season with lemon juice and paprika. Chill until firm.

Mould as desired. Cover with sliced olives. Chill. Serve with sliced lemon.

AVOCADO AND PRAWN SALAD STARTER

2 avocados
½ pound cooked, cleaned prawns
Sauce:
4 fluid ounces mayonnaise
2 fluid ounces chilli pickle
¼ teaspoon grated onion
1 tablespoon finely chopped green
    pepper
1½ teaspoons Worcestershire sauce
1 tablespoon lemon juice
¼ teaspoon salt
Dash of Tabasco sauce

Prepare sauce by combining all sauce ingredients. Chill until ready to serve.

Cut avocados into halves, lengthwise, and peel if desired. Place each avocado half on lettuce leaf. Place prawns over cut side of fruit. Serve with sauce. Serves 4.

TOMATO-GRAPEFRUIT SALAD

4 tomatoes, peeled
½ bunch watercress
2 grapefruit, peeled and sectioned
Pimiento strips
Mayonnaise, salad dressing, or
    French dressing

For each serving place a tomato, whole, quartered or sliced, on watercress on a small plate. Surround the tomato with grapefruit sections. Garnish with canned pimiento strips.

Serve with mayonnaise, salad dressing, or French dressing. Serves 4.

Tossed Salads and Vegetable Salads

BASIC TOSSED SALAD

This is the simplest of all bowl salads. Any number of fresh or cooked vegetables may be used. Choose one or several kinds of following greens: lettuce, chicory, cos lettuce, endive, escarole, watercress, green dandelions, or raw spinach.

Add any of following: sliced or chopped radishes, onions, celery, green pepper, cucumber, tomato, carrot, bits of leftover runner beans, beetroots, carrots, peas, sliced cauliflower, etc.

Be sure greens are crisp, clean, and dry. Wash them thoroughly in cold water, then dry by shaking in a towel. No salad should ever be watery.

Break greens into desired pieces. Add chopped or sliced vegetables. Mix in salad dressing, using two forks, taking care not to break the vegetables. Serve on lettuce leaves or in individual salad bowls.

For a suggestion of garlic or onion, rub bowl, before adding ingredients, with a freshly cut surface of either.

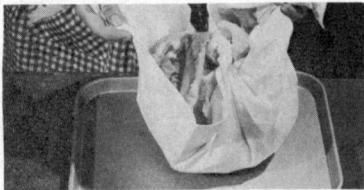

Tie washed greens in a dry towel and shake well before storing.

Store cleaned salad vegetables in refrigerator to chill them.

For tossed salads, tear salad greens to bite-size pieces.

Add dressing to salad greens just before serving.

ITALIAN SALAD BOWL

1 clove garlic
1 2-ounce can rolled anchovy fillets
4 tablespoons olive or other salad oil
1 tablespoon tarragon vinegar
1 tablespoon fresh lemon juice
1 teaspoon dry mustard
½ teaspoon salt
Freshly ground black pepper
1 tablespoon capers
2 large potatoes
1 1-pound can runner beans
Lettuce
1 or 2 tomatoes
Black olives

Peel garlic and mash with 2 anchovies. Add oil, vinegar, lemon juice, seasonings, and capers. Allow to stand 1 hour.

Cook potatoes in jackets until tender; peel and dice. Drain beans, add potatoes and pour dressing over them; toss to coat well and chill in refrigerator at least 1 hour.

Just before serving, toss again. Garnish with a ruffle of lettuce, tomatoes cut into wedges, black olives, and remaining anchovies. Serves 4 to 6.

TOSSED GREENS SALAD BOWL WITH DRESSING

1 small clove garlic, if desired
4 fluid ounces salad oil
3 tablespoons vinegar
¾ teaspoon salt
⅛ teaspoon black pepper
½ teaspoon sugar
½ teaspoon dry mustard
½ teaspoon paprika
1 medium head round lettuce, broken into 1½-inch pieces
4 large cos lettuce leaves, cut into 1½-inch lengths
¼ bunch watercress, stems removed

Have all salad ingredients except seasonings chilled. Rub inside of salad bowl with cut surface of garlic clove and then discard garlic.

Add next 7 ingredients and beat with fork until well blended. Break round and cos lettuce into salad bowl in alternate layers. Add watercress.

Toss ingredients lightly until each piece of salad green is coated with dressing. Serve immediately. Serves 6.

RUNNER BEAN AND RADISH SALAD

Use 12 ounces cooked slivered runner beans, 1 teaspoon chopped chives, and 2 ounces thinly sliced crisp radishes tossed with a few greens and French dressing. If desired, add a few tablespoons crumbled Roquefort cheese.

Italian Salad Bowl

GREEK SALAD

Cut 1 round lettuce and the following vegetables very fine: 3 peeled tomatoes, 4 spring onions, ¾ large cucumber, 2 green peppers, 1 bunch watercress.

Toss mixture with 3 tablespoons vinegar, 1 teaspoon salt, and 12 black olives.

Pour 6 tablespoons olive oil over all; allow to stand ¼ hour to ripen before serving. Serves 6.

CAESAR SALAD

1 clove garlic
4 fluid ounces salad oil
½ round lettuce
½ head curly endive
3 ounces croutons
1 2-ounce can anchovy fillets
3 or 4 tomatoes, diced
1 beaten egg
1 tablespoon Worcestershire sauce
4 tablespoons lemon juice
½ teaspoon black pepper
½ teaspoon salt
2 ounces grated Parmesan cheese

Crush garlic and add to salad oil. Break lettuce into large wooden salad bowl. Tear endive.

Add croutons, anchovies, and tomatoes. Strain oil to remove garlic and pour over vegetables.

Combine remaining ingredients and beat well. Pour over salad and toss lightly. Serves 4 to 6.

Croutons: Work 1 teaspoon brown sauce or Worcestershire sauce into 4 ounces butter and spread on slices of stale bread.

Cut into cubes and brown in the oven or in a frying pan. Sprinkle lightly with salt and use as a garnish for Caesar Salad.

Caesar Salad

Grapefruit Spinach Salad Oriental

GRAPEFRUIT SPINACH SALAD ORIENTAL

10 ounces raw spinach, washed and drained
1 4-ounce can sliced mushrooms, drained
1 5-ounce can water chestnuts, diced
2 grapefruits, sectioned and diced
4 tablespoons salad oil
2 tablespoons vinegar
2 tablespoons grapefruit juice
1 tablespoon soy sauce
¼ teaspoon Tabasco sauce
¼ teaspoon salt
¼ teaspoon dry mustard

Coarsely tear spinach into large salad bowl. Add mushrooms, water chestnuts, and grapefruit.

Mix oil, vinegar, grapefruit juice, soy sauce, Tabasco, salt, and dry mustard. Toss with spinach mixture. Serves 6 to 8.

HEARTY GARDEN SALAD BOWL

6 tablespoons garlic French dressing
3 tablespoons mayonnaise
1 1-pound can mixed vegetables
1 small onion, thinly sliced
2 ounces chopped celery
2 ounces canned pimiento strips
2 hard-boiled eggs, diced
5 to 6 ounces slivered canned tongue
Salt and pepper

Combine French dressing and mayonnaise. Add drained mixed vegetables, onion, and celery. Chill about 1 hour to blend flavours.

Add pimiento, eggs, and tongue. Mix gently. Add salt and pepper to taste. Chill. Serve on crisp lettuce leaves. Serves 4 to 6.

Hearty Garden Salad Bowl

RAW VEGETABLE SALAD

1½ ounces grated cucumber
1½ ounces grated raw beetroot
2 teaspoons wine vinegar
¼ teaspoon sugar
1 ounce grated raw carrots
1 ounce grated or chopped celery or apple
4 fluid ounces soured cream or yoghurt
¼ teaspoon salt
Black pepper
¼ teaspoon dry mustard or curry powder
1 tablespoon lemon juice

Sprinkle cucumbers and beetroots with vinegar and sugar. Allow to stand while preparing other ingredients.

Add carrots and celery or apple and chill.

Mix sour cream, salt, pepper, mustard or curry powder, and lemon juice. Blend with vegetables just before serving. Serve on any salad greens. Serves 4 to 5 as a dinner salad.

Luncheon Salad: Serve Raw Vegetable Salad with cottage cheese as a luncheon main dish, in which case portions would be reduced to 3.

Starter Salad: Prepare Raw Vegetable Salad and garnish servings with anchovies to use as starter salad. Serves 8.

TOSSED SALAD, WINE DRESSING

1 head of lettuce, cut up
2 tomatoes, cut in eighths
1 stalk celery, cut in strips
3 carrots, cut in strips
2 spring onions, sliced
½ unpeeled cucumber, sliced thin
Watercress
4 fluid ounces salad oil
2 tablespoons lemon juice
1 tablespoon sugar
½ teaspoon salt
⅛ teaspoon black pepper
4 fluid ounces Burgundy or claret

Combine lettuce, tomatoes, celery, carrots, onions, cucumber, and watercress in a bowl.

Mix salad oil through salad before bringing to the table.

Blend lemon juice, salt, pepper, and wine in small bowl at table. Pour over salad; toss lightly. Serves 6.

COMBINATION SALAD

6 ounces cooked runner beans
2 ounces grated raw carrots
2 ounces celery strips
6 ounces shredded lettuce
1 hard-boiled egg
French dressing

Combine runner beans, raw carrots, celery strips, and lettuce. Mix lightly.

Arrange sliced egg on vegetables. Serve with French dressing. Serves 5.

Vegetable and Egg Combination Salad: Increase eggs to 3 and add 1½ ounces chopped green peppers to Combination Salad recipe.

BEAN SPROUTS SALAD BOWL

Use 2 ounces fresh bean sprouts, 2 ounces chopped celery, ½ sliced cucumber, 1 ounce sliced radishes, and 4 or 5 rings of green pepper. Toss with French dressing seasoned with a little soy sauce.

RAW BEETROOT SALAD

Use 12 ounces minced raw beetroot and 8 fluid ounces piccalilli. Toss with French dressing or thin mayonnaise and a few leaves of lettuce.

CUCUMBER AND CARROT SALAD

Use ½ cucumber (unpeeled and sliced), 1 green pepper (cut in strips), 3 grated carrots, 2 ounces chopped celery, and ½ small head of lettuce or other greens. Toss with thinned mayonnaise.

LUNCHEON SALAD BOWL WITH CHEESE AND HAM

Chopped lettuce
10 dried figs, cooked and sliced
4 slices Gruyère cheese, cut into strips
5 slices ham, cut into strips
2 oranges, peeled and sectioned
French dressing

Make a bed of chopped lettuce in bottom of salad bowl. Toss figs with cheese, ham, oranges, and additional lettuce.

Garnish with whole figs, orange sections, and ham strips rolled up. Serve with thick French dressing. Serves 5.

Luncheon Salad Bowl with Cheese and Ham

Miscellaneous Vegetable Salads

ARTICHOKE SALAD

8 canned artichoke hearts, drained
8 fluid ounces French dressing
Leaf lettuce
8 anchovy fillets
4 thin strips canned pimiento
Freshly ground black pepper
Salad dressing

Cut the artichoke hearts in half lengthwise and marinate in French dressing for several hours. Drain.

Arrange on crisp lettuce and top each serving with two anchovy fillets and a strip of pimiento. Season with pepper. Serve with salad dressing. Serves 4.

MARINATED CUCUMBERS

Wash and slice 1 large chilled, unpeeled cucumber in very thin slices. Sprinkle with 2 teaspoons salt and 6 tablespoons sugar.

Add 6 fluid ounces vinegar. Then press slices with the back of spoon until salad is quite juicy.

SIMPLE ASPARAGUS SALAD

Drain and chill cooked or canned asparagus tips. Marinate $\frac{1}{2}$ to 1 hour in French or other desired dressing.

Arrange 4 to 6 tips on tomato slices over crisp lettuce on individual plates. Serve with French dressing.

STRIPED TOMATO SALAD

Remove stems from unpeeled tomatoes and make 4 or 5 parallel cuts through each almost to the bottom.

Put a generous spoonful of well seasoned cottage cheese between the slices. Serve on leaves of Webb's Wonder lettuce. If desired, cottage cheese may be seasoned with chives, spring onions, or garlic.

Striped Tomato Salad

VEGETABLE SALAD PARISIENNE

12 ounces cooked peas
12 ounces cooked runner beans
12 ounces cooked sliced carrots
1½ ounces chopped spring onion
tops
1½ ounces chopped parsley
3 fluid ounces vinegar
2 teaspoons seasoned salt
½ teaspoon sugar
6 fluid ounces salad oil
6 to 8 lettuce cups
8 fluid ounces soured cream

Combine drained peas, beans, and carrots in a bowl with spring onions and parsley.

In a screw-top, pint-size jar combine vinegar, seasoned salt, and sugar. Add oil and shake thoroughly. Pour over vegetables and toss until well coated. Marinate 1 hour or longer.

When ready to serve, drain vegetables, saving the marinade. Fill lettuce cups, topping with soured cream which has been seasoned to taste with part of the marinade. Garnish with a top sprinkling of seasoned salt. Serves 6 to 8.

WILTED LETTUCE SALAD

6 ounces leaf lettuce
1 teaspoon sugar
½ teaspoon salt
⅛ teaspoon black pepper
6 rashers streaky bacon
4 tablespoons vinegar
2 tablespoons sweet or soured cream
(optional)
2 hard-boiled eggs, sliced

Wash, drain, and tear lettuce into warm serving bowl. Sprinkle with sugar, salt, and pepper. Mix with fork and allow to stand about 10 minutes to wilt slightly.

Cut bacon in small pieces and fry until crisp. Add vinegar and cream and bring to boil. Pour over lettuce, mixing lightly with fork.

Serve immediately, garnished with sliced hard-boiled eggs. Serves 6.

MARINATED TOMATOES

4 to 6 tomatoes
1 clove garlic
1 tablespoon chopped chives
4 tablespoons highly seasoned
French dressing
2 sprigs parsley, chopped
1 teaspoon mixed dried herbs
(mint, tarragon, and basil)

Wash tomatoes and cut in large chunks. Drain if necessary. Place in bowl.

Add remaining ingredients and toss lightly. Cover and marinate in refrigerator several hours. Remove garlic before serving. Serves 4.

Vegetable Salad Parisienne

WATERCRESS SALAD

Wash 2 bunches watercress thoroughly. Remove yellow leaves. Mix with 4 fluid ounces French dressing and serve at once.

Onion rings may be mixed with the watercress. Serves 4.

LUNCHEON SALAD WITH WINE-CHEESE DRESSING

Lettuce or other salad greens
½ peeled tomato
2 or 3 stalks cooked broccoli
2 anchovy fillets
2 devilled egg halves
1 canned artichoke heart, halved

To assemble salad, line a salad plate with crisp salad greens. Place tomato half, cut-side-up, in centre of plate; top tomato with broccoli stalks; lay anchovy fillets crisscross over broccoli.

Arrange devilled egg halves and artichoke heart round tomato. Serve with wine-cheese dressing (below). Serves 1.

Wine-Cheese Dressing:
8 fluid ounces vegetable oil
4 fluid ounces Sauternes or other
white wine
2 fluid ounces wine vinegar
2 ounces grated Parmesan cheese
2 raw eggs
1 teaspoon salt
½ teaspoon each: onion salt, garlic
salt, coarsely ground black
pepper, and paprika
¼ teaspoon Worcestershire sauce

Combine all ingredients in mixing bowl. Beat with rotary beater until well blended.

If dressing is not to be used at once, store it in covered jar in refrigerator and shake well just before serving. Makes about ¾ pint dressing.

Luncheon Salad with Wine-Cheese Dressing

FRENCH CHICORY SALAD

Wash about ½ pound or 4 heads chicory thoroughly. Cut into quarters. Drain and place 4 quarters on individual salad plates.

Garnish plates with sprigs of watercress. Serve salad with Lorenzo dressing. Serves 4.

CUCUMBERS WITH SOURED CREAM

Peel and slice 1½ cucumbers. Add 1½ teaspoons salt, ⅛ teaspoon pepper, 3 tablespoons chopped chives or spring onions, 8 fluid ounces soured cream, and 2 tablespoons lemon juice. Chill about 10 minutes. Serves 4 to 6.

CARROT AND RAISIN SALAD

Combine 12 ounces grated carrots, ¼ teaspoon salt, and 5 ounces seedless raisins.

Add 4 fluid ounces mayonnaise and mix lightly. Serve on lettuce. Serves 6.

CARROT AND APPLE SALAD

Coarsely dice 3 unpeeled apples. Combine with 8 ounces grated carrots and 1 tablespoon grated onion.

Add 4 fluid ounces sweet or freshly soured cream blended with 2 tablespoons lemon juice, ¾ teaspoon salt, and ⅛ teaspoon pepper. Mix well. Serve on lettuce. Serves 6.

CELERY VICTOR

4 hearts of celery (1½ pounds)
8 fluid ounces chicken broth
¼ teaspoon Aromat
4 fluid ounces French dressing
Anchovies
Tomato wedges
Lettuce or watercress

Wash celery thoroughly without separating stalks. Cut lengthwise into 2 or 4 pieces, depending on size. Cut off most of leafy tops.

Place celery in pressure cooker with broth and Aromat. Cook at 15-pound pressure for 6 to 8 minutes. Or simmer for ½ hour in ordinary pan. Remove and drain.

Place celery in shallow dish; pour French dressing over and marinate 1 hour, turning occasionally. Chill.

Arrange celery with two strips of anchovies over each heart, with tomato wedges, on watercress or lettuce.

Serves 6 to 8.

ASPARAGUS AND DEVILLED EGG SALAD

Cut 6 hard-boiled eggs in half lengthwise. Remove the yolks.

Mash or sieve the egg yolks. Blend in 3 tablespoons of mayonnaise, and season with salt and pepper.

Fill a piping tube with the egg yolk mixture.

Arrange lettuce on individual salad plates and on each plate place, alternately, 3 groups of cooked asparagus tips and 3 hard-boiled egg white halves, radiating the asparagus tips from the centre. Fill the egg whites with the egg yolk mixture by forcing it through the piping tube.

Place a spoonful of mayonnaise on the centre of each salad. Serve as a main dish for lunch or supper.

TURKISH AUBERGINE SALAD

3   medium aubergines
6   tablespoons olive oil
Salt
Juice of 1 lemon
1   tablespoon vinegar
2   medium tomatoes, sliced
2   green peppers, sliced and seeded
1   medium onion, chopped
10 black olives

Put aubergines on rotisserie or hold with tongs and grill, preferably over charcoal fire, but gas flame will do. Skin must be allowed to burn black as this gives a delicious smoked flavour to salad.

Skin aubergines while still hot (the skin will come off like that of a scalded tomato).

Place aubergines in bowl containing olive oil and sprinkle with salt and lemon juice. Mash.

Add vinegar and beat smooth. Shape into a form and place on serving dish. Decorate with tomatoes, peppers, onion, and black olives. Serves about 6.

Variation: Mayonnaise can be used in place of olive oil, vinegar, and lemon juice.

GREEN BEANS PARMESAN

Cook 8-ounce packet of frozen French-style green beans as label directs. Drain and cool.

Mix 1 small chopped onion, 4 tablespoons olive oil, 3 tablespoons wine vinegar, 1 tablespoon chopped parsley, and 1 ounce grated Parmesan cheese. Pour over beans. Chill.

Serve on lettuce leaves. Serves 4.

Variations: Cut French or runner beans, broccoli, or asparagus are also good in this salad.

MARINATED BROCCOLI SALAD

Cook 8-ounce packet of frozen broccoli as label directs. Drain and cool.

Rub a small bowl with cut clove of garlic. Put 2 tablespoons oil in bowl. Add juice of 1 lemon and small pinch each of tarragon and oregano. Season and pour over broccoli.

Chill. Serve on lettuce leaves. Serves 3.

Variations: Also try marinated asparagus, cauliflower, French or runner beans, peas, or peas and carrots.

Celery Victor

SWEETCORN AND TOMATO SALAD

Use 2 tomatoes (cut in chunks), 3½ ounces whole kernel sweetcorn, 2 tablespoons chopped green pepper, and about 3 ounces lettuce. Toss with French dressing.

FRESH TOMATO RELISH

Chop 2 pounds tomatoes, 2 medium green peppers, 2 peeled medium onions; drain slightly.

Add 2 teaspoons salt, 1 teaspoon each dry mustard and celery salt, 4 tablespoons each vinegar and salad oil; mix; chill: Makes 2½ pounds.

STUFFED TOMATO SALADS

Select medium-sized smooth tomatoes. Scald and peel tomatoes. Cut a slice from top and remove some of the pulp.

Sprinkle inside with salt, invert, and place in refrigerator 30 minutes to chill. Fill with stuffing. Serve on lettuce leaves.

Avocado Stuffing: Mix diced avocado with chopped celery hearts. Moisten with French dressing.

Cabbage Stuffing: Mix 8 ounces shredded cabbage, ¼ teaspoon celery salt, ¼ teaspoon salt, and 2 tablespoons French dressing.

Chicken Stuffing: Mix diced cooked chicken, diced cucumber, and chopped tomato pulp. Moisten with mayonnaise.

Cottage Cheese and Chives: Mix cottage cheese and chopped chives. Stuff tomatoes.

Top with a spoonful of desired dressing and stuffed olives.

Pineapple-Cheese Stuffing: Combine finely chopped fresh or canned pineapple, tomato pulp, cream cheese, and chopped watercress. Moisten with mayonnaise.

Crabmeat Stuffing: Mix flaked crabmeat, diced celery, grated carrot, tomato and cucumber pulp. Moisten with mayonnaise.

Other Suggested Stuffings: Waldorf salad, egg salad, tuna fish, or any meat salad.

Red tomatoes filled with a variety of stuffings appeal to both eyes and appetite.

DUTCH ASPARAGUS SALAD

2 pounds fresh asparagus
½ pound streaky bacon, cut into tiny squares
3 to 4 tablespoons wine vinegar
1 teaspoon sugar
Salt
Black pepper, freshly ground
2 hard-boiled eggs, sliced
2 spring onions
1 head round lettuce

Prepare and cook whole asparagus spears until tender. Chill.

Fry tiny bacon squares until crisp and brown. Remove browned bacon and stir vinegar, sugar, and seasonings into hot bacon fat.

Arrange chilled asparagus on lettuce-lined serving dish. Cover with sliced eggs. Sprinkle with bacon and finely cut spring onions. Pour hot dressing over salad. Serve immediately. Serves 6.

CUCUMBER "BOATS"

1½ cucumbers
5 ounces elbow macaroni, cooked
1 12-ounce can luncheon meat, cubed
2 ounces grated carrots
1 ounce chopped green pepper
4 fluid ounces mayonnaise
2 tablespoons vinegar
2 tablespoons horseradish
Salt and pepper

Cut cucumbers in half lengthwise. Scoop out pulp from each half, leaving a shell ¼ inch thick.

Chop pulp and combine with macaroni, luncheon meat, carrot, and green pepper.

Blend together mayonnaise, vinegar, and horseradish. Add to meat mixture and toss lightly. Season to taste with salt and pepper. Pile salad into cucumber shells. Serves 6.

CAULIFLOWER SALAD BOWL

1 medium head cauliflower
6 fluid ounces French dressing
Lettuce
1 spring onion, chopped
2 teaspoons lemon juice
1 tablespoon milk
4 fluid ounces mayonnaise
Slices of cucumber
Tomato wedges

Remove leaves and all of woody base and wash head of cauliflower. Cook whole in small amount of salted water in covered saucepan about 15 minutes or until just tender.

Chill. Marinate in French dressing ½ hour.

Place head of cauliflower in salad bowl lined with lettuce. Combine spring onion, lemon juice, milk, and mayonnaise and pour over cauliflower.

Garnish with cucumber slices and tomato wedges. Serves 6.

Dutch Asparagus Salad

KIDNEY BEAN MEDLEY SALAD

12 ounces drained cooked or canned red kidney beans
3 fluid ounces tart French dressing
1 small onion, sliced in rings
1 ounce chopped celery
2 ounces chopped sweet pickles
Salt and pepper to taste

Mix beans and dressing; chill an hour or more. Turn beans in the dressing occasionally so they absorb the flavour.

Just before serving, add rest of ingredients. Mix lightly. Season to taste. Serve in lettuce cups, garnished with slices of hard-boiled egg. Serves 4 to 6.

CALIFORNIA VEGETABLE SALAD

Stone 2 ounces black olives and combine with 10 ounces finely shredded cabbage or 8 ounces coarsely grated carrot, 2 tablespoons diced green sweet pepper, and 1 ounce thinly sliced spring onion.

Toss together lightly with 4 tablespoons mayonnaise seasoned with 1 teaspoon Worcestershire sauce, ½ teaspoon salt, ¼ teaspoon dill seed, and black pepper to taste. Serves 4.

CARROT, EGG, AND CELERY SALAD

Use 9 ounces cooked diced carrots, 3 ounces diced celery, 1 chopped hard-boiled egg, lettuce, and ½ teaspoon grated onion. Toss with thinned cooked dressing.

BEANS AND PEAS SALAD BOWL

Use 6 ounces cooked runner beans, 6 ounces cooked peas, 2 ounces sliced celery, 2 ounces chopped apple, and about 3 ounces lettuce. Toss with French dressing.

Cauliflower Salad Bowl

September Salad Bowl: Wedges of rosy tomatoes and crisp green leaves of lettuce heaped in a big bowl is popular with almost everyone. Mayonnaise is the favourite dressing for this tomato and lettuce combination but many other salad dressings are good here, too.

AUBERGINE AND PEPPER SALAD

1 medium aubergine
3 sweet red peppers
1 small onion, chopped
4 tablespoons garlic French dressing
Salt and pepper

Wash aubergine and peppers. Cook in hot oven (400°F. Mark 6) until tender when pierced with a fork, about 30 minutes for aubergine and 20 minutes for peppers. Cool.

Cut aubergine in half. Scoop out pulp and break up with spoon. Remove seeds from peppers and cut into ¼-inch slices.

Add remaining ingredients and mix well. Chill and serve on lettuce. Serves 4.

CARROT AND GREEN PEPPER SALAD

Combine 12 ounces grated carrots with 3 ounces chopped green pepper, and 3 mint leaves, chopped.

Moisten with mayonnaise. Serve in lettuce cups. Serves 6.

HARICOT BEAN AND RADISH SALAD

Use 9 ounces well seasoned cooked haricot beans, 2 ounces sliced radishes, about 3 ounces of shredded lettuce or other greens, and a few stoned olives. Toss with French dressing seasoned with onion juice.

Luncheon Salad Bowl

KIDNEY BEAN SALAD

1 pound cooked red kidney beans
4 ounces diced celery
4 hard-boiled eggs, diced
4 spring onions, with tops, sliced thin
2 tablespoons piccalilli or chopped sweet pickle
6 ounces diced cooked cold potato
2 teaspoons chopped parsley
Salt and pepper
Cooked dressing or mayonnaise

Combine ingredients with salt and pepper to taste and chill for several hours before serving. The dressing for this salad should be on the sharp side, so if mayonnaise is used, add a little vinegar and some prepared horseradish.

Sliced radishes and diced cucumbers may also be added, but, if used, should be combined with the other ingredients shortly before serving. Serves 8.

BROCCOLI AND EGG SALAD

Use 8 ounces cooked broccoli (chilled), 4 chopped hard-boiled eggs, 4 tablespoons crumbled Roquefort cheese, and thinned salad dressing.

SWEETCORN SALAD BOWL

Use 12 ounces drained whole kernel sweetcorn, 2 tablespoons chopped green pepper, 1 tablespoon grated onion, ½ chopped canned pimiento, and 1 chopped hard-boiled egg. Toss with thinned cooked dressing and lettuce.

CHINESE CELERY CABBAGE SALAD

Place 8 ounces shredded Chinese celery cabbage on crisp outer leaves.

Serve with Thousand Island dressing or spicy mayonnaise. Serves 4.

LUNCHEON SALAD BOWL

2 pounds fresh asparagus
2 hard-boiled eggs
½ cucumber
3 spring onions
2 tomatoes
1 small head lettuce
3 ounces sliced black olives
Wine vinegar French dressing

Wash asparagus, break off tough ends and cook in small amount of boiling salted water until tender. Drain and cool.

Slice eggs. Peel and slice cucumber. Slice onions very thin. Cut tomatoes into wedges. Tear lettuce into bite-sized pieces in salad bowl.

Arrange asparagus stalks, tomato, and cucumber in groups over lettuce as shown in picture. Sprinkle onions over all. Centre with egg slices and sliced olives. Serve with wine vinegar French dressing. Serves 5.

HOW TO PREPARE A PICNIC TOSSED SALAD

Here is what to do if you'd like to serve a crisp, cold tossed vegetable salad in all its glory far from home:

1. Wash and separate leaves from a head of lettuce. Dry lettuce in a kitchen towel and keep wrapped.

2. Assemble and wash 2 large tomatoes, ½ cucumber, ½ dozen or so radishes, 1 whole uncut avocado. Pack in plastic food containers.

3. Hard-boil two or three eggs and chill.

4. Carry these ingredients to the picnic with large wooden bowl, fork and spoon, individual serving dishes of wood or paper, and bottle of dressing.

5. When ready to serve picnic meal, tear lettuce leaves into salad bowl, slice vegetables and eggs into bowl, and season with salt and pepper.

6. Drizzle on a bought French dressing or your homemade variety which you've prepared ahead and stored in a screw-top jar.

GRAPEFRUIT ASPARAGUS SALAD

On bed of endive, chicory, or lettuce, centre 5 cooked or canned asparagus stalks. Arrange 5 grapefruit segments on each side of asparagus and garnish with strips of canned pimiento.

Serve with mayonnaise made with lemon juice. Serves 1.

A buffet style salad is an ideal accompaniment for a barbecue or outdoor supper. Combine round, cos or Webb's Wonder lettuce, torn into bite-size pieces, in a large salad bowl. Surround with a selection of garnishes (chopped pimiento, onion rings, anchovies, black olives, sliced cucumber, and cottage cheese), and a choice of dressings.

Cole Slaws

COLE SLAW—MASTER RECIPE

Sometimes erroneously called cold slaw, the name of this popular salad is derived from the Dutch words for cabbage and salad.

Use fresh, tender cabbage. Red cabbage may be used or equal amounts of red and white cabbage. Remove and discard the wilted outer leaves and the hard core from a small firm head of cabbage. Shred the cabbage extra-fine, using a chef's knife or grater, cutting only as much as is needed for immediate use. To avoid last minute rush, toss cabbage with ice cubes; place in refrigerator 1 hour. Remove ice; drain well and dry between towels.

If desired, to 1 pound shredded cabbage add 1 ounce chopped green pepper or 2 tablespoons grated onion, or 4 ounces grated raw carrots and 2 ounces raisins.

Immediately before serving, moisten by tossing with one of the following dressings:
● Cooked dressing or salad dressing; French dressing; soured cream dressing.
● Mix 2 to 3 tablespoons sugar, 3 tablespoons vinegar, 2 tablespoons salad oil, and 1 teaspoon salt. Stir until sugar dissolves.
● Mix 6 tablespoons mayonnaise or salad dressing, 1 tablespoon vinegar, 2 teaspoons sugar, ½ teaspoon salt, and ½ teaspoon celery seed. Stir until sugar dissolves.
● Mix 4 fluid ounces salad dressing, 2 tablespoons vinegar, and 1 teaspoon French mustard.

For an outdoor meal, serve cole slaw in a hollowed-out cabbage surrounded by hard-boiled "penguin" eggs. Pieces of black olive form the wings and trim. They can be attached with cocktail sticks or unflavoured gelatine which has been softened in a small amount of cold water and melted over low heat. A skewered whole olive is used for each head.

DUTCH SLAW

8 ounces chopped streaky bacon
4 tablespoons lemon juice
1 teaspoon salt
4 fluid ounces mayonnaise
1 pound finely shredded white cabbage
1½ ounces chopped green pepper
½ ounce chopped parsley
1 ounce chopped celery
2 tablespoons grated onion

Fry bacon until crisp. Remove from pan.

Mix 2 ounces bacon dripping, lemon juice, and salt. Add to mayonnaise and blend.

Pour over combined vegetables and bacon and toss lightly. Chill before serving. Serves 6.

APPLE COLE SLAW WITH SOURED CREAM DRESSING

8 fluid ounces soured cream
1 tablespoon vinegar
2 teaspoons French mustard
½ teaspoon onion powder
¼ teaspoon salt
Dash of cayenne pepper
1 pound shredded white cabbage
4 ounces diced red apple
1 teaspoon celery salt

Combine soured cream, vinegar and seasonings. Mix thoroughly.

Pour over cabbage, apple, and celery seed. Toss lightly. Garnish with paprika. Serves 8.

PINEAPPLE SLAW

1 pound shredded white cabbage
2 tablespoons chopped green pepper
2 ounces diced unpeeled apple
4 slices pineapple
1 teaspoon salt
1 tablespoon sugar
4 fluid ounces vinegar
Lettuce
4 ounces grated carrots

Combine cabbage, green pepper, apple, and 2 slices pineapple, cut into sections.

Mix salt, sugar, and vinegar, and add. Place in a bowl lined with lettuce leaves.

Top with grated carrots and remaining drained pineapple slices cut into halves. Serves 4.

HONEY COLE SLAW

Beat 8 fluid ounces cold soured cream until thick. Add 2 fluid ounces honey, 1 teaspoon salt, and 2 teaspoons celery salt. Pour over 1 pound finely shredded cabbage.

RIO GRANDE SLAW

Add salt and celery salt to shredded cabbage. Pour heated barbecue sauce over the mixture, toss and serve while hot.

For colour and flavour contrasts, make several types of cole slaw for a party cole slaw dish.

PENNSYLVANIA PEPPER CABBAGE

8 ounces shredded white cabbage
1 green pepper, finely chopped
1 teaspoon salt

Mix shredded cabbage, pepper, and salt and allow to stand about 1 hour.

Drain off all liquid. Pour hot salad dressing (below) over the cabbage and mix well. Serve at once. Serves 4 to 5.

Hot Salad Dressing:
3 rashers streaky bacon
1 tablespoon flour
4 fluid ounces vinegar
1 tablespoon sugar
½ teaspoon dry mustard
½ teaspoon salt
⅛ teaspoon black pepper
1 egg yolk, beaten

Cut bacon in small bits and fry until crisp. Remove from frying pan and put aside.

Blend flour into fat and brown. Add vinegar and stir until it thickens.

Mix together sugar, mustard, salt, and pepper and add to the mixture. Pour over the beaten egg yolk and mix well.

Put on heat again and cook 1 minute longer. Add bacon bits when ready to use.

CABBAGE AND CARROT SLAW
(Master Recipe)

6 ounces grated carrots
1 pound shredded white cabbage
¼ teaspoon salt
2 teaspoons sugar
1 tablespoon vinegar
3 tablespoons mayonnaise

Combine carrots, cabbage, salt, sugar, and vinegar. Moisten with mayonnaise. Mix lightly.

Arrange on crisp lettuce. Sprinkle with chopped parsley or paprika. May be garnished with orange slices. Serves 6.

Cabbage and Apple Salad: In master recipe, substitute 6 ounces thinly sliced unpeeled tart red apples for carrots.

Cabbage, Carrot and Celery Salad: In master recipe, decrease shredded cabbage to 8 ounces. Add 4 ounces thinly sliced celery.

Bull's Eye Salad

BULL'S EYE SALAD

2 large tomatoes
½ pound white cabbage
3 large carrots
2 tablespoons chopped chives
1 cucumber
1 head escarole, curly endive, or
    cos lettuce
Mayonnaise

Double an 18-inch strip of grease-proof paper lengthwise and then double again. Lap ends to form circle about 5 inches in diameter and fasten with cocktail stick.

Cut slice from stem end of tomatoes so they will stand flat. Cut in eighths and stand up inside paper. Fill centre with mayonnaise and garnish with chopped chives.

Radiate greens from tomatoes to edge of plate. Place ring of crisp shredded cabbage round tomatoes, half slices of unpeeled cucumber, and shredded carrots.

Garnish with cucumber twists, by cutting through each slice from centre. Turn one cut edge to right, the other to left and fasten with stick. Stand in iced water ½ hour and remove stick. Remove greaseproof paper. Serves 6.

CABBAGE SALAD IN PIMIENTO CUPS

6 to 8 ounces finely chopped cab-
    bage
½ tablespoon chopped onion
1 tablespoon chopped green pepper
2 tablespoons vinegar
Salt and pepper
½ teaspoon celery salt
6 ounces chopped, drained tomato
4 tablespoons salad dressing
8 canned pimientos

Combine cabbage, onion, and green pepper; add vinegar and seasonings. Allow to stand 1 hour; drain.

Add tomato and salad dressing; toss lightly. Fill pimientos. Serves 8.

CABBAGE AND ONION SALAD

Shred cabbage. Cut onions into very thin rings. Season with salt, celery salt, pepper, and paprika.

Mix with mayonnaise or French dressing. Serve on cabbage leaf.

HOT SLAW

Combine in saucepan 2 slightly beaten egg yolks, 4 tablespoons cold water, 4 tablespoons vinegar, ½ ounce butter or margarine, 1 tablespoon sugar, and ½ teaspoon salt.

Cook on low heat, stirring constantly until mixture thickens.

Add 1 pound shredded cabbage and reheat. Serves 5.

HERB COLE SLAW

1 pound finely shredded cabbage
½ teaspoon salt
¾ teaspoon dried thyme
2 tablespoons chopped parsley
4 fluid ounces French dressing

Toss cabbage with salt, thyme, and parsley. Then toss well with French dressing. Serve at once. Serves 4.

MEXICAN SLAW

Crisp a small head of cabbage by removing a few of the outer leaves, then cutting in half, and standing in iced water ½ hour. Shake out water well, and shred.

Dice cold cooked ham or tongue, celery, green pepper, and canned pimiento. Sprinkle with salt.

Mix salad with mayonnaise which has been thinned with sweet or soured cream.

Line a serving dish with outside leaves of cabbage and fill centre with slaw. Squeeze ½ lemon over all.

SOURED CREAM SLAW

4 fluid ounces mayonnaise
2 fluid ounces soured cream
½ teaspoon salt
½ teaspoon sugar
1 teaspoon tarragon vinegar
1 pound shredded cabbage

Combine mayonnaise, soured cream, salt, sugar, and vinegar.

Toss with shredded cabbage until well coated. Serve after chilling thoroughly. Serves 6.

RED CABBAGE SLAW

8 ounces red cabbage, shredded
3 tart red apples, diced
4 ounces grated carrot
1½ ounces brown sugar
3 tablespoons vinegar
2 tablespoons French dressing

Combine cabbage, apple, and carrot. Mix sugar, vinegar, and dressing and pour over salad.

Toss lightly until dressing coats salad. Serves 6.

VEGETABLE AND APPLE SALAD

4 ounces grated raw carrots
4 ounces shredded cabbage
4 ounces diced celery
4 ounces thin apple strips

Dash of salt
Salad dressing
Lettuce

Toss vegetables, apples, and a dash of salt with salad dressing to moisten. Chill. Serve in crisp lettuce cups. Serves 6.

ITALIAN PEPPER SLAW

1 clove garlic
8 ounces finely shredded cabbage
1 ounce chopped green pepper
1 ounce chopped canned pimiento
½ teaspoon salt
½ teaspoon celery salt
Dash of cayenne pepper
Dash of paprika
1 tablespoon soft breadcrumbs
2 tablespoons tomato purée
2½ teaspoons water
¼ teaspoon salt
⅛ teaspoon sugar
2½ teaspoons vegetable oil
2 teaspoons cider or malt vinegar

Rub salad bowl with cut garlic clove. Put vegetables, ½ teaspoon salt, celery salt, cayenne pepper, and paprika in bowl.

Mix remaining ingredients thoroughly. Pour over contents of salad bowl. Toss. Serves 6.

HOT CABBAGE SALAD— WINE DRESSING

4 frankfurters
2 ounces butter or margarine
1 large or 2 small onions
6 fluid ounces chablis, hock,
    Sauternes, riesling, or any
    white wine
2 tablespoons sugar
1 tablespoon flour
½ teaspoon salt
¼ teaspoon black pepper
8 ounces shredded cabbage

Split frankfurters and sauté in butter or margarine until lightly browned. Remove to hot serving dish.

Sauté onion until yellow. Combine wine, sugar, flour, salt, and pepper in small covered jar and shake vigorously until well blended. Add to onions in frying pan and cook, stirring constantly, until smooth and slightly thickened.

Add cabbage and cook, mixing constantly with wine dressing for about 6 minutes.

Serve topped with sautéed frankfurters and garnish with spring onions. Serves 4.

*Hot Cabbage Salad
with Wine Dressing*

Potato, Macaroni, Rice Salads

Hot potato salad, attractively garnished, is equally tempting in summer or winter.

MASTER POTATO SALAD

- 1¼ pounds diced cooked potatoes, cooked in jackets
- 1 tablespoon grated onion
- 3 tablespoons French dressing
- 1 tablespoon chopped parsley
- 1 teaspoon salt
- ¼ teaspoon paprika
- Mayonnaise

Combine ingredients, except mayonnaise, tossing lightly with a fork. Chill 3 to 4 hours.

Just before serving add mayonnaise, mixing carefully. Serve on lettuce or watercress. Serves 6.

Potato Salad Variations

Potato Salad with Celery: To master potato salad, add 4 ounces diced celery.

Potato-Egg Salad: To master potato salad, add 4 ounces diced celery and 4 chopped hard-boiled eggs.

Gourmet Potato Salad: To master potato salad, add 4 fluid ounces tartar sauce and 3 fluid ounces piccalilli and stuffed olives, finely chopped.

Potato Salad with Carrots: To master potato salad, add 4 ounces diced celery and 4 ounces grated raw carrot.

Potato Salad with Cabbage: To master potato salad, add 4 ounces finely cut cabbage.

Potato Salad with Nuts: To master potato salad, add 4 ounces diced celery and 3 ounces salted peanuts, chopped Brazil nuts, or toasted hazelnuts.

Potato Salad with Cucumber: To master potato salad, add 4 ounces diced celery and ½ diced cucumber.

Cornucopia Potato Salads: Roll thin slices of bologna sausage to form cornucopias. Fill with potato salad.

Moulded Potato Salad Ring: Pack potato salad into medium-sized ring mould. Chill.

Unmould on bed of greens. Garnish with assorted sliced cold meats, radish roses, and quartered tomatoes.

HOT POTATO SALAD

- 1 large onion, finely chopped
- 2½ pounds thinly sliced cooked potatoes
- 2 tablespoons chopped parsley
- 5 to 6 fluid ounces malt vinegar
- 3 fluid ounces hot water
- 1 teaspoon sugar
- 1 slightly beaten egg
- 3 fluid ounces vegetable oil
- 1½ teaspoons salt
- Few grains black pepper
- 1½ teaspoons Aromat

Combine onions, potatoes, and parsley.

Combine vinegar and water; heat to boiling; add sugar; stir until dissolved.

Add hot mixture slowly to egg. Add salad oil, salt, pepper, and Aromat.

Beat vigorously with rotary egg beater until well blended.

Pour over potato mixture; stir with fork until thoroughly mixed. Heat gently or allow to stand in warm place 10 to 15 minutes. Serves 6 to 8.

MASTER MACARONI SALAD

- 6 ounces elbow macaroni, cooked and chilled
- ½ green pepper, finely chopped
- 1½ tablespoons grated onion
- 2 ounces chopped celery
- 6 tablespoons French dressing
- Lettuce
- Mayonnaise or cooked dressing

Combine macaroni, green pepper, onion, celery, and French dressing. Chill.

Arrange on lettuce and garnish with mayonnaise or cooked dressing. Serves 6.

Macaroni Salad Variations

Macaroni Salad with Hard-Boiled Eggs: Slice and add 3 hard-boiled eggs to master macaroni salad.

Macaroni Salad with Tuna Fish: In master macaroni salad, use a little less macaroni. Add a 7-ounce can flaked tuna fish. Use additional mayonnaise.

Macaroni Salad with Vegetables: To master macaroni salad, add 6 ounces mixed cooked or canned carrots, peas, and diced runner beans. If desired, marinate vegetables first.

Baked Bean Salad: Follow master macaroni salad recipe and substitute cold, cooked haricot beans for macaroni.

Red Bean Salad: Follow master recipe and substitute cold cooked red kidney beans for macaroni.

HOT DUTCH POTATO SALAD

- 4 rashers streaky bacon
- 1 medium onion, chopped
- 1½ ounces chopped green pepper
- 4 tablespoons vinegar
- 1 teaspoon salt
- ⅛ teaspoon black pepper
- 1 teaspoon sugar
- 1 slightly beaten egg
- 2 pounds hot, cooked, cubed potatoes
- 1 chopped canned pimiento
- 3 hard-boiled eggs, diced

Cut bacon into strips and fry. Add onion and green pepper. Cook 3 minutes.

Add vinegar, salt, pepper, sugar, and beaten egg. Cook slightly.

Add cubed potatoes, pimiento, and hard-boiled eggs. Blend lightly. Serve hot. Serves 8.

Note: If desired, dilute vinegar with 3 tablespoons water.

WESTERN RICE SALAD BOWL

- 1 garlic clove, peeled
- 1¼ pounds canned bean sprouts, drained and rinsed
- 3 ounces thinly sliced unpeeled radishes
- 4 to 5 ounces diced unpeeled cucumber
- 4 ounces thinly sliced celery
- 2 to 3 ounces chopped watercress
- 2 small mild onions, chopped
- 1 ounce chopped green pepper
- 6 to 8 ounces cold cooked rice
- 1 to 1½ teaspoons Aromat
- 8 fluid ounces mayonnaise
- Soy sauce (optional)

Rub salad bowl with garlic. Have all vegetables and rice well chilled; layer them into bowl in order given.

Blend Aromat into mayonnaise; pour over top layer of salad (which should be rice). Lift and toss carefully to blend but not crush.

Taste and if salt is needed try adding soy sauce. Serves 6 to 8.

Cold Cuts with Macaroni Salad

HAWAIIAN POTATO SALAD

4 hard-boiled eggs
6 ounces hot cooked rice
1 large potato, hot, mashed
4 tablespoons French dressing
½ teaspoon salt
2 tablespoons chopped canned
   pimiento
1 tablespoon chopped green pepper
1 tablespoon finely chopped onion
1 tablespoon chopped parsley

Press 2 of the hard-boiled eggs through a sieve and combine with rice and potatoes. Blend in French dressing. Chill.

Just before serving, add remaining ingredients. If desired, add more seasoning. Garnish with remaining eggs, sliced or sieved, and parsley. Serves 4.

SOURED CREAM POTATO SALAD

2 pounds sliced cooked potato
2 ounces chopped celery
1 onion, chopped
4 radishes, sliced
4 tablespoons French dressing
8 fluid ounces soured cream
Salt, pepper, and cayenne pepper
Chopped fresh dill

Combine potato, celery, onion, and radishes. Pour French dressing over mixture, and allow to stand in refrigerator for several hours.

Just before serving, fold in soured cream. Season to taste. Sprinkle with chopped dill. Serves 4.

MACARONI AND CHICKEN SALAD

3 ounces diced cooked chicken
4 ounces elbow macaroni, cooked
1 tablespoon grated onion
2 ounces cooked mushrooms
1 teaspoon salt
¼ teaspoon black pepper
6 fluid ounces cooked salad dressing or mayonnaise
Curly endive
2 tomatoes, quartered

Combine all ingredients except endive and tomatoes. Place in refrigerator about 2 hours to chill.

Wash endive thoroughly and arrange it in 9-inch crinkle-edge glass pie dish.

Place salad mixture on endive and garnish with quartered tomatoes.
Serves 6 to 8.

Macaroni and Chicken Salad

EL PATIO POTATO SALAD

3 to 4 medium potatoes
4 tablespoons Sauternes wine
3 spring onions
2 ounces whole or stoned black
   olives
3 ounces chopped celery
2 tablespoons chopped parsley
Salt and pepper
6 tablespoons mayonnaise
1 teaspoon vinegar

Boil potatoes in salted water until tender. Drain and cool sufficiently to handle. Peel and dice. Pour wine over potatoes and allow to stand until cold.

Slice onions thin. Cut olives into large pieces, removing stones first.

Add onions, olives, celery, and parsley to potatoes. Season with salt and pepper.

Blend mayonnaise and vinegar; pour over salad mixture and mix lightly. Serves 4.

BOLOGNA SAUSAGE CUPS WITH POTATO SALAD

Sauté bologna sausage slices with skin on in a small amount of butter or margarine until they form well-shaped cups.

Remove skins. Pile potato salad into bologna sausage cups and arrange on a large dish. Garnish with sliced tomatoes on lettuce leaves.

*Bologna Sausage Cups With
Potato Salad*

RAINBOW MACARONI SALAD

8 ounces elbow macaroni
4 tablespoons French dressing
1 ounce sliced spring onion
½ diced canned pimiento
2-3 ounces finely chopped sweet
   pickle
2 ounces thinly sliced carrots
2 tablespoons French mustard
Mayonnaise, salt, and pepper

Cook macaroni in boiling, salted water until tender. Drain and rinse with cold water. Add French dressing and chill for several hours, if possible.

Add remaining ingredients, using about 8 fluid ounces mayonnaise and salt and pepper to taste; mix thoroughly but lightly. Chill several hours.

Serve in lettuce lined bowl; sprinkle with chopped fresh parsley and top with hard-boiled egg slices, if desired. Serves 8.

*Chinese
Salad Bowl*

CHINESE SALAD BOWL

10 ounces rice
12 ounces cooked peas
1 8-ounce can water chestnuts
1 8-ounce can bean sprouts
1 head Chinese cabbage or escarole
4 fluid ounces mayonnaise
4 fluid ounces soured cream
1 teaspoon celery salt
½ teaspoon Aromat
6 ounces roast pork, cut in thin
   strips

Cook rice according to directions on packet. Chill; place in salad bowl. Add peas.

Drain water chestnuts: slice: add. Drain bean sprouts; add. Tear cabbage or escarole leaves into small pieces; add.

Combine mayonnaise, soured cream, celery salt, and Aromat; beat well; pour into salad bowl.

Toss until all ingredients are well mixed. Scatter strips of pork on top. Serves 6 to 8.

LUNCHEON RICE SALAD

1 pound cooked rice, chilled
4 fluid ounces French dressing
2-3 ounces chopped onion (spring
   onions preferred)
1 head lettuce
Grated sharp cheese (optional)
1 pound pickled beetroots
Watercress or other greens to garnish
4 whole tomatoes, peeled and
   quartered
1 canned pimiento, cut in thin strips
Egg slices and radish roses to
   garnish

Pour French dressing over rice and toss lightly with fork. Allow to stand 1 hour, then drain thoroughly.

Add chopped onion and mould in timbales (glass fruit cups make a nice size mould).

Unmould timbales of rice in centre of lettuce cups. Sprinkle with grated cheese if desired; garnish with pickled beetroots, watercress, peeled and quartered tomatoes, and top the rice with thin strips of pimiento. Egg slices and radish roses may be added. Mayonnaise may accompany this salad if desired. Serves 6.

Luncheon Rice Salad

Fish and Shellfish Salads

MASTER FISH SALAD

Use cooked or canned fish. Cut into $\frac{1}{4}$- to $\frac{1}{2}$-inch cubes or flake. Toss lightly with mayonnaise or cooked salad dressing. Add salt, if necessary.

Chill and serve in salad bowl or individual plates. Garnish with dressing, crisp greens, cooked or raw vegetables.

Apple and Fish Salad: Use 12 ounces flaked fish and 8 ounces diced tart apple.

Cucumber and Fish Salad: Use 12 ounces flaked fish, 2 ounces each of diced cucumber and celery, $\frac{1}{2}$ shredded head lettuce, 1 finely chopped small onion, and a few diced radishes.

Seafood Salad: Use 6 ounces cooked or canned prawns, 4 ounces flaked canned crabmeat, and 2 ounces diced tart apple. Marinate in French dressing.

Lobster Salad: Use 1 pound cooked or canned lobster meat and 4 ounces chopped celery. Marinate in French dressing for 20 minutes. Mix with mayonnaise.

PRAWN SALAD

    4 fluid ounces sharp mayonnaise
    1 tablespoon lemon juice
    12 ounces canned or cooked prawns
    1 pound canned peas
    3 sliced hard-boiled eggs
    3 ounces thinly sliced celery
    Lettuce
    3 stuffed olives
    Lemon wedges

Thin mayonnaise with lemon juice and 2 tablespoons liquid from prawns. Add drained peas, eggs, and celery. Mix gently.

Place on lettuce leaves. Garnish with sliced stuffed olives and lemon wedges. Serves 6.

Variations: Crabmeat, lobster, salmon, tuna fish, or flaked fish may be used instead of prawns.

PRAWN SALAD—GUEST STYLE

    1 pound prawns
    2 ounces diced celery
    16 sliced black olives
    1 hard-boiled egg, chopped
    4 fluid ounces soured cream
    2 fluid ounces mayonnaise
    1 tablespoon lemon juice

Salt and pepper to taste
Dash of cayenne pepper

Shell, cook, and chill prawns. Combine chilled prawns with remaining ingredients.

Serve on mixed greens, preferably with thin-sliced whole meal or salty rye bread. Serves 5 to 6.

CRAB LOUIS

    Whole lettuce leaves
    Shredded lettuce leaves
    8 ounces cooked or canned crabmeat
    2 hard-boiled eggs, sliced
    Chopped chives
    4 fluid ounces French dressing
    4 fluid ounces chilli pickle
    2 tablespoons mayonnaise
    $\frac{1}{2}$ teaspoon Worcestershire sauce
        (optional)
    Salt and pepper to taste

Arrange lettuce leaves round the inside of a salad bowl. Place some shredded lettuce leaves on bottom.

Heap crabmeat on top of shredded lettuce. Garnish with slices of hard-boiled egg. Sprinkle with chopped chives.

Mix remaining ingredients in another bowl and pour over salad. Serves 4.

BUFFET TUNA FISH SALAD

    1 small head lettuce
    2 7-ounce cans tuna fish
    3 hard-boiled eggs, halved
    3 whole canned pimientos
    6 green pepper rings
    6 spring onions
    12 radishes
    4 carrots, quartered lengthwise
    12 black olives
    12 cucumber slices

Cover large serving dish with lettuce. Place tuna fish in centre. Surround with remaining ingredients. Serve with Tangy Salad Dressing (below). Serves 6.

Tangy Salad Dressing: Blend together 4 fluid ounces mayonnaise, $\frac{1}{2}$ teaspoon salt, 1 teaspoon lemon juice, and 2 teaspoons Worcestershire sauce.

Lobster and Macaroni Salad

LOBSTER AND MACARONI SALAD

    6 (3 to 5 ounce) lobster tails
    8 ounces macaroni shells
    1-2 ounces green pepper, finely
        diced
    2 ounces celery, finely diced
    1 teaspoon onion juice
    3 ounces stuffed olives, sliced
    4 fluid ounces mayonnaise
    2 fluid ounces tomato ketchup
    $\frac{1}{2}$ teaspoon aromatic bitters
    Salt and pepper to taste

Cook lobster tails. Remove shells and dice meat.

Cook macaroni shells according to packet directions. Drain in colander and rinse with cold water. Chill.

Mix together macaroni, lobster, green pepper, celery, onion juice, and olives. Combine mayonnaise, ketchup, and bitters and add to salad. Toss all together lightly but thoroughly. Add salt and pepper to taste. Chill well.

At serving time, decorate bowl with empty lobster shell. Serves 6.

OYSTER SALAD

    1 pint oysters
    $\frac{1}{4}$ teaspoon celery salt
    $\frac{1}{2}$ ounce butter or margarine
    1 ounce chopped lettuce
    2 hard-boiled eggs, chopped
    2 ounces diced celery
    1 canned pimiento, chopped
    1 teaspoon grated onion
    1 teaspoon lemon juice
    4 fluid ounces mayonnaise or salad
        dressing
    $\frac{1}{2}$ teaspoon salt
    $\frac{1}{8}$ teaspoon black pepper
    Lettuce

Drain oysters. Add celery salt and cook in butter until edges begin to curl. Chill and dice oysters.

Combine all ingredients and serve on lettuce cups. Garnish with paprika. Serves 6.

SALMON COTTAGE CHEESE SALAD

    8 ounces flaked salmon
    8 ounces cottage cheese
    2 ounces chopped celery
    2 ounces chopped sweet pickle
    Salad dressing

Combine all ingredients. Chill. Serve on lettuce. Serves 6.

Buffet Tuna Fish Salad

West Coast Salad with Mushroom Dressing

WEST COAST SALAD WITH MUSHROOM DRESSING

1   head Webb's Wonder lettuce
2   fluid ounces wine vinegar
4   fluid ounces olive or salad oil
1½ teaspoons salt
1   teaspoon paprika
Freshly ground black pepper
1   small clove garlic, crushed
½   pound fresh mushrooms, sliced
½   pound cooked, cleaned prawns
4   ounces cooked or canned lobster
      or crabmeat
4   ounces sliced celery
1   10-ounce packet frozen
      asparagus, cooked
1   10-ounce packet frozen fresh
      peas, cooked
2   hard-boiled eggs, sliced
2   tomatoes, cut in wedges

Wash lettuce in cold water and drain well. Place in polythene bag or transparent polythene wrap; refrigerate.

Combine vinegar, oil, salt, paprika, pepper, and garlic in bowl; mix well. Add mushrooms, chill 1 hour.

Half an hour before serving, separate lettuce leaves. Line salad bowl; shred remaining lettuce into bottom of bowl. Arrange prawns, lobster, celery, drained asparagus, and peas in rows over lettuce. Spoon mushrooms onto salad.

Stir the dressing and pour over salad. Garnish with egg slices and tomato wedges. Chill. Toss lightly before serving. Serves 6 to 8.

Salmon Hollandaise Mould

SALMON AND CUCUMBER SALAD

8   ounces diced cucumber
4   ounces sliced celery
1   teaspoon Aromat
1   1-pound can salmon
1   tablespoon capers (optional)
4   fluid ounces mayonnaise
Melon balls
Celery salt dressing (below)

Combine cucumber and celery; sprinkle with Aromat; toss well to mix. Allow to stand while preparing remaining ingredients and dressing.

Flake salmon, removing skin and bones; add capers. Combine with cucumber mixture and mayonnaise.

Serve on lettuce leaves; garnish with melon balls. Serve dressing separately. Serves 4 to 6.

Celery Salt Dressing:
4   fluid ounces mayonnaise
4   fluid ounces soured cream
1   teaspoon celery salt
¼   teaspoon Aromat
2   tablespoons tomato ketchup

Combine all ingredients; mix well.

Salmon and Cucumber Salad

SALMON HOLLANDAISE MOULD

Hollandaise Sauce:
2   egg yolks
Dash of cayenne pepper
4   ounces butter or margarine,
      melted
3   tablespoons lemon juice

Beat egg yolks until thick and lemon coloured; stir in pepper. Blend in 1½ ounces butter, a little at a time, beating constantly.

Slowly beat in remaining butter with lemon juice.

Mould:
34 cream crackers, finely crushed
1   1-pound can salmon, well drained
8   ounces chopped celery
½   medium onion, chopped
½   teaspoon salt
¼   teaspoon black pepper
Hollandaise sauce (above)

Combine all ingredients; blend well. Pack into 2-pint mould; chill.

When ready to serve, unmould on bed of endives and garnish with olives and lemon wedges. Serves 6 to 8.

SWEDISH HERRING SALAD

3   1-pound cans ocean herring or
      3 kippers
1½ pounds diced cooked beetroots
3   medium apples, finely chopped
1   medium onion, chopped
4   ounces chopped dill pickle
3   hard-boiled eggs, chopped
French dressing
1   hard-boiled egg, sliced
Watercress

Drain canned herring. (Soak kippers in cold water 1 hour; drain; cook until tender in boiling water.)

Remove skin and bones; cut into small pieces.

Combine all ingredients, mixing lightly with French dressing.

Decorate with slices of hard-boiled egg and sprigs of watercress. Serves 12.

GRAPEFRUIT SALMON SALAD

2   grapefruits
1   1-pound can salmon
4   fluid ounces mayonnaise
2   fluid ounces chilli pickle
½   teaspoon Aromat

Halve grapefruits, making scalloped edge if desired. Spoon out pulp; remove all membrane with scissors.

Drain salmon; flake, removing skin. Combine salmon and grapefruit pulp.

Combine mayonnaise, chilli pickle, and Aromat; add to salmon mixture; toss to mix. Fill grapefruit shells.

Serve on watercress or other salad greens. Serves 4.

PRAWN ARTICHOKE SALAD

2   pounds medium-sized prawns,
      cooked, shelled, and
      cleaned
2   10-ounce packets frozen artichoke
      hearts, cooked and drained
2   8-ounce cans mandarin oranges,
      drained
1   head Webb's Wonder lettuce,
      shredded

Combine all ingredients. Place in a salad bowl. Chill well. Just before serving toss with French dressing. Serves 6.

Prawn Artichoke Salad

-BB

LOBSTER SALAD

1 pound diced, boiled rock lobster-
    tail meat
4 tablespoons French dressing
2 tablespoons grated Spanish onion
6 ounces diced celery
8 tablespoons mayonnaise
½ teaspoon salt
⅛ teaspoon paprika
Lettuce leaves
Canned pimiento strips
Green olives
Lemon wedges

Stir together lobster meat and French dressing. Chill thoroughly.

Add onion and celery. Stir in mayonnaise until all ingredients are well mixed, with salt and paprika. Correct seasoning if necessary.

Line salad bowl with crisp lettuce leaves. Pile salad in centre.

Garnish with pimiento strips, green olives, and additional mayonnaise if desired. Serve with lemon wedges. Serves 4.

CURRIED TUNA FISH-RICE SALAD

6 ounces pre-cooked rice
8 fluid ounces water
¼ teaspoon salt
8 fluid ounces mayonnaise
2 teaspoons curry powder
2 tablespoons diced canned
    pimiento
1 teaspoon salt
½ teaspoon Aromat
6 ounces cooked peas
1 6½-ounce can tuna fish

Combine rice, water, and the ¼ teaspoon salt in saucepan. Mix just until all rice is moistened. Bring quickly to boil over high heat, fluffing rice gently once or twice with fork (do not stir). Cover; remove from heat; allow to cool to room temperature.

Blend mayonnaise and curry powder; add pimiento, the 1 teaspoon salt, and Aromat; add remaining ingredients and rice; toss well to mix. Chill.

Serve on lettuce with additional mayonnaise. Serves 6.

Note: If the brand of tuna fish already contains monosodium glutamate, slightly less Aromat will be needed.

Curried Tuna Fish-Rice Salad

SALMON SALAD TROPICAL

2 sliced or diced, ripe firm
    bananas
4 ounces drained, diced, canned
    pineapple
about 12 ounces canned cooked,
    flaked salmon
2-4 ounces diced celery
2 tablespoons chopped, sweet pickle
1 teaspoon salt
1 tablespoon mayonnaise or salad
    dressing
1 tablespoon French mustard
Lettuce
Salad greens for garnish

Combine bananas and pineapple. Add salmon, celery, pickle, and salt.

Mix together mayonnaise or salad dressing and mustard and add to salad mixture. Mix lightly.

Combine 2 or 3 crisp lettuce leaves to form a cup and arrange on each salad plate. Fill each lettuce cup with salad mixture.

Garnish salad with crisp salad greens. Serves 4 to 6.

Variations of Salmon Salad Tropical

Tuna Fish and Banana Salad: In place of salmon, use 1 7-ounce or 1 12-ounce can flaked tuna fish.

Chicken Salad Tropical: In place of salmon, use 6 to 9 ounces diced cooked chicken.

Note: When canned salmon or tuna is used, drain and mix liquid with mayonnaise or salad dressing. One tablespoon lemon juice may be added to mayonnaise or salad dressing, if desired.

For additional colour and texture contrast, cold cooked peas, crisp carrot strips or radishes may be arranged on each salad.

PRAWN BOUQUET SALAD

1 pound fresh or frozen prawns
4 medium-sized tomatoes
3 radishes, sliced
Lettuce
Coral Dressing (below)

Cook and clean prawns. Chill. Arrange tomatoes, prawns, and radishes on beds of shredded lettuce to form red and pink bouquet. Serve with Coral Dressing. Serves 3.

Coral Dressing:

8 tablespoons mayonnaise
2 tablespoons tomato ketchup
½ teaspoon Worcestershire sauce
1 teaspoon horseradish
Dash of Tabasco sauce
¼ teaspoon salt
⅛ teaspoon black pepper
1 tablespoon lemon juice

Blend ingredients. Chill.

Egg and Cheese Salads

TOMATO ROSE SALAD

Peel one firm tomato for each tomato rose salad.

Slightly soften 3 ounces of cream cheese with milk.

Form a row of petals on the upper side of each tomato by pressing level teaspoons of the softened cheese against the side of the tomato, then drawing the teaspoon down with a curving motion.

Make a second row of petals on the lower side of the tomato, placing each of these petals between the two petals above it on the top row.

Place each tomato on watercress on a salad plate. Press hard-boiled egg yolk through a sieve onto the centre of the tomato. Serve with French dressing.

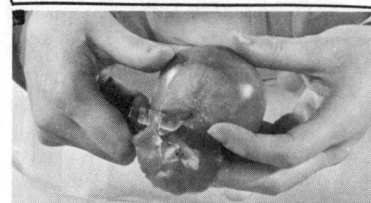

Cottage Cheese and Vegetable Salad

COTTAGE CHEESE AND VEGETABLE SALAD

1 clove garlic (optional)
1 pound cottage cheese
1 teaspoon salt
Paprika
2 tablespoons chopped chives or spring onion
2 tablespoons chopped canned pimiento
1 ounce chopped celery
1 cucumber
1 medium-sized onion
2 large tomatoes
2 carrots
French dressing
Lettuce

Rub mixing bowl with cut clove of garlic. Add cottage cheese, salt, and paprika. Fold in chopped chives, pimiento, and chopped celery. Turn into bowl that has been rinsed in cold water; chill in refrigerator.

Unmould on centre of large salad plate; surround with watercress, thin cucumber slices, onion rings, carrot flowers, and tomato wedges. Serve with French dressing. Serves 6.

Variation: The cottage cheese mixture can be served in whole tomatoes in lettuce cups, topped with toasted almonds or peanuts. French dressing is served with it.

CHEESE AND ANCHOVY STARTER SALAD

8 ounces Roquefort or blue cheese
3 ounces cream cheese
½ teaspoon grated onion
1½ teaspoons French mustard
Dash of Tabasco sauce
4 thick slices tomato
4 leaves lettuce
8 rolled anchovies

Blend the 2 cheeses with onion, mustard, and Tabasco sauce. When smooth, pack into piping tube.

Place slice of tomato on lettuce leaf on small salad plate. Pipe cheese spread into mound on tomato slice. Top with 2 rolled anchovies.

Serve with crisp crackers or Melba toast. Serves 4.

SIMPLE COTTAGE CHEESE SALADS

Season 1 pound cottage cheese with salt and pepper to taste. Add single cream to form desired consistency.

Serve on lettuce leaves topped with French dressing or vary as suggested below. Serves 6.

Cottage Cheese with Chives: Season and cream as above. Add 1 ounce chopped chives. Serves 6.

Cottage Cheese with Olives: Add whole or sliced stuffed olives to seasoned, creamed cottage cheese.

Cottage Cheese with Orange Wedges: Combine 6 ounces orange wedges with 12 ounces seasoned, creamed cottage cheese. Flavour with a little chopped fresh mint. Serves 6.

Cottage Cheese with Raisins and Green Pepper: To 12 ounces seasoned, creamed cottage cheese add 3 ounces seedless raisins and 1 ounce chopped green pepper.

If desired, use mayonnaise instead of cream with the cottage cheese. Serves 6.

Cottage Cheese with Fresh Strawberries: Fold 4 ounces fresh strawberries into 12 ounces seasoned, creamed cottage cheese. Flavour with a little chopped fresh mint. Serves 6.

EGG-OLIVE TIMBALES WITH SEAFOOD DRESSING

6 ounces stoned black olives
12 hard-boiled eggs
2 canned pimientos
2 spring onions
2 tablespoons soured cream
2 tablespoons mayonnaise
½ teaspoon salt
½ teaspoon seasoned salt
Endive or other salad greens
Seafood Dressing (below)
Whole stoned black olives for garnish
Seafood Dressing:
6 tablespoons mayonnaise
6 tablespoons soured cream
6 tablespoons chilli pickle
Juice of 1 lemon
6 ounces cooked, cleaned prawns, crabmeat, or lobster

Slice olives into rings. Arrange 3 overlapping slices in bottom of each of 6 lightly greased individual casseroles.

Peel eggs and grate on medium fine grater. Chop pimientos and spring onions. Combine with eggs, soured cream, mayonnaise, salt, seasoned salt, and remaining sliced olives and toss lightly. Spoon into casseroles and press down lightly. Chill several hours.

Unmould onto plate garnished with endive. Garnish with Seafood Dressing and whole black olives.

Seafood Dressing: Blend together mayonnaise, soured cream, chilli pickle, and lemon juice. Fold in prawns or other seafood. Chill thoroughly before serving. Serves 6.

ANCHOVY CHEESE SALAD

1 2-ounce can anchovies, drained
1 teaspoon finely cut chives
1 pound creamed cottage cheese
Crisp lettuce leaves
6 small tomatoes, peeled and sliced

Chop ⅔ of the anchovies into small pieces. Cut ⅓ into long strips for garnish.

Add chives and anchovy pieces to cottage cheese, and mix lightly.

Cover and place in refrigerator for at least ½ hour to blend flavours.

Arrange lettuce cups on large round serving dish.

Put mound of cottage cheese in centre and overlap tomato slices on lettuce round edge.

Place strips of anchovies on top of cheese as a garnish.

Serve mayonnaise or French dressing on the side. Serves 6.

MOULDED EGG SALAD

8 hard-boiled eggs
4 ounces finely diced celery
4 tablespoons salad dressing
1 teaspoon Worcestershire sauce
1 tablespoon lemon juice
1 teaspoon grated onion
Salt and pepper
6 thick slices of tomato
Lettuce
Paprika
Celery curls

Chop eggs coarsely. Add celery, dressing, and seasoning. Season to taste with salt and pepper. Press into large or individual moulds and chill.

Unmould on tomato slices placed in a bed of lettuce. Sprinkle with paprika. Garnish with celery curls and additional dressing if desired. Serves 6.

Egg-Olive Timbales with Seafood Dressing

Meat and Poultry Salads

CHICKEN, TURKEY, OR DUCK SALAD

12 ounces diced cooked or canned chicken, turkey, or duck
8 ounces diced celery
8 fluid ounces mayonnaise or salad dressing
Salt and pepper
Lemon juice
Lettuce or other greens

Combine chicken, celery, and salad dressing. Season to taste with salt, pepper, and lemon juice.

Chill and serve on lettuce or other greens.

If desired, canned pimiento strips, sliced olives, sliced cucumbers, browned almonds, or marinated asparagus tips may be used for a garnish. Serves 4.

With French Dressing: Marinate chicken in French dressing. Chill. Drain and combine with other ingredients. Blend with mayonnaise, if desired. Season to taste.

Chicken Salad Variations

Chicken-Nut Salad: Add 1 to 2 ounces slivered toasted almonds just before serving.

Avocado-Chicken Salad: Add 4 ounces diced avocado. If desired, serve in halved avocados.

Cranberry-Chicken Salad: Garnish or serve salad with cranberry sauce.

Egg-Vegetable-Chicken Salad: Add 2 chopped hard-boiled eggs, 2 tablespoons chopped green pepper, and 1 teaspoon finely grated onion.

Grape-Chicken Salad: Add 4 ounces fresh seedless grapes.

Pineapple-Chicken Salad: Add 8 ounces diced fresh or canned pineapple.

Ham and Chicken: Substitute half diced cooked ham for half the chicken.

Note: A 4-pound drawn bird yields about 1½ pounds cooked chicken; a 10-pound drawn turkey yields about 3 pounds cooked turkey.

Ham and Orange Salad Bowl

CHICKEN AND MUSHROOM SALAD

Use 12 ounces diced cooked chicken, 2 ounces sautéed button or sliced mushrooms, and 2 ounces diced celery. Moisten with desired dressing.

CHICKEN WITH NUTS AND OLIVES SALAD

Use 12 ounces diced cooked chicken, 2 ounces diced celery, 3 ounces sliced black olives, and 2 ounces sliced toasted almonds. Moisten with mayonnaise.

CHICKEN AND SWEETBREADS SALAD

Use 12 ounces diced cooked chicken, 4 ounces diced cooked sweetbreads, and 2 ounces chopped cucumber. Moisten with mayonnaise.

CHICKEN-FRUIT-NUT SALAD

Use 12 ounces diced cooked chicken, 2 ounces chopped celery, 4 ounces diced pineapple (or 2 ounces whole grapes or cherries), and 2 ounces sliced toasted almonds. Moisten with mayonnaise.

CHICKEN-TOMATO SALAD

Use 6 ounces diced cooked chicken, 1 ounce diced crisp-fried bacon and 6 ounces diced tomato. Moisten with desired dressing.

CHICKEN-TONGUE SALAD

Use 6 ounces diced cooked chicken, 6 ounces diced cooked tongue, 2 ounces chopped celery, and 3 ounces chopped stuffed olives. Moisten with desired dressing.

MEAT SALAD

In master recipe for Chicken Salad, substitute any kind of diced cooked meat for chicken. For large groups, veal may be economically combined with chicken. For 25 servings, use 4½ pounds meat and/or chicken or turkey and 2 pounds diced celery.

HAM AND ORANGE SALAD BOWL

1 clove garlic (optional)
10 ounces cubed ham
8 ounces orange sections
4 ounces chopped celery
2 ounces chopped walnuts
6 tablespoons grated onion (optional)
6-8 tablespoons mayonnaise
2 tablespoons single cream
1 tablespoon vinegar
Dash of black pepper

Rub salad bowl with garlic. Mix ham, orange sections, celery, walnuts, and onion in bowl.

Combine other ingredients; then add to ham mixture and toss. Serves 6 to 8.

Chilled Chicken Salad Pie

CHILLED CHICKEN SALAD PIE

1 baked and chilled, 9-inch pastry case, made with pastry mix or 4 ounces plain flour, ½ teaspoon salt, 3 ounces margarine and 3 to 4 tablespoons cold water

Chicken Salad Filling:
12 ounces cooked chicken, cut into pieces
3 ounces grated Cheddar cheese
2 ounces diced celery
1 9-ounce can drained crushed pineapple
1 ounce blanched slivered almonds or chopped walnuts
½ teaspoon paprika
½ teaspoon salt
4 fluid ounces mayonnaise
4 fluid ounces whipping cream
2 fluid ounces mayonnaise
Grated carrot

Combine cooked chicken, Cheddar cheese, celery, crushed pineapple, almonds or walnuts, paprika, salt, and mayonnaise. Toss lightly. Turn into cooled baked pastry case.

Whip whipping cream until thick and stiff. Fold in extra mayonnaise. Spread over salad in pastry case, leaving 1 inch of salad round edge uncovered.

Garnish with grated carrot. Chill until serving time, at least 30 minutes. Serves 6.

CHEF'S SALAD BOWL

Line a salad bowl with cos lettuce; fill in centre with bite-sized pieces of endive or any combination of greens.

Arrange strips of ham, turkey, and Cheddar cheese in groups on top of chicory, with tomato wedges and thinly sliced unpeeled cucumber between. Top with wedges of hard-boiled eggs.

Carry to the table for all to see, then toss with your best French dressing and serve.

Dutch Salad

DUTCH SALAD

    2 medium red apples
    10 ounces diced, cooked beef
    1 large dill pickle, chopped
    1½ pounds diced, cooked potatoes
    1 medium onion, finely chopped
    2 tablespoons vegetable oil
    3 tablespoons vinegar
    4 tablespoons mayonnaise
    Halved hard-boiled eggs
    Pickled beetroots

Wash and core apples; do not peel; dice. Combine with beef, pickle, potatoes, and onion.

Combine oil, vinegar, and mayonnaise; pour over apple mixture; toss to mix well. Serve on bed of lettuce, garnished with halved hard-boiled eggs and pickled beetroots. Serves 8.

CHICKEN LIVER AND EGG SALAD

    3 onions, finely chopped
    1½ ounces chicken fat or 3 table-
         spoons vegetable oil
    ½ pound chicken livers
    4 hard-boiled eggs
    2 stalks celery, finely chopped
    Salt and pepper

Sauté onions in melted fat until lightly browned. Remove onions. Sauté livers until tender.

Chop livers with eggs and celery. Mix with browned onions. Season with salt and pepper.

Moisten with fat in which onions were fried. Serve on lettuce leaves. Serves 6.

HAM SALAD

    1 pound cubed, cooked ham, cut
         into ½-inch cubes
    15 radishes, sliced thin
    8 sweet pickles, sliced thin
    2 hard-boiled eggs, chopped
    4 fluid ounces cooked salad
         dressing
    4 fluid ounces mayonnaise
    1 teaspoon French mustard
    ½ teaspoon salt
    ⅛ teaspoon black pepper
    Hard-boiled egg slices

Combine ham, radishes, pickles, and chopped hard-boiled eggs.

Blend salad dressing and mayonnaise; season with mustard, salt, and pepper. Stir salad ingredients into dressing.

Pile salad into lettuce cups placed in individual bowls or on large serving dish.

Garnish each serving with hard-boiled egg slices. Serves 6.

MEAT SALAD BOWL
(Master Recipe)

    1 small onion, sliced
    1 small head lettuce
    2 tomatoes, cut in wedges
    12 ounces cooked or canned peas
    16 sliced, stuffed olives
    5 ounces cooked meat, cut in strips
    1 teaspoon salt
    8 fluid ounces French dressing

Separate onion rings. Tear lettuce into bite-sized pieces. Arrange vegetables and meat on lettuce. Sprinkle with salt. Add dressing. Toss lightly. Serves 6.

Variations: Tongue, beef, veal, lamb, duck, turkey, liver, or chicken may be used for the meat. Cabbage may be used in place of celery.

Tuna Fish or Salmon Salad Bowl: Use tuna fish or salmon in place of the meat. Omit onion. Add 4 ounces chopped celery.

RICE AND CHICKEN SALAD WITH ORANGES

    1 ounce butter or margarine
    6 ounces uncooked rice
    ¾ pint warm water or chicken
         broth
    ½ teaspoon salt
    12 ounces diced, cooked chicken
    4 ounces diced celery
    10-12 ounces orange sections
    4 fluid ounces French dressing
    ½ teaspoon salt
    1 head lettuce

In a 3½-pint saucepan, melt butter or margarine. Add rice and cook until grains are a brownish colour. Stir occasionally.

Add water slowly, add salt and bring to vigorous boil. Turn heat as low as possible. Cover and leave over low heat 20 minutes. Chill rice.

Add chicken, celery, orange sections (save some for garnish), French dressing, and salt to chilled rice. Toss.

Place in lettuce cups or line a bowl or serving dish with lettuce and place rice and chicken salad on lettuce. Garnish with remaining orange sections. Serves 8 to 10.

HORNS OF PLENTY

    1 tablespoon dried onion flakes
    2 tablespoons table wine or broth
    1 tablespoon chopped canned
         pimiento
    ⅛ teaspoon garlic powder, or 1
         crushed garlic clove
    2 tablespoons sweet pickle relish
    2 tablespoons wine vinegar
    3 tablespoons vegetable oil
    ¼ teaspoon salt
    ¼ teaspoon sugar
    1 or 2 1 pound cans runner beans
    Sliced cooked ham or turkey
    Spiced peaches

Measure dried onion flakes into wine. Combine all ingredients except runner beans, ham, and spiced peaches. Drain beans; combine with marinade and allow to stand several hours.

When ready to serve, roll ham or turkey into cornucopias; hold together with cocktail sticks if necessary. Fill each cornucopia with beans. Serve as salad or first course with hot or cold spiced peaches. Serves 6 as starters or 12 for salads.

Note: Marinade is sufficient for 1 or 2 cans green beans. To serve Horns of Plenty hot, heat marinade gently with drained beans. Spoon into hot ham or turkey cornucopias.

Horns of Plenty may be served as a salad or first course, hot or cold. They are especially good accompanied by hot or cold spiced peaches.

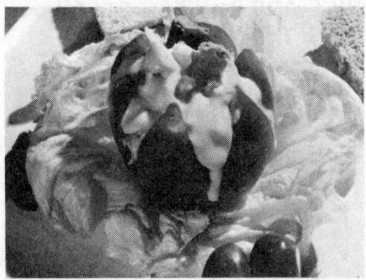

For a summer luncheon serve chicken salad in a tomato.

MEAL-IN-ITSELF SALAD BOWL

1 clove garlic, if desired
4 fluid ounces vegetable oil
2 tablespoons vinegar
¾ teaspoon salt
⅛ teaspoon black pepper
½ teaspoon dry mustard
¼ teaspoon paprika
½ head lettuce, torn into 1½-inch
    pieces
2 tablespoons chopped green pepper
2 ounces sliced celery
2 ounces thinly sliced raw cauli-
    flowerets
6 ounces cooked asparagus tips
1 hard-boiled egg, cut in eighths
½ pound cooked ham or salami, cut
    in thin strips

Have all salad ingredients chilled. Rub inside of salad bowl with cut surface of garlic clove and then discard garlic.

Stir in vegetable oil and vinegar. Add seasonings and beat with fork until well mixed.

Combine remaining ingredients in order given. Toss lightly until each piece of salad is coated with dressing. Serve immediately. Serves 6 to 8.

CHICKEN SALAD—CALIFORNIA STYLE

3 avocados, halved
2 fluid ounces orange juice
12 ounces cooked diced chicken
4 ounces diced celery
2 oranges, sectioned and diced
4 fluid ounces mayonnaise
3 tablespoons chilli pickle
⅛ teaspoon paprika
1 teaspoon salt
2 tablespoons chopped canned
    pimiento
Lettuce

Brush halved avocados with orange juice. Combine chicken and celery with diced oranges; mix well.

Blend mayonnaise, chilli pickle, and seasonings; fold into chicken mixture, mixing until thoroughly blended.

Fill cavity of avocados with chicken salad. Top with chopped pimiento. Serve on bed of lettuce. Garnish with additional orange sections. Serves 6.

PORK SALAD

12 ounces cubed cooked pork
4 ounces diced pared apples
6 ounces chopped celery
1 teaspoon grated onion
4 tablespoons chopped parsley
4 tablespoons chopped green
    pepper
1 teaspoon salt
4 tablespoons cooked salad dressing
4 tablespoons mayonnaise
4 tablespoons soured cream
1 tablespoon lemon juice
8 ounces cranberry sauce
Lettuce

Combine pork, apples, celery, onion, parsley, and green pepper.

Blend together salt, salad dressing, mayonnaise, soured cream, and lemon juice. Mix dressing lightly with meat and vegetables.

Serve salad on crisp lettuce. Garnish with cranberry sauce. Serves 4.

TONGUE AND VEGETABLE SALAD

5 ounces cooked tongue
1 pound canned or cooked
    vegetables
4 ounces thinly sliced celery
1 tablespoon chopped onion
2 tablespoons chopped sweet pickle
4 fluid ounces sharp mayonnaise
1 head lettuce
1 hard-boiled egg, sliced

Cut tongue in strips. Drain chilled vegetables.

Combine tongue, vegetables, onion, and pickles with mayonnaise. Chill 1 hour to blend flavours.

Serve in lettuce cups. Garnish each serving with a slice of egg. Serves 6.

Variations: Use cooked or canned chicken, canned tuna fish, salmon, or other cooked fish instead of tongue.

Snappy Sauerkraut Salad: Add 6 ounces sauerkraut to tongue and vegetable salad with the mixed vegetables.

Florida Chicken Salad

FLORIDA CHICKEN SALAD

1 pound can and 1 8-ounce can
    orange and grapefruit
    sections
12 ounces diced cooked chicken
4 ounces diced celery
2 tablespoons lime or lemon juice
4 tablespoons mayonnaise
¼ teaspoon salt
⅛ teaspoon black pepper
Lettuce

Drain citrus sections thoroughly. Add drained sections to chicken and celery in mixing bowl.

Mix together lime or lemon juice, mayonnaise, and seasonings. Add to salad and toss lightly.

Serve with lettuce and garnish with additional fruit sections.

Serves 5 to 6.

CHICKEN SALAD—GUEST STYLE

12 ounces diced, cooked or canned
    chicken
4 ounces chopped celery
5 ounces seedless grapes, or black
    grape halves with pips
    removed
2 ounces browned almonds
4 fluid ounces mayonnaise
Crisp lettuce

Combine chicken, celery, grapes, and nuts. Chill.

Add mayonnaise and toss lightly. Serve in lettuce cups. Serves 4 to 6.

*Chicken Salad—
California Style*

Salads with Fruit

WALDORF SALAD

Combine 8 ounces cubed apples, 1 ounce chopped nuts, and 4 ounces cubed celery.

Moisten with 4 fluid ounces mayonnaise. Mix lightly with 2 forks. Serve on lettuce. Serves 5.

WALDORF SALAD SPECIAL

6 apples
2 tablespoons lemon juice
6 ounces chopped celery
2 ounces chopped walnuts or pecans
6 fluid ounces mayonnaise or cooked salad dressing
4 fluid ounces double cream, whipped
Apple slices and whole nuts for garnish

Wash, core, and dice apples coarsely without peeling. Sprinkle apples with lemon juice and toss quickly to prevent discolouration.

Add chopped celery and nuts and blend well. Fold mayonnaise or cooked salad dressing into whipped cream. Gently mix dressing with fruit.

Place in large bowl. Garnish with apple slices and nuts. Serves 8.

APPLE AND GRAPE SALAD

3 unpeeled red apples, diced
5 ounces halved black grapes with pips removed
Mayonnaise or salad dressing
Lettuce
2 ounces grated Cheddar cheese

Combine the apples and grapes and toss with sufficient mayonnaise or salad dressing to moisten and season well.

For each serving place a mound of the salad on lettuce on a salad plate; sprinkle generously with cheese.

Serve with additional mayonnaise or salad dressing. Serves 4.

APPLE-CARROT-RAISIN SALAD

Combine bite-sized pieces of unpeeled red apple with grated carrot and raisins. Serve with mayonnaise.

Avocado-Fruit Cocktail Salad: Fill avocado halves with chilled drained fruit cocktail. Sprinkle fruit with a few drops of lemon juice. Serve on crisp lettuce.

APPLE-CUCUMBER SALAD

6 ounces diced unpeeled red apples
6 ounces diced peeled cucumbers
½ teaspoon salt
Dash of black pepper
4 tablespoons pineapple or lemon juice
6 tablespoons mayonnaise or salad dressing
1 ounce chopped walnuts
Lettuce

Season the apples and cucumbers with salt and pepper; sprinkle with the pineapple or lemon juice.

Add the mayonnaise or salad dressing and walnuts.

Serve in crisp lettuce cups. Serves 4.

APPLE AND PINEAPPLE SALAD

6 ounces diced unpeeled red apples
French dressing
6 slices pineapple
Lettuce

Toss apples with enough French dressing to moisten. For each serving, place a slice of pineapple on lettuce, with a mound of the apple salad in the centre. Serves 6.

TOMATO SLICES FILLED WITH AVOCADO

Peel, then mash, avocado and season with lemon juice, grated onion, salt, and paprika. Spread the mixture between slices of tomato.

Garnish with a bit of mayonnaise and arrange individual servings on lettuce.

STUFFED AVOCADO SLICES

2 avocados
2 tablespoons lemon juice
Salt
4 tablespoons single cream
8 ounces cream cheese
2 ounces finely chopped sweet pickles
2 tablespoons chopped spring onion
1 tablespoon chopped parsley
½ teaspoon salt
6 slices pineapple
Lettuce
French dressing

Cut each avocado into halves lengthwise; remove the stone, and peel. Sprinkle inside and out with lemon juice and salt.

Gradually add the cream to the cream cheese, blending until smooth. Add the pickles, onion, parsley, and salt.

Fill the cavity of each avocado half with the cheese filling, spreading it well to the sides. Put the halves together and wrap in greaseproof paper; chill.

Slice crosswise into rings. For each serving place a slice of pineapple on lettuce on a salad plate; top with a stuffed avocado slice. Serve with French dressing. Serves 6.

Colourful, piquant Ambassador Salad makes an impressive main dish for lunch.

AMBASSADOR SALAD WITH ONION DRESSING

2 large or 3 small avocados
Crisp lettuce leaves
1½ dozen cooked scampi
6 hard-boiled eggs
12 cooked asparagus spears
Tiny tomatoes
Black olives
Onion Dressing (below)

Cut avocados in halves lengthwise; remove stones and skin. Cut avocados crosswise into thick half circles (you will need 18).

Arrange crisp lettuce on salad plates. Alternate 3 avocado pieces and 3 scampi in centre of plate. Arrange 2 hard-boiled egg halves and 2 asparagus spears on salad; garnish with tiny whole tomatoes and black olives. Serve with Onion Dressing. Serves 6.

Onion Dressing:
4 tablespoons wine vinegar
2 teaspoons dried onion flakes
¼ teaspoon paprika
4 fluid ounces vegetable oil
1 teaspoon soy sauce
2 drops Tabasco sauce
½ teaspoon dry mustard
⅛ teaspoon dried dill (optional)
½ teaspoon salt

Combine all ingredients in a covered jar. Shake to blend. Allow to stand at least 1 hour before using.

AVOCADO-ORANGE SALAD

3 oranges, peeled and sliced
1 Spanish onion, thinly sliced
French dressing
2 large avocados
2 tablespoons lemon juice
Lettuce

Marinate the orange and onion slices in the French dressing, in the refrigerator, for several hours. Drain.

Cut the avocados in half lengthwise; remove the stones, peel and slice. Sprinkle with lemon juice to prevent darkening.

For each serving place alternate slices of orange, onion, and avocado on lettuce.

Serve with the French dressing drained from the oranges and onion. Serves 6 to 8.

AVOCADO-CREAM CHEESE SALAD

2 medium-sized avocados
8 ounces cream cheese
1 teaspoon grated onion
½ teaspoon celery salt

Peel avocados, halved lengthwise, and hollow out stem ends slightly. Sprinkle inside and out with lemon juice and salt.

Combine cheese, onion, and celery salt, and blend thoroughly. Fill halves with cheese mixture and press two filled halves together. Wrap in greaseproof paper and chill thoroughly. Cut into thick lengthwise slices and lay on lettuce garnished salad plates.

Allow one filled oval to each serving. Top with mayonnaise if desired. Serves 8.

Variations: Filling may be varied in flavour with chopped capers; chopped celery; green pepper or sweet pickles; chopped green or black olives; chopped chives; chopped salted nuts; chopped canned pimiento; finely chopped pineapple.

SUMMER SALAD

On a large tray, arrange mounds of grapefruit sections, halved grapes, strawberries, banana slices, and small scoops of cottage cheese.

Allow each person to make his own selection of fruit, crisp salad greens and lots of savoury biscuits. Serve with lemon allspice dressing (below).

Note: Cut grapefruit in half and then section. Shells may then be used as novel serving dishes.

Lemon Allspice Dressing:
4 fluid ounces mayonnaise
1½ ounces icing sugar
3 tablespoons lemon juice
⅛ teaspoon salt
¼ teaspoon allspice
4 fluid ounces double cream
      whipped

Blend mayonnaise with sugar, lemon juice, salt, and allspice. Fold in whipped cream. Makes 12 fluid ounces.

Egg and Grapefruit Salad

AVOCADO-CANTALOUPE RINGS

2 avocados
Lemon juice
1 cantaloupe or other melon, peeled
Leaf lettuce
4 ounces stoned sweet cherries
French dressing, sweetened

Cut the avocados in half lengthwise; remove the stones and peel. Cut in thin slices and dip in lemon juice.

For each serving cut thin slices of the melon and alternate with the avocado slices on lettuce on a salad plate.

Fill centre with cherries. Serve with sweetened French dressing. Serves 4.

GUACAMOLE (AVOCADO) SALAD

2 small avocados
½ to 1 tablespoon onion juice
1 chopped canned pimiento
Juice of 1 lemon
½ teaspoon salt
⅛ teaspoon black pepper
Lettuce
2 tomatoes, quartered
Paprika

Peel and mash avocados. Add onion juice, pimiento, lemon juice, and salt and pepper to taste. Blend well.

Arrange lettuce in nests on 4 salad plates. Pile avocado mixture in each lettuce nest.

Garnish with tomatoes. Sprinkle paprika on top of each salad. Serves 4.

EGG AND GRAPEFRUIT SALAD

2 tablespoons lemon juice
6 ounces diced celery
2 large firm grapefruit
6 hard-boiled eggs
½ teaspoon salt
4 tablespoons mayonnaise
Paprika
2 olives (optional)

Pour lemon juice over celery placed in chilled bowl. Refrigerate while preparing other ingredients.

Peel and separate grapefruit sections, keeping as whole as possible and free from membrane.

Slice 1 hard-boiled egg, and set aside for garnish.

Add the 5 eggs, coarsely chopped, salt, half the mayonnaise, and the grapefruit to celery. Mix gently with 2 forks. Add more seasoning if desired. Pile into prepared grapefruit shells or lettuce cups.

Garnish top with egg slices. Finish with a dash of paprika. Place on chilled plates and serve promptly. Serve salad dressing separately if desired. Serves 4.

Note: Green celery makes an especially colourful salad. If used, add chopped olives to salad mixture. Pink grapefruit is especially nice.

APPLE CUPS

Use red-skinned unpeeled apples. Wash apples. Cut off a thin slice from stem end. Core without cutting through bottom of apple. With spoon, scoop out apple to form a cup.

Fill with any of the following. Serve on crisp lettuce.

1. Combine equal amounts of chopped celery, peas, and chopped nuts. Moisten with mayonnaise.

2. Mix fruit salad with French dressing.

3. Add chopped celery and nuts to any fruit-flavoured jelly. Fill apple cups; chill until set. Serve topped with a soured cream dressing.

4. Combine chopped cooked chicken with halved purple grapes, chopped celery, and chopped nuts; moisten with mayonnaise. Top with dressing.

FIG AND PEACH SALAD

Arrange a peach half in a crisp cup-shaped lettuce leaf on each plate, using shredded lettuce underneath to hold cup in place.

Cut a fig in half and place, narrow end pointing inward, beside the peach.

Cut remaining figs coarsely with scissors, and mix with about ¼ pint mayonnaise, 1 ounce sliced celery, and 1 tablespoon lemon juice. Pile a spoonful of this in each peach half and put a dot of it on figs. Decorate with walnut halves and serve.

Variation: For a luncheon salad, put a big spoonful of cottage cheese under peach, serve with cinnamon toast or hot rolls, and you have a complete meal.

FRUIT AND VEGETABLE CHEESE SALAD

2 red apples, cut in wedges
8 ounces cubed pineapple or 1 large orange, sliced
1 small bunch purple grapes, cut in halves, or berries in season
2 or 3 tomatoes, cut in slices
1 cucumber, cut in strips
1 small bunch spring onions or sliced Spanish onion
Salad greens (chicory, watercress, or lettuce)
12 ounces grated Cheddar cheese

Arrange wedges of apple in a semi-circle on one side of large round serving plate or tray. In centre of the half-circle, pile pineapple cubes. At each side, place grapes.

On opposite side, arrange vegetables on bed of salad greens. Fill centre of plate with grated Cheddar cheese.

Garnish with parsley. Serve with soured cream salad dressing. Serves 6.

GRAPE CLUSTER SALAD

Blend cream cheese with a small amount of milk. For each salad place a pear half, round side up, on lettuce on a salad plate. Spread it with the cream cheese.

Cut purple grapes in half lengthwise, and arrange them, cut side down, on each cream cheese-covered pear, to resemble a bunch of grapes. Put a bit of grape stem in the large end of each pear.

Serve with French dressing.

STUFFED PEACH SALAD

4 tablespoons milk
3 ounces cream cheese
2 ounces chopped walnuts
2 ounces chopped sultanas
8 peach halves
8 large cooked prunes, stoned
Leaf lettuce
French dressing

Gradually add milk to cream cheese, blending until smooth. Add nuts and raisins and mix well.

Fill centres of peaches with mixture.

For each salad, arrange 2 stuffed peach halves and 2 stoned prunes on lettuce. Serve with French dressing. Serves 4.

Cottage Cheese Coronation Salad

ROSE PETAL SALAD

4 slices pineapple
Lettuce
3 ounces cream cheese
Milk
4 radishes, thinly sliced
French dressing

For each serving, place a slice of pineapple in a lettuce cup.

Soften the cream cheese slightly with a small amount of milk and place a rounded scoop in the centre of each pineapple slice.

Press thin radish slices into the cheese to resemble rose petals. Serve with French dressing. Serves 4.

LANAI SALAD

3 ounces cream cheese
4 tablespoons mayonnaise
2 tablespoons pineapple syrup
1 banana, sliced
4 maraschino cherries, cut in
quarters
1 ounce chopped walnuts
4 slices pineapple, drained

Mix cream cheese, mayonnaise, and pineapple syrup together until smooth. Fold in banana slices, cherries, and nuts.

Arrange drained pineapple slices on a bed of crisp lettuce. Pile cheese-fruit mixture on top. Serves 4.

COTTAGE CHEESE CORONATION SALAD

This easy-to-make salad combines a serving of cottage cheese with a canned peach half, cut as a crown, with red and green maraschino cherries as crown jewels.

Make individual nests of endive or leaf lettuce for a very attractive setting and add a sprig of watercress.

PARTY SALAD

3 ounces cream cheese
1 tablespoon mayonnaise
2 1-pound cans sliced pineapple
1 ounce finely chopped parsley
8 ounces watermelon wedges
8 ounces cantaloupe wedges
2 bananas
Leaf lettuce or escarole
8 ounces black grapes

Mix cheese and mayonnaise; spread on edges of chilled pineapple slices. Roll edges in parsley.

Combine chilled watermelon and cantaloupe wedges.

Cut peeled bananas in half and into strips.

Outline a serving dish with lettuce, and group the fruit attractively. Garnish with French dressing. Serves 8. **Note:** When melons are not available, use such fruits as apples, pears, or plums.

PEAR-CHEESE SALAD

Arrange pear halves on lettuce leaves. Top with mayonnaise, then a sprinkle of grated Cheddar cheese.

COTTAGE CHEESE WITH FRESH FRUIT

1 pound cottage cheese
1 teaspoon salt
1 teaspoon lemon juice
1 ounce chopped walnuts
Lettuce
1 melon, cut in round slices
2 oranges
2 bananas
8 ounces fresh sweet cherries or
strawberries
3 pineapple slices

Add salt and lemon juice to cottage cheese. Fold in part of chopped nuts. Turn into bowl that has been rinsed in cold water and place in refrigerator to chill.

Just before serving, unmould on large salad plate; surround with crisp lettuce leaves or lettuce cups filled with fresh fruits—melon rounds, orange sections, banana slices (soaked in lemon or pineapple juice), pineapple sections, and red cherries or strawberries. Serves 6.

Cottage Cheese with Fresh Fruit

GEORGIA SALAD

8 ounces drained canned fruit cocktail (or coarsely diced peaches)
1 banana, diced
1 ounce finely diced celery
4 fluid ounces salad dressing
Lettuce

Combine the fruit, celery, and salad dressing; toss until well blended. Serve on lettuce. Serves 4.

QUICK ORANGE SALAD

12 peeled orange slices
Leaf lettuce
Mayonnaise or salad dressing
4 maraschino cherries

For each portion arrange 3 orange slices on lettuce. Garnish with mayonnaise or salad dressing and a cherry.
Serve as a starter salad. Serves 4.

PEACH-PINEAPPLE DAISIES

Arrange leaf lettuce in 5 separate nests on a large round serving plate.

Place a slice of canned pineapple in each lettuce nest.

On each slice of pineapple place 4 slices of canned peaches, petal fashion.

Place a spoonful of salad dressing in the centre of each daisy.

Garnish each daisy with a maraschino cherry.

PINEAPPLE SALADS

Pineapple-Apricot: Arrange pineapple slices on lettuce. Top each slice with an apricot half.

Pineapple-Apple: Alternate half slices of pineapple with lengthwise slices of unpeeled red apples on lettuce.

Pineapple-Cream Cheese: Arrange pineapple slices on lettuce. Garnish with watercress and cream cheese that has been formed into balls and rolled in chopped nuts.

Pineapple-Cottage Cheese: Arrange mounds of cottage cheese on lettuce leaves. Surround each mound with pineapple slices, cut in quarters.

Pineapple-Banana: Arrange pineapple chunks and thick slices of banana (dip in pineapple syrup and roll in finely chopped nuts) on lettuce. Garnish with maraschino cherries.

Pineapple Chunks 'n' Cherries: Arrange drained canned pineapple chunks and dark sweet cherries on lettuce.

Pineapple-Banana-Nut: Arrange drained canned pineapple slices on lettuce. Place banana slices (which have been dipped in pineapple syrup) atop the pineapple and sprinkle with salted peanuts.

Pineapple Salads

HONEYDEW RING SALAD

6 slices honeydew melon, peeled
Lettuce
8 ounces cantaloupe balls
4 ounces fresh raspberries
8 ounces seedless grapes
Fresh mint
4 tablespoons olive oil
4 tablespoons lime juice

Place melon slices on lettuce, and fill centres with other fruits, combined.

Garnish with mint; serve with mixed oil and juice. Serves 6.

CANTALOUPE RINGS

Lettuce
4 peeled cantaloupe rings
2 ounces raspberries
4 ounces seedless grapes
4 ounces red plums, diced
3 ounces watermelon balls
Cream cheese dressing

Cover large individual dishes with crisp lettuce. Arrange the cantaloupe rings on the lettuce.

Toss the raspberries, grapes, plums, and watermelon balls lightly together. Heap in the cantaloupe rings.

Serve with cream cheese dressing. Serves 4.

WINE FRUIT SALAD

Prepare sliced bananas, pineapple, and orange sections. Cover with dressing made by blending 4 ounces sugar, 6 tablespoons sherry, and 2 tablespoons madeira.

Allow to stand in a cold place for an hour before serving. May be served as a sweet.

Old-Fashioned Salad

OLD-FASHIONED SALAD

1 large orange
8 ounces halved black grapes with
    pips removed
8 ounces diced fresh or canned
    pineapple
4 ounces diced tart apple
¼ pint whipping cream
1½ tablespoons fresh lemon juice
1 tablespoon sugar
Few grains salt
Lettuce
Clusters of black grapes for garnish

Peel and section orange. Combine with grapes, pineapple, and apple.

Whip cream until stiff. Add lemon juice, sugar, and salt, and blend gently. Fold into fruit mixture. Garnish with crisp lettuce and tiny clusters of black grapes. Serves 4 to 6.

EASY FRUIT WALDORF

2 1-pound cans fruit cocktail
2 ounces sliced celery
2 ounces chopped walnuts
Lettuce
Mayonnaise or cream dressing

Drain fruit cocktail well and mix lightly with celery and walnuts.

Serve on lettuce and top with mayonnaise. Serves 6.

Variation: Instead of mayonnaise, serve lemon-honey dressing separately, to be spooned over the fruit at the table. Make dressing by combining equal parts lemon juice and honey.

SPICED PEACH SALAD

4 fluid ounces wine vinegar
1 teaspoon cloves
1 stick cinnamon
4 ounces sugar
6 canned peach halves
3 ounces cream cheese
1 teaspoon lemon juice
1 ounce chopped walnuts

Put vinegar in saucepan; add spices and sugar and cook 3 minutes. Pour over drained peaches. Chill 3 hours.

Drain and fill peach cavities with cream cheese seasoned with lemon juice and mixed with chopped walnuts.

Arrange on lettuce and garnish with mayonnaise. Serves 6.

FRESH GRAPEFRUIT WINTER SALADS

Arrange on lettuce-covered salad plate.

Poinsettia: On 5 or 6 grapefruit segments arranged flower-petal fashion, place thin strips of canned pimiento. Centre with 4 or 5 small pimiento cheese balls; sprinkle with paprika. Serve mayonnaise separately. Serves 1.

Grapefruit-Banana: Alternate 6 grapefruit segments with 6 banana slices, rolled in chopped nuts, coconut, or sweet biscuit crumbs. Serve with any desired dressing. Serves 1.

Grapefruit-Apple: Alternate 6 grapefruit segments with 6 wedges of unpeeled, red-skinned apple. Serve with grapefruit French dressing. Serves 1.

Holiday: Fill centre of an individual ring mould of cranberry jam with 4 or 5 avocado or banana balls. Round base arrange 6 or 7 grapefruit segments. Garnish with endives. Serve grapefruit French dressing separately.

If canned cranberry jam is used, cut in inch-thick slices and cut out centre with biscuit cutter to simulate ring moulds. Serves 1.

FRESH GRAPEFRUIT SUMMER SALADS

Arrange on lettuce-covered salad plate.

Fruit-Cheese Luncheon Plate: Fill a peach or pear half with cream or cottage cheese, moistened with fruit mayonnaise. Circle with 5 or 6 grapefruit segments. Garnish with cube of red jam. Serve fruit mayonnaise separately. Serves 1.

Grapefruit, Pear and Grape: Combine 2 ounces each of grapefruit pieces, diced pear, and seedless grapes. Serve with fruit mayonnaise. Serves 1.

Grapefruit-Egg: Cut a devilled egg in 6 lengthwise slices. Alternate these with grapefruit segments. Garnish with sliced stuffed olives. Serve with mayonnaise. Serves 1.

Grapefruit-Melon: Arrange 6 grapefruit segments in flower-petal pattern, alternately with long fingers of cantaloupe or honeydew melon. (Marinate melon slices first in sweetened grapefruit juice.) Serve with sweet grapefruit French dressing. Serves 1.

MELON BALL SALAD

1 cantaloupe
Lettuce
8 ounces watermelon balls
6 ounces honeydew melon balls
Sprigs of mint
Mayonnaise, sweetened

Slice the cantaloupe into rings about an inch thick. Peel each ring and place on lettuce on a salad plate.

Fill each ring with watermelon and honeydew balls. Garnish with sprigs of mint.

Serve with sweetened mayonnaise. Serves 4.

GRAPEFRUIT-MELON BALL SALAD

2 grapefruits, peeled and sectioned
Lettuce
6 ounces watermelon or cantaloupe
    balls

For each serving arrange grapefruit sections, petal fashion, on crisp lettuce on a salad plate.

Fill the centre with melon balls and serve with a sweetened dressing. Serves 4 to 6.

FLOWER PETAL SALAD

2 oranges, peeled and sectioned
2 grapefruits, peeled and sectioned
Lettuce
Mayonnaise or salad dressing
4 walnut halves

For each salad arrange alternate orange and grapefruit sections, petal fashion, on lettuce on a salad plate.

Place a spoonful of mayonnaise or salad dressing in the centre. Garnish with a walnut half. Serves 4.

Grapefruit sections encircled by orange slices and Spanish onion rings make an eye-catching and delicious salad served with a fruit dressing.

WATERMELON BOWL CENTREPIECE

½ watermelon
8 ounces cantaloupe balls
8 ounces pineapple chunks
4 ounces bilberries
Lettuce leaves
French dressing

With a melon scoop, remove the centre from half of a short thick watermelon.

Toss together the watermelon and cantaloupe balls, pineapple chunks, and bilberries.

Place the watermelon bowl on lettuce leaves on a round serving dish and fill it with the mixed fruit. Serve the salad with French dressing. Serves 4 to 6.

CARLTON FRUIT SALAD

4 ounces grapefruit sections
6 ounces orange sections
2 ounces black grapes, cut in half and with pips removed
Lettuce
Honey French dressing

Combine the grapefruit and orange sections and the grapes. Place in a mound on lettuce. Serve with honey French dressing. Serves 4.

FRUIT SALAD DELIGHT

8 peach halves
4 ounces bilberries
Leaf lettuce
4 ounces watermelon balls
4 ounces honeydew melon balls
12 peeled cantaloupe slices
Mayonnaise or salad dressing

For each serving, place 2 peach halves filled with bilberries opposite each other on lettuce arranged on a salad plate.

Between the peaches on one side of the plate place a mound of melon balls, and opposite it place 3 cantaloupe slices, petal fashion.

Garnish the centre of the plate with mayonnaise or salad dressing. Serves 4.

For an appetizing luncheon plate: Combine cottage cheese and chopped dried figs (4 figs to 1 pound cheese). Place a mound of cottage cheese-fig mixture on each lettuce-lined plate. Garnish each plate with 2 whole dried figs, pineapple spears, orange slices, and strawberries or cherries.

PACIFIC SALAD COOLER

For each serving, peel two seedless oranges and cut them into thin cartwheel-like slices.

Arrange two melon slices on a bed of lettuce that has been placed on a large salad or luncheon plate.

Take the cartwheel slices of oranges and form two semi-circles with them, overlapping each slice, at one end of plate.

For a bright touch of colour, add several large strawberries, sliced, and tucked in round the edge of the orange slices and several at one side of plate.

Drop a large scoop of lemon water ice in centre and serve immediately.

Serve hot rolls or cinnamon toast plus tall glasses of fresh lemonade and you'll have a complete summer lunch.

Pacific Salad Cooler

PEACH 'N' COTTAGE CHEESE

Place drained halves of canned peaches cut-side-up on lettuce. Top with cottage cheese to which chives have been added.

WINTER PEAR WALDORF SALAD

8 ounces diced, peeled pears or 4 ounces each diced pear and unpeeled red apple
2 tablespoons lemon juice
1 teaspoon sugar
4 fluid ounces mayonnaise
4 ounces thinly sliced celery
2 ounces coarsely chopped walnuts

Toss fruit with lemon juice, sugar, and 1 tablespoon mayonnaise.

Just before serving, add celery, walnuts, and remaining mayonnaise. Toss and serve on crisp lettuce. Sprinkle with French dressing. Serves 6.

Variations: Substitute, for pears, cubes of fresh or canned pineapple or banana or 1 large orange, sliced, and 5 ounces grapes, or 8 ounces apple, plus 2½ ounces raisins or fresh dates.

Coconut Waldorf: Substitute shredded coconut for nuts.

A citrus salad of orange slices and grapefruit sections served with cottage cheese and a garnish of strawberries make an attractive low calorie luncheon.

GOLDEN SALAD

4 pineapple slices
Leaf lettuce
2 oranges, peeled and sectioned
1 grapefruit, peeled and sectioned
6 maraschino cherries, sliced
Watercress
Mayonnaise or salad dressing

For each serving, place a slice of pineapple on lettuce on a salad plate.

Arrange alternate orange and grapefruit sections on the pineapple, with thin slices of maraschino cherry between the sections.

Garnish each salad with watercress. Serve with mayonnaise or salad dressing. Serves 4.

COTTON BLOSSOM SALAD

4 red apples
4 large oranges
1 pound cottage cheese
1 teaspoon grated orange rind
2 ounces chopped maraschino cherries
4 fluid ounces soured cream
½ teaspoon salt
Watercress
Mayonnaise or salad dressing

Wash apples, quarter, core, and slice thin. Peel oranges and remove sections.

Combine cottage cheese, orange rind, cherries, soured cream, and salt; mix well.

Place ring of crisp watercress round edge of large round plate. Place alternate slices of apple and orange sections in a ring on watercress. Pile cottage cheese mixture in centre.

Serve with mayonnaise or salad dressing. Serves 6.

Cotton Blossom Salad

FESTIVE SALAD

3 well-beaten egg yolks
4 fluid ounces single cream
2 fluid ounces lemon juice
⅛ teaspoon salt
1 1-pound and 1 8-ounce can sweet cherries, stoned
1 1-pound can pineapple, cut in small pieces
6 ounces almonds, blanched and slivered
½ pound marshmallows, cut in pieces
8 fluid ounces whipping cream, whipped

Combine egg yolks, 4 fluid ounces cream, lemon juice, and salt. Place in top of double boiler and cook over boiling water, stirring constantly until thick.

Cool mixture. Fold fruit, nuts, and marshmallows into cooled sauce. Then fold in whipped cream.

Pour into large shallow pan or bowl and chill for several hours or overnight.

Serve on lettuce with cherry garnish. This salad may be served as a sweet, if desired. Serves 12.

CLUB PLATE

6 oranges, peeled and sliced
3 bananas, cut in sixths
12 ounces melon or avocado balls
1 pound cottage cheese
3 ounces cream cheese
Walnuts
Lettuce

Arrange fruits, cottage cheese, and walnut bonbons (below) on lettuce for individual servings. Serve with lemon French dressing. Serves 6.

Walnut Bonbons: Place balls of cream cheese between walnut halves.

BLUSHING PEAR

Drain canned pear halves and put 2 halves together with softened cream cheese. If desired, sprinkle paprika on one side to make a blush.

Top with cream cheese and a short strip of green pepper or a leaf of watercress for a stem. Stand upright on lettuce or other salad greens.

Blushing Pear

SALAD BUFFET PLATTER

Here are eight delightful salads made from a variety of canned fruits. Back row: ready-to-serve fruits for salad; fruit cocktail moulded in lemon gelatine with walnuts; orange and grapefruit sections with cheese topped with a walnut; apricot halves put together with cream cheese.

Front row: a pear half filled with grated cheese; pineapple slices topped with coconut and maraschino cherries; a peach half filled with cream cheese and raisins; cottage cheese topped with pineapple chunks. These are all ideal salads to serve with the main course.

CRANBERRY-PEACH SALAD

Place a slice of canned jellied cranberry sauce on endive. Round it make a ring of overlapping canned peach slices.

Top cranberry sauce with a spoonful of cottage cheese. Serve mayonnaise separately.

PEACH BOWL SALAD

Mix drained canned sliced peaches, sliced celery, sliced stuffed olives, and shredded lettuce to taste. Toss with French dressing or mayonnaise.

Cottage Cheese Showcap with Fruit Salad Cups

BANANA GRAPEFRUIT SALAD

3 grapefruit sections, fresh or canned
1 fully ripe banana
Lettuce
Berries or cherries

Arrange overlapping grapefruit sections along centre section of salad plate. Peel banana and slice crosswise into pieces about ¼-inch thick. Arrange 2 rows of overlapping banana slices round sides of plate.

Garnish the centre with crisp lettuce leaves and berries or cherries, if desired. Serve with a sweet or tart dressing. Serves 1.

Note: Pink and white grapefruit sections combined make an especially attractive salad arrangement.

If desired, orange sections may be used in place of, or combined with, the grapefruit sections.

COTTAGE CHEESE SNOWCAP WITH SALAD CUPS

1 pound cream-style cottage cheese
½ teaspoon salt
1 teaspoon grated lemon rind
2 tablespoons lemon juice
2 ounces slivered, candied ginger

Combine ingredients, reserving a little ginger to garnish top of cottage cheese, and blend. Turn into a chilled bowl.

Serve with chilled fruit salad cups: Wash and drain 9 individual lettuce cups. On 3 cups place peach halves with centres filled with bilberries; alternate grapefruit and orange sections on 3 other cups. Fill 3 remaining cups with pineapple cubes and halved strawberries.

Arrange cups on a large serving dish round a snowcap of cottage cheese. Serves 9.

SALAD BOATS

2 pineapples
10 ounces grape halves
2 large bananas, sliced
8 ounces cottage cheese
Watercress

Cut pineapples in half and scoop out centre. Remove core and cut in bite-sized pieces.

Mix pineapple with grape halves and banana. Pile back into pineapple shell.

Divide cottage cheese in four balls; place one on each salad. Garnish with watercress. Serve with cream crackers. Serves 4.

PEAR DESSERT SALAD

2 large fresh pears
1 tablespoon lemon juice
1 pound cottage cheese
2 to 4 tablespoons soured cream
2 to 4 tablespoons chopped
       preserved ginger
⅛ teaspoon salt
Lettuce or other salad greens
Mayonnaise

Cut pears into quarters, core, and slice. Brush cut surfaces with lemon juice.

Mix cheese, soured cream (enough to soften), ginger, and salt.

Place lettuce on individual plates and top with a mound of cheese. Insert pear slices.

Serve with mayonnaise and a garnish of any other fresh fruits, if desired. Serves 4.

CURRIED APPLE-ONION-PEPPER SALAD

Combine strips of apple with thin onion rings and crisp slivers of red and green peppers. Serve with mayonnaise seasoned with curry powder.

SUMMER CLUSTERS

For each serving place a slice of pineapple on endive. Cover it with a slice of peeled orange. Place 3 slices of fluted banana on orange.

Quarter fresh strawberries and place between banana slices round edge of orange.

Garnish centre with a whole strawberry. Serve with salad dressing.

Summer Clusters

FRESH SALAD OF FRUIT

1 large honeydew melon
Lettuce
4 tablespoons lemon juice
4 medium peaches, peeled and
       halved
4 bananas, sliced diagonally
½ pound fresh sweet cherries,
       stoned
Mayonnaise

Have all ingredients chilled. Cut honeydew melon into halves lengthwise. Remove seeds and cut halves into 4 lengthwise boat-shaped pieces. Peel and place on lettuce cups.

Drizzle lemon juice over peach halves and banana slices. Place a peach half in each slice of melon. Add several banana slices. Top with a few sweet cherries. Serve with mayonnaise. Serves 8.

PINEAPPLE-CUCUMBER SALAD

1 unpeeled cucumber, scored, thinly
       sliced
4 pineapple slices
Lettuce
French dressing

For each serving place overlapping slices of cucumber on a slice of pineapple and place on crisp lettuce. Serve with French dressing. Serves 4.

CALIFORNIA FRUIT PLATE

3 ripe pears
1 melon, cut in 6 slices
2 ounces bilberries
1 lime, cut in sixths
Lettuce

Halve and core ripe, chilled pears. Cut melon in 6 slices; remove skin and pips. Scallop edge with paring knife or score with fork.

Place a melon slice on each dish; put a pear half in the centre of each melon slice. In core cavity of pear put a few ripe bilberries.

Add a wedge of lime for dessert plate or line plate with crisp lettuce for salad. Serves 6.

PINEAPPLE AND CHEESE SALAD

4 pineapple slices
Lettuce
2 ounces grated Cheddar cheese
French dressing

For each serving, place a slice of pineapple on lettuce on a salad plate, with a mound of grated cheese in the centre of the pineapple. Serve with French dressing. Serves 4.

FRUIT IN COTTAGE CHEESE RING

Drain a chilled can of mixed fruit. Add slice of celery for crunchiness.

Spoon cottage cheese in a ring on lettuce-covered plates. Put fruit in centre.

Sunshine Cottage Cheese Salad

SUNSHINE COTTAGE CHEESE SALAD

1 pound creamed cottage cheese
½ teaspoon salt
1 teaspoon grated lemon rind
2 tablespoons lemon juice
3 tablespoons grated orange rind
3 large oranges, peeled, sliced
1 head lettuce or other salad greens
Fresh strawberries

Add salt, lemon rind, lemon juice, and 2 tablespoons orange rind to cottage cheese; stir lightly to blend. Turn into greased bowl and chill.

Wash and drain crisp lettuce and arrange on plate. Turn out cottage cheese in centre of plate, sprinkling remaining orange rind on top.

Surround cottage cheese mound with overlapping sliced oranges and whole fresh strawberries. Serves 6.

AVOCADO RING

Cut avocado in half and peel thinly. Remove stone and fill cavity with pineapple or pimiento cream cheese. Press halves together; wrap in greaseproof paper. Chill.

Cut into slices ¼-inch thick. Arrange 2 or 3 slices in lettuce cup. Serve with French dressing.

CRANBERRY COTTAGE CHEESE

Combine 12 ounces cottage cheese with 8 ounces well drained cranberry sauce and 1 ounce chopped walnuts. Serve with mayonnaise.

Rainbow Salad: For a warm-weather luncheon, serve a fruit salad, buffet style. This one gives you time to enjoy your own party. Combine 2 pounds cottage cheese, 6 ounces chopped dates, 2 ounces coarsely chopped walnuts, and 1 tablespoon sugar. Place in centre of lettuce-lined plate. Surround with assorted fresh fruits. Serve with rolls.

Frozen Salads

Frozen salads are especially suitable when the thermometer soars in summer or when much of the food preparation must be done well in advance. When the salad is frozen, you simply cut it in squares or slice, place a serving on a bed of lettuce and garnish with a little salad dressing.

Frozen Grapefruit Salad

TO FREEZE SALADS

(1) Turn the mixture into freezer trays or other moulds and place in freezing compartment of refrigerator or in the freezer. Set refrigerator at coldest point. Freeze until firm.

(2) Pack mixture into greased mould. Seal tightly with tin foil or adhesive tape. Cans with lids, such as baking powder cans, make good moulds. Pack mould in 5 parts ice to 1 part salt and leave for about 4 hours or until firm.
Note: Do not freeze salad long enough for fruits to become frozen or icy.

FROZEN FRUIT-CHEESE SALAD

1 1-pound and 1 8-ounce can fruit
   cocktail
1 teaspoon unflavoured gelatine
2 tablespoons lemon juice
3 ounces cream cheese
4 tablespoons mayonnaise
Dash of salt
6 fluid ounces whipping cream,
   chilled
4 ounces sugar
2 ounces chopped nuts

Drain fruit cocktail. soften gelatine in lemon juice, then dissolve over hot water. Blend cream cheese with mayonnaise and salt. Stir in gelatine.

Whip cream until stiff, adding sugar gradually during last stages of beating. Fold in cheese mixture, nuts, and fruit cocktail. Pour into freezer tray that has been lined with greaseproof paper.

Freeze until firm with refrigerator set at coldest setting (approximately 4 hours).

Turn out on serving dish, remove paper, cut into thick slices. Garnish with watercress. Serves 8.
Note: Allow the salad to stand at room temperature for a few minutes just before serving. The flavour and texture are much better.

Frozen Fruit-Cheese Salad

FROZEN BANANA SALAD

4 ripe bananas
2 tablespoons lemon juice
8 fluid ounces whipping cream,
   whipped
4 fluid ounces mayonnaise
½ pound marshmallows, cut in pieces
3 canned pimientos, puréed, and
   juice
¾ teaspoon salt

Slice bananas and mix with lemon juice. Fold in whipped cream, mayonnaise, marshmallows, and pimientos. Add salt.

Mix well and turn into freezer trays. Freeze until stiff, about 3 hours.

To serve, cut into squares. Serve on lettuce or watercress with French dressing. Serves 6.

FROZEN ROQUEFORT CHEESE SALAD

4 ounces Roquefort cheese
2 tablespoons cream cheese
1 teaspoon lemon juice
4 ounces celery, finely chopped
Chopped onion or chives
Paprika
8 fluid ounces whipping cream,
   whipped

Blend Roquefort and cream cheese with lemon juice, using a silver fork. Add remaining ingredients, folding in whipped cream. Freeze. Serves 6.

FROZEN CREAM CHEESE AND FRUIT SALAD

3 ounces cream cheese
4 fluid ounces mayonnaise
4 fluid ounces whipping cream,
   whipped
2 to 3 ounces seedless grapes
1 ounce red maraschino cherries
1 8-ounce can crushed pineapple,
   drained
2 ounces diced marshmallows
   (about 14)

Blend cheese and mayonnaise until smooth. Fold in whipped cream, fruits, and marshmallows.

Turn into freezer tray. Freeze until firm. Serve on lettuce. Serves 6.

EASY FROZEN SALAD

Freeze overnight 1 1-pound can fruit cocktail or other canned fruit.

Immerse can in hot water a few seconds. Open both ends. Push frozen fruit through and slice.

Or pour fruit into freezer tray and freeze. Turn out and cut into slices. Serve at once on lettuce with mayonnaise. Serves 6.

FROZEN GRAPEFRUIT SALAD

8 ounces cream cheese
8 fluid ounces soured cream
¼ teaspoon salt
4 ounces sugar
1 grapefruit, sectioned
1 avocado, diced
5 ounces seedless grapes, halved
2 ounces chopped walnuts

Soften cream cheese; blend in soured cream. Add salt and sugar and stir until well blended. Add grapefruit sections, avocado, grapes, and nuts.

Pour into 9×5-inch loaf tin and freeze until firm. Slice and serve on lettuce with French dressing. Serves 6 to 8.

FROZEN DELIGHT SALAD

8 fluid ounces whipping cream,
   whipped
2 fluid ounces mayonnaise
1 teaspoon unflavoured gelatine
3 tablespoons syrup from pineapple
8 ounces crushed canned pineapple
3 ounces chopped black olives
2 ounces chopped celery
½ teaspoon prepared horseradish
Salt
Lettuce

Fold mayonnaise into whipped cream. Soften gelatine in cold syrup and heat over hot water until dissolved. Cool slightly and fold into cream mixture.

Fold in pineapple, olives, celery, horseradish, and salt to taste.

Pour into refrigerator tray and freeze. Stir occasionally during freezing. When firm, cut into squares and serve on lettuce. Serves 8.

CALIFORNIA FROZEN SALAD

3 ounces cream cheese
3 tablespoons mayonnaise
⅛ teaspoon salt
8 fluid ounces whipping cream,
   whipped
1 ounce chopped kumquats
1 ounce chopped dates
1 ounce chopped maraschino
   cherries
2 ounces crushed pineapple
1 tablespoon finely chopped
   preserved ginger
2 ounces chopped blanched almonds

Blend cheese smoothly with mayonnaise; add salt. Fold in whipped cream and fruit and ginger mixture.

Pour into freezer tray; sprinkle almonds over top. Freeze. Serve on crisp lettuce. Serves 8.

Frozen Cranberry Loaf

FROZEN CRANBERRY LOAF

    3 ounces finely ground toast
          crumbs
    3 ounces brown sugar
    1 teaspoon cinnamon
    ½ teaspoon nutmeg
    ¼ teaspoon allspice
    ¼ teaspoon cloves
    ¼ teaspoon ginger
    1½ ounces melted butter or
          margarine
    1 1-pound can jellied cranberry
          sauce
    4 fluid ounces whipping cream
    3 ounces cream cheese
    Green food colouring

Mix first 7 ingredients together. Work in melted butter. Press mixture evenly against sides and bottom of a freezer tray. Chill in freezing compartment for at least 1 hour.

Crush jellied cranberry sauce with a fork and spread over crumb crust.

Whip cream. Soften cream cheese and whip with cream. Tint green with green food colouring. Spread whipped cream-cheese mixture over cranberry sauce.

Place in freezing compartment and freeze until firm. Slice to serve. Serves 8.

FROSTED STRAWBERRY SALAD

    8 ounces strawberries
    8-10 ounces marshmallows, cut
          small
    6 ounces cream cheese
    6 fluid ounces mayonnaise
    8 fluid ounces whipping cream,
          whipped
    Endive

Wash and top berries; reserve some for garnish and slice remaining ones.

Combine sliced berries with marshmallows and allow to stand while preparing other ingredients.

Mash cream cheese with fork and blend in mayonnaise. Fold in whipped cream. Fold in berry mixture and pour into freezer tray or loaf tin and freeze until firm.

Unmould on serving tray; garnish with endives and whole strawberries. Slice and serve with additional mayonnaise, if desired. Serves 6 to 8.

FROZEN CHICKEN SALAD

    1 teaspoon unflavoured gelatine
    2 tablespoons cold water
    6 fluid ounces mayonnaise
    9 ounces cold diced cooked chicken
    1 ounce chopped blanched almonds
    2 ounces grapes, halved
    ⅛ teaspoon salt
    6 fluid ounces whipping cream,
          whipped

Soften gelatine in cold water 5 minutes, then dissolve over boiling water.

Cool and combine well with mayonnaise. Add other ingredients, folding in whipped cream last.

Turn into freezer tray and freeze. Slice and serve on lettuce. Serves 6.

FROZEN PEACH SALAD

    1 1-pound and 1 8-ounce can peach
          halves
    ½ ounce butter or margarine
    1½ tablespoons flour
    1 tablespoon sugar
    ¼ teaspoon salt
    4 fluid ounces syrup from peach
          halves
    2 fluid ounces orange juice
    1 stiffly beaten egg white
    2 fluid ounces evaporated milk,
          whipped

Place 8 drained peach halves cut-side-down in freezer tray.

Melt butter; add flour and blend. Add sugar, salt, peach syrup, and orange juice. Cook, stirring constantly, until thick and smooth.

Fold in stiffly beaten egg white. Cool. Dice remaining peaches and add to mixture. Fold in whipped evaporated milk. Pour over peaches. Freeze until firm.

Cut in squares and place in lettuce cups, peach half up. Place a maraschino cherry in centre of each peach. Serves 8.

FROZEN TOMATO MOUSSE

    1 pound canned tomatoes
    2 teaspoons vinegar
    ½ teaspoon grated onion
    ½ teaspoon salt
    ½ teaspoon celery salt
    ½ teaspoon allspice
    1 tablespoon unflavoured gelatine
    12 ounces whipping cream,
          whipped stiff

Simmer tomatoes, vinegar, and seasoning 15 minutes and strain carefully.

Add gelatine, which has been softened 5 minutes in 4 tablespoons cold water, and stir until dissolved.

Cool and, when partially congealed, fold in cream. Turn into freezer tray and freeze. Serve on bed of watercress. Garnish with cucumber slices. Serves 6.

FROZEN FRUIT SALAD

Finely cut fruit from 1 pound can mixed fruit.

Combine with 4 fluid ounces fruit salad dressing or honey dressing and 4 fluid ounces whipping cream, whipped. Freeze. Serves 6.

FROSTY FRUIT CREAM

    3 ounces cream cheese
    1 tablespoon lemon juice
    ⅛ teaspoon salt
    2 ounces sugar
    8 ounces diced canned peaches,
          well drained
    4 ounces fresh bilberries, washed
    ¾ pint soured cream
    Endives
    Bilberry cream dressing

Set refrigerator control at coldest point.

Allow cream cheese to soften at room temperature. Gradually stir in lemon juice, salt, and sugar. Add peaches and bilberries, stirring until well blended. Fold in soured cream.

Pour into freezer tray lined with greaseproof paper or aluminium foil. Fold ends of paper or foil over top of fruit salad. Freeze until firm, about 1½ to 2 hours.

Unmould on chilled serving dish on bed of endives. If desired, garnish with additional peaches and bilberries and serve with bilberry cream dressing. Serves 6.

Bilberry Cream Dressing:
    1 tablespoon lemon juice
    1 to 2 tablespoons sugar
    ⅛ teaspoon salt
    1 ounce crushed bilberries
    8 fluid ounces soured cream

Add lemon juice, sugar, and salt to bilberries, mixing well. Fold in soured cream. Chill. Makes ½ pint.

Frosty Fruit Cream

Moulded Salads, Aspics, Mousses

GELATINE SALAD HINTS

Please read about gelatine in **Ingredients—How to Use Them.**

Gelatine moulded salads are especially suitable when you entertain a crowd and much of the food preparation has to be done well in advance. They are not tricky to prepare, but a few "do's" and "don'ts" may be helpful.

● Use syrup from canned fruits as part of liquid in gelatine salads for added flavour.

● For large moulds, cut liquid to 14 fluid ounces for 1 packet fruit-flavoured gelatine, or 1 tablespoon unflavoured gelatine.

● Chill gelatine until slightly thickened (unbeaten egg white consistency) before adding solid ingredients. Carefully fold well drained fruits and vegetables into thickened gelatine, distributing them evenly.

● A gelatine salad may be moulded in several ways—in large ring or fancy mould, in individual moulds, or in shallow pan.

● To mould fruits or vegetables in definite pattern, arrange in thin layer of slightly thickened gelatine. Chill until firm, then add balance of gelatine.

● To make moulded layered salads, be sure each layer is firm before adding next layer.

● Prepare large gelatine moulds a day ahead of serving, so they will be thoroughly set before unmoulding.

● Fill moulds as full as possible for easy unmoulding.

Gelatine Moulds with Vegetables

CARDINAL SALAD

1 packet lemon-flavoured gelatine
8 fluid ounces hot water
6 fluid ounces beetroot juice
3 tablespoons vinegar
½ teaspoon salt
1 tablespoon prepared horseradish
2 teaspoons grated onion
3 ounces diced celery
6 ounces cooked diced beetroots
Mayonnaise

Dissolve gelatine in hot water. Add beetroot juice, vinegar, salt, horseradish, and onion. Chill until partly set.

Fold in celery and beetroots. Pour into mould rinsed in cold water and chill.

Serve on watercress garnished with mayonnaise. Serves 6.

FRUITED COLESLAW SALAD MOULD

1 1-pound can fruit cocktail
1 packet lemon-flavoured gelatine
18 fluid ounces boiling water
3 tablespoons lemon juice
¼ teaspoon salt
4 ounces finely shredded raw cabbage
Mustard Dressing (below)

Drain fruit cocktail thoroughly.

Dissolve lemon gelatine in boiling water. Add lemon juice and salt; chill until mixture begins to thicken.

Stir in 10 ounces well-drained fruit cocktail (saving remainder for garnish) and the cabbage. Turn into a lightly greased mould or individual moulds and chill until firm.

Unmould, garnish with fruit cocktail, and serve with Mustard Dressing. Serves 6 to 8.

Mustard Dressing: Blend 2 fluid ounces mayonnaise, 4 fluid ounces soured cream, ¼ teaspoon salt, ½ teaspoon French mustard, and 1½ teaspoons lemon juice together until smooth.

EASY ASPIC
(Master Recipe)

1 tablespoon unflavoured gelatine
4 fluid ounces cold canned mixed vegetable juices
½ pint hot canned mixed vegetable juices

Soften gelatine in the cold vegetable juices. Add hot vegetable juice and stir until dissolved. Pour into individual moulds and chill until firm.

Unmould on lettuce and serve with mayonnaise or French dressing. Serves 4.

Variations
Ring Mould: For ring mould double the recipe and pour into 2-pint ring mould. Unmould and fill centre with chicken, turkey, or tuna fish salad. Serves 8.

Seafood Aspic: Make Easy Aspic. Chill until the mixture is the consistency of unbeaten egg white.

Fold in 6 ounces diced prawns, 4 ounces crabmeat, 8 ounces lobster, and 2 ounces diced celery. Serves 6.

Olive Cucumber Aspic: Make Easy Aspic. Chill until the mixture is the consistency of unbeaten egg white.

Fold in 16 sliced stuffed olives and 4 ounces diced cucumber. Serves 6.

Perfection Aspic: Make Easy Aspic. Chill until the mixture is the consistency of unbeaten egg white.

Fold in 4 ounces finely shredded cabbage, 6 ounces diced celery, and 2 tablespoons chopped green pepper. Serves 6.

Fruited Slaw Salad Mould

TOMATO ASPIC
(Master Recipe)

2 tablespoons unflavoured gelatine
4 fluid ounces cold water
1¼ pounds canned tomatoes
1 tablespoon grated onion
1 tablespoon sugar
1 teaspoon salt
4 peppercorns
½ bay leaf
4 cloves
2 tablespoons lemon juice

Soften gelatine in cold water 5 minutes.

Cook tomatoes and seasonings (except lemon juice) 5 to 10 minutes. Strain.

Pour ¾ pint hot tomato mixture over softened gelatine.

Add lemon juice and pour into moulds rinsed with cold water. Chill.

Unmould on lettuce. Serve with mayonnaise or cooked dressing. Serves 6.

Tomato Aspic Ring: Prepare master tomato aspic. Pour into large ring mould or individual small moulds. Chill until firm.

Unmould and fill centre with chicken, tuna fish, or salmon salad.

Tomato Aspic with Celery and Peas: Prepare master tomato aspic; add 6 ounces canned peas and 4 ounces diced celery to thickened aspic.

Tomato Aspic with Cottage Cheese: Prepare master tomato aspic; fill moulds only ⅔ full of tomato aspic.

When firm, complete filling moulds with seasoned cottage cheese. Unmould with cottage cheese on the bottom.

Tomato Aspic with Cucumber: Prepare master tomato aspic and add 8 ounces diced cucumber to thickened aspic.

To Chill Individual Salad Moulds: Place individual salad moulds in bun tins and partially fill. Place in refrigerator and add remaining liquid.

HORSERADISH MOULD WITH COLE SLAW

1 tablespoon unflavoured gelatine
2 fluid ounces cold water
4 fluid ounces boiling water
4 fluid ounces mayonnaise or salad
  dressing
3 fluid ounces prepared horseradish
¼ teaspoon salt
¼ teaspoon paprika
4 fluid ounces whipping cream,
  whipped
1 small head red cabbage,
  shredded
1 ounce diced green pepper
2 tablespoons diced canned
  pimiento
Mayonnaise or salad dressing
Salt and pepper

Soften gelatine in cold water. Add boiling water and stir until dissolved. Combine with mayonnaise or salad dressing, horseradish, salt, and paprika.

Fold in the whipped cream. Pour into a 2-pint mould; chill until firm.

Toss cabbage with green pepper, pimiento, and just enough mayonnaise or salad dressing to moisten. Season to taste with salt and pepper.

Unmould the gelatine on a serving dish; surround with cole slaw. Serve with mayonnaise or salad dressing. Serves 4 to 6.

CUCUMBER AND OLIVE MOULD

2 packets lime-flavoured gelatine
1 pint 4 fluid ounces hot water
½ teaspoon salt
2 ounces sliced stuffed olives
4 ounces cubed cucumber, drained
8 ounces crushed, canned pineapple,
  drained

Dissolve gelatine in hot water. Add salt. Place slices of stuffed olives on the bottom of a 2½-pint ring mould. Add enough gelatine to cover. Chill until firm.

Chill remaining gelatine until slightly thickened. Add cucumber and pineapple and pour into the mould. Chill until firm.

Unmould and surround with crisp lettuce. Serve with salad dressing. Serves 8 to 10.

BROCCOLI SALAD MOULD

1 tablespoon unflavoured gelatine
2 fluid ounces cold water
8 fluid ounces hot stock or bouillon
6 fluid ounces mayonnaise
¼ teaspoon salt
⅛ teaspoon black pepper
12 ounces chopped cooked broccoli
2 hard-boiled eggs, chopped
2 hard-boiled eggs, sliced
Lettuce

Soften gelatine in cold water 5 minutes. Dissolve in very hot stock. Chill until slightly thickened.

Fold in mayonnaise and seasonings,

mixing until well blended. Fold in broccoli and chopped eggs. Turn into 2-pint mould. Chill until firm.

Unmould on large serving dish. Garnish with lettuce and sliced hard-boiled eggs. Serves 6.

TOMATO ASPIC IN GREEN PEPPER SLICES

5 large green peppers
1½ tablespoons unflavoured
  gelatine
4 fluid ounces cold water
1 pint tomato juice
4 fluid ounces tomato purée
2 teaspoons salt
¼ teaspoon black pepper
4 ounces chopped celery
Lettuce
4 ounces thin strips Cheddar cheese
Salad dressing

Cut a slice from the top of each pepper. Remove the seeds and membrane and place in iced water until crisp. Drain well.

Soften gelatine in cold water and dissolve it over hot water. Add tomato juice and purée, and the seasonings. Chill until slightly thickened.

Fold in the celery. Fill the pepper shells and chill until the aspic is firm. Cut each pepper into ½-inch slices.

For each serving place 3 slices on lettuce. Garnish with strips of cheese and serve with salad dressing. Serves 8 to 10.

TOMATO SALAD MOULD

2 tablespoons unflavoured gelatine
4 fluid ounces cold water
8 fluid ounces condensed tomato
  soup, undiluted, heated
8 ounces cream cheese
8 fluid ounces mayonnaise or salad
  dressing
4 ounces chopped celery
1 ounce chopped green pepper
1 tablespoon chopped onion
Salt and black pepper

Soften gelatine in cold water and dissolve in hot soup. Gradually add to cream cheese, blending until smooth. Chill until slightly thickened.

Fold in mayonnaise or salad dressing and chopped vegetables. Season to taste.

Pour into a 2-pint mould and chill until firm.

Unmould and garnish with crisp lettuce. Serve with mayonnaise or salad dressing. Serves 6 to 8.

MOULDED BEETROOT SALAD

1 packet lemon-flavoured gelatine
16 fluid ounces hot water
2 fluid ounces vinegar
12 ounces diced cooked beetroots,
  drained

1 ounce chopped celery
1 tablespoon prepared horseradish
½ teaspoon salt

Dissolve gelatine in hot water. Add vinegar, and chill until slightly thickened. Add beetroots, celery, horseradish, and salt. Pour into 4 or 6 individual moulds and chill until firm. Unmould and garnish with endive. Serve with mayonnaise or salad dressing. Serves 4 to 6.

LAYERED TOMATO ASPIC SALAD

First Layer—Tomato Aspic:
1 bay leaf
Dash of Tabasco sauce
1 small onion, finely chopped
½ teaspoon salt
2 pints tomato juice
3 tablespoons unflavoured gelatine
6 fluid ounces water
2 tablespoons vinegar

Place bay leaf, Tabasco sauce, onion, salt, and tomato juice in 3-pint saucepan. Bring to boil on high heat; lower heat, and cook 10 minutes.

Soften gelatine in water 5 minutes; dissolve in juice mixture, add vinegar, and strain. Cool slightly.

Pour ¾ pint of aspic mixture in lightly greased 9½ × 5¼ × 2¾-inch loaf tin. Chill in refrigerator until firm, about 60 to 70 minutes.

Cool remaining aspic mixture for later use, but do not allow to congeal.

Second Layer—Cottage Cheese:
3 ounces cream cheese
12 ounces drained cottage cheese
1½ teaspoons salt
2 tablespoons finely chopped
  parsley
1 tablespoon finely chopped onion
2 tablespoons aspic mixture

Mix cream cheese, cottage cheese, salt, parsley, onion, and aspic mixture. Spread over firm layer of aspic in loaf tin.

Third Layer—Tomato Aspic:
Pour remaining aspic mixture over cottage cheese layer and chill in refrigerator about 1 hour or until firm.

Fourth Layer—Chopped Ham Salad:
5 ounces very finely chopped ham
  or luncheon meat
4 fluid ounces mayonnaise
1 ounce finely chopped celery
1 ounce finely chopped green
  pepper
1 teaspoon French mustard
1 tablespoon unflavoured gelatine
2 fluid ounces cold water

Combine meat, mayonnaise, celery, green pepper, and mustard.

Soften gelatine in water 5 minutes. Heat on low heat until gelatine is dissolved, add slowly to meat mixture; mix.

Spread over firm aspic in tin. Chill until firm. Serves 8 to 10.

The bright colour of the moulded salad ring filled in the centre with a salad of contrasting colour makes an appetizing sight.

MASTER VEGETABLE SALAD MOULD

1 tablespoon unflavoured gelatine
2 fluid ounces cold water
8 fluid ounces hot water
2 fluid ounces mild vinegar
1 tablespoon lemon juice
½ teaspoon salt
2 tablespoons sugar
⅛ teaspoon black pepper
6-8 ounces diced vegetables (below)
1 tablespoon grated onion

Use raw or cooked vegetables. Add more sugar if desired.

Soften gelatine in cold water 5 minutes. Dissolve in hot water. Add vinegar, lemon juice, salt, sugar, and pepper. Cool until syrupy.

Fold in vegetables. Turn into mould that has been rinsed in cold water. Chill until firm.

Unmould on lettuce. Serve with desired dressing. Serves 6.

Vegetable Salad Mould Variations

1. 2 ounces diced celery, 2 ounces diced cucumber, 1 ounce sliced radishes, and 2 tablespoons chopped green pepper.

2. 2 ounces shredded raw cabbage, 2 ounces grated raw carrots, 1 ounce diced apples, and 1 ounce chopped nuts.

3. 4 ounces shredded raw cabbage, 2 ounces chopped celery, and 2 tablespoons chopped green pepper or pimiento.

4. 2 ounces each chopped celery, grated raw carrots, and cooked peas.

5. 4 ounces shredded raw cabbage and 2 ounces sliced green olives.

6. 3 ounces each shredded raw cabbage and grated raw carrots.

Vary the fruit (or vegetable) filling with the season so your family will enjoy ring moulds the year round.

7. 3 ounces each canned asparagus tips, canned peas, grated raw carrots, and 2 tablespoons chopped canned pimiento.

8. 3 ounces each cubed pickled beetroots and chopped celery.

9. 2 ounces each chopped celery, diced cooked beetroots and shredded raw cabbage.

10. 4 ounces cooked peas and 3 ounces chopped roasted peanuts.

11. 2 ounces each diced celery, and diced or grated carrots, raw or cooked, and 4 ounces canned broad beans.

12. 4 ounces each canned red kidney beans and peas, 2 ounces chopped celery, 1 ounce chopped green pepper, and 1 tablespoon grated onion.

Moulded 'Kraut Cooler

MOULDED 'KRAUT COOLER

2 3-ounce packets lemon-flavoured gelatine
8 fluid ounces boiling water
16 fluid ounces cold water
4 fluid ounces soured cream
1 1-pound 4-ounce can sauerkraut, drained and cut into short lengths
1 large red apple, cored and diced
4 ounces diced cucumber
4 tablespoons grated onion

Dissolve gelatine in boiling water; add cold water and soured cream. Beat until well blended. Chill in refrigerator until slightly thickened.

Fold in sauerkraut and remaining ingredients; mix well and turn into 3-pint mould. If desired a layer of clear gelatine may be poured in bottom of mould. Chill in refrigerator until firm.

Unmould and garnish with cucumber slices and apple wedges. Serves 4 to 6.

EASY TOMATO ASPIC

1 packet lemon-flavoured gelatine
1 8-ounce can tomato sauce
8 fluid ounces hot water
½ teaspoon salt
1 tablespoon lemon juice

Dissolve gelatine in hot water. Stir until dissolved.

Add tomato sauce, salt, and lemon juice. Mix thoroughly. Chill until syrupy. Pour into moulds and chill until firm. Unmould on crisp lettuce leaves.

Serves 4.

SUNSET SALAD

1 tablespoon unflavoured gelatine
2 fluid ounces cold water
1 egg yolk
½ teaspoon salt
8 fluid ounces pineapple juice
2 tablespoons lemon juice
4 fluid ounces chilled evaporated milk
8 ounces shredded cabbage
8 ounces chopped canned pineapple
2 ounces grated carrots

Soak gelatine in cold water for at least 5 minutes.

Beat egg yolk, add salt, pineapple juice, and lemon juice. Bring to the boil, stirring constantly. Remove from heat, add gelatine and stir until gelatine is dissolved. Cool until mixture begins to thicken.

Whip the evaporated milk and fold the gelatine, cabbage, pineapple, and carrot into the milk. Pour into moulds that have been rinsed with cold water.

Serve on lettuce. Serves 8.

LEMON VEGETABLE MOULD

Dissolve 1 packet lemon-flavoured gelatine in 8 fluid ounces hot water. Add 8 fluid ounces cold water and 1 tablespoon lemon juice. Cool.

Add 4 ounces shredded raw cabbage, 3 ounces cooked peas, 3 ounces cooked diced carrots, and ¼ teaspoon salt.

Mix well. Pour into moulds and chill. Serves 4 to 6.

ALMOND TOMATO MOULD SALAD

14 fluid ounces tomato juice
1 tablespoon pickling spices
¼ teaspoon salt
1 packet lemon-flavoured gelatine
2 tablespoons lemon juice
1 teaspoon grated onion
1 teaspoon Worcestershire sauce
¼ teaspoon oregano
2 ounces diced cucumber
2 ounces diced celery
1 ounce blanched almonds, chopped

Heat tomato juice, spices, and salt to boiling point; strain. Add gelatine and stir until dissolved. Chill until slightly thickened.

Add remaining ingredients. Pour into 2-pint mould and chill until firm.

Tomato Mould Salad

Christmas Tree Salads

CHRISTMAS TREE SALADS

1 tablespoon unflavoured gelatine
2 fluid ounces cold water
1 1-pound can jellied cranberry
    sauce, crushed with a fork
4 ounces finely shredded cabbage
1 ounce diced celery
2 ounces chopped walnuts
Soft cream cheese, tinted green

Place gelatine in a bowl. Add cold water. Allow to stand 2 minutes.

Place bowl with gelatine in pan of boiling water. Heat until gelatine is dissolved. Mix with crushed cranberry sauce, cabbage, celery, and nuts.

Spoon into cone-shaped paper cups supported in small glasses. Chill until firm. Place on lettuce and peel off paper cups. Trim with softened cream cheese. Makes 4 to 6 salads.

JELLIED COLE SLAW

1 packet lemon-flavoured gelatine
8 fluid ounces hot water
1 small onion, grated
8 ounces crushed pineapple, with
    juice
1 chopped canned pimiento
3 tablespoons wine vinegar
¼ green pepper, finely chopped
¼ teaspoon salt
⅛ teaspoon black pepper
8 ounces shredded cabbage

Place gelatine in bowl and add hot water. Stir until gelatine dissolves. Mix in remaining ingredients.

Pour mixture into 10×6×2-in oven tin, then chill until set.

Cut into squares; arrange on lettuce. Serve salad dressing separately. Serves 6.

TOMATO RELISH SLICES

4 large firm tomatoes, peeled
1 tablespoon unflavoured gelatine
2 fluid ounces cold water
8 ounces cream cheese
1 tablespoon chopped celery
1 tablespoon chopped green pepper
1 tablespoon chopped pickle
1 tablespoon chilli pickle
¼ teaspoon salt
¼ teaspoon paprika

Cut a thin slice from the stem end of each tomato. Scoop pulp out carefully and drain upside down.

Soften gelatine in cold water; dissolve over hot water.

Gradually add to the cream cheese, blending until smooth. Add celery, green pepper, pickle, chilli pickle, salt, and paprika.

Pour into the tomato shells and chill until firm.

Slice with a sharp knife and arrange on crisp lettuce. Serve with mayonnaise. Serves 6.

CUCUMBER SALAD MOULD

1 packet lime-flavoured gelatine
16 fluid ounces hot water
1 tablespoon lemon juice or vinegar
1 teaspoon grated onion
½ teaspoon salt
Dash of pepper
4 ounces finely chopped cucumber

Dissolve gelatine in hot water. Add lemon juice or vinegar and seasoning. Chill.

When slightly thickened, fold in cucumber. Turn into square baking tin and chill until firm.

Cut into squares and serve on lettuce. Serves 4 to 6.

Pineapple and Carrot: Use orange-flavoured gelatine with grated carrot and pineapple instead of cucumber.

Pineapple and Cucumber: Substitute 4 ounces crushed canned pineapple for 2 ounces cucumber.

JELLIED GREEN PEPPER RINGS

4 large green peppers
1 packet lemon-flavoured gelatine
16 fluid ounces boiling water
4 ounces chopped celery
4 ounces chopped raw carrots
4 ounces shredded cabbage
4 ounces drained chopped cucum-
    bers

Cut the stem ends from green peppers; remove seeds.

Dissolve gelatine in boiling water. When gelatine is cool and somewhat thickened, add remaining ingredients.

Spoon gelatine-vegetable mixture into pepper shells and chill until firm.

Cut each pepper into 6 crosswise slices. For each portion of salad, place 2 slices on crisp lettuce.

Garnish with a radish rose and serve with mayonnaise. Serves 6.

TEXAS BUFFET MOULD

2 tablespoons unflavoured gelatine
4 fluid ounces cold water
16 fluid ounces boiling water
3 fluid ounces mild vinegar
2 tablespoons lemon juice
4 ounces sugar
1 teaspoon salt
8 ounces chopped celery
3 ounces diced raw carrots
4 ounces finely chopped cabbage
2 canned pimientos, finely chopped
1 red apple, unpeeled, diced

Soften gelatine in cold water and dissolve it in boiling water. Add vinegar, lemon juice, sugar, and salt. Chill until slightly thickened.

Fold in celery, carrots, cabbage, pimientos, and apple. Pour into 3-pint mould and chill until firm.

Unmould and surround with crisp lettuce. Serve with mayonnaise or salad dressing. Serves 10 to 12.

ASPARAGUS AND TOMATO MOULD

Simmer ¾ pint tomato juice, bit of bay leaf, 1 clove, ½ teaspoon salt, and ½ onion (sliced) 15 minutes.

Add 1 tablespoon unflavoured gelatine soaked in 4 tablespoons cold water. Dissolve. Strain and cool mixture.

When slightly thickened, add 8 ounces tender cooked or canned asparagus cut into ½-inch pieces. Turn into moulds and chill. Serves 4 to 6.

Pineapple Cucumber Mould

PINEAPPLE CUCUMBER MOULD

Pineapple Layer:
8 ounces crushed canned pineapple
   (not drained)
1 packet lemon-flavoured gelatine
½ teaspoon salt
2 ounces finely grated carrots

Cucumber Layer:
1 tablespoon unflavoured gelatine
2 fluid ounces cold water
8 fluid ounces mayonnaise
4 fluid ounces single cream
½ teaspoon salt
1 tablespoon grated onion
2 ounces finely chopped celery
2 ounces grated cucumber, drained

Pineapple Layer: Drain pineapple. Add enough water to syrup to make ¾ pint liquid. Heat to boiling; dissolve gelatine in it.

Chill to the consistency of unbeaten egg whites. Add salt, carrots, and crushed pineapple.

Turn into a 2½-pint ring or fancy mould. Chill until firm.

Cucumber Layer: Soften gelatine in cold water; dissolve over hot water.

Combine remaining ingredients. Add gelatine and blend. If desired, tint pale green. Pour over pineapple layer.

Chill until firm. Unmould and garnish with watercress. Serves 8 to 10.

CUCUMBER AND SOURED CREAM SALAD MOULD

1 tablespoon unflavoured gelatine
2 fluid ounces cold water
4 fluid ounces hot water
2 ounces sugar
4 ounces grated cucumber, well
   drained
8 fluid ounces soured cream
2 tablespoons lemon juice
1 tablespoon grated onion and juice
½ teaspoon salt
**Cucumber slices, black olives, and
   watercress**

Soften gelatine in cold water. Combine hot water and sugar and heat to boiling point. Add softened gelatine, stirring until dissolved. Chill until slightly thickened.

Fold in cucumber, soured cream, lemon juice, onion juice, and salt. Pour into mould and chill until firm.

Unmould and garnish with thin slices

of cucumber, black olives, and parsley or watercress. Serves 4.

PERFECTION SALAD

1 tablespoon unflavoured gelatine
2 fluid ounces cold water
8 fluid ounces hot water
2 ounces sugar
½ teaspoon salt
1 tablespoon lemon juice
2 fluid ounces vinegar
2 ounces finely shredded cabbage
4 ounces finely diced celery
1 canned pimiento, finely chopped
   or 2 tablespoons chopped red
   or green pepper

Soften gelatine in cold water in top of double boiler. Add hot water, sugar, and salt. Stir over boiling water until dissolved.

Add lemon juice and vinegar. Chill until mixture is consistency of unbeaten egg whites.

Stir in vegetables. Pour into mould. Chill until firm.

Unmould on lettuce. Garnish with mayonnaise. Or, cut salad into cubes and serve in green pepper cases. Serves 6.

JELLIED CABBAGE AND PINEAPPLE SALAD

First Layer:
2 tablespoons unflavoured gelatine
4 fluid ounces cold water
½ pint boiling water
4 ounces sugar
1 teaspoon salt
4 fluid ounces syrup drained from
   pineapple slices
4 fluid ounces vinegar
2 fluid ounces lemon juice
2 pineapple slices
Second Layer:
Canned pimiento
12 ounces finely shredded cabbage
4 ounces diced celery
1 ounce diced green pepper
1 diced canned pimiento
1 or 2 slices pineapple, diced
Mayonnaise

Add gelatine to cold water; allow to stand 5 minutes, then add boiling water, sugar, and salt; stir until dissolved. Add syrup drained from pineapple slices, vinegar, and lemon juice.

Pour a thin layer of this into an 8×4×4-inch loaf tin; chill until almost firm; arrange 2 slices of pineapple over the gelatine, centre with pimiento, chill until firm.

Mix shredded cabbage, celery, green pepper, pimiento, and diced pineapple; add, then fold in remaining gelatine. Pour over pineapple in tin; chill. Unmould and serve with mayonnaise. Serves 6 to 8.

Note: If you prefer to mould this in a ring, use pineapple chunks in place of slices, arranging them attractively in the mould or mixing them with the cabbage.

RING MOULDS WITH SALAD

1 tablespoon unflavoured gelatine
2 fluid ounces cold water
8 fluid ounces boiling water
1 tablespoon vinegar
1 tablespoon grated onion
2 tablespoons chopped parsley
6 hard-boiled eggs, chopped
2 tablespoons salad dressing
1 teaspoon salt
Dash of freshly ground pepper
Dash of paprika
Chicken, prawn, or vegetable salad

Soften gelatine in cold water and dissolve it in boiling water. Add the vinegar and chill until slightly thickened.

Combine onion, parsley, eggs, salad dressing, and seasonings. Add the gelatine. Pour into 4 individual ring moulds and chill until firm.

Unmould and fill the centres with chicken, prawn or vegetable salad. Garnish with endive or watercress. Serves 4.

HOME GARDEN BARBECUE SALAD

1 packet lemon-flavoured gelatine
½ pint hot water
1 8-ounce can tomato sauce
1½ tablespoons vinegar
½ teaspoon salt
Few grains black pepper
4 ounces diced cucumber
3 ounces sliced radishes
2 ounces sliced spring onions
1 teaspoon Aromat

Dissolve gelatine in hot water. Add tomato sauce, vinegar, salt, and pepper. Chill until consistency of mayonnaise.

Meanwhile combine vegetables; sprinkle with Aromat; toss well to mix.

Fold into gelatine mixture; pour into greased ring mould. Chill until firm.

Unmould; fill centre with lettuce. Serve with mayonnaise. Serves 4 to 6.

Home Garden Barbecue Salad

Gelatine Moulds with Meat and Poultry

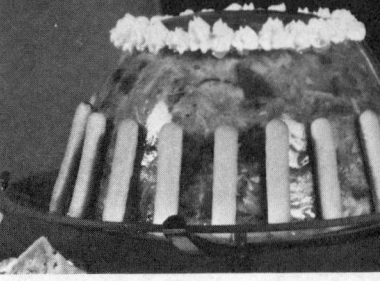

Lemon Chicken Mould. A tasty, versatile mould to serve as a starter spread or salad with crisp savoury biscuits.

MEAT LOAF MOULD
(With Leftover Meats)
1 tablespoon unflavoured gelatine
6 fluid ounces cold water
1 10½-ounce can condensed consommé
2 tablespoons lemon juice
¼ teaspoon salt
5 ounces finely diced leftover meat (lamb, veal, beef, pork, chicken, etc.)
2 ounces chopped celery
2 tablespoons chopped green pepper (optional)

Soften gelatine in 2 fluid ounces cold water. Combine soup with remaining 4 fluid ounces water and bring to boil.

Add softened gelatine and stir until dissolved. Add lemon juice and salt. Cool.

When mixture begins to thicken, fold in meat and celery and green pepper if used.

Turn into 1½-pint mould, loaf tin, or individual moulds that have been rinsed in cold water. Chill.

Unmould on lettuce. Serve with mayonnaise. Serves 6.

Variations: 12 fluid ounces boiling water and 2 stock cubes may be used instead of canned consommé. Homemade soup stock may also be used, in which case you would soften gelatine in 2 fluid ounces cold water and dissolve it in 12 fluid ounces hot soup.

Any desired combination of leftover vegetables such as sweetcorn, runner beans, cabbage, carrots, peas, etc., may be used instead of celery.

JELLIED HAM MOULD
2 tablespoons unflavoured gelatine
2 tablespoons cold water
1¾ pints consommé
1 tablespoon prepared horseradish
2 teaspoons French mustard
1 tablespoon grated onion
Dash of black pepper
1 pound minced cooked ham (or minced luncheon meat)

Soak gelatine in cold water. Heat con-

Jellied Ham Mould

sommé and add gelatine, stirring until dissolved. Cool.

Add horseradish, mustard, onion, and pepper. Place in refrigerator.

When mixture begins to thicken, stir in ham. Pour into ring mould, loaf tin, or decorative mould, which has been well rubbed with vegetable oil or rinsed with cold water. Serves 6 to 8.

MOULDED CHICKEN SALAD
1 tablespoon unflavoured gelatine
2 tablespoons lemon juice
2 chicken stock cubes
½ teaspoon salt
¾ pint hot water
3 fluid ounces mayonnaise
1 diced, peeled avocado
6 ounces diced, cooked chicken
3 ounces diced apples
Lettuce

Soften gelatine in lemon juice.

Dissolve stock cubes and salt in hot water; add gelatine. Cool to consistency of unbeaten egg white.

Fold in mayonnaise, avocado, chicken, and apples. Pour into 6 small moulds; refrigerate until firm. Unmould on crisp lettuce. Serves 4.

Moulded Chicken Salad

HAM MOUSSE
1 tablespoon unflavoured gelatine
2 tablespoons cold water
4 fluid ounces boiling water
1 teaspoon dry mustard
½ teaspoon salt
1 tablespoon prepared horseradish
½ teaspoon brown sugar
Dash of cayenne pepper
10 ounces minced cooked ham
8 fluid ounces whipping cream, whipped

Soften gelatine in cold water. Dissolve in boiling water. Chill until partially thickened.

Mix remaining ingredients except cream together. Add gelatine and mix lightly. Fold in cream.

Turn into mould. Chill until firm. Unmould and garnish with crisp lettuce, pickles, and radishes. Serves 6.

LEMON CHICKEN MOULD
1 chicken stock cube
8 fluid ounces boiling water
1 tablespoon unflavoured gelatine
12 ounces chopped, cooked chicken
1½ teaspoons salt
⅛ teaspoon black pepper
1 tablespoon lemon juice
1 ounce finely chopped celery
2 tablespoons finely chopped onion
2 tablespoons finely chopped sweet pickle
2 tablespoons chopped parsley
2 tablespoons chopped pimiento

Dissolve stock cube in boiling water. Remove and cool 4 tablespoons stock.

Soften gelatine in cooled stock. Add to remaining stock and stir until dissolved. Cool until mixture starts to thicken.

Add remaining ingredients. Pour into 2½-pint mixing bowl. Cool. Unmould.

Glaze: Dissolve 1 3-ounce packet lemon-flavoured gelatine in 8 fluid ounces hot water. Cool. Pour into mixing bowl.

Put chicken mould back into bowl pushing down gently to force gelatine up sides of mould. Chill.

Unmould. Garnish with rosettes of softened cream cheese and serve with assorted savoury biscuits.

HAM AND CABBAGE MOULDS
1 tablespoon unflavoured gelatine
2 fluid ounces cold water
½ pint hot water
1 tablespoon vinegar
½ teaspoon salt
6 fluid ounces mayonnaise or salad dressing
1 teaspoon French mustard
8 ounces cubed cooked ham
4 ounces shredded cabbage
2 tablespoons grated onion

Soften gelatine in cold water. Add hot water and stir to dissolve. Add vinegar and salt. Cool to room temperature.

Stir in mayonnaise and mustard. Chill until partially set.

Fold in ham, cabbage, and onion. Pour into fruit cups. Chill until firm. Serves 5.

Jellied Chicken Loaf

JELLIED CHICKEN LOAF

9 slices cooked chicken breast
2 tablespoons unflavoured gelatine
4 tablespoons cold water
1¾ pints chicken stock
1 pound diced cooked chicken
2 ounces diced pimiento
8 ounces diced celery
12 ounces cooked peas
4 tablespoons lemon juice
2 tablespoons Worcestershire sauce
Salt

Arrange chicken slices in well-greased loaf tin (9×5×3 inches).

Soften gelatine in cold water; dissolve in hot chicken stock. Cool; pour ¼ pint over chicken, chill until set.

Add diced chicken and rest of ingredients to remainder of gelatine mixture. Fill tin. Chill until firm, invert to unmould. Garnish as desired. Serves 8 to 10.

TOMATO-HAM SALAD MOULD

1½ tablespoons unflavoured gelatine
6 fluid ounces water
1 chicken stock cube
12 fluid ounces condensed tomato soup
1 tablespoon finely chopped onion
10 ounces minced cooked ham or luncheon meat
2 ounces chopped celery
2 ounces chopped canned pimiento
4 fluid ounces chilled evaporated milk, whipped
2 tomatoes, thinly sliced
2 hard-boiled eggs
4 fluid ounces mayonnaise
1 teaspoon mustard-with-horse-radish
Lettuce

Tomato-Ham Salad Mould

Soften gelatine in 3 fluid ounces cold water. Mix stock cube with rest of water and dissolve in hot soup.

Add onion and minced meat and cool until slightly thickened.

Fold in celery, pimiento, and stiffly whipped evaporated milk. Turn into heart-shaped mould (2½ pints) rinsed in cold water and chill until firm.

Unmould and surround with lettuce. Form heart outline with sliced egg white on top of mould. Fill with mayonnaise mixed with mustard-with-horseradish and arrange thinly sliced tomatoes round edge. Serves 6.

BUFFET PARTY LOAF

1 1-pound and 1 8-ounce can fruit cocktail, well-drained
2 tablespoons unflavoured gelatine
2 tablespoons vinegar
½ teaspoon cinnamon
⅛ teaspoon ground cloves
Syrup from fruit cocktail
2 12-ounce cans ham-type luncheon meat, very finely chopped
2 ounces celery, very finely chopped
1 ounce green pepper or olives, finely chopped
4 fluid ounces mayonnaise-type salad dressing
1 tablespoon French mustard
½ teaspoon salt

Arrange drained fruit cocktail in 9×5×3-inch loaf tin. Add gelatine, vinegar, cinnamon, cloves to cold syrup; dissolve over hot water. Carefully pour 2 fluid ounces dissolved gelatine over fruit.

Mix ham, celery, green pepper, or olives. Mix salad dressing with mustard, salt, rest of dissolved gelatine. Add to ham mixture; mix well.

Spread on fruit; chill until firm (at least 4 hours). Serves 8 to 10.

CHICKEN IN ASPIC (NORWEGIAN)

1 ready-to-cook chicken (3 to 3½ pounds), jointed
4 ounces diced carrot, celery, and onion
1 tip bay leaf
4 peppercorns
2 cloves
1 tablespoon salt
4 tablespoons unflavoured gelatine
4 fluid ounces cold water
1½ pints chicken broth
About 1 teaspoon salt
¼ teaspoon ground ginger
¼ teaspoon white pepper
1 tablespoon brandy or 2 tablespoons sherry
12 ounces cooked peas, drained

Cook chicken several hours in advance of preparing this dish as follows: Place in saucepan, with vegetables and spices tied in muslin, the salt and 1¼

pints boiling water. Simmer, covered, until meat is tender, 2½ to 3 hours.

Remove meat and strain broth. Chop meat, discarding skin and bones.

Meanwhile soften gelatine in 4 fluid ounces cold water about 5 minutes. Add to boiling chicken broth and stir until gelatine is dissolved. Season rather highly. Add more seasoning if necessary. Add brandy. Chill until syrupy.

Pour layer of broth in 3-pint mould. When almost firm, add chicken, broth, and peas, chilling each layer before adding next. Fill mould with remaining broth. Chill several hours or overnight.

Unmould. Serve with mayonnaise, garnishing as desired. Serves 12 to 14.

TWO-TONE JELLIED CHICKEN DINNER

Chicken Salad Layer:

1 tablespoon unflavoured gelatine
6 fluid ounces cold chicken broth
¼ teaspoon salt
¼ teaspoon Aromat
1 tablespoon lemon juice
6 fluid ounces mayonnaise
6 ounces diced steamed chicken
3 tablespoons finely diced green pepper
3 ounces thinly sliced celery

Pour gelatine into top of double saucepan; add cold chicken broth; dissolve over hot water. Cool.

Add salt, Aromat, and lemon juice; add slowly to mayonnaise, blending well. Stir in chicken, green pepper, and celery.

Turn into 2½-pint mould; chill until almost firm.

Vegetable Aspic Layer:

1 tablespoon unflavoured gelatine
¾ pint cold canned mixed vegetable juice
¼ teaspoon Aromat

Pour gelatine into top of double saucepan. Add vegetable juice and Aromat; dissolve over hot water. Chill to consistency of unbeaten egg white.

Spoon on top of first layer; chill until firm. Garnish with lettuce, cucumber slices, and radish roses. Serves 8.

Two-Tone Jellied Chicken Dinner

MOULDED CHICKEN AND TONGUE SLICES

1 tablespoon unflavoured gelatine
3 tablespoons cold water
¾ pint chicken stock
2 teaspoons grated onion
1½ teaspoons salt
⅛ teaspoon black pepper
½ teaspoon Aromat
¼ teaspoon ground poultry seasoning
8 to 12 ounces cooked smoked
   tongue, sliced
12 ounces diced cooked chicken
3 ounces chopped celery
4 fluid ounces mayonnaise

Soften gelatine in cold water. Heat chicken stock with onion and seasonings to boiling; dissolve softened gelatine in hot mixture. Strain a little hot gelatine liquid over bottom of loaf tin; chill until firm.

Arrange overlapping slices of tongue on top of firm gelatine. Cover tongue slices with additional gelatine. Chill.

Layer chicken and celery alternately on top of tongue.

Stir mayonnaise into remaining gelatine; mix well and pour over chicken and celery. Chill until firm.

Unmould on bed of crisp watercress. Garnish with thinly sliced cucumber, radish roses, and olives. Serves 6 to 8.

GARLIC SAUSAGE MOUSSE

1 tablespoon unflavoured gelatine
2 fluid ounces cold water
6 fluid ounces mayonnaise
6 ounces garlic sausage spread
1½ teaspoons grated onion
2 ounces chopped celery
1 ounce chopped green pepper
2 ounces chopped sweet pickles

Soften gelatine in cold water; dissolve over hot water.

Blend mayonnaise with garlic sausage, onion, celery, green pepper, and pickles.

Stir in dissolved gelatine. Pour mixture into a pint mould; chill until firm.

Unmould and garnish with lettuce. Surround with chilled frankfurters and slices of corned beef. Serves 6 to 8.

Devilled Ham Mousse

CHICKEN ALMOND MOUSSE

1½ tablespoons unflavoured gelatine
1¼ pints chicken stock or broth
1 teaspoon salt
¼ teaspoon black pepper
1 teaspoon grated onion
⅛ teaspoon paprika
3 egg yolks
2 ounces finely chopped almonds
12 ounces diced cooked chicken
8 fluid ounces whipping cream,
   whipped

Soften gelatine in 4 fluid ounces cold chicken stock. Add salt, pepper, onion, and paprika to remaining stock and heat.

Stir a little of hot stock into egg yolks. Mix well and return to double boiler. Cook over hot water until smooth and thick. Strain if necessary.

Stir in and blend softened gelatine. Cool until partially thickened.

Fold in nuts, chicken, and whipped cream. Turn into ring mould. Chill until firm.

Unmould on serving dish. Fill centre with crisp lettuce. Garnish with tomato wedges. Serves 6.

Variation: Vary seasonings by adding a little horseradish and dry mustard.

CHICKEN MOUSSE

1 tablespoon unflavoured gelatine
2 fluid ounces cold water
4 fluid ounces milk, scalded
1 10½ ounce can condensed cream
   of chicken soup
12 ounces minced cooked chicken
2 fluid ounces mayonnaise
1 tablespoon grated onion
½ teaspoon salt
¼ teaspoon black pepper
8 fluid ounces whipping cream

Soak gelatine in cold water 5 minutes; dissolve in hot milk. Combine with undiluted soup, chicken, mayonnaise, onion, salt and pepper; blend well. Chill until almost set.

Whip cream stiff; fold into chicken mixture. Pour into 2½-pint mould rinsed with cold water. Chill about 4 hours or until set.

Unmould just before serving and garnish with mayonnaise. Accompany with marinated asparagus, cranberry sauce, and savoury crackers. Serves 8.

PRESSED CHICKEN LOAF

1 3½- to 4-pound chicken
1 carrot
1 slice onion
1 whole clove
2 peppercorns
2 teaspoons salt
1 tablespoon unflavoured gelatine
2 fluid ounces cold water

1 ounce chopped parsley
6 hard-boiled eggs, sliced

Cut chicken in pieces. Cover with hot water; add carrot, onion, and seasonings. Cook slowly until tender. Remove chicken and cook stock down to ¾ pint.

Soften gelatine in cold water. Chop carrot cooked with chicken and combine with parsley. Arrange egg slices on bottom of well greased loaf tin. Alternate layers of chicken, egg, and parsley-carrot mixture.

Dissolve softened gelatine in hot stock. Pour over arrangement in loaf tin. Cover with greaseproof paper. Place weight on top to hold chicken mixture in stock. Chill overnight.

Unmould. Garnish with crisp lettuce. Slice for serving. Serves 6 to 8.

CHICKEN SAUTERNES SOUFFLÉ SALAD

1 packet lemon-flavoured gelatine
8 fluid ounces hot water
4 fluid ounces Sauternes or other
   white wine
1 tablespoon lemon juice
4 fluid ounces mayonnaise
½ teaspoon salt
4 to 5 drops Tabasco sauce
6 ounces diced, cooked chicken
2 ounces diced celery
1½ ounces browned, slivered,
   blanched almonds

Dissolve gelatine in hot water. Add wine, lemon juice, mayonnaise, salt, and Tabasco. Blend well with rotary beater.

Pour into freezer tray. Quick-chill in freezing unit (without changing control) 20 to 25 minutes, or until firm about 1 inch from edge but soft in centre.

Turn mixture into bowl and whip with rotary beater until fluffy. Fold in chicken, celery, and almonds. Pour into individual moulds.

Chill until firm in refrigerator (not freezing unit) 30 to 60 minutes.

Unmould and garnish with lettuce. Serve with additional mayonnaise, if desired. Serves 4.

Chicken Mousse

Gelatine Moulds with Fish and Shellfish

PRAWN MOULDS

1 packet lime-flavoured gelatine
8 fluid ounces hot water
1 teaspoon salt
1 teaspoon dry mustard
1 tablespoon prepared horseradish
1 tablespoon lemon juice
8 fluid ounces soured cream
1 tablespoon chopped chives
8 ounces cooked or canned prawns
4 ounces drained grated cucumber
4 tablespoons chopped parsley

Dissolve gelatine in hot water. Cool. Add salt, mustard, horseradish, lemon juice, and soured cream. Chill until slightly thickened.

Add chives, prawns, cucumber, and parsley. Pour into 6 or 8 individual moulds. Chill until firm.

Unmould on crisp lettuce. Garnish with watercress. Serves 6 to 8.

SEA GARDEN SALAD

1 pound fillet of halibut or other white fish
½ teaspoon Aromat
2 packets lime-flavoured gelatine
1¼ pints hot water
8 fluid ounces pineapple juice
2 tablespoons lime juice
8 ounces diced canned pineapple
2 ounces seedless grapes (optional)
4 ounces diced melon

"Poach" fish in water to cover to which Aromat has been added, about 10 minutes or until done. Drain; cool; break into small chunks.

Dissolve gelatine in hot water; add pineapple juice and lime juice. Chill to consistency of unbeaten egg white.

Fold in fruits and fish. Turn into lightly greased mould. Chill until firm.

Unmould on lettuce. Serve with mayonnaise. Serves 6 to 8.

Double Decker Salmon Loaf

DOUBLE DECKER SALMON LOAF

Salmon Layer:
1 tablespoon unflavoured gelatine
½ pint cold water
4 ounces chopped celery
1 7¾ ounce can salmon
1 tablespoon grated onion
4 fluid ounces sharp mayonnaise
1 tablespoon French mustard
Consommé Layer:
1 tablespoon unflavoured gelatine
4 fluid ounces cold water
1 10½ ounce can condensed consommé
2 tablespoons lemon juice
Few dashes Tabasco sauce

Salmon Layer: Soften gelatine in 2 fluid ounces cold water 5 minutes. Heat remaining water to boiling and pour over gelatine; stir until dissolved.

Add celery, flaked salmon, onion, mayonnaise, and mustard. Season with salt if needed. Mix well and pour into a loaf tin and chill. When almost firm, begin consommé layer.

Consommé Layer: Soften gelatine in cold water for 5 minutes. Add hot consommé and stir until dissolved. Add lemon juice and Tabasco sauce. Cool. Pour over salmon mixture.

Chill until firm. Unmould on serving dish. Serves 6 to 8.

Variation: Tuna fish may be used instead of salmon.

TUNA FISH-COTTAGE CHEESE MOULD SAUTERNES

2 tablespoons unflavoured gelatine
2 fluid ounces cold water
8 fluid ounces Sauternes, Rhine, or other white wine
8 fluid ounces undiluted evaporated milk
8 fluid ounces mayonnaise
1 pound cottage cheese with chives
1 6½-ounce can tuna fish
4 ounces finely diced celery
2 tablespoons chopped parsley
Salt and pepper to taste

Soften gelatine in mixture of cold water and 2 fluid ounces wine for 5 minutes; dissolve over boiling water.

Add remaining wine, milk, and mayonnaise; beat until well blended. Chill until slightly thickened.

Add remaining ingredients and mix well. Pour into a greased fish mould or loaf tin; chill until firm.

Unmould and surround with crisp lettuce and serve with French dressing or mayonnaise. Serves 8.

Sea Garden Salad

TUNA FISH MOUSSE

2 tablespoons unflavoured gelatine
4 fluid ounces cold water
8 fluid ounces mayonnaise
2 6½- or 7-ounce cans tuna fish
2 ounces chopped cucumber
3 tablespoons chopped stuffed olives
2 fluid ounces lemon juice
1½ teaspoons prepared horseradish
2 teaspoons onion juice
¼ teaspoon salt
¼ teaspoon paprika
8 fluid ounces whipping cream, whipped

Soften gelatine in cold water. Dissolve over boiling water and stir into mayonnaise.

Flake tuna fish and add with remaining ingredients except cream. Mix well.

Fold in whipped cream. Pour into 2½-pint mould. Chill until firm. Unmould on crisp lettuce. Serves 8.

Prawn Mousse: Substitute cooked or canned flaked prawns for tuna.

Tuna Fish-Cottage Cheese Mould Sauternes

LOBSTER IN ASPIC

2½ tablespoons unflavoured gelatine
4 fluid ounces cold water
¾ pint boiling water
1½ teaspoons salt
4 tablespoons sugar
2 fluid ounces lemon juice
4 fluid ounces lobster liquid or cold water
1 pound shredded, cooked lobster
4 ounces blanched almonds

Soak gelatine in cold water 5 minutes. Add boiling water, salt, sugar, and lemon juice. Cool.

Add lobster liquid, shredded lobster and blanched almonds. Pour into a mould that has been dipped in cold water. Chill until firm. Unmould and serve on lettuce. Serves 6.

SALMON AND CUCUMBER MOUSSE

1 tablespoon unflavoured gelatine
2 fluid ounces cold water
1 stock cube
4 fluid ounces boiling water
4 fluid ounces mayonnaise
1 teaspoon Worcestershire sauce
1 tablespoon onion, grated
1 tablespoon vinegar
1 teaspoon salt
¼ teaspoon black pepper
1 pound flaked cooked or canned salmon
6 ounces diced cucumber
4 fluid ounces whipping cream, whipped

Soften gelatine in cold water. Dissolve stock cube in boiling water and add to gelatine. Stir until gelatine dissolves.

Allow to cool. Add mayonnaise, Worcestershire, onion, vinegar, salt, and pepper. Blend well and chill until thick.

Beat with rotary egg beater until light and foamy. Fold in salmon, cucumber, and whipped cream.

Turn into 2-pint fish-shaped mould. Chill until firm. Serve on lettuce with slices of cucumber. Serve with mayonnaise. Serves 4.

LEMON-TUNA FISH MOUSSE

1 packet lemon-flavoured gelatine
¾ pint boiling water
2 tablespoons vinegar
1 tablespoon grated onion
1 7-ounce can tuna fish, drained and flaked
1 ounce chopped green pepper
1 canned pimiento, chopped
½ teaspoon salt
2 teaspoons prepared horseradish
8 fluid ounces whipping cream, whipped

Dissolve gelatine in boiling water; add vinegar and onion; chill until partially firm.

Combine remaining ingredients, except cream; fold into gelatine mixture. Fold in whipped cream.

Pour into greased 2-pint mould; chill until firm. Unmould on lettuce. Serves 4 to 6.

JELLIED FISH SALAD

1 tablespoon unflavoured gelatine
4 tablespoons cold water
½ teaspoon salt
½ teaspoon celery salt
4 tablespoons vinegar
4 tablespoons water
2 eggs, beaten
1 pound flaked cooked or canned fish

Soften gelatine in cold water. Add seasonings, vinegar, and water to eggs. Cook over boiling water until thick-ened, stirring constantly.

Add gelatine and stir until it is dissolved.

Add fish and mix thoroughly. Pour into individual moulds, or large ring mould and chill. Serves 6.

MOULDED TUNA FISH LOAF

1 tablespoon unflavoured gelatine
2 fluid ounces cold water
8 fluid ounces hot water
6 fluid ounces mayonnaise or salad dressing
1 tablespoon lemon juice
1 tablespoon French mustard
2 6½- or 7-ounce cans tuna fish, flaked
4 ounces thinly sliced celery
1½ ounces diced cucumber
1 tablespoon thinly sliced spring onions

Soften gelatine in cold water. Add hot water and stir to dissolve gelatine. Cool to room temperature.

Blend in mayonnaise, lemon juice, and mustard. Chill until partially set.

Fold in tuna fish, celery, cucumber, and onion. Pour into 9×5×3-inch loaf tin. Chill until firm.

Garnish with tomato slices and lemon wedges, if desired. Serves 4 to 6.

PRAWN SALAD MOULD

2 tablespoons unflavoured gelatine
1 pint cold water
8 fluid ounces boiling water
2 fluid ounces lemon juice
½ teaspoon salt
1 teaspoon Worcestershire sauce
1 or 2 drops Tabasco sauce
1 teaspoon grated onion
1 pound prawns, cooked and cleaned
4 ounces diced celery
1½ ounces diced green pepper
2 ounces sliced pimiento stuffed olives
Devilled eggs
Sliced olives

Soften gelatine in 8 fluid ounces cold water. Add 8 fluid ounces boiling water and stir until gelatine is dissolved.

Add remaining water and lemon juice. Stir in salt, Worcestershire, Tabasco, and onion.

Pour thin layer of gelatine mixture into 2-pint mould and arrange prawns in it. Chill until set.

Chill remaining gelatine mixture until slightly thickened, then fold in celery, pepper, and olives. Carefully pour over prawns. Chill until firm.

Unmould and garnish with additional sliced olives, devilled eggs, and lettuce. Serve with mayonnaise or soured cream dressing. Serves 6.

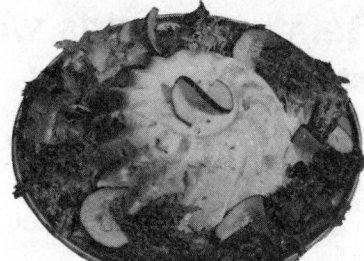

Tuna Fish Soufflé Salad

MOULDED SEAFOOD OR VEGETABLE SALAD TO FREEZE

1 tablespoon unflavoured gelatine
3 fluid ounces cold water
1 6-ounce can frozen lemonade concentrate
4 tablespoons tomato ketchup
8 fluid ounces soured cream

Soak gelatine in cold water, then heat in top of double boiler until dissolved. Remove from double boiler.

Add concentrate for lemonade, ketchup and soured cream.

Freeze plain in mould or containers; or add 6 ounces of any cooked seafood, poultry, meat, or cooked vegetables, and freeze.

TUNA FISH SOUFFLÉ SALAD

1 packet lemon-flavoured gelatine
8 fluid ounces hot water
4 fluid ounces cold water
4 fluid ounces mayonnaise
1 tablespoon lemon juice
¼ teaspoon salt
Dash of black pepper
3 ounces flaked tuna fish
¼ cucumber, diced
1 hard-boiled egg, diced
1 tablespoon chopped onion

Dissolve gelatine in hot water. Mix in cold water, mayonnaise, lemon juice, salt, and pepper.

Pour into freezer tray. Quick-chill in freezing unit 15 to 20 minutes, or until firm about 1 inch from edge but soft in centre.

Turn into bowl and whip with rotary egg beater. Fold in remaining ingredients; pour into 2-pint mould. Chill in refrigerator until firm (about 60 minutes). Unmould onto a bed of endives; garnish with cucumber slices. Serves 4 to 6.

Prawn Salad Mould

Moulded Prawn and Egg Buffet Style

MOULDED PRAWN AND EGG BUFFET STYLE

Prawn Salad:
1 tablespoon unflavoured gelatine
4 fluid ounces cold water
2 tablespoons lemon juice
½ teaspoon salt
¼ teaspoon Worcestershire sauce
⅛ teaspoon Tabasco sauce
6 fluid ounces salad dressing
1½ teaspoons grated onion
2 ounces finely diced celery
1 ounce finely diced green pepper
1 chopped canned pimiento
12 ounces fresh, frozen or canned
    prawns cut in small pieces

Sprinkle gelatine on cold water to soften. Place over boiling water and stir until gelatine is dissolved.

Add lemon juice, salt, Worcestershire sauce, and Tabasco sauce. Cool.

Add salad dressing; mix in remaining ingredients. Turn into large or individual moulds and chill until firm. Serves 6.

Egg Salad: Follow recipe for prawn salad increasing salt to 1 teaspoon and substituting 4 hard-boiled eggs (chopped) for the prawns. Serves 6.

Note: To serve 12 from either mould as illustrated in picture, double all ingredients and turn into 2½-pint mould.

TUNA FISH LUNCHEON MOULD

1 tablespoon unflavoured gelatine
4 fluid ounces cold water
8 fluid ounces mayonnaise
3 fluid ounces lemon juice
3 ounces diced celery
1 ounce diced green pepper
Salt and pepper
2 6½-ounce cans grated or flaked
    tuna fish

Soften gelatine in cold water and dissolve it over hot water. Combine mayonnaise and lemon juice and add to celery, green pepper, seasonings, and tuna which have been tossed together.

Add gelatine to mixture, and mix lightly. Pour into ring mould and chill until firm.

Unmould ring on endive arranged on large round serving dish. Fill centre with radish roses. Serves 6 to 8.

MASTER SOUFFLÉ SALAD

Ingredients:
1 packet lemon flavoured gelatine
8 fluid ounces hot water
4 fluid ounces cold water
3 tablespoons vinegar or canned
    lemon juice
4 fluid ounces mayonnaise
¼ teaspoon salt
dash of black pepper
4 ounces chopped celery
4 tablespoons chopped parsley
1½ tablespoons grated onion

Choose One:
1 1-pound can salmon, drained and
    flaked
2 7-ounce cans tuna, drained and
    flaked
1 12-ounce can luncheon meat,
    chopped
1 1-pound can peas, peas and
    carrots, or mixed vegetables,
    drained. (Use 8 fluid ounces
    hot tomato juice in place of
    hot water.)
1 12-ounce can boned chicken,
    diced
2 6-ounce cans boned turkey, diced
1 12-ounce can tongue

Dissolve gelatine in hot water. Add cold water, vinegar or lemon juice, mayonnaise, salt, and pepper; blend well with rotary beater; pour into freezer tray.

Chill in freezing unit 15 to 20 minutes, or until firm round edges but soft in centre.

Turn into bowl; whip with rotary beater until fluffy; fold in remaining ingredients. Pour into 2-pint mould or 6 individual moulds.

Chill (not in freezing unit) 30 to 60 minutes, or until firm. Unmould; garnish with watercress. Serves 6.

Note: For Fruit Soufflé Salad, omit pepper, parsley, and onion; reduce salt to ⅛ teaspoon and vinegar to 1 tablespoon. Choose 1- or 1½-pound can fruit cocktail, peaches, apricots, grapefruit sections, or pears. Use syrup drained from fruit as part of liquid. Follow same directions.

CANADIAN SALMON MOULD

2 tablespoons unflavoured gelatine
4 fluid ounces cold water
8 fluid ounces hot chicken broth or
    stock
8 fluid ounces salad dressing or
    mayonnaise
3 tablespoons chilli pickle
2 tablespoons lemon juice
1 tablespoon grated onion
½ teaspoon Worcestershire sauce
Dash of cayenne pepper
½ teaspoon Aromat
Salt to taste
8 ounces canned or cooked salmon
4 ounces finely diced celery
2 ounces sliced stuffed olives

Soften gelatine in cold water; dissolve in hot chicken broth.

Cool slightly. Add slowly to mayonnaise, blending well after each addition.

Add chilli pickle, lemon juice, onion, Worcestershire sauce, cayenne, Aromat, and salt. Chill to consistency of unbeaten egg whites.

Flake salmon; fold in with celery and olives. Turn into a greased 2-pint mould; chill until firm.

Unmould on crisp lettuce. Serve with any desired dressing. Serves 8.

Variations: Use 1 packet lemon- or lime-flavoured gelatine instead of unflavoured gelatine. Substitute water for chicken broth.

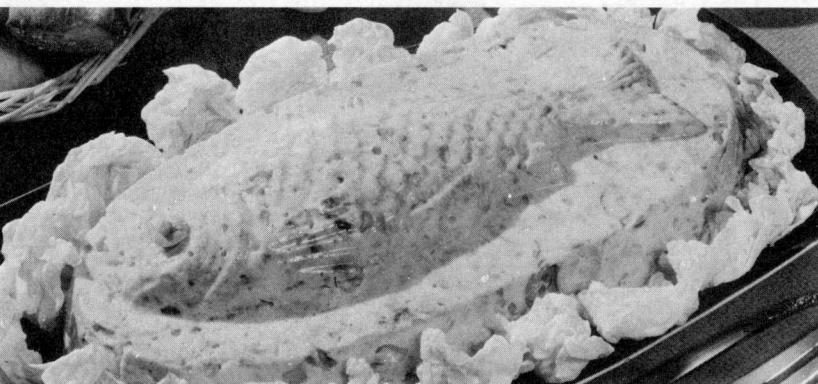

Canadian Salmon Mould

AVOCADO AND TUNA FISH LOAF

Tuna Fish Layer:
1 tablespoon unflavoured gelatine
4 fluid ounces cold water
6 fluid ounces boiling water
3 tablespoons lemon juice
1 teaspoon salt
1 7-ounce can tuna fish, flaked
4 ounces diced celery
1 diced canned pimiento

Sprinkle gelatine on cold water to soften. Add boiling water and stir until gelatine is dissolved.

Add lemon juice and salt. Chill until mixture is consistency of unbeaten egg white. Fold in flaked tuna fish, celery, and pimiento.

Turn into a 9×5×3-inch loaf tin; chill until almost firm.

Avocado Layer:
1 tablespoon unflavoured gelatine
6 fluid ounces cold water
1 teaspoon sugar
2 tablespoons lemon juice
1 large avocado, peeled and mashed
4 fluid ounces soured cream
4 fluid ounces mayonnaise
1 teaspoon salt
⅛ teaspoon Tabasco sauce

Sprinkle gelatine on cold water to soften. Place over boiling water and stir until gelatine is dissolved.

Add sugar and 1 tablespoon lemon juice.

Chill until mixture is consistency of unbeaten egg white.

Immediately after mashing avocado, add remaining tablespoon lemon juice, soured cream, mayonnaise, salt, and Tabasco. Fold in gelatine mixture.

Turn on top of almost firm first layer; chill until firm.

Unmould; if desired, garnish with additional avocado slices, black and stuffed olives. Serves 8.

Avocado and Tuna Fish Loaf

PRAWN PARTY RING SALAD

2 tablespoons unflavoured gelatine
6 fluid ounces cold water
12 fluid ounces hot water
2 fluid ounces honey
¾ teaspoon salt
3 fluid ounces lemon juice
8 fluid ounces mayonnaise
8 ounces cooked prawn pieces
4 ounces chopped celery
1 tablespoon grated onion
2 tablespoons chopped parsley
2 tablespoons chopped pimiento
Endives
Spinach leaves
Cooked whole prawns
Pimiento strips
8 fluid ounces mayonnaise
½ teaspoon grated lemon rind
2 teaspoons lemon juice
Thin lemon slices

Soften gelatine in cold water. Add hot water, honey, salt, and lemon juice. Chill.

Stir mixture into 8 fluid ounces mayonnaise. Pour 4 fluid ounces of mixture in an 8½-inch ring mould. Chill until firm.

To remaining mixture add prawn pieces, celery, onion, parsley, and pimiento. Chill until beginning to thicken. Pour into ring mould and chill until firm.

Unmould on serving dish. Place endive and spinach leaves in centre of mould. Garnish with whole prawns and additional endive and spinach leaves. Place pimiento strips on top of mould in a pattern.

Combine 8 fluid ounces mayonnaise with lemon rind and juice. Serve salad garnished with thin slices of lemon. Serves 6.

SALMON MOUSSE

1 tablespoon unflavoured gelatine
2 fluid ounces cold water
8 fluid ounces mayonnaise
4 fluid ounces single cream or top of milk
2 tablespoons lemon juice
1 teaspoon salt
4 ounces finely chopped celery
2 ounces finely chopped sweet pickles
1 tablespoon grated onion
2 teaspoons prepared horseradish
1 1-pound can salmon, drained and flaked

Soften gelatine in cold water; dissolve over hot water.

Combine remaining ingredients. Add gelatine and blend. Pour into a 2-pint mould. Chill until firm.

Unmould and garnish with parsley, devilled eggs, and slices of lemon. Serves 6 to 8.

Prawn Party Ring Salad

MOULDED KING CRAB SALAD

2 6-ounce packets frozen king crabmeat
4 ounces chopped celery
2 fluid ounces French dressing
1 packet lemon-flavoured gelatine
12 fluid ounces hot water
4 fluid ounces lemon juice
½ teaspoon salt
Watercress or parsley
4 fluid ounces mayonnaise or salad dressing

Thaw crabmeat and remove any cartilage. Marinate crabmeat and celery in French dressing.

Dissolve gelatine in hot water. Add lemon juice and salt. Place about ⅓ of the gelatine in a ring mould; chill until almost congealed.

Arrange crabmeat and celery attractively over the gelatine base and cover with remaining gelatine. Chill until firm.

Unmould on round serving dish and garnish with watercress or parsley. Fill centre with mayonnaise. Serves 6.

PRAWN-AVOCADO ASPIC

1 tablespoon unflavoured gelatine
2 tablespoons cold water
8 fluid ounces boiling water
1 large avocado, peeled and sieved
1½ tablespoons lemon juice
¾ teaspoon salt
½ teaspoon Worcestershire sauce
dash of Tabasco sauce
1 canned pimiento, diced
6-8 ounces cooked or canned prawns, cleaned

Soften gelatine in cold water. Dissolve in boiling water. Add avocado, seasonings, and pimiento. Chill until mixture begins to thicken.

Add prawns and turn into mould rinsed in cold water. Chill until firm. Unmould on lettuce. Serves 6.

Salmon Mousse

Gelatine Moulds with Cheese

Pineapple Cheese Mould

CHRISTMAS SALAD MOULD

1st Layer:

1 tablespoon unflavoured gelatine
4 fluid ounces cold water
6 fluid ounces hot water
½ teaspoon salt
1 tablespoon lemon juice
8 ounces cream cheese, softened
green pepper: cut in shape of holly
    leaves (about 8)
pimiento: cut in shape of holly
    berries (about 12)

Soften gelatine in cold water; add hot water and salt. Stir until gelatine dissolves. Add lemon juice and cream cheese; mix until smooth.

Pour 3 tablespoons in bottom of 9-inch ring mould. Press green pepper holly leaves and pimiento berries alternately in design on bottom of mould.

Chill until firm, then add remaining gelatine mixture and chill.

2nd Layer:

1½ pints tomato juice
1 tablespoon chopped onion
1 teaspoon salt
dash of cayenne pepper
2 tablespoons unflavoured gelatine
4 fluid ounces cold water
1 teaspoon Worcestershire sauce
1 teaspoon lemon juice
2 ounces chopped celery

Combine tomato juice, onion, salt, and cayenne. Simmer 15 minutes.

Soften gelatine in cold water. Add Worcestershire sauce, lemon juice, softened gelatine, and celery to tomato juice mixture. Cool and pour over cream cheese layer.

Chill. Unmould. Fill centre with leaves of lettuce. Serves 8 to 10.

Christmas Salad Mould

PINEAPPLE CHEESE MOULD

1 tablespoon unflavoured gelatine
2 fluid ounces cold water
1 8-ounce can crushed pineapple
1 tablespoon lemon juice
½ teaspoon salt
4 ounces grated mild Cheddar
    cheese
8 fluid ounces whipping cream,
    whipped
strawberries
endive

Soften gelatine in cold water. Heat 4 fluid ounces juice from crushed pineapple and, when hot, add to gelatine.

Cool until partially thickened, then fold in 8 ounces well-drained crushed pineapple, the lemon juice, salt, cheese, and the whipped cream.

Pour into a round greased ring mould and return to refrigerator until firm. Unmould onto large round serving dish. Garnish with strawberries and endive. Serve with salad dressing. Serves 6.

BUFFET PARTY MOULD

1¼ pounds canned crushed pine-
    apple
1 3-ounce packet lime-flavoured
    gelatine
6 ounces cream cheese
1 chopped canned pimiento
8 fluid ounces whipping cream,
    whipped
4 ounces diced celery
4 ounces chopped walnuts

Heat pineapple to boiling point; add gelatine and stir until dissolved. Chill until partially set.

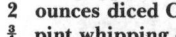

Soften cream cheese; stir in pimiento; add to gelatine mixture and blend. Fold in whipped cream, celery, and nuts.

Pour into 2½-pint fluted mould. Chill until firm. Serves 6 to 8.

ROQUEFORT-CREAM CHEESE MOULD

8 ounces Roquefort or blue cheese
6 ounces cream cheese
1 tablespoon unflavoured gelatine
4 fluid ounces whipping cream,
    whipped

Mash cheeses to a smooth paste.

Soften gelatine in 4 fluid ounces cold water and stir over hot water until dissolved.

Add cheese paste to whipped cream and stir in gelatine. Turn into mould rinsed in cold water. Chill until firm. Serve with mayonnaise or French dressing. Serves 6 to 8.

BLUE CHEESE-COTTAGE CHEESE MOULDS

1 packet lemon-flavoured gelatine
8 fluid ounces boiling water
4 fluid ounces cold water
4 tablespoons mayonnaise
12 ounces cottage cheese
1 ounce crumbled blue cheese

Dissolve gelatine in hot water. Add cold water. Chill until of a jelly-like consistency.

Beat with a rotary beater until frothy. Add mayonnaise, cottage cheese, and blue cheese and mix well.

Pour into individual moulds which have been greased or dipped in cold water. Makes 8 individual moulds.

SPRING BEAUTY SALAD

1½ tablespoons unflavoured gelatine
3 tablespoons cold water
8 ounces cottage cheese, sieved
4 ounces Cheddar cheese, grated
1 teaspoon salt
⅛ teaspoon white pepper
2 tablespoons chopped canned
    pimiento
2 tablespoons chopped green
    pepper
2 ounces diced Cheddar cheese
¾ pint whipping cream, whipped

Soften gelatine in cold water 5 minutes and dissolve over hot water.

Soften cottage cheese with a little single cream and press through sieve. Add grated cheese, gelatine, seasonings, pimiento, pepper, and diced cheese. (Some of diced cheese may be sprinkled in bottom of mould.)

Fold in stiffly beaten cream. Turn mixture into wet mould and chill.

Serve on large round plate with centre filled with fresh fruit or vegetable salad. Garnish with crisp lettuce, endive, or watercress. Serves 6.

Spring Beauty Salad

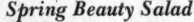

APPLE AND CHEESE LAYERED MOULD

1 packet lemon-flavoured gelatine
¾ pint boiling water
2 tablespoons lemon juice
½ teaspoon salt
1 diced red apple
1 teaspoon sugar
3 ounces cream cheese
2 ounces chopped nuts

Dissolve gelatine in boiling water. Add 1 tablespoon lemon juice and salt. Chill.

Combine apple, sugar, and remaining lemon juice. When gelatine mixture is slightly thickened, fold apples into half the mixture. Turn into mould and chill until firm.

Place remaining gelatine mixture in a bowl of crushed ice and beat with a rotary beater until thick and fluffy like whipped cream. Fold in mashed cheese and nuts. Pour over gelatine-apple layer and chill until firm.

To serve, cut in slices and arrange on lettuce leaves. Top with mayonnaise or any desired dressing. Serves 6.

CRANBERRY-COTTAGE CHEESE SALADS

1 tablespoon unflavoured gelatine
4 tablespoons cold water
1 1-pound can cranberry sauce (jellied or whole)
2 teaspoons prepared horseradish
¾ teaspoon dry mustard
4 tablespoons lemon juice
1 teaspoon grated lemon rind
¼ teaspoon salt
pinch of cayenne pepper
4 tablespoons cottage cheese

Place gelatine in a basin. Add cold water. Allow to stand 2 minutes. Place the basin in pan of boiling water until gelatine dissolves.

Combine cranberry sauce and gelatine. Stir in other ingredients, beating slightly to blend.

Spoon into moulds which have been rinsed in cold water. Chill until firm.

Unmould and serve garnished with endive. Serves 4 to 6. An excellent accompaniment for fish.

Cranberry-Cottage Cheese Salads

LAYERED CHEESE AND FRUIT SALAD

First Layer—Fruit Gelatine:
¾ pint hot water
2 packets lime-flavoured gelatine
¾ pint pear juice drained from 1 1-pound can of pears (add water to make up to ¾ pint)
2 medium bananas
16 to 20 halves of maraschino cherries

Heat water in 3-pint saucepan until it boils. Remove from heat and add lime gelatine. Stir until dissolved, add pear juice and water mixture; cool.

Pour ¼ pint of gelatine mixture into lightly greased 9×5×3-inch loaf tin, and chill in refrigerator until firm. Chill remaining mixture in refrigerator, but do not allow to congeal.

Arrange banana slices on firm gelatine in two outside rows lengthwise of the tin, and cherries, cut-side-up, in two centre rows. Pour 12 fluid ounces cooled gelatine mixture slowly down the side of tin, being careful not to disturb fruit arrangement. Place in refrigerator, and chill until firm.

Second Layer—Cream Cheese:
9 ounces cream cheese
4 fluid ounces mayonnaise
2 tablespoons fruit gelatine mixture
2 ounces finely chopped salted peanuts
1½ ounces chopped cherries

Beat cream cheese at a medium speed on electric mixer until light and fluffy. Add mayonnaise and gelatine mixture; fold in nuts and cherries.

Spread in an even layer over firm fruit gelatine in loaf tin.

Third Layer—Fruit Gelatine:
8 ounces diced canned pears

Add diced pears to remaining gelatine mixture, and pour over cheese layer.

Chill layered salad in refrigerator until firm. Serves 8 to 10.

TOMATO CHEESE MOULD

1 tablespoon unflavoured gelatine
2 fluid ounces cold water
16 fluid ounces canned tomato sauce
2 teaspoons finely chopped onion
salt and pepper
8 ounces Cheddar cheese, grated

Soften gelatine in cold water and dissolve over hot water.

Add to tomato sauce and onion. Season to taste. Chill until slightly thickened.

Fold in grated cheese. Pour into 4 or 6 individual moulds. Chill until firm; unmould on lettuce and serve with mayonnaise or salad dressing. Serves 4 to 6.

Moulded Plum and Cottage Cheese Salad

MOULDED PLUM AND COTTAGE CHEESE SALAD

1 1-pound can purple plums
1 packet orange-flavoured gelatine
plum syrup plus water to make 8 fluid ounces
8 ounces creamed cottage cheese
2 ounces chopped celery
2 ounces chopped walnuts
2 tablespoons lemon juice
4 fluid ounces evaporated milk, chilled until icy cold

Drain plums and save syrup. Cut plums in halves; remove and discard stones. Place plum halves fairly close together in the bottom of an 8-inch ring mould or in 8 individual moulds. If any plum halves remain, use them for some other purpose.

Empty gelatine into a medium-sized mixing bowl. Heat syrup and water to boiling. Add to gelatine and stir until gelatine is dissolved.

Chill gelatine until it begins to thicken, then add cottage cheese, celery, nuts, and lemon juice.

Whip milk until it will hold a stiff peak. Fold into chilled gelatine mixture. Spoon carefully over plums. Chill until firm, about 2 to 3 hours.

Unmould on chilled serving plate. Garnish with orange or grapefruit segments, if desired. Serves 6 to 8.

SUPERB SALAD MOULDS

2 fluid ounces milk
8 ounces cream cheese
4 ounces grated Cheddar cheese
½ teaspoon salt
¼ teaspoon paprika
1 tablespoon unflavoured gelatine
2 fluid ounces cold water
8 fluid ounces whipping cream, whipped
6 pineapple slices

Gradually add the milk to the cream cheese, blending until smooth. Add the grated cheese, salt, and paprika.

Add the gelatine which has been softened in the cold water and dissolved over hot water. Chill until slightly thickened.

Fold in the whipped cream. Pour into 6 individual moulds. Chill until firm. For each serving, place a slice of pineapple on crisp watercress. Unmould a gelatine salad in the centre of each pineapple. Serves 6.

Emerald Mould

EMERALD MOULD

1 3-ounce packet lime-flavoured
    gelatine
12 fluid ounces hot water
1 1¼-pound can crushed pineapple,
    well drained
1 teaspoon peppermint essence
1 tablespoon unflavoured gelatine
4 tablespoons cold water
1 pound cream cheese, softened
4 ounces sugar
2 eggs
½ teaspoon vanilla essence

Dissolve lime-flavoured gelatine in hot water. Chill until syrupy. Fold in crushed pineapple and peppermint essence. Pour half of mixture into a lightly greased 2-pint mould. Chill until set.

Soften unflavoured gelatine in cold water. Dissolve over hot water. Add to softened cream cheese. Stir in sugar, eggs, and vanilla. Beat until smooth. Pour half of cheese mixture over gelatine layer in mould. Chill until firm.

Repeat layers, chilling after each addition. Serves 8 to 10.

CREAMY CHEESE SALAD MOULD

1 tablespoon unflavoured gelatine
2 fluid ounces cold water
3 eggs
¾ pint milk
¼ teaspoon salt
6 ounces diced Cheddar cheese
¾ teaspoon onion juice
2 ounces sliced stuffed olives
2 ounces chopped sweet pickles
2 ounces finely diced celery
1 tablespoon vinegar or pickle juice
lettuce, endive, or watercress
paprika

Creamy Cheese Salad Mould

Soften gelatine in cold water.

Beat eggs, add milk and salt, and cook over boiling water, stirring constantly, until mixture thickens slightly.

Remove from heat and stir in softened gelatine until dissolved. Add remaining ingredients (except lettuce and paprika) until well mixed, not until cheese melts.

Decorate large or individual moulds with additional olive and pickle slices. Pour in a little of gelatine mixture (not enough to float garnish) and chill until firm.

Then add remainder of mixture and chill until whole mould is firm.

Unmould on crisp salad greens, on one large or individual plates. Garnish with paprika. Serves 6 to 8.

RED AND WHITE SALAD

1 tablespoon unflavoured gelatine
4 fluid ounces water
1 10½-ounce can condensed tomato
    soup
1 teaspoon grated onion
8 ounces creamy cottage cheese

Soften gelatine in cold water. Heat soup; mix in softened gelatine and grated onion.

Pour into 1 large or 4 individual moulds that have been rinsed with cold water. Chill until firm.

Unmould on lettuce. Serve with top knot of cottage cheese. Serves 4.

Red and White Salad

OLIVE SALAD LOAF

2 tablespoons unflavoured gelatine
2 fluid ounces cold water
8 fluid ounces tomato sauce
2 tablespoons vinegar
½ teaspoon salt
1 pound cottage cheese
6 ounces black olives
4 fluid ounces mayonnaise
4 ounces finely chopped celery
1 ounce finely chopped green
    pepper
1 diced canned pimiento

Soften gelatine in cold water. Heat tomato sauce to boiling. Add gelatine and stir until it is dissolved.

Blend in vinegar and salt. Cool to room temperature.

Force cottage cheese through sieve. Cut olives into large pieces.

Blend cheese, olives, mayonnaise, celery, green pepper, and pimiento into gelatine mixture. Turn into loaf tin (about 9×5×3 inches), and chill until firm.

Unmould on lettuce to serve. Serves 8 to 10.

PINEAPPLE-COTTAGE CHEESE MOULD

2 teaspoons unflavoured gelatine
3 tablespoons cold water
8 fluid ounces pineapple juice or
    pineapple juice plus water
2 tablespoons lemon juice
2 tablespoons sugar
pinch of salt
1 8- or 9-ounce can drained crushed
    pineapple
1 ounce finely chopped celery
3 ounces cottage cheese

Sprinkle gelatine on cold water and soak a few minutes.

Heat fruit juices; add sugar, salt, and gelatine. Stir until gelatine is dissolved.

Chill until thick enough to hold solid food in place. Stir in pineapple, celery, and cottage cheese. Chill until firm. Serves 4.

LEMON-WALNUT-COTTAGE CHEESE MOULDS

1 packet lemon-flavoured gelatine
8 fluid ounces boiling water
4 fluid ounces cold water
12 ounces cottage cheese
2 fluid ounces mayonnaise
1 ounce chopped walnuts
1 tablespoon lemon juice

Dissolve gelatine in boiling water. Add cold water. Chill until of a jelly-like consistency.

Beat with rotary beater until frothy. Add mayonnaise, cottage cheese, walnuts, and lemon juice. Mix ingredients well.

Pour into individual moulds that have been greased or dipped in cold water. Makes 8 individual moulds.

Olive Salad Loaf

Gelatine Moulds with Fruit

WALDORF SALAD MOULD

1 packet lemon-flavoured gelatine
¾ pint hot water
1 tablespoon vinegar
½ teaspoon salt
6 ounces cooking apples, diced
2 ounces coarsely chopped walnuts
3 ounces diced celery
endive

Dissolve gelatine in hot water. Add vinegar and salt.

Cover bottom of 2-pint mould with a thin layer of gelatine. Chill until firm.

Chill remaining gelatine until slightly thickened. Add apples, nuts, and celery. Pour into mould. Chill until firm.

Unmould on serving plate. Surround with endive. Serve with a cream cheese dressing. Serves 4 to 6.

Prepare a Waldorf Salad Mould in a ring and fill the centre with cottage cheese garnished with apple slices dipped in lemon juice to prevent fruit from darkening. Garnish with nuts.

GINGER ALE-LEMON MOULD

Dissolve 1 packet lemon-flavoured gelatine in 4 fluid ounces boiling water. When cool, add 12 fluid ounces ginger ale.

Chill until slightly thickened and fold in 8 ounces diced mixed fruits (fresh or canned and drained), 1 ounce chopped celery, and 1 ounce chopped nuts. Pour into moulds and chill. Serves 6.

APPLE-LIME MOULD

Dissolve 1 packet lime-flavoured gelatine in 8 fluid ounces hot water. Add 14 ounces sweetened, unflavoured apple sauce. Pour into moulds and chill. Serves 4 to 6.

Two-Tone Rainbow Salad

INDIVIDUAL PEACH AND BLACKBERRY RINGS

1 packet lemon-flavoured gelatine
8 fluid ounces boiling water
6 fluid ounces liquid from canned peaches
1 1-pound can sliced peaches
4 ounces sweetened fresh, frozen, or canned blackberries

Dissolve gelatine in boiling water. Add peach liquid and mix. Pour a small amount into the bottom of 8 well greased individual ring moulds. Allow to stand until partially set.

Press three peach slices into the bottom of each mould.

Chill remaining gelatine until partially set.

Add the blackberries and any remaining peaches, chopped.

Pour on top of the peach slices in the moulds. Chill until set.

Unmould on mounds of cottage cheese which have been arranged on lettuce. Fill the centres with additional cottage cheese. Serves 8.

Individual Peach and Blackberry Rings

TWO-TONE RAINBOW SALAD

1 1½-pound can fruit cocktail
1 packet fruit-flavoured gelatine
1 tablespoon lemon juice
3 ounces cream cheese or 8 ounces cottage cheese
mayonnaise

Drain fruit cocktail and measure syrup; add water to make 16 fluid ounces liquid. Heat to boiling and dissolve gelatine in hot liquid. Add lemon juice.

Arrange drained fruit cocktail in a 2-pint ring mould. Pour in 8 fluid ounces of gelatine mixture; chill until firm.

Meanwhile, mix together until smooth the remaining gelatine and cream cheese (or cottage cheese). Pour over firm gelatine and fruit mixture in the mould and chill. Turn out upside-down on plate and serve with mayonnaise. Serves 6 to 8.

Lemonade Layered Salad With Melon Balls

LEMONADE LAYERED SALAD WITH MELON BALLS

First Layer:
1 tablespoon unflavoured gelatine
2 fluid ounces cold water
4 fluid ounces hot water
1 6-ounce can frozen lemonade concentrate
4 fluid ounces salad dressing

Soak gelatine in cold water 5 minutes. Add hot water and stir until gelatine is completely dissolved. Add undiluted lemonade concentrate. Mix.

Then add salad dressing and stir, or whip with rotary beater, until dressing and gelatine are thoroughly blended.

Pour into 5×9-inch loaf tin which has been rinsed with cold water or greased. Chill in refrigerator until firm before adding second layer.

Second Layer:
1 tablespoon unflavoured gelatine
2 fluid ounces cold water
4 fluid ounces hot water
4 tablespoons frozen lemonade concentrate
2 tablespoons maraschino cherry juice
8 fluid ounces ginger ale (allow to settle for accurate measurement)
2 ounces sliced maraschino cherries
16 melon balls (fresh or frozen)
additional melon balls and sprigs of mint for garnish

Soak gelatine in cold water 5 minutes. Add hot water and stir until gelatine is completely dissolved.

Add lemonade concentrate, cherry juice, and ginger ale, stirring well. Chill until mixture begins to thicken, then add sliced cherries and melon balls and mix well.

Pour mixture on top of chilled first layer of salad. Chill until firm.

Unmould on serving dish and, before serving, garnish.

MOULDED CRUSHED PINE-APPLE

Dissolve 1 packet lemon-flavoured gelatine in ¾ pint hot water. Chill until slightly thickened.

Fold in 4 ounces drained crushed canned pineapple, 4 ounces diced unpeeled red apple, and 1 ounce chopped walnuts.

Turn into individual moulds. Chill until firm; unmould. Serves 4 to 6.

Hidden Apricot Salad

MASTER FRUIT SALAD MOULD

1 tablespoon unflavoured gelatine
2 fluid ounces cold water
8 fluid ounces hot fruit juice or water
2 fluid ounces lemon juice
2 ounces sugar
¼ teaspoon salt
6 to 12 ounces canned or fresh fruit (below)

Soften gelatine in cold water 5 minutes. Add hot fruit juice or water and stir until dissolved.

Add lemon juice, sugar, and salt. Chill until syrupy.

Fold in diced fruits. Rinse mould in cold water. Line bottom with thinly sliced fruits. Pour in thickened mixture. Chill until firm.

Unmould on lettuce. Serve with desired dressing. Serves 6.

Master Fruit Salad Mould Variations

1. 2 ounces diced apples, 2 ounces cut-up orange segments, 2 ounces chopped dates, and 1 ounce chopped nuts.

2. 2 ounces each diced grapefruit and orange sections, and 4 ounces diced canned pineapple.

3. 3 ounces each diced orange sections, diced pears, and peaches, fresh or canned.

4. 3 ounces diced apple, 2 ounces chopped celery, and 1 ounce chopped nuts.

5. 4 ounces diced canned pineapple, and 2 ounces each diced apple and sliced strawberries.

6. 4 ounces diced canned pineapple, and 2 ounces each grated raw carrot and shredded cabbage.

7. 4 ounces diced pears, fresh or canned, and 3 ounces diced cucumber.

8. 6 ounces diced canned pineapple and 3 ounces diced raw cucumber.

9. 2 ounces each sliced bananas, diced orange sections, and green grapes.

Harvest Fruits In Wine Jelly

10. 2 ounces each sliced red cherries, diced melon, and diced orange sections.

11. 6 ounces of cantaloupe and honeydew melon balls.

HIDDEN APRICOT SALAD

2 1-pound cans apricot halves, drained
1 packet orange-flavoured gelatine
8 fluid ounces boiling apricot syrup
4 fluid ounces water
3 ounces cream cheese, softened
1 tablespoon thick salad dressing
8 fluid ounces evaporated milk

Drain and save syrup from apricot halves. Measure 8 fluid ounces apricot syrup and heat to boiling. Dissolve gelatine in hot syrup. Stir in water and allow to cool slightly.

Meanwhile, fill drained apricot halves with a mixture of cream cheese and salad dressing. Put the halves together and place whole apricots in bottom of a 2-pint ring mould.

Stir evaporated milk into cooled gelatine mixture. (Mixture may be a little curdled but becomes smooth when chilled.) Pour gelatine mixture over stuffed apricots. Refrigerate until firm. To serve, unmould and garnish with lettuce.

HARVEST FRUITS IN WINE JELLY

1 packet lime-flavoured gelatine
1 packet lemon-flavoured gelatine
¾ pint hot water
juice of 2 fresh limes
8 fluid ounces Sauternes, Rhine, Chablis, or any white wine
6 fluid ounces boiled salad dressing
2 ounces diced unpeeled apples
2 ounces diced fresh pears
2 ounces seedless grapes
2 ounces walnuts
lettuce
fruits for garnish

Dissolve gelatine in hot water. Cool. Add lime juice and wine. Chill slightly.

Divide in 2 portions. Add salad dressing to first half of gelatine mixture and allow to set slightly.

Rinse a ring mould in cold water and pour enough of second half of gelatine mixture in mould to just cover bottom. Put in refrigerator to set slightly.

Arrange a design of fruits and nuts on the layer of gelatine. Add remaining fruits to rest of gelatine and pour over design layer. Chill.

Whip gelatine salad dressing mixture with rotary beater until smooth. Pour into ring mould. Chill until firm.

Unmould on large round plate. Fill centre of ring with crisp lettuce. Garnish plate with pears and grapes. Serves 8.

MOULDED PINEAPPLE-CUCUMBER SALAD CHABLIS

2 tablespoons unflavoured gelatine
4 fluid ounces cold water
1 9-ounce can crushed pineapple
12 fluid ounces dry white wine
2 tablespoons lemon juice
4 ounces sugar
1 teaspoon salt
1 green pepper, finely chopped
4 ounces finely diced cucumber

Soften gelatine in cold water 5 minutes.

Drain pineapple and to the juice add wine, lemon juice, and enough water to make ¾ pint liquid. Bring this to boil; add soaked gelatine, sugar, and salt; stir until gelatine and sugar are dissolved; chill until slightly thickened.

Fold in drained pineapple, green pepper, and cucumber; pour into ring mould or individual moulds; chill until firm.

Unmould and surround with crisp lettuce or endive, and serve with mayonnaise. Serves 6.

DELLA ROBBIA WREATH

2 tablespoons plain gelatine
4 fluid ounces cold water
2 1-pound cans fruit cocktail
3 fluid ounces lemon juice
8 ounces canned cranberry sauce
endive

Soften gelatine in cold water. Drain syrup from fruit cocktail and add water, if necessary, to make 1 pint. Heat. Add gelatine to syrup mixture and stir until dissolved. Add lemon juice.

Pour a little of the gelatine mixture into 9-inch ring mould; chill until partially set; arrange a wreath of fruit cocktail in it. Chill until firm.

Divide remaining gelatine mixture into two equal parts. To one part, add cranberry sauce; to the other, fruit cocktail.

Spoon cranberry portion into ring mould; chill until firm. Spoon fruit cocktail into ring mould; chill until firm. Unmould on bed of endive. Makes one 9-inch ring mould.

Della Robbia Wreath

CRANBERRY SALAD MOULD

8 ounces sugar
8 fluid ounces water
8 ounces fresh cranberries
1 tablespoon unflavoured gelatine
4 fluid ounces cold water
½ teaspoon salt
2 ounces diced celery
2 ounces chopped walnuts

Make cranberry sauce by combining sugar and water. Boil 5 minutes. Add cranberries. Cook without stirring until all skins pop open, about 5 minutes.

Soften gelatine in cold water. Add to hot cranberries with salt. Stir until gelatine is dissolved. Strain.

Chill until mixture is consistency of unbeaten egg whites.

Stir in celery and chopped nuts. Pour into individual moulds. Chill until firm.

Unmould on lettuce. Garnish with whole walnuts. Serve with mayonnaise. Serves 6.

Variation: Canned cranberry jelly (1 pound) may be used in place of fresh cranberry sauce. Either may also be used without straining.

SPICY FRUIT RING

1½ pounds canned fruit cocktail
1   3-inch stick cinnamon
1   teaspoon whole cloves
1   teaspoon whole allspice
2   tablespoons unflavoured gelatine
6   tablespoons lemon juice

Drain fruit cocktail. Simmer syrup with spices 10 minutes. Strain out spices, measure syrup and add water to make 1 pint 8 fluid ounces liquid. Heat.

Soften gelatine in lemon juice and dissolve in hot liquid. Cool until slightly thickened.

Fold in fruit cocktail. Turn into 8½-inch ring mould and chill until firm.

Unmould and garnish with endive. Fill ring with chicken salad. Garnish with avocado balls and slivered almonds. Serves 8.

Spicy Fruit Ring

AVOCADO SALAD RING MOULD

1½ tablespoons unflavoured gelatine
2   fluid ounces cold water
1   pint tomato juice
2   bay leaves
5   cloves
½   small onion, chopped
½   teaspoon salt
black pepper
few drops of Tabasco sauce
2   avocados
2   ounces diced celery
lettuce

Soften gelatine in cold water. Combine tomato juice, bay leaves, cloves, onion, salt, pepper, and Tabasco sauce. Boil 5 minutes and strain. Add softened gelatine and stir until dissolved. Cool.

When gelatine begins to set, stir in 1 cubed avocado and celery. Mould in ring mould.

To serve, fill centre of ring with lettuce and remaining avocado, sliced. Serve with desired dressing. Serves 6 to 8.

Variations:

Substitute any flavoured gelatine mould, and vary form of avocado pieces as desired.

Emerald Mould: Lime gelatine, sliced stuffed olives and cocktail onions, and diced cucumbers.

Waldorf Mould: Lemon gelatine, diced apple, finely cut celery, and a few walnuts or almonds.

Seafood Mould: Lime or lemon gelatine with lemon juice and condiments, and seafood.

Nectar Mould: Apricot, plum, nectarine, or strawberry gelatine base, bananas, and pineapple.

SELF-LAYERING SALAD

2   packets orange-flavoured gelatine
¾   pint hot water
¾   pint cold water
¼   teaspoon almond essence
1½   pounds sliced canned peaches, drained
3   medium bananas, sliced

Empty orange gelatine into 3-pint bowl. Add hot water and stir until gelatine has dissolved.

Add cold water and almond essence to gelatine mixture. Cool and pour into a lightly greased 9×5×3-inch loaf tin.

Add peaches and banana slices to gelatine mixture. Be sure bananas are coated with gelatine mixture. Stir to distribute fruit evenly. Chill in refrigerator until firm.

Peaches will sink to bottom of loaf tin and bananas will float, making a self-layered salad. Serves 6 to 8.

Party Fruit Ring Mould

PARTY FRUIT RING MOULD

2   packets lemon-flavoured gelatine
12 fluid ounces hot water
16 fluid ounces fruit syrup (drained from peaches and pineapple)
peach halves, canned, drained
pineapple slices, canned, drained
dark sweet cherries, canned, drained
watercress

Dissolve gelatine in hot water. Add fruit syrup and chill mixture until slightly thickened.

Pour ¼ pint gelatine into the bottom of an 8-inch ring mould (2½ pints) and chill until almost firm.

Set pineapple slices in gelatine with a dark sweet cherry in the centre and pour in gelatine just to cover. Chill until firm.

Stand peach halves upright against sides of mould and place cherries above pineapple slices.

Pour in gelatine to half cover peaches and chill until firm.

Add remaining gelatine and chill thoroughly. Unmould and garnish with watercress. Serve with a whipped cream dressing. Serves 6 to 8.

SPICED PEACH SOUFFLÉ SALAD

12 fluid ounces peach juice from canned peaches
4   whole cloves
¼   teaspoon cinnamon
2   tablespoons vinegar
2   tablespoons sugar
1   packet orange-flavoured gelatine
mayonnaise
1¼ pounds chopped canned peaches

Combine peach juice, cloves, cinnamon, vinegar, and sugar. Heat just to boiling.

Empty gelatine into small bowl. Pour hot liquid through fine sieve and over gelatine; stir until gelatine is dissolved.

Add mayonnaise and blend at a medium to high speed on mixer or with rotary beater.

Pour into freezer tray. Chill in freezer compartment of refrigerator about ½ hour or until set but not frozen.

Empty mixture into small mixer bowl and beat at a high speed until smooth and fluffy. Fold in chopped peaches.

Pour into 2-pint lightly greased mould. Chill in vegetable compartment of refrigerator until firm, about 1 hour. Serves 6 to 8.

Tawny Salad Moulds

TAWNY SALAD MOULDS

1   1½-pound can fruit cocktail
1½ tablespoons unflavoured
      gelatine
3   tablespoons lemon juice
1   6-ounce can frozen orange juice
lettuce

Drain syrup from fruit cocktail, measure, and add water to make 12 fluid ounces liquid. Heat.

Soften gelatine in 3 fluid ounces cold water and dissolve in hot syrup. Stir in lemon juice and undiluted orange juice. Cool until slightly thickened.

Fold in fruit cocktail. Turn into moulds and chill until firm.

Unmould on to lettuce and garnish with additional fruit cocktail as desired. Makes 8 6-fluid-ounce moulds.

BANANA GELATINE SALAD

1   packet fruit-flavoured gelatine or
      1 tablespoon unflavoured
      gelatine
2   ripe bananas
parsley
salad dressing

Mix gelatine according to packet directions. Chill only until slightly thickened.

Partly fill 1-pint mould with gelatine. Peel bananas, slice and arrange on top of gelatine. Fill mould with remaining gelatine. Chill until firm.

Unmould. Garnish with additional slices of ripe bananas or other fruit if desired. Garnish with parsley. Serve with soured cream, mayonnaise, or a tary French dressing.

Serves 4 to 6.

Note: Four to six individual moulds may be used in place of 1 large mould.

Banana Gelatine Salad

APPLE SALAD MOULD

1   packet cherry-flavoured gelatine
8   fluid ounces hot water
½   teaspoon cinnamon
6   fluid ounces boiling water
2   ounces chopped peeled apples
2   ounces chopped celery
2   ounces chopped walnuts

Dissolve gelatine in hot water. Add cinnamon to boiling water. Add to gelatine. Chill until slightly thickened.

Add apples, celery, and walnuts. Pour into 6 or 8 individual moulds; chill until firm.

Unmould and surround with crisp lettuce. Serve with a sweet dressing. Serves 6 to 8.

AVOCADO-GRAPEFRUIT SALAD

1   packet lemon-flavoured gelatine
¾   pint hot water
1   avocado, peeled and sliced
1   grapefruit, peeled and sectioned
lettuce
thin cantaloupe slices
French dressing

Dissolve the gelatine in the hot water. Cool. Arrange avocado slices and grapefruit sections in the bottom of a 2-pint mould. Add enough gelatine to cover and chill until firm.

Chill the remaining gelatine until slightly thickened and fold in the remaining avocado slices and grapefruit sections. Pour over the firm gelatine in the mould. Chill until firm.

Unmould and surround with lettuce. Garnish with cantaloupe slices. Serve with French dressing. Serves 4.

WHITE BEAUTY MOULD

4   slightly beaten egg yolks
8   fluid ounces milk
1   teaspoon unflavoured gelatine
2   tablespoons lemon juice
¾   pint whipping cream, whipped
1¼ pounds canned pineapple chunks,
      drained
1   1-pound can sweet cherries,
      stoned and halved
12 ounces (about 48) marshmallows,
      cut in quarters
8   ounces chopped blanched
      almonds

Mix egg yolks with milk in double boiler; cook, stirring constantly, until thick.

Soften gelatine in lemon juice; dissolve in hot mixture. Cool slightly. Fold in whipped cream and remaining ingredients.

Turn into 11 × 7 × 1½-inch baking tin and chill until firm. Cut in squares. Cut each square in half diagonally.

Serve 2 of the triangles on each plate on a bed of endive. Serves 6 to 8.

RASPBERRY FRUIT RING

1   packet raspberry-flavoured
      gelatine
¾   pint hot water
8   ounces canned sweet cherries,
      stoned
8   ounces canned pineapple chunks
8   ounces orange sections

Dissolve gelatine in hot water. Chill until slightly thickened.

Add well drained fruit. Pour into a 2-pint ring mould and chill until firm.

Unmould and garnish with endive. Fill centre with mayonnaise or salad dressing. Serves 6 to 8.

GREENGAGE-LIME MOULD

Dissolve 1 packet lime-flavoured gelatine in 8 fluid ounces hot water. Add 8 fluid ounces greengage juice and water, and 1 pound canned greengages. Chill. Serves 4 to 6.

GINGER ALE-GRAPE MOULD

Dissolve 1 packet lemon-flavoured gelatine in 8 fluid ounces hot grape juice. Cool. Add 8 fluid ounces ginger ale. Turn into moulds and chill. Serves 4 to 5.

STRAWBERRY BAVARIAN SLIMMER

1   packet strawberry-flavoured gela-
      tine
2   ounces sugar
1   8-ounce packet frozen straw-
      berries, thawed and drained
3   fluid ounces iced water
1   tablespoon lemon juice
1   ounce non-fat dried milk

Combine gelatine and sugar. Make gelatine according to label directions, using 8 fluid ounces hot water. Add 4 fluid ounces berry syrup. Cool.

Add berries and chill until slightly thickened.

Combine iced water and lemon juice, sprinkle non-fat dried milk over top. Beat until stiff, 8 to 10 minutes.

Fold into thickened gelatine mixture. Turn into 2-pint mould and chill until firm. Serves 8.

Strawberry Bavarian Slimmer

TOP-AND-BOTTOM FRUIT LOAF

2 packets fruit-flavoured gelatine
¾ pint boiling apricot juice and water
2 tablespoons lemon juice
¾ pint cold water
12 ounces drained canned apricots, cut small
5 ounces seeded grape halves
6 ounces sliced apples
2 firm bananas, sliced

Dissolve gelatine in hot apricot juice (measure juice drained from apricots and add water to measure ¾ pint; heat to boiling). Add lemon juice and cold water. Cool completely but do not chill.

Lightly grease loaf tin (9×5×3-inches); place apricots and grapes in layer over bottom. Pour in cooled gelatine.

Place sliced apples and bananas in layer on top, pressing fruit just below surface of gelatine. Chill until firm. Fruits will stay in place with layer of clear gelatine between.

Cut in slices and serve on watercress with a fruit salad dressing. Serves 8.

EASTER BONNET SALAD

2 packets lime-flavoured gelatine
1 pint 12 fluid ounces boiling water
lettuce
8 fluid ounces mayonnaise
3 tablespoons orange juice
maraschino cherries

Dissolve gelatine in boiling water. Pour 1 pint 4 fluid ounces into a 7-inch round mould which has been rinsed in cold water. Place in refrigerator to set.

Allow remaining liquid to chill until thick and syrupy. Whip with a rotary beater until light and fluffy. Pile into a 5-inch round mould and allow to set until firm.

Unmould plain gelatine on a bed of lettuce. Unmould whipped gelatine on top of larger mould.

With a piping tube, decorate "bonnet" with 2 fluid ounces mayonnaise. Garnish with maraschino cherries.

Serve with 6 fluid ounces mayonnaise combined with orange juice. Fresh fruit makes a delicious accompaniment. Serves 6 to 8.

Easter Bonnet Salad

GRAPEFRUIT-SAUTERNES MOULD

2 tablespoons unflavoured gelatine
water
2 large or 3 medium grapefruit
4 fluid ounces honey
dash of salt
6 fluid ounces Sauternes
3 fluid ounces lemon juice
lettuce

Soften gelatine in 4 fluid ounces cold water 5 minutes.

Peel grapefruit, and cut in segments, reserving all juice. Add enough water to juice to make ¾ pint; heat to boiling.

Add gelatine, and stir until dissolved. Add honey, salt, Sauternes, and lemon juice; blend well. Cool until mixture begins to thicken.

Fold in grapefruit segments.

Pour into greased 3-pint ring mould; chill until firm.

Unmould on to lettuce. Serve with French dressing. Serves 6.

GOLDEN SALAD MOULD

1 tablespoon unflavoured gelatine
2 fluid ounces cold water
2 ounces sugar
¼ teaspoon salt
8 fluid ounces hot pineapple syrup or juice
2 fluid ounces cold orange juice
2 fluid ounces vinegar
3 ounces coarsely grated raw carrots
4 ounces orange sections, chopped
12 ounces drained canned pineapple, cut into small pieces
lettuce

Soften gelatine in cold water. Add sugar, salt, and hot pineapple syrup. If necessary add water to pineapple syrup to complete measurement. Stir until dissolved.

Add orange juice and vinegar. Chill to consistency of unbeaten egg whites. Stir in carrots, oranges, and pineapple.

Pour into mould. Or, if individual moulds are used, place 1 teaspoon clear jelly in bottom of each. When nearly firm, place on it 1 tablespoon mayonnaise. When this is firm fill moulds with salad mixture. Chill until firm.

Unmould on lettuce. Decorate with pineapple. Serve with mayonnaise or salad dressing, if desired. Serves 6.

CHERRY-OLIVE MOULD

Dissolve 1 packet cherry-flavoured gelatine in 8 fluid ounces hot water. Add 8 fluid ounces cherry juice and cold water.

When slightly thickened, add 10 ounces stoned red cherries, 2 ounces chopped pickle, and 1 ounce sliced stuffed olives. Chill. Serves 6.

Cranberry-Orange Salad

CRANBERRY ORANGE SALAD

1 tablespoon unflavoured gelatine
2 tablespoons cold water
8 fluid ounces orange juice, heated to boiling
6 fluid ounces evaporated milk, chilled until icy cold
1 teaspoon lemon juice
12 ounces cranberry sauce

Soak gelatine in cold water and dissolve in hot orange juice. Chill until mixture is of a jelly-like consistency.

Meanwhile, chill a bowl, beater and evaporated milk in freezer tray until ice crystals form round edge.

Beat evaporated milk in chilled bowl until it forms peaks; add lemon juice, and beat until stiff. Fold whipped evaporated milk and cranberry sauce into gelatine.

Pour into a greased star-shaped mould and chill until set.

Unmould on lettuce and garnish with orange slices and cranberry sauce. Serves 6.

GUACAMOLE RING MOULD

2 tablespoons unflavoured gelatine
4 fluid ounces cold water
½ pint hot water
6 tablespoons lemon juice
2 tablespoons sugar
½ teaspoon salt
3 avocados, sieved
6 fluid ounces mayonnaise

Soften gelatine in cold water and dissolve in hot water. Add lemon juice, sugar, and salt. Cool.

Add avocado and mayonnaise and stir only until blended. Turn into 2-pint ring mould and chill until firm.

Unmould and garnish with avocado slices and parsley. Fill centre with marinated fruits. Serves 10.

Ginger Guacamole Ring Mould: Fold 3 ounces minced preserved ginger or chutney in with mayonnaise. Fill centre with poultry or fruit salad.

Zesty Guacamole Ring Mould: Omit sugar from recipe and add 1 teaspoon chilli seasoning, juice of 1 clove garlic, 1 teaspoon grated onion, and 1 green or red pepper, chopped. Serve with fish, meat, poultry, or vegetable salad.

SALAD MOULD WITH CURRY MAYONNAISE

1 packet orange-flavoured gelatine
8 fluid ounces boiling water
4 fluid ounces orange juice
2 fluid ounces grapefruit juice
1 tablespoon lemon juice
3 ounces orange sections
3 ounces grapefruit sections
8 fluid ounces mayonnaise
1 to 2 teaspoons curry powder

Dissolve gelatine in boiling water. Cool.

Add fruit juices, and allow to stand until partially thickened.

Add orange and grapefruit sections. Pour into mould rinsed in cold water, and chill until firm.

Unmould and serve with mayonnaise combined with curry powder. Serves 4.

GRAPEFRUIT-CUCUMBER SALAD

1 packet lemon-flavoured gelatine
12 fluid ounces hot water
½ teaspoon salt
1 tablespoon lemon juice
1 grapefruit, peeled and diced
4 ounces peeled, diced cucumber, drained
2 ounces chopped celery
1 tablespoon chopped pimiento

Dissolve gelatine in hot water. Add salt and lemon juice. Chill until slightly thickened.

Add grapefruit, cucumber, celery, and pimiento. Pour into a 2-pint mould and chill until firm.

Unmould and surround with crisp lettuce. Serve with soured cream dressing. Serves 4 to 6.

GRAPEFRUIT MOULDS WITH AVOCADO

1 packet lime-flavoured gelatine
¾ pint hot water
1 grapefruit, peeled and sectioned
1 avocado
lettuce
mayonnaise or salad dressing

Dissolve the gelatine in the hot water. Pour into 4 individual moulds in each of which place 2 sections of grapefruit. Chill until firm.

Cut the avocado in half crosswise; remove the stone; peel and slice.

Unmould each serving on lettuce on a salad plate and surround with slices of avocado.

Garnish the slices with mayonnaise or salad dressing forced through a piping tube. Serves 4.

PINEAPPLE-COTTAGE CHEESE SALAD

Dissolve 1 packet lemon- or lime-flavoured gelatine in 8 fluid ounces hot water. Add 8 fluid ounces cold water. Cool.

Add 8 ounces seasoned cottage cheese and 4 ounces drained crushed canned pineapple. Pour into mould rinsed in cold water and chill until firm.

Unmould on crisp lettuce and garnish with mayonnaise. Serves 6.

STUFFED CHERRY SALAD MOULD

3 ounces cream cheese
2 ounces chopped nuts
8 ounces drained stoned sweet cherries
1 packet lemon-flavoured gelatine
8 fluid ounces hot cherry juice
8 fluid ounces grapefruit juice
1 grapefruit, peeled and sectioned
leaf lettuce

Combine cream cheese and nuts. Stuff cherries with this mixture.

Dissolve gelatine in hot cherry juice. Add grapefruit juice.

Arrange cherries and grapefruit sections in bottom of 2-pint mould; add enough gelatine to cover and chill until firm.

Chill remaining gelatine until slightly thickened. Pour into mould. Chill until firm.

Unmould and garnish with lettuce. Serve with sweetened mayonnaise. Serves 4 to 6.

GRAPEFRUIT-CHEESE MOULD

1½ tablespoons unflavoured gelatine
12 fluid ounces unsweetened grapefruit juice
4 fluid ounces lime or lemon juice
4 ounces sugar
2 ounces finely diced celery
3 ounces cream cheese

Soften gelatine in 4 fluid ounces of grapefruit juice. Dissolve over hot water. Add to the remaining grapefruit juice. Add the lime juice and sugar. Chill until slightly thickened.

Add the celery to half of this gelatine mixture and pour into a 2-pint ring mould. Chill until firm.

Gradually add the remaining gelatine mixture to the cream cheese, blending until smooth. Chill until slightly thickened. Pour over the firm gelatine in the mould. Chill until firm.

Unmould on a serving dish and garnish with watercress. Serve with mayonnaise or salad dressing. Serves 4 to 6.

COTTAGE CHEESE AND CANTALOUPE SOUFFLÉ SALAD

1 packet lime-flavoured gelatine
8 fluid ounces hot water
4 fluid ounces cold water
1 tablespoon lemon juice
4 fluid ounces mayonnaise
8 ounces cottage cheese
6 ounces diced cantaloupe

Empty gelatine into small bowl; pour hot water over it and stir until dissolved.

Add cold water, lemon juice, and mayonnaise. Blend ingredients at a medium to high speed on mixer or with rotary beater.

Pour into freezer tray. Chill in freezer compartment of refrigerator about ½ hour or until set but not frozen. Empty mixture into small bowl and beat at high speed until smooth and fluffy.

Fold in cottage cheese and cantaloupe. Pour into 2-pint lightly greased mould. Chill in vegetable compartment of refrigerator until firm, about 1 hour. Serves 6 to 8.

CRANBERRY-LEMON MOULD

Dissolve 1 packet lemon-flavoured gelatine in 8 fluid ounces boiling water.

Put 4 ounces raw cranberries through vegetable mill and add 8 fluid ounces orange juice and 4 ounces sugar. Add to cooled gelatine.

Pour into mould and chill. Serves 6.

PEACH AND GRAPE EMERALD SALAD

2 packets lime-flavoured gelatine
8 fluid ounces boiling water
8 fluid ounces liquid from canned peach slices
¾ pint cold water
1 1-pound can sliced peaches
5 ounces black or white grapes, seeded and halved
1 red maraschino cherry

Dissolve gelatine in boiling water. Add peach liquid and cold water and mix well. Pour a small amount of this mixture into bottom of a well greased 2½-pint mould. Allow to chill until partially set.

When set, press peaches into gelatine in bottom of mould and place a cherry in centre. Chill remaining gelatine until partially set also.

Dice any peach pieces that are not used in decoration. Then add sliced grapes and diced peach slices. Pour into mould and chill until set.

Unmould on a serving plate and surround with lettuce leaves filled with cottage cheese. Serves 8 to 10.

Peach and Grape Emerald Salad

Miscellaneous Gelatine Moulds

MACARONI AND CHEESE MOULD

1 tablespoon unflavoured gelatine
4 fluid ounces cold water
6 fluid ounces hot water
4 ounces grated Cheddar cheese
1 tablespoon lemon juice
2 teaspoons grated onion
1 teaspoon salt
2 tablespoons chopped parsley
1 tablespoon chopped pimiento
2 ounces diced celery
8 ounces macaroni, cooked and broken
4 fluid ounces mayonnaise or salad dressing

Soften gelatine in cold water. Add hot water. Stir constantly until gelatine is dissolved.

Add grated cheese. Stir until cheese has softened.

Stir in lemon juice, grated onion, and salt. Chill until mixture is consistency of unbeaten egg whites.

Stir in remaining ingredients. Pour into 1 large or 6 individual moulds. Chill until firm. Unmould on to lettuce. Serves 6.

ASPARAGUS-EGG MOULD

1 tablespoon unflavoured gelatine
2 fluid ounces cold water
8 fluid ounces hot asparagus liquid
½ teaspoon salt
⅛ teaspoon black pepper
1 tablespoon grated onion
2 tablespoons lemon juice
1 pound diced cooked or canned asparagus
4 hard-boiled eggs
4 ounces chopped celery
8 fluid ounces soured cream

Soften gelatine in cold water and dissolve in hot asparagus liquid. Add salt, pepper, onion, and lemon juice. Cool.

When mixture begins to thicken, fold in asparagus, 3 chopped eggs, celery, and soured cream.

Slice remaining hard-boiled egg and place round side of rinsed mould. Pour asparagus mixture into mould. Chill until firm.

Unmould and garnish with sliced tomatoes. Serve with French dressing. Serves 4 to 6.

Asparagus-Egg Mould

CREAMY RAISIN MUSTARD RING

6 ounces sugar
1 tablespoon unflavoured gelatine
2 tablespoons dry mustard
1 teaspoon salt
4 eggs
4 fluid ounces mild vinegar
8 fluid ounces water
1 teaspoon prepared horseradish
1 tablespoon lemon juice
5 ounces raisins, coarsely chopped
2 tablespoons finely chopped spring onions
2 tablespoons finely chopped canned pimiento
2 ounces finely chopped celery
8 fluid ounces whipping cream

Combine sugar, gelatine, mustard, and salt. Blend in beaten eggs, vinegar, and water. Cook over simmering water until mixture thickens, about 15 minutes; stir frequently to keep smooth. Add horseradish, lemon juice, and raisins.

Cool. When mixture begins to jell, fold in vegetables and stiffly beaten cream. Spoon into 2½-pint ring mould. Chill until firm. Unmould on serving plate. Serves 8.

EGG SALAD MOULD

2 tablespoons unflavoured gelatine
8 fluid ounces cold water
12 fluid ounces mayonnaise or salad dressing
juice of 1 lemon
½ teaspoon salt
2 drops Tabasco sauce
1 teaspoon grated onion
12 hard-boiled eggs
½ ounce chopped parsley
1½ ounces finely chopped green pepper or celery

Soften gelatine in cold water. Dissolve over boiling water. Cool slightly.

Add mayonnaise, lemon juice, salt, Tabasco sauce, and grated onion.

Place centre slices of hard-boiled egg round inside of greased 2- to 3-pint ring mould.

Separate remaining yolks and whites of eggs. Sieve yolks. Chop whites.

Combine yolks and ½ the gelatine mixture; place as a layer in ring mould. Then add parsley and green pepper as a layer. Cover with egg whites mixed with remaining ½ of gelatine mixture. Chill until set.

Unmould on large serving plate. Fill centre of ring with chicken or vegetable salad. Garnish with watercress. Serve with French dressing. Serves 6 to 8.

Creamy Raisin Mustard Ring

HAM AND MACARONI MOULD

4 ounces macaroni
1 tablespoon unflavoured gelatine
2 fluid ounces cold water
1 ounce butter or margarine
2 tablespoons flour
¾ pint milk
½ teaspoon salt
4 tablespoons pickle juice
½ teaspoon Worcestershire sauce
2 ounces chopped or sliced stuffed olives
4 ounces chopped sweet pickles
5 ounces diced celery
1 pound minced cooked ham
3 hard-boiled eggs, sliced

Cook macaroni in salted boiling water until tender (about 20 minutes). Drain and rinse thoroughly with cold water; drain.

Soak gelatine in cold water.

Melt butter, blend in flour; add milk, and cook over direct heat, stirring constantly, until sauce boils and thickens; add salt. Remove from heat and stir in softened gelatine until dissolved.

Add pickle juice and Worcestershire sauce, and cool.

Combine cold macaroni with olives, pickles, celery, ham, and eggs, reserving a few centre slices of egg and a few olive slices for garnishing. Add cold sauce and mix lightly with other ingredients.

Rinse a 2½-pint mould with cold water and arrange reserved egg and olive slices in the bottom in any desired pattern. Pack the salad mixture into mould and chill until firm.

When ready to serve, unmould on to chilled serving plate and garnish with pickle slices and lettuce. Serves 6.

Ham and Macaroni Mould

SALAD DRESSINGS

HINTS ABOUT SALAD DRESSINGS

We have suggested suitable dressings for individual salads in most cases. We advise, however, experimenting with variations of the master recipes to suit the ingredients and your individual taste. The dressing as well as garnishes should enhance the salad with contrasts in colour, flavour, and texture.

What type of dressing to choose — sweet or tart, thick or thin — may be determined by your family's taste. Main-dish salads made with meat, fish, poultry, eggs, beans, cheese or potatoes usually call for a mayonnaise-type or cooked salad dressing. But some of these more substantial salads are good with tart French dressing.

Tart French dressing is the most likely choice for vegetable salads and vegetable-fruit combinations. But some vegetable salads may well take a mayonnaise or cooked dressing.

Reserve sweet, clear French dressings for salads with fruit. Mayonnaise made milder with whipped cream or thinned and sweetened with fruit juice is good for these salads too.

MAYONNAISE
(Master Recipe)

- 1 whole egg or 2 egg yolks
- 1 teaspoon dry mustard
- 1 teaspoon salt
- 1 teaspoon olive oil
- Black pepper
- Cayenne pepper
- Dash of paprika
- 12 fluid ounces cold olive or vegetable oil
- 2 tablespoons vinegar or lemon juice

Combine the first 7 ingredients and beat thoroughly. Add oil 1 tablespoon at a time, beating thoroughly after each addition, until half the oil is added.

Then add remaining oil in larger quantities, and lastly add vinegar or lemon juice. Makes ¾ pint.

Note: If mayonnaise should curdle, wash the beater, beat 1 egg yolk in another bowl, and very slowly add the curdled mayonnaise to the egg yolk, beating constantly to form new emulsion.

MAYONNAISE VARIATIONS

Use these variations with homemade or bought mayonnaise.

Caper Mayonnaise: To 8 fluid ounces mayonnaise, add a scant 2 ounces finely chopped well-washed capers.

Caviar Mayonnaise: To 8 fluid ounces mayonnaise add 1 tablespoon caviar.

Horseradish Caviar Mayonnaise: To 8 fluid ounces mayonnaise add 1 tablespoon each of drained horseradish and caviar.

Anchovy Caviar Mayonnaise: To 8 fluid ounces mayonnaise, add 4 washed, dried, and finely chopped anchovy fillets and 1 tablespoon caviar.

Chilli Mayonnaise: To 8 fluid ounces mayonnaise add 2 fluid ounces chilli pickle, 1½ tablespoons vinegar, ¾ tablespoon Worcestershire sauce, and ¼ teaspoon chopped chives. Serve with fish salads.

Chutney Mayonnaise: To 8 fluid ounces mayonnaise add 1½ tablespoons chopped chutney.

Cranberry Mayonnaise: To 8 fluid ounces mayonnaise add 2 tablespoons well-beaten cranberry jelly or sauce and 1 teaspoon grated orange rind.

Curry Mayonnaise: To 8 fluid ounces mayonnaise, add and blend well ½ to 1 teaspoon curry powder, 1 crushed parlic clove, ¼ teaspoon ginger, 1 tablespoon lime juice, and 1 teaspoon honey. Serve with fish.

Green Mayonnaise: Colour mayonnaise with green food colouring or spinach juice.

Honey Cream Dressing: Blend ¼ teaspoon dry mustard with 1 tablespoon honey and ½ teaspoon lemon juice. Add to mayonnaise. For salads with fruit.

Horseradish Mayonnaise: To 8 fluid ounces mayonnaise add 3 tablespoons prepared horseradish. Serve with cold beef.

Ideal Salad Dressing: To 8 fluid ounces mayonnaise add 2 tablespoons condensed tomato soup, ½ tablespoon lemon juice, 1 teaspoon Worcestershire sauce, and 1½ teaspoons icing sugar.

Nippy Mayonnaise: To 8 fluid ounces mayonnaise add 3 teaspoons prepared horseradish, 3 teaspoons French mustard and 1 small chopped sweet pickle. Serve with tomato salads, lettuce, or a tossed salad.

Piquante Mayonnaise: To 8 fluid ounces mayonnaise add 2 tablespoons each finely chopped olives and pickles and 1 teaspoon each chopped onion and chives.

Ravigote Mayonnaise: Mix and chop 1 ounce watercress, 1 ounce parsley, 2 teaspoons chives, 1 tablespoon capers, and 4 anchovies.

Force mixture through fine sieve and add to 8 fluid ounces mayonnaise. Serve with fish and vegetable salads.

Red Beetroot Mayonnaise: To 8 fluid ounces mayonnaise add 1 tablespoon strained beetroot juice and 2 tablespoons finely chopped cooked beetroot.

Red Mayonnaise: Tint mayonnaise with red food colouring.

Roquefort Mayonnaise: To 8 fluid ounces mayonnaise add 2 tablespoons crumbled Roquefort cheese, a few drops Worcestershire sauce, 1 tablespoon French dressing, and 1 tablespoon finely chopped chives.

Rum Cream Mayonnaise: To 8 fluid ounces mayonnaise add 1 teaspoon rum, mixed with 4 fluid ounces whipped cream, and add 1 ounce chopped toasted almonds. Serve with fruit salads.

Russian Dressing: To 8 fluid ounces mayonnaise add 1 chopped hard-boiled egg, 2 fluid ounces chilli pickle and 2 tablespoons chopped green pepper.

MAYONNAISE VARIATIONS

Spicy Mayonnaise: To 8 fluid ounces mayonnaise add ¼ teaspoon each Worcestershire sauce, paprika, and dry mustard. Serve with fish, meat, or vegetable salads.

Thousand Island Dressing: To 8 fluid ounces mayonnaise add 2 tablespoons chilli pickle, 2 tablespoons chopped green pepper, 2 tablespoons canned pimiento, and 2 tablespoons chopped sweet pickle. Serve with vegetable salads.

Whipped Cream Mayonnaise: Fold 8 fluid ounces mayonnaise into 4 fluid ounces double cream, whipped. For salads with fruit.

Whipped Cream Fruit Mayonnaise: Fold into 8 fluid ounces mayonnaise, 4 fluid ounces double cream, whipped, 1 ounce chopped almonds and 2 ounces redcurrant jelly.

GREEN MAYONNAISE
(Sauce Verte)

Use ¾ pint mayonnaise; blend in 2 tablespoons parsley, 1 tablespoon chives, 2 tablespoons tarragon, 1 teaspoon dill, and 1 teaspoon chervil, all finely chopped. Allow to stand in a cool place for 2 hours to blend flavours. Serve with cold fish or shellfish or vegetables. Makes about ¾ pint.

FRUIT MAYONNAISE
3 fluid ounces grapefruit juice
4 fluid ounces mayonnaise
1½ teaspoons sugar

Blend thoroughly. Serves 8.

COOKED DRESSING
(Master Recipe)

¼ tablespoon salt
2 tablespoons sugar
1 tablespoon flour
¾ teaspoon dry mustard
Few grains cayenne pepper
2 slightly beaten eggs
1 ounce butter or margarine
6 fluid ounces milk
2 fluid ounces vinegar or lemon
    juice

Sift dry ingredients; add eggs, butter, milk, and vinegar very slowly.

Stir and cook over boiling water until mixture begins to thicken. Strain and cool. Makes about 8 fluid ounces.

Note: For a thinner dressing use 1 egg yolk. Store, covered, until ready to use.

Cooked Dressing Variations

Almond and Cucumber Dressing: To cooled dressing add 2 ounces diced cucumber and 1 ounce blanched and finely chopped almonds. Serve with salads with fruit.

Banana Nut Dressing: To 2 fluid ounces cooked dressing add 3 tablespoons peanut butter and 1 mashed banana. Thin with a little cream, if necessary. Serve with fruit salads.

Chutney Dressing: To 6 fluid ounces cooked dressing add 2 tablespoons chopped chutney and 2 fluid ounces whipped cream. For fruit or vegetable salads.

Cream Dressing: In master recipe omit butter; use 8 fluid ounces single cream instead of milk.

Fruit Dressing: In master recipe increase flour to 2 tablespoons. Substitute 8 fluid ounces orange juice for milk.

Ham Salad Dressing: To 8 fluid ounces cooked dressing add 2 to 3 ounces chopped ham and 1 tablespoon chopped green pepper. For any vegetable or green salad.

Honey Dressing: In master recipe, substitute 3 tablespoons honey for sugar.

Peanut Butter Dressing: Prepare master recipe. Blend 2 ounces peanut butter with hot dressing after removing from heat.

Sardine Cooked Dressing: Skin, bone, and mash 6 sardines. Mix with 1 tablespoon lemon juice. Add to 8 fluid ounces cooked dressing. For fish or vegetable salad.

Soured Cream Dressing Prepare master recipe. Fold in 8 fluid ounces whipped soured cream when cool.

Toasted Nut Dressing: Prepare master recipe. Add 1 to 2 ounces toasted chopped nuts when cool. Serve with potato, tomato, or plain fruit salads.

Whipped Cream Dressing: Prepare master recipe. Fold in 4 fluid ounces double cream, whipped, when cool.

SOURED CREAM DRESSING

8 fluid ounces thick soured cream
1 tablespoon lemon juice
1 tablespoon prepared horseradish
2 tablespoons sugar
½ teaspoon salt
⅛ teaspoon dry mustard

Whip soured cream; fold in remaining ingredients. Serve at once. Makes about ¾ pint.

SOURED CREAM-CURRY DRESSING FOR SALADS WITH FRUIT

¼ to ½ teaspoon curry powder
1 teaspoon sugar
1 tablespoon lemon juice
2 tablespoons mild vinegar
8 fluid ounces soured cream

Blend curry, sugar, lemon juice, and vinegar, then stir into soured cream. Makes about 8 fluid ounces.

LOW CALORIE SALAD DRESSING

16 artificial sweetening tablets
2 beaten eggs
2 tablespoons cornflour
½ teaspoon dry mustard
1 teaspoon celery salt
Salt and pepper
2 fluid ounces lemon juice
¾ pint water

Add crushed artificial sweetening tablets to eggs and mix well. Add cornflour, dry mustard, celery salt, salt, and pepper. Add lemon juice and mix well.

Add water. Cook over medium heat, stirring constantly, until mixture begins to thicken. Cool. Makes 40 tablespoons dressing, each containing 5 calories.

Tomato Salad Dressing: To 8 fluid ounces of low calorie salad dressing, add 8 fluid ounces tomato juice, 1 teaspoon grated onion, 8 artificial sweetening tablets, crushed, and 1 teaspoon cornflour.

Mix well and cook over medium heat, stirring constantly, until mixture thickens. Cool. Makes 32 tablespoons dressing, each containing 5 calories.

Thousand Island Dressing: To 8 fluid ounces low calorie salad dressing, add 4 ounces each chopped canned pimiento, chopped olives, and chopped dill pickle, and 4 fluid ounces chilli pickle or tomato ketchup.

Finely chop 1 hard-boiled egg and add to mixture. Makes 32 tablespoons, each containing 10 calories.

LOW CALORIE SALAD DRESSING

8 fluid ounces tomato juice
2 tablespoons vegetable oil
1 tablespoon Worcestershire sauce
¼ teaspoon salt
2 tablespoons vinegar
½ small onion, grated
2 tablespoons chopped parsley
¼ teaspoon black pepper

Combine all ingredients. Chill. Shake thoroughly for serving.

BLUE CHEESE DRESSING

8 fluid ounces vegetable oil
4 fluid ounces malt or cider vinegar
1½ teaspoons salt
Few grains cayenne pepper
¼ teaspoon paprika
1½ teaspoons sugar
2 ounces crumbled or chopped
    blue cheese

Combine all ingredients except cheese and beat with rotary beater.

Add cheese. Store in covered jar in refrigerator. Stir or shake well before using. Makes 12 fluid ounces.

MASTER ITALIAN DRESSING

1 clove garlic
½ teaspoon dry mustard
½ teaspoon salt
4 tablespoons wine vinegar
4 fluid ounces olive oil

Cut garlic clove in half. Mix mustard, salt, garlic, and vinegar thoroughly. Add oil and stir until all ingredients are blended.

Store in covered jar in cold place. Shake well just before using. Makes 6 fluid ounces.

Variations of Italian Dressing

Roquefort Cheese Italian Dressing: Crumble 2 ounces Roquefort cheese into dressing just before using.

Gorgonzola Cheese Dressing: Crumble 2 ounces Gorgonzola cheese into dressing just before using.

Other Variations: Most of the variations of French or cooked dressing may be used.

LEMON-SHERRY DRESSING FOR SALADS WITH FRUIT

2 fluid ounces lemon juice
⅛ teaspoon salt
2 ounces sugar
2 tablespoons dry sherry

Blend lemon juice, salt, and sugar until sugar has dissolved. Add sherry. Makes about 8 fluid ounces.

YOGHURT SALAD DRESSING

8 fluid ounces yoghurt
1 teaspoon unsweetened lemon juice
2 to 3 teaspoons prepared mustard
¼ teaspoon onion salt
½ teaspoon liquid artificial sweetener

Combine ingredients in jar. Mix well. Cover and store in refrigerator. Serve with tossed salad or potato salad. Makes 8 fluid ounces.

Celery Salt Dressing: Add 1 teaspoon celery salt.

Chive Bacon Dressing: Add 2 tablespoons chopped chives. If desired, add 2 rashers crisp, crumbled streaky bacon. Serve with or on vegetables, jacket potatoes, salads. Makes about 8 fluid ounces.

SALAD DRESSING WITH CREAM CHEESE

3 ounces cream cheese
6 fluid ounces single cream
2 tablespoons redcurrant jelly
1 tablespoon lemon juice

Soften the cream cheese with a fork and beat until smooth. Slowly blend in remaining ingredients. Chill 1 hour before serving. Makes about ½ pint.

WHIPPED CREAM DRESSING (Master Recipe)

8 fluid ounces double cream
¼ teaspoon salt
2 tablespoons lemon juice or vinegar
Few grains of black pepper

Beat cream until stiff. Fold in other ingredients very slowly. Chill and add to salad just before serving.

Whipped cream dressing may be used as a sweet or savoury dressing by the addition of flavourings and seasonings. It may be delicately tinted with a very small amount of liquid food colouring.

Whipped Cream Dressing

Variations

Anchovy Cream Dressing: Add 3 anchovy fillets, washed, dried, and finely chopped, with 1 teaspoon grated lemon rind to 8 fluid ounces whipped cream dressing just before serving.

Caviar Cream Dressing: Add 1 tablespoon red or black caviar and a few drops onion juice to 8 fluid ounces whipped cream dressing just before serving.

Ginger Cream Dressing: Add 1 teaspoon chopped, candied ginger and 1 teaspoon grated lemon rind to 8 fluid ounces whipped cream dressing just before serving.

Savoury Cream Dressing: Add ¼ teaspoon anchovy paste and a little chopped parsley and chives to 8 fluid ounces whipped cream dressing just before serving.

Horseradish Cream Dressing: Fold 2 tablespoons grated fresh horseradish into 8 fluid ounces whipped cream dressing just before serving. Omit vinegar in master recipe if bottled horseradish is used.

Jam Cream Dressing: Add 5 ounces tart red jelly, such as redcurrant, cranberry, or raspberry, to 8 fluid ounces whipped cream dressing before serving.

Mustard Cream Dressing: In master recipe, beat in 1 tablespoon prepared mustard as cream begins to thicken. Add salt to taste.

Nut Cream Dressing: Add 3 tablespoons chopped nuts to 8 fluid ounces whipped cream dressing before serving.

California Cream Dressing: Add 1 tablespoon each chopped dates, figs, and raisins to 8 fluid ounces whipped cream dressing just before serving.

Pepper Cream Dressing: Add 1 ounce finely chopped green pepper and 2 tablespoons finely chopped canned pimiento to 8 fluid ounces whipped cream dressing before serving.

GREEN GODDESS DRESSING

8 fluid ounces mayonnaise
1 clove garlic, crushed
3 anchovies, chopped
1 ounce finely cut chives or spring onions with tops
1 ounce chopped parsley
1 tablespoon tarragon vinegar
1 tablespoon fresh lemon juice
½ teaspoon salt
Black pepper, coarsely ground
8 fluid ounces soured cream, whipped

Combine ingredients, folding in the whipped soured cream after the other ingredients have been blended.

Tear round lettuce into bite-sized pieces and toss with a generous amount of dressing. Makes ¾ pint.

GARLIC DRESSING

10 to 11 fluid ounces vegetable oil
4 fluid ounces malt vinegar
4 cloves garlic, peeled and halved
1½ teaspoons salt
1 teaspoon sugar
½ teaspoon dry mustard

Combine ingredients in a jar or bottle. Cover, shake well, and store in refrigerator for several hours to blend flavours.

Shake well before serving. Makes ¾ pint.

TOMATO SALAD DRESSING

1 clove garlic, peeled
1 slice soft bread
1 1-pound can tomatoes
3 fluid ounces vegetable oil
2 tablespoons vinegar
½ teaspoon salt
¼ teaspoon black pepper
1 teaspoon sugar
2 teaspoons Angostura bitters

Cut garlic in 3 or 4 pieces and insert in bread. Allow to stand half an hour and remove garlic.

Mix tomatoes, oil, vinegar, and seasonings. Add bread and beat until thoroughly mixed. Serve as a dressing for a tossed green salad.

Tomato Salad Dressing

MASTER FRENCH DRESSING

¼ teaspoon dry mustard
⅛ teaspoon freshly ground pepper
¾ teaspoon salt
2 fluid ounces malt vinegar
¼ to ½ teaspoon paprika
1 teaspoon sugar
6 fluid ounces vegetable oil

Measure all ingredients into a mixing bowl or glass jar. Beat with a fork or rotary beater or cover jar tightly and shake to mix thoroughly.

French dressing may be made in larger quantities and stored in the refrigerator. Always shake well just before serving. Makes 8 fluid ounces.

Variations of French Dressing

Chiffonade Dressing: To master recipe add following, finely chopped: 2 tablespoons parsley, 2 hard-boiled eggs, 2 tablespoons chopped red pepper, 1 tablespoon each chopped olives and cucumber pickle, and ¼ teaspoon paprika.

Chutney French Dressing: In master recipe, use half lemon juice and half vinegar. Add 2 ounces finely chopped chutney.

Cottage Cheese French Dressing: To master recipe add 2 to 4 ounces cottage cheese and shake.

Cream French Dressing: To master recipe add 2 tablespoons fresh or soured cream.

Cream Cheese French Dressing: Mash 3 ounces cream cheese. Stir in French dressing to form a smooth paste. Add to remainder of French dressing and shake well.

Cucumber French Dressing: To master recipe add 4 ounces well drained, grated cucumber. Serve very cold with fish salads.

Curry French Dressing: To master recipe add ¾ teaspoon curry powder before beating.

Egg-Cheese French Dressing: To master recipe add 1 hard-boiled egg (finely chopped), 4 tablespoons grated Cheddar cheese, 1 tablespoon each chopped parsley and chives, and 1 tablespoon each chopped green pepper and canned pimiento.

Foamy French Dressing: Prepare cream French dressing and fold in 1 egg white, beaten until dry but not stiff.

Fruit French Dressing: In master recipe, substitute 2 fluid ounces orange juice for 2 fluid ounces vinegar. Add 1 tablespoon lemon juice. May be sweetened with additional sugar, golden syrup or honey.

Garlic French Dressing: Before preparing master recipe, peel and rub clove of garlic over bottom of bowl. If desired, clove of garlic may be left in dressing about 1 hour.

Ginger French Dressing: To master recipe add 1½ tablespoons finely chopped preserved ginger. Use on salads with fruit.

Grapefruit French Dressing: Use grapefruit juice instead of vinegar in master recipe.

Honey French Dressing: In master recipe, omit mustard and pepper. Add 4 fluid ounces strained honey and beat until frothy. Use on salads with fruit.

Horseradish French Dressing: To master recipe add 2 tablespoons horseradish before serving.

Lemon French Dressing: In master recipe, substitute lemon juice for vinegar.

Lime French Dressing: In master recipe, use equal parts lime and lemon juice, or 3 tablespoons lime and 1 tablespoon lemon juice instead of vinegar.

Mint French Dressing: To master recipe add 1 tablespoon chopped mint.

Olive French Dressing: To master recipe add 8 chopped olives before serving.

Roquefort French Dressing: Crumble 4 ounces Roquefort cheese and add to French dressing before serving.

Spanish Dressing: To master recipe add ½ teaspoon chilli seasoning.

Spicy French Dressing: To master recipe add 2 tablespoons French mustard and 2 teaspoons Worcestershire sauce.

Swiss Dressing: To master recipe add 1 ounce grated Gruyère cheese and ¼ teaspoon Worcestershire sauce.

Tarragon French Dressing: In master recipe, use tarragon vinegar.

Tomato French Dressing: To master recipe add 2 teaspoons tomato juice and a few drops onion juice.

Vinaigrette French Dressing: Follow master recipe. Before beating, add 1 tablespoon chopped pickles, 1 tablespoon chopped capers, 1 tablespoon chopped green olives, 1 tablespoon chopped canned pimiento, 1 teaspoon grated onion, and 1 teaspoon dry mustard.

"TRADITIONAL" FRENCH DRESSING

Many food experts insist this is the only "genuine" French dressing. To 4 fluid ounces vinegar (wine, cider, or malt vinegar) add ¾ teaspoon salt and ½ teaspoon ground white pepper. Stir well with a fork and add 12 fluid ounces olive oil. Beat the mixture with fork until it thickens.

For a garlic flavour, hang a garlic clove by a thread into the bottle containing the vinegar for at least 3 or 4 days before making the dressing.

SPECIAL FRENCH DRESSING

1 clove garlic, finely grated
4 ounces sugar
3 fluid ounces mild vinegar
1 teaspoon Worcestershire sauce
1 small onion, grated
6 fluid ounces tomato ketchup
1 teaspoon salt
16 fluid ounces vegetable oil

Mix in order given and beat thoroughly. Pour into 2-pint jar. Store in cool place.

LOUIS DRESSING

4 fluid ounces chilli pickle
4 fluid ounces mayonnaise or salad dressing
4 fluid ounces creamy French dressing
1 teaspoon Worcestershire sauce

Slowly stir chilli pickle into mayonnaise. Add French dressing and Worcestershire sauce. Mix well.

Serve with lettuce and tomato salads. Makes 12 fluid ounces.

LORENZO DRESSING

4 fluid ounces French dressing
2 tablespoons chopped watercress
2 tablespoons chilli pickle
1 teaspoon chopped canned pimiento
1 teaspoon chopped chives or onion

Blend ingredients thoroughly and serve over tossed salad. Makes 6 fluid ounces.

BLENDER MAYONNAISE

1 egg
¼ teaspoon dry mustard
½ teaspoon salt
2 teaspoons lemon juice or wine vinegar
6 fluid ounces vegetable oil or equal amounts of vegetable and olive oil

Combine egg, mustard, and salt in container of electric blender. Cover and blend at high speed for 5 seconds.

Pour in lemon juice or vinegar and then, blending at low speed, pour in oil as slowly as possible. If the mayonnaise thickens too much at any point, add a few more drops of lemon juice or vinegar. Makes about 8 fluid ounces.

SANDWICHES

Sandwich Hints

Bread for Sandwiches

There are numerous different kinds of bread available from bakers', including the long, hard-crusted loaves of Italian and French white bread, and the odd-shaped and unusually flavoured loaves to be found at many small bakers'. Rolls, bap rolls, scones, and fruit breads are all excellent for sandwiches.

● For more interesting sandwiches, use different kinds of bread in the same sandwich.

● To facilitate slicing and spreading of ordinary sandwiches, use day-old bread of firm texture.

● For rolled sandwiches, use very fresh bread.

● For very thin, dainty sandwiches, buy unsliced bread and cut with a razor-sharp knife into slices not more than ¼-inch thick. If many sandwiches are to be made, sharpen knife frequently.

● When a lot of sandwiches are to be made without crust, cut the crust from the loaf before slicing. However, sandwiches will stay moist longer if the crust is left on, and there'll be no waste.

● For fancy sandwiches to be cut with a biscuit cutter, slice the bread lengthwise.

Butter for Sandwiches

● Cream butter or margarine until soft before spreading. Never melt butter. To facilitate creaming, keep butter at room temperature for about an hour.

● Butter prevents the sandwich from becoming soggy when a moist filling is used.

● For savoury sandwiches, soften butter with mayonnaise; for sweet sandwiches, with a little cream or whipped cream.

Sandwich Fillings

● Sandwich fillings are often a blend of the cook's ingenuity and whatever there is to hand. The recipes and hints that follow should serve as suggestions—starting points for your imagination. An infinite variety of fillings will be developed from them.

● For additional fillings, refer to the spreads in the appetizer and salad sections. The canapé spreads should be used for dainty, attractive tea sandwiches.

● Use a variety of fillings for contrast in colour, flavour, shape, and texture.

● Vegetables, such as cucumber, sliced tomato, and lettuce, should be prepared and added just before serving.

● Sliced fillings such as meat and cheese should be cut very thin and arranged to fit the sandwich.

● For colour in fillings, add chopped canned pimiento, green pepper, parsley, olives, or pickles.

To Keep Sandwiches

● If possible, avoid making sandwiches with moist fillings in advance, since the bread tends to become soggy.

● If sandwiches must be made in advance, wrap in greaseproof paper or slightly dampened cloth.

● To keep sandwiches for an hour or longer, wrap first in greaseproof paper, then in a damp cloth, and place in refrigerator.

● To prevent an interchange of flavours from various fillings, wrap each type separately in greaseproof paper.

● Ribbon, chequerboard, loaf, and other sandwiches, which have to be chilled or even frozen in the refrigerator, should always be well wrapped to preserve the flavour and prevent drying out.

Keep Frozen Sandwiches to Hand

● Sandwich fillings made of sliced cooked meat, meat loaf, chicken, or cheese can be frozen.

● Sandwich spreads also lend themselves to freezing—especially those made of chopped or minced meat, chicken, canned fish (tuna, salmon, etc.), cheese, peanut butter.

● All sandwich fillings should be thoroughly chilled before being used.

● Butter both slices of bread before adding the filling. This will prevent the filling soaking into the bread.

● Work quickly and wrap each sandwich separately in moisture-vapour-proof freezer paper, excluding as much air as possible. Seal or tape and freeze.

● Sandwiches may be stored 2 to 3 months.

● When making sandwiches for the freezer, include a variety of breads such as white, whole meal, rye, raisin, or other family preferences.

● Pack sandwiches, straight from freezer, in lunch bags.

Vary not only the bread and fillings but also the way you cut the sandwiches.

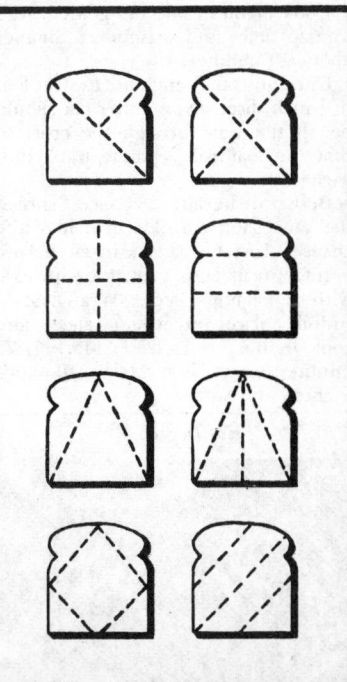

Hot Sandwiches

PICNIC ITALIANOS

1 loaf French bread
8 ounces garlic sausage spread
3 tomatoes, sliced
½ teaspoon oregano
4 1-ounce slices Cheddar or
    Mozzarella cheese

Split bread in two lengthwise. Spread cut slices generously with garlic sausage. Top with tomato slices, sprinkle with oregano, then add cheese slices.

Cook in moderate oven (375°F. Mark 5) until cheese is melted and sandwiches thoroughly heated. Serves 8 to 10.

Suggestions: These may be cooked over an open fire when wrapped in aluminium foil. Especially popular with men and teenagers. For spicier flavour add chilli pickle or tomato ketchup to cheese.

BARBECUED SANDWICHES

(1) Heat sliced roast beef, pork, ham, turkey, or meat loaf in barbecue sauce. Serve in toasted guns. (2) Cover toasted buns with cold or hot sliced meat and pour hot barbecue sauce over buns.

HOT DOG LOAF

½ small onion, chopped
2 tablespoons vegetable oil
1 8-ounce can tomato sauce
1 tablespoon French mustard
2 teaspoons brown sugar
2 teaspoons vinegar
1 teaspoon Worcestershire
    sauce
1 loaf French bread
2 ounces grated mild
    Cheddar cheese
15 frankfurters, halved
    crosswise

Cook onion in oil until golden. Add tomato sauce and seasonings. Simmer about 10 minutes.

Cut ends off French bread. Cut loaf in ¼-inch slices. Every other cut should be all the way through the crust so that the loaf will separate into sandwiches.

Between the attached slices, spread the sauce and sprinkle in half of the cheese. Insert 3 frankfurter halves, letting uncut ends protrude. Sprinkle with remaining cheese. Wrap loaf in tinfoil, place on baking sheet and cook in hot oven (425°F. Mark 7) 25 minutes. Serve hot. Makes 10 sandwiches.

Picnic Italianos

OPEN-FACE SANDWICHES
(Italian Style)

½ pound minced beef
½ pound sausage meat
8 thin slices Mozzarella
    cheese
8 slices French bread
oregano

Mix beef and sausage and shape in 8 thin patties. Grill under medium heat until well browned on both sides.

Put a slice of cheese on each slice of bread. Sprinkle with oregano. Grill until cheese is slightly melted.

While still hot, press a meat patty on each slice.

Makes 8 small sandwiches.

CHICKEN SANDWICH ROYAL

8 slices buttered toast
slices of cooked chicken
slices of tomato
salt
4 ounces grated Cheddar cheese
2 teaspoons Worcestershire sauce

Lay slices of buttered toast on grill pan. Place sliced chicken on toast. Place slices of tomato on the chicken. Sprinkle with salt.

Spread thickly with grated cheese mixed with Worcestershire sauce.

Grill quickly until cheese is melted and browned. Serve at once. Makes 8.

CHEESE AND HAM SAND-WICHES

4 ounces cooked ham, minced or
    chopped
1 clove garlic, crushed
1 8-ounce can tomato sauce
4 ounces Cheddar cheese, grated
1 slightly beaten egg
dash of cayenne pepper

Combine all ingredients in top of double saucepan and cook until cheese melts, stirring constantly. Serve on toasted bread. Serves 6.

HOT ROAST BEEF SAND-WICHES

Make sandwiches with toasted bread and slices of roast beef.

Serve on hot plates, with hot gravy poured over the sandwiches. Garnish with a sprig of parsley and pickles.

CURRY FRIED PORK
SANDWICHES

2 fluid ounces vinegar
4 to 6 slices cooked pork
3 tablespoons flour
2 teaspoons curry powder
½ teaspoon salt
½ ounce margarine
4 slices bread
butter or margarine

Pour vinegar over pork. Allow to stand 15 to 20 minutes.

Combine flour, curry powder, and salt. Drain pork slices and dip in flour mixture. Fry in melted margarine until crisp.

Place between slices of buttered bread. Serve hot. Serves 2.

SAUTÉED MEAT SANDWICHES

Moisten minced leftover meat with thick white sauce or gravy. Place between slices of bread. Brown on each side in hot fat.

BAKED BEANS AND SALAMI

4 ounces salami
1 1-pound can baked beans
2 tablespoons chilli pickle
2 tablespoons French mustard
½ teaspoon grated onion

Cut salami into small bits and combine with remaining ingredients. Mash with a fork.

Spread between slices of bread. Grill the sandwiches, turning to brown both sides.

For Chicken Rarebit Sandwiches, arrange toast in a shallow over dish; top with thick slices of chicken. Cover with cheese sauce; sprinkle lightly with paprika. Heat under grill only until cheese sauce begins to brown lightly.

Hot Dog Loaf

Cheese Strata

CHEESE STRATA

Arrange 6 slices of bread (crusts trimmed) in bottom of rectangular dish.

Place a slice of processed Cheddar cheese on each slice of bread. Cover with 6 slices of bread (crusts trimmed).

Beat 4 eggs. Add 1 pint milk and salt and pepper.

Pour egg and milk mixture over bread and cheese sandwiches. Allow to stand an hour.

Cook in slow oven (325°F. Mark 3) about 40 minutes. Serve plain or with your favourite jam.

SOUFFLÉD CHEESE SANDWICH

4 to 6 slices bread
½ teaspoon salt
3 eggs, separated
dash of black pepper
dash of paprika
2 ounces grated sharp Cheddar cheese

Toast bread (crust removed, if desired) on one side.

Add salt to egg whites and beat until stiff.

Add pepper and paprika to yolks. Beat until light. Add cheese and fold into beaten egg whites.

Heap on untoasted side of bread. Place on greased baking sheet. Bake in moderate oven (350°F. Mark 4) for 15 minutes or until puffy and delicately browned. Serve at once.

Makes 4 to 6 sandwiches, depending upon size of slice and thickness of egg mixture desired.

SAUTÉED TOMATO AND CHEESE

Spread slices of bread with spicy mayonnaise.

Put a slice of tomato and a slice of Cheddar cheese between each 2 slices.

Dip in an egg-milk mixture; fry as for French toast.

WESTERN SANDWICH

For each sandwich, fry 1 tablespoon grated onion in butter until slightly browned.

Add 1 tablespoon chopped cooked ham and stir in 1 slightly beaten egg.

Cook slowly until firm and season with salt and pepper. Serve hot.

OLIVE-CHEESE SANDWICHES

6 ounces black olives
6 ounces grated Cheddar cheese
6 tablespoons mayonnaise
½ teaspoon minced onion
½ teaspoon Worcestershire sauce
6 round rolls
butter or margarine
tomatoes

Cut olives in small pieces. Blend with cheese, mayonnaise, onion, and Worcestershire sauce.

Make 2 cuts part way through each roll from top to bottom, and spread cut edges lightly with butter, then quickly with cheese-olive mixture.

Cut tomatoes in halves and then into thin slices. Put a half slice in each cut.

Place rolls on baking sheet. Cook in moderate oven (375°F. Mark 5) about 15 minutes. Serve at once. Makes 6 rolls.

Olive-Cheese Sandwiches

CHEESE BARBECUE

Grind together 1 pound Cheddar cheese, ½ green pepper, 1 medium onion, 2 hard-boiled eggs, and 4 ounces stuffed olives.

Add 1 5-ounce can condensed tomato soup and 1 ounce melted butter. Mix well.

Spread on halves of rolls or rye bread and grill.

GRILLED COTTAGE CHEESE SANDWICHES

Season cottage cheese with salt and paprika.

Spread on buttered toast. Top with bacon rashers and grill slowly until bacon is crisp.

BACON, CHEESE AND TOMATO DOUBLE DECKERS

12 slices white bread
3 ounces butter or margarine
12 slices Cheddar cheese
6 slices tomato
salt
12 rashers streaky bacon

Trim crusts from white bread slices and toast on one side. Spread untoasted side generously with butter.

Cover 6 slices each with a slice of cheese and remaining 6 slices of bread.

Put slices of peeled tomato on top of second bread slice, add salt and then top with a slice of cheese.

Place in moderate oven until cheese begins to soften.

Place 2 slices of partly grilled bacon on top. Place under low grill; heat until cheese is thoroughly melted and bacon is crisp.

Makes 6 double decker sandwiches.

ROAST TURKEY SANDWICH PUFF

8 slices buttered bread
thin slices cooked turkey
thin slices Cheddar cheese
3 eggs, slightly beaten
12 fluid ounces milk
4 fluid ounces sherry
salt, celery salt, and pepper

Prepare 4 turkey-cheese sandwiches, using bread, turkey, and cheese. Arrange sandwiches in a greased shallow oven pan.

Mix together eggs, milk, sherry, and seasonings. Pour mixture over sandwiches and allow to stand for hour or so. Cook in slow oven (325°F. Mark 3) 1 hour.

To serve, separate sandwiches with a sharp knife and lift on to plates with a broad spatula. Serves 4.

Variations: Slices of cooked chicken or ham may be substituted for the turkey in this recipe.

WAFFLE-GRILLED CHEESE SANDWICHES

For each sandwich, place 1 slice of processed Cheddar cheese between 2 slices of bread.

Brush top and bottom of sandwich with melted butter or margarine.

Put sandwiches in waffle iron until bread is golden brown, and cheese is melted.

Waffle-Grilled Cheese Sandwiches

BARBECUED TUNA BURGERS

1 clove garlic, crushed
½ ounce butter or margarine
1 8-ounce can tomato sauce
2 tablespoons vinegar
1 tablespoon brown sugar
½ teaspoon salt
½ teaspoon dry mustard
½ teaspoon chilli seasoning
1 7-ounce can tuna fish, drained
    and flaked
4 hamburger buns or bap rolls, split

Cook garlic in butter or margarine 1 minute; add remaining ingredients, except tuna fish and buns; simmer 5 minutes. Add tuna; heat thoroughly.

Toast buns; spoon barbecued tuna over buns. Makes 4 sandwiches.

HOT FISH SANDWICHES

½ ounce margarine
1½ tablespoons chopped green pepper
1 tablespoon grated onion
2 slightly beaten eggs
2 fluid ounces milk
½ teaspoon salt
4 ounces flaked canned or cooked
    fish
toasted rolls

Heat margarine and cook green pepper and onion in it until they are tender.

Combine remaining ingredients and add to vegetables. Cook over low heat or boiling water, stirring constantly, until thick and creamy. Serve hot on toasted rolls. Makes 4.

SOUFFLÉED PRAWN SANDWICH

8 slices white bread
2 eggs, separated
4 ounces Cheddar cheese, grated
dash of black pepper
dash of paprika
1 pound prawns, cleaned

Trim crusts from bread; toast lightly and cut in half. Beat egg yolks.

Melt cheese in top of double saucepan. Gradually add to the beaten egg yolks. Add seasonings and fold this mixture into stiffly beaten egg whites. Arrange toast triangles in 4 individual or 1 large greased casserole. Top with cleaned prawns, then the sauce.

Cook in slow oven (325°F. Mark 3) until brown and puffy. Serves 4.

SALMON SANDWICH FONDUE

1 8-ounce can salmon
4 ounces minced celery
4 tablespoons mayonnaise
1 tablespoon French mustard
¼ teaspoon salt
12 thin slices whole wheat bread
6 slices Cheddar cheese
3 beaten eggs
1 pint milk
2 teaspoons Worcestershire sauce
½ teaspoon Aromat

Drain salmon; flake, removing bones; add celery.

Blend mayonnaise, mustard, and salt; add to salmon mixture; mix well.

Spread between bread slices to make 6 sandwiches. Arrange sandwiches in shallow oven dish; top each with slice of cheese.

Combine eggs, milk, Worcestershire sauce, and Aromat. Pour over sandwiches.

Cook in slow oven (325°F. Mark 3) 45 minutes. Makes 6 sandwiches.

FRENCH-TOASTED TUNA FISH CHEESE SANDWICHES

1 7-ounce can tuna fish
1 teaspoon lemon juice
2 ounces diced celery
3 tablespoons mayonnaise
2 ounces butter or margarine
12 slices bread
6 slices Cheddar cheese
2 eggs, beaten
½ teaspoon salt
8 fluid ounces milk
1 ounce butter or margarine

Combine tuna fish, lemon juice, celery, and mayonnaise.

Butter slices of bread on one side; spread 6 buttered slices with tuna fish mixture.

Top each with a slice of cheese and place remaining slices on top; chill.

Combine eggs, salt, and milk; stir to blend. Dip each sandwich in mixture to coat both sides.

Melt butter in frying pan or on griddle over medium heat and lightly brown sandwiches on both sides, turning only once. Serve immediately. Serves 6.

Fish-Finger Buns: Prepare frozen fish fingers according to packet directions. Split frankfurter buns and toast. On each bun half, place a lettuce leaf and two fish fingers. Put a heaped tablespoon of tartare sauce on the fingers. Cover with remaining bun halves. Serve while fish fingers are warm.

OYSTER CLUB SANDWICHES

12 rashers streaky bacon
1 pint oysters
2 ounces plain flour
½ teaspoon salt
⅛ teaspoon black pepper
12 lettuce leaves
12 slices tomato
4 fluid ounces mayonnaise
18 slices buttered toast

Fry bacon and drain on absorbent paper.

Drain oysters, roll in flour seasoned with salt and pepper. Fry in bacon fat. When brown on one side, turn and brown on other side. Cooking time is about 5 minutes. Drain on absorbent paper.

Arrange lettuce, oysters, bacon, tomatoes, and mayonnaise between 3 slices of toast. Fasten with cocktail sticks.

FISH ROLL GRILL

12 long frankfurter rolls
6 large sardines or 6 soused her-
    ring fillets
1 egg white, beaten stiff
6 fluid ounces mayonnaise
2 tablespoons chopped onion
melted butter or margarine

Pull rolls apart lengthwise. Fit sardines or split herring fillets on lower half of roll.

Beat egg white stiff and fold into mayonnaise. Place a line of this mixture on top of fish. Sprinkle finely chopped onion over mayonnaise.

Brush top halves of roll with melted butter or margarine. Arrange both kinds of halves on baking sheet.

Place under grill or in very hot oven (450°F. Mark 8) until lightly browned and both fish and rolls are piping hot. Garnish with radishes and spring onions. Serves 6.

Souffléed Prawn Sandwich

Cheese-Ham Rolls

CHEESE-HAM ROLLS

1 tablespoon finely chopped onion
2 tablespoons chilli pickle
2 tablespoons chopped green pepper
2 tablespoons piccalilli
2 ounces garlic sausage spread
6 ounces grated processed cheese
8 frankfurter rolls

Combine onion, chilli pickle, green pepper, piccalilli, garlic sausage and cheese. Cut rolls in half and place 3 tablespoons cheese-garlic sausage mixture between matched halves.

Wrap and seal each filled roll in aluminium foil. Heat in moderate oven (350°F. Mark 4) for 8 to 10 minutes, or until cheese melts. Makes 8 cheese-ham rolls.

CHEESE CLUB SANDWICH

Melt ½ pound sharp Cheddar cheese in chafing dish or top of double saucepan. Add 3 fluid ounces milk gradually, stirring until sauce is smooth.

Add ½ teaspoon salt, ¼ teaspoon pepper, 1 teaspoon Worcestershire sauce, and ⅛ teaspoon dry mustard.

Trim crusts from 12 slices white bread and toast slices on both sides.

For each sandwich, spread toast slice with mayonnaise, cover with peeled sliced tomatoes and second toast slice spread with mayonnaise on both sides; add 2 slices grilled bacon and a lettuce leaf. Cover with third toast slice spread with mayonnaise.

Cut diagonally and serve each sandwich with generous amount of hot cheese sauce. Garnish with pickles. Makes 4.

GRILLED HAM, CHICKEN AND PICKLE SANDWICHES

4 slices bread, toasted on 1 side
butter or margarine
4 slices cooked or canned chicken
4 slices cooked or canned ham
thin slices dill pickles
4 slices processed cheese

Spread untoasted side of bread with butter or margarine.

Place slice of chicken, then slice of ham on each.

Cover with a layer of pickle, then slice of cheese. Grill until cheese melts. Serve hot. Makes 4.

EGG 'N' BACON SQUARE

Combine 4 chopped hard-boiled eggs, 1 ounce chopped green pepper, ½ teaspoon salt, and enough Thousand Island salad dressing to moisten.

Spread egg mixture over 4 slices whole wheat bread. Top with 1 ounce grilled streaky crumbled bacon.

Place under grill 3 minutes.

TURKEY SANDWICH GRILL

6 ounces chopped cooked turkey
4 ounces finely diced celery
1 tablespoon sweet pickle
6 tablespoons mayonnaise or salad dressing
salt and pepper
6 slices buttered toast
4 ounces grated cheese

Combine turkey, celery, pickle, and mayonnaise. Season to taste with salt and pepper.

Spread turkey mixture on each slice of toast. Sprinkle cheese over each.

Place in hot oven (425°F. Mark 7) or under grill to melt cheese, 2 to 5 minutes.

Serve with a dot of chilli pickle and a sprig of parsley on each sandwich.

If desired, serve with triangles of additional toast, grilled tomatoes and crisp bacon. Makes 6 sandwiches.

CRANBERRY MEAT SANDWICH

Toast bread. Place a slice of grilled or roast meat on each slice of bread. Pour over gravy, if desired. Top with generous spoonful of hot cranberry sauce.

CHEESE SAUCE OVER MEAT SANDWICHES

Melt 4 ounces grated Cheddar cheese in 8 fluid ounces medium white sauce. Pour over any meat sandwich.

SWISS LOAF

1 1-pound loaf unsliced bread
2 ounces butter or margarine
2 to 3 ounces finely chopped onion
2 fluid ounces chilli pickle
1 tablespoon celery salt
8 1-ounce slices Gruyère cheese

With a sharp knife, make 9 equal diagonal slices in loaf, almost through to the bottom crust.

Melt butter in frying pan; add onion and sauté about 5 minutes. Add chilli pickle and celery salt and heat 5 minutes. Remove from heat.

Spread onion mixture and put 1 slice cheese between each slice of bread. Place loaf on baking sheet. Pour remaining onion mixture over top.

Heat in a moderate oven (350°F. Mark 4) for 20 minutes. Serves 8.

TURKEY RED DEVILS

buttered toast
sliced sharp cheese
sliced tomatoes
sliced cooked turkey
1 10½-ounce can condensed cream of mushroom soup
¼ pint broth, milk, or water
Cayenne pepper and mustard (optional)
paprika

Arrange on a shallow oven pan for individual servings—toast topped with the cheese, tomato seasoned with salt and pepper, and the turkey.

Blend soup with broth and season. Top each sandwich with 3 or 4 spoonfuls of the soup. Sprinkle with paprika.

Place in hot oven (425°F. Mark 7) until cheese begins to melt and top is browned, about 15 minutes. The diluted mushroom soup is enough for 4 or 5 sandwiches.

BACON, CHEESE AND TOMATO SANDWICHES

Trim the crusts from slices of bread and toast them on one side. Spread the untoasted sides with mayonnaise.

Place a slice of peeled tomato on each slice of toast.

Place a slice of processed Cheddar cheese on each slice of tomato.

Arrange two slices of partly grilled bacon on each slice of cheese. Place under moderate grill until the cheese melts.

Serve piping hot, and see if it doesn't become one of your family's favourite sandwiches.

Party Sandwiches

HUMPTY-DUMPTY

From a slice of whole wheat bread, cut an egg-shaped piece attached at bottom end to a small rectangle of bread. Spread egg-shaped section with filling and cover with an egg-shaped piece cut from white bread.

Decorate Humpty-Dumpty egg face with diamond shaped cucumber peel for eyes, a strip of raisin for the nose, pimiento cut in half-moon shape for mouth, and a strip of pimiento for belt.

To simulate a wall on which egg is sitting, pipe cream cheese across the rectangular section of bread, representing the cement between the bricks of a wall. Pipe cream cheese on the wall for Humpty-Dumpty's legs.

SAILING BOATS

Cut a slice of whole wheat bread into the shape of a sailing boat; butter and spread with filling.

Cut two sails for each boat from white bread and place them on the whole wheat bread, leaving a narrow strip of filling showing between sails for the boat's mast.

Cut the hull of the boat from whole wheat bread and place it over filling. Cut a flag of pimiento and place it at the top of the mast.

To simulate portholes and waves, pipe cream cheese on the lower part of the hull.

For added interest and colour, coconut that has been tinted green with food colouring may be placed on the cream cheese waves.

FACES

With a biscuit cutter, cut slices of whole wheat and white bread into circles, about 2½ inches in diameter. Butter the bread circles and spread a filling between each two.

To make the face, pipe cream cheese round the top of circle, and sprinkle grated carrot over the cream cheese to simulate hair.

Use strips of raisins for eyebrows and nose, diamond-shaped cucumber peel or green pepper for eyes, and pimiento cut in half-moon shape for mouth.

Children's Sandwich Tray

COTTAGES

Remove crusts from slices of whole wheat bread and cut off top corners to form a pointed roof. Each sandwich requires two slices of whole wheat bread cut in the above shape. Butter the first slice and spread with sandwich filling.

It is suggested that red jam or meat be used as filling to make colourful windows and door.

From second slice, cut door and windows, and place it over first slice.

Decorate house by piping cream cheese shutters at sides of windows and along edge of roof.

CLOWNS

From a slice of whole wheat bread, cut a round clown's head with a cone-shaped hat on one side. Butter and spread with filling.

Place a circle of white bread over the filling for the face, and a triangle of whole wheat for the hat.

Trim the hat and hair sections of the clown face with cream cheese. Sprinkle the "cheese hair" with coconut that has been tinted green with food colouring.

Cut round eyes from black olives, a half-moon-shaped mouth from pimiento, and tiny triangles of pimiento for cheeks.

Lily Sandwiches

LILY SANDWICHES

Cut thinly sliced fresh bread into 2¾-inch rounds. Roll over each round with a rolling pin to remove the "spring" of the bread.

Spread each round with a cheese spread, softened at room temperature, and place a carrot strip in the centre to represent the stamen. Fold over at one edge to form a lily and pinch together to hold in place.

Put a parsley stem on the end of each lily, to represent the stem.

MOSAICS

From the centre of slices of buttered whole wheat and white breads, cut out a small design with a biscuit cutter.

Reverse cut-outs, placing the white bread cut-out into the whole wheat slice and the whole wheat bread cut-out into the white bread slice.

Place each slice, buttered side down, on alternate slices of white or whole wheat bread spread with a sandwich filling. Trim crusts from sandwiches. Use raisins to decorate.

Different cut-outs, such as stars, rabbits, or hearts, may be used for variety.

TEA SANDWICHES

Cut an equal number of slices of white and whole wheat bread. Cut into desired shapes with fancy biscuit cutters.

Cut fancy designs in half of the slices of white and whole wheat bread.

Spread whole slices of bread with desired sandwich filling. Top spread slices with cut-out slices.

The shapes cut out of the white bread in forming fancy designs may be fitted into the cuts made in the dark bread, and vice versa.

RIBBON SANDWICHES

Start with 2 slices white bread and 2 slices whole wheat.

Stack these alternately (light-dark-light-dark) with a filling of softened butter or margarine, cream cheese, meat or fish spread, or jam between each slice.

Press stack firmly together and slice crusts from all sides.

Wrap tightly in greaseproof paper and chill in refrigerator for several hours.

Just before serving cut stack down into ¼ inch thick ribbon slices.

...bon Sandwiches

Little Layers

...equerboard Sandwiches

Roll-ups

...alentine Sandwiches

Pinwheels

PINWHEELS

Using an unsliced loaf of bread, cut crusts off all sides.

Cut into lengthwise slices about ¼ inch thick.

Run rolling pin lightly over the slices to make the bread easy to handle and less likely to crack.

Spread with softened butter or margarine, then if desired with a spread.

Arrange stuffed olives, pickles, or frankfurters across short end of bread.

Roll up tightly as you do a Swiss roll. Wrap rolls individually in greaseproof paper or aluminium foil, twisting ends securely. Chill several hours or overnight.

To serve cut each chilled roll down into ¼ to ½ inch slices.

LITTLE LAYERS

Cut crusts from slices of sandwich bread. Spread with softened butter or margarine.

Cut into circles with a 2½-inch biscuit cutter.

Use three rounds for each sandwich. Cover bottom round with pimiento cheese spread. Top with another circle of bread and spread with chopped eggs and mayonnaise. Now place a buttered circle, plain-side-up, on top.

Coat sandwiches all over with cream cheese, moistened with a little cream.

CHEQUERBOARD SANDWICHES

Prepare 2 stacks as directed for ribbon sandwiches.

Cut each stack into ½-inch slices. Then put 3 alternating slices together, with softened butter or a spread between, so that light and dark breads alternate to form a chequerboard design.

Wrap each block in greaseproof paper and chill for several hours.

To serve, remove from refrigerator and with a sharp knife, immediately cut each block crosswise into chequerboard slices, ½ inch thick.

ROLL-UPS

Cut crusts from thin-sliced white or whole wheat bread. Lightly flatten out with rolling pin.

Spread with softened butter or margarine to keep bread from getting soggy.

Place asparagus tip, celery heart, or watercress sprig across one end of slice.

Roll up each slice Swiss-roll fashion into a tight roll.

Cover with a damp cloth until serving time. Serve roll-ups whole or cut in half.

VALENTINE SANDWICHES

Trim crusts from slices of bread, then with a heart-shaped biscuit cutter, cut out a heart design from the centre of each slice.

Spread half of the "hearts" with sandwich filling and top with a matching heart.

Let the remaining portion of the bread, from which the heart was taken, serve as half of a second sandwich to eliminate waste of bread. Just trim the edges of the two slices to be sure they are the same size.

CARD PARTY SANDWICHES

Slice bread thinly. Spread with any desired sandwich filling and place a second slice on top of the first. Press lightly together, then cut out with biscuit cutters in the form of hearts, diamonds, clubs, and spades.

Garnish top with tiny pieces of pimiento cut in heart or diamond shapes, or with pieces of black olives cut to form spades or clubs.

For a children's party, serve tiny sandwiches cut in animal shapes.

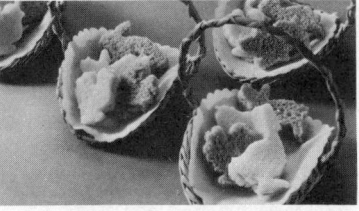

Garnish heart-shaped sandwiches with tiny hearts cut from cranberry or red-currant jelly.

Party glamour is added to the snack tray by a patterned arrangement of the sandwiches.

Many of these tiny finger sandwiches can be prepared ahead of time, chilled in the refrigerator and brought to the serving table freshly sliced.

Sandwich Loaves

SHERRY-CHEESE SANDWICH LOAF

Remove all crusts from a day-old 12-inch loaf of sandwich bread. (If only a longer loaf is available, slice off the extra bread and reserve for other purposes.) Cut the loaf lengthwise into 4 slices of equal thickness; keep slices in order.

Place bottom slice on a serving plate or tray; spread with softened butter or margarine, then with Filling 1 (below). Butter both sides of the next slice; press in place over bottom slice; spread with Filling 2 (below). Butter both sides of the third slice; press in place; spread with Filling 3 (below). Butter bottom of the top slice; press in position.

Spread Sherry-Cheese Coating (below) over top and sides of loaf.

If desired, decorate top of loaf with slices of stuffed olive, strips of pimiento, green pepper, etc.

Chill in the refrigerator for several hours. Before serving, garnish serving plate with bunches of parsley or watercress or crisp lettuce leaves. Slice crosswise with a sharp knife and serve with forks.

Filling 1: Mix 8 ounces garlic sausage spread, 2 ounces finely chopped celery and enough mayonnaise to moisten.

Filling 2: Peel 2 medium-sized tomatoes; slice crosswise in very thin slices. Arrange slices on the bread; spread with mayonnaise; sprinkle with salt and pepper.

Filling 3: Grate or chop 4 hard-boiled eggs. Mix eggs with 2 ounces cottage cheese, enough mayonnaise to moisten, and seasonings to taste.

Sherry-Cheese Coating: Blend ½ pound cream cheese with 5 ounces strong cheese spread. Gradually beat in about 4 fluid ounces sherry (enough to make a fluffy mixture that will spread easily). Season with ¼ teaspoon each Worcestershire sauce and French mustard, and salt to taste.

Sherry-Cheese Sandwich Loaf

TULIP SANDWICH LOAF

½ pound cold boiled ham
½ pound Cheddar cheese
6 sweet pickles
mayonnaise
1 loaf unsliced sandwich bread
9 ounces cream cheese
cream
4 ounces canned pimientos
1 green pepper

Mince ham and grate cheese. Combine ham, cheese, and chopped pickles and add enough mayonnaise to moisten.

Remove crusts from loaf of bread. Cut a ½- to ¾-inch-thick slice of bread the length of the loaf. Remove centre of remaining loaf, so there is a box made of bread having ½- to ¾-inch-thick sides and bottom.

Spread inside of loaf of bread and one side of slice generously with softened butter. Put sandwich filling inside loaf and put top slice on with butter side down.

Soften the cream cheese with a small amount of cream until you have a spreading consistency. Cover loaf with cream cheese.

Cut small tulips and leaves from the pimiento and green pepper and decorate the sides of the loaf.

Chill for at least one hour and when ready to serve cut in one-inch slices. Serves 12 to 15.

CHEESE-COATED SALMON LOAF

1 large loaf bread
butter or margarine
1 8-ounce can salmon
3 tablespoons chopped pickles
mayonnaise
2 large tomatoes
salt and pepper to taste
½ green pepper, chopped
4 ounces grated raw carrots
2 ounces chopped celery
12 ounces cream cheese
12 fluid ounces single cream

Remove crusts from bread. Cut into four slices lengthwise. Spread each slice with softened butter.

Drain and flake salmon. Combine with chopped pickles, moisten with mayonnaise, and spread on first slice.

Cover second slice of bread with sliced tomatoes. Season.

Combine green pepper with mayonnaise. Spread over sliced tomatoes.

Combine grated carrots and chopped celery. Season with salt and pepper, moisten with mayonnaise, and spread on third slice of bread.

Put the four slices together, press into loaf shape, wrap tightly in greaseproof paper. Chill.

Tulip Sandwich Loaf

Spread top and sides with cream cheese softened with cream. Keep in refrigerator until ready to serve.

Garnish with radish roses, parsley, carrot strips, stuffed olives, pimiento, etc. Cut into 1-inch-thick slices.

BAKED TUNA FISH OR SALMON SANDWICH LOAF

1 medium loaf white or whole wheat bread
1 6-ounce can tuna fish or salmon
3 hard-boiled eggs, chopped
1 10½-ounce can condensed mushroom soup
½ teaspoon celery salt
¼ teaspoon onion salt
dash of black pepper
2 fluid ounces vegetable oil
3 fluid ounces milk

Remove crusts from the loaf of bread and slice lengthwise in thirds.

Combine tuna fish and eggs and moisten with 3 fluid ounces mushroom soup. Season with celery and onion salt and pepper. Spread between bread slices.

Brush top and sides of loaf with melted oil. Place in moderate oven (375°F. Mark 5) 20 minutes or until lightly browned.

Add milk to remaining soup; heat and serve as a sauce. Serves 6.

MEAT STUFFED RYE LOAF

1 large onion, sliced
1 ounce dripping
½ pound minced beef
½ ounce chopped parsley
1 carrot, grated
2 teaspoons salt
1 tablespoon chilli pickle
¼ teaspoon black pepper
¼ teaspoon paprika
1 loaf rye bread, unsliced
1 medium onion, grated

Cook sliced onion in fat until lightly browned. Add beef, and cook until browned. Add parsley, carrot, and seasonings; cook 5 minutes.

Cut a slice from one end of bread, and put aside; take out soft centre of bread, and mix with meat mixture. Add grated onion, ¼ pint water; mix well; stuff into loaf. Put back cut slice, and fasten with cocktail sticks.

Place in moderate oven (350°F. Mark 4) 25 minutes. Slice to serve. Serves 4.

SALMON SALAD SURPRISE LOAF

1 large loaf day-old white bread, unsliced
4 hard-boiled eggs, chopped
1 1-pound 4-ounce can red salmon, flaked and boned
1 tablespoon grated lemon rind
1 tablespoon lemon juice
1 ounce finely chopped celery
1½ teaspoons salt
6 fluid ounces mayonnaise or salad dressing
1 tablespoon chopped green pepper
2 tablespoons sliced green olives

With a sharp knife, remove the crusts from a loaf of bread to make an even, box-shaped loaf. Cut a lengthwise slice from the top (see below).

Hollow out the centre of the loaf, leaving side walls and bottom at least ½ inch thick. Place on a baking sheet. (Save centre of loaf for breadcrumbs or stuffing.)

Combine chopped eggs, flaked salmon, lemon rind, lemon juice, celery, salt, mayonnaise, pepper, and olives.

Loaf Topping:
1 tablespoon unflavoured gelatine
1 tablespoon diluted vinegar
8 fluid ounces mayonnaise or salad dressing
¼ teaspoon cayenne pepper
½ teaspoon Worcestershire sauce
1 hard-boiled egg, sliced
3 sliced olives

Mix gelatine with vinegar and dissolve over hot water. Slowly combine mayonnaise and dissolved gelatine. Add pepper and Worcestershire sauce.

To Complete Salmon Salad Surprise Loaf: Fill centre of the loaf of bread with salmon salad. Cover with top slice of bread. Spread top and sides of loaf with topping mixture. Garnish with sliced egg and olives.

Cover finished loaf with heavy greaseproof paper to prevent discolouration of mayonnaise from moisture.

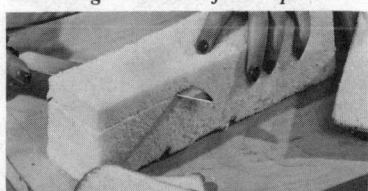

1. Remove crusts from loaf of bread. Cut a lengthwise slice from top.

2. Hollow out centre of the loaf, leaving side walls and bottom at least half an inch thick. Fill centre of loaf.

Place in refrigerator for 12 hours. To serve: cut 1-inch slices. Serves 8.

HAM 'N' EGG SALAD SANDWICH LOAF

Remove crusts from small loaf of unsliced bread, leaving top rounded. Cut in 3 lengthwise slices.

Spread bottom slice with egg filling (below); cover with middle slice. Spread with ham filling (below). Cover with rounded top slice.

Wrap in greaseproof paper. Chill. Coat thinly with mayonnaise.

Garnish with "flowers" made of pimiento strips and capers and sprays of endive. Cut in slices to serve. Serves 8.

Egg Filling:
4 hard-boiled eggs, chopped
2 tablespoons chopped green pepper
few grains black pepper
¼ teaspoon Aromat
2 tablespoons mayonnaise

Combine all ingredients; mix well.

Ham Filling:
¼ pound cooked ham, minced
3 tablespoons chopped celery
few grains black pepper
¼ teaspoon Aromat
1½ tablespoons mayonnaise

Combine all ingredients; mix well.

POOR BOY SANDWICH

This hearty snack, native to New Orleans, Louisiana, U.S.A., is made in dozens of different ways, depending on one's taste and what is available.

A medium-long, thin loaf of French bread is slit in half lengthwise and generously buttered. Then the loaf is sliced in three or four, not quite through the bottom crust. A different kind of filling goes in each section.

3. Spread top and sides with topping mixture. Garnish and cover with greaseproof paper. Chill in refrigerator 12 hours.

Salmon Salad Surprise Loaf

Ham 'n' Egg Salad Sandwich Loaf

Fried oysters almost invariably go in one part. The other sections can be filled with slices of well seasoned tomato with a rasher of grilled bacon, another with sausage, chicken salad, fried egg with hot chilli pepper, or chopped green pepper and onion, and so on, using any appetizing tidbit desired.

HOT CHICKEN SALAD LOAF

1 1-pound loaf day-old white bread, unsliced
½ ounce soft butter or margarine
9 ounces chopped, cooked chicken
3 ounces finely chopped celery
2 teaspoons chopped onion
1½ teaspoons chopped parsley
4 fluid ounces mayonnaise or salad dressing
¼ teaspoon salt
dash of black pepper

With a sharp knife, remove crusts from loaf of bread to make an even, box-shaped loaf. Cut a lengthwise slice from the top.

Hollow out the centre of loaf, leaving sides and bottom at least ½ inch thick. Spread butter on inside walls of the cavity. (Save centre of loaf for breadcrumbs or stuffing.)

Combine chicken, celery, onion, parsley, mayonnaise, salt, and pepper. Fill centre of the loaf with chicken salad.

Cover with top slice of bread. Wrap loaf in heavy greaseproof paper. Chill in refrigerator for 6 hours.

Loaf Topping: Beat 2 egg whites until stiff. Fold in 4 tablespoons mayonnaise and a dash of salt.

To Complete Loaf: Unwrap and spread top and sides of loaf with topping mixture. Place on baking sheet and brown in very hot oven (450°F. Mark 8) 10 minutes. Serve hot and cut crosswise into 6 sections. Serve with whole cranberry sauce. Serves 6.

GOURMET SANDWICH LOAF

4 hard-boiled eggs
6 ounces finely chopped cooked turkey
2 ounces chopped sweet pickles or pickle relish
1 10½-ounce can cream of mushroom soup
salt and pepper
12 slices bread
1 ounce softened butter or margarine
2 fluid ounces milk

Chop 2 of the eggs. Combine with turkey, pickles, and half of the soup. Season to taste with salt and pepper.

Trim crusts from bread and cut slices in half to make 24 pieces. Place 6 pieces of bread close together on baking sheet or heat-proof serving dish. Spread with turkey mixture. Top with layer of bread.

Repeat until there are 3 layers of turkey and 4 layers of bread. Brush top with softened butter.

Place in moderate oven (375°F. Mark 5) until lightly browned, 15 minutes.

Blend milk with remaining soup. Heat to boiling. Add remaining chopped eggs. Pour over 6 sandwiches.

TEA SANDWICH LOAF

Prepare the following sandwich fillings: salmon salad, olive and nut, and egg salad.

Remove crusts from an unsliced loaf of white bread and cut lengthwise into five slices.

Spread each bread slice with softened butter. Spread salmon salad between first and second slices of bread; olive and nut between second and third slices; egg salad between third and fourth slices; a sharp processed cheese spread topped with a layer of tomatoes between fourth and fifth slices.

Press loaf firmly together. Wrap in greaseproof paper and chill for an hour.

Coat top and sides of loaf with cream cheese softened with cream. Arrange chopped parsley, sliced cucumber, and a fish-shaped slice of pimiento on top

Turkey 'n' Cranberry Rounds

of loaf. Garnish serving dish with lemon wedges, tomato slices, and parsley. Cut into thick slices when serving.

MINCEMEAT PARTY LOAVES

1 pound cream cheese
9 ounces mincemeat
4 fluid ounces water
32 slices white bread, cut 3 inches square
5 ounces cream cheese spread
8 ounces cranberry sauce, drained
4 fluid ounces single cream

Allow cream cheese to soften at room temperature. Place mincemeat in small saucepan. Add water. Place over low heat and stir until mincemeat is thoroughly broken up. Increase heat and boil briskly for 3 to 5 minutes or until mixture is dry, stirring frequently. Chill.

To make each loaf, spread about 2 tablespoons of mincemeat on a slice of bread, about 1½ tablespoons of cheese spread on second slice of bread and about 2 tablespoons of cranberry sauce on third slice of bread. Pile spread bread slices one on top of the other. Top with fourth slice of plain bread.

Wrap in greaseproof paper and chill in refrigerator. Repeat procedure for each loaf. Meanwhile beat cream cheese until light and fluffy. Gradually add cream, blending until smooth and fluffy Coat each loaf on all sides and top. Garnish with crystallized fruit.

Return to refrigerator and chill. To serve, slice diagonally. Makes 8 3-inch square loaves.

TURKEY 'N' CRANBERRY ROUNDS

18 slices bread
2 ounces softened butter or margarine
1 pound jellied cranberry sauce
4 ounces diced turkey
3 tablespoons sliced olives
3 tablespoons chopped pickles
1 ounce diced celery
1 tablespoon grated onion
3 tablespoons mayonnaise
½ teaspoon salt
8 ounces cream cheese, softened

Cut bread slices into rounds the size of cranberry slices. Spread with softened butter or margarine.

Cut jellied cranberry sauce into 6 slices. Place a slice on 6 rounds of bread.

Top each with 2nd round of bread. Spread 2nd round with turkey filling made by combining turkey, olives, pickles, celery, onion, mayonnaise and salt.

Top with 3rd bread round. Coat with cream cheese. Serves 6.

YULE LOG SANDWICH

Prepare the following fillings: garlic sausage-peanut butter; egg-bacon; avocado-pineapple; cheese-prawn; cranberry-cheese.

Remove crusts from an unsliced loaf of white bread and cut lengthwise into 5 slices.

Butter slices and spread each with one of the first four fillings above. Stack and top with 5th bread slice.

Press loaf firmly together. Wrap in greaseproof paper and chill for 1 hour.

Frost top and sides of loaf with cranberry-cheese mixture, making lengthwise ridges with a spatula.

Garnish platter with cinnamon pear halves set on lettuce leaves, with canned cherries for bell clappers. Cut into thick slices to serve.

Sandwich Fillings for Yule Log

Garlic Sausage-Peanut Butter: Combine 3 ounces peanut butter, 3 ounces garlic sausage spread, 4 tablespoons mayonnaise, 3 tablespoons chopped dill pickle.

Egg-Bacon: Combine 2 chopped hard-boiled eggs, 1 to 2 ounces chopped cooked bacon, 3 tablespoons mayonnaise.

Avocado Pineapple: Combine 3 ounces mashed avocado, 2 tablespoons drained crushed pineapple, 1 teaspoon lemon juice, 1 tablespoon mayonnaise, and a dash of salt.

Cheese-Prawn: Combine 4 ounces pimiento cream cheese, ½ teaspoon chilli pickle, 3 ounces finely chopped cooked prawns, and ½ teaspoon lemon juice.

Cranberry-Cheese: Combine 6 ounces cream cheese with 6 ounces strained cranberry sauce, mixing with a rotary beater until smooth.

A delicious sandwich loaf makes a good party food and is easy to make. For a Christmas party, the pimiento tree arranged on the cream cheese frosting adds a festive note.

Fish and Shellfish Sandwiches

SARDINE-PICKLE FILLING

1 4-ounce can sardines packed in
oil, drained, flaked
1 dill pickle, chopped, or 2 tablespoons plus 1 teaspoon sweet
pickle relish
1 tablespoon softened butter or
margarine
1 teaspoon French mustard
1 tablespoon salad dressing or
mayonnaise

Combine ingredients and spread on
toast. Makes spread for 4 sandwiches.

TUNA FISH AND COLESLAW SUBMARINES

2 tablespoons mayonnaise or salad
dressing
2 tablespoons chilli pickle
1 tablespoon lemon juice
dash of salt
1 7-ounce can tuna fish, drained
and flaked
2 small loaves or 1 large loaf French
bread
4 ounces coleslaw, well drained

Blend mayonnaise or salad dressing,
chilli pickle, lemon juice, and salt; add
tuna fish; toss lightly.

Split French bread lengthwise almost
through; spread with additional mayonnaise or salad dressing; line with
lettuce, if desired.

Fill first with tuna mixture, then with
coleslaw. Cut in serving slices. Serves 4.

SARDINE-EGG FILLING

Combine 1 can drained, mashed sardines and 2 chopped hard-boiled eggs.
Moisten with lemon juice to taste.

*Danish Open Sandwiches: A colourful
open sandwich buffet would make a
pleasant lunch-time or supper snack.
Your imagination is the only limit
when it comes to the filling. Pictured
here are toppings of roast beef with
horseradish, egg and asparagus, and
prawns with fresh dill. Each roll half
was spread with mayonnaise glaze
before the toppings were added.*

*To make mayonnaise glaze: Soften 1
tablespoon unflavoured gelatine in 4
tablespoons cold water. Stir in 8 fluid
ounces mayonnaise and heat, stirring
constantly, until gelatine is dissolved.*

EGG-CRABMEAT-ALMOND SANDWICH BARS

3 ounces cream cheese
2 tablespoons milk
2 tablespoons chopped, toasted
almonds
1 hard-boiled egg, chopped
1 ounce flaked crabmeat
¼ teaspoon celery salt
2 tablespoons mayonnaise or salad
dressing
1 teaspoon lemon juice
3 lengthwise slices whole wheat
bread (from unsliced loaf)
2 ounces soft butter or margarine

Combine cream cheese, milk, and
almonds. Combine chopped egg, crabmeat, celery salt, mayonnaise, and
lemon juice.

Spread each slice of bread with butter. Spread cheese-almond mixture on
1 slice of bread; top with second slice,
buttered-side-up.

Spread egg-crabmeat mixture on
second slice of bread; top with third
slice, buttered-side-down.

Press loaf together gently. Wrap in
greaseproof paper, twisting ends of
paper; chill.

To serve: unwrap and cut sandwich
loaf in half lengthwise. Cut each lengthwise strip into 16 sections. Makes 32.

SALMON SALAD FILLING

10 ounces flaked salmon
1 ounce chopped celery
1 tablespoon chopped green pepper
2 tablespoons salad dressing

Combine salmon, celery, and green
pepper. Add salad dressing and mix
thoroughly. Makes filling enough for
6 sandwiches.

SALMON BOATS

1 8-ounce can salmon, drained and
flaked
4 ounces diced celery
4 tablespoons salad dressing
2 hard-boiled eggs, chopped
½ teaspoon onion salt
⅛ teaspoon black pepper
6 frankfurter rolls
lettuce

Combine salmon, celery, salad dressing, eggs, and seasonings.

Split 6 frankfurter rolls; line with
lettuce; spoon salmon salad into rolls.
Makes 6 salad rolls.

TUNA FISH AND EGG FILLING

Combine 7 ounces flaked tuna fish,
and 2 chopped hard-boiled eggs, with
1½ ounces chopped stuffed olives.
Moisten with mayonnaise.

*Lobster Party Sandwiches: Flaked
cooked lobster was combined with
chopped celery and grated onion, then
moistened with mayonnaise to make the
topping for the half slices of whole
wheat bread.*

ANCHOVY FILLING

4 ounces mashed anchovies or
anchovy paste
2 ounces chopped olives
2 ounces butter or margarine

Mix ingredients together to form a
smooth paste. Store in refrigerator.
Makes 8 ounces.

FLAKED FISH FILLING

6 ounces flaked cooked fish
1 tablespoon chopped celery
1 tablespoon chopped pickles
(sweet or sour)
3 tablespoons mayonnaise
½ tablespoon horseradish
¼ teaspoon salt
⅛ teaspoon black pepper

Combine all ingredients and mix
well.

PRAWN SPECIAL FILLING

8 ounces chopped, cooked or canned
prawns
3 tablespoons chopped celery
¼ teaspoon salt
1 teaspoon lemon juice
mayonnaise

Combine all ingredients well and
moisten with mayonnaise.

SARDINE FILLING

Mix sardines with chopped hard-
boiled eggs, grated cheese, butter, and
lemon juice. Season with curry powder.

SALAD FILLED ROLLS

4 ounces black olives
2 hard-boiled eggs
1 7-ounce can tuna fish
3 ounces chopped celery
4 fluid ounces mayonnaise
6 long, thin rolls
butter or margarine
lettuce

Cut olives into large pieces. Dice
eggs. Drain oil from tuna fish and flake
coarsely. Combine olives, eggs, tuna
fish and celery and blend lightly with
mayonnaise.

Cut rolls in half, leaving one side
attached, and hollow slightly. Butter
inside, and heap with filling. Tuck a
crisp lettuce leaf inside each roll.
Serves 6.

Cheese and Egg Sandwiches

EGGS AND LIVER FILLING

4 chopped, hard-boiled eggs
3 ounces cooked liver
salt and pepper
prepared horseradish
mayonnaise

Combine hard-boiled eggs with chopped cooked liver. Season with salt and pepper and prepared horseradish. Moisten with mayonnaise.

DEVILLED EGG FILLING

3 hard-boiled eggs
3 teaspoons chopped parsley
3 teaspoons vinegar
$\frac{1}{8}$ teaspoon dry mustard
$\frac{1}{4}$ teaspoon salt
$\frac{1}{8}$ teaspoon black pepper

Chop hard-boiled eggs fine. Combine with parsley, vinegar, dry mustard, salt, and pepper. Blend well.

EGG-CELERY FILLING

3 hard-boiled eggs
salt and pepper
2 ounces finely chopped celery
mayonnaise or prepared sandwich
     spread

Chop hard-boiled eggs well. Season with salt and pepper. Mix with celery and mayonnaise or prepared sandwich spread. Makes 4 sandwiches.

EGG-MAYONNAISE FILLING

3 hard-boiled eggs
2 ounces chopped black olives
4 tablespoons mayonnaise
$\frac{1}{4}$ teaspoon French mustard
$\frac{1}{4}$ teaspoon salt
black pepper to taste

Chop eggs and blend with remaining ingredients. Makes about 8 ounces.

EGG-HAM FILLING

Combine 4 chopped hard-boiled eggs and 2 to 4 ounces chopped boiled ham. Moisten with mayonnaise.

EGG-BACON FILLING

4 chopped hard-boiled eggs
6 rashers crisp bacon, chopped
3 tablespoons chopped olives
$\frac{1}{4}$ teaspoon salt
mayonnaise

Combine hard-boiled eggs, bacon, olives, and salt. Moisten with mayonnaise.

EGG AND WATERCRESS FILLING

Mix chopped hard-boiled egg, watercress, and mayonnaise.

EGGS AND SPINACH FILLING

Mix chopped hard-boiled eggs with half the amount of spinach.

CREAMY CHEESE FILLING

4 tablespoons mayonnaise
8 to 9 ounces cream cheese
1 ounce chopped green pepper
1½ teaspoons grated onion

Blend all ingredients to spreading consistency. Makes about 10 ounces.

CREAMY CHEESE-OLIVE FILLING

3 ounces cream cheese
1 to 2 tablespoons milk or cream
2 ounces chopped black olives
dash of Tabasco sauce
salt to taste

Soften cheese and gradually blend in milk to make spreading consistency. Blend in olives and seasonings to taste. Makes about 6 ounces.

COTTAGE CHEESE-CUCUMBER FILLING

½ cucumber
1 tablespoon grated onion
½ teaspoon salt
1 pound cottage cheese
dash of black pepper

Peel cucumber and grate or grind, then mix with onion and salt. Place in sieve over a bowl until just ready to make sandwiches.

Mix well with cottage cheese and dash of pepper. Additional salt to taste may be added. Makes 8 to 10 sandwiches.

ROQUEFORT-OLIVE SWIRL SANDWICHES

3 tablespoons cream cheese
2 tablespoons grated Roquefort
     cheese
½ tablespoon milk
4 slices white bread
2 or 3 black olives

Combine cream cheese, Roquefort cheese, and milk. Cut each slice of bread into 4 1½-inch circles with a biscuit cutter. Spread 1 teaspoon cheese mixture on each circle.

Garnish top of each sandwich with slivers of black olives arranged in a swirl pattern. Makes 16.

COTTAGE CHEESE-GREEN PEPPER FILLING

½ pound dry cottage cheese
3 fluid ounces evaporated milk
1 teaspoon salt
$\frac{1}{8}$ teaspoon black pepper
3 tablespoons chopped green pepper
1 tablespoon grated onion

Cream cottage cheese with evaporated milk until smooth. Add salt, pepper, green pepper, and grated onion. Mix well. Makes 5 sandwiches.

Flower Sandwiches

FLOWER SANDWICHES

white bread
pimiento cheese spread
cream cheese
milk
sliced stuffed olives
small squares green pepper
slivers of green pepper

Cut thinly sliced bread with biscuit cutter. Spread half of the slices with pimiento cheese spread and the stem with cream cheese softened with milk.

Top the centres of the flowers with olive slices or small squares of green pepper. Decorate the leaves and stems with slivers of green pepper.

CHERRY-CHEESE ROLLS

3 ounces cream cheese
2 tablespoons chopped maraschino
     cherries
1 ounce soft butter or margarine
20 maraschino cherries
2 lengthwise thin slices white
     bread (cut from unsliced
     sandwich loaf)

Combine cream cheese and chopped cherries. Spread each slice of bread with butter, then with cheese-cherry mixture.

Cut each slice in half crosswise. Place a row of five cherries across width of each half slice of bread, pressing cherries firmly together end to end.

Roll each half slice of bread as for Swiss roll, starting at cherry end, being careful to keep first turn firm and cherries in place.

Wrap each roll in greaseproof paper, twisting ends of paper. Place on a flat surface so that roll rests on last turn of bread; chill.

To serve: unwrap and cut each roll into 6 slices. Makes 24.

Meat and Poultry Sandwiches

HAM-OLIVE PINWHEELS

6 tablespoons minced boiled ham
2 tablespoons mayonnaise
1 teaspoon prepared horseradish
1 loaf sandwich bread, unsliced
2 ounces butter
6 stuffed olives

Combine ham, mayonnaise, and horseradish. Remove crusts from bread.

Cut bread lengthwise into slices ¼-inch thick. Spread with softened butter and with ham mixture.

Place olives in a line crosswise at one end of the bread; roll bread starting at the end of slice.

Wrap roll in a damp cloth or grease-proof paper and place in refrigerator for several hours.

When ready to serve cut crosswise into slices any thickness desired. This makes sufficient filling for 1 full-length slice of bread which will cut into 8 thin pinwheels.

Other Meat or Fish Fillings: Use minced cooked or canned chicken or turkey or canned or cooked fish instead of ham.

Peanut Butter Filling: Omit horseradish and substitute 3 ounces peanut butter for the ham.

Cream Cheese Filling: Spread with a mixture of cream cheese and just enough chilli pickle to give the cheese a spreading consistency.

ROLLED CHICKEN SAND-WICHES
(For a Crowd)

8 to 9 ounces soft cream cheese
12 ounces finely minced cooked chicken
2 ounces finely diced celery
1 ounce chopped parsley
4 fluid ounces Sauternes or other dry white wine
2 teaspoons grated onion
1 teaspoon Worcestershire sauce
salt to taste
softened butter or margarine
36 to 40 thin slices very fresh white bread, crusts trimmed

Blend cheese, chicken, celery, and parsley. Gradually beat in wine. Add onion and seasonings.

Spread bread with butter, after rolling lightly with rolling pin, and spread with filling. Roll up like Swiss roll.

Place seam-side-down on dish or shallow pan. Cover with greaseproof paper, then wrap in damp towel and chill ½ hour or longer before serving. Makes 36 to 40.

TURKEY OR CHICKEN CLUB SANDWICHES

Spread a slice of toast with butter and mayonnaise. Add layer of thin sliced cooked chicken or turkey. Top with another buttered slice of toast.

Then add grilled rashers of streaky bacon, slices of tomato and a leaf of lettuce. Cover with third slice of toast. Skewer together with cocktail sticks and cut into quarters.

MINCED BEEF FILLINGS

1. Cook minced beef with chopped celery and onion. Mix with a little horseradish and salad dressing.
2. Cook minced beef with a little chopped onion. Mix with chilli pickle and mayonnaise.
3. Cooked minced beef mixed with pickle and mayonnaise.
4. Slice each of meat loaf, tomato, and cheese, spread with French mustard.
5. Slice meat loaf, pickle, sliced hard-boiled egg, and salad dressing.

MINCED HAM FILLING

4 fluid ounces vinegar
1 teaspoon French mustard
½ teaspoon salt
1½ ounces light brown sugar
1 egg, well beaten
8 ounces minced, cooked ham

Combine all ingredients except ham, and cook, stirring constantly, until boiling. Boil 5 minutes.

Cool, then add ham and mix well. Spread between buttered slices of white or whole wheat bread. Serve with pickle.

ZESTY CHICKEN LIVER FILLING

3 rashers streaky bacon
½ pound chicken livers
¼ pound chopped mushrooms
1 tablespoon grated onion
¾ teaspoon salt
dash of black pepper
8 slices rye bread

Fry bacon until crisp. Remove from frying pan.

In bacon drippings, sauté chicken livers with mushrooms until tender.

Turn into chopping bowl with bacon; finely chop. Add onion, salt, and pepper. Blend well. Makes 4 sandwiches.

HAM-CABBAGE FILLING

Combine chopped cooked or canned ham and chopped or finely shredded cabbage. Moisten with mayonnaise or salad dressing. Season with French mustard.

Sandwich Trees: Sandwich trees are a delightfully different way to feed a group—large or small. Cut bread into rounds of 4 sizes from 1¾ to 3¾ inches in diameter. Spread one of the larger rounds with your favourite sandwich spread. Top with round of the same size. Repeat the rounds. Build trees with sandwiches of graduated rounds. Top with parsley or tiny bread star. Each tree makes 4 servings.

HAM SALAD FILLING

½ pound baked ham or luncheon meat
8 ounces sweet pickles or pickle relish
4 hard-boiled eggs
1 teaspoon lemon juice
about ¼ pint mayonnaise

Mince meat and sweet pickles; chop hard-boiled eggs (chop whites very finely). Add lemon juice. Mix with mayonnaise. Makes 6 to 8 sandwiches.

CHICKEN-BLACK OLIVE FILLING

Combine 6 ounces chopped cooked chicken with 2 ounces chopped celery and 2 ounces black olives, chopped. Moisten with mayonnaise.

CREAM CHEESE-GARLIC SAUSAGE RIBBON SAND-WICHES

3 ounces garlic sausage spread
3 ounces cream cheese
2 lengthwise slices white bread (cut from unsliced 1½-pound loaf)
1 lengthwise slice whole wheat bread (cut from unsliced 1½-pound loaf)
1½ ounces soft butter or margarine

Combine garlic sausage spread and cream cheese. Spread each slice of bread with butter. Spread half of the cheese-ham mixture on 1 slice of white bread; top with whole wheat slice, butter-side down.

Spread the remaining mixture on whole wheat bread. Top with second slice of white bread, buttered side down.

Wrap in greaseproof paper, twisting ends of paper; chill. To serve: unwrap and cut sandwich loaf crosswise into 16 sections. Makes 16.

Meal-in-itself Sandwich

MEAL-IN-ITSELF SANDWICH

For each serving, butter a large round slice of rye bread. Place butter-side-up on plate.

First put on several leaves of lettuce, then a layer of thin slices of Gruyère or Emmenthal cheese.

Then add large lettuce cup, reverse side up. Cover it with slices of breast of chicken. Now pour Thousand Island dressing over all.

Top with a tomato slice, then a hard-boiled egg slice. Garnish sandwich with crisp, hot bacon rashers, black olives, and parsley.

BOLOGNA SAUSAGE-EGG FILLING

½ pound bologna sausage
2 ounces chopped pickles
4 fluid ounces mayonnaise
½ teaspoon grated onion
dash of Tabasco sauce
2 tablespoons pickle juice
3 chopped hard-boiled eggs
½ teaspoon salt

Mince bologna sausage and mix well with remaining ingredients. Makes 7 sandwiches.

SALAMI-BEAN FILLING

½ pound salami, finely chopped
8 ounces canned baked beans, drained
2 teaspoons grated onion
2 tablespoon chilli pickle
2 teaspoons French mustard
1 teaspoon prepared horseradish

Place salami, baked beans, onion, chilli pickle, mustard, and horseradish in mixing bowl. Mash well with fork. Makes about 1 pound.

TONGUE-OLIVE FILLING

Combine 8 ounces chopped cooked or canned tongue with 3 ounces chopped stuffed olives. Moisten with mayonnaise or salad dressing.

BACON-PICKLE FILLING

Grill 6 rashers streaky bacon until crisp. Crumble and combine with 4 ounces chopped dill pickle, and 4 tablespoons mayonnaise. Makes 4 sandwiches.

HAM-CHUTNEY FILLING

Combine minced cooked or canned ham and chutney. Moisten with mayonnaise or salad dressing.

HAM-CHEESE FILLING

8 ounces Cheddar cheese
½ teaspoon Aromat
about ¼ pint tomato ketchup
2 or 3 slices boiled ham

Coarsely grate cheese. Add Aromat and enough ketchup for spreading consistency. Cut ham into ¼-inch strips and use for tops. Makes filling for 4 to 6 sandwiches.

CORNED BEEF FILLING

1 ounce mature Cheddar cheese
2 tablespoons mayonnaise
4 ounces cooked corned beef
6 tablespoons chopped sweet pickles
2 teaspoons grated onion
1 teaspoon French mustard
¼ teaspoon salt
⅛ teaspoon black pepper

Grate cheese and blend thoroughly with mayonnaise until smooth and soft. Add chopped corned beef and other ingredients.

Spread on half slices of buttered whole wheat and white bread. A slice of tomato and crisp lettuce may be added to each sandwich. Makes 12 sandwiches.

LIVER SAUSAGE FILLING

4 tablespoons sweet pickles
2 ounces liver sausage
2 ounces cream cheese.

Blend ingredients well. Makes spread for 3 to 4 sandwiches.

MINCED LIVER FILLING

8 ounces minced, cooked liver
1 teaspoon chopped pickles
1 tablespoon pickle juice
4 tablespoons mayonnaise
dash of Tabasco sauce (optional)
salt and pepper to taste

Combine all ingredients and mix thoroughly. Makes 5 sandwiches.

SALAMI-EGG FILLING

Combine chopped salami and hard-boiled egg. Top with sliced onion or tomato.

HAM FILLING

3 ounces sliced cooked ham
3 ounces cream cheese
1 teaspoon horseradish
1 tablespoon grated onion
black pepper

Cut ham slices into thin strips with scissors. Combine with remaining ingredients. Makes 4 sandwiches.

HAM-CUCUMBER FILLING

Combine 5-ounces minced, cooked ham, 1 ounce diced cucumber, 3 tablespoons mayonnaise, and salt to taste. Mix well.

CHICKEN SALAD FILLING

1 pound chopped cooked chicken or turkey
4 ounces chopped celery
1 canned pimiento, chopped
6 large stuffed olives, chopped
salad dressing to moisten

Mix all ingredients and season to taste.

Spread liberally between slices of light or dark bread. A leaf of lettuce may be added. For 12 sandwiches.

Note: The same mixture may be used for salad if meat and celery is chopped more coarsely.

MOCK PÂTÉ FILLING

Blend liver sausage with cream cheese. Season with grated onion.

PORK-EGG-PICKLE FILLING

Combine chopped canned pork luncheon meat, chopped hard-boiled egg and pickles. Moisten with mayonnaise or salad dressing.

LIVER-EGG FILLING

10 ounces cooked pigs' liver
2 hard-boiled eggs
1 small onion, chopped
½ ounce dripping
4 fluid ounces single cream or top of milk
salt and pepper
few drops Tabasco sauce

Steam liver 25 minutes in large saucepan.

Cool and mince. Chop eggs coarsely. Brown onion in the dripping. Mix all ingredients well. Keep in a cool place.

Sandwiches for lunch can be made more fun for children and adults alike if cut sometimes into triangles, on the diagonal, or into strips.

These sandwich filling ingredients freeze well: cooked egg yolk; peanut butter; cooked or canned meat, poultry, or fish; Roquefort or blue cheese; meat mastes' olives; pickles. Not recommended' mayonnaise; jam; whites of hard-boiled egg; lettuce, tomatoes; cucumber; celery; watercress.

848

ALMOND

MINT

ORANGE

Many elegant dishes owe their special appeal to a fine subtly seasoned sauce, and many simply cooked foods become superb party fare when served with a classic sauce or one of its interesting variations. The art of making sauces was developed in France, hence many sauces have French names. In French cookery, the word sauce means any liquid or semi-liquid adjunct that complements a dish. This includes, of course, the gravy in a stew and the white or cream sauce on a vegetable. It also encompasses salad dressings, melted butter dressings, the savoury butters for hors d'oeuvres, marinades for meats and other foods, and other additions to whet the appetite.

In this section are the most versatile, the most commonly used, and the most famous sauces for meats, poultry, fish, game, and vegetables. Salad dressings, sweet sauces, and savoury butters are given in separate sections.

Many sauces are prepared with the dishes they are intended to complete—dishes that create their own sauce in the cooking; therefore many sauces are given with specific recipes throughout this book. For a complete list of the sauces contained in this book, consult the index.

Bought sauces are often used to flavour homemade varieties. They have a very definite place in the store cupboard, and are often used as a convenient accessory in cooking and for the most part they have developed from sauces once laboriously made in the home or restaurant kitchen.

As long as there are good cooks, new sauces will continue to be invented, and new variations will be given to old ones; therefore do not hesitate to apply your imagination and creative abilities in the creation of your own variations of the standard classics.

Special Butters

CLARIFIED BUTTER

This is merely melted butter with the sediment removed. To make clarified butter, place butter in a fireproof cup and stand the cup in hot water. When completely melted, remove from heat, let stand for a few minutes to allow the milk solids to settle to the bottom. Pour off fat and discard the milky sediment.

KNEADED BUTTER OR BEURRE MANIÉ

This is butter and flour kneaded together and used as a thickening agent for sauces rather than a real sauce or butter. Knead or cream together butter and flour in equal proportions. Whisk into hot gravy, sauce, or other liquid to be thickened. Simmer, but do not boil sauce after adding kneaded butter, just long enough to thicken sauce and dispel the floury taste.

BROWN BUTTER (BEURRE NOISETTE)

This is melted butter cooked slowly until light brown. A better flavour and appearance will be obtained if clarified butter is used. Use with vegetables such as asparagus and broccoli, and with fish.

BROWN BUTTER SAUCE

Brown slowly but do not burn, 2 ounces butter or margarine, stirring constantly. Add 2 teaspoons lemon juice and ¼ teaspoon salt.

ALMOND BUTTER

Blanch 1 ounce chopped almonds in boiling water; remove skins. Pound almonds to a smooth paste, adding 1 teaspoon water if necessary. Cream 2 ounces butter and blend in almonds. If desired, rub through a fine sieve. Use in cream sauces.

BLACK BUTTER (BEURRE NOIR)

This is melted butter cooked until it is very dark brown. A better flavour will be obtained if clarified butter is used. If desired, flavour to taste with lemon juice or vinegar. Use with vegetables, sweetbreads and brains.

BLACK BUTTER SAUCE

2 ounces butter or margarine
4 sprigs parsley, stems removed
2 tablespoons lemon juice

Melt butter and when very hot add parsley. Fry until crisp and brown.

When butter is brown but not burnt, pour into serving dish.

Heat lemon juice until hot and add to butter before serving.

GREEN BUTTER

2 spring onions finely chopped
1 teaspoon chopped chervil
1 teaspoon chopped tarragon
6 to 8 spinach leaves, chopped
1 tablespoon chopped parsley
2 ounces butter, creamed

Combine all ingredients except butter; cover with boiling water and cook 5 minutes. Drain and dry well in a teacloth.

Rub through a fine sieve or pound in a mortar or basin. Blend with creamed butter. Use for fish or to give sauces a green colour.

MAÎTRE D'HÔTEL BUTTER

Cream 4 ounces butter. Add 1 tablespoon chopped parsley and gradually blend in 3 tablespoons lemon juice, ½ teaspoon salt, and ⅛ teaspoon pepper. Serve with grilled fish. Makes about 5 fluid ounces of sauce.

COLBERT BUTTER

To 4 fluid ounces maître d'hôtel butter add ½ teaspoon melted beef essence or meat glaze, and ¼ teaspoon chopped tarragon.

LOBSTER OR PRAWN BUTTER

Dry the shells from 1 pound prawns or from 1 large cooked lobster in a slow oven for a short time. Pound the shells in a mortar until they are pulverized or put them through a food mill so they are broken up as fine as possible.

Melt 4 ounces butter in the top of a double saucepan over (not in) hot water. Add the shells with 2 tablespoons water. (If you are using lobster shell, add also the coral if available.) Simmer 10 to 12 minutes. Do not let the butter boil.

Strain the butter through fine muslin into a basin of ice water. Set basin in refrigerator until butter hardens. Skim off the butter and store in covered jar in refrigerator to use in recipes for fish or shellfish sauces, or serve with shellfish.

DRAWN BUTTER

Drawn butter is melted butter, used as a sauce. It is sometimes thickened.

DRAWN BUTTER SAUCE

3 ounces butter or margarine
1½ ounces flour
12 fluid ounces vegetable or fish stock
½ teaspoon salt
⅛ teaspoon pepper
1 teaspoon lemon juice

Melt half the butter. Add flour and blend until smooth. Gradually add stock.

Bring to boiling point, stirring constantly. Cook 3 minutes. Add seasonings and remaining butter.

Drawn Butter with Anchovy: Season drawn butter sauce to taste with anchovy paste.

Drawn Butter with Capers: Add 1 tablespoon drained capers to drawn butter sauce.

Drawn Butter with Egg: Add 2 sliced hard-boiled eggs to drawn butter sauce.

Drawn Butter with Seafood: Add 2 to 3 ounces cooked or tinned prawns or other seafood to drawn butter sauce.

PAPRIKA BUTTER

Melt 1 ounce butter (clarified butter is preferred) in a saucepan. Cook 2 tablespoons finely chopped onion in it until light brown. Blend in 1 teaspoon paprika and cool.

Cream 2 ounces butter and blend into the paprika mixture. Strain through a fine sieve. Serve with fish or poultry or for finishing a paprika sauce.

MUSTARD BUTTER FOR FISH

Melt 2 ounces butter and add to it a little at a time 1½ teaspoons prepared English or French mustard.

BERÇY BUTTER

2 teaspoons finely chopped spring onions
6 fluid ounces dry white wine
2 ounces butter
2 teaspoons chopped parsley
salt and pepper

Simmer onions and wine in a saucepan until reduced to about ¼ original quantity. Cool.

Cream butter with parsley and blend into wine-onion mixture. Season to taste with salt and pepper. Serve with grilled meat.

MARCHAND DE VIN BUTTER

Prepare Berçy butter using dry red wine instead of white wine. Use only 1 teaspoon chopped parsley. Use with grilled meat.

LEMON BUTTER

Combine 2 to 3 tablespoons lemon juice with 4 ounces melted butter or margarine. Add 1 tablespoon chopped parsley and a dash of paprika.

Quick Sauces with Tinned Soups

Condensed soups when heated may be the right consistency for the sauce you want. Use such soups as asparagus, celery, mushroom, tomato, etc.

Vary the seasonings by using about 2 tablespoons sherry, a little salt, pepper, chilli powder, cayenne pepper or Tabasco sauce, Worcestershire sauce, curry powder, dry mustard, etc.

If the sauce is too thick, dilute with a little milk or stock.

Ready-to-serve soups may be thickened with a roux made of flour blended with melted butter, but be sure to cook several minutes after blending in the roux. Specific examples of such sauces are given in this section.

QUICK CREOLE SAUCE

1 small finely chopped onion
¾ ounce finely chopped green pepper
1 ounce melted lard or oil
4 fluid ounces water
1 can condensed tomato soup
1 teaspoon vinegar
black or cayenne pepper to taste
dash of Tabasco sauce

Cook onion and green pepper until tender in lard or oil.

Add remaining ingredients and cook over low heat about 10 minutes.

Use with rice, seafood, roast meats, or as a hot "dipping" sauce. Makes about ¾ pint.

QUICK TOMATO SAUCE

1 can (about 10 ounces) condensed tomato soup
¼ bay leaf
4 whole cloves
1 sprig parsley

Combine and heat thoroughly. Strain before serving.

QUICK À LA KING SAUCE

1 finely chopped green pepper
½ ounce butter or margarine
1 can condensed cream of mushroom soup
1 pimiento, chopped

Sauté green pepper in melted butter. Add to heated mushroom soup with pimiento.

QUICK SPANISH SAUCE

2 tablespoons finely chopped onion
1 tablespoons finely chopped green pepper
1 ounce lard or bacon dripping
1 can condensed tomato soup
1 to 2 ounces cooked mushrooms, optional

Cook onion and green pepper until tender in lard or dripping.

Stir in soup and mushrooms; continue cooking over low heat about 5 minutes.

This sauce is especially good with omelets, meat, or cooked rice. Makes about ¾ pint.

QUICK MUSHROOM SAUCE

Combine 1 can condensed cream of mushroom soup with 4 fluid ounces hot milk. Heat thoroughly. Serve at once.

QUICK ONION SAUCE

Heat 1 can onion soup. Blend in a little flour to thicken it and cook a few minutes.

If desired, add a little grated cheese just before serving.

QUICK HOT MUSTARD SAUCE

Blend 1 can condensed cream of celery soup, 4 fluid ounces milk, and 2 tablespoons prepared English mustard; heat well.

Serve over broccoli, asparagus, cauliflower, carrots, or with tongue, ham, corned beef. Makes about ¾ pint.

SAUCES WITH DRIED SOUPS

Interesting time-saving sauces may be made from the dried packet soups although they take a little longer than the tinned soups. For a well-flavoured base, use about half the liquid called for normally. These packet mixes are particularly suitable in making casserole dishes; however, do not season until the dish has cooked for at least 20 minutes and you have tasted it.

Cold Sauces

AÏOLI SAUCE

A famous French sauce of the mayonnaise type, with a strong garlic flavour, sometimes called garlic mayonnaise.

2 or 3 large garlic cloves
2 egg yolks
7 or 8 tablespoons olive oil
1 teaspoon strained lemon juice
scant
few drops cold water
salt and freshly-milled pepper

Skin and crush the garlic cloves in a mortar to pulp; combine with egg yolks. Beat in the olive oil, drop by drop at first, increasing to a thin stream as the sauce begins to thicken.

Blend well, stirring constantly, and when half the oil has been beaten in, alternate with the remaining oil the lemon juice and a few drops of cold water.

Adjust seasonings to taste with salt and freshly-milled pepper. Serve very cold with poached fish and boiled beef. Makes about 4 fluid ounces.

Note: If the sauce should curdle, place another egg yolk into a bowl and beat the curdled sauce into it very very slowly.

GRIBICHE SAUCE (VINAIGRETTE AND EGG MAYONNAISE)

3 hard-boiled eggs
½ teaspoon salt
1 teaspoon French mustard, optional
dash of pepper
12 fluid ounces olive oil
4 fluid ounces vinegar
1½ ounces chopped gherkins
1 tablespoon mixed chopped parsley, chervil, tarragon, and chives

Separate the eggs and crush the yolks in a bowl until smooth. Blend in salt, mustard, and pepper.

Add oil a few drops at a time, beating constantly, until about 1 ounce has been added. Then add the oil in a thin stream while beating constantly. Add vinegar a little at a time when the mixture starts to get too thick.

Chop the egg whites finely. Press out all of the moisture from the gherkins. Blend these into the sauce along with the mixed herbs. Serve with fish and coat meat. Makes about 1¼ pints.

ASPIC GLAZE FOR MEATS

1 tablespoon unflavoured gelatine powder
4 fluid ounces cold meat or vegetable stock
16 fluid ounces hot meat or vegetable stock
seasonings to taste

Dissolve gelatine in stock over hot water. Season to taste.

Chill until somewhat thickened, then use as a glaze for cold meats, fish, and hors d'oeuvres.

RAVIGOTE SAUCE

Ravigote sauce may be any of several sauces flavoured with vinegar: a French dressing with chopped onion, capers, tarragon, sometimes hard-boiled egg, and other seasonings; a hot white sauce with herbs; a highly seasoned mayonnaise containing anchovy fillets.

A popular version of a cold sauce is given below.

RAVIGOTE OR VINAIGRETTE SAUCE

8 fluid ounces olive oil
3 fluid ounces tarragon vinegar
1 tablespoon capers
1 tablespoon chopped onion
2 to 3 sprigs chopped parsley
salt and pepper
1 hard-boiled egg, sieved or chopped fine

Combine ingredients and mix thoroughly.

Serve with cold meats, vegetables, vegetable salads, and fish. Makes about 12 fluid ounces.

GELATINE MAYONNAISE OR MAYONNAISE CHAUD-FROID

2 tablespoons unflavoured gelatine powder
4 fluid ounces cold water
8 rounded tablespoons mayonnaise

Mix gelatine in cold water then stir over hot water until the gelatine is dissolved.

Add mayonnaise and blend well. This sauce is used to bind salad mixtures which are to be moulded.

It is used to coat cold fish, lobster, poultry, and meat, and to make decorations adhere.

CHAUD-FROID SAUCE

Chaud-froid is a French term meaning, literally, hot-cold. It is thick cooked white sauce cooled and jellied as a coating for meats and fish.

1½ ounces butter
2 ounces flour
1 pint, 12 fluid ounces clear chicken or turkey stock
2 tablespoons gelatine powder
4 fluid ounces cold water
2 egg yolks
4 fluid ounces cream

Melt butter in a saucepan and stir in the flour. In another pan bring stock to a boil; add all at once to butter-flour mixture, stirring vigorously. When mixture is thickened and smooth, cook

5 minutes over low heat.

Stir gelatine into cold water and add to sauce. Stir until gelatine is dissolved. Remove from heat.

Beat egg yolks with cream and slowly stir into hot sauce. Heat but do not boil. Cool but do not chill. Makes about 2 pints.

RÉMOULADE SAUCE

Rémoulade sauce is mayonnaise seasoned with various ingredients such as mustard, chopped gherkins, chopped herbs, and capers. It is served with fried fish or with cold fish and shellfish.

1½ ounces finely chopped gherkins
2 tablespoons finely chopped capers
1 tablespoon prepared mustard
1 tablespoon mixed finely chopped parsley, tarragon, chervil, and chives
8 rounded tablespoons mayonnaise

Press all moisture out of gherkins and capers. Add with remaining ingredients to mayonnaise.

TARTARE SAUCE

Tartare (or tartar) sauce may be a cold sauce made of mayonnaise with lemon juice and various other ingredients as given below; or it may be a hot version made of white sauce with similar additions. Both are served with fried or grilled fish or shellfish.

4 rounded tablespoons mayonnaise
½ ounce chopped gherkins
1 teaspoon chopped onion
1 tablespoon capers (optional)
1 tablespoon chopped ripe olives
1 tablespoon minced parsley
1 hard-boiled egg, chopped
1 tablespoon chopped green pepper
lemon juice

Blend ingredients and add lemon juice to thin slightly and sharpen flavours. Makes about 12 ounces.

CHINESE MUSTARD

Stir 6 tablespoons boiling water into 2 tablespoons dry mustard. Add ½ teaspoon salt and 2 teaspoons olive oil. For additional yellow colouring, add some turmeric.

Chaud-froid glaze is often used to decorate a cold baked ham.

Marinades and Barbecued Sauces

A marinade is a liquid in which food is soaked (marinated) for added flavour and tenderness. Marinades usually include oil, an acid (wine, vinegar, or lemon juice), and spices and herbs. The length of time depends upon the food in question. The marinade is also used to baste meats and fish during cooking.

A commonly used marinade is the basic recipe for French or Vinaigrette dressing or one of the variations given in the salad dressing section. For a variety of marinades as well as additional barbecue sauces, see barbecue cooking section. For a complete listing of all in this book, see Index.

COOKED MARINADE FOR MEATS

1 pint, 12 fluid ounces water
12 fluid ounces vinegar
2 onions, chopped
1 carrot, chopped
1 clove garlic
3 or 4 sprigs parsley
12 peppercorns, bruised
1 tablespoon salt

Combine all ingredients in a saucepan. Bring to a boil; reduce heat and simmer gently for 1 hour.

Let cool, then pour over meat to be marinated. Store the cold marinade and meat in a cool place or in the refrigerator. Turn the meat occasionally. After removing the meat from the marinade, wipe it carefully with a dry cloth before cooking.

WINE MARINADE

8 fluid ounces dry wine (see note below)
8 fluid ounces olive oil
2 or 3 cloves garlic, halved
2 tablespoons dried herbs such as marjoram, rosemary, or thyme
½ ounce chopped parsley
¼ teaspoon freshly-milled pepper

Mix ingredients and use for meat and poultry.

Note: Use white wine with poultry and veal, red for other meats. If desired, add 4 fluid ounces orange or pineapple juice when using with chicken or duck.

FRENCH DRESSING MARINADE

8 fluid ounces French dressing
1 clove garlic, crushed
1 teaspoon chopped parsley
dash each of dried tarragon and thyme

Mix ingredients and use for fish, lamb, veal, chicken, or vegetables. The French dressing should preferably be made with wine vinegar.

UNCOOKED MARINADE FOR MEATS

1 large onion, thinly sliced
2 large carrots, thinly sliced
2 to 4 shallots, chopped
3 sprigs parsley
1 teaspoon salt
8 peppercorns, bruised
2 sticks celery, chopped
1 clove garlic
2 bay leaves
2 cloves
pinch of thyme
16 fluid ounces red or white wine
4 fluid ounces olive oil

Mix all ingredients together and pour over the meat to be marinated. Store in a cool place or in the refrigerator, turning the meat occasionally. When ready to cook, wipe the meat with a cloth and reserve the marinade, which is often used in cooking the meat.

SOY SAUCE MARINADE FOR STEAK

8 fluid ounces soy sauce
1½ ounces brown sugar
1 tablespoon ground ginger

Combine ingredients; pour over steak and marinate, covered, in refrigerator 2 to 3 hours.

BARBECUE SAUCE

1 medium onion, chopped
1 ounce lard or dripping
2 tablespoons lemon juice
8 fluid ounces water
2 ounces chopped celery
½ teaspoon dry mustard
2 tablespoons vinegar
2 tablespoons brown sugar
4 tablespoons tomato ketchup
2 tablespoons Worcestershire sauce
⅛ teaspoon pepper
1 teaspoon salt

Brown onion in hot fat. Add remaining ingredients and simmer gently 20 to 30 minutes. Pour over meat before cooking or baste meat during roasting.

Use over baked or grilled chicken, frankfurters, braised beef, steaks, hamburgers, etc. Makes about 16 ounces.

LEMON BARBECUE SAUCE

1 clove garlic
½ teaspoon salt
2 fluid ounces olive oil
4 fluid ounces lemon juice
2 tablespoons grated onion
¼ teaspoon black pepper
1 teaspoon Worcestershire sauce

Mash garlic with salt in basin; stir in remaining ingredients.

Chill 24 hours. Especially good for chicken. Makes 6 ounces.

For a barbecued taste, spoon barbecue sauce over chicken towards end of grilling.

QUICK BARBECUE SAUCE 1

1 can condensed cream of tomato soup, undiluted
India relish (see Index)
1 small finely chopped onion
1 tablespoon Worcestershire sauce
½ ounce flour

Combine soup, relish, onion, and Worcestershire. Blend in flour, stirring constantly, over low heat.

Bring to boiling point and simmer 3 minutes.

Use for barbecued meat, poultry, or fish, or serve hot with meat or fish, on frankfurters, etc.

QUICK BARBECUE SAUCE 2

1 small finely chopped onion
1½ ounces finely chopped celery
½ clove garlic, minced
1½ ounces melted lard or oil
1 can condensed tomato soup
2 tablespoons brown sugar
2 tablespoons Worcestershire sauce
2 tablespoons lemon juice or vinegar
2 teaspoons prepared English mustard
4 drops Tabasco sauce, if desired

Cook onion, celery, and garlic until soft in lard in heavy frying pan.

Add remaining ingredients; stir well and simmer 10 minutes.

Excellent on grilled steaks, chops, chicken, baked spareribs, meat loaf or with hot dogs or hamburgers. Makes about 1 pint of sauce.

TOMATO KETCHUP BARBECUE SAUCE

2 medium onions, chopped
2 ounces lard or dripping
½ clove garlic, grated
2 rounded tablespoons tomato ketchup
1 stock cube dissolved in 8 fluid ounces water
2 tablespoons Worcestershire sauce
salt and pepper to taste

Cook onion in lard until golden; add rest of ingredients. Simmer for 30 minutes.

Use to baste turkey, chickens, spareribs, and hamburgers. Makes about 1 pint.

Basic Sauces

WHITE SAUCE (Basic Recipe)

Every cook should learn to make a perfect white sauce, often called cream sauce, although it is usually made with milk. It is used for creaming foods like fish, poultry, and vegetables. It is the basis of many dishes such as cream soups, soufflés, and scalloped dishes, and also is the basis for many other sauces.

Thin White Sauce:
½ ounce butter
½ ounce flour
¼ teaspoon salt
8 fluid ounces milk, cream, or stock

Medium White Sauce:
1 ounce butter
1 ounce flour
¼ teaspoon salt
8 fluid ounces milk, cream, or stock

Thick White Sauce:
1½ ounces butter
1½ to 2 ounces flour
¼ teaspoon or more salt
8 fluid ounces milk, cream, or stock

Use methods 1, 2, or 3 (below). Makes about 8 fluid ounces sauce.

Method 1: Melt butter; stir in flour and salt. Cook until mixture bubbles.

Remove from heat; add liquid, and stir until smooth.

Cook in double saucepan or over low heat until mixture thickens, stirring constantly or not at all.

Method 2: Melt butter and remove from heat. Add flour and salt. Stir until smooth.

Add liquid gradually, stirring constantly over low heat until mixture thickens.

Method 3: Stir enough liquid into flour and salt to form a thin smooth paste.

Scald remainder of liquid in double saucepan. Add flour paste to hot liquid, stirring constantly until mixture thickens.

Cover and cook 20 minutes longer. Stir in butter just before serving.

To keep hot and prevent skin from forming over sauce, place over hot water and cover tightly.

WHITE SAUCE USES

Thin Sauce: Use as base for cream soups and other sauces.

Medium Sauce: Use for creamed and scalloped dishes, and gravies.

Thick Sauce: Use for croquettes and soufflés.

WHITE SAUCE VARIATIONS

Anchovy Egg Sauce: To 8 fluid ounces thin white sauce add ¼ teaspoon anchovy paste. Boil the mixture, stirring it constantly, for 3 minutes. Remove the saucepan from the heat and add 2 hard-boiled eggs, finely chopped.

Asparagus Sauce: Add 4 ounces cooked or tinned asparagus, cut into small pieces, to hot medium white sauce. Serve with omelets or soufflés.

Caper Sauce: Add 3 to 4 tablespoons chopped capers and 1 teaspoon lemon juice to white sauce. Serve with fish.

Cheese Sauce: Add 2 to 4 ounces chopped or grated Cheddar cheese and a dash of Worcestershire sauce or paprika (optional) to white sauce.

Stir over hot, not boiling, water until cheese is melted. Serve with fish, eggs, macaroni, or rice.

Cheese-Olive Sauce: Prepare thin white sauce; omit salt. Add 2 to 4 ounces chopped or grated Cheddar cheese and 8 sliced stuffed olives to white sauce.

Stir over hot, not boiling, water until cheese is melted. Serve with macaroni, rice, or vegetables.

Cheese-Tomato Sauce: Use 4 fluid ounces tomato juice or strained tomatoes and 4 fluid ounces milk in preparing medium sauce.

Add 1 ounce grated or finely cut Cheddar cheese to hot sauce. Stir until melted. Serve over cauliflower.

Cold Chiffon Sauce: Stir 1 egg yolk into 8 fluid ounces medium white sauce. Add salt and pepper to taste. Let sauce stand for 10 minutes and add 2 tablespoons tarragon vinegar. Cool and fold in 1 stiffly beaten egg white. Serve well chilled with cold fish.

Rich Cheese Sauce: To 8 fluid ounces thick white sauce, add 2 well beaten egg yolks, and 1 ounce grated cheese. Heat in double saucepan over hot water without boiling until cheese melts.

Chivry Sauce: Combine 4 fluid ounces dry white wine, 1 teaspoon each chopped chives, chervil, and tarragon, and 1 tablespoon chopped watercress in a saucepan; cook until it is reduced to a third of original quantity.

Add 16 fluid ounces medium white sauce and rub through a fine sieve.

Cook 1 tablespoon chopped spinach with a teaspoon of chopped tarragon and chervil in a little water for a few minutes. Rub through a fine sieve; add to the sauce to colour it. Use for eggs and poultry.

Crab Sauce: Remove bony particles from 2 to 4 ounces flaked tinned crab and add to seasoned medium white sauce.

Flavour with 1 tablespoon dry white wine if desired.

Cream Onion or Celery Sauce: Sauté 1 small finely chopped onion or celery in ½ ounce butter or margarine. Add to 8 fluid ounces medium white sauce.

Creole Sauce: Use tomato juice or strained tomatoes for the liquid.

Sauté chopped onion, chopped green pepper, and chopped celery in the butter before flour is added.

Curry Sauce Add ¼ to ½ teaspoon curry powder with dry ingredients. Serve with chicken, lamb, rice or fish.

Dill Sauce: Add 3 tablespoons minced fresh dill to 8 fluid ounces hot, seasoned medium white sauce.

Egg Sauce: Add 2 chopped hard-boiled eggs to white sauce, additional salt, and a dash of paprika. Serve with fish.

Goldenrod Sauce: Add 2 chopped hard-boiled egg whites to 8 fluid ounces seasoned medium white sauce. Pour over fish and sprinkle with chopped hard-boiled egg yolks.

Green Pea Sauce: Add 3 ounces hot cooked or tinned peas and 1 tablespoon chopped pimiento to hot medium white sauce. Serve with omelets or salmon or tuna loaf.

Horseradish Sauce: Add 2 to 4 tablespoons prepared drained horseradish, and ¼ to ½ teaspoon prepared English mustard to white sauce. Serve with boiled beef or corned beef.

A perfect white sauce is smooth, glossy, satiny.

Lobster or Prawn Sauce: Add 2 to 4 ounces tinned or cooked lobster meat or prawns, cut into small pieces, to seasoned medium white sauce.

For added flavour, add a tablespoon dry white wine. Serve with omelets, baked, grilled or poached fish.

Milanese Sauce: Use 4 fluid ounces veal stock and 4 fluid ounces milk in preparing medium white sauce.

Add 2 tablespoons grated Parmesan cheese to the thickened sauce. Serve with veal.

Mock Hollandaise Sauce: To 4 fluid ounces well-seasoned white sauce, add equal amount of mayonnaise and enough lemon juice to sharpen. Serve on asparagus and other green vegetables.

Mushroom Sauce: Add 3 to 6 ounces sliced cooked or tinned mushrooms to white sauce. Serve with chicken or vegetables.

Mustard Sauce: Add 1 tablespoon prepared English mustard to white sauce. Serve with fish or tongue.

Oyster Sauce: Gently cook 3 to 6 ounces small oysters in their own liquid until they plump and the edges begin to curl, about 3 minutes.

Add to hot medium white sauce. Serve with omelets, fish cakes, and timbales.

Paprika Sauce: Add ½ to 1 teaspoon paprika with dry ingredients. Season with ¼ teaspoon onion juice, if desired. Serve with noodles, macaroni, or chicken.

Pimiento Sauce: Add ½ of a small tin chopped pimiento to white sauce; 1 ounce chopped green pepper may be added, if desired. Serve with fish or vegetables.

Hot Ravigote Sauce: Combine 3 fluid ounces dry white wine, 3 fluid ounces vinegar, and 6 finely chopped shallots in a saucepan; cook until reduced to a third of original quantity.

Add ¾ pint medium white sauce and simmer gently for 4 to 6 minutes. Remove from heat; add 1 ounce butter and 1 teaspoon mixed chopped chives, chervil, and tarragon. Serve with fish or poultry.

Wine-Egg Sauce: To 12 fluid ounces medium white sauce, add 1 teaspoon Worcestershire sauce, 4 chopped hard-boiled eggs, and 2 tablespoons sherry or dry white wine. Blend thoroughly and serve hot on fish.

Dutch Sauce: Add a little cold water to a slightly beaten egg yolk, and stir slowly into the white sauce.

Cook for a minute over hot water, stirring constantly. Add a few drops of lemon juice. Serve over vegetables, meat or poultry.

WHITE SAUCE MIX WITH DRIED MILK
(Basic Recipe)

8 ounces dried milk
8 ounces all-purpose flour
8 ounces butter or margarine

Combine all ingredients with pastry fork until mixture is coarse and flaky.

Store in covered jars in refrigerator. Makes about 3¼ pints medium sauce.

This basic mix can be used for thin, medium, or thick white sauces. Just measure the required amount into a saucepan; add water and cook until thickened, adding the desired seasonings.

Thin White Sauce: Use 2 ounces mix with 8 fluid ounces water.

Medium White Sauce: Use 4 ounces mix with 8 fluid ounces water.

Thick White Sauce: Use 6 ounces mix with 8 fluid ounces water.

HOLLANDAISE SAUCE
(Basic Recipe)

This queen of sauces makes a superb dish out of the plainest and most simply cooked vegetables. It is a favourite with fish, grilled or roasted meats and poultry, and in such special dishes as Eggs Benedict.

The name is derived from the French term, *hollandaise*, the feminine of *hollandais*, meaning of Holland, a country famous for its butter which is used so liberally in this rich sauce.

Béarnaise sauce, which may be considered a special variation of Hollandaise sauce, was named in honour of the gourmet king, Henry IV of France.

2 ounces butter
4 egg yolks
2 tablespoons lemon juice
¼ teaspoon salt
dash of cayenne pepper
2 fluid ounces boiling water

Divide butter into 3 sections. Beat egg yolks and lemon juice together. Add 1 piece of butter and cook in double saucepan, stirring constantly until mixture begins to thicken.

Remove from cooker, add second piece of butter, and stir rapidly.

Then add remaining butter and continue to stir until mixture is completely blended. Add salt, cayenne pepper, and boiling water.

Return to double saucepan; cook until thickened, stirring constantly. Serve at once.

Note: Sauce may separate if cooked too long, or at too high a temperature, or if permitted to stand too long before serving. To smooth, beat in 1 table-spoon boiling water and a little lemon juice drop by drop, with a whisk.

Hollandaise Sauce Variations

Béarnaise Sauce: Reduce lemon juice to 1½ tablespoons. Add 1 teaspoon each chopped tarragon and chopped parsley, 1 tablespoon tarragon vinegar, and 1 teaspoon onion juice or ½ teaspoon onion salt. Serve with baked or grilled fish.

Chive Hollandaise Sauce: Add 1½ tablespoons finely chopped chives to sauce. Serve with vegetables.

Cucumber Hollandaise Sauce: Add 4 to 5 ounces drained, chopped cucumber to sauce. Serve with fish.

Dill Hollandaise Sauce: Add 1 tablespoon chopped dill to sauce.

Mint Hollandaise Sauce: Add 1 tablespoon finely chopped mint to sauce.

LIQUIDIZER HOLLANDAISE SAUCE

4 ounces butter
3 egg yolks (at room temperature)
2 tablespoons lemon juice
¼ teaspoon salt
pinch of cayenne pepper

Heat butter to bubbling but do not brown. Combine in the liquidizer the egg yolks, lemon juice, salt, and cayenne pepper. Blend these ingredients at low speed for a few seconds.

Add hot butter gradually and blend a few seconds longer until the sauce is smooth and thickened. Makes about 8 fluid ounces.

MALTAISE SAUCE

Prepare 8 fluid ounces Hollandaise sauce. Just before serving add 2 or 3 tablespoons orange juice and 1 teaspoon grated orange rind. This sauce should be pink; hence, if desired, add 1 or 2 drops pink food colouring. Use with asparagus.

MOUSSELINE SAUCE

Prepare Hollandaise sauce. Just before serving over fish or vegetables, fold in an equal quantity of whipped cream or egg white. Serve hot or cold.

Hollandaise sauce makes a superb dish out of the plainest and most simply cooked vegetables and it is popular with meats, poultry, and fish.

FIGARO SAUCE

Prepare 1 cup Hollandaise sauce. Beat in very slowly 2 to 3 ounces warm tomato purée. Fold in 1 tablespoon finely chopped parsley. Correct seasoning with salt to taste and a few grains cayenne pepper.

VELOUTÉ SAUCE
(Basic Recipe)

Velouté is French for velvety. Velouté sauce is a basic French sauce from which many other famous sauces are derived such as the variations given here. Fish, chicken, or veal stock is used in its preparation, depending on how it is to be used. For example, in Normandy (or Normande) sauce, fish or shellfish stock is used because it is to be served with seafood. Allemande sauce is a smooth yellow sauce served on eggs, fish, meats, and vegetables, and also on chicken and fish cakes and croquettes. Soubise sauce contains onions and is served with meat, especially lamb and veal.

1 ounce butter or margarine
1 ounce flour
8 fluid ounces fish, chicken, or veal stock
salt to taste
dash of white pepper
⅛ teaspoon nutmeg (optional)

Melt butter over low heat. Blend in flour. Remove from heat and gradually stir in stock.

Return to heat and cook, stirring constantly, until smooth and thick. Blend in seasonings.

If desired, strain through a very fine sieve. Serve hot over croquettes, baked fish, etc. Makes about 8 fluid ounces.

Velouté Sauce Variations

Allemande Sauce: Stir into strained velouté sauce 1 well beaten egg, 1 teaspoon lemon juice, and 2 tablespoons cream or finely grated Parmesan cheese.

Anchovy Velouté Sauce: Omit salt and use fish stock in basic recipe.

Blend 1½ teaspoons anchovy paste into flour and butter mixture.

Add 1 tablespoon finely chopped parsley just before serving.

Caper Velouté Sauce: Prepare basic recipe. Add 1 teaspoon capers to strained sauce. Serve with lamb or vegetables.

If serving with fish, substitute fish stock for chicken or veal stock.

Fish Velouté Sauce: Use fish stock in basic recipe.

Normandy Sauce: Use fish stock in basic recipe. Beat a little hot sauce into 2 slightly beaten egg yolks and beat into remaining sauce. Blend in 1 tablespoon lemon juice, salt, pepper, and cayenne pepper to taste.

Parsley Sauce: Add 2 tablespoons finely chopped parsley to strained Allemande sauce.

Soubise Sauce (Onion Sauce): Cover 3 medium-sized onions with boiling water and cook until soft. Drain and rub onion pulp through a sieve into velouté sauce.

Add 4 fluid ounces single cream and stir to boiling.

Remove from heat and stir in ½ ounce butter. Season with salt to taste.

Sauce Poulette: Add 2 ounces sliced cooked mushrooms to strained Allemande sauce.

SUPRÊME SAUCE

16 fluid ounces rich chicken stock
3 or 4 mushrooms or stems and peelings of mushrooms
8 fluid ounces Velouté sauce
8 fluid ounces single cream
salt and pepper

Cook chicken stock with mushrooms until it is reduced to ⅓ the original quantity.

Combine with Velouté sauce; bring to the boil and reduce to scant ½ pint.

Gradually add cream, stirring constantly. Season to taste with salt and pepper. Serve with eggs, fish, and poultry. Makes about 12 fluid ounces.

BASIC BROWN SAUCE

The basic brown sauce is also known as Spanish sauce or Sauce Espagnole. It is used as the basis of many other sauces and as an ingredient in various dishes. A good quality clear brown beef stock should be used. Throughout the preparation very slow simmering is required for gradual reduction, and retention of flavour.

4 ounces fat (beef, veal, or pork dripping)
1 carrot, coarsely chopped
2 onions, coarsely chopped
4 ounces flour
about 3 pints brown beef stock
1 clove garlic
2 sticks celery
3 sprigs parsley
1 bay leaf
pinch of thyme
4 fluid ounces tomato juice or 1 rounded tablespoon tomato ketchup

Melt fat in a large heavy saucepan. Add carrot and onions and cook until they just start to turn golden, shaking the pah for even cooking.

Add flour and cook, stirring frequently, until the flour takes on a good brown colour (hazelnut-brown) and the carrots and onions are also brown.

Add 1 pint of the boiling stock, the garlic, celery, parsley, bay leaf, and thyme. Cook, stirring constantly, until the mixture thickens, then add 1 pint more of stock.

Simmer very slowly over low heat, stirring occasionally, until the mixture is reduced to about 1 pint. This should take 1 to 1½ hours. As it cooks, skim off the excess fat rising to the surface. Add tomato juice and cook a few minutes longer, then strain through a fine sieve.

Add remaining stock and continue cooking slowly until the sauce is reduced to about 1½ pints, skimming the surface from time to time as needed. Cool, stirring occasionally.

Store in a covered jar in the refrigerator. If not used within a week, recook it, put in another jar, and return to refrigerator. A little good melted fat over the top will seal it and help keep it a little longer.

Variations: For a richer sauce, cook 3 ounces chopped salt pork along with the carrot and onions. When adding the final beef stock also add 4 fluid ounces gravy or juice from roast beef.

BROWN ONION SAUCE

1 ounce butter
2 onions, finely chopped
3 fluid ounces dry white wine or vinegar
8 fluid ounces basic brown sauce
1 teaspoon finely chopped parsley

Melt butter in a saucepan; add onions and cook until golden brown. Add wine and simmer until reduced to half.

Add brown sauce and simmer 15 minutes. Just before serving stir in parsley. Use with meat, especially leftovers, and vegetables. Makes ½ pint.

DIABLE SAUCE
(Brown Devil Sauce)

3 shallots or spring onions, finely chopped
7 or 8 peppercorns, finely crushed
3 fluid ounces dry white wine
8 fluid ounces basic brown sauce
1 teaspoon Worcestershire sauce
1 teaspoon chopped parsley

Combine shallots, peppercorns, and wine; cook until reduced to one-third.

Add brown sauce, Worcestershire sauce, and parsley. Serve with grilled food. Makes about ½ pint.

MADEIRA SAUCE 1

Prepare 16 fluid ounces basic brown sauce and simmer gently until reduced to ½ pint. Add 3 fluid ounces Madeira and bring again just to boiling point but do not allow to boil, or the flavour of the wine will be impaired. Serve with game, beef, veal, ham, or poultry.

BASIC BROWN SAUCE
(Quick Method)

2 ounces butter or fat
2 ounces flour
¾ pint meat, vegetable, or fish stock
1 teaspoon salt
⅛ teaspoon pepper

Melt butter, blend in flour and cook until browned, stirring constantly.

Gradually add stock, stirring until mixture boils and thickens.

Add salt and pepper; cook 3 minutes longer, stirring constantly.

Serve with meat, poultry, fish or vegetables. Makes ¾ pint.

Brown Sauce Variations

Creole Brown Sauce: Sauté small chopped onion and 1½ ounces chopped green pepper in butter before adding flour.

Dill Brown Sauce: Add to brown sauce 2 tablespoons wine or cider vinegar and chopped dill to taste. Serve with veal or lamb.

Giblet Gravy: Substitute dripping for other fat. Add chopped cooked chicken or turkey giblets to gravy.

Mushroom Brown Sauce: Sauté 2 ounces sliced mushrooms and 1 teaspoon chopped onion in butter before adding flour.

Olive Brown Sauce: Add about 12 sliced green or black olives to brown sauce.

Pan Gravy: In basic brown sauce substitute pan dripping for other fat. Use water or stock.

Piquant Brown Sauce: Simmer together for a few minutes 2 tablespoons each tarragon vinegar and finely chopped green pepper, 1 teaspoon each chopped onion and chopped capers. Add to brown sauce with 2 tablespoons chopped gherkin.

Serve with fish, beef, veal, or tongue. If used with fish, use fish stock when preparing basic brown sauce.

Port Brown Sauce: To ⅓ pint brown sauce add 2 tablespoons port. Simmer about 5 minutes.

Savoury Horseradish Brown Sauce: Add 3 to 4 tablespoons prepared horseradish and 1 tablespoon prepared English mustard to brown sauce.

Spanish Brown Sauce: Sauté 1 small chopped onion, 1½ ounces chopped green pepper, 1 ounce sliced mushrooms in butter before adding flour.

Substitute tomato juice or stewed tomatoes for 8 fluid ounces stock. Serve with rice, spaghetti, or meat balls.

BÉCHAMEL SAUCE
(Basic Recipe)

This name is often applied to plain white sauce or to any sauce based on it. However, the original or true Béchamel is made of chicken or veal stock, cream or milk, flour, and butter and is usually seasoned with onions. Use it with any of the variations suggested for white cause. It is said to have originated with the Marquis de Béchamel, maître d'hôtel of Louis XIV.

A famous variation is Mornay sauce, believed to be named after Philippe de Mornay, premier of France under Henry IV.

12 fluid ounces chicken or veal
  stock
1 sprig parsley
6 celery leaves
½ small onion, chopped
¼ bay leaf
6 whole black peppers
1½ ounces butter or margarine
1½ ounces flour
few grains cayenne pepper
¼ teaspoon salt
few grains nutmeg
8 fluid ounces scalded milk

Simmer stock with parsley, celery leaves, onion, bay leaf, and whole black peppercorns for 20 minutes.

Strain and measure. If necessary, add water to make 8 fluid ounces.

Melt butter over low heat and blend in flour and seasonings. Gradually add hot stock and scalded milk.

Bring to boiling point and let boil 2 minutes or until thick and smooth.

Strain through fine sieve. Serve on chicken croquettes, chicken mousse, or fried chicken. Makes about ¾ pint.

Béchamel Sauce Variations

Fish Béchamel Sauce: Substitute fish stock for chicken or veal stock.

Stir a little hot stock into 1 slightly beaten egg and beat into remaining sauce. Blend in 1 tablespoon lemon juice.

Mornay Sauce: Add 2 to 4 tablespoons grated Parmesan cheese to sauce. Serve with vegetables or fish.

Yellow Béchamel Sauce: Stir 1 slightly beaten egg yolk into sauce.

Mushroom Béchamel Sauce: Sauté 2 ounces sliced mushrooms in butter 5 minutes before blending in flour.

PAPRIKA SAUCE OR HUNGARIAN SAUCE

8 fluid ounces Béchamel sauce
1 tablespoon finely chopped onion
1 ounce butter
2 teaspoons paprika

Prepare Béchamel sauce. Sauté onion in ½ ounce butter, drain well and add to sauce. Add paprika, then put through a fine sieve. Add ½ ounce butter. Serve with fish, poultry, lamb, and veal.

AURORE SAUCE

Prepare ¾ pint Béchamel sauce and add to it 3 tablespoons very red tomato purée. Boil slightly before putting through a fine sieve. Then add ½ ounce butter. Serve with fish or poultry.

TOMATO SAUCE
(Basic Recipe)

16 ounces canned tomatoes
2 slices onion
1 teaspoon caster sugar
1 bay leaf
2 whole allspice
2 whole cloves
butter or dripping
flour
salt and pepper

Simmer tomato, onion, sugar, and spices 10 minutes. Strain through fine sieve and measure the liquid.

For each half pint liquid blend 1 ounce flour and 1 ounce melted butter. Add to tomato juice; season with salt and pepper, and stir until thickened.

Continue to cook over hot water 5 to 10 minutes. Serve hot over croquettes, meat loaf, or spaghetti.

Tomato Sauce Variations

Tomato-Cheese Sauce: Add 2 ounces grated cheese to tomato sauce. Cook until cheese is melted.

Tomato-Lobster Sauce: Add 4 ounces chopped cooked or tinned lobster meat to tomato sauce. Use prawns or lobster sauces over cooked spaghetti or macaroni.

Tomato-Meat Sauce: Brown tiny meat balls in butter before blending in flour. Serve with spaghetti or noodles in casserole.

Tomato-Prawn Sauce: Add 3 to 4 ounces tinned or cooked cleaned prawns to tomato sauce.

Tomato-Sherry Sauce: Add 4 tablespoons sherry to tomato sauce.

CHINESE SWEET-SOUR SAUCE

4 fluid ounces pineapple juice
2 fluid ounces malt vinegar
3 tablespoons groundnut or cooking
  oil
1½ ounces (according to taste) brown
  sugar
1 teaspoon soy sauce
½ teaspoon pepper

Combine ingredients and heat. Serve with fish, shellfish, and meats. For other Chinese sweet-sour sauces, see recipes in index.

FRENCH
COOKERY

Coq au Vin (Chicken with Wine)

Chicken with Grape Garnish
(Chicken Veronique)

Mushrooms and Onions in Wine Sauce
Frozen Peas-French Style

BASIC BÉARNAISE SAUCE

8 fluid ounces dry white wine
1 tablespoon tarragon vinegar
1 tablespoon finely chopped shallots
    or spring onion
1 sprig parsley
2 sprigs tarragon, chopped
1 sprig chervil, chopped
2 peppercorns, bruised
3 egg yolks
8 ounces melted butter

Combine in top of double saucepan the wine, vinegar, shallots, parsley, tarragon, chervil, and peppercorns. Cook over direct heat until reduced to $\frac{2}{3}$ of original volume.

Allow to cool, then place over, not in, hot water and add a little egg yolk and then a little melted butter, combining well before next addition. Continue alternating additions until all butter and eggs are added. When finished the sauce should have the consistency of double cream. Note: All of the egg and butter may not be needed to arrive at this consistency.

Strain through a fine sieve before serving, and correct the seasoning with salt to taste and a dash of cayenne pepper. If desired, 1 teaspoon each of chopped chervil and tarragon leaves may be added. Serve with any grilled steak. It is also a luxurious choice for eggs and fish. Makes a generous $\frac{1}{2}$ pint.

VALOIS SAUCE

To $\frac{1}{2}$ pint Béarnaise sauce, add 1 teaspoon melted beef essence to give a light brown colour. Serve with eggs or grilled chicken.

CHORON SAUCE

To $\frac{1}{2}$ pint Béarnaise sauce, add 3 ounces tomato purée. Use with fish, chicken, or meat.

CREOLE SAUCE 2

1 small chopped onion
1 ounce butter or margarine
1 tablespoon flour
16 ounces tinned tomatoes
2 ounces chopped celery
1 green pepper, chopped
4 tablespoons chopped cooked ham
    or streaky bacon
chopped parsley
salt and pepper to taste

Cook onion in butter for a few minutes. Sprinkle flour over onion and quickly stir in tomatoes, celery, and green pepper. Simmer about 20 minutes.

Add ham or bacon, parsley, and salt and pepper. Serve with omelets, spaghetti and fish. Makes about 1 pint sauce.

TOMATO SAUCE
(Italian Style)

2 large chopped onions
3 cloves garlic, chopped
3 tablespoons olive oil
2 pounds tinned Italian tomatoes
2 6-ounce cans tomato paste
about $\frac{3}{4}$ pint water or meat stock
1 bay leaf
$\frac{1}{2}$ teaspoon salt
$\frac{1}{2}$ teaspoon oregano or $\frac{1}{4}$ teaspoon
    each oregano and basil

Sauté onion and garlic in olive oil until brown, stirring often.

Add tomatoes, tomato paste, water or stock, bay leaf, salt, and pepper. Simmer, uncovered, stirring occasionally, about 2 hours. Add additional water as needed.

Add oregano and basil and continue cooking about 15 minutes. The sauce should be thick. Makes about $2\frac{1}{2}$ pints.

HUNTER'S SAUCE OR CHASSEUR SAUCE

1 to 2 ounces butter
2 ounces sliced mushrooms
$\frac{1}{4}$ teaspoon salt
few grains pepper
2 shallots or spring onions, finely
    chopped
4 fluid ounces red wine
8 fluid ounces basic brown sauce
2 tablespoons tomato sauce or purée
1 teaspoon chopped parsley or $\frac{1}{2}$
    teaspoon each of chopped
    parsley and chopped tarragon

Melt butter in a saucepan; add mushrooms, salt, and pepper; sauté until mushrooms are lightly browned. Add shallots or spring onions and wine; simmer until reduced to about half.

Add brown sauce, tomato sauce, and parsley. Simmer about 5 minutes. Adjust the seasoning. Serve with poultry, game, and red meat. Makes about $\frac{3}{4}$ pint.

HOT RAVIGOTE SAUCE 2

3 fluid ounces dry white wine
3 fluid ounces vinegar
5 or 6 shallots, finely chopped
$\frac{3}{4}$ pint rich white sauce
1 ounce butter
1 teaspoon mixed herbs (chopped
    chives, chervil, and tarragon)

Combine wine, vinegar, and shallots in a saucepan; cook until reduced to $\frac{1}{3}$ original quantity.

Add white sauce; boil gently 5 or 6 minutes. Remove from heat and add butter and herbs. Serve with fish, light meat, and poultry. Makes about 1 pint.

CHEESE SAUCE 2

1 ounce butter or margarine
1 ounce flour
8 fluid ounces milk
1 egg yolk, well beaten
$\frac{1}{2}$ teaspoon dry mustard
$\frac{1}{8}$ teaspoon pepper
$\frac{3}{4}$ teaspoon salt
few grains cayenne pepper or
    paprika
1 ounce grated Parmesan cheese

Melt butter and blend in flour. Add milk slowly, stirring constantly. Cook over hot water until smooth and thick.

Pour over egg yolk, stirring constantly.

Season to taste. Add cheese. Serve with vegetables, fish, macaroni, or rice.

SOUR CREAM SAUCE

about 1 ounce butter
2 small onions, finely chopped
4 fluid ounces dry white wine
8 fluid ounces heavy sour cream,
    scalded
salt and pepper
about 1 teaspoon lemon juice (op-
    tional)

Melt butter in a saucepan; add onions and fry until soft but not brown. Add wine and cook until the mixture is reduced to about half, stirring occasionally.

Pour in scalded sour cream, stirring constantly, and stir until thoroughly blended. Simmer very gently 5 minutes but do not let mixture boil after adding sour scream or it will curdle.

Strain sauce through fine sieve and season with salt and pepper to taste. For a sourer effect add lemon juice to taste. Serve with fish, chicken, or light meat. Makes about $\frac{1}{2}$ to $\frac{3}{4}$ pint.

BORDELAISE SAUCE

A famous brown sauce usually served with steak.

1 ounce butter or margarine
1 ounce flour
$\frac{3}{4}$ pint brown stock or consommé
2 cloves garlic, chopped fine
2 tablespoons chopped onion
bit of bay leaf
2 tablespoons chopped ham
2 slices carrot
2 tablespoons chopped parsley
8 whole black peppercorns
1 tablespoon Worcestershire sauce
1 tablespoon tomato ketchup
2 tablespoons sherry

Melt butter. Stir in flour until lightly browned. Add remaining ingredients except sherry and simmer 8 minutes.

Strain sauce and season with sherry, salt and pepper to taste. Makes about $\frac{3}{4}$ pint.

Sauces for Meats and Poultry

POIVRADE SAUCE
(Pepper Sauce)

A dark-brown sauce with black pepper served with meat and game, especially venison.

2   ounces cooking or olive oil
1   carrot, chopped
1   onion, chopped
3   sprigs parsley
1   bay leaf
pinch of thyme
2   fluid ounces wine vinegar
4   fluid ounces liquid from
       marinade used for the meat
       or game (see note below)
1   pint, 4 fluid ounces basic brown
       sauce
10 peppercorns
4   fluid ounces dry red wine
salt and pepper

Heat oil in saucepan; fry in it the carrot and onion until golden brown. Add parsley, bay leaf, thyme, vinegar, and 2 ounces marinade liquid. Simmer gently until reduced to ⅓.

Add brown sauce; bring to the boil, reduce heat and simmer for 1 hour.

Add peppercorns and simmer 5 minutes more. Strain sauce into another saucepan and add remaining marinade liquid. Cook slowly for 30 minutes, then add wine. Correct seasoning with salt and freshly-milled pepper to make a hot sauce. Serve with meat and game. Makes about 1¼ pints.
Note: If the meat or game was not marinated, see index for basic uncooked marinade for meat or game.

GRAND VENEUR SAUCE

Add 1 tablespoon truffles, diced or cut into julienne strips, to Poivrade sauce. The sauce may be thickened with the blood of a hare or rabbit. Add the blood slowly, rotating the pan to swirl it into the sauce. Do not boil the sauce after adding the blood.

QUICK BROWN SAUCE OR GRAVY

½ clove garlic
1 ounce butter
1 ounce flour
8 ounces tinned consommé or 2
       stock cubes dissolved in 8
       fluid ounces boiling water
salt and pepper
other seasoning as desired, such as
       Worcestershire sauce, dry
       sherry, tomato ketchup,
       lemon juice, and dried herbs

Rub a saucepan with garlic. Melt butter, blend in flour. Stir in stock. Bring to boiling point, stirring constantly. Season to taste with salt and pepper, and other seasonings as desired. Makes about ½ pint.

SAUCE ROBERT

There is also a commercial Sauce Robert on the market, used for flavouring many dishes, but the sauce found on many menus is often made this way.

1 small finely chopped onion
½ ounce butter
3 fluid ounces dry white wine
1 tablespoon vinegar
8 fluid ounces basic brown sauce
2 tablespoons tomato sauce or tomato
       purée (optional)
1 tablespoon finely chopped gherkin
1 teaspoon prepared English mustard
¼ teaspoon caster sugar

Cook onion in melted butter in a saucepan until onion is golden brown. Add wine and vinegar and cook until reduced to about ¾ of original quantity.

Add brown sauce and tomato sauce; simmer gently 10 to 15 minutes. Just before serving, stir in gherkins, mustard, and sugar. Serve with meat. Makes about ½ pint.

BREAD SAUCE

1 onion
6 whole cloves
¾ pint milk
few grains cayenne pepper
1 teaspoon salt
3 ounces fresh fine breadcrumbs

Stud onion with cloves. Place onion and milk in a saucepan. Add cayenne pepper and salt. Bring to boiling point. Cook 5 minutes.

Strain and add breadcrumbs. Taste and add more salt if necessary.

Serve with roast poultry or game. If a richer sauce is desired, add a little butter or cream.

MARCHAND DE VIN SAUCE
(Wine Merchant's Sauce)

3   ounces butter
6   chopped shallots, or 1 medium
       chopped onion
6   fluid ounces dry red wine
12 fluid ounces basic brown sauce
       or tinned beef gravy
2   tablespoons lemon juice

Melt 2 ounces butter. Slowly stir in onions and cook until soft, about 5 minutes. Add wine and simmer uncovered until the liquid is reduced to about 2 ounces, about 20 minutes.

Add brown sauce and lemon juice; heat and stir in remaining butter piece by piece. Serve with grilled steak or roast beef. Makes about ¾ pint.

Mushroom steak sauce is a quick topping for steaks, chops, and hamburgers.

MUSHROOM STEAK SAUCE

1   6-ounce can sliced mushrooms
2   fluid ounces water
few drops Tabasco sauce
¼   teaspoon Aromat or mixed herbs
1½ teaspoons cornflour

Place all ingredients in small saucepan. Mix well. Bring to boil, stirring constantly. Salt to taste. Serve over steaks, chops, or grilled hamburgers. Makes about 8 fluid ounces sauce.

ROSEMARY SAUCE

Heat 2 fluid ounces dry red wine to boiling point. Remove from heat and add ¼ teaspoon dried rosemary. Cover and let stand 5 to 10 minutes. (Note: if desired, a mixture of rosemary and other dried herbs may be used such as thyme, basil, bay leaf, sage, and marjoram.)

Strain the herb-flavoured wine into 8 fluid ounces basic brown sauce. Serve with game. Makes about ½ pint.

CRANBERRY GAME SAUCE

1 teaspoon cinnamon
¼ teaspoon ground cloves
pinch of nutmeg
3 tablespoons caster sugar
grated rind of 1 lemon
4 fluid ounces port
1 pound whole cranberry sauce

Simmer above ingredients together for 5 minutes. Stir 1 tablespoon cornflour into spice-wine mixture. Heat thoroughly, stirring until mixture thickens slightly.

To keep hot until serving time, place saucepan over pan of boiling water. Serving suggestions: with small game, pork chops, or baked ham.

REDCURRANT JELLY SAUCE

8 ounces redcurrant jelly
2 tablespoons vinegar
1 teaspoon dry mustard
¼ teaspoon ground cloves
¼ teaspoon cinnamon

Heat jelly until melted. Add other ingredients and simmer 10 minutes. Serve hot with ham or baked tinned meat. Makes about 8 fluid ounces.

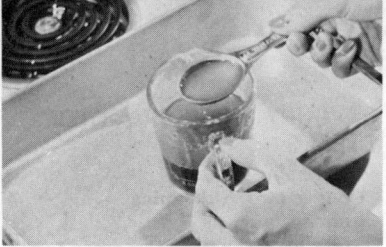

TO PREPARE GRAVY WITH PAN DRIPPINGS

1. Measure the fat and dripping to be used.

2. Measure and add flour, stirring until well blended.

3. Gradually add stock or other liquid called for in recipe.

4. Cook over low heat, stirring until thick and smooth.

HOW TO BROWN FLOUR FOR GRAVY

Spread flour in pan and place in slow oven (300°F. Mark 2). Stir frequently to prevent burning; 20 to 25 minutes are required to brown 24 ounces.

Flour may be browned in a frying pan on top of cooker. Watch carefully to avoid burning flour.

Store browned flour in a tightly covered jar.

FLOUR PASTE FOR THICKENING SAUCES AND GRAVIES

A thin paste will give better results. The usual proportions are about 1 part water to 2 parts flour.

Blend flour and cold water together, then stir as much as required into boiling stock or dripping. Cook until sauce thickens.

ROAST BEEF GRAVY

Skim fat from the roast drippings, leaving about 4 tablespoons in pan. Add 3 to 4 ounces flour and stir over moderate heat until flour is thoroughly browned. Do not add water until the flour is thoroughly browned.

Gradually add ¾ pint water or stock. Cook, stirring until gravy is smooth and thickened. Season to taste with salt and pepper.

POT ROAST GRAVY

Measure amount of pot roast liquid left in roasting pan. Add to this enough water, soup, stock, or water in which vegetables have been cooked to make the desired amount of gravy.

For each ½ pint of liquid, measure 1½ ounces flour and make a smooth paste by adding enough cold water to blend. The water must be cold to prevent lumping. Use a spoon or egg whisk to thin flour paste.

Add paste gradually to pot roast liquid, stirring constantly over moderate heat. Bring to the boil and simmer 2 or 3 minutes.

GIBLET GRAVY

Chop cooked giblets finely and save liquid in which they were cooked.

Skim off excess fat in roasting pan, leaving about 4 fluid ounces for 1½ pints of gravy.

Add 2 ounces flour and stir until smooth over low heat.

Gradually add 1½ pints stock, using water if there isn't enough. Stir constantly to keep gravy smooth as it thickens.

Add chopped giblets, and salt and pepper, to season. For thinner gravy, add more liquid.

COUNTRY GRAVY

¾ pint milk
1 ounce flour
4 tablespoons dripping
salt and pepper

This is milk gravy made after frying chicken, salt pork, or sausages.

Make a smooth thin paste with a little of the milk and flour.

Add paste to hot dripping, stirring constantly.

Add remaining milk, stir and cook until gravy is smooth and thickened. Season to taste.

SOUR CREAM GRAVY

Prepare gravy according to any of given recipes. Add 4 fluid ounces sour cream for each 8 fluid ounces of gravy, just before removing from heat.

Cook just long enough to heat sour cream. Do not boil as sour cream will curdle.

WINE GRAVY

Make gravy according to any of given recipes. Add 1 fluid ounce wine for each 8 fluid ounces of gravy and cook only long enough to heat through.

Use red wine for beef gravy and white wine for veal.

MADEIRA SAUCE 2

½ pint basic brown sauce
2 fluid ounces Madeira or dry sherry
1 teaspoon beef essence
1 ounce butter
additional fluid ounce Madeira

Prepare brown sauce, then simmer gently until reduced to about 6 or 7 fluid ounces. Add 2 fluid ounces Madeira or dry sherry and beef essence. Simmer gently 5 to 10 minutes.

Add butter bit by bit, swirling it in by moving the pan in a circular motion. Keep hot, but do not let sauce boil after adding butter.

Finally add additional Madeira, swirling it in the same way. Serve with sautéed fillets of beef. Makes about ½ pint.

Note: This sauce may be made in the same pan in which you have sautéed the meat. Pour off the fat from pan, then proceed as above.

PÉRIGUEUX SAUCE

Make Madeira sauce and add 1 tablespoon chopped truffles and a little liquid from truffles to it. Add ½ ounce butter, swirling it in by moving the pan in a circular motion. Keep hot but do not let sauce boil after adding butter. Use with croquettes, eggs, and chicken.

PERIGOURDINE SAUCE

This sauce is usually very similar to Sauce Périgueux; however the truffles are diced finely instead of chopped.

PIQUANT SAUCE

½ ounce butter
2 tablespoons finely chopped onion
2 tablespoons dry white wine or vinegar
½ pint basic brown sauce
1 tablespoon tomato purée
2 tablespoons finely chopped gherkin
1 sprig chopped parsley

Melt butter in a saucepan; add onion and cook until lightly browned. Add wine and simmer until liquid is almost evaporated. Add brown sauce and tomato sauce and simmer 10 minutes.

Just before serving, add gherkin and parsley. Adjust the seasoning with salt. This is good for reheating leftover meat. Makes about ½ pint.

CREAM GRAVY FOR FRIED CHICKEN

Pour off all but 2 tablespoons fat from the pan in which chicken has been fried. Stir in ½ ounce flour and when the mixture is well blended, pour in slowly, stirring constantly and scraping in the brown bits, 8 fluid ounces single cream. When the sauce boils, taste for seasoning and add salt and pepper if required. Pour over fried chicken.

ORANGE SAUCE FOR ROAST DUCK OR GOOSE

5 ounces caster sugar
¼ teaspoon salt
1 ounce cornflour
8 fluid ounces boiling water
½ ounce butter or margarine
juice and grated rind of 2 oranges

Mix sugar, salt, and cornflour. Pour hot water over mixture, stirring constantly. Cook until thick and clear.

Add butter, orange juice, and grated rind just before removing from heat. Stir well and serve with duck. Makes about ¾ pint.

GINGER SAUCE

5 crushed ginger biscuits
3 ounces brown sugar
2 ounces vinegar
1 teaspoon onion juice
8 fluid ounces hot water
1 lemon, sliced
1¼ ounces raisins

Mix ingredients in saucepan and heat, stirring constantly, until smooth and fairly thick. Serve with boiled tongue. Makes a generous ½ pint.

HORSERADISH SAUCE

½ ounce butter or margarine
½ ounce flour
8 fluid ounces milk
2 rounded tablespoons prepared horseradish
1 tablespoon lemon juice
salt and pepper
1 tablespoon minced pimiento

Melt butter and blend in flour. Slowly add milk, stirring constantly until the mixture boils.

Add drained horseradish to lemon

Raisin sauce is an attractive garnish for smoked tongue.

juice, seasonings, and pimiento. Add to cream sauce and serve hot. Serve with "boiled" meat and poultry. Makes a generous ½ pint.

CURRY SAUCE

1 ounce butter or margarine
1 medium onion, chopped
1 ounce flour
1 teaspoon curry powder
8 fluid ounces beef stock consommé

Melt butter; add onion and let cook until tender.

Stir in flour; let it brown slightly, then add curry and liquid. Cook and stir until sauce is thickened and smooth.

A hint of garlic may be added to this sauce by cooking a clove with onion for 1 minute. Serve with veal, lamb, or poultry. Makes about 8 fluid ounces.

CUMBERLAND SAUCE

1 tablespoon port
grated rind of 1 lemon
juice of 1 lemon
grated rind of 1 orange
1 tablespoon icing sugar
1 teaspoon prepared mustard
5 ounces melted redcurrant jelly

Combine ingredients and blend well. If the jelly is very stiff, dilute with 1 or 2 tablespoons hot water. Serve with any cold meat or game. Makes about ¼ pint.

MINT SAUCE FOR LAMB

1 to 1½ ounces caster sugar
2 fluid ounces hot water
4 fluid ounces malt vinegar
1 ounce chopped fresh mint leaves
3 tablespoons lemon juice
½ teaspoon salt

Dissolve sugar in water. Add vinegar. Bring to boil.

Pour over fresh mint leaves. Add lemon juice and salt.

Let stand ½ to 1 hour before straining and serving with lamb. Makes about 8 ounces sauce.

RAISIN SAUCE FOR TONGUE AND HAM

3 ounces brown sugar
1½ teaspoons dry mustard
½ ounce cornflour
12 fluid ounces water
2 fluid ounces vinegar
1½ ounces raisins
½ ounce butter or margarine

Combine dry ingredients; slowly add water and vinegar.

Add raisins and cook over low heat, stirring constantly, until thickened.

Cook 10 minutes longer to plump raisins, then add butter or margarine.

SAVOURY ONION GRAVY FOR STEAKS

4 large sliced onions
1 ounce lard or dripping
1 ounce flour
¾ pint meat stock
1 tablespoon Worcestershire sauce
salt and pepper to taste

Cook onions in hot lard until golden; stir in flour.

Add meat stock, Worcestershire, salt and pepper, and cook, stirring constantly, over low heat until thick.

Cover and simmer 10 minutes. Makes 6 to 8 servings.

Note: 2 stock cubes dissolved in ¾ pint hot water may be used instead of meat stock.

CHINESE BROWN GRAVY

3 ounces dripping from roast beef, ham, or chicken
3 ounces flour
2 tablespoons soy sauce
1 teaspoon Chinese brown gravy sauce*
1 teaspoon salt
dash of pepper
4 fluid ounces cold water
12 fluid ounces hot water

Mix flour and dripping in bottom of pan. Add sauces, salt, pepper, and cold water. Crush lumps and mix thoroughly.

Add hot water. Stir well and cook to smooth paste.

Pour in hot gravy boat and serve with egg foo yong, cooked or fried rice, scones, potatoes, dumplings, egg noodles, chops, roast beef, pork, or veal. Makes ¾ pint.

Variations: One beef or chicken stock cube may be added, and mushroom juice may be used instead of hot water, if available. Add more flour if thicker gravy is desired. Add more water if thinner gravy is desired.

*Note: Chinese brown gravy sauce may be purchased in most large grocery stores.

WINE SAUCE FOR ROAST CHICKEN

2 fluid ounces sweet white wine
juice of 1 orange
1 ounce butter or margarine, melted
1 stick celery, chopped
1 small onion, sliced

Combine all ingredients, and pour over breast of dressed and stuffed chicken in roasting pan.

Roast at 325°F. Mark 3 until tender, basting with wine sauce at 20 minute intervals. Strain dripping in pan for gravy. Makes enough for one 4-pound chicken.

Sauces for Fish and Shellfish

NEWBURG SAUCE

½ ounce butter
1 teaspoon Worcestershire sauce
½ ounce flour
¾ pint single cream
2 egg yolks, well beaten
2 fluid ounces sherry

Melt butter. Stir in Worcestershire sauce and flour. Gradually stir in cream. Cook over low heat, stirring constantly until smooth and thickened.

At this point add cooked and cleaned lobster, prawns, crab meat, flaked fish, or tuna fish.

When ready to serve, gradually beat in egg yolks and sherry. Reheat slightly and adjust seasoning. Serve over vol-au-vent cases or toast triangles. Makes about ¾ pint sauce, enough for 4 servings of seafood.

Variation: For chicken à la king, to this amount of sauce add 6 ounces cooked peas, 1 4-ounce can mushrooms, 2 tablespoons chopped pimiento, and 15 to 16 ounces diced cooked chicken.

BERÇY SAUCE

1½ ounces butter
1 teaspoon finely chopped shallot
4 fluid ounces white wine
½ ounce flour
¼ teaspoon salt
few grains pepper
1 sprig chopped parsley

Cook shallot in ½ ounce melted butter until soft and brown. Add wine and cook until reduced by half.

Meanwhile cream remaining butter with flour and cook over low heat, stirring until well blended.

Add to wine sauce and mix together until well blended. Add salt, pepper, and parsley.

This sauce is used with fish. Place the fish in a baking-dish. Cover with sauce and bake in oven. Serve from the dish.

HOT MAYONNAISE SAUCE

3 rounded tablespoons mayonnaise
3 fluid ounces milk
¼ teaspoon salt
dash of white pepper
few grains cayenne pepper
1 tablespoon chopped parsley or
    chives or ⅓ teaspoon dried
    basil or tarragon

Combine mayonnaise and milk in top of double saucepan. Heat over, not in, boiling water, stirring until smooth, about 5 minutes.

Stir in salt, pepper, and cayenne pepper, then remove from heat. Stir in parsley or chives. Serve with hot fish or vegetables. Makes about ½ pint.

BURGUNDY SAUCE OR SAUCE BOURGUIGNONNE

1 small carrot
1 small onion
1 small celeriac
1½ ounces unsalted butter
pinch of thyme
bit of bay leaf
8 fluid ounces red Burgundy
12 fluid ounces fish stock
1 clove garlic
salt and pepper

Cut vegetables into very small pieces. Brown them in 1 ounce melted butter in a heavy saucepan. Add thyme, bay leaf, wine, 4 fluid ounces fish stock, and garlic. Cook over moderate heat until the sauce is reduced to half its original quantity. Then add remaining fish stock and simmer gently 15 to 20 minutes.

Strain the liquid through a fine sieve, pressing gently to force some of the pulp through. Season to taste with salt and pepper. Just before serving, stir in ½ ounce butter. Strain again and serve with fish. Makes about a generous ½ pint.

SAUCE MEUNIÈRE

Heat 2 to 3 ounces butter or margarine until it is brown.

Stir in 1 teaspoon lemon juice and pour over food already sprinkled with chopped parsley.

PRAWN SAUCE FOR FISH

¾ pint medium white sauce
4 ounces cooked or tinned prawns,
    cleaned
2 ounces canned or sautéed fresh
    mushrooms
1 ounce finely chopped celery
8 chopped olives
2 tablespoons chopped parsley
1 teaspoon Worcestershire sauce

Prepare white sauce and season well to taste; add remaining ingredients and heat just to boiling point.

Serve in sauce dish with baked or peached fish; or place fish on a plate and pour sauce over it. Makes about 1¼ pints.

Variations: A well-seasoned, thickened tomato sauce may be substituted for the medium white sauce. Other ingredients may be varied as desired.

WATERCRESS SAUCE (MAYONNAISE)

To 3 rounded tablespoons mayonnaise, add ¼ bunch finely chopped watercress, 1 tablespoon lemon juice, and salt and pepper to taste. Use with cold fish and shellfish. Makes about ½ pint.

NANTUA SAUCE

2 fluid ounces double cream, scalded
8 fluid ounces medium white sauce
salt and pepper
1 ounce lobster or prawn butter
finely chopped cooked prawns

Add scalded cream to white sauce; blend well and put through a fine sieve into a saucepan.

Heat without boiling; add salt and pepper to taste, then stir in lobster or prawn butter. Garnish the sauce with finely chopped cooked prawns or lobster. Serve with fish.

Note: Instead of prawn or lobster butter, you may use ½ ounce finely ground shellfish and ½ ounce butter made into a smooth paste.

ANCHOVY SAUCE FOR FISH

Prepare 8 fluid ounces thin white sauce; add to it 3 anchovy fillets, washed and pounded to a paste. Blend well with the sauce.

ANCHOVY BUTTER SAUCE

Add ½ ounce anchovy paste to Maître d'Hôtel Butter with the lemon juice.

GARLIC OR ONION BUTTER SAUCE

Heat 2 ounces butter or margarine and 1 clove garlic or 1 very small chopped onion. Press through a sieve.

ALMOND BUTTER SAUCE

Sauté 2 ounces shredded blanched almonds in 2 ounces butter or margarine until lightly browned, stirring constantly. Serve with fish. Makes about 3 ounces.

SOUR CREAM-CUCUMBER SAUCE

4 fluid ounces thick sour cream
4 ounces diced, unpeeled cucumber
½ teaspoon salt
4 drops onion juice

Whip sour cream until smooth; add cucumber, salt, and onion juice. Serve with fish. Makes ½ pint.

HORSERADISH BUTTER SAUCE

Combine 2 to 4 tablespoons horseradish with 4 ounces melted butter or margarine.

PARSLEY BUTTER SAUCE

Combine 2 to 3 sprigs finely chopped parsley with 4 ounces melted butter or margarine.

Add 1 teaspoon lemon juice, ½ teaspoon salt, and ⅛ teaspoon pepper.

CHIVES OR CHERVIL BUTTER SAUCE

Heat 2 ounces butter or margarine and add 2 tablespoons minced chervil or 1 tablespoon minced chives.

Sauces for Vegetables

BUTTER SAUCE FOR CANNED OR BOILED VEGETABLES

Drain vegetables and boil the vegetable liquid until it is reduced by half. Add to it melted butter and seasonings to taste.

SOUR CREAM SAUCE FOR BAKED POTATOES

8 fluid ounces sour cream
1 teaspoon Worcestershire sauce
½ teaspoon Aromat
dash of Tabasco sauce
½ teaspoon salt
freshly-milled black pepper to taste
chopped chives

Blend all ingredients except chives. Garnish with latter. Makes ½ pint.

POLONAISE SAUCE

3 ounces butter
1 ounce fine breadcrumbs
few drops lemon juice
1 teaspoon chopped parsley

Heat butter gently until it begins to brown slightly. Add breadcrumbs and cook until the crumbs are brown and the butter has stopped bubbling. Add lemon juice and parsley and serve immediately as a garnish for vegetables. If desired, sprinkle the vegetables with finely chopped egg.

Variation: If desired, 1 tablespoon finely chopped onion may be cooked in the butter until onion is transparent, before adding breadcrumbs.

SOUR CREAM SAUCE
(Mock Hollandaise)

2 egg yolks
6 fluid ounces sour cream
1 tablespoon lemon juice
½ teaspoon minced parsley
⅛ teaspoon salt
¼ teaspoon paprika

Beat egg yolks and cream together in top part of double saucepan.

Place over simmering water and cook, stirring constantly, until mixture is of custard consistency.

Remove from heat and add remaining ingredients. Serve at once with vegetables or fish.

French butter pecan sauce is quick, tasty, and simple.

VINAIGRETTE

The traditional French vinaigrette is classic French salad dressing (oil, vinegar, salt, and pepper) but English vinaigrette usually refers to any of several variations for vegetables, and sometimes for meats and fish. In the recipe given here change the proportions or add other herbs, as desired. This version may be served cold or hot. The recipe is excellent served cold over a green salad. Cooked vegetables served with this sauce are also excellent cold.

1 teaspoon salt
½ teaspoon paprika
⅛ teaspoon pepper
½ tablespoon dry mustard
½ teaspoon sugar
1 tablespoon tarragon vinegar
2 tablespoons cider vinegar
3 fluid ounces olive oil or cooking oil
1 tablespoon chopped gherkins
1 tablespoon chopped stuffed olives
1 teaspoon minced onion

Mix all ingredients together and beat well.

Heat to boiling point and serve with vegetables such as spinach, broccoli, artichokes, and asparagus.

ALMOND BUTTER FOR VEGETABLES

To 2 ounces melted butter or margarine add 2 tablespoons chopped salted almonds and 1 tablespoon lemon juice.

Serve over green beans, Brussels sprouts, or broccoli.

QUICK HOLLANDAISE SAUCE

Heat 2 rounded tablespoons mayonnaise over very low heat; stir in 1 teaspoon lemon juice and ⅛ teaspoon Tabasco sauce. Serve with vegetables.

MINT BUTTER FOR VEGETABLES

To 2 ounces butter or margarine, add 1 tablespoon chopped fresh mint leaves. Serve on peas, carrots, or a combination of the two.

FRENCH BUTTER PECAN SAUCE

4 ounces butter, melted
2 tablespoons chopped chives
⅛ teaspoon salt
¼ teaspoon pepper
¼ teaspoon marjoram
2 to 4 tablespoons lemon juice
2 ounces chopped pecans (or walnuts)

Combine ingredients; heat to blend flavours. Serve over cooked vegetables. Makes 8 fluid ounces or enough for 4 10-ounce packets of frozen vegetables.

Any one of a number of simple sauces made with butter can be used to add flavour and enjoyment to fresh or frozen vegetables. One of the most popular is lemon butter: butter melted until bubbling, then flavoured with lemon juice and grated lemon rind.

ORANGE BUTTER FOR BEETROOT

To 2 ounces butter or margarine, add 3 tablespoons orange juice and 1 tablespoon grated orange rind.

Simmer for a few minutes over low heat and serve over beetroot.

MOCK HOLLANDAISE SAUCE

1. Place an 8-ounce packet of cream cheese (which has been standing at room temperature until soft) in the top of double saucepan. Cream it with a spoon.

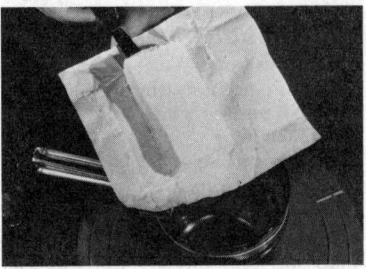

2. Add 2 egg yolks, one at a time, blending thoroughly after each addition.

Slowly add 2 tablespoons lemon juice and a dash of salt.

3. Place over hot water just until the sauce is heated through. Pour over hot cooked asparagus placed on toast triangles.

4. Serve hot. A delicious sauce, too, for broccoli and cauliflower.

SOUFFLÉS

Long considered the final test of an accomplished cook, the soufflé is often held in awe by many people who entertain an exaggerated idea of the difficulties of its composition. The classic French soufflé is actually easy to prepare and has a simple, even thrifty base: butter, flour, and milk for cream sauce, ¼ pound cheese or almost any leftover, and eggs.

Today, this dish can be simplified even more: a can of condensed soup, cheese, and eggs make a main dish soufflé; a packet of pudding mix, some milk, and eggs make the most delectable—and impressive—of sweet courses.

HINTS ON MAKING SOUFFLÉS

● The secret of a soufflé is primarily the proper whisking of the eggs and the incorporation of these beaten eggs into the basic mixture.

● Use eggs at room temperature; however yolks aren't as likely to break if you separate them from the whites while still cold from the refrigerator.

● If you let egg whites warm to room temperature before whisking, they'll fluff up better.

● French chefs always beat an extra egg white into a soufflé for lightness, that is, 4 whites to every 3 yolks.

● Many good cooks add ¼ teaspoon cream of tartar to whites while whisking—as insurance for a well risen soufflé.

● Egg yolks are whisked until thick and lemon-coloured.

● Egg whites are beaten until stiff but still glossy—never until dry.

● Underbeaten eggs make a small, unstable soufflé; overbeaten eggs will produce a tough soufflé.

● The ready and waiting hot sauce is slowly stirred into the beaten egg yolks. This way the yolks are smoothly blended with the sauce.

The size, shape, and preparation of the dish will influence the quality of the soufflé. A straight-sided dish gives maximum volume.

● The *cooled* sauce mixture is *folded* very gently into the beaten egg whites. A blending fork or metal spoon is just the thing for this. Take your time, and gently lift up-and-over in high strokes.

● Soufflés may be prepared in advance, with the exception of the beating of the egg whites, which must be done immediately before the soufflé is put into the oven.

● For a 3- or 4-egg soufflé, use a 2½-pint dish; for a large soufflé with more than 4 eggs, use a 3½-pint dish.

● For highest rise, butter or oil the bottom only, but not the sides of a baking dish. The mixture will cling to the dry sides and make a taller and more uniform soufflé.

● For extra height, tie a folded band of greaseproof paper around the outside of soufflé dish like a collar to support the rise. Pour soufflé mixture in almost to the top of dish.

● To bake a soufflé with a "top hat", pour the soufflé mixture into the baking dish, then run a teaspoon all around, 1 inch from the edge and about 1 inch deep. This crease will cause the crust to break at this point and form a taller centre.

● For a sweet crust soufflé, butter the baking dish and sprinkle with sugar before filling.

● When making a soufflé in a ring mould with the intention of inverting the contents when done, butter the ring mould well. Then fill with soufflé mixture and set in larger pan with 1 inch of hot, not boiling, water. This will facilitate turning out the soufflé from the mould and will give it a uniform consistency. For serving, fill the centre of the turned out, inverted mould.

● Once done, serve soufflés promptly, because they begin falling as soon as they start cooling. It is better to let your family or guests wait for the soufflé than to let the soufflé do the waiting. If your meal is delayed, turn the oven temperature to very low (250°F. Mark ½) and leave the soufflé in the oven—but not more than an extra 10 or 15 minutes.

● Soufflés may be cooked in a double saucepan over, not in, simmering water. Grease well both the pot and the lid. Pour in the soufflé mixture. Cover it and cook about 45 minutes to 1 hour. Turn out onto a hot plate.

Testing for doneness: the knife inserted in centre should come out clean.

With the constant oven temperatures of today's modern cookers, it is easier to succeed than to fail in making a perfect soufflé. Check the temperature of your oven with an oven thermometer. Periodic adjustments should be made by regular servicing.

Main-Course Soufflés

FISH SOUFFLÉ

15 ounces leftover cooked fish,
 flaked (or use 1 can drained
 tinned salmon or tuna fish)
1 tablespoon lemon juice
salt and pepper to taste
½ teaspoon paprika
pinch of nutmeg
3 ounces breadcrumbs, fresh
6 fluid ounces milk
4 eggs, separated

Sprinkle flaked fish with lemon juice
and mix in seasonings.

Combine breadcrumbs and milk;
heat to just boiling point, and add to
fish.

Beat egg yolks until light yellow in
colour; combine with fish and breadcrumb mixture.

Finally, add egg whites which have
been beaten until stiff but not dry.

Pour into buttered baking dish. Set
into a pan with hot water and bake in
moderate oven (350°F. Mark 4) until
set, about 40 to 45 minutes.

Serve immediately in baking dish
with an egg sauce, tomato sauce, or
lobster sauce. Serves 6.

EASY ASPARAGUS-CHEESE SOUFFLÉ
(Quick Main Dish Soufflé)

1 can condensed cream of
 asparagus soup
4 ounces grated Cheddar cheese
6 eggs, separated

Heat soup slowly; add cheese and
cook, stirring constantly until cheese is
melted. Add slightly beaten egg yolks;
cool. Fold stiffly beaten egg whites into
soup mixture.

Pour into an ungreased 3½-pint casserole. Bake in a slow oven (300°F.
Mark 2) for 1 to 1¼ hours or until
soufflé is golden brown. Serve immediately. Serves 6.

Easy Chicken Soufflé: Follow recipe
for Easy Asparagus Cheese Soufflé except use cream of chicken soup; omit
cheese and use instead 6 ounces finely
diced cooked chicken.

Easy Celery Salmon Soufflé: Follow
recipe for Easy Asparagus Cheese
Soufflé except use cream of celery soup
instead of asparagus; omit cheese and
use instead, 7 ounces finely flaked salmon, drained.

Easy Mushroom Cheese Soufflé: Follow recipe for Easy Asparagus Cheese
Soufflé except use cream of mushroom
soup instead of cream of asparagus.

"TOP HAT" CHEESE SOUFFLÉ

2 ounces butter or margarine
2 ounces flour
1 teaspoon salt
dash of cayenne pepper
12 fluid ounces milk
½ pound processed Cheddar cheese,
 sliced
6 eggs, separated

Melt the butter or margarine in the
top of a double saucepan placed over
boiling water. Remove from the boiling water, and blend in the flour, salt,
and cayenne pepper.

Gradually add the milk, blending
well. Return to the boiling water and
cook, stirring constantly, until the sauce
is thick and smooth.

Add the sliced cheese and continue
cooking, stirring frequently, until the
cheese has melted.

Remove from the heat and slowly
add the beaten egg yolks, blending
them in well.

Slightly cool the mixture, then pour
onto the stiffly beaten whites of the
eggs, folding the mixture thoroughly
together. Pour into an *ungreased* 3½-
pint casserole.

Run the tip of a teaspoon around in
the mixture one inch from the edge of
the casserole, making a slight depression. This forms the "top hat" on the
soufflé as it bakes and puffs up.

Bake in a slow oven (300°F. Mark 2)
1¼ hours. Serve immediately. Serves 6.

RICE AND CHEESE SOUFFLÉ

about 16 ounces cooked rice
⅛ to ¼ pound finely grated Cheddar
 cheese
½ ounce melted butter or margarine
2 beaten egg yolks
8 fluid ounces milk
½ teaspoon salt
⅛ teaspoon paprika
few grains cayenne pepper
1 tablespoon grated onion
 (optional)
1 teaspoon Worcestershire sauce
 (optional)
3 sprigs chopped parsley
 (optional)
2 egg whites
⅛ teaspoon salt

Combine rice, cheese, melted butter, egg yolks, milk, salt, paprika,
cayenne, onion, Worcestershire sauce,
and parsley.

Beat egg whites and salt until stiff.
Fold them into the rice mixture.
Bake the soufflé in a moderate oven
(350°F. Mark 4) for about 25 minutes.
Serves 4.

"TOP HAT" CHEESE SOUFFLÉ

1. Make a white sauce, using the butter, flour, milk, salt, and cayenne.

2. When the sauce is thickened and smooth, add the sliced cheese; stir until cheese melts.

3. Remove from the heat and add the beaten egg yolks while stirring con-stantly. Cool the mixture slightly.

4. Fold the cheese sauce into the egg whites whisked until stiff but not dry, cutting and folding the mixture thor-oughly together.

5. Pour into ungreased 3½-pint casserole. With a teaspoon draw a line around the casserole one inch in from the edge to form a "top hat".

6. Bake 1¼ hours in slow oven (300°F. Mark 2) and serve immediately.

LIQUIDISER CHEESE AND VEGETABLE SOUFFLÉ

This recipe may be used for any vegetable soufflé. Use 6 ounces of a raw vegetable such as carrots or 8 to 12 ounces of a leafy vegetable such as spinach.

6 fluid ounces milk
2 ounces soft butter
4 egg yolks
2 ounces cubed cheese
6 ounces diced raw carrot
2 ounces flour
1 onion slice
1 teaspoon salt
⅛ teaspoon pepper
4 egg whites, stiffly beaten

Combine all ingredients except egg whites in electric liquidiser; blend until vegetable is pulped. Turn into saucepan and cook over moderate heat, stirring until thickened.

Cool slightly, then fold in stiffly beaten egg whites. Turn into greased baking dish; sprinkle with paprika. Bake in slow oven (325°F. Mark 3) 50 minutes to 1 hour. Serve immediately by itself or with a mushroom or tomato sauce. Serves 5.

SWEET POTATO SOUFFLÉ

14 ounces cooked, mashed sweet potatoes (or swedes or turnips)
6 fluid ounces hot milk
3 ounces butter or margarine
1 teaspoon grated lemon rind
¾ teaspoon salt
few grains pepper
3 stiffly beaten egg whites

To mashed sweet potatoes add hot milk and butter; beat until fluffy. Add lemon rind, salt and pepper.

Fold in egg whites beaten stiff but not dry.

Pile lightly into a greased casserole. Bake in a hot oven (400°F. Mark 6) 30 to 35 minutes, or until puffy and browned. Serves 6.

OYSTER SOUFFLÉ

¾ pint oysters
1½ ounces butter or margarine
1½ ounces flour
8 fluid ounces milk
1 teaspoon salt
⅛ teaspoon pepper
dash of nutmeg
3 eggs, separated

Drain and chop oysters. Melt butter and blend in flour. Add milk and bring to boiling point, stirring constantly. Cook 3 minutes.

Add oysters, seasonings, and beaten egg yolks.

Beat egg whites until stiff but not dry. Fold into oyster mixture. Pour into buttered casserole.

Set in pan of hot water and bake in moderate oven (350°F. Mark 4) until brown, about 30 minutes. Serves 6.

BASIC CHEESE SOUFFLÉ

2 ounces butter or margarine
2 ounces flour
8 fluid ounces milk
¼ pound sharp cheese, grated
¼ teaspoon dry mustard
⅛ teaspoon pepper
¾ teaspoon salt
4 eggs, separated

Melt butter, add flour, blend well and cook over low heat until bubbly.

Add cold milk all at once and cook, stirring constantly, until thickened throughout. Add cheese to white sauce and stir until melted and well blended.

Add mustard, pepper, and sauce to egg yolks whisking constantly.

Add salt to egg whites and beat until shiny and whites leave peaks that fold over when whisk is withdrawn.

Pour yolk-cheese mixture gradually over egg whites folding at the same time. Pour into an *ungreased* 2½-pint casserole.

Circle mixture with a spoon about 1-inch from side of casserole and about 1-inch deep.

Set in a pan of hot water and bake in slow oven (325°F. Mark 3) until puffy, delicately browned, and knife inserted in centre comes out clean, 60 to 75 minutes. Serve promptly. Serves 4.

Variations of Cheese Soufflé

Chicken, Turkey, Salmon, or Tuna Soufflé: Omit cheese. Stir 5 to 7 ounces finely chopped cooked meat and 1 tablespoon chopped onion into yolks before combining with hot sauce.

Increase seasonings as needed with salt and add grated rind of 1 lemon and 1 tablespoon lemon juice. Serve plain or with gravy, or mushroom sauce.

Chive Cheese Soufflé: Add ½ teaspoon finely chopped chives and 1 teaspoon finely chopped parsley with the stiffly beaten egg whites.

Mushroom Cheese Soufflé: Sauté 1 ounce finely chopped mushrooms in butter for a few minutes. Add with stiffly beaten egg whites.

Spinach or Carrot Soufflé: Omit cheese. Stir 4 to 8 ounces finely chopped raw spinach or grated raw carrot and 1 tablespoon chopped onion into yolks before combining with hot sauce. Increase salt to 1¼ teaspoons. Cheese, parsley, or tomato sauce is a good accompaniment.

It is always advisable to serve a soufflé the minute it is baked. A soufflé firm enough to stand without falling is not delicate enough to be perfect.

"TOP HAT" SPINACH SOUFFLÉ

6 ounces chopped fresh spinach, uncooked (8 ounces chopped frozen spinach, thawed but uncooked, may also be used)
2 ounces butter or margarine
1 ounce all-purpose flour
8 fluid ounces milk
2 ounces grated sharp cheese
3 beaten egg yolks
½ teaspoon salt
dash pepper
3 egg whites
¼ teaspoon salt

Prepare spinach, wash and drain thoroughly.

Melt butter or margarine in top of double saucepan. Blend in flour. Add milk. Cook over hot water, stirring constantly, until thick. Stir in cheese. Remove from heat.

Blend in egg yolks to which a little of the hot mixture has been added. Fold in ½ teaspoon salt, pepper, and drained spinach. Place over hot water.

Beat egg whites with ¼ teaspoon salt until stiff but not dry. Fold in hot spinach mixture gently but thoroughly.

Pour into ungreased 2½-pint casserole. Place casserole inside pan of hot water; water should be level with top of soufflé mixture. With a palette knife, mark a circle around top of soufflé about 1 inch in from edge and ½ inch deep.

Bake in moderate oven (375°F. Mark 5) 35 to 40 minutes or until firm to the touch. Serve immediately or, if it must wait a few minutes, leave in oven with heat turned off. Serves 4 to 6.

"Top Hat" Spinach Soufflé: The baking of a soufflé has much to do with its quality. Do not place the dish in hot water unless the recipe calls for it, as in this case. The water will keep the soufflé moist and soft, and in other cases it is preferable to have it crisp and crusty.

LOBSTER SOUFFLÉ

2½ ounces butter or margarine
2½ ounces flour
½ teaspoon salt
½ teaspoon paprika
12 fluid ounces milk
5 eggs, separated
12 ounces finely flaked, cooked
    lobster meat
1 tablespoon ketchup
1 teaspoon Worcestershire sauce

Melt butter. Blend in flour, salt, and paprika. Add milk gradually and cook, stirring constantly, until smooth and thickened.

Remove from heat and whisk in egg yolks, one at a time.

Stir in lobster meat, ketchup, and Worcestershire sauce. Fold in stiffly beaten egg whites.

Turn into greased 2½-pint casserole. Bake in hot oven (425°F. Mark 7) about 25 minutes. Serve at once. Serves 4 to 6.

CHESTNUT SOUFFLÉ

1 ounce flour
½ teaspoon salt
⅛ teaspoon pepper
about 6 to 8 ounces mashed
    cooked chestnuts
4 fluid ounces milk
3 egg whites

Mix the flour, salt, and pepper and add to the chestnuts. Mix well. Add the milk, stirring until smooth.

Whisk the egg whites stiff and fold lightly into the chestnut mixture.

Pour the mixture into a 1½-pint ungreased casserole. Bake in slow oven (325°F. Mark 3) about 30 minutes, or until firm. Serves 4.

CHICKEN-RICE SOUFFLÉ DELUXE

1½ ounces butter or margarine
1½ ounces flour
8 fluid ounces double cream
salt and pepper
3 eggs, separated
6 ounces cooked rice
6 to 7 ounces finely chopped
    cooked or canned chicken
2 ounces finely chopped ham
1 small onion, finely chopped
2 ounces grated Swiss or
    Parmesan cheese

Melt the butter; blend in flour and add cream slowly, cooking until smooth and thickened.

Remove from the heat and stir in the egg yolks and then the rice, chicken, ham, onion, and cheese. Season.

Whip the egg whites until stiff and fold in gently.

Turn into a greased baking dish, preferably one with straight sides, and bake in a moderate oven (350°F. Mark 4) until the top is lightly browned and springs back when gently touched with the finger. Serves 4 to 6.

INDIVIDUAL CHEESE CRUMB SOUFFLÉS

8 fluid ounces milk, scalded
4½ ounces fine, soft breadcrumbs
6 ounces grated sharp Cheddar
    cheese
½ teaspoon salt
¼ teaspoon paprika (optional)
½ teaspoon baking powder
4 eggs, separated

Pour scalded milk over crumbs and cheese. Add seasoning and baking powder.

Pour part of mixture into beaten egg yolks. Add egg mixture to remainder of sauce.

Fold in stiffly beaten egg whites. Turn into individual baking dishes.

Bake in moderate oven (350°F. Mark 4) until delicately browned and firm to touch, about 30 minutes. Serve at once. Serves 6.

Variations of Cheese Crumb Soufflé

Chicken or Veal Soufflé: Substitute finely chopped cooked chicken or veal for cheese and add 1 ounce finely chopped celery, if desired.

Ham Soufflé: Substitute finely chopped ham for cheese and add ¼ teaspoon mustard, if desired.

Salmon Soufflé: Substitute about 10 ounces finely flaked canned salmon for cheese. Add 1 ounce finely chopped green pepper, 2 teaspoons lemon juice, and ½ teaspoon onion juice.

TOMATO SOUFFLÉ

2 slices bread
4 fluid ounces milk
5 fresh tomatoes
1 ounce butter or margarine
1 teaspoon onion juice
salt and pepper
4 egg yolks, slightly beaten
5 egg whites, stiffly beaten
2 tablespoons grated cheese

Trim crusts from bread and soak in the milk. Mix bread and milk to a paste.

Peel, finely chop and sieve the tomatoes.

Melt the butter in a saucepan. Add tomatoes, onion juice, bread, and salt and pepper to taste. Cook, stirring until ingredients are thoroughly incorporated.

Remove from heat, stir in whisked egg yolks, and cool.

Fold in egg whites and pour into a well buttered soufflé dish.

Sprinkle grated cheese on top. Bake in moderate oven (350°F. Mark 4) for 35 to 40 minutes. Sprinkle with paprika. Serves 4.

BACON SOUFFLÉ

½ to ¾ pound fried streaky bacon
6 slices bread
5 beaten eggs
¾ teaspoon salt or more*
¼ teaspoon dry mustard
paprika
16 fluid ounces milk

Finely chop bacon and cook until light brown. Drain.

Grease casserole with bacon fat. Arrange bread in layers in casserole, sprinkling the cooked bacon and some bacon fat over each layer. Reserve some bacon for the top.

Add seasonings and milk to eggs and pour over bread. Sprinkle reserved bacon over top.

Bake in moderate oven (350°F. Mark 4) until puffy and knife inserted in centre comes out clean, about 1 hour. Serve from casserole. Serves 6 to 8.

*Note: Depending upon saltiness of bacon.

OLIVE RICE SOUFFLÉ

about 30 black olives
3 eggs, separated
4 fluid ounces milk
1 teaspoon salt
1 teaspoon Worcestershire sauce
1 teaspoon grated onion
6 ounces chopped raw spinach
4 ounces grated Cheddar cheese
18 ounces cooked rice
2 ounces melted butter or
    margarine

Cut olives into large pieces. Separate eggs and beat yolks slightly. Combine with olives and all remaining ingredients except egg whites.

Fold in stiffly beaten egg whites.

Turn into 2½-pint baking dish. Bake in moderate oven (350°F. Mark 4) about 35 minutes. Serves 5 to 6.

CRAB SOUFFLÉ

1 6½-ounce can crab meat
8 fluid ounces thick white sauce
1 tablespoon lemon juice
4 eggs, separated
1½ teaspoons grated onion
1 tablespoon finely chopped
    parsley
½ teaspoon paprika
¼ teaspoon cream of tartar

Pick over crab meat to remove cartilage and shred finely.

To white sauce add crab meat, lemon juice, egg yolks beaten until thick and lemon-coloured, onion, parsley, and paprika. Cool.

Beat egg whites until frothy; add cream of tartar and continue beating until stiff but not dry. Fold into crab meat mixture.

Turn into a 2½-pint greased casserole. Bake in slow oven (325°F. Mark 3) about 1 hour. Serves 4 to 6.

INDIVIDUAL CHEESE SOUFFLÉS

1 ounce butter or margarine
1 ounce flour
⅓ teaspoon bicarbonate of soda
1 teaspoon salt
2 teaspoons Worcestershire sauce
¼ teaspoon paprika
4 fluid ounces milk
4 ounces grated cheese
4 eggs, separated

Melt butter; add flour, soda, salt, Worcestershire sauce, and paprika and stir until well blended.

Add milk gradually, stirring constantly over boiling water until sauce thickens.

Remove from heat and stir in grated cheese and egg yolks, whisked until thick and lemon coloured. Then fold in stiffly beaten egg whites.

Bake in individual paper cases or in well buttered ramekins which can be sent to the table. Bake in moderate oven (350°-375°F. Marks 4-5) about 12 minutes.

Serve immediately. Makes 8 to 10 small soufflés.

HAM SOUFFLÉ

1 ounce melted butter or margarine
1 ounce flour
16 fluid ounces milk
3 eggs, separated
4 ounces dry breadcrumbs
12 ounces minced cooked ham
1 tablespoon chopped parsley
salt and pepper to taste

Prepare a sauce of butter, flour, and milk.

Whisk egg yolks and mix with crumbs, ham, and sauce. Add parsley, salt, and pepper.

Fold in stiffly beaten egg whites. Turn into greased baking dish.

Bake in slow oven (300°F. Mark 2) until set in centre, about 1 hour. Serves 6.

MUSHROOM AND HAM SOUFFLÉ

16 fluid ounces thick white sauce
1½ ounces grated Cheddar cheese
2½ ounces minced celery
1½ tablespoons minced pimiento
2 ounces mushrooms, cooked
3½ ounces chopped boiled ham
4 eggs, separated
¾ teaspoon curry powder
1½ teaspoons grated onion

To white sauce add cheese, celery, pimiento, mushrooms, ham, well beaten egg yolks, curry powder, and onion. Mix well, then fold in egg whites beaten stiffly but not dry.

Turn into a greased casserole and place in a pan of hot water.

Bake in moderate oven (350°F. Mark 4) about 30 to 45 minutes, or until nicely browned. Serves 6.

BUDGET CHICKEN SOUFFLÉ

1 ounce butter or margarine
1 ounce flour
1 can (about 10 ounces) cream of chicken soup, undiluted
3 eggs, separated

Melt butter in saucepan; stir in flour. Add soup; heat slowly, stirring until mixture bubbles and is thickened. Cool slightly.

Whisk egg whites until stiff but not dry.

Add soup mixture gradually to slightly beaten egg yolks. Fold in egg whites.

Spoon into 1½ pint casserole. Place casserole in pan of warm water.

Bake in slow oven (325°F. Mark 3) for 1 hour or until knife, when inserted, comes out clean. Serves 4 to 5.

Note: For 4 to 5 individual soufflés: Bake as above for 30 to 45 minutes.

POTATO SOUFFLÉ WITH CHEESE

1½ pounds hot mashed potatoes
2 egg yolks
1 ounce butter or margarine
4 fluid ounces hot cream
1 teaspoon salt
⅛ teaspoon paprika
2 egg whites
⅛ teaspoon salt
1½ ounces dry grated cheese, preferably Parmesan

Combine mashed potatoes, egg yolks, butter, cream, 1 teaspoon salt, and paprika; beat well.

Shape these ingredients into a mound in a fireproof dish.

Whip egg whites and ⅛ teaspoon salt until stiff. Fold in grated cheese. Spread mixture lightly on mound.

Bake in slow oven (325°F. Mark 3) about 15 minutes. Serves 6.

VEGETABLE SOUFFLÉ

½ tablespoon finely chopped onion
½ tablespoon finely chopped green pepper
1 tablespoon finely chopped celery
1 ounce melted lard or dripping
1 ounce flour
4 fluid ounces milk
½ teaspoon salt
pepper to taste
4 ounces finely chopped cooked vegetables
2 eggs, separated

Brown onion, green pepper, and celery lightly in lard.

Blend in flour and add milk. Cook over low heat, stirring constantly, until thickened. Season with salt and pepper.

Stir vegetables into sauce; add hot mixture to beaten egg yolks.

Beat egg whites stiff but not dry. Fold in vegetable mixture. Pour into greased baking dish.

Bake in slow oven (325°F. Mark 3) 40 to 50 minutes or until set. Serves 4.

CHICKEN LIVER SOUFFLÉ

½ pound chicken livers
1 tablespoon finely chopped onion
2½ ounces butter or margarine
3 rashers crumbled cooked streaky bacon
1½ ounces flour
8 fluid ounces milk or chicken stock
3 eggs, separated
salt and pepper

Sauté chicken livers with onion in 1 ounce butter. Mash slightly with a fork and add bacon.

Melt remaining butter in another pan; stir in flour and blend well. Add the milk or chicken stock and stir constantly until thickened and smooth.

Remove from the heat. Add chicken-livers-and-bacon mixture and whisked egg yolks.

Fold in stiffly beaten egg whites and turn into a greased baking dish with straight sides.

Bake in moderate oven (350°F. Mark 4) 45 to 50 minutes or until the top is delicately brown and springs back when gently touched. Serves 4.

MAIZE SOUFFLÉ

16 fluid ounces milk
1½ ounces maize flour
½ ounce butter or margarine
2 ounces or more grated cheese
1 teaspoon salt
¼ teaspoon paprika
few grains cayenne pepper
3 eggs, separated

Heat milk to boiling point and stir in maize flour and butter. Reduce heat and stir in cheese. Cook these ingredients to consistency of porridge.

Season them with salt, paprika, and cayenne pepper. Add whisked egg yolks. Cook and stir for 1 minute. Cool these ingredients.

Whip egg whites until stiff, then fold in.

Bake in an ungreased 7-inch baking dish in moderate oven (350°F. Mark 4) until it is slightly crusty, about 45 minutes. In Italy bits of ham and seafood are added to the batter which is baked until it is very crisp. Serves 3.

Vegetable Soufflé

Sweet Soufflés

GRAND MARNIER SOUFFLÉ

1½ ounces butter
1½ ounces flour
6 fluid ounces milk
3 tablespoons orange marmalade
4 egg yolks, lightly beaten
2 fluid ounces Grand Marnier
6 egg whites

Butter a 2½ pint soufflé dish or casserole and sprinkle bottom and sides with sugar.

Melt butter in a saucepan; stir in flour. Add milk gradually, stirring with a wire whisk, and cook over low heat until mixture thickens. Stir in marmalade and egg yolks. Add Grand Marnier.

Beat egg whites until stiff and gently fold into soufflé mixture. Pour soufflé mixture into prepared dish. Bake in moderate oven (375°F. Mark 5) until puffy and golden brown, 30 to 45 minutes. Serves 4 to 5.

VANILLA SOUFFLÉ
(Basic Recipe)

1½ ounces plain flour
4 ounces caster sugar
⅛ teaspoon salt
8 fluid ounces milk
4 eggs, separated
¼ teaspoon cream of tartar
1 teaspoon vanilla

Combine flour, sugar, and salt in a saucepan. Stir in milk a little at a time.

Cook over low heat, stirring constantly, until mixture is smooth and thick.

Whisk egg yolks until thick and yellow; slowly fold in the milk mixture.

Beat egg whites until foamy; sprinkle the cream of tartar over them and continue beating until stiff but not dry. Fold into the first mixture with vanilla.

Pour into an ungreased 2½ pint casserole. Bake in slow oven (325°F. Mark 3) 50 to 60 minutes, or in a hot oven (425°F. Mark 7) about 25 minutes or until well browned, using a lower shelf in the oven.

The long slow baking makes a soufflé of even moistness throughout; quick baking gives a thicker crust and a soft moist interior. Serve immediately from the baking dish. Serves 6.

Vanilla Soufflé Variations

Butterscotch Pecan Soufflé: In Vanilla Soufflé, substitute 4 ounces brown sugar for caster sugar; add 1 ounce butter or margarine.

Fold in 4 ounces finely chopped pecans or walnuts with the thickened milk mixture.

Chocolate Soufflé: In Vanilla Soufflé, stir 2 ounces melted cooking chocolate into thickened milk mixture before stirring into egg yolks.

Pineapple Soufflé: In Vanilla Soufflé, substitute 8 fluid ounces pineapple juice for milk. Omit vanilla; add 1 tablespoon lemon juice and ½ teaspoon lemon rind. Fold in about 5 ounces well drained crushed pineapple with the thickened milk mixture.

Orange Soufflé: In Vanilla Soufflé, substitute 8 fluid ounces orange juice for milk. Omit vanilla; add 1 tablespoon lemon juice and 1 tablespoon grated orange rind.

Lemon Soufflé: In Vanilla Soufflé, reduce milk to 5 fluid ounces. Add 3 fluid ounces lemon juice when thickened. Omit vanilla; add 1 teaspoon grated lemon rind.

STRAWBERRY SOUFFLÉ

6 ounces strawberries
4 ounces caster sugar
2 tablespoons kirsch or brandy
2 ounces butter or margarine
3 eggs, separated
3 ounces soft breadcrumbs

Slice strawberries; add 2 ounces sugar and liquor and let stand until needed. Drain berries, reserving half for soufflé and remainder of berries and juice for sauce.

Cream butter with remaining 2 ounces sugar until fluffy. Add well whisked egg yolks, then crumbs and half the strained berries.

Beat egg whites until stiff and fold into mixture.

Turn into 2½ pint casserole which has been greased only on the bottom or which has been buttered all over and sprinkled with sugar.

Set in pan of hot water and bake in moderate oven (350°F. Mark 4) until firm, about 45 minutes. Serve with reserved berry and juice mixture. Serves 4 to 5.

FRESH PEACH SOUFFLÉ

about 8 or 9 ounces mashed peaches
1½ tablespoons lemon juice
2 ounces caster sugar
4 beaten egg yolks
⅛ teaspoon salt
1 tablespoon grated orange rind
4 stiffly beaten egg whites
cream

Peel and mash ripe peaches to make required amount. (Or use an equal amount of tinned puréed baby food peaches or other raw or canned fruit.)

Add lemon juice, sugar, egg yolks, salt, and orange rind to peaches. Fold in egg whites.

Place the mixture in a 7-inch baking dish. Bake in slow oven (325°F. Mark 3) for about 45 minutes. Serve hot with cream. Serves 5.

PRUNE SOUFFLÉ
(Basic Recipe)

2 ounces caster sugar
6 to 7 ounces mashed prunes
2 teaspoons lemon juice
5 egg whites

Combine sugar and prunes and heat until sugar has dissolved. Add lemon juice.

Beat egg whites until frothy. Fold in.

Turn into a baking dish and bake in moderate oven (350°F. Mark 4) about 40 minutes.

When done, sprinkle with icing sugar. Serve at once from baking dish with cream. Serves 4.

Variations of Prune Soufflé

Apple Soufflé: Substitute 9 ounces thick apple sauce for prunes.

Apricot Soufflé: Substitute mashed apricots for prunes. Add ¼ teaspoon almond essence with lemon juice.

Cherry Soufflé: Substitute mashed sweet cherries for prunes and cherry brandy for lemon juice.

Peach Soufflé: Substitute mashed peaches for prunes. Add ¼ teaspoon almond essence with lemon juice.

HAZELNUT SOUFFLÉ

3 eggs, separated
1½ ounces caster sugar
1½ ounces flour
⅛ teaspoon salt
3 ounces hazelnuts
8 fluid ounces milk
1½ ounces butter or margarine
½ teaspoon vanilla or 1 tablespoon rum
8 fluid ounces double cream, whipped
caramel or coffee flavouring or essence

Whisk egg yolks until light. Gradually whisk in sugar, flour, and salt.

Put hazelnuts through a grinder. Pour milk over them and heat to just below the boiling point.

Stir in egg mixture. Stir and cook these ingredients over low heat to permit the yolks to thicken slightly. Stir in butter.

Cool, then beat in vanilla or rum.

Beat egg whites until stiff; fold into first mixture.

Bake in a buttered dish in slow oven (325°F. Mark 3) for about 30 minutes. Serve hot or cold with whipped cream flavoured with caramel or coffee. Serves 4 to 5.

ORANGE SOUFFLÉ 2

2 ounces butter or margarine
6 tablespoons all-purpose flour
dash of salt
8 fluid ounces milk
1 6-ounce can frozen orange juice
    concentrate
4 fluid ounces water
1½ teaspoons grated lemon rind
6 eggs, separated
2 ounces caster sugar
1 recipe orange sauce (see below)

Melt butter; blend in flour and salt. Gradually stir in milk; cook over low heat, stirring constantly, until thick.

Combine 2 fluid ounces of the orange juice concentrate (reserve remainder for orange sauce), water, and lemon rind. Stir into hot mixture.

Whisk egg yolks until thick and lemon coloured; gradually add hot mixture; mix well.

Beat egg whites until soft peaks form; gradually add sugar, beating until stiff peaks form.

Fold yolk mixture into egg whites. Pour into ungreased straight-sided 2½ pint casserole around which has been tied a 6-inch collar of buttered greaseproof paper.

Set baking dish in shallow pan, filling pan to 1 inch with hot water.

Bake in slow oven (325°F. Mark 3) about 1½ hours, or until mixture does not adhere to knife. Serve at once with orange sauce. Serves 8.

Orange Sauce: Combine 4 ounces caster sugar, 1½ tablespoons cornflour, and dash of salt.

Stir in reserved orange juice concentrate (4 ounces) and 8 fluid ounces water. Cook, stirring constantly, until thick.

Remove from heat; stir in ½ ounce butter or margarine. Serve warm in a jug. Makes about 12 fluid ounces.

QUICK PUDDING SOUFFLÉ

1 packet blancmange or pie filling
    (vanilla, butterscotch, or
    chocolate flavour)
8 fluid ounces milk
3 eggs, separated
pinch of salt

Combine in saucepan blancmange or pie filling and milk. Cook and stir over medium heat until mixture thickens and boils. Remove from heat.

Whisk egg yolks and add pudding gradually, stirring constantly.

Beat egg whites with a pinch of salt until stiff enough to stand in soft peaks. Carefully fold in egg yolk mixture.

Pour into greased and sugar-sprinkled 2½ pint baking dish. Bake in moderate oven (350°F. Mark 4) for 45 minutes, or until firm. Serves 6 to 8.

LEMON SOUFFLÉ 2

4 eggs, separated
2 fluid ounces hot water
8 ounces caster sugar
½ teaspoon salt
2 teaspoons grated lemon rind
2 ounces lemon juice

Whisk yolks until thick; add water gradually and continue beating. Add sugar gradually, beating thoroughly after each addition.

Add salt and lemon rind and juice; fold in stiffly beaten egg whites.

Turn into 2½ pint dish, buttered on the bottom.

Place in pan of hot water and bake in moderate oven (350°F. Mark 4) 30 to 45 minutes, or until firm. Serve at once with lemon sauce. Serves 6.

TOP-OF-THE-COOKER CHOCOLATE SOUFFLÉ

5 fluid ounces milk
2½ ounces granulated sugar
1 ounce cooking chocolate
⅛ teaspoon salt
½ teaspoon vanilla
2 eggs, unbeaten

In double saucepan, heat milk with sugar, chocolate, salt, and vanilla until chocolate melts. With egg whisk, beat until smooth.

Break eggs into cup; add to chocolate mixture; whisking 1 minute.

Cook, covered, over boiling water 35 minutes without removing cover. Serve hot or cold, as is or with single cream. Serves 4.

ALMOND AND STRAWBERRY SOUFFLÉ

3 ounces almonds
1 tablespoon sugar
3 ounces crushed strawberries
2½ ounces caster sugar
6 fluid ounces hot milk
2 tablespoons flour
2 fluid ounces cold milk
½ ounce unsalted butter or
    margarine
4 egg yolks, well beaten
6 egg whites, stiffly beaten

Blanch almonds by steeping in boiling water for 5 minutes, then cut lengthwise into slivers.

Add 1 tablespoon sugar to crushed strawberries. Dissolve 2½ ounces sugar in hot milk.

Blend flour in cold milk and add gradually to the hot milk, stirring over the heat for about 2 minutes, or until thick and creamy.

Remove from heat and stir in butter and well whisked egg yolks. Cool.

Fold in strawberries and three quarters of the almonds, then fold in egg whites. Pour into greased baking dish;

sprinkle top with remaining almonds. Bake in moderate oven (350°F. Mark 4) for 30 minutes. Sprinkle top with icing sugar. Serves 6.

PINEAPPLE-MACAROON SOUFFLÉ

1½ ounces butter or margarine
1½ ounces flour
8 ounces crushed pineapple
3 ounces dry crushed macaroons
3 eggs, separated
⅛ teaspoon salt
2 tablespoons caster sugar
½ teaspoon vanilla

Melt butter over low heat. Stir in flour. When blended, stir in pineapple.

Then when thick and smooth, stir in macaroons and egg yolks. Permit the yolks to thicken slightly. Cool the mixture.

Beat egg whites with salt until stiff. Gradually beat in sugar and vanilla. Fold this into the soufflé mixture.

Bake it in a 7-inch baking dish in a slow oven (325°F. Mark 3) for about 30 minutes. Serves 4.

MOCHA SOUFFLÉ

1½ ounces butter or margarine
1 ounce plain flour
2½ ounces caster sugar
2 teaspoons cocoa
5½ fluid ounces milk
2½ fluid ounces strong fresh coffee
4 eggs, separated
¼ teaspoon salt
¼ teaspoon vanilla

Melt butter in saucepan; gradually stir in flour combined with sugar and cocoa. Cook, stirring constantly, until mixture bubbles.

Then slowly stir in milk mixed with coffee. Cook, stirring constantly, until thick and smooth. Let cool.

Then stir in well whisked egg yolks, salt, and vanilla. Gently fold in stiffly beaten egg whites.

Turn into 2½ pint casserole, greased on bottom only. Put casserole in pan of hot water.

Bake in slow oven (325°F. Mark 3) until done, 50 to 60 minutes. Serve at once. Serves 6.

Mocha Soufflé

SOUPS

Soups should be an important part of any low-cost menus, not only because they are highly nutritious, but because to delicious soups may be added food ingredients which the average cook may normally discard.

The water in which meat, fish, and vegetables are simmered, as well as the liquids from canned vegetables, contain precious vitamins and minerals and should be used as a liquid in the preparation of soups. They can be saved and stored in the refrigerator for future use.

Scraps of raw or cooked vegetables, fish, meats, and bones should be used in soups together with the addition of the lower-priced cuts of meats. Inexpensive meat cuts have essentially the same nutritive values as the higher-priced cuts. To obtain the full flavour from such soups, always simmer or boil these soups in closely covered saucepans. A helpful hint to keep in mind is that soups made from these leftover ingredients may very often be improved with the addition of a can of bought soup.

SOUP-MAKING HINTS

There are innumerable ways to vary soups and there are many enticing names but, basically, soups are divided into just a few groups.

Soups made from white stock have veal or poultry as a base.

Soups made from brown stock have dark meat as a base.

Bouillon is a clear soup made from beef stock.

Consommé is made from beef, chicken, veal, and vegetables.

Chowders are thick soups made from fish, meat, and vegetables.

Broth is the liquid resulting from meat which has been simmered slowly in water.

The cream soups (purées and bisques) contain both milk and butter, as well as the vegetables after which they are named.

COOKING SOUPS AT HIGH ALTITUDES

Since liquids boil at lower temperatures at high altitudes, soups will require longer cooking periods above 2,500 feet.

HOW TO REMOVE EXCESS FAT FROM SOUP

The easiest method is to chill the soup so that the fat congeals on the surface and can be scraped off.

If the soup is still simmering, use a long-handled spoon and draw it over the surface, dipping up a thin layer of fat. The remaining fat can be removed when the cooking is done. If the soup is still hot, let it settle for 5 minutes so that the fat will rise to the surface. Then tip the saucepan so that the heavier fat deposit will collect at one side and can be more easily spooned off. When you have taken off as much as you can, roll up a paper towel and use one end to skim off fat. When the end is coated with fat, cut it off and continue the process until the last floating fat globules have been blotted off.

SOUP GARNISHING HINTS

The finishing touch—a colourful garnish—is liked by everyone and should not be forgotten when serving soups. Here are some suggestions.

For Chowders and Meat Soups: Chopped parsley, thin slices of lemon for fish chowder; thin slices of frankfurters in bean and pea soups. See other suggestions with specific recipes.

For Clear Soups: Finely chopped parsley; chives; thin slices of lemon; balls or slices of avocado; thin, cooked celery rings or celery leaves; sautéed mushroom slices; thinly sliced olive rings; julienne carrots; string beans; rice; macaroni in small shapes.

For Cream Soups: Salted whipped cream alone or with chopped parsley or chopped nuts; toast croûtons; chopped pimiento; chopped chives; puffed cereals; raw grated carrots; thick soured cream; crumbled crisp bacon; grated cheese.

FRITTER GARNISH FOR SOUP

1 egg
¾ teaspoon salt
2 ounces flour
2 tablespoons milk or water

Beat egg until light. Add salt, flour, and milk.

Pour through colander into deep hot fat (365°F.). Fry until brown. Drain on paper. Serve in hot soup.

CUSTARD FOR SOUP

1 egg
4 fluid ounces milk or stock
pinch of salt
pinch of nutmeg (optional)
pinch of paprika

Beat egg slightly. Add milk or stock and seasonings. Pour into small buttered ovenproof dish.

Set in pan of hot water and bake in slow oven (325°F. Mark 3) until it is set.

Remove from dish and cut into diamonds or fancy shapes. Drop into soup just before serving it.

Royal Custard: Add 3 egg yolks and proceed as above.

CHICKEN FORCEMEAT FOR SOUP (Quenelles)

2 ounces fine dry breadcrumbs
4 fluid ounces milk
1 ounce butter or margarine
1 stiffly beaten egg white
salt
few grains cayenne
slight grating of nutmeg
6 ounces raw breast of chicken

Cook breadcrumbs and milk to a paste. Add butter, egg white, and seasonings.

Add chicken which has been pounded and forced through a purée strainer or mincer. Form into small balls and cook in soup.

CHEESE PUFF BALLS

2 ounces grated Parmesan cheese
1 tablespoon flour
¼ teaspoon salt
Dash of cayenne or paprika pepper
2 egg whites, stiffly beaten
3 tablespoons dry breadcrumbs

Mix cheese, flour, salt, and pepper; fold into egg whites. If too crumbly to mould, add a few drops of milk.

Shape in small balls; roll in crumbs and fry in hot deep fat (375°F. Mark 5) about 1 minute, or until golden brown. Drain on absorbent paper. Makes 18 balls.

FAROLA PUFFS FOR SOUP

1 ounce butter or margarine
3 tablespoons uncooked farola
½ teaspoon baking powder
1 well beaten egg yolk
pinch of salt
pinch of grated nutmeg
boiling water or soup

Cream the butter or margarine. Mix farola with baking powder and work into the creamed butter. Add egg yolk, salt, and nutmeg.

Drop by ¼ teaspoonfuls into simmering water or soup. Cook about 10 minutes.

Remove with a slotted spoon if cooked in water. The puffs will double or triple in size. Makes 20 small puffs.

WHIPPED CREAM GARNISH

4 fluid ounces double cream
2 tablespoons horseradish
pinch of paprika

Whip cream. Fold in horseradish and paprika.

Place a spoonful of the mixture on top of each individual serving of soup.

Variations: Omit horseradish and paprika; place a spoonful of whipped cream on top of each serving and garnish with paprika and chopped parsley.

Or add a pinch of cayenne or curry powder to the whipped cream instead of horseradish and paprika.

With Eggs: Fold equal amount of whipped cream into stiffly beaten egg whites to make a fluffy and less rich garnish for soups.

With Colour: Add 1 tablespoon tomato purée or puréed pimiento to give whipped cream garnish an attractive pink colour. Use with white or green soups.

TOASTED BREAD ANIMALS

Cut animal shapes out of bread with biscuit cutters. Butter and toast a golden brown under the grill. Serve to children with their soup.

EGG DROP FOR SOUP

1 beaten egg
dash of salt
3 tablespoons flour
2 fluid ounces cold water

Stir all ingredients together until smooth. Drop slowly from end of spoon into boiling soup.

Cover. Cook 5 minutes and serve hot.

Variation: Pour well beaten egg gradually into boiling soup just before serving.

Quick Hot Soups

Many soup variations are made possible by combining two prepared soups of different yet harmonizing flavours. The addition of herbs, cream, or perhaps wine (madeira or sherry), finely chopped onions, chives, parsley, etc., will improve the flavours as well as seasoning such as curry powder, Worcestershire, or Tabasco sauce.

Delightful, appetizing combinations result from personal experiments in "mixing and matching" these soups.

Condensed soups are also used as cooking sauces and in preparing main dishes such as casseroles and meat loaves, to enhance the flavour of homemade soups and in recipes calling for soup stock.

The "can" measure in preparing "Quick Change" combinations is your soup can.

QUICK MINESTRONE

1 can vegetable soup
2 cans hot water
1 can baked beans in tomato sauce
2 tablespoons macaroni
1 clove garlic, finely sliced
grated Parmesan cheese

Combine all ingredients. Cook until macaroni is tender, about 12 minutes.

Serve with grated Parmesan cheese sprinkled over each bowl.

CHICKEN CORN CHOWDER

Prepare 1 10¾-ounce can condensed cream of chicken soup according to label directions. Add 1 packet frozen sweetcorn.

Cover and cook until corn is tender. Add 1 ounce pimiento strips and 4 rashers diced, cooked bacon

TOMATO SOUP WITH SHERRY

To 1 10¾-ounce can condensed tomato soup add 1 can water; heat to boiling; add 3 fluid ounces sherry, heat and serve with lemon slices. Serves 4.

Onion Soup Italienne

ONION SOUP ITALIENNE

1 can (10¾-ounces) condensed onion soup
1½ teaspoons Worcestershire sauce
½ ounce butter or margarine
1 egg, well beaten
3 tablespoons flour
¼ teaspoon salt
1 tablespoon grated Parmesan cheese

Prepare onion soup according to directions on the can. Heat and add Worcestershire sauce.

Cream butter. Blend in egg, flour, salt, and Parmesan cheese. Drop batter by tiny teaspoonfuls into simmering soup. Simmer 5 minutes. Serves 2.

QUICK PRAWN BISQUE

Sauté 1 green pepper cut into rings in 1 ounce melted butter. Add 1 packet frozen prawns and cook until lightly browned.

Add 1 can condensed tomato soup and 4 fluid ounces single cream. Heat to serving temperature.

HO-HO SOUP

2 10½-ounce cans beef broth
1½ soup cans water
1 12-ounce can vegetable juice cocktail
2 tablespoons soy sauce
3 tablespoons vinegar
¼ teaspoon pepper
1½ ounces thinly sliced carrots
1 ounce chopped green beans
3 ounces chopped cooked chicken
3 eggs, beaten

Combine all ingredients except eggs. Bring to the boil. Simmer about 10 minutes. Stir in beaten eggs. Serve at once with salty crackers. Serves 6 to 8.

Ho-Ho Soup: A whimsical version of an Oriental chicken-vegetable soup. It's nutritious and fun to serve in Chinese rice bowls.

CURRY-AVOCADO SOUP
½ ounce butter or margarine
1 to 1½ teaspoons curry powder
1 can (10½ ounces) condensed
    chicken consommé
8 fluid ounces milk or single cream
1 slightly beaten egg yolk
1 medium avocado

In saucepan, melt butter or margarine; stir in curry powder; add consommé. Bring to boil; cover and simmer 10 minutes.

Combine milk or cream with egg yolk and stir into soup.

Mash half the avocado and coarsely chop the other half; add both to soup. Heat, stirring constantly; serve hot or chill thoroughly before serving. Serves 4.

QUICK TUNA SOUP
1 can (10¾ ounces) condensed
    cream of mushroom soup
1 can (10½ ounces) condensed
    cream of asparagus soup
16 fluid ounces milk or 8 fluid
    ounces milk and 8 fluid
    ounces single cream
1 7-ounce can tuna fish, drained
    and flaked
chopped parsley or chives

Blend soups and milk, or milk and cream; add tuna. Heat slowly, but do not boil. Sprinkle with parsley or chives. Serves 4.

SALMON CHOWDER
1 can cream of tomato soup
1 can cream of mushroom soup
12 fluid ounces milk
2 tablespoons grated onion
1 1-pound can white potatoes,
    drained and quartered
1 8-ounce can peas, drained
1 1-pound can salmon, drained
    and flaked
8 fluid ounces single cream

Blend tomato soup, mushroom soup, milk, and onion; heat. Add potatoes, peas, and salmon; heat thoroughly, stirring carefully.

Just before serving, add cream; heat but do not boil. Serves 6.

ASPARAGUS AND MUSHROOM SOUP
Combine 1 can each asparagus and mushroom soups. If using condensed soups, dilute with milk. Heat and garnish with chopped pimiento.

BEEF-CELERY SOUP
Mix 1 can cream of celery soup and 1 can beef soup. Stir well.

Blend in 2 cans of water. Simmer about 5 minutes.

CREOLE TOMATO SOUP
Combine 1 can tomato soup, 1 can chicken gumbo soup, and 2 cans water. Simmer about 5 minutes.

PUMPKIN-TOMATO SOUP
In a saucepan, combine 1 10¾-ounce can of condensed tomato soup with an equal amount of milk.

Add 4 ounces canned pumpkin, ¼ teaspoon salt, ¼ teaspoon allspice, and a dash each of pepper and thyme; blend well. Heat and serve.

EASY HERBED TOMATO SOUP
½ teaspoon dried basil
1 teaspoon celery salt
4 whole cloves
1 tablespoon finely chopped onion
½ teaspoon salt
pinch of pepper
12 fluid ounces water
1 can (10¾ ounces) condensed
    tomato soup, undiluted

Combine all ingredients except soup. Simmer, uncovered, about 10 minutes.

Then add soup; heat and serve with crisp crackers. Serves 4.

QUICK HEARTY MAIN-DISH CHOWDER
Combine 1 1-pound can corned beef hash, 1 10¾-ounce can condensed tomato soup, 1 soup can milk, and 1 8-ounce can peas.

Heat, stirring often; dilute with additional milk, if desired.

Serve in big bowls with crackers. Serves 4 to 5.

BACON-CLAM CHOWDER
Combine 1 can each clam chowder and cream of celery soup.

Add 1 can milk, ½ teaspoon grated onion, 1 tablespoon chopped parsley, and pinch of thyme. Heat to boiling and simmer a few minutes.

Garnish with generous spoonful of crumbled cooked bacon.

VEGETABLE SOUP, PEASANT STYLE
Combine 1 can vegetable soup, 1 can bean with bacon soup, and 2 cans water.

Simmer about 5 minutes.

CREAM OF TOMATO AND BEAN SOUP WITH FRANKFURTERS
Combine 1 can each tomato and bean soup.

Add 2 cans milk and ¼ pound frankfurters, sliced. Heat.

OLD-FASHIONED VELVET
Stir 1 can cream of mushroom soup; add 2 cans water slowly, stirring constantly.

Blend in 1 can chicken noodle soup. Heat without boiling.

FISH MONGOLE SOUP
Combine 1 can each tomato and pea soup. Add 2 cans milk or water and 1 cup flaked cooked fish.

Bring to boiling point and add 2 tablespoons sherry, if desired.

Quick Bean Soup

QUICK BEAN SOUP
1 packet onion soup mix
6 peppercorns
1 bay leaf
12 fluid ounces beef gravy
1 1-pound can beans in tomato
    sauce
2 tablespoons tomato purée or
    ketchup

Prepare onion soup mix as directed on packet, adding the peppercorns and bay leaf. Add remaining ingredients to onion soup and bring to boiling point; simmer for 5 minutes. Serves 5 to 6.

TOMATO CHICKEN-NOODLE SOUP
Combine 1 can each tomato and chicken noodle soup. Add 1 can water and dash of garlic salt.

Heat to boiling point and simmer a few minutes.

GREEN PEA AND MUSHROOM SOUP
Mix 1 can green pea soup and 1 can cream of mushroom soup. Stir well.

Slowly add 1 can water, then 1 can milk. Heat thoroughly without boiling.

QUICK FRENCH ONION SOUP
2 ounces butter or margarine
4 large onions, thinly sliced
6 beef bouillon cubes
2½ pints boiling water
1 teaspoon Worcestershire sauce
2 teaspoons salt
½ teaspoon paprika
pinch of pepper
2 hard rolls
grated Parmesan cheese

Melt butter or margarine in large frying pan and cook onions until golden.

Pour dissolved bouillon cubes over cooked onions. Add Worcestershire sauce, salt, paprika, and pepper. Bring to boiling point but, for fuller flavour, do not boil.

Pour soup into medium-sized earthenware casserole. For that final French touch, cut rolls into thin slices and sprinkle each slice with cheese. Float these on top of soup.

Slide casserole under grill, and grill until cheese turns a rich brown colour. Serve at once. Serves 6.

Cottage Cheese Soup: A savoury blend that just dares you to be different.

COTTAGE CHEESE SOUP

1 10¾-ounce can condensed cream
   of celery soup
1 soup can milk
2 tablespoons chopped onion
½ ounce butter or margarine
½ teaspoon paprika
pinch of cayenne pepper
pinch of nutmeg
8 ounces cottage cheese
2 tablespoons chopped pimiento

Combine soup and milk. Heat. Sauté onion in butter 5 minutes. Add to soup. Add remaining ingredients and heat but do not boil. Serves 4.

VEGETABLE AND BEEF SOUP

½ pound minced beef
1 small onion, finely chopped
1½ ounces fresh white breadcrumbs
2 fluid ounces milk
1 egg
½ teaspoon salt
dash of pepper
1 packet vegetable soup mix with
   noodles

Combine all ingredients, except soup mix. Shape in 1-inch balls; brown.

Prepare soup mix according to packet directions. Add beef balls; simmer 5 minutes. Serves 4.

FOUR-SEASON HEARTY SOUP

Prepare 1 can (10¾ ounces) condensed cream of asparagus soup according to label directions.

Drain 1 12-ounce packet frozen oysters, and cook oysters in 3 tablespoons melted butter until edges curl.

Add oysters and oyster liquid to asparagus soup. Heat to serving temperature. Top with Parmesan toast strips.

VEGETABLE AND BEEF NOODLE

Combine 1 can vegetable soup, 1 can beef noodle soup and 1½ cans water. Simmer about 5 minutes.

CHICKEN WATERCRESS SOUP

Combine 1 can cream of chicken soup with 1 can milk; heat almost to boiling.

Add ½ cup chopped watercress; simmer a few minutes.

CLAM CHOWDER CREOLE

Combine equal parts clam chowder and chicken gumbo creole.

Chilled Soups

To most people, at one time a cold creamed soup meant Vichyssoise in the most elegant, high-priced restaurants or made with lots of trouble at home. It is not only possible but easy to make good cold soups at home with little effort and at slight expense—in infinite varieties. Many of the recipes given below require only a few minutes preparation.

There are a few points to remember. Canned soups, served cold, are much lighter in flavour than when heated. In some cases they can take double the usual amount of seasoning to make them delicious.

Chill the ingredients thoroughly and use a rotary beater, electric blender, or electric mixer for combining.

Use the soup can for measuring.

To keep the soup cold on the table, put it in a bowl and set in a larger bowl filled with ice. Bowls or serving dishes of copper are ideal because they remain cold.

VICHYSSOISE
(Cream of Potato and Leek Soup)

Although many people think of Vichyssoise as a classic French dish, the original rich cream soup of potatoes and leeks, served chilled and sprinkled with finely chopped chives, was created in 1941 by Louis Diat, then chef of the Ritz-Carlton Hotel, in New York.

4 large potatoes
3 leeks
16 fluid ounces chicken stock
½ ounce butter or margarine
2 teaspoons salt
¼ teaspoon white pepper
16 fluid ounces milk
8 fluid ounces cream
4 tablespoons chopped chives
½ teaspoon paprika

Peel and dice potatoes; cook with diced leeks (using green tops also) in stock until very soft (about 20 minutes). Put through a fine strainer.

To this purée add butter, seasonings, milk and cream and reheat.

Serve cold or hot with chopped chives on top and a garnish of paprika. If served cold, more milk or cream may be needed on serving. Two medium white onions may be used instead of leeks. Serves 6.

CHILLED CREAM OF ASPARAGUS SOUP

Combine 2 10¾-ounce cans condensed cream of asparagus soup and 2 cans single cream or rich milk.

Season with ¼ teaspoon each of paprika, garlic salt, and marjoram, and freshly ground pepper to taste. Garnish with chopped chives. Serves 6.

CHILLED CREAM OF CHICKEN SOUP

Combine 2 10¾-ounce cans condensed cream of chicken soup and 2 cans single cream or rich milk.

Season with salt and freshly ground pepper to taste. Garnish with chopped chives. Serves 6.

CHILLED TOMATO SOUP

Stir 2 10¾-ounce cans condensed tomato soup; add 1 can single cream and 1 can milk gradually, stirring constantly.

Chill 4 hours. Garnish with parsley. Serves 4.

BORSHT (Chilled Beet Soup)

Borsht may be any of a variety of soups originating in Russia, but popularly it refers to a beetroot soup made with or without meat and served either hot or cold. Citric acid or lemon juice is sometimes added. Beetroot borsht is usually served with soured cream. Cabbage and spinach borsht are other versions. Also spelled borsch, borscht, bortsch, and borshch, the last of these being the closest to the Russian pronunciation.

2 young beetroots
3¼ pints water
salt and pepper to taste
juice of 1 lemon
sugar to taste
2 eggs

Use dark red beetroots. Wash, peel, and grate. Add to water with salt and pepper, to taste. Cook until tender.

Add lemon juice and about 1 tablespoon sugar. Cool. Soup should have distinctly sweet-sour taste. Since beetroots vary in sugar content, amount of seasonings is added accordingly. Beat eggs slightly and blend slowly with cooled borsht. May be served hot or ice cold topped with a tablespoon of soured cream.

Sliced hard-boiled eggs and chopped cucumber are also used as a garnish. A small sprig of fresh dill added to beetroots while cooking enhances flavour. If desired, serve with hot boiled potatoes. Serves 8.

BLENDER BORSHT

8 fluid ounces stock or bouillon
8 fluid ounces beetroot liquid
2 tablespoons soured cream
2 teaspoons lemon juice
½ pound cooked or canned sliced
   beetroots
½ teaspoon salt
dash of pepper
about 1 tablespoon thin lemon peel
4 fluid ounces soured cream

Put all ingredients except the soured cream in container. Blend until smooth, about 2 minutes.

Chill thoroughly. Serve topped with soured cream. Serves 3.

SCHAV BORSHT (SORREL SOUP)

Schav is the Yiddish term for this highly favoured Jewish dish.

- 1½ pounds sorrel
- 1½ pints water
- 2½ ounces sugar
- 1 tablespoon vinegar
- 2 tablespoons lemon juice
- 1 teaspoon salt
- 2 lightly beaten eggs
- 4 fluid ounces soured cream

Wash sorrel thoroughly in cold water; remove stems and chop finely. Combine sorrel, water, and sugar in a saucepan; bring to boiling point. Lower heat and simmer 10 minutes. Add vinegar, lemon juice, and salt. Leave to cool.

Mix eggs and soured cream until blended. Add to sorrel and mix thoroughly. Chill and serve very cold with a hot boiled potato per serving, or sliced hard-boiled eggs. Makes about 2½ pints.

Spinach Borsht: Substitute spinach for sorrel.

COLD YOGURT SOUP (TURKISH STYLE)

- 3 medium cucumbers
- ¼ teaspoon salt
- 1 clove garlic (optional)
- 1 tablespoon vinegar
- 1 teaspoon chopped dill (optional)
- ¾ pint yogurt
- 2 tablespoons olive oil
- 1 tablespoon chopped mint leaves or ½ teaspoon dried mint leaves

Peel cucumbers, quarter lengthwise, and slice about ⅛ inch thick. Place in bowl and sprinkle with salt.

Rub another bowl with garlic and swish vinegar around in it to collect flavour, then add dill and yogurt.

Stir until mixture is consistency of thick soup, if necessary, adding 3 tablespoons cold water.

Pour over cucumbers and stir. Pour into individual serving dishes, sprinkle with olive oil, and garnish with chopped mint. Serves 6.

CHILLED SPINACH SOUP

Melt 1 ounce butter, blend in 2 tablespoons flour, ½ teaspoon onion salt, and ½ teaspoon salt.

Add 16 fluid ounces single cream gradually and cook, stirring constantly, until thickened.

Add 1 packet frozen chopped spinach. Cover and cook until spinach is tender. Chill thoroughly.

Jellied Soups

Some canned bouillons and consommés will jell when thoroughly chilled in the refrigerator. Others require the addition of gelatine. If a canned bouillon or consommé, ready-to-serve or condensed will jell upon chilling, it is usually so stated on the label.

The cans should be stored in the refrigerator for several hours or preferably overnight. Most rich, concentrated home-made bouillons or consommés will jell when thoroughly chilled.

JELLIED CONSOMMÉ OR BOUILLON

When using a consommé or bouillon which requires the addition of gelatine, allow 1 teaspoon gelatine for each ½ pint of bouillon or consommé.

Soften the gelatine in a little cold water (1 tablespoon to a teaspoon gelatine). Then add hot bouillon or consommé and stir until gelatine is dissolved. Season to taste.

Pour into a bowl; chill until firm. Just before serving, cut into cubes or break up lightly with a fork. Pile lightly in chilled soup bowls. Serve with lemon slices.

CANNED MADRILÈNE

Chill in the can. Turn out into a chilled bowl, whip with a fork and serve at once in chilled bowls.

Top each serving with 1½ to 2 tablespoons soured cream, or a little chopped parsley, chives or fresh dill, basil or chervil.

ORANGE JELLIED SOUP

- ½ tablespoon (½ envelope) gelatine
- 2 tablespoons cold water
- 2 fluid ounces boiling water
- 2 ounces sugar
- 8 fluid ounces orange juice (about 2 oranges)
- pinch of salt
- 2 teaspoons lemon juice
- 2 whole oranges

Soften gelatine in cold water for 5 minutes and dissolve in boiling water.

Add sugar, orange juice, salt, and lemon juice.

Peel and divide oranges into segments; add to gelatine mixture. Fill soup bowls about half full and place in refrigerator to chill.

JELLIED MADRILÈNE

- 2 tablespoons (2 envelopes) gelatine
- 2 fluid ounces cold water
- 5 chicken bouillon cubes
- 1¾ pints boiling water
- 2 teaspoons aromatic bitters
- 6 tablespoons finely chopped chives

Jellied Madrilène

Soak gelatine 5 minutes in cold water. Dissolve bouillon cubes in boiling water. Add gelatine and stir until dissolved. Add bitters and chill until mixture begins to set. Stir in the chopped chives and chill until set.

Beat slightly with a fork and pile into soup cups. Top with soured cream, if wished. Serves 4 to 6.

GAZPACHO

There are many versions of this Spanish dish that is a cross between a soup and a salad. The jellied version given here will be a colourful, refreshing addition to any menu. Spoon it into lettuce-lined bowls and serve it with assorted cold meat and hot rolls for a simple bit of luxury eating. For a more formal occasion, present it as a first course. Served in soup bowls or small dishes bedded in crushed ice, it makes a good appetizer.

JELLIED GAZPACHO

- 1 tablespoon (1 envelope) gelatine
- 18 fluid ounces canned tomato juice
- 2 tablespoons wine vinegar
- 2 tablespoons olive oil
- ½ teaspoon salt
- few drops Tabasco sauce
- dash of black pepper
- 1 pound cooked or canned green beans, drained
- 1 medium cucumber, peeled and chopped
- 1 ounce diced green pepper
- 1 small onion, finely chopped
- 2½ ounces canned mushrooms, sliced and drained

Add gelatine to tomato juice in a small saucepan. Heat several minutes over low heat, stirring frequently until gelatine is dissolved. Stir in vinegar, oil, and seasonings. Cool slightly.

While tomato mixture is cooling, combine remaining ingredients in a large bowl. Stir in tomato mixture. Chill 4 to 5 hours or until mixture will mound up on a spoon. Serve cold in soup bowls or lettuce-lined salad bowls. Garnish with dollops of soured cream and chopped chives, if wished.

Gazpacho

Creamed Soups

CREAM OF VEGETABLE SOUP
(Master Recipe)

1½ ounces butter or margarine
2 or 3 medium-sized onion slices
3 tablespoons flour
1½ teaspoons salt
few grains pepper
1¼ pints milk
about 16 fluid ounces vegetables
    and cooking liquid (see
    below)
2½ fluid ounces cream (optional)

Melt butter in a saucepan; add onion and cook gently until soft but not browned, about 5 minutes.

Stir in flour and seasonings. Remove from heat and slowly add milk, stirring until well blended.

Place over low heat and cook until smooth and thick, stirring constantly.

Add vegetables and cooking liquid prepared as directed below.

Heat thoroughly and add cream if wished. Sprinkle each portion with chopped parsley, watercress, or chives or a dash of paprika. Serves 6.

Cream of Vegetable Soup Variations

With Leftover Vegetables: Reheat vegetables singly or in combination in vegetable cooking liquid or in milk until soft enough to put through electric blender.

Measure pureé or finely chopped vegetables and add cooking liquid or milk to make 16 fluid ounces.

Cream of Asparagus Soup: Follow master recipe, increasing butter to 2 ounces and flour to 4 tablespoons.

Use 2 pounds of asparagus cut in 1-inch lengths. Cook covered in 2½-3 fluid ounces boiling salted water until very tender.

Save asparagus tips for garnish and put remainder through a sieve. Add cooking liquid to make 16 fluid ounces of purée.

Cream of Carrot Soup: Follow master recipe. Use 12 ounces grated carrots, which have been cooked covered in 8 fluid ounces boiling salted water for 5 to 10 minutes.

Cream of Celery Soup: Follow master recipe. Use ½ pound finely chopped or diced celery. Cook covered in 8 fluid ounces milk in top of double boiler or over low heat until very tender. Add cooking liquid to make up to 16 fluid ounces.

Cream of Corn Soup: Follow master recipe. Use 2 cans creamed sweetcorn and press it through a sieve.

Cream of Spinach Soup: Use 1 pound raw spinach. Cook until tender in the water which clings to the leaves after washing.

Put through sieve. Follow master recipe, increasing butter to 2 ounces and flour to 4 tablespoons.

Cream of Watercress Soup: Use 2 bunches of watercress. Wash and chop coarsely. Cook covered in 8 fluid ounces boiling salted water until tender.

Put through sieve and add cooking liquid to make 16 fluid ounces. Follow master recipe, increasing butter to 2 ounces and flour to 4 tablespoons.

Cream of Mushroom Soup: Use ¼ pound fresh mushrooms. Wash and chop finely; cook gently in 2 ounces butter with 1 teaspoon grated onion until tender, about 10 minutes.

Follow master recipe, adding 1 to 2 teaspoons lemon juice, if wished.

Cream of Lima Bean Soup: Use ¾ pound cooked or canned lima beans and liquid. Put through sieve and follow master recipe.

Cream of Onion Soup: Use 2 large or 3 medium onions, very finely sliced or chopped. Cook gently in 2 ounces butter until tender, about 15 minutes, but do not brown. If wished, put through sieve. Follow master recipe.

Cream of Pea Soup: Use 12 ounces fresh frozen peas or canned peas. Cook fresh peas in 1 cup boiling salted water, frozen peas according to packet directions until very tender.

Heat canned peas in their own liquid about 10 minutes. Put peas through a sieve. Follow master recipe.

Cream of Potato Soup: Use 12 ounces diced, cooked potatoes and 1 tablespoon chopped pimiento. Do not put through sieve. Follow master recipe.

CHESTNUT SOUP—FRENCH STYLE

1 pound chestnuts
bouquet garni (see below)
¼ teaspoon thyme
salt and pepper
16 fluid ounces chicken stock
4 fluid ounces double cream,
    scalded
2½ fluid ounces sherry

Prepare chestnuts: cut gash on flat sides; place in extremely hot oven (500°F. Mark 10) for about 6 minutes, or until shells may be easily removed, taking care not to burn them. Remove shells and skins with a sharp knife.

Put chestnuts in a saucepan with bouquet garni, ¼ teaspoon thyme, and just enough water to cover nuts. Season with salt and pepper to taste. Cover and boil gently until nuts are soft, 20 to 25 minutes.

Discard bouquet garni and put chestnuts and liquid through a fine sieve into another saucepan. Add chicken stock; bring to boiling point and stir in scalded cream. Adjust seasoning to taste and if the soup is too thick add more chicken stock. Let soup boil up once, then stir in sherry.

If wished, serve garnished with whipped cream sprinkled with crumbled roast chestnuts. Makes about 1½ pints.

Bouquet Garni: Wrap in a piece of muslin and tie securely: 8 sprigs parsley, 3 sprigs green celery tops, 2 whole cloves, and 1 bay leaf.

PUMPKIN SOUP

2 pounds cooked fresh or canned
    pumpkin
1¼ pints milk, scalded
½ ounce butter
1 tablespoon granulated sugar or 2
    tablespoons brown sugar
⅛ teaspoon saffron
2½ ounces ham, cut in match-stick
    strips
salt and pepper to taste
nutmeg and cinnamon to taste, if
    wished

Combine pumpkin with scalded milk; add remaining ingredients. Heat to serving temperature but do not boil. Serve immediately. Makes about 4 cups.

ALMOND SOUP

½ pound blanched whole almonds
2 tablespoons dried flaked onion
1¼ pints water
3 tablespoons chicken stock base*
¼ teaspoon salt
½ teaspoon coriander seed
12 fluid ounces milk
grated orange rind

Finely grind almonds in a grinder or blender. In a saucepan, combine ground almonds, onion, water, chicken stock base, salt, and coriander. Simmer 30 minutes.

Remove from heat; strain and gradually stir in milk. Heat gently until thoroughly hot. Serve hot or cold, garnished with grated orange rind. Makes 4 large servings or 8 small servings.

***Note:** 1¼ pints chicken broth and 5 chicken bouillon cubes may be substituted.

Almond soup is served hot or cold.

CREAM OF TOMATO SOUP

20 ounces canned tomatoes
2 slices onion
1 bay leaf
1 teaspoon salt
$\frac{1}{4}$ teaspoon pepper
$\frac{1}{4}$ teaspoon cinnamon
$\frac{1}{8}$ teaspoon cloves
1 ounce butter or margarine
2 tablespoons flour
16 fluid ounces milk

Combine tomatoes, onion, and seasonings. Simmer 10 minutes, then strain.

Make white sauce; melt butter; blend in flour. Gradually add milk and cook over low heat until slightly thick, stirring constantly.

Just before serving, slowly add hot, strained tomatoes to white sauce, stirring constantly. Do not reheat. Serves 6.

MUSHROOM BISQUE

1 pound mushrooms
1$\frac{1}{4}$ pints water
1 slice onion
$\frac{1}{2}$ teaspoon salt
1$\frac{1}{2}$ ounces butter or margarine
1 ounce flour
16 fluid ounces milk
salt and pepper
paprika
1 egg yolk
2$\frac{1}{2}$ fluid ounces double cream, whipped

Clean and chop mushrooms. Add water, onion, and $\frac{1}{2}$ teaspoon salt. Simmer $\frac{1}{2}$ hour. Press through a medium sieve.

Melt butter and blend in flour. Gradually add milk and cook over hot water, stirring occasionally until thick.

Add the sieved mushrooms, season with salt, pepper, and paprika to taste.

Beat egg yolk and gradually add to mushroom mixture. Serve with whipped cream. Serves 4 to 6.

POTATO CARROT CHOWDER

1 white onion, finely chopped
2 ounces butter or margarine
12 ounces diced raw potatoes
1$\frac{1}{4}$ pints boiling water
1 teaspoon salt
$\frac{1}{4}$ teaspoon paprika
1 tablespoon flour
16 fluid ounces milk, scalded
2 carrots, diced and cooked

Sauté onion in 1 ounce butter in large saucepan until lightly browned.

Add potatoes, boiling water, salt, and paprika. Boil about 15 minutes or until potatoes are soft.

Blend flour with remaining butter and gradually add milk, stirring constantly until smooth and thickened.

Add to potato mixture. Add carrots. Cook 5 minutes, stirring until smooth. Serves 6.

CORN AND POTATO CHOWDER
(Master Recipe)

1 medium onion, finely chopped
1$\frac{1}{2}$ ounces fat
1$\frac{1}{4}$ pints boiling water
3 medium-sized potatoes, cubed
dash of pepper
1$\frac{1}{2}$ teaspoons salt
10$\frac{1}{2}$ ounces canned sweetcorn
1$\frac{1}{4}$ pints scalded milk

Sauté onions in fat until lightly browned. Add boiling water, potatoes, and seasonings. Cook until potatoes are tender, about 15 minutes.

Add sweetcorn and milk. Heat to boiling point, but do not boil. Serves 6.

Variations of Corn and Potato Chowder

Bean Chowder: Substitute $\frac{3}{4}$ pound canned lima beans for sweetcorn and diced carrots for potatoes.

Fish Chowder: Substitute 1$\frac{1}{2}$ pounds fish (haddock or cod) for sweetcorn. Add fish with potatoes and cook until both are tender. Then add milk, heat, and serve.

Additional fish bones or heads may be used, if wished.

Potato Soup: Omit sweetcorn. Cook 2 tablespoons chopped celery leaves with potatoes.

Garnish each serving with a little butter and a dash of paprika.

BLENDER BISQUES
(Master Recipe)

16 fluid ounces milk
1 tablespoon flour
1 ounce butter or margarine
1 teaspoon salt
dash of pepper
1 ounce diced celery or 3 sprigs parsley
1 thin slice raw onion, optional
cooked or canned fish, seafood, or meat

Combine all ingredients in container. Blend until smooth.

Heat over low heat, stirring occasionally, until mixture reaches boiling point. Serves 3 to 4.

Variations of Blender Bisques

Crab Bisque: Use 3 ounces cooked or canned crabmeat.

Fish Bisque: Use 3 ounces cooked or canned fish flakes.

Lobster Bisque: Use 3$\frac{1}{2}$ ounces cooked or canned lobster meat.

Oyster Bisque: Use 3 or 4 raw oysters.

Salmon Bisque: Use 3$\frac{1}{2}$ ounces cooked or canned salmon.

Shrimp Bisque: Use 3 ounces cooked or canned shrimp.

Meat Bisque: Use 3 ounces diced cooked leftover chicken, beef, lamb, veal, or ham. Substitute 8 fluid ounces stock for 8 fluid ounces milk.

BLENDER CREAM SOUP
(Master Recipe)

16 fluid ounces milk
2 tablespoons flour
1 ounce butter or margarine
1 teaspoon salt
dash of pepper
1 thin slice onion
few sprigs of parsley or 1 ounce diced raw celery
raw, canned, or cooked vegetables, cut up into small pieces

Put all ingredients in blender and blend until smooth. Heat over low heat, stirring occasionally, until mixture boils.

If cooked leftover food is used, season after blending. Frozen vegetables do not have to be defrosted before blending. Serves 3 to 4.

Variations of Blender Cream Soup

Asparagus Cream Soup: Use 4 ounces asparagus tips.

Carrot Cream Soup: Use 4 ounces diced raw or canned carrots.

Corn Cream Soup: Use 7 ounces raw or canned corn.

Cucumber Cream Soup: Use 8 ounces raw, sliced, unpeeled cucumber.

Mushroom Cream Soup: Use 6 whole sautéed mushrooms.

Pea Cream Soup: Reduce flour to 1 tablespoon. Use 6 ounces fresh or canned peas.

Spinach Cream Soup: Use 1 pound raw spinach or 4 ounces cooked or canned spinach.

CREAM OF CHICKEN SOUP

1 ounce butter or margarine
2 tablespoons flour
16 fluid ounces heated chicken stock
8 fluid ounces scalded milk or cream
salt and pepper

Melt butter and blend in flour. Add stock and milk or cream. Cook 5 minutes, stirring constantly.

Season to taste and remove from heat to avoid curdling. Serves 4.

With Egg Yolk: Use only 1 tablespoon flour. Beat an egg yolk slightly. Slowly pour hot soup over it. Strain and serve at once.

HAM AND CORN CHOWDER

$\frac{1}{2}$ large onion, sliced
4 ounces melted butter or margarine
20 ounces canned creamed sweetcorn
4 fluid ounces single cream
6 ounces chopped cooked ham
$\frac{1}{4}$ teaspoon salt
pinch of pepper

Sauté onion slices in melted butter until tender. Add sweetcorn, single cream, cooked ham, salt, and pepper. Heat to serving temperature. Serve with celery croûtons. Serves 4 to 5.

Fish and Shellfish Soups

LOBSTER BISQUE
(Master Recipe)

1½ ounces butter or margarine
4 tablespoons flour
1 teaspoon salt
pinch of pepper
1¼ pints milk
8 fluid ounces bouillon
6 ounces canned lobster meat
1 medium-sized onion, sliced
1 sprig parsley
4 fluid ounces single cream

Melt butter in saucepan. Stir in flour, salt, and pepper. Add milk and bouillon gradually, stirring constantly, and simmer over low heat until mixture thickens.

Add lobster, onion, and parsley. Cover and simmer 10 minutes. Remove from heat.

Strain, pressing as much of the meat as possible through a sieve. Add cream and reheat. Serves 6.

Lobster Bisque Variations

Crab Bisque: Substitute canned crabmeat for lobster.

Prawn Bisque: Remove black line and wash 6 ounces canned or cooked prawns. Substitute in Lobster Bisque.

Clam Bisque: Substitute canned minced clams for lobster.

SEAFOOD SOUP

2 ounces butter or margarine
1 large onion, chopped
1 green pepper, chopped
8 ounces canned sliced mushrooms
1 clove garlic, crushed
1 pint canned tomato juice
6 fluid ounces water
2 chicken bouillon cubes
½ teaspoon oregano
5 ounces canned lobster
10 ounces frozen, cooked prawns
1 6½-ounce can crabmeat

Melt butter or margarine. Sauté next 4 ingredients 5 minutes. Stir in tomato juice, water, bouillon cubes, and oregano. Cook over low heat 15 minutes.

Add lobster, prawns, and crabmeat. Heat. Serve with crackers. Serves 6 to 8.

Seafood Soup: From the sea comes a bounty of succulent foods. Three of them combine to make one of the heartiest and best of soups. It's a meal in itself—served with crisp crackers.

CLAM CHOWDER, NEW ENGLAND AND MANHATTAN

Clam chowder fanciers in America are divided into two uncompromising schools. New Englanders are firm in their insistence on milk or cream in chowder; those who prefer Manhattan chowder claim that any chowder worth its salt must contain tomatoes. How New England chowder got its name is obvious. How Manhattan chowder got its name is more mysterious. For chowder with tomatoes is eaten with gusto not only in Manhattan, but all over the United States.

2 pounds canned clams
6 tablespoons chopped bacon
1 large onion, sliced
1 pound potatoes, diced
½ teaspoon salt
¼ teaspoon pepper
16 fluid ounces hot water
1⅗ pints milk
8 crackers

Drain clams, saving juice. Chop clams.

Cook bacon in a large saucepan until crisp. Add onions and brown slightly.

Add potatoes, salt, pepper, and water; cook 10 minutes.

Add clams, milk, and clam juice; cook until potatoes are tender, about 10 minutes.

Pour chowder over crumbled crackers in serving bowls. Serves 6.

Manhattan Clam Chowder: Follow recipe for New England Clam Chowder, substituting 2 ounces diced celery for same quantity of potatoes, and canned tomatoes or tomato juice for milk. Add 1 teaspoon thyme.

GULF STATES OYSTER GUMBO

2 ounces butter or margarine
1½ tablespoons finely chopped onion
1 pint oysters
1½ pints fish stock or canned clam broth
6 ounces cooked or canned okra
16 ounces cooked or canned tomatoes
salt and pepper
2 tablespoons flour

Cook onion in 1 ounce melted butter until lightly browned.

Add oysters and their liquid, stock, okra, tomatoes, and salt and pepper to taste. Bring slowly to boiling point.

Add a smooth paste made of 1 ounce butter and 2 tablespoons flour. Stir until smooth. Serves 4 to 6.

CLAM BROTH

Wash and scrub clams in shell with a brush. Place in deep saucepan. Add 4 fluid ounces water for each quart clams. Cover tightly and cook until clams open wide, 20 to 30 minutes.

Let stand 10 to 15 minutes so that any sediment will settle. Strain through muslin. Season to taste.

Serve hot or cold. Chop clams and use for canapé spread or other recipes.

Clam Broth Variations

Clam and Tomato Broth: Combine equal quantities of clam broth and tomato juice or tomato bouillon. Season with celery salt.

Clam and Chicken Frappé: Combine 12 fluid ounces clam broth and 1 pint highly seasoned chicken stock. Freeze to mush. Serve in chilled bowls.

Clam and Chicken Broth: Combine equal quantities of clam broth and chicken stock. Either or both may be fresh or canned. Season to taste with salt and pepper. Garnish with chopped chives or parsley.

TURTLE SOUP

It is a timesaver to buy canned or frozen turtle meat; however, if you want to prepare your own, see Index.

¾ pound diced fresh turtle meat
3¼ pints beef stock
1 bay leaf
1½ tablespoons lemon juice
1 clove mace
few drops Tabasco sauce
salt and pepper
sherry
2 hard-boiled egg whites, chopped

Combine turtle meat, stock, bay leaf, mace, lemon juice, and Tabasco sauce. Bring to boiling point. Simmer until turtle meat is tender.

Remove bay leaf and mace. Season with salt and pepper.

Add 1 tablespoon sherry to each serving and garnish with chopped egg white. Serves 8.

LOBSTER STEW

1 2-pound lobster, boiled
2 ounces butter or margarine
1¾ pints milk
1 slice onion
1 teaspoon salt
paprika

Cut lobster meat into small pieces. Sauté lightly without browning in melted butter.

Scald milk with onion slice. Discard onion; add lobster meat and seasonings. Heat thoroughly.

If wished, lobster coral or liver may be rubbed through a sieve and added at the last minute. Serves 4.

BOUILLABAISSE

Bouillabaisse is an elaborate seafood chowder or stew made of many kinds of fish and shellfish (generally five or six), olive oil, tomatoes, garlic, and usually saffron; it is sometimes seasoned with wine. True bouillabaisse can be made only on the Mediterranean coast of France, since it depends on local varieties of fish. Similar dishes to which the same name is applied are also popular elsewhere. Our version given below includes ingredients available everywhere.

6 fluid ounces salad oil
1 carrot, finely chopped
3 onions, finely chopped
3 pounds various fish fillets
1 bay leaf
8 fluid ounces tomato pulp
$1\frac{1}{4}$ pints fish stock or water
1 dozen oysters or clams
6 ounces cooked prawns or lobster meat
2 pimientos, finely chopped
2 teaspoons salt
$\frac{1}{3}$ teaspoon paprika
2 tablespoons lemon juice
toast
2 tablespoons finely chopped parsley

Use a combination of several kinds of fish such as flounder, haddock, perch, sole, whiting, or cod.

Heat oil in large heavy saucepan and cook carrot and onions 5 minutes. Add fish, cut into small pieces, and bay leaf. Cook 5 minutes then add tomato pulp and fish stock.

Cover and simmer, without actually boiling, about 20 minutes or until fish is tender.

Add oysters or clams, shrimp or lobster meat, pimientos, seasonings, and lemon juice. Heat thoroughly.

Serve in soup plates, ladling the Bouillabaisse over toast in plates and sprinkling parsley over the surface. Serves 6.

FISH BISQUE
(Master Recipe)

12 fluid ounces thin white sauce
1 slice onion
4-5 ounces canned or cooked fish
lemon juice
whipped cream (optional)

Add onion to white sauce. Add flaked or chopped fish and heat thoroughly.

Press through a sieve. Heat carefully. Season to taste.

Just before serving, add a few drops lemon juice. If wished, garnish with whipped cream to which a few grains of salt has been added, and, if wished, a sprinkling of paprika. Serves 3.

Variations: Vary by adding a dash of Tabasco sauce or $\frac{1}{2}$ teaspoon Worcestershire sauce. If wished, 2 ounces cooked celery may be added before pressing through sieve.

QUICK PRAWN GUMBO

1 medium-sized onion, chopped
$\frac{1}{2}$ green pepper, chopped
$1\frac{1}{2}$ ounces butter or margarine
$1\frac{3}{4}$ pints chicken stock or consommé
6 ounces cooked or canned okra, cut in small pieces
20 ounces canned tomatoes
6 ounces cooked or canned prawns
1 teaspoon arrowroot

Cook onion and green pepper in melted butter until soft, about 5 minutes. Add stock, okra, and tomatoes and simmer gently 20 minutes.

Add prawns, and the arrowroot mixed with a little water. Heat thoroughly, and bring to the boil.

Season to taste with salt and pepper. Garnish with finely chopped parsley. Serves 6.

Quick Crab Gumbo: Substitute canned crabmeat for prawns.

OYSTER STEW

2 ounces butter or margarine
1 pint shelled oysters with liquid
$1\frac{3}{4}$ pints milk
1 teaspoon salt
pinch of pepper
$1\frac{1}{2}$ tablespoons flour

Heat 1 ounce butter with oysters and oyster liquid in top part of a double boiler.

Combine $1\frac{1}{2}$ pints milk, 1 ounce butter, salt, and pepper in a saucepan; heat to scald milk.

Stir flour into remaining milk and blend well. Add to the scalded milk mixture; cook over low heat, stirring constantly, until it thickens.

Pour over the hot oysters and place stew over, not in, hot water for 15 minutes before serving. Serves 4 to 6.

PLANTATION CHOWDER

3 medium onions, sliced
2 green peppers, cut into small pieces
3 large carrots, diced
4 fluid ounces olive oil
3 frozen lobster tails, cut into 1-inch pieces (shell on)
$\frac{1}{2}$ pound deveined frozen prawns
1 pound frozen fish fillets
water to cover (2 pints)
$\frac{1}{2}$ pound cooked tomatoes
$1\frac{1}{2}$ teaspoons salt
$\frac{1}{4}$ teaspoon pepper
12 ounces rice, cooked
saffron (optional)

Sauté vegetables in oil in a large saucepan. Add lobster tails, prawns, then fish fillets. Add water, tomatoes, and seasonings. Cover and cook to boiling. Reduce heat and simmer 20 minutes.

Meanwhile, boil the rice until tender. Add saffron for colour and flavour, if wished. In individual bowls, serve fish and soup, topped with scoops of freshly cooked rice.

NEW ENGLAND FISH CHOWDER

$1\frac{1}{2}$ pounds fresh cod, haddock, or any other large fish
12 ounces diced potatoes
4 ounces diced carrots
$1\frac{1}{4}$ pints water
1 onion, chopped
2 tablespoons flour
16 fluid ounces milk
$\frac{1}{2}$ teaspoon Aromat
salt and pepper
6 crackers
1 ounce butter or margarine

Cut fish into small pieces; remove bones and skin. Cook fish, potatoes, and carrots in water 15 minutes.

Fry salt pork until crisp; remove and drain.

Sauté onion in pork fat; add flour and stir until well blended. Gradually add milk. Add to fish mixture. Add Aromat and salt and pepper to taste. Stir frequently and simmer 10 minutes longer.

Add more seasoning if necessary. Add crackers and butter. Serve at once. Serves 6.

SCALLOP STEW

$1\frac{3}{5}$ pints milk
8 fluid ounces cream
$2\frac{1}{2}$ ounces butter or margarine
1 tablespoon sugar
$\frac{1}{2}$ teaspoon Worcestershire sauce
1 pound scallops

Heat milk and cream in double boiler.

Melt butter in a frying pan, and add sugar and Worcestershire sauce.

Crush scallops, cut off the hard pieces and dice. Add to mixture in frying pan. Simmer until tender.

Pour heated milk and cream over cooked scallops. Season to taste with salt and pepper. Serves 6.

Plantation Chowder

OYSTER STEW, WHITE WINE

1 ounce butter or margarine
1 pint oysters
¾ pint milk
8 fluid ounces Chablis, Hock,
    Sauternes, Riesling or any
    white wine
8 fluid ounces cream

Melt butter or margarine. Add oysters and cook until edges begin to curl. Season with salt and pepper.

Scald milk and oyster liquid. Add to oysters. Heat to boiling point.

Remove from heat; add wine gradually. Finally add the cream. Reheat and serve very hot. Serves 4.

SOUTHERN CRAYFISH BISQUE

2 dozen crayfish
1½ pints water
2 onions
2 carrots
2 sticks celery
4 sprigs parsley
¼ teaspoon thyme
5 tablespoons dry breadcrumbs
milk
1½ ounces butter or margarine
2 tablespoons flour
salt and pepper
1 beaten egg

Prepare crayfish for soup by soaking in cold salted water (1 tablespoon salt to 1¾ pints water) for 30 minutes. Wash and scrub under running water to remove all the dirt.

When cleaned, place in a large saucepan with the water, 1 onion, the carrots, celery, half the quantity of parsley, and the thyme. Allow to come to a boil and simmer for 25 minutes.

Drain off the water from the crayfish and set aside for later use.

Remove all the meat from the heads and bodies of the crayfish; set aside the heads, which are to be stuffed.

Moisten the breadcrumbs with the milk. Chop crayfish meat and add to the moistened crumbs.

Finely chop the remaining onion; melt the butter, add the onion and 1 tablespoon of flour. Add 1 tablespoon of the broth and the remainder of the parsley. Season with salt and pepper to taste.

Simmer slowly for a few minutes; add the crayfish and crumb mixture and cook 2 minutes longer.

Remove from stove and allow to cool slightly. Stir in the beaten egg. Fill the crayfish heads with this mixture.

Roll the heads in flour and fry in butter until nicely browned. Drain on paper and keep warm while preparing the stock.

Melt the rest of the butter; add the remainder of the flour and stir until smooth.

Strain reserved stock in order to remove celery and carrots. Add the broth to the butter and flour. Cook slowly for 12 minutes; season with more salt and pepper if desired. Before serving, add the stuffed crayfish heads.

Serves 4 to 5.

CREOLE PRAWN GUMBO

1 slice (½ pound) raw ham, cut in
    small pieces
2 pounds okra, cut in ¾-inch pieces
2 medium-sized onions, chopped
2 sticks celery with leaves,
    chopped
½ chopped green pepper, seeds and
    membrane removed
2 cloves garlic, finely chopped
1 sprig fresh thyme or ⅓ teaspoon
    dried thyme
1 bay leaf
¾ pound skinned fresh tomatoes
    or 1 15-ounce can tomatoes
2½ pints water
2 pounds fresh prawns
2 tablespoons chopped parsley
boiled rice

Sauté ham lightly in a frying pan. Sauté okra slowly in ham fat for 10 minutes. (If you use canned okra, do not sauté.) Add onion and sauté for the last 2 minutes.

Add celery, green pepper, garlic, thyme, bay leaf, tomatoes, and water. If a thick gumbo is desired use less water.

Shell and remove black veins from prawns. Let the soup boil, then reduce heat and add ham, prawns, and parsley. Simmer 30 minutes.

Serve with boiled rice. Serves 8 to 10 as a main dish or 10 to 12 as a soup.

VELOUTINE DE CRUSTACES

6 medium oysters with liquid
3-4 scallops, diced
10 canned little neck clams
5 or 6 celery leaves
16 fluid ounces chicken broth
2 tablespoons quick-cooking
    tapioca
2 egg yolks
4 fluid ounces single cream
salt to taste
½ teaspoon Aromat
dash of pepper
½ ounce butter or margarine

Cook oysters, scallops, and celery leaves in oyster liquid for 5 minutes; strain.

Skim liquid; add chicken broth; heat to boiling. Add tapioca; cook until thickened (about 10 minutes).

Beat egg yolks with cream; add to chicken broth while stirring. Add remaining ingredients with oysters, scallops and clams; heat to boiling point

but do not boil.

Serve hot in soup bowls; keep hot if for sauce; spoon hot into pastry shells if for entrée.

Garnish with finely chopped chives or sprinkle of paprika. Makes 4 to 6 servings.

CLAM CHOWDER À LA CAPE COD

4 dozen medium hard-shelled
    clams
2½ pints cold water
1 2-inch cube salt pork, diced
1 large onion, very finely chopped
4 medium-sized potatoes, diced
salt and pepper
¾ pint milk
8 fluid ounces single cream

Wash and scrub clams thoroughly. Place in a deep saucepan with cold water. (Water should almost cover clams.) Boil clams gently until shells open, about 10 minutes.

Strain broth through muslin and save. Remove clams from shells, clean and finely chop.

Fry salt pork in deep saucepan. Add onion and cook slowly until it begins to turn golden brown.

Add clams and broth. Skim well, if necessary. Add potatoes and season to taste with salt and pepper. Cook until potatoes are tender.

Remove from heat and slowly add milk and cream which have been heated. Serve at once. Serves 8 to 10.

MARTHA WASHINGTON'S CRAB SOUP

2 hard-boiled eggs
1 ounce butter or margarine
2 tablespoons flour
grated rind of ½ lemon
2 pints milk, scalded
¾ pound crabmeat, cooked or
    canned
8 fluid ounces cream
2 teaspoons Worcestershire sauce
8 fluid ounces sherry or madeira
salt and pepper

Mash yolks of boiled eggs to a paste with butter, flour, and grated lemon rind.

Add chopped egg whites. Pour hot milk over mixture. Place over low heat and simmer 5 minutes, stirring constantly.

Add crabmeat and cream; bring to boiling point.

Add Worcestershire sauce and wine. Season to taste with salt and pepper. Heat through but do not boil after wine has been added. Serves 6 to 8.

Note: This is a modern adaptation of the original early American recipe.

Stocks and Soups Made with Meat

BEEF OR BROWN SOUP STOCK (Master Recipe)

A good stock is the basis of countless thousands of dishes. The preparation is relatively easy; it can be made in large quantities and frozen for later use.

- 5 pounds beef knuckle
- 4¾ pints cold water
- 1 medium onion, sliced
- 2 carrots, sliced
- 1 medium turnip, diced
- 4 sticks celery (with leaves), cut into ½-inch pieces
- ½ teaspoon black peppercorns
- 5 whole cloves
- 1 small bay leaf
- 3 sprigs parsley
- 1 tablespoon salt

Have beef knuckle cut in several pieces. Cut meat from bone and cut in cubes. Brown meat cubes.

Put meat and bone into a large saucepan; add water and leave to stand for 1 hour to draw out juices.

Bring to boil; skim and reduce heat to simmering. Cook slowly 4 to 5 hours.

Add vegetables and seasonings during last hour of cooking.

Strain stock. Chill. Remove layer of fat when stock is chilled. Makes about 3¼ pints.

CONSOMMÉ

Follow recipe for Brown Soup Stock. Substitute 2 pounds lean beef (cut in 1-inch cubes), 1 pound marrowbone (cracked), and 2 pounds veal knuckle (cut in pieces), for beef knuckle.

Sauté vegetables in ½ ounce butter until lightly browned before adding to stock.

Chicken stock or chicken bones may be added to the pan. Makes about 3¼ pints consommé.

CONSOMMÉ PRINCESS

Serve consommé with shredded chicken and new green peas.

CONSOMMÉ ROYALE

Garnish each serving of consommé with royal custard (see Index) diced or cut in fancy shapes.

HOW TO CLARIFY STOCK

For 1½-1¾ pints of stock, combine 2 tablespoons water with 1 egg white and shell. Add to cold stock. Heat stock and stir constantly until it boils. Boil 5 to 10 minutes without stirring.

Let stand 15 to 20 minutes at back of stove for stock to settle. Strain through two thicknesses of muslin.

VEAL OR WHITE STOCK

Follow recipe for Beef or Brown Soup Stock and substitute 4 to 5 pounds of knuckle of veal or poultry or a combination of both for beef.

Do not brown meat. Cover with cold water and proceed as directed.

LAMB OR MUTTON STOCK

Follow recipe for Beef or Brown Soup Stock and substitute 4 to 5 pounds lamb or mutton for beef.

Do not brown meat. Remove any excess fat from meat before cooking.

BOUILLON

Prepare brown stock. Cool and clarify as directed.

CONSOMMÉ JARDINIÈRE

Cut vegetables into fancy shapes with vegetable cutters.

Cook and serve in the consommé, allowing about ½ pound vegetables to 2 pints stock.

CONSOMMÉ MACEDOINE

Add cubed cooked vegetables in various colours to stock and reheat.

TOMATO BOUILLON

Combine 1 pint bouillon and 1 pint tomato juice; stir well and heat to boiling point. Pour into soup bowls. Top with slightly salted whipped cream. Sprinkle with chopped parsley.

BEEF JUICE OR TEA FOR INVALIDS AND CHILDREN

Cut 1 pound lean steak into small cubes. Put in a 2-pound glass jar. Add 8 fluid ounces cold water and a pinch of salt.

Cover jar tightly and place in a pan of cold water, using as much water as possible without upsetting the jar.

Slowly bring the water in pan to boiling point and boil gently for 1 hour.

Remove jar and place on a rack to cool as quickly as possible.

Strain the juice and store in refrigerator until ready to heat and serve.

MADRILÈNE

- 12 fluid ounces chicken stock or bouillon
- 12 fluid ounces beef stock or bouillon or use cube or canned bouillon
- 12 fluid ounces tomato juice
- 4 ounces chopped celery
- 2 ounces chopped carrot
- 4 ounces chopped leeks
- salt and pepper

Mix bouillons and tomato juice; bring to the boil.

Add vegetables and simmer 30 minutes. Taste, and add more salt and pepper if needed. Strain. Reheat. Serve hot or chilled. Serves 5 to 6.

Minestrone

MINESTRONE (Italian Vegetable Soup)

This Italian thick vegetable soup appears in countless versions; however all of them include a pasta and usually dried beans or peas. It is usually served with grated Parmesan cheese.

- ¼ pound bacon or bacon ends, chopped
- 2 medium onions, sliced
- 1 clove garlic, finely chopped
- 2 ounces chopped celery and leaves
- 1 carrot, sliced
- 2-3 tablespoons chopped parsley
- 2 ounces chopped escarole or endive
- 5 ounces chopped cabbage
- 6 ounces dried beans, cooked
- 20 ounces canned tomatoes
- 4 ounces canned chickpeas
- ½ teaspoon dried basil
- ¼ teaspoon oregano
- salt
- ½ teaspoon Aromat (optional)
- 2 ounces macaroni
- cayenne
- 1 pound hot Italian sausage, sliced and cooked
- grated Parmesan cheese

Brown bacon and onions in a large saucepan. Add remaining raw vegetables; cook 10 minutes, stirring occasionally.

Add 2½ pints water, beans, tomatoes, chickpeas, herbs, ½ teaspoon Aromat, and 2 teaspoons salt. Bring to the boil; cover and simmer 30 minutes.

Add macaroni, and cook 10 minutes, or until tender. Add salt and cayenne to taste. Serve topped with sausage and cheese. Makes about 4¾ pints.

MUSHROOM CONSOMMÉ

- ¾ pound mushrooms
- 2½ pints brown stock or 2 cans condensed consommé made up to 2½ pints with water

Wash mushrooms. Remove stems and chop them finely; slice caps.

Place chopped stems and stock in a saucepan; cover and simmer about 30 minutes. Strain, chill and remove excess fat.

Simmer sliced mushroom caps in ½ pint of the stock until tender, about 10 minutes. Combine with remaining stock and reheat. Serves 6 to 8.

QUICK STOCK, BOUILLON, OR CONSOMMÉ

For quick stock, bouillon, or consommé, use one of the following: canned clear soup directly from the can; canned condensed soup diluted with an equal amount of water; 1 or 2 bouillon cubes dissolved in ½ pint boiling water, or 1 to 2 teaspoons beef extract or meat concentrate dissolved in ½ pint boiling water.

PEPPER POT

1 pound fresh honeycomb tripe
1½ ounces butter or dripping
4¾ pints cold water
1 pound stewing lamb or mutton, trimmed of fat
¼ pound lean salt pork
1 small bay leaf
1 clove
1 sprig each parsley, thyme, and marjoram
12 ounces mixed vegetables
6 ounces diced potatoes

Use a variety of vegetables in season, making up the 12 ounces with equal parts of beans, carrots, and celery; peas, onions, and beans; tomato, aubergine, and onion, etc.

Wash tripe, drain well, and cut into cubes. Brown in a large saucepan in butter or dripping.

Add water, meat (cut into small pieces), salt pork, and seasonings tied together in a piece of muslin. Cover tightly, bring to boiling point and simmer 2 hours.

Add vegetables and potatoes and cook until tender.

Cool, skim off fat and season to taste with salt and pepper. Thicken with a paste made of 3 to 5 tablespoons flour blended with 1½-2½ ounces butter. Bring to boiling point.

If a rich effect is desired, pour boiling soup over 2 egg yolks, while stirring constantly. Serves 6 to 8.

Pepper Pot: The birthplace of many American traditions—Philadelphia—is also the home of this flavourful and hearty soup, hence it is often called Philadelphia Pepper Pot. There are many versions but one ingredient—tripe—is in every one of them or it is not a true pepper pot.

CHICKEN SOUP STOCK

1 4- to 4½-pound chicken, cut up
2½ pints cold water
2 small onions, sliced
2 sticks celery, diced
1 carrot, sliced
3 sprigs parsley
1 teaspoon salt
dash of pepper
4 black peppercorns

Put chicken in a large saucepan and cover with cold water. Bring to boiling point and skim.

Add vegetables and seasonings, and simmer until chicken is tender.

Remove chicken and strain stock. Cool. Place stock in refrigerator until needed.

Before using chicken stock, remove film of fat from top. The chicken stock may be used for sauces or as a soup base. Makes 1¾-2 pints.

Use the chicken meat in chicken salad, chicken loaf, or soufflé.

CHICKEN NOODLE SOUP

Heat 1¾ pints chicken stock in top of double boiler.

Add 6 ounces noodles and cook until noodles are tender, about 25 to 30 minutes. Serves 6.

CHICKEN RICE SOUP

Heat 1¾ pints chicken stock in top of double boiler. Add 8 ounces rice; cook until rice is fluffy, about 40 minutes. Serves 6.

MULLIGATAWNY SOUP

This is an East Indian curry-flavoured soup with apples and vegetables. Some versions of this dish are made with mutton instead of chicken.

2 ounces butter or other fat
½ pound raw diced chicken
1 apple, thinly sliced
1 small onion, diced
1½ ounces diced celery
1½ ounces diced carrot
1 green pepper, finely chopped
1 ounce flour
1 teaspoon curry powder
1 blade mace
3 cloves
1 8-ounce can tomatoes
2 tablespoons finely chopped parsley
1 teaspoon salt
½ teaspoon pepper
2½ pints rice, cooked
2½ pints chicken stock
4 ounces rice, cooked

Cook chicken, apple, and vegetables (except tomatoes and parsley) in butter until brown.

Add remaining ingredients (except rice) in order given. Simmer gently 1 hour.

Strain and pick out pieces of chicken. Press vegetables through a sieve.

Return chicken and vegetables to soup. Adjust seasoning. Place cooked rice in bowls and pour over the hot soup. Serves 6 to 8.

COCK-A-LEEKIE (From Scotland)

This famous Scottish soup sometimes appears on menus as cockie-leekie.

2 bunches leeks
1 3½- to 4-pound chicken
1½ teaspoons salt
½ teaspoon pepper
½ teaspoon nutmeg
1¾ pints veal stock or water
1 dozen prunes

Wash leeks and cut off green tops. Slice white parts in ½-inch pieces. Place half the sliced leeks in a large saucepan with closely-fitting lid.

Cut chicken into serving pieces and place on top of leeks. Add remaining leeks and seasonings. Cover with stock. Bring to rolling boil and skim the top.

Cover well and simmer until chicken is tender, about 1½ hours.

Add prunes 30 minutes before end of cooking time.

Remove meat from bones and place in soup bowls. Pour soup over chicken. Serves 6 to 8.

SPLIT PEA SOUP

½ pound dried split peas
4¾ pints water
1 large onion, chopped
2 stalks celery
sprig of parsley (optional)
ham bones or small shank end of ham
salt and pepper

Soak peas overnight in cold water to cover.

Combine peas, onion, celery, parsley, ham bones or shank, and additional water to make 4¾ pints. Cover and simmer until peas are tender, 3 to 4 hours.

Rub vegetables through a sieve or leave some of the peas whole. Skim off excess fat. Season to taste with salt and pepper.

If wished, thicken soup with a paste made of 3 tablespoons flour and 1½ ounces butter. If necessary, dilute with additional water or milk.

Serve with croûtons or slices of frankfurters if wished. Garnish with julienne strips of cooked carrot. Serves 6 to 8.

Variations of Split Pea Soup

Purée Mongole: Use yellow split peas and at end dilute with strained cooked tomatoes instead of water or milk.

Black Bean Soup: Use dried black beans instead of peas. Garnish each portion with a slice of lemon and a slice of hard-boiled egg.

Soup St. Germain: Add 3 or 4 lettuce leaves with the peas. Serve with croûtons.

CHICKEN BROTH

Use a 3- to 4-pound ready-to-cook boiling chicken. Clean, remove skin and fat and cut in pieces.

Cover with 3¼ pints cold water; heat slowly to boiling point. Skim, then cover and simmer until tender, about 3 hours. Add 1 teaspoon salt after 2 hours of cooking.

Remove fat and strain as for clear soup. Season to taste and serve hot. Makes about 1¾ pints broth.

Note: If desired, 2 tablespoons tapioca, sago, rice or pearl barley soaked overnight, may be cooked with the broth.

The chicken meat, cut from the bones, may be used in salads, creamed, or in other dishes calling for cooked chicken meat.

PETITE MARMITE PARISIENNE

This is a French meat-and-vegetable soup traditionally served in small individual casseroles (marmites). Beef marrow is often added just before serving and the soup may be garnished with toast or bread crusts and grated cheese. There are innumerable versions of this soup. Either the recipe below or the one for Pot-au-Feu are suitable for serving in this way. If individual casseroles are used, after filling them with soup, sprinkle on grated cheese and brown under a grill.

3¼ pints meat stock
6 to 8 chicken wings or pieces of
     chicken
6 cubes of beef (¾-inch)
1 small onion, split and grilled
     with a clove in each half
2 carrots
2 sticks celery
1 white turnip
1 bunch leeks, cut 1-inch long and
     thick as a pencil
⅛ head cabbage
salt and pepper to taste
1 tablespoon Aromat
6 marrow bone rings (sawn ¼-inch
     thick)
French bread crusts, toasted
grated Parmesan cheese
sprinkle of chopped chervil

Put meat stock in stew pot and bring slowly to boil. Add chicken, beef, and onion; simmer about 30 minutes.

Add carrots, celery, turnip, and leeks, and continue to simmer.

Parboil cabbage in salted water; drain and wash in cold water. When rest of vegetables are nearly cooked, add cabbage, correct seasoning and add Aromat.

Remove from heat and place in earthenware pot designed for petite marmite.

You can float marrow bone rings in pot or bring slowly to the boil in a more shallow dish with stock, to be lifted later to individual serving.

Serve with bread crust and cheese. Sprinkle with chervil. Serves 6 to 8.

POT-AU-FEU
(French Boiled Dinner)

Pot-au-Feu means, literally, pot on the fire or stock pot. This meat-and-vegetable soup is considered a French national dish. The meat, although cooked with the soup, may be served as a separate course.

4 pounds lean beef with bone
     (brisket, rump, shin, chuck,
     or round)
4¾ pints cold water
1 tablespoon salt
bouquet garni (see below)
12 ounces chopped mixed
     vegetables
3 large carrots, quartered
6 cabbage wedges
6 leeks, white part only
6 potatoes, whole or quartered

For the bouquet garni, tie in a muslin bag 1 bay leaf, ¼ teaspoon thyme, ½ teaspoon black peppercorns, 3 cloves, 4 sprigs parsley, and a few celery leaves.

For the mixed vegetables, use onion, carrots, white turnips, and parsnips.

Place meat, water, salt, and bouquet garni in a large saucepan. Bring to boiling point, skimming often. Lower heat and simmer until meat is almost tender, 4 hours or longer.

Add chopped vegetables and those cut into larger pieces. Simmer until larger pieces are tender, about 45 minutes.

To serve, remove meat to a hot serving dish and surround with large pieces of vegetables. Keep warm.

Serve the broth with chopped vegetables as a first course. Refrigerate the remainder. Chill and remove fat. Use for stock. Serves 6 or more.

Note: If a fatty piece of meat is used, it is better to make it a day earlier. Chill and remove fat before serving.

QUEBEC PEA SOUP

1 pound dried whole peas
4 quarts cold water
½ pound fat back salt pork or 1 ham
     bone
3 tablespoons chopped onion
salt and pepper
parsley or savory

Wash peas and soak overnight in cold water.

Add salt pork and chopped onion. Bring soup gradually to boiling point. Then simmer slowly about 3 hours or until peas are tender and mealy, which gives a thick, velvety soup.

Remove pork. Before serving, add salt, if needed, pepper, and parsley or savory to taste. Makes 12 servings.

Note: If pea soup is made in a pressure cooker, use the recipe given above, reducing water to 3¼ pints and cooking 1 hour at 10-pound pressure. Remove from heat and allow pressure to drop gradually until it is completely down.

OXTAIL SOUP

2 oxtails
flour
1½ ounces fat
1 teaspoon salt
½ teaspoon black peppercorns
dash of cayenne
1 bay leaf
2 ounces chopped celery
1 medium onion or leek, chopped
1 carrot, diced
4 fluid ounces tomato purée
1 teaspoon Worcestershire sauce
chopped parsley
salt and pepper

Have oxtails cut in pieces and roll them in 2 ounces flour. Brown in 1 ounce fat in a large saucepan.

Add 3¼ pints water, salt, pepper, cayenne, and bay leaf. Bring to the boil and skim. Cover and simmer 3 hours, or until meat is tender.

Strain broth. Cool and remove fat. Separate meat from bones.

To broth and meat, add celery, onion, and carrot. Bring to boil. Reduce heat and simmer 30 minutes.

Add tomato purée and simmer 10 minutes.

Brown 2 tablespoons flour in a frying pan; blend in remaining 1 ounce fat. Add to soup and bring to boil.

Add Worcestershire and parsley. Season to taste. Makes about 1¾ pints.

SCOTCH BROTH

3 ounces pearl barley
3 pounds lamb or mutton
1 ounce butter or margarine
1 ounce each celery, carrots,
     turnips, onions, or leeks,
     diced
salt and pepper
finely chopped parsley

Soak pearl barley for 2 hours or overnight in cold water.

Put meat and cold water to cover in a large saucepan. Bring to boiling point and add barley. Simmer until meat is tender, about 1½ to 2 hours.

Sauté vegetables in butter and add to soup for last half hour. Add salt and pepper to taste. Add more boiling water if soup is too thick. Add parsley just before serving. Serves 6 to 8.

Note: For the meat, use the inexpensive cuts such as breast, neck, or flank. Soaked split peas may be added with the barley. Rice may be substituted for barley. Add with the vegetables.

French Onion Soup

WON TON SOUP

Won ton is a Chinese name for small cases of noodle dough stuffed with various mixtures. Although here they are boiled, then served in a chicken soup, the same won tons are often fried in deep oil until golden brown.

Dough:
8 ounces plain flour
1 teaspoon salt
1 large egg
about 2½ fluid ounces water

Mix and sift flour and salt into mixing bowl. Beat egg slightly and stir into flour.

Add water, a little at a time, mixing until dough is smooth and right for rolling.

Turn out on a lightly floured board and knead until smooth, turning and folding over a few times. Cover and leave to stand 15 to 20 minutes.

Roll out paper-thin and cut into 3-inch squares.

Filling:
1 pound finely minced cooked pork
1 beaten egg
1 tablespoon soy sauce
½ teaspoon salt
¼ teaspoon pepper

Mix pork and remaining ingredients smoothly together. Place 1 teaspoon of mixture in the centre of each square. Fold squares in half diagonally to form triangles and press edges together with a fork.

Drop filled won tons a few at a time into 1½-2 pints boiling salted water and cook until they float to the surface, about 15 minutes. Remove with slotted spoon and drain.

Soup:
2½ pints chicken stock
2 tablespoons chopped spring onions
2 tablespoons soy sauce

Heat stock. Place filled cooked won tons in bowls. Sprinkle with spring onions. Season each bowl with a little soy sauce. Pour on hot stock. Serves 4.
Variations: Cooked minced beef or prawns may be substituted for pork in won ton filling. Two ounces finely chopped celery and ½ pound spinach may be added to chicken stock, in which case cook 1 minute when heating the stock before serving.

FRENCH ONION SOUP

1 ounce butter or margarine
2-3 large onions, thinly sliced (depending upon desired thickness)
2 pints meat stock, canned bouillon, or diluted bouillon cubes
salt and pepper to taste
4 ounces finely grated Cheddar or Parmesan cheese
croûtons or French bread

Melt butter in a saucepan; add onions and sauté until lightly browned, about 5 minutes.

Add stock and simmer, covered, about 20 minutes or until onions are just tender.

Season with salt and pepper. Pour into soup bowls; sprinkle with grated cheese and place croûtons on top. If using French bread, place slices around edge of soup. Makes about 6 8-ounce bowls of soup.

CHICKEN OKRA GUMBO (Creole)

1 ounce butter or margarine
1 3- to 3½-pound chicken
1½ to 2 pounds ham slices
1 onion, chopped
½ red chilli, seeded
1 sprig thyme or parsley, chopped
6 large tomatoes, peeled and chopped
1 pound okra
4¾ pints boiling water
1 bay leaf
salt and cayenne
1¼ pounds rice, boiled

Heat butter. Add the chicken and ham, both of which have been cut up into pieces. Cook, covered, about 10 minutes.

Add onion, red pepper, thyme, and solid part of tomatoes, reserving juice. Simmer a few minutes; stir often.

Wash okra well, remove stems and cut into ½-inch slices. Add to onion mixture and simmer, stirring constantly until brown.

Add the reserved tomato juice, boiling water, and bay leaf. Add salt and cayenne to taste. Simmer about 1 hour. Serve with boiled rice. Serves 8 to 10.

Note: Okra quickly burns, and should be watched and frequently stirred during browning. The traditional New Orleans gumbo is highly seasoned, so add cayenne generously.

The Creoles of the Crescent City make many different gumbos, thickening them with powdered filé (sassafras) or with okra. Chicken gumbo, like the above, is done with either. Okra is often used to thicken crab and shrimp gumbos.

Of the thick soup, that is the gumbo, it has been said:

"It is an original conception, a something *sui generis* in cooking, peculiar to New Orleans alone, and to the manner born."

BLENDER ONION SOUP

2 sliced onions
2 ounces butter or margarine
¾ pint beef or chicken stock
2 small sprigs celery leaves
2 sprigs parsley

Sauté onions in hot fat in a covered frying pan over low heat until golden brown, about 25 minutes. Uncover and sauté 5 minutes longer. Cool and put in blender with other ingredients. Blend about 30 seconds.

Reheat and serve with toast rounds and grated Parmesan cheese. Serves 3.

BLENDER WATERCRESS SOUP

1 bunch watercress
1¼ pints chicken stock
2 tablespoons flour
knob (just under ½ ounce) of butter or margarine
½ teaspoon salt

Put watercress, ½ pint stock, flour, fat, and salt in container. Blend thoroughly, about ½ minute.

Heat remaining stock. Add blended mixture. Bring to boiling point. Strain, if wished. Serves 4.

AVOCADO SOUP

1¾ pints beef or chicken stock (canned or cubes and water may be used)
1 large avocado, peeled
3 tablespoons finely chopped parsley
salt
3 tablespoons sherry

Heat stock to boiling point in top part of double boiler over direct heat. Keep hot over hot water.

Put avocado pulp through sieve.

Stir avocado pulp, chopped parsley, salt to taste, and sherry into hot stock just before serving. Serves 4.
Note: Do not heat soup with avocado pulp over direct heat. The flavour of avocado is spoiled by too much heat.

CLARET BOUILLON

Heat 1 pint beef bouillon to boiling point. Remove from heat and add 6 fluid ounces claret. Serve at once in soup bowls and garnish with chopped parsley.

WHAT TO DO IF SOUP IS TOO SALTY

Add a few slices raw potato to the soup. Let the soup boil until potatoes are done. They will absorb excess salt.

RUSSIAN CABBAGE SOUP

1½ pounds flank steak
4 pints water
1 tablespoon salt
pepper to taste
1¼ pounds canned tomatoes or chopped fresh tomatoes
1 large onion
1 bay leaf (optional)
½ clove garlic, finely chopped (optional)
1 medium cabbage
2 tablespoons sugar
1 tablespoon vinegar or lemon juice

Place meat and water in an 8-pint saucepan. Add salt, pepper, tomatoes, onion, bay leaf, and garlic. Bring to boiling point; reduce heat and simmer 1½ hours.

Shred cabbage coarsely and add. Add sugar, vinegar, and a little more salt to taste. Simmer gently for another 1½ hours. Serve hot. Serves 4 to 6.

Note: If desired, top each portion with a heaped tablespoon of soured cream.

CLEAR TOMATO SOUP WITH CHEESE

2 medium-sized onions, sliced
1½ ounces butter or margarine
20 ounces canned tomatoes
½ teaspoon salt
¼ teaspoon pepper
½ teaspoon oregano
1¼ pints beef bouillon or beef stock
4 ounces Cheddar cheese, grated

Sauté onion in butter until clear. Add tomatoes and cook 5 minutes longer.

Add seasonings and bouillon or stock. Simmer for 10 minutes.

Strain. Serve with grated Cheddar cheese. Serves 4.

Note: If meat stock is not available, prepare bouillon using 1¼ pints of boiling water and 3 beef bouillon cubes.

QUICK CHICKEN GUMBO

1½ ounces butter or margarine
1 onion, finely chopped
½ green pepper, finely chopped
1¾ pints chicken stock or consommé
6 ounces cooked or canned okra
1 15-ounce can tomatoes
about 1½ teaspoons salt
about ¼ teaspoon pepper
6 ounces finely diced cooked or canned chicken

Cook onion and green pepper in melted butter until tender, about 5 minutes.

Add stock and remaining ingredients. Simmer gently about 20 minutes. Serves 6.

CHINESE WATERCRESS SOUP

1 loin pork chop
1½ pints water
¼ pound pig's liver
1 tablespoon soy sauce
½ tablespoon oil
1 bunch watercress, coarsely chopped
1 slightly beaten egg
salt

Shred meaty portion of chop and simmer in water with bone until meat is tender.

While meat is cooking, cut liver into shreds. Add soy sauce and oil to it and leave it to marinate.

Add watercress to pork chop and cook 5 minutes. Add liver in its marinade and bring to the boil. Add egg.

Reduce heat and cook until egg is poached. Add salt to taste. Serves 4.

CANADIAN CHEESE BISQUE

1½ pints clear chicken or veal stock
1 tablespoon finely chopped carrot
1 tablespoon finely chopped celery
2 tablespoons flour
1 ounce butter or margarine
½ pound strong Cheddar cheese, grated
pinch of pepper
½ teaspoon salt
½ teaspoon Worcestershire sauce
1 tablespoon finely chopped green pepper
½ pint beer, heated

To the stock add carrot and celery.

Make a roux by blending the flour, butter, and cheese. Stir into the stock and whip until smooth and blended.

Season with pepper, salt, and Worcestershire sauce.

Lastly add the green pepper, then set on top of stove until ready to serve, whereupon add the beer, heated. Blend together and serve. Serves 6.

EGG AND LEMON SOUP (Greece)

3¼ pints soup stock (below)
4-8 ounces uncooked rice
3 egg yolks
1 tablespoon cornflour
8 fluid ounces milk
juice of ½ lemon
½ ounce butter or margarine, melted
1 teaspoon chopped parsley
salt and pepper to taste

(To make stock: Cut 1½ to 2 pounds of lean lamb in pieces, add 3¼ pints water, 3 teaspoons salt, 4 carrots, 1 onion, 2 potatoes, and 1 celeriac if available. The vegetables should be sliced or cut in pieces before adding. Simmer until meat is tender, then strain off the stock and chill.)

Remove fat from stock, measure, and add water to make 3¼ pints. Heat to boiling point. Wash rice and add to hot stock. Cook until rice is tender (about 30 minutes). Mix egg yolks with cornflour and milk and stir into soup. When the mixture has thickened slightly, remove from heat and stir in lemon juice slowly to avoid curdling. Add butter, chopped parsley, salt, and pepper to soup and serve immediately. Serves 8 to 12.

FAMILY VEGETABLE SOUP

bones and scraps from roast rib or leg of lamb
4 pints cold water
1 medium onion, sliced
2 sticks celery (with leaves), sliced

Place above ingredients in a large saucepan. Simmer 1¼ hours.

4 ounces pearl barley
2 medium white turnips, diced
2 medium potatoes, diced
4 medium carrots, diced
6 ounces sliced celery
1 ounce finely chopped parsley
2 teaspoons salt
¼ teaspoon pepper
1 to 1½ teaspoons Aromat
⅛ teaspoon powdered cloves
⅛ teaspoon thyme

At end of 1¼-hours first simmering add the pearl barley. Continue cooking, at a gentle boil, until barley is swollen and tender, about 1 to 1¼ hours.

Remove bones from stock. If soup is not to be finished for immediate serving, chill stock to congeal fat on top, then remove it. Otherwise skim off fat from stock; bring to boil and add all remaining ingredients.

Simmer gently until vegetables are tender, about 15 minutes.

Meanwhile remove all meat from bones; chop or dice.

soup meat
2 cans condensed tomato soup
1 teaspoon sugar
Aromat, as needed

Add soup meat, tomato soup, and sugar. Heat soup thoroughly. Correct seasoning with Aromat.

Vegetable Soup, Family Style

UKRAINIAN BORSHT

2½ pounds soup meat
soup bones
1 pound beetroots cleaned and
    quartered
1 large onion
1 small can tomato purée
3 cloves garlic, crushed
2 tablespoons lemon juice
2 ounces sugar
2 to 3 tablespoons salt
½ teaspoon paprika
pinch of pepper
3¼ pints water
3 pounds cabbage, quartered

Combine all ingredients, except cabbage, in a large pot. Cover and simmer slowly for 2 hours or until meat is tender.

Put cabbage wedges on top and simmer about another hour until cabbage is done.

Serve with soured cream and plenty of crisp crackers. Makes about 10 servings but most people will want more than one. If there's any left, it's just as delicious reheated for another meal.

MUSHROOM AND BARLEY SOUP
(With Dried Mushrooms)

¼ pound pearl barley
1½ pints bouillon
1 ounce dried mushrooms
1 onion, diced
1 carrot, diced
few sprigs of parsley
few sprigs of dill
2 bay leaves
6 ounces diced cooked soup meat

Cook the pearl barley in water until tender. Combine bouillon, cooked barley, and dried mushrooms, which have been washed and cut into pieces, onion, and carrot.

Wrap the parsley and dill around the bay leaves and tie into a bouquet; add to saucepan.

Simmer gently until vegetables are tender, then remove bouquet. Add the soup meat and serve hot. Serves 4 to 6.

YETCAMEIN

Boil 4½ ounces of fine noodles or vermicelli in 1½ pints rich chicken, beef, or other broth for 4 minutes.

Divide noodles and broth into serving bowls.

Garnish with halves of hard-boiled eggs, sliced cold roast pork or chicken, and sprinkle with chopped parsley or spring onions. Flavour individual portions to taste with soy sauce. Serves 3.

TOMATO-RICE SOUP

Cook 4 ounces rice and 1 ounce diced celery in 1½ pints chicken broth until tender.

Add 1 can (10¾ ounces) condensed tomato soup, 1 red chilli, and salt to taste. Heat and remove pepper pod before serving. Serves 6.

BEEF BROTH

Use 3 to 4 pounds beef (shin, chuck, or neck); cut in pieces and crack bone.

Combine with 1½ pints cold water; bring slowly to a boil, skim, then cover and simmer about 4 hours. Add ½ teaspoon salt after 2 hours of cooking.

Remove fat and strain. Reheat and serve in hot bowls, or chill and serve as a jelly. Makes about ¾ pint broth.

TURKEY BONE SOUP

bones of 1 turkey
3¼ pints cold water
1 carrot, sliced
1 stick celery, chopped
1 teaspoon chopped onion
1 sprig parsley
¼ bay leaf
3 black peppercorns
½ teaspoon salt

Place all ingredients in a large saucepan. Bring to the boil and simmer, covered, 2 hours; strain. Makes about 2½ pints soup.

Miscellaneous Meatless Soups

FRENCH VEGETABLE SOUP
(Potage Julienne)

2 potatoes
2 turnips
2 carrots
2 sticks celery
3 cabbage leaves
2 spring onions
½ pound string beans
6 ounces sweet green peas
2½ pints water
1½ teaspoons salt
1 ounce butter or margarine

Cut the vegetables in thin, matchlike strips; cook all vegetables for 1 hour in boiling water to which you have added salt and butter. Liquid should be reduced to half its volume.

For a *crème julienne*, press the cooked vegetables through a sieve and add 4-8 fluid ounces single cream or rich milk just before serving. Serves 6 to 8.

MUSHROOM STOCK

This is a good way to use up mushroom skins and stalks. Combine with chopped onion, celery pieces and leaves, sliced carrots, and chopped parsley.

Cover with cold water; simmer for 30 minutes.

Strain the stock and when ready to use season with salt, pepper, and sherry.

MEATLESS MINESTRONE
(Italian Vegetable Soup)

6 ounces white haricot beans
    (soaked overnight in cold
    water)
2 pints cold water
¼ teaspoon salt
2 ounces butter or 4 tablespoons oil
1 clove garlic, finely chopped
1 tablespoon onion, finely chopped
2 tablespoons parsley, finely chopped
3 ounces or more celery, finely chopped
¼ teaspoon salt
¼ teaspoon pepper
8 fluid ounces fresh or canned
    tomato pulp
6 ounces coarsely chopped cabbage
2 ounces macaroni, cooked
salt and paprika
1 ounce or more grated Parmesan
    cheese

Drain the beans and add the cold water. Simmer the beans until tender.

Add boiling water, if needed, and ¼ teaspoon salt.

Heat oil or butter in a saucepan. Sauté the garlic, onion, parsley, and celery in the oil or butter until golden brown. Add ¼ teaspoon salt, pepper, tomato pulp, and cabbage. Bring to boiling point and combine with the cooked beans.

Add cooked macaroni. Simmer 15 minutes longer. Add salt and paprika, if needed. Serve in bowls and sprinkle with Parmesan cheese. Makes about 6 bowls of soup.

MEATLESS LENTIL SOUP

12 ounces lentils (soaked overnight in cold water)
1 onion, diced
1 ounce fat
1 carrot, diced
3 sticks celery, diced
1 teaspoon salt
¼ teaspoon pepper
3¼ pints hot water
finely chopped parsley

Drain the lentils and add diced onion browned in fat. Stir over heat 5 minutes.

Add carrot, celery, salt, and pepper and hot water. Simmer slowly until lentils are tender, about 45 minutes.

Rub through a sieve. Bring to the boil and serve hot garnished with parsley. Serves 6 to 8.

Lentil Soup Variations

Lentil and Barley Soup: Add 3 ounces pearl barley with the lentils.

Lentil Soup With Frankfurters: Slice frankfurters into pieces about ½ inch thick. Cook in 1 pint of soup stock. Serve soup with sliced frankfurters.

Lentil Soup With Meat: Add soup bone and 1½ to 2 pounds soup meat. Simmer until meat is tender.

SPAGHETTI, MACARONI, NOODLES, AND OTHER PASTA

PASTA

Pasta is a general term covering all the Italian thin-dough products, such as macaroni, spaghetti, and noodles. Some are usually made fresh, such as cappelletti and ravioli; most are dried, and it is estimated that more than 150 shapes are made commercially. They taste different because they look different, but the dough is the same for all. Many stories tell of the origins of pasta; these include tales of ancient Romans eating pasta with cheese and, on the other hand, of Marco Polo's bringing it home from China. Actually, the Mongols are believed to have introduced it into Europe when they invaded Germany in the 13th century; similar products have been used in Asia for thousands of years.

Pasta dough is made by adding water, with or without salt, to semolina or flour, or a mixture of these. The quality depends almost entirely on the wheat used. Pastas made from durum wheat break with a clean, sharp edge and keep their shape when cooked. Egg pastas, which include noodles and egg vermicelli, are made of a similar dough with the addition of a government-specified amount of whole eggs or egg yolks.

Baked or boiled, served with all sorts of sauces or with plain butter, pasta is an integral part of the Italian diet. It cooks quickly and easily, its bland flavour blends well with other foods, and it needs only a green salad to make a well-rounded meal.

Sauces for Pasta

BUTTER SAUCE FOR SPAGHETTI OR OTHER PASTA

Finely chop a generous handful of fresh parsley picked from the stems. Add the parsley and ¼ pound butter to 1 pound of any cooked and well drained pasta, which has been kept steaming hot.

Toss quickly until the butter is completely melted. Sprinkle with grated Parmesan cheese and toss until the cheese is well blended with the pasta. Serve very hot. Serves 5 to 6.

MARINARA SAUCE FOR SPAGHETTI

2 onions, sliced
1 clove garlic
4 tablespoons olive oil
1¼ pounds cooked or canned
     tomatoes seasoned with basil
2 anchovy fillets, cut into small
     pieces
¼ teaspoon sugar
salt and pepper to taste
¼ teaspoon oregano

Sauté onions and garlic in olive oil for about 5 minutes. Discard garlic and stir the tomatoes into the seasoned oil.

Cook over high heat for 5 minutes; lower the heat and simmer for 1 hour.

Add anchovy fillets, sugar, and salt and pepper to taste. Simmer for 10 minutes longer. Add oregano.

Pour the sauce over 1 pound cooked spaghetti on a hot platter and sprinkle with grated Parmesan cheese. Serves 6.

ITALIAN TOMATO-MEAT SAUCE

1 clove garlic or 1 onion, finely
     chopped
2 fluid ounces olive or salad oil
1 large can tomatoes
6 ounces tomato purée
16 fluid ounces water
1 teaspoon salt
pinch of cayenne pepper
½ pound minced beef
½ pound minced veal
2 tablespoons chopped parsley
4 tablespoons chopped celery tops

Cook garlic or onion in 2 tablespoons oil 5 minutes. Add tomatoes, tomato purée, water, and seasonings, and simmer while meat is cooking.

Cook meat in remaining oil in a heavy frying pan. Stir and cook until redness is gone.

Combine meat and sauce and simmer 2 hours. Add parsley and celery tops and simmer 1 hour more.

Serve sauce on cooked spaghetti and sprinkle with grated Parmesan cheese. Serves 6.

WHITE CLAM SAUCE FOR SPAGHETTI

1 medium onion, chopped
1 clove garlic, finely chopped
1 tablespoon chopped parsley
2 tablespoons olive oil
1 can (10½ ounces) minced clams
½ teaspoon salt
pinch of pepper

Cook onion, garlic, and parsley in hot oil 5 minutes.

Add clams with liquid and seasonings. Simmer 5 minutes. Serves 4.

RED CLAM SAUCE FOR PASTA

2 tablespoons olive oil
2 cloves garlic, finely chopped
1 onion, chopped
2 sticks celery, chopped
1 16-ounce can tomatoes
6 ounces tomato purée
12 fluid ounces water
¼ teaspoon thyme
¼ teaspoon basil
½ teaspoon oregano
salt and pepper
16 fluid ounces canned or bottled
    clam juice
10 ounces finely chopped clams,
    fresh or canned
2 ounces butter
1 ounce chopped parsley

Heat oil in heavy saucepan add garlic, onion, and celery; sauté until onion is golden brown.

Add tomatoes, tomato purée, water, thyme, basil, oregano, and salt and pepper to taste. Bring to boiling point; reduce heat and simmer gently, uncovered, 1 hour. Add clam juice after half an hour.

About 5 minutes before serving add clams and cook gently. Stir in butter and parsley. Correct seasoning to taste with salt and pepper. Heat until the butter melts. Serve with freshly cooked pasta. Makes about 2½ pints.

GREEN SAUCE FOR SPAGHETTI

2½ ounces butter or margarine
1 clove garlic, finely chopped
1½ ounces finely chopped
    parsley
grated Parmesan cheese

Melt butter in saucepan over low heat. Add garlic and cook until lightly browned. Pour over hot cooked spaghetti.

Add parsley and about 2 ounces grated cheese. Toss well and serve with additional cheese. Serves 4.

CHICKEN LIVER SAUCE FOR SPAGHETTI

1 medium onion, finely chopped
2 cloves garlic, finely chopped
4 tablespoons olive or salad oil
20 ounces canned tomatoes
6 ounces tomato purée
¾ pint water
2 teaspoons salt
¼ teaspoon pepper
¼ teaspoon chicken seasoning
1 bay leaf
½ pound chicken livers
1 ounce canned sliced mushrooms

Cook onion and garlic in 2 tablespoons hot oil until yellow. Add tomatoes, tomato paste, water, and seasonings.

Cut livers into small pieces and cook in remaining oil until browned. Add with mushrooms and liquid to tomato mixture.

Simmer uncovered over low heat, 2 hours, stirring occasionally. Serves 6.

PRAWN SAUCE FOR PASTA

2 medium onions, chopped
2 tablespoons olive oil
2 garlic cloves, finely chopped
2 pounds canned Italian-style
    tomatoes
1½ pounds prawns, shelled and cut
    in small pieces
pinch of oregano
salt and pepper

Sauté onion in hot oil in a heavy saucepan until it is just golden brown. Add garlic and cook over very low heat about 3 minutes.

Add tomatoes and cook uncovered over moderately high heat about 12 minutes. Add prawns and oregano. Lower heat and simmer about 5 minutes. Add salt and pepper to taste. Serve with freshly cooked spaghetti or other pasta. Makes about 4 servings.

Other Seafood: Substitute for the prawns any of the following: crabmeat, lobster meat in small pieces; raw oysters in small pieces (whole if very small), raw clams in small pieces and without juice, young squid cut in very thin slices, octopus cut in bite-size pieces. With squid and octopus, it will be necessary to cook about 15 minutes longer.

QUICK TOMATO SOUP SAUCE FOR SPAGHETTI

1 medium onion, finely chopped
1 clove garlic, finely chopped
2 tablespoons salad oil
1 can (10¾ ounces) condensed
    tomato soup
4 fluid ounces water
½ teaspoon salt
dash of pepper
dash of Worcestershire sauce

Cook onion and garlic in hot oil until yellowed.

Add remaining ingredients and bring to boiling point.

Lower heat and simmer 5 minutes. Serves 4.

ITALIAN SAUSAGE SAUCE FOR SPAGHETTI

1 pound hot or mild Italian
    sausage
water
1 medium onion, chopped
1 tablespoon chopped parsley
20 ounces canned tomatoes
2 8-ounce cans tomato sauce
1 bay leaf
salt and pepper

Cut sausage into 1-inch pieces. Cook in a large pan in 2 fluid ounces water until water evaporates and sausage begins to brown, about 10 minutes.

Add onion and parsley, and cook until onion is yellow. Add 2 fluid ounces water and remaining ingredients.

Bring to boiling point and simmer, uncovered, 1¼ hours, stirring occasionally. Serves 6.

ITALIAN SPAGHETTI AND MEAT BALLS

2 medium onions, chopped
2 cloves garlic, finely chopped
2 tablespoons salad oil
1¾ pounds canned tomatoes
½ ounce chopped parsley
pinch of dried basil
½ teaspoon thyme
2½ teaspoons salt
¼ teaspoon pepper
¼ teaspoon dried red pepper
6 ounces tomato purée
meat balls (below)
1 pound spaghetti, cooked
grated Parmesan cheese

Cook onion and garlic in oil 5 minutes.

Add tomatoes and simmer, uncovered, 20 minutes, or until oil comes to surface of sauce.

Add 8 fluid ounces water, parsley, seasonings, and tomato purée; bring to boil.

Add meat balls; cover, and simmer at least 2 hours. Add more seasonings, if wished.

Serve over hot, drained spaghetti; sprinkle with cheese. Serves 6.

Meat Balls:
½ pound minced beef
½ pound minced pork
2 medium onions, finely chopped
1 clove garlic, finely chopped
½ ounce chopped parsley
2 ounces grated Parmesan cheese
2 ounces fine, dry breadcrumbs
1 egg
2 teaspoons salt
½ teaspoon pepper
2 tablespoons salad oil

Combine all ingredients except oil; mix thoroughly. Add a little water if mixture seems dry.

Shape in 24 balls, and brown slowly in hot oil.

CHILLI MEAT SAUCE

3 small onions, chopped
1 pound minced beef
20 ounces canned tomatoes
2 teaspoons chilli powder
2 teaspoons salt

Brown onions and minced beef in a frying pan for a few minutes, stirring with a fork to break meat into bits.

Add remaining ingredients and simmer gently for 45 minutes. Serves 6.

Note: This sauce is excellent on spaghetti, rice, potatoes or frankfurters.

MUSHROOM-TOMATO SAUCE FOR SPAGHETTI

1 pound mushrooms, sliced
1 medium onion, chopped
1 clove garlic, finely chopped
2 fluid ounces olive oil
20 ounces canned tomatoes
¼ teaspoon dried basil
⅛ teaspoon dried red pepper
1 teaspoon salt

Cook mushrooms, onion, and garlic in hot oil in a large saucepan about 10 minutes, or until mushrooms are browned. Stir frequently.

Add remaining ingredients. Bring to boiling point. Lower heat and simmer, uncovered, 1 hour, stirring occasionally. Serves 6.

MEAT SAUCE WITH BLACK OLIVES

1 pound minced lean beef
2 fluid ounces olive oil
1 large onion, chopped
1 clove garlic, finely chopped (optional)
1 ounce chopped green sweet pepper
1¾ pounds canned tomatoes
½ bay leaf
2 teaspoons salt
1 teaspoon chilli powder
½ teaspoon basil
¼ teaspoon black pepper
about 20 stoned black olives

Brown meat in olive oil. Add onion, garlic and green pepper to meat and cook until lightly browned.

Stir in tomatoes and seasonings and simmer 1 hour or longer.

If sauce becomes too thick, add water as needed.

Quarter half of olives and add with remaining olives to sauce a few minutes before serving, heating thoroughly. Serves 6.

EASY SPAGHETTI AND MEAT BALLS

1 medium-sized onion, chopped
1 clove garlic, finely chopped
2 ounces fat
1 teaspoon salt
1 pound minced beef
1 8-ounce can tomato sauce
8 fluid ounces water
¼ teaspoon pepper
2 teaspoons Worcestershire sauce
8 ounces spaghetti, cooked
grated cheese

Lightly brown onion and garlic in hot oil or dripping.

Add salt to meat, mix lightly, form into 8 meat balls. Brown in fat in pan.

Add tomato sauce, water, and seasoning. Cover and simmer 40 minutes.

Pour sauce over hot spaghetti. Sprinkle with cheese. Serves 4.

SPAGHETTI SAUCE A LA MASI

2 ounces butter or margarine
1 medium-sized onion, chopped
1 large clove garlic, finely chopped
1½ pounds minced steak
1 small bunch celery hearts and leaves, finely chopped
2 medium-sized carrots, finely chopped
12 ounces tomato purée
12 fluid ounces water
1¾ pounds canned plum tomatoes
1 tablespoon chopped parsley
1 tablespoon rosemary
1½ tablespoons sweet basil
1½ tablespoons salt
1 teaspoon pepper

Cook onion and garlic in melted butter in a heavy saucepan until onion is golden.

Add minced beef and cook until browned.

Add remaining ingredients in order listed and simmer slowly until sauce has thickened, about 4 hours. Serves 10.

Note: The "secret ingredient" in this as well as other old-time Italian spaghetti sauce recipes is the long, slow simmering.

ITALIAN HERBED TOMATO SAUCE FOR SPAGHETTI

3 medium onions, finely chopped
3 cloves garlic, finely chopped
2 fluid ounces olive oil
1¾ pounds canned tomatoes
6 ounces tomato purée
8 fluid ounces dry red wine
1 teaspoon salt
pepper
1 bay leaf
¼ teaspoon basil
¼ teaspoon thyme or oregano
bouillon or water

Sauté onions and garlic in olive oil until lightly browned, stirring often.

Add remaining ingredients and, to develop a complete blending of flavour, simmer 2 to 3 hours, adding bouillon or water as needed. The sauce should be thick. Strain if wished. Adjust seasonings.

Serve over cooked spaghetti or use as an ingredient in such dishes as aubergine parmigiana, meat loaf, soups, and stews. Makes about 1½ pints.

Herbed Meat Tomato Sauce: Brown ½ pound chopped beef in the fat before adding onions and garlic.

SPAGHETTI WITH GARLIC SAUCE

Sauté 3 finely chopped garlic cloves in 2½ fluid ounces olive oil, salad oil, or butter or margarine, for 3 minutes, stirring constantly so that the garlic does not brown. Pour over hot drained cooked spaghetti (8-ounce packet). Lift with fork to distribute the oil and garlic throughout.

TOMATO MEAT SAUCE WITH WINE FOR SPAGHETTI

2 fluid ounces olive oil or salad oil
2 onions, finely chopped
1 clove garlic
1 pound minced beef
1 pound canned tomatoes or 4 fresh tomatoes, cut in pieces
6 ounces tomato purée
salt and pepper
16 fluid ounces red wine
1 can (7½ ounces) mushrooms

Sauté onion and garlic in oil until lightly browned.

Remove garlic. Add minced beef and cook, stirring frequently until well browned. Add tomatoes and tomato purée, salt and pepper to season. Add 2 fluid ounces red wine.

Allow mixture to simmer in a covered frying pan until thick.

Add another 2 fluid ounces wine, then continue cooking and adding wine as sauce thickens. Simmer at least 1 hour.

Add mushrooms about 10 minutes before the end of the cooking period. Serves 6.

SPAGHETTI WITH SEAFOOD SAUCE

2 ounces butter or margarine
1 medium-sized onion, chopped
1 medium-sized green pepper, chopped
4 ounces chopped celery
2 8-ounce cans tomato sauce
8 fluid ounces water
½ teaspoon marjoram
½ pound prawns, shelled and deveined
½ pound lobster meat
salt and pepper to taste
1 tablespoon salt
4¾ pints boiling water
8 ounces spaghetti

Melt butter; add onion, green pepper, and celery. Sauté until tender, stirring occasionally.

Add tomato sauce, water, and marjoram, and heat to boiling point, stirring occasionally. Simmer, uncovered, for 20 minutes.

Add prawns and lobster. Cook, covered, 10 minutes, or until tender. Season with salt and pepper.

Meanwhile, add 1 tablespoon salt to rapidly boiling water. Gradually add spaghetti so that water continues to boil. Cook, uncovered, stirring occasionally, until tender. Drain in colander. Serve seafood sauce over spaghetti. Serves 4 to 6.

Antipasto Salad, Pizza for
Hors d'oeuvres

ITALIAN
COOKERY

Chicken Cacciatore

Spaghetti with Seafood Sauce

Miscellaneous Pasta Recipes

HOW TO BOIL MACARONI, SPAGHETTI, AND NOODLES

Directions on the packet give definite method and time for the product.

If directions are not available, allow about 3¼ pints rapidly boiling water and 4 teaspoons salt for 10-15 ounces uncooked macaroni, spaghetti, or noodles.

Break long sticks of macaroni or spaghetti into short pieces or use small macaroni, shells, or other small shapes.

Drop into rapidly boiling salted water. Bring back to the boil as quickly as possible and keep at an active boil.

For most products, boil 9 to 12 minutes or to desired degree of softness. Do not overcook.

Drain in a strainer, rinse, and drain again.

If long spaghetti sticks are to be served whole or unbroken, boil by placing one end in the boiling water and gradually coiling in the remainder as the sticks soften.

In most recipes spaghetti, macaroni, and noodles may be used interchangeably. Macaroni and spaghetti double in bulk on cooking.

Serve hot at once or use boiled macaroni, noodles, and spaghetti in other recipes.

A variety of sauces for spaghetti is included in this section. Many of the sauces for fish, meats, poultry and vegetables may also be used.

SPINACH NOODLES (GREEN NOODLES)

3 tablespoons spinach purée, dried
1 beaten egg
¼ teaspoon salt
8 ounces plain flour

Combine spinach purée, egg, and salt. Stir flour in gradually. Knead until smooth. Place dough in a covered dish for ½ hour.

Roll into paper-thin sheets. Spread out on cloths to dry.

Before they are too dry to handle, fold over into a roll and cut into very thin shreds. Toss apart and permit them to dry thoroughly.

Store in a glass jar until ready to use.

BUTTERED NOODLE RING

Boil ½ pound noodles. Rinse with hot water and drain.

Add 2 ounces butter and stir well. Pack in a ring mould.

Unmould on a serving dish. Fill centre and garnish as above. Serves 6.

HOME-MADE NOODLE DOUGH

about 8 ounces plain flour
½ teaspoon salt
2 eggs
2 or 3 teaspoons cold water

Sift flour with salt into a mixing bowl or onto a board. Make a "well" in the centre.

Drop in eggs and combine with a fork, adding spoonfuls of water as necessary to form a ball of dough that is compact but not hard.

Knead dough until as smooth and elastic as possible, about 5 minutes.

Roll out on a lightly floured board. Use the rolling pin from the outer edges toward the centre, turning the board as necessary for easier rolling.

When the dough is rolled evenly thin, let stand 20 minutes in order to dry so that it will not stick together when rolled up.

Roll up lightly and use a very sharp knife to slice ⅛ inch thick, or ¼ inch thick for broad noodles.

Toss the noodles lightly to separate them and spread on lightly floured surface. Let dry thoroughly at room temperature, about 2 hours, then store in covered jars.

Note: Do not try to make noodle dough in damp weather, especially if you are a novice at it.

To Cook Home-made Noodles: Drop by handfuls into boiling soup or boiling, salted water and cook 10 minutes.

Noodle Puffs: Prepare noodle dough and roll out as for noodles; leave to stand until almost dry.

Fold dough in two and cut through both thicknesses with a small floured cutter (thimble size), pressing well so that the edges stick together.

Fry in deep hot fat until brown. They should puff up like small balls. Serve in hot soup.

Noodle Squares: Roll noodle dough out thin as for noodles.

When dry, cut into 3-inch strips.

Place on top of each other and cut in ½-inch strips crosswise.

Pile up again and cut to form ½-inch squares. Dry and store as for noodles.

Cook in boiling soup for 15 minutes.

BUTTERED NOODLES

Boil 8 ounces noodles in 4¾ pints boiling salted water until tender. Drain in a colander and rinse with hot water.

Add 1½ ounces butter, salt and pepper, to taste. Stir gently. Serve as soon as butter melts. Serves 4 to 6.

Noodle Cheese Custard Ring with Vegetables

NOODLE CHEESE CUSTARD RING WITH VEGETABLES

8 ounces fine noodles
8 fluid ounces milk, scalded
3 beaten eggs
6 ounces grated sharp Cheddar cheese
1 teaspoon salt
few grains pepper
½ teaspoon Aromat
1 bunch carrots, sliced and cooked
6 ounces lima beans, cooked
2½ ounces butter or margarine, melted
2 ounces chopped peanuts

Cook noodles in boiling salted water until tender; drain; rinse with cold water.

Pour scalded milk over eggs; add to noodles with cheese and seasonings.

Pour into greased 9-inch ring mould; set mould in a pan of hot water. Bake in slow oven (325°F. Mark 3) 45 minutes.

Unmould on serving plate. Fill centre with hot vegetables.

Melt butter or margarine; add peanuts; cook until butter begins to brown; pour over vegetables and top of noodle ring. Serves 6.

Note: When cooking vegetables, add ¼ teaspoon Aromat to cooking water.

BAKED NOODLE RING

8 ounces noodles
1 ounce dry breadcrumbs
4 ounces grated Cheddar cheese
1 pint milk
4 slightly beaten eggs
1 teaspoon salt
1 teaspoon Worcestershire sauce

Cook noodles in boiling salted water. Drain in colander, rinse, and drain again.

Put alternate layers of noodles, crumbs, and cheese in a greased ring mould.

Combine milk, eggs, salt, and Worcestershire sauce; pour over noodles.

Set in a pan of hot water.

Bake in moderate oven (350°F. Mark 4) about 45 minutes. Serves 6.

Note: Cheese may be omitted and 1½ ounces butter added.

LUKSHEN KUGEL
(Broad Noodle Pudding)

Lukshen Kugel is Yiddish for noodle pudding; this is a traditional broad noodle pudding which has always been a popular dish in many versions among European Jews.

8 ounces broad noodles
1½ ounces fat
3 eggs, separated
1 teaspoon cinnamon
¼ teaspoon nutmeg
4 ounces chopped seedless raisins
4 ounces sugar
pinch of salt

Boil, drain, and rinse noodles. Add fat, well beaten egg yolks, and remaining ingredients, lastly folding in stiffly beaten egg whites.

Mix well and pour into a greased casserole.

Bake in moderate oven (350°F. Mark 4) about 45 minutes, or until browned. Serves 4 to 6.

Lukshen Kugel Variations

With Almonds: Reduce raisins to 3 ounces. Add 1 ounce chopped almonds.

With Apples and Nuts: Use only 1¼ ounces raisins. Add 2½ ounces sliced, peeled apple and 1 ounce chopped nuts.

With Breadcrumbs: Sprinkle with 3 tablespoons fried or dry breadcrumbs before baking.

With Crackling: Omit nutmeg. Use only ¼ teaspoon cinnamon.

Substitute 2 ounces chopped crackling for raisins. Use chicken fat for the fat.

With Prunes or Apricots: Substitute chopped dried prunes or apricots for raisins.

Add 1 tablespoon lemon juice and ¼ teaspoon grated lemon rind.

FRIED NOODLES

1 pound fine egg noodles (vermicelli)
peanut oil for deep frying

Add noodles to boiling salted water and boil 3 to 5 minutes. Drain and dry.

Drop noodles, one quarter of amount at a time, into hot deep fat (375°F.), separating them so they will brown on all sides. Drain on absorbent paper.

FRIED NOODLE RINGS

10 ounces fine dry noodles
1 teaspoon salt
fat for deep frying

Cook noodles in boiling salted water until tender. Drain but do not wash the noodles.

Place in individual ring moulds.

Chill until firm. Remove from ring moulds.

Fry in deep fat heated to 365°F. (or when an inch cube of bread browns in 60 seconds) 2 to 3 minutes. Drain on absorbent paper.

Place in oven to reheat just before serving. Serve with creamed seafood, creamed chicken, or chow mein. Serves 6.

NOODLE SQUARES

Cook noodles in boiling salted water until tender. Drain and place in a greased baking dish to about 1 inch thickness.

Pour a mixture of 1 beaten egg and a cup of milk over noodles. Season with salt and bake in a slow oven (325°F. Mark 3) until firm. Allow to stand a while before cutting into squares.

BAKED SOUR CREAM NOODLE RING

4 ounces broad noodles
8 fluid ounces sour cream
1 slightly beaten egg
8 ounces cottage cheese
½ teaspoon salt
dash of pepper
2 ounces butter or margarine, melted

Cook, drain, and rinse noodles. Combine with remaining ingredients and turn into a buttered ring mould.

Bake in slow oven (300°F. Mark 2) about 1½ hours.

Unmould and fill centre with creamed mushrooms, or fish, as wished. Serves 4.

POPPY SEED NOODLES

8 ounces broad noodles
3 tablespoons poppy seeds
2 ounces blanched, browned almonds, chopped
½ ounce butter or margarine, melted
1 teaspoon lemon juice
½ teaspoon salt
pinch of white pepper
sprig parsley, finely chopped

Boil, drain, and rinse noodles.

Blend poppy seeds and almonds with butter. Add remaining ingredients. Mix lightly with hot noodles. Serves 6.

NOODLE BASKETS

Noodle baskets are used to serve creamed foods and are available in some food delicatessens. To make them at home 2 small strainers are needed, one about 3 inches in diameter and another about ⅜-inch smaller to fit into the larger one and allowing space for the swelling of the noodles.

Prepare noodle dough (see Index) and when it is dry cut into ¼-inch strips.

Dip the strainers in hot fat to keep from sticking, then line with noodle strips in criss-cross fashion. Cut off any ragged edges and place the smaller strainer over the noodle basket. Fry in deep hot fat (375°F. Mark 5) until lightly browned. Remove basket from strainer and continue with others. Use immediately or let cool and reheat them briefly, without the strainers, in hot fat before using.

SPEEDY GREEN NOODLES DE LUXE

½ pound green noodles
12 ounces canned spaghetti meat sauce
1 teaspoon Worcestershire sauce
1 clove garlic
2 tablespoons red wine
grated Parmesan cheese

Cook noodles in 3¼ pints boiling salted water (½ tablespoon salt) until tender, about 10 to 12 minutes. Drain.

Heat spaghetti sauce with Worcestershire sauce, garlic, and red wine.

Pile noodles on garlic-rubbed plates. Pour sauce in centre. Sprinkle liberally with cheese. Serves 4.

MACARONI WITH CHEESE AND OLIVE SAUCE

½ pound uncooked macaroni
2 ounces butter or margarine
3 tablespoons flour
1 pint milk
½ pound grated Cheddar cheese
1 teaspoon salt
pinch of pepper
2-4 ounces sliced, stuffed green olives

Cook macaroni in boiling salted water until tender. Drain and run hot water through macaroni.

Melt butter; add flour and blend until smooth. Add milk and cook in top of double boiler until sauce thickens, stirring constantly.

Reserve a little cheese to garnish top and add remaining cheese with seasonings to white sauce. Stir until cheese is melted. Add sliced olives.

Arrange macaroni on warm serving plate. Pour sauce over it. Garnish top with grated cheese.

Serve with grilled tomatoes on buttered toast rounds. Serves 6.

Macaroni with Cheese and Olive Sauce

KREPLACH

Kreplach is a Yiddish term for noodle dough cut into small squares; filled with meat or cheese, and other fillings; folded into triangular turnovers; cooked, and served in soups or sometimes fried. It is a traditional Jewish dish.

1 recipe home-made noodle dough filling (below)

Roll out noodle dough very thinly on a lightly floured board. Cut into 3-inch squares.

Place a heaped teaspoon of the filling on each square. Moisten edges lightly with water, and fold over diagonally to form triangles. Press edges firmly together with a fork. These may be wrapped and frozen.

To cook, drop the kreplach one at a time into a large saucepan of rapidly boiling water to which $\frac{1}{2}$ teaspoon salt has been added. Cover pan and cook 20 minutes. Remove with a draining spoon.

Serve in clear soup or serve meat or kashe kreplach with meat gravy, cheese kreplach with soured cream. Makes 12 to 18 3-inch kreplach.

Note: If bite-size $1\frac{1}{2}$-inch kreplach are made, cook only 10 to 15 minutes.

Chicken Filling for Kreplach:
8 ounces finely chopped cooked chicken
1 slightly beaten egg
1 tablespoon finely chopped parsley
1 teaspoon onion juice
salt and pepper to taste

Mix together and use as filling for kreplach.

Variations: Other cooked leftover meat may be substituted for chicken. Crackling (greben) may be combined with leftover chicken, seasoned to taste, and used as a filling.

Cheese Filling for Kreplach:
1 pound dry cottage cheese
1 slightly beaten egg
1 tablespoon sugar
$\frac{1}{4}$ teaspoon cinnamon
$\frac{1}{4}$ teaspoon salt
1 ounce seedless raisins (optional)

Blend ingredients together.

Chicken Liver and Egg Filling for Kreplach:

Grill chicken livers under moderate heat until tender. Combine with as many shelled hard-boiled eggs as wanted and chop together in wooden chopping bowl or put through medium blade of mincer.

Season with salt and pepper, poultry seasoning, and finely chopped parsley. Blend into a smooth mixture before using.

CAPPELLETTI

Moist stuffed pasta that takes its name from a resemblance to little hats. Cappelletti are served with sauce or in soups.

Stuffing:
1 chicken breast, raw
1 ounce butter or margarine
1 pound Ricotta cheese
1 whole egg, unbeaten
1 egg yolk, unbeaten
pinch of nutmeg
salt and pepper to taste
3 tablespoons grated Parmesan cheese

Pasta (Dough):
1 pound plain flour
3 slightly beaten eggs
$\frac{1}{2}$ ounce butter or margarine
lukewarm water

To prepare stuffing, brown chicken breast in 1 ounce butter.

Chop meat very finely and to it add a mixture of the Ricotta cheese, 1 unbeaten egg, 1 unbeaten egg yolk, nutmeg, salt, and pepper to taste. Add Parmesan cheese and mix well.

To make dough, sift flour onto centre of a board. Stir into its centre the 3 slightly beaten eggs. Add $\frac{1}{2}$ ounce butter and enough lukewarm water (less than 8 fluid ounces) to form a firm dough. Knead well until smooth and manageable.

Cut dough in half and roll into thin sheets on a lightly floured board. Cut into rounds with a biscuit cutter.

To prepare the cappelletti, place 1 teaspoon stuffing in the centre of each round. Fold one side over to form a little hat. Press edges gently but firmly to prevent filling from falling out.

When all the ingredients are used, drop the cappelletti into 8-9 pints of rapidly boiling salted water. Cook about 5 minutes or until dough is tender.

Drain and put on a hot serving dish. Serve with any plain Italian-style tomato sauce and grated Parmesan cheese.

These cappelletti may also be boiled in chicken broth and served in the soup.

MACARONI CAMP-STYLE

8 ounces macaroni
$\frac{1}{2}$ pound grated Cheddar cheese
2 fluid ounces tomato ketchup or sauce
3 tablespoons Worcestershire sauce
salt and pepper to taste
6 ounces hot melted butter or margarine

Cook macaroni in boiling salted water until tender. Drain and spread out on a hot large platter.

Sprinkle with cheese, tomato ketchup or sauce, and Worcestershire sauce. Add salt and pepper to taste.

Pour over the hot melted butter and toss with 2 forks until sauce is creamy. Serve at once. Serves 6.

RAVIOLI

Ravioli is an Italian speciality. Small pillows of thinly rolled noodle dough are filled with chopped spinach, meat, cheese, or other forcemeat and cooked in stock or boiling salted water. They are served with butter and cheese or with a sauce and may also be baked with cheese and tomato sauce.

6 ounces plain flour
1 egg yolk
water to make a stiff dough
1 ounce fine dry breadcrumbs
1 egg
3 ounces chopped cooked spinach
chicken stock
salt and pepper
2 ounces grated Parmesan cheese
4 tablespoons tomato purée
12 fluid ounces water
2 tablespoons flour

Sift flour onto a board. Make a depression in the centre and drop in the egg yolk. Moisten with enough warm water to make a stiff dough.

Knead until the mixture is smooth, cover, and leave to stand 10 minutes.

Roll paper-thin and cut with a pastry cutter into strips 3 inches wide and as long as the pastry.

Mix crumbs, egg, and spinach. Moisten with stock and season with salt and pepper.

Place spoonfuls of the spinach mixture on the lower half of each strip about 2 inches apart. Fold the upper half of the strip over the lower part. Press pastry together along the edges and between mounds of filling. Cut apart with pastry cutter.

Drop into boiling stock and cook 10 minutes.

Remove to serving dish, placing ravioli in layers with the cheese and covering with tomato sauce made by cooking the tomato purée, water, and flour together until smooth and thickened, or serve any tomato spaghetti sauce. Serves 4 to 6.

Macaroni Camp-Style

CHEESE NOODLE RING

8 ounces fine noodles
8 fluid ounces milk, scalded
3 eggs, beaten
6 ounces grated Cheddar cheese
1 teaspoon salt
few grains pepper
½ teaspoon Aromat
1 bunch carrots, sliced and cooked
6 ounces lima beans, cooked
2½ ounces butter or margarine
2 ounces chopped unsalted peanuts

Cook noodles in boiling salted water until tender; drain; rinse with cold water. Pour scalded milk over eggs; add to noodles with cheese and seasonings. Pour into greased 9-inch ring mould; set in pan of hot water. Bake in slow oven (325°F. Mark 3) until firm, 45 minutes.

Unmould on serving plate. Fill centre with hot carrots and lima beans.

Melt butter; add peanuts; cook until butter begins to brown; pour over vegetables and top of noodle ring. Serves 6.

ARGENTINE TAGLIARINI AND BEEF

2 fluid ounces olive oil
1 large onion, chopped
1½ pounds steak, cut into 2-inch strips
½ green pepper, cut in small strips
4 tablespoons fresh mushrooms, chopped
8 fluid ounces claret or other dry red wine
½ pound hot boiled tagliarini (see below)
grated cheese (optional)

Heat oil in a frying pan. Add onion and cook until clear only. Add steak and green pepper and cook until steak is brown all over.

Add mushrooms and wine. Simmer, covered, until beef is tender.

Strain this sauce over tagliarini; mix well, adding grated cheese if desired. Spread on a hot serving dish; put beef on top; serve. Serves 6.

Note: Tagliarini are a very fine strip-type Italian paste, a third the width of ordinary noodle strips. They may be bought in well-stocked supermarkets or in Italian grocers or delicatessens.

CHILLI SPAGHETTI OR MACARONI

1 ounce butter or margarine
3 tablespoons chopped onion
1 ounce diced green pepper
½ pound lean minced beef
20 ounces canned tomatoes
6 ounces tomato purée
1 teaspoon salt
2 teaspoons chilli powder
1 15-ounce can kidney beans, drained
½ pound spaghetti or macaroni, cooked

Cook onion and green pepper until tender in melted butter in a frying pan.

Add beef and cook until lightly browned.

Add tomatoes, tomato purée, salt, and chilli powder. Simmer over low heat, stirring occasionally, for 20 minutes.

Add kidney beans to chilli mixture; heat thoroughly and serve over cooked, drained spaghetti or macaroni. Serves 6.

CREAMY MACARONI PATTIES

2 ounces margarine
5 tablespoons flour
8 fluid ounces milk
1 teaspoon salt
½ pound grated cheese
4 ounces macaroni, cooked
1 tablespoon chopped parsley
1 teaspoon scraped onion
fine dry breadcrumbs
1 egg
1 tablespoon water
4 tablespoons fat

Melt margarine. Blend in flour. Add milk and salt. Stir until smooth and thickened.

Remove from heat. Add grated cheese and stir until cheese is melted.

Add macaroni, cut into small pieces, parsley, and onion.

Turn into a well-greased baking tin. Chill until firm.

Cut into patties. Dip in fine crumbs, then in beaten egg which has been diluted with water, then again in crumbs.

Fry in hot fat until brown. Serve with tomato sauce. Serves 5.

Macaroni Croquettes: Prepare above recipe. Shape into croquettes when chilled.

Fry in deep fat (375°F.) until browned. Drain on absorbent paper. Serve with cheese sauce.

SPAGHETTI GABRIELE

4 fluid ounces olive oil
4 ounces butter or margarine
3 cloves garlic, finely chopped
1 onion, sliced
2 ounces chopped celery
2 ounces chopped parsley
8 ounces canned mushrooms, drained
½ pound coarsely minced beef
½ pound coarsely minced pork
½ pound coarsely minced veal
1¼ pounds canned tomatoes
6 ounces tomato purée
½ teaspoon ground allspice
½ teaspoon black pepper
1 tablespoon salt
1 teaspoon thyme
1½ pounds spaghetti, cooked
2 teaspoons grated Parmesan cheese
1 tablespoon chopped parsley

Heat olive oil and melt 2 ounces butter or margarine in a large heavy frying pan. Add garlic, onions, celery, 2 ounces parsley, mushrooms, and meat. Sauté until meat is lightly browned.

Add tomatoes and tomato purée; cook over low heat, stirring occasionally, 1 hour.

Add allspice, pepper, 1 tablespoon salt, and thyme; mix thoroughly.

Place hot cooked spaghetti in saucepan; add 2 ounces butter or margarine, cheese, and 1 tablespoon parsley. Cover; leave to stand 2 to 3 minutes.

Add small amount of sauce to spaghetti mixture; blend well. Serve spaghetti with remaining sauce. Serves 8 to 10.

TURKEY SPAGHETTI SUPREME

2 ounces butter or margarine
1 ounce chopped green pepper
1 ounce plain flour
16 fluid ounces turkey broth or chicken bouillon
8 fluid ounces milk
1 teaspoon salt
pinch of pepper
3 tablespoons chopped canned pimiento
8 ounces spaghetti, cooked
12 ounces diced boned cooked turkey or chicken
3 ounces canned mushrooms, drained
grated Parmesan cheese

Melt butter or margarine over low heat and cook green pepper until tender.

Blend in flour. Add turkey or chicken broth and milk. Cook, stirring constantly, until mixture thickens. Season with 1 teaspoon salt and pepper. Add pimiento.

Add half the sauce to drained spaghetti and mix well. Turn onto a large serving dish.

Add turkey or chicken and mushrooms to remaining sauce and heat.

Pour turkey or chicken mixture into centre of spaghetti on serving dish; sprinkle with Parmesan cheese.

Serves 4 to 6.

Oven Main Dishes

MANICOTTI

Manicotti is an Italian word which means literally "little muffs". These may be thin rectangles or rounds of noodle dough stuffed with meat or cheese filling, rolled up, and baked in a sauce, but more commonly manicotti refers to a pipelike macaroni about 1 inch across similarly filled and baked. Tufoli, a similarly shaped macaroni product, may be used instead of manicotti.

Sauce:
- 1 pound minced beef
- 2 fluid ounces olive or salad oil
- 1 small onion, chopped
- 1 large clove garlic, finely chopped
- 12 ounces tomato purée
- 16 fluid ounces water
- 1½ teaspoons salt
- dash of pepper
- 2 tablespoons chopped parsley
- 4 teaspoons basil
- 1 teaspoon aniseed (optional)

Filling:
- ¾ pound fresh ricotta cheese or ¾ pound cream-style cottage cheese
- 1½ ounces grated Parmesan cheese
- 1 beaten egg
- 2 tablespoons chopped parsley
- ¼ teaspoon salt
- dash of pepper
- ½ pound manicotti shells
- additional grated Parmesan cheese

Sauce: Sauté meat in hot oil until lightly browned. Add remaining sauce ingredients (next 9 ingredients). Simmer uncovered, stirring occasionally, about 45 minutes.

Filling: Combine next 6 ingredients. Mix lightly but thoroughly.

Cook manicotti in a large quanity of boiling salted water until half done, about 10 minutes. Drain and rinse in cold water. Return to pot and toss with small amount of melted butter to prevent sticking.

Using a teaspoon or piping bag with a plain nozzle, stuff manicotti with filling.

Pour half the tomato-meat sauce into a baking tin. Arrange manicotti in a layer, overlapping slightly. Cover with remaining sauce. Sprinkle with grated cheese.

Bake in moderate oven (350°F. Mark 4) 25 to 30 minutes. Serves 6 to 8.

MACARONI-BEEF CASSEROLE
- 1 pound lean minced beef
- 1 small onion, chopped
- 2 tablespoons cooking oil
- 2 fluid ounces dry white wine
- 1 8-ounce can tomato sauce
- 1 teaspoon salt
- ¼ teaspoon cinnamon
- ¾ ounce margarine or butter
- 1½ tablespoons flour
- 12 fluid ounces milk
- 1 egg, well beaten
- 1 tablespoon fresh breadcrumbs
- ½ pound macaroni, cooked just tender, drained
- 3 ounces grated Parmesan cheese

Cook beef and onions in oil until meat is lightly browned. Add wine, tomato sauce, salt, and cinnamon. Simmer 10 minutes.

Melt butter in saucepan; add flour and stir until blended. Slowly add milk and cook, stirring until smooth and thickened.

Add egg and breadcrumbs to meat mixture.

Put half of macaroni into a 4-pint greased baking dish. Sprinkle macaroni with ⅓ of the grated Parmesan cheese and spread with meat mixture. Add remaining macaroni and sprinkle with another ⅓ grated Parmesan. Pour white sauce over all and sprinkle with remaining cheese. Bake in hot oven (400°F. Mark 6) 30 minutes. Serves 6 to 8.

MACARONI PARMIGIANA
- 2 cloves garlic, finely chopped
- 2 tablespoons olive oil
- 1 8-ounce can tomato sauce
- 20 ounces canned tomatoes
- 1 small onion, finely chopped
- 1½ teaspoons salt
- ¼ teaspoon pepper
- 1½ teaspoons oregano
- 8 ounces macaroni
- 1 pound cottage cheese
- ½ pound Mozzarella or Gruyère cheese, thinly sliced
- 2 ounces grated Parmesan cheese

Brown garlic in oil. Stir in tomato sauce, tomatoes, onion, salt, pepper, and oregano.

Cover and simmer until thickened, about 15 to 20 minutes.

Cook macaroni until tender. Drain. Fill a 4½-pint casserole with alternate layers of macaroni, cottage cheese, Mozzarella or Gruyère cheese, tomato mixture, and Parmesan cheese.

Bake in moderate oven (375°F. Mark 5) 20 to 25 minutes. Serves 6 to 8.

Macaroni-Beef Casserole

LASAGNE WITH BEEF AND SAUSAGE

Lasagne are a type of very broad noodle. They are prepared like macaroni. The dish that is popularly called lasagne should be more specifically called lasagne imbottite: stuffed noodles, made by layering cooked noodles in a baking dish with tomato sauce, meat, and cheese and cooking it in the oven. The recipe that follows is a popular version of this dish. It is sometimes called lasagna, which is the singular form of the word.

- ½ pound minced beef
- ½ pound sausage meat
- 1 clove garlic, crushed
- 1 small onion, chopped
- 2 ounces chopped celery
- 12 ounces tomato purée
- 1¼ pints hot water
- 2 teaspoons sugar
- 2 teaspoons salt
- ½ teaspoon sage
- 1 pound lasagne noodles, cooked
- ½ pound ricotta cheese
- ½ pound Mozzarella cheese, thinly sliced

Cook meat until crumbly. Add garlic, onion, and celery; cook until tender.

Stir in tomato purée, water, and seasonings. Blend well. Cover and simmer 50 minutes. Drain off extra fat.

Arrange alternate layers of cooked noodles, sauce, and cheese in greased 13 × 9 × 2-inch baking tin, ending with Mozzarella.

Bake in moderate oven (375°F. Mark 5) 25 to 30 minutes, or until cheese melts.

Leave to stand out of oven 5 minutes. Cut into squares. Serves 6 to 8.

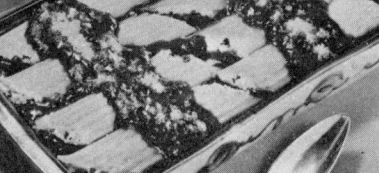

Manicotti

Lasagne with Beef and Sausage

MACARONI-VEGETABLE-MEAT CASSEROLE
(Master Recipe)

8 ounces broken macaroni
2½ pints boiling water
2½ teaspoons salt
½ ounce butter or margarine
1 tablespoon flour
¼ teaspoon pepper
6 fluid ounces vegetable liquid
6 fluid ounces evaporated milk
4 ounces grated Cheddar cheese
½ pound minced cooked meat (see below)
4 ounces drained vegetable, freshly cooked or canned (see below)
2 ounces dry breadcrumbs or crushed cornflakes
1 ounce butter or margarine, melted

Cook macaroni until tender in boiling salted water, using 1½ teaspoons salt. Drain and rinse with hot water.

Melt butter; blend in flour, 1 teaspoon salt, and pepper. Stir in vegetable liquid slowly. Stir and boil 2 minutes. Stir in milk and heat well. Remove from heat.

Add drained macaroni, grated cheese, meat, and vegetable; pour into 3½-pint greased casserole.

Sprinkle top with mixture of breadcrumbs or cornflakes and melted butter.

Bake in moderate oven (375°F. Mark 5) until crumbs are brown (10 minutes). Serves 6.

Variations: Substitute ½ pound noodles or spaghetti for macaroni.

Use ham, corned beef, bologna sausage, frankfurters, or tongue.

Use carrots, green beans, peas, or celery.

LASAGNE AL FORNO
(Italian Baked Cheese and Noodles)

½ pound lasagne (very broad noodles)
3 tablespoons finely chopped green pepper
1 large onion, chopped
2 fluid ounces olive oil
1 8-ounce can tomato sauce
½ teaspoon sugar
salt and pepper
¾ pound Mozzarella cheese
2 ounces grated Parmesan cheese

Cook noodles in boiling salted water and drain.

Brown green pepper and onion in hot oil and add tomato sauce and seasonings.

Place alternate layers of drained noodles and thin slices of Mozzarella cheese in a casserole, sprinkling each layer with Parmesan cheese and sauce.

Sprinkle top with Parmesan cheese.

Bake in moderate oven (250°F. Mark 4) until cheese is well browned, about 15 minutes. Serves 4 to 6.

NOODLE CASSEROLE SUPREME

8 ounces wide noodles
1½ ounces butter or margarine
1 large onion, chopped
1 can (15 ounces) whole tomatoes
1 tablespoons Worcestershire sauce
2 tablespoons sugar
8 ounces cottage cheese
8 fluid ounces soured cream
2 tablespoons finely cut chives
1 ounce grated Parmesan cheese

Cook noodles as directed on packet; put in greased 3½-pint casserole.

Melt butter in a saucepan, add onion and cook over medium heat until tender.

Stir in tomatoes, Worcestershire sauce, and sugar; bring to boil.

Remove from heat and stir in cottage cheese, soured cream, and chives. Pour over noodles in casserole; sprinkle with Parmesan cheese.

Bake in moderate oven (350°F. Mark 4) for 25 to 30 minutes. Serves 8.

SPAGHETTI AND TOMATO CASSEROLE

8 ounces thin spaghetti
1 green pepper, chopped
1 small onion, finely chopped
2 ounces butter or margarine
20 ounces canned tomatoes
6 ounces tomato purée
6 fluid ounces water
1 teaspoon salt
pinch of pepper
½ pound sharp processed cheese, grated
2 ounces sliced black olives

Cook spaghetti in boiling salted water until tender. Drain thoroughly.

Sauté green pepper and onion in butter 5 minutes. Add tomatoes, tomato purée, water, seasonings, and half of cheese. Blend thoroughly.

Place in greased casserole. Sprinkle with remaining cheese. Bake in moderate oven (350°F. Mark 4) 30 minutes. Garnish with olives. Serves 6.

CHESTERFIELD PIE
(Old-Time Southern Hunt Speciality)

4 ounces macaroni, cooked
4 ounces grated Cheddar cheese
1½ ounces fresh breadcrumbs
3 tablespoons finely chopped green pepper
3 tablespoons finely chopped onion
2 ounces butter or margarine
8 fluid ounces milk
1 teaspoon salt
3 eggs, separated
1 pound creamed chicken
1 tablespoon finely chopped parsley

Cook macaroni the previous day or the morning you plan to serve the dish. Drain, and while hot, add cheese, crumbs, pepper, onion, butter, milk, and salt.

Cool. Place, covered, in refrigerator until ready to bake.

Then add beaten egg yolks. Fold in stiffly beaten egg whites. Pour into well greased 8-inch ring mould.

Place mould in a shallow pan of water in slow oven (300°F. Mark 2) about 20 minutes.

Remove from water and continue baking 10 to 15 minutes longer or until skewer inserted in centre comes out clean.

Unmould onto a serving dish and fill centre of ring with creamed chicken. Garnish with parsley. Serves 6 to 8.

SALAMI-SPAGHETTI DINNER

6 ounces spaghetti
2 ounces margarine
1 ounce flour
1¼ teaspoons salt
pinch of pepper
½ teaspoon dry mustard
1 teaspoon Worcestershire sauce
16 fluid ounces milk
1 tablespoon finely chopped onion
3 ounces grated Cheddar cheese
6 ounces diced salami
2 ounces slivered sweet pickle

Cook spaghetti in boiling salted water until tender. Drain and rinse.

Melt margarine in saucepan. Stir in flour, salt, pepper, mustard, and Worcestershire sauce. Mix until smooth.

Gradually add milk, stirring constantly until sauce thickens and comes to the boil.

Fold in onion, cheese, salami, and pickle. Fold into spaghetti.

Pour into well-greased 3½-pint baking dish or into 6 individual dishes. Bake in moderate oven (350°F. Mark 4) 25 minutes.

If wished, garnish with grated cheese and a cluster of salami "flowers". Make the "flowers" by folding thin slices of salami. Fasten with wooden cocktail sticks and insert strips of cheese and pickle in the centre. Serves 6.

Salami-Spaghetti Dinner

Baked Macaroni and Cheese

BAKED MACARONI AND CHEESE
(Master Recipe)

2 teaspoons grated onion
½ pound grated cheese
16 fluid ounces medium white sauce
8 ounces macaroni
2 ounces buttered crumbs
paprika

Add onion and half the grated cheese to white sauce. Blend well.

Cook macaroni, drain, and rinse Place in alternate layers with sauce in buttered casserole.

Sprinkle with crumbs, remaining cheese, and paprika.

Bake uncovered in moderate oven (375°F. Mark 5) about 25 minutes, or until crumbs are browned. Serves 6 to 8.

BAKED MACARONI VARIATIONS

Baked Macaroni with Ham or Corned Beef: Follow master recipe for baked macaroni and cheese.

Before baking, add 6 ounces chopped cooked ham or corned beef. If cheese is omitted, dot meat with butter.

Baked Macaroni with Sausage: Follow master recipe for baked macaroni and cheese.

Substitute 8-10 ounces chopped cooked sausage for the cheese.

Baked Macaroni and Hard-Boiled Eggs: Alternate layers of cooked macaroni and slices of hard-boiled egg.

Cover with medium white sauce and bake.

Baked Macaroni with Tomato Sauce: Omit onion and paprika in master recipe.

Substitute tomato sauce for white sauce.

Baked Italian Macaroni: Add sautéed finely chopped onion and garlic to tomato sauce.

Pour it over cooked macaroni and sprinkle Parmesan cheese on top. Bake.

Baked Spanish Macaroni: Add 1 ounce chopped green pepper which has been fried until soft in 1 tablespoon oil, and 1 tablespoon each of finely chopped onion, celery, and pimiento to 16 fluid ounces tomato sauce.

Pour it over cooked macaroni and bake.

NOODLES ROMANOFF

8 ounces cottage cheese
8 fluid ounces soured cream
6 ounces noodles, cooked
1 teaspoon finely chopped onion
1 small clove garlic, finely chopped
1 teaspoon Worcestershire sauce
½ teaspoon salt
1 ounce grated cheese

Mix together gently the cottage cheese, soured cream, hot, cooked noodles. Add onion, garlic, and seasonings.

Place in greased 3½-pint casserole. Sprinkle with cheese.

Bake in moderate oven (350°F. Mark 4) 40 minutes. Serve hot. Serves 6.

MACARONI BAKED WITH SOURED CREAM

6 ounces macaroni
3 tablespoons melted butter or margarine
8 fluid ounces soured cream
2 ounces grated cheese

Cook macaroni in boiling salted water. Drain and toss with melted butter.

Turn into greased baking dish. Make a well in the centre. Pour in soured cream. Sprinkle grated cheese over all.

Bake in hot oven (400°F. Mark 6) until top is brown. Serves 4.

CANELLONI ALLA GRUCCI

Canelloni is an Italian term for pasta stuffed with meat and baked with tomato or cheese sauce.

5½ ounces flour
1 egg plus 1 egg yolk
pinch of salt

Blend flour, egg and egg yolk, and salt to make a smooth paste. Roll the dough out very thinly and cut into 3½-inch squares. Drop the squares into boiling salted water and cook for 8 minutes, or until tender but somewhat firm. Drain and place them on a cloth.

Filling:
6 chicken livers
1 onion, finely chopped
1 clove garlic, finely chopped
1½ ounces butter
½ pound cubed cooked chicken or veal
¼ teaspoon thyme
salt and pepper
2 eggs, slightly beaten

Topping:
12 fluid ounces tomato sauce, slightly heated
grated Parmesan cheese

Pan-fry chicken livers with onion and garlic in butter about 5 minutes, or until delicately coloured. Put this mixture and the cooked meat through

a mincer, using the fine blade; season with thyme and salt and pepper to taste. Blend with the eggs.

Put a little of this filling on each noodle square and roll each one to make a tube.

Arrange the canelloni, side by side, in a large shallow baking dish. Cover with heated tomato sauce; sprinkle generously with grated cheese. Brown under grill. Serves 5 to 6.

MACARONI-TOMATO-GREEN PEPPER CASSEROLE

8 ounces macaroni
3 tablespoons chopped onion
1 ounce butter or margarine
20 ounces canned tomatoes
1 teaspoon salt
3 medium green peppers
2 ounces grated Cheddar cheese

Cook macaroni in boiling salted water until tender. Drain thoroughly.

Cook onion in butter until soft and yellow. Add tomatoes and simmer about 5 minutes.

Add drained macaroni and salt. Mix well and simmer 10 minutes longer.

Cut peppers into quarters. Wash, remove white membranes and boil about 5 minutes in salted water (1 teaspoon salt to 1½ pints water).

Drain peppers and arrange in bottom of greased casserole. Fill casserole with macaroni-tomato mixture. Sprinkle top with grated cheese.

Bake in hot oven (400°F. Mark 6) until cheese is nicely browned, about 15 minutes. Serves 5 to 6.

ITALIAN SPAGHETTI CASSEROLE

2 tablespoons chopped onion
1 clove garlic, finely chopped
4 tablespoons chopped green pepper
2 fluid ounces salad oil
¼ pound minced beef
¼ pound minced pork
20 ounces canned tomatoes
6 ounces tomato purée
2 ounces sliced mushrooms
1 teaspoon sugar
about 1 teaspoon salt
dash of pepper
½ teaspoon chilli powder
4 fluid ounces red wine (claret or burgundy)
3 ounces spaghetti, cooked
4 ounces grated Parmesan cheese

Lightly brown onion, garlic, and green pepper in hot oil. Add beef and pork; brown lightly.

Add tomatoes, tomato purée, mushrooms, and seasonings. Cover and simmer 30 minutes.

Add wine, spaghetti and cheese. Turn into casserole. Bake (325°F. Mark 3) 30 minutes. Serves 6.

Cheese Macaroni with Chopped Eggs

MACARONI-FRANKFURTER LOAF

8 ounces macaroni
1½ ounces margarine
3 tablespoons soya flour or 2 table-
    spoons plain flour
2 teaspoons salt
8 fluid ounces milk
2 well beaten eggs
4 ounces grated Cheddar cheese
2 teaspoons prepared mustard or 1
    teaspoon dry mustard
6 to 8 large frankfurters

Cook macaroni in boiling salted water until tender; drain.

Melt margarine; blend in flour and salt, then gradually add milk, stirring until thickened.

Pour a little of the hot sauce into beaten eggs, mix and then combine with remaining sauce. Add cheese and mustard and stir until cheese is melted. Mix the sauce with cooked, drained macaroni.

Pour a layer in the bottom of a well greased loaf tin (9×5×3 inches).

Lay 3 or 4 frankfurters on top, lengthwise. Add another layer of macaroni, then the remaining frankfurters, and top with another layer of macaroni.

Bake in hot oven (400°F. Mark 6) 45 minutes. Keep top covered with grease-proof paper during most of cooking time to prevent drying.

Turn out on a serving dish and garnish with tomato wedges. When cut, there will be 4 to 5 circles of frankfurters in each slice. Serves 5 to 8.

Coronado Shell Casserole

CHEESE MACARONI WITH CHOPPED EGGS

2 ounces butter or margarine
1 tablespoon chopped onion
1 ounce flour
16 fluid ounces milk
salt and pepper to taste
2 tablespoons chopped parsley
2 tablespoons chopped canned
    pimiento
½ teaspoon Worcestershire sauce
½ pound grated cheese
5 hard-boiled eggs, chopped
8 ounces macaroni, cooked

Melt butter or margarine over low heat; add onion and sauté until tender. Add flour and blend.

Gradually add milk and cook, stirring constantly, until sauce thickens.

Add salt, pepper, parsley, pimiento, Worcestershire sauce, and cheese. Stir until cheese is melted.

Combine chopped eggs with cooked macaroni and cheese sauce. Turn into 6 individual casseroles or a 2½-pint casserole.

Bake in moderate oven (350°F. Mark 4) 20 minutes, or until sauce begins to bubble. If wished, garnish with strips of pimiento. Serves 4 to 6.

CORONADO SHELL CASSEROLE

8 ounces macaroni shells
2 ounces butter or margarine
1 ounce flour
1 pint 8 fluid ounces tomato juice
1¼ teaspoons salt
dash of cayenne
1 pound prawns, cooked, shelled
    and deveined
3-4 ounces peas cooked
2 ounces grated cheese

Add 1 tablespoon salt to 4½ pints rapidly boiling water.

Gradually add macaroni shells so that water continues to boil.

Cook, uncovered, stirring occasionally, until tender.

Drain in colander.

Melt butter or margarine over low heat; add flour and blend.

Gradually add tomato juice and cook until thickened, stirring constantly.

Add 1¼ teaspoons salt, cayenne, prawns and peas; mix well.

Fold in macaroni shells. Turn into greased 3½-pint casserole.

Top with grated cheese.

Bake in moderate oven (375°F. Mark 5) 25 minutes, or until cheese is melted and golden brown. Serves 6.

ITALIAN MACARONI CASSEROLE

8 ounces macaroni, cooked
1 onion, thinly sliced
½ pound Mozzarella cheese, sliced
2 teaspoons salt
freshly ground pepper
4 fluid ounces mayonnaise
8 fluid ounces single light cream
3 hard-boiled eggs
1 rasher crisp, cooked bacon,
    crumbled
1 tablespoon chopped canned
    pimientos
Mayonnaise to moisten

In a shallow 3½-pint baking dish, arrange alternate layers of cooked macaroni, onion slices, and cheese slices. Season with salt and pepper.

Blend the mayonnaise and cream until smooth; pour over macaroni mixture.

Cover and bake in moderate oven (350°F. Mark 4) 35 minutes.

Uncover and arrange stuffed eggs on top. Bake 10 minutes longer. Serve piping hot. Serves 6.

To Make Stuffed Eggs: Halve hard-boiled eggs lengthwise; remove yolks.

Combine egg yolks, bacon, pimiento, and mayonnaise to moisten; mix lightly but thoroughly. Refill egg whites with mixture.

NOODLES AMANDINE

8 ounces egg noodles
1 ounce butter or margarine
3 ounces blanched almonds, slivered
2 ounces butter or margarine
2 tablespoons flour
8 fluid ounces single cream
8 fluid ounces milk
1½ teaspoons salt
white pepper, freshly ground
1 ounce grated Cheddar cheese

Cook noodles in 4½ pints boiling salted water (1 tablespoon salt) until tender. Drain in colander.

Meanwhile, melt 1 ounce butter or margarine over low heat. Add slivered almonds and sauté until golden brown.

Melt 2 ounces butter or margarine over low heat. Add flour, blending well. Slowly stir in cream and milk. Cook, stirring constantly, until sauce is thickened. Add 1½ teaspoons salt and pepper.

Combine cooked noodles, sauce, and half the almonds; mix lightly but thoroughly. Turn into greased 3½-pint casserole.

Mix together remaining almonds and grated cheese; sprinkle across top of casserole in diagonal lines.

Bake in moderate oven (350°F. Mark 4) 20 minutes. Serves 4 to 6.

STUFFINGS FOR FISH, MEAT, AND POULTRY

HINTS FOR MAKING STUFFINGS

The type of stuffing or dressing to use depends upon the kind of fish, meat, or poultry.

As a general rule, the more rich and oily the meat, the more simple and fruity the stuffing. That's why oysters, sausage, or other rich mixtures are generally used for dry-meated chicken or turkey, and stuffings including chopped apples, prunes, cranberries, pineapple, etc. are used for duck, goose, pork, and similar meat.

Stuffings may be dry or crumbly, or moist and compact, depending upon the amount of liquid used. When a stuffing is used inside poultry, the meat juice will increase the moisture.

All stuffings expand during cooking, therefore stuff lightly and bake any excess stuffing in a separate baking dish. Cover with bacon, salt pork, or poultry fat or pour a little meat stock over the stuffing. Bake slowly with the meat for at least an hour.

The seasonings given in the following recipes may be varied in accordance with personal taste; however, it is wise to remember to use only spices and herbs with full strength and fragrance.

Always taste the stuffing before using and add required seasoning.

Many stuffing recipes call for "day-old" bread, yet, today, bakery bread has "first day" freshness even after several days in the home bread bin. If bread is soft when a dry stuffing is desired, toast the bread slices or cubes in the oven until lightly browned. Soft breadcrumbs and cracker crumbs are likely to make a compact stuffing.

For hints on preparing crumbs for stuffings, see breadcrumbs in Index.

DO'S AND DON'TS FOR STUFFING POULTRY

● If stuffing is made before using, do not stuff the bird until just before it goes into the oven.
● Refrigerate the cleaned bird and the stuffing separately in a covered container.
● If you want to freeze the bird, do it with an unstuffed cavity.
● Stuffing may be frozen in a separate container.
● The bird takes a long time to defrost. Stuffing which is in the separate container requires much less time and should be used as soon as it is thawed.
● If there is stuffing left after the bird has been carved and served, take out stuffing and refrigerate separately.
● Do not let stuffing stay in the bird while it stays in the refrigerator.
● Cooked stuffing should be used within 3 days. Reheat only enough for 1 meal.
● Fresh sausage meat used in a stuffing always should be browned in a frying pan or otherwise thoroughly cooked before being added to the stuffing mixture.
● Some recipes call for cubes of ham. For these recipes make certain that ham is cooked before being used in stuffing.
● Cook giblets in water before using in stuffing.
● If meat stock is used in stuffing, make certain the stock is well refrigerated during the period between the making of the stock and the use in the stuffing. Do not make the stock more than 24 hours before stuffing the bird.

AMOUNT OF STUFFING TO MAKE

Allow about 3 ounces stuffing for each pound ready-to-cook weight of poultry. Allow 2 to 3 ounces stuffing per serving of meat.

MINT STUFFING FOR LAMB

1½ tablespoons chopped onion
3 tablespoons chopped celery and leaves
4 tablespoons fat
1 ounce fresh mint leaves
9 ounces soft breadcrumbs
salt and pepper to taste

Cook onion and celery for a few minutes in fat. Then stir in mint leaves and breadcrumbs. Season with salt and pepper.

Mix all ingredients together until hot. Makes stuffing for 3- to 4-pound boned shoulder of lamb. For a rolled shoulder, use half the recipe.

WILD RICE AND MUSHROOM STUFFING

1 pound wild rice
3 teaspoons chopped onion
2 ounces sliced mushrooms
2 ounces fat or cooking oil
1 teaspoon salt
dash of pepper

Wash rice and cover with salted water. Bring to boil and cook until tender, about 20 minutes. Drain.

Brown onion and mushrooms in hot fat. Mix with rice, salt, and pepper. Makes enough for 4- to 5-pound bird.

Wild Rice and Chestnut Stuffing: In above recipe omit mushrooms. Boil, peel, and chop ½ pound chestnuts. Mix with other ingredients.

Wild Rice and Mushroom Stuffing is a favourite with poussins.

BREAD STUFFING
(Basic Recipe)

1 pound stale bread cubes
¼ teaspoon pepper
1 teaspoon salt
¼ teaspoon thyme or marjoram
½ to 1 teaspoon poultry seasoning
1 ounce finely chopped onion
1 tablespoon melted fat

Combine bread, seasonings, and onion. Slowly add fat, tossing lightly with a fork until blended.

For a more moist stuffing slowly add up to 3 fluid ounces hot water or stock. Makes about 1 pound stuffing. Allow 3 ounces for each pound of poultry.

Bread Stuffing Variations

Celery Stuffing: To basic recipe add 4 ounces finely chopped celery.

Chestnut Stuffing: To basic recipe add 2 ounces finely chopped celery and 1 pound of boiled, chopped chestnuts.

Corn Bread Stuffing: In basic recipe, substitute corn bread crumbs for bread cubes.

Giblet Stuffing: To basic recipe add chopped, cooked giblets. Use giblet stock for moistening.

Mushroom Stuffing: Sauté 1 ounce sliced mushrooms in the fat and add to basic recipe.

Oyster Stuffing: To basic recipe add ½ pint chopped, drained oysters.

Parsley Stuffing: To basic recipe add 2 to 3 tablespoons chopped parsley.

Prune Stuffing: Omit thyme or marjoram and prepare half of basic recipe for bread stuffing.

Remove stones from ½ pound cooked prunes and add with 4 ounces diced apple.

Raisin Stuffing: To basic recipe add 2½ ounces seedless raisins.

Sage Stuffing: In basic recipe, omit thyme or marjoram. Add 1 tablespoon crumbled sage leaves.

Sausage Stuffing: To basic recipe add 2 ounces fried sausage meat, well drained.

PINEAPPLE STUFFING FOR LAMB

9 ounces soft white breadcrumbs
9 ounces rye breadcrumbs
¾ teaspoon cinnamon
½ teaspoon salt
4 ounces drained, crushed pineapple
1 tablespoon melted butter or margarine

Combine crumbs, cinnamon, pineapple, and salt. Add butter or margarine and mix well.

Use with 14- to 16-rib crown roast of lamb.

BASIC SAVOURY STUFFING

4 ounces chopped celery
1 ounce chopped parsley
1 ounce chopped onion
3 ounces fat
1 pound breadcrumbs
½ to 1 teaspoon salt
⅛ teaspoon pepper
1 teaspoon savoury seasoning

Cook celery, parsley, and onion in hot fat for a few minutes. Add breadcrumbs and seasonings. Mix well. Makes stuffing for 5- to 6-pound bird.

Savoury Stuffing Variations

Savoury Bacon Stuffing: Dice ½ pound bacon and fry until crisp. Drain on paper. Add with the dry ingredients in basic recipe. Use for poultry, fish, or fresh pork.

Savoury Chestnut Stuffing: To basic recipe add 1 pound of cooked, chopped chestnuts. To prepare chestnuts, boil in water 15 minutes, peel off shells and brown skin while still hot.

Savoury Corn Bread Stuffing: In basic recipe, use crumbled stale corn bread instead of breadcrumbs. Use for poultry, veal, or other meat.

Savoury Hazelnut, Walnut, Pecan, or Almond Stuffing: Add 4 ounces of any of these chopped nuts to basic recipe.

RICE STUFFING

2 tablespoons chopped onion
1 tablespoon chopped parsley
4 ounces chopped celery and leaves
2 tablespoons fat
1 pound cooked rice (brown, white, or wild)
½ teaspoon savoury seasoning
salt and pepper to taste

Cook onion, parsley, and celery in fat a few minutes. Add rice and seasoning. Stir until well mixed and hot.

Use as stuffing in chicken, duck or other poultry or in boned cuts of meat.

ONION STUFFING

6 medium-sized onions, minced
4 fluid ounces melted butter or margarine
9 ounces soft breadcrumbs
1½ teaspoons sage
¾ teaspoon salt
¼ teaspoon pepper
3 tablespoons minced parsley
2 tablespoons water
2 well beaten eggs

Sauté onions lightly in melted butter. Add crumbs, sage, salt, pepper, parsley and water and cook until lightly browned.

Remove from heat and stir in eggs. Makes about 1 pound of stuffing for 1 4- to 5-pound bird.

All stuffings expand during cooking, so do not pack too firmly and leave space for the mixture to swell and stay light.

MASHED POTATO OR SWEET POTATO STUFFING

12 ounces hot mashed potatoes
3 ounces soft breadcrumbs
3 tablespoons melted fat or salad oil
1 lightly beaten egg
3 tablespoons chopped onion
1 teaspoon chopped parsley

Use white or sweet potatoes. Season well while mashing.

Combine all ingredients. Moisten with stock if mixture is dry. Makes 12 ounces stuffing for veal or lamb breast or shoulder.

GRATED RAW POTATO STUFFING

6 medium raw potatoes
1 onion, grated
2 eggs
2 ounces flour
dash of pepper
1 teaspoon salt
minced parsley
4 fluid ounces hot melted fat or cooking oil

Peel and grate raw potatoes. Squeeze out excess water.

Mix all ingredients, adding hot melted fat last. Let mixture stand a few minutes before stuffing. Makes stuffing for 4- to 5-pound breast of veal.

CHESTNUT STUFFING

1 pound boiled chestnuts
2 fluid ounces cream
4 fluid ounces melted butter or margarine
4 ounces dry breadcrumbs or cracker crumbs
about 1 teaspoon salt
about ⅛ teaspoon pepper
1 ounce chopped celery (optional)
2 tablespoons chopped parsley (optional)

Shell and skin chestnuts. Cook in boiling water until soft.

Put chestnuts through ricer or vegetable mill. Combine with other ingredients. Makes about 12 ounces or enough for 3½- to 4-pound chicken.

Chestnut-Oyster Stuffing: Use part oysters and part chestnuts in above recipe.

BASIC STUFFING FOR FISH

2-4 ounces melted butter or
 margarine
1 tablespoon grated onion
8 ounces breadcrumbs or cubes
½ teaspoon salt
⅛ teaspoon pepper
1 tablespoon lemon juice
1 tablespoon chopped parsley
1 teaspoon capers (optional)

Amount of butter depends upon type of fish. Use smaller amount with lean fish, larger amount with fat fish.

Add onion and crumbs to melted butter. Stir over low heat until crumbs brown slightly.

Add and mix remaining ingredients. If desired, ¼ teaspoon sage or thyme may be substituted for capers. Makes stuffing for 3- to 4-pound fish.

Variations of Fish Stuffing

Bacon Stuffing: In basic stuffing substitute for the butter 3 to 6 slices bacon, diced and browned but not crisp.

Cucumber Stuffing: In basic stuffing reduce breadcrumbs or cubes to 4½ ounces. Add 4 to 5 ounces drained chopped cucumbers.

Pickle Stuffing: To basic stuffing add 2 to 3 ounces chopped drained sweet or dill pickles.

PRAWN STUFFING FOR FISH

2 tablespoons butter or margarine
½ tablespoon water
1 teaspoon anchovy paste
3 ounces soft breadcrumbs
4 ounces finely cut cooked prawns
¼ teaspoon grated onion
1 tablespoon lemon juice
2 teaspoons chopped stuffed olives

Heat butter, water, and anchovy paste together until butter is melted.

Add to crumbs and mix in remaining ingredients. This is especially good with stuffed trout.

CELERY-ONION STUFFING FOR FISH

3 tablespoons lard or margarine
1 ounce chopped onion
2 ounces chopped celery
12 ounces toasted ½-inch bread
 cubes
2 tablespoons minced parsley
1 tablespoon lemon juice
½ teaspoon salt
¼ teaspoon sage
3 tablespoons milk or water

Melt lard in a frying pan; add onion and celery and sauté until tender.

Pour over toasted bread cubes, adding parsley, lemon juice, salt, and sage. Add milk and mix well. Makes stuffing for 1 4- to 5-pound fish.

CRACKER STUFFING

1½ ounces chopped onion
4 ounces butter or margarine
1 pound cream cracker crumbs
¾ teaspoon salt
few grains of pepper
2 tablespoons chopped parsley
4 fluid ounces water

Cook onion in butter or margarine until lightly browned. Mix with crumbs, salt, pepper, and parsley. Add water and mix well.

Makes stuffing for 4 to 5 pounds chicken or fish.

APPLE STUFFING

2 ounces chopped celery and leaves
2 ounces chopped onion
1 ounce chopped parsley
2 to 3 tablespoons melted fat
5 tart apples, diced
4 ounces sugar
salt and pepper to taste
3 ounces soft breadcrumbs

Cook celery, onion, and parsley a few minutes in half of fat. Remove from pan.

Put remaining fat in pan and add apples. Sprinkle apples with sugar. Cover and cook until tender.

Remove cover and cook until apples are candied.

Combine with vegetables, breadcrumbs, and seasonings. Use with goose, duck, lamb, beef, or other meats.

CORN BREAD STUFFING

2½ ounces diced bacon
2 ounces butter or margarine
2 ounces minced onion
4 ounces diced celery
1 teaspoon salt
¼ teaspoon pepper
1 teaspoon Aromat
1 teaspoon poultry seasoning
8 ounces corn bread, cubed or
 crumbled
4 ounces white bread cubes,
 thoroughly dried

Heat bacon and butter in heavy skillet over low heat until butter melts. Add onion and celery; fry gently until bacon is lightly browned.

Add seasonings. Combine with corn bread and white bread cubes in bowl; mix thoroughly.

Makes enough stuffing for 5- to 6-pound capon or roasting chicken.

Corn Bread Stuffing Variations

1. Reduce onion to 1½ ounces and celery to 2 ounces; add 3 ounces finely chopped pecans or blanched almonds.

2. Omit celery and add 4 ounces peeled and chopped boiled chestnuts.

3. Omit celery and add 4 ounces raisins and 4 ounces finely chopped walnuts.

PRUNE STUFFING FOR CROWN ROAST OF PORK

6 ounces prunes
6 ounces breadcrumbs
4 ounces diced celery
1 medium onion, finely chopped
1 ounce finely chopped green
 pepper
salt and pepper
8 fluid ounces meat stock

Cook prunes until tender. Drain and cut in small pieces, removing stones.

Add crumbs, celery, onion, and green pepper. Season to taste with salt and pepper. Moisten with stock. Makes stuffing for 10- to 12-rib crown.

PRUNE STUFFING BALLS

10 ounces cooked prunes
1 ounce finely chopped onion
4 ounces thinly sliced celery
4 ounces butter or margarine
12 ounces soft stale breadcrumbs
½ teaspoon salt
¼ teaspoon sage or poultry
 seasoning
⅛ teaspoon black pepper
2 eggs
hot water

Cut prunes from stones into pieces. Cook onion and celery very slowly in butter 10 minutes. Pour over bread, tossing to blend. Sprinkle with salt, sage, and pepper.

Beat eggs well; mix with bread. Blend in prunes lightly.

Sprinkle with 1 to 4 tablespoons hot water, depending on moisture of bread. Mixture should not be wet, just moist enough to hold together.

Shape lightly into 12 balls and place on greased baking sheet.

Bake in moderate oven (350°F. Mark 4) 25 to 30 minutes, or until crisp and lightly browned. Serve hot with roast pork or lamb. Serves 6.

Give your next roast pork or lamb a lift by serving these "Prune Stuffing Balls". Just add the chopped, stoned prunes to a barely moistened bread stuffing, shape into balls and bake. Good with turkey, too.

ORANGE STUFFING FOR DUCKS OR GOOSE

6 ounces butter or margarine
2 ounces chopped onion
6 ounces chopped celery
8 fluid ounces boiling water
2 teaspoons salt
2 teaspoons poultry seasoning
½ teaspoon pepper
2 tablespoons grated orange rind
2 tablespoons minced parsley
1 pound toasted bread cubes
2 oranges, peeled and diced

Sauté onion in butter. Cook celery in water until tender. Add seasonings, orange rind, and parsley.

Add to cooked onions with bread cubes and oranges. Mix well and stuff goose or ducks. Makes stuffing for 2 ducks or 10- to 12-pound goose.

QUICK SAVOURY RICE STUFFING

2 ounces butter or margarine
10 ounces pre-cooked rice
4 ounces diced celery
2 tablespoons chopped celery leaves
1 ounce chopped onion
2 tablespoons chopped parsley
1 teaspoon salt
½ teaspoon sage
⅛ teaspoon pepper
12 fluid ounces chicken stock

Melt butter in saucepan. Add rice and sauté until lightly browned, stirring constantly.

Add celery, celery leaves, onion, parsley, and seasonings Sauté 2 or 3 minutes longer.

Then add chicken stock. Bring quickly to the boil over high heat, uncovered, fluffing rice gently with a fork. (Do not stir.) Cover and remove from heat. Let stand 10 minutes.

Makes 12 ounces stuffing, enough for chicken, duck, or half turkey.

POTATO STUFFING FOR GOOSE OR DUCKLINGS

4 ounces bacon or salt pork dripping
4 ounces chopped onion
2 ounces chopped celery
10 medium potatoes, cooked and riced
4 slices bread, crumbled
2 beaten eggs
1 tablespoon poultry seasoning
1 teaspoon salt
¼ teaspoon pepper
1½ teaspoons Aromat

Melt fat in frying pan; add onions and celery; cook until soft but not brown.

Combine remaining ingredients; add contents of frying pan; mix well.

Makes enough stuffing for one 10- to 12-pound goose or two 5- to 6-pound ducklings.

BROWN RICE-SAUSAGE STUFFING

½ pound pork sausage meat
1 medium-sized onion, chopped
1 tart apple, peeled and diced
4 ounces chopped celery, including a few leaves
1 teaspoon salt
dash of pepper
½ teaspoon sage or poultry seasoning
½ pound raw brown rice
16 fluid ounces water

In a heavy frying pan or casserole, cook sausage until lightly browned, stirring occasionally to keep loose. Drain off all except 3 tablespoons fat.

Mix in onion, apple, and celery; simmer about 5 minutes longer.

Add seasonings, rice, and water. Stir to mix and loosen browned bits. Cover tightly and cook over low heat until almost done, about 30 minutes. Do not stir. Makes stuffing for 4- to 5-pound bird.

PENNSYLVANIA DUTCH STUFFING

12 ounces hot mashed potatoes
1 well beaten egg
1 pound dry bread cubes
3 tablespoons butter or other fat
1 ounce chopped parsley
2 ounces chopped onion
1 teaspoon salt
½ teaspoon poultry seasoning
pepper to taste

Combine potatoes and egg. Sauté bread cubes in butter. Combine potato mixture with bread.

Stir in remaining ingredients. Mix well. Makes 1¼ pounds of stuffing for 6-pound turkey.

HAMBURGER STUFFING FOR POULTRY OR CABBAGE LEAVES

½ pound minced beef
2 tablespoons fat
1 teaspoon salt
¼ teaspoon pepper
2 ounces finely chopped onion
4 ounces finely chopped celery
¼ teaspoon poultry seasoning
2 slightly beaten eggs
2 fluid ounces water
1½ pounds bread cubes

Fry meat in hot fat in heavy frying pan. Add salt, pepper, onion, celery, and poultry seasoning. Continue cooking until onion is transparent.

Beat eggs and water. Add egg mixture to bread cubes. Stir in meat mixture. Makes stuffing for 6-pound roasting chicken.

Variations: Use as stuffing for cabbage leaves or pack in 9×9×2-inch pan. Top with strips of salt pork or bacon and bake in moderate oven (375°F. Mark 5) 30 minutes.

FRUITED BRAZIL NUT STUFFING

1 pound bread cubes
6 tablespoons melted butter or margarine
6 ounces chopped tart apples
6 ounces chopped cooked prunes
5 ounces chopped Brazil nuts
2½ teaspoons salt
¼ teaspoon pepper
1 teaspoon poultry seasoning
4 fluid ounces bouillon or broth

Combine ingredients and mix lightly. Use to stuff half a turkey or a goose, duck, or chicken. Makes about 1 pound.

CORN STUFFING FOR POULTRY

1 pound canned corn
½ pound breadcrumbs
2 eggs
1 tablespoon finely minced green pepper
1 ounce chopped mushrooms
⅔ teaspoon salt
¼ teaspoon pepper
2 tablespoons fat

Mix all ingredients thoroughly. If too dry, add a little stock. If too moist, add a little more breadcrumbs. Makes stuffing for 4- to 5-pound bird.

HAM STUFFING RING

2 ounces finely chopped onion
4 ounces butter or margarine
½ pound mushrooms, diced
1 pound dry breadcrumbs
12 ounces minced ham
1 ounce chopped parsley
2 teaspoons poultry seasoning
¼ teaspoon pepper
1 egg
1 cup milk

Sauté onion in butter or margarine until transparent; add mushrooms and cook 5 minutes longer.

Combine with breadcrumbs, ham, parsley, poultry seasoning, and pepper.

Beat egg; blend in milk. Lightly stir into crumb mixture.

Pile into well oiled 9-inch ring mould. Bake in slow oven (325°F. Mark 3) about 50 minutes.

Unmould by running knife around sides. Fill centre of ham ring with broccoli and serve to accompany roast capons or small turkeys stuffed with small white onions. Makes about 10 servings.

Ham Stuffing Ring

Spicy Cheese-Olive Loaf

FRENCH TOAST
(Basic Recipe)

2 eggs
dash of salt
1 tablespoon sugar
6 fluid ounces milk
6 slices white bread

Beat eggs slightly. Add salt, sugar, and milk. Dip bread into milk mixture.

Cook on hot, well-greased girdle or frying pan. Brown on one side. Turn and brown on other side, or fry in deep hot fat 1 to 2 minutes, or until browned.

Serve with syrup, jam, or cinnamon and sugar mixture.

Variations:

French Toast Fingers: Cut slices of bread into fingers about 1 inch wide. Prepare as French toast. Serve with icing sugar, jam, or jelly.

Hawaiian French Toast: In basic recipe substitute 6 fluid ounces pineapple juice for milk. Serve toast on half slices of heated pineapple.

Honey French Toast: In basic recipe add 3 ounces honey to milk mixture of French toast.

Orange French Toast: In basic recipe substitute 6 fluid ounces orange juice and 1 teaspoon orange rind for milk. Serve with honey.

TOAST CORNUCOPIAS

Remove crusts from thin-sliced bread. Spread each slice on both sides with softened butter, sprinkle with garlic salt. Roll to form cornucopias and fasten each with toothpick. Stuff centres with crusts so that cornucopias will retain rounded shape. Toast in moderate oven (350°F. Mark 4) 20 to 25 minutes or until golden. Remove crusts in cornucopias and fill centres with parsley sprigs.

SPICY CHEESE-OLIVE LOAF

1 (1-pound) loaf unsliced wholemeal bread
4 ounces grated Cheddar cheese
4 ounces finely chopped olives
2 tablespoons minced onion
4 ounces soft butter or margarine
2 teaspoons prepared mustard

Cut the unsliced loaf lengthwise. Cut each half loaf almost through the bottom crust, into 6 slices.

Combine cheese with remaining ingredients; spread mixture between slices of bread. Wrap loaf in foil. Heat in a not-too-hot part of the grill until piping hot and crusty. Or just place unwrapped on a baking sheet and heat in a hot oven (400°F. Mark 6) about 12 minutes.

GARLIC BREAD

1 loaf French bread
1 clove garlic
¼ pound butter or margarine

Cut the loaf in 1½-inch slices, cutting diagonally almost through the bread.

Crush garlic and heat in butter or margarine. Let mixture stand a few minutes so garlic permeats butter, then remove garlic and spread the butter over cut surfaces of bread.

Wrap loaf in foil and place in hot oven (400°F. Mark 6) 12 to 15 minutes, or until heated through.

HOW TO REHEAT BREAD OR ROLLS

Put the bread or rolls in a paper bag. Close the bag and place in a hot oven (425°F. Mark 7) for 5 minutes.

Or put the bread or rolls in a hot covered double saucepan over boiling water for about the same amount of time. If the bread is old, it may be sprinkled with water.

IDEAS WITH TOAST AND BREAD

TEA TOAST

Cut bread very thin. If desired, remove crusts, cut slices into halves or strips. Spread hot toast with butter, then with desired mixture. Place under grill long enough to melt sugar, about 2 minutes.

Cinnamon Toast: Use 1½ teaspoons cinnamon and 2 tablespoons brown sugar.

Honey Cinnamon Toast: Use mixture of honey and cinnamon to taste.

Honey Toast
Use strained honey.

Maple Toast: Use maple sugar.

Orange Toast: Use mixture of ½ tablespoon grated orange rind, 2 tablespoons orange juice, and 2 ounces sugar.

TOMATO FRENCH TOAST

2 eggs
4 fluid ounces condensed tomato soup
½ teaspoon salt
½ teaspoon paprika
6 slices bread

Beat eggs until blended; then beat in tomato soup, salt, and paprika. Dip bread in this mixture; fry in melted butter until browned. Serve alone or with a cheese sauce.

ROLL BASKETS

Hollow out small rolls. Spread the hollows with melted butter. Toast in slow oven (300°F. Mark 2) until crisp.

VANILLA BAKED TOAST

Cut slices of bread into thirds. Combine 4 fluid ounces milk, 1 tablespoon sugar, and ½ teaspoon vanilla.

Brush surface of bread. Toast in slow oven (300°F. Mark 2) until crisp, dry, and golden.

BREAD BASKETS (CROUSTADES)

Trim crusts from 1 large loaf unsliced white bread. Cut bread into blocks 2×3×2-inches.

With sharp knife, cut centres from blocks of bread to fashion baskets.

Brush baskets with melted butter or margarine. Place on a baking sheet and toast under a pre-heated grill to a light golden brown. Serve with creamed foods.

Note: Use the leftover bread trimmings for breadcrumbs.

SAVOURY CROÛTONS

Cut bread in small cubes. Fry in small amount of butter, margarine, or dripping until brown, stirring constantly.

Sprinkle with curry powder, marjoram, chilli seasoning, onion salt, or garlic salt.

MILK TOAST

Place hot buttered toast in cereal bowl. Serve with scalded milk seasoned with salt and pepper. Allow about 4 fluid ounces per slice.

MELBA TOAST

Cut stale bread into ¼-inch slices. Bake in slow oven (300°F. Mark 2) until brown and dry, 15 to 20 minutes.

SEEDED FRENCH BREAD

Slice French bread and spread generously with softened butter or margarine.

Sprinkle slices with caraway, poppy, or sesame seed.

Bake in hot oven (400°F. Mark 6) until lightly browned, about 10 minutes.

TOASTED CHEESE ROLLS

Split, butter, and toast long rolls; sprinkle with grated Cheddar cheese and return to moderate oven (350°F. Mark 4) until cheese melts. Serve warm.

TOAST CUPS

Trim crusts from ¼-inch thick slices of fresh bread. Brush with melted butter.

Press each slice into ramekin dish so that bread forms a cup. Bake in moderate oven until crisp and brown, 15 to 20 minutes.

Prawns In Toast Cups

BREAD CUBES OR CRUMBS

Soft Breadcrumbs: Tear a fresh slice of bread into small pieces with the fingers.

Soft Bread Cubes: Stack two or three slices of bread on a bread board and with a sharp knife, using a sawing motion, cut sliced bread into strips of desired width. Cut again in opposite direction to form cubes of even size.

Toasted Bread Cubes: Arrange soft bread cubes on a baking sheet. Place baking sheet under a pre-heated grill (400°F.) or in a slow oven (300°F. Mark 2) and toast until bread cubes are golden brown on all sides, turning occasionally.

Dry Breadcrumbs: Put dry breads through a mincer, using fine mincing screen. Tie a paper bag on the blade end of the mincer so that crumbs will drop into bag as they are ground. If fine breadcrumbs are desired, sift the crumbs through a sieve and store the coarse dry and fine dry crumbs in covered separate containers.

Fried Breadcrumbs: Melt 2 ounces butter in a frying pan. When hot, add 4 ounces dry breadcrumbs. Stir constantly until crumbs are golden brown.

SLIM JIM BREAD STICKS

Quarter frankfurter rolls lengthwise. Spread cut sides, or all sides, with soft butter or margarine.

Roll in one of these: minced parsley, chives, or nuts, poppy seeds, or grated Parmesan cheese. Bake in hot oven (425°F. Mark 7) 5 to 10 minutes.

GARLIC BREAD SQUARES

Cut unsliced loaf of bread into 2-inch squares.

Mix thoroughly ¼ clove garlic, mashed, and 2 ounces butter or margarine. Spread mixture on outside of squares.

Bake on baking sheet in very hot oven (450°F. Mark 8) 10 minutes.

PAIN PERDUE (LOST BREAD)

6 slices bread (not too thick)
4 fluid ounces milk
2 tablespoons sugar
⅛ teaspoon salt
1 teaspoon vanilla
3 egg yolks, beaten
butter
caster sugar

Remove crusts and dampen bread slightly in milk to which sugar, salt, and vanilla are added. Bread must not break.

Dip in beaten yolks, coating evenly. Fry to a golden brown in hot butter. Drain.

Serve on napkin generously sprinkled with caster sugar.

Making Soft Breadcrumbs

Making Soft Bread Cubes

Toasted Bread Cubes

Making Dry Breadcrumbs

SALT STICKS

Cut sliced white bread in ½-inch strips. Brush with melted butter or margarine.

Toast in hot oven (400°F. Mark 6) until lightly browned, 8 to 10 minutes. Sprinkle with coarse salt.

CHEESE FOLD-UPS

Remove crusts from bread slices and spread with butter or margarine. Sprinkle lightly with grated cheese.

Fasten opposite corners together with wooden cocktail sticks. Bake the fold-ups in very hot oven (450°F. Mark 8) 10 minutes.

NIPPY CHEESE FINGERS

Mix a Cheddar cheese spread with butter or margarine. Remove crusts from bread slices; spread and cut in strips. Bake in moderate oven (350°F. Mark 4) 10 minutes.

French Toast and Peaches

Fresh, canned or frozen peaches can be used to make an unusual snack for lunch, supper or even breakfast.

It's simply hot French toast layered with cottage cheese and lightly sweetened peaches.

SHERRIED FRENCH TOAST

2 slightly beaten eggs
¼ teaspoon salt
4 fluid ounces sherry
5 or 6 slices bread (stale bread is best)

Mix eggs, salt, and sherry in a shallow dish.

Dip bread slices quickly into mixture, coating both sides.

Brown slowly in hot fat in a heavy frying pan. Serve hot, sprinkled with sugar. Serves 2 to 3.

BREAD CONFECTIONS

1 large can sweetened condensed milk
1 teaspoon vanilla
6 ounces desiccated coconut
orange food colouring
1 loaf day-old bread, thinly sliced
orange marmalade

Combine sweetened condensed milk and vanilla in a small bowl. Put coconut into a jar, add a drop or two of orange food colouring, being careful not to add too much; cover jar and shake until coconut is evenly coloured; put onto a flat pudding plate.

Cut two 2-inch rounds from each slice of bread. Spread half the rounds with sweetened condensed milk mixture; then spread with marmalade. Top each spread round with a plain bread round. Dip one flat surface and sides of each sandwich in sweetened condensed milk mixture; drain; dip in coloured coconut. Put on ungreased baking sheet, plain surface down. Continue until all circles are coated.

Bake in slow oven (325°F. Mark 3) 12 to 15 minutes; do not let coconut brown. Remove at once from baking sheet. Cool. Makes 21.

ROLLS IN LOAF

Trim side and top crusts from a loaf of unsliced white bread.

Cut through the centre of the loaf, just to the lower crust, but not through it. Then make crosswise cuts, spacing them so that the "rolls" will be even in size.

Brush with melted margarine or butter and toast in a moderate oven (375°F. Mark 5) until the edges of the loaf are golden brown. Serve hot.

PEANUT BUTTER BREAD FINGERS

2½ tablespoons peanut butter
8 fluid ounces milk
½ teaspoon salt
¼ teaspoon pepper
1 egg, slightly beaten
12 slices bread

Cream together peanut butter and milk. Add salt and pepper, then add slightly beaten egg.

Remove crusts from bread slices and cut into narrow strips. Dip in the mixture and sauté in butter.

TOASTED CHEESE RINGS

Cut rings from bread slices with doughnut or pastry cutter; brush with melted butter or cooking oil, then dip into grated cheese. Place in moderate oven (350°F. Mark 4) until light brown.

ONION-CARAWAY RYE LOAF

With a sharp knife, cut a loaf of caraway rye bread in diamonds without cutting through bottom crust.

Season softened butter or margarine with salt and grated onion; spread generously around diamonds of bread. Bake in hot oven (400°F. Mark 6) for 10 minutes, or until loaf is hot.

TOAST STRIPS

Cut slices ⅓-inch thick. Remove crusts. Spread butter on both sides. Cut slices in ½-inch strips. Lightly brown under grill.

TOAST POINTS

Remove crusts from ½-inch thick slices of bread. Toast. While hot, cut into 4 triangles. Use as a garnish.

GARLIC BREAD STRIPS

Brush thin slices of rye bread with melted butter to which garlic salt has been added. Cut in thin strips. Toast in hot oven (400°F. Mark 6) until lightly browned, about 5 minutes.

SAVOURY STUFFED ROLLS

Cut circle, ¾ inch from edge of baps. Remove centre with fork, leaving about ¼ inch on bottom.

Fry until brown a small amount of chopped onion in a generous amount of margarine or dripping. Add a few leaves of marjoram and thyme, the bread crumbs, and some chopped parsley. Stuff baps with mixture.

Heat in moderate oven (375°F. Mark 5) for 8 to 10 minutes, or until hot.

HOT PUMPERNICKEL SLICES

With a sharp knife, slice day-old round loaf of pumpernickel or rye bread ⅛ to ¼ inch thick. Tie together with string. Spread softened butter or margarine over top.

Heat in hot oven (400°F. Mark 6) for 10 minutes, or until heated through and crust is crisp. Put in serving basket, and remove string.

FRENCH TOASTED MATZOS

6 eggs
½ teaspoon salt
2 tablespoons butter, chicken fat, or salad oil
4 matzos
sugar and cinnamon
grated lemon rind, optional

Beat eggs very light; add salt. Heat butter in frying pan. Break matzos into large equal-sized pieces. Dip each piece in the beaten egg. Fry until lightly browned on both sides. Serve hot, sprinkled with sugar and cinnamon and, if desired, with grated lemon rind.

Bread Confections

HONEY-FRUIT BUNS

Split and toast buns. Spread with softened butter. Put a slice of pineapple or slices of banana and a little honey on each.

Grill until topping is lightly browned.

CELERY BREAD STICKS

Trim crusts of ⅜-inch thick slices of bread. Brush both sides of bread slices with butter.

Cut each slice into 6 equal size strips. Roll strips in celery salt.

Place on a baking sheet. Toast in moderate oven (350°F. Mark 4) 15 minutes.

CHEESE FRENCH TOAST

3 eggs
1¼ pints milk
½ teaspoon salt
12 slices day-old bread
3 ounces butter
5 ounces grated Cheddar cheese

Beat eggs slightly; add milk and salt and blend thoroughly. Dip bread slices in mixture.

Melt butter in a frying pan; add soaked bread slices and cook until a delicate brown on one side.

Turn, sprinkle grated cheese over top of each slice and cook until underside is a delicate brown and cheese is melted.

Serve hot with crisp bacon or sausage for luncheon or supper. Serves 6.

CRUSTY CHEESE LOAF

Cut crusts from top and side of unsliced sandwich loaf. Slice to, but not through, bottom crust.

Spread top and sides of slices with mixture of 4 ounces butter or margarine and two 5 ounce jars Cheddar cheese spread.

Tie loaf together with string; place in baking pan. Bake in hot oven (400°F. Mark 6) 20 minutes.

FRENCH OVEN TOAST

2 eggs, beaten
½ teaspoon salt
2 tablespoons sugar
8 fluid ounces milk
½ teaspoon almond extract
12 slices bread

Combine beaten eggs, salt, sugar, milk, and almond extract. Dip sliced bread into mixture.

Place slices on well greased baking sheet and brown in extremely hot oven (500°F. Mark 10). Turn toast over after 10 minutes and brown on the other side. Serve with honey or maple syrup. Makes 6 servings—2 slices per serving.
Note: This toast may be reheated satisfactorily.

GARLIC BREAD STICKS

Add 2 cloves cut garlic to 4 fluid ounces melted butter or margarine and let stand 15 minutes. Remove garlic.

Brush 12 or more Italian bread sticks or sticks cut from stale bread with flavoured butter or margarine.

Place in moderate oven (375°F. Mark 5) until hot, crisp, and delicately browned.

For stronger flavour touch sticks with cut side of garlic and proceed as above.

Bread for the Barbecue

BARBECUE BREAD HINTS

Bread and rolls are easy to reheat; for convenience, butter the bread indoors, then warm on the grill outside. Simply slice bread and wrap in foil, either the whole loaf or a couple of pieces to a package. Heat on or near the fire.

French or rye bread can be split lengthwise or cut in diagonal slices almost to bottom crust, spread with your choice of spreads, wrapped in foil and put in a not-too-hot part of the grill.

Rolls may be split and spread with a filling before wrapping in foil and heating.

SAVOURY SPREADS FOR BREAD AND ROLLS

Garlic Butter: Mash 1 to 2 cloves garlic or use garlic press; cream into 4 ounces butter or margarine.

Cheese-Parsley Butter: Combine 4 ounces butter or margarine with 1 ounce each of grated Cheddar, Gruyère or Emmenthal cheese and minced parsley.

Onion Butter: Chop a small bunch of spring onions (scallions), including some tops, and mix with 4 ounces butter or margarine.

Sesame-Onion Butter: Toast 1 ounce sesame seeds; mix with onion butter.

Herb Butter: Cream 4 ounces butter or margarine with 2 tablespoons of fresh rosemary, tarragon, or basil. If desired, add a little chopped onion.

HOT ROLLS AND MUFFINS

Put muffins or rolls in large can. Place can on side on grill or hot coals. Roll occasionally until rolls are heated through.

TOASTED ROLLS AND MUFFINS

Split and spread with butter or marmarine or one of the savoury spreads. Toast on grill in hinged wire griller or on skewers.

Or toast by placing buttered side down in frying pan on grill. (Muffins are good this way.)

CHEESE BREAD CHUNKS

Spread thick slices of French bread with butter or margarine mixed with grated Parmesan cheese. Toast on skewers over coals.

HERBED FRENCH OR ITALIAN BREAD

Cut a long loaf of French or Italian bread in half lengthwise.

Mix 4 ounces softened butter or margarine with 2 ounces chopped parsley, 1 ounce chopped spring onions, and 2 finely chopped garlic cloves. Spread on the two bread halves.

Sandwich the two halves together and wrap in foil. Heat on the grill.

POPPY SEED BREAD

Buy a Farmhouse loaf unsliced and cut in thick slices down to, but not through, the bottom crust. Stand on a large sheet of foil.

Mix softened butter with poppy seeds, or sugar and cinnamon, if preferred. Spread the cut slices.

Bring the foil up over the bread and wrap, but leave opening at top for steam to escape.

Heat for about 20 minutes on the grill over medium heat. Tip over on both sides for part of time for even heating. Serve from foil.

GRILLED BUNS

Split buns crosswise (Bath buns are especially good). Spread with soft butter or margarine. Toast in heavy frying pan or on girdle.

French Bread with Savoury Spread Heat the prepared bread in a foil wrapper in a not-too-hot part of the grill.

VEGETABLES

A variety of attractively garnished vegetables makes a colourful and appetizing side dish.

PREPARATION HINTS

● The tightly grown or curled vegetables (cabbage, cauliflower, Brussels sprouts, leeks, artichokes) should be soaked briefly in salted cold water before cooking.

● Some vegetables need a stiff brush to get them clean (potatoes, beetroot, swedes, salsify or oyster plant); others require a soft brush or "hand rubbing" (asparagus, mushrooms, celery). Still others need several washings in clear, cool water (all the leafy vegetables and salad plants).

● If they are to be cooked whole, do not peel beetroot. Leave at least 2 inches of top on each beetroot to prevent "bleeding". When tender, drain and rinse quickly with cold water, then slip off skins.

● Wash and pick over the garden herbs and vegetables used for garnishes (chives, parsley, mint, celery leaves, etc.) as carefully as you do the vegetables they are to garnish. Have them crisp if they are used in sprigs, sprays, bunches, or tufts. If they are to be cut fine to sprinkle over a vegetable, snip them with scissors.

● Husk and remove silk from sweetcorn just before cooking; in fact, have the water at a galloping boil before exposing sweetcorn to the air. Cook quickly and do not overcook.

   Trim stems to ½-inch length and remove coarse, discoloured outer leaves from artichokes; cut off about ½ inch of tops to expose inner leaves. Clean carefully. Cook *head-down* in slightly acidulated boiling water (lemon juice or vinegar) until stem is tender. Drain upside down.

QUICK SEASONING IDEAS

● Slivered, chopped, or sliced nuts (almonds, hazelnuts, Brazil nuts, peanuts, walnuts, macadamias, etc.) as a garnish.

● A sliver or two of garlic heated in the butter for vegetables, then removed.

● Chopped or riced hard-boiled egg for garnish or to mix with fried breadcrumbs.

● Snipped parsley or chives stirred into the butter or margarine, or the cream sauce.

● Sour cream, lemon juice, or herb vinegars, for pleasing tartness.

● Condensed canned soups to use for easy sauces.

● Caraway, or dry-toasted sesame seeds to sprinkle on.

● A *little* crushed thyme, oregano, or marjoram for tomatoes and greens. Fresh snipped chervil or tarragon for peas, beans, greens.

HOW TO SHORTEN COOKING TIME

● By removing all inedible or "woody" portions: such as root ends of asparagus, tough mid ribs of kale, coarse outer leaves of cabbage, Brussels sprouts, etc.

● By peeling and slitting thick stems such as broccoli (or cook and serve stems as a separate vegetable).

● By shredding (cabbage, carrots, turnips, etc.) or grating coarsely (beetroot, carrots swedes, etc.).

● By cubing (potatoes, turnips, etc.); slicing (onions, carrots, celery, etc.); cutting into match-size strips called Julienne (the root vegetables especially; also celery, green beans, potatoes, etc.).

● By separating cauliflower into flowerets.

● By dividing or cutting large vegetables into individual servings; cabbage into wedges, small vegetables or stem-types tied in portions, etc.

HINTS ABOUT COOKING VEGETABLES

● Clean and keep them cool until cooking time . . . do not *soak* in water unless directed.

● Avoid scraping or peeling if possible . . . if removing the skin is necessary, peel *thinly*.

● Use freshly *boiling* water and as little of it as possible—none at all for delicate greens . . . enough water clings to leaves or the vegetable itself is "watery" enough to cook without additional water.

● Boil vegetables gently and cook them only until crisply tender. Vegetables should never be limp or soggy, faded or unattractive looking. The testing fork should meet a little resistance when put into the vegetables.

● Cover most vegetables to speed up cooking. Too slow cooking keeps the vegetables in contact with water or steam unnecessarily long.

● Do **not** use bicarbonate of soda to "set" the colour. Properly cooked vegetables will retain their colour.

● Heavy-bottom saucepans with covers, and with bases that fit firmly and completely over the cooking heat, permit cooking in a minimum amount of water and in a minimum time.

● Cook frozen vegetables according to directions on the packet. Measure the water—don't guess. Avoid over-cooking and reduce heat immediately. Never let the vegetable "cool down with the cooker".

● Canned vegetables are already cooked—do *not* cook them further. Heat, but do not boil. Add seasonings; serve immediately. Or, drain liquid from vegetable into saucepan; boil down to about 2 to 4 fluid ounces. Add vegetable and seasonings; heat and serve.

● Do not throw away the water or juice from cooked vegetables . . . if it is not served with the vegetable, save it for soups, sauces, casseroles—or drink it.

Vegetable-Cheese Casserole

Basic Recipes for Vegetables

VEGETABLE CROQUETTES
(Basic Recipe)

½ pint thick white sauce
1 pound cooked or canned
  chopped vegetables, well drained
1 tablespoon chopped onion
2 tablespoons chopped parsley
1 or 2 eggs
salt, pepper, paprika, or other
  desired seasoning
½ pound sifted seasoned breadcrumbs
1 egg
2 tablespoons milk or water

Prepare the sauce and, when it is smooth and boiling, stir in vegetables.

Heat to boiling point, remove from the heat and beat in 1 or 2 eggs.

Cook and stir over low heat to permit the eggs to thicken slightly. Season to taste.

Other seasonings may be used such as a choice of ½ teaspoon curry powder, ½ teaspoon dried herbs, 1 teaspoon Worcestershire sauce, ½ teaspoon Tabasco sauce, etc.

Spread the mixture in a dish. Let cool, then shape it as desired. Roll croquettes in seasoned breadcrumbs, then in 1 egg beaten slightly with milk or water, and again in breadcrumbs.

Be sure to cover the entire croquette with the egg mixture to prevent the fat from penetrating. Let the croquettes dry for about 2 hours.

Fry a few at a time in deep hot fat (390°F.) until delicately browned, 3 to 5 minutes. Drain on absorbent paper. To reheat, place in a hot oven (400°F. Mark 6).

Serve with tomato, mushroom, or other desired sauce. Serves 6.

Vegetable Soufflé

SCALLOPED VEGETABLES
(Basic Recipe)

1 to 1½ pounds cooked or canned
  vegetables
12 fluid ounces medium white sauce
2 ounces fried breadcrumbs
paprika

Arrange prepared vegetables in alternate layers with white sauce. Sprinkle top with fried breadcrumbs, topped with a dash of paprika.

Bake in moderate oven (375°F. Mark 5) until browned, about 25 minutes. Serves 4 to 6.

Note: Almost any vegetables may be used singly or in combination. A good combination is carrots, cauliflower, and green beans. Or, asparagus tips or broccoli with small white onions or new potatoes.

Vegetables Au Gratin (Scalloped Vegetables with Cheese): In basic recipe, alternate layers of grated Cheddar cheese with vegetables or mix 2 ounces grated cheese with fried breadcrumbs and sprinkle top before baking.

Curried Scalloped Vegetables: In basic recipe, season the white sauce with curry powder to taste.

VEGETABLE SOUFFLÉ
(Basic Recipe)

3 eggs, separated
4 to 8 fluid ounces thick white
  sauce, seasoned
¼ to ½ teaspoon chopped onion
6 ounces drained cooked vegetables
  (chopped, mashed, puréed)

Beat yolks until thick and lemon coloured; stir into white sauce and add vegetables.

Fold in stiffly beaten egg whites. Turn into ungreased casserole.

Bake in slow oven (325°–350°F. Mark 3-4) 30 to 45 minutes.

Serve at once with cream sauce or cheese sauce, if desired. Serves 4 to 6.
Note: Vegetable may be increased to 8 ounces, if desired.

VEGETABLE-CHEESE CASSEROLE

2 Spanish onions, sliced
    (about 9 ounces)
12 ounces sliced carrots
1 pound processed cheese
    spread
about 14 ounces cracker crumbs
    (cream crackers, finely rolled)
¼ teaspoon pepper
½ teaspoon whole thyme
4 ounces chopped pimentos

Cook onions and carrots until tender. Drain. Heat cheese spread over boiling water. Combine crumbs with pepper and thyme.

Layer vegetables, melted cheese, and crumb mixture in a greased shallow 2-quart baking dish. Sprinkle with chopped pimentos.

Bake, covered, 15 minutes in moderate oven (350°F. Mark 4), then 15 minutes uncovered. Serves 6 to 8.

VEGETABLE LOAF

2 tablespoons melted fat (lard,
    butter, or margarine)
1 large onion, chopped
4 ounces grated raw carrots
4 ounces grated raw carrots
4 ounces finely chopped walnuts
    or mixed nuts
4 ounces dry wholemeal- or rye-
    breadcrumbs
1 teaspoon salt
1 teaspoon poultry seasoning
2 beaten eggs
½ pint evaporated milk or cream

Fry onions over low heat in melted fat until light brown.

Add celery, carrots, nuts, crumbs, and seasonings; cook and stir over low heat about 5 minutes.

Beat eggs; stir in cream or evaporated milk. Combine the two mixtures.

Turn into a well greased loaf pan. Bake in moderate oven (350°F. Mark 4) until nicely browned, about 40 to 45 minutes.

Turn out on a heated platter. Surround with cooked green peas; garnish with sliced hard-boiled eggs. Serve with mushroom or tomato sauce. Condensed cream of mushroom soup, heated just before serving, makes a good sauce. Serves 4 to 6.

Vegetable-Cheese Fondue

VEGETABLES **907**

VEGETABLE-CHEESE FONDUE

½ pint milk
3 ounces soft breadcrumbs
1 tablespoon butter or margarine
¼ teaspoon salt
few grains paprika
few grains pepper
¼ teaspoon Aromat
¼ pound Cheddar cheese
3 eggs, separated
6 ounces green peas

Scald milk; combine with crumbs, butter or margarine, salt, paprika, pepper, and Aromat. Grate cheese; add.

Add unbeaten egg yolks; mix well. Add peas. Beat egg whites stiff; fold in.

Bake in greased casserole in moderate oven (350°F. Mark 4) 45 minutes. Serve at once.

Serves 6.

Note: Any cooked vegetable may be used instead of peas.

VEGETABLE CASSEROLE
(Basic Recipe)

5 ounces cooked or canned peas, drained
5 ounces cooked or canned sliced carrots, drained
5 ounces cooked or canned green beans, drained
6 ounces cooked or canned diced celery, drained
2 tablespoons grated onion
12 fluid ounces medium white sauce
2 ounces fried breadcrumbs or 2 ounces grated cheese
paprika

Put peas, carrots, beans, and celery in layers in greased casserole, sprinkling each layer with grated onion. Pour sauce over vegetables.

Top with fried breadcrumbs and a dash of paprika or with grated cheese.

Bake in moderate oven (375°F. Mark 5) about 25 minutes. Serves 6 to 8.

Vegetable Casserole Variations

Vegetable Casserole with Canned Soup: Follow basic recipe, substituting for white sauce 1 large can condensed

cream of asparagus or mushroom soup diluted with 2½ fluid ounces milk.

Or, omit white sauce and diced celery, and use 1 large can condensed cream of celery soup diluted with 2½ fluid ounces milk.

Vegetable Pie: Follow recipe for vegetable casserole. Omit crumbs or cheese topping. Cover casserole with plain pastry, biscuit dough, or toasted bread cubes.

Vegetable Casserole with Mushrooms: Follow recipe for vegetable casserole, adding grilled or fried whole button or sliced mushrooms to top of casserole before sprinkling with breadcrumbs.

VEGETABLE COVER BATTER

4 ounces sifted flour
¼ teaspoon salt
1 slightly beaten egg
½ pint milk
1 tablespoon melted fat or cooking oil

Sift flour with salt. Mix egg, milk, and fat; gradually add to flour, beating with rotary beater until smooth.

Use for dipping cauliflower, aubergine, and other vegetables.

Dip pieces of vegetable into the batter. Fry in deep hot fat (365°-375°F.) 2 to 5 minutes. Makes 10 fluid ounces batter.

CREAMED VEGETABLES
(Basic Recipe)

10 ounces cooked or heated canned vegetables, drained
½ pint hot medium white sauce

Add hot vegetables to sauce or heat in sauce or place hot vegetables in serving dish and pour white sauce over vegetables.

If desired, add a little grated onion to sauce. Garnish with a little chopped parsley. Serves 4 to 6.

TO BRAISE OR "PAN" VEGETABLES

Use a covered pan or frying pan. Put in 2 to 4 tablespoons butter, margarine, bacon fat, or salt pork fat. Add a small amount of water or stock, and the vegetable. Cover tightly; cook slowly on direct heat or in moderate oven. Depending upon type and flavour of fat used, add salt to taste when vegetable is done.

You can *braise*: cabbage, chard, turnip, and other greens (omit water); celery, leeks; sweetcorn (cut from cob); French beans, peas, spring onions, aubergine, vegetable marrows, and okra.

TO STEAM VEGETABLES

Use a rack or perforated steamer insert over rapidly boiling water. Season after cooking.

Note: Portions of prepared vegetables may be seasoned and buttered first, then wrapped securely in foil or tied in parchment paper, then steamed or boiled. This method is excellent for retaining all the natural juices.

For easier serving, certain vegetables may be tied in individual servings with thick clean cotton string before cooking: asparagus, celery, leeks, spring onions, whole snap beans, etc.

TO DEEP FRY VEGETABLES

Cut large vegetables in pieces to facilitate cooking. Season both the vegetable and the breading mix with Aromat. Pre-heat fat to correct temperature (see recipe directions) and bring fat to correct temperature again before putting in another batch of vegetables. Serve immediately after cooking. Cooked vegetables are usually seasoned first; others, like chipped potatoes, are sprinkled with salt after cooking.

You can *deep fry*: potatoes, parsnips, onions (rings), asparagus, aubergines, green tomatoes, vegetable marrows, carrots, okra, and cauliflower.

TO GRILL VEGETABLES

Choose firm vegetables that will slice well and hold their shape, such as aubergine, tomatoes (green or red), celeriac, and parsnips, previously parboiled and drained. Season with salt, pepper, and Aromat. Brush or dot with fat. Grill under a moderate heat.

TO BOIL VEGETABLES

Start with boiling water. Add salt. Use high heat until steam appears around edge of cover, then lower heat to a gentle boil until vegetables are just done. Count time from moment water comes to boil again after vegetable is put in.

TO BAKE VEGETABLES

Allow 2 to 3 times longer cooking than for boiling. Some vegetables will require more liquid, or must be covered for part of the baking time. Pierce potatoes when done to let steam escape.

You can *bake*: large onions, tomatoes, potatoes, aubergine, vegetable marrow, winter squash (Hubbard), corn on the cob, and courgettes.

FROZEN VEGETABLES WITH HERBS

Cook 1 packet frozen mixed vegetables as label directs.

Meanwhile, melt 2 tablespoons butter or margarine; add a pinch of marjoram, thyme, or savory. Pour over drained vegetables and season to taste. Serves 3 to 4.

Variations: These herbs also add flavour to peas, peas and carrots, succotash, or green beans.

ARTICHOKES (Globe)

Really an unopened flower bud that grows on a thistle-like plant, the globe artichoke is native to the Mediterranean region and was popular in Italy as early as 1466. Nowadays almost all the artichokes available in Britain are grown in France, Belgium or Holland.

Artichokes have a delicate nut-like flavour. Though they may be stuffed and are sometimes pickled, they are usually boiled and served hot or cold as indicated below.

Selection: Allow 1 per serving. Size not important to quality and flavour. Choose compact, heavy globular buds which yield slightly to pressure. A good artichoke has large, tightly closed leaf scales. Freshness indicated by green colour.

Preparation: Prepare just before cooking. If unusually large, split each in half lengthwise to make 2 servings. Cut off 1 inch of the top, cutting straight across with a sharp knife. Cut off stem about 1 inch from base, leaving a stub. Pull off any loose leaves around the bottom. With scissors, clip off tip of each leaf.

Cooking Time: 20 to 45 minutes.

Cooking—Western Style: drop into boiling salted water. Season by adding a small clove of garlic, 1 thick slice of lemon, 1 tablespoon olive or other cooking oil for *each* artichoke. Add a small piece of bay leaf if desired.

Cover and boil until leaf can be pulled easily from stalk, or stem can be easily pierced with a fork—20 to 45 minutes. Remove carefully from water. Drain. Cut off stub.

Serving as a Hot Vegetable: Place upright on plate. Serve with hot melted butter or margarine, mayonnaise, or Hollandaise sauce. Put sauce in crisp lettuce cups, small crinkled paper cups or tiny ramekin dishes.

Serving as a Salad: drain and chill cooked artichoke. Place upright on salad plate. Serve with mayonnaise blended with fresh lemon juice and prepared mustard. Artichokes are often served as a starter.

How to Eat: Pull off the leaves (petals) one by one and dip the base (the light-coloured end) into the sauce. Eat only the tender part of the leaf by drawing it between the teeth. Discard the remaining less-tender tip.

Continue with leaf after leaf until you come to the fuzzy centre or "choke."

Remove the small "choke" with a knife and fork and discard it. Cut the heart into bite-sized pieces with a fork, dip in sauce and eat.

ARTICHOKES — ITALIAN STYLE

4 large or 8 small artichokes
3 tablespoons olive oil
2 onions, chopped
2 cloves garlic, chopped
2 tablespoons chopped parsley
4 ounces chopped celery
8 anchovies, chopped
4 tablespoons grated Parmesan cheese
3 ounces fine soft breadcrumbs
3 tablespoons capers
¼ teaspoon pepper
salt to taste

Wash artichokes well. Cut off about ¼ of tops and stems. Remove bottom leaves. Stand in 1½ inches of boiling salted water. Add stems. Cover and cook 30 minutes. Drain. Peel and chop stems and reserve.

Sauté onion and garlic in 1 tablespoon oil until yellow. Add chopped stems, parsley, celery, anchovies, cheese, crumbs, capers, and pepper. Add salt to taste.

Spread the leaves of the cooked artichokes apart and remove choke. Fill centre with stuffing and put a little stuffing at base of large leaves.

Place in baking dish. Cover bottom of dish with ¼ inch of water. Pour remaining 2 tablespoons oil over artichokes.

Cover and bake in moderate oven (350°F. Mark 4) until base of leaves is very tender. Baste occasionally with dripping in pan or more oil. Serves 4.

ARTICHOKE HEARTS

Globe artichokes stripped of leaves and chokes. These bottoms of artichokes are delicately flavoured and may be cooked fresh or purchased canned. They are delicious in salads or served with mayonnaise or Hollandaise sauce.

Globe Artichokes

FRIED ARTICHOKE BOTTOMS OR HEARTS

Drain cooked artichoke hearts; dip in 1 well beaten egg mixed with 1 tablespoon milk, then dip in fine, dried breadcrumbs.

Fry in deep hot fat (365°F.) 5 minutes. Drain. Serve with tartar sauce; 2 or 3 hearts make 1 serving.

Or cut each heart in half and sauté lightly in unsalted butter or margarine. Sprinkle with a few drops of lemon juice. Serve hot.

ARTICHOKE FRITTERS

3 eggs, well beaten
½ teaspoon salt
½ teaspoon pepper
½ pint evaporated milk
1 small onion, chopped fine
½ clove garlic, chopped fine
2 ounces grated Parmesan cheese
2 ounces flour
1 teaspoon baking powder
6 cream crackers, crushed fine
2 packets frozen artichoke hearts, coarsely chopped

Combine all ingredients and let stand approximately 10 minutes. Drop by teaspoons into hot deep fat (375°F.) and cook until brown and crisp. Serves 6.

ARTICHOKES — JERUSALEM

The Jerusalem artichoke is a root or tuber vegetable of the sunflower family. It has no connection with Jerusalem or with true artichokes; the first part of its name is a corruption of the Italian word for sunflower, and the second part arose from a fancied resemblance in taste. It looks like a small, gnarled white potato but is sweeter and more watery, having a taste somewhat similar to that of a cooked chestnut. The boiled tubers may be eaten hot, with various sauces, or diced and served cold in a salad.

Selection: Allow 1 pound for 6.

Preparation: Wash, peel, leave whole or slice. Cook until tender in boiling salted water, 15 to 25 minutes, or in pressure cooker 2 minutes. Overcooking toughens this vegetable. Drain; add 2 ounces butter or margarine, 2 tablespoons lemon juice, 2 tablespoons finely chopped parsley, ¼ teaspoon cayenne, and a few grains pepper. Cook 3 minutes more.

Mayonnaise and sliced olives heated in top of double saucepan, then poured over cooked asparagus on toast makes a delightful side dish.

ASPARAGUS

Of its two types, white and green asparagus, the latter is generally imported in Great Britain. The green type is an early spring crop and is usually cut just as soon as the tips of the stalks come above ground about eight inches. The white asparagus is the same variety, but it is clipped while most of the stalk is still below ground.

Selection: Buy 2 pounds for 4 servings. The stalk should be green and tender for almost its entire length. It should be fresh and firm with close, compact tips.

Preparation: Cut off tough ends and remove large scales along the stalk that hold grit. If stalks are peeled, they are as tender as the tips and will cook in the same length of time.

Peeled stalks may be placed horizontally in the saucepan in which they cook, but unpeeled stalks should be tied together and placed upright.

Wash the vegetable thoroughly but gently until no sand remains. A soft brush helps.

Cooking Time: 10 to 20 minutes.

Boiled Whole Stalks: Stand unpeeled stalks upright in the bottom of a double boiler. Add boiling salted water to 1-inch depth. Cover tightly with upper part of double boiler and boil until just tender, 10 to 20 minutes.

Drop peeled stalks into a saucepan which holds boiling salted water to a depth of 1 inch. Cover pan tightly and boil until just tender, 10 to 15 minutes.

Boiled 1-inch Lengths: Cook, covered, in 1-inch boiling salted water for 10 to 15 minutes, or until tender.

Steamed: Cook in steamer 7 to 15 minutes, or until tender.

Pressure cooked: Stand in pressure pan; add water to just cover bottom and cook to 15-pound pressure or ½ minute. Lower pressure immediately.

Serving: Remove from water carefully to avoid breaking tips. Serve at once with melted butter or margarine, white sauce, or Hollandaise sauce.

ASPARAGUS AU GRATIN

Follow basic recipe for scalloped vegetables with cheese.

DEEP FRIED ASPARAGUS

Use fresh cooked or canned asparagus tips. Drain and dip in egg and fine crumbs or flour. Chill.

Fry a few at a time in deep hot fat (380°F.) until delicately brown, about 3 minutes. Drain on paper.

With Cheese: Mix grated Parmesan or Cheddar cheese with the crumbs used for dipping, using half cheese and half crumbs.

SCALLOPED ASPARAGUS

Follow basic recipe for scalloped vegetables, using 2-inch lengths of cooked or canned asparagus. Add diced hard-boiled eggs and 1 or 2 tablespoons chopped pimiento.

ASPARAGUS SOUFFLÉ

Follow basic recipe for vegetable soufflé.

ASPARAGUS WITH PARMESAN CHEESE

Cook 1 bunch asparagus by a method given above and drain well.

Lay in a shallow ovenproof baking dish.

Sprinkle with freshly ground pepper, 3 tablespoons butter, and 1 ounce grated Parmesan cheese. Brown lightly under grill. Serves 4.

ASPARAGUS À LA GOLDENROD

Cook 1 pound asparagus. Add 3 hard-boiled eggs, sliced in 12 fluid ounces cheese sauce.

Serve hot on buttered toast. If desired, add 1 ounce chopped black olives. Serves 6.

CREAMED ASPARAGUS

Cut cooked asparagus into 1-inch pieces. Heat in medium white sauce. Serve on toast.

Diced hard-boiled eggs may be added to sauce. Garnish with chopped parsley and pimento strips.

Canned asparagus with cream sauce and garnish of sliced hard-boiled eggs.

BAMBOO SHOOTS

Edible bamboo shoots are the tender young stalks of a species of bamboo plant. They resemble asparagus spears in appearance. Freshness, crispness, and a good green colour are general indications of quality. They are commonly available canned, ready to use, and are often pickled in vinegar. Japanese bamboo shoots can be pickled in saké vinegar.

BEAN SPROUTS

Young edible soybean sprouts are commonly used in so-called "Chinese" dishes. To cook fresh sprouts, add 1 pound bean sprouts to 6 fluid ounces boiling water. Cover and simmer until almost soft, just long enough to remove the raw bean flavour. Season with salt or soy sauce.

BEANS — GREEN

Green beans are sometimes called string beans because they have to have the strings removed before using; however, nowadays varieties are usually available that only have to have the ends snipped off. Some varieties are green, some are flat and some are round but all are equally good. Selection depends upon personal taste. The fresh beans found on the market all year are in reality varieties of the kidney bean, picked while the seeds are tiny.

Selection: Buy 1½ pounds for 4 servings. They should be clean, firm, crisp, tender and free from blemishes.

Preparation: Young, tender beans need only to be washed and have the ends nipped off. Cut crosswise into inch lengths, or sliver them lengthwise for French beans. For older beans (runner bean size) remove strings and cut them diagonally in thin slices.

Cooking Time: 10 to 20 minutes.

Cooking: Cook, covered, in ½ inch of boiling salted water. Allow 15 to 20 minutes for cut beans; 10 minutes for French beans.

Serving: Season with salt and pepper and butter or margarine. For variety, bacon or ham dripping or crumbled crisp-cooked bacon will add a good flavour.

To Serve Raw: Reserve a few young beans to cut into mixed green salads.

GREEN BEANS WITH ALMONDS

Arrange cooked and seasoned green beans in a buttered casserole. Add a thin white sauce. Cover with slivered almonds.

Bake in hot oven (400°F. Mark 6) until almonds are browned.

OLD-FASHIONED BEANS AND BACON

¼ pound bacon, diced
1 ounce chopped onion
1½ pounds fresh beans
2 medium-sized potatoes, diced
6 fluid ounces water
1½ teaspoons salt
⅛ teaspoon pepper

Brown the bacon. Add onion and let brown slightly.

Add to other ingredients and bring to boil. Lower heat and cook until beans are tender, 25 to 30 minutes. Serves 5.

Note: If canned beans are used, simmer only 20 minutes.

SWEET AND SOUR GREEN BEANS

1 pound canned green beans
3 rashers bacon, diced
3 tablespoons sweet pickle juice

Drain beans; cook bean liquid until 3 fluid ounces remains. Fry bacon until crisp.

Add beans, bacon, and pickle juice to hot liquid. Simmer to blend flavours, about 15 minutes. Serves 4 to 5.

SAUTÉED BEANS

Cook and season 1½ pounds beans cut in strips.

Drain and cook in 2 ounces butter or margarine about 5 minutes, stirring frequently. Serve hot.

ITALIAN GREEN BEAN CASSEROLE

12 ounces canned green beans
1 tablespoon dried chopped onion
pinch garlic powder, or ½ clove garlic, finely chopped
3 eggs beaten
3 ounces soft stale breadcrumbs
¼ teaspoon oregano
⅛ teaspoon pepper
½ teaspoon salt
2 ounces grated Parmesan cheese

Drain beans, reserving 4 fluid ounces liquid. Combine liquid with all remaining ingredients, mixing well. Add beans and mix lightly.

Turn into 1½-pint baking dish. Bake in moderate oven (350°F. Mark 4) about 35 minutes, until set in centre. Serve at once, from baking dish. Serves 4 to 5.

Italian Green Bean Casserole

BEANS—ITALIAN STYLE

Cook 1 pound beans until tender. Then simmer 10 minutes longer with 8 fluid ounces tomato soup, 1 clove garlic (to be removed at end of cooking period), 2 tablespoons butter or margarine, and salt and pepper to taste.

SCALLOPED BEANS

Follow basic recipe for Scalloped Vegetables.

GREEN BEANS À LA FRANCAISE

Cook covered in 3 tablespoons butter until tender: 1 medium onion, sliced; 1 stick celery, diced; 1 small carrot, chopped.

Add 12 ounces green beans and 1 bouillon cube dissolved in 2 tablespoons hot water. Simmer until vegetables are tender but not mushy. Be sure vegetables retain their crispness when you serve them.

GREEN BEANS AND MUSHROOMS

Wash and slice ¼ pound fresh mushrooms. Chop ½ small onion and cook with mushrooms in 1 tablespoon butter or margarine 5 minutes.

Add 1 packet frozen green beans, 3 fluid ounces boiling water, and ½ teaspoon salt. Bring to boil; cover, and cook 8 to 12 minutes, or until beans are just tender.

Add 2 fluid ounces double cream to undrained vegetables and season to taste. Heat well. Serves 4.

Variations: Peas or asparagus are also good cooked with mushrooms.

MUSTARD BUTTERED GREEN BEANS

Cook 12 ounces green beans in boiling, salted water until tender; drain.

Melt 2 ounces butter or margarine and season to taste with prepared mustard. Pour over green beans. Serves 6.

BROAD BEANS

Broad beans are a long, round, velvety-podded variety held in high esteem by epicures.

Selection and Preparation: Same as for green lima beans. (See p.912)

Cooking Time: 20 to 25 minutes.

Cooking: Follow directions for cooking green lima beans. Add a clove of garlic while cooking or season with onion.

Serving: Same as for green lima beans.

DRIED BEANS—BOILED

There are many varieties of dried beans; the best known in the average grocery are lima, haricot, kidney, soya, yellow eye, and black.

Preparation: In general to prepare them, pick over and discard any discoloured beans.

Cover with 1¾ pints water to each 8 ounces of beans. Soak overnight. Bring to the boil in same water. Skim. Simmer until tender but not mushy. Add salt when beans are about half done.

Cooking time: The time will vary depending on size and type of beans. Dried limas cook in about 45 minutes, soya beans 2 to 3 hours, some types of soya beans as much as 4 to 6 hours, other beans 1 to 3 hours. Add water from time to time as it cooks away.

Some types of dried beans are available treated to eliminate the soaking. Follow directions on packet for these.

Pressure Cooked Beans: Cook limas 20 minutes, kidney beans 15 minutes, soya beans 40 minutes.

Note: Dried beans swell to double or more in bulk as they cook.

Serving: To serve as boiled beans, season with salt and pepper to taste. Dress with butter, margarine, or a little olive oil. Or, add a small amount of fat meat —salt pork, bacon, or ham bone with some meat left on for the last hour of cooking. Chopped fresh parsley is a good addition to a serving of boiled beans.

Boiled beans are good hot or cold; they are useful in salad mixtures, as sandwich filler, and in other recipes. One serving of hot boiled beans is usually about 3 ounces.

PINTO BEAN

A speckled, pink bean related to the kidney bean and common in Mexico and the U.S. Southwest. It is used dried. Also called Mexican beans.

PURÉE OF DRIED BEANS OR LENTILS

Wash well. Soak overnight in cold water to cover. (Specially treated beans should be prepared in accordance with directions on packet.)

If the beans are strong in flavour, drain and add fresh water. Otherwise cook in the water in which they were soaked to conserve minerals and vitamins.

Season with salt (about 1 teaspoon to 12 ounces beans). Simmer covered until tender, about 1½ to 2 hours. Add water as needed in small amounts.

Drain and put through purée strainer. Season to taste with salt, pepper, and melted butter or margarine.

FRIJOLES

Frijoles is a Spanish term which means literally, beans; specifically, Mexican-style beans, cooked with chilli and sometimes with tomatoes, Frijoles refritos: refried (that is, twice-fried) beans, which after cooking are lightly fried, then mashed and fried again.

FRIJOLES, SOUTHWESTERN STYLE

Pick over and wash 1 pound pink Mexican beans; soak overnight in water to cover.

Remove seeds and ribs from 6 to 8 dry Mexican chilli peppers (a variety of red pepper or pimento, grown in Mexico and in other warm parts of the world).

Wash peppers; add to beans; simmer, covered, 2 to 3 hours, or until tender enough to mash easily, adding 2 teaspoons salt while cooking. Also add more water if necessary during cooking.

Drain while hot, saving the liquid.

Heat 4 ounces bacon dripping in a heavy frying pan. Add some of the beans and mash thoroughly with a potato masher. Blend in some bean liquid, then add more beans and mash them. Continue until all beans and liquid are used; cook, stirring constantly, until thick and creamy.

Serve with tortillas which have been reheated quickly on a dry girdle or frying pan. Serves 4 to 6.

Mexican Frijoles: Use small red beans, and omit the red chilli peppers from above recipe.

Frijoles Refritos (Refried Beans): Simply heat the already mashed and fried beans in additional bacon dripping or lard, stirring constantly, until they are thoroughly hot and completely dry.

Variations: Many people like to add chopped onion, green pepper, and garlic to pink or red beans after they have cooked for an hour or so. Some like to use canned tomatoes in place of part of the water ordinarily used. Some like to add 1 to 2 tablespoons chilli powder for each pound of beans. Some add browned meat balls, or bits of ham or other meat.

MEXICAN STEWED BEANS

1 pound washed pinto (or kidney) beans
2 teaspoons salt
cold water
1 tablespoon bacon fat
1 onion, chopped
2 cloves garlic, chopped
3 seeded green peppers, chopped

Combine in saucepan pinto or kidney beans, salt, and cold water to cover. Bring to boil.

Meanwhile, heat bacon fat in another pan. Add onion, garlic, and green peppers. Cook until lightly browned.

Turn the cooking beans into this pan with enough of their water to cover. Cook gently until soft, or about 1½ hours, adding water as necessary.

At moment of serving there should be only enough liquid to make a moist dressing and not enough for a watery sauce.

Note: This is one of the commonest daily dishes of Mexico. The recipe is varied by substituting for the green peppers, *Chile Ancho Pulp,* or pulp from any of the many kinds of chile peppers available.

SOYA BEANS

The soya bean is the seed of any of several hundred plants that have been cultivated in the Orient for probably 5,000 years. It is the most nutritious of legumes, with a high content of good-quality protein. Soya beans are not eaten much fresh in the Western world but are grown for flour, oil, feed, and other commercial products. In the Far East they are a basic food. They are ground into meal, pressed into cakes, fermented into cheeses, and boiled and crushed to make a sort of milk.

GREEN SOYA BEANS

Fresh green soya beans are very similar to fresh green peas in appearance and flavour. Use young vegetable soya beans (not the field type) while pods are still green.

To shell, drop the pods in boiling water. Cover and let stand 5 minutes. Drain and cool slightly. Press the beans out of pods by squeezing with thumb and forefinger.

Cook beans in lightly salted boiling water until tender, 10 to 25 minutes. (Use ½ pint water to 1 pound beans.) Some varieties cook more quickly than others.

If desired, they may be cooked in the pods 25 to 30 minutes, cooled and shelled. The shelled beans may be cooked 5 to 10 minutes more before being served. Or they may be steamed instead of boiled.

To serve, follow recipes for fresh or canned lima beans, or season simply with salt and pepper to taste and melted butter, or serve with crisply fried bacon or salt pork.

DRIED SOYA BEANS

Dried soya beans (either the vegetable or field type) should be prepared and served in practically the same way as other dried beans, except that most of the varieties require a longer period of cooking. They should always be soaked overnight.

After soaking overnight, drain, add fresh water, and simmer. 8 ounces of dried beans will make about 1 pound of cooked soya beans. Some varieties will cook tender in about 2 hours. The field varieties require additional cooking time.

With a pressure cooker at 15 pounds pressure the cooking time required is from 15 to 30 minutes. 1½ pints of water to 8 ounces of beans may be used. The vegetable type softens more quickly than the field type of soya bean.

To bake soya beans, first simmer them about 2 hours. After adding such seasonings as salt pork, tomato sauce, mustard, brown sugar, or black treacle, and a couple of tablespoons of flour, bake for 3 to 4 hours in a slow oven.

Dried soya beans may be substituted for other dried beans, haricot, pea, lima, etc. in other recipes (see index).

CHEESE LIMA BAKE

4 tablespoons butter
3 tablespoons flour
1 teaspoon salt
¾ pint milk
4 ounces grated Cheddar cheese
diced pimento
1 teaspoon grated onion
6 black olives
1¼ pounds cooked dried lima beans
    (8 ounces uncooked)

Make cream sauce by melting butter, blending in flour and salt. Add milk slowly and cook and stir over low heat until mixture thickens. Add cheese and stir until melted. Stir in pimento, onion, and ripe olives cut from stones in large pieces.

Pour over drained beans in buttered 1½-quart casserole. Bake in moderate oven (350°F. Mark 4), until browned and bubbly on top, about 30 to 35 minutes. Serves 6.

Note: Addition of 2½ ounces chopped ham makes a good variation. If desired, prepare and serve in individual casseroles.

Cheese Lima Bake

BEANS—GREEN LIMAS

Lima beans are flat and kidney shaped, the smaller sizes being known as butter beans.

Selection: Buy 3 pounds (purchased in the pod) for 4 servings. Pods should be well-filled, crisp, fresh and dark green in colour. The shelled bean should be plump and have a tender skin which is green or greenish-white in colour.

Preparation: Wash pods and then shell beans just before cooking. For ease of shelling cut off thin outer edge of pod with a sharp knife or scissors—then slip out the beans.

Cooking Time: 20 to 25 minutes.

Cooking: Cook, covered, in about 1 inch boiling, salted water 20 to 25 minutes.

Serving: Season with salt, pepper, and butter or margarine or cream.

SCALLOPED FRESH LIMA BEANS

Follow basic recipe for scalloped vegetables.

BAKED BARBECUED LIMAS

1 pound large dry limas
½ pound diced salt pork
1 chopped large onion
1 chopped clove garlic
2 tablespoons cooking oil
1 tablespoon chilli powder
1 large can condensed tomato soup
1 teaspoon Worcestershire sauce
1 teaspoon soy sauce
2 teaspoons prepared mustard
2 ounces brown sugar
2 fluid ounces lemon juice
¾ teaspoon salt

Soak limas several hours or overnight in 2½ pints water. Bring to boil. Add salt pork and boil gently until nearly tender, about 30 to 45 minutes.

Fry onion and garlic in hot oil about 5 minutes. Sprinkle with chilli powder; mix well.

Stir in tomato soup, 12 fluid ounces cooking liquid from limas, Worcestershire sauce, soy sauce, mustard, brown sugar, lemon juice, and salt. Heat to boiling.

Pour over beans in earthenware casserole. Top with some salt pork. Bake in moderate oven (350°F., Mark 4) 1 to 1½ hours. Serves 6.

Baked Barbecued Limas

CHILLI LIMA BEANS

Cook ½ pound canned lima beans as label directs.

Cook 1 small, chopped onion in 3 tablespoons bacon fat, butter, or margarine until yellowed. Add 2½ fluid ounces of chilli sauce and a dash of cayenne.

Drain beans, add sauce and heat well. Serves 3.

Variations: Green beans, cauliflower, succotash, or sweet corn can be substituted for lima beans.

LIMA BEANS AND SPRING ONIONS

Cook ½ pound canned lima beans as label directs.

Meanwhile, slice 6 spring onions with tops. Cook in 2 tablespoons butter or margarine 2 minutes. Add ¼ teaspoon paprika.

Drain beans; add spring onions and season. Serves 3.

Variations: Peas, peas and carrots, spinach, green beans, or kale are good with spring onions, too.

LIMAS IN MUSHROOM SAUCE

Cook ½ pound canned lima beans as label directs. Drain, reserving 12 fluid ounces liquid.

Add to lima beans 1 tablespoon chopped onion, 1 teaspoon Worcestershire sauce, 1 can condensed cream of mushroom soup, bean liquid, and salt and pepper to taste. Heat well.

Serves 4 to 5.

Variations: Succotash, asparagus, or green beans can also be prepared this way.

DRIED LIMA BEANS IN TOMATO SAUCE

8 ounces dried lima beans
1¼ pints water
¾ teaspoon salt
2 ounces chopped onion
8 ounces cooked or canned tomatoes
4 rashers bacon

Wash beans. Add water, boil 2 minutes, then remove from heat and let soak 1 hour. Or, add water and let soak overnight in a cool place.

Add ½ teaspoon salt to beans and boil gently in the same water 45 minutes. Drain.

To bake, put onion and beans in a greased baking dish. Add tomatoes and rest of salt. Arrange bacon strips on top.

Bake in moderate oven (350°F., Mark 4) until beans are tender and most of the liquid has been absorbed, 45 minutes to 1 hour. Serves 4.

Top-of-Stove Method: Soak, boil, and drain beans as above. Chop bacon and brown it with the onion in a frying pan.

Add beans, tomatoes, and salt. Boil gently until beans are tender, stirring occasionally to keep from sticking, about 30 minutes. Add a little water or tomato if the mixture gets too dry.

BEETROOT

Selection: Beetroot are marketed with or without tops; the autumn crop, which is sometimes stored, being the one usually sold with only the root part remaining.

Fresh, prime quality beetroot should have a good globular shape, with a smooth, firm flesh. Those of medium size are less likely to be tough. In the early crop, a poor appearance of the leaves is no certain indication of inferiority, for beetroot tops deteriorate rapidly without affecting the root quality.

Preparation: Cut off all but about 2 inches of the tops. Wash beetroot well.

Cooking Time: 30 to 45 minutes.

Cooking: Cook whole beetroot, covered, in boiling salted water to cover until tender—30 to 45 minutes. Very old, woody beetroot will never cook tender.

Serving: Drain. Pour cold water over beetroot and rub off skins. Serve small beetroot whole; slice or dice large ones. Reheat with butter or margarine, salt, pepper, and a little fresh lemon juice or vinegar.

To Serve Raw Beetroot: Shred fine and add to salad.

CITRUS HARVARD BEETROOT

2 tablespoons sugar
1 tablespoon cornflour
¼ teaspoon salt
1 can (1 pound) grapefruit sections
2 fluid ounces vinegar
1 can (1 pound) tiny whole or sliced beetroot, drained

Combine sugar, cornflour, and salt in saucepan. Drain grapefruit sections; stir syrup into cornflour mixture with vinegar.

Place over medium heat and cook, stirring constantly, until mixture comes to the boil. Boil ½ minute.

Add drained beetroot; heat to serving temperature. Remove from heat. Add grapefruit sections. Serves 6.

Citrus Harvard Beetroot

EASY PICKLED BEETROOT

Slice cooked beetroot and cover with mild cider or white wine vinegar or 8 fluid ounces vinegar boiled 5 minutes with 4 ounces sugar. Serve lukewarm or cold.

BEETROOT TOPS

Beetroot tops contain valuable food elements and are highly palatable. Cut them off, wash and cook them as you do spinach.

HARVARD OR SWEET-SOUR BEETROOT

- **4 ounces sugar**
- **2 tablespoons flour**
- **2 fluid ounces water**
- **4 fluid ounces vinegar**
- **½ teaspoon salt**
- **2 tablespoons butter or margarine**
- **1¼ pounds cooked, diced beetroot**

Mix sugar and flour; add water and vinegar. Cook on medium heat until thick, about 10 minutes.

Add salt, butter and then beetroot. Cover and continue cooking about 10 minutes. Serves 4 to 5.

BEETROOT IN ORANGE BUTTER

Wash 6 medium-sized beetroot. Cook whole beetroot until tender, remove peel, and shred or chop fine.

Place in casserole. Add 3 tablespoons butter or margarine, 2 fluid ounces orange juice, 1 teaspoon grated orange rind, and ½ teaspoon salt.

Cover and bake in moderate oven (350°F. Mark 4) until well heated. Serves 6.

BRAISED SHREDDED BEETROOT

Peel and shred 1 pound young beetroot. Combine with 3 tablespoons butter or margarine in heavy saucepan.

Cover tightly. Simmer 3 to 5 minutes, stirring several times. Season with salt and pepper. Serves 4.

DEVILLED BEETROOT

Heat 3 tablespoons butter or margarine, 2 tablespoons vinegar, ⅓ teaspoon salt, ¼ teaspoon each paprika and dry mustard, 1 tablespoon sugar, and 1 teaspoon Worcestershire sauce.

Pour over 1¼ pounds cooked, diced beetroot, heat and serve. Serves 6.

Serve a Broccoli Casserole with Mushroom-Cheese Sauce and a topping of crisp onion rings.

BROCCOLI

Italian broccoli, which was cultivated as far back as the 16th century, is a first cousin of cauliflower and is served in practically the same way.

Selection: Buy 1½ pounds for 4 servings. Broccoli should be fresh and clean with stalks that are firm and tender. It should have tightly closed green flower buds in compact clusters or heads; there should be no yellow evident in the buds.

Preparation: Wash well and trim off a bit of the end of the stems, but do not remove the stems. The whole stalk is edible. If any of the stems are more than 1 inch in diameter, it is well to make lengthwise gashes through them (about 4 or 6) almost to the flowerets. The stalks will then cook as quickly as the flower buds.

Cooking Time: 10 to 15 minutes.
Cooking: Drop the prepared broccoli into a small amount of boiling salted water. Cover and cook quickly until just tender—10 to 15 minutes.

Serving: Remove broccoli carefully from water to avoid breaking flower buds. Serve at once seasoned with salt, pepper, and melted butter or margarine or with lemon or almond butter, or with Hollandaise or cheese sauce.

To Serve Raw Broccoli: Use the flowerets in lettuce and tomato salad or serve as an hors-d'oeuvre.

BROCCOLI CASSEROLE WITH MUSHROOM-CHEESE SAUCE

- **1½ pounds fresh broccoli spears**
- **4 ounces grated Cheddar cheese**
- **6 fluid ounces evaporated milk**
- **1 large can condensed cream of mushroom soup**
- **1 3½-ounce can deep fried onion rings**

Turn on oven and set at very hot (425°F. Mark 7). Place broccoli spears in shallow 2-quart baking dish. Cover (no water necessary) and bake near centre of oven for 25 to 30 minutes or until tender when pierced with fork.

Remove from oven and lower oven temperature to moderate (350°F. Mark 4). Sprinkle grated cheese over broccoli spears. Mix evaporated milk and mushroom soup until smooth and pour over broccoli. Top with onion rings. Return to oven and bake 15 minutes more uncovered.

Variations: Follow recipe for Broccoli Casserole, except in place of broccoli, use 1 medium head cauliflower, broken apart; 2 pounds fresh asparagus spears; or 1½ pounds fresh green beans.

BROCCOLI WITH PARMESAN CHEESE

Cook broccoli. Season with melted butter or margarine. Serve Parmesian cheese separately to be sprinkled over broccoli.

CREAMED BROCCOLI

Add ½ pound cooked broccoli to 1½ pints medium white sauce. Heat thoroughly.

SCALLOPED BROCCOLI

Follow basic recipe for Scalloped Vegetables.

BROCCOLI SOUFFLÉ

Follow basic recipe for Vegetable Soufflé.

Broccoli with Mock Hollandaise sauce, garnished with slivered almonds.

BROCCOLI WITH SLIVERED ALMONDS

Cook broccoli. Sauté slivered almonds in butter or margarine until browned. Add drained broccoli and heat thoroughly. Season and serve.

BRUSSELS SPROUTS

Brussels sprouts receive their name from the Belgian city of Brussels, where they were first grown in the 13th century.

Selection: Buy 1 pound for 3 servings. Brussels sprouts should resemble firm, miniature heads of cabbage. They should be compact and bright green in colour.

Preparation: Remove any loose or discoloured leaves. Cut off a bit of the stem end. Wash thoroughly in cold water.

Cooking Time: 8 to 10 minutes.
Cooking: Cook, covered, in 1 inch of boiling salted water only until tender, about 8 to 10 minutes.

Serving: Serve at once seasoned with pepper and a generous amount of melted butter or margarine or serve with Hollandaise sauce.

BRUSSELS SPROUTS WITH CHESTNUTS

Add 4 ounces chopped, boiled, peeled and skinned chestnuts to 1½ pounds cooked sprouts.

Melted butter or margarine, or cream sauce may be added. Serves 6.

BRUSSELS SPROUTS WITH CHEESE

Heat 1½ pounds cooked drained sprouts in the top part of a double saucepan with 3 ounces grated cheese. Mix. Serves 6.

CREAMED BRUSSELS SPROUTS

Add 8 fluid ounces medium white sauce to 10 ounces cooked sprouts. Heat thoroughly. If desired, add 2 ounces diced crisp bacon.

BRUSSELS SPROUTS WITH MUSHROOMS

Add 2 ounces chopped, sautéed mushrooms to 1½ pounds cooked sprouts. Mix well. Serves 6.

DEEP FRIED BRUSSELS SPROUTS

Cook sprouts until barely tender. Drain well and dip in egg and crumbs.

Fry in deep hot fat (375°F.) until delicately browned, about 3 minutes. Drain on absorbent paper.

BRUSSELS SPROUTS IN CASSEROLE

Season cooked sprouts with melted butter or margarine. Put in casserole. Sprinkle with fried breadcrumbs. Bake in moderate oven (350°F. Mark 4) until crumbs are brown.

DEVILLED BRUSSELS SPROUTS

Cook 1 packet frozen sprouts as label directs.

Meanwhile, melt 3 tablespoons butter or margarine; add ¾ teaspoon prepared mustard, ¼ teaspoon salt, ½ teaspoon Worcestershire, and dash of cayenne. Pour over drained sprouts. Serves 3.

Variations: Prepare devilled cauliflower or green beans in the same way.

Brussels sprouts: This picture shows how "sprouts" grow on their stalk. They are gathered as they become ready from the bottom of the stalk upwards.

CABBAGE

Selection: There are numerous common varieties of cabbage but the quality characteristics are generally the same for all types. Well-trimmed, reasonably solid heads that are heavy for their size and show no discoloured veins are your best buy. Early or new cabbage is not so firm as some of the Autumn and Winter strains which are suitable for storing. One of the most unusual-looking varieties is called Savoy cabbage. Its yellowish, crimped leaves form a head usually not much harder than that of Iceberg or Webb's Wonder lettuce. Another novel type is celery cabbage also called Chinese cabbage, which has some of the characteristics of both romaine and cabbage. This variety is used principally for salads and its long, oval shaped head should be firm, fresh, and well blanched.

All fresh raw cabbage is very rich in vitamin C and has a fair content of vitamin B_1. Like so many other vegetables, it is also a good source of several important minerals.

Cooking Hint: The typical cabbage odour can be appreciably decreased by dropping a whole walnut into the water in which the vegetable is cooked.

CABBAGE — GREEN

Preparation: Wash well. Cut into wedges and remove the core, or shred for cooking.

Cooking Time: 5 to 15 minutes.

To Cook Wedges: Cook, covered, 10 to 15 minutes, or until just barely tender, in 1 inch of boiling salted water or the water in which a ham or brisket was cooked.

To Cook Shreds: Cook rapidly, uncovered, in a small amount (not more than ½ inch) of boiling salted water for about 5 minutes, or until just crisply tender.

Serving: Serve at once while hot. Season with pepper and butter or margarine.

To Serve Cabbage Raw: See Salads.

CABBAGE — RED

Selection And Preparation: Same as for Green Cabbage.

Cooking Time: 8 to 12 minutes.

Cooking: Follow directions for cooking Green Cabbage but add 2 tablespoons fresh lemon juice or vinegar to the cooking water to retain the cherry red colour of the cabbage.

Serving: Serve at once while hot. Season with salt, pepper and melted butter or margarine.

To Serve Raw: Same as for Green Cabbage. See Salads.

Properly cooked, well-seasoned vegetables attractively served with sauces can be a meal on their own.

This triple vegetable platter features cabbage with cheese sauce, tomato halves stuffed with seasoned cottage cheese, and buttered green beans.

CREAMED CABBAGE

Heat cooked cabbage in cream or white sauce. Season with grated cheese or curry powder, if desired.

SCALLOPED CABBAGE

Put creamed cabbage in buttered baking dish. Cover with fried breadcrumbs.

Bake in moderate oven (350°F. Mark 4) until brown. If desired, add grated cheese to crumbs.

FRIED CABBAGE

Brown drained, cooked cabbage lightly in dripping.

SWEDISH STYLE CABBAGE

Heat, but do not boil 4 fluid ounces sour cream and ½ teaspoon caraway seeds together. Mix with 1 pound cooked, drained cabbage. Serves 4.

BUTTERED CABBAGE

Add 1½ to 2 tablespoons melted butter or margarine to 6 ounces of drained, cooked cabbage.

SWEET AND SOUR CABBAGE

1 medium cabbage, red or white
salt and pepper
3 small sour apples, sliced
2 tablespoons fat
boiling water
2 tablespoons flour
3 tablespoons lemon juice
4 tablespoons brown sugar

Shred cabbage very fine. Season with salt and pepper.

Add cabbage and apples to melted fat in pan. Pour over boiling water to cover and simmer until tender.

Sprinkle with flour; add lemon juice and sugar. Simmer 10 minutes longer. Serves 6.

Note: Vinegar may be substituted for lemon juice. If red cabbage is used, pour boiling water over several times before cooking. More sugar and lemon juice or vinegar may be added according to taste.

BRAISED CABBAGE

Melt 2 tablespoons butter; add 1¼ pounds shredded green or white cabbage, salt and freshly ground pepper to taste.

Cover tightly and cook, stirring a few times, until just tender. Add water only if necessary. Serves 4.

BAVARIAN CABBAGE

Sauté 1 tablespoon chopped onion in 2 tablespoons bacon dripping 5 minutes.

Add 2 tablespoons vinegar and 1 tablespoon brown sugar. Mix with 1 pound drained, boiled cabbage. Serves 4.

DUTCH STYLE CABBAGE

Heat together over boiling water, 1 well beaten egg, 1 tablespoon butter or margarine, ½ teaspoon salt, and 2 fluid ounces thick cream or evaporated milk.

Mix with 1 pound drained, boiled cabbage. Serves 4.

CHEESED CABBAGE

Melt 2 ounces grated Cheddar cheese in 4 fluid ounces thin white sauce, then mix with 1 pound boiled, drained cabbage. Serves 4.

SOUTHERN WILTED CABBAGE

Use 1 medium head raw cabbage, shredded. Cook 4 rashers chopped bacon in frying pan until crisp.

Add 2 tablespoons sugar, 1 teaspoon salt, few grains pepper, and 2 fluid ounces vinegar.

When hot pour over shredded cabbage. Add 1 ounce chopped parsley and serve immediately. Cabbage will be crisp, though warm.

DEVILLED CABBAGE

1 large head green cabbage (2½ pounds), shredded
1 teaspoon prepared mustard
½ teaspoon salt
1 teaspoon sugar
3 tablespoons butter or margarine
1 tablespoon lemon juice

Cook cabbage in covered pan in rapidly boiling salted water about 5 to 7 minutes, until just tender; drain.

Meanwhile, mix remaining ingredients in saucepan. Heat slowly, stirring to blend. Pour over hot cabbage, mixing lightly. Serves 6.

Don't be afraid of using the more unusual vegetables; try them once and you may want to have them often.

CELERY OR CHINESE CABBAGE

One pound celery cabbage makes 4 servings.

To Boil: Wash and cook whole celery cabbage in water to cover for 15 to 20 minutes; or shred and cook in ½ pint water to 1½ pounds cabbage with ½ teaspoon salt. Cover the saucepan in each case.

To serve: Drain cooked cabbage; serve with 2 tablespoons butter or margarine per 6 ounces of cooked cabbage, or 1 tablespoon butter or margarine per serving if cooked whole.

Or dress the cooked cabbage with a cream sauce or with Hollandaise sauce, using 2 tablespoons of either per serving.

To Serve Raw: Celery cabbage is popular in salads. Wash and chill it as for any other green.

CARDOON

Cardoon is a vegetable related to the artichoke. It is a tall, thistle-like plant, greenish olive in colour. Outwardly it resembles coarse prickly celery, although the taste is not similar. The stalks of this plant have at times attained a height of eight feet or more, although this is unusual. Cardoon is popular in France. It has a pleasant, though rather bitter flavour. The roots and leafstalks are usually cooked and eaten in soups; it may be served as a vegetable or used in stews. It is best when boiled and served in a salad.

Wash and scrape. Cut into short lengths (2 to 3 inches). Cook, covered, until tender in boiling salted water, 15 to 20 minutes, or pressure cook 2 to 3 minutes. Drain and serve with melted butter or margarine.

Cardoon—Italian Style: Cook 10 to 15 minutes. Drain and roll in fine crumbs. Sauté in hot olive oil. Serve with well seasoned tomato sauce.

CARROTS

The carrot owes its chief claim of nutritional fame to the extraordinary amount of vitamin A, also termed "carotene," found in its roots. About 4 ounces of raw carrots can supply over twice the amount needed daily by the average person.

Selection: Brightly coloured carrots that have a well-shaped firm flesh are best eating. Usually these are smooth, clean, and free from straggling rootlets. The condition of the green tops in most instances will help you to judge edibility in the early crops. This is no sure guide however, as tops may be damaged in handling without hurting the quality of the roots. Storage carrots are sold with their tops off, but green-topped carrots can usually be found in the shops throughout the year.

Buy 1¼ pounds for 3 servings.

Preparation: Remove tops. Scrape or peel carrots thinly with a knife—or scrub well with a stiff brush. Leave whole, dice, cut into slices or strips, or shred.

Cooking Time: 5 to 20 minutes.

Cooking: Cook, covered, in 1 inch of boiling salted water. Boil gently about 5 minutes for shredded carrot, 10 to 20 minutes for cut pieces, and 15 to 20 minutes for whole carrots.

For Variety: Add finely cut spring onion or grated dry onion to carrots while they are cooking.

Serving: Serve with a sprinkling of parsley and season with salt, pepper, and butter or margarine or serve with lemon butter or with white sauce. Carrots may be mashed and served hot seasoned with pepper and melted butter or margarine.

CANDIED CARROTS

Cut cooked carrots in halves or quarters, if large. Melt 4 ounces butter in heavy pan; add 3 ounces brown sugar. Stir until melted; add carrots and cook until well glazed.

CARROT PUFF

1½ ounces seedless raisins
3 tablespoons butter or margarine
4 tablespoons flour
½ pint milk
1 teaspoon salt
1 teaspoon prepared horseradish
½ pound grated raw carrots
4 ounces grated Cheddar cheese
2 eggs, separated

Rinse and drain raisins. Melt butter and blend in flour. Add milk and cook and stir until mixture boils and is thick.

Add salt, horseradish, carrots, cheese, and raisins, and stir over low heat until cheese is melted. Remove from heat.

Beat egg whites until stiff. Beat yolks lightly. Stir yolks into cooked mixture. Fold in whites.

Turn into greased 1-quart baking dish. Bake in slow oven (325°F. Mark 3) 1 hour. Serves 5 or 6.

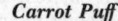
Carrot Puff

OVEN GLAZED CARROTS

Scrape 6 medium-sized carrots and cut in long strips lengthwise. Cook until barely tender.

Place carrots in baking dish. Combine 6 ounces brown sugar, 3 tablespoons butter or margarine, and 4 fluid ounces water in a saucepan. Cook until sugar is dissolved and pour over carrots.

Bake in moderate oven (350°F. Mark 4) until glazed, basting occasionally, about 20 minutes. Serves 6.

OVEN GLAZED MINT CARROTS

Add 2 tablespoons fresh, chopped mint to melted butter or margarine and follow recipe for Oven Glazed Carrots.

CARROT RING OR MOULD

1 pound mashed cooked carrots
2 teaspoons chopped onion or onion juice
2 tablespoons melted butter or margarine
2 well beaten eggs
1 tablespoon flour
½ pint rich milk or thin cream
salt, pepper, paprika

Mix ingredients, adding seasonings to taste.

Pack into buttered ring mould. Place in shallow pan of hot water and bake in moderate oven (350°F. Mark 4) 40 to 50 minutes.

Serve ring filled with green beans, peas, or Brussels sprouts, or as a main dish with creamed chicken. Serves 6.
Carrot Ring with Cheese: Use 12 ounces carrots; add 6 ounces grated Parmesan cheese and 4 ounces breadcrumbs.

SCALLOPED CARROTS

Follow basic recipe for Scalloped Vegetables. Small cooked white onions may be added.

CARROTS BAKED WITH ROAST

Scrape whole carrots and place around meat roast 1 hour before roast is done. Baste with dripping.

RICED (MASHED) CARROTS

Put cooked carrots through potato ricer. Season with butter, salt, and pepper. Sprinkle with chopped parsley.

CREAMED CARROTS AND CELERY

Cube cooked carrots; add finely cut cooked celery. Heat in medium white sauce.

SAUTÉED CARROTS

Use cooked carrots cut into long thin strips. Dip in slightly beaten egg and cream cracker crumbs.

Sauté in small amount of butter or margarine in hot frying pan until well browned. Serve at once.

CARROT TIMBALES

3 tablespoons butter or margarine
2 teaspoons chopped onion
2 tablespoons flour
8 fluid ounces single cream or evaporated milk
12 ounces mashed, cooked carrots
2 well beaten eggs
½ teaspoon salt
⅛ teaspoon ground mace

Melt butter or margarine; sauté onion in it 3 minutes.

Add flour and blend well; add cream or milk slowly, stir and simmer 5 minutes. Let cool.

Add carrots; mix well and add eggs, salt, and mace.

Pour into 6 greased ramekin dishes place in a shallow baking pan half full of hot water.

Bake in moderate oven (350°F. Mark 4) 25 minutes. Serves 6.

MINTED CARROTS

Top drained cooked carrots with melted butter or margarine to which chopped fresh mint has been added.

CAULIFLOWER

Selection: Cauliflower should have bright green leaves, denoting freshness. If it passes this test, make sure the head is white or creamy white, clean and solidly formed. Size of the head does not affect quality nor do the leaves you occasionally find growing through the curds. However, the small flowers in the head must not have started to grow or the cauliflower will be of inferior eating quality. Yellowed, withered leaves are indicative of age, particularly if the head is of "ricy" appearance.
Preparation: Before cooking soak it for 10 minutes or up to an hour, if desired, with the head down in cold water to which has been added a teaspoonful each of vinegar and salt. This will freshen the head and draw out any hidden worms if left in this water for about an hour. This same treatment can be given to cabbage, sprouts, and other vegetables. To cook, remove the green stalks. Leave the head whole or separate into flowerets.
Cooking Time: 8 to 30 minutes.
Cooking: Cook, covered, in 1 inch of boiling salted water only until tender when tested with a fork. Flowerets will require no more than 8 to 15 minutes; a whole head of cauliflower will require 20 to 30 minutes.
Serving: Serve hot with butter or margarine or serve with cheese sauce, almond butter, or Hollandaise sauce.
To Serve Raw Cauliflower: Break into flowerets and serve as an hors d'oeuvre. Use as an appetizer with a "dunking" sauce. Add to vegetable salads.

Cauliflower and Asparagus au Gratin

CAULIFLOWER AND ASPARAGUS AU GRATIN

1 medium-sized cauliflower
6 ounces grated Cheddar cheese
¾ pint medium white sauce
½ pound asparagus tips, or 1 bunch fresh cooked asparagus
1 ounce breadcrumbs

Break cauliflower into flowerets and cook in boiling salted water; drain well.

Add grated cheese to hot white sauce and blend thoroughly.

Place cooked cauliflower in buttered casserole. Surround with cooked asparagus and cover with sauce. Sprinkle top with fried breadcrumbs or dot with butter.

Bake in slow oven (325°F. Mark 3) 20 to 30 minutes, until heated through and crumbs are brown. Serves 6.

CAULIFLOWER WITH MUSHROOMS

Sauté ¼ pound diced mushrooms in butter. Add to cooked flowerets of 1 medium head. Serve on toast with cheese sauce. Serves 6.

CAULIFLOWER WITH CHEESE CRUMB TOPPING

Use large head of hot, cooked cauliflower. Sprinkle top with fried breadcrumbs, then a generous amount of grated Cheddar cheese.

Place in oven or under moderate grill to brown crumbs and melt cheese. Serves 6.

CREAMED CAULIFLOWER

Combine ½ pint medium white sauce with about ½ pound cooked flowerets. Heat thoroughly and sprinkle with paprika.

SCALLOPED CAULIFLOWER

Follow basic recipe for Scalloped Vegetables.

CAULIFLOWER À LA CREOLE

Add 1 teaspoon salt and dash of pepper to 8 ounces canned tomatoes. Cook until most of liquid has evaporated.

Place 1 pound of cauliflower flowerets in buttered casserole. Pour over canned tomatoes.

Sprinkle with 4 ounces grated Cheddar cheese and 1 ounce soft breadcrumbs. Dot with butter.

Bake in slow oven (325°F. Mark 3) 12 to 20 minutes. Serves 5.

CELERIAC (CELERY ROOT)

Celeriac, also known as celery root, or knob celery, is a type of celery with a root somewhat like a turnip. The root is the only edible portion, and is used for salads and sometimes for cooking as a vegetable. The quality characteristics of celeriac are the same as those of other root vegetables. Buy 1½ pounds for 4 servings.

Preparation: Cut away leaves and root fibres. Scrub well but do not peel before cooking.

Cooking Time: 40 to 60 minutes.

Cooking: Cook, covered, in boiling salted water until tender, from 40 to 60 minutes.

Serving: Peel the cooked root. Slice and serve hot with melted butter or margarine and pepper or with white sauce or Hollandaise sauce.

To serve Raw Celeriac: Peel, then slice very thin and season with salt, pepper, and vinegar to serve as a relish.

CREAMED CELERIAC

Combine with medium white sauce (2 roots of cereriac, boiled to ½ pint sauce). Serve hot. Garnish with parsley.

FRIED CELERIAC

Cook, drain and chill thoroughly. Dip into beaten egg and breadcrumbs.

Fry in small amount of fat until browned on all sides. Season with salt and pepper.

CELERY

Celery is a vegetable which grew wild for centuries before most people were aware of its food value. Authorities generally agree that to Italians is due the credit for "domesticating" celery and beginning its cultivation for table use. Celery is probably native to England, as old textbooks mention it as "smallage". Celery still grows in a wild state in ditches and country lanes.

Selection: Buy 1 medium head for 4 servings. The branches should be crisp and topped with fresh leaves. Home-grown celery is self-blanching or white. Green celery is imported in the winter months and is more common in the U.S.A.

Preparation: Remove leaves and trim roots. Wash thoroughly, using a brush to remove sand. Dice outer branches. Reserve inner branches to serve raw.

Cooking Time: 15 to 20 minutes; in pressure cooker, cook 2 to 3 minutes.

Cooking: Cook diced celery, covered, in 1 inch of boiling salted water for 15 to 20 minutes.

Serving: Season with salt, pepper, and melted butter or margarine and serve hot, or serve with white sauce.

CREAMED CELERY

Combine with medium white sauce (2 large bunches celery to ½ pint sauce). Serve hot. If desired, sprinkle with chopped toasted almonds. Serves 4.

For variety, add 1 or 2 green peppers, seeded, precooked, and cut in small pieces.

BRAISED CELERY

Clean, cut off leaves, and cut 1 bunch celery into 3-inch pieces.

Heat 2 tablespoons cooking oil in frying pan. Brown celery lightly.

Add ½ pint meat stock or consommé. Cook slowly until stock is reduced about ¼ pint. Season with salt and pepper.

CELERY AU GRATIN

Follow basic recipe for Scalloped Vegetables with Cheese.

CELERY VINAIGRETTE

1 head celery
4 fluid ounces olive or cooking oil
3 fluid ounces wine or tarragon vinegar
1 tablespoon chopped parsley
1 tablespoon chopped chives or 1 teaspoon grated onion
2 tablespoons finely chopped green pepper
½ teaspoon salt
dash of pepper

Wash celery and cut into pieces about 6 inches long. Cook in boiling salted water until tender but not soft; drain and cool.

Combine oil with vinegar, parsley, chives or onion, green pepper, salt and pepper; pour over celery. Let stand in refrigerator 2 to 3 hours.

To serve, lift out celery; save oil mixture to use again. Serves 4 to 5.

Green Beans Vinaigrette: In above recipe use 1 pound cooked whole green beans instead of celery.

CHERVIL

Salad chervil is a leafy vegetable generally used like parsley. Turnip-rooted chervil, sometimes called parsnip chervil, is cultivated for its edible root which is cooked and served like parsnips. See also **Chervil**, in **Herbs**.

CHICK-PEAS (GARBANZOS)

The chick-pea is the dried seed of a bushy plant of the pea family with short, hairy pods. The seeds are round, wrinkled, and somewhat larger than peas. There are white, black, and red varieties; the white is considered the best. Chick peas originated in the Mediterranean area, and are popular in Spain, south-western France and North Africa. They are used in soups, baked like beans, or coated with sugar and eaten as a confection. Chick-peas are available canned.

To prepare dried chick-peas, soak and cook in 3 times their volume of water until tender, seasoning as you do any dried beans; they will require about 2 hours. One pound will serve 5 to 6.

CHICORY

Chicory, the blanched heads of which are known as chicons, in which form it is usually seen in the shops, is also called French or Belgian Endive or Witloof Chicory, particularly in the United States and France. This has caused a confusion of names because there is a green-leafed salad vegetable, which is also blanched, known in both the U.K. and U.S.A. as Endive (see Endive). Chicory has a delicate bitter-sweet flavour; it can be eaten raw as a salad and is also delicious cooked in a variety of ways.

CHICORY WITH LEMON-EGG SAUCE

4 large (or 8 small) heads chicory
½ pint chicken bouillon
2 eggs, separated
2 fluid ounces lemon juice

When large heads of chicory are used, cut in half lengthwise, beginning at the root end. Arrange chicory carefully in a large heavy frying pan, cut side up. Add bouillon; cover, bring to the boil and simmer gently until tender and transparent, but not overcooked, 10 to 15 minutes.

Meanwhile with a rotary beater, beat egg whites until frothy but not stiff; add egg yolks and continue beating until blended. Then add lemon juice gradually, and beat until thick and smooth.

When chicory is done remove it to a deep preheated vegetable dish

Measure hot bouillon and add enough boiling water to make 6 fluid ounces. Pour hot liquid gradually into the egg mixture, then return to pan and cook over very low heat, stirring gently until thickened (or heat in double boiler). Pour sauce over chicory and serve garnished with sprigs of parsley or watercress. Serves 4.

CORN (SWEET CORN)

Also known as Indian corn it was cultivated by the Peruvians before the arrival of the Spanish settlers in South America. Many Indian legends were woven about this "all inclusive food" which in the days of the early settler, had a mixture of red, white, yellow, and black kernels on each ear. Careful breeding since then has produced the present day scientifically developed hybrids that now represent almost all commercially grown sweet corn types.

Selection: Sweet corn may be either while or yellow. In best quality, the husk is a fresh green colour while the kernels are tender, milky, and sufficiently large to leave no space between the rows. They should be just firm enough to puncture rather easily when slight pressure is applied. Ears generally should be filled to the tip, with no rows of missing kernels. If you see cobs with kernels that are very soft and very small, you can be quite sure that the sweet corn is immature. When young sweet corn is cooked just after picking it is naturally sweet and has a delicious flavour. Even a few hours off the stalk brings about changes that lessen this choice eating flavour.

MEXICAN SWEET CORN CUSTARD

1 ounce chopped onion
1 ounce diced green pepper
3 tablespoons butter or bacon fat
3 tablespoons chopped pimento
14 ounces whole kernel sweet corn
2 eggs, slightly beaten
1 teaspoon sugar
1 pint hot milk
1¾ teaspoons salt
⅛ teaspoon pepper

Cook chopped onion and green pepper in melted butter for 3 minutes; add with pimento to corn.

Beat eggs slightly, add sugar and hot milk; add seasonings and sweet corn mixture.

Pour into a well greased 2½-pint casserole. Place in a pan of hot water and bake in slow oven (325°F. Mark 3) 1 hour and 15 minutes, or until a clean knife inserted in the centre comes out clean. Serves 6.

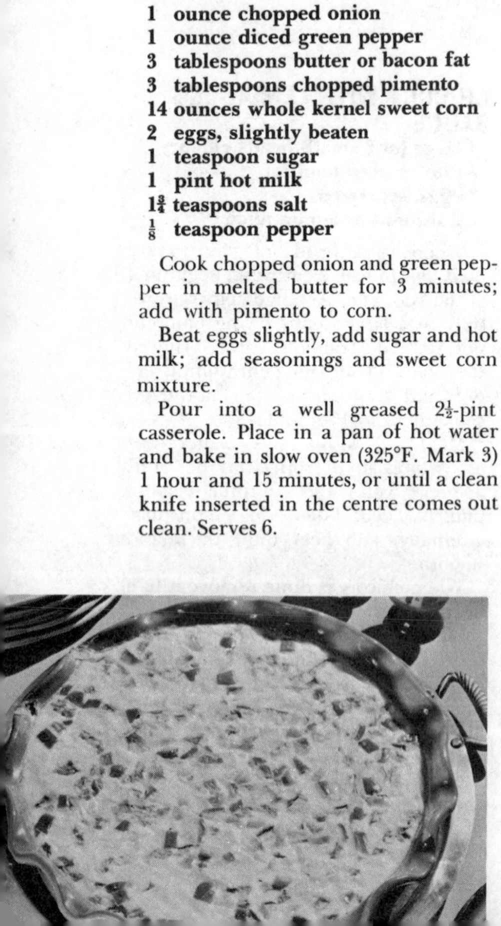

CORN-ON-THE-COB

Selection: Allow 1 or 2 ears per person. Cobs should be well filled with plump, milky kernels. The husks should be fresh and green.

Preparation: Just before serving, remove husks and silk.

Cooking Time: 3 to 5 minutes.

Cooking: Line the bottom of a pan with some of the corn husks. Put in ears of sweet corn. Cook, covered, in unsalted boiling water from 3 to 5 minutes.

Serving: Lift sweet corn from water and serve at once with salt, pepper, and plenty of butter or margarine.

SWEET CORN PUDDING

2 tablespoons butter or margarine
2 tablespoons flour
1½ teaspoons salt
½ teaspoon sugar
⅛ teaspoon pepper
1½ pints milk
1 teaspoon grated onion
4 slightly beaten eggs
12 ounces frozen sweet corn
2 tablespoons chopped pimento

Melt butter. Add flour, salt, sugar, and pepper, mixing well to blend. Add milk gradually, stirring until smooth. Cook and stir over medium heat until thickened.

Remove from heat. Add onion, eggs, and sweet corn and mix well. Carefully stir in pimento. Spoon into 2½ pint baking dish.

Place in pan of hot water and bake, uncovered, in moderate oven (350°F. Mark 4) until firm, about 1 hour. Serves 6 to 8.

SWEET CORN FRITTERS

4 ounces flour
1 teaspoon salt
1 teaspoon baking powder
2 eggs
2 fluid ounces milk
1 tablespoon melted lard
11 ounces cooked whole kernel sweet corn

Sift flour, salt, and baking powder into bowl. Beat eggs with milk; add melted fat and whole kernel sweet corn and combine two mixtures lightly.

Drop from teaspoon into deep fat heated to 365°F. (or when an inch cube of bread browns in 60 seconds).

Fry until brown and cooked in centre about 4 to 5 minutes. Drain on absorbent paper.

Makes 8 medium fritters.

ROAST SWEET CORN

Place ears of corn with husk in hot oven (400°F. Mark 6). Bake until corn is tender, about 15 minutes.

Mexican sweet corn custard may be baked either in one large casserole or in individual ramekin dishes or casseroles.

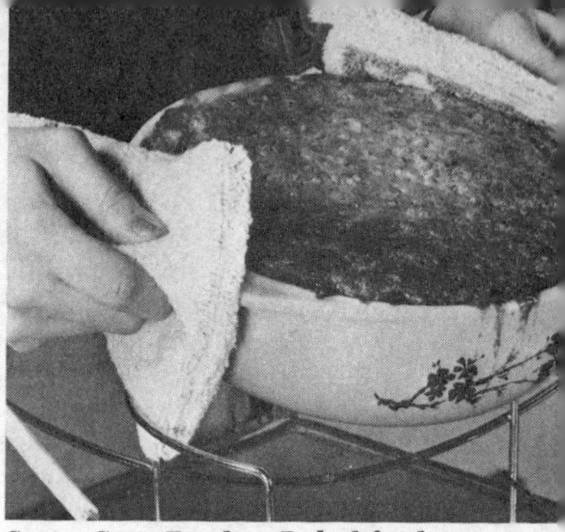

Sweet Corn Fondue: Baked fondue must be served immediately—like a soufflé—so plan to have the rest of the meal on the table when your fondue comes out of the oven.

SWEET CORN FONDUE

½ pint milk
½ pound cream cracker crumbs, finely rolled
½ pound grated sharp Cheddar cheese
2 12-ounce cans sweet corn, drained
1 ounce chopped green pepper
4 ounces chopped pimentos
2 tablespoons chopped celery
1 tablespoon chopped onion
1 teaspoon salt
½ teaspoon dry mustard
4 eggs, separated

Scald milk, add cracker crumbs, and next 8 ingredients.

Beat egg yolks; stir into crumb mixture. Beat egg whites. Fold into crumb mixture.

Pour into a buttered 2½-pint baking dish. Bake in moderate oven (350°F. Mark 4) 1¼ to 1½ hours or until brown. Serve immediately. Serves 8.

SWEET CORN PATTIES (MOCK OYSTERS)

1 pound grated fresh sweet corn
2 beaten eggs
2 ounces cream cracker crumbs
2 ounces sifted flour
½ teaspoon baking powder
1 teaspoon salt
¼ teaspoon pepper

Grate sweet corn on coarse grater or cut tips from kernels with sharp knife and scrape cobs with dull edge of knife.

Add eggs, cracker crumbs, and flour sifted with baking powder. Add salt and pepper.

Drop from tablespoon into 1 inch of cooking oil, hot enough to brown bread cube in 40 seconds. Turn once.

Makes 18 small patties.

STEWED FRESH SWEET CORN

Combine sweet corn cut from cob with small amount milk or water. Cover and simmer until sweet corn is just tender, 5 to 6 minutes. Season to taste with salt, pepper, and butter or margarine.

Chuck Wagon Sweet Corn Cakes

SCALLOPED SWEET CORN
(Basic Recipe)

4 tablespoons butter or margarine
2 tablespoons flour
½ pint liquid (use liquid drained
    from sweet corn plus single
    cream or evaporated milk)
1 teaspoon salt
⅛ teaspoon pepper
2 beaten eggs
12 ounces canned whole kernel
    sweet corn, drained
1 tablespoons chopped pimento
2 ounces dry breadcrumbs
paprika

Melt 2 tablespoons butter. Blend in flour. Gradually add liquid and cook until thickened, stirring constantly. Season with salt and pepper.

Remove from heat and slowly add beaten eggs, stirring constantly. Mix in sweet corn and pimento. Turn into greased casserole.

Combine crumbs with 2 tablespoons melted butter and sprinkle over top. Add a sprinkling of paprika.

Set in shallow pan of water. Bake in moderate oven (350°F. Mark 4) 45 to 50 minutes. Serves 4 to 5.

Scalloped Sweet Corn Variations

Scalloped Sweet Corn with Sausage Meat or Bacon: Omit butter in preparing sauce. Cook ½ pound sausage meat or 4 rashers bacon in saucepan until browned and crisp. Blend in flour and continue as directed in basic recipe.

Scalloped Sweet Corn with Clams: Add 4 ounces drained, minced canned or fresh clams just before adding eggs in basic recipe.

Scalloped Sweet Corn with Dried Beef: Frizzle 4 ounces dried beef in the butter before blending in flour in basic recipe. Decrease salt to ½ teaspoon.

Scalloped Sweet Corn with Ham: Add 1 small can devilled ham or 2 to 3 ounces chopped cooked minced ham just before adding eggs in basic recipe.

Scalloped Sweet Corn with Mushrooms: Lightly brown 2 ounces chopped or sliced mushrooms in the butter before blending in flour in basic recipe.

CHUCK WAGON SWEET CORN CAKES

2 ounces flour, sifted
2 teaspoons baking powder
½ teaspoon salt
8 ounces cooked rice
7 ounces canned whole kernel
    sweet corn, drained
1 egg, beaten
about 3 tablespoons milk

Sift together flour, baking powder, and salt. Stir in rice, sweet corn, and egg. Mix thoroughly. Add enough milk to make a thin batter. Mix thoroughly.

Cook on hot girdle or in a frying pan in a liberal amount of cooking fat. Cook on both sides until golden brown. Makes 10 cakes.

CREOLE SWEET CORN

1 onion, chopped
2 tablespoons butter or margarine
1 pound peeled, chopped tomatoes
1 teaspoon sugar
1 teaspoon salt
¼ teaspoon pepper
1 pound sweet corn cut from cob
    (about 6 to 8 ears)
½ medium green pepper, chopped

Fry onion in butter until tender and lightly browned. Add tomatoes, sugar, and seasonings; simmer 10 minutes.

Add sweet corn and green pepper; simmer 5 minutes longer. Serves 6.

STEAMED SWEET CORN IN THE HUSK

Remove outer husks from sweet corn; turn back inner husks and remove silk. Replace inner husks over cob and tie. Let stand in cold water in large, heavy kettle about 15 to 20 minutes.

Drain; cover and cook over medium heat until cover gets hot. Turn heat very low and continue cooking until sweet corn is tender, about 15 minutes. Serve with butter or margarine and salt.

GRILLED SWEET CORN

Drain boiled corn-on-the-cob. Spread generously with butter or margarine. Place on rack in preheated grill. Use high flame, turning ears to brown. Sprinkle with salt.

SQUAW SWEET CORN

3 rashers bacon, diced
1¾ pounds canned sweet corn
½ teaspoon salt
dash of pepper
3 slightly beaten eggs
6 buttered toast rounds

Fry bacon until crisp, add sweet corn and heat thoroughly.

Add seasonings to eggs and pour over sweet corn. Cook slowly, stirring occasionally until eggs are cooked. Serve on toast. Serves 6.

CUCUMBERS

Selection: A good guide in buying cucumbers is to remember that those which are firm, fresh, and bright green are best. The shade of colour is important, as the older ones tend to be of a rather deep black-green or sometimes yellow. Poor quality is also indicated by an outside rind that has a decided "give" to it when slight pressure is applied.

Preparation: Peel thinly and cut into thick slices.

Cooking Time: 10 to 15 minutes.

Cooking: Cook, covered, in a small amount of boiling salted water until tender, from 10 to 15 minutes.

Serving: Season with melted butter or margarine and pepper. Serve hot.

To Serve Raw: Do not peel if skins are tender. Slice, cover with vinegar and season with salt, pepper, and finely sliced onion or see recipes and serving suggestions in appetizers and salads.

FRIED (SAUTÉED) CUCUMBERS

Peel and cut in slices at least ¼ inch thick. Dry on paper towels. Sprinkle with salt, pepper, and flour.

Brown in butter or margarine, or dip in crumbs, then in slightly beaten egg, and again in crumbs and fry in deep hot fat (385°F.). Drain on paper towels.

BAKED STUFFED CUCUMBERS

4 large cucumbers
2 tablespoons chopped onion
2 tablespoons chopped parsley
4 tablespoons butter or margarine
4 ounces breadcrumbs
8 fluid ounces tomato pulp
1 teaspoon salt
pepper

Wash and peel cucumbers if the skin is tough. Cut in half lengthwise. Scoop out as much of seed portion as possible without breaking the fleshy part.

Parboil cucumber shells in lightly salted water 10 minutes. Drain.

Meanwhile cook onion and parsley in fat. Add other ingredients and cucumber pulp. Cook this mixture 5 minutes.

Fill cucumber shells with hot stuffing. Place in shallow baking dish. Add a little water to keep them from sticking.

Bake in moderate oven (350°F. Mark 4) 15 minutes, or until stuffing has browned on top. Serve in baking dish.

Serves 4 to 6.

DANDELION

When used as a food, dandelions usually are served as a salad green. However, cooked dandelion leaves are an excellent source of vitamin A, 2 ounces supplying more than enough of this element to meet the normal daily requirements.

Good quality is characterized by a fresh green appearance and comparatively large, tender leaves. See **Greens.**

DANDELION SALAD

½ pound young dandelion leaves
3-4 spring onions
2 tomatoes
French dressing

Wash and dry the leaves and chop them coarsely. Add the thinly sliced onions and mix lightly with the dressing. Put in a salad bowl and arrange the peeled thinly sliced tomatoes overlapping slightly round the edge.

DANDELION LEAVES WITH BACON

1½ pounds young dandelion leaves
4 rashers bacon
4 fluid ounces wine vinegar
salt

Wash the leaves and cut into coarse shreds, then drain well. Dice the bacon and fry gently until crisp. Gradually add the vinegar and when it is hot, put in the dandelion leaves. Cover and cook slowly until the leaves are soft and look wilted. Add a little salt if necessary, depending on the bacon used.

EGGPLANT OR AUBERGINE

Native to the tropics, but widely grown in the United States and Europe, the aubergine has a white or purple colour, depending on the variety. Aubergines are at their best in July and August but are usually obtainable throughout the year.
Selection: Purple aubergines should be of a clear, dark glossy colour that covers the entire surface. Heaviness and firmness of flesh are also important. Watch the size of aubergines you buy. A good rule to follow is to choose pear-shaped aubergines from 3 to 6 inches in diameter. Buy one medium aubergine (about 1½ pounds) for 4 servings.
Preparation: It is not necessary to peel aubergines unless the skin is tough. Do not soak in salt or in salt water before cooking. Wash well.

GRILLED AUBERGINE

Cut aubergine into ½- to ¾-inch slices. Brush with melted butter or margarine or bacon dripping.

Place under a hot grill. Grill about 5 minutes, or until brown. Turn and brown other side.

Season and serve hot. Serve with grilled meat.

SCALLOPED AUBERGINE

1 medium aubergine
4 tablespoons butter or margarine
2 tablespoons chopped green pepper
2 tablespoons chopped onion
1 pound cooked or canned
tomatoes
1 teaspoon salt
pepper to taste
4 ounces bread cubes

Peel aubergine if necessary and cut into small even pieces.

Brown green pepper and onion in 2 tablespoons butter in frying pan.

Add tomatoes, salt, pepper, and aubergine; simmer 10 minutes. Pour into greased baking dish.

Melt rest of butter and mix with bread cubes. Spread over top of aubergine mixture.

Bake in moderate oven (350°F. Mark 4) 20 minutes, or until aubergine is tender and bread cubes are brown. Serves 4.

AUBERGINE AU GRATIN

1 large aubergine
2 eggs, slightly beaten
about 7 ounces cream cracker
crumbs, (finely rolled)
4 fluid ounces olive oil or cooking
oil
¾ pint tomato sauce
1 clove garlic, chopped
1 tablespoon chopped parsley
¼ teaspoon basil
1 teaspoon oregano
6 ounces Mozzarella cheese

Peel aubergine, cut crosswise, making ¼-inch slices. Dip slices in egg, then into dry crumbs (about 4 ounces). Sauté in oil until golden brown. Drain well.

Combine tomato sauce, remaining crumbs, and next 4 ingredients. Simmer gently 20 minutes, stirring frequently.

Alternate slices of aubergine, sauce, and slices of cheese in a 1-quart baking dish. Bake in moderate oven (350°F. Mark 4) 30 minutes. Serves 4 to 6.

STUFFED AUBERGINE

2 small aubergines, cut in half
1 ounce diced green pepper
1 ounce diced onion
1 ounce diced celery
1 tablespoon cooking oil
1 large can condensed tomato soup
8 ounces cooked rice
½ teaspoon salt
dash of pepper
dash of thyme
18 cream crackers, finely crushed
(about 6 ounces crumbs)
butter or margarine

Simmer aubergines in salted boiling water until almost tender, about 10 minutes.

Sauté green pepper, onion, and celery in oil until golden brown. Combine with tomato soup, rice, salt, pepper, and thyme.

Scoop out centre of aubergines; leave ½-inch layer of pulp around edges. (Save pulp scooped out of aubergines and add to spaghetti sauce another day.)

Sprinkle 2 tablespoons cream cracker crumbs over bottom of each shell. Fill with rice mixture. Spread remaining crumbs over top; dot with butter or margarine.

Bake in moderate oven (375°F. Mark 5) 30 minutes. Serves 4.

PAN FRIED (SAUTÉED) AUBERGINE

Cut aubergine into ½- or 1-inch slices. Peel if necessary.

Dip in flour, or dip in fine dry breadcrumbs, then in an egg beaten with 2 tablespoons of milk, then dip in flour or crumbs again.

Season and fry slowly in a small amount of hot fat until browned on one side and rather transparent looking. Turn and brown on other side. Serve hot.

BAKED AUBERGINE

Marinate sliced aubergine in French dressing for 15 minutes. Drain or spread with softened butter.

Bake in hot oven (400°F. Mark 6) until tender, about 15 minutes, turning once. Sprinkle with lemon juice.

Aubergine au Gratin

DEEP FRIED AUBERGINE

Peel aubergine if necessary and cut in ¼-inch slices crosswise.

Sprinkle with salt and pepper and dip in flour. Dip in egg which has been beaten with 2 tablespoons of milk. Roll in fine, dry breadcrumbs until completely covered.

Fry in hot deep fat from 2 to 4 minutes, or until golden brown.

Drain. Season with salt and pepper. Serve hot.

AUBERGINE CASSEROLE
(Italian Style)

1 aubergine
1 well beaten egg
3 fluid ounces milk
½ teaspoon salt
½ pound Mozzarella cheese, sliced
3 tomatoes, sliced
oregano, salt, pepper
1 tablespoon olive oil

Wash aubergine thoroughly, then slice ¼ inch thick without peeling.

Dip slices into batter made by blending egg, milk, and salt. Brown in frying pan in which 2 tablespoons dripping or fat have been heated.

Place several slices of fried aubergine in bottom of casserole.

Place thin slices of cheese and tomato on top of aubergine. Sprinkle with oregano, using about ½ teaspoon per layer. Season with salt and pepper.

Repeat procedure until aubergine is used. Pour olive oil on top of last layer of cheese.

Cover and bake in moderate oven (350°F. Mark 4) about 30 minutes, removing cover for last 10 minutes of cooking.

If desired, a garlic flavouring can be given by adding crushed clove of garlic to the melted dripping in which aubergine slices are browned. Serves 6.

ENDIVE, ESCAROLE

Endive, which is a green salad plant, is available in two types—the curly-leaved which is the most popular, and the broad-leaved. Batavia and Escarole are similar plants which can be prepared like Endive.

Curly endive grows in a bunchy head, with narrow, ragged-edge leaves which curl at the ends. The centre of the head is a yellowish white and has a milder taste than the darker green outer leaves which tend to be slightly bitter. If this centre is not so white as desired when the endive is purchased, it can be further bleached by covering overnight with a damp cloth.

There is another variety of endive

with broad leaves (Batavian endive) that do not curl at the tips. It is the type which is almost universally marketed as escarole.

Witloof chicory is a rather tightly folded plant that grows upright in a thin, elongated stalk with creamy-white, smooth tapering leaves 1 to 2 inches wide, rather than flat or bushy like endive or escarole. This vegetable is usually bleached a decided white while growing.

BRAISED ENDIVE

3-4 endive
3 tablespoons lemon juice
4 fluid ounces chicken stock
1 tablespoon sugar
3 tablespoons butter
1 tablespoon flour

Wash and blanch the endive for about 10 minutes, then drain, cut in halves and put in a greased ovenproof dish. Add the lemon juice, stock, salt, sugar and 2 tablespoons of the butter. Bring to the boil, then cover. Simmer gently for about 25 minutes. Remove the endive, put into a hot serving dish and keep hot. Reduce the liquid left in pan. Mix the remaining butter with the flour and stir a little at a time into the liquor in the pan. Pour over the endive and serve immediately.

FLORENCE FENNEL

Florence Fennel, also called sweet fennel or finocchio, is similar in appearance to celery but has a spicy licorice flavour. It should be tender and have a well-developed bulb when bought in the fresh state. This edible type of fennel should not be confused with the variety that is grown only for the oil that is secreted by its leaves.

Selection: Buy 1 medium-sized bulb per serving.

Preparation: Scrape the bulb. Cut bulb and stalk into 1-inch slices.

Cooking Time: 15 to 20 minutes.

Serving: Serve hot seasoned with salt, pepper, melted butter or margarine, and fresh lemon juice.

Cooking: Cook, covered, in a small amount of boiling salted water 15 to 20 minutes, or until just tender.

To Serve Raw: Serve like celery. Cut heads in quarters or eighths, or scrape the bulb, slice thin and use in salads.

BAKED FENNEL

2 young fennel roots
2 tablespoons milk
1½ ounces butter
2 tablespoons grated Parmesan cheese

Remove any coarse outside leaves and cook in boiling salted water until tender—about 20 minutes. Cut vertically into 4 slices and arrange in a shallow fireproof dish in which half the butter has been melted. Pour the milk over, sprinkle with cheese and dot with the remaining butter. Cook in a moderately hot oven (400°F. Mark 6), until golden brown, about 20 minutes.

FENNEL SICILIANA

3 roots fennel
2 tablespoons oil
½ small onion, finely chopped
½ clove garlic
salt, black pepper
¼ pint chicken stock
2-3 tablespoons grated Parmesan cheese

Wash and trim the fennel and cut into quarters. Heat the oil in a sauté pan, add the onion and sauté for five minutes. Add the crushed garlic and fennel and sauté for a further ten minutes, shaking the pan frequently. Add a little salt and pepper and the stock. Cover and cook over low heat for about fifteen minutes or until the fennel is tender. Sprinkle with the cheese and brown under a hot grill.

FENNEL JARDINIÈRE

3 heads fennel
1 clove garlic, chopped
1 onion, sliced
1 carrot, sliced or 3 ounces green peas
4 fluid ounces consommé, chicken stock, or water
salt
1 tablespoon melted butter or olive oil

Cut tops off fennel and remove any outer discoloured stalks. Wash well. Cut each head into quarters or sixths, leaving stalks attached at root end.

Combine fennel, garlic, onion, carrot or peas, consommé, stock or water, and salt. Cook, covered, until tender, about 15 minutes.

Drain or serve in stock with butter or olive oil. Serves 4.

GREENS

Use young tender beetroot tops; carrot tops—add to other greens; kale; spring greens; outer leaves of endive and escarole; outer leaves of lettuce; radish tops—add to other greens; chard; turnip tops, and dandelion leaves.

Selection: Buy 2 pounds of greens for 4 servings. Select greens which are fresh, crisp, tender and have a good bright fresh colour.

Preparation: Same as for spinach (which see).

Cooking Time: 5 to 25 minutes, depending on variety.

Cooking: Follow directions for cooking spinach. Allow 5 to 15 minutes for beetroot tops; 15 to 20 minutes for endive, escarole, lettuce, chard; 10 to 15 minutes for spring greens; 15 to 25 minutes for turnip tops and kale.

Serving: Season with salt, pepper, and butter or margarine. Small pieces of bacon may be crisped and served mixed with greens.

GREENS WITH BACON DRESSING

1½ to 2 pounds greens (dandelion, young beetroot, chard, spinach, escarole, or a mixture of these)
1 ounce spring onions, chopped
4 rashers bacon
2 tablespoons vinegar
½ teaspoon dry mustard
1½ teaspoons sugar
salt and pepper
2 hard-boiled eggs, sliced

Pick over greens, removing any tough stems. Wash thoroughly, lifting them from one water to another until no sand remains.

Cook in small amount salted water until tender and drain well.

Chop if leaves are large. Add spring onions.

Cook bacon until crisp. Remove and set aside. To fat in pan, add vinegar, mustard, sugar, and salt and pepper to taste.

Add to hot vegetables. Turn into serving dish. Garnish with egg slices and reserved bacon, crumbled. Serves 4.

KALE

Kale (or Borecole) is a large, hardy, curly leafed green of the cabbage family, inexpensive and usually available throughout the winter. Dark green kale is best but a few leaves with slightly browned edges are not objectionable, as they can readily be trimmed.

Cut off the root and wash thoroughly. Remove heavy stems from leaves. For 1 pound kale, add ½ pint water and ½ teaspoon salt. Cover and cook 15 to 20 minutes.

Drain, chop, and add 2 tablespoons butter or margarine.

Or add lemon juice and butter or margarine to the hot cooked kale. Mix. Sprinkle the top with chopped hard-boiled egg.

CREAMED KALE

Cook 1 pound kale. Add 6 fluid ounces medium white sauce to drained, chopped kale instead of butter or margarine.

KALE—COUNTRY STYLE

Cook 1 pound kale in ½ pint boiling water. Drain and chop. Put back in saucepan.

Add 3 tablespoons bacon fat and 1 tablespoon pickle relish. Heat well and season to taste. Serves 3.

Variations: Other greens or green beans may be prepared in the same way.

KOHLRABI

Kohlrabi is a vegetable of the cabbage family with a turnip-like thickened bulb or root. It should be young, small, and tender, as the large overgrown specimens are tough and woody. The young tender leaves are eaten as greens.

Selection: Allow 1 medium-sized kohlrabi per person. Look for small or medium-sized kohlrabi with fresh tops.

Preparation: Remove leaves. Peel and cut into cubes or slices.

Cooking Time: 25 minutes.

Cooking: Cook, covered, in a small amount of boiling salted water until tender, about 25 minutes.

Serving: Serve hot, seasoned with pepper and melted butter or margarine or with white sauce.

Kohlrabi may be diced, cooked, and served with boiled chestnuts or with grilled mushrooms. A topping of grated nuts offers an unusual and delicious touch to a dish of kohlrabi.

MASHED KOHLRABI

Mash the cooked bulbs; season with salt, pepper, and butter or margarine.

KOHLRABI PATTIES

Mash the cooked bulbs; season with salt and pepper. Form into small patties; dip in seasoned flour and fry in butter or margarine.

SCALLOPED KOHLRABI

Follow basic recipe for Scalloped Vegetables.

LEEKS

This member of the onion family has a mild onion flavour and, although highly acceptable when cooked alone, it is most often combined with other vegetables. Part of the green top, as well as the lower white section, is used.
Selection: Buy 2 bunches for 4 servings.
Preparation: Cut off green tops to within 2 inches of the white part. Wash.
Cooking Time: 15 minutes; in pressure saucepan, cook 2 or 3 minutes.
Cooking: Cook, covered, in boiling salted water until just tender, about 15 minutes.
Serving: Drain and serve hot, seasoned with pepper and melted butter or margarine.

CREAMED LEEKS

Follow basic recipe for Creamed Vegetables.

LEEKS AU GRATIN

Arrange cooked stalks in baking dish. Season with salt and pepper. Sprinkle with grated cheese. Place under grill to melt cheese.

LENTILS

The lentil is the dried seed of a plant of the pea family, round and flattish in shape and purplish green to red in colour. Lentils have been used since biblical times. They are prepared and cooked like dried beans or peas and may be substituted for them in many dishes. One pound of lentils serves 6 to 8.
Cooking: Wash, drain, cover with water and soak overnight. Then drain, cover with water and simmer until tender, 20 to 30 minutes.

Serve with butter or margarine and lemon juice, or use in combination with other foods.
Savoury Lentils: Add 1 or 2 slices of fat salt pork to the cooking lentils; lower the heat and simmer lentils slowly.

Remove pork before serving. Garnish the cooked lentils with chopped parsley.

Just a bit of effort makes the simplest vegetable plate look appetizing.

LETTUCE

While there are several types of lettuce which are commercially important, the variety known as *Iceberg* or *Webb's Wonder* is by far the most popular and widely known. Available the year round, this is a tight-headed variety of lettuce, medium green on the outside with a very pale green heart. When making your selection at the grocery, look for heads that are heavy for their size with leaves clean and free from burned or rusty-looking tips. Along with freshness of appearance, weight and solidity are the best indications of all-round good quality in lettuce.

Round lettuce, sometimes called "Butterhead", is another rather well-known variety of lettuce. This type forms heads somewhat softer and lighter than Iceberg and is not so crisp in texture. Round lettuce is medium in size with light green outer leaves and light yellow leaves inside.

Romaine, or *cos*, has a green, elongated head of moderate firmness with a coarser leaf and stronger flavour than Iceberg lettuce. The long stiff leaves are usually medium dark to dark green on the outside and become greenish white near the centre.

Leaf lettuce, as its name implies, grows with leaves loosely branching from its stalk and has a crisp texture. It is popular in the United States.

Corn salad, a lettuce-like vegetable, is also known as lamb's lettuce or fetticus. Its leaves are generally used in the fresh state but are also sometimes cooked as greens.

Although lettuce is usually regarded as a salad green or garnish — one of the most popular — it may be cooked in simple ways. The French often cook lettuce, mainly by braising.

BRAISED LETTUCE

    3 small lettuce hearts or 1 large
        heart, quartered
    2 tablespoons butter or margarine
    salt and pepper
    pinch of nutmeg
    1 tablespoon lemon juice

Soak lettuce in cold water 1 hour. Drain. Tie firmly with string. Cook in boiling salted water 10 minutes. Drain and cut off string.

Melt butter in heavy frying pan; add lettuce, season and cook slowly 35 minutes. Pour lemon juice over lettuce. Serves 2 to 3.

MOREL

Morel is a member of the truffle family; this edible fungus is usually classed with the mushrooms since it grows above ground, whereas truffles grow underground.

MUSHROOMS

Many edible varieties of mushrooms are known, but the cultivated mushrooms on the market belong, almost entirely, to a single species. There is no need to worry about mushrooms bought in the shops; however it's dangerous to collect wild mushrooms. There is no simple way to identify the edible types and some poisonous mushrooms so closely resemble edible types that they even fool the experts.

Selection: Buy 1 pound for 4 to 6 servings. Buy clean, firm, moist, white to creamy-white mushrooms which are free of spots.

Preparation: Clean by brushing well. Do not wash unless loam clings to them. If it's necessary to wash mushrooms, wash quickly; do not soak. Do not peel unless skin is tough and brown. If you have to peel, save the skin to make mushroom soup. Leave whole, or remove stems and chop fine, leaving caps whole.

Cooking Time: 8 to 10 minutes.

Cooking (Sautéed): Cook in a covered frying pan in 2 ounces butter or margarine for 8 to 10 minutes. Season with salt and pepper.

Serving: Serve as a hot vegetable, or combine with other freshly cooked hot vegetables — peas, green beans, or green limas, etc.

CREAMED MUSHROOMS

Proceed as for sautéed mushrooms, blending in 2 teaspoons flour for each ½ pound mushrooms. Add ½ pint thin cream when half done.
vegetables — peas, green beans, or green limas, etc.

CREAMED CANNED MUSHROOMS

Use 4 ounces canned mushrooms to ½ pint medium white sauce. Heat thoroughly. Serve very hot on toast.

GRILLED MUSHROOMS

Clean mushrooms, removing stems. Chop stems and season with salt and pepper.

Place caps gill-side-down under moderate grill 2 to 3 minutes. Turn and season with salt and pepper.

Fill hollows with chopped seasoned stems and dot with butter. Grill a few minutes longer.

Lift carefully from grill so that juices are not lost. Serve on buttered toast.

DRIED MUSHROOMS — CHINESE STYLE

    ½ pound dried mushrooms
    1½ pints cold water
    3 teaspoons soy sauce
    1 teaspoon salt
    2 teaspoons sugar (optional)

Wash the mushrooms several times in cold water, then cover with boiling water and soak 15 minutes.

Drain; add cold water, soy sauce, salt, and sugar; bring to a boil and cook over high heat 10 minutes. Reduce heat and simmer 50 minutes. Refrigerate in covered jar for use in Chinese-style recipes.

MUSHROOM CROQUETTES

    4 fluid ounces thick white sauce
    ½ teaspoon Worcestershire sauce
    ⅛ teaspoon curry powder
    1 slightly beaten egg
    2 tablespoons cream cracker crumbs
    2 ounces chopped mushrooms
    ½ teaspoon salt
    ¼ teaspoon paprika

Prepare the thick white sauce. Remove from heat and add remaining ingredients.

Shape into croquettes and chill thoroughly.

Fry in deep hot fat (360°F.) until brown. Makes about 6.

MUSHROOMS AND ONIONS IN WINE SAUCE

    ½ pound fresh mushrooms, sliced
    ½ pound small pearl onions, peeled
    2 ounces butter or margarine
    2 tablespoons chopped parsley
    ¼ teaspoon grated nutmeg
    2 tablespoons flour
    ½ pint chicken broth or cube or
        canned bouillon
    2 fluid ounces Madeira or sherry

Sauté mushrooms and onions in butter 5 minutes. Add parsley and nutmeg; cover and simmer 5 minutes.

Blend in flour until well mixed. Add broth and simmer, stirring 5 minutes.

Add wine. Heat and serve with steamed rice or on buttered toast. Serves 4.

Mushrooms and Onions in Wine Sauce

MUSHROOMS — DRIED

To give dried mushrooms the texture and flavour of fresh mushrooms, they should be soaked 2 to 12 hours. They can then be used just like fresh or canned mushrooms.

They may also be crushed and used dried as a flavouring. 1 tablespoon crushed dried mushrooms equals 1 ounce fresh mushrooms in flavour. Add them to cooked dishes about 15 minutes before removing from the heat.

MUSHROOMS BAKED IN CREAM

Cut stems from cleaned large mushrooms. Place in shallow buttered baking dish, smooth side down.

Sprinkle with salt and pepper. Dot with butter. Pour a little cream or top of milk around them.

Bake in very hot oven (450°F. Mark 8) 10 minutes. Serve on dry toast, with cream remaining in pan poured over.

MUSHROOMS STUFFED WITH HAM

1 pound fresh mushrooms
5 ounces chopped ham
4 fluid ounces thick cream sauce
breadcrumbs

Remove stems from washed mushrooms and put both cups and stems in a buttered baking dish in a hot oven for 5 minutes.

Chop the cooked stems with the ham; add the cream sauce and fill the mushroom cups.

Sprinkle the tops with breadcrumbs and return to the oven for 7 or 8 minutes.

MUSHROOMS STUFFED WITH CRAB

Use 8 large mushrooms and 2 ounces crabmeat. Combine crabmeat, 2 tablespoons cream, and seasonings.

Remove stems of mushrooms, wash and peel. Grill rounded-side up 5 minutes. Turn, fill each with crabmeat mixture.

Cover with cheese and crumbs. Grill again 5 minutes.

CHEESE-STUFFED MUSHROOMS

Fill cavities of fresh mushroom caps with small pieces of sharp Cheddar cheese. Dot with butter.

Grill slowly until cheese melts and mushrooms are cooked through. Spear each with a pick. Serve hot.

STUFFED MUSHROOM CAPS

8 ounces medium-sized mushroom caps
3 ounces cooked pork sausage meat
2 tablespoons burgundy wine
dash of red pepper

Scoop out centre of mushrooms: fill with a mixture of sausage meat, wine, and pepper.

Place under grill until tender. Spear with cocktail sticks to serve hot.

NETTLES

Nettles is the common name for a family of plants and shrubs. Some of them provide edible leaves which are cooked like spinach and considered nourishing and tasty. A soup is sometimes prepared from young nettle leaves.

OKRA

Okra are the sticky green pods of a tall, originally African plant. Okra is used chiefly in soups and stews. It is widely eaten in the Near East, South America, the southern United States and West Africa. It is indispensable to a gumbo (see index) and is often called by this name. It may also be cooked as a vegetable.

Selection: Buy 1 pound for 4 servings. Buy young, tender, clean pods which snap easily. Choose small- to medium-sized pods, from 2 to 4 inches in length.

Preparation: Wash well and cut off stems. Leave small pods whole and cut large pods into ½-inch slices.

Cooking Time: 10 minutes.

Cooking: Cook, covered, in a small amount of boiling salted water until just tender, about 10 minutes.

Serving: Season with pepper, a dash of vinegar, and melted butter or margarine. Serve hot.

FRIED (SAUTÉED) OKRA

Wash and dry okra thoroughly before cutting into ½-inch pieces.

Heat 3 or 4 tablespoons fat in heavy frying pan. Add okra, cover and cook 10 minutes, stirring frequently to prevent burning.

Remove cover and cook until tender and lightly browned. Serve at once.

STEWED OKRA AND TOMATOES

2 tablespoons bacon dripping or other fat
1 small onion, chopped
1 pound sliced okra
1 pound cooked or canned tomatoes
½ teaspoon salt
pepper

Melt fat in frying pan. Brown onion and okra slightly, stirring as it cooks. Add tomatoes and salt. Cook over moderate heat until vegetables are tender and mixture is thick, about 20 minutes. Stir occasionally to prevent sticking.

Season with pepper and more salt if needed. Serves 4.

Variation: Add 3 tablespoons rice with the tomatoes. Cook until rice is tender, 20 to 30 minutes. Add a little water if needed.

ONIONS — DRY

There are several different varieties of dry onion of which the domestic is probably the most common. This variety is medium size, globular in shape and may be either red, yellow, or white.

Spanish onions are another mild variety, globe shaped and considerably larger than the domestic. They may be either white or yellowish brown.

Onions of any of the above varieties are often called "boilers" when they range from 1 to 1½ inches in diameter. Any which are still smaller than that are termed "picklers."

Selection: When selecting onions, look for those that are well shaped and dry enough to crackle. Thin necks and bright hard bulbs are two other indications of quality. Avoid those with a wet, soggy feeling at the neck, as this is usually, although not invariably, a sign that decay is starting, if not already present. Buy 1½ pounds for 4 servings. Buy bright, clean, hard, well shaped onions with dry skins.

Preparation: Peel. To avoid weeping when peeling onions, pour boiling water over them, rinse in cold water, and then slip off skins. Leave whole for boiling.

Cooking Time: 15 to 35 minutes.

Cooking: Drop peeled onions into several inches of boiling salted water. Boil small onions 15 to 20 minutes and large ones 30 to 35 minutes, or add to other vegetables while they are cooking.

Serving: Drain. Serve hot seasoned with salt, pepper, and butter or margarine, or with medium white sauce.

Creamed onions with a difference: just add a few sautéed mushrooms and seasoning to the medium white sauce before combining with the boiled onions.

Onion Cheese Squares

ONION CHEESE SQUARES

4 tablespoons butter
3 large onions, sliced
4 eggs, slightly beaten
1½ pints scalded milk
1 teaspoon salt
½ teaspoon celery salt
¼ teaspoon paprika
6 ounces grated Cheddar cheese
2 ounces sliced pimento
6 ounces dry breadcrumbs
1 ounce chopped parsley

Melt butter, add onion and cook over low heat until tender.

Beat eggs slightly and gradually add hot milk, while stirring. Add onions and remaining ingredients and blend.

Turn mixture into a buttered baking dish, 6×10×2 inches and bake in a slow oven (325°F. Mark 3), over hot water 50 to 60 minutes. Cut into squares. Serves 6 to 8.

STUFFED ONIONS

6 large onions
½ green pepper, chopped
½ pound mushrooms or 4 ounces cooked meat, poultry, fish or shellfish
4 tablespoons butter or margarine
½ pound cooked rice, soft bread-crumbs, or mashed potatoes
salt, pepper, and any other season-ing desired (soy sauce, curry powder)
1 ounce sifted breadcrumbs or grated Parmesan cheese

Peel onions without cutting off root end (in order to keep them whole) and boil in salted water until almost tender. Drain, cut a slice from top of each and remove centres, leaving a rim of 3 or 4 layers of onion. Chop slices and centres.

While onions are boiling, lightly sauté the pepper and mushrooms (or a substitute) in 2 tablespoons butter.

Add rice (or alternative), seasonings, and chopped onion. Fill onion shells.

Sprinkle tops with sifted crumbs or cheese and dot with bits of remaining butter.

Place in a pan that has a film of water over the bottom and bake in a moderate oven (375°F. Mark 5) until tops are brown, about 15 minutes. Serves 6.

SAUTÉED OR SMOTHERED ONIONS

1½ pounds large onions or small boilers
3 tablespoons butter or margarine
salt
freshly ground pepper

Peel large onions and cut into wedges or thick slices. The small boilers are easy and almost odourless to peel if they are first boiled about 1 minute and then drained and rinsed with cold water. Leave the onions whole if they are even in size.

Melt fat in a saucepan with a tight-fitting cover or in a pressure saucepan. Add onions and salt and pepper to taste.

Cover and cook until onions are tender, about 20 minutes, adding a drop of water and stirring onions once if closure is loose and steam escapes.

In the pressure saucepan, cook at 15-pound pressure about 3 minutes. Reduce pressure quickly.

If desired, serve sprinkled with chopped parsley or paprika.
Serves 3 to 4.

Smothered Mixed Vegetables: Substitute green beans, celery, carrots, or other vegetables for part of the onions in above recipe.

OLIVE-ONION FLAN

2 ounces black olives
2 large onions, thinly sliced
2 tablespoons butter or margarine
2 eggs
½ pint thick sour cream
1 teaspoon salt
⅛ teaspoon black pepper
pastry for 9-inch flan
paprika

Cut olives from stones into large pieces. Cook onions slowly in butter in covered pan 5 to 10 minutes, until transparent.

Beat eggs, add sour cream, salt, and pepper, and beat again. Stir in onions and olives, and turn into pastry-lined flan tin. Sprinkle with paprika.

Bake in hot oven (425°F. Mark 7) 10 minutes. Reduce heat to moderate (350°F. Mark 4) about 25 to 30 minutes longer, or until set in centre. Serve hot. Serves 6 to 8.

DEEP FRIED ONION RINGS

2 pounds large Spanish onions
6 fluid ounces milk
2 ounces flour
fat for deep frying

Cut cleaned onions into ¼-inch slices and separate into rings. Dip onion rings in milk and then in seasoned flour.

Fry in deep hot fat (365°F.), or when an inch cube of bread browns in 60 seconds. Fry onion rings, a few at a time, until well browned (about 3 minutes). Drain on absorbent paper.
Serves 4 to 5.

SCALLOPED ONIONS

Put 8 ounces cooked onions (quar-tered) in buttered baking dish. Cover with ½ pint medium white sauce.

Sprinkle with buttered cream cracker crumbs. Bake in hot oven (400°F. Mark 6) until crumbs are brown.

If desired, sprinkle with grated cheese before adding white sauce.

ONIONS BAKED IN CREAM

Cut large sweet onions in thin slices. Arrange in baking dish. Sprinkle with salt and pepper. Pour over cream to cover.

Bake in slow oven (325°F. Mark 3) until tender.

GRILLED ONIONS

Slice large mild onions ½ inch thick. Put in shallow buttered pan. Season with salt and pepper. Dot with butter.

Grill until tender (about 15 min-utes), turning once with spatula.

SPRING ONIONS (SCALLIONS)

A young green onion that has not developed a bulb.

Selection: Buy 2 bunches for 4 serv-ings (cooked). Spring onions are marketed in bunches. Buy onions with crisp, green tops and with medium-sized, well-formed necks well-blanched 2 to 3 inches from the root.

Preparation: Wash well and remove any loose layers of skin.

Cooking Time: 8 to 10 minutes.

Cooking: Cook in a small amount of boiling salted water until barely ten-der, 8 to 10 minutes, or chop and cook with other vegetables.

Serving: Carefully remove from water and serve hot seasoned with freshly ground pepper and melted butter or margarine.

To Serve Raw: Trim tops, remove any loose skin and wash well. Serve whole and crisp as an hors-d'oeuvre. Use chopped or cut fine in salads.

Deep Fried Onion Rings

HEART OF PALM

Heart of palm is a very delicate vegetable from the tender centre head of the cabbage palmetto tree. It is available in cans and is used chiefly in salads.

PARSNIPS

Parsnips are one of the hardiest vegetables on the market and grow well under either warm or quite cold temperatures. However, many authorities state that the parsnip's flavour is not really brought out until it has been stored for some time at a temperature close to 32°F.

Selection: Buy 1½ pounds for 4 servings (2 per person). Buy smooth, firm, well-shaped parsnips, small to medium in size.

Preparation: Scrape or peel. Leave whole or cut into halves, quarters, or slices.

Cooking Time: 30 minutes.

Cooking: Cook, covered, in a small amount of boiling salted water until tender, about 30 minutes.

Serving: Season with salt, pepper, and melted butter or margarine and serve hot with a sprinkling of chopped parsley.

MASHED PARSNIPS

Mash boiled parsnips or press through ricer. For 1¼ pounds parsnips add 4 fluid ounces hot milk, 3 to 4 tablespoons butter or margarine, salt and pepper to taste. Beat until fluffy.

PARSNIP PATTIES

Mash cooked parsnips. Season with butter or margarine, salt, and pepper.

Shape in small, flat, rounded cakes. Roll in flour. Sauté in butter.

FRENCH FRIED PARSNIPS

Cut raw parsnips into very thin slices. Fry in deep hot fat (380°F.) until delicately brown. 7 to 8 minutes.

PARSNIP SOUFFLÉ

Follow basic recipe for Vegetable Soufflé.

Carrot and Parsnip duo: carrots and parsnips are generously coated with butter, sprinkled with parsley and chives and flavoured with seasoned salt.

SAUTÉED (FRIED) PARSNIPS

Use young boiled parsnips, cut in sixths, lengthwise. Brown lightly in butter or margarine. Season with salt and pepper.

To Glaze: Sprinkle with brown sugar, then sauté.

PARSNIP CARAMEL

Scrape parsnips. Cook 20 minutes and drain.

Arrange in shallow baking dish. Sprinkle with brown sugar. Bake in hot oven (400°F. Mark 6) 20 minutes.

PARSNIP FRITTERS

Cut cooked parsnips in 3-inch pieces. Dip in fritter coating batter.

Fry in deep hot fat (385°F.) until browned.

GLAZED PARSNIPS

Cook 12 medium-sized parsnips until nearly tender. Heat 2 tablespoons butter or margarine, 2½ ounces sugar, and 1 tablespoon water in frying pan. Add parsnips and cook until glazed and golden brown. Serves 6.

PARSNIPS BAKED WITH BACON

Cook 12 parsnips. Place in buttered casserole. Sprinkle with salt, pepper, and 1 tablespoon sugar. Cover with 6 strips bacon.

Bake in moderate oven (375°F. Mark 5) until bacon is crisp and parsnips are heated through. Garnish with parsley. Serves 6.

GREEN PEAS

Selection: Buy 3 pounds for 4 servings. Look for bright green, fresh-looking pods somewhat velvety to the touch.

Preparation: Prepare and serve peas as soon as possible after marketing. Shell and wash just before cooking. Reserve a few pods to cook with the peas.

Cooking Time: 8 to 12 minutes.

Cooking: Cook peas, covered, in 1 inch boiling salted water for 8 to 12 minutes. Drop in a few of the pods for flavour.

Serving: Remove the pods. Season with pepper and with butter or margarine. Try adding a sprinkling of chopped fresh mint leaves for variety. Serve at once while the colour is bright and the flavour is fresh and sweet.

MINTED PEAS

Add sprigs of mint to boiling water with peas. When cooked, remove mint. Drain and season with salt and butter.

PURÉE OF GREEN PEAS

Put cooked or canned peas through sieve or vegetable mill.

Beat until light and smooth with hot milk or cream. Season to taste. Keep hot in double boiler. Dust with paprika before serving.

Curried peas and eggs: Canned or frozen green peas and quartered hard-boiled eggs in a rich cream sauce make a pretty but simple lunch or supper treat. Add a bit of curry powder to the sauce. Serve with a basket of toasted buns.

MUSHROOM BUTTERED PEAS AND ONIONS

Cook 12 small pearl onions and 9 ounces peas separately in boiling salted water. Drain.

Melt 2 ounces butter over low heat. Add 1 ounce cooked, diced mushrooms and 1 teaspoon grated onion. Cook slowly until mushrooms are lightly browned.

Combine peas and onions in bowl and pour sauce over. Serves 6.

SAVOURY PEAS AND CARROTS

Cook 1 packet frozen peas and carrots as label directs.

Cook 1 small chopped onion in 3 tablespoons butter or margarine until yellowed. Add 5 chopped stuffed olives.

Drain vegetables and add onion mixture. Season with salt and pepper to taste. Serves 3 to 4.

PEAS AND NOODLES SUPREME

1 8-ounce packet noodles
¾ pint seasoned medium white sauce
1 pound peas

Cook noodles in boiling salted water until tender. Drain and blanch with boiling water.

Combine cooked noodles and white sauce. Heat. Place in individual baking shells or ramekins. Top with heated, seasoned peas. Serves 5 to 6.

Variations: 2 ounces grated cheese and/or 1 ounce sautéed mushrooms may be added to the sauce.

Peas and Noodles Supreme

CREAMED PEAS

Follow basic recipe for Creamed Vegetables.

FROZEN PEAS—FRENCH STYLE

Put 2 fluid ounces boiling water, ½ teaspoon each of salt and sugar, and 1 packet frozen peas in saucepan. Add 1 small peeled onion, 1 sprig parsley, and 1 or 2 lettuce leaves.

Bring to boil, breaking up peas with fork. Cook slowly about 8 minutes, or until peas are tender.

Remove onion, parsley, and lettuce before serving. Serves 3.

SNOW PEAS

Snow peas, also called podded peas, sugar peas, and Chinese peas, are often used as an ingredient in various Chinese style recipes. They can usually be found only in Chinese shops. To prepare them, wash, cut off the ends and string, and cook in the same way as green beans just until crisply tender.

BOILED DRIED PEAS

Soak dried peas 6 hours or longer in cold water.

Drain and simmer in salted water until tender, about ½ hour.

Dried peas may be substituted in practically all recipes calling for dried beans, although black treacle is omitted in baked dried peas. Dried peas need salt to bring out their flavour.

PURÉE OF SPLIT PEAS

10 ounces dried peas
water to cover
ham bone or ½ pound salt pork
1 large onion, quartered
1 stalk celery, quartered
2 tablespoons butter or margarine

Wash peas; soak overnight in water to cover.

Drain and add to ham bone or pork in a large kettle. Add water to cover. Add onion and celery. Simmer until peas are tender.

Force through a sieve. Serve purée with melted butter or margarine whipped into it. Serves 4.

HOPPING JOHN

Hopping john is a dish of dried peas (sometimes dried black-eyed peas), salt pork, rice, and bacon dripping; believed to be native to South Carolina.

12 ounces dried peas, soaked overnight
¼ pound salt pork or other seasoning meat
8 ounces uncooked rice
3 tablespoons bacon dripping

Boil the peas with salt pork until tender, 1½ to 2 hours, or 30 minutes in a pressure cooker.

Add the peas and 12 fluid ounces of the water in which they were cooked to rice and dripping. Cook over slow heat for 1 hour. Serves 6.

Note: Dried black-eyed peas may be used in above.

BOILED BLACK-EYED PEAS

1 pound dried black-eyed peas
½ pound salt pork, cut into cubes
2 pints boiling water
1 teaspoon salt

Cover peas with cold water and soak overnight.

Drain peas; add salt pork, boiling water, and salt. Simmer for 2 hours, or until peas are done.

Serve with some of the "pot likker" in which the peas were cooked. Serves 6.

PEPPERS

Peppers, which are believed to have originated in South America, are available on the market the year round. The Sweet Pepper is the most popular variety and may be bought either green or red, according to the stage of maturity desired. Best quality peppers are well shaped, thick walled, and firm, with a uniform glossy colour. Pale colour and soft seeds are signs of immaturity, while sunken, blister-like spots on the surface indicate that decay may set in rather quickly.

Chilli, Pimento, and Cayenne are varieties of hot peppers which are often dried and sold in strings.

FRIED GREEN PEPPERS

Remove seeds from 6 large green peppers, and cut in eighths. Cover with boiling water. Cover and cook 3 minutes; drain.

Fry peppers slowly in 2 fluid ounces hot dripping until lightly browned. Season to taste with salt and pepper. Serves 4.

TO PREPARE PEPPERS FOR STUFFING

Cut off stem ends of peppers. If very large, cut into half lengthwise. Remove seeds and inner white ribs.

Parboil by dropping into boiling water. Remove from heat and let stand in the water about 5 minutes.

Drain well, stuff with desired filling, and bake as directed.

MEAT AND RICE STUFFED PEPPERS

½ pound cooked rice
10 ounces chopped cooked meat
1 tablespoon chopped onion
1 beaten egg
salt and pepper
6 green peppers
breadcrumbs

Combine and mix rice, meat, onion, and egg. Season to taste.

Stuff prepared peppers. Cover with crumbs and dot with fat.

Place upright in baking dish. Surround peppers with water or stock about ¼ inch in depth.

Bake until peppers are tender and tops browned, 30 to 40 minutes. Serves 6.

Variation: Substitute 7 ounces canned or cooked sweet corn for 10 ounces meat.

SALMON STUFFED PEPPERS

6 green peppers
1 1-pound can salmon
1 onion, grated
2½ ounces soft breadcrumbs
6 fluid ounces milk
1 teaspoon salt
1 beaten egg
2 teaspoons lemon juice
fried breadcrumbs

Combine all ingredients. Mix well. Stuff prepared peppers. Top with fried breadcrumbs.

Bake in moderate oven (375°F. Mark 5) until just tender, 15 to 20 minutes. Do not allow peppers to brown. Serves 6.

CORNED BEEF HASH STUFFED PEPPERS

4 large or 6 small green peppers
1 1-pound can corned beef hash
1 ounce chopped onion
3 tablespoons sweet pickle relish
2 tablespoons vinegar
4 fluid ounces chilli sauce
1 tablespoon brown sugar
1 teaspoon prepared mustard
⅛ teaspoon Tabasco sauce

Fill prepared peppers with corned beef hash.

Combine remaining ingredients and bring to a boil. Reduce heat and simmer 5 minutes.

Place filled peppers in casserole. Pour over sauce.

Cover. Bake in hot oven (400°F. Mark 6) 30 minutes.

Serves 4 to 6.

For added flavour, top cooked beef and rice stuffed peppers with grated cheese or fried breadcrumbs and brown under the grill just before serving.

SWEET CORN AND BACON STUFFED PEPPERS

6 large green peppers
4 rashers bacon
1 tablespoon butter or margarine
2 tablespoons finely diced onion
2 tablespoons flour
1 teaspoon sugar (optional)
1½ teaspoons salt
¼ teaspoon pepper
12 fluid ounces milk, scalded
14 ounces cooked sweet corn
1½ ounces soft breadcrumbs
1 slightly beaten egg

Wash peppers. Cut a slice from side of each and remove seeds and fibrous parts. Cover with boiling water and simmer 5 minutes.

Meanwhile, cook bacon, drain and dice. Melt butter in saucepan; add onion and cook until tender. Add flour, sugar, and seasonings and blend. Add milk gradually and cook over low heat until thickened, stirring constantly.

Add sweetcorn, crumbs, and bacon, and stir into beaten egg. Fill green pepper shells.

Bake in pan of hot water, in slow oven (325°F. Mark 3) 45 minutes or until filling is set. Serve with cheese sauce. Serves 6.

STUFFED GREEN PEPPERS — TOP OF STOVE METHOD

4 large green peppers
8 ounces minced, cooked meat
(ham, tongue, lamb, pork, beef, or veal)
2 ounces rice
1 ounce chopped onion
1½ teaspoons salt
¼ teaspoon pepper
⅓ pint tomato sauce
½ pint water or vegetable cooking water
dash of cayenne
2 basil leaves, or pinch of dry basil, if desired

Cut off tops and remove seeds from peppers.

Mix meat, rice, onion, salt, and pepper. Stuff peppers about ¾ full.

Stand upright in small, heavy saucepan with tight-fitting lid. Pour combined sauce, water, and seasonings over peppers.

Cover and cook very slowly until rice is tender, about 40 minutes. If necessary, add a little more water. Serves 4.

DEEP FRIED PEPPER RINGS

Slice peppers in thin rings. Cover with boiling water and cook 5 minutes. Drain.

Dip in egg slightly beaten with 1 tablespoon water, then in fine crumbs. Fry, a few at a time, in deep hot fat (370°F.). Drain on paper towels.

CHEESE STUFFED GREEN PEPPERS

6 green peppers
1 pound cooked rice
4 fluid ounces milk
2 tablespoons chopped pimento
1 tablespoon finely chopped parsley
1 tablespoon grated onion
1 teaspoon salt
⅛ teaspoon pepper
2 tablespoons melted butter or margarine
6 ounces diced Cheddar cheese

Prepare peppers for stuffing by cutting off tops. Remove fibres and seeds. Drop into boiling, salted water and simmer gently 5 minutes. Drain.

Combine cooked rice, milk, pimento, parsley, grated onion, salt, pepper, melted butter, and diced cheese.

Fill peppers with cheese stuffing. Place upright in baking dish; add 4 fluid ounces hot water.

Bake in moderate oven (350°F. Mark 4) 30 minutes, or until peppers are tender. Serves 6.

HUNGARIAN STUFFED PEPPERS

6 green peppers (plump, uniform)
1 pound minced beef
2 ounces chopped onion
1 egg
8 ounces uncooked rice
1 teaspoon salt
pepper
1 10½-ounce can tomato soup
1 tablespoon flour

Cut tops off green peppers. Use scissors to remove centre and all seeds.

Combine minced beef, onion, egg, rice, salt, and pepper. Mix well and stuff loosely into green peppers (allow for rice to swell).

Place upright in a casserole. Pour tomato soup mixed with 2 cans of water into casserole.

Bake in moderate oven (350°F. Mark 4) at least 1 hour or until rice is tender. (If rice is boiled 10 minutes before combining with meat, 1 hour baking is adequate.)

Remove peppers to hot platter. Combine flour and sour cream and stir into tomato sauce in casserole. Stir and boil to thicken. Pour over peppers. Serves 6.

OTHER STUFFINGS FOR PEPPERS

A vast variety of stuffings can be used besides those already given. In fact, you can make them up yourself. Here are a few suggestions:

1. Tomatoes combined with leftover meats, properly herbed and seasoned.

2. Mashed potatoes seasoned with diced onion or chopped chives and blended with cream or a beaten egg.

3. Leftover spaghetti, tomatoes, and cheese make another combination.

Cheese Stuffed Peppers

POTATOES

Potatoes are native to South America and were first brought to England (from North America) in the 16th century. White potatoes, contrary to popular belief, are not an exceptionally fattening food. As a matter of fact, one medium-size potato contains no more calories than a large apple or single scone of average size.

Furthermore, the potato is a fair source of vitamins B_1, C, and G and, in addition, has an abundant content of iron, phosphorus, and other health-giving minerals. With such a wealth of food values it is therefore obvious that potatoes more than deserve their position as the backbone of our national vegetable diet.

Selection: New potatoes, always characterized by a thin, feathery skin which may be either red or white, are ideally suited for boiling or mashing. The Arran Pilot is a good general purpose early potato, while the Maris Peer is excellent in July, August and September. Maincrop potatoes are available from September or October onwards. The best all-purpose variety is the King Edward, while Desirée is also a well-flavoured potato.

Good quality white potatoes are generally clean, firm, and free from cuts, growth cracks, and other unsightly knobs or surface defects. If you choose those that are well shaped and have shallow eyes, your waste in preparation will be kept to a minimum. "Sunburnt" potatoes, characterized by a green colour on part of their surface, should be avoided, as they are usually bitter-tasting. Also watch out for frost-damaged potatoes which generally have a watery appearance or show a black ring near the surface when cut across.

The best way to get the most food value from potatoes is to cook them in their jackets. So, if possible, start with potatoes boiled in their jackets, whether you have them mashed, creamed, parslied, or hashed brown. Boiling in the skins conserves even more vitamins than baking potatoes.

Monday—*Scalloped potatoes*
Tuesday—*Potatoes cooked in milk*
Wednesday—*Franconia potatoes*
Thursday—*Creamy mashed potatoes*
Friday—*Buttered parsley potatoes*
Saturday—*Creamed potatoes with chives*

BOILED POTATOES

Wash and scrub with brush if potatoes are to be boiled in their skins.

Cook in boiling salted water in covered pan until tender, 20 to 40 minutes.

Drain and shake in pan over low heat until potatoes are dry and mealy.

Boiled Potato Variations

Boiled New Potatoes: Scrub with brush or scrape, but do not peel. Cook as above for 25 to 30 minutes.

Cheese Potatoes: Cover hot boiled potatoes with cheese sauce or sprinkle grated cheese over potatoes. Add cream and heat.

Parsley Potatoes: For each 5 or 6 potatoes, sprinkle 3 tablespoons chopped parsley and 2 tablespoons melted butter or margarine over cooked, peeled potatoes.

Potatoes and Carrots: Cook an equal amount of sliced carrots and potatoes together until done. Season and add cream and butter.

Potatoes and Onions: Cook an equal amount of sliced or whole onions and potatoes together until done. Season with cream and butter or margarine.

Potatoes and Peas: Cook whole new potatoes with new peas. Serve creamed.

Quick Browned Potatoes: Sprinkle hot boiled potatoes with flour. Brown in hot fat.

Savoury Potatoes: Season hot boiled potatoes with cream and paprika.

Creamed Potatoes: Use cooked sliced or diced potatoes. Prepare thin white sauce.

If potatoes are cold, reheat in sauce. Add chopped pimento and sprinkle with chopped parsley.

POTATOES COOKED IN MILK

1¼ pounds finely diced raw potato
6 fluid ounces milk
1 teaspoon salt
dash of pepper

Mix all ingredients in top part of double boiler.

Cover and cook over boiling water about 45 minutes. Serves 4.

MASHED POTATOES

Boil potatoes. Force through a ricer or mash well. Season to taste with salt and pepper.

Add 2½ fluid ounces hot milk or potato liquid and 3 tablespoons butter, margarine, sour cream, or sour milk for every 5 potatoes. Beat well until light and fluffy.

To keep hot, set over pan of hot water or pile lightly in casserole and place in slow oven (325°F. Mark 3).

Mashed Potato Variations

Baked Potato Puff: Add 1 egg yolk to 14 ounces riced potatoes. Beat well.

Fold in 1 stiffly beaten egg white.

Place in greased baking pan and bake in moderate oven (350°F. Mark 4) until browned.

Mashed Cheese Potatoes: Add 2 ounces grated cheese to 14 ounces mashed potatoes.

Sprinkle grated cheese and paprika on top. Brown in moderate oven (350°F. Mark 4).

Duchess Potatoes: Add 2 tablespoons butter or margarine, ½ teaspoon salt, and 2 slightly beaten egg yolks to 1-1¼ pounds hot riced or mashed potatoes.

Mix thoroughly. Shape into patties or croquettes.

Place in greased shallow baking dish. Brown in very hot oven (450°F. Mark 8). Serves 4 to 6.

Mashed Potato Cakes: Combine 14 ounces seasoned, mashed potatoes with one egg.

Shape into four patties. Dip in flour.

Fry until well browned in hot lard about ¼ inch deep in heavy frying pan. Serves 4.

Mashed Potatoes with Fried Onions: Prepare mashed potatoes. Before serving, cover with sliced fried onions.

Mayonnaise Potatoes: Prepare mashed potatoes, substituting a little mayonnaise for butter or margarine called for in recipe.

Beat until light and fluffy. Season to taste.

Parsley Mashed Potatoes: Beat finely chopped parsley into mashed potatoes.

Pimento Potatoes: Add diced pimento to hot mashed potatoes.

Potato Cakes with Meat: Add 4 ounces minced leftover cooked meat to 14 ounces mashed potatoes. Form into cakes. Fry until browned.

Potato Nests: Make a cavity in centre of mashed potato mound. Fill with creamed carrots or peas.

Yellow Mashed Potatoes: Rice or mash together boiled potatoes and boiled carrots.

For a well-baked potato, wrap a scrubbed, dried and greased baking potato in foil. Bake at from 350° to 425°F. Mark 4 to 7 for 40 to 50 minutes, while baking other foods. Keep inside foil until ready to serve—it will keep hot and moist.

BAKED POTATOES

Scrub potatoes, dry, rub skins with soft butter or margarine.

Bake in pre-heated very hot oven (450°F. Mark 8) until tender, 45 to 60 minutes.

Remove from oven, cut 2 crossed slits on one side, and pinch potato until it opens at slit.

Put a lump of butter or margarine in opening; sprinkle with paprika.

Baked Stuffed Potatoes: Bake as above, then cut in half lengthwise.

Carefully scoop out potato without breaking skin.

Mash potato with butter or margarine, salt, pepper, and enough milk or potato water to give a fluffy texture.

Pile mixture into shell, sprinkle with grated cheese and paprika. Return to oven to brown.

Baked Stuffed Potatoes with Eggs: Prepare as above and, for every potato, add 1 chopped, hard-boiled egg to the mixture.

Baked Stuffed Potatoes with Meat, Fish, or Vegetables: Omit milk in baked stuffed potatoes. Combine potato with any leftover creamed fish or vegetables, or cooked poultry or meat moistened with fat.

Baked Stuffed Potatoes with Mushrooms: For every potato add 1 tablespoon chopped or sliced sautéed mushrooms to the mixture.

Stuffed Baked Potatoes

POTATOES ANNA

- 6 medium-sized potatoes (about 2 pounds), peeled and thinly sliced
- 6 tablespoons butter
- 1½ teaspoons salt
- ¼ teaspoon pepper
- grated onion
- grated Parmesan cheese

Lightly grease a 10-inch frying pan with a heat-resistant handle or a shallow casserole, with tight fitting cover. Arrange the potatoes in slightly overlapping spirals until the bottom of the pan is filled.

Dot with bits of butter. Add a sprinkling of salt, pepper, grated onion, and grated Parmesan cheese. Repeat with 2 additional layers.

Cover pan and bake in hot oven (425°F. Mark 7) 30 minutes. Remove cover and bake 5 minutes longer. To serve, invert on platter. Serves 6.

SCALLOPED POTATOES
(Basic Recipe)

- 6 medium potatoes
- 3 tablespoons butter or margarine
- 2 tablespoons flour
- 1½ pints milk
- 1 teaspoon salt
- ¼ teaspoon pepper
- 2 tablespoons chopped onion

Peel potatoes and slice thin.

Melt butter in saucepan; blend in flour. Slowly add milk; cook over medium heat until thickened, stirring constantly.

Put half the potatoes in greased 1½-pint casserole. Cover with half the sauce, seasonings, and onion. Add remaining potatoes, seasoning, and onion. Top with remaining sauce.

Cover and bake in moderate oven (350°F. Mark 4) about 1 hour. Uncover and bake until top is browned. Serves 4 to 6.

Scalloped Potato Variations

Scalloped Potatoes with Cheese (Au Gratin): Prepare as in basic recipe. Sprinkle each layer with cheese. Or, cheese may be melted in white sauce.

Scalloped Potatoes with Seafood: Prepare as in basic recipe. Add cooked or canned fish such as finnan haddie, salmon, prawns, lobster, herring, smoked salmon, crabmeat, etc. in layers with potatoes. Season to taste.

Scalloped Potatoes with Meat: Pre-peel as in basic recipe. Add cooked diced or sliced leftover meat, dried beef, corned beef, frankfurters, bacon, or ham.

If desired, bake a slice of ham or minced meat patties with the potatoes, placing it on the bottom of casserole, on the top, or between layers.

FRANCONIA POTATOES
(Roast Potatoes)

Peel potatoes. Cut in half or quarter large potatoes. Place in roasting tin with meat which is being roasted about 1¼ hours before meat finishes cooking.

Turn and baste occasionally during cooking so that they brown evenly on all sides.

To shorten cooking time, cook potatoes in boiling salted water 10 to 15 minutes before placing in roasting tin; allow 45 minutes to 1 hour for roasting.

Variations: Potatoes may be dipped into melted fat, then rolled in dry breadcrumbs and roasted in separate tin.

BAKED POTATOES WITH SOUR CREAM

- 3 ounces chopped onions
- 3 tablespoons butter or margarine, melted
- 12 fluid ounces sour cream
- 2 eggs, slightly beaten
- 1 pound sliced, cooked potatoes
- ½ teaspoon salt
- ⅛ teaspoon pepper
- 4 ounces cornflakes or cornflake crumbs
- 1 ounce grated Cheddar cheese

Cook onions in 2 tablespoons butter until golden brown. Combine sour cream and eggs.

Place half the potatoes in greased individual casseroles or 1½-quart baking dish. Spread half the onions over potatoes; pour on half the sour cream mixture. Repeat layering, using remaining potatoes, onions, and sour cream mixture. Sprinkle with salt and pepper.

If using cornflakes, crush into fine crumbs. Combine cornflake crumbs, cheese, and remaining butter. Sprinkle cornflake crumb mixture over potatoes. Bake in moderate oven (350°F. Mark 4) about 25 minutes. Serves 6 to 8.

HASHED-BROWN POTATOES

Chop enough cold boiled or baked potatoes to make 1½ pounds. Add 3 tablespoons flour and 2 fluid ounces milk; mix well. Season with salt and pepper to taste.

Heat 2 tablespoons bacon fat in heavy 9-inch frying pan. Add potatoes and pack with spatula into a large cake. Cook over medium heat until potato is brown and crusty, shaking pan to keep potato from sticking. Turn out onto flat plate.

Wipe pan free of crumbs. Add 1 tablespoon fat. Slide potato back into hot pan to brown other side.

Cook until brown, packing edges with spatula and shaking pan. Serves 4.

Variations: Add a little chopped onion or chopped parsley with the salt and pepper.

POTATOES O'BRIEN

Combine 1 pound cooked, chopped potatoes, 1 ounce each of chopped green pepper and onion, and 1 tablespoon diced pimento.

Fry until golden brown in hot fat about ¼ inch deep in heavy frying pan. Serves 4.

POTATO CHIPS

Wash, peel, and cut potatoes into lengthwise strips, about ½ inch thick.

Soak in cold water 1 hour. Drain, dry thoroughly between towels.

Heat pan of deep fat, hot enough to brown a small piece of bread in 60 seconds (375°F.).

Fry about 4 ounces of sliced potatoes at one time until lightly browned. Drain on absorbent paper.

Just before serving, return to hot fat (375°F. Mark 5) and fry until crisp and brown.

Drain on absorbent paper and sprinkle with salt. Serve at once.

Variations

Lattice Potatoes: Cut potatoes with a lattice vegetable cutter. Fry as above.

Potato Balls: Cut potatoes into tiny balls with ball cutter. Fry as above.

Potato Chips: Cut potatoes into thin slices. Fry as above.

Saratoga Chips: Cut potatoes into very thin slices. Soak in cold water, drain, and plunge into boiling water.

Drain, dry, and fry as above.

PAN FRIED POTATOES

Cut peeled potatoes in ⅛-inch slices. Fry over low heat in heavy frying pan in bacon dripping or other fat. Season with salt and pepper.

After potatoes are browned, turn and fry slowly on the other side. Do not cover.

Baked Potatoes with Sour Cream

Fried Potato Balls

FRIED POTATO BALLS

1 pound cornflakes, golden
    crumbs or cornflake crumbs
½ pound cottage cheese, drained
1 ounce finely chopped onion
1 egg, well-beaten
1¼ pounds mashed potatoes
1 teaspoon salt
⅛ teaspoon pepper
⅛ teaspoon paprika
¼ teaspoon dry mustard
2 teaspoons grated horseradish
2 eggs
2 tablespoons milk

If using cornflakes, crush into fine crumbs.

Combine cottage cheese, onion, beaten egg, potatoes, seasonings, and horseradish; mix well. Shape into small balls, 1½ inches in diameter.

Beat eggs and milk together. Roll balls in cornflake crumbs, then in egg-milk mixture; roll again in crumbs.

Fry in deep hot fat (375°F.) about 2 minutes, or until crisp and well-browned. Serve with horseradish flavoured sour cream, if desired. Makes about 2 dozen balls, 1½ inches in diameter.

FRIED POTATO BALLS 2

14 ounces hot mashed potatoes
2 slightly beaten eggs
1 teaspoon baking powder
¼ teaspoon salt
⅛ teaspoon paprika
1 tablespoon chopped parsley

Combine all ingredients and beat well.

Drop by teaspoonfuls into deep hot fat (390°F.). Cook until golden brown. Drain on absorbent paper. Serve hot.

SOUFFLÉED POTATO SLICES

Select medium-sized baking potatoes of uniform size. Peel and cut on slant in slices about ⅛ inch thick. Dry between towels.

Fry, a few at a time, in medium hot, deep fat (275°-300°F.) 5 minutes, keeping potatoes in motion.

Then lift basket and plunge quickly into very hot, deep fat (400°-425°F.) 1 to 2 minutes, or until puffed and browned, keeping potatoes moving. They should puff at once when dropped into very hot fat.

Hold basket over pan for fat to drip, then turn out on absorbent paper to drain. Sprinkle with salt. Serve at once.

The type of potato and the quick change from a medium hot to a very hot fat are important in making these slices.

POTATO BASKETS

Cut 2 peeled potatoes in very fine strips. Soak in cold water, drain, and dry well.

Fry in deep fat heated to 365°F. (or when an inch cube of bread browns in 60 seconds) 2 minutes. Sprinkle with salt and press into patty tins.

Brown in hot oven (400°F. Mark 6) 7 to 8 minutes. Makes 4 baskets.

BAKED POTATO WAFERS

4 to 6 large potatoes
4 ounces butter or margarine
salt and pepper

Select large potatoes and rub them with butter after scrubbing them well. Cut, without peeling, into slices ⅛ inch thick.

Place in large frying pan in which butter has been melted. Sprinkle with salt and pepper and brown slightly on both sides at a low temperature.

Cover and continue cooking over low heat 20 minutes, or until slices are tender. Serves 6.

OVEN-FRIED (TOASTED) POTATOES

Cut potatoes as for chipped potatoes. Rinse in cold water. Drain and dry on absorbent paper.

Arrange on shallow baking dish. Brush generously with melted butter or margarine.

Bake in very hot oven (450°F. Mark 8) until golden brown and tender, turning occasionally, 35 to 40 minutes. Sprinkle with salt.

COTTAGE FRIED POTATOES

Cook potatoes in jackets. Remove skins and slice or dice.

Fry in hot fat, turning frequently, until brown and crisp. Season with salt and pepper.

Lyonnaise-Potatoes: Proceed as above, frying thinly sliced onions with the potatoes.

BUTTER BROWNED POTATO BALLS

6 large potatoes
4 ounces butter or margarine,
    melted
salt and pepper

Peel potatoes and cut with a round ball cutter. Cook them in melted butter in large frying pan until golden

brown and cooked through. A medium temperature is best for butter cooking.

Sprinkle with salt and pepper and serve at once. Serves 4 to 6.

POTATOES WITH SOUR CREAM

6 medium potatoes
1 pint sour cream
3 tablespoons finely chopped onion
salt and pepper

Boil potatoes in jackets until tender. Peel, cool enough to handle, and cut into pieces.

Warm cream and onion, being careful not to heat cream to point where it curdles.

Add potatoes. Season to taste with salt and pepper and serve, if desired, with a garnish of parsley. Serves 6.

CHEESED POTATOES

8 medium new potatoes
2 ounces butter or margarine
2 tablespoons chopped chives
1 teaspoon salt
⅛ teaspoon paprika
2 ounces grated Cheddar cheese

Cook potatoes in jackets; drain and return to low heat, 2 to 3 minutes, shaking gently until they are hot and mealy. Turn into hot serving dish.

Meanwhile, melt butter, add chopped chives, seasonings, and cheese. Pour hot cheese mixture over potatoes. Sprinkle with extra chives and a dash of paprika. Serves 6.

BAKED POTATOES WITH MUSHROOM SAUCE

1 can (12 fluid ounces) condensed
    cream of mushroom soup
3 fluid ounces milk
4 medium potatoes, baked
2 tablespoons butter or margarine
black pepper

Pour soup into saucepan and stir well; blend in milk. Simmer about 2 minutes.

Split hot potatoes and dot each with ½ tablespoon butter. Sprinkle with pepper. Pour sauce in and over each potato. Serves 4.

Baked Potato Wafers
Butter Browned Potato Balls
Potatoes with Butter Sauce

GERMAN POTATO PIE

6 to 8 large raw potatoes
¼ small onion, grated
3 eggs, well beaten
½ pint hot milk
6 tablespoons butter or margarine, melted
2½ teaspoons salt

Peel and grate potatoes. Combine with remaining ingredients, blending well. Pour into well greased shallow casserole, about 7 × 12 inches.

Bake in moderate oven (350°F. Mark 4) until set, about 1 hour and 15 minutes. Serves 6.

POTATO SPINACH PUFF

1 pound (2 large) potatoes
salt
1 large packet frozen chopped spinach
2 tablespoons cream
2 tablespoons butter or margarine
1 egg
pepper and nutmeg

Peel potatoes and cut in quarters. Cook in boiling salted water until tender. Drain and put through ricer.

Meanwhile, cook spinach as directed on packet. Drain and add to potatoes.

Add cream, butter, and egg; beat until light and fluffy. Season to taste with salt, pepper, and nutmeg.

Pile into 1-quart casserole. Bake in hot oven (400°F. Mark 6) 15 minutes. Serves 4.

SURPRISE POTATOES

Foil-bake potatoes. Divide potatoes lengthwise, allowing about ⅔ for the lower half.

Scoop out centres and whip up to feathery lightness with hot milk, butter, and seasonings.

Heap the filling nicely in the larger potato skin shell, discarding the smaller one. Sprinkle with paprika and melted butter.

Wrap these stuffed potatoes in foil and store in freezer. When ready to serve, place direct from freezer in moderate oven (375°F. Mark 5) and heat 30 minutes. Serve them in the foil, turning it back at the table. These potatoes may also be stored in the refrigerator for short periods and heated in 25 minutes when not frozen.

Surprise Potatoes

POTATO CHEESE CROQUETTES

14 ounces cold mashed potatoes
1 beaten egg
4 ounces grated Cheddar cheese
salt to taste
¾ teaspoon Aromat
2 ounces fine dry breadcrumbs
4 fluid ounces milk

Break up potatoes. Beat egg in blender until frothy. Add potato pieces gradually, beating at medium speed until blended.

Stir in cheese, salt, and Aromat. Shape as desired. Dip into crumbs, then into milk, and again into crumbs.

Fry in shallow hot fat until golden brown on all sides. Serves 4 to 6.

BEEF-STUFFED BAKED POTATOES

4 baking potatoes
½ pound minced beef
2 tablespoons chopped onion (or sliced spring onion or chives)
2 tablespoons butter or margarine
1 teaspoon salt
2 ounces grated cheese

Scrub potatoes and bake in very hot oven (450°F. Mark 8) for 45 to 55 minutes, or until tender when pierced with a fork.

Fry minced beef and onion in butter in a frying pan.

Cut a slice from top of each potato and scoop out inside. Mash thoroughly. Add the meat, butter, and onion mixture to the potatoes and whip until light and fluffy.

Pile lightly into potato shells and top each with shredded cheese. Return to very hot oven to reheat and melt cheese. Serves 4.

CASSEROLE-BAKED POTATOES

12 small potatoes
½ to 1 teaspoon salt
6 fluid ounces butter or margarine, melted

Wash potatoes, peel and wash again. Pat dry with absorbent paper or towel.

Place in oven-glass casserole. Salt well and add butter. Cover.

Bake in moderate oven (350°F. Mark 4) until browned and tender, about 1 hour. Turn potatoes several times, or shake the casserole so they turn themselves, to make sure they brown evenly. Serves 6.

BAKED MASHED POTATOES

10 ounces mashed potatoes
2 tablespoons butter or margarine
1 egg
4 fluid ounces hot milk or cream
salt and pepper to taste

Combine ingredients, beat well, and place in greased baking dish.

Sprinkle with a little paprika and bake in moderate oven (375°F. Mark 5) until top is lightly browned. Serves 4 to 6.

Potato Cheese Croquettes

POTATO CHEESE PUFFS

1¼ pounds hot mashed potatoes
4 fluid ounces thick cream, whipped
2 ounces grated Cheddar cheese

Mash potatoes with salt and butter or margarine to taste, and enough milk to give a light fluffy consistency. Place in buttered ramekin dishes.

Whip cream, add cheese, and mix well. Spread over potatoes.

Bake in moderate oven (350°F. Mark 4) about 15 minutes, or until browned. Serves 6.

POTATOES FRIED WITH BACON

Fry 4 rashers bacon in heavy frying pan; remove and crumble.

Peel 4 large potatoes; slice very thin. Place in bacon dripping; add 1 teaspoon salt and ¼ teaspoon pepper.

Fry until almost tender and quite brown. Then cover and move to edge of grill. Add bacon bits and fry until tender. Serves 4 to 6.

CRISPY-TOPPED CHEESE POTATOES

3 tablespoons melted butter or margarine
4 medium-sized boiled potatoes
4 ounces cornflakes, finely crushed
4 ounces finely grated cheese
½ teaspoon paprika
1 teaspoon salt

Pour 2 tablespoons butter or margarine into shallow baking pan.

Cut potatoes into ½-inch slices and place close together in pan. Brush tops with remaining butter or margarine.

Crush cornflakes into fine crumbs; combine with cheese, paprika, and salt; sprinkle over potatoes.

Bake in hot oven (425°F. Mark 7) about 15 minutes. Serves 6.

Crispy-Topped Cheese Potatoes

Panned Potatoes

PANNED POTATOES

2 ounces butter or margarine
10 to 12 small potatoes
4 tablespoons flour
2 to 3 teaspoons salt
1 large onion, sliced
paprika

Melt butter or margarine in frying pan with tight-fitting cover.

Peel and slice potatoes thin. Arrange ½-inch-thick layer in frying pan and sprinkle with flour, salt, and onion.

Continue layers until frying pan is nearly full. Arrange onion slices on top. Sprinkle with paprika.

Cover and cook slowly until potatoes are tender but not mushy.

If desired, loosen around edge with knife, cover frying pan with large plate and invert. Potatoes will come out in one piece, or cut and serve in wedges. Serves 6.

POTATOES AU GRATIN

1¼ pounds diced cold cooked potatoes
6 tablespoons butter or margarine
3 tablespoons flour
12 fluid ounces milk
¼ pound sharp Cheddar cheese, grated
salt and pepper
2 ounces soft breadcrumbs

Put potatoes in shallow baking dish.

Melt 3 tablespoons butter in a saucepan; blend in flour. Add milk gradually and cook, stirring constantly, until smooth and thickened. Add cheese and stir until melted. Season to taste.

Pour over potatoes and mix lightly.

Melt remaining 3 tablespoons butter and mix with crumbs. Sprinkle over contents of baking dish.

Put in grill under medium heat and grill until golden brown. Serves 4.

POTATOES—SPANISH STYLE

Measure 1 pound thinly sliced peeled raw potatoes into 1½-pint casserole.

Blend ¾ pint tomato sauce, 1 medium onion, chopped, 1 finely chopped garlic clove, 1½ teaspoons salt, dash of pepper, and 1 teaspoon paprika.

Pour sauce over potatoes, stirring lightly. Cover with tight-fitting lid.

Bake in moderate oven (375°F. Mark 5) until potatoes are tender, 1 hour. Serves 6.

QUICK SCALLOPED POTATOES WITH HAM

6 large potatoes
1 large onion, sliced
5 ounces diced cooked ham
1 teaspoon salt
¼ teaspoon pepper
1 pint evaporated milk, diluted with 4 fluid ounces hot water
2 ounces crisp breadcrumbs
2 tablespoons melted butter or margarine

Boil potatoes with skins on for just 5 minutes. Peel and slice potatoes.

Place half the potatoes in 1½-quart buttered baking dish. Arrange sliced onion and ham on top of potatoes. Add remaining potatoes.

Add seasonings to milk diluted with hot water and pour over potatoes.

Mix crumbs and melted butter and sprinkle on top. Bake in moderate oven (350°F. Mark 4) 30 minutes. Serves 4 to 6.

Variations: Substitute ½ pound chipped beef or other cooked meat for ham. Potatoes may be used without boiling, but increase baking time to 45 minutes.

SCALLOPED POTATOES WITH SAUSAGE AND TOMATOES

12 ounces raw sliced potatoes
6 diced sausages
4 tablespoons flour
1 teaspoon salt
⅛ teaspoon pepper
3 tablespoons chopped onion
12 fluid ounces milk
3 slices tomato
parsley, if desired

Arrange about half the potato slices and diced sausages in well-greased 1½-quart casserole. Sprinkle with half the flour, salt, pepper, and onion.

Repeat. Pour milk over ingredients. Top with tomato slices. Cover.

Bake in moderate oven (350°F. Mark 4) ¾ hour. Remove cover and bake another ½ hour, or until done.

If desired, garnish with sprigs of parsley for serving. Serves 3 to 4.

IRISH POTATO PUFF

2 ounces butter or margarine
3 ounces breadcrumbs
1 teaspoon salt
1 tablespoon grated lemon rind
1 teaspoon lemon juice
3 egg yolks
½ pint milk
3 egg whites, beaten stiff
1¼ pounds mashed potatoes
1 ounce grated cheese

Combine butter and crumbs. Mix until well blended. Press on bottom and sides of round baking dish.

Combine salt, lemon rind, lemon juice, and egg yolks. Blend well and stir in milk.

Fold in egg whites and gently fold mixture into mashed potatoes. Fill baking dish and stir in half of grated cheese. Sprinkle remaining cheese on top.

Bake in moderate oven (350°F. Mark 4) ½ hour, or until firm and delicate brown on top. Serve hot. Serves 6.

BAKED CREAMED POTATO RING

2½ pounds diced, cooked potatoes
1 medium onion, chopped
¾ pint thick white sauce
2 beaten eggs
¾ teaspoon Aromat
4 ounces grated sharp Cheddar cheese

Combine potatoes and onion.

Pour hot white sauce over beaten eggs; add Aromat. Add cheese; stir over low heat until cheese melts.

Combine cheese mixture and potato mixture; mix well. Pack into heavily greased 10-inch ring mould.

Set in pan of hot water. Bake in moderate oven (350°F. Mark 4) 45 minutes.

To unmould, run knife around edges, invert on large plate, then invert again on serving plate so that browned top will be uppermost.

Fill centre with buttered Brussels sprouts. Serves 6.

POTATO KUGEL

6 medium potatoes
1 small onion
3 eggs
½ teaspoon salt
dash of pepper
about 3 ounces flour
4 tablespoons lard

Peel and grate raw potatoes; squeeze out excess liquid. Grate onion into the potatoes.

Add eggs, salt, pepper, and just enough flour to make a batter that will drop from a spoon.

Heat lard in baking dish; mix into batter. Turn batter into greased baking pan.

Bake in moderate oven (375°F. Mark 5) until nicely browned and crisp at edges, 30 to 40 minutes. Serves 6.

Potato Kugel

PUMPKIN

Pumpkin, a member of the same gourd family as marrow, is usually classified as a vegetable. It is used chiefly for pies and has a golden yellow colour when ripe. Size and shape have little to do with a pumpkin's flavour, although the smaller ones have less waste and usually a more tender flesh. They are a good source of vitamin A.

In general, pumpkin is prepared for mashing or other use by boiling like winter squash. Cut pumpkin into small pieces and peel.

Pressure Cooked: Place on rack in pressure cooker with 4 fluid ounces water. Cook at 15-pound pressure 10 to 12 minutes. Estimate time by how hard it was to cut pumpkin into pieces. Cool cooker at once under running water. Drain pumpkin. This yields a drier product than boiling.

Boiled: Cover cut-up pumpkin with water. Cover and cook until tender, 30 minutes or longer. Drain well.

Baked: Cut pumpkin in half. Remove seeds and fibrous matter. Place it cutside down in a pan with a small amount of water. Bake in slow oven (325°F. Mark 3) until tender, 1 hour or longer. This yields a dry product.

RADISHES

Good quality in fresh radishes is not indicated by the condition or colour of the leaves but by the root, which should be smooth, crisp, and firm, never soft or spongy. The long, white, mild-flavoured ones are called "Icicles" but the small, red "button" variety is more popular.

RADISHES — RED

Selection: Buy 2 bunches for 4 servings. Buy well-formed, smooth, firm, crisp radishes with fresh, bright green tops.

Preparation: Wash and remove roots. If radishes are large remove leaves. Remove only damaged leaves of small radishes.

Cooking Time: 5 to 10 minutes.

Cooking: Cook whole in a small amount of boiling salted water in a tightly covered saucepan. The small ones and their tops will be done in about 5 minutes. The larger ones will take about 10 minutes.

Serving: Serve piping hot drenched with melted butter or margarine.

To Serve Raw: Serve crisp and cold as an hors d'oeuvre. Add thin slivers to vegetable or green salads.

SALSIFY (OYSTER PLANT)

Salsify (oyster plant or vegetable oyster) is similar in appearance and quality characteristics to parsnips except that the tops look like heavy grass. It also resembles the parsnip in that its flavour is improved after exposure to cold temperatures. It is also known as oyster plant or vegetable oyster because when cooked it tastes somewhat like an oyster.

Preparation: Wash, scrape and cut into small pieces. Place in cold water, adding 1 teaspoon vinegar or lemon pieces to 1½ pints of water to prevent discoloration. Drain.

Cooking: Cover with boiling water. (Do not salt before cooking.) Cover and cook until tender, 20 to 40 minutes (10 minutes in pressure saucepan).

Drain and add melted butter, and season with salt and pepper to taste.

SAUTÉED SALSIFY

Boil salsify and drain. Roll in seasoned flour or breadcrumbs. Sauté in fat until brown on all sides, 7 to 10 minutes.

CREAMED SALSIFY

Reheat boiled salsify in medium white sauce. Sprinkle with chopped parsley.

SALSIFY PATTIES OR FRITTERS

Mash cooked salsify. Season with butter, salt, and pepper.

Shape in small flat cakes. Roll in flour. Brown in butter.

SALSIFY WITH EGGS

2-3 roots of salsify
lemon juice
4 eggs
1½ ounces butter
2 tablespoons cream
salt, pepper
fried croûtons

Cook the salsify in boiling salted water to which a squeeze of lemon juice has been added. Drain and cut into small dice. Heat half the butter in a sauté pan until foamy, add the salsify and shake over moderate heat for four to five minutes. Season well and add one teaspoon of lemon juice. Beat the eggs, add cream and seasoning. Pour into the pan with the salsify and cook gently, stirring with a fork. When creamy and just set, turn on to a serving dish and surround with the croûtons.

SORREL

Sorrel, which is usually cooked as a green, is a member of the buckwheat family, identifiable by its arrow-shaped leaves. Buy and handle sorrel as you would spinach, with which it is usually cooked to add flavour. Sorrel is also sometimes known as sour grass.

SAUERKRAUT

Sauerkraut is German for sour cabbage; shredded cabbage fermented in a brine of its own juice.

Boiled: One pound serves 4. Drain sauerkraut. Cover with boiling water or stock. Cook slowly, uncovered, 30 to 35 minutes.

Drain and season to taste with salt, butter, and, if needed, pepper. If desired, season with 1 teaspoon caraway or celery seed and 1 to 2 tablespoons brown sugar.

Note: If sauerkraut is very salty, it should be drained, rinsed in cold running water and drained again before cooking.

SAUERKRAUT WITH WINE

Drain sauerkraut. Add 12 fluid ounces white or red wine per pound. Cook slowly until tender.

SAUERKRAUT WITH ONIONS

Dice 1 onion and sauté in 2 tablespoons fat until soft.

Add drained sauerkraut, stir well, cover, and cook slowly at least 30 minutes on top of stove or in oven. Season to taste.

SAUERKRAUT AND FRANKFURTERS

2 tablespoons bacon dripping or margarine
1 medium-sized onion, chopped
1 medium-sized green pepper, chopped
1 pound sauerkraut
½ pound canned tomatoes
1 teaspoon brown sugar
½ pound canned okra
1 pound frankfurters

In a large heavy frying pan, melt dripping or margarine over low heat. Add onion and green pepper; sauté 5 minutes.

Stir in sauerkraut, tomatoes, and sugar; mix thoroughly. Add okra and mix lightly.

Arrange frankfurters on top. Cover and cook over low heat 20 minutes. Serve piping hot. Serves 4 to 6.

Sauerkraut and Frankfurters

Baked Spinach Casserole

SPINACH

Spinach has been cultivated for many centuries and was introduced into Europe by the Moors. Today spinach, because of its wealth of natural food values, is one of our most commonly used vegetables. Both the crinkly-leaf and flat-leaf types are good for cooking. Incidentally, you won't have to wash spinach so much as usual if a little salt is dissolved in the first water you use.

Selection: Buy 2 to 2½ pounds for 4 servings. Look for well-developed plants with fresh, crisp, clean leaves of good green colour. If you buy spinach in cellophane bags, washed and ready to cook, be sure it is young and fresh. Frozen or canned spinach is not as crisp as fresh spinach.

Preparation: Cut off root ends and any damaged leaves. Wash at least 3 times to remove sand unless it is packaged, washed spinach.

Cooking Time: 3 to 10 minutes.

Cooking: Cook, covered, using only the water that clings to the leaves after washing. Boil 3 to 10 minutes. Chop or leave in sprays or cut through several times.

Serving: Serve at once seasoned with salt, pepper, butter or margarine, and a little vinegar or fresh lemon juice.

To Serve Raw: Use crisp and chilled in mixed green salads.

SPINACH WITH ALMONDS

Cook 1 packet frozen chopped spinach as label directs.

Cook 2 tablespoons chopped and blanched almonds in 2 tablespoons butter or margarine until lightly browned. Add 2 teaspoons lemon juice. Pour over drained spinach. Season with salt and pepper to taste. Serves 3.

Spinach Ring

BAKED SPINACH CASSEROLE

2 10-ounce packets frozen chopped spinach
2 tablespoons chopped onion
3 tablespoons butter or margarine
3 tablespoons flour
1 pint milk
3 hard-boiled eggs, finely chopped
2 teaspoons salt
¼ teaspoon pepper
⅛ teaspoon nutmeg
4 ounces cornflakes or cornflake crumbs
2 ounces grated Cheddar cheese
2 tablespoons butter or margarine, melted
paprika

Cook spinach according to directions on packet; drain thoroughly.

Cook onion in butter until transparent. Stir in flour. Add milk gradually, stirring constantly. Cook until thickened, stirring occasionally. Fold in spinach and eggs; season with salt, pepper, and nutmeg.

Spread in greased shallow baking dish. If using cornflakes, crush into fine crumbs. Combine cornflake crumbs with cheese and butter; sprinkle over spinach. Sprinkle with paprika.

Bake in moderate oven (375°F. Mark 5) about 20 minutes. Serves 6.

CREAMED SPINACH

Cook 1 packet of frozen chopped spinach as label directs.

Melt 2 tablespoons butter or margarine; blend in 1½ tablespoons flour and dash of nutmeg. Stir in ½ pint milk. Add 1 chicken bouillon cube and 1 teaspoon grated onion. Cook, stirring constantly, until thickened.

Add to hot, drained spinach. Season to taste. Serves 3.

Variations: Cream other frozen greens in the same way.

SPINACH RING

3 packets frozen chopped spinach
3 tablespoons butter
3 tablespoons flour
6 fluid ounces milk
1½ teaspoons salt
2 teaspoons aromatic bitters

Thaw spinach and put in colander. Drain off all water by pressing with spoon.

Make cream sauce of butter, flour, and milk. Add salt and bitters. This will make a thick sauce. Add drained spinach and cook over low heat for 5 minutes.

Grease ring mould with butter or cooking oil and press spinach mixture into it evenly. Put ring in hot water to keep warm. Turn spinach ring out on a round platter. Fill ring with creamed chicken. Serves 6 to 8.

Spinach Timbales

SPINACH TIMBALES

1½ pounds chopped cooked spinach
3 lightly beaten eggs
2 fluid ounces cream
2 tablespoons melted butter
2½ ounces soft, fine breadcrumbs
½ teaspoon salt

Combine ingredients and mix well. Fill buttered ramekin dishes or dariole moulds ⅔ full. Place in shallow baking pan of hot water. Bake in moderate oven (350°F. Mark 4) about 40 minutes, or until firm.

Unmould. Serve with white sauce. Place a slice of hard-boiled egg on top of each timbale. Serves 6.

SQUASH

The term squash refers to any of a number of edible gourds closely related to the pumpkin. The name is of American Indian origin. Squashes fall into 2 categories—summer and winter. Summer squash are used when they are young, before the rind hardens. The skin of summer squashes should be tender enough not to need paring. They may be boiled, steamed, baked, or fried. The most common squash grown in Great Britain is the Vegetable Marrow (Bush Green).

Winter squash have hard shells and will keep all winter in a warm, dry room. They are often halved and baked; they may then be mashed or eaten from the shell. If cooked in any other way they must be pared, and they need more cooking time than the summer squashes. All squashes are good stuffed.

WINTER SQUASH

Varieties: Banana, Hubbard, Acorn, Des Moines, Table Queen, or Danish. The pumpkin can also be prepared in the same way as winter squash.

Selection: Buy 3 pounds for 4 servings. All winter squash should be very heavy for its size. The rind should be very hard, and the flesh thick and bright orange in colour.

Preparation: Wash, cut into individual servings, and remove seeds.

Cooking Time: 30 to 60 minutes.

Cooking—Baked: Season with salt, pepper, butter or margarine, bacon or ham dripping, and bake, covered, in a hot oven (400°F. Mark 6) until tender.

Allow 30 minutes for banana squash, 45 to 60 minutes for Hubbard squash, and 30 to 40 minutes for acorn squash.
Serving: Remove from rind, mash, add additional seasonings, if necessary, or serve the individual pieces on the "half shell".

WINTER SQUASH—BAKED IN SQUARES

Cut in pieces about 3 inches square. Remove seeds and stringy portion.

Place in a greased shallow pan. Sprinkle with salt and pepper. Pour melted butter or margarine over top.

Cover and bake in moderate oven (350°F. Mark 4) 1 hour, or until squash is tender. Serve hot.

MASHED WINTER SQUASH

Cut in pieces, remove seeds and stringy portions. Peel and cut into small serving pieces.

Cook rapidly in small amount boiling salted water, covered, until tender, 20 to 30 minutes.

Drain, mash, and season to taste with salt, pepper, and butter.

STUFFED ACORN SQUASH

Fill baked or boiled squash with tomatoes Creole, creamed ham, or creamed chicken. Sprinkle with fried breadcrumbs, if desired. Brown in oven.

Or, fill hot baked or boiled squash with creamed or buttered spinach or other vegetables and serve very hot.

HAM-STUFFED ACORN SQUASH

7   ounces cream cracker crumbs
4   fluid ounces water
10 ounces chopped, cooked ham
1   tablespoon prepared mustard
¼   teaspoon pepper
2   eggs, beaten
3   acorn squash

Combine all ingredients except squash; mix well.

Cut 3 acorn squash in half lengthwise. Remove seeds and fill cavity with stuffing. Bake in covered dish in moderate oven (350°F. Mark 4) 1 hour, or until squash are tender. Serves 6.

Stuffed Acorn Squash: This delicious ham and cream cracker crumb stuffing brings out the delicate flavour of Acorn Squash. Serve with a crisp tossed salad.

SUMMER SQUASH

Varieties: 1. White—Cymling, patty-pan or scalloped. 2. Yellow—Straight neck or crookneck. 3. Light Green—Custard pie. 4. Dark Green—Courgettes. 5. Vegetable marrow.
Selection: Buy 2 pounds for 4 servings. Summer squash must be extremely young, fresh and heavy for its size. The skin may be smooth or warty (depending on variety) but must be very tender.
Preparation: Wash but do not peel. Remove stem and blossom ends. Cut into ½-inch slices or cubes.
Cooking Time: 10 to 15 minutes.
Cooking: Cook, covered, in a very small amount of boiling salted water until tender, 10 to 15 minutes.
Serving: Serve hot seasoned with salt, pepper, and butter or margarine. For variety, add ketchup or tomato sauce or a dash of French dressing, or mash and season with butter, salt, and pepper.

BROWNED SUMMER SQUASH SLICES

Wash squash. Do not peel unless skin is quite tough; cut into slices about ½-inch thick. Sprinkle with salt and pepper; dip in flour to coat lightly.

Brown slices in small amount of butter or margarine (about 10 minutes); serve sizzling hot.

FRENCH FRIED SUMMER SQUASH

Cut in ½-inch pieces. Season with salt and pepper. Dip in fine crumbs, then in egg, lightly beaten with 1 tablespoon water, and again in crumbs.

Fry in deep hot fat (375°F.) and drain.

CREAMED SUMMER SQUASH

Cut in cubes; cook until nearly done but still firm. Drain and reheat in cream. Season to taste.

BAKED COURGETTES

Cut courgettes in half, lengthwise. Place cut-side-up in buttered baking dish. Dot with butter or bits of bacon. Season with salt and pepper.

Bake in moderate oven (375°F. Mark 5) until tender, about 30 minutes. Allow 1 small courgette per serving. Serve with Hollandaise or tomato sauce.
Courgettes Baked with Tomato: Scoop out some of centre. Fill with tomato, cut in pieces. Season and bake as above.

STUFFED COURGETTES

6   medium-size courgettes
12 ounces canned whole kernel sweetcorn, drained
2   teaspoons seasoned salt

Stuffed Courgettes

2   eggs, beaten
1   ounce chopped chives
2   ounces grated sharp Cheddar cheese

Scrub courgettes well. Cut off ends; do not peel. Cook whole in boiling water about 5 to 7 minutes.

Cut courgettes in half lengthwise. With tip of spoon carefully remove flesh from shells. Chop into small pieces; then combine with corn, seasoned salt, eggs, and chives.

Pile mixture lightly into courgette shells. Place in 2-quart oblong baking dish. Sprinkle with grated cheese. Bake, uncovered, in moderate oven (350°F. Mark 4) 30 minutes or until brown on top. Serves 6.

COURGETTES—ITALIAN STYLE

Cook 1 sliced onion in butter or margarine until yellow. Add 1 pound courgettes, sliced; cook and stir 5 minutes.

Add 8 ounces fresh or canned tomatoes; season with salt and pepper. Cover and cook 5 minutes. Lower heat and cook until tender, about 25 minutes.
Variation: Or place in casserole; sprinkle with grated cheese and bake in moderate oven (375°F. Mark 5) until brown. Serves 4.

SHERRIED SQUASH

1   pound winter squash, fresh or canned, cooked and mashed
¾   teaspoon salt
¼   teaspoon celery salt
dash of pepper
1½ tablespoons sherry
1   tablespoon butter or margarine, melted
⅛   teaspoon nutmeg

Combine squash, salt, celery salt, pepper, and wine; pile in greased shallow 1-quart baking dish. Brush with melted butter; sprinkle with nutmeg.

Place in preheated grill 5 to 7 minutes or in moderate oven (375°F. Mark 5) 15 to 20 minutes until heated. Serves 6.
Sherried Sweet Potatoes: In place of squash, use 1 pound sweet potatoes cooked and mashed.

SUCCOTASH

A mixture of sweetcorn and lima beans. Both the dish and the name are of American Indian origin.

Combine equal parts cooked lima beans and cooked sweetcorn kernels. Season with butter and salt. Reheat. Canned limas and canned or frozen sweetcorn are excellent for succotash.

SUCCOTASH 2

1 pound cooked or canned, drained
    whole kernel sweetcorn
1 pound fresh or canned green
    limas, cooked and drained
3 tablespoons butter or margarine
salt and pepper
4 fluid ounces single cream or top
    of milk

Combine vegetables in double saucepan. Add butter, seasonings, and cream; heat thoroughly. Serves 6.

SWEDES

The swede is a large, yellow fleshed, strong-flavoured turnip with a good content of vitamin B_1. In Europe, it is usually regarded as cattle feed, but it makes an excellent vegetable if not overcooked. The tops, which are not eaten, show first signs of deterioration and, consequently, are usually trimmed off before they are placed on sale. The roots of good quality swedes should be smooth skinned, firm, and heavy for their size.

Stored turnips are generally treated with an edible wax to make them keep better. This comes off when the root is peeled, of course. For cooking methods, see **Turnips.**

SWEET POTATOES

Cultivated from ancient times by the Aztecs, sweet potatoes were introduced into Europe in the 16th century and spread from there to Asia.

There are two types of sweet potatoes—one is light-coloured, dry, and mealy (Jersey); the other moist, soft, and sugary (Nancy Hall or Porto Rico). In southern states of North America the latter type is commonly called a yam. The true yam, however, belongs to another plant family (see Index).

Baked Sweet Potatoes with Prune Filling

Disregard colour in sweet potato buying, but remember that thick, chunky, medium-sized sweets which taper toward the ends are preferable. Avoid those with any sign of decay, as such deterioration spreads rapidly, affecting the taste of the entire potato, even in portions not immediately adjacent to the decayed area. Buy bright, clean potatoes that are free from blemishes.

SWEET POTATOES—BOILED IN JACKETS

Wash and scrub sweet potatoes. Cook whole in boiling salted water, covered, about 30 minutes, or until tender. Drain.

Peel, and season with butter or meat dripping, salt and pepper to taste.

MASHED SWEET POTATOES

Peel hot cooked sweet potatoes (6 medium-sized make 6 servings). Mash thoroughly and quickly. Add seasoning and butter or margarine.

Beat in hot milk a little at a time until sweet potatoes are fluffy and smooth.

Variations:

1. Shape seasoned mashed sweet potatoes into mounds with small well in centre. Brown in hot oven (425°F. Mark 7).

Fill well with cranberry sauce or jelly, and serve hot.

2. Use orange juice in place of milk, add a little grated orange rind, butter or margarine, and a few raisins.

If desired, place in baking dish, top with meringue, and brown lightly in moderate oven (350°F. Mark 4). Serve hot.

PAN-FRIED SWEET POTATOES

Boil sweet potatoes in jackets, peel, and slice. Add salt and pepper to taste.

Fry in hot fat in large frying pan, turning occasionally until nicely browned.

BAKED SWEET POTATOES

Select medium-sized or large sweet potatoes. Scrub thoroughly, removing any imperfections, and rub skins all over with a little fat of any kind.

Bake in hot oven (400°F. Mark 6) until potatoes are soft, from 40 to 60 minutes, according to size.

Remove from oven and cut lengthwise, then crosswise to allow steam to escape. Pinch the potatoes, pressing up the pulp so that it will show.

To save time in baking sweet potatoes, they may be parboiled for 15 minutes.

Serve plain, or with a dusting of paprika and a small pat of butter or margarine on each potato.

BAKED SWEET POTATOES WITH PRUNE FILLING

6 medium-sized sweet potatoes
    (about 3 pounds)
10 ounces chopped prunes
¼ teaspoon salt
½ teaspoon nutmeg
2 ounces butter
6 whole plump stoned prunes

Cut off both ends of sweet potatoes and bake in hot oven (400°F. Mark 6) 40 to 45 minutes.

Remove and cool slightly. Cut off tops, scoop out with teaspoon, leaving shells. Mash sweet potatoes, add chopped prunes, salt, nutmeg, and butter; blend well. Refill shells.

Reheat for serving in moderate oven (350°F. Mark 4) 15 minutes. Make a small indentation in top centre of each sweet potato and place a warm stoned prune on each. Serves 6.

BAKED STUFFED SWEET POTATOES

4 medium sweet potatoes
3 tablespoons butter or margarine
½ teaspoon salt
about 2 fluid ounces milk or thin
    cream

Wash potatoes, dry and bake in hot oven (400°F. Mark 6) about 40 minutes, or until soft when tested with a vegetable knife.

Cut a slice from the top of each potato. Scoop out pulp and run it through a potato ricer or vegetable mill. Reserve shells.

Whip pulp until fluffy with 2 tablespoons butter, salt, and milk or cream, using enough liquid to make mixture about as soft as mashed white potatoes.

Fill shells, and brush with remaining tablespoon of butter, melted. Return to oven and bake until lightly browned. Serves 4.

Variations of
Baked Stuffed Sweet Potatoes

Sweet Potato Puffs: Fold 1 stiffly beaten egg white into mashed potato before filling shells.

Sweet Potato Boats: Add 1 of the following to the mashed sweet potato mixture before filling shells: 4 rashers of crisp bacon, crumbled; 4 ounces chopped cooked chicken or ham; 1 ounce chopped nuts, raisins, or well drained chopped pineapple.

SWEET POTATO PATTIES

Shape cold mashed sweet potatoes into small patties.

Roll in breadcrumbs or crushed dry breakfast cereal. Brown on both sides in a little fat.

Variations: Add to the mashed sweet potatoes, chopped cooked leftover meat or finely chopped apple.

SCALLOPED SWEET POTATOES AND APPLES
(Basic Recipe)

Place alternate layers of sliced cooked sweet potatoes and sliced raw apples in a greased baking dish.

Sprinkle apple layers with sugar and a little salt. Dot with fat.

Add just enough hot water to cover bottom of dish. Apples and sweet potatoes do not take up liquid.

Bake covered in moderate oven (375°F. Mark 5) 30 to 40 minutes, or until apples are tender.

If desired, uncover the dish for last 15 to 20 minutes of cooking and top with crushed dry breakfast cereal or breadcrumbs mixed with a little fat.

Sliced raw sweet potatoes may be used but require longer baking.

Variations: Substitute peeled orange slices, cranberry sauce (not jelly), or sliced fresh pears for apples. With pears, use brown sugar instead of granulated for added flavour. Top with breadcrumbs and bake 20 to 30 minutes.

SCALLOPED SWEET POTATOES WITH ORANGE JUICE

Omit apples and water in basic recipe. Pour over sweet potatoes 3 to 4 fluid ounces orange juice containing a little grated orange rind. Top with breadcrumbs, and bake about 20 minutes.

SCALLOPED SWEET POTATOES WITH HAM

Follow recipe for scalloped sweet potatoes and apples. For a main dish, use chopped cooked ham in place of apples. Omit sugar and breadcrumbs. Bake until heated through, 20 to 30 minutes.

SCALLOPED SWEET POTATOES WITH PEANUTS

Substitute chopped roasted peanuts for apples in basic recipe. Omit fat and crumbs, and, if nuts are salted, omit salt. Bake 20 to 30 minutes.

Cranberry Candied Sweet Potatoes

OLD-FASHIONED SWEET POTATO PONE

6 medium sweet potatoes
1 pound sugar
2 ounces butter or margarine
3 beaten eggs
1 teaspoon cinnamon
1 teaspoon allspice
1 teaspoon ground cloves
1 teaspoon nutmeg
12 ounces sultanas

Cook potatoes until tender. Peel and place in single layer in casserole.

Blend sugar and butter; mix in remaining ingredients. Pour over potatoes.

Bake in moderate oven (350°F. Mark 4) until very hot, about 45 minutes. Serves 6.

SWEET POTATOES WITH MARSHMALLOWS

Boil 4 to 6 medium sweet potatoes until tender, but not soft.

Drain, peel, and put through ricer or mash with fork. Add milk, butter, 4 tablespoons chopped walnut kernels, brown sugar, and salt to taste.

Turn mixture into buttered baking dish, allowing enough room between layer of potatoes and top of dish for a layer of marshmallows, which swell and spread during cooking.

Bake in slow oven (325°F. Mark 3) until marshmallows are puffed and browned. Serve in baking dish. Serves 6.

LOUISIANA CASSEROLED SWEET POTATOES

Arrange 6 whole cooked Louisiana sweet potatoes in a buttered baking dish. Cover with 12 ounces honey. Dot with 4 ounces butter or margarine. Sprinkle with a few drops lemon juice.

Bake in moderate oven (350°F. Mark 4) 15 to 20 minutes, basting potatoes occasionally with syrup. Serves 6.

CRANBERRY CANDIED SWEET POTATOES

4 medium sweet potatoes, cooked and peeled, fresh or canned
4 ounces canned whole cranberry sauce
3 tablespoons lemon juice
6 ounces golden syrup
1 tablespoon melted butter or margarine

Cut sweet potatoes in half lengthwise. Place in greased shallow baking tin. Combine cranberry sauce and lemon juice; mix well. Spread cranberry mixture over sweet potatoes.

Combine golden syrup and butter or margarine. Pour over sweet potato mixture.

Bake in moderate oven (350°F. Mark 4) 25 minutes, basting occasionally with syrup mixture. Serves 4.

TOMATOES

It may surprise you to learn that tomatoes, once known as "love apples", are actually a fruit, not a vegetable, and that only a generation ago, many people thought they were poisonous. However, it is hardly conceivable that anyone labours under such a misapprehension today, as it is well known that this delicious red-ripe fruit is one of the richest sources of vitamins C and A.

Selection: Buy 2 pounds for 4 servings. Tomatoes should be firm, well-formed and not overripe.

Preparation: Wash well. The skin is edible, but if necessary, peel. Keep tomatoes covered and refrigerated after peeling.

To Peel: Dip in boiling water for about $\frac{1}{2}$ minute, then into cold water to chill; skin can be removed easily; or hold tomato on a fork over flame until skin blisters and splits. Peel.

Cooking Time: 10 minutes.

Cooking: Cut peeled tomatoes into quarters. Simmer gently, covered, for about 10 minutes. Use no water.

Serving: Season with chopped onion, salt, pepper, and butter or margarine.

CHERRY TOMATO

A miniature red or yellow tomato about the size of a small plum, often no more than 1 inch in diameter.

PLUM TOMATO

The small Italian tomatoes shaped like plums; they can be used in any recipes calling for tomatoes.

BAKED OR GRILLED TOMATOES

3 medium tomatoes, cut in half
1 teaspoon salt
$\frac{1}{8}$ teaspoon pepper
2 ounces fried breadcrumbs
2 ounces grated Cheddar cheese

Season each tomato half with salt and pepper. Blend crumbs and cheese, and sprinkle on each tomato half.

Arrange in baking pan and bake in moderate oven (375°F. Mark 5) 15 minutes, or grill 8 to 10 minutes, under low heat. Serves 6.

FRIED RIPE OR GREEN TOMATOES

Slice 6 medium-sized ripe or green tomatoes about $\frac{1}{2}$-inch thick. Dip in mixture of 2 ounces fine, dry breadcrumbs or flour, $\frac{1}{2}$ teaspoon salt, and a little pepper.

Cook in small amount fat until brown on both sides.

If desired, dip tomatoes in beaten egg, then in flour or breadcrumbs before cooking. Serves 6.

Tomatoes Provençale

TOMATOES PROVENÇALE

4 ounces black olives
8 large firm tomatoes
3 tablespoons olive or cooking oil
2 ounces chopped onion
2 chopped cloves garlic
1 pound pork sausagemeat
½ teaspoon salt
small pinch of pepper
2 tablespoons chopped parsley

Stone and chop olives, leaving 8 whole. Wash tomatoes; cut a slice off the bottom and with a cocktail stick, put whole olive in top of each.

Scoop out tomatoes; turn upside down to drain on absorbent paper.

Heat oil in frying pan; add onion and garlic; cook until soft and golden. Add sausagemeat and brown slowly for about 15 minutes.

Drain off fat. Stir in seasonings, parsley, and chopped olives; fill tomatoes.

Place in baking dish. Bake in moderate oven (375°F. Mark 5) 15 to 20 minutes. Top with tomato slices for last 5 minutes of cooking time. Serves 6 to 8.

SCALLOPED RIPE OR GREEN TOMATOES

1½ pounds sliced fresh or canned tomatoes
1 ounce chopped onion
2 tablespoons chopped green pepper, optional
1 teaspoon salt
pepper
sugar, optional—½ teaspoon for ripe or canned tomatoes, 1 tablespoon for green tomatoes
6 ounces soft breadcrumbs
2 tablespoons fat

Mix together tomatoes (ripe or green), onion, green pepper, salt, pepper, and sugar if used.

Place in baking dish alternate layers of tomato mixture and breadcrumbs, ending with breadcrumbs. (For a thinner mixture, omit 3 ounces of the breadcrumbs.) Dot with fat.

Bake in moderate oven (375°F. Mark 5) 20 to 30 minutes for ripe tomatoes, about 45 for green.

If liked, sprinkle 2 ounces grated cheese over the top for the last 10 to 15 minutes of cooking. Serves 6.

Variations: For a change, combine ripe tomatoes with other vegetables. Reduce tomatoes to 1 pound and add 1 pound cooked whole-kernel sweet corn; or 1 pound shredded cabbage; or 1 medium-sized aubergine, peeled and cut in ½-inch pieces; or 4 medium-sized onions, sliced or quartered, in place of the chopped onion. Mix all together.

Cover and bake until vegetables are tender—with sweet corn, 20 to 30 minutes; with onions, about 1 hour; with cabbage or aubergine the scallop will need 45 to 50 minutes.

RIPE OR GREEN STEWED TOMATOES

Remove stem ends and cut 6 medium ripe or green tomatoes into quarters (peel ripe tomatoes, if preferred). Add 1 tablespoon chopped onion for flavour, if liked. Cover and cook until soft, 10 to 20 minutes for ripe tomatoes, 20 to 35 for green. Add a little water to green tomatoes, if needed.

Season with 1 teaspoon salt; a little pepper; sugar, if liked—½ teaspoon for ripe tomatoes, 1 tablespoon for green; and 1 tablespoon fat.

For variety, add 1½ ounces soft breadcrumbs before serving or toasted bread cubes. Serves 6.

Stewed Canned Tomatoes: Season canned tomatoes in the same way as fresh ripe ones, and heat through (if onion is added cook until onion is tender).

Stewed Tomatoes with Onions or Celery: Cook together half as much sliced onion or chopped celery as ripe tomatoes. Season as above.

Cook, covered, until onion or celery is soft, about 20 minutes. This is an excellent way to use the outer stalks of celery that are not good for eating raw.

BAKED STUFFED TOMATOES
(Basic Recipe)

Choose smooth, medium-sized tomatoes. Cut thin slice from stem ends; remove seeds and pulp; discard seeds.

Drain off most of the juice. Sprinkle tomatoes with salt, turn upside down and, if possible, leave to stand 30 minutes or longer.

Add an equal quantity of breadcrumbs to pulp. Season with salt and pepper, and a few drops onion juice. If liked, finely chopped onion and green pepper may also be added. Stuff tomatoes with mixture.

Place in buttered pan; sprinkle with additional fried breadcrumbs. Bake in hot oven (400°F. Mark 6) 20 minutes.

STUFFING VARIATIONS FOR BAKED TOMATOES

This is an excellent way to use up small amounts of leftover seafood, meat, poultry and vegetables.

Sauté a little chopped onion in butter or margarine; add chopped or minced meat, some of the tomato pulp, and breadcrumbs. Season to taste.

For a firmer stuffing, stir in 1 lightly beaten egg.

Other suggested stuffings:

Prawn Stuffing: Cut canned, or freshly cooked, cleaned prawns into 2 or 3 pieces; add a little cream, cheese or curry sauce. Fill tomatoes.

Top with fried breadcrumbs. Bake in moderate oven (350°F. Mark 4) until top is brown.

Curried Leftover Meat Stuffing: Use any leftover cooked meat, ham etc. Put through vegetable mill.

Bind with a little meat stock; season to taste with curry powder and a little grated onion. Fill tomatoes.

Top with fried breadcrumbs. Bake in moderate oven (350°F. Mark 4) until top is brown.

Mixed Vegetable Stuffing: Chop leftover cooked vegetables (cucumber, onion, green pepper, peas, cauliflower, etc.). Mix with a little cream sauce or cheese sauce. Fill tomatoes.

Top with fried breadcrumbs. Bake in moderate oven (350°F. Mark 4) until top is brown.

Creole Rice Stuffing: Sauté chopped onion in butter or margarine. Add cooked rice, tomato pulp and seasoning to taste. Fill tomatoes.

Top with fried breadcrumbs. Bake until top is brown.

Sweet Corn Stuffing: Fry gently 1 tablespoon chopped onion and 1 tablespoon green pepper in 2 tablespoons butter or margarine. Add 1 pound drained whole-kernel sweet corn, 2 ounces fine breadcrumbs, 2 well beaten eggs and ½ teaspoon salt.

Fill tomatoes. Bake until tops are brown.

Sweet Corn and Green Pepper Stuffing: Use sweet corn cut from cob. Mix with cooked, chopped green pepper, season with salt, pepper and flavour with onion. Fill tomatoes.

Top with fried breadcrumbs. Bake until top is brown.

Broccoli Stuffing: Dip cooked broccoli tips in melted butter or margarine. Fill tomatoes.

Top with fried breadcrumbs. Bake in moderate oven until top is brown.

Green Pea Stuffing: Fry gently 1 tablespoon grated onion and 1 ounce finely chopped celery in 2 tablespoons butter or margarine.

Add ¾ pound cooked peas and the pulp which has been scooped out of the tomatoes. Mix well. Fill tomatoes. Bake.

Creole Stuffed Tomatoes

CREOLE STUFFED TOMATOES

3 rashers bacon
1 ounce chopped green pepper
1 ounce chopped onion
6 medium tomatoes
½ pound whole-kernel sweet corn
1 teaspoon celery salt

Fry bacon in frying pan until crisp. Drain and set aside. Remove fat in pan, leaving about 1 tablespoon. Sauté green pepper and onion gently.

Meanwhile prepare tomatoes by removing top slice and centre core from each. Scoop out pulp.

Add pulp, sweet corn and celery salt to vegetables in frying pan. Heat thoroughly. Crumble bacon and add to vegetable mixture, saving some of the bacon for garnish.

Fill tomato cups and top with remaining bacon. Bake in shallow dish in moderate oven (350°F. Mark 4) 15 to 20 minutes. Serves 6.

TOMATOES CREOLE

1 green pepper, shredded
1 large onion, chopped
2 tablespoons chopped celery
2 tablespoons butter or margarine
4 to 6 large tomatoes, skinned and sliced

Cook pepper, onion, and celery in melted butter until soft.

Add tomatoes and cook slowly until soft. Season to taste with salt and pepper. Serves 4 to 5.

SWISS CHARD

Swiss chard is a form of beetroot that is grown for the tops only. Like all salad greens, it is important that the leaves are fresh, crisp and of a good green colour. They are an excellent source of vitamin A and have a fair content of C and G. See **Greens**.

Selection and Preparation: One pound serves 3 to 4. Use young chard; wash thoroughly in 4 or 5 waters to remove sand and dirt.

Cooking: It usually needs no more water than that which clings to the leaves. Cover pan and cook over low heat 10 to 15 minutes. The liquid should be entirely absorbed.

If the leaves are old or have heavy white stalks, cut these off and cook them separately from the leaves. Cut the stalks into 2-inch lengths; cover with boiling salted water and simmer until tender, about 25 minutes.

Serving: Chop the cooked leaves; add 1 tablespoon melted butter or margarine and ¼ teaspoon salt per pound.

Serve with melted butter or margarine, hollandaise sauce, or hot mayonnaise as a dressing. Garnish with hard-boiled egg.

SWISS CHARD CASSEROLE

Use the centre mid ribs; wash and trim them to a suitable length. Put in a casserole with a knob of butter, 1 onion, peeled and grated, salt, pepper and about 2 tablespoons water. Cover and cook in a moderate oven (375°F. Mark 5) for about 1 hour. Make a thick cheese sauce and pour over; sprinkle with grated cheese and breadcrumbs, dot with butter and return to oven until browned on top.

TURNIPS

Turnips originated in Southern Europe where, during the earliest times, they were cultivated for medicinal purposes as well as for food. In fact, it was then popularly believed that broth made from turnips was good for gout and that turnip could be made into an excellent scouring soap for beautifying the face and hands. Modern research indicates that turnips are a good source of several vitamins, the fresh green tops being particularly rich in A and C.

Turnips are generally sold with tops removed, although those from early crops are sometimes sold in bunches with tops on. The tops should be young, fresh and green. Good winter turnips of the purple-top variety should have all the characteristics of good root vegetables—smooth skin, firmness and a good weight for their size. The eating quality of turnip tops depends largely on their freshness when purchased.

Turnips can be made sweeter and their flavour greatly improved by adding a teaspoonful of sugar to the cooking water.

Preparation: Turnips and swedes are cooked the same way. Scrub and peel as thinly as possible before cooking. Leave whole, cut into large pieces or dice. Save the green tops to use as another vegetable.

Cooking Time: 15 to 30 minutes.

Cooking: Cook, covered, in a small amount of boiling, salted water. Allow 20 to 30 minutes for whole turnips and 15 to 20 minutes for sliced or diced turnips.

Serving: Season with salt and pepper and add butter or margarine. Or mash, add a little hot milk and margarine or butter and season.

Raw: Thin strips of turnip are a good addition to the hors-d'oeuvre dish.

CREAMED TURNIPS OR SWEDES

Reheat diced, cooked turnips or swedes in a little double cream.

TURNIP SOUFFLÉ

Follow basic recipe for Vegetable Soufflé.

GLAZED TURNIPS

Cook 8 small or ¾ pound diced turnips until tender. Drain.

Place in frying pan with 3 tablespoons butter or margarine, 3 tablespoons golden syrup and 1 blade of mace. Cook slowly until lightly browned, turning often. Serves 6.

TURNIPS EN CASSEROLE

Put cubed raw turnip in casserole. Dot with butter or margarine. Season with salt and pepper.

Add water or consommé to cover bottom of dish. Bake in moderate oven (350°F. Mark 4) until soft, about 40 minutes.

TRUFFLES

A truffle is a small, fleshy fungus that grows underground, usually in woodlands close to the roots of trees. It is found in several parts of Europe but is valued most highly in France. The several varieties vary in colour from grey or brown to nearly black; those of Périgord are especially esteemed. Their pungent, aromatic flavour makes them a good garnish and sauce ingredient. Because they have not been successfully cultivated and must usually be rooted out by pigs or dogs trained to scent them, they are expensive. Truffles are available in cans or jars, imported from France.

UDO

Udo is the Japanese name for the spikenard, a perennial herb of the valerian family. Its blanched shoots resemble celery and are used like asparagus.

YAMS

A yam is the starchy tuberous root of several tropical or subtropical climbing herbs or shrubs. The sweet potato, though commonly so called in parts of North America, is not a yam. True yams, which often grow to 30 pounds or more, are grown in the West Indies, some Central and South American countries, and other parts of the world and to a limited extent in the southern United States. They are baked, boiled, or ground into flour and are also fed to livestock.

SPECIAL COOKING AIDS

Pressure Cooking

The wide variety of pressure cookers developed in recent years attests to the popularity of this versatile utensil. A pressure cooker is a saucepan in which food is cooked at temperatures above the normal temperature of boiling water. In ordinary top-of-the-stove cooking the boiling point of water (212°F.) is the highest temperature that can be reached. In a pressure cooker, the temperature is raised above boiling point by the pressure of steam; the heat is driven through the food at a much faster rate and in that way the cooking time is cut. For example, at 5 pounds pressure the temperature in the cooker is 228°F., at 10 pounds pressure it is 240°F., and at 15 pounds pressure it is 250°F.

Pressure cookers have regulators with which the pressure and temperature can be kept at the required level. And they have safety valves intended to release steam (if the regulator clogs) before a dangerous pressure is reached. The pressure cooker as we know it today is different in size and weight from the big pressure canners. It is, therefore, used for different purposes and handled differently. For canning, a large cooker of 3-gallon capacity is more practical than the pressure cookers that range in size from 7 to 10 pints.

The pressure cooker is not only a timesaver; it also conserves the vitamin content of food, because air and light are excluded during the cooking period. Minerals, too, are conserved because those minerals which are soluble in water are contained in the small amount of water used in pressure cooking, and the cooking water that is left may be used in gravies, sauces or soups.

GENERAL RULES FOR USING A PRESSURE COOKER

1. Before you use a pressure cooker for the first time, study the instruction booklet thoroughly and follow the manufacturer's directions with great care. They have been worked out in the maker's laboratories to insure safety in operation and the best possible results. Your cooker is a mechanically designed precision tool and cannot be operated by guesswork.

2. Make sure that the valve opening is properly cleaned and clear of any particles of food.

3. Put in the trivet or omit as directed. Use the exact amount of water or other liquid specified in the recipe.

4. Fill the cooker no more than $\frac{2}{3}$ or $\frac{3}{4}$ full of solid food, using $\frac{2}{3}$ for a lever or spring top cooker, $\frac{3}{4}$ for the solid dome types. Under no circumstances should the food touch the top of the cooker as this might clog the valve opening or block the safety plug. Note, however, that some manufacturers stipulate that their cookers should never be filled more than $\frac{2}{3}$ full of any kind of food.

5. Fill the cooker **no more than half full** of soup, liquids, or cereals.

6. Unless you are cooking a boiled or stewed dish, use just enough water or liquid to come to the top of the trivet, not over it.

7. Be sure that a steady stream of cold air with steam is coming out of the valve before pressure is built up. This takes from 2 to 4 minutes according to the size of the cooker, and the temperature of the liquid and food when put in.

8. Don't start cooking in a pressure cooker unless the lid is tight and well adjusted.

9. Remember that, unless the heat is reduced after pressure is reached, a continuous escape of steam causes so much loss of moisture that food cooks dry and burns.

10. Count pressure-cooking time given in a recipe from the time when the indicator, weight or gauge shows the required pressure.

11. It may be desirable to use a timer to keep close track of minutes—particularly to avoid overcooking frozen foods or fresh fruits.

12. Regulate the heat under the cooker so the pressure will stay even. If it tends to rise, even when the heat is lowered, place an asbestos pad under the cooker. The cause is probably that the valve tube is clogged or the heat is too high. If pressure starts to drop during the cooking period, it usually means that all moisture has been exhausted from the cooker. This is usually due to excess heat.

13. If you're called away while using the pressure cooker, turn off the heat or push cooker off the ring. Return it to the heat when you return.

14. When the cooking time is up, turn off the heat. Reduce pressure to 0, according to the manufacturer's directions. Foods tend to overcook if allowed to stand in the cooker after pressure cooking. There are some foods, however, such as dried vegetables, puddings, cereals and some casserole dishes which have a better texture if the pressure is reduced gradually. You will be able to determine this by experience and personal preference.

15. Always tilt the lid of a pressure cooker when removing it so that any steam left is directed away from your face.

16. **Never attempt to force a cover off.** If you feel any resistance, that means the cooker has not been completely cooled. You could scald yourself if the lid is prematurely removed while steam pressure remains in pot. That's why some cookers are so constructed

as to make it impossible to remove the lid until all pressure has been exhausted. If you feel any resistance, follow the manufacturer's directions in immersing the pan in cold water or allowing cold water to run over it for a while before opening it. Food in a cooker cooled to just the point where it can be opened is usually the right temperature for serving.

HOW TO ADAPT YOUR OWN RECIPES TO PRESSURE COOKING

You don't have to acquire a whole set of new recipes for your pressure cooker. Most manufacturers supply a book of instructions and recipes giving cooking time, amount of water to be added, recipes, etc., but you are not limited. You can easily adapt your favourite recipes.

In general, remember to cook things only ⅓ as long, and for most foods such as meats, vegetables, stews, etc., add only the amount of liquid you want in the finished food. As a general rule, 4 tablespoons is sufficient for foods requiring less than 10 minutes to cook and 8 tablespoons for foods which take up to 20 minutes.

WHAT PRESSURE TO USE

The recipes and charts in this book are designed as a general guide. If they differ from the instructions in the booklet provided by the manufacturer of your cooker it is wise to follow those instructions because the maker knows best how his cooker performs.

Some of the cookers have a pressure gauge so that 5, 10 or 15 pounds pressure may be used. Others are keyed to 15 pounds. If you have a pressure cooker with various weights, that is, if a choice is possible from 5 to 15 pounds, you may want to use the following table which is recommended by some manufacturers: 5 pounds for fruits and vegetables, 10 pounds for meats and dried vegetables, and 15 pounds for fresh vegetables, soups and one-dish meals. Other manufacturers recommend a standard 15 pound pressure, claiming that similar results are obtained at this higher pressure.

Most recipes and all charts in this book use a consistent 15 pound pressure. If you follow this plan you will find it unnecessary to learn a number of different timings.

CARE OF PRESSURE COOKERS

1. When the pressure cooker is new, rinse in hot soapy water. To make cleaning easier, pour warm water into cooker as soon as you remove the food. After each use wash thoroughly in fairly hot, soapy water. Scald and dry thoroughly. Store uncovered to prevent accumulation of stale odours.

2. To remove food stains, add 1 heaped teaspoon cream of tartar to 1 pint water and bring to pressure.

3. The steam control valves and weights do not require cleaning and should **never be immersed in water**. Handle indicator control or weight carefully. Dropping it may damage it.

4. When the valve tube needs cleaning use a very tiny brush or a pipe cleaner, or force water through the valve tube to rinse it.

5. Keep the smooth edge of the cooker free of chips. Avoid hitting the edge of the cooker with utensils such as knives or spoons. A marred uneven edge will allow steam to escape and with it precious vitamins and minerals.

6. Keep the cover away from direct heat such as gas ring, electric ring or oven. Direct heat affects the gasket in such a way that it may not create a perfect seal and pressure will not be built up in the cooker.

7. Keep the cover clean and store right side up and not on the pressure cooker.

8. Never pour cold water inside a dry, overheated cooker: the sudden temperature change may crack or warp the metal.

9. If your cooker has a gauge, get it checked periodically for accuracy.

HINTS FOR PRESSURE COOKING MEAT, POULTRY, GAME

The primary advantage of pressure cooking meat is that you can use the cheaper cuts or older boiling poultry and they can be stewed or pot roasted to make a tender, juicy dish in a relatively short time. It is questionable, however, whether you should prepare steak, chops, or high-quality joints in this manner. We certainly would not recommend it. The pressure cooker, for example, cannot give you the fine flavour of meat cooked by direct heat as in grilling.

Most types of meat are usually browned in the pressure cooker or frying pan before being pressure cooked. It improves the flavour and helps to seal in the juices; however, to avoid unnecessary shrinkage browning should be done slowly. In browning meat before pressure cooking we suggest that you use as little fat as possible. If more than 1 ounce is used, pour off any excess fat after the meat is browned. With some finished dishes it is often better to brown and crisp the meat under a moderate grill or in the oven after pressure cooking.

It is very difficult to give the exact time for pressure cooking meat. The cut and quality, the size and shape, the amount and distribution of fat, bones, etc., must all be taken into consideration as well as whether your family likes meat undercooked, medium or well done. In general, a thick, chunky piece of meat will require more time than a thin one, and the larger the amount of fat and the smaller the amount of bone the more minutes per pound will be required for pressure cooking.

FROZEN MEAT AND POULTRY

It is advisable to defrost any large cuts of meat before pressure cooking or it may cook unevenly. In general, meat does not have to be defrosted before cooking; however, it will require a much longer cooking period. Allow ½ to ¾ as much time again as given in the recipes and add about double the amount of water or other liquid.

Whole poultry should be entirely defrosted. Poultry pieces should be defrosted only to the point where they can be separated from one another.

CONDENSED RECIPE HINTS

It is very important to watch timing very carefully. An additional minute or two may represent many minutes of ordinary cooking.

If you want to use a lower pressure than the standard pressure of 15 pounds that is followed in these recipes, then

---

PRESSURE COOKING AT HIGH ALTITUDES

As the altitude increases the boiling point of water decreases. At sea level the boiling point of water is 212°F. If your pressure cooker has an adjustable gauge, use the following table. Increase the pressure according to the altitude but do not alter the cooking time. No adjustment is needed for altitudes below 2,000 feet.

Elevation Above Sea Level	Boiling Point of Water	Increased Pressure
Below 2,000 feet	212°F.	nil
Above 2,000 feet	208°F.	1 pound
Above 3,000 feet	206°F.	2 pounds
Above 4,000 feet	204°F.	2 pounds
Above 5,000 feet	202°F.	3 pounds
Above 6,000 feet	201°F.	3 pounds
Above 7,000 feet	199°F.	4 pounds

consult the directions supplied by the manufacturer of your cooker.

The directions that follow are intended as a guide so that you can make your own combination of dishes. You merely take into consideration the difference in cooking time of the various foods.

For example, if the meat takes 1 hour, the potatoes 15 minutes, and another vegetable only 5 minutes, you reduce pressure to 0 after 45 minutes of cooking and add the potatoes. Cook at 15 pounds pressure an additional 10 minutes. Reduce pressure to 0 again and add the second vegetable. Cook at 15 pounds pressure 5 minutes, or a total of 1 hour.

Season pressure cooked foods lightly, since very little liquid is used. You can always season to taste later. You can substitute tomato juice or stock for water and, of course, you can use other seasonings but use them lightly until you have gained experience. For suggestions about seasonings see the index for other recipes.

Cooking time in the following condensed recipes begins when pressure reaches 15 pounds.

Unless you are making a stewed dish always use a trivet in the cooker.

CONDENSED RECIPES
Cook at 15-Pound Pressure

CORNED BEEF
Use 3 to 4 pounds. Soak in cold water before cooking to remove excess salt. Drain. Place on trivet in cooker. Add ¾ pint water. Cook 20 to 25 minutes per pound. For additional flavouring, add a bay leaf, several peppercorns and 1 small sliced onion.

Near the end of cooking time, pour off all but ⅓ pint water and add potatoes and cabbage wedges.

BEEF OLIVES
Use 1½ pounds stewing steak. Cut into serving pieces. Season meat lightly. Spread with stuffing. Roll and tie. Brown on all sides in fat. Place on trivet. Add ¼ pint boiling water or tomato juice.

Near the end of cooking period, potatoes, carrots and onions can be added. Total cooking time 35 to 45 minutes.

BRAISED RIBS
Season lightly. Brown well in hot fat. Add ½ pint tomato juice. Cook 20 to 25 minutes.

BEEF STEW
Cut 2 pounds beef into 1-inch cubes. Season lightly. Brown in hot fat. Add ¾ pint hot water. Cook 25 minutes. Near end of cooking period add mixed vegetables.

POT ROAST
Use 3 to 4 pounds topside or rump. Season lightly. Pound flour into surface. Brown on all sides in hot fat. Add ¼ pint hot water, 1 medium-sized onion (chopped), 1 bay leaf, salt and pepper. Place on trivet. Cook 10 minutes per pound.

Add other vegetables near end of cooking period.

BRAISED STEAK
Use 2 pounds topside, cut ¾ inch thick. Season lightly. Pound with flour. Brown slowly on both sides in hot fat. Add ¼ pint tomato juice. Cook 25 minutes. Add vegetables near end of cooking period.

SHOULDER OF PORK
Brown slowly on all sides in hot fat. Pour off excess fat. Season lightly. Add ¼ pint hot water. Cook 15 to 18 minutes per pound. When tender, crisp in oven.

SPARERIBS
Use 2 pounds spareribs. Brown slowly in hot fat. Season lightly. Add 2 tablespoons hot water. Cook 15 minutes. To brown, brush with barbecue sauce and brown under low grill.

HAM SHANK
Brown lightly in hot fat. Season lightly. Add ¼ pint hot water. Cook 20 minutes. Near end of cooking period add cabbage wedges or sauerkraut.

HAM OR BACON JOINT
Use a half or whole ham or a joint of bacon. Cover with cold water. Soak 2 hours or more. Discard water. Place on trivet in cooker. Add ¾ pint hot water or cider. Cook 12 minutes per pound.

To roast, remove rind and excess fat. Cover with glaze and brown in hot oven.

KNUCKLE OF HAM
Place a 1- to 3-pound ham knuckle on trivet in cooker. Add ½ pint hot water. Cook 35 minutes. Reduce pressure and remove meat. Cook cabbage and swedes in broth.

KNUCKLE OF VEAL
Split knuckle. Brown slowly in hot fat. Add 4 tablespoons hot water. Cook 20 minutes.

VEAL STEW
Brown floured veal cubes in hot fat. Season lightly. Add ½ pint hot water. Cook 15 to 20 minutes. Add vegetables near end of cooking period.

VEAL OLIVES
Use ½-inch-thick slices. Stuff, season and roll up. Tie and roll in flour. Brown in hot fat. Add 4 tablespoons hot water. Cook 15 minutes.

STUFFED BREAST OF LAMB
Stuff and roll up a boned breast of lamb. Brown in hot fat. Season lightly. Add ¼ pint hot water and 1 small chopped onion. Cook 20 to 25 minutes. After removing meat to a warm place, add thickening and colouring to stock for gravy.

LAMB STEW
Cut meat into 1-inch cubes. Season lightly. Roll in flour. Brown on all sides in hot fat. Add ½ pint hot water for 2 pounds meat. Cook 20 minutes. Add vegetables near end of cooking period.

LAMB, SCRAG END OF NECK
Brown in hot fat. Season lightly. Add ½ pint hot water or tomato juice. Cook 20 minutes.

OX TONGUE, SMOKED
Add ¾ pint hot water. Cook 25 minutes per pound.
Note: If tongue is to be served cold, skin and allow to cool in seasoned liquid. If tongue is to be served hot, remove and skin while cooking vegetables in part of tongue liquid.

OX TONGUE, CORNED
Add ¾ pint hot water. Cook 20 minutes per pound.

OX TONGUE, FRESH
Add ¾ pint hot water. Cook 15 minutes per pound.

BRAISED OXTAIL
Cut into 1½-inch pieces. Brown in hot fat. Season lightly. Add ¾ pint water. Cook 45 minutes.

BRAISED OX HEARTS
Remove veins. Stuff if liked. Brown on all sides in 1 ounce hot fat. Season lightly. Add ½ pint hot water or tomato juice. Cook 25 minutes per pound.

CHICKEN FRICASSÉE
Dredge serving-sized pieces with seasoned flour. Brown on all sides in hot fat. Add ¼ pint hot water. Cook 30 to 40 minutes.

STEWED CHICKEN
Use a large boiling chicken. Joint. Add ¾ pint hot water. Cook 30 to 40 minutes. Use for creamed chicken, salads, moulds, etc. Use the liquid in sauces.

BRAISED OR JUGGED HARE
Joint and clean thoroughly. Brown in hot fat. Add 4-8 tablespoons hot brown stock. Cook 30 to 40 minutes. If young, cook the shortest time, using only 4 tablespoons hot stock.

RABBIT
Clean and cut into serving-sized pieces. Season and flour. Brown in hot fat. Add ½ pint hot water. Cook 15 minutes.

Pressure-Cooked Soups

RULES FOR PRESSURE-COOKED SOUPS

A much smaller amount of liquid is used in cooking soups in the pressure cooker than by the usual methods because soup is cooked without evaporation.

Soup is cooked at 15-pound pressure: in that way, the full flavour and the essential nutrients are quickly extracted from the bones, meat and other ingredients.

Your pressure cooker should not be filled more than half full of liquid ingredients or two-thirds full of liquids and solids unless the manufacturer's directions state otherwise. If your recipe calls for more liquids than your pressure cooker should hold, or if the result is too highly concentrated, it can always be diluted at serving time with boiling water, vegetable juices or milk.

Less seasoning is needed in pressure-cooked soup, so season lightly. That, too, can be adjusted later.

Bones should be cracked open so that all the flavour is extracted in the cooking.

A minimum amount of fat should be used because fat tends to clog the valve tube. All excess fat should be trimmed from meat or poultry used in pressure-cooked soups.

To make a clear soup in which vegetables are to be cooked, calculate the cooking time of the vegetables according to the chart and add them when the soup is partly cooked. Reduce the pressure, strain the soup, and add the vegetables, then pressure cook until the vegetables are tender.

Your favourite recipes may be adapted to the pressure cooker. Read the instructions above about quantities of liquids and solids and cut the usual time of each step in your recipes to about one-sixth. Note, too, that vegetables should be added towards the end of the cooking time; otherwise they may be overcooked and too soft.

CHICKEN SOUP

    a 3-pound chicken
    1 teaspoon salt
    1 stick celery, chopped
    1 medium-sized carrot, diced
    1 small onion, diced
    2½ pints boiling water

Cut chicken into serving pieces. (Wings, necks, and backs make excellent soup.) Put chicken in cooker. Add remaining ingredients. Cover and cook at 15-pound pressure for 15 minutes.

Reduce pressure. Strain soup. Remove skin and bones from chicken. Cut meat into tiny pieces and serve in soup. Serves 6 to 8.

BROWN SOUP STOCK

    1½ pounds lean beef, cut into 1-inch
         cubes
    1 ounce melted fat
    2 to 3 ounces diced onion
    1 ounce diced carrot
    1 small bay leaf
    1½ teaspoons salt
    small pinch black pepper
    1 ounce chopped celery with
         leaves
    1 teaspoon chopped parsley
    2½ pints boiling water

Brown meat in pressure cooker in the melted fat. Add onion, carrot, bay leaf, salt, pepper, celery, parsley and water.

Adjust cover. Cook at 15-pound pressure 15 minutes.

Reduce pressure. Uncover and strain. Adjust seasoning. Serve as clear soup, consommé, or store in refrigerator for soup stock. After soup is made, diced or julienned vegetables, pasta, diced meat, etc., may be served in it. Serves 6.

ECONOMY SOUP STOCK

    1½ pounds small bones, cracked
    1 teaspoon salt
    2½ pints water

Place bones, salt and water in cooker. Cook at 15-pound pressure for 20 minutes. Reduce pressure. Strain soup. Serves 6.

CREOLE GUMBO

    1½ ounces bacon or other dripping
    8 ounces cut okra
    1 large onion, chopped
    2 cloves garlic, chopped
    1 medium-sized green pepper,
         chopped
    1 8-ounce can tomato purée
    2 ounces crabmeat
    1 teaspoon thyme
    2 tablespoons flour
    ½ pint oysters with liquid
    1½ pints water
    3 tablespoons diced ham
    2 bay leaves
    1 teaspoon chopped parsley
    1 teaspoon salt
    ½ teaspoon cayenne pepper

Heat cooker. Brown okra lightly in fat in cooker. Combine remaining ingredients in cooker and mix well.

Cover and cook at 15-pound pressure for 15 minutes. Reduce pressure.

Serves 6 to 8.

HARICOT BEAN SOUP

    8 ounces haricot beans
    1 ham or bacon bone
    1 onion, chopped
    2 carrots, sliced
    2 sticks celery, chopped
    2 tablespoons chopped green
         pepper
    4 fluid ounces tomato purée
    small pinch dried mustard
    1 clove
    2 peppercorns
    1¾ pints water

Wash beans. Cover with water and soak overnight.

Drain. Put all ingredients in cooker. Season with salt and pepper to taste. Cook at 15-pound pressure for 30 minutes. Serves 6.

VEGETABLE SOUP

    1 pound lean meat
    1 small bone
    1½ pints water
    2 teaspoons salt
    2 ounces washed rice or barley
    1 pound fresh or canned tomatoes
    1½ ounces diced potatoes
    1 ounce diced carrots
    1 ounce cut green beans
    1 ounce diced celery
    1 tablespoon chopped parsley

Combine all ingredients except parsley in cooker. Cook 20 minutes at 15-pound pressure. Reduce pressure. Decorate soup with parsley. Serves 4 to 6.

FRENCH ONION SOUP

    1 ounce butter or margarine
    4 large onions, thinly sliced
    1½ pints brown soup stock
    4 slices crisp, buttered toast
    2 ounces grated Parmesan cheese

Brown onions in melted butter in cooker. Add stock. Cover and cook at 15-pound pressure for 4 minutes.

Place toast in heated bowls. Pour soup over and sprinkle with Parmesan cheese. Serves 4.

Creole Gumbo

Packed Lunches

TIPS FOR AN EASIER PACKED LUNCH

1. Plan your lunch menus at the same time that you are planning your other family meals so you get more balanced meals in both. This will save you time and effort and help you make a better packed lunch.

2. Aim to prepare some food (such as sandwich fillings, egg custards, puddings, biscuits, stewed fruit) the day before while you are cooking other meals to save your time in the morning (store in the refrigerator or freezer until needed).

3. Keep a lunch-packing area on a convenient table, or a cupboard for frequently used utensils, spices, grease-proof paper, string, etc. assembled together.

4. Wash and air lunch box daily to prevent food odours and flavours from developing.

5. Soften butter well before spreading. Spread on both slices of bread to prevent the filling from soaking in.

6. Spread fillings to edge of bread, but do not allow to run over edge.

7. Cut sandwiches in different simple shapes for variety.

8. Wrap foods separately in grease-proof paper or aluminium foil.

9. Pack heavy foods in bottom of container or bag, with lighter ones on top, to prevent crushing.

10. Small salt and pepper shakers are useful. Cover top with paper and rubber band to prevent spilling. Plastic food containers give good protection to moist foods.

11. Include paper napkins with the lunch.

12. Remember: foods with variety in flavour, colour and texture add to the interest and variety of the meal and help to prevent boring lunches.

SANDWICHES

Sandwiches are usually the basis of the lunch. Use whole wheat bread rather than plain white bread. If you use white bread, be sure it is "enriched" as it helps to supply some of the same minerals and vitamins found in the whole grain.

Make your sandwich fillings tasty and interesting. Most fillings are nicer if ingredients are chopped or minced and combined with salad dressing or some other binder to make a good consistency to spread. Slices of cold meat and cheese are often dry and unappetizing on their own.

Use a variety of loaves such as whole wheat, cracked wheat, rye and raisin bread. Savoury biscuits — cream crackers, digestive biscuits or starch-reduced wafers — also make good sandwiches. Spread the bread with butter to prevent filling from soaking into it.

Filling Preparations

You will want to vary the flavour of sandwiches with different seasonings such as mustard, tomato ketchup, horseradish, paprika, olives, pickles, onions, pimiento or pepper, parsley, celery or celery salt. Salad dressing should be combined with most fillings to hold the mixture together. Suggested combinations are:

1. Minced meat (ham, beef, heart, liver) with horseradish, pickles.
2. Minced meat, egg, pickles, with tomato ketchup.
3. Sliced cold meat, pickles.
4. Salmon, pickles, tomato ketchup.
5. Chopped egg, celery, green pepper, lemon juice.
6. Chopped egg, pickles, olives.
7. Chopped egg, cheese, crisp bacon.
8. Cream or cottage cheese, nuts, chopped raisins.
9. Cream or cottage cheese, pimiento, onion juice, green pepper.
10. Cream cheese and jam.
11. Cream or cottage cheese, grated pineapple or dried fruit purée.
12. Peanut butter and chopped raisins mixed with fruit juice.
13. Peanut butter and grated raw carrots.
14. Peanut butter and apple sauce or fruit jam.
15. Peanut butter and honey.
16. Baked beans (mashed), tomato ketchup, pickles.
17. Apple, celery, carrot, raisins.
18. Apple, celery, nuts.
19. Minced cabbage, carrots, peanuts, lemon juice.
20. Chopped prunes, raisins, nuts.

VEGETABLES AND FRUIT

Raw vegetables and fruit add interest as well as vitamins to the lunch menu.

Wrap freshly washed vegetables in greaseproof paper, aluminium foil or polythene bags to keep them crisp. Good vegetables to serve raw are: carrots, cabbage, celery, lettuce, spinach, onions, radishes, cauliflower, tomatoes and cucumbers.

Wrap lettuce for sandwiches separately, so that it can be placed in bread at the time of eating to prevent wilting.

SOUPS

Soups provide something hot and make the meal more satisfying.

If you have a thermos flask, hot soups are good. These may be clear broth, plain vegetable or any creamed soup. Heat the flask well with hot water before adding the soup to help retain heat.

TO FINISH OFF THE MEAL

Raw fruit is always good. Simple desserts are more nutritious than rich ones. Heavy desserts such as pies, rich cakes and puddings tend to make one feel sluggish after lunch. However, they may be served occasionally to an active working person. Stewed fruit, egg custards, simple puddings and plain cake or biscuits are usually preferable.

Occasional surprises such as a few small pieces of chocolate, crystallized fruit and dried fruit relieve the monotony of a packed lunch. Avoid too many sweets for the child or overweight person.

Always include an orange, an apple or some other fresh fruit.

Dried fruit washed and wrapped in greaseproof paper.

Cooked fruit in covered plastic food container.

Wholesome biscuits and cakes made with whole-grain cereals, fruits and nuts.

Egg custards and other milk puddings in covered plastic food container.

DRINKS

You will always want to include milk in some form. Milk is the best possible beverage for a packed lunch. It is a necessary food for both children and adults, and there is no substitute for it in the diet. Include it as a drink or in cream soups, egg custards or puddings.

Fruit juices and tomato juice also offer good variety.

A thermos flask is necessary to keep beverages hot or cold. Rinse with hot or cold water first to help maintain temperature.

A WORD OF WARNING — AVOID FOOD POISONING

Some foods, such as meat, salads and egg dishes, spoil very quickly if not kept cool enough. Be especially careful with these in hot weather — or use sandwich fillings made of safe ingredients such as peanut butter, jam, diced vegetables or fruit.

Do not pack devilled eggs or potato salads. Bacteria develops very rapidly in these dishes in warm temperatures and can cause poisoning.

SALT IN SUMMER IS IMPORTANT

For the man who does hard active work, put in a little extra salt in hot weather. Losing a lot of salt through perspiration may cause heat cramps.

Cooking at High Altitudes

The housewife who moves into a high-altitude region soon finds that she must make changes in her everyday recipes. The lower air pressure at high altitudes means that water boils at a lower temperature. Foods boiled or steamed fail to reach as high a cooking temperature as they do at lower levels, and they take longer to cook. Changes in atmospheric pressure necessitate many modifications in cooking procedures. Among these are an increase in the cooking times for most vegetables, a lowering in the end-point temperatures in making sweets and cake icings, and modifications of rich dough mixtures.

Fortunately, much research has been done to eliminate the mysteries of high-altitude cookery by a number of organizations as well as by housewives in high-altitude areas working under the direction of various experiment stations and commercial food companies. A housewife can readily obtain the results of these experiments in booklet form. The information offered in this section, as well as in the Pressure Cooking section, will give a brief résumé of this information and in that way prepare her for the problems she will encounter and show her how to overcome them.

CAKES

The most perplexing problem that confronts a housewife at high altitudes is that of baking, especially cakes. Since the air pressure is lower, the leavening gas expands more and causes a coarse, crumbly result that may even collapse.

As the pressure decreases (with the increase in elevation) a correspondingly smaller weight of carbon dioxide or other leavening gas is required to perform the same amount of leavening. This applies to all flour mixtures, whether they are leavened with carbon dioxide, as in the case of butter cakes, baking powder scones, quick breads and yeast breads; or with air, as in angel food and sponge cakes; or with steam, as in cream puffs.

The structure of a cake is very delicate, and increased pressure resulting from expanded carbon dioxide within the cells causes them to expand too much. This makes the texture too coarse; if the cells are expanded still more, they will rupture and a collapsed cake will result. To produce a satisfactory cake at a high altitude, less baking powder must be used. For cakes made with soured milk and bicarbonate of soda, less soda should be used.

Liquid at high altitudes evaporates to a greater extent, causing the sugar solution in the batter to become more concentrated. Excessive sugar in the cell walls weakens the structure and makes them more apt to collapse. Thus reducing the sugar in a cake recipe gives stronger cell walls and makes the cake less likely to collapse.

In general, for 5,000 feet, a reduction of $\frac{1}{2}$ teaspoon baking powder, $2\frac{1}{2}$ teaspoons sugar and an increase of $\frac{1}{2}$ to 1 tablespoon liquid for a cake containing 8 ounces flour is recommended. Contrary to popular opinion, there are no set rules for modification of cake recipes for high altitudes. The changes that are necessary depend on the type of cake and the relationship of the ingredients to one another.

In angel food cakes, the leavening is air, and care must be taken not to beat too much air into the egg whites. They should be beaten until they form peaks which just fall over. The sugar should be reduced by about 1 tablespoon for each 1,000 feet of altitude. A higher baking temperature for a shorter time is more satisfactory. Less sugar and more liquid should be used for sponge cake. The eggs or egg yolks should not be overbeaten and if baking powder is required, the amount should be reduced.

QUICK BREAD

With scones, buns and other quick bread the baking powder may be decreased slightly but the structure of the product is such that it will withstand the increased pressure quite well.

For Yorkshire pudding the amount of egg in the batter should be increased and the fat reduced. This makes a stronger batter which will be able to retain the steam long enough for a crust to form. Yorkshire pudding made by sea-level recipes loses the steam too fast, by both expansion and evaporation, and turns out more like buns.

Cream puff batter, being heavier, holds the steam well and does not require any correction for high altitude.

YEAST BREAD

Yeast bread dough rises more rapidly at high altitudes, and it may become over-puffed if it is not watched carefully and allowed to rise only until it is doubled in bulk. Less yeast may be used, but most bakers prefer to let the dough rise for a shorter time. Flour dries out more quickly at higher altitudes; therefore it may be necessary to use more liquid to compensate for this loss and to make the dough the proper consistency.

BISCUITS

Biscuits usually do not need adjustment for high altitudes. A slight reduction in baking powder and sugar may improve them.

PASTRY

Pastry is not affected by high altitudes except for the faster rate of evaporation. Therefore, slightly more liquid may be required.

DOUGHNUTS

Doughnuts made from sea-level recipes are frequently found to be cracked, too high in fat absorption, and too hard and brown. To remedy this difficulty, the sugar should also be reduced.

HIGH-ALTITUDE DOUGHNUTS

1   ounce lard
$\frac{1}{2}$ pound sugar
2   eggs
8   fluid ounces soured milk or
     buttermilk
1   teaspoon bicarbonate of soda
16 to 18 ounces sifted plain flour
$1\frac{1}{2}$ teaspoons baking powder
1   teaspoon salt
1   teaspoon nutmeg

Cream lard and sugar. Add eggs and beat well. Add soured milk.

Sift dry ingredients and add to first mixture. Mix well, chill.

Roll out and fry in hot deep fat (350°F.). Makes about 42.

Smoke Cooking

This is a method of cooking which uses hot smoke in place of direct heat, giving to meat, poultry and fish that wonderful flavour that is characteristic of some Chinese barbecued foods and a variety of expensive foods often found in delicatessens.

Smoke cooking is an ancient art regaining popularity now that portable smoke ovens are on the market.

Cooking times and methods vary with the type of oven used, the heat of the fire and the distance of the smoking rack or hooks from the firebox. The manufacturer's directions accompanying your oven should be followed.

In general, the ovens consist of a firebox and a chimney.

After the fire is started and the oven warmed, food is suspended in the chimney and cooked by the hot air and smoke which escapes past it.

The temperature is controlled by a lid with an adjustable damper.

The fire should be made with hardwoods (chips or sawdust) such as hickory, oak or hard maple, or fruit woods (apple, cherry, lemon, etc.) to give the foods their characteristic smoke flavour.

To smoke-cook foods in a barbecue-oven with a hood, start with a charcoal fire, then when it burns down to even glowing embers, add slightly dampened hickory or fruit tree chips or sawdust.

Place the food on the grill or spit, close the hood tightly and allow it to cook. Remember that this is a slow process and can't be hurried.

In all smoke cooking care must be taken to avoid overcooking as there is a tendency for the food to dry out. For this reason fatty foods are most suitable. And it's usually best to soak the food in a marinade for several hours or overnight to add flavour and to temper the smoky taste.

Chafing Dishes

Chafing dish or fondue cookery is fun, and almost anything that can be made in a frying pan or double saucepan can also be made in many chafing dishes.

TYPES OF CHAFING DISHES

You'll find chafing dishes in many handsome designs from tiny ones for individual servings to jumbo sized for more than 20.

They come with different kinds of heating devices. For cooking at the table, most people prefer a heat you can adjust, such as the methylated spirits burner, bottled heat and the electric unit with heat control.

Some chafing dishes are actually a double saucepan (bain-marie) with water pan and a cooking pan (blazer). The cooking pan can be used directly over the flame for browning or for foods that don't require the gentle heat of the bain-marie. Other chafing dishes are the deep-pot type with just one pan.

Then there are food warmers, often pottery casseroles, heated by candle or methylated spirits. These keep cooked food at serving temperature on the table or sideboard. You may also use a double saucepan chafing dish for the same purpose.

CHAFING-DISH COOKING HINTS

● Plan a simple first course such as a large salad to keep your guests busy while you play chef.

● So you won't keep hungry guests waiting too long while you cook, choose a quick-to-prepare recipe.

● Memorize the recipe thoroughly. If necessary, rehearse it in advance.

● Get most of the preparations out of the way before the guests arrive. Measure out all ingredients carefully in the kitchen.

● Arrange all ingredients and utensils you'll need on a tray near the chafing dish. Put the chafing dish on another tray.

● And remember, part of the fun is collecting pretty tiny dishes and pans to hold these ingredients. Choose conversation pieces that will help to make your meal attractive.

● Cook silently. Use long wooden spoons for stirring.

● It's wise to fill the methylated spirits burner beneath the chafing dish well before lighting. And if you must refuel while cooking, carry the whole thing to the kitchen sink.

Cooking for Two

Cooking for two, despite its romantic implications, often poses a problem because most recipes give quantities for 4, 6 or 8 servings. For a smaller number of servings, the amount of each ingredient in such recipes as casseroles, salads and vegetable dishes may be cut to a half or a third. Pies can be prepared as individual tarts. It's best, however, to bake whole recipes for bread and cakes, then freeze half or more. Left-over cake can be turned into a variety of enticing puddings. Many of these are included in this book.

In many sections of this book you'll find certain types of popular recipes specifically marked "for two". In general, you'll save money and time if you plan several meals at once when you cook for two. You can then make use of small joints as well as such items as half a ham or a small turkey. Leftovers present the minimum problem since they make easily prepared casseroles, meat pies and sandwiches.

BUYING and COOKING GUIDE for SMALL JOINTS of MEAT (Roasted at 325°F. Mark 4, Oven Temperature)			
Meat to Buy	*Weight*	*Time: Minutes Per Pound*	*Meat Thermometer Reading*
Beef: Standing Rib (short cut)	2½-3 lbs (1 rib roast)	20 25 30	140°F. (rare) 160°F. (medium) 170°F. (well done)
Beef: Rolled Rib	2½-3 lbs (3-4 inches thick)	30-35 35-40 40-45	140°F. (rare) 160°F. (medium) 170°F. (well done)
Veal: Shoulder, boned and rolled	3½-4 lbs	55-60	170°F.
Veal: Breast, rolled and stuffed	1 breast (about 4 lbs)	45	170°F.
Veal: Loin	3-4 lbs	55-60	170°F.
Lamb: Shoulder, boned and rolled	3-3½ lbs	40	175°F. (medium) 180°F. (well done)
Fresh Pork: Small joint	2-2½ lbs	40	185°F.
Fresh Pork: Spareribs	2-2½ lbs	1½-2 hours (total time)	
Fresh Pork: Fillet	2 thick pieces fillet	1½ hours (total time)	185°F.
Smoked Ham: Slice	1-2 inches thick	1-2 hours (total time depending on thickness)	
Bacon Joint	1½ lbs	1 hour (total time)	170°F.

For any cook, beginner or expert, a meat thermometer is a wise investment. It tells you at a glance whether meat is rare, medium or well done.

Ways to Use Leftovers

SOME OF THE DISHES IN WHICH LEFTOVERS CAN BE USED

Egg whites
Egg custards
Fruit fools
Meringue
Soufflés

**Hard-boiled
egg or yolk**
Casserole dishes
Garnishes
Salads
Sandwiches

Soured cream
Cakes, biscuits
Sweet sauces
Meat stews
Pie fillings
Salad dressings
Sauces for vegetables

**Cooked meat,
poultry, fish**
Casserole dishes
Meat patties
Meat pies
Salads
Sandwiches
Stuffed vegetables

**Cooked rice, noodles,
macaroni, spaghetti**
Casseroles
Meat or cheese loaves
Timbales

Egg yolks
Cakes
Blancmanges
Egg custards or sauces
Pie fillings
Salad dressings
Scrambled eggs

**Cooked runner beans,
lima beans, sweetcorn,
peas, carrots**
Meat and vegetable pies
Soups
Salads
Stews
Stuffed peppers
Stuffed tomatoes
Vegetables in cheese sauce

Cooked potatoes
Croquettes
Fried or creamed potatoes
Meat-pie crusts
Potatoes in cheese sauce
Stews or chowders

**Cooked leaf vegetables,
chopped**
Creamed vegetables
Soups
Meat loaves
Meat patties
Omelettes
Soufflés

**Cooked or canned
fruits**
Fruit cups
Fruit sauces
Jellies
Quick bread recipes
Upside-down cakes
Yeast bread recipes

**Cooked wheat, oat
or corn cereals**
Fried cereals
Meat loaves or patties
Sweet puddings

Cake or biscuits
Brown Betty
Refrigerator cake
Toasted, with sweet
  topping for puddings

Bread
Slices, for
  French toast
Dry crumbs, in
  Brown Betty
  Croquettes
  Fried chops
Soft crumbs, in
  Meat loaves
  Stuffings

Soured milk
Cakes, biscuits
Quick bread recipes

HINTS FOR USING LEFTOVER MEAT

With leftover meat the possibilities are almost limitless. With the price of meat as high as it is, it is wise to see that none is wasted. Some families like a joint and feel that although the initial cost is high, it goes farther than steaks, chops or even hamburgers or stewing meat.

Hash need not be looked down on when planning menus. With proper handling it can become a far more sophisticated dish than cartoonists or comedians would like us to believe. It can be well-seasoned, dry minced meat, or it can be moistened with leftover gravy, milk, cream (even soured cream), cream sauce or soup—with or without onions, peppers, potatoes or chopped vegetables.

A piece of meat from making soup or some leftover stew can emerge as an attractive and tasty dish if it is minced, seasoned, moistened with gravy or soup, and used to fill the centre of a straight-sided oven dish or casserole which has been buttered and lined with cooked rice or vermicelli. Cook in a moderate oven until heated through. Turn out on to a serving dish and sprinkle with chopped parsley or chives. Serve with leftover gravy, tomato or mushroom sauce poured round the mound of meat and rice (or noodles).

Another variation is to make the minced meat—and it need not be just one meat; it can be a combination of different types of meat, or meat and vegetables—into pasties or pinwheels. Use either shortcrust pastry or a scone dough.

For the pasties roll the pastry into a rectangle. Shape the minced meat mixture into a roll about 1½ inches in diameter. Place it along the edge of the rectangle of pastry and roll until the meat is covered by the pastry. Cut into suitable lengths. Place on a greased pan and bake until the pastry is browned.

The pinwheels are made and cut like a Swiss roll. Spread the pastry or dough with the meat mixture, roll up, cut in slices about one inch thick, place on greased baking sheet or pan, and bake. Serve with stewed tomatoes, tomato ketchup, gravy or mushroom sauce.

Pieces of meat from the bone of a joint can be added to a spaghetti sauce or minced and made into a sandwich filling.

Bits of chopped ham, chicken or veal are delicious added to an omelette or scrambled eggs, or cut into small strips and added to a dressed salad.

Meat pies from stews, with shortcrust pastry, scone dough or mashed potato topping, are always popular. Try a well seasoned pasty in a packed lunch instead of the usual sandwich.

HINTS FOR USING LEFTOVER VEGETABLES AND FRUIT

Reheated cooked vegetables are apt to be unattractive, lacking in flavour and vitamins. Make a casserole by adding freshly boiled and diced celery and onion to the leftover vegetables and topping with an undiluted can of cream soup—chicken, tomato or mushroom—or grated cheese and breadcrumbs.

Leftover broccoli, Brussels sprouts or cauliflower can be placed in a shallow dish, topped with a cheese spread and browned under the grill. Placed on a slice of boiled ham or cold chicken, this could be an easily prepared main course and a welcome change.

Cold vegetables well marinated in a French dressing and served with lettuce or added to a mixed salad will take the place of separate vegetables and salad. Freshly diced tomato added to this dish improves its appearance.

Almost any combination of cooked or cooked and raw vegetables can be blended and used in soups or sauces. Finely chopped, they may be added to salad dressings, meat loaves, croquettes or hamburgers. Again they might be reseasoned—with onion, celery salt, chives, parsley, Worcester sauce, a herb, such as tarragon—and a little thick cream sauce added. Shape as croquettes, dip in egg and breadcrumbs, and cook or sauté . . . thus giving the leftover a new personality.

For stuffing peppers, tomatoes, marrows, aubergines or cabbage leaves, the possible combinations of vegetables, breadcrumbs, rice and meat are limited only by the cook's imagination. As in all leftovers, if it tastes good before it is cooked, it will taste better afterwards. Flavour is important all along the line.

Leftover Salad

Salads pose a problem only when prepared as a large salad. A small amount of dressed salad is often left over. This is good chopped and added to mayonnaise when serving a sliced tomato, cucumber or potato salad. The dressed salad can also be mixed with a sandwich spread, or even added to a soup (French dressing included).

Tomato aspic is just as delicious served hot as a soup. If necessary, make it go further with a beef or chicken consommé or stock cube. It can also be added to vegetable soup.

Leftover Fruit

If some mixed fruit salad is left over and cannot be used attractively in a fruit cup, it can be stewed with added sugar and used as a tutti-frutti sauce — or cooked until thick and used as jam for toast or as filling for a sponge. Grated lemon or orange rind will improve the flavour of any fruit combination.

Cooked chopped fruit may be added to mincemeat.

Fruit juices, fresh or canned, should be saved and used in gelatine salads, sweets and drinks.

HINTS FOR USING LEFTOVER SWEETS AND CAKES

A sponge cake which has become too dry can appear as a party trifle.

Slice and toast the cake or break it into crumbs. Place in a dish, add custard, chill and top with jam, whipped cream or coconut. Fruit may be combined with the crumbs.

A crumble crust for a pie is delicious when made from cake or biscuit crumbs, either plain, spiced or chocolate. It is easier to crumble cakes or biscuits when they are not too dry. Place on paper napkins in a shallow pan and allow to dry in a low oven. Sift or roll well for even crumbs and store in the refrigerator or a cool, dry place.

An elaborate trifle is easily made with angel food or sponge cake. If there is only a piece or two left make it in individual dishes. Make a pattern of fruit in the bottom of the dish, using sliced peaches, canned pineapple, cherries, grapes, orange segments or just well drained fruit salad. Cover the fruit with broken pieces of cake. Pour over this a warm jelly made with fruit juice. Place in the refrigerator to chill. Serve with cream, custard or chopped fruit.

Fruit Bettys made with crumbled cake instead of bread will cut down on the sugar and butter needed.

Cake crumbs with a little brown sugar and cinnamon added are good as a topping on a fruit flan.

Fine, sifted sponge-cake crumbs with white sugar and grated lemon rind, sprinkled lightly on a lemon chiffon pie, make a change from whipped cream and are kinder to the figure and the purse. When used as a topping, chocolate crumbs, nuts and a pinch of cinnamon give a pleasing texture combination to blancmanges and pies.

Frequently, when making pies, there will be a little leftover filling. If it is of a blancmange or egg custard type, it can be baked without a crust so that any member of the family who cannot eat pastry can still enjoy the sweet.

If there is a little leftover shortcrust pastry, cut it in rounds with a large biscuit cutter, bake and store to use another day to top stewed fruit.

A little extra pie filling, such as lemon meringue or any of the blancmange-type fillings, may be thinned with either fruit juice, milk or cream and put into sundae glasses for another meal, or used undiluted as a cake filling. A little leftover fruit from pie-making can be used in a turnover or a tart.

Too many times a little fresh fruit is allowed to spoil when it might be used. Cook it for sauce or jam, use it in fruit fools, jellies, or add it to girdle cakes, waffles or scones.

Leftover pancakes spread with jam, rolled up, reheated in the oven and sprinkled with icing sugar or served with a lemon sauce will make a pleasant sweet.

HINTS FOR USING LEFTOVER BREAD

Leftover bread is perhaps the most wasted item of food in many homes — yet it has innumerable uses. If bread and butter puddings are not popular with members of the family, the bread can be used for any number of fruit Bettys.

Fine breadcrumbs (made by drying the bread in a warm oven, then putting it through a mincer or blender) are handy for coating chops. Breadcrumbs, salt, pepper and a generous amount of paprika make a good combination for breadcrumbing veal escalopes and other meat.

Fish, sliced liver or sliced aubergine brushed with melted fat and then dusted with this mixture can be baked quickly in a very hot oven (500°F Mark 10) for 12 to 15 minutes. This combination emerges looking and tasting better than when fried; furthermore, it is much less greasy.

Bread cut into tiny squares, or crumbled, dried and mixed with herbs and stored, saves time when stuffing poultry. Again, you can cut the crusts from not too dry, thinly sliced bread and make waffle toast in a waffle iron. Or dry it completely in the oven and store for use with soups and salads as Melba toast.

Wine Cookery

Cooks everywhere are beginning to catch up with their French counterparts, who have known this little kitchen secret all along: to make a mundane dish sensational, add a little wine. Even old standbys like stews and spaghetti bolognese become subtle mellow dishes with a touch of wine. For wine, like salt and pepper, complements the natural flavour of foods. And wine also blends with foods to create something new and richer in the way of flavour.

There is no trick to cooking with wine. At first you may feel safer if you follow a recipe. But in many cases you don't need one. When you add your seasonings, pour in a little wine as well; taste, and continue adding wine a little at a time until it tastes just right. (The alcohol burns off as heat is applied, just as it does from vanilla essence.)

While almost any wine can be used with almost any food, there are natural "taste harmonies" between certain wines and foods. Take sherry, for instance. Its flavour harmonizes with a variety of foods, with soups and with fish. It's delicious, too, in many chicken dishes and in sauces for ham and other meat. And it's a natural in sauces for puddings and stewed fruit.

White table wines, such as Sauternes and Rhine wine, are delicate in flavour — the perfect complement to the delicate flavours of fish, chicken, lamb and veal.

The red table wines, such as burgundy and claret, being more robust in flavour, go well with red meat. They're excellent, too, in spaghetti and cheese dishes. And you can improve the flavour and texture of inexpensive cuts of meat by marinating them in red wine for several hours before cooking.

The dessert wines, such as port, muscatel and tokay, give extra flavour to sweets and fruit dishes.

You'll find wines are versatile, too. You can substitute one wine for another in a recipe as long as you use the same type of wine. For instance, in a recipe calling for Sauternes you can use Chablis or any other white table wine. The same thing applies to red wines — any claret can be substituted for burgundy.

Cooking for Large Numbers

HINTS ON PLANNING FOR AND SERVING LARGE NUMBERS

● The first step to consider if you are on a committee planning a meal for a large group is to select a thoroughly dependable chairman with whom people like to work. She will have to delegate the work to her assistants and see that they carry it out.

● The various jobs will include the shopping and budgeting, the preparation of the food in the kitchen, arrangements for the dining room—laying and decorating the tables, serving the incidentals such as butter and water, waiting at table and the final clearing up.

● Planning the menu is the next step. Make sure that the food you select is suitable for the group you are serving. Choose dishes that are most generally liked by the greatest number of people, keeping in mind the fact that an all-man group may like one thing, an all-woman group something else, and that a church supper requires quite different food from what would be included in a menu for teenagers.

● Decide upon the type of meal, keeping in mind the cost of each item and any extras.

● Simplify the work by choosing food that can be prepared in advance and will require the minimum of last-minute effort.

● Choose foods that are in season and readily available.

● Bear in mind the cooking facilities as well as the refrigeration. Avoid dishes that can't be made on the available equipment.

● If the equipment is inadequate perhaps some dishes can be prepared at the homes of committee members and brought in ready to be served. Select food that can be easily prepared.

● Consider contrasts in colour, flavour, shape and texture. For example, don't serve split pea soup if peas are to be included in the main dish, or tomatoes if tomato soup is to be the starter.

● Be prepared for extra guests. Have a supply of canned food on hand.

● And finally, organize the meal as simply as possible, whether it's a buffet or a sit-down affair, doing everything that can be done in advance, and leaving time for the things that must be done at the last minute such as putting bread and butter on the tables, tossing the salad, etc.

APPROXIMATE QUANTITIES NEEDED TO SERVE FIFTY PEOPLE

	Size of Helping	Approximate amount to buy for 50
BEVERAGES		
Coffee	1 cup	1 to 1¼ pounds
Cocoa	1 cup	½ pound
Fruit punch	2 to 3 punch glasses	3 gallons
Tea, hot	1 cup	5 ounces
Tea, iced	1 glass	½ pound
Fruit juice	1 tumbler	10½ pints
DAIRY PRODUCTS AND EGGS		
Butter or margarine	1 to 1½ pats	1½ pounds
Cheese, hard	1 to 2 ounces	4¾ pounds
Cheese, cottage	3 to 5 ounces for salad 3 ounces if part of main course	8 to 12½ pounds
Cheese, cream	½ ounce per sandwich	1½ pounds
Cheese, Gruyère (12 to 20 slices per pound)	1 slice per sandwich	4 pounds
Cream, for the sweet	2 to 4 tablespoons	2½ to 5 pints
for coffee	1 tablespoon	1½ pints
Cream, whipping, for decoration	1 tablespoon	1½ pints
Ice cream, bulk	¼ pint	13 pints
Ice cream, brick	¼ pint	13 pints
Eggs, for scrambling	1½ to 2 eggs	75 to 100 eggs
Milk	1 glass	16 pints
FRUIT		
Canned	1 fruit cup	13 to 14 1-pound cans
Apples for pie	6 to 7 portions per pie	15 pounds
Fruit for shortcake	2 ounces	6 to 7 pounds
Frozen fruit for pie	6 to 7 portions per pie	10 pounds
Frozen fruit for topping for ice cream	1½ ounces	5 pounds
Raspberries for sauce	1 ounce	3 pounds
FISH AND SHELLFISH		
Fish, with tail, head, bones and skin	½ pound	25 pounds
Fish, without tail or head	¼ pound	14 pounds
Fish fillets	¼ pound	14 pounds
Lobster, fresh or canned	2 to 3 ounces for salad	18 to 20 pounds live or 3 pounds canned
Oysters, for cocktail	6 to 8 raw	8 pints
Oysters, for stew	about ½ pint stew	8 to 10 pints
Oysters, scalloped	about ¼ pint scalloped	8 to 10 pints
Prawns, fresh or canned	8 to 10 prawns for cocktail	8 pounds fresh, shelled or canned
Tuna fish, canned	about 4 portions per can	12 to 13 7-ounce cans
POULTRY (Dressed Weight)		
Chicken, roast	¼ pound	30 to 35 pounds
Chicken, fried	¼ or ½ chicken	13 to 25 chickens weighing 2½ to 3½ pounds
Chicken for dishes using chopped cooked meat	5 to 6 ounces	20 to 25 pounds
Turkey, roast	2½ ounces	35 to 40 pounds
Turkey for dishes using chopped cooked meat	5 to 6 ounces	16 pounds

APPROXIMATE QUANTITIES NEEDED TO SERVE FIFTY PEOPLE

	Size of helping	Approximate amount to buy for 50
MEAT (uncooked weight)		
Beef		
Frying steak, ½-inch thick	3 ounces	20 pounds
Liver	3 ounces	13 pounds
Chuck steak	3 ounces	20 pounds
Steaks to grill	4 to 4½ ounces	18 to 20 pounds
Stew with vegetables	5½ ounces	12 pounds
Swiss steak, ¾-inch thick	3½ ounces	16 pounds
Veal		
Breadcrumbed veal cutlets	3 ounces	12½ pounds
Escalopes	3½ ounces	12½ pounds
Cutlets and chops	3 ounces	12½ to 15 pounds
Lamb		
Chops	2 each	25 pounds
Roast leg	2½ ounces	25 pounds (4 legs)
Pork		
Ham, cured, baked, on bone	3 ounces	25 pounds
Ham, cured, boned	3 ounces	15 pounds
Pork chops	1 each	10 to 15 pounds
Roast loin with bone	4 ounces	20 to 25 pounds
Roast, fresh ham	3 ounces	20 pounds
Sausages	2 each	12½ pounds
Sausage meat	4 to 5 ounce patty	12½ pounds

VEGETABLES

	Size of helping	Approximate amount to buy for 50
Canned vegetables	2 to 3 ounces	13 to 14 1-pound cans
Dried vegetables:		
Kidney beans	4 ounces	5½ pounds
Broad beans	5 ounces	6 pounds
Haricot beans	6 ounces	6 pounds
Split peas	4 ounces	5 pounds
Fresh vegetables:		
Beetroots	3 ounces	13 to 14 pounds
Cabbage, to cook	2½ to 3 ounces	12 pounds
Cabbage, for cole slaw	1 to 2 ounces	8 pounds
Carrots	3 ounces	12½ pounds
Cauliflower	3 ounces	28 to 32 pounds
Celery curls	1 piece	2 medium heads
Courgettes or marrows	3 ounces	10 to 12 pounds
Lettuce	1½ to 2 ounces	8 to 10
Lettuce, for garnish	2 or 3 leaves	4 to 5
Potatoes, jacket	6 ounces	20 pounds
Potatoes, mashed	5 ounces	15 pounds
Radishes	2 each	10 bunches
Tomatoes, sliced	3 slices	10 to 12½ pounds
Frozen vegetables	2¼ to 2½ ounces	8 to 10 pounds or 13 to 17 packets of 10 to 12 ounces each

APPROXIMATE QUANTITIES OF READY-TO-EAT FOOD FOR FIFTY PEOPLE

	Quantity for 50
Baked beans	16 pounds
Drinks	16 to 19 pints
Cakes, sponge angel food	4 7-inch cakes 4 7-inch cakes
Cooked vegetables	12½ pounds
Cooked potatoes	12½ pounds
Fruit cup	3½ pints
Gravy and sauces	3¼ pints
Pies	8 pies (6 to 7 portions per pie)
Potato crisps	3 pounds
Salad	6 pounds

APPROXIMATE QUANTITIES OF FOOD NEEDED TO SERVE FIFTY PEOPLE

MISCELLANEOUS

	Size of helping	Approximate amount to buy for 50
Bread:		
1 pound loaf	1½ slices	5 loaves
Hard rolls	1 to 1½ each	4½ to 6½ dozen
Soft rolls	1½ to 2 each	6 to 8½ dozen
Cream crackers	2 each	1 pound
Jam	2 tablespoons	3 pounds
Macaroni	6 ounces	6 pounds
Noodles	6 ounces	4 pounds
Salad dressing	1½ to 2 tablespoons	1¾ to 2½ pints
Spaghetti	6 ounces	6 pounds
Sugar, lump	1 to 2 lumps	1½ pounds
Sugar, granulated	1½ teaspoons	¾ pound

TABLE SETTING AND SERVICE

Family Meals

Have you ever stopped to think that your family as well as your friends are your guests when they sit down at table? The trouble you have taken to plan and prepare the meal can mean just as much to them. An attractive table and a well-planned menu make everyone happy.

Mealtime is often the only time in the day when the whole family is together. There are many ways to make it a sociable and friendly hour of relaxation amid the day's activities.

You'll also find it easier to train the children to have good table manners if you make each meal a pleasant occasion. Good manners and social poise come through everyday practice. So put a bowl of flowers on your lunch table, a gay tablecloth on your dinner table, or occasionally use your best china—just for the family's enjoyment. These little things count a good deal at mealtimes.

And when special occasions—bank holidays, dinner parties, or cocktail parties—come along, every member of your family will be at ease. They will be able to make your guests feel that they are really part of a friendly family circle.

FAMILY STYLE SERVICE

One of the most popular ways of serving meals is the "family-style" meal. It's informal and easy to hand the food round in serving dishes at table. Even for dinner parties, family-style service may be the one you prefer to use.

But there's much you can do to make your table, and this way of serving meals, colourful, inviting and appropriate to the occasion. There's a tradi-tional way to lay this kind of table, a correct and convenient way to serve your family and guests, and a hundred and one ideas for using your china, glasses and cutlery to arrange a pretty table with an interesting centrepiece.

Perhaps you're so used to using the dishes nearest to hand, or the same old tablecloths, that you've forgotten about some of the little extras that will brighten up your table. Now is the time to bring them out.

SELECTING THE TABLE COVERING

Tablecloths are made from numerous materials—linen, rayon, or cotton damask, or plain or fancy cloths. And what a variety of colours they come in, from traditional white to pastels or deep rich tones.

Polythene, vinyl, nylon and paper tablecloths or place mats are real time-savers when it comes to cleaning and laundering. But choose them just as carefully as you would a more expensive cloth. You can do wonders with a pretty background even if it's for your everyday breakfast table.

Sometimes it is a problem to get things to match. All of us acquire dishes or cutlery, tablecloths or glasses at different times. Here's a simple rule —if your china has a design or pattern on it, use plain cloths as much as possible. If it is on the plain side, you can have more pattern in your table-cloth. This gives the tablecloth a chance to perform its real duty—to be a pretty background for your china and glasses.

Use a pad of felt or cotton under your tablecloth. It protects the table top and improves the appearance and feel of the cloth. Another thing— your tablecloth will look best if it hangs 10 to 12 inches over the edge of the table.

For those special occasions, you may want to use a lace cloth, or a sheer linen or embroidered one. In this case, lay it straight on the table with no cloth underneath. Use mats under hot dishes. Lace cloths can have more of an overhang than damask.

PLACE MATS

Up to now you may not have used place mats very often. But they're a good idea for family meals as well as dinner parties. They are decorative, easy to clean and often less expensive than a cloth. They come in a wide variety of materials, textures and designs.

When buying linen mats, choose them large enough to hold a dinner plate, side plate, cup and saucer and tumbler or wine glass, as well as the cutlery. Lay the place mat close to and parallel to the edge of your table.

SEATING ARRANGEMENTS

Before you lay your table, you'll want to know the correct places for your family and guests to sit. Perhaps you have a traditional place for everyone now. But once in a while change is a good thing. Then, too, you'll want to know the most convenient place for everyone to sit when you are entertaining.

Usually the host and hostess sit at the ends of the table, hostess next to the kitchen for convenience. A female guest of honour will sit on the host's right; the male guest of honour sits on the hostess's right.

Or try other seating arrangements. When there are four or six at the table omit the two end places and seat your family or guests along the sides. Place the decorations at the ends. Or try a horseshoe arrangement with one end or side left open. You'll find it adds an unusual touch to put an interesting decoration at that end or side of the table.

Make sure that each person has plenty of room, both for appearance and comfort. Twenty-four to thirty inches between the centre of each place setting is comfortable.

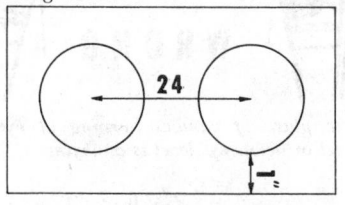

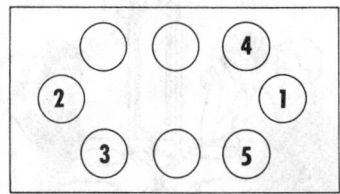

1. Hostess 2. Host 3. Female guest of honour 4. Male guest of honour

HOW TO LAY THE TABLE

Now you are going to be an artist. Whether you use your everyday or your best china, you are going to arrange a pretty table. Remember, first, the tablecloth—one that fits the occasion.

The area for each person, together with the necessary cutlery, glasses, napkins and china is called a "cover". Mark each cover with a plate. Space the plates evenly and directly opposite each other, one inch from the edge of the table.

Now place the cutlery beside the plate in order of its use, beginning from the outside.

Place forks on the left, with prongs up.

Place knives on the right, with sharp edges towards the plate.

Put spoons on the right of the knife

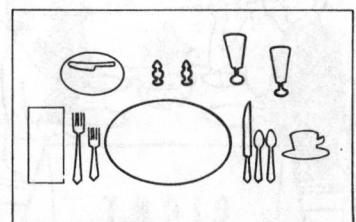

The area for each person, together with the necessary cutlery, glasses, napkin and china, is called a "cover."

facing upwards. Line the pieces of cutlery parallel to each other, with the handles even and one inch from the edge of the table.

The dessert fork and spoon can be either placed across the top of or beside the plate, or brought in with the sweet.

Lay only those pieces of cutlery required by the menu.

Place the glass at the tip of the knife. If that crowds the setting or forces the glass off the place mat, put the glass slightly to the right of the tip of the knife. Place a second glass, if used, to the right of the first glass and slightly forward.

Lay the napkin to the left of the forks one inch from the edge of the table. Fold it simply in a square or rectangle. Or roll the napkin up and place it in a napkin ring on the side plate.

Put salt cellars and pepper pots at the top of the plate, or between every two covers in line with the glasses.

CREATE A BALANCED PICTURE

Now that you've laid your table, stand back and look at it. Of course, you haven't added a centrepiece yet, nor are there dishes of food on the table. But just for a moment look at your table as if you were the guest.

Why does it look nice? Because a convenient table is also an attractive table! All table arrangements have certain features in common. They are our guide lines.

When you plan your china, glasses, cutlery and decorations so that they go together, they form a pleasing picture. And when you arrange your table to

The simple pattern is set off beautifully by the textured place mat in a contrasting colour.

give that balanced look, from centre-piece to serving dish, serving actually becomes easier.

GIVE THE TABLE BALANCE

Have you ever noticed how crowding all the serving dishes toward the centre of the table, or even at one end, makes the table look top-heavy or lopsided? It's out of balance. Try moving a few of the dishes outwards, or down the table. By filling up the empty spaces you will achieve that feeling of balance.

Offset the bulk or weight of a large dish at one end of the table by a similar one at the other end. Or use two smaller dishes for the same purpose. You'll create a feeling of harmony if you place one cover opposite another and arrange the serving dishes to balance each other.

Key the colours of your table scheme to that of your dining room.

CREATING COLOUR HARMONY

Of course, you'll want to use colour. Colour schemes are easier to develop when you start with what you have. For a start, the colours in your dining room itself are something to think about. But suppose you have a mixed collection of linen, china and glasses. What can you do with them?

Suppose you have:

White tablecloth. Blue (or other plain) tablecloth. Pale green linen or cotton place mats. Clear cut glass wineglasses. Blue glass tumblers. Set of pink and white porcelain dishes. Or a set of gold band china or semiporcelain. Red and white peasant crockery. Or plain but brightly coloured crockery.

You may not have any or all of these, of course. But for the moment, let's suppose you have. These are the makings of several attractive table arrangements.

The green linen, pink china and clear glasses were made for each other. The blue cloth, with red and white crockery and blue tumblers are just right for breakfast and lunch.

For dinner parties—the white cloth, white china, or slender glasses with your shining silver will be just right. Then you can plan for colour in the flowers, food and accessories. Or try the green place mats with your white china and cut glass.

Perhaps you would like more colour as a background for your white china—then choose a coloured cloth made of linen or rayon. Even dye a white tablecloth the colour you want. It will do wonders for your china and your table.

Numerous combinations, as you can see, will give a pleasing effect if you remember a few simple rules. Let one colour predominate, use a medium amount of a second colour, and just a touch of a third. Contrasting colours are pretty together if you use neutral colours such as cream, grey or beige with smaller amounts of brighter, contrasting colours.

GIVE THE TABLE HARMONY

It's the little things that give harmony to your table. You may not have noticed that you've chosen china and glasses and cutlery that go well together. They are in keeping or in harmony with each other.

And note that you've placed the china and cutlery parallel to, or at right angles to, the lines of your table. This gives the harmony of line you want. Even a round lace mat will fit into the picture if you place it so the threads are parallel to the edge of the table. Avoid diagonal lines by turning the handles of carafes or jugs, bowls and cups parallel to the edges of your table as well.

MAKE EVERY TABLE SETTING DIFFERENT

There is no reason why our tables should look alike day after day. It's the difference that makes mealtime more interesting. Do use gaily coloured crockery and linen for your breakfast table, lunch in the garden or supper on the patio. It's the appropriateness that counts. Try a centrepiece of vegetables, fruits or hardy annuals such as zinnias or hollyhocks.

For dinner parties and special occasions bring out your best lace or fine linen or damask tablecloth. Lay your table with your nicest china and glasses and cutlery. Then select flowers in keeping with this feeling of festivity. Try roses or lilac, dahlias, lilies of the valley or sweet peas, just to mention a few. Perhaps you will wish to use cut glass or silver candlesticks or china figurines.

Here is your chance to make a table that will be remembered by your family and friends.

CHOOSING A CENTREPIECE— THAT ADDED TOUCH

You really don't need to be an artist to plan a pretty table. Try a single flower, floating in a low container, for your centrepiece. Or perhaps use a china figurine surrounded by a few sprigs of greenery.

For special dinner parties make a low arrangement of flowers in the centre with candles at each end. Or try a cluster of candles for the centrepiece. Or a few glass balls with greenery.

Keep the central arrangement low so that your guests can see each other. About 10 inches is the highest it can be without becoming a nuisance. If unsure, you can always sit down to see if the centrepiece obstructs the view.

If you use candles, they should stand above eye level so that their light is not annoying. Fourteen to sixteen inches above the table is comfortable. Use enough candles to give good light, or don't use them at all. A minimum of four is necessary. Use candles only in the late afternoon or evening.

All too often we tend to overdecorate. It's really too much work, and the decoration overshadows the rest of the table arrangement and the food.

CENTREPIECE HINTS

The glare of candles burning at eye level or below eye level is annoying.

Flame should be 14 to 16 inches above the table. Use at least four candles or none at all.

Tall flower arrangements interfere with vision across the table.

Keep flowers low so that everyone can see and speak freely across the table.

FINAL CHECK LIST

Now that you've worked out your table, you will want to check up all those last-minute jobs that need doing just before you invite your guests to the table.

● Check the table setting with your menu to be sure that all the necessary items are on the table.

● Have extra cutlery ready to use on the sideboard or side table.

● Make the dining room comfortable by adjusting lights, heating and ventilation.

● Place chairs round the table with front edges even with the edge of the table.

● Pour the wine either just before the meal is announced or just after your guests have taken their places at the dinner table.

● Place butter on the table.

● Salad can also be put on the table before the meal is announced.

● Bread and rolls go on the table just before the meal is served, or, if hot, are brought in immediately afterwards.

● You may have the first course on the table when the guests are seated, or you may prefer to serve it immediately afterwards. Choose the method of serving that keeps the food at its best.

● Place serving implements beside the dish of food, not in it.

How to Serve "Family" Style

Many things, such as family traditions and customs, will influence the way you serve family meals.

Probably you use the style which has already been mentioned. Assume everything is ready and the family is seated at table.

You should serve the woman on your right first, with the first course, if there is one, or with the main dish.

The potatoes and vegetables are followed by gravy or sauce, bread and extras such as pickles.

Hand the food round to the left or to the right, whichever is easier. However, once it is decided, all food should go in the same direction. Suppose you decide to hand round to the right. The person nearest a dish of food puts the serving cutlery in the dish and offers it to the person on his right. That person helps himself and hands the dish to the next person on his right. Each dish goes round the table and is returned to its original place.

The success of this type of service depends on the cooperation of all members of the family in handing round food and in foreseeing the needs and wishes of others.

A sidetable or trolley near the hostess is a great help in holding the water jug or bottle of wine, cider or beer, and extra bread or rolls, under a suitable cover. While you may wish to leave the sweet in the kitchen until you are ready to serve it, you may also place it on the side table or trolley. With thoughtful planning no member of the family will need to leave the table to wait on the others.

Following the main course, the serving dishes and individual plates can be handed to the hostess, who stacks them on the side table or trolley, or they can be removed by a member of the family.

The sweet can be served on individual plates and handed to the guests. Or the plates can be handed round first followed by the sweet, so the guests can serve themselves.

Traditional Service —Another Way to Serve

You will want your children to be used to waiting at table and to being waited on by other accepted methods apart from the one already described. So you must know something about other ways of serving family meals.

For instance, a more formal style can be used for family occasions as well as for dinner or lunch parties.

This is how it is done:

All food is served by the host or hostess at the table. The host normally serves the meat, potatoes and vegetables, while the hostess serves the soup or other first course, the salad, if any, and the sweet. The host normally pours the wine or other drink. The hostess serves the coffee at the end of the meal.

If necessary, you should rearrange the host's china and cutlery to make room for the main serving dish and carving knife and fork. The dish should go straight in front of him, with the vegetable dishes on either side so that they're in easy reach. The plates should be piled up in front of him.

Who should be served first? The answer to this much-debated question is a matter of opinion, but the most usual sequence is for the female guest on the host's left to be served first, followed by all the other women; if there is a woman "guest of honour" or a much older woman present, it is customary for her to be served first. Children are normally served after grown-ups.

Assuming that there is no guest of honour and everyone is much the same age, the host passes the first plate to the woman on his left, the next one to the woman to her left and so on. The host and hostess normally serve themselves last.

1. Stack of plates 2. Meat dish 3 and 4. Vegetable dishes 5. Serving cutlery

Arrangement of serving dishes for family meals. 1. Hostess 2. Host 3. Centrepiece 4. Serving plates 5. Serving cutlery 6. Meat 7. Gravy or sauce 8. Potatoes 9. Green vegetables 10. Rolls 11 and 12. Pickles or other extras.

The hostess serves the salad. So the salad bowl, or tray containing individual salads, is placed before her. Salad plates and large salad servers should be provided. The hostess may serve the salad while the host is serving meat and vegetables. The order in which she serves the guests is similar to the order in which the host serves from his end of the table.

Bread or hot rolls and gravy or sauce are handed round the table, always in the same direction.

The hostess indicates when all are ready to eat by picking up her knife and fork.

At the end of the course the food is removed, beginning with the dish of meat, or main dish, the other serving dishes, then the individual plates and cutlery, and finally everything including salt and pepper. Leave only glasses and cutlery to be used for the last course.

SERVING THE SWEET

The hostess usually serves the sweet. It may be placed before her, or she may transfer it from a sideboard.

RUSSIAN-STYLE SERVICE

You may like to arrange the food on the plates and place them on the table before the family is seated, or they can be brought in by a member of the family and placed before each person.

You probably make use of this method often, when serving soup, salad and sweet, when it is served in individual portions to each member of the family.

COMPROMISE SERVICE

There are times when you may want to use a combination of these different methods of serving. We call it compromise service.

The main course, meat and vegetables, is served at the table by the host and hostess. This gives the host an opportunity to carve the chicken, turkey, or joint at table. The family, too, will enjoy seeing the meat or main dish before it is cut for serving.

First, however, you may prefer to serve the soup in the kitchen and place the individual bowls before each person. The salad can also be arranged on individual plates and placed beside each guest.

The compromise service helps make the sweet rather special. After the main course is finished, any left-overs and used dishes are removed, and the sweet is brought on in individual portions.

This style combines the convenience of doing much of the serving in the kitchen with the hospitable gesture of serving the main course at table.

Tips on Service

A little practice will make it easy for you to serve everyday meals or give dinner parties correctly.

Here are some points to remember:

● Place and remove dishes from the left with your left hand.

● Offer food such as rolls or pickles to the left with your left hand.

● Serve or pour drinks from the right with your right hand.

● Refill glasses during the meal without moving the glass. Use a napkin to catch the drips.

● Handle dishes and plates by the outer edge. Do not place your thumb over the rim.

● When a meal is served in courses, remove everything relating to one course before serving the next one.

● Remove leftover food first, then used plates and dishes from individual covers, then clean plates and unused cutlery.

● Remove one cover at a time.

● Do not stack dishes in front of guests or family members.

● Remove the hostess's plate first, then work round the table beginning on her right.

● If the hostess removes the plates and dishes, she begins on her right and removes her own things last.

● Brush any crumbs off the table with a folded napkin and a plate.

Good Table Manners

The basis of all good manners is consideration for others, whether you are eating at home or in a restaurant or at friends'. Attention to the following points will help your family to be more considerate of others, and to be at ease in any gathering:

● Be punctual for meals.

● Give attention to personal grooming before meals. Hands and face should be clean and hair combed.

● Boys and men should remain standing until women and girls are seated. They should seat the ladies.

● Sit down from left side of chair.

● If grace is said, the head is bowed and the hands are kept in the lap.

● The hostess unfolds her napkin first, takes up knife, fork or spoon and indicates that it is time to begin eating.

ORDER OF SERVICE WHEN HOST SERVES

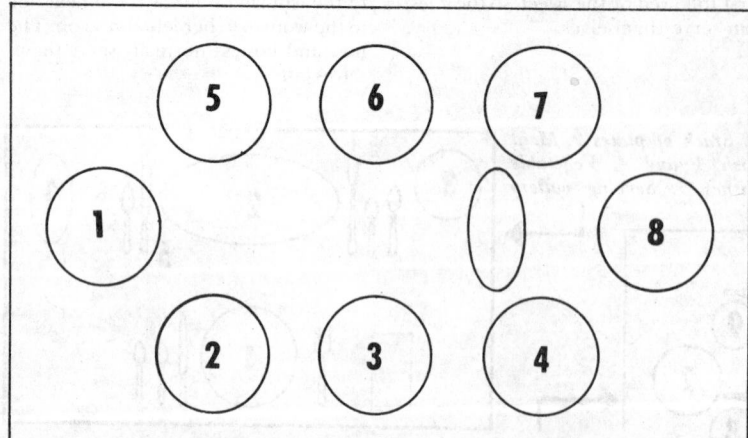

Order of service
1. Hostess receives first plate of food. 2. Person receiving second plate of food. 3, 4, 5, 6, and 7. Receive plates of food in that order. 8. Host serves himself last.

• Sit up straight at the table.

• Keep elbows at your sides, not resting on the table while eating. Don't let elbows interfere with your neighbour.

• If you want something that is out of reach, ask someone to pass it to you. Never stretch out in front or across anyone.

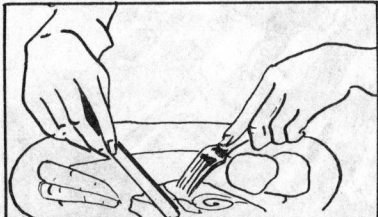

• In cutting food hold the knife in your right hand, the fork in the left, prongs down. Grasp the handles firmly and naturally. The ends of the handles rest in the palms of your hands and are not seen. Extend your index fingers along the handles to steady and guide the knife and fork.

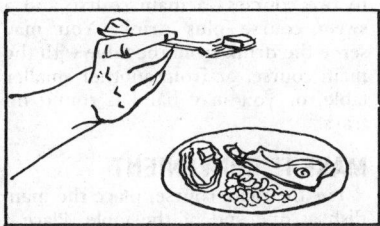

• Carry food to your mouth with the fork in your left hand, prongs down. Don't put food on the back of the fork.

• Use a fork rather than a spoon whenever possible.

• When eating soup, dip towards the back of the dish and sip from side of spoon. When eating other food with a spoon, dip towards you and take food from end of spoon.

• Use a spoon to stir and test the temperature of a hot drink. Do not leave the spoon standing in the cup. Lay it on the saucer. Never drink from a cup with a spoon in it.

• When cutlery has been used, lay it on the plate, pointing away from you, never on the tablecloth or propped up on the edge of the plate.

• If food or drink is too hot, leave it until it has cooled. Never blow on it.

• Do not drink while you have food in your mouth.

• Keep your mouth closed while eating. Never talk with food in your mouth.

• Eat slowly and quietly. Never appear greedy.

• Never hold food on the fork or spoon while talking. Having once picked it up, eat it promptly.

• In handing your plate for a second helping leave knife and fork on plate side by side so that there is no danger of their slipping off.

• If you are asked to choose between two dishes, do so at once. If not, take what is served without comment.

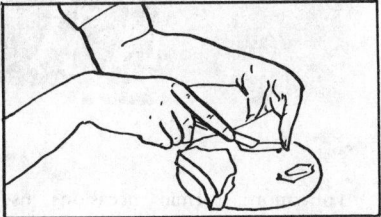

• To butter bread, break off a small piece, hold it on the plate and spread the butter. Do not butter a whole slice at a time. Do not bite from a whole slice of bread. Break it into small pieces as you go.

• Do not pick up and hold a dish while eating. Do not tip a dish to scrape out the last bit of food.

• Do not eat while passing food to other guests.

• Take only the portion of food into the mouth that can be eaten at once.

• Things eaten with the fingers include: bread, olives, pickles, radishes, nuts, celery, strips of carrot, potato crisps, biscuits, cake (that isn't sticky), corn on the cob and chocolates.

• Fish bones, like other bones taken into the mouth, are removed by taking between the finger and thumb and removing between compressed lips.

• The stones of stewed prunes or cherries that are eaten with a spoon are made as clean and dry as possible in the mouth, then dropped into the spoon with which you are eating and put on the edge of the plate. Pips and skin may be removed with the finger and thumb with lips closed, or you may drop stones or pips into the cupped hand, held close to the lips.

• If finger bowls are used, dip only the tips of the fingers of one hand in at a time. Wipe on the napkin.

• Leave your plate in front of you when you have finished eating.

• Leave the napkin on the lap until the hostess places hers on the table just before rising. Then leave it on the left of the plate.

• Rise from the left side of the chair. If necessary, push chair close to table so that others can get past.

• Do not use toothpicks in the presence of others.

• If you must cough or sneeze at the table, cover your mouth and nose with your handkerchief, not the napkin.

• If you must leave the table in the midst of the meal, ask the hostess's permission and go quietly.

How to Make the Most of Meal Times

"Take time to live a little every day" might be a good slogan for every family. "Breaking bread" together can bring your family closer together and help each member to understand and appreciate the others more.

It is important that at least one meal a day, perhaps the evening meal, be observed as a daily family hour.

Serve the meal as leisurely as your family's activities will permit. Allow a spirit of happy companionship to prevail. Keep the conversation pleasant. Petty troubles and unpleasant topics can spoil any meal. They may have to be talked out at some later time, but never allow unpleasant issues to spoil the pleasure of your family at meal time. Correcting children at the table should also be kept to the minimum.

Encourage everyone to join in the conversation. The opinions expressed by members of the family during the gay as well as the more serious moments of the meal hour will have a direct influence on the attitudes and thinking of your children.

Remember special days—birthdays and anniversaries. They are opportunities for family pleasures to be cherished a lifetime.

Share responsibility as well as fun. Let the children begin early to help serve meals. Avoid assigning only routine tasks such as peeling potatoes and washing up. Give children responsibilities that bring out their skill, and they will be glad to help.

Buffets

Buffet meals create a friendly, informal atmosphere. Guests usually enjoy moving round to talk to each other, and serving themselves at an attractive table. Best of all, a buffet is easier to prepare and to serve than the usual type of dinner party.

While this seems to suggest that buffet service is just for informal occasions, you can also make it more elaborate for weddings, anniversaries and receptions.

Plan a buffet breakfast or a one o'clock lunch. Or even carry over this idea for tea parties in the late afternoon, and for early or late suppers.

Even church or club suppers, when the number of people to be served is indefinite, run smoothly when served buffet style.

FIT THE OCCASION

Choose a theme that fits the occasion. It may be a Guy Fawkes party with guys and bonfires; a New Year's Eve supper; a meal after a football match with appropriate decorations; a family reunion, or perhaps a family or neighbourhood supper for new neighbours.

Make your table attractive with table cloth, dishes and centrepiece appropriate to each other and to the food you are serving. Peasant cloths and napkins, brightly coloured crockery and wooden salad bowls go together for informal affairs. Or you may prefer to use an uncovered table. Your decoration might be fruit, vegetables, nuts or garden flowers such as zinnias, marigolds and chrysanthemums. If you want to use candlesticks, choose ones in pottery, wood, pewter, brass or copper in keeping with the other decorations.

For more formal occasions use your best linen and your nicest china, glasses and cutlery. You may want to use a cloth that covers the table, but small mats also make interesting backgrounds. Use roses, daffodils, antirrhinums, nasturtiums, chrysanthemums or other delicate flowers for your floral centrepiece. And use your silver or cut-glass candlesticks if you ish.

PLAN A PRETTY TABLE

Whatever the setting, your table is the centre of interest. Originally the term "buffet" applied to service from the buffet or sideboard. Now we generally use the dining table but the idea is the same, and often the sideboard is used in addition to the table.

Place your table to give the best use of space or to create an attractive effect. It may be in the centre of the room, at one end or at the side. Or you may decide to push the table against the wall. This limits the amount of table edge space, but you can create interesting and unusual decorations at the back of the table against the wall.

CREATE A PICTURE

When you are ready to lay your table, what are the artistic rules to remember? There is balance. Make sure that no area of your table is cluttered or overloaded while the rest of it looks bare. Arrange the plates, food, cutlery, napkins and decorations so that the table has a restful, orderly appearance.

Use colours that go together and set off the food. They may be soft pastels or bright, rich tones. The decorations need not always be flowers and candles. You could use figurines, vegetables, fruit, nuts, gourds, grasses, wild flowers or pine cones.

Your menu and the way you serve it will determine the way you arrange the food, china and cutlery. There are many ways to serve a buffet meal. We shall discuss these as we go along.

For the meal itself, limit your menu to two courses—a main course and a sweet course plus drink. You may serve the drink from the table with the main course, or from another smaller table, or you may hand it round on trays.

MAKE IT CONVENIENT

For the main course, place the main dish at one end of the table. Place a stack of six or eight plates near it. Bring in other plates as you need them. The serving implements belong beside the appropriate dish of food. If only a spoon is needed, place it on the right. If both spoon and fork are required, place the spoon on the right and the fork on the left of the dish of food.

Here is a suggested buffet menu. Note the arrangement and where the serving implements are placed.

Chicken Loaf   Curry Sauce
Buttered Peas   Fluffy Jacket Potatoes
Hot Rolls
Lemon Meringue Pudding
with Digestive Biscuit Topping
Wine, cider, beer
or fruit squash

Place food such as salad, vegetables, rolls and sandwiches along the side of the table. Put them near the edge within easy reach of your guests.

You may like to arrange the food in individual portions, such as slices of meat loaf or individual pies. In this way the serving dishes or plates will still look attractive even after several people have helped themselves. The meat dish and salad can be adapted to produce individual servings or portions.

If you serve the wine or other drink with the main course, place it at the end of the table opposite the main dish.

Arrange the glasses in an orderly and convenient manner.

Arrange cutlery and napkins on the other side of the table so that they can be picked up last.

If your table looks crowded, serve the drinks from a small table or trolley near by. You may also use this for trays, napkins and cutlery.

Ask your guests to move round the table either to the left or to the right as you wish. This will depend upon the arrangement of the table and the rooms. Moving to the left is generally more logical, and allows the right hand to be nearest the table—which makes it easier for guests to help themselves.

THREE WAYS TO SERVE

Buffet service may be informal, semi-formal or formal. There is clearly no distinct line between them. Your choice will depend upon the occasion, the number of guests you have, whether they are young or older, the facilities in your home and the amount of help you have.

Of course, the type of service you choose will depend on the seating arrangements you've planned. At women's parties, it's simpler to let your guests hold the filled plates on their laps. Trays are a good idea, however: they make lap service somewhat easier.

If there are men present, provide small tables. Most men are not good at holding plates or trays on their laps, nor do they enjoy it. Small tables for holding glasses are helpful, but card tables for the complete meal are

Arrangement when coffee is served from a side table

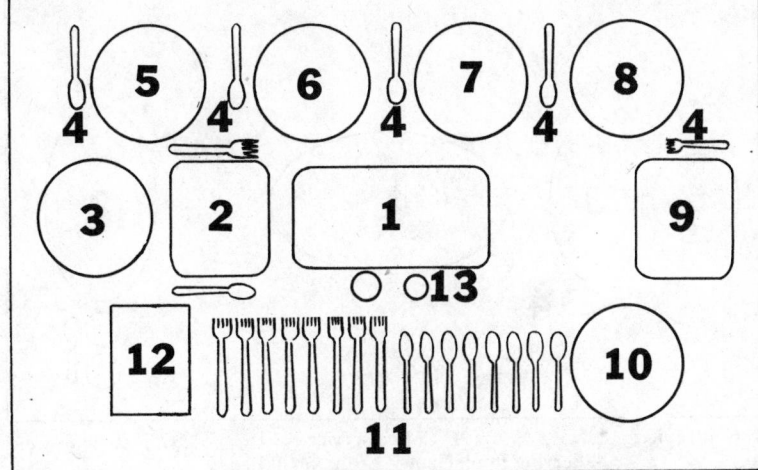

1. Centrepiece
2. Main dish
3. Stack of plates
4. Serving implements
5-6. Vegetable dishes
7-8. Salads
9. Mustard, oil and vinegar
10. Rolls and bread
11. Cutlery
12. Napkins
13. Salt and pepper

preferable.

Cover the tables with informal cloths or place mats in keeping with the china and cutlery you have chosen for the buffet. Or use bare tables with mats for hot or very cold dishes. Arrange the cutlery, napkins and glasses on the small tables. Pour the drink at the tables.

Coffee pot, coffee cups, cream and sugar can be left on the main table or distributed among the small tables.

While there are no set rules for serving a buffet meal, there are certain features of the different types of service to keep in mind.

ENTERTAINING A SMALL GROUP

When you entertain a relatively small group, keep the buffet informal. This works best when your guests know each other and all feel free to help themselves. Keep the menu simple, and the service as easy and as informal as possible.

You (the hostess) announce the meal and invite your guests to help themselves. Ask them to come to the table a few at a time. Avoid a long queue.

Each guest takes a plate and moves round the table in the direction indicated, choosing the food he wants. The drink, cutlery and napkin are taken last. Then the guests find a seat for themselves.

Second helpings are always in order. Part of the charm of a buffet is the freedom your guests have to choose the food each especially enjoys.

If you prefer, hand the serving dishes to your guests for second helpings. Also hand round the rolls again, or invite your guests to go back to the table for them.

After the main course has been eaten and second helpings have been offered, clear the table of the first course and arrange the sweet course. Ask your guests to place their first-course plates on the buffet table. Then invite them to help themselves to the sweet. They can also help themselves to coffee at this point.

When your guests have finished, they place their used plates on the side table. This must be kept orderly and cleared. This is easier if your guests stack their plates up.

Table arrangement for the main course

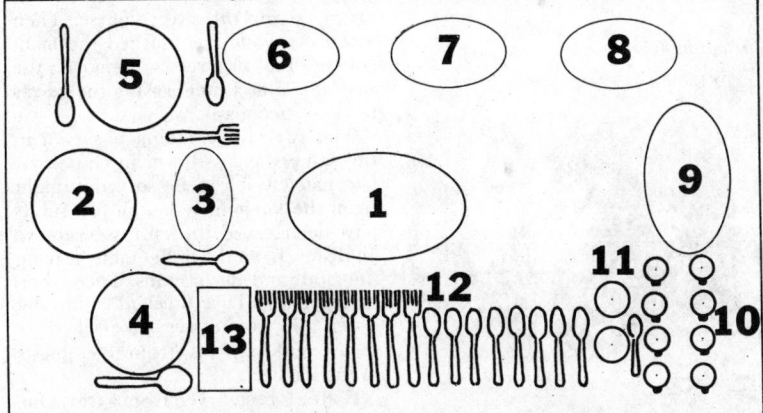

1. Centrepiece
2. Plates
3. Main Dish
4. Vegetable
5. Gravy or Sauce
6. Vegetables
7. Rolls
8. Mustard, oil and vinegar, salt and pepper
9. Coffee service
10. Cups
11. Cream and sugar, spoon
12. Cutlery

Table arrangement for the sweet course

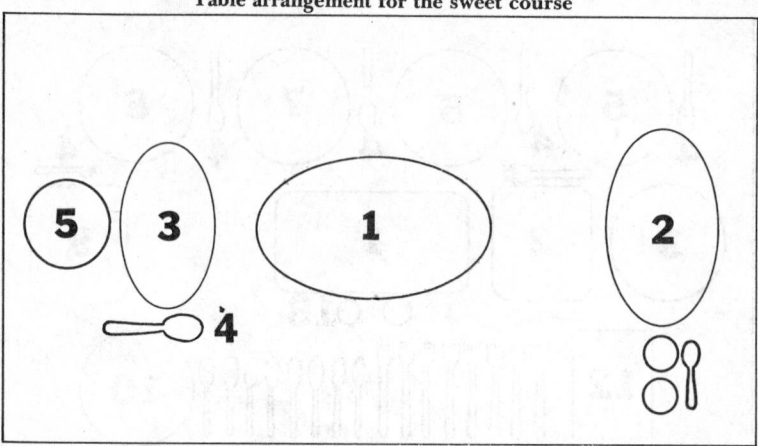

1. Centrepiece 2. Coffee service 3. The sweet 4. Serving implements 5. Small plates

There are several ways to serve the sweet course:

(1) Place it on the table as in the case of the informal buffet. Your guests will help themselves.

(2) Serve it at the table. A friend of the hostess can do the serving.

(3) Carry it from the kitchen to your guests. If this is done, waitresses or young friends of the hostess remove two main-course plates from the guests, taking the plates to the kitchen and returning with two sweets. It speeds up the service if each waitress carries two plates at a time as she removes the empty plates and returns with the filled ones.

The helpers leave the table after they have finished serving the food to the guests. They help themselves and join the other guests.

FOR MORE SPECIAL OCCASIONS

There are many occasions when you will wish to offer a semi-formal buffet

—a lunch or supper for a group of friends, a meal to celebrate an anniversary, or perhaps a wedding breakfast for a member of your family or a friend.

The semi-formal service differs from the informal in that you can ask one or two friends to assist at the buffet table. One may sit at one end of the table and serve the main dish, and perhaps a second dish or salad. Another friend may be seated at the opposite end of the table to pour the drinks.

Your guests will help themselves to other food and to cutlery and napkins. This service is convenient, as it's sometimes difficult to help oneself while holding a plate.

FOR VERY SPECIAL OCCASIONS

A wedding reception, an anniversary party, or a party in honour of some special guest is the perfect occasion for a formal buffet. This is a little less formal than a formal dinner, and easier

if you want to have a large number of guests. If your home is not large enough you may decide to hire a room at a hotel or club. The management will then help you with your buffet.

When you entertain at home, use your best linen, china and silver, and lay your table with great care. Choose the flowers, candles and other decorations with equal attention to attractiveness and suitability.

Seat your guests in the dining room and rooms adjoining. This time they will not go to the table to help themselves. Put the plates, napkins and cutlery on the buffet or service table to avoid overcrowding the table. Arrange duplicate dishes of food at either end of the table.

Two friends of the hostess, seated at opposite ends of the table, serve the food. The filled plates are then taken by waitresses or other friends of the hostess to the seated guests. This is the procedure for the formal service:

The waitress takes two empty plates from the service table and places one (left hand, left side) before the person serving. The waitress takes the filled plate (left hand, left side) and places the empty one (right hand, left side) in its place. She then goes to the service table and places a fork on the plate and a napkin under it and carries it to the guest. She hands it to the guest with the handle of the fork to the guest's right. She then takes another empty plate from the service table and continues to exchange empty plates for filled ones, which she hands to the guests until all are served.

Rolls or bread should be handed round twice.

Trays are used to hand round glasses of wine or other drinks.

When all the guests have been served, the buffet table is cleared and arranged for the sweet course. Then when everyone has finished the main course the waitresses remove the plates, two at a time, asking the guests to keep their napkins.

The sweet or pudding is served in the same way as the main course, or alternatively it can be served straight from the kitchen. When all the guests have been served, the waitresses remove all dishes from the buffet table, leaving the cloth and decorations. Then when all the guests have finished eating the sweet, the waitresses take all dirty plates and napkins from the guests to the kitchen.

Coffee is best served from a tray. One waitress carries a tray of filled cups while a second one follows behind with a second tray containing cream, sugar and coffee spoons for those who want them.

Main course for semi-formal buffet

THE "POTLUCK" MEAL

"Potluck" meals, where each person contributes one dish of food, are a convenient way to share the responsibility for feeding a large group. They have become popular for all-day club meetings, church socials, or community or family get-togethers.

This type of meal will work out better if you do some planning beforehand as to what type of food each person or family shall bring. Menus usually include main dishes, vegetable dishes, salads, sandwiches or rolls and a sweet. The hostess usually provides the drinks.

Make sure that you have a table large enough to hold the food without crowding. The hostess provides a suitable tablecloth, a simple centrepiece or decoration and all necessary serving dishes and serving implements.

You can avoid much confusion and delay by organizing your group before going to the kitchen to prepare the meal. Ask:

● Two women to help organize the drinks.
● Two women to arrange the dining table and supervise placing of food for the first course.
● Two women to arrange the sweet course.
● Two women to help the hostess to make and serve the coffee.
● Two women to supervise the clearing away after the meal, and to see that the hostess's kitchen is left neat and tidy.

Arrangement of "potluck" table

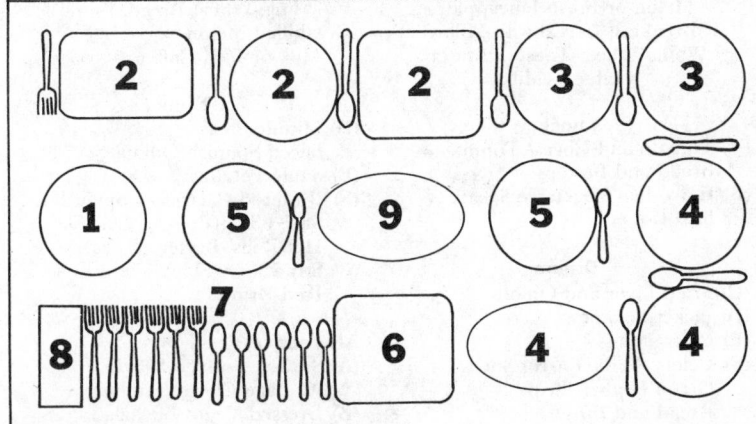

1. Plates
2. Main dishes
3. Vegetables
4. Salads
5. Mustard, oil and vinegar, salt and pepper
6. Sandwiches or rolls
7. Cutlery
8. Napkins
9. Centrepiece

Make the sweet course special

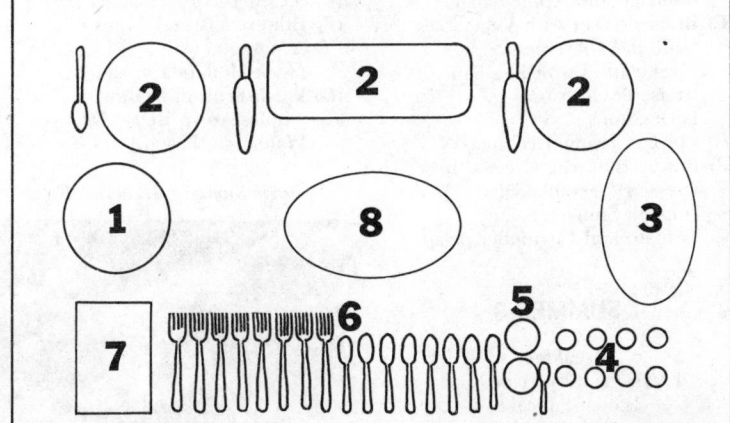

1. Small plates
2. Choice of sweets
3. Coffee service
4. Coffee cups
5. Cream and sugar
6. Cutlery
7. Napkins
8. Centrepiece

SERVING LUNCH

Often the potluck table looks rather disorganized. It is easy to achieve logical order if each woman is told where to place her dish of food. (See diagram.) Place the serving implements on the table beside the dishes.

Very often one is confronted with many dishes of the same kind. Plan to place only enough food on the table at one time to give variety to your meal. For example, serve one or two protein dishes, two or three vegetable dishes, two or three salads and sandwiches at the beginning of the meal. As the food disappears replenish with fresh dishes of food.

When the meal is ready, the hostess invites the guests to help themselves. Some groups may be accustomed to saying grace before their meal. In that case, the hostess can call on someone to give the blessing or lead the guests in saying grace.

If there are one or more guests of honour present, they should be among the first to be served. The guests, in small groups, start at the end of the table where the main dishes are placed. Each person moves round the table to the left, choosing whatever dishes he or she fancies.

Drinks can be poured at one end of the table or they can be served from a small table or a buffet. Or they can be put on a tray and handed round after the guests are seated. The same is true of coffee. Cream and sugar can be taken with the coffee or handed round later.

Guests should feel free to return to the buffet table for second helpings or the hostess may hand round extra dishes.

SERVING THE SWEET

When the main course is finished, the dessert committee clears the table and arranges the sweets. Then the guests are invited to go back to the table and help themselves. They can also help themselves to coffee, or it may be poured at their tables. After the meal is finished each woman assembles her own dishes to take home.

The clearing-away committee clears the table, and prepares the hostess's dishes for washing. The kitchen should be left looking neat and tidy.

MENUS

Balanced Menus for Each Season

The following daily menus for each season of the year outline appetizing, nutritious meals which are for the most part modestly priced but varied and nourishing. The basic menus have alternative choices so if you feel like a change, look for a letter to the left of the item on the menu, and substitute a dish marked with the same letter under "Alternatives".

BALANCED MENUS
SUMMER 1

Breakfast
Melon
Corn Flakes   Milk
Raisin Bread   Butter
Coffee   Milk

Lunch
(A) Cream of Carrot and Potato Soup
Cheese Biscuits
(B) Tuna Fish Salad on
Thick Tomato Slices
Bread and Butter, Lemonade

Dinner
(C) Stuffed Green Peppers
(Rice and Meat Stuffing)
Tomato Sauce
(D) Corn-on-the-Cob
(E) Vegetable Salad Bowl
Whole-Wheat Bread, Butter
(F) Fresh Fruit, Coffee

Alternatives:
(A) Vegetable Chowder or
Cream of Celery Soup
(B) Sliced Tomatoes and Lettuce
Salad; Waldorf Salad
(C) Carrot Meat Loaf with
Tomato Sauce; Stuffed Cabbage
Rolls; Ham with Raisin Sauce
(D) Hot Potato Salad
(E) Beetroot and Lettuce Salad
(F) Rhubarb Pie

SUMMER 2

Breakfast
Tomato Juice,
Melon or Fresh Pineapple
Breakfast Cereal with Milk
Whole-Wheat Toast   Butter
Coffee   Milk

Lunch
(A) Tomato and Cheese Fondue
Bread and Butter
(B) Individual Vegetable Salads
Iced Coffee

Dinner
(C) Fried Liver and Onions
(D) Jacket Potatoes
(E) Courgettes
(F) Celery Curls, Carrot Sticks,
Green Pepper Strips
Bread and Butter,
Ice Cream, Cold Fruit Squash

Alternatives:
(A) Fluffy Omelet with Cheese Sauce
Welsh Rarebit
Scrambled Eggs on Toast
Ham and Cheese Sandwich
(B) Health Salad
Cabbage and Apple Salad
(C) Braised Liver with Vegetables
Stuffed Aubergines
Liver Patties with Egg Sauce
Braised Spareribs
Pork Chops
(D) Chips; Creamed Potatoes
(E) Buttered Spring Greens; Broccoli
(F) Dressed Vegetable Salad
Dressed Spinach Salad
Tomato and Cucumber Salad

SUMMER 3

Breakfast
Fresh Fruit or Fruit Juice
Scotch Pancakes
with Syrup
Bacon
Coffee   Milk

Lunch
(A) Cold Plate (Sliced Eggs, Cheddar
Cheese, Bologna Sausage)
(B) Potato Salad
Whole-Wheat Bread, Butter
(C) Chilled Melon
Milk or Iced Coffee

Dinner
(D) Minute Steak
Sliced Spanish Onions
(E) Sauté Potatoes
(F) Buttered Carrots or Spinach
Sliced Tomatoes or Cole Slaw
Hot Rolls, Butter
(G) Strawberry Shortcake
Iced Drink

Alternatives:
(A) Stuffed Tomato Salad
(Cottage Cheese Stuffing)
(B) Dressed Vegetable Salad
Apple and Celery Salad
Kidney Bean Salad
Macaroni Salad
(C) Stewed Fresh Fruit
(D) Grilled Frankfurters
Grilled Lamb or Beef Patties
Fried Lamb Chops
Fishcakes
(E) Steamed New Potatoes
(F) Buttered Broad Beans,
Asparagus with
Mock Hollandaise Sauce
(G) Fresh Fruit in Season;
Apple Brown Betty; Orange
Water Ice; Peach Pie

Basic Summer Breakfast No. 1

SUMMER 4

Breakfast
Fresh Fruit Cup
Fruit Scones
Bacon   Butter
Coffee   Milk

Lunch
(A) Grilled Cheese Sandwiches
with Tomato Slices
(B) Waldorf Salad
1875ffENCY OF COOKERY   (963)

Dinner
(C) Fried Chicken with Cream Sauce
(D) Creamed Potatoes
(E) Sliced Carrots and Green Beans
(F) Hors-d'oeuvre Plate (Celery, Green
Pepper, Tomato, Pickles);
Cracked Wheat Bread, Butter
(G) Peach Shortcake
Coffee or Iced Fruit Squash

Alternatives:
(A) Grilled Cottage Cheese
Sandwiches
(B) Grapefruit or Orange Salad
(C) Chicken Fricassée
Stewed Chicken with Noodles
Chicken Curry with Steamed Rice
(D) Parsley Potatoes
Boiled New Potatoes
(E) Buttered Spring Greens or Broccoli
Spinach Moulds; Carrots and
Runner Beans au Gratin
(F) Tomato Stuffed with Cole Slaw
(G) Fresh Fruit Pie
Rhubarb Strawberry Flan;
Lemon Water Ice

AUTUMN 1

Breakfast
Fresh Fruit
Cooked Breakfast Cereal
with Raisins, Milk
Toast   Butter   Jam
Coffee   Hot Cocoa

Lunch
(A) Meat Salad Bowl
Rolls and Butter
Fruit in Season
Milk or Hot Coffee

Dinner
(B) Country-Style Roast Chicken;
Cream Sauce
(C) Buttered Swedes or Carrots
Roast Potatoes
(D) Dressed Salad
(E) Chocolate Cake
Coffee or Tea

Alternatives:
(A) Tuna Fish or Salmon Salad
Egg and Vegetable Salad
(B) Roast Duck with Apple Stuffing
Stewed Chicken with Dumplings
Oven-Braised Steak
with Roast Potatoes
(C) Sweetcorn and Broad Beans
(combined);
Buttered Carrots and Peas
(D) Moulded Vegetable Salad;
Cranberry Mould;
Combination Salad
(E) Rhubarb Betty; Egg Custard;
Apple Crumble

AUTUMN 2

Breakfast
Canned Grapefruit Segments
or Citrus Fruit Salad
Breakfast Cereal with Milk
Scrambled or Fried Eggs
Buttered Toast
Coffee   Milk   Hot Cocoa

Lunch
(A) Cream of Tomato Soup
Water Biscuits
(B) Pineapple and Cheese Salad
Bread and Butter
Milk

Dinner
(C) Spaghetti Bolognese with
Grated Parmesan Cheese
(D) Vegetable Salad with
Vinaigrette Dressing
Hot French Bread with
Garlic Butter
(E) Orange Mousse;
Coffee or Tea

Alternatives:
(A) Cream of Celery Soup or
Cream of Asparagus Soup
(B) Cabbage and Carrot Salad
Apple and Carrot Salad
(C) Lamb, Beef or Veal Stew with
Dumplings, Meat Loaf with
Tomato Sauce; Lamb Chops
with Vegetable Gravy;
Potato Cakes with
Cooked Meat and Gravy
(D) Lettuce with Thousand Island
Dressing; Dressed Tomato Salad;
Grapefruit Salad; Tomato Aspic
with Cottage Cheese Salad
(E) Peach Shortcake with Cream;
Fruit Jelly with Vanilla Sauce;
Lemon Pudding;
Butterscotch Blancmange

AUTUMN 3

Breakfast
Orange, Grapefruit or Tomato Juice
Porridge
with Milk and Brown Sugar
Toast
Marmalade
Coffee   Milk   Hot Cocoa

Lunch
(A) French Onion Soup
with Croûtons
(B) Hors-d'oeuvre Plate (Assorted
Vegetables and Sliced Hard-
boiled Egg);
Whole-Wheat Bread, Butter
Stewed Pears or Fruit Salad
Milk or Coffee

Dinner
(C) Grilled Hamburger with
Onion Rings
(D) Chips
(E) Buttered Cabbage
(F) Cole Slaw
(G) Bread and Butter Pudding
Coffee or Tea

Alternatives:
(A) Vegetable Soup
Fish Soup
(B) Egg and Celery Salad on Lettuce
Tomato Aspic Salad with
Sliced Hard-boiled Egg
(C) Fried Gammon Steaks; Meat Loaf
with Mashed Potatoes
Minced Beef and Vegetable
Casserole
(D) Creamed Potatoes
(E) Buttered Broccoli
Brussels Sprouts
(F) Watercress Salad;
Cos Lettuce Salad
(G) Rice Pudding
Chocolate Bread Pudding
Blackberry and Apple Pie
Sliced Peaches

AUTUMN 4

Breakfast
Fresh Plums
Grapefruit Juice; Orange Wedges
Bacon and Eggs
Hot Rolls or Whole-Wheat Toast
Butter
Coffee   Milk   Hot Cocoa

Lunch
(A) Vegetable Soup
Cheese Biscuits
(B) Cottage Cheese and Cucumber
Sandwiches on
Whole-Wheat Bread
(C) Fresh Fruit in Season;
Sultana Biscuits, Milk

Dinner
(D) Veal Olives and Boiled Potatoes
(E) Scalloped Tomatoes
(F) Orange and Coconut Salad
Hot Rolls or
Maize Flour Scones
(G) Fruit Crumble
Coffee or Tea

Alternatives:
(A) Minestrone Soup
Split Pea Soup
with Croûtons

(B) Cottage Cheese and Green Pepper
or Egg and Celery Sandwiches
(C) Canned Fruit; Stewed Fruit
(D) Stuffed Breast of Lamb with
Roast Potatoes; Beef Chow
Mein with Steamed Rice; Ham
Loaf with Jacket Potatoes;
Pork Chops with Mashed
Potatoes
Spareribs with Roast Potatoes
(E) Buttered Spinach
Broccoli with Brown Butter Sauce
(F) French Salad Bowl
Orange and Vegetable Salad Bowl
(G) Butterscotch Blancmange
Plain Blancmange

WINTER 1

Breakfast
Orange Juice or Tomato Juice
Bacon and Egg
Fruit Scones
or Fresh Hot Croissants
Butter
Milk   Coffee

Lunch
(A) Puffy Cheese Omelet
Buttered Parsnips
Whole-Wheat Bread, Butter
Canned Fruit, Milk

Dinner
(B) Breadcrumbed Veal Cutlet with
Tomato Sauce
Mashed Potatoes
(C) Buttered Carrots
(D) Round Lettuce with French
Dressing;
Whole-Wheat Scones or
Hot Rolls
(E) Fruit Crumble
Coffee or Tea

Alternatives:
(A) Grilled Cheese Sandwiches
Baked Eggs au Gratin
(B) Roast Chicken with Celery
Stuffing; Chicken Fricassée;
Chicken Tetrazzini;
Stuffed Veal Steak and Roast
Potatoes; Fried Plaice
with Paprika Potatoes
(C) Okra and Tomatoes;
Steamed Marrow
Stewed Tomatoes
(D) Pear and Celery Salad;
Citrus Salad Bowl; Cabbage Salad
(E) Baked Apples with Cream;
Apple Dumplings
Orange Mousse

WINTER 2

Breakfast
Baked Apple
Grapefruit or Orange Juice
Poached or Scrambled Eggs
Buttered Toast
Coffee   Cocoa   Milk

Lunch
(A) Split Pea Soup with Croûtons
(B) Grilled Tomato and Cheese
Sandwiches
(C) Stewed Apples
Milk or Coffee

Dinner
(D) Escalloped Fish
(E) Jacket Potatoes
(F) Buttered Broccoli
(G) Dressed Vegetable Salad
Hot Whole-Wheat Scones
(H) Peach Flan
Coffee or Tea

Alternatives:
(A) Haricot Bean Soup;
Cream of Mushroom Soup
(B) Egg Sandwiches
(C) Stewed Dried Fruit; Bananas
and Cream
(D) Baked Fish Fillets; Salmon or
Tuna Fish Loaf; Fried Fish or
Scallops with Mashed Potatoes
(E) Potato Pancakes; Potato Puffs
(F) Buttered Brussels Sprouts;
Stewed Tomatoes; Buttered
Beetroots
(G) Lettuce and Spinach Salad
Carrot and Green Pepper Salad
(H) Rice Pudding
Tapioca Cream Pudding
Butterscotch Bread Pudding

WINTER 3

Breakfast
Stewed Fruit or Fruit Juice
Porridge
with Milk and Brown Sugar
Sausages and Tomatoes
Coffee   Cocoa   Milk

Lunch
(A) Hot Bacon Rolls
(B) Gelatine Salad with Fruit
Cocoa or Milk

Dinner
(C) Roast Leg of Lamb with Gravy;
Roast Potatoes
(D) Mint Carrots or Buttered Peas
(E) Beetroot Salad
Whole-Wheat Scones or
Hot Rolls
(F) Apple Pie
Coffee or Cocoa

Alternatives:
(A) Waffles with Bacon
Tomato Rarebit on Toast
Grilled Cheese Sandwiches
with Bacon
(B) Mixed Salad with Fruit
Peach and Cottage Cheese Salad
(C) Beef Hot Pot with Mashed
Potatoes; Roast Veal with Jacket
Potatoes; Roast Shoulder of Pork
with Sage and Onion Stuffing and
Mashed Potatoes
Braised Steak with Celery Stuffing
and Jacket Potatoes
(D) Brussels Sprouts
Braised Marrow
Glazed Carrots
(E) Lettuce with Roquefort Dressing
Chef's Salad
(F) Lemon Pie
Steamed Fruit Pudding

WINTER 4

Breakfast
Grapefruit or Fruit Juice
French toast
Coffee   Cocoa   Milk

Lunch
(A) Cheese Omelet
Bread and Butter
Lettuce Salad with Mayonnaise
(B) Bananas and Cream
Biscuits, Milk

Dinner
(C) Lambs' Liver Loaf
(D) Sauté Potatoes
(E) Buttered Beetroots or Parsnips
(F) Cole Slaw with Green Pepper
French Bread and Butter
(G) Sago Pudding
Coffee or Tea

Alternatives:
(A) Shirred Eggs in Toast Cups
Scrambled Eggs on Toast
Baked Eggs au Gratin
(B) Canned Raspberries or
Redcurrants with Cream
(C) Baked Pork Chops with
Creamed Potatoes; Braised Liver
and Vegetables; Braised Oxtail
with Jacket Potatoes;
Beef Casserole
with Fluffy Mashed Potatoes
(D) Boiled Potatoes or
Fluffy Mashed Potatoes
(E) Buttered Marrow
(F) Waldorf Salad; Lettuce
with French Dressing
(G) Lemon Chiffon Pie
One-Egg Cake
Egg Custard and Biscuits

Basic Spring Breakfast No. 1

SPRING 1

Breakfast
Grapefruit Cup
Filled with
Fresh Grapefruit Sections
and Halved Black Grapes
Shredded Wheat   Milk
Coffee or Tea

Lunch
(A) Buttered Asparagus on Toast;
Radishes, Spring Onions
(B) Pear and Cottage Cheese Salad;
Whole Wheat Bread, Butter,
Milk or Coffee

Dinner
(C) Baked Ham;
Roast Potatoes
(D) Buttered Green Peas
(E) Cabbage and Pineapple Salad;
Hot Rolls
(F) Gingerbread with Lemon Sauce

Alternatives:
(A) French or Runner Beans;
Runner Beans au Gratin
(B) Chocolate Blancmange;
Orange Blancmange
(C) Roast Hand of Pork with Roast
Potatoes; Steak with Potatoes
au Gratin; Stuffed Breast of
Veal with Roast Potatoes;
Shoulder of Lamb with Jacket
Potatoes
(D) Buttered Carrots; Asparagus
(E) Mixed Salad;
Carrot and Pineapple Salad
with Vinaigrette Dressing
(F) Apple Pie with Custard
Rhubarb Pie

SPRING 2

Breakfast
Blended Orange and Grapefruit Juice
Poached Eggs on Toast
Coffee   Milk   Cocoa   Tea

Lunch
(A) Poached Eggs in Cream Sauce;
Sliced Carrots, Sliced Tomatoes
(B) Rice Pudding; Biscuits, Milk

Dinner
(C) Meat Pie
(D) Fruit Salad;
Whole Wheat Bread, Butter
(E) Hot Gingerbread;
Coffee; Milk

Alternatives:
(A) Creamed Eggs on Toast;
Baked Eggs au Gratin;
Macaroni Cheese
(B) Blancmange
Coconut Egg Custard; Junket
(C) Shepherd's Pie; Steak and
Kidney Pie; Macaroni or Spaghetti
and Meat Casserole;
Chicken en Casserole
Raw Cabbage and Green Pepper
Salad
Cabbage and Carrot Salad
(E) Simnal Cake; Fresh Fruit
Shortcake; Stewed Rhubarb with
Ginger

SPRING 3

Breakfast
Fruit Juice
Puffed Rice Cereal
Toast and Marmalade
Milk   Coffee   Tea

Lunch
(A) Cream of Tomato Soup
(B) Egg Sandwiches
(C) Canned Fruit
Biscuits, Milk, Coffee

Dinner
(D) Lamb or Beef Burgers
Spanish Rice, Buttered Peas
(E) Dressed Carrot and Pineapple
Salad;
French Bread
Gingerbread Upside-Down Cake

Alternatives:
(A) Cabbage with Soured Cream
Creamed Butter Beans
(B) Grilled Cheese and Bacon
Sandwich; Bologna Sausage and
Hard-Boiled Egg Sandwich
(C) Stewed Prunes; Prune Whip
(D) Braised Pork Chops with
Parsley Potatoes; Barbecued
Frankfurters with Sauté
Potatoes; Fried Liver and
Onions with Mashed Potatoes;
Fried Plaice with Fried Potatoes
(E) Lettuce with Soured Cream
Dressing; Cos Lettuce and
French Dressing

SPRING 4

Breakfast
Orange Slices or Stewed Fruit
Crisp Whole-Wheat Cereal with Milk
Fluffy Omelet
Cinnamon Toast
Coffee   Tea   Milk

Lunch
(A) Cream of Mushroom Soup
(B) Grilled Tomato and Bacon
Sandwich;
Sliced Raw Carrot; Spring
Onions,
Fresh or Stewed Fruit Salad

Dinner
(C) Fish Cakes with Cheese Sauce;
Mashed, Boiled or Sauté
Potatoes; Buttered Broccoli,
Asparagus or Peas
(D) Cole Slaw;
Whole-Wheat Bread, Butter
(E) Swiss Roll

Alternatives:
(A) Any Cream of Vegetable Soup
(B) Cream Cheese and Chives
Sandwich
(C) Baked Fish with Egg Sauce;
Grilled Fish;
Chilli Con Carne;
Fried Steak
(D) Grapefruit and Carrot
Moulded Salad;
Moulded Vegetable Salad
(E) Gooseberry Crumble; Sliced Fresh
Pineapple; Lemon Water Ice

SPECIAL OCCASION MENUS

New Year's Eve Dinner
Minted Fruit Cup
Celery   Olives
Roast Goose
with Apple and Prune Stuffing
Mashed Potatoes
Green Peas in Onion Cups
Lettuce Hearts with Russian Dressing
Hot Mince Pies   Cheese
Coffee

New Year's Eve Buffet Supper
Celery   Olives
Baked Ham   Pineapple Rings
Potato Puffs
Asparagus Tips
with Hollandaise Sauce
Lobster Salad
Green Salad with Fresh Fruit
Hot Buttered Rolls
Cheesecake
Salted Nuts   Crystallized Fruit

Ringing In the New Year
Cheese Board   Assorted Savoury
Biscuits
Stuffed Celery, Olives, Radishes,
Carrot Curls
Stuffed Dates   Salted Nuts
Chocolates
Christmas Cake   Biscuits   Fruit
Punch Bowl   Coffee

Christmas Dinner 1
Tomato Juice, Hot or Chilled
French Bread
Stuffed Celery
Roast Turkey
with
Oyster Dressing   Giblet Gravy
Roast Potatoes
Buttered Brussels Sprouts
Spiced Peaches or Pears
Hot Rolls   Butter
Christmas Pudding   Brandy Butter
Cheese   Nuts   Raisins   Coffee

Christmas Dinner 2
Melon Cocktail
Roast Duck
with Apple and Celery Stuffing
Courgettes
Sliced Onions in Cream Sauce
Roast Jerusalem Artichokes
Avocado and Tangerine Salad
Fresh Fruit Salad   Cream   Coffee

Easter Dinner
Melon
Roast Leg of Lamb
Mint Sauce
Buttered New Potatoes and Peas
Green Salad with Roquefort Dressing
Hot Rolls
Apple Pie   Custard
Nuts   Coffee

Fork Lunch 1
Macaroni, Ham and Tomato Casserole
Buttered Broccoli
Rolls
Peach Crumble   Coffee

Fork Lunch 2
Tomato Juice Cocktail
Spaghetti Bolognese
with
Grated Cheese
French Bread
Green Salad with Italian Dressing
Biscuit Tortoni   Coffee

Fork Lunch 3
Prawn and Macaroni Salad
in Tomato Aspic Ring
Buttered Green Beans
Crisp Poppyseed Rolls
Lemon Meringue Pie   Coffee

After Afternoon Bridge Party
Fresh Fruit Salad
with Lemon Sorbet Topping
Hot Fruit Scones
Nuts   Chocolates
Coffee

Tea
Assorted Sandwiches
Victoria Sponge   Chocolate Cake
Chocolates   Nuts
Tea or Chocolate

French Dinner
French Onion Soup
with Croûtons and Grated Cheese
or
Clear Consommé with Sherry
Beef À la Mode
or
Chicken Sauté Chasseur
Braised Celery   Potato Croquettes
Rolls or French Bread
Sugared Fresh Strawberries
or Fresh Pineapple Slices
or
Napoleons or Other French Pastries
Red or White Wine   Coffee

Italian Dinner
Antipasto
(shredded lettuce, tomato slices, fennel
wedges, pimiento slices, Italian salami
slices, stuffed and black olives, anchovy
fillets)
Oil and Vinegar
Ministrone
with Grated Parmesan Cheese
Italian Bread
Veal Scallopine or Chicken Cacciatore
Biscuit Tortoni or Zabaglione
or Pears in Red Wine
Red Wine   Espresso Coffee

Chinese Dinner
Clear Chicken Soup
or Meat Broth with Egg
or Chicken Subgum Soup
Egg Rolls (Frozen) with Mustard Sauce
Prawns and Green Peppers
or Beef with
Tomatoes and Green Peppers
Sweet and Pungent Pork
Steamed Rice
Preserved Kumquats or
Almond Biscuits
Tea   Rice Wine

Latin-American Dinner
Kidney Bean Soup
or
Chilled Mixed Vegetable Soup
Arroz Con Pollo (Chicken with Rice)
Tamales (canned or homemade)
Mexican Chocolate-Coffee
(made of half hot coffee and half

hot cocoa, flavoured with cinnamon)
or
Iced Mexican Coffee

Buffet Supper
Tomato Juice Cocktail
Baked Ham
Pineapple Slices
Jacket Potatoes
Dressed Green Salad   Buttered Rolls
Fruit Flan   Coffee
or
Sliced Cold Baked Ham
and Tongue
Sliced Tomatoes   Sliced Cucumbers
Potato Salad
Buttered Rolls
Moulded Vegetable Salad Mayonnaise
Petits Fours   Coffee

Vegetarian Dinners
or Suppers
Fish Chowder Cheese Biscuits Butter
Cottage Cheese
Green Pepper Chutney
Dressed Vegetable Salad
Baked Apples with Custard
Coffee

2.
Baked Fish with Lemon Sauce
Boiled Potatoes   Buttered Broccoli
Lettuce
with Cottage Cheese Dressing
Bread   Butter
Chocolate Blancmange
Coffee

3.
Macaroni Cheese
Runner Beans with Butter
Breadcrumb Sauce
Tomato Pickle
Hot Rolls   Butter
Cole Slaw
Fruit Crumble
Coffee

4.
Fish au Gratin
Buttered Beetroots
Buttered Green Beans
Green Salad
Dark Rye Bread   Butter
Lemon Blancmange
Coffee

PURNELL'S
COMPLETE
COOKERY

INDEX

NOTES

NOTES

NOTES

NOTES

NOTES